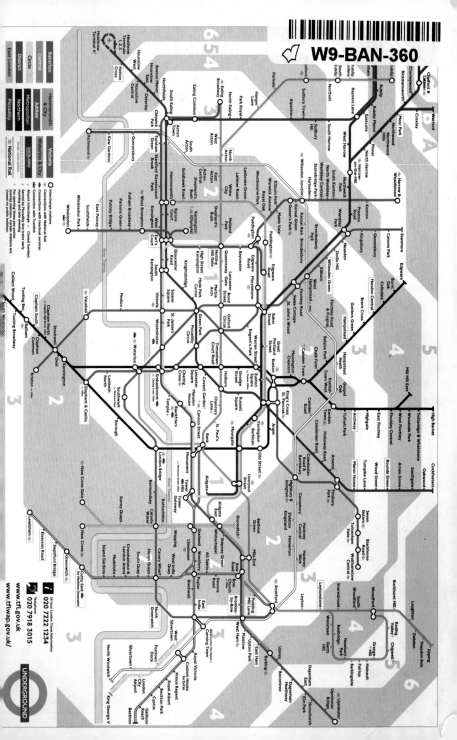

W9-BAN-360

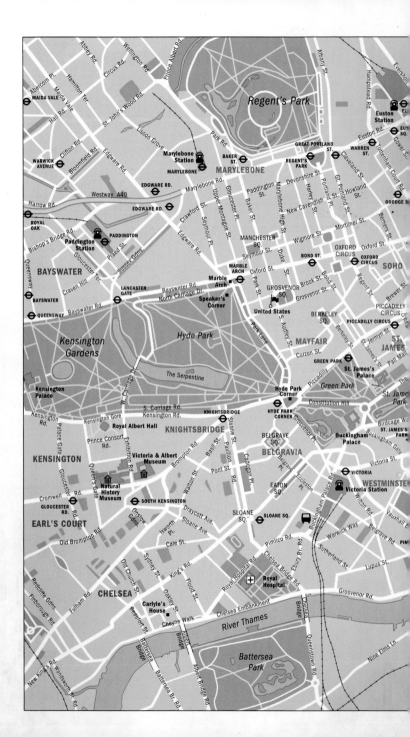

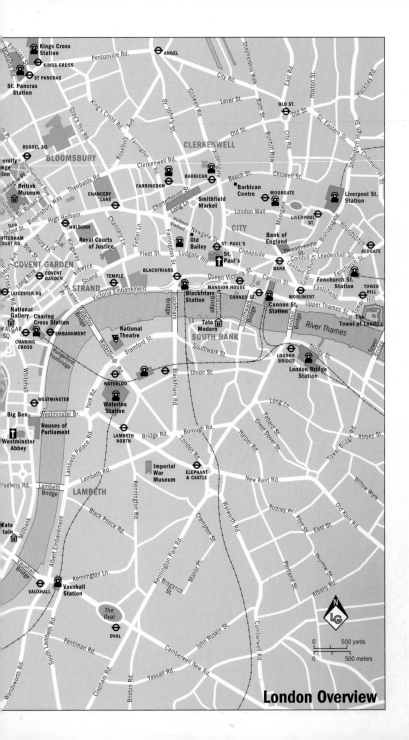

London Overview

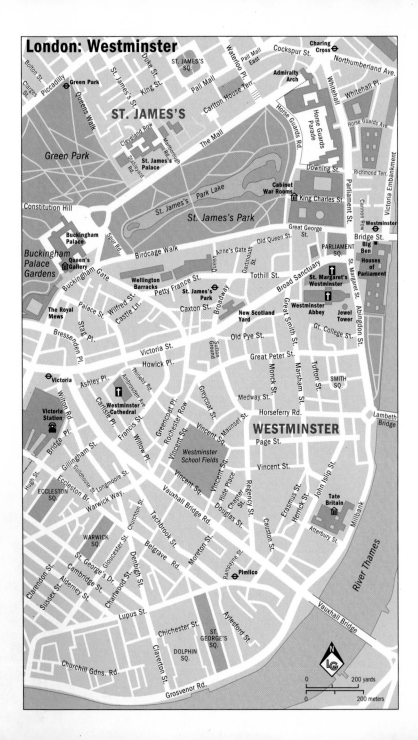

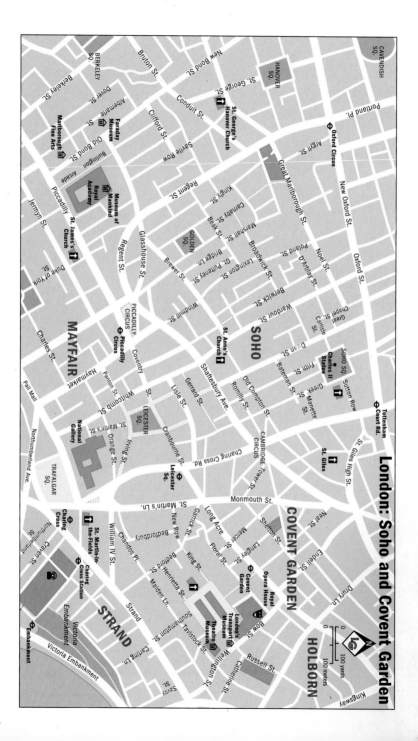

London: Soho and Covent Garden

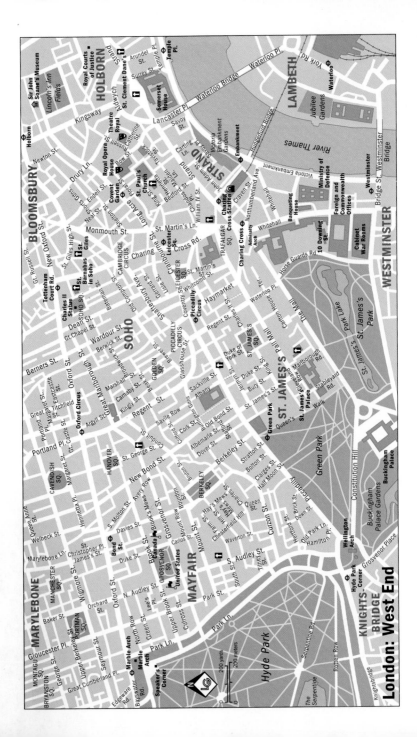

London: West End

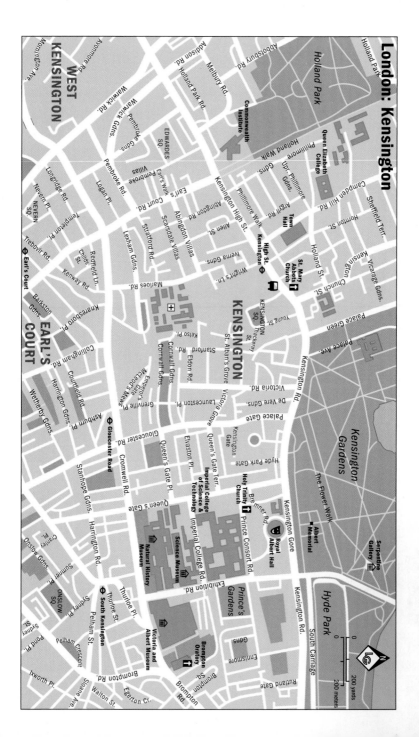

London: Kensington

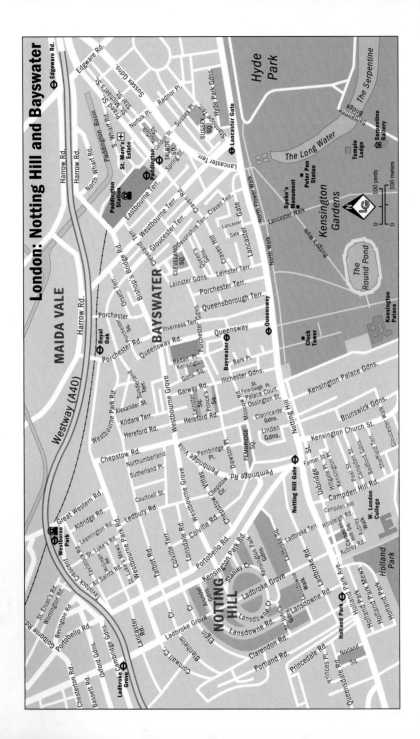

London: Notting Hill and Bayswater

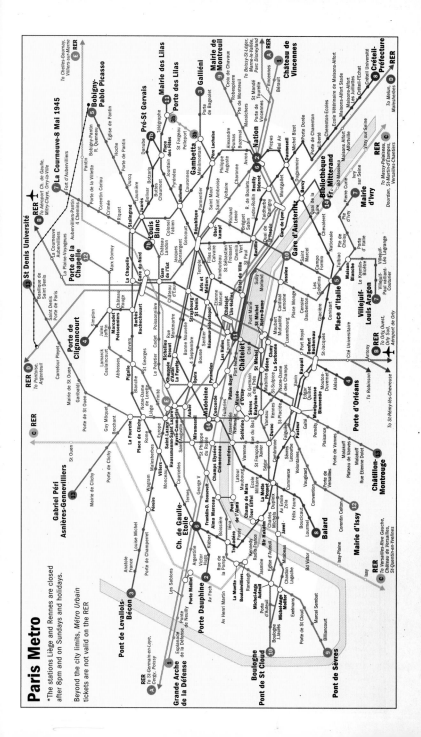

Paris Metro

*The stations Liège and Rennes are closed after 8pm and on Sundays and holidays.

Beyond the city limits, *Métro Urbain* tickets are not valid on the RER

Paris: Overview and Arrondissements

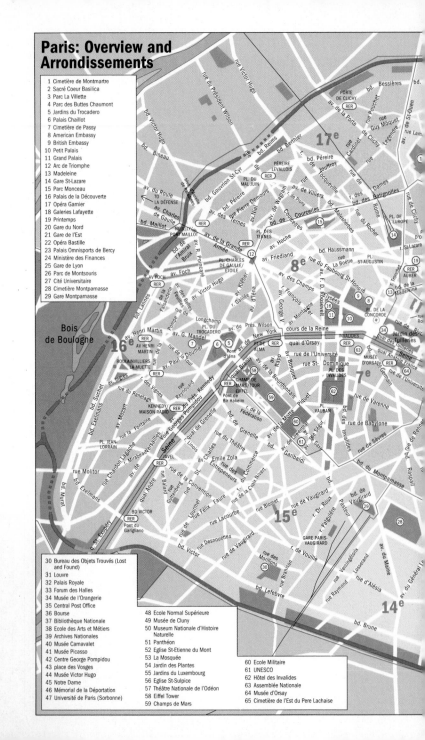

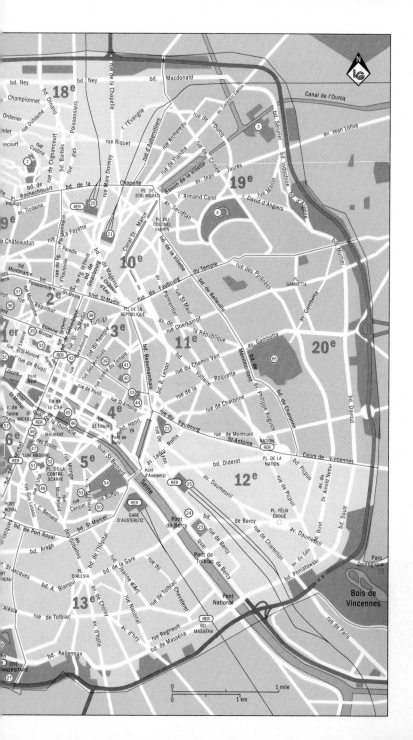

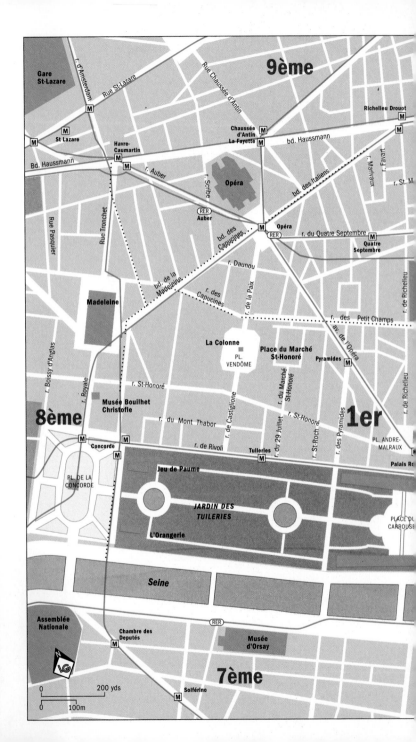

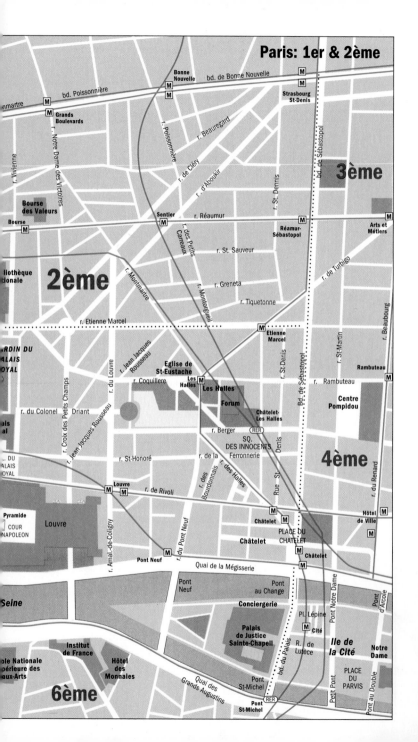

Paris: 1er & 2ème

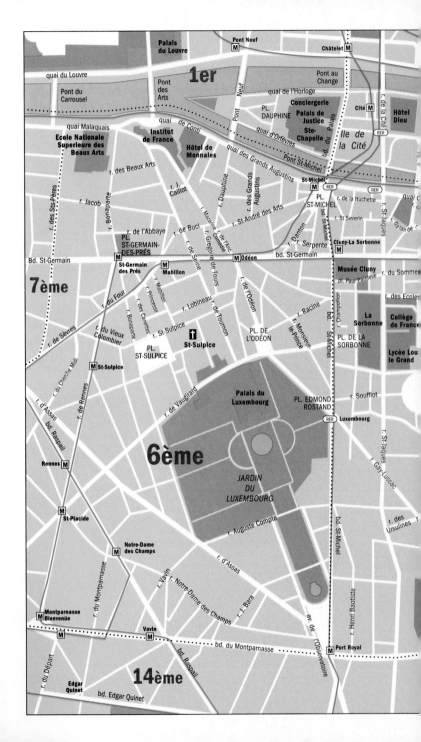

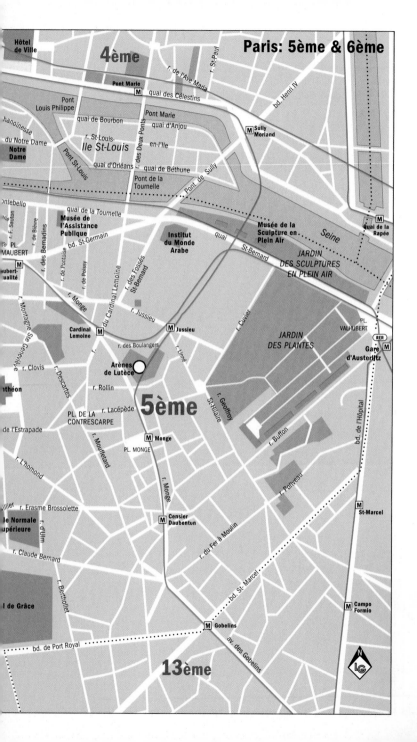

Paris: 5ème & 6ème

Hôtel de Ville

4ème

r. St-Paul

r. de l'Ave Maria

Pont Marie M quai des Célestins

bd. Henri IV

Pont Louis Philippe

quai de Bourbon

Pont Marie

quai d'Anjou

M **Sully Morland**

hanoinesse

du Notre Dame

Notre Dame

r. St-Louis- **Ile St-Louis** en-l'Ile

quai d'Orléans quai de Béthune

Pont St-Louis

r. des Deux Ponts

Pont de Sully

Quai de la Rapée M

Pont de la Tournelle

Seine

ontebello

quai de la Tournelle

Musée de l'Assistance Publique

r. de Bièvre

bd. St-Germain

r. des Fossés St-Bernard

Institut du Monde Arabe

quai

Musée de la Sculpture en Plein Air

St-Bernard

JARDIN DES SCULPTURES EN PLEIN AIR

arie

PL. MAUBERT

r. des Bernardins

r. de Pontoise

r. de Poissy

r. du Cardinal Lemoine

aubert-ualité M

r. Monge

r. Jussieu

M **Jussieu**

r. Cuvier

PL. VALHUBERT

RER

Cardinal Lemoine M

r. des Boulangers

Gare d'Austerlitz M

r. Montagne Ste Geneviève

r. Clovis

r. Descartes

Arènes de Lutèce ⭘

r. Rollin

r. Linné

JARDIN DES PLANTES

r. Geoffroy St-Hilaire

5ème

r. de l'Hôpital

nthéon

PL. DE LA CONTRESCARPE

r. Lacépède

r. Buffon

de l'Estrapade

r. Mouffetard

M **Monge**

PL. MONGE

r. Poliveau

r. L'homond

r. Monge

illiet

r. Erasme Brossolette

r. d'Ulm

le Normale upérieure

M **Censier Daubenton**

M **St-Marcel**

r. Claude Bernard

r. du Fer à Moulin

r. Berthollet

l de Grâce

bd. St-Marcel

M **Campo Formio**

bd. de Port Royal

M **Gobelins**

av. des Gobelins

13ème

N LG

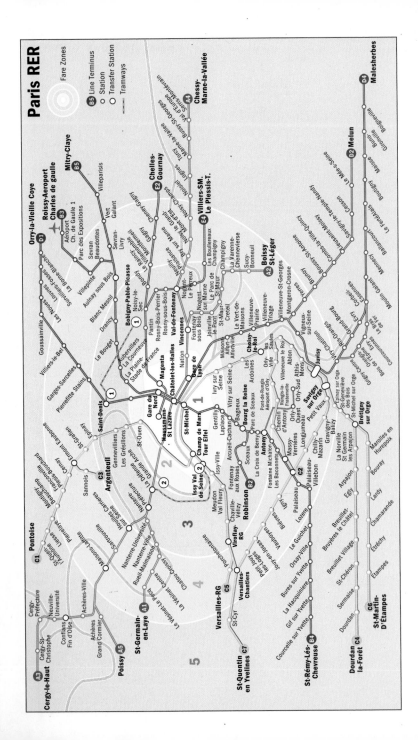

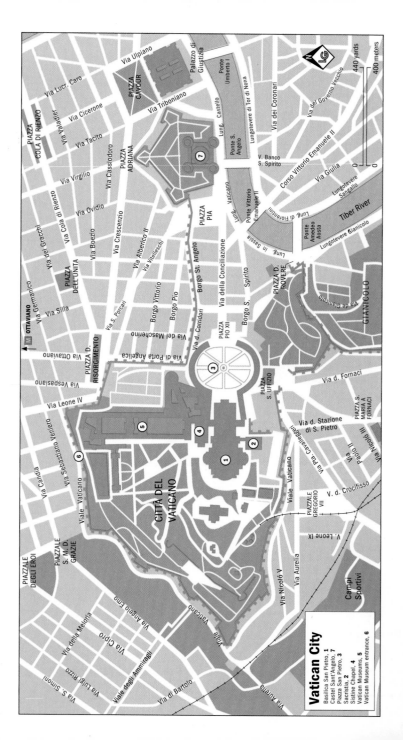

Vatican City

Basílica San Pietro, **1**
Castel Sant'Angelo, **7**
Piazza San Pietro, **3**
Sacristia, **2**
Sistine Chapel, **4**
Vatican Museums, **5**
Vatican Museum entrance, **6**

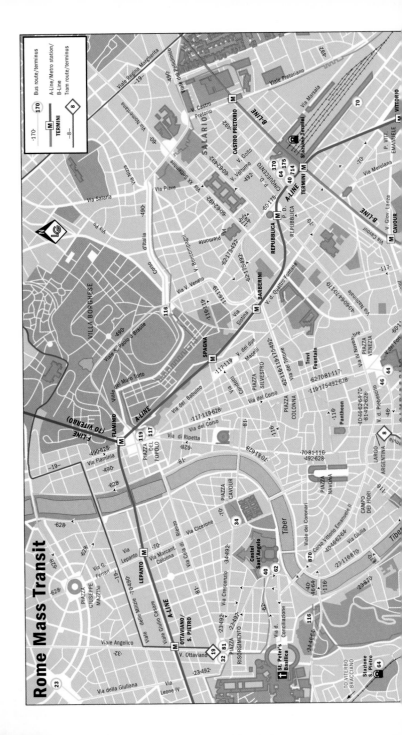

Rome Mass Transit

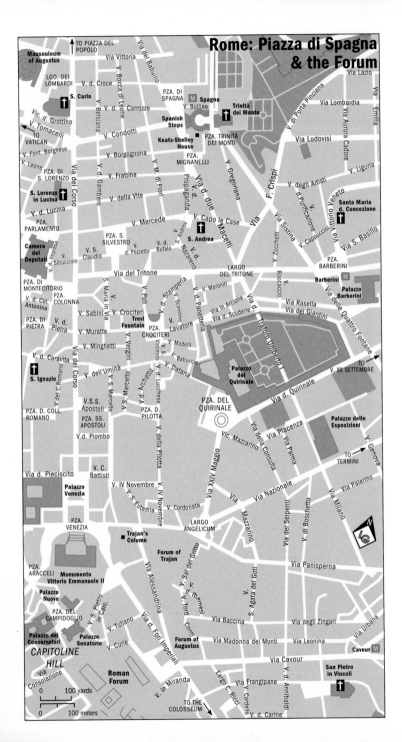

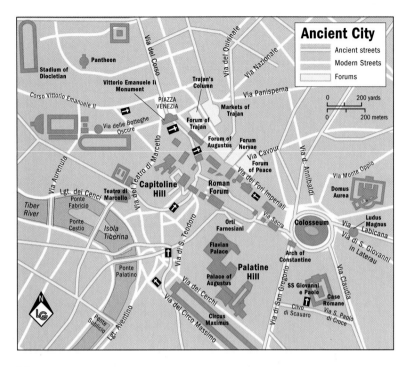

Ancient City

Ancient streets
Modern Streets
Forums

0   200 yards
0   200 meters

Stadium of Diocletian
Pantheon
Corso Vittorio Emanuele II
Vittorio Emanuele II Monument
Trajan's Column
Via del Corso
Via del Quirinale
Via Nazionale
Via Panisperna
PIAZZA VENEZIA
Markets of Trajan
Forum of Trajan
Via delle Botteghe Oscure
Forum of Augustus
Forum Nervae
Via Cavour
Forum of Peace
Via dei Fori Imperiali
Via d. Annibaldi
Via Monte Oppio
Domus Aurea
Via Aurenula
Lgt. dei Cenci
Ponte Fabricio
Teatro di Marcello
Via del Teatro di Marcello
Capitoline Hill
Roman Forum
Via Sacra
Colosseum
Via Labicana
Ludus Magnus
Tiber River
Ponte Cestio
Isola Tiberina
Orti Farnesiani
Via di S. Teodoro
Flavian Palace
Arch of Constantine
Via di S. Giovanni in Laterau
Ponte Palatino
Palace of Augustus
Palatine Hill
SS Giovanni e Paolo
Via Claudia
Via del Cerchi
Ponte Sublicio
Lgr. Aventino
Via del Circo Massimo
Circus Maximus
Clivo di Scauaro
Via S. Paolo in Croce
Case Romane
Via di San Gregorio

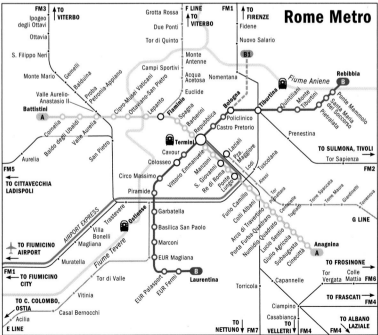

Rome Metro

FM3
TO VITERBO
Ipogeo degli Ottavi
Ottavia
S. Filippo Neri
Monte Mario
Gemelli
Balduina
Valle Aurelio-Anastasio II
Battistini
Cornelia
Baldo degli Ubaldi
Valle Aurelia
Aurelia
Proba Petronia Appiano
Cipro-Musei Vaticani
Ottaviano-San Pietro
San Pietro

F LINE
TO VITERBO
Grotta Rossa
Due Ponti
Tor di Quinto
Monte Antenne
Campi Sportivi
Acqua Acetosa
Euclide
Lepanto
Flaminio
Spagna
Barberini
Repubblica

FM1
TO FIRENZE
Fidene
Nuovo Salario
Nomentana
B1
Bologna
Policlinico
Castro Pretorio

Tiburtina
Quintiliani
Monte Tiburtini
Prenestina

Fiume Aniene
Santa Maria del Soccorso
Pietralata

Rebibbia
B
Ponte Mammolo

TO SULMONA, TIVOLI
Tor Sapienza

FM2

FM5
TO CITTAVECCHIA LADISPOLI

AIRPORT EXPRESS
Trastevere
Ostiense
Villa Bonelli
Magliana
Muratella
Fiume Tevere

Termini
Cavour
Colosseo
Circo Massimo
Piramide
Garbatella
Basilica San Paolo
Marconi
EUR Magliana

Vittorio Emmanuele
Manzoni
S. Giovanni
Re di Roma
Ponte Lungo

Laziali
Pza. Maggiore
Lodi
Furio Camillo
Colli Albani
Arco di Travertino
Porta Furba Quadraro
Numidio Quadrato
Lucio Sestio
Giulio Agricola
Subaugusta
Cinecittà

Tuscolana
Alessi
Tor Papattara
Centocelle
Togliatti
Tor Spaccata
Torre Maura
Giardinetti
Torrenova

G LINE

Anagnina
A
TO FROSINONE

FM6
Tor Vergata
Colle Mattia

FM1
TO FIUMICINO CITY

TO FIUMICINO AIRPORT

Tor di Valle

EUR Palasport
EUR Fermi
EUR Magliana
B
Laurentina

Torricola
Capannelle

TO FRASCATI
FM4

Vitinia
Casal Bernocchi
Acilia
E LINE
TO C. COLOMBO, OSTIA

TO NETTUNO
FM7

Ciampino
Casabianca
TO VELLETRI
FM4

FM4

TO ALBANO LAZIALE

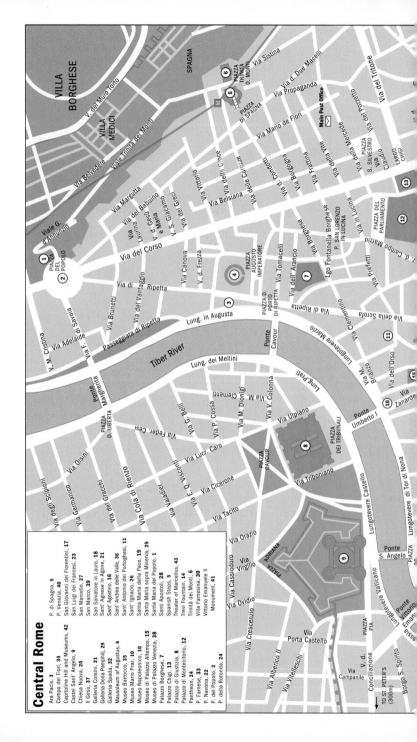

Central Rome

Ara Pacis, **3**
Campo dei Fiori, **34**
Capitoline Hill and Museums, **42**
Castel Sant' Angelo, **9**
Chiesa Nuova, **20**
Il Gesù, **37**
Galleria Corsini, **31**
Galleria Doria Pamphilj, **29**
Galleria Spada, **32**
Mausoleum of Augustus, **4**
Museo Barrocco, **35**
Museo Mario Praz, **10**
Museo Napoleonico, **10**
Museo di Palazzo Altemps, **15**
Museo di Palazzo Venezia, **38**
Palazzo Borghese, **7**
Palazzo Chigi, **13**
Palazzo di Giustizia, **8**
Palazzo di Montecitorio, **12**
Pantheon, **24**
P. Farnese, **33**
P. Navona, **22**
P. del Popolo, **2**
P. della Rotonda, **24**

P. di Spagna, **5**
P. Venezia, **40**
San Giovanni dei Fiorentini, **17**
San Luigi dei Francesi, **23**
San Marcello, **27**
San Marco, **39**
San Salvatore in Lauro, **18**
Sant' Agnese in Agone, **21**
Sant' Agostino, **16**
Sant' Andrea delle Valle, **36**
Sant' Antonio dei Portoghesi, **11**
Sant' Ignazio, **26**
Santa Maria della Pace, **19**
Santa Maria sopra Minerva, **25**
Santa Maria del Popolo, **1**
Santi Apostoli, **28**
Spanish Steps, **5**
Theater of Marcellus, **43**
Trevi Fountain, **14**
Trinità dei Monti, **6**
Villa Farnesina, **30**
Vittorio Emanuele II
Monument, **41**

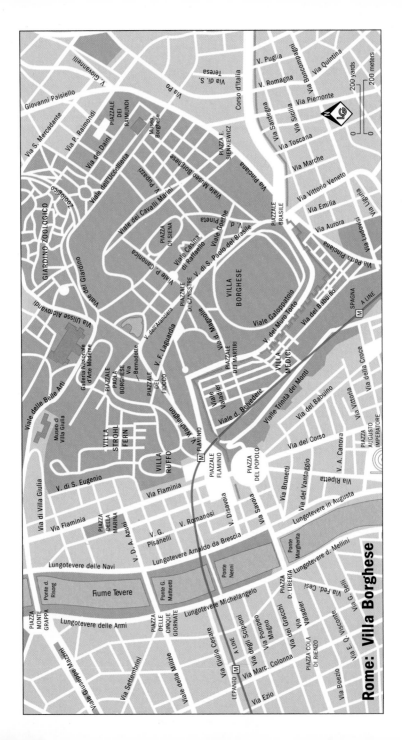

Rome: Villa Borghese

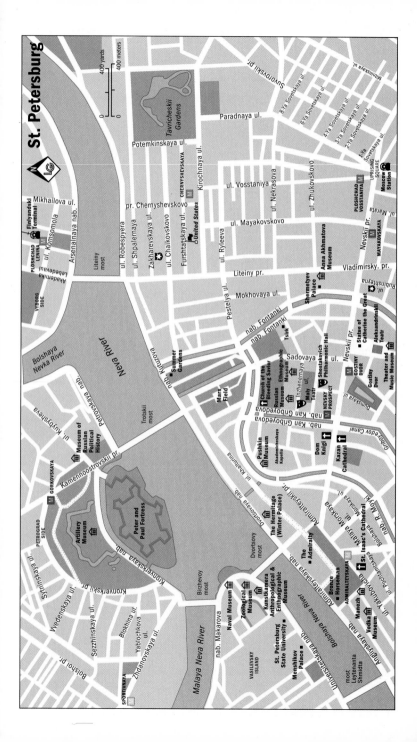

Moscow

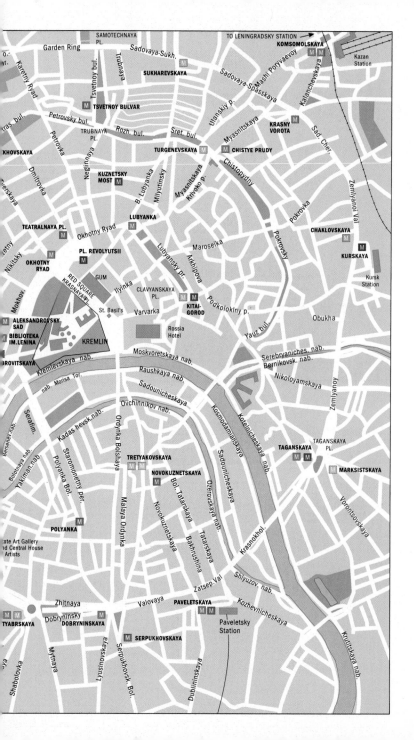

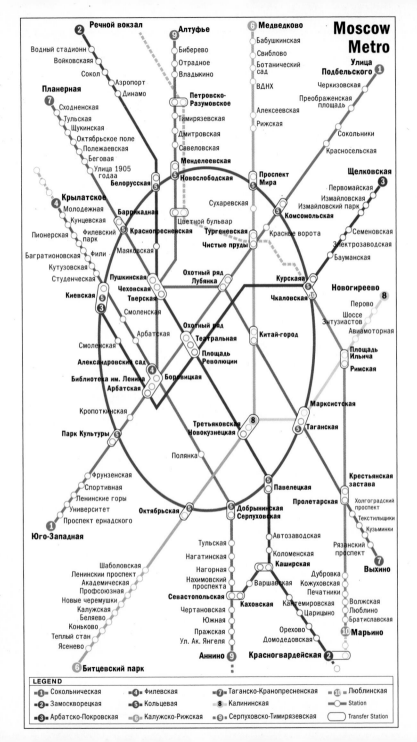

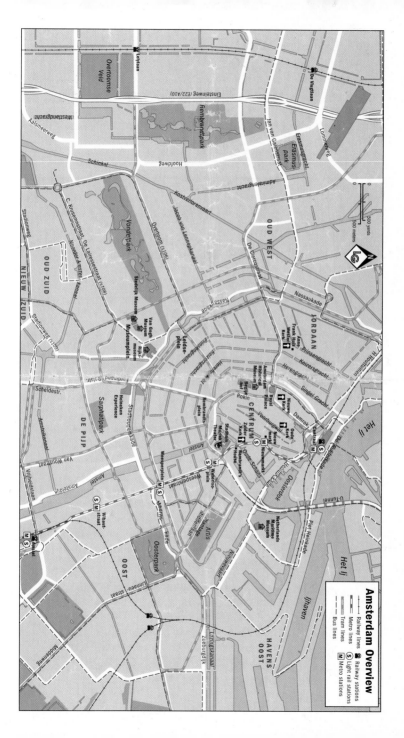

Amsterdam Overview

- Railway lines
- Metro lines
- Light rail lines
- Tram lines
- Bus lines
- ■ Railway stations
- Ⓢ Light rail stations
- Ⓜ Metro stations

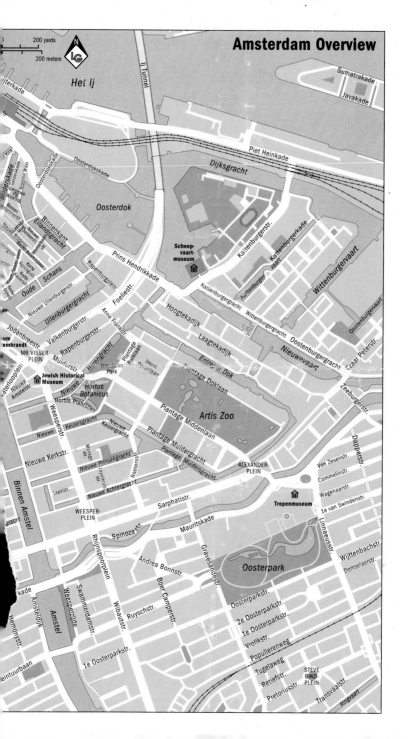

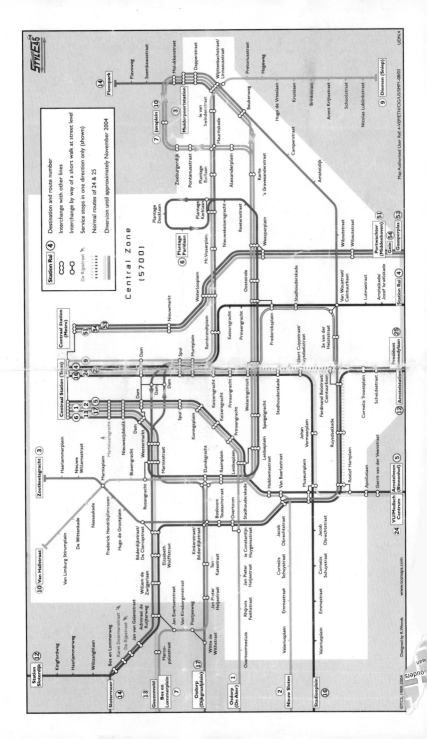

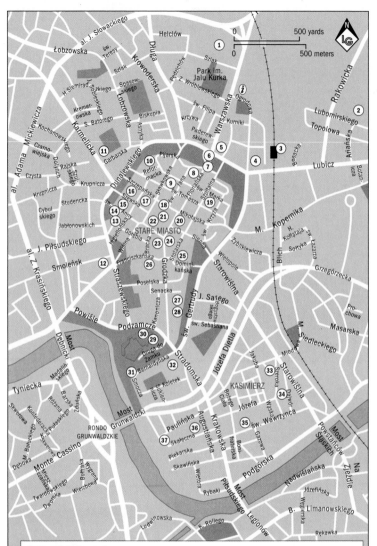

Central Kraków

Akademia Ekonomiczna, **2**
Almatur Office, **24**
Barbican, **6**
Bernardine Church, **32**
Bus Station, **4**
Carmelite Church, **11**
Cartoon Gallery, **9**
City Historical Museum, **17**
Collegium Maius, **13**
Corpus Christi Church, **35**
Czartoryski Art Museum, **8**
Dominican Church, **25**
Dragon Statue, **31**

Filharmonia, **12**
Franciscan Church, **26**
Grunwald Memorial, **5**
Jewish Cemetery, **33**
Jewish Museum, **34**
Kraków Glowny Station, **3**
Monastery of the
  Reformed Franciscans, **10**
Muzeum Historii Fotografii, **23**
Orbis Office, **19**
Pauline Church, **37**
Police Station, **18**
Politechnika Krakowska, **1**

St. Andrew's Church, **28**
St. Anne's Church, **15**
St. Catherine's Church, **36**
St. Florian's Gate, **7**
St. Mary's Church, **20**
St. Peter and Paul Church, **27**
Stary Teatr (Old Theater), **16**
Sukiennice (Cloth Hall), **21**
Town Hall, **22**
University Museum, **13**
Wawel Castle, **29**
Wawel Cathedral, **30**

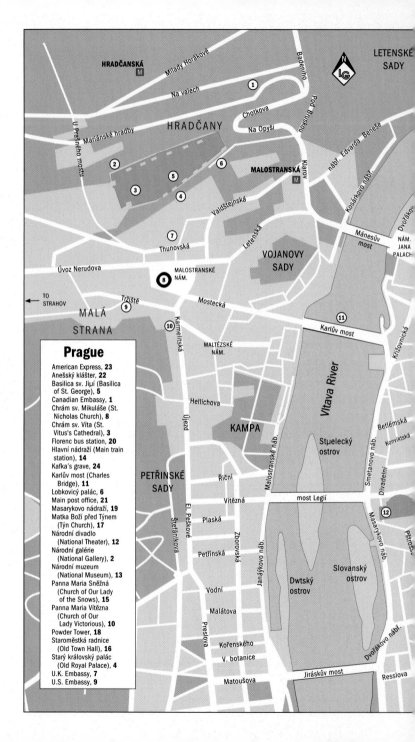

HRADČANSKÁ Ⓜ

LETENSKÉ SADY

Miladv Horákové

Na valech

Chotkova

HRADČANY

Na Opyši

Badeniho

Pod Bruskou

U Prašného mostu

Mariánské hradby

① ② ⑤ ⑥

MALOSTRANSKÁ Ⓜ

③ ④

Klarov

nábř. Edvarda Beneše

Kosárkovo nábř.

Valdštejnská

⑦

Thunovská

Letenská

Mánesův most

NÁM. JANA PALACH

VOJANOVY SADY

Úvoz Nerudova

MALOSTRANSKÉ NÁM.

⑧

TO STRAHOV

Tržiště ⑨

Mostecká

Karlův most ⑪

MALÁ STRANA

⑩

Karmelitská

MALTÉZSKÉ NÁM.

Vltava River

Křižovnická

Hellichova

Újezd

KAMPA

Střelecký ostrov

Betlémská

Konviktská

Malostranské nábř.

Smetanovo nábř.

Divadelní

PETŘINSKÉ SADY

Říční

Vítězná

most Legií

⑫

Masarykovo nábř.

Pštross...

El. Peškové

Plaská

Petřínská

Zborovská

Janáčkovo nábř.

Dvtský ostrov

Slovanský ostrov

Štefánikova

Preslova

Vodní

Malátova

Kořenského

V. botanice

Dvořákovo nábř.

Matoušova

Jiráskův most

Resslova

Prague

American Express, **23**
Anežský klášter, **22**
Basilica sv. Jiljí (Basilica of St. George), **5**
Canadian Embassy, **1**
Chrám sv. Mikuláše (St. Nicholas Church), **8**
Chrám sv. Víta (St. Vitus's Cathedral), **3**
Florenc bus station, **20**
Hlavní nádraží (Main train station), **14**
Kafka's grave, **24**
Karlův most (Charles Bridge), **11**
Lobkovický palác, **6**
Main post office, **21**
Masarykovo nádraží, **19**
Matka Boží před Týnem (Týn Church), **17**
Národní divadlo (National Theater), **12**
Národní galérie (National Gallery), **2**
Národní muzeum (National Museum), **13**
Panna Maria Sněžná (Church of Our Lady of the Snows), **15**
Panna Maria Vítězna (Church of Our Lady Victorious), **10**
Powder Tower, **18**
Staroměstská radnice (Old Town Hall), **16**
Starý královský palác (Old Royal Palace), **4**
U.K. Embassy, **7**
U.S. Embassy, **9**

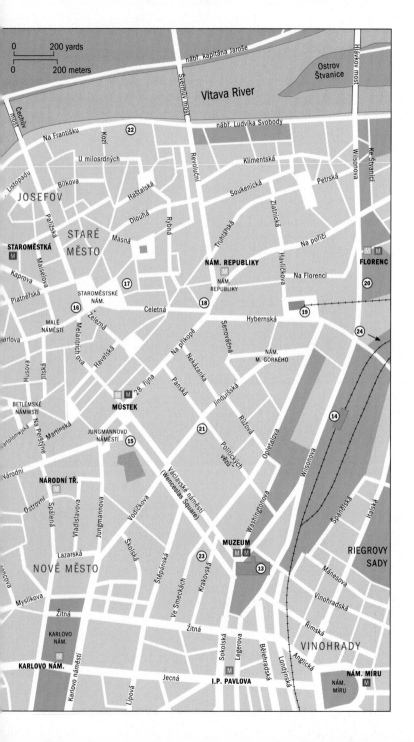

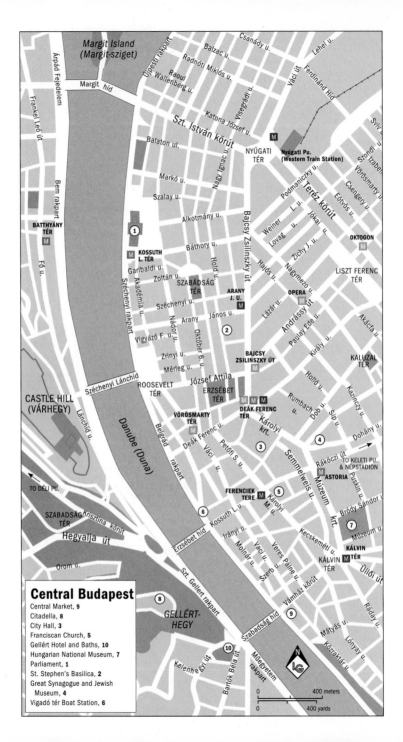

Central Budapest

Central Market, **9**
Citadella, **8**
City Hall, **3**
Franciscan Church, **5**
Gellért Hotel and Baths, **10**
Hungarian National Museum, **7**
Parliament, **1**
St. Stephen's Basilica, **2**
Great Synagogue and Jewish
  Museum, **4**
Vigadó tér Boat Station, **6**

Margit Island
(Margit-sziget)

Árpád Fejedelem

Margit híd

Frankel Leó út

Bem rakpart

Fő u.

BATTHYÁNY
TÉR
Ⓜ

CASTLE HILL
(VÁRHEGY)

TO DÉLI PU.

SZABADSÁG
TÉR

Hegyalja út

Orom u.

Kelenhegyi út

Bartók Béla út

GELLÉRT-
HEGY

Krisztina körút

Széchenyi Lánchíd

Lánchíd u.

Danube (Duna)

Belgrád rakpart

Szt. Gellért rakpart

Műegyetem
rakpart

Üpesti rakpart

Csanády u.

Balzac u.

Radnóti Miklós u.

Raoul
Wallenberg u.

Katona József u.

Visegrádi u.

Szt. István körút

Balaton ul.

Markó u.

Szalay u.

Nagy Ignác u.

Alkotmány u.

Báthory u.

NYÚGATI
TÉR

Ⓜ Nyúgati Pu.
(Western Train Station)

Lehel u.

Váci út

Ferdinánd híd

Sviv

Szondi

Szondi Izabell

Vörösmarty u.

Csengery u.

Eötvös u.

Podmaniczky u.

Teréz körút

Jókai u.

Weiner

Lovag

L. u.

OKTOGON
Ⓜ

KOSSUTH
L. TÉR
Ⓜ

Garibaldi u.

Zoltán u.

Akadémia u.

Széchenyi rakpart

SZABÁDSÁG
TÉR

Hold u.

Bajcsy Zsilinszky út

Haós u.

Zichy J. u.

Nagymező u.

ARANY
J. U.
Ⓜ

OPERA
Ⓜ

Andrássy út

LISZT FERENC
TÉR

Akácfa u.

Széchenyi u.

Nádor u.

Arany

Október 6 u.

János u.

Vigyázó F. u.

Zrinyi u.

Mérleg u.

Lázár u.

Paulay Ede u.

Király u.

KALUZAL
TÉR

②

BAJCSY
ZSILINSZKY ÚT
Ⓜ

ROOSEVELT
TÉR

József Attila

ERZSÉBET
TÉR

Holló u.

Rumbach u.

Dob u.

Síp u.

Kazinczy u.

Dohány u.

VÖRÖSMARTY
TÉR
Ⓜ

DEÁK FERENC
TÉR
Ⓜ Ⓜ Ⓜ

Károlyi
krt.

④

Deák Ferenc u.

Petőfi S. u.

Váci u.

③

Semmelweis u.

Rákóczi út

TO KELETI PU.
& NÉPSTADION

ASTORIA
Ⓜ

Múzeum

Puskin u.

Bródy Sándor u.

FERENCIEK
TERE
Ⓜ

Károlyi
M. u.

⑤

⑥

Kossuth L. u.

Irányi u.

Váci u.

Veres Pálne u.

Szerb u.

Molnár u.

Kecskeméti u.

⑦

Múzeum krt.

KÁLVIN
TÉR

KÁLVIN Ⓜ TÉR

Üllői út

Ráday u.

Erzsébet híd

Vámház körút

⑧

⑨

Szabadság híd

Mátyás u.

Lónyay u.

Közraktár u.

⑩

0   400 meters

0   400 yards

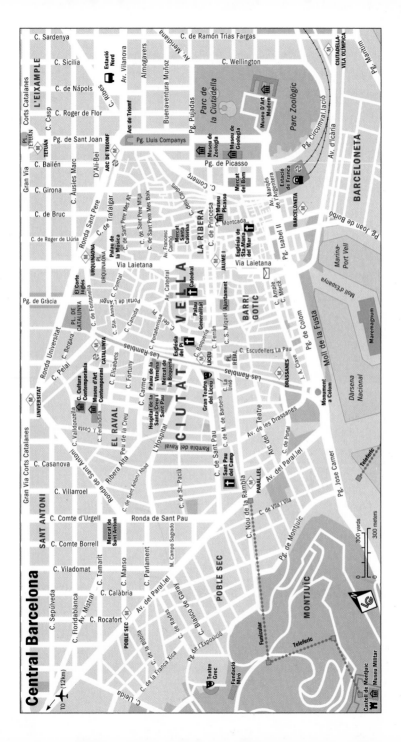

Barcelona Metro

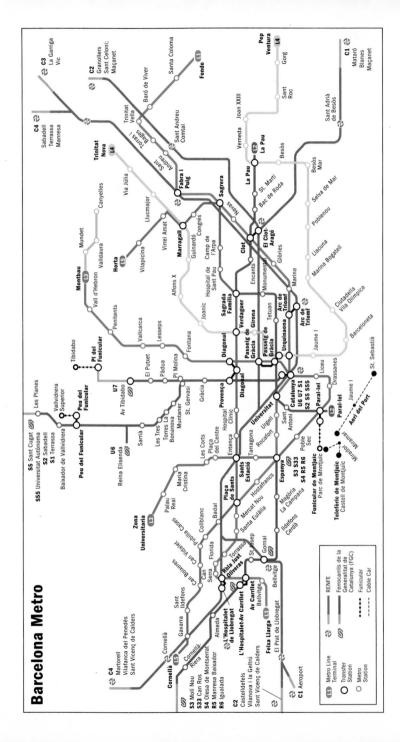

Berlin Transit

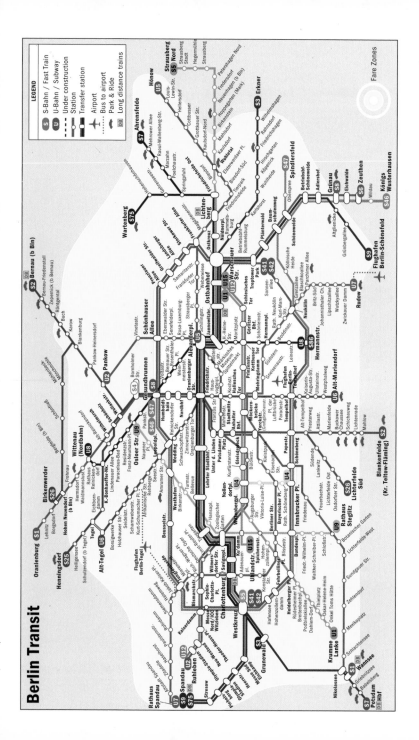

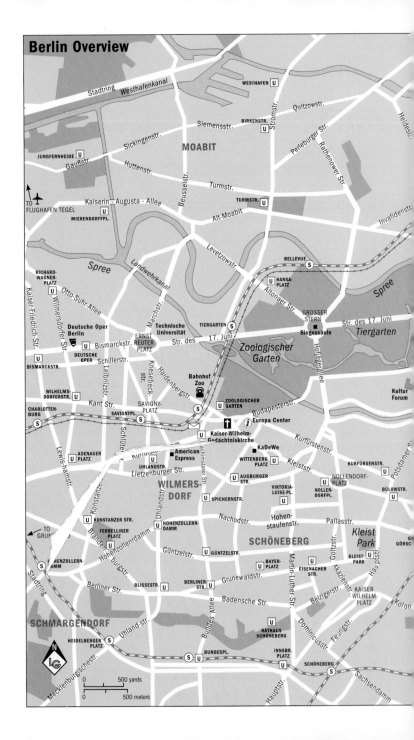

Berlin Overview

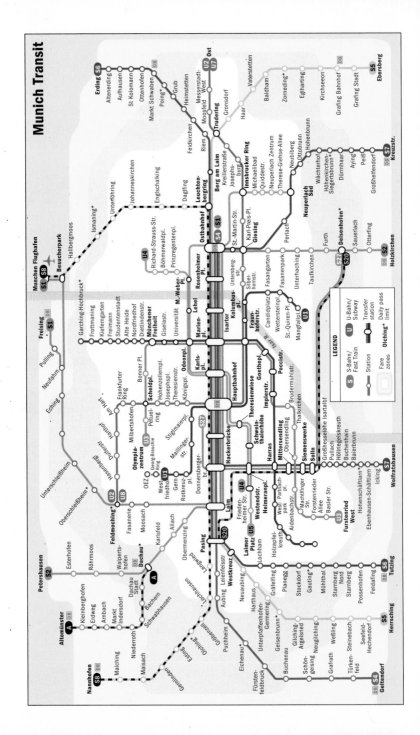

Munich Transit

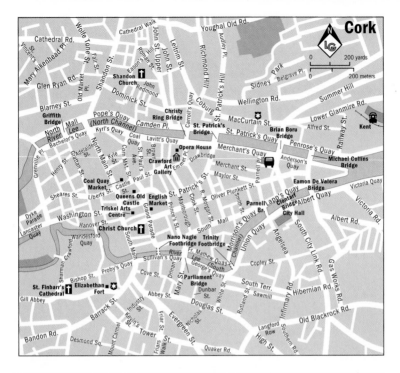

Cork

Cathedral Rd.
Cathedral Walk
Youghal Old Rd.
Wolfe Tone St.
Cathedral Rd.
John St. Upper
John St.
Audley Pl.
Leitrim St.
Richmond Hill
St. Vincent's
Mary Aikenhead Pl.
Fair Hill
John Redmond
Roman St.
Shandon St.
Sidney Park
Belgrave Pl.
Glen Ryan Rd.
Old Market Pl.
Shandon Church
John St.
Wellington Rd.
Summer Hill
Dominick St.
Coburg St.
Blarney St.
Pope's Quay (North Channel)
Camden Pl.
Carroll's Quay
MacCurtain St.
Lower Glanmire Rd.
Griffith Bridge
North Mall
Christy Ring Bridge
St. Patrick's Bridge
St. Patrick's Quay
Brian Boru Bridge
Alfred St.
Kent
River Lee
Bachelor's Quay
Kyrl's Quay
Lavitt's Quay
Penrose's Quay
Railway St.
Grenville Pl.
North Main St.
Coal Quay
Opera House
Merchant's Quay
Anderson's Quay
Michael Collins Bridge
Henry St.
Sheares St.
Corn Mkt. St.
Drawbridge
Emmet Pl.
Merchant St.
Maylor St.
Crawford Art Gallery
Coal Quay Market
St. Paul's St.
Castle St.
St. Patrick's St.
Oliver Plunkett St.
Eamon De Valera Bridge
Lapp's Quay
Victoria Quay
Liberty St.
Adelaide St.
Queens Old Castle
English Market
Cook St.
R. Morgan St.
Parnell Pl.
Lapp's Quay Br.
Clontarf Bridge
Albert Quay
Victoria Quay
Dyke Parade
Washington St.
Triskel Arts Centre
Grand Parade
Marlborough St.
Prince's St.
Morrison's Quay
City Hall
Albert Rd.
Lancaster Quay
Hanover St.
Christ Church
South Mall
Union Quay
Gas Works Rd.
Wandesford Quay
South Main St.
Nano Nagle Footbridge
Trinity Footbridge
Fr. Mathew Quay
Angelsea
South City Link Rd.
Sharman Crawford
Bishop St.
Sullivan's Quay
Lee (South Channel)
George's Quay
Copley St.
Proby's Quay
St. Finbarr's Cathedral
Elizabethan Fort
Mary St.
Drinan St.
White St.
South Terr.
Sawmill
Hibernian Rd.
Old Blackrock Rd.
Gill Abbey
Cove St.
Parliament Bridge
Dunbar St.
Rutland St.
Infirmary Rd.
Barrack St.
Industry St.
Abbey St.
Nicholas St.
Douglas St.
Langford Row
Southern Rd.
Bandon Rd.
Desmond Sq.
Kevin's Tower
Mount Carmel
Friars Walk
Friar St.
Evergreen St.
Quaker Rd.
High St.

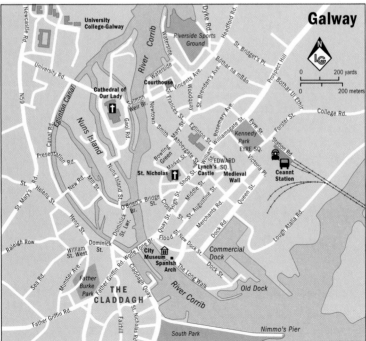

Galway

Newcastle Rd.
University College-Galway
Dyke Rd.
Waterside
River Corrib
Riverside Sports Ground
St. Bridger's Pl.
Prospect Hill
University Rd.
Waterside
Bóthar na mBán
Bóthar Ui Eithir
N59
Courthouse
St. Vincents Ave.
St. Brendan's Ave.
College Rd.
Cathedral of Our Lady
Salmon Weir Br.
Newtown Smyth
Frances St.
St. Brendan's Ave.
Forster St.
Canal Rd.
Eglinton Canal
Nuns Island
Gaol Rd.
Eglinton St.
Rosemary Ave.
Kennedy Park
EYRE SQ.
Station Rd.
Presentation Rd.
Bowling Green
Williamsgate St.
William St.
Victoria Pl.
Ceannt Station
St. Mary's Rd.
Helens St.
New Rd.
Mill St.
Nuns Island St.
Abbeygate
Market St.
St. Nicholas
St. EDWARD SQ.
Lynch's Castle
Medieval Wall
Lough Atalia Rd.
Henry St.
O'Brien's Bridge Br.
Dominick St. Lwr.
Shop St.
Middle St.
Queen St.
Raleigh Row
William St. West
Quay St.
Cross St.
High St.
St. Augustine St.
Merchants Rd.
Dock Rd.
Sea Rd.
Munster Ave.
Dominick St.
Wolfe Tone Br.
Flood St.
New Dock St.
Dock St.
Commercial Dock
Father Burke Park
Father Griffin Rd.
City Museum
Spanish Arch
The Long Walk
Old Dock
THE CLADDAGH
Claddagh Quay
River Corrib
Fairhill
St. Nicholas Rd.
South Park
Nimmo's Pier

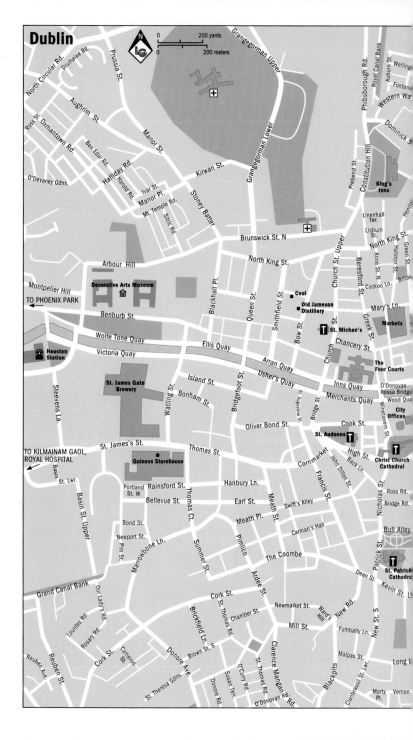

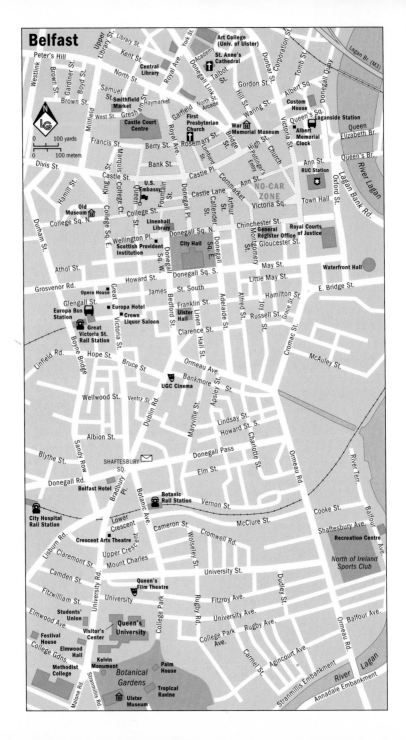

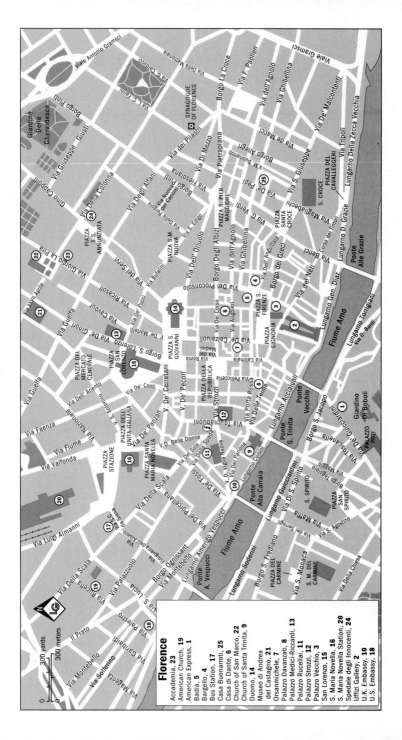

Florence

Accademia, 23
American Church, 19
American Express, 1
Badia, 5
Bargello, 4
Bus Station, 17
Casa Buonarroti, 25
Casa di Dante, 6
Church of San Marco, 22
Church of Santa Trinità, 9
Duomo, 14
Museo di Andrea
del Castagno, 21
Orsanmichele, 7
Palazzo Davanzati, 8
Palazzo Medici-Riccardi, 13
Palazzo Rucellai, 11
Palazzo Strozzi, 12
Palazzo Vecchio, 3
San Lorenzo 15
S. Maria Novella 16
S. Maria Novella Station, 20
Spedale degli Innocenti, 24
Uffizi Gallery, 2
U.K. Embassy, 10
U.S. Embassy, 18

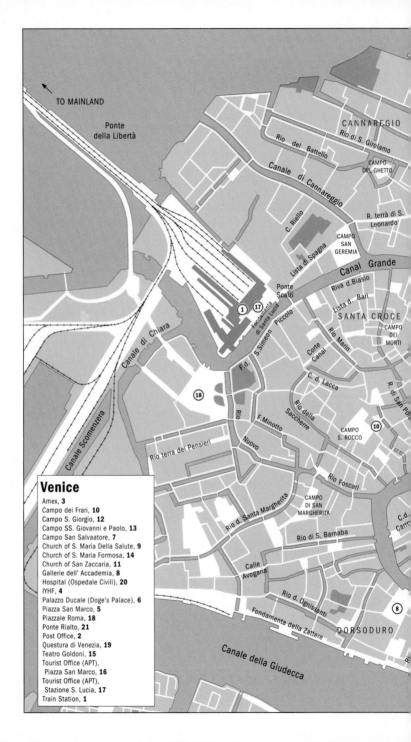

Venice

Amex, **3**
Campo dei Frari, **10**
Campo S. Giorgio, **12**
Campo SS. Giovanni e Paolo, **13**
Campo San Salvaatore, **7**
Church of S. Maria Della Salute, **9**
Church of S. Maria Formosa, **14**
Church of San Zaccaria, **11**
Gallerie dell' Accademia, **8**
Hospital (Ospedale Civili), **20**
IYHF, **4**
Palazzo Ducale (Doge's Palace), **6**
Piazza San Marco, **5**
Piazzale Roma, **18**
Ponte Rialto, **21**
Post Office, **2**
Questura di Venezia, **19**
Teatro Goldoni, **15**
Tourist Office (APT),
 Piazza San Marco, **16**
Tourist Office (APT),
 Stazione S. Lucia, **17**
Train Station, **1**

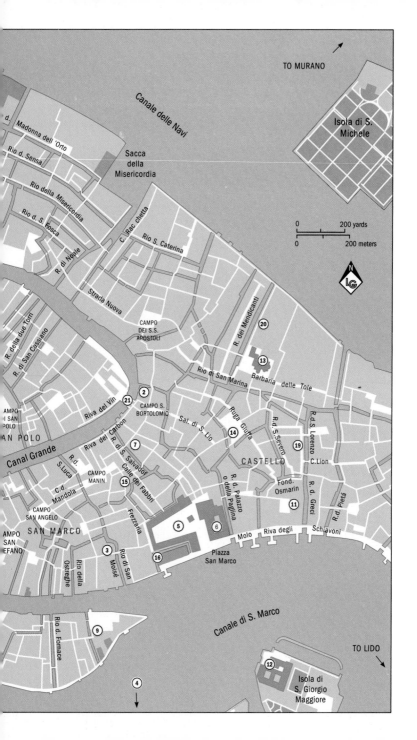

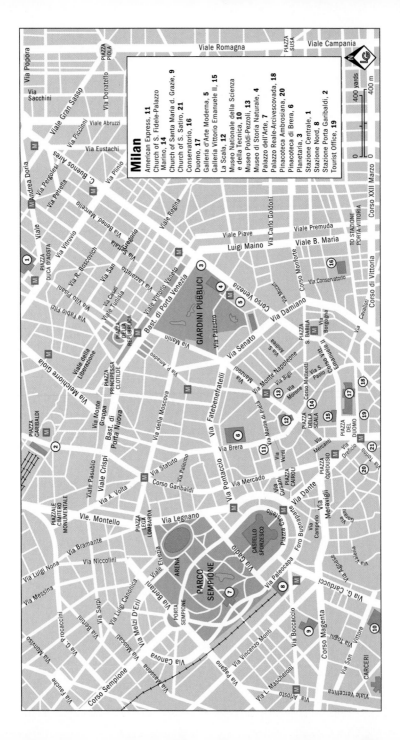

Milin

American Express, **11**
Church of S. Fidele-Palazzo Marino, **14**
Church of Santa Maria d. Grazie, **9**
Church of S. Satiro, **21**
Conservatorio, **16**
Duomo, **17**
Galleria d'Arte Moderna, **5**
Galleria Vittorio Emanuele II, **15**
La Scala, **12**
Museo Nazionale della Scienza e della Tecnica, **10**
Museo Poldi-Pezzoli, **13**
Museo di Storia Naturale, **4**
Palazzo dell'Arte, **7**
Palazzo Reale-Arcivescovada, **18**
Pinacoteca Ambrosiana, **20**
Pinacoteca di Brera, **6**
Planetaria, **3**
Stazione Centrale, **1**
Stazione Nord, **8**
Stazione Porta Garibaldi, **2**
Tourist Office, **19**

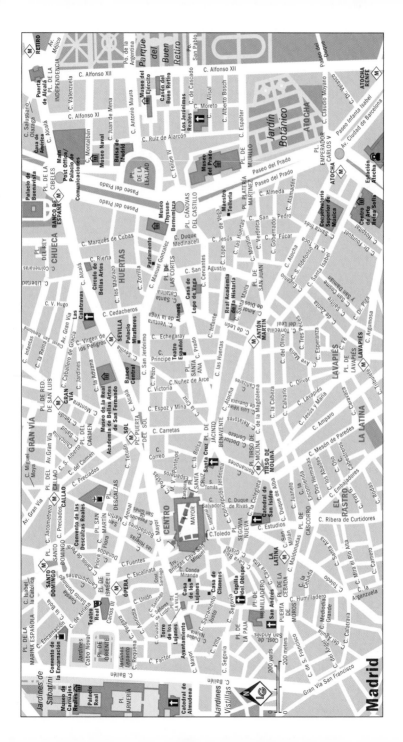

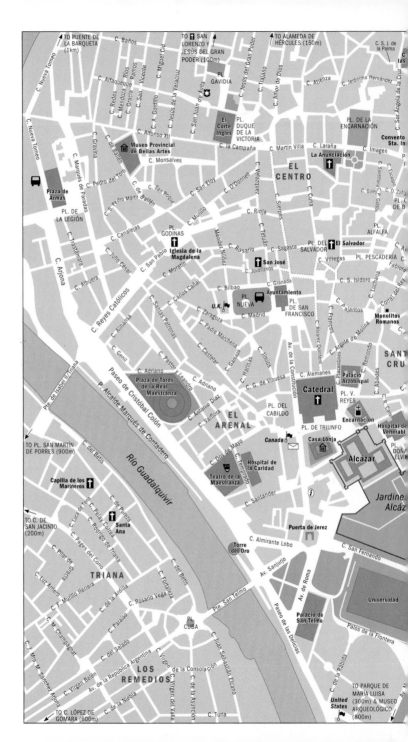

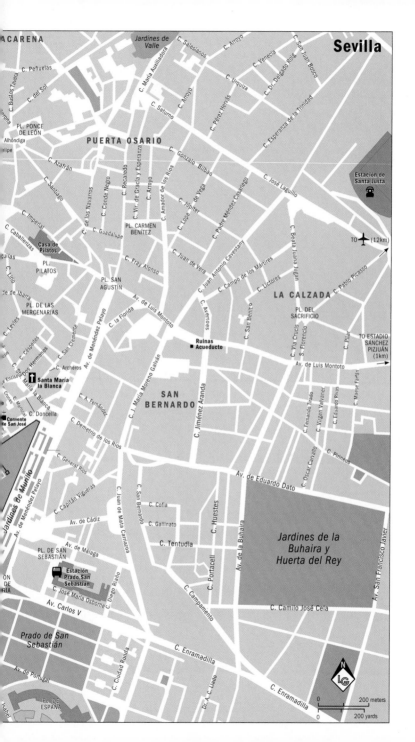

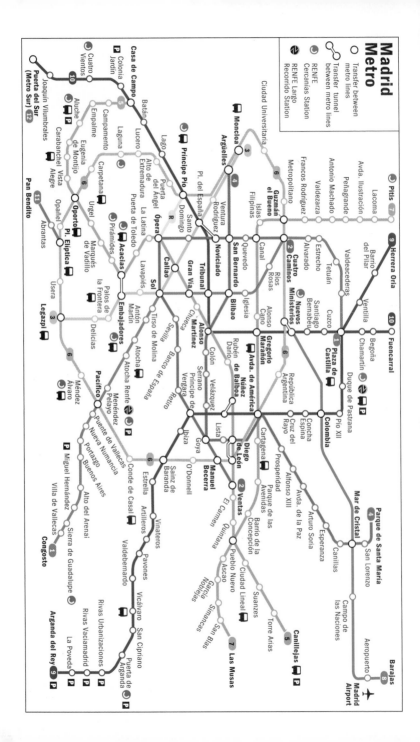

LET'S GO

■ THE RESOURCE FOR THE INDEPENDENT TRAVELER

"The guides are aimed not only at young budget travelers but at the independent traveler; a sort of streetwise cookbook for traveling alone."

—The New York Times

"Unbeatable; good sight-seeing advice; up-to-date info on restaurants, hotels, and inns; a commitment to money-saving travel; and a wry style that brightens nearly every page."

—The Washington Post

"Lighthearted and sophisticated, informative and fun to read. [Let's Go] helps the novice traveler navigate like a knowledgeable old hand."

—Atlanta Journal-Constitution

"A world-wise traveling companion—always ready with friendly advice and helpful hints, all sprinkled with a bit of wit."

—The Philadelphia Inquirer

■ THE BEST TRAVEL BARGAINS IN YOUR PRICE RANGE

"All the dirt, dirt cheap."

—People

"Anything you need to know about budget traveling is detailed in this book."

—The Chicago Sun-Times

"Let's Go follows the creed that you don't have to toss your life's savings to the wind to travel—unless you want to."

—The Salt Lake Tribune

■ REAL ADVICE FOR REAL EXPERIENCES

"The writers seem to have experienced every rooster-packed bus and lunar-surfaced mattress about which they write."

—The New York Times

"A guide should tell you what to expect from a destination. Here Let's Go shines."

—The Chicago Tribune

"[Let's Go's] devoted updaters really walk the walk (and thumb the ride, and trek the trail). Learn how to fish, haggle, find work—anywhere."

—Food & Wine

LET'S GO PUBLICATIONS

TRAVEL GUIDES

Alaska 1st edition **NEW TITLE**
Australia 2004
Austria & Switzerland 2004
Brazil 1st edition **NEW TITLE**
Britain & Ireland 2004
California 2004
Central America 8th edition
Chile 1st edition
China 4th edition
Costa Rica 1st edition
Eastern Europe 2004
Egypt 2nd edition
Europe 2004
France 2004
Germany 2004
Greece 2004
Hawaii 2004
India & Nepal 8th edition
Ireland 2004
Israel 4th edition
Italy 2004
Japan 1st edition **NEW TITLE**
Mexico 20th edition
Middle East 4th edition
New Zealand 6th edition
Pacific Northwest 1st edition **NEW TITLE**
Peru, Ecuador & Bolivia 3rd edition
Puerto Rico 1st edition **NEW TITLE**
South Africa 5th edition
Southeast Asia 8th edition
Southwest USA 3rd edition
Spain & Portugal 2004
Thailand 1st edition
Turkey 5th edition
USA 2004
Western Europe 2004

CITY GUIDES

Amsterdam 3rd edition
Barcelona 3rd edition
Boston 4th edition
London 2004
New York City 2004
Paris 2004
Rome 12th edition
San Francisco 4th edition
Washington, D.C. 13th edition

MAP GUIDES

Amsterdam
Berlin
Boston
Chicago
Dublin
Florence
Hong Kong
London
Los Angeles
Madrid
New Orleans
New York City
Paris
Prague
Rome
San Francisco
Seattle
Sydney
Venice
Washington, D.C.

COMING SOON:
Road Trip USA

EUROPE

2004

TABBY GEORGE EDITOR

EMILIE S. FITZMAURICE ASSOCIATE EDITOR
DAVID HAMBRICK ASSOCIATE EDITOR
PAUL G. KOFOED ASSOCIATE EDITOR
MATTHEW C. LYNCH ASSOCIATE EDITOR
REBECCA PARGAS ASSOCIATE EDITOR
CHRISTOPHER J. REISIG ASSOCIATE EDITOR

RESEARCHER-WRITERS
SLOAN J. EDDLESTON
DAVID HAMMER
DEFNE OZGEDIZ

TIM SZETELA MAP EDITOR
MATTHEW HUDSON MANAGING EDITOR

ST. MARTIN'S PRESS ❧ NEW YORK

Maps by David Lindroth copyright © 2004 by St. Martin's Press.

Distributed outside the USA and Canada by Macmillan.

ISBN: 0-312-31984-3

First edition
10 9 8 7 6 5 4 3 2 1

Let's Go: Europe is written by Let's Go Publications, 67 Mount Auburn Street, Cambridge, MA 02138, USA.

ABOUT LET'S GO

GUIDES FOR THE INDEPENDENT TRAVELER

Budget travel is more than a vacation. At *Let's Go*, we see every trip as the chance of a lifetime. If your dream is to grab a knapsack and a machete and forge through the jungles of Brazil, we can take you there. Or, if you'd rather enjoy the Riviera sun at a beachside cafe, we'll set you a table. If you know what you're doing, you can have any experience you want—whether it's camping among lions or sampling Tuscan desserts—without maxing out your credit card. We'll show you just how far your coins can go, and prove that the greatest limitation on your adventure is not your wallet, but your imagination. That said, we understand that you may want the occasional indulgence after a week of hostels and kebab stands, so we've added "Big Splurges" to let you know which establishments are worth those extra euros, as well as price ranges to help you quickly determine whether an accommodation or restaurant will break the bank. While we may have diversified, our emphasis will always be on finding the best values for your budget, giving you all the info you need to spend six days in London or six months in Tasmania.

BEYOND THE TOURIST EXPERIENCE

We write for travelers who know there's more to a vacation than riding double-deckers with tourists. Our researchers give you the heads-up on both world-renowned and lesser-known attractions, on the best local eats and the hottest nightclub beats. In our travels, we talk to everybody; we provide a snapshot of real life in the places you visit with our sidebars on topics like regional cuisine, local festivals, and hot political issues. We've opened our pages to respected writers and scholars to show you their take on a given destination, and turned to lifelong residents to learn the little things that make their city worth calling home. And we've even given you Alternatives to Tourism—ideas for how to give back to local communities through responsible travel and volunteering.

OVER FORTY YEARS OF WISDOM

When we started, way back in 1960, Let's Go consisted of a small group of well-traveled friends who compiled their budget travel tips into a 20-page packet for students on charter flights to Europe. Since then, we've expanded to suit all kinds of travelers, now publishing guides to six continents, including our newest guides: *Let's Go: Japan* and *Let's Go: Brazil*. Our guides are still annually researched and written entirely by students on shoe-string budgets, adventurous travelers who know that train strikes, stolen luggage, food poisoning, and marriage proposals are all part of a day's work. Even as you read this, work on next year's editions is well underway. Whether you're reading one of our new titles, like *Let's Go: Puerto Rico* or *Let's Go Adventure Guide: Alaska*, or our original best-seller, *Let's Go: Europe*, you'll find the same spirit of adventure that has made *Let's Go* the guide of choice for travelers the world over since 1960.

GETTING IN TOUCH

The best discoveries are often those you make yourself; on the road, when you find something worth sharing, please drop us a line. We're Let's Go Publications, 67 Mt. Auburn St., Cambridge, MA 02138, USA (feedback@letsgo.com).

For more info, visit our website: www.letsgo.com.

V

HOW TO USE THIS BOOK

If you're reading this, you're probably about to embark on a grand tour of Europe—maybe your first, maybe your seventeenth. For the 44th year in a row, *Let's Go: Europe* is here to guide you to the grandest cathedrals, the cleanest hostels, and the finest €1.20 wines. Things are changing in Europe: You can now travel between half the countries on the continent without so much as pulling out your passport, and you're more likely to come across an Internet terminal than a coin-operated pay phone. It's a pretty different place than you may remember—but we've been keeping up. Whether you're a long-time expat or an international newbie, the freshly reformatted and always updated *Let's Go: Europe 2004* will tell you everything you need to know.

ORGANIZATION. *Let's Go: Europe* is arranged to make the information you need easy to find. The **Discover** chapter offers highlights of the region, tips on when to travel (including a calendar of festivals), and suggested itineraries. **Essentials** details the nitty-gritty of passports, money, communications, and more–everything you'll need to plan your trip and stay safe on the road. The **Transportation** section will get you to and around Europe, while **Alternatives to Tourism** gives advice on how to work or volunteer your way across the continent. Next come 36 jam-packed **country chapters,** from Andorra to Ukraine; each begins with essential information on traveling in that specific country. At the back is a **language appendix** (p. 1051), a crash course in local dialects to help you navigate along your way.

PRICE RANGES AND RANKINGS. Our researchers list establishments in order of value from best to worst. Our absolute favorites are denoted by the *Let's Go* thumbs-up (🖑). Since the best value does not always mean the cheapest price, we have incorporated a system of **price ranges** (❶❷❸❹❺) into our coverage of accommodations and restaurants. At a glance, you can compare the cost of a night's stay in towns a mile apart or halfway across the country. The price ranges for each country can be found in the introductory sections of each chapter, and for more information on what to expect from each ranking, see **p. 22**.

NEW FEATURES. Long-time readers will notice a number of other changes in our series, most notably the sidebars that accompany much of our coverage. At the end of the book, you'll find a series of longer **Scholarly Articles** focused on issues affecting Europe as a whole. Whether read on a long train ride or a quiet hostel, we hope these articles will entertain as well as inform.

ENJOY YOUR TRIP. Need we say more?

A NOTE TO OUR READERS The information for this book was gathered by *Let's Go* researchers from May through August of 2003. Each listing is based on one researcher's opinion, formed during his or her visit at a particular time. Those traveling at other times may have different experiences since prices, dates, hours, and conditions are always subject to change. You are urged to check the facts presented in this book beforehand to avoid inconvenience and surprises.

CONTENTS

GREECE (ELLAV) 492

HUNGARY (MAGYARORSZÁG) 527

ICELAND (ÍSLAND) 549

REPUBLIC OF IRELAND AND NORTHERN IRELAND 561

MAPS

ACKNOWLEDGMENTS

TEAM EUROPE THANKS: Matt Hudson, for being everything good and right in a managing editor—trusting, competent, and supportive to the end. Our mapper Tim, for careful work and a calm presence. Our beloved podmates, Eastern Europe, who preached Cyrillic like a preacher, full of ecstasy and fire. Europe RWs Dave, Defne, and Sloan, for outstanding attitude, excellent research, and valued friendship. Prod for so, so much help. Country guides, whose hard work and dedication made this book possible—and so much better.

TABBY THANKS: Above all my AEs, who made a top-notch team and dear friends: Becca for constant cheerfulness; Chris for smart work; Dave, whose patience is limitless; Emilie, the most can-do person I know; Matt for breaking the tension at all the right moments; and Paul for vegan-tastic chillness and a grounding perspective. Matt Hudson, an outstanding ME and a better friend. Mom, Dad, and Maggie for so much love; all of my friends, who fill my life with happiness.

EMILIE THANKS: Tabby, for her expert navigation and graceful leadership; Becca, Chris, Dave, Matt & Paul, for making me forget I was at work; my RWs, Dave, Defne, and Sloan, for their unfaltering devotion to the books; EEUR, for keeping us sane late at night; my family, for conceiving me in the spirit of travel; and always Dan, who is the sunlight in my growing.

DAVE THANKS: Tabby for dedication and supportive leadership; Chris, Emilie, Paul, Matt L., and Becca for making this a wonderful experience; the EEUR team for help and humor; Betsy and John for friendship and fun times; Mom and Dad for love; and Amy for being a fantastic and fabulous sister.

MATT THANKS: Tabby for commandeering the ship/train; Chris, Emilie, Paul, Becca, and Dave for being good neighbors; Mom, Dad, Adam and Abbie for everything; Christine for countless lunches, Thompson for Euro-advice, Leigh for always keeping in touch, and Ravs for always keeping it real.

PAUL THANKS: Tabby for bumps and sets; the boat crew for blood-curdling monkeys, communal food, and wisdom; Mom and Dad for roadtrips and words, background and foreground; Russ, Seana, and Eric for family matters; Reid, who likes to ride his bicycle; Wendy: Yawp!; and Ruthy, for the spring in my step.

BECCA THANKS: Tabby for amazing dedication; the W/EUR team—Chris, Dave, Emilie, Matt H., Matt L., and Paul—for being fabulous; HPF and my roomies for belly-aching laughs; Jorge for walks; Dan for duets; Mama, Papa, Rafa, Ate Rica & Mike, for patience (Mahal ko kayo!); and George, ever curious, forever listening.

CHRIS THANKS: Tabby for always leading by example; thank you for this incredible opportunity; Becca, Dave, Emilie, Matt, Matt H., and Paul—you made this a great summer; may you never have to format again. Pat, for sanity through it all; Mom and John, for always being there; And Gena, always my silver lining.

TIM THANKS: The Europod for leading me through this continent; Mapland for all of the work you've put into making and editing the maps throughout this guide. And thanks always to April, Tony, Rachel, Mom, and Dad.

RESEARCHER-WRITERS

David Hammer *Finland and Sweden*

A savvy traveler and veteran warrior of the road, Dave brought a keen eye and keener wit to his coverage of Sweden and Finland. Moving with ease from cosmopolitan Stockholm and Helsinki to the pristine wilds above the Arctic Circle, Dave took his coverage in stride, whether scoping the hottest bars or playing golf under the midnight sun.

Defne Ozgediz *Iceland and Norway*

Satisfying a long-held Scandinavian fascination, Defne trekked through Norway and Iceland, hunting down popular nightspots, unpopulated wilderness, and elusive sights with indefatigable spirit and grace. Traveling past glaciers and volcanoes, from the peaks of mountains to the base of a fjord, Defne sent in pristine, thorough research.

REGIONAL EDITORS AND RESEARCHER-WRITERS

LET'S GO: AMSTERDAM

Andrew A. M. Crawford	*Editor*
Miranda I. Lash	*Associate Editor*
Irin Carmon	*Researcher-Writer*
John Hulsey	*Researcher-Writer*
Linda Li	*Researcher-Writer*

LET'S GO: AUSTRIA AND SWITZERLAND

Patrick Blanchfield	*Editor*
Chris Townsend	*Associate Editor*
Brent A. Butler	*Researcher-Writer*
Alison Giordano	*Researcher-Writer*
Helen Human	*Researcher-Writer*
Patrick Salisbury	*Researcher-Writer*
Lacey Whitmire	*Researcher-Writer*

LET'S GO: BARCELONA

Stef Levner	*Editor*
Megan Moran-Gates	*Associate Editor*
Scott Michael Coulter	*Researcher-Writer*
Emilie Faure	*Researcher-Writer*
Manuela S. Zoninsein	*Researcher-Writer*

LET'S GO: BRITAIN

Tiffany Hsieh — *Researcher-Writer*

LET'S GO: PARIS

Abigail K. Joseph	*Editor*
Megan Moran-Gates	*Associate Editor*
William Lee Adams	*Researcher-Writer*
Neasa Coll	*Researcher-Writer*
Brendan McGeever	*Researcher-Writer*

LET'S GO: ROME

Matthew W. Mahan	*Editor*
Miranda I. Lash	*Associate Editor*
Vedran Lekic	*Researcher-Writer*
Michael Squire	*Researcher-Writer*
Elizabeth Thrall	*Researcher-Writer*

LET'S GO: SPAIN, PORTUGAL, AND MOROCCO

Catherine M. Phillips	*Editor*
Kathryn A. Russon	*Associate Editor*
R. Kang-Xing Jin	*Associate Editor*
Peter M. Brown	*Researcher-Writer*
Megan Creydt	*Researcher-Writer*
Marla B. Kaplan	*Researcher-Writer*
Caroline Luis	*Researcher-Writer*
Naresh Ramarajan	*Researcher-Writer*
Chris Starr	*Researcher-Writer*
Sarah Thomas	*Researcher-Writer*

LET'S GO: WESTERN EUROPE

Sloan Eddleston	*Researcher-Writer*

CONTRIBUTING WRITERS

Derek Glanz   *Knockin' on EU's Door (p. 1061)*

Derek Glanz is currently earning a Ph.D. in political science and was an editor for *Let's Go: Spain and Portugal 1998*.

Jeremy Faro   *With or Without EU (p. 1062)*

Jeremy Faro is is currently a master's student in European Studies and has worked in the past on *Let's Go: Britain & Ireland*.

Publishing Director
Julie A. Stephens
Editor-in-Chief
Jeffrey Dubner
Production Manager
Dusty Lewis
Cartography Manager
Nathaniel Brooks
Design Manager
Caleb Beyers
Editorial Managers
Lauren Bonner, Ariel Fox,
Matthew K. Hudson, Emma Nothmann,
Joanna Shawn Brigid O'Leary,
Sarah Robinson
Financial Manager
Suzanne Siu
Marketing & Publicity Managers
Megan Brumagim, Nitin Shah
Personnel Manager
Jesse Reid Andrews
Researcher Manager
Jennifer O'Brien
Web Manager
Jesse Tov
Web Content Director
Abigail Burger
Production Associates
Thomas Bechtold, Jeffrey Hoffman Yip
IT Directors
Travis Good, E. Peyton Sherwood
Financial Assistant
R. Kirkie Maswoswe
Associate Web Manager
Robert Dubbin
Office Coordinators
Abigail Burger, Angelina L. Fryer,
Liz Glynn
Director of Advertising Sales
Daniel Ramsey
Senior Advertising Associates
Sara Barnett, Daniella Boston
Advertising Artwork Editor
Julia Davidson, Sandy Liu
President
Abhishek Gupta
General Manager
Robert B. Rombauer
Assistant General Manager
Anne E. Chisholm

PRICE RANGES >> EUROPE

①②③④⑤

Our researchers list establishments in order of value from best to worst; our favorites are denoted by the *Let's Go* thumbs-up (☒). Since the best value does not always come at the cheapest price, we have incorporated a system of price ranges to tell you how an establishment compares to others in the same country on a strictly cost-related basis. Our price ranges are based on a rough estimation of what you will pay. For **accommodations,** we base our price range on the cheapest amount a single traveler can spend for a one-night stay. For **restaurants** and other dining establishments, we approximate the average amount that you will pay for a meal in that restaurant. The table below tells you what you will *typically* find in Europe at the corresponding price range; keep in mind that a particularly expensive ice cream stand may still only be marked a ❷, depending on what you will spend.

ACCOMMODATIONS	WHAT YOU'RE *LIKELY* TO FIND
❶	Camping; most dorm rooms, such as you'll find in HI or other hostels, or university dorm rooms. Expect bunk beds and a communal bath; you may have to provide or rent towels and sheets.
❷	Upper-end hostels or small hotels. You may have a private bathroom, or there may be a sink in your room and a communal shower in the hall.
❸	A small room with a private bath. Should have decent amenities, such as a phone and TV. Breakfast may be included in the price of the room.
❹	Similar to 3, but may have more amenities or be in a more convenient or touristed area.
❺	Large hotels or upscale chains. If it's a 5 and it doesn't have the perks you want, you've paid too much.
FOOD	**WHAT YOU'RE *LIKELY* TO FIND**
❶	Mostly street-corner stands, pizza places, or fast-food joints. Occasionally a sit-down meal in Eastern Europe, rarely in Western Europe.
❷	Sandwiches, appetizers at a bar, or low-priced entrees. You may have the option of sitting down or getting take-out.
❸	Mid-priced entrees, possibly coming with soup or salad. A tip will bump you up a couple dollars, since you'll probably have a waiter or waitress.
❹	A somewhat fancy restaurant or a steakhouse. Either way, you'll have a special knife. Few restaurants in this range have a dress code, but some may look down on t-shirt and jeans.
❺	Upscale restaurant, generally specializing in regional fare, with a decent wine list. Slacks and dress shirts may be expected.

DISCOVER EUROPE

The most popular tourist destination in the world, Europe offers as many unique journeys as it has travelers to take them. The continent's fame is age-old, and some things never change. Aspiring writers still spin impassioned romances in Parisian alleyways; a glass of *sangría* at twilight on the Plaza Mayor tastes as sweet as ever; and iconic treasures, from the onion domes of St. Basil's cathedral to the behemoth slabs of Stonehenge, inspire wonder in another generation. But against this ancient backdrop plays a continent at the beginning of a new act. With the emergence of the European Union, these distinct nations are more intimately connected than ever before.

The results are impressive: Emerging cities like Kraków and Stockholm challenge the elder statesmen of Rome, Prague, and Vienna for international prominence and travelers' attention. New cultural showpieces like Bilbao's Guggenheim and London's Tate Modern complement timeless galleries and architectural shrines like the Louvre and the Hermitage, and fashion-forward locals and a constant influx of students keep the nightlife as hot as the innumerable beaches. Whether it's the pubs of Dublin, the upscale bistros of Lyon, the calm hills of Switzerland, or the dazzling beaches of Croatia's Dalmatian Coast that call to you, *Let's Go: Europe 2004* has the answer.

Average Temp. and Precipitation	January			April			July			October		
	°C	°F	in	°C	°F	in	°C	°F	in	°C	°F	in
Amsterdam	5/1	41/34	3.1	11/4	53/40	1.5	20/12	69/55	2.9	13/7	57/46	4.1
Athens	12/6	55/44	1.9	18/11	66/52	0.9	31/22	89/73	0.2	22/15	73/60	2.1
Berlin	1/-3	35/26	1.6	12/2	54/37	1.6	22/13	73/56	2.0	13/5	56/42	1.0
Budapest	2/-3	36/25	1.2	15/5	60/41	1.5	26/15	79/59	2.3	15/6	59/43	1.4
Copenhagen	2/-1	37/30	1.7	9/2	49/36	1.6	20/12	69/55	2.6	11/6	53/44	2.1
Dublin	7/2	46/37	2.5	11/5	52/41	1.9	18/12	66/54	2.6	12/7	55/46	2.9
Kraków	0/-5	33/22	1.3	12/3	54/38	1.9	21/12	71/55	3.5	12/4	55/40	1.7
London	7/2	45/36	2.4	12/5	55/41	1.7	22/13	72/56	1.8	14/7	58/46	2.9
Madrid	10/0	51/32	1.8	17/5	63/42	1.8	32/16	90/61	0.4	20/8	68/47	1.8
Moscow	-6/-11	21/11	1.4	9/1	49/34	1.5	21/12	71/55	3.2	7/0	45/33	2.0
Paris	6/1	43/34	0.2	13/5	57/42	0.2	23/14	75/58	0.2	15/7	59/46	0.2
Prague	1/-4	34/24	0.8	12/2	54/36	1.4	22/12	72/54	2.6	12/3	54/39	1.2
Rome	12/3	55/39	3.2	17/8	63/47	2.6	28/18	83/66	0.6	21/13	71/56	4.5
Stockholm	0/-5	31/22	1.2	8/0	47/31	1.1	21/12	70/54	2.5	8/3	48/38	2.0
Vienna	2/-2	36/27	1.5	13/5	57/41	2.0	25/15	77/59	2.9	13/6	57/43	1.9

WHAT TO DO

Let's be honest—we've never met you, we don't know where we'd take you on our first date, and we certainly don't know what'll make your dream vacation. So we've compiled a few launching pads from which you can start drawing up a custom itinerary: **Themed categories** to let you know where to find your museums, your mountains, your madhouses; **Let's Go Picks** to point you toward some of the quirkiest gems you could uncover; and **suggested itineraries** to outline the common paths across Europe. After getting a general idea of the continent, turn to the country-specific **Discover** sections at the beginning of each chapter for more detailed info.

MUSEUM MANIA

Europe's most precious artifacts reside in her museums; nearly every city houses a sculpture, a painting, or a relic recognized the world over. **London** (p. 144) is packed with artistic gems, not least of which are the imperialist spoils at the British Museum and the striking Tate Modern Gallery. On the other side of the Channel, **Paris** (p. 327) is equally well-stocked—although you could spend half your life at the Louvre, you'd have to take some breaks to visit the Musée d'Orsay, the Musée Rodin, and the endearingly garish Pompidou Centre. For museums designed with as much artistic inspiration as their collections, try Spain's Guggenheim Museum in **Bilbao** (p. 977), and the Dalí Museum in **Figueres** (p. 968). **Madrid** (p. 908) preserves the world's largest collection of paintings in the Prado, while the Reina Sofía shelters Picasso's overpowering *Guernica*.

Florence (p. 667) was the home of the Renaissance and still retains many of its masterworks in the Uffizi and the Accademia. The Vatican Museums in **Rome** (p. 603) house the Sistine Chapel and other priceless works of sculpture and art. Celebrate Germany's reunification at the East Side Gallery in **Berlin** (p. 416), built around the longest remaining stretch of the Wall. **Munich** (p. 475) boasts the technological Deutsches Museum and the twin Pinakotheks; if those don't raise your spirits, try **Hamburg**'s Erotic Art Museum (p. 449). The biggest sin you could commit in **Amsterdam** (p. 737) would be to overlook the Rijksmuseum and the van Gogh Museum. **Moscow**'s Kremlin once contained the secrets to an empire; it still holds the legendary Fabergé eggs (p. 869). The Hermitage, in **St. Petersburg,** has the world's largest art collection (p. 880). **Budapest**'s Museum of Fine Arts houses little-seen but nonetheless spectacular works by Raphael, Rembrandt, and the rest of the usual suspects (p. 539). And lastly, the finest museum in the Baltics is the Occupation Museum in **Rīga** (p. 698), detailing the lengthy Soviet occupation.

⊠ LET'S GO PICKS: NOT YOUR MIDDLE SCHOOL FIELD TRIP

HEY NOW, YOU'RE A ROCK STAR: Experience sex, drugs, and rock 'n' roll at Copenhagen's **Museum Erotica** (p. 281), Liverpool's **The Beatles Story** (p. 191), and Amsterdam's **Cannabis College** (p. 748).

CRIME AND PUNISHMENT: First hit Rome's **Museo Criminologico** (p. 626), which displays the tools of Italy's terrorists, spies, and druggies; then head to the **Museo Della Tortura** (p. 677) in San Gimignano, Italy, for a lesson in Medieval torture devices.

BEST-HUNG EXHIBITS: Reykjavik's **Phallalogical Museum** (p. 557) has the manhoods of over 100 mammals and will soon acquire its first human specimen.

MOST MEMORABLE (UNTIL THE MORNING): Learn as you drink at Dublin's **Guinness Brewery** (p. 572) and Moscow's **Russian Vodka Museum** (p. 882).

RUINS AND RELICS

For those who prefer to meet history outside of a museum case, Europe's castles, churches, and ruins are a dream come true. In **London** (p. 144), royals wander around Buckingham Palace, while choirboys croon at Westminster Abbey. Venture away from the city to ponder the mysteries of **Stonehenge** (p. 178). Nobody could miss **Paris**'s (p. 327) breathtaking Cathédrale de Notre-Dame. Elsewhere in France, the *châteaux* of the **Loire Valley** (p. 364) and Normandy's fortified abbey of **Mont-St-Michel** (p. 359) are must-sees, as is the fortress of **Carcassonne** (p. 375). Man-made treasures are strewn throughout Spain, including the largest Gothic cathedral in the world in **Seville** (p. 934) and the luxurious Palacio Real in **Madrid** (p. 908). **Barcelona** (p. 952) sports fanciful Modernism, headlined by Antoni Gaudí's La Sagrada Familia and Park Gaudí. Muslim-infused Andalucía offers the mosque in **Córdoba** (p. 929) and the Alhambra in **Granada** (p. 944). And although Morocco is not *technically* in Europe, **Fez**'s Bou Inania Madrasa (p. 728) competes with any attraction north of Gibraltar.

Germany's marvels include the cathedral at **Cologne** (p. 457) and the pure gold tea house at **Potsdam**'s breathtaking Schloß Sanssouci (p. 439). Go a little crazy in Mad King Ludwig's castles (p. 485), or try to figure out Denmark's **Kværndrup** (p. 288) and the optical illusion that makes the castle of Egeskov Slot float on water. **Rome** (p. 603) practically invented architecture as we know it, beginning with the Pantheon, Colosseum, and Forum. In Greece, the crumbling Acropolis—the foundation of Western civilization—towers above **Athens** (p. 496). Journey to the navel of the ancient world to learn your fate from the oracle at **Delphi** (p. 505) or the temple of Apollo on **Delos** (p. 519). **Prague** Castle (p. 260) has been the seat of the Bohemian government for 1000 years, but the kaleidoscopic onion domes of St. Basil's Cathedral in **Moscow** (p. 869) are the true emblem of Eastern Europe.

■ LET'S GO PICKS: PEOPLE MAKE THE DARNDEST THINGS

REALLY, REALLY, RIDICULOUSLY NOT NEW: Ireland's **Newgrange** tomb, and the bones inside it, have been around since the 4th millennium BC (p. 575).

MOST LIKELY TO BE GONE TILL NOVEMBER: Sweden's **IceHotel** melts away each April, only to be built anew by the craftiest team of ice sculptors in the world (p. 1009).

BEST WAY TO JUST EAT IT: Head to the Szabó Marzipan **Museum and Confectionary** in Budapest, where it don't matter if you're black or a **white chocolate statue of Michael Jackson** (p. 541).

BADDEST TO THE BONE: See what remains of Évora's **Capela dos Ossos** (Chapel of Bones; p. 834), built by Franciscan monks from the bones of 5000 people.

THE GREAT OUTDOORS

You've seen the Eiffel Tower. You've been to the British Museum. Now it's time to heed the call of the wild. Britain brims with national parks; our favorite is the **Lake District** (p. 196). For jagged peaks and crashing waves, head north to Scotland; the **Outer Hebrides** (p. 219) are particularly breathtaking. Ireland's **Ring of Kerry** (p. 582) is home to secluded Irish villages, and **Killarney National Park** (p. 581) features spectacular mountains. The majestic Pyrenees are the setting for Spain's **Parque Nacional de Ordesa** (p. 970). **Grenoble** (p. 395), in the French Alps, brims with hiking opportunities and tempts skiers with some of the world's steepest slopes. North of Sicily, the **Aeolian Islands** (p. 691) boast pristine beaches, dramatic volcanoes, and bubbling thermal springs. The dramatic **Tatra** mountain range stretches across Eastern Europe; the trails from the Slovak Republic's **Starý Smokovec** (p. 892) are especially rewarding. Get lost in Europe's largest national park, **Hohe Tauern** (p. 102), and then ski in style at Austria's **Kitzbühel** (p. 106). For fresh Swiss Alpine air, conquer the **Matterhorn** (p. 1029) or take up adventure sports in **Interlaken** (p. 1027). Soak up the scenery of southern Germany, then hike through the eerie **Black Forest** (p. 474), which inspired the Brothers Grimm. Western **Norway** (p. 764) is splintered by dramatic fjords and glaciers, all open for exploration. At the end of your trip, soak your weary feet in the warm mineral mud of Iceland's **Blue Lagoon** (p. 558).

▨ LET'S GO PICKS: LIVING ON THE EDGE

BEST WAYS TO HANG OUT: Cliff-diving is so much more fun when you're naked, according to Corfu's **Pink Palace** (p. 515). And be sure to stop and smell the roses, albeit very, very carefully, in **Lokrum**'s nudist botanical garden (p. 245).

SO HOT RIGHT NOW. If you can't take the heat, then don't tour the active volcano on the Italian island of **Stromboli** (p. 692).

THE FAST AND THE FURIOUS: Get your heart rate up fleeing the angry *toros* during the festival of **San Fermines** (Running of the Bulls; p. 973) in Pamplona.

BEST PLACE TO GO TO EXTREMES. Try sky diving, paragliding, canyoning, river rafting, or bungee jumping in **Interlaken**, Switzerland (p. 1027).

BACKPACKERS GONE WILD

When the museums close and the sun sets over the mountains, Europe's wildest parties are just beginning. **Edinburgh** (p. 204) has the highest concentration of pubs in Europe, but it's often overlooked for the offerings of **Dublin** (p. 566). When you're all crawled out, join the students of **Oxford** (p. 181) for a night of punting. Or, for a completely different scene, try sipping a strawberry daiquiri on the beach in Portugal's **Lagos** (p. 835), or along Spain's **Costa del Sol,** where hip clubs line the beaches of **Marbella** (p. 943). Don't miss the **Balearic Islands**—there are clubs on **Ibiza** (p. 980) that open at eight in the morning. For the true Spanish experience, join *la Movida* in **Madrid** (p. 908) or try getting into the chic clubs of **Barcelona** (p. 952). Afterward, flaunt your way to the one and only **French Riviera** (p. 382), then let dynamic **Milan** (p. 649) introduce you to Italian style. Head to the Greek islands for the beautiful beaches of **Corfu** (p. 515) and for **Ios** (p. 520), a frat party run amok. The best beaches in Europe, however, lie along Croatia's **Dalmation Coast** (p. 241). **Prague** (p. 250) and **Munich** (p. 475) know that discriminating drinkers don't need a beach to get sloshed, and **Amsterdam** (p. 737)... trust us, it knows everything it needs—and more than you want—to know.

▨ LET'S GO PICKS: BACKPACKERS GONE WILD II

BREAKFAST OF CHAMPIONS: The ragers at **Space** (p. 980) in Ibiza, Spain, begin at 8am and don't stop until 5am the next morning.

EU COME HERE OFTEN? In **Brussels**, Belgium (p. 116), official seat of the European Parliament, a different country throws an international bash each week.

BETTER THAN DRINKIN' ALONE: Join hordes of revelers for Munich's **Oktoberfest** (p. 475); the five million liters of beer aren't going to drink themselves.

SHORTEST DISTANCE BETWEEN KEG AND BED: The bungalow city of **Na Vlachovce** in Prague (p. 250), combines the best of two worlds, offering cozy bedding in romantic two-person *Budvar* barrels.

FÊTES! FESTAS! FESTIVALS!

COUNTRIES	APR. – JUNE	JULY – AUG.	SEPT. – MAR.
AUSTRIA AND SWITZERLAND	Vienna Festival (mid-May to mid-June)	Salzburger Festspiele (late July to late Aug.) Open-Air St. Gallen (late June)	Fasnacht (Basel; Mar. 1-3) Escalade (Geneva; early Dec.)
BRITAIN AND IRELAND	Bloomsday (Dublin; June 16) Wimbledon (London; late June)	Edinburgh Int'l Festival (Aug.15-Sept. 4) Fringe Festival (Aug. 3-25)	Matchmaking Festival (Lisdoonvarna; Sept.) St. Patrick's Day (Mar. 13)
CROATIA	World Festival of Animated Film (Zagreb; May)	Int'l Folklore Festival (July) Dubrovnik Summer Fest. (July and Aug.)	Int'l Puppet Festival (Sept.) Zagreb Fest (Nov.)
CZECH REPUBLIC	Prague Spring Festival (May)	Český Krumlov Int'l Music Fest (Aug.)	Int'l Organ Fest (Olomouc; Sept.)
FRANCE	Cannes Film Festival (May)	Festival d'Avignon (July-Aug.) Bastille Day (July 14) Tour de France (July)	Carnevale (Nice, Nantes; Feb.)
GERMANY	May Day (Berlin; May 1) Christopher St. Day (late June)	Love Parade (Berlin; mid-July) Rhine in Flames Festival (Rhine Valley; Aug. 9)	Fasching (Munich; Jan. 7-Feb. 4) Oktoberfest (Munich; Sept. 18-Oct. 3)
HUNGARY	Golden Shell Folklore (Siófok; June)	Sziget Rock Fest (Budapest; July) Baroque Festival (Eger; July)	Eger Vintage Days (Sept.) Festival of Wine Songs (Pécs; Sept.)
ITALY	Maggio Musicale (Florence; late Apr. to mid-June) Scoppio del Carro (Florence; Easter Su)	Il Palio (Siena; July 2 and Aug. 16) Umbria Jazz Festival (July)	Carnevale (late Feb.) Festa di San Gennaro (Naples; Dec. 16, Sept. 19, May 7) Dante Festival (Ravenna; mid-Sept.)
THE NETHERLANDS	Queen's Day (Apr. 30) Holland Festival (June)	Gay Pride Parade (Aug.)	Flower Parade (Aalsmeer; Sept.) Cannabis Cup (Nov.)
POLAND	Int'l Short Film (Kraków; May) Festival of Jewish Culture (Kraków; June)	Street Theater (Kraków; July) Highlander Folklore (Zakopane; Aug.)	Kraków Jazz Fest (Oct.) Nat'l Blues Music (Toruń; Nov.)
PORTUGAL	Burning of the Ribbons (Coimbra; early May)	Feira Internacional de Lisboa (June) Feira Popular (mid-July)	Carnival (Mar. 4) Semana Santa (Apr. 4-11)
SCANDINAVIA	Midsummer (June 21-23) Bergen Festival (May 21-June 1) Norwegian Wood (Oslo; early June)	Quart Music Festival (Kristiansand; early July) Savonlinna Opera Festival (July 2-July 29)	Helsinki Festival (Aug. 22-Sept. 7)
SPAIN	Feria de Abril (Seville; late Apr.)	San Fermines (Pamplona; July 6-14)	Semana Santa (Apr. 4-11) Las Fallas (Valencia; Mar.) Carnaval (Mar.)

DISCOVER

SUGGESTED ITINERARIES
THE BASIC TOUR (1 OR 2 MONTHS)

THE BEST OF EUROPE IN 1 MONTH

Start in **London** (3 days; p. 144), spinning from theater to museum to club, then chunnel to rejuvenating **Paris** (3 days; p. 327). Sample the cuisine of **Lyon** (1 day; p. 398) en route to animated **Barcelona** (2 days; p. 952). Graze the Mediterranean shoreline, hitting the French Riviera in **Nice** (1 day; p. 385) and strolling by the Renaissance art of **Florence** (2 days; p. 667). Discover the one and only **Rome** (3 days; p. 603) before gliding through **Venice** (2 days; p. 633). Break out the clubbing clothes in **Milan** (1 day; p. 649), then don your banker's suit in **Geneva** (1 day; p. 1030). Continue north for a frothy pint in **Munich** (2 days; p. 475) and a cup of coffee in **Vienna** (2 days; p. 80), before following the crowds to enrapturing **Prague** (2 days; p. 250) and hip **Kraków** (2 days; p. 805). Overwhelm yourself in sprawling **Berlin** (2 days; p. 416). Indulge in the goods of **Amsterdam** (2 days; p. 737), then recuperate with a final day in **Brussels** (p. 116).

THE BEST OF EUROPE IN 2 MONTHS

From **London** (4 days; p. 144), catch a cheap flight to energetic **Dublin** (2 days; p. 566). Get studious in **Oxford** (1 day; p. 181), then take in the natural beauty of the **Cotswolds** (1 day; p. 185) en route to elegant **Bath** (2 days; p. 178). Meet the continent in the museums and cafes of **Paris** (4 days; p. 327), and the gorgeous châteaux of the **Loire Valley** (1 day; p. 364). Venture south to worldly **Madrid** (2 days; p. 908) and then hook around to otherworldly **Barcelona** (3 days; p. 952). After a night in **Marseille** (1 day; p. 379), soak in the Riviera's rays at **Nice** (1 day; p. 385). Continue on to the orange roofs of **Florence** (2 days; p. 667) and pause at stunning **Siena** (1 day; p. 676) en route to **Rome** (3 days; p. 603). Wind through **Venice** (2 days; p. 633) on your way to posh **Milan** (1 day; p. 649). Stop in **Lyon** (1 day; p. 398) for your trip's best meal before heading to international **Geneva** (1 day; p. 1030). Scale the Swiss Alps around **Zermatt** (1 day; p. 1029) and **Interlaken** (1 day; p. 1027). Move on to cultured **Zürich** (1 day; p. 1019) and classical **Salzburg** (1 day; p. 94) before taking in an opera in **Vienna** (2 days; p. 80). Go south toward Croatia's beautiful **Dalmatian Coast** and up-and-coming **Dubrovnik** (2 days; p. 243). Soak in the baths of **Budapest** (2 days; p. 531) and then turn back westward to historical **Kraków** (2 days; p. 805). **Prague** (3 days; p. 250) and gorgeous **Český Krumlov** (1 day; p. 267) may convince you never to leave Central Europe, but it's onward for a beer in **Munich** (2 days; p. 475) and a sobering daytrip to nearby **Dachau** (1 day; p. 484). The **Romantic Road** (2 days; p. 489) will steer you to **Berlin** (3 days; p. 416). Head north to cosmopolitan **Copenhagen** (2 days; p. 275) and drop down to restless **Hamburg** (2 days; p. 449). Take a last wild breath in **Amsterdam** (3 days; p. 737), then top off your trip in peaceful **Brussels** (1 day; p. 116).

THE MEDITERRANEAN (37 DAYS)

From **Madrid,** take the high-speed train to flower-filled **Seville** (2 days; p. 934) before partying in the Costa del Sol resort town of **Marbella** (1 day; p. 943). Skip inland to **Granada** (2 days; p. 944), where you'll wind your way through the Moorish Albaicín to the Alhambra. From **Valencia** (2 days; p. 949), island hop in the **Balearic Islands** between the foam parties at **Ibiza** and **Formentera** (2 days; p. 980). Ferry to vibrant **Barcelona** (3 days; p. 952), saving time for a daytrip out to **Costa Brava** and the Dalí museum in **Figueres** (1 day; p. 968). Head to France, stopping first in fortified **Carcassonne** (1 day; p. 375) and then Roman **Arles** (1 day; p. 378). Papal riches await in **Avignon** (1 day; p. 377), culinary delights in **Marseille** (1 day; p. 379). Move on to the glittery Côte d'Azur, soaking in the celebrity of flashy **Cannes** (1 day; p. 383) and the Riviera's capital, **Nice** (2 days; p. 385). If you have any money left, blow it at the world-famous **Monte-Carlo** casino (1 day; p. 391). Take a break from your vacation in Italy's restful **Finale Ligure** (2 days; p. 659) and snap photos in **Pisa** (1 day; p. 678) before David-hopping through **Florence**'s magnificent art collections (3 days; p. 667). Check out the two-tone *duomo* of

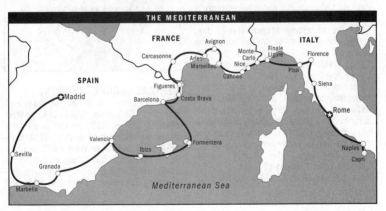

THE MEDITERRANEAN

FRANCE — Avignon — Monte-Carlo — Finale Ligure — ITALY — Florence
Carcassonne — Arles — Nice — Pisa
Marseilles — Cannes
SPAIN — Figueres — Siena
Madrid — Barcelona — Costa Brava
Valencia — Rome
Ibiza — Formentera
Sevilla — Naples
Granada — Capri
Marbella
Mediterranean Sea

Siena (2 days; p. 676) and find a forum for all things ancient in **Rome** (4 days; p. 603). From **Naples** (2 days; p. 682), home of pizza and pickpockets, finish off your trip in sun-drenched **Capri** (2 days; p. 688). Or, continue your journey using the Greece and Turkey itinerary.

THE ENGLISH CHANNEL (29 DAYS)
After visiting **London** (4 days; p. 144), punt on the Isis in **Oxford** (1 day; p. 181). From there, explore elegant **Bath** (1 day; p. 178) before strolling in the quaint **Cotswolds** (1 day; p. 185). Check out Shakespeare's hometown, **Stratford-upon-Avon** (1 day; p. 184). Breeze through **Manchester** (1 day; p. 189) on your way to Beatles worship in **Liverpool** (1 day; p. 190). Cross the Irish Sea to **Dublin** (2 days; p. 566), home to James Joyce and Guinness, and then discover the charming villages of rural Ireland in the **Ring of Kerry** (2 days; p. 582). From **Galway** (1 days; p. 586), a center of Irish culture, forge on to neighborly **Belfast** (2 days; p. 590). From there, it's back across the Irish Sea to Stranraer, trainbound for historic **Edinburgh** (2 days; p. 204) and the sublime **Lake District** (2 days; p. 196). Head back to London and hop a train for carefree **Paris** (4 days; p. 327). Use **Tours** (2 days; p. 366) as a hub for exploring the fertile **Loire Valley** before pressing on to **Rennes** (1 day; p. 360). The fortified island of **Mont-St-Michel** (1 day; p. 359) gives you a chance to stretch your legs and imagination before you settle into the seaside paradise of **St-Malo** (2 days; p. 361). A train will whisk you back to Paris and your homebound airline of choice. But should your craving *française* persist, a train to **Marseille** (p. 379) leaves you at the heart of the Mediterranean itinerary.

CENTRAL EUROPE (31 DAYS)
Begin in glamorous, Bohemian **Prague** (3 days; p. 250), then stop in stately **Wrocław** (1 day; p. 812) on the way to the seaport of **Gdańsk** (1 day; p. 816). Continue to no-nonsense **Warsaw** (2 days; p. 796), then to trendy **Kraków** (2 days; p. 805). Hike in the Tatra Mountains surrounding **Zakopane** (2 days; p. 811) and

Starý Smokovec (1 day; p. 892). Next, visit vibrant **Budapest** (3 days; p. 531), followed by the warm, shallow waters of **Lake Balaton** (2 days; p. 547). Wander the streets of **Zagreb** (2 days; p. 237), then stop over in **Sarajevo** (2 days; p. 135) before returning to Croatia to explore the heavenly islands of the **Dalmatian Coast** (3 days; p. 241), between Dubrovnik and Split. Continue on to lovely **Ljubljana** (2 days; p. 898), then experience the grandeur of **Vienna** (3 days; p. 80), ending up in blossoming **Bratislava** (2 days; p. 888).

GREECE AND TURKEY (28 DAYS)

Get off the ferry at **Corfu** (1 day; p. 515), beloved by literary luminaries and partiers alike, then continue on to **Patras** (1 day; p. 506). Discover the mysteries of love in the ruins of **Corinth** (1 day; p. 509), and a jumble of things ancient and modern in chaotic **Athens** (2 days; p. 496). Party all night long in the **Cyclades**—fast-paced **Mykonos** (p. 518), sacred **Delos** (p. 519), and the earthly paradise of **Santorini** (4 days; p. 520). Catch the ferry to **Crete,** where chic **Iraklion** and **Knossos,** home to the Minotaur, await (2 days; p. 521). Base yourself in **Rethymno** or **Hania** and hike the spectacular **Samaria Gorge** (2 days; p. 522). Backtrack to Iraklion to catch the ferry to the Dodecanese, hitting historical **Rhodes** (2 days; p. 525) and partying in **Kos** (1 day; p. 525).

THE BALTIC SEA (22 DAYS)

Begin in the bustling, medieval streets of **Tallinn** (2 days; p. 298), then relax on the tranquil and secluded **Estonian Islands** (4

days; p. 302). Move on to lively **Tartu,** the oldest city in the Baltics (2 days; p. 302), before immersing yourself in glitzy **Rīga** (2 days; p. 696). Head down the coast of Lithuania to **Palanga, Klaipėda,** and dreamy **Nida** (3 days; p. 711). Continue to up-and-coming **Vilnius** (2 days; p. 706), one of the many "New Pragues," then wake up from the night train in **Moscow**'s historic Red Square (4 days; p. 862). Cap it off spending some time in **St. Petersburg,** home of the ornate delights of the Hermitage (3 days; p. 874). Connect to the Scandinavian route via Helsinki.

SCANDINAVIA (21 DAYS)

From modern **Copenhagen** (4 days; p. 275), daytrip to the glorious Elsinore castle in **Helsingør** (1 day; p. 284). Head to Sweden through **Malmö** (1 day; p. 1002) to reach luxurious **Gothenburg** (2 days; p. 1004). Zip to Norway's bustling capital,

DISCOVER

Oslo (2 days; p. 769), and take the Oslo-Bergen railway to inspiring **Bergen** (2 days; p. 778) before plunging into the natural wonders that are **Sognefjord** (1 day; p. 785) and **Geirangerfjord** (1 day; p. 787). Head back to Oslo to catch the night train to Sweden's **Stockholm** (2 days; p. 989), the jewel of Scandinavia's cities. Take a daytrip to **Uppsala** (1 day; p. 998), home of Sweden's oldest university. Hop on the ferry to Finland's **Helsinki** (2 days; p. 308), where east meets west, and end your travels gazing at the scenic marvels surrounding **Savonlinna** (2 days; p. 318). Ferry to Estonia's Tallinn (p. 298) to link with the Baltic Sea itinerary.

ESSENTIALS

ENTRANCE REQUIREMENTS.
Passport (p. 11): Almost always required to visit a European country.
Visa (p. 12): Typically, Western European countries require visas for citizens of South Africa, but not for citizens of Australia, Canada, Ireland, New Zealand, the UK, or the US (for stays shorter than 90 days). Eastern European countries are more likely to require visas. Belarus and Russia require invitations to obtain visas. For specific details, see individual country chapters.
Immunizations (p. 19): Travelers to Europe should be up to date on vaccines for measles, mumps, rubella, diphtheria, tetanus, pertussis, polio, haemophilus influenza B, hepatitis A, and hepatitis B.
Work Permit (p. 12): Required for all foreigners planning to work in Europe, except for citizens of countries in the EU.
Driving Permit (p. 59): Drivers in Europe need an International Driving Permit.

DOCUMENTS AND FORMALITIES

Information on European **consular services** at home, foreign consular services in Europe, and specific entry requirements is located in individual country chapters; it can also be found at at www.towd.com or www.embassyworld.com.

PASSPORTS

REQUIREMENTS. Citizens of Australia, Canada, Ireland, New Zealand, South Africa, the UK, and the US need valid passports to enter European countries and to reenter their own country. Most countries do not allow entrance if the holder's passport expires in under six months. Returning home with an expired passport is illegal and may result in a fine.

NEW PASSPORTS. Citizens of Australia, Canada, Ireland, New Zealand, the UK, and the US can apply for a passport at most post offices, passport offices, or courts of law. Citizens of South Africa can apply for a passport at any Home Affairs office. Any new passport or renewal application must be filed well in advance of the departure date, although most passport offices offer rush services for a very steep fee.

PASSPORT MAINTENANCE. Be sure to photocopy the page of your passport with your photo, as well as any other important documents. Carry one set of copies in a safe place, apart from the originals, and leave another set at home. Consulates also recommend that you carry an expired passport or an official copy of your birth certificate in a part of your baggage separate from other documents.

If you lose your passport, immediately notify the local police and the nearest embassy or consulate of your home government. To expedite its replacement, you will need to know all information previously recorded and show ID and proof of citizenship. In some cases, a replacement may take weeks to process, and it may be valid only for a limited time. Any visas stamped in your old passport will be irretrievably lost. In an emergency, ask for immediate temporary traveling papers that will permit you to reenter your home country. More detailed info regarding lost and stolen passports is available at www.usembassy.it/cons/acs/passport-lost.htm.

ONE EUROPE. The idea of European unity has come a long way since 1958, when the European Economic Community (EEC) was created in order to promote solidarity and cooperation. Since then, the EEC has become the European Union (EU), with political, legal, and economic institutions spanning 15 member states: Austria, Belgium, Denmark, Finland, France, Germany, Greece, Ireland, Italy, Luxembourg, The Netherlands, Portugal, Spain, Sweden, and the UK. In 1999, the EU established **freedom of movement** across 15 European countries—the entire EU minus Ireland and the UK, but plus Iceland and Norway. This means that border controls between participating countries have been abolished and visa policies harmonized. While you're still required to carry a passport (or government-issued ID card for EU citizens) when crossing an internal border, once you've been admitted into one country, you're free to travel to all participating states. Britain and Ireland have also formed a **common travel area,** abolishing passport controls between the UK and the Republic of Ireland. This means that the only time you'll see a border guard within the EU is while traveling between the British Isles and the Continent.

VISAS, INVITATIONS, WORK PERMITS

VISAS. Some countries require a visa—a stamp, sticker, or insert in your passport specifying the purpose of your travel and the permitted duration of your stay—in addition to a valid passport for entrance. Most standard visas cost US$10-70, are valid for one to three months, and must be validated within six months to one year from the date of issue. Many countries grant double-entry visas for a premium. The **Center for International Business and Travel** (CIBT; US ☎800-925-2428; www.cibt.com) secures visas for travel to almost any country for a service charge.

The requirements in the chart below apply only to tourist stays shorter than 90 days. If you plan to stay longer than 90 days, or if you plan to **work or study abroad** (p. 65), your requirements will differ. In any case, check with the nearest embassy or consulate of your desired destination for up-to-date information. US citizens can also consult www.travel.state.gov/foreignentryreqs.html.

Note that the following countries are not listed in this chart: **Andorra, Austria, Belgium, Denmark, Finland, France, Germany, Greece, Iceland, Italy, Liechtenstein, Luxembourg, Morocco, The Netherlands, Norway, Portugal, Slovenia, Spain, Switzerland,** and **Sweden.** These require visas of South Africans, but not for nationals of Australia, Canada, Ireland, New Zealand, the UK, or the US (for stays shorter than 90 days). Also not listed are the **UK, Ireland,** and **Switzerland,** which do not require visas for any of the seven nationalities listed above (including South Africans) for stays shorter than 90 days. Travelers to **Andorra** should contact a French or Spanish embassy with any inquiries, while those going to **Liechtenstein** should contact a Swiss embassy.

INVITATIONS. In addition to a visa, **Belarus** and **Russia** require that visitors from any country obtain an invitation from a sponsoring individual or organization. See country chapters to learn how to acquire invitations. Requirements can change rapidly, so double-check with the appropriate consulate in your home country.

IDENTIFICATION

When you travel, carry two or more forms of identification on your person, including at least one photo ID; a passport combined with a driver's license or birth certificate is usually adequate. Never carry all your forms of ID together; split them up in case of theft or loss, and keep photocopies in your luggage and at home.

DO I NEED A VISA? FOR STAYS OF FEWER THAN 90 DAYS:		AUS	CAN	IRE	NZ	SA	UK	US
	BELARUS	Y*	Y*	Y*	Y*	Y*	Y*	Y*
	BOSNIA	N	N	N	N	Y*	N	N
	BULGARIA	N¹	N¹	N¹	N¹	Y*	N¹	N¹
	CROATIA	N	N	N	N	Y⁰	N	N
	CZECH REP.	Y	Y	N	N	Y	N	N
	ESTONIA	N	Y*	N	N	Y*	N	N
	HUNGARY	Y	N	N	N	Y	N	N
	LATVIA	N	N	N	N	Y	N	N
	LITHUANIA	N	N	N	N	Y	N	N
	POLAND	Y	Y	N	Y	Y	N	N
	ROMANIA	Y	N	N²	Y	Y	N²	N²
	RUSSIA	Y*	Y*	Y*	Y*	Y*	Y*	Y*
	SLOVAK REP.	N	N	N	N	N	N	N¹
	SLOVENIA	N	Y	N	N	Y	N	N
	UKRAINE	Y*	Y	Y	Y*	Y*	Y	Y*

KEY: Y tourist visa required; **Y*** invitation required; **Y⁰** proof of travel required; **N** tourist visa not required; **N¹** visa required for stays longer than 30 days; **N²** visa required for stays longer than 90 days.

ESSENTIALS

TEACHER, STUDENT, AND YOUTH IDENTIFICATION. The **International Student Identity Card (ISIC),** the most widely accepted form of student ID, provides discounts on some sights, accommodations, and transport; access to a 24hr. emergency helpline (in North America call ☎877-370-ISIC; elsewhere call US collect ☎+1 715-345-0505); and insurance benefits for US cardholders (see **Insurance,** p. 22). Applicants must be degree-seeking students of a secondary or post-secondary school and must be at least 12 years old. Because of the proliferation of fake ISICs, some services (particularly airlines) require additional proof of student identity.

The **International Teacher Identity Card (ITIC)** offers teachers the same insurance coverage as well as similar but limited discounts. For travelers who are 25 years old or under but are not students, the **International Youth Travel Card** (**IYTC**) also offers many of the same benefits as the ISIC. Similarly, the **International Student Exchange ID Card (ISE)** provides discounts, medical benefits, and the ability to purchase student airfares.

Each of these identity cards costs US$22 or equivalent. ISIC and ITIC cards are valid for roughly one and a half academic years; IYTC cards are valid for one year from the date of issue. Many student travel agencies (p. 43) issue the cards; for a list of issuing agencies, or for more info, contact the **International Student Travel Confederation (ISTC),** Herengracht 479, 1017 BS Amsterdam, The Netherlands (☎+31 20 421 28 00; www.istc.org).

CUSTOMS

Upon entering a country, you must declare certain items from abroad and pay a duty on the value of those articles if they exceed the allowance established by that country's customs service. Note that goods and gifts purchased at duty-free shops abroad are not exempt from duty or sales tax; "duty-free" merely means that you need not pay a tax in the country of purchase. Duty-free allowances were abolished for travel between EU member states on June 30, 1999, but still exist for those arriving from outside the EU. Upon returning home, you must declare all articles acquired abroad and pay a duty on the value of articles in excess of your home country's allowance. In order to expedite your return, make a list of any valuables brought from home and register them with customs before traveling, and be sure to keep receipts for all goods acquired while abroad.

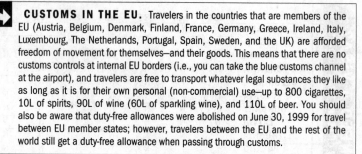

CUSTOMS IN THE EU. Travelers in the countries that are members of the EU (Austria, Belgium, Denmark, Finland, France, Germany, Greece, Ireland, Italy, Luxembourg, The Netherlands, Portugal, Spain, Sweden, and the UK) are afforded freedom of movement for themselves—and their goods. This means that there are no customs controls at internal EU borders (i.e., you can take the blue customs channel at the airport), and travelers are free to transport whatever legal substances they like as long as it is for their own personal (non-commercial) use—up to 800 cigarettes, 10L of spirits, 90L of wine (60L of sparkling wine), and 110L of beer. You should also be aware that duty-free allowances were abolished on June 30, 1999 for travel between EU member states; however, travelers between the EU and the rest of the world still get a duty-free allowance when passing through customs.

MONEY

CURRENCY AND EXCHANGE

As a general rule, it's cheaper to convert money in Europe than at home. However, you should bring enough foreign currency for the first few days of a trip to avoid being cashless if you arrive after bank hours or on a holiday.

When changing money abroad, try to go only to banks or change bureaus that have at most a 5% margin between their buy and sell prices. Since you lose money with every transaction, convert large sums (unless the currency is depreciating rapidly), but no more than you'll need. Use **ATM, debit,** or **credit cards** for the lowest exchange rates.

If you use traveler's checks or bills, carry some in small denominations (the equivalent of US$50 or less) for times when you are forced to exchange money at disadvantageous rates, but bring a range of denominations since charges may be levied per check cashed. Store your money in a variety of forms; ideally, at any given time you will be carrying some cash, some traveler's checks, and an ATM and/or credit card. All travelers should also consider carrying some US dollars (about US$50 worth), which are often preferred by local tellers.

For more info on currency and exchange rates, see individual country chapters.

THE EURO. The official currency of 12 members of the EU—Austria, Belgium, Finland, France, Germany, Greece, Ireland, Italy, Luxembourg, The Netherlands, Portugal, and Spain—is now the euro. The currency has some important—and positive—consequences for travelers hitting more than one euro-zone country. First, money-changers across the euro-zone are obliged to exchange money at the official, fixed rate, and at no commission (though they may still charge a small service fee). Second, euro-denominated traveler's checks allow you to pay for goods and services across the euro-zone, again at the official rate and commission-free. At the time of printing, **€1=US$1.093=CAD$1.513=AUS$1.707= NZ$1.911=ZAR7.992.** For more info, check a currency converter site such as www.xe.com or www.europa.eu.int.

CREDIT, DEBIT, AND ATM CARDS

Where they are accepted, credit cards often offer superior exchange rates—up to 5% better than the retail rate used by banks and other currency exchange establishments. Credit cards may also offer services such as insurance or emergency help, and are sometimes required to reserve hotel rooms or rental cars. **MasterCard** (a.k.a. EuroCard or Access in Europe) and **Visa** (a.k.a. Carte Bleue or Barclaycard) are widely-accepted; **American Express** cards work at some ATMs and at AmEx offices and major airports.

Automatic Teller Machine (ATM) cards are commonplace in Europe. Depending on the system that your home bank uses, you can most likely access your personal bank account from abroad. ATMs get the same wholesale exchange rate as credit cards, but there is often a limit on the amount of money you can withdraw per day (around US$500), and unfortunately computer networks sometimes fail. There is typically also a surcharge of US$1-5 per withdrawal.

Debit cards are as convenient as credit cards but have a more immediate impact on your funds. A debit card can be used wherever its associated credit card company (usually MasterCard or Visa) is accepted, yet the money is withdrawn directly from the holder's checking account. Debit cards often also function as ATM cards and can be used to withdraw cash from associated banks and ATMs throughout Europe. Ask your local bank about obtaining one.

The two major international money networks are **Cirrus** (to locate ATMs US ☎800-424-7787 or www.mastercard.com) and **Visa/PLUS** (to locate ATMs US ☎800-843-7587 or www.visa.com). Most ATMs charge a transaction fee that is paid to the bank that owns the ATM.

PIN NUMBERS AND ATMS. To use a cash or credit card to withdraw money from a cash machine (ATM) in Europe, you must have a four-digit Personal Identification Number (PIN). If your PIN is longer than four digits, ask your bank whether you can just use the first four, or whether you'll need a new one. Credit cards don't usually come with PINs, so if you intend to hit up ATMs in Europe with a credit card to get cash advances, call your credit card company before leaving to request one. People with alphabetic, rather than numerical, PINs may also be thrown off by the lack of letters on European cash machines. The following handy chart gives the corresponding numbers to use: 1=QZ; 2=ABC; 3=DEF; 4=GHI; 5=JKL; 6=MNO; 7=PRS; 8=TUV; and 9=WXY. Note that if you mistakenly punch the wrong code into the machine three times, it will swallow your card for good.

TRAVELER'S CHECKS

Traveler's checks are a relatively safe and convenient means of carrying funds. American Express and Visa are the most widely recognized brands. Many banks and agencies sell them for a small commission. Check issuers provide refunds if the checks are lost or stolen, and many provide services such as toll-free refund hotlines, emergency message services, and stolen credit card assistance. They are readily accepted across Europe. Ask about toll-free refund hotlines and the location of refund centers when purchasing checks, and always carry emergency cash.

American Express: Checks available with commission at select banks, at AmEx offices, and online (www.americanexpress.com; US residents only). AmEx cardholders can also purchase checks by phone (☎888-269-6669). *Cheques for Two* can be signed by either of 2 people traveling together. For purchase locations or more info contact AmEx's service centers: in the US and Canada ☎800-221-7282; in the UK ☎0800 587 6023; in Australia ☎800 68 80 22; in ☎New Zealand 0508 555 358; elsewhere US collect ☎+1 801-964-6665.

Visa: Checks available (generally with commission) at banks worldwide. For the location of the nearest office, call Visa's service centers: in the US ☎800-227-6811; in the UK ☎0800 51 58 84; elsewhere UK collect ☎+44 020 7937 8091.

GETTING MONEY FROM HOME

If you run out of money while traveling, the easiest and cheapest solution is to have someone back home make a deposit to your credit card or cash (ATM) card. Failing that, consider one of the following options.

WIRING MONEY. It is possible to arrange a **bank money transfer,** which means asking a bank back home to wire money to a bank in Europe. This is the cheapest way to transfer cash, but it's also the slowest, usually taking several days or more. Note that some banks may only release your funds in local currency, potentially sticking you with a poor exchange rate; inquire about this in advance. Money transfer services like **Western Union** are faster and more convenient than bank transfers—but also much pricier. Western Union has many locations worldwide. To find one, visit www.westernunion.com, or call: in Australia ☎ 800 501 500, in Canada ☎ 800-235-0000, in New Zealand ☎ 800 27 0000, in South Africa ☎ 0860 100 031, in the UK ☎ 0800 83 38 33, or in the US ☎ 800-325-6000. Money transfer services are also available at **American Express** and **Thomas Cook** offices.

US STATE DEPARTMENT (US CITIZENS ONLY). In dire emergencies only, the US State Department will forward money within hours to the nearest consular office, which will then disburse it according to instructions for a US$15 fee. If you wish to use this service, you must contact the Overseas Citizens Service division of the US State Department (☎ 202-647-5225; Su, nights, and holidays ☎ 202-647-4000).

COSTS

The cost of your trip will vary considerably depending on where you go, how you travel, and where you stay. The most significant expenses will probably be your round-trip (return) **airfare** to Europe (p. 43) and a **railpass** or **bus pass** (p. 51). Before you go, spend some time calculating a reasonable per-day budget that will meet your needs.

STAYING ON A BUDGET. To give you a general idea, the typical first-time, under-26 traveler planning to spend most of their time in Western Europe and then tack on a quick jaunt into Eastern Europe, sleeping in hostels and traveling on a two-month unlimited Eurail pass, can probably expect to spend about US$2000, plus cost of plane fare (US$300-800), railpass (US$882), and backpack (US$150-400). Don't forget to factor in emergency reserve funds (at least US$200).

SAVING MONEY. Some simple ways to save include searching out opportunities for free entertainment, splitting accommodation and food costs with trustworthy fellow travelers, and buying food in supermarkets rather than eating out. Bring a **sleepsack** (p. 23) to save on sheet charges in hostels, and do your **laundry** in the sink (unless you're explicitly prohibited from doing so). With that said, don't go overboard with your budget obsession. Though staying within your budget is important, don't do so at the expense of your health or a great travel experience.

TAXES. The EU imposes a **value-added tax (VAT)** on goods and services, usually included in the sticker price. Non-EU citizens visiting Europe may obtain a **refund** for taxes paid on *unused* retail goods, but not for taxes paid on services. As the VAT is 15-25%, it might be worthwhile to file for a refund. To do so, you must obtain **Tax-free Shopping Cheques,** available from shops sporting the Europe Tax-free Shopping logo, and save your receipts. Upon leaving the EU, present your goods, invoices, and passport to customs and have your checks stamped. Then go to an ETS cash refund office or file for a refund once back home. Keep in mind that goods must be taken out of the country within three months of the end of the month of purchase, and that some stores require minimum purchase amounts to become eligible for a refund.

TIPPING AND BARGAINING

In most European countries, the 5-10% gratuity is already included in the food service bill, but an additional 5-10% tip for very good service is often also polite. Note that in Germany, the tip is handed directly to the server instead of being left on the table. For other services such as taxis or hairdressers, a 10-15% tip is recommended. Watch other customers to guage what is appropriate. Bargaining is useful in Greece and outdoor markets in Italy, Britain, and Ireland. See individual country chapters for more specific information.

SAFETY AND SECURITY

PERSONAL SAFETY

EXPLORING. Respecting local customs (in many cases, dressing more conservatively) may placate would-be hecklers. Familiarize yourself with your surroundings before setting out. Check maps in shops and restaurants rather than on the street. Never admit that you are traveling alone, and be sure someone at home knows your itinerary. When walking at night, stick to busy, well-lit streets and avoid dark alleyways. If you feel uncomfortable, leave as quickly as possible.

SELF-DEFENSE. There is no sure-fire way to avoid all the threatening situations you might encounter when you travel, but a good self-defense course will give you concrete ways to react to unwanted advances. **Impact, Prepare, and Model Mugging** can refer you to local self-defense courses in the US (☎800-345-5425). Visit the website at www.impactsafety.org for a list of nearby chapters. Group workshops (2-3hr.) start at US$50; full courses (20-24hr.) run US$350-500.

TERRORISM AND CIVIL UNREST. In the wake of 9/11, exercise increased vigilance near embassies and be wary of big crowds and demonstrations. Keep an eye on the news, heed travel warnings, and comply with security measures.

Overall, risks of civil unrest tend to be localized and rarely directed toward tourists. Though the peace process in Northern Ireland is progressing, tension tends to surround the July "marching season." Notoriously violent separatist movements include ETA, a Basque group that operates in France and Spain, and FLNC, a Corsican separatist group in France. The November 17 group in Greece is known for anti-Western acts, though they do not target tourists. For now, it is safest to avoid conflict-ridden Macedonia, Serbia, Montenegro, and Bosnia-Herzegovina.

TRAVEL ADVISORIES. The following government offices provide travel info and advisories by phone or via the web:

Australian Department of Foreign Affairs and Trade: ☎13 0055 5135; www.dfat.gov.au.

Canadian Department of Foreign Affairs and International Trade (DFAIT): In Canada and the US ☎800-267-6788; www.dfait-maeci.gc.ca. Call for their free booklet, *Bon Voyage...But.*

New Zealand Ministry of Foreign Affairs: ☎64 4439 8000; www.mft.govt.nz.

United Kingdom Foreign and Commonwealth Office: ☎087 0606 0290; www.fco.gov.uk.

US Department of State: ☎888-407-4747; www.travel.state.gov. For the booklet *A Safe Trip Abroad,* call ☎202-512-1800.

FINANCIAL SECURITY

PROTECTING YOUR VALUABLES. There are a few steps you can take to minimize the financial risk associated with traveling. First, **bring as little with you as possible.** Second, buy a combination **padlock** to secure your belongings either in your pack or in a hostel or train station locker. Third, **carry as little cash as possible.** Keep your traveler's checks and ATM/credit cards in a **money belt**—not a "fanny pack"—along with your passport and ID cards. Finally, **keep a small cash reserve separate from your primary stash.** This should be about US$50 sewn into or stored in the depths of your pack, along with your traveler's check numbers and important photocopies.

CON ARTISTS AND PICKPOCKETS. In large cities **con artists** often work in groups and employ small children. Beware of certain classic scams, including sob stories that require money, rolls of bills "found" on the street, and mustard spilled (or gum spit) onto your shoulder to distract you while they snatch your bag. Don't ever let your bags out of sight. Beware of **pickpockets** in city crowds, especially on public transportation. Also, be alert in public telephone booths: If you must say your calling card number, do so very quietly; if you punch it in, make sure no one can look over your shoulder. Cities such as Rome, Paris, London, Moscow, and Amsterdam have higher rates of petty crime.

ACCOMMODATIONS AND TRANSPORTATION. Never leave your belongings unattended; crime can occur in even the most demure-looking hostel or hotel. Be particularly careful on **buses** and **trains,** as sleeping travelers are easy prey for thieves. When traveling with others, sleep in shifts. When alone, never stay in an empty compartment; use a lock to secure your pack to the luggage rack. Try to sleep on top bunks with your luggage stored above you (if not in bed with you), and keep important documents and other valuables on your person. If traveling by **car,** don't leave valuables in sight while you are away.

DRUGS AND ALCOHOL

Drug and alcohol laws vary widely throughout Europe. In The Netherlands you can buy "soft" drugs on the open market; in much of Eastern Europe drug possession may lead to a heavy prison sentence. If you carry **prescription drugs,** you must carry both a copy of the prescriptions themselves and a note from a doctor, especially at border crossings. **Public drunkenness** is culturally unacceptable and against the law in many countries; it can also jeopardize your safety.

> **!** **TROUBLE WITH THE LAW.** Travelers who run into trouble with the law, knowingly or not, do not retain the rights of their home country; instead, they have the same rights as a citizen of the country they are visiting. The law mandates that police notify the embassy of a traveler's home country if he or she is arrested. In custody, a traveler is entitled to a visit from a consular officer. US citizens should check the Department of State's website (www.travel.state.gov/arrest.html) for more info.

HEALTH AND INSURANCE

BEFORE YOU GO

In your **passport,** write the names of any people you wish to be contacted in case of a medical emergency, and list any allergies or medical conditions. While most prescription and over-the-counter **drugs** are available throughout Europe, matching a prescription to a foreign equivalent is not always easy, safe, or possible, so carry up-to-date, legible prescriptions or a statement from your doctor stating the medication's trade name, manufacturer, chemical name, and dosage. See www.rxlist.com to figure out what to ask for at the pharmacy counter. While traveling, be sure to keep all medication with you in your carry-on luggage. For tips on packing a basic **first-aid kit** and other health essentials, see p. 23.

IMMUNIZATIONS AND PRECAUTIONS. Travelers over two years old should be sure that the following vaccines are up to date: MMR (for measles, mumps, and rubella); DTaP or Td (for diptheria, tetanus, and pertussis); IPV (for polio); and Hib (for haemophilus influenza B). For travelers going to Eastern or Southern Europe, the hepatitis A and typhoid vaccines are recommended; those in contact with blood or other fluids should also consider HBV shots (for hepatitis B). Some countries may deny entrance to travelers arriving from parts of South America and sub-Saharan Africa without a certificate of vaccination for yellow fever. For more **region-specific information** on vaccination requirements, as well as recommendations on immunizations and prophylaxis, consult the CDC (see below) in the US or the equivalent in your home country.

USEFUL ORGANIZATIONS AND PUBLICATIONS. The US **Centers for Disease Control and Prevention (CDC;** US ☎877-394-8747; www.cdc.gov/travel) maintains an international travelers' hotline and an informative website. The **World Health Organization (WHO;** www.who.int/ith) provides disease maps and the free booklet *International Travel and Health.* For the most in-depth country recommendations and a list of travel medicine providers, register with **Travel Health Online** (www.tripprep.com). Consult the appropriate government agency of your home country for consular info sheets on health, entry requirements, and other issues for various countries (see the listings in the box on **Travel Advisories,** p. 17).

For info on medical evacuation services and travel insurance firms, see the US government's website (www.travel.state.gov/medical.html) or the **British Foreign and Commonwealth Office** (www.fco.gov.uk). For detailed info on travel health, including a country-by-country overview of diseases, try the *International Travel Health Guide,* by Stuart Rose, MD (US$12.95; www.travmed.com).

MEDICAL ASSISTANCE ON THE ROAD. While health care systems in Western Europe tend to be quite accessible and of high quality, medical care varies greatly across Eastern and Southern Europe. Major cities such as Prague and Budapest will have English-speaking medical centers or hospitals for foreigners, whereas English-speaking facilities are nearly non-existent in relatively untouristed countries like Belarus or Latvia. Tourist offices may have names of local doctors who speak English. In general, medical service in these regions is not up to Western standards; though basic supplies are always there, specialized treatment is not. Private hospitals tend to have better facilities than state-operated ones. All EU citizens can receive free first-aid and emergency services by presenting an **E111 form** (available at post offices).

If you are concerned about access to medical support while traveling, contact one of these services: **GlobalCare, Inc.** (US ☎800-860-1111; www.globalems.com), which provides 24hr. international medical assistance, support, and medical evacuation resources; or the **International Association for Medical Assistance to Travelers (IAMAT;** US ☎716-754-4883, Canada ☎416-652-0137; www.iamat.org), which has free membership, lists English-speaking doctors worldwide, and offers detailed info on immunization requirements and sanitation. If your regular insurance policy does not cover travel abroad, you may wish to purchase more coverage (p. 22).

Those with medical conditions (diabetes, allergies, epilepsy, heart conditions) may want to get a stainless-steel **Medic Alert** ID tag (first year US$35, US$20 thereafter), which identifies the condition and gives a 24hr. collect-call number. Contact the Medic Alert Foundation (US ☎888-633-4298; www.medicalert.org).

For emergencies and quick info on health and other travel warnings, contact a passport agency, embassy, or consulate abroad; US citizens can also call the **Overseas Citizens Services** (US ☎ 202-647-5225; after-hours US ☎ 202-647-4000).

ONCE IN EUROPE

ENVIRONMENTAL HAZARDS

Heat exhaustion and dehydration: Heat exhaustion can lead to fatigue, headaches, and wooziness. Avoid it by drinking plenty of fluids, eating salty foods (e.g. crackers), and avoiding dehydrating beverages (that contain alcohol or caffeine). Continuous heat stress can eventually lead to heatstroke, characterized by fever, severe headache, and extreme confusion. Victims should be cooled off with wet towels and taken to a doctor.

High altitude: Allow your body a couple of days to acclimate before exerting yourself above 8000 ft. Alcohol is more potent and UV rays are stronger at high elevations.

Hypothermia and frostbite: A rapid drop in body temperature is the clearest sign of overexposure to cold. Victims may also shiver, feel exhausted, have poor coordination or slurred speech, hallucinate, or suffer amnesia. *Do not let hypothermia victims fall asleep.* To avoid hypothermia, keep dry, wear layers, and stay out of the wind. When the temperature is below freezing, watch out for frostbite. If skin turns white, waxy, and cold, do not rub the area. Drink warm beverages, get dry, and slowly warm the area with dry fabric or steady body contact until a doctor can be found.

INSECT-BORNE DISEASES

Many diseases are transmitted by insects—mainly mosquitoes, fleas, ticks, and lice—especially when hiking and camping in wet or forested areas. **Mosquitoes** are most active from dusk to dawn. Wear pants and long sleeves, tuck pants into socks, and sleep in a mosquito net. Use insect repellents such as DEET and spray gear and clothing with permethrin. **Ticks** can give you **Lyme disease,** which is marked by a two-inch bull's-eye on the skin. If you find a tick attached to your skin, grasp it with tweezers as close to the skin as possible and apply slow, steady traction. Left untreated, Lyme disease can cause problems in joints, the heart, and the nervous system. Antibiotics are effective if administered early. Ticks can also give you **encephalitis,** a viral infection. Symptoms can range from headaches and flu-like symptoms to swelling of the brain, but the risk of contracting the disease is relatively low.

FOOD- AND WATER-BORNE DISEASES

Unpeeled fruit and vegetables and tap water should be safe throughout most of Europe, particularly Western Europe. In Southern and Eastern Europe, be cautious of ice cubes and anything washed in tap water, like salad. Other sources of illness are raw meat, shellfish, unpasteurized milk, and sauces containing raw eggs. Buy bottled water, or purify your own water by bringing it to a rolling boil or treating it with **iodine tablets,** especially in Morocco, where food- and water-borne diseases are a common cause of illness.

Traveler's diarrhea: Results from drinking untreated water or eating uncooked foods. Symptoms include nausea, bloating, and urgency. Try quick-energy, non-sugary foods with protein and carbohydrates to keep your strength up. Over-the-counter antidiarrheals (e.g. Imodium) may counteract the problems. The most dangerous side effect is dehydration; drink sweetened, uncaffeinated beverages, and eat salted crackers. If you develop a fever or your symptoms don't go away after 4-5 days, consult a doctor. Consult a doctor immediately for treatment of diarrhea in children.

Hepatitis A: A viral liver infection acquired primarily through contaminated water. An intermediate risk in Eastern Europe, most prevalent in rural areas. Symptoms include fatigue, fever, loss of appetite, nausea, dark urine, jaundice, vomiting, aches and pains, and light stools. Ask your doctor about the vaccine (Havrix or Vaqta) or an injection of immune globulin (IG).

Mad Cow Disease: The human variant, Cruetzfeldt-Jakob disease (nvCJD), is an invariably fatal brain disease. Even in the UK, where the risk is highest, only 1 in 10 billion servings of meat are contaminated. Milk and milk products do not pose a risk.

Parasites: Microbes, tapeworms, etc. that hide in unsafe water and food. **Giardiasis,** for example, is acquired by drinking untreated water from streams or lakes. Symptoms include swollen glands or lymph nodes, fever, rashes or itchiness, and digestive problems. To avoid parasites, boil water, wear shoes, and eat only cooked food.

OTHER INFECTIOUS DISEASES

Hepatitis B: A viral infection of the liver transmitted via bodily fluids or needle-sharing. Symptoms may not surface until years after infection. A three-shot vaccination sequence is recommended for health-care workers, sexually-active travelers, and anyone planning to seek medical treatment abroad; it must begin six months before traveling.

Hepatitis C: Like hepatitis B, but transmitted primarily through exchanges of blood. IV drug users, recipients of blood transfusions and tattoos, those with occupational exposure to blood, and hemodialysis patients are at the highest risk, but the disease can also be spread through sexual contact or by sharing items like razors and toothbrushes that may have traces of blood.

Rabies: Transmitted through the saliva of infected animals; fatal if untreated. By the time symptoms (thirst and muscle spasms) appear, the disease is in its terminal stage. If you are bitten, wash the wound thoroughly, seek immediate medical care, and try to have the animal located. A rabies vaccine, which consists of 3 shots given over a 21-day period, is available but only semi-effective.

AIDS, HIV, AND STIS

For detailed info on **Acquired Immune Deficiency Syndrome (AIDS)** in Europe, call the CDC's 24hr. hotline at US ☎ 800-342-2437, or contact the **Joint United Nations Programme on HIV/AIDS (UNAIDS)** (Switzerland ☎ 22 791 3666; www.unaids.org). Belarus, Bulgaria, Hungary, Russia, Slovak Republic and Ukraine screen incoming travelers for HIV, primarily those planning extended visits for work or study, and deny entrance to those who test HIV-positive. Contact the country's consulate or the CDC in the US (p. 19) for more info.

Sexually-transmitted infections (STIs) such as **gonorrhea, chlamydia, HPV, syphilis,** and **herpes** are easier to catch than HIV and can be just as deadly. Hepatitis B and C can also be transmitted sexually (p. 21). Though condoms may protect you from some STIs, oral or even tactile contact can lead to transmission of others. If you think you may have contracted an STI, see a doctor immediately.

WOMEN'S HEALTH

Women traveling in unsanitary conditions are vulnerable to **urinary tract and bladder infections,** common and very uncomfortable bacterial conditions that cause a burning sensation and painful (sometimes frequent) urination. Over-the-counter medicines can sometimes alleviate symptoms, but if they persist, see a doctor.

Vaginal yeast infections may flare up in hot and humid climates. Wearing loosely fitting clothing and cotton underwear will help, as will over-the-counter remedies like Monistat or Gynelotrimin. Bring supplies from home if you are prone to infection, as they may be difficult to find on the road.

Since **tampons, pads,** and reliable **contraceptive devices** are sometimes hard to find when traveling, bring supplies with you.

ESSENTIALS

INSURANCE

Travel insurance generally covers four basic areas: medical problems, property loss, trip cancellation/interruption, and emergency evacuation. Although your regular insurance policies may well extend to travel-related accidents, you should consider purchasing travel insurance if the cost of potential trip cancellation/interruption or emergency medical evacuation is greater than you can absorb. Prices for travel insurance purchased separately generally run about US$50 per week for full coverage, while trip cancellation/interruption may be purchased separately at a rate of about US$5.50 per US$100 of coverage.

   Medical insurance (especially university policies) often covers costs incurred abroad; check with your provider. **US Medicare** does not cover foreign travel. Canadians are protected by their home province's health insurance plan for up to 90 days after leaving the country; check with the provincial Ministry of Health or Health Plan Headquarters for details. Australians traveling in Finland, Italy, The Netherlands, Sweden, or the UK are entitled to many of the services that they would receive at home as part of the Reciprocal Health Care Agreement. **Homeowners' Insurance** (or your family's coverage) often covers theft during travel and loss of travel documents (passport, plane ticket, railpass, etc.) up to US$500.

   ISIC and **ITIC** (p. 13) provide basic insurance benefits, including US$100 per day of in-hospital sickness for up to 60 days, US$3000 of accident-related medical reimbursement, and US$50,000 for emergency evacuation. Cardholders have access to a toll-free 24hr. helpline (run by insurance provider **TravelGuard**) for medical, legal, and financial emergencies overseas (US and Canada ☎877-370-4742, elsewhere call US collect ☎715-342-4104). **American Express** (US ☎800-338-1670) grants most cardholders automatic car rental insurance (collision and theft, but not liability) and ground travel accident coverage of US$100,000 on flight purchases made with the card.

INSURANCE PROVIDERS. STA (p. 43) offers a range of plans that can supplement your basic coverage. Other US and Canadian providers include **Access America** (☎866-807-3982; www.accessamerica.com), **Travel Guard** (☎800-826-4919; www.travelguard.com), and **International Student Insurance (ISI;** ☎877-328-1565). The UK has **Columbus Direct** (☎084 5330 8518; www.columbusdirect.net), and Australia has **AFTA** (☎02 9264 3299; www.afta.com.au).

PACKING

Pack light: Lay out only what you absolutely need, then take half as many clothes and twice as much money. If you plan to do a lot of hiking, also see **Camping and the Outdoors** (p. 28) for tips on what to pack.

LUGGAGE. If you plan to cover most of your itinerary by foot, a sturdy **frame backpack** is unbeatable. (For the basics on buying a pack, see p. 29.) Toting a **suitcase** or **trunk** is fine if you plan to live in one or two cities and explore from there, but a very bad idea if you're going to be moving around a lot. In addition to your main piece of luggage, a **daypack** (a small backpack or courier bag) is a must.

CLOTHING. No matter when you're traveling, it's always a good idea to bring a **warm jacket** or wool sweater, a **rain jacket** (Gore-Tex is both waterproof and breathable), sturdy shoes or **hiking boots,** and **thick socks. Flip-flops** or waterproof sandals are must-haves for grubby hostel showers. You may also want to add one outfit beyond jeans and a t-shirt, and maybe a nicer pair of shoes if you have the room. If you plan to visit any religious or cultural sites, remember that you'll need something besides tank tops and shorts to be respectful.

SLEEPSACK. Some hostels require that you either provide your own linen or rent sheets from them. Save cash by making your own sleepsack: Fold a full-size sheet in half the long way, then sew it closed along the long side and one short side. Remember: a sleeping bag is *not* a sleepsack, and will not pass for one.

ELECTRONICS. In Europe, electricity is 230V AC, enough to fry any 120V North American appliance. Americans and Canadians should buy an adapter (which changes the shape of the plug; US$10) and a converter (which changes the voltage; US$10-15). Don't make the mistake of using only an adapter (unless appliance instructions state otherwise). New Zealanders, South Africans, and Australians won't need a converter, but will require an adapter. The website www.kropla.com/electric.htm has comprehensive info on what you'll need.

FIRST-AID KIT. For a basic first-aid kit, pack: Bandages, pain reliever, antibiotic cream, a thermometer, a Swiss Army knife, tweezers, moleskin, decongestant, motion-sickness remedy, upset-stomach or diarrhea medication (Pepto Bismol or Imodium), an antihistamine, sunscreen, insect repellent, and burn ointment.

FILM. Film and developing in Europe are expensive, so consider bringing enough film for your entire trip and developing it at home. Less serious photographers may want to bring a **disposable camera** or two rather than an expensive permanent one. Despite disclaimers, airport security X-rays *can* fog film, so buy a lead-lined pouch at a camera store or ask security to hand-inspect it. Always pack film in your carry-on luggage, since higher-intensity X-rays are used on checked luggage.

OTHER USEFUL ITEMS. For safety purposes, you should bring a **money belt** and small **padlock**. Basic **outdoors equipment** (plastic water bottle, compass, waterproof matches, pocketknife, sunglasses, sunscreen, hat) may also prove useful. Quick repairs of torn garments can be done with a needle and thread; also consider bringing electrical tape for patching tears. Other things you're liable to forget: an **umbrella**, sealable **plastic bags** (for damp clothes, soap, food, etc.), an **alarm clock**, safety pins, rubber bands, a flashlight, **earplugs**, and garbage bags.

IMPORTANT DOCUMENTS. Don't forget your passport, traveler's checks, ATM and/or credit cards, and adequate ID (p. 12). Also check that you have any of the following that might apply to you: a hosteling membership card (p. 24); driver's license; travel insurance forms; and/or rail or bus pass (p. 50).

ACCOMMODATIONS

HOSTELS

In the summer Europe is overrun by young budget travelers, many of whom frequent hostels, which allow people from around the world to meet and learn about places to visit. Hostels are generally laid out dorm-style, often with large single-sex rooms and bunk beds, a common bathroom, and a lounge down the hall. Some offer private rooms for families and couples. Other amenities may include kitchens and utensils, bike or moped rentals, storage areas, Internet access, and laundry facilities. There can be drawbacks: some hostels close during certain daytime "lockout" hours, have a curfew, don't accept reservations, impose a maximum stay, or, less frequently, require chores. A bed in a hostel averages around US$10-25 in Western Europe and US$5-15 in Eastern Europe.

HOSTELLING INTERNATIONAL

Joining the youth hostel association in your own country (see below) automatically grants you membership privileges in **Hostelling International (HI)**, a federation of national hostelling associations. HI's umbrella organization's website (www.iyhf.org), which lists the web addresses and phone numbers of all national associations, is a great place to begin researching hostelling in a specific region. HI hostels are scattered throughout Europe and are typically less expensive than private hostels. Many accept reservations via the **International Booking Network** (US ☎202-783-6161; www.hostelbooking.com). Other comprehensive hostelling websites include www.hostels.com and www.hostelplanet.com. All of these sites offer online reservations, but still call a few days ahead to confirm.

Most HI hostels also honor **guest memberships.** You'll get a blank card with space for six validation stamps; each night you'll pay a nonmember supplement (one-sixth the membership fee) and earn one guest stamp. Six stamps grants you full membership. This system works well in most of Western Europe, but in some countries you may need to remind the hostel reception. Most student travel agencies (p. 43) sell HI cards, as do the national hostelling organizations listed below. All prices listed below are valid for **one-year memberships.**

Australian Youth Hostels Association (AYHA), Level 3, 10 Mallett St., Camperdown NSW 2050 (☎02 9565 1699; www.yha.org.au). AUS$52, under-18 AUS$16.

Hostelling International-Canada (HI-C), 400-205 Catherine St., Ottawa, ON K2P 1C3 (☎800-663-5777 or 613-237-7884; www.hihostels.ca). CDN$35, under-18 free.

Hostelling International Northern Ireland (HINI), 22-32 Donegall Rd., Belfast BT12 5JN, Northern Ireland (☎048 9031 5435; www.hini.org.uk). UK£10, under-18 UK£6.

Youth Hostels Association of New Zealand (YHANZ), P.O. Box 436, Level 1 Moore-house City, 166 Moorehouse Ave., Christchurch 1 (☎03 379 9970; yha.org.nz). NZ$40, under-18 free.

Hostels Association of South Africa, 3rd fl. 73 St. George's House, P.O. Box 4402, Cape Town 8001 (☎021 424 2511; www.hisa.org.za). ZAR79, under-18 ZAR40.

Youth Hostels Association (England and Wales) Ltd., Trevelyan House, Dimple Rd., Mat-lock, Derbyshire DE4 3YH, UK (☎016 2959 2600; www.yha.org.uk). UK£13.50, under-18 UK£6.75.

An Óige (Irish Youth Hostel Association), 61 Mountjoy St., Dublin 7 (☎01 830 4555; www.irelandyha.org). IR€25, under-18 IR€10.50.

Scottish Youth Hostels Association (SYHA), 7 Glebe Crescent, Stirling FK8 2JA (☎017 8689 1400; www.syha.org.uk). UK£6, under-18 UK£2.50.

Hostelling International-American Youth Hostels (HI-AYH), 733 15th St. NW, #840, Washington, D.C. 20005 (☎202-783-6161; www.hiayh.org). US$28, under-18 free.

OTHER TYPES OF ACCOMMODATIONS

HOTELS, GUESTHOUSES, AND PENSIONS. In Northern Europe, **hotels** generally start at a hefty US$35 per person. Elsewhere, couples and larger groups can get by fairly well. You'll typically share a hall bathroom; a private bathroom or hot shower will cost extra. Some hotels offer "full pension" (all meals) or "half pen-sion" (no lunch). Smaller **guesthouses** and **pensions** are often cheaper than hotels. Many hotels now offer online reservations. Be sure to indicate your night of arrival and the number of nights you plan to stay. The manager will send a confir-

mation and may request payment for the first night. Not all establishments take reservations, and few accept checks in foreign currency. For letters, enclosing two **International Reply Coupons** will ensure a prompt reply (each US$1.75; available at any post office).

BED AND BREAKFASTS (B&BS). For a cozy alternative to impersonal hotel rooms, B&Bs (private homes with rooms available to travelers) range from the acceptable to the sublime. B&Bs are particularly popular in Britain and Ireland, where rooms average UK£20/€30 per person. For more info on B&Bs, see InnFinder () or InnSite (www.innsite.com).

UNIVERSITY DORMS. Many colleges and universities open their residence halls to travelers when school is not in session; some do so even during term-time. Getting a room may take a couple of phone calls and require advanced planning, but rates tend to be low, and many offer free local calls.

HOME EXCHANGES. Home exchange offers the traveler various types of homes (houses, apartments, condominiums, villas, even castles in some cases), plus the opportunity to live like a native and to cut costs. For more information, contact **HomeExchangecCom** (☎ 800-877-8723; www.homeexchange.com) or **Intervac International Home Exchange** (☎ 800-756-4663; www.intervac.com).

CAMPING AND THE OUTDOORS

Organized campgrounds exist just outside most European cities. Showers, bathrooms, and a small restaurant or store are common; some have more elaborate facilities. Prices are low, usually running US$5-15 per person plus additional charges for tents and/or cars. While camping is cheaper than hostelling, the cost of transportation to the campsites can add up. Some parks or public land allow **free camping**, but check local regulations before you set up camp.

USEFUL PUBLICATIONS AND RESOURCES. An excellent resource for travelers planning on camping or spending time in the outdoors is the **Great Outdoor Recreation Pages** (www.gorp.com). Campers heading to Europe should consider buying an **International Camping Carnet.** Similar to a hostel membership card, it's required at a few campgrounds and provides discounts at others. It is available in North America from the **Family Campers and RVers Association** (www.fcrv.org) and in the UK from **The Caravan Club** (see below). For info about camping, hiking, and biking, contact the publishers listed below to receive a **free catalog.**

The Caravan Club, East Grinstead House, East Grinstead, West Sussex RH19 1UA (UK ☎ 013 4232 6944; www.caravanclub.co.uk). For UK£30, members receive equipment discounts, a 700-page directory and handbook, and a monthly magazine.

The European Federation of Campingsite Organizations, EFCO Secretariat, 6 Pullman Court, Great Western Rd., Gloucester GL1 3ND (UK ☎ 014 5252 6911; www.campingeurope.com). The website has links to campsites in most European countries.

CAMPING AND HIKING EQUIPMENT

WHAT TO BUY... Good camping equipment is both sturdy and light. It is generally more expensive in Australia, New Zealand, and the UK than in North America.

Sleeping Bag: Most sleeping bags are rated by season ("summer" 30-40°F at night; "four-season" or "winter" often means below 0°F). They are made either of **down** (warmer and lighter, but more expensive and miserable when wet) or of **synthetic** material (heavier, more durable, and warmer when wet). Prices range from US$80-210 for a summer synthetic to US$250-300 for a good down winter bag. **Sleeping bag pads** include foam pads (US$10-20), air mattresses (US$15-50), and Therm-A-Rest self-inflating pads (US$45-80). Bring a **stuff sack** to store your bag and keep it dry.

Tent: The best tents are free-standing (with their own frames and suspension systems), set up quickly, and require staking only in high winds. Low-profile dome tents are the best all-around. Good 2-person tents start at US$90, 4-person at US$300. Seal the seams of your tent with waterproofer, and make sure it has a rain fly. Other tent accessories include a **battery-operated lantern,** a **plastic groundcloth,** and a **nylon tarp.**

Backpack: Internal-frame packs mold better to your back, keep a lower center of gravity, and flex adequately to allow you to hike difficult trails. **External-frame packs** are more comfortable for long hikes over even terrain, as they keep weight higher and distribute it more evenly. Make sure your pack has a strong padded hip-belt to transfer weight to your legs. Any serious backpacking requires a pack of at least 4000 cubic inches, plus 500 cubic inches for sleeping bags in internal-frame packs. Sturdy backpacks cost anywhere from US$125-420. This is one area in which it doesn't pay to economize. Fill up any pack with something heavy and walk around the store with it to get a sense of how it distributes weight before buying it. Either buy a **waterproof backpack cover,** or store all of your belongings in plastic bags inside your pack.

Boots: Be sure to wear hiking boots with good **ankle support.** They should fit snugly and comfortably over one or two pairs of wool socks and thin liner socks. Break in boots over several weeks first to avoid blisters.

Other Necessities: Synthetic layers, like those made of polypropylene, and a **pile jacket** will keep you warm even when wet. A **"space blanket"** will help you to retain your body heat and doubles as a groundcloth (US$5-15). Plastic **water bottles** are virtually shatter- and leak-proof. Bring **water-purification tablets** for when you can't boil water. For those places that forbid fires or the gathering of firewood (virtually every orga-

ESSENTIALS

nized campground in Europe), you'll need a **camp stove** (the classic Coleman starts at US$40) and a propane-filled **fuel bottle** to operate it. Also, don't forget a **first-aid kit, pocketknife, insect repellent, calamine lotion,** and **waterproof matches** or a **lighter.**

...AND WHERE TO BUY IT. The mail-order/online companies listed below offer lower prices than many retail stores, but a visit to a local camping or outdoors store will give you a good sense of the look and weight of certain items.

Campmor, 28 Parkway, P.O. Box 700, Upper Saddle River, NJ 07458 (US ☎888-226-7667; elsewhere US ☎201-825-8300; www.campmor.com).

Discount Camping, 880 Main North Rd., Pooraka, South Australia 5095, Australia (☎08 8262 3399; www.discountcamping.com.au).

Eastern Mountain Sports (EMS), 1 Vose Farm Rd., Peterborough, NH 03458 (☎888-463-6367 or 603-924-9571; www.ems.com).

L.L. Bean, Freeport, ME 04033 (US and Canada ☎800-441-5713; UK ☎0800 891 297; elsewhere, call US ☎207-552-3028; www.llbean.com).

Mountain Designs, 51 Bishop St., Kelvin Grove, Queensland 4059, Australia (☎07 3856 2344; www.mountaindesigns.com).

Recreational Equipment, Inc. (REI), Sumner, WA 98352 (☎800-426-4840 or 253-891-2500; www.rei.com).

YHA Adventure Shop, 152-160 Wardour St., London WIF 8YA, UK (☎020 7025 1900; www.yhaadventure.com).

CAMPERS AND RVS

Renting an RV is more expensive than tenting or hosteling, but it's cheaper than staying in hotels and renting a car (see **Renting,** p. 60), and the convenience of bringing along your own accomodations makes it an attractive option, although navigating some streets may prove difficult. Rates vary widely by region, season

(July and Aug. are the most expensive months), and type of RV. **Motorhome.com** (www.motorhome.com/rentals.html) lists rental companies for several European countries. **Auto Europe** (US ☎ 888-223-5555; UK ☎ 0800 169 9797; www.autoeurope.com) rents RVs in Britain, France, and Germany.

ORGANIZED ADVENTURE TRIPS

Organized **adventure tours** offer another way of exploring the wild. Activities include hiking, biking, skiing, canoeing, kayaking, rafting, climbing, photo safaris, and archaeological digs. Tourism bureaus can suggest parks, trails, and outfitters; stores and organizations that specialize in camping and outdoor equipment like REI and EMS are also good resources (see above). The **Specialty Travel Index** (☎ 888-624-4030 or 415-455-1643; www.specialtytravel.com) compiles tours worldwide.

 ENVIRONMENTALLY RESPONSIBLE TOURISM. The idea behind responsible tourism is to leave no trace of human presence behind. A camp-stove is a safer way to cook than using vegetation, but if you must make a fire, keep it small and use only dead branches or brush. Make sure your campsite is at least 150 ft. (50m) from water supplies or bodies of water. If there are no toilet facilities, bury human waste (but not paper) at least four inches (10cm) deep and above the high-water line, and 150 ft. or more from any water supplies and campsites. Pack your trash in a plastic bag and carry it until you reach the next trash receptacle. For more info, contact any of the organizations listed below.

Earthwatch, 3 Clock Tower Pl. #100, Box 75, Maynard, MA 01754 (☎ 800-776-0188 or 978-461-0081; www.earthwatch.org).

International Ecotourism Society, 733 15 St. NW #1000, Washington, D.C. 20005 (☎ 202-347-9203; www.ecotourism.org).

National Audubon Society, Nature Odysseys, 700 Broadway, New York, NY 10003 (☎ 212-979-3000; www.audubon.org).

Tourism Concern, Stapleton House, 277-281 Holloway Rd., London N7 8HN, UK (☎ 020 7753 3330; www.tourismconcern.org.uk).

COMMUNICATION

BY MAIL

SENDING MAIL HOME FROM EUROPE. Airmail is the best way to send mail home from Europe. From Western Europe to North America, airmail averages seven days; from Central or Eastern Europe, allow anywhere from seven days to three weeks. In Russia, Ukraine, and Belarus, your mail will probably be opened and may not be sent. **Aerogrammes,** printed sheets that fold into envelopes and travel via airmail, are available at post offices. Write "par avion" (or *por avion, mit Luftpost, via aerea,* etc.) on the front. Most post offices will charge exorbitant fees or simply refuse to send aerogrammes with enclosures. **Surface mail** is by far the cheapest and slowest way to send mail. It takes one to three months to cross the Atlantic and two to four to cross the Pacific—so it's good for items you won't need to see for a while, such as souvenirs or other articles you've acquired along the way that are weighing down your pack. Check the beginning of each chapter for more specific info on postal service in each country.

SENDING MAIL TO EUROPE. Mark envelopes "airmail" in your country's language; otherwise, your letter or postcard will not arrive. In addition to the standard postage system, **Federal Express** (Australia ☎ 13 26 10; Canada and US ☎ 800-247-4747; New Zealand ☎ 0800 733 339; UK ☎ 0800 123 800; www.fedex.com) has express mail services from most home countries to Europe.

Australia: www.auspost.com.au/pac. Allow 5-7 days for regular airmail to Europe. Postcards up to 20g cost AUS$1 and letters up to 50g cost AUS$1.65; packages up to 0.5kg AUS$14, up to 2kg AUS$50.

Canada: http://www.canadapost.ca/personal/rates/default-e.asp. Allow 4-7 days for regular airmail to Europe. Postcards and letters up to 30g cost CDN$1.25; packages up to 0.5kg CDN$10.65, up to 2kg CDN$35.55.

Ireland: www.letterpost.ie. Allow 2-3 days for regular airmail to the UK and Western Europe. Postcards and letters up to 50g cost €0.41 to the UK, €0.71 to the continent. **International Swiftpost** zips letters to some major European countries for an additional €3.60 on top of priority postage.

New Zealand: www.nzpost.net.nz/nzpost/control/ratefinder. Allow 6-12 days for airmail to Europe. Postcards cost NZ$1.50; letters up to 200g NZ$2-5; small parcels up to 0.5kg NZ$17.23, up to 2kg NZ$55.25.

UK: www.royalmail.com/international/calculator. Allow 2-3 days for airmail to Europe. Letters up to 20g cost UK£0.38; packages up to 0.5kg UK£2.78, up to 2kg UK£9.72. **UK Swiftair** delivers letters a day faster for an extra UK£3.30.

US: www.usps.com. Allow 4-7 days for regular airmail to Europe. Postcards/aerogrammes cost US$0.70; letters under 1oz. US$0.80; packages under 1lb. US$14; larger packages up to 5lb. $22.75. **Global Express Mail** takes 3-5 days; ½lb. costs US$23, 1lb. US$26. **US Global Priority Mail** delivers flat-rate envelopes to Europe in 4-6 days for US$5-9.

RECEIVING MAIL IN EUROPE. There are several ways to pick-up letters while traveling abroad. Mail can be sent via **Poste Restante** (General Delivery; *Lista de Correos, Fermo Posta, Postlagernde Briefe*, etc.) to almost any city or town in Europe with a post office. See individual country chapters to find out how to address *Poste Restante* letters. The mail will go to a special desk in the central post office, unless you specify a post office by street address or postal code. It's best to use the largest post office, since mail may be sent there regardless. It is usually safer and quicker, though more expensive, to send mail express or registered. Bring your passport (or other photo ID) for pick-up; there may be a small fee. If the clerks insist that there is nothing for you, check under your first name as well. *Let's Go* lists post offices in the **Practical Information** section for each city and most towns.

American Express travel offices offer a free **Client Letter Service** (mail held up to 30 days and forwarded upon request) for cardholders who contact them in advance. Address the letter as you would for Poste Restante. Some offices offer these services to non-cardholders (especially AmEx Traveler's Cheque holders), but call ahead. *Let's Go* lists AmEx office locations for most large cities in **Practical Information** sections; for a complete, free list, call US ☎ 800-528-4800.

BY TELEPHONE

TIME DIFFERENCES. All of Europe falls within three hours of **Greenwich Mean Time (GMT).** For more info, consult the **time zone chart** on the inside back cover. GMT is five hours ahead of New York time, eight hours ahead of Vancouver and

San Francisco time, two hours behind Johannesburg time, 10 hours behind Sydney time, and 12 hours behind Auckland time. Some countries ignore **daylight savings time;** fall and spring switchover times vary.

PLACING INTERNATIONAL CALLS. To call Europe from home or to call home from Europe, dial:

1. The **international dialing prefix.** To dial out of **Australia,** dial 0011; **Canada** or the **US,** 011; the **Republic of Ireland, New Zealand,** or the **UK,** 00; **South Africa,** 09. See the inside back cover for a full list of dialing prefixes.
2. The **country code** of the country you want to call. To call **Australia,** dial 61; **Canada** or the **US,** 1; the **Republic of Ireland,** 353; **New Zealand,** 64; **South Africa,** 27; the **UK,** 44. See the back cover for a full list of country codes.
3. The **city/area code.** Let's Go lists the city/area codes for cities and towns opposite the city or town name within each country's chapter, next to a ☎. If the first digit is a zero (e.g., 020 for London), omit the zero when calling from abroad (e.g., dial 20 from Canada to reach London).
4. The **local number.**

ESSENTIALS

CALLING HOME FROM EUROPE. A **calling card** is probably cheapest. Calls are billed collect or to your account. *Let's Go* has recently partnered with **ekit.com** to provide a calling card that offers a number of services, including email and voice messaging. Before purchasing a calling card, be sure to compare rates, and make sure it serves your needs; for instance, a local phonecard is generally better for local calls. For more info, visit www.letsgo.ekit.com. You can also purchase cards from your national telecommunications companies. Keep in mind that phone cards can be problematic in Russia, Ukraine, Belarus, and Slovenia—double-check with your provider before setting out. You can often make **direct international calls** from pay phones, but without a calling card, you may need to continually add more change. Where available, **prepaid phone cards** and occasionally major credit cards can be used for direct international calls, but they are still less cost-efficient. Placing a **collect call** through an international operator is a more expensive alternative.

CALLING WITHIN EUROPE. Many travelers are opting to buy mobile phones for placing calls within Europe. (For more info, see **Cell Phones in Europe** below.) Beyond that, perhaps the easiest way to call within a country is to use a coin-operated phone. However, much of Europe has switched to a **prepaid phone card** system, and in some countries you may have a hard time finding any coin-operated phones at all. Prepaid phone cards (available at newspaper kiosks and tobacco stores), which carry a certain amount of phone time depending on the card's denomination, usually save time and money in the long run. The computerized phone will tell you how much time, in units, you have left on your card. Another kind of prepaid telephone card comes with a Personal Identification Number (PIN) and a toll-free access number. Instead of inserting the card into the phone, you call the access number and follow the directions on the card. These cards can be used to make international as well as domestic calls. Phone rates tend to be highest in the morning, lower in the evening, and lowest on Sunday and at night.

BY EMAIL AND INTERNET

Email is popular and easily accessible in most of Europe. Take advantage of **web-based email accounts.** If you don't already have one, free services (e.g., www.hotmail.com and www.yahoo.com) are a convenient option, although they can be sus-

CELL PHONES IN EUROPE. Cell phones are an increasingly popular option for travelers calling within Europe. In addition to greater convenience and safety, mobile phones often provide an economical alternative to expensive landline calls. Unlike North America, virtually all areas of Europe receive excellent coverage, and the widespread use of the **Global System for Mobiles (GSM)** allows one phone to function in multiple countries. A small chip called a **Subscriber Identity Module Card (SIM or "smart card")** can be purchased from carriers in any European country to provide a local number for any GSM phone. However, some companies lock their phones to prevent switches to competitor carriers, so inquire about using the phone in other countries before buying. Phones in Europe cost around US$100, and instead of requiring a service contract, they often run on prepaid minutes that are easily purchased in many locations. Frequently, incoming calls are free. For more info about GSM phones, try these sites: www.vodafone.com, www.orange.co.uk, www.roadpost.com, www.cellularabroad.com, www.t-mobile.com, and www.planetomni.com.

ceptible to spam. While it's sometimes possible to forge a remote link with your home server, in most cases this is a much slower and more expensive option. Travelers with laptops can call an Internet service provider via a **modem,** and long-distance phone cards specifically intended for such calls can defray normally high phone charges; check with your long-distance provider to see about this option. A handful of large European cities (e.g., Paris) are in the process of making **wireless Internet** available in a variety of public places. **Internet cafes** and the occasional free Internet terminal at a public library or university are listed in the **Practical Information** sections of major cities. For lists of additional cybercafes in Europe, check www.cybercaptive.com or www.netcafeguide.com.

SPECIFIC CONCERNS

WOMEN TRAVELERS

Women traveling on their own inevitably face some additional safety concerns, but it's still possible to be adventurous without taking undue risks. If you are concerned, consider staying in hostels with **single rooms** that lock from the inside or in religious organizations with rooms for women only. Communal **showers** in some hostels are safer than others; check them before settling in. Stick to centrally located accommodations and avoid solitary late-night treks or public transportation rides. Always carry extra money for a phone call, bus, or taxi. **Hitchhiking** is never safe for women, or even for two women traveling together. Choose **train compartments** occupied by women or couples; ask the conductor to put together a women-only compartment if he or she doesn't offer to do so first. Look as if you know where you're going and approach older women or couples for directions if you're lost or uncomfortable.

In general, the less you look like a tourist, the better. Consider wearing skirts rather than shorts to blend in; avoid baggy jeans, T-shirts, and sneakers, since they may make it obvious that you're a foreigner. Try to dress conservatively, especially in rural areas. Wearing a conspicuous **wedding band** may help prevent unwanted overtures; some travelers report that carrying pictures of a "husband" or "children" is extremely useful to help document marriage status.

Your best answer to verbal harassment is no answer at all. The extremely persistent can often be dissuaded by a firm, loud, and very public "Go away!" in the appropriate language (see **Language Basics,** p. 1051). Don't hesitate to seek out a police officer or passerby if you are being harassed or feel threatened. Memorize the emergency numbers in places you visit, and consider carrying a whistle or airhorn on your keychain. A **self-defense course** will both prepare you for a potential attack and raise your awareness and confidence (p. 17). It's also a good idea to be conscious of the health concerns that women face when traveling (p. 21).

USEFUL ORGANIZATIONS

Journeywoman, 50 Prince Arthur Av., Toronto, Canada, M5R 1B5 (Canada ☎416-929-7654; www.journeywoman.com). Posts an online newsletter and other resources providing female-specific travel tips.

Women Traveling Together, 1642 Fairhill Drive, Edgewater, MD 21037 (US ☎410-956-5250; www.women-traveling.com). Places women in small groups to explore the world.

PUBLICATIONS

Active Women Vacation Guide, Evelyn Kaye. Blue Panda Publications (US$18).

A Foxy Old Woman's Guide to Traveling Alone: Around Town and Around the World, Jay Ben-Lesser. Crossing Press (US$11).

A Journey of One's Own: Uncommon Advice for the Independent Woman Traveler, Thalia Zepatos. Eighth Mountain Press (US$17).

Gutsy Women: More Travel Tips and Wisdom from the Road, Marybeth Bond. Travelers' Tales Guides, Inc. (US$13).

Safety and Security for Women Who Travel, Sheila Swan. Travelers' Tales Guides, Inc. (US$13).

The Single Woman's Travel Guide, Jacqueline Simenauer, Doris Walfield. Kensington Publishing (US$13).

SOLO TRAVELERS

There are many benefits to traveling alone, among them greater independence and more opportunities to interact with native residents. On the other hand, a solo traveler is more vulnerable to harassment and street theft. Lone travelers need to be well-organized and look confident at all times. Try not to stand out as a tourist, and be especially careful in deserted or very crowded areas. If questioned, never admit you are traveling alone. Maintain regular contact with someone at home who knows your itinerary. The **Travel Companion Exchange,** P.O. Box 833, Amityville, NY 11701 (US ☎631-454-0880; www.travelcompanions.com) links solo travelers with companions who have similar travel habits; subscribe to their bimonthly newsletter for more info (US$48). **Contiki Holidays** (☎888-CONTIKI; www.contiki.com) offers a variety of European packages designed for 18- to 35-year-olds. Tours include accommodations, transportation, guided sightseeing, and some meals; most average about $65 per day. The books and organizations listed below provide info and services for the lone traveler.

USEFUL ORGANIZATIONS

American International Homestays, P.O. Box 1754, Nederland, CO 80466 (US ☎303-258-3234; www.aihtravel.com). Arranges lodgings with host families across the world.

Connecting: Solo Travel Network, 689 Park Road, Unit 6, Gibsons, BC V0N 1V7 (US ☎604-886-9099; www.cstn.org; membership US$35, internet membership US$25). Offers solo travel tips, host information, and individuals looking for travel companions.

PUBLICATIONS

Traveling Solo, Eleanor Berman. Globe Pequot Press (US$18).

Travel Alone & Love It: A Flight Attendant's Guide to Solo Travel, Sharon B. Wingler. Chicago Spectrum Press (US$15).

OLDER TRAVELERS

Senior citizens are eligible for discounts on transportation, museums, theaters, restaurants, and accommodations. If you don't see a senior citizen price listed, ask, and you might be surprised. However, keep in mind that some hostels, particularly in Germany, do not allow guests over age 26; so call ahead to check. The following books and organizations offer more info for older travelers.

TOUR AGENCIES

ElderTreks, 597 Markham St., Toronto, ON M6G 2L7 (Canada ☎800-741-7956; www.eldertreks.com). Adventure travel programs for ages 50+ in Finland, Iceland, and Transylvania.

Elderhostel, 11 Ave. de Lafayette, Boston, MA 02111 (US ☎877-426-8056; www.elderhostel.org). Organizes one- to four-week "educational adventures" throughout Europe on varied subjects for ages 55+.

The Mature Traveler, P.O. Box 15791, Sacramento, CA 95852 (US ☎800-460-6676; www.thematuretraveler.com). Deals, discounts, and travel packages for the 50+ traveler. Subscription US$30.

Walking the World, P.O. Box 1186, Fort Collins, CO 80522 (US ☎800-340-9255; www.walkingtheworld.com). Organizes trips for 50+ travelers to many places in Europe.

PUBLICATIONS

No Problem!: Worldwise Travel Tips for Mature Adventurers, by Janice Kenyon. Orca Book Publishers (US$16).

Unbelievably Good Deals and Great Adventures That You Absolutely Can't Get Unless You're Over 50, by Joan Rattner Heilman. McGraw-Hill/Contemporary Publishing (US$13).

BI-GAY-LESBIAN TRAVELERS

Attitudes toward bisexual, gay, and lesbian travelers are particular to each region in Europe. Acceptance is generally highest in large cities and The Netherlands, and generally lower in eastern nations. Listed below are contact organizations, mail-order bookstores, and publishers that offer materials addressing some specific concerns. **Out and About** (www.planetout.com) offers a biweekly newsletter as well as a comprehensive website.

USEFUL ORGANIZATIONS

Giovanni's Room, 1145 Pine St., Philadelphia, PA 19107 (US ☎215-923-2960; www.queerbooks.com). An international lesbian/feminist and gay bookstore with mail-order service (carries many of the publications listed below).

International Lesbian and Gay Association (ILGA), 81 r. Marché-au-Charbon, B-1000 Brussels, Belgium (☎02 502 2471; www.ilga.org). Provides political info, such as the homosexuality laws of specific countries.

PUBLICATIONS

*Damron Men's Travel Guide, Damron Women's Traveler, Damron's Accommodations,*and *Damron Amsterdam Guide.* Damron Travel Guides (US$16-22). For more info, call US ☎ 800-462-6654 or visit www.damron.com.

Ferrari Guides' Gay Travel A to Z, Ferrari Guides' Men's Travel in Your Pocket, and *Ferrari Guides' Inn Places.* Ferrari Publications (US$16-20).

Spartacus International Gay Guide 2003-2004, Bruno Gmunder Verlag (US$33).

The Gay Vacation Guide: The Best Trips and How to Plan Them, Mark Chesnut. Kensington Publishing Corp. (US$15).

TRAVELERS WITH DISABILITIES

European countries vary in accessibility to travelers with disabilities. Some national and regional tourist boards provide directories on the accessibility of various accommodations and transportation services. If these services are not available, contact institutions of interest directly. It is essential that those with disabilities inform airlines, hotels, restaurants, and other facilities of their needs when making reservations, as some time may be needed to prepare special accommodations. **Guide dog owners** should inquire as to the quarantine policies of each destination country. At the very least, you will need to provide a certificate of immunization against rabies.

Rail is probably the most convenient form of transportation for disabled travelers in Europe: Many stations have ramps, and some trains have wheelchair lifts, special seating areas, and specially equipped toilets. In general, the countries with the most **wheelchair-accessible rail networks** are: Denmark, France, Germany, Ireland, Italy, The Netherlands, Sweden, and Switzerland. Austria, Poland, and Britain offer accessibility on selected routes. Greece and Spain's rail systems have limited accessibility. For those who wish to rent cars, some major **car rental agencies** (Hertz, Avis, and National) offer hand-controlled vehicles.

USEFUL ORGANIZATIONS

Mobility International USA (MIUSA), P.O. Box 10767, Eugene, OR 97440 (US ☎ 541-343-1284, voice and TDD; www.miusa.org). Sells *A World of Options: A Guide to International Educational Exchange, Community Service, and Travel for Persons with Disabilities* (US$35).

Moss Rehab ResourceNet (www.mossresourcenet.org). An Internet resource for international travel accessibility and other travel-related tips for those with disabilities.

Society for Accessible Travel and Hospitality (SATH), 347 Fifth Ave., #610, New York, NY 10016 (US ☎ 212-447-7284; www.sath.org). An advocacy group that publishes free online travel info and the travel magazine *OPEN WORLD* (US$18, free for members). Annual membership US$45; students and seniors US$30.

TOUR AGENCIES

Accessible Europe, Viale Londra, Rome, Italy 00142 (Italy ☎ 067 158 2945; www.accessibleurope.com). A European travel group that specializes in arranging individual and group vacations and tours for the physically disabled.

The Campanian Society, P.O. Box 167, Oxford, OH 45056 (US ☎ 513-524-4846; www.campanian.org). An excellent organization that specializes exclusively in arranging group vacations for the visually impaired. Special emphasis is placed on its educational component, via tactile experience, audio description, and lectures.

The Guided Tour Inc., 7900 Old York Rd., #114B, Elkins Park, PA 19027 (US ☎800-783-5841 or 215-782-1370; www.guidedtour.com). Organizes travel programs for persons with developmental and physical challenges around Ireland, London, and Rome.

PUBLICATIONS

European Holidays and Travel Abroad, Royal Association for Disability and Rehabilitation (US$5).

Around the World Resource Guide, Patricia Smither. Access for Disabled American Publishing (US$20).

Wheelchair Around the World, Patrick D. Simpson. Ivy House Publishing Group (US$25).

MINORITY TRAVELERS

In general, minority travelers will find a high level of tolerance in large cities; the small towns and the countryside are more unpredictable. Travelers with darker skin may face regional intolerance, though most minority travelers, especially those of African or Asian descent, will usually meet with more curiosity than hostility. Anti-Semitism is still a problem in many countries and anti-Muslim sentiment has increased in many places; travelers of Arab ethnicity may be treated suspiciously. Sad to say, it is generally best to be discreet about your religion. Skinheads are on the rise in Europe, and minority travelers, especially Jews and blacks, should regard them with caution. Still, attitudes will vary from country to country and town to town; travelers should use common sense—consult **Safety and Security** (p. 17) for tips on how to avoid unwanted attention.

TRAVELERS WITH CHILDREN

Needless to say, family vacations often require a slower pace and more planning; not all establishments are built for children. If you pick a B&B or a small hotel, call ahead and verify that it's child-friendly. If you rent a car, make sure the rental company provides a car seat for younger children. **Always have your child carry some sort of ID** in case of an emergency, or in case he or she gets lost.

Museums, tourist attractions, accommodations, and restaurants often offer discounts for children. Children under two generally fly for 10% of the adult airfare on international flights (this does not necessarily include a seat). International fares are usually discounted 25% for children from two to 11. Check with your airline, though, to confirm their specific child policy.

DIETARY CONCERNS

Vegetarians should have no problem finding suitable cuisine in most of Western Europe. Particularly in city listings, *Let's Go* notes many restaurants that offer good vegetarian selections. For info on vegetarian and vegan options throughout Europe, check www.vegdining.com.

Travelers who keep **kosher** should contact synagogues in larger cities for info on food options. Your own synagogue or college Hillel should have access to lists of Jewish institutions across the globe. If you are strict in your observance, you may have to prepare your own food on the road. The website www.kashrut.com/travel provides contact info and further resources, while www.shamash.org/kosher catalogues kosher restaurants worldwide.

USEFUL ORGANIZATIONS

North American Vegetarian Society, P.O. Box 72, Dolgeville, NY 13329 (US ☎518-568-7970; www.navs-online.org). Offers resources and publications.

The Vegan Traveller (www.vegan-traveller.com). An internet resource center with info on a number of vegan establishments throughout Europe.

PUBLICATIONS

The Vegan Travel Guide: Places to Stay and Places to Eat for Vegans, Vegetarians, and the Dairy Intolerant, The Vegan Society (US$9).

Vegetarian Europe, Alex Bourke (US$17).

OTHER RESOURCES

Let's Go tries to cover all aspects of budget travel, but we can't include *everything*. Listed below are organizations and websites for your own research.

TRAVEL PUBLISHERS AND BOOKSTORES

Adventurous Traveler Bookstore, 702 H St. NW, Ste. 200, Washington, D.C. 20001 (US☎202-654-8017; www.adventuroustraveler.com), offers information and gear for outdoor and adventure travel.

Hippocrene Books, Inc., 171 Madison Ave., New York, NY 10016 (☎212-685-4371; orders 718-454-2366; www.hippocrenebooks.com). Publishes travel guides, as well as foreign language dictionaries and learning guides. Free catalog.

Hunter Publishing, 130 Campus Dr., Edison, NJ 08818 (☎800-255-0343; www.hunter-publishing.com). Has an extensive catalog of travel guides and diving and adventure travel books.

Rand McNally, 8255 N. Central Park Ave., Skokie, IL 60076 (☎800-275-7263; elsewhere call US ☎847-329-6656; www.randmcnally.com), publishes a number of comprehensive road atlases (from US$10).

THE WORLD WIDE WEB

Almost every aspect of budget travel is accessible via the web. With a few minutes at the keyboard, you can make a hostel reservation, get advice from other travelers, or find out exactly how much a train from Paris to Munich costs.

Listed below are some budget travel sites to start off your surfing; other relevant websites are listed throughout the book. Because web-site turnover is high, use search engines (such as www.google.com) to strike out on your own.

LEARNING THE ART OF BUDGET TRAVEL

Backpacker's Ultimate Guide: www.bugeurope.com. Tips on packing, transportation, and where to go. Also tons of country-specific travel info.

Backpack Europe: www.backpackeurope.com. Helpful tips, a bulletin board, and links.

How to See the World: www.artoftravel.com. A compendium of great travel tips, from cheap flights to self-defense to interacting with local culture.

Travel Library: www.travel-library.com. A fantastic set of links for general information and personal travelogues.

TripSpot: www.tripspot.com/europefeature.htm. An outline of links to help plan trips, transportation, accommodations, and packing.

ESSENTIALS

DESTINATION GUIDES

Atevo Travel: www.atevo.com/guides/destinations. Detailed introductions, transportation tips, and suggested itineraries. Free travel newsletter.

Columbus Travel Guides: www.travel-guides.com/region/eur.asp. Well-organized site with info on geography, governments, communication, health precautions, economies, and useful addresses.

In Your Pocket: www.inyourpocket.com. Extensive virtual guides to select Baltic and Eastern European cities.

MyTravelGuide: www.mytravelguide.com. Country overviews, with everything from history to transportation to local newspapers and weather.

OTHER HELPFUL PAGES

CIA World Factbook: www.odci.gov/cia/publications/factbook/index.html. Vital statistics on European geography, governments, economies, and politics.

Lycos: http://travel.lycos.com. General introductions to cities and regions throughout Europe, accompanied by links to applicable history, news, and local tourism sites.

WWW.LETSGO.COM Our website, www.letsgo.com, now includes introductory chapters from all our guides and a wealth of information on a monthly featured estination. As always, our website also has info about our books, a travel forum buzzing with stories and tips, and additional links that will help you make the most of a trip to Europe.

TRANSPORTATION

GETTING TO EUROPE

BY PLANE

When it comes to airfare, a little effort can save you a bundle. If your plans are flexible enough to deal with the restrictions, courier fares are the cheapest. Standby seats and tickets bought from consolidators are also good deals, but last-minute specials, charter flights, and airfare wars often generate even lower rates. The key is to hunt around, be flexible, and ask persistently about discounts. Students, seniors, and those under 26 should never pay full price for a ticket.

AIRFARES

Airfares to Europe peak between mid-June and early September; holidays are also expensive. The cheapest times to travel are November to mid-December and early January to March. Midweek (Monday to Thursday morning) round-trip flights run US$40-50 cheaper than weekend flights, but they are generally more crowded and less likely to permit frequent-flier upgrades. Flights without a fixed return date ("open return") or those that arrive and depart from different cities ("open jaw") can be pricier. Patching one-way flights together is the most expensive way to travel. Flights between Europe's capitals or regional hubs—London, Paris, Amsterdam, and Frankfurt—tend to be cheaper. For deals on continental flights to England and other destinations in Europe, try **Ryanair** (www.ryanair.com), **Basiq** (www.basiqair.com), and **Sterling European** (www.sterlingticket.com). For deals flying from England, try Ryanair flights departing from London's **Stansted Airport.**

If Europe is only one stop on a more extensive globe-hop, consider a round-the-world (RTW) ticket. Tickets usually include at least five stops and are valid for about a year; prices range from US$1200-5000. Try **Northwest Airlines/KLM** (US ☎800-447-4747; www.nwa.com) or **Star Alliance,** a consortium of 22 airlines including United Airlines (US ☎800-241-6522; www.star-alliance.com).

BUDGET AND STUDENT TRAVEL AGENCIES

While knowledgeable agents specializing in flights to Europe can make your life easier and help you save, they get paid on commission, so they may not spend the time to find you the lowest possible fare. Travelers holding **ISIC and IYTC cards** (p. 13) qualify for big discounts from student travel agencies. Most flights from budget agencies are on major airlines, but in peak season some may sell seats on less reliable chartered aircraft.

CTS Travel, 30 Rathbone Pl., London W1T 1GQ, UK (☎020 7290 0630; www.ctstravel.co.uk). A British student travel agency with offices in 39 countries including the US, Empire State Building, 350 Fifth Ave., Ste. 7813, New York, NY 10118 (☎877-287-6665; www.ctstravelusa.com).

STA Travel, 7890 S. Hardy Dr., Ste. 110, Tempe, AZ 85284 (☎800-781-4040, 24hr. reservations and info; www.sta-travel.com). A student and youth travel organization with over 150 offices worldwide (check their website for a listing of all offices), including US offices in Boston, Chicago, L.A., New York, San Francisco, Seattle, and Washington, D.C. Tickets, travel insurance, railpasses, and more. In the UK, 11 Goodge St., **London** W1T 2PF (☎020 7436 7779); in New Zealand, Shop 2B, 182 Queen St., **Auckland** (☎09 309 0458); in Australia, 366 Lygon St., **Carlton** Vic 3053 (☎03 9349 4344).

Travel CUTS (Canadian Universities Travel Services Limited), 187 College St., Toronto, ON M5T 1P7 (☎416-979-2406; www.travelcuts.com). Offices in Canada, the US, and elsewhere. Also in the UK, 295-A Regent St., **London** W1B 2H9 (☎020 7255 2191).

USIT, 19-21 Aston Quay, Dublin 2 (☎01 602 1600; www.usitworld.com). Ireland's leading student/budget travel agency has 22 offices throughout Northern Ireland and the Republic of Ireland. Offers programs to work in North America.

Wasteels, Skoubogade 6, 1158 Copenhagen K. (☎3314 4633; www.wasteels.com). A huge chain with 180 locations across Europe. Sells Wasteels BIJ tickets discounted 30-45% off regular fare, 2nd-class international point-to-point train tickets with unlimited stopovers for those under 26 (sold only in Europe).

✈ FLIGHT PLANNING ON THE INTERNET.

Many airline websites offer special last-minute deals, although some may require membership logins or email subscriptions. Try www.icelandair.com, www.air-france.com, www.lufthansa.de, and www.britishairways.com. (For a great set of links to practically every airline in every country, see www.travelpage.com.)

Other websites do the legwork and compile the deals for you—try www.best-fares.com, www.flights.com, www.lowestfare.com, www.onetravel.com, and www.travelzoo.com.

■ **StudentUniverse** (www.studentuniverse.com), **STA** (www.sta-travel.com), and **Orbitz.com** provide quotes on student tickets, while **Expedia** (www.expedia.com) and **Travelocity** (www.travelocity.com) offer full travel services. **Priceline** (www.price-line.com) allows you to specify a price, and obligates you to buy any ticket that meets or beats it; be prepared for antisocial hours and odd routes. **Skyauction** (www.skyauc-tion.com) allows you to bid on both last-minute and advance-purchase tickets.

An indispensable resource on the Internet is the *Air Traveler's Handbook* (www.cs.cmu.edu/afs/cs/user/mkant/Public/Travel/airfare.html), a comprehensive listing of links to everything you need to know before you board a plane.

One last note: To protect yourself, make sure any website you use has a secure server before handing over any credit card details.

COMMERCIAL AIRLINES

The commercial airlines' lowest regular offer is the **APEX** (Advance Purchase Excursion) fare, which provides confirmed reservations and allows "open-jaw" tickets. Generally, reservations must be made seven to 21 days ahead of departure, with seven- to 14-day minimum-stay and up to 90-day maximum-stay restrictions. These fares carry hefty cancellation and change penalties (fees rise in summer). Book peak-season APEX fares early; by May you will have a hard time getting your desired departure date. Use **Expedia** (www.expedia.com) or **Travelocity** (www.trav-elocity.com) to get an idea of the lowest published fares, then use the resources outlined here to try and beat those fares. Low-season fares should be appreciably cheaper than the **high-season** (mid-June to August) ones listed here.

TRAVELING FROM NORTH AMERICA

Basic round-trip fares to Europe are generally cheapest from the East Coast and range from roughly US$200-750: to Frankfurt, US$300-750; London, US$200-600; Paris, US$250-700. Standard commercial carriers like American (☎800-433-7300; www.aa.com) and United (☎800-241-6522; www.ual.com) will probably offer the most convenient flights, but they may not be the cheapest, unless you manage to grab a special promotion or airfare war ticket. You will probably find flying one of the following "discount" airlines a better deal, if any of their limited departure points is convenient for you.

Icelandair: US ☎800-223-5500; www.icelandair.com. Stopovers in Iceland for no extra cost on most transatlantic flights. New York to Frankfurt May-Sept. US$500-780; Oct.-May US$390-$450.

Finnair: US ☎800-950-5000; www.us.finnair.com. Cheap round-trip fares from San Francisco, New York, and Toronto to Helsinki. Connections throughout Europe.

Martinair: US ☎800-627-8462; www.martinairusa.com. Fly from California or Florida to Amsterdam mid-June to mid-Aug. US$880; mid-Aug. to mid-June US$730.

TRAVELING FROM THE UK AND IRELAND

Because many carriers fly from the British Isles to the continent, we only include discount airlines or those with cheap specials here. The **Air Travel Advisory Bureau** in London (☎020 7636 5000; www.atab.co.uk) provides referrals to travel agencies and consolidators that offer discounted airfares out of the UK.

Aer Lingus: Ireland ☎081 836 5000; UK ☎084 5084 4444; www.flyaerlingus.com. Round-trip tickets from Dublin, Shannon, and Cork to Amsterdam, Brussels, Düsseldorf, Frankfurt, Madrid, Milan, Munich, Paris, Rome, Stockholm, and Zurich (€40-135).

British Midland Airways: UK ☎087 0607 0555; www.flybmi.com. Departures from throughout the UK. Discounted online fares including London to Brussels (UK£83), Madrid (UK£118), Milan (UK£126), and Paris (UK£84).

easyJet: UK ☎087 0600 0000; www.easyjet.com. London to Amsterdam, Athens, Barcelona, Geneva, Madrid, Nice, and Zurich (from UK£30). Online ticketing.

KLM: UK ☎087 0507 4074; www.klmuk.com. Cheap round-trip tickets from London and elsewhere direct to Amsterdam, Brussels, Frankfurt, and Zurich; via Amsterdam Schiphol Airport to Düsseldorf, Milan, Paris, Rome, and elsewhere.

Ryanair: Ireland ☎081 830 3030; UK ☎087 0156 9569; www.ryanair.ie. From Dublin, London, and Glasgow to destinations in France, Germany, Ireland, Italy, Scandinavia, and elsewhere. Deals from as low as UK£9 on limited weekend specials.

TRAVELING FROM AUSTRALIA AND NEW ZEALAND

Air New Zealand: New Zealand ☎0800 737 000; www.airnz.co.nz. From Melbourne, Auckland, and elsewhere to Frankfurt, London, Paris, Rome, and beyond.

Qantas Air: Australia ☎13 13 13; New Zealand ☎0800 808 767; www.qantas.com.au. Flights from Australia and New Zealand to London AUS$2400-3000.

Singapore Air: Australia ☎13 10 11; New Zealand ☎0800 808 909; www.singaporeair.com. Flies from Auckland, Sydney, Melbourne, and Perth to Amsterdam, Brussels, Frankfurt, London, and more.

Thai Airways: Australia ☎13 0065 1960; New Zealand ☎093 770 268; www.thaiair.com. Auckland, Sydney, and Melbourne to Rome, Frankfurt, London, and more.

TRAVELING FROM SOUTH AFRICA

Air France: South Africa ☎0860 340 340; www.airfrance.com/za. Johannesburg to Paris; connections throughout Europe.

British Airways: South Africa ☎0860 011 747; www.british-airways.com/regional/sa. Johannesburg to London; connections to the rest of Western Europe from ZAR3400.

Lufthansa: South Africa ☎0861 842 538; www.lufthansa.co.za. From Cape Town, Durban, and Johannesburg to Germany and elsewhere.

Virgin Atlantic: South Africa ☎0113 403 400; www.virgin-atlantic.co.za. Flies to London from both Cape Town and Johannesburg.

AIR COURIER FLIGHTS

Those who travel light should consider courier flights. Couriers help transport cargo on international flights by using their checked luggage space for freight. Usually, couriers must travel with carry-ons only and must deal with complex flight restrictions. Most flights are round-trip with short fixed-length stays (usually one week) and a limit of one ticket per issue. Most flights also operate only out of major gateway cities, mostly in North America. Generally, you must be over 21 (in some cases 18). In summer, the most popular destinations usually require an advance reservation of about two weeks (you can usually book up to two months ahead). Super-discounted fares are common for "last-minute" flights (three to 14 days ahead).

TRAVELING FROM NORTH AMERICA. Round-trip courier fares from the US to Europe run about US$200-500. Most flights leave from New York, Los Angeles, San Francisco, or Miami in the US; and from Montreal, Toronto, or Vancouver in Canada. The organizations below provide their members with lists of opportunities and courier brokers worldwide for an annual fee (typically US$50-60). Alternatively, you can contact a courier broker directly; most charge registration fees.

Air Courier Association, 350 Indiana St., Ste. 300, Golden, CO 80401 (US ☎800-282-1202; elsewhere call US ☎303-279-3600; www.aircourier.org). Ten departure cities throughout the US and Canada to London, Madrid, Paris, Rome, and throughout Western Europe (high-season US$150-360). One-year membership US$39.

International Association of Air Travel Couriers (IAATC), P.O. Box 980, Keystone Heights, FL 32656 (☎352-475-1584; www.courier.org). From nine North American cities to Western European cities, including London, Madrid, Paris, and Rome. One-year membership US$45-50.

Global Courier Travel, P.O. Box 3051, Nederland, CO 80466 (☎866-470-3061; www.globalcouriertravel.com). Searchable online database. Departures from the US and Canada to Amsterdam, Athens, Brussels, Copenhagen, Frankfurt, London, Madrid, Milan, Paris, and Rome. Lifetime membership US$40, 2 people US$55.

FROM THE UK, IRELAND, AUSTRALIA, AND NEW ZEALAND. The minimum age for couriers from the **UK** is usually 18. **Brave New World Enterprises,** P.O. Box 22212, London SE5 8WB (www.courierflights.com) publishes a directory of all the companies offering courier flights in the UK (UK£10, in electronic form UK£8). **Global Courier Travel** (see above) also offers flights from London and Dublin to continental Europe. **British Airways Travel Shop** (☎087 0240 0747; www.batravelshops.com) arranges some flights from London to destinations in continental Europe (specials may be as low as UK£60; no registration fee). From **Australia** and **New Zealand, Global Courier Travel** (see above) often has listings from Sydney and Auckland to London and occasionally Frankfurt.

STANDBY FLIGHTS

Traveling standby requires considerable flexibility in arrival and departure dates and cities. Companies dealing in standby flights sell vouchers rather than tickets, along with the promise to get you to your destination (or near your destination) within a certain window of time (typically one to five days). You call in before your specific window of time to hear your flight options and the probability that you will be able to board each flight. You can then decide which flights you want to try to make, show up at the appropriate airport at the appropriate time, present your voucher, and board if space is available. Vouchers can usually be bought for both one-way and round-trip travel. You may receive a monetary refund only if every available flight within your date range is full; if you opt not to take an available (but perhaps less convenient) flight, you can only get credit toward future travel. Carefully read agreements with any company offering standby flights. To check on a company's service record in the US, call the Better Business Bureau (☎212-533-6200; www.bbb.org). It is difficult to receive refunds, and vouchers will not be honored when an airline fails to receive payment in time.

TICKET CONSOLIDATORS

Ticket consolidators, or **"bucket shops,"** buy unsold tickets in bulk from commercial airlines and sell them at discounted rates. The best place to look is in the Sunday travel section of any major newspaper, where many bucket shops place tiny ads. Call quickly, as availability is typically very limited. Not all bucket shops are reliable, so insist on a receipt that gives full details of restrictions and refunds, and pay by credit card (in spite of the 2-5% fee) so you can stop payment if you never receive your tickets. For more info, see www.travel-library.com/air-travel/consolidators.html. Keep in mind that these are just suggestions to get you started in your research; *Let's Go* does not endorse any of these agencies. As always, be cautious, and research companies before giving them your credit card number.

TRAVELING FROM NORTH AMERICA. Travel Avenue (☎800-333-3335; www.travelavenue.com) searches for the best available published fares and then uses several consolidators to attempt to beat that fare. **NOW Voyager,** 74 Varick St., Ste. 307, New York, NY 10013 (☎212-431-1616; www.nowvoyagertravel.com) arranges discounted flights, mostly from New York, to Barcelona, London, Madrid, Milan, Paris, and Rome. Other consolidators worth trying are **Pennsylvania Travel** (☎877-251-6866; www.patravel.com), **Rebel** (☎800-227-3235; www.rebeltours.com), and **Cheap Tickets** (☎800-377-1000; www.cheaptickets.com). Yet more consolidators on the web include the **Internet Travel Network** (www.itn.com), **Flights.com** (www.flights.com), and **TravelHUB** (www.travelhub.com).

TRAVELING FROM THE UK, AUSTRALIA, AND NEW ZEALAND. In the UK, the **Air Travel Advisory Bureau** (☎020 7636 5000; www.atab.co.uk) has the names of reliable consolidators and discount flight specialists. From Australia and New Zealand, look for consolidator ads in the travel section of the *Sydney Morning Herald.*

CHARTER FLIGHTS

Charters are flights a tour operator contracts with an airline to fly extra loads of passengers during peak season. Charter flights fly less frequently than major airlines, make refunds particularly difficult, and are almost always fully booked. Schedules and itineraries may also change or be cancelled at the last moment (as late as 48 hours before the trip, and without a full refund), and check-in, boarding, and baggage claim are often pretty slow. However, they can also be cheaper.

Discount clubs and **fare brokers** offer members savings on last-minute charter and tour deals. Study contracts closely; you don't want to end up with an unwanted overnight layover. **Travelers Advantage,** Trumbull, CT (☎203-365-2000; www.travelersadvantage.com; US$60 annual fee includes discounts and cheap flight directories) specializes in European travel and tour packages.

BY CHUNNEL FROM THE UK

Traversing 27 miles under the sea, the Chunnel is undoubtedly the fastest, most convenient, and least scenic route from England to France.

BY TRAIN. Eurostar, Eurostar House, Waterloo Station, London SE1 8SE (UK ☎0990 186 186; US ☎800-387-6782; elsewhere call UK ☎020 7928 5163; www.eurostar.com; www.raileurope.com) runs frequent trains between London and the continent. Ten to 28 trains per day run to Paris (3hr., US$75-159 2nd-class), Brussels (4hr., US$75-159 2nd-class), and Eurodisney. Routes include stops at Ashford in England, and Calais and Lille in France. Book at major rail stations in the UK, at the office above, by phone, or on the web.

BY BUS. Both **Eurolines** and **Eurobus** provide bus-ferry combinations (p. 58).

BY CAR. Eurotunnel, Customer Relations, P.O. Box 2000, Folkestone, Kent CT18 8XY (UK ☎080 0096 9992; www.eurotunnel.co.uk) shuttles cars and passengers between Kent and Nord-Pas-de-Calais. Round-trip fares for vehicle and all passengers range from UK£100-210 with car, UK£259-636 with campervan. Same-day round-trip costs UK£110-150, five-day round-trip UK£139-195. Book online or via phone. Travelers with cars can also look into sea crossings by ferry (see below).

BY BOAT FROM THE UK AND IRELAND

The fares below are **one-way** for **adult foot passengers** unless otherwise noted. Though standard round-trip fares are usually just twice the one-way fare, **fixed-period returns** (usually within five days) are almost invariably cheaper. Ferries run **year-round** unless otherwise noted. **Bikes** are usually free, although you may have to pay up to UK£10 in high season. For a **camper/trailer** supplement, you will have to add UK£20-140 to the "with car" fare. A directory of ferries in this region can be found at www.seaview.co.uk/ferries.html.

P&O Stena Line: UK ☎087 0600 0611; from Europe, call UK ☎130 486 4003; www.posl.com. **Dover** to **Calais, France** (1¼hr., 30 per day, UK£24).

Hoverspeed: UK ☎087 0240 8070; www.hoverspeed.co.uk. **Dover** to **Calais** (35-55min., every hr., UK£24) and **Ostend, Belgium** (2hr., 5-7 per day, UK£28). **Newhaven** to **Dieppe, France** (2¼-4¼hr., 1-3 per day, UK£28).

DFDS Seaways: UK ☎087 0533 3000; www.dfdsseaways.co.uk. **Harwich** to **Hamburg** (20hr.) and **Esbjerg, Denmark** (19hr.). **Newcastle** to **Amsterdam** (14hr.); **Kristiansand, Norway** (19hr.); and **Gothenburg, Sweden** (22hr.).

Brittany Ferries: UK ☎087 0366 5333; France ☎08 25 82 88 28; www.brittany-ferries.com. **Plymouth** to **Roscoff, France** (6hr.; in summer 1-3 per day, off-season 1 per week; UK£20-58) and **Santander, Spain** (24-30hr., 1-2 per week, round-trip UK£80-145). **Portsmouth** to **St-Malo** (8¾hr., 1-2 per day, €23-49) and **Caen, France** (6hr, 1-3 per day, €21-44). **Poole** to **Cherbourg, France** (4¼hr., 1-2 per day, €21-44). **Cork** to **Roscoff, France** (13½hr., Apr.-Sept. 1 per week, €52-99).

P&O North Sea Ferries: UK ☎087 0 29 6002; www.ponsf.com. Daily ferries from **Hull** to **Rotterdam, The Netherlands** (13½hr.) and **Zeebrugge, Belgium** (14hr.). Both UK£38-48, students UK£24-31, cars UK£63-78. Online bookings.

Fjord Line: Norway ☎55 54 88 00; UK ☎019 1296 1313; www.fjordline.no. **Newcastle** to **Stavanger** (19hr.) and **Bergen** (26hr.), **Norway** (UK£50-110, students £25-110). Also from **Bergen** to **Egersund, Norway** and **Hanstholm, Denmark.**

Irish Ferries: Ireland ☎189 031 3131; France ☎01 44 88 54 50; UK ☎087 0517 1717; www.irishferries.ie. **Rosslare, Ireland** to **Cherbourg** and **Roscoff, France** (17-18hr., Apr.-Sept. 1-9 per week, €60-120, students €48) and **Pembroke, UK** (3¾hr., €25-39/€19). **Holyhead, UK** to **Dublin** (2-3hr., round-trip £20-31/£15).

Stena Line: UK ☎412 3364 6826; www.stenaline.co.uk. **Harwich** to **Hook of Holland** (5hr., UK£26). **Fishguard** to **Rosslare** (1-3½hr.; UK£18-21, students £14-17). **Holyhead** to **Dublin** (4hr., UK£23-27/£19-23) and **Dún Laoghaire, Ireland** (1-3½hr., £23-27/£19-23). **Stranraer** to **Belfast** (1¾-3¼hr., UK£14-36/£10).

GETTING AROUND EUROPE

Fares on all modes of transportation are either **one-way** (single) or **round-trip** (return). **"Period returns"** require a return trip within a specific number of days. **"Day returns"** require a same-day return trip. Unless stated otherwise, *Let's Go* always lists one-way fares for trains and buses. Round-trip fares on trains and buses in Europe are simply double the one-way fare.

BY PLANE

Budget flights are increasingly common and have come to rival trains for affordable and convenient continental travel. Student travel agencies sell cheap tickets, and budget fares are frequently available in the spring and summer on high-volume routes between Northern Europe and areas of Greece, Italy, and Spain; consult budget travel agents and local newspapers. For info on cheap flights from Britain to the continent, see **Traveling from the UK,** p. 46.

The **Star Alliance European Airpass** offers low Economy Class fares for travel within Europe to more than 200 destinations in 43 countries. The pass is available to transatlantic passengers on Star Alliance carriers, including Air Canada, Austrian Airlines, BMI British Midland, Lufthansa, Mexicana, Scandinavian Airlines System, Thai Airways, United Airlines, and Varig, as well as on certain partner airlines. Prices are based on mileage between destinations.

In addition, a number of European airlines offer coupon packets that considerably discount the cost of each flight leg. Most are available only as tack-ons to their transatlantic passengers, but some are available as stand-alone offers. Most must be purchased before departure, so research in advance.

Austian Airlines: US ☎ 800-843-0002; www.austrianair.com/greatdeals/europe_airpass.html. "European Airpass" available in the US to Austrian Airlines transatlantic passengers (min. 3 cities; max. 10). Prices based on distance.

BMI: www.flybmi.com. "Discover Europe Airpass" permits travelers to change departure dates and times allowing for flexible travel among any of 25 European destinations.

Europe by Air: US ☎ 888-387-2479; www.europebyair.com. Coupons good on 30 partner airlines to 150 European cities in 30 countries. Must be purchased prior to arrival in Europe. US$99 each, excluding airport tax. Also offers 15- and 21-day unlimited passes; US$699-899.

Iberia: US ☎ 800-772-4642; www.iberia.com. "EuroPass" allows Iberia passengers flying from the US to Spain to tack on additional destinations in Europe.

KLM/Northwest: US ☎ 800-800-1504; www.nwavacations.com. "Passport to Europe," available to US transatlantic passengers, connects 90 European cities (3-city min., 12-city max.). US$100 each.

Lufthansa: US ☎ 800-399-5838; www.lufthansa.com. "Discover Europe" available to US travelers on transatlantic Lufthansa flights (3 cities min., 9 max.). US$119 each for the first three cities, US$99 each for additional cities.

Scandinavian Airlines: US ☎ 800-221-2350; www.scandinavian.net. One-way coupons for travel within Scandinavia, the Baltics, or all of Europe. US$75-155, 8 coupons max. Most are available only to transatlantic Scandinavian Airlines passengers, but some United and Lufthansa passengers also qualify.

BY TRAIN

Trains in Europe are generally comfortable, convenient, and reasonably swift. Second-class compartments, which seat two to six, are great places to meet fellow travelers. For long trips, make sure you are in the correct car, as trains sometimes split at crossroads. Towns listed in parentheses on European train schedules require a train switch at the town listed immediately before the parenthesis. For safety tips on train travel, see p. 18.

You can either buy a **railpass,** which allows you unlimited travel within a particular region for a given period of time, or rely on buying individual **point-to-point** tickets as you go. Almost all countries give students or youths (usually defined as anyone under 26) direct discounts on regular domestic rail tickets, and many also sell a student or youth card that provides 20-50% off all fares for up to a year.

RESERVATIONS. While seat reservations (usually US$3-10) are required only for selected trains, you are not guaranteed a seat without one. You should strongly consider reserving in advance during peak holiday and tourist seasons (at the very latest, a few hours ahead). You will have to purchase a **supplement** (US$10-50) or special fare for high-speed or high-quality trains such as Spain's AVE, Cisalpino trains in Switzerland/Italy/Germany, Finland's Pendolino S220, Italy's ETR500 and Pendolino, Germany's ICE, and certain French TGVs. InterRail holders must also purchase supplements (US$10-25) for trains like EuroCity, InterCity, Sweden's X2000, and many French TGVs; supplements are unnecessary for Eurailpass and Europass holders.

OVERNIGHT TRAINS. On night trains, you won't waste valuable daylight hours traveling, and you can avoid the hassle and expense of staying at a hotel. However, the main drawbacks include discomfort, sleepless nights, and the lack of scenery. **Sleeping accommodations** on trains differ from country to country, but typically you can either sleep upright in your seat (for free) or pay for a separate space. **Couchettes** (berths) typically have four to six seats per compartment (about US$20 per person); **sleepers** (beds) in private sleeping cars offer more privacy and comfort, but are considerably more expensive (US$40-150). If you are using a railpass valid only for a restricted number of days, inspect train schedules to maximize the use of your pass: an overnight train or boat journey uses up only one of your travel days if it departs after 7pm.

SHOULD YOU BUY A RAILPASS? Railpasses were conceived to allow you to jump on any train in Europe, go wherever you want whenever you want, and change your plans at will. In practice, it's not so simple. You still must stand in a line to validate your pass, pay for supplements, and fork over cash for seat and couchette reservations. More importantly, railpasses don't always pay off. If you are planning to spend extensive time on trains, hopping between big cities, a railpass will probably be worth it. But in many cases, budget flights or point-to-point tickets (especially if you are under 26) may prove a cheaper option.

You may find it tough to make your railpass pay for itself in Belgium, Greece, Ireland, Italy, Luxembourg, The Netherlands, Portugal, Spain, Eastern Europe, or the Balkans, where train fares are reasonable, distances short, or buses preferable. If, however, the total cost of your trips nears the price of the pass, the convenience of avoiding ticket lines may be worth the difference.

MULTINATIONAL RAILPASSES

EURAILPASS. Eurail is valid in most of Western Europe: Austria, Belgium, Denmark, Finland, France, Germany, Greece, Hungary, Ireland, Italy, Luxembourg, The Netherlands, Norway, Portugal, Spain, Sweden, and Switzerland. It is not valid in the UK. Standard **Eurailpasses,** valid for a consecutive given number of days, are best for those planning to spend extensive time on trains every few days. **Flexipasses,** valid for any 10 or 15 days within a two-month period, are more cost-effec-

Rail prices and times are subject to wide variation, and student or other discounts may be available. This map gives only a general picture of train travel in Europe. Consult *Thomas Cook's European Timetable* for accurate schedule info.

0   300 miles
0   300 kilometers

N

Shetland Islands

Orkney Islands

SCOTLAND

North Sea

Bergen

DENMARK

Glasgow $47 3½hr.

Belfast   Edinburgh

NORTHERN IRELAND

$22 2½hr.

Dublin

GREAT BRITAIN

ENGLAND

Hamburg

IRELAND

$122 5hr.

$130 5¼hr.

WALES

Cardiff

NETHERLANDS

$79 6hr.

London

Amsterdam

$46 3hr.

$108 7hr.

ATLANTIC OCEAN

$109-149 3hr.

$33 2½hr.

GERMANY

Brussels   Cologne $10 ½hr.

BELGIUM

Bonn $36 2hr.

$109-149 3hr.

$68 1¾hr.

$108 7hr.

Frankfurt

Paris   LUXEMBOURG

$91 3½hr.

Nantes

$84 4½hr.

$130 8½hr.

$60 3hr.

$78 2¼hr.

$78 3¾hr.

Zurich

$66 4¼hr.

Bay of Biscay

SWITZERLAND   Bern

Santiago de Campostela

Bordeaux

$99 10½-14hr.

Lyon

$19 2hr.

Geneva

$16 1½hr.

San Sebastián

FRANCE

Milan   Verona

$48 3hr.

$27 3hr.

$21 2½hr.

$52 7½hr.

$39 1½hr.

$84 7¼hr.

Marseille

Nice

$36 2¾hr.

Florence

PORTUGAL

ANDORRA

$64 7hr.

MONACO

$27 2hr.

Lisbon

$50 10½hr.

Madrid

$56 7hr.

Corsica (Fr.)

$48-85 1¾hr.

$39 1½hr.

Barcelona

SPAIN

$31 3½hr.

Palma

Seville $10-23 1½hr.   Córdoba

Valencia

Sardinia (It.)

$23 4½hr.   Granada

Balearic Islands (Sp.)

$27 4½hr.

Algeciras

Tangier   GIBRALTAR

Mediterranean Sea

Rabat

MOROCCO

Algiers

ALGERIA

Tunis

TUNISIA

Rail Planner

tive for those traveling longer distances less frequently. The **Selectpass,** which replaces the Europass, allows five to 15 travel days within a two-month period, in three to five pre-selected, contiguous countries. (For the purpose of the Selectpass, Belgium, The Netherlands, and Luxembourg are considered one country.) **Saverpasses** provide first-class travel for travelers in groups of two to five (prices are per person). **Youthpasses** provide parallel second-class perks for those under 26. Youth and Saver versions of all passes are available.

Passholders receive a timetable for major routes and a map with details on ferry, steamer, bus, car rental, hotel, and Eurostar (see p. 48) discounts. Passholders often also receive reduced fares or free passage on many bus and boat lines.

EURAILPASSES	15 DAYS	21 DAYS	1 MONTH	2 MONTHS	3 MONTHS
Eurailpass	US$588	US$762	US$946	US$1338	US$1654
Eurailpass Saver	US$498	US$648	US$804	US$1138	US$1408
Eurailpass Youth	US$414	US$534	US$664	US$938	US$1160

SELECTPASSES	5 DAYS	6 DAYS	8 DAYS	10 DAYS	15 DAYS
Selectpass: 3-country	US$356	US$394	US$470	US$542	N/A
4-country	US$398	US$436	US$512	US$584	N/A
5-country	US$438	US$476	US$552	US$624	US$794
Saver: 3-country	US$304	US$336	US$400	US$460	N/A
4-country	US$340	US$372	US$436	US$496	N/A
5-country	US$374	US$406	US$470	US$530	US$674
Youth: 3-country	US$249	US$276	US$329	US$379	N/A
4-country	US$279	US$306	US$359	US$409	N/A
5-country	US$307	US$334	US$387	US$437	US$556

FLEXIPASS	10 DAYS IN 2 MONTHS	15 DAYS IN 2 MONTHS
Flexipass	US$694	US$914
Flexipass Saver	US$592	US$778
Flexipass Youth	US$488	US$642

SHOPPING AROUND FOR A EURAIL PASS. Eurail passes are designed by the EU itself and can be bought only by non-Europeans, almost exclusively from non-European distributors. These passes must be sold at uniform prices determined by the EU. However, some travel agents tack on a US$10 handling fee, and others offer certain bonuses with purchase, so shop around. Also, keep in mind that pass prices usually go up each year, so if you're planning to travel early in the year, you can save by purchasing before January 1 (you have three months from the purchase date to validate your pass in Europe).

It is best to buy your Eurail or Europass before leaving; only a few places in major European cities sell them, and at a marked-up price. You can get a replacement for a lost pass only if you have purchased insurance on it under the Pass Protection Plan (US$14). Passes are available through travel agents and student travel agencies like STA (p. 43). Several companies specialize in selecting and distributing appropriate railpasses; try **Rail Europe** (US ☎ 888-382-7245; www.raileurope.com) or **Railpass.com** (US ☎ 877-724-5727; www.railpass.com).

OTHER MULTINATIONAL PASSES. If your travels will be limited to one area, regional passes are often good values. The new **France'n Italy pass** lets you travel in France and Italy for four days in a two-month period (standard US$239, saver US$209, youth US$199). The **Scanrail pass,** which covers rail travel in Denmark, Finland, Norway, and Sweden, is available both in the UK and the US (five days of

2nd-class travel in a two month period US$286, under-26 US$199, seniors US$253; 10 days in two months US$382/267/339; 21 consecutive days US$443/309/392). The **Benelux Tourrail pass** for Belgium, Luxembourg, and The Netherlands is available in the UK, in the US, and at train stations in Belgium and Luxembourg, but not in The Netherlands (five days of 2nd-class travel in a one month period US$163, under-26 US$109). The **Balkan Flexipass** is valid for travel in Bulgaria, Greece, Macedonia, Montenegro, Romania, Serbia, and Turkey (five, ten, or 15 days of travel in a one month period US$175/306/368; under-26 US$104/182/221; seniors US$141/244/294). The **European East pass** covers Austria, the Czech Republic, Hungary, Poland, and the Slovak Republic (five days of travel in a one month period US$158).

INTERRAIL PASS. If you have lived for at least six months in any European country, **InterRail passes** prove an economical option. There are eight InterRail **zones**. The pass allows either 21 consecutive days or one month of unlimited travel within one, two, three, or all of the eight zones; the cost is determined by the number of zones the pass covers (UK£219-379). The **Under-26 InterRail pass** (UK£149-265) provides the same services as the InterRail pass, as does the new **Child pass** (ages 4-11 UK£110-190). Passholders receive **discounts** on rail travel, Eurostar journeys, and most ferries to Ireland, Scandinavia, and the rest of Europe. Most exclude **supplements** for high-speed trains. Tickets and info are available from travel agents, at major train stations, or online (www.railpassdirect.co.uk).

DOMESTIC RAILPASSES

If you are planning to spend a significant amount of time in one country or region, a national pass will probably be more cost-efficient than a multinational pass. Several national passes offer companion fares, allowing two adults traveling together to save about 50% on the price of one pass. However, they are often limited and, unlike Eurail, don't provide free or discounted travel on many private railways and ferries. Some of these passes can be bought only in Europe, some only outside of Europe; check with a railpass agent or with national tourist offices.

NATIONAL RAILPASSES. The domestic analogs of the Eurailpass, national railpasses (called "flexipasses" in some countries) are valid either for a given number of consecutive days or for a specific number of days within a given period. Usually, they must be purchased before you leave your home country. Though national passes will usually save frequent travelers money, in some cases (particularly in Eastern Europe) you may find that they are actually more expensive than point-to-point tickets. Regional passes are also available for areas where the main pass is not valid. For more info, contact Rail Europe (p. 54).

EURO DOMINO. Like the InterRail pass, the **Euro Domino pass** is available to anyone who has lived in Europe for at least six months; however, it can only be used in one country. The pass is available for three to eight days of travel within a one-month period in one of 29 European countries plus Morocco. **Supplements** for many high-speed trains (e.g., French TGV, German ICE, and Swedish X2000) are included, though you must pay for **reservations.** The pass must be bought within your country of residence. Contact your national rail company for more info.

RAIL-AND-DRIVE PASSES

In addition to simple railpasses, many countries (as well as Europass and Eurail) offer rail-and-drive passes, which combine car rental with rail travel—a good option for travelers who wish both to visit cities accessible by rail and to make side trips into the surrounding areas.

TRANSPORTATION

DISCOUNTED RAIL TICKETS

For travelers under 26, BIJ tickets (e.g., **Wasteels, Eurotrain,** and **Route 26**) are great alternatives to railpasses. Available for international trips within Europe, travel within France, and most ferry services, they knock 20-40% off regular second-class fares. Issued for a specific international route between two points, they must be used in the direction and order of the designated route and must be bought in Europe. However, tickets are good for 60 days after purchase and allow a number of stopovers along the normal direct route of the train journey. The equivalent for those over 26, **BIGT** tickets provide a 20-30% discount on first- and second-class international tickets for business travelers, temporary residents of Europe, and their families. Both types of tickets are available from European travel agents, at Wasteels or Eurotrain offices (usually in or near train stations), or directly at the ticket counter in some stations. For more info, see www.wasteels.com.

> **FURTHER RESOURCES ON TRAIN TRAVEL.**
> **Point-to-Point Fares and Schedules:** www.raileurope.com/us/rail/ fares_schedules/index.htm. Allows you to calculate whether buying a railpass would save you money.
> **European Railway Servers:** http://mercurio.iet.unipi.it/misc/timetabl.html. Links to railway servers throughout Europe.
> **Info on Rail Travel and Railpasses:** www.eurorail.com; www.raileurope.com.
> *Thomas Cook European Timetable,* updated monthly, covers all major and most minor train routes in Europe. In the US, order it from Forsyth Travel Library. (☎800-367-7984; www.forsyth.com. US$28.95.) In Europe, find it at any Thomas Cook Money Exchange Center. Alternatively, buy directly from Thomas Cook (www.thomascookpublishing.com).
> *On the Rails Around Europe: A Comprehensive Guide to Travel by Train,* Melissa Shales. Thomas Cook Ltd. (US$18.95).
> *Europe By Eurail 2003,* Laverne Ferguson-Kosinski. Globe Pequot Press (US$18.95).

BY BUS

Though European trains and railpasses are extremely popular, buses may prove a better option. In Spain, Hungary, and the Baltics, buses are on par with trains; in Britain, Greece, Ireland, and Portugal, bus networks are more extensive, more efficient, and often more comfortable than train routes; and in Iceland and parts of northern Scandinavia, bus service is the only ground transportation available. In the rest of Europe, scattered offerings from private companies can be inexpensive but sometimes unreliable. Often cheaper than railpasses, **international bus passes** typically allow unlimited travel on a hop-on, hop-off basis between major European cities. In general, these services tend to be more popular among non-American backpackers.

Eurolines, 4 Cardiff Rd., LU1 1PP Luton (UK☎015 8241 5841; www.eurolines.com). The largest operator of Europe-wide coach services, Eurolines offers unlimited peak-season 30-day (UK£259, under-26 UK£209) or 60-day (UK£299/229) travel between 30 major European cities in 16 countries; off-season prices are lower. Euroexplorers minipasses offer stops at select cities across Europe (UK£55-75).

Busabout, 258 Vauxhall Bridge Rd., London SW1V 1BS (UK ☎020 7950 1661; www.busabout.com) covers 60 European cities. Sells 2 week, consecutive-day passes (US$339, students US$309) and season passes (US$1149/1039). Flexipasses valid for 7 days out of 1 month (US$339/309) or 24 days out of 4months (US$909/809) also available.

BY CAR

Cars offer speed, freedom, access to the countryside, and an escape from the town-to-town monotony of trains. Before setting off, know the laws of the countries in which you'll be driving (e.g., both seat belts and headlights must be on at all times in Scandinavia, and remember to keep left in Ireland and the UK). For an informal primer on European road signs and conventions, check out www.travlang.com/signs. Scandinavians and Western Europeans use unleaded **gas** almost exclusively, but it's not available in many gas stations in Eastern Europe.

SAFETY. Cheaper rental cars tend to be less reliable and harder to handle on difficult terrain. Less expensive 4WD vehicles in particular tend to be more top-heavy and are more dangerous when navigating bumpy roads. Road conditions in Eastern Europe are often poor, and many travelers prefer public transportation. Western European roads are generally excellent, but keep in mind that each area has its own hazards. In Scandinavia, for example, you'll need to watch for moose and elk (particularly in low light), while on the Autobahn, cars driving 150kph will probably pose more of a threat. Road conditions fluctuate with seasons; winter weather will make driving difficult in some countries, while in others, spring thaws cause flooding due to melted ice. Roads in mountainous areas are often steep and curvy, and may be closed in the winter. The **Association for Safe International Road Travel (ASIRT),** 11769 Gainsborough Rd., Potomac, MD 20854 (US ☎301-983-5252; www.asirt.org) can provide specific info about road conditions. ASIRT considers road travel to be relatively safe in most of Western Europe and slightly less safe in developing nations due to poorly maintained roads and inadequately enforced traffic laws. Carry emergency equipment with you (see **Driving Precautions,** p. 60) and know what to do in case of a breakdown.

DRIVING PERMITS AND CAR INSURANCE

INTERNATIONAL DRIVING PERMIT (IDP). If you plan to drive a car while in Europe, you must be over 18 and have an International Driving Permit (IDP), although certain countries (such as the UK) allow travelers to drive with a valid American or Canadian license for a limited number of months. It may be a good idea to get one anyway, in case you're in an accident or stranded in a smaller town where the police may not speak English; info on the IDP is also printed in French, Spanish, Russian, German, Arabic, Italian, Scandinavian, and Portuguese.

Your IDP, valid for one year, must be issued in your own country before you depart. An application for an IDP usually requires one or two passport photos, a valid local license, and a fee (about US$10). To apply, contact the national or local branch of your home country's automobile association.

CAR INSURANCE. If you rent, lease, or borrow a car, you will need a **green card,** or **International Insurance Certificate,** to certify that you have liability insurance and that it applies abroad. Green cards can be obtained at car rental agencies, from car dealers (for those leasing cars), from some travel agents, and at some border crossings. Rental agencies may require the purchase of theft insurance in countries that are considered high-risk. Remember that if you are driving a conventional vehicle on an **unpaved road,** you are almost never covered by insurance; ask about this before leaving the rental agency. Always ask if prices quoted include tax and **insurance** against theft and collision; some credit card companies cover the deductible on collision insurance, allowing their customers to decline the collision damage waiver. Be aware that cars rented on **Ameri-**

can **Express** or **Visa/Mastercard Gold or Platinum** credit cards in Europe might *not* carry the automatic insurance that they would in some other countries; check with your credit card company.

> **DRIVING PRECAUTIONS.** When traveling in the summer or in the desert, bring substantial amounts of water (5L of water per person per day) for drinking and for the radiator. For long drives to unpopulated areas, register with police before beginning your trek, and again upon arrival at your destination. Check with the local automobile club for details. When traveling long distances, make sure tires are in good condition and have enough air, and get good maps. A compass and a car manual can also be very useful. You should always carry a spare tire and a jack, jumper cables, extra oil, flares, a flashlight, and heavy blankets (in case your car breaks down at night or in the winter). If you don't know how to change a tire, learn before heading out, especially if you are planning to travel in deserted areas. Blowouts on dirt roads are exceedingly common. If you do have a breakdown, stay with your car; if you wander off, there's less likelihood that trackers will find you.

RENTING A CAR

Although a single traveler won't save by renting a car, four usually will. If you can't decide between train and car travel, you may benefit from a combination of the two; RailEurope and other railpass vendors offer rail-and-drive packages (p. 57). Fly-and-drive packages are also often available from travel agents or airline/rental agency partnerships.

You can rent a car from a US-based firm (e.g., Alamo, Avis, Budget, or Hertz) with European offices, from a European-based company with local representatives (Europcar), or from a tour operator (Auto Europe, Europe By Car, and Kemwel Holiday Autos) that will arrange a rental for you from a European company at its own rates. Multinationals offer greater flexibility, but tour operators often strike better deals. Rates vary widely by country; expect to pay US$80-400 per week, plus tax (5-25%), for a tiny car. Reserve ahead and pay in advance if possible. Picking up your car in Belgium, Germany, or The Netherlands is usually cheaper than renting in Paris. Particularly during the summer, rental in parts of Eastern Europe and Scandinavia, as well as in Denmark, Ireland, and Italy, might be more expensive; some companies charge extra fees for traveling into Eastern Europe. It is always less expensive to reserve a car from the US than from Europe.

Some chains allow you to choose a drop-off location different from your pickup city, but there is often a minimum rental period and an extra charge. Expect to pay more for larger cars and for 4WD. Cars with **automatic transmission** are far more expensive than manuals (stick shift), and are more difficult to find in most of Europe. It is virtually impossible to obtain an automatic 4WD. Many rental packages offer unlimited kilometers, while others offer 200km per day with a surcharge of around US$0.15 per kilometer after that. Return the car with a full tank of **gasoline** to avoid high fuel charges in the end. Gas is generally most expensive in Scandinavia; in any country, fuel tends to be cheaper in cities than in outlying areas.

Ask about discounts and check the terms of insurance, particularly the size of the deductible. Minimum age varies from country to country but is usually 21-25; some companies charge those aged 21-24 additional insurance. In general, all you need to rent a car is a license from home and proof that you've had it for a year. Car rental in Europe is available through these agencies:

Auto Europe: US and Canada ☎888-223-5555; www.autoeurope.com.

Avis: Australia ☎ 136 333; Canada ☎800-272-5871; New Zealand ☎0800 655 111; UK ☎087 0606 0100; US ☎800-230-4898; www.avis.com.

Budget: US and Canada ☎800-527-0700; UK ☎014 4228 0181; www.budgetrentacar.com.

Europe by Car: US ☎800-223-1516; www.europebycar.com.

Europcar International: France ☎55 66 83 00; US ☎877-506-0070; www.europcar.com.

Hertz: Australia ☎9698 2555; Canada ☎800-263-0600; UK ☎087 0844 8844; US ☎800-654-3001; www.hertz.com.

Kemwel: US ☎877-820-0668; www.kemwel.com.

LEASING A CAR

For longer trips, leasing can be cheaper than the daily cost of renting; it is often the only option for those ages 18-21. The cheapest leases are agreements to buy the car and then sell it back to the manufacturer at a prearranged price. As far as you're concerned, though, it's a lease and doesn't entail enormous financial transactions. Leases generally include insurance coverage and are not taxed. The most affordable ones usually originate in Belgium, France, or Germany. Expect to pay around US$1100-1800 (depending on the size of the car) for 60 days. Contact **Auto Europe, Europe by Car,** or **Kemwel** (see above) for more info.

BUYING A CAR

If you're brave and know what you're doing, **buying** a used car or van in Europe and selling it just before you leave can provide the cheapest wheels for longer trips. Check with consulates for import-export laws concerning used vehicles, registration, and safety and emission standards.

BY FERRY

Most European ferries are slow but inexpensive and quite comfortable; even the cheapest ticket typically includes a reclining chair or couchette. Plan ahead and reserve tickets in advance, or you may spend days waiting in port for the next sail. Fares jump sharply in July and August—ask for discounts. ISIC holders (p. 13) can often get student fares, and Eurailpass holders (p. 51) get many discounts and free trips. Occasional port taxes should run less than US$10. For more info, consult the *Official Steamship Guide International* (available at travel agencies), or www.youra.com/ferry.

ENGLISH CHANNEL AND IRISH SEA FERRIES. Ferries are frequent and dependable. The main route across the **English Channel,** from England to France, is Dover-Calais. The main ferry port on the southern coast of England is Portsmouth, which has connections to France and Spain. Ferries also cross the **Irish Sea,** connecting Northern Ireland with Scotland and England, and the Republic of Ireland with Wales. For more info on sailing (or "hovering") in this region, see **By Boat from the UK and Ireland,** p. 49, or www.ferrybooker.com.

NORTH AND BALTIC SEA FERRIES. Ferries in the **North Sea** are reliable and cheap. For info on ferries heading across the North Sea to and from the UK, see p. 49. **Baltic Sea** ferries service routes between Poland and Scandinavia.

Polferries: Poland ☎48 94 35 52 102; www.polferries.se. Ferries run from Poland to Denmark and Sweden.

Color Line: Norway ☎47 22 94 44 00; www.colorline.com. Offers ferries from Norway to Denmark, Germany, and Sweden.

Silja Line: US sales ☎800-533-3755; Finland ☎09 18041; www.silja.com. Helsinki to Stockholm (16hr.); Tallinn, Estonia (3hr., June to mid-Sept.); and Rostock, Germany (23-25hr., June to mid-Sept.). Also Turku to Stockholm (10hr.).

DFDS Seaways: US ☎800-533-3755; www.seaeurope.com. Offers routes within Scandinavia and between Scandinavia and England, Germany, Holland, and Poland.

MEDITERRANEAN AND AEGEAN FERRIES. Mediterranean ferries run from France and Spain to Morocco. Reservations are recommended, especially in the summer. Shop around—many companies operate on erratic schedules, with similar routes and varying prices. Beware of lines that don't take reservations. For more info, see p. 722.

Companies such as **Superfast Ferries** (US ☎954-771-9200; www.superfast.com) offer routes across the **Adriatic and Ionian Seas** from Ancona and Bari, Italy to Patras and Igoumenitsa, Greece, as well as to Split and Dubrovnik, Croatia. **Eurail** is valid on certain ferries between Brindisi, Italy and Patras, Greece. Countless ferry companies operate these routes simultaneously; websites such as www.ferries.gr list various schedules. See specific country chapters for more info.

BY BICYCLE

Biking can be a very enjoyable way to explore Europe. Many airlines will count your bike as your second free piece of luggage; a few charge extra (up to US$110 one-way). Bikes must be packed in a cardboard box with the pedals and front wheel detached; airlines often sell **bike boxes** at the airport (US$10). Most ferries let you take your bike for free or for a nominal fee, and you can always ship your bike on trains. If your touring will be confined to one or two regions, renting a bike beats bringing your own. Some youth hostels rent bicycles for low prices. In Switzerland, train stations rent bikes and often allow you to drop them off elsewhere; check train stations throughout Europe for similar deals.

EQUIPMENT. In addition to **panniers** to hold your luggage, you'll need a good **helmet** (from US$25) and a U-shaped **Citadel** or **Kryptonite lock** (from US$30). For equipment, **Bike Nashbar**, 6103 State Rte. 446, Canfield, OH 44406 (US ☎800-627-4227; www.nashbar.com), beats all competitors' offers and ships anywhere in the US or Canada. For more info, purchase *Europe by Bike*, by Karen and Terry Whitehill. (US ☎800-553-4453; www.mountaineersbooks.org. US$14.95.)

BIKE TOURS. If you'd rather not strike out on your own, **Blue Marble Travel** (Canada ☎519-624-2494; France ☎42 36 02 34; US ☎215-923-3788; www.bluemarble.org) offers bike tours throughout Europe for small groups of travelers ages 20-49. **CBT Tours** (☎800-736-2453; www.cbttours.com) offers full-package biking, mountain biking, hiking, and multisport tours (US$1500-2500) to Belgium, the Czech Republic, England, France, Germany, Italy, Ireland, The Netherlands, Scotland, and Switzerland. **Cycle Rides** (UK ☎012 2542 8452; www.cycle-rides.co.uk) offers various one- to two-week tours throughout Europe. **EURO Bike and Walking Tours** (☎800-321-6060; www.eurobike.com) gives dozens of six-day to five-week bike tours across Central and Western Europe.

BY MOPED AND MOTORCYCLE

Motorized bikes and **mopeds** use little gas, can be put on trains and ferries, and are a good compromise between the cost of car travel and the limited range of bicycles. However, they're uncomfortable for long distances, dangerous in the rain, and unpredictable on rough roads and gravel. Always wear a helmet and never ride with a backpack. If you've never been on a moped before, a twisting Alpine road is not the place to start. Expect to pay about US$20-35 per day; try auto repair shops, and remember to bargain. **Motorcycles** can be much more expensive and normally require a license, but are better for long distances. Before renting, ask if the quoted price includes tax and insurance to avoid unexpected fees. Do not offer your passport as a deposit; if you have an accident or experience mechanical failure you may not get it back until all repairs are covered. Pay ahead of time instead. For more info, try: *Motorcycle Journeys through the Alps and Corsica,* by John Hermann (US$24.95); *Motorcycle Touring and Travel,* by Bill Stermer (US$19.95); or *Europe by Motorcycle,* by Gregory W. Frazier (US$19.95).

BY FOOT

Europe's grandest scenery can often be seen only by foot. *Let's Go* describes many daytrips in town listings for the pedestrian-inclined, but native inhabitants, hostel proprietors, and fellow travelers are often the best source of tips. Many European countries have hiking and mountaineering organizations; alpine clubs in Austria, Germany, Italy, and Switzerland, as well as tourist organizations in Scandinavia, provide simple accommodations in idyllic settings.

BY THUMB

Let's Go strongly urges you to consider the risks before choosing to hitchhike. We do not recommend hitchhiking as a safe means of transportation, and none of the information presented here is intended to do so.

Never hitchhike before carefully considering the risks involved. Hitchhiking means entrusting your life to a stranger, and risking theft, assault, sexual harassment, and unsafe driving. Despite the dangers, there are advantages to hitchhiking when it is safe: It allows you to meet local people and get where you're going, especially in Northern Europe and Ireland, where public transportation is spotty. The choice, however, remains yours.

Conscientious hitchhikers avoid getting in the back of two-door cars (or any car they wouldn't be able to get out of in a hurry) and never let go of their backpacks. If you ever feel threatened, insist on being let off immediately. Acting as if you are going to open the car door or vomit will usually get a driver to stop. Hitchhiking at night can be particularly dangerous; experienced hitchhikers stand in well-lit places and expect drivers to be leery of nocturnal thumbers. For women traveling alone, hitchhiking is just too dangerous. A man and a woman are a safer combination; two men will have a harder time getting a ride.

Experienced hitchhikers pick a spot outside of built-up areas, where drivers can stop, return to the road without causing an accident, and have time to look over potential passengers as they approach. Hitchhiking (or even standing) on superhighways is usually illegal: One may only thumb at rest stops or at the entrance ramps to highways. Most Europeans signal with an open hand, not a thumb; many write their destination on a sign in large, bold letters and draw a smiley-face under it. Finally, success will depend on appearance. Drivers prefer hitchhikers who are neat and wholesome-looking, and are often wary of people wearing sunglasses.

Britain and **Ireland** are the easiest places in Europe to get a lift. Hitchhiking in **Scandinavia** is slow but steady. Hitchhiking in **Southern Europe** is generally mediocre; **France** is the worst. In some **Central and Eastern European** countries, drivers may expect to be paid. Most Western European countries offer a **ride service,** which pairs drivers with riders; the fee varies according to destination. **Eurostop International (Verband der Deutschen Mitfahrzentralen** in Germany and **Allostop** in France) is one of the largest ride service providers in Europe. Riders and drivers can enter their names on the Internet through the **Taxistop** website (www.taxistop.be). Not all organizations screen drivers and riders; ask in advance.

ALTERNATIVES TO TOURISM

In 2002, nearly 700 million trips were made across international borders, and that number is projected to rise to one billion by 2010; that's quite a change from the 1.7 million trips taken when *Let's Go: Europe* was first published in 1961. The dramatic rise in tourism has created an interdependence between the economy, environment, and culture of Europe and the tourists it hosts. In fact, no continent hosts more: with over 400 million arrivals last year, Europe welcomes a larger number of visitors anually than all other destinations combined.

At *Let's Go*, we aim to foster a mutually beneficial relationship between traveler and destination. We've watched the growth of the "ignorant tourist" stereotype with dismay, knowing that the majority of travelers care passionately about the state of the communities and environments they explore—but also knowing that even conscientious tourists can inadvertently damage natural wonders and cultural enclaves. We feel the philosophy of **sustainable travel** is among the most important travel tips we can impart to our readers. Through sensitivity to local communities, today's travelers can be a powerful force in preserving and restoring this fragile world.

Two rising trends in sustainable travel are ecotourism and community-based tourism. **Ecotourism** focuses on the conservation of natural habitats and the promotion of local economies without exploitation or overdevelopment. **Community-based tourism** aims to channel tourist dollars into the local economy by emphasizing tours and cultural programs run by members of the host community, often to the benefit of disadvantaged groups. **Volunteer** opportunities range from conservation to humanitarian projects, and can be completed on an infrequent basis or as the main component of your trip.

There are many other ways to integrate with the communities you visit. **Studying** at a college or language program is one popular option. Many travelers also structure trips around the **work** they can get along the way, which often consists of odd jobs as they go or full-time stints in larger cities.

For more info about sustainable tourism visit www.worldsurface.com, which features photos and personal stories of volunteer experiences. More general info is available at www.sustainabletravel.org. For those who would prefer hands-on involvement, Earthwatch International, Operation Crossroads Africa, and Habitat for Humanity offer fulfilling volunteer opportunities around the world.

VOLUNTEERING

Many people who volunteer in Europe do so on a short-term basis at organizations that make use of drop-in or once-a-week volunteers. The best way to find opportunities that match up with your interests is to check with local or national volunteer centers, which generally provide extensive lists of options.

More intensive volunteer services may charge you a fee to participate. These costs can be surprisingly hefty (although they frequently cover airfare and most, if not all, living expenses). Most people choose to go through a parent organization that takes care of logistical details and frequently provides a group environment and support system. There are two main types of organizations—religious and secular—although there are rarely restrictions on participation in either.

TIPS FOR SUSTAINABLE TRAVEL

Reduce, reuse, recycle: use electronic tickets, recycle papers and bottles wherever possible, and avoid using containers made of Styrofoam.

Conserve water by opting out of frequent changes of towels and sheets.

Reduce electricity consumption by using hotels that favor fluorescent or other low-energy lighting.

Fill out the comment form typically found in guest rooms and suggest specific steps to improve the hotel's environmental practices.

Travel by train when feasible. Rail travel requires only half the energy per passenger mile that planes do.

When renting a car, ask whether fuel-efficient vehicles are available. Honda and Toyota produce vehicles that use hybrid engines powered by electricity and gasoline, thus reducing emissions of carbon dioxide.

Be thoughtful in your purchases. Take care not to buy souvenir objects made from trees in old-growth or endangered forests, such as teak, or items made from endangered species, like ivory or tortoise jewelry.

Opportunities for volunteer work are more abundant in Eastern Europe than in other areas of the continent. Habitat for Humanity and Peace Corps placements, for example, are not usually available in Western Europe.

ONLINE DIRECTORIES

www.alliance-network.org. Umbrella website bringing together various international service organizations from around the world.

www.idealist.org. Provides extensive listings of service opportunities.

www.volunteerabroad.com. Searchable database of opportunites around the world.

www.worldvolunteerweb.org. Lists organizations and events around the world.

PROGRAMS

COMMUNITY DEVELOPMENT

Cross-Cultural Solutions, 47 Potter Ave., New Rochelle, NY 10801 (☎800-380-4777; crossculturalsolutions.org). 2- to 12-week education and social service placements in Russia and many other countries. 17+. From US$2000.

Elderhostel, Inc., 11 Ave. de Lafayette, Boston, MA 02111-1746 (☎877-426-8056; fax 877-426-2166; www.elderhostel.org). Sends volunteers age 55 and over to destinations in Europe to work in conservation, research, teaching, and other programs.

Global Volunteers, 375 E. Little Canada Rd., St. Paul, MN 55117 (☎800-487-1074). A variety of 1- to 3-week volunteer programs throughout Europe. Fees range from US$1295-2395 including room and board but not airfare.

Habitat for Humanity International, 121 Habitat St., Americus, GA 31709 (☎229-924-6935, ext. 2551; www.habitat.org). Volunteers build houses in over 87 countries. Program durations range from 2 weeks to 3 years. Short-term programs in Europe, including airfare, room, board, and insurance, cost from US$1800-2600.

Peace Corps, Office of Volunteer Recruitment and Selection, 1111 20th St., NW, Washington, D.C. 20526 (☎800-424-8580; www.peacecorps.gov). Various opportunities throughout the developing world including Morocco and parts of Eastern Europe.

Service Civil International Voluntary Service (SCI-IVS), SCI USA Main Office, 5474 Walnut Level Rd., Crozet, VA 22932 (☎206-350-6585; www.sci-ivs.org). Arranges placement in outdoor work camps throughout Europe. 18+. Registration fee US$175.

CONSERVATION

Archaeological Institute of America, 656 Beacon St., Boston, MA 02215 (☎617-353-9361; www.archaeological.org). The *Archaeological Fieldwork Opportunities Bulletin*, available on the organization's website, lists field sites throughout Europe.

Business Enterprises for Sustainable Travel, (www.sustainabletravel.org). Supports travel that helps communities preserve natural and cultural resources and create sustainable livelihoods. Has listings of local programs, innovative travel opportunities, and internships.

Club du Vieux Manoir, Abbaye Royale du Moncel, 60700 Pontpoint, France (☎03 44 72 33 98; cvmclubduvieuxmanoir.free.fr). Offers year-long and summer programs restoring castles and churches throughout France. €14 membership/insurance fee; €16 per day, including food and tent.

Earthwatch Institute, 3 Clocktower Pl., Ste. 100, Box 75, Maynard, MA 01754 (☎800-776-0188; www.earthwatch.org). Arranges 1- to 3-week programs to promote conservation of natural resources. Fees vary based on program location and duration: costs average $1700 plus airfare.

Eco-Centre Caput Insulae-Beli, Beli 4, 51559 Beli, Island of Cres, Croatia (☎/fax 51 840 525; www.caput-insulae.com). Spend 2 weeks protecting the natural, cultural, and historical heritage of the island of Cres, Croatia.

The National Trust, Volunteering and Community Involvement Office, Rowan, Kembrey Park, Swindon, Wiltshire, SN2 8YL, UK (☎08706 095 383; www.nationaltrust.org.uk/volunteers). Arranges numerous volunteer opportunities, including Working Holidays.

World Wide Opportunities on Organic Farms (WWOOF), Main Office, P.O. Box 2675, Lewes BN7 1RB, UK (www.wwoof.org). Arranges volunteer work with organic and eco-conscious farms around the world.

World Wildlife Federation of Finland, (www.wwf.fi/work_camps.html). Offers conservation work camps throughout Finland.

HEALTH

AIDS Take Care, Schlossstr. 15, 82269 Getendorf/Munich, Germany (☎8193 93000; fax 950754). Supports AIDS education and patient treatment throughout the world.

Doctors Without Borders, 333 7th Ave., 2nd fl., New York, NY 10001 (☎212-679-6800; www.doctorswithoutborders.org/volunteer). Medical and non-medical volunteer assignments wherever there is need.

Mental Health Ireland, Mensana House, 6 Adelaide St., Dún Laoghaire, Co. Dublin, Ireland (☎01 284 1166; www.mentalhealthireland.ie). Volunteer activities include fundraising, housing, "befriending," and promoting mental health in various regions of Ireland. Opportunities listed in their online newsletter, *Mensana News*.

HUMANITARIAN AND SOCIAL SERVICES

Balkan Sunflowers, (www.ddh.nl/org/balkansunflower). An organization aiding refugees in Albania, FYR Montenegro, and Kosovo. Programs generally last about 6 weeks and volunteers often work with children.

Coalition for Psychotrauma and Peace, Gunduliceva 18, 32000 Vukovar, Croatia (☎/fax 32 441 975; www.cwwpp.org). Work in a group for 1½-2 years in education and health care related to long-term conflict stress in Bosnia, Croatia, and Serbia.

Oxfam International, 266 Banbury Rd., Ste. 20, Oxford, OX2 7DL, UK (☎18 65 31 39 39; www.oxfam.org). Runs poverty relief campaigns.

Simon Wiesenthal Center, 64 av. Marceau, 75008 Paris, France (☎01 47 23 76 37; www.wiesenthal.org). Fights anti-Semitism and Holocaust denial throughout Europe. Small, variable donation required for membership.

UNICEF, (www.unicef.org). Volunteers recruited through the US Fund for UNICEF, 333 E. 38th St., 6th fl., New York, NY 10016 (☎800-367-5437). Offices in Belarus, Bosnia, Croatia, Macedonia, Moldova, Montenegro, Romania, Russia, Ukraine, and Serbia.

United Nations High Commission for Refugees (UNHCR), Case Postale 2500, CH-1211 Genève 2 Dépôt, Switzerland (☎22 739 8111; www.unhcr.org). Gladly provides advice on how and where to help.

Volunteers for Peace, 1034 Tiffany Rd., Belmont, VT 05730 (☎802-259-2759; www.vfp.org). Arranges placement in work camps throughout Europe. Membership required for registration. Programs average US$200-500 for 2-3 weeks.

ALTERNATIVES TO TOURISM

Before handing your money over to any volunteer or study aborad program, it's a good idea to get the names of **previous participants** and ask them about their experience, as some programs sound much better on paper than in reality. The **questions** below are a good place to start:

-How many people participate in the program and what are they typically like? How old are they? To what extent does the program promote group interaction?

-Are room and board included? Will you be expected to share a room or a bathroom? What are the meals like? How well do they handle dietary restrictions?

-Is transportation included? Are there any additional expenses?

-How much free time will you have? Will you be able to travel?

-What kind of safety network is in place? Will you still be covered by your home insurance? Does the program have an emergency plan?

STUDYING ABROAD

Study-abroad programs range from basic language and culture courses to college-level classes, often for credit. In order to choose a program that best fits your needs, you will want to research all you can before making your decision—determine costs and duration, as well as what kind of students participate in the program and what sort of accommodations are provided.

In programs that have large groups of students who speak the same language, there is a trade-off. You may feel more comfortable in the community, but you will not have the same opportunity to practice a foreign language or to befriend other international students. For accommodations, dorm life provides a better opportunity to mingle with fellow students, but there is less of a chance to experience the local scene. If you live with a family, there is a potential to build lifelong friendships with natives and to experience day-to-day life in more depth, but conditions can vary greatly from family to family.

UNIVERSITIES

Some American schools still require students to pay them for credits obtained elsewhere. Most university-level study-abroad programs are meant as language and culture enrichment opportunities, and therefore are conducted in the local language. Still, many programs do offer classes in English and beginner- and lower-level language courses. Those relatively fluent in a foreign language, on the other hand, may find it cheaper to enroll directly in a university abroad, although getting college credit may be more difficult. The following is a list of organizations that can help place students in university programs abroad or have their own branches in Europe.

ONLINE DIRECTORIES

The following websites are good resources for finding programs that cater to your particular interests. Each has links to various study-abroad programs broken down by a variety of criteria, including desired location and focus of study.

www.studyabroad.com. A great starting point for finding college or high school level programs in foreign languages or specific academic subjects. Also maintains a page of links to several other useful websites.

www.petersons.com/stdyabrd/sasector.html. Lists summer and full-year study-abroad programs at accredited institutions that usually offer cross-credit.

www.westudyabroad.com/europe.htm. Lists language and college-level programs in a number of European countries.

PROGRAMS

American Institute for Foreign Study, River Plaza, 9 W. Broad St., Stamford, CT 06902 (☎800-727-2437, ext. 5163; www.aifsabroad.com). Organizes programs for college study at universities in Austria, Britain, the Czech Republic, France, Ireland, Italy, The Netherlands, Poland, Russia, and Spain.

American Field Service (AFS), 71 W. 23rd St., 17th fl., New York, NY 10010 (☎212-807-8686; www.afs.org), has branches in over 50 countries. Summer-, semester-, and year-long homestay exchange programs for high school students and graduating seniors in the Czech Republic, Hungary, Latvia, Russia, and the Slovak Republic. Community service programs also offered for young adults, 18+. Teaching programs available for current and retired teachers. Financial aid available.

American School of Classical Studies (ASCSA), Souidias 54, 10676 Athens, Greece (☎210 72 36 313; www.ascsa.org). Offers a variety of archaeological and classical studies programs to undergraduates, graduate students, and doctoral candidates. Visit the website to find a list of publications and links to other archaeological programs.

Arcadia University for Education Abroad, 450 S. Easton Rd., Glenside, PA 19038 (☎866-927-2234; www.arcadia.edu/cea). Operates programs in Britain, Greece, Ireland, Italy, and Spain. Costs range from US$2300 (summer) to US$31,000 (full-year).

The British Council, 10 Spring Gardens, London SW1A 2BN, UK (☎0207 930 8466; www.britishcouncil.org). Invaluable source of info for those wishing to study in the UK.

Central College Abroad, Box 0140, 812 University, Pella, IA 50219 (☎800-831-3629 or 641-628-5284; www.central.edu/abroad). Offers internships, as well as summer-, semester-, and year-long programs in Austria, Britain, France, The Netherlands, and Spain. US$30 application fee.

Council on International Educational Exchange (CIEE), 7 Custon House St., 3rd fl., Portland, ME 04101 (☎800-407-8839; www.ciee.org). Sponsors academic, internship, volunteer, and work programs in Belgium, Britain, the Czech Republic, France, Hungary, Italy, The Netherlands, Poland, Russia, Spain, and Turkey.

International Association for the Exchange of Students for Technical Experience (IAESTE), 10400 Little Patuxent Pkwy. Ste. 250, Columbia, MD 21044 (☎410-997-2200; www.aipt.org). 8- to 12-week programs in Britain, Finland, France, Germany, Ireland, Sweden, and Switzerland for college students who have completed 2 years of technical study. US$25 application fee.

International Association of Students in Economic and Business Management (AIESEC), (http://us.aieseconline.net). The "world's largest student organization," with 43 locations throughout the US. Places students in international "traineeships." US$45 non-refundable application fee. Program $US455.

Institute for the International Education of Students (IES), 33 N. LaSalle St., 15th fl., Chicago, IL 60602 (☎800-995-2300; www.IESabroad.org). Offers year-long, semester, and summer programs in Austria, England, France, Germany, Ireland, Italy, The Netherlands, and Spain for college students. Internship opportunities. US $50 application fee. Scholarships available.

The International Kitchen, 1 IBM Plaza, 330 N. Wabash #3005, Chicago, IL 60611 (☎312-726-4525; www.theinternationalkitchen.com). Leading provider of cooking school vacations to Italy and France. Traditional cooking instruction in beautiful settings for groups of 8-12. Program locations include Amalfi Coast, Liguria, and Tuscany. Courses run 2-7 nights. Prices vary.

School for International Training, College Semester Abroad, Admissions, Kipling Rd., P.O. Box 676, Brattleboro, VT 05302 (☎888-272-7881; www.sit.edu). Socially-themed semester-long programs in the Balkans, the Czech Republic, France, Germany, Ireland, The Netherlands, Russia, Spain, and Switzerland. US$12,050-13,700. Also runs **Experiment in International Living** (☎800-345-2929; www.usexperiment.org), 3- to 5-week summer programs that offer high school students cross-cultural homestays, community service, ecological adventures, and language training in Britain, France, Germany, Ireland, Italy, Poland, Spain, and Switzerland. US$2700-5000.

Youth for Understanding International Exchange (YFU), 6400 Goldsboro Rd., Ste. 100, Bethesda, MD 20817 (☎866-493-8872; www.yfu.org). Places US high school students with host families throughout Europe for a year, semester, or summer. US$75 application fee plus $500 enrollment deposit.

LANGUAGE SCHOOLS

Unlike American universities, language schools are often independently run international or local divisions of foreign universities that rarely offer college credit. Language schools are a good alternative to university study if you desire a more intense focus on the language or a slightly less-rigorous courseload. These programs are also good for high school students that might not feel comfortable with older students in a university program.

Eurocentres, 101 N. Union St., Ste. 300, Alexandria, VA 22314 (☎703-684-1494; www.eurocentres.com) or in Europe, Head Office, Seestr. 247, CH-8038 Zurich, Switzerland (☎41 1 485 50 40; fax 481 61 24). Language programs for beginning to advanced students with homestays in Britain, France, Germany, Italy, and Spain.

Language Immersion Institute, 75 South Manheim Blvd., SUNY-New Paltz, New Paltz, NY 12561 (☎845-257-3500; www.newpaltz.edu/lii). 2-week summer language courses and some longer overseas courses in France, Italy, and Spain. Program fees are around US$1000 for a 2-week course.

LanguagesPLUS, 413 Ontario St., Toronto, Ontario M5A 2V9, Canada (US ☎888-526-4758; international 416-925-7117; www.languagesplus.com), runs 2- to 12-week programs in Britain, France, Germany, Ireland, Italy, and Spain. 18+. US$350-3000; includes tuition and accommodations with host families or apartments.

WORKING

WORK AND STUDY VISA INFORMATION. Work and study visas for most countries can be acquired only with the help of a sponsoring organization in that country; non-EU nationals looking for work may have a hard time getting permission, and, if they do secure a permit, it may be valid for only 3-6 months. The organizations listed under **Long-Term Work** (see p. 71) may be able to find sponsors, while the **Center for International Business and Travel** (CIBT; see p. 12) can help expedite the visa process. Study-abroad programs or universities should have no problems sponsoring study visas; check before applying to an institution. Citizens of the EU are free to work in any EU member country, but they may need special permits. Contact the consulate of the country in which you want to work for more info.

As with volunteering, work opportunities tend to fall into two categories. Some travelers want long-term jobs that allow them to get to know another part of the world as a member of the community, while other travelers seek out short-term jobs to finance the next leg of their travels. International English-language newspapers, such as the International Herald Tribune (www.int.com), often list long- and short-term job opportunities in their classifieds sections.

Acquiring the appropriate work permits will be much easier for EU citizens than for others. Non-EU citizens planning to work in Europe must carefully research country-specific requirements and limitations before their departure.

LONG-TERM WORK

If you're planning to spend a substantial amount of time (more than three months) working in Europe, search for a job well in advance. International placement agencies are often the easiest way to find employment abroad, especially for teaching English. **Internships,** usually for college students, are a good way to segue into working abroad, although they are often unpaid or poorly paid (many say the experience, however, is well worth it). Be wary of advertisements or companies that claim the ability to get you a job abroad for a fee—often times the listings are out of date, or available online or in newspapers. It's best, if going through an organization, to use one that's reputable. Some good ones include:

Council Exchanges, 633 Third Ave., New York, NY (☎800-407-8839; www.councilexchanges.org). Charges a US$300-475 fee for arranging 3- to 6-month work authorizations in France, Germany, and Ireland.

Escapeartist.com, (http://jobs.escapeartist.com). International employers post directly to this website; various European jobs advertised.

Fruitful Ltd., Unit 3 Ind. Est., Honeybourne, Evesham, Worcester, WR117QF, UK (☎01386 83255; www.fruitfuljobs.com). Sets up farm work for backpackers and students in the UK; online application available.

International Co-operative Education, 15 Spiros Way, Menlo Park, CA 94025 (☎650-323-4944; www.icemenlo.com). Finds summer jobs for students in Belgium, Finland, Germany, and Switzerland. Costs include a US$200 application fee and a US$600 placement fee.

International Employment Gazette, 423 Townes St., Greenville, SC 29601 (☎800-882-9188; www.intemployment.com). An online subscription service that publishes available overseas jobs every 2 weeks. US$20 per month.

ResortJobs.com, (www.resortjobs.com). Searchable database of service and entertainment jobs at resorts around the world.

StepStone, UK office: StepStone ASA, 2 Bell Court, Leapale Lane, Guildford, Surrey GU1 4LY (☎44 14 83 73 94 50; fax 44 14 83 73 94 99; www.stepstone.com). An online database covering international employment openings for most of Europe. Several search options and a constantly changing list of openings.

TEACHING ENGLISH

Teaching jobs abroad are rarely well-paid, although some private American schools can pay competitive salaries. Volunteering as a teacher is also a popular option; programs often provide a daily stipend to help with living expenses. In almost all cases, you must have at least a bachelor's degree to be a full-fledged teacher, although college undergraduates can get summer positions tutoring.

Many schools require teachers to have a **Teaching English as a Foreign Language** (TEFL) certificate. This does not necessarily exclude you from finding a teaching job, but certified teachers often find higher paying jobs. Native English speakers working in private schools are most often hired for immersion classrooms where only English is spoken. Those volunteering or teaching in public schools, or poorer areas, are more likely to be working in both English and the local language. Placement agencies or university fellowship programs are the best resources for finding teaching jobs in Europe. The alternative is to make contacts directly with schools or just to try your luck once you get there. The following organizations specialize in placing teachers in Europe.

Central European Teaching Program (CETP), 3800 NE 72nd Ave., Portland, OR 97213 (www.ticon.net/~cetp). College graduates only. Half- or full-year periods in Hungary and Romania. $2500 (full-year) or $1250 (half-year) placement fee.

International Schools Services (ISS), 15 Roszel Rd., Box 5910, Princeton, NJ 08543 (☎609-452-0990; www.iss.edu). Hires teachers for more than 200 schools worldwide. Teaching experience recommended. 2-year commitment expected.

Teaching English as a Foreign Language (TEFL), TEFL Professional Network Ltd., 72 Pentyla Baglan Rd., Port Talbot SA12 8AD, UK (www.tefl.com). Maintains the most extensive database of openings throughout Europe. Offers job training and certification.

AU PAIR WORK

Au pairs are typically women, aged 18-27, who work as live-in nannies, caring for children and doing light housework in foreign countries in exchange for room, board, and a small spending allowance or stipend. Most former au pairs speak favorably of the experience as a chance to get to know a country without the high expenses of traveling. Drawbacks, however, include long hours and somewhat mediocre pay: au pairs in Europe typically work 25-35 hours per week and receive $200-350 per month. Much of the au pair experience really does depend on the host family. The agencies below help place au pairs.

Accord Cultural Exchange, 3145 Geary Blvd., San Francisco, CA 94118 (☎415-386-6203; www.aupairsaccord.com).

Au Pair in Europe, P.O. Box 68056, Blakely Postal Outlet, Hamilton, Ontario, Canada L8M 3M7 (☎905-545-6305; www.princeent.com/aupair).

Childcare International, Ltd., Trafalgar House, Grenville Pl., London NW7 3SA, UK (☎44 020 8906 3116; www.childint.co.uk).

Working Abroad, InterExchange, 161 Sixth Ave., New York, NY 10013 (☎212-924-0446; www.interexchange.org).

SHORT-TERM WORK

Traveling for long periods of time can get expensive, so picking up odd jobs for a few weeks at a time is a good way to subsidize the next leg of a trip. Another option is to work several hours a day at a hostel in exchange for free or discounted room and/or board. Most often, these short-term jobs are found by word of mouth, or simply by talking to the owner of a hostel or restaurant. Due to the high turnover in the tourism industry, places are often eager for help.

The availability and legality of temporary work vary widely across Europe. If you are interested in working your way through the continent, we recommend picking up *Let's Go* city and country guides. These books contain thorough information on local work opportunities at specific hostels and restaurants, and are updated yearly.

FURTHER READING ON ALTERNATIVES TO TOURISM

Alternatives to the Peace Corps: A Directory of Third World and U.S. Volunteer Opportunities, by Joan Powell. Food First Books, 2001 (US$10).

How to Get a Job in Europe, by Matherly and Sanborn. Planning Communications, 2003 (US$23).

How to Live Your Dream of Volunteering Oversees, by Collins, DeZerega, Heckscher, and Lappe. Penguin Books, 2002 (US$17).

International Directory of Voluntary Work, by Victoria Pybus. Peterson's Guides and Vacation Work, 2003 (US$20).

International Jobs, by Kocher and Segal. Perseus Books, 2003 (US$19).

Overseas Summer Jobs 2002, by Collier and Woodworth. Peterson's Guides and Vacation Work, 2002 (US$18).

Work Abroad: The Complete Guide to Finding a Job Overseas, by Hubbs, Griffith, and Nolting. Transitions Abroad Publishing, 2002 ($20).

Work Your Way Around the World, by Susan Griffith. Worldview Publishing Services, 2003 (US$20).

Invest Yourself: The Catalogue of Volunteer Opportunities. The Commission on Voluntary Service and Action (☎718-638-8487).

ANDORRA

The forgotten country sandwiched between France and Spain, Andorra (pop. 65,000; 464 sq. km), has had its democratic constitution for only ten years; it spent its first 12 centuries caught in a tug-of-war between the Spanish Counts of Urgell, the Church of Urgell, and the French King. Catalán is the official language, but French and Spanish are widely spoken. Because of Andorra's diminutive size, one day can include sniffing aisles of duty-free perfume, hiking through a pine-scented valley, and relaxing in a luxury spa.

▰▱ TRANSPORTATION AND PRACTICAL INFORMATION

The only way to get to Andorra is by car or bus. All traffic from Spain enters through the town of La Seu d'Urgell; the gateway to France is Pas de la Casa. **Andor-Inter/Samar** buses (Andorra ☎82 62 89; Madrid ☎914 68 41 90; Toulouse ☎561 58 14 53) run from Andorra la Vella to **Madrid** (9hr.; Tu and F-Su 11am, W-Th and Su 10pm; €35). **Alsina Graells** (Andorra ☎82 65 67) and **Eurolines** (3¼hr., 5 per day, €19) run to **Barcelona** (4hr., 5 per day, €18). To go anywhere else in Spain, first go to the town of La Seu d'Urgell on a **La Hispano-Andorra** bus (☎82 13 72; 30min., 5-7 per day, €2.50), departing from Av. Meritxell 11. From La Seu, Alsina Graells buses continue into Spain via Puigcerdà (1hr., 2 per day, €3.60). **Driving** in Andorra la Vella is an adventure for some, but navigating the streets, which often lack signs, can be maddening; it's best to ditch the car in a parking lot as soon as possible. Intercity buses connect the villages along the three major highways that converge in Andorra la Vella, and the country's cities can be seen in a single day via public transportation. **Bus** stops are easy to find; rides cost €0.70-1.70; and all buses make every stop in the city. Making an international **telephone call** in Andorra requires a STA *teletarjeta* (telecard) from the tourist office (p. 74) or the post office (€3 minimum). For directory assistance dial ☎111 or 119 (international). *Let's Go* uses the same **price diversity** range in Andorra as in Spain (p. 907).

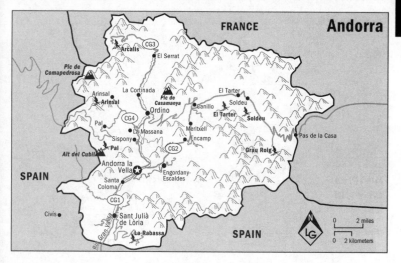

ANDORRA LA VELLA

Andorra la Vella (pop. 20,760), the country's capital, is effectively a single road flanked by shop after duty-free shop. This city is anything but *vella* (old); the old buildings have been upstaged by shiny new stores. After shopping, you're best off escaping to the countryside.

PRACTICAL INFORMATION. There are several **tourist offices** scattered throughout Andorra la Vella; the largest is on Pl. de la Rotonda. From Spain, take Av. Meritxell until it crosses the river. At the bridge Pl. de la Rotonda will be on your right. Their multilingual staff offers free *Sports Activities* and *Hotels i Restaurants* guides. (☎82 71 17. July-Aug. open M-Sa 9am-9pm, Su 9am-7pm. Sept.-June open daily 9:30am-1:30pm, 3:30-7:30pm.) In a **medical emergency** call ☎116 or the **police**, Prat de la Creu 16 (☎87 20 00). For **weather and ski conditions**, call Ski Andorra (☎86 43 89). **Internet** is available at **Future@Point**, C. de La Sardana 6. (☎82 82 02. €1.20/15min. Open M-Sa 10am-11pm, Su 10am-10pm. MC/V.)

ACCOMMODATIONS AND FOOD. The friendly **Hostal del Sol ❶**, Pl. Guillemó 3, provides decent rooms. From Spain, take Av. Príncep Benlloch until you pass the **Teatre Comunal.** At the intersection, bear left onto C. Doctor Nequi. Watch for the fountain on your left. (☎82 37 01. €13 per person. MC/V.) You don't exactly rough it at **Camping Valira ❶**, Av. Salou, which has video games, hot showers, and a pool. (☎82 23 84. €4.50 per person, per tent, and per car. Call ahead.) Try the cheese shop extravaganza **La Casa del Formatge ❷**, C. les Canals 4. From Spain, take your first left after Pl. Príncep Benlloch, and then turn left on C. les Canals. (Open M-F 10am-8pm, Sa 9:30am-9pm, Su 9:30am-7pm.)

EXCURSIONS. The best thing to do in Andorra la Vella is drop your bags in a hostel and get out. **Caldea-Spa,** bordering **Escaldes-Engordany,** is the largest in Europe, with luxurious treatments and prices to match. (☎80 09 99. €25 for 3hr., plus fees. Open daily 9am-11pm.) The **MicroArt Museum,** located within the Caldea-Spa complex, houses a collection of miniature art. (Open daily 9am-9pm. €3.) If you have no patience for the miniscule, visit **Canillo**'s colossal **Palau de Gel D'Andorra,** a recreational complex with a swimming pool and an ice-skating rink,

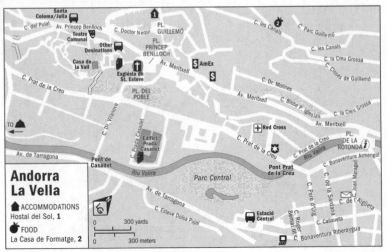

Andorra La Vella

▲ ACCOMMODATIONS
Hostal del Sol, **1**

🍴 FOOD
La Casa de Formatge, **2**

which hosts "ice disco" and "ice-rink go-carts" by night. (☎80 08 40. Open daily 10am-11:30pm; each facility has its own hours. €5.50-8 each. €12.20 for all in 1 day. Equipment rental €2.30-€4.50.) For shopping, check out one of the supermarket monstrosities in Santa Coloma, or the **Grans Magatzems Pyrénées,** Av. Meritxell 11, the country's biggest department store, where an entire aisle is dedicated to chocolate bars. (Open Sept.-July M-F 9:30am-8pm, Sa 9:30am-9pm, Su 9:30am-7pm; Aug. and holidays M-Sa 9:30am-9pm, Su 9:30am-7pm.)

■ **HIKING AND THE OUTDOORS.** The tourist office brochure *Sports Activities* has 52 suggested hiking itineraries, as well as cabin and *refugios* listings. La Massana is home to Andorra's tallest peak, **Pic Alt de la Coma Pedrosa** (2946m). For organized hiking trips, try the **La Rabassa Sports and Nature Center** (☎32 38 68) in southwest Andorra. In addition to *refugio*-style accommodations, the center has mountain biking, guided hikes, horseback riding, archery, and other field sports.

■ **SKIING.** With five outstanding resorts, Andorra offers skiing opportunities galore. (Nov.-Apr.; €30-40.) **Pal** (☎73 70 00), 10km from La Massana, is accessible by bus from La Massana (5 per day, €1.50). Seven buses run daily from La Massana to nearby **Arinsal** (€1). On the French border, **Pas de la Casa Grau Roig** (☎80 10 60) offers 600 hectares of skiable land, lessons, medical centers, night skiing, and 27 lifts serving 48 trails for all levels of ability. **Soldeu-El Tarter** (☎89 05 00) occupies 840 hectares of skiable area; **free buses** pick up skiers from their hotels in Canillo. The more horizontal **La Rabassa** (☎32 38 68) is Andorra's only cross-country ski resort, offering sleighing, skiing, and horse rides. Call **SKI Andorra** (☎86 43 89; www.skiandorra.ad) or the tourist office with any questions.

ANDORRA

AUSTRIA
(ÖSTERREICH)

At the peak of Habsburg megalomania, the Austrian Empire was one of the largest in history, encompassing much of Europe from Poland and Hungary in the east to Spain in the west. Although the mighty empire crumbled during World War II, Austria remains a complex, multiethnic country. Drawing on centuries of Habsburg political maneuvering, Austria has become a skillful mediator between Eastern and Western Europe, connecting its eight bordering countries. Today, Austria owes much of its allure to the overpowering Alps, which dominate two-thirds of its surface. The mention of Austria evokes images of onion-domed churches set against snow-capped alpine peaks, castles rising from lush meadows of golden flowers, and 12th-century monasteries towering over the majestic Danube.

FACTS AND FIGURES

Official Name: Republic of Austria.

Capital: Vienna.

Major Cities: Graz, Innsbruck, Salzburg.

Population: 8,030,000.

Land Area: 83,858 sq. km.

Time Zone: GMT +1.

Language: German.

Religions: Roman Catholic (74%), Protestant (5%), Muslim (4%), other (17%).

DISCOVER AUSTRIA

In Austria's capital, Vienna (p. 80), drink up the cafe culture, stare down works by Klimt and other Secessionist artists, and listen to a world-famous opera for a mere pittance. An easy stopover between Munich and Vienna, Salzburg (p. 94) would

make a fitting child of the two; its beer gardens are as uplifting as its orchestras. Hike around and above historic Hallstatt (p. 100) in the nearby Salzkammergut region, or explore the expanses of the vast Hohe Tauern National Park (p. 102), including the Krimml Waterfalls (p. 102). Farther west, Innsbruck (p. 103) is a great jumping-off point for skiers and hikers into the snow-capped peaks of the Tyrolean Alps. For superior skiing, head to Kitzbühel (p. 106).

ESSENTIALS

WHEN TO GO

November to March is peak ski season; prices in western Austria double and travelers need reservations months in advance. The situation reverses in the summer, when the flatter eastern half fills with vacationers. Sights and accommodations are cheaper and less crowded in the shoulder season (May-June and Sept.-Oct.). However, some Alpine resorts close in May and June—call ahead. The Vienna State Opera, the Vienna Boys' Choir, and many major theaters throughout Austria don't have any performances during July and August.

DOCUMENTS AND FORMALITIES

VISAS. EU Citizens do not need a visa. Citizens of Australia, Canada, New Zealand, South Africa, and the US do not need a visa for stays of up to 90 days.

EMBASSIES. All foreign embassies in Austria are in Vienna (p. 84). Austrian embassies at home include: **Australia,** 12 Talbot St., Forrest, Canberra ACT 2603 (☎(612) 6295 1533; www.austriaemb.org.au); **Canada,** 445 Wilbrod St., Ottawa, ON K1N 6M7 (☎613-789-1444; www.austro.org); **Ireland,** 15 Ailesbury Court, 93 Ailesbury Rd., Dublin 4 (☎(353) 1 269 4577); **New Zealand,** Level 2, Willbank House, 57 Willis St., Wellington (☎04 499 6393; austria@ihug.co.nz); **South Africa,** 1109 Duncan St., Momentum Office Park, Brooklyn, Pretoria 0011 (☎(012) 45 29 155; autemb@mweb.co.az); **UK,** 18 Belgrave Mews West, London SW1X 8HU (☎(020) 7235 3731; www.austria.org.uk); **US,** 3524 International Ct. NW, Washington, D.C. 20008 (☎202-895-6700; www.austria.org).

TRANSPORTATION

BY PLANE. The only major international airport is Vienna's Schwechat Flughafen (VIE). European flights also land in Linz, Innsbruck, Salzburg, Graz, and Klagenfurt. From London-Stansted, **Ryanair** flies to the latter three (☎3531 249 7851; www.ryanair.com).

BY TRAIN. The **Österreichische Bundesbahn** (ÖBB), Austria's federal railroad, operates an efficient system with fast and comfortable trains. **Eurail, InterRail,** and **Europe East** are valid in Austria; however, they do not guarantee a seat without a reservation (US$11). The **Austrian Railpass** allows three days of travel within any 15-day period on all rail lines; it also entitles holders to 40% off on bike rental at train stations (2nd-class US$107, each additional day US$15).

BY BUS. The efficient Austrian bus system consists mainly of orange **Bundes-Buses,** which cover areas inaccessible by train. They usually cost about as much as trains, but railpasses are not valid. Buy tickets at the station or from the driver. For bus info, call ☎(0222) 711 01 between 7am-7pm.

BY CAR. Driving is a convenient way to see more isolated parts of Austria, but gas is costly, an international license is required, and some small towns prohibit cars. The roads are well-maintained and well-marked, and Austrian drivers are quite careful. **Mitfahrzentrale** (ride-sharing services) in larger cities pair drivers with riders for a small fee. Riders then negotiate fares with the drivers. Be aware that not all organizations screen their drivers or riders; ask in advance.

BY BIKE. Bikes are a great way to get around Austria; roads are generally smooth and safe. Many train stations rent bikes and allow you to return them to any participating station. Consult local tourist offices for bike routes and maps.

TOURIST SERVICES AND MONEY

EMERGENCY	**Police:** ☎ 133. **Ambulance:** ☎ 144. **Fire:** ☎ 122.

TOURIST OFFICES. Virtually every town has a tourist office marked by a green "i" sign. Most brochures are available in English. Visit www.austria-tourism.at for more Austrian tourist info.

MONEY. On January 1, 2002, the **euro** (€) replaced the **Schilling** (ATS) as the unit of currency in Austria. For more info, see p. 14. As a general rule, it's cheaper to exchange money in Austria than at home. Railroad stations, airports, hotels, and most travel agencies offer exchange services, as do banks and currency exchanges. If you stay in hostels and prepare most of your own food, expect to spend anywhere from €30-60 per person per day. Accommodations start at about €12, while a basic sit-down meal usually costs around €10. Menus will say whether service is included (*Preise inclusive* or *Bedienung inclusiv*); if it is, you don't have to **tip.** If it's not, leave a tip up to 10%. Austrian restaurants expect you to seat yourself, and servers will not bring the bill until you ask them to do so. Say *Zahlen bitte* (TSAHL-en BIT-uh) to settle your accounts, and don't leave tips on the table. Be aware that some restaurants charge for each piece of bread that you eat during your meal. Don't expect to bargain except at flea markets and the Naschmarkt in Vienna. Austria has a 10-20% **value-added tax (VAT),** which is applied to purchased goods. You can get refunds for purchases of over €75 at one store.

COMMUNICATION

TELEPHONES. Wherever possible, use a calling card for international phone calls, as the long-distance rates for national phone services are often exorbitant. Prepaid phone cards and major credit cards can be used for direct international calls, but they are still less cost-efficient. For info on cell phones, see p. 36. Direct dial access numbers include: **AT&T,** ☎ (0800) 20 02 88; **British Telecom,** ☎ (0800) 20 02 09; **Canada Direct,** ☎ (0800) 20 02 17; **Ireland Direct,** ☎ (0800) 40 00 00; **MCI,** ☎ (0800) 20 02 35; **Sprint,** ☎ (0800) 20 02 36; **Telecom New Zealand,** ☎ (0800) 20 02 22; **Telkom South Africa,** ☎ (0800) 20 02 30.

PHONE CODES	**Country code:** 43. **International dialing prefix:** 00 (from Vienna, 900). From outside Austria, dial int'l dialing prefix (see inside back cover) + 43 + city code + local number. To call **Vienna** from outside Austria, dial int'l dialing prefix + 43 + 1 + local number.

MAIL. Letters take 1-2 days within Austria. Airmail to North America takes 4-7 days, up to 9 days to Australia and New Zealand. Mark all letters and packages "mit Flugpost." Aerogrammes are the cheapest option. *Let's Go* lists the addresses for mail to be held (*Postlagernde Briefe*) in the practical information of big cities.

LANGUAGE. German is the official language. English is the most common second language; outside of cities and among older residents, English is less common. For basic German words and phrases, see p. 1055.

ACCOMMODATIONS AND CAMPING

AUSTRIA	❶	❷	❸	❹	❺
ACCOMMODATIONS	under €9	€9-15	€16-30	€31-70	over €70

Always ask if your lodging provides a **guest card** (*Gästekarte*), which grants discounts on activities, museums, and public transportation. The **Österreiches Jugendherbergsverband-Hauptverband** (ÖJH) runs the over 80 HI **hostels** in Austria. Because of the rigorous standards of the national organizations, these are usually very clean and orderly. Most charge €12-22 per night for dorms; non-HI members usually pay a surcharge. **Independent hostels** vary in quality, but often have more personality and foster a more lively backpacking culture. **Hotels** are expensive (singles €40-100; doubles €80-150). The cheapest have *Gasthof, Gästehaus,* or *Pension-Garni* in the name. Renting a **Privatzimmer** (room in a family home) is an inexpensive and friendly option. Rooms range from €20-50 a night; contact the local tourist office for a list. Slightly more expensive, **Pensionen** are similar to American and British bed-and-breakfasts. **Camping** in Austria is less about getting out into nature than about having a cheap place to sleep; most sites are large plots glutted with RVs and are open in summer only. Prices run €4-6 per person and €4-8 per tent. In the high Alps, hikers and mountaineers can retire to the famously well-maintained system of **mountain huts** (*Hütten*).

HIKING AND SKIING. Nearly every town has **hiking** trails in its vicinity; consult the local tourist office. Trails are usually marked with either a red-white-red marker (only sturdy boots and hiking poles necessary) or a blue-white-blue marker (mountaineering equipment needed). Most mountain hiking trails and mountain huts are open only from late June to early September because of snow in the higher passes. Western Austria is one of the world's best **skiing** regions; the areas around Innsbruck and Kitzbühel are saturated with lifts and runs. High season normally runs from mid-December to mid-January and from February to March. Tourist offices provide information on regional skiing and can suggest budget travel agencies that offer ski packages.

FOOD AND DRINK

AUSTRIA	❶	❷	❸	❹	❺
FOOD	under €5	€5-10	€11-16	€17-25	over €25

Loaded with fat, salt, and cholesterol, traditional Austrian cuisine is a cardiologist's nightmare but a delight to the palate. Staple foods include pork, veal, sausage, eggs, cheese, bread, and potatoes. Austria's best known dish, *Wienerschnitzel*, is a breaded meat cutlet (usually veal or pork) fried in butter. Vegetarians should look for *Spätzle* (noodles), *Eierschwammerl* (yellow mushrooms), or anything with the word "Vegi" in it. The best supermarkets are Billa and Hofer, where you can buy cheap rolls, fruits, and veggies. Natives nurse their sweet tooth with *Kaffee und Kuchen* (coffee and cake). Try *Sacher Torte*, a rich chocolate cake layered with marmalade; *Linzer Torte*, a light yellow cake with currant jam; *Apfelstrudel;* or just about any pastry. Austrian beers are outstanding—try *Stiegl Bier*, a Salzburg brew; *Zipfer Bier* from Upper Austria; and Styrian *Gösser Bier*.

HOLIDAYS AND FESTIVALS

Holidays: Just about everything closes down on public holidays, so plan accordingly. New Year's Day (Jan. 1); Epiphany (Jan. 6); Good Friday (Apr. 9); Easter Monday (Apr. 12); Labor Day (May 1); Ascension (May 20); Corpus Christi (June 19); Assumption Day (Aug. 15); Austrian National Day (Oct. 26); All Saints' Day (Nov. 1); Immaculate Conception (Dec. 8); Christmas (Dec. 25); Boxing Day (Dec. 26).

Festivals: Vienna celebrates **Fasching** (Carnival) during the first 2 weeks of February. Austria's most famous summer music festivals are the **Wiener Festwochen** (mid-May to mid-June; p. 91) and the **Salzburger Festspiele** (late July to late Aug.; p. 99).

VIENNA (WIEN)   ☎01

From its humble origins as a Roman camp along the Danube, Vienna (pop. 1,500,000) was catapulted by war, marriage, and Habsburg maneuvering into the political lynchpin of the continent. Meanwhile, music saved its soul; the melodies of Mozart and Beethoven, Mahler and Schönberg have made Vienna an everlasting arbiter of high culture. So high, at times, that it seemed inflated; during its *fin-de-siècle* coffeehouse phase, bohemian Viennese self-mockingly referred to their city as the "merry apocalypse." This smooth veneer of Straussian waltzes and *Gemütlichkeit* (good nature) concealed a darker side expressed in Freud's theories, and later in Musil's *Man Without Qualities*. Although the city has a reputation for living absent-mindedly in its grand past, the recently opened *MuseumsQuartier*, an ultra-modern venue for architecture, film, theater, and dance, proves that Vienna is still writing its own dynamic brand of history.

✈ INTERCITY TRANSPORTATION

Flights: The **Wien-Schwechat Flughafen** (VIE; ☎ 700 72 22 33) is home to **Austrian Airlines** (☎ 051 76 60; www.aua.com). The airport is 18km from the city center; the cheapest way to reach the city is S7 Flughafen/Wolfsthal, which stops at **Wien Mitte** (30min., every 30min. 5am-11pm, €3). The heart of the city, **Stephansplatz**, is a short Metro ride from Wien Mitte on the U3 line. The **Vienna Airport Lines Shuttle Bus**, which runs between the airport and the City Air Terminal, at the Hilton opposite Wien Mitte, is more convenient, but also more expensive. (☎ 93 00 00 23 00. Every 20min. 6:30am-11:10pm, every 30min. midnight-6am; €5.80.) **Buses** connect the airport to the *Südbahnhof* and *Westbahnhof* (see below) every 30min. 8:25am-6:55pm and every hr. from 5:30-8:25am and 6:55pm-12:10am.

Trains: Vienna has two main train stations with international connections. For general train info, dial ☎ 05 17 17 (24hr.) or check www.oebb.at.

Westbahnhof, XV, Mariahilferstr. 132. Most trains head west, but a few go east and north. To: **Amsterdam** (14½hr., daily, €159); **Berlin Zoo** (11hr., daily, €123); **Budapest** (3-4hr., 3 per day, €38); **Hamburg** (9½hr., 2 per day, €125); **Innsbruck** (5-6hr., 2 per day, €49); **Munich** (4½hr., 5 per day, €63); **Paris** (14hr., 2 per day, €13); **Salzburg** (3½hr., every hr., €37); **Zurich** (9¼hr., 3 per day, €78). **Info counter** open daily 7am-10pm.

Südbahnhof, X, Wiedner Gürtel 1a. Trains go south and east. To: **Graz** (2¾hr., every hr., €27); **Kraków** (7-8hr., 3 per day, €46); **Prague** (4½hr., 5 per day, €46); **Rome** (14hr., daily, €101); **Venice** (9-10hr., 3 per day, €72). **Info counter** open daily 6:30am-9pm.

Buses: Buses in Austria are seldom cheaper than trains; compare prices before buying a ticket. **City bus terminals** at Wien Mitte/Landstr., Hütteldorf, Heiligenstadt, Floridsdorf, Kagran, Erdberg, and Reumannpl. **BundesBuses** run from these stations. Ticket counters open M-F 6am-5:50pm, Sa-Su 6am-3:50pm. Many international bus lines also have agencies in the stations. For info, call BundesBus (☎ 711 01; 7am-10pm).

Hitchhiking and Ride Sharing: Hitchhikers headed for Salzburg take U4 to Hütteldorf; the highway is 10km farther. Hitchhikers traveling south often ride tram #67 to the last stop and wait at the rotary near Laaerberg. *Let's Go* does not recommend hitchhiking.

ORIENTATION

Vienna is divided into 23 **districts** (*Bezirke*). The first is the *Innenstadt* (city center), defined by the **Ringstraße** on three sides and the Danube Canal on the fourth. The Ringstraße (or "Ring") consists of many different segments, each with its own name, such as Opernring or Kärntner Ring. Many of Vienna's major attractions are in District I and immediately around the Ringstraße. Districts II-IX spread out from the city center following the clockwise traffic of the Ring. The remaining districts expand from yet another ring, the **Gürtel** ("belt"). Like the Ring, this major thoroughfare has numerous segments, including Margaretengürtel, Währinger Gürtel, and Neubaugürtel. Street signs indicate the district number in Roman or Arabic numerals *before* the street and number. **Let's Go includes district numbers for establishments in Roman numerals before the street address.**

LOCAL TRANSPORTATION

Public transportation: call ☎ 790 91 00 for general info. The **subway** (U-Bahn), **tram** (Straßenbahn), **elevated train** (S-Bahn), and **bus** lines operate under one ticket system. A **single fare** (€2 on board; €1.50 in advance from a ticket machine, ticket office, or tobacco shop) lets you travel to any destination in the city and switch from bus to U-Bahn to tram to S-Bahn, as long as your travel is uninterrupted. To **validate a ticket,** punch it in the machine upon entering the first vehicle, but don't stamp it again when you switch trains. Otherwise, plainclothes inspectors may fine you €60. Other ticket options (available at the same places as pre-purchased single tickets) are a **24hr. pass** (€5), a **3-day "rover" ticket** (€12), a **7-day pass** (€12.50; valid M 9am to the next M 9am), or an **8-day pass** (€24; valid any 8 days, not necessarily consecutive; valid also for several people traveling together). The **Vienna Card** (€16.90) offers free travel for 72hr. as well as discounts at sights and events. Regular trams and subway cars stop running between midnight and 5am. **Nightbuses** run every 30min. along most routes; "N" signs designate night bus stops. (Single fare €1.50; day transport passes not valid.) A complete night bus schedule is available at bus counters in U-Bahn stations.

Taxis: ☎ 313 00, 401 00, 601 60, or 814 00. Stands at *Westbahnhof, Südbahnhof,* Karlspl. in the city center, and by the Bermuda Dreieck for late-night revelers. Accredited taxis have yellow-and-black signs on the roof. Rates generally run €2 plus €0.20 per km; slightly more expensive holidays and from 11pm-6am.

Car Rental: Avis, I, Opernring 3-5 (☎ 587 62 41). Open M-F 7am-8pm, Sa 8am-2pm, Su 8am-1pm. **Hertz** (☎ 700 73 26 61), at the airport. Open M-F 7:15am-11pm, Sa 8am-8pm, Su 8am-11pm.

Bike Rental: Pedal Power, II, Ausstellungsstr. 3 (☎ 729 72 34). Rents bikes (€4 per hr., €32 for 24hr. with delivery) and offers bike tours (€19-23). Student and Vienna Card discounts. Open May-Oct. daily 8am-8pm. Pick up *Vienna By Bike* at the tourist office.

> ▼ **CRIME IN THE CITY.** Vienna is a gentle giant, but it still knows crime. Pickpockets abound on the U-Bahn, and **Karlsplatz** is home to many pushers and junkies. Be especially cautious in districts **X** and **XIV,** as well as in **Prater Park** and in Vienna's Red Light District, which covers sections of the Gürtel.

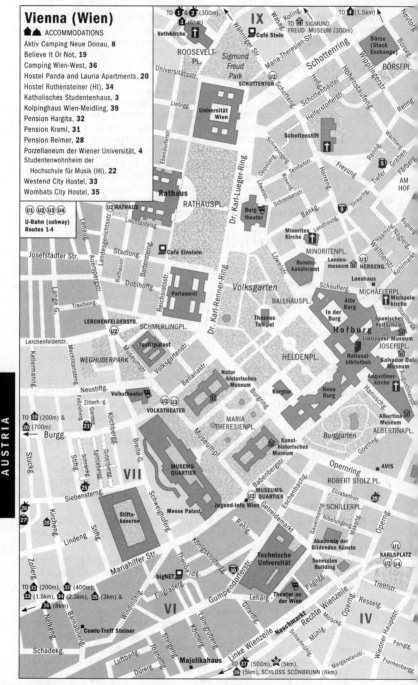

Vienna (Wien)

▲▲ ACCOMMODATIONS

Aktiv Camping Neue Donau, **8**
Believe It Or Not, **19**
Camping Wien-West, **36**
Hostel Panda and Lauria Apartments, **20**
Hostel Ruthensteiner (HI), **34**
Katholisches Studentenhaus, **3**
Kolpinghaus Wien-Meidling, **39**
Pension Hargita, **32**
Pension Kraml, **31**
Pension Reimer, **28**
Porzellaneum der Wiener Universität, **4**
Studentenwohnheim der
  Hochschule für Musik (HI), **22**
Westend City Hostel, **33**
Wombats City Hostel, **35**

(U1) (U2) (U3) (U4)
**U-Bahn (subway)
Routes 1-4**

FOOD
A Tavola, 16
Café Nil, 26
Café Willendorf, 37
Centimeter, 25
DO&CO, 13
Elsäßer Bistro, 2
Ma Crêperie, 14
Maschu Maschu, 7
OH Pot, OH Pot, 1
Smutny, 29

Trzesniewski, 12
Vegetasia, 24
Wrenkh, 11

CAFÉS
Café Central, 9
Café Hawelka, 15
Café Sperl, 30
Demel, 10
Hotel Sacher, 23
Kleines Café, 17

BARS
Benjamin, 6
Cato, 5
Das Möbel, 21
Europa, 27

NIGHTLIFE
Porgy & Bess, 18
U-4, 38

AUSTRIA

Eßling.
Gonzaga.
elinkag.
Franz Josefs Kai
Obere Donaustr.
Heinrichsg.
Werdertorg.
RUDOLFSPL.
Salzgries
Gölsdorfg.
CONCORDIAPL.
Salztorbr.
Wippingerstr.
Schwed.
Marla am Gestade
Fischerg.
Vorstr.
Marc-Aurel-Str.
Salztog
MORZINPL.
Martenbr.
Shakespeare & Co.
Sterne.
Rabensteig
Salzgries
SCHWEDENPL.
Ferdinand-Str.
Fischerg.
TO 8 (6km)
Untere Donaustr.
Salvatorg.
Ruprechtskirche
Seitenstetten.
SCHWEDENPL.
Donaukanal
Aspernbr.
(Danube Canal)
Judisches Museum
Altes Rathaus
Kammerspiele
Griecheng.
DDSG Ferry Docks
Franz Josefs Kai
Ob
JUDENPL.
bigNET
Judeng.
Stadt-tempel
JULIUS-RAAB-PL.
Radetzkystr.
Reischst.
Kirche am Hof
HOHER MARKT
Bauernmkt.
Fleischmarkt
Rotg.
Ireland
Köllnerhof.
Canada
Postsparkasse
Finanzlandes Direktion
Landskrong.
Lichtensteg.
Wiesingerstr.
Regierungs-gebaude
eterskirche
Steindl.
Tuchlauben
Brandstätte
Bauernmkt.
Kärnner.
Lichtenstr.
Rotenturmstr.
Sonnenfelsg.
Schönlaterng.
Dominikanerbastei
Rosenbursenstr.
Wien Fluß
PETERSPL.
Graben
Jasomirstr.
STEPHANSPL.
Bäckerstr.
Wollzeile
Alte Universität
Predigerg.
Falkestr.
Maxerg.
Goldschm.
Haas Haus
STOCK-IM-EISENPL.
Stephansdom
Schulerstr.
Postg.
DR. KARL LUEGERPL.
Biberstr.
Stubenring
Museum für angewandte Kunst (MAK)
TAXI
Wien-Mitte Bahnhof
Bräuners.
Dorotheerg.
Spiegelg.
STEPHANSPL.
Lilleng.
Weihburg.
Blutg.
Grünangerg.
Kumpfg.
Zedlitzg.
Riemerg.
Stubenbastei
Weiskirchnerstr.
STUBENTOR
Plankeng.
Spiegelg.
Seilerg.
AmEx
FRANZIS-KANERPL.
Singerstr.
Cobdeng.
Liebenbg.
Parkring
LANDSTRASSE/WIEN MITTE
Landstr.
NEUERMARKT
Kapuziner Kirche
Himmelpfortg.
Ballg.
Weihburg.
Sellerstätte
Coburgbastei
Gartenbau-promenade
City Air Terminal
Monument gegen Hitler
Führichg.
Haus der Musik
Johannesg.
Wien Fluß
Am Stadtpark
Invalidenstr.
Maysederg.
Annag.
Seiler-stätte
Stadtpark
Ungarg.
Philharm.
nikerstr.
Hotel Sacher
Krugerstr.
Schellingg.
Fichteg.
Hegelg.
Johannesg.
TO 24 (700m)
Linkebahng.
Rechte Bahng.
taatsoper
Kärntner Str.
Walfischg.
Fichtg.
Mahlerstr.
Schwarzenbergstr.
U4 STADTPARK
Am Heumarkt
Beatrixg.
Opern-Passage
Kärntner Ring
Schubertring
Christg.
BEETHOVENPL.
RUDOLF-SALLINGERPL.
Bayerng.
Grimmelshauseng.
Gottfried-Keller-G.
Reisnerstr.
Bösendorferstr.
bigNET
Akademiestr.
Dumbastr.
Canovag.
Pestalozig.
Lothringer Str.
Am Heumarkt
Lagerg.
Ölzeltg.
Salesianerg.
KARLSPL.
Künstlerhaus
Musikverein
Friedrichstr.
Konzerthaus
Akademietheater
Iszststr.
Traung.
Marokkaneng.
Am Modena-Park
Resselpark
KARLSPL.
Historisches Museum der Stadt Wien
Australia
Daffingerstr.
Veithg.
Neulingg.
LG
Technische Universität
Karlskirche
Rennweg
Schwarzenbergdenkmal
Palais Schwarzenberg
Strohg.
UK
0   250 yards
0   250 meters
Karlsg.
Argentinierstr.
Gußhausstr.
Schwindg.
Pr. Eugenstr.
Zäunerg.
TO SCHLOSS BELVEDERE
(200m) & WIEN SCHWECHAT (25km)

⚡ PRACTICAL INFORMATION

Main Tourist Office: I, Albertinapl. (☎21 11 40). Follow Operng. up 1 block from the Opera House. The staff gives a free map of the city and the pamphlet *Youth Scene*, and books rooms for a €3 fee plus a 1-night deposit. Open daily 9am-7pm.

Embassies and Consulates: Australia, IV, Mattiellistr. 2 (☎512 85 80). **Canada,** I, Laurenzerberg 2 (☎531 38 30 00). **Ireland,** I, Rotenturmstr. 16 (☎715 42 46). **New Zealand,** XIX, Karl-Tomay-g. 34 (☎318 85 05). **South Africa,** XIX, Sandg. 33 (☎32 06 49 30). **UK,** III, Jauresg. 10 (☎716 13 51 51). **US,** IX, Boltzmanng. 16 (☎313 39).

Currency Exchange: The 24hr. exchange at the **main post office** has excellent rates and an €8 fee for up to US$1100 in traveler's checks. Otherwise, **ATMs** are your best bet.

American Express: I, Kärntnerstr. 21-23 (☎515 40), down the street from Stephanspl. Cashes AmEx and Thomas Cook (min. €7 commission) checks, sells theater tickets, and holds mail for 4 weeks. Open M-F 9am-5:30pm, Sa 9am-noon.

Bi-Gay-Lesbian Resources: Pick up the *Vienna Gay Guide* (www.gayguide.at), *Extra Connect,* or *Bussi* from any tourist office or gay bar, cafe, or club. **Rosa Lila Villa,** VI, Linke Wienzeile 102 (☎587 17 89), is a favored resource and social center for homosexual Viennese and visitors alike. Friendly staff speaks English. Open M-F 5-8pm.

Laundromat: Most hostels offer laundry service for €4-6. **Schnell und Sauber,** VII, Westbahnhofstr. 60. Wash €4.50, dry €1 per 20min. Soap included. Open 24hr.

EMERGENCY AND COMMUNICATION

Police: ☎133. **Ambulance:** ☎144. **Fire:** ☎122.

Medical Assistance: Allgemeines Krankenhaus (hospital), IX, Währinger Gürtel 18-20 (☎404 00 19 64). **Emergency care:** ☎141.

24hr. Pharmacy: ☎15 50. Consulates have lists of English-speaking doctors, or call **Wolfgang Molnar** (☎330 34 68).

Internet Access: bigNET.internet.cafe, I, Kärntnerstr. 61 or I, Hoher Markt 8-9 (€3.70 per 30min.). **Jugend-Info des Bundesministeriums,** I, Franz-Josefs-Kai 51. Open M-F 11am-6pm. **Cafe Stein,** IX, Wahringerstr. 6-8 (€4 per 30min.).

Post Offices: Hauptpostamt, I, Fleischmarkt 19. Open 24hr. Branches throughout the city and at the train stations; look for the yellow signs with the trumpet logo. Address mail to be held: SURNAME, Firstname, *Postlagernde Briefe,* Hauptpostamt, Fleischmarkt 19, A-1010 Wien AUSTRIA. **Postal Codes:** 1st district A-1010, 2nd A-1020, 3rd A-1030, etc., to the 23rd A-1230.

🏠 ACCOMMODATIONS AND CAMPING

Hunting for cheap rooms in Vienna during peak tourist season (June-Sept.) can be unpleasant; call for reservations at least five days in advance. Otherwise, plan on calling between 6 and 9am to put your name down for a reservation. If full, ask to be put on a waiting list. The summer crunch for budget rooms is slightly alleviated in July, when university dorms convert into makeshift hostels.

HOSTELS

▨ **Hostel Ruthensteiner (HI),** XV, Robert-Hamerlingg. 24 (☎893 42 02). Exit *Westbahnhof,* turn right onto Mariahilferstr., and continue until Haidmannsg. Turn left, then right on Robert-Hamerlingg. Knowledgeable staff, spotless rooms, a rose-filled courtyard, and a kitchenette. Breakfast €2.50. Sheets included (except for 10-bed dorms). Internet €2 for 25min. 4-night max. stay. Reception 24hr. "The Outback" summer dorm €11; 4- to 10-bed dorms €10-12; singles €18-22; doubles €36-44. AmEx/MC/V. ❷

Wombats City Hostel, XIV, Grang. 6 (☎897 23 36). Exit *Westbahnhof*, turn right on Mariahilferstr., right on Rosinag., and left on Grang. While near train tracks and auto-body shops, Wombats compensates with a pub and other perks. Internet €1 per 12min. Bike or in-line skate rental €8 per day. 2-, 4-, and 6-bed dorms €14-36 per person. ❷

Believe It Or Not, VII, Myrtheng. 10, Apt. #14 (☎526 46 58). Take U6 to Burgg./ Stadthalle, then bus #48A (dir.: Ring) to Neubaug. Walk back on Burgg. 1 block and take the 1st right on Myrtheng. A converted apartment, with kitchen and 2 bunkrooms. Min. 2-night stay. Reception 8am-1pm. Easter-Oct. €12.25; Nov.-Easter €7.50-10. ❶

Hostel Panda, VII, Kaiserstr. 77. (☎522 25 55). U6: Burgg. Small, old-fashioned, *Jugendstil*, co-ed rooms. Kitchen and TV. Check-in until 11pm. Bring lock for lockers. Dorms Easter-Oct. €12.50; Nov.-Easter €9. €3.50 surcharge for 1-night stays. ❷

Westend City Hostel, VI, Fügerg. 3. Near Westbahnhof. Exit on Äussere Mariahilferstr., cross the large intersection, go right on Mullerg. and left on Fügerg. Very plain, but its location is ideal. Breakfast included. Internet €2.60 per 30min. Reception 24hr. Check-out 10:30am. Curfew 11:30pm. 12-bed dorms €16; 8-10 bed dorms €17; 4-6 bed dorms €18; singles €38.50; doubles €23. ❷

Kolpinghaus Wien-Meidling, XIII, Bendlg. 10-12 (☎813 54 87). U6: Niederhofstr. Head right on Niederhofstr. and take the 4th right onto Bendlg. Institutional hostel with 202 beds. Breakfast €3.80. Showers in all rooms. Reception 24hr. Check-out 9am. 8- and 10-bed dorms €11.40; 4- and 6-bed dorms €12.80-14.60. AmEx/MC/V. ❷

HOTELS AND PENSIONS

▨**Pension Hargita,** VII, Andreasg. (☎526 19 28). U3: Zieglerg. and exit on Andreasg. Hardwood floors, seafoam walls, cozy beds, and quiet. Breakfast €3. Reception 8am-10pm. Singles €31, with shower €50; doubles €45/52; triples €63/71. MC/V. ❹

Pension Kraml, VI, Brauerg. 5 (☎587 85 88). U3: Zierierg. Exit on Otto-Bauerg., take 1st left, then 1st right. Near the Naschmarkt. Large rooms, a lounge, and cable TV. Breakfast included. Singles €26; doubles €48, with shower €65; triples €65/85. Apartment with bath €100-115 for 3-5 people. ❸

Lauria Apartments, VII, Kaiserstr. 77, Apt. #8 (☎522 25 55). From *Westbahnhof*, take tram #5 to Burgg. The 'Breakfast Club' meets Vienna in this small, but comfortable cluster of apartments. Fully equipped kitchens. Lockers and TV included. 2-night min. Reception 8am-2pm. Lockout 10am-2pm. Dorms €13; singles €35; doubles €46, with shower €60; triples €75-120. ❷

Pension Reimer, IV, Kircheng. 18 (☎523 61 62). Centrally located with huge, comfortable rooms that are always clean. Breakfast included. Singles €31-38; doubles €50-56, with bath €60-64. ❹

UNIVERSITY DORMITORIES

From July through September, many university dorms become hotels, usually with singles, doubles, and a few triples and quads. These rooms don't have much in the way of character, but showers and sheets are standard, and their cleanliness and relatively low cost make them particularly suited to longer stays.

Studentenwohnheim der Hochschule für Musik, I, Johannesg. 8 (☎514 84). Walk 3 blocks down Kärntnerstr. from Stephansdom and turn left on Johannesg. Music student clientele; 23 practice rooms equipped with grand pianos (€5 per hr.). Breakfast included. Reception 24hr. Reserve in advance. Singles €33-36; doubles €58-70; triples €66; quads €80; quints €100. ❹

Porzellaneum der Wiener Universität, IX, Porzellang. 30 (☎317 728 20). From *Süd-bahnhof*, take tram D (dir.: Nußdorf) to Fürsteng. Great location in the student district. Reception 24hr. Call ahead. Singles €16-18; doubles €30-35; quads €56-64. ❸

Katholisches Studentenhaus, XIX, Peter-Jordanstr. 29 (☎369 55 85). U6: Nußdorfer-str., then bus #35A or tram #38 to Hardtg. In a calm, quiet district. Free Internet. Reception daily until 10pm. Singles €18; doubles €30. ❸

CAMPING

Wien-West, Hüttelbergstr. 80 (☎914 23 14). Take U4 to Hütteldorf, then bus #14B or 152 (dir.: Campingpl.) to Wien West. Crowded but clean. 8km from the city center. Hikes go through the Vienna Forest. Laundry, groceries, and cooking facilities. Reception daily 7:30am-9:30pm. Open Apr.-Oct. €5-6 per person, €3 per tent. ❶

Aktiv Camping Neue Donau, XXII, Am Kleehäufel 119 (☎202 40 10), is 4km from the city center and adjacent to Neue Donau beaches. U1: Kaisermühlen, then bus #91a to Kleehäufel. Boat and bike rentals. Laundry, supermarket, kitchen, and showers. Open mid-May to mid-Sept. €5.50 per person, €3 per tent. ❶

◘ FOOD

The Viennese don't eat to live, they live to eat. The restaurants near Kärntnerstr. are generally expensive—a cheaper area is the neighborhood north of the university, near the Votivkirche (U2: Schottentor), where Universitätsstr. and Währing-erstr. meet. Cafes with cheap meals also line **Burggasse** in district VI. The area radiating from the Rechte and Linke Wienzeile near Naschmarkt (U4: Ketten-brückeg.) has cheap restaurants. The **Naschmarkt** has the city's biggest market, while **Brunnenmarkt** (U6: Josefstädterstr.) has a Turkish flair. Supermarket chains include **Zielpunkt, Hofer,** and **Spar.** Kosher groceries are available at the **Kosher Supermarket,** II, Hollandstr. 10 (☎216 96 75).

INSIDE THE RING

▩ **DO&CO,** I, Stephanspl. 12, 7th fl. (☎535 39 69). Set above the Stephansdom, this modern gourmet restaurant offers both traditional Austrian dishes and other interna-tional specialties like Thai noodles and Uruguay beef (€19-23.50). Reservations recom-mended. Open daily noon-3pm and 6pm-midnight. ❹

▩ **Ma Crêperie,** I, Grünangerg. 10. Off Singerstr. near Stephanspl. The sensual decor of this restaurant complements the sumptuous crepes, both sweet and savory (€3-18). Try the *Himbeer* (raspberry) soda (€2). Open daily 11am-midnight. AmEx/MC/V. ❸

▩ **Wrenkh,** I, Bauernmarkt 10. The delicious and creative cuisine at this strictly vegetarian restaurant ranges from Japanese springrolls to spinach gnocchi (€4-18) and fresh fruit juices to original mixed drinks (€3-8). Open daily 11:30am-11pm. AmEx/MC/V. ❷

Trzesniewski, I, Dorotheerg. 1, 3 blocks down the Graben from Stephansdom. This famous stand-up establishment has been serving petite open-faced sandwiches for over 80 years. A filling lunch (6 sandwiches and a mini-beer) costs about €5. This was Kafka's favorite place to eat. Open M-F 8:30am-7:30pm, Sa 9am-5pm. ❷

Smutny, I, Elisabethstr. 8. Off Karlspl. A delicious traditional Austrian restaurant offering schnitzel and goulash. Entrees €5-8. ❷

A Tavola, I. Weihburgg. 3. U1: Stephansplatz. Walk down Härtnerstr. and make a left onto Weihburgg. Enjoy homemade pasta dishes with beef, seafood, or pheasant (€8-16) in the romantic, candlelit vaults of the city tavern. Italian wines by the glass (€3-5). Open M-Sa noon-2:30pm and 6pm-midnight. AmEx/MC/V. ❸

Maschu Maschu, I, Rabensteig 8. In Bermuda Dreieck. Filling and super-cheap falafel and schwarma (€3 each). Open M-W 11:30am-midnight, Th-Sa 11:30am-3am. ❶

OUTSIDE THE RING

🔊 **OH Pot, OH Pot,** IX, Währingerstr. 22. U2: Schottentor. This adorable eatery serves filling "pots," stew-like veggie or meat concoctions (€7-10). Fusion fare from Chilean to Ethiopian. Open M-F 10am-3pm and 6pm-midnight, Sa-Su 6pm-midnight. AmEx/MC/V. ❷

Centimeter, IX, Liechtensteinstr. 42. Tram D to Bauernfeldpl. This chain offers huge portions of greasy Austrian fare and an unbelievable selection of beers. You pay by the centimeter. Open M-F 10am-2am, Sa 11am-2am, Su 11am-midnight. AmEx/MC/V. ❷

Elsäßer Bistro, IX, Währingerstr. 32. U2: Schottentor. In the palace that houses the French Cultural Institute—walk into the garden and follow your nose to an extravagant meal (€14) and exquisite French wines. Open M-F 11am-3pm and 6:30-11pm. ❹

Vegetasia, III, Ungarg. 57. Take the O tram to Neulingg. A vegetarian nirvana, this cozy Taiwanese restaurant offers seitan and many forms of soy. Lunch buffet M-Sa €6.50. Open daily 11:30am-3pm and 5:30-11:30pm. Closed Tu evenings. AmEx/MC/V. ❷

Café Nil, VII, Siebensterng. 39. Enjoy vegetarian dishes (€6-12) with tortured writers at this Middle Eastern haunt. Breakfast until 3pm. Open daily 10am-midnight. ❷

Café Willendorf, VI, Linke Wienzeile 102. Take U4 to Pilgramg. and look for the pink building which also houses the **Rosa Lila Villa,** the center of gay life in Vienna. Artsy fare (€7-13), relaxed atmosphere. Open M-Th 6pm-1am, F-Sa 6pm-2pm. ❸

⬛ COFFEEHOUSES

In Vienna, the coffeehouse is not simply a place to resolve your midday caffeine deficit. For years these establishments were havens for artists, writers, and thinkers who stayed into the night: Peter Altenberg, "the cafe writer," scribbled lines; Oskar Kokoschka brooded alone; exiled Lenin and Trotsky played chess; Theodor Herzl planned for a Zionist Israel; and Kafka came to visit the Herrenhof. The original literary haunt was **Café Griensteidl,** but after it was demolished the torch passed to **Café Central** and then to **Café Herrenhof.** Cafes still exist under all these names, but only Café Central looks like it used to. Most also serve hot food, but don't order anything but pastries with your

Melange (Viennese coffee) unless you want to be really gauche. The most serious dictate of coffeehouse etiquette is that you linger; the waiter (*Herr Ober*) will serve you when you sit down, then leave you to sip, read, and cogitate. When you're ready to leave, just ask to pay: *"Zahlen bitte!"* Vienna has many coffeehouses; the best are listed below.

🛇 **Café Central,** I, at the corner of Herreng. and Strauchg. inside Palais Fers. Arched ceilings, wall frescoes, and every bit the Mecca of the cafe world. Open M-Sa 8am-10pm, Su 10am-6pm. AmEx/MC/V.

🛇 **Kleines Café,** I, Franziskanerpl. 3. Turn off Kärtnerstr. onto Weihburg. and follow it to the Franziskanerkirche. This tiny, cozy cafe features courtyard tables and salads that are minor works of art (€6.50). Open M-Sa 10am-2am, Su 1pm-2am.

Demel, I, Kohlmarkt 14. 5min. from the Stephansdom down Graben. The most lavish Viennese *Konditorei,* Demel was confectioner to the imperial court until the Empire dissolved. All of the chocolate is made fresh every morning, and the desserts are legendary. Open daily 10am-7pm. AmEx/MC/V.

Café Sperl, VI, Gumpendorferstr. 11. U2: Museumsquartier. Walk 1 block on Getreidemarkt and turn right on Gumpendorferstr. One of Vienna's oldest and most elegant cafes. Coffee €2-4.50. Cake €2.50-4. Sept.-June live piano Sa after 5pm. Open July-Aug. M-Sa 7am-11pm; Sept.-June M-Sa 7am-11pm, Su 11am-8pm.

Café Hawelka, I, Dorotheerg. 6, off Graben. Well-worn and glorious. Josephine and Leopold Hawelka put this legendary cafe on the map in 1939. Today, at 90 and 92 years respectively, they still make a mean *Buchteln* (bohemian doughnut with plum marmelade; fresh at 10pm; €3). Open M and W-Sa 8am-2am, Su 4pm-2am.

Hotel Sacher, I, Philharmonikerstr. 4, behind the opera house. This historic site has served world-famous *Sachertorte* for years. Cafe open daily 11am-11:30pm. Bakery open daily 9am-11:30pm. AmEx/MC/V.

🗺 SIGHTS

Vienna's streets are by turns stately, cozy, scuzzy, and grandiose; expect contrasts around every corner. To wander on your own, grab the brochure *Vienna from A to Z* (with Vienna Card €4) from the tourist office. The range of available **tours** is overwhelming—there are 42 themed walking tours alone, detailed in the brochure *Walks in Vienna*. Contact **Vienna-Bike,** IX, Wasag. (☎319 12 58), for **bike rental** (€5) or **cycling tours** (€20). **Bus tours** (from €30) are given by **Vienna Sightseeing Tours,** III, Stelzhamerg. 4/11 (☎712 46 83), and **Cityrama,** I, Börgeg. 1. (☎534 13).

INSIDE THE RING

District I is Vienna's social and geographical epicenter; with its Romanesque arches, Gothic portals, *Jugendstil* apartments, and modern *Haas Haus*, it's also a gallery of the history of aesthetics.

STEPHANSPLATZ, GRABEN, AND PETERSPLATZ. Right in the heart of Vienna, this square is home to the massive **Stephansdom** (St. Stephen's Cathedral), Vienna's most treasured symbol. For a view of Vienna, take the elevator up the North Tower or climb the 343 steps of the South Tower. *(North Tower open Apr.-June and Sept.-Oct. daily 8:30am-4pm. €3.50. South Tower open daily 9am-5:30pm. €2.50.)* Downstairs, skeletons of thousands of plague victims fill the **catacombs.** The **Gruft** (vault) stores all of the Habsburg innards. *(Tours M-Sa every 30min. 10-11:30am and 1-4:30pm, Su and holidays 1:30-4:30pm. €3.)* From Stephanspl., follow **Graben** for a landscape of *Jugendstil* architecture, including the **Ankerhaus** (#10), Otto Wagner's red-marble **Grabenhof,** and the underground public toilet complex designed by Adolf Loos. Graben leads to **Petersplatz** and the 1663 **Pestsaüle** (Plague Column), which was built in celebration of the passing of the Black Death. *(U1 or 3: Stephanspl.)*

HOHER MARKT AND STADTTEMPEL. Once both a market and an execution site, **Hoher Markt** was the heart of the Roman encampment, Vindobona. Roman ruins lie beneath the shopping arcade across from the fountain. *(From Stephanspl., walk down Rotenturmstr. and turn left on Lictenstr. Open Su and Tu-Sa 9am-12:15pm and 1-4:40pm. €1.80, students €0.70.)* The biggest draw is the 1914 *Jugendstil* **Ankeruhr** (clock), whose 3m figures—from Marcus Aurelius to Maria Theresia—rotate past the Viennese coat of arms accompanied by the tunes of their times. *(1 figure per hr. At noon all figures appear. Follow Judeng. from Hoher Markt to Ruprechtspl.)* Hidden on Ruprechtspl. at Seitenstetteng. 2, the **Stadttempel** is the only synagogue in Vienna to escape Nazi destruction during *Kristallnacht. (Bring passport. Open M-Th. Free.)*

AM HOF AND FREYUNG. Once a medieval jousting square, **Am Hof** now houses the **Kirche am Hof** (Church of the Nine Choirs of Angels) and **Collalto Palace,** where Mozart gave his first public performance. *(From Stephanspl., walk down Graben until it ends, go right and continue on Bognerg.; Am Hof is on the right.)* Just west of Am Hof is **Freyung,** the "square" with the **Austriabrunnen** (Austria Fountain) in the center. *Freyung* (sanctuary) took its name from the **Schottenstift** (Monastery of the Scots), where fugitives could claim asylum in medieval times. It was once used for public executions, but the annual **Christkindl market** held here blots out such unpleasant memories with baked goods and Christmas cheer.

HOFBURG. The sprawling **Hofburg** was the winter residence of the Habsburgs. Construction began in 1275, and additions continued until the end of the family's reign in 1918. Coming through the Michaelertor, you'll first enter the courtyard called **In der Burg** (within the fortress). On your left is the red-and-black-striped **Schweizertor** (Swiss Gate), erected in 1552. The **Silberkammer,** on the ground floor, displays the gold, silver, goblets, and 100 ft. gilded candelabra that once adorned the imperial table. *(Open 9am-5pm. €7, students €6.)*

Behind the Schweizertor lies the **Schweizerhof,** the inner courtyard of the **Alte Burg** (Old Fortress), which stands on the same site as the original 13th-century palace. Take a right at the top of the stairs for the Gothic **Burgkapelle** (chapel), where the members of the **Wiener Sängerknaben (Vienna Boys' Choir)** raise their heavenly voices every Sunday (p. 92). Beneath the stairs is the entrance to the **Weltliche und Geistliche Schatzkammer,** containing the Habsburg jewels, crowns, and Napoleon's cradle. *(Open M and W-Su 10am-6pm. €7, students €5. Free audio guide available in English.)* Northeast of the Alte Burg, the **Stallburg** is home to the Lipizzaner stallions and the **Spanische Reitschule** (Spanish Riding School). The cheapest way to see the steeds is to watch them train. *(From mid-Feb. to June and late Aug. to early Nov. Tu-F 10am-noon, except when the horses tour. Tickets sold at the door at Josefspl., Gate 2. €11.60, children €5.)*

Built between 1881 and 1913, the **Neue Burg** is the youngest wing of the palace. The double-headed golden eagle crowning the roof symbolizes the double empire of Austria-Hungary. Today, the Neue Burg houses Austria's largest library, the **Österreichische Nationalbibliothek.** *(Open July-Aug. and Sept. 23-30 M-F 9am-3:45pm, Sa 9am-12:45pm; closed Sept. 1-22; Oct.-June M-F 9am-7pm, Sa 9am-12:45pm.)*

High masses are still held in the 14th-century **Augustinerkirche** (St. Augustine's Church) on Josefspl. The hearts of the Habsburgs are stored in urns in the **Herzgrüftel.** *(To reach Hofburg, head through the Michaelertor in Michaelerpl. Mass 11am. Open M-Sa 10am-6pm, Su 11am-6pm. Free.)*

AUSTRIA

OUTSIDE THE RING

Some of Vienna's most famous modern architecture is outside the Ring, where 20th-century designers found more space to build. This area is also home to a number of Baroque palaces and parks that were once beyond the city limits.

KARLSPLATZ AND NASCHMARKT. Karlspl. is home to Vienna's most beautiful Baroque church, the **Karlskirche,** an eclectic masterpiece combining a Neoclassical portico with a Baroque dome and towers on either side. *(U1, 2, or 4 to Karlspl. Open M-F 7:30am-7pm, Sa 8:30am-7pm, Su 9am-7pm. Free.)* West of Karlspl., along Linke Wienzeile, is the colorful **Naschmarkt** food bazaar. On Saturdays, the Naschmarkt becomes a massive flea market. *(Open M-F 6am-6:30pm, Sa 6am-2pm.)*

SCHLOß BELVEDERE. The **Schloß Belvedere** was originally the summer residence of Prince Eugène of Savoy, one of Austria's greatest military heroes. The grounds, stretching from Schwarzenberg Palace to the *Südbahnhof,* contain three excellent museums (p. 90) and an equal number of spectacular sphinx-filled gardens. *(Take tram D or #71 one stop past Schwarzenbergpl.)*

SCHLOß SCHÖNBRUNN. From its humble beginnings as a hunting lodge, **Schönbrunn** ("beautiful brook") was Maria Theresia's favorite residence. The **Grand Tour** passes through the **Great Gallery,** where the Congress of Vienna met, and the **Hall of Mirrors,** where 6-year-old Mozart played. If you take the shorter **Imperial Tour,** you'll miss these. *(U4: Schönbrunn. Palace open July-Aug. daily 8:30am-7pm; Apr.-June and Sept.-Oct. 8:30am-5pm; Nov.-Mar. 8:30am-4:30pm. Imperial Tour €8, students €7.40. Grand Tour €10.50/8.60. Audioguides included.)* As impressive as the palace itself are the classical **gardens** behind it, which extend nearly four times the length of the palace and contain the **Schmetterlinghaus** (Butterfly House) and a hodgepodge of other attractions. *(Park open 6am-dusk. Free.)*

ZENTRALFRIEDHOF. The Viennese like to describe the Central Cemetery as half the size of Geneva but twice as lively. **Tor I** (Gate 1) leads to the old **Jewish Cemetery.** Many of the headstones are cracked and neglected because the families of most of the dead have left Austria. Behind **Tor II** (Gate 2) are Beethoven and Strauss, and an honorary monument to Mozart, whose true resting place is an unmarked pauper's grave in the **Cemetery of St. Mark,** III, Leberstr. 6-8. **Tor III** (Gate 3) leads to the Protestant section and the new Jewish cemetery. *(XI, Simmeringer Hauptstr. 234. Take S7 to Zentralfriedhof or tram #71 from Schwarzenbergpl. Open May-Aug. daily 7am-7pm; Mar.-Apr. and Sept.-Oct. 7am-6pm; Nov.-Feb. 8am-5pm.)*

🏛 MUSEUMS

Vienna owes its vast selection of masterpieces to the acquisitive Habsburgs and to the city's own crop of art schools and world-class artists. An exhaustive list is impossible to include here, but the tourist office's free *Museums* brochure lists all opening hours and admission prices. All museums run by the city of Vienna are **free on Friday** before noon (except on public holidays). If you're going to be in town for a while, invest in the **Museum Card** (ask at any museum ticket window).

📱 ÖSTERREICHISCHE GALERIE (AUSTRIAN GALLERY). The Upper Belvedere houses European art of the 19th and 20th centuries, including Klimt's *The Kiss.* The Lower Belvedere contains the **Austrian Museum of Baroque Art** and the **Austrian Museum of Medieval Art,** which showcase an extensive collection of sculptures and altarpieces. *(III, Prinz-Eugen-Str. 27, in the Belvedere Palace behind Schwarzenbergpl. Walk up from the Südbahnhof, then take tram D to Schloß Belvedere or tram #71 to Unteres Belvedere. Both Belvederes open Tu-Su 10am-6pm. €7.50, students €5.)*

KUNSTHISTORISCHES MUSEUM (MUSEUM OF FINE ARTS). The world's 4th-largest art collection features Venetian and Flemish paintings, Classical art, and an Egyptian burial chamber. The **Ephesos Museum** exhibits findings of excavations in Turkey, the **Hofjagd- und Rustkammer** is the 2nd-largest collection of arms in the world, and the **Sammlung alter Musikinstrumente** includes Beethoven's harpsichord and Mozart's piano. *(U2: Museumsquartier. Across from the Burgring and Heldenpl. on Maria Theresia's right. Open Tu-Su 10am-6pm. €9, students €6.50. 1st audio guide free.)*

MUSEUMSQUARTIER. At 60 sq. km, it's one of the ten biggest art districts in the world. Central Europe's largest collection of modern art, the ■ **Museum Moderner Kunst,** highlights Classical Modernism, Pop Art, Photo Realism, Fluxus, and Viennese Actionism in a building made from basalt lava. 20th-century masters include Kandinsky, Klee, Magritte, Miró, Motherwell, Picasso, Pollock, and Warhol. *(Open Su, Tu-W, and F-Sa 10am-7pm; Tu 10am-7pm; Th 10am-9pm. €8, students €6.50.)* The **Leopold Museum** has the world's largest Schiele collection, plus works by Egger-Lienz, Gerstl, Klimt, and Kokoschka. *(Open M, W-Th, and Sa-Su 10am-7pm, F 10am-9pm; €9, students €5.50.)* Themed exhibits of contemporary artists fill **Kunsthalle Wien.** *(Open M-W and F-Su 10am-7pm, Th 10am-10pm. Exhibition Hall 1 €6.50, students €5; Exhibition Hall 2 €5/3.50; both €8/6.50; students €2 on M. Take U2 to Museumsquartier.)*

ALBERTINA. First an Augustinian monastery and then the largest of the Habsburg residences, the Albertina now houses the **Collection of Graphic Arts.** Michelangelo, Picasso, and Dürer are among the diamonds in the rough of 65,000 drawings and 1 million prints. *(Open M-Tu and Th-Su 10am-6pm, W 10am-9pm.)*

HISTORISCHES MUSEUM DER STADT WIEN (VIENNA HISTORICAL MUSEUM). This collection of historical artifacts and paintings documents Vienna's evolution from a Roman encampment, through the Turkish siege, to the subsequent 640 years of Habsburg rule. *(IV, Karlspl., to the left of the Karlskirche. Open Su and Tu-Sa 9am-6pm. €3.50, students €1.50. Free after 3pm on F.)*

KUNST HAUS WIEN. Artist-environmentalist Friedenreich Hundertwasser built this museum without straight lines—even the floor bends. In addition to his work, it hosts contemporary art from around the world. *(III, Untere Weißgerberstr. 13. U1 or 4 to Schwedenpl., then tram N to Hetzg. Open daily 10am-7pm. €8, students €6; M half-price.)*

ENTERTAINMENT AND FESTIVALS

While Vienna offers all the standard entertainment in the way of theater, film, and festivals, the heart of the city beats to music. All but a few of classical music's marquee names lived, composed, and performed in Vienna. Mozart, Beethoven, and Haydn wrote their greatest masterpieces in Vienna, creating the **First Viennese School;** a century later, Schönberg, Webern, and Berg teamed up to form the **Second Viennese School.** Every Austrian child must learn to play an instrument during schooling, and the Vienna **Konservatorium** and **Hochschule** are world-renowned conservatories. All year, Vienna has performances ranging from the above-average to the sublime, with many accessible to the budget traveler. Note that the venues below have **no performances in July and August.**

Vienna hosts an array of important annual festivals, mostly musical. The **Vienna Festwochen** (mid-May to mid-June) has a diverse program of exhibitions, plays, and concerts. (☎58 92 20; www.festwochen.or.at.) The Staatsoper and Volkstheater host the annual **Jazzfest Wien** during the first weeks of July, featuring many famous acts. (☎503 5647; www.viennajazz.org.) The Social Democrats host the late-June **Donauinsel Fest** which draws millions of party-goers annually for fireworks and rock, jazz, and folk concerts. From mid-July to mid-August, the **Im-Puls**

Dance Festival (☎523 55 58; www.impuls-tanz.com) attracts some of the world's greatest dance troupes and offers seminars to enthusiasts. In mid-October, the annual city-wide film festival, the **Viennale,** kicks off.

Staatsoper, I, Opernring 2 (www.wiener-staatsoper.at). Vienna's premiere opera performs nearly every night Sept.-June. No shorts allowed. 500 standing-room tickets are available for every performance (1 per person; €2-3.50), but plan on getting there 2hr. before curtain. The box office (Bundestheaterkasse; ☎514 44 78 80), I, Hanuschg. 3, around the corner from the opera, sells tickets in advance. Seats €10-180. Open M-F 8am-6pm, Sa-Su 9am-noon, 1st Sa of each month 9am-5pm.

Wiener Philharmoniker (Vienna Philharmonic Orchestra) plays in the **Musikverein,** Austria's premiere concert hall. Even if you only want standing room tickets, visit the box office (Bösendorferstr. 12 or www.wienerphilharmoniker.at) well in advance.

Wiener Sängerknaben (Vienna Boys' Choir) sings during mass every Su at 9:15am (mid-Sept. to the first week of June) in the Hofburgkapelle (U3: Herreng.). Despite rumors to the contrary, standing room is free; arrive before 8am.

◼ NIGHTLIFE

With one of the highest bar-to-cobblestone ratios in the world, Vienna is a great place to party, whether you're looking for a quiet evening with a glass of wine or a wild night in a disco. Take U1 or 4 to Schwedenpl., which will drop you within blocks of the **Bermuda Dreieck** (Bermuda Triangle), an area packed with lively, crowded clubs. If you make it out, head down **Rotenturmstraße** toward Stephansdom or walk around the areas bounded by the Jewish synagogue and Ruprechtskirche. Slightly outside the Ring, the streets off **Burggasse** and **Stiftgasse** in District VII and the **university quarter** (Districts XIII and IX) have tables in outdoor courtyards and loud, hip bars.

Viennese nightlife starts late, often after 11pm. For the scoop, pick up a copy of the indispensable **Falter** (€2), which prints listings of everything from opera and theater to punk concerts and updates on the gay and lesbian scene.

U-4, XII, Schönbrunnerstr. 222. (www.clubnet.at). U4: Meidling Hauptstr. In the late 80s, U-4 hosted Nirvana and Hole before they were famous. 2 dance areas and multiple bars. Check in advance for theme nights. Cover €8. Open daily 10pm-5am.

Europa, VII, Zollerg. 8. Buy a drink, sidle back to the neon-lit alcoves, and strike a pose. The hip 20-something crowd hangs out late after long nights of clubbing. Mai Tai €6.50. Open daily 9am-5am.

Das Möbel, VII, Burgg. 10. U2 or 3 to Volkstheater. Metal couches, car-seat chairs, and Swiss-army tables are filled by an artsy crowd. Open M-F noon-1am, Sa-Su 10am-1am.

Cato, I, Tiefer Graben 19. U3: Herreng. Turn right on Strauchg. and continue onto Tiefer Graben. By night's end the warm hostess, Anna Maria, will have you singing. Try the Sekte Cuvee, a dry spirit from Burgenland (€4). Open Su-Th 6pm-2am, F-Sa 6pm-4am.

Porgy & Bess, I, Riemerg. 11. (www.porgy.at). U1: Stubentor. The best jazz club in Vienna. Prices vary—shows generally €15-20. Open M-Sa 7pm-late, Su 8pm-late. MC/V.

Benjamin, I, Salzgries 11. Punk rock and tequila shots (€1.60). Open daily 7pm-2am.

STYRIA (STEIERMARK)

Many of southern Austria's folk traditions live on in this, "the Green Heart of Austria." Even its largest city, Graz, remains relatively untouristed. Circumnavigate crumbling medieval strongholds, salivate at the Lipizzaner studs, and drink of the wine from the Styrian vine.

GRAZ
☎ 0316

Graz's under-touristed *Altstadt* has an unhurried Mediterranean feel, picturesque red-tiled roofs, and Baroque domes. The second largest of Austria's cities, Graz (pop. 226,000) offers a sweaty, energetic nightlife thanks to the 45,000 students at Karl-Franzens-Universität.

TRANSPORTATION. From the **Hauptbahnhof**, trains run to: Innsbruck (6hr., 7 per day, €44); Munich (6½hr., 4 per day, €63); Salzburg (4¼hr., €37); Vienna *Südbahnhof* (2½hr., 16 per day, €25); and Zurich (10hr., 10pm, €74).

PRACTICAL INFORMATION. From the train station, go down Annenstr. and cross the main bridge to reach **Hauptplatz,** the center of town. Five minutes away is **Jakominiplatz,** the hub of the public transportation system. **Herrengasse,** a pedestrian street lined with cafes and boutiques, connects the two squares. The **University** is tucked away past the *Stadtpark*, in the northeast part of Graz. The **tourist office,** Herreng. 16, has free city maps and a walking guide of the city. The staff offers English-language **tours** of the *Altstadt* (2hr.; Apr.-Oct. Su, Tu-W, and F-Sa 2:30pm; €7.50) and makes room reservations for free. (☎807 50. Open June-Sept. M-F 9am-7pm, Sa 9am-6pm, Su 10am-4pm; Oct.-May M-F 9am-6pm, Sa 9am-3pm, Su 10am-3pm.) **Postal Code:** A-8010.

ACCOMMODATIONS AND FOOD. In Graz, most hotels, guesthouses, and pensions are pricey and far from the city center. Luckily, the web of local transportation provides a reliable and easy commute to and from the outlying neighborhoods. To reach **Jugendgästehaus Graz (HI) ❸,** Idlhofg. 74, from the station, cross the street, head right on Eggenberger Gürtel, turn left on Josef-Huber-G., then take the first right; the hostel is through the parking lot on your right. Buses #31 and 32 run here from Jakominipl. (☎71 48 76. All rooms with bath. Breakfast included. Laundry €3. **Internet** €1.50 per 20min. Reception daily 7am-10pm. Dorms €19.50; singles €26.50; doubles €42.50. Discount for longer stays. MC/V.) **Hotel Strasser ❸,** Eggenberger Gürtel 11, is 5min. from the train station. Exit, cross the street, and head right on Eggenberger Gürtel. (☎71 39 77. Breakfast included. Singles €29, with shower €36; doubles €45/54; triples with shower €66. AmEx/DC/MC/V.)

Find an inexpensive meal on **Hauptplatz,** where concession stands sell sandwiches, *Wurst* (€1.50-3), and other fast food. Cheap student hangouts line **Zinzendorfgasse** near the university. **Braun de Praun ❹,** Morellenfeldg. 32, is unafraid of a little culinary experimentation. Main dishes include curry pork with glazed banana and almond-raisin rice (€12.50) and chicken "mexicano" (€12.50), but the numerous local dishes, Biergarten ambience, and Lederhosen-clad waiters keep it firmly rooted in Graz. (☎32 20 03. Open M-Sa 8am-2am. AmEx/MC/V.) **Gasthaus Alte Münze ❸,** Schloßbergpl. 8, serves scrumptious Styrian specialties in a traditional setting. (Open M and Su 10am-7pm, Tu-Sa 8am-midnight.) A grocery store, **Merkur,** is to your left as you exit the station. (Open M-Th 8am-7pm, F 7:30am-7:30pm.)

SIGHTS AND NIGHTLIFE. The tourist office, in the **Landhaus,** is itself a sight; the building was remodeled by architect Domenico dell'Allio in 1557 in the Lombard style. The **Landeszeughaus** (Provincial Arsenal), Herreng. 16, details the history of Ottoman attacks on the arsenal and has enough spears, muskets, and armor to outfit 28,000 burly mercenaries. (Open Su and Tu-Sa 10am-6pm. €1.50.) North of Hauptpl., the wooded **Schloßberg** (Castle Mountain) rises 123m above Graz. The hill is named for the castle that stood there from 1125 until 1809, when it

AUSTRIA

was destroyed by Napoleon's troops. Even without the castle, it remains a beautiful city park. Climb the zig-zagging stone steps of the **Schloßbergstiege,** built by Russian prisoners during WWI, for sweeping views of the vast Styrian plain.

The hub of after-hours activity is the so-called **Bermuda Triangle,** an area of the old city behind Hauptpl. and bordered by Mehlpl., Färberg., and Prokopig. At **Kulturhauskeller,** Elisabethstr. 30, the dance music throbs. (No sports or military clothing. 19+. Cover €2. Open Tu-Sa 9pm-late.) At the artsy grad-student hangout, **Café Harrach,** Harrachg. 26, most everyone tosses back white wine spritzers. (Open M-F 9am-midnight, Sa-Su 5pm-midnight.)

⚡ DAYTRIP FROM GRAZ: LIPIZZANER STUD FARM. The **Gestüt Piber** (Piber Stud Farm) is home to the world-famous **Lippizaner** horses, whose delicate footwork and snow white coats are the pride of the Spanish Riding School in Vienna. Born either solid black or brown, they become progressively paler, reaching a pure white color sometime between the age of five and ten. The rolling green hills of Piber are home to the mares, their foals, and trained stallions in retirement. On a 1hr. tour of the stud farm, you can see the horses up close in the stables and visit the carriage house and the Lippizaner museum in the 300-year-old Piber castle. (☎ 03144 33 23. Open Apr.-Oct. daily 9-10:30am and 1:30-3:30pm. €10, students €5.) The horse farm is 1km outside **Köflach.** Take the **train** from Graz (50 min., 8 per day 6am-2pm, €5.40), then the **bus** (€1.60) to Piber. Sign up at the tourist office in Graz for a ride and English-language tour. (Sa 2pm. €24, children €9.)

SALZBURGER LAND AND UPPER AUSTRIA

Salzburger Land derives its name from the German *Salz* (salt), and it was this white gold that first drew visitors to the region. Combined with Upper Austria, this region encompasses the shining lakes and rolling hills of the Salzkammergut, where Salzburg and Hallstatt are among the more enticing destinations.

SALZBURG ☎ 0662

Backdropped by mountains and graced with Baroque wonders, Salzburg (pop. 140,000) offers both spectacular sights and a rich musical culture. Mozart's birthplace and the setting of *The Sound of Music*, Salzburg now carries on this legacy with aplomb. The city's adoration of classical music and the arts reaches a dizzying climax every summer during the **Salzburger Festspiele,** a five-week music festival featuring hundreds of operas, plays, and open-air performances.

▐ TRANSPORTATION

Trains: Hauptbahnhof, in Südtirolerpl. (24hr. reservations ☎ 05 17 17). To: **Graz** (4hr., 8 per day, €37); **Innsbruck** (2hr., 11 per day, €30); **Munich** (2hr., 30 per day, €26); **Vienna** (3½hr., 26 per day, €37); **Zurich** (6hr., 7 per day, €65).

Public Transportation: Get bus info. at the **Lokalbahnhof** (☎ 44 80 61 66), next to the train station. Single tickets (€1.70) available at automatic machines or from the drivers. Books of **five tickets** (€7), **daypasses** (€3.20), and **week passes** (€9) available at

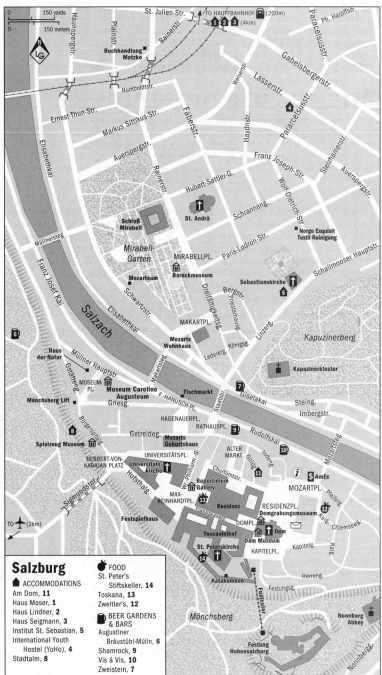

0 150 yards
0 150 meters

Salzburg

🏠 ACCOMMODATIONS
Am Dom, **11**
Haus Moser, **1**
Haus Lindner, **2**
Haus Seigmann, **3**
Institut St. Sebastian, **5**
International Youth
   Hostel (YoHo), **4**
Stadtalm, **8**

🍴 FOOD
St. Peter's
   Stiftskeller, **14**
Toskana, **13**
Zweitler's, **12**

🍺 BEER GARDENS
& BARS
Augustiner
   Bräustübl-Mülln, **6**
Shamrock, **9**
Vis á Vis, **10**
Zweistein, **7**

AUSTRIA

machines, the ticket office, or *Tabak* shops (newsstand/tobacco shops). Punch your ticket when you board in order to validate it or risk a €36 fine. Buses usually make their last run at 10:30-11:30pm, but **BusTaxi** fills in when the public buses stop. Get on at Hanuschpl. or Theaterg. and tell the driver where you need to go (every 30min. Su-Th 11:30pm-1:30am, F-Sa 11:30pm-3am; €3 for anywhere within the city limits).

✦ ✷ ❓ ORIENTATION AND PRACTICAL INFORMATION

Just a few kilometers from the German border, Salzburg covers both banks of the **Salzach River.** Two hills abut the river: the **Mönchsberg** over the **Altstadt** (old city) on the south side and the **Kapuzinerberg** by the **Neustadt** (new city) on the north side. The *Hauptbahnhof* is on the northern side of town beyond the *Neustadt;* buses #1, 5, 6, 51, and 55 connect it to downtown. On foot, turn left out of the station onto Rainerstr. and follow it straight under the tunnel and on to Mirabellpl.

Tourist Office, Mozartpl. 5 (☎88 98 73 30), in the *Altstadt.* From the station, take bus #5, 6, 51, or 55 to Mozartsteg, head away from the river and curve right around the building into Mozartpl. The office gives free hotel maps, guided tours of the city (daily 12:15pm, €8), and sells the **Salzburg Card,** which grants admission to all museums and sights as well as unlimited public transportation (24hr. card €19; 48hr. €27; 72hr. €33). Room reservation service €2.20. Open daily 9am-6pm.

Currency Exchange: Banks have better rates than AmEx offices but often charge higher commissions. The station exchange is open M-F 8:30am-5pm, Sa 8:30am-2:30pm.

Emergencies: Police: ☎133. **Ambulance:** ☎144. **Fire:** ☎122.

Pharmacies: Elisabeth-Apotheke, Elisabethstr. 1a (☎87 14 84). Pharmacies in the city center open M-F 8am-6pm, Sa 8am-noon. There are always 3 pharmacies open for emergencies; check the list on the door of any closed pharmacy.

Internet Access: Internet Café, Mozartpl. 5 (☎84 48 22), near the tourist office. €0.15 per min. Open Sept.-June daily 9am-10pm, July-Aug. 9am-midnight. **Piterfun Internetc@fe,** Ferdinand-Porsche-Str. 7, across from the train station, has a rave ambience. 15min. €1.80, 30min. €2.90, 60min. €5. Open daily 10am-10pm.

Post Office: At the train station (☎88 30 30). Address mail to be held: Firstname SURNAME, *Postlagernde Briefe*, Bahnhofspostamt, **A-5020** Salzburg, AUSTRIA. Open M-F 7am-8:30pm, Sa 8am-2pm, Su 1-6pm.

⌂ ACCOMMODATIONS

Although hostels are plentiful, other housing in the city center is expensive; other affordable options lie on the outskirts of town or just outside it on **Kasern Berg.**

IN SALZBURG

Be wary of hotel hustlers at the station. Instead, ask for the tourist office's list of *Privatzimmern* (private rooms) or the *Hotel Plan* (which has info on hostels). From mid-May to mid-September, hostels fill by mid-afternoon; call ahead, and be sure to make reservations during the *Festspiele* (p. 99).

◪ **Stadtalm,** Mönchsberg 19c (☎ 84 17 29). Take bus #1 to *Mönchsbergaufzug*, go through the stone arch on the left to the Mönchsberglift (elevator) and ride up (daily 9am-11pm, round-trip €2.40). At the top, turn right, climb the steps, and follow the signs. The view is princely. Breakfast included. Shower €0.80 per 4min. Reception 9am-9pm. Curfew 1am. Open Apr.-Sept. Dorms €13. AmEx/MC/V. ❷

Institut St. Sebastian, Linzerg. 41 (☎87 13 86). From the station, bus #1, 5, 6, 51, or 55 to *Mirabellpl.*; continue in the same direction as the bus, turn left onto Bergstr., and left again onto Linzerg.; the hostel is through the arch. Breakfast included. Sheets €2 for dorms. Laundry €3. Reception 8am-noon and 4-9pm. Dorms €15; singles €21, with shower €33; doubles €40/54; triples €60/69; quads €72/84. ❷

International Youth Hotel (YoHo), Paracelsusstr. 9 (☎87 96 49). Frat-party atmosphere; a no-frills place to crash. Breakfast €3-4. Happy Hour 6-7pm. Sheets €5 deposit. Dorms €15; doubles €20, with shower €23; quads €68/80. MC/V. ❷

Am Dom, Goldg. 17 (☎84 27 55). Unbeatable location on the square. Historic, wood-paneled, traditional Austrian hotel. Singles €68; doubles €94. MC/V. ❹

OUTSIDE OF SALZBURG

The rooms on **Kasern Berg** are officially outside Salzburg, which means the tourist office can't recommend them, but the personable hosts and bargain prices make these *Privatzimmer* (rooms in a family home) a terrific housing option. Expect rolling fields and a reliance on public transportation. All northbound trains run to Kasern Berg (4min.; every 30min. 6:15am-11:15pm; €1.60; Eurail valid). Get off at Salzburg-Maria Plain and take the only road uphill. Most don't accept credit cards.

Haus Lindner, Panoramaweg 5 (☎45 66 81). Offers homey rooms, some with mountain views. Breakfast included. Call for pickup from the station. €16 per person. ❷

Haus Moser, Turnerbühel (☎45 66 76). Climb up the steep hidden stairs on the right side of Kasern Berg road across from German Kapeller. A charming couple offers comfortable rooms in their cozy, dark-timbered home. Breakfast and laundry included. €15 per person. Cheaper after 1st night. ❷

Haus Seigmann, Kasern Bergstr. 66 (☎45 00 01). Snug comforters and balconies overlooking the valley. Afternoon tea served on the hillside patios. About €15 per person (negotiable). Reservations recommended in the summer. MC/V. ❷

🍴 FOOD

Countless beer gardens and pastry-shop patios make Salzburg a great place for outdoor dining. Local specialties include *Salzburger Nockerl* (egg whites, sugar, and raspberry filling baked into three mounds that represent the three hills of Salzburg), *Knoblauchsuppe* (a rich cream soup loaded with croutons and garlic), and the world-famous *Mozartkugeln* (hazelnuts coated in marzipan, nougat, and chocolate). **Supermarkets** cluster on the Mirabellpl. side of the river, and **open-air markets** are held on Universitätpl. (Open M-F 6am-7pm, Sa 6am-1pm.)

Zwettler's, Kaig. 3. Near the tourist office on Mozartpl. Try the tasty *Spinatnockerl* (spinach baked into a pan with cheese and parsley, €6.50) or the classic *Wienerschnitzel* (€9.70). For added excitement local customers yell suggestions to the chef on the second floor. Open daily 6pm-1am, during the *Festspiele* also 11am-2pm. ❸

St. Peter's Stiftskeller, St.-Peter-Bezirk 1/4. Tucked away behind the fortress at the foot of the cliffs is the oldest restaurant in Central Europe, established in 803. Most dishes run €18-20. Open M-F 11am-midnight, during the *Festspiele* until 1am. MC/V. ❹

Toskana, Sigmund Haffnerg. 11. College cafeteria with the cheapest eats in the *Altstadt*. Entrees €4. Open July-Aug. M-F 9am-3pm; Sept.-June M-Th 9am-5pm, F 9am-3pm. ❶

👁 SIGHTS

THE ALTSTADT

FESTUNG HOHENSALZBURG. Built between 1077 and 1681 by the ruling archbishops, Hohensalzburg Fortress, which looms over Salzburg from atop Mönchsberg, is the largest completely preserved castle in Europe—partly because it was never successfully attacked. The castle contains formidable Gothic state rooms, the fortress organ (nicknamed the "Bull of Salzburg" for its off-key snorting), and a watchtower that affords an unmatched view of the city and mountains. The **Burgmuseum** inside the fortress displays medieval instruments of torture and has side-by-side histories of Salzburg, the fortress, and the world. (Take the trail or the Festungsbahn funicular up to the fortress from Festungsg. Funicular every 10min. 9am-9pm. Ascent €5.60, round-trip €8.50; includes entrance to fortress. Grounds open mid-June to mid-Sept. daily 8:30am-8pm; mid-Sept. to mid-Mar. 9am-5pm; mid-Mar. to mid-June 9am-6pm. Interior open mid-June to mid-Sept. daily 9am-5:30pm; mid-Sept. to mid-Mar. 9am-4:30pm; mid-Mar. to mid-June 9:30am-5pm. If you walk up, entrance to fortress is €3.60; **combo ticket** including fortress, castle interiors, and museums €7.20.)

MOZARTS GEBURTSHAUS. Mozart's birthplace holds an impressive collection of the child genius' belongings, including his first viola and violin and a pair of keyboardish instruments. Several rooms recreate his young years as a traveling virtuoso. Come before 11am to avoid the crowd. (Getreudeg. 9. Open July-Aug. daily 9am-6:30pm; Sept.-June 9am-5:30pm. €5.50, students and seniors €4.50.)

TOSCANINIHOF, CATACOMBS, AND THE DOM. Steps lead from **Toscaninihof,** the courtyard of **St. Peter's Monastery,** up the Mönchsberg cliffs. **Stiftskirche St. Peter,** a church within the monastery, features a marble portal from 1244. In the 18th century, the building was remodeled in Rococo style. (Open daily 9am-12:15pm and 2:30-6:30pm.) Near the far end of the cemetery, against the Mönchsberg, is the entrance to the **Catacombs.** In the lower room (St. Gertrude's Chapel), a fresco commemorates the martyrdom of Thomas á Beckett. (Open May-Sept. Tu–Su 10:30am-5pm; Oct.-Apr. W-Su 10:30am-3:30pm. €1, students €0.60.) The exit at the other end of the cemetery leads to the immense baroque **Dom** (cathedral), where Mozart was christened in 1756 and later worked as concert master and court organist. The square leading out of the cathedral, **Domplatz,** features a statue of the Virgin Mary and figures representing Wisdom, Faith, the Church, and the Devil. (Free, but donation requested.)

RESIDENZ. The archbishops of Salzburg have resided in the magnificent Residenz since 1595. Stunning baroque **Prunkräume** (state rooms) have gigantic ceiling frescoes, gilded furniture, Flemish tapestries from the 1600s, and ornate stucco work. A **gallery** exhibits 16th- to 19th-century art. (Open daily 10am-5pm. €7.30, students €5.50; audio guide included.)

FESTSPIELHAUS. Once the riding school for the archbishops' horses, it now hosts many of the big-name events of the *Festspiele* in its two opera houses. (☎84 90 97. Down Wiener-Philharmonikerg. from Universitätspl. Tours at 2pm. €5, under 13 €2.90.) Opposite the *Festspielhaus,* the **Rupertinum Gallery** exhibits modern painting, sculpture, and photography in a graceful building remodeled by Friedensreich Hundertwasser. (☎80 42 23 36. Open mid-July to Sept. Su, Tu and Th-Sa 9am-5pm, W 10am-9pm; Oct. to mid-July Su, Tu and Th-Sa 10am-5pm, W 10am-9pm. €8, students €4.50.)

THE NEUSTADT

MIRABELL PALACE AND GARDENS. Mirabellpl. holds the marvelous **Mirabell Schloß,** which the supposedly celibate Archbishop Wolf Dietrich built for his mistress and their ten children in 1606. Behind the palace, the delicately cultivated **Mirabellgarten** is a maze of seasonal flower beds and groomed shrubbery. The Mirabellgarten contains a wooden, moss-covered shack called the **Zauberflötenhäuschen,** where Mozart allegedly composed *The Magic Flute* in just five months.

MOZARTS WOHNHAUS. Mozart moved here at age 17 with his family, staying from 1773-1780. Hear excerpts from his music alongside original scores. *(Makartpl. 8. Open July-Aug. daily 9am-6:30pm; Sept.-June 9am-5:30pm.)*

ENTERTAINMENT

Max Reinhardt, Richard Strauss, and Hugo von Hofmannsthal founded the renowned **Salzburger Festspiele** in 1920. Ever since, Salzburg has become a musical mecca from late July to the end of August. On the eve of the festival's opening, over 100 dancers don regional costumes and perform a *Fackeltanz* (torchdance) on Residenzpl. Operas, plays, films, concerts, and tourists overrun every available public space. Info and tickets for *Festspiele* events are available through the *Festspiele Kartenbüro* (ticket office) and *Tageskasse* (daily box office) in Karajanpl., against the mountain and next to the tunnel. (Open M-F 9:30am-3pm; July 1-July 22 M-Sa 9:30am-5pm; July 23-end of festival daily 9:30am-6:30pm.)

Even when the *Festspiele* are not on, many other concerts and events occur around the city. The **Salzburg Academy of Music and Performing Arts** performs a number of concerts on a rotating schedule in the **Mozarteum** (next to the Mirabell gardens), and the **Dom** has a concert program in July and August. (€8.75, students €7.30.) In addition, from May through August there are **outdoor performances**, including concerts, folk-singing, and dancing, around the Mirabellgarten. The tourist office has leaflets on scheduled events, but an evening stroll through the park might answer your questions just as well. **Mozartplatz** and **Kapitelplatz** are also popular stops for talented street musicians and touring school bands.

PUBS AND BEER GARDENS

Munich may be known as the world's beer capital, but much of that liquid gold flows south to Austria's pubs and *Biergärten* (beer gardens). These lager oases cluster in the city center by the Salzach River. The more boisterous stick to Rudolfskai between the Staatsbrücke and Mozartsteg. Elsewhere, especially along Chiemseeg. and around Anton-Neumayr-Pl., you can throw back a few drinks in a more reserved *Beisl* (pub). Refined bars with older patrons can be found along Steing. and Giselakai on the other side of the river. The gargantuan ▨**Augustiner Bräustübl-Mülln,** Augustinerg. 4, has been serving home-brewed beer, *Biergarten* style, since 1621. (Open M-F 3-11pm, Sa-Su 2:30-11pm.) Settle into an armchair at the chic **Vis à Vis,** Rudolfskai 24.

NO WORK, ALL PLAY

START YOUR ENGINES.

At the end of May Salzburg shuts down in recognition of *Christi Himmelfahrt,* the Catholic holiday of the Ascension. Although the holiday is a celebration of Jesus's return to heaven, part of Salzburg's observance may seem surprising. At the end of May, antique race cars pour into Residenzpl., revving their engines and parading around town for three days. In 2003 the Gaisberg Race for classic motor cars, which ran from 1929 to 1969, was resurrected by a group of farsighted politicians and antique car lovers. The race is a "regularity contest," meaning that racers try to match their own times. The 8652m course runs from the city center to the Gaisberg, one of three hills overlooking Salzburg. Beaming from their cars, models 1910 to 1970, the owners make the 672m climb. The event allows car collectors a chance to show off their babies, and gives Salzburgers and tourists an excuse to gather in the *Altstadt* and see some really cool cars. While admiring the competitors' automobiles, spectators enjoy the live music and the food stands set up around the edges of Residenzpl.

In 2004, *Christi Himmelfahr* falls on Thursday, May 20. The festivities last for three days, through Saturday. For more info, check out the Gaisberg Race's site www.src.co.at.

(Open daily 7:30pm-4am.) A relaxed and friendly Irish pub, **Shamrock**, Rudolfskai 11, has plenty of room and nightly live music. (Open Su noon-2am, M-Th 3pm-2am, F-Sa noon-4am.) **Zweistein**, Giselakai 9, is the center of Salzburg's gay and lesbian scene. (Open M-W 6pm-4am, Th-Su 6pm-5am.)

DAYTRIPS FROM SALZBURG

HELLBRUNN. Just south of Salzburg lies the unforgettable **Lustschloß Hellbrunn**, a sprawling estate with a large palace, fish ponds, flower gardens, and the **Wasserspiele**, elaborate water-powered figurines and a booby-trapped table that spouts water on surprised guests. Pictures of you getting sprayed are available at the end of the tour. (Open May-June and Sept. daily 9am-5:30pm; July-Aug. 9am-10pm; Apr. and Oct. 9am-4:30pm. Ticket for castle tour, gardens, and Wasserspiele €7.50, students €5.50.) Take bus #55 (dir.: Rif; 30 min.) to Hellbrun from the train station, Mirabellpl., or Mozartsteg.

After you dry off, continue on bus #55 to St. Leonhard, where Charlemagne supposedly rests under Untersberg Peak, prepared to return and reign over Europe when duty calls. A cable car glides over the rocky cliffs to the summit, and from there hikes lead off into the distance. On top is a memorial cross and unbelievable mountain scenery. (Open July-Sept. daily 8:30am-5:30pm; Mar.-June and Oct. 8:30am-5pm; Dec.-Feb. 9am-4pm. Round-trip €17.)

HALLSTATT   ☎06134

Teetering on the banks of the Hallstättersee, tiny Hallstatt (pop. 960) seems to defy gravity by clinging to the face of a stony slope. It is easily the most striking lakeside village in the Salzkammergut, if not in all of Austria.

■ TRANSPORTATION. Buses are the cheapest way (€12) to get to Hallstatt from Salzburg, but require layovers in both Bad Ischl and Gosaumühle. The **train station,** across the lake, is not staffed. All trains come from Attnang-Puchheim in the north or Stainach-Irdning in the south. **Trains** run hourly to Bad Ischl (30min., €3) and Salzburg via Attnang-Puchheim (2½hrs., €17).

⊠ PRACTICAL INFORMATION. The **tourist office,** Seestr. 169, finds rooms and offers help with the town's confusing system of street numbers. (☎82 08. Open July-Aug. M-F 9am-5pm, Sa 10am-4pm, Su 10am-2pm; Sept.-June M-Tu and Th-F 9am-noon and 2-5pm, W 9am-noon.) There is an **ATM** next to the post office. The **post office,** Seestr. 160, is below the tourist office. (Open M-Tu and Th-F 8am-noon and 1:30-5:30pm, W 8am-noon.) **Postal Code:** A-4830.

⌂☐ ACCOMMODATIONS AND FOOD. To reach **Gästehaus Zur Mühle ❷**, Kirchenweg 36, from the tourist office, walk uphill, heading for a short tunnel at the upper right corner of the square; it's right at the end of the tunnel by the waterfall. (☎83 18. Breakfast €2.50. Reception 10am-2pm and 4-10pm. Closed Nov. Dorms €10.) **Frühstückspension Sarstein ❸**, Gosamühlstr. 83, offers glorious views as well as a beachside lawn. From the ferry landing, turn right on Seestr. and walk 10min. (☎82 17. Breakfast included. Showers €1 per 10min. Singles €18; doubles €36.) To get to **Camping Klausner-Höll ❶**, Lahnstr. 201, turn right out of the tourist office and follow Seestr. for 10min. (☎832 24. Breakfast €4-8. Showers included. Laundry €8. Gate closed daily noon-3pm and 10pm-7:30am. Open mid-Apr. to mid-Oct. €5.80; tent €3.70; car €2.90.) The cheapest eats are at the **Konsum supermarket** across from the bus stop; the butcher's counter prepares sandwiches on request. (Open M-Tu and Th-F 7:30am-noon and 3-6pm, W and Sa 7:30am-noon.)

🔲 🔌 **SIGHTS AND HIKING.** Back when Rome was still a village, the "white gold" from the salt mines made Hallstatt a world-famous settlement; the 2500-year-old **Salzbergwerk** is the oldest salt mine in the world. Take the guided tour (1hr., in English and German), and zip down a wooden mining slide on a burlap sack to an eerie lake deep inside the mountain. (☎200 2400. Open daily May-Sept. 9:30am-4:30pm; Oct. 9:30am-3pm. €14.50; students €8.70.) In the 19th century, Hallstatt was also the site of an immense and well-preserved Iron Age archaeological find. The **charnel house** next to St. Michael's Chapel is a bizarre repository filled with the remains of over 610 villagers dating from the 16th century on; the latest were added in 1995. The dead were previously buried in the mountains, but villagers soon ran out of space and transferred older bones to the charnel house to make room for more corpses. From the ferry dock, follow the signs marked *Katholische Kirche*. (Open daily June-Sept. 10am-6pm; May and Oct. 10am-4pm. €1.)

Hallstatt offers some of the most spectacular day hikes in the Salzkammergut. The tourist office offers an excellent Dachstein **hiking guide** in English (€6), which details 38 hikes in the area, as well as **bike** trail maps (€7). The **Salzbergwerk hike** is a simple 1hr. gravel hike leading to the salt-mine tour; walk to the Salzbergbahn and take the road to the right upward, turning at the black and yellow Salzwelten sign. The **Waldbachstrub Waterfall hike** is a light 1¾hr. walk along a tumbling stream and up to a spellbinding waterfall. From the bus station, follow the brown Malerweg signs near the supermarket and continue to follow them until the Waldbachstrub sign appears (about 40min.). The waterfall is in the **Echental,** a valley carved out millennia ago by glaciers and now blazed with trails leading deep into the valley. The **Gangsteig,** a slippery, primitive stairway, carved into the side of a cliff, requires sturdy hiking shoes and a strong will to climb.

📕 **DAYTRIPS FROM HALLSTATT: DACHSTEIN ICE CAVES.** Above **Obertraun,** opposite the lake from Hallstatt, the famed **Riesenhöhle** (Giant Ice Cave) is part of the largest system of ice caves in the world. Slide by its frozen waterfalls and palaces on a sheet of green ice. The Riesenhöhle and the **Mammuthöhle** (Mammoth Cave) are up on the mountain, while the **Koppenbrüllerhöhle,** a giant spring, is in the valley. Mandatory tours are offered in English and German; you'll be assigned to a group at the Schönbergalm station. The cave temperatures are near freezing, so wear good footwear and something warm. (☎ (06131) 84 00. Open May to mid-Oct. daily 9am-5pm. Admission to each cave €8, children €4.80.)

From Hallstatt, walk to the Lahn station by heading down Seestr. with the lake to your left, and catch the **bus** to Obertraun (10min., every hr. 9am-5pm, €1.40). Stop at Dachstein, then ride the cable car up to Schönbergalm to reach the ice and mammoth caves. (Every 15min. 8:40am-5:30pm, round-trip €13.) The Koppenbrüller cave is a 15min. walk from the Dachstein bus stop in Obertraun.

GRÜNAU   ☎07616

Poised below the picturesque **Totes Gebirge** (Dead Mountains), Grünau (pop. 2100) is ideal for almost any kind of outdoor activity. The real reason to visit is ◪**The Treehouse ❷**, Schindlbachstr. 525, a backpacker's dream resort. The incredibly friendly staff organizes adventure tours, including **canyoning** (€50), **bungee jumping** (€95, only on weekends), and **horseback riding** (€9.50 per hr.). To strike out on your own, rent a **mountain bike** (€6 per day) or ask the staff about **hiking** trails. For winter visitors, the ski lift is a 5min. walk from the front door, and snow gear (jackets, snowsuits, gloves, etc.) is provided free of charge. Day ski-lift passes are €20.50, and **skis** and **snowboards** are available for rent (€13 and up).

Regular **trains** service Grünau from Wels, on the Vienna-Salzburg rail line (1hr., 6:45am-8:45pm, €6). Call ahead to The Treehouse to be picked up free of charge. Rooms feature private showers and goosedown blankets, and amenities include a

TV room with hundreds of English-language movies, book-exchange library, sauna, basketball and tennis courts, **Internet** (€0.10 per min.), and two in-house bars for nighttime revelry. (☎84 99. Breakfast included. 3-course dinners €7. 6-bed dorms €14.50; doubles €37; triples €51.50; quads €66. AmEx/MC/V.)

HOHE TAUERN NATIONAL PARK

The enormous Hohe Tauern range, part of the Austrian Central Alps and the largest national park in Europe, boasts 246 glaciers and 304 mountains over 3000m. Preservation is a primary goal, so there are no large campgrounds or recreation areas. The best way to explore this rare preserve is to take one of the many hikes, which range from pleasant ambles to difficult mountain ascents. *An Experience in Nature*, available at park centers and most area tourist offices, plots and briefly describes 84 different hikes. The center of the park is Franz-Josefs-Höhe and the Pasterze glacier, which hovers right above the town of Heiligenblut. Aside from the skiing and hiking, the main tourist attractions are the Krimml Waterfalls, in the northwestern corner near Zell am See, and the Großglockner Hochalpenstraße, a high mountain road that runs between Heiligenblut and Bruck.

▐ TRANSPORTATION. Trains arrive in **Zell am See** from: Innsbruck (1½-2hr., 3:45am-9:25pm, €20); Kitzbühel (45min., 7:15am-11:30pm, €8.10); and Salzburg (1½hr., 1-2 per hr., €13). From Zell am See, a rail line runs west along the northern border of the park, terminating in Krimml (1½hr., 6am-10:55pm, €6.80); a bus also runs directly to the Höhe (2hr., 2 per day, €10). The park itself is crisscrossed by **bus** lines that operate on a complicated timetable.

FRANZ-JOSEFS-HÖHE. This tourist center, stationed above the Pasterze glacier, has an amazing view of the Großglockner (3798m). The Höhe has its own **park office** in the parking area. (☎(04824) 27 27. Open daily 10am-4pm.) The free elevator next to the info center leads to the **Swarovski Observation Center**, a crystal-shaped building with binoculars for viewing the surrounding terrain. (Open daily 10am-4pm. Free.) The **Gletscherweg** (3hr.) hike is like walking on the moon.

HEILIGENBLUT. The closest town to the highest mountain in Austria and a great starting point for hikes, Heiligenblut (pop. 1,200) is a convenient base for exploration of the region. Heiligenblut can be reached by **bus** from Franz-Josefs-Höhe (30min., €3.60) and Lienz (1 hr., 2-6 per day, €6). The **tourist office**, Hof 4, up the street from the bus stop, dispenses info about rooms, hikes, and park transportation. (☎04824 20 01 21. Open July-Aug. M-F 8:30am-6pm, Sa 9am-noon and 4-6pm; Sept.-June M-F 8:30am-noon and 2:30-6pm, Sa 9am-noon and 4-6pm.) To reach the **Jugendgästehaus Heiligenblut (HI) ❸**, Hof 36, take the path down from the wall behind the bus stop parking lot. (☎04824 22 59. Breakfast included. Reception daily 7-10am and 5-9pm. Dorms €20, under-27 €15; singles €27/22.)

KRIMML. Over 400,000 visitors per year arrive here to see the extraordinary Krimml Waterfalls, a set of three cascades spanning 380m. (8am-6pm €1.50; free after 6pm.) These waterfalls are usually enjoyed as a daytrip from Zell am See; **buses** run from Zell am See (1½ hr., 5:45am-8:55pm, €7.50) to *Maustelle Ort*, the start of the path to the falls. The trail, called the **Wasserfallweg** (4km), maintains a constant upward pitch. The first set of falls are accessible almost directly from the entrance; it's about 30min. from the first to the second set of falls, and an additional 30min. to the third set. To reach the **tourist office**, Oberkrimml 37, follow the road from the Krimml Ort bus stop and turn right down the hill in front of the church. (☎723 90. Open M-F 8am-noon and 2:30-5:30pm, Sa 8:30-10:30am.)

TYROL (TIROL)

Tyrol's mountains overwhelm the average mortal with their superhuman scale. Craggy summits rising in the northeast and south cradle four-star resorts and untouched valleys like the Ötzal and Zillertal. In eastern Tyrol, the mighty Hohe Tauern range is protected as a national park. The region is a mountain playground, and Innsbruck is its swing set.

INNSBRUCK   ☎ 0512

The 1964 and 1976 winter Olympics were held in Innsbruck (pop. 128,000), bringing international recognition to this beautiful mountain city. The nearby Tyrolean Alps await skiers and hikers, and the tiny cobblestone streets of the *Altstadt* are peppered with fancy facades and relics of the Habsburg Empire.

▐▌ TRANSPORTATION AND PRACTICAL INFORMATION

Trains: Hauptbahnhof, Südtirolerpl. (☎05 17 17). To: **Munich** (2hr., 13 per day, €32); **Rome** (8½-9½hr., 2 per day, €60); **Salzburg** (2½hr., 13 per day, €30); **Vienna Westbahnhof** (5½-7hr., 10 per day, €47); **Zurich** (4hr., 4 per day, €44).

Public Transportation: The **IVB** Office, Stainerstr. 2 (☎530 17 99), near Maria-Theresien-Str., has bus schedules. Open M-F 7:30am-6pm. The main bus station is in front of the entrance to the train station. Most buses stop running at 10:30 or 11:30pm, but 3 *Nachtbus* lines continue through the night.

Tourist Office: Innsbruck Tourist Office, Burggraben 3, 3rd fl. (☎598 50). Off the end of Museumstr. Sells maps (€1) and the **Innsbruck Card,** which provides unlimited access to public transportation and most museums. (24hr. card €21, 48hr. €26, 72hr. €31). Open M-F 8am-6pm, Sa 8am-noon.

Police: ☎133. **Ambulance:** ☎144 or 142. **Fire:** ☎122.

Internet Access: International Telephone Discount, Bruneckstr. 12 (☎59 42 72 61). Turn right from the *Hauptbahnhof;* it's on the left, just past the end of Südtirolerpl. €0.11 per min. Open daily 9am-11pm.

Post Office: Maximilianstr. 2 (☎500 79 00). Open M-F 7am-11pm, Sa 7am-9pm, Su 8am-9pm. Address mail to be held: Firstname SURNAME, *Postlagernde Briefe,* Hauptpostamt, Maximilianstr. 2, **A-6020** Innsbruck AUSTRIA.

▐ ACCOMMODATIONS

Inexpensive accommodations are scarce in June, when some hostels close. The opening of student dorms to backpackers in July and August somewhat alleviates the crush. Visitors should join the free **Club Innsbruck** by registering at any Innsbruck accommodation. Membership gives discounts on skiing, bike tours, and the club's hiking program.

Pension Paula, Weiherburgg. 15 (☎29 22 62). Take bus D to *Schmelzerg.* and head uphill. Escape the city rumble. Beautiful views across the valley. Breakfast included. Singles €27, with shower €33; doubles €45/54; triples €60/70; quads €80. ❸

Gasthof Innbrücke, Instr. 1 (☎28 19 34). From the *Altstadt,* cross the Innbrücke. The 575-year-old inn has a riverside and mountain view. Breakfast included. Singles €27, with shower €35; doubles €45/60; quads €110. ❸

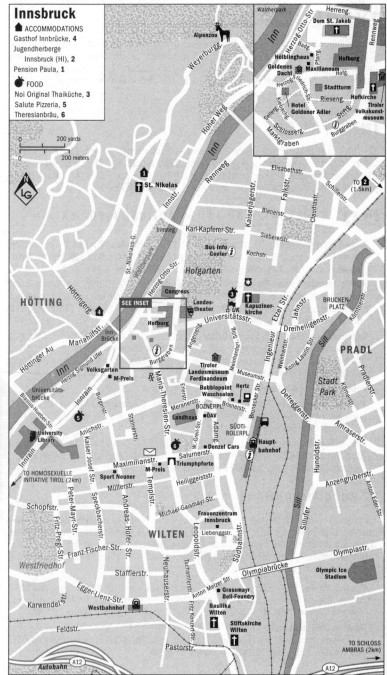

Innsbruck

🏠 **ACCOMMODATIONS**
Gasthof Innbrücke, **4**
Jugendherberge
  Innsbruck (HI), **2**
Pension Paula, **1**

🍎 **FOOD**
Noi Original Thaiküche, **3**
Salute Pizzeria, **5**
Theresianbräu, **6**

0   200 yards
0   200 meters

Walterpark

Herreng.

Dom St. Jakob

Inn

Herzog-Otto-Str.
Badg.
Pfarr.
Rennweg

Hölblinghaus
Hofburg
Goldenes Dachl
Maximilianeum
Hofg.

Herzog-Friedrich-Str.
Stadtturm

Kiebach.
Rieseng.
Hofkirche

Seilerg.
Hotel Goldener Adler
Stift.
Tiroler Volkskunst-museum

Schlosserg.
Maktgraben
Burggraben

Alpenzoo

Weyerburgg.

Hoher Weg

Inn

Rennweg

St. Nikolas

Innstr.

Elisabethstr.

Schillerstr.

TO 2 (1.5km)

Kaiserjägerstr.
Falkstr.
Claudiastr.

Karl-Kapferer-Str.
Blenerstr.

Innsteg

St-Nikolaus-G.

Walterpark

Sieberstr.

Bus Info Center

Kochstr.

Hofgarten

HÖTTING

Höttingerg.

Herzog-Otto-Str.

Congress
Landes-theater

Landhaus

SEE INSET

Hofburg

UK
Universitätsstr.

Kapuziner-kirche

Etzel Str.
Jahnstr.

BRÜCKEN-PLATZ

Körnerstr.

Mariahilfstr.
Inn-Brücke

Burggraben

Dreiheiligenstr.

Ingenieur

Weinhartstr.

König Laurin Str.

PRADL

Höttinger Au

Inn

Herzog Sigmund Ufer

Volksgarten
M-Preis

Maria-Theresien-Str.

Angerzelle
Sille

Meinhardstr.

Tiroler Landesmuseum Ferdinandeum

Museumstr.

Brunecker Str.

Defreggerstr.

Stadt Park

Pradlerstr.

Universitäts-brücke

Blasius-Hueber-Str.

Innrain

Burgerstr.

Stainerstr.

Erlerstr.

Bubblepoint Waschsalon
Hertz

Meranerstr.
BOZNERPL.
Brixnerstr.

Adams.

Amraserstr.

University Library

Anichstr.

Kaiser Josef Str.

Landhaus
ÖAV

W.-Greil-Str.

SÜDTI-ROLERPL.

Hunoldstr.

Silluifer

Anzengruberstr.

Anton Eder-Str.

Innrain

TO HOMOSEXUELLE INITIATIVE TIROL (2km)

Salurnerstr.
Denzel Cars

Haupt-bahnhof

Maximilianstr.
M-Preis
Triumphpforte

Sport Neuner

Heiliggeiststr.

Müllerstr.

Templstr.

Andreas-Hofer-Str.

Michael-Gaismayr-Str.

Schopfstr.

Peter-Mayr-Str.

Fritz-Pregl-Str.

Speckbacherstr.

Leopoldstr.

Frauenzentrum Innsbruck

Liebenggstr.

Südbahnstr.

WILTEN

Westfriedhof

Franz-Fischer-Str.

Stafflerstr.

Neuhauserstr.

Tschamlerstr.

Anton Melzer Str.

Olympiabrücke

Olympiastr.

Olympic Ice Stadium

Egger-Lienz-Str.

Karwendel Str.

Westbahnhof

Feldstr.

Basilika Wilten

Grassmayr Bell-Foundry

Stiftskirche Wilten

Pastorstr.

TO SCHLOSS AMBRAS (2km)

Autobahn
A12

A12

AUSTRIA

Jugendherberge Innsbruck (HI), Reichenauer Str. 147 (☎34 61 79). From the train station, take tram 3 to *Sillpark* and bus O to *Jugendherberge*. Bike rental €11 per day. Breakfast included. Reception daily 5-10pm. 6-bed dorms €12; 4-bed dorms €15; singles with shower €28; doubles with shower €41. Nonmembers add €3. ❷

🍴 FOOD

From the *Altstadt*, cross the Inn River to Innstr., in the university district, for ethnic restaurants and cheap pizzerias. There are **M-Preis Supermarkets** at Museumstr. 34 and across from the train station. (Open M-F 7:30am-6:30pm, Sa 7:30am-5pm.)

🍺 Theresianbräu, Maria-Theresien-Str. 51. Try the dark house lager and traditional meals such as *Käsespatzl* (homemade noodles with cheese; €6.80). Open M-W 10:30am-1am, Th-Sa 10:30am-2am, Su 10:30am-midnight. MC/V. ❷

Salute Pizzeria, Innrain 35. A popular student hangout with the best and least expensive pizza in town (€3-8). Pasta €4.50-6.50. Salad €3-4.50. Open 11am-midnight. ❷

Noi Original Thaiküche, Kaiserjägerstr. 1. Cooks up Thai soups (€4-8.40) and spicy dishes from the wok (€8-11). Open M-F 11:30am-3pm and 6-11pm, Sa 6-11pm. ❷

🎫 SIGHTS

Inside the **Goldenes Dachl** (Golden Roof) on Herzog-Friedrich-Str., the tiny **Maximilianeum** commemorates emperor Maximilian I. (Open May-Sept. daily 10am-6pm; Oct.-Apr. 10am-12:30pm and 2-5pm. €3.65, students €1.45.) A block behind the Goldenes Dachl rise the two towers of the **Dom St. Jakob,** which displays *trompe l'oeil* ceiling murals. (Open Apr.-Sept. daily 7:30am-7:30pm; Oct.-Mar. 8am-6:30pm. Free.) The entrance to the grand **Hofburg** is behind and to the right of the Dom. (Open daily 9am-5pm. €5.45, students €3.65.) Across Rennweg sits the **Hofkirche** which holds larger-than-life bronze statues of saints and Roman emperors, including some by Dürer. (Open M-Sa 9am-5pm, Su noon-5pm. €2.20, students €1.45.) Up Rennweg past the Dom, the **Hofgarten** is a beautiful park complete with ponds, a concert pavilion, and an oversized chess set.

🥾 ⛷ HIKING AND SKIING

A **🎿Club Innsbruck** membership (see Accommodations, above) lets you in on one of the best deals in Austria. The club's excellent and very popular **hiking** program provides free guides, transportation, and equipment (including boots). Participants meet in front of the Congress Center (June-Sept. daily 9am), board a bus, and return after a moderate hike around 4 or 5pm. To hike on your own, take the J-line bus to *Patscherkofel Seilbahnen* (20min.). The lift provides access to moderate 1½-5hr. hikes near the bald summit of the Patscherkofel. (Open 9am-noon and 12:45-4:30pm; round-trip €15.) For Club-Innsbruck-led **ski excursions,** take the complimentary ski shuttle (schedules at the tourist office) to any cable car. The **Innsbruck Gletscher Ski Pass** (available at all cable cars) is valid for all 59 lifts in the region (with Club Innsbruck membership: 3-day €85, 6-day €150). The tourist office also rents **ski equipment** (€19-32 per day).

🔆 DAYTRIPS FROM INNSBRUCK

SCHLOß AMBRAS. In the late 16th century, Ferdinand II transformed a royal hunting lodge into one of Austria's most beautiful castles, **Schloß Ambras,** and filled it with vast collections of art, armor, weapons, and trinkets. Don't miss the

AUSTRIA

famous **Spanischer Saal** (Spanish Hall) and the impressive **Portrait Gallery** (open in summer only). The **gardens** outside vary from manicured shrubs with modern sculptures to shady, forested hillsides. (Schloßstr. 20. Open Apr.-Oct. daily 10am-5pm; Dec.-Mar. closed Tu. Apr.-Oct. €7.50, students €5.50; Dec.-Mar. €4.50/3.) From Innsbruck, take tram 3 or 6 (dir.: Igls) to Schloß Ambras (20min., €1.60).

KITZBÜHEL
☎ 05356

Everyone in Kitzbühel (pop. 8,500) is merely catching his breath before the next run; the town's **ski area,** the **Ski Circus,** is one of the best in the world. A one-day **ski pass** (€33) or a 3- or 6-day summer **vacation pass** (€35/48) include all 64 lifts and the shuttles that connect them; purchase either at any lift. In the summer, 77 **hiking trails** snake up the mountains; trail maps are free at the tourist office.

Trains leave from the *Hauptbahnhof* for Innsbruck (1hr., every 2hr., €12); Salzburg (2½hr., 9 per day, €21); and Vienna (6hr., 3 per day, €42). To reach the *Fußgängerzone* (pedestrian zone) from the *Hauptbahnhof*, head straight down Bahnhofstr.; turn left at the main road, turn right at the traffic light, and follow the road uphill. The **tourist office,** Hinterstadt 18, is near the *Rathaus* in the *Fußgängerzone*. (☎ 62 15 50. Open July-Aug. and Christmas to mid-Mar. M-F 8:30am-6:30pm, Sa 8:30am-noon and 4-6pm, Su 10am-noon and 4-6pm; Nov.-Christmas and mid-Mar. to June M-F 8:30am-12:30pm and 2:30-6pm, Sa 8:30am-noon.) Make sure to pick up a free **guest card,** which provides guided hikes (Jun.-Oct. M-F 8:45 am) and informative tours (M 10am) in English. **Hotel Haselberger ❹,** Maurachfeld 4, is seconds from the *Hahmennkammerbahn* ski lift. (☎ 628 66. Breakfast included. In summer €35 per person; in winter €44. AmEx/MC/V.) Nearby **Chizzo ❸,** Josef Herold-Str. 2, helps skiers recuperate with hearty Tyrolean fare. (Open daily 11am-midnight.) **SPAR supermarket,** Bichlstr. 22, is at the intersection with Ehrenbachg. (Open M-F 8am-7pm, Sa 7:30am-1pm.) **Postal Code:** A-6370.

BELARUS (БЕЛАРУСЬ)

Flattened by the Germans during WWII, then exploited by the Soviets until 1990, Belarus has become the unwanted stepchild of Mother Russia. While Minsk evokes the glory days of the USSR, the unspoiled countryside harkens back to an earlier era of agricultural beauty. For those willing to endure the difficulties of travel in Belarus, the country presents a unique look at a people in transition.

FACTS AND FIGURES

Official Name: Republic of Belarus.
Capital: Minsk.
Major Cities: Brest, Gomel, Hrodna.
Population: 10,300,000.

Land Area: 207,600 sq. km.
Time Zone: GMT +2.
Language: Belarussian, Russian.
Religions: Orthodox (80%).

BELARUS

ESSENTIALS

DOCUMENTS AND FORMALITIES

VISAS. To visit Belarus, you must secure a visa, an invitation, and medical insurance. With an **official invitation** from an acquaintance in Belarus, you can obtain a single-entry (5-day service US$100, next day US$180), double-entry (US$200/380), triple-entry (US$300/580), or multiple-entry (5-day service $350). Or, try **Alatan Tour** (www.alatantour.com) or **SMOK Travel** (www.smoktravel.com) for invitations and visa services. Obtain a **visa** at an embassy or consulate by submitting your passport, the application, a check or money order, and a recent passport photo. **Transit visas** (US$40), valid for 48 hours, are issued at consulates and at the border. Belarus requires documentation of **medical insurance** or the purchase of insurance at the port of entry (US$1 for a one-day stay, US$15 for 30 days, US$28 for 60 days, and up to US$85 for a year).

EMBASSIES. Foreign embassies are in Minsk (p. 110). Embassies at home include: **Canada,** 130 Albert St., Ste. 600, Ottawa, ON K1P 5G4 (☎613-233-9994; fax 233-8500); **South Africa,** 327 Hill Street, Arcadia 0083; mail to: PO Box 4107, Pretoria 0001 (☎2712-430-7664; fax 342-6280); **UK,** 6 Kensington Ct., London, W8 5DL (☎020 7937 3288; fax 7361 0005; visas 090 6641 0140); **US,** 1619 New Hampshire Ave. NW, Washington, D.C. 20009 (☎202-986-1606; www.belarusembassy.org).

TRANSPORTATION

The national airline, **Belavia** (www.belavia.net), flies into Minsk from many European capitals; **Lufthansa** also offers daily flights from Frankfurt. However, Minsk's airports often fail to meet Western safety standards; entering by train or bus is better. Some international train tickets must be paid partly in Belarussian rubles; **Eurail** is not valid. All immigration and customs formalities are done on the trains.

TOURIST SERVICES AND MONEY

EMERGENCY	Police: ☎02. Ambulance: ☎03. Fire: ☎01.

Belintourist (p. 110) is a helpful resource. Hotel Belarus in Minsk has a **private travel agency.** There are few **ATMs** outside Minsk, and traveler's checks are rarely accepted. Carry plenty of **hard cash;** Russian rubles (which cannot be exchanged abroad), euros, and US dollars are preferred. In Belarus, posted prices often omit the final three zeros; *Let's Go* prices follow that convention, and because **inflation** is rampant, many prices are listed in US dollars.

BELARUSSIAN RUBLES		
AUS$1 = 1335.89BR	1000BR = AUS$0.75
CDN$1 = 1495.38BR	1000BR = CDN$0.67
EUR€1 = 2270.96BR	1000BR = EUR€0.44
NZ$1 = 1195.67BR	1000BR = NZ$0.84
UK£1 = 3292.09BR	1000BR = UK£0.30
US$1 = 2086.51BR	1000BR = US$0.48
ZAR1 =283.83BR	1000BR = ZAR3.52

BELARUS

COMMUNICATION

PHONE CODES	Country code: 375. **International dialing prefix:** 810. From outside Belarus, dial international dialing prefix (see inside back cover) + 375 + city code + local number.

Avoid the mail system—almost everything is opened by the authorities and often discarded. Local calls require **tokens** sold at kiosks or **magnetic cards** available at the post office and some hotels (from 1500BR). International calls must be placed at the telephone office and paid for in advance, in cash. Calls to the US and Western Europe cost US$1-3 per minute. International access numbers include: **AT&T Direct, ☎ 8800 101; MCI WorldPhone** (☎ 8800 104); and **NZ Direct** (☎ 8800 641). Email is easy and cheap; check the local post office for **Internet** access.

ACCOMMODATIONS AND FOOD

BELARUS	❶	❷	❸	❹	❺
ACCOMMODATIONS	under US$12	US$12-20	US$21-28	US$29-55	over US$55
FOOD	under US$2	US$2-5	US$6-10	US$11-20	over US$20

Keep all receipts from hotels; when exiting the country, you may have to produce them to avoid fines. **Hotels** are very cheap for Belarussians and reasonable for citizens of CIS member countries, but outrageous for foreigners; desk clerks will request your passport, making it impossible to pass as a native. To find a **private room,** look for postings at train stations, or ask taxi drivers, who may know of a lead. The *babushki* (older women) at train stations are usually willing to feed and house you for US$10 or less. **Camping** facilities in Belarus are extremely limited. However, camping is permitted outside towns anywhere in the countryside. Belarussian cuisine consists of what farmers can either grow or fatten: potatoes, bread, chicken, and pork. If you guess at a menu, you'll probably receive bread, sausage, and a vegetable.

SAFETY AND SECURITY

Medical care in Belarus is inadequate at best. There is a severe shortage of even the most basic health supplies, such as antibiotics, vaccines, and anesthetics. Travelers with **existing health problems** are at high risk in Belarus. If a **medical emergency** occurs, try to make it to the nearest major city in Western Europe. A medical evacuation to the United States may cost up to US$50,000. Although Belarus was greatly affected by the 1986 Chernobyl accident, it is now possible to travel through formerly contaminated areas. *Let's Go* does not cover any affected regions, but it is important to be aware of certain safety considerations: Avoid cheap **dairy products,** which may come from contaminated areas—opt instead for something German or Dutch—and stay away from **mushrooms** and **berries,** which collect radioactivity. Drink bottled water; **tap water** may be contaminated.

HOLIDAYS

Holidays: New Year's Day (Jan. 1); Orthodox Christmas (Jan. 7); International Women's Day (Mar. 8); Constitution Day (Mar. 15); Good Friday (Apr. 9); Catholic Easter (Apr. 11); Victory Day (May 9); Labor Day (May 11); Independence Day (July 3); Remembrance Day (Nov. 2); October Revolution Day (Nov. 7); Catholic Christmas (Dec. 25).

BELARUS

MINSK (МІНСК) ☎ 8017

If you're looking for a true Soviet city, skip Moscow and head to Minsk (pop. 1,800,000). Completely rebuilt after WWII in the "grand" Stalinist style, Minsk's ubiquitous gray concrete high-rises sprouting from flat expanses sometimes make for surreal cityscapes. Since the dissolution of the USSR, only a handful of streets have been renamed, and Lenin's statue still presides over Independence Square. President Lukashenka's recent heavy-handed reforms have improved transportation and cleaned up the city, bringing hope to a populace living in the rubble of Communism. However, in this city of concrete and police, everyone is asking whether the government is really giving Minsk a new face or just a new facade.

◨◪ TRANSPORTATION AND PRACTICAL INFORMATION. Trains depart from Chigunachny Vokzal (Чыгуначны Вокзал; ☎225 54 10, international 225 86 67), on pl. Privakzalnaya, for: Brest (5hr., 8 per day, 11,000BR); Hrodna (8hr., daily, 15,300BR); Kyiv (9hr., daily, 30,000BR); Moscow (10-11hr., 15 per day, 30,000BR); St. Petersburg (17hr., 6 per day, 35,000BR); and Vilnius (4hr., 5 per day, 25,000BR); trains also run to Berlin, Kaliningrad, and Warsaw. Tickets are sold on the first floor of the new M.C. Escher-esque train station building, or at **Belinturist** (see below). **Buses** go from Avtovakzal Tsentralny (Автовакзал Центральны; ☎227 37 25), vul. Babruyskaya 6 (Бабруйская), next to the train station, to: Bialystok (8hr., 2 per day, 25,000BR); Hrodna (4-5 hr., 2-3 per hr., 15,000BR); and Vilnius (4hr., 4 per day, 12,000BR). To get to the center of town, walk up vul. Leningradskaya from the square and go left on Sverdlova (Свердлова) to reach pl. Nezalezhnastsi; from there, pr. Skaryny will take you through the center. The English-speaking staff at **Belinturist** (Белінтурiст), pr. Masherava 19, next to Gastsinitsa Yubileyny, can give info. (☎226 90 56; www.belintourist.by. M-red: Nyamiha. First-floor ticket office open M-F 8am-1pm and 2-8pm, Sa-Su 9am-5pm. Second-floor info office open M-Th 10am-6pm, F 10am-4:30pm.) **Embassies: UK,** vul. Karla Marksa 37 (Карла Маркса; ☎210 59 20; fax 229 23 11. Open M-F 9am-1pm and 2-5:30pm.); **US,** vul. Staravilenskaya 46 (☎210 12 83; fax 234 78 53. Open M-F 8:30am-5:30pm.) A **pharmacy,** Apteka 13, is at pr. Skaryny 16. (Open 24hr.; ring bell on the right for late night service.) **Ekomedservis** (Экомедсервис), at vul. Talstogo 4 (Толстого), is a hospital. (☎207 74 74; in **emergencies** call toll-free ☎003 for an ambulance.) All **phone numbers** have seven digits and start with a "2"; add an initial "2" to any six-digit numbers. Check email and make phone calls at **Beltelekom** (Белтелеком), vul. Karla Marksa 39. (☎219 06 79; www.beltelecom.by. 815BR per 30min. Open 24hr.)

◨◲ ACCOMMODATIONS AND FOOD. To get to **Gastsinitsa 40 Let Pobedy** ❷ (Лет Победы), vul. Azgura 3 (Азгура), from the train station, take any tram to vul. Zakharova. Get off and turn right, then right again. (☎236 79 63. "Deluxe" rooms include a lounge plus fridge and TV. Ring bell after hours. Singles 35,000BR; doubles 70,000BR. Cash only.) **Gastsinitsa Yubileny** ❹, pr. Masherava 19, next to Belinturist, is more expensive, but centrally located. (☎226 90 24; fax 226 91 71. Breakfast included. ATM outside. Currency exchange in the lobby. Singles with bath US$50; doubles US$62.) Take bus #81 from the train station to the building with a star on the top (30min.) and walk 200m to reach Soviet-style **Gastsinitsa Zvezda** ❸ (Звезда), pr. Gazety Izvestiya 47. (Газеты Известия; ☎272 75 97. Ring bell after 11pm. Singles 47,000BR; doubles 109,000BR.) Private rooms are also a good option; ask older women waiting at the train station. Serving Belarussian specialties, **Krinitsa** ❷ (Криница), vul. Lenina 2 (Леніна), is between M-red/blue: Kupalavskaya and Nyamiga. (Entrees US$3.50-7. Open daily noon-4pm and 5pm-midnight.) Watch chefs prepare your food on a flaming grill at **Grill-Bar Pechki-Lav-ochki** ❸ (Печки-Лавочки), F. Skaryny 22, near M-red/blue: pl. Kastrytchitskaya.

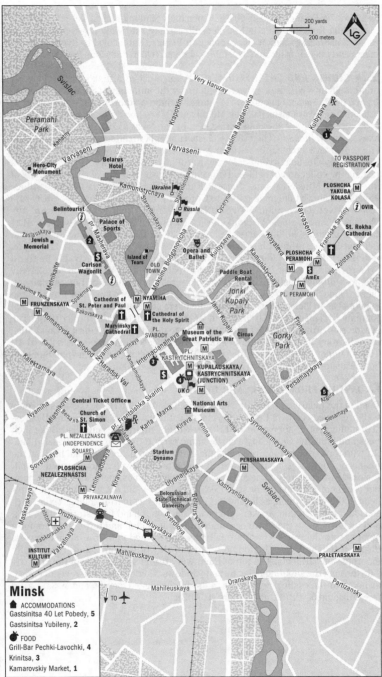

Minsk

🏠 ACCOMMODATIONS
Gastsinitsa 40 Let Pobedy, **5**
Gastsinitsa Yubileny, **2**

🍴 FOOD
Grill-Bar Pechki-Lavochki, **4**
Krinitsa, **3**
Kamarovskiy Market, **1**

(☎227 78 79. Entrees 8000-25,000BR. Open daily 8am-midnight.) Get off at M-blue: pl. Yakuba Kolasa, take a left on Very Kharuzhey, and walk down one block to reach **Kamarovskiy Market** (Камаровский Рынак; Kamarovskiy Rynak), where meats and piles of fruits and vegetables abound. (Open daily 9am-7pm.)

◎ ♫ SIGHTS AND ENTERTAINMENT. After most of Minsk's buildings were obliterated in WWII, the city was rebuilt under the influence of Stalin. The crimson **Church of St. Simon,** Savetskaya 15, stands behind a statue of the saint slaying a dragon. The **Jewish memorial,** vul. Melnikaite (Мельникайте), commemorates the 5000 Jews who were shot and buried here by the Nazis in 1942. (M-blue: Frunzenskaya; фрунзенская.) The ■**State Museum of Folk Architecture and Peasant Life** (Белорусский Государственный Музей Народной Архитектуры и Быта; Belorusskiy Gosudarstvennyy Muzey Narodnoy Arkhitektury i Byta) features a fascinating collection of nailless 17th-century houses and churches near the site of 9th-century Minsk. (M-blue: Institut Kultury. The museum is near the village Azyatso (Азяцо); take minibus #81 to Gorodishe and mention "muzey" (MOO-zay) to the driver. Open Su and Tu-Sa 10am-4:30pm. 10,000BR.) The **National Arts Museum** (Нацыянальны Мастацкі Музей Распублікі Беларусь; Natsyanalny Mastatski Muzey Raspubliki Belarus), pr. Lenina 20, brims with fantastic Russian and Belarussian art. (M-red/blue: Kastrytchnitskaya. Open Su-M and W-Sa 11am-7pm. 5000BR.) The grim **Museum of the Great Patriotic War** (Музей Велікой Отечественной Войны; Muzey Velikoy Otechestvennoy Voyny), at pr. Skaryny 25a, M-red/blue: Kastrytchnitskaya, celebrates the heroism of Belarussian soldiers. (Open Su and Tu-Sa 10am-5pm. 3000BR.) Walk down vul. F. Skarny past the 40m obelisk in **Victory Square,** to reach the **Opera and Ballet Theater,** vul. Paryzhskai Kamuny 1 (Парыжскай Камуны), one of the best ballets in the former USSR. The season runs from September to May; purchase tickets at the Central Ticket Office at pr. Skoriny 13 or the theater box office. (M-blue: Nyamiha; Нямiга. ☎234 01 41. Tickets under US$7. Ticket office open M-F 9:30am-8pm, Sa 10am-7pm, Su noon-5pm. Theater box office open Su and Tu-Sa 11:30am-7:30pm.)

♫ DAYTRIP FROM MINSK: MIR CASTLE.

Deep in the Belarussian countryside, the 16th-century **Mir** (Мир) Castle is the only well-preserved castle in the country. In 2000, the castle became the first Belarussian monument to appear on UNESCO's World Cultural Heritage list. Duke Ilich began building the Gothic-style castle in the early 16th century. The Radzivil family, who took over in 1568, preferred the ways of the Renaissance and finished the job accordingly. Despite thick earthen ramparts and a water moat surrounding it, the castle was severely damaged by warfare several times, including the little number Napoleon's troops did on it in 1812. Luckily, they did not take the stone ram's head in the wall, which, as legend has it, keeps the castle from falling. Today, artisans and construction workers are giving the ram a hand by restoring the castle and its environs to their former grandeur. Climb the tall and tortuous stairs for a glimpse into the castle's past: a small museum, located in one of the five towers, displays relics of yore, including weapons, clay pots, coins, and traditionally embroidered garments. The top of the tower affords a great view of the countryside through the shooting holes-turned-windows. Guided tours are recommended, as much of the castle's beauty lies in its rich history. (Open Su and W-Sa. Castle free. Museum 5000BR. Guided tours 10,000BR.)

BELGIUM

(BELGIQUE, BELGIË)

Situated between France and Germany, Belgium rubs shoulders with some of Western Europe's most powerful cultural and intellectual traditions. Travelers too often mistake Belgium's subtlety for dullness, but its cities offer some of Europe's finest art and architecture, and its castle-dotted countryside provides a beautiful escape for hikers and bikers. While Brussels, the nation's capital and home to the head offices of NATO and the European Union, is a flagship for international cooperation, regional tension persists within Belgium's borders between Flemish-speaking Flanders and French-speaking Wallonie. But some things transcend politics: from the deep caves of the Ardennes to the white sands of the North Sea coast, Belgium's diverse beauty is even richer than its chocolate.

FACTS AND FIGURES

Official Name: Kingdom of Belgium.

Capital: Brussels.

Major Cities: Antwerp, Ghent, Charleroi.

Population: 10,300,000.

Land Area: 32,547 sq. km.

Time Zone: GMT +1.

Language: Flemish, French, German.

Religions: Roman Catholic (75%).

DISCOVER BELGIUM

Starting out in the northern region of Flanders, take in the old city and diverse museums of **Brussels** (p. 116), then spend at least two days in **Bruges** (p. 123), a majestic town with Gothic beauty unparalleled elsewhere in Europe. Spend a day

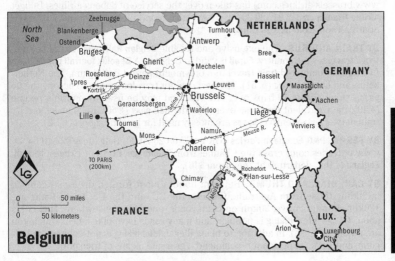

Belgium

in bustling **Antwerp** (p. 127), then dance the night away in energetic **Ghent** (p. 129). For a more leisurely pace, head south to the Wallonie region to hike and bike around the Ardennes in **Namur** (p. 131) and **Dinant** (p. 131).

ESSENTIALS

WHEN TO GO

Belgium, temperate and rainy, is best visited May to September, when temperatures average 13-21°C (54-72°F) and precipitation is the lowest. Winter temperatures average 0-5°C (32-43°F). Bring a sweater and umbrella whenever you go.

DOCUMENTS AND FORMALITIES

VISAS. EU citizens may stay in Belgium for as long as they like. Citizens of Australia, Canada, New Zealand, South Africa, and the US do not need a visa for stays of up to 90 days.

EMBASSIES. All foreign embassies are in Brussels (p. 116). For Belgian embassies at home: **Australia,** Arkana St., Yarralumla, Canberra, ACT 2600 (☎02 62 70 66 66; fax 62 70 66 06); **Canada,** 80 Elgin St., 4th fl., Ottawa, ON K1P 1B7 (☎613-236-7267; fax 613-236-7882); **Ireland,** 2 Shrewsbury Rd., Ballsbridge, Dublin 4 (☎353 269 20 82; fax 283 84 88); **New Zealand,** Willis Corroon House, 12th fl., Willeston St. 1-3, PB 3379, Wellington (☎04 472 95 58; fax 471 27 64); **South Africa,** 625 Leyds St., Muckleneuk, Pretoria 0002 (☎12 44 32 01; fax 12 44 32 16); **UK,** 103-105 Eaton Sq., London SW1W 9AB (☎020 470 37 00; www.belgium-embassy.co.uk); **US,** 3330 Garfield St NW, Washington, D.C. 20008 (☎202-333-6900; www.diplobel.org/us).

TRANSPORTATION

BY PLANE. Several major airlines fly into **Brussels** from Europe, North America, and Africa. **SN Brussels Airlines** (Belgium ☎070 35 11 11, UK ☎0870 735 23 45; www.brussels-airlines.com) has taken over the service of Sabena airlines. Budget airline **RyanAir** (☎353 819 30 30 30; www.ryanair.com) flies into Charleroi Brussels South Airport from across Europe.

BY TRAIN AND BUS. The extensive and reliable **Belgian Rail** (www.b-rail.be) network traverses the country. **Eurail** is valid in Belgium. A **Benelux Tourrail pass** allows five days of unlimited **train** travel in a one-month period in Belgium, The Netherlands, and Luxembourg (p. 51). The best deal for travelers under 26 may be the **Go pass,** which allows 10 trips over one year and may be used by multiple people (€40); the equivalent for those over 26 is the **Rail pass** (€60). Belgium's intercity train network is extensive; **buses** are mostly used for local transport (€1-2).

BY FERRY. P&O European Ferries (UK ☎087 05 20 20 20, Belgium ☎027 10 64 44; www.poferries.com) cross the Channel from **Zeebrugge,** north of Bruges, to **Hull, England** (11hr., departure at 7pm, from £46).

BY CAR, BIKE, AND THUMB. Belgium honors most foreign driver's licenses, including those from Australia, Canada, the EU, and the US. **Speed limits** are 120kph on motorways, 90kph on main roads, and 50kph elsewhere. **Fuel** costs about €1 per liter. **Biking** is popular, and many roads have bike lanes (which you are required to use). In addition to being illegal, **hitchhiking** is not common in Belgium, and *Let's Go* does not recommend it as a safe means of transport.

TOURIST SERVICES AND MONEY

EMERGENCY	Police: ☎ 101. Ambulance: ☎ 105. Fire: ☎ 100.

TOURIST OFFICES. **Bureaux de Tourisme,** marked by green-and-white or blue signs labelled "i," are supplemented by **Infor-Jeunes/Info-Jeugd,** a service that helps young people secure accommodations. For info, contact the main office of the **Belgian Tourist Office,** Grasmarkt 63 (☎ 025 04 30 90; www.visitbelgium.com). The weekly English-language *Bulletin* (€2.15) lists everything from movies to job openings.

MONEY. On January 1, 2002, the **euro** (€) replaced the **Belgian Franc** as the unit of currency in Belgium. The Belgian Franc can still be exchanged at a rate of 44.34BF to €1. For exchange rates and more info on the euro, see p. 14. Expect to pay €13-16 for a hostel bed, €23-50 for a hotel room, €7-13 for a day's groceries, and €5-13 for a cheap restaurant meal. A barebones day in Belgium might cost €19-30; a slightly more comfortable day might cost €32-45. The European Union imposes a **value-added tax (VAT)** on goods and services purchased within the EU, which is included in the price (p. 16). Restaurants and taxis include a **service charge** (16%) in the price. Rounding up is also common practice.

BUSINESS HOURS. **Banks** are generally open Monday through Friday 9am-4pm, but some take a lunch break noon-2pm. **Stores** are open Monday to Saturday 10am to 6 or 7pm; during summer some shops are open Sunday. Most **sights** are open Sundays but closed Mondays except in Bruges and Tournai, where museums are closed Tuesday or Wednesday. Most stores close on holidays; museums stay open during all except for Christmas, New Year's, and Armistice Day (Nov. 11).

COMMUNICATION

PHONE CODES	Country code: 32. International dialing prefix: 00.

TELEPHONES. Most public phones require a phone card (€5), available at post offices, supermarkets, and magazine stands. Coin-operated phones are rare and more expensive. Calls are cheapest from 6:30pm-8am and on weekends. Mobile phones are an increasingly popular and economical alternative (p. 36). For **operator assistance** within Belgium, dial ☎ 12 07 or 13 07; for **international assistance,** ☎ 12 04 or 13 04 (€0.25). **International direct dial** numbers include: **AT&T,** ☎ 0800 100 10; **British Telecom,** ☎ 0800 100 24; **Canada Direct,** ☎ 0800 100 19 or 0800 700 19; **Ireland Direct,** ☎ 0800 10 353; **MCI,** ☎ 0800 100 12; **Sprint,** ☎ 0800 100 14; **Telecom New Zealand,** ☎ 0800 100 64; **Telkom South Africa,** ☎ 0800 100 27; **Telstra Australia,** ☎ 0800 100 61.

MAIL. A postcard or letter (up to 50g) sent to a destination within Belgium costs €0.41-0.49, within the EU €0.47-.52, and to the rest of the world €0.74-.84. Most post offices open Monday to Friday 9am to 4 or 5pm (sometimes with a midday break) and sometimes on Saturdays 9 or 10am to noon or 1pm.

INTERNET ACCESS. There are cybercafes in the larger towns and cities in Belgium. Many hostels offer Internet access. Expect to pay €1.50-6 per hr.

LANGUAGES. Belgium is a multilingual nation, with several official languages. Flemish (a variation of Dutch) is spoken in Flanders, the northern half of the country; French is spoken in Wallonie, the southern region; and German is spoken in a small enclave in the west. Both Flemish and French are spoken in Brussels. Most people, especially in Flanders, speak English. For basic French words and phrases, see p. 1054; for German, see p. 1055.

BELGIUM

ACCOMMODATIONS AND CAMPING

BELGIUM	❶	❷	❸	❹	❺
ACCOMMODATIÓNS	under €10	€10-17	€18-26	€27-33	over €33

There is a wide range of accommodations throughout Belgium; however, **hotels** are fairly expensive, with "trench-bottom" singles from €22 and doubles around €30-35. Belgium's 31 **HI youth hostels,** which charge about €13 per night, are generally modern and many boast cheap bars. **Private hostels,** however, often cost about the same but are much nicer. Most receptionists speak some English, and reservations are a good idea, particularly in the summer and on weekends. **Campgrounds** charge about €4 per night. An **international camping card** is not required in Belgium.

FOOD AND DRINK

BELGIUM	❶	❷	❸	❹	❺
FOOD	under €5	€5-8	€8-10	€11-15	over €15

Belgian cuisine, a combination of French and German traditions, is praised throughout Western Europe, but an authentic evening meal may cost as much as that night's accommodations. Seafood, fresh from the coast, is served in a variety of dishes. **Moules** or **mosselen** (steamed mussels), regarded as the national dish, are usually tasty and reasonably affordable (€14 is the cheapest, usually €17-20). Often paired with mussels are **frites** (french fries), actually a Belgian invention, which they dip in mayonnaise and consume in abundance. Belgian **beer** is both a national pride and a national pastime; more varieties—over 300, ranging from ordinary **Pilsners** to religiously brewed **Trappist** ales—are produced here than in any other country. Prices range from as little as €1 for regular or quirky blonde up to €3 for other varieties. Leave room for Belgian **waffles** (*gaufres*)—soft, warm, glazed ones on the street (€1.50) and thin, crispier ones piled high with toppings at cafes (€2-5)—and for the famous brands of **chocolate,** from Leonidas to Godiva.

HOLIDAYS & FESTIVALS

Holidays: New Year's Day (Jan. 1); Easter (Apr. 11); Easter Monday (Apr. 12); Labor Day (May 1); Ascension Day (May 20); Whit Sunday and Monday (May 30-31); Independence Day (July 21); Assumption Day (Aug. 15); All Saints Day (Nov. 1); Armistice Day (Nov. 11); Christmas (Dec. 25).

Festivals: Ghent hosts the **Gentse Feesten,** also know as 10 Days Off (July 17-26). Wallonie hosts a slew of quirky and creative carnivals, including the **Festival of Fairground Arts** (late May), **Les Jeux Nautiques** (early Aug.), the **International French-language Film Festival** (early Sept.), and the **International Bathtub Regatta** (mid-Aug.).

BRUSSELS (BRUXELLES, BRUSSEL) ☎02

Beyond the international traffic resulting from the city's association with NATO and the EU, Brussels (pop. 1.2 million) has a relaxed and witty local character best embodied in its two boy heroes, Tintin and the Mannekin Pis. In the late 1920s, cartoonist Hergé created a comic strip hero, Tintin, who, followed by his faithful white dog Snowy, righted international wrongs long before Brussels became the capital of the EU. The cherubic Mannekin Pis perpetually pees three blocks from the Grand Place, ruining any semblance of formality created by international poli-

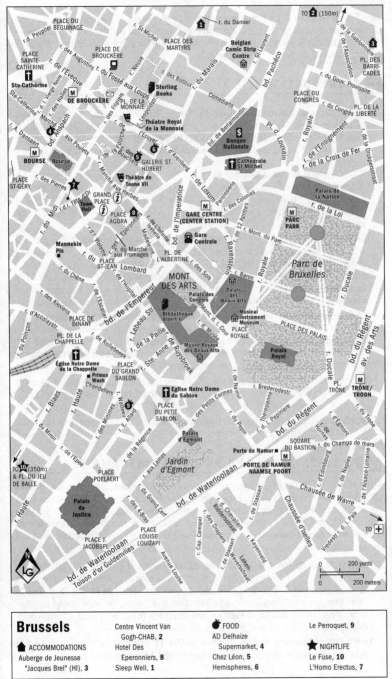

Brussels

ACCOMMODATIONS
Auberge de Jeunesse
"Jacques Brel" (HI), **3**

Centre Vincent Van
Gogh-CHAB, **2**
Hotel Des
Eperonniers, **8**
Sleep Well, **1**

FOOD
AD Delhaize
Supermarket, **4**
Chez Léon, **5**
Hemispheres, **6**

Le Perroquet, **9**

NIGHTLIFE
Le Fuse, **10**
L'Homo Erectus, **7**

BELGIUM

tics. The museums of Brussels are rich with collections of Flemish masters, modern art, and antique sculptures, but you don't need to go inside for a visual feast—many of the city's restaurants, lounges, and movie theaters were built in the style of Art Nouveau architect Victor Horta.

⌐ TRANSPORTATION

Flights: Brussels International Airport (BRU; ☎ 753 42 21 or 723 31 11; www.brusselsairport.be) is 14km from the city. See www.flysn.be for info on **SN Brussels Airline,** the Belgian national carrier. Trains run to the airport from Gare du Midi (25min., every 20min., €2.50), stopping at Gare Centrale and Gare du Nord. Another option is to take bus #12 to the airport (every 30min.; 5am-11pm, Sept.-June until midnight; €3). **Charleroi Brussels South** (CRL; ☎ 71 25 12 11; www.charleroi-airport.com) is 46km outside the city, between Brussels and Charleroi. Buses run to the airport from r. de France just outside the Gare du Midi in Brussels (2½hr. before every flight, €10). Buses head to Brussels and Charleroi from outside the main terminal 30min. after each flight (€10).

Trains: Info ☎ 555 25 55. All international trains stop at the **Gare du Midi;** most also stop at the **Gare Centrale** (near Grand Place) or the **Gare du Nord** (near the Botanical Gardens). To: **Amsterdam** (3hr.; M-F €57, Sa-Su €38); **Antwerp** (45 min.; M-F €11, Sa-Su €7); **Bruges** (45min.; M-F €22, Sa-Su €14); **Cologne** (2¾hr.; €36, under-26 €18); **Luxembourg City** (1¾hr., €31); **Paris** (1½hr.; €66, under-26 €33). **Eurostar** goes to **London** (2¾hr.; from €79, under-26 from €60, Eurail and Benelux railpass discount).

Public Transportation: The **Métro (M), buses,** and **trams** run daily 6am-midnight. 1hr. ticket €1.40, day pass €3.70, 5 trips €6.40, 10 trips €9.20. All three are run by the **Société des Transports Intercommunaux Bruxellois (STIB),** Gare du Midi (☎ 515 20 00; www.stib.irisnet.be). Open M-F 7:30am-5:30pm. **Branch offices** at the *Porte de Namur* and *Rogier* metro stops. Open M-Sa 10am-6pm.

Bus: De Boeck offers a tourist bus that allows you to get on and off at any of 14 major sites. Tickets are good for 24hr.; purchase them aboard the big blue bus. (☎ 513 77 44; www.brussels-city-tours.com. €14, students €12.)

Hitchhiking: Hitchhiking is illegal on highways in Belgium. *Let's Go* does not recommend hitchhiking as a reliable means of transport.

◼◼ 🛈 ORIENTATION AND PRACTICAL INFORMATION

Most major attractions are clustered around **Grand Place,** between the **Bourse** (Stock Market) to the west and the **Parc de Bruxelles** to the east. Two **Métro** lines circle the city, while efficient trams run north to south. Signs in Brussels list both the French and Flemish street names. *Let's Go* gives the French name for all addresses. A **tourist passport** (*Carte d'un Jour;* €7.45), which includes two days of public transit and discounted museum admissions, is sold at the BITC (see below).

Tourist Offices: National, Belgian Tourist Office, Grasmarkt 63 (☎ 504 30 90; www.visitbelgium.com), one block from Grand Place. Books rooms all over Belgium and offers the free copies of *What's On.* Open July-Aug. M-F 9am-7pm, Sa-Su 9am-1pm and 2-7pm; Sept.-June M-F 9am-6pm, Sa-Su 9am-1pm and 2-6pm; Nov.-Apr. closed Su afternoon. **Brussels International-Tourism and Congress** (BITC; ☎ 513 89 40; www.brusselsinternational.be), on Grand Place, in the Town Hall.

Tours: City Sightseeing, in Gare Centrale (☎ 466 11 11), offers a 1½hr. bus tour that passes all the major attractions. Daily 10am-8pm. €12, students €11.

Budget Travel: Infor-Jeunes Bruxelles, 155 r. Van Arteveld (☎514 41 11; bruxelles@inforjeunes.be). Budget travel info for students. Open M-F 10am-5:30pm.

Embassies and Consulates: Australia, 6-8 r. Guimard, 1040 (☎286 05 00; fax 230 68 02). **Canada,** 2 av. Tervuren, 1040 (☎741 06 11; fax 741 06 43). **Ireland,** 50 r. Wiertz 1050 (☎235 66 76; fax 230 53 12). **New Zealand,** 1 de Meeussquare, 1000 (☎512 10 40). **South Africa,** 26 r. de la Loi (☎285 44 00; fax 285 44 02). **UK,** 85 r. d'Arlon, 1040 (☎287 62 11; fax 287 63 55). **US,** 27 bd. du Régent, 1000 (☎508 21 11; www.usinfo.be). Open M-F 9am-noon.

Currency Exchange: Many exchange booths near Grand Place stay open until 11pm. Most banks and booths charge a commission (€2.50-3.75) to cash checks. **CBC-Automatic Change,** 7 Grand-Place (☎547 12 11) exchanges cash and checks and is open 24hr. Exchange booths are also available in the train stations.

Bi-Gay-Lesbian Resources: Call ☎736 26 81 for info on local events. Staffed Tu 8-10pm, W and F 8-11pm. The tourist office offers a guide to gay nightlife.

English-Language Bookstore: Sterling Books, Wolvengracht 38 (r. du Fossé aux Loups). Open M-Sa 10am-7pm, Su noon-6:30pm.

Laundromat: Primus Wash, 50 r. Haute, around the corner from the Jeugdherberg Bruegel. Gare Centrale. Wash €3.50, dry €0.50 per 10min. Open daily 7am-11pm.

Emergencies: Medical: ☎100. **Police:** ☎101. **From a Mobile Phone:** ☎112.

Pharmacy: Neos-Bourse Pharmacie (☎218 06 40), bd. Anspach at r. du Marché aux Polets. M: Bourse. Open M-Sa 8:30am-6:30pm.

Medical Assistance: Free Clinic, 154a Chaussée de Wavre (☎512 13 14). Ignore the name—you'll have to pay. Open M-F 9am-6pm, Sa 10am-noon. **Centre Hospitalier Universitaire St. Pierre,** 322 r. Haute (☎535 31 11). **Medical Services,** (☎479 18 18). Doctors on call 24hr.

Internet Access: easyEverything, pl. de Brouckère (www.easyeverything.com). Approx. €1.50 per hr., rates vary by time of day. Open 9am-1:30am.

Post Office: pl. de la Monnaie, Centre Monnaie, 2nd fl. (☎226 21 11). M: de Brouckère. Open M-F 8am-6pm, Sa 9:30am-3pm. Address mail to be held: Firstname SURNAME, *Poste Restante,* pl. de la Monnaie, **1000** Bruxelles, BELGIUM.

▐ ACCOMMODATIONS

Accommodations can be difficult to find in Brussels, especially on weekends and in June and July. In general, accommodations are well-kept and centrally located. If a hotel or hostel is booked, the staff will usually call other establishments on behalf of prospective guests.

Sleep Well, 23 r. du Damier (☎218 50 50; www.sleepwell.be), near Gare du Nord. M: Rogier. Nice, newly refurbished rooms and a grand lobby. Breakfast included. Internet €2 per 30min. Lockout 11am-3pm. Dorms €14-19; singles €26; doubles €41; triples €60. Reduced price after 1st night. 5% ISIC discount. ●

Centre Vincent Van Gogh-CHAB, 8 r. Traversière (☎217 01 58; www.ping.be/chab). M: Botanique. Exit on r. Royale, head right and turn right onto Chausée d'Haecht which becomes r. Traversière. Newly renovated clean rooms, chic lobby. Breakfast included. Sheets €3.60. Laundry €4.50. Internet access. Reception daily 7:30am-2am. Under-35 only. Dorms €12-14; singles €22; doubles €32. ●

Auberge de Jeunesse "Jacques Brel" (HI), 30 r. de la Sablonnière (☎218 01 87), on pl. des Barricades. M: Botanique. Follow r. Royale, with the botanical gardens to your right, and take the 1st left onto r. de la Sablonnière. Clean, spacious rooms. Breakfast included. Sheets €3.25. Reception daily 8am-1am. HI members only. Dorms €13; singles €23; doubles €35; triples €44. ●

Hotel Des Eperonniers, 1 r. des Eperonniers (☎513 53 66). Great location close to Grand Place. Well-kept rooms. Breakfast €3.75. Reception daily 7am-midnight. Singles €40-55; doubles €47-70. ❺

FOOD

Inexpensive restaurants cluster around **Grand Place,** and **Rue du Marché aux From-ages,** to the south of Grand Place, offers cheap Middle Eastern food. Shellfish, paella, and other seafood are served up on **Rue des Bouchers,** a sight of its own at night with narrow streets and sparkling lights. Cheaper seafood can be found at the small restaurants on **Quai aux Briques,** in the Ste-Catherine area behind pl. St-Géry. **Belgaufra** peddles waffles from nearly every streetcorner, and **Panos** offers quick and tasty sandwiches across the city. The giant **AD Delhaize supermarket** is on the corner of bd. Anspach and r. du Marché aux Polets. (M: Bourse. Open M-Th, Sa 9am-9pm, F 9am-4pm, Su 9am-6pm.)

Chez Léon, 18 r. des Bouchers. Serving seafood and other local dishes for over a century. *Moules frites* €13-22. Open daily noon-11pm. ❹

Maison Antoine, 1 pl. Jourdan. M: Schuman. From the rotary, walk down r. Froissart; it's the brown kiosk in the middle of pl. Jourdan. The best *frites* in town. Also offers tasty sandwiches and fried kebabs. Cones of *frites* (€1.60-1.80) with a huge selection of sauces (€0.50 each). Open Su-Th 11:30am-1am, F-Sa 11:30am-2am. ❶

Le Perroquet, 31 r. Watteau. Sit down for lunch, an afternoon beer, or a late-night pastry. Selection of salads and delicious pitas from €5. Open daily 10:30am-1am. ❷

Hemispheres, 65 r. de l'Ecuyer. Delicious Middle Eastern and Asian cuisine. Vegetarian meals €7-10. Open M-F noon-3pm and 6:30-10:30pm, Sa 6:30pm-midnight. ❸

SIGHTS

GRAND PLACE AND ENVIRONS. Victor Hugo once called the gold-trimmed **Grand-Place** "the most beautiful square in the world." During the flower display (around Aug. 15), it's especially easy to see why. A flower market fills the place each morning, and at night the **Town Hall** is illuminated by 800 multi-colored floodlights set to classical music. *(Apr.-Aug. and Dec. daily around 10 or 11pm. Tours available. Inquire at the Town Hall for info. ☎279 43 65.)* Three blocks behind the Town Hall, on the corner of r. de l'Etuve and r. du Chêne, is Brussels's most giggled-at sight, the **Mannekin Pis,** a statue of an impudent boy (with an apparently gargantuan bladder) continuously urinating. The most commonly told story claims that it commemorates a boy who ingeniously defused a bomb destined for Grand Place. In reality, the fountain was installed to supply the neighborhood with drinking water during the reign of Archduke Albert. Locals have created hundreds of outfits for him, dressing him in the ritual coats of different organizations and regions, each with a strategically placed hole for his you-know-what. In the glorious **Galerie Saint-Hubert** arcade, one block behind Grand Place, you can window-shop for everything from square umbrellas to marzipan frogs.

MONT DES ARTS. The ▦**Musées Royaux des Beaux-Arts** houses the **Musée d'Art Ancien,** the **Musée d'Art Moderne,** a sculpture gallery, and temporary exhibitions. Together the museums showcase a huge collection of Belgian art spanning the centuries, including Bruegel the Elder's *Landscape with the Fall of Icarus* and pieces by Rubens and Brussels native René Magritte. Other masterpieces not to be missed are David's *Death of Marat* and paintings by Delacroix, Ingres, Gauguin, van Gogh, and Seurat. The panoramic view of Brussels's cityscape from the fourth floor of the 19th-century wing is alone worth the admission fee.

(3 r. de la Régence. M: Parc. ☎ 508 32 11. Open Su and Tu-Sa 10am-5pm. Some wings close noon-2pm. €5, students €3.50; 1st W of each month 1-5pm free. Audioguide €2.50.)

BELGIAN COMIC STRIP CENTRE. This museum, in the "Comic Strip Capital of the World," pays homage to *les bandes dessineés* with hundreds of Belgian comics. The **museum library,** in a renovated Art Nouveau warehouse, features a reproduction of Tintin's rocket ship and works by over 700 artists. For Tintin souvenirs, check out the museum store or the Tintin Boutique near Grand Place. *(20 r. des Sables. M: Rogier. From Gare Centrale, take bd. de l'Impératrice until it becomes bd. de Berlaimont, and turn left onto r. des Sables. ☎ 219 19 80. Open Su and Tu-Sa 10am-6pm. €6.20, students €5.)*

PARKS AND SQUARES. The **Botanical Gardens** on r. Royale are beautiful in summer. The **Parc de Bruxelles,** just behind Gare Centrale, and the **Parc Leopold,** amidst the EU buildings, are pleasantly green sanctuaries that provide a nice spot for a walk or jog. The charming hills around the **Place du Grand Sablon** are home to antique markets, art galleries, and cafes. Around **Place au Jeu de Balle,** you can practice the fine art of bargaining at the morning **flea market.**

OTHER SIGHTS. The enormous **Musées Royaux d'Art et d'Histoire** showcases artifacts from a wide variety of eras—Roman torsos without heads, Syrian heads without torsos, and Egyptian caskets with feet. The eerily illuminated *Salle au Tresor* (Treasure Room) and the Greco-Roman collection are the museum's main attractions. *(10 Parc du Cinquantenaire. M: Mérode. From the station, it's next to the big arch. ☎ 741 72 11. Open Tu-F 9:30am-5pm, Sa-Su 10am-5pm. €4, students €3.)* Next door, the **Royal Museum of the Army and Military History** contains a huge exhibit of WWI relics, including tanks, cannons, and uniforms, that bring to life the most important moments in Belgian history. *(3 Parc du Cinquantenaire. ☎ 737 78 33. Open Su and Tu-Sa 9am-noon and 1-4:45pm. Free.)* The **European Parliament Building** has been called the *Caprice des Dieux* ("Whim of the Gods"), perhaps because of its exorbitant cost. A quick tour allows you to visit the Parliament floor. *(43 r. Wiertz. M: Schuman. ☎ 284 34 53; www.europarl.eu.int. Tours M-Th 10am and 3pm, F 10am.)* **Mini-Europe,** an open-air exhibit of European landmarks replicated at one-twenty-fifth of their actual size, may be a perfect solution for travelers pressed for time. Also housed in the **Bruparck** entertainment complex are the **Kinepolis cinema and IMAX,** (the largest movie theater in Europe), and the **Oceade** water park. *(☎ 478 08 50; www.bruparck.com. Hours vary, but generally open daily*

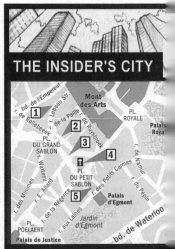

THE INSIDER'S CITY

THE HEART OF BRUSSELS

Antique galleries, beautiful buildings, and the best chocolate shop in the city make up a quintessentially Belgian neighborhood.

1 The splendid **Hotel Frison,** r. Lebeau 37, designed by Art Nouveau architect Victor Horta in 1894, now houses the **Gallery J. Visser.**

2 Splurge on some of the best chocolate in the city at **Wittamer,** pl. du Grand Sablon 6.

3 Surrounded by 16th- to 19th-century houses, the **Place du Grand Sablon** is enlivened every Saturday by an antique market.

4 View the stained glass windows of the flamboyantly Gothic **Cathédral de Notre Dame du Sablon,** r. Bodenbroeck 6.

5 The bronze statues on the balustrades around **Place du Petit Sablon,** r. de la Régence, depict the ancient trades of Brussels, while the fountain memorializes the fight against Spanish tyranny.

9:30am-5pm. Call or check website for info.) Twentieth-century master architect Victor Horta's graceful home, today the **Musée Horta,** shows off his pioneering Art Nouveau style. *(25 r. Américaine. M: Horta. Take a right out of the stop, walking uphill on ch. de Waterloo (7min.), then turn left onto ch. de Charleroi and right onto r. Américaine. ☎543 04 90. Open Su and Tu-Sa 2-5:30pm. €5, students €3.70.)*

ENTERTAINMENT AND NIGHTLIFE

For information on events, check the weekly *What's On,* available from the tourist office. The flagship of Brussels's theater network is the beautiful **Théâtre Royal de la Monnaie,** on pl. de la Monnaie. The theater is renowned throughout the world for its opera and ballet. Its performance of the opera *Muette de Portici* in August 1830 inspired the audience to take to the streets and begin the revolt that led to Belgium's independence. (M: de Brouckère. Info ☎229 12 00, tickets 70 233 939; www.lamonnaie.be. Tickets €8-75.) The **Théâtre Royal de Toone VII,** 21 petite r. des Bouchers, is a seventh generation puppet theater that stages marionette performances, a distinctly Belgian art form. The theater also houses a unique bar. (☎513 54 86. Shows generally in French; German, Flemish, and English available upon request. Tu-Sa 8:30pm. €10, students €7.) In summer, **concerts** are held on Grand Place, on pl. de la Monnaie, and in the parc de Bruxelles.

On summer nights, **Grand Place** and the **Bourse** come to life with street performers and live concerts. Students crowd in bars and hopping cafes around **Place Saint Géry. Le Fuse,** 208 r. Blaes, is one of Belgium's trendiest clubs. (Open daily 10pm-late.) Gay nightlife centers around r. des Pierres; **L'Homo Erectus,** 57 r. des Pierres, is always hot. (Open Su-Th 1pm-3am, F-Sa 1pm-5am.)

DAYTRIPS FROM BRUSSELS

WATERLOO. At Waterloo, the Allied troops, commanded by the Duke of Wellington, and the Prussians, led by Marshal Blücher, encountered the French army on June 18th, 1815. It took only nine hours to defeat Napoleon, but 50,000 men were killed in the process. **The Lion's Mound** *(Butte Du Lion),* 5km outside of town, is a huge hill that overlooks the site of Napoleon's last battle. (Open Apr.-Sept. daily 9:30am-6:30pm; Oct. 9:30am-5:30pm; Nov.-Feb. 10:30am-4pm; Mar. 10am-5pm. €1.) **Guides 1815** offers a guided walking tour of the battlefields leaving from the Lion's Mound Visitors Center. (1hr. Apr.-Sept. Sa-Su only. €3.) The informative **Musée Wellington,** 147 ch. de Bruxelles, was the British general's headquarters and is now home to battle artifacts. (Open Apr.-Sept. daily 9:30am-6:30pm; Oct.-Mar. 10:30am-5pm. €5, students €4. Audioguide included.)

Waterloo Station is far from most sights. The best option is to take a **train** from Brussels's Gare du Midi to Braine L'Alleud station (15min., every hr., €3), and return on **bus** W, hopping off at *Eglise* (a church in the center of Waterloo near the Musée Wellington) and *Route de Nivelles* (a gas station near Lion's Mound). The reverse route is also possible. Across the street from the Musée Wellington is the **tourist office,** 218 ch. de Bruxelles. (☎02 354 99 10. Open Apr.-Sept. daily 9:30am-6:30pm; Oct.-Mar. 10:30am-5pm.) There are several cheap restaurants along Chaussée de Bruxelles, including **L'Amusoir ❷,** 121 ch. de Bruxelles. (Lunch €7.35. Open daily noon-2:30pm and 6pm-10:30pm.)

MECHELEN (MALINES). Just north of Brussels, Mechelen (pop. 78,000), once the ecclesiastical capital of Belgium, is best known today for its abundance of treasure-filled churches and its grim role in the Holocaust. The stately **St. Rum-**

bold's Cathedral, down Consciencestr. from the Centraal station, features gorgeous stained-glass windows and the Gothic St. Rumbold's Tower, which rises 97m over the Grote Markt and houses two carillons (sets of 49 bells) that offer recitals. (Climb the tower July-Aug. M 2:15pm and 7:15pm, Tu-Su 2:15pm; June and Sept. M 7:15pm, Sa-Su and holidays 2:15; €2.50. Carillon recitals June-Sept. M 11:30am and 8:30pm, Sa 11:30am, Su 3pm.) Architectural gems, including the Stadhuis (city hall), line the Grote Markt. (Stadhuis open daily July-Aug. Required tour 2pm.) The 15th-century Church of St. John boasts Rubens's magnificent 17th-century triptych *The Adoration of the Magi*. (Open Su and T-Sa 1:30-5pm.) To reach the Jewish Museum of Deportation and Resistance, 153 Goswin de Stassartstr, follow Wollemarkt from behind St. Rumbold's; it becomes Goswin de Stassartstr. The museum is housed in the 18th-century military barracks used as a temporary holding spot for Jews en route to Auschwitz-Birkenau during the Holocaust. (Open Su-Th 10am-5pm, F 10am-1pm. Free. Tours by request.) The botanical gardens along the Dilje River are a great place to stop for a picnic.

Trains arrive from Brussels (15min., every 5-10min., €3.30) and Antwerp (15min., every 5-15min., €2.90). The tourist office near the Stadhuis books rooms. (☎015 29 76 55; www.mechelen.be. Open Easter-Oct. M-F 8am-6pm, Sa-Su 9:30am-12:30pm and 1:30-5pm; Nov.-Easter reduced hours.) Restaurants cluster around the Grote Markt. Try the white *asperge* (asparagus), a regional specialty. Postal Code: 2800.

FLANDERS (VLAANDEREN)

In Flanders, the Flemish-speaking part of Belgium, you can sample the nightlife in Antwerp, relax in romantic Bruges, and sate your castle-cravings in Ghent. Historically, the mouth of the Schelde River at Antwerp provided the region with a major port, and the production and trade of linen, wool, and diamonds created great prosperity. During it's Golden Age in the 16th century, Flanders's commercial centers were among the largest cities in Europe and its innovative artists inspired the Northern Renaissance. Today, the well-preserved cities of Flanders, rich in masterful oil painting and inspiring Gothic architecture, are Belgium's biggest attractions.

BRUGES (BRUGGE) ☎050

Famed for its lace and native Jan van Eyck, Bruges (pop. 116,000) is also the most touristed city in Belgium and one of the most romantic cities in Europe. Canals carve their way through rows of stone houses and cobblestone streets to reveal the breathtaking Gothic Markt. The city remains one of the best-preserved examples of Northern Renaissance architecture. Its beauty, however, belies the destruction sustained in World War I; eight decades after the war, farmers still uncover 200 tons of artillery every year as they plough their fields.

TRANSPORTATION AND PRACTICAL INFORMATION

Bruges is enclosed by a circular canal, with its main train station, Stationsplein, just beyond its southern extreme. The compact historic district is entirely accessible on foot. The dizzying Belfort (belfry) towers high over the center of town, presiding over the handsome Markt. The windmill-lined Kruisvestraat and serene Minnewater Park are great for a walk or a jog.

BELGIUM

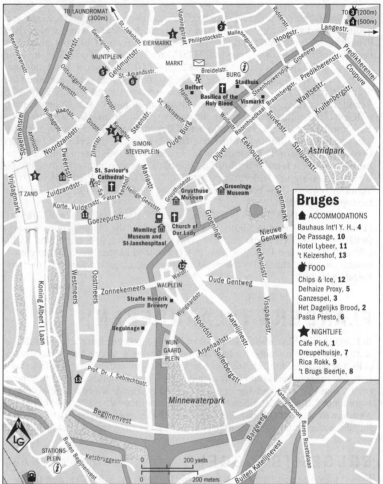

Bruges

🏠 ACCOMMODATIONS

Bauhaus Int'l Y. H., **4**
De Passage, **10**
Hotel Lybeer, **11**
't Keizershof, **13**

🍴 FOOD

Chips & Ice, **12**
Delhaize Proxy, **5**
Ganzespel, **3**
Het Dagelijks Brood, **2**
Pasta Presto, **6**

⭐ NIGHTLIFE

Cafe Pick, **1**
Dreupelhuisje, **7**
Rica Rokk, **9**
't Brugs Beertje, **8**

Trains: Leave from **Stationsplein** (☎38 23 82; open daily 4:30am-11pm), a 15min. walk south of the city, for: **Brussels** (50min., 2-6 per hr., €11); **Antwerp** (1¼hr., 2-6 per hr. €12); **Ghent** (25min., 3-10 per hr., €4.80); **Ostend** (17min., 3-5 per hr., €3); **Zee-brugge** (10min., every hr., €2.20).

Bike Rental: At the train station (☎30 23 29). €6.50 per half-day, €9 per day. **'t Koffie,** off the Markt by the belfry. €6 four hours, €9 per day; students €6 per day. Open daily 9am-11pm. Many hostels and hotels also rent bikes for around €9 per day.

Tourist Office: Burg 11 (☎44 86 86; www.brugge.be). From the train station, head left to 't Zand, turn right on Zuidzandstr., and walk through the Markt to Breidelstr. (20min.). Books rooms (€2.50 service fee, €20 deposit) and sells maps (€0.20) and info guides (€1). Open Apr.-Sept. M-F 9:30am-6:30pm, Sa-Su 10am-12:30pm and 2-6:30pm; Oct.-Mar. M-F 9:30am-5pm, Sa-Su 9:30am-1pm and 2-5:30pm. **Branch** office at the train station. Open Tu-Sa 10am-1pm and 2-4pm.

BELGIUM

ATMs: Two in the Markt, Vlamingstr. 18 and 78, and at Simon Stevenplein.

Luggage Storage: At the train station. €1.50-3.30. **Lockers** at the tourist office. €1. Only accessible during regular hours.

Laundromat: Belfort, Ezelstr. 51. Wash €2.50-3.50, dry €1. Open daily 7am-10pm.

Emergencies: ☎ 100. **Police:** ☎ 101. Police station at Hauwerstr. 7 (☎ 44 88 44).

Pharmacies: Apotheek Dryepondt, Wollestr. 7. Open M-F 9am-12:30pm and 2-6:30pm, Sa until 6pm. **Apotheek K. Dewolf,** Zuidzandstr. 1. Open M-F 9am-12:30pm and 2-6:30pm, Sa until 6pm.

Hospitals: A. Z. St.-Jan (☎ 41 21 11; not to be confused with Oud St-Janshospitaal, a museum), St.-Lucas (☎ 36 91 11), St.-Franciscus Xaverivskliniek (☎ 47 04 70). Call tourist office for doctors on call.

Internet Access: The Coffee Link, Mariastr. 38 (☎ 34 99 73), in the Oud St-Janshospitaal. €1.25 for first 15min., €0.07 per min. thereafter. Open daily 10am-8pm. Many hostels (see below) also offer access open to all.

Post Office: Markt 5. Address mail to be held: Firstname SURNAME, *Poste Restante*, Markt 5, **8000** Brugge, BELGIUM. Open M-F 9am-7pm, Sa 9:30am-12:30pm.

▌ ACCOMMODATIONS

Despite Bruges's popularity, reasonably-priced accommodations are available just blocks from the city center. Reserve in advance, as rooms can be hard to come by on weekends.

▨ **De Passage,** Dweersstr. 26 (☎ 34 02 32). Ideal location, super-friendly service, and a popular cafe. Free beer with dinner, and a free t-shirt after a 3-night stay. Breakfast €3. Reception daily 8:30am-11pm. Dorms €12; singles €22; doubles €40. ❷

▨ **Hotel Lybeer,** Korte Vuldersstr. 31 (☎ 33 43 55; hotellybeer@hotmail.com). Great location. Old-fashioned charm with modern comforts. Backpacker-friendly. Breakfast included. Free Internet access. Reception daily 7:30am-midnight. Singles €25; doubles €43; triples €57; quads €89. ❸

't Keizershof, Oostmeers 126 (☎ 33 87 28; hotel.keizershof@12move.be). Pretty, comfortable rooms on a quiet street. Breakfast included. Laundry €8. Singles €25; doubles €38; triples €60; quads €70. ❸

Bauhaus International Youth Hotel, Langestr. 133-137 (☎ 34 10 93; info@bauhaus.be). Cybercafe and popular bar. Nearby laundromat. Breakfast €2. Reception Su-Th 8am-1am, F-Sa 8am-3am. Dorms €11-23; doubles €25-35. ❷

Camping: St-Michiel, Tillegemstr. 55 (☎ 38 08 19). From the station, take bus #7 to Jagerstr. Face the road, head left and then turn left on Jagerstr. Bear left at the first intersection, staying on Jagerstr. and going around the rotary to Tillegemstr. €2.90 per person, €3.40 per tent. Showers €2. ❶

▐ FOOD

Inexpensive food can be hard to find in Bruges, but seafood lovers should splurge at least once on Belgium's famous *mosselen* (mussels; usually €15-22) or buy fresh (raw) seafood at the **Vismarkt.** From the Burg, cross the river and turn left. (Open Tu-Sa 8am-1pm.) **Delhaize Proxy,** Noordzandstr. 4, has groceries. (Open M-Sa 9am-7pm.) **Ganzespel ❷,** Ganzestr. 37, serves up generous and delicious portions of traditional Belgian fare. (Menu €7.35. Entrees €5-15. Open Su and W-Sa 6-10pm.) **Pasta Presto ❷,** St. Amandsstraat. 17, has nicely priced Italian fare. (Pasta with choice of nine sauces €2.50. Open M and W-Su 11:30am-9:30pm.) **Het Dagelijks Brood ❷,** Philipstockstr. 21, serves sandwiches, quiches, salads, pastries, and organic yogurt at a big wooden table. (Open M, W-Su 7:30am-6pm.) **Chips and Ice ❷**, Katelijnestr. 32, has the cheapest sandwiches (€2.25-3) around. (Open daily 9:30am-7pm.)

🅖 SIGHTS

Lined with gorgeous canals, and small enough to be explored on a short walk, Bruges is best seen on foot. Avoid visiting Bruges on Mondays, when all the museums are closed. If you plan to visit many museums, consider a cost-saving combination ticket (€15; includes admission to five museums of your choice).

MARKT AND BURG. Over the **Markt** looms the **Belfort,** an 88m medieval bell tower. During the day, climb its dizzying 366 steps for a great view; return at night, when the tower serves as the city's torch. *(Belfort open Su and Tu-Sa 9:30am-5pm. Tickets sold until 4:15pm. €5, students €3. Bell concerts Oct.-June 15 W and Sa-Su 2:15pm; June 15-Sept. Su only.)* Behind the Markt, the **Burg** is dominated by the massive, yet finely detailed Gothic facade of the **Stadhuis** (City Hall). Inside, the building's attractions include paintings, wood carvings, and a gilded hall where many residents of Bruges still get married. *(Open Su and Tu-Sa 9:30am-4:30pm. €2.50, students €1.50. Audioguide included.)* Hidden in a corner of the Burg next to the Stadhuis, the **Basilica of the Holy Blood** houses a relic that allegedly holds the blood of Christ. *(Basilica open Apr.-Sept. daily 9:30-11:50am and 2-5:50pm; Oct.-Mar. 10am-noon and 2-4pm; closed W afternoon. Free. Worship of the Relic F 11:50am, 5:50pm, 10-11am, and 3-4pm. €1.50.)*

MUSEUMS. From the Burg, follow Wollestr. left and then head right on Dijver to reach the **Groeninge Museum,** which has a comprehensive collection of Belgian and Dutch paintings from the last six centuries. Highlights include Hieronymous Bosch's fantastically lurid 🖼 *Last Judgment,* and works by Bruges-based Jan Van Eyck and Bruges-born Hans Memling. *(Dijver 12. Open Su and Tu-Sa 9:30am-5pm; €8, students €5.)* Formerly a palace, the nearby **Gruuthuse Museum** houses a large collection of intricate 16th- and 17th- century tapestries, along with other artifacts dating to the 6th century. The museum's small chapel, which protrudes into the Church of Our Lady (see below), was built so that the Palace residents could attend church services from the comfort of their home. *(Dijver 17. Open Su and Tu-Sa 9:30am-5pm; €6, students €4.)* Continue on Dijver as it becomes Gruuthusestr. and walk under the stone archway to enter the **Memling Museum,** housed in **St-Janshospitaal,** one of the oldest surviving medieval hospitals in Europe. The museum reconstructs everyday life in the hospital and has several paintings by Hans Memling. *(Mariastr. 38. Open Su and Tu-Sa 9:30am-5pm; €8, students €5.)*

OTHER SIGHTS. The 14th century **Church of Our Lady,** at Mariastr. and Gruuthusestr., contains Michelangelo's *Madonna and Child* as well as frescoed fragments of the 16th-century tombs of Mary of Burgundy and Charles the Bold. *(Open M-F 9am-12:20pm and 1:30-4:50pm, Sa 9am-12:30pm and 1:30-3:50pm, Su 1:30-4:50pm. Church free. Tomb viewing €2.50, students €1.50.)* Beer aficionados will enjoy the informative tour (and free sample) at the **Straffe Hendrik Brewery,** a beer museum and brewery built in 1856. *(From the Church of Our Lady, turn left, follow Mariastr., turn right onto Wijngaardstr., and turn right onto Welplein. Tours 45min. Apr.-Sept. 11am, noon, 2, 3, and 4pm; Oct.-Mar. 11am and 3pm.)* A short hike away, the 230-year-old windmill **St-Janshuismolen** is still used to grind flour in the summer months. *(From the Burg, follow Hoogstr., which becomes Langestr., and turn left at the end on Kruisvest. It's the second windmill. Open May-Sept. daily 9:30am-12:30pm and 1:30-5pm. €1, students €0.50.)* The **Minnewater** (Lake of Love), on the southern end of the city, is a beautiful park perfect for an afternoon picnic; you'd never know it was once used as an ammunition dump.

NIGHTLIFE

The best nighttime activity in Bruges is a walk through the city's romantic streets and over its cobblestoned bridges. There are some more lively late-night options, however, including the popular **bar** at the Bauhaus Hostel (see above) or the 300 varieties of beer at **'t Brugs Beertje**, Kemelstr. 5, off Steenstr. (Open Su-Tu and Th 4pm-1am, F-Sa 4pm-2am.) Next door, the candlelit **Dreupelhuisje** serves tantalizingly fruity *jenever*, a flavored Dutch gin. Be careful—the flavors mask a very high alcohol content. (Open Su, Tu and Th-Sa 6pm-1am.) Behind the Markt, **Cafe Pick** is a lively spot popular with young locals, and often offers late-night happy hour specials. (Open Su-Tu 10:30am-2am, W-Sa 10:30am-late. 2 for 1 beer special W and F 11pm-midnight, 2 for 1 spirits Su 10pm-midnight.) A 20-something crowd dances to pulsing music at **Rica Rokk**, 't Zand 6. (Beer from €1.60. Open daily 9:30am-5am.)

DAYTRIPS FROM BRUGES

OSTEND (OOSTENDE). On the coast of the North Sea, Ostend is a beach town with a promenade lined with restaurants and bars. The pier and **Viserkaai** (Fisherman's Quay) mark the entrance to the harbor that brings in most of the fresh fish sold in the country. Near the bustling **Vitrap** (Fishmarket), vendors set up stands selling steaming bowls of *caricoles* (sea snails) and fresh seafood galore. To get to the main **beach,** cross the bridge directly in front of the station, turn right on Visserkaai and follow the promenade for 20min.

Trains run to Ostend from Bruges (15min., 3 per hr., €3). To get to the **tourist office** (☎70 11 99; www.oostende.be), follow the directions to the beach, but walk on the promenade for only 10min. and turn left onto Langestr.; follow it to the end. Don't even bother asking for a menu at **Taverne Koekoek ❶**, Langestr. 38-40, because they only do one thing: perfectly spiced, divine rotisserie chicken. (Half-chicken €4.90. Open 24hr.)

ANTWERP (ANTWERPEN, ANVERS)   ☎0 3

Home to the Golden Age master painter Rubens, Antwerp (pop. 450,000) is distinctly cosmopolitan. Its main street, the Meir, showcases trendy clothing, diamond jewelry, and delectable chocolate.

TRANSPORTATION AND PRACTICAL INFORMATION. Trains go from Berchem Station to: Amsterdam (2hr., €24); Brussels (1hr., €6); and Rotterdam (1hr., €16). To get from Berchem station to the **tourist office,** Grote Markt 15, take tram #8 (all trams €1) to Groenplaats. (☎232 01 03; www.visitantwerpen.be. Open M-Sa 9am-6pm, Su 9am-5pm). **Postal Code:** 2000.

ACCOMMODATIONS AND FOOD. To get to ⬛**Bed & Breakfast 26,** Pelgrimsstr. 26, from Groenpl., take Reyndersstr. away from Hilton, and turn right onto Pelgirmsstr.; it's the third building on left. Beautiful rooms, appealing showers, and a personable owner. (☎42 83 69. M: Groenpl. Breakfast included. Reserve in advance. Singles €25, with private bath €35; doubles €50/60.) The **New International Youth Hotel and Hostel ❷**, Provinciestr. 256, is a 15min. walk from the train station, on the corner of De Boeystr. and Provinciestr. Or, take tram #2 or 15 to Plantin, follow Plantin de Moretus under the bridge, and turn right on Baron Joostensstr., left on Van Den Nestlei, and right on De Boeystr. Rooms are clean and carpeted. (☎230 05 22. Breakfast included. Sheets €3.50. No lockout. Dorms €14; singles €29; doubles €44-55; quads €71-85.) To get to the conveniently located

Scoutel ❹, Stoomstr. 3, from Centraal station, turn left on Pelikaanstr., take first left under bridge; once through, the entrance is on the right. (☎226 46 06; www.vvksm.be. Breakfast and sheets included. Reception daily 8am-7pm. Singles €27, under-26 €25; doubles €44/39; quads €71/62.) Farther from the center is **Jeugdherberg Op-Sinjoorke (HI) ❷**, Eric Sasselaan 2. From Groenplaats, take tram #2 (dir.: Hoboken) to *Bouwcentrum*. From the tram stop, walk toward the fountain, take a left, and follow the yellow signs. (☎238 02 73; www.vjh.be. Breakfast included. Reception 7am-10am, 4pm-midnight. Lockout 10am-4pm. Dorms €13; doubles €18. Nonmembers add €3.) You can **camp** near the Jeugdherberg Op-Sinjoorke at the well-kept **Sted. Kamp Vogelzangan ❶**. Follow the directions above to *Bouwcentrum*; when you get off the tram, walk away from the fountain, and take the first left; the campground is on the left. (Max. stay 28 days. Open Apr.-Sept. 3. €2.50 per person, €1 per car; €1.25 per tent. Electricity €2.50. No credit cards.) The **Grote Markt** and **Groenplaats** are surrounded by numerous restaurants. **Suiker-rui**, off Grote Markt, is the street for those seeking seafood. For hearty pizza (€4.50-10) and friendly, multilingual service just off Groenpl., visit **Pizzeria Ristorante Da Giovanni ❷**, Jan Blomstr. 8. (Open daily 11am-1am. 20% student discount.) **Spaghettiworld ❸**, Oude Koornmarkt 3, has funky decor and a large selection of large, inexpensive pasta dishes. (Pasta €7-12. Open Su 4-11pm, Tu-F 7am-11pm, Sa noon-11pm.) The **GB Supermarkt** is off Groenpl. (Open M-Th and Sa 8:30am-8pm, F 8:30am-9pm.)

🔊📷 **SIGHTS AND NIGHTLIFE.** Many of Antwerp's best sights are free. Its main street, the **Meir,** is great for window shopping. In the city's historic center, the **Cathedral of Our Lady,** Groenpl. 21, boasts a magnificent Gothic tower and Rubens's *Descent from the Cross.* (Open M-F 10am-5pm, Sa 10am-3pm, Su 1-4pm. €2.) Nearby, the dignified Renaissance **Stadhuis** (City Hall) is well worth visiting. (Tours by request only ☎220 80 20. €0.75.) Take tram #11 to see the fanciful and eclectic Golden Age mansions lining the **Cogels Osylei.**

If you're museum-bound, try to plan your trip to Antwerp on Friday; admission is free at all museums. A stroll down the promenade by the Schelde River leads to the 13th-century **Steen Castle,** which houses the extensive collections of the **National Maritime Museum.** (Open Su and Tu-Sa 10am-4:45pm. €4, students €2.) The **Royal Museum of Fine Arts,** Leopold De Waelpl. 1-9, has one of the world's finest collections of Old Flemish Master paintings. (Open Su and Tu-Sa 10am-5pm. €8, under-25 €2.) The **Mayer van den Bergh Museum,** Lange Gasthuisstr. 19, formerly a private collection with works from the 14th to 16th centuries, showcases Bruegel's *Mad Meg.* (Open Su and Tu-Sa 10am-5pm. €4, students €2.) The **Rubens Huis,** Wapper 9, off Meir, was built by Antwerp's favorite son and is filled with his works. (Open Su and Tu-Sa 10am-5pm. €5, students €2.50.) The **Diamant Museum,** Kon. Astridplein 19, explores every facet of the precious gem, from its unique creation to Antwerp's historic role as the world's diamond center. (Open May-Oct. daily 10am-6pm; Nov.-Apr. 10am-5pm. €5, students €3. Audioguide included.)

Although mostly in Dutch, *Weekly Up* magazine (free at any tourist office) provides nightlife and movie information. Bars abound behind the cathedral, but a trendy scene has emerged in the southern part of the city, near the Royal Arts Museum. For live jazz and a chill atmosphere, visit **De Muze,** Melkmarkt 15, a bar that has remained popular since the 60s. Sample the local *elixir d'Anvers* (a strong, sugary drink) amidst traditionally dressed Flemish bartenders in the candlelit, 15th-century **Pelgrom,** Pelgrimstr. 15. (Open daily noon-late.) Over 600 Flemish religious figurines hang out with drinkers at **'t Elfde Gebod,** Torfburg 10, next to the cathedral. (Beer €1.75-3. Open M-F noon-1am, Sa-Su noon-2am.) Gay nightlife clusters around **Van Schoonhovenstraat,** just north of Centraal Station.

GHENT (GENT)   ☎ 09

Once the heart of the Flemish textile industry, modern Ghent (pop. 225,000) celebrates the memory of its industrial past. Awe-inspiring buildings in the city's main square stand in proud testament to its former grandeur, and the **Gentse Feesten,** the "10 Days Off" celebration, commemorates the first vacation granted to laborers in 1860. During the festivities, the streets fill with performers, live music, carnival rides, great food and loads and loads of beer; the celebration also brings 11 nights of international DJs. (July 17-26, 2004. Info ☎269 46 00.)

🖪🔁 TRANSPORTATION AND PRACTICAL INFORMATION. Trains run from St-Pietersstation (accessible by tram #1 or 12) to: Antwerp (40min., €7); Brussels (40min., €6.60); and Bruges (20min., €4.80). The **tourist office,** Botermarkt 17A, is in the crypt of the belfry. (☎266 52 32. Open Apr.-Oct. daily 9:30am-6:30pm; Nov.-Mar. 9:30am-4:30pm.) **Postal Code:** 9000.

🖪🔁 ACCOMMODATIONS AND FOOD. To reach **De Draeke (HI) ❷,** St-Widostr. 11, from the station, take tram #1, 10, or 11 to Gravensteen (15min.). Facing the castle, head left over the canal, then go right on Gewad and turn right on St-Widostr. In the shadow of a castle, it's the only hostel in town. (☎233 70 50. Breakfast and sheets included. Internet €0.08 per min. Reception daily 7am-11pm. Dorms €16; singles €24; doubles €38. Nonmembers add €3.) For a listing of private rooms, visit the tourist office. To get to **Camping Blaarmeersen ❶,** Zuiderlaan 12, take bus #9 from St-Pietersstation and ask the driver to connect you to bus #38 to Blaarmeersen. When you get off, take the first street on your left to the end. (☎266 81 60. Open Mar. to mid-Oct. In summer, €4 per person, €4 per tent; off-season, €3.30 per person, €3.30 per tent.) **Oudburg,** near Patershol, has many inexpensive kebob and pita restaurants. Also try **St-Pietersnieuwstraat,** by the university. **Magazyne ❶,** Penitentenstr. 24, is a great place for cheap and hearty fare, with good vegetarian options. (Open M-F noon-2pm and 6-11pm, Sa-Su 6-11pm.) **Pain Perdu ❸,** Walpoortstr. 9, serves tasty sandwiches and salads. (Open M-F 8:30am-6:30pm, Sa 9am-6:30pm, Su 9am-2:30pm.)

🖪🔁 SIGHTS AND NIGHTLIFE. The **Leie canal** runs through the center of the city and wraps around the **Gravensteen,** St-Veerlepl. 11, a medieval fortress whose shadowy halls and spiral staircases will give you chills before you even reach the crypt, dungeon, and torture chamber. (Open Apr.-Sept. daily 9am-5:15pm; Oct.-Mar. 9am-4:15pm. €6, students €1.20.) The castle is near the historic **Partershol** quarter and **Vrijmarkt,** a network of funky and well-preserved 16th- to 18th-century houses. A block away on Limburgstr., the elaborately decorated 14th- to 16th-century **🖪Saint Bavo's Cathedral** boasts van Eyck's *Adoration of the Mystic Lamb* and Rubens's *St. Bavo's Entrance into the Monastery of Ghent.* (Cathedral open Apr.-Oct. daily 8:30am-6pm; Nov.-Mar. M-Sa 8:30am-5pm, Su 1-6pm. Free. Crypt and *Mystic Lamb* open Apr.-Oct. M-Sa 9:30am-5pm, Su 1-5pm; Nov.-Mar. M-Sa 10:30am-4pm, Su 1-4pm. €2.50. Audioguide included.) Walk across **Saint Michael's Bridge** and along the **Graslei,** a medieval port-street, to see the handsomely preserved guild houses. The **🖪Church of St. Nicholas,** absolutely striking from the exterior, is also worth a look inside. (Open M 2:30-5pm, Tu-Su 10am-5pm. Free.) The **Museum voor Sierkunst** (Museum of Decorative Arts), nearby on Jan Breydelstr., has a large collection of Art Nouveau designs as well as more contemporary furniture. (Open Su and T-Sa 9:30am-5pm. €2.50, students €1.20.) The **Museum voor Schone Kunsten** (Museum of Fine Arts), in Citadel Park, has a collection of 14th- to 16th-century Flemish works. (Open Su and Tu-Sa 10am-6pm. €2.50, students €1.20.) The **Stedelijk Museum voor Actuele Kunst** (SMAK; Municipal Museum for Contemporary Art) is also located in Citadel Park. (Open Su and Tu-Sa 10am-6pm. €5, students €2.50). **Korenmarkt** and **Vrijdagmarkt** are filled with restaurants and pubs. Beer-lovers flock to **Dulle Griet,** in Vrijdagmarkt, which serves over 250 types of beer. (Open M 4:30pm-12:30am, Tu-Sa noon-12:30am, Su noon-7:30pm.)

YPRES (IEPER)   ☎ 57

"We are the dead. Short days ago/We lived, felt dawn, saw sunset glow/Loved and were loved, and now we lie/In Flanders fields." Canadian soldier John McCrae wrote these famous lines during WWI at the Battle of Ypres Salient. What the Germans believed would be a quick, sweeping victory quickly became a vicious stalemate that defined the horrors of WWI; chemical warfare was used for the first time in Western history. In four years of intense fighting, 450,000 people died here. Ypres (pop. 35,000), once a medieval textile center, was completely destroyed by the long combat, but was rebuilt as a near-perfect replica of its former self. Today, the town is surrounded by over 150 **British cemeteries** and filled with memorial sites, drawing soldiers' families as well as many British tourists and school groups.

In the **Cloth Hall,** one of the grand medieval guild halls that preside over **Grote Markt,** the **Flanders Field Museum,** Grote Markt 34, documents the gruesome history and bloody battles of the Great War. (Open Apr.-Sept. daily 10am-6pm; Oct.-Mar. Su and Tu-Sa 10am-5pm. €7.50.) Next door stands the splendid Gothic **Saint Martin's Cathedral.** Cross the street in front of St. Martin's and head right to reach the Anglican **Saint George's Memorial Church,** Elverdingsestr. 1. Each brass plaque and kneeling pillow in the church commemorates a specific individual or unit. (Both churches open daily except during services. Free.) Across the *markt,* the names of 54,896 British soldiers who were lost in the trenches are inscribed on the somber **Menin Gate.** At 8pm each evening, the **Last Post** bugle ceremony honors those who defended Ypres. You can easily walk the circumference of Ypres along the old ramparts. From Menin Gate, take the **Rose Coombs Walk** to visit the nearby **Ramparts Cemetery,** where row upon row of white crosses face the river. The battlefields are largely inaccessible by foot, so **car tours** are a good, if pricey option. Two companies, **Flanders Battlefield Tours** (☎360 460. www.ypres-fbt.be; €16-22), and **Salient Tours** (☎214 657. www.salienttours.com; €15- 21), offer informative tours that traverse the surrounding battlefields.

Trains run to: Bruges via Courtrai (2hr., €9); Ghent (1hr., €8.50); and Brussels (1½hr., €14). To get to the **Visitors Center,** housed in the Cloth Hall in Grote Markt from the train station, head straight down Stationsstr., turn left onto Tempelstr., then turn right onto Boterstr. (☎22 85 84; www.ieper.be. Open Apr.-Sept. M-Sa 9am-6pm, Su 10am-6pm; Oct.-Mar. M-Sa 9am-5pm, Su 10am-5pm.) **The Hortensia ❺,** Rijselsestr. 196, is a bed & breakfast with great rooms and a friendly owner. From the Grote Markt, turn onto Rijselsestr. and continue for 10min. (☎21 24 06. Singles €46, doubles €54, triples €69.) Many restaurants line the **Grote Markt,** including **I'nt Klein Stadhuis ❸,** a traditional pub and restaurant with a terrace. The **Super GB** grocery store is at Vandepeereboomplein 15. (Open M-Sa 9am-7pm.)

WALLONIE

Wallonie, the French-speaking region of Belgium, enjoys less wealth than its Flemish counterpart; nonetheless, its bigger towns boast interesting histories, partially thanks to their oft-coveted citadels. The towns in the **Ardennes** offer a relaxing hideaway, with hiking trails through deep forests and beautiful landscapes. The most exceptional area lies in the southeast corner, where gorgeous train rides sweep through peaceful farmland. Although nature-lovers will probably want to spend a night in this part of the Wallonie wilderness, those pressed for time can enjoy the scenery from a train on the way to Brussels, Paris, or Luxembourg.

TOURNAI
☎069

The first city liberated by Allied forces, Tournai's (pop. 68,000) medieval old town has a history of being bounced between various empires; it was once a Roman trading post and the former capital of Gaul. The city's most spectacular sight is the 800-year-old **Cathedral of Our Lady,** known for its five steeples and **treasure room.** (Treasure room open in summer daily 10am-noon and 2-5pm, Su until 7:15pm; off-season 10:15-11:45am and 2-3:30pm. €1.) Climb the **belfry** for a stunning view. (Open Mar.-Oct. Su 11am-1pm and 2-6:30pm, Tu-Sa 10am-1pm and 2-5:30pm; Nov.-Feb. Su 2-5pm, Tu-Sa 10am-noon; €2.) Designed by Victor Horta, the **Museum of Fine Arts,** encloses St-Martin, is an Art Nouveau building that houses a small collection of Flemish paintings. (Open Apr.-Oct. M and W-Su 9:30am-noon and 2-4:30pm; Nov.-Mar. M and W-Sa 10am-noon and 2-5pm, Su 2-5pm. €3, students €2.)

Trains arrive at pl. Crombez (☎88 62 23) from Brussels's Gare du Midi (1hr., €9.60). To get to the **tourist office,** 14 Vieux Marché Aux Poteries, exit the station, walk straight to the city center (10min.), and go around the left side of the cathedral. (☎22 20 45; www.tournai.be. Open Apr.-Oct. M-F 8:30am-6pm, Sa-Su 10am-noon and 2-6pm; Nov.-Mar. M-F 8:30am-6pm, Sa-Su 2-6pm. To get to the **Auberge de Tournai (HI) ❷,** 64 r. St-Martin, continue straight up the hill from the tourist office or take bus #7 or 88 (€1.10) from the station. (☎21 61 36. Breakfast and sheets included. Reception daily 8am-noon and 5-10pm. Reservations required during off-season. Closed Jan. Dorms €13; singles €23; doubles €36. Nonmembers add €2.50.) The area around **Grand Place** has plenty of options for cheap food.

NAMUR
☎081

The quiet and friendly city of Namur (pop. 105,000), in the heart of Wallonie, is the last sizable outpost before the wilderness of the Ardennes. Given the proximity of opportunities for **hiking, biking, caving,** and **kayaking,** it is the most convenient base for exploration. The foreboding **citadel,** on top of a cliff to the south, was built by the Spanish in the Middle Ages, expanded by the Dutch in the 19th century, the site of a bloody battle in WWI, and occupied until 1978. (Open daily 11am-5pm. €6.)

Trains link Namur to Brussels (1hr., €6.60). Two **tourist offices,** one a few blocks left of the train station at sq. Leopold (☎24 64 49; open daily 9:30am-6pm), and the other in the **Hôtel de Ville,** r. de Fer (☎24 64 44, www.ville.namur.be; open M-F 8am-4:30pm), help plan excursions. To enjoy a lake-front view, take bus #3 to the **Auberge Félicien Rops (HI) ❷,** 8 av. Félicien Rops. (☎22 36 88; namur@laj.be. Bikes €13 per day. Breakfast and sheets included. Laundry €6.50. Reception daily 7:30am-1am. Lockout 11am-3pm. Dorms €13-15. Nonmembers add €2.50.) To **camp** at **Les Trieux ❶,** 99 r. des Tris, 6km away in Malonne, take bus #6. (☎44 55 83. Open Apr.-Oct. €2.50 per person, €3.75 per tent.) Restaurants cluster in the small square of **Place Marché-aux-legumes** on r. St-Jean.

DINANT
☎082

The tiny town of Dinant (pop. 13,000) boasts wonders disproportionate to its size. An imposing **citadel** towers over the Meuse River. (☎22 36 70. Citadel open Mar.-Sept. daily 10am-6pm. Required tour in French and Dutch, 45min., every 35min., €5.50.) Bring a jacket to tour the cascade-filled caves of the **Grotte Merveilleuse,** 142 rte. de Phillippeville. Rich with stalagmites and stalagtites, the cave lives up to its name—it is indeed marvellous. (Open Apr.-Oct. daily 10-11am and 1-5pm; Nov.-Mar. 11am and 1-4pm. Tours every hr. €5, students €4.50.) The ▨**Leffe Abbey,** a brew of beer and religion, offers enlightening tours for the adventurous beer pilgrim. (Tours May-Aug. Su and W 3pm.) Dinant is also a good base for **outdoor** excursions. **Dakota Raid Adventure,** r. Cousot 6 (☎22 32 43), leads rock-climbing and kayaking daytrips in the area. Dinant is accessible by **train** from Brussels (1hr., €9.60) or by **bike** from Namur; on summer weekends, take a one-way river cruise from Namur (3hr.). With your back to the train station, turn right, take the first left, and then the very next left to reach the **tourist office,** Quai Cadoux 8 (☎22 28 70), which plans excursions and books rooms.

▶ **DAYTRIP FROM DINANT: ROCHEFORT .** Rochefort (pop. 10,000), a charming town with hospitable residents, is hidden within the rolling hills and woods of the Lesse Valley. Hike up to the crumbled **Château Comtal** for a breathtaking view of the Northern Ardennes. (☎084 21 44 09. Site open Apr.-Oct. daily 10am-6pm. €1.80.) Also visit the **Grotte de Lorette,** one of Wallonie's many spectacular caves. (☎084 21 20 80. Tours July-Aug. daily 10:30am-noon and 1-5:30pm, every 45min.) To reach Rochefort, take the **train** from Namur to Jemelle (40min., every 40min., €6.60) and **bus** #29 from Jemelle (every hr., usually 34min. after the hr., €1.10). The **tourist office,** 5 r. de Behogne, sells hiking maps. (☎084 34 51 72. Open M-F 8am-5pm, Sa-Su 9:30am-5pm.)

BOSNIA AND HERZEGOVINA (BOSNA I HERCEGOVINA)

> **❗** In June 2002, the US State Department reiterated its **Travel Warning** against unnecessary travel to certain regions in Bosnia, particularly the Republika Srpska. For updates, consult http://travel.state.gov/travel_warnings.html.

The mountainous centerpiece of the former Yugoslavia, Bosnia and Herzegovina defied odds throughout the centuries to stand as an independent nation today. Bosnia's distinctiveness, as well as its troubles, spring from its role as a mixing ground for Muslim Bosniaks, Catholic Croats, and Orthodox Serbs. In Sarajevo, the country's cosmopolitan capital, the ideal of tolerance is at least verbally maintained, but ethnic tensions continue in the countryside. The past decade has not been kind to Bosnia—the country's lush valleys are now punctuated by abandoned houses and gaping rooftops—however, its resilient people are optimistic, and in this period of peace, reconstruction has begun.

FACTS AND FIGURES

Official Name: Bosnia and Herzegovina.

Capital: Sarajevo.

Major Cities: Mostar.

Population: 3,500,000 (48% Bosniak, 37% Serb, 14% Croat, 1% other).

Land Area: 51,129 sq. km.

Languages: Bosnian, Serbian, Croatian.

Time Zone: GMT +1.

Religions: Muslim (43%), Orthodox (30%), Catholic (18%), other (9%).

ESSENTIALS

DOCUMENTS AND FORMALITIES

VISAS. Citizens of Australia, Canada, Ireland, New Zealand, the UK, and the US may visit Bosnia visa-free for up to three months; **visas** are required for citizens of South Africa. A valid passport is required to enter and leave the country. Visas include: single-entry (valid for 30 days, €31), multiple-entry (90 days, €57), and multiple-entry (more than 90 days, €72). There are occasional police checkpoints within Bosnia; you must **register** with the police within 48 hours of arrival—accommodations will usually do it for you. It is also a good idea to register with your embassy upon arrival and keep your papers with you at all times. Bosnian visas are not available at the border; there is no fee for crossing.

EMBASSIES. Foreign embassies in Bosnia are in Sarajevo (p. 135). Bosnian embassies at home include: **Australia,** 5 Beale Crescent, Deakin, ACT 2600 (☎02 6232 4646; www.bosnia.webone.com.au); **Canada,** 130 Albert St. Ste. 805, Ottawa, ON K1P 5G4 (☎613-236-0028; fax 236-1139); **South Africa,** 25 Stella St., Brooklyn 0181; mail to: P.O. Box 11464, Hatfield 0028 (☎012 346 5547; bih@mweb.co.za); **UK,** 5-7 Lexam Gardens, London W8 5JJ (☎020 7373 0867; fax 7373 0871); **US,** 2109 E St. NW, Washington, D.C. 20037 (☎202-337-1500; www.bhembassy.org); **US Consulate,** 866 UN Plaza Ste. 580, New York, NY 10017 (☎212-593-1042).

TRANSPORTATION

Buses are reliable, uncrowded, and clean, but Balkan driving can be nervewracking. Commercial **plane** service into Sarajevo is limited and expensive; **Croatia Airlines** has regular service to Sarajevo from Zagreb. **Railways** are not functional and should not be considered an option. Also avoid driving, biking, and hitchhiking.

TOURIST SERVICES AND MONEY

Bosnia and Herzegovina

EMERGENCY	Police: ☎92. Ambulance: ☎94. Fire: ☎93.

The Bosnian **convertible mark** (KM), introduced in 1998, is fixed to the euro at a rate of 1KM to €0.51. The Croatian **kuna** was named an official Bosnian currency in 1997; while not legal tender in Sarajevo, it is accepted in the western (Croatian) area of divided Mostar. The old Bosnian *dinar* is no longer valid currency. Change your money back to euros when you leave, as the convertible mark is inconvertible outside Bosnia. Banks are the best places to exchange money; some in Sarajevo cash traveler's checks. **Western Union** in Sarajevo has a very helpful English-speaking staff. **ATMs** are available in Sarajevo. If you travel outside of Sarajevo, bring euros with you. **Tip** waitstaff only for excellent service.

CONVERTIBLE MARKS		
AUS$1 = 1.15KM	1KM = AUS$0.87
CDN$1 = 1.28KM	1KM = CDN$0.78
EUR€1 = 1.96KM	1KM = EUR€0.51
NZ$1 = 1.02KM	1KM = NZ$0.98
UK£1 = 2.82KM	1KM = UK£0.35
US$1 = 1.79KM	1KM = US$0.58
ZAR1 = 0.24KM	1KM = ZAR4.11

COMMUNICATION

PHONE CODES	**Country code:** 387. **International dialing prefix:** 00. From outside Bosnia-Herzegovina, dial int'l dialing prefix (see inside back cover) + 387 + city code + local number.

TELEPHONES AND INTERNET ACCESS. Phones are troublesome and expensive; the best option is to call collect from the Sarajevo post office. The **AT&T** direct access number is ☎00 800 0010. **Internet** access is becoming widely available.

MAIL. Yellow-and-white "PTT" signs indicate post offices; service is becoming increasingly efficient. Mail to Europe takes three to five days, to North America seven to ten days. Address mail to be held: Firstname SURNAME, *Post Restante*, Zmaja od Bosne 88, Sarajevo 71000 BOSNIA AND HERZEGOVINA.

ACCOMMODATIONS AND FOOD

BOSNIA	❶	❷	❸	❹	❺
ACCOMMODATIONS	under 35KM	35-40KM	41-50KM	51-60KM	over 60KM
FOOD	under 4KM	4-6KM	7-10KM	11-14KM	over 14KM

Accommodations options are limited in Bosnia—**hotels** are usually the only choice, and run €15-30 per night. **Private rooms** exist only in Sarajevo, and usually cost the same as cheaper hotels (€15-25). **Camping** should be avoided except through special organizations. Cheap **meals** average €2-5.

SAFETY AND SECURITY

Hundreds of thousands of **land mines** and **unexploded ordnance** (UXO) cover the country, many on road shoulders and in abandoned houses. Outside Sarajevo, **NEVER set foot off the pavement;** stay on paved roads and hard-covered surfaces. Do not pick up any objects from the ground. The **Mine Action Center** (MAC), Zmaja od Bosne 8 (☎667 310; www.bhmac.org), has more info. In Sarajevo, finding **medical help** and supplies is not difficult; your embassy is the best resource. Peacekeeping has brought English-speaking doctors, but not insurance; you must pay cash.

HOLIDAYS

Holidays: New Year's (Jan. 1); Orthodox Christmas (Jan. 7); Orthodox New Year's (Jan. 14); Independence Day (Mar. 1); Easter (Apr. 11-12); Labor Day (May 1); All Saints' Day (Nov. 1); All Souls' Day (Nov. 2); National Day (Nov. 25); Christmas (Dec. 25).

SARAJEVO ☎033

Sarajevo lives again thanks to the warmth and spirit of the people in this "big village" (pop. 496,000). While glimpses of the destruction this city faced during the brutal 1992-1995 siege by Bosnian Serbs are unavoidable, rejuvenation is well under way. Reconstruction projects are methodically attempting to heal the physical scars. The lively marketplace of the old Turkish Quarter, a burgeoning arts scene, and an enthusiastic nightlife all promise a return to the prewar glory that attracted visitors from around the world and won the city the privilege of hosting the 1984 Olympic Games. Optimistic about the way their city is changing, the residents of Sarajevo are never aloof—cafe owners, shopkeepers, and even taxi drivers welcome today's visitors like old friends.

! The following outlying areas of Sarajevo were battlegrounds during the war and still contain land mines: Grbavica, Lukavica, Illidža, and Dobrinja.

🚍🚊 TRANSPORTATION AND PRACTICAL INFORMATION. Buses (☎53 28 74) run from Kranjčevića 9, behind the Holiday Inn at the corner with Halida Kajtaza, to: Dubrovnik (7hr., daily, 42KM); Frankfurt (15hr., daily, 192KM); Ljubljana (10hr., 3 per week, 72KM); Split (7hr., 4 per day, 32KM); Vienna (13hr., daily, 74KM); and Zagreb (9hr., 3 per day, 51KM). Turn left from the station and walk on Kranjčevića for 20min. to reach the city's main street, **Maršala Tita,** or take a cab (7-8KM). To reach the tourist bureau, **Turistička Zajednica,** Zelenih Beretki 22a, bear right past the Eternal Flame on Maršala Tita; when you see the church on your left, take a right down Strossmajerova, then turn left onto Zelenih Beretki. (☎22 07 24. Open M-Sa 9am-8pm, Su 10am-6pm.) **Embassies** include: **Canada,**

BOSNIA AND
HERZEGOVINA

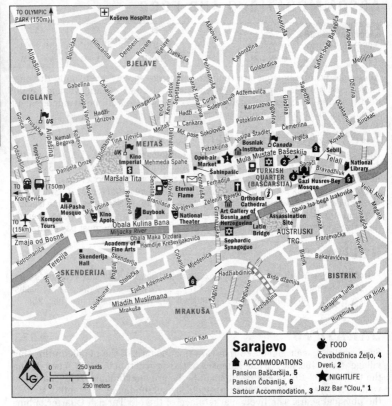

TO OLYMPIC
PARK (150m)

Koševo Hospital

BJELAVE

CIGLANE

MEJTAŠ

Kino
Imperial
Mehmeda Spahe

Maršala Tita

All-Pasha
Mosque

Kompou
Tours

Kino
Apolo

Obala Kulina Bana

Buybook

National
Theater

Miljacka River

Academy of
Fine Arts

Hamdije Kreševljakovića

Skenderija
Hall

SKENDERIJA

MRAKUŠA

Mladih Muslimana

Cicin han

Bošnjak
Institute
Canada
Mula Mustafe Bašeskija
Sebilj
Telali
National
Library
Saraci

Open-air
Market
Šahinpašić
TURKISH
QUARTER
(BAŠČARŠIJA)
Gazi Husrev-Bey
Mosque
Bravadžiluk
Ferhadija

Eternal
Flame
Zelenih Beretki
Orthodox
Cathedral

Art Gallery of
Bosnia and
Herzegovina
Latin
Bridge
Assassination
Site
AUSTRIJSKI
TRG.

Sephardic
Synagogue
BISTRIK

Sarajevo

▲ ACCOMMODATIONS
Pansion Baščaršija, 5
Pansion Čobanija, 6
Sartour Accommodation, 3

🍅 FOOD
Čevabdžinica Željo, 4
Dveri, 2

★ NIGHTLIFE
Jazz Bar "Clou," 1

0   250 yards
0   250 meters

Grbavička 4 (☎22 20 33; open M-F 8:30am-5pm.); citizens of **New Zealand** should contact the embassy in Rome (p. 606); **UK**, Tina Ujevica 8 (☎44 44 29; open M-F 8:30am-5pm); and **US**, Alipašina 43 (☎44 57 00; www.usembassy.ba; open M-F 2-3:30pm, Tu and Th 8am-noon). **Australians** should contact the embassy in Vienna (p. 84). **Central Profit Banka,** Zelenih Beretki 24, cashes **traveler's checks** and changes money. (Open M-F 8am-7pm, Sa 8am-noon.) **ATMs** are at Ferhadija 9 and Maršala Tita 17. There are several **Internet** cafes along Ferhadija (2-3KM per hr.). **Postal Code:** 71120.

⌐⌐⌐ ACCOMMODATIONS AND FOOD. Relatively cheap **private rooms** (30-50KM) are all over town; ask a taxi driver at the station for help if you arrive late. Walk down Ferhadija away from the Eternal Flame, go right onto Gazi Huzrev-Begova, and take the third left onto Veliki Čurčiluk; ▼**Pansion Baščaršija** ❹, Veliki Čurčiluk 41, is 2 blocks up on the left. (☎23 21 85 or 21 01 53. Singles 60KM; doubles 100KM; triples 120KM.) Just before the intersection with Kovaći, **Sartour Accommodation** ❷, Mula Mustafe Bašeskije 63, operates two excellent guesthouses. (☎23 86 80. Singles 40KM; doubles 80KM. Cash only.) To reach modern **Pansion Čobanija** ❺, Čobanija 29, from the Eternal Flame, take the first left onto Kulovića, which crosses the river to become Čobanija. (☎44 17 49; fax 20 39 37. Reserve ahead by fax. Singles 80KM; doubles 120KM.) Hidden in a small alley, 🏠**Dveri ❸**, Prote Bakovice 12, serves authentic Bosnian food, and has vegetarian options. From Baščaršija, walk up Ferhadija and turn right at the first side street; the alley is on your left. (Entrees 7-15KM. Open M-Sa 11am-4pm and 7-11pm.) Scour the Turkish Quarter for **čevabdžinića** (kebab) shops; **Čevabdžinića Željo ❷**, Kundurdžiluk 19, is the most popular. (Čevap 4KM. Open daily 8am-10:30pm.)

🔲 **SIGHTS.** The **Eternal Flame,** where Maršala Tita splits into Ferhadija and Mula Mustafe Bašeskije, was lit in 1945 as a memorial to all Sarajevans who died in WWII; its homage to South Slav unity now seems painfully ironic. Within the city center, reconstruction has hidden most signs of the recent siege, but the glaring **treeline** in the hills still marks the war's front lines; Bosnians trapped in Sarajevo cut down all the safely available wood for winter heat. From Maršala Tita, walk toward the river to Obala Kulina Bana and turn left to find the **National Library,** at the tip of the Turkish Quarter. Once Sarajevo's most beautiful building, the library was firebombed on August 25, 1992, the centennial of its construction. As the building burned, citizens risked their lives to salvage the library's treasures, but most of the collection was destroyed. Walk toward the center to the second bridge on Obala Kulina Bana, where Serbian terrorist Gavrilo Princip shot the Austrian Archduke Franz Ferdinand on June 28, 1914, triggering WWI.

The places of worship for various religions huddle together in the city center. Walk right at the Eternal Flame on Ferhadija, which becomes Sarači, to find the 16th-century **Gazi Husrev-Bey mosque,** Sarači 12, one of Sarajevo's most famous buildings. Inside, brightly-colored Bosnian carpets compliment intricate designs on the walls and dome. (Women must cover their head and shoulders. Open daily 9am-noon, 2:30-4pm, and 5:30-7pm. 1KM.) The low, red-roofed buildings surrounding the mosque make up **Baščaršija,** the Turkish Quarter, whose centerpiece is its traditional bazaar. At Mula Mustafe Bašerskije 23, directly across from the Catholic Cathedral, **The Bosniak Institut** (Bošnjački Institut) seeks to link the past with the present. This former *hamam* houses an impressive collection of Bosniak artwork, artifacts, clothing, and furniture, while a library containing periodicals, monographs, manuscripts, and over 100,000 books related to the history of the Bosnian Muslim community fills the six floors of the high-rise. (☎ 27 98 00. Open July-Aug. daily 8am-2pm; Sept.-June Sa 8am-2pm. Free.) The **National Museum** and the **History Museum** are at Zmaja od Bosne 3 and 5, respectively. The former, one of the Balkans's most famous museums, just received a facelift, though some exhibits will continue to be under construction until early 2004; the latter houses contemporary art, much of which pertains to the recent siege of the city. (National Museum open Tu-F, Su 10am-2pm. 5KM, students 1KM. History Museum open M-F 9am-2pm, Sa-Su 9am-1pm. Free.) Next to the National Museum, the shattered tower of the **Parliament Building** is a shocking reminder of what most of Sarajevo looked like following the recent war. In 1992, a peace rally began from Parliament and marched on ul. Vrbanja across the bridge; Serb snipers opened fire, causing the first casualties of the war. A small monument to the victims can now be found at the side of the bridge.

🔲🔲 **ENTERTAINMENT AND NIGHTLIFE.** Sarajevo has begun a steady ascent toward its former position as the cultural capital of the Balkans. For a monthly schedule of theater, opera, ballet, and concert events, stop by the Tourist Information Center (p. 135) and pick up a **Program of Cultural Events** (Program Kulturnih Događaja). Sarajevo's revived **National Theater** (Narodno Pozorište Sarajevo), Obala Kulina Bana 9, hosts theater, opera, ballet, and concert events. From the

Eternal Flame, walk down Maršala Tita to Kulovića and take a left; one block down on the left is Pozorišni Trg (Theater Square); enter on Branilaca Sarajeva. (☎22 16 82; www.npsa.org. Box office open daily 9am-noon and 4-7:30pm.) Every summer in July, the Turkish Quarter hosts the **Turkish Nights** (Baščaršija Noci) featuring open-air music, theater, and film. In late August, the **Sarajevo Film Festival** rolls into theaters throughout the city. (☎22 15 16; www.sff.ba. Box office open in summer M-F 9am-6pm. 4-5KM per film.) Sarajevo also holds the annual **Sarajevan Winter** (Sarajevska Zima; ☎20 79 48) from February 7 to March 21; this celebration of art and culture persisted even through the siege. **Futura 2004** features techno and house raves in mid to late July. There are always underground events going on; the best way to find out about them is by word of mouth. Cafes along **Ferhadija** and **Maršala Tita** are popular, but the best nightlife is found in clubs along **Štrosmajerova** and basement bars on **Baščaršija.** At Mula Mustafe Bašeskije 5, through an unmarked door near the Eternal Flame, ▩**Jazz Bar "Clou"** plays the best music in town and hosts local bands on Friday and Saturday nights. (Beer 3-4KM. Open daily 8:30pm-5am.)

BRITAIN

Having spearheaded the Industrial Revolution, colonized two-fifths of the globe, and won every foreign war in its history but two, Britain seems intent on making the world forget its tiny size. But this small island nation is just that: small. The rolling farms of the south and the rugged cliffs of the north are only a day's train ride apart, and peoples as diverse as London clubbers, Cornish miners, Welsh students, and Gaelic monks all occupy a land area half the size of Spain. Beyond the stereotypical snapshots of Merry Olde England—gabled cottages with flowery borders, tweed-clad farmers shepherding their flocks—Britain today is a cosmopolitan destination driven by international energy. Though the sun may have set on the British Empire, its legacy survives in multicultural urban centers and a dynamic arts and theater scene. Brits eat kebab as often as they do scones, and five-story dance clubs in post-industrial settings draw as much attention as fairy-tale country homes with picturesque views.

Travelers should be aware that names hold political force. "Great Britain" refers to England, Scotland, and Wales; the term "United Kingdom" refers to these nations as well as Northern Ireland. *Let's Go* uses the term "Britain" to refer to England, Scotland, and Wales because of legal and currency distinctions.

FACTS AND FIGURES

Official Name: United Kingdom of Great Britain and Northern Ireland.
Capital: London.
Major Cities: Cardiff, Glasgow, Edinburgh, Liverpool, Manchester.
Population: 60,000,000.

Land Area: 241,590 sq. km
Time Zone: GMT.
Language: English; also Welsh, Scottish, and Gaelic.
Religions: Anglican and Roman Catholic (72%), Muslim (3%), other (25%).

DISCOVER BRITAIN

London (p. 144) brims with cultural wonders. Don't miss a trip to Tate Modern, which mixes the work of Andy Warhol with that of Monet in a dizzying cultural blender. Southwest of London, the lovely **Winchester** (p. 177) celebrates Jane Austen; prehistoric **Stonehenge** (p. 178) and the cathedral at **Salisbury** (p. 177) sit close by. The rich and famous of Georgian England once flocked to **Bath** (p. 178) for Roman-style healing; visitors head there today for both the ruins and the elegantly preserved mansions. *Let's Go* can't promise that a visit to **Oxford** (p. 181), **Cambridge** (p. 187), and the Shakespeare-crazy **Stratford-Upon-Avon** (p. 184) will make you smarter, but the fascinating history of the three towns makes it worth a try. All you need is love in **Liverpool** (p. 190), which basks in Beatle-mania, and all you'll need is a camera in the dramatic **Lake District National Park** (p. 196). In Wales, commune with nature in **Snowdonia National Park** (p. 201) while in **Cardiff** (p. 198) experience the city's revitalization firsthand at one of is many theaters, clubs, or pubs. Farther north in Scotland, enjoy the cultural capitals of **Edinburgh** (p. 204) and **Glasgow** (p. 212), then head to **Loch Ness** (p. 217), where Nessie is said to await.

ESSENTIALS

WHEN TO GO

It may be wise to plan around the high season (June-Aug.). Spring or autumn (Apr.-May and Sept.-Oct.) are more appealing times to visit; the weather is still reasonable and flights are cheaper, though there may be fewer services in rural areas. If you intend to visit the large cities and linger indoors at museums and theaters, the off season (Nov.-Mar.) is most economical. Keep in mind, however, that sights and accommodations often close or run reduced hours, especially in rural regions. Another factor to consider is hours of daylight—in Scotland, summer light lasts almost to midnight, but in winter the sun may set as early as 3:45pm. Regardless of when you go, it will rain; have warm, waterproof clothing on hand.

DOCUMENTS AND FORMALITIES

VISAS. EU citizens do not need a visa. Citizens of Australia, Canada, New Zealand, South Africa, and the US do not need a visa for stays up to six months.

EMBASSIES. Foreign embassies for Britain are in London 144. For British embassies and high commissions at home, contact: **Australia,** British High Commission, Commonwealth Ave., Yarralumla, Canberra, ACT 2606 (☎02 6270 6666; www.uk.emb.gov.au); **Canada,** British High Commission, 80 Elgin St., Ottawa, ON K1P 5K7 (☎613 237 1530; www.britain-in-canada.org); **Ireland,** British Embassy, 29 Merrion Rd., Ballsbridge, Dublin 4 (☎01 205 3700; www.britishembassy.ie); **New Zealand,** British High Commission, 44 Hill St., Thorndon, Wellington 1 (☎04 924 2888; www.britain.org.nz); **South Africa,** British High Commission, 91 Parliament St., Cape Town 8001 (☎021 405 2400); **US,** British Embassy, 3100 Massachusetts Ave. NW, Washington, D.C. 20008 (☎202-588-6500; www.britainusa.com).

TRANSPORTATION

BY PLANE. Most flights into Britain that originate outside Europe land at London's Heathrow and Gatwick airports (p. 144). Some fly directly to regional airports such as Manchester or Edinburgh (p. 204).

BY TRAIN. For info on getting to Britain from the Continent, see p.48. Britain's train network is extensive. Prices and schedules often change; find up-to-date information from **National Rail Inquiries** (☎(08457) 484 950) or online at **Railtrack** (www.railtrack.co.uk; schedules only). The **BritRail Pass,** only sold outside Britain, allows unlimited travel in England, Wales, and Scotland (8-day US$270, under 26 US$219; 22-day US$515, under 26 US$360); in Canada and the US, contact **Rail Europe** (Canada ☎800-361-7245; US ☎877-456-7245; www.raileurope.com). Rail discount cards, available at rail stations and through travel agents, grant 33% off most fares and are available to those ages 16-25 and full-time students (£18), seniors (£18), and families (£20). **Eurail** is not valid in Britain.

BY BUS. The British distinguish between **buses,** which cover short local routes, and **coaches,** which cover long distances; *Let's Go* uses the term "buses" to refer to both. **National Express** (☎(08705) 808 080; www.gobycoach.co.uk) is the principal long-distance coach service operator in Britain, although **Scottish Citylink** (☎(08705) 505 050) has coverage in Scotland. **Discount Coachcards** (£9) are available for seniors over 50, students, and young persons ages 16-25; they reduce fares on National Express by about 30%. The **Tourist Trail Pass** offers unlimited travel for a number of days within a given period (2 days out of 3 £49, students, seniors, and children £39; 5 of 30 £85/£69; 8 of 30 £135/£99; 15 of 30 £190/£145).

BY FERRY. Several ferry lines provide service between Britain and the Continent. Ask for discounts; ISIC holders can sometimes get student fares, and Eurail passholders can get reductions and free trips. Book ahead June through August. For information on boats from Wales to Dublin and Rosslare, Ireland, see p. 198; from Scotland to Belfast, see p. 203; from England to the Continent, see p. 49.

BY CAR. To drive, you must be 17 and have a valid license from your home country. Britain is covered by a high-speed system of **motorways** ("M-roads") that connect London with other major cities. Visitors may not be accustomed to driving on the left, and automatic transmission is rare (and more expensive) in rental cars. Roads are well-maintained, but parking in London is impossible and traffic is slow.

BY BIKE AND BY THUMB. Much of Britain's countryside is well suited for **bik-ing.** Many cities and villages have bike rental shops and maps of local cycle routes. Large-scale Ordnance Survey maps, often available at tourist offices, detail the extensive system of long-distance **hiking** paths. Tourist offices and National Park Information Centres can provide extra information about routes. Hitchhiking is illegal on M-roads; *Let's Go* does not recommend hitchhiking.

TOURIST SERVICES AND MONEY

EMERGENCY	Police: ☎999. Ambulance: ☎999. Fire: ☎999.

TOURIST OFFICES. The **British Tourist Authority** (BTA; www.visitbritain.com) is an umbrella organization for the separate tourist boards outside the UK. **Tourist offices** within Britain usually stock maps and information on sights and accommodations.

MONEY. The **pound sterling** is the main unit of currency in the United Kingdom. It is divided into 100 pence, issued in standard denominations of 1p, 2p, 5p, 10p, 20p, 50p, and £1 in coins, and £5, £10, £20, and £50 in notes. Scotland has its own bank notes, which can be used interchangeably with English currency, though you may have difficulty using Scottish £1 notes outside Scotland. Expect to spend any-where from £25-50 per day. London in particular is a budget-buster, with the bare minimum for accommodations, food, and transport costing £30-40. **Tips** in restau-rants are often included in the bill, sometimes as a "service charge." If gratuity is not included, you should tip 10-15%. Tipping the barman in pubs is not at all expected, though a waiter should be tipped. Taxi drivers should receive a 10-15% tip, and bellhops and chambermaids usually expect somewhere between £1 and £3. Aside from open-air markets, don't expect to **bargain.** The European Union imposes a **value-added tax (VAT)** on goods and services purchased within the EU, which is included in the price (p. 16).

AUS$1 = UK£0.41	UK£1 = AUS$2.41
CDN$1 = UK£0.46	UK£1 = CDN$2.20
EUR€1 = UK£0.69	UK£1 = EUR€1.44
NZ$1 = UK£0.37	UK£1 = NZ$2.70
ZAR1 = UK£0.09	UK£1 = ZAR11.70
US$1 = UK£0.64	UK£1 = US$1.57

BRITISH POUNDS

COMMUNICATION

PHONE CODES	**Country code: 44. International dialing prefix: 00.** From outside Britain, dial int'l dialing prefix (see inside back cover) + 44 + city code + local number.

TELEPHONES. Most public pay phones in Britain are run by **British Telecom (BT).** BT no longer offers phonecards, but chargecards can be purchased that bill directly to your credit card. Public phones charge a minimum of 10p and don't accept 1p, 2p, or 5p coins. Mobile phone are an increasingly popular and eco-nomical alternative (p. 36). For **operator assistance,** dial ☎192. International direct dial numbers include: **AT&T,** ☎0800 013 0011; **British Telecom,** ☎0800 345 144; **Canada Direct,** ☎0800 890 016; **MCI,** ☎0800 890 222; **Sprint,** ☎0800 890 877; and **Telkom South Africa,** ☎0800 890 027.

MAIL. To send a postcard or letter within Europe costs £0.37; a postcard to any other international destination costs £0.40, while a letter costs £0.65. Address mail to be held according to the following example: Firstname SURNAME, *Poste Restante*, New Bond St. Post Office, Bath BA1 1A5, UK.

INTERNET ACCESS. Britain is one of the world's most wired countries. Cybercafes can be found in larger cities. They cost £4-6 per hour, but you often pay for only the time used, not for the whole hour. Online guides to cybercafes in Britain and Ireland, updated daily, include the **Cybercafe Search Engine** (http://cybercaptive.com) and **Cybercafes.com** (www.cybercafes.com).

ACCOMMODATIONS AND CAMPING

BRITAIN	❶	❷	❸	❹	❺
ACCOMMODATIONS	under £10	£10-19	£20-30	£31-59	over £60

Hostels are run by the **Youth Hostels Association (YHA) of England and Wales** (www.yha.org.uk) and the **Scottish Youth Hostels Association** (SYHA; www.syha.org.uk). Unless noted as "self-catering," the YHA hostels listed in *Let's Go* offer cooked meals at standard rates (breakfast £3.20, small/standard packed lunch £2.80/£3.65, evening meal £4.15, and children's meals £1.75-2.70). Hostel dorms will cost around £9 in rural areas, £13 in larger cities, and £15-20 in London. You can book **B&Bs** by calling directly, or by asking the local tourist office to help you find accommodations. Tourist offices usually charge a 10% deposit on the first night's or the entire stay's price, deductible from the amount you pay the B&B proprietor; often a flat fee of £1-3 is added on. **Campsites** tend to be privately owned and cost £3-10 per person per night. It is illegal to camp in national parks.

FOOD AND DRINK

BRITAIN	❶	❷	❸	❹	❺
FOOD	under £5	£5-9	£10-14	£15-20	over £21

Most Britons like to start their day off heartily with the famous, cholesterol-filled, meat-anchored English breakfast, served in most B&Bs across the country. The best native dishes for lunch or dinner are roasts—beef, lamb, and Wiltshire hams—and puddings, including the standard Yorkshire. The ploughman's lunch, served in pubs, consists of cheese, bread, and pickles. Fish and chips (french fries) are traditionally drowned in malt vinegar and salt. To escape English food, try Chinese, Greek, or Indian cuisine. British "tea" refers to both a drink and a social ritual. The refreshment is served strong and milky. An afternoon tea might include cooked meats, salad, sandwiches, and pastries. Cream tea, a specialty of Cornwall and Devon, includes toast, shortbread, crumpets, scones, jam, and clotted cream.

HOLIDAYS AND FESTIVALS

Holidays: New Year's Day (Jan. 1); Good Friday (Apr. 9); Easter Sunday and Monday (Apr. 11 and 12); May Day (May 1); Bank Holiday (May 31); and Christmas (Dec. 25).

Festivals: One of the largest festivals in the world is the **Edinburgh International Festival** (Aug. 15-Sept. 4); also highly recommended is the **Fringe Festival** (Aug. 3-25). Manchester's Gay Village hosts **Mardi Gras** (late Aug.). Muddy fun abounds at the **Glastonbury Festival,** Britain's biggest homage to rocks (June 27-29).

ENGLAND

In a land where the stately once prevailed, conservatism has been booted in two successive elections and a wild profusion of the avant-garde has emerged from hallowed academic halls. The country that once determined the meaning of "civilised" now takes many of its cultural cues from former fledgling colonies. The vanguard of art, music, film, and eclecticism, England is a youthful, hip nation looking forward. But traditionalists can rest easy; for all the moving and shaking in the large cities, around the corner there are handfuls of quaint towns, dozens of picturesque castles, and scores of comforting cups of tea.

LONDON   ☎ 020

London offers the visitor a bewildering array of choices: Leonardo at the National or Hirst at Tate Modern; tea at Brown's or chilling in the Fridge; Rossini at the Royal Opera or Les Mis at the Palace; Bond Street couture or Covent Garden cutting-edge—you could spend your entire stay just deciding what to do and what to leave out. The London "buzz" is continually on the move—every few years a previously disregarded neighborhood explodes into cultural prominence. In the 1960s Soho and Chelsea swung the world; the late 80s saw grunge rule the roost from Camden; and in the 90s the East End unleashed Damien Hirst and the Britpack artists. More recently, South London has come to prominence with the cultural rebirth of the South Bank and the thumping nightlife of a recharged Brixton.

✈ INTERCITY TRANSPORTATION

Flights: Heathrow (LON; ☎(0870) 000 0123) is London's main airport. The **Piccadilly Line** heads from the airport to central London (45min.-1hr.; every 4-5min.; £3.70, under-16 £1.50). The expensive **Heathrow Express** train speeds to Paddington (15min.; every 15min.; £14, round-trip £25). From **Gatwick Airport** (LGW; ☎(0870) 000 2468), the **Gatwick Express** heads to Victoria (30min., every 15min., round-trip £22), as do cheaper **Connex** commuter trains (40min.; £8.20, round-trip £17).

Trains: London has 8 major stations: **Charing Cross** (serves south England); **Euston** (the northwest); **King's Cross** (the northeast); **Liverpool St.** (East Anglia); **Paddington** (the west and south Wales); **St. Pancras** (the Midlands and the northwest); **Victoria** (the south); and **Waterloo** (the south, the southwest and the Continent). All stations are linked by the Underground (Tube). Itineraries involving a change of stations in London usually include a cross-town transfer by Tube. Get info at the station ticket office or from the **National Rail Enquiries Line** (☎(08457) 484 950; www.britrail.com).

Buses: Long-distance buses (known as **coaches** in the UK) arrive in London at **Victoria Coach Station,** 164 Buckingham Palace Rd. (☎7730 3466). Tube: Victoria. Some services stop at nearby **Eccleston Bridge,** behind Victoria train station.

◆ ORIENTATION

The heart of London is the vaguely defined **West End,** which stretches east from Park Lane to Kingsway and south from Oxford St. to the River Thames; within this area you'll find aristocratic **Mayfair,** the shopping streets around **Oxford Circus,** the bars and clubs of **Soho,** and the street performers and boutiques of **Covent Garden.**

Heading east of the West End, you'll pass legalist **Holborn** before hitting the ancient **City of London** (a.k.a. "the City"), the site of the original Roman settlement and home to St. Paul's Cathedral and the Tower of London. The City's eastern border jostles the ethnically diverse, working-class **East End.**

Westminster encompasses the grandeur of **Trafalgar Square** and extends south along the Thames; this is the heart of royal and political London, with the Houses of Parliament, Buckingham Palace, and Westminster Abbey. Farther west lies rich, snooty **Chelsea.** Across the river from Westminster and the West End, the **South Bank** has an incredible variety of entertainment and museums, from Shakespeare's Globe Theatre to the Tate Modern. The enormous expanse of **Hyde Park** lies to the west of the West End; along its southern border lies chic **Knightsbridge**, home to Harrods and Harvey Nicks, and posh **Kensington.** North of Hyde Park is the media-infested **Notting Hill** and the B&B-filled **Bayswater.** Bayswater, Mayfair, and **Marylebone** meet at Marble Arch, on Hyde Park's northeast corner; from there, Marylebone stretches west to meet academic **Bloomsbury**, north of Soho and Holborn. **Camden Town, Islington, Hampstead,** and **Highgate** lie to the north of Bloomsbury and the City. A good street atlas is essential for efficient navigation; the best is ■ *London A to Z,* available at bookstores and newsstands (£5).

■ LOCAL TRANSPORTATION

Public Transportation: Run by Transport for London (TfL; 24hr. info ☎ 7222 1234; www.tfl.gov.uk). Pick up maps at all Tube stations; TfL **Information Centres** at Euston; Heathrow Terminals 1, 2, and 3; Liverpool St.; Oxford Circus; Paddington; Piccadilly Circus; St. James's Park; and Victoria also offer guides.

Underground: The Underground (a.k.a. the **Tube**) network is divided into 6 concentric zones; fares depend on the number of zones crossed. Buy your ticket before you board and pass it through automatic gates at both ends of your journey. A one-way trip in Zone 1 costs £1.60. The Tube runs approx. 5:30am-12:30am, depending on the line; always check the last train times. See the color maps section of this book.

Buses: Divided into 4 zones. Zones 1-3 are identical to the Tube zones. Fares 70p-£1. Buses run 6am-midnight, after which a limited network of **Night Buses,** prefixed by an "N," take over.

Passes: The **Travelcard** is valid for travel on all TfL services. Daily, weekend, weekly, monthly, and annual cards. 1-day Travelcard from £5.10 (Zones 1-2). Passes expire at 4:30am the morning after their printed expiration date.

Licensed Taxicabs: An illuminated "taxi" sign on the roof of a black cab signals availability. Expensive, but drivers know their stuff. Tip 10%. For pick-up (min. £2 extra charge), call **Computer Cabs** (☎ 7286 0286), **Dial-a-Cab** (☎ 7253 5000), or **Radio Taxis** (☎ 7272 0272).

Minicabs: Private cars. Cheaper than black cabs, but less reliable—stick to a reputable company. **Teksi** (☎ 7267 0267) offers 24hr. pick-up anywhere in London.

■ PRACTICAL INFORMATION

TOURIST, FINANCIAL, AND LOCAL SERVICES

Tourist Offices: Britain Visitor Centre, 1 Regent St. (www.visitbritain.com). Tube: Oxford Circus. Open M 9:30am-6:30pm, Tu-F 9am-6:30pm, Sa-Su 10am-4pm. **London Visitor Centres** (www.londontouristboard.com). Tube branches at: **Heathrow Terminals 1, 2,** and **3** (open Oct.-Aug. daily 8am-6pm; Sept. M-Sa 9am-7pm and Su 8am-6pm); **Liverpool St.** (open June-Sept. M-Sa 8am-7pm, Su 8am-6pm; Oct.-May daily 8am-6pm); **Victoria** (open Easter-Sept. M-Sa 8am-8pm, Su 8am-6pm; Oct.-Easter daily 8am-6pm); **Waterloo** (open daily 8:30am-10:30pm).

BRITAIN

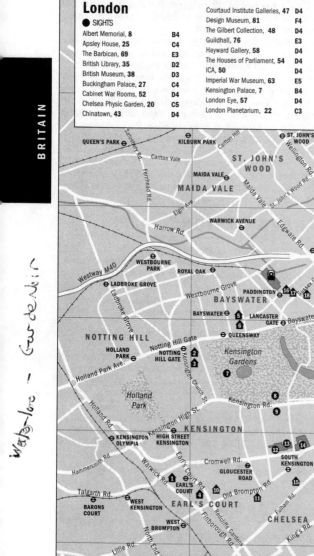

London

● SIGHTS

Albert Memorial, **8**	B4
Apsley House, **25**	C4
The Barbican, **69**	E3
British Library, **35**	D2
British Museum, **38**	D3
Buckingham Palace, **27**	C4
Cabinet War Rooms, **52**	D4
Chelsea Physic Garden, **20**	C5
Chinatown, **43**	D4
Courtaud Institute Galleries, **47**	D4
Design Museum, **81**	F4
The Gilbert Collection, **48**	D4
Guildhall, **76**	E3
Hayward Gallery, **58**	D4
The Houses of Parliament, **54**	D4
ICA, **50**	D4
Imperial War Museum, **63**	E5
Kensington Palace, **7**	B4
London Eye, **57**	D4
London Planetarium, **22**	C3
London Transport Museum, **42**	D3
Madame Tussaud's, **23**	C3
Marble Arch, **19**	C3
Millennium Bridge, **72**	E4
Monument, **77**	F4
Museum of London, **70**	E3
National Gallery, **45**	D4
National Portrait Gallery, **44**	D4
Natural History Museum, **12**	B5
National Gallery, **45**	D4
Royal Academy, **32**	D4
Royal Albert Hall, **9**	B4
Royal Courts of Justice, **61**	E3

BRITAIN

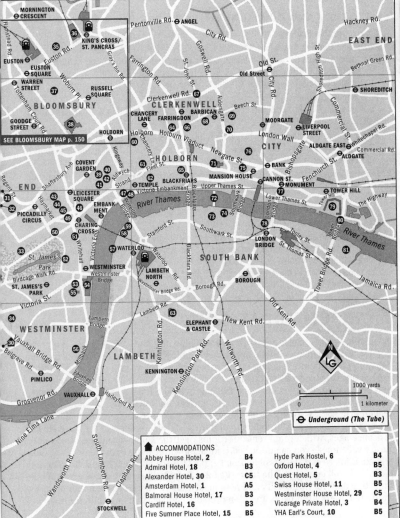

The Royal Hospital, 21	C5	St. Paul's Cathedral, 71	E3	The Temple, 62	E3
The Royal Mews, 28	C4	St. Paul's Church, 41	D3	Theatre Royal, Dury Lane, 40	D3
Royal Opera House, 39	D3	Savile Row, 31	D3	Tower Bridge, 80	F4
St. Bartholomew the Great, 68	E3	Science Museum, 13	B5	The Tower of London, 79	F4
St. Bride's, 65	E3	Shakespeare's Globe		Trafalgar Square, 49	D4
St. Ethelreda's, 64	E3	Theatre, 74	E4	University College London, 37	D3
St. James's Palace, 33	D4	Sir John Soane's Museum, 60	E3	Victoria and Albert Museum, 14	B5
St. John's Square, 67	E3	Smithfield Market, 66	E3	The Wallace Collection, 24	C3
St. Margaret's Westminster, 53	D4	South Bank Centre, 59	D4	The Wellington Arch, 26	C4
St. Martin-in-the-Fields, 46	D4	Southwark Cathedral, 78	E4	Westminster Abbey, 55	D4
St. Mary-le-Bow, 75	E3	Tate Britain, 54	D5	Westminster Cathedral, 34	D5
St. Pancras Station, 36	D2	Tate Modern, 73	E4	Whitehall, 51	D4

⊖ Underground (The Tube)

⌂ ACCOMMODATIONS			
Abbey House Hotel, 2	B4	Hyde Park Hostel, 6	B4
Admiral Hotel, 18	B3	Oxford Hotel, 4	B5
Alexander Hotel, 30	C5	Quest Hotel, 5	B3
Amsterdam Hotel, 1	A5	Swiss House Hotel, 11	B5
Balmoral House Hotel, 17	B3	Westminster House Hotel, 29	C5
Cardiff Hotel, 16	B3	Vicarage Private Hotel, 3	B4
Five Sumner Place Hotel, 15	B5	YHA Earl's Court, 10	B5

Embassies: Australia, Australia House, Strand (☎7379 4334). Tube: Temple. Open M-F 9:30am-3:30pm. **Canada,** MacDonald House, 1 Grosvenor Sq. (☎7258 6600). Tube: Bond St. Open M-F 9am-5pm. **Ireland,** 17 Grosvenor Pl. (☎7235 2171). Tube: Hyde Park Corner. Open M-F 9:30am-4:30pm. **New Zealand,** New Zealand House, 80 Haymarket (☎7930 8422). Tube: Piccadilly Circus. Open M-F 10am-5pm. **South Africa,** South Africa House, Trafalgar Sq. (☎7451 7299). Tube: Charing Cross. Open M-F 9am-5pm. **US,** 24 Grosvenor Sq. (☎7499 9000). Tube: Bond St. Open M-F 8:30am-5:30pm. Phones answered 8am-10pm.

Financial Services: The best rates for **currency exchange** are found at banks, such as **Barclays, HSBC, Lloyd's,** and **National Westminster** (NatWest). **Branches** open M-F 9:30am-4:30pm. Call ☎(0800) 521 313 for the nearest **American Express** location.

Bi-Gay-Lesbian Resources: London Lesbian and Gay Switchboard (☎7837 7324). 24hr. advice and support service.

EMERGENCY AND COMMUNICATIONS

Emergency: Medical, Police, and **Fire** ☎999; no coins required.

Hospitals: Charing Cross (☎8846 1234), on Fulham Palace Rd.; enter on St. Dunstan's Rd. Tube: Baron's Ct. or Hammersmith. **Royal Free** (☎7794 0500), on Pond St. Tube: Belsize Park. **St. Thomas's** (☎7928 9292), on Lambeth Palace Rd. Tube: Waterloo. **University College Hospital** (☎7387 9300), on Grafton Way. Tube: Warren St.

Pharmacies (Chemists): Most pharmacies keep standard hours (usually M-Sa 9:30am-5:30pm). Late-night and 24hr. chemists are rare; one 24hr. option is **Zafash Pharmacy,** 233 Old Brompton Rd. (☎7373 2798). Tube: Earl's Ct.

Police: London is covered by two police forces: The **City of London Police** (☎7601 2222) for the City, and the **Metropolitan Police** (☎7230 1212) for the rest. There is at least one police station in each borough open 24hr. Call to locate the nearest one.

Internet Access: Try the ubiquitous **easyEverything** (☎7241 9000). Locations include: 9-16 Tottenham Court Rd. (Tube: Tottenham Court Rd.); 456/459 The Strand (Tube: Charing Cross); 358 Oxford St. (Tube: Bond St.); 9-13 Wilson Rd. (Tube: Victoria); 160-166 Kensington High St. (Tube: High St. Kensington). Prices (from £1 per hr.; £2 min. charge) vary with demand. All open 24hr.

Post Office: Post offices are everywhere; call ☎(08457) 740 740 for locations. When sending mail to London, be sure to include the full postal code, since London has 7 King's Roads, 8 Queen's Roads, and many other opportunities for misdirected mailings. The largest office is the **Trafalgar Square Post Office,** 24-28 William IV St. (☎7484 9304). Tube: Charing Cross. All mail sent *Poste Restante* to unspecified post offices ends up here. Open M-Th and Sa 8am-8pm, F 8:30am-8pm. **Postal Code:** WC2N 4DL.

▐ ACCOMMODATIONS

No matter where you plan to stay, it is essential to plan ahead, especially in summer; London accommodations are almost always booked solid. Be sure to check the cancellation policy before handing over the deposit; some are non-refundable. **Hostels** are not always able to accommodate every written request for reservations, much less on-the-spot inquiries, but they frequently hold a few beds—it's always worth checking. Sheets are included at all YHA hostels, but towels are not; buy one from reception ($3.50). YHA hostels also sell discount tickets to theaters and major attractions. No YHA hostels have lockouts or curfews. The best deals in town are **student residence halls,** which often rent out rooms over the summer and, less frequently, Easter vacations—you can often get a single for a little more than the price of a hostel bed. Book as early as possible. Don't expect luxury, although rooms are generally clean and well equipped. The term **"Bed and Breakfast"** encompasses accommodations of wildly varying quality and personality, often with little relation to price. Be aware that in-room showers are often prefabricated units jammed into a corner.

BAYSWATER

The streets between **Queensway** and **Paddington** station house London's highest concentration of cheap accommodations, with countless hostels, B&Bs, and budget hotels. The neighborhood is fairly central, with plenty of nearby restaurants, but accommodations vary in quality—be sure to see a room first.

HOSTELS

Hyde Park Hostel, 2-6 Inverness Terr. (☎7229 5101; www.astorhostels.com). Tube: Queensway or Bayswater. Crowded backpacker hostel with flimsy mattresses, but tons of fun. Big dorms are more spacious. Kitchen, bar, and lounge available. Continental breakfast and sheets included. Laundry facilities. Internet access. Ages 16-35 only. Reserve at least 2 weeks ahead. Dorms £11-17.50; doubles £42-45. MC/V. ❷

Quest Hostel, 45 Queensborough Terr. (☎7229 7782; www.astorhostels.com). Tube: Queensway or Bayswater. Offers good beds and more personal space, but dorms without bath could be 2 floors from a shower. Kitchen available. Continental breakfast and sheets included. Laundry facilities. Dorms £14-16; doubles £40. MC/V. ❷

B&BS AND HOTELS

Admiral Hotel, 143 Sussex Gdns. (☎7723 7309; www.admiral-hotel.com). Tube: Paddington. Beautifully kept B&B. 19 summery, non-smoking rooms with bath and tea kettle. Singles £45; doubles £65; triples £90; quads £100; quints £120. MC/V. ❹

Balmoral House Hotel, 156-157 Sussex Gdns. (☎7723 4925; www.balmoralhousehotel.co.uk). Tube: Paddington. Classy establishment with low prices. All rooms with bath, kettle, and hair dryer. English breakfast included. Singles £40; doubles £65; triples £80; quads £100; quints £120. MC/V (5% surcharge). ❹

Cardiff Hotel, 5-9 Norfolk Sq. (☎7723 9068; www.cardiff-hotel.com). Tube: Paddington. All rooms have kettle and phone. Enthusiastic staff and elegant, reasonably sized rooms. Singles are small. English breakfast included. 48hr. cancellation policy. Singles with shower £49, with bath £55-69; doubles with bath £79; triples with bath £90; quads with bath £110. MC/V. ❹

BLOOMSBURY AND MARYLEBONE

Bloomsbury's proximity to Soho makes it well suited for those who want to stay near nightlife. The neighborhood is also close to the British Museum and plenty of cheap restaurants. Many B&Bs are on busy roads, so be wary of noise levels. The area becomes seedier closer to King's Cross.

HOSTELS AND STUDENT RESIDENCES

▨ The Generator, Compton Pl. (☎7388 7655; www.the-generator.co.uk), off 37 Tavistock Pl. Tube: Russell Sq. In a former police barracks, this is the ultimate party hostel. Basement dorms have lockers and military-style bathrooms. Bar and cafeteria. Internet access. Dorms are 18+. Reserve ahead for weekends. Dorms £15-17; singles £42; doubles £53; triples £68; quads £90. MC/V. ❷

▨ Ashlee House, 261-265 Gray's Inn Rd. (☎7833 9400; www.ashleehouse.co.uk). Tube: King's Cross St. Pancras. Not the best neighborhood, but convenient to nightlife. Quiet and friendly. Steel bunks crammed into clean, bright rooms. Kitchen available. Continental breakfast included. Towels £1. Laundry facilities. Internet access. Dorms £15-19; singles £36; doubles £48. Oct.-Apr. reduced prices. ❷

Indian YMCA, 41 Fitzroy Sq. (☎7387 0411; www.indianymca.org). Tube: Warren St. Standard rooms with desk, phone, and shared bathrooms. Continental breakfast and Indian dinner included. Laundry facilities. Reservations essential. Dorms £20; singles £34; doubles £49, with bath £55. AmEx/MC/V. ❸

BRITAIN

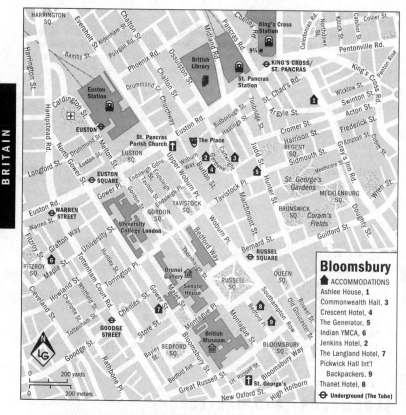

Bloomsbury

📍 ACCOMMODATIONS

Ashlee House, **1**
Commonwealth Hall, **3**
Crescent Hotel, **4**
The Generator, **5**
Indian YMCA, **6**
Jenkins Hotel, **2**
The Langland Hotel, **7**
Pickwick Hall Int'l
  Backpackers, **9**
Thanet Hotel, **8**
⊖ Underground (The Tube)

Pickwick Hall International Backpackers, 7 Bedford Pl. (☎7323 4958). Tube: Russell Sq. or Holborn. 3- to 4-bed single-sex "dorms." Rooms are clean and recently redecorated by the friendly owner. No smoking, no food in dorms, no guests. Kitchen available. Continental breakfast and sheets included. Laundry facilities. Reception 8am-10pm. Reserve 6 weeks ahead for summer. Singles £25; doubles £50 with bathroom; triples £66 with bathroom. Discounts for longer stays. AmEx/MC/V. ❶

International Student House, 229 Great Portland St. (☎7631 8300; www.ish.org.uk). Tube: Great Portland St. A thriving international metropolis. 3 bars, cafeteria, fitness center. Continental breakfast included with private rooms; with dorms £2. Laundry facilities. Internet access. Key deposit £10. Reserve at least 1 month ahead. Dorms £12; singles £31, with bath £33; doubles £50/52; triples £60; quads £72. MC/V. ❷

Commonwealth Hall, 1-11 Cartwright Gdns. (☎7685 3500; cwh@lon.ac.uk). Tube: Russell Sq. Basic student-residence singles. English breakfast included. July-Aug. reserve at least 3 months ahead; no walk-ins. Open Easter (Mar. 22-Apr. 26) and mid-June to mid-Sept. Singles £23, with dinner £27; UK students £20 (dinner included). MC/V. ❸

B&BS AND HOTELS

▓ **Jenkins Hotel,** 45 Cartwright Gdns. (☎7387 2067; www.jenkinshotel.demon.co.uk), enter on Barton Pl. Tube: Euston. Bright, airy, non-smoking rooms with antique-style furniture, phone, fridge, hair dryer, and safe. Guests can use tennis courts. English breakfast included. Reserve 1-2 months ahead. Singles £52, with bath £72; doubles with bath £85; triples with bath £105. MC/V. ❹

▓ **The Langland Hotel,** 29-31 Gower St. (☎7636 5801; www.langlandhotel.com). Tube: Goodge St. Family atmosphere, and sparkling bathrooms cleaned twice a day. All rooms with fan. Singles £40, with bath £55; doubles £50/75; triples £70/90; quads £90/110; quints £100. Discounts for students and in off-season. AmEx/MC/V. ❹

Crescent Hotel, 49-50 Cartwright Gdns. (☎7387 1515; www.crescenthoteloflondon.com). Tube: Russell Sq. Artistic rooms in a family-run atmosphere. All rooms with phone and wash stand. Singles £46, with bath £51-73; doubles with bath £89; triples with bath £99; quads with bath £108. Discounts for longer stays. MC/V. ❹

Thanet Hotel, 8 Bedford Pl., Russell Sq. (☎7636 2869; www.thanethotel.co.uk). Tube: Russell Sq. or Holborn. Bright, clean rooms in this family-run B&B have hair dryer, kettle, phone, and TV. Rooms at the back have a view of the garden. All rooms have private bath. English breakfast included. Reserve 1 month in advance. Singles £69; doubles £94; triples £102; quads £112. AmEx/MC/V. ❺

CLERKENWELL

City University Finsbury Residences, 15 Bastwick St. (☎7040 8811; www.city.ac.uk/ems). Tube: Barbican. Student residence with a tower-block facade but renovated interior. Short walk to City sights, Islington restaurants, and Clerkenwell nightlife. Breakfast included. Dinner £4.70. Open June to mid-Sept. Dorms £21, students £19. MC/V. ❸

KENSINGTON

▓ **Five Sumner Place Hotel,** 5 Sumner Pl. (☎7584 7586; www.sumnerplace.com). Tube: South Kensington. The amenities of a luxury hotel with the charm of a converted Victorian, plus an unbeatable location. Spacious rooms have large windows, private bath, fridge, phone, and hair dryer. English breakfast included. Book 1 month ahead in summer. Singles £85; doubles £130. AmEx/MC/V. ❺

▓ **Swiss House Hotel,** 171 Old Brompton Rd. (☎7373 2769; www.swiss-hh.demon.co.uk). Tube: Gloucester Rd. or South Kensington. Large rooms all with phone, fan, and bath. Continental breakfast included; English breakfast £6.50. In summer, reserve 1 month ahead. Singles £51-71; doubles £89-104; triples £120; quads £134. AmEx/MC/V. ❹

Vicarage Private Hotel, 10 Vicarage Gate (☎7229 4030; www.londonvicaragehotel.com). Tube: High St. Kensington. Beautifully kept house with charming rooms. English breakfast included. Reserve 2 months ahead. Singles £46, with bath £75; doubles £76/100; triples £95/130; quads £102/140. ❹

Abbey House Hotel, 11 Vicarage Gate (☎7727 2594; www.abbeyhousekensington.com). Tube: High St. Kensington. Spacious pastel rooms with desk and sink. Very helpful staff. English breakfast included. Singles £45; doubles £74; triples £90; quads £100. Winter discounts. ❹

EARL'S COURT

West of fashionable Kensington, Earl's Court feeds on budget tourism. The area is especially popular with Australian travelers. Be careful at night, and be cautious of guides trying to lead you from the station to a hostel. Some B&Bs conceal grimy rooms behind fancy lobbies and well-dressed staff; always ask to see a room.

Oxford Hotel, 24 Penywern Rd. (☎7370 1161; www.the-oxford-hotel.com). 3min. from the Connex train to Heathrow or Gatwick. Large rooms with enormous windows afford grand views of the gardens. Continental breakfast included. Reserve 2-3 weeks ahead. Singles with shower £36, with bath £50; doubles £57/67; triples £69/79; quads £87/93; quints £105/115. Discounts for longer stays. AmEx/MC/V. ❹

Amsterdam Hotel, 7 Trebovir Rd. (☎7370 2814; www.amsterdam-hotel.com). Tube: Earl's Court. Suites include kitchenette and lounge. All rooms have private bath, kettle, and phone. Continental breakfast included. Singles £74-82; doubles £84-98; triples £108-112. Suites: studios £98-101; doubles £102-115; triples £129-140; 2-bedroom £150-160. Discounts for longer stays. AmEx/MC/V. ❺

YHA Earl's Court, 38 Bolton Gdns. (☎7373 7083; earlscourt@yha.org.uk). Tube: Earl's Court. Rambling Victorian townhouse better equipped than most YHAs. Garden. Bright single-sex dorms. Breakfast included for doubles. Sheets included. Reserve at least 1 month ahead. Dorms £19; doubles £52; quads £76. AmEx/MC/V. ❷

THE WEST END

High Holborn Residence, 178 High Holborn (☎7379 5589; www.lse.ac.uk/vacations). Tube: Holborn. Comfortable and modern, this is the London School of Economics' best student residence. Suites of 4-5 rooms share phone, kitchen, and bath. Continental breakfast included. Laundry facilities. Open mid-June to late Sept. Singles £30; doubles £48, with bath £58; triples with bath £68. MC/V. ❸

YHA Oxford Street, 14-18 Noel St. (☎(0870) 770 5984; www.yha.org). Tube: Oxford Circus. Limited facilities, but an unbeatable location for Soho nightlife. Continental breakfast £3.40. Reserve 1 month ahead. Dorms £24, under-18 £20; doubles £26. ❸

WESTMINSTER

Quiet **Pimlico,** south of Victoria station, is full of budget hotels; **Belgrave Road** has the highest number. Quality tends to improve farther from the station. Though the area is fairly close to major sights such as Parliament and Buckingham Palace, there's little in the way of restaurants or nightlife.

Alexander Hotel, 13 Belgrave Rd., SW1V 1RB (☎7834 9738; www.alexanderhotel.co.uk). Tube: Victoria. Rooms are lavishly furnished with quality fittings, oak dressers, and comfy beds. Sunny breakfast room. Prices vary according to demand. Singles £45; doubles £65; triples from £75; quads and quints £120. MC/V. ❹

Westminster House Hotel, 96 Ebury St. (☎7730 7850; www.westminsterhousehotel.co.uk). Tube: Victoria. The welcoming proprietors keep the 10 rooms spotless. Almost all with private bath. English breakfast included. Singles £50, with bath £55; doubles £70/80; triples with bath £90; quads with bath £100. AmEx/MC/V. ❹

⬛ FOOD

Forget stale stereotypes: In terms of quality and choice, London's restaurants offer a gastronomic experience as diverse, stylish, and satisfying as you'll find, albeit an expensive one. An entree under £10 is regarded as "cheap"; add drinks and service and you're nudging £15. Special offers at lunchtime and in the early evening make it possible to dine in style and stay on budget. For the best ethnic food, head to the source: Whitechapel for Bengali *baltis*, Islington for Turkish *meze*, Marylebone for Lebanese *schwarma*, and Soho for Cantonese *dim sum*.

BAYSWATER

▨ **Aphrodite Taverna,** 15 Hereford Rd. (☎ 7229 2206). Tube: Bayswater. The owners' 20 years of experience is everywhere apparent in this warm Greek restaurant. Entrees £7-10. Chef specials £10-24. The cafe next door has some cheaper specialties. Restaurant open M-Sa noon-midnight. Cafe open daily 8am-5pm. AmEx/MC/V. ❷

▨ **La Bottega del Gelato,** 127 Bayswater Rd. (☎ 7243 2443). Tube: Queensway. Now in his 70s, Quinto Barbieri still makes the best *gelati* this side of the Rubicon. Scoops from £1.60. Open daily 10am-7pm, later in summer. Cash only. ❶

BLOOMSBURY AND MARYLEBONE

▨ **ECCo (Express Coffee Co.),** 46 Goodge St. (☎ 7580 9250). 11-inch thin-crust pizzas, made to order, cost an incredible £3.50. Sandwiches and baguettes from £1.50. Rolls 50p. Buy any hot drink before noon and get a free croissant. Pizzas available after noon. Open M-Sa 7am-11pm, Su 9am-11pm. ❶

▨ **Mandalay,** 444 Edgware Rd. (☎ 7258 3696). Tube: Edgware Rd. Looks ordinary, tastes extraordinary; this Burmese restaurant's wall is plastered with awards. Great lunch specials (curry and rice £3.70; 3-courses £5.90). Entrees £3-5. No smoking. Open M-Sa noon-2:30pm and 6-10:30pm. AmEx/MC/V. ❶

Patogh, 8 Crawford Pl. (☎ 7262 4015). Tube: Edgware Rd. Out of proportion portions in the tiny Iranian space; order 'bread' and get a 14 in. flatbread with sesame seeds and subtle spices, just £1.50. Entrees £4-6. Open daily noon-midnight. Cash only. ❶

THE CITY OF LONDON

▨ **Cafe Spice Namaste,** 16 Prescot St. (☎ 7488 9242). Tube: Tower Hill. The standard-bearer for a new breed of Indian restaurants. The menu features Goan and Parsee specialities. Meat dishes are pricey (£11-13), but vegetarian meals are a bargain (£7-8). Open M-F noon-3pm and 6:15-10:30pm, Sa 6:30-10pm. AmEx/MC/V. ❷

Futures, 8 Botolph Alley (☎ 7623 4529), off Botolph Ln. Tube: Monument. Suits besiege this tiny takeaway for breakfast (pastries 80p, porridge £1) and later for a variety of vegetarian dishes (£2-4). Open M-F 7:30-10am and 11:30am-3pm. ❶

HOLBORN AND CLERKENWELL

▨ **Bleeding Heart Tavern** (☎ 7404 0333), corner of Greville St. and Bleeding Heart Yard. Tube: Farringdon. Laid-back upstairs pub and cozy restaurant below. Restaurant decor provides a romantic backdrop to hearty English fare, including spit-roasted pork with crackling. Entrees £8-10. Open M-F noon-2:30pm and 6-10:30pm. AmEx/MC/V. ❷

St. John, 26 St. John St. (☎ 7251 0848). Tube: Farringdon. St. John has won countless prizes for its eccentric English cuisine. Prices in the posh restaurant are high (entrees from £13), but you can enjoy similar bounty in the smokehouse bar. Excellent lamb sandwich £5. Roast bone-marrow salad £6. A bakery at the back of the bar churns out fresh loaves for £2.50. Open M-Sa 11am-11pm. MC/V. ❷

KENSINGTON AND EARL'S COURT

▨ **Zaika,** 1 Kensington High St. (☎ 7795 6533). Tube: High St. Kensington. London's best Indian restaurant: Elegant decor, attentive service, and sophisticated food. Appetizers £3-10. Entrees £13-23. Desserts £4-5. 2-course min. for dinner. Lunch fixed menu £12 for 2 courses, £14 for 3. 5-course dinner menu £38, with wine £57. Reservations recommended. Open M-Sa noon-2:45pm and 6:30-10:45pm, Su 6:30-9:45pm. MC/V. ❸

KNIGHTSBRIDGE AND BELGRAVIA

▨ Jenny Lo's Teahouse, 14 Eccleston St. (☎ 7259 0399). Tube: Victoria. Stripped-down Chinese fare at communal tables. *Cha shao* (pork noodle soup) £5.50. Teas (from 65p) are blended in-house and served in hand-turned stoneware. £5 min. Open M-F 11:30am-3pm and 6-10pm, Sa noon-3pm and 6-10pm. ❷

NOTTING HILL

▨ George's Portobello Fish Bar, 329 Portobello Rd. (☎ 8969 7895). Tube: Ladbroke Grove. Choose from the fillets on display or ask them to fry up a new one (£4-5), add a generous helping of chunky chips (£1), and wolf it down outside (no inside seating). Open M-F 11am-midnight, Sa 11am-9pm, Su noon-9pm. ❷

▨ Books for Cooks, 4 Blenheim Crescent (☎ 7221 1992). Tube: Ladbroke Grove. The Chef-owner "tests" recipes from new titles. Offerings change daily, but rely on the cakes (£2). Kitchen open M-Sa 10am-2:30pm. Bookstore open Tu-Sa 10am-6pm. MC/V. ❶

THE SOUTH BANK

▨ Cantina del Ponte, 36c Shad Thames (☎ 7403 5403), Butlers Wharf. Tube: Tower Hill or London Bridge. Amazing riverside location and high-quality Italian food. Bargain fixed menu £11 for 2 courses, £13.50 for 3 (available M-F noon-3pm and 6-7:30pm). Pizzas £7-8. Entrees £12-15. Live Italian music Tu and Th evenings. Open M-Sa noon-3pm and 6-10:45pm, Su noon-3pm and 6-9:45pm. AmEx/MC/V. ❸

▨ Tas, 72 Borough High St. (☎ 7403 7200; Tube: London Bridge) and 33 The Cut (☎ 7928 2111; Tube: Southwark). Stylish and affordable Turkish food. Stews and baked dishes—many vegetarian—outshine the kebabs. Entrees £6-8. Live music from 7:30pm. Reservations essential. Open M-Sa noon-11:30pm, Su noon-10:30pm. AmEx/MC/V. ❷

THE WEST END

▨ busaba eathai, 106-110 Wardour St. (☎ 7255 8686). Tube: Tottenham Court Rd. Wildly popular Thai eatery. Great food (£5-8) at shared tables in a cozy, wood-paneled room. Open M-Th noon-11pm, F-Sa noon-11:30pm, Su noon-10pm. AmEx/MC/V. ❷

▨ Mô, 23 Heddon St. (☎ 7434 3999). Tube: Piccadilly Circus. A little piece of Morocco. Enjoy *tapas*-style dishes £6-7.50. Wash it down with sweet mint tea (£2). Arrive early to avoid lines. Open M-W 11am-11pm, Th-Sa noon-midnight. AmEx/MC/V. ❷

Mr. Kong, 21 Lisle St. (☎ 7437 7341). You can't go wrong at Mr. Kong. Deep-fried Mongolian lamb £6.50. Pig's knuckles £9. £7 min. Open daily noon-3am. AmEx/MC/V. ❷

Café Emm, 17 Frith St. (☎ 7437 0723). Generous portions in an unpretentious bistro setting. Entrees (£6-8) range from enormous salads to rump steak. Open M-Th noon-2:30pm and 5:30-10:30pm, F noon-2:30pm and 5-11:30pm, Sa 1-4pm and 5-11:30pm, Su 1-4pm and 5-11:30pm. ❷

WESTMINSTER

▨ Goya, 34 Lupus St. (☎ 7976 5309). Tube: Pimlico. Corner bar where earnest Spanish waiters serve delicious *tapas* to a chattering crowd. Most *tapas* £4-5; 2-3 per person is enough. Open daily noon-11:30pm. AmEx/MC/V. ❸

NORTH LONDON

▨ Tartuf, 88 Upper St. (☎ 7288 0954). Tube: Angel. Have a fantastic cutlery-free experience with an Alsatian *tarte flambée* (£5-6), a cross between a crepe and a pizza, only much tastier. Before 3pm get 1 savory and 1 sweet *tarte* for £7. All-you-can-eat £12. Open M-Th 6-11pm, Sa noon-midnight, Su noon-11pm. MC/V. ❷

▨ **Gallipoli,** 102 Upper St., and **Gallipoli Again,** 120 Upper St. (☎7359 0630). Tube: Angel. Tiled walls and hanging lamps complement Turkish delights like "Iskender Kebap": Grilled lamb with yogurt and marinated pita bread (£6). Make reservations F-Sa. Open M-Th 10:30am-11pm, F-Sa 10:30am-midnight, Su 10:30am-11pm. MC/V. ❷

Le Crêperie de Hampstead, 77 Hampstead High St. Tube: Hampstead. Watch as delicate crepes like Mushroom Garlic Cream (£3) and Banana Butterscotch Cream Dream (£2.60) are prepared before your eyes. 40p extra gets you gooey Belgian chocolate instead of syrup. Open M-Th 11:45am-11pm, F-Su 11:45am-11:30pm. Cash only. ❶

Carmelli Bakery, 128 Golders Green Rd. (☎8455 2074). Tube: Golders Green. The golden, egg-glazed *challah* (£1.30-1.90) is considered the best in London; the bagels and sinfully good pastries (£1.50) aren't far behind. Packed F afternoons. Hours vary, but usually open daily 6am-1am, Th and Sa open 24hr. ❶

SOUTH LONDON

▨ **Bug** (☎7738 3366) in the crypt of St. Matthew's Church, Brixton Hill. Tube: Brixton. Eerie lighting gives a gothic atmosphere. Prices for the mostly vegetarian and fish entrees are high (£9-11), but Sunday's "Bug Roast" gets you 2 courses for £13.50. Reservations essential. Open Su 1-9pm, Tu-Th 5-11pm, F-Sa 5-11:30pm. MC/V. ❸

Café Bar and Juice Bar, 407 Coldharbour Ln. (☎7738 4141). Tube: Brixton. Plop into a deep leather chair or perch atop a (surprisingly ergonomic) upended bucket in the makeshift bar. Exceptional smoothies, soups, organic quiches, and generous open sandwiches all £4-4.50. Open daily 10am-midnight. MC/V. ❷

WEST LONDON

▨ **Café Zagora,** 38 Devonshire Rd. (☎8742 7922). Tube: Turnham Green. From the Tube, walk south to Chiswick High St.; turn right, then left onto Devonshire Rd. Oozes elegance, from the attentive, discreet service to the warm North African interior. Inexpensive Lebanese-Moroccan cuisine. Appetizers £2.50-4. Entrees £6.50-13. Excellent desserts £3.50. Open daily 5-11pm. MC/V. ❷

AFTERNOON TEA

Afternoon tea is a ritual as much as a meal. It involves a long afternoon of sandwiches, scones, pastries, and restrained conversation. The main attraction of afternoon tea is the chance to lounge in sumptuous surroundings and mingle with the upper crust for a few hours. Most **major hotels** and hoity-toity **department stores** serve tea, but for the ultimate experience, take tea at **Brown's ❺**, Albemarle St. (☎7493 6020. Tube: Green Park.). Brown's was London's first luxury hotel and serves tea (£23) M-F at 3 and 4:45pm, Sa-Su 3-4:45pm; dress is smart casual.

◎ SIGHTS

ORGANIZED TOURS

The classic London **bus tour** is on an open-top double-decker; in good weather, it's undoubtedly the best way to get a good overview of the city. Tickets for the **Big Bus Company,** 48 Buckingham Palace Rd., are valid for 24hr. on three hop-on, hop-off routes, with 1hr. walking tours and a short Thames cruise included. (☎7233 9533; www.bigbus.co.uk. Tube: Victoria. £16, children £6.) For a more in-depth account, you can't beat a **walking tour** led by a knowledgeable guide. **Original London Walks** is the biggest walking-tour company, running 12-16 walks per day, from the "Beatles Magical Mystery Tour" to the nighttime "Jack the Ripper's Haunts" and guided visits to larger museums. Most walks last 2hr. and start from Tube stations. (☎7624 3978; www.walks.com. £5, students and seniors £4. Under-16 free.)

HE LOCAL STORY

THE STRONG SILENT TYPE

After 18 years of stony silence, Simon Knowles of the Queen's Guard finally speaks out.

G: Your uniforms look pretty heavy. Are they comfortable?

A: They're not comfortable at all. The uniform weighs about 3 stone about 45 lb.] in all.

G: How do you overcome the tches, sneezes, and bees?

A: Inherent discipline is instilled in every British soldier during training. We know not to move a muscle while on parade no matter what the provocation or distraction—unless, of course, it is a security matter. But our helmets are akin to wearing a boiling kettle on your head; to relieve the pressure, sometimes we use the back of our sword blade to ease the back of the helmet forward.

G: How do you make the time pass while on duty?

A: The days are long. Smarter men work on horseback in the boxes in shifts from 10am-4pm; less smart men work on foot from 7am-8pm. Some guys count the number of buses that drive past. Unofficially, here are lots of pretty girls around here, and we are allowed to move our eyeballs.

G: What has been your funniest distraction attempt?

A: One day a taxi pulled up, and out hopped 4 Playboy bunnies, who then posed for a photo shoot ight in front of us. You could call hat a distraction if you like.

WESTMINSTER

The City of Westminster, now a borough of London, has been the seat of British power for over a thousand years. William the Conqueror was crowned in Westminster Abbey on Christmas Day, 1066, and his successors built the Palace of Westminster that would one day house Parliament.

BUCKINGHAM PALACE

Originally built for the Dukes of Buckingham, Buckingham House was acquired by George III in 1762 and converted into a full-scale palace by George IV. During the summer opening of the **State Rooms**, visitors have access to the **Throne Room**, the **Galleries** (with works by Rubens and Rembrandt), and the **Music Room**, where Mendelsohn played for Queen Victoria, among others. In the opulent **White Room**, the large mirrored fireplace hides a door used by the Royal Family at formal dinners. Since 2001, Queen Elizabeth has also allowed visitors into the **gardens.** *(The Mall; entrance to State Rooms on Buckingham Palace Rd. Tube: Victoria, Green Park, or St. James's Park.* ☎ *7839 1377. State Rooms open Aug.-Sept. daily 9:30am-4:30pm. Ticket Office in Green Park* ☎ *7321 2233. Open late July to Sept. £12, students and seniors £10, under-17 £6.)*

CHANGING OF THE GUARD. The Palace is protected by a detachment of Foot Guards in full dress uniform. Accompanied by a band, the "New Guard" starts marching down Birdcage Walk from Wellington Barracks around 10:30am, while the "Old Guard" leaves St. James's Palace around 11:10am. When they meet at the gates of the palace, the officers touch hands, symbolically exchanging keys, *et voilà*, the guard is changed. Show up well before 11:30am and stand directly in front of the palace, or use the steps of the Victoria Monument as a vantage point. For a less-crowded close-up of the marching guards, stand along the Mall between the Victoria Memorial and St. James's Palace. *(Daily Apr.-Oct., varies Nov.-Mar. Dependent on whether the Queen is in residence, the weather, and state functions. Free.)*

OTHER PALACE SIGHTS. The **Royal Mews**' main attraction is the collection of coaches, from the "glass coach" used to carry Diana to her wedding to the four-ton Gold State Coach and the carriage horses. *(Buckingham Palace Rd. Tube: St. James's Park or Victoria. Open Apr.-Sept. M-Th 11am-4pm. £5.)*

WESTMINSTER ABBEY

On December 28, 1065, Edward the Confessor, the last Saxon King of England, was buried in the church of the West Monastery; a year later, the Abbey saw the coronation of William the Conqueror, thus establishing the Abbey's twin traditions as the figurative birthplace and literal resting place of royalty. It was this connection that allowed Westminster, uniquely among England's great monasteries, to escape wholesale destruction by Henry VIII. Early English kings are buried around the Confessor's tomb in the **Shrine of St. Edward,** behind which the **Coronation Chair** stands at the entry to the Tudor **Lady Chapel. Poet's Corner** begins with Geoffrey Chaucer, buried in 1400; plaques at his feet commemorate writers, as does the stained-glass window above. At the center of the Abbey, the **Sanctuary** holds the altar, where coronations and royal weddings are held. The simple grave of **Winston Churchill** is just beyond the **Tomb of the Unknown Warrior.** The **Old Monastery** houses the **Great Cloister,** from which passages lead to the **Chapter House,** the **Pyx Chamber,** and the **Abbey Museum,** which features an array of royal funeral effigies. *(Parliament Sq.; enter the Old Monastery and cloister from Dean's Yard, behind the Abbey. ☎ 7222 5152. Tube: Westminster. Abbey open M-Tu and Th-F 9:30am-3:45pm, W 9:30am-7pm, Sa 9:30am-1:45pm, Su for services only. £6, students, seniors, and under-16 £4. Services free. Museum open daily 10:30am-4pm. Chapter House open Apr.-Oct. daily 9:30am-4:45pm; Nov.-Mar. 10am-4pm. Chapter House £1. Cloisters open daily 8am-6pm. Cloisters free.)*

THE HOUSES OF PARLIAMENT

The Palace of Westminster, as the building in which Parliament sits is officially known, has been at the heart of English governance since the 11th century, when Edward the Confessor established his court here. Highlights include the ostentatious **House of Lords,** which is dominated by the **Throne of State.** In contrast is the restrained **House of Commons,** with simple green-backed benches under a plain wooden roof. With seating for only 437 out of 635 MPs, things get hectic when all are present. *(Parliament Sq. Tube: Westminster. ☎ 7219 4272. Debates open to the public while Parliament is in session (Oct.-July). M-Th after 6pm and F are least busy. Advance tickets required for Prime Minister's Question Time (W 3-3:30pm). Lords usually sits M-W from 2:30pm, Th 3pm, occasionally F 11:30am; closing times vary. Commons sits M-W 2:30-10:30pm, Th 11:30am-7:30pm, F 9:30am-3pm. Free. Tours Aug.-Sept. M-Sa 9:15am-4:30pm; reserve through Firstcall (☎ (0870) 906 3773). £7, students £3.50.)*

OUTSIDE THE HOUSES. A statue of Oliver Cromwell stands in front of the midpoint of the complex, **Westminster Hall,** the only statue to survive the 1834 fire. During its centuries as a court of law, famous defendants included Saint Thomas More and Charles I. The **Clock Tower** is universally miscalled **Big Ben,** which actually refers only to the bell within; it's named after the robustly proportioned Sir Benjamin Hall, who served as Commissioner of Works when the bell was cast in 1858.

OTHER WESTMINSTER SIGHTS

WHITEHALL. Whitehall is synonymous with the British civil service. From 1532 until a fire in 1698, it was the main royal palace. Nearby, King James St. leads to the ▓**Cabinet War Rooms** (p 167). Current Prime Minister Tony Blair lives on **Downing Street,** separated from Whitehall by steel gates. The Prime Minister traditionally lives at #10, but Blair's family is so big that he's had to swap with the Chancellor, Gordon Brown, at #11.

WESTMINSTER CATHEDRAL. Westminster, London's first Catholic cathedral after Henry VIII espoused Protestantism, was started in 1887; in 1903, money ran out, leaving the interior only partially completed. The blackened brick domes contrast dramatically with the swirling marble of the lower walls and the magnificence of the side chapels. An elevator carries visitors up the striped 90m **bell tower.** *(Cathedral Piazza, off Victoria St. Tube: Victoria. Cathedral open daily 7am-7pm. Suggested donation £2. Bell tower open daily 9am-5pm. £3, students and seniors £1.50.)*

TRAFALGAR SQUARE AND THE STRAND

John Nash suggested the design of **Trafalgar Square** in 1820 to commemorate Nelson's 1805 victory over Napoleon's navy at the Battle of Trafalgar. But it took years to take on its current appearance: Nelson only arrived in 1843, the bronze lions in 1867. The reliefs at the column's base are cast from captured French and Spanish cannons. Every December, the square hosts a giant **Christmas Tree,** donated by Norway to thank the British for assistance against the Nazis. *(Tube: Charing Cross.)*

ST. MARTIN-IN-THE-FIELDS. James Gibbs's 1720s creation was the model for countless Georgian churches in Britain and America. It's still the Queen's parish church; look for the royal box to the left of the altar. The **crypt** downstairs has a life of its own, home to a cafe, bookshop, art gallery, and the **London Brass Rubbing Centre.** *(St. Martin's Ln., in the northeast corner of Trafalgar Sq. Tube: Leicester Sq. Brass Rubbing Centre open M-Sa 10am-6pm. Rubbings £3-15.)*

THE CITY OF LONDON

Until the 18th century, the City *was* London; the rest was merely outlying villages. Yet its modern appearance belies a 2000-year history; what few buildings survived the Great Fire of 1666 and WWII bombings are now overshadowed by giant temples of commerce. Of the 300,000 who work here, only 8000 people call the City home. The **City of London Information Centre,** in St. Paul's Churchyard, offers acres of leaflets and maps, sells tickets to sights and shows, and provides info on a host of traditional municipal events. *(☎7332 1456. Tube: St. Paul's. Open Apr.-Sept. daily 9:30am-5pm; Oct.-Mar. M-F 9:30am-5pm, Sa 9:30am-12:30pm.)*

ST. PAUL'S CATHEDRAL

Christopher Wren's masterpiece is the fifth cathedral to occupy the site; the original was built in AD 604. After three designs were rejected by the bishops, Wren, with Charles II's support, just started building—sneakily, he had persuaded the king to let him make "necessary alterations" as work progressed, and the building that emerged in 1708 bore little resemblance to the model Charles II had approved.

With space to seat 2500 worshippers, the **nave** is festooned with monuments to great Britons; the tombs, including those of Nelson, Wellington, and Florence Nightingale, are all downstairs, in the **crypt.** Christopher Wren lies beneath the epitaph *Lector, si monumentum requiris circumspice* ("Reader, if you seek his monument, look around"). To see the inside of the second-tallest freestanding **dome** in Europe (after St. Peter's in the Vatican), climb the 259 steps to the **Whispering Gallery.** From here, 119 more steps lead to **Stone Gallery,** on the outer base of the dome, and it's another 152 to the summit's **Golden Gallery.** *(St. Paul's Churchyard. ☎7246 8348; www.stpauls.co.uk. Tube: St. Paul's. Open M-Sa 8:30am-4pm; open for worship daily 7:15am-6pm. £6, students and seniors £5, children £3. Worshippers free. Audio tours £3.50, students and seniors £3. 1½hr. tours M-F 4 per day; £2.50, students £2.)*

THE TOWER OF LONDON

The Tower of London, palace and prison of English monarchs for over 900 years, is steeped in blood and history. Conceived by William the Conqueror in 1067 to provide protection *from* rather than *to* his new subjects, the original wooden palisade was replaced by a stone structure in 1078 that over the next 20 years would grow into the **White Tower.** Colorfully dressed Yeomen Warders, or "Beefeaters" (a reference to their former daily allowance of meat), serve as guards and guides.

From the western entrance near the **Middle Tower,** you pass over the old moat, now a garden, entering the **Outer Ward** though **Byward Tower.** Just beyond Byward Tower is a massive **Bell Tower,** dating from 1190; the curfew bell has been rung nightly for over 500 years. **Traitor's Gate** was built by Edward I for his personal use, but it is now associated with the prisoners who passed through it on their way to execution at **Tower Green.** Some of the victims are buried in the **Chapel Royal of St. Peter and Vincula,** including Catholic martyr Saint Thomas More and Henry VIII's wives Catherine Howard and Anne Boleyn. **White Tower** is now home to a huge display of arms and armor from the Royal Armory. Across the green is the **Bloody Tower,** so named because Richard III allegedly imprisoned and murdered his nephews here before usurping the throne in 1483.

The most famous sights in the Tower are the **Crown Jewels.** While the eye is naturally drawn to the **Imperial State Crown,** featuring the Stuart Sapphire along with 16 others, 2876 diamonds, 273 pearls, 11 emeralds, and a mere five rubies, don't miss the **Sceptre with the Cross,** topped with the First Star of Africa, the largest quality-cut diamond in the world. Other famous gems include the **Koh-i-Noor,** set into the **Queen Mother's Crown;** legend claims the stone will bring luck only to women. Many retired crowns and other treasures are displayed in the **Martin Tower,** at the end of **Wall Walk.** (Tower Hill. ☎ 7709 0765; www.hrp.org.uk. Tube: Tower Hill. Open Mar.-Oct. M-Sa 9am-5:30pm, Su 10am-5:30pm; Nov.-Feb. M 10am-4:30pm, Tu-Sa 9am-4:30pm. £12, students and seniors £9. Tickets also sold at Tube stations; buy them in advance to avoid horrendous lines. Audio tours £3. 1hr. tours every 90min. M-Sa 9:30am-3:30pm, Su 10am-3:30pm. Free.)

OTHER CITY OF LONDON SIGHTS

■ **MONUMENT.** Raised in 1677, Christopher Wren's 202 ft. column stands exactly that distance from Pudding Lane where the Great Fire started in 1666. The view from the top is astounding. (Monument St. Tube: Monument. Open daily 9:30am-5pm. £2.)

ALL HALLOWS-BY-THE-TOWER. Holding its own against a vast new Norman Foster development, All Hallows bears the marks of its longevity with pride. The undercroft is home to an array of archaeological finds, including Roman pavements and some striking Celtic carvings. (Byward St. Tube: Tower Hill. Church open M-F 9am-5:45pm, Sa-Su 10am-5pm. Crypt open M-Sa 10:30am-4pm, Su 1-4pm.)

GUILDHALL. In this vast Gothic hall, representatives from the City's 102 guilds, from the Fletchers (arrow-makers) to the Information Technologists, meet at the **Court of Common Council,** under the Lord Mayor. The Court meets the third Thursday of every month. (Off Gresham St. Tube: St. Paul's. Open May-Sept. daily 10am-5pm, Sa-Su 10am-4pm; Oct.-Apr. closed Su. Free.)

TOWER BRIDGE. This iconic symbol of London is often mistaken for its plain upriver sibling, London Bridge—the story goes that when an Arizona millionaire bought the previous London Bridge and shifted it stone-by-stone to the US, he thought he was getting Tower Bridge. The **Tower Bridge Experience** offers a cutesy introduction to the history and technology of the unique lifting mechanism, though the view isn't all it's cracked up to be. (Tube: Tower Hill. Open daily 9:30am–6pm; last admission 5pm. £4.50, students and seniors £3.)

WREN CHURCHES. Aside from St. Paul's Cathedral, the City's greatest architectural treasures are the 22 surviving churches designed by Christopher Wren to replace those lost in the Great Fire of 1666. The most famous is **St. Mary-le-Bow.** For the past 800 years, the Archbishop of Canterbury has sworn in bishops in the 11th-century crypt, whose "bows" (arches) gave the church its epithet. (On Cheapside, near Bow Ln. Tube: St. Paul's. Open M-F 7:30am-6pm. Free.) **St. Stephen Walbrook,** built from 1672-1679, was Wren's personal favorite. A plain exterior gives no inkling of the wide dome that floats above Henry Moore's 1985 mysterious free-form altar. (39 Walbrook. Tube: Bank. Organ concert F 12:30pm. Open M-Th 9am-4pm. Free.)

BRITAIN

THE SOUTH BANK

From the Middle Ages until Cromwell's arrival, the South Bank was London's center of amusement; banished from the strictly regulated City, all manner of illicit attractions sprouted in "the Borough" at the southern end of London Bridge. Today, the South Bank is once again at the heart of London entertainment, with some of the city's top concert halls, theaters, cinemas, and galleries.

LONDON EYE. At 135m, the London Eye is the world's biggest observational wheel. The ellipsoid glass "pods" give uninterrupted views at the top of each 30min. revolution; on clear days, Windsor is visible to the west. *(Jubilee Gardens, between County Hall and the Festival Hall. Tube: Waterloo. Open late May to early Sept. daily 9:30am-10pm; Apr. to early May and late Sept. 10:30am-8pm; Oct.-Mar. 10:30am-7pm; Ticket office, on the corner of County Hall, open daily 8:30am-6:30pm. £11, under-16 £6.)*

THE SOUTH BANK CENTRE. Sprawling on either side of Waterloo Bridge, this concrete complex is Britain's premier cultural center. Its nucleus is the **Royal Festival Hall,** a classic piece of white 1950s architecture. Nearby, the **Purcell Room** and **Queen Elizabeth Hall** host smaller concerts, while just behind, the spiky ceiling of the **Hayward Gallery** shelters excellent modern art exhibitions. The **National Film Theatre,** on the embankment beneath the bridge, offers London's most varied cinematic fare, while the **National Theatre** (p. 168) can show you how one of the world's largest theaters operates with a backstage tour. *(Between Hungerford and Waterloo Bridges. Tube: Waterloo. Tours M-Sa 10:15am, 12:15, and 5:15pm. £5, students £4.30.)*

TATE MODERN AND THE MILLENNIUM BRIDGE. Squarely opposite each other on Bankside are the biggest success and most abject failure of London's millennial celebrations. **Tate Modern** (p. 166), created from the shell of the Bankside power station, is as visually arresting as its contents are thought-provoking. The **Millennium Bridge,** built to link the Tate to the City, was completed six months too late for the Y2K festivities and, following a literally shaky debut, has only recently been stabilized. *(Queen's Walk, Bankside. Tube: Southwark.)*

SHAKESPEARE'S GLOBE THEATRE. In the shadow of Tate Modern, the half-timbered Globe, opened in 1997, sits just 200m from where the original burned down in 1613. Try to arrive in time for a tour of the theater itself, given on mornings during the performance season and 10am-5pm otherwise. Tours include the **Rose Theatre,** where both Shakespeare and Marlowe performed; not much of it is left. *(Bankside. Tube: Southwark. Open May-Sept. daily 9am-noon and 1-4pm; Oct.-Apr. 10am-5pm. £8, students £6.50. See also p. 168.)*

OTHER SOUTH BANK SIGHTS. The giant **HMS Belfast** was used in the bombardment of Normandy during D-Day and then to support UN forces in Korea before graciously retiring in 1965. Dozens of narrow passages, steep staircases, and ladders make exploring the boat a physical challenge. *(At the end of Morgans Ln., off Tooley St. Tube: London Bridge. Open Mar.-Oct. daily 10am-6pm; Nov.-Feb. 10am-5pm. £6, students and seniors £4.40.)* **Vinopolis** is a Dionysian fantasy land offering patrons an interactive tour of the world's wine regions. *(1 Bank End. Tube: London Bridge. Open M and Sa 11am-9pm, Tu-F and Su 11am-6pm. £11.50, seniors £10.50.)*

BLOOMSBURY AND MARYLEBONE

Marylebone's most famous resident (and address) never existed. 221b Baker St. was the fictional lodging house of Sherlock Holmes, but 221 Baker St. is actually the headquarters of the Abbey National Bank. Bloomsbury's intellectual reputation was bolstered in the early 20th century when Gordon Sq., east of Marylebone, resounded with the philosophizing and womanizing of the **Bloomsbury Group,** an early 20th-century coterie of intellectuals that included John Maynard Keynes, Bertrand Russell, Lytton Strachey, and Virginia Woolf.

■**BRITISH LIBRARY.** Since its 1998 opening, the new British Library has won acclamation from visitors and users alike. The library houses a dramatic glass cube containing the 65,000 volumes of George III's **King's Library,** and a stunning display of books and manuscripts, from the 2nd-century *Unknown Gospel* to Joyce's handwritten draft of *Finnegan's Wake. (96 Euston Rd. ☎ 7412 7332. Tube: King's Cross. Open M and W-F 9:30am-6pm, Tu 9:30am-8pm, Sa 9:30am-5pm, Su 11am-5pm. Free. Tours M, W, F-Sa 3pm, also Sa 10:30am. £5, students and seniors £3.50. Tours including reading rooms Tu 6:30pm, Su 11:30am and 3pm. £6, £4.50. Reservations recommended.)*

■**REGENT'S PARK.** London's most attractive and popular park, with a wide range of landscapes from soccer fields to formal gardens. The exclusive-sounding **Inner Circle** road separates the flower-filled **Queen Mary's Gardens** from the park without. On the northern edge of the Inner Circle, ■**St. John's Lodge Gardens**—a blaze of lavender entered through an easy-to-miss gate on the Inner Circle itself—remain open to the public. *(500 acres stretching from Marylebone Rd. to Camden Town. Tube: Baker St., Regent's Park, Great Portland St., or Camden Town. Open daily 6am-dusk. Free.)*

ACADEMIA. The strip of land along **Gower Street** and immediately to its west is London's academic heartland. Established in 1828, **University College London** was the first in Britain to admit Catholics, Jews, and women. The embalmed body of founder **Jeremy Bentham** has been on display in the South Cloister since 1850. *(Main entrance on Gower St. South Cloister entrance through the courtyard. Tube: Warren St.)* Now the administrative headquarters of the University of London, **Senate House** was the model for the Ministry of Truth in *1984;* George Orwell worked there as part of the BBC propaganda unit in WWII. *(At the southern end of Malet St. Tube: Goodge St.)*

HOLBORN AND CLERKENWELL

Squeezed between the capitalism of the City and the commercialism of the West End, Holborn is historically the home of two of the world's least-loved professions—lawyers and journalists.

INNS OF COURT. These venerable institutions house the chambers of practicing barristers and provide apprenticeships for law students. Most were founded in the 13th century when a royal decree barred the clergy from the courts, giving rise to a class of professional advocates. Most impressive of the four Inns is the ■**Temple,** south of Fleet St. *(Between Fleet St., Essex St., Victoria Embankment, and Temple Ave./Bouvier St. Numerous passages lead from these streets into the Temple. Tube: Temple.)* The 12th-century **Temple Church** is the finest round church in England. *(Open W-Th 11am-4pm, Sa 10am-2:30pm, Su 12:45-4pm. Free.)* Shakespeare premiered *Twelfth Night* in front of Elizabeth I in **Middle Temple Hall,** whose large wooden dining table is made from the hatch of Sir Francis Drake's *Golden Hinde.* According to Shakespeare's *Henry VI,* the red-and-white flowers of the War of the Roses were plucked in **Middle Temple Garden,** south of the hall. *(Garden open May-Sept. M-F noon-3pm. Free.)*

■**ST. ETHELDREDA'S.** The mid-13th-century church of St. Etheldreda is the sole surviving edifice of its age in London, barely: The upper church was badly damaged in WWII. Inside, the surprisingly high ceiling swallows up the bustle of the streets, and the enormous stained-glass windows make this one of London's most beautiful churches. *(Ely Pl. Tube: Farringdon. Open daily 7:30am-7pm. Free.)*

SOMERSET HOUSE. A magnificent Palladian structure completed in 1790, Somerset House was London's first intended office block. Originally home to the Royal Academy and the Royal Society, the building now harbors the magnificent ◾**Courtauld Institute** (p. 167). From mid-December to mid-January, the central **Fountain Courtyard** is iced over to make an open-air rink. *(On the Strand. Tube: Charing Cross. Courtyard open daily 7:30am-11pm. Free. Tours Sa 1:30 and 3:45pm. £2.80.)*

KENSINGTON

Nobody took much notice of Kensington before 1689, when the newly crowned William III and Mary II moved into Kensington Palace. Then, in 1851, the Great Exhibition brought in enough money to finance the museums and colleges of South Kensington. Now the neighborhood is home to London's most expensive stores, including Harrods and Harvey Nichols, and it's hard to imagine the days when the area was known for its taverns and its highwaymen.

KENSINGTON PALACE. Remodeled by Christopher Wren for William III and Mary II, parts of the palace are still in use today as a royal residence. Princess Diana lived here until her death. The **Royal Ceremonial Dress Collection** features 19th-century court costumes along with the Queen's demure evening gowns and some of Diana's sexier numbers. Hanoverian economy is evident in the *trompe l'oeil* decoration in the **State Apartment,** carried out by William Kent for George I. *(On the western edge of Kensington Gardens; enter through the park. Tube: High St. Kensington. Open Mar.-Oct. daily 10am-6pm; Nov.-Feb. 10am-5pm. £11, students and seniors £8.)*

HYDE PARK AND KENSINGTON GARDENS. Surrounded by London's wealthiest neighborhoods, giant Hyde Park has served as the model for city parks around the world, including Central Park in New York and Bois de Boulogne in Paris. **Kensington Gardens,** to the west, is contiguous with Hyde Park. The 41-acre **Serpentine** was created in 1730; innumerable people pay to row and swim here. At the northeastern corner of the park, near Marble Arch, proselytizers, politicos, and flat-out crazies dispense their knowledge to bemused tourists at **Speaker's Corner** on Sundays. *(Tube: Queensway, Lancaster Gate, Marble Arch, Hyde Park Corner, or High St. Kensington. Hyde Park open daily 5am-midnight. Kensington Gardens open dawn-dusk. Both free.)*

KNIGHTSBRIDGE

APSLEY HOUSE AND WELLINGTON ARCH. Apsley House, with the convenient address of "No. 1, London," was bought in 1817 by the Duke of Wellington. On display is Wellington's outstanding collection of art, much of it given in gratitude by European royalty following the battle of Waterloo. *(Hyde Park Corner. Tube: Hyde Park Corner. Open Su and Tu-Sa 11am-5pm. £4.50, students £3. Seniors and children free.)* Across from Apsley House, the **Wellington Arch** was built in 1825. In 1838 it was dedicated to the Duke of Wellington; later, to the horror of its architect, Decimus Burton, an enormous statue of the Duke was placed on top. The arch offers scenic views. *(Hyde Park Corner. Tube: Hyde Park Corner. Open Apr.-Sept. Su and W-Sa 10am-5:30pm; Oct. Su and W-Sa 10am-5pm; Nov.-Mar. Su and W-Sa 10am-4pm. £2.50, students and seniors £2.)*

THE WEST END

MAYFAIR AND ST. JAMES'S

Home to Prince Charles, the Ritz, and exclusive gentlemen's clubs, this is London's aristocratic quarter. On **Jermyn Street,** one block south of Piccadilly, stores cater to the tastes of the English squire, with hand-cut suits and hunting gear.

BURLINGTON HOUSE. The only one of Piccadilly's aristocratic mansions that stands today, Burlington House was built in 1665. Today, it houses numerous regal societies, including the **Royal Academy,** heart of the British artistic establishment and home to some excellent exhibitions (p. 167).

ST. JAMES'S PALACE. Built in 1536, St. James's is London's only remaining purpose-built palace; Prince Charles lives here. The only part of the palace open to the public is the **Chapel Royal,** open for Sunday services from October to Easter at 8:30 and 11am. *(Between the Mall and Pall Mall. Tube: Green Park.)* From Easter to September, services are held in **Queen's Chapel,** across Marlborough Rd.

SOHO

Soho's first settlers were French Huguenots fleeing religious persecution in the 17th century. These days, a concentration of gay-owned restaurants and bars has turned **Old Compton Street** into the heart of gay London.

PICCADILLY CIRCUS. In the glow of lurid neon signs, five of the West End's major arteries merge and swirl round the **Statue of Eros,** dedicated to the Victorian philanthropist, Lord Shaftesbury. Eros originally pointed down Shaftesbury Ave., but recent restoration work has put his aim significantly off. *(Tube: Piccadilly Circus.)*

LEICESTER SQUARE. Amusements at this entertainment nexus range from London's largest cinema to the **Swiss Centre** glockenspiel, whose atonal renditions of Beethoven's *Moonlight Sonata* are enough to make even the tone-deaf weep. *(Rings M-F noon, 6, 7, and 8pm; Sa-Su noon, 2, 4, 5, 6, 7, and 8pm.)* Be true to your inner tourist by having your name engraved on a grain of rice and sitting for a caricature. *(Tube: Leicester Sq. or Piccadilly Circus.)*

CHINATOWN. The pedestrian, tourist-ridden **Gerrard Street,** with dragon gates and pagoda-capped phone booths, is the heart of London's tiny slice of Canton, but gritty **Lisle Street,** one block to the south, has a more authentic feel. Chinatown is most exciting during the raucous Chinese New Year in February. *(Between Leicester Sq., Shaftesbury Ave., and Charing Cross Rd.)*

COVENT GARDEN

The Covent Garden piazza, designed by Inigo Jones in the 17th century, is one of the few parts of London popular with locals and tourists alike. On the very spot where England's first Punch and Judy show was performed, street entertainers delight the thousands who flock here year round. *(Tube: Covent Garden.)*

THE ROYAL OPERA HOUSE. The Royal Opera House reopened in 2000 after a major expansion. After wandering in the ornate lobby of the original 1858 theater, head up to the enormous **Floral Hall.** Then take the escalator to reach the **terrace,** which offers scenic views. *(Bow St. ☎ 7304 4000. Open daily 10am-3:30pm. Backstage tours M-Sa 10:30am, 12:30, and 2:30pm. Reservations essential. £8, students and seniors £7.)*

NORTH LONDON

CAMDEN TOWN

An island of good, honest tawdriness in an increasingly affluent sea, Camden Town has thrown off attempts at gentrification thanks to the ever-growing **Camden Markets.** On weekends, the market presents a variety of life unmatched even by **London Zoo,** just up the **Regent's Canal** from the market's center.

LONDON ZOO. Thousands of little critters from around the world run freely, their guardians trying frantically to keep up, as the animals look on with indifference from their enclosures. For daily activities, check the *Daily Events* leaflet. *(Main* *gate on Outer Circle, Regent's Park. Tube: Camden Town. 12min. walk from the Tube station or a quick jaunt on bus #274. Open Apr.-Oct. daily 10am-5:30pm; Nov.-Mar. 10am-4:30pm. £12, students and seniors £10.20, under-16 £9.)*

HAMPSTEAD

Hampstead first caught the attention of well-heeled Londoners in the 17th century. In the 1930s, residents such as Barbara Hepworth, Aldous Huxley, Piet Mondrian, and Sigmund Freud lent the area a cachet that grows to this day.

HAMPSTEAD HEATH. Hampstead Heath is one of the last remaining commons in England, open to all since 1312. **Parliament Hill** is the highest open space in London, with excellent views of the city. Farther north, ■**Kenwood House** is a picture-perfect 18th-century country estate, designed by Robert Adams for the first Earl of Mansfield and home to the impressive **Iveagh Bequest** of Old Masters, including works by Botticelli, Rembrandt, Turner, and Vermeer. *(Tube: Hampstead. A 20min. walk from the station. Kenwood House open Apr.-Sept. daily 8am-8:30pm; Oct.-Mar. 8am-4pm.)*

EAST LONDON

THE EAST END AND DOCKLANDS

Whitechapel is the oldest part of the East End. In the 19th century, it was thronged with Jewish refugees from Eastern Europe; today it's the heart of London's Bangladeshi community, which centers around **Brick Lane. Christ Church,** on Commercial St., opposite Spitalfields market, is Nicholas Hawksmoor's largest, and considered by many to be his masterpiece; it is slowly being restored to its former glory. *(Tube: Liverpool St. Open M-F 12:30-2:30pm.)*

GREENWICH

Greenwich's position as the "home of time" is connected to its maritime heritage—the Royal Observatory, site of the Prime Meridian, was founded to produce starcharts once essential to navigation. The most pleasant way of getting to Greenwich is by boat. **Westminster Passenger Association** boats head from Westminster Pier. *(1hr., call ☎7930 9033 for schedule. Round-trip £6.30.)* TfL Travelcard holders get 33% off riverboat fares. The **Greenwich Tourist Information Centre** is in Pepys House, 2 Cutty Sark Gdns. *(☎(0870) 608 2000. Open daily 10am-5pm.)*

ROYAL OBSERVATORY. Charles II founded the Royal Observatory in 1675 to develop a method for calculating longitude at sea; the **Prime Meridian** (which marks 0° longitude) started out as the axis along which the astronomers' telescopes swung. Next to the Meridian is Christopher Wren's **Flamstead House,** whose **Octagon Room** features long windows designed to accommodate telescopes. The **Observatory Dome,** next to the Meridian Building's telescope display, houses a 28 in. telescope constructed in 1893. It hasn't been used since 1954, but you can get a peek at the stars at the **Planetarium.** *(Greenwich Park. Open daily 10am-5pm. Free.)*

CUTTY SARK. Even landlubbers will appreciate the **Cutty Sark,** the last of the great tea clippers. Launched in 1869, she was the fastest ship of her time, making the trip to and from China in only 120 days. *(King William Walk, by Greenwich Pier. Open daily 10am-5pm; last admission 4:30pm. £4; students, seniors, and under-16 £3.)*

WEST LONDON

■**HAMPTON COURT PALACE.** Although a monarch hasn't lived here for 250 years, Hampton Court still exudes regal charm. Cardinal Wolsey built the first palace here in 1514, showing the young Henry VIII how to act the part of a ruler. In 1689, William III and Mary II employed Christopher Wren to bring Hampton Court up to date. In addition to touring the sumptuous rooms of the palace, including Henry's **State Apartments** and William's **King's Apartments,** be sure to leave time for the vast gardens, including the devilishly difficult **maze.** Take the train from Waterloo (35min., every 30min., round-trip £4) or a boat from Westminster Pier (4hr.; 4 per day; £10, round-trip £14); to leave time to see the palace, take the boat one way and return by train. *(Open mid-Mar. to late Oct. M 10:15am-6pm, Tu-Su 9:30am-6pm; mid-Mar. closes 4:30pm. £11, students £8.30. Maze only £3. Gardens only free.)*

KEW GARDENS. The Kew Gardens (a.k.a. the Royal Botanic Gardens) feature thousands of flowers, fruits, trees, and vegetables from around the globe. The three **conservatories,** housing a staggering variety of plants ill-suited to the English climate, are the highlight of the gardens. Most famous is the steamy **Palm House.** The **Temperate House** is the largest ornamental glasshouse in the world. The interior of the **Princess of Wales Conservatory** is divided into 10 different climate zones, including one entirely devoted to orchids. *(Main entrance at Victoria Gate. Tube: Kew Gardens. Open Apr.-Aug. M-F 9:30am-6:30pm, Sa-Su 9:30am-7:30pm; Sept.-Oct. daily 9:30am-6pm; Nov.-Jan. 9:30am-4:15pm; Feb.-Mar. 9:30am-5:30pm. £6.50, "late entry" (45min. before the glasshouses close) £5.50; students and seniors £5.50.)*

🏛 MUSEUMS

Centuries spent as the capital of an empire, together with a decidedly English penchant for collecting, have given London a spectacular set of museums. Art lovers, history buffs, and amateur ethnologists won't know which way to turn when they arrive. And there's even better news for museum lovers: in celebration of the Queen's Golden Jubilee, all major museums are free indefinitely.

▓ BRITISH MUSEUM

The funny thing about the British Museum is that there's almost nothing British in it. The **Western Galleries** house the most famous items in the collection. Room 4 harbors Egyptian sculpture, including the **Rosetta Stone,** and Room 18 is entirely devoted to the Athenian **Elgin Marbles.** Other highlights include giant Assyrian and Babylonian **reliefs,** the Roman **Portland Vase,** and bits and bobs from two Wonders of the Ancient World, the **Temple of Artemis** at Ephesus and the **Mausoleum of Halikarnassos.** The **Northern Galleries** feature artifacts from the ancient Near East, including the **Oxus Treasure** from Iran. The northern wing also houses the excellent African and Islamic galleries, the giant Asian collections, and the Americas collection. The upper level of the **South** and **East Galleries** is dedicated to ancient and medieval Europe, some of which is actually British. *(Great Russell St., Bloomsbury. Rear entrance on Montague St. ☎ 7323 8000; www.thebritishmuseum.ac.uk. Tube: Tottenham Court Rd., Russell Sq., or Holborn. Great Court open M-W and Su 10am-5:30pm, Th-Sa 9am-9pm. Galleries open daily 10am-5:30pm. Suggested donation £2. Temporary exhibitions average £7, students £3.50. Audio tours £2.50. 1½hr. highlights tour M-Sa 10:30am and 1pm; Su 11am, 12:30, 1:30, 2:30, and 4pm. £7, students £4.)*

▓ NATIONAL GALLERY

The National Gallery was founded by an Act of Parliament in 1824, with 38 paintings displayed in a townhouse; it grew so rapidly in size and popularity that a new gallery was constructed in 1838. The new **Sainsbury Wing** houses the oldest, most fragile paintings, including the 14th-century English *Wilton Diptych*, Botticelli's *Venus and Mars*, and the *Leonardo Cartoon*, a detailed preparatory drawing by Leonardo da Vinci for a never-executed painting. The **West Wing** displays paintings from 1510-1600 and is dominated by Italian High Renaissance and early Flemish art. Highlights include versions of the *Madonna and Child* by Raphael and Michelangelo. The **East Wing,** home to paintings from 1700-1900, is the most popular in the gallery, thanks to an array of Impressionist works including van Gogh's *Sunflowers* and Cézanne's *Bathers. (Main entrance on north side of Trafalgar Sq., Westminster.* ☎ *7747 2885; www.nationalgallery.org.uk. Tube: Charing Cross or Leicester Sq. Open M-Tu and Th-Sa 10am-6pm; W 10am-9pm, Sainsbury Wing special exhibitions until 10pm. Free; some temporary exhibitions £5-7, students £2-3. Audio tours free; suggested donation £4. 1hr. gallery tours start at Sainsbury Wing info desk daily 11:30am and 2:30pm, W also 6:30pm. Free.)*

■ TATE MODERN

Since opening in May 2000, Tate Modern has been credited with single-handedly reversing the long-term decline in museum attendance in Britain. The largest modern art museum in the world, its most striking aspect is the building, formerly the Bankside power station. The Tate has been criticized for its controversial curatorial method, which groups works according to themes rather than period or artist: The four divisions are **Landscape/Matter/Environment** and **Still Life/Object/Real Life** on level 3 and **Nude/Body/Action** and **History/Memory/Society** on level 5. Even skeptics admit that this arrangement throws up some interesting contrasts, such as the nascent geometry of Cézanne's *Still Life with Water Jug* overlooking the checkerboard tiles of Carl André's *Steel Zinc Plain.* The main achievement of the thematic display is that it forces visitors into contact with an exceptionally wide range of art. It's now impossible to see the Tate's more famous pieces, which include Marcel Duchamp's *Large Glass* and Picasso's *Weeping Woman,* without also confronting challenging and invigorating works by little-known contemporary artists. *(Bankside, The South Bank. Main entrance on Holland St.* ☎ *7887 8006; www.tate.org.uk. Tube: Blackfriars. Open Su-Th 10am-6pm, F-Sa 10am-10pm. Free. Special exhibitions £5-7; students £4-6. Audio tours £1.)*

TATE BRITAIN

The original Tate opened in 1897 as a showcase for modern British art. Before long, it had expanded to include contemporary art from all over the world, as well as British art from the Middle Ages on. Despite many expansions, it was clear that the dual role was too much for one building; the problem was resolved with the relocation of almost all the contemporary art to the new Tate Modern at Bankside (see above). At the same time, the original Tate was rechristened and rededicated to British art. The **Clore Gallery** continues to display the Turner Bequest of 282 oils and 19,000 watercolors; other painters featured heavily are William Blake, John Constable, Lucien Freud, David Hockney, and Dante Gabriel Rossetti. Despite the Tate Modern's popular explosion, the annual **Turner Prize** for contemporary art is still held here. *(Millbank, near Vauxhall Bridge, Westminster.* ☎ *7887 8008; www.tate.org.uk. Tube: Pimlico. Open daily 10am-5pm. Free. Special exhibitions £3-9. Audio tours £3. Highlights tour M-F 11:30am, Sa 3pm. Free.)*

VICTORIA & ALBERT MUSEUM

Founded in 1852 to encourage excellence in art and design, the V&A is the largest museum of the decorative arts in the world. The subject of a £31 million renovation, the vast **British Galleries** hold a series of recreated rooms from every period between 1500 and 1900. If you only see one thing in the museum, make it the **Raphael Gallery,** hung with paintings commissioned by Leo X in 1515. The V&A's **Asian** collections are particularly formidable—if the choice of objects occasionally seems to rely on national cliches (Indian carvings, Persian carpets, Chinese porcelain, Japanese ceramics), it says more about how the V&A has formed opinion than followed it. The **upper levels** are mostly arranged in specialist galleries devoted to everything from jewelry to musical instruments to stained glass. The six-level **Henry Cole wing** is home to a collection of **British paintings,** including some 350 works by Constable and numerous Turners. Also on display are a number of Rodin bronzes, donated by the artist, and a collection of **miniature portraits.** *(Main entrance on Cromwell Rd., Kensington. ☎ 7942 2000; www.vam.ac.uk. Tube: South Kensington. Open M-Tu and Th-Su 10am-5:45pm, W and last F of month 10am-10pm. Free. Tours daily 10:30, 11:30am, 1:30, and 2:30pm. Gallery talks daily 1pm. Free.)*

OTHER MUSEUMS AND GALLERIES

British Library Galleries, 96 Euston Rd. (☎ 7412 7332). Tube: King's Cross. A stunning display of texts, from the 2nd-century *Unknown Gospel* to the Beatles' hand-scrawled lyrics. Other highlights include a Gutenberg Bible and pages from da Vinci's notebooks. Open M and W-F 9:30am-6pm, Tu 9:30am-8pm, Sa 9:30am-5pm, Su 11am-5pm. Free.

Museum of London, London Wall, The City of London (☎ 7600 3699). Tube: Barbican. Enter through the Barbican. The engrossing collection traces the history of London from its foundations to the present day, with a particular focus on Roman objects. Open M-Sa 10am-6pm, Su noon-6pm; last admission 5:30pm. Free.

Courtauld Institute, Somerset House, The Strand, Westminster (☎ 7848 2526). Tube: Charing Cross. Small, outstanding collection. 14th- to 20th-century abstractions, focusing on Impressionism. Manet's *A Bar at the Follies Bergères,* van Gogh's *Self Portrait with Bandaged Ear,* and Cézanne's *The Card Players.* Open M-Sa 10am-6pm. £5, students £4. Free M 10am-2pm.

Natural History Museum, on Cromwell Rd., Kensington (☎ 7942 5000). Tube: South Kensington. Cathedral-like building home to an array of minerals and stuffed animals. Highlights include a frighteningly realistic T-Rex and the engrossing, interactive *Human Biology* gallery. Open M-Sa 10am-5:50pm, Su 11am-5:50pm. Free.

Royal Academy of Art, Burlington House, Piccadilly, The West End (☎ 7300 8000). Tube: Piccadilly Circus. Founded in 1768 as both an art school and meeting place for Britain's foremost artists. Outstanding exhibitions on all manner of art. Open M-Th and Sa-Su 10am-6pm, F 10am-10pm. Around £7; seniors £6, students £5.

Design Museum, 28 Shad Thames, Butler's Wharf (☎ 7403 6933). Tube: Tower Hill or London Bridge. This thoroughly contemporary museum explores the development of mass-market design with a constantly changing selection of objects; most fun are the dozens of funky chairs that you can try out. Open daily 10am-5:45pm, last admission 5:15pm. £6, families £16, concessions £4.

Dulwich Picture Gallery, Gallery Rd., Dulwich (☎ 8693 5254). 10min. from North or West Dulwich rail station, or bus P4 from Tube: Brixton. Designed by Sir John Soane, this marvelous array of Old Masters was England's first public art gallery. Rubens and van Dyck feature prominently, as does Rembrandt's *Portrait of a Young Man.* Open Su 11am-5pm, Tu-F 10am-5pm, Sa 11am-5pm. £4, seniors £3. Students and children free; free for all F.

Cabinet War Rooms, Clive Steps, Westminster (☎ 7766 0130). Tube: Westminster. The rooms where Churchill and his staff lived and worked from 1939 to 1945. Highlights include a room containing the top-secret trans-atlantic hotline—known as Churchill's personal toilet. Open Apr.-Sept. daily 9:30am-6pm; Oct.-Mar. 10am-6pm. £7, students £5.50.

⛶ ENTERTAINMENT

The West End is the world's theater capital, supplemented by an adventurous "Fringe" and a justly famous National Theatre. New bands spring eternal from the fountain of London's many music venues. Whatever you're planning to do, the listings in *Time Out* (£2.20, every W) are indispensable.

THEATER

The stage for a dramatic tradition over 800 years old, London theaters maintain unrivaled breadth of choice. At a **West End** theater (a term referring to all the major stages, whether or not they're actually in the West End), you can expect a professional (if mainstream) production and top-quality performers. **Off-West End** theaters tend to present more challenging works, while remaining as professional as their West End brethren. The **Fringe** refers to scores of smaller venues, often just rooms in basements with a few benches and a team of dedicated amateurs. **tkts,** on the south side of Leicester Sq., is run jointly by London theaters and is the only place where you can be sure your discount tickets are genuine. You can only buy on the day of the performance, in person and in cash, and with no choice in seating. There's no way of knowing in advance which shows will have tickets, but you can expect a wide range. There's a ₤2.50 booking fee per ticket but no limit on the number you can buy. (Open M-Sa 10am-7pm, Su noon-3pm. Most tickets ₤15-25.)

WEST END AND REPERTORY COMPANIES

▨ **Shakespeare's Globe Theatre,** 21 New Globe Walk (☎7401 9919). Tube: Southwark or London Bridge. A faithful reproduction of the original 16th-century playhouse. Opt for backless wooden benches or stand as a "groundling." For **tours,** see p. 160. Performances mid-May to late Sept. Su 6:30pm, Tu-Sa 7:30pm; June Su 1 and 6:30pm. Tu-Sa 2 and 7:30pm. Box office open M-Sa 10am-6pm, and at 8pm on performance days. Seats £12-27, concessions £10-24; standing £5.

Barbican Theatre, main entrance on Silk St. (☎7638 8891). A huge, futuristic auditorium with steeply raked, forward-leaning balconies. Hosts touring companies and short-run shows, as well as frequent contemporary dance performances. **The Pit** is largely experimental, while **Barbican Hall** houses the London Symphony Orchestra (p. 170). Tickets £6-30. Student and senior standbys from 9am day of performance.

National Theatre, just down-river of Waterloo bridge (info ☎7452 3400, box office 7452 3000; www.nationaltheatre.org.uk). Tube: Waterloo or Embankment. At the forefront of British theater since opening under the direction of Laurence Olivier in 1976. The **Olivier** stage seats 1080, the **Lyttelton** is a proscenium stage, and the **Cottesloe** offers flexible staging for experimental dramas. Box office open M-Sa 10am-8pm. Tickets £10-30; from 10am day of performance £10; standby (2hr. before curtain) £15; standing places, only if all seats sold, £6. Concessions available.

Royal Court Theatre, Sloane Sq. (☎7565 5000). Called "the most important theater in Europe," dedicated to new writing and innovative interpretations of classics. Main stage £7.50-26; concessions £9; standing room 1hr. before curtain 10p. Upstairs £12.50-15, concessions £9. M all seats £7.50.

MAJOR FRINGE THEATERS

The Almeida, Almeida St. (☎7359 4404). Tube: Angel or Highbury & Islington. Top fringe in London, if not the world. Hollywood stars, including Kevin Spacey and Nicole Kidman, queue up to prove their acting cred here. Show times and prices to be announced.

Donmar Warehouse, 41 Earlham St. (☎7369 1732). Tube: Covent Garden. Serious contemporary theater. £14-35; concessions standby £12, 30min. before curtain.

Young Vic, 66 The Cut (☎7928 6363). Tube: Waterloo. With only 8 rows of seats surrounding the flat stage, Vic can be unnervingly intimate. Box office open M-Sa 10am-8pm. £19, seniors £12.50, students and children £4-9.50.

CINEMA

The heart of the movie-going is **Leicester Square** (p. 163), where the latest releases premiere a day before hitting the city's chains. The dominant mainstream cinema chain is **Odeon** (☎(0870) 5050 007). Tickets to West End cinemas begin at £8; weekday matinees before 5pm are usually cheaper. For less mainstream offerings, try the ◼**Electric Cinema,** 191 Portobello Rd. (Tube: Ladbroke Grove), for the combination of Baroque stage splendor and a big screen. For an special experience, choose a armchair or 2-seat sofa. (☎7908 9696; tickets 7229 8688. Late-night reruns Sa 11pm; classics, recent raves, and double bills Su 2pm. M £7.50, Su and Tu-Sa £12.50; 2-seat sofa M £20, Su and Tu-Sa £30; Su double bills £7.50.) ◼**Riverside Studios,** Crisp Rd. (Tube: Hammersmith) shows a wide and extraordinary range of excellent foreign and classic films. (☎8237 1111; £5.50, concessions £4.50.)

COMEDY

Capital of a nation famed for its sense of humor, London takes comedy seriously. Check listings in *Time Out* or a newspaper to get up to speed. Summertime giggle-seekers should note that London empties of comedians in **August,** when most head to Edinburgh to take part in the annual festival; that means **July** provides plenty of comedians trying out their material. A young Robin Williams performed frequent impromptu acts at the ◼**Comedy Store,** 1a Oxendon St. (Tube: Piccadilly Circus), the UK's top comedy club. (TicketMaster ☎(0870) 060 2340. Shows Su and Tu-Sa 8pm, F-Sa 8pm and midnight. Book ahead. 18+. £12-15, concessions £8.) East London's ◼**Comedy Cafe,** 66 Rivington St., merits a health warning: Prolonged exposure may lead to uncontrollable laughter. (☎7739 5706. Reserve F-Sa. Cover Th £5, F £10, Sa £14. Shows daily at 9pm.)

MUSIC

ROCK AND POP

Birthplace of the Stones, the Sex Pistols, Madness, and the Chemical Brothers, home to Madonna (sort of) and McCartney, London is a town steeped in rock.

◼ **The Water Rats,** 328 Grays Inn Rd. (☎7837 7269). Tube: King's Cross St. Pancras. Pub-cafe by day, stomping ground for top new talent by night. Cover £5, with band flyer £4. Open for coffee M-F 8am-noon. Music M-Sa 8pm-late.

Brixton Academy, 211 Stockwell Rd. (Ticketweb ☎7771 2000). Tube: Brixton. 1929 ex-theater; sloping floor ensures everyone can see the band. Covers all bases, from the Pogues to Senegalese stars. 4300 capacity. Box office open only on performance evenings. £15-30. Cash only at the door.

Dublin Castle, 94 Parkway (☎8806 2668). It's madness in the back room every Tu, with a blur of record execs and talent scouts on the lookout for the next big thing at *Club Fandango*. 3 bands nightly 8:45-11pm; doors open 8:30pm. £5, students £4.

Forum, 9-11 Highgate Rd. (☎7284 1001; box office 7344 0044). Tube: Kentish Town. Turn right and cross the road. Lavish Art Deco theater with great sound and views. Bjork, Jamiroquai, Oasis, Van Morrison, and others have played this 2000-capacity space.

CLASSICAL

Home to four world-class orchestras, three major concert halls, two opera houses, and two ballet companies, London is ground zero for serious music—and there's no need to break the bank. To hear some of the world's top choirs for free, head to Westminster Abbey (p. 156) or St. Paul's Cathedral (p. 158) for **Evensong.**

Barbican Hall (see **Barbican Theatre,** p. 168). Tube: Barbican. One of Europe's leading concert halls. Home to the **London Symphony Orchestra.** Tickets £6-33.

English National Opera, the Coliseum, St. Martin's Ln. (☎7632 8300; www.eno.org). Tube: Charing Cross or Leicester Sq. In London's largest theater, re-opening in January 2004 for its centennial celebration. Known for innovative productions of the classics and contemporary, avant-garde work. Box office open M-Sa 10am-8pm. £5-55; under-18 half-price with adult. Cheap standbys bookable on performance days, by phone from 9am.

The Proms, at the Royal Albert Hall. This summer season of classical music has been held since 1895, with concerts every night from mid-July to mid-Sept. "Promenade" refers to the tradition of selling dirt-cheap standing tickets, but it's the presence of up to 1000 dedicated prommers that gives the concerts their unique atmosphere. Tickets (£5-30) go on sale in May; standing room (£4) from 1½hr. before the concert.

Royal Opera House, Bow St. (☎7304 4000). Tube: Covent Garden. Known as "Covent Garden" to the aficionado, the Opera House is also home to the **Royal Ballet.** Box office open daily 10am-8pm. Best seats start at £100, but standing room and restricted-view upper balcony can be under £5. Concessions standby 4hr. before curtain £12.50-15. 67 seats from 10am day of performance £10-40.

South Bank Centre, on the South Bank (☎7960 4201). Tube: Waterloo or Embankment. All manner of serious music is on the program here; the **London Philharmonic** is the orchestra-in-residence for the **Royal Festival Hall.** Tickets for all events at the Festival Hall box office (open daily 11am-8 or 9pm); **Queen Elizabeth Hall** and **Purcell Room** box offices open 45min. before curtain. Some concessions; standbys may also be released 2hr. before performance (check ☎7921 0973).

Wigmore Hall, 36 Wigmore St. (☎7935 2141; www.wigmore-hall.org.uk). Tube: Oxford Circus. London's premier chamber music venue, in a beautiful setting with excellent acoustics. Occasional jazz. £1 fee for phone bookings. Concerts most nights 7:30pm, no concerts July-Aug. £8-20, student and senior standbys 1hr. before curtain £8-10 (cash only). Daytime concerts Su 11:30am (£10) and M 1pm (£8, seniors £6).

JAZZ, FOLK, AND WORLD

This isn't Chicago, but top **jazz** clubs still pull in big-name performers. **Folk** (which in London usually means ◪**Irish trad**) and **world** music keep a lower profile, mostly restricted to pubs and community centers.

◪ **606 Club,** 90 Lots Rd. (☎7352 5953; www.606club.co.uk). Hard to find; look for the brick arch with a light bulb and ring the doorbell. The intrepid will be rewarded with brilliant British and European jazz in a smoky basement venue. Open M-W 7:30pm-late, Th 8pm-late, F-Sa 8pm-2am, Su 8pm-midnight.

Ronnie Scott's, 47 Frith St. (☎7439 0747). Tube: Tottenham Court Rd. or Piccadilly Circus. London's oldest and most famous jazz club. 2 bands alternate 4 sets M-Sa, opener at 9:30pm and headline around 11pm. Reservations essential. Food £5-25. Cocktails £7-8. Cover M-Th £15, F-Sa £25, Su £8-12; students M-W £10. Box office open M-Sa 11am-6pm. Club open M-Sa 8:30pm-3am, Su 7:30-11pm. AmEx/MC/V.

⌐ SHOPPING

London has always been a trading city, its wealth and power built upon two millennia of commerce. London's economy is truly international—and thanks to the eclectic nature of Londoners' tastes, the range of goods is unmatched anywhere.

DEPARTMENT STORES

■ **Hamley's,** 188-189 Regent St. (☎7734 3161). Tube: Bond St. 7 floors filled with every conceivable toy and game; dozens of strategically placed product demonstrations. Open M-F 10am-8pm, Sa 9:30am-8pm, Su noon-6pm. AmEx/MC/V.

Selfridges, 400 Oxford St. (☎(0870) 837 7377). Tube: Bond St. The total department store. Covers everything from traditional tweeds to space-age clubwear. 14 eateries, hair salon, **bureau de change,** and hotel. Open M-W 10am-7pm, Th-F 10am-8pm, Sa 9:30am-7pm, Su noon-6pm. AmEx/MC/V.

Harrods, 87-135 Old Brompton Rd. (☎7730 1234). Tube: Knightsbridge. The only thing bigger than the bewildering store is the mark-up on the goods—no wonder only tourists and oil sheikhs actually shop here. Open M-Sa 10am-7pm. AmEx/MC/V/your soul.

Harvey Nichols, 109-125 Knightsbridge (☎7235 5000). Tube: Knightsbridge. Bond St., Rue St-Honoré, and Fifth Avenue all rolled up into 5 floors of the best new fashion. Open M-Tu and Sa 10am-7pm, W-F 10am-8pm, Su noon-6pm. AmEx/MC/V.

MAJOR CHAINS

As with any large city, London retailing is dominated by chains. Most have a flagship on or near Oxford St. Branches have slightly different hours, but almost all the stores listed below are open daily 10am-7pm, starting at noon on Su and staying open an hour later on Thursday night.

■ **Karen Millen** (☎(01622) 664 032). 8 locations including 262-264 Regents St. (Tube: Oxford Circus) and 22-23 James St. (Tube: Covent Garden). Best known for embroidered brocade suits and evening gowns, but edging towards a more casual line.

■ **Lush** (☎(01202) 668 545). 6 locations, including Garden Piazza (Tube: Covent Garden) and 40 Carnaby St. (Tube: Oxford Circus). All-natural cosmetics that look good enough to eat; soap is hand-cut from blocks masquerading as cakes and cheeses (£3-5) and guacamole-like facial masks are scooped from tubs.

FCUK (☎7529 7766). Flagship at 396 Oxford St. (Tube: Bond St.) Home of the advertising coup of the 90s, FCUK offers an extensive collection of items with their vaguely offensive, mildly subversive moniker. AmEx/MC/V.

Muji (☎7287 7323). Flagship at 41 Carnaby St. (Tube: Oxford Circus.) Minimalist lifestyle stores, with a Zen take on everything from clothes to kitchenware. AmEx/MC/V.

■ NIGHTLIFE

The **West End**—especially **Soho**—is the scene of much of Central London's afterdark action, from the glitzy Leicester Sq. tourist traps, like the Hippodrome and Equinox, to semi-secret underground clubs. The other major axes of London nightlife are East London's **Shoreditch** and **Hoxton** (known as Shoo) and South London's **Brixton,** which is quickly becoming London's top neighborhood for nightlife.

PUBS

Pubs might close at 11pm, but they're still an essential part of the London social scene. There are thousands of pubs in London; these are some of our favorites.

■ **Ye Olde Mitre Tavern,** 1 Ely Ct. Between Ely Pl. and Hatton Garden. Tube: Chancery Ln. To find the alley where this pub hides, look for the street lamp on Hatton Garden bearing a sign of a mitre. This classic pub was built in 1546 by the Bishop of Ely. With dark oak beams and spun glass, the two pint-sized rooms are perfect for nestling up to a bitter. Arguably London's finest pub. Open M-F 11am-11pm.

■ **The Wenlock Arms,** 26 Wenlock Rd. Tube: Old St. or Angel. One of the best-kept secrets in London, this fantastic pub is the real deal, with an unbeatable array of real ales and the best hot salt beef sandwich in the city (£3). Food served "until we run out of bread." Open Tu-F 11am-7pm, Sa 10am-4pm. MC/V.

■ **Ye Olde Cheshire Cheese,** Wine Office Ct. By 145 Fleet St. Tube: Blackfriars or St. Paul's. One-time haunt of Charles Dickens, Theodore Roosevelt, and Mark Twain. Open M-F 11am-11pm, Sa 11am-3pm and 5:30-11pm, Su noon-3:30pm. AmEx/MC/V.

The Eagle, 159 Farringdon Rd. Tube: Farringdon. The original gastropub. The Eagle offers tasty Mediterranean dishes (£10) and a down-to-earth atmosphere that appeals to both tourists and locals. Open M-F 12:30-3pm and 6:30-10pm, Sa 12:30-2:30pm and 6:30-10:30pm, Su 12:30-3:30pm. MC/V.

The Royal Oak, 44 Tabard St. Tube: Borough. Voted the Best Pub of 2003 by the Campaign for Real Ale, the Royal Oak is one of the most pleasant establishments in London. Open M-F 11:30am-11pm. MC/V.

BARS

An explosion of **club-bars** has invaded the previously forgotten gap between pubs and clubs, offering seriously stylish surroundings and top-flight DJs together with plentiful lounging space. Club-bars are usually open from noon or early evening, allowing you to skip the cover charge by arriving early and staying put. They tend to close earlier than clubs, usually between midnight and 2am.

■ **Filthy MacNasty's Whisky Café,** 68 Amwell St. Tube: Angel. This Irish pub is frequented by a galaxy of stars—the drop-in list includes Johnny Depp, Ewan McGregor, Kate Moss, and U2. Live music most Th. Occasional readings fulfill the erudite bad-boy atmosphere. 32 different whiskies (around £2). Open M-Sa noon-11pm, Su noon-10:30pm.

■ **The Market,** 240A Portobello Rd. Tube: Ladbroke Grove. The loudest spot on Portobello, The Market has a rowdy, unpretentious atmosphere. Cuban punch £3. Jazz Su 5-8pm. Open M-Sa 11am-11pm, Su noon-12:30am.

Freud, 198 Shaftesbury Ave. The sand-blasted walls occasionally echo to live jazz (M starting at 4pm). Cocktails from £3.40. Bottled beers less than £3. Light meals noon-4:30pm (£3.50-6). Open M-Sa 11am-11pm, Su noon-10:30pm. MC/V.

NIGHTCLUBS

Every major DJ in the world either lives in London or makes frequent visits. The UK has taken the lead in developing and experimenting with new types of dance music. Even weekly publications have trouble keeping up with the club scene—*Time Out* (W, £2.20), the Londoner's clubbing bible, only lists about half the happenings any given night. To stay on top of things, comb through *Time Out*, which also prints the "TOP" pass, giving you discounts on the week's shenanigans.

Working out how to get home afterwards is crucial; the Tube and regular buses stop shortly after **midnight,** and after **1am** black cabs are rare. If there's no convenient **Night Bus** home, ask the club if they can order a **minicab** for you; otherwise, order your own before you leave. Although it's technically illegal for minicabs to ply for hire, many will stop; of course, there's no guarantee that the driver is reputable. Agree on a price before you get in, and never ride alone.

DRESS. Clubs tend to fall into one of two categories: those for dancing, and those for posing. In the former, dress codes are generally relaxed, though women are usually expected to make more of an effort. At posers' clubs, however, dress is crucial. If you're not sure what to wear, call the club beforehand.

■ **Fabric,** 77a Charterhouse St. Tube: Farringdon. One of London's premier clubs, Fabric is as large and loud as it gets, featuring a vibrating main dance floor that is actually one giant speaker. Cover F £12, Sa-Su £15.

Tongue&Groove, 50 Atlantic Rd. Tube: Brixton. Soak up the brothel chic—huge black leather sofas and red lighting—and anticipate ecstatic early-morning partying. Cover £3-4. Open daily 9pm-5am.

Bug Bar, Crypt, St. Matthew's Church. Tube: Brixton. The antithesis of most self-labeled "cool" nightspots, the intimate space in this whitewashed former church crypt holds an extremely laid-back, friendly crowd. Cover under £7. Open W-Th 7pm-1am, F-Sa 8pm-3am, Su 7pm-2am.

Strawberry Moons, 15 Heddon St. Tube: Piccadilly Circus or Oxford Circus. Eccentric club with theatrical lighting effects, an animatronic talking moose head, a "time machine," and a staff that performs impromptu dance routines. Cover under £10. Open M and W 5pm-11pm, Tu and Th-Sa 5pm-3am.

Scala, 275 Pentonville Rd. (☎ 7833 2022, tickets 0870 060 0100). Tube: King's Cross. The huge main floor embraces its movie-theater past: DJs spin from the projectionist's box, tiered balconies make great people-watching, and giant screens pulse with wild visuals. Dress up. Cover £7-13.

Ministry of Sound, 103 Gaunt St. Tube: Elephant and Castle. Take the exit for South Bank University. Mecca for serious clubbers worldwide—arrive before it opens or queue all night. Emphasis on dancing rather than decor, with a massive main room, smaller second dance floor, and overhead balcony bar. Dress well—*no* jeans or sneakers, especially on Saturdays. Friday garage and R&B (10:30pm-5am; £12); Sa US and vocal house (11pm-8am; £15).

◪ **DAYTRIP FROM LONDON: WINDSOR AND ETON.** The town of Windsor and the attached village of Eton are consumed by two bastions of the British class system, **Windsor Castle** and **Eton College.** Within the ancient stone walls of Windsor Castle lie some of the most sumptuous rooms and rarest artwork in Europe. When the Queen is home, the Royal Standard flies in place of the Union Jack. During these times, large areas of the castle are unavailable to visitors, usually without warning. The **Changing of the Guard** takes place in front of the Guard Room at 11am on most days. (24hr. info ☎ 01753 831 118. Castle open Apr.-Oct. daily 10am-4pm; Nov.-Mar. 10am-3pm. £11.50, seniors £9.50, under-17 £6, families £29.) **Eton College,** founded by Henry VI in 1440, is still England's preeminent public (or private in the American system) school. The best way to see Eton, 10min. down Thames St. from the town center, across the river, is to wander around the schoolyard, a central quad complete with a statue of Henry VI. (☎ 01753 671 177. Open July-Aug. and late Mar. to mid-Apr. daily 10:30am-4:30pm; other times 2-4:30pm. £3, under-16 £2.25.)

Two train stations are near Windsor Castle; follow the signs. **Trains** (☎ 08457 484 950) pull into Windsor and Eton Central from London Paddington via Slough (50min., 2 per hr., round-trip £6.90). Trains arrive at Windsor and Eton Riverside from London Waterloo (50min., 2 per hr., round-trip £6.90). Green Line **buses** (☎ 8668 7261) make the trip from London, leaving from Eccleston Bridge (#700 and 702; 1-1½hr., round-trip £5.50-6.70).

SOUTHERN ENGLAND

Southern England's history has deep continental roots. Early Britons settled the pastoral counties of Kent, Sussex, and Hampshire after crossing the Channel. Later, William the Conqueror left his mark in the form of awe-inspiring cathedrals, many built around settlements begun by Romans. During World War II, German bombings uncovered long-buried evidence of an invasion by Caesar. This historic landscape has in turn had a profound influence on the country's national identity, inspiring such British literati as Geoffrey Chaucer, Jane Austen, and E.M. Forster. For detailed info on transport options to the Continent, see p. 48.

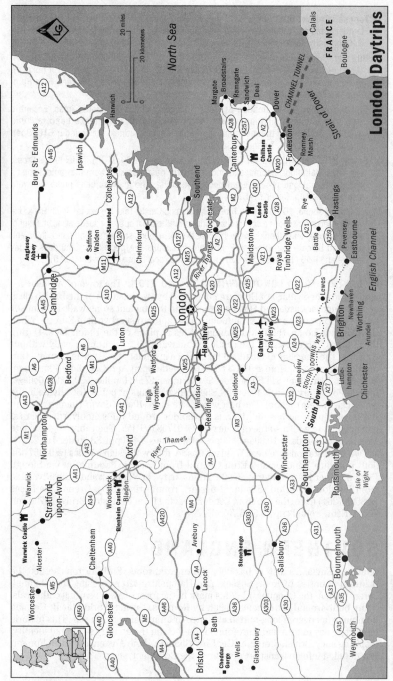

BRITAIN

London Daytrips

20 miles
20 kilometers

North Sea

FRANCE

Calais
Boulogne

CHANNEL TUNNEL

Strait of Dover

English Channel

A12
Harwich
Bury St. Edmunds
A45
Ipswich
A45
Colchester
London-Stansted
A120
Saffron Walden
Anglesey Abbey
A11
Chelmsford
A10
Cambridge
A45
A12
A127
Southend
River Thames
Rochester
A2
M2
Maidstone
A20
A21
Margate
Broadstairs
Ramsgate
Sandwich
Deal
Dover
A28
A257
A2
Canterbury
Chilham Castle
M20
Folkestone
Romney Marsh
A20
A28
Rye
Hastings
A21
Battle
A259
Pevensey
Eastbourne
Leeds Castle
Royal Tunbridge Wells
A22
A21
A25
Lewes
Newhaven
Worthing
Brighton
A23
A22
A23
M25
M11
M25
Luton
A6
A428
Bedford
A5
M1
A6
A43
Northampton
A43
A41
Watford
High Wycombe
Windsor
Reading
M4
M3
Guildford
A3
A24
Crawley
Gatwick
M23
SOUTH DOWNS WAY
South Downs
Amberley
Arundel
A32
Little-hampton
A27
Chichester
Heathrow
London
M40
A40
A34
Oxford
Woodstock
Blenheim Castle
Bladon
A420
A40
Cheltenham
A40
A46
M5
Gloucester
M50
Worcester
M5
A40
Bristol
Bath
A4
Lacock
A36
Avebury
Stonehenge
A303
A4
A36
Salisbury
A30
A303
A30
A31
A35
Bournemouth
A35
Weymouth
A31
A3
Southampton
A33
Winchester
A3
Portsmouth
Isle of Wight
Cheddar Gorge
Wells
Glastonbury
M4
Warwick
Warwick Castle
Alcester
Stratford-upon-Avon
M1
Northampton
A41
A4
Thames
River Thames

CANTERBURY   ☎ 01227

Archbishop Thomas à Becket met his demise at ▓**Canterbury Cathedral** in 1170 after an irate Henry II asked, "Will no one rid me of this troublesome priest?" Later, in his famed *Canterbury Tales*, Chaucer captured the irony of tourists visiting England's most famous execution site. (☎ 762 862. Open M-Sa 9am-5pm, Su 12:30-2:30pm and 4:30-5:30pm. ₤3, students ₤2. Audio tour ₤2.50.) **The Canterbury Tales,** on St. Margaret's St., is a museum that simulates the journey of Chaucer's pilgrims. (☎ 479 227. Open July-Aug. daily 9am-5:30pm; Mar.-June and Sept.-Oct. 9:30am-5:30pm; Nov.-Feb. Su-F 10am-4:30pm, Sa 9:30am-5:30pm. ₤6, students ₤5.50.) On Stour St., the **Canterbury Heritage Museum** tells the history of Canterbury from medieval times to WWII. (☎ 452 747. Open June-Oct. M-Sa 10:30am-5pm, Su 1:30-5pm; Nov.-May M-Sa 10:30am-5pm. ₤2.60, students ₤1.70.) For a quiet break, walk to the riverside gardens of England's first Franciscan friary, **Greyfriars,** Stour St. (Open in summer M-F 2-4pm. Free.)

Trains from London Victoria arrive at Canterbury's **East Station** (1¾hr., 2 per hr., day return ₤17), while trains from London Charing Cross and Waterloo arrive at **West Station** (1½hr., every hr., day return ₤17). National Express **buses** (☎ (08705) 808 080) arrive from London at St. George's Ln. (2hr., 2 per hr., ₤11). The **tourist office** is in the Buttermarket, 12-13 Sun St., and books rooms for a ₤2.50 fee and 10% deposit. (☎ 378 100. Open M-Sa 9:30am-5pm, Su 10am-4pm.) **B&Bs** cluster near West Station, around **High Street,** and on **New Dover Road.** For a relaxing stay, try ▓**Kipps, A Place to Sleep ❷,** 40 Nunnery Fields, home to a social, yet not overbearing, atmosphere. The friendly management offers a kitchen, comfortable lounge, and a great movie selection. (☎ 786 121. Laundry ₤3. Key deposit ₤10. Internet ₤1 per 30min. Dorms ₤11-13; singles ₤18; doubles ₤30.) The **YHA Canterbury ❷,** 54 New Dover Rd., is in a beautiful old house. (☎ 462 911. Kitchen available. **Bureau de change.** Breakfast included. Internet ₤2.50 per 30min. Reception 7:30-10am and 1-11pm. Book at least 2 weeks ahead in summer. Dorms ₤15, under-18 ₤12.) **The Camping and Caravanning Club Site ❶,** on Bekesbourne Ln., has good facilities. (☎ 463 216. Electricity and showers. ₤4-5.50 per person. ₤5 per tent.) ▓**Marlowe's ❷,** 55 St. Peter's St., serves an eclectic mix of English and Mexican food. (Entrees €7-10. Open M-Sa 9am-10:30pm, Su 10am-10:30pm.) There's a **Safeway** supermarket on St. George's Pl. (☎ 769 335. Open M-F 8am-8pm, Su 10am-4pm.) **Postal Code:** CT1 2BA.

BRIGHTON   ☎ 01273

According to legend, the future King George IV sidled into Brighton (pop.180,000) for some decidedly common hanky-panky around 1784. Today, Brighton is still the unrivaled home of the "dirty weekend"—it sparkles with a tawdry luster all its own. Before indulging, check out England's long-time obsession with the Far East at the excessively ornate **Royal Pavilion,** on Pavilion Parade, next to Old Steine. Rumor has it that King George IV wept tears of joy upon entering it, proving that wealth does not give you taste. (☎ 290 900. Open daily Apr.-Sept. 9:30am-4:30pm; Oct.-Mar. 10am-4:30pm. Admission ₤5.80, students ₤4. Guided tours daily 11:30am-2:30pm.) Around the corner on Church St. stands the **Brighton Museum and Art Gallery,** showcasing Art Nouveau paintings, English pottery, and Art Deco pieces, as well as an informative historical exhibit that thoroughly explains the phrase "dirty weekend." (Open Tu 10am-7pm, W-Sa 10am-5pm, Su 2-5pm. Free.) Before heading out to the rocky **beach,** stroll the **Lanes,** a jumble of 17th-century streets that form the heart of Old Brighton.

Brighton has plenty of nightlife options; for tips, pick up *The Punter* or *What's On* at music stores, newsstands, and pubs. Purify yourself at ▓**Font and Firkin,** Union St., in the Lanes, where the altar in this former parish house now honors the gods of rock. Live entertainment and good food make this a place worthy of devo-

BRITAIN

tion. (Music W, F-Sa. Open M-Sa 11:30am-11pm, Su noon-10:30pm.) Sample the dark rum concoction at the trendy pub **Mash Tun,** 1 Church St., which attracts an eclectic student crowd. (Open M-Sa noon-11pm, Su noon-10:30pm.) Most **clubs** are open M-Sa 9pm-2am. Brighton native Fatboy Slim still mixes occasionally at **The Beach,** 171-181 King's Rd., a popular shore-side club. (Cover £4-10.) **Casablanca,** on Middle St., plays live jazz to a predominantly student crowd. **Event II,** on West St., is crammed with the down-from-London crowd looking for thrills. Gay clubbers flock to the zany **Zanzibar,** 129 James St., for drinks and nightly entertainment.

Trains (☎(08457) 484 950) leave from Brighton Station at the northern end of Queen's Rd. for London (1¼hr., 6 per hr., £12) and Portsmouth (1½hr., every hr., £12). National Express **buses** (☎(08705) 808 080) arrive at Pool Valley from London (2hr., 15 per day, round-trip £8). The **tourist office** is at 10 Bartholomew Sq. (☎(0906) 711 2255; www.visitbrighton.com. Open Apr.-Sept. M-F 9am-5pm, Sa 10am-5pm; Oct.-Mar. M-F 9am-5pm, Sa 10am-5pm, Su 10am-4pm.) Rest at **Baggies Backpackers** ❷, 33 Oriental Pl., which has exquisite murals, frequent live music, and many spontaneous parties. Head west of West Pier along King's Rd., and Oriental Pl. is on the right. (☎733 740. Dorms £12; doubles £30.) The rowdy **Brighton Backpackers Hostel** ❷, 75-76 Middle St., features a downstairs lounge that functions as an all-night party spot. A quieter annex faces the ocean. (☎777 717. Dorms £11-12; doubles £25-30.) **Bombay Aloo** ❶, 39 Ship St., is an inventive Indian/vegetarian restaurant that serves an unbeatable all-you-can-eat special. (Vegetarian special £5. Entrees £3-7. Open noon-midnight.) **Postal Code:** BN1 1BA.

PORTSMOUTH   ☎023

Set Victorian seaside holidays against prostitutes, drunkards, and a lot of bloody cursing sailors, and the 900-year history of Portsmouth (pop. 190,500) will emerge. On the **seafront,** visitors relive D-Day, explore warships, and learn of the days when Britannia truly ruled the waves. War buffs and historians will want to plunge head first into the unrivaled ▨**Portsmouth Historic Dockyard,** in the Naval Base, which houses a fleet of Britain's most storied ships, including Henry VIII's *Mary Rose,* the HMS *Victory,* and the HMS *Warrior.* The entrance is next to the tourist office on the Hard. (Ships open Mar.-Oct. daily 10am-5:30pm; Nov.-Feb. 10am-4:45pm. Individual site tickets £9.50. Combination ticket £15, seniors and children £12.) The ▨**D-Day Museum,** on Clarence Esplanade, leads visitors through life-size dioramas of the 1944 invasion. (Open Apr.-Sept. daily 10am-5:30pm; Oct.-Mar. 10am-5pm. £5, students £3, seniors £3.75.)

Trains (☎(08457) 484 950) run to Southsea Station, on Commercial Rd., from London Waterloo (1½hr., 4 per hr., £21). National Express **buses** (☎(08705) 808 080) arrive from London (2½hr., every 2hr., £17) and Salisbury (2½hr., every 2hr., £17). The **tourist office** is on the Hard, next to the dockyard. (☎9282 6722; www.visitportsmouth.co.uk. Open daily 9:30am-5:45pm.) Moderately priced B&Bs (around £20) clutter **Southsea,** 2½km east of the Hard along the coast. Take any Southsea bus and get off at the Strand to reach the ▨**Portsmouth and Southsea Backpackers Lodge** ❶, 4 Florence Rd., which offers immaculate rooms, energetic owners, and a pan-European crowd. (☎/fax 9283 2495. Internet £1 per 30min. Dorms £12; doubles £26, with bath £29.) **Birchwood Guest House** ❷, 44 Waverly Rd., has bright, spacious rooms, an ample breakfast, and a lounge with digital cable and a bar. (☎9281 1337. Prices vary with season; call for rates.) The owner of the **Brittania Guest House** ❸, 48 Granada Rd., loves to share his maritime interests with guests. (☎814 234. Breakfast included. Singles £20; doubles £40-45.) **Country Kitchen** ❶, 59a Marmion Rd., serves savory vegetarian entrees. (£4-6. Open daily 9:30am-5pm.) **Pubs** near the Hard provide weary sailors with galley fare and grog. **Postal Code:** PO1 1AA.

WINCHESTER
☎ 01962

Having once been the center of William the Conqueror's kingdom, Winchester (pop. 32,000) revels in its storied past. Duck under the archway, pass through the square, and behold the 900-year-old **Winchester Cathedral,** 5 the Close. The 169m long cathedral is the longest medieval building in Europe; the interior holds magnificent tiles and Jane Austen's tomb. The 12th-century Winchester Bible also resides in the library. (☎857 225. Cathedral open daily 7:15am-5:30pm; east end closes 5pm. Suggested donation £3.50, students £2.50. Free tours 10am-3pm.) About 25km north of Winchester is the meek village of **Chawton,** where Jane Austen lived. It was in her cottage that she penned *Pride and Prejudice, Emma, Northanger Abbey,* and *Persuasion,* among others. Many of her manuscripts are on display. Take Hampshire **bus** #X64 (M-Sa 11 per day, round-trip £5.30), or the London and Country bus #65 from the bus station (Su); ask to be let off at the Chawton roundabout, and follow the signs. (☎0142 083 262. Open Mar.-Dec. daily 11am-4pm; Jan.-Feb. Sa-Su only, call for hours. £4, seniors £3, under-18 50p.)

Trains (☎08547 484 950) arrive at Winchester's Station Hill, at City Rd. and Sussex St., from London Waterloo (1hr., 3 or 4 per hr., £20) and Portsmouth (1hr., every hr., £7). National Express **buses** (☎08705 808 080) run from London via Heathrow (1½hr., 7 per day, £12) and Oxford (2½hr., 2 per day, £6.80). The **tourist office,** the Guildhall, Broadway, is across from the bus station. (☎840 500; www.winchester.gov.uk. Open May-Sept. M-Sa 9:30am-5:30pm, Su 11am-4pm; Oct.-Apr. M-Sa 10am-5pm.) Just a 10min. walk from town is the **Farrells B&B ❸,** 5 Ranelagh Rd., off Christchurch Rd. With large, well-kept rooms, friendly owners, and furniture a mother would rave about, this B&B feels instantly welcoming. (☎/fax 869 555. Singles £22, with bath £25; doubles £44.) The **YHA Winchester ❶,** 1 Water Ln., is located in an 18th-century watermill, and offers creative bed arrangements between the mill's roof beams. (☎853 723. Kitchen available. Lockout 10am-5pm. Curfew 11pm. Open from late Mar. to early Nov. daily; late Nov. to early Mar. weekends only. Dorms £11, students £10, under-18 £7.) **Royal Oak ❶,** on Royal Oak Passage, next to Godbegot House off High St., is yet another pub touting itself as the UK's oldest. The locally brewed hogshead cask ale (£1.75) is delicious. (Pub food £3-6. Open daily 11am-11pm.) A **Sainsbury's** supermarket is on Middle Brook St., off High St. (Open M-Sa 7am-8pm, Su 11am-5pm.) **Postal Code:** SO23 8WA.

SALISBURY
☎ 01722

Salisbury (pop. 37,000) centers around ■**Salisbury Cathedral** and its astounding 123m spire. The bases of the pillars actually bend inward under 6400 tons of limestone; the chapel houses the oldest functioning mechanical clock, which has ticked 500 million times in the last 600 years. (☎555 120. Open June-Aug. M-Sa 7:15am-8:15pm, Su 7:15am-6:15pm; Sept.-May daily 7:15am-6:15pm. Suggested donation £3.50, students and seniors £2.50. Check for free tour times.) The roof and tower tours are worthwhile. (May-Sept. M-Sa 11am, 2, 3pm, Su 4:30pm; June-Aug. also M-Sa 6:30pm. £3, students £2. Call ahead.) Nearby, one of 4 surviving copies of the **Magna Carta** rests in the **Chapter House.** (Open June-Aug. M-Sa 9:30am-5:30pm, Su noon-5:30pm; Sept.-May daily 9:30am-5:30pm. Free.)

Trains arrive at South Western Rd. from London (1½hr., every hr., £22-30) and Winchester (1½hr., £9.90). National Express **buses** (☎08705 808 080) pull into 8 Endless St. from London Victoria (2¾hr.; 4 per day; £12.20, round-trip £14); Wilts & Dorset buses (☎336 855) arrive from Bath (#X4; every hr. from 7am-6pm, £4). The **Tourist Information Centre** is on Fish Row in the Guildhall. (☎334 956. Open June-Sept. M-Sa 9:30am-6pm, Su 10:30am-4:30pm; Oct.-Apr. M-Sa 9:30am-5pm; May M-Sa 9:30am-5pm, Su 10:30am-4:30pm.) From the TIC, head left on Fish Row, turn right on Queen St., go left on Milford St., and then under the overpass to find the

YHA Salisbury ❷, in Milford Hill House, on Milford Hill, which offers 4 kitchenettes, a TV lounge, and a cafeteria. (☎327 572. Breakfast included. Internet access £2.50 per 30min. Lockout 10am-1pm. Reservations recommended. Dorms £15; under-18 £12.) **Matt and Tiggy's ❷**, 51 Salt Ln. just up from the bus station, is a welcoming 450-year-old house with warped floors and exposed ceiling beams. (☎327 443. Dorms £11-12.) At ▨**Harper's "Upstairs Restaurant" ❷**, 6-7 Ox Rd., inventive international and English dishes (£6-10) make hearty meals and the "8B48" (2 courses for £8 before 8pm) buys a heap of food. (Open M-F noon-2pm and 6-9:30pm, Sa noon-2pm and 6-10pm, Su 6-9pm.) **Postal Code:** SP1 1AB.

🗗 DAYTRIP FROM SALISBURY: STONEHENGE AND AVEBURY. A sunken colossus amid swaying grass and indifferent sheep, **Stonehenge** stands unperturbed by winds whipping at 80km per hour and legions of people who have visited for over 5000 years. The monument has retained its present shape since about 1500 BC; before that it was a complete circle of 7m-tall stones weighing up to 45 tons. Though fantastical attributions of Stonehenge's erection, ranging from Merlin to extraterrestrials, have helped build an attractive mythology around the site, the more plausible explanation—Neolithic builders using still unknown methods—is perhaps the most astonishing of all. You may admire Stonehenge for free from nearby Amesbury Hill, 2½km up A303, or pay admission at the site. (☎01980 624 715. Open daily June-Aug. 9am-7pm; mid-Mar. to May and Sept. to mid-Oct. 9:30am-6pm; mid-Oct. to mid-Mar. 9:30am-4pm. £4.40, students £3.30.) For those looking for less touristy stone circles, the neighboring megaliths at **Avebury** are a good alternative. With stones that date from 2500 BC, Avebury's titans are older and larger than their favored cousins at Stonehenge. Wilts & Dorset **buses** (☎336 855) connect from Salisbury's center and train station, and run to both sites (#3, 5, and 6; round-trip £4-6). An **Explorer** ticket (£6) allows travel all day on any bus.

BATH
☎01225

A place of pilgrimage and an architectural masterwork, Bath (pop. 83,000) has been a must-see for travelers since AD 43. In 1701, Queen Anne's trip to the springs re-established the city as a prominent meeting place for artists, politicians, and intellectuals, and the city quickly became a social capital second only to London. No longer an upper-crust resort, today Bath now plays host to crowds of tourists eager to appreciate its historic sites and still-preserved elegant charm.

🗗🗗 TRANSPORTATION AND PRACTICAL INFORMATION. Trains leave from Bath for: Bristol (15min., 4 per hr., £4.60); Exeter (1¼hr., every hr., £23); and London Paddington (1½hr., 2 per hr., £32). National Express **buses** (☎(08705) 808 080) run to London (3hr., every hr., £14) and Oxford (2hr., daily, £11). The train and bus stations are near the south end of Manvers St.; walk toward the town center and turn left on York St. to reach the **tourist office**, in Abbey Chambers. (☎(0870) 444 6442. Open May-Sept. M-Sa 9:30am-6pm, Su 10am-4pm; Oct.-Apr. M-Sa 9:30am-5pm, Su 10am-4pm.) **Postal Code:** BA1 1AJ.

🗗🗗ACCOMMODATIONS AND FOOD. Many **B&Bs** cluster on Pulteney Rd., Pulteney Gdns., and Crescent Gdns. The **International Backpackers Hostel ❷**, 13 Pierrepont St., which has musically themed rooms, is up the street from the stations. (☎446 787. Laundry £2.50. **Internet** access. Dorms £12; doubles £30.) To get to the friendly **Toad Hall Guest House ❸**, 6 Lime Grove, go across Pulteney Bridge and through Pulteney Gdns. (☎423 254. Breakfast included. Singles £22-25; doubles £40-45.) **Marlborough House ❹**, 1 Marlborough Ln., has themed rooms ranging in style from Georgian to the orientalist "Bamboo." (☎318 175. Breakfast included. Singles £33-43; doubles £75-85.) To reach **Newton Mill Camping ❶**, 4km west on Newton Rd., take bus #5 from the station to Twerton and ask to be let off at the campsite. (☎333 909. Showers free. Tents £4.30-12.) **Demuths Restaurant ❸**, 2 North Parade Passage, has creative vegetarian dishes; the chocolate fudge cake (£4.80) is delicious. (Entrees £8-12. Open Su-F 10am-5:30pm and 6:30-9:30pm, Sa 9am-5:30pm and 6-10:30pm.) Fantastic pan-Asian noodles at **f.east ❷**, 27 High St., range from £7-9. (Open M-Sa noon-11pm, Su noon-5pm.) **Guildhall Market,** between High St. and Grand Parade, has fresh fruit and vegetables. (Open daily 9am-5:30pm.)

■ **SIGHTS.** For 400 years, Bath flourished as a Roman city, its bubbling hot springs making the town a pilgrimage site for those seeking religious miracles and physical healing. The ■**Roman Baths Museum** showcases the complexity of Roman architecture and engineering, which included central heating and internal plumbing. (Open July-Aug. daily 9am-10pm; Apr.-June and Sept. 9am-6pm; Oct.-Mar. 9:30am-5pm; last admission 1hr. before closing. Admission £8.50, seniors and students £7.50, children £4.80. Audio tour included.) Nearby, the towering 15th-century **Bath Abbey** has a whimsical west facade with several angels climbing ladders up to heaven and, curiously enough, two climbing down. (Open Apr.-Oct. M-Sa 9am-6pm, Su 1-2:30pm and 4:30-5:30pm; Nov.-Mar. M-Sa 9am-4pm, Su between services. Requested donation £2.50.) Head north up Stall St., turn left on Westgate St., and turn right on Saw Close to reach Queen Sq.; **Jane Austen** lived at #13. Continue up Gay St. to **The Circus,** where Thomas Gainsborough, William Pitt, and David Livingstone lived. To the left down Brock St. is the **Royal Crescent,** a half-moon of Gregorian townhouses bordering **Royal Victoria Park.** The **botanical gardens** nurture 5000 species of plants. (Open M-Sa 9am-dusk, Su 10am-dusk. Free.) The dazzling **Museum of Costume,** on Bennet St. left of the Circus, will satisfy any fashion fetish. (Open daily 10am-5pm. £6; joint ticket with Roman Baths £11.)

GLASTONBURY ☎01458

The seat of Arthurian legend and the reputed cradle of Christianity in England, Glastonbury (pop. 6,900) is an amalgam of myth and religion. Legend has it that Joseph of Arimathea founded ■**Glastonbury Abbey,** on Magdelene St., in AD 63. The abbey was destroyed during the English Reformation, but the colossal pile of ruins that remains still invokes the grandeur of the original church. For Arthurian buffs, **Glastonbury Tor** is a must-see. Once an island, the 160m Tor is reputedly the site of the Isle of Avalon, where King Arthur sleeps until his country needs him. To reach the Tor, take the bus in summer (£1), or turn right at the top of High St. onto Lambrook, which becomes Chilkwell St.; turn left onto Wellhouse Ln. and follow the path up the hill. On your way, visit the **Chalice Well,** on Chilkwell St., where it is said that Joseph of Arimathea washed the Holy Grail. Legend holds that the well once ran red with Christ's blood. Pilgrims of a different sort flock to the annual summertime **Glastonbury Festival,** Britain's largest music event. The week-long concert takes place at the end of June and has featured some of the world's biggest bands. (Tickets ☎(0115) 912 9129; www.glastonburyfestivals.co.uk.)

No trains serve Glastonbury, but First **buses** (☎(01934) 429 336) run from Bath via Wells (1¼hr., every hr., £4). From the bus stop, turn right on High St. to reach the **tourist office,** the Tribunal, 9 High St., which books rooms for a £3 fee. (☎832 954; fax 832 949. Open Apr.-Sept. Su-Th 10am-5pm, F-Sa 10am-5:30pm; Oct.-Mar. Su-Th 10am-4pm, F-Sa 10am-4:30pm.) **Glastonbury Backpackers ❷**, at the corner of Magdalene St. and High St., has a lively cafe bar and friendly staff; both compliment a great location. (☎833 353. Breakfast £2-5. **Internet** £1 per 30min. Dorms £12; doubles £30, with bath £35.) **Postal Code:** BA6 9HG.

THE CORNISH COAST

With lush cliffsides stretching out into the Atlantic, Cornwall's terrain doesn't feel quite like England. Indeed, its isolation made it a favored place for Celtic migration in the face of Saxon conquest; though the Cornish language is no longer spoken, the area remains protective of its distinctive past. England's southwest tip has some of the broadest, sandiest beaches in northern Europe, and the surf is up year-round, whether or not the sun decides to break through.

NEWQUAY. Known to the locals as "the new California," Newquay (pop. 30,000) is an incongruous slice of surfer culture in the middle of Cornwall. Winds descend on **Fistral Beach** with a vengeance, creating what some consider the best surfing conditions in Europe. The enticing **Lusty Glaze Beach** beckons from the bay side. Drink up at **The Chy**, 12 Beach Rd., a chic loft with the hippest interior in Newquay. (open M-Sa 10am-2am, Su 10am-12:30am.) Then, dance at **Tall Trees**, 12 Beach Rd. (Cover £2-6. Open mid-Mar. to mid-Sept. M-Sa 9pm-2am; mid-Sept. to mid.-Mar. W-Sa 9pm-2am.) All **trains** (☎(08457) 484 950) to Newquay come from Par (50min., 4-5 per day, £4.30). From Par, trains connect to Plymouth (1hr., 15 per day, £6.80) and Penzance (2hr., 12 per day, £9.10). First (☎(0870) 608 2608) **buses** arrive from St. Ives (2¼hr., 4 per day, £4.50). National Express (☎(08705) 808 080) runs to London (6hr., 2-4 per day, £32). The **tourist office** is on Marcus Hill, a block from the bus station. (☎(01637) 854 020. Open June-Sept. M-Sa 9:30am-5:30pm, Su 9:30am-3:30pm; Oct.-May M-F 9:30am-4:30pm, Sa 9:30am-12:30pm.) **Original Backpackers ❷**, 16 Beachfield Ave., has a fantastic location off Bank St. and near Central Sq., facing the beach. (☎(01637) 874 668. £12 per person, £49 per week.)

PENZANCE. Penzance is the very model of an ancient English pirate town. A Benedictine monastery, **St. Michael's Mount**, was built on the spot where St. Michael appeared in AD 495. The interior is modest, but the grounds are lovely and the 30-story views are captivating. (Open July-Aug. 10:30am-5:30pm and most weekends; Apr.-Oct. M-F 10:30am-5:30pm; Nov.-Mar. M, W, and F by guided tours only. £4.80.) During low tide, visitors can walk to the mount; during high tide, take ferry bus #2 or 2A to Marazion Sq. and catch a ferry (£1). Penzance boasts an impressive number of art galleries; pick up the *Cornwall Gallery Guide* (£1) at the tourist office. **Trains** (☎(08457) 484 950) go to London (5½hr., 7 per day, £56) and Plymouth (2hr., every hr., £11). National Express (☎(08705) 808 080) **buses** also run to London (8hr., 8 per day, £29) and Plymouth (3hr., 2 per hr., £6). The **tourist office** is between the train and bus stations on Station Rd. (☎(01736) 362 207. Open May-Sept. M-Sa 9am-5:30pm, Su 10am-1pm; Oct.-Apr. M-F 9am-5pm, Sa 10am-1pm.) **❷Blue Dolphin Penzance Backpackers ❷**, on Alexandra Rd., is relaxed and well-kept. (☎(01736) 363 836; fax 363 844. **Internet** 5p per min. Dorms £10; doubles £24.) **❷The Turk's Head ❸**, 49 Chapel St., is a pub once sacked by pirates.

ST. IVES. St. Ives (pop. 11,400) is 15km north of Penzance, on a spit of land edged by pastel beaches and azure waters. The town drew a colony of painters and sculptors in the 1920s; Virginia Woolf's *To the Lighthouse* is thought to refer to the Godrevy Lighthouse in the distance. The *Cornwall Gallery Guide* (£1) will help you navigate the dozens of galleries here, but St. Ives's real attractions are its beaches. **❷Porthminster Beach**, downhill from the train station, is a magnificent stretch of white sand and tame waves. **Trains** (☎(08457) 484 950) to St. Ives usually pass through or change at **St. Erth** (15min., every hr., £1.60), though direct service is occasionally available. National Express (☎(08705) 808 080) **buses** go to Plymouth (3hr., 4 per day) and Penzance (20min., 4 per day). First (☎(0870) 608 2608) buses #15, 16, and X17 go to Penzance (30min., 2 per hr., £2.40); bus #301 runs to Newquay (2¼hr., 4 per day, £4.50). The **tourist office** is in The Guildhall on Street-an-Pol. From the stations, walk down to the foot of Tregenna Hill and turn right. (☎(01736) 796 297. Open Easter-Sept. M-Sa 9:30am-6pm, Su 10am-4pm; Oct.-Easter M-F 9am-5pm.) **St. Ives International Backpackers ❷**, The Stenmack, is in a 19th-century Methodist church. (☎(01736) 799 444. **Internet** £1 per 15min. Dorms £9-13.)

EAST ANGLIA AND THE MIDLANDS

The rich farmland and watery flats of East Anglia stretch northeast from London, cloaking the counties of Cambridgeshire, Norfolk, and Suffolk, as well as parts of Essex. Literally England's newest landscape, the vast plains of the fens were drained as late as the 1820s. Mention of The Midlands inevitably evokes grim urban images, but there is a unique heritage and quiet grandeur to this smoke-stacked pocket. Even Birmingham, the region's much-maligned center, has its saving graces, among them a lively nightlife and the Cadbury chocolate empire.

OXFORD   ☎01865

A near millennium of scholarship at Oxford has seen the education of 25 British prime ministers as well as numerous other world leaders. Academic pilgrims can delve into the basement room of Blackwell's Bookstore, explore the impeccable galleries of the Ashmolean Museum, or stroll through the perfectly maintained quadrangles of Oxford's 39 colleges. Secluded from the touring crowds, these quiet destinations reveal Oxford's history and irrepressible grandeur.

TRANSPORTATION AND PRACTICAL INFORMATION

Trains run from Botley Rd., which is down Park End, to London Paddington (1hr., 2-4 per hr., round-trip £15). **Buses** depart from Gloucester Green. **Oxford CityLink** (☎785 400) goes to: London Victoria (1¾hr.; 3 per hr.; round-trip £10, students £7.50); Gatwick (2hr.; every hr. daytime, every 2 hr. at night; round-trip £21); and Heathrow (1½hr., 2 per hr., day return £14). Most local buses board on the streets around Carfax and have fares between 80p and £1.20. The **tourist office,** 15-16 Broad St., books rooms for a £4 fee and runs 2hr. walking tours for £6-7. (☎726 871. Open M-Sa 9:30am-5pm, Su 10am-3:30pm.) You can access the **Internet** at **Pickwick Papers,** 90 Gloucester Green, near the bus station. (£1 per 30min. Open M 5am-7pm, Tu-Sa 5am-9pm, Su 7am-6pm.) **Postal Code:** OX1 1ZZ.

ACCOMMODATIONS

In summer, book at least one week ahead. **B&Bs** line the main roads out of town. On Banbury Rd. (bus #2A, 2C, or 2D), B&Bs are located in the 300s; cheaper ones lie in the 200s and 300s on Iffley Rd. (bus #3 or 4 to "Rose Hill"), and on Abingdon Rd. in south Oxford (bus #16). Expect to pay £25 per person. Take the "Rose Hill" bus from the bus station, train station, or Carfax Tower to reach **▨Heather House ❹,** 192 Iffley Rd., which offers sparkling, modern rooms, replete with TV, phone, coffee, and tea in every room. (☎249 757. Singles £33; doubles £66. Reduced rates for longer stays.) **Oxford Backpacker's Hotel ❷,** 9a Hythe Bridge St., has a lively backpacker atmosphere, fostered by an inexpensive bar, pool table, and constant music. Linen provided, but no towels. (☎721 761. Internet 50p per 10 min. Dorms £13-14.) The **YHA Youth Hostel ❷,** 2a Botley Rd., immediately to the right of the train station, is in a superb location with bright surroundings. Facilities include kitchen, lockable wardrobes, and towels (£1). Most rooms have 4-6 bunks. (☎727 275. Breakfast included. 4-6 bunk dorms £19,

BRITAIN

Oxford

★ NIGHTLIFE
Freud, 2

○ COLLEGES
All Souls College, T
Balliol College, H
Brasenose College, S
Christ Church, Z
Corpus Christi
   College, AA
Exeter College, O
Hertford College, P
Jesus College, N
Keble College, B
Lincoln College, R
Magdalen College, X
Harris Manchester
   College, K
Mansfield College, F
Merton College, BB
New College, Q
Nuffield College, L
Oriel College, V
Pembroke College, Y
Queen's College, U
Regent's Park
   College, C
Somerville College, A
St. Catherine's
   College, DD
St. Cross College, D
St. Hilda's College, CC
St. John's College, E
St. Peter's College, M
Trinity College, I
University College, W
Wadham College, J
Worcester College, G

⬥ ACCOMMODATIONS
Heather House, 13
Newton House, 11
Oxford Backpackers
   Hostel, 6
YHA Youth Hostel, 5

● FOOD
Chiang Mai, 10
Heroes, 8
Kazbar, 12
Mick's Cafe, 4
The Nosebag, 7

▯ PUBS
The Eagle and Child, 3
The Old Bookbinders, 1
Turf Tavern, 9

under-18 £14, students £1 off.) The recently renovated **Newton House ❹**, 82-84 Abingdon Rd., about 0.75km from town, has an affable proprietress and dark wardrobes that await Narnia fans. (☎240 561. Doubles £58-64.) **Oxford Camping and Caravaning ❶**, 426 Abingdon Rd., offers a cheap alternative for the backpacker planning to stay more than one night. (☎244 088. Toilet and laundry facilities. Pitch fee £4.60. Electricity fee £2.60. Open 7am-11pm. £3.80-5 per person; nonmembers an additional £5.65.)

FOOD

Oxford students tired of cafeteria food keep cheap restaurants in business. **Kebab vans** roam Broad St., High St., Queen St., and St. Aldate's St. (kebabs £2-5). Across Magdalen Bridge, try restaurants along the first four blocks of Cowley Rd. **Kazbar ❶**, 25-27 Cowley Rd., is a favorite *tapas* bar among locals. (£5 lunch special includes two *tapas* and a drink, served until 4pm. Open M-F noon-11pm.) **The Nosebag ❷**, 6-8 St. Michael's St., has a gourmet menu served cafeteria-style with good veggie options. (Lunch under £6.50; dinner under £8. Open M-Th 9:30am-10pm, F-Sa 9:30am-10:30pm, Su 9:30am-9pm.) The chic **Chiang Mai ❷**, 130a High St., tucked down an alley, is a popular Thai restaurant; The jungle curry with rabbit (£7) is great. (Open M-Sa noon-2pm and 6-11pm, Su noon-1pm and 6-10pm. Reservations recommended.) **Heroes ❶**, 8 Ship St., is filled with students feeding on sandwiches and freshly baked breads. (Sandwiches £2-4. Open M-F 8am-9pm, Sa 8:30am-6pm, Su 10am-5pm.) Despite its small size, **Mick's Cafe ❶**, next to the train station on Cripley Rd., serves up large English breakfasts of bigger value. (Breakfast £2.70-5. Open M-F 6am-2pm, Sa 7am-1pm, Su 8am-1pm.) **The Covered Market,** between Market St. and Carfax, sells produce and deli goods. (Open M-Sa 8am-5:30pm.)

SIGHTS

The tourist office's *Welcome to Oxford* guide (£1) lists the colleges' public visiting hours. Start by hiking up the 99 steps of **Carfax Tower** for a great view of the city. (Open Apr.-Oct. M-F 10am-5pm, Su 11am-5pm. £1.20.) Just down St. Aldate's St. from Carfax, **Christ Church College** has Oxford's grandest quad and its most socially distinguished students. The **Christ Church Chapel** also serves as the university's cathedral. It was here that the Reverend Charles Dodgson (better known as Lewis Carroll) first met Alice Liddell, the dean's daughter; the White Rabbit can be spotted fretting in the hall's stained glass. (Open M-Sa 9:30am-11:45am and 2:30-4pm, no entry after 4pm, Su 9:45am-11:45am, 2:30-4:45pm. Services Su 8, 10, and 11:15am, and 6pm; weekdays 6pm. £4, students £3.) From Carfax, head up Cornmarket St., which becomes Magdalen St., to get to the imposing **Ashmolean Museum**, Beaumont St., houses works by van Gogh, Matisse, Monet, Michelangelo, Rodin, and da Vinci. Opened in 1683, the Ashmolean was Britain's first public museum, and still possesses one of its finest collections. From Carfax, head up Cornmarket St., which becomes Magdalen St.; Beaumont St. is on the left. (Open Tu-Sa 10am-5pm, Su 2-5pm. Th open until 7:30pm in the summer. Free.) **Bodleian Library,** on Catte St. off of High St., is Oxford's principal reading and research library that boasts over 5 million books; no one has ever been permitted to check one out. (Open M-F 9am-6pm, Sa 9am-1pm. Tours £3.50.) Next to the Bodleian is the **Sheldonian Theatre,** a Romanesque auditorium designed by a teenaged Christopher Wren. The Sheldonian houses graduation ceremonies conducted in Latin, as well as world-class opera performances. The cupola affords a picturesque view of Oxford's spires. (Open M-Sa 10am-12:30pm and 2-4:30pm. £1.50, children £1.) You could browse for days at **Blackwell's Bookstore,** 53 Broad St., which according to the *Guinness Book of Records* is the world's largest room devoted to bookselling. (☎333 606. Open M and W-Sa 9am-6pm, Tu 9:30am-6pm, Su 11am-5pm.)

♫ ▮ **ENTERTAINMENT AND NIGHTLIFE**

Punting on the River Thames (known in Oxford as the Isis) or on the River Cherwell (CHAR-wul) is a traditional Oxford pastime. Punters receive a tall pole, a small oar, and an advisory against falling into the water. **Magdalen Bridge Boat Company,** just under Magdalen Bridge, rents boats. (☎202 643. £12 per hr.; deposit £30 plus ID. Open Apr.-Oct. daily 7:30am-9pm. Cash only.) Music and drama at Oxford are cherished arts. Attend a concert or Evensong service at one of the colleges—the **New College Choir** is one of the best boy choirs around (www.new.ox.ac.uk/choir). The **Oxford Playhouse,** 11-12 Beaumont St., is a venue for bands, dance troupes, and both amateur and professional plays. (☎798 600. Standby tickets available for seniors and students.) The **City of Oxford Orchestra,** the city's professional orchestra, plays a subscription series in the Sheldonian and in college chapels during the summer. (☎744 457. Tickets £10-20).

Pubs far outnumber colleges in Oxford. The 13th-century ▮**Turf Tavern** on Bath Pl., off Holywell St., is the most popular student bar, tucked within an alley of an alley. (Open M-Sa 11am-11pm, Su noon-10:30pm. Kitchen open noon-7:30pm.) Walk up Walton St. and take a left at Jericho St. to reach **The Old Bookbinders,** 17-18 Victor St., a crowded little pub full of locals. Occasional beer fests feature over 25 ales. (Open M-Sa until 11pm, Su 10am-10:30pm.). **The Eagle and Child,** 49 St. Giles, moistened the tongues of C.S. Lewis and J.R.R. Tolkien for 25 years; *The Chronicles of Narnia* and *The Hobbit* were first read aloud here. (Open M-Sa noon-11pm, Su noon-10:30pm.) Although pubs in Oxford tend to close down by 11pm, nightlife lasts until 3am; grab *This Month in Oxford* at the tourist office. **Walton Street** and **Cowley Road** host late-night clubs, as well as many ethnic restaurants and offbeat shops. **Freud,** 119 Walton St., in a former church, is a cafe by day and collegiate cocktail bar by night. (Open Su-Tu 11am-midnight, W-Sa 11am-2am.)

STRATFORD-UPON-AVON ☎01789

Former native William Shakespeare is the area's industry; you'll find even the vaguest connections to the Bard fully exploited. Beyond the "Will Power" t-shirts, though, the aura of Shakespeare remains—in the quite grace of the Avon and the pin-drop silence before a soliloquy in the Royal Shakespeare Theatre.

▮ **HENCE, AWAY!** Thames **trains** (☎08457 484 950) arrive from: Birmingham (1hr., every hr., £3.80); London Paddington (2¼hr., 7 per day, £23); and Warwick (25min., 7 per day, £2.80). National Express (☎08705 808 080) runs **buses** from London Victoria (3hr., 3 per day, £13).

▮ **WHO IS'T THAT CAN INFORM ME.** The **tourist office,** Bridgefoot, across Warwick Rd., offers maps and a free accommodations guide. (☎293 127. Open Apr.-Oct. M-Sa 9am-5pm, Su 10:30am-4:30pm; Nov.-Mar. M-Sa 9am-5pm.) Surf the **Internet** at **Cyber Junction,** 28 Greenhill St. (£3 per 30min., £5 per hr.; students £2.50/4.) **Postal Code:** CV37 6PU.

▮▮ **TO SLEEP, PERCHANCE TO DREAM...AND FOOD.** To B&B or not to B&B? Bed and Breakfasts line Evesham Place, Evesham Road, Grove Road, and Shipston Road, but reservations are still a must. The **YHA Stratford ❷,** Wellsbourne Rd., is located 3km from Clopton Bridge. Follow B4086 35min. from the town center, or take bus X18 from Bridge St. The hostel includes B&B amenities like breakfast, a kitchen, and Internet access (£1 per 15min.), all housed within a gorgeous 200 year-old house. (☎297 093. Midnight lockout. Dorms £17, under-18 £12.) **Carl-**

ton Guest Houes ❸, 22 Evesham Pl., has spacious rooms and spectacular service. (☎293 548. Singles £20-26; doubles £40-52.) **Melita Hotel ❹**, 37 Shipston Rd., is an upscale B&B that offers its patrons a lovely garden and an "honesty bar," where guests can help themselves to a drink. (☎292 432. Breakfast included. Singles £39; doubles £72.) **Riverside Caravan Park ❶**, Tiddington Rd., 1½km east of Stratford on B4086, has **camping** with beautiful but crowded views of the Avon. (☎292 312. Open Easter-Oct. Free electricity and showers. Tent and up to 4 people £10.)

Opposition ❸, 13 Sheep St., is a bistro that receives rave reviews from locals for its varied cuisine. The lasagne (£9) and lamb steak (£12) are definitely worth a try. (Open M-Sa noon-2pm and 5-10pm, Su noon-2pm and 6-9pm.) **Hussain's Indian Cuisine ❷**, 6a Chapel St., has fantastic *chicken tikka masala;* keep an eye out for regular Ben Kingsley. (Lunch £6. Main dishes from £6.50. Open M-W 5pm-midnight, Th-Su 12:30-2:30pm and 5pm-midnight.) A great place for delicious breads, sandwiches, and pastries is **Le Petit Croissant ❶**, 17 Wood St. (Baguettes from 80p. Sandwiches £1.80-2.50. Open M-Sa 8:30am-6pm.) A **Safeway** supermarket is on Alcester Rd. (Open M-W and Sa 8am-9pm, Th-F 8am-10pm, Su 10am-4pm.)

◙ ♫ **DRINK DEEP ERE YOU DEPART (FOR THE SIGHTS).** Traffic at the Shakespeare sights peaks around 2pm, so try to hit them before 11am or after 4pm. Die-hard fans can buy a ticket for admission to all five official Shakespeare properties: Anne Hathaway's cottage, Mary Arden's House and Countryside Museum, Shakespeare's Birthplace, New Place and Nash's House, and Hall's Croft (£13, students and seniors £12). You can also buy a ticket that covers only the latter three sights (£9, students and seniors £8). **Shakespeare's Birthplace,** on Henley St., is part period re-creation and part exhibition of Shakespeare's life and works. (Open summer M-Sa 9am-5pm and Su 9:30am-5pm; mid-season M-Sa 10am-5pm and Su 10:30am-5pm; winter M-Sa 10am-4pm and Su 10:30am-4pm.) **New Place,** on High St., was Stratford's finest home when Shakespeare bought it in 1597. Only the foundation remains—it can be viewed from **Nash's House,** which belonged to the husband of Shakespeare's granddaughter. **Hall's Croft** and **Mary Arden's House** also capitalize on connections to Shakespeare's extended family, but also provide exhibits of what life was like in Elizabethan times. Pay homage to Shakespeare's grave in the **Holy Trinity Church,** on Trinity St. (Admission £1).

Get thee to a performance by the world-famous ▨**Royal Shakespeare Company;** recent sons include Kenneth Branagh and Ralph Fiennes. Tickets for all three theaters—the Royal Shakespeare Theatre, the Swan Theatre, and the Other Place— are sold through the box office in the foyer of the Royal Shakespeare Theatre, on Waterside. (☎403 403, 24hr. ticket hotline ☎(0870) 609 1110; www.rsc.org.uk. Open M-Sa 9:30am-8pm. Tickets £5-40; highly demanded student standbys £8-12. Tours M-Sa 1:30, 5:30pm, and Su noon, 1, 2, 3, 5:30pm. £4, students and seniors £3.)

THE COTSWOLDS

The Cotswolds have deviated little from their etymological roots - "Cotswolds" means "sheep enclosure in rolling hillsides." Grazing sheep and cattle roam 2,000 square kilometers of vivid, verdant hills, which hide tiny towns barely touched by modern times. These old Roman settlements and tiny Saxon villages, hewn from the famed Cotswold stone, demand a place on any itinerary, although their relative inaccessibility via public transportation will necessitate extra effort to get there.

▐ **TRANSPORTATION.** Useful gateway cities are Cheltenham, Oxford, and Bath. **Moreton-in-Marsh** is one of the bigger villages and has **trains** to Oxford (30min., every hr., £7.90) and London (1½hr., every 1-2hr., £25). The Cotswolds are much easier to reach by **bus.** *Getting There,* a pamphlet that details bus information in

The Cotswolds, is available free from the Cheltenham tourist office. **Pulham's Coaches** (☎ (01451) 820 369) run from Cheltenham to Moreton-in-Marsh (1hr.; M-Sa 8 per day, Su daily; £1.70) via Stow-on-the-Wold (50min., £2).

Local roads are perfect for biking. **The Toy Shop,** on High St. in Moreton-in-Marsh, rents bikes. (☎ (01608) 650 756. Open M and W-Sa 9am-1pm and 2-5pm. £12 per day.) Visitors can also experience the Cotswolds as the English have for centuries by treading footpaths from village to village. **Cotswold Way,** spanning 160km from Bath to Chipping Camden, gives hikers glorious vistas of hills and dales. The *Cotswold Events* booklet lists anything from music festivals and antique markets to cheese-rolling and woolsack races along the Cotswold Way. A newer way of seeing the region, the **Cotswold Experience** is a full-day bus tour that starts in Bath and visits five of the most scenic villages. (☎ (01225) 477 101. £22, students £18.)

WINCHCOMBE, MORETON-IN-MARSH, STOW-ON-THE-WOLD. 10km north of Cheltenham on A46, **Sudeley Castle,** once the manor of King Ethelred the Unready, crowns the town of **Winchcombe.** (Open Mar.-Oct. daily 11am-5pm. £6.70.) The Winchcombe **tourist office** is in Town Hall. (☎ (01242) 602 925. Open Apr.-Oct. M-Sa 10am-5pm, Su 10am-4pm, closed 1-2pm; Nov.-Mar. sa-Su 10am-4pm.) With a train station, relatively frequent bus service, and bike shop, **Moreton-in-Marsh** is a convenient base for exploring the Cotswolds. The **tourist office** is in the District Council Building. (☎ (01608) 650 881. Open M 8:45am-4pm, Tu-W 8:45am-5:15pm, Th 8:45am-7:30pm, F 8:45am-4:45pm, Sa 9:30am-1pm.) **Warwick House B&B ❸,** on London Rd., offers many luxuries, including a pleasant garden and access to a nearby gym. Book 2 weeks in advance. (☎ (01608) 650 733. www.snoozeandsizzle.com. Singles £21-25; doubles £42-50.) **Stow-on-the-Wold,** the self-proclaimed "Heart of the Cotswolds," sits atop a hill, offering visitors fine views and a sense of the Cotswold pace of life. The **tourist office** is in Hollis House on The Square. (☎ (01451) 831 082. Open Easter-Oct. M-Sa 9:30am-5:30pm; Nov.-Easter M-Sa 9:30am-4:30pm.) The **YHA youth hostel ❷** is near the tourist office on The Square. (☎ (01451) 830 497. Open mid Feb.-Oct. daily; Nov.-Dec. F-Sa. Dorms £13, under-18 £9.)

BIRMINGHAM
☎ 0121

As the industrial heart of the Midlands, Birmingham (pop. 1.2 million) is steadily overcoming its reputation for lack of urban charm. At night, the city truly comes alive, fueled by world-class entertainers and a young university crowd. Twelve minutes south of town by rail lies ■**Cadbury World,** an unabashed celebration of the famed chocolate company. Take a train from New St. to Bournville, or bus #83, 84, or 85 from the city center. (☎ 451 4159. Open daily 10am-3pm; closed certain days, so call ahead to confirm. £8.80, students and seniors £7, children £6.60.) The **Birmingham Jazz Festival** (☎ 454 7020) brings over 200 jazz singers and instrumentalists to town during the first 2 weeks of July; book through the tourist office. **Broad St.** is lined with trendy cafe-bars and clubs. Pick up the bimonthly *What's On* to discover the hotspots. **Stoodibakers,** 192 Broad St., has a dark decor set against a futuristic warehouse motif. Dress trendy. (Cover £4 F-Sa after 9:30pm.) A thriving gay-friendly scene has arisen in the area around **Essex St.** Head to **Nightingale,** Kent. St, for a predominantly gay clientele enjoying 2 dance floors, 5 bars, and a jazz lounge. (Cover £6 Sa. Open Su-Th 5pm-2am, F 5pm-4am, Sa 5pm-7am.)

Birmingham is the center of a web of train and bus lines between London, central Wales, southwest England, and all destinations north. **Trains** arrive in New St. Station (☎ (08457) 484 950) from: Liverpool Lime St. (1½hr., 1-2 per hr., £19); London Euston (2hr., 4 per hr., £30); Manchester Piccadilly (2½hr., every hr., £19); and Oxford (1¼hr., 2 per hr., £19). National Express **buses** (☎ 08705 808 080) arrive in Digbeth Station from: Cardiff (3hr., 3 per day, £19); Liverpool (2½hr., every hr., round-trip £9.30); London (3hr., every hr., £13); and Manchester (2½hr., every 2hr., round-trip £10). The **tourist office,** in the Bullring, makes room reservations. (☎202 5099. Open M-Sa 9:30am-5:30pm, Su 10:30am-4:30pm.) Despite its size, Birmingham has no hostels, and inexpensive B&Bs are rare. **Hagley Road** is your best bet. To reach **Wentworth Hotel ❹,** 103 Wentworth Rd., turn right onto Lonsdale Rd. from Harbone swimming bath and then left onto Wentworth Rd. The hotel provides luxurious baths in most rooms, a comfy lounge, and bar downstairs. (☎427 4546. Breakfast included. Singles £32; doubles £54.) **Thai Edge ❸,** 7 Oozells Sq., serves up big portions of delicious Thai specialities. (Entrees £6-15. Open Su-Th 5:30pm-11:30pm, F-Sa-5:30pm-midnight.) **Postal Code:** B2 4AA.

CAMBRIDGE   ☎01223

In contrast to metropolitan Oxford, Cambridge is determined to retain its pastoral academic robes. As the tourist office will tell you, the city manages (rather than encourages) visitors. No longer the exclusive preserve of upper-class sons, the university now welcomes women and state-school pupils; during May Week, which marks term's end, Cambridge shakes off its reserve with gin-soaked glee.

▐▀▐▌ TRANSPORTATION AND PRACTICAL INFORMATION. Trains (☎(08457) 484 950) run from Station Rd. to London King's Cross (45min., 2 per hr., £16) and London Liverpool St. (1¼hr., 2 per hr., £16). **Buses** run from Drummer St.; **National Express** (☎(08705) 808 080) goes to London Victoria (2hr., 2 per hr., from £9), and **Stagecoach Express** (☎(01604) 676 060) runs to Oxford (3hr., every hr., from £6). The **tourist office,** on Wheeler St., is just south of Market Sq. (☎(09065) 862 526; calls cost 60p per min. Open Apr.-Oct. M-F 10am-5:30pm, Sa 10am-5pm, Su 11am-4pm; Nov.-Mar. M-F 10am-5:30pm, Sa 10am-5pm.) **Postal Code:** CB2 3AA.

▐▀▐▌ ACCOMMODATIONS AND FOOD. Many of the **B&Bs** around **Portugal Street** and **Tenison Road** are open only in summer. Check the list at the tourist office or pick up their guide to lodgings (50p). ◪**Warkworth Guest House ❹,** Warkworth Terr., is an elegantly decorated home with sunny, ensuite rooms. They also provide packed lunches on request. (☎363 682. Singles from £40; doubles from £60.) Two blocks from the train station, **Tenison Towers Guest House ❸,** 148 Tenison Rd., is impeccably clean, and has airy rooms filled with fresh flowers. (☎566 511. Singles £20-25; doubles £40-50.) **YHA Cambridge ❷,** 97 Tenison Rd., has a welcoming atmosphere. (☎354 601. Kitchen available. **Bureau de change.** Breakfast £3.50. Laundry facilities. **Internet** 50p per 7min. Call in advance. Dorms £16, under-18 £12.) **Home from Home B&B ❸,** 78 Milton Rd., offers apartments including decked-out kitchens and enormous lounges, in addition to spotless B&B singles and doubles. (☎323 555. Singles £35-40; doubles £50-60; apartments £350 per week.) Take Cambus #118 from Drummer St. to reach **Highfield Farm Touring Park ❶,** Long Rd., Comberton. (☎262 308. Showers included. £7 per tent, with car £8.75.)

◪**Dojo's Noodle Bar ❶,** 1-2 Mill Ln., whips out enormous plates of noodles for less than £6. (Open M-Th noon-2:30pm and 5:30-11pm, F-Su noon-4pm and 5:30-11pm.) **Rainbow's Vegetarian Bistro ❷,** 9a King's Parade, is a creative nook featuring delicious international vegetarian fare. (All entrees £7.30. Open M-Sa 11am-11pm.) **Market Square** has cheap fruits and vegetables. (Open M-Sa 9:30am-4:30pm.)

▐▀▐▌ SIGHTS AND ENTERTAINMENT. Cambridge is an architect's dream—it packs some of the most breathtaking examples of English architecture into less than 3 square kilometers. It's most exciting to behold during the university's three eight-week terms: Michaelmas (Oct.-Dec.), Lent (Jan.-Mar.), and Easter (Apr.-June). **Trinity College** houses the stunning **Wren Library,** on Trinity St., home to A.A. Milne's handwritten manuscript of *Winnie the Pooh* and the equally great original

BRITAIN

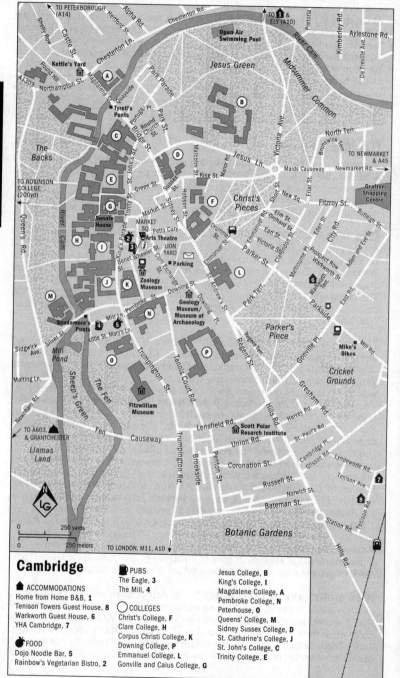

Cambridge

🏠 **ACCOMMODATIONS**
Home from Home B&B, **1**
Tenison Towers Guest House, **8**
Warkworth Guest House, **6**
YHA Cambridge, **7**

🍺 **PUBS**
The Eagle, **3**
The Mill, **4**

◯ **COLLEGES**
Christ's College, **F**
Clare College, **H**
Corpus Christi College, **K**
Downing College, **P**
Emmanuel College, **L**
Gonville and Caius College, **G**

🍎 **FOOD**
Dojo Noodle Bar, **5**
Rainbow's Vegetarian Bistro, **2**

Jesus College, **B**
King's College, **I**
Magdalene College, **A**
Pembroke College, **N**
Peterhouse, **O**
Queens' College, **M**
Sidney Sussex College, **D**
St. Catharine's College, **J**
St. John's College, **C**
Trinity College, **E**

copy of Isaac Newton's *Principia*. (Chapel and courtyard open daily 10am-5pm. Free. Wren Library open M-F noon-2pm. Easter-Oct. £2, students £1. Nov.-Easter free.) **King's College,** south of Trinity on King's Parade, is E.M. Forster's alma mater. Rubens's magnificent *Adoration of the Magi* hangs behind the altar of the its spectacular Gothic chapel. (Open M-Sa 9:30am-4:30pm, Su 10am-5pm. Tours arranged through the tourist office. £3.50, students £2.50.) The **⊠Fitzwilliam Museum,** on Trumpington St., displays Egyptian, Greek, and Asian treasures. (Open Su 2:15-5pm, Tu-Sa 10am-5pm. Suggested donation £3. Guided tours £3.)

The best source of info on student activities is the newspaper *Varsity* (20p); the tourist office also has useful brochures. **Punts** (gondola-like boats) are a favorite form of entertainment in Cambridge. Beware that punt-bombing—jumping from bridges into the river alongside a punt, thereby tipping its occupants into the Cam—has evolved into an art form. **Tyrell's,** at Magdalene Bridge, rents boats. (☎(01480) 394 941. £12 per hr. plus a £40 deposit.) Even more traditional than punting is **pub-crawling;** most pubs are open from 11am to 11pm. The oldest pub in Cambridge is **The Eagle,** 8 Benet St. **The Mill,** 14 Mill Ln., off Silver St. Bridge, claims a riverside park as its own for punt- and people-watching.

NORTHERN ENGLAND

The north's innovative music and arts scenes are world-famous: Liverpool and Manchester alone produced four of *Q Magazine's* ten biggest rock stars of the century. Its principal urban areas may have grown out of the wool and coal industries, bearing 19th-century scars to prove it, but their newly refurbished city centers have redirected their energies toward accommodating visitors. Find respite from city life in the Peak District to the east or the Lake District to the north.

MANCHESTER ☎0161

The Industrial Revolution transformed the once unremarkable village of Manchester (pop. 2.5 million) into Britain's second-largest urban area. Though dodgy in parts, the city is undergoing a gradual gentrification and is accessible to the street smart. Thousands are drawn to its vibrant arts and nightlife scenes, proving that it's not just the pretty who are popular.

◪◪ TRANSPORTATION AND PRACTICAL INFORMATION. Trains leave **Piccadilly Station,** on London Rd., and **Victoria Station,** on Victoria St., for: Birmingham (1¾hr., 2 per hr., £17); Chester (1hr., every hr., £8); Edinburgh (4hr., every hr., £46); Liverpool (50min., 2 per hr., £7.80); London Euston (2½-3½hr., every hr., £49); and York (40min., 2 per hr., £18). National Express **buses** (☎(0870) 580 8080) go from Chorlton St. to London (4-5hr., 7 per day, £19) and Liverpool (50min., every hr., £5). **Piccadilly Gardens** is home to about 50 local bus routes; pick up a route map at the tourist office. **Manchester Visitor Centre,** in the Town Hall Extension on Lloyd St., provides maps and books accommodations for £2.50, plus a 10% deposit. (☎234 3157; 24hr. info (0891) 715 533. Open M-Sa 10am-5pm, Su 10:30am-4:30pm.) Check **email** at **Internet Exchange,** 1-3 Piccadilly Sq., on the 2nd fl. of Coffee Republic. (£1 per hr. with £2 membership, non-members £1 per 15min. Open M-F 7:30am-6:30pm, Sa 8am-6:30pm, Su 9:30am-5:30pm.) **Postal Code:** M1 1NS.

◪◪ ACCOMMODATIONS AND FOOD. The elegant **Jury's Inn Manchester ❸,** 56 Bridgewater St., offers enormous and economical triples, luxurious baths, and professional service. (☎953 8888. £73 per room includes one single and one double bed.) Take bus #33 from Piccadilly Gardens toward Wigan to reach the swanky

YHA Manchester ❷, Potato Wharf, Castlefield. (☎(0870) 770 5950. Lockers £1-2. Laundry £1.50. Internet 50p per 6min. Reception open 7am-11pm. Dorms £19; doubles £32-42.) ❧**Tampopo Noodle House ❷**, 16 Albert Sq., is a chic Manchester favorite. (Entrees £3-8. Open daily noon-11pm.) At **Gaia ❸**, 46 Sackville St., skilled chefs fuse British and Mediterranean cuisines. (Entrees £8-13. Open Su-Th noon-midnight, F-Sa noon-2am.) Check out **Portland Street** for lots of cheap restaurants.

◫ ♫ SIGHTS AND ENTERTAINMENT. The exception to Manchester's unspectacular buildings is the neo-Gothic **Manchester Town Hall** on Albert St. Nearby is the domed **Central Library,** one of the largest municipal libraries in Europe and the architectural jewel of the city. In the **Museum of Science and Industry,** on Liverpool Rd. in Castlefield, working steam engines provide a dramatic vision of Britain's industrialization. (Open daily 10am-5pm. Museum free. Special exhibit £3-5.) The **Manchester United Museum and Tour Centre,** on Sir Matt Busby Way at the Old Trafford football stadium, revels in everything that is the football team Manchester United. Follow the signs up Warwick Rd. from the Old Trafford Metrolink stop. (Open daily 9:30am-5pm. Museum £5.50. Tours every 10min. 9:40am-4:30pm.) Manchester's biggest draws are its artistic offerings, most notably its theater and music scenes; the **Royal Exchange Theatre,** on St. Ann's Sq., regularly puts on Shakespearean and original works. (☎833 9333. Box office open M-Sa 9:30am-7:30pm. Tickets £7-24; student discounts in advance.) **Bridgewater Hall,** on Lower Mosley St., is Manchester's premier venue for orchestral concerts. (☎907 6255. Box office open M-Sa 10am-6pm, until 8pm on performance days.)

Come nightfall, try the lively **The Lass O'Gowrie,** 36 Charles St., for good food at even better prices. (Kitchen open M-F noon-5pm and Sa-Su noon-3pm. Lunch £2-5. Open M-Sa 11am-11pm, Su noon-10:30pm.) **Musicbox,** on Oxford Rd., is a popular underground club that hosts weekly events. (Cover £5-8. Open Th-Sa from 10pm.) Manchester's gay nightlife centers around the vibrant **Gay Village,** northeast of Princess St.; bars line **Canal Street,** the village's center. Enthusiastic crowds pack **Essential,** 8 Minshull St., arguably the most popular club in the Gay Village. (Cover £3-8. Open F 10:30pm-5am, Sa 10:30pm-6am, Su 10:30pm-3am.)

LIVERPOOL
☎ **0151**

Legendary nightlife, a multitude of free museums, and restaurants on every block make Liverpool, hometown of the Beatles, a great destination for travelers. Scousers—as Liverpudlians are colloquially known—are usually happy to introduce you to their dialect and to discuss the relative merits of Liverpool's two football teams.

◫ ♫ TICKET TO RIDE. Trains (☎(08457) 484 950) arrive at Lime Street Station from: Birmingham (1¾hr., 2-5 per day, £19); Chester (45min., 2 per hr., £3.40); London Euston (3hr., 10-24 per day, £49); and Manchester Piccadilly (1hr., 2-3 per hr., £7.50). National Express **buses** (☎(08705) 808 080) head from Norton Street Coach Station to: Birmingham (2½hr., 5 per day, £9.30); London (4½hr., 5-6 per day, £19); and Manchester (1hr., 1-2 per hr, £5). The Isle of Man Steam Packet Company (☎(08705) 523 523) runs **ferries** from Princess Dock to Dublin.

⚑ HELP! The main **tourist office,** in Queen Square Centre, gives away the handy *Visitor Guide to Liverpool and Merseyside,* and books beds for a 10% deposit. (☎(0906) 680 6886; calls charged 25p per min. Open M and W-Sa 9am-5:30pm, Tu 10am-5:30pm, Su 10:30am-4:30pm.) Expert guide Phil Hughes runs personalized **Beatles tours** (☎228 4565) for the lucky eight that fit in his van. Surf the **Internet** for free at the **Central Library,** on William Brown St. (Open M-Th 9am-8pm, F 9am-7pm, Sa 9am-5pm, Su noon-4pm.) **Postal Code:** L1 1AA.

▐▐ A HARD DAY'S NIGHT. Budget hotels are mostly located around **Lord Nelson Street,** next to the train station, and **Mount Pleasant,** one block from Brownlow Hill. At **▇Embassie Backpackers ❶,** relax by using some of the numerous amenities (including a pool table, three lounges, and a kitchen), or simply sit back for a chat over free toast, tea, or a pint. (☎ 707 1089. Laundry facilities. Dorms £14 for the first night, £13 for each additional night.) Clean rooms and a relaxing bar await at **Aachen Hotel ❸,** 89-91 Mt. Pleasant, the winner of numerous awards. (☎ 709 3477. Breakfast included. Singles £28-38; doubles £46-54.) **YHA Liverpool ❷,** 24 Tabley St., off The Wapping, has upscale rooms on three Beatles-themed floors. (☎ 709 8888. Kitchen available. Breakfast included. Laundry facilities. Internet access. Dorms £19, under-18 £14.) The **International Inn ❷,** 4 South Hunter St., is clean and fun. Enjoy the lounge and adjoining cafe. (☎ 709 8135. Dorms £15; doubles £36.)

Trendy cafes and well-priced Indian restaurants line **Bold Street** and **Hardman Street,** while fast-food joints crowd **Hardnon Street** and **Berry Street.** Many eateries stay open until 3am. **▇Country Kitchen ❶,** Drury Ln., dishes out cheap and delicious meals. Toasties, salads, and pasta cost a mere £1, and soup is just 75p. (☎ 236 0509. Open daily 7:30am-3:30pm.) **Simply Heathcotes ❹,** 25 The Strand, Beetham Plaza, is simply elegant. Try the breaded veal escalope. (Entrees around £15. Open M-F noon-2:30pm and 6-10pm, Sa 6-11pm, Su noon-2:30pm and 6-9:30pm.) **Tavern Co. ❷,** in Queen Sq., near the tourist office, serves burritos and taco salads (£5-7) in a wine-bar atmosphere. (Open M-Sa noon-11pm, Su 10:30am-10:30pm.)

◼ MAGICAL MYSTERY TOUR. The tourist office's **Beatles Map** (£2.50) leads visitors through Beatles-themed sights, including **Strawberry Fields** and **Penny Lane.** At Albert Dock, **The Beatles Story** pays tribute to the group's work with a re-creation of the Cavern Club and a yellow submarine. (Open Apr.-Oct. daily 10am-6pm; Nov.-Mar. 10am-5pm. £8, students £5.50.) The intimate Liverpool branch of the **Tate Gallery,** also on Albert Dock, contains a select range of 20th-century artwork. (Open Su and Tu-Sa 10am-6pm. Free. Special exhibits £4.) The Anglican **Liverpool Cathedral,** on Upper Duke St., boasts the highest Gothic arches ever built and the heaviest bells in the world. Climb to the top of the 100m tower for a view stretching to Wales. (Cathedral open daily 8am-6pm. Suggested donation £2.50. Tower open M-Sa 11am-4pm, weather permitting. £2.50.) Neon-blue stained glass casts a glow over the interior of the **Metropolitan Cathedral of Christ the King,** on Mt. Pleasant. Note the many modern sculptures that fill the chapels. (Open in summer M-F 7:30am-6pm, Sa-Su 8:30am-6pm; off-season M-F 8am-6pm, Sa 8:30am-6pm, Su 8:30am-5pm. Free.) The **Liverpool** and **Everton football clubs**—intense rivals—both offer tours of their grounds. Bus #26 runs from the city center to both stadiums. (Book ahead. Everton ☎ 330 2277; tour £5.50. Liverpool ☎ 260 6677; tour £8.50.)

◼ COME TOGETHER. Consult the *Liverpool Echo,* an evening paper sold by street vendors, for up-to-date information on nightlife. **Slater Street** in particular brims with £1 pints, while on weekend nights, the downtown area—especially **Mathew Street, Church Street,** and **Bold Street**—overflows with young clubbers. John Lennon once said that the worst thing about fame was "not being able to get a quiet pint at the Phil." Fortunately, the rest of us can sip in solitude at **The Philharmonic,** 36 Hope St. (Open M-Sa noon-11pm, Su noon-10:30pm.) **The Jacaranda,** on Slater St., the site of the Beatles' first paid gig, has live bands and a dance floor. (Open M-Sa noon-2am, Su noon-10:30pm.) **Medication,** in Wolstonholme Sq., offers the wildest student night in town. (Students only; bring ID. Cover £5. Open W 10am-2am.) **The Cavern Club,** 10 Matthew St., is on the site where the Fab Four gained prominence; today it draws locals for live bands. (No cover until 10pm, 10-11pm £2, 11pm-2am £4. Club open M-W 6pm-midnight, Th 6pm-2am, F-Sa 6pm-2:30am. Pub open M-Sa from noon, Su noon-11:30pm.)

HE LOCAL STORY

ONCE HAD A BAND, OR SHOULD I SAY, THEY ONCE HAD ME

Allan Williams, owner of The Jacaranda Coffee Bar in Liverpool, was the first manager of the world's favorite mop-heads. According to Williams, the Beatles were coffee bar bums who skipped lectures to hang out at the Jac, eating their beloved "bacon-butty" sandwiches and listening to the music they would come to dominate. Williams also recalled that when Pete Best kept the beat (not that interloper, Ringo), the group was smuggled into Hamburg as "students," then deported when a 17-year-old George Harrison was busted for hanging out at 18+ clubs. Here are more of Williams's memories.

LG: How did you meet the Beatles?

A: My wife and I had a coffee bar club. Because I was a rock 'n' roll promoter, all the groups used to come to my place, mainly 'cuz I let them rehearse for free in the basement. I only knew [the Beatles] as coffee bar layabouts—they were always bummin' free coffee off of anybody... I had complaints about the obscene graffiti that the girls were writing about the groups, and here these lads were from the art school and they could paint. I said, "Will you decorate the ladies' toilets for me?" And the way they decorated them, I'd have preferred the graffiti, to be honest with you. They were just *throwing* paint on them as if they were Picassos.

PEAK DISTRICT NATIONAL PARK

A green cushion among England's industrial giants of Manchester, Sheffield, and Nottingham, Britain's first national park sprawls across 1400sq. km of rolling hills and windswept moors, offering a playground for its 22 million urban neighbors.

⚡ TRANSPORTATION AND PRACTICAL INFORMATION. The invaluable *Peak District Timetable* (60p), available at tourist offices, has transport routes and a map. Two **train** lines originate in Manchester and enter the park from the west: one stops at Buxton, near the park's edge (1hr., every hr., £5.70), and the other crosses the park (1½hr., 9-17 per day) via Edale (£6.70), Hope, and Hathersage, terminating in Sheffield (£11). Trent (☎(01773) 712 2765) **bus** TP, the "Transpeak," departs from Manchester to Nottingham (3hr., 6 per day), stopping at Buxton, Bakewell, Matlock, Derby, and other towns in between. First PMT (☎(01782) 207 999) #X18 leaves from Sheffield for Bakewell (45min., M-Sa 5 per day). First Mainline (☎(01709) 515 151) #272 and Stagecoach East Midland (☎(01246) 211 007) #273 and 274 depart from Sheffield to Castleton (40-55min., 12-15 per day). The **Derbyshire Wayfarer,** available at tourist offices, allows one day of train and bus travel through the Peak District as far as Sheffield and Derby (£7.50).

The **National Park Information Centres** (NPICs) at Bakewell, Castleton, and Edale offer walking guides. Info is also available at **tourist offices** in Buxton (☎(01298) 25 106) and Matlock Bath (☎(01629) 55 082). There are 20 **YHA Youth Hostels ❷** in the park (Dorms £8-15). For Bakewell, Castleton, and Edale, see below; the Buxton YHA, Harpur Hill Rd., can be reached at ☎(0870) 770 5738, while the Matlock YHA, 40 Bank Rd., can be contacted at ☎(01629) 582 983. To stay at the 13 **YHA Camping Barns ❶** throughout the park (£4 per person), book ahead at the **Camping Barns Reservation Office,** 6 King St., Clitheroe, Lancashire BB7 2EP (☎(0870) 770 6113). The park operates six **Cycle Hire Centres** (£12.50 per day); a free brochure, *Peak Cycle Hire,* available at NPICs, includes phone numbers, hours, and locations.

CASTLETON. The main attraction in Castleton (pop. 705) is ◪**Treak Cliff Cavern,** which hides seams of Blue John, a mineral found only in these hills. (40min. tours every 15-30min. Open Easter-Oct. daily from 10am, last tour between 4-5pm.; Nov.-

Feb. 10am-3:20pm; Mar.-Easter 10am-4:20pm. £5.60, students £4.50.) Castleton lies 3.2km west of **Hope.** The Castleton **NPIC** is on Buxton Rd. (☎ (01433) 620 679. Open Apr.-Oct. daily 10am-1pm and 2-5:30pm; Nov.-Mar. Sa-Su 10am-5pm.) **YHA Castleton ❷** is in Castleton Hall, a pretty country house in the heart of town. (☎ (01433) 620 235. Kitchen available. **Internet** access. Book 2-3 weeks in advance. Open Feb. to late Dec. Dorms £12-14, under-18 £9-10.)

BAKEWELL AND EDALE. The town of Bakewell, 50km southeast of Manchester, is the best base from which to explore the region; several scenic walks through the **White Peaks** begin nearby. Bakewell's **NPIC** is in Old Market Hall, at Bridge St. (☎ (01629) 813 227. Open Mar.-Oct. daily 9:30am-5:30pm; Nov.-Feb. 10am-5pm.) The cozy **YHA Bakewell ❷**, on Fly Hill, is 5min. from the town centers. (☎ (01629) 812 313. Open Mar.-Oct. M-Sa; Nov.-Feb. daily. Dorms £11, under-18 £7.)

The northern Dark Peak area contains some of the wildest and most rugged hill country in England. The area around **Edale** is spectacular, and the National Park Authority's *8 Walks Around Edale* (£1.20) details nearby trails. The town offers little other than a church, cafe, pub, school, and the nearby **YHA youth hostel ❷**, Rowland Cote. (☎ (01433) 670 302. Dorms £11.50, under-18 £8.30.)

YORK ☎ 01904

Although its well-preserved city walls have foiled many, York (pop. 105,000) fails to impede its present-day hordes of visitors. Today, marauders brandish cameras instead of swords, and the plunder is now York's compact collection of rich historical sights, including Britain's largest Gothic cathedral.

⛃ TRANSPORTATION AND PRACTICAL INFORMATION. Trains leave from Station Rd. for: Edinburgh (2½hr., 2 per hr., £60); London King's Cross (2hr., 2 per hr., £64); Manchester Piccadilly (1½hr., 2 per hr., £17); and Newcastle (1hr., 2 per hr., £18). National Express **buses** (☎ (08705) 808 080) depart from Rougier St. for: Edinburgh (5½hr., daily, £36); London (5hr., 3 per day, £31); and Manchester (2¾hr., 3 per day, £12). To reach the **tourist office,** in Exhibition Sq., follow Station Rd., which turns into Museum St., go over the bridge, and turn left on St. Leonard's Pl. (Open June-Oct. M-Sa 9am-6pm, Su 10am-5pm; Nov.-May 9am-5pm.) **Cafe of the Evil Eye,** 42 Stonegate, has **Internet** access (£2 per hr.). **Postal Code:** YO1 8DA.

LG: Sort of Pollock-style...

A: Heh. Yeah...

LG: And how did you become their manager?

A: I put this big rock 'n' roll show on. They came and saw me the next day and said, "Hey Al? When are you going to do something for us like?" And I said to them, "Look, there's no more painting to be done." And they said, "No, we've got a *group.*" I said, "I didn't know that." And they said, "Well, will you manage us?" By then I had got to know them, and they were quite nice personalities—very witty. And I go, "Oh yeah, this could be fun." And then I managed them.

Williams felt that it was their stint in Hamburg, and not Liverpool, that made the Beatles. He describes his falling out with the group as a disagreement over—what else?—contract disputes and general rock-star ingratitude.

A: I wrote them a letter saying that they appeared to be getting more than a little swell-headed and "Remember, I managed you when nobody else wanted to know you. But I'll fix it now so that you'll never ever work again."

LG: Uh-oh.

A: So that's my big mistake, yeah. Heh. And on that note, we'll finish.

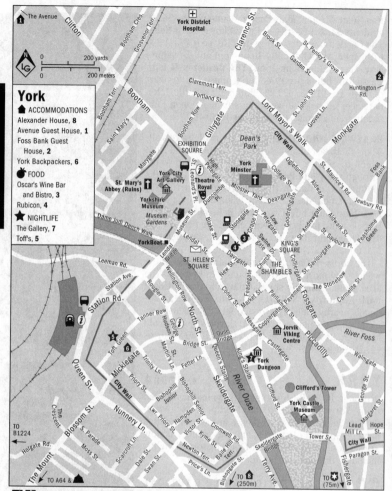

York District
Hospital

0   200 yards
0   200 meters

York

🏠 **ACCOMMODATIONS**
Alexander House, **8**
Avenue Guest House, **1**
Foss Bank Guest
    House, **2**
York Backpackers, **6**

🍴 **FOOD**
Oscar's Wine Bar
    and Bistro, **3**
Rubicon, **4**

⭐ **NIGHTLIFE**
The Gallery, **7**
Toff's, **5**

🏠🍴**ACCOMMODATIONS AND FOOD. B&Bs** are concentrated on the side streets along **Bootham** and **Clifton,** in the Mount area down **Blossom Street,** and on **Bishopsthorpe Road,** south of town. Book ahead in summer, when competition for all types of accommodations can be fierce. 🏠**York Backpackers ❶,** 88-90 Mickle-gate, has a fun atmosphere in a stately 18th-century mansion. Their "Dungeon Bar" is open five nights per week, long after the pubs close. (☎627 720; fax 339 350. Internet £1 per 20min. Dorms £13-14; doubles £34.) 🏠**Avenue Guest House ❷,** 6 The Avenue, off Clifton, is immaculate and comfortable. (☎620 575; www.ave-nuegh.fsnet.co.uk. Singles £20-22; doubles £38-42, with bath £42-46.) **Alexander House ❹,** 94 Bishopsthorpe Rd., 5min. from the train station, has luxurious rooms with flowers and king-sized beds. (☎625 016. Singles £55-59; doubles £65-70.) **Foss Bank Guest House ❸,** 16 Huntington Rd., reachable by bus #12 or 13 from the train station, offers comfortable beds and some particularly swanky doubles. (☎635 548. Singles £22-25; doubles £42-52. Discount for *Let's Go* users.)

Oscar's Wine Bar and Bistro ❷, 8 Little Stonegate, combines a chic courtyard and lively mood with massive portions of pub favorites. (☎652 002. Open M-Sa 11:30am-11pm, Su noon-10:30pm.) **Rubicon ❷,** 5 Little Stonegate, has exotic international options, as well as vegan and gluten-free dishes. (☎676 076. Sandwiches £4.50. Entrees £7-9. Open daily 11:30am-10pm.) Fruits and vegetables are available at **Newgate market,** between Parliament St. and Shambles. (Open Apr.-Dec. M-Sa 9am-5pm, Su 9am-4:30pm; Jan.-Mar. M-Sa 9am-5pm.)

◨ ◧ **SIGHTS AND NIGHTLIFE.** The best introduction to York is the 4km walk along its **medieval walls.** Beware of the tourist stampede, which slows only in the early morning and just before the walls and gates close at dusk. A free 2hr. **walking tour** is offered daily by the **Association of Voluntary Guides** (☎630 284); tours leave from the York City Art Gallery, across from the tourist office. Everyone and everything in York converges at the enormous ◧**York Minster.** Half of all the medieval stained glass in England glitters here; the **Great East Window** depicts the beginning and end of the world in over 100 scenes. (Cathedral open daily 9am-6pm. £4.50, concessions £3. Tours 9:30am-3:30pm.) The ◧**York Castle Museum,** at the Eye of York, between Tower St. and Piccadilly St. in a former debtor's prison, is arguably Britain's premier museum dedicated to everyday life. (Open daily 9:30am-5pm. £6, concessions £3.50.) The **Jorvik Viking Centre,** on Coppergate, is one of the busiest places in York; visit early or late to avoid lines, or call at least 24hr. in advance. Visitors pass through the York of AD 948, with authentic artifacts and painfully accurate smells. (☎643 211. For advance booking, call ☎543 403. Open Apr.-Oct. 9:30am-5pm; Nov.-Mar. 10am-4pm. £7.20, concessions £6.10.) The **Yorkshire Museum** presents Roman, Anglo-Saxon, and Viking artifacts, as well as the £2.5 million **Middleham Jewel** from circa 1450. (Enter from Museum St. or Marygate. Open daily 10am-5pm. £4, concessions £2.50. Gardens and abbey free.)

The monthly *What's On* and *Artscene* guides, available at the tourist office, publish info on live music, theater, cinema, and exhibitions. **The Gallery,** 12 Clifford St., has two dance floors and six bars. (Cover £1.50-7.50. Open daily 9:30pm-2:30am.) **Toff's,** 3-5 Toft Green, plays mainly dance and house music. (Cover £3.50-7. Open M-Sa 10pm-2am. Gay-friendly "Alternative Sundays" 9pm-1am.)

NEWCASTLE-UPON-TYNE ☎0191

The largest city in the northeast, Newcastle (pop. 278,000) has emerged into the 21st century determined to forge itself a new identity. Ambitious building efforts have lent the city genuine daytime energy, and its nightlife is hotter than ever as locals, students, and tourists continue to flock to its pubs and cafes. A combination of hoary old and resilient new, Newcastle's monuments blend well with the city. The largely intact **Castle Garth Keep,** at the foot of St. Nicholas St., is all that remains of the 12th-century New Castle complex. Oddly enough, the city derives its name from a castle that existed over 100 years earlier. (☎232 7938. Open Apr.-Sept. daily 9:30am-5:30pm; Oct.-Mar. 9:30am-4:30pm. Admission £1.50, concessions 50p.) The **BALTIC Centre for Contemporary Art,** housed in a renovated grain warehouse, is the largest center for contemporary art outside of London. This stunning yet simplistically designed museum rises seven stories above the Tyne and showcases current artists at the cutting edge of their fields. (☎478 1810. Open M-W and F-Sa 10am-7pm, Th 10am-10pm, Su 10am-5pm. Free.) Treat yourself to an evening at the lush gilt-and-velvet **Theatre Royal,** 100 Grey St., undoubtedly northern England's premier stage. The **Royal Shakespeare Company** makes a month-long stop here each fall, complementing other top-notch performances. (☎232 2061. Call for performance times.) Rowdy **Bigg Market** features the highest concentration of pubs in England, while **Quayside** (KEY-side) is slightly more relaxed and attracts local students. **Chase,** 10-15 Sandhill, is a flashy pub, while nearby **Offshore 44,** 40 Sandhill, has a tropical theme. (Both open M-Sa 11am-11pm and Su noon-6pm.) The hottest dance club is **The Tuxedo Princess,** on a cruise ship under the Tyne Bridge. (Open M and W-Sa 7:30pm-2am.) For a happening gay and lesbian scene, head to Waterloo St. for a night of drinking and dancing at **The Powerhouse.** (Open M, Th, and Su 10:30pm-2am, F-Sa 10pm-3am.)

Trains leave from Neville St. for Edinburgh (1½hr., approx. every hr., £36) and London King's Cross (3½hr., every hr., £83). National Express **buses** (☎(08705) 808 080) leave Percy St. for Edinburgh (3hr., 4 per day, £14) and London (7hr., 4 per day, £24). The **tourist office** is on 132 Grainger St., facing Grey's Monument. (☎277 8000. Open June-Sept. M-W and F 9:30am-5:30pm, Th 9:30am-7:30pm, Sa 9am-5pm, Su 10am-4pm; Oct.-May M-W and F 9:30am-5:30pm, Th 9:30am-7:30pm, Sa 9am-5pm.) To get to the friendly **YHA Newcastle** ❷, 107 Jesmond Rd., take the Metro to Jesmond, turn left onto Jesmond Rd., and walk past the traffic lights. Call well in advance. (☎281 2570. **Internet** access. Open mid-Jan. to mid-Dec. Dorms £12, under-18 £8.30.) **University of Northumbria** ❷, Sandyford Rd., offers standard dorm accommodations, but its proximity to the city center is a plus. Some rooms come with partial kitchen. (☎227 3215. Breakfast included. Open June-Aug. Singles midweek £23, weekends £28.) **Gershwins** ❷, 54 Dean St., is a cool underground grotto restaurant that serves continental cuisine at a great price. (2-course dinner with wine £7-11. Open M-Sa 11:30am-2:30pm and 5:30-10:30pm.) **Postal Code:** NE1 7AB.

LAKE DISTRICT NATIONAL PARK

Quite possibly the loveliest place in England, the Lake District owes its beauty to a thorough glacier-gouging during the last ice age. Jagged peaks and windswept fells stand in desolate splendor as hillside rivers pool in serene mountain lakes. Use Windermere, Ambleside, Grasmere, and Keswick as bases from which to ascend into the hills—the farther west you go from the A591, which connects these towns, the more countryside you'll have to yourself.

The **National Park Visitor Centre** is in **Brockhole,** halfway between Windermere and Ambleside. (☎(015394) 46 601. Open Apr.-Oct. daily 10am-5pm.) **National Park Information Centres** book accommodations and dispense free information and town maps. Although B&Bs line every street in every town and there's a hostel around every bend, lodgings do fill up in summer; book ahead.

⌐ TRANSPORTATION. Trains (☎(08457) 484 950) run to Oxenholme, the primary gateway to the lakes, from: Birmingham (2½hr., 1 every 2hr., £42); Edinburgh (2½hr., 6 per day, £39); London Euston (4hr., 11-16 per day, £63); and Manchester Piccadilly (1½hr., 9-10 per day, £13). A short line covers the 16km between Windermere and Oxenholme (20min., every hr., £3.20). There is also direct service to Windermere from Manchester Piccadilly (2hr., 1-6 per day, £13). National Express **buses** (☎(08705) 808 080) arrive in Windermere from Birmingham (4½hr., daily, £25) and London (7½hr., daily, £26), and continue north through Ambleside and Grasmere to Keswick. **Stagecoach in Cumbria** (☎(0870) 608 2608) is the primary operator of bus service in the region; a complete timetable, *The Lakeland Explorer*, is available at tourist offices. An **Explorer** ticket offers unlimited travel on all area Stagecoach buses (1-day £7.50, children £5.30; 4-day £17/13). The Ambleside YHA Youth Hostel offers a convenient **minibus** service (☎(01539) 432 304) between hostels (2 per day, £2.50) as well as free service from the Windermere train station to the Windermere and Ambleside hostels.

WINDERMERE AND BOWNESS. **Windermere** and its sidekick **Bowness-on-Wind-ermere** fill to the gills with vacationers in summer, when sailboats and waterski-ers swarm the lake. At **Windermere Lake Cruises** (☎(01539) 443 360), at the north end of Bowness Pier, boats sail north to Waterhead Pier in Ambleside (30min., round-trip £6.40) and south to Lakeside (40min., round-trip £6.60). Lakeland Experience **buses** to Bowness (#599; 3 per hr., £1) leave from the train station. The **tourist office** is next door. (☎(01539) 446 499. Open July-Aug. daily 9am-7:30pm; Easter-June and Sept.-Oct. 9am-6pm; Nov.-Easter 9am-5pm.) The local **National Park Information Centre**, on Glebe Rd., is beside Bowness Pier. (☎(01539) 442 895. Open July-Aug. daily 9:30am-6pm; Apr.-June and Sept.-Oct. daily 9am-5:30pm; Nov.-Mar. F-Su 10am-4pm.) **Brendan Chase ❷**, 1-3 College Rd., is family friendly, with large and attractive rooms. (☎(01539) 445 638. Singles £13-25, dou-bles £26-50.) To get to the spacious **YHA Windermere ❷**, Bridge Ln., 1.5km north of Windermere off A591, catch the YHA shuttle from the train station. This hostel offers panoramic views of the lake, and rents bikes. (☎(01539) 443 543. Open Feb.-Nov. daily; early Dec. F-Sa only. Dorms £12, under-18 £8.30.) **Camp** at **Park Cliffe ❷**, Birks Rd., 7km south of Bowness. Take bus #618 from Windermere. (☎(01529) 531 344. £11-12 per tent.)

AMBLESIDE. About 2km north of Lake Windermere, Ambleside offers an attractive and convenient starting place for a day's trip to just about anywhere in the park. Splendid views of higher fells can be had from the top of **Loughrigg** (a moderately difficult 11km round-trip hike); 1.5km from town is the lovely waterfall **Stockghyll Force.** The tourist office has guides to these and other walks. Lakeslink **bus** #555 (☎(01539) 432 231) leaves from Kelsick Rd. for Gras-mere, Keswick, and Windermere (every hr., £2-6.50). The **tourist office** is located in the Central Building on Market Cross. (☎(01539) 432 582. Open daily 9am-5pm.) To reach the **National Park Information Centre,** on Waterhead, walk south on Lake Rd. or Borrans Rd. from town to the pier. (☎(01539) 432 729. Open Eas-ter-Oct. daily 9:30am-5:30pm.) Bus #555 conveniently stops in front of ☒**YHA Ambleside ❷**, 1.5km south of Ambleside and 5km north of Windermere, an extremely social spot with superbly refurbished rooms, great food, and swim-ming off their pier. (☎(01539) 432 304. Bike rentals. **Internet** £2.50 per 30min. Dorms £14, under-18 £10.)

GRASMERE. The peace that Wordsworth enjoyed in the village of Grasmere is still tangible on quiet mornings. The 17th-century **Dove Cottage,** 10min. from the center of town, was Wordsworth's home from 1799 to 1808 and remains almost exactly as he left it; next door is the outstanding **Wordsworth Museum.** (Both open mid-Feb. to mid-Jan. daily 9:30am-5pm. £5.50, students £4.70.) The **Word-sworth Walk** (9.5km) circumnavigates the two lakes of the Rothay River, passing the cottage, the poet's grave in St. Oswald's churchyard, and **Rydal Mount,** where Wordsworth lived until his death. (Rydal open Mar.-Oct. daily 9:30am-5pm; Nov.-Feb. W-M 10am-4pm. £4, students £3.25.) **Bus** #555 stops in Grasmere every hour on its way south to Ambleside or north to Keswick. The combined **tourist office** and **National Park Information Centre** is on Redbank Rd. (☎(01539) 435 245. Open Easter-Oct. daily 9:30am-5:30pm; Nov.-Easter F-Su 10am-4pm.) **YHA Butterlip How ❷**, 140m up Easedale Rd., is situated in a large Victorian house, and has **Internet** access. (Open Mar.-Oct. Su and Tu-Sa; Nov.-Feb., call for availability. £13, under-18 £9.) Sarah Nelson's famed **Grasmere Gingerbread Shop ❶**, a staple since 1854, is a bargain at 30p in Church Cottage, outside St. Oswald's Church. (Open Easter-Nov. M-Sa 9:15am-5:30pm, Su 12:30-5:30pm; closes earlier in winter.)

KESWICK. Between towering Skiddaw peak and the northern edge of Lake Derwentwater, Keswick (KEZ-ick) rivals Windermere as the Lake District's tourist capital. A standout 6km day-hike from Keswick culminates with the eerily striking **Castlerigg Stone Circle,** a 5000-year-old neolithic henge. Another short walk hits the beautiful **Friar's Crag,** on the shore of Derwentwater, and **Castlehead,** a viewpoint encompassing the town, the lakes, and the peaks beyond. Both of these walks are fairly easy, although they do have their more strenuous moments. Maps and information on these and a wide selection of other walks are available at the **National Park Information Centre,** in Moot Hall, Market Sq. (☎(01768) 772 645. Open Apr.-Oct. daily 9:30am-5:30pm; Nov.-Mar. 9:30am-4:30pm.) **YHA Derwentwater ❷,** in Barrow House, Borrowdale, is in a 200-year-old house with its own waterfall. Take bus #79 (every hr.) 3km south out of Keswick. (☎(01768) 777 246. Open Feb. to early Oct. daily; Dec.-Jan. F-Sa only. Dorms £11.50, under-18 £8.)

WALES

Wales may border England, but if many of the 2.9 million Welsh people had their way, it would be floating oceans away. Ever since England solidified its control over the country with the murder of Prince Llywelyn ap Gruffydd in 1282, relations between the two have been marked by a powerful unease. Wales clings steadfastly to its Celtic heritage, as the Welsh language endures in conversation, commerce, and literature. As coal, steel, and slate mines fell victim to Britain's faltering economy in the mid-20th century, Wales turned its economic eye from heavy industry to tourism. Travelers come for the sandy beaches, grassy cliffs, brooding castles, and dramatic mountains that typify the rich landscape of this corner of Britain.

◀ FERRIES TO IRELAND

Irish Ferries (☎(08705) 171 717; www.irishferries.ie) sail to Dublin, Ireland, from Holyhead (2-3½hr., 3-4 per day, round-trip £40-65) and to Rosslare, Ireland, from Pembroke (4hr., round-trip £25-39, students £19). **Stena Line** (☎(08705) 707 070; www.stenaline.co.uk) runs from Holyhead to Dublin (4hr., £24-28) and Dún Laoghaire, Ireland (1-3½hr., £26).

CARDIFF (CAERDYDD) ☎029

The "Come on, Cardiff!" signs that flutter all around the city speak to the vigor with which Cardiff (pop. 325,000) is trying to reinvent itself. Formerly the main port of call for Welsh coal, Cardiff is now the port of arrival for a colorful international population. Climb the Norman keep of the flamboyant ▨**Cardiff Castle** for a sweeping view of the city, then tour its beautifully restored interior. (Open Mar.-Oct. daily 9:30am-6pm; Nov.-Feb. 9:30am-4:30pm. £5.50, students £4.20.) Nearby, the **National Museum and Gallery,** at Cathay's Park, next to the Civic Center, houses an eclectic mix of exhibits from an excellent Impressionist collection to a dazzling audio-visual exhibit on the evolution of Wales. (Open Su and Tu-Sa 10am-5pm. Free.) For a place to relax after sight-seeing, ▨**Europa Cafe,** 25 Castle St., across from the castle, is a comfortable coffeehouse with good drinks. (Beverages £1-3. Open Su-Tu 11am-6pm, W-Sa 11am-11pm.) If you're looking to gear up, Cardiff's downtown is filled with numerous pubs and nightspots. Try **The Owain Glyndwr** in St. John's Square for its classic Cardiff pub ambiance. (Open M-Th 11am-11pm, F-Sa noon-1am.) **Clwb Ifor Bach** (the Welsh Club), 11 Womanby St., is a manic, three-tiered club with everything from Motown tunes to video games. (Cover £2.50-10. Open M-Th until 2am, F-Sa until 3. Closed some Mondays, so call ahead.)

Trains (☎(08457) 484 950) arrive at Central Station, Central Sq., from: Bath (1-1½hr., 1-3 per hr., £12); Edinburgh (7hr., 7 per day, £96); and London Paddington (2hr., every hr., £47). National Express **buses** ((08705) 808 080) leave from Wood St. for London Victoria (3½hr., 6 per day, £17) and Manchester (5½hr., 4 per day, £25). The **tourist office** is at 16 Wood St., across from the bus station. (☎2022 7281. Open July-Aug. M-Sa 9am-6pm, Su 10am-4pm; Sept.-June M-Sa 9am-5pm, Su 10am-4pm.) **Internet Exchange** is located at 8 Church St., by St. John's Church. (£4 per hr. Open M-Th 9am-9pm, F-Sa 9am-8pm, Su 11am-7pm.) The best (and more expensive) **B&Bs** are on Cathedral Rd. (take bus #32 or walk 15min. from the castle); better bargains await on side streets. To get to the colorful ◼**Cardiff International Backpacker** ❷, 98 Neville St., from the train station, go west on Wood St., turn right on Fitzham Embankment, and turn left onto Despenser St. Happy Hour (Su-Th 7-9pm) and great amenities make this hostel a young backpacker's heaven. (☎2034 5577. Kitchen available. Internet £1 per 15min. Dorms £15; doubles £36; triples £44.) **Anned Lon** ❸, 157-159 Cathedral Rd., provides a peaceful respite from the city. (☎2022 3349. No smoking. Singles £30; doubles £45.) For quick food and a wide variety of options, head to the lively **Central Market,** in the arcade between St. Mary St. and Trinity St. **Postal Code:** CF10 2SJ.

WYE VALLEY ☎01291

Crossing and recrossing the oft-troubled Welsh-English border, the Wye River (Afon Gwy) cuts through a tranquil valley, its banks riddled with trails, abbeys, and castles rich in legend. The past is palpable in the towns and clusters of homes and farms, from Tintern Abbey to the George Inn Pub.

▣ TRANSPORTATION

The valley is best entered from the south, at Chepstow. **Trains** go to Chepstow from Cardiff and Newport (40min., 7-8 per day). National Express **buses** (☎(08705) 808 080) arrive from Cardiff (50min., 7 per day) and London (2¼hr., 10 per day). There is little Sunday bus service in the valley. For schedules, pick up *Discover the Wye Valley on Foot and by Bus* in tourist offices.

Hiking grants the most stunning views of the valley. The 219km **Wye Valley Walk** treks north from Chepstow, through Hay-on-Wye, and on to Prestatyn along wooded cliffs and farmland. **Offa's Dyke Path** consists of more than 293km of hiking and biking paths along the length of the Welsh-English border. For information, consult the **Offa's Dyke Association** (☎(01547) 528 753).

CHEPSTOW AND TINTERN. Chepstow's strategic position at the mouth of the river and the base of the English border made it an important fortification in Norman times. **Castell Casgwent,** Britain's oldest datable stone castle, offers stunning views of the Wye from its tower walls. (☎624 065. Open June-Sept. daily 9:30am-6pm; Oct. and Apr.-May daily 9:30am-5pm; Nov.-Mar. M-Sa 9:30am-4pm, Su 11am-4pm. £4, students £3.) **Trains** arrive on Station Rd.; **buses** stop in front of Somerfield supermarket. Purchase tickets at **The Travel House,** 9 Moor St. (☎623 031. Open M-Sa 9am-5:30pm.) The **tourist office** is on Bridge St. (☎623 772. Open Apr.-Oct. daily 10am-5:30pm; Nov.-Mar. 10am-4:30pm.) Visit **Mrs. Presley** ❸, 30 Kingsmark Ave., for beautiful rooms and a conservatory. (☎624 466. Singles £20; doubles £40.) **Postal Code:** NP16 5DA.

Eight kilometers north of Chepstow on A466, the haunting arches of ◼**Tintern Abbey** "connect the landscape with the quiet of the sky"—as described in Wordsworth's famous poem, written just a few kilometers away. (☎689 251. Open June-Sept. daily 9:30am-6pm; Apr.-May and Oct. daily 9:30am-5pm; Nov.-Mar. M-Sa 9:30am-

4pm, Su 11am-4pm. £2.50.) A 2½km. hike will get you to **Devil's Pulpit,** from which Satan is said to have tempted the monks as they worked in the fields. A couple kilometers to the north on A466, the **tourist office** is housed in a train carriage at the Old Station. (☎689 566. Open Apr.-Oct. daily 10:30am-5:30pm.) **YHA St. Briavel's Castle ❷,** 6.5km northeast of Tintern across the English border, occupies a 12th-century fortress. While a unique experience, St. Briavel's is somewhat remote, and should only be booked by those willing to walk uphill. From A466 (bus #69 from Chepstow) or Offa's Dyke, follow signs for 3.25km from the edge of the bridge. (☎(01594) 530 272. Dorms £11.55, under-18 £8.30.) The cozy **Holmleigh B&B ❷** is near the edge of Tintern Village on A466. (☎689 521. £16.50 per person.) Try **The Moon and Sixpence ❷,** next to Holmleigh B&B, for an astonishing array of dishes in a traditional pub atmosphere.

BRECON BEACONS NATIONAL PARK

The *Parc Cenedlaethol Bannau Brycheiniog* encompasses 837 dramatic square kilometers of barren peaks, well-watered forests, and windswept moors. The park is divided into four regions: **Brecon Beacon,** where King Arthur's fortress is thought to have once stood; **Fforest Fawr,** with the spectacular waterfalls of Ystradfellte; the eastern **Black Mountains;** and the remote western **Black Mountain** (singular). Brecon, on the fringe of the park, makes a pleasant touring base.

▐ TRANSPORTATION. Trains (☎08457 484 950) run from London Paddington to Abergavenny at the park's southeastern corner and to Merthyr Tydfil on the southern edge. National Express (☎08705 808 080) **bus** #509 runs from London (5hr., daily, £19) via Cardiff (1¼hr., £3). Stagecoach Red and White (☎01633 838 856) buses arrive from Abergavenny and Newport (#21; M-Sa, 6 per day; £3-4.50.)

BRECON (ADERHONDDU). Just north of the mountains, Brecon is the park's best hiking base. **Buses** arrive at the **Bulwark** in the central square. The **tourist office** is in the Cattle Market parking lot; walk through Bethel Square off Lion St. (☎(01874) 622 485. Open daily 9:30am-5pm.) The **National Park Information Centre** (☎(01874) 623 156) is in the same building. **Mulberry House ❷,** 3 Priory Hill, is in a former monks' habitation. (☎624 461. £18 per person.) Camp at **Brynich Caravan Park ❶,** 2.5km east on the A40, signposted from the A40-A470 roundabout. (☎(01874) 623 325. Open Easter-Oct. £5 per person, £11 for 2 people with car.)

FFOREST FAWR. Rivers tumble through rapids, gorges, and spectacular falls near Ystradfellte, about 11km southwest of the Beacons. The **YHA Ystradfellte ❶** is a perfect launching pad for those willing to walk there. (☎01639 720 301. Open mid-July to Aug. daily; Apr. to mid-July and Sept.-Oct. M-Tu and F-Sa. Dorms £9, students £8, under-18 £6.50.) From the hostel, 16km of trails pass **Fforest Fawr,** the headlands of the Waterfall District, on their way to the touristy **Dan-yr-Ogof Show-caves** (Open Apr.-Oct. daily 10:30am-5pm. £8.50, children £5.50.) Stagecoach Red and White **bus** #63 (1½hr., 2-3 per day) stops at the hostel and caves via Brecon.

THE BLACK MOUNTAINS. Located in the easternmost section of the park, the Black Mountains are a group of long, lofty ridges offering 130sq. km of solitude, linked by unsurpassed ridge-walks. Begin forays from **Crickhowell,** or travel the eastern boundary along **Offa's Dyke Path,** which is dotted with a handful of impressive ruins. The **YHA Capel-y-ffin ❶** (kap-EL-uh-fin), along Offa's Dyke Path, is 13km from Hay-on-Wye. Take Stagecoach Red and White **bus** #39 to Brecon, stop before Hay, and walk uphill. (☎01873 890 650. Lockout 10am-5pm. Open July-Sept. daily; Oct.-Dec. and Mar.-June M-Tu and F-Sa. Dorms £9, students £8, under-18 £6.)

THE BRECON BEACONS. These peaks at the center of the park lure hikers with pastoral slopes. The most convenient route to the top begins at **Storey Arms** (a carpark on A470) and offers views of **Llyn Cwm Llwch** (HLIN koom hlooch), a 610m deep glacial pool. Because this route is the most convenient, however, it is also the most overcrowded. Consult guides at the National Park Information Centres (in Brecon or Abergavenny) for recommendations on alternate trails.

ST. DAVID'S (TYDDEWI)   ☎01437

An evening walk in St. David's (pop. 1,700), a major medieval pilgrimage site, inevitably leads to ◪**St. David's Cathedral,** where visitors and locals gather to watch the sunset. Its history dates to the 6th century, when it was built with hopes that the defendable church would offer some protection from marauding pirates. Legend has it that the bones of St. David are still kept in the cathedral's relinquary. (Cathedral open daily 6am-5:30pm. Suggested donation ₤2.) The **Bishop's Palace,** across the stream from the cathedral, features over 150 carvings of fantastic beasts and human heads. (☎720 517. Open June-Sept. daily 9:30am-6pm; Apr.-May and Oct. 9:30am-5pm; Nov.-Mar. M-Sa 9:30am-4pm, Su noon-2pm. ₤2.)

To reach St. David's from Cardiff, take the **train** to Haverfordwest (2½hr., 2 per day), and then take Richards Bros. **bus** #411 (50min., 2-5 per day). The **tourist office** is on the Grove. (☎720 392; www.stdavids.co.uk. Open Easter-Oct. daily 9:30am-5:30pm; Nov.-Easter M-Sa 10am-4pm.) Beautiful **Alandale ❸**, 43 Nun St., has friendly proprietors who serve up filling breakfasts. (☎720 404. Singles ₤28; doubles ₤56.) For excellent Welsh food, head to **Cartref ❷**, in Cross Sq. Try the Celtic pie (₤9.30), an incredible Welsh dish that combines cheese, oats, flan, and bread. (Lunch ₤3-4. Dinner from ₤10. Open June-Aug. daily 11am-3pm and 6-8:30pm; Mar.-May 11am-2:30pm and 6:30-8:30pm.) **Postal Code:** SA62 6SW.

SNOWDONIA NATIONAL PARK

Snowdonia's craggy peaks actually yield surprisingly diverse terrain—pristine mountain lakes etch glittering blue outlines onto fields of green, while desolate slate cliff-faces slope into thickly wooded hills. Rough and handsome, England and Wales's highest mountains stretch across 2175 square kilometers, from forested Machynlleth to sand-strewn Conwy. Although these lands lie largely in private hands, endless public footpaths accommodate droves of visitors.

▉❼ TRANSPORTATION AND PRACTICAL INFORMATION. Trains (☎ (08457) 484 950) stop at several large towns on the park's outskirts, including Conwy (p. 203). The **Conwy Valley Line** runs through the park from Llandudno through Betws-y-Coed to Blaenau Ffestiniog (1hr., 2-7 per day). At Blaneau Ffestiniog the Conwy Valley Line connects with the narrow-gauge **Ffestiniog Railway** (p. 202), which runs through the mountains to Porthmadog, meeting the Cambrian Coaster to Llanberis and Aberystwyth. **Buses** run to the interior of the park from Conwy and Caernarfon; consult the *Gwynedd Public Transport Maps and Timetables*, available in all regional tourist offices. The **Snowdonia National Park Information Headquarters**, Penrhyndeudraeth, Gwynedd (☎(01766) 770 274), provides hiking info and can best direct you to the eight quality **YHA hostels** in the park and the region's other **tourist offices** (www.gwynedd.gov.uk).

◪ HIKING. The highest peak in England and Wales, **Mount Snowdon** (*Yr Wyddfa;* "the burial place") is the park's most popular destination, measuring 1085m. Six paths of varying difficulties wind their way up Snowdon; tourist offices and National Park Information Centres can provide guides on these ascents.

BRITAIN

Weather on Snowdonia's exposed mountains shifts unpredictably. No matter how beautiful the weather is below, it will be cold and wet in the high mountains. Pick up the *Ordnance Survey Landranger* Map #115 (£6) and *Outdoor Leisure* Map #17 (£7), as well as individual path guides at tourist offices and park centers. Contact **Mountaincall Snowdonia** (☎ (09068) 500 449; 36-48p per min.) for local forecasts and ground conditions. Weather forecasts are also posted in Park Information Centres.

LLANBERIS. Llanberis owes its outdoorsy bustle to the popularity of Mt. Snowdon, whose ridges and peaks unfold just south of town. The immensely popular **Snowdon Mountain Railway** has been taking visitors to Snowdon's summit since 1896. (☎ (0870) 458 0033. Open mid-Mar. to Oct. Round-trip £18.) KMP (☎ (01286) 870 880) **bus** #88 runs from Caernarfon (25min., 1-2 per hr., £1.50). The **tourist office** is at 41b High St. (☎ (01286) 870 765. Open Easter-Oct. daily 9:30am-5:30pm; Nov.-Easter Su, W, and F-Sa 11am-4pm.) Plenty of sheep keep hostelers company at the **YHA Llanberis ❷.** (☎ (0870) 770 5928. Curfew 11:30pm. Open Apr.-Oct. daily; Nov.-Mar. Su-Th. Dorms £11.50, under-18 £8.30.)

HARLECH   ☎ 01766

This tiny coastal town just south of the Llyn Peninsula commands panoramic views of sea, sand, and Snowdonian summits. High above the sea and sand dunes is ▧**Harlech Castle,** another of Edward I's Welsh castles; this one served as the insurrection headquarters of Welsh rebel Owain Glyndŵr. (Open June-Sept. daily 9:30am-6pm; May and Oct. 9:30am-5pm; Nov.-Mar. M-Sa 9:30am-4pm, Su 11am-4pm. £3, students £2.50.) Harlech lies midway on the Cambrian Coaster line; **trains** arrive from Machynlleth (1¼-1¾hr., 3-7 per day, £8.20) and connect to Pwllheli and other spots on the Llyn Peninsula. The **Day Ranger** pass allows unlimited travel on the Coaster line for one day (£4-7). The **tourist office**, 1 Stryd Fawr, doubles as a **Snowdonia National Park Information Centre.** (☎ 780 658. Open daily 10am-1pm and 2-6pm.) Enjoy spacious rooms and breakfast served in a glassed-in patio with views of the ocean and castle at **Arundel ❷,** Stryd Fawr. Call ahead for pick-up. (☎ 780 637. Singles £15; doubles £30.) At the **Plâs Cafe ❷,** Stryd Fawr, guests linger over long afternoon tea (£1-4) and sunset dinners (from £7) while enjoying sweeping ocean views from the grassy patio. (☎ 780 204. Open Mar.-Oct. daily 9:30am-8:30pm; Nov.-Feb. 9:30am-5:30pm.) **Postal Code:** LL46 2YA.

LLYN PENINSULA   ☎ 01766

The seclusion and sublime tranquility of the Llyn have brought visitors to reverence since the Middle Ages, when holy men made pilgrimages across it on their way to Bardsey Island, just off the western tip of the peninsula. Today, sun worshippers make the pilgrimage to the endless beaches that line the southern coast. **Porthmadog,** on the southeastern part of the peninsula, is the main gateway. This travel hub's principal attraction is the charming **Ffestiniog Railway** (☎ 516 073; call for hours.), which runs from Harbour Station on High St. into the hills of Snowdonia (1¼hr., 2-10 per day, round-trip £14). **Trains** run from Aberystwyth (1½-2hr., 3-7 per day). TrawsCambria **bus** #701 travels once a day to Aberystwyth (2hr.) and Cardiff (7hr.). Express Motors bus #1 stops in Porthmadog on its way from Blaenau Ffestiniog to Caernarfon (M-Sa every hr. until 10:25pm). The **tourist office** is on High St. by the harbor. (☎ 512 981. Open Easter-Oct. daily 10am-6pm; Nov.-Easter 10am-5pm.) The birthplace of Lawrence of Arabia is now the huge and comfortable **Snowdon Backpackers Hostel ❷,** complete with an upscale cafe and bar. (☎ 515 354. Dorms £12-13; doubles £29-33.) **Postal Code:** LL49 9AD.

CAERNARFON
☎ 01286

Majestic and fervently Welsh, the walled city of Caernarfon (car-NAR-von) has a world-famous castle at its prow and mountains in its wake. Built by Edward I beginning in 1283, the ▓**Caernarfon Castle** was left unfinished when Eddie ran out of money, yet it is still an architectural feat. (☎ 677 617. Open June-Sept. daily 9:30am-6pm; Apr.-May and Oct. daily 9:30am-5pm; Nov.-Mar. M-Sa 9:30am-4pm, Su 11am-4pm. £4.50, students £3.50.) Arriva Cymru **buses** #5 and 5x arrive from Conwy (☎ (08706) 082 608; 1¼hr., 1-3 per hr.). TrawsCambria bus #701 arrives daily from Cardiff (7½hr.). National Express bus #545 arrives daily from London (☎ (08705) 808 080; 9hr, daily). The **tourist office** is on Castle St. (☎ 672 232. Open Apr.-Oct. daily 9:30am-5:30pm; Nov.-Mar. Th-Tu 9:30am-4:30pm.) ▓**Totter's Hostel ❷**, 2 High St., has huge rooms, free bikes, a comfortable living room, and a full kitchen. (☎ 672 963. Dorms £11.) **Hole-in-the-Wall Street** offers a tremendous collection of bistros, cafes, and restaurants from which to choose. Try the Welsh lamb (£11) at **Stones Bistro ❸**, 4 Hole-in-the-Wall St., a crowded, candle-lit eatery near Eastgate. (Open Tu-Sa 6-11pm.) **Postal Code:** LL55 2ND.

CONWY
☎ 01492

The central attraction of this tourist mecca is the 13th-century ▓**Conwy Castle,** another link in Edward I's chain of impressive North Wales fortresses. (Open June-Sept. daily 9:30am-6pm; Apr.-May and Oct. 9:30am-5pm; Nov.-Mar. M-Sa 9:30am-4pm, Su 11am-4pm. £3.50, students £3. Tours £1.) Arriva Cymru **buses** #5 and 5X stop in Conwy on their way to Caernarfon from Bangor (☎ (08706) 082 608; 1-2 per hr.). National Express buses (☎ (08705) 808 080) arrive from: Liverpool (2¾hr., daily); Manchester (4hr., daily); and Newcastle (10hr., daily). The **tourist office** is at the castle entrance. (☎ 592 248. Open Easter-Oct. daily 9:30am-6pm; Nov.-Easter Th-Sa 10am-4pm.) For a good night's sleep, try the ▓**Swan Cottage ❷**, 18 Berry St. Tucked into an old 16th-century building near the center of town, this cottage has cozy rooms and timber ceilings. (☎ 596 840. Singles £17; doubles £34.) **Bistro Conwy ❷** serves truly inspired Welsh fare on humble wooden plates. (☎ 596 326. Lunch £5-9. Dinner £13. Open Su-M 11:30am-2pm, Tu-Th 11:30am-2pm and 7-9pm, F-Sa 11:30am-2pm and 7-9:30pm.) **Postal Code:** LL32 8DA.

SCOTLAND

A little over half the size of England but with just a tenth of the population, Scotland possesses open spaces and wild natural splendor its southern neighbor cannot hope to rival. The craggy, heathered Highlands, the silver beaches of the west coast, and the luminescent mists of the Hebrides elicit any traveler's awe, while farmlands to the south and peaceful fishing villages on the east coast harbor a gentler beauty. Scotland at its best is a world apart from the rest of the UK. Before reluctantly joining with England in 1707, the Scots defended their independence, bitterly and heroically, for hundreds of years. Since the union, they have nurtured a separate identity, retaining control of schools, churches, and the judicial system. In 1999, the Scots finally regained a separate parliament, which gave them more power over domestic tax laws and strengthened their national identity.

▶ TRANSPORTATION

Bus travel from London is generally cheaper than **train** fares. **British Airways** (☎ (08457) 773 3377) sells a limited number of APEX round-trip tickets from £70. **British Midland** (☎ (0870) 607 0555) also offers a round-trip Saver fare from London to Glasgow (from £70). Scotland is linked by **ferry** to Northern Ireland. From **Stranraer,** Stena Line (☎ (08705) 707 070) sails to Belfast (£15-24).

In the **Lowlands** (south of Stirling and north of the Borders), train and bus connections are frequent. In the **Highlands,** trains snake slowly on a few restricted routes, bypassing the northwest almost entirely, and many stations are unstaffed or nonexistent—buy tickets on board. A great money-saver is the **Freedom of Scotland Travelpass.** It allows unlimited train travel as well as transportation on most Caledonian MacBrayne ferries, with discounts on some other ferry lines. Purchase the pass *before* traveling to Britain, at any BritRail distributor (p. 141). Buses tend to be the best way to travel; **Scottish Citylink** (☎(08705) 505 050) provides most intercity service. **MacBackpackers** (☎(0131) 558 9900; www.macbackpackers.com) and **HAGGiS** (☎(0131) 557 9393; www.radicaltravel.com) run hop-on/hop-off tours that let you travel Scotland at your own pace.

EDINBURGH ☎0131

A city of elegant stone set among rolling hills and ancient volcanoes, Edinburgh (ED-in-bur-ra; pop. 500,000) is the jewel of Scotland. Since David I granted it burgh (town) status in 1130, Edinburgh has been a site of cultural significance—the seeds of the Scottish Reformation were sown here as well as the philosophies of the Scottish Enlightenment. The medieval Stuarts made Edinburgh a center of poetry and music. That tradition lives on today during the festivals each August, when the city becomes a theatrical, musical, and literary magnet, drawing international talent and enthusiastic crowds. At the beginning of the 21st century, Edinburgh's star appears only to be on the rise. Today's city continues to be a cultural beacon, its medieval spires calling travelers to the cosmopolitan mecca beneath.

TRANSPORTATION

Flights: Edinburgh International Airport (EDI; ☎333 1000), 11.25km west of the city center. **Lothian Buses' Airlink** (☎555 6363) runs shuttles to the airport from Waverley Bridge (25min., £3.30). **Airsaver** gives you 1 trip on Airlink plus 1 day unlimited travel on local Lothian Buses (£4.20, children £2.50).

Trains: Waverley Station straddles Princes St., Market St., and Waverley Bridge. Trains (☎(08457) 484 950) arrive from: **Aberdeen** (2½hr.; M-Sa every hr., Su 8 per day; £32); **Glasgow** (1hr., 2 per hr., £7.80-8.60); **Inverness** (3½hr., every 2hr., £32); **London King's Cross** (4¾hr., 2 per hr., £83-89); **Stirling** (50min., 2 per hr., £5.30).

Buses: The **bus station** is on the east side of St. Andrew's Sq. **National Express** (☎(08705) 808 080) arrives from **London** (10hr., 5 per day, £29). **Scottish Citylink** (☎(08705) 505 050) arrives from: **Aberdeen** (4hr., every hr., £15); **Glasgow** (1hr., 2-4 per hr., £3.80); and **Inverness** (4½hr., 8-10 per day, £15). A bus-ferry route via Stranraer goes to **Belfast** (2 per day, £20) and **Dublin** (daily, £28).

Public Transportation: Lothian Buses (☎555 6363; www.lothianbuses.co.uk) provide most services. Exact change required (50p-£1). Buy a 1-day **Daysaver** ticket (all day M-F £2.50; after 9:30pm M-F and all day Sa or Su £1.80) from any driver or from the **Travelshops** on Hanover St. and Waverley Bridge. **Night buses** cover selected routes after midnight (£2). **First Edinburgh** also operates locally. **Traveline** (☎(0800) 232 323) has info on all public transport.

Bike Rental: Biketrax, 11 Lochrin Pl. (☎228 6633). Mountain bikes £10 per day. Open M-F 9:30am-6pm, Sa 9:30am-5pm, Su noon-5pm.

BRITAIN

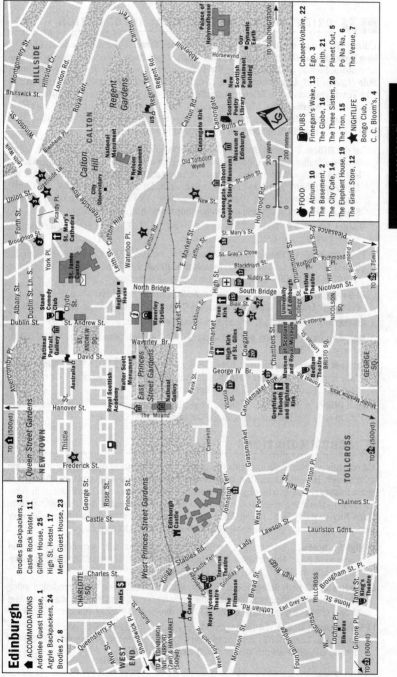

Edinburgh

◆ ACCOMMODATIONS
Ardenlee Guest House, 1
Argyle Backpackers, 24
Brodies 2, 8

Brodies Backpackers, 18
Castle Rock Hostel, 11
Gifford House, 25
High St. Hostel, 17
Merlin Guest House, 23

● FOOD
The Atrium, 10
The Basement, 2
The City Cafe, 14
The Elephant House, 19
The Grain Store, 12

🍺 PUBS
Finnegan's Wake, 13
The Globe, 16
The Three Sisters, 20
The Tron, 15

★ NIGHTLIFE
Bongo Club, 9
C. C. Bloom's, 4

Cabaret-Voltaire, 22
Ego, 3
Faith, 21
Planet Out, 5
Po Na Na, 6
The Venue, 7

BRITAIN

■ 🔲 ORIENTATION AND PRACTICAL INFORMATION

Edinburgh is a glorious city for walking. **Princes Street** is the main thoroughfare in **New Town,** the northern section of Edinburgh. From there you can view the impressive stone facade of the towering **Old Town,** the southern half of the city. **The Royal Mile** (Castle Hill, Lawnmarket, High St., and Canongate) is the major road in the Old Town and connects **Edinburgh Castle** in the west to the **Palace of Holyroodhouse** in the east. **North Bridge, Waverley Bridge,** and **The Mound** connect Old and New Town. Greater Edinburgh stretches well beyond Old and New Town; **Leith,** 3.2km northeast, is the city's seaport on the Firth of Forth.

Tourist Office: 3 Princes St. (☎473 3800), Waverley Market, on the north side of the Waverley Station complex. Books rooms for a £3 fee and 10% deposit, and offers excellent free maps and pamphlets. **Bureau de change.** Open July-Aug. M-Sa 9am-8pm, Su 10am-8pm; Sept. and May-June M-Sa 9am-7pm, Su 10am-7pm; Oct.-Apr. M-W 9am-5pm, Th-Sa 9am-6pm, Su 10am-5pm. In summer, look for the blue-jacketed **Guiding Stars,** who roam the city and can answer questions in several languages.

Budget Travel: STA Travel, 27 Forrest Rd. (☎226 7747). Open M-W 10am-6pm, Th 10am-7pm, F 10am-5:30pm, Sa 10am-5pm.

Financial Services: Thomas Cook, 52 Hanover St. (☎226 5500). Open M-F 9am-6pm, Sa 9am-5:30pm and Su 11am-5pm. **American Express,** 139 Princes St. (☎718 2505 or ☎(08706) 001 600). Open M-F 9am-5:30pm, Sa 9am-4pm.

Bi-Gay-Lesbian Resources: Pick up *Gay Information* at the tourist office or drop by the **Edinburgh Lesbians, Gays, and Bisexuals Centre,** 58a Broughton St. (☎478 7069).

Emergency: ☎999 or 112; no coins required. **Police:** 5 Fettes Ave. (☎311 3131).

Hospital: Royal Infirmary of Edinburgh, Old Dalkeith Rd. (**emergencies** ☎536 4000, otherwise ☎536 1000).

Internet Access: easyInternet Cafe, 58 Rose St. (☎220 3577). £1 per 30min. Open daily 8am-11pm. **Internet Cafe,** beside Platform 1, Waverley Station. £1 per 20min. Open M-F 7:30am-9pm, Sa-Su 8am-9pm.

Post Office: (☎556 9546), in the St. James Shopping Centre, New Town. Open M 9am-5:30pm, Tu-F 8:30am-5:30pm, Sa 8:30am-6pm. **Postal Code:** EH1.

🔺 ACCOMMODATIONS

Edinburgh accommodations run the gamut and offer good options for every type of traveler. In the city center, **hostels** and **hotels** are the only options; **B&Bs** and **guest houses** reside on the city's outer edges. It's a good idea to book ahead in summer, and absolutely essential to be well ahead of the game during festival-time (late July to early Sept.). The TIC's booking service can help during those busy periods when many people sublet their apartments for longer stays.

■ **High St. Hostel,** 8 Blackfriars St. (☎557 3984). Good facilities, party atmosphere, and convenient Royal Mile location have made this hostel a long-time Edinburgh favorite. Continental breakfast £1.90. Dorms £11-13. ❷

■ **Brodies 2,** 93 High St. (☎556 6770). Currently the best value accommodation along the Royal Mile. Offers a luxurious common room, a spotless kitchen, stainless steel showers, and heavenly beds. Dorms £11-17; doubles £34-45; quads from £55. ❷

■ **Merlin Guest House,** 14 Hartington Pl., Bruntsfield (☎229 3864), southwest of the Royal Mile. Comfortable, well-priced rooms in a leafy-green neighborhood. £15-23 per person; student discounts available in the off-season. ❷

Ardenlee Guest House, 9 Eyre Pl. (☎556 2838), at the northern edge of New Town. Walk or take northbound bus #23 or 27 from Hanover St. to the corner of Dundas St. and Eyre Pl. Near the Royal Botanic Garden, this friendly guest house offers large, comfortable rooms. No smoking. £30-40 per person. ❸

Castle Rock Hostel, 15 Johnston Terr. (☎225 9666), just steps from the castle. Regal views and top-notch common areas. Continental breakfast £1.60. Internet 80p per 30min. Dorms £11-13. ❷

Brodies Backpackers, 12 High St. (☎/fax 556 6770; www.brodieshostels.co.uk). Under the same management as Brodies 2. Relaxed, fun environment at this relatively small Royal Mile hostel. Free Internet. Dorms £11-17; £59-89 per week. ❷

Gifford House, 103 Dalkeith Rd. (☎667 4688), Newington. Take bus #33 from Prince St. Offers enormous rooms for families with good views of Arthur's Seat. Singles £25-60; doubles £45-80; family rooms £80-140. ❸

Argyle Backpackers, 14 Argyle Pl. (☎667 9991; argyle@sol.co.uk), next to the Meadows and south of the Royal Mile. 2 renovated townhouses with a lovely little back garden. Internet access. Dorms £10-15; doubles £30-40. ❷

⬛ FOOD

Edinburgh boasts an increasingly wide range of cuisines and restaurants. If it's traditional fare you're after, the capital won't disappoint, with everything from haggis at the neighborhood pub to "modern Scottish" at the city's top restaurants. If you're looking for cheap eats, many **pubs** offer student discounts in the early evening. Takeaway shops on **South Clerk Street, Leith Street,** and **Lothian Road** have well-priced Chinese and Indian fare. There's also a **Sainsbury's supermarket,** 9-10 St. Andrew's Sq. (☎225 8400. Open M-Sa 7am-10pm, Su 10am-8pm).

The City Cafe, 19 Blair St. (☎220 0125). Right off the Royal Mile behind the Tron Kirk, this Edinburgh institution is popular with the young and stylish. Relaxed by day, a flashy pre-club spot by night. Incredible shakes immortalized in *Trainspotting*. Burgers £4-6. Food served M-Th 11am-11pm, F-Su 11am-10pm. Drinks until 1am. ❷

The Basement, 10a-12a Broughton St. (☎557 0097). Draws a lively mix of locals to its candle-lit cavern. Menu changes daily. Well-known for Mexican fare Sa-Su and Thai cuisine on W nights. Vegetarian options available. 2-course lunch £7. Dinner £10-12. Reservations recommended. Food served daily noon-10pm. Drinks until 1am. ❸

Restaurant Martin Wishart, 54 The Shore (☎553 3557), Leith. Showcases exquisite modern French cuisine, which can be sampled in a 5-course tasting menu (£48). The 3-course lunch special (£19) will also leave you more than satisfied. Make reservations 2 weeks in advance. Open Tu-Sa noon-2pm and 7-9:30pm. ❺

The Atrium, 10 Cambridge St. (☎228 8882). A hot Edinburgh eatery, serving modern Scottish fare. Reservations essential. Open M-F noon-2pm and 6-10pm, Sa 6-10pm. ❹

The Grain Store, 30 Victoria St. (☎225 7635). Only a minute walk from the Royal Mile, The Grain Store offers an extensive wine menu and prepares French cuisine using local Scottish produce. 2-course dinner £20. Reservations recommended. Open M-Th noon-2pm and 6-10pm, F-Sa noon-3pm and 6-11pm, Su 6-10pm. ❹

The Elephant House, 21 George IV Bridge (☎220 5355). A perfect place to chill, chat, or pore over stacks of newspapers. Author J.K. Rowlings made her first notes for the *Harry Potter* series here. Tea and coffee under £5. Open daily 8am-11pm. ❶

La Tasca, 9 South Charlotte St. (☎558 8894). *Tapas* bar with good music and a decor that hits the mark. A native staff will happily help you choose from dozens of small dishes (£2-3 each). Open daily noon-11pm. ❶

◉ SIGHTS

A boggling array of Edinburgh tour companies tout themselves as "the original" or "the scariest," but the most worthwhile is the ▦**Edinburgh Literary Pub Tour.** Led by professional actors, this alcohol-sodden 2hr. crash course in Scottish literature meets outside the Beehive Inn in the Grassmarket. (☎226 6665. June-Sept. daily 7:30pm; Nov.-Mar. F 7:30pm; Oct. and Apr.-May Th-Su 7:30pm. £8, students £6.) Of the many tours exploring Edinburgh's dark and gristly past, the **City of the Dead Tour** and its promised one-on-one encounter with the MacKenzie Poltergeist is most popular. (40 Candlemaker Row. ☎225 9044. Apr.-Oct. daily 8:30, 9:15, and 10pm; Nov.-Mar. 7:30 and 8:30pm. £6, concessions £5.)

THE OLD TOWN AND THE ROYAL MILE

Edinburgh's medieval center, the fascinating **Royal Mile** defines **Old Town** and passes many classic and worthwhile sights. The Old Town once packed thousands of inhabitants into a scant few square miles, with narrow shop fronts and slum buildings towering to a dozen stories.

▦**EDINBURGH CASTLE.** Perched atop an extinct volcano and dominating the city center, the castle is a testament to Edinburgh's past strategic importance. The castle is the result of centuries of renovation and rebuilding; the most recent additions date to the 1920s. The **One O'Clock Gun** fires daily (except Su) at 1pm. *(Open Apr.-Oct. daily 9:30am-6pm; Nov.-Mar. 9:30am-5pm. Last admission 45min. before closing. £8.50, seniors £6.25, children £2. Under-5 free. Audio tours £3.)*

ALONG THE ROYAL MILE. Near the Castle, through Mylne's Close, the **Scottish Parliament** convenes in the **Church of Scotland Assembly Hall;** guests are welcome to watch the MPs debate. The **Visitors Centre** is nearby, at the corner of the Royal Mile and the George IV Bridge. *(☎348 5411. Sept.-June. Tickets must be reserved in advance. Free. Visitor Centre open M-F 10am-5pm. Free.)* In 2004, the Scotland's seat of government will move to the **new Scottish Parliament Building** at Holyrood. The new structure was designed by late Catalan architect Enric Miralles. *(Off Holyrood Rd. Open daily 10am-4pm. Free.)* The 17th-century **Lady Stair's House** contains the **Writer's Museum,** featuring memorabilia and manuscripts belonging to three of Scotland's greatest literary figures: Robert Burns, Sir Walter Scott, and Robert Louis Stevenson. *(Lawnmarket St. Open M-Sa 10am-5pm; during festival season M-Sa 10am-5pm, Su 2-5pm. Free.)* At the beautiful ▦**High Kirk of St. Giles** (St. Giles Cathedral), Scotland's principal church, John Knox delivered the fiery Presbyterian sermons that drove Mary, Queen of Scots, into exile. Now it offers free concerts year-round. *(Where Lawnmarket becomes High St. Open Easter to mid-Sept. M-F 9am-7pm, Sa 9am-5pm, Su 1-5pm; mid-Sept. to Easter M-Sa 9am-5pm, Su 1-5pm. Suggested donation £1.)* The 17th-century **Canongate Kirk,** at the end of the Mile, is the resting place of economist Adam Smith; royals used to worship here when in residence. *(Same hours as the High Kirk. Free.)*

THE PALACE OF HOLYROODHOUSE. This Stewart palace sitting at the base of the Royal Mile beside Holyrood Park remains Queen Elizabeth II's official Scottish residence; as a result, only parts of the ornate interior are open to the public. On the palace grounds lie the 12th-century ruins of **Holyrood Abbey,** which was built by David I in 1128 and was ransacked during the Scottish Reformation. *(Open Apr.-Oct. daily 9:30am-6pm; Nov.-Mar. M-Sa 9:30am-4:30pm; last admission 45min. before closing. Closed during official residences. £7.50, concessions £6. Free audio guide.)*

OTHER SIGHTS IN THE OLD TOWN. The ▦**Museum of Scotland** and the connected **Royal Museum,** on Chambers St., just south of the George IV Bridge, are not to be missed. The former houses a definitive collection of Scottish artifacts in a stunning contemporary building; the latter contains a varied mix of art and natural history. *(Open M and W-Sa 10am-5pm, Tu 10am-8pm, Su noon-5pm. Free.)* Just across the street stands the statue of Greyfriar's loyal pooch, Bobby, marking the entrance to **Greyfriar's Kirk,** built in 1620 and surrounded by a beautiful and supposedly haunted churchyard. *(Off Candlemaker Row. Gaelic services Su 12:30pm, English 11am. Open Apr.-Oct. M-F 10:30am-4:30pm, Sa 10:30am-2:30pm; Nov.-Mar. Th 1:30-3:30pm. Free.)*

THE NEW TOWN

Edinburgh's New Town is a masterpiece of Georgian design. James Craig, a 23-year-old architect, won the city-planning contest in 1767; his rectangular grid of three parallel streets (**Queen, George,** and **Princes**) linking two large squares (**Charlotte** and **St. Andrew**) reflects the Scottish Enlightenment's belief in order.

THE GEORGIAN HOUSE AND THE WALTER SCOTT MONUMENT. The elegantly restored Georgian House gives a fair picture of how Edinburgh's elite lived 200 years ago. *(7 Charlotte Sq. From Princes St., turn right on Charlotte St. and take the second left. Open Apr.-Oct. daily 10am-5pm; Nov.-Dec. and Mar. 11am-3pm. £5, students £3.80.)* The ▊**Walter Scott Monument** is a Gothic "steeple without a church;" climb the 287-step staircase for far views stretching out to Princes St., the castle, and the surrounding city. *(On Princes St., between The Mound and Waverley Bridge. Open Mar.-Oct. M-Sa 9am-6pm, Su 10am-6pm; Nov.-Feb. daily 9am-3pm. £2.50.)*

THE NATIONAL GALLERIES

Edinburgh's National Galleries of Scotland form an elite group, with excellent collections housed in stately buildings and connected by a free shuttle every hour. The flagship is the ▊**National Gallery of Scotland,** on The Mound, which houses a superb collection of works by Renaissance, Romantic, and Impressionist masters, as well as a fine spread of Scottish art. The **Scottish National Portrait Gallery,** 1 Queen St., north of St. Andrew's Sq., features the faces of famous Scots. Take the free shuttle, bus #13 from George St., or walk to the **Scottish National Gallery of Modern Art,** 75 Belford Rd., west of town, and the new **Dean Gallery,** 73 Belford Rd., specializes in Surrealist and Dadaist art. *(All open M-W and F-Su 10am-5pm, Th 10am-7pm; longer hours during festival season. Free.)*

GARDENS AND PARKS

Just off the eastern end of the Royal Mile, ▊**Holyrood Park** is a true city oasis, a natural wilderness replete with hills, moorland, and lochs. **Arthur's Seat,** the park's highest point, affords stunning views of the city and countryside. The walk to the summit takes about 45min. The lovely **Royal Botanic Gardens** are north of the city center. Take bus #23 or 27 from Hanover St. *(Open Apr.-Sept. daily 10am-7pm; Oct. and Mar. 10am-6pm; Nov. and Feb. 10am-4pm. Free.)*

🎵 ENTERTAINMENT

The summer sees an especially joyful string of events—music in the gardens, plays and films, and *ceilidhs*—even before the Festival comes to town. In winter, shorter days and the crush of students promote a flourishing nightlife. For the most up-to-date info on what's going on, check out *The List* (£2.20), a comprehensive bi-weekly guide to events, available from any local newsstand.

THEATER, FILM, AND MUSIC. The **Festival Theatre,** 13-29 Nicholson St., stages ballet and opera, while the affiliated **King's Theatre,** 2 Leven St., hosts comedy, drama, musicals, and opera. Tickets range from £8 matinees to £52 operas. (☎ 529 6000. Box office open M-Sa 10am-6pm.) **The Stand Comedy Club,** 5

York Pl., has nightly acts. (☎558 7272. Tickets £1-8.) The **Filmhouse,** 88 Lothian Rd., offers quality European, arthouse, and Hollywood cinema. (☎228 2688. Tickets £3.50-5.50.) Thanks to an abundance of students, Edinburgh's live music scene is alive and well. For a run-down of upcoming acts, look to *The List.* Free live jazz can be found at **Henry's Jazz Bar,** 8 Morrison St. (Open W-Su 8pm-3am. £5.) **The Venue,** 15 Calton Rd. (☎557 3073), and **The Liquid Room,** 9c Victoria St. (☎225 2528), often host rock and progressive shows. **Whistle Binkie's,** 4-6 South Bridge, off High St., is a subterranean pub with live music most nights. (Open daily until 3am.)

🎵 NIGHTLIFE

PUBS

Edinburgh claims to have the highest density of pubs anywhere in Europe. Pubs directly on the Royal Mile usually attract a mixed crowd, while students tend to loiter in the Old Town just to the south.

■ **The Tron,** 9 Hunter Sq., behind the Tron Kirk. Wildly popular for its incredible deals. Frequent live music on 3 hopping floors. Students and hostelers get £1 drinks on W nights. Alcoves downstairs make for a perfect night with friends. Open daily 11:30am-1am.

The Globe, 13 Niddry St. This backpacker's abode is recommended up and down the Royal Mile. A great place to relax and meet fellow travelers. Hosts DJs and karaoke. Open Su-Th 4pm-1am, F-Sa noon-1am.

Finnegan's Wake, 9b Victoria St. Promotes the Irish way with several stouts on tap and live Irish music every weekend. Open daily 1pm-1am.

The Three Sisters, 139 Cowgate. Loads of space for dancing, drinking, and socializing. Three themed bars (Irish, Gothic, and Style) and an outdoor beer garden draw a boisterous, young crowd. Open daily 9am-1am.

CLUBS

Club venues are constantly closing down and reopening under new management; consult *The List* for updated info. Clubs cluster around the historically disreputable **Cowgate,** just downhill from and parallel to the Royal Mile; most close at 3am.

Cabaret-Voltaire, 36-38 Blair St. Hosting a wide range of live music, dance, and art, this innovative club throws a great party. Cover free-£15, depending on events.

Bongo Club, 14 New St. Noted for its hip-hop. Sa is incredibly popular. Cover free-£10.

The Venue, 17-23 Calton Rd. 3 dance floors host top live gigs. Cover £2-8.

Po Na Na, 26 Frederick St. Moroccan-themed and glamorous. Plays an eclectic mix of disco, funk, and lounge music. Cover £2-5.

Faith, 207 Cowgate. This purple-hued club housed in an old church specializes in R&B, and runs the very popular Chocolate Sunday each week. Cover free-£6.

GAY AND LESBIAN

The Broughton St. area of the New Town (better known as the **Broughton Triangle**) is the center of Edinburgh's gay community.

Planet Out, 6 Baxter's Pl. Start off the night at this mellow club. All drinks £1 on M. Open M-F 4pm-1am, Sa-Su 2pm-1am.

C.C. Bloom's, 23-24 Greenside Pl., on Leith St. A friendly gay club with no cover. M-Sa dancing, Su karaoke. Open M-Sa 6pm-3am, Su 8pm-3am.

Ego, 14 Picardy Pl. Hosts several gay nights, including **Joy** (1 Sa per month). Cover £10.

☉ FESTIVALS

Edinburgh has special events year-round, but the real show is in August when the city is *the* place to be in Europe. What's commonly referred to as "the Festival" actually encompasses a number of independently organized events. For more info on all the festivals, check out www.edinburghfestivals.co.uk. The **Edinburgh International Festival** (Aug. 15-Sept. 4 in 2004), the largest of them all, features a kaleidoscopic program of music, drama, dance, and art. Most tickets (£7-57, 50% discount for students) are sold beginning in April, but you can usually get tickets at the door; look for half-price tickets starting at 9am on performance days at **The HUB,** Edinburgh's Festival Centre, Castlehill. (☎473 2000. Open M-Sa.) Around the established festival has grown a less formal ■**Fringe Festival** (Aug. 8-30 in 2004), which now includes over 600 amateur and professional companies presenting theater, comedy, children's shows, folk and classical music, poetry, dance, and opera events that budget travelers may find more suitable for their wallets (usually free-£10). Contact the **Fringe Festival Office,** 180 High St. (☎226 0000; www.edfringe.com. Open June-Aug. daily.) Another August festival is the **Military Tattoo** (Aug. 6-28 in 2004), spectacle of military bands, bagpipes, and drums. For tickets (£9-31), contact the **Tattoo Ticket Sale Office,** 33-34 Market St. (☎225 1188; www.edintattoo.co.uk). The excellent **Edinburgh International Film Festival** is also in August at The Filmhouse (☎229 2550; tickets on sale starting late July), while the **Edinburgh Jazz and Blues Festival** is from July 23 to August 1 in 2004 (☎467 5200; tickets on sale in June). The fun doesn't stop for the long, dark winter: **Hogmanay,** Edinburgh's traditional New Year's Eve festival, is a serious street party with a week of associated events (www.edinburghshogmanay.org).

▶ DAYTRIP FROM EDINBURGH

ST. ANDREWS. Golf overruns the small city of St. Andrews, where the rules of the sport were formally established. The **Old Course** frequently hosts the British Open. (☎(01334) 466 666 for reservations or enter a same-day lottery for starting times. Apr.-Oct. £90 per round; Nov.-Mar. £56.) The budget option, still lovely, is the nine-hole **Balgove Course** for £7-10. If you're more interested in watching than playing, visit the **British Golf Museum,** next to the Old Course, which details the ancient origins of the game. (☎(01334) 460 046. Hours change seasonally; call for info. £4, students £3.) **St. Andrews Cathedral** was the center of

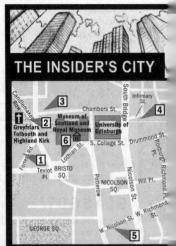

THE INSIDER'S CITY

EDINBURGH UNIVERSITY PUB CRAWL

Oscar Wilde once said that "nothing worth knowing can be taught." For a real Edinburgh education, pick up a thing or two on the *Let's Go* pub crawl.

1 Live folk music at **Sandy Bell's** will prime you for the evening ahead. (25 Forrest Rd. Open daily 11am-1am.)

2 **Greyfriars Bobby** is a student favorite. (34 Candlemaker Row. Open daily 11am-1am.)

3 **Beluga Bar** is *the* spot for the stylish scholar set. (30a Chambers St. Open daily 9am-1am.)

4 **Oxygen Bar** cuts a cool profile with a smart decor. (3-5 Infirmary St. Open M-Sa 10am-1am, Su 11am-1am.)

5 Catch a little sun at **Pear Tree House**'s beer garden. (38 W. Nicolson St. Open daily 11am-midnight, F-Sa until 1am.)

6 Laid-back **Negociants** serves great food until 2:15am. (45-47 Lothian St. Open M-Sa 9am-3am, Su 10am-3am.)

Scottish religion before and during the Middle Ages. The nearby **St. Andrews Castle** hides secret tunnels and bottle-shaped dungeons. (Cathedral and castle open Apr.-Sept. daily 9:30am-6:30pm; Oct.-Mar. 9:30am-4:30pm. Joint ticket £4.)

Trains (☎(08457) 484 590) stop 11km away in Leuchars (1hr., every hr., £8.10), where buses #94 and 96 (£1.60) depart for St. Andrews. **Buses** (☎(01383) 621 249) pull in from Edinburgh (bus #X59 or X60; 2hr.; M-Sa 1-2 per hr. until 6:45pm, fewer on Su; £5.70) and Glasgow (#X24, change at Glenrothes to #X59; 2½hr., M-Sa every hr., £5.50). To get from the bus station to the **tourist office,** 70 Market St., turn right on City Rd. and take the first left. (☎(01334) 472 021; www.standrews.com. Open Apr.-June M-Sa 9:30am-5:30pm, Su 11am-4pm; July-Aug. M-Sa 9:30am-7pm, Su 10:30am-5pm; Sept. M-Sa 9:30am-6pm, Su 11am-4pm; Oct.-Mar. M-Sa 9:30am-5pm.) **Internet** access is across the street at **Costa Coffee,** 83 Market St. (£1 per 20min. Open M-Sa 8am-6pm, Su 10am-5:30pm.) B&Bs line **Murray Place** and **Murray Park** near the bus station. **St. Andrews Tourist Hostel ❷,** St. Mary's Pl., has a great location and has sparkling facilities. (☎(01334) 479 911. Dorms £12; family room £40-48.)

GLASGOW ☎0141

Scotland's largest metropolitan area, Glasgow (pop. 700,000) has re-invented itself several times, and the mark of each era remains today. It rose to prominence during the Victorian period, exploiting heavy industry to become the world's leading center of shipbuilding and steel production, as evidenced by the soot and cranes that once littered the River Clyde. Yet Glasgow's urbanization had its positive side as well, the legacy of which can be observed in the grand architecture that still characterizes the city centre. Across the river, the daring curves of a new multi-million pound Science Centre shimmer brilliantly. Free museums and international cuisine add cosmopolitan flair, separating the city from its industrial past. At night, Glasgow's pubs explode as Scotland's largest student population and its football-mad locals live up to their national reputation for nighttime fun.

▐ TRANSPORTATION

Flights: Glasgow Airport (GLA; ☎887 1111), 15km west in Abbotsinch. Citylink buses connect to **Buchanan Station** (25min., 6 per hr., £3.30).

Trains: Central Station, on Gordon St. (U: St. Enoch), leave for **London King's Cross** (5-6hr., every hr., £82) and **Stranraer** (2½hr., 3-8 per day, £16). From **Queen St. Station,** on George Sq. (U: Buchanan St.), trains go to: **Aberdeen** (2½hr., 11-24 per day, £31); **Edinburgh** (50min., 2 per hr., £7.40); **Inverness** (3¼hr., 5 per day, £31). Bus #88 runs between the 2 stations (4 per hr., 50p).

Buses: Buchanan Station (☎(0870) 608 2608), on Hanover St., 2 blocks north of Queen St. Station. **Scottish Citylink** (☎(08705) 505 050) to: **Aberdeen** (4hr., every hr., £26); **Edinburgh** (1¼hr., 2-3 per hr., £6); **Inverness** (3½-4½hr., every hr., £26); **Oban** (3hr., 2-3 per day, £12). **National Express** (☎(08705) 808 080) buses arrive daily from **London** (8hr.; every hr.; £22, round-trip £28).

Public Transportation: The circular **Underground** (U) subway line, a.k.a. the "Clockwork Orange," runs M-Sa 6:30am-11pm, Su 11am-5:30pm. 90p. The **Discovery Ticket** is good for one day of unlimited travel. M-F after 9:30am, Su all day. £1.70.

✳ ▐ ORIENTATION AND PRACTICAL INFORMATION

George Square is the center of town. Sections of **Sauchiehall Street, Argyle Street,** and **Buchanan Street** are pedestrian areas. **Charing Cross,** where Bath St. crosses M8 in the northwest, is a useful landmark. The vibrant **West End** revolves around **Byres Road** and **Glasgow University,** 1½km northwest of the city center.

BRITAIN

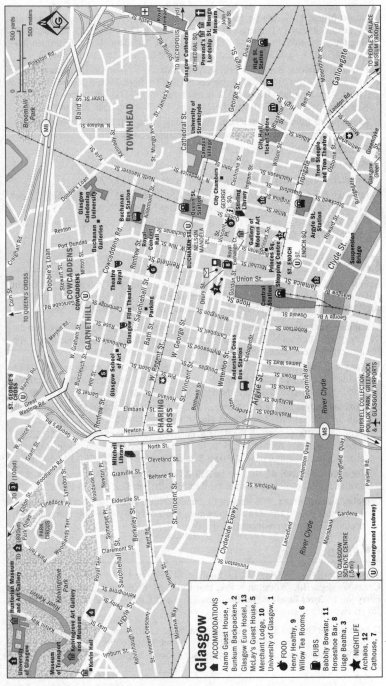

Glasgow

▲ ACCOMMODATIONS
Alamo Guest House, 4
Bunkum Backpackers, 2
Glasgow Euro Hostel, 13
McLay's Guest House, 5
Merchant Lodge, 10
University of Glasgow, 1

🍴 FOOD
Henry Healthy, 9
Willow Tea Rooms, 6

🍺 PUBS
Babbity Bowster, 11
Horseshoe Bar, 8
Uisge Beatha, 3

★ NIGHTLIFE
Archaos, 12
Cathouse, 7

Ⓤ Underground (subway)

Tourist Office: 11 George Sq. (☎204 4400), south of Queen St. Station, and northeast of Central Station. U: Buchanan St. Books rooms for a £2 fee plus 10% deposit. **Walking tours** depart M-Tu and Th-F 2:30 and 6pm, Su 10:30am (1½hr., £5). Open July-Aug. M-Sa 9am-8pm, Su 10am-6pm; Sept.-June M-Sa 9am-7pm, Su 10am-6pm.

Financial Services: Banks are plentiful and **ATMs** are on every corner. **Thomas Cook,** 15 Gordon St. (☎204 4484), inside Central Station. Open M-Sa 8:30am-5:30pm, Su 10am-4pm. **American Express,** 115 Hope St. (☎(08706) 001 060). Open July-Aug. M-F 8:30am-5:30pm, Sa 9am-5pm; Sept.-June M-F 8:30am-5:30pm, Sa 9am-noon.

Laundromat: Coin-Op Laundromat, 39-41 Bank St. (☎339 8953). U: Kelvin Bridge. Wash £2. Dry 20p per 5min. Open M-F 9am-7:30pm, Sa-Su 9am-5pm.

Emergency: ☎999; no coins required.

Police: 173 Pitt St. (☎532 2000).

Hospital: Glasgow Royal Infirmary, 84-106 Castle St. (☎211 4000).

Internet Access: easyInternet Cafe, 57-61 St. Vincent St. (☎222 2365). £1 per 40min.-3hr. depending on time of day. Open daily 7am-10:45pm.

Post Office: 47 St. Vincent St. (☎204 3688). Open M-F 8:30am-5:45pm, Sa 9am-5:30pm. **Postal Code:** G2 5QX.

▐ ACCOMMODATIONS

Reserve B&Bs and hostels in advance, especially in August. If rooms are booked in Glasgow, consider staying at the **SYHA Loch Lomond** (p. 216). Most B&Bs cluster on **Argyle Street** in the university area or on **Westercraigs Road,** east of the Necropolis.

Bunkum Backpackers, 26 Hillhead St. (☎581 4481). Though located away from the city centre, Bunkum is minutes away from the vibrant West End. Spacious dorms with comfortable beds. Lockers. Laundry £1.50. Dorms £12 per day. ❷

Glasgow Euro Hostel, (☎222 2828; www.euro-hostels.com), on the corner of Clyde St. and Jamaica St. Convenient to the city centre, this hostel also offers a dining room and bar. Breakfast included. Laundry facilities. Internet access. Dorms from £13.80. ❶

Merchant Lodge, 52 Virginia St. (☎552 2424). Originally a tobacco store, this upscale B&B is convenient and comfortable. Singles £35; doubles £55; triples £70. ❸

University of Glasgow, No. 3 The Square, Conference & Visitor Services (☎330 5385). Enter the university from University St. and turn right into the square. Summer housing at several dorms. Office open M-F 9am-5pm. Student dorms £14; B&B £17.50. ❷

Alamo Guest House, 46 Gray St. (☎339 2395), across from Kelvingrove Park at its southern exit. Beautiful location in the West End. Singles £23; doubles £40-46. ❸

McLay's Guest House, 268 Renfrew St. (☎332 4796). With 3 dining rooms and satellite TV, this posh B&B looks and feels more like a hotel. Singles £24, with bath £26; doubles £40/48; family room £55/65. ❸

▐ FOOD

The area bordered by Otago St. in the west, St. George's Rd. in the east, and along Great Western Rd., Woodlands Rd., and Eldon St. brims with cheap kebab-and-curry joints. **Byres Road** and **Ashton Lane,** a tiny cobblestoned alley parallel to Byres Rd., thrive with cheap, trendy cafes.

Ashora, 108 Elderslie St. Just west of several hostels on Berkeley St., this award-winning restaurant features cheap, delicious Indian food. Lunch buffet £2.95, dinner buffet £5.95. Lunch served 11am-2pm. Open daily 11am-midnight. ❶

Willow Tea Rooms, 217 Sauchiehall St. Upstairs from Henderson the Jewellers. A Glasgow landmark. Sip one of 31 kinds of tea. £1.70 per pot. High tea £8.80. Open M-Sa 9am-4:30pm, Su noon-4:15pm. ❷

La Tasca, 39 Renfield St. (☎204 5188), is a popular Spanish *tapas* bar where the *sangria* is not to be missed. *Tapas* £3-8. Open daily noon-midnight. ❶

Cul-de-Sac Restaurant, 44-46 Ashton Ln. Turn from Byres Rd. onto Ashton Ln., and bear right. 3-course dinners include vegetable dishes, meat *cassoulet,* and haggis (£13-20). Open M-Sa noon-10:30pm, Su 12:30-10:30pm. ❸

Henry Healthy, Queen St. (☎227 2791), just south of George Sq. A great place for a quick snack or lunch. Soup 80p. Sandwiches £1.60. Open M-Sa 7:30am-3pm. ❶

BRITAIN

📷 SIGHTS

Glasgow is a budget sightseer's paradise, with splendid architecture, grand museums, and chic galleries that are often free to visitors. Your first stop should be to the Gothic 🔲**Glasgow Cathedral,** the only full-scale cathedral spared the fury of the 16th-century Scottish Reformation. (Open Apr.-Sept. M-Sa 9:30am-6pm, Su 2-5pm; Oct.-Mar. M-Sa 9:30am-4pm, Su 2-4pm. Free.) On the same street is the **St. Mungo Museum of Religious Life and Art,** 2 Castle St., which surveys every religion from Islam to Yoruba. (Open M-Sa 10am-5pm, Su 11am-5pm. Free.) Behind the cathedral is the spectacular **Necropolis,** a terrifying hilltop cemetery. (Open 24hr. Free.)

In the West End, **Kelvingrove Park** lies on the banks of the River Kelvin. In the southwest corner of the park, at Argyle and Sauchiehall St., sits the magnificent **Kelvingrove Art Gallery and Museum,** which shelters works by van Gogh, Monet, and Rembrandt. Due to renovation, the museum's collection is on display at the new **Open Museum,** 161 Woodhead Rd., until construction is completed in 2006. (Museum open M-Th and Sa 10am-5pm, F and Su 11am-5pm. Free.) Farther west rise the Gothic edifices of the **University of Glasgow.** The main building is on University Ave., which runs into Byres Rd. While walking through the campus, stop by the **Hunterian Museum,** home to the death mask of Bonnie Prince Charlie, or see 19th-century Scottish art at the **Hunterian Art Gallery,** across the street. (U: Hillhead. Open M-Sa 9:30am-5pm. Free.) Several buildings designed by Charles Rennie Mackintosh, Scotland's most famous architect, are open to the public; the **Glasgow School of Art,** 167 Renfrew St., reflects a uniquely Glaswegian Modernist style. (Tours July-Aug. M-F 11am and 2pm; Sa-Su 10:30am, 11:30am, and 1pm. Sept.-June M-F 11am and 2pm, Sa 10:30am. £5, students £3.)

🎵 📷 ENTERTAINMENT AND NIGHTLIFE

Glaswegians have a reputation for partying hard. *The List* (£2.20 at newsstands) has detailed nightlife and entertainment listings for both Glasgow and Edinburgh. The infamous **Byres Road** pub crawl slithers past the University of Glasgow area, starting at Tennant's Bar and proceeding toward the River Clyde. 🔲**Uisge Beatha,** 232 Woodlands Rd., serves over 100 kinds of malt whiskey. (Whiskey £1.30-1.60. Open M-Th 11am-11pm, F-Sa 11am-midnight, Su 12:30-11pm.) Go to 🔲**Babbity Bowster,** 16-18 Blackfriar St., for football talk and good drinks. (Open M-Sa 10am-midnight, Su 11am-midnight.) **Horseshoe Bar,** 17-21 Drury St., boasts the longest continuous bar in the UK. (Open M-Sa 11am-midnight, Su 12:30pm-midnight.) At the club **Archaos,** 25 Queen St., students drink 2-for-1 whiskeys. (Cover £3-7. Open Su, Tu, and Th-Sa 11pm-3am.) Indie music pleases younger crowds at **Cathouse,** 15 Union St., a 3-story club. (Cover £3-5, student £1-4. Open W-Su 11pm-3am.)

STIRLING ☎ 01786

The third point of a strategic triangle completed by Glasgow and Edinburgh, Stirling has historically presided over north-south travel in the region; it was once said that "he who controlled Stirling controlled Scotland." At the 1297 Battle of Stirling Bridge, **William Wallace** (of *Braveheart* fame) overpowered the English army, enabling Robert the Bruce to finally overthrow the English at **Bannockburn,** 3km south of town. To reach Bannockburn, take bus #51 or 52 from Murray Pl. in Stirling. (Visitors center open Apr.-Oct. daily 10am-5:30pm; Feb.-Mar. and Nov.-Dec. 10:30am-4pm. £3.50, children £2.60. Battlefield open year-round.) **Stirling Castle** has superb views of the Forth valley and recalls a history both of royal residence and military might. (Open Apr.-Oct. daily 9:30am-6pm; Nov.-Mar. 9:30am-5pm. £7.50, concessions £5.50.) **Argyll's Lodging,** a 17th-century mansion below the castle has been impressively restored. (Open Apr.-Sept. daily 9:30am-6pm; Oct.-Mar. 9:30am-5pm. £3.30, concessions £2.50. Free with castle admission.) The 19th-century **Wallace Monument Tower,** on Hillfouts Rd., 2.5km from town, offers incredible views. You can also admire the 1.5m sword William Wallace wielded against King Edward I. Take bus #62 or 63 from Murray Pl. (Open July-Aug. daily 9:30am-6pm; Sept. 9:30am-5pm; Oct. and Mar.-May 10am-5pm; Nov.-Feb. 10:30am-4pm; June 10am-6pm. £5, concessions £3.80.)

Trains run from Goosecroft Rd. (☎ (08457) 484 950) to: Aberdeen (2hr.; M-Sa every hr., Su 6 per day; £31); Edinburgh (50min., 2 per hr., £5.30); Glasgow (40min., 1-3 per hr., £5.40); Inverness (3hr., 3-4 per day, £31); and London King's Cross (5½hr., every hr., £44-84). **Buses** also run from Goosecroft Rd. to: Edinburgh (1¼hr., every hr., £4); Fort William (2¾hr., daily, £15); Glasgow (40min., 2-3 per hr., £4); and Inverness (3¾hr., every hr., £13). The **tourist office** is at 41 Dumbarton Rd. (☎ 475 019. Open July-Aug. M-Sa 9am-7:30pm, Su 9:30am-6:30pm; Sept.-Oct. and Apr.-May daily 9am-5pm; Nov.-Mar. M-F 10am-5pm, Sa 10am-4pm.) At the clean and friendly **Willy Wallace Hostel ❷,** 77 Murray Pl., a delightful staff fosters a fun atmosphere. (☎ 446 773. **Internet** access. Dorms £9-13.) The comfortable **Forth Guest House ❸,** 23 Forth Pl., is near the train station. (☎ 471 020. All rooms with bath. Singles £20-40; doubles £20-45.) **Postal Code:** FK8 2BP.

LOCH LOMOND ☎ 01389

Immortalized by the famous ballad, the pristine wilderness surrounding Loch Lomond continues to inspire; lush bays, wooded islands, and bare hills compliment the beauty of Britain's largest lake. Hikers adore the **West Highland Way,** which snakes along the entire eastern side of the Loch and stretches north 152km from Milngavie to Fort William. At the southern tip of the lake is **Balloch,** the area's largest tourist center. Attractions and services at the new **Loch Lomond Shores** in Balloch include a giant-screen film about the loch, a **National Park Gateway Centre,** a tourist office, and bike and canoe rentals. (☎ 722 406. Shores open June-Sept. 10am-6pm, Oct.-May 10am-5pm. £5.) One of the best introductions to the area is a Sweeney's Cruises **boat tour,** which leaves from the tourist office's side of the River Leven in Balloch (1hr.; every hr. 10am-5:30pm; £5.20, children £2.50).

Trains arrive on Balloch Rd. from Glasgow Queen St. (45min., 2 per hr., £3.20). Scottish Citylink **buses** (☎ (08705) 505 050) arrive from Glasgow (45min., 3-5 per day, £3.60). First (☎ (0141) 423 6600) buses arrive from Stirling (1½hr., 4 per day, £3.80). **Tourist offices** are at Loch Lomond Shores (see above) and in the Old Station Building. (☎ 753 533. Open July-Aug. daily 9:30am-6pm;

June-Sept. 9:30am-5:30pm; Apr.-May and Oct. 10am-5pm.) The ▓SYHA **Loch Lomond ②**, 3km north of town, is one of Scotland's largest hostels. From the train station, follow the main road for 800m; at the roundabout, turn right, continue 2.5km, turn left at the sign for the hostel, and it's a short way up the hill. (☎850 226. Dorms £12-14, under-18 £10-12.) Camp at the luxurious **Lomond Woods Holiday Park ①**, on Old Luss Rd., up Balloch Rd. from the tourist office. (☎750 000. Spa facilities. Bikes £10 per day. Reception 8:30am-8pm. Tent and two people £9-15; additional guests £2.)

THE TROSSACHS   ☎01877

The most accessible tract of Scotland's wilderness, the Trossachs has long been praised for its rich green mountains and misty lochs. The A821 winds through the heart of the area between **Aberfoyle** and **Callander,** the region's main towns. It also passes near **Loch Katrine,** the Trossachs's original lure and the setting of Scott's *The Lady of the Lake.* A pedestrian road traces the loch's shoreline, while the popular Steamship Sir Walter Scott **cruises** from the Trossachs Pier (1-3 per day, round-trip £5.80-6.80). Above the loch hulks **Ben A'an'** (461m); the rocky 1hr. hike up begins a mile from the pier, along A821. The **Rob Roy and Trossachs Visitor Centre** in Callander is a combined tourist office and exhibit on the 17th-century hero who is buried nearby. (☎330 342. Open June-Aug. daily 9am-6pm; Sept. 10am-6pm; Oct.-Dec. and Mar.-May 10am-5pm; Jan.-Feb. Sa-Su 11am-4:30pm. £3.25.)

From Callander, First (☎(01324) 613 777) **buses** run to Stirling (45min., 8 per day, £3) and Aberfoyle (45min., 4 per day, £2.50). **Postbuses** reach some remoter areas of the region; find timetables at tourist offices or call the **Stirling Council Public Transport Helpline** (☎(01786) 442 707). About 2km south of Callander on Invertrossachs Rd. is **Trossachs Backpackers ②**, a comfortable hostel with an attractive setting. (☎331 100. **Internet** access. Dorms £12.50; singles £15.) Camp at **Trossachs Holiday Park ①**, outside Aberfoyle. (☎382 614. Open Mar.-Oct. £10-14 per person.)

INVERNESS AND LOCH NESS   ☎01463

In 565, St. Columba repelled a savage sea beast as it attacked a monk; whether a prehistoric leftover or cosmic wanderer, the monster has captivated the world's imagination ever since. ▓**Loch Ness** still guards its secrets 7.5km south of Inverness. Tour agencies often are the most convenient ways to see Nessie's home; **Guide Friday** offers a 3hr. bus and boat tour. (☎224 000. May-Sept. daily 10:30am and 2:30pm. £15, students and seniors £12, children £7.) Or let **Kenny's Tours** take you around the entire loch and back to Inverness on a minibus. (☎252 411. Tours 10:30am-5pm. £13, students £10.) Five kilometers south on A82, visit ▓**Urquhart Castle** (URK-hart), one of the largest in Scotland before it was blown up in 1692 to prevent Jacobite occupation. Alleged photos of Nessie have since been taken from the ruins. (☎(01456) 450 551. Open June-Aug. daily 9:30am-6:30pm; Apr.-May and Sept. daily 9:30am-5:45pm; Oct.-Mar. M-Sa 9:30am-3:45pm. Admission £5.) The Jacobite cause died in 1746 on **Culloden Battlefield,** east of Inverness, when Bonny Prince Charlie lost 1200 men in 40min. To get there, take Highland County bus #12 from the post office at Queensgate (round-trip £2). Just 2.5km south of Culloden, the stone circles and chambered cairns (mounds of rough stones) of the **Cairns of Clava** recall civilizations of the Bronze Age. Bus #12 will also take you to **Cawdor Castle,** home of the Cawdors since the 15th century; don't miss the maze. (Open May-Sept. daily 10am-5pm. £6.50, students and seniors £5.30, children £3.50.)

BRITAIN

Trains (☎(08457) 484 950) run from Academy St. in Inverness's Station Sq. to: Aberdeen (2¼hr., 7-10 per day, £19); Edinburgh (3½-4hr., 5-7 per day, £31); Glasgow (3½hr., 5-7 per day, £31); and London (8hr., 3 per day, £84-110). Scottish Citylink **buses** (☎(08705) 505 050) run from Farraline Park, off Academy St., to Edinburgh and Glasgow (both 4½hr., 10-12 per day, £15). To reach the **tourist office,** Castle Wynd, from the stations, turn left on Academy St. and then right onto Union St. (☎234 353. **Bureau de change** and **Internet** £1 per 20min. Open mid-June to Aug. M-Sa 9am-7pm, Su 9:30am-5pm; Sept. to mid-June M-Sa 9am-5pm, Su 10am-4pm.) **Bazpackers Backpackers Hotel ❶,** 4 Culduthel Rd., has a homey atmosphere and great views of the city. (☎717 663. Reception 7:30am-midnight. Dorms £12; doubles £15.) A minute's walk from the city center, **Felstead ❸,** 18 Ness Bank, is a spacious B&B with comfortable beds. (☎321 634. Singles £28-36; doubles £56-72.) Try the **Lemon Tree ❶,** 18 Inglis St., for fabulously cheap and tasty soups (£1.80) and baked goods. (Open M-Sa 8:30am-5:45pm.)

THE INNER HEBRIDES

ISLE OF SKYE

Often described as the shining jewel in the Hebridean crown, Skye possesses unparalleled natural beauty, from the serrated peaks of the Cuillin Hills to the rugged northern tip of the Trotternish Peninsula.

◧ TRANSPORTATION. The tradition of ferries carrying passengers "over the sea to Skye" ended with the **Skye Bridge,** which links Kyle of Lochalsh, on the mainland, to Kyleakin, on the Isle of Skye. **Trains** (☎(08457) 484 950) arrive at Kyle of Lochalsh from Inverness (2½hr., 2-4 per day, £15). Skye-Ways (☎(01599) 534 328) runs **buses** from: Fort William (2hr., 3 per day, £11); Glasgow (5½hr., 3 per day, £19); and Inverness (2½hr., 2 per day, £11). **Pedestrians** can traverse the Skye Bridge's 2.5km footpath or take the **shuttle bus** (2 per hr., £1.70). **Buses** on the island are infrequent and expensive; pick up the handy *Public Transport Guide to Skye and the Western Isles* (£1) at a tourist office.

KYLE OF LOCHALSH AND KYLEAKIN. Kyle of Lochalsh and Kyleakin (Ky-LAACK-in) bookend the Skye Bridge. The former, on the mainland, has an **ATM,** tourist office, and train station, making it of practical value to travelers. Kyleakin, though short on amenities, boasts three hostels, countless tours, and a backpackers' atmosphere. **◧MacBackpackers Skye Trekker Tour,** departing from the hostel in Kyleakin, offers either a 1-day tour emphasizing the history and legends of the the island and a 2-day eco-conscious hike into the Cuillin hills, with all necessary gear provided. (☎(01599) 534 510. Call ahead. 1-day £15, 2-day £45.) Located between Kyle of Lochalsh and Inverness, **Eilean Donan Castle** is the restored 13th-century seat of the MacKenzie family. If you don't bring a camera, you'll definitely stand out; Eilean Donan Castle is the most photographed monument in Scotland. (☎(01599) 555 202. Open Apr.-Oct. daily 10am-5:30pm; Nov. and Mar. 10am-3pm. £4, students £3.20.) To enjoy the incredible sunset views from the quiet Kyleakin harbor, climb to the memorial on the hill behind the SYHA hostel. A slippery scramble to the west takes you to the small ruins of **Castle Moil.** Cross the bridge behind the hostel, turn left, follow the road to the pier, and take the gravel path. The Kyle of Lochalsh **tourist office** is on the hill above the train station. (☎(01599) 534 276. Open May-Oct. M-Sa 9am-5:30pm.) The friendly owners of **◧Dun Caan Hostel ❷,** in Kyleakin, have masterfully renovated a 200-year-old cottage. (☎(01599) 534 087. **Bikes** £10 per day. Book ahead. Dorms £10.)

SLIGACHAN. Renowned for their hiking and cloud and mist formations, the **Cuillin Hills** (COO-leen), the highest peaks in the Hebrides, are visible from nearly every part of Skye, beckoning hikers and climbers. *Walks from Sligachan and Glen Brittle* (£1), available at tourist offices, hotels, and campsites, suggests routes. West of Kyleakin, the smooth, conical Red Cuillin and the rough, craggy Black Cuillin Hills meet in Sligachan, a hiker's hub in a jaw-dropping setting. Don't be misled by the benign titles 'hills'; the Cuillins are great for experienced hikers, but can be risky for beginners. For accommodations, try the **Sligachan Hotel ❹**, a classic hill-walker and climber's haunt. (☎ (01478) 650 204. Breakfast included. Singles £30-40; doubles £60-80.) **Camp** at **Glenbrittle Campsite ❶**, in Glenbrittle at the foot of the Black Cuillins. Take bus #53 (M-Sa 2 per day) from Portree or Sligachan to Glenbrittle. (☎ (01478) 640 404. Open Apr.-Sept. £4 per person.)

PORTREE. The island's capital, Portree, has busy shops and an attractive harbor. **Dunvegan Castle**, the seat of the clan MacLeod, holds the record for the longest-inhabited Scottish castle, with continual residence since the 13th century. The castle holds the **Fairy Flag**, a 1,500-year-old silk, and **Rory Mor's Horn**, capable of holding 2 liters of claret. Traditionally, the new MacLeod chief must drain the horn in one draught. Present lord John MacLeod emptied it in just under two minutes. Buses (1-3 per day) arrive from Portree. (☎ (01478) 521 206. Open Apr.-Oct. daily 10am-5:30pm; Nov.-Mar. 11am-4pm. £6. Gardens only £4.) **Buses** to Portree from Kyle of Lochalsh (5 per day, £7.80) stop at Somerled Sq. The **tourist office** is on Bayfield Rd. (☎ (01478) 612 137. Open July-Aug. M-Sa 9am-7pm, Su 10am-4pm; Apr.-June and Sept.-Oct. M-F 9am-5pm, Su 10am-4pm; Nov.-Mar. M-Sa 9am-4pm.) **Portree Independent Hostel ❷**, The Green, has many amenities, an enthusiastic staff, and gregarious guests. (☎ (01478) 613 737. **Internet** £1 per 20min. Dorms £11; doubles £23.)

THE OUTER HEBRIDES

The landscape of the Outer Hebrides is extraordinarily beautiful and astoundingly ancient. Much of its rock is more than half as old as the Earth itself, and long-gone inhabitants have left a collection of tombs, standing stones, and other relics. The culture and customs of the Hebridean people seem equally storied, rooted in religion and a love of tradition. While tourism has diluted some old ways, you're still more likely to get an earful of Gaelic here than anywhere else in Scotland.

◪ TRANSPORTATION. Caledonian MacBrayne (☎ (01475) 650 100) **ferries** serve the Western Isles, from Ullapool to Lewis and from Skye to Harris and North Uist. Find schedules in *Discover Scotland's Islands with Caledonian MacBrayne*, free from tourist offices. You'll also want to pick up the *Lewis and Harris Bus Timetables* (40p). Inexpensive **car rental** (from £20 per day) is possible throughout the isles. The terrain is hilly but excellent for **cycling.**

LEWIS AND HARRIS. Despite its 20,000 inhabitants, the island of **Lewis** is desolate; its landscape flat, treeless, and speckled with lochs. Mists shroud miles of moorland and fields of peat, nearly hiding Lewis's many archaeological sites, most notably the ◪**Callanish Stones,** an extraordinary Bronze Age circle. (☎ (01851) 621 422. Visitors center open Apr.-Sept. M-Sa 10am-7pm; Oct.-Mar. 10am-4pm. Exhibit £1.80. Stones free.) CalMac **ferries** sail from Ullapool, on the mainland, to **Stornoway** (pop. 8,000), the largest town in northwestern Scotland (M-Sa 2 per day; £14, round-trip £24). To get to the Stornoway **tourist office,** 26 Cromwell St., turn left from the ferry terminal, then right onto Cromwell St. (☎ (01851) 703 088. Open Apr.-Oct. M-Sa 9am-6pm or until the last ferry; Nov.-Mar. M-F 9am-5pm.) The best place to lay your head is **Fair Haven Hostel ❷**, over the surf shop at the intersection of Francis St. and Keith St. From the pier, turn left onto Shell St., which becomes South Beach, then turn right on Kenneth St. and right again onto Francis St. The meals here are better than in town. (☎ (01851) 705 862. Dorms £10, with three meals £20; doubles £15 per person.)

Harris is technically the same island as Lewis, but they're entirely different worlds. The deserted flatlands of Lewis, in the north, give way to another, more rugged and spectacular kind of desolation—that of Harris's steely gray peaks. Toward the west coast, the **Forest of Harris** (ironically, a treeless, heather-splotched mountain range) descends to yellow beaches bordered by indigo waters and *machair*—sea meadows of soft grass and summertime flowers. Essential *Ordnance Survey* hiking maps can be found at the tourist office in **Tarbert**, the biggest town on Harris. **Ferries** arrive in Tarbert from Uig on Skye (M-Sa 2 per day; £9, round-trip £16). The **tourist office** is on Pier Rd. (☎ (01859) 502 011. Open Apr. to mid-Oct. M-Sa 9am-5pm and for late ferry arrivals; mid-Oct. to Mar. for arrivals only.) **Rockview Bunkhouse ❶**, on Main St., is less than 5min. west of the pier, on the north side of the street. (☎ (01859) 502 211. Dorms £9.)

BULGARIA (БЪЛГАРИЯ)

The history of Bulgaria's people is not as serene as its landscape. Once the most powerful state in the Balkans, Bulgaria fell to the Turks in the late 14th century. During its 500 years under Ottoman rule, Bulgaria's nobles were obliterated and its peasants were enserfed. At the same time, however, underground monasteries were preserving the nation's culture. This paved the way for the National Revival of the 1870s, when education spread and much of the majestic architecture now gracing Bulgaria's cities was built. Today, the country struggles with a flagging economy and a lack of full European recognition, problems heightened by the recent Balkan wars. Nonetheless, travelers should not pass over Bulgaria's beautiful coastline, lush countryside, and lovely monasteries.

FACTS AND FIGURES

Official Name: Republic of Bulgaria.

Capital: Sofia.

Major Cities: Varna, Burgas, Ruse.

Population: 7,600,000.

Land Area: 110,910 sq. km.

Time Zone: GMT +2.

Language: Bulgarian.

Religions: Orthodox (84%).

DISCOVER BULGARIA

Bulgaria is a convenient trip from Greece. In **Sofia** (p. 225), admire Orthodox Churches and wander cobblestone alleyways. **Rila Monastery** (p. 229), in the highest mountains on the Balkan Peninsula, is the masterpiece of Bulgarian religious art. **Plovdiv** (p. 229) shelters Roman ruins and art museums, and is only 30min. from the splendid **Bachkovo Monastery** (p. 230). The **Black Sea Coast** (p. 231) is full of raucous discos and deserted beaches. On your way to the coast from western Bulgaria, stop in **Veliko Turnovo** (p. 230), the most beautiful town in the country.

ESSENTIALS

WHEN TO GO

Year-round, Bulgaria is milder than other Balkan countries due to the proximity of the Mediterranean and Black Seas. Spring and fall weather is generally ideal, as winter can be quite cold. For the Black Sea Coast, summer is the best time to visit.

DOCUMENTS AND FORMALITIES

VISAS. Citizens of Australia, Canada, New Zealand, and the US may stay without visas for up to 30 days. Citizens of the EU may visit visa-free for up to 90 days. Citizens of South Africa and all travelers staying more than 30 days must obtain a 90-day visa from their local embassy or consulate.

EMBASSIES. Foreign embassies in Bulgaria are in Sofia (p. 227). Bulgarian embassies at home include: **Australia** (consulate), 4 Carlotta Rd., Double Bay, Sydney, NSW 2028; mail to: P.O. Box 1000, Double Bay, NSW 1360 (☎00612 932 77581; www.users.bigpond.com/bulcgsyd); **Canada**, 325 Stewart St., Ottawa, ON K1N 6K5 (☎613-789-3215; mailmn@storm.ca); **Ireland**, 22 Bulington Rd., Dublin 4 (☎01 660 3293; fax 01 660 3915); **South Africa,** 1071 Church St., Hatfield, Pretoria 0083; mail to: P.O. Box 26296, Arcadia (☎012 342 37 20; embulgsa@iafrica.com); **UK**, 186-188 Queensgate, London SW7 5HL (☎020 7584 9400; www.bulgarianembassy.org.uk); **US**, 1621 22nd St. NW, Washington, D.C. 20008 (☎202-387-0174 or 387-7969; www.bulgaria-embassy.org).

TRANSPORTATION

BY PLANE. All flights to Sofia connect through England or Western Europe. Budget travelers might want to fly into a nearby capital—Athens or Bucharest—and take a bus to Sofia.

BY TRAIN. Bulgarian trains run to Hungary, Romania, and Turkey and are most useful for travel in the north; **Rila** is the main international train company. The train system is comprehensive but slow, crowded, and old. There are three types of trains: Express (експрес; ekspres), fast (бърз; burz), and slow (пътнически; putnicheski). Avoid *putnicheski* like the plague—they stop at anything that looks inhabited. *Purva klasa* (първа класа; first-class seating) is very similar to *vtora klasa* (втора класа; second-class) and not worth the extra money.

BY BUS. Buses are better for travel in eastern and western Bulgaria and are often faster than trains—they are also less frequent and less comfortable. Buses head north from Ruse, to İstanbul from anywhere on the Black Sea Coast, and to Greece from Blagoevgrad. For long distances, **Group Travel** and **Etap** offer modern buses with air-conditioning, bathrooms, and VCRs at prices 50% higher than trains. Some buses have set departure times; others leave when full. Grueling local buses stop everywhere and are a bumpy (and in the summer, hot) ride.

BY TAXI. Yellow taxis are everywhere; some Black Sea towns can be reached only by cab. Refuse to pay in euros or US dollars and insist on a metered ride (*"sus apparata"*); ask the distance and price per kilometer to do your own calculations.

BY FOOT AND BY THUMB. Cars, not pedestrians, have the right of way in Bulgaria; faithfully obey crosswalk signs, and cross roads quickly. Hitchhiking is rare because drivers hardly ever stop, but it is generally safe if precautions are taken. *Let's Go* does not recommend hitchhiking.

TOURIST SERVICES AND MONEY

EMERGENCY	Police: ☎166. Ambulance: ☎150. Fire: ☎160.

TOURIST OFFICES. Tourist offices are fairly common, as are local travel agencies. The staffs are helpful and usually speak English. In big hotels, you can often find an English-speaking receptionist and maps.

MONEY. The **lev** (lv; plural *leva*) is the standard monetary unit; there are 100 stotinki in a lev. It is illegal to exchange money on the street. **Banks** are the most reliable way to exchange money, and they can cash traveler's checks and give Visa cash advances; use exchange bureaus only when banks are closed. Credit cards are rarely accepted except in larger hotels and expensive resorts. **ATMs** give the best exchange rate and are common throughout Bulgaria; they usually accept MasterCard, Visa, Plus, and Cirrus. Restaurant meals cost 6lv on average. **Tipping** is not obligatory, as most people just round up to the nearest lev, but 10% doesn't hurt. A 7-10% service charge will occasionally be added for you; always check the bill or the menu. Tipping taxi drivers usually means rounding up to the nearest half-lev. Bargaining for fares is not done, but make sure there is a meter or agree on a price.

BUSINESS HOURS. Businesses open at 8 or 9am and there is a one-hour lunch break between 11am and 2pm. Banks are usually open 8:30am to 4pm, but some close at 2pm. *Vseki den* (всеки ден; every day) usually means Monday through Friday, and "non-stop" doesn't always mean open 24 hours.

LEVA		
	AUS$1 = 1.13LV	1LV = AUS$0.88
	CDN$1 = 1.28LV	1LV = CDN$0.78
	EUR€1 = 1.94LV	1LV = EUR€0.52
	NZ$1 = 1.01LV	1LV = NZ$0.99
	UK£1 = 2.80LV	1LV = UK£0.36
	US$1 = 1.77LV	1LV = US$0.56
	ZAR1 = 0.24LV	1LV = ZAR4.13

COMMUNICATION

PHONE CODES	**Country code: 359. International dialing prefix: 00.** From outside Bulgaria, dial int'l dialing prefix (see inside back cover) + 359 + city code + local number.

TELEPHONES AND INTERNET ACCESS. For local and international calls, it's best to buy a phone card. There are two brands: **Bulfon** (orange) and **Mobika** (blue), which work only at telephones of the same brand. Cards are sold at kiosks and bookstores. Bulfon is better and more prevalent. Making international telephone calls from Bulgaria can be a challenge. **Payphones** are ludicrously expensive; opt for the phones in a telephone office. If you must make an international call from a pay phone, purchase a 400 unit card for 20lv—units run out very quickly. To call collect, dial ☎01 23 for an international operator. The Bulgarian phrase for collect call is *za tyahna smetka* (за тяхна сметка). International direct access numbers include: **AT&T,** ☎00 800 0010; **BT Payphones,** ☎00 800 9727; and **MCI,** ☎00 800 0001. **Internet** access is widespread and cheap, around 1lv per hr.

MAIL. Overseas mail requires a Bulgarian return address, and costs: 0.60lv for any European destination; 0.90lv for the US; 0.80-1lv for Australia, New Zealand, or South Africa. Write "С въздушна поща" for airmail. *Poste Restante* is unreliable; address mail to be held: Firstname SURNAME, *Post Restante*, Gen. Gurko 6, Sofia 1000, BULGARIA.

LANGUAGES. Bulgarian is a South Slavic language similar to Russian; learning the Cyrillic alphabet (p. 1051) is helpful. English is spoken mostly by young people and in tourist areas. German is understood in many places.

> **YES AND NO.** To indicate "yes" and "no," Bulgarians shake their heads in the opposite directions from Brits and Yankees. If you are uncoordinated, it's easier to just hold your head still and say *dah* or *neh*.

ACCOMMODATIONS AND CAMPING

BULGARIA	❶	❷	❸	❹	❺
ACCOMMODATIONS	under 20lv	21-35lv	36-50lv	51-70lv	over 70lv

Upon crossing the border, citizens of South Africa may receive a **statistical card** to document where they sleep. **Foreigner registration** is required as of March 2002 in response to 9/11. If you are staying in Bulgaria for more than 48 hours, you must be registered with the police. The hotel/hostel you are staying in will do this for you, and may ask for your passport, but should return it immediately. Keep the registration with your passport, and make sure you are re-registered every time you change accommodations. If you are staying with friends, register yourself with the **Bulgarian Registration Office;** see the consular section of your embassy for details.

Private rooms are indicated by частни квартири (*tschastnee kvartiri*) signs. Rooms can be arranged through **Balkantourist** (www.balkantourist.bg) or other tourist offices for US$6-12 per night (be sure to ask for a central location), or from individuals in train and bus stations. Be careful if alone, and don't hand over any money until you've checked the place out. *Babushki* are your best bet, but try to bargain them down. Bulgarian **hotels** are classed on a star system; rooms in one-star hotels are almost identical to those in two- and three-star hotels, but have no private bathrooms. Hotels are usually US$9-50 per night, although foreigners are often charged more. The majority of Bulgarian **youth hostels** are in the countryside. Outside major towns, most **campgrounds** provide tent space or spartan bungalows.

FOOD AND DRINK

BULGARIA	❶	❷	❸	❹	❺
FOOD	under 4lv	4-8lv	9-14lv	15-18lv	over 18lv

Tap water is generally safe for drinking. Bulgaria is known for cheese and yogurt; try *shopska salata* (шопска салата), a mix of tomatoes, peppers, and cucumbers with feta cheese, or *tarator* (таратор), a cold soup made with yogurt, cucumber, garlic, and sometimes walnuts. Baklava and *sladoled* (сладолед; ice cream) are sold in *sladkarnitsy* (сладкарници). Fruit and vegetables are sold in a *plod-zelenchuk* (плод-зеленчук; fruit store), *pazar* (пазар; market), or on the street. Kiosks sell *kebabcheta* (кебабчета; sausage burgers), sandwiches, pizzas, and *banitsa sus sirene* (баница със сирене; cheese-filled pastries). *Skara* (скара; grill restaurants) serve *kavarma* (каварма), meat dishes with onions, spices, and egg. In restaurants, seat yourself and ask for the bill when you are finished.

SAFETY AND SECURITY

Public bathrooms (Ж for women, M for men) are often holes in the ground; pack a small bar of soap and toilet paper, and expect to pay 0.05-0.20lv. The sign "Аптека" (apteka) denotes a **pharmacy.** There is always a late-night pharmacy in larger towns; its address is posted on the doors of the others. **Emergency care** is far better in Sofia than in the rest of the country; services at the Pirogov State Hospital are free, some doctors speak English, and the tourist office will send someone to translate. Don't buy **alcohol** from street vendors, and watch out for homemade liquor—there have been cases of poisoning and contamination. The Bulgarian government recently recognized **homosexuality,** but acceptance is slow in coming.

HOLIDAYS

Holidays: New Year's Day (Jan. 1); Baba Marta (Mar. 1); Liberation Day (Mar. 3); Good Friday (Apr. 9); Easter (Apr. 11); Labor Day (May 1); St. George's Day (May 6); Education and Culture Day and Day of Slavic Heritage (May 24); Festival of the Roses (June 6); Day of Union (Sept. 6); Independence Day (Sept. 22); Christmas (Dec. 24-26).

SOFIA (СОФИЯ)　　　　　　　☎02

A history of assimilation has left Bulgaria unsure of its identity. In Sofia (pop. 1,100,000), spray-painted skateboarding ramps front the iron Soviet Army monument, while *babushkas* tote their loaves of bread home in *Harry Potter* shopping bags. Although the McDonald's arches keep surfacing, the dome of St. Alexander Nevsky Cathedral is still Sofia's most visible golden landmark, and there are plenty of places to find traditional Bulgarian food, folk music, and handmade souvenirs.

◧ TRANSPORTATION

Flights: Airport Sofia (☎79 80 35). Bus #84 goes to Eagle Bridge (Орлов Мост), a 10min. walk from the city center. Calling a cab (see below) is cheaper than hailing one; a ride to the city center should cost no more than 5lv.

Trains: Tsentralna Gara (Централна Гара; Central Train Station), Knyaginya Maria Luiza St. (Мария Луиза). **Ticket office** (☎931 11 11) open M-F 7am-7pm. To **Burgas** (7 per day, 8.20-12lv) and **Plovdiv** (9 per day, 3.80-5.40lv). Left of the main entrance, **Rila Travel Bureau** (Рила; ☎932 33 46) sells tickets to **Athens** (daily, 65-90lv) and **Budapest** (daily, 110-135lv). Open daily 6am-11pm.

Buses: Private buses, which leave from the parking lot across from the train station, are usually cheap and fast. **Group Travel** (☎32 01 22) sends buses to: **Burgas** (2 per day, 7lv); **Varna** (3 per day, 9lv); **Veliko Tarnovo** (4 per day, 9lv). Arrive 30-45min. before departure to get a seat. Open daily 6:30am-9pm.

Local Transportation: Trams, trolleybuses, and buses cost 0.45lv per ride. Day-pass 2lv; 5-day pass 9lv. Buy tickets at kiosks with signs reading "Билети" (*bileti;* tickets), or from the driver. Punch them on board to avoid a 5lv fine. If you put your backpack on a seat, you might be required to buy a second ticket. Trams #1 and 7 run to pl. Sv. Nedelya; #9 and 12 head down Hristo Botev (Христо Ботев) and Vitosha bul. (Витоша). Officially, public transportation runs 5:30am-11:00pm, but rides are scarce after 9pm.

Taxis: Taxi S-Express (☎912 80), **OK Taxi** (☎973 21 21), and **INEX** (☎919 19) are reliable. At night, take cabs. Fares are 0.40-0.45lv per km, slightly more after 10pm. Drivers almost never speak English. Make sure the meter is on to avoid bargaining.

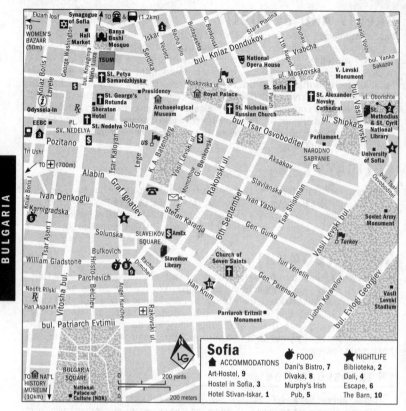

Sofia

ACCOMMODATIONS
Art-Hostel, **9**
Hostel in Sofia, **3**
Hotel Stivan-Iskar, **1**

FOOD
Dani's Bistro, **7**
Divaka, **8**
Murphy's Irish Pub, **5**

NIGHTLIFE
Biblioteka, **2**
Dali, **4**
Escape, **6**
The Barn, **10**

✚ ⓘ ORIENTATION AND PRACTICAL INFORMATION

The city center, **pl. Sveta Nedelya** (Света Неделя), is a triangle formed by the Tsurkva (church) Sv. Nedelya, the wide Sheraton Hotel, and the department store Tsentralen Universalen Magazin (TSUM). **Bul. Knyaginya Maria Luiza** (Княгиня Мария Луиза) connects pl. Sveta Nedelya to the train station. Bul. Vitosha, one of the main shopping and nightlife thoroughfares, links pl. Sveta Nedelya to **pl. Bulgaria** and the huge, concrete **Natsionalen Dvorets Kultura** (Национален Дворец Култура; NDK, National Palace of Culture). On your right as you go down bul. Maria Luiza, historic **bul. Tsar Osvoboditel** (Цар Освободител; Tsar the Liberator) leads to **Sofia University.** The monthly *Sofia City Guide* (2.40lv, available at the Sheraton Hotel and at tourist centers) is an English publication with loads of tourist info. **Maps** are also available in the Sheraton Hotel (open 24hr.) and the open-air book market at Slaveikov Sq. (Славейков) on Graf Ignatiev (Граф Игнатиев).

TOURIST, FINANCIAL, AND LOCAL SERVICES

▨ **Tourist Office: Odysseia-In/Zig Zag Holidays,** bul. Stamboliiskii 20-B (Стамболийски; ☎980 51 02; http://zigzag.dir.bg). From pl. Sv. Nedelya, head down Stamboliiskii and take the 2nd right on Lavele; Odysseia is halfway down on the left, 2 floors up. Consultation 5lv per session. Open M-Sa 9am-6:30pm.

Embassies: Australian Consulate, Trakia Str. 37 (☎98 11 721). **Canada,** Assen Zlatarov Str. 11 (☎943 37 04). Citizens of **New Zealand** should contact the British Embassy. **South Africa,** ul. Gendov, bl. 1 (☎971 21 38). Open M and Th 10am-noon. **UK,** ul. Moskovska 9 (Московска; ☎933 92 22). Register either by phone or in person upon arrival in Bulgaria. Open M-Th 8am-12:30pm and 2-5pm, F 9am-noon. **US,** ul. Suborna 1a (Суборна; ☎937 51 004), 3 blocks from pl. Sv. Nedelya behind the Sheraton Hotel. Open M-F 8:30am-1pm and 2-5pm. Consular section at Kapitan Andreev 1 (Капитан Андреев; ☎963 20 22), behind the NDK. Open M-F 9am-5pm.

Currency Exchange: Bulbank (Булбанк), pl. Sv. Nedelya 7 (☎923 21 11), cashes traveler's checks with a minimum US$3 fee and gives Visa cash advances for a 4% commission. Open M-F 8:30am-6:30pm.

American Express: D. Ignatij 21, 2nd fl. (☎988 49 53), on the left past the post office heading toward Slaveikov Sq. Issues (1% commission) and cashes (3.5% commission) AmEx Traveler's Cheques. Open daily M-F 9am-6pm, Sa 9am-noon.

Luggage Storage: Downstairs at the central train station. 0.80lv per piece. Claim bags 30min. before departure. Open daily 5:30am-midnight.

EMERGENCY AND COMMUNICATIONS

Emergency: Police: ☎166. **Ambulance:** ☎150. **Fire:** ☎160.

24hr. Pharmacies: Apteka #7, pl. Sv. Nedelya 5 (☎950 25). **Purva Chastna Apteka** (Първа Частна Аптека; ☎952 26 22), Tsar Asen 42, near Neofit Rilski.

Medical Assistance: State-owned hospitals offer foreigners free emergency aid. **Pirogov Emergency Hospital,** bul. Gen. Totleben 21 (Ген. Тотлебен; ☎515 31), opposite Hotel Rodina. Take trolley #5 or 19 from city center. Open 24hr.

Telephones: Ul. Stefan Gurko 4. Turn right from the post office onto Vasil Levski then left onto Gurko; white building 1 block down. Phone, fax, photocopy, email, Internet access.

Internet Access: Stargate, Pozitano 20 (Позитано), 30m on left if facing Hostel Sofia. 1lv per hr. Open 24hr.

Post Office: Gen. Gurko 6 (Гурко). Send international mail at windows #6-8; Poste Restante at window #12. Open M-Sa 7am-8:30pm, Su 8am-1pm. Address mail to be held: Firstname SURNAME, *Poste Restante*, Gen. Gurko 6, Sofia **1000,** BULGARIA.

▐▌◖ ACCOMMODATIONS AND FOOD

Big hotels are rarely worth the exorbitant price; hostels or private rooms are the best option. ▨**Hostel in Sofia ❶,** Pozitano 16 (Позитано), has a great location and a friendly staff. From pl. Sv. Nedelya, walk down Vitosha, and go right on Pozitano. (☎/fax 989 85 82; hostelsofia@yahoo.com. Breakfast included. Kitchen available. Reception 24hr. US$10 per person.) The spacious new **Art-Hostel ❷,** ul. Angel Kunchev 21A (Ангел Кънчев), is part hostel, part art gallery. From pl. Sv. Nedelya, take Vitosha to William Gladstone (Уилям Гладстон), turn left, and after two blocks turn right onto Angel Kunchev. (☎987 05 45 or 980 91 30; www.art-hostel.com. Kitchen, bar, tea room, and garden. Internet access. Reception 24hr. 20lv per person.) To get to **Hotel Stivan-Iskar ❸,** ul. Iskar 11B, walk up bul. Maria Luiza and turn right on ul. Ekzah Iosif (Екзарх Йосиф), then walk two blocks and turn right on Bacho Kiro, then left on Iskar. (☎986 67 50; www.hoteliskar.com. Breakfast €2. Check-out noon. Doubles €25-37; apartment with fridge €50-55.)

Cheap meals are easy to find. The large **markets**—the **Women's Bazaar** (Жени Пазар) and **Hali** (Хали)—lie across bul. Maria Luiza from TSUM. ▨**Dani's Bistro ❸,** Angel Kunchev 18A (Ангел Кьнчев), is a quiet street side cafe known for its friendly staff and simple, savory fare. (☎987 45 48.) Facing McDonald's in pl. Slaveikov, take the left side street and continue right at the fork to **Divaka ❶**, ul. William Gladstone 54, which serves huge salads (1.50-3.50lv) and sizzling veggie and meat *sacheta* (4.50lv) on iron plates. (☎989 95 43. Open 24hr.) **Murphy's Irish Pub ❷**, Karnigradska 6 (Кърниградска), is a friendly haven for homesick English-speakers. (☎980 28 70. Entrees from 6.50lv. Live music F. Open daily noon-12:30am.)

👁 SIGHTS

PLOSHAD ALEXANDER NEVSKY. In the city center stands Sofia's pride and joy, the gold-domed **St. Alexander Nevsky Cathedral** (Александр Невски; Sv. Aleksandr Nevsky), which was erected in memory of the 200,000 Russians who died in the 1877-78 Russo-Turkish War. Through a separate entrance left of the main church, the **crypt** contains a spectacular array of painted icons and religious artifacts from the past 1500 years. *(Cathedral open daily 7am-7pm; free. Crypt open M and W-Su 10:30am-6:30pm; 3lv, students 1.5lv.)*

AROUND PLOSHAD SVETA NEDELYA. The focal point of pl. Sveta Nedelya, the **Cathedral of St. Nedelya** (Катедрален Храм Св. Неделя; Katedralen Hram Sv. Nedelya) is filled with frescoes blackened by soot from the candles lit by visitors. The church is a reconstruction of a 14th-century original destroyed by a bomb detonated in an attempt on Tsar Boris III's life in 1925. Sunday liturgy shows off the church's great acoustics. *(Open daily 7am-6pm.)* In the courtyard behind the Sheraton Hotel stands the 4th-century **St. George's Rotunda** (Св. Георги; Sv. Georgi), which is adorned with beautiful 11th- to 14th-century murals. *(In summer, open daily 8am-6pm; in winter, 8am-5pm.)* Walk up bul. Maria Luiza and take a left on Ekzarh Iosif to reach the **Synagogue of Sofia** (Софийска Синагога; Sofiiska Sinagoga), Sofia's only synagogue, where a museum upstairs outlines the history of Jews in Bulgaria. *(Open M-F 9am-5pm. Weekly services F 7pm, Sa 10am. Synagogue 2lv; museum free.)*

ALONG BULEVARD TSAR OSVOBODITEL. Historical bul. Tsar Osvoboditel stretches between the **House of Parliament** and the **Royal Palace.** Midway sits the exquisitely ornamented **St. Nicholas Russian Church** (Св. Николай; Sv. Nikolai), which is topped with Russian Orthodox onion domes. *(Open daily 9am-10:30pm.)*

MUSEUMS. The Royal Palace houses the **National Museum of Ethnography** (Национален Етнографски Музей; Natsionalen Etnograficheski Muzey), which is devoted to folk history, art, and crafts. *(Open Su and Tu-Sa 10am-5:30pm. 3lv, students 1.50lv.)* It also houses the **National Art Gallery** (Национална Художествена Галериа; Natsionalna Hudozhestvena Galeriya). *(Open Su and Tu-Sa 10:30am-6:30pm. 3lv, students 1.50lv.)* To reach the **National History Museum,** Residence Boyana, Palace 1 (Национален Исторически Музей; Natsionalen Istoricheski Muzey), take minibus #21, trolley #2 or bus #63 or 111 to *Boyana.* The museum traces Bulgarian culture and holds archaeological treasures. *(Open daily 9:30am-6pm. 10lv, students 5lv.)*

🎵 🎭 ENTERTAINMENT AND NIGHTLIFE

Half a dozen theaters lie on **Rakovski** (Раковски), Bulgaria's theater hub. A left on Rakovski leads to the columns of the **National Opera House,** Rakovski 59. (☎987 13 66. Shows Tu-Sa 6pm. Box office open M-Tu 9:30am-2pm and 2:30-6:30pm, W-F 8:30am-7:30pm, Sa 10:30am-6:30pm, Su 10am-6pm. Tickets 5-20lv.)

At night, smartly dressed Sofians roam the main streets, filling the outdoor bars along **bulevard Vitosha** and the cafes around the **National Palace of Culture.** For the younger set, nightlife centers around the University of Sofia at the intersection of

Vasil Levski and Tsar Osvoboditel. Hidden away at Hambara, Sklada, 22 Sixth September, ◼The Barn (Хамбара) is a former communist newspaper turned tavern. (Open 8pm-late.) Dance with Sofia's beautiful people at **Escape,** Angel Kunchev 1. (Cover 3lv. Open W-Sa 10:30pm-4am.) **Dali,** behind the University on Hristo Georgiev, is the best Latin club in town. (☎946 51 29. Men 3lv, women free. Call ahead to reserve a table, 10lv per person. Open daily 8pm-5am.) **Biblioteka** (Библиотека), in St. Cyril and Methodius Library, has live bands and Karaoke. (Cover Sa 4lv, Su-F 3lv. Open daily 8:30pm-6am.)

◣ DAYTRIP FROM SOFIA

RILA MONASTERY. Holy Ivan of Rila built the 10th-century Rila Monastery (Рилски Манастир; Rilski Manastir), Bulgaria's largest and most famous monastery, as a refuge from worldly temptation. The monastery sheltered the arts of icon painting and manuscript copying during the Byzantine and Ottoman occupations, and remained a bastion of Bulgarian culture during five centuries of foreign rule. Today's monastery, decorated with 1200 brilliantly-colored **frescoes,** was built between 1834 and 1837; little remains from the earlier structure. Maps and suggested hiking routes through **Rila National Park** are on signs outside the monastery.

To get to the monastery, take **tram** #5 from Hostel Sofia to Ovcha Kupel Station (Овча Къпел) and take the **bus** to Rila Town (2hr., 2 per day, 5lv). From Rila Town, catch the bus to the monastery (30min., 3 per day, 1.50lv). **Hotel Tsarev Vruh ❷** (Царев Врьх), 100m down the path that follows the river from behind the monastery, has private baths and phones. (☎/fax (07054) 22 80. Breakfast US$2. Rooms US$22.) Inquire at room #170 in the monastery about staying in a spartan, but heated, **monastic cell ❷.** (☎ (07054) 22 08. Curfew midnight. US$15 per person.) Behind the monastery is a cluster of restaurants, cafes, and a mini-market.

KOPRIVSHTITSA. Todor Kableshkov's 1876 "letter for blood," urging rebellion against Ottoman rule, incited the War of Liberation in this little village in the Sredna Gora mountains. Today, Koprivshtitsa (КОПРИВЩИЦА; pop. 2,600) is a historical center and home to Bulgaria's popular **folk festival,** which attracts international throngs. The well-preserved **National Revival houses** were built by the town's first settlers. Many homes have enclosed verandas and delicate woodwork, and six have been turned into **museums** of history and ethnography; buy tickets and maps at the tourist office. (5lv, students 3lv. Open daily 9am-5:30pm.)

Trains go to Plovdiv (3½hr., 45 per day, 2.60-3.20lv) via Karlovo and Sofia (2hr., 3 per day, 5lv). **Private buses** also go to Plovdiv (2½hr., daily, 46lv) and Sofia (2hr., 2 per day, 46lv). Backtrack along the river bisecting town to reach the main square, where the **tourist office** sells an invaluable map (2lv) and rents mountain bikes for 3lv per hr. (☎(07184) 21 91. Open daily 10am-6pm.) The office also arranges **private rooms** in the center of town. (Rooms US$7-10.) Small **hotels,** often with "Kushta" (Къща) in the name, are also easy to find (15-20lv).

PLOVDIV (ПЛОВДИВ) ☎032

Although Plovdiv (pop. 376,000) is smaller than Sofia, it is widely hailed as the cultural capital of Bulgaria. Plovdiv's historical and cultural treasures are concentrated among the **Trimondium** (three hills) of **Stariya Grad** (Стария Град; Old Town). Stariya Grad is filled with churches and National Revival houses. To reach the 2nd-century Roman ◼**Amphitheater** (Античен Театр; Antichen Teatr) from pl. Tsentralen (Централен), take a right off Knyaz Aleksandr (Княз Александр) onto Suborna (Съборна), then go right up the steps along Mitropolit Paisii to the steps next to the music academy. This marble masterpiece from the early Roman occupation of the Balkans currently serves as a popular venue for concerts and shows, hosting the **Festival of the Arts** in the summer and early fall, and the **Opera Festival** in June. (Amphitheater open daily 9am-7pm. 3lv.) Return to Knyaz Aleksandr and follow it to the end to pl. Dzhumaya (Джумая), home to the **Dzhumaya Mosque** and the ancient **Philipopolis Stadium**, which still has an intact gladiator's entrance. (Both free.) At the end of Suborna, the **Museum of Ethnography** (Етнографски Музей; Etnografski Muzey) has *kukerski maski* (masks used to scare away evil spirits) and other Bulgarian artifacts. (Open Su, Tu-Th and Sa 9am-noon and 2-5pm, F 2-5:30pm. 3lv, students 2lv.)

Trains go to: Burgas (5hr., 7 per day, 6-8.20lv); Sofia (2½hr., 14 per day, 7lv); and Varna (5½hr., 3 per day, 7.80-10.80lv). Buy tickets at **Rila**, bul. Hristo Botev 31a. (Open M-F 8am-7:30pm, Sa 8am-2pm.) **Buses** from Sofia (2hr., every 30 min., 0.80lv) arrive at Yug (Юг) station, bul. Hristo Botev 47, opposite the train station (☎62 69 37). An up-to-date map is absolutely essential; street vendors sell good **Cyrillic maps** for 3lv. Check email at **Speed**, Kryaz Aleksander 12, on the left before the mosque. (1.20lv per hr. Open 24hr.) It is important to make reservations for rooms in Plovdiv in the summer. ■**Bed and Breakfast Queen Mary Elizabeth ❶**, Gustav Vaigand Str. 7, is clean, backpacker-friendly, and cheap. (☎62 93 06. From Ruski, turn left onto Gustav Vaigand; it's on the right side, 100m down. Free laundry. Reception 24 hr. Shared bathroom. A/C. 10lv per person.) **Hotel Bulgaria ❺**, Patriarch Evtimii 13, has private baths, TV, A/C, and a fitness center. (☎63 35 99. www.hotelbulgaria.net. Reception 24hr. Singles €50.) **Postal Code:** 4000.

◗ DAYTRIP FROM PLOVDIV: BACHKOVO MONASTERY. In the Rodopi mountains, 28km south of Plovdiv is Bulgaria's second-largest monastery, **Bachkovo Monastery** (Бачковски Манастир; Bachkovski Manastir), built in 1083. The main church holds the **Icon of the Virgin Mary and Child** (икона Света Богородица; Ikona Sveta Bogoroditsa), which is said to have miraculous healing power. (Open daily 7am-8pm. Free.) Well-maintained hiking paths lie uphill from the monastery. **Buses** run from Plovdiv's Yug station to Asenovgrad (25min., every 30min., 0.80lv), as do **trains** (25min., 17 per day, 0.80lv). From Asenovgrad, take a bus headed to Luki (Лъки); the monastery is the third stop (20 min., 4 per day, 0.60lv).

VELIKO TARNOVO (ВЕЛИКО ТЪРНОВО)   ☎062

Picturesque Veliko Tarnovo (pop. 75,000), on the steep hills above the Yantra River, has been watching over Bulgaria for 5000 years. For centuries, the city has been the center of Bulgarian politics; its residents led the national uprising against Byzantine rule in 1185, and revolutionaries wrote the country's first constitution here in 1879. The remains of the ■**Tsarevets** (Царевец), a fortress that once housed the royal palace and a cathedral, span a hillside outside the city. (Open daily 7am-7pm. 4lv.) Climb uphill to the beautiful **Church of the Ascension** (Църква Възнесениегосподне; Tsurkva Vuzneseniegospodne), which was restored for the 1300th anniversary of Bulgaria in 1981. (Open daily 7am-6:30pm. 8lv.) From the center, go down Nezavisimost, which becomes Nikola Pikolo, and turn right at ul. Ivan Vazov (Иван Вазов) to reach the **National Revival Museum** (Музей на Възраждането; Muzey na Vuzrazhdaneto), which documents Bulgaria's 19th-century National Revival movement. (Open M and W-Su 8am-noon and 1-6pm. 4lv.) On summer evenings, there is often a ■**sound-and-light show** above Tsarevets Hill. (20min. show starts between 9:45 and 10pm.)

All **trains** stop at nearby Gorna Oryahovitsa (Горна Оряховица; 20min., 10 per day, 0.50lv), where connecting trains leave for: Burgas (6hr., 5 per day, 7lv); Sofia (5hr., 9 per day, 8.30lv); and Varna (4hr., 4 per day, 7.30lv). Minibuses and city bus #10 go from the station to **ploshad Maika Bulgaria** (Майка Българиа), the town center. Just off the square is the **tourist office,** Hristo Botev 5. (Maps 2.50lv. Open M-Sa

9am-6pm.) Check **email** at nearby **Bezanata** (Безаната), Otets Paisii 10. (0.90lv per hr., 60lv after 10pm. Open 24hr.) ◪**Hotel Comfort** ❸, Panayot Tipografov 5 (Панайот Типографов), has an amazing view of Tsarevets. From Stambolov, turn left on Rakovski (Раковски), turn left onto the small square, and look for the signs. (☎287 28. Singles 40lv; doubles 100-120lv.) **Hotel Trapezitsa (HI)** ❶, Stefan Stambolov 79, has rooms with private bathrooms; from the town center, walk down Nezavisimost toward the post office and follow the street to the right. (☎6 20 61. Singles 18lv; doubles 30lv.) **Postal Code:** 5000.

BLACK SEA COAST

The Black Sea, the most popular vacation spot in Bulgaria, is covered with tiny fishing villages and secluded bays, as well as pricey resorts. Along the coast, you will run into more tourists than in any other part of Bulgaria, along with higher (but still reasonable) prices.

VARNA (ВАРНА)   ☎052

Visitors are drawn to Varna (pop. 290,000) by its expansive beaches, Mediterranean-like climate, and frequent summer festivals. Go right on bul. Primorski (Приморски) from the train station to reach the **beaches** and **seaside gardens.** Despite Varna's sprawl, most sights are within a 30min. walk of one another. In the city's old quarter, **Grutska Makhala** (Гръцка Махала), the well-preserved ruins of the ◪**Roman Thermal Baths** (Римски Терми; Rimski Termi) sit on San Stefano. (Open Su and Tu-Sa 10am-5pm. 3lv, students 2lv.) The **Archaeological Museum** (Археологически Музей; Arkheologicheski Muzey), in the park on Maria Luiza, has the world's oldest gold artifacts. (Open in summer Su and Tu-Sa 10am-6pm; off-season Tu-Sa 10am-5pm. 4lv.) Varna's cultural events include the **International Jazz Festival** in late August and **Varna Summer,** a chamber music festival from June to July. For schedules and tickets, check the **Festival and Congress Center,** on bul. Primorski, which also has cafes and a cinema; the international film festival **"Love is Folly"** takes place there from August to September.

Trains depart from near the commercial harbor for: Plovdiv (7hr., 3 per day, 8-11lv) and Sofia (8hr., 6 per day, 14lv). **Buses,** at Ul. Vladislav Varenchik (Владислав Варенчик), go to Burgas (2½hr., M-Sa 5 per day, 6lv) and Sofia (6hr., 16 per day, 19lv). **Megatours,** in the Hotel Cherno More, Slivnitsa 33, has tourist info. (Open June-Sept. M-F 9am-7pm, Sa 9am-3pm; Oct.-May M-F 9am-7pm, Sa 9am-2pm.) **Astra Tour,** near track #6 at the train station, finds private rooms that are typically US$12-14 per person. (☎60 58 61; atratur@mail.vega.bg. Open in summer daily 6am-10pm.) **Hotel Trite Delfina** ❸ (Трите Делфина; Three Dolphins), ul. Gabrovo 27, is close to the train station. Go up Simeon from the station and take a right on Gabrovo. (☎60 09 11. Call ahead. Singles 50lv; doubles 60lv.)

▶ **DAYTRIP FROM VARNA: BALCHIK.** The houses in the quiet fishing village of Balchik (Балчик) are carved into chalky cliffs. From pl. Ribarski (Рибарски), turn right and walk along Primorska (Приморска) or along the beach boardwalk (20min.) to reach Romanian Queen Marie's ◪**Summer Palace,** where you can sit on a marble throne and explore the botanical garden. (Open daily 8am-8pm. 5lv, children 1lv.) Take a taxi (4lv) from pl. Ribarski to the mud baths of **Tuzlata,** 7km north, for a grand bath (грязни баия; grazni banya)—cover yourself in mud, then bask in the sun while it dries. (Open in summer daily 8:30am-7pm. 3lv.) If you decide to stay the night, **Tourist Agency Chayka** (Чайка) on pl. Ribarski 2, arranges private rooms. (☎7 20 53; www.bgtur.hit.bg. Rooms from US$8. Open in summer daily 8am-8pm.) **Minibuses** run from Mladost station in Varna (40min., every hr. 6:30am-7:30pm, 3lv).

BURGAS (БУРГАС)   ☎056

Though mostly used as a transport hub for the Southern Black Sea Coast, Burgas (pop. 230,000) also has its own pleasant beaches and seaside gardens. The bus and train stations are near the port at pl. Garov (Гаров). **Trains** go to Sofia (6-8hr., 5 per day, 11lv) and Varna (5hr., 4 per day, 7lv). From a stop to the left as you face the train station, **minibuses** run to the coastal resorts. Many smaller resorts don't have places to change money. **Bulbank**, across the street from Hotel Bulgaria on Aleksandrovska, cashes traveler's checks and has an **ATM**. (Open M-F 8:30am-4pm.) If you stay overnight, **Primoretz Tourist Bourgas**, across from the train station, can secure a room. (☎84 27 27. Open daily M-F 7am-7pm. Rooms from 11lv per person.) Or, go up Aleksandrovska from the station, take a right on Bogoridi (Богориди), pass the Hotel Bulgaria, and take the second left on Lermontov to **Hotel Mirage ❸** (Мираж), Lermontov 18. (☎84 56 57. Doubles 40lv.) **Postal Code:** 8000.

◪ DAYTRIPS FROM BURGAS: NESEBUR AND SOZOPOL. A charming, popular resort town, Nesebur (Несебър; pop. 10,000) is atop the peninsula at the south end of Sunny Beach. A walk through the ancient **Stariya Grad** (Old Town) begins along the 3rd-century stone **fortress walls.** The Byzantine gate and port date from the 5th century. The **Archaeological Museum** (Археологически Музей; Arkheologicheski Muzey), to the right of the town gate, displays ancient ceramics and relics. (Open May-Oct. M-F 9am-12:30pm and 1-7pm, Sa-Su 9am-1pm and 2-5pm; Nov.-Apr. M-F 9am-5pm. 2.50lv.) From the center, take Mitropolitska to reach the 10th-century **Temple of John the Baptist** (Йоан Кръстител; Yoan Krustitel), a UNESCO-protected site that is now an art gallery. (Open daily 10am-10pm. Free.) The 13th-century **Church of Christ the Almighty** (Христос Пантократор; Hristos Pantokrator) in the main square doubles as an art gallery in summer. (Open daily 9am-9pm.) Along the harbor, street kiosks sell fruit, nuts, and small meals. **Buses** go to Burgas (40min., every 40min., 6am-9pm, 3lv).

Sozopol (Созопол), settled in 610 BC, was once the resort of choice for Bulgaria's artistic community, and is still a haven for the creative set. Take a **boat cruise** (7 and 8:15pm; 5lv) from the seaport behind the bus station to get a closer look at the two nearby islands, **St. Peter** and **St. Ivan.** To explore some less-crowded beaches, rent a motorbike near the New Town beach and cruise along the shoreline (10lv per hr.). **Minibuses** arrive from Burgas (45min., every 30min. 6am-9:30pm, 2lv). Turn left on Apolonia (Аполония) to reach **Old Town.** To get to the **New Town,** go right from the station and bear left at the fork onto Republikanska (Републиканска). If you walk until Republikanska runs into a pedestrian street and then go down the blocked street, you'll reach **Imperial Tour**, Ropotamo St. 5., which arranges private rooms as well as trips to Istanbul. (☎4167, fax 2463. Open daily 9am-10pm. Singles 10-12lv per person; doubles 20-24lv.) After walking into Old Town, take the right-most fork along the seacoast to reach popular **Orfei ❸** (Орфеи), which offers a panoramic view and a long list of seafood specialities. (☎35 17. Open daily 10am-midnight.)

CROATIA (HRVATSKA)

Croatia is a land of unearthly beauty, endowed with thick forests, barren mountains, and crystal-clear waters. Positioned at the convergence of the Mediterranean, the Alps, and the Pannonian Plain, the country has been historically situated on dangerous political divides—between the Frankish and Byzantine empires in the 9th century, the Catholic and Orthodox churches since the 11th century, Christian Europe and Islamic Turkey from the 15th to the 19th centuries, and between its own fractious ethnic groups in the past decade. Although economic recovery from the recent war has been difficult, it is easy to forget the political tensions of Croatia's past; now that the country is independent for the first time in 800 years, Croatians and visitors can enjoy the extraordinary landscape in peace.

FACTS AND FIGURES

Official Name: Republic of Croatia.

Capital: Zagreb.

Major Cities: Split, Dubrovnik.

Population: 4,400,000 (78% Croat, 12% Serb, 1% Bosniak, 9% other).

Land Area: 56,414 sq. km.

Time Zone: GMT +1.

Language: Croatian.

Religions: Catholic (77%), Orthodox (11%), Muslim (1%), other (11%).

DISCOVER CROATIA

Croatia's lively capital, **Zagreb** (p. 237), boasts relaxing Mediterranean breezes, Habsburg splendor, and the hippest cafe scene in the Balkans. **Pula** (p. 240), the 2000-year-old heart of the Istrian Peninsula, has impressive Roman ruins. The true highlight of Croatia, however, is the dazzling **Dalmatian Coast** (p. 241), where pristine beaches and azure waters meet. Bask on the sands of **Split** (p. 242) on the central coast, then visit **Dubrovnik** (p. 243), which George Bernard Shaw called "paradise on earth" for its stunning seascapes and walled city center.

ESSENTIALS

WHEN TO GO

Croatia's mild Mediterranean climate means that there is no wrong time to visit. The high season (July-Aug.) brings crowds to the coast; travelers will find lower prices and more breathing room in June and September.

DOCUMENTS AND FORMALITIES

VISAS. Citizens of Australia, Canada, Ireland, New Zealand, the UK, and the US do not need visas for stays of up to 90 days. Visas are required of South African citizens. All visitors must **register** with the police within 48 hours of arrival, regardless of the length of their stay. Hotels, campsites, and accommodations agencies should automatically register you, but those staying with friends or in private rooms must register themselves to avoid fines or expulsion. Police may check passports anywhere. There is no entry fee at the border.

EMBASSIES. Foreign embassies in Croatia are all in Zagreb (p. 237). Croatian embassies at home include: **Australia,** 14 Jindalee Crescent, O'Malley ACT 2606 (☎02 6286 6988; croemb@bigpond.com.au); **Canada,** 229 Chapel St., Ottawa, ON

Croatia

K1N 7Y6 (☎613-562-7820; www.croatiaemb.net); **New Zealand** (consulate), 291 Lincoln Rd., Henderson, Auckland; mail to: P.O. Box 83-200, Edmonton, Auckland (☎09 836 5581; cro-consulate@xtra.co.nz); **South Africa,** 1160 Church St., Colbyn, 0083; mail to: Pretoria; P.O. Box 11335, Hatfield 0028 (☎012 342 1206; fax 342 1819); **UK,** 21 Conway St., London W1P 5HL (☎020 7387 2022; amboffice@croatianembassy.co.uk; Consular Department ☎020 7387 1144; consulardept@croatianembassy.co.uk); **US,** 2343 Massachusetts Ave. NW, Washington, D.C. 20008 (☎202-588-5899; www.croatiaemb.org).

TRANSPORTATION

BY PLANE. Zagreb (ZAG) is the main entry point; **Croatia Airlines** flies from many cities, including Frankfurt, London, New York, Paris, and Toronto, to Zagreb, Dubrovnik, or Split. Rijeka, Zadar, and Pula have tiny international airports.

BY TRAIN AND BY BUS. Trains travel to Zagreb from Budapest, Ljubljana, Venice, and Vienna. Train connections are *very* slow, and nonexistent south of Split. *Odlazak* means departures, *dolazak* arrivals. For domestic travel, **buses** work best. Tickets are cheaper if you buy them on board.

BY BOAT. If you're on the coast, take one of the ferries run by **Jadrolinija** (www.jadrolinija.hr), which sail the Rijeka-Split-Dubrovnik route with island stops. Ferries also run from Split to Ancona, Italy, and from Dubrovnik to Bari, Italy. A basic ticket provides only a place on the deck. Cheap beds sell out fast, so purchase tickets in advance. If you have a basic ticket, *run* to get a bed.

BY CAR AND BY THUMB. You can rent a car (350-400kn per day) in larger cities, but parking and gas can be expensive. Rural roads are in poor condition; in the Krajina region and other conflict areas, drivers should be wary of off-road land mines. *Let's Go* does not recommend hitchhiking in Croatia.

TOURIST SERVICES AND MONEY

EMERGENCY	Police: ☎092. Ambulance: ☎094. Fire: ☎093.

TOURIST OFFICES AND MONEY. Even small towns have a branch of the excellent, English-speaking tourist board **turistička zajednica** (www.htz.hr). Accommodations are handled by private tourist agencies (*turistička/putnička agencija*), the largest of which is **Atlas**. Croatia's monetary unit is the **kuna** (kn), which is divided into 100 *lipa;* the *kuna* is virtually impossible to exchange abroad, except in Bosnia, Hungary, and Slovenia. The South African *rand* is not exchangeable in Croatia. Banks usually have the best rates, and most give MasterCard or Visa cash advances. Credit cards are widely accepted and **ATMs** are common. **Tipping** is not expected, but some round up to the nearest whole *kuna*. In some cases, the establishment will do it for you. Bargaining is acceptable only for informal transactions.

KUNA		
	AUS$1 = 4.39KN	1KN = AUS$0.23
	CDN$1 = 4.90KN	1KN = CDN$0.20
	EUR€1 = 7.47KN	1KN = EUR€0.13
	NZ$1 = 3.91KN	1KN = NZ$0.26
	UK£1 = 10.78KN	1KN = UK£0.09
	US$1 = 6.86KN	1KN = US$0.15
	ZAR1 = 0.93KN	1KN = ZAR1.07

COMMUNICATION

PHONE CODES	**Country code: 385. International dialing prefix: 00.** From outside Croatia, dial int'l dialing prefix (see inside back cover) + 385 + city code + local number.

TELEPHONES. Post offices usually have public phones; pay after you talk. All payphones require phone cards (*telekarta*), sold at newsstands and post offices. 50 "impulses" cost 23kn (1 impulse equals 3min. domestic, 36 seconds international; 50% discount 10pm-7am and Sundays and holidays). Calls to the US and Europe are expensive (20kn per min.). International direct dial numbers include: **AT&T,** ☎0800 22 01 11; **BT Direct,** ☎0800 22 10 44; **Canada Direct,** ☎0800 22 01 01; and **MCI Worldphone,** ☎0800 22 01 12.

MAIL. *Avionski* and *zrakoplovom* both indicate airmail. *Poste Restante* mail is held for 30 days at the main post office. Address mail to be held: Firstname SURNAME, *Poste Restante*, Pt. Republike 28, 2000, Dubrovnik, CROATIA.

LANGUAGE. Croatian is written in Roman characters. Street designations on maps often differ from those on signs by "-va" or "-a" because of grammatical declensions. Young Croatians often know some English, but the most common second language is German. For basic Croatian words and phrases, see p. 1052.

ACCOMMODATIONS AND CAMPING

CROATIA	❶	❷	❸	❹	❺
ACCOMMODATIONS	under 90kn	90-140kn	141-200kn	201-300kn	over 300kn

Croatia only has six youth hostels (in Zagreb, Pula, Zadar, Dubrovnik, Šibenik, and Punat); for info, contact the **Croatian Youth Hostel Association,** Savska 5, 10000 Zagreb (☎01 482 92 94; www.nncomp.com/hfhs). Camping is usually a good, cheap option; for info, contact the **Croatian Camping Union,** HR-52440 Poreč, Pionirska 1 (☎52 451 3 24; www.camping.hr). **Private rooms** are also affordable; look for *sobe* signs, especially near transportation stations. Agencies generally charge 30-50% more if you stay fewer than three nights. All accommodations are subject to a tourist tax of 5-10kn. If you opt for a hotel, call in advance, especially during summer.

FOOD AND DRINK

CROATIA	❶	❷	❸	❹	❺
FOOD	under 30kn	30-60kn	61-120kn	121-200kn	over 200kn

Croatian cuisine is defined by the country's varied geography; in continental Croatia, east of Zagreb, heavy meals featuring meat and creamy sauces dominate. *Purica s mlincima* (turkey with pasta) is the regional dish near Zagreb. Also popular is the spicy Slavonian *kulen,* which is considered one of the world's best sausages by the panel of German men who decide such things. On the coast, textures and flavors change with the presence of seafood and Italian influence. In this region, don't miss out on *lignje* (squid) or *Dalmatinski pršut* (Dalmatian smoked ham). If your budget is tight, *slane sardele* (salted sardines) are a tasty substitute. Croatia has excellent wines; price is usually the best indicator of quality. *Šlivovica* is a hard-hitting plum brandy found in many small towns. *Karlovačko* and *Ožujsko* are the two most popular beers.

SAFETY AND SECURITY

Although Croatia is no longer at war, travel to the Slavonia and Krajina regions remains dangerous due to **unexploded landmines.** Croatians are friendly toward foreigners and sometimes a little too friendly to female travelers; going out in public with a companion will help ward off unwanted advances. Croatians are just beginning to accept homosexuality; discretion may be wise. Pharmacies are generally well stocked with Western products.

HOLIDAYS AND FESTIVALS

Holidays: New Year's Day (Jan. 1); Epiphany (Jan. 6); Easter (Apr. 11-12); May Day (May 1); Corpus Christi (June 10); Anti-Fascist Struggle Day (June 22); Statehood Day (June 25); National Thanksgiving Day (Aug. 5); Assumption (Aug. 15); Independence Day (Oct. 8); All Saints' Day (Nov. 1); Christmas (Dec. 25-26).

Festivals: Zagreb hosts many festivals: street performers swarm in for **Cest is D'best** in June; the **International Children's Festival** in late June and early July features a children's derby and puppet performances; the **International Folklore Festival** in July is the premier gathering of European folk dancers and singing groups. On Korčula Island, the **Festival of**

Sword Dances (Festival Viteških Igara) takes place from July-Aug. **Dubrovnik Summer Festivals** in July and Aug. feature theater, ballet, opera, classical music, and jazz.

ZAGREB ☎ 01

Despite its spacious boulevards, sprawling public parks, and stern Habsburg architecture, Croatia's capital (pop. 750,000) maintains a distinctive small-town charm. Mediterranean breezes blow past magnificent churches and lively outdoor cafes, and the external scars of recent civil war have all but vanished.

⊑ TRANSPORTATION. Trains leave the Glavni Kolodvor (main station), Trg Kralja Tomislava 12 (☎06 033 34 44, international info 378 25 32) for: Budapest (7hr., 4 per day, 180kn); Ljubljana (2½hr., 4 per day, 90kn); Venice (7hr., 2 per day, 303kn); Vienna (6½hr., 2 per day, 341kn); and Zurich (8hr., daily, 639kn). To reach the main square, Trg bana Josipa Jelačića, from the train station, cross the street, walk along the left side of the park until it ends, then follow Praška. **Buses** (☎060 313 333) head from the Autobusni Kolodvor (bus station), Držiceva bb, to: Dubrovnik (11hr., 17 per day, 170kn); Ljubljana (2hr., 2 per day, 90kn); Sarajevo (9hr., 3 per day, 196kn); Split (6½-8½hr., 29 per day, 120kn); and Vienna (8hr., 2 per day, 170kn). To reach Trg b. Jelačića, exit on Držićeva, turn left, continue past Trg Žrtava Fašizma, and turn left onto Jurišićeva.

⊓ PRACTICAL INFORMATION. The tourist office is at Trg b. Jelačića 11. (☎481 40 51; www.zagreb-touristinfo.hr. Open M-F 8:30am-8pm, Sa 9am-5pm, Su 10am-2pm.) All foreigners staying in private accommodations must register within two days of arrival. In Zagreb, register at the **Department for Foreign Visitors,** room 103 at the central police station, Petrinjska 30. Use Form 14. (☎456 36 23. Open M-F 8am-4pm.) Hotels and hostels register guests automatically, bypassing this frustrating process. Find **Internet** access at **Charlie Net,** Gajeva 4. (☎488 02 33. Open M-Sa 8am-10pm. 16kn per hr.) **Postal Code:** 10000.

⌐⌐ ACCOMMODATIONS AND FOOD. Few rooms in Zagreb are cheap. ⊠**Ravnice Youth Hostel ❷,** 1. Ravnice 38d, is impeccably clean and just a 20min. tram ride from the city center. Take tram #11 or 12 from Trg bana Jelačića, tram #4 from the train station, or tram #7 from the bus station (dir.: Dubrava or Dubec). Get off at the (unmarked) Ravnice stop, one block past football stadium "Dinamo," and the second-to-last stop on the tram line. (☎233 23 25; fax 234 56 07. Kitchen available.

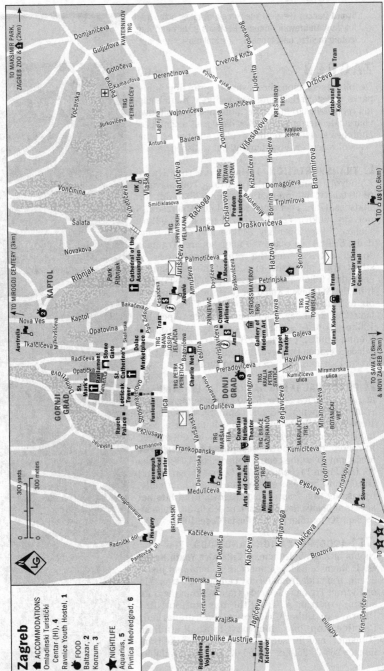

CROATIA

Zagreb

▲ ACCOMMODATIONS
Omladinski Turistički
Centar (HI), **4**
Ravnice Youth Hostel, **1**

🍴 FOOD
Baltazar, **2**
Konzum, **3**

★ NIGHTLIFE
Aquarius, **5**
Pivnica Medvedgrad, **6**

Laundry 15kn. Dorms 99kn. Internet 16kn per hr.) **Omladinski Turistićki Centar (HI) ❶,** Petrinjska 77, is well-located; from the train station, walk right on Branimirova, and Petrinjska is on the left. (☎484 12 61; fax 484 12 69. Reception 24hr. Dorms 67kn; singles 149kn, with bath 202kn; doubles 204/274kn. Nonmembers add 5kn.) For traditional Croatian meat dishes, try ⬛**Baltazar ❷,** Nova Ves 4. (Entrees 35-80kn. Open daily noon-midnight.) **Konzum,** on the corner of Preradovićeva and Hebrangova, has groceries. (Open M-F 7am-8pm, Sa 7am-3pm.)

◙ **SIGHTS.** The best way to see Zagreb is on foot. From Trg b. Jelačica, take Ilica, then turn right on Tomiceva. The funicular (3kn) allows easy access to many sights on the hills of Gornji Grad (Upper Town). **Lotršćak Tower** provides a spectacular view of the city. (Open May-Sept. Su and Tu-Sa 11am-8pm. 5kn.) The elegant **St. Catherine's Church** is right of the tower. (Open Su-F 7am-11pm, Sa 7am-6:30pm.) Follow ul. Cirilometodska to Markov Trg; the colorful roof tiles of Gothic **St. Mark's Church** (Crkva Sv. Marka) depict the coats of arms of Croatia, Dalmatia, and Slavonia on the left and of Zagreb on the right. Visible from anywhere in Zagreb, the striking neo-Gothic bell towers of the 11th-century **Cathedral of the Assumption** loom over Kaptol Hill. (Open daily 10am-5pm. Free.) Take a short bus ride (8min., every 15 min.) from Kaptol to **Mirogoj,** the country's largest and most beautiful cemetery; Croatia's first President, Franjo Tudjman, is buried beyond the grand mausoleum at the entrance. (Open M-F 6am-8pm, Su 7:30am-6pm. Free.)

Zagreb's museums focus on the best Croatian artwork. The ⬛**Museum of Arts and Crafts,** Trg Maršala Tita 10, has an eclectic mix of ornately-designed works from the 15th century onward. (Open Tu-F 10am-6pm, Sa-Su 10am-1pm. 20kn, students 10kn.) The **Gallery of Modern Art,** Herbrangova 1, features rotating exhibitions of Croatia's best artists in a small, attractive gallery. (Open Su 10am-1pm, Tu-Sa 10am-6pm. Prices vary with each exhibit.) The **Mimara Museum,** Rooseveltov Trg 5, contains a vast and varied collection ranging from prehistoric Egyptian art to Manet, Raphael, Rembrandt, Renoir, Rubens, and Velasquez. (Open Su 10am-2pm, Tu-W and F-Sa 10am-5pm, Th 10am-7pm. 20kn, students 15kn.)

⬛ ▣ **FESTIVALS AND NIGHTLIFE.** Zagreb is host to an impressive collection of festivals. Each year kicks off with a **blues festival** in January. In late June, streets burst with performances for the annual Zagreb street festival **Cest is d'Best** ("The Streets are the Best"), and the **Eurokaz Avant-Garde Theaters Festival.** During the first three weeks of June, the Kerempuh Satirical Theater, Ilica 31, hosts **Satire Days,** showing various satirical plays almost daily. Folklore fetishists will flock to Zagreb in mid-July 2004 for the 38th **International Folklore Festival,** the premier gathering of European folk dancers and singing groups. The huge **International Puppet Festival** occurs at the beginning of September and the end of October sees Zagreb's **International Jazz Days.** Mid-December is brightened by the colorful **Christmas Fair.** For up-to-date info and schedules, check out www.zagreb-touristinfo.hr.

Dance and swim at the lakeside club ⬛**Aquarius,** on Lake Jarun. Take tram #17 to Srednjaci, the third unmarked stop after Studenski dom "S. Radić" (15min.). Cross the street, follow any dirt path to the lake, and walk left along the boardwalk. Aquarius is the last building. (☎364 02 31. Cover 30kn. Club open Su and Tu-Sa 10pm-4am. Cafe open daily 9am-9pm.) The best and cheapest beer is chugged at **Pivnica Medvedgrad,** Savska 56. (Beer 16kn per liter. Open M-Sa 10am-midnight, Su noon-midnight.)

▣ **DAYTRIP FROM ZAGREB: TRAKOŠČAN CASTLE.** Built in the 13th century as a defense tower, Trakoščan was acquired by the Drašković nobility, who enlarged and refurbished it, retaining ownership of the castle until WWII. Today, family portraits, tapestries, a collection of firearms and suits of armor from the

CROATIA

15th through the 19th centuries are on display. Leave time to wander around the quiet lake and to hike through the hills surrounding the castle. The restaurant at the bottom of the hill is expensive, so bring a sandwich or get a hot dog or hamburger at the cafe. (Castle open April-Oct. daily 9am-6pm; Nov.- Mar. daily 9am-3pm. Free guided tours in English; call ahead. 20kn, students 10kn. English booklet 20kn.) **Buses** run from the Zagreb bus station to Varaždin (1¾hr., 20 per day, 40kn), where a local bus (1½ hr.; M-F 1daily, Sa-Su 7 per day; 22kn) can take you to Trakošćan. Leave early in order to make the connection and still have plenty of time at the castle. (☎042 79 62 81. Last bus back from Trakošťan to Varaždin leaves M-F 9pm, Sa-Su 5pm.)

NORTHERN COAST

As you approach the coast from Zagreb, you'll encounter the islands of the Gulf of Kvarner, which are blessed by long summers and gentle breezes; Rab also boasts rare sand beaches. The Roman ruins at Pula sit farther north along the coast on the Istrian Peninsula, where the Mediterranean laps at the foot of the Alps.

PULA   ☎052

If you get to visit only one city in Istria, it should be Pula—not only for its cool, clear water, but also for its winding medieval corridors, outdoor cafes, and breathtaking Roman ■amphitheater. The second largest in the world, is often used as a concert venue. (Open daily 8am-9pm. 16kn, students 8kn.) To get there from the bus station, take a left on Istarska. Following Istarska in the opposite direction will bring you to the **Arch of the Sergians** (Slavoluk obitelji Sergii), dating from 29 BC; go through the gates and down bustling **ulica Sergijevaca** to the **Forum,** which holds the remarkably well-preserved **Temple of Augustus** (Augustov hram.), built between 2 BC and AD 14. To reach the private coves of Pula's **beaches,** buy a bus ticket from any newsstand (8kn) and take bus #1 to the Stója campground. ■**Fort Bourguignon,** Zlatne Stijene 6c, is a cafe, nightclub, and art gallery located in an old stone fortress. Take bus #2 or 7 from Giardini to the last stop; walk toward the sea, curving left. (Open M-F 8am-midnight, Sa 11am-4am, Su 6am-noon.)

Trains (☎54 19 82) run from Kolodvorska 5 to Ljubljana (7½hr., 3 per day, 127kn) and Zagreb (7hr., 4 per day, 112-125kn). **Buses** (☎50 29 97) go from Trg Istarske Brigade to Dubrovnik (15hr., daily, 366kn); Trieste, Italy (3hr., 4 per day, 98kn); and Zagreb (5-6hr., 15 per day, 136kn). The **tourist office,** Forum 3, can help find private rooms. (☎21 29 87; www.pulainfo.hr. Open M-Sa 9am-midnight, Su 10am-6pm.) To get to the **Omladinski Hostel (HI) ①**, Zaljev Valsaline 4, take bus #2 (dir.: Veruda) from the bus station and ask the driver to let you off, then follow the signs. (☎39 11 33. Call ahead. Singles 63-97kn.) **Postal Code:** 52100.

⚡ DAYTRIP FROM PULA: BRIJUNI ARCHIPELAGO. Scenic Brijuni Archipelago is one of Croatia's most fascinating and beautiful regions. The largest island in the archipelago, **Veli Brijun** has been the site of a Roman resort, a Venetian colony, and the residence of former Yugoslav president Josip Brož Tito. A guided tour is the best way to see the island. The **Brijuni Agency,** Brijunska 10, in Fazana, has the lowest rates. (☎52 58 83. Tours daily 11:30am; call at least one day in advance. Round-trip ferry and 4hr. tour 180kn. Open daily 8am-7pm.)

RAB   ☎051

Beautiful Rab Town on Rab Island is filled with old churches, whitewashed stone houses, and the scent of rosemary from backyard gardens. The best way to experience Rab Town is to stroll along **Gornja Ulica.** The street runs from the remains of **St. John's Church** (Crkva sv. Jvana), a Roman basilica, to **St. Justine's Church** (Crkva sv. Justine), which houses a museum of Christian art. (Open daily 10am-12:30pm and 7:30-10pm. 5kn.) The top of the bell tower at **St. Mary's Church** (Crkva sv. Marije) is a great place for viewing sunsets, or for peering into the garden that the nuns maintain. (Open daily 7:30pm-10pm. 5kn.) **Beaches** are scattered all over Rab Island; ask at the tourist office for transportation info. Most sand beaches (some of the few in Croatia) are on the north end of the island, while rocky beaches lie on the west side and pebble beaches on the east.

   Buses arrive from Zagreb (5½hr., M-Sa 4 per day, 127kn). The friendly **tourist office** is on the other side of the bus station. (☎77 11 11. Open daily 8am-10pm.) **Katurbo ②**, M. de Dominisa, between the bus station and the town center, arranges private rooms. (☎72 44 95; katurbo-tourist-agency@ri.tel.hr. Open July-Aug. daily 8am-9pm; Sept.-June 8am-1pm and 4-9pm. Singles 80-120kn. 30% discount on stays longer than 3 nights.) **Hotel Istra ④** has clean, modern rooms. (☎72 41 34. 190-320kn per person.) Walk east along the bay 2km from the bus station to reach **Camping Padova ①**. (☎72 43 55. 20-32kn per person, 18-26kn per tent. Registration 4.50kn.) Restaurant 🍴**St. Maria ②**, Dinka Dokule 6, serves Hungarian specialties in a medieval courtyard. (Entrees 50-90kn. Open daily 11am-2pm and 4pm-midnight.) There's a **supermarket** in the basement of Merkur, Palit 71, across from the tourist office. (Open daily 7am-9pm.) **Postal Code:** 51280.

DALMATIAN COAST

After his last visit to Dalmatia, George Bernard Shaw wrote: "The gods wanted to crown their creation and on the last day they turned tears, stars and the sea breeze into the isles of Kornati." Shaw's words speak to the entire Dalmatian Coast—a stunning seascape of unfathomable beauty set against a backdrop of dramatic mountains. With more than 1100 islands, Dalmatia is not only Croatia's largest archipelago, but also has the cleanest and clearest waters in the Mediterranean.

TROGIR   ☎021

In Trogir (pop. 1,500), made up of tiny Trogir Island and Čiovo Island, medieval buildings crowd into winding streets and palmed promenades open onto well-maintained parks and the calm, blue sea. On Trogir Island, the beautiful Renaissance **North Gate** forms the entrance to **Stari Grad** (Old Town), which earned a coveted place on the UNESCO World Heritage List in 1997. Most sights, including the **Cathedral of St. Lawrence** (Crkva sv. Lovre), are in **Trg Ivana Pavla,** the central square. The **City Museum of Trogir,** which is housed in two buildings, contains many examples of Trogir's storied stone-carving tradition. The **lapidary,** through the arch directly in front of the North Gate, features stone sculpture. (Open M-Sa 9am-noon and 6-9pm. 10kn, students 5kn.) The other part of the museum is in the convent of St. Nicholas, off Kohl-Genscher past Trg Ivana Pavla. (Open M-Sa 9am-12:30pm and 3-7:30pm.) At the tip of the island lie the remains of the **Fortress of Kamerlengo,** which now serves as an open-air cinema. (Open M-Sa 9am-11pm. 10kn. Students free. Movies 20kn.) Trogir's best beaches lie on **Čiovo Island,** accessible from Trogir Island by the Čiovski bridge, past Trg Ivana Pavla.

Buses from Zagreb stop in front of the station on the mainland on their way south to Split (30min., 2-3 per hr., 22kn). Local bus #37 also runs from Trogir to Split (30min., 2-3 per hr., 18kn). Across Čiovski bridge, **Atlas,** Obala kralja Zvonimira 10, has bus schedules. (☎88 42 79. Open M-Sa 8am-9pm, Su 8am-noon.) The **tourist office,** Trg Ivana Pavla 2, gives out free maps of the city. (☎88 14 12. Open M-Sa 8am-9pm, Su 8-noon.) **Cipko ❶,** Gradska 41, across from the cathedral and through an archway, arranges private rooms. (☎88 15 54. Open daily 8am-8pm. July-Aug. singles 84-92kn; tourist tax 7.50kn. May-June and Sept. 70-73/5.50kn.) To reach beachside **Prenoćište Saldun ❶,** Sv. Andrije 1, cross Čiovski bridge and take Put Balana up the hill, keeping right; Saldun is at the top. (☎80 60 53. Call ahead. Singles 76kn; tax 6kn.) Luxurious waterfront **Vila Sikaa ❺,** Obala Kralja Zvonimira 13, is across Čiovski Bridge. (☎88 12 23; stjepan.runtic@st.tel.hr. Call ahead. Singles 420-470kn; doubles 450-600kn.) **Bistro Lučica ❸,** Kralja Tomislava, across Čiovski bridge and to the right, grills delightful meat and seafood. (35-120kn. Open M-F 9am-midnight, Sa-Su 4pm-midnight.) **Čiovka supermarket** is next to Atlas. (Open M-Sa 5:30am-9pm, Su 6:30am-8pm.) Cafes line **Kohl-Genscher. Postal Code:** 21220.

SPLIT   ☎021

This palatial city by the sea is more of a cultural center than a beach resort; Split boasts a wider variety of activities and nightlife than its neighbors. The **Stari Grad** (Old Town), wedged between a high mountain range and palm-lined waterfront, sprawls around a luxurious **palace** where Roman Emperor Diocletian, known for his violent persecution of Christians, spent his summers. The **cellars** of the city are near the entrance to the palace, across from the taxis on **Obala hrvatskog narodnog preporoda;** turn in either direction to wander around this haunting labyrinth. (Open daily 10am-7pm. 8kn.) Through the cellars and up the stairs is the open-air **peristyle.** The Catholic **cathedral** on the right side of the peristyle is the oldest in the world; ironically, it was once Diocletian's mausoleum. The view from atop the adjoining **Bell Tower of St. Dominus** (Zvonik sv. Duje) is incredible. (Cathedral and tower open daily 8:30am-9:30pm. Tower 5kn.) A 25min. walk away along the waterfront, the **Meštrović Gallery** (Galerija Ivana Meštrovića), Šetaliste Ivana Meštrovića 46, features a collection by Croatia's most famous modern sculptor. (Open June-Aug. Su 9am-2pmTu-Sa 9am-1pm and 5-8pm; Sept.-May Su 10am-2pm, Tu-Sa 10am-4pm. 15kn, students 10kn.)

Buses (☎33 84 83; schedules ☎(050) 32 73 27) go to: Dubrovnik (4½hr., 17 per day, 110kn); Ljubljana (11hr., daily, 236kn); Sarajevo (7½hr., 6 per day, 180kn); and Zagreb (8hr., every 30min., 107-120kn). **Ferries** (☎33 83 33) head from the terminal across from the train and bus stations to Dubrovnik (8hr., 5 per week, 115kn) and Ancona, Italy (10hr., 4 per week, 329kn). From the bus station, follow Obala kneza Domagoja (also called Riva) until it runs into Obala hrvatskog narodnog preporoda, which runs roughly east-west. The **tourist office** is at Obala hrv. 12. (☎34 71

00. Open M-F 8am-9pm, Sa 8am-10pm, Su 8am-1pm.) The **Daluma Travel Agency,** Obala kneza domagoja 1, near the bus and train stations, helps find private rooms. (☎33 84 84; www.tel.hr/daluma-travel. May-Oct. singles 150kn; doubles 240kn; Nov.-Apr. singles 100-120kn. Open M-F 8am-8pm, Sa 8am-2pm.) To get from the stations to **Prenoćište Slavija ❹,** Buvinova 2, follow Obala hrv., turn right on Trg Braće Radića, then go right on Mihovilova širina; signs lead up the stairs. (☎34 70 53. Breakfast included. Singles 220kn, with shower 280kn; doubles 290/360kn.) There is a **supermarket** at Svačićeva 4. (Open daily 7am-10pm.) To reach ▧**Jugo Restoran ❷,** Uvala Baluni bb, face the water on Obala hrv. and walk right along the waterfront for 10min., following the curves onto Branimirova Obala. (Entrees 30-65kn. Open daily 9am-midnight.) The closest **beach** to downtown Split is sandy **Bačvice,** a nighttime favorite for local skinny dippers and the starting point of a great strip of waterfront bars. **Postal Code:** 21000.

BRAČ ISLAND: BOL ☎021

Central Dalmatia's largest island, Brač is an ocean-lover's paradise. Most visitors come here for **Zlatni rat,** a peninsula of white pebble beach and emerald waters, just a short walk from the town center of Bol. The 1475 **Dominican Monastery,** on the eastern tip of Bol, displays Tintoretto's altar painting of the Madonna with Child. (Open daily 10am-noon and 5-7pm. 10kn.) The **ferry** from Split docks at Supetar (1hr., 7-13 per day, 23kn). From there, take a **bus** to Bol (1hr., 5 per day, 15kn). The last bus back to the ferry leaves at 5:50pm. From the bus station, walk left for 5min. to reach the **tourist office,** Porad bolskich pomorca bb, on the far side of the small marina. (☎63 56 38; tzo-bol@st.tel.hr.) **Adria Tours,** Obala Vladimira Nazora 28, to the right facing the sea from the bus station, rents small motorcycles (120kn per half-day, 200kn per day) and cars (400kn per day including mileage), and also books rooms. (☎63 59 66; www.tel.hr/adria-tours-bol. 60-170kn per person. Open daily 8am-9pm.) There are five **campsites** around Bol; the largest is **Kito ❶,** Bračka cesta bb, on the road into town. (☎63 55 51. Open May-Sept. 46kn per person with tent included.) **Postal Code:** 21420.

KORČULA ☎020

Within sight of the mainland are the macchia thickets and slender cypress trees of Korčula. Marco Polo was born here, among sacred monuments and churches dating from the time of the Apostles. The **Festival of Sword Dances** clangs into town July-Aug. (60kn; tickets available at tourist office). **Buses** from Korčula board a ferry to the mainland and head to: Dubrovnik (3½hr., daily, 75kn); Sarajevo (6½hr., 4 per week, 145kn); Split (5hr., daily, 90kn); and Zagreb (11-13hr., daily, 209kn). **Ferries** run to Dubrovnik (3½hr., 5 per week, 64kn) and Split (4½hr., daily, 74kn). To reach the **tourist office,** face the water and walk left around the peninsula to Hotel Korčula; the office is next door. (Open M-Sa 8am-3pm and 5-9pm, Su 9am-1pm.) **Private rooms** are the only budget lodgings available; shopping around is a good idea. **Marko Polo,** Biline 5, can also arrange rooms. (☎71 54 00; www.korcula.com. Singles 87-150kn; doubles 210-263kn. Open daily 8am-9pm.) ▧**Adio Mare ❸,** Marka Pola bb, serves authentic local specialties. (Entrees 40-80kn. Open M-Sa 5:30pm-midnight, Su 6pm-midnight.) **Postal Code:** 20260.

DUBROVNIK ☎020

George Bernard Shaw once wrote: "Those who seek Paradise on earth should come to Dubrovnik." Nearly scarless despite recent wars, the city continues to draw visitors with azure waters and golden sunsets over its 14th-century marble walls. If you make it as far south as Dubrovnik, you might never leave.

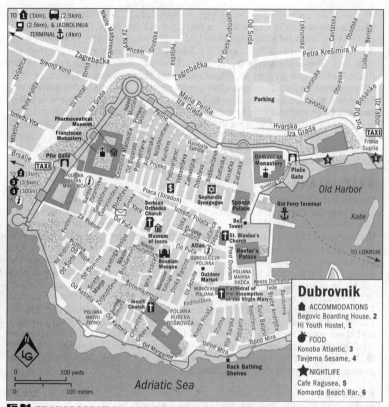

Dubrovnik

🏠 ACCOMMODATIONS
Begovic Boarding House, **2**
HI Youth Hostel, **1**

🍴 FOOD
Konoba Atlantic, **3**
Tavjerna Sesame, **4**

⭐ NIGHTLIFE
Cafe Ragusea, **5**
Komarda Beach Bar, **6**

📧📱 **TRANSPORTATION AND PRACTICAL INFORMATION.** Jadrolinija **ferries** (☎41 80 00) depart from opposite Obala S. Radica 40 for Bari, Italy (9hr., 5 per week, 329kn) and Split (8hr., daily, 115kn). **Buses** (☎35 70 88) run to: Sarajevo (6hr., 2 per day, 160kn); Split (4½hr., 16 per day, 103kn); Trieste (15hr., daily, 325kn); and Zagreb (11hr., 7 per day, 175kn). To reach Stari Grad, walk around the bus station, turn left on Ante Starčevića, and follow it uphill to the Old Town's western gate (25min.). To reach the ferry terminal, head left from the station and then bear right. All local buses *except* #5, 7, and 8 go to Stari Grad's Pile Gate (7kn at kiosks, 10kn from driver.) From the bus stop at Pile Gate, walk up Ante Starčevića away from Stari Grad to reach the **Tourist Board**, Ante Starčevića 7, which has free maps and pamphlets. (☎42 75 91. Open June-Sept. M-Sa 8am-8pm; Oct.-May 8am-3pm.) **Turistička Zajednica Grada Dubrovnika,** Cvjete Zuzoric 1/2, gives out the free, invaluable *City Guide.* (☎32 38 87. Open June-Aug. M-F 8am-4pm, Sa 9am-3pm, Su 9am-noon; Sept.-May M-F 8am-4pm.) **Postal Code:** 20000.

📧📱 **ACCOMMODATIONS AND FOOD.** For two people, a **private room** is cheapest; arrange one through the Tourist Board (above; 80-150kn) or **Atlas ❷,** Lučarica 1, next to St. Blasius's Church. (☎44 25 28; www.atlas-croatia.com. Open June-Aug. M-Sa 8am-9pm, Su 8am-1pm; Sept.-May M-Sa 8am-7pm. Singles 100-150kn; doubles 120-180kn.) For cheaper rooms, try haggling with the women around the ferry and bus terminals. To get to cozy ◨Begovic Boarding House ❷, Primorska 17, from the bus station, take bus #6 toward Dubrava and tell the driver you want to get off at post office Lapad. Facing the pedestrian walkway, turn right at the intersection. Go left at the fork, and take the first right onto Primorska. (☎43 51 91. July-Aug. rooms 100kn; Sept.-June 80kn.) The HI youth hostel ❶, b. Josipa Jelačića 15/17 is one of the best in Croatia. From the bus station, walk up Ante Starčevića, turn right at the lights (10min.), take a right on b. Josipa Jelačića, and look for the hidden HI sign on your left. (☎42 32 41. Dorms 70-100kn.) Konoba Atlantic ❷, Kardinala Stopinga 42, serves up some of the best pasta in Croatia (28-45kn). To get there, take bus #6 to post office Labad and walk straight on the walkway; take a right on the staircase just before the Hotel Kompas, which will take you up to the restaurant. (Open daily noon-11pm.) Tavjerna Sesame ❸, Dante Alighiera bb, specializes in fresh pasta dishes. From Pile Gate, walk on Ante Starčevića toward the hostel. (Entrees 60-95kn. Open M-Sa 8am-11pm, Su 10am-11pm.) Behind St. Blasius's Church, on Gundulićeva Poljana, is an open air market. (Open daily 7am-8pm.) Supermarket Mediator, Od puča 4, faces the market. (Open M-Sa 6:30am-9pm, Su 7am-9pm.)

◨ SIGHTS. Stari Grad (Old Town) is full of churches, museums, monasteries, palaces, and fortresses. The most popular sights are along Placa. The entrance to the staggering city walls (gradske zidine) lies just inside the Pile Gate, on the left. Set aside an hour for the 2km walk along the top. (Open daily 9am-7pm. 15kn.) The 14th-century Franciscan Monastery (Franjevački samostan), next to the city wall entrance on Placa, houses the oldest working pharmacy in Europe and a pharmaceutical museum. (Open daily 9am-6pm. 6kn.) The Cathedral of the Assumption of the Virgin Mary (Riznica Katedrale) dominates Buničeva Poljana. Its treasury holds religious relics, including the "Diapers of Jesus." (Cathedral open daily 6:30am-8pm. Free. Treasury open M-Sa 9am-7pm, Su 11am-5:30pm. 5kn.) To reach the 19th-century Serbian Orthodox Church (Pravoslavna Crkva) and its Museum of Icons (Muzej Ikona), Od Puča 8, walk from Pile Gate down Placa, go right on Široka, and then turn left on Od Puča. (Church open daily 8am-noon and 5-7pm. Free. Museum open M-Sa 9am-1pm. 10kn.)

> **⚠ WATCH YOUR STEP.** As tempting as it may be to stroll in the hills above Dubrovnik or wander the unpaved paths on Lopud, both may still be laced with **landmines.** Stick to the paved paths and beach.

◨ BEACHES. Right outside the fortifications of Stari Grad are a number of rock shelves for sunning and swimming. To the left of the cathedral entrance on Pobijana and through a small door into the wall is a great place to watch sunsets. (Open 9am-8pm.) For a truly surreal seaside experience, take a swim in the cove at the foot the old Hotel Libertas. The hotel was damaged during the war, then abandoned for lack of tourists; it now looks like a post-apocalyptic movie set. Dubrovnik's youth gather to swim in the pristine water and to play soccer in the old swimming pool. The nearby island of Lokrum features a nude beach. Ferries shuttle to and from the Old Port (20min.; 9am and every 30min. 10am-8pm; round-trip 25kn). Once there, stroll through the nature preserve.

◨◨ FESTIVALS AND NIGHTLIFE. Dubrovnik becomes a cultural mecca and crazy party from mid-July to mid-August during the Dubrovnik Summer Festival (Dubrovački Ijetni Festival). The festival office on Placa has schedules and tickets. (☎42 88 64; www.dubrovnik-festival.hr. Open daily for info 8:30am-9pm, tickets 9am-2pm and 3-7pm. 50-300kn.) Off-season, contact the head office (☎32 34 00).

Dubrovnik is lively by night, but the scene is usually based in Old Town bars rather than in disco clubs. There are often live bands playing in summer, and many bars stay open until 4 or 5am. Crowds gravitate to Stari Grad and the cafes on Buničeva Poljana. Another great center of nightlife is outside the city walls on B. Josipa Jela̅ica by the youth hostel, otherwise known as **Bourbon Street.** The foreboding, sinister exterior of **Komarda Beach Bar,** Lazareti, hides a disco, a bar with its own bit of coastline, art space, and even a theater. (Open M-W 10pm-2am, Th-Sa 10pm-5am, Su 10pm-1am.) **Cafe Ragusea,** just past Ploče Gate on the right, offers fresh air, a live DJ, and an incredible view of the old harbor. (Beer 7.50kn. Mixed drinks 25-47kn. Open daily 8am-3am.)

▶ DAYTRIP FROM DUBROVNIK: LOPUD ISLAND. Less than an hour from Dubrovnik is Lopud, an enchanting island of the Elafiti Archipelago. The tiny village is dotted with white buildings, chapels, and parks, stretching along the island's waterfront *(obala)*. A short walk along the shore leads to an abandoned **monastery,** which is great for exploring—just be careful of crumbling floors. The island's highlight is its **beach,** Plaža Šunj. Arguably the best beach in Croatia, this cove has one thing that most of the Dalmatian Coast lacks—sand.

Ferries run from Dubrovnik to the Elafiti islands (50min.; in summer M-Sa 4 per day, Su daily; round-trip 30kn). The beach is on the opposite side of the island from the village. Facing the water, walk left for 5min. and turn left onto the road between the high wall and the palm park; look for the "Konoba Barbara" sign and continue over the hill for 15min., keeping right when the path forks.

CZECH REPUBLIC (ČESKÁ REPUBLIKA)

From the Holy Roman Empire through the USSR, the Czechs have long stood at a crossroads of international affairs. Unlike many of their neighbors, the citizens of this small, landlocked country have rarely resisted as armies marched across their borders, often choosing to fight with words instead of weapons; as a result, Czech towns and cities are among the best-preserved and most beautiful in Europe. Today, the Czechs face a different kind of invasion, as enamored tourists sweep in to savor the magnificent capital, the welcoming locals, and the world's best beers.

FACTS AND FIGURES

Official Name: Czech Republic.
Capital: Prague.
Major Cities: Brno, Ostrava.
Population: 10,300,000.
Land Area: 78,866 sq. km.
Time Zone: GMT +1.
Language: Czech.
Religion: Roman Catholic (40%), Atheist (40%), Protestant (5%), other (15%).

DISCOVER THE CZECH REPUBLIC

From the medieval alleys of Staré Město and its fabulous Baroque and Art Nouveau architecture to the world's best beer, **Prague** (p. 250) is truly the starlet of Central Europe. At nearby **Kutná Hora** (p. 264), human femurs and crania hang from the ceilings and chandeliers. In Western Bohemia, international crowds flock to **Karlovy Vary** (p. 265) for its summer film festival and for its *Becherovka*, a local herb liqueur with "curative powers" rivaled only by those of the local hot springs. In Southern Bohemia, **Český Krumlov** (p. 267) charms visitors with its 13th-century castle, a summer medieval festival, and great nightlife.

ESSENTIALS

WHEN TO GO

Since the country is mobbed in summer, spring and fall are the best times to visit, although spring can be rainy. Winters are cold, damp, and snowy.

DOCUMENTS AND FORMALITIES

VISAS. Citizens of Ireland, New Zealand, and the US may visit the Czech Republic without a visa for up to 90 days, UK citizens for up to 180 days. Australians, Canadians, and South Africans must obtain 30-day tourist visas. Visas are available at embassies or consulates, but not at the border. Single-entry visas and transit visas cost US$52 for Australians, US$56 for Canadians, and US$30 for citizens of most other countries, while 90-day multiple-entry visas cost US$52/112/112. Travelers on a visa must **register** with the Czech Immigration Police within three days of arrival; hotels register their guests automatically.

EMBASSIES. All foreign embassies are in Prague (p. 250). Czech embassies at home include: **Australia,** 8 Culgoa Circuit, O'Malley, Canberra, ACT 2606 (☎02 6290 1386; canberra@embassy.mzv.cz); **Canada,** 251 Cooper St., Ottawa, ON K2P OG2 (☎613-562-3875; ottawa@embassy.mzv.cz); **Ireland,** 57 Northumberland Rd., Balls-

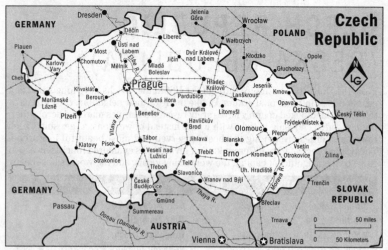

bridge, Dublin 4 (☎01 668 1135; dublin@embassy.mzv.cz); **South Africa,** 936 Pretorius St., Arcadia 0083, Pretoria; mail to: P.O. Box 13671, Hatfield 0028, Pretoria 0001 (☎012 431 2380; www.mzv.cz/pretoria); **UK,** 26 Kensington Palace Gardens, London W8 4QY (☎020 7243 1115; www.czechembassy.org.uk); and **US,** 3900 Spring of Freedom St. NW, Washington, D.C. 20008 (☎202-274-9123; www.mzv.cz/washington).

TRANSPORTATION

BY PLANE AND BY TRAIN. Many major carriers fly into Prague's Ruzyně airport, but the best way to enter and travel through the Czech Republic is by train. **Eastrail** is accepted, but **Eurail** is only valid up to the Czech border. The fastest international trains are EuroCity and InterCity (*expresní,* marked in blue on schedules). Rychlík, or *zrychlený vlak,* are fast domestic trains (marked in red). Avoid slow *osobní* trains (marked in white). Seat reservations (*místenka;* 10Kč) are recommended on express and international trains and for all first-class seating.

BY BUS. Buses are efficient and convenient for domestic travel, but schedules are often confusing. **ČSAD** runs national and international bus lines. Consult the timetables posted at stations or buy your own schedule (25Kč) from kiosks.

BY CAR AND BY TAXI. Roads in the Czech Republic are well-maintained and **roadside assistance** is usually available. In addition to an international Driving Permit, US citizens must have a US driver's license. **Taxis** are a safe means of travel, though many tourists complain of exorbitant rates, especially in Prague. Phoning a taxi company is generally more affordable than flagging a cab on the street.

BY THUMB. Although it is a common way for young people to travel in the Czech Republic, *Let's Go* does not recommend hitchhiking.

TOURIST SERVICES AND MONEY

| **EMERGENCY** | Police: ☎158. Ambulance: ☎155. Fire: ☎150. |

TOURIST OFFICES. CKM (www.ckm-praha.cz), a national student tourist agency, books hostel beds and issues ISIC and HI cards. **Municipal tourist offices** provide info on sights and events, provide lists of accommodations, and often book rooms.

MONEY. The Czech unit of currency is the **koruna** (crown; Kč), plural *koruny*. Banks offer good exchange rates; **Komerční banka** and **Česká spořitelna** are common chains. **ATMs,** which have the best exchange rates, are everywhere; look for the red-and-black "*Bankomat*" signs. Traveler's checks can be exchanged almost everywhere, though rarely without commission. MasterCard and Visa are accepted at most high-priced establishments, but rarely at hostels. To **tip,** add 10-20% to the cost of your meal and tell the waiter the new amount; simply leaving *koruny* on the table is considered rude.

BUSINESS HOURS. Banks are usually open Monday to Friday 8am to 4pm, shops Monday to Friday 9am to 5pm and Saturday 9am to noon. Almost all museums and galleries close on Mondays.

CZECH KORUNY		
AUS$1 = 19.11Kč	10Kč = AUS$0.52	
CDN$1 = 21.31Kč	10Kč = CDN$0.47	
EUR€1 = 32.44Kč	10Kč = EUR€0.31	
NZ$1 = 17.07Kč	10Kč = NZ$0.59	
UK£1 = 46.59Kč	10Kč = UK£0.21	
US$1 = 29.54Kč	10Kč = US$0.34	
ZAR1 = 4.03Kč	10Kč = ZAR2.48	

COMMUNICATION

PHONE CODES — **Country code: 420. International dialing prefix: 00.** From outside the Czech Republic, dial int'l dialing prefix (see inside back cover) + 420 + city code + local number.

TELEPHONES AND INTERNET ACCESS. Card-operated phones (175Kč per 50 units; 320Kč per 100 units) are simpler to use than coin phones. **Phone cards** are sold at most *Tábaks* and *Trafika* (convenience stores). Calls run 8Kč per minute to Australia, Canada, the UK, or the US; and 12Kč per minute to New Zealand. Dial ☎1181 for English info or ☎0800 12 34 56 for the international operator. International access codes include: **AT&T** (☎00 42 000 101); **British Telecom** (☎00 420 04412); **Canada Direct** (☎00 42 000 151); **MCI** (☎00 42 000112); **South Africa** (☎00 420027 01); **Sprint** (☎0042 087 187); **Telkom Telstra Australia** (☎0042 0061 01). **Internet** access is readily available throughout the Czech Republic, with rates around 2Kč per minute.

MAIL. The Czech Republic has an efficient postal system. A postcard to the US costs 9Kč, to Europe 7Kč. When sending by airmail, stress that you want it to go on a *letecky* (plane). Go to the customs office to send international packages heavier than 2kg. Address mail to be held: Firstname SURNAME, *Poste Restante*, Jindřišská 14, 1 110 00 Praha, CZECH REPUBLIC.

LANGUAGES. Czech is a Western Slavic language, most closely related to Slovak and Polish. English is widely understood, and German phrases may be useful, especially in the western spas. Russian is also commonly understood but is not always welcome. For Czech words and phrases, see p. 1052.

ACCOMMODATIONS AND CAMPING

CZECH REPUBLIC	❶	❷	❸	❹	❺
ACCOMMODATIONS	under 320Kč	320-500Kč	501-800Kč	801-1200Kč	over 1200Kč

Hostels are consistently clean and safe; **university dorms** are the cheapest lodgings in July and August, with two- to four-bed rooms running 250-400Kč per person. **Pensions** are the next most affordable option; expect to pay 600Kč, including breakfast. **Hotels** start at around 1000Kč. From June to September reserve rooms at least one week ahead in Prague, Český Krumlov, and Brno. If you can't keep a reservation, always call to cancel. **Private homes,** indicated by *Zimmer frei* signs at train stations, are not nearly as popular (or as cheap) as in the rest of Eastern Europe. **Campgrounds** are strewn throughout the countryside, though most are open only mid-May to September.

FOOD AND DRINK

CZECH REPUBLIC	❶	❷	❸	❹	❺
FOOD	under 80Kč	80-110Kč	111-150Kč	151-200Kč	over 200Kč

Thick, pasty *knedlíky* dough is a staple of Czech meals. The national meal, known as *vepřo-knedlo-zelo*, consists of *vepřové* (roast pork), *knedlíky*, and *zelí* (sauerkraut). If you're in a hurry, try *párky* (frankfurters) or *sýr* (cheese) from food stands. Vegetarian restaurants serving *bez masa* (meatless) dishes are uncommon; at most restaurants, vegetarian options will be limited to *smažený sýr* (fried cheese) or *saláty* (salad). Ask for *káva espresso* rather than *káva* to avoid the mud that Czechs call coffee. The most beloved dessert is *koláč*—a tart with poppy-seed jam or sweet cheese. *Plzeňský Prazdroj* (Pilsner Urquell) is the most prominent beer, but many Czechs are loyal to *Budvar* or *Krušovice*.

HOLIDAYS AND FESTIVALS

Holidays: New Year's Day (Jan. 1); Easter (Apr. 9-11); May Day (May 1); Liberation Day (May 8); Cyril and Methodius Day (July 5); Jan Hus Day (July 6); St. Wenceslas Day (Sept. 28); Independence Day (Oct. 28); Day of Student Struggle for Freedom and Democracy (Nov. 17); Christmas (Dec. 24-25).

Festivals: The **Spring Festival** (mid-May to early June) attracts international classical music lovers to Prague. In June, Český Krumlov hosts the boisterous **Five-Petaled Rose Festival,** which features music, dancing, and a jousting tournament. **Masopust** is a version of Mardi Gras celebrated across the country from Epiphany to Ash Wednesday.

PRAGUE (PRAHA)

According to legend, Countess Libuše stood above the Vltava and declared, "I see a grand city whose glory will touch the stars." Medieval kings, benefactors, and architects fulfilled the prophecy, building soaring cathedrals and lavish palaces that reflected the status of Prague (pop. 1,200,000) as capital of the Holy Roman Empire. Prague's maze of alleys spawned legends of demons and occult

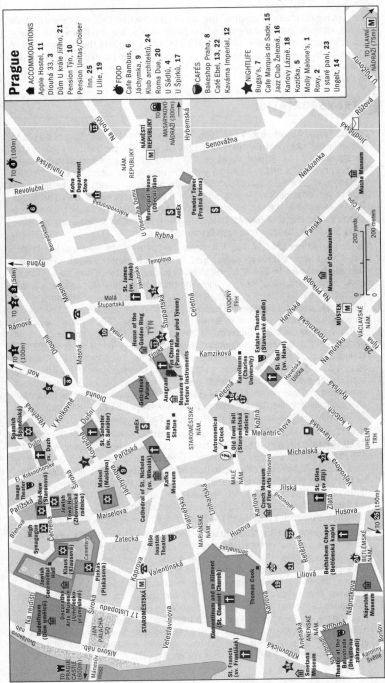

Prague

▲ ACCOMMODATIONS
Apple Hostel, **11**
Dlouhá 33, **3**
Dům U krále Jiřího, **21**
Pension Týn, **10**
Pension Unitas/Cloiser
Inn, **25**
U Lilie, **19**

🍴 FOOD
Café Bambus, **6**
Jáchymka, **9**
Klub architektů, **24**
Roma Due, **20**
U Sádlů, **4**
U Špirků, **17**

☕ CAFÉS
Bakeshop Praha, **8**
Café Ebel, **13, 22**
Kavárna Imperial, **12**

★ NIGHTLIFE
Bugsy's, **7**
Cafe Marquis de Sade, **15**
Jazz Club Železná, **16**
Karlovy Lázně, **18**
Kozička, **5**
Molly Malone's, **1**
Roxy, **2**
U staré paní, **23**
Ungelt, **14**

CZECH REPUBLIC

forces, giving this "city of dreams" the dark mystique that inspired Franz Kafka's tales of paranoia. Yet since the fall of the Iron Curtain, hordes of foreigners have flooded the city; in summer, tourists pack streets so tightly that crowd-surfing seems a viable method of transportation. Walk a few blocks away from the major sights, however, and you'll be a lone backpacker among cobblestone alleys and looming churches.

■ TRANSPORTATION

Flights: Ruzyně Airport (☎220 113 259), 20km northwest of the city. Take bus #119 to Metro A: Dejvická (daily 6am-midnight; 12Kč, luggage 6Kč per bag); buy tickets from kiosks or machines. **Airport buses** (☎220 114 296) run from outside Metro stops (6am-9pm every hr.; Nám. Republiky 90Kč, Dejvická 60Kč). **Cedaz** (☎220 114 296; cedaz@email.cz) offers a shared door-to-door shuttle service. Tickets from the airport are sold at the Cedaz kiosk in the main arrivals hall; tickets to the airport can be booked in advance via phone or email. To/from: central Prague, 360Kč (1-4 people), 720Kč (5-8 people); outer Prague, 720Kč (1-8 people). **Taxis** to the airport are extremely expensive (400-600Kč); try to settle on a price before starting out.

Trains: Domestic ☎224 224 200; International ☎224 615 249; www.cdrail.cz. Prague has 4 main terminals. **Hlavní nádraží** (☎224 224 200; Metro C: Hlavní nádraží) and **Nádraží Holešovice** (☎224 613 249; Metro C: Nádraží Holešovice) are the largest and cover most international service. Domestic trains leave from **Masarykovo nádraží** (☎224 61 51 54; Metro B: Nám. Republiky), on the corner of Hybernská and Havlíčkova, and from **Smíchovské nádraží** (☎224 61 72 55); Metro B: Smíchovské nádraží). International trains run to: **Berlin** (5½hr., 5 per day, 1400Kč); **Bratislava** (4½-5½hr., 7 per day, 450Kč); **Budapest** (7-9hr., 5 per day, 1300Kč); **Kraków** (8½hr., 4 per day, 820Kč); **Moscow** (31hr., daily, 3000Kč); **Munich** (7-9hr., 4 per day, 1650Kč); **Vienna** (4½hr., 4 per day, 900Kč); **Warsaw** (9½hr., 4 per day, 1290Kč). **BIJ Wasteels** (☎224 617 454; www.wasteels.cz), on the 2nd fl. of Hlavní nádraží, to the right of the stairs, sells discounted international tickets to those under 26, and also books couchettes and bus tickets. Open M-F 8am-6pm, Sa 8am-3pm. Wasteels tickets are also available from the **Czech Railways Travel Agency** (☎224 239 464; fax 224 223 600) at Nádraží Holešovice. Open M-F 9am-5pm, Sa-Su 8am-4pm.

Buses: Schedule info (☎900 149 044; www.jizdnirady.cz or www.vlak.cz). The state-run **ČSAD** (Česká státní automobilová doprava; Czech National Bus Transport; ☎257 319 555) has several bus terminals. The biggest is **Florenc**, Křižíkova 4 (☎ 900 119 041). Metro B or C: Florenc. Info office open daily 6am-9pm. Buy tickets in advance. To: **Berlin** (8hr., daily, 850Kč); **Budapest** (8hr., daily, 1550Kč); **Paris** (18hr., daily, 2200Kč); **Sofia** (26hr., 4 per day, 1600Kč); **Vienna** (8½hr., daily, 600Kč). 10% ISIC discount. The **Tourbus** office (☎224 210 221; www.eurolines.cz), at the terminal, sells tickets for **Eurolines** and airport buses. Open M-F 8am-8pm, Sa 9am-8pm, Su 9am-7pm.

Public Transportation: Buy **Metro, tram,** or **bus** tickets from newsstands, *tabák* kiosks, machines in stations, or **DP** (*Dopravní Podnik;* transport authority) kiosks. The basic 8Kč ticket is good for 15min. on a tram (or 4 stops on the Metro); the 12Kč ticket is valid for 1hr. during the day, with unlimited connections between buses, trams, and Metro in any one direction. Large bags require an extra 6Kč ticket. Validate tickets in machines above escalators or face a 400Kč fine. Before paying a fine, look for the inspector's badge and get a receipt. The three Metro lines run daily 5am-midnight: A is green on maps, B is yellow, C is red. **Night trams** #51-58 and **buses** #501-513 run all night after the last Metro (every 30min.; look for dark blue signs with white lettering at bus stops). The tourist office in the Old Town Hall sells **multi-day passes** valid for the entire network. (Open 24hr. 70Kč, 3-day 200Kč, 7-day 250Kč.)

Taxis: Radiotaxi (☎224 916 666) or **AAA** (☎ 221 111 111). 30Kč flat rate plus 22Kč per km. Hail a cab anywhere on the street, but call one of the above numbers to avoid getting ripped off. To avoid the taxi scams that run rampant throughout the city, always ask for a receipt (*"Prosím, dejte mi paragon"*) with distance traveled and price paid.

ORIENTATION

Shouldering the river **Vltava**, greater Prague is a mess of suburbs and maze-like streets. Fortunately, nearly everything of interest to the traveler lies within the compact downtown. The Vltava runs south-northeast through central Prague, separating **Staré Město** (Old Town) and **Nové Město** (New Town) from **Malá Strana** (Lesser Side). On the right bank of the river, **Staroměstské Náměstí** (Old Town Square) is the heart of Prague. From the square, the elegant **Pařížská ulice** (Paris Street) leads north into **Josefov**, the old Jewish ghetto in which only six synagogues and the Old Jewish Cemetery remain. South of Staré Město, Nové Město houses **Václavské Náměstí** (Wenceslas Square), the administrative and commercial core of the city. West of Staroměstské nám., the picturesque **Karlův most** (Charles Bridge) spans the Vltava, connecting the Staré Město with **Malostranské náměstí** (Lesser Town Square). **Pražský Hrad** (Prague Castle) looks over Malostranské nám. from **Hradčany** hill.

Prague's **train station,** Hlavní nádraží, and Florenc bus station lie northeast of Václavské nám. All train and bus terminals are on or near the excellent Metro system. To get to Staroměstské nám., take the Metro A line to *Staroměstská* and head down Kaprova away from the river. Kiosks and bookstores sell an indexed *plán města* (map), which is essential for newcomers to the city.

PRACTICAL INFORMATION

TOURIST AND FINANCIAL SERVICES

Tourist Offices: Green "i"s mark tourist agencies, which book rooms and sell maps, bus tickets, and guidebooks. **Pražská Informační Služba** (PIS; Prague Info Service; ☎221 714 170; www.pis.cz) is in the Staré Město Hall. Additional branches at Na plíkopě 20 and Hlavní nádraží (open in summer M-F 9am-7pm, Sa-Su 9am-5pm; off-season M-F 9am-6pm, Sa 9am-3pm), as well as the tower by the Malá Strana side of the Charles Bridge (open Apr.-Oct., daily 10am-6pm; closed Nov.-Mar.).

Budget Travel: CKM, Manesova 77 (☎222 721 595; www.ckm-praha.cz). Metro A: Jiřího z Poděbrad. Budget air tickets for those under 26. Also books accommodations (dorms from 250Kč). Open M-Th 10am-6pm, F 10am-4pm.

Passport Office: Foreigner Police Headquarters, Olšanská 2 (☎261 441 111). Metro A: Flora. From the Metro, turn right on Jičínská with the cemetery on your right and go right again on Olšanská. Or take tram #9 from Václavské nám. toward Spojovací and get off at Olšanská. For a **visa extension,** get a 90Kč stamp inside. Line up in front of doors #2-12, and prepare to wait up to 2hr. Little English spoken. Open M-Tu and Th 7:30-11:30am and 12:15-3pm, W 8am-12:15pm and 1-5pm, F 7:30-11:30am.

Embassies: Canada, Mickiewiczova 6 (☎272 101 800). Metro A: Hradčanská. Open M-F 8:30am-12:30pm. **Ireland,** Tržiště 13 (☎257 530 061). Metro A: Malostranská. Open M-F 9:30am-12:30pm and 2:30-4:30pm. **South Africa,** Ruská 65 (☎267 311 114). Metro A: Flora. Open M-F 8am-4:30pm. **UK,** Thunovská 14 (☎257 402 111; www.britain.cz). Metro A: Malostranská. Open M-F 9am-noon. **US,** Tržiště 15 (☎257 530 663; emergency ☎253 12 00; www.usembassy.cz). Metro A: Malostranská. Open M-F 9am-4:30pm. **Australia** (☎251 018 350) and **New Zealand** (☎222 514 672) have consuls, but citizens should contact the UK embassy in an emergency.

Currency Exchange: Exchange counters are everywhere and their rates vary wildly. Never change money on the street. **Chequepoints** are convenient and open late, but usually charge commission. **Komerční banka,** Na příkopě 33 (☎222 432 111), buys notes and checks for a 2% commission. Open M-W 9am-6pm, Th-F 9am-5pm. **ATMs** ("Bankomats") abound and can offer the best rates, but sometimes charge large fees.

American Express: Václavské nám. 56 (☎222 432 422). Metro A or C: Muzeum. The **ATM** outside takes AmEx cards. Grants MC/V cash advances for a 3% commission. Open daily 9am-7pm. **Branches** on Mostecká 12 (☎257 313 638; open daily 9:30am-7:30pm), Celetná 17 (☎/fax 224 818 274; open daily 8:30am-7:15pm), and Staroměstské nám. 5 (☎224 818 388; open daily 9am-7:30pm).

LOCAL SERVICES

Luggage Storage: Lockers in all train and bus stations take two 5Kč coins. If these are full, or if you need to store your cargo longer than 24hr., use the luggage offices to the left in the basement of **Hlavní nádraží** (15-30Kč per day; open 24hr.) or halfway up the stairs at **Florenc** (25Kč per day; open daily 5am-11pm).

Laundromat: Laundry Kings, Dejvická 16 (☎233 343 743), 1 block from Metro A: Hradčanská. Cross the tram and railroad tracks, and turn left. Very social. Internet access 55Kč per 30min. Wash 60Kč per 6kg, dry 15Kč per 8min. Open M-F 6am-10pm, Sa-Su 8am-10pm.

EMERGENCY AND COMMUNICATION

Medical Assistance: Na Homolce (Hospital for Foreigners), Roentgenova 2 (☎257 272 142; after-hours 257 772 025; www.homolka.cz). Bus #168 and 184. Open M-F 8am-4pm. 24hr. emergency service. **American Medical Center,** Janovského 48 (☎220 807 756). Major foreign insurance accepted. On call 24hr. Appointments M-F 9am-4pm. Average consultation 50-200Kč.

24hr. pharmacy: U. Lékárna Andwla, Štefánikova 6 (☎257 320 918). Metro B: Anděl.

Telephones: Phone cards sell for 175Kč per 50 units and 320Kč per 100 units at kiosks, post offices, and some exchange places; don't let kiosks rip you off.

Internet Access: Prague is an Internet nirvana. ▓**Bohemia Bagel,** Masna 2 (www.bohemiabagel.cz). Metro A: Staroměstská. 1.5Kč per min. Open M-F 7am-midnight, Sa-Su 8am-midnight. **Cafe Electra,** Rašínovo nábřeží 62 (☎224 922 887; www.electra.cz). Metro B: Karlovo nám. Exit on the Palackého nám. side. Extensive menu. Internet access 80Kč per hr. Open M-F 9am-midnight, Sa-Su 11am-midnight.

Post Office: Jindřišská 14 (☎221 131 445). Metro A or B: Můstek. Airmail to the US takes 7-10 days. Open daily 2am-midnight. For *Poste Restante,* address mail to be held: Firstname SURNAME, *Poste Restante,* Jindřišská 14, Praha 1 **110 00,** CZECH REPUBLIC.

▐ ACCOMMODATIONS AND CAMPING

Although hotel prices are through the roof, rates in the glutted hostel market have stabilized at around 300-600Kč per night. Reservations are a must at hotels, which can be booked solid months in advance, and are a good idea at the few hostels that accept them. Most accommodations have 24hr. reception and require check-out by 10am. A growing number of Prague residents rent affordable rooms.

ACCOMMODATIONS AGENCIES

Many room hawkers at the train station offer legitimate deals, but some will rip you off. Apartments go for around 600-1200Kč per day, depending on proximity to the city center. Haggling is possible. If you don't want to bargain on the street, try a **private agency**. Ask where the nearest tram, bus, or Metro stop is, and don't pay until you know what you're getting; ask for details in writing. You can often pay in euros or US dollars, but prices are lower if you pay in Czech crowns. Some travel agencies book lodgings as well (p. 253). **AveTravel,** on the second floor of Hlavní nádraží, books rooms starting at 800Kč per person and hostels from 290Kč. (☎224 223 226; www.avetravel.cz. Open daily 6am-11pm. AmEx/MC/V.)

HOSTELS

If you tote a backpack in Hlavní nádraží or Holešovice, expect to be bombarded by hostel runners. Many accommodations are university dorms that free up from June to August, and often you'll be offered free transportation. These rooms are convenient options for those arriving in the middle of the night without reservations. If you prefer more than just a place to sleep, smaller establishments are a safer bet. It's a good idea to call as soon as you know your plans, even if only the night before you arrive or at 10am when they know who's checking out. In Prague, the staff typically speaks English, and hostels rarely have curfews.

▨ **Hostel Boathouse,** Lodnická 1 (☎241 770 057; www.aa.cz/boathouse), south of the city center. Take tram #21 from Národni south toward Sídliště. Get off at Černý Kůň (20min.) and follow the yellow signs. As Věra the owner says, "This isn't a hostel, it's a crazyhouse." Look for the name of this book's editor on the wall. Summer camp vibe. Hot breakfast or dinner 70Kč. Dorms 300-320Kč. ❶

▨ **Penzion v podzámčí,** V podzámčí 27 (☎241 444 609; www.sleepinprague.com), south of the city center. From Metro C: Budějovická, take bus #192 to the 3rd stop (*Nad Rybníky*). Homey, with kitchen and laundry facilities. Dorms Sept.-June 280Kč, July-Aug. 300Kč; doubles 640/720Kč; triples 900/990Kč. ❶

▨ **Dlouhá 33,** (☎224 826 662). Metro B: Nám. Republiky. Follow Revoluční toward the river, turn left on Dlouhá. Unbeatable location in Staré Město; in the same building as the Roxy (p. 263), but soundproof. Book 2-3 weeks in advance in summer. Open year-round. Dorms 370-430Kč; doubles 1240Kč; triples 1440Kč. ISIC discount 40Kč. ❷

Apple Hostel, Krádlodvorská 16 (☎224 231 050; www.applehostel.cz). Metro B: Nám. Republiky. At the corner of Revoluční and Nám. Republiky, across from Kotva department store. Brand new hostel with a social atmosphere, helpful staff, and a prime location in the heart of Staré Město. Breakfast included. Internet access 1Kč per min. Mar.-Oct. 4-bed dorms 450Kč, Nov.-Feb. 350Kč; 5-bed dorms 440/340Kč; 7-bed dorms 420/320Kč. Singles 1950/1150Kč; doubles 1240/1040Kč. ❷

Hostel U Melounu, Ke Karlovu 7 (☎/fax 224 918 322; www.hostelmelounu.cz), in Nové Město. Metro C: I.P. Pavlova. Follow Sokolská and go right on Na Bojišt then left onto Ke Karlovu. A historic building with great facilities. Breakfast included. Reservations accepted. Dorms 380Kč; singles 500Kč; doubles 840Kč. ISIC discount 30Kč. ❷

Husova 3, (☎222 220 078), in Staré Město. Metro B: Národní třída. Turn right on Spálená (which becomes Na Perštýně after Národní), and again on Husova. Open July-Aug. only. Dorms 400Kč. ❷

Střelecký ostrov, (☎224 932 999), on an island beneath Legií bridge in Staré Město. Metro B: Národní třída. Open mid-June to mid-Sept. Spacious dorms 300Kč. ❶

Ujezd, (☎257 312 403), across Most Legií bridge in Staré Město. Metro B: Národní třída. Sports facilities and park. Open mid-June to mid-Sept. Dorms 220Kč. ❶

Pension Týn, Týnská 19 (☎/fax 224 808 333; backpacker@razdva.cz), in Staré Město. Metro A: Staroměstská. From the Old Town Square, head down Dlouhá, bear right at Masná then right onto Týnská. A quiet getaway located in the center of Staré Město. Immaculate facilities. Dorms 400Kč; doubles 1100Kč. ❷

Welcome Hostel, Zíkova 13 (☎224 320 202; www.bed.cz), outside the center. Metro A: Dejvická. Cheap, tidy, spacious, and convenient university dorm. Near airport shuttle stop. Singles 400Kč; doubles 540Kč. 10% ISIC discount. ❷

Welcome Hostel at Strahov Complex, Vaníčkova 5 (☎233 359 275), outside the center. Take bus #217 or 143 from Metro A: Dejvická to Koleje Strahov. Newly renovated high-rise dorms near Prague Castle. A little far, but there's always space. Singles 300Kč; doubles 440Kč. 10% ISIC discount. ❶

HOTELS AND PENSIONS

As tourists colonize Prague, hotels are upgrading their service and their prices; budget hotels are now quite scarce. Call several months ahead to book a room in summer and confirm by fax with a credit card.

▓ **Dům U krále Jiřího,** Liliová 10 (☎222 220 925; www.kinggeorge.cz), in Staré Město. Metro A: Staroměstská. Exit onto Nám. Jana Palacha, walk down Křížovnická toward the Charles Bridge and turn left onto Karlova; Liliová is the first right. Gorgeous rooms with private bath. Breakfast included. May-Dec. singles 2000Kč; doubles 3300Kč. Dec.-May 1500/2700Kč. ❺

U Lilie, Liliová 15 (☎222 220 432; www.pensionville.cz), in Staré Město. Metro A: Staroměstská. See directions for Dům U krále Jiřího (above). Lovely courtyard. Breakfast included. Singles with showers 1850Kč; doubles 2150-2800Kč. ❺

Hotel Kafka, Cimburkova 24 (☎/fax 222 781 333), outside the center. From Metro C: Hlavní nádraží, take tram #5 (dir.: Harfa), 9 (dir.: Spojovací), or 26 (dir.: Nádraží Hostivař); get off at *Husinecká*. Head uphill along Seifertova then go left on Cimburkova. Locals frequent nearby beer halls. Breakfast included. Apr.-Oct. singles 1700Kč; doubles 2300Kč. Nov.-Mar. 1000/1300Kč. MC/V for 5% commission. ❺

Pension Unitas/Cloister Inn, Bartolomějská 9 (☎224 221 802; www.unitas.cz), in Staré Město. Metro B: Národní třída. Cross Národní, head up Na Perštýně away from Tesco, and turn left on Bartolomějská. Renovated rooms in the cells of the former Communist prison where Václav Havel was incarcerated. Breakfast included. Singles 1100Kč; doubles 1400Kč; triples 1750Kč. ❹

CAMPING

Campsites can be found in both the outskirts and the centrally located Vltava islands. Bungalows must be reserved in advance, but tent space is generally available without prior notice. Tourist offices sell a guide to sites near the city (15Kč).

Sokol Troja, Trojská 171 (☎/fax 233 542 908), north of the center in the Troja district. Metro C: Nádraží Holešovice. Take bus #112 to Kazanka. Similar places line the road. July-Aug. 130Kč per person, 90-180Kč per tent; Oct.-June 70-150Kč per tent. Private rooms available. July-Aug., singles 320Kč; doubles 640Kč. Oct.-June 290/580Kč. ❶

Caravan Park, Císařská louka 599 (☎257 318 681; fax 257 318 387), on the Císařská louka peninsula. Metro B: Smíchovské nádraží, then any of the buses numbered in the 300s to Lihovar. Alternatively, a ferry service leaves every hr. on the hour from the small landing 1 block over from Smíchovské nádraží (10Kč). Small, tranquil camping ground on the banks of the Vltava river. Clean facilities, friendly staff, convenient cafe and currency exchange on premises. 95Kč per person, 90-140Kč per tent. ❶

◨ FOOD

The nearer you are to the center, the more you'll pay. Away from the center, pork, cabbage, dumplings, and a half-liter of beer costs about 50Kč. You will be charged for everything the waiter brings to the table; check your bill carefully. Most restaurants accept only cash. Outlying Metro stops become markets in the summer. **Tesco,** Národní třída 26, has **groceries** right next to metro B: Národní třída. (Open

M-F 7am-10pm, Sa 8am-8pm, Su 9am-8pm.) Look for the **daily market** in Staré Město where Havelská and Melantrichova intersect. After a night out, grab a *párek v rohlíku* (hot dog) or a *smažený sýr* (fried cheese sandwich) from a Václavské nám. vendor, or a gyro from a stand on Spálená or Vodíčkova.

RESTAURANTS

▨ **Jáchymka,** Jáchymova 4 (☎224 819 621). From the Old Town Square, walk up Pařížská and take a right on Jáchymova. A favorite among locals, Jáchymka serves heaping portions of traditional Czech cuisine in a lively, informal atmosphere. Try the goulash with dumplings (95Kč) or one of their massive meat escalopes (80-185Kč). Or for lighter fare, try the salmon with pasta and vegetables (195Kč). Open daily 11am-11pm. ❸

▨ **Radost FX,** Bělehradská 120, is both a dance club and a late-night cafe with an imaginative menu and great vegetarian food. Metro C: I.P. Pavlova. Entrees 105-170Kč. Brunch Sa-Su 95-140Kč. Open daily 11am-late. See also Clubs and Discos, p. 263. ❸

U Sádlů, Klimentskà 2 (☎224 813 874; www.usadlu.cz). Metro B: Nám. Republiky. From the square, walk down Revoluční toward the river, then go right on Klimentskà. Medieval themed restaurant with bountiful portions; call ahead. Czech-only menu lists traditional meals (115-245Kč). Open daily 11am-midnight. ❸

Klub architektů, Betlémské nám. 52A, in Staré Město. Metro B: Národní třída. A 12th-century cellar with 20th century ambience. Veggie options 90-100Kč. Meat dishes 150-290Kč. Open daily 11:30am-midnight. MC/V. ❸

U Švejků, Újezd 22, in Malá Strana. Metro A: Malostranská. Head down Klárov and go right onto Letenská. Bear left through Malostranské nám. and follow Karmelitskà until it becomes Újezd. Named after the lovable Czech cartoon hero from Hasek's novel *The Good Soldier Svejk,* and decorated with scenes from the book. Daily accordion music after 7pm. Entrees 98-148Kč. Open daily 11am-midnight. AmEx/MC/V. ❸

Velryba (The Whale), Opatovická 24, in Nové Město. Metro B: Národní třída. Cross the tram tracks and follow Ostrovní, then go left onto Opatovická. Relaxed cafe-restaurant with downstairs art gallery. Entrees 80-140Kč. Open M-Th 11am-midnight, F 11am-2am. Cafe and gallery open M-F noon-midnight, Sa 5pm-midnight, Su 3-10pm. ❷

Kajetanka, Hradcanské nám., in Malá Strana. Metro A: Malostranská. Walk down Letenská through Malostranské nám.; climb Nerudova until it curves to Ke Hradu, continue up the hill. Terrace cafe with a spectacular view. Meat dishes 129-299Kč, salads 49-69Kč. Open in spring and summer daily 10am-8pm; off-season 10am-6pm. ❹

Cafe Bambus, Benediktska 12, in Staré Město. Metro B: Nám. Republiky. An African oasis with an international menu. Entrees 55-228Kč. Czech pancakes 55-75Kč. Open M-Th 10am-1am, F 10am-2am, Sa 11am-2am, Su 11am-11pm. ❷

U Špirků, ul. Kožná 12, in Staré Město. Metro A: Staroměstská. Authentic Czech decor and some of the city's best food at incredibly low prices. Entrees about 100Kč. Open daily 11am-midnight. ❶

Roma Due, Liliová 18. Metro A: Staroměstská. Perfect to cap off a night out. Pasta 89-155Kč until 10pm. Pizza 99-150Kč until 5am. Open 24hr. ❸

CAFES AND TEAHOUSES

▨ **Cafe Ebel,** Týn 2 (☎224 895 788; www.ebelcoffee.cz). Metro A or B: Staroměstská. Under the Ungelt arches. The best coffee in town and an affordable continental breakfast. Additional location at Retezova 9. Open daily 9am-10pm.

▨ **Bakeshop Praha,** Kozí 1 (☎222 316 823; info@bakeshop.cz). From the Old Town Square, follow Dlouhá to the intersection of Kozí. Mouthwatering breads, pastries, muffins, salads, sandwiches, and quiches and a multitude of espresso and tea drinks. Additional location at Lázenska 19, off Mostécka in Malá Strana. Open daily 7am-7pm.

■ **Kavarná Imperial,** Na Poříčí 15. Metro B: Nám. Republiky. Pillared cafe with a courtly air. Live jazz F-Sa 9pm. Open M-Th 9am-midnight, F-Sa 9am-1am, Su 9am-11pm.

The Globe Coffeehouse, Pštrossova 6. Metro B: Národní třída. At the Globe Bookstore. Exit Metro left on Spálená, turn right on Ostrovní, then left to Pštrossova. Fruit smoothies (45-60Kč), black coffee (25Kč), and English speakers trying to make a love connection (priceless). Open daily 10am-midnight.

U Malého Glena, Karmelitská 23. Metro A: Malostranská. Take tram #12 to Malostranské nám. Their motto is: "Eat, Drink, Drink Some More." Killer margaritas 90Kč. Daily jazz or blues 9pm. Cover 100-150Kč. Open daily 10am-2am.

U zeleného čaje, Nerudova 19. Metro A: Malostranská. Follow Letenská to Malostranské nám.; stay right of the church. Over 60 varieties of fragrant tea to please the senses and calm the mind. Sandwiches 25-89Kč. Open daily 11am-10pm.

Kavárna Medúza, Belgická 17. Metro A: Nám. Míru. Walk down Rumunská and turn left at Belgická. Cafe masquerading as an antique shop. Fluffed-up Victorian seats and lots of coffee (19-30Kč). Open M-F 11am-1am, Sa-Su noon-1am.

👁 SIGHTS

One of the only major Central European cities unscathed by WWII, Prague is a well-preserved blend of labyrinthine alleys and Baroque architecture. You can easily escape the crowds by venturing away from **Staroměstské náměstí, Karlův Most** (Charles Bridge), and **Václavské náměstí.** Compact central Prague is best explored on foot. There are plenty of opportunities for exploration in the back alleys of **Josefov,** the hills of **Vyšehrad,** and the maze of streets in **Malá Strana.**

NOVÉ MĚSTO (NEW TOWN)

Established in 1348 by Charles IV, Nové Město has become the commercial center of Prague, complete with American chain stores.

WENCESLAS SQUARE. Not so much a square as a boulevard running through the center of Nové Město, Wenceslas Square (Václavské náměstí) owes its name to the Czech ruler and saint **Wenceslas** (Václav), whose statue is in front of the National Museum (Národní muzeum). Wenceslas has presided over a century of turmoil and triumph, witnessing no fewer than five revolutions from his pedestal: The declaration of the new Czechoslovak state in 1918, the invasion by Hitler's troops in 1939, the arrival of Soviet tanks in 1968, the self-immolation of Jan Palach in protest of the Soviet invasion, and the 1989 Velvet Revolution. The square stretches from the statue past department stores, thumping discos, posh hotels, sausage stands, and glitzy casinos. **Radio Free Europe,** which gives global news updates and advocates peace, has been broadcasting from its glass building behind the National Museum since WWII. (*Metro A or C: Muzeum.*)

FRANCISCAN GARDEN AND VELVET REVOLUTION MEMORIAL. Monks somehow manage to preserve the immaculate and serene **rose garden** (Františkánská zahrada) in the heart of Prague's bustling commercial district. A plaque under the arcades halfway down Národní, across from the Black Theatre, memorializes the hundreds of citizens beaten by police on November 17, 1989. A subsequent wave of mass protests led to the total collapse of Communism in Czechoslovakia during the Velvet Revolution. (*Metro A or B: Můstek. Enter through the arch to the left of Jungmannova and Národní, behind the statue. Open daily mid-Apr. to mid-Sept. 7am-10pm; mid-Sept. to mid-Oct. 7am-8pm; mid-Oct. to mid-Apr. 8am-7pm. Free.*)

THE DANCING HOUSE. American architect Frank Gehry (of Guggenheim-Bilbao fame; p. 979) built the undulating "Dancing House" (Tančící dům) at the corner of Resslova and Rašínovo nábřeží. Since its 1996 unveiling, it has been called an eyesore by some, and a shining example of postmodern design by others. *(Metro B: Karlovo nám. As you walk down Resslova toward the river, the building is on the left.)*

STARÉ MĚSTO (OLD TOWN)

Getting lost among the narrow roads and old-world alleys of Staré Město is probably the best way to appreciate the 1000-year-old neighborhood's charm.

CHARLES BRIDGE. Thronged with tourists and the hawkers who feed on them, the Charles Bridge (Karlův Most) is Prague's most recognizable landmark. On each side of the bridge, defense towers offer splendid views of the city and of the river. Five stars and a cross mark the spot where the St. Jan Nepomucký was tossed over the side of the bridge for guarding the queen's extramarital secrets from a suspicious King Wenceslas IV. *(Metro A: Malostranská on the Malá Strana side and Metro A: Staroměstská on the Staré Město side. Open daily 10am-10pm. 40Kč, students 30Kč.)*

OLD TOWN SQUARE. The heart of Staré Město is Staroměstské náměstí (Old Town Square), surrounded by eight magnificent towers. Next to the grassy knoll stands the **Old Town Hall** (Staroměstské radnice). The multi-facaded building is missing a piece of the front facade where the Nazis partially demolished it in the final week of WWII. Crowds gather on the hour to watch the **astronomical clock** chime, releasing a procession of apostles accompanied by a skeleton symbolizing Death. *(Metro A: Staroměstská or Metro A or B: Můstek. Town Hall open in summer M 11am-5:30pm, Tu-Su 9am-5:30pm. Clock tower open daily 10am-6pm. 40Kč, students 30Kč.)* Opposite the Old Town Hall, the spires of **Týn Church** (Matka Boží před Týnem) rise above a mass of medieval homes. The famous astronomer Tycho Brahe is buried inside. Brahe died when he overindulged at one of Emperor Rudolf's lavish dinner parties, where it was unacceptable to leave the table unless the Emperor himself did so. Because he was forced to stay seated, his bladder burst. The bronze statue of theologian **Jan Hus,** the country's most famous martyr, stands in the middle of the square. In front of the Jan Hus statue sits the flowery **Goltz-Kinský Palace,** the finest of Prague's Rococo buildings. *(Open Tu-F 10am-6pm; closes early in summer for daily concerts.)*

POWDER TOWER AND MUNICIPAL HOUSE. One of the original eight city gates, the Gothic **Powder Tower** (Prašná Brána) looms at the edge of Nám. Republiky as the entrance to Staré Město. A steep climb to the top rewards you with expansive views. Next door, on the site of a former royal court, is the **Municipal House** (Obecnídům), where the Czechoslovak state declared independence on October 28, 1918. *(Nám. Republiky 5. Metro B: Nám. Republiky. Tower open July-Aug. daily 10am-10pm; Apr.-June and Sept.-Oct. daily 10am-6pm. House open daily 10am-6pm. Guided tours Sa noon and 2pm. 150Kč.)*

JOSEFOV

Josefov, the oldest Jewish settlement in Central Europe, lies north of Staroměstské nám., along Maiselova. In 1180, Prague's citizens built a 12 ft. wall around the area. The closed neighborhood bred exotic tales, many of which centered around Rabbi Loew ben Bezalel (1512-1609) and his legendary *golem*—a mud creature that supposedly came to life to protect Prague's Jews. The city's Jews remained clustered in Josefov until WWII, when the ghetto was vacated as the residents were deported to death camps. Ironically, Hitler's wish to create a "museum of an extinct race" sparked the preservation of Josefov's cemetery and synagogues. Although it's only a fraction of its former size, there's still a Jewish

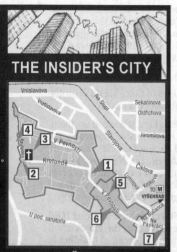

THE INSIDER'S CITY

VYŠEHRAD

The former haunt of Prague's 19th-century Romantics, Vyšehrad is a storehouse of nationalist myths and imperial legends. Quiet paths wind among crumbling stone walls offering respite from Prague's busy streets. (Metro C: Vyšehrad.)

1 Stroll by **St. Martin Rotunda,** Prague's oldest building.

2 Indulge in an elegant Czech meal at **Na Vyšehradě** (open daily 10am-10pm).

3 The **cemetery** holds the remains of the Czech Republic's most famous citizens.

4 Walk along the **castle walls** to enjoy Prague from new heights.

5 Relax in the sun with ice cream from **Obcerstveni Penguin** (open daily 11am-7pm).

6 A small **gallery** exhibits the work of local disabled children (open daily 10am-5pm).

7 Pass through the **Tábor Gate** to reach **Nad Vyšehradem,** a popular beer hall (open M-Th 10am-10pm, F-Su 11am-11pm).

community living in Prague today. (*Metro A: Staroměstská. Synagogues and cemetery open Apr.-Oct. Su-F 9am-6pm; Nov.-Mar. 9am-4:30pm. Closed Jewish holidays. All six synagogues except Starnová charge 250Kč, students 170Kč. Starnová Synagogue 200/140Kč.*)

THE SYNAGOGUES. The **Maisel Synagogue** (Maiselova synagoga) displays artifacts from the Jewish Museum's collections. *(On Maiselova, between Široká and Jáchymova.)* At the time of publication, **Pinkas Synagogue** (Pinkasova) was under repair due to recent flooding. To reach it, turn left down Široká to reach this sobering 16th-century memorial to the 80,000 Czech Jews killed in the Holocaust. Upstairs is an exhibit of drawings made by children in the Terezín camp. Backtrack up Široká and go left on Maiselova to visit the oldest operating synagogue in Europe, the 700-year-old **New Synagogue** (Staronová). Further up Široká on Dušní is the **Spanish Synagogue** (Španělská), which has an ornate Moorish interior.

OLD JEWISH CEMETERY. The Old Jewish Cemetery (Starý židovský hřbitov) remains Josefov's most-visited site. Between the 14th and 18th centuries, 20,000 graves were laid in 12 layers. The striking clusters of tombstones result from a process in which the older stones rose from underneath. Rabbi Loew is buried by the wall opposite the entrance. (*At the corner of Široká and Žatecká.*)

MALÁ STRANA

A seedy hangout for criminals and counter-revolutionaries for nearly a century, the cobblestone streets of Malá Strana have become prized real estate. Malá Strana is centered around **Malostranské Náměstí** and its centerpiece, the Baroque **St. Nicholas's Cathedral** (Chrám sv. Mikuláše), whose towering dome is one of Prague's most prominent landmarks. *(Metro A: Malostranská; follow Letenská to Malostranské nám. Open daily 9am-4:45pm. 50Kč, students 25Kč.)* Along Letenská, a wooden gate opens into the beautiful **Wallenstein Garden** (Valdštejnská zahrada), one of Prague's best-kept secrets. *(Letenská 10. Metro A: Malostranská. Open Apr.-Oct. daily 10am-6pm. Free.)* **Church of Our Lady Victorious** (Kostel Panna Marie Vítězné) is known for the famous wax statue of the **Infant Jesus of Prague,** said to bestow miracles on the faithful. *(Metro A: Malostranská. Follow Letecká through Malostranské nám. and continue onto Karmelitská. Open daily 8:30am-7pm. Museum open M-Sa 9:30am-5:30pm, Su 1-6pm. Free.)*

PRAGUE CASTLE (PRAŽSKÝ HRAD)

Prague Castle has been the seat of the Bohemian government for over 1000 years. From Metro A: Hradčanská, cross the tram tracks and turn left onto

Tychonova, which leads to the newly renovated **Royal Summer Palace**. The main castle entrance is at the other end of the lush **Royal Garden** (Královská zahrada), where the Singing Fountain spouts and chimes. Before exploring, pass the main gate to see the **Šternberg Palace**, which houses art from the National Gallery. (*Metro A: Malostranská. Take trams #22 or 23 to Pražský Hrad and go down U Prašného Mostu. Open Apr.-Oct. daily 9am-5pm; Nov.-Mar. 9am-4pm. Buy tickets opposite St. Vitus's Cathedral, inside the castle walls. 1-day ticket valid at Royal Crypt, Cathedral and Powder Tower, Old Royal Palace, and the Basilica. 220Kč, students 110Kč.*)

ST. VITUS'S CATHEDRAL. Inside the castle walls stands the colossal St. Vitus's Cathedral (Katedrála sv. Víta), which looks Gothic but was in fact finished in 1929, 600 years after construction began. To the right of the high altar stands the silver **Tomb of St. Jan Nepomucký**. In the main church, the walls of **St. Wenceslas's Chapel** (Svatováclavská kaple) are lined with precious stones and a painting cycle depicting the legend of Wenceslas. Climb the 287 steps of the **Great South Tower** for the best view of the city, or descend underground to the **Royal Crypt**, which holds the tomb of Charles IV.

OLD ROYAL PALACE. The Old Royal Palace (Starý Královský Palác) is to the right of the cathedral, behind the Old Provost's House and the statue of St. George. The lengthy **Vladislav Hall** once hosted jousting competitions. Upstairs is the **Chancellery of Bohemia**, where the Second Defenestration of Prague took place.

ST. GEORGE'S BASILICA AND ENVIRONS. Behind the cathedral and across the courtyard from the Old Royal Palace stands St. George's Basilica (Bazilika sv. Jiří). The **National Gallery of Bohemian Art**, which has art ranging from Gothic to Baroque, is in the adjacent convent. (*Open Tu-Su 10am-6pm. 100Kč, students 50Kč.*) **Jiřská** street begins to the right of the basilica. Halfway down, tiny **Golden Lane** (Zlatá ulička) heads off to the right; alchemists once worked here, and Kafka later lived at #22.

OUTER PRAGUE

The city's outskirts are packed with greenery, churches, and panoramic vistas, all peacefully tucked away from hordes of tourists. **Vyšehrad** is the former haunt of Prague's 19th-century Romantics; quiet walkways wind between crumbling stone walls to one of the Czech Republic's most celebrated sites, **Vyšehrad Cemetery,** home to the remains of composer Antonín Dvořák. The oldest monastery in Bohemia, **Břevnov Monastery,** was founded in AD993 by King Boleslav II and St. Adalbert, each of whom was guided by a divine dream to build a monastery atop a bubbling stream. The stream leads to a pond to the right of **St. Margaret's Church** (Bazilika sv. Markéty) within the complex. (*From Metro A: Malostranská, take tram #22 uphill to Břevnovský klášter. Church open daily 7:30am-6pm.*) The traditional **Prague Market** (Pražskátrznice) has acres of stalls selling all kinds of wares. (*Take tram #3 or 14 from Nám. Republiky to Vozovna Kobylisy and get off at Pražskátrznice. Open daily.*)

🏛 MUSEUMS

The city's museums often have striking facades but mediocre collections. Still, a few quirky museums are worth a visit.

MUCHA MUSEUM. The museum is devoted to the work of Alfons Mucha, the Czech Republic's most celebrated artist, who composed some of the pioneering brushstrokes of the Art Nouveau movement. (*Panská 7. Metro A or B: Můstek. Walk up Václavské nám. toward the St. Wenceslas statue. Go left onto Jindřišská and again onto Panská. ☎221 451 333; www.mucha.cz. Open daily 10am-6pm. 120Kč, students 60Kč.*)

MUSEUM OF MEDIEVAL TORTURE INSTRUMENTS. The collection and highly detailed explanations are guaranteed to nauseate. *(Mostécka 21. Metro A: Malostranská. Follow Letenská from the Metro and turn left on Mostécka. Open daily 10am-10pm. 120Kč, students 100Kč.)* In the same building, the **Exhibition of Spiders and Scorpions** shows live venomous spiders and scorpions in their natural habitats. *(Open daily 10am-10pm. 100Kč, children 80Kč.)*

NATIONAL GALLERY. The massive collection of the National Gallery (Národní Galerie) is spread around nine different locations; the notable Šternberský palác and Klášter sv. Jiří are in the **Prague Castle** (see p. 260). The **Trade Fair Palace and the Gallery of Modern Art** (Veletržní palác a Galerie moderního umwní) exhibits an impressive collection of 20th-century Czech and European art. *(Dukelských hrinů 47. Metro C: Holešovice. All open Su and T-Sa 10am-6pm. 150Kč, students 70Kč.)*

MUSEUM OF COMMUNISM. This new gallery is committed to exposing the flaws of the Communist system that suppressed the Czech people from 1948-1989. It features 3-D objects, a model factory, and an interrogation office. *(Na Příkopě 10. Metro A: Můstek. Open daily 9am-9pm. 180Kč, students 140Kč.)*

🎵 ENTERTAINMENT

For concerts and performances, consult *Threshold, Do města-Downtown* (both free at many cafes and restaurants), *The Pill,* or *The Prague Post.* Most performances start at 7pm and offer standby tickets 30min. beforehand. Between mid-May and early June, the **Prague Spring Festival** draws musicians from around the world. For tickets, try **Bohemia Ticket International,** Malé nám. 13, next to Čedok. (☎224 227 832; www.ticketsbti.cz. Open M-F 9am-5pm, Sa 9am-2pm.) The **National Theater** (Národní divadlo), Národní 2/4, stages drama, opera, and ballet. (☎114 901 448. Metro B: Národní třída. Box office open M-F 10am-6pm, Sa-Su 10am-12:30pm, 3-6pm, and 30min. before performances. 100-1000Kč.) **Estates Theater** (Stavovské divadlo), Ovocný trg 1, is on the pedestrian Na Příkopě. (Metro A or B: Můstek.) Mozart's *Don Giovanni* premiered here; shows today are mostly classic theater. Use the National Theater box office, or show up 30min. before the performance. The **Marionette Theater** (Říše loutek), Žatecká 1, stages a hilarious marionette version of *Don Giovanni.* (Metro A: Staroměstská. Performances June-July Su-Tu and Th-Sa 5 and 8pm. Box office open daily 10am-8pm. 490Kč, students 390Kč.)

🍷 NIGHTLIFE

With some of the best beers in the world on tap, it's no surprise that pubs and beer halls are Prague's most popular nighttime hangouts. Tourists have overrun the city center, so authentic pub experiences are now largely restricted to the suburbs and outlying Metro stops. Although dance clubs abound, Prague is not a clubbing city—locals prefer the many jazz and rock hangouts scattered about the city.

BARS

▨ **Vinárna U Sudu,** Vodičkova 10. Metro A or B: Můstek. Cross Václavské nám. to Vodičkova and follow the curve left. Infinite labyrinth of cavernous cellars. Red wine 120Kč per 1L. Open M-F 1pm-midnight, Sa-Su 2pm-midnight.

▨ **Kozička** (The Little Goat), Kozí 1. Metro A: Staroměstská. This giant cellar bar is always packed; you'll know why after your first 0.5L of *Krušovice* (18Kč). Czech 20-somethings stay all night. Open M-F noon-4am, Sa-Su 6pm-4am.

U Fleků, Křemencova 11. Metro B: Národní třída. Turn right on Spálená away from Národní, right on Myslíkova, and then right again on Křemencova. The oldest beer hall in Prague. Home-brewed beer 49Kč. Open daily 9am-11pm.

Pivnice u Sv. Tomáše, Letenská 12 (☎257 531 835). Metro A: Malostranská. Walk downhill on Letenská. While meat roasts on a spit, the mighty dungeons echo with boisterous revelry and gushing toasts. Order meats a day in advance, 350-400Kč. Beer 40Kč. Live brass band daily 7-11pm. Open daily 11:30am-midnight. MC/V.

Bugsy's, Parížská 10. Sophisticated, American style speakeasy serving the tastiest mixed drinks in town. Cocktail menu so thick it's hardcover (60-200Kč). When the upscale munchies hit, sushi awaits. Open daily 7pm-2am. Live Jazz M nights.

Cafe Marquis de Sade, Melnicka 5. Metro B: Nám. Republiky. Spacious bar decorated in rich red velvet. Happy Hour M-F 4-6pm. Velvet beer 27-35Kč. Open daily noon-2am.

Zanzibar, Saská 6. Metro A: Malostranská. Head down Mostecká toward the Charles Bridge, turn right on Lázeňská, and turn left on Saská. The tastiest, priciest, and most exotic cocktails this side of the Vltava (110-150Kč). Open daily 5pm-3am.

Molly Malone's, U obecního dvora 4. Metro A: Staroměstská. Overturned sewing machines serve as tables in this pub. Small groups can head to the loft. Guinness 80Kč. Open Su-Th 11am-1am, F-Sa 11am-2am.

Jo's Bar and Garáž, Malostranské nám. 7. Metro A: Malostranská. All-Anglophone with foosball, darts, cards, and a DJ. Beer 30Kč during Happy Hour (6-10pm). Open daily 11am-2am.

CLUBS AND DISCOS

■ **Radost FX,** Bělehradská 120 (www.radostfx.cz). Metro C: I.P. Pavlova. Plays the hippest techno, jungle, and house. Creative drinks. Cover 80-150Kč. Open M-Sa 10pm-late.

Jazz Club Železná, Železná 16. Metro A or B: Staroměstská. Vaulted cellar bar showcases live jazz daily. Beer 30Kč. Cover 120-150Kč. Shows 9-11:30pm. Open daily 3pm-1am. AmEx/MC/V.

Roxy, Dlouhá 33. Metro B: Nám. Republiky. In the same building as the Dlouhá 33 Traveler's Hostel (p. 255). Experimental DJs and theme nights. Crowds hang out on the huge staircases. Cover 100-350Kč. Open M-Tu and Th-Sa 9pm-late.

Karlovy Lázně, Novotného lávka 1. Four levels of themed dance floors under the Charles Bridge. Cover 100Kč, 50Kč before 10pm and after 4am. Open daily 9pm-late.

Palác Akropolis, Kubelíkova 27 (www.palacakropolis.cz). Metro A: Jiřího z Poděbrad. Head down Slavíkova and turn right onto Kubelíkova. Live bands several times a week. Top Czech act *Psí vojáci* is an occasional visitor. Open daily 10pm-5am.

U staré paní, Michalská 9. Metro A or B: Můstek. Some of Prague's finest jazz vocalists in a tiny yet classy venue. Shows daily 9pm-midnight. Cover 160Kč, includes 1 drink. Open for shows 7pm-2am.

Ungelt, Tyn 2. Metro A: Staroměstská. Subterranean vault with live jazz daily from 9pm-midnight. (Cover 160Kč). Or, listen from the pub for free. Open daily noon-midnight.

GAY AND LESBIAN NIGHTLIFE

At any of the places below, you can pick up a copy of *Amigo* (69Kč), the most thorough guide to gay life in the Czech Republic with a lot in English, or *Gaýčko* (60Kč), a glossier piece of work written mostly in Czech.

Friends, Náprstkova 1 (☎221 635 408; www.friends-prague.cz). Lively cellar bar in the heart of Staré Město. Slightly touristy but always busy. Friendly, English-speaking bartenders are good sources for info on hot spots. Czech music party W nights. Internet access 2Kč per min (4-8pm). Open daily 3pm-3am.

Tingl Tangl, Karolíny Světlé 12. Metro B: Národní třída. Under the archway on the left, this gay club draws a diverse crowd for its cabarets. Cover 120Kč. Open W-Sa 9pm-5am, with shows after midnight.

A Club, Milíčova 25. Metro C: Hlavní nádraží. Take tram #5, 9, 26, or 55 uphill and get off at Lipsanká. A favorite lesbian nightspot. Men are free to enter, but expect funny looks. Beer 20Kč. Open daily 7pm-6am.

◪ DAYTRIPS FROM PRAGUE

TEREZÍN (THERESIENSTADT). In 1941, when Terezín became a concentration camp, Nazi propaganda films touted the area as a resort where Jews would live a normal life. In reality, over 30,000 died here, some of starvation and disease, others in death chambers; another 85,000 Jews were transported to death camps further east. The **Ghetto Museum,** around the corner, to the left of the bus stop in town, sets Terezín in the wider context of WWII. (Open Apr.-Sept. daily 9am-6pm; Oct.-Mar. 9am-5:30pm. Tickets to museum, barracks, and small fortress 180Kč, students 160Kč.) Across the river is the **Small Fortress,** which was used as a Gestapo prison. (Open Apr.-Sept. daily 8am-6pm; Oct.-Mar. 8am-4:30pm.) The **cemetery** has tributes left by the victims' descendants. Men should cover their heads when visiting. (Open Mar.-Nov. Su-F 10am-5pm. Free.) The furnaces of the **crematorium** are temporarily closed due to flooding. Terezín has been repopulated to about half of its former size; families now live in the barracks and supermarkets occupy former Nazi offices. A **bus** runs from Prague Florenc station (1hr., 9 per day, 59Kč); get off at the Terezín stop, where the **tourist office** sells a 30Kč map. (Open Su and Tu-Sa 9am-12:30pm and 1-4pm.)

KUTNÁ HORA. East of Prague, the former mining town of Kutná Hora (Mining Mountain) has a history as morbid as the **bone church** that has made the city famous. Founded in the late 13th century when lucky miners hit a vein of silver, the city boomed with greedy diggers, but the Black Plague halted the fortune-seekers dead in their tracks. When the graveyard became overcrowded, the Cistercian Order built a chapel to hold bodies. In a fit of whimsy (or insanity), one monk began designing floral shapes out of pelvises and crania; he never finished, but the artist František Rint eventually completed the project in 1870 with the bones of over 40,000 people, including femur crosses and a grotesque chandelier made from every kind of bone in the human body. (Open Apr.-Oct. daily 8am-6pm; Nov.-Mar. 9am-noon and 1-4pm. 30Kč, students 20Kč.) Take a **bus** (1½hr., 6 per day, 54-64Kč) from Prague Florenc station. Exit left onto Benešova, continue through the rotary until it becomes Vítězná, then go left on Zámecká.

KARLŠTEJN. A gem of the Bohemian countryside, Karlštejn is a turreted fortress built by Charles IV in the 14th century to store his crown jewels and holy relics. (Open July-Aug. Su and Tu-Sa 9am-6pm; May-June and Sept. 9am-5pm; Apr.-Oct. 9am-4pm; Nov.-Mar. 9am-3pm. 7-8 English tours per day; 200Kč, students 100Kč.) The **Chapel of the Holy Cross** is inlaid with precious stones and 129 apocalyptic paintings by medieval artist Master Theodorik. (☎(02) 74 00 81 54; reservace@spusc.cz. Open Su and Tu-Sa 9am-5pm. Tours by reservation only; 300Kč, students 100Kč.) The area also has beautiful **hiking** trails. A **train** runs to Praha-Hlavní (45min., every hr., 55Kč). To reach the castle, turn right out of the station and go left over the modern bridge; turn right, then walk through the village.

MĚLNÍK. Fertile Mělník is known for its wine-making, supposedly perfected about 1000 years ago when St. Wenceslas, the patron saint of Bohemian wine-makers, was initiated in its vineyards. In one day, you can tour the stately Renaissance castle, sample its homemade wines, and lunch in the old schoolhouse overlooking the Říp Valley. Wine tasting (110Kč) with Martin, the wine master, is available by reservation. (☎206 62 21 21; www.lobkowicz-melnik.cz. Castle open daily 10am-6pm. Tours 60Kč, students 40Kč.) Buses run from Prague Holešovice (45min., every 30min., 32Kč). From the station, make a right onto Bezručova and head up the left fork onto Kpt. Jaroše, to the town center. Enter the Old Town Square; the castle is down Svatovaclvska to your left.

ČESKÝ RÁJ NATIONAL PRESERVE. The narrow sandstone pillars and deep gorges of **Prachovské skály** (Prachovské Rocks) make for climbs and hikes with stunning views. Prachovské skály also boasts the **Pelíšek** rock pond and the ruins of the 14th-century rock castle **Pařez**. (Open Apr.-Oct. daily 8am-5pm; swimming May-Aug. 25Kč, students 10Kč.) The 588 acres of the park are interwoven by a dense network of **trails**; both green and yellow signs guide hikers to additional sights, while triangles indicate vistas off the main trails. Red signs mark the "Golden Trail," which connects Prachovské skály to **Hrubá Skála** (Rough Rock), a rock town surrounding a hilltop castle from which hikers enjoy the best view of the sandstone rocks. From the Hrubá Skála castle, the red trail leads up to what remains of **Wallenstein Castle** (Valdštejnský hrad). **Buses** run from Prague-Florenc station to **Jičín** (1¾hr., 7 per day, 86Kč), where other buses go to Prachovské Skály and Český Ráj (15min., several per day, 9Kč). Buses to Český Ráj sometimes run less frequently than scheduled; you can also walk from Jičín along a relatively easy 6km trail beginning at Motel Rumcajs, Koněva 331.

WEST AND SOUTH BOHEMIA

West Bohemia overflows with curative springs; over the centuries, emperors and intellectuals alike have soaked in the waters of Karlovy Vary (also known as Carlsbad). Those seeking good beer visit the *Pilsner Urquell* brewery in Plzeň or the *Budvar* brewery in České Budějovice. More rustic than West Bohemia, South Bohemia is filled with brooks, virgin forests, and castle ruins.

KARLOVY VARY (CARLSBAD)

A stroll through the spa district or into the hills of Karlovy Vary (pop. 55,000) reveals why this lovely town developed into one of the great "salons" of Europe, frequented by Johann Sebastian Bach, Peter the Great, Sigmund Freud, and Karl Marx. Although older Germans and Russians seeking the therapeutic powers of the springs are the main visitors, film stars from around the world and fans from around the country also fill the town for the International Film Festival each July.

▐▌ TRANSPORTATION AND PRACTICAL INFORMATION. Buses, much more convenient than trains, run from Dolní nádraží, on Západní, to Plzeň (1½hr., 12 per day, 60-80Kč) and Prague (2½hr., 25 per day, 100-130Kč); buy tickets on board. To reach the town center from the bus station, turn left on Západní, continue past the Becher building, and bear right on T. G. Masaryka, which runs parallel to the other main thoroughfare, Dr. Davida Bechera. For a Centrum **taxi,** call ☎353 223 000. **Infocentrum,** Lazenska 1, next to Mill Colonnade, sells maps (35-169Kč) and theater tickets (60-400Kč) and books rooms (from 400Kč) in town. (☎353 224 097. Open Jan.-Oct. M-F 8am-6pm, Sa-Su 10am-6pm; Nov.-Dec. M-F 7am-5pm.) *Promenáda*, a monthly booklet with event schedules and other info, is available here and at kiosks throughout town (15Kč). The **post office** is at T. G. Masaryka 1. (Open M-F 7:30am-7pm, Sa 8am-1pm, Su 8am-noon.) **Postal Code:** 360 01.

⌂⍟ ACCOMMODATIONS AND FOOD. City Info ❸, T. G. Masaryka 9, which has an English-speaking staff, offers pension singles from 600Kč and hotel doubles from 860Kč. (☎353 223 351. Open daily 9am-6pm.) Next to the post office at the corner of Zahradní and T.G. Masaryka, ⌗**Pension Romania ❸**, Zahradní 49 offers luxurious, modern rooms right on the Teplá. (☎353 222 822. Breakfast included. Singles 800Kč; doubles 1430Kč, with view of river 1580Kč; triples 1845Kč. Students 715Kč. Oct.-Dec. 15-30% discount.) Follow the directions from the bus station to T.G. Masaryka and bear right at the post office to reach **Hotel Kosmos ❹**, Zahradní 39, in the center of the spa district. (☎353 225 476. Singles from 850Kč; doubles from 950Kč. Oct.-Apr. 100Kč reduction.) Karlovy Vary is known for its sweet *oplatky* (spa wafers); try them at a street vendor (5Kč). Trendy **Retro ❷**, T.G. Masaryka 18, has a diverse menu. (Entrees 70-200Kč. Open M-Th 10am-1am, F-Sa 10am-3am, Su 11am-1am.) The **supermarket**, Horova 1, is in the large building with the "Městská tržnice" sign, behind the local bus station. (Open M-F 6am-7pm, Sa 7am-5pm, Su 9am-5pm.)

◙⍟ SIGHTS AND ENTERTAINMENT. The **spa district**, which overflows with springs, baths, and colonnades, starts at the Victorian **Bath 5** (Lázně 5), Smetanovy Sady 1, across the street from the post office. (☎353 222 536; www.spa5.cz. Thermal baths 355Kč. Underwater massages 495Kč. Reserve ahead. Pool and sauna open M-F 8am-9pm, Sa 8am-6pm, Su 10am-6pm. 90Kč.) Mlýnské nábř. follows the Teplá River to **Bath 3**, which offers full-body massages for 755Kč. (Treatments daily 7-11:30am and noon-2:30pm.) Next door, the imposing **Mill Colonnade** (Mlýnská kolonáda) shelters five springs. Farther down is the **Zawojski House**, Trižiště 9, a cream-and-gold Art Nouveau building that now houses Živnostenská Banka. Two doors down, **Strudel Spring** (Vřídlo pramen), inside the **Strudel Colonnade** (Vřídelní kolonáda), is Karlovy Vary's hottest and highest-shooting spring, spouting 30L of 72°C (162°F) water each second. (Open daily 6am-7pm.)

Follow Stará Louka to find signs pointing you to the funicular (every 15min. 9am-7pm; 30Kč, round-trip 50Kč), which leads to the **Diana Observatory** and a magnificent panorama of the city. (Observatory tower open daily 9am-7pm. 10Kč.) *Promenáda* (see above) lists each month's concerts and performances, including info about the **International Film Festival**, which screens independent films in early July. Tickets sell out quickly; go to the box office early. **Routes Berlin**, Jaltská 7, off Bechera, attracts a hip young crowd with live music and a seductive red interior. (Mixed drinks 35-70Kč. Open daily noon-midnight.)

◪ DAYTRIP FROM KARLOVY VARY: PLZEŇ. A beer lover's perfect day begins at Plzeň's legendary ⌗**Pilsner Urquell Brewery** (Měšťanský Pivovar Plzeňský Prazdroj), where knowledgeable guides lead visitors to the fermentation cellars for samples. After the tour, take a lunch break at the on-site beerhouse **Na spilce**, which pours *Pilsner* for 20Kč per pint. The entrance to the complex is across the Radbuza River from Staré Město, where Pražská becomes U Prazdroje. (70 min. tours June-Aug. daily 10:30am and 12:30, 2, and 3:30pm; Sept.-May 12:30pm. 120Kč, students 60Kč.) From the square, go down Pražská and turn left on Perlová to visit the ⌗**Brewery Museum**, Veleslavínova 6, which traces the history of brewing from ancient times. (Open daily 10am-6pm. 60Kč, students 30Kč.) Stroll through the town center and the **Kopecký gardens** (Kopeckého sady) at the end of Františkánská, then cap off the day with dinner at **U Salzmannů ❸**, Pražská 8, the city's oldest beerhouse. (Entrees 72-179Kč. Beer 20Kč. Open M-Sa 11am-11pm, Su 11am-10pm.) **Buses** leave from Husova 58 for Karlovy Vary (1¾hr., 17 per day, 59-76Kč) and Prague (2hr., every hr., 60-66Kč). To reach the main square, turn left on Husova, which becomes Smetanovy sady, then turn left on Bedřicha Smetany (15min.).

ČESKÉ BUDĚJOVICE

České Budějovice (pop. 99,000) is a great base for exploring the surrounding region's many attractions. The town was known as Budweis in the 19th century, inspiring the name of the popular but pale North American Budweiser, which bears little relation to the malty local *Budvar*. Today, rivalry still lingers between Anheuser-Busch and the **Budvar Brewery,** Karoliny Světlé 4, which can be reached from the center by buses #2 and 4. (Tours 9am-4pm. English tours 92Kč, students 70Kč.) **Staré Město** (Old Town) centers around the gigantic **Náměstí Přemysla Otakara II** and is surrounded by colorful Renaissance and Baroque buildings. More than 100 motorcycles dating from the early 1900s to today are displayed at the **Museum of Motorcycles** in Piaristicke Nám. (Open Su and Tu-Sa 10am-1:30pm and 2-6pm. 40Kč, students 20Kč.)

Buses run to: Brno (4½hr., 6 per day, 170-220Kč); Český Krumlov (45min., 15 per day, 26Kč); and Prague (2½hr., 10 per day, 120-144Kč). **Trains** leave from opposite the bus station. The TIC **tourist office,** Nám. Otakara II 2, books private rooms. (☎/fax 635 94 80; infocb@c-budejovice.cz. Open May-Sept. M-F 8:30am-6pm, Sa 8:30am-5pm, Su 10am-4pm; Oct.-Apr. M-F 9am-5pm, Sa 9am-3pm.) To reach the center of town from the train station, turn right on Nádražní, take a left at the first crosswalk, and follow the pedestrian street Lannova třída, which becomes Kanovnická. To reach the beautifully furnished **AT Penzion ❸,** Dukelská 15, from Nám. Otakara II, make a right down Dr. Stejskala. At the first intersection, turn left and follow Siroka, veering right on Dukelská. Follow Dukelská past Na Sadech and Alesova. (☎386 351 598. Rooms with private baths, TV, and fridge. Breakfast 50Kč. Singles 600Kč; doubles 800Kč.) **Večerka grocery** is at Palachého 10; enter on Hroznova. (Open M-F 7am-8pm, Sa 7am-1pm, Su 8am-8pm.) Under Grand Hotel Zvon, the brewhouse **Česká Rychta ❸,** Nám. Otakara II 30, has a patio overlooking the square. (Entrees 68-265Kč. Open M-Sa 10am-midnight, Su 10am-11pm.) **Postal Code:** 37001.

🔁 DAYTRIPS FROM ČESKÉ BUDĚJOVICE: HLUBOKÁ NAD VLTAVOU.

Hluboká's extraordinary **castle** owes its appearance to Eleonora Schwarzenberg, who, after visiting England in the mid-19th century, turned the castle into a fairy-tale stronghold modeled after Windsor Castle. A 45min. tour winds through 12 of the castle's 141 ornate rooms. (Open July-Aug. daily 9am-noon and 12:30-5pm; Apr. and Sept.-Oct. Su and Tu-Sa 9am-4:30pm; May-June Su and Tu-Sa 9am-5pm. English tours 150Kč, students 80Kč. Czech tours 80/40Kč.) **Buses** run from České Budějovice (25min., 14Kč) frequently during the week but less often on weekends; look for buses with Týn nad Vltavou as their final destination, and get off at *Pod Kostolem.* Head left on Nad parkovištěm, take a right onto Zborovskám, and then turn right onto Bezručova and head uphill, bearing right at the fork.

ČESKÝ KRUMLOV

This once hidden gem of the Czech Republic has finally been discovered—some might say besieged—by tourists seeking refuge from Prague's hectic pace and overcrowded streets. Český Krumlov (pop. 15,000) still won't disappoint those who wander its medieval streets, raft down the meandering Vltava, and explore the enormous 13th-century castle that looms over it all. Days could be spent exploring and enjoying this UNESCO-protected town and its surrounding hills. Apart from hiking, horseback riding, and kayaking, the town lures visitors with affordable accommodations and burgeoning nightlife.

■ ▨ TRANSPORTATION AND PRACTICAL INFORMATION. Frequent **buses** arrive from České Budějovice (45min., 12-25 per day, 26Kč) and Prague (3hr., 8 per day, 120-145Kč). To get to the main square, **Náměstí Svornosti,** head up the path from the back of the terminal, to the right of stops #20-25. Go downhill at its intersection with Kaplická, then cross the highway and head onto Horní, which leads into the square. The **tourist office,** Nám. Svornosti 1, books rooms in pensions (from 600Kč) as well as cheaper private rooms. (☎380 704 622; www.ckrumlov.cz/infocentrum. Open July-Aug. daily 9am-8pm; May-June and Sept. daily 9am-7pm; Oct.-Apr. 9am-6pm.) **Postal Code:** 38101.

▨ ▣ ACCOMMODATIONS AND FOOD. To reach ▨**Krumlov House ❶,** Rooseveltova 68, which is run by an American expat couple, follow the directions to the square from the station; turn left from onto Rooseveltova after the lights and follow the signs. (☎380 711 935; www.krumlevhostel.com. Dorms 250Kč; doubles 600Kč; suites 750Kč.) The comfy beds at **Hostel 99 ❶,** Věžní 99, were acquired from a 4-star hotel. From Nám. Svornosti, head down Radniční, which becomes Latrán; at the red and yellow gate, turn right onto Věžní. (☎380 712 812; www.hostel99.com. Bike rental. Dorms 300Kč; doubles 700Kč.) Take Panská off of Nám. Svornosti and turn right on Soukenická to reach the conveniently located **Traveller's Hostel ❶,** Soukenická 43, one of the most social hostels in town. (☎380 711 345; www.travellers.cz. Kitchen, lounge, satellite TV, pool table, and foosball for guest use. Laundry 100Kč. **Internet** access 1.5Kč per min. 4-8 bed dorms 270Kč, 7th night free.) From the right-hand corner of Nám. Svornosti, across from the tourist office, angle left onto Kájovská. Just down the street is **Na louži ❷,** Kájovská 66, which serves generous portions of Czech dishes. (Entrees 59-135Kč. Veggie options 54-71Kč. Open daily 10am-10pm.) **Krcma v Šatlavské ❸,** Horní 157, just off the square on the corner of Šatlavská and Masná, features big hunks of meat cooked over a roaring wooden fire. (Meat 95-210Kč. Open daily noon-midnight.) Get groceries at **NOVA,** Linecká 49. (Open M-Sa 7am-6pm, Su 8am-6pm.)

◉ ▣ SIGHTS AND NIGHTLIFE. From Nám. Svornosti, take Radniční across the Vltava as it becomes Latrán to reach the main entrance of the **castle,** whose stone courtyards are free to the public. Two tours cover different parts of the lavish interior, including a frescoed ballroom, a splendid Baroque theater, and Renaissance-style rooms. The eerie galleries of the **crypts** showcase distorted sculptures. Climb the 162 steps of the tower for a fabulous view. (Castle open June-Aug. Su and Tu-Sa 9am-noon and 1-6pm; May and Sept. 9am-noon and 1-5pm; Apr. and Oct. 9am-noon and 1-4pm. 1hr. English tours 140-50Kč, students 70-75Kč. Crypts open June-Aug. daily 10am-5pm. 20Kč, students 10Kč. Tower open June-Aug. daily 9am-5:30pm; May and Sept. 9am-4:30pm; Apr. and Oct. 9:30am-4:30pm. 30Kč, students 20Kč.) The castle gardens also host the outdoor **Revolving South Bohemia Theater,** where operas and plays are performed in Czech during the summer. (Open June-early Sept. Shows at 9:30pm. Tickets 224-390Kč; purchase at the tourist office.) The Austrian painter Egon Schiele (1890-1918) lived in Český Krumlov—until residents ran him out for painting burghers' daughters in the nude. The ▨**Egon Schiele International Cultural Center,** Široká 70-72, displays his work, along with paintings by other 20th-century Central European artists. (Open daily 10am-6pm. 180Kč, students 105Kč.)

Rybárška is lined with lively bars and cafes, including **U Hada** (Snake Bar), Rybárška 37 (open M-Th 7pm-3am, F-Sa 7pm-4am, Su 7pm-2am) and **U baby,** Rooseveltova 66 (open Su and Tu-Sa 6pm-late).

CZECH REPUBLIC

⚑ OUTDOORS. Whether you'd like to float down the Vltava in a kayak or a canoe or bike through the Bohemian countryside to the 13th century **Zlatá Koruna** monastery, stop by **Vltava,** Kájovská 62 for equipment rental and info. Go horseback riding at **Jezdecký klub Slupenec,** Slupenec 1; from the center, follow Horní to the highway, take the second left on Křížová, and take the red trail to Slupenec. (☎ 380 711 052; www.jk-slupenec.cz. 250Kč per hr. Call ahead. Open Tu-Sa 9am-6pm.)

MORAVIA

Wine-making Moravia makes up the easternmost third of the Czech Republic. Home to the country's finest folk-singing and two leading universities, it's also the birthplace of a number of Eastern European notables, including Tomáš G. Masaryk, first president of Czechoslovakia, psychoanalyst Sigmund Freud, and chemist Johann Gregor Mendel, who founded modern genetics in a Brno monastery.

BRNO

The country's second-largest city, Brno (pop. 388, 900) has been an international marketplace since the 13th century. Today, global corporations compete with family-owned produce stands, while historic churches soften the glare of casinos and clubs. The result is a dynamic city that epitomizes the modern Czech Republic.

⌘🔁 TRANSPORTATION AND PRACTICAL INFORMATION. Trains (☎ 542 214 803) go to: Bratislava (2hr., 8 per day, 250Kč); Budapest (4½hr., 2 per day, 945Kč); Prague (3hr., 16 per day, 294Kč); and Vienna (2hr., daily, 536Kč). From the main exit, cross the tram lines on Nádražní, walk left, and then go right on Masarykova to reach **Náměstí Svobody,** the main square. **Buses** (☎ 543 217 733) leave from the corner of Zvonařka and Plotní for Prague (3hr., several per day, 112-167Kč) and Vienna (2½hr., 3 per day, 250Kč). The **tourist office** (Kulturní a informační centrum města Brna), Radnická 8, inside the town hall, books rooms (from 400Kč). From Nám. Svobody, head down Masarykova and turn right onto Průchodní. (☎ 542 211 090; fax 42 21 07 58. Open M-F 8am-6pm, Sa-Su 9am-5pm.) **Internet Center Cafe,** Masarykova 2/24, has speedy computers in the center of town. (40Kč per hr. Open daily 8am-midnight.) **Postal Code:** 601 00.

📍🏠 ACCOMMODATIONS AND FOOD. From the train station, take Masarykova and turn right on Josefská; at the fork, veer right onto Novobranská to reach the new, centrally located **Hotel Astorka ❸,** at #3. (☎ 542 510 370; astorka@jamu.cz. Open July 1-Sept. 31. Doubles 840Kč per person, students 420Kč; triples 930/474Kč.) The beautifully furnished rooms in **Pension U Leopolda ❸,** Jeneweinova 49, have private baths. Take tram #12 or bus #A12 to *Komarov,* go left on Studnici, and turn right on Jeneweinova. (☎ 545 233 036. Singles 775Kč; doubles 1250Kč; triples 1450Kč.) **Fischehabsburgr Cafe ❸,** Masarykova 8/10, is an uber-sleek hotspot with ingenious entrees (85-199Kč), massive salads (53-140Kč), and phenomenal breakfasts. (Open M-F 8am-10pm, Sa 9am-11pm, Su 10am-10pm.) Enjoy a Czech feast in a medieval atmosphere at **Dávně Časy ❸,** Starobrněnská 20, up Starobrněnská from Zelny trh. (Entrees 95-219Kč. Open daily 11am-11pm.) A **Tesco supermarket** is behind the train station. (Open M-F 7am-8pm, Sa 7am-7pm, Su 8am-6pm.)

🎦🎵 SIGHTS AND NIGHTLIFE. In the 18th century, monks at the **Capuchin Monastery Crypt** (Hrobka Kapucínského kláštera), just left of Masarykova from the train station, developed a burial technique that preserved more than 100 bodies. (Open May-Sept. M-Sa 9am-noon and 2-4:30pm, Su 11-11:45am and 2-4:30pm. 40Kč, students 20Kč.) From Nám. Svobody, take Zámečnická and go right on Panenská; after Husova, head uphill to reach ■**Špilberk Castle** (Hrad Špilberk), which earned a reputation as the cruelest prison in Habsburg Europe. (Open May-Sept. Su and Tu-Sa 9am-6pm; Oct. and Apr. 9am-5pm; Nov.-Mar. Su and W-Sa 9am-5pm. 100Kč, students 50Kč.) The newly expanded **Mendelianum**, Mendlovo nám. 1a, documents the life and work of Johann Gregor Mendel, who founded modern genetics in a Brno monastery. (Open Su and Tu-Sa 10am-6pm. 80Kč, students 40Kč.) In summer, **techno raves** are announced by posters. After performances in the attached Merry Goose Theater, artsy crowds gather at **Divadelní hospoda Veselá husa**, Zelný trh. 9. (Open M-F 11am-1am, Sa-Su 3pm-1am.) Students frequent dance club **Mersey**, Minská 14. Take tram #3 or 11 from *Česká* to *Tábor*. (Beer 20Kč. Open M-Sa 8pm-late.)

⚡ DAYTRIPS FROM BRNO

MORAVSKÝ KRAS. The Moravský Kras cave network lies in the forested hills of Southern Moravia. The tour of ■**Punkevní** passes magnificent stalactites and stalagmites to emerge at **Stepmother Abyss** (Propast Macocha), then finishes with a chilly boat ride down the eerie underground **Punkva River.** (Tours Apr.-Sept. 8:20am-3:50pm; Jan.-Mar. and Oct.-Dec. 8:40am-2pm. Buy tickets at the Skalní Mlýn bus stop or at the entrance; arrive early, as tours sell out quickly. 100Kč, students 50Kč.) BVV in Brno, Starobrněnská 20, organizes afternoon tours of Punkevní. (☎542 217 745. 640Kč per person, 4 person minimum.) Other caves in the area are also open to visitors, and the Moravský Kras Reserve has many leisurely **hiking trails.** For a great view of Stepmother Abyss, take a **cable car** (60Kč, students 40Kč) to the top. A **train** runs from Brno to Blansko (30min., 7 per day, round-trip 43Kč). Take the bus (15min., 5 per day, 8Kč) from the Blansko station to Skalní Mlýn or hike the 8km green trail where there is a ticket and **info office** (☎516 410 024; www.cavemk.cz) for the caves.

TELČ. The town's Italian aura results from the crew of artists and craftsmen that the town's ruler imported from Genoa in 1546. As you cross the cobblestone footbridge to the main square—flanked by long arcades of peach gables and timeworn terra-cotta roofs—it's easy to see why UNESCO designated the gingerbread town a World Heritage Monument. Two tours of Telč's **castle** are available. The more interesting *trasa A* leads you through Renaissance hallways, past the old chapel, and under extravagant ceilings; *trasa B* goes through rooms decorated in later styles. (Open May-Aug. Su and Tu-Sa 9am-noon and 1-5pm; Mar.-Apr. and Sept.-Oct. closes 1hr. earlier. Tours 70Kč, students 35Kč; English tour 140Kč.) Rent a **rowboat** from Půjčovna lodí to view the castle and town from the swan-filled lake. (Open June 20-Aug. daily 10am-6pm. 20Kč per 30min.) **Buses** running between Brno and České Budějovice stop at Telč (2hr., 8 per day, 88Kč). From the station, follow the walkway and turn right on Tyršova, left on Masarykovo, and pass under the archway on the right to reach **Náměstí Zachariáše Hradce,** the main square. The **tourist office**, Nám. Zachariáše Hradce 10, is in the town hall. (☎567 243 145; www.telc-etc.cz. Open June-mid Sept. M-F 8am-5pm, Sa-Su 10am-5pm; mid-Sept.-May M-F 8am-3pm.)

DENMARK
(DANMARK)

Like Thumbelina, the heroine of native son Hans Christian Andersen's fairy tales, Denmark has a tremendous personality crammed into a tiny body. Located between Sweden and Germany, the country is the geographic and cultural bridge between Scandinavia and continental Europe, made up of the Jutland peninsula and the islands of Zealand, Funen, Lolland, Falster, and Bornholm, as well as some 400 smaller islands, some of which are not inhabited. With its Viking past behind it, Denmark now has one of the most comprehensive social welfare structures in the world, and liberal immigration policies have diversified the erstwhile homogeneous population. Today, Denmark has a progressive youth culture that beckons travelers to the hip pub scene in Copenhagen. Contrary to the suggestion of a certain English playwright, very little seems to be rotten in the state of Denmark.

FACTS AND FIGURES

Official Name: Kingdom of Denmark.
Capital: Copenhagen.
Major Cities: Aalborg, Århus, Odense.
Population: 5,370,000.

Land Area: 42,394 sq. km.
Time Zone: GMT +1.
Languages: Danish, Faroese, and Greenlandic.
Religions: Evangelical Lutheran (91%).

DISCOVER DENMARK

Begin in chic, progressive **Copenhagen** (p. 275), where you can cruise the canals, party until dawn, and ponder Kierkegaard. Daytrip north to the fabulous **Louisiana** museum (p. 283) and **Elsinore** (p. 284), Hamlet's castle, or shoot west to **Roskilde** (p. 285) and the fascinating Viking Ship Museum. If you time it right, you'll hit the massive **Roskilde Festival,** when rock takes over the city. For some of the best beaches in Denmark, ferry to the island of **Bornholm** (p. 285). Move west over the Storebæltsbro bridge to the island of **Funen** (p. 287), including **Odense** (p. 287), the hometown of Hans Christian Andersen, then head south to the stunning 16th-century castle **Egeskov Slot** (p. 288). From the southern end of Funen, hop on a ferry to the idyllic island of **Ærø** (p. 288), a throwback to the Denmark of several centuries ago. Cross the Lillebælt to Jutland, where laid-back **Aalborg** (p. 293) delights with students and culture, then play with blocks at **Legoland** (p. 291). On your way back down south, stop in historic **Ribe** (p. 292).

ESSENTIALS

WHEN TO GO

Denmark is best visited May to September, when days are sunny and temperatures average 10-16°C (50-61°F). Winter temperatures average 0°C (32°F). Although temperate for its northern location, Denmark is often windy, and nights can be chilly, even in summer; pack a sweater.

DOCUMENTS AND FORMALITIES

VISAS. EU citizens do not need a visa. Citizens of Australia, Canada, New Zealand, South Africa, and the US do not need a visa for stays of up to 90 days.

EMBASSIES AND CONSULATES: All foreign embassies in Denmark are in Copenhagen (p. 275). Danish embassies abroad include: **Australia,** 15 Hunter St., Yarralumla, Canberra, ACT 2600 (☎(02) 62 73 21 95; fax 62 73 38 64). **Canada,** 47 Clarence St., Ste. 450, Ottawa, ON K1N 9K1 (☎613-562-1811; www.trade-comm.com/danish). **Ireland,** 121 St. Stephen's Green, Dublin 2 (☎(01) 475 64 04; www.denmark.ie). **New Zealand,** 45 Johnston St., PO Box 10874, Wellington (☎(04) 471 05 20; fax 471 05 21). **South Africa,** PO Box 11439, Hatfield, Pretoria 0028 (☎(012) 430 94 30; www.denmark.co.za). **UK,** 55 Sloane St., London SW1X 9SR (☎(020) 7333 0200; www.denmark.org.uk). **US,** 3200 Whitehaven St. NW, Washington, D.C. 20008-3683 (☎202-234-4300; www.denmarkemb.org).

TRANSPORTATION

BY PLANE. Kastrup Airport in Copenhagen (CPH; www.cph.dk) handles international flights from cities around the world, mostly by Air France, British Airways, Delta, Icelandair, KLM, Lufthansa, SAS, and Swiss Air. **Billund Airport** (BLL; ☎76 50

50 50; www.billund-airport.dk) handles flights to other European cities. SAS (Scandinavian Airlines; US ☎800-221-2350; www.scandinavian.net), the national airline company, offers youth, spouse, and senior discounts to some destinations.

BY TRAIN AND BY BUS. The state-run rail line in Denmark is **DSB;** visit www.dsb.dk/journey_planner to use their extremely helpful ⚡**journey planner.** **Eurail** is valid on all state-run routes. The **Scanrail pass,** purchased outside Scandinavia, is good for rail travel through Denmark, Finland, Norway, and Sweden, as well as many discounted ferry and bus rides. The Scanrail pass is also available for purchase within Scandinavia, with restrictions on the number of days spent in the country of purchase. See p. 54 for more info or visit www.scanrail.com or www.railpass.com/eurail/passes/scanrail.htm. Remote towns are typically served by buses from the nearest train station. The national **bus** network is reliable and fairly cheap. You can take buses or trains over the **Øresund bridge** from Copenhagen to Malmö, Sweden.

BY FERRY. Railpasses include discounts or free rides on many Scandinavian ferries. The free *Vi Rejser* newspaper, at tourist offices, can help you sort out the dozens of smaller ferries that serve Denmark's outlying islands, although the best bet for overcoming language barriers is just to ask at the station. For info on ferries from Copenhagen to Norway, Poland, and Sweden, see p. 277. For more on connections from Bornholm to Germany and Sweden, see p. 285, and from Jutland to England, Norway, and Sweden, see p. 289.

BY CAR. Roads are toll-free, except for the **Storebæltsbro** (Great Belt Bridge; 210kr) and the **Øresund bridge** (around 220kr). Speed limits are 50kph (30mph) in urban areas, 80kph (50mph) on highways, and 110kph (68mph) on motorways. **Service centers** for motorists, called *Info-terias*, are spaced along Danish highways. **Gas** averages 6.50kr per liter. Watch out for bikes, which have the right-of-way. Driving in cities is discouraged by high parking prices and numerous one-way streets. For more info on driving in Denmark, contact the **Forenede Danske Motorejere** (FDM), Firskovvej 32, Box 500, 2800 Kgs. Lyngby (☎70 13 30 40; www.fdm.dk).

BY BIKE AND BY THUMB. Flat terrain, well-marked bike routes, bike paths in the countryside, and raised bike lanes on most streets in towns and cities make Denmark a cyclist's dream. You can rent **bikes** (55-65kr per day) from some tourist offices, rental shops, and a few train stations. The **Dansk Cyklist Forbund** (Danish Cycle Federation), Rømersg. 7, 1362 Copenhagen K (☎33 32 31 21; www.dcf.dk), can hook you up with longer-term rentals. For info on bringing your bike on a train (which costs 50kr or less), pick up *Bikes and Trains* at any train station. **Hitchhiking** on motorways is illegal and uncommon. *Let's Go* does not recommend hitchhiking as a safe means of transport.

TOURIST OFFICES. Contact the tourist board in Denmark at Islands Brygge 43, 2300 Copenhagen S (☎32 88 99 00; www.visitdenmark.dt.dk). **Tourist Boards** at home include: **UK,** 55 Sloane St., London SW1X 9SY (☎7259 5959; www.dtb.dt.dk); **US,** 18th fl., 655 3rd Ave., New York, NY 10017 (☎212-885-9700; www.goscandinavia.com). Additional tourist info and helpful ⚡**maps** can be found at www.krak.dk.

MONEY. The Danish unit of currency is the **krone** (kr), which is divided into 100 *øre*. The easiest way to get cash is from **ATMs;** cash cards are widely accepted, and many machines give advances on credit cards. Denmark has a high cost of living; expect to pay 85-130kr for a hostel bed, 300-850kr for a hotel room, 75-150kr for a day's groceries, and 40-100kr for a cheap restaurant meal. A barebones day in Denmark might cost 250-350kr; a slightly more comfortable day might cost 400-600kr. The European Union imposes a **value-added tax (VAT)** on goods and services purchased within the EU, which is included in the price (see

p. 16). Denmark's VAT is one of the highest in Europe (25%). Non-EU citizens can get a VAT refund upon leaving the country for purchases in any one store that total over 300kr. There are no hard and fast rules for **tipping**, but it's always polite to round up to the nearest 10kr in restaurants and for taxis. In general, service at restaurants is included in the bill, although tipping up to 15% is becoming common in Copenhagen.

DANISH KRONE (KR)		
	AUS$1 = 4.44KR	10KR = AUS$2.25
	CDN$1 = 4.88KR	10KR = CDN$2.05
	EUR€1 = 7.43KR	10KR = EUR€1.35
	NZ$1 = 3.98KR	10KR = NZ$2.51
	ZAR1 = 0.91KR	10KR = ZAR10.96
	UK£1 = 10.73KR	10KR = UK£0.93
	US$1 = 6.83KR	10KR = US$1.46

BUSINESS HOURS. Shops are normally open Monday to Thursday from about 9 or 10am to 6pm and Friday until 7 or 8pm; they are usually open Saturday mornings. Shops in Copenhagen stay open all day Saturday. Regular **banking** hours are Monday to Friday 9:30am-4pm, Thursday until 6pm.

COMMUNICATION

PHONE CODES   **Country code: 45. International dialing prefix: 00.**

TELEPHONES. There are no separate city codes; include all digits for local and international calls. Buy phone cards at post offices or kiosks (30kr for 30 units; 50kr for 53 units ; 100kr for 110 units). **Mobile phones** are an increasingly popular and economical alternative (p. 30). For domestic directory info, call ☎118; international info, ☎113; collect calls, ☎141. International direct dial numbers include: **AT&T,** ☎8001 0010; **Canada Direct,** ☎80 01 00 11; **Ireland Direct,** ☎80 01 03 53; **MCI,** ☎8001 0022; **Sprint,** ☎800 10 877; **Telecom New Zealand,** ☎80 01 0064; **Telkom South Africa,** ☎8001 0027; **Telstra Australia,** ☎80 88 0543.

MAIL. Mailing a postcard/letter to Australia, Canada, New Zealand, the US, or South Africa costs 6.25kr; to elsewhere in Europe 5.25kr. Domestic mail costs 4kr.

LANGUAGES. Danish is the official language of Denmark. Faroese is spoken in the Faroe Islands; Greenlandic is spoken in Greenland. The Danish add æ (pronounced like the "e" in "egg"), ø (pronounced like the "i" in "first"), and å (sometimes written as *aa;* pronounced like the "o" in "lord") to the end of the alphabet; thus Århus would follow Viborg in an alphabetical listing of cities. *Let's Go* indexes these under "ae," "o," and "a." Nearly all Danes speak flawless English, but a few Danish words might help break the ice: try *skal* (skoal), or "cheers." Danish has a distinctive glottal stop known as a *stød.* For basic Danish phrases, see p. 1053.

ACCOMMODATIONS AND CAMPING

DENMARK	❶	❷	❸	❹	❺
ACCOMMODATIONS	under 85kr	86-120kr	121-200kr	200-300kr	over 300kr

While Denmark's hotels are generally expensive (300-850kr per night), the country's more than 100 HI youth hostels (*vandrehjem*) are cheap , well-run, and have no age limit. They are also given an official ranking of one to five stars, based on facilities and service. Sheets cost about 45-50kr. Breakfast usually runs 45kr and dinner 65kr. Dorms run about 100kr per night; nonmembers add 25kr. Reception desks normally close for the day around 8 or 9pm, although some are open 24hr. Reservations are highly recommended, especially in summer and near beaches. Many Danish youth hostels are filled by school groups in summer, so it's important to make reservations well in advance. Make sure to arrive before check-in to confirm your reservation. For more info, contact the Danish Youth Hostel Association, Vesterbrog. 39, in Copenhagen. (☎31 31 36 12; www.danhostel.dk. Open M-Th 9am-4pm, F 9am-3pm.) Tourist offices offer the *Danhostel* booklet, which also has more information, and many book rooms in private homes (125-175kr).

Denmark's 525 official **campgrounds** (about 60kr per person) rank from one-star (toilets and drinking water) to three-star (showers and laundry) to five-star (swimming, restaurants, and stoves). You'll need either a **Camping Card Scandinavia**, available at campgrounds (1-year 80kr), or a **Camping Card International.** Campsites affiliated with hostels generally do not require this card. If you only plan to camp for a night, you can buy a 24hr. pass (20kr). The **Danish Camping Council** (*Campingradet;* ☎39 27 80 44) sells the campground handbook *Camping Denmark* and passes. Sleeping in train stations, in parks, or on public property is illegal.

FOOD AND DRINK

DENMARK	❶	❷	❸	❹	❺
FOOD	under 40kr	40-70kr	71-100kr	101-130kr	over 130kr

A "Danish" in Denmark is a *wienerbrød* ("Viennese bread"), found in bakeries alongside other flaky treats. For more substantial fare, Danes favor open-faced sandwiches called *smørrebrød*. Herring is served in various forms, though usually pickled or raw with onions or a curry mayonnaise. For cheap eats, look for lunch specials (*dagens ret*) and all-you-can-eat buffets (*spis alt du kan* or *tag selv buffet*). National beers include Carlsberg and Tuborg; bottled brew tends to be cheaper. A popular alcohol alternative is *snaps* (or *aquavit*), a clear distilled liquor flavored with fiery spices, usually served chilled and unmixed. Many vegetarian (*vegetarret*) options are the result of Indian and Mediterranean influences, but salads and veggies (*grønsager*) can be found on most menus.

HOLIDAYS AND FESTIVALS

Holidays: New Year's (Jan. 1); Easter Holidays (Apr. 8-12); Queen's Birthday (Apr. 16); Worker's Day (May 1); Great Prayer Day (May 7); Ascension Day (May 20); Whit Sunday and Monday (May 30-31); Constitution Day (June 5); Midsummer Eve (June 23); Christmas (Dec. 24-26).

Festivals: Danes celebrate **Fastelavn** (Carnival) in Feb. and Mar. The **Roskilde Festival** is an immense, open-air rock festival held in Roskilde in late June. In early July, the **Copenhagen Jazz Festival** hosts a week of concerts, many free.

COPENHAGEN (KØBENHAVN)

Copenhagen (pop. 1,800,000) combines the swan ponds, gingerbread houses, and *Lille Havfrue* (Little Mermaid) of Hans Christian Andersen's fairy tales with the cosmopolitan style, world-class museums, and round-the-clock nightlife of Europe's largest cities, all the while maintaining a friendly, distinctly Danish charm. Denmark's capital embodies the youthful, laid-back, and progressive attitude that pervades this country of islands.

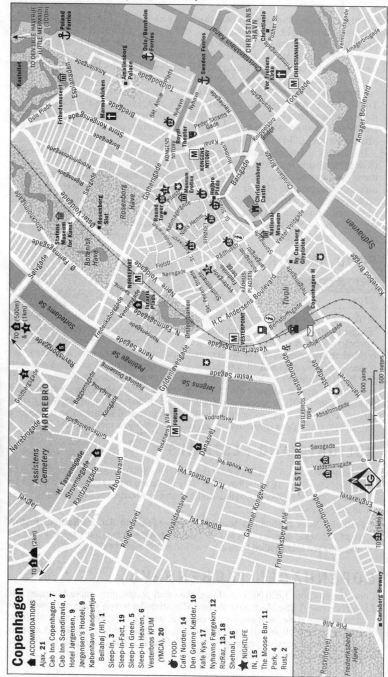

Copenhagen

⛺ ACCOMMODATIONS
Ajax, 21
Cab Inn Copenhagen, 7
Cab Inn Scandinavia, 8
Hotel Jørgensen, 9
Jørgensen's Hostel, 9
København Vandrerhjen
Bellahøj (HI), 1
Sleep-In, 3
Sleep-In-Fact, 19
Sleep-In Green, 5
Sleep-In Heaven, 6
Vesterbros KFUM
(YMCA), 20

🍴 FOOD
Café Norden, 14
Den Grønne Kælder, 10
Kafe Kys, 17
Nyhavns Færgekro, 12
RizRaz, 13, 18
Shehnai, 16

★ NIGHTLIFE
IN, 15
The Moose Bar, 11
Park, 4
Rust, 2

⌐ TRANSPORTATION

Flights: Kastrup Airport (CPH; ☎32 47 47 47; www.cph.dk). **Trains** connect the airport to København H (13min., every 10min., 25kr). RyanAir flies cheaply into nearby **Sturup Airport** in Malmö, Sweden (MMX; ☎+46 40 613 1000) from London and Frankfurt. **Flybuses** depart for København H 30min. after RyanAir arrivals (45min., 100kr).

Trains: Trains stop at **København H** (Hovedbanegården or Central Station; domestic travel ☎70 13 14 15; international reservations ☎70 13 14 16; info ☎33 14 17 01). For travel within the country, www.dsb.dk is indispensable. Fares depend on seat availability; for the cheapest tickets, book at least 14 days in advance, travel with a partner, or use your Wildcard (under-26 only). Approximate fares to: **Berlin** (9hr., daily, 800kr); **Hamburg** (4½hr., 5 per day, 519kr); **Oslo** (9hr., 3 per day, 800kr); **Stockholm** (5½hr., 4-5 per day, 1100kr). Seat reservations (23-51kr) are mandatory.

Ferries: Scandinavian Seaways (☎33 42 33 42; www.dfds.dk) departs daily for **Oslo** (16hr.; 480-735kr, under-26 315-570kr). **Polferries** (☎33 11 46 45; www.polferries.dk) set out from Ndr. Toldbod, 12A (off Esplanaden) for **Świnoujście, Poland** (10hr.; Su-M and W 8am, Th-F 7:30pm; 340kr, with ISIC 285kr).

Public Transportation: Buses (info ☎36 13 14 15; www.hur.dk) run daily 7am-9:30pm. **Trains** (info ☎33 14 17 01) run 6:30am-11pm. Buses and **S-trains** (subways and suburban trains; M-Sa 5am-12:30am, Su 6am-12:30am) operate on a zone system. To travel any distance, you must buy a minimum of a 2-zone **ticket** (15kr, additional zones 7.50kr). For extended stays or travel in Zealand, the best deal is the **rabatkort** (rebate card; 95kr), available from kiosks and bus drivers, which offers 10 2-zone tickets at a discount; just "clip" the ticket as you embark. For longer travel, you can clip the ticket more than once or purchase a *rabatkort* with more zones. Tickets and clips allow 1hr. of transfers. The **24hr. pass** (90kr), available at any train station, grants unlimited bus and train transport in Northern Zealand, as do both Copenhagen Cards (see below). **Night buses,** marked with an "N," run 12:30-5:30am on limited routes and charge double fare; they also accept the 24hr. pass. Copenhagen's newly renovated **Metro** system is efficient and convenient.

Taxis: ☎35 35 35 35 or 38 77 77 77. Base fare 23kr; add 10-13kr per km. København H to Kastrup Airport costs around 200kr.

Bike Rental: City Bike (www.citybike.dk) lends bikes from 120 racks all over the city for a 20kr deposit. Anyone can return your bike and claim your deposit; lock up your bike or return it to the rack when not in use. **Københavns Cykler,** Reventlowsg. 11 (☎33 33 86 13; www.rentabike.dk), in København H. 75kr per day, 340kr per week; 500kr deposit. Open July-Aug. M-F 8am-5:30pm, Sa 9am-1pm, Su 10am-1pm.

Hitchhiking and Ridesharing: Hitchhiking is not common in Denmark. *Let's Go* does not recommend hitchhiking. For info on ridesharing, check out www.nice.person.dk or www.useit.dk. Always exercise caution when traveling with strangers.

■♣ ⍰ ORIENTATION AND PRACTICAL INFORMATION

Copenhagen lies on the east coast of the island of **Zealand** (Sjælland), across the Øresund Sound from Malmö, Sweden. The 28km **Øresund bridge and tunnel,** which opened July 1, 2000, established the first "fixed link" between the two countries. Copenhagen's main train station, København H, lies near the city's heart. North of the station, **Vesterbrogade** passes **Tivoli** and **Rådhuspladsen,** the central square, then cuts through the city center as **Strøget** (STROY-yet), the world's longest pedestrian thoroughfare. As it heads east, Strøget goes through a series of names: **Frederiksberggade, Nygade, Vimmelskaftet, Amagertorv,** and **Østergade.**

TOURIST, FINANCIAL, AND LOCAL SERVICES

Tourist Offices: Wonderful Copenhagen, Bernstorffsg. 1 (☎70 22 24 42; www.visit-copenhagen.dk). Head out the main exit of København H and go left, past the back entrance to Tivoli. Open May-Aug. M-Sa 9am-8pm, Su 10am-6pm; Sept.-Apr. M-F 9am-4:30pm, Sa 9am-1:30pm. **Use It,** Rådhusstr. 13 (☎33 73 06 20; www.useit.dk). From the station, follow Vesterbrog., cross Rådhuspl. onto Frederiksbergg., and turn right on Rådhusstr. Indispensable info geared toward budget travelers. Pick up a copy of *Play Time,* a comprehensive budget guide to the city. Provides daytime luggage storage, has free **Internet** access (20min. max.), finds lodgings, and holds mail. Open mid-June to mid-Sept. daily 9am-7pm; mid-Sept. to mid-June M-W 11am-4pm, Th 11am-6pm, F 11am-2pm. The **Copenhagen Card** (24hr. card 159kr), sold in hotels, tourist offices, and train stations, grants free admission to most major sights and discounts on others, but is not worth it unless you're visiting 5 museums or more in one day. The **Copenhagen Card Plus** (72hr. card 395kr) includes even more museums, provides unlimited bus and train travel in Northern Zealand, and offers discounts on ferries to Sweden, but also requires significant museum-hopping to justify the cost.

Budget Travel: Kilroy Travels, Skinderg. 28 (☎70 15 40 15). Open M-F 10am-5:30pm, Sa 10am-2pm. **Wasteels Rejser,** Skoubog. 6 (☎33 14 46 33). Open M-F 9am-5pm, Sa 10am-2pm.

Embassies and Consulates: Australia, Dampfaergevej 26, 2nd fl. (☎70 26 36 76). **Canada,** Kristen Bernikowsg. 1 (☎33 48 32 00). **Ireland,** Østerbaneg. 21 (☎35 42 32 33; fax 35 43 18 58). **New Zealanders** should contact their embassy in Brussels (see p. 123). **South Africa,** Gammel Vartovvej 8 (☎39 18 01 55; www.southafrica.dk). **UK,** Kastelsvej 36-40 (☎35 44 52 00). **US,** Dag Hammarskjölds Allé 24 (☎35 55 31 44; www.usembassy.dk).

Currency Exchange: Numerous locations, especially on Strøget. 25kr commission standard. **Forex,** in København H. 20kr commission on cash, 10kr per traveler's check. Open daily 8am-9pm. **The Change Group,** Østerg. 61. 35kr commission minimum. Open May-Sept. M-Sa 8:45am-8pm, Su 10am-6pm; Oct.-Apr. daily 10am-6pm.

Luggage Storage: Free at **Use It** (above) and most hostels. At **København H,** 30kr per bag per day; 10-day maximum. Lockers 25-35kr per 24hr.; 3 day maximum. Open M-Sa 5:30am-1am, Su 6am-1am.

Laundromats: Look for **Vascomat** and **Møntvask** chains. At Borgerg. 2, Nansensg. 39, Vendersg. 13, and Istedg. 45. Wash and dry 40-50kr. Most open daily 7am-9pm.

Bi-Gay-Lesbian Resources: Landsforeningen for Bøsser and Lesbiske (National Association for Gay Men and Women), Teglgårdsstr. 13 (☎33 13 19 48; www.lbl.dk). Open M-F 11am-4pm. The monthly *Out & About,* which lists clubs, cafes, and organizations, is available at gay clubs and the tourist office. Also check out www.copenhagen-gay-life.dk. The city hosts the **Danish Mermaid Parade** (www.danishpride.dk) in August.

EMERGENCY AND COMMUNICATIONS

Emergencies: ☎112. **Police:** ☎33 14 14 48. Headquarters are at Polititorvet.

24-Hour Pharmacy: Steno Apotek, Vesterbrog. 6c (☎33 14 82 66). Open 24hr.; ring the bell. Across from the Banegårdspl. exit of København H.

Medical Assistance: Doctors on Call (☎70 27 57 57). **Emergency rooms** at **Amager Hospital,** Kastrup 63 (☎32 34 32 34), and **Bispebjerg Hospital,** Bispebjerg Bakke 23 (☎35 31 35 31).

Internet Access: Free at **Use It** (above). **Copenhagen Hovedbibliotek** (Central Library), Krystalg. 15 (☎33 73 60 60). Free. Open M-F 10am-7pm, Sa 10am-2pm. **Boomtown,** Axeltorv 1 (☎33 32 10 32). 20kr per 30min., 30kr per hr. Open 24hr.

Post Office: In København H. Address mail to be held: SURNAME Firstname, Post Denmark, Hovedbanegårdens Posthus, Hovedbanegården, **1570** Copenhagen V. DENMARK. Open M-F 8am-9pm, Sa 9am-4pm, Su 10am-4pm. **Use It** (see tourist offices, above) also holds mail. Address mail to: Firstname SURNAME, *Poste Restante*, Use It, 13 Rådhusstr., **1466** Copenhagen K, DENMARK.

▛ ACCOMMODATIONS

Comfortable and inexpensive accommodations can be hard to find near the city center, where most hostels are converted gymnasiums or warehouses, packed with up to 200 beds. On the upside, many hostels feature a lively social scene. The price jump between hostels and hotels is significant. In summer (especially during holidays and festivals, particularly Roskilde), it is wise to reserve well in advance.

HOSTELS

Jørgensen's Hostel, Rømersg. 11 (☎33 13 81 86), 20min. from København H, 10min. from Strøget, next to Israels Pl. M: Nørreport. Go right along Vendersg.; it's on the left. Central location. 6-12 beds per room. Breakfast included. Sheets 30kr. Max. stay 5 nights. Lockout 11am-3pm. Under-35 only. No reservations. Dorms 135kr. ❸

Sleep-In-Fact, Valdemarsg. 14 (☎33 79 67 79; www.sleep-in-fact.dk). From the main exit of København H, turn left on Vesterbrog., then left again on Valdemarstr. (10min.). Comfortable and clean rooms in a factory-turned-hostel. 30 beds per room. Bikes 50kr per day. Breakfast included. Sheets 30kr. Internet 5kr for first 5min., 20kr per 30min. thereafter. Reception daily 6am-3am. Open late June-Aug. Dorms 120kr. ❸

Sleep-In Heaven, Struenseg. 7 (☎35 35 46 48; morefun@sleepinheaven.com), in Nørrebro. M: Forum. From København H, take bus #250S two stops (dir.: Buddinge; every 10min.) to *H.C. Ørsteds Vej*. 30-86 beds per room. Lively social atmosphere. Close to nightlife. Breakfast 40kr. Free lockers. Sheets 30kr. Internet 20kr per 30min. Reception 24hr. Under-35 only. Dorms 110kr; doubles 450kr. ❷

Sleep-In, Blegdamsvej 132 (☎35 26 50 59). From København H, take bus #1A (dir.: Hellerup; 15min., every 5-7min.) to *Trianglen* and walk down Blegdamsvej. Popular hostel in a huge warehouse. Near lively Østerbro and Nørrebro nightlife. Kitchen available. Sheets 30kr. Internet 6kr per 15min. Reception 24hr. Lockout noon-4pm. Open June 28-Aug. No reservations. Dorms 90kr. ❷

Vesterbros KFUM (YMCA), Valdemarsg. 15 (☎33 31 15 74). Across the street from Sleep-In-Fact (see above). Friendly staff, homey atmosphere, and fewer beds per room come at the cost of an early curfew. Breakfast 25kr. Kitchen available. Sheets 15kr. Reception daily 8:30-11:30am, 3:30-5:30pm, and 8pm-12:30am. Curfew 12:30am. Open late June-early Aug. Dorms 85kr. ❷

Sleep-In Green, Ravnsborgg. 18, Baghuset (☎35 37 77 77). M: Nørreport. From there, take bus #5A. The lackluster exterior belies clean rooms inside this eco-friendly hostel. 30 beds per room. Internet 20kr per 30min. Organic breakfast 30kr. Sheets included; pillow and blanket 30kr. Reception 24hr. Open early May-Sept. Dorms 95kr. ❷

Ajax, Bavnehøj Allé 30 (☎33 21 24 56). From København H, take bus #10 (dir.: CF Richvej) to Bavnehøj Allé. Or, take the S-train to *Sydhavn*, walk north on Enghavevej with the train tracks on your right, and turn left on Bavnehøj Allé. Pleasantly off the beaten track. The rental tents may be the best deal in town. Breakfast 25kr. Kitchen available. Sheets 20kr. Internet 15kr for first 30min., 25kr per hr. Reception daily 8am-midnight. Open July to mid-Aug. Dorms 70kr; singles and doubles 200kr; triples 300kr; quads 350kr. **Camping** 50kr; tent rental 10kr. ❶

København Vandrerhjem Bellahøj (HI), Herbergvejen 8 (☎38 28 97 15; www.danhostel.dk/bellahoej), in Bellahøj. Take bus #2A (dir.: Tingbjerg; 15min., every 5-10min.) to Fuglsang Allé. Turn right onto Fuglsang Allé; it's on the right after 50m.

Quiet, clean, and modern hostel 5km from the city center. Breakfast 45kr. Sheets 35kr. Laundry 35kr. Internet 1kr per min. Reception 24hr. Lockout 10am-2pm. Open Feb.-Dec. Dorms 95kr; doubles 300kr; triples 390kr; quads 460kr; 5-person rooms 475kr; six-person rooms 570kr. Nonmembers add 30kr. ❷

HOTELS

Hotel Jørgensen, Rømersg. 11 (☎33 13 81 86; www.hoteljorgensen.dk). Same owner-ship and location as Jørgensen's Hostel. Small rooms in a great location. Breakfast included. Reception 24hr. Singles 475-575kr; doubles 575-700kr; triples 900kr. ❺

Cab Inn Scandinavia, Vodroffsvej 55 (☎35 36 11 11, www.cabinn.com). From Køben-havn H, take bus #2A (dir.: Tingbjerg; 5min., every 5min.) to Vodroffsvej. Sister hotel **Cab Inn Copenhagen** is 5min. away at Danasvej 32-34 (☎33 21 04 00). Small, com-fortable, modern rooms. Breakfast 50kr. Reception 24hr. Singles 510kr; doubles 630kr; triples 750kr; quads 870kr. ❺

Hotel Rye, Ryesg. 115 (☎35 26 52 10; www.hotelrye.dk). Take bus #1A (dir.: Hellerup; 15min., every 5-7min.) or 14 to *Trianglen,* then turn right off Osterbrog. onto Ryesg. Cozy hotel that provides a kimono and slippers in your room and homemade buns at breakfast. Shared showers. Breakfast included. Reception daily 8am-9pm. Singles 500kr; doubles 700kr; triples 900kr; quads 1000kr. ❺

CAMPING

Bellahøj Camping, Hvidkildevej 66 (☎38 10 11 50), 5km from the city center. Take bus #2A from København H (dir.: Tingbjerg; 15min., every 5-10min.) to Primulavej. Kitchen, cafe, and market. Showers included. Reception 24hr. Open June-Aug. 59kr per person; rental tents 100kr per person. ❶

◨ FOOD

Among the Viking's legacies is Copenhagen's love-it-or-hate-it pickled herring. Around **Kongens Nytorv,** elegant cafes serve the truly Danish *smørrebrød* (open-faced sandwich) for about 40kr. All-you-can-eat buffets (29-70kr) are popular, especially on Strøget. **Fakta** and **Netto supermarkets** are budget fantasies; there are several in the Nørreport area (S-train: Nørreport) and around the city. (Most open M-F 9am-8pm, Sa 10am-4pm.) Open-air **markets** provide fresh fruits and veggies; try the one at **Israels Plads** near Nørreport Station. (Open M-Th 9am-5:30pm, F 9am-6:30pm, Sa 9am-3pm.) **Fruit stalls** line Strøget and the side streets to the north.

Nyhavns Færgekro, Nyhavn 5. Upscale fisherman's cottage atmosphere along the canal. Lunch on 10 styles of all-you-can-eat herring (89kr) or pick just one style (45kr). Dinner from 150kr. Open daily 9:30am-11:30pm. ❹

Café Norden, Østerg. 61, on Strøget and Nicolaj Pl., in sight of the fountain. A chic cafe in the heart of Strøget. Great for people-watching. Sandwiches 69-89kr. Salads 92-95kr. Brunch 110kr. Kitchen open Su-Th until 9pm, F until 10pm. Open M-Sa 9am-mid-night, Su 10am-midnight. ❸

RizRaz, Kompagnistr. 20 and Store Kannikestr. 19. Extensive vegetarian and mediterra-nean buffet. Lunch buffet 59kr. Dinner 69kr. Open daily 11:30am-midnight. ❷

Kafe Kys, Læderstr. 7, on a quiet street running south of and parallel to Strøget. Plenty of vegetarian options, tasty sandwiches, and salads (48-75kr). Kitchen closes daily at 10:30pm. Open M-Th 11am-1am, F-Sa 11am-2am, Su 11am-midnight. ❷

Shehnai, Vimmelskaftet 39. An Indian restaurant that serves a tasty all-you-can-eat pizza and salad buffet (29kr), in addition to traditional dishes. Tandoori chicken 20kr. Indian buffet 49kr. Open 11am-11pm. ❶

Den Grønne Kælder, Pilestr. 48. Popular vegetarian and vegan dining in a casual atmosphere. Sandwiches 40kr. Lunch 65kr. Dinner 85kr. Open M-Sa 11am-10pm. ❷

◉ SIGHTS

Compact Copenhagen is best seen on foot or by bike. Various **walking tours** are detailed in *Play Time* (at **Use It**), covering all sections of the city. Opposite Kongens Nytorv is the multi-colored and picturesque Nyhavn, the "new port" where Hans Christian Andersen wrote his first fairy tale. On a nice day, take the 6.4km walk along the five lakes (*Sø*) that border the western end of the city center. The lakes, as well as the Rosenborg Have, are great places for a **picnic.** Wednesday is the best day to visit museums, as most are free.

CITY CENTER. The first sight you'll see as you exit the train station is **Tivoli,** the famous 19th-century **amusement park.** Christian VIII ordered the creation of the park in 1843, convinced that "when the people are enjoying themselves they forget about politicking." Heed the king and lose yourself in the festive ambience, replete with beautiful fountains, town-fair-style games, and, of course, roller coasters. *(www.tivoligardens.com. Open mid-June to mid-Aug. Su-Th 11am-midnight, F-Sa 11am-1am; off-season reduced hours. Admission 65kr, children 30kr. Rides 15-60kr. Admission with unlimited rides 180kr, children 120kr.)* Across the street from the back entrance of Tivoli, the beautiful ◧**Ny Carlsberg Glyptotek** boasts a fine collection of ancient and Impressionist art and sculpture, complete with an enclosed Mediterranean garden. *(Dantes Pl. 7. Open Su and Tu-Sa 10am-4pm. 40kr. Free W and S or with ISIC.)* Follow Denmark's changing face since the beginning of man at the **National Museum.** *(Ny Vesterg. 10. ☎33 13 44 11. Open Su and Tu-Sa 10am-5pm. 50kr, students 40kr. W free.)* **Christiansborg Castle** features subterranean ruins, still-in-use royal reception rooms, and the *Folketing* (Parliament) chambers. To see the magnificent tapestries given to the Queen for her 50th birthday, take the tour. *(Prins Jørgens Gård. ☎33 92 64 92. Ruins open daily 9:30am-3:30pm. 25kr. Required castle tours May-Sept. daily 11am, 1, and 3pm; Oct.-Apr. Su, Tu, Th, and Sa 3pm. 45kr, students 35kr.)* Satisfy your carnal curiosity at the **Museum Erotica,** where various exhibits offer peeks into the sex lives of the famous, the history of prostitution, and kinky art from around the world. *(☎33 12 03 11; www.museumerotica.dk. Open May-Sept. daily 10am-11pm; Oct.-Apr. Su-Th 11am-8pm, F-Sa 10am-10pm.)*

CHRISTIANSHAVN. Climb the awe-inspiring golden spire of **Vor Frelsers Kirke** (Our Savior's Church) for a great view of both the city and the water. *(Sankt Annæg. 29. M: Christianshavn or bus #48. Turn left onto Prinsesseg. Church open Mar.-Nov. daily 11am-4:30pm; Dec.-Feb. 10am-2pm. Free. Tower open Mar.-Nov. M-Sa 11am-4:30pm, Su noon-4:30pm. 20kr.)* The "free city" of **Christiania,** in the southern section of Christianshavn, was founded in 1971 by youthful squatters in abandoned military barracks. Today it is inhabited by a thriving group of artists and alterna-thinkers carrying 70s activism and free love into the new millennium. At Christmas, there is a fabulous **market** with curiosities from all over the world. The aptly named **Pusher Street** features stands that sell all kinds of hash and marijuana. Beware, however, as possession of even small amounts can get you arrested. If you *must,* keep consumption limited to the premises. Always ask before taking pictures, never take pictures on Pusher St. itself, and exercise caution in the area at night. *(Main entrance on Prinsesseg. From København H, take bus #48.)*

FREDERIKSTADEN. Edvard Eriksen's **Lille Havfrue** (Little Mermaid), the tiny but touristed statue at the opening of the harbor, honors Hans Christian Andersen's version of the tale. *(S-train: Østerport; turn left out of the station, left on Folke Bernadottes Allé, right on the path bordering the canal, left up the stairs, and then right along the street. Open* *daily 6am-dusk.)* Head back along the canal and turn left across the moat to reach **Kastellet**, a 17th-century fortress that's now a park. Cross through Kastellet to the fascinating **Frihedsmuseet** (Museum of Danish Resistance), which documents the German occupation from 1940-1945, during which the Danes helped over 7000 Jews escape to Sweden and committed about 4000 acts of sabotage. *(At Churchill-parken. ☎33 13 77 14. Open May to mid-Sept. Su 10am-5pm, Tu-Sa 10am-4pm; mid-Sept. to Apr. Su 11am-4pm, Tu-Sa 11am-3pm. 40kr, students 30kr. W free. English tours May to mid-Sept. Tu, Th, and Su 2pm. Free.)* From the museum, walk south down Amalieg. to reach the lovely ▧ **Amalienborg Palace,** residence of Queen Margrethe II and the royal family. Most of the interior is closed to the public, but the apartments of Christian VII are open, including the gaudy, original studies of 19th-century Danish kings. The changing of the guard takes place at noon on the brick plaza. *(☎33 12 08 08; www.rosenborg-slot.dk. Open May-Oct. daily 10am-4pm; Nov.-Apr. Su and Tu-Sa 11am-4pm. 45kr, students 25kr; combined ticket with Rosenborg Slot (see below) 80kr.)* The gorgeous 19th-century **Marmokirken** (Marble Church), opposite the palace, features an ornate interior, Europe's third-largest dome, and a spectacular view. *(Fredriksg. 4. Open M-Tu and Th 10am-5pm, W 10am-6pm, F-Su noon-5pm. Free. Dome open mid-June to Aug. daily 1 and 3pm; Sept. to mid-June Sa-Su 1 and 3pm. 20kr.)* A few blocks north, **Statens Museum for Kunst** (State Museum of Fine Arts) displays an eclectic collection of Danish and international art in a beautifully designed building. *(Sølvg. 48-50. S-train: Nørreport. Walk up Øster Voldg. ☎33 74 84 94; www.smk.dk. Open Su, Tu, and Th-Sa 10am-5pm, W 10am-8pm. 50kr, under-25 35kr. W free.)* Opposite the museum, **Rosenborg Slot,** built from 1606-1634 by King Christian IV as a summer residence, hoards royal treasures, including the **crown jewels.** *(Øster Voldg. 4A. S-train: Nørreport. Walk up Øster Voldg. ☎33 15 32 86. Open June-Aug. daily 10am-5pm; May and Sept. 10am-4pm; Oct. 11am-3pm; Nov.-Apr. Su and Tu-Sa 11am-2pm. 60kr, students 30kr.)* Nearby, stroll through the 13,000 plant species in the **Botanisk Have** (Botanical Gardens); make sure to visit the **Palm House.** *(Gardens open June-Aug. daily 8:30am-6pm, Sept.-May Su and Tu-Sa 8:30am-4pm. Palm House open June-Aug. daily 10am-3pm; Sept.-May Su and Tu-Sa 10am-3pm. Free.)*

OTHER SIGHTS. A trip to the **Carlsberg Brewery** will reward you with a wealth of ale-related knowledge and, more importantly, free samples. *(Ny Carlsbergvej 140. Take bus #26 to Bjerregårdsvej (dir.: Ålholm Pl.; 11min., every 10min.) and walk back the way the bus came to turn right onto Ny Carlsbergvej. ☎33 27 13 14; www.carlsberg.com. Open Su and Tu-Sa 10am-4pm. Free.)*

🎵 🎭 ENTERTAINMENT AND FESTIVALS

For events, consult *Copenhagen This Week.* The **Royal Theater** is home to the world-famous Royal Danish Ballet; the box office is located at Tordenskjoldsg. 7. (Open M-Sa 10am-6pm.) For same-day half-price tickets, head to the **Tivoli ticket office,** Vesterbrog. 3. (☎33 15 10 12. Open mid-Apr. to mid-Sept. daily 10am-8pm; mid-Sept. to mid-Apr. 9am-7pm.) Call **Arte,** Hvidkildevej 64 (☎38 88 22 22), to ask about student discounts. Tickets for a variety of events are sold online at www.billetnet.dk. During the world-class **Copenhagen Jazz Festival** (☎33 93 20 13; www.cjf.dk) in mid-July, the city teems with free outdoor concerts. Other festivals include the **Swingin' Copenhagen** festival in late May (www.swinging-copenhagen.dk) and the **Copenhagen Autumn Jazz** festival in early November.

🎧 NIGHTLIFE

In Copenhagen, weekends often begin on Wednesday, clubs rock until 5am, and then the "morning pubs" open up. On Tuesday and Thursday, most bars and clubs have reduced covers and cheap drinks. The city center, **Nørrebro,** and **Østerbro** reverberate with hip, crowded bars. Fancier options abound along **Nyhavn,** but loads of Danes just bring beer and sit on the pier. Copenhagen is known for its progressive view on homosexuality, but its gay and lesbian scene is surprisingly calm.

▨ **Park,** Østerbrog. 79, in the Østerbro. An enormous, enormously popular club with 2 packed dance floors, a live music hall, and a rooftop patio. Beer 40kr. Cover Th-Sa 60kr. Restaurant open Tu-Sa 11am-10pm. Club open Th-Sa 11am-5am, Su-Tu 11am-midnight, W 11am-2am.

▨ **Rust,** Guldbergsg. 8, in Nørrebro. More intimate than other area nightclubs, with a chic, yet chill ambience. Expect lines after 1am. Cover W 35kr, Th 30kr, F-Sa 50kr. No cover (but no crowd) before 11pm. Open W-Sa 10pm-5am.

The Moose Bar, on Sværtevej. Low on ambiance, high on local spirit. Cheap Happy-Hour specials. Happy Hour Tu, Th, and Sa 9pm-6am. 2 pints 30kr. 2 mixed drinks 25kr. Open Su-M, and W 11am-2am, Tu and Th-Sa 11am-6am.

IN, Nørreg. 1. Steep cover comes with free champagne and wine once inside. Lively and popular club after hours. 18+. Th cover men 130kr, women 80kr; F-Sa 165kr. Open W 10pm-4am, Th 11pm-6am, F 11pm-8am, Sa 11pm-10am.

PAN Club and Café, Knabrostr. 3. Gay cafe, bar, and disco. Cover F-Sa 50kr. Cafe open W-Th 9pm, F-Sa 10pm; disco opens 11pm and gets going around 1am.

▨ DAYTRIPS FROM COPENHAGEN

Stunning castles and white sand beaches hide in Northern and Central Zealand. Trains offer easy access to many attractive sights within an hour of Copenhagen.

HUMLEBÆK AND RUNGSTED. Humlebæk distinguishes itself with the spectacular ▨**Louisiana Museum of Modern Art,** 13 Gl. Strandvej, named for the three wives (all named Louisa) of the estate's original owner. Featuring works by Calder, Lichtenstein, Picasso, and Warhol, Louisiana is an engulfing experience; the building and its sculpture-studded grounds overlooking the sea are themselves worth the trip. Follow signs 1.5km north from the Humlebæk station, or take bus #388 (dir.: Helsingør; every 20min., 15kr) to *Louisiana*. (☎ 49 19 07 19. Open M-Tu and Th-Su 10am-5pm, W 10am-10pm. 72kr, students 65kr.) The quiet harbor town of **Rungsted** is where Karen Blixen (pseudonym Isak Dinesen) wrote *Out of Africa*. The **Karen Blixen Museum,** Rungsted Strandvej 111, details her life. Follow the street leading out of the train station and turn right on Rungstedsvej, then right again on Rungsted Strandvej; or, take bus #388 and tell the driver your destination. (☎ 45 57 10 57. Open May-Sept. Su and Tu-Sa 10am-5pm; Oct.-Apr. W-F 1-4pm, Sa-Su 11am-4pm. 35kr. Audioguide 25kr.) Both Humlebæk (45min., every 20min., 53kr or 4 clips) and Rungsted (30min., every 20min., 53kr or 4 clips) are on the Copenhagen-Helsingør **rail** line. The **tourist office** kiosk is on the corner by the museum.

HILLERØD. Hillerød is home of the moated ▨**Frederiksborg Slot;** with its exquisite Baroque gardens, brick ramparts, and dazzling Great Hall, it is the most impressive of Northern Zealand's castles. To get there from the station, cross the street onto Vibekeg. and follow the signs; at the main plaza, walk to the pond and follow it to reach the castle. (☎ 48 26 04 39. Castle open Apr.-Oct. daily 10am-5pm; Nov.-Mar. 11am-3pm. 60kr, students 50kr. Gardens open May-Aug. daily 10am-9pm; Sept. and Apr. 10am-7pm; Oct. and Mar. 10am-5pm; Nov.-Feb. 10am-4pm. Free.) Hillerød is at the end of **S-train** lines A and E (40min., every 15min., 53kr or 4 clips).

CHARLOTTENLUND AND KLAMPENBORG. Charlottenlund and Klampenborg, on the coastal line, feature topless **beaches.** To get to the beach from the Charlottenlund station, follow the signs for the "Danmark Akvarium," which is next to the

DENMARK

beach. The Klampenborg beach is somewhat bigger. Less refined than Tivoli, **Bakken,** the world's oldest amusement park, delivers more thrills. From the Klampenborg train station, turn left, cross the overpass, and head through the park. (☎ 39 63 73 00; www.bakken.dk. Open late March to late Aug. Hours vary; consult the website. Free admission. Rides 10-35kr each; unlimited rides 199kr.) Bakken borders the **Jægersborg Deer Park,** the royal family's former hunting grounds. It is still home to wooded paths, the **Eremitage** summer chateau, and over 2000 deer. Charlottenlund (18min., every 20min., 23kr or 3 clips) and Klampenborg (22min., every 20min., 30kr or 4 clips) are on **S-train** lines C and F+.

HELSINGØR AND HORNBÆK. Helsingør, 5km from the coast of Sweden, was formerly a strategic Danish stronghold. The fortified 15th-century **Kronborg Slot** was captured and ransacked by the Swedes in 1658, only to be returned two years later. Also known as **Elsinore,** the castle is the setting for Shakespeare's *Hamlet* (although neither the historical "Amled" nor the Bard ever came to visit). A statue of Viking chief Holger Danske sleeps in the castle's spooky casemates; according to legend, he will awake to face any threat to Denmark's safety. The castle also houses the **Danish Maritime Museum,** which contains a sea biscuit from 1852. From the train station, turn right and follow the signs along the waterfront. (☎ 49 21 30 78; www.kronborg.dk. Open May-Sept. daily 10:30am-5pm; Apr. and Oct. Su and Tu-Sa 11am-4pm; Nov.-Mar. Su and Tu-Sa 11am-3pm. Castle and casemates 40kr. Maritime Museum 30kr. Combination ticket 60kr. Guided 45min. tour of castle daily 2pm. Free.) Helsingør is at the end of the northern **train** line (55min., every 20min., 53kr or 4 clips). The **tourist office,** Havnepl. 3, is in the Kulturhuset, the large brick building across from the station. (☎ 49 21 13 33. Open mid-June to Aug. M-Th 9am-5pm, F 9am-6pm, Sa 10am-3pm; Sept. to mid-June M-F 9am-4pm, Sa 10am-1pm.) To reach the gorgeous beachfront **Helsingør Vandrerhjem Hostel (HI) ❷,** Ndr. Strandvej 24, take bus #340 (8min., every hr.). Or, take the train toward Hornbæk, get off at *Hojstrup,* and follow the path across the park; it's on the other side of the street. (☎ 49 21 16 40; www.helsingorhostel.dk. Breakfast 45kr. Sheets 40kr. Reception daily 8am-noon and 3-9pm. Curfew 11pm. Open Feb.-Nov. Dorms 110kr; doubles 300kr; triples 400kr. Nonmembers add 30kr.)

Hornbæk, a small, untouristed fishing town near Helsingør, offers beautiful beaches. The town hosts a wild harbor festival on the fourth weekend in July. **Bus** #340 runs from Helsingør to Hornbæk (25min., every 1-2hr., 23kr). The **tourist office,** Vestre Stejlebakke 2A, in the public library, has a listing of local B&Bs. Turn right from the station onto Havnevej, left onto Ndr. Strandvej, then right through the alley just before the Danske bank. (☎ 49 70 47 47; www.hornbaek.dk. Open M-Tu and Th 2-7pm, W and F 10am-5pm, Sa 10am-2pm.)

ISHØJ. The small harbor town of Ishøj, just south of Copenhagen, is home to the **Arken Museum of Modern Art,** Skovvej 100, which features temporary exhibitions by notable artists; Edward Munch and Gerhard Richter have both been featured. (☎ 43 54 02 22; www.arken.dk. Open Su, Tu and Th-Sa 10am-5pm, W 10am-9pm. 55kr, students 35kr.) Take bus #128 (every hr., 14kr) or follow the signs from the station (45min. walk). From Copenhagen take **S-train** lines A or E. **Ishøj Strand Vandrerhjem ❷,** Ishøj Strandvej 13, is near the beach. (☎ 43 53 50 15. Breakfast 45kr. Sheets 40kr. **Internet** 2kr per min. Reception daily 8am-noon and 2-9:30pm. Dorms 100kr; singles and doubles 370-400kr. **Camping** 62kr per person.)

MØN. To see what Hans Christian Andersen once called the most beautiful spot in Denmark, head south of Copenhagen to the isle of Møn. The gorgeous **Møns Klint** (chalk cliffs) guard the northeastern section of the island. A scenic 3km hike from the cliffs, **Liselund Slot** sits in a beautiful park with peacocks and pastel farm houses. To get to either site, take bus #632 from Stege (30min., 3 per day, 12kr), or hike from the hostel (3km). To get to Møn, take the **train** from Copenhagen to Vordingborg (1½hr., 97kr), then bus #62 or 64 to Stege (45min., 36kr). The **Møns Turistbureau,** Storeg. 2, is next to the bus stop in Stege. (☎55 86 04 00; www.moentouristbureau.dk. Open June 15-Aug. M-F 9:30am-4:30pm, Sa 9am-6pm, Su 11am-1pm; Sept.-June 14 M-F 9:30am-4:30pm, Sa 9am-noon.) Stay at the lakeside **Youth Hostel (HI) ❷,** Langebjergvej 1. From mid-July to Aug., take the infrequent bus #632 to the campsite stop, backtrack, then take the first road on the right. From Sept. to mid-July, take bus #52 to Magleby and walk 2.5km left down the road. (☎55 81 20 30. Breakfast 45kr. Sheets 30-45kr. Reception daily 8am-noon and 4-8pm. Dorms 100kr; singles and doubles 280kr.)

ROSKILDE
☎46

Roskilde (pop. 53,000), in central Zealand, served as Denmark's capital when King Harald Bluetooth built the country's first Christian church here in AD 980. These days, Roskilde is famous for the ■**Roskilde Music Festival,** the largest outdoor concert in Northern Europe, where performers such as Coldplay, REM, U2, Bob Dylan, and Bob Marley have taken the stage. (www.roskilde-festival.dk. July 1-4, 2004.) The ornate sarcophagi of the red-brick ■**Roskilde Domkirke,** in Domkirkepl., house the remains of generations of Danish royalty. (☎35 16 24. Open Apr.-Sept. M-F 9am-4:45pm, Sa 9am-noon, Su 1-2pm; Oct.-Mar. Su 12:30-3:45pm, Tu-Sa 10am-3:45pm. 15kr, students 10kr. English tours mid-June to mid-Aug. M-F 11am and 2pm, Sa 11am, Su 2pm.) The **Viking Ship Museum,** Vindeboder 12, near Strandengen along the harbor, houses remnants of five ships sunk circa AD 1060 and salvaged in the late 1960s. From the tourist office, take the pleasant walk downhill through the park or take bus #607 (dir.: Boserup; free with train ticket). Book a ride on an authentic Viking ship, but be prepared to take an oar—conquest is no spectator sport. (☎30 02 00; www.vikingeskibsmuseet.dk. Museum open daily 9am-5pm. In summer 60kr, off-season 45kr. Boat trip 90kr, 50kr with museum ticket.)

Trains depart for Copenhagen (25-30min., every 15min., 52kr). The **tourist office,** Gullandsstr. 15, sells festival tickets and books rooms for a 25kr fee and a 10-15% deposit. From the train station, turn left on Jernbaneg., right on Allehelgansg., and left again on Bredg.; the office is at the corner of Bredg. and Gullandsstr. (☎31 65 65. Open mid-June to Aug. M-F 9am-6pm, Sa 10am-2pm; Apr. to mid-June M-F 9am-5pm, Sa 10am-1pm; Sept.-Mar. M-Th 9am-5pm, F 9am-4pm, Sa 10am-1pm.) The **Youth Hostel (HI) ❷,** Vindeboder 7, is on the harbor next to the Viking Museum shipyard. Book *far* in advance during the festival. (☎35 21 84; www.danhostel.dk/roskilde. Kitchen available. Breakfast 45kr. Sheets 40kr. Reception daily 8am-noon and 4-10pm. Dorms 100kr. Nonmembers add 30kr.) **Roskilde Camping ❶,** Baunehøjvej 7, is on the beach; take bus #603 (15kr) toward Veddelev to *Veddelev Byg.* (☎75 79 96. Reception daily 8am-9pm. Open Apr. to mid-Sept. 64kr per person.)

BORNHOLM

In an area ideal for bikers and nature-lovers, Bornholm's red-roofed cliffside villas may seem Mediterranean, but the flowers and half-timbered houses are undeniably Danish. The unique round churches (half the round churches in Denmark are in Bornholm) were both places of worship and fortresses for waiting out pirate attacks. The sandiest and longest **beaches** are at **Dueodde,** on the island's southern tip. For more info, check out www.bornholm.info.

■ **TRANSPORTATION. Trains** from Copenhagen to Ystad, Sweden are timed to meet the **ferry** from Ystad to Rønne, Bornholm's capital. (Train ☎70 13 14 15; 1¾hr., 5-6 per day; ferry 1½hr.; trip 205kr, under-26 180kr.) A cheaper option is the combo

NO WORK, ALL PLAY

ROSKILDE ROCKS

In AD 800, Vikings put the small town of Roskilde on the map by sailing to continental Europe and annihilating the feudal order. Over a millennium later, the tiny town is taking Europe by storm with its annual Roskilde Music Festival, again challenging any semblance of law and order.

Headliners Coldplay, Metallica, REM, U2, Bob Dylan, and Björk have all graced the enormous Orange Stage, but 70,000 international fans don't trek to Roskilde for only the big-name acts. Northern Europe's largest outdoor music festival is not just a concert; it's a week-long, Woodstock-esque musical experience. Although the festival technically begins on Thursday, the gates open four days earlier, offering revelers less hygiene and more hijinks. With five stages showcasing local and international bands, rhythm and communal atmosphere flow nonstop all week.

Attendees wear wrist bands in lieu of tickets, and the most devoted fans sport their bracelets year-round like badges of honor—those boasting 5 years' worth are offered free admission.

At the end of the seven days, unbathed, dehydrated, and sated music-lovers have new friends—and 358 days to recover.

Roskilde reconvenes July 1-4, 2004. For ticket info, see www.roskilde-festival.dk.

bus/ferry route (bus ☎56 95 18 66; 1½hr., 4-6 per day; ferry 1½hr.; trip 195/145kr.) Overnight ferries from Copenhagen to Rønne leave at 11:30pm and arrive in Rønne at 6:30am (224kr, add 76kr for a dorm-style bed). **Bornholmstrafikken** (Rønne ☎56 95 18 66; www.bornholmferries.dk) offers the combo train/ferry and bus/ferry routes. **Scandlines** operates ferries from Fährhafen Sassnitz in Germany. (☎+49 383 926 44 20. 3½hr., 1-2 per day, 90-130kr.) Bornholm has an efficient local BAT **bus** service. (☎56 95 21 21. 36-45kr, 24hr. pass 110kr.) Bus #7 makes a circuit of the entire island; it starts at Rønne and end at Hammershus, stopping at towns and attractions along the way. There are numerous well-marked cycling paths between all the major towns; the **bike** ride from Rønne to Sandvig is about 28km.

RØNNE. Tiny but charming Rønne (pop. 14,000), on the southwest coast, is Bornholm's principal port of entry. The town serves mainly as an outpost for biking trips through the surrounding fields, forests, and beaches. Rent a **bike** from **Bornholms Cykeludlejning**, next door to the tourist office at Ndr. Kystvej 5. (☎56 95 13 59. Reserve ahead in July. 60kr per day. Open May-Sept. daily 7am-4pm and 8:30-9pm.) The **tourist office**, Ndr. Kystvej 3, books private rooms (140-195kr) for free. (☎56 95 95 00. Open June-Aug. M-Sa 9am-5pm, Su 10am-3pm; Aug.-Feb. M-F 9am-4pm; Mar.-May M-F 9am-4pm, Su 10am-4pm.) The **HI Youth Hostel** ❸, Arsenalvej 12, is in a wooded area near the coastline. From the ferry, walk 3min. down Snellemark to the red BAT terminal and take bus #23 or 24. (☎56 95 13 40. Breakfast 45kr. Kitchen available. Sheets 55kr. Reception daily 8am-noon and 4-5pm. Open mid-June to mid-Aug. Dorms 100kr. Nonmembers add 30kr.) **Galløkken Camping** ❶, Strandvejen 4, is near the city center and the beach. (☎56 95 23 20. Bikes 55kr per day. Reception 7:30am-noon and 2-9pm. Open mid-May to Aug. 58kr per person.) Get groceries at **Kvickly,** opposite the tourist office. (Open mid-June to late Aug. daily 9am-8pm; Sept. to early June M-F 9am-8pm, Sa 8am-5pm, Su 10am-4pm.)

SANDVIG AND ALLINGE. On the tip of the spectacular northern coast, the white-sand and rock beaches in these two small towns attract bikers and bathers. A few kilometers from central Allinge is **Hammershus**, northern Europe's largest castle ruin. Take bus #1, 2, or 7. Set in a field of waving grass, the whitewashed **Østerlars Rundkirke** is the largest of the island's four uniquely fortified round churches. Take bus #3 or 9 to *Østerlars Kirke.* Many pleasant trails originate in Sandvig; the rocky area around **Hammeren,** northeast of the town, is a 2hr. walk that can only be covered on foot. The **Nordbornholms Turistbureau**, Kirkeg. 4, in Allinge, finds rooms. (☎56 48 00 01. Open mid-June to mid-Aug. M-F 10am-5pm, Sa 10am-3pm; mid-Aug. to mid-June 10am-5pm, Sa 10am-noon.) Rent **bikes** at the **Sandvig Cykeludlejning**, Strandvejen 121. (☎56 48 00 60. 55kr per day. Open June-Aug. M-F 9am-4pm, Sa 9am-2pm, Su 10am-1pm.) Many local families rent rooms; look for signs on Strandvejen between Sandvig and Allinge. Just outside Sandvig is the lakeside **Sandvig Vandrerhjem (HI) ❸**, Hammershusvej 94. (☎56 48 03 62. Breakfast 45kr. Sheets 60kr. Reception daily 9-10am and 4-6pm. Open Apr.-Oct. Dorms 100kr; singles 250kr; doubles 350kr.) **Sandvig Familie Camping ❶**, Sandlinien 5, has sites on the sea. (☎56 48 04 47. Bikes 50kr per day, 200kr per week. Reception daily 8am-11pm. Open Apr.-Oct. 50kr per person, 15kr per tent.) **Riccos ❶**, Strandg. 8, a pleasant cafe near the sea, offers free **Internet** access. (Open 7am-10pm.)

FUNEN (FYN)

Situated between Zealand to the east and the Jutland Peninsula to the west, the island of Funen is Denmark's garden. This remote breadbasket is no longer isolated from the rest of Denmark—a bridge and tunnel now connect it to Zealand. Pick up maps (75kr) of the bike paths covering the island at Funen tourist offices.

ODENSE

Most tourists are drawn to Odense (OH-n-sa; pop. 185,000) by the legacy of Hans Christian Andersen and his fairytales. At **Hans Christian Andersen's Hus**, Hans Jensens Str. 37-45, you can learn about the great author's eccentricities, listen to his timeless children's tales, and follow his rags-to-riches rise to fame. From the tourist office, walk right on Vesterg., then turn left on Torveg. and right on Hans Jensens Str. (☎65 51 46 20. Museum open mid-June to Aug. daily 9am-7pm; Sept. to mid-June Su and Tu-Sa 10am-4pm. English performances W-Th 3pm. 40kr.) A few scraps of Andersen's own ugly-duckling childhood are on display at **H. C. Andersen's Barndomshjem** (Childhood Home), Munkemøllestr. 3-5. (☎66 14 88 14. Open mid-June to Aug. daily 10am-4pm; Sept. to mid-June Su and Tu-Sa 11am-3pm. 10kr.) At the **Carl Nielsen Museum**, Claus Bergs G. 11, listen to the works of the most famous Danish musician. (☎66 14 88 14. Open Su noon-4pm, Th-F 4-8pm. 15kr.) Walk down Vesterg. to the eclectic **Brandts Klædefabrik**, Brandts Passage 37 and 43, a former cloth mill that houses the **Museum of Photographic Art**, the **Graphic Arts Museum**, and a **contemporary art** gallery. (☎66 13 78 97. All open July-Aug. daily 10am-5pm; Sept.-June Su and Tu-Sa 10am-5pm. 25-30kr, combination ticket 50kr.)

Trains arrive from Copenhagen (1½hr., 197kr) and from Svendborg via Kværndrup (40min., 55kr). **Buses** depart from behind the train station. The **tourist office**, on Rådhuspl., books rooms for a 35kr fee and sells the **Odense Adventure Pass**, good for admission to museums, discounts on plays, and unlimited public transport (24hr. pass 110kr, 48hr. pass 150kr). From the train station, take Nørreg., which becomes Asylg., and turn left at the end on Vesterg.; it's on the right. (☎66 12 75 20; www.visitodense.com. Open June 15-Aug. M-F 9:30am-7pm, Sa 10am-5pm, Su 10am-4pm; Sept.-June 14 M-F 9:30am-4:30pm, Sa 10am-1pm.) The library in the station has free **Internet**, but you must reserve a slot in advance. (Open Apr.-Sept. M-Th 10am-7pm, F 10am-4pm, Sa 10am-2pm; Oct.-Mar. M-Th 10am-7pm, Sa-Su 10am-4pm.) Rent **bikes** next door to the station at **Rolsted Cykler.** (85kr per day, 300kr deposit. Open M-Th 10am-5:30pm, F 10am-7pm, Sa 10am-2pm.) The fabulous **Danhostel Odense City (HI) ❹** is attached to the station. (☎63 11 04 25. Kitchen available. Breakfast 45kr. Sheets 50kr. Laundry 40kr. Internet 10kr per 15min. Reception daily 8am-noon and 4-8pm. Call ahead. Dorms 115kr; singles 310-360kr;

doubles 360-460kr; triples 420-460kr; quads 460kr. Nonmembers add 30kr.) To reach **DCU Camping ❷**, Odensevej 102, take bus #21, 22, or 23 (dir.: Højby) and ask the driver to drop you off. (☎66 11 47 02. Pool. Reception daily 7am-10pm. Open late Mar. to Sept. 58kr per person, 20kr per tent.) Get groceries at **Aktiv Super,** at the corner of Nørreg. and Skulkenborgg. (Open M-F 9am-7pm, Sa 9am-4pm.)

🖪 **DAYTRIP FROM ODENSE: KVÆRNDRUP.** Just 30min. south of Odense on the Svendborg rail line is Kværndrup, home to 🖾**Egeskov Slot,** a stunning 16th-century castle that appears to float on the surrounding lake. Spend at least two hours in the magnificent Renaissance interior and grounds, which include a bamboo labyrinth and motorcycle museum. (Castle open July daily 10am-7pm, W until 11pm; May-June and Aug.-Sept. 10am-5pm. Grounds open July daily 10am-8pm; June and Aug. 10am-6pm; Apr.-May and Sept. 10am-5pm. Grounds, maze, and museums 75kr, with castle 130kr.) Take the Svendborg-bound **train** from Odense to Kværndrup; from the station, go right and continue to Bøjdenvej, the main road. Wait for bus #920 (every hr.; 18kr, free with connecting train ticket), or turn right and walk 2km through wheat fields to the castle. The **tourist office,** Egeskovg. 1, is up the street from the castle. (☎62 27 10 46. Open July daily noon-8pm; June and Aug. noon-6pm; Sept. and Apr.-May noon-5pm.)

SVENDBORG AND TÅSINGE

On Funen's southern coast, an hour from Odense by train, Svendborg (pop. 43,000) is a harbor town and a departure point for ferries to the south Funen islands. On the adjacent island of Tåsinge (pop. 6,000), the regal 17th-century **Valdemars Slot,** built by Christian IV for his son, boasts a yachting museum, Scandinavia's largest hunting museum, a toy museum, and a beach. (☎62 22 61 06. Open May-Aug. daily 10am-5pm; Sept. Su and Tu-Sa 10am-5pm; Apr. and Oct. Sa-Su 10am-5pm. Castle 60kr, combination ticket 110kr.)

Several **trains** from Odense to Svendborg are timed to meet the **ferry** (☎62 52 40 00) to Ærøskøbing; ferries depart behind the train station. The **tourist office,** on Centrum Pl., books ferries and rooms. From the train station, go left on Jernbaneg., then right on Brog., which becomes Gerritsg., and right on Kyseborgstr.; it's in the plaza on the right. (☎62 21 09 80. Open late June-Aug. M-F 9:30am-6pm, Sa 9:30am-3pm; Sept.-late June M-F 9:30am-5pm, Sa 9:30am-12:30pm.) To get from the station to the **Youth Hostel (HI) ❷**, Vesterg. 45, a five-star on the Danhostel scale, turn left on Jernbaneg. and walk with the coast to your left, then go right onto Valdemarsg., which becomes Vesterg. (☎62 21 66 99; dk@danhostel-svendborg.dk. Bikes 50kr per day. Kitchen available. Breakfast 45kr. Sheets 50kr. Laundry 30kr. Reception M-F 8am-8pm, Su 8am-noon and 4-8pm. Dorms 115kr; singles and doubles 375kr. Nonmembers add 30kr.) To get to **Carlsberg Camping ❶**, Sundbrovej 19, take bus #800, 801, or 910 from the ferry terminal to *Bregninge Tasinge*. (☎62 22 53 84; www.carlsbergcamping.dk. Reception daily 7:30am-10pm. Open Apr.-Sept. 59kr per person.) Pick up groceries at **Kvickly,** Gerritsg. 33. (Open M-F 9am-8pm, Sa 8am-5pm.) **Postal Code:** 5700.

ÆRØ

The wheat fields, harbors, and hamlets of Ærø (EH-ruh), a small island off the southern coast of Funen, quietly preserve an earlier era of Danish history. Cows, rather than real estate developers, lay claim to the beautiful land, and bikes are the ideal way to explore the Island's three towns, Ærøskøbing, Marstal, and Søby.

🖪 **TRANSPORTATION. Ferries** (☎62 52 40 00) run between Ærøskøbing and Svendborg (1¼hr.; 6 per day; one-way 79kr, round-trip 132kr; buy tickets on board). From Mommark, on Jutland, you can sail to Søby (1hr.; 2-5 per day, Oct.-Mar. W-Su only; 85kr; call ahead), on Ærø's northwestern shore. **Bus** #990 travels between Ærøskøbing, Marstal, and Søby (20kr, day pass 60kr).

ÆRØSKØBING. Due to economic stagnation followed by conservation efforts, the town of Ærøskøbing appears today almost as it did 200 years ago. Rosebushes, half-timbered houses, and a quaint town center attract German boaters and vacationing Danes. The **tourist office,** Vesterg. 1, opposite the ferry landing, books rooms for a 25kr fee. (☎62 52 13 00; www.arre.dk. Open mid-June to Aug. M-F 9am-5pm, Sa 9am-2pm, Su 9:30am-12:30pm; Sept. to mid-June M-F 9am-4pm, Sa 9:30am-12:30pm.) Rent **bikes** from the hostel or **Pilebækken Cykel & Servicestation,** Pilebæken 11. (☎62 52 11 10. 45kr per day.) To get to the **Youth Hostel (HI) ❷,** Smedevejen 15, turn left on Smedeg., which becomes Nørreg., Østerg., and finally Smedevejen. (☎62 52 10 44. Breakfast 40kr. Kitchen available. Sheets 40kr. Bikes 45kr per day. Reception daily 8am-noon and 4-8pm. Check-in 6pm. Open Apr.-Sept. Dorms 100kr; singles and doubles 260kr. Nonmembers add 30kr. No credit cards.) **Ærøskøbing Camping ❶,** Sygehusvejen 40b, is 10min. to the right along Sygehusvejen, off Vestre Allé as you leave the ferry. (☎62 52 18 54. Reception daily 8am-noon and 3-10pm. Open May-Sept. 54kr per person.) Stock up at **Netto,** across from the ferry landing. (Open M-F 9am-7pm, Sa 8am-5pm.) **Postal Code:** 5970.

JUTLAND (JYLLAND)

The Jutland peninsula, homeland of the Jutes who joined the Anglos and Saxons in the conquest of England, is Denmark's largest landmass. Beaches and campgrounds mark the area as prime summer vacation territory, while verdant hills, marshlands, and sparse forests add color and texture.

◧ FERRIES TO ENGLAND, NORWAY, AND SWEDEN

From **Frederikshavn** (see p. 293), on the northern tip of Jutland, **Stena Line** ferries (☎96 20 02 00; www.stenaline.com) leave for Gothenburg, Sweden (2-3¼hr.; 100-125kr, 50% Scanrail discount) and Oslo, Norway (8½hr.; 145-255kr, with Scanrail 90kr). **Color Line** (☎99 56 20 00; www.colorline.com) sails to Larvik, Norway (6¼hr.; 180-410kr, students and seniors 50% discount). Color Line boats also go from Hirtshals, on the northern tip of Jutland, to Oslo (8-8½hr., 180-410kr) and Kristiansand, Norway (2½-4½hr., 160-350kr).

ÅRHUS

Århus (ORE-hoos; pop. 280,000), Denmark's second-largest city, bills itself as "the world's smallest big city." With small-town charm and a lively downtown, many find that this laid-back student and cultural center fits just right.

◧◪ TRANSPORTATION AND PRACTICAL INFORMATION. Trains run from

Århus to: Aalborg (1¾hr., 2 per hr., 138kr); Copenhagen (3hr., 2 per hr., 273kr); Fredericia (1hr., 2 per hr., 105kr); and Frederikshavn (2½hr., every hr., 180kr). All major **buses** leave from the train station or from outside the tourist office. To get to the **tourist office,** exit the train station and go left across Banegardspl., then take the first right on Park Allé. They book private rooms (200-300kr) for a 25kr fee and sell the **Århus pass,** which includes unlimited public transit and admission to most museums and sights (1-day 97kr, 2-day 121kr). If you're not going to many museums, consider the **24hr. Tourist Ticket** (50kr), also available at the tourist office, which offers unlimited bus transportation. (☎89 40 67 00; www.visitaarhus.com. Open mid-June to early Sept. M-F 9:30am-6pm, Sa 9:30am-5pm, Su 9:30am-1pm; May to mid-June M-F 9:30am-5pm, Sa 10am-1pm; early Sept.-Apr. M-F 9am-4pm, Sa 10am-1pm.) The main **library,** on Vesterg. 55 in Mølleparken, has free **Internet** access. (Open May-Sept. M-Th 10am-7pm, F 10am-6pm, Sa 10am-2pm; Oct.-Apr. M

10am-10pm, Tu-Th 10am-8pm, F 10am-6pm, Sa 10am-3pm, Su noon-4pm.) After hours, try **Boomtown NetCafe,** Åboulevarden 21, along the canal. (☎89 41 39 30. Open Su-Th 10am-2am, F-Sa 10am-8am. 20kr per 30min., 30kr per hr.) The **post office,** Banegardspl. 1A, is next to the train station. **Postal Code:** 8000.

🏠🍴 ACCOMMODATIONS AND FOOD. Popular with backpackers, **Århus City Sleep-In ❸,** Havneg. 20, is 10min. from the train station and in the middle of the city's nightlife. From the train station, follow Ryesg., which becomes Sønderg., all the way to the canal. Take the steps or elevator down to Åboulevarden, cross the canal, and turn right; at the end of the canal, turn left on Mindebrog., then left again on Havneg. (☎86 19 20 55; www.citysleep-in.dk. Bikes 50kr per day; deposit 200kr. Kitchen available. Breakfast 40kr. Sheets 40kr; deposit 30kr. Laundry 25kr. Key deposit 50kr. Internet 20kr per hr. Reception 24hr. Dorms 105kr; doubles 320-360kr. Credit card surcharge 4.75%.) **Hotel Guldsmeden ❺,** Guldsmedg. 40, has gorgeous rooms in the center of town. The annex in the back has the cheapest rooms. From the tourist office, continue along Park Allé, which becomes Immervad, and veer left onto Guldsmedg. at the intersection of Vesterg. (☎86 13 45 50; www.hotelguldmeden.dk. Breakfast included. Reception daily 7am-midnight. Singles 495-895kr; doubles 745-995kr.) **Blommehaven Camping ❶,** Ørneredevej 35, is a camper's resort located in the Marselisborg forest south of the city, near the beach. In summer, take bus #19 from the station to the grounds; off-season, take bus #6 to *Hørhavevej.* (☎86 27 02 07; info@blomme-haven.dk. Reception daily 8am-noon and 2-10pm. Open Apr.-Aug. 62kr per person, 20kr per site. Add 80kr without camping card.) **Frederiksgade** has a few restaurants with all-you-can-eat buffets. Get groceries at **Netto,** in St. Knuds Torv. (Open M-F 9am-8pm, Sa 8am-5pm.)

📷🎭 SIGHTS AND ENTERTAINMENT. The **Århus Kunstmuseum,** on Vennelyst-parken, houses modern Danish art. (☎86 13 52 55. Open Su and Tu-Sa 10am-5pm, W until 8pm. 40kr, students 30kr.) Just outside town is the **Moesgård Museum of Prehistory,** Moesgård Allé 20, which chronicles Århus's history from 4000 BC through the Viking age and displays the famous mummified **◙Grauballe Man.** Take bus #6 from the train station to the end. (Open Apr.-Sept. daily 10am-5pm; Oct.-Mar. Su and Tu-Sa 10am-4pm. 45kr, students 35kr.) The **Prehistoric Trail** is a beautiful walk that leads from behind the museum to a sandy **beach** (3km). In summer, bus #19 (last bus 10:18pm) returns from the beach to the Århus station. West of the town center, the open-air **Den Gamle By,** Viborgvej 2, re-creates traditional Danish life with actors in authentic garb and original (but relocated) Danish buildings. From the center, take bus #3, 14, 25, or 55. (☎86 12 31 88. Open June-Aug. daily 9am-6pm; off-season reduced hours. 75kr; students 60kr. Grounds free after hours.) The exquisite rose garden of **Marselisborg Slot,** Kongevejen 100, Queen Margrethe II's summer getaway, is open to the public. From the train station, take bus #1, 18, or 19. (Palace and rose gardens closed in July and whenever the Queen is in residence. Changing of the guard daily at noon when the Queen is in residence.) To get to **Tivoli Friheden,** Skovbrynet 1, a smaller version of the amusement park in Copenhagen, take bus #4 or 19. (☎86 14 73 00; www.frihe-den.dk. Hours and dates vary, but usually open May to mid-Aug. 1-9pm. 35kr admission; unlimited rides 160kr.)

Århus hosts an acclaimed **jazz festival** (July 10-17, 2004; www.jazzfest.dk). The **Århus Festuge** (☎89 31 82 70; www.aarhusfestuge.dk), from the last weekend in August to early September, is a rollicking celebration of theater, dance, and music. Throughout the year, **Åboulevarden,** in the heart of town, hops with trendy cafes and bars. **Waxies,** Frederiksg. 16, is a popular pub with a young crowd. (Open Su-W 11am-2am, Th-Sa 11am-5am.)

▶ DAYTRIP FROM ÅRHUS: BILLUND. Billund is best known as the home of ▦**Legoland,** an amusement park filled with spectacular sculptures made from over 50 million Lego pieces. "Lego" is an abbreviation of the Danish *leg godt* ("have fun playing"), and young and old will have no trouble doing just that. Don't miss the bone-rattling **Power Builder,** most intense ride in the park. (☎ 75 33 13 33; www.legoland.com. Park open July to mid-Aug. daily 10am-9pm; June and late Aug. daily 10am-8pm; Apr.-May and Sept.-Oct. reduced hours. Day pass 170kr, under-13 150kr. Free entrance 30min. before rides close.) To get there, take the **train** from Århus to Vejle (45min., every hr.), then take **bus** #912 (dir.: Grinsted) to the park.

SILKEBORG AND RY

Closest to Jutland's wilderness, Silkeborg and Ry both offer a prime base for canoeing, biking, and hiking. Silkeborg (pop. 38,000) is a bit bigger with a bit less charm, but offers more conveniences. The **Silkeborg Museum** boasts the **Tollund Man,** a 2500-year-old body found preserved in a local bog. (Open May to late Oct. daily 10am-5pm; late Oct. to Apr. M-Tu and Th-F 10am-5pm, W and Sa-Su noon-4pm. 40kr.) **Trains** run from Silkeborg to Århus (2 per hr., 39kr) and Ry (2 per hr., 25kr). Visit the **tourist office** for more info on outdoor activities. (☎ 86 82 19 11; www.silkeborg.com. Open mid-June to Aug. M-F 9am-5pm, Sa 9am-3pm, Su 9:30am-12:30pm; Sept. to mid-June M-F 9am-4pm, Sa 9am-noon.) The **Silkeborg Vandrerhjem (HI) ❶** is near downtown and the water. (☎ 86 82 36 42. Breakfast 45kr. Sheets 40kr. Laundry. Reception daily 8am-noon and 4-8pm. Dorms June-Aug. only 75kr. Quads 440kr; 6-person rooms 660kr.)

Smaller and more charming, Ry (pop. 4,800) is an excellent, if less developed, base for exploration. Rent canoes from **Ry Kanofart,** Kyhnsvej 20, and bikes from **Ry Mosquito Cykel Center,** Skangerborgvej 19. (Kanofart ☎ 86 89 11 67. 60kr per hr., full-day 300kr. Open May-Aug. daily 9am-6pm. Cykel Center ☎ 86 89 14 91. Open M-Th 8am-5:30pm, F 8am-6pm, Sa 8am-noon.) The helpful **tourist office** sells maps, including one to **Himmelbjerget Tower,** one of Denmark's highest points. (☎ 86 89 34 22; www.visitry.com. Open July M-F 6:15am-4pm, Sa 10am-2pm; June and Aug. M-F 6:15am-4pm, Sa 10am-2pm; Sept.-May M-F 6:15am-4pm, Sa 10am-noon.)

FREDERICIA

Now known primarily as a major railway junction, Fredericia (pop. 49,000) was built between 1650 and 1657 by King Frederik III following his defeat in the Thirty Years War. Convinced the country needed better protection, Frederik outfitted the town with moated and cannon-strewn **ramparts.** In the Battle of Fredericia in 1849, the ramparts helped the Danes ward off enemy troops from the south with sweet vindication. For a great view, climb the **White Water Tower,** across the street from the tourist office. (Open late June to mid-Aug. daily 10am-4pm; May to late June and mid-Aug. to Sept. 11am-4pm. 10kr.)

Trains go to Århus (1¾hr., 105kr) and Copenhagen (2hr., 241kr). To get to the **tourist office,** Danmarksg. 2A, go left across the plaza, and then turn right on Vesterbrog, and right again on Danmarksport. (☎ 75 92 13 77; www.visitfredericia.dk. Open mid-June to Aug. M-F 9am-6pm, Sa 9am-2pm; Sept. to mid-June M-F 10am-5pm, Sa 10am-1pm.) The library, on the corner of Danmarksg. and Prinsesseg, has free **Internet** access. (Open M-Th 10am-7pm, F 10am-5pm, Sa 10am-2pm.) **Fredericia Vandrerhjem and Kursuscenter (HI) ❷,** Vestre Ringvej 98, is situated on a beautiful lake. From the station, go across the plaza, turn left on Vejlevej, go under the bridge, turn right on the first road past the lake, walk for 10min., then take the path on the right. (☎ 75 92 12 87; www.fredericia-danhostel.dk. Breakfast 45kr. Sheets 55kr. Reception daily 8am-noon and 4-8pm. Dorms 118kr; doubles 420-472kr. Credit card surcharge 4.75%.) **Postal Code:** 7000.

D E N M A R K

RIBE

Aware of their town's historic value, the government of Ribe (pop. 8,000) forged preservation laws in 1899 forcing residents to maintain the character of their houses and to live in them year-round. The result is a magnificently preserved medieval town, beautifully situated on the salt plains near Jutland's west coast. For a great view, climb the 248 steps through the clockwork and huge bells of the 12th-century **cathedral tower**. (☎75 42 06 19. Open July to mid-Aug. M-Sa 10am-5:30pm, Su noon-5:30pm; May-June and mid-Aug. to Sept. M-Sa 10am-5pm, Su noon-5pm; Apr. and Oct. M-Sa 11am-6pm, Su noon-4pm; Nov.-Mar. daily 11am-3pm. 12kr.) Next to the *Radhus*, **Von Støckens Plads,** a former debtor's prison, houses a small museum on medieval torture. (☎76 88 11 22. Open June-Aug. daily 1-3pm; May and Sept. M-F 1-3pm. 15kr.) Follow the **night watchman** on his rounds for an English and Danish tour of town beginning in the Torvet. (35min.; June-Aug. 8 and 10pm; May and Sept. 10pm. Free.) South of town, the open-air **Ribe Vikingcenter,** Lustrupvej 4, re-creates a Viking town, complete with a farm and a marketplace. (☎75 41 16 11. Open July-Aug. daily 11am-4:30pm; May-June and Sept. M-F 11am-4pm. 60kr.) Take bus #711 to the **Vadehavscentret** (Wadden Sea Center), Okholmvej 5 in Vestervedsted, which gives *Mandøbus* tours of the marshes on the nearby island of Mandø. (Sea Center ☎75 44 61 61. Open Apr.-Oct. daily 10am-5pm; Feb.-Mar. and Nov. 10am-4pm. 50kr. Tours ☎75 44 51 07. May-Sept. daily. 50kr.)

Trains run to Bramming (25min., every hr., 30kr) and Esbjerg (40min., every hr., 50kr). The **tourist office,** Torvet 3, books rooms for a 20kr fee. From the train station, walk down Dagmarsg.; it's on the right in the main square. (☎75 42 15 00; www.ribe.dk. Open July-Aug. M-F 9:30am-5:30pm, Sa 10am-5pm, Su 10am-2pm; off-season reduced hours.) Access the **Internet** at **Gamer's Gateway,** Saltg. 20. (☎76 88 03 37. 25kr per hr. Open M-Tu 3pm-midnight, W-Su noon-midnight.) **Ribe Vandrerhjem (HI)** ❶, Sct. Pedersg. 16, offers **bike** rentals (60kr per day). From the station, cross the Viking Museum parking lot, bear right, walk down Sct. Nicolajg. to the end, then turn right on Saltg. and immediately left on Sct. Petersg. (☎75 42 06 20. Breakfast 45kr. Sheets 45kr. Laundry 45kr. Reception daily 8am-noon and 4-6pm. Open Feb.-Nov. Dorms 90kr; singles 250kr; doubles 325kr. Credit card surcharge 4%.) **Ribe Camping** ❶, Farupvej 2, is 1.5km from the town center. Take bus #715 (every 1½hr.) from the station to *Gredstedbro*. (☎75 41 07 77. 65kr per person; 2-person cabins 325kr.) **Seminarievej** is home to a number of supermarkets. Restaurants cluster around the cathedral. **Postal Code:** 6760.

VIBORG

Sights cluster around the cobblestone center of this well-preserved provincial town (pop. 30,000). The mid-19th-century granite **Viborg Cathedral,** Sct. Mogensg. 4, is covered with spectacular, colorful frescoes. (Open June-Aug. M-Sa 10am-5pm, Su noon-5pm; Apr.-May and Sept. M-Sa 11am-4pm, Su noon-4pm; Oct.-Mar. M-Sa 11am-3pm, Su noon-3pm.) A short trip outside of Viborg is the ▓**Mønsted Kalkgruber,** Kalkvaerksvej 8, a beautiful limestone cave shaped by subterranean rivers. Though there is no direct public transportation, the visit is worth the trek. Take bus #28 (every 1-2hr., 20kr) from Viborg to Mønsted and follow the signs for 1.5km. (Open daily Apr.-Oct. 10am-5pm. 45kr.)

Trains run to Århus (1½hr., every hr., 97kr.). To get to the **tourist office,** Nytorv 9, from the station, go straight across the rotary and onto Jernebaneg., turn right onto Sct. Mathiasg., go through part of the shopping area, and turn left into the main square. (☎87 25 30 75. Open mid-June to Aug. M-F 9am-5pm, Sa 9am-2pm; mid-May to mid-June M-F 9am-5pm, Sa 9:30am-12:30pm; Sept. to mid-May M-F 9am-4pm, Sa 9:30am-12:30pm.) Alongside a lake lie the **Youth Hostel (HI) and Viborg**

Sø Camping ❷, Vinkelvej 36. Take bus #707 from the station to *Vinkelvej* and continue walking along the road for 10min. (Hostel ☎86 67 17 81; viborg@danhostel.dk. Kitchen available. Breakfast 45kr. Laundry. Reception daily 7:30am-noon and 2-10pm. Dorms 100kr. Camping ☎86 67 13 11; viborg@dcu.dk.) Pick up groceries at **Netto** on Vesterbrog. (Open M-F 9am-8pm, Sa 8am-5pm.)

AALBORG

Modern Aalborg (OLE-borg; pop. 160,000) is a laid-back student haven located near the remains of the earliest known Viking settlement. **Lindholm Høje,** Vendilavej 11, is the site of 700 ancient Viking graves and a museum detailing life in Viking times. Take bus #6 or 25 (13kr) from outside the tourist office. (☎96 31 04 28. Graves open 24hr. Museum open mid-Apr. to Oct. daily 10am-5pm; Nov. to mid-Apr. M and W-Sa 10am-5pm, Tu 10am-4pm, Su 11am-4pm. 30kr, students 15kr.) The **Budolfi Church,** on Alg., has a brilliantly colored interior. From the tourist office, turn left onto Østeråg. and right on Alg. (Open May-Sept. M-F 9am-4pm, Sa 9am-2pm; Oct.-Apr. M-F 9am-3pm, Sa 9am-noon.) At the corner of Alg. and Molleg., an elevator descends to the ruins of the **Franciscan Friary.** (Open in summer daily 10am-5pm; off-season Su and Tu-Sa 10am-5pm. 20kr.) For a more exhilarating drop, head to the roller coasters at **Tivoliland,** on Karolinelundsvej, a smaller cousin of Copenhagen's famous amusement park. (Open July-Aug. daily 10am-10pm; Sept. and Apr. daily noon-8pm; May-June daily noon-9pm. Entrance 50kr. Rides 10-40kr.) Centuries ago, untamed Aalborg was beyond the northern reach of the king's soldiers and considered "north of law and justice"—at night, watch Aalborg's students carry on the city's wild past in the bars along **Jomfru Ane Gade.**

Trains arrive from Århus (1¾hr., every hr., 140kr) and Copenhagen (5hr., 2 per hr., 300kr). From the station, cross J.F.K. Pl. and turn left on Østeråg., which becomes Østeråg., to find the **tourist office,** Østeråg. 8. (☎98 12 60 22; www.visitaalborg.com. Open July M-F 9am-5:30pm, Sa 10am-4pm; late June and Aug. M-F 9am-5:30pm, Sa 10am-1pm; Sept. to mid-June M-F 9am-4:30pm, Sa 10am-1pm.) The library has free **Internet** access. (☎99 31 44 00. Open June-Aug. M-F 10am-8pm, Sa 10am-2pm; Sept.-May M-F 10am-8pm, Sa 10am-3pm.) After hours, try **Net City,** Nytorv 13a. (Open Su-Th 11am-3am, F-Sa 11am-8am. 20kr per hour.) **Aalborg Vandrerhjem and Camping (HI) ❷,** Skydebanevej 50, has private cabins and hostel dorms alongside a beautiful fjord. Take bus #8 (dir.: Fjordparken) right to the door, or take bus #2 or 9 and walk. (☎98 11 60 44. Laundry 20kr. Reception daily mid-June to mid-Aug. 7:30am-11pm; mid-Jan. to mid-June and mid-Aug. to mid-Dec. 8am-noon and 4-9pm. Dorms 85-100kr; singles 250-398kr; doubles 325-398kr. Camping 49kr.) **Ved Stranden** is lined with cheap eateries. **Postal Code:** 9000.

FREDERIKSHAVN

Despite noble efforts to woo tourists with its hospitality, Frederikshavn (pop. 35,000) is best known for its **ferry** links (p. 289). The **tourist office,** Skandia Torv 1, is inside the Stena Line terminal south of the rail station. (☎98 42 32 66; www.frederikshavn.dk. Open July to mid-Aug. M-Sa 8:30am-7pm, Su 8:30am-5pm; June and late Aug. daily 8:30am-5pm; Sept.-May M-F 9am-4pm, Sa 11am-2pm.) From the tourist office, walk left to reach the bus and train stations. To get from the station to the **Youth Hostel (HI) ❶,** Buhlsvej 6, walk right on Skipperg. for 10min., then turn left onto Norreg., and follow the signs. (☎98 42 14 75; www.danhostel.dk/frederikshavn. Reception in summer daily 8am-noon and 4-9pm. Call ahead. Closed Jan. Dorms 70-90kr; singles 150-200kr; doubles 210-270kr.) **Postal Code:** 9900.

SKAGEN

Perched on Denmark's northernmost tip, sunny Skagen (SKAY-en; pop. 10,000) is a beautiful summer retreat amid long stretches of sea and white sand dunes. With houses painted in vibrant "Skagen yellow" and roofs covered in red tiles with white edges—supposedly decorated to welcome local fisherman home from sea—Skagen is a colorful and pleasant vacation spot. In nearby **Grenen,** the powerful currents of the North and Baltic Seas violently collide. Stand with one foot in each ocean, but don't try to swim in these dangerous waters; every year people are carried out to sea. To get to Grenen, take bus or 79 from the Skagen station to *Gammel* (12kr) or walk 3km down Fyrvej; turn left out of the train station and bear left when the road forks. About 13km south of Skagen is the spectacular and enormous **Råberg Mile** (MEE-lay; sand dune), formed by a 16th-century storm. The vast faux-desert migrates 15m east each year. Take bus #79 or the train from Skagen to *Hulsig*, then walk along Kandestedvej. From here, you can swim along 60km of **beaches.** Skagen has a large annual **music festival** the last weekend in June.

Nordjyllands Trafikselskab (☎98 44 21 33) runs **buses** and **trains** to Frederikshavn (1hr.; 42kr, with Scanrail 21kr). Biking is by far the best way to experience Skagen's charm, including Grenen and the Råberg Mile; rent **bikes** at **Skagen Cyke-lUdlejning,** Banegardspl., next to the bus station. (☎98 44 10 70. 5kr per day. 200kr deposit. Open daily 8am-8pm.) The **tourist office** is in the station. (☎98 44 13 77; www.skagen.dk. Open July-Aug. M-Sa 9am-6pm, Su 10am-4pm; Sept.-May M 9am-5pm, Tu-Th 9am-4pm, F 9am-3pm, Sa 10am-1pm; June M-Sa 9am-5pm, Su 10am-6pm.) The only **Internet** access is at the Skagen library, Sct. Laurentii Vej 23. (Free. Open M and Th 10am-6pm; Tu-W and F 1-6pm, Sa 10am-1pm.) The **Skagen Ny Vandrerhjem ❷,** Rolighedsvej 2, is popular among vacationing Danish families. From the station, turn right on Chr. X's Vej, which becomes Frederikshavnvej, then left on Rolighedsvej. (☎98 44 22 00; www.danhostelnord.dk/skagen. Breakfast 45kr. Kitchen available. Sheets 50kr. Reception daily 9am-noon and 4-6pm. Open Mar.-Nov. Dorms 115kr; singles 250-400kr; doubles 300-500kr. No credit cards.) Bus #79 passes several **campgrounds.** Get groceries at **Fakta,** Chr. X's Vej.

ESTONIA (EESTI)

Happy to sever its Soviet bonds, Estonia has quickly revived ties with its Nordic neighbors. As a result, Finnish tourism and investment have proven a revitalizing force. The material wealth that has accumulated in Tallinn, however, masks the declining living standards that lurk outside of big cities, as well as the chagrin of the ethnically Russian minority over Estonia's Finnish leanings. Still, having overcome successive centuries of domination by the Danes, Swedes, and Russians, Estonians are now proud to take their place as members of modern Europe.

FACTS AND FIGURES

Official Name: Republic of Estonia.

Capital: Tallinn.

Major Cities: Pärnu, Tartu.

Population: 1,400,000.

Land Area: 45,226 sq. km.

Time Zone: GMT +2.

Languages: Estonian (official); Russian.

Religions: Evangelical Lutheran, Russian Orthodox, Estonian Orthodox.

ESSENTIALS

WHEN TO GO

The best time to visit is from May to September. During summer, Estonia's climate is mild due to its proximity to the Baltic Sea. Winters, however, can be severe.

DOCUMENTS AND FORMALITIES

VISAS. Citizens of Australia, Ireland, New Zealand, and the US do not need a visa for up to 90 days in a six-month period, UK citizens for 180 days in a year. Canadians and South Africans must obtain a visa, but may use a Latvian or Lithuanian

visa to enter the country (30-day single-entry visa €14, 90-day multiple-entry €66). Visa extensions are not granted, and visas cannot be purchased at the border. For visa info, consult the **Estonian Ministry of Foreign Affairs** (www.vm.ee/eng).

EMBASSIES. Foreign embassies are all in Tallinn (p. 299). Estonian embassies at home include: **Australia,** 86 Louisa Rd., Birchgrove NSW, 2041 (☎02 9810 7468; eestikon@ozemail.com.au); **Canada,** 958 Broadview Ave., Ste. 202, Toronto, ON M4K 2R6 (☎416 461 0764; estconsu@ca.inter.net); **Ireland,** 24 Merlyn Park, Ballsbridge, Dublin 4 (☎01 269 1552; asjur@gofree.indigo.net); **South Africa,** 16 Hofmeys St., Welgemoed, Belville 7530 (☎021 913 3850; fax 913 2579); **UK,** 16 Hyde Park Gate, London SW7 5DG (☎020 7589 3428; www.estonia.gov.uk); **US,** 1730 M St. NW, 503 Washington, D.C. 20036 (☎202 588 0101; www.estemb.org).

TRANSPORTATION

BY PLANE, TRAIN, AND FERRY. Several international airlines offer flights to Tallinn; try **SAS** or **AirBaltic.** If you're coming from another Baltic state or Russia, trains may be even cheaper than ferries—which connect to Finland, Sweden, and Germany—but expect more red tape when crossing the border.

BY BUS. Domestically, buses are the best means of transport, as they are cheaper and more efficient than trains. It's even possible to ride buses from the mainland to island towns (via ferry) for less than the price of the ferry ride. During the school year (Sept.-June 25), students receive half-price bus tickets. Internationally, buses can be a painfully slow choice as clearing the border may take hours.

BY BIKE AND BY TAXI. On the islands, bike rentals (around 100EEK per day) are an excellent means of exploration. Taxis are safe; the average rate is 7EEK per km.

BY THUMB. *Let's Go* does not recommend hitchhiking. Those who choose to do so should stretch out an open hand. Or, call the **Vismutar** (☎8290 010 50) agency, which will match you with a driver going in your direction 24hr. before you leave.

TOURIST SERVICES AND MONEY

EMERGENCY Police: ☎110. Ambulance and Fire: ☎112.

TOURIST OFFICES. Most towns have tourist offices with English-speaking staff. Small info booths, marked with a green "i," sell maps and give away brochures.

MONEY. The unit of currency is the **kroon** (EEK), divided into 100 *senti*. Prices and exchange rates are relatively stable. **Hansapank** and **Eesti Ühispank** cash traveler's checks. Credit cards are widely accepted, and **ATMs** are common. When making a purchase, cash is not passed between hands, but placed in a tray on the counter. **Tipping** is uncommon, but a service charge may be included in the bill.

KROON		
AUS$1 = 9.21EEK		1EEK = AUS$0.11
CDN$1 = 10.31EEK		1EEK = CDN$0.10
EUR€1 = 15.65EEK		1EEK = EUR€0.06
NZ$1 = 8.24EEK		1EEK = NZ$0.12
UK£1 = 22.69EEK		1EEK = UK£0.04
US$1 = 14.38EEK		1EEK = US$0.07
ZAR1 = 1.96EEK		1EEK = ZAR0.51

COMMUNICATION

PHONE CODES	**Country code:** 372. **International dialing prefix:** 800. From outside Estonia, dial int'l dialing prefix (see inside back cover) + 372 + city code + local number.

TELEPHONES AND INTERNET ACCESS. The phone system in Estonia is a little chaotic. Tallinn numbers all begin with the number 6 and have 7 digits, while numbers in smaller towns often have only 5 digits. Tallinn, unlike other Estonian cities, has no city code. The 0 listed in parentheses before each city code should only be dialed when placing calls within Estonia. Payphones require **digital cards,** available at banks and newsstands. Cards come in denominations of 30, 50, and 100EEK. International calls can be made at post offices. Calls to the Baltic states cost 5EEK per minute, to Russia 10EEK. Phoning the US costs US$1-4 per minute. International access codes include: **AT&T** (☎0 800 12 001); **British Telecom** (☎800 10442); **Canada Direct** (☎0800 12011); **MCI** (☎0800 1122). **Internet** access is common, and usually costs 30-60EEK per hour.

MAIL. To Europe, an airmail letter costs 7.50EEK and a postcard 6EEK; to the rest of the world, 8/7.50EEK. For *Poste Restante*, address envelope: Firstname SURNAME, *Poste Restante*, Narva mnt. 1, Tallinn 10101, ESTONIA.

LANGUAGES. Estonians speak the best English in the Baltic states; most young people also know Finnish or Swedish, but German is more common among the older set. Russian used to be mandatory, but many Estonians resist its use, except along the eastern border.

ACCOMMODATIONS AND CAMPING

ESTONIA	❶	❷	❸	❹	❺
ACCOMMODATIONS	under 200EEK	200-400EEK	401-550EEK	551-600EEK	over 600EEK

Tourist offices have accommodations listings and can often arrange beds. There is little distinction between hotels, hostels, and guesthouses. For info on HI hostels, contact the **Estonian Youth Hostel Association,** Narva Mantee 16-25, 10121, Tallinn (☎6461 455; www.baltichostels.net). Some **hostels** are part of larger hotels, so ask for the cheaper rooms. Note that even some upscale **hotels** have hall baths. **Homestays** are inexpensive, but the cheapest hostels can be a better deal. The word *võõrastemaja* (guesthouse) often implies that a place is less expensive. **Camping** is a great option on the islands, but camping outside designated areas is illegal.

FOOD AND DRINK

ESTONIA	❶	❷	❸	❹	❺
FOOD	under 40EEK	40-80EEK	81-100EEK	101-140EEK	over 140EEK

Much to the dismay of vegetarians and those trying to keep kosher, *schnitzel* (a breaded and fried pork fillet) appears on nearly every menu, and most cheap Estonian cuisine is fried and doused with sour cream. Estonian specialties include the typical Baltic *seljanka* (meat stew) and *pelmenid* (dumplings), as well as smoked salmon and trout. Bread is usually dark and dense. A delicious, common dessert is pancakes with cheese curd and berries. The national brew *Saku* and the darker *Saku Tume* are excellent, but local beers, like Kuressaare's *Saaremaa*, are less consistent. Carbonated *Värska* mineral water is particularly salty.

ESTONIA

HOLIDAYS AND FESTIVALS

Holidays: New Year's Day (Jan. 1); Independence Day (Feb. 24); Good Friday (Apr. 9); Easter (Apr. 11); May Day (May 1); Pentecost (May 30); Victory Day (June 23); Midsummer (June 24); Restoration of Independence (Aug. 20); Christmas (Dec. 25-26).

Festivals: The **National Song Festival** (July 2004), Estonia's biggest event, occurs only once every five years. The Tallinn festival honors Estonian folk music, culminating in a gigantic celebration featuring Estonians in native dress swilling local brews while singing their hearts out. Conductors and musical groups from around the world are drawn to **Pärnu** for its summer film and music festivals.

TALLINN   ☎0

In the heart of Tallinn (pop. 371,000), cosmopolitan shops contrast with the serene Vanalinn (Old Town), where German spires, Danish towers, and Russian domes rise above the sea. Tourists from all over Europe are quickly falling in love with the city's ethnic restaurants, vibrant nightlife, and low prices.

▐ TRANSPORTATION

Trains: Toompuiestee 35 (☎615 68 51; www.evrekspress.ee). Trams #1 and 5 connect the station to the center. English spoken at the info desk. To **Moscow** (16½hr., daily, 49-1391EEK) and **St. Petersburg** (10hr., even-numbered days daily, 217-372EEK).

Buses: Lastekodu 46 (☎680 09 00), 1.5km southeast of Vanalinn. Take tram #2 or 4 or bus #2 to the city center. Buy tickets at the station or from the driver. **Eurolines** (www.eurolines.ee) runs to: **Rīga** (5½hr., 6 per day, 200EEK); **St. Petersburg** (8-9hr., 7 per day, 180-220EEK); and **Vilnius** (10½hr., 2 per day, 400EEK).

Ferries: (☎631 85 50). At the end of Sadama, 15min. from the city center. 4 different terminals. Boats, hydrofoils, and catamarans cross to **Helsinki. Eckerö Line,** Terminal B (☎631 86 06; www.eckeroline.ee; 3½hr., daily.) **Nordic Jet Line,** Terminal C (☎613 70 00; www.njl.info; 1½hr., 6 per day, 295-595EEK.) **Silja Line,** Terminal D (☎611 66 61; www.silja.ee; 1½hr.; 5 per day; 250-530EEK; students 200-480EEK.) **Tallink,** Terminals A and D (☎640 98 08; www.tallink.ee; 3¼hr.; 3 per day; 315-345EEK, students 284-310EEK. Express ferries 1½hr.; 7 per day; 235-425EEK, students 212-384EEK.)

Public Transportation: Buses, trams, and **trolleybuses** cover the entire metropolitan area 6am-midnight. Buy tickets (*talong*; 10EEK) from kiosks around town and validate them in the metal boxes on board or risk a 600EEK fine.

Taxis: Silver Takso (☎648 23 00) or **Tulika Takso** (☎12 00). 5.5-7EEK per km. Call ahead to avoid the 8-50EEK "waiting fee."

✳ ▐ ORIENTATION AND PRACTICAL INFORMATION

Tallinn's **Vanalinn** (Old Town) is surrounded by the major streets Rannamäe tee, Mere pst., Pärnu mnt., Kaarli pst., and Toompuiestee. Vanalinn is divided into the larger, busier **All-linn** (Lower Town) and **Toompea**, a fortified rocky hill. Enter Vanalinn through the 15th-century **Viru ärarad,** the main gates in the city wall, located across from **Hotel Viru,** Tallinn's central landmark. To reach Vanalinn from the ferry terminal, walk 15min. along Sadama, which becomes Põhja pst., and turn left on Pikk through **Paks Margareeta** (Fat Margaret) gate. To get to **Raekoja plats** (Town Hall Square), the center of All-linn, from the train station, cross under Toompuiestee and continue straight on Nunne; turn left on Pikk and then take a right on Kinga.

Tallinn

🏠 ACCOMMODATIONS   🍎 FOOD   ⭐ NIGHTLIFE
Hotell G9, **6**   Cafe Illusion, **5**   Club Hollywood, **10**
Oldhouse Guesthouse, **1**   Elevant, **4**   Nimeta Baar, **9**
Tallinn Old Town   Olde Hansa, **7**   Pegasus, **8**
   Backpackers, **2**   Troika, **3**

Tourist Office: Kullassepa 4/Niguliste 2 (☎645 77 77; www.tourism.tallinn.ee). Offers city **maps** and sells *Tallinn In Your Pocket* (35EEK). Open July-Aug. M-F 9am-8pm, Sa-Su 10am-6pm; Sept. M-F 9am-6pm, Sa-Su 10am-5pm; Oct. M-F 9am-5pm, Sa 10am-3pm; May-June M-F 9am-7pm, Sa-Su 10am-5pm.

Embassies: For more info, contact the Estonian Foreign Ministry (www.vm.ee). **Canada,** Toom-Kooli 13 (☎627 33 11; canembt@uninet.ee). Open M, W, and F 9am-noon. **UK,** Wismari 6 (☎667 47 00; www.britishembassy.ee). Open Tu-Th 2:30-4:30pm. **US,** Kentmanni 20 (☎668 81 00; www.usemb.ee). Open M-F 9am-noon and 2-5pm.

Currency Exchange: Throughout the city. **ATMs** are on nearly every street in Vanalinn.

American Express: Suur-Karja 15 (☎626 62 11; www.estravel.ee). Books hotels and tours. Sells airline, ferry, and rail tickets. Arranges visas. Open June-Aug. M-F 9am-6pm, Sa 10am-5pm; Sept.-May M-F 9am-6pm, Sa 10am-3pm.

Emergencies: Police, Ambulance, Fire: ☎0112.

Pharmacy: Raeapteek, Raekoja pl. 11 (☎631 48 30). In business since 1422. Open M-F 9am-7pm, Sa 9am-5pm.

Internet Access: Central Library, Estonia pst. 8. Free, but you may have to wait. Open M-F 11am-7pm, Sa 10am-5pm. **@5 Internet Cafe,** Gonsiori 2, in the Kaubamaja department store. 40EEK per hr. Open M-F 9am-9pm, Sa 9am-8pm, Su 10am-6pm.

Post Office: Narva mnt. 1. (☎661 66 16), opposite Hotel Viru. Open M-F 7:30am-8pm, Sa 8am-6pm, Su 9am-3pm. Address mail to be held: Firstname SURNAME, *Poste Restante*, Narva mnt. 1, Tallinn **10101**, ESTONIA.

🏠 🛏 ACCOMMODATIONS AND FOOD

Hostels fill fast, so book ahead. **Rasastra**, Mere pst. 4, 2nd fl., finds private rooms. (☎661 62 91; www.bedbreakfast.ee. Singles 260EEK; doubles 480EEK; triples 650EEK. Apartments from 800EEK. Open daily 9:30am-6pm.) 🏠**Oldhouse Guesthouse ❷**, Uus 22/1, has small, immaculate rooms. From Raekoja pl., follow Viru and turn left on Uus. (☎641 14 64; www.oldhouse.ee. Dorm 290EEK; singles 450EEK; doubles 650EEK; quads 1300EEK. Apartments 950-2000EEK. 10% ISIC discount.) **Tallinn Old Town Backpackers ❷**, Uus 14, right before Oldhouse Guesthouse is small, clean, and modern. (☎051 711 337; www.balticbackpackers.com. Sheets 25EEK. Dorms 220EEK. Nonmembers add 5EEK.) **Hotell G9 ❸**, Gonsiori 9 is a short walk from Vanalinn. (☎62 67 100; www.hotelg9.ee. Phones, satellite TVs, and showers. Singles 500EEK; doubles 600EEK; triples 750EEK.)

🍴**Cafe Illusion ❷**, Muurivahe 50/Uus 3 is hidden between the walls of the 24.2m-high Hellemann's Tower. For the best deal, order your food from the cafe menu and eat at the very top of the tower. (Cafe entrees 50-85EEK; restaurant entrees 89-179. Open daily 10am-11pm.) Extravagant **Troika ❹**, Raekoja pl. 15, has a different Russian menu each day. (Entrees 98-252EEK. Live music daily 7-10pm. Open daily 10am-11pm.) **Elevant ❸**, Vene 5, serves tasty, creative Indian fare. (Entrees 84-278EEK. Open daily noon-11pm.) **Olde Hansa ❺**, Vana turg 1, is a popular medieval-themed restaurant near Raekoja pl. (Entrees 148-540EEK. Open daily 11am-midnight.) Buy groceries at **Rimi supermarket**, Aia 7, between Uus and Aia. Head toward the bus station on Lastekodu to reach the **central market**, Keldrimäe 9.

👁 SIGHTS

ALL-LINN. Enter Vanalinn through the Viru gate and head up Viru to reach **Raekoja plats** (Town Hall Square), where beer flows in outdoor cafes and local troupes perform throughout the summer. In July, classical music concerts are held each weekend in the town hall, Europe's oldest; buy tickets at the tourist office. *(Town Hall open July-Aug. M-F 10am-2pm. 30EEK, students 20EEK. Tower open May 15-Sept. 15 daily 11am-6pm. 25/15EEK.)* Take Mündi out of the square, turn right on Pühavaimu, and then left on Vene to reach the **Tallinn City Museum** (Tallinna Linnamuuseum), Vene 17. The visitor-friendly museum charts the city's history from its founding in 1219. *(Open May-Sept. Su-M and W-Sa 10:30am-5:30pm; Oct.-Apr. 11am-4:30pm. 25EEK, students 10EEK.)* Continue up Vene, turn left on Olevimägi, and turn right on Pikk for a view of the medieval city's north towers. Head to the other end of Pikk and turn left on Rataskaevu to see **St. Nicholas Church** (Niguliste kirik) and its mighty spire. The church also houses an exquisite silver treasury. *(Open Su and W-Sa 10am-5pm. Organ music Sa-Su 4-4:30pm. Museum 35 EEK, students 20EEK.)*

TOOMPEA. Toompea's **Lossi plats** (Castle Square) is dominated by the onion domes of golden **Aleksander Nevsky Cathedral.** *(From Raekoja pl., head down Kullassepa, right on Niguliste, and uphill on Lühike jalg. Open daily 8am-8pm. Services 9am and 6pm.)* Directly behind **Toompea Castle**, the current seat of the Estonian Parliament (closed to the public), an Estonian flag tops **Tall Hermann** (Pikk Hermann), Tallinn's tallest tower and most impressive medieval fortification. The spires of 13th-century **Toomkirik** tower over Toompea; to reach the cathedral, take either Piiskopi or Toom-Kooli to Kiriku pl. *(Open Su and Tu-Sa 9am-5pm. Services Su 10am.)*

ESTONIA

Next door is the **Art Museum of Estonia** (Eesti Kunstimuuseum), Kiriku pl. 1, which features 19th- to 20th-century Estonian art. *(Open Su and W-Sa 11am-6pm. Museum 20EEK, students 5EEK.)*

KADRIORG. Among the quiet paths, shady trees, and fountains of Kadriorg Park is Peter the Great's ◧**Kadriorg Palace,** whose sumptuous grand hall is considered to be one of the best examples of Baroque architecture in Northern Europe. *(www.ekm.ee. Open May-Sept. Su and Tu-Sa 10am-5pm; Oct.-Apr. Su and W-Sa 10am-5pm. 35EEK, students 20EEK.)* The grounds also have two superb art museums, as well as the **Peter the Great Museum** in his temporary residence. The museum holds many of the tsar's original furnishings, as well as an imprint of his extremely large hand. *(Mäekalda 2. From Vanalinn, follow Narva mnt. and at the fork veer right on Weizenbergi (20-30min.); or, take tram #1 or 3 to Kadriorg. Open mid-May-Sept. Su and W-Sa 10:30am-5:30pm. 10EEK, students 5EEK.)*

ROCCA-AL-MARE. On the peninsula of Rocca-al-Mare, 10km west of the city center, is the **Estonian Open-Air Museum** (Eesti Vabaõhumuuseum). The park is filled with 17th- to 20th-century wooden mills and homesteads collected from all over the country. Estonian folk troupes perform here regularly. *(Vabaõhumuuseumi 12. Take bus #21 or tram #7 (25min.) to the zoo stop. Open May-Oct. daily 10am-6pm; Nov.-Apr. 10am-5pm; Oct. 10am-4pm. 28EEK, students 12EEK. Last Tu of each month free.)*

▮ ▮ ENTERTAINMENT AND NIGHTLIFE

Pick up *Tallinn This Week* at the tourist office (free). The **Estonia Concert Hall** and the **Estonian National Opera** are both at Estonia pst. 4. (Concert Hall ☎614 77 60; www.concert.ee. Box office open M-F noon-7pm, Su 1hr. before curtain. Tickets 30-150EEK. Opera ☎626 02 60; www.opera.ee. Box office open daily noon-7pm. Tickets 30-270EEK.) On summer Sundays, all of Tallinn converges on the beach of **Pirita** on the outskirts of the city. (Take bus #1, 1a, 8, 34, or 38 from the post office to *Pirita.*) During **Old Town Days,** held in the first week of June, the city fills with open-air concerts. The first week of July brings **Beersummer,** a celebration of all that foams. Vanalinn is packed with bars; ◧**Club Hollywood,** Vana-Posti 8, is the final destination of any young Estonian's night out. A very large dance floor holds up to 1000 people and world-famous DJs frequent the club. (Cover 40-100EEK. W women free. Open W-Th 10pm-4am, F-Sa 10pm-5am.) **Pegasus,** Harju 1, is a futuristic, trendy bar that offers sushi and an impressive list of mixed drinks. (Open M-Th 8am-1am, F 8am-2am, Sa 11am-2am.) **Nimeta Baar,** Suur-Karja 4/6. (Beer 32EEK. Happy Hour 6pm. Open Su-Th 11am-2am, F-Sa 11am-4am.)

▮ DAYTRIP FROM TALLINN: PÄRNU

Breezy Pärnu (pop. 45,000), famous for its mud baths, beaches, and festivals, is the summer capital of Estonia. At the **Mudaravila** health resort, Ranna pst. 1, you can get hosed with mud or covered with compresses for 100-150EEK. (www.mudaravila.ee. Open M-F 8am-3pm.) Take a break from relaxing to visit Pärnu's **Museum of New Art,** Esplanaadi 10, which exhibits unorthodox contemporary art. (Open daily 9am-9pm. 15EEK, students 10EEK.) The clean water of the white-sand **beach** warms up in July and August. At night, crowds dance on the beach at **Sunset Club,** Ranna pst. 3. (Open Su-Th 10pm-4am, F-Sa 10pm-6am.)

Buses (☎(044) 720 02; Eurolines ☎278 41) go from Ringi 3 to: Rīga (3½hr., 6-8 per day, 110-150EEK); Tallinn (2hr., 42 per day, 30-85EEK); and Tartu (2½hr., 21 per day, 50-95EEK). **Rattapood,** Riia 95 (☎324 40), rents **bikes** for 75EEK per day. (Open M-F 10am-6pm, Sa 10am-2pm.) The **tourist office,** Rüütli 16, gives out the invaluable

ESTONIA

Pärnu In Your Pocket for free. (☎(044) 730 00; www.parnu.ee. Open May 15-Sept. 15 M-F 9am-6pm, Sa 9am-4pm, Su 10am-3pm; Sept. 16-May 14 M-F 9am-5pm.) **Tanni-Vakoma Majutusbüroo,** Hommiku 5, behind the bus station, arranges **private rooms.** (☎(044) 310 70. Open May-Aug. M-F 10am-8pm, Sa-Su 10am-3pm. 130-330EEK.) **Trahter Postipoiss ❷,** Vee 12, serves small, delicious portions of Russian delicacies, as well as fish and meat dishes. (☎(044) 648 64. Entrees 45-175EEK. F-Sa live music and dancing 9pm. Open Su-Th noon-midnight, F-Sa noon-2am.) Cafeteria-style **Georg ❶,** Rüütli 43, is packed with locals. (Entrees under 35EEK. Open M-F 7:30am-10pm, Sa-Su 9am-10pm.)

TARTU   ☎027

Tartu (pop. 110,000), the oldest city in the Baltics, is home to prestigious **Tartu University** (Tartu Ülikool). Tartu's social center is **Raekoja plats** (Town Hall Square), built in 1775. From there, follow Ülikooli behind the town hall to the university's main building at Ülikooli 18. In the attic is the ▩**student lock-up** (*kartser*), which until 1892 was used to detain rule-breaking students; their drawings and inscriptions are still visible. (Open M-F 11am-5pm. 5EEK, students 4EEK.) The **Tartu City Museum** (Tartu Linnamuuseum), Narva mnt. 23, details Tartu's history and hosts concerts. (Open Su and Tu-Sa 11am-6pm. 20EEK, students 5EEK.) **Cathedral Hill** (Toomemägi) features statues, an observatory, and the ruins of the **Cathedral of St. Peter and Paul** (Toomkirik).

Buses (☎477 227) leave from Turu 2, on the corner with Riia, 300m southeast of Raekoja pl. along Vabaduse, for: Pärnu (4hr., 20 per day, 50-95EEK); Rīga (5hr., daily, 190EEK); St. Petersburg (9hr., daily, 160EEK); and Tallinn (2-3hr., 46 per day, 50-80EEK). Some routes offer 30-50% ISIC discounts. **Trains** (☎615 68 51), generally less reliable than buses, go from the intersection of Kuperjanovi and Vaksali, 1.5km from the center, to Tallinn (2½-3½hr., 3 per day, 70EEK). Public buses #5 and 6 run from the train stop to the city center and then to the bus station. From the bus station, follow Riia mnt. and turn right on Ülikooli to reach Raekoja pl. Pick up the helpful *Tartu Today* (15EEK) at the **tourist office,** Raekoja pl. 14. (☎442 111; www.visitestonia.com. Open June-Aug. M-F 9am-5pm, Su 10am-2pm; Sept.-May M-F 9am-5pm, Sa 10am-3pm.) ▩**Ülüôpilaselamu Hostel ❷,** Pepleri 14, has cheerful, modern rooms with private baths. From the bus station, take Vadabuse toward town, turn left on Vanemuise, then take a left on Pepleri. (☎42 76 08; janikah@ut.ee. Singles 250EEK; doubles 400EEK.) The tavern **Püssirohu Kelder ❸,** Lossi 28, has an international menu. (Live music Tu-Sa 9 or 10pm. Open M-Th noon-2am, F-Sa noon-3am, Su noon-midnight.) ▩**Wilde Irish Pub ❸,** Vallikraavi 4, serves Irish and Estonian dishes. (Entrees 49-170EEK. Live music Tu and F-Sa 9 or 10pm. Open Su-Tu noon-midnight, W-Th noon-1am, F-Sa noon-3am.) **Postal Code:** 51001.

ESTONIAN ISLANDS

Afraid that Estonia's 1500 islands would serve as an escape route to the West, the Soviets cordoned them off from foreign and mainland influence; the islands now remain a preserve for all that is distinctive about Estonia.

SAAREMAA. Kuressaare (pop. 16,000), the largest town of the island of Saaremaa, is making a comeback with summer tourists but remains quiet and tranquil. Head south from Raekoja pl. (Town Hall Square) along Lossi, through the park, and across the moat to reach the 1260 ▩**Bishopric Castle** (Piiskopilinnus). Inside, the eclectic **Saaremaa Museum** chronicles the island's history. (Open May-Aug. daily 10am-7pm; Sept.-Apr. Su and W-Sa 11am-6pm. 30EEK, students 15EEK.) Rent a **bike** (135EEK per day) at **Oü Bivarix,** Tallinna 26, near the bus station, to pedal to the beaches of Southwest Saaremaa (8-12km) or to **Karujärve Lake** in West Saaremaa (23km).

Direct **buses** (☎(045) 316 61) leave from Pihtla tee 2, at the corner with Tallinna, for Pärnu (3½hr., 5 per day, 99-120EEK) and Tallinn (3-4hr., 11 per day, 100-160EEK). The **tourist office,** Tallinna 2, in the town hall, has maps (10EEK) and arranges private rooms. (☎(045) 331 20; www.visitestonia.com. Open May-Sept. 15 M-F 9am-7pm, Sa 9am-5pm, Su 10am-3pm; Sept. 16-Apr. M-F 9am-5pm.) **Sug Hostel ❷,** Kingu 6, is your best bet for low-priced accommodations. (☎(045) 54 388. Open June-Aug. singles 210-250EEK; doubles 300-350EEK; quads 480-580EEK.)

HIIUMAA. By restricting access to Hiiumaa (pop. 11,500) for 50 years, the Soviets unwittingly preserved the island's rare plant and animal species. Creek-laced **Kärdla** (pop. 4,000) is the island's biggest town. To explore the interesting sights along the coast, rent a **bike** (150EEK per day) from **Kerttu Sport,** Sadama 15, across the bridge from the bus station. (☎(046) 321 30. Open M-F 10am-6pm, Sa 10am-3pm.) Bike west from Kärdla toward Kõrgessaare to the spooky **Hill of Crosses** (Ristimägi; 6km) and turn right to reach the **Tahkuna Lighthouse** (11km), brought from Paris in 1874. Return to the main road and turn right again toward Kõrgessaare; continue 20km past the town to reach the impressive 16th-century **Kõpu Lighthouse,** which offers a panoramic view of the Baltic Sea. (20EEK, students 10EEK.) The whole trip is 38km; buses travel the same route. The tiny island of **Kassari** is attached to Hiiumaa by a land bridge from Käina, which can be reached from Kärdla by local buses or a 22km bike ride. The island's most beautiful sight is the 1.3m-wide ▓**Sääretirp** peninsula, covered in wild strawberry and juniper bushes and jutting 3km into the sea.

Ferries run between Saaremaa's Triigi port and Hiiumaa's Sõru port (1hr.; 3 per day; 50EEK, students 30EEK). Direct **buses** run from Sadama 13 (☎(046) 320 77), north of Kärdla's main square, Keskväljak, to Tallinn (4½hr., 2-3 per day, 140EEK). The **tourist office,** Hiiu 1, in Keskväljak, sells maps (5-40EEK) and *The Lighthouse Tour* (20EEK), an indispensable guide. (☎(046) 222 32; www.hiiumaa.ee. Open May-Sept. M-F 9am-6pm, Sa-Su 10am-3pm; Oct.-Apr. M-F 10am-4pm.) ▓**Eesti Posti Puhkekeskus ❶,** Posti 13, has modern rooms and clean shared baths. From Keskväljak, turn onto Uus to reach Posti; look for the pink building on the left. (☎(046) 918 71. Call ahead. Singles 150EEK.) Käina boasts Hiiumaa's best restaurant, ▓**Lilia Restoran ❸,** Hiiu mnt. 22, which serves high-society dishes at budget prices. (Entrees 50-120EEK. Open daily 11am-11pm.)

ESTONIA

FINLAND (SUOMI)

After seven centuries in the crossfire between warring Sweden and Russia, Finland gained autonomy in 1917 and never looked back. Hearty nationalism is expressed in typical Finnish fashion—with a heavy dose of modesty and prudence. Although politically and socially neutral, Finland is a country with dramatic natural extremes and cutting-edge architecture and design. Endless summer nights contrast with dark winter days, and provincial seaside towns stand against bustling, modern Helsinki.

FACTS AND FIGURES

Official Name: Republic of Finland.
Capital: Helsinki.
Major Cities: Oulu, Tampere, Turku.
Population: 5,200,000.

Land Area: 305,000 sq. km.
Time Zone: GMT +2.
Languages: Finnish, Swedish.
Religions: Evangelical Lutheran (89%).

DISCOVER FINLAND

Hugging the Russian border, vibrant **Helsinki** (p. 308) mixes Orthodox cathedrals, Lutheran churches, sleek 20th-century architecture, and grand 19th-century avenues. Stroll along the river in **Turku** (p. 315), Finland's oldest city. For stunning scenery, head to the Lake District's **Savonlinna** (p. 318) and the **Punkaharju Ridge** (p. 319). Check out the quirky museums in **Tampere** (p. 317) before traveling north into **Lapland** (p. 320), Europe's last great wilderness.

ESSENTIALS

WHEN TO GO

The long days of Finnish summers make for a tourist's dream, although the situation reverses in winter. After coming out of the two-month *kaamos* (polar night) without any sunlight, winter-sport fanatics start hitting the slopes in early February; the skiing continues into March and April. The temperature averages about 15-25°C (60-77°F) in the summer and dips as low as -20°C (-5°F) in the winter.

DOCUMENTS AND FORMALITIES

VISAS. EU citizens do not need a visa. South Africans need a visa for stays of any length. Citizens of Australia, Canada, New Zealand, and the US do not need a visa for stays of up to 90 days, but this three-month period begins upon entry into any Nordic country; for more than 90 days in any combination of Denmark, Finland, Iceland, Norway, and/or Sweden, you will need a visa.

EMBASSIES AND CONSULATES. Foreign embassies are in Helsinki (p. 308). Finnish embassies at home include: **Australia,** 12 Darwin Ave., Yarralumla, ACT 2600 (☎26 273 38 00; www.finland.org.au); **Canada,** 55 Metcalfe St., Ste. 850, Ottawa, ON K1P 6L5 (☎613-236-2389; www.finemb.com); **Ireland,** Russell House, Stokes Pl., St. Stephen's Green, Dublin 2 (☎01 478 1344; fax 01 478 3727); **South Africa,** P.O. Box 443, Pretoria 0001 (☎012 343 0275; fax 012 343 3095); **UK,** 38 Chesham Pl., London SW1X 8HW (☎020 7838 6200; www.finemb.org.uk); **US,** 3301 Massachusetts Ave. NW, Washington, D.C. 20008 (☎202-298-5800; www.finland.org).

TRANSPORTATION

BY PLANE. Finnair (Finland ☎(09) 818 83 33; US ☎800-950-5000; UK ☎870 241 4411; www.finnair.com) flies from 50 international cities and also covers the domestic market. Finnair gives a domestic discount of up to 50% for ages 17-24, and has summer and snow rates that reduce fares by up to 60%.

BY TRAIN. Eurail is valid in Finland. The national rail company is **VR Ltd., Finnish Railways** (☎30 72 09 00; www.vr.fi). Efficient trains run at typically high Nordic prices; seat reservations (€2.20-8.40) are not required except on the faster *InterCity* and *pendolino* trains. A **Finnrail pass** gives three (€114), five (€154), or 10 travel days (€208) in a one-month period. Purchased in Scandinavia, the **Scanrail pass** allows unlimited rail travel through Denmark, Finland, Norway, and Sweden, and many free or discounted ferry rides. (5 days within 15 days €270; 21 consecutive days €418.) However, only three of those days can be used in the country of purchase, so a **Scanrail pass** purchased at home (p. 54) is more economical for those traveling mainly within Finland.

BY BUS. Buses are the only way to reach some smaller towns or to travel past the Arctic Circle. **Expressbus** covers most of Finland (☎0200 4000; www.expressbus.com). **Pohjollan Liikenne** (www.pohjollanliikenne.fi) runs a daily bus between Helsinki and St. Petersburg. ISIC cardholders can buy a **student card** (€5.40 plus passport-sized photo), at bus stations, which provides a 50% discount on tickets. Some drivers will give the student discount to those with a student ID. **Railpasses** are valid on buses when trains are not in service.

BY FERRY. Viking Line (Helsinki ☎(09) 123 51; Stockholm ☎08 452 40 00) runs from Stockholm to Helsinki, Mariehamn on Åland, and Turku. Scanrail holders get 50% off on Viking; Eurailers ride free. **Silja Line** (Helsinki ☎(09) 180 41; Stockholm ☎08 452 50 00; www.silja.com/english) sails from Stockholm to Helsinki, Mariehamn, and Turku. **Birka Lines** (Mariehamn ☎(018) 270 27; Stockholm ☎08 702 72 30; www.birkacruises.com) sails daily from Mariehamn to Stockholm.

BY CAR. A valid driver's license is required to operate a car. Driving conditions are good, but be wary of reindeer crossings and winter hazards. Drive on the right side of the road. For info on renting a car in Europe, see p. 60.

BY BIKE AND BY THUMB. Finland has 10,000km of beautiful **cycling** paths. Rental rates average €5-15 per day or €35-50 per week. **Hitchhikers** find more rides in Finland than elsewhere in Scandinavia, but the language barrier is more likely to be a problem. *Let's Go* does not recommend hitchhiking as a safe means of transport.

TOURIST SERVICES AND MONEY

EMERGENCY	Police: ☎122. Ambulance: ☎123. Fire: ☎124.

TOURIST OFFICES. The **Finnish tourist boards** (☎09 417 6911; www.mek.fi) offer a comprehensive website. Contact the tourist office of the region you plan to visit.

MONEY. The official currency of Finland is the **euro**. The **markka** can still be exchanged at a rate of 5.95mk to €1. For exchange rates and more info on the euro, see p. 14. Banks exchange currency and accept ATM cards. **Forex** offices and **ATMs** offer the best exchange rates. Orange "Otto" bank machines accept Cirrus, MC, Visa, and bank cards. Food runs €10-17 per day if you're shopping in grocery stores; meals generally cost at least €6 for lunch and €10 for dinner. Restaurants include a 15% gratuity in the meal price, although an extra 10% **tip** is not uncommon for good service. Round the fare up to the nearest euro for cab drivers. A normal tip for bellhops, train porters, and sauna and coatroom attendants is €1-2. The European Union imposes a **value-added tax (VAT)** on goods and services purchased within the EU, which is included in the price (p. 16).

BUSINESS HOURS. Most shops are open Monday to Friday from 9am until 8 or 9pm, and Saturday from 9am until 3 or 6pm. Some shops are open on Sundays from noon until 9pm. Banks are typically open Monday to Friday 9am-4:30pm.

COMMUNICATION

PHONE CODES	Country code: 358. International dialing prefix: 00. From outside Finland, dial the int'l dialing prefix (see inside back cover) + 358 + city code + local number.

TELEPHONES. To make a long-distance call within Finland, dial 0 and the number. Local and long-distance calls within Finland usually cost €0.55; **Finncards** are available from R-kiosks and post offices in €5, and €10 denominations. **Mobile phones** phones are extremely popular in the land of Nokia; prepaid cell phone cards are widely available and can be used to make international calls. For more info on cell phones in Europe, see p. 36. For domestic info, call ☎118. For international info, call ☎020 208. International direct dial numbers include: **AT&T,** ☎0800 1100 15; **British Telecom,** ☎0800 11 04 40; **Canada Direct,** ☎0800 1100 11; **Ireland Direct,** ☎0800 11 03 53; **MCI,** ☎08001 102 80; **Sprint,** ☎0800 11 02 84; **Telecom New Zealand,** ☎0800 11 06 40; **Telkom South Africa,** ☎0800 11 02 70; and **Telstra Australia,** ☎0800 11 00 610.

MAIL. Mail service is fast and efficient. Postcards and letters under 50g cost €0.60 within Finland, €0.80 within the EU, and €1.10 outside Europe. Letters under 20g going outside Finland cost €0.60. *Poste Restante* service is offered at all local post offices.

LANGUAGES. Finnish is spoken by most of the population. In Helsinki, about 90% of the city speaks English, and Swedish is officially spoken as well. Sami (Lappish) is spoken by about 1700 people in northern Finland. Although there are fewer English speakers in smaller towns, English is widely spoken and the language barrier shouldn't pose a problem. Some town names take a modified form on train and bus schedules. For example, "To Helsinki" is *"Helsinkiin,"* while "From Helsinki" is *"Helsingistä."* For Finnish words and phrases, see p. 1054.

ACCOMMODATIONS AND CAMPING

FINLAND	①	②	③	④	⑤
ACCOMMODATIONS	under €10	€11-20	€21-45	€46-70	over €70

Finland has over 100 **youth hostels** (*retkeilymaja*; RET-kay-loo-MAH-yah), although only 50 are open year-round. Prices average €10-50 per person; nonmembers add €2.50. Most have laundry facilities and a kitchen; some have saunas and rent bicycles, boats, or ski equipment. The **Finnish Youth Hostel Association** (SRM; Suomen Retkeilymaja-järjestö; ☎ (09) 565 71 50; www.srmnet.org) is Finland's HI affiliate. **Hotels** are often exorbitant (over €50); *kesähotelli* (summer hotels) operate from June to August and cost about €18.50 per person. The **Finland Tourism Board** (see above) keeps a database of booking agencies for year-round and summer hotels. **Private room** rental is not particularly common. Local tourist offices can help you find the cheapest accommodations. About 350 **campgrounds** are scattered throughout the country, 70 of which are open year-round (tent sites €7-20 per night; *mökit* (small cottages) from €26). International Camping Cards (ICC; €5 at campsites) earn discounts at most campgrounds. For a campground guide, contact the **Finnish Campingsite Association** (☎ (09) 622 628 23; www.camping.fi). You may camp for free for one or two nights almost anywhere as long as you respect the flora, fauna, and the owner's privacy, and pick up all garbage.

FOOD AND DRINK

FINLAND	①	②	③	④	⑤
FOOD	under €8	€8-15	€16-20	€21-30	over €30

A *kahvila* serves food, coffee, and beer; a *grilli* is a fast-food stand. A *ravintola* (restaurant) may be anything from a cafeteria to a pub. The best budget dining is at all-you-can-eat lunch buffets (€6-10), often found at otherwise pricey restaurants. Kebab and pizza joints are cheap (from €4), but their quality varies. The cheapest supermarkets are Alepa, Euromarket, Valintatalo, and K Markets. The Finns are proud of their fish, including *taimen* (trout), *silakka* (Baltic herring), and *lohi* (salmon). Finnish dietary staples include rye bread, potatoes, sour milk, Karelian pastries, and *viili* (yogurt). Reindeer meat, roasted or in a stew, is on some menus. In summer, blueberries, cranberries, lingonberries, and Arctic cloudberries are picked for desserts, wines, vodka, and other liquors. You must be 18 to purchase beer and wine, 20 for hard liquor; the minimum age in bars is usually 18, but can be as high as 25. Outside bars and restaurants, all alcohol stronger than light beer must be purchased at state-run Alko liquor stores.

HOLIDAYS AND FESTIVALS

Holidays: New Year's Day (Jan. 1); Epiphany (Jan. 6); Good Friday (Apr. 9); Easter (Apr. 11-12); May Day (May 1); Ascension Day (May 20); Midsummer (June 21-23); All Saints' Day (Nov. 1); Independence Day (Dec. 6); Christmas Day (Dec. 25); Boxing Day (Dec. 26).

Festivals: Naantali (p. 316) hosts a well-known **Chamber Music Festival** in June. Virtually the entire country shuts down during **Midsummer,** when Finns party all night to the light of *kokko* (bonfires) and the midnight sun. Each Midsummer, thousands of Finns head for the beaches of Rauma (p. 316) for its annual **Rock Festival.** Savonlinna's (p. 318) **Opera Festival** (early July to early Aug.), in Olavinlinna Castle, is Finland's largest cultural event. The **Pori Jazz Festival** draws huge crowds and top

FINLAND

musicians (July 12-20). Finland's biggest rock festival, **Ruisrock**, takes place in Turku (p. 315) each July. The **Helsinki Festival** (Aug. 22-Sept. 7) fills the city with concerts, dance performances, plays, and operas.

HELSINKI (HELSINGFORS) ☎09

With all the appeal of a big city but none of the grime, Helsinki's (pop. 560,000) broad avenues, grand architecture, and green parks make it a model of successful urban planning. The city distinguishes itself with a decidedly multicultural flair: Lutheran and Russian Orthodox cathedrals stand almost face-to-face, and youthful energy mingles with old-world charm. Baltic Sea produce fills the marketplaces and restaurants, while St. Petersburg and Tallinn are only a short cruise away.

⊏ TRANSPORTATION

Flights: Helsinki-Vantaa Airport (HEL; ☎02 00 46 36). Buses #615 and 616 (less direct) run frequently between the airport and the train station square (every 20 min., 5:20am-12:20am, €3). A **Finnair bus** shuttles between the airport and the Finnair building at Asemaaukio 3, next to the train station (35min., every 15min. 5am-midnight, €5).

Trains: ☎(030) 072 09 00. Reserve for all long-distance routes. To: **Moscow** (14hr., 5:40pm, €83); **Rovaniemi** (10-13hr., 5-8 per day, €66-71); **St. Petersburg** (5hr., 2 per day, €50); **Tampere** (2hr., 6am-10pm, €17-27); **Turku** (2hr., 12 per day, €17-27).

Buses: ☎020 040 00; The station is between Salomonk. and Simonk.; from the Mannerheimintie side of the train station, take Postik. past the statue of Mannerheim. Cross Mannerheimintie onto Salomonk.; the station will be to your left. To: **Lahti** (1½hr., 2 per hr., €17); **Tampere** (2½hr., every hr., €18); **Turku** (2½hr., 2 per hr., €21).

Ferries: For route options, see p. 305. **Silja Line,** Mannerheimintie 2 (☎980 07 45 52 or 091 80 41). Take tram #3B or 3T from the city center to the Olympic terminal. **Viking Line,** Mannerheimintie 14 (☎12 35 77). **Tallink,** Erottajank. 19 (☎09 22 83 11).

Local Transportation: ☎010 01 11. **Metro, trams,** and **buses** run 5:30am-11pm; major tram and bus lines, including tram #3T, run until 1:30am. There is one Metro line (running approximately east to west), 10 tram lines, and many more bus lines. **Night buses,** marked with an N, run after 1:30am. Single-fare tickets are €2 on buses and trams or from machines at the Metro station; cheaper advance tickets (€1.70) are available at R-kiosks and at the **City Transport** office in the Rautatientori Metro station (open in summer M-Th 7:30am-6pm, F 7:30am-4pm; off-season M-Th 7:30am-7pm, F 7:30am-5pm, Sa 10am-3pm). Tickets are valid for 1hr. (transfers free); punch your ticket on board. The **Tourist ticket,** a convenient bargain for a 5-day stay, is available at City Transport and tourist offices and provides unlimited bus, tram, Metro, and local train transit (1-day €4.80, 3-day €9.60, 5-day €15; 50% child discount). The city also provides over 300 free **green bikes** at major destinations throughout the city; simply deposit a €2 coin in the lock and retrieve it upon returning the bike to any location.

◼✳ 🔢 ORIENTATION AND PRACTICAL INFORMATION

Sea surrounds Helsinki on the east and west, and the city center is bisected by two lakes. Water shapes everything in the Finnish capital, from relaxing city beaches to gorgeous parks around the lakes. Helsinki's main street, **Mannerheimintie**, passes between the bus and train stations on its way to the city center, eventually crossing **Esplanadi**. This tree-lined promenade leads east to **Kauppatori** (Market Square) and the beautiful South Harbor. Both Finnish and Swedish are used on all street signs and maps; *Let's Go* uses the Finnish names.

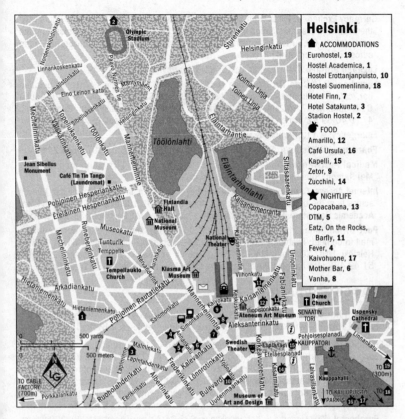

Helsinki

♠ ACCOMMODATIONS
Eurohostel, 19
Hostel Academica, 1
Hostel Erottanjanpuisto, 10
Hostel Suomenlinna, 18
Hotel Finn, 7
Hotel Satakunta, 3
Stadion Hostel, 2

● FOOD
Amarillo, 12
Café Ursula, 16
Kapelli, 15
Zetor, 9
Zucchini, 14

★ NIGHTLIFE
Copacabana, 13
DTM, 5
Eatz, On the Rocks,
 Barfly, 11
Fever, 4
Kaivohuone, 17
Mother Bar, 6
Vanha, 8

Tourist Offices: City Tourist Office, Pohjoisesplanadi 19 (☎91 69 37 57; www.hel.fi). From the train station, walk 2 blocks down Keskusk. and turn left on Pohjoisesplanadi. Open May-Sept. M-F 9am-8pm, Sa-Su 9am-6pm; Oct.-Apr. M-F 9am-6pm, Sa-Su 10am-4pm. The **Finnish Tourist Board,** Eteläesplanadi 4 (☎41 76 93 00; www.mek.fi), has info covering all of Finland. Open May-Sept. M-F 9am-5pm, Sa-Su 11am-3pm; Oct.-Apr. M-F 9am-5pm. **Hotellikeskus** (Hotel Booking Center; ☎22 88 14 00), in the train station, books rooms for a €5.05 fee in person or for free by phone. Open June-Aug. M-F 9am-7pm, Sa-Su 10am-6pm; Sept.-May M-F 9am-6pm, Sa 9am-5pm. The **Helsinki card,** sold at the tourist office, Hotellikeskus, central R-kiosks, and most hotels, provides unlimited local transportation and free or discounted admission to most museums, although it may only be economical for those visiting many sites (24hr. card €24, 48hr. €32, 72hr. €38). **Finnsov Tours,** Eerikink. 3, arranges trips to Russia and expedites the visa process. (Open M-F 8:30am-5pm.)

Embassies: Canada, Pohjoisesplanadi 25B (☎17 11 41; www.canada.fi). Open M-F 8:30am-noon and 1-4:30pm. **Ireland,** Erottanjank. 7A (☎64 60 06). **South Africa** Rahapajank. 1A 5 (☎68 60 31 00). **UK,** Itäinen Puistotie 17 (☎22 86 51 00; www.ukembassy.fi). Also handles diplomatic matters for **Australians** and **New Zealanders.** Open M-F 8:30am-5pm. **US,** Itäinen Puistotie 14A (☎17 19 31; www.usembassy.fi). Open M-F 8:30am-5pm.

Currency Exchange: Forex, with 5 locations in Helsinki. Best rates in the city. Hours vary; the **branch** in the train station is open 8am-9pm. **Exchange,** Kaivok. 6, across from the train station. €3.50 fee to convert foreign money to euros, no fee to convert back from euros. €6 fee per traveler's check.

Luggage Storage: Train station lockers €1-3 per day.

Laundromat: ▧**Cafe Tin Tin Tango** (☎27 09 09 72), Töölöntorink. 7, a combination bar, cafe, laundromat, and sauna. Laundry €3.40. Sandwiches €4.50-5.30. Sauna €17. Open M-F 7am-2am, Sa-Su 10am-2am. More typical is **Easywash,** Runebergink. 47 (☎40 69 82). Open M-Th 10am-9pm, F 10am-6pm, Sa 10am-4pm.

Emergency: ☎112. **Police:** ☎100 22.

Pharmacy: Yliopiston Apteekki, Mannerheimintie 96 (☎41 78 03 00). Open 24hr.

Medical Assistance: 24hr. medical advice **hotline** (☎100 23). 24hr. medical clinic **Mehilainen,** Runebergink. 47A (☎431 44 44).

Internet Access: Cable Book Library, Mannerheimintie 22-24, in the Lasipalatsi mall directly across from the bus station. Free 30min. slots. Open M-Th 10am-8pm, Sa-Su noon-6pm. **Academic Bookstore,** Keskusk. 2. Free 15min. slots. Open M-F 9am-9pm, Sa 9am-6pm.

Post Office: Mannerheiminaukio 1A (☎98 00 71 00). Open M-F 9am-6pm. Address mail to be held: Firstname SURNAME, *Poste Restante*, Mannerheiminaukio 1A, **00100** Helsinki, FINLAND. Open M-F 9am-6pm. **Branch** at Helsinki 10, Elielinaukio 2F (☎04 51 49 48), also handles *Poste Restante.* Open M-F 9am-9pm, Sa-Su 10am-6pm.

■ ACCOMMODATIONS

Helsinki's hotels tend to be expensive, but budget hostels are often quite nice. In June and July, it's wise to make reservations a few weeks in advance.

▧**Hostel Erottanjanpuisto (HI),** Uudenmaank. 9 (☎64 21 69). Head right from the train station, turn left on Mannerheimintie, bear right onto Erottajank., and turn right on Uudenmaank. In 19th-century building in the heart of the city. Well-kept rooms, friendly staff, and an unbeatable location. Breakfast €5. Kitchen available. Lockers €2. Internet €1 per 10min. Reception 24hr. Reserve in advance. In summer, dorms €20; singles €44; doubles €55; off-season reduced prices. Nonmembers add €2.50. ❷

Eurohostel (HI), Linnank. 9, Katajanokka (☎622 04 70; www.eurohostel.fi). 200m from the ferry terminal. From the train station, head right to Mannerheimintie and take tram #2 or 4 to *Katajanokka.* From Uspensky Cathedral, head down Kanavank., turn left on Pikku Satamank., and bear right on Linnank. This well-run hostel feels like a hotel, with bright rooms, non-smoking floors, a cafe, and a sauna. Breakfast €5. Kitchen available. Sheets included. Internet €1 per 10min. Reception 24hr. Dorms €20; singles €34. Nonmembers add €2.50. ❷

Hotel Satakunta (HI), Lapinrinne 1A (☎69 58 52 31; ravintola.satakunta@sodexho.fi). Take the Metro to *Kampi* and walk downhill, or take bus #55 or 55a and tell the driver your destination. Spacious, well-equipped private rooms, and minimalist dorms close to the city center. Breakfast included. Sheets €5. Laundry €5.50. Internet €6 per hr. Reception 24hr. Check-in 2pm. Check-out noon. Open June-Aug. Dorms €12; singles €33; doubles €48; triples €58; quads €67. Nonmembers add €2.50. ❶

Hostel Academica (HI), Hietaniemenk. 14A (☎13 11 43 34; hostel.academica@hyy.fi). Take tram #3T to Kauppakorkeakoulu, go left on Lapuank., and turn right on Hietaniemenk. Breakfast €5. Sheets €4.50. Reception 24hr. Check-in 2pm. Check-out noon. Open June-Aug. Dorms €16; singles €41; doubles €58; triples €71; quads €84. ❷

Stadion Hostel (HI), Pohj. Stadiontie 3B (☎49 60 71; fax 49 64 66). Take tram #7A or 3 to *Auroran Sairaala.* Walk down Pohj. Stadiontie toward the white tower for 250m, following the signs. The hostel, on the far side of the stadium, is a converted athletic space popular with school groups. Live music acts playing in the stadium can be heard from the rooms. Breakfast and sheets €5. Kitchen available. Lockers €1. Laundry €2.50. Internet €1 per 15min. Lockout noon-4pm. Reception June to early Sept. daily 7am-3am; mid-Sept. to May 8-10am and 4pm-2am. Dorms €12; singles €24; doubles €34. Nonmembers add €2.50. ❷

Hostel Suomenlinna (HI), Iso Mustasaari (☎684 74 71; fax 79 44 81), by the main quay on Suomenlinna. Comfortable, tasteful rooms in an old brick building on Suomenlinna's western island. Breakfast €3. Sheets included. Reception 9am-11pm. Dorms €18; doubles and triples €25. Nonmembers add €2.50. ❷

Hotel Finn, Kalevank. 3B (☎68 44 360; fax 68 44 36 10). From the train station, go right, then turn left on Mannerheimintie, and then turn right onto Kalevank. The hotel is on the 6th fl. The basic rooms may be somewhat pricey, but the hotel's location is simply unbeatable. Breakfast included. Singles €55, with shower 65; doubles €65/80. ❹

Rastila Camping, 12km east of the city center (☎321 65 51). Take the Metro east to *Rastila*; the campsite is 100m to the right. Beach access, toilets, showers, and kitchen. Reception mid-May to mid-Sept. 24hr; mid-Sept. to mid-May daily 8am-10pm. 1 person with tent €9, 2 people with tent €14; 2-person cabins €40; 4-person cabins €62. Summer hostel: dorms €17; singles €26; doubles €43; triples €63. ❶

🍴 FOOD

Restaurants and cafes are easy to find on **Esplanadi** and the streets branching off from **Mannerheimintie** and **Uudenmaankatu.** Cheaper options surround the **Hietalahti** flea market. An **Alepa supermarket** is under the train station. (Open M-F 7:30am-10pm, Sa 9am-10pm, Su 10am-10pm.) Freshly-cooked fish and farm-fresh berries are sold at the open-air markets of **Kauppatori,** by the port. (Open June-Aug. M-Sa 6:30am-2pm and 3:30-8pm; Sept.-May M-F 7am-2pm.)

Kapelli, Eteläesplanadi 1, at the Unionk. end of Esplanadi park. Frequented by well-heeled Bohemians since 1837. The outdoor cafe serves salads and sandwiches (€5-8). The restaurant inside is pricier. Kitchen closes at 1am. Open daily 9am-2am. ❶

Zetor, Kaivok. 10, in Kaivopiha, the mall directly opposite the train station. The dishes' names are cheeky and the farm-inspired decor is cheekier, but the Finnish fare is absolutely delicious. Homemade beer €4. Entrees €7-21. 22+ after 9pm. Open Su-M 3pm-1am, Tu-Th 3pm-3am, F 3pm-4am, Sa 1pm-4am. ❷

Café Ursula, Kaivopuisto park. Delicious meals in an idyllic setting on the edge of the Baltic Sea. Sandwiches €4-6. Salads €8-9. Open daily 9am-midnight. ❶

Lappi, Annank. 22. The fantastic Lappish cuisine makes this the perfect place to sample regional specialties like reindeer, elk, lingonberries, and arctic char. Entrees from €17. Open M-F noon-10:30pm, Sa-Su 1-10:30pm. ❸

Amarillo, Mikonk. 9. Surprisingly cheap Tex-Mex dishes served in a trendy atmosphere. At night, the 3 bars make this one of Helsinki's hotspots. Entrees from €6. Open M-Tu 11am-1am, W-Th 11am-3am, F-Sa 11am-4am, Su 11am-11pm. ❶

Zucchini, Fabianink. 4, near the tourist office. A casual *kasvisravintola* (vegetarian restaurant). Daily lunch special €7.20. Open Aug.-June M-F 11am-4pm. ❶

👁 SIGHTS

Home to bold new designs and polished Neoclassical works, Helsinki reflects Finnish architect Alvar Aalto's statement, "Architecture is our form of expression because our language is so impossible." Much of the layout and architecture of the old center, however, is the brainchild of a German. After Helsinki became

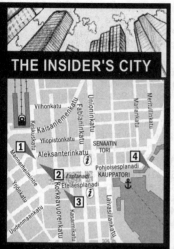

THE INSIDER'S CITY

AALTO'S HELSINKI

Finnish Modernist Alvar Aalto's mark on Helsinki's cityscape goes far beyond the magnificent Finlandia Hall. Many of Aalto's other buildings are in easy walking distance of the center of Helsinki.

1 Rautaulo (Iron House), Keskusk. 3. The stark facade conceals a light-filled atrium meant to recall Italian piazzas.

2 Academic Bookstore, Pohjoisesplanadi 39. With a facade similar to the nearby Rautaulo, the bookstore contains a cafe perched at the top of a stone staircase.

3 Savoy Restaurant Interior, Eteläesplanadi 14. This top-notch eatery may be too pricey for the budget traveler, but the Aalto-decorated interior, inspired by country houses, is gorgeous.

4 Stora Enso Headquarters, Kanavak. 1. One of Aalto's most controversial works, this ultra-Modernist "sugar cube" overlooks the South Harbor.

the capital of the Grand Duchy of Finland in 1812, Carl Engel designed a grand city modeled after St. Petersburg. Today, Art Nouveau (*Jugendstil*) and Modernist structures give Helsinki a unique cosmopolitan feel. Most of the major sights are packed tightly into the compact center of the city, making the city ideal for walking tours; pick up *See Helsinki on Foot* from the tourist office for suggested routes. Trams #3T and 3B loop around the major sights in about an hour in opposite directions, providing a cheap alternative to sightseeing buses. Helsinki is dotted with parks, including **Kaivopuisto** in the south, **Töölönlahti** to the north, and **Esplanadi** and **Tahtitorninvuori** in the center of town.

SUOMENLINNA. This 18th-century Swedish military fortification consists of five beautiful interconnected islands used to repel attacks on Helsinki. The old fortress's dark passageways are great to explore, and the islands house a number of related museums. Especially worthwhile are the **Suomenlinna Museum,** which covers the history of the island fortress, and the **Ehrensvärd Museum,** formerly the commandant's residence. (*www.suomenlinna.fi. Museums open May-Aug. daily 11am-5pm; Sept.-Apr. reduced hours. €5.50, students €2.50. Ferries depart from Market Sq. every 20min. 8am-11pm; round-trip €4.*)

SENAATIN TORI (SENATE SQUARE). The square and its gleaming white **Tuomiokirkko** (Dome Church) showcase Engel's work and exemplify the splendor of Finland's Russian period. (*At Aleksanterink. and Unionink. in the city center. Church open June-Aug. M-Sa 9am-midnight, Su noon-midnight; Sept.-May M-Sa 9am-6pm, Su noon-6pm.*)

USPENSKINKATEDRAADI (USPENSKY ORTHODOX CATHEDRAL). Just opposite Senate Sq., this beautiful red-brick cathedral evokes images of Russia with its ornate interior and golden onion domes. The cathedral's lofty heights also provide an excellent perch from which to survey the city. (*Follow Esplanadi to Kauppatori. Open M and W-Sa 9:30am-4pm, Tu 9:30am-6pm, Su 9:30am-3pm.*)

SUOMEN KANSALLISMUSEO (NATIONAL MUSEUM OF FINLAND). The museum displays intriguing bits of Finnish culture, from Gypsy and Sami costumes to woven *ryijyt* (rugs), as well as a magnificent roof mural by Akseli Gallen-Kallela. (*Mannerheimintie 34, up the street from the Finnish Parliament House. Open Su and Th-Sa 11am-6pm, Tu-W 11am-8pm. €4.*)

ART MUSEUMS. Ateneum Taidemuseo, Finland's largest art museum, offers a comprehensive look at Finnish art from the 1700s to the 1960s. (*Kaivok. 2,* *opposite the train station. Open Tu and F 9am-6pm, W-Th 9am-8pm, Sa-Su 11am-5pm. €5.50; special exhibits €7.50.)* **Kiasma** picks up where Ateneum leaves off, showcasing great modern art in a funky silver building. *(Mannerheiminaukio 2. Open Su and W-Sa 10am-8:30pm, Tu 9am-5pm. €5.50, students €4.)* The **Museum of Art and Design** presents the work of well-established Finnish designers alongside exciting creations by young artists. *(Korkeavuorenk. 3. Open June-Aug. daily 11am-6pm; Sept.-May Su, Tu and Th-Sa 11am-6pm, W 11am-8pm. €7.)*

KAAPELI (CABLE FACTORY). Situated in a rather empty industrial area at the western end of the city, this mammoth building (formerly used by Nokia) now houses three museums, dozens of artists' studios and galleries, and various performance areas. Especially worthwhile is the **Finnish Museum of Photography,** with dramatic photographs from the past century. The complex also hosts major cultural events. *(Tallbergink. 1. Take the Metro to Ruoholahti and walk 5 blocks down Itämerenk., or take tram #8 to the end of the line. Theatre/Photography museums open Su and Tu-Sa noon-7pm; combined ticket €4.)*

FINLANDIA TALO. Home to the Helsinki Philharmonic and the Radio Symphony Orchestra, this magnificent white-marble concert hall stands testament to the skill of the Finnish architect Alvar Aalto, who also designed the interior and furnishings. *(Mannerheimintie 13E. ☎ 402 41; www.finlandia.hel.fi. Tours in summer daily 1:30pm.)*

TEMPPELIAUKIO KIRKKO. This stunning church, designed in 1969 by Tuomo and Timo Suomalainen, was hewn from a hill of rock, with only the roof visible from the outside. Inside, its huge domed ceiling appears to be supported by rays of sunshine. *(Lutherink. 3. Walk away from the main post office on Paasikivenaudio, which becomes Arkadiagatan, then turn right on Fredrikinatu and follow it to the end. Open M-F 10am-8pm, Sa 10am-6pm, Su noon-1:45pm and 3:15-5:45pm. Services in English Su 2pm.)*

JEAN SIBELIUS MONUMENT. Dedicated in 1967 by sculptor Eila Hiltunen to one of the 20th-century's greatest composers, the Sibelius monument looks like a stormcloud of organ pipes ascending to heaven. A well-touristed spot in a scenic area, the monument and its surrounding park make a great place for an afternoon picnic. *(On Mechelinink. in Sibelius park. Catch bus #24 (dir.: Seurasaari) from Mannerheimintie; get off at Rasjasaarentie and the monument will be behind you on the left.)*

SEURASAARI. A quick walk across the beautiful white bridge from the mainland brings you to the many paths of the island of Seurasaari, a repository of old churches and farmsteads transplanted from all over the country. An open-air museum allows entrance into many of the island's historical buildings. Visit during Midsummer to witness the *kokko* (bonfires) and Finnish revelry in its full splendor. *(Take bus #24 from Erottaja, outside the Swedish Theater, to the last stop. The island is always open for hiking. Museum open M-F 9am-3pm, Sa-Su 11am-5pm. €3.40. Children free.)*

🎵 🎭 ENTERTAINMENT AND NIGHTLIFE

Helsinki's parks are always animated; daily afternoon jazz fills the **Esplanadi** park in July (www.kultturi.hel.fi/espanlava), and concerts rock **Kaivopuisto** park (on the corner of Puistok. and Ehrenstromintie, in the southern part of town) and **Hietani-emi beach** (down Hesperiank. on the western shore). The free English-language papers *Helsinki This Week*, *Helsinki Happens*, and *City* list popular cafes, bars, nightclubs, and events; pick up copies at the tourist office.

Bars and clubs, ranging from laid-back neighborhood pubs to sleek discos, line **Mannerheiminkatu, Uudenmaankatu,** and nearby streets. The bars and beer terraces start filling up in the late afternoon; most clubs don't get going until midnight and stay hopping until 4am. Age limits at clubs range from 20 to 23;

only rarely are they lower or higher. With the exception of licensed restaurants and bars, only the state-run liquor store **Alko** can sell alcohol more potent than light beer. (Branch at Mannerheimintie 1, in Kaivopiha across from the train station. Open M-F 9am-8pm, Sa 9am-6pm.) For sheer touristy novelty, nothing can beat the red **Pub Tram** that runs throughout the city, stopping at major sights and selling beer. (Beer €5. Open daily 3-8pm.) East of the train station, the scene flourishes around **Yliopistonkatu** and **Kaisaniemenkatu.** The hottest spot is on Mikonk., where three popular bar/clubs share a terrace: international **Eatz** (no cover), edgy **On the Rocks** (23+, cover €6-7), and chic **Barfly** (F-Sa cover €7). **Copacabana,** Yliopistonk. 5, has salsa dancing each Sunday. (F-Sa cover €7-8.50. Open daily 6pm-4am.) A student crowd gathers at **Vanha,** Mannerheimintie 3, in the Old Students' House. (F-Sa cover €2. Open M-Th 11am-1am, F 11am-2am, Sa 11am-4am.) **DTM** (Don't Tell Mama), Annank. 32, is a popular gay club that draws a mixed crowd to foam parties and drag bingo. (www.dtm.fi. 22+. F-Sa cover €5. Open M-Sa 9am-4am, Su noon-4am.) Wednesday night turns **Kaivohuone,** in Kaivopuisto park, into a swimming pool party. (Cover €4-10.) Brand-new **Fever,** Annank. 32, draws a chic crowd who boogie to pop and hip-hop. (23+. Cover €2. Open M-F 3pm-4am, Sa-Su 9pm-4am.) **Mother Bar,** Eerikink. 2, is a relaxed lounge with nightly techno. (Open M-Th 11:30am-midnight, F-Sa 2pm-3am.) Finland's best DJs play six-hour sets at the roving **Club Unity,** Finland's longest-running club night. (www.clubunity.org.)

◪ DAYTRIPS FROM HELSINKI

PORVOO. Porvoo, the nation's most photographed town (pop. 44,000) hugs the Porvoo River and follows Old King Rd., which passes from Helsinki to Russia. In 1809, Tsar Alexander I granted Finland autonomy at the Porvoo **cathedral** in the old town. (Open May-Sept. M-F 10am-6pm, Sa 10am-2pm, Su 2pm-5pm; Oct.-Apr. Tu-Sa 10am-2pm, Su 2-4pm. Free.) The former home of **Johan Ludvig Runeberg,** Aleksanterink. 3, is closed for renovations until 2004; its sculpture exhibition, however, remains open. (Open May-Aug. M-Sa 10am-4pm, Su 11am-5pm; Sept.-Apr. W-Su 11am-3pm. €4.) **Buses** roll into Porvoo from Helsinki (1hr., every 15min., €8). The helpful **tourist office,** Rihkamak. 4, gives out maps and finds accommodations for free. (☎019 520 23 16; www.porvoo.fi. Open mid-June to Aug. M-F 9am-6pm, Sa-Su 10am-4pm; Sept. to mid-June reduced hours.)

HANKO. Occupying a peninsula at the southernmost tip of Finland, seaside Hanko (pop. 10,000) makes for an excellent change of pace from the bustle of Helsinki or Turku. The villas lining the coastline reflect the decadence of the long-gone Russian nobility. Choose from over 30km of **beaches;** those along Appelgrenintie are the most popular. **Trains** arrive from Helsinki (2hr., 6 per day, €19) and Turku (2hr., 6 per day, €22), both via Karjaa, as do **buses** (2¼hr., 5 per day, €14). Superfast **ferries** run daily from Hanko to Rostock, Germany (21hr., 9pm, €70). The **tourist office,** Raatihuoneentori 5, helps book rooms, often in converted villas. (☎019 220 34 11; www.hanko.fi. Open June-July M-F 9am-5pm, Sa 10am-4pm; Apr.-May and Aug. M-F 9am-5pm; Sept.-Mar. M-F 8am-4pm.)

LAHTI. World-class winter sports facilities make Lahti a popular winter destination. All year round, the **Ski Museum** has ski-jump and biathalon simulators. (Open M-F 10am-5pm, Sa-Su 11am-5pm. €4.30, students €3.) The extensive network of cross-country **ski trails** (100km) is hikable in the summer. Rising more than 200m, the tallest of three **ski jumps** is accessible by a chairlift/elevator combination. (Open in summer M-F 10am-5pm; €5, with ski museum €6.) Lahti also serves as a transportation hub, with **buses** to Jyväskylä (3hr., €16) and Savon-linna (4hr., €21). **Trains** go to: Helsinki (1½-2hr., every hr., €12-17); Savonlinna (3-3½hr., 5 per day, €35); St. Petersburg, Russia (4hr., 2 per day, €38); and Tam-pere (2hr., 15 per day, €22). The **tourist office**, Aleksanterink. 16, provides **Inter-net** access; walk up Raututienk. seven blocks and turn left on Aleksanterink. (☎03 814 45 66; www.lahtitravel.fi. Open in summer M-F 9am-6pm, Sa 10am-2pm; off-season M-F 9am-5pm.)

TURKU (ÅBO)   ☎02

Finland's oldest city, Turku (pop. 163,000) became the capital in 1809 when Tsar Alexander I snatched the country from Sweden and granted it autonomy. Soon after the capital moved to Helsinki in 1812, the worst fire in Scandinavian history devoured Turku's wooden buildings. In 2004, the rebuilt cultural and academic center celebrates its 775th birthday.

⌨️ TRANSPORTATION AND PRACTICAL INFORMATION. Trains arrive from Helsinki (2hr., 12 per day, €22-27) and Tampere (2hr., 11 per day, €20-25). Seaw-ind, Viking, and Silja Line **ferries** head to Åland and Stockholm (see p. 305); to get to the terminal, hop on the train (3 per day) to *satama* (harbor), or catch bus #1 from Kauppatori (€2). The **tourist office**, Aurak. 2, has accommodations info and offers 15min. of free **Internet** access. (☎262 74 44; www.turkutouring.fi. Open June-Aug. M-F 8:30am-6pm, Sa-Su 9am-4pm; Sept.-May M-F 8:30am-6pm, Sa 10am-3pm.)

▐▐ ACCOMMODATIONS AND FOOD. The spacious and well-run ▐Hostel **Turku (HI) ❶,** Linnank. 39, is on the river between the ferry terminals and the train station. From the station, walk west four blocks on Ratapihank., turn left on Puis-tok., and make a right on Linnank. at the river. (☎262 76 80; fax 262 76 75. Break-fast €4.50. Kitchen available. Lockers. Sheets €4.50. Laundry €2. Reception daily 7am-midnight. Curfew 2am. Reserve in advance. Dorms €11; doubles €32; quads €46. Nonmembers add €2.50.) For well-kept rooms in a peaceful setting, try the nun-run **Bridgettine Sisters' Guesthouse ❸,** Ursinink. 15A, near the corner of Puutar-hak. (☎250 19 10; birgitta.turku@kolubus.fi. All rooms with bath. Reception 8am-9pm. Singles €42; doubles €61; triples €80.) Take bus #8 from Eerikink. to **Ruis-salo Camping ❶,** on Ruissalo Island. (☎262 51 00. Reception 7am-11pm. Open June-Aug. Electricity €3.50. €9 per person with tent, €8 per extra person.) Produce fills **Kauppatori** (open M-Sa 7am-2pm) and **Kauppahalli,** (open M-Th 8am-5pm, F 8am-2pm, Sa 8am-2pm) on Eerikink.

◼️◻️ SIGHTS AND ENTERTAINMENT. The **Turku Cathedral** towers above Cathedral Square. (Open daily 9am-7pm.) The 700-year-old **Turun Linna** (Turku Castle), 3km from the town center, contains a **historical museum** with dark pas-sageways, medieval artifacts, and Iron-Age dioramas. Catch bus #1 (€2) from Market Square. (Open mid-Apr. to mid-Sept. daily 10am-6pm; mid-Sept. to mid-Apr. Su and Tu-Sa 10am-3pm. €6.50, children €4.50.) The nearby **Forum Mari-num,** Linnank. 72, is a top-notch maritime museum. (Open May-Sept. daily 11am-7pm; Oct.-Apr. Su and Tu-Sa 10am-6pm. €10.) **Luostarinmäki,** the only neighborhood to survive the 1827 fire, now houses an interactive open-air **handicrafts museum.** (Open mid-Apr. to mid-Sept. daily 10am-6pm; mid-Sept. to mid-Apr. Su and Tu-Sa 10am-3pm. €3.40, children €2.60.) The collections of the **Turun Taidemuseo** (Art Museum), which include vibrant *Kalevala* paintings by Akseli Gallen-Kallela, return to their permanent home in **Puolalanmäki,** at the northern tip of Aurank., in spring 2004. (Open Tu-Th 11am-7pm, F-Su 10am-

4pm. €3.50-5.50.) The excellent ⬛Aboa Vetus Ars Nova, located in an old residence in the city center, houses two museums: An archaeological museum and a modern art museum directly above it. (Open May-Sept. 15 daily 11am-7pm; Sept. 16-Dec. 1 and Jan. 2-Apr. Su and Th-Sa 11am-7pm. €7, students €6.)

Turku is known throughout Finland for its pubs and breweries, many of which are housed in unusual spaces: an old apothecary (**Pub Uusi Apteeki,** Kaskenk. 1), a 19th-century girls' school (**Brewery Restaurant Koulu,** Eerikink. 18), and a public restroom (**Restaurant Puutorin Vessa,** Puutori). In summer, Turku's nightlife centers around the river, where Finns and tourists alike crowd the boats docked by the banks to dance and drink. Posh **Prima,** Aurak. 16, is the best place for late-night clubbing; it features two sleek dancefloors, a bar, and a basement Indian restaurant. (Cover F-Sa €3-5. Club open W-Th and Su 11pm-4am, F-Sa 10pm-4am. Bar open M-Tu 10am-1am, W-Sa 10am-4am, Su noon-4am. Restaurant open daily 5-10pm.) Ruissalo Island hosts the hard-rock **Ruisrock** in mid-July. (☎ (0600) 07 08 09; www.ruisrock.fi.)

▓ **DAYTRIP FROM TURKU: NAANTALI.** Naantali (pop. 13,000), an enclave of old wooden houses 15km west of Turku, is awakened each summer by vacationing Finns. Mannerheimink. leads to the **Old Town,** whose buildings date to the late 18th century. Across the harbor is the Finnish president's fortress-like summer home, **Kultaranta;** if the flag's up, keep an eye out for her. During the summer, hordes of Finnish tots, parents in tow, descend upon Naantali's main attraction, the fantasy theme park **Moomin World,** where kids can interact with author Tove Janssen's various creations. It's like *The Birds,* but with children. (☎02 511 11 11. Open June to mid-Aug. daily 10am-7pm. €13-17.) The most traditional summer event is **Sleepyhead Day** (July 27), when the residents of Naantali get up at 6am and proceed to crown the year's Sleepyhead and throw him or her into the harbor. **Buses** #11, 110, and 111 run to Naantali from Turku (30-45min., €3.50). The **tourist office,** Kaivotori 2, books accommodations. From the bus station, walk southwest on Tullik. to Kaivok. (☎02 435 98 00; www.naantalinmatkailu.fi. Open June to mid-Aug. M-F 9am-6pm, Sa-Su 10am-3pm; mid-Aug. to May M-F 9am-4:30pm.)

RAUMA   ☎02

Farther up the Baltic Coast lies the culturally bustling town of Rauma (pop. 37,000), known for its distinct lace and dialect. **Old Rauma,** a wooden town consisting of over 600 buildings, is a UNESCO World Heritage site. Many islands in Rauma's **archipelago** are excellent for hiking; try **Kuuskajaskari,** a former military fortress. (Ferries depart twice daily in summer. 30min., €7.) The hugely popular **Finnish Rock Festival** (www.raumanmerenjuhannus.com) takes place each Midsummer. **Buses** depart every hour for Pori (1hr.; €14, students €7) and Turku (2hr.; €16, students €8). To reach the **tourist office,** Valtak. 2, walk down Nortamonk. and turn right. (☎834 45 51; www.rauma.fi. Open June-Aug. M-F 8am-6pm, Sa 10am-3pm, Su 11am-2pm; Sept.-May M-F 8am-4pm.) **Kesahotelli Rauma ❶,** Satamak. 20, is a summer hotel and hostel. (☎824 01 30. Breakfast and sheets €3 each. Reception daily 7am-10pm. Dorms €9.50; singles €33; doubles €52.)

PORI   ☎02

Each July the coastal town of Pori (pop. 76,000) overflows with tourists attending the **Pori Jazz Festival.** (July 17-25. Info ☎626 22 00; tickets 626 22 15; www.porijazz.fi. Tickets €7-60. Some events free.) Head to the **Pori Art Museum,** on the corner of Etelärantak. and Raatihuonek., for first-class modern art. (Open Su and Tu-Sa 11am-6pm, W until 8pm. €5, students €2.50.) The nearby **Satakunnan Museum,** Hallitusk. 11, has exhibits on the area's history and wildlife. (Open Su, Tu, and Th-

Sa 11am-5pm, W 11am-8pm. €4, students €2.) In a graveyard 1.5km west of the center, on Maantiek., the gorgeous **Juselius Mausoleum** is adorned with frescoes by Akseli Gallen-Kallela and his son Jorma. (☎623 87 46. Open May-July noon-3pm.) Take bus #2 to **Repossaari** fishing village and the gorgeous **Yteri beach,** one of Finland's best. **Trains** run to Helsinki (3½-4hr.; 5-8 per day; €27-30, students €14-15), some via Tampere (1½hr., 5-7 per day, €14/7). **Buses** go to Tampere (2hr., 4 per day, €15) and Turku (2hr., 6-7 per day, €20). The **tourist office,** Hallitusk. 9A, designed by Carl Engel, helps find rooms. (☎621 12 73; www.pori.fi. Open June-Aug. M-F 8am-6pm; Sept.-May 8am-4pm.) Be sure to sample a **Poriburger,** an amalgam of fried sausage, pickles, and condiments, from one of the local merchants surrounding the **Kauppatori;** wash it down with **Porin Karhu** beer, brewed in the city.

TAMPERE ☎03

The smokestacks of Tampere's (pop. 192,000) now-defunct factories still line the city's waterways. Today, however, quirky museums, expansive beaches, energetic nightlife, and frequent cultural festivals eclipse Tampere's industrial past.

▐▌ TRANSPORTATION AND PRACTICAL INFORMATION. Trains head to: Helsinki (2hr., 2 per hr., €18-25); Oulu (4-5hr., 8 per day, €48-53); and Turku (2hr., 11 per day, €19-24). **Boats** (☎212 48 04) sail to towns in the surrounding Lake Region. The **tourist office,** Verkatehtaank. 2, and its army zipping around town on green scooters, offers incredible service and free **Internet.** Amazingly, the office also lends out free handheld computers to navigate the city and look up info wirelessly. From the train station, walk up Hämeenk. four blocks, and turn left before the bridge. (☎31 46 68 00; www.tampere.fi. Open June-Aug. M-F 8:30am-8pm, Sa-Su 10am-5pm; Sept.-May M-F 8:30am-5pm.)

▐▌ ACCOMMODATIONS AND FOOD. Tampeeren NNKY (HI) ❷, Tuomiokirkonk. 12, offers rooms near the cathedral overlooking the city. From the train station, walk down Hämeenk. and make a right on Tuomiokirkonk. (☎254 40 20. Breakfast €5. Sheets €4.50. Reception 8-10am and 4-11pm. Dorms €11-13; singles €29; doubles €39. Nonmembers add €2.50. Cash only.) Bus #1 (€2) goes to **Camping Härmälä ❷,** which overlooks Lake Pyhäjärvi. (☎265 13 55. Open early May-late Aug. Tents €13.50-15; cabins €27-60.) Restaurants cluster around **Hämeenkatu.** The gastronomically bold can try the local delicacy *mustamakkara,* a black sausage, available at Tampere's **Kauppahalli,** Hämeenk. 19, the largest market hall in Scandinavia. (Open M-F 8am-6pm, Sa 8am-4pm.) The city's oldest pizzeria, **Napoli ❶,** Aleksanterink. 31, serves 100 different varieties. (Pizza €6.30-11. Open M-Th 11am-10pm, F 11am-11pm, Sa noon-11pm, Su 1-11pm.) The laid-back brewery **Plevna Panimoravintola ❷,** Itäinenk. 8, in an old mill, serves local specialties. (Open M-Th 11am-1am, F-Sa 11am-2am, Su noon-11pm.)

◙ ▐ SIGHTS AND ENTERTAINMENT. Tampere's collection of museums can only be described as eccentric. The **Spy Museum,** Hatanpäänvaltatie 42, exhibits a variety of sneaky devices. (Open M-F noon-6pm, Sa-Su 10am-4pm. €6, students €4.) A defiant proletarian spirit burns at the last existing **Lenin Museum,** Hämeenpuisto 28, 3rd fl. The building itself is a historical relic; it was the site of the first conference of Lenin's revolutionary party, and of the first meeting of Lenin and Stalin. (Open M-F 9am-6pm, Sa-Su 11am-4pm. €4, students €2.) The **Amuri Museum of Workers' Housing,** Makasiinink. 12, shows the housing conditions of workers between 1882 and 1973. (Open early May to mid-Sept. Su and Tu-Sa 10am-6pm. €4, students €1.) Other museums include the **Shoe Museum,** inside the Vapriiki Museum Center, and the **Museum of Dolls and Costumes,** Puistokuja 1. (Both open

Su and Tu-Sa 9am-5pm. €5.) More conventionally, the **Vapriikki Museum Center,** Veturiaukio 4, has exhibitions on Tampere's history. Admission includes the **Finnish Ice Hockey Museum.** (Both open Tu and Th-Su 10am-6pm, W 11am-8pm. €4.)

For an authentic Finnish **beach** experience—which involves jumping from a hot sauna into chilly water—take bus #2 to **Rauhaniemi.** (Sauna open M and W 6-10pm, F 3-9pm, Sa 2-10pm. €4.50.) Bus #27 goes to **Pyynikki forest park,** which offers walking trails through wooded hills. Take the stairs or ride an elevator to the top of the **observation tower** for a panoramic view. (Open daily 9am-8pm. €1.) For an even more spectacular sight, take the elevator up the 124m **Näsinuela** in the **Särkänniemi** amusement complex. (www.sarkanniemi.fi. Tower open daily 11am-midnight. €4 admission; rides €3.50.)

The **Short Film Festival** screens works from 30 countries each March. (☎ 223 51 88; www.tampere.fi/festival/film.) In August the **International Theater Festival,** transforms Tampere's streets into stages. (☎ 223 10 66; www.tampere.fi.)

🖪 **NIGHTLIFE. Hämeenkatu** and the surrounding streets are energetic at night, and many hotels host discos. **Cafe Europa,** Aleksanterink. 29, serves meals and drinks in a candlelit bohemian lounge. (Beer €4. 20+ after 6pm. Dancing W-Sa 9pm-close. Open Su-Th noon-2am, F-Sa noon-3am.) **Telakka,** Tullikamarinaukio 3, houses a bar, restaurant, club, and theater in an old warehouse near the train station. (Live music F-Sa. Open M-Th 11am-2am, F 11am-3am, Sa noon-3am, Su noon-2am.) **Doris,** Aleksanterink. 20, is a popular rock club featuring live acts most nights. (Open Su and Tu-Th 9pm-3am, F-Sa 10pm-3am.)

SAVONLINNA

☎ 015

Savonlinna (pop. 28,000) sits amid a chain of islands in the heart of Finland's lake region. The tsarist aristocracy was the first to discover Savonlinna as a vacation spot, turning it into a fashionable spa town. The elegant **Olavinlinna Castle,** built to reinforce the border against those tsars in 1475, has impressively towering spires. From Kauppatori (Market Square), follow the docks along the water that hugs Linnank. as it winds between old wooden houses en route to the castle. (Open June to mid-Aug. daily 10am-5pm; mid-Aug. to May 10am-3pm. English tours every hr. €5.) Each July, the city is deluged with over 70,000 visitors attending the world-class **Savonlinna Opera Festival,** staged in the castle. (July 9-Aug. 7. ☎ 37 67 50; www.operafestival.fi. Tickets from €37; book far in advance.) The secluded **Sulosaari** island is a peaceful retreat two footbridges past Kauppatori.

Trains run from Savonlinna to Helsinki (5hr., 3 per day, €43); when arriving, hop off at *Savonlinna-Kauppatori,* in the center of town, rather than at the distant *Savonlinna* station. The **tourist office,** Puistok. 1, across the bridge from the market, has info about the region's parks and daytrips. (☎ 51 75 10; www.travel.fi/fin/savonlinna. Open June-Aug. daily 8am-8pm; Sept.-May M-F 9am-5pm.) Savonlinna has many hotels and hostels, but advance booking is absolutely necessary in July, when every place fills up for the opera festival. **Vuorilinna Hostel (HI) ❷,** on Kylpylaitoksentie, offers well-equipped student apartments. (☎ 739 54 30; fax 27 25 24. Breakfast €6. Kitchen available. Sheets €5. Reception 7am-11pm. Open June-Aug. Dorms €20; singles €31; doubles €57. Nonmembers add €2.50.) **Malakias Hostel (HI) ❷,** Pihlajavedenkuja 6, offers rooms 2km from the city center. Go right on Olavink. from the tourist office and bear left on Tulliportink., or take bus #3. (☎ 53 32 83. Breakfast €6. Sheets €5. Reception 7am-11pm. Open June to mid-Aug. Dorms €20; singles €42-54, with bath €54-71; doubles €57-71/71-81. Nonmembers add €2.50.) Bars and cafes line **Olavinkatu** and the marketplace area, and summer terraces off **Linnankatu** look out over the castle. **Panimoravintola Huvila ❷,** Puistok. 4, serves hearty meals by the lake. The restaurant also has a microbrewery with four home-brewed beers on tap. From Kauppatori, cross the bridge and turn left on Puistok. (Entrees from €12.50. Open daily 11am-3am.)

🔁 DAYTRIPS FROM SAVONLINNA: PUNKAHARJU AND THE RETRETTI.
About 30min. from Savonlinna by **bus** (7 per day, €4.50), the surreal **Retretti Art Center** is a set of massive caves displaying beautiful glassworks, dream-like installations, and fabulous rotating exhibits. The center also holds concerts. (Open July daily 10am-6pm; June and Aug. 10am-5pm. €15, students €9.) In the nearby **Punkaharju Nature Conservation Area**, trails trace the breathtaking 🔁**Punkaharju Ridge**, a narrow stretch of forests flanked on both sides by water. The **METLA Research Park** is home to an arboretum and the insightful **Lusto Finnish Forest Museum.** (Open June-Aug. daily 10am-7pm; May and Sept. 10am-5pm; Oct.-Dec. and Feb.-Apr. Su and Tu-Sa 10am-5pm. €7, students €6.) The Punkaharju **tourist office**, Kauppatie 20, has more info on the Conservation Area. (☎734 12 33; www.punkaharju.fi.)

OULU   ☎08

Flower-lined avenues and the warm winds of the Gulf of Bothnia lend Oulu (pop. 124,000) a relaxed feel. The island of **Pikisaari**, whose multi-colored cottages and azure seaside make an ideal setting for picnics, is near the city center; take the footbridge at the end of Kaarlenväylä. Huge banana plants, 5m cactuses, and other exotic flora flourish at the university's **Botanical Gardens,** Kaitoväylä 5, a 15min. ride on buses #4, 6, or 19. (Open June-Aug. Tu-F 8am-3pm, Sa-Su 11am-3pm; Sept.-May Su noon-3pm, Tu-F 8am-3pm, Sa noon-3pm. €1.70. Gardens open in summer daily 8am-8pm; off-season 7am-5pm.) The **Tietomaa**, Nahkatehtaank. 6, has interactive science exhibits, a huge IMAX theater, and the pants of the world's heaviest man. (Open July daily 10am-8pm; Aug.-June M-F 10am-6pm. €10, students €8.40.) Nightlife spills out of the pavilion on **Kirkkokatu**, the terraces lining **Otto Karhin Park,** and the club-lined **Asemakatu.** Among Oulu's many summer festivals is the **X Oulu Music Video Festival,** held in late August, where fierce competitors frantically rock out for the air guitar world championship.

All **trains** between northern and southern Finland pass through Oulu, heading south to Helsinki (6-7hr., 5-6 per day, €55-65) and north to Rovaniemi (2½hr., 4 per day, €22). The **tourist office,** Torik. 10, provides info on the Ostrobothnia region. Take Hallitusk., then the second left after passing through the park. (☎55 84 13 30; www.oulutourism.fi. Open mid-June to mid-Aug. M-F 9am-6pm, Sa 10am-3pm; mid-Aug. to mid-June M-F 9am-4pm.) The friendly **Oppimestari Summer Hotel ❸,** Nahkatehtaank. 3, offers bright student dorms in the summer. From the train station, cross Rautatienk. straight onto Asemak. After four blocks, turn right on Isok., which becomes Kasarmintie, and turn right again onto Nahkatehtaank. (☎884 85 27; www.merikoski.fi/hotel. Breakfast and sheets included. Laundry €3. Singles €35; doubles €50.) For those staying longer than one night, a better value is the University of Oulu's summer housing, which rents out flats for €60 per week. (☎553 40 48; housing@oulu.fi. Reserve in advance.) Bus #5 (€2) goes to **Nallikari Camping ❷,** which has colorful bungalows. (☎55 86 13 50; fax 55 86 17 13. €11-16 per person; 4-person cabins €29.) Cheap food is easy to find; as in many university towns, it's hard to walk 10m without passing a pizza or kebab joint.

KUOPIO   ☎017

Kuopio (pop. 87,000) eastern Finland's largest city, is a center of religion and culture in the midst of a region known for its natural beauty. The archbishop of the Finnish Orthodox Church resides here, and the **Orthodox Church Museum,** Karjalank. 1, houses a collection of textiles and icons. (Open May-Aug. Su and Tu-Sa 10am-4pm; Sept.-Apr. M-F noon-3pm, Sa-Su noon-5pm. €5, students €2.55.) A 2km hike leads to the **Puijo Tower,** which has a lovely view. From Kauppatori, walk away from the water on Puijonk. and continue up the hill. (Open May-Sept.

FINLAND

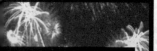

O WORK, ALL PLAY

ORTH HER WEIGHT IN EXTRA GOLD

Some can lay claim to struggling through marathons; others can boast of having stared down Pamplona's raging bulls. Only a select few, however, can brag of having carried their wife through 250m of obstacles. Every year, the small towns of Iisalmi and Sonkajärvi, located on the railway between Oulu and Kuopio, become a center for beer-soaked festivities and one of the strangest races in the world.

In early July, the Olvi brewery, one of Finland's largest, sponsors a Beer Festival in Iisalmi. As the golden brew flows through Iisalmi's streets, a much less conventional phenomenon is taking place in Sonkajärvi. The party starts on a Friday with the Finnish Barrel Rolling Contest, really just a warm-up for the main event: The International Wife-Carrying Championship. Admittedly, it's a bit of a misnomer—the competing pair do not, in fact, need to be man and wife, so long as the woman weighs at least 49kg. The race itself is run in heats. The men must navigate the course's obstacles and water trap without dropping the woman. In 2003, a team of Estonians (who traditionally dominate the field), posted an impressive time of 1 minute. And the prize? Aside from the pride of excellence in wife-carrying, the winner's reward matches his skill—he receives his wife's weight in beer.

daily 9am-10pm. €3.) The **Kuopio Dance Festival** (www.kuopiodancefestival.fi) draws crowds in mid-June, while oenophiles toast early July's **Wine Festival.**

Trains travel to Helsinki (5½hr., 9 per day, €41-51) and Oulu (4½hr., 6 per day, €34-45). The **tourist office,** Haapaniemenk. 17, has a stand at the train station that provides info, as well as roving staff members throughout the city. To get to the main office from the station, go right on Asemak., and turn left on Haapaniemenk. (☎18 25 84; www.kuopioinfo.fi. Open mid-June to mid-Aug. M-F 9:30am-6pm; mid-Aug. to May 9:30am-4pm.) Close to the train station, **Retkeilymaja Virkkula ❷,** Asemak. 3, offers bare-bones schoolhouse accommodations with rooms that remain unlocked at all times. (☎263 18 39. Breakfast €5. Sheets €5. Open mid-June to July. Reception 6am-9pm. Dorms €14.) **Rauhalahti Hostel ❹,** Katiskaniementie 8, at a spa 5km from the city center, is near walking trails, a beach, and the **Jatkaukamppa sauna,** the world's largest steam sauna. (☎473 473, fax 473 470. Breakfast, sheets, and sauna included. Reception 24hr. Singles €57; doubles €66. Sauna open June-Aug. Tu and F; Sept.-May Tu only.) **Muikkuravintola Sampo ❷,** Kauppak. 13, is renowned throughout Finland for its *Muikku,* a local whitefish. (Entrees €9-12. Open M-Th 11am-midnight, F-Sa 11am-1am, Su noon-midnight.) Fresh produce and fish are available at **Kauppatori,** the market in the center of town. (Open daily 7am-3pm.)

ROVANIEMI   ☎016

Just south of the Arctic Circle, the capital of Finnish Lapland (pop. 23,000) is a gateway to the northern wilderness. The **Arktikum,** housed in a beautiful glass corridor at Pohjoisranta 4, has a treasure trove of info on Arctic peoples, culture, landscapes, and wildlife. (Open mid-June to mid-Aug. daily 9am-7pm; early June and late Aug. daily 9am-6pm; Sept.-May Su and Tu-Sa 9am-6pm. €10, students €8.50.) The Arctic Circle passes through **Santa Claus's Village,** home to the world's favorite fat man. Take bus #8 (€2.70) from the train station. (Open June-Aug. and Dec. to mid-Jan. daily 9am-7pm; Sept. 9am-5pm; Oct.-Nov. and Jan.-May 10am-5pm.) The **Ranua Wildlife Park,** 80km south of Rovaniemi, has 3km of paths through the fenced-in territory of Arctic elk, bears, and wolves. (Open June to mid-Aug. daily 9am-8pm; mid-Aug. to Sept. and May 10am-6pm; Oct.-Apr. 10am-4pm. €10, children €8.50.) **Lapland Safaris,** Koskik. 1 (☎331 12 00), offers longboat river cruises in summer and husky safaris in winter (€59-153).

Trains go south to Helsinki (10hr.; 4 per day; €71, students €36) via Oulu (2½hr.; €22/11) and to Kuopio (8hr.; 3-4 per day; €54/27). **Buses** run to destinations throughout northern Finland, and to North Cape, Norway (11hr, daily, €101). The staff of the **tourist office,** Rovak. 21, combs the town on yellow mopeds. (☎34 62 70; www.rovaniemi.fi. Open June-Aug. M-F 8am-6pm, Sa-Su 10am-4pm; Sept.-May M-F 8am-4pm.) The no-frills **Tervashonka Hostel (HI) ❷,** Hallitusk. 16, is the cheapest accommodation in town. (☎34 4 6 44. Reception daily 8-10am and 5-10pm. Breakfast €5. Sheets €3. Dorms €14; singles €32; doubles €36. Nonmembers add €2.50.) Straight uphill from the station is the pleasant **Matka Borealis ❸,** Asemiesk. 1, a sunny guesthouse with comfortable rooms. (☎342 01 30; personal.inet.fi/business/matkaborealis. Breakfast, sheets, and sauna included. Kitchen available. Singles €40; doubles €52; triples €70; apartments from €110.) Dozens of restaurants, cafes, beer terraces, and bars can be found on **Koskikatu,** and many of the street's large hotels host discos.

FRANCE

The French celebrate the senses like no one else: The vineyards of Bordeaux, the savory dishes of Dijon, the sun-soaked shores of the Riviera, and the crisp air of the Alps combine for an exhilarating experience. France welcomes over 70 million visitors to its cities, chateaux, mountains, and beaches each year, making it the most popular tourist destination in the world. Yet to the French, it is only natural that outsiders should flock to their beloved homeland, so steeped in history, rich in art and architecture, and magnificently endowed with diverse landscapes. The fruits of France include the rich literature of Hugo, Proust, and Camus; the visionary art of Rodin, Matisse, and Monet; and the philosophical insight of Voltaire, Sartre, and Derrida. From the ambition of Napoleon to the birth of existentialism and postmodernism, the French occupied the driver's seat of history for many centuries. While France may no longer control the course of world events, it nonetheless remains among the most influential forces in Western history.

FACTS AND FIGURES

Official Name: French Republic.
Capital: Paris.
Major Cities: Lyon, Marseilles, Nice.
Population: 60,000,000.

Land Area: 547,030 sq. km.
Time Zone: GMT+1
Language: French.
Religions: Roman Catholic (90%).

DISCOVER FRANCE

Paris—ah, Paris. Aside from the requisite croissant-munching, tower-climbing activities, don't miss the less heralded sights. A stroll down the **Champs-Elysées** (p. 345), through the youthful **Latin Quarter** (p. 342), or into medieval **Montmartre** (p. 345) will reveal the unique magic of the city. When you've had your fill, leave time for daytrips to extravagant **Versailles** (p. 356) and the Gothic cathedral in **Chartres** (p. 356). The story of William the Conqueror is depicted in the tapestry at nearby **Bayeux** (p. 358), which serves as a good base for exploring the **D-Day beaches** (p. 359) of Normandy. The majestic abbey of **Mont-St-Michel** (p. 359) rises from the sea above shifting sands between Normandy and Brittany, while the chateau-studded **Loire Valley** (p. 364) brings visitors back to the days of royal intrigue and excess. Sweep down to wine-filled **Bordeaux** (p. 369) before exploring the *vieille ville* of **Carcassonne** (p. 375) with its spectacular medieval ramparts. To see Provence's **Camargue** (p. 378), an untamed flatland of bulls, wild horses, and flamingoes, stay in **Arles** (p. 378), whose picturesque streets once enchanted van Gogh. Arles also has the largest Roman amphitheater in France, but its sister in **Nîmes** (p. 376) is even more well-preserved. The seven popes who called nearby **Avignon** (p. 377) home in the 15th century left behind an impressive palace. A bustling city with an international flavor, **Marseilles** (p. 379) is the gateway to the **French Riviera** (p. 382), famous for its beauty and decadence. **Nice** (p. 385), with its excellent museums and nightlife, is the first stop on most itineraries, but its rocky beaches will have you seeking better sand strips in more secluded towns. The star-studded beach enclaves of **Cannes** (p. 383) and **St-Tropez** (p. 382) are also worth a look. In the shadow of Mont Blanc lies **Chamonix** (p. 396), which features fantastic skiing and mountain climbing. Then stop over in

France

BRITAIN — Dover, Folkestone, Portsmouth, Plymouth — Calais, Dunkerque — BELGIUM — Brussels, Lille, Boulogne

English Channel (La Manche) — Somme R., Arras, Amiens — LUX., GERMANY

Channel Islands — Cherbourg — Le Havre, Rouen — Reims, Metz

Roscoff, Paimpol, St-Malo — Bayeux, Caen — Seine R., Epernay, Nancy, Strasbourg

Brest, St-Brieuc, Dinan — Paris — Marne R.

Quimper, Rennes — Le Mans, Chartres — Troyes, Mulhouse

Angers, Blois, Amboise — Orléans, Fontainebleau — Semur-en-Auxois, Dijon, Besançon — SWITZ., Bern

Quiberon, Belle Ile, Nantes, Saumur, Tours — Loire R., Bourges, Nevers, Beaune — Lake Geneva, Geneva — THE ALPS

Ile d'Yeu — Poitiers, Vienne R. — Cluny, Annecy, Chamonix, Mont Blanc

ATLANTIC OCEAN — La Rochelle, Rochefort, Saintes — Limoges, Clermont-Ferrand, Vichy, Lyon — Grenoble — ITALY

Gironde R., Cognac, Angoulême — Périgueux, Les Eyzies — CEVENNES MTS., Rhône R.

Bay of Biscay — Bordeaux, Garonne R., Dordogne R., Sarlat

TGV Line — Chunnel

Cap Corse, Calvi, Bastia, CORSICA, Corte, Ajaccio, Porto-Vecchio, Bonifacio, SARDINIA (ITALY)

Cahors, Montauban, Albi, Avignon, Nîmes, Arles, Aix-en-Provence — Menton, MONACO, Nice, Cannes, CÔTE D'AZUR

Bayonne, Biarritz, St-Jean-Pied-de-Port, Lourdes, Cauterets — Toulouse, Montpellier, Marseille, Toulon, St-Tropez

PYRENEES — Carcassonne, Aude R., Perpignan, Golfe du Lion — Mediterranean Sea

SPAIN — ANDORRA

0 ——— 120 miles
0 ——— 120 kilometers

the modern metropolis of **Lyon** (p. 398) before exploring the mix of French and German culture in **Strasbourg** (p. 404), home to an amazing Gothic cathedral and the beginning of **La Route du Vin** (p. 405). If sparkling varieties of wine are more to your liking, head to **Reims** (p. 408) and **Épernay** (p. 409), home to the world's most famous producers of champagne.

ESSENTIALS

WHEN TO GO

In July, Paris starts to shrink; by August it is devoid of Parisians, animated only by tourists and the pickpockets who love them. The French Riviera fills with Anglophones from June to September. On the other hand, the rest of France teems with Frenchmen during these months, especially along the Atlantic coast. Early summer and autumn are the best times to visit Paris—the city has warmed up but not completely emptied out. The north and west have cool winters and mild summers, while the less-crowded center and east have a more continental climate. From December to February, the Alps provide some of the best skiing in the world, while the Pyrenees offer a calmer, if less climatically dependable, alternative.

DOCUMENTS AND FORMALITIES

VISAS. For stays shorter than 90 days, only citizens of South Africa need a short-stay visa (30-day visa costs ZAR217; 90-day ZAR260). For stays longer than 90 days, all non-EU citizens need long-stay visas (€95).

EMBASSIES. Foreign embassies in France are in Paris (p. 330). For French embassies at home, contact: **Australia,** Consulate General, Level 26, St. Martins Tower, 31 Market St., Sydney NSW 2000 (☎02 92 61 57 79; www.consulfrance-sydney.org.); **Canada,** Consulate General, 1 pl. Ville Marie, 26th fl., Montréal, QC H3B 4SE (☎514-878-4385; www.consulfrance-montreal.org); **Ireland,** Consulate Section, 36 Ailesbury Rd., Ballsbridge, Dublin 4 (☎01 260 16 66; www.ambafrance.ie); **New Zealand,** 34-42 Manners St., P.O. Box 11-343, Wellington (☎04 384 25 55; www.ambafrance.net.nz); **South Africa,** Consulate General at Johannesburg, 191 Jan Smuts Ave., Rosebank; mailing address P.O. Box 1027, Parklands 2121 (☎011 778 5600, visas 778 5605; www.consulfrance-jhb.org.); **UK,** Consulate General, 21 Cromwell Rd., London SW7 2EN (☎020 7838 2000; www.ambafrance-uk.org.); **US,** Consulate General, 4101 Reservoir Rd. NW, Washington, D.C. 20007 (☎202-944-6195; www.consulfrance-washington.org).

MONEY. On January 1, 2002, the **euro** (€) replaced the **franc** as the unit of currency in France. For more information, see p. 14. **Tips** are always included in meal prices in restaurants and cafes, and in drink prices at bars and clubs; look for the phrase *service compris* on the menu or just ask. If service is not included, tip 15-20%. Even when service is included, it is polite to leave a *pourboire* of up to 5% at a cafe, bistro, restaurant, or bar.

TRANSPORTATION

BY PLANE. The two major international airports in Paris are **Roissy-Charles de Gaulle** (CDG; to the north) and **Orly** (ORY; to the south). For information on cheap flights from the UK to Paris, see p. 46.

BY TRAIN. The French national railway company, **SNCF** (☎08 36 35 35 35; www.sncf.fr), manages one of Europe's most efficient rail networks. **TGV** (*train à grande vitesse,* or high-speed) trains, the fastest in the world, run from Paris to major cities in France, as well as to Geneva and Lausanne, Switzerland. **Rapide** trains are slower; local **Express** trains are, oddly, the slowest option. SNCF offers a wide range of discounted round-trip tickets called *tarifs Découvertes*. Get a calendar from a train station detailing *période bleue* (blue period), *période blanche* (white period), and *période rouge* (red period) times and days; blue gets the most discounts, while red gets none. Those under 25 have two great options: The **Découverte 12-25** (€41.20) gives a 25% discount for any blue-period travel; and the **Carte 12-25** (€41.20), valid for a year, is good for 25-50% off all TGV trains, 50% off all non-TGV trips that started during a blue period, and 25% off non-TGV trips starting in a white period. Tickets must be validated in the orange machine at the entrance to the platforms at the *gare* (train station) and revalidated at any connections on your trip. Seat reservations, recommended for international trips, are mandatory on EuroCity (EC), InterCity (IC), and TGV trains. All three require a ticket supplement and reservation fee.

Eurail is valid in France. The SNCF's **France Railpass** grants four days of unlimited rail travel in France in any 30-day period (US$210; companion travelers US$171 each; up to 6 extra days US$30 each); the parallel **Youthpass** provides those under 26 with four days of unlimited travel within a two-month period (US$140; up to 6 extra days US$18 each). The **France Rail 'n' Drive pass** combines three days of rail travel with two days of car rental (US$245; companion travelers US$175 each; extra rail days US$31 each, extra car days US$37).

BY BUS. Within France, long-distance buses are a secondary transportation choice, as service is relatively infrequent. However, in some regions buses are indispensable for reaching out-of-the-way towns. Bus services operated by the SNCF accept railpasses. *Gare routière* is French for "bus station."

BY FERRY. Ferries across the English Channel (*La Manche*) link France to England and Ireland. The shortest and most popular route is between **Dover** and **Calais,** and is run by **P&O Stena Line, SeaFrance,** and **Hoverspeed** (p. 49). Hoverspeed also travels from **Dieppe** to **Newhaven,** England. **Brittany Ferries** (☎08 25 82 88 28; www.brittanyferries.co.uk) travels from **Caen** (p. 358) and **St-Malo** (p. 361) to **Portsmouth.** For more info on English Channel ferries, see p. 49. For info on ferries from **Nice** and **Marseilles** to **Corsica,** see p. 392.

BY CHUNNEL. Traversing 27 miles under the sea, the Chunnel is undoubtedly the fastest, most convenient, and least scenic route from England to France. There are two types of passenger service. **Eurostar** runs a frequent train service from London to Paris and Brussels, with stops at Ashford in England and Calais and Lille in France. Book reservations in UK, by phone, or over the web. (UK ☎0990 186 186; US ☎800-387-6782; elsewhere ☎020 7928 5163; www.eurostar.com.) Eurostar tickets can also be bought at most major travel agencies. **Eurotunnel** shuttles cars and passengers between Kent and Nord-Pas-de-Calais. (UK ☎08705 35 35 35; France ☎03 21 00 61 00; www.eurotunnel.co.uk.)

BY CAR. Unless you are traveling in a group of three or more, you won't save money traveling long distance by car rather than train, thanks to highway tolls, high gasoline cost, and rental charges. If you can't decide between train and car travel, get a **Rail 'n' Drive pass** from railpass vendors (see above). The French drive on the right-hand side of the road; France maintains its roads well, but the landscape itself often makes the roads a menace, especially in twisting Corsica.

BY BIKE AND BY THUMB. Of all Europeans, the French may be alone in loving cycling more than soccer. Drivers usually accommodate bikers on the wide country roads, and many cities banish cars from select streets each Sunday. Renting a bike (€8-19 per day) beats bringing your own if your touring will be confined to one or two regions. Many consider France the hardest country in Europe to get a lift. *Let's Go* does not recommend hitchhiking. In major cities, ride-sharing organizations such as **Eurostop International,** or **Allostop** in France (www.allostop.com), pair drivers and riders, though not all of them screen.

TOURIST SERVICES

EMERGENCY	Police: ☎122. Ambulance: ☎123. Fire: ☎124.

TOURIST OFFICES. The extensive French tourism support network revolves around **syndicats d'initiative** and **offices de tourisme;** and in the smallest towns, the **Mairie,** the mayor's office; all of which *Let's Go* labels "tourist office." All three distribute maps and pamphlets, help you find accommodations, and suggest excursions to the countryside. For up-to-date events and regional info, see www.francetourism.com.

FRANCE

COMMUNICATION

PHONE CODES	**Country code: 33. International dialing prefix: 00.** France has no city codes. From outside France, dial int'l dialing prefix (see inside back cover) + 33 + local number (drop the leading zero).

TELEPHONES. When calling from abroad, drop the leading zero of the local number. French payphones only accept stylish *Télécartes* (phonecards), available in 50-unit (€7.50) and 120-unit (€15) denominations at *tabacs*, post offices, and train stations. *Décrochez* means pick up; you'll then be asked to *patientez* (wait) to insert your card; at *numérotez* or *composez* you can dial. Use only public France Télécom payphones, as privately owned ones charge more. An expensive alternative is to call collect *(faire un appel en PCV)*; an English-speaking operator can be reached by dialing the appropriate service provider listed below. The information number is ☎ 12; for an international operator, call ☎ 00 33 11. For information on purchasing a **cell phone**, see p. 36. International direct dial numbers include: **AT&T,** ☎ 0 800 99 00 11; **British Telecom,** ☎ 0 800 99 02 44; **Canada Direct,** ☎ 0 800 99 00 16 or 99 02 16; **Ireland Direct,** ☎ 0 800 99 03 53; **MCI,** ☎ 0 800 99 00 19; **Sprint,** ☎ 0 800 99 00 87; **Telecom New Zealand,** ☎ 0 800 99 00 64; **Telkom South Africa,** ☎ 0 800 99 00 27; **Telstra Australia,** ☎ 0 800 99 00 61.

MAIL. Mail can be held for pickup through *Poste Restante* to almost any city or town with a post office. Address letters to be held according to the following example: SURNAME Firstname, *Poste Restante*, 52 r. du Louvre, 75001 Paris, France. Mark the envelope HOLD.

INTERNET ACCESS. Most major post offices and some branches now offer Internet access at special "cyberposte" terminals; you can buy a rechargeable card that gives you 50min. of access at any post office for €8. Note that *Let's Go* does not list "cyberposte" locations. Most large towns in France have a cybercafe. Rates and speed of connection vary widely; occasionally there are free terminals in technologically-oriented museums or exhibition spaces. **Cybercafé Guide** (www.cyberiacafe.net/cyberia/guide/ccafe.htm#working_france) lists cybercafes in France.

LANGUAGE. Contrary to popular opinion, even flailing efforts to speak French will be appreciated, especially in the countryside. Be lavish with your *Monsieurs*, *Madames*, and *Mademoiselles*, and greet people with a friendly *bonjour* (*bonsoir* in the evening). For basic French vocabulary and pronunciation, see p. 1054.

ACCOMMODATIONS AND CAMPING

FRANCE	❶	❷	❸	❹	❺
ACCOMMODATIONS	under €15	€16-25	€26-35	€36-55	over €55

Hostels generally offer dormitory accommodations in large, single-sex rooms with four to 10 beds, though some have as many as 60. At the other end of the scale, many offer private singles and doubles. In France, a bed in a hostel averages around €7.65-15.25. The **French Hostelling International (HI)** affiliate (p. 24), **Fédéraion Uniedes Auberges de Jeunesse** (FUAJ), operates 178 hostels within France. Some hostels accept reservations through the International Booking Network (p. 24). Two or more people traveling together will often save money by staying in cheap hotels rather than hostels. The French government employs a four-star hotel ratings system. *Gîtes d'étapes* are rural accommodations for cyclists, hikers, and other ramblers in less-populated areas. Expect *gîtes* to provide beds, a kitchen facility, and a resident caretaker. After 3000 years of settled history, true wilderness in France is hard to find. It's illegal to camp in most public spaces, including national parks. Instead, look forward to organized *campings* (campsites), where you'll share your splendid isolation with vacationing families and all manner of programmed fun. Most campsites have toilets, showers, and electrical outlets, though you may have to pay extra for such luxuries (€2-6); you'll often need to pay a fee for your car, too (€3-8). Otherwise, expect to pay €8-15 per site.

FOOD AND DRINK

FRANCE	❶	❷	❸	❹	❺
FOOD	under €5	€6-10	€11-15	€16-25	over €25

French chefs cook for one of the most finicky clienteles in the world. The largest meal of the day is *le déjeuner* (lunch). A complete French meal includes an *apéritif* (drink), an *entrée* (appetizer), a *plat* (main course), salad, cheese, dessert, fruit, coffee, and a *digestif* (after-dinner drink). The French drink wine with virtually every meal; *boisson comprise* entitles you to a free drink (usually wine) with your meal. Most restaurants offer a *menu à prix fixe* (fixed-price meal) that costs less than ordering *à la carte*. The *formule* is a cheaper, two-course version for the hurried luncher. Odd-hour cravings between lunch and dinner can be satisfied at *brasseries*, the middle ground between casual cafes and structured restaurants. *Service compris* means the tip is included in *l'addition* (check). It's easy to get satisfying dinner for under €10 with staples such as cheese, pâté, wine, bread, and chocolate; for a picnic, get fresh produce at a *marché* (outdoor market) and then hop between specialty shops. Start with a *boulangerie* (bakery) for bread, proceed to a *charcuterie* (butcher) for meats, and then *pâtisseries* and *confiseries* (pastry and candy shops) to satisfy a sweet tooth. When choosing a cafe, remember that you pay for its location—those on a major boulevard are more expensive than smaller places a few steps down a side street. Prices are cheaper at the *comptoir* (counter) than in the *salle* (seating area). For supermarket shopping, look for the chains Carrefour, Casino, Monoprix, and Prisunic.

HOLIDAYS AND FESTIVALS

Holidays: New Year's Day (Jan. 1); Easter Monday (Apr. 12); Labor Day (May 1); L'Anniversaire de la Liberation (May 8); Ascension Day (May 20); Whitmonday (May 31); Bastille Day (July 14); Feast of the Assumption (Aug. 15); All Saints' Day (Nov. 1); Armistice Day (Nov. 11); and Christmas (Dec. 25).

Festivals: Most festivals take place in summer. The **Cannes Film Festival** (May; www.festival-cannes.com) is mostly for directors and stars, but provides good people watching. The **Festival d'Avignon** (July-Aug.; www.festival-avignon.com) is famous for its theater. **Bastille Day** (July 14) is marked by military parades and fireworks nationwide. Although you may not be competing in the **Tour de France** (3rd or 4th Su in July; www.letour.fr), you'll enjoy all the hype. A **Vineyard Festival** (Sept., in Nice; www.nice-coteazur.org/americain/tourisme/vigne/index.html) celebrates the grape harvest with music, parades, and wine tastings.

PARIS

City of light, city of love, unsightly city, invisible city—Paris somehow manages to do it all. From alleys that shelter the world's best bistros to broad avenues flaunting the highest of *haute couture*, from the centuries-old stone of Notre Dame's gargoyles to the futuristic motions of the Parc de la Villette, from the masterpieces of the Louvre to the installations of avant-garde galleries, Paris presents itself as both a harbor of tradition and a hotbed of impulse.

Paris has been a center of commerce, culture, and conflict for centuries—and in the midst of it all, this city became the Western world's symbolic capital of romance, revolution, heroism, and hedonism. No wonder it's the world's most heavily touristed city—or that intellectuals in the later 20th century, in inimitable French style, started to question whether "Paris" had become nothing more than a conglomeration of illusions in the imagination of the tourist. You might find yourself wondering the same thing, as you sit in some perfect sidewalk cafe with a view of the Eiffel Tower, sipping an espresso or savoring a croissant, surrounded by beautiful people in brooding black: Can this place exist? But it does. Paris seems, incredibly, to live up to its mythical reputation and utterly defy it; it is at once a living monument to the past and a city driving the present.

■ INTERCITY TRANSPORTATION

Flights: Aéroport Roissy-Charles de Gaulle (CDG; ☎01 48 62 22 80; www.parisairports.com), 23km northeast of Paris, services most transatlantic flights. For flight info, call the 24hr. English-speaking information center. **Aéroport d'Orly** (ORY; English recording ☎01 49 75 15 15), 18km south of Paris, is used by charters and many continental flights. The cheapest and fastest ways to get into the city are by **RER** or **bus.**

Trains: There are 6 train stations in Paris. Each part of the Métro system services a different geographic region.

Gare d'Austerlitz: To the Loire Valley, southwestern France (Bordeaux, Pyrenees), Spain, and Portugal. TGV to southwestern France leaves from Gare Montparnasse. To Barcelona (9hr., daily, €97) and Madrid (12-13hr., 4 per day, €102).

Gare de l'Est: To eastern France (Champagne, Alsace, Lorraine, Strasbourg), Luxembourg, parts of Switzerland (Basel, Lucerne, Zürich), southern Germany (Frankfurt, Munich), Austria, Hungary, and Prague. To: Luxembourg (4hr., 10 per day, €50); Munich (9hr., 14 per day, €130); Prague (16hr., daily, €180); Strasbourg (4hr., 13 per day, €39); Vienna (13hr., 5 per day, €180); Zürich (6-7hr., 10 per day, €110).

Gare de Lyon: To southern France (Lyon, Provence, Riviera), parts of Switzerland (Bern, Geneva, Lausanne), Italy and Greece. To: Florence (13hr., 4 per day, €145); Geneva (4hr., 7 per day, €69); Lyon (2hr., 23 per day, €35); Marseilles (4-5hr., 18 per day, €84); Nice (6hr., 8 per day, €60); Rome (15hr., 4-5 per day, €160).

Gare du Nord: Trains to northern France, Belgium, Britain, The Netherlands, Scandinavia, and northern Germany (Cologne, Hamburg). To: Amsterdam (4-5hr., 6 per day, €87); Brussels (1½hr., 28 per day, €66); Cologne (4hr., 7 per day, €78); London (by the Eurostar Chunnel; 3hr., 12-28 per day, up to €299).

Gare Montparnasse: To Brittany and southwestern France on the TGV. To Rennes (2hr., 30 per day, €46).

Gare St-Lazare: To Normandy. To Caen (2hr., 9 per day, €27) and Rouen (1-2hr., 13 per day, €18).

Buses: Gare Routière Internationale du Paris-Gallieni, 28 av. du Général de Gaulle, just outside Paris in Bagnolet. M: Gallieni. **Eurolines** (☎01 43 54 11 99; www.eurolines.fr) sells tickets to most destinations in France and neighboring countries.

■ ORIENTATION

The **Ile de la Cité** and **Ile St-Louis** sit at the center of the city, while the **Seine,** flowing east to west, splits Paris into two large expanses: The **Rive Gauche (Left Bank)** to the south and the **Rive Droite (Right Bank)** to the north. The Left Bank, with its older architecture and narrow streets, has traditionally been considered bohemian and intellectual, while the Right Bank, with grand avenues and designer shops, is more ritzy. Administratively, Paris is divided into 20 **arrondissements** (districts; e.g. 1*er*, 6*ème*) that spiral clockwise around the Louvre. Well-known sites are packed into the central *arrondissements* (1*er* through 8*ème*), though the peripheral ones should not be overlooked. Refer also to this book's **color maps** of the city.

RIVE GAUCHE (LEFT BANK). The **Latin Quarter,** encompassing the 5*ème* and parts of the 6*ème* around the **Sorbonne** and the **Ecole des Beaux-Arts** (School of Fine Arts), has been home to students for centuries; the animated **boulevard St-Michel** is the boundary between the two *arrondissements*. The lively **rue Mouffetard** in the 5*ème* is quintessential Latin Quarter. The area around east-west **boulevard St-Germain,** which crosses bd. St-Michel just south of pl. St-Michel in the 6*ème*, is known as **St-Germain des Prés.** To the west, the gold-domed **Invalides** and the stern Neo-classical **Ecole Militaire,** which faces the **Eiffel Tower** across the **Champ-de-Mars,** recall the military past of the 7*ème* and northern 15*ème*, now full of traveling businesspeople. South of the Latin Quarter, **Montparnasse,** in the 14*ème*, eastern 15*ème*, and southwestern 6*ème*, lolls in the shadow of its tower. The glamorous **boulevard du Montparnasse** belies the surrounding residential districts. The eastern Left Bank, the 13*ème*, is a new hot spot, centered on **place d'Italie.**

RIVE DROITE (RIGHT BANK). The **Louvre** and **rue de Rivoli** occupy the sight- and tourist-packed 1*er* and the more business-oriented 2*ème*. The crooked streets of the **Marais,** in the 3*ème* and 4*ème*, escaped Baron Haussmann's redesign of Paris and now support many diverse communities. From **place de la Concorde,** at the western end of the 1*er*, **avenue des Champs-Elysées** bisects the 8*ème* as it sweeps up toward the **Arc de Triomphe** at **Charles de Gaulle-Etoile.** South of the Etoile, old and new money fills the exclusive 16*ème*, bordered to the west by the **Bois de Boulogne** park and to the east by the Seine and the **Trocadéro,** which faces the Eiffel Tower across the river. Back toward central Paris, the 9*ème*, just north of the 2*ème*, is defined by the sumptuous **Opéra.** East of the 9*ème*, the 10*ème* hosts cheap lodgings and the **Gare du Nord** and **Gare de l'Est.** The 10*ème*, 3*ème*, and the 11*ème*, which claims the newest hip nightlife in Paris (in **Bastille**), meet at **place de la République.** South of Bastille, the 12*ème* surrounds the **Gare de Lyon,** petering out at the **Bois de Vincennes.** East of Bastille, the party atmosphere gives way to the quieter, more residential 20*ème* and 19*ème*, while the 18*ème* is home to the quaint and heavily touristed **Montmartre,** which is capped by the **Sacré-Cœur.** To the east, the 17*ème* begins in the red-light district of **Pigalle** and bd. de Clichy, and grows more elegant toward the Etoile, the **Opéra Garnier,** and the 16*ème*. Continuing west along the *grande axe* defined by the Champs-Elysées, the skyscrapers of **La Défense,** Paris's newest quarter, loom across the Seine from Bois de Boulogne.

▐ LOCAL TRANSPORTATION

Public Transportation: The efficient **Métropolitain,** or **Métro (M),** runs 5:30am-12:30am. Lines are numbered and are generally referred to by their number and final destinations; connections are called *correspondances.* **Single-fare tickets** within the city €1.30; *carnet* (packet) of 10 €9.60. Buy extras for when ticket booths are closed (after 10pm) and hold onto your ticket until you exit. The **RER** (Réseau Express Régional), the commuter train to the suburbs, serves as an express subway within central Paris; changing to and getting off the RER requires sticking your validated ticket into a turnstile. Watch the signboards next to the RER tracks and check that your stop is lit up before riding. **Buses** use the same €1.30 tickets (bought on the bus; validate in the machine by the driver), but transfer requires a new ticket. Buses run 6:30am-8:30pm, *Autobus de Nuit* until 1am, and *Noctambus* (3-4 tickets) every hr. 1:30-5:30am at stops marked with the bug-eyed moon between the Châtelet stop and the *portes* (city exits). The **Mobilis** pass covers the Métro, RER, and buses only (€5 for a 1-day pass in Zones 1 and 2). A weekly pass (carte orange hebdomadaire) costs €13.75 and expires every Su; photo ID required. Refer to this book's **color maps** of Paris's transit network.

Taxis: Alpha Taxis (☎01 45 85 85 85). **Taxis 7000** (☎01 42 70 00 42). Cabs are expensive and take 3 passengers (there is a €2.45 surcharge for a 4th). The meter starts running when you phone. Cab stands are near train stations and major bus stops.

Car Rental: Rent-a-Car, 79 r. de Bercy (☎01 43 45 98 99). Open M-Sa 8:30am-6pm.

Bike Rental: Paris à velo, 2 r. de Fer-à-Moulin, 5ème (☎01 43 37 59 22). M: Censier-Daubenton. Bike rental €14 per day. Open M-Sa 10am-12:30pm and 2-7pm.

🛂 PRACTICAL INFORMATION

TOURIST AND FINANCIAL SERVICES

Tourist Office: Bureau d'Accueil Central, 127 av. des Champs-Elysées, 8ème (☎08 92 68 31 12; www.paris-touristoffice.com). M: Georges V. Open in summer daily 9am-8pm; off-season M-Sa 9am-8pm Su 11am-7pm.

Embassies: Australia, 4 r. Jean-Rey, 15ème (☎01 40 59 33 00; www.austgov.fr). M: Bir-Hakeim. Open M-F 9:15am-noon and 2-4:30pm. **Canada,** 35 av. Montaigne, 8ème (☎01 44 43 29 00; www.amb-canada.fr). M: Franklin-Roosevelt. Open M-F 9am-noon and 2-5pm. **Ireland,** 12, av. Foch, 16ème (☎01 44 17 67 00; www.irlande-tourisme.fr). M: Trocadéro. Open M-F 9:30am-1pm and 2:30-5:30pm. **New Zealand,** 7ter r. Leonardo de Vinci, 16ème (☎01 45 01 43 43; www.nzembassy.com/france). M: Victor-Hugo. Open July-Aug. M-Th 8:30am-1pm and 2-5:30pm, F 8:30am-2pm; Sept.-June M-F 9am-1pm and 2-5:30pm. **South Africa,** 59 quai d'Orsay, 7ème (☎01 53 59 23 23; www.afriquesud.net). M: Invalides. Open M-F 8:30am-5:45pm; visa services 9am-noon. **UK,** 18bis r. d'Anjou, 8ème (☎01 44 51 31 00; www.amb-grandebretagne.fr). M: St-Augustin. Open M and W-F 9:30am-12:30pm and 2:30-5pm, Tu 9:30am-4:30pm. **US,** 2 r. St-Forentin, 1er (☎01 43 12 22 22; www.amb-usa.fr). M: Concorde. Open M-F 9am-12:30pm and 1-6pm; notarial services Tu-F 9am-noon. Skip the long line; go to the right and tell them you are there for American services.

Currency Exchange: Hotels, train stations, and airports offer poor rates but have extended hours; Gare de Lyon, Gare du Nord, and both airports have booths open 6:30am-10:30pm. Most **ATMs** accept **Visa** ("CB/VISA") and **MasterCard** ("EC"). Crédit Lyonnais ATMs take **AmEx;** Crédit Mutuel and Crédit Agricole ATMs are on the **Cirrus** network; and most Visa ATMs accept **PLUS**-network cards.

American Express: 11 r. Scribe, 9ème (☎01 47 14 50 00), opposite the back of the Opéra. M: Opéra or Auber. Mail held for cardholders and AmEx Traveler's Cheque holders. Open M-Sa 9am-6:30pm; exchange counters open Su 10am-5pm.

LOCAL SERVICES

English-Language Bookstore: Shakespeare and Co., 37 r. de la Bûcherie, 5ème, across the Seine from Notre-Dame. M: St-Michel. A Paris fixture for anglophones, with a quirky, wide selection of new and used books. Open daily noon-midnight.

Gay and Lesbian Services: Centre Gai et Lesbien, 3 r. Keller, 11ème (☎01 43 57 21 47). M: Ledru Rollin or Bastille. Info hub for all gay services and associations in Paris. English spoken. Open M-Sa 2-8pm, Su 2-7pm. **Les Mots à la Bouche,** 6 r. Ste-Croix de la Bretonnerie, 4ème (☎01 42 78 88 30; www.motsbouche.com), is Paris's largest gay and lesbian bookstore and serves as an unofficial info center. M: Hôtel-de-Ville. Open M-Sa 11am-11pm, Su 2-8pm.

Laundromats: Laundromats are everywhere, especially in the 5*ème* and 6*ème*. **Arc en Ciel,** 62 r. Arbre Sec, 1*er* (☎01 42 41 39 39), does dry cleaning. M: Louvre.

EMERGENCY AND COMMUNICATIONS

Emergencies: Ambulance: ☎15. **Fire:** ☎18. **Police:** ☎17. For non-emergencies, head to the local *gendarmerie* (police force) in each *arrondissement*.

Crisis Lines: Rape, SOS Viol (☎08 00 05 95 95). Call free anywhere in France for counseling (medical and legal). Open M-F 10am-7pm. **SOS Help!** (☎01 46 21 46 46). Anonymous, confidential English-speaking crisis hotline. Open daily 3-11pm.

Hospitals: Hôpital Américain de Paris, 63 bd. Hugo, Neuilly (☎01 46 41 25 25). M: Port Maillot, then bus #82 to the end of the line. **Hôpital Franco-Britannique de Paris,** 3 r. Barbès, in the Parisian suburb of Levallois-Perret (☎01 46 39 22 22). M: Anatole France. Has some English speakers, but don't count on it. **Hôpital Bichat,** 46 r. Henri Buchard, 18*ème* (☎01 40 25 80 80). M: Port St-Ouen. Emergency services.

24 hr. Pharmacies: Every *arrondissement* has a **pharmacie de garde** which opens in emergencies. The locations change, but their names are posted on every pharmacy's door. **Pharmacie Dhéry,** in the Galerie des Champs 84, av. des Champs-Elysées, 8*ème* (☎01 45 62 02 41). M: George V. Open 24hr. **British & American Pharmacy,** 1 r. Auber, 9*ème* (☎01 42 65 88 29). M: Auber or Opéra. Open daily 8am-8:30pm.

Telephones: To use the phones, you'll need to buy a **phone card** (télécarte), available at post offices, Métro stations, and *tabacs*. For **directory info,** call ☎12.

Internet Access: Internet cafes are widespread throughout the city.

Artefak, 42 r. Volta, 3*ème* (☎01 44 59 39 58). M: Arts et Metiers or Temple. Early-bird special (before 1pm) €2 per hr.; regular €3 per hr. Open daily 10pm-2am.

Le Jardin de l'Internet, 79 bd. St-Michel, 5*ème* (☎01 44 07 22 20). RER: Luxembourg. €2.50 per hr. Open daily 9am-11pm.

Le Sputnik, 14-16 r. de la Butte-aux-Cailles, 13*ème* (☎01 45 65 19 82). M: Place d'Italie. €1 for 15min., €4 per hr.

Taxiphone, 343 r. des Pyrénées, 20*ème* (☎01 43 15 68 25). M: Pyrénées or Jourdain. €3 per hr. Open daily noon-10pm.

Post Office: Poste du Louvre, 52 r. du Louvre, 1*er* (☎01 40 28 20 40). M: Louvre. Open 24hr. Address mail to be held: SURNAME Firstname, *Poste Restante,* 52 r. du Louvre, 75001 Paris, FRANCE. **Postal Codes:** 750xx, where "xx" is the *arrondissement* (e.g., 75003 for any address in the 3*ème*).

⚑ ACCOMMODATIONS

High season in Paris falls around Easter and from May to October, peaking in July and August. Paris's hostels skip many standard restrictions (sheets, curfews, etc.) and tend to have flexible maximum stays. The city's six HI hostels are for members only. The rest of Paris's dorm-style beds are either private hostels or quieter *foyers* (student dorms). Hotels may be the most practical accommodations for the majority of travelers. Expect to pay at least €25 for a single or €35 for a double in the cheapest, luckiest of circumstances. In cheaper hotels, few rooms have private baths; hall showers cost about €2.50 per use. Rooms fill quickly after morning check-out (10am-noon), so arrive early or reserve ahead. Most hostels and *foyers* include the **taxe de séjour** (€1-1.50 per person per day) in listed prices, but some do not. If you haven't reserved ahead, tourist offices (see p. 330) and the organizations below can book rooms.

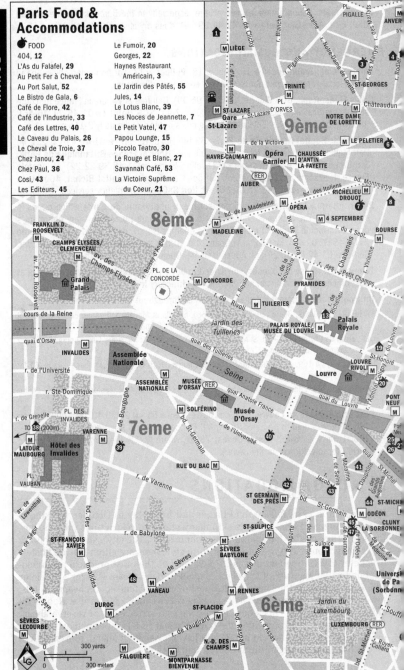

Paris Food & Accommodations

FOOD

404, **12**	Le Fumoir, **20**
L'As du Falafel, **29**	Georges, **22**
Au Petit Fer à Cheval, **28**	Haynes Restaurant
Au Port Salut, **52**	Américain, **3**
Le Bistro de Gala, **6**	Le Jardin des Pâtés, **55**
Café de Flore, **42**	Jules, **14**
Café de l'Industrie, **33**	Le Lotus Blanc, **39**
Café des Lettres, **40**	Les Noces de Jeannette, **7**
Le Caveau du Palais, **26**	Le Petit Vatel, **47**
Chez Janou, **24**	Papou Lounge, **15**
Chez Paul, **36**	Piccolo Teatro, **30**
Le Cheval de Troie, **37**	Le Rouge et Blanc, **27**
Cosi, **43**	Savannah Café, **53**
Les Editeurs, **45**	La Victoire Suprême
	du Coeur, **21**

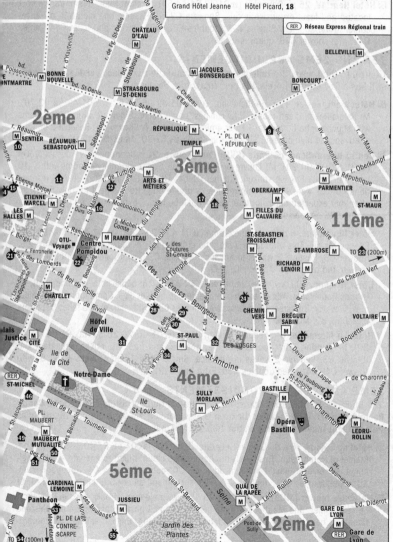

ACCOMMODATIONS
Auberge de Jeunesse "Jules Ferry" (HI), 9
Cambrai Hôtel, 2
Centre International de Paris (BVJ): Paris Louvre, 19
Centre International de Paris (BVJ): Quartier Latin, 50
Le Fauconnier, 35
Le Fourcy, 34
Grand Hôtel Jeanne d'Arc, 32
Hôtel du Champs de Mars, 38
Hôtel d'Esmeralda, 46
Hôtel Europe-Liège, 1
Hôtel Henri IV, 25
Hôtel du Marais, 17
Hôtel Marignan, 49
Hôtel La Marmotte, 10
Hôtel Montebello, 48
Hôtel Montpensier, 13
Hôtel de Nesle, 41
Hôtel Picard, 18
Hôtel St-André des Arts, 44
Hôtel St-Jacques, 51
Hôtel du Séjour, 16
Hôtel Tiquetonne, 11
Hôtel Vivienne, 8
Maubuisson, 31
Modern Hôtel, 23
Perfect Hôtel, 4
Woodstock Hostel, 5
Young and Happy (Y&H) Hostel, 54

RER Réseau Express Régional train

ACCOMMODATIONS SERVICES

La Centrale de Réservations (FUAJ-HI), 4 bd. Jules Ferry, 11ème. (☎01 43 57 02 60; fax 01 40 21 79 92). M: République. Open daily 8am-10pm.

OTU-Voyage (Office du Tourisme Universitaire), 119, r. St-Martin 4ème (☎08 20 81 78 17 or 01 49 72 57 19 for groups). €1.53 service charge. Open M-F 9:30am-7pm, Sa 10am-noon and 1:30-5pm. Also at 2 r. Malus, 5ème (☎01 44 41 74 74). M: Place Monge. Open M-Sa 9-6pm.

ILE DE LA CITÉ

▨ **Hôtel Henri IV,** 25 pl. Dauphine (☎01 43 54 44 53). M: Pont Neuf. One of Paris's best located and least expensive hotels. Showers €2.50. Reserve one month in advance, earlier in the summer. Singles €23; doubles €30, with shower and toilet €54; triples €41, with shower €48; quads €48. ❷

1ER AND 2ÈME ARRONDISSEMENTS

Central to the **Louvre,** the **Tuileries,** the **Seine,** and the ritzy **place Vendôme,** this area still has a few budget hotels. It's best to avoid r. St-Denis.

▨ **Hôtel Montpensier,** 12 r. de Richelieu, 1er (☎01 42 96 28 50; fax 01 42 86 02 70). M: Palais-Royal. Clean rooms, lofty ceilings, bright decor. Small elevator. TVs in rooms with shower or bath. Internet €1 per 4min. Breakfast €7. Shower €4. Reserve 2 months in advance in high season. Singles and doubles €57-89. AmEx/DC/MC/V. ❺

▨ **Centre International de Paris (BVJ): Paris Louvre,** 20 r. Jean-Jacques Rousseau, 1er (☎01 53 00 90 90). M: Louvre or Palais-Royal. Bright, dorm-style rooms with 2-10 beds per room. English spoken. Internet €1 per 10min. Lockers €2. Weekend reservations up to 1 week in advance; reserve by phone only. Rooms held for only 5-10min. after your expected check-in time; call if you'll be late. Doubles €28 per person; other rooms €25 per person. ❷

Hôtel Tiquetonne, 6 r. Tiquetonne, 2ème (☎01 42 36 94 58; fax 01 42 36 02 94). M: Etienne-Marcel. This affordable 7-story hotel is a study in faux finishes. Breakfast €5. Shower €5. Reserve 2 weeks in advance. Singles €28, with toilet €38; doubles with shower and toilet €46. AmEx/MC/V. ❸

Hôtel Vivienne, 40 r. Vivienne, 2ème (☎01 42 33 13 26; paris@hotel-vivienne.com). M: Grands Boulevards. Adds a touch of refinement to budget digs. Some rooms with balconies. Elevator. Breakfast €6. Singles with shower €50, with shower and toilet €78; doubles €65/80. MC/V. ❹

Hôtel La Marmotte, 6 r. Léopold Bellan, 2ème (☎01 40 26 26 51; fax 01 21 42 96 20). M: Sentier. Quiet rooms with TVs, phones, and free safe-boxes. Breakfast €4. Shower €3. Reserve 2 weeks in advance. Singles and 1-bed doubles €28-35, with shower €42-54; 2-bed doubles €60. Extra bed €12. ❸

3ÈME AND 4ÈME ARRONDISSEMENTS

The Marais's 17th-century mansions now house budget hotels close to the **Centre Pompidou** and the **Ile St-Louis;** the area is also convenient for sampling nightlife, as Paris's night buses converge in the 4ème at M: Châtelet.

▨ **Hôtel du Séjour,** 36 r. du Grenier St-Lazare, 3ème (☎/fax 01 48 87 40 36). M: Etienne-Marcel or Rambuteau. This family-run hotel offers clean, bright rooms and a warm welcome. Reserve at least 1 week in advance. 20 rooms. Showers €4. Reception 7am-10:30pm. Singles €31; doubles €43, with shower and toilet €55, third person €23. ❸

▨ **Hôtel des Jeunes (MIJE)** (☎01 42 74 23 45; www.mije.com). Books beds in Le Fourcy, Le Fauconnier, and Maubuisson (see below), 3 small hostels located on cobblestone streets in beautiful old Marais residences. No smoking. English spoken. Restaurant.

Internet €0.15 per min. Public phones and free lockers (with a €1 deposit). Ages 18-30 only. 7-day max. stay. Reception 7am-1am. Lockout noon-3pm. Curfew 1am. Quiet after 10pm. Breakfast, shower, and sheets included. Arrive before noon the first day of reservation (call in advance if you'll be late). Groups may reserve a year in advance. Individuals should reserve at least 1 week in advance. 5-bed (or more) dorms €24-26; singles €40-47; doubles €60-72; triples €78-93; quads €100-108. ❷

Le Fourcy, 6 r. de Fourcy, 4ème. M: St-Paul or Pont Marie. From M: St-Paul, walk opposite the traffic down r. François-Miron and turn left on r. de Fourcy. The hostel surrounds a large courtyard ideal for meeting travelers. Light sleepers should avoid rooms on the social courtyard.

Le Fauconnier, 11 r. du Fauconnier, 4ème. M: St-Paul or Pont Marie. From M: St-Paul, take r. du Prevôt, turn left on r. Charlemagne, and turn right on r. du Fauconnier. Ivy-covered building steps away from the Seine and Ile St-Louis.

Maubuisson, 12 r. des Barres, 4ème. M: Hôtel-de-Ville or Pont Marie. From M: Pont Marie, walk opposite traffic on r. de l'Hôtel-de-Ville and turn right on r. des Barres. A half-timbered former girls' convent on a silent street by the St-Gervais monastery.

Grand Hôtel Jeanne d'Arc, 3 r. de Jarente, 4ème (☎01 48 87 62 11; www.hoteljeanne-darc.com). M: St-Paul or Bastille. Bright, clean hotel with pleasant lounge and breakfast area. Recently renovated rooms with showers, toilets, and TVs. 2 wheelchair-accessible rooms on the ground floor. Breakfast €5.80. Reserve 2-3 months in advance. Singles €55-64; doubles €67-92; triples €107; quads €122. Extra bed €12. MC/V. ❹

Hôtel Picard, 26 r. de Picardie, 3ème (☎01 48 87 53 82; fax 01 48 87 02 56). M: République. In a superb location with a friendly, helpful staff. TVs in rooms with showers. Wheelchair accessible. Breakfast €4.50. Hall showers €3. Reserve 2 weeks ahead Apr.-Sept. Singles €33, with shower €41, with shower and toilet €51; doubles €40-43, with shower €52, with bath €63; triples €59-82. 5% *Let's Go* discount. MC/V. ❸

Hôtel du Marais, 16 r. de Beauce, 3ème (☎01 42 72 30 26; hotelmarais@voila.fr). M: Temple or Filles-de-Calvaire. Simple but spotless rooms in a great location near an open-air market. Take the small stairs above the cafe owned by the same friendly man. Curfew 2am. 3rd fl. showers €3. Singles with sink €25; doubles €33. ❷

5ÈME AND 6ÈME ARRONDISSEMENTS

The lively Latin quarter and St-Germain-des-Prés offer proximity to the **Notre-Dame,** the **Panthéon,** the **Jardin du Luxembourg,** and the bustling student cafe culture.

🏨 **Young and Happy (Y&H) Hostel,** 80 r. Mouffetard, 5ème (☎01 45 35 09 53; www.youngandhappy.fr). M: Monge. A funky, lively hostel with laid-back staff, clean rooms, and commission-free currency exchange. Breakfast included. Sheets €2.50, towels €1. Laundry facilities. Lockout 11am-4pm. Curfew 2am. 25 rooms, a few with showers and toilets. Dorms from €20 per person; doubles from €23 per person; off-season (Jan.-Mar.) prices €2 less per night. ❷

🏨 **Hôtel de Nesle,** 7 r. du Nesle, 6ème (☎01 43 54 62 41; www.hoteldenesle.com). M: Odéon. Walk up r. de l'Ancienne Comédie, take a right onto r. Dauphine, and then take a left on r. du Nesle. Friendly staff and sparkling rooms. Singles €50-69; doubles €69-99. Extra bed €12. AmEx/MC/V. ❹

Hôtel St-André des Arts, 66 r. St-André-des-Arts, 6ème (☎01 43 26 96 16; hsaintand@minitel.net). M: Odéon. Country inn feeling. New bathrooms, free breakfast, and very friendly owner. Reservations recommended. Singles €63; doubles €80-85; triples €100; quads €110. MC/V. ❺

Hôtel St-Jacques, 35 r. des Ecoles, 5ème (☎01 44 07 45 45; hotelstjacques@wanadoo.fr). M: Maubert-Mutualité or RER: Cluny-La Sorbonne. Spacious, faux-elegant rooms with balconies, renovated bathrooms, and TVs. English spoken. Internet access. Breakfast €7. Singles €49, with toilet and shower €75; doubles with toilet and shower €85, some with bath €112. AmEx/MC/V.

Hôtel Marignan, 13 r. du Sommerard, 5ème (☎01 43 54 63 81; www.hotel-marignan.com). M: Maubert-Mutualité. The privacy of a hotel and the welcoming atmosphere of a hostel. Free laundry facilities and kitchen access. Hall showers open until 11pm. Breakfast €3. Internet access. Singles €42-45; doubles €60, with shower and toilet €80-86; triples €90-110; quads €100-130. 15% discount mid-Sept. to Mar. for stays longer than 5 nights. AmEx/MC/V. ❹

Hôtel d'Esmeralda, 4 r. St-Julien-le-Pauvre, 5ème (☎01 43 54 19 20; fax 01 40 51 00 68). M: St-Michel. Rooms are clean but creaky, and tend to have an ancient, professorial feel about them. Great location. Breakfast €6. Singles €35, with shower and toilet €65; doubles €90; triples €110; quads €120. ❸

Centre International de Paris (BVJ): Paris Quartier Latin, 44 r. des Bernardins, 5ème (☎01 43 29 34 80; fax 01 53 00 90 91). M: Maubert-Mutualité. Boisterous, generic hostel with large cafeteria. English spoken. Internet €1 per 10min. Breakfast included. Showers in rooms. Lockers €2. Dorms €25; singles €30; doubles €54; triples €81. ❷

7ÈME AND 8ÈME ARRONDISSEMENTS

▓ **Hôtel du Champs de Mars,** 7 r. du Champs de Mars, 7ème (☎01 45 51 52 30; www.hotel-du-champs-de-mars.com). M: Ecole Militaire. Just off av. Bosquet. Elegant rooms. Reserve 1 month ahead and confirm by fax or email. Small elevator. Singles and doubles with shower €68-74; triples with bath €94. MC/V. ❺

▓ **Hôtel Montebello,** 18 r. Pierre Leroux, 7ème (☎01 47 34 41 18; fax 01 47 34 46 71). Behind the unremarkable facade are clean, cheery rooms with full baths. Reserve at least 2 weeks in advance. Breakfast €3.50. Singles €37; doubles €42-45. ❸

Hôtel Europe-Liège, 8 r. de Moscou, 8ème (☎01 42 94 01 51; fax 01 43 87 42 18). M: Liège. Clean and fresh rooms and a lovely interior courtyard. Reserve 15 days in advance. All have TV, hair dryer, phone, and shower or bath. 2 wheelchair-accessible rooms on the ground floor. Breakfast €7. Singles €68; doubles €84. AmEx/MC/V. ❺

9ÈME AND 10ÈME ARRONDISSEMENTS

▓ **Perfect Hôtel,** 39 r. Rodier, 9ème (☎01 42 81 18 86; perfecthotel@hotmail.com). This hotel almost lives up to its name, with hotel-quality rooms at hostel prices. Breakfast free for *Let's Go* users. Singles €30, with shower and toilet €50; doubles €36/50; triples €53/65. MC/V. ❸

▓ **Cambrai Hôtel,** 129bis bd. de Magenta, 10ème (☎01 48 78 32 13; fax 01 48 78 43 55; www.hotel-cambrai.com). M: Gare du Nord. Clean rooms with high ceilings and TVs. Breakfast €5. Showers €3. Singles €30, with toilet €35, with shower €41, with full bath €48; doubles with shower €46, with full bath €54, with twin beds and full bath €60; triples €80; 4-person family suite €90; 5-person €110. AmEx/MC/V. ❷

Woodstock Hostel, 48 r. Rodier, 9ème (☎01 48 78 87 76; www.woodstock.fr). M: Anvers. Funky atmosphere. Communal kitchen and safe-deposit box. International staff; English spoken. Breakfast included. Sheets €2.50, towels €1. Showers on every floor are free (and clean). Internet €1 per 10min. Call ahead to reserve a room. Max. stay 1 week. Curfew 2am. Lockout 11am-4pm. Dorms €20; doubles €23. ❷

11ÈME AND 12ÈME ARRONDISSEMENTS

These hotels are close to hopping bars and clubs, but be careful at night.

▓ **Modern Hôtel,** 121 r. de Chemin-Vert, 11ème (☎01 47 00 54 05; www.modern-hotel.fr). M: Père Lachaise. Newly renovated, with spotless marble bathrooms. All rooms have a hair dryer, modem connection, and safe-deposit box. Breakfast €5. Singles €60; doubles €70-75; triples €85; quads €95. Extra bed €15. AmEx/DC/MC/V. ❺

▓ **Hôtel Printania,** 91 av. du Dr. Netter, 12ème (☎01 43 07 65 13; fax 01 43 43 56 54). M: Porte de Vincennes. Mini-fridges, large soundproof windows, and faux-marble floors. Breakfast €4.60. Reserve at least 2 weeks in advance; confirm reservations by fax. Doubles with sink and *bidet* €39, with shower and bath €48, with TV €54; triples with shower, bath, and TV €61. AmEx/MC/V. ❷

Auberge de Jeunesse "Jules Ferry" (HI), 8 bd. Jules Ferry, 11ème (☎01 43 57 55 60; auberge@easynet.fr). M: République. Walk east on r. du Faubourg du Temple and turn right on the far side of bd. Jules Ferry. Wonderful location, party atmosphere. Breakfast and showers included. Lockers €1.55. 1 week max. stay. Internet access in lobby. Lockout 10am-2pm. No reservations; arrive by 8am. Dorms €20; doubles €39. MC/V. ❶

Centre International du Séjour de Paris: CISP "Ravel," 6 av. Maurice Ravel, 12ème (☎01 44 75 60 00; www.cisp.asso.fr). M: Porte de Vincennes. Large, clean rooms (most with fewer than 4 beds) with art exhibited all around. Breakfast, sheets, and towels included. Reception 6:30am-1:30am; you can arrange to have the night guard let you in after 1:30am. Reserve at least a month ahead by phone or email. 8-bed dorm with shower and toilet in hall €16; 2- to 4-bed dorm €20; singles with shower and toilet €30; doubles with shower and toilet €48. AmEx/MC/V. ❷

13ÈME TO 15ÈME ARRONDISSEMENTS

Just south of the Latin Quarter, Montparnasse mixes intellectual charm with thriving commercial centers and cafes.

Hôtel de Blois, 5 r. des Plantes, 14ème (☎01 45 40 99 48; fax 01 45 40 45 62). M: Mouton-Duvernet. Elegant rooms. TVs, hair dryers, and big, clean baths. Breakfast €5. Reserve 10 days ahead. Singles €39, with shower €43, with shower and toilet €45, with bath and toilet €51; doubles €41/45/47/56; triples €61. AmEx/MC/V. ❹

Ouest Hôtel, 27 r. de Gergovie, 13ème (☎01 45 42 64 99; fax 01 45 42 46 65). M: Pernety. A clean hotel with modest furnishings. Charming dining room. Breakfast €5. Hall shower €5 (sometimes long waits). Singles €22-28; 1-bed doubles €28, with shower €37; 2-bed doubles €34/39. MC/V. ❷

FIAP Jean-Monnet, 30 r. Cabanis, 14ème (☎01 43 13 17 00; reservations ☎01 43 13 17 17; www.fiap.asso.fr). M: Glacière. 500-bed student center offers spotless rooms with phone, toilet, and shower. Breakfast included; add €1.60 for buffet. Curfew 2am. Reserve 2-4 weeks in advance. Be sure to specify if you want a dorm bed or you will be booked for a single. €15 deposit per person per night by check or credit card. Wheelchair accessible. Rooms cleaned daily. Check-in after 2:30pm. Check-out 9am. 3-month maximum stay. Dorms €22; singles €50; doubles €64; quads €112. MC/V. ❷

Three Ducks Hostel, 6 pl. Etienne Pernet, 15ème (☎01 48 42 04 05; www.3ducks.fr). M: Félix Faure. Aimed at young Anglo travelers. Shower and breakfast included. Sheets €2.30, towels €0.75. Internet access in lobby. Reception daily 8am-2am. Lockout daily 11am-5pm. 1 week max. stay. Reserve with credit card a week ahead. Mar.-Oct. dorm beds €22; doubles €50. Nov.-Feb. reduced prices. MC/V. ❷

🍴 FOOD

In Paris, life is about eating. Establishments range from the famous repositories of *haute cuisine* to corner *brasseries*. Inexpensive bistros and *crêperies* offer the breads, cheeses, wines, pâtés, *pôtages*, and pastries central to French cuisine. *Gauche* or gourmet, French or foreign, you'll find it in Paris. **CROUS (Centre Regional des Oeuvres Universitaires et Scolaires),** 39 av. Georges Bernanos, 5ème, has information on university restaurants, which are a cheap way to get a great meal. (M: Port-Royal. Open M-F 9am-5pm.) To assemble a picnic, visit the specialty shops of the **Marché Montorgeuil,** 2ème, **rue Mouffetard,** 5ème, or the **Marché Bastille** on bd. Richard-Lenoir (M: Bastille; open Th and Su 7am-1:30pm).

ILE DE LA CITÉ AND ILE ST-LOUIS

Le Caveau du Palais, 19 pl. Dauphine, Ile de la Cité (☎01 43 26 04 28). M: Cité. A chic, intimate restaurant serving traditional French food from an old-style brick oven. Reservations recommended. Open daily noon-3pm and 7-10:30pm. MC/V. ❹

FRANCE

Le Rouge et Blanc, 26 pl. Dauphine, Ile de la Cité (☎01 43 29 52 34). M: Cité. Simple, friendly *provençale* bar and bistro. *Menus* €17 and €22. A la carte *plats* €14-20. On sunny days, tables are set out along the sidewalk. Open M-Sa 11am-3pm and 7-10:30pm. Closed when it rains. MC/V. ❹

1ER AND 2ÈME ARRONDISSEMENTS

Cheap options surround **Les Halles,** 1*er* and 2*ème*. Near the **Louvre,** the small streets of the 2*ème* teem with traditional bistros.

▨ **Papou Lounge,** 74 r. Jean-Jacques Rousseau, 1*er* (☎01 44 76 00 03). M: Les Halles. Papou's cuisine is both flavorful (rumsteak €13) and inventive (tuna tartar with strawberries €13.50). Lunch special €10. Beer €3.30. Open daily 10am-2am; food served noon-4:30pm and 7pm-midnight. MC/V. ❸

▨ **Jules,** 62, r. Jean-Jacques Rousseau, 1*er* (☎01 40 28 99 04). M: Les Halles. This restaurant feels like home. Subtle blend of modern and traditional French cooking; selections change by season. 4-course *menu* €21-29 includes terrific cheese course. Open M-Sa noon-2:30pm and 7-10:30pm. AmEx/MC/V. ❹

Les Noces de Jeannette, 14 r. Favart and 9 r. d'Amboise, 2*ème* (☎01 42 96 36 89). M: Richelieu-Drouot. Elegant bistro. 3-course *menu* €28. Reservations recommended. Open daily noon-1:30pm and 7-9:30pm. ❺

La Victoire Suprême du Coeur, 41 r. des Bourdonnais 1*er* (☎01 40 41 93 95). M: Châtelet. All vegetarian, and very tasty. Meals marked with a "V" can be made vegan. 2-course lunch *menu* €11. Open M-F 11:45am-3pm and 6:40-10pm, Sa noon-3pm and 6:40-10pm. MC/V. ❷

Le Fumoir, 6 r. de l'Amiral Coligny, 1*er* (☎01 42 92 05 05). M: Louvre. Decidedly untouristy types drink their chosen beverage in deep leather sofas. Serves one of the best brunches in Paris (€20). Coffee €2.50. Open daily 11am-2am. AmEx/MC/V. ❸

3ÈME AND 4ÈME ARRONDISSEMENTS

The Marais offers chic bistros, kosher delis, and couple-friendly cafes.

▨ **Chez Janou,** 2 r. Roger Verlomme, 3*ème* (☎01 42 72 28 41). M: Chemin-Vert. Hip and friendly restaurant lauded for its reasonably priced gourmet food. Main courses such as *thon à la provençale* (€14) are delightful, as are the desserts (€6). Open daily noon-3pm and 8pm-midnight. ❸

▨ **Au Petit Fer à Cheval,** 30 r. Vieille-du-Temple, 4*ème* (☎01 42 72 47 47). M: Hôtel-de-Ville or St-Paul. An oasis of *chèvre, kir,* and *Gauloises,* and a loyal local crowd. Excellent house salads (€3.50-10). Desserts €4-7. Open daily 10am-2am; food served noon-1:15am. MC/V. ❷

L'As du Falafel, 34 r. des Rosiers, 4*ème* (☎01 48 87 63 60). M: St-Paul. Amazing falafel; special €5. Tiny but delicious lemonade €3.50 per glass. Open Su-F 11:30am-11:30pm. MC/V. ❶

Piccolo Teatro, 6 r. des Ecouffes (☎01 42 72 17 79). M: St-Paul. A romantic vegetarian hideout. Weekday lunch *menus* at €8.20, €9.90, or €13.30. Entrees €3.60-7.10. *Plats* €7.70-12.50. Open Tu-Sa noon-3pm and 7-11:30pm. AmEx/MC/V. ❷

404, 69 r. des Gravilliers, 3*ème* (☎01 42 74 57 81). M: Arts et Métiers. Classy, comfortable North African restaurant. Mouth-watering couscous (€13-23) and *tagines* (€13-19). Lunch *menu* €17. Open daily noon-2:30pm and 8pm-midnight. AmEx/MC/V. ❸

Georges, on the 6th fl. of the Centre Pompidou (☎01 44 78 47 99). Ultra-sleek, Zen-cool, in-the-spotlight cafe. Open M and W-Su noon-2am. ❸

5ÈME AND 6ÈME ARRONDISSEMENTS

The way to the Latin Quarter's heart is through its cafes. Tiny low-priced restaurants and cafes pack the quadrangle bounded by bd. St-Germain, bd. St-Michel, r. de Seine, and the Seine river. **Rue de Buci** harbors Greek restaurants and a street market, and **rue Gregoire de Tours** has cheap, greasy spoons for a quick bite.

Savannah Café, 27 r. Descartes (☎01 43 29 45 77). M: Cardinal Lemoine. This cheerful yellow restaurant prides itself on its flavorful Lebanese food. *Entrées* €7-12.50. *Formule* €23. Open M-Sa 7-11pm. MC/V. ❹

Comptoir Méditerranée, 42 r. du Cardinal Lemoine (☎01 43 25 29 08). Savannah's little sister around the corner has takeout and lower prices. Open M-Sa 11am-10pm. ❷

Au Port Salut, 163bis r. St-Jacques (☎01 46 33 63 21). M: Luxembourg. 3 floors of traditional French cuisine. Fabulous 3-course *menus* change with the season (€12.50 and €22). Open Tu-Sa noon-2:30pm and 7-11:30pm. MC/V. ❸

Le Petit Vatel, 5 r. Lobineau (☎01 43 54 28 49). M: Mabillon. Fresh selection of Mediterranean-French specialties like *catalan pamboli* (bread with puréed tomatoes, ham, and cheese), all a very reasonable €10. Non-smoking. Lunch *menu* €11. Vegetarian options always available. Open Tu-Sa noon-2:30pm and 7-10:30pm. ❷

Les Editeurs, 4 carrefour d'Odéon (☎01 43 26 67 76). Les Editeurs pays homage to St-Germain's literary pedigree with books filling its plush red and gold dining rooms. Coffee €2.50, *pressions* €4.50, cocktails €9. *Croque Monsieur* €9.50. Happy Hour daily 6-8pm (cocktails €6-8). Open daily 8am-2am. AmEx/MC/V. ❷

Café de Flore, 172 bd. St-Germain (☎01 45 48 55 26). M: St-Germain-des-Prés. From the Métro, walk against traffic on bd. St-Germain. Sartre composed *Being and Nothingness* here. In the contemporary feud between Café de Flore and Les Deux Magots, Flore reportedly snags more of the local intellectuals. Espresso €4. Pastries €6-10.50. Open daily 7:30am-1:30am. AmEx/MC/V. ❸

Le Jardin des Pâtés, 4 r. Lacépède (☎01 43 31 50 71). M: Jussieu. From the Métro, walk up r. Linné and turn right on r. Lacépède. As calming and pleasant as the Jardin des Plantes around the corner. A menu of organic food is heavy on pâté (€7-12.50), pasta, and vegetables. Open daily noon-2:30pm and 7-11pm. MC/V. ❷

Così, 54 r. de Seine (☎01 46 33 35 36). M: Mabillon. From the Métro, walk down bd. St-Germain and make a left onto r. de Seine. Enormous, tasty, inexpensive sandwiches on fresh, brick-oven bread. Sandwiches €5.20-7.60. Open daily noon-11pm. ❷

7ÈME AND 8ÈME ARRONDISSEMENTS

Le Lotus Blanc, 45 r. de Bourgogne, 7ème (☎01 45 55 18 89). M: Varenne. Delicious Vietnamese fare. Lunch and all-day *menus* €9-29. Vegetarians will appreciate the great veggie *menu* (€6.50-12.50). Reservations encouraged. Open M-Sa noon-2:30pm and 7-10:30pm. Closed 2 weeks in Aug. AmEx/MC/V. ❸

Escrouzailles, 36 r. du Colisée, 8ème (☎01 45 62 94 00). M: Franklin D. Roosevelt. Several comfortable yellow-walled dining rooms; fine yet relaxed dining. Choose from lists of entrees (€8) such as *foie gras*, *plats* (€12) such as the rack of lamb with zucchini, and delicious desserts (€6). Plenty of vegetarian options. Open M-Sa noon-2:30pm and 7:30-10:30pm. MC/V. ❷

Café des Lettres, 53 r. de Verneuil, 7ème (☎01 42 22 52 17). M: Solférino. This Scandinavian cafe offers unique tastes in a fantastic atmosphere. Patrons enjoy platters of smoked salmon and *blindis* (€16) and other Danish seafood dishes (€12.50-20). Coffee €2.50, beer €5-6. Open M noon-3pm, Tu-F noon-11pm, Sa noon-7pm. ❸

Le Paris, 93 av. des Champs-Elysées, 8ème (☎01 47 23 54 37). M: George V. Snobby, but the terrace is the ideal space for people-watching and sipping tea. At night, the cafe turns into a bar with a live DJ. Coffee €3.50, tea €5.50, glass of wine €5.50-7. Sandwiches €10-12.50. Soup €7. Open daily 8am-6am. ❸

Bagel & Co., 31 r. de Ponthieu (☎01 42 89 44 20). M: Franklin D. Roosevelt. One of the only cheap options in the 8ème. A New York-inspired deli; bagel and specialty sandwiches €3-5. Vegetarian, kosher options. Open M-F 7:30am-9pm, Sa 10am-8pm. AmEx/MC/V. ❶

9ÈME TO 11ÈME ARRONDISSEMENTS

Meals close to the Opéra cater to the after-theater and movie crowd and can be quite expensive. **Rue Faubourg-Montmartre** is packed with cheap eateries.

▣ **Haynes Restaurant Américain,** 3 r. Clauzel, 9ème (☎01 48 78 40 63). M: St-Georges. An expat center famous for its "original American Soul Food." Very generous portions, most under €16. Vocal jazz concerts F nights; funk and groove Sa nights (€6 cover). Open Tu-Sa 7pm-12:30am. AmEx/MC/V. ❸

▣ **Le Bistro de Gala,** 45 r. du Faubourg-Montmartre, 9ème (☎01 40 22 90 50). M: Grands Boulevards. Spacious bistro lined with film posters; the reputed hangout of some of Paris's theater elite. The price of the *menu* is predictably high (€26-36), but definitely worth it. Reservations recommended. Open M-F noon-2:30pm and 7-11:30pm, Sa 7-11:30pm. AmEx/MC/V. ❺

Chez Paul, 13 r. de Charonne, 11ème (☎01 47 00 34 57). M: Bastille. Paul's fun staff serves a delicious menu. Extensive appetizer list; great *steak au poivre* with *au gratin* potatoes (€13). Reservations are a must during peak hours. Open daily noon-2:30pm and 7pm-2am; food served until 12:30am. AmEx/MC/V. ❸

Cantine d'Antoine et Lili, 95 quai de Valmy, 10ème (☎01 40 37 34 86). M: Gare de l'Est. Canal-side cafe-bistro with tasty, light fare. Pasta salads €6. Salads €6.50. Prices cheaper for takeout. Open Su-Tu 11am-8pm, W-Sa 11am-1am. AmEx/MC/V. ❶

Café de l'Industrie, 16 r. St-Sabin, 11ème(☎01 47 00 13 53). M: Breguet-Sabin. This happening cafe could double as a museum of French colonial history. Quality food, including a €9 lunch *menu*. Coffee €2, *vin chaud* €4. Salads €7-7.50. After 10pm, add €0.60. Open Su-F 10am-2am; lunch served noon-2pm. ❷

12ÈME TO 14ÈME ARRONDISSEMENTS

The 13ème is a budget gourmand's dream, with scores of Asian restaurants packing Paris's **Chinatown,** south of pl. d'Italie on av. de Choisy, and numerous affordable French restaurants in the **Butte-aux-Cailles** area. The 14ème is bordered at the top by the busy **boulevard du Montparnasse,** which is lined with a diverse array of restaurants. Rue du Montparnasse, which intersects with the boulevard, has reasonably priced *crêperies.* **Rue Daguerre** is lined with vegetarian-friendly restaurants. Inexpensive restaurants cluster on **rue Didot, rue du Commerce, rue de Vaugirard,** and **boulevard de Grenelle.**

▣ **Café du Commerce,** 39 r. des Cinq Diamants, 13ème (☎01 53 62 91 04). M: Place d'Italie. Traditional food with a twist. Dinner (€15.50) and lunch (€10.50) *menus* both feature options like *boudin antillais* (spiced bloodwurst), and *fromage blanc aux kiwis.* Open daily noon-3pm and 7pm-2am, Sa and Su brunch noon-4pm. Reservations recommended for dinner. AmEx/MC/V. ❸

▣ **Tricotin,** 15 av. de Choisy, 13ème (☎01 45 84 74 44). M: Porte de Choisy. This Asian eatery, one of the best in Chinatown, serves delicious food from Cambodia, Thailand, and Vietnam. The *vapeur* foods are specialties here—see if you can eat just one order of steamed shrimp ravioli (€3.40). Open daily 9:30am-11:30pm. MC/V. ❶

Chez Papa, 6 r. Gassendi, 14ème (☎01 43 22 41 19). M: Denfert-Rochereau. Delicious dishes are often served straight from the pot in which they were cooked. Hearty *menu* (€9.20) served M-F until 4pm. Also in the 8ème (29 r. de l'Arcade; ☎01 42 65 43 68), 10ème (206 r. Lafayette; ☎01 42 09 53 87), and 15ème. (101 r. de la Croix Nivert; ☎01 48 28 31 88). Open daily 10am-1am. AmEx/MC/V. ❷

Le Cheval de Troie, 71 r. de Charenton, 12*ème* (☎01 43 44 24 44). M: Bastille. Savory Turkish food in an appealing setting. Dinner *menu* €16. Open M-Sa noon-2:30pm and 7-11:30pm. MC/V. ❹

15ÈME AND 16ÈME ARRONDISSEMENTS

▨ **Thai Phetburi**, 31 bd. de Grenelle, 15*ème* (☎01 41 58 14 88; www.phetburi-paris.com). M: Bir-Hakeim. Award-winning food, friendly service, low prices, and a relaxing atmosphere. Open M-Sa noon-2:30pm and 7-10:30pm. AmEx/MC/V. ❷

▨ **La Rotunde de la Muette**, 12 Chaussée de la Muette, 16*ème* (☎01 45 24 45 45). M: La Muette. Hip cafe in a beautiful *fin-de-siècle* building overlooking the tree-lined Chaussée de la Muette. Sandwiches €5-9.60. Salads €4-9.15. AmEx/MC/V. ❷

Byblos Café, 6 r, Guichard, 16*ème* (☎01 42 30 99 99). M: La Muette. This airy, modern, Lebanese restaurant serves cold *mezzes* (think Middle Eastern *tapas*) that are good for pita-dipping. *Menu* €15. Vegetarian options available. Open daily 11am-3pm and 5-11pm. AmEx/MC/V. ❸

Aux Artistes, 63 r. Falguière, 15*ème* (☎01 43 22 05 39). M: Pasteur. One of the 15*ème*'s coolest spots, this lively cafe draws a mix of professionals, students, and artists. Lunch *menu* €9.20, dinner *menu* €12.50. Open M-F noon-2:30pm and 7:30pm-midnight, Sa 7:30pm-midnight. ❸

18ÈME TO 20ÈME ARRONDISSEMENTS

In the 18*ème*, charming bistros and cafes lie near **rue des Abbesses** and **rue Lepic**. The 20*ème*'s **Belleville** offers great traditional dining.

▨ **Refuge des Fondues**, 17 r. des Trois Frères, 18*ème* (☎01 42 55 22 65). M: Abbesses. Only 2 main dishes: *Fondue bourguignonne* (meat fondue) and *fondue savoyarde* (cheese fondue). *Menu* €15. Reserve a table or show up early. Open daily 6:30pm-2am (no new diners after 12:30am). Closed Aug. ❸

▨ **Café Flèche d'Or**, 102 r. de Bagnolet, 20*ème* (☎01 43 72 04 23; www.flechedor.com). M: Alexandre Dumas. In a defunct train station, this bar/cafe/performance space serves North African, French, Caribbean, and South American cuisine with nightly jazz, ska, folk, salsa, and samba (cover €5-6). Dinner *menus* €12-15. Bar/cafe open daily 10am-2am; dinner daily 8pm-1am. MC/V. ❸

L'Endroit, 67 pl. du Dr. Félix Lobligeois, 17*ème* (☎01 42 29 50 00). M: Rome. As cool by day as it is at night, L'Endroit must be, well, *the* place to go in the 17*ème*. Long menu packed with things like melon and *jambon* (€10.80), salads (€10.70), and toasted sandwiches (€10). Open daily noon-2am. MC/V. ❷

Lao Siam, 49 r. de Belleville, 19*ème* (☎01 40 40 09 68). M: Belleville. Every bite is worth writing about—you'll forget that you came so far out of your way. Open daily noon-3pm and 6:30-11:30pm. MC/V. ❷

◖ SIGHTS

While seeing all there is to see in Paris is a daunting, if not impossible, task, you can make a solid dent in a reasonable amount of time. In a few hours, you can walk from the heart of the Marais in the east to the Eiffel Tower in the west, passing most major monuments along the way. A solid day of wandering will show you how close the medieval Notre Dame is to the modern Centre Pompidou and the funky Latin Quarter to the royal Louvre, and why you came here in the first place.

ILE DE LA CITÉ AND ILE ST-LOUIS

ILE DE LA CITÉ. If any one place is the heart of Paris, it is this small island. In the 3rd century BC, when it was inhabited by the *Parisii*, a Gallic tribe of hunters, sailors, and fishermen, the Ile was all there was to Paris. Today, all distance-points in France are measured from *kilomètre zéro*, a sundial in front of Notre-Dame.

CATHÉDRALE DE NOTRE DAME DE PARIS. This 12th- to 14th-century cathedral, begun under Bishop Maurice Sully, is one of the world's most famous and beautiful examples of medieval architecture. After the Revolution, the building fell into disrepair and was even used to shelter livestock until Victor Hugo's 1831 novel *Notre Dame de Paris* (a.k.a. *The Hunchback of Notre Dame*) inspired citizens to lobby for restoration. The intricately carved, apocalyptic facade and soaring, apparently weightless walls, effects produced by brilliant Gothic engineering and optical illusions, are inspiring even for the most church-weary. The cathedral's biggest draws are its enormous stained-glass **rose windows** that dominate the north and south ends of the transept. A staircase inside the towers leads to a perch from which gargoyles survey the city. *(M: Cité. ☎01 53 40 60 87; crypt 01 43 29 83 51. Cathedral open daily 8am-6:45pm. Towers July-Aug. 9am-7:30pm; Sept.-June reduced hours. Admission €6.10, ages 18-25 €4.10. Tours begin at the booth to the right as you enter. In English W-Th noon, Sa 2:30pm; in French M-F noon, Sa 2:30pm. Free. Treasury open M-Sa 9:30am-12:30pm and 1:30-5:30pm, Su 1:30-5:30pm; last ticket at 5pm. €2.50, students €2. Crypt open daily 10am-5:30pm. €3.90, under-27 €2.20.)*

■**STE-CHAPELLE AND CONCIERGERIE.** Within the courtyard of the **Palais de Justice,** which has housed Paris's district courts since the 13th century, the opulent, Gothic **Ste-Chapelle** was built by Saint Louis (Louis IX) to house his most precious possession, Christ's crown of thorns, now in Notre Dame. No mastery of the lower chapel's dim gilt can prepare the visitor for the **Upper Chapel,** where twin walls of stained glass glow and frescoes of saints and martyrs shine. *(4 bd. du Palais. M: Cité. Within Palais de la Cité. Open daily Apr.-Sept. 9:30am-6pm. €6.10, seniors and ages 18-25 €4.10. Under-18 free.)* Around the corner is the **Conciergerie,** one of Paris's most famous prisons; Marie-Antoinette and Robespierre were imprisoned here during the Revolution. *(Entrance on bd. du Palais, to the right of Palais de Justice. M: Cité. Open daily Apr.-Sept. 9:30am-6:30pm; Oct.-Mar. 10am-5pm. €6.10, students €4.10.)*

ILE ST-LOUIS. The Ile St-Louis is home to some of Paris's most privileged elite, like the Rothschilds and Pompidou's widow, and formerly Voltaire, Baudelaire, and Marie Curie. Paris's best ice cream is at ■**Berthillon,** 31 r. St-Louis-en-Ile. *(M: Pont Marie. Open Sept. to mid-July; take-out W-Su 10am-8pm; eat-in W-F 1-8pm, Sa-Su 2-8pm.)*

THE LATIN QUARTER AND ST-GERMAIN-DES-PRÉS: 5ÈME AND 6ÈME ARRONDISSEMENTS

The student population is the soul of the Latin Quarter named for prestigious *lycées* and universities that taught in Latin until 1798. Since the violent student riots in May 1968, many artists and intellectuals have migrated to the cheaper outer *arrondissements*, and the *haute bourgeoisie* have moved in. The 5*ème* still presents the most diverse array of bookstores, cinemas, bars, and jazz clubs in the city. Designer shops and cutting edge art galleries lie near **St-Germain-des-Prés.**

BOULEVARD ST-MICHEL AND ENVIRONS. At the center of the Latin Quarter, bd. St-Michel, which divides the 5*ème* and 6*ème*, is filled with cafes, restaurants, bookstores, and clothing boutiques. **Place St-Michel,** to the north, is packed with students, often engaged in a protest of some sort, and lots of tourists. *(M: St-Michel.)*

LA SORBONNE. Founded in 1253 by Robert de Sorbon as a dormitory for 16 poor theology students, the Sorbonne is one of Europe's oldest universities. Visitors can stroll through the **Chapelle de la Sorbonne** (entrance off of the pl. de la Sorbonne), an impressive space which houses temporary exhibitions on the arts and letters. Nearby **place de la Sorbonne,** off bd. St-Michel, boasts a flavorful assortment of cafes, bookstores, and—during term-time—students. (*45-7 r. des Ecoles. M: Cluny-La Sorbonne or RER: Luxembourg. Walk away from the Seine on bd. St-Michel and turn left on r. des Ecoles to see the main building.*)

RUE MOUFFETARD. South of pl. de la Contrescarpe, **rue Mouffetard** plays host to one of the liveliest street markets in Paris, and, along with **rue Monge,** binds much of the Latin Quarter's student social life. (*M: Cardinal Lemoine or Place Monge.*)

JARDIN DU LUXEMBOURG. South along bd. St-Michel, the formal French gardens of the Jardin du Luxembourg are perfect for strolling and reading; they're also home to the most famous *guignol* puppet theater. (*RER: Luxembourg; main entrance is on bd. St-Michel. Open Apr.-Oct. daily 7:30am-9:30pm; Nov.-Mar. 8:15am-5pm.*)

PANTHÉON. The **crypt** of the Panthéon, which occupies the highest point on the Left Bank, houses the tombs of Louis Braille, Victor Hugo, Jean Jaurès, Rousseau, Voltaire, and Emile Zola; you can spy each tomb from behind locked gates. The Panthéon also houses **Foucault's Pendulum,** which proves the rotation of the earth. (*Pl. du Panthéon. M: Cardinal Lemoine. From the Métro, walk down r. Cardinal Lemoine and turn right on r. Clovis; walk around to the front of the building to enter. Open daily in summer 10am-6pm; off-season 10am-6pm; last admission 5:15pm. Admission €7, students €4.50. Under-18 free. Free entrance first Su of every month Oct.-Mar. Guided tours in French leave from inside the main door daily at 2:30 and 4pm.*)

BOULEVARD ST-GERMAIN. Most famous as the ex-literati hangout of Existentialists (who frequented the Café de Flore, p. 339) and Surrealists like André Breton (who preferred the Deux Magots), the bd. St-Germain is stuck somewhere in between nostalgia for its intellectual cafe-culture past and an unabashed delight with all things fashionable and cutting edge. (*M: St-Germain-des-Prés.*)

EGLISE ST-GERMAIN-DES-PRÉS. Scarred by centuries of weather, revolution, and war, the Eglise St-Germain-des-Prés, begun in 1163, is the oldest standing church in Paris. (*3 pl. St-Germain-des-Prés. From the Métro, walk into pl. St-Germain-des-Prés to enter the church from the front. Open daily 8am-8pm. Info office open M 2:30-6:45pm, Tu-Sa 10:30am-noon and 2:30-6:45pm.*)

JARDIN DES PLANTES. Opened in 1640 to grow medicinal plants for King Louis XIII, the garden now features science museums, rosaries, and a zoo, which Parisians raided for food during the Prussian siege of 1871. (*M: Gare d'Austerlitz or Jussieu. ☎01 40 79 37 94. Open daily 7:30am-8pm; off-season 7:30am-5:30pm.*)

7ÈME ARRONDISSEMENT

EIFFEL TOWER. Built in 1889 as the centerpiece of the World's Fair, the *Tour Eiffel* has come to symbolize the city. Despite criticism, tacky souvenirs, and Gustave Eiffel's own sentiment that "France is the only country in the world with a 300m flagpole," the tower is unfailingly elegant and commands an excellent view of the city. At night, when the lights are turned on, it will win over even the most jaded tourist. (*M: Bir-Hakeim or Trocadéro. ☎01 44 11 23 23; www.tour-eiffel.fr. Open daily mid-June through Aug. 9am-midnight; Sept.-Dec. 9:30am-11pm (stairs 9:30am-6pm); Jan. through mid-June 9:30am-11pm (stairs 9:30am-6:30pm). Elevator to 1st fl. €3.70; 2nd fl. €7; 3rd fl. €10.20. Stairs to 1st and 2nd fl. €3. Last access to top 30min. before closing.*)

FRANCE

INVALIDES. The tree-lined **Esplanade des Invalides** runs from the impressive **Pont Alexandre III** to the gold-leaf domed **Hôtel des Invalides.** The Hôtel, built for veterans under Louis XIV, now houses the **Musée de l'Armée** and **Napoleon's Tomb.** The **Musée Rodin** (see p. 347) is nearby on r. Varenne. (M: Invalides, Latour Maubourg, or Varenne.)

LOUVRE AND OPÉRA: 1ER, 2ÈME, AND 9ÈME ARRONDISSEMENTS

AROUND THE LOUVRE. World-famous art museum and former residence of kings, the **Louvre** (see p. 346) occupies about one-seventh of the 1er arrondissement. **Le Jardin des Tuileries,** at the western foot of the Louvre, was commissioned by Catherine de Médicis in 1564 and improved by André Le Nôtre (designer of the gardens at Versailles) in 1649. (M: Tuileries. ☎ 01 40 20 90 43. Open daily Apr.-Sept. 7am-9pm; Oct.-Mar. 7:30am-7:30pm. Tours in English from the Arc de Triomphe du Carrousel.) Three blocks north along r. de Castiglione, **place Vendôme** hides 20th-century offices and luxury shops behind 17th-century façades. Look out for Napoleon on top of the column in the center of the place—he's the one in the toga. (M: Tuileries or Concorde.) The **Palais-Royal** was commissioned in 1632 by Cardinal Richelieu, who gave it to Louis XIII. In 1784, the buildings enclosing the palace's garden became galeries, the prototype of a shopping mall. The revolutions of 1789, 1830, and 1848 all began with angry crowds in the same garden. (M: Palais-Royal/Musée du Louvre or Louvre-Rivoli.)

OPÉRA. Located north of the Louvre in the 9ème arrondissement, Charles Garnier's grandiose **Opéra Garnier** was built under Napoleon III in the eclectic style of the Second Empire. Gobelin tapestries, gilded mosaics, a 1964 Marc Chagall ceiling, and a six-ton chandelier adorn the magnificent interior. (M: Opéra. General info ☎ 08 36 69 78 68, tours 01 40 01 22 63; www.opera-de-paris.fr. Concert hall and museum open Sept. to mid-July daily 10am-5pm, last entry 4:30pm; mid-July to Aug. 10am-6pm, last entry 5:30pm. Concert hall closed during rehearsals; call ahead. Admission €6; ages 10-16, students, and over 60 €3. English tours daily at noon and 2pm. €10; students €8.)

MARAIS: 3ÈME AND 4ÈME ARRONDISSEMENTS

The Marais became the most chic place to live with Henri IV's construction of the elegant **Place des Vosges** at the beginning of the 17th century; several remaining mansions, including Victor Hugo's, now house museums. Today, the streets of the Marais are the center of the city's Jewish and gay communities as well as fun, hip restaurants and shops. The **rue des Rosiers** (M: St-Paul) is packed with kosher delis and falafel counters. At the confluence of the 1er, 2ème, 3ème, and 4ème, the **Centre Pompidou** (see p. 347), a museum and cultural center, looms like a colorful factory over the vast place, where artists, musicians, and pickpockets gather. Be cautious at night. (M: Rambuteau; take r. Rambuteau to pl. Georges Pompidou. Or, from M: Chatelet-Les Halles, take r. Rambuteau or r. Aubry le Boucher.)

BASTILLE: 11ÈME AND 12ÈME ARRONDISSEMENTS

Further east, Charles V built the **Bastille** prison to guard the eastern entrance to his capital. When it became a state prison under Louis XIII, it housed religious heretics and political undesirables. On July 14, 1789, revolutionaries stormed the Bastille, searching for gunpowder and political prisoners. By 1792, nothing was left of the prison but its outline on the place. Today, the **July Column** stands at one corner of the place to commemorate those who died in the Revolution. On July 14, 1989, François Mitterrand inaugurated the glittering (and, some say, hideous) **Opéra Bastille** to preside over the place. (130 r. de Lyon. Look for the words "Billeterie" on the building. M: Bastille. ☎ 01 40 01 19 70; www.opera-de-paris.fr. 1hr. tour almost every day, usually at 1 or 5pm; call ahead. €10, under-26 €5.)

CHAMPS-ELYSÉES AND ENVIRONS: 8ÈME AND 16ÈME ARRONDISSEMENTS

PLACE DE LA CONCORDE. Paris's most famous public square lies at the eastern end of the Champs-Elysées. Built between 1757 and 1777 for a monument to Louis X, the area soon became the **place de la Révolution,** site of the guillotine that severed 1343 necks from their blue-blooded bodies. After the Reign of Terror, the square was renamed *concorde* (peace). The huge, rose-granite, 13th-century BC **Obélisque de Luxor** depicts the deeds of Egyptian pharaoh Ramses II. Given to Charles X by the Viceroy of Egypt, it is Paris's oldest monument. *(M: Concorde.)*

CHAMPS-ELYSÉES. Stretching west and anchored by the Arc de Triomphe on one end and the pl. de Concorde on the other, the legendary **avenue des Champs-Elysées** is lined with luxury shops, chain stores, cafes, and cinemas. The avenue is the work of Baron Haussmann, who was commissioned by Napoleon III to convert Paris into a grand capital with broad avenues, wide sidewalks, new parks, elegant housing, and sanitary sewers. The city's most elegant shopping is on **avenue Montagne** and **rue Faubourg St-Honoré.**

ARC DE TRIOMPHE. Napoleon commissioned the Arc de Triomphe, at the western terminus of the Champs-Elysées, in 1806 in honor of his Grande Armée. In 1940, Parisians were brought to tears as Nazis goose-stepped through the Arc; on August 26, 1944, British, American, and French troops liberating the city from Nazi occupation marched through to the roaring cheers of thousands. The terrace at the top has a fabulous view. The **Tomb of the Unknown Soldier** has been under the Arc since November 11, 1920. It bears the inscription, "Here lies a French soldier who died for his country, 1914-1918," but represents the 1,500,000 men who died during WWI. *(On pl. Charles de Gaulle. M: Charles-de-Gaulle-Etoile. Open Apr.-Sept. daily 10am-11pm; Oct.-Mar. 10am-10:30pm. €7, ages 18-25 €4.50. Under-17 free.)*

THE MADELEINE. Mirrored by the Assemblée Nationale across the Seine, the Madeleine—formally called **Eglise Ste-Marie-Madeleine** (Mary Magdalene)—was begun in 1764 by Louis XV and modeled after a Greek temple. Construction was halted during the Revolution, when the Cult of Reason proposed transforming the building into a bank, a theater, or a courthouse. Characteristically, Napoleon decreed that it should become a temple to the greatness of his army, but Louis XVIII shouted, "It shall be a church!" Completed in 1842, the structure stands alone in the medley of Parisian churches, distinguished by four ceiling domes that light the interior, 52 exterior Corinthian columns, and a curious altarpiece. *(Pl. de la Madeleine. M: Madeleine. ☎01 44 51 69 00. Open daily 7:30am-7pm.)*

MONTMARTRE AND PERE-LACHAISE: 18ÈME, 19ÈME, AND 20ÈME ARRONDISSEMENTS

MOUNTING MONTMARTRE. Montmartre, comprised mostly of one very large hill, is one of the few Parisian neighborhoods Baron Haussmann left intact when he redesigned the city and its environs. During its Belle Epoque heyday from 1875 to 1905, it attracted bohemians like Toulouse-Lautrec and Erik Satie as well as performers and impresarios like Aristide Bruant. Later, Picasso, Modigliani, Utrillo, and Apollinaire came into its artistic circle. Nowadays, Montmartre is a mix of upscale bohemia (above r. des Abbesses) and sleaze (along bd. de Clichy). The northwestern part of the area retains some village charm, with breezy streets speckled with interesting shops and cafes. *(Funicular runs cars up and down the hill every 2min. Open 6am-12:30am. €1.30 or Métro ticket. M: Anvers or Abbesses.)*

BASILIQUE DU SACRÉ-COEUR. The Basilique du Sacré-Coeur crowns the butte Montmartre like an enormous white meringue. Its onion dome is visible from almost anywhere in the city, and its 112m bell tower is the highest point in Paris, offering a view that stretches up to 50km. *(35 r. du Chevalier de la Barre. M: Anvers, Abbesses, or Château-Rouge. ☎01 53 41 89 00. Open daily 7am-10:30pm. Wheelchair accessible through back. Free. Dome and crypt open daily 9am-6:45pm. €5.)* Nearby, **place du Tertre** is full of touristy cafes and amateur artists.

CIMETIÈRE PÈRE LACHAISE. The Cimetière Père Lachaise, located in the 20ème, holds the remains of Balzac, Sarah Bernhardt, Colette, Danton, David, Delacroix, La Fontaine, Haussmann, Molière, Proust, and Seurat within its peaceful, winding paths and elaborate sarcophagi. Foreigners buried here include Modigliani, Gertrude Stein, and Oscar Wilde, but the most visited grave is that of Jim Morrison. French Leftists make ceremonious pilgrimage to the **Mur des Fédérés** (Wall of the Federals), where 147 revolutionaries were executed and buried. *(16 r. du Repos. M: Père-Lachaise. Open Mar.-Oct. M-F 8am-6pm, Sa 8:30am-6pm, Su and holidays 9am-6pm; Nov.-Feb. M-F 8am-5:30pm, Sa 8:30am-5:30pm, Su and holidays 9am-5:30pm. Last entrance 15min. before closing. Free.)*

PERIMETER SIGHTS

LA DÉFENSE. Outside the city limits, west of the 16ème, the skyscrapers and modern architecture of La Défense make up Paris's newest (unofficial) *arrondissement*, home to the headquarters of 14 of France's top 20 corporations. The **Grande Arche**, inaugurated in 1989, completes the *axe historique* running through the Louvre, pl. de la Concorde, and the Arc de Triomphe. There's yet another stunning view from the top. Trees, shops, and sculptures by Miró and Calder line the esplanade. *(M/RER: La Défense. Arch open daily 10am-8pm. €7.50; under-18, students, and seniors €5.50.)*

BOIS DE BOULOGNE. Popular by day for picnics, this 846-hectare (roughly 2,000-acre) park was until recently home to many drug dealers and prostitutes at night and is not the best bet for nighttime entertainment. *(On the western edge of the 16ème. M: Porte Maillot, Sablons, Pont de Neuilly, or Porte Dauphine.)*

🏛 MUSEUMS

The **Carte Musées et Monuments** grants immediate entry to 70 Paris museums (no waiting in line) and will save you money if you plan to visit three or more museums and major sights per day. It's available at major museums and Métro stations. (1-day €22; 3-days €38; 5-days €52.)

MUSÉE DU LOUVRE. A short list of its masterpieces includes the *Code of Hammurabi*, Jacques-Louis David's *The Oath of the Horatii*, Vermeer's *Lacemaker*, and Delacroix's *Liberty Leading the People*. Oh, yeah, and there's that lady with the mysterious smile, too—the *Mona Lisa*. Enter through I.M. Pei's controversial glass **Pyramid** in the Cour Napoléon, or skip lines by entering directly from the Métro. When visiting the Louvre, strategy is everything. The Louvre is organized into three different wings: Sully, Richelieu, and Denon. Each is divided into different sections according to the artwork's date, national origin, and medium. The color-coding and room numbers on the free maps correspond to the colors and numbers on the plaques at the entrances to every room within the wing. *(1er. M: Palais-Royal-Musée du Louvre. ☎01 40 20 51 51; www.louvre.fr. Open M and W 9am-9:30pm, Th-Su 9am-5:30pm. Closed Tu. Last entry 45min. before closing, but people are asked to leave 15-30min. before closing. Admission M and W-Sa 9am-3pm €7.50, M and W-Sa 3pm-close and Su €5. Under-18 and first Su of the month free.)*

MUSÉE D'ORSAY. While considered the world's premier Impressionist collection, the museum is dedicated to presenting all major artistic movements between 1848 and WWI. On the ground floor, works from Classicism and Proto-Impressionism are on display, including Manet's *Olympia*, a painting that caused a scandal when it was unveiled in 1865. Other highlights include: Monet's *La Gare St-Lazare* and *Cathédrale de Rouen* series, Renoir's *Le bal du Moulin de la Galette* (*The dance at the Moulin de la Galette*), Edgar Dégas's *La classe de danse* (*The Dance Class*), Whistler's *Portrait of the Artist's Mother*, and paintings by Sisley, Pissaro, and Morisot. Over a dozen diverse works by van Gogh follow, including his tormented *Portrait de l'Artiste*. Cézanne's works experiment with the soft colors and geometric planes that would open the door to Cubism. (*62 r. de Lille. 7ème. M: Solférino; RER: Musée d'Orsay. ☎01 40 49 48 14; www.musee-orsay.fr. Open June 20-Sept. 20 Tu-W and F-Su 9am-6pm, Th 9am-9:45pm; Sept. 21-June 19 Tu-W and F-Su 10am-6pm, Th 10am-9:45pm. Closed M. Last ticket sales 45min. before closing. €7, ages 18-25 and Su €5. Under-18 and first Su of every month free. Tours in English Tu-Sa 11:30am, 2:30pm. €5.50.*)

CENTRE NATIONAL D'ART ET DE CULTURE GEORGES-POMPIDOU. This inside-out building has inspired debate since its opening in 1977. The exterior is a sight, with chaotic colored piping and ventilation ducts, but it's an appropriate shell for the Fauves, Cubists, and Pop and Conceptual works inside. (*Pl. Georges-Pompidou, 4ème. M: Rambuteau or Hôtel-de-Ville. ☎01 44 78 12 33. Centre open W-M 11am-10pm; museum open W-M 11am-9pm, last tickets 8pm. Permanent collection €5.50, students and over-60 €3.50. 1st Su of month free.*)

MUSÉE RODIN. The 18th-century Hôtel Biron holds hundreds of sculptures by Auguste Rodin (and by his student and lover, Camille Claudel), including the *Gates of Hell, The Thinker, Burghers of Calais,* and *The Kiss.* (*77 r. de Varenne, 7ème. M: Varenne. ☎01 44 18 61 10; www.musee-rodin.fr. Open Tu-Su Apr.-Sept. 9:30am-5:45pm; Oct.-Mar. 9:30am-4:45pm. €5; seniors, 18-25, and Su €3.*)

MUSÉE PICASSO. This museum follows Picasso's career from his early work in Barcelona to his Cubist and Surrealist years in Paris and Neoclassical work on the Riviera. (*5 r. de Thorigny, 3ème. M: Chemin Vert. ☎01 42 71 63 15. Open Apr.-Sept. M and W-Su 9:30am-6pm; Oct.-Mar. 9:30am-5:30pm; last entrance 30min. before closing. Admission €5.50, Su and ages 18-25 €4. Under-18 free.*)

MUSÉE DE CLUNY. One of the world's finest collections of medieval art, the Musée de Cluny is housed in a medieval monastery built on top of Roman baths. Works include the **La Dame et La Licorne** (The Lady and the Unicorn), a studding medieval tapestry series. (*6 pl. Paul Painlevé, 5ème. M: Cluny-La Sorbonne. ☎01 53 73 78 00. Open M and W-Sa 9:15am-5:45pm; last ticket sold at 5:15pm. €6.70; students, under-25, over-60, and Su €5.20; under-18 free.*)

MUSÉE MARMOTTAN MONET. This hunting-lodge-turned-mansion features an eclectic collection of Empire furniture, Impressionist Monet and Renoir canvases, and medieval illuminations. (*2 r. Louis-Boilly, 16ème. M: La Muette. Follow Chaussée de la Muette (which becomes av. Ranelagh) through the Jardin du Ranelagh. ☎01 44 96 50 33. Open Tu-Su 10am-6pm. €6.50, students €4.*)

LA VILLETTE. This vast urban renewal project encloses a landscaped park, a science museum, a planetarium, a conservatory, a concert/theater space, a high-tech music museum, and more. (*19ème. M: Porte de la Villette or Porte de Pantin. Music museum open Su 10am-6pm, Tu-Sa noon-6pm. €6.10, students €4.60, under-18 €2.30. Science museum open Su 10am-7pm, Tu-Sa 10am-6pm. €7.50, under-25 €5.50.*)

INVALIDES MUSEUMS. The resting place of Napoleon also hosts the **Musée de l'Armée,** which celebrates French military history, and the **Musée de l'Ordre de la Libération,** on bd. de Latour-Maubourg, which tells the story of the Resistance fighters. *(Esplanade des Invalides, 7ème. M: Invalides. ☎01 47 05 04 10. Open daily Apr.-Sept. 10am-6pm; Oct.-Mar. 10am-5pm; last ticket sales 30min. before closing. Admission to all 3 museums €7, students €5. Under-18 free. MC/V.)*

PALAIS DE TOKYO. Part of the magnificent Palais houses the **Musée d'Art Moderne de la Ville de Paris,** one of the world's foremost collections of 20th-century art. *(M: Iéna. 11 av. du Président Wilson, 16ème. ☎01 53 67 40 00. Wheelchair-accessible. Open Tu-F 10am-5:30pm, Sa-Su 10am-6:45pm. Admission to permanent exhibitions free; special exhibits admission varies, expect approximately €5, students €2.20-3.)* On the other side, the **site creation contemporaine** displays several exhibits a year of exciting, controversial contemporary art. *(Open Tu-Su noon-midnight. Admission varies with exhibit, expect approximately €5, with reduced student, youth, and senior prices. Free admission for art students.)*

INSTITUT DU MONDE ARABE. Featuring art from the Maghreb and the Near and Middle East, the riverside facade is shaped like a boat, representing the migration of Arabs to France. *(1 r. des Fossés St-Bernard, 5ème. M: From the Métro, walk down r. Jussieu away from the Jardin des Plantes. ☎01 40 51 38 38. M: Jussieu. Open Tu-Su 10am-7pm; library open Tu-Sa 1-8pm. €4.)*

MUSÉE DE LA MODE ET DU COSTUME. With 30,000 outfits and 70,000 accessories, the museum has no choice but to showcase fashions of the past three centuries. A fabulous place to see the history of Parisian fashion, society, and *haute couture. (10 av. Pierre I-de-Serbie, 16ème, in the Palais Galliera. M: Iéna. ☎01 56 52 86 00. Open Tu-Su 10am-6pm; last entrance 5:30pm. €7, students and seniors €5.50.)*

▣ ENTERTAINMENT

Paris's cabarets, cinemas, theaters, and concert halls can satisfy all tastes and desires. The bibles of Parisian entertainment, the weekly *Pariscope* and the *Officiel des Spectacles* (both €0.40), on sale at any kiosk or *tabac*, have every conceivable listing. *Pariscope* includes an English-language section.

For listings of **free concerts,** check *Paris Selection*, free at tourist offices. Free concerts are often held in churches and parks, especially during summer festivals, and are extremely popular, so plan to arrive at the host venue early. The **American Church in Paris,** 65 quai d'Orsay, 7*ème*, sponsors free concerts (Sept.-May Su 6pm; ☎01 40 62 05 00; M: Invalides or Alma Marceau). **Eglise St-Germain-des-Prés** also has free concerts; check the info booth just inside the door for times. **Eglise St-Merri,** 78 r. St-Martin, 4*ème*, is also known for its free concerts (Sept.-July Sa 9pm, Su 4pm; M: Hôtel de Ville); contact Accueil Musical St-Merri, 76 r. de la Verrerie, 4*ème* (☎01 42 71 40 75; M: Châtelet). Concerts take place W-Su in the **Jardin du Luxembourg's** band shell, 6*ème* (☎01 42 34 20 23); show up early for a seat or prepare to stand. Occasional free concerts are held in the **Musée d'Orsay,** 1 r. Bellechasse, 7*ème* (☎01 40 49 49 66; M: Solférino).

OPERA AND THEATER

Opéra de la Bastille, pl. de la Bastille, 12*ème* (☎08 92 69 78 68; www.opera-de-paris.fr). M: Bastille. Opera and ballet with a modern spin. Tickets can be purchased by Internet, mail, fax, phone (M-Sa 9am-7pm), or in person (M-Sa 11am-6:30pm). Rush tickets for students under-25 and seniors 15min. before show. For wheelchair access, call 2 weeks ahead (☎01 40 01 18 08). Tickets €60-105. MC/V.

Opéra Garnier, pl. de l'Opéra, 9*ème* (☎ 08 92 89 90 90; www.opera-de-paris.fr). M: Opéra. Hosts symphonies, chamber music, and the Ballet de l'Opéra de Paris. Tickets available 2 weeks before shows. Box office open M-Sa 11am-6pm. Last-minute discount tickets available 1hr. before showtime. For wheelchair access, call 2 weeks ahead (☎01 40 01 18 08). Tickets €19-64. AmEx/MC/V.

Opéra Comique, 5 r. Favart, 2ème (☎01 42 44 45 46; www.opera-comique.com). M: Richelieu-Drouot. Operas on a lighter scale—from Rossini to Offenbach. Box office open M-Sa 11am-7pm. Tickets €29-112. Student rush tickets available 15min. before show.

La Comédie Française, 2 r. de Richelieu, 1er (☎01 44 58 15 15; www.comedie-francaise.fr). M: Palais-Royal. Founded by Molière, now the granddaddy of all French theaters. Expect wildly gesticulated slapstick farce; you don't need to speak French to understand the jokes. Tickets €4.50-30, under-27 €4.50-7.50. Rush tickets for students (€9) available 1hr. before show. Handicapped patrons and their guests are asked to make reservations in advance (tickets €11). AmEx/MC/V.

Bouffes du Nord, 37bis bd. de la Chapelle, 10ème (☎01 46 07 34 50; www.bouffes-dunord.com). M: La Chapelle. This experimental theater headed by British director Peter Brook and Stephen Lissner produces cutting-edge performances and concerts and offers occasional productions in English. Closed Aug. Box office open M-Sa 11am-6pm. Concerts €18.50, under 26 and over 60 €12; plays €14-24.50. Wheelchair-accessible, but you must call in advance.

La Cartoucherie, route du Champ de Manoeuvre, 12ème. M: Château de Vincennes; a free shuttle departs every 15min. beginning 1hr. before performances, from the station. This 19th-century weapons factory has housed cutting-edge, socially conscious, and refreshingly democratic theater since 1970. The internationally renowned theater is home to 5 collectives, 2 studios, and 7 performance spaces. Most shows €15-20. For more info, visit www.la-tempete.fr/theatre/cartoucherie.html, or check *Pariscope*.

JAZZ AND CABARET

■ **Au Duc des Lombards,** 42 r. des Lombards, 1er (☎01 42 33 22 88; www.jazzvalley.com/duc). M: Châtelet. Still the best in French jazz, with occasional American soloists, and hot items in world music. Three sets each night. Cover €12-23. Beer €5-8. Mixed drinks €9. Music 9:30pm-1:30am. Open M-Sa 8pm-2am. MC/V.

Aux Trois Mailletz, 56 r. Galande, 5ème (☎01 43 54 00 79; before 5pm 01 43 25 96 86). M: St-Michel. Basement houses a crowded cafe featuring world music and jazz vocals. Upper floor is packed with a mix of well-dressed students and forty-somethings. €12.20-19 cover for club on weekends; no cover for bar. Grog €9 at bar. Mixed drinks €12.50. Bar open daily 5pm-dawn; *cave* 10pm-dawn.

Au Lapin Agile, 22 r. des Saules, 18ème (☎01 46 06 85 87). M: Lamarck-Coulaincourt. Picasso, Verlaine, and Renoir; now audiences crowd in for comical poems and songs. Open Tu-Su 9pm-2am. Cover €25; includes 1 drink. Su-F students €18.

CINEMA

There are scores of cinemas throughout Paris, particularly in the Latin Quarter and on the Champs-Elysées. The two big theater chains—**Gaumont** and **UGC**—offer *cartes privilèges* discounts for five visits or more. Most cinemas offer student, senior, and family discounts. On Monday and Wednesday, prices drop by about €1.50 for everyone. Check *Pariscope* or *l'Officiel des Spectacles* (available at any newsstand, €0.40) for weekly film schedules, prices, and reviews.

■ **Cinémathèque Française,** pl. du Trocadéro, 16ème (☎01 45 53 21 86; recorded info 01 47 04 24 24 lists all shows; www.cinemathequefrancaise.com). M: Trocadéro. At the Musée du Cinéma in the Palais de Chaillot; enter through the Jardins du Trocadéro. Also at 42 bd. Bonne Nouvelle, 10eme. M: Bonne Nouvelle. A must for film buffs. 2-3 classics, near-classics, or soon-to-be classics per day. Foreign films usually in V.O. Buy tickets 20min. early. Open W-Su 5-9:45pm. €4.70, students €3.

Les Trois Luxembourg, 67 r. Monsieur-le-Prince, 6ème (☎01 46 33 97 77). M: Cluny. High-quality independent, classic, and foreign films, all in V.O. €6.40, students €5.

La Pagode, 57bis r. de Babylone, 7ème (☎01 45 55 48 48). M: St-François-Xavier. A pseudo-Japanese pagoda built in 1895 and reopened as a cinema in 2000, La Pagode screens foreign and independent films. Stop in at the cafe between shows. Tickets €7.30; over-60, under-21, students and M and W €5.80. MC/V.

🛍 SHOPPING

Like its food, nightlife, and conversation, Paris's fashion is an art. From the wild wear near r. Etienne-Marcel to the boutiques of the Marais to the upscale shops of St-Germain-des-Prés, everything Paris touches turns to gold. The great *soldes* (sales) of the year begin after New Year's and at the very end of June, with the best prices at the beginning of February and the end of July. And if at any time of year you see the word *braderie* (clearance sale) in a store window, march in without hesitation.

ETIENNE-MARCEL AND LES HALLES (1ER AND 2ÈME). Fabrics are cheaper here, and the style is younger, especially around **rue Tiquetonne.** A stroll down **rue Etienne-Marcel** will delight shoe fetishists. **Forum Les Halles** and the streets that surround it offer everything you'll need for an urban warrior aesthetic. *(M: Les Halles).*

MARAIS (3ÈME AND 4ÈME). Shopping in the Marais is a complete aesthetic experience: boutiques of all colors and flavors pop out along medieval streets and among welcoming, tree-shaded cafes (M: St-Paul or Hôtel-de-Ville). What the Marais does best is independent designer shops selling truly unique creations, as well as vintage stores that line **rue Vieille-du-Temple, rue de Sévigné, rue Roi de Sicile** and **rue des Rosiers.** The best selection of affordable-chic menswear in Paris can be found here, especially along **rue Ste-Croix-de-la-Bretonnerie,** in stores catering to a largely gay clientele—but anyone who wants to absorb a bit of Euro-style should check them out. Most stores are open on Sundays. *(M: St-Paul or Hôtel de Ville.)*

LATIN QUARTER AND ST-GERMAIN-DES-PRÉS (5ÈME AND 6ÈME). Although you can find plenty of chain clothing stores around **boulevard St-Michel** and numerous little boutiques selling chic scarves and jewelry, bookstores of all kinds are where the 5*éme* really stands out. Post-intellectual, materialistic St-Germain-des-Prés, meanwhile, particularly the triangle bordered by **boulevard St-Germain, rue St-Sulpice** and **rue des Sts-Pères,** is saturated with high-budget names.

CHAMPS-ELYSÉES AREA (8ÈME). The 8*ème* is not exactly wallet-friendly, but it is perfect for a day of window shopping. Take a break from the exhausting Champs-Elysées and walk along **avenue Montaigne** to admire the great couture houses; their collections change every season, but are always innovative, gorgeous, and jaw-droppingly expensive—and the window displays won't disappoint. Check out **Chanel** at no. 42, **Christian Dior** at no. 30, **Emanuel Ungaro** at no. 2, and **Nina Ricci** at no. 39. **Rue du Faubourg Saint-Honoré** is home to **Lanvin** at no. 22, **Jean-Paul Gaultier** at no. 30, and other boutiques. Around the **Madeleine,** you'll find **Burberry** and some big American names. Back on the **Champs-Elysées,** you can purchase everything from CDs (check out the **Virgin Megastore,** open until midnight) to perfumes to chocolates, usually until a much later hour than in the rest of Paris. Sale season on the Champs is a great time to pillage the collections and come home with money to spare. *(M: Charles de Gaulle-Etoile or Franklin D. Roosevelt).*

MONTMARTRE (18ÈME). The 18*ème* has some of the city's most eclectic shopping: Stroll around **rue de Lavieuville** (don't miss **Spree** at no. 16; ☎01 42 23 41 40) for funky independent designer wares. In the **Goutte d'Or** area, meanwhile, cheap fabric and clothing stores abound. *(M: Abbesses).*

DEPARTMENT STORES

Au Printemps, 64 bd. Haussmann, 9ème (☎01 42 82 50 00). M: Chaussée d'Antin-Lafayette or Havre-Caumartin. Also at 30 pl. d'Italie, 13ème (☎01 40 78 17 17), M: Place d'Italie; and 21-25 cours de Vincennes, 20ème (☎01 43 71 12 41), M: Porte de Vincennes. One of the two biggies in the Parisian department store scene. Oo-la-la your way through endless *couture*. Haussmann open M-W and F-Sa 9:35am-7pm, Th 9:35am-10pm. Other locations open M-Sa 10am-8pm. AmEx/MC/V.

Galeries Lafayette, 40 bd. Haussmann, 9ème (☎01 42 82 34 56). M: Chaussée d'Antin. Also at 22 r. du Départ, 14ème (☎01 45 38 52 87), M: Montparnasse. Chaotic (the equivalent of Paris's entire population visits here each month), but carries it all. Haussmann open M-W and F-Sa 9:30am-7:30pm, Th 9:30-9pm; Montparnasse open M-Sa 9:45am-7:30pm. AmEx/MC/V.

Samaritaine, 67 r. de Rivoli, on the quai du Louvre, 1er (☎01 40 41 20 20). M: Pont Neuf, Châtelet-Les Halles, or Louvre-Rivoli. 4 large, historic Art Deco buildings between r. de Rivoli and the Seine, connected by tunnels and bridges. The rooftop observation deck provides one of the best views of the city; take the elevator to the 9th floor and climb the spiral staircase. Open M-W and F-Sa 9:30am-7pm, Th 9:30am-10pm. AmEx/MC/V.

Au Bon Marché, 22 r. de Sèvres, 7ème (☎01 44 39 80 00). M: Sèvres-Babylone. Paris's oldest department store, Bon Marché has it all, from scarves to smoking accessories and designer clothes to home furnishings. Open M-W and F 9:30am-7pm, Th 10am-9pm, Sa 9:30am-8pm. AmEx/MC/V.

▧ NIGHTLIFE

CAFES AND BARS

LES HALLES AND MARAIS (1ER, 2ÈME, 3ÈME, 4ÈME)

▨ **Banana Café,** 13-15 r. de la Ferronnerie, 1er. M: Châtelet. This *très branché* (way cool) evening arena is the most popular gay bar in the 1er, and draws an extremely mixed group. Legendary theme nights. Happy Hour 6-9pm. Beer M-F €5.18, Sa-Su €6.71. Open daily 4pm-dawn. AmEx/MC/V.

▨ **Le Champmeslé,** 4 r. Chabanais, 1er. M: Pyramides or Quatre Septembre. This welcoming lesbian bar is Paris's oldest and most famous. Mixed crowd in the front, but women-only in back. Beer €4. Mixed drinks €8. Popular cabaret show Th 10pm (first drink is €8). Monthly art exhibits. Open M-Th 2pm-2am, F-Sa 2pm-2am. MC/V.

L'Apparement Café, 18 r. des Coutures St-Gervais, 3ème. M: St-Paul. Beautiful wood and red lounge with games and a calm, young crowd. Late-night meals €10-13.

Chez Richard, 37 r. Vieille-du-Temple, 4ème. M: Hôtel-de-Ville. A hot spot to people-watch on weekends, but during the week it's ideal for chilling, with hip bartenders and smooth beats. Happy Hour 6-8pm for cocktails. Beer €4-6. Mixed drinks €9. Open daily 6pm-2am. AmEx/MC/V.

Lizard Lounge, 18 r. du Bourg-Tibourg, 4ème. M: Hôtel-de-Ville. A happening, split-level space for students and twenty-somethings. Happy Hour upstairs 6-8pm, throughout the bar 8-10pm. Beer €6.20. "Lizard Juice" €7.50. Open daily noon-2am. Serves food noon-3pm and 7-10:30pm, Sa-Su brunch noon-4pm. MC/V.

The Flann O'Brien, 6 r. Bailleul, 1er. M: Louvre-Rivoli. Arguably the best Irish bar in Paris, Flann is often packed, especially on live music nights (F-Su). Go for the Guinness and stay for the reportedly good "crack" downstairs (that's Irish for good fun). Demi €4, full pint €6. Open daily 6pm-5am.

FRANCE

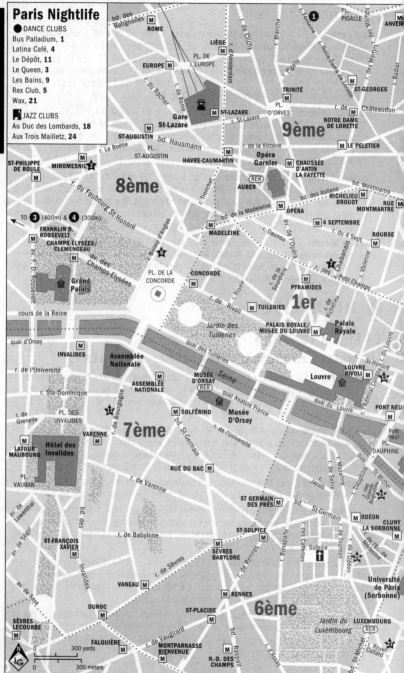

Paris Nightlife

● DANCE CLUBS
Bus Palladium, 1
Latina Café, 4
Le Dépôt, 11
Le Queen, 3
Les Bains, 9
Rex Club, 5
Wax, 21

▣ JAZZ CLUBS
Au Duc des Lombards, 18
Aux Trois Mailletz, 24

FRANCE

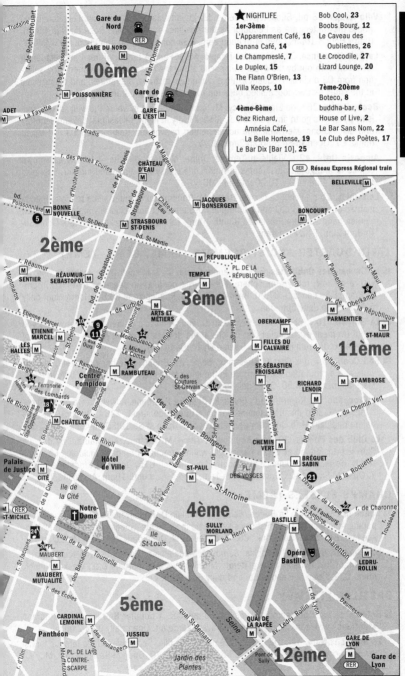

★ NIGHTLIFE

1er-3ème
L'Apparement Café, 16
Banana Café, 14
Le Champmeslé, 7
Le Duplex, 15
The Flann O'Brien, 13
Villa Keops, 10

4ème-6ème
Chez Richard,
    Amnésia Café,
    La Belle Hortense, 19
Le Bar Dix [Bar 10], 25

Bob Cool, 23
Boobs Bourg, 12
Le Caveau des
    Oubliettes, 26
Le Crocodile, 27
Lizard Lounge, 20

7ème-20ème
Boteco, 8
buddha-bar, 6
House of Live, 2
Le Bar Sans Nom, 22
Le Club des Poètes, 17

RER Réseau Express Régional train

Villa Keops, 58 bd. Sébastopol, 3ème. M: Etienne-Marcel. Stylish, candlelit couch bar where the waiters are as beautiful as the designer drinks. Divine Rose du Nile €8.50. Happy Hour 8-10pm. Open M-Th noon-2am, F-Sa noon-4am, Su 4pm-3am. AmEx/MC/V.

La Belle Hortense, 31 r. Vieille-du-Temple. M: St-Paul. A breath of fresh intellectual air for those worn out by the *hyper-chic* scene along the rest of the *rue*. Varied wine selection from €3 a glass. Frequent exhibits, readings, lectures, signatures, and discussions in the small leather-couch-filled back room. Open daily 5pm-2am. MC/V.

Boobs Bourg, 26 r. de Montmorency. M: Rambuteau. This is where the well-spiked, stylishly punk girls go to find each other. Always lively at night, occasional daytime lectures and discussions. Men welcome accompanied by women. Beer on tap €3.80. Mixed drinks €7. Open Tu-Su 5:30pm-2am. MC/V.

Amnésia Café, 42 r. Vieille-du-Temple, 3ème. M: Hôtel-de-Ville. A largely gay crowd comes to lounge on plush sofas in Amnésia's classy wood-paneled interior. Espresso €2. *Kir* €4. Open daily 10:30am-2am. MC/V.

Le Duplex, 25 r. Michel Le Comte, 3ème. M: Rambuteau. A great place to make friends instead of trouble. Small and intimate atmosphere. Not an exclusively male bar, but few women hang out here. Beer €2.60 until 10pm, €3.50 after. Cocktails €7.30. Open Su-Th 8pm-2am, F-Sa 8pm-4am.

LATIN QUARTER AND ST-GERMAIN (5ÈME, 6ÈME, 7ÈME)

■ **Le Caveau des Oubliettes,** 52 r. Galande, 5ème. M: St-Michel. Three scenes in one, all with a mellow, funky atmosphere. Free *soirée boeuf* (jam session) Su-Th 10:30pm-1:30am; F-Sa concerts €7.50. Beer €3.70-4.10. Rum cocktail €3.80. Happy Hour daily 5-9pm. Open daily 5pm-2am.

■ **Le Bar Dix,** 10 r. de l'Odéon, 6ème. M: Odéon. A classic student hangout where you might overhear existentialist discussions in the downstairs cellar. After a few glasses of *sangria* (€3), you might join in. Open daily 5:30pm-2am.

■ **Bob Cool,** 15 r. des Grands Augustins, 6ème. M: Odéon. Laid-back clientele, friendly vibe, and a reputation among those in the know for being one of the best bars in Paris. Mexican *mezcal* €8.50. Open daily 5pm-2am.

Le Crocodile, 6 r. Royer-Collard, 6ème. M: Cluny-La Sorbonne. A lively crowd of 20-somethings packs into this unassuming bar on a quiet side street. 238 tasty cocktails (€8, before midnight M-Th €6) from which to choose. Open M-Sa 10:30pm-4am.

Le Club des Poètes, 30 r. de Bourgogne, 7ème. M: Varenne. A restaurant by day, Le Club is transformed at 10pm each night when a troupe of readers, including Rosnay's family, bewitch the audience with poetry. Lunch *menu* €15. Drinks €9, for students €5-7. Open M-Sa noon-2:30pm and 8pm-1am; food served until 10pm. AmEx/MC/V.

CHAMPS-ELYSÉES (8ÈME)

■ **House of Live,** 124 r. La Boétie, 8ème. M: Franklin D. Roosevelt. This friendly and happening American bar has first-class live music most nights. Snack bar has good ol' Yankee fare. Beer €6. Mixed drinks €6.80. Coffee €2-4. Open daily 9am-5am. AmEx/MC/V.

buddha-bar, 8 r. Boissy d'Anglas, 8ème. M: Madeleine or Concorde. Gorgeous bar and restaurant frequented by the glitterati. Mixed drinks and martinis €12. Weekday lunch *menu* €32. Open M-F noon-3pm and daily 6pm-2am.

BASTILLE (11ÈME)

■ **Boteco,** 131 r. Oberkampf, 11ème. M: Parmentier. A popular Brazilian bar-restaurant with trendy waitstaff, jungle decor, and avant-garde art. Open daily 9am-2am.

Le Bar Sans Nom, 49 r. de Lappe, 11ème. M: Bastille. Seductive lounge famous for its inventive cocktails (€8.50). Beer €5-6.20. Shots €6.20. Open M-Sa 7pm-2am. MC/V.

MONTPARNASSE (13ÈME, 14ÈME)

☒ **L'Entrepôt,** 7-9 r. Francis de Pressensé, 14ème. M: Per-nety. Proving that intellectualism and good times go together: Cinema, restaurant, art gallery, and bar. Concerts F-Sa; usually around €5. Beer €2.50. Su brunch 11:30am-4:30pm (€15). Food served noon-3pm and 7:30-11:30pm. Open M-Sa 9am-midnight (though usually stays open later), Su 11:30am-midnight.

Batofar, facing 11 quai François-Mauriac, 13ème. M: Quai-de-la-Gare. This barge/bar/club has made it big with the electronic music crowd and has a friendly vibe. Open Tu-Th 9pm-3am, F-Sa until 4am. Cover €6.50-9.50 usually includes first drink. MC/V.

La Folie en Tête, 33 r. de la Butte-aux-Cailles, 13ème. M: Corvisart. *The* artsy axis mundi of the 13ème. Crowded concerts on Sa nights, usually Afro-Caribbean music (€8); no concerts July-Aug. Beer €2.50. Happy Hour 6-8pm. Open M-Sa 6pm-2am. MC/V.

MONTMARTRE AND PIGALLE (9ÈME, 17ÈME, 18ÈME)

☒ **L'Endroit,** 67 pl. du Dr. Félix Lobligeois, 17ème. M: Rome. Hip, young 17èmers come for the snazzy bar and idyllic location. Beer €4.50-5.10. Wine €3.50-4. Mixed drinks €6. Open daily noon-2am. MC/V.

Chez Camille, 8 r. Ravignan, 18ème. M: Abbesses. Small, trendy, bright yellow bar on the safe upper slopes of Montmartre. Beer €2.20-3.30. Wine from €2.80. Mixed drinks €6.50. Open M 11am-2pm, Tu-Sa 9am-2am, Su 9am-8pm.

DANCE CLUBS

LES HALLES AND MARAIS (1ER, 2ÈME, 3ÈME, 4ÈME)

Les Bains, 7 r. du Bourg l'Abbé, 3ème. M: Etienne-Marcel or Réaumur-Sébastopol. Look for the long line of people. Ultra-selective, super-crowded, and expensive. Madonna and Mick Jagger have stopped in. Cover (includes first drink) Su-Th €16, F-Sa €19. Drinks €11. Clubbing daily 11pm-6am. AmEx/MC/V.

Le Dépôt, 10 r. aux Ours, 3ème. M: Etienne-Marcel. A veritable pleasure complex for gay men. Dance for inspiration then take your boy toy of the night to one of the rooms in the downstairs labyrinth. Women welcome after 11pm on the upstairs dance floor. Cover (includes first drink); M-Th €7.50, F €10, Sa €12, Su €10. Open daily 2pm-8am.

Rex Club, 5 bd. Poissonnière, 2ème. M: Bonne-Nouvelle. A non-selective club which presents very selective DJ line-ups. One of the best sound systems in Paris. Large dance floor and lots of seats. Shots €4-5. Beer €5-7. Cover €8-13. Open Th-Sa 11:30pm-6am.

THE HIDDEN DEAL

CAB FARE

When it comes to grabbing a late night snack in Paris, the options are about as plentiful as French military victories. The paucity of after-hours dining options exists for good reason: At 2am perhaps the only people awake are club-goers and taxi-drivers. While the former group stumbles home, the latter group can be found chowing down at a club all their own. If you find yourself roming the streets of Paris in the wee hours with a sudden case of the hunger pangs, join them for some fabulously inexpensive, if culinarily unspectacular, nighttime eats.

Taxi Club ❹, 8 r. Etienne Marcel, 1er, (☎01 42 36 28 30) is at the intersection with r. de Turbigo. Look for the taxis. While far from gourmet, this quirky cafe attracts taxi-drivers with its cheap beer (€2.10-2.30) and cheaper coffee (€1). Customers dig in to breakfast served round-the-clock (omelette paysanne €4), a wide variety of meats (grilled chicken €4.20), and the most expensive item on the menu: the plat du jour, a whopping €7. As if the cheap grub weren't appealing enough, the club has perfected the tacky-chic look: White Christmas lights, picnic-style table cloths, and mounted objects that were once attached to taxis. As a bonus, once you're done with your midnight munching, a cab driver is just a table away. Open daily 11am-2am. and 4am-6am.

FRANCE

CHAMPS-ELYSÉES (8ÈME)

▨ **Latina Café,** 114 av. des Champs-Elysées. M: George V. Draws one of the largest night-club crowds on the Champs with an energetic world music mix. Drinks €9-11. Women get in free Su-Th, men pay €7 cover which includes a drink. €16 cover F-Sa includes first two drinks. Cafe open daily 7:30pm-2am, club open daily 11:30am-6:30am.

Le Queen, 102 av. des Champs-Elysées. M: George V. Drag queens, superstars, models, moguls, and go-go boys get down to the mainstream rhythms of a 10,000 gigawatt sound system. Cover Su-Th €12, includes one drink. F-Sa €18. All drinks €9. Open daily midnight-dawn. AmEx/MC/V.

BASTILLE (11ÈME)

▨ **Wax,** 15 r. Daval, 11ème. M: Bastille. Always free and fun. Set up in a concrete bunker, with retro orange, red and white couches, this bar/club has DJ competitions and its own magazine. Funk and electronic music. Open daily 6pm-2am. Closed Su in summer months. Drinks €4-9.50. AmEx/MC/V.

Nouveau Casino, 109 r. Oberkampf, 11ème. M: Parmentier or Ménilmontant. This latest hot spot is drawing in the crowds of the 11ème. Each night offers a different form of entertainment, ranging from concerts (rock, electronic, house, or drum and bass), clubbing, video shows, and modern art exhibits.

MONTMARTRE AND PIGALLE (9ÈME, 17ÈME, 18ÈME)

Bus Palladium, 6 r. Fontaine, 9ème. M: Pigalle, Blanche, or St-Georges. Getting past the bouncers can be tough. A trendy, beautiful crowd rocks this rock 'n' roll club. Cover €16. Tu free cover and drinks for ladies. Drinks €13. Open Tu-Sa 11pm-6am. AmEx/V.

Folies Pigalle, 11 pl. Pigalle, 9ème. M: Pigalle. The largest and wildest club in the sleazy Pigalle *quartier*—definitely not for the faint of heart. Popular among both gay and straight clubbers. Very crowded, even at 4am. Open Su 5pm-6am, Tu-Th midnight-6am, F-Sa midnight-noon. €20 cover; includes first drink. Drinks €10. AmEx/MC/V.

▨ DAYTRIPS FROM PARIS

VERSAILLES. Louis XIV, the Sun King, built and held court at Versailles' extraordinary palace, 12km west of Paris. The incredibly lavish chateau embodies the extravagance of the Old Regime, especially in the **Hall of Mirrors** and fountain-filled **gardens.** (Chateau open May-Sept. Tu-Su 9am-6:30pm; Oct.-Apr. Tu-Su 9am-5:30pm. €7.50, over-60 and after 3:30pm €5.30 (entrance A). Audio (1hr., €4) and guided tours at entrances C and D (1-2hr.; €4, under-18 €2.70), respectively. Gardens open dawn-dusk; €3, under 18 and after 6pm free.) A **shuttle** (round-trip €5, ages 3-12 €3) runs behind the palace to the **Grand** and **Petit Trianons,** and to Marie Antoinette's peasant fantasy, the **Hameau.** (Both Trianons Open Nov.-Mar. Tu-Sa noon-5:30pm; Apr.-Oct. noon-6pm. €5. Under-18 free.) Take any RER C5 **train** beginning with a "V" from M: Invalides to the Versailles Rive Gauche station (30-40min., every 15min., round-trip €5). Buy your RER ticket before getting to the platform; a Métro ticket will not get you through the RER turnstiles at Versailles.

CHARTRES. Chartres's stunning **Cathédrale Notre-Dame** is one of the most beautiful surviving creations of the Middle Ages. Arguably the finest example of early Gothic architecture in Europe, the cathedral retains several of its original 12th-century stained-glass windows; the rest of the windows and the magnificent sculptures on the main portals date from the 13th century, as does the carved floor in the rear of the nave. You can enter the 9th-century **crypt** only from La Crypte, opposite the cathedral's south entrance. (☎02 37 21 75 02; www.cathedrale-chartres.com. Open Easter through Oct. daily 8am-8pm, Nov. through Easter daily 8:30am-7pm. No casual visits during mass. North Tower open May-Aug. M-Sa 9:30am-noon and 2-5:30pm, Su 2-5:30pm; Sept.-Apr. M-Sa 9:30am-noon and 2-4:30pm, Su 2-4:30pm. Tower admission €4, ages 18-25 €2.50. Under-18 and some Su free.) **Trains** run from Paris's Gare Montparnasse (1hr., every hr., €23). From the station, walk straight, turn left into the pl. de Châtelet, turn right on r. Ste-Même, then turn left on r. Jean Moulin.

GIVERNY. Today, Monet's house and gardens in Giverny are maintained by the **Fondation Claude Monet.** From April to July, Giverny overflows with roses, holly-hocks, poppies, and the heady scent of honeysuckle. The water lilies, the Japanese bridge, and the weeping willows seem to be plucked straight from Monet's paint-ings. Monet's thatched-roof house holds his collection of 18th- and 19th-century Japanese prints. The accompanying **Musée d'Art Américain** houses work by Ameri-can Impressionists Butler, Breck, and others. (84 r. Claude Monet. ☎ 02 32 51 28 21; www.fondation-monet.com. Open Apr.-Oct. Tu-Su 9:30am-6:30pm. Admission €5.50, students €4. Gardens €4.) **Trains** run infrequently from Paris-St-Lazare to Vernon, the station nearest Giverny (round-trip €21). When you purchase your ticket, check the timetables or ask for the **bus** schedules for travel from Vernon to Giverny. (Buses ☎ 02 32 71 06 39. 10min.; 4-6 per day; €2, round-trip €4.)

NORMANDY (NORMANDIE)

Fertile Normandy is a land of fields, fishing villages, and cathedrals. Vikings seized the region in the 9th century, and invasions have twice secured Normandy's place in military history: in 1066, William of Normandy conquered England; on D-Day, June 6, 1944, Allied armies began the liberation of France on Normandy's beaches.

ROUEN

However strongly Gustave Flaubert may have criticized his home in *Madame Bovary*, Rouen (pop. 108,000) is no provincial town. The pathos of the Joan of Arc story and the Gothic splendor of Rouen's churches have always entranced artists and writers, and today a younger crowd populates the *vieille ville*. The most famous of Rouen's "hundred spires" are those of the ▨**Cathédrale de Notre-Dame,** in pl. de la Cathédrale, one of which is the tallest in France (151m). The facade incor-porates nearly every style of Gothic architecture. (Open M 2-7pm, Tu-Sa 7:45am-7pm, Su 8am-6pm.) The **Musée des Beaux-Arts,** 26 bis r. Jean Lecanuet, down r. Jeanne d'Arc from the train station, houses a worthwhile collection from the 16th to 20th centuries, including works by Monet and Renoir. (☎ 02 35 71 28 40. Open M and W-Su 10am-6pm. €3, ages 18-25 and groups €2, under-18 free.) Combining the disparate themes of Flaubert (who was raised on the premises) and medical his-tory, the **Musée Flaubert et d'Histoire de la Médicine,** 51 r. de Lecat, down r. de Crosne from pl. de Vieux Marché, contains strange paraphernalia on both sub-jects. (☎ 02 35 15 59 95. Open Tu 10am-6pm, W-Sa 10am-noon and 2-6pm. €2.20, ages 18-25 €1.50, medical students and under-18 free.)

Trains leave r. Jeanne d'Arc for Lille (3hr., 5 per day, €27) and Paris (1½hr., every hr., €17). From the station, walk down r. Jeanne d'Arc and turn left on r. du Gros Horloge to reach pl. de la Cathédrale and the **tourist office,** 25 pl. de la Cathédrale. (☎ 02 32 08 32 40; fax 02 32 08 32 44. Open May-Sept. M-Sa 9am-7pm, Su 9:30am-12:30pm and 2-6pm; Oct.-Mar. M-Sa 9am-6pm, Su 10am-1pm and 2pm-6pm.) Check email at **Place Net,** 37 r. de la République, near the Église St-Maclou. (€4 per hr. Open M-Sa 11am-midnight, Su 2-10pm.) ▨**Hôtel Normandya ❷,** 32 r. de Courdier, near the train station, is run by a friendly couple and offers comfortable, well-decorated rooms. (☎ 02 35 71 46 15. Singles €20; doubles €22.) Cheap eateries crowd **place du Vieux-Marché** and the **Gros Horloge** area. **Monoprix supermarket** is at 73-83 r. du Gros Horloge. (Open M-Sa 8:30am-9pm.) **Postal Code:** 76000.

CAEN

Although Allied bombing leveled three-quarters of its buildings during WWII, Caen (pop. 120,000) has skillfully rebuilt itself into a vibrant university town. Its biggest draw is the powerful ■**Mémorial de Caen.** The best of Normandy's WWII museums, it features footage of the war, displays on pre-war Europe, a haunting testament to the victims of the Holocaust, and a new wing exploring the Cold War. Take bus #2 to *Mémorial.* (☎ 02 31 06 06 44; www.memorial-caen.fr. Open mid-July to Aug. daily 9am-8pm; Sept. to mid-July reduced hours. €17, students €15.) Flanking the ruined chateau of Caen's most famous denizen, the twin abbeys **Abbaye-aux-Hommes,** off r. Guillaume le Conquérant, and **Abbaye-aux-Dames,** off r. des Chanoines, hold the tombs of William the Conqueror and his wife. (Abbaye-aux-Hommes open 9:15am-noon and 2-6pm; €1.55, students €0.80. Abbaye-aux-Dames open M-Sa 8am-5:30pm, Su 9:30am-12:30pm; free.)

Trains run to: Paris (2½hr., 12 per day, €26); Rennes (3hr., 3 per day, €27); Rouen (2hr., 5 per day, €19); and Tours (3½hr., 2 per day, €27). **Bus Verts** (☎ 08 10 21 42 14) covers the beaches and the rest of Normandy. The **tourist office,** pl. St-Pierre, offers free maps. (☎ 02 31 27 14 14; www.ville-caen.fr. Open July-Aug. M-Sa 9am-7pm, Su 10am-1pm and 2-5pm; Sept.-June M-Sa 9:30am-1pm and 2-6pm, Su 10am-1pm.) **Hôtel de l'Univers ❸,** 12 quai Vendeuvre, has reasonable prices and a convenient location. From the train station, follow av. 6 Juin to its end and turn right. All rooms have a shower, TV, and telephone. (☎ 02 31 85 46 41. Singles €28, doubles €33. AmEx/V.) **Hôtel du Château ❹,** 5 av. 6 Juin, has large, bright rooms. (☎ 02 31 86 15 37; fax 02 31 86 58 08. Singles and doubles €35, with shower €45. Oct.-Easter reduced prices. MC/V.) Ethnic restaurants, *crêperies,* and *brasseries* line the **quartier Vaugueux** near the chateau, as well as the streets between **Église St-Pierre** and **Église St-Jean.** Get your groceries at **Monoprix supermarket,** 45 bd. du Maréchal Leclerc. (Open M-Sa 9am-8:30pm.) At night Caen's old streets come to life. **Rue de Bras, rue des Croisiers,** and **rue St-Pierre** are especially popular. **Postal Code:** 14000.

BAYEUX

Relatively untouched by the war, beautiful Bayeux (pop. 15,000) is an ideal base for exploring the nearby D-Day beaches. However, visitors should not miss its 900-year-old ■**Tapisserie de Bayeux,** 70m of embroidery that relates the tale of William the Bastard's invasion of England and his earning of a more respectable name—"the Conqueror." The tapestry is displayed in the **Centre Guillaume le Conquérant,** on r. de Nesmond. (Open May-Aug. daily 9am-7pm; mid-Mar. to Apr. and Sept. to mid-Oct. 9am-6:30pm; mid-Oct. to mid-Mar. 9:30am-12:30pm and 2-6pm. €7.40, students €3.) Nearby is the original home of the tapestry, the extraordinary **Cathédrale Notre-Dame.** (Open July-Aug. M-Sa 8am-7pm, Su 9am-7pm; Sept.-June M-Sa 8:30am-noon and 2:30-7pm, Su 9am-12:15pm and 2:30-7pm. Free.) The **Musée de la Bataille de Normandie,** bd. Fabian Ware, recounts the D-Day landing and subsequent 76-day battle. (Open May to mid-Sept. 9:30am-6:30pm; mid-Sept. to Apr. 10am-12:30pm and 2-6pm. Closed early Jan. €5.70, students €2.60.) The **British Cemetery** across the street provides a strikingly simple yet moving wartime record.

Trains (☎ 02 31 92 80 50) leave pl. de la Gare for: Caen (20min., 15 per day, €5.20) and Paris (2½hr., 12 per day, €28). To reach the **tourist office,** pont St-Jean, turn left on the highway (bd. Sadi-Carnot), bear right, follow the signs to the *centre ville,* and follow r. Larcher to r. St-Martin. (☎ 02 31 51 28 28; www.bayeux-tourism.com. Open June-Aug. M-Sa 9am-7pm, Su 9am-1pm and 2-6pm; Sept.-May reduced hours.) From the tourist office, turn right onto r. St-Martin, follow through several name changes, and turn left onto r. Général de Dais to reach the ▩**Family Home/Auberge de Jeunesse (HI) ❶**, 39 r. Général de Dais. (☎02 31 92 15 22; fax 02 31 92 55 72. Dorms €16. Nonmembers €18.) Follow r. Genas Duhomme to the right and continue straight for **Camping Municipal ❶**, on bd. d'Eindhoven. (☎02 31 92 08 43. Open May-Sept. €3 per person, €3.60 per tent and car.) Get **groceries** at **Champion**, on bd. d'Eindhoven. **Postal Code:** 14400.

D-DAY BEACHES

On June 6, 1944, over one million Allied soldiers invaded the beaches of Normandy in the first of a chain of events that liberated France and led to the downfall of Nazi Europe. Today, reminders of that first devastating battle can be seen in somber gravestones, remnants of German bunkers, and the pockmarked landscape.

🛈 **TRANSPORTATION.** Reaching and exploring the D-Day beaches can be difficult without a car. That said, many of the sites are accessible from Caen and Bayeux with **Bus Verts** (☎08 10 21 42 14); ask about the special "D-Day" line. A day pass (€17) takes you to four major sites. **Utah Beach** is accessible only by car or foot from **Ste-Mère-Église.** Take a **train** from Bayeux to Caretan (30min., 10 per day, €6.60) and then a **bus** from Caretan to Ste-Mère-Eglise (15min.; 12:50pm, return 6:35pm; €2.90). English-language **Victory Tours** leave from behind the Bayeux tourist office. (☎02 31 51 98 14; www.victory-tours.com. 4hr. tour 12:30pm, €31; 8hr. tour 9am, €54. Reserve ahead.)

BEACHES NEAR BAYEUX. At **Utah Beach,** near Ste-Marie du Mont, the Americans headed the western flank of the invasion. The **Musée du Débarquement** here shows how 836,000 troops, 220,000 vehicles, and 725,000 tons of equipment came ashore. (☎02 33 71 53 35. Open June-Sept. daily 9:30am-7pm; Oct.-May reduced hours. €4.50.) The most difficult landing was that of the First US Infantry Division at **Pointe du Hoc.** The Pointe is considered a military cemetery because many who perished are still there, crushed beneath collapsed concrete bunkers. **Omaha Beach,** next to Colleville-sur-Mer and east of the Pointe du Hoc, is perhaps the most famous beach and the severe losses suffered there bestowed the moniker "bloody Omaha." Overlooking the beach, 9387 graves stretch across the American Cemetery. (Open daily 9am-5pm.) Ten kilometers north of Bayeux and just east of Omaha is **Arromanches**, a small town at the center of **Gold Beach,** where the British built the artificial Port Winston in a single day to provide shelter while the Allies unloaded their supplies. The **Arromanches 360° Cinéma** combines images of modern Normandy with those of D-Day. Turn left on r. de la Batterie from the museum and climb the steps to get there. (Open June-Aug. daily 9:40am-6:40pm; Sept.-May reduced hours. Closed Jan. €3.70, students €3.30.)

MONT-ST-MICHEL

Rising like a vision from the sea, the fortified island of Mont-St-Michel (pop. 42) is a dazzling labyrinth of stone arches, spires, and stairways that climb up to the **abbey.** Adjacent to the abbey church, **La Merveille,** a 13th-century Gothic monastery, encloses a seemingly endless web of passageways and chambers. (Open May -Aug. daily 9am-7pm; Sept.-Apr. 9:30am-6pm. €7, ages 18-25 €4.50.) The Mont is most stunning at night, but plan carefully—there is no late-night public transport off the island. Mont-St-Michel is best visited as a daytrip via a Courriers Bretons **bus,** 104 r. Couesnon in Pontorson (☎02 33 60 11 43), from Rennes (1½hr., 3-6 per day, €11) or St-Malo (1½hr., 2-4 per day, €9). Hotels on Mont-St-Michel are expensive, starting at €50 a night. The **Pontorson tourist office,** pl. de l'Église, helps visitors find affordable accommodations (☎02 33 60 20 65; fax 02 33 60 85 67. Open

July-Aug. M-F 9am-12:30pm and 2-6:30pm, Sa 10am-12:30pm and 3-6:30pm; Sept.-June reduced hours.) The cheapest beds are at the **Centre Dugusclin (HI) ❶**, r. Général Patton. (☎/fax 02 33 60 18 65. Dorms €8.) **Postal Code:** 50116.

BRITTANY (BRETAGNE)

Lined with spectacular beaches, wild headlands, and cliffs gnawed by the sea into long crags and inlets, Brittany fiercely maintains its Celtic traditions despite Paris's age-old effort to assimilate the province. Britons fled Anglo-Saxon invaders between the 5th and 7th centuries for this beautiful, wild peninsula, and in the 800 years that followed, they defended their independence from Frankish, Norman, French, and English invaders. Breton traditions, dating from centuries of freedom, linger in the pristine islands off the Atlantic coast, and lilting *Brezhoneg* (Breton) is spoken at pubs and ports in the western part of the province.

RENNES

The throbbing heart of Brittany, Rennes (pop. 210,000) has a well-earned reputation as the party capital of northwestern France, but the city is more than just a rocking good time. Its *vielle ville* is as charming as any of France's small medieval towns, cobblestones, half-timbered houses, and all. Unlike many of its neighbors, Rennes is not sagging under history's awesome weight; this is, first and foremost, a city dedicated to life in the moment.

⧉ TRANSPORTATION. Trains leave from pl. de la Gare (☎02 99 29 11 92) for: Brest (2¼hr., every hr., €27); Caen (3hr., 8 per day, €28); Paris (2hr., every hr., €47); and St-Malo (1hr., 15 per day, €11). **Buses** (☎02 99 30 87 80) leave the train station for Angers (2½-3hr., 3-4 per day, €16) and Mont-St-Michel (2½hr., 1-2 per day, €12). Local **buses** run daily 5am-8pm; lines in areas with hopping nightlife run as late as midnight. A **Métro** line runs through Rennes on the same ticket (€1).

⧉ PRACTICAL INFORMATION. To get from the train station to the **tourist office**, 11 r. St-Yves, take av. Jean Janvier to quai Chateaubriand, turn left, walk along the river until you reach r. George Dottin, then turn right onto r. St-Yves. (☎02 99 67 11 11; fax 02 99 67 11 10. Open Apr.-Sept. M-Sa 9am-7pm, Su and holidays 11am-6pm.) Access the **Internet** at **Neurogame**, 2 r. de Dinan. (☎02 99 65 53 85; www.neurogame.com. €3 per hr. Open M-Th 2pm-1am, F-Sa 2pm-3am. The **post office** (☎02 99 01 22 11) is at 27 bd. du Colombier, near the train station. **Postal Code:** 35032.

⧉⧉ ACCOMMODATIONS AND FOOD. The **Auberge de Jeunesse (HI) ❶**, 10-12 Canal St-Martin, provides cheap and decent lodging. Take the Métro (dir.: Kennedy) to *Ste-Anne*. Follow r. St-Malo downhill to the river, bear left onto r. St-Martin, and the hostel will be on the right. (☎02 99 33 22 33; fax 02 99 59 06 21. Breakfast included. Reception 7am-11pm. Dorms €13. MC/V.) **Hotel d'Angleterre ❷**, 19 r. Marechal Joffre, can't be beat for location. Take the Métro (dir.: Kennedy) to *pl. de la République*, walk towards the river and turn right onto r. Jean Jaurès; the hotel is on the right. (☎02 99 79 38 61; fax 02 99 79 43 85. Breakfast €5. Reception 7am-10:30pm. Singles €21-37; doubles €32-44; triples €41-46. MC/V.) **Camping Municipal des Gayeulles ❶**, deep within Parc les Gayeulles, is packed with activities. Take bus #3 (dir.: St-Laurent) from pl. du Colombier (left of the train station) to *Piscine/Gayuelles*. Follow the paths and signs to the campground. (☎02 99 36 91 22. Reception mid-June to mid-Sept. 7:30am-1pm and 2-8pm; mid-Sept. to mid-June 9am-12:30pm and 4:30-8pm. Electricity €2.60. €3 per person; €1.60 per car. MC/V.) **Rue St-Malo** has many ethnic restaurants. Inside the *vielle ville* are traditional *brasseries* and cheap kebab stands. In general, the best food is found on the outskirts of the city center. The upscale ▧**Café Breton ❷**, 14 r. Nantaise, serves Breton cuisine at reasonable prices. (☎ 02 99 30 74 95. Open M and Sa noon-4pm, Tu-F noon-3pm and 7-11pm.)

🖥 🎟 **SIGHTS AND ENTERTAINMENT.** Excellent examples of medieval architecture are near the tourist office on **rue de la Psalette** and **rue St-Guillaume.** At the end of r. St-Guillaume, turn left onto r. de la Monnaie to visit the imposing **Cathédrale St-Pierre,** which was begun in 1787. The center of attention is its carved and gilded altarpiece depicting the life of the Virgin. (Open daily 9:30am-noon and 3-6pm.) Across the street from the cathedral, the **Portes Mordelaises,** down an alley bearing the same name, are the former entrances to the city and the last vestiges of the medieval city walls. The **Musée des Beaux-Arts,** 20 quai Émile Zola, houses a small but stunningly varied collection. (☎ 02 99 28 55 85 40. Open Su-M and W-Sa 10am-noon and 2-6pm. €5, students €2.50. Under-18 free.) Across the river and up r. Gambetta is the lush **Jardin du Thabor,** considered to be among the most beautiful gardens in France. Concerts are often held here; a small gallery on the north side exhibits local artwork on a rotating basis. (Open June-Sept. 7:15am-9:30pm.)

With enough bars for a city twice its size and a collection of clubs that draws students from Paris and beyond, Rennes is a partygoer's weekend mecca. Look for action in **place Ste-Anne, place St-Michel,** and the radiating streets. ▧**Delicatessen,** 7 allée Rallier du Baty, is tucked around the corner from pl. St-Michel in a former prison, having swapped jailhouse bars for dance cages to become one of Rennes' hottest clubs. (Cover €10 Th-Sa after 1:30am, F-Sa €14 after 1:30am. Open Tu-Sa midnight-5am.) **Le Zing,** 5 pl. des Lices, packs the house with the young and beautiful. (☎ 02 99 79 64 60. Opens daily at 2pm, active from midnight until 2am.)

ST-MALO

St-Malo (pop. 52,000) manages to merge the best of northern France. Combining miles of warm, sandy beaches and crystal blue waters with a charming, walled *vielle ville* that holds numerous *créperies*, boutiques, and cafes, St-Malo makes for the ultimate oceanside getaway. To the east is the **Grand Plage,** the city's most popular beach. The slightly more secluded **Plage de Bon Secours** lies to the west and features the curious **Piscine de Bon-Secours,** three cement walls that hold in a pool's worth of warm salt water even when the tide recedes. The best view of St-Malo is from its **ramparts,** which once kept out invaders but now attract tourists in droves. All entrances to the city have stairs leading up to the old walls; the view from the north side reveals a series of small islands leading out into the sea.

Trains run from pl. de l'Hermine to: Dinan (1hr., 5 per day, €8); Paris (5hr., 3 per day, €50); and Rennes (1hr., 8-12 per day, €11). As you exit the station, cross bd. de la République and follow esplanade St-Vincent to the **tourist office,** near the entrance to the *vielle ville.* (☎ 02 99 56 64 48; www.saint-malo-tourisme.com. Open July-Aug. M-Sa 9am-7:30pm, Su 10am-6pm; Sept.-June reduced hours.) The 247-bed **Auberge de Jeunesse (HI) ❶,** 37 av. du Révérend Père Umbricht, is near the beach. From the train station, take bus #5 (dir.: Parame or Davier) or bus #1 (dir.: Rotheneuf) to *Auberge de Jeunesse.* (☎ 02 99 40 29 80; fax 02 99 40 29 02. Reception 24hr. Dorms €13.) Overlooking Plage de Bon Secours, **Les Chiens de Guet ❸,** 4 pl. de Guet, has bright, elegant rooms and a great location within the city walls. (☎ 02 99 40 87 29; fax 02 99 56 08 75. Breakfast €5. Doubles €31; quads €66. Closed mid-Nov. to Jan. AmEx/MC/V.) The most interesting eateries lie closer to the center of the *vielle ville;* those near the entrances are often generic and overpriced. **Champion supermarket,** on av. Pasteur, is near the hostel. (Open M-F 8:30am-1pm and 3-7:30pm, Sa 8:30am-7:30pm, Su 9:30am-noon.) **Postal Code:** 35400.

DINAN

Perhaps the best-preserved medieval town in Brittany, Dinan's (pop. 10,000) cobblestone streets are lined with 15th-century houses inhabited by traditional artisans. On the ramparts, the 13th-century **Porte du Guichet** is the entrance to the **Château de Dinan**, also known as the **Tour de la Duchesse Anne**. Climb to the terrace to look over the town or inspect the galleries of the 15th-century **Tour de Coëtquen**, which houses a collection of funerary ornaments. (Open June-Sept. daily 10am-6:30pm; Oct.-May reduced hours. €3.90, ages 12-18 €1.50.) On the other side of the ramparts from the chateau is the **Jardin du Val Cocherel**, which holds bird cages and a chessboard scaled for life-sized pieces. (Open daily 8am-7:30pm.) A long, picturesque walk down the steep r. de Petit Fort will lead you to the **Maison d'Artiste de la Grande Vigne**, 103 r. du Quai. This former home of painter Yvonne Jean-Haffen (1895-1993), is a work of art, with exhibitions of her work, murals adorning the walls, and a picturesque garden that would be any artist's dream. (☎02 96 87 90 80. Open May 2-6pm, June-Sept. 2-6:30pm. €2.50, students €1.60.)

Trains run from the pl. du 11 Novembre 1918 to Paris (3hr., 8 per day, €50) and Rennes (1hr., 8 per day, €12). To get from the station to the **tourist office**, r. du Château, bear left across pl. 11 Novembre to r. Carnot, turn right on r. Thiers, turn left into the *vieille ville*, and bear right onto r. du Marchix, which becomes r. de la Ferronnerie; it will be on your right. (☎02 96 87 69 76; www.dinan-tourisme.com. Open mid-June to mid-Sept. M-Sa 9am-7pm, Su 10am-12:30pm and 2:30-6pm; mid-Sept. to mid-June M-Sa 9am-12:30pm and 2-6pm.) **Internet** access is available at **Arospace Cybercafe**, 9 r. de la Chaux, off r. de l'Horloge. (☎02 96 87 04 87. Open Tu-Sa 10am-12:30pm, 1:30-7pm. €1.50 per 15 min.) To reach the **Auberge de Jeunesse (HI) ❶**, in Vallée de la Fontaine-des-Eaux, turn left as you exit the station and cross the tracks, then turn right, and follow the tracks downhill for 1km before turning right again; it will be on your right. (☎02 96 39 10 83. Reception 8am-noon and 5-8pm. Curfew 11pm. Dorms €8.50.) **Hôtel du Théâtre ❶**, 2 r. Ste-Claire, is in the heart of the *vieille ville*. (☎02 96 39 06 91. Singles €15; doubles €21.) Get **groceries** at **Monoprix** on r. du Marchix. (Open M-Sa 9am-7:30pm.) **Rue de la Cordonnerie** and **place des Merciers** have inexpensive *brasseries*. **Postal Code: 22100.**

ST-BRIEUC. As most locals will tell you, St-Brieuc (pop. 48,000) is much more of a commercial center than a tourist trap. The university students help make the city vibrant; its lively bar scene is one of the best in the region. Situated between the Côte d'Emeraude and the Côte de Granite Rose, it is a perfect base for daytrips to the scenic countryside. **Trains** arrive from Dinan (1hr., 2-3 per day, €8.60) and Rennes (1hr., 15 per day, €15). From the station on bd. Charner, walk straight down r. de la Gare and bear right at the fork to reach pl. de la Résistance and the **tourist office**, 7 r. St-Gouéno. (☎02 96 33 32 50; fax 02 96 61 42 16. Open July-Aug. M-Sa 9am-7pm, Su 10am-1pm; Sept.-June M-Sa 9am-noon and 1:30-6pm.) The ⚫**Youth Hostel ❶** is in a 15th-century house 3km from town; take bus #2 (dir.: Centre Commercial les Villages) and get off at the last stop, turn around and take the first left onto r. du Brocéliande; follow it to its end and turn left onto r. du Vau Méno. Turn right onto r. de la Ville Guyomard, where you'll find the hostel on the left. (☎02 96 78 70 70.) Breakfast included. Reception 9:30am-noon, 2-7pm and 8-8:30pm. Dorms €3. MC/V.) Bars and outdoor cafes cluster in the area behind the tourist office and along the small **rue Fardel** behind the Cathédrale St-Etienne; **rue des Trois Frères le Goff** is lined with inexpensive Moroccan, Italian, Chinese, Mexican, and Indian restaurants. **Postal Code: 22000.**

CAP FRÉHEL. The rust-hued cliffs of **Cap Fréhel** mark the northern point of the Côte d'Emeraude. Catch a CAT **bus** from St-Brieuc (1½hr.; 3-4 per day; €7.20, students €5.80) and follow the red- and white-striped markers along the **GR34 trail** on the edge of the peninsula. There's also a scenic 1½hr. walk to **Fort La Latte**, a 13th-century castle complete with drawbridges. To reach the **Auberge de Jeunesse Cap Fréhel (HI) ❶**, in La Ville Hadrieux in Kerivet, get off the bus one stop after Cap Fréhel at *Auberge de Jeunesse*, take the only road that branches from the stop, and follow the fir-tree hostel signs. (☎02 96 41 48 98; mid-Sept. to Apr. 02 98 78 70 70. Breakfast €3. Open May-Sept. Dorms or camping €7.)

PAIMPOL. Paimpol (pop. 8200), northwest of St-Brieuc at the end of the Côte de Granite Rose, offers easy access to nearby islands, beaches, and hiking trails. **Trains** (1hr., 4-5 per day, €10) and CAT **buses** (1¼hr.; 8 per day; €7.20, students €5.80) leave av. Général de Gaulle for St-Brieuc. From the station, turn right onto av. de Général de Gaulle and bear left at the roundabout; the **tourist office** will be on the left, and the port will be to the right. (☎02 96 20 83 16; www.paimpol-goelo.com. Open June-Sept. M-Sa 9:30am-7:30pm, Su 10am-6pm; Oct.-May M-Sa 9:30am-12:30pm and 1:30-6:30pm.) **Hôtel Le Goelo ❸**, quai Duguay Trouin, has comfortable rooms, some overlooking the port. From the tourist office, walk towards the water and take the first right; the hotel is just ahead. (☎02 96 20 82 74. Breakfast €4.60. Singles €25, with shower and toilet €31; doubles €34-42; triples €54. MC/V.) **Rue des 8 Patriots** is the best bet for restaurants. **Postal Code:** 22500.

BREST

Brest (pop. 156,000) was transformed into a somber wasteland in 1944 by Allied bombers driving out the occupying German flotilla. However, the city has begun to show signs of life; Brest features a number of pleasant daytime cafes and a new summer concert series, as well as one of the largest aquariums around. Brest's **château** was the only building in the town to survive WWII, and is now the world's oldest active military institution, as well as home to the **Musée de la Marine**, off r. de Château, which highlights the local maritime history. (Open Apr.-Sept. daily 10am-6:30pm; Oct.-Mar. M and W-Su 10am-noon and 2-6pm. €4.60, students €3.) The newly renovated **Océanopolis**, at port de Plaisance, has tropical, temperate, and polar pavilions and a coral reef accessible by a glass elevator. From the Liberty terminal, take bus #7 (dir.: Port de Plaisance; M-Sa every 30min. until 7:30pm; €1) to *Océanopolis*. (☎02 98 34 40 40. Open Apr.-Aug. daily 9am-6pm; Sept.-Mar. Su 10am-6pm, Tu-Sa 10am-5pm. €15.)

    Trains (☎02 98 31 51 72) leave pl. du 19*ème* Régiment d'Infanterie for Nantes (4hr., 6 per day, €35); Quimper (30min., 5 per day, €14); and Rennes (1½hr., 15 per day, €27). From the station, av. Georges Clemenceau leads to the intersection of r. de Siam and r. Jean Jaurès, and the **tourist office**, at pl. de la Liberté. (☎02 98 44 24 96. Open July-Aug. M-Sa 9:30am-7pm, Su 10am-noon; Sept.-June M-Sa 10am-12:30pm and 2-6pm.) Access the **Internet** at @cces.cibles, 31 av. Clemenceau. (☎02 98 33 73 07. €3 per hr. Open M-Sa 11am-1am, Su 2-11pm.) For the luxurious ⚑**Auberge de Jeunesse (HI) ❶**, 5 r. de Kerbriant, 4km away near Océanopolis, take bus #7 (dir.: Port de Plaisance) from opposite the station to its final stop (M-Sa until 7:30pm, Su until 6pm; €1); with your back to the bus stop, go left toward the beach, take an immediate left, and follow the signs to the hostel. (☎02 98 41 90 41. Reception M-F 7-9am and 5-8pm, Sa-Su 7-10am and 6-8pm. Curfew July-Aug. midnight; Sept.-June 11pm; ask for a key. Dorms €12.) **Kelig Hôtel ❷**, 12 r. de Lyon, has clean, relatively spacious rooms. (☎02 98 80 47 21. Breakfast €6. Singles €24-37; doubles €27-40; triples €44-47. AmEx/MC/V.) The area at the end of **rue de Siam**, near the port, has a variety of restaurants. **Postal Code:** 29200.

QUIMPER

With a central waterway crisscrossed by pedestrian footbridges decorated with colorful flowers, Quimper (pop. 63,000) has the feel of a mini-Paris. The magnificent dual spires of the **Cathédrale St-Corentin**, built between the 13th and 15th centuries, mark the entrance to the old quarter from quai St-Corentin. (Open M-Sa 8:30am-noon and 1:30-6:30pm, Su 8:30am-noon, except during mass, and 2-6:30pm.) The **Musée Départemental Breton**, 1 r. du Roi Gradlon, through the cathedral garden, offers exhibits on local history, archaeology, and ethnography. (Open June-Sept. daily 9am-6pm; Oct.-May Su 2-5pm, Tu-Sa 9am-noon and 2-5pm. €4, students €2.50.) At night, head to one of the several cafes near the cathedral, or to the Irish pub 🔖**Molly Malone's**, pl. St-Mathieu, on r. Falkirk. (☎02 98 53 40 42. Beamish stout €3.10, pint €5.40. Open daily 11am-1am.)

Trains go to Brest (1½hr., 4 per day, €14) and Rennes (2¼hr., 10 per day, €28). From the train station, go right onto av. de la Gare and follow the river Odet, keeping it on your right; it will become bd. Dupleix and lead to pl. de la Résistance. The **tourist office** will be on your left. (☎02 98 53 04 05; www.quimper-tourisme.com. Open July-Aug. M-Sa 9am-7pm, Su 10am-1pm and 3-5:45pm; Sept.-June reduced hours.) Access the **Internet** at **CyberCopy**, 3 bd. Amiral Kerguelen (☎02 98 64 33 99. €4.50 per hr. Open M 1-7pm, Tu-F 9am-7pm, Sa 9am-3pm.) To reach the **Centre Hébergement de Quimper (HI)** ❶, 6 av. des Oiseaux, take bus #1 from pl. de la Résistance (dir.: Kermoysan) to *Chaptal* (last bus 7:30pm). The hostel will be 50m up the street on your left. (☎02 98 64 97 97; quimper@fuaj.org. Breakfast €3.25. Sheets €3. Dorms €8.40. HI members only.) **Hôtel Le Derby** ❸, 13 av. de la Gare, facing the train station, has well-decorated rooms, all with bath. (☎02 98 52 06 91; fax 02 98 53 39 04. Breakfast €5.40. Extra bed €4. Singles €28; doubles €38; Oct.-Apr. €3 discount.) The lively **Les Halles** (covered markets), off r. Kéréon on r. St-François, always has shops with bargains on produce, seafood, meats, and cheeses. (Open M-Sa 7am-8pm, Su 9am-1pm.) **Postal Code** 29200.

LOIRE VALLEY (VAL DE LOIRE)

The Loire, France's longest and most celebrated river, meanders to the Atlantic through a valley overflowing with gentle vineyards and majestic chateaux. Loire vineyards produce some of France's best wines, and the soil is among the country's most fertile. It is hardly surprising that a string of French (and English) kings chose to station themselves in opulent chateaux by these waters rather than in the commotion of their capital cities.

▌ TRANSPORTATION

Faced with such widespread grandeur, many travelers plan over-ambitious itineraries—two chateaux a day is a reasonable limit. Biking is the best way to explore the region, since trains to chateaux are infrequent. The city of Tours is the region's best **rail** hub, although the chateaux Chambord and Cheverny aren't accessible by train. Many stations distribute the invaluable *Châteaux pour Train et Vélo* booklet with train schedules and **bike** and **car rental** information.

ORLÉANS

A pleasant gateway from Paris into the Loire, Orléans (pop. 117,000) clings tightly to its historical connection to Joan of Arc. Most of Orléans's highlights are near **Place Ste-Croix.** Joan of Arc triumphantly marched down nearby **Rue de Bourgogne**, the city's oldest street, in 1429. The **Musée des Beaux-Arts**, 1 r. Ferdinand Rabier, has a fine collection of French, Italian and Flemish works. (☎02 38 79 21 55. Open M 1:30-6pm, Tu-Sa 10am-noon and 1:30-6pm. €3, students €1.50.) The **Église St-Paterne**, pl. Gambetta, is a massive showcase of modern stained glass. The stunning windows of **Cathédrale Sainte-Croix,** pl. Ste-Croix, depict Joan's dramatic story. (Open July-Aug. daily 9:15am-7pm; Sept.-June reduced hours.)

Trains arrive at the Gare d'Orléans on pl. Albert 1er from: Blois (30min., every hr. 7am-9pm, €8.40); Paris (1¼hr., 3 per hr., €15); and Tours (1hr., 2 per hr., €14.10). To get from the station to the **tourist office,** 6 r. Albert 1er, go left under the tunnel to pl. Jeanne d'Arc; it's across the street. (☎02 38 24 05 05; fax 02 38 54 49 84. Open May-Sept. Tu-Sa 9:30am-1pm and 2-6pm; Oct.-Apr. reduced hours.) To reach the **Auberge de Jeunesse (HI) ❶**, 1 bd. de la Motte Sanguin, take bus RS (dir.: Rosette) or SY (dir.: Concyr/La Bolière) from pl. Jeanne d'Arc to Pont Bourgogne; follow bd. de la Motte and it'll be up on the right. (☎02 38 53 60 06. Breakfast €3.40. Sheets €3.20. Reception M-F 8am-7pm, Sa-Su 9-11am and 5-7pm. Dorms €8.) **Les Halles Châtelet,** pl. du Châtelet, is a market attached to the Galeries Lafayette. (Open Su 7am-1pm, Tu-Sa 7am-7pm.) In the back of the mall, buy groceries in **Carrefour** at pl. Jeanne d'Arc. (Open M-Sa 8:30am-9pm.) **Rue de Bourgogne** and **rue Sainte Catherine** have a variety of eateries. **Postal Code:** 45000.

BLOIS

Blois (pop. 50,000) is one of the Loire's most popular and historical cities. Home to monarchs Louis XII and François I, Blois's **chateau** was the Versailles of the late 15th and early 16th centuries; today it exemplifies the progression of French architecture from the 13th to the 17th century. Housed within are excellent museums: The recently renovated **Musée de Beaux-Arts,** featuring a 16th-century portrait gallery; the **Musée d'Archéologie,** showcasing locally excavated glass and ceramics; and the **Musée Lapidaire,** preserving sculpted pieces from nearby chateaux. (☎02 54 90 33 33. Open July-Aug. daily 9am-7:30pm; Apr.-June and Sept. 9am-6pm; Oct.-Mar. 9am-12:30pm and 2-5:30pm. €6, students €4.) At night the seemingly tame Blois lights up. Move from the cafes of **Place de la Résistance** to 🖪**Le Blue Night,** 15 r. Haute, for a selection of over 100 international beers served in a bar that resembles a medieval chapel. (Open daily 6pm-4am.)

Trains leave pl. de la Gare for: Orléans (30min., 14 per day, €8.40); Paris (1¾hr., 8 per day, €20) via Orléans and Tours (1hr., 13 per day, €8.20). **Transports Loir-et-Cher** (TLC; ☎02 54 58 55 44) sends **buses** from the station and pl. Victor Hugo to nearby chateaux (45min.; 2 per day; €10, students €8.). Or, rent a **bike** from **Amster Cycles,** 7 r. de Desfray, one block from the train station, for the hour-long ride to the valley. (☎02 54 74 30 13. €13 per day. Open M-Sa 9:15am-1pm and 2-6:30pm, Su 10am-1:30pm and 3-6:15pm.) To reach the **tourist office,** 3 av. Jean Laigret, take a left on av. Jean Laigret out of the train station. (☎02 54 90 41 41; www.loiredeschateaux.com. Open Apr.-Oct. Su-M 10am-7pm, Tu-Sa 9am-7pm; Nov.-Mar. reduced hours.) 🖪**Hôtel du Bellay ❷**, 12 r. des Minimes, is at the top of porte Chartraine, 2min. above the city center. This family-run establishment offers spotless, comfortable rooms and personal attention. (☎02 54 78 23 62; fax 02 54 78 52 04. Breakfast €4.20. Closed Jan. 5-25. Singles and doubles €24; triples €45; quads €55. MC/V.) **Le Pavillon ❷**, 2 av. Wilson, has clean and bright rooms. Take bus line 3A from the station; the hotel can also be reached on foot in 20min. (☎02 54 74 23 27; fax 02 54 74 03 36. Breakfast €5.25. Singles €24-38; quads €50. MC/V.) Fragrant *pâtisseries* entice from **rue Denis Papin,** while **rue Drussy, rue St-Lubin,** and **place Poids du Roi** have a number of dining options. **Postal Code:** 41000.

▶ DAYTRIPS FROM BLOIS: CHAMBORD AND CHEVERNY. Built from 1519 to 1545 to satisfy François I's egomania, **Chambord** is the largest and most extravagant of the Loire chateaux. With 440 rooms, 365 fireplaces, and 83 staircases, the chateau rivals Versailles in grandiosity. To cement his claim, François stamped 700 of his trademark stone salamanders throughout this "hunting lodge" and built a spectacular double-helix staircase in the center of the castle. (☎02 54 50 40 00. Open Apr.-Sept. 9am-6:45pm; Oct.-Mar. reduced hours. €7, ages 18-25 €4.50. Under-18 free.) Take TLC **bus** #2 from Blois (45min., 2 per day, €10) or **bike** south from Blois on D956 for 2-3km, and then turn left on D33 (1hr.).

Cheverny and its manicured grounds are unique among the major chateaux. Its magnificent furnishings include elegant tapestries and delicate Delft vases. Fans of Hergé's *Tintin* books may recognize Cheverny's Renaissance facade as the inspiration for Marlinspike, Captain Haddock's mansion. The **kennels** hold 70 mixed English Poitevin hounds who stalk stags in hunting expeditions. (☎02 54 79 96 29. Open July-Aug. daily 9:15am-6:45pm. Hunting Oct.-Mar. Tu and Sa. Off season reduced hours. €6, students €4.) Cheverny is 45min. south of Blois by **bike** and on the route of TLC **bus** #2 (see above).

AMBOISE

Amboise (pop. 11,000) is guarded by the parapets of the 15th-century **chateau** that six security-minded French kings called home. In the **Logis de Roi**, the main part of the chateau, intricate 16th-century Gothic chairs stand over 2m tall to prevent any attacks from behind. The jewel of the grounds is the 15th-century **Chapelle St-Hubert**, the final resting place of **Leonardo da Vinci**. (☎02 47 57 00 98. Open Apr.-Nov. daily 9am-6pm; Dec.-Mar. reduced hours. €7, students €6.) Four hundred meters away is **Clos Lucé** manor, where Leonardo da Vinci spent the last three years of his life. Inside are his bedroom, library, drawing room, and chapel, but the main attraction is a collection of 40 machines created from da Vinci's visionary designs and built with materials contemporaneous to da Vinci's lifetime. (☎02 47 57 62 88. Open Mar.-Oct. daily 9am-7pm; Nov.-Feb. reduced hours. €11, students €9.)

Trains leave bd. Gambetta for: Blois (20min., 20 per day, €5.40); Orléans (1hr., 6 per day, €13); Paris (2½hr., 7 per day, €24); and Tours (20min., 11 per day, €4.30). To reach the **tourist office** on quai du Général de Gaulle, take a left once outside the train station, following r. Jules-Ferry and cross both bridges past the residential Ile d'Or. (☎02 47 57 09 28; fax 02 47 57 14 35. Open July-Aug. M-Sa 9am-8pm, Su 10am-6pm; Sept.-June reduced hours.) The **Centre International de Séjour Charles Péguy (HI) ❶**, on Ile d'Or, sits on an island in the middle of the Loire. Some rooms have a view of the chateau. (☎02 47 30 60 90; fax 02 47 30 60 91. Breakfast €2.60. Sheets €3.10. Reception M-F 3-7pm. Dorms €8.60.) **Postal Code:** 35400.

TOURS

Tours (pop. 253,000) works best as a base for nearby Loire chateaux, but its fabulous nightlife and collection of sights should not be missed. The **Cathédrale St-Gatien**, on r. Jules Simon, has dazzling stained glass and an intricate facade. (Cathedral open daily 9am-7pm. Free. Cloister open Easter-Sept. 9:30am-12:30pm and 2-6pm; Oct.-Mar. Su, W-Sa 9:30am-12:30pm and 2-5pm. €2.50.) At the **Musée du Gemmail**, 7 r. du Murier, works of *gemmail* (a fusion of enameled shards of brightly colored glass) glow in rooms of dark velvet. (Open Apr.-Nov. Su and Tu-Sa 10am-noon and 2-6:30pm. €4.60, students €3.) At night, **place Plumereau** (or just plain pl. Plum) is the place to be, with cheerful students sipping drinks and chatting at cafes and bars.

Trains leave pl. du Général Leclerc for Bordeaux (2½hr., 4 per day, €34) and Paris (2¼hr., 7 per day, €25). To reach the **tourist office,** 78-82 r. Bernard Palissy, from the station, walk through pl. du Général Leclerc, cross bd. Heurteloup and take a right. (☎02 47 70 37 37; www.ligeris.com. Open mid-Apr. to mid-Oct. M-Sa 8:30am-7pm, Su 10am-12:30pm and 2:30-5pm; mid-Oct. to mid-Apr. reduced hours.) Access the **Internet** at Cyber Gate, 11 r. de Président Merville. (☎02 47 05 95 94. €1 per 15min., €5 for 1hr. of access, a sandwich, and a beverage. Open M 1-10pm, Tu-Sa 11am-midnight, Su 2-10pm.) The owners of ◪**Hôtel Regina ❸**, 2 r. Pimbert, make you feel like family. It's close to beautiful river strolls and good restaurants. (☎02 47 05 25 36; fax 02 47 66 08 72. Breakfast €4.30. Singles and doubles €20-24; triples €23-36. MC/V.) **Foyer des Jeunes Travailleurs ❷**, 16 r. Bernard Palissy, is centrally located. (☎02 47 60 51 51. Singles €17; doubles €31.) Try **place Plumereau** and **rue Colbert** for great restaurants, cafes, and bars. **La Souris Gourmande ❷**, 100 r. Colbert, is a friendly restaurant specializing in regional cheese dishes and fondues. (Open Tu-Sa noon-2pm and 7-10:30pm.) **Postal Code:** 37000.

⟐ DAYTRIPS FROM TOURS: CHENONCEAU AND LOCHES. Perhaps the most exquisite chateau in France, Chenonceau arches gracefully over the Cher river. A series of women created the beauty that is the chateau: first Catherine, the wife of a tax collector; then Diane de Poitiers, the lover of Henri II; and then Henri's widowed wife, Catherine de Médici. The part of the chateau bridging the Cher marked the border between occupied and Vichy France during WWII. (☎02 47 23 90 07. Open mid-Mar. to mid-Sept. daily 9am-7pm; off-season reduced hours. €8, students €6.50.) **Trains** from Tours roll into the station in front of the castle. (30min., 6 per day, €5.10). Fil Vert **buses** also leave from Tours (1¼hr, 2 per day, €2.10) and Amboise (20 min., 2 per day, €1).

Surrounded by a walled medieval town that merits a visit in itself, the chateau of **Loches** consists of two structures at opposite ends of a hill. To the north, the 11th-century keep and watchtowers changed roles from keeping enemies out to keeping them in when Charles VII made it a state prison, complete with suspended cages. While the floors in the three-story tower to the south have fallen out, the walls and stairs remain; you can climb the staircase and take in a view of the village below. The **Logis Royal** (Royal Lodge) honors the famous ladies who held court here, including Charles VII's lover Agnès Sorel, the first officially declared Mistress of the King of France. (☎02 47 59 01 32. Open Apr.-Sept. daily 9am-7pm; Oct.-Mar. 9:30am-5pm. Logis Royal €3.80, students €2.70.) **Trains** and **buses** run from Tours to Loches (50 min., 13 per day, €7).

ANGERS

From illustrious aristocratic origins, Angers (pop. 160,000) has grown into a sophisticated modern city. Behind the massive stone walls of the **Château d'Angers,** on pl. Kennedy, the medieval Dukes of Anjou ruled the surrounding area and a certain island across the Channel. The 13th-century chateau remains a well-preserved haven of medieval charm in a city filled with shops and sights. Inside the chateau is the 14th-century **Tapisserie de l'Apocalypse,** the world's largest tapestry. (Open May to mid-Sept. daily 9:30am-7pm; mid-Sept. to Apr. 10am-5:30pm. €5.50, students €3.50.) Angers's other woven masterpiece is the 1930 **Chant du Monde** ("Song of the World"), in the **Musée Jean Lurçat,** 4 bd. Arago. (☎02 41 24 18 45. Open mid-June to mid-Sept. daily 9:30am-6:30pm; mid-Sept. to mid-June Su and Tu-Sa 10am-noon and 2-6pm. €3.50.) The **Musée Cointreau** offers tours of the factory where it makes the famous liqueur, a native of Angers since its creation in 1849, followed by a free tasting. Take bus #7 from the train station to *Cointreau*. (Open July-Aug. daily 10:30am-6:30pm; Sept.-June reduced hours. €5.50)

From r. de la Gare, **trains** leave for Paris (2-4hr., 3 per day, €44) and Tours (1hr., 12 per day, €14). **Buses** run from pl. de la République to Rennes (3hr., 2 per day, €16). To get from the station to the **tourist office,** at pl. du Président Kennedy, exit straight onto r. de la Gare, turn right at pl. de la Visitation on r. Talot, and turn left on bd. du Roi-René; it's on the right, across from the chateau. (☎02 41 23 50 00; www.angers-tourisme.com. Open June-Sept. M-Sa 9am-6:30pm, Su 10am-5pm; Oct.-May reduced hours.) Access the **Internet** at **Cyber Espace,** 25 r. de la Roë. (☎02 41 24 92 71. €3.85 per hr. Open M-Th 9am-10pm, F-Sa 9am-midnight, Su 2-8pm.) **Hôtel de l'Univers ❷,** 2, pl. de la Gare, near the train station, has comfortable rooms. (☎02 41 88 43 58; fax 02 41 86 97 28. Breakfast €5.60. Singles and doubles €25-50.) Walk further down r. de la Gare for the spacious **Royal Hôtel ❷,** 8 bis pl. de la Visitation. (☎ 02 41 88 30 25; fax 02 41 81 05 75. Breakfast €4.60. Singles and doubles €26-42. AmEx/MC/V.) Cheap food is abundant along **rue St-Laud** and **rue St-Aubin.** Grab groceries in **Galeries Lafayette,** at r. d'Alsace and pl. du Ralliement. (Open M-Sa 9:30am-7:30pm.) **Postal Code:** 49052.

PÉRIGORD AND AQUITAINE

Périgord presents seductive images: green countryside splashed with yellow sunflowers, white chalk cliffs, golden white wines, and plates of black truffles. The region has long been popular; first settled 150,000 years ago, the area around Les Eyzies-de-Tayac has produced more stone-age artifacts than anywhere on earth.

PÉRIGUEUX

Rich with tradition and gourmet cuisine, the lovely old quarters of Périgueux (pop. 65,000) have preserved significant architecture from the city's past, which goes back to Gallo-Roman times. The towering steeple and five massive cupolas of the **Cathédrale St-Front** dominate Périgueux from above the Isle river. Fifteen-hundred years of rebuilding, restoration, rethinking, and revision have produced the largest cathedral in southwestern France. (Open daily 8am-noon and 2:30-7pm.) Just down r. St-Front, the **Musée du Périgord,** 22 cours Tourny, houses one of France's most important collections of prehistoric artifacts, including a set of 2m mammoth tusks. (Open Apr.-Sept. M and W-F 10:30am-6pm, Sa-Su 1-6pm; Oct.-Mar. reduced hours. €4, students €2. Under-18 free.) The **Musée Gallo-Romain,** 20 r. du 26 Régiment d'Infanterie, has built an intricate walkway over the excavated ruins of the *Domus de Vésone,* once the home of a wealthy Roman merchant. (Open July-Aug. daily 10am-7pm; Sept.-June Su and Tu-Sa 10am-12:30pm and 2-6pm. €5.50.)

Trains leave r. Denis Papin for: Bordeaux (1½hr., 12 per day, €17); Paris (4-6hr., 12 per day, €57); and Toulouse (4hr., 8 per day, €33). The **tourist office,** 26 pl. Francheville, has free maps. From the station, turn right on r. Denis Papin, bear left on r. des Mobiles-de-Coulmierts, which becomes r. du Président Wilson, and take the next right after the Monoprix; it will be on the left. (☎ 05 53 53 10 63; www.ville-perigueux.fr. Open M-Sa 9am-1pm and 2-6pm.) Across from the train station, **Hôtel des Voyageurs ❶,** 26 r. Denis Papin, has clean, bright rooms. (☎/fax 05 53 53 17 44. Breakfast €3.20. Singles €13; doubles €15, with shower €18.) ▨**Au Bien Bon ❸,** 15 r. Aubergerie, serves exceptional regional cuisine. (☎ 05 53 09 69 91. *Menu* €10-14. Open M 7:30-10pm, Tu-Sa noon-2pm and 7:30-10pm.) **Monoprix supermarket** is on pl. de la République. (Open M-Sa 8:30am-8pm.) **Postal Code:** 24070.

SARLAT

The golden medieval *vieille ville* of Sarlat (pop. 11,000) has been the focus of tourist and movie cameras; Gérard Depardieu's *Cyrano de Bergerac* was filmed here. Today, its narrow 14th- and 15th-century streets fill with flea markets, dancing violinists, and purveyors of *gâteaux aux noix* (cakes with nuts) and golden Monbazillac wines. **Trains** go to Bordeaux (2½hr., 4 per day, €19) and Périgueux (3hr., 2 per day, €12). Sarlat **Buses** runs locally on two almost identical routes around town. Line A stops at the train station; line B at the roundabout one block away, down r. Dubois. (☎ 05 53 59 01 48. M-Sa 8:30am-5pm.) The **tourist office,** r. Tourny in the Ancien Eveche, can arrange accommodations. (☎ 05 53 31 45 45. Open Apr.-Oct. M-Sa 9am-7pm, Su 10am-noon and 2-6pm; Nov.-Mar. M-Sa 9am-noon and 2-7pm.) Sarlat's **Auberge de Jeunesse ❶,** 77 av. de Selves, is 40min. from the train station, but only 10min. from the *vieille ville.* From the *vieille ville,* go straight on r. de la République, which becomes av. Gambetta, and bear left at the fork onto av. de Selves. (☎ 05 53 59 47 59. Reception 6am-8:30pm. Open mid-Mar. to Nov. Reserve ahead. Dorms €10. **Camping** €6.) **Champion supermarket** is near the hostel on rte. de Montignac; continue following av. de Selves away from the *centre ville*. (Open M-Sa 9am-7:30pm, Su 9am-noon.) **Postal Code:** 24200.

▓ DAYTRIPS FROM SARLAT AND PÉRIGUEUX

CAVE PAINTINGS. The most spectacular cave paintings ever discovered line the **Caves of Lascaux,** near the town of **Montignac,** 25km north of Sarlat. They were discovered in 1940 by a couple of teenagers, but were closed in 1963—the hordes of tourists had fostered algae and micro-stalactites that ravaged the paintings. **Lascaux II** duplicates the original cave in the same pigments used 17,000 years ago. Although they may lack ancient awe and mystery, the new caves—filled with paintings of 5m tall bulls, horses, and bison—manage to inspire a wonder all their own. The **ticket office** (☎ 05 53 35 50 10) shares a building with Montignac's **tourist office** (☎ 05 53 51 82 60), on pl. Bertram-de-Born. (Ticket office open 9am until sold-out. €7.70.) The **train** station nearest Montignac is at Le Lardin, 10km away. From there, you can call a **taxi** (☎ 05 53 50 86 61). During the school year (Sept.-June), **CFTA** (☎ 05 55 86 07 07) runs buses from Périgueux (1½hr., daily, €6.10) and Sarlat (20 min., 3 per day, €4.60).

At the **Grotte de Font-de-Gaume,** 1km outside **Les Eyzies-de-Tayac** on D47, amazing 15,000-year-old paintings are still open for viewing. (☎ 05 53 06 86 00; www.leseyzies.com/grottes-ornees. Open mid-May to mid-Sept. Su-F 9am-5:30pm; mid-Sept. to mid-May reduced hours. Reserve in advance. €6.10, ages 18-25 €4.10. Under-18 free. Tours available in English.) Get more info at the **Point Accueil Prehistoire,** across from the post office, on the main street through town. (☎ 06 86 66 54 43. Open daily 9:15am-1:30pm and 3-7pm.) The **tourist office** is located at pl. de la Mairie, before the Point Accueil. (☎ 05 53 06 97 05; www.leseyzies.com. Open July-Aug. M-Sa 9am-8pm, Su 10am-noon and 2-6pm; Sept.-June reduced hours.) From Les Eyzies-de-Tayac, **trains** go to Périgueux (30min., 5 per day, €8.10) and Sarlat (1hr., 3 per day, €9.20) via Le Buisson.

THE DORDOGNE VALLEY. Steep, craggy cliffs and poplar tree thickets overlook the slow-moving turquoise waters of the Dordogne River, 15km south of Sarlat. The town of **Castelnaud-La-Chapelle,** 10km southwest of Sarlat, snoozes in the shadow of its pale yellow **chateau.** (☎ 05 53 31 30 00. Open July-Aug. daily 9am-8pm; May-June and Sept. 10am-6pm; mid-Nov. to Feb. Su-F 2-5pm. €6.40.) The town of **Domme** was built by King Philippe III in 1280 on a high dome of solid rock. Over 70 Templar Knights were imprisoned by King Philip IV in the **Porte des Tours.** The graffiti they scrawled upon the walls with their bare hands and teeth still remains. Consult the **tourist office,** pl. de la Halle, for tours and more info on exploring the region. (☎ 05 53 31 71 00. Open July-Aug. daily 10am-7pm; Sept.-June 10am-noon and 2-6pm.) To get to and around the valley, you'll need to rent a car or be prepared for a good bike workout. Many outfits along the Dordogne rent **canoes** and **kayaks.** At the Pont de Vitrac, near Domme, you can find them at **Canoës-Loisirs** (☎ 05 53 28 23 43) and **Périgord Aventure et Loisirs** (☎ 05 53 28 23 82).

BORDEAUX

Enveloped by emerald vineyards, Bordeaux (pop. 280,000) toasts the ruby wine that made it famous. Not just a mecca for wine connoisseurs, this spirited, diverse university town also has vibrant nightlife, a stunning opera house, and some of France's best food. Construction of a new transit system, currently disrupts the center of the city, but is expected to be complete by 2004.

■■ TRANSPORTATION AND PRACTICAL INFORMATION. Trains leave Gare St-Jean, r. Charles Domercq (☎ 05 56 33 11 06), for: Nice (9-10hr., 5 per day, €70); Paris (3½hr., 15-25 TGV per day, €58); and Toulouse (2-3hr., 11 per day, €27). From the train station, take bus #7 or 8 (dir.: Grand Théâtre) to pl. Gambetta and walk toward the Monument des Girondins to reach the **tourist office,** 12 cours du 30 juillet, which arranges winery tours. (☎ 05 56 00 66 00; www.bordeaux-tourisme.com. Open July-Aug. M-Sa 9am-7:30pm, Su 9:30am-6:30pm; Oct.-June reduced hours.) **Postal Code:** 33065.

■■ ACCOMMODATIONS AND FOOD. With its sunny rooms, all of which contain a bathroom, TV and phone, it's no wonder that **Hôtel Studio ❷**, 26 r. Huguerie, is a favorite among backpackers. (☎ 05 56 48 00 14; fax 05 56 81 25 71. Breakfast €4. **Internet** access €2.25 per hr. for hotel clientele, €4.50 for guests. Singles and doubles €16-27; triples €31; quads €38. MC/V.) **Hôtel de la Boétie ❷**, 4 r. de la Boétieis run by the same family and offers similar amenities. Check in is around the corner at Hôtel Bristol, 4 r. Bouffard. (☎ 05 56 81 76 68; fax 05 56 81 24 72. Breakfast €4. Singles €20-24; doubles €28; triples €31; quads €38. MC/V.) The newly renovated **Auberge de Jeunesse (HI) ❶**, 22 cours Barbey, is in a seedy area near the train station making the 30min. from the *centre ville* a little harrowing at night. (☎ 05 56 33 00 70; fax 05 56 33 00 71. Breakfast included. HI members €17, nonmembers add €1.60. MC/V.) For the **Hôtel Boulan ❷**, 28 r. Boulan, take bus #7 or 8 from the station to cours d'Albret. (☎ 05 56 52 23 62; fax 05 56 44 91 65. Breakfast €3.50. Singles €19; doubles €26. MC/V.)

Bordelais take their food as seriously as their wine. Hunt around **rue St-Remi** and **place St-Pierre** for splendid regional specialties, including oysters, beef braised in wine sauce, and the cake *canelé de Bordeaux.* **La Casuccia ❷**, 49 r. Saint Rémi, is perfect for an intimate dinner or a casual outing. (☎ 05 56 51 17 70. Open Su 7-11:30pm, Tu-Sa noon-3pm and 7-11:30pm. MC/V.) Stock up at **Auchan supermarket,** at the Centre Meriadeck on r. Claude Bonnier. (☎ 05 56 99 59 00. Open M-Sa 8:30am-10pm.)

■■ SIGHTS AND ENTERTAINMENT. Near the tourist office, on pl. de Quinconces, the elaborate fountains of the **Monument aux Girondins** commemorate revolutionary leaders from towns bordering the Gironde river. Retrace your steps to the breathtaking **Grand Théâtre,** on pl. de la Comédie, to see a performance or take a tour. (☎ 05 56 00 66 00. Tours €5, students €4.) Follow r. Ste-Catherine from the pl. de la Comédie, facing the theater, to reach the Gothic **Cathédrale St-André,** in pl. Pey-Berland. (Open Apr.-Oct. daily 8-11am and 2-5:30pm; Nov.-Mar. W and Sa 2:30-5:30pm. €4, under-25 and seniors €2.50.) Its bell tower, the **Tour Pey-Berland,** juts 50m into the sky. Climb the 229 spiraling steps for a beautiful view of the city. (☎ 05 56 81 25 26. Open daily June-Sept. 10am-6:30pm; Oct.-May Su and Tu-Sa 10am-noon and 2-5pm. €4, under-25 and seniors €2.50.) Walking toward the river along cours d'Alsace, turn left onto quai Richelieu for the **place de la Bourse,** whose pillars and fountains reflect Bordeaux's grandeur. The impressive **Musée des Beaux Arts,** 20 cours d'Albret, near the cathedral, began as a place to display Napoleon's spoils of war and now contains great works by artists such as Picasso, Seurat, Matisse, and Titian. (Open M and W-Su 11am-6pm. Permanent collection €4, joint pass for permanent and temporary collections €5.50, students free.)

A haven for the young, Bordeaux boasts a seemingly endless list of lively bars and nightclubs, including a gay scene rivaled only by that of Paris. For an overview of Bordeaux nightlife, pick up a copy of *Clubs and Concerts* at the tourist office. **Place de la Victoire** and **place Gambetta** are year-round hot spots. **El Bodegon,** on pl. de la Victoire, has theme nights and free giveaways on weekends. (Beer €2.50. Open M-Sa 7am-2am, Su 2pm-2am.)

🖪 DAYTRIP FROM BORDEAUX: ST-ÉMILION. Just 35km northeast of Bordeaux, St-Émilion (pop. 2,850) is home to viticulturists who have been refining their technique since Roman times. Today, they gently crush hectares of grapes to produce 23 million liters of wine annually. Vineyards aside, the medieval-style village itself is a pleasure to visit, with its winding narrow streets and cafe-lined square. The **Église Monolithe** is the largest subterranean church in Europe. The **tourist office**, at pl. des Créneaux, near the church tower, rents **bikes** (€14 per day) and offers guided tours (€9) of the local chateaux. (☎05 57 55 28 28. Open July-Aug. daily 9:30am-8pm; Sept.-June reduced hours.) **Trains** run from Bordeaux to St-Émilion (30min., 4 per day, €7).

THE PAYS BASQUE AND GASCONY

South of Aquitaine, the forests recede and the mountains of Gascony begin, shielded from the Atlantic by the Basque Country. Long renowned as fierce fighters, the Basques continue to struggle to maintain their identity, with some separatists claiming that they are an independent people rather than a part of France or Spain. The Gascons, meanwhile, have long considered themselves French. Today, people come to Gascony to be healed: millions of believers descend on Lourdes hoping for miracle cures, while thousands of others undergo natural treatments in the *thermes* of the Pyrenees.

BAYONNE

The pace of life in Bayonne (pop. 43,000) has not changed for centuries. Here the word for walk is *flâner*, meaning "to stroll," rather than *marcher* or even *se promener*. Towering above it all, the Gothic 13th-century **Cathédrale Ste-Marie** marks the leisurely passing of the time with the tolling of its bells. (Open June-Sept. M-Sa 7:30am-noon and 3-7pm, Su 3:30-8pm; Oct.-May reduced hours.) The **Musée Bonnat**, 5 r. Jacques Laffitte, in Petit-Bayonne, contains works by Degas, El Greco, and Goya. (Open May-Oct. M and W-Su 10am-6:30pm; Nov.-Apr. reduced hours. €5.50, students €3.) The **Harmonie Bayonnaise** orchestra holds traditional Basque **concerts** in pl. de Gaulle. (July-Aug. Th at 9:30pm. Free.)

   Trains depart from the station in pl. de la République, running to: Bordeaux (2hr., 9 per day, €22); Toulouse (4hr., 5 per day, €32); and San Sebastián, Spain (1½hr., 6 per day, €8). Local STAB **buses** depart from the Hôtel de Ville for Biarritz (every 30-40min.; last bus M-Sa 8pm, Su 7pm; €1.20). The **tourist office**, on pl. des Basques, finds rooms. From the train station, take the middle fork onto pl. de la République, veer right over pont St-Esprit, pass through pl. Réduit, cross pont Mayou, and turn right on r. Bernède which becomes av. Bonnat. The tourist office is on the left. (☎05 59 46 01 46; www.bayonne-tourisme.com. Open July-Aug. M-Sa 9am-7pm, Su 10am-1pm; Sept.-June M-F 9am-6:30pm, Sa 10am-6pm.) The **🖪Hôtel Paris-Madrid ❷**, on pl. de la Gare, has cozy rooms and friendly proprietors. (☎05 59 55 13 98. Breakfast €4. Reception 6am-12:30am. Singles and doubles €16-22; triples and quads €44.) Get groceries at **Monoprix supermarket,** 8 r. Orbe. (Open M-Sa 8:30am-7:30pm.) **Postal Code:** 64100.

BIARRITZ

A playground for the wealthy since the 19th century, Biarritz (pop. 29,000) can still put a dent in the wallet, but its free **beaches** make it an option for budget travelers as well. Surfers ride the waves and bathers soak up the sun at **Grande Plage,** while bathers repose *au naturel* just to the north at the less-crowded **Plage Miramar.** A short **hike** to **Pointe St-Martin** affords a priceless view of the water.

BASQUE ME NO QUESTIONS

In Bayonne, the capital of France's Basque region, restaurants post signs reading "Euskara badikigu." Years of Latin lessons won't help you discover that this means "Basque spoken here," for Basque is the only non-Indo-European language spoken in Western Europe. Basque might not be the language of Babel, as believed in the 18th century, but Basques are tied to an ancient past—geneticists recently found a link between Basques and Celts. Recent talk of Basque identity, however, has focused on the the ETA (Basque Homeland and Liberty), a radical movement based in Spain that organizes attacks in the name of independence. As violence continues in Spain, France has cracked down on ETA training cells and imprisoned members for acts of terrorism.

Only 10% of French Basques vote for Basque parties, and even fewer support the ETA's radical ideology. How has France escaped Spain's problems? French Basques did not experience the cultural oppression that their Spanish counterparts did under Franco, and scholars suggest that tolerance toward French Basque culture has actually aided in their assimilation with the larger nation. The Pays Basque remains on the middle ground, balancing its cultural identity between extremes of separatism and assimilation.

Trains leave from Biarritz-la-Négresse (☎ 05 59 23 04 84), 3km from town, for Bordeaux (2hr., 7 per day, €26) and Paris (5hr., 5 TGVs per day, €67). The **tourist office**, 1 sq. d'Ixelles, finds accommodations. (☎ 05 59 22 37 10; fax 05 59 24 97 80. Open July-Aug. daily 8am-8pm; Sept.-June reduced hours.) The 🏠**Auberge de Jeunesse (HI) ❶**, 8 r. de Chiquito de Cambo, has a friendly staff and lakefront location at the *Francis Jammes* stop on bus line #2. (☎ 05 59 41 76 00; fax 05 59 41 76 07. **Internet** access €2.50 per 30min. Dorms €13. Amex/MC/V.) **Hôtel Barnetche ❷**, 5 bis r. Charles-Floquet, is one of the best values in the *centre ville*. (☎ 05 59 24 22 25; www.hotel-barnetche.fr. Breakfast €6. Reception 7:30am-10:30pm. Open May-Sept. Dorms €17; singles €35; doubles €58.) Cheap eateries can be found along **Rue Mazagran** and **Place Clemenceau**. Stock up at **Shopi supermarket**, 2 r. du Centre, is just off r. Gambetta. (Open 9am-12:45pm and 3:30-5pm.) **Postal Code:** 64200.

🔁 DAYTRIP FROM BIARRITZ: ST-JEAN-DE-LUZ.

The vibrant seaport of St-Jean-de-Luz lures visitors with the **Maison Louis XIV**, pl. Louis XIV, which temporarily housed the Sun King. (Open July-Aug. M-Sa 10:30am-12:30pm and 2:30-6:30pm, Su 2:30-6:30pm; Sept.-June closes 5:30pm. €4.50. Tours every 30min.) The village's earlier days of piracy funded its unique buildings, exemplified in the **Église St-Jean-Baptiste**, r. Gambetta, built to resemble a fishing boat. (Open daily 10am-noon and 2-6pm.) **Trains** roll in to bd. du Cdt. Passicot from Biarritz (15min., 10 per day, €2.50) and Bayonne (30min., 7 per day, €3.90). ATCRB **buses** (☎ 05 59 08 00 33), across from the train station, also run to Bayonne (35min., 7-13 per day, €3.60) and Biarritz (25min., 7-13 per day, €2.80). The **tourist office** is at pl. Foch. (☎ 05 59 26 03 16 05; fax 05 59 26 21 47. Open July-Aug. M-Sa 9am-7pm, Su 10:30am-1pm and 3-7pm; Sept.-June reduced hours). **Postal Code:** 64500.

LOURDES

In 1858, 14-year-old Bernadette Soubirous saw the first of 18 visions of the Virgin Mary in the Massabielle grotto in Lourdes (pop. 16,300). Today five million visitors from across the globe make the pilgrimage each year. To get to **La Grotte de Massabielle** and the three **basilicas**, follow av. de la Gare, turn left on bd. de la Grotte, and follow it to the right and across the river Gave. Processions depart daily from the grotto at 5pm and 8:45pm. (No shorts or tank tops. Grotto open daily 5am-midnight. Basilicas open Easter to Oct. daily 6am-7pm; Nov.-Easter 8am-6pm.)

Trains leave the station, 33 av. de la Gare, for: Bayonne (2hr., 5 per day, €18); Bordeaux (3hr., 7 per day, €28); Paris (7-9hr., 5 per day, €86); and Toulouse (2½hr., 8 per day, €21). To reach the **tourist office,** on pl. Peyramale, turn right onto av. de la Gare, bear left onto av. Marasin, cross a bridge above bd. du Papacca, and climb uphill. The office is to the right. (☎05 62 42 77 40; lourdes@sudfr.com. Open May-Oct. M-Sa 9am-7pm; Nov.-Apr. reduced hours.) The newly-renovated **Hôtel du Commerce ❸,** 11 r. Basse, faces the tourist office. (☎05 62 94 59 23; hotel-commerce-et-navarre@wanadoo.fr. Breakfast €3.80. July to mid-Oct. singles €32; doubles €38; triples €45; mid-Oct. to June reduced prices. MC/V.) **Camping and Hôtel de la Poste ❶,** 26 r. de Langelle, 2min. from the post office, offers a campground and attached hotel. (☎05 62 94 40 35. Open Easter to mid-Oct. Electricity €2.50. Showers €1.30. €2.50 per person, €3.60 per site.) The cheapest eateries are near the tourist office, away from the touristy main strip. **Postal Code:** 65100.

CAUTERETS

Nestled in a narrow, breathtaking valley on the edge of the **Parc National des Pyrenees Occidentales** is tiny, friendly Cauterets (pop. 1,300). Cauterets's hot sulfuric *thermes* have long been instruments of healing; for more info, contact **Thermes de Cesar,** av. Docteur Domer. (☎05 62 92 51 60. Open M-F 9am-12:30pm and 2-5pm.) Today, most visitors come to ski and hike. For **hiking** info and advice, head to Parc National des Pyrenees (see below). **Skilys,** rte. de Pierrefitte, on pl. de la Gare, rents **bikes** and **skates.** (☎05 62 92 52 10. Bikes €15.30 per day. Open in winter daily 8am-7:30pm; off-season 9am-7pm.)

SNCF **buses** run from pl. de la Gare to Lourdes (1hr., 6 per day, €6). The **tourist office,** on pl. Foch, has free maps of ski trails. (☎05 62 92 50 27; www.cauterets.com. Open July-Aug. daily 9:30am-12:30pm and 1:30-7pm; Sept.-June reduced hours.) ▧**Gite d'Etape UCJG ❶,** av. du Docteur Domer, has a great location and friendly staff. From the Parc National office, cross the street and turn left uphill on a footpath underneath the funicular depot. (☎05 62 92 52 95. Open June 15-Sept. 15. Dorms €8; camping and tent rental €6.50.) **Postal Code:** 65110.

▶ **DAYTRIP FROM CAUTERETS: THE PYRENEES.** The striking **Parc National des Pyrenees** shelters thousands of endangered animals in its snow-capped mountains and lush valleys. Touch base with the friendly and helpful **Parc National Office,** Maison du Parc, pl. de la Gare, before braving the wilderness; they have tons of info on the park and the 15 trails beginning and ending in Cauterets. The trails in the park are designed for wide range of skill levels, from novice hiker to rugged outdoorsman. (☎05 62 92 62 97; www.parc-pyranees.com. Open June-Aug. daily 9:30am-noon and 3-7pm; Sept.-May M-Tu and F-Su 9:30am-12:30pm and 3-6pm, Th 3-6pm.) From Cauterets, the **GR10** winds through **Luz-St-Saveur,** over the mountain, and then on to **Gavarnie,** another day's hike up the valley; this is also known as the **circuit de Gavarnie.** One of the most spectacular trails follows the GR10 to the turquoise **Lac de Gaube** and then to the end of the glacial valley (2hr. past the lake) where you can spend the night at the **Refuges Des Oulettes ❶,** the first shelter past the lake. (☎05 62 92 62 97. Open June-Sept. €13.)

LANGUEDOC-ROUSSILLON

An immense region called Occitania once stretched from the Rhône Valley to the foothills of the Pyrenees. It was eventually integrated into the French kingdom, and its Cathar religion was severely persecuted by the Crown and Church. Their *langue d'oc* dialect of French faded, and in 1539, the northern *langue d'oïl* became official. Latent nationalism lingers, however, in vibrant cities like Toulouse and Pérpignan. Many locals speak Catalán, a relative of *langue d'oc*, and feel a stronger cultural connection with Barcelona than Paris.

TOULOUSE

Sassy, headstrong Toulouse—*la ville en rose* (city in pink)—provides a breath of fresh air along with stately architecture and a vibrant twenty-something scene. A rebellious city during the Middle Ages, Toulouse (pop. 350,000) has always retained an element of independence, pushing the frontiers of knowledge as a university town and the prosperous capital of the French aerospace industry.

▣▨ TRANSPORTATION AND PRACTICAL INFORMATION. Trains leave Gare Matabiau, 64 bd. Pierre Sémard, for: Bordeaux (2-3hr., 14 per day, €27); Lyon (6½hr., 3-4 per day, €48); Marseilles (4½hr., 8 per day, €39); and Paris (8-9hr., 4 per day, €75). To get from the station to the **tourist office,** r. Lafayette, in sq. Charles de Gaulle, turn left along the canal, turn right on allée Jean Jaurès, bear right around pl. Wilson, and turn right on r. Lafayette; it's in a park near r. d'Alsace-Lorraine. You can also take the Métro to *Capitole.* (☎ 05 61 11 02 22; www.mairie-toulouse.fr. Open Jun.-Sept. M-Sa 9am-7pm, Su 10am-1pm and 2-6pm; Oct.-May reduced hours.) Surf the **Internet** at **Espace Wilson Multimedia,** 7 allée du Président Roosevelt. (€3 per hr. Open M-F 10am-7pm, Sa 10am-6pm.) **Postal Code:** 31000.

▨▣ ACCOMMODATIONS AND FOOD. While it lacks a youth hostel, Toulouse has a number of well-located budget hotels. To reach the spacious ▨**Hôtel des Arts ❷**, 1bis r. Cantegril off r. des Arts, take the Métro (dir.: Basso Cambo) to *pl. Esquirol.* Walk down r. de Metz, away from the river; r. des Arts is on the left. (☎ 05 61 23 36 21; fax 05 61 12 22 37. Breakfast €4. Singles €15-21, with shower €23-25; doubles €25/26-28. MC/V.) Antoine de St-Exupéry always stayed in room #32 at the **Hôtel du Grand Balcon ❸**, 8 r. Romiguières. (☎/fax 05 61 62 77 59. Breakfast €4. Singles and doubles €26, with bath €36; triples with bath €45.) Take bus #59 to *Camping* to **camp** at **Pont de Rupé ❶**, 21 chemin du Pont de Rupé. (☎ 05 61 70 07 35. €9, €3 per additional person.) **Markets** line **place des Carmes** and **place Victor Hugo.** (Open Su and Tu-Sa 6am-1pm.). A cross between a restaurant, an art gallery and a small theater, **Le Grand Rideau ❸**, 75 r. du Taur, serves regional food in a three-course lunch (€9) and an evening *menu* (€14.) in an eclectic atmosphere. (☎ 05 61 23 90 19. Open M noon-2pm, Tu-F noon-2pm and 7pm-midnight.)

▣▨ SIGHTS AND ENTERTAINMENT. The **Capitole,** the brick palace next door to the tourist office, is the city's most prominent monument. (Open M-F 8:30am-noon and 1:30-7pm, Sa-Su 10am-noon and 2-6pm.) Rue du Taur leads to the **Basilique St-Sernin,** the longest Romanesque structure in the world; its **crypt** houses ecclesiastical relics gathered from Charlemagne's time. (Church open July-Sept. M-Sa 8:30am-6:15pm, Su 8:30am-7:30pm; Oct.-June reduced hours. Free. Crypt open July-Sept. M-Sa 10am-6pm, Su 11:30-6pm; Oct.-June reduced hours. €2.) Backtrack to the pl. du Capitole, take a right on r. Romiguières, and turn left on r. Lakanal to get to the **Réflectoire des Jacobins,** 69 r. Pargaminières, which has exhibitions of archaeological artifacts and modern art. (Open daily 10am-7pm. €5.) Nearby on r. Lakanal, a 13th-century southern Gothic **church** holds the remains of St. Thomas Aquinas in an elevated, underlit tomb. (Open daily 9am-7pm.) Retracing your steps on r. de Metz takes you to the restored **Hôtel d'Assézat,** at pl. d'Assézat on r. de Metz, which houses the **Fondation Bemberg,** an impressive array of Bonnards, Gauguins, and Pisarros. (Open Su, Tu and F-Sa 10am-12:30pm and 1:30-6pm. €2.80.) Toulouse has something to please almost any nocturnal whim, although nightlife is liveliest when students are in town. Numerous cafes flank **place St-Georges** and **place du Capitole,** and late-night bars line **rue St-Rome** and **rue des Filatiers.** The best dancing is at **Bodega-Bodega,** 1 r. Gabriel Péri, just off bd. Lazare Carnot. (Cover €6 Th-Sa 10pm-2am. Open Su-F 7pm-2am, Sa 7pm-6am.)

CARCASSONNE

When approaching breathtaking Carcassonne (pop. 45,000), you realize that Beauty may have fallen in love with the Beast in this fairy-tale city. However, its charm is no secret; the narrow streets of the *cité* are flooded with tourists. Its walls and fortifications date back to the 1st century. Built as a palace in the 12th century, the **Château Comtal,** 1 r. Viollet-le-Duc, became a citadel after royal take-over in 1226. (Open June-Sept. daily 9am-7:30pm; Apr.-Oct. reduced hours. €6.10, under-25 €4.10.) Turned into a fortress after the city was razed during the Hundred Years' War in 1355, the Gothic **Cathédrale St-Michel,** r. Voltaire, in bastide St-Louis, still has fortifications on its southern side. (Open M-Sa 7am-noon and 2-7pm, Su 9:30am-noon.) The evening is the best time to experience the *cité* without the crowds. Although nightlife is limited, several bars and cafes along **boulevard Omer Sarraut** and **place Verdun** are open late. Locals dance all night at **La Bulle,** 115 r. Barbacane. (☎04 68 72 47 70. Cover €9, includes 1 drink. Open F-Sa until dawn.)

Trains (☎04 68 71 79 14) depart behind Jardin St-Chenier for: Marseilles (3hr., every 2hr., €36); Nice (6hr., 5 per day, €47); Nîmes (2½hr., 12 per day, €25); and Toulouse (50min., 24 per day, €14). Shops, hotels, and the train station are in the **bastide St-Louis,** once known as the *basse ville* (lower city). Free **shuttles** run from sq. Gambetta to the more touristed *cité.* From the station, walk down av. de Maréchal Joffre, which becomes r. Clemenceau; after pl. Carnot, turn left on r. Verdun, which leads to sq. Gambetta and the **tourist office,** 15 bd. Camille Pelletan. (☎04 68 10 24 30; www.carcassonne-tourisme.com. Open July-Aug. daily 9am-7pm; Sept.-June 9am-1pm and 2-6pm.) The ⬛**Auberge de Jeunesse (HI) ❶,** r. de Vicomte Trencavel, is in the *cité,* has a great view of the castle late at night. (☎04 68 25 23 16; carcassonne@fuaj.org. Sheets €2.70. **Internet** €3 per hr. Dorms €13. HI members only. MC/V.) **Hôtel Le Cathare ❷,** 53 r. Jean Bringer, is near the post office in the lower city. (☎04 68 25 65 92. Reception 8am-7pm. Singles and doubles €18, with shower €26; triples €46-53. MC/V.) **Camping de la Cité ❷,** rte. de St-Hilaire, 2km from town across the Aude, has a pool and a grocery store. A shuttle runs there from the train station. (☎04 68 25 11 77. Reception 8am-9pm. Open Mar.-Oct. €17 per site, €4.80 per person.) The regional speciality is *cassoulet* (a stew of white beans, herbs, and meat). Restaurants on **rue du Plo** have *menus* under €10, but save room for *crêperies* around **place Marcou** for dessert. **Postal Code:** 11000.

MONTPELLIER

Capital of Languedoc and a bustling college town, Montpellier (pop. 230,000) has earned a reputation as the most light-hearted city in southern France, with superb shopping and nightlife. The gigantic **Musée Fabre,** 39 bd. Bonne Nouvelle, is undergoing renovations until 2006, but part of its substantial collection is on display on a rotating basis at the **pavillion** on the opposite side of Esplanade Charles de Gaulle from the museum. (☎04 67 66 13 46. Open Su and Tu-Sa 1-7pm. Hours vary, call in advance. €3, students €1.) Bd. Henri IV leads to the **Jardin des Plantes,** France's first botanical garden. (Open June-Sept. M-Sa noon-8pm, Oct.-May M-Sa noon-6pm.) At sundown, **rue de la Loge** fills with vendors, musicians, and stilt-walkers. The most animated bars are scattered along **place Jean-Jaurès.** The popular **Barberousse "Bar A Shooters,"** 6 r. Boussairolles, just off pl. de la Comédie, sells 73 flavors of rum. (Rum €2. Beer €3. Open M-Sa 6pm-2am.) Gay nightlife is prominent in Montpellier, with establishments scattered throughout the *vielle ville.*

Trains leave pl. Auguste Gibert for Avignon (1¼hr., 10 per day, €13); Marseilles (1¾hr., 9 per day, €21); Paris (3½hr., 12 per day, €84); and Toulouse (2½hr., 10 per day, €29). From the train station, r. Maguelone leads to **place de la Comédie,** Montpellier's modern center. The **tourist office,** 30 allée Jean de Lattre de Tassigny, is to the right. (☎04 67 60 60 60; www.ot-montpellier.fr. Open July-Aug. M-F 9am-

7:30pm, Sa 9:30am-6pm, Su 9:30am-1pm and 2:30-6pm; Sept.-May reduced hours.) Access the Internet at **Cybercafé www**, 12 bis r. Jules Ferry, across from the train station. (€1.50 per hr. Open daily 9am-1am.) To reach the **Auberge de Jeunesse (HI) ❶**, 2 impasse de la Petite Corraterie, walk from pl. de la Comédie onto r. de la Loge. Turn right onto r. Jacques Cœur and walk until you reach impasse de la Petite Corraterie, just before bd. Louis Blanc, and turn right. The hostel has sunny rooms and large windows. (☎04 67 60 32 22; montpellier@fuaj.org. Breakfast €3. Lockout 10am-1pm. Curfew 2am. Dorms €8.40. MC/V. **Hotel d'Angleterre ❸**, 7 r. Maguelone, is comfortable and centrally located. (☎04 67 58 59 50; www.hotel-d-angle-terre.com. Breakfast €5.50. Singles with shower €28; doubles €28-50. Amex/MC/V.) French cuisine dominates Montpellier's *vielle ville*, while a number of ethnic restaurants have taken hold on **rue des Écoles Laïques**. Get groceries at **Supermarket INNO**, in the basement of the Polygone commercial center, just past the tourist office. (Open M-Sa 9am-8:30pm.) **Postal Code:** 34000.

PROVENCE

Carpets of olive groves and vineyards unroll along hills dusted with lavender, sunflowers, and mimosas, while the fierce winds of the *mistral* carry the scent of sage, rosemary, and time well-spent. Generations of writers and artists have found inspiration in Provence's varied landscape—from the Roman arena and cobblestoned elegance of Arles to Cézanne's lingering footsteps in Aix-en-Provence, life unfolds along Provence's shaded paths like a bottomless glass of *pastis*.

NÎMES

Southern France flocks to Nîmes (pop. 132,000) for the *férias*, celebrations featuring bullfights, flamenco dancing, and other hot-blooded fanfare. Yet Nîmes's star attractions are its incredible Roman structures. The magnificent **Les Arènes** is a well-preserved first-century Roman amphitheater that still holds bullfights and concerts. (☎04 66 76 72 77. Open M-F 10am-6pm. €4.50, students €3.20.) North of the arena stands the exquisite **Maison Carrée**, a rectangular temple built in the first century BC. (☎04 66 36 26 76. Open June-Sept. daily 9am-7pm; Oct.-May 10am-6pm.) Across the square, the **Carrée d'Art** houses an excellent collection of contemporary art. (☎04 66 76 35 70. Open Tu-Su 10am-6pm. €4.50, students €3.20.) Along the canals to the left, off pl. Foch, the **Jardins de la Fontaine** hold the Roman ruins of the **Temple de Diane** and the **Tour Magne**. (Garden open Apr.-Sept. daily 7:30am-10pm; Oct.-Mar. 8am-6:30pm; free. Tower open July-Aug. daily 9am-7pm; Sept.-June 9am-5pm; €2.40, students €2.)

Trains chug from bd. Talabot to: Arles (20min., 13 per day, €6.30); Marseilles (1¼hr., 20 per day, €12); and Toulouse (3hr., 8 per day, €30). **Buses** (☎04 66 29 52 00) depart from behind the train station for Avignon (1½hr., 2-8 per day, €6.70). The **tourist office** is at 6 r. Auguste, just off pl. Comédie and near the Maison Carrée. (☎04 66 58 38 00; fax 04 66 58 38 01. Open July-Aug. M-F 8am-8pm, Sa 9am-7pm, Su 10am-6pm; May and Sept. reduced hours.) The newly renovated ▨**Auberge de Jeunesse (HI) ❶** is 4.5km from quai de la Fontaine, at 257 chemin de l'Auberge de la Jeunesse, off chemin de la Cigale. Take bus #2 (dir.: Alès or Villeverte) to *Stade, Route d'Alès* and follow the signs uphill; after buses stop running, call for pick-up. This comfortable, well-kept hostel is well worth the trek. (☎04 66 68 03 20; fax 04 66 68 03 21. Breakfast €3.20. Sheets €2.80 per week. **Internet** access €3.80 per hr. Mar.-Sept. 4- to 6-bed dorms €9.50. **Camping** €5.50. Members only. MC/V.) Stock up at **Marché U supermarket**, 19 r. d'Alès, downhill from the hostel. (Open M-Sa 8am-12:45pm and 3:30-8pm.) **Postal Codes:** 30000 and 30900.

☒ DAYTRIP FROM NÎMES: PONT DU GARD. In 19 BC, Augustus's close friend and advisor Agrippa built an aqueduct to channel water 50km to Nîmes from the Eure springs near Uzès. The architectural fruit of this 15-year project remains in the Pont du Gard, spanning the gorge of the Gardon River and towering over sunbathers and swimmers. A great way to see the Pont du Gard is to start from **Collias,** 6km toward Uzès. Here **Kayak Vert** rents canoes, kayaks, and bikes. (☎66 22 80 76. Canoes and kayaks €14 per day, kayak/canoe rental and shuttle €16, bikes €17 per day. 15% discount for students or with stay at the hostel in Nîmes.) STDG **buses** (☎04 66 29 27 29) run to the Pont du Gard from Avignon (45min., 7 per day, €5) and Nîmes (30min., 2-5 per day, €4.75). **Camping le Barralet ❶,** r. des Aires in Collias, offers a pool and hot showers. (☎04 66 22 84 52; fax 04 66 22 89 17. Closed Oct.-Feb. €6-8 per person. Mar.-June and Sept. reduced prices. MC/V.)

AVIGNON

Known to most as the home of the bridge made famous by the children's song, the city of Avignon (pop. 100,000) also hosts Europe's most prominent theater festival. A reminder of Avignon's brief stint as the center of the Catholic Church, the 14th-century golden **🖾Palais des Papes** keeps watch over the city with its gargoyles. Although Revolutionary looting stripped the interior of its lavish furnishings, the giant rooms and their frescoed walls are still remarkable. (☎04 90 27 50 74. Open July-Sept. daily 9am-8pm; Apr.-June and Oct. 9am-7pm; Nov. to Mar. 9:30am-5:45pm. €7.50.) The most prestigious theatrical gathering in Europe, the **🖾Festival d'Avignon** appears in at least 30 different venues, from factories to cloisters to palaces. (☎04 90 14 14 14; www.festival-avignon.com. July-early Aug. Tickets up to €30. Some shows free. Reservations accepted from mid-June. Standby tickets available 45min. before shows; 50% student discount.) The also well-established, more experimental **Festival OFF** also takes place in July. (OFFice on pl. du Palais. ☎01 48 05 01 19; www.avignon-off.org. Tickets purchased at the venue or the OFFice; not available over the phone. Tickets €0-16.) Tickets are not necessary to experience the festivals; free theatrical performances often spill into the streets, especially at night. During the festival most eateries stay open late as well. **Place des Corps Saints** has a few lively bars.

Trains (☎04 90 27 81 89) run from porte de la République to: Arles (30min., 19 per day, €5.70); Marseilles (1¼hr., 15 per day, €16); Nîmes (30min., 12 per day, €7.10); and Paris (TGV 3½hr., 13 per day, €80). **Buses** leave from bd. St-Roch, to the right of the train station, for Arles (45min., 5 per day, €7.80) and Marseilles (2hr., 5 per day, €16). From the train station, walk through porte de la République to cours Jean Jaurès to reach the **tourist office,** 41 cours Jean Jaurès (☎04 32 74 32 74; www.ot-avignon.fr. Open Apr.-Sept. M-Sa 9am-6pm, Su 10am-5pm.; Oct.-Mar. reduced hours.) Take an **Internet** break at **Webzone,** 3 r. St-Jean le Vieux, at pl. Pie. (☎04 32 76 29 47. €4 per hr. Open daily 9am-midnight.) Avignon's hotels and *foyers* usually have room; although they fill up fast during festival season; book well ahead or try staying in Arles or Nîmes. The **Foyer YMCA/UCJG ❶,** 7bis chemin de la Justice, is across the river in Villeneuve. From the station, turn left and follow the city wall, cross pont Daladier and Ile Barthelasse, walk straight ahead, and turn left on chemin de la Justice; it will be up the hill on your left. (☎04 90 25 46 20; www.ymca-avignon.com. Reception 8:30am-noon and 1:30-6pm. *Demi-pension* obligatory in July. Dorms €15. AmEx/MC/V.) The **Hôtel Splendid ❸,** 17 r. Perdiguier, near the tourist office, lives up to its name. (☎04 90 86 14 46; fax 04 90 85 38 55. Breakfast €5. Reception 7am-11pm. Singles €30-34; doubles €40-46. MC/V.) **Camp** at **Pont d'Avignon ❶,** 300 Ile de la Barthelasse. (☎04 90 80 63 50; fax 04 90 85 22 12. Reception daily 8am-10pm. Open Mar. 27-Oct. 28. €15 per person with tent or car, €4 per extra person. Off-season reduced prices.) **Rue des Teinturiers** hosts a number of restaurants. A **Petit Casino supermarket** is on r. St-Agricol. (Open M-F 8am-8pm, Sa-Su 9am-8pm.) **Postal Code:** 84000.

FRANCE

ARLES

The beauty and ancient history of Arles (pop. 35,000) have made it a Provence favorite. A reminder of Arles's former position as the capital of Roman Gaul, the great Roman arena, **Les Arènes**, is still used for bullfights. (€4, students €3.) The city's Roman past comes back to life in the excellent **Musée d'Arles Antique**, on av. de la 1er D.F.L. (Open daily Mar.-Oct. 9am-7pm; Nov.-Feb. 10am-5pm. €5.40, students €3.80.) The **Fondation Van Gogh**, 26 Rond-Point des Arènes, houses tributes to the master painter by artists, poets, and composers. (Open daily 10am-7pm. €5, students €3.50.) The contemporary **Musée Réattu**, r. du Grand Prieuré, houses 57 drawings with which Picasso honored Arles in 1971. (Open May-Sept. daily 10am-noon and 2-6:30pm; Oct.-Apr. reduced hours. €4, students €3.) The city celebrates **Fête d'Arles** in costume the last weekend in June and the first in July.

Trains leave av. P. Talabot for: Avignon (20min., 17 per day, €5.50); Marseilles (1hr., 20 per day, €11); Montpellier (1hr., 5 per day, €12); and Nîmes (30min., 8 per day, €6.30). **Buses** (☎ 04 90 49 38 01) depart from next to the station for Avignon (45min., M-Sa 6 per day, €8.10) and Nîmes (1hr., M-Sa 6 per day, €5.20). To get to the **tourist office**, esplanade Charles de Gaulle on bd. des Lices, turn left from the station, walk to pl. Lamartine, turn left and follow bd. Emile Courbes to the big intersection, and then turn right on bd. des Lices. (☎ 04 90 18 41 20; fax 04 90 18 41 29. Open daily Apr.-Sept. 9am-6:45pm; Oct.-Mar. reduced hours.) To get from the tourist office to the **Auberge de Jeunesse (HI) ❶**, on av. Maréchal Foch, cross bd. des Lices and follow the signs down av. des Alyscamps. (☎ 04 90 96 18 25; fax 04 90 96 31 26. Breakfast included. Reception 7-10am and 5-11pm. Lockout 10am-5pm. Curfew midnight; in winter 11pm. Reserve ahead Apr.-June. Dorms €14; €12 after 1st night.) **Hôtel le Rhône ❸**, 11 pl. Voltaire, has pastel-painted rooms and an inviting breakfast loft. (☎ 04 90 96 43 70; fax 04 90 93 87 03. Breakfast €5. Singles and doubles €26-39, with shower €30-33; triples with shower €36, with toilet €43. MC/V.) Take the Starlette bus to Clemencau and then take bus #2 (dir.: Pont de Crau) to Hermite for **Camping-City ❶**, 67 rte. de Crau. (☎ 04 90 93 08 86. Reception 8am-8pm. Open Apr.-Sept. €4 per person, €3 per car.) **Monoprix supermarket** is on pl. Lamartine by the station. (Open M-Sa 8:30am-8pm.) **Place du Forum** and **place Voltaire** have many cafes. **Postal Code:** 13200.

▶ DAYTRIP FROM ARLES: THE CAMARGUE. Between Arles and the Mediterranean coast stretches the Camargue. Pink flamingos, black bulls, and the famous white Camargue horses roam freely across this flat expanse of protected wild marshland. The **Parc Ornithologique de Pont de Gau**, along D570, offers views of birds and grazing bulls. (Open Apr.-Sept. daily 9am-dusk; Oct.-Mar. 10am-dusk. €5.50.) The best way to see the Camargue is on horseback; call the **Association Camarguaise de Tourisme Equestre** (☎ 04 90 97 10 10; €12 per hr, €33 per half-day) for more info. Other options include jeep safaris (☎ 04 90 97 89 33; 2hr. trip €31, 4hr. trip €37) and boat trips (☎ 04 90 97 84 72; 1½hr., 3 per day, €10). Biking is another way to see the area, and informative trail maps are available from the **tourist office** in Stes-Maries-de-la-Mer, 5 av. Van Gogh. (☎ 04 90 97 82 55. Open July-Aug. daily 9am-8pm; Sept.-June reduced hours.) Arles runs **buses** to Stes-Maries-de-la-Mer (1hr., 5 per day, €4.80), the region's largest town.

AIX-EN-PROVENCE

Famous for festivals, fountains, and former residents Paul Cézanne and Victor Vasarely, Aix (pop. 137,000) caters to tourists without being ruined by them. The **Chemin de Cézanne**, 9 av. Paul Cézanne, features a self-guided walking tour, including the artist's studio. (☎ 04 42 21 06 53. Open June-Sept. daily 10am-6:30pm; Oct.-May reduced hours. €5.50, students €2.) The **Fondation Vasarely**, av. Marcel-Pagnol, in Jas-de-Bouffan, designed by artist Victor Vasarely, is a must-see for modern art fans. (☎04 42 20 01 09. Open July-Sept. daily 10am-7pm; Oct.-June 10am-1pm and 2-6pm. €7, students €4.) **Cathédrale St-Sauveur,** r. Gaston de Saporta, on pl. de l'Université, is a dramatic mix of Romanesque, Gothic, and Baroque carvings and reliefs. (☎04 42 23 45 65. Open daily 9am-noon and 2-6pm.) In June and July, Aix's **International Music Festival** brings in operas and concerts. (☎04 42 17 34 34; www.aix-en-provence.com/festartlyrique. Tickets from €6.) Aix also hosts a two-week **dance festival** (☎04 42 23 41 24; tickets €10-38). Tickets are available at the tourist office. **Rue Verrerie** is lined with bars and clubs. **The Red Clover,** 30 r. de la Verrerie, is a lively bar with an overflowing international crowd. (Open daily 8am-2am.) **Bistro Aixois,** 37 cours Sextius, packs in students. (Open daily 6:30pm-4am.)

　　Trains, at the end of av. Victor Hugo, run to Marseilles (35min., 21 per day, €5.70). **Buses** (☎04 42 91 26 80), av. de l'Europe, also run frequently to Marseilles (30min., almost every 10min., €4). From the train station, follow av. Victor Hugo, bearing left at the fork, until it feeds into La Rotonde. On the left is the **tourist office,** 2 pl. du Général de Gaulle, which books rooms for free and stocks maps and guides. (☎04 42 16 11 61; www.aixenprovencetourism.com. Open July-Aug. daily 8:30am-8pm; Sept.-June reduced hours.) You can surf the **Internet** at **Millenium,** 6 r. Mazarine, off cours Mirabeau. (☎04 42 27 39 11. €3 per hr. Open daily 10am-11pm.) The excellent **Hôtel du Globe ❹,** 74 cours Sextius, is 5min. from *centre ville.* (☎04 42 26 03 58; fax 04 42 26 13 68. Singles €35, with bath €40; doubles €50/59; triples €63-69; quads €89.) **Hôtel des Arts ❸,** 69 bd. Carnot, has compact modern rooms. (☎04 42 38 11 77; fax 04 42 26 77 31. Breakfast €4.30. Singles and doubles €31-44. MC/V.) To **camp** at **Arc-en-Ciel ❶,** on rte. de Nice, take bus #3 from La Rotonde to Trois Sautets or Val St-André. (☎04 42 26 14 28. €5.20 per person, €5.80 per tent.) The roads north of **cours Mirabeau** are packed with reasonably priced restaurants, as is **rue Verrerie,** off r. des Cordiliers. You can choose from three **Petit Casinos supermarkets** at: 3 cours d'Orbitelle (open M-Sa 8am-1pm and 4-7:30pm); 16 r. Italie (open M-Sa 8am-7:30pm, Su 8:30am-12:30pm); and 5 r. Sapora (open M and W-Sa 8:30am-7:30pm, Su 8:30am-12:30pm). **Postal Code:** 13100.

MARSEILLES (MARSEILLE)

France's third-largest city, Marseilles (pop. 800,000), is steeped in history yet thoroughly modern. Underneath its seemingly rough, fiesty exterior is a world of cultural diversity and international flavor. The city that Alexandre Dumas once called "the meeting place of the entire world" remains a major center for immigration and international influence.

◫ TRANSPORTATION

Flights: Aéroport Marseilles-Provence (MRS; ☎04 42 14 14 14). Flights to **Lyon** and **Paris.** Buses connect airport to Gare St-Charles (3 per hr. 5:30am-9:50pm, €8.50).

Trains: Gare St-Charles, pl. Victor Hugo (☎08 36 35 35 35). To: **Lyon** (1½hr., 12 per day, €47); **Nice** (2½hr., 12 per day, €25); **Paris** (3hr., 17 per day, €68).

Buses: Gare Routière, pl. Victor Hugo (☎04 91 08 16 40), ½ a block from the train station. Open M-Sa 6:30am-6:30pm, Su 7:30am-6:30pm. To: **Avignon** (2hr., 5 per day, €15); **Cannes** (2¼-3hr., 4 per day, €21); **Nice** (2¾hr., daily, €23).

Ferries: SNCM, 61 bd. des Dames (☎08 91 70 18 01; www.sncm.fr). Ferries to **Corsica** (€26-52) and **Sardinia** (€41-67). Open M-F 8am-6pm, Sa 8am-noon and 2-5:30pm.

Local Transportation: RTM, 6-8 r. des Fabres (☎04 91 91 92 10). Tickets sold at bus and Métro stations (day pass €3.85; 6- to 12-ride **Carte Liberté** €6.50-13). **Métro** runs M-Th 5am-9pm and F-Su 5am-12:30am.

Taxis: (☎04 91 02 20 20). 24hr. €20-30 from the train station to most hostels.

⚡🛈 ORIENTATION AND PRACTICAL INFORMATION

Although the city is divided into 16 *arrondissements*, Marseilles is understood by neighborhood names and major streets. **La Canebière** is the main artery, funneling into the **vieux port,** with its upscale restaurants and nightlife, to the west. North of the *vieux port*, working-class residents pile into the hilltop neighborhood of **Le Panier,** east of which lies the **Quartier Belsunce,** the hub of the city's Arab and African communities. A few blocks to the southeast, **Cours Julien** has a younger, countercultural feel to it. Both **Métro** lines go to the train station; line #1 (blue) goes to the *vieux port.* The thorough **bus** system is essential to get to beaches, stretching along the coast southwest of the *vieux port.*

Tourist Office: 4 La Canebière (☎04 91 13 89 00; fax 04 91 13 89 20). Has brochures of walking tours, free maps, accommodations service, and RTM day pass. Offers city tours (€6.50) daily at 10am and 2pm, as well as frequent excursions. Open July-Aug. M-Sa 9am-8pm, Su 10am-6pm; Oct.-June M-Sa 9am-7pm, Su and holidays 10am-5pm.

Currency exchange: La Bourse, 3 pl. Général de Gaulle (☎04 91 13 09 00). Good rates and no commission. Open M-F 8:30am-6:30pm, Sa 9am-5:30pm.

Police: 2 r. du Commissaire Becker (☎04 91 39 80 00). Also in the train station on esplanade St-Charles (☎04 91 14 29 97). Dial ☎17 in **emergencies.**

Internet Access: Internet cafes in Marseilles generally run from €2-5 per hr.

Cyber Café de la Canebière, 87 r. de la Canebière. €2 per hr. Open daily 9am-11pm.

Info Café, 1 quai Rive Neuve. €3.80 per hr. Open M-Sa 8:30am-10pm.

Le Rezo, 68 cours Julien. €4.60 per hr. Open M-F 9:30am-8pm, Sa 10am-10pm.

Post Office: 1 pl. Hôtel des Postes (☎04 91 15 47 00). Follow La Canebière toward the sea and turn right onto r. Reine Elisabeth as it becomes pl. Hôtel des Postes. Address mail to be held: Firstname SURNAME, *Poste Restante,* 1 pl. Hotel des Postes, **13001** Marseilles, FRANCE.

🏠 ACCOMMODATIONS

Marseilles has a range of hotel options, from the pricey hotels near the *vieux port* to the less reputable but cheap hotels in the Quartier Belsunce. Hotels listed here prioritize safety and location. The two hostels are located far from the city center, which offers an escape from the fast pace of the city, but bus access is infrequent in the summer. Most places fill up quickly on weekends and in the summer, so call at least a week in advance.

Hôtel du Palais, 26 r. Breteuil (☎04 91 37 78 86; fax 04 91 37 91 19). Kind owner rents large, cheery rooms at a good value. Soundproofed rooms have A/C, TV, and shower. Breakfast €5. Singles €38; doubles €45; triples €53. Extra bed €8. MC/V. ❹

Auberge de Jeunesse Bonneveine (HI), impasse Bonfils (☎04 91 17 63 30; fax 04 91 73 97 23), off av. J. Vidal. From the station, take Métro line #2 to Rond-Point du Prado, and transfer to bus #44 to *pl. Bonnefon.* At the bus stop, walk back toward the traffic circle and turn left at av. J. Vidal, then turn onto impasse Bonfils. A well-organized hostel with an international crowd. Reception 9am-noon. Curfew 1am. Closed Dec. 22-Feb. Dorms €14 first night, €12 thereafter; doubles €17/15. Members only. MC/V. ❶

Auberge de Jeunesse Château de Bois-Luzy (HI), allée des Primevères (☎/fax 04 91 49 06 18). Take bus #8 (dir.: Saint-Julien) from La Canebière to Felibres Laurient, walk uphill and make the first left; the hostel will be on your left. The beautiful, 19th-century chateau used to house a count and countess. Breakfast €3. Dinner €7.50. Sheets

€1.80. Reception 7:30am-noon and 5-10:30pm. Lock-out noon-5pm. Dorms €11 first night, €8 thereafter; singles €15/12; doubles €12/9. Members only. ❶

Hôtel Saint-Louis, 2 r. des Recollettes (☎04 91 54 02 74; fax 04 91 33 78 59). Pretty, high-ceilinged rooms painted in cheerful colors, just off noisy La Canebière. Some rooms with balcony, nearly all with satellite TV. Breakfast €5. Reception 24hr. Singles €30; doubles €38-45; triples €53. Extra bed €7. AmEx/V. ❸

⬛ FOOD

For the city's famed seafood and North African fare, explore the *vieux port*, especially **place Thiers** and **cours d'Estienne d'Orves,** where one can eat *al fresco* for as little as €9. For a more artsy crowd and cheaper food, head up to **cours Julien,** northeast of the harbor. **Ivoire Restaurant ❷,** 57 r. d'Aubagne, near cours Julien, serves up inexpensive but tasty West African cuisine. (☎04 91 33 75 33. Open daily noon-midnight.) For a taste of Provence with some modern flair, try **Le Su du Haut ❸,** 80 cours Julien. (☎04 91 92 66 64. Open W-Sa noon-2am.) You can pick up groceries at **Monoprix supermarket,** across from the AmEx office on La Canebière. (Open M-Sa 8:30am-8:30pm.)

⬛ SIGHTS

Marseilles in all its glory can be seen from the steps of the **Basilique de Notre Dame de la Garde.** Its golden statue of the Madonna, affectionately known as *"la bonne mère,"* towers 230m above the city. (☎04 91 13 40 80. Open in summer 7am-8pm; off-season 7am-7pm.) The chilling catacombs of the fortified **Abbaye St-Victor,** on r. Sainte at the end of quai de Rive Neuve, contain an array of pagan and Christian relics, including the remains of 3rd-century martyrs. (☎04 96 11 22 60. Open daily 9am-7pm. Crypts €2.) Take a boat out to the **Château d'If,** the dungeon immortalized in Dumas's *Count of Monte Cristo,* or explore the windswept quarantine island of **Ile Frioul.** (Boats ☎04 91 55 50 09. Departures from quai des Belges; 20min., both islands €15.) Also worth a visit is **La Vieille Charité,** 2 r. de la Charite, an old poorhouse and orphanage that now shelters Egyptian, prehistoric, and classical collections. (☎04 91 14 58 80. Open June-Sept. Tu-Sa 11am-6pm; Oct.-May reduced hours. Temporary exhibits €3, permanent €2; students with ID half-price.) Bus #83 (dir.: Rond-Point du Prado) takes you from the *vieux port* to Marseilles's **public beaches.** Catch it on the waterfront side of the street and get off just after it rounds the statue of David (20-30min.). Beaches **plage du Prado** and **plage de la Corniche** offer clear water and plenty of space.

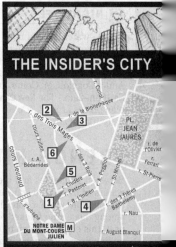

THE INSIDER'S CITY

STAYING THE COURS

An eclectic collection of murals, vintage shops, bookstores and cafes, cours Julien is one of Marseille's most interesting neighborhoods and the perfect place to find a bargain.

1 Cartoonish humor and bright colors make up the impressive **murals** on rue **Crudère** and rue **Pastoret** .

2 Black Music, 2 r. de la Bibliothèque, has a wide collection of classical and contemporary music by black artists.

3 Kaleidoscope, 3 r. des Trois Mages, offers a sweet selection of used records.

4 Tiny Baluchon Boutique, 11 r. des Trois Rois, features the best vintage threads.

5 Immerse yourself in paperbacks at Librairie du Cours Julien on cours Julien.

6 La Passerelle, 26 r. des Trois Mages, features a large selection of comic books and a snappy little cafe-bar.

FRANCE

⬛ NIGHTLIFE

People-watching and nightlife center around **place Thiers** and **cours Julien.** Local and international DJs spin at ⬛**Trolleybus,** 24 quai de Rive Neuve, a mega-club in an 18th-century warehouse. (Beer from €5. Mixed drinks €6.50. Cover Sa €10, includes 1 drink. Open W-Sa 11pm-7am.) The underwater-themed **Le Poulpason,** 2 r. André Poggioli, M: Cours Julien, has live music and DJs. (Drinks €2.50-5. Open W-Sa 10pm-2am.) The **New Can Can,** 22 r. Beauvau, is one of the more popular gay/lesbian places around. (Cover F-Sa €13 after midnight, €8 Sa before midnight. Open daily 10pm-6am.)

FRENCH RIVIERA (CÔTE D'AZUR)

Between Marseilles and the Italian border, the sun-drenched beaches and warm waters of the Mediterranean form the backdrop for this fabled playground of the rich and famous. F. Scott Fitzgerald, Cole Porter, Picasso, Renoir, and Matisse are among those who flocked to the coast in its heyday. Despite the Riviera's glorious past, this choice stretch of sun and sand is a curious combination of high-handed millionaires and low-budget tourists. High society steps out yearly for the Cannes Film Festival and the Monte-Carlo Grand Prix, both in May. Less exclusive are Nice's raucous *Carnaval* in February and various summer jazz festivals.

> **!** Most women who have traveled on the Riviera have a story to tell about men in the big beach towns. Unsolicited pick-up techniques range from subtle invitations to more, uh, bare displays of interest. Brush them off with a biting "laissez-moi tranquille!" ("leave me alone") or stony indifference, but don't be shy about enlisting the help of passersby or the police to fend off Mediterranean Don Juans.

ST-TROPEZ

Nowhere do the glitz and glamour of the Riviera shine more than in St-Tropez. The "Jewel of the Riviera" unfailingly attracts Hollywood stars and curious backpackers to its exclusive clubs and nude beaches. Unfortunately, the beaches in St-Tropez are difficult to reach without a car. The **shuttle** (*navette municipale*) leaves pl. des Lices for **Les Salins,** a secluded sunspot, and **plage Tahiti** (*Capon-Pinet* stop), the first of the famous **plages des Pampelonne.** (Shuttle runs M-Sa, €1.). Take a break from the sun at the **Musée de l'Annonciade,** pl. Grammont, which showcases Fauvist and neo-Impressionist paintings. (Open June-Sept. M and W-Sa 10am-1pm and 4-9pm; Oct. and Dec.-May reduced hours. €5.50, students €3.50.)

Les Bateaux de St-Raphaël **ferries** (☎04 94 95 17 46), at the old port, serve St-Tropez from St-Raphaël (1hr., 2-5 per day, €10). Sodetrav **buses** (☎04 94 97 88 51) leave av. Général Leclerc for St-Raphaël (2hr., 8-14 per day, €8.40). The **tourist office,** on quai Jean Jaurès, has schedules of the shuttle transport and a *Manifestations* guide that lists local events. (☎04 94 97 45 21; www.ot-saint-tropez.com. Open July-Aug. daily 9:30am-8:30pm; Sept.-June reduced hours.) Budget hotels do not exist in St-Tropez, and the closest youth hostel is in Fréjus (see below). **Camping** is the cheapest option—**Kon Tiki ❶** has a choice location near the northern stretch of the Pampelonne beaches. Campers can soak up sun by day and the beach's wild nightlife (including Kon Tiki's own bar) by night. (☎04 94 55 96 96; fax 04 94 55 96 95. Open Apr. to mid-Oct. July-Aug. two people, tent and car €35; off-season reduced prices.) If you prefer not to camp, one of the most budget-friendly and central hotels is **Lou Cagnard ❹**, 18 av. Paul Roussel. (☎04 94 97 04 24; fax 04 94

97 09 44. Breakfast €8. Open Jan.-Oct. Singles and doubles €43-54, with toilet €55-92. MC/V.) The **vieux port** and the streets behind the waterfront are lined with charmingly pricey restaurants, so create your own meal at **Monoprix supermarket,** 9 av. du Général Leclerc. (Open July-Aug. daily 8am-10pm; Sept.-June 8am-7:50pm.)

ST-RAPHAËL AND FRÉJUS

The twin cities of St-Raphaël and Fréjus provide an excellent base for exploring the Riviera thanks to cheap accommodations, convenient transport, and proximity to the sea. In St-Raphaël, the boardwalk turns into a carnival and golden beaches stretch along the coast, while Fréjus trades sandy shores for Roman ruins. The first weekend in July brings the **Compétition Internationale de Jazz New Orleans** (☎04 98 11 89 00). In Fréjus, the **Roman amphitheater,** on r. Henri Vadon, holds frequent concerts and bullfights twice a year. (Open Apr.-Oct. M and W-Sa 10am-1pm and 2:30-6:30pm, Su 8am-7pm; Nov.-Mar. M and W-F 10am-noon and 1:30-5:30pm, Sa 9:30am-12:30pm and 1:30-5:30pm, Su 8am-5pm. Bullfights €22-61. Contact the tourist office for a concert schedule.)

St-Raphaël sends **trains** every 30min. to Cannes (25min., €5.30) and Nice (1hr., €8.80). **Buses** leave from behind the train station in St-Raphaël for Fréjus (25min., every hr., €1.40) and St-Tropez (1½hr., 11 per day, €8.40). The **tourist office,** on r. Waldeck Rousseau, is opposite the train station. (☎04 94 19 52 52; www.saint-raphael.com. Open July-Aug. daily 9am-7pm; Sept.-June M-Sa 9am-12:30pm and 2-6:30pm.) Take bus #6 from St-Raphaël to pl. Paul Vernet to get to the **Fréjus tourist office,** 325 r. Jean Jaurès. (☎04 94 51 83 83; www.ville-frejus.fr. Open July-Aug. M-Sa 10am-noon and 2:30-6:30pm, Su 10am-noon and 3-6pm; Sept.-June M-Sa 9am-noon and 3-6pm.) Take av. du 15*ème* Corps d'Armée from the Fréjus tourist office and turn left on chemin de Councillier after the next roundabout to reach the ▧**Auberge de Jeunesse de St-Raphaël-Fréjus (HI) ❶,** a clean, friendly hostel with a beautiful, secluded location. (☎04 94 52 93 93; youth.hostel.frejus.st.raphael@wanadoo.fr. Sheets €2.70. Reception 8-10am and 6-8pm. Lockout 10am-6pm. Curfew July-Aug. midnight; Sept.-June 10pm. Open Feb.-Nov. Dorms €13. Camping €10 per person with tent.) In St-Raphaël, the **Hôtel les Pyramides ❸,** 77 av. Paul Doumer., is on a calm street just minutes from the waterfront. To get there, leave the station to the left, make a right onto av. Henri Vadon, and take the first left onto av. Paul Doumer. (☎04 98 11 10 10; www.saint-raphael.com/pyramides. Breakfast €7. Open Mar. 15-Nov. 15. Reception 7am-9pm; access code after hours. Singles €26; doubles €36-55; triples €56; quads €66. Extra bed €13. MC/V.) St-Raphaël's **Monoprix supermarket** is on 14 bd. de Félix Martin, off av. Alphonse Karr near the train station. (Open M-Sa 8:30am-7:30pm.) **Postal Codes:** St-Raphaël: 83700; Fréjus: 83600.

CANNES

With its legendary **Festival International du Film** each May, Cannes (pop. 70,000) has more associations with stardom than any other place on the coast. None of the festival's 350 screenings are open to the public, but the sidewalk show is free. For the other 11 months of the year, Cannes is among the most approachable of the Riviera's glam-towns. A palm-lined boardwalk, gorgeous sandy beaches, and innumerable boutiques ensure that anyone can sport the famous Cannes style. The best window-shopping along the Riviera lies along **rue d'Antibes** and **boulevard de la Croisette.** Farther west, the **Eglise de la Castre** and its courtyard stand on the hill on which *vieux Cannes* was built. Of Cannes's three **casinos,** the most accessible is **Le Casino Croisette,** 1 jetée Albert Edouard, next to the Palais des Festivals. (No shorts, jeans, or t-shirts. Jackets required for men. 18+ with ID. Cover €10. Gambling daily 8pm-4am; slots open at 10am.) If you want to get into one of Cannes's elite nightspots, dress to kill. Just as fun and half the price, cafes and bars near the waterfront stay open all night. Nightlife thrives around **rue Dr. G. Monod.**

Coastal **trains** depart from 1 r. Jean-Jaurès for: Antibes (15min., €2.30); Marseilles (2hr., €23); Monaco (1hr., €7.80); Nice (40min., €5.20); and St-Raphaël (25min., €4.10). The **tourist office,** 1 bd. de la Croisette, helps find accommodations. (☎04 93 39 24 53; www.cannes.fr. Open July-Aug. daily 9am-8pm; Sept.-June M-F 9am-7pm.) There is a **branch** office at the train station. (Open M-Sa 9am-7pm.) Access the **Internet** at **CyberCafé Institut Riviera Langue,** 26 r. de Mimont. (€4 per hr. Open daily 9am-10pm.) Hostels are 10-20min. farther from the beach than other lodgings, but are the cheapest options in town. The **Hostel Les Iris ❷,** 77 bd. Carnot, thrives under the care of friendly, English-speaking owners who have converted an old hotel into a clean, bright hostel with firm beds, a terrace for lounging and dining, and TV. (☎/fax 04 93 68 30 20. Dorms €18. MC/V.) **Hotel Mimont ❸,** 39 r. de Mimont, is two streets behind the train station, off bd. de la République. (☎04 93 39 51 64; fax 04 93 99 65 35. Singles €29; doubles €37; triples €51. AmEx/MC/V.) **Hôtel de Bourgogne ❸,** 11 r. du 24 août, has well-maintained rooms in the heart of town. (☎04 93 38 36 73; fax 04 92 99 28 41. Breakfast €5. Singles €30-50; doubles €40-55; triples €65-80; off-season reduced prices. AmEx/MC/V.) Stock up at **Monoprix supermarket,** in Champion, 6 r. Meynadier. (Open M-Sa 8:30am-7:30pm.) The pedestrian zone around **rue Meynadier** has inexpensive restaurants. **Postal Code:** 06400.

ANTIBES

Blessed with beautiful beaches and a charming *vieille ville*, Antibes (pop. 78,000) is less touristy than Nice and more relaxed than St-Tropez; with access to top-notch nightlife in neighboring **Juan-les-Pins**, it has become an undisputed jewel of the Riviera. The **Musée Picasso,** in the Château Grimaldi, on pl. Mariejol, displays works by the former Antibes resident and his contemporaries. (Open mid-June to mid-Sept. Su and Tu-Sa 10am-6pm; mid-Sept. to mid-June 10am-noon and 2-6pm. €6, students €3.) The two main public **beaches** in Antibes are **Plage du Ponteil** and the adjacent **Plage de la Salis.** Come summer, the young and hip Juan-Les-Pins is synonymous with wild nightlife. Frequent **buses** and **trains** run from Antibes, although walking between the two along bd. Wilson is also an option. Boutiques remain open until midnight, cafes until 2am, and nightclubs past dawn. **Discothèques** are generally open from 11pm to 5am. (Cover approx. €15, usually includes 1 drink.) ▓**Milk,** on av. Gallice, fills with a spunky crowd. (Cover €16. Open July-Aug. daily midnight-5am; Sept.-June F-Sa only.) In psychedelic **Whisky à Gogo,** 5 r. Jacques Leonetti, a young crowd dances the night away amid waterfilled columns. (Cover €16. Open Apr. to mid-Oct. daily 12:30-5:30am.)

Trains leave av. Robert Soleau for: Cannes (20min., 20 per day, €2.10); Marseilles (2¼hr., 10 per day, €24); Nice (15min., 20 per day, €3.50). **Buses** leave 200 pl. de Gaulle for Cannes (20min., every 20min. €2.50) and Nice (45min., every 20min., €4.10). Exit the station, turn right on av. Robert Soleau, and follow the signs to the **tourist office** at 11 pl. de Gaulle. (☎04 92 90 53 00; www.antibes-juanlespins.com. Open July-Aug. daily 9am-7pm; Sept.-June M-F 9am-12:30pm and 1:30-6pm, Sa 9am-noon and 2-6pm.) For the distant-but-beautiful ▓**Relais International de la Jeunesse (Caravelle 60) ❶,** take bus #2A (every 40min. 6:50am-7:30pm, €1.15) from pl. Guynemer in Antibes. (☎04 93 61 34 40. Reception daily 8-10am and 5:30pm-10:30pm. Dorms €14.) Rather than make the trek back to Antibes, crash in Juan-Les-Pins at **Hôtel Parisiana ❹,** 16 av. de L'Estérel, which has bright rooms with excellent amenities. (☎04 93 61 27 03; fax 04 93 67 97 21. Breakfast €5. Singles €35; doubles €49; triples €59; quads €67. Sept.-May reduced prices. AmEx/MC/V.) The **Marché Provençal,** on cours Masséna, is considered one of the best markets on the Côte d'Azur. (Open Su and Tu-Sa 6am-1pm.) **Postal Code:** 06600.

NICE

Sun-drenched and spicy, Nice (pop. 380,000) is the unofficial capital of the Riviera. Its pumping nightlife, top-notch museums, and bustling beaches are unerring tourist magnets. During the annual three-week February **Carnaval,** visitors and *Niçois* alike ring in the spring with wild revelry, grotesque costumes, and raucous song and dance. Prepare to have more fun than you'll remember.

▗ TRANSPORTATION

Flights: Aéroport Nice-Côte d'Azur (NCE; ☎08 20 42 33 33). **Air France,** 10 av. Félix Faure (☎08 02 80 28 02), serves **Paris** (€93, under-25, over-60, and couples €46).

Trains: Gare SNCF Nice-Ville (☎04 93 82 62 11), on av. Thiers. Open 5am-12:15am. To: **Cannes** (45min., every 15-45min., €5); **Marseilles** (2¾hr., every 30-90min., €24); **Monaco** (15min., every 10-30min., €3); **Paris** (5½hr., 6 per day, €76).

Buses: 5 bd. Jean Jaurès (☎04 93 85 61 81). Open M-Sa 8am-6:30pm. To: **Cannes** (1½hr., every 20min., €6) and **Monaco** (40min., every 15min., €3.40).

Ferries: Corsica Ferries, Port du Commerce (☎04 92 00 42 93; www.corsicaferries.com). Take bus #1 or 2 (dir.: Port) from pl. Masséna. To **Corsica** (€20-40).

Public Transportation: Sunbus, 10 av. Félix Faure (☎04 93 16 52 10), near pl. Leclerc and pl. Masséna. Individual tickets €1.30. Long treks to museums, the beach, and hostels make passes a bargain (day pass €4, 8-ticket *carnet* €8.30, 7-day pass €17). The tourist office provides **Sunplan** bus maps, schedules, and route info.

Bike and Scooter Rental: JML Location, 34 av. Auber (☎04 93 16 07 00), opposite the train station. Bikes €11 per day, €42 per week. Scooters €37 per day, €196 per week. Credit card deposit required. Open June-Sept. daily 9am-6:30pm; Oct.-May M-Sa 8am-1pm and 2-6:30pm. MC/V.

✶ ⑦ ORIENTATION AND PRACTICAL INFORMATION

Avenue Jean-Médecin, on the left as you exit the train station, and **boulevard Gambetta,** on the right, run directly to the beach. **Place Masséna** is 10min. down av. Jean-Médecin. Along the coast, **promenade des Anglais** is a people-watching paradise. To the southeast, past av. Jean-Médecin and toward the bus station, is **Vieux Nice.** Women should not walk alone after sundown, and everyone should exercise caution at night around the train station, *Vieux Nice,* and promenade des Anglais.

THE LOCAL LEGEND

YOU CANNES NEVER LEAVE

A few short days in celebrity-filled Cannes makes most visitors wish they were just a bit more glamorous. In 1800, however, Cannes was little more than a tiny fishing village, inhabited by the monks of St-Honorat abbey. The city was transformed by the 1834 arrival of Lord Henry Brougham, an member of British Parliament. Lord Brougham was headed to Nice, in hopes that a warm Mediterranean climate would mend his daughter's failing health. He found the city under quarantine due to a sudden cholera epidemic, and was forced to spend the night in Cannes. Thirty-four years later, Brougham was still there. He had built a lovely chateau, planted grass seeds imported from England, and done a fair bit of entertaining. Well-connected Brougham drew both English and French elites to his frequent dinner parties, including Lord Byron and King Louis Philippe of France: Cannes rapidly gained a reputation for being *the* place for the European aristocracy to winter. Villas and luxury hotels transformed the Croisette from a simple seaside dirt path into a posh boulevard. Guy de Maupassant joked wryly: "I met three princes one after the other on the Croisette!" Cannes transformed from the quiet haunt of monks and fishermen to a playground for the rich and famous in just a few decades, and it has never looked back.

FRANCE

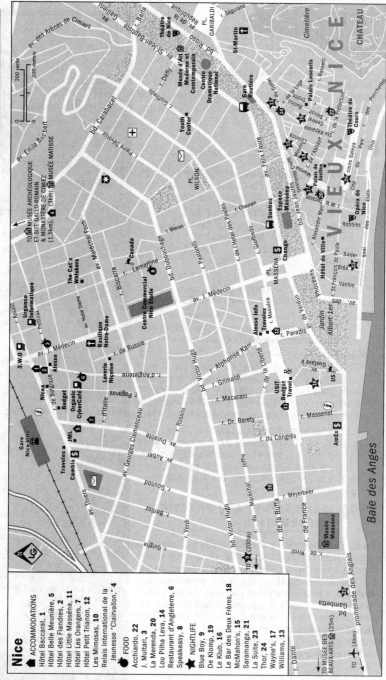

Nice

▲ ACCOMMODATIONS

Hôtel Baccarat, **1**
Hôtel Belle Meunière, **5**
Hôtel des Flandres, **2**
Hôtel Little Masséna, **11**
Hôtel Les Orangers, **7**
Hôtel Petit Trianon, **12**
Les Mimosas, **10**
Relais International de la
  Jeunesse "Clairvallon," **4**

🍴 FOOD

Acchiardo, **22**
J. Multari, **3**
La Merenda, **20**
Lou Pilha Leva, **14**
Restaurant d'Angleterre, **6**
Speakeasy, **8**

★ NIGHTLIFE

Blue Boy, **9**
De Klomp, **19**
Le Klub, **16**
Le Bar des Deux Frères, **18**
McMahon's, **15**
Saramanga, **21**
La Suite, **23**
Thor, **24**
Wayne's, **17**
Williams, **13**

FRANCE

Tourist Office: Av. Thiers (☎08 92 70 74 07; www.nicetourism.com), by the train station. Makes same-day hotel reservations; best chances of getting a room are between 9 and 11am. Ask for *Nice: A Practical Guide,* and a map. Open June-Sept. M-Sa 8am-8pm, Su 9am-6pm; Oct.-May M-Sa 8am-7pm.

Consulates: Canada, 10 r. Lamartine (☎04 93 92 93 22). Open M-F 9am-noon. **UK,** 26 av. Notre Dame (☎04 93 62 13 56). Open M, W, and F 9:30-11:30am. **US,** 7 av. Gustave V (☎04 93 88 89 55). Open M-F 9-11:30am and 1:30-4:30pm.

American Express: 11 promenade des Anglais (☎04 93 16 53 53). Open 9am-8:30pm.

Laundromat: Laverie Niçoise, 7 r. d'Italie (☎04 93 87 56 50). Beside Basilique Notre-Dame. Open M-Sa 8:30am-12:30pm and 2:30-7:30pm. Wash €4. Dry €2 per 20min.

Police: (☎04 93 17 22 22). At the opposite end of bd. M. Foch from av. Jean-Médecin.

Hospital: St-Roch, 5 r. Pierre Devoluy (☎04 92 03 33 75).

Internet Access: Teknosoft, 16 r. Paganini, (☎04 93 16 89 81), has 14 computers with English keyboards. Open daily 9am-10pm. €2 per 30min. **Alexso Info,** 1 r. de Belgique (☎04 93 88 65 02), has 12 computers and 8 English keyboards. €0.90 per 10min. Open daily 10am-8pm.

Post Office: 21 av. Thiers (☎04 93 82 65 22), near the train station. Open M-F 8am-7pm, Sa 8am-noon. Address mail to be held: Firstname SURNAME, *Poste Restante, Recette Principale,* Nice 06000, FRANCE. **Postal Code:** 06033 Nice Cedex 1.

ACCOMMODATIONS

To sleep easy, come to Nice with reservations. Hotels fill up quickly, especially in the summertime, so book at least a few weeks in advance. The city has two clusters of budget hotels: near the train station and near *vieux Nice.* Those by the station are newer but less conveniently located, and the walk home at night can be unsettling for those travelling alone. Hotels closer to *vieux Nice* are more convenient but tend to be less modern.

Hôtel Belle Meunière, 21 av. Durante (☎04 93 88 66 15; fax 04 93 82 51 76), directly across from the train station. Birds chirp in the courtyard of this converted mansion and backpackers become fast friends over free breakfast. Luggage storage €2. Laundry €5.50-9.50. Dorms €14-19; doubles €48; triples €57; quads €76. MC/V. ●

Relais International de la Jeunesse "Clairvallon," 26 av. Scudéri (☎04 93 81 27 63; clajpaca@cote-dazur.com), 4km out of town in Cimiez. Take bus #15 to Scudéri (dir.: Rimiez; 20min., every 10min.). Join 160 fellow backpackers in the luxurious villa of a deceased marquis. TV and swimming pool (open 5-7pm). Laundry €4. Check-in 5pm. Lockout 9:30am-5pm. Curfew 11pm. No reservations. Dorms €14. ●

Hôtel Little Masséna, 22 r. Masséna (☎04 93 87 72 34). Small but functional rooms with TV and kitchenette. Owners are young and friendly. Singles and doubles €28-48. Extra person €6.10. Oct.-May reduced prices. MC/V. ●

Hôtel Petit Trianon, 11 r. Paradis (☎04 93 87 50 46), off r. Masséna. This budget oasis in an otherwise expensive part of town has humble but elegant rooms. Singles €15; doubles €31; triples €60. Extra bed €8. MC/V. ●

Hôtel des Flandres, 6 r. de Belgique (☎04 93 88 78 94). Large rooms with high ceilings and private bathrooms. Breakfast €5. Dorms €17; singles €35-45; doubles €45-51; triples €60; quads €67. Extra bed €12. MC/V. ●

Hôtel Notre Dame, 22 r. de la Russie (☎04 93 88 70 44), 1 block west of av. Jean-Médecin. Spotless, quiet rooms. Breakfast €4. Singles €39; doubles €45; triples €57; quads €60. Extra bed €10. MC/V. ●

FRANCE

Hôtel Les Orangers, 10bis av. Durante (☎04 93 87 51 41; fax 04 93 82 57 82). Bright rooms, all with showers and fridges. Free luggage storage. Closed Nov. Dorms €16; singles €20-26; doubles €38-40; triples €54; quads €60. MC/V. ❷

Les Mimosas, 26 r. de la Buffa (☎04 93 88 05 59). Close to the beach and r. Masséna. Renovated rooms. Singles €29-34; doubles €37-49; triples €50-59; quads €60-68. ❸

Hôtel Baccarat, 39 r. d'Angleterre (☎04 93 88 35 73), 2nd right off r. de Belgique. Large rooms in homey, secure atmosphere. 3- to 5-bed dorms €18; singles €29; doubles €44. AmEx/MC/V. ❷

◗ FOOD

Restaurants in Nice range from four-star establishments to outdoor terraces to tiny holes-in-the-wall. Expensive gourmet establishments line r. Masséna, which offer nothing cheaper than a €9 pizza. Av. Jean-Médecin features reasonable *brasseries* and *panini* vendors, and gems hide amid the tourist traps on *Vieux Nice*.

■ **La Merenda,** 4 r. de la Terrasse. Those lucky enough to get a table can savor the work of a culinary master who abandoned a 4-star hotel to open this 12-table gem. Amazing value for the area (*Plats* €10-15). The only constant on the menu is its exotic flair, fried zucchini flowers, oxtail, tripe, and veal head. Reserve in the morning in person. Open M-F noon-1:30pm and 7-9:30pm. ❸

■ **Le Restaurant d'Angleterre,** 25 r. d'Angleterre (☎04 93 88 64 49), near the train station. This local favorite serves delicious French specialties in an intimate setting. Try and finish the *menu Sâge:* bread, large salad, main course, side dish, dessert, and an after-dinner cordial (€11.50). Open Tu-Sa 11:30am-1:45pm and 6:45-10pm. ❸

■ **Lou Pilha Leva,** 13 r. du Collet (☎04 93 80 29 33). Get a lot of *niçois* food for little money. Pizza slices €3, *moules* (mussels) €5. Open daily 8am-11pm. ❶

Speakeasy, 7 r. Lamartine (☎04 93 85 59 50). Delectable and affordable vegan options. Open M-Sa for lunch noon-2:15pm. ❷

Acchiardo, 38 r. Droite (☎04 93 85 51 16), in *Vieux Nice.* Surprisingly reasonable pastas from €6. Open M-F noon-1:30pm and 7-10pm. ❶

J. Multari, 58 bis av. Jean-Médecin. This graceful *salon de thé*, bakery, and sandwich shop serves excellent fare at budget prices. Try a sandwich on a fresh baguette (€3.10), salad (€3), or pizza (€1.45). Open M-Sa 6am-8:30pm. ❶

◎ SIGHTS

Many visitors to Nice head straight for the beaches and don't retreat from the sun and water until the day is done. Whatever dreams you've had about Nice's beach, though, the hard reality is an endless stretch of rocks; bring a beach mat if you plan to soak up the sun in comfort. Contrary to popular opinion, there are things in Nice more worthwhile than a long, naked sunbath on a bunch of pebbles. Nice's **promenade des Anglais,** named after the English expatriates who built it, is a sight in itself. At the **Négresco,** one of many luxury hotels lining the boulevard, the staff still dons top hats and 19th-century uniforms. If you follow the promenade east of bd. Jean Jaurès, you'll stumble upon **Vieux Nice,** a medieval *quartier* whose twisting streets and sprawling terraces draw massive crowds. *Vieux Nice* hosts a number of lively morning markets, including a fish frenzy at **place St-François.** The **Église St-Martin,** pl. Augustine, is the city's oldest church and site of Italian revolutionary Garibaldi's baptism. Farther down the promenade is **Le Château,** a hillside park crowned with the remains of an 11th-century cathedral. (Open daily 7am-8pm.)

Even devoted sunbathers will have a hard time passing by Nice's first-class museums. Walk 15min. north of the train station onto av. du Dr. Ménardor bus #15 (dir.: Rimiez) to the ◙Musée National Message Biblique Marc Chagall, which showcases Chagall's 17 moving *Message Biblique* paintings. (Open July-Sept. M and W-Su 10am-6pm; Oct.-June 10am-5pm. €5.50, under-26 €4.) Higher up the hill is the ◙Musée Matisse, 164 av. des Arènes de Cimiez, in a 17th-century Genoese villa. Take bus #15, 17, 20, or 22 to Arènes. The museum's collection of paintings is small, but the bronze reliefs and dozens of cut-and-paste *tableaux* are dazzling. (Open Apr.-Sept. W-M 10am-6pm; Oct.-Mar. 10am-5pm. €3.80, students €2.30.) Matisse, along with Raoul Dufy, is buried nearby in a cemetery beside the **Monastère Cimiez,** which contains a museum of Franciscan art and lovely gardens. (Museum open M-Sa 10am-noon and 3-6pm. Church open daily 9am-6pm. Cemetery and gardens open daily 8am-6pm.) Check out the onion-domed **Cathédrale Orthodoxe Russe St-Nicolas,** 17 bd. du Tzarevitch, west of bd. Gambetta near the train station, which was funded by Czar Nicolas II. (Open June-Aug. daily 9am-noon and 2:30-6pm; reduced hours Sept.-May. €1.80.)

Closer to *Vieux Nice,* the **Musée d'Art Moderne et d'Art Contemporain,** on promenade des Arts, on av. St-Jean Baptiste near pl. Garibaldi, features avant-garde works by French and American provocateurs, including works by Lichtenstein, Warhol, and Klein. Take bus #5 (dir.: St-Charles) from the station to *Garibaldi.* (Open Su and Tu-Sa 10am-6pm. €4, students €2.50.) Traditionalists will enjoy the **Musée de Beaux Arts,** 33 av. Baumettes, off bd. Francois Grosso. The museum's collection of French academic painting is overshadowed by rooms devoted to Van Dongen and Raoul Dufy. From the train station, take bus #38 to Chéret or bus #12 to Grosso. (Open Tu-Su 10am-noon and 2-6pm. €3.80, students €2.30.)

◨ NIGHTLIFE

Nice's **Jazz Festival,** in mid-July at the Parc et Arènes de Cimiez near the Musée Matisse, attracts world-famous performers. (☎08 20 80 04 00; www.nicejazzfest.com. €30.) Nice's **Carnaval** in late February gives Rio a run for its money with three weeks of parades, outlandish costumes, fireworks, and parties.

The party crowd swings long after St-Tropez and Antibes have called it a night. The bars and nightclubs around r. Masséna and *Vieux Nice* pulsate with dance and jazz. The dress code at all bars and clubs is simple: look good. Most pubs will turn you away if they catch you wearing shorts, sandals, or a baseball cap. To experience Nice's nightlife without spending a euro, head down to the **promenade des Anglais,** where street performers, musicians, and pedestrians fill the beach and boardwalk. For more info pick up the free brochure *l'Excés* (www.exces.com) at the tourist office and in some bars.

BARS

◙ **McMahon's,** 50 bd. Jean Jaurès. Join the locals and expats who lap up Guinness and shoot pool at this friendly Irish pub. Happy Hour daily 3-9pm (pints €3, wine €2). Karaoke on Th, request DJ and free shots on Sa. Open daily 3pm-2am.

Thor, 32 cours Saleya. Svelte blonde bartenders pour pints for a youthful crowd in this raucous Scandinavian pub. Daily live music starting at 10pm. Happy Hour 6-9pm (pints €4). Open daily 6pm-2am.

Le Bar Des Deux Frères, 1 r. du Moulin. A young crowd tosses back tequila (€3.10) and beer (€5) amid red curtains and smoky tables at this local favorite. Open Th-Sa 6pm-3:30am, Su-M 10pm-2:30am.

L'Havane, 32 r. de France. This hip Latin bar caters to a mainly local mid-20s crowd and features live salsa bands nightly. Open daily 5pm-2:30am.

De Klomp, 6 r. Mascoinat. 40 types of whiskey (from €6.50) and 18 beers on tap (pints €7). A variety of live music every night. Happy Hour 5:30-9:30pm. Open M-Sa 5:30pm-2:30am, Su 8:30pm-2:30am.

Williams, 4 r. Centrale. When other bars close up, Williams keeps the kegs flowing. Karaoke nights M-Th. Live music F-Sa. Open 9pm-7am.

Wayne's, 15 r. de la Préfecture. Common denominators for this wild, crowded bar: Young and on the prowl. Open noon-1am.

CLUBS

▨ **Saramanga,** 45-47 promenade des Anglais. A tropical theme reigns in Nice's hottest club, replete with exotic drinks, Hawaiian shirts, and fire-juggling showgirls. Cover €15. Open F-Sa 11pm-5am.

La Suite, 2 r. Brea. This *petite boîte* attracts a funky, well-dressed, moneyed crowd. Cover €13. Open T-Su 11pm-2:30am.

Blue Boy, 9 r. Jean-Baptiste Spinetta, in west Nice. Though far from town, Blue Boy's foam parties make it Nice's most popular gay club. Sa cover €9. Foam parties on W, June-Sept. Open daily 11pm-6am.

Le Klub, 6 r. Halévy. Popular gay club caters to well-tanned crowd. Cover €11. Open T-Su 11:30pm-6am.

▶ DAYTRIPS FROM NICE

THE CORNICHES

Rocky shores, pebble beaches, and luxurious villas glow along the Corniches, between hectic Nice and high-rolling Monaco. More relaxing than their glamorous neighbors, these tiny towns have interesting museums, ancient finds, and breathtaking countryside. The train offers a glimpse of the coast up close, while bus rides on the high roads allow bird's-eye views of the steep cliffs and crashing sea below.

VILLEFRANCHE-SUR-MER. The town's narrow streets and pastel houses have enchanted Aldous Huxley, Katherine Mansfield, and many other artists. Strolling from the train station along quai Ponchardier, a sign to the *vieille ville* points to the spooky 13th-century **rue Obscure,** the oldest street in Villefranche. At the end is the **Chapelle St-Pierre,** decorated by Jean Cocteau, former resident, filmmaker, and jack-of-all-arts. (☎04 93 76 90 70. Call ahead for hours. €2.) **Trains** run from Nice. (7min., every hr., €1.30.) To get to the **tourist office** from the train station, exit on quai 1, head inland on av. G. Clemenceau, and continue straight when it becomes av. Sadi Carnot; it will be at the end of the street. (☎04 93 01 73 68. Open July-Aug. daily 9am-7pm; Sept.-June reduced hours.)

ST-JEAN-CAP-FERRAT. A lovely town with an even lovelier beach, St-Jean-Cap-Ferrat is the trump card of the Riviera. The **Fondation Ephrussi di Rothschild,** just off av. D. Semeria, is a stunning Italian villa that houses the collections of the Baroness de Rothschild, including Monet canvases, Gobelins tapestries, and Chinese vases. The seven lush gardens reflect different parts of the world. (Open July-Aug. daily 10am-7pm; Sept.-Nov. 1 and Feb. 15-June 10am-6pm; Nov. 2-Feb. 14 M-F 2-6pm, Sa-Su 10am-6pm. €8, students €6.) The town's beautiful **beaches** have earned the area the nickname *"presqu'île des rêves"* (peninsula of dreams). The tiny **tourist office,** 59 av. Denis Séméria, is half-way along the winding street that runs from Nice and Monaco to the port. (☎04 93 76 08 90; fax 04 93 76 16 67. Open July-Aug. M-Sa 8:30am-6:30pm; Sept.-June reduced hours.) Two buses per day run from Nice via Villefrance-sur-Mer (9:10 am and 12:15 pm, €1.60).

FRANCE

EZE. Three-tiered Eze owes its fame to the pristine medieval town in the middle tier. It features the **Porte des Maures,** which served as a portal for a surprise attack by the Moors, and the **Eglise Paroissial,** containing sleek Phonecian crosses mixed with Catholic gilt. (Open daily 9am-7pm.) The best views are 40min. up the **Sentier Friedrich Nietzsche,** a windy trail where its namesake found inspiration; the path begins in Eze Bord-du-Mer, 100m east of the train station and tourist office, and ends near the base of the medieval city, by the **Fragonard parfumerie.** Frequent **trains** run from Nice (15min., every hr., €2).

MONACO

Monaco (pop. 7,200) has money—lots of it—invested in ubiquitous surveillance cameras, high-speed luxury cars, and sleek yachts. At Monaco's spiritual heart is its famous casino in Monte-Carlo, a magnet for the wealthy and dissolute since 1885. The sheer spectacle of it all is worth a daytrip from Nice.

> **CALLING TO AND FROM MONACO** — Monaco's country code is 377. To call Monaco from France, dial 00377, then the 8-digit Monaco number. To call France from Monaco, dial 0033, and drop the first zero of the French number.

▐▌ TRANSPORTATION AND PRACTICAL INFORMATION. Trains run to: Antibes (1hr., every 30min., €7); Cannes (65min., every 30min., €7); and Nice (25min., every 30min., €3). **Buses** (☎93 85 61 81) leave av. Princesse Alice, near the tourist office, for Nice (45min., every 15min., €3.70). Follow the signs in the new train station for Le Rocher and Fontvieille to the **avenue Prince Pierre** exit; it's close to **La Condamine** quarter, Monaco's port, which has a morning market and cafes. To the right of La Condamine rises the *vieille ville,* **Monaco-Ville.** Leaving the train station onto bd. Princess Charlotte or pl. St-Devote leads to **Monte-Carlo** and the casino. **Bus #4** links the train station to the casino in Monte-Carlo; buy tickets on board. (€1.40, €3.30 for a *carte* of 4). At the **tourist office,** 2a bd. des Moulins, a friendly, English-speaking staff provides city plans, an events guide, and hotel reservations free of charge. (☎92 16 61 16; www.monaco-congres.com. Open M-Sa 9am-7pm, Su 10am-noon.) Access the **Internet** at **Stars 'N' Bars,** 6 quai Antoine 1*er.* (€5 per 30min. Open daily 10am-midnight.) **Postal Code:** 06500.

▐▌ ACCOMMODATIONS AND FOOD. There's no need to stay in Monaco, since it is easily accessible from nearby (and less expensive) coastal towns. **Beausoleil,** in France, has several reasonable options and is a 5min. walk from the beach or 10min. from the casino. **Hôtel Diana ❸,** 17 bd. du Général Leclerc, has clean rooms. (☎04 93 78 47 58; www.monte-carlo.mc/hotel-diana-beausoleil. Singles €32; doubles €55; triples €63. Amex/MC/V.) Not surprisingly, Monaco has little budget fare. Fill a picnic basket at the fruit and flower **market** on pl. d'Armes at the end of av. Prince Pierre (open daily 6am-1pm), or at the huge **Carrefour** in Fontvieille's shopping plaza (☎92 05 57 00; open M-Sa 8:30am-10pm).

▐▌ SIGHTS AND ENTERTAINMENT. The extravagant **Monte-Carlo Casino,** at pl. de Casino, is where Richard Burton wooed Elizabeth Taylor and Mata Hari shot a Russian spy. The slot machines open at 2pm, while blackjack, craps, and roulette open at noon (cover €10). The exclusive *salons privés,* where such French games as *chemin de fer* and *trente et quarante* begin at noon, will cost you an extra €10 cover. Next door, the more relaxed **Café de Paris** opens at

10am and has no cover. All casinos have **dress codes** (no shorts, sneakers, sandals, or jeans), and the *salons privés* require coat and tie. Guards are strict about the **21 age minimum;** bring a passport as proof. High above the casino is the **Palais Princier,** the occasional home of Prince Rainier and his tabloid-darling family. When the flag is down, the prince is away and visitors can tour the small but lavish palace, which includes Princess Grace's official state portrait and the chamber where England's King George III died. (☎93 25 18 31. Open June-Sept. 9:30am-6:20pm; Oct. 10am-5pm. €6, students €3.) Next door, the **Cathédrale de Monaco,** at pl. St-Martin, is the burial site of the Grimaldi family and the site of Prince Rainer and Princess Grace's 1956 wedding; Princess Grace lies behind the altar in a tomb marked simply with her Latinized name, "Patritia Gracia." (Open Mar.-Oct. daily 7am-7pm; Nov.-Feb. 7am-6pm.) The **Private Collection of Antique Cars of H.S.H. Prince Rainier III,** on les Terraces de Fontvielle, showcases 105 of the most glamorous cars ever made. (☎92 05 28 56. Open daily 10am-6pm. €6, students and ages 8-14 €3.) The **Musée Océanographique** on av. St-Martin, once directed by Jacques Cousteau, holds the most exotic and bizarre oceanic species. (☎93 15 36 00; www.oceano.mc. Open Apr.-Sept. daily 9am-7pm; Oct.-Mar. 10am-6pm. €11, students €6.) Monaco's nightlife has two centers. **La Condamine,** near the port, is less expensive and caters to a younger clientele. Bars and clubs near the casino are more expensive. **Café Grand Prix,** at 1 quai Antoine 1*er,* serves up live music to a mixed crowd. (Open daily 10am-5am.)

CORSICA (LA CORSE)

The colorful island of Corsica has a colorful history—having been controlled by Phoenicia, Rome, Carthage, Pisa, and Genoa before becoming part of France. Ever since Corsicans have been divided over the issue of allegiance to France—among those who side with the French was officer Carlo-Maria Buonaparte, father to the island's favorite son, Napoleon. Today a substantial faction still seeks greater autonomy. Many are reluctant, however, as Corsica's economy is highly dependent on France; tourists flock there for summer sun and winter skiing.

▐▀ TRANSPORTATION

Air France and its subsidiary Compagnie Corse Méditerranée (CCM) fly to Bastia and Ajaccio from Paris (round-trip from €170, students €140); Nice (€120, students €98); and Marseilles (€128, students €104). In Ajaccio, the Air France/CCM office is at 3 bd. du Roi Jérôme (☎08 20 82 08 20). **Ferry** travel between the mainland and Corsica can be a rough trip. High-speed ferries (3½hr.) run between Nice and Corsica. Overnight ferries from Marseilles take upwards of 10 hours. The **Société National Maritime Corse Méditerranée** (☎08 91 70 18 01; www.sncm.fr) sends ferries from Marseilles (€35-53, under 25 €20-40) and Nice (€30-41, under 25 €15-26) to Bastia and Ajaccio. In summer, nine boats cross between Corsica and the mainland each day, and only three out of season. SNCM schedules and fees are available at travel agencies and ports. **Corsica Ferries** (☎08 25 09 50 95; www.corsicaferries.com) has similar destinations and prices and also crosses from Livorno and Savona in Italy to Bastia (€16-33). **SAREMAR** (☎04 95 73 00 96) and **Moby Lines** (☎04 95 73 00 29) run from Santa Teresa in Sardinia to Bonifacio. (€6.80-15 per person.) **Train** service in Corsica is slow, limited to the half of the island north of Ajaccio, and doesn't accept rail passes. **Buses** provide more comprehensive service; call **Eurocorse Voyages** (☎04 95 21 06 30) for more info.

▨ HIKING

Hiking is the best way to explore the island's mountainous interior. The **GR20** is an extremely difficult 14- to 15-day 200km trail that crosses the island. The popular **Mare e Monti** (10 days) and **Da Mare a Mare Sud** (4-6 days) trails are shorter and less challenging. The **Parc Naturel Régional de la Corse**, 2 Sargent Casalonga, in Ajaccio (☎ 04 95 51 79 10), publishes maps and a guide to *gîtes d'étapes* (rural lodgings).

AJACCIO (AIACCIU)

One of the few Corsican towns with true urban energy, Ajaccio (pop. 60,000) has excellent museums and nightlife to compliment its palm trees and yellow sunlit buildings. Inside the ▨**Musée Fesch**, 50-52 r. Cardinal Fesch, you'll find an impressive collection of 14th- to 19th-century Italian paintings gathered by Napoleon's uncle Fesch, a merchant during the Revolution who later turned to the cloth and spent his worldly wealth acquiring artistic treasures. Also within the complex is the **Chapelle Impériale**, the final resting place of most of the Bonaparte family—though Napoleon himself is buried in a modest tomb in Paris. (Open July-Aug. M 1:30-6pm, Tu-Th 9am-6:30pm, F 9am-6:30pm and 9pm-midnight, Sa-Su 10:30am-6pm; Sept.-June reduced hours. Museum €5.40, students €3.80; chapel €1.50/0.75.) Napoleon's first home, the **Musée National de la Maison Bonaparte**, r. St-Charles, between r. Bonaparte and r. Roi-de-Rome, is now a warehouse of memorabilia. (Open Apr.-Sept. M 2-6pm, Tu-Su 9am-noon and 2-6pm; Oct.-Mar. M 2-4:45pm, Tu-Su 10am-noon and 2-4:45pm. €4, ages 18-25 €2.60. Under-18 free.) Several lively bars crowd around **boulevard Pascal Rossini.**

Trains (☎ 04 95 23 11 03) leave pl. de la Gare, for Bastia (4hr., 4 per day, €24) and Corte (2hr., 2 per day, €13). The **tourist office** is at 3 bd. du Roi Jérôme. (☎ 04 95 51 53 03; www.tourisme.fr/ajaccio. Open July-Aug. M-Sa 8am-8:30pm, Su 9am-1pm and 4-7pm; Sept.-June reduced hours.) The serene and centrally located ▨**Hôtel Kallisté ❹** is at 51 cours Napoléon. (☎ 04 95 51 34 45; www.cyrnos.com. Singles in Aug. €56; doubles €69; triples €89. Reduced prices off-season. AmEx/MC/V.) To camp at **Les Mimosas ❶**, take bus #4 from cours Napoléon to *Brasilia* and walk straight to the roundabout, take a left on chemin de la Carrossaciai and follow the signs. (☎ 04 95 52 01 17. Electricity €2.80. July-Aug. €4.80 per person, €2 per tent or car. Prices 10% lower Apr.-June and Sept. to mid-Oct.) Pizzerias, bakeries, and one-stop *panini* shops can be found on **rue Cardinal Fesch;** at night, patios on the festive quai offer affordable seafood and pizza. Get groceries at **Monoprix**, 31 cours Napoléon. (Open M-Sa 8am-7:15pm.) **Postal Code:** 20000.

BONIFACIO (BONIFAZIU)

The fortified city of Bonifacio (pop. 3,000) rises like a majestic sand castle atop jagged limestone cliffs; **Marina Croisières** offers **boat tours** of the hidden coves and grottoes. (☎ 04 95 73 09 77. €11-21.) All the companies by the port run frequent ferries (30min.) to the pristine sands of **Iles Levezzi,** a nature reserve with beautiful reefs perfect for **scuba diving.** To explore the *haute ville*, head up the steep montée Rastello, the wide staircase halfway down the port, where excellent views of the ridged cliffs to the east await. Continue up montée St-Roch to the lookout at **Porte des Gênes**, a drawbridge built by invaders. Then walk to the **place du Marche** to see Bonifacio's famous cliffs and the **Grain de Sable.**

Eurocorse Voyages (☎ 04 95 21 06 30) runs **buses** to Ajaccio (3½hr., 2-3 per day, €21) as well as Porto Vecchio (30min., 1-4 per day, €6.50), where connections can be made to Bastia. To reach the **tourist office,** at the corner of av. de Gaulle and r. F. Scamaroni, walk along the port and then up the stairs before the *gare maritime*. (☎ 04 95 73 11 88; www.bonifacio.com. Open May to mid-Oct. daily 9am-8pm; mid-Oct. to Apr. M-F 9am-noon and 2-6pm, Sa 9am-noon.) Finding affordable rooms is difficult in summer; avoid visiting in August, when prices soar. Try **Hôtel** des Étrangers ❹, av. Sylvère Bohn. (☎04 95 73 01 09; fax 04 95 73 16 97. Singles and doubles €50-72; triples €72; quads €82. MC/V.) **Camp** at **L'Araguina,** av. Sylvère Bohn, at the entrance to town between Hôtel des Étrangers and the port. (☎04 95 73 02 96; fax 04 95 73 57 04. Open mid-Mar. to Oct. Electricity €2.80. Laundry €5. €5.30-5.60 per person, €1.90 per car or tent.) **Postal Code:** 20169.

BASTIA

Bastia (pop. 40,000), Corsica's second largest city, constantly bustles with the arrival and departure of ferries from the mainland and Italy. More than just a stop mid-transit, Bastia has some lovely sights of its own in addition to being the perfect gateway to the must-see Cap Corse. The 14th-century **Citadel,** also called Terra Nova, has beautiful views of the sea. The **Oratoire de St-Roch,** on r. Napoleon, is a jewel-box of a church with crystal chandeliers and meticulous *trompe l'oeil* decoration. The neoclassical towers of the **Église St-Jean Baptiste,** pl. de l'Hôtel de Ville, cover an immense interior with gilded domes. **Shuttle buses** leave pl. de la Gare for the **Bastia-Poretta Airport** (30min., €8). **Trains** (☎04 95 32 80 61) also leave pl. de la Gare for Ajaccio (4hr., 4 per day, €24) and Calvi (3hr., 2 per day, €18). Eurocorse **buses** (☎04 95 21 06 30) leave r. Nouveau Port for Ajaccio (3hr., 2 per day, €17). The **tourist office,** pl. St-Nicholas, has indispensable copies of the bus schedule. (☎04 95 54 20 40; fax 04 95 31 81 34. Open daily 8am-noon and 2-6pm.) The **Hôtel Central ❷,** 3 r. Miot, has large, well-kept rooms. (☎04 95 31 71 12; fax 04 95 31 82 40. Breakfast €5.50. Singles €35-50; doubles €40-80. AmEx/MC/V.) To reach **Les Orangiers camping ❶,** take bus #4 from the tourist office to *Licciola-Miomo.* (☎04 95 33 24 09. Open May to mid-Oct. Electricity €3.50. €4.50 per person, €2.50 per tent, €5 per car.) Inexpensive cafes crowd **place St-Nicolas.**

▶ **DAYTRIP FROM BASTIA: CAP CORSE.** North of Bastia stretches the gorgeous Cap Corse peninsula, a necklace of tiny former fishing villages strung together by a narrow road of perilous curves and breathtaking views. The Cap is a dream for **hikers;** every forest and cliff lays claim to some decaying Genoese tower or hilltop chapel. If you don't have access to or funds for a car, the cheapest and most convenient way to see Cap Corse is to take **bus** #4 from pl. St-Nicolas in Bastia, which goes to: Erbalunga (20min., €2); Macinaggio (50min., €6.40); and Marina di Siscu (30min., €2.30). Ask politely and the driver will drop you off wherever you feel the urge to explore. However, most buses serve only the coast; you'll have to hike or hitchhike to the inland villages. While *Let's Go* wholeheartedly endorses hiking, it does not recommend hitchhiking.

CORTE

The most dynamic of Corsica's inland towns, Corte combines breathtaking natural scenery with a boisterous collegiate spirit. Sheer cliffs, snow-capped peaks, and breathtaking gorges create a dramatic backdrop for the island's only university, whose students keep prices surprisingly low. The town's *vieille ville,* with its steep streets and stone **citadel,** has always been a bastion of patriotism. At the top of r. Scolisca is the engaging **La Musée de la Corse,** which also provides entrance to the higher fortifications of the citadel. (Open June-Sept. daily 10am-8pm; Nov.-May reduced hours. Museum and citadel €3-5.30, students €2.30-3.) Corte's mountains and valleys feature numerous spectacular trails. Choose from **hiking** (weather ☎08 92 68 02 20), **biking,** and **horseback riding.** Rent **horses** at **Ferme Equestre Albadu,** 1.5km from town on N193. (☎04 95 46 24 55. €14 per hr., €69 per day.)

Trains (☎04 95 46 00 97) leave from the rotary, where av. Jean Nicoli and N193 meet, for: Ajaccio (2hr., 4 per day, €13) and Bastia (1½hr., 4 per day, €11). Eurocorse Voyages runs **buses** to Ajaccio (1¾hr., M-Sa 2 per day, €12) and Bastia (1¼hr., M-Sa 2 per day, €10). To reach the *centre ville* from the train station, turn right on D14 (av. Jean Nicoli), cross two bridges, and follow the road until it ends at **cours Paoli,** Corte's main drag. A left turn leads to **place Paoli,** the town center; at the *place's* top right corner, climb the stairs of r. Scolisca to reach the citadel and the **tourist office,** which has hiking maps and info. (☎04 95 46 26 70; www.corte-tourisme.com. Open July-Aug. daily 9am-8pm; May-June and Sept. M-Sa 9am-noon and 2-6pm; Oct.-May M-F 9am-noon and 2-6pm.) The youthful **Hôtel-Residence Porette ❷,** 6 allée du 9 septembre, offers functional and clean rooms and a nice garden. Bear left from the train station to the stadium and follow it around for another 100m. (☎04 95 45 11 11; fax 04 95 61 02 85. Breakfast €5. Singles €21, with bath €29; doubles €29/39; triples €54.) **Place Paoli** is the spot to find sandwiches and pizza, while **rue Scolisca** and the surrounding citadel streets abound with inexpensive local cuisine. The huge **Casino supermarket** is near the train station, on allée du 9 septembre. (Open mid-June to Aug. daily 8:30am-7:45pm; Sept. to mid-June M-F 8:30am-12:30pm and 3-7:30pm, Sa 8:30am-7:30pm.) **Postal Code: 20250.**

THE ALPS (LES ALPES)

Nature's architecture is the real attraction of the Alps. The curves of the Chartreuse Valley rise to rugged crags in the Vercors range and ultimately crescendo at Europe's highest peak, Mont Blanc. Winter skiers enjoy some of the world's most challenging slopes. In the summer, hikers take over the mountains for endless vistas and clear air. Skiing arrangements should be made well in advance; Chamonix and Val d'Isère are the easiest bases. TGV trains whisk you from Paris to Grenoble or Annecy; scenic trains and slower buses service Alpine towns from there. The farther into the mountains you want to go, the harder it is to get there, although service is more frequent during ski season (Dec.-Apr.).

GRENOBLE

Grenoble (pop. 156,000) has the eccentric cafes and shaggy radicals of any university town, but also boasts snow-capped peaks and sapphire-blue lakes cherished by athletes and aesthetes alike.

▉❼ TRANSPORTATION AND PRACTICAL INFORMATION. Trains leave pl. de la Gare for: Annecy (2hr., 18 per day, €14); Lyon (1½hr., 27 per day, €16); Marseilles (2½-4½hr., 15 per day, €33); Nice (5-6½hr., 5 per day, €48); and Paris (3hr., 6 per day, €59-74). **Buses** leave from the left of the station for Geneva, Switzerland (3hr., daily, €26). From the station, turn right into pl. de la Gare, take the third left on av. Alsace-Lorraine, and follow the tram tracks on r. Félix Poulat and r. Blanchard to reach the **tourist office,** 14 r. de la République. (☎04 76 42 41 41; www.grenoble-isere.info. Open M-Sa 9am-6:30pm, Su 10am-1pm and 2-5pm.) **E-toile** has **Internet** access. (☎04 76 00 13 60. €3.50 per hr. Open M-F 10am-11pm, Sa-Su 10am-midnight.) **Postal Code: 38000.**

▉❑ ACCOMMODATIONS AND FOOD. From the tourist office, follow pl. Ste-Claire to pl. Notre-Dame and take r. du Vieux Temple on the far right to reach **Le Foyer de l'Etudiante ❶,** 4 r. Ste-Ursule, a stately building with large rooms that serves as a dorm during most of the year, but opens to travellers during July and August. (☎04 76 42 00 84; www.multimania.com/foyeretudiante. Sheets €8. Laundry €2.20. Free Internet access. July-Aug. three-night min. for room; five-night max. for dorm. Dorms €8; singles €14; doubles €22.) **Hôtel de la Poste ❷,** 25 r. de la Poste, near the pedestrian zone, has amazing rooms. (☎/fax 04 76 46 67 25. Singles €22-26; doubles €28; triples €32; quads €37. MC/V.) To reach **Camping Les 3 Pucelles ❶,** 58 r. des Allobroges in Seyssins, take tram A (dir.: Fontaine-La Poya) to *Louis Maisonnat,* then take bus #51

FRANCE

(dir.: Les Nalettes) to *Mas des Iles;* it's on the left. (☎ 04 76 96 45 73; fax 04 76 21 43 73. One person, tent, and car €7.50; extra person €2.80.) Grenoble has many affordable restaurants, some with student discounts. Regional restaurants cater to locals around **place de Gordes,** while Asian eateries abound between pl. Notre-Dame and the river and along **rue Condorcet.** *Pâtisseries* and North African joints congregate around **rue Chenoise** and **rue Lionne,** between the pedestrian area and the river. Cafes and restaurants cluster around **place Notre-Dame** and **place St-André,** in the heart of the *vieille ville.* **Monoprix supermarket** is opposite the tourist office. (Open M-Sa 8:30am-7:30pm.)

◨ ⚠ SIGHTS AND THE OUTDOORS. *Téléphériques* (cable cars) depart from quai Stéphane-Jay every 10min. for the 16th-century **Bastille,** a fort that hovers above town. Enjoy the views from the top, then descend via the **Parc Guy Pape,** which crisscrosses through the fortress and deposits you just across the river from the train station. (Open July-Aug. M 11am-12:15am, Tu-Su 9:15am-12:15am; Sept.-June reduced hours. One-way €3.80, round-trip €5.50; students €3/4.40.) Cross the Pont St-Laurent and go up Montée Chalemont for the **Musée Dauphinois,** 30 r. Maurice Gignoux, with its futuristic exhibits on the people of the Alps and the history of skiing. (Open June-Sept. M and W-Su 10am-7pm; Oct.-May 10am-6pm. €3.20. Under-25 free.) The **Musée de Grenoble,** 5 pl. de Lavelette, has one of France's most prestigious collections of art. (Open July-Sept. M, Th-Su 10am-6pm, W 10am-9pm; Oct.-June M and Th-Su 11am-7pm, W 11am-10pm. €4, students €2.) Grenoble's proximity to the slopes is another attractive aspect of the city. The biggest and most developed **ski areas** are to the east in **Oisans;** the **Alpe d'Huez** boasts 220km of trails. (Tourist office ☎ 04 76 11 44 44. €33 per day, €171 per week.) The **Belledonne** region, northeast of Grenoble, has lower elevation and prices. **Chamrousse** is the biggest and most popular ski area (lift tickets €23 per day, €79-113 per week). Only 30min. from Grenoble by **bus** (€8.70), the resort also makes for a hiker's ideal daytrip in summer. Grenoble boasts plenty of funky cafes, bars and clubs; most are in the area between **place St-André** and **place Notre-Dame.**

CHAMONIX

The site of the first winter Olympics in 1924, Chamonix (pop. 10,000) is the ultimate ski town, with soaring mountains and the toughest slopes in the world. The town itself combines the dignity of Mont Blanc, Europe's highest peak (4807m), with the exuberant spirit of energetic travelers.

◨ ⯀ TRANSPORTATION AND PRACTICAL INFORMATION. Trains leave av. de la Gare (☎ 04 50 53 12 98) for: Annecy (2½hr., 7 per day, €17); Geneva, Switzerland (2½hr., 7 per day, €21); Lyon (4hr., 6 per day, €30); and Paris (6½hr., 9 per day, €50-70). Société Alpes Transports **buses** (☎ 04 50 53 01 15) leave the train station for Annecy (2¼hr., daily, €15) and Geneva, Switzerland (1½hr., 2 per day, €29-32). **Local buses** (€1.50) connect to ski slopes and hiking trails. From the station, follow av. Michel Croz, turn left on r. du Dr. Paccard, and take the first right to reach pl. de l'Eglise and the **tourist office,** 85 pl. du Triangle de l'Amitié. (☎ 04 50 53 00 24; www.chamonix.com. Open July-Aug. daily 8:30am-7:30pm; Sept.-June reduced hours.) **Compagnie des Guides,** in Maison de la Montagne facing the tourist office-leads ski trips and hikes. (☎ 04 50 53 00 88; www.cieguides-chamonix.com. Open Jan.-Mar. and July-Aug. daily 8:30am-noon and 3:30-7:30pm; Sept.-Dec. and Apr.-June reduced hours.) Access the **Internet** at **Cybar,** 80 r. des Moulins. (☎ 04 50 53 69 70. €1 per 10min. Open daily 11am-1:30am.) **Postal Code:** 74400.

◨ ⬚ ACCOMMODATIONS AND FOOD. Chamonix's *gîtes* (mountain hostels) and dorms are cheap, but they fill up fast; call ahead. From the train station, walk down av. Michel Croz and take a right onto r. Joseph Vallot for the ▨**Red Mountain**

Lodge ❷, 435 r. Joseph Vallot. The fun-loving, English-speaking staff keeps guests happy with plush furnishings, views of Mont Blanc, and frequent barbeques for €12. (☎04 50 53 94 97; fax 04 50 53 82 64. Reception 8am-noon and 5-7pm. Dorms €16; doubles €40, with bath €50; triples €60/75.) Gîte le Vagabond ❶, 365 av. Ravanel le Rouge, near the town center, has a friendly atmosphere and a climbing wall. (☎04 50 53 15 43; gitevagabond@hotmail.com. Breakfast €5. Laundry €7.70. Internet €0.15 per min. Reception 8-10:30am. 4- to 8-bunk dorms €13. Credit card deposit. MC/V.) Turn left from the base of the Aiguille du Midi *téléphérique*, continue past the main roundabout, and look right to camp at L'Ile des Barrats ❶, on rte. des Pélerins. (☎/fax 04 50 53 51 44. Reception July-Aug. daily 8am-10pm; May-June and Sept. 9am-noon and 4-7pm. Open Feb. to mid-Oct. Electricity €2.80. €5 per person, €4.60 per tent, €2 per car.) Restaurants in Chamonix cluster around the town center. Rue du Docteur Paccard is a good bet, as is rue des Moulins, which also boasts Chamonix's most popular nightclubs and bars. Get groceries at Super U, 117 r. Joseph Vallot. (Open M-Sa 8:15am-7:30pm, Su 8:30am-noon.)

⛰️🎿 HIKING AND SKIING. Whether you've come to climb up the mountains or ski down them, you're in for a challenge. Wherever you go, be cautious—the mountains here are as wild and steep as they are beautiful. The Aiguille du Midi *téléphérique* (cable car) offers a pricey, knuckle-whitening ascent over forests and snowy cliffs to a needlepoint peak at the top, revealing a fantastic panorama from 3842m. (☎04 50 53 40 00. €34.) Bring your passport to continue by gondola to Helbronner, Italy for views of three countries and the Matterhorn and Mont Blanc peaks; pack a picnic to eat on the glacier (May-Sept., round-trip €18). Chamonix has 350km of hiking; the tourist office has a map with departure points and estimated length for all trails, some of which are accessible by cable car, which can save time and energy. Hikes generally either head into the north, facing mountains with their jagged peaks and snow fields, or to the south, with wildflowers, blue lakes, and views of Mt. Blanc. Sunken in a valley, Chamonix is surrounded by mountains ideal for skiing. To the south, Le Tour-Col de Balme, above the village of Le Tour, is ideal for beginner and intermediate skiers (☎04 50 54 00 58. Day pass €25.) On the northern side of the valley, Les Grands Montets is the *grande dame* of Chamonix skiing, with advanced terrain and remodeled snowboarding facilities. (☎04 50 53 13 18. Day pass €32.)

ANNECY

With narrow cobblestone streets, winding canals, and a turreted castle, Annecy (pop. 50,000) appears more like a fairy-tale fabrication than a modern city. The Palais de l'Isle, located in the beautiful *vielle ville*, is a 13th-century chateau that served as a prison for Resistance fighters during WWII. (Open June-Sept. daily 10am-6pm; Oct.-May M and W-Su 10am-noon and 2-5pm. €3.10, students €0.80.) The shaded Jardins de l'Europe are the town's pride and joy. Although it may be hard to tear yourself away from the charming city, Annecy's Alpine forests boast excellent hiking and biking trails, and its clear, crystalline lake is a popular spot for windsurfing and kayaking, particularly along the free plage d'Albigny. One of the best hikes begins at the Basilique de la Visitation, near the hostel. An exquisite 16km scenic *piste cyclable* (bike route) hugs the lake along the eastern coast.

Trains arrive at pl. de la Gare from: Chamonix (2½hr., 7 per day, €17); Grenoble (2hr., 12 per day, €15); Lyon (2hr., 9 per day, €18); Nice (7hr., 2 per day, €55); and Paris (4hr., 8 per day, €58-73). Autocars Frossard buses (☎04 50 45 73 90) leave from next to the station for Geneva, Switzerland. (1¼hr., 6 per day, €9) and Lyon (3½hr., 2 per day, €17). From the train station, take the underground passage to r. Vaugelas, go left and continue for four blocks, and enter the Bonlieu shopping mall to reach the tourist office, 1 r. Jean Jaurès, in pl. de la Libération. (☎04 50 45 00 33; www.lac-annecy.com. Open July-Aug. M-Sa 9am-6:30pm, Su 9am-12:30pm and 1:45-6:30pm;

Sept.-June daily 9am-12:30pm and 1:45-6pm.) In summer, you can reach the clean and beautifully located **⚑Auberge de Jeunesse "La Grande Jeanne" (HI) ❶**, on rte. de Semnoz, via the *ligne d'été* (dir.: Semnoz) from the station (€1); otherwise, take bus #1 (dir.: Marquisats) from the station to *Hôtel de Police*, turn right on av. du Tresum, and follow signs pointing to Semnoz. (☎04 50 45 33 19; fax 04 50 52 77 52. Breakfast included. Sheets €2.70. Reception daily 8am-10pm. Dorms €13. AmEx/MC/V.) Caring managers and spacious rooms await at **Hôtel Savoyard ❷**, 41 av. de Cran. From the train station, exit left, walk around the station on r. Brobigny to av. Berthollet, and turn left again on av. de Cran. (☎04 50 57 08 08. Breakfast €4. Open May-Oct. Singles and doubles €20, with bath €27-35; triples €25/31-41; quads with bath €41.) **Camping Bélvèdere ❶**, 8 rte. de Semnoz, is near the youth hostel. (☎04 50 45 48 30. Open mid-Apr. to mid-Oct. €13 for 2 people, tent, and car.) **Place Ste-Claire** has morning **markets** (Su, Tu and F 8am-noon) and some of the best restaurants in the city. A **Monoprix supermarket** fills the better part of pl. de Notre-Dame. (Open M-Sa 8:30am-7:30pm.) **Postal Code:** 74000.

LYON

Laid-back Lyon (pop. 1,200,000), usually a stopping point between the north and south, elicits cries of "forget Paris" from weary backpackers. Culinary capital, former center of the silk trade and French Resistance, and ultramodern city, Lyon is friendlier than that other French metropolis. It also has a few more centuries of history, having been a major crossroads since Augustus ordered the construction of roads connecting the provincial capital of Gaul to Italy. *Vieux Lyon* recalls the city's wealthy past with ornate 16th-century townhouses. This city is also a stomping ground for world-renowned chefs and an incubator for new culinary genius. If the way to your heart is through your stomach, Lyon will have you at *bon apètit.*

▤ TRANSPORTATION

Flights: Aéroport Lyon-Saint-Exupéry (LYS; ☎04 72 22 72 21), 25km east of Lyon. 50 daily flights to Paris. The TGV stops at the airport, and is cheaper than flying. **Sato-buses/Navette Aéroport** (☎04 72 68 72 17) shuttle passengers to Gare de Perrache, Gare de la Part-Dieu, and subway stops Jean Mace, Grange-Blanche, and Mermoz Pinel (every 20min., €8.20). **Air France** is at 17 r. Victor Hugo, 2ème (☎04 20 82 08 20).

Trains: Trains passing through Lyon stop only at **Gare de la Part-Dieu**, bd. Marius Vivier-Merle (M: Part-Dieu), in the business district on the east bank of the Rhône. Trains terminating at Lyon also stop at **Gare de Perrache**, pl. Carnot (M: Perrache). TGV trains to Paris stop at both. **SNCF** info and reservation desk at Part-Dieu open M-F 9am-7pm, Sa 9am-6:30pm; Perrache open M-Sa 9am-7pm. To: **Dijon** (2hr., 6 per day, €21); **Geneva,** Switzerland (2hr., 13 per day, €19); **Grenoble** (1¼hr., 21 per day, €18); **Marseilles** (3hr., 17 per day, €39); **Nice** (6hr., 12 per day, €48); **Paris** (2hr., 26 TGVs per day, €54-68); and **Strasbourg** (5½hr., 9 per day, €39).

Buses: On the lowest level of the Gare de Perrache, at the train station, and at Gorge de Loup in the 9ème (☎04 72 61 72 61 for all three). Perrache station open daily 5am-12:30am. Domestic companies include **Philibert** (☎04 78 98 56 00) and **Transport Verney** (☎04 78 70 21 01), but it's almost always cheaper, faster, and simpler to take the train. **Eurolines** (☎04 72 56 95 30; fax 04 72 41 72 43) travels out of France.

Local Transportation: TCL (☎04 78 71 70 00), has info offices at both train stations and major *Métro* stops. Pocket maps are available from the tourist office or any TCL branch. Tickets are valid for all methods of mass transport, including the *Métro*, buses, funiculars, and trams. 1hr. single-fare ticket €1.40; carnet of 10 €11, students €9. The *Ticket Liberté* day pass (€3.80) allows unlimited use of all mass transit for the day. The efficient **Métro** runs 5am-midnight. **Buses** run 5am-9pm (a few until midnight).

FRANCE

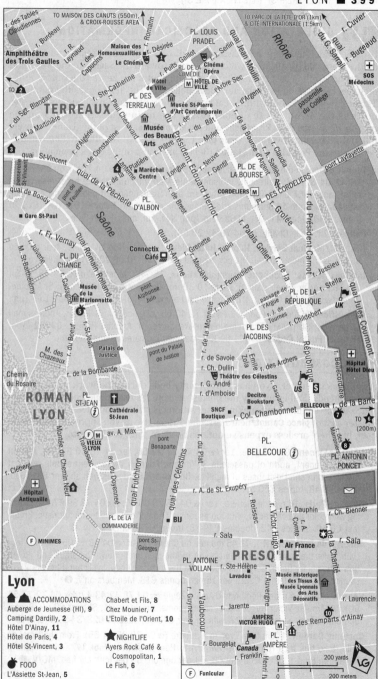

Lyon

ACCOMMODATIONS
Auberge de Jeunesse (HI), 9
Camping Dardilly, 2
Hôtel D'Ainay, 11
Hôtel de Paris, 4
Hôtel St-Vincent, 3

FOOD
L'Assiette St-Jean, 5

Chabert et Fils, 8
Chez Mounier, 7
L'Etoile de l'Orient, 10

NIGHTLIFE
Ayers Rock Café &
Cosmopolitan, 1
Le Fish, 6

(F) Funicular

FRANCE

⚡🛈 ORIENTATION AND PRACTICAL INFORMATION

Lyon is divided into nine **arrondissements** (districts). The 1*er*, 2*ème*, and 4*ème* lie on the **presqu'île** (peninsula), which juts south toward the **Saône** (to the west) and the **Rhône** (to the east) rivers. Starting in the south, the 2*ème* (the *centre ville*) includes the **Gare de Perrache** and **place Bellecour**. The 1*er* houses the nocturnal Terraux neighborhood, with its cafes and popular student-packed bars. Farther north is the 4*ème* and the **Croix-Rousse**. The main pedestrian roads on the *presqu'île* are **rue de la République** and **rue Victor Hugo**. West of the Saône, **Fourvière Hill** and its basilica overlook **Vieux Lyon** (5*ème*). East of the Rhône (3*ème* and 6-8*ème*) lies the **Part-Dieu** train station (3*ème*) and most of the city's population.

Tourist Office: In the Tourist Pavilion, at pl. Bellecour, 2*ème* (☎04 72 77 69 69; fax 04 78 42 04 32). M: Bellecour. Indispensable *Map and Guide*, free hotel reservation office, and SNCF desk. The **Lyon City Card** authorizes unlimited public transport along with admission to 14 museums and various tours. Valid for: 1 day €15, 2 days €25, or 3 days €30. Open May-Oct. M-Sa 9am-7pm; Nov.-Apr. daily 10am-6pm.

Police: 47 r. de la Charité (☎04 78 42 26 56).

Hospital/Medical Service: Hôpital Hôtel-Dieu, 1 pl. de l'Hôpital, 2*ème*, near quai du Rhône, is the most central. The city hospital line (☎08 20 08 20 09) will direct you.

Internet Access: Taxiphone Communications, 15-17 r. Montebello (☎04 78 14 54 25). €3 per hr. Open daily 8:30am-10:30pm. **Connectix Café,** 19 quai St-Antoine, 2*ème* (☎04 72 77 98 85). €7 divisible card allows 1hr. of use. Open M-Sa 11am-7pm.

Post Office: Pl. Antonin Poncet 2 (☎04 72 40 65 22), near pl. Bellecour. Address mail to be held: SURNAME Firstname, *Poste Restante,* pl. Antonin Poncet, **69002** Lyon, FRANCE. **Postal Codes:** 69001-69009; last digit indicates *arrondissement*.

🛏 ACCOMMODATIONS

As a financial center, Lyon has fewer empty beds during the work week than on the weekends. Fall is actually the busiest season; it's easier and cheaper to find a place in the summer, but making reservations is still a good idea. Budget hotels cluster east of **place Carnot**, near Perrache. Prices rise as you approach **place Bellecour,** but there are less expensive options north of **place des Terreaux.**

▩ Hôtel St-Vincent, 9 r. Pareille, 1*er* (☎04 78 27 22 56; fax 04 78 30 92 87). Just off quai St-Vincent, north of passerelle St-Vincent. Friendly owners rent simple, elegant rooms within short distances of nightlife. Breakfast €6. Singles with shower €31; doubles €38-48; triples €50-53. MC/V. ❸

Hôtel de Paris, 16 r. de la Platière, 1*er* (☎04 78 28 00 95; fax 04 78 39 57 64). Bursting with color and character, with rooms ranging from the classic to the futuristic. Breakfast €6.50. Singles €42; doubles €49-75; triples €78. AmEx/MC/V. ❹

Auberge de Jeunesse (HI), 41-45 montée du Chemin Neuf (☎04 78 15 05 50). M: Vieux Lyon. Take the funicular from *Vieux Lyon* to Minimes, walk down the stairs and go left down the hill for 5min. Gorgeous views from the *terrasse* and a lively bar. Sheets €2.70. Laundry €4.50. Internet €2.25 per 15min. Dorms €13. Members only. ❶

Hôtel d'Ainay, 14 r. des Remparts d'Ainay, 2*ème* (☎04 78 42 43 42; fax 04 72 77 51 90). M: Ampère-Victor Hugo. Basic, sunny rooms. Breakfast €4. Shower €2.50. Reception 6am-10pm. Singles €24-27, with shower €33-38; doubles €28/34-39. MC/V. ❷

Camping Dardilly, 10km from Lyon in a suburb (☎04 78 35 64 55). From the Hôtel de Ville, take bus #19 (dir.: Ecully-Dardilly) to Parc d'Affaires. Pool, TV, and restaurant. Reception 8am-10pm. Electricity €3. €3 per person; €6 per tent; car free. MC/V. ❶

🍴 FOOD

The galaxy of Michelin stars adorning the city's restaurants confirms what the locals proudly declare—this is the gastronomic capital of the Western world. But if *haute cuisine* doesn't suit your wallet, try one of Lyon's many **bouchons,** cozy restaurants serving local cuisine for low prices. They can be found in the **Terraux** district, along **rue des Marronniers** and **rue Mercière** (both in the 2*ème*), and on **rue St-Jean.** Ethnic restaurants are near **rue de la République,** in the 2*ème*.

Chez Mounier, 3 r. des Marronniers, 2*ème* (☎04 78 37 79 26). This tiny place satisfies a discriminating local clientele with generous traditional specialties. 4-course *menus* €9.60-15.10. Open Su noon-2pm, Tu-Sa noon-2pm and 7-10:30pm. ❸

Chabert et Fils, 11 r. des Marronniers, 2*ème* (☎04 78 37 01 94). One of the better-known *bouchons* in Lyon. For dessert, try the delicious *Guignol.* Lunch *menus* start at €8-12.50. Open daily noon-2pm and 7-11pm. MC/V. ❷

L'Assiette St-Jean, 10 r. St-Jean, 5*ème* (☎04 72 41 96 20). An excellent *bouchon,* with unusual, somewhat archaic decor. House specialty *gâteau de foies de volaille* (chicken liver) €6.60. *Menus* €13-27.50. Open in summer Su and Tu-Sa noon-2pm and 7-10:30pm. Closed Tu in winter. AmEx/MC/V. ❸

L'Etoile de l'Orient, 31 r. des Remparts d'Ainay, 2*ème* (☎04 72 41 07 87). M: Ampère-Victor Hugo. Be sure to have some tea at this intimate Tunisian restaurant, run by an exceedingly warm couple. Tajine lamb €11.50. Couscous dishes €11-13. *Menus* €10-25. Open M noon-2pm, Tu-Su noon-2pm and 7-11pm. ❸

🎇 SIGHTS

VIEUX LYON. Nestled along the Saône at the bottom of the Fourvière Hill, the cobblestone streets of *Vieux Lyon* wind between lively cafes and magnificent medieval and Renaissance **townhouses** (M: Vieux Lyon). The townhouses are graced with **traboules,** tunnels that lead from the street through a maze of courtyards. *(Tours in summer daily 2pm. €9, students €5.)* The southern end of *Vieux Lyon* is dominated by the 12th-century **Cathédrale St-Jean,** at pl. St-Jean, and its 14th-century astronomical clock, which can calculate Church feast days until 2019. *(Open M-F 8am-noon and 2-7:30pm, Sa-Su 8am-noon.)*

FOURVIÈRE AND ROMAN LYON. From the corner of r. du Bœuf and r. de la Bombarde in *Vieux Lyon,* climb the stairs to reach the **Fourvière Hill,** the nucleus of Roman Lyon. (M: Fourvière.) Continue up via the rose-lined **chemin de la Rosarie,** through a garden to the **esplanade Fourvière,** where a model of the cityscape points out local landmarks. Most prefer to take the funicular (*la ficelle*) from av. A. Max in *Vieux Lyon,* off pl. St-Jean, to the top of the hill. Behind the esplanade is the **Basilique Notre-Dame de Fourvière,** with multicolored mosaics, gilded pillars, and elaborate carvings. *(Open daily 8am-7pm.)* Set back into the hillside as you walk down from the church, you'll find the **Musée Gallo-Romain,** 17 r. Cléberg, 5*ème,* and its huge collection of arms, pottery, statues, and jewelry. Check out the bronze tablet inscribed with a speech by Lyon's favorite son, Emperor Claudius. *(Open Mar.-Oct. Su and Tu-Sa 10am-6pm; Nov.-Feb. reduced hours. €3.80, students €2.30. Th free.)*

LE PRESQU'ÎLE AND LES TERREAUX. Monumental squares, statues, and fountains mark the **Presqu'île,** the lively area between the Rhône and the Saône. The heart is **place Bellecour,** a sea of red gravel lined with shops and flower stalls. The pedestrian **rue Victor Hugo** runs south from pl. Bellecour; to the north, the crowded **rue de la République** is the urban artery of Lyon. It terminates at **place Louis Pradel** in the 1*er,* at the tip of the **Terreaux** district. Across the square at pl. Louis Pradel is the spectacular 17th-century **Hôtel de Ville.** In pl. des Terreaux is the huge **Musée des Beaux-Arts,** second only to the Louvre with a comprehensive archaeological wing, works by Spanish and Dutch masters, and a sculpture garden. *(Open Su-M and W-Sa 10:30am-6pm. €3.80, under-26 €2. Students with ID free.)*

EAST OF THE RHÔNE AND MODERN LYON. Lyon's newest train station and monstrous space-age mall form the core of the ultramodern Part-Dieu district. The **Centre d'Histoire de la Résistance et de la Déportation,** 14 av. Bertholet, 7*ème,* documents the Lyon-based resistance to the Nazis. *(M: Jean Mace. Open Su-M and W-Sa 9am-5:30pm. €3.80, students €2.)* The futuristic **Cité Internationale de Lyon,** quai Charles de Gaulle, 6*ème,* has a commercial complex housing offices, shops, theaters, Interpol's world headquarters, and the **Musée d'Art Contemporain.** *(Take bus #4 from M: Foch. Open Su-M and W-Sa noon-7pm. €3.80, students €2.)*

🎵🎭 ENTERTAINMENT AND NIGHTLIFE

At the end of June is the two-week **Festival du Jazz à Vienne,** which welcomes jazz masters to Vienne, a medieval town south of Lyon, accessible by bus or train. (☎04 74 85 00 05. Tickets €26, students €24.) **Les Nuits de Fourvière** is a three-month summer music festival held in the ancient Théâtre Romain and Odéon. (☎04 72 32 00 00. Tickets and info at the Théâtre Romain and the FNAC shop on r. de la République. €10-35.) The biennial **Festival de Musique du Vieux Lyon,** 5 pl. du Petit Collège, 5*ème,* draws artists worldwide between mid-Nov. and mid-Dec. to perform in the churches of *Vieux Lyon.* (☎04 78 42 39 04. Tickets €15-36.)

Nightlife in Lyon is fast and furious; the city is crawling with nightclubs. The best and most accessible spots are a strip of **riverboat dance clubs** by the east bank of the Rhône. 📍**Le Fish,** 21 quai Augagner, is the choice spot for *Lyonnais* youth. (€11-13 cover after 11pm. Open W-Th 10pm-5am, F-Sa 10pm-6am.) **Ayers Rock Café,** 2 r. Desirée, and **Cosmopolitan,** next door, are packed with students. (Ayers open M-Sa 6pm-3am. Cosmopolitan open M-Sa 8pm-3am.) The city guide from the tourist office lists gay and lesbian nightlife; the most popular spots are in the 1*er.*

BERRY-LIMOUSIN

Too often passed over for beaches and big cities, Berry-Limousin offers peaceful countryside and fascinating towns. Bourges served as the capital of France and benefited from King Charles VII's financier, Jacques Coeur, who built a lavish string of chateaux through the area. The region later became an artistic and literary breeding ground, home to Georges Sand, Auguste Renoir, and Jean Giraudoux.

BOURGES

In 1433, Jacques Coeur chose Bourges (pop. 80,000) as the site for one of his many chateaux. You'll see more of the unfurnished **Palais Jacques-Coeur** than he ever did, since he was imprisoned for embezzlement before its completion. (Open July-Aug. daily 9:30am-5:45pm; Sept.-June reduced hours. €6.10, ages 18-24 €4.10, under-18 free.) Inquire at the tourist office about excursions to other chateaux along the **Route Jacques Coeur.** The 📍**Cathédrale St-Etienne,** has stunning stained-glass that illuminates the white marble interior with deep reds and blues. The cathedral is free, but tickets are necessary to enter the simple **crypt** and scenic **tower.** (Open Apr.-Sept. daily 8:30am-7:15pm; Oct.-Mar. 9am-5:45pm. Closed Su morning. Crypt and tower €5.50, students €3.50.) As you exit the cathedral, head right on r. des 3 Maillets and turn left on r. Molière for the **promenade des Remparts,** which offers a quiet stroll past ramparts and flowery gardens.

Trains leave from the station at pl. Général Leclerc (☎02 48 51 00 00) for Paris (2½hr., 5-8 per day, €24) and Tours (1½hr., 10 per day, €17). From the station, follow av. H. Laudier, which turns into av. Jean Jaurès; bear left onto r. du Commerce, and continue down r. Moyenne to reach the **tourist office**, 21 r. Victor Hugo. (☎02 48 23 02 60; www.ville-bourges.fr. Open Apr.-Sept. M-Sa 9am-7pm, Su 10am-7pm; Oct.-Mar. reduced hours.) **Hôtel St-Jean ❷**, 23 av. Marx-Dormoy, has clean rooms, all with showers, and friendly owners. (☎02 48 24 70 45; fax 02 48 24 79 98. Breakfast €4. Singles €22-28; doubles €26-34; triples €43.) To get to the **Auberge de Jeunesse (HI) ❶**, 22 r. Henri Sellier, bear right from r. du Commerce on to r. des Arènes, which becomes r. Fernault, cross at the intersection to r. René Ménard, follow it to the right, and turn left at r. Henri Sellier. (☎02 48 24 58 09. Breakfast €3.30. Sheets €2.80. Reception daily 8am-noon and 5-10pm. Dorms €8.40.) **Place Gordaine, rue des Beaux-Arts, rue Moyenne**, and **rue Mirabeau** are lined with eateries. The **Leclerc supermarket** is on r. Prado off bd. Juraville. (Open M-F 9:15am-7:20pm, Sa 8:30am-7:20pm.) **Postal Code:** 18000.

BURGUNDY (BOURGOGNE)

What the Loire Valley is to chateaux, Burgundy is to churches. During the Middle Ages, it was the heart of the religious fever sweeping Europe: abbeys swelled in size and wealth, and towns eager for pilgrim traffic built magnificent cathedrals. Today, Burgundy's production of some of the world's finest wines and most delectable dishes, like *coq au vin* and *bœuf bourguignon*, have made this region the homeland of Epicureans worldwide.

DIJON

Dijon (pop. 160,000) isn't just about the mustard. The capital of Burgundy is a charming city with numerous gardens, a couple of good museums, and many fine wines. The diverse **Musée des Beaux-Arts** occupies the east wing of the colossal **Palais des Ducs de Bourgogne**, in pl. de la Libération at the center of the *vieille ville*. (☎03 80 74 52 70. Open May-Oct. W-M 9:30am-6pm; Nov.-Apr. W-M 10am-5pm. €3.40; students with ID free, Su free.) The brightly-tiled **Cathédrale St-Bénigne**, in pl. St-Bénigne, has a spooky circular crypt. (☎03 80 30 39 33. Open 9am-7pm. Crypt €1.) Next door, the **Musée Archéologique**, 5 r. Dr. Maret, features Gallo-Roman sculptures and Neolithic housewares. (☎03 80 30 88 54. Open June-Sept. Tu-Su 9am-6pm; Oct.-May Tu-Su 9am-noon and 2-6pm; €2.20; students free; Su free.) Get your **Grey Poupon** at the Maille Boutique, 32 r. de la Liberté, where *moutarde au vin* has been made since 1747. (☎03 80 30 41 02. Open M-Sa 9am-7pm. MC/V.)

From the train station at cours de la Gare, **trains** chug to: Lyon (2hr., 7 per day, €21); Nice (7-8hr., 6 per day, €57); Paris (1½hr., 20 per day, €26). The **tourist office**, in pl. Guillaume Darcy, is a straight shot down av. Maréchal Foch from the station. (☎03 80 44 11 44. Open May-Oct. daily 9am-7pm; Nov.-Apr. 10am-6pm.) ◪**Hôtel Montchapet ❸**, 26-28 r. Jacques Cellerier, 10min. north of av. Première Armée Française, off pl. Guillaume Darcy, is bright and comfortable. (☎03 80 53 95 00; www.hotelmontchapet.com. Breakfast €5. Reception 7am-10:30pm. Check-out 11am. Singles €26-39; doubles €36-46.) To get to the huge **Auberge de Jeunesse, Centre de Rencontres Internationales (HI) ❶**, 1 av. Champollion, take bus #5 (or night bus A) from pl. Grangier to Epirey. (☎03 80 72 95 20; fax 03 80 70 00 61. Breakfast included. Dorms €15; singles €28. MC/V.) **Rue Amiral Boussin** has charming cafes, while reasonably priced restaurants line **rue Mongue**. Fend for yourself at the **supermarket** in the basement of the Galeries Lafayette department store, 41 r. de la Liberté. (Open M-Sa 8:15am-7:45pm.) **Postal Code:** 21000.

▶ **DAYTRIP FROM DIJON: BEAUNE.** Wine has poured out of the well-touristed town of **Beaune** (pop. 24,000), just south of Dijon, for centuries. Surrounded by the famous Côte de Beaune vineyards, the town itself is packed with wineries offering free *dégustations* (tastings). The largest of the cellars belongs to ▧**Patriarche Père et Fils,** 5-7 r. du Collège, a 5km labyrinth of corridors packed with over four million bottles. (☎03 80 24 53 78. Open daily 9:30-11:30am and 2-5pm. €9.) The **tourist office,** 1 r. de l'Hôtel-Dieu, lists *caves* (cellars) that offer tours. (☎03 80 26 21 30; fax 03 80 26 21 39. Open mid-June to mid-Sept. M-Sa 9:30am-8pm, Su 10am-6pm; mid-Sept. to mid-June reduced hrs.) **Trains** run from Dijon (25min., 37 per day, €5.70).

ALSACE-LORRAINE AND FRANCHE-COMTÉ

As first prize in the endless Franco-German border wars, France's northeastern frontier has had a long and bloody history. Heavily influenced by its tumultuous past, the entire region now maintains a fascinating blend of French and German in the local dialects, cuisine, and architecture. Alsace's well-preserved towns offer half-timbered Bavarian houses flanking tiny crooked streets and canals, while Lorraine's elegant cities spread to the west among wheat fields. In Franche-Comté, the Jura mountains offer some of France's finest cross-country skiing.

STRASBOURG

Right near the Franco-German border, Strasbourg (pop. 450,000) has spent much of its history being annexed by one side or another. Today, German is often heard on its streets, and *winstubs* sit next door to *pâtisseries*. It is also the joint center, along with Brussels, of the European Union. With its rich culture and bustling university, Strasbourg combines cosmopolitan elegance with youthful energy.

▣▨ TRANSPORTATION AND PRACTICAL INFORMATION. Strasbourg is a major rail hub. **Trains** (☎03 88 22 50 50) go to: Luxembourg (2½hr., 14 per day, €27); Frankfurt (3hr., 18 per day, €47); Paris (4hr., 16 per day, €38); and Zürich (3hr., 18 per day, €35). The **tourist office,** 17 pl. de la Cathédrale, makes hotel reservations for a €1.60 fee plus deposit. (☎03 88 52 28 28. Open daily 9am-7pm.) There is also a branch at pl. de la Gare, near the train station (☎03 88 32 51 49). Get on the **Internet** at **Net computer,** 14 quai des Pêcheurs. (€2 per hr. Open M-F 10am-10pm, Sa and Su noon-10pm.) **Postal Code:** 67000.

▛▟ ACCOMMODATIONS AND FOOD. Make reservations or arrive early to find reasonable accommodations. ▧**CIARUS** (Centre International d'Accueil de Strasbourg) ❷, 7 r. Finkmatt, has large, spotless facilities. From the train station, take r. du Maire-Kuss to the canal, turn left, and follow quais St-Jean, Kléber, and Finkmatt; turn left on r. Finkmatt, and it's on the left. (☎03 88 15 27 88; www.ciarus.com. Breakfast included. Check-in 3:30pm. Check-out 9am. Curfew 1am. Dorms €16-18; singles €38. MC/V.) **Hôtel Kléber** ❹, 29 pl. Kléber, sits on the central pl. Kléber and has spacious, classy rooms. (☎03 88 32 09 53; www.hotel-kleber.com. Breakfast €6. Reception daily 7am-midnight. Singles €32-57; doubles €36-66; triples €66-73. AmEx/MC/V.) **Hôtel le Grillon** ❸, 2 r. Thiergarten, is 1 block from the station toward the city center, has large rooms above a bar where guests get a free drink with *Let's Go.* (☎03 88 32 71 88; www.grillon.com. Breakfast €7.50. **Internet** access free for 15min., €1 per 15min. thereafter. Singles €29, with shower €38-53; doubles €37/44-59. D/MC/V.) Informal *Winstubs* serve Alsatian specialties such as *choucroute garnie* (spiced sauerkraut served with meats); try the **La Petite France** neighborhood, especially along r. des Dentelles. Explore **place de la Cathédrale, rue Mercière,** or **rue du Vieil Hôpital** for restaurants, and **place Marché Gayot,** off r. des Frères, for lively cafes. For groceries, swing by the **ATAC,** 47 r. des Grandes Arcades, off pl. Kléber. (Open M-Sa 8:30am-8pm.)

🔲 📷 **SIGHTS AND ENTERTAINMENT.** The tower of the ornate Gothic 🏰**Cathédrale de Strasbourg** climbs 142m skyward. Inside, the **Horloge Astronomique** demonstrates the wizardry of 16th-century Swiss clockmakers. While you wait for the clock to strut its stuff—apostles troop out of the clockface while a cock crows to greet Saint Peter daily at 12:30pm—check out the **Pilier des Anges** (Angels' Pillar), a masterpiece of Gothic sculpture. You can climb the **tower** in front of the clock like the young Goethe, who scaled its 330 steps regularly to cure his fear of heights. (Cathedral open M-Sa 7-11:40am and 12:40-7pm, Su 12:45-6pm. Tickets for the clock on sale 8:30am in cathedral and 11:45am at south entrance; €0.80. Tower open Apr.-Oct. M-F 9am-5:30pm; Nov.-Mar. reduced hours. €3, students €1.50.) **Palais Rohan,** 2 pl. du Château, houses three small but excellent museums: the **Musée des Beaux-Arts, Musée des Arts Décoratifs,** and **Musée Archéologique.** (All open M and W-Su 10am-6pm. €4 each, students €2.50.) Take bus #23, 30, or 72 for **L'Orangerie,** Strasbourg's most spectacular park; free concerts play in the summer at the Pavilion Joséphine (Su-Tu and Th-Sa 8:30pm.) **Strasbourg** has bars everywhere. **Pl. Kléber** attracts a student crowd, while **rue des Frères** and the tiny **place du Marché Gayot** wake up with a mixed crowd after 10pm.

LA ROUTE DU VIN

Since the Middle Ages, the wines of Alsace have been highly prized—and priced. The vineyards of Alsace flourish along a 170km corridor known as La Route du Vin (Wine Route) that begins at **Strasbourg** (p. 404) and stretches south along the foothills of the Vosges, passing through 100 towns along the way to Mulhouse. Hordes of tourists are drawn each year to the beautifully preserved medieval villages along the route—and to the free *dégustations* (tastings) along the way.

Colmar (p. 406) and Sélestat (p. 405) offer excellent bases and fascinating sights, but don't miss smaller, less-touristed villages. The most accessible towns from Strasbourg are **Molsheim,** a medieval university center, and **Barr,** an old town with a vineyard trail that leads through the hills. The more famous towns lie to the south: The most visited sight in Alsace, the **Château de Haut Koenigsbourg,** towers over **Kintzheim;** and the 16th-century walled hamlet of **Riquewihr,** the Route's most popular village, with many of Alsace's best-known wine houses. To help plan your tour, pick up the 📷*Alsace Wine Route* brochure from a tourist office.

📧 **TRANSPORTATION.** Strasbourg, the northern terminus of the Wine Route, is a major rail hub, easily accessible from France, Germany, and Luxembourg. **Trains** from Strasbourg hit many of the towns along the northern half of the Route, including: Barr (50min., 10 per day, €5.50); Colmar (40min., 36 per day, €10); and Sélestat (30min., 20 per day, €6.50). Trains also run to Colmar from Sélestat, (15min., 20 per day, €3.70). **Bus** lines pepper the southern half of the Route, running from Colmar to Kaysersberg (20min., every hr., €2.30), Riquewihr (30min., 10 per day, €3), and many other small towns on the Route. From Mulhouse, head to nearby Basel, Switzerland (20min., 7 per day, €6.50); go to Paris (4½hr., 8 per day, €45), or return to Strasbourg (1hr., 14 per day, €14).

SÉLESTAT. Sélestat (pop. 17,200), between Colmar and Strasbourg, is a charming town often overlooked by tourists on their way to larger Route cities. The **Bibliothèque Humaniste,** 1 r. de la Bibliothèque, founded in 1452, contains a fascinating collection of ancient documents produced during Sélestat's 15th-century humanistic boom. (Open July-Aug. M and W-F 9am-noon and 2-6pm, Sa 9am-noon and 2-5pm, Su 2-5pm; Sept.-June closed Su. €3.50, students €2.) The **tourist office,** 10 bd. Général Leclerc, in the Commanderie St-Jean, rents **bikes** (€12.50 per day). From the train station, go straight on av. de la Gare, through pl. Général de Gaulle, to av. de la Liberté. Turn left onto bd. du Maréchal Foch, which veers right and becomes bd. Général Leclerc; the office is a few blocks down on your right.(☎03 88 58 87 20; www.selestat-tourisme.com. Open

July-Aug. M-F 9am-noon and 1:30-6:45pm, Sa 9am-noon and 2-5pm, Su 11am-3pm; Sept.-June. reduced hours M-Sa, closed Su.) The ▧**Hôtel de l'Ill ❷**, 13 r. des Bateliers, has bright rooms. (☎03 88 92 91 09. Breakfast €5. Reception daily 7am-3pm and 5-11pm. Singles €23; doubles €38; triples €55. MC/V.) **Camping Les Cigognes ❶** is on the south edge of the *vieille ville*. (☎03 88 92 03 98. Reception July-Aug. 8am-noon and 3-10pm; May-June and Sept.-Oct 8am-noon and 3-7pm. Open May-Oct. July-Aug. €9.20 per person, €13 per 2 or 3 people; reduced prices Sept.-Oct. and May-June.) The cobbled **rue des Chevaliers** has a wide variety of restaurants. **Postal Code:** 67600.

COLMAR. The bubbling fountains, crooked lanes, and pastel houses of Colmar (pop. 68,000) evoke an intimate charm despite the packs of tourists. The collection of **Musée Unterlinden,** 1 r. d'Unterlinden, ranges from Romanesque to Renaissance, including Grünewald's *Issenheim Altarpiece.* (Open May.-Oct. daily 9am-6pm; Nov.-Apr. M and W-Su 9am-noon and 2-5pm. €7, students €5.) The **Église des Dominicains,** on pl. des Dominicains, has Colmar's other major masterpiece, Schongauer's *Virgin in the Rose Bower.* (Open Apr.-Dec. daily 10am-1pm and 3-6pm. €1.30.) To get to the **tourist office,** 4 r. d'Unterlinden, from the train station, turn left on av. de la République (which becomes r. Kléber) and follow it to the right to pl. Unterlinden. (☎03 89 20 68 92; www.ot-colmar.fr. Open July-Aug. M-Sa 9am-7pm, Su 9:30am-2pm; Sept.-June reduced hours.) To reach the **Auberge de Jeunesse (HI) ❶,** 2 r. Pasteur, take bus #4 (dir.: Logelbach) to *Pont Rouge.* (☎03 89 80 57 39. Breakfast included. Sheets €3.50. Reception July-Aug. daily 7-10am and 5pm-midnight; Sept.-June 7-10am and 5-11pm. Lockout 10am-5pm. Curfew midnight. Open mid-Jan. to mid-Dec. Dorms €12; singles €17; doubles €28. Members only. MC/V.) **Hôtel Kempf ❸,** 1 av. de la République, has large rooms right in the middle of the *vielle ville.* (☎03 89 41 21 72; fax 03 89 23 06 94. Breakfast €6. Shower €2.50. Open early Feb. to mid-Jan; closed two weeks June-July. Singles and doubles €28, with shower €35; triples with bath €55. MC/V.) Take bus #1 (dir.: Horbourg-Wihr) to *Plage d'Ill* for **Camping de l'Ill ❶,** on rte. Horbourg-Wihr. (☎03 89 41 15 94. Reception July-Aug. daily 8am-10pm; Feb.-June and Sept.-Nov. 8am-8pm. Open Feb.-Nov. Electricity €2.40. €3 per person, €1.80 per child; €3.30 per site.) **Monoprix supermarket** is on pl. Unterlinden. (Open M-F 8am-8pm, Sa 8am-8pm.) **Grand Rue** has a multitude of *brasseries* and other tasty options. **Postal Code:** 68000.

BESANÇON

Surrounded by the river Doubs on three sides and by a steep bluff on the fourth, Besançon (pop. 120,000) has intrigued military strategists from Julius Caesar to the great military engineer Vauban 1800 years later. Today, Besançon boasts a smart, sexy student population and an impressive number of museums and discos. See the city's Renaissance buildings from high up in the Vauban's **citadel,** at the end of r. des Fusilles de la Résistance. Within the citadel, the **Musée de la Résistance et de la Déportation** chronicles the Nazi rise to power and the German occupation of France. Other sights include a natural history museum, a zoo, an aquarium, and a folk arts museum. (☎03 81 65 07 54. Open July-Aug. daily 9am-7pm; Sept.-June reduced hours. Closed Tu Nov.-Easter. €7, students €6.) The **Cathédrale St-Jean,** beneath the citadel, holds two treasures: The white marble **Rose de St-Jean** and the intricate 19th-century **Horloge Astronomique.** (Open M and W-Su 9am-6pm. €2.50. Students and under-18 free.) The **Musée des Beaux-Arts et d'Archéologie,** on pl. de la Révolution, houses an exceptional collection ranging from ancient Egyptian mummies to works by Matisse, Picasso, and Renoir. (☎03 81 87 80 49. Open M and W-Su 9:30am-12:30pm and 2-6pm. €3. Students free, Su and holidays free.) The area between **rue Claude Pouillet** and **rue Pont Battant** buzzes with nightlife. ▧**Carpe Diem,** 2 pl. Jean Gigoux, is a hotspot that brings together students and non-students for drinks and discussion, with events and concerts held regularly. (☎03 81 83 11 18. Beer €2. Open M-Th 7am-1am, F-Sa 7am-2am, Su 8am-

11pm. MC/V.) Shoot pool at the surprisingly hip **Pop Hall**, 26 r. Proudhon. (☎03 81 83 01 90. Beer €2. Open Su-Th 2pm-1am, F-Sa 2pm-2am.)

Trains pull up at the station on av. de la Paix (☎08 36 35 35 35) from: Dijon (1hr., 22 per day, €12); Paris (2hr., 8 per day, €43); and Strasbourg (3hr., 10 per day, €27). Monts Jura **buses**, 9 r. Proudhon (☎03 81 21 22 00), go to Pontarlier (1hr., 6 per day, €8). From the station, walk downhill; turn onto av. Maréchal Foch, and continue to the left as it becomes av. de l'Helvétie, until you reach pl. de la Première Armée Française. The *vieille ville* is across the pont de la République; the **tourist office**, 2 pl. de la Première Armée Française, is in the park to the right. (☎08 20 32 07 82; www.besancon-tourisme.com. Open Apr.-Sept. M 10am-7pm, Tu-Sa 9am-7pm, Su 10am-noon; Oct.-Mar. reduced hours.) Check **email** at **T@cybernet**, 18 r. de Pontarlier. (☎03 81 81 15 74; www.tacybernet.com. €3.60 per hr. Open M-Sa 11am-10pm, Su 2-8pm. MC/V.) For the **Foyer Mixte de Jeunes Travailleurs (HI) ❷**, 48 r. des Cras, take bus #7 or night line A (both €0.90) from pl. Flore (dir.: Orchamps, 3-5 per hr.). To get to pl. Flore bus stop, cross the parking lot of the train station and head down the stairs. Take the road in front of you that heads slightly to the left (av. de la Paix), and keep to the left as the road bends and turns into r. de Belfort. Turn right onto av. Carnot, walk for a block until you see the green lights of the pharmacy in pl. Flore, and take a sharp left onto r. des Chaprais. This friendly hostel has concerts, movies, and other special events, as well as free Internet access in the lobby. (☎03 81 40 32 00; fax 03 81 40 32 01. Singles €17; doubles €25. AmEx/MC/V.) **Hôtel du Nord ❸**, 8-10 r. Moncey, has clean rooms in a quiet but central location. (☎03 81 81 35 56; fax 03 81 81 85 96. Breakfast €4.60. Singles and doubles with shower or bath €30-52; triples and quads with shower €54. AmEx/D/MC/V.) A variety of restaurants line **rue Claude-Pouillet**. Buy groceries at **Monoprix supermarket**, 12 Grande Rue. (Open M-Sa 8:30am-8pm.)

▶ DAYTRIP FROM BESANÇON: PONTARLIER AND THE JURA. The sedate town of **Pontarlier** (pop. 18,400) is a good base from which to explore the oft-overlooked **Haut-Jura Mountains**. The Jura are best known for **cross-country skiing;** nine trails cover every skill level. (Day pass €6, under-17 €3.50; available at the Le Larmont and Le Malmaison trails.) Le Larmont is the closest Alpine ski area (☎03 81 46 55 20). In summer, **fishing, hiking,** and **mountain biking** are popular. Monts Jura **buses** (☎81 39 88 80) run to Besançon (1hr., 6 per day, €8). The **tourist office,** 14 bis r. de la Gare, has guides and maps. (☎03 81 46 48 33; fax 03 81 46 83 32. Open July-Aug. M-Sa 9am-6pm, Su 10am-noon; Sept.-June M-Sa 9am-6pm.) **Postal Code:** 25300.

ON THE MENU

THE GOÛT DU VIN

Being in France and drinking wine go hand in hand. Perhaps in a less heralded wine region you could avoid looking like an amateur, but the wine lists along the Route du Vin are a bit more daunting. It's time to learn if that wine was a *première cuvée* or just a bouquet of walnuts and old socks:

Gewurztraminer: This dry, aromatic white wine has been called "The Emperor of Alsatian wines." Drink it as an apéritif with foie gras, pungent cheeses, or Indian, Mexican, or Asian cuisine.

Riesling: Considered one of the world's finest white wines, Riesling is fruity, very dry, and accompanies white meats, *choucroute*, and fish.

Sylvaner: From an Austrian grape, Sylvaner is a light, slightly sparkling white wine that goes well with seafood and salads.

Muscat: A sweet and highly fruity white wine, often an apéritif.

The Pinot family: Pinot Blanc is an all-purpose white wine for chicken, fish, and all sorts of appetizers; **Pinot Gris** is a smoky, strong white wine that can often take the place of a red wine in accompanying rich meats, roasts, and game; and **Pinot Noir**, the sole red wine of the Alsatian bunch, tastes of cherries and complements red meats.

NANCY

Nancy (pop. 100,000) has always been passionate about beauty: the town that spawned the art-nouveau "Nancy school" is today the artistic and intellectual heart of modern Lorraine. The elaborate ◪**Place Stanislas** houses three neoclassical pavilions, with *son-et-lumière* (sound and light) spectacles held nightly at 10pm in July and August. The collection in the **Musée des Beaux-Arts**, 3 pl. Stanislas, spans from the 14th century to today. (☎03 83 85 30 72. Open Su-M and W-Sa 10am-6pm. €4.80, students €2.30. W and 1st Su of the month students free.) Portals of pink roses lead into the aromatic **Roseraie,** in the relaxing **Parc de la Pépinière,** just north of pl. de la Carrière. (Open May-Sept. 6:30am-11:30pm; Oct.-Apr. reduced hours. Free.) Nancy has a vibrant arts and nightlife scene; check www.nancybynight.com for info on everything from theater to concerts to clubs. **Rue Stanislas** and **Grand Rue** are great places to grab a drink.

Trains (☎03 83 22 12 46) depart from the station at pl. Thiers for Paris (3hr., 14 per day, €36) and Strasbourg (1hr., 17 per day, €19). Follow r. Raymond Poincaré away from the station, through a stone archway, and continue straight to pl. Stanislas and the **tourist office.** (☎03 83 35 22 41; www.ot-nancy.fr. Open Apr.-Sept. M-Sa 9am-7pm, Su 10am-5pm; Oct.-Mar. M-Sa 9am-6pm, Su 10am-1pm.) Access the **Internet** at **E-café,** r. des Quatre Eglises. (☎03 83 35 47 34. €5.40 per hr. Open M-Sa 9am-9pm, Su 2-8pm.) **Centre d'Accueil de Remicourt (HI) ❶**, 149 r. de Vandoeuvre, is in Villiers-les-Nancy, 4km away. From the station, take bus #122 to *St-Fiacre* (dir.: Villiers Clairlieu; 2 per hr.; confirm route with the driver); head downhill from the stop, turn right on r. de la Grange des Moines, which turns into r. de Vandoeuvre. Signs point to Château de Remicourt. (☎03 83 27 73 67. Reception 9am-9pm. Dorms €13; doubles €29. MC/V.) **Hôtel Flore ❸**, 8 r. Raymond Poincaré, near the train station, is bright and homey. (☎03 83 37 63 28. Reception 7:30am-2am. Singles €26-32; doubles €37-40; triples €43. AmEx/MC/V.) Restaurants line **rue des Maréchaux, place Lafayette,** and **place St-Epvre.** A **SHOPI** market sits at 26 r. St-Georges. (Open M-Sa 9am-8pm. MC/V.) **Postal Code:** 54000.

CHAMPAGNE AND THE NORTH

Legend has it that at the moment he discovered Champagne, Dom Perignon exclaimed, "Come quickly, I am drinking the stars!" Since then everyone from Napoleon to John Maynard Keynes has proclaimed its virtues. The term "champagne" is fiercely guarded; the name can only be applied to wines made from regional grapes and produced according to a rigorous, time-honored method. As you head further north to the ferry ports, don't overlook the intriguing Flemish culture of Arras and the world-class art collections of Lille.

REIMS

Reims (pop. 185,000) sparkles with the champagne of its famed caves, the beauty of its architectural masterpieces, and the excitement of its nightlife. The **Cathédrale de Notre-Dame,** built with golden limestone quarried in the Champagne *caves,* features sea-blue stained-glass windows by Marc Chagall. (☎03 26 77 45 25. Open daily 7:30am-7:30pm. €6, students €3.50.) Enter the adjacent **Palais du Tau,** at pl. du Cardinal Luçon, for dazzling 16th-century tapestries. (☎03 26 47 81 79. Open May-Aug. Su and Tu-Sa 9:30am-6:30pm; Sept.-Apr. reduced hours. €6.10, students €4.10.) The firm of **Champagne Pommery,** 5 pl. du Général Gouraud, boasts the largest *tonneau* (vat) in the world, and the best tour of the Champagne caves in Reims. (☎03 26 61 62 56. Tours by reservation. €7, students €3.50.) For good deals on champagne, look for sales on local brands and check prices at supermarkets. Good bottles start at €9.50. The small schoolroom where Germany surrendered to the Allies during WWII is now the **Musée de la Reddition,** 12 r. Franklin Roosevelt, a potent time capsule for the momentous event it witnessed. At night, people congregate in the cafes and bars of **place Drouet d'Erlon.**

Trains (☎ 03 26 88 11 65) leave bd. Joffre for Épernay (25min., 16 per day, €5.20). Paris (1½hr., 11 per day, €21). To get from the train station to the **tourist office**, 2 r. Guillaume de Machault, follow the right-hand curve of the rotary to pl. Drouet d'Erlon, turn left onto r. de Vesle, turn right on r. du Tresor, and it's on the left before the cathedral. (☎ 03 26 77 45 00; www.tourisme.fr/reims. Open mid-Apr. to mid-Oct. M-Sa 9am-7pm, Su 10am-6pm; mid-Oct. to mid-Apr. M-F 9am-noon and 2-6pm, Sa 9am-6pm, Su 10am-5pm.) The ◪**Centre International de Séjour/Auberge de Jeunesse (HI) ❶**, on chaussée Bocquaine, has bright, comfortable rooms. Cross the park in front of the station, following the right-hand side of the traffic circle. Turn right onto bd. Général Leclerc, follow it to the canal and cross the first bridge (pont de Vesle) on your left. Bocquaine is the first left. (☎ 03 26 40 52 60; fax 03 26 47 35 70. Dorms €10; singles €15, with shower €26; doubles €22/30; triples with shower €36. Nonmembers add €2. AmEx/MC/V.) The sunny and spotless **Au Bon Accueil ❷**, 31 r. Thillois, is just off the central pl. d'Erlon. (☎ 03 26 88 55 74; fax 03 26 05 12 38. Breakfast €4.50. Singles €18-27; doubles €30-39. MC/V.) **Place Drouet d'Erlon** is crowded with cafes, restaurants, and bars. **Monoprix supermarket** is at r. de Vesle and r. de Talleyrand. (Open M-Sa 8:30am-9pm.) **Postal Code: 51100.**

ÉPERNAY

Épernay (pop. 30,000), at the juncture of three wealthy grape-growing regions, is appropriately ritzy. The aptly named **avenue de Champagne** is distinguished by its palatial mansions, lush gardens, and swanky champagne companies. **Moët & Chandon,** 20 av. de Champagne, produces the king of all wines: Dom Perignon. (☎ 03 26 51 20 20. Open late Mar.-early Nov. daily 9:30-11:30am and 2-4:30pm; early Nov. to late Mar. M-F 9:30-11:30am and 2-4:30pm. 1hr. tour with one glass €7.50.) Ten minutes away is **Mercier,** 70 av. de Champagne, the self-proclaimed "most popular champagne in France," which gives tours in rollercoaster-like cars. (☎ 03 26 51 22 22. Open Mar.-Nov. daily 9:30-11:30am and 2-5pm; Dec. 1-19 and Jan. 13-Mar. Su-M and Th-Sa 9:30-11:30am and 2-4:30pm. 30min. tours €6.)

Trains leave cour de la Gare for Paris (1¼hr., 18 per day, €18) and Reims (25min., 16 per day, €5.20). From the station, walk straight ahead through pl. Mendès France, go one block up r. Gambetta to the central **place de la République,** and turn left on av. de Champagne to reach the **tourist office,** 7 av. de Champagne. (☎ 03 26 53 33 00. Open Easter-Oct. 15 M-Sa 9:30am-noon and 1:30-7pm, Su 11am-4pm; Oct. 16-Easter M-Sa 9:30am-5:30pm.) Épernay caters to the champagne set—budget hotels are rare. ◪**Hôtel St-Pierre ❷**, 14 av. Paul-Chandon, is the best budget bet, with spacious, antique-furnished rooms. (☎ 03 26 54 40 80; fax 03 26 57 88 68. Breakfast €5. Reception 7am-10pm. Singles and doubles €21, with shower €25-32. MC/V.) **Rue Gambetta** has ethnic eateries, while the area around **place des Arcades** and **place Hugues Plomb** is dotted with delis and bakeries. **Postal Code: 51200.**

TROYES

While the city plan of Troyes (pop. 56,000) resembles a champagne cork, this city shares little with its grape-crazy northern neighbors. Gothic churches, 16th-century mansions, and an abundance of museums attest to the city's colorful role in French history, dating back to the Middle Ages. The enormous **Cathédrale St-Pierre et St-Paul,** pl. St-Pierre, down r. Clemenceau past the town hall, has stunning stained glass that has remarkably survived several fires and other disasters. (Open daily 10am-noon and 2-5pm. Closed M morning.) The **Musée d'Art Moderne,** on pl. St-Pierre, has over 2000 works by French artists, including Degas, Rodin, and Seurat. (Open Tu-Su 11am-6pm. €6, students €0.80; W free.) Cinemas and pool halls rub elbows with chic boutiques on **rue Emile Zola.** On warm nights, *Troyens* fill the cafes and taverns of **rue Champeaux** and **rue Mole** near pl. Alexandre Israel.

Trains run from av. Maréchal Joffre to Paris (1½hr., 14 per day, €8.60). The **tourist office,** 16 bd. Carnot, near the station, helps reserve rooms. (☎03 25 82 62 70; www.ot-troyes.fr. Open M-Sa 9am-12:30pm and 2-6:30pm.) ▨**Les Comtes de Champagne ❸,** 56 r. de la Monnaie, is housed in a 16th-century mansion and has large, airy rooms. (☎03 25 73 11 70; www.comtesdechampagne.com. Reception 7am-10pm. Singles from €28; doubles from €32; triples from €50; quads from €55.) **Camping Municipal ❶,** 2km from Troyes, on N60, has showers and laundry facilities. Take bus #1 (dir.: Pont St-Marie) and ask to be let off at the campground. (☎03 25 81 02 64. Open Apr. to mid-Oct. €4 per person, €5.50 per tent or car.) *Crêperies* and inexpensive eateries lie near **rue Champeaux,** in *quartier* St-Jean, and on **rue Général Saussier,** in *quartier* Vauluisant. You can stock up at **Monoprix supermarket,** 78 r. Emile Zola. (Open M-Sa 8:30am-8pm.) **Postal Code: 10000.**

▶ DAYTRIPS FROM TROYES: LES GRANDS LACS. About 30km from Troyes are the freshwater lakes of the Forêt d'Orient. While **Lake Orient** welcomes sunbathers, swimmers, and windsurfers; **Lake Temple** is reserved for fishing and bird-watching; and **Lake Amance** roars with speedboats from **Port Dierville.** The **Comité Départemental du Tourisme de l'Aube,** 34 quai Dampierre, provides free brochures on various activities. (☎03 25 42 50 00; fax 03 25 42 50 88. Open M-F 8:45am-noon and 1:30-6pm.) The Troyes tourist office has bus schedules for the Grands Lacs.

LILLE

A longtime international hub with a rich Flemish ancestry and exuberant nightlife, Lille (pop. 175,000) exudes big-city charm without the hassle. The impressive **Musée des Beaux-Arts,** on pl. de la République, boasts a wide display of 15th- to 20th-century French and Flemish masters. (M: République. Open M 2-6pm, W-Th and Sa-Su 10am-6pm, F 10am-7pm. €4.60, students €3.) Housed in a renovated interior pool, aptly named **La Piscine,** 23 r. de L'Esperance (M: Gare Jean Lebas), has a collection that includes paintings from the 19th and early 20th centuries, vases and stained glass. (Open Tu-Th 11am-6pm, F 11am-8pm, Sa-Su 1-8pm.) The **Vielle Bourse** (Old Stock Exchange), on pl. Général de Gaulle, epitomizing the Flemish Renaissance, houses flower and book markets. (Markets Su and Tu-Sa 9:30am-7:30pm.) At night, students flock to the pubs along **rue Solférino** and **rue Masséna,** while the **vielle ville** has a more sophisticated scene.

Trains leave from Gare Lille Flandres, on pl. de la Gare (M: Gare Lille Flandres), for Brussels, Belgium (1½hr., 20 per day, €22) and Paris (1hr., 21 per day, €34-45). Gare Lille Europe, on r. Le Corbusier (M: Gare Lille Europe; ☎08 36 35 35 35), sends **Eurostar** trains to London, Brussels, and Paris and all TGVs to the south of France and Paris. From Gare Lille Flandres, walk straight down r. Faidherbe and turn left through pl. du Théâtre and pl. de Gaulle; behind the huge war monument is the **tourist office,** pl. Rihour (M: Rihour), which offers free maps and currency exchange. (☎03 20 21 94 21; fax 03 20 21 94 20. Open M-Sa 9:30am-6:30pm, Su 10am-noon and 2-5pm.) To reach the friendly and spacious **Auberge de Jeunesse (HI) ❶,** 12 r. Malpart, from Gare Lille Flandres, circle left around the station, turn right onto r. du Molinel, take the second left on r. de Paris, and take the 3rd right onto r. Malpart. (☎03 20 57 08 94; fax 03 20 63 98 93. M: Mairie de Lille. Sheets €2.75. Key deposit €10. Reception 7-11am and 3pm-1am. Check-out 10am. Curfew 1am. Open Feb. to mid-Dec. Dorms €13.) The spotless **Hôtel Faidherbe ❸,** 42 pl. de la Gare (M: Gare Lille Flandres), is noise-proof. (☎03 20 06 27 93; fax 03 20 55 95 38. Singles and doubles €28-42; triples €50. 10% *Let's Go* discount. AmEx/MC/V.) Restaurants and markets line **rue de Béthune, rue Léon Gambetta** and **place du Théâtre.** A huge **Carrefour supermarket** is next to the Gare Lille Europe train station in the EuraLille shopping center. (Open M-Sa 9am-10pm.) **Postal Code: 59000.**

⊠ DAYTRIPS FROM LILLE: ARRAS AND VIMY. The town hall of Arras (pop. 80,000), in the gorgeous **Hôtel de Ville,** is built over the eerie **Les Boves** tunnels, which have sheltered both medieval chalk miners and WWI soldiers (Contact tourist office for tours. €3.80, students €2.30.) **Trains** leave pl. Maréchal Foch for Lille (45min., 20 per day, €8.80). From the train station, walk across pl. Foch to r. Gambetta, turn left on r. Desire Delansorne, turn left, and walk two blocks to reach the **tourist office,** on pl. des Héros, in the Hôtel de Ville. (☎ 03 21 51 26 95. Open May-Sept. M-Sa 9am-6:30pm, Su 10am-1pm and 2:30-6:30pm; Oct.-Apr. reduced hours.) The countryside surrounding Arras is dotted with war cemeteries and unmarked graves. The vast limestone **Vimy Memorial,** 12km from Arras, honors the more than 66,000 Canadians killed in WWI. The morbid yet beautiful park, whose soil came from Canada, is dedicated to the crucial victory at Vimy Ridge in 1917. Stay on the marked paths, as there are still undetonated mines in the area. The kiosk by the trenches is the starting point for an **underground tour** of the crumbling tunnels dug by British and Canadian soldiers. (☎ 03 21 59 19 34. Memorial open dawn-dusk. Tunnel tours Apr. to mid-Nov. 10am-6pm. Free) The closest town, **Vimy,** is 3km away. **Buses** run from Arras to Vimy (20min., 8 per day M-Sa, €2.40).

CALAIS

Calais (pop. 80,000) is the liveliest of the Channel ports, and with the Chunnel next door, English is spoken as often as French. Rodin's famous sculpture **The Burghers of Calais** stands in front of the **Hôtel de Ville,** at the juncture of bd. Jacquard and r. Royale. Follow r. Royale to the end of r. de Mer for Calais's wide, gorgeous **beaches.** See p. 49 for schedules and prices to **Dover,** England. During the day, free **buses** connect the ferry terminal and train station, Gare Calais-Ville, on bd. Jacquard, from which **trains** leave for: Boulogne (45min., 8 per day, €6.30); Lille (1¼hr., 8 per day, €14); and Paris-Nord (3¼hr., 6 per day, €40). To reach the **tourist office,** 12 bd. Clemenceau, from the train station, turn left, cross the bridge; it's on your right. (☎ 03 21 96 62 40; fax 03 21 96 01 92. Open M-Sa 9am-7pm, Su 10am-1pm.) The renovated **Centre Européen de Séjour/Auberge de Jeunesse (HI) ❶,** av. Maréchal Delattre de Tassigny, is near the beach. (☎ 03 21 34 70 20; fax 03 21 96 87 80. Dorms €14.50. Nonmembers add €1.50.) The quiet **Hotel Bristol ❸,** 13-15 r. du Duc de Guise, is off the main road. (☎ 03 21 34 53 24. Singles €25; doubles €36. MC/V.) **Markets** are held on pl. Crèvecoeur and on pl. d'Armes (both W and Sa); or look for **Prisunic supermarket,** 17 bd. Jacquard. (Open M-Sa 8:30am-7:30pm, Su 10am-7pm.) **Postal Code:** 62100.

BOULOGNE-SUR-MER

With its refreshing breeze and lavish floral displays, Boulogne (pop. 46,000) is by far the most attractive Channel port. The huge **Château-Musée,** r. de Bernet, houses an eclectic collection that includes Napoleon's second-oldest hat. (Open M and W-Sa 10am-12:30pm and 2-5pm, Su 10am-12:30pm and 2:30-5:30pm. €3.50, students €2.50.) Boulogne also has a huge aquarium, **Le Grand Nausicaa,** bd. Ste-Beuve. (Open July-Aug. daily 9:30am-8pm; Sept.-June reduced hours. €12, students €8.50.) **Trains** leave Gare Boulogne-Ville, bd. Voltaire, for: Calais (30min., 18 per day, €6.40); Lille (2½hr., 11 per day, €18); Paris-Nord (2-3hr., 11 per day, €26-47). From the train station, turn right on bd. Voltaire, turn left on bd. Danou and follow it to pl. Angleterre; continue past pl. de France and pl. Frédéric Sauvage onto r. Gambetta for the **tourist office,** 24 quai Gambetta. (☎ 03 21 10 88 10; fax 03 21 10 88 11. Open July-Aug. M-Sa 9am-7pm, Su 10am-1pm and 3-6pm; Sept.-June reduced hours.) The fantastic ⊠**Auberge de Jeunesse (HI) ❶,** 56 pl. Rouget de Lisle, is across from the station. (☎ 03 21 99 15 30; fax 03 21 80 45 62. **Internet** €2 per 40min. Reception in summer daily 8am-1am; off-season 8am-midnight. Curfew 1am. Dorms €15. Nonmembers add €3. MC/V.) **Champion supermarket,** on r. Daunou, is in the Centre Commercial de la Liane mall. (Open M-Sa 8:30am-8pm.) **Postal Code:** 62200.

GERMANY
(DEUTSCHLAND)

Germany is a nation saddled with an incredibly fractured past. Steeped deeply in Beethoven's fiery orchestration and Goethe's Faustian whirlwind, modern Germany must also contend with the legacy of xenophobia and genocide left by Hitler and the Third Reich. Even now, more than a decade after the fall of the Berlin Wall, Germans are still fashioning a new identity for themselves. After centuries of war and fragmentation, Germany finds itself a wealthy nation at the forefront of both European and global politics. Its medieval castles, snow-covered mountains, and funky metropolises make Germany well worth a visit.

FACTS AND FIGURES

Official Name: Federal Republic of Germany.

Capital: Berlin.

Major Cities: Cologne, Frankfurt, Hamburg, Munich.

Population: 83,030,000.

Land Area: 357,021 sq. km.

Time Zone: GMT + 1.

Language: German.

Religions: Protestant (38%), Roman Catholic (34%), Muslim (2%), unaffiliated or other (27%).

DISCOVER GERMANY

Sprawling over an area eight times the size of Paris, **Berlin** (p. 416) is the palpitating cultural and political heart of the country. **Dresden** (p. 440) is nearly as intense, with a jumping nightlife and thoroughly palatial feel. To the north, reckless **Hamburg** (p. 449), Germany's second-largest city, fuses the burliness of a port town with cosmopolitan flair, while **Cologne** (p. 457) worships in the world's tallest Gothic cathedral. **Koblenz** (p. 468), to the south, is the gateway to the castles and wine towns of the **Rhine Valley.** Germany's oldest and most prestigious university sits below the ruins of a castle in **Heidelberg** (p. 469). From there, live out your favorite Grimms' fairy tales in the **Black Forest** (p. 474) or follow the **Romantic Road** (p. 489) along the western edge of Bavaria. No trip to Germany would be complete without visiting the Bavarian capital of **Munich** (p. 475), which takes bucolic merriment to a frothy head with its excellent museums and jovial beer halls.

ESSENTIALS

WHEN TO GO

Germany's climate is temperate, with rain year-round (especially in summer). The cloudy, moderate months of May, June, and September are the best time to go, as there are fewer tourists and the weather is pleasant. Germans head to vacation spots en masse in early July with the onset of school vacations. Winter sports gear up November to April; skiing high-season is mid-December to March.

DOCUMENTS AND FORMALITIES

VISAS. South Africans require a visa. Citizens of Australia, Canada, the EU, New Zealand, and the US do not need a visa for stays of up to 90 days.

EMBASSIES. All foreign embassies are in Berlin (p. 416). German embassies at home include: **Australia,** 119 Empire Circuit, Yarralumla, Canberra, ACT 2600 (☎(02) 62 70 19 11); **Canada,** 1 Waverly St., Ottawa, ON K2P OT8 (☎(613) 232-1101); **Ireland,** 31 Trimleston Ave., Booterstown, Blackrock, Co. Dublin (☎(01) 269 30 11); **New Zealand,** 90-92 Hobson St., Thorndon, Wellington (☎(04) 473 60 63); **South Africa,** 180 Blackwood St., Arcadia, Pretoria, 0083 (☎(012) 427 89 00); **UK,** 23 Belgrave Sq., London SW1X 8PZ (☎(020) 7824 1300); and **US,** 4645 Reservoir Rd., Washington, D.C. 20007 (☎202-298-8140).

GERMANY

TRANSPORTATION

BY PLANE. Most flights land in Frankfurt; Berlin, Munich, and Hamburg also have international airports. **Lufthansa,** the national airline, has the most flights in and out of the country, but they're not always the cheapest option. Flying within Germany is usually more expensive and less convenient than taking the train.

BY TRAIN. The **DB (Deutsche Bahn)** network (in Germany ☎ (0180) 599 66 33; www.bahn.de) is Europe's best but also one of its most expensive. **RE** (Regional-Express) and the slightly slower **RB** (RegionalBahn) trains include a number of rail networks between neighboring cities. **IR** (InterRegio) trains, covering larger networks between cities, are speedy and comfortable. **D** trains are foreign trains that serve international routes. **EC** (EuroCity) and **IC** (InterCity) trains zoom between major cities every hour from 6am-10pm. You must purchase a *Zuschlag* (supplement) for IC or EC trains (€3.60). **ICE** (InterCityExpress) trains approach the luxury and kinetics of an airplane, running at speeds up to 280km per hour. On all trains, second-class compartments are clean and comfortable.

Designed for tourists, the **German Railpass** allows unlimited travel for four to 10 days within a four-week period. Non-Europeans can purchase German Railpasses in their home countries and—with a passport—in major German train stations (2nd-class 4-day pass €180, 10-day €316). The **German Rail Youth Pass** is for those under 26 (4-day pass €142, 10-day €216). A **Schönes-Wochenende-Ticket** (€28) gives up to five people unlimited travel on any of the slower trains (RE or RB) from 12:01am Saturday or Sunday until 3am the next day. Single travelers often find larger groups who will share their ticket for a fraction of the purchase cost.

BY BUS. Bus service between cities and to outlying areas runs from the local **ZOB** (*Zentralomnibusbahnhof*), which is usually close to the main train station. Buses are often slightly more expensive than trains for comparable distances. Railpasses are not valid on any buses other than a few run by Deutsche Bahn.

BY CAR. German road conditions are generally excellent. It's true, there is no set speed limit on the *Autobahn*, only a recommendation of 130kph (80mph). Germans drive fast. Watch for signs indicating right-of-way (usually designated by a yellow triangle). The *Autobahn* is marked by an intuitive "A" on signs; secondary highways, where the speed limit is usually 100kph (60mph), are accompanied by signs bearing a "B." Germans drive on the right side of the road; in cities and towns, speed limits hover around 30-60kph (20-35mph). Germans use mainly unleaded gas; prices run around €4.30 per gallon, or €1.10 per liter. **Mitfahrzentralen** are agencies that pair up drivers and riders for a small fee; riders then negotiate payment for the trip with the driver.

BY BIKE. Cities and towns have designated bike lanes, often on the sidewalk. *Germany by Bike*, by Nadine Slavinski (Mountaineers Books, 1994; US$15), details 20 tours throughout the country.

TOURIST SERVICES AND MONEY

EMERGENCY	Police: ☎ 110. **Ambulance** and **Fire:** ☎ 112.

TOURIST OFFICES. Every city in Germany has a tourist office, usually near the *Hauptbahnhof* (main train station) or *Marktplatz* (central square). All are marked by a thick lowercase "i" sign. Many offices book rooms for a small fee. The tourist info website for Germany is www.germany-tourism.de.

MONEY. On January 1, 2002, the **euro** (€) replaced the **Deutschmark** (DM) as the unit of currency in Germany. For more info, see p. 14. As a general rule, it's cheaper to exchange money in Germany than at home. If you stay in hostels and prepare your own food, expect to spend anywhere from €20-40 per person per day. **Tipping** is not practiced as liberally in Germany as elsewhere—most Germans just round up €1. Note that tips in Germany are not left lying on the table, but handed directly to the server when you pay. If you don't want any change, say *"Das stimmt so"* (das SHTIMMT zo). Germans rarely bargain except at flea markets. Most goods and services bought in Germany will automatically include a 7 or 16% **value-added tax (VAT)**; see p. 16 for more info.

COMMUNICATION

PHONE CODES	Country code: 49. International dialing prefix: 00.

TELEPHONES. Most public phones accept only telephone cards. You can pick up a *Telefonkarte* (phone card) in post offices, at kiosks, or at selected Deutsche Bahn counters in major train stations. **Mobile phones** are an increasingly popular and economical alternative (p. 36). There is no standard length for telephone numbers. The smaller the city, the more digits in the city code, while individual phone numbers have between three and 10 digits. International direct dial numbers include: **AT&T,** ☎800 22 55 288; **British Telecom,** ☎800 89 00 49; **Canada Direct,** ☎800 888 00 14; **Ireland Direct,** ☎08000 800 353; **MCI,** ☎800 88 88 000; **Sprint,** ☎800 888 00 13; **Telecom New Zealand,** ☎800 080 00 64; **Telkom South Africa,** ☎800 180 00 27; **Telstra Australia,** ☎800 08 00 061.

MAIL. *Let's Go* lists the addresses for mail to be held (*Postlagernde Briefe*) in the practical information sections of big cities. Address mail to be held according to the following example: Firstname SURNAME, *Postlagernde Briefe*, Postamt in der Joachimstaler Str. 7, 10706 Berlin, Germany. The mail will go to the main post office unless you specify another by street address or postal code. Air mail usually takes 3-7 days to North America, Europe, and Australia; 6-12 days to New Zealand.

INTERNET ACCESS. Most German cities (as well as a surprising number of smaller towns) have at least one Internet cafe with web access for about €1-5 per 30min. Some German universities have banks of computers hooked up to the Internet in their libraries, though ostensibly for student use.

LANGUAGE. Many people in Western Germany speak English; this is less common in the East. The letter ß is equivalent to a double *s*. For basic German words and phrases, see p. 1055.

ACCOMMODATIONS AND CAMPING

GERMANY	❶	❷	❸	❹	❺
ACCOMMODATIONS	under €14	€14-19	€20-35	€36-60	over €60

Germany currently has about 600 **hostels**—more than any other nation on Earth. Official hostels in Germany are overseen by **DJH** (*Deutsches Jugendherbergswerk*), Bismarckstr. 8, 32756 Detmold, Germany (☎(05231) 740 10; www.djh.de). DJH has recently initiated a growing number of **Jugendgästehäuser,** youth guest houses that have more facilities and attract slightly older guests. DJH publishes *Jugendherbergen in Deutschland,* a guide to all federated German hostels. The cheapest **hotel-style** accommodations are places with *Pension, Gasthof, Gästehaus,* or *Hotel-Garni* in the name. Hotel rooms start at €20 for singles and €25 for doubles; in large cities, expect to pay nearly twice as much. *Frühstück* (break-fast) is almost always available and often included. The best bet for a cheap bed is often a **Privatzimmer** (a room in a family home). This option works best if you have a rudimentary knowledge of German. Prices generally run €15-30 per person. Travelers over 26 who would pay higher prices at youth hostels will find these rooms within their budget range. Reservations are made through the local tourist office or through a private *Zimmervermittlung* (room-booking office) for free or a €1-4 fee. Germans love **camping;** over 2600 campsites dot the outskirts of even the most major cities. Facilities are well maintained and usually provide showers, bathrooms, and a restaurant or store. Camping costs €3-6 per person, with addi-tional charges for tents and vehicles. Blue signs with a black tent on a white back-ground indicate official sites.

FOOD AND DRINK

GERMANY	❶	❷	❸	❹	❺
FOOD	under €4	€4-6	€7-12	€13-20	over €20

The typical German breakfast consists of coffee or tea with *Brötchen* (rolls), *Wurst* (cold sausage), and *Käse* (cheese). The main meal of the day, *Mittagessen* (lunch), includes soup, broiled sausage or roasted meat, potatoes or dumplings, and a salad or vegetable side dish. *Abendessen* or *Abendbrot* (dinner) is a reprise of breakfast, only beer replaces coffee and the selection of meats and cheeses is wider. Many older Germans indulge in a daily ritual of *Kaffee und Kuchen* (coffee and cake) at 3 or 4pm. To eat on the cheap, stick to the daily *Tagesmenü*, buy food in supermarkets, or, if you have a student ID, head to a university *Mensa* (cafeteria). Fast-food *Imbiß* stands also offer cheap fare; try the delicious Turkish *Döner*, something like a gyro. The average German beer is maltier and more "bread-like" than Czech, Dutch, or American beers; an affectionate German slang term for beer is *Flüßige Brot* ("liquid bread").

HOLIDAYS AND FESTIVALS

Holidays: Epiphany (Jan. 6); Good Friday (Apr. 9); Easter Sunday and Monday (Apr. 11-12); Labor Day (May 1); Ascension Day (May 29); Whit Sunday and Monday (May 30-31); Corpus Christi (June 10); Assumption Day (Aug. 15); Day of German Unity (Oct. 3); All Saints' Day (Nov. 1); Christmas (Dec. 25-26).

Festivals: Check out **Fasching** in Munich (Jan. 7-Feb. 24; see p. 475), the **Berlinale Film Festival** (Feb. 5-15; see p. 436), **Karneval** in Cologne (Feb. 19-24; see p. 461), **Christopher Street Day** in Berlin and other major cities (late June), the **Love Parade** in Berlin (mid-July; see p. 3), **Oktoberfest** in Munich (Sept. 18-Oct. 3; see p. 475), and the **Christmas Market** in Nuremberg.

BERLIN ☎ 030

Don't wait any longer to see Berlin (pop. 3.4 million). The city is nearing the end of a massive transitional phase, developing from a reunited metropolis reeling in the aftermath of the Cold War to the epicenter of the EU—and the Berlin of five or even two years from now will be radically different from the Berlin of today. Ger-many is the industrial leader of the continent, and when the Lehrter *Stadtbahnhof* (Europe's largest train station) opens in 2004, this city will essentially become its capital too. However, in the wake of the Nazi regime, some Germans question their own ability—and right—to govern. The problem of *"Mauer im Kopf"* ("wall in the head"), the psychological division between East and West Germany, is felt here more than anywhere else. Still, Berliners have always been more progressive than the rest of their countrymen, a tendency that prompted Hitler's famous proclamation: "Berliners are not fit to be German!"As a result, the atmosphere is the most diverse and tolerant in the country, with a famous gay and lesbian scene and an almost non-existent racial crime rate. But the real reason to visit is the almost palpable tension between past and future. No other city is currently poised to attain such geopolitical importance, and the air is taut with hope and foreboding.

◪ INTERCITY TRANSPORTATION

Flights: For info on all 3 airports, call ☎(0180) 500 01 86. The city is transitioning from 3 airports to 1 (Flughafen Schöneweld), but for now **Flughafen Tegel** (TXL) remains Berlin's main international airport. Express bus X9 from *Bahnhof Zoo*, bus #109 from *Jakob-Kaiser-Pl.* on U7, bus #128 from *Kurt-Schumacher-Pl.* on U6, or bus TXL from *Potsdamer Platz*. **Flughafen Schöneweld** (SXF), southeast of Berlin, has intercontinental flights. S9 or S45 to *Flughafen Berlin Schöneweld*. **Flughafen Tempelhof** (THF), Berlin's smallest airport, has intra-German and European flights. U6 to *Pl. der Luftbrücke*.

Train Stations: Trains to and from Berlin are serviced by **Zoologischer Garten** (almost always called **Bahnhof Zoo**) in the West and **Ostbahnhof** in the East. Most trains go to both stations, but some connections to cities in former East Germany only stop at *Ostbahnhof*. For **info** call ☎(0180) 599 66 33 or visit www.bahn.de. Trains run every hour to: **Cologne** (4¼hr., €98); **Frankfurt** (4hr., €106); **Hamburg** (2½hr., €45); **Leipzig** (2hr., €34); **Munich** (6½-7hr., €102). One per 2hr. to: **Dresden** (2¼hr., €22); **Rostock** (2¾hr., €34). International connections to: **Amsterdam** (6½hr.); **Brussels** (7½hr.); **Budapest** (12hr.); **Copenhagen** (7½hr.); **Kraków** (8½-11hr.); **Moscow** (27-33hr.); **Paris** (9hr.); **Prague** (5hr.); **Rome** (17½-21hr.); **Stockholm** (13-16hr.); **Vienna** (9½hr.); **Warsaw** (6hr.); **Zurich** (8½hr.). Times and prices change frequently—check at the computers in the stations. Under Deutsche Bahn's new pricing system, prices depend on when you book. If you book at the last minute, you'll get the prices we list; for the cheapest tickets, book at least three weeks in advance. The **Euraide** counter has info in English, sells tickets, and often has the shortest lines.

Buses: ZOB, the central bus station (☎301 03 80), by the *Funkturm* near Kaiserdamm. U2 to *Kaiserdamm* or S4, 45, or 46 to *Witzleben*. Open M-F 6am-7:30pm, Sa-Su 6amnoon. Check *Zitty* and *Tip* for deals on long-distance buses. **Gullivers,** Hardenbergpl. 14 (☎0800 4855 4837; www.gullivers.de), by the bus parking lot in *Bahnhof Zoo*. To: **Paris** (14hr., €59) and **Vienna** (10½hr., €49). Open daily 9am-2:30pm and 3-7pm. Buses are slower and less comfortable than trains, but often cheaper.

Mitfahrzentralen: Berlin has many ride-sharing centers; check the magazines *Zitty*, *Tip*, and *030* for addresses and phone numbers. Larger ones include: **Citynetz,** Joachimstaler Str. 17 (☎194 44; www.mtz-citynetz.de). U9 or 15 to *Kurfürstendamm*. To: **Hamburg** or **Hanover** (€17), **Frankfurt** (€29). Open M-F 9am-8pm, Sa-Su 9am-7pm. **Mitfahrzentrale Zoo,** (☎194 40; www.mfzoo.de) on the U2 platform at *Bahnhof Zoo*. Open M-F 9am-8pm, Sa-Su 10am-6pm. **Mitfahr2000,** has branches at Joachimsthaler Str. 1, (☎19 20 00), Yorckstr. 52 (☎194 2000) and Oderberger Str. 45 (☎440 9392; www.mitfahr2000.de). Open daily 8am-8pm.

◪ ORIENTATION

Berlin is an immense conglomeration of what were once two separate and unique cities. The former East contains most of Berlin's landmarks and historic sites, as well as an unfortunate number of pre-fab concrete socialist architectural experiments. The former West functioned for decades as a small, isolated, Allied-occu-

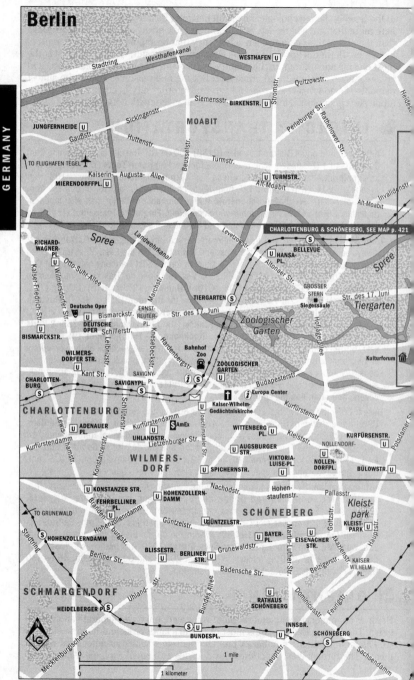

Berlin

Westhafenkanal

Stadtring

WESTHAFEN U

Quitzowstr.

Siemensstr. BIRKENSTR. U

Stromstr.

Perleburger Str.

Rathenower Str.

Heidestr.

Sickingenstr.

JUNGFERNHEIDE U

Gaußstr.

Huttenstr.

MOABIT

Beusselstr.

Turmstr.

Invalidenstr.

TO FLUGHAFEN TEGEL

Kaiserin– Augusta– Allee

MIERENDORFFPL. U

Alt-Moabit

U TURMSTR.

Alt-Moabit

Alt-Moabit

CHARLOTTENBURG & SCHÖNEBERG, SEE MAP p. 421

Spree

Landwehrkanal

Levetzowstr.

RICHARD-
WAGNER-
PL. U

Otto-Suhr-Allee

BELLEVUE S

U HANSA-
PL.

Altonaer Str.

Spree

Wilmersdorfer Str.

Kaiser-Friedrich-Str.

Marchstr.

TIERGARTEN S

GROSSER
STERN

Siegessäule

Str. des 17. Juni

Tiergarten

Deutsche Oper

U Bismarckstr.

ERNST-
REUTER-
PL.

Str. des 17. Juni

Zoologischer
Garten

Hofjägerallee

Kulturforum

DEUTSCHE
OPER U

Schillerstr.

Leibnizstr.

Knesebeckstr.

Hardenbergstr.

BISMARCKSTR. U

WILMERS-
DORFER STR.
U

Kant Str.

SAVIGNY-
PL.

Bahnhof
Zoo

ZOOLOGISCHER
GARTEN U

Budapesterstr.

CHARLOTTEN-
BURG S

SAVIGNYPL. S

Schlüterstr.

i S

i Europa Center

CHARLOTTENBURG

Kaiser-Wilhelm-
Gedächtniskirche

Kurfürstenstr.

Lewishamstr.

ADENAUER
PL. U

Kurfürstendamm

AmEx S

Joachimstaler Str.

WITTENBERG
PL. U

Kleiststr.

KURFÜRSTENSTR.
U

Potsdamer Str.

Konstanzerstr.

UHLANDSTR. U

Lietzenburger Str.

AUGSBURGER
STR. U

NOLLENDORF-
PL.

Kurfürstendamm

WILMERS-
DORF

U SPICHERNSTR.

VIKTORIA-
LUISE-PL.

U NOLLEN-
DORFPL.

BÜLOWSTR. U

U KONSTANZER STR.

FEHRBELLINER
PL. U

U HOHENZOLLERN-
DAMM

Nachodstr.

Hohen-
staufenstr.

Pallasstr.

Kleist-
park

TO GRUNEWALD

Brandenburgischestr.

Hohenzollerndamm

SCHÖNEBERG

Goltzstr.

Akazienstr.

KLEIST-
PARK U

Stadtring

Hohenzollerndamm

Güntzelstr.

U GÜNTZELSTR.

Martin-Luther-Str.

Haupstr.

S HOHENZOLLERNDAMM

U BAYER-
PL.

U EISENACHER
STR.

KAISER
WILHELM
PL.

Berliner Str.

BLISSESTR. U

BERLINER
STR. U

Grunewaldstr.

Belzigerstr.

SCHMARGENDORF

Uhland-str.

Badensche Str.

Dominicusstr.

Feurigstr.

HEIDELBERGER PL. S

Bundes Allee

U RATHAUS
SCHÖNEBERG

Mecklenburgischestr.

S U
BUNDESPL.

INNSBR.
PL. U

SCHÖNEBERG S

Haupstr.

Sachsendamm

N

0   1 mile

0   1 kilometer

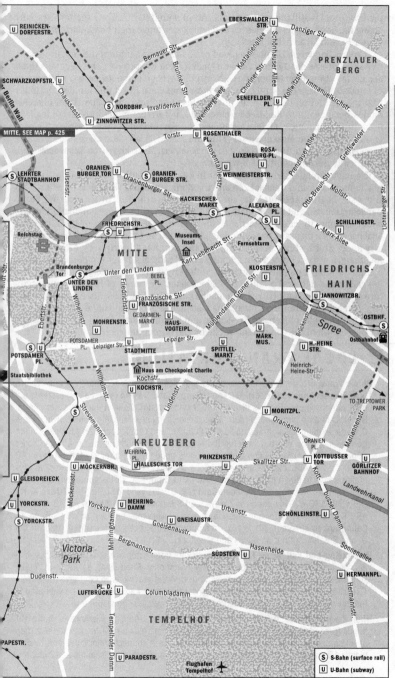

pied state and is still the commercial heart of united Berlin. The situation is rapidly changing, however, as businesses and embassies move their headquarters to Potsdamer Pl. and Mitte in the East.

The vast **Tiergarten,** Berlin's beloved park, lies in the center of the city; the grand, tree-lined **Straße des 17. Juni** runs through it from west to east and becomes **Unter den Linden** at the **Brandenburg Gate.** North of the Gate is the **Reichstag,** while south of the Gate **Ebertstraße** winds to glitzy **Potsdamer Platz.** Unter den Linden continues east through **Mitte,** the location of countless historical sites. The street changes names once again, to **Karl-Liebknecht-Straße,** before emptying into **Alexanderplatz,** home to Berlin's most visible landmark, the **Fernsehturm** (TV tower). At the east end of Mitte is the **Museumsinsel** (Museum Island). Cafe- and shop-lined **Oranienburgerstraße** cuts through the area of northeastern Mitte known as **Scheunenviertel,** historically Berlin's center of Jewish life.

The commercial district of West Berlin lies at the southwest end of the Tiergarten, centered around **Bahnhof Zoo** and the **Kurfürstendamm** (Ku'damm for short). To the east is **Breitscheidplatz,** marked by the bombed-out **Kaiser-Wilhelm-Gedächtniskirche,** and **Savignyplatz,** one of many pleasant squares in **Charlottenburg,** which is home to cafes, restaurants, and *Pensionen.* Southeast of the Ku'damm, **Schöneberg** is a pleasant residential neighborhood and the traditional nexus of the city's gay and lesbian community. At the southeast periphery of Berlin lies **Kreuzberg,** a district home to an exciting mix of radical leftists and punks as well as a large Turkish population. Northeast of the city is **Prenzlauer Berg,** a former working-class area, and east of Mitte is **Friedrichshain,** the center of Berlin's counterculture and nightlife. Berlin is rightly called a collection of towns, not a homogeneous city, as each neighborhood maintains a strong sense of individual identity: Every year, for example, citizens of Kreuzberg and Friedrichshain battle with vegetables for possession of the Oberbaumbrücke on the border between them.

▐ LOCAL TRANSPORTATION

Public Transportation: It is impossible to tour Berlin on foot—fortunately, the extensive **bus, Straßenbahn** (streetcar), **U-Bahn** (subway), and **S-Bahn** (surface rail) systems will take you anywhere. Berlin is divided into 3 transit zones. **Zone A** encompasses central Berlin, including Tempelhof airport. Almost everything else falls into **Zone B,** while **Zone C** contains the outlying areas, including Potsdam and Oranienburg. An **AB ticket** is the best deal, as you can buy regional Bahn tickets for the outlying areas. A single ticket (*Einzelfahrschein*) for the combined network is good for 2hr. after validation (Zones AB or BC €2.25, ABC €2.60). However, since single tickets are pricey, it almost always makes sense to buy a pass: a **Tageskarte** (AB €5.60, ABC €6) is good from validation until 3am the next day; the **WelcomeCard** (AB €19) is valid for 72hr.; the **7-Tage-Karte** (AB €23, ABC €29) is good for 7 days; and the **Umweltkarte Standard** (AB €58.50, ABC €72.50) is valid for one calendar month. Tickets may be used on any S-Bahn, U-Bahn, bus, or streetcar. **Bikes** require a supplemental ticket and are permitted on the U- and S-Bahn, but not on buses and streetcars.

Purchasing and Validating Tickets: Buy tickets from *Automaten* (machines), bus drivers, or ticket windows in the U- and S-Bahn stations. When using an *Automat*, make your selection before inserting money; note that the machines will not give more than €10 change and that some machines do not take bills. All tickets must be validated in the box marked *hier entwerfen* before boarding, or you may be slapped with a €40 fine.

Night Transport: U- and S-Bahn lines shut down from 1-4am on weeknights, but **night buses** (preceded by the letter N) run every 20-30min.; pick up the *Nachtliniennetz* map at a *Fahrscheine und Mehr* office. **Clubshuttle** buses connect major clubs and hostels nightly 10pm-6am. A €16 ticket is good one week and includes discounts at 12 clubs.

GERMANY

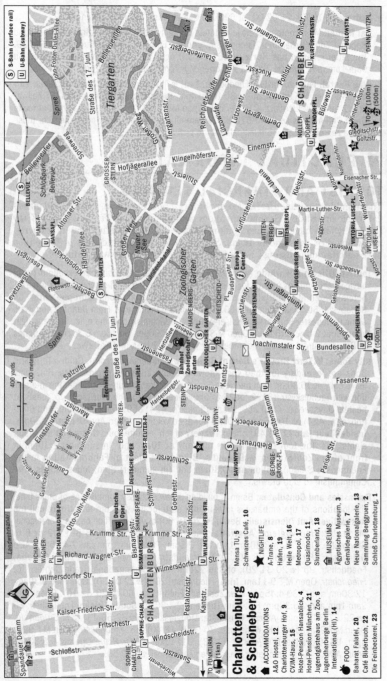

Charlottenburg & Schöneberg

⬤ ACCOMMODATIONS
A&O Hostel, 12
Charlottenburger Hof, 9
CVJM-Haus, 15
Hotel-Pension Hansablick, 4
Hotel-Pension München, 21
Jugendgästehaus am Zoo, 6
Jugendherberge Berlin
International (HI), 14

● FOOD
Baharat Falafel, 20
Café Bilderbuch, 22
Die Feinbeckerei, 23

Mensa TU, 5
Schwarzes Café, 10

★ NIGHTLIFE
A-Trane, 8
Hafen, 19
Heile Welt, 16
Metropol, 17
Quasimodo, 11
Slumberland, 18

▥ MUSEUMS
Ägyptisches Museum, 3
Gemäldegalerie, 7
Neue Nationalgalerie, 13
Sammlung Berggruen, 2
Schloß Charlottenburg, 1

Taxis: ☎26 10 26, 21 02 02, or 690 22. Call at least 15min. in advance.

Car Rental: Most companies have counters at Tegel and Schönefeld airports and around Bahnhof Zoo, *Ostbahnhof*, Friedrichstr., and the Europa Center at Budapester Str. 39. The latter location has **Hertz** (☎261 10 53) open M-F 7am-8pm, Sa 8am-4pm, Su 9am-1pm; and **Avis** (☎230 93 70) open M-F 7am-7pm, Sa 9am-2pm.

Bike Rental: Fahrradstation, Friedrichstr. 141, is in the Friedrichstr. S-Bahn station. €15 per day. Open M-F 8am-8pm, Sa-Su 10am-4pm. **Prenzleberger Orangebikes,** 37 Kollwitz Pl. U2 to *Senefelderplatz.* €10 per day. Open M-F 2:30-7pm, Sa 10am-7pm. **Deutsche Bahn Call-A-Bikes** (☎0800 522 55 22) are all over the city. Only convenient for those with a cell phone, as you must call both to pick up and drop off.

🛈 PRACTICAL INFORMATION

TOURIST AND FINANCIAL SERVICES

The monthly magazine *Berlin Programm* (€1.50) lists opera, theater, and classical music schedules. German-speakers should spring for *Tip* (€2.50) or *Zitty* (€2.30), which have the most comprehensive listings for film, theater, concerts, and clubs. For gays and lesbians, *Siegessäule, Sergej,* and *Gay-yellowpages* have entertainment listings. For info in English, check out www.berlin.de.

Tourist Offices: 🟦 **EurAide** (www.euraide.com), in *Bahnhof Zoo,* has excellent travel advice, recommends hostels for free, and makes train and hotel reservations (€4 fee for hotels). Open M-F 8:30am-noon and 1-4pm, Sa 8:30am-noon. **Europa-Center,** on Budapester Str., has city maps (€0.50) and free transit maps. From *Bahnhof Zoo,* walk along Budapester Str. past the Kaiser-Wilhelm-Gedächtniskirche; the office is on the right after about 2 blocks (5min.). Open M-Sa 8:30am-8:30pm, Su 10am-6:30pm. **Branches** at Brandenburg Gate, the Alexanderplatz Television Tower, and KaDeWe.

City Tours: 🟦 **Terry Brewer's Best of Berlin** (www.brewersberlin.com). Guides Terry and Boris are legendary for their vast knowledge and engaging personalities. 5hr. tours leave daily at 10:30am from the Neue Synagoge on Oranienburger Str., near the intersection with Tucholskystr. (S1, 2, or 25 to *Oranienburger Str.*). The tour picks up guests at hostels Odyssee (p. 426) at 9:15am, Circus (p. 424) at 9:40am and 2pm, and Clubhouse (p. 424) at 10:15am. €10. An abridged version offered Apr.-Oct. at 12:30pm. **Insider Tour** (☎692 31 49) offers a variety of fun, erudite tours that hit all the major sights. The 4hr. tour (€9.50) picks up daily at 10am and (in summer) 2:30pm in front of the Zoo Station McDonald's. **Bike tours** meet at Fahhradstation in the Friedrichstr. S-Bahn station at 10:30am and (in summer) 3pm; focus ranges from Communism to club crawls.

Embassies and Consulates: Berlin is building a new embassy complex. As of press time, the locations of the embassies remain in a state of flux. For the latest info, call the **Auswärtiges Amt Dienststelle Berlin** (☎20 18 60) or visit its office on the Werderscher Markt. U2: *Hausvogteipl.* **Australia,** Friedrichstr. 200 (☎880 08 80). U2 or 6 to *Stadtmitte.* Open M-Th 8:30am-1pm and 2-5pm, F 8:30am-1pm and 2-4:15pm. Also Uhlandstr. 181 (☎880 08 80). U15: *Uhlandstr.* Open M-F 8:30am-1pm. **Canada,** Friedrichstr. 95 (☎20 31 20), on the 12th fl. of the International Trade Center. U6: *Friedrichstr.* Open M-F 9-11am. **Irish,** Friedrichstr. 200 (☎22 07 20). Open M-F 9:30am-12:30pm and 2:30-4:45pm. **New Zealand,** Friedrichstr. 60 (☎20 62 10). Open M-Th 9am-1pm and 2-5:30pm; F at 9am-1pm and 2-4:30pm. **South African,** Friedrichstr. 60 (☎22 07 30). South African Consulate: Douglasstr. 9 (☎82 50 11). S7: *Grunewald.* Open M-F 9am-noon. **UK,** Wilhelmstr. 70 (☎20 18 40). U6: *Friedrichstr.* Open M-F 9am-4pm. **US,** Clayallee 170 (☎832 92 33). U1: *Oskar-Helene-Heim.* Open M-F 8:30am-noon. Advice M-F 2-4pm; after hours emergencies, call ☎830 50.

Currency Exchange: The best rates are usually at offices that exclusively exchange currency and traveler's checks—look for **Wechselstube** signs at major train stations and squares. **ReiseBank,** at *Bahnhof Zoo* (open daily 7:30am-10pm) and *Ostbahnhof* (open M-F 7am-10pm, Sa 8am-8pm, Su 8am-noon and 12:30-4pm), has worse rates.

American Express: Main Office, Bayreuther Str. 37 (☎21 47 62 92). U1, 2, or 15 to *Wittenbergpl.* Holds mail and offers banking services. No commission on AmEx traveler's checks. Open M-F 9am-7pm, Sa 10am-1pm. The **branch office,** Friedrichstr. 172 (☎20 45 57 21). U6: *Französische Str.* has the same hours.

LOCAL SERVICES

Luggage Storage: In **Bahnhof Zoo.** Lockers €0.50-2 per day, depending on size. 72hr. max. If lockers are full, try **Gepäckaufbewahrung** (€2 per piece per day). Open daily 6:15am-10:30pm. 24hr. lockers are available at **Ostbahnhof** and **Alexanderplatz.**

Bookstores: Marga Schöler Bücherstube, Knesebeckstr. 33, between Savignypl. and the Ku'damm. S3: *Savignypl.* Off-beat and contemporary reading material in English. Open M-W 9:30am-7pm, Th-F 9:30am-8pm, Sa 9:30am-4pm. **Dussman,** Friedrichstr. 90. U6: *Friedrichstr.* Huge store; books in English on the 2nd fl. Open M-Sa 10am-10pm.

Bi-Gay-Lesbian Resources: Lesbenberatung, Kulmer Str. 20a (☎215 20 00), offers lesbian counseling. Open M-Tu and Th 4-7pm, F 2-5pm. The gay equivalent is **Schwulenberatung,** Mommsenstraße 45 (☎194 46), in Charlottenburg.

Laundromat: Waschcenter Schnell und Sauber has locations in **Charlottenburg,** Leibnizstr. 72 (S3: *Savignypl.*); **Schöneberg,** Wexstr. 34 (U9: *Bundespl.*); **Kreuzberg,** Mehringdamm 32 (U6: *Mehringdamm*); **Mitte,** Torstr. 115 (U8: *Rosenthaler Pl.*). Wash €2-4 for 6kg, dry €0.50 per 15min. Open daily 6am-11pm.

EMERGENCY AND COMMUNICATIONS

Emergency: Police: ☎110. **Ambulance and Fire:** ☎112.

Pharmacies: Pharmacies are ubiquitous. **Europa-Apotheke,** Tauentzienstr. 9-12 (☎261 41 42), is near *Bahnhof Zoo.* Open M-F 6am-8pm, Sa 9am-4pm.

Medical Assistance: The American and British embassies list English-speaking doctors. **Emergency doctor** (☎31 00 31); **Emergency dentist** (☎89 00 43 33). Both 24hr.

Internet Access: Some cafes have America Online internet stations, free for customers. Also try: **Netlounge,** Auguststr. 89. U-Bahn: *Oranienburgerstr.* €1.50 per hr. Open noon-midnight. **Easy Everything,** the corner of Kurfürstendamm and Meineckestr., fuses Dunkin' Donuts and the Internet (finally!). €1.50-2.50 per hr. Open daily 6am-2:30am. **Com Line,** Innsbrückerstr. 56, in Schöneberg. €1 per hr. Open 24hr.

Post Offices: Joachimstaler Str. 7, down Joachimstaler Str. from *Bahnhof Zoo.* Open M-Sa 8am-midnight, Su 10am-midnight. Most neighborhood branches open M-F 9am-6pm, Sa 9am-noon. Address mail to be held: Firstname SURNAME, *Postlagernde Briefe,* Postamt in der Joachimstaler Str. 7, 10706 Berlin GERMANY.

⌐ ACCOMMODATIONS

Thanks to the ever-growing hostel and hotel industry, same-day accommodations aren't impossible to find. Failing to make a reservation will, however, limit your options. For longer visits, the various **Mitwohnzentrale** can arrange for you to house-sit or sublet an apartment from €250 per month; for more info, contact **Home Company Mitwohnzentrale,** Joachimstaler Str. 17. (☎194 45. U9 or 15 to *Kurfürstendamm.* Open M-F 9am-6pm, Sa 11am-2pm.) For long stays or on weekends, reservations are essential. During the **Love Parade,** call at least two months ahead for a choice of rooms and at least two weeks ahead for any bed at all. Some hostels increase prices that weekend by up to €10 per night.

HOTELS, HOSTELS, AND PENSIONS

MITTE

▨ **Mitte's Backpacker Hostel,** Chausseestr. (☎102 28 39 09 65). U6: *Zinnowitzer Str.* Look for the giant orange sign on the wall outside. The apex of hostel hipness, with gregarious English-speaking staff and themed rooms. Bikes €10 per day. Kitchen available. Sheets €2.50. Staff does laundry for €5. Internet access €6 per hr. Reception 24hr. Dorms €15-18; singles €20-30; doubles €40-60; €1-2 cheaper in winter. ❷

▨ **Circus,** Rosa-Luxemburg-Str. 39 (☎28 39 14 33). U2: *Rosa-Luxemburg-Pl.* Circus was designed with the English-speaking traveler in mind. Laundry, Internet, info on nightlife, and a disco ball in the lobby. A second **Circus** at Rosenthaler Pl. on Weinbergersweg 1a, has similar facilities and the same prices. Sheets €2. Reception and bar open 24hr. Confirm reservations 1 day before arrival. 6-8 bed dorms €15; 4-5 bed dorms €18; singles €32; doubles €48; triples €60. Cheaper in winter. ❷

Honigmond, Tieckstr. 12 (☎284 45 50). U6: *Zinnowitzer Str.* Old-fashioned and well-furnished rooms with canopy beds. Breakfast €3-9. Check-in 3pm-1am; if checking in after 8pm, call beforehand. Singles €45-70; doubles €65-85, with bath €90-145. ❸

Clubhouse Hostel, Kalkscheunestr. 2 (☎28 09 79 79). U6: *Oranienburger Tor.* Enter the courtyard from Johannisstr. 2 or Kalkscheunestr. In the center of the Oranienburger Str. nightlife. Sheets €2. Internet €0.50 per 5min. Reception and bar open 24hr. 8-10 bed dorms €14; 5-7 bed dorms €17; singles €32; doubles €46. ❷

TIERGARTEN

Jugendherberge Berlin International (HI), Kluckstr. 3 (☎261 10 98). U1 to *Kurfürstenstr.,* then walk up Potsdamer Str., go left on Pohlstr., and right on Kluckstr. Big, clean, and modern. Bikes €10 per day. Large breakfast and sheets included. Internet available. Reception and cafe open 24hr. Dorms €23, under-27 €19. ❷

Hotel-Pension Hansablick, Flotowstr. 6 (☎390 48 00). S3, 5, 7, 9, or 75 to *Tiergarten.* Some rooms have balconies overlooking the Spree; all have bath, minibar, phone, and cable TV. Riverboat tours stop 200m away. Breakfast included. Reception 24hr. Singles €82, doubles €101-121. Mention *Let's Go* for a 5% discount. ❹

SCHÖNEBERG AND WILMERSDORF

Studentenhotel Meininger 10, Meininger Str. 10 (☎78 71 74 14). U4 or bus #146 to *Rathaus Schöneberg.* Walk toward the Rathaus tower on Freiherr-vom-Stein-Str., turn left onto Martin-Luther-Str., then right on Meininger Str. A hostel for the students, by the students. Breakfast included. 24hr. reception. Co-ed dorms €12.50; 3- to 4-bed dorms €21; singles €33; doubles €46. Flash a copy of *Let's Go* for a 5% first night discount. ❶

CVJM-Haus, Einemstr. 10 (☎264 10 88). U1: *Nollendorfpl.* It's fun to stay at the German YMCA, despite its institutional atmosphere. Unlike most hostels, here you usually get your own room. Breakfast included. Sheets €4. Reception M-F 8am-5pm. Quiet time 10pm-7am. Book well ahead. Dorms and singles €21, doubles €42. ❸

Hotel-Pension München, Güntzelstr. 62 (☎857 91 20). U9: *Güntzelstr.* Like visiting a smartly done apartment—the rooms are simple and bright and the halls are pinned with contemporary *Berliner* art. Breakfast included. Singles €40, with bath €56; doubles with bath €70-80; triples €90; quads €105. ❹

CHARLOTTENBURG

Jugendgästehaus am Zoo, Hardenbergstr. 9a (☎312 94 10), opposite the Technical University Mensa. Bus #145 to *Steinpl.,* or take the short walk from *Bahnhof Zoo* down Hardenbergstr. Push open the front door and hike four flights of stairs—unless

(GERMANY)

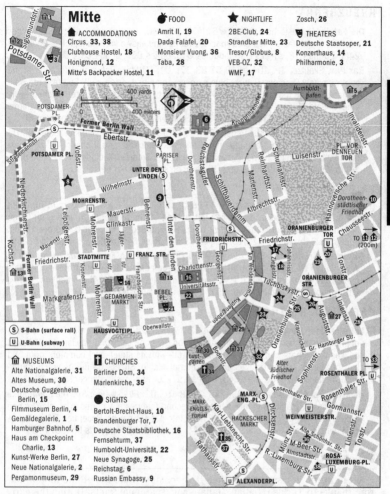

Mitte

🏠 ACCOMMODATIONS
Circus, **33, 38**
Clubhouse Hostel, **18**
Honigmond, **12**
Mitte's Backpacker Hostel, **11**

🍎 FOOD
Amrit II, **19**
Dada Falafel, **20**
Monsieur Vuong, **36**
Taba, **28**

⭐ NIGHTLIFE
2BE-Club, **24**
Strandbar Mitte, **23**
Tresor/Globus, **8**
VEB-OZ, **32**
WMF, **17**

Zosch, **26**

🍷 THEATERS
Deutsche Staatsoper, **21**
Konzerthaus, **14**
Philharmonie, **3**

Ⓢ S-Bahn (surface rail)
Ⓤ U-Bahn (subway)

🏛 MUSEUMS
Alte Nationalgalerie, **31**
Altes Museum, **30**
Deutsche Guggenheim
Berlin, **15**
Filmmuseum Berlin, **4**
Gemäldegalerie, **1**
Hamburger Bahnhof, **5**
Haus am Checkpoint
Charlie, **13**
Kunst-Werke Berlin, **27**
Neue Nationalgalerie, **2**
Pergamonmuseum, **29**

✝ CHURCHES
Berliner Dom, **34**
Marienkirche, **35**

● SIGHTS
Bertolt-Brecht-Haus, **10**
Brandenburger Tor, **7**
Deutsche Staatsbibliothek, **16**
Fernsehturm, **37**
Humboldt-Universität, **22**
Neue Synagoge, **25**
Reichstag, **6**
Russian Embassy, **9**

GERMANY

the elevator's working. Reception 9am-midnight. Check-in 10am. Check-out 9am. Lockout 10am-2pm. No curfew. Dorms €19, under-27 €16; singles €27/24; doubles €46/43. ❷

A&O Hostel, Joachimstaler Str. 1, (☎0800 2 22 57 22), 40m from *Bahnhof Zoo*. The crowded lobby feels like a cross between a frat and a fast-food restaurant, but the rooms are clean. Sheets €3. Reception 24hr. No curfew. Dorms €10, with shower €18-20; singles €35; doubles €68. Cheaper in winter. ❷

Charlottenburger Hof, Stuttgarter Pl. 14 (☎32 90 70). U7: *Wilmersdorfer Str.* Mondrian-themed ceilings match the Kandinsky prints on the walls. Every room has a phone, TV, and computer with free Internet (DSL). Pricier rooms have whirlpools. Reception 24hr. Singles €75, doubles €85, quads €125. ❹

KREUZBERG

Die Fabrik, Schlesische Str. 18 (☎611 71 16; www.diefabrik.com). U1: *Schlesisches Tor.* This former factory features spacious rooms and easy access to nightlife. Reception 24hr. Dorms €18; singles €36; doubles €49; triples €66; quads €80. ❷

Bax Pax, Skalitzer Str. 104 (☎69 51 83 22). U1: *Görlitzer Bahnhof.* A location at the start of mighty Oranienstr., fuzzy blue carpets, and a bed inside a VW Bug (ask for room 3) make for the mellow good times you'd expect in a Kreuzberg hostel. Kitchen available. Sheets €2.50. Internet €6 per hr. Reception 24hr. Big dorms €15; 6-7 bed dorms €16; 4-5 bed dorms €18; singles €30; doubles and triples €20-30 per person. ❷

Pension Kreuzberg, Großbeerenstr. 64 (☎251 13 62; www.pension-kreuzberg.de). U6 or night bus #N19 to *Mehringdamm.* Gorgeous staircases and a cheery yellow breakfast room. Lively neighborhood, even for Kreuzberg. Breakfast included. Reception 8am-10pm. Singles €40; doubles €52. Larger rooms €22.50 per person. ❸

FRIEDRICHSHAIN

Sunflower Hostel, Helsingforser Str. 17 (☎44 04 42 50). U1: *Warschauer Str.* Turn right out of the station and take your first left coming off the bridge; hug the river for 5min. Airy, relaxed feel. The staff is a trove of insider knowledge. Internet €1.50 per 15min. Reception 24hr. Dorms €13-15; singles €35; doubles €45; triples €57; quads €68. ❷

Odyssee, Grünberger Str. 23 (☎29 00 00 81). U5 to *Frankfurter Tor* or U1 to *Warschauer Str.* A rarity: hip AND spotless. Someone sinks a lot of money into this place, but at €13 a night, it isn't you. Bar open until dawn. 24hr. reception. Dorms €13; doubles €45, with shower €52; triples €57; quads €68. ❷

PRENZLAUER BERG

🏠 **Lette'm Sleep Hostel,** Lettestr. 7 (☎44 73 36 23). U2: *Eberswalder Str.* Follow the trail of graffiti to the spray-painted gangsta bear on the door. Lette'm Sleep isn't just "tucked between" the bars and cafes on Helmholtzpl.—with its street-level common room and laid back staff, it practically *is* one. Kitchen available. Sheets €3 in dorms. Free Internet. Dorms €15-16; doubles €48; triples €57. Lower prices for longer stays. ❷

Alcatraz, Schönhauserallee 133a (48 49 68 15). U2: *Eberswalder Str.* The main building has small, graffitied rooms, while the second features airy dorms in an old German brewery. Free bike loan. Kitchen facilities. Internet €3 per hr. Reception 24hr. Dorms €13; singles from €40; doubles from €44; triples from €59; quads from €74. ❶

🎇 FOOD

Food in Berlin is less German than it is cosmopolitan; the ethnic food is terrific thanks to Turkish, Indian, Italian, and Thai immigrants. During the early summer, expect an onslaught of *Spargel* (asparagus). Berlin's dearest culinary tradition, however, is breakfast, a gloriously civilized institution served well into the afternoon in cafes. Relax over a *Milchkaffee*, a bowl of coffee with foamed milk.

Typical Berlin street food is Turkish. Their *Imbiß* stands are a late-night lifeline; many are open 24 hours. The *Döner Kebap*—shaved roast lamb or chicken stuffed into toasted flatbread and topped with vegetables—has cornered the fast-food market, with falafel running a close second. Quality Indian and Italian eateries also abound, and of course the city has its share of *Currywurst* and bratwurst.

Aldi, Plus, Edeka, and **Penny Markt** are the cheapest supermarket chains, followed by the pricier **Bolle, Kaiser's,** and **Reichelt.** Supermarkets are usually open M-F 9am-6pm and Sa 9am-4pm, though some are open as late as 8pm on weekdays. *Bah-*

nhof Zoo's **open-air market** fires up Saturday mornings on Winterfeldtpl., but almost every neighborhood has one. For cheap veggies and huge wheels of *Fladenbrot*, hit the **Turkish market**, in Kreuzberg along Maybachufer on the Landwehrkanal, every Friday. Take U8 to *Schönleinstr.*

MITTE

Monsieur Vuong, Alte Schonhauser Str. 46. U2: *Rosa Luxembourg Platz.* People who live here have this strange obsession with Monsieur Vuong's glass noodle salad (€6.50). It's odd. Really, no one orders anything else. Other things €6-9. Open M-Sa noon-midnight, Su 4pm-midnight. ❷

Taba, Torstr. 164. U8: *Rosenthaler Pl.* A roomy Brazilian restaurant and bar. Dishes are pricey, but the vast, €6.50 buffet on M and Th is tasty and filling. Live music F-Su, occasionally charges cover after 10pm. Open Su and Tu-Sa from 7pm. ❹

Amrit II, Oranienburgerstr. 50. S1: *Oranienburgerstr.* Indian entrees run high (€9) but can be shared. The original location in Kreuzberg, Oranienstr. 202, has same hours. ❸

Dada Falafel, Linienstr. 132. S1 or S2 to *Oranienburgertor.* "*Ich habe soviel getanzt dass ich ganz und gar hungrig bin.*" (I have danced so much that I am hungry.) "*Was willst du essen?*" (What do you want to eat?) "*Falafel.*" (Falafel.) "*Lass uns zu Dada gehen.*" (Then let us go to Dada.) Serves the business crowd by day and the clubgoers by night. Falafel/schwarma sandwiches €3. Open Su-Th 10am-2am, F-Sa until 4am. ❶

SCHÖNEBERG

Die Feinbeckerei, Vorbergstr. 2. U7: *Kleistpark.* The menu has "schwabish" and "not schwabish" sections; *Let's Go* recommends ordering from the schwabish one. Southern German cuisine, unassuming and full of carbohydrates. Try the cheese Spätzle with herbs (€6.50). Open daily noon-midnight. ❸

Baharat Falafel, Winterfeldtstr. 37. U1: *Nollendorfpl.* This ain't no greasy Döner stand—it's all about falafel. Five plump chick-pea balls in a fluffy pita, covered with veggies and heavenly sesame, mango, or chili sauce (€3-4). Wash it down with fresh-squeezed *Gute-Laune Saft* (good mood juice). Open daily 8am-4am. Closed the last week in July. ❷

Café Bilderbuch, Akazienstr. 28. U7: *Eisenacher Str.* Fringed lamps, oak bookcases and fat viridian sofas give Café Bilderbuch the feel of a Venetian library. Tasty brunch baskets served around the clock (€8). Oct.-Apr. you can swing or tango at Sunday afternoon *Tantzee.* Open M-Th 9am-1am, F-Sa 9am-2am, Su 10am-1am. ❸

KREUZBERG

Café V, Lausitzer Pl. 12. U1: *Görlitzer Bahnhof.* Top-of-the-line, bottom of the food chain. Berlin's oldest vegetarian restaurant also serves fish. Try the *Spinatballchen mit Käse Sauße* (€7) or any of the equally tasty specials (€6-7). Open daily 10am-2am. ❸

Abendmahl, Muskauer Str. 9 (☎612 51 70). U1: *Görlitzer Bahnhof.* A favorite of gay and lesbian Berliners. Sorrel cream soup and fish carpaccio are trumped by macabre deserts—the "Last Date" is ice cream shaped like coffins. Open daily from 6pm. ❹

Weinhaus Hoff, Reichenberger Str. 116 (☎342 08 13). U1: *Gorlitzer Bahnhof.* Delicious Swabian specialties in an out-of-the-way restaurant lined with wine bottles. Pork fillet with mushroom cream and *Spätzle* €7.50. Open M-Sa 4pm-midnight. ❸

Blue Nile, Tempelhofer Ufer 6 (☎25 29 46 55). U1: *Möcknerbrücke.* It's hard to get to and the food takes an age, but with a flask of honey wine (€2.50), you won't mind a bit. All the meals at this Ethiopian restaurant are served on *injera*, a traditional spongy sourdough bread. Vegetarian or meat combos €7-12. Open 3pm-midnight. ❸

PRENZLAUER BERG

🟨 **Café-Restaurant Miró,** Raumerstr. 29. U2: *Eberswalder Str.* The kind of place where the food looks almost as good as it tastes. Generous portions of delectable Mediterranean cuisine. Breakfast €3-8. Soup €3. Open 10am-midnight. ❸

La Bodeguita del Medio, Husemanstr. 10. U2: *Eberswalderstr.* A Cuban *tapas* bar, decorated by customer scrawlings that cover the tables, walls, and ceilings. Aside from the *tapas* (€4-8) there's not really a menu—they cook new dinner specials every day. Sa-Su dinner buffet (€9.50) starting at 7pm. Open daily 4pm-late. ❸

The Chop Bar, Pappalallee 29. A friendly West African restaurant. Try the *Jassa Djin* (€7), a tasty mackerel dish, or any one of the vegetarian options (€6.50-8). Open Su-Th 4-11pm, F-Sa 4pm-midnight. ❸

Li Do, Knaackstr. 30. U2: *Senefelderpl.* Essential East German chic. Try a blini burger (€8; lox and buckwheat pancakes) or more filling pasta (€5). Open daily 9am-late. ❷

CHARLOTTENBURG

Mensa TU, Hardenbergstr. 34, 10min. from *Bahnhof Zoo.* The mightiest of Berlin's *Mensen.* Vegetarian options. Meals €2-4. Cafeteria downstairs has longer hours and higher prices. *Mensa* open M-F 11:00am-3pm. Cafeteria open M-F 8am-5pm. ❶

Schwarzes Café, Kantstr. 148. S3: *Savignypl.* Exposed brick walls, frescoes, and absinthe give Schwarzes a bohemian feel. It's *always* open (except Tu 3am-10am). Prices are a bit high, but breakfasts are cheaper and served around the clock (€6-8). ❸

🅖 SIGHTS

Most of central Berlin's major sights are along the route of **bus #100,** which travels from *Bahnhof Zoo* to Prenzlauer Berg, passing by the Siegessäule, Brandenburg Gate, Unter den Linden, the Berliner Dom, and Alexanderplatz. There are only a few places to see remnants of the **Berlin Wall:** a narrow band stands in Potsdamer Platz; the popular Haus Am Checkpoint Charlie guards another piece; the sobering Documentation Center in Prenzlauer Berg preserves an entire city block; and an embellished section in Friedrichshain has become the East Side Gallery.

MITTE

Mitte was once the heart of Berlin and has most of the city's imperial architecture. The district was split down the middle by the wall and much of it fell into disrepair, but the wave of revitalization that swept post-wall Berlin hit Mitte first.

UNTER DEN LINDEN

Unter den Linden is one of the best known boulevards in Europe and the spine of Imperial Berlin. During the Cold War it was known as the "idiot's mile" because it was often all that visitors saw, giving them little idea of what the city was really like. Beginning in Pariser Platz in front of the Brandenburger Tor, the street runs east through Bebelplatz and the Lustgarten, interspersed with huge dramatic squares. *(S1: Unter den Linden. Bus #100 runs the length of the boulevard every 4-6 minutes.)*

🟨 **BRANDENBURGER TOR.** Built during the reign of Friedrich Wilhelm II as an image of peace to replace its medieval predecessor, the gate became the enduring symbol of the Cold War East-West division. Situated directly in the center of the city, it was the heart of no-man's land for decades. Today the Brandenburg gate is the most powerful emblem of reunited Germany and Berlin.

RUSSIAN EMBASSY. Rebuilding the edifices of the rich and famous wasn't a huge priority in the workers' state. One exception was this massive structure, which covers almost an entire block. *(Unter den Linden 55.)*

DEUTSCHE STAATSBIBILIOTHEK AND HUMBOLDT-UNIVERSITÄT. The stately library's shady, ivy-covered courtyard provides a pleasant respite from the surrounding urban bustle. *(Unter den Linden 8. Open M-F 9am-9pm, Sa 9am-5pm. €0.50. Free Internet.)* Just beyond the *Staatsbibliothek* lies Humboldt University, which saw Hegel, Einstein, the Brothers Grimm, Bismarck, and Karl Marx. In the wake of the post-1989 shift, in which "tainted" departments were radically revamped or simply shut down, international scholars have descended upon the university to take part in its dynamic renewal. *(Unter den Linden 6.)*

BEBELPLATZ. On May 10, 1933 Nazi students burned nearly 20,000 books here by "subversive" authors such as Heinrich Heine and Sigmund Freud—both Jews. A plaque in the center of the square is engraved with Heine's eerily prescient 1820 quote: *Nur dort wo man Bücher verbrennt, verbrennt man am Ende auch Menschen.* ("Wherever books are burned, ultimately people are burned as well.")

TIERGARTEN

Once a hunting ground for Prussian monarchs, the lush **Tiergarten** park greens the center of Berlin from *Bahnhof Zoo* to the Brandenburg Gate. **Straße des 17. Juni,** bisecting the park from west to east, is the site of demonstrations.

■**THE REICHSTAG.** The Reichstag is the current home of Germany's governing body, the *Bundestag.* History has long been made here, from Philipp Scheidemann's 1918 proclamation "*Es lebe die Deutsche Republik*" ("Long live the German Republic") to the fire that Adolf Hitler used to declare a state of emergency and seize power. *(Open daily 8am-midnight; last entrance at 10pm. Free.)*

SIEGESSÄULE. In the heart of the Tiergarten, the slender 70m victory column commemorates Prussia's defeat of France in 1870. The statue at the top—the goddess of victory—was made from melted-down French cannons. Climb its 285 steps for a panorama or leave your mark on the graffiti-covered interior, which has become a forum of expression for the world's touring youth. *(Großer Stern. Take bus #100 to Großer Stern. Open Apr.-Nov. M 1-6pm, Tu-Su 9am-6pm. €1.20, students €0.60.)*

POTSDAMER PLATZ

Potsdamer Platz was designed with the primary purpose of moving troops. After reunification, Potsdamer Pl. was chosen to become the commercial center of united Berlin and promptly achieved infamy as the city's largest construction site. Today, its wildly postmodern architectural designs are by turns sickening and sublime. The central complex, overlooking Potsdamer Str., includes the **Deutsche Bahn headquarters,** the glossy ■**Sony Center,** and a glass recreation of Mt. Fuji. Take in a movie, go window-shopping, or just sit and marvel. *(U2: Potsdamer Pl.)*

MUSEUMSINSEL AND ALEXANDERPLATZ

After crossing the Spree, Unter den Linden becomes Karl-Liebknecht-Str. and cuts through the **Museumsinsel** (Museum Island), home to five major museums and the **Berliner Dom.** Take S3 to *Hackescher Markt.* Karl-Liebknecht-Str. continues into the monolithic **Alexanderplatz.**

BERLINER DOM. This bulky, multi-domed cathedral, one of Berlin's most recognizable landmarks, proves that Protestants can be as excessive as Catholics. Built during the reign of Kaiser Wilhelm II, it recently emerged from 20 years of restoration after being damaged in a 1944 air raid. Look for the Protestant icons (Calvin, Zwingli, and Luther) that adorn the interior, or bask in a glorious view of Berlin from the tower. *(Open M-Sa 9am-8pm, Su noon-8pm; closed during services 6:30-7:30pm. Combined admission to Dom, crypt, tower, and galleries €5, students €3. Free organ recitals W-F at 3pm. Frequent concerts in summer; buy tickets in the church or call ☎ 20 26 91 36.)*

O WORK, ALL PLAY

THE LOVE PARADE

Every year on the 3rd weekend n July, the Love Parade brings Berlin to its knees—trains run late, streets fill with litter, and German eenagers dye their hair, drop ecstasy, and get down en masse. What started in 1988 as a DJ's birthday party of 150 people has mutated into an annual corporate-echno-Woodstock—half a million attended in 2004. A huge parade" takes place on Saturday, nvolving a procession of tractor-railers loaded with blasting speakers and topped by gyrating bodies that slowly works it from Ernst-Reuter-Pl. to the Branden-burg Gate. The city-wide party urns the Str. des 17. Juni into a riotous dance floor and the Tier-garten into a den of iniquity. To celebrate the licentious atmo-sphere, the BVG offers a "No-Limit-Ticket," useful for getting rom venue to venue during the weekend's 54hr. of nonstop party-ng (€5, condom included). Club prices skyrocket as the best DJs are imported for the frantic, beat-humping weekend.

Some have proclaimed that the Love Parade is dying, down to barely a third of the attendence it enjoyed in the late-90s. But tell hat to anyone who's ever been here, they'll tell you it's an experi-ence they'll never forget. Unless hey partied too hard, of course.

(The 16th Love Parade will take place the weekend of July 10, 2004.)

ALEXANDERPLATZ. Formerly the heart of Weimar Berlin, the plaza was transformed in East German times into a wasteland of concrete-block classics. In the 1970s, the drear was interrupted by neon signs with declarations like "Medical Instruments of the DDR—Distributed in All the World!" in order to satisfy the people's need for bright lights. Today chain stores like **Kaufhof** serve as a backdrop for the affairs of bourgeois German shoppers, tourists, and punks.

MARIENKIRCHE. The church is gothic, the altar and pulpit are rococo, and the tower is neo-romantic. Relatively undamaged during the war, this little church still holds relics from other nearby churches which used it as a shelter. Knowledgeable guides explain them and the painting collection from the Dürer and Cranach schools. *(Open M-Th 10am-4pm, Sa-Su noon-4pm.)*

FERNSEHTURM. The tremendous and bizarre TV tower, the tallest structure in Berlin at 368m, was originally intended to prove East Germany's technological capabilities; as a result, the tower has acquired some colorful politically-infused nicknames, among them the perennial favorite "Walter Ulbricht's Last Erection." *(Open daily Mar.-Oct. 9am-1am; Nov.-Feb. 10am-midnight. €6.50, under-16 €3.)*

SCHEUNENVIERTEL AND ORANIENBURGER STRAßE

Northwest of Alexanderpl., around the streets of Oranienburger Str. and Große Hamburger Str., lies the **Scheunenviertel.** Once the center of Berlin's Orthodox Jewish community, the neighborhood harbors evidence of Jewish life back to the 13th century, though the Jews were twice expelled from the city; once for 100 years in in 1573, then again during WWII. In the past few years several Judaica-oriented bookstores and kosher restaurants have opened. Take U6 to *Oranienburger Tor.*

NEUE SYNAGOGE. This huge, "oriental-style" building, modelled after the Alhambra, was destroyed by bombing but restored by international funding. Exhibits chronicle the history of Berlin's Jews. *(Oranienburger Str. 30. Open Su-M 10am-8pm, Tu-Th 10am-6pm, F 10am-2pm. Museum €5, students €3. Dome €1.50, students €1.)*

OTHER SIGHTS IN MITTE

BERTOLT-BRECHT-HAUS. If anyone personifies the political and aesthetic contradiction that is Berlin, it is **Bertolt Brecht.** "There is a reason to prefer Berlin to other cities," the playwright declared. "What is bad today can be improved tomorrow." The **Brechtforum**

sponsors exhibits and lectures. *(Chausseestr. 125. U6: Zinnowitzer Str. Mandatory tour in German every 30min. Tu-F 10-11:30am, Th 10-11:30am and 5-6:30pm, and Sa 9:30am-1:30pm. Tours every hr. Su 11am-6pm. €3, students €1.50.)*

CHARLOTTENBURG

Welcome to Berlin—you're probably in Charlottenburg! Berlin's main shopping strip, the Ku'damm, is heavy with tourist traffic and upscale department stores. Most things in Charlottenburg are expensive, but the sights and tourist services around *Bahnhof Zoo* bring most travelers through.

AROUND BAHNHOF ZOO. During the city's division, West Berlin centered around *Bahnhof Zoo*, the station that inspired U2's "Zoo TV" tour. (The U-Bahn line U2 runs through the station—clever, no?) The surrounding area is a spectacle of department stores and peepshows intermingled with souvenir shops and G-rated attractions. Many of the animals at the renowned **Zoologischer Garten** live in open air habitats, and its flamingo flock is not confined at all. *(Open May-Sept. daily 9am-6:30pm; Oct.-Feb. 9am-5pm; Mar.-Apr. 9am-5:30pm. €9, students €7, children €4.50; combo ticket to zoo and aquarium €14/11/7.)* Within the walls of the Zoo, but independently accessible, the **Aquarium** has insects and reptiles as well as miles of fish. Check out the psychedelic jellyfish tanks, filled with translucent sea nettles. *(Budapester Str. 32. €9, students €7, children €4.50.)*

KAISER-WILHELM-GEDÄCHTNISKIRCHE. Nicknamed "the rotten tooth" by Berliners, the jagged edges of this shattered church are a reminder of the destruction caused by WWII. Inside, a small exhibit shows pictures of the city in ruins. In the summer, Berlin's street performers, salesmen, foreigners, and young people gather in front of the church to hang out, sell watches, and play bagpipes and sitars. *(☎218 50 23. Exhibit open M-Sa 10am-4pm. Church open daily 9am-7pm.)*

SCHLOß CHARLOTTENBURG. Commissioned by Friedrich I, this broad Baroque palace occupies a park in northern Charlottenburg. The grounds include the furnished **Altes Schloß** *(open Tu-F 9am-5pm, Sa-Su 10am-5pm; €8, students €5; Required tour.)*; the marbled receiving rooms of the **Neuer Flugel** *(open Tu-F 10am-6pm, Sa-Su 11am-6pm; €5, students €4)*; the **Neuer-Pavillon,** a museum dedicated to Prussian architect Karl Friedrich Schinkel *(open Su and Tu-Sa 10am-5pm; €2, €1.50)*; the **Belvedere,** a small building with the royal family's porcelain collection *(open Apr.-Oct. Su and Tu-Sa 10am-5pm, Nov.-Mar. Tu-F noon-4pm and Sa-Su noon-5pm; €2, students €1.50)*; and the **Mausoleum** *(open Apr.-Oct. Su and Tu-Sa 10am-noon and 1-5pm; €1)*. Stroll the **Schloßgarten** *(open Su and Tu-Sa 6am-10pm; free)* behind the main buildings, an elysium of small lakes, footbridges, and fountains. *(U7: Richard-Wagner-Pl, then walk 15min. down Otto-Suhr-Allee. Entire complex €7, students €5. Family card €20.)*

OLYMPIA-STADION. The Olympic Stadium is one of the most prominent legacies of the Nazi architectural aesthetic. It was erected for the 1936 Olympic Games, in which Jesse Owens, an African-American, trounced Nazi racial theories by winning four gold medals. The stadium is under construction until late 2004, but the *Glockenturm* (bell tower) gives a great view of it. *(Glockenturm open April-Oct. 9am-6pm. S5 or 7 to Pichelsburg, turn left onto Shirwindter All and left again onto Passenheimerstr.)*

KREUZBERG

Kreuzberg is West Germany's dose of counter-culture. Anti-government protests are still frequent; the most prominent is the annual May 1st demonstration. Home to a large ethnic population, the district has recently seen a wave of gentrification that has brought an influx of prepsters and government workers.

■**HAUS AM CHECKPOINT CHARLIE.** This eccentric museum at the famous border-crossing has become one of Berlin's most popular attractions. It's a clutter of artwork, newspaper clippings, and the devices used to breach the wall. The exhibits detail how women curled up in loudspeakers, men attempted to crawl through spiked gates, and student groups dug tunnels with their fingers, all in an attempt to reach the West. On the street is the station itself, overshadowed by photos of an American and a Russian soldier looking into "enemy" territory. *(Friedrichstr. 43. U6: Kochstr. Museum open daily 9am-10pm. €7.50, students €4.50.)*

ORANIENSTRAßE. The May Day parades start on Oranienplatz, the site of frequent riots in the 1980s. Radicals jostle shoulders with Turkish families, while an anarchist punk faction and a boisterous gay population can make things contentious after hours. *(U1: Kottbusser Tor or Görlitzer Bahnhof.)*

FRIEDRICHSHAIN AND LICHTENBERG

As the alternative scene follows the low rents eastward, Friedrichshain is becoming the new temple of hipness. Relatively unrenovated since reunification, the district retains its pre-fab apartments and large stretches of the wall. Simon-Dach-Str. is cluttered with cafes and 20-somethings. The grungier Rigärstr. is a stronghold of Berlin's legendary alternative scene, home to squatter bars and makeshift clubs.

■**EAST SIDE GALLERY.** The longest remaining portion of the wall, this 1.3km stretch is the world's largest open-air art gallery, unsupervised and open at all hours. The murals are not remnants of Cold War graffiti but rather the efforts of an international group of artists who gathered in 1989 to celebrate the fall of the wall. It was thought that the wall would be destroyed and the paintings lost, but in 2000, with the wall still standing, many of the same artists repainted their work, covering the scrawlings of tourists; unfortunately, the new paintings are again being graffitied over. *(Along Mühlenstr. U1: Warschauer Str., and walk back toward the river.)*

FORSCHUNGS- UND GEDENKSTÄTTE NORMANNENSTRAßE. In the suburb of Lichtenberg is the most hated and feared building of the DDR regime—the headquarters of the East German secret police, the **Staatssicherheit** or **Stasi.** On January 15, 1990, a crowd of 100,000 Berliners stormed the building in protest. During the Cold War, some 6 million dossiers on citizens of the DDR were kept here. Since a 1991 law made the records public, the files have rocked Germany, exposing informants—and wrecking careers, marriages, and friendships—at all levels of society. *(Ruschestr. 103, Haus 1. U5: Magdalenenstr. From the Ruschestr. exit, walk up Ruschestr. and take a right on Normannenstr. Open Su and Sa 2-6pm, Tu-F 11am-6pm. €3, students €1.50.)*

PRENZLAUER BERG

Everything in Prenzlauer Berg used to be something else. Plush brunches unfold every Sunday in what were butcher shops; a former power plant stages exhibitions about furniture; and kids cavort in breweries-turned-nightclubs. Relics of Prenzlberg's past life are disappearing, but cafe owners know shabby chic when they see it: Plenty of advertisements for cabbage and mismatched sofas remain.

■**DOKUMENTATIONSZENTRUM DER BERLINER MAUER.** A museum, chapel, and entire city block of the Berlin Wall form a controversial memorial to "victims of the communist tyranny." The museum assembles a record of all things related to the wall. *(Bernauer Strasse 111. U8: Bernauer Str. Open Su and W-Sa 10am-5pm. Free.)*

JÜDISCHER FRIEDHOF. Prenzlauer Berg was one of the major centers of Jewish Berlin, especially during the 19th and early 20th centuries. The ivied Jewish cemetery on Schönhauser Allee contains the graves of composer Giacomo

Meyerbeer and painter Max Liebermann. *(Open M-Th 8am-4pm, F 8am-3pm. Men must cover their heads before entering the cemetery.)* Nearby stands the **Synagoge Rykestraße,** one of Berlin's loveliest. *(Rykestr. 53.)*

🏛 MUSEUMS

Berlin is one of the world's great museum cities, with collections of art and arti-facts encompassing all subjects and eras. The **Staatliche Museen zu Berlin (SMB)** runs over 20 museums in four major regions—the **Museumsinsel, Kulturforum, Char-lottenburg,** and **Dahlem**—and elsewhere in Mitte and around the Tiergarten. Single admission is €6, €3 for students; the *Drei-Tage-Karte* (€10, students €5) is valid for three consecutive days. Both can be bought at any SMB museum. Admission is free the first Sunday of every month. Unaffiliated museums are smaller and more specialized, dealing with everything from Käthe Kollwitz to the cultural history of marijuana. *Berlin Programm* (€1.60) lists museums and galleries.

SMB MUSEUMS

MUSEUMSINSEL (MUSEUM ISLAND)

The Museumsinsel holds the treasure hoard of the former DDR in five separate museums, separated from the rest of Mitte by two arms of the Spree River. Some are being renovated; the **Bodenmuseum** will be closed until 2005 and the **Neues Museum** until 2008. *(S3, 5, 7, 9 or 75 to Hackescher Markt or bus #100 to Lustgarten. ☎ 20 90 55 55. All SMB museums open Su and Tu-Sa 10am-6pm, Th until 10pm unless noted. All offer free audio tours in English. Admission to each is €6, students €3 unless noted. All sell a 3-day card good for admission to every museum; €10, students €5.)*

⊠ PERGAMONMUSEUM. One of the world's great ancient history museums. The museum is named for Pergamon, the city in present-day Turkey from which the enormous Altar of Zeus (180 BC) in the main hall was taken. The museum features pieces of ancient Mediterranean and Near Eastern history from as far back as the 10th century BC. *(Kupfergraben.)*

ALTE NATIONALGALERIE. After extensive renovations, this renowned museum is again open to art-lovers. Everything from German Realism to French Impression-ism and Caspar David Friedrich to Karl Friedrich Schinkel. *(Am Lustgarten.)*

ALTES MUSEUM. This surprisingly untouristed museum contains the *Antiken-sammlung*, a permanent collection of ancient Greco-Roman decorative art.

TIERGARTEN-KULTURFORUM

The **Tiergarten-Kulturforum** is a complex of museums at the eastern end of the Tier-garten, near the Staatsbibliothek and Potsdamer Pl. Students and local fine arts aficionados throng through the buildings and on the multi-leveled courtyard in front. *(U2: Potsdamer Pl. Walk down Potsdamer Str., the museums will be on your right on Matthäikirchpl. ☎ 20 90 55 55. Hours and prices same as above.)*

⊠ GEMÄLDEGALERIE. One of Germany's most famous museums, and rightly so. It houses a stunning and enormous collection by Italian, German, Dutch, and Flemish masters, including works by Botticelli, Dürer, Raphael, Rembrandt, Rubens, Titian, and Vermeer. *(Stauffenbergstr. 40. ☎ 266 29 51.)*

⊠ HAMBURGER BAHNHOF/MUSEUM FÜR GEGENWART. Berlin's foremost col-lection of contemporary art features Warhol, Beuys, Kiefer, and some in-your-face temporary exhibits in the bright, airy spaces of a converted train station. The enor-mity of the exhibition space lends itself to outrageous sculptures. *(Invalidenstr. 50-51. U6: Zinnowitzer Str. Open Su and Sa 11am-6pm, Tu-F 10am-6pm. €6, students €3.)*

GERMANY

NEUE NATIONALGALERIE. This sleek building, designed by Mies van der Rohe, has interesting temporary exhibits and a permanent collection of Ernst, Kirchner, Munch, Warhol, and contemporary art. *(Potsdamer Str. 50, just past the Kulturforum.)*

KUNSTBIBLIOTHEK. A stellar collection of lithographs and drawings by Renaissance masters, including Dürer and Goya, and Botticelli's illustrations for the *Divine Comedy. (Library open M 2-8pm, Tu-F 9am-8pm. Tours Su at 3pm. Free.)*

CHARLOTTENBURG

The area surrounding **Schloß Charlottenburg** is home to a number of excellent museums. Take bus #145 to *Luisenpl./Schloß Charlottenburg* or U7 to *Richard-Wagner-Pl.* and walk about 15min. down Otto-Suhr-Allee.

■**ÄGYPTISCHES MUSEUM.** This stern Neoclassical building contains a famous collection of ancient Egyptian art—hulking sarcophogi, mummified cats, a massive temple gateway, and the famous bust of **Queen Nefertiti** (1350 BC), considered one of the most stunning sculptures on earth. *(Schloßstr. 70. Across Spandauer Damm from the palace. Open Su and Tu-Sa 10am-6pm. €8, students €4.)*

SAMMLUNG BERGGRUEN. A substantial collection of Picasso, Paul Klee, Alberto Giacometti, French Impressionists, and African masks. *(Schloßstr. 1. Across the street from the Ägyptisches Museum. Open Su and Tu-Sa 10am-6pm. €6, students €3.)*

DAHLEM

■**ETHNOLOGISCHES MUSEUM.** The Ethnology Museum richly rewards a trek to Dahlem. The exhibits range from ancient Central American stonework to African elephant tusk statuettes to enormous boats from the South Pacific. The smaller **Museum für Indisches Kunst** (Museum for Indian Art), housed in the same building, features ornate shrines and bright murals. *(U1 to Dahlem-Dorf and follow the "Museen" signs. ☎830 14 38. Open Su-Sa 11am-6pm, Tu-F 10am-6pm. €3, students €1.50.)*

INDEPENDENT (NON-SMB) MUSEUMS

DEUTSCHE GUGGENHEIM BERLIN. A joint venture of Deutsche Bank and the Guggenheim Foundation features rotating exhibits of contemporary art. *(Unter den Linden 13. ☎202 09 30. Open daily 11am-8pm. €3, students €2.50. M free.)*

KUNST-WERKE BERLIN. This former margarine factory has studio space, a matrix of rotating contemporary exhibitions, a cafe, and an independent bookstore. *(Auguststr. 69. U6: Oranienburger Tor. ☎243 45 90; www.kw-berlin.de. Exhibitions open Su and Tu-Sa noon-6pm, Th until 8pm. €4, students €2.)*

FILMMUSEUM BERLIN. This new museum chronicles the development of German film, with a special focus on older films like *Metropolis* and whole rooms devoted to such superstars as Leni Riefenstahl and Marlene Dietrich. *(Potsdamer Str. 2; 3rd and 4th fl. of the Sony Center. U2: Potsdamer Pl. Tickets sold on the ground floor. Open Su and Tu-Sa 10am-6pm, Th until 8pm. €6, students €4, children €2.50.)*

JÜDISCHES MUSEUM BERLIN. Built from Daniel Libeskind's winning design, the zinc-plated structure that houses this museum is a fascinating architectural experience. None of the walls are parallel, and the jagged hallways end in windows overlooking "the void." Wander through the labyrinthine "Garden of Exile" or experience the chill of being shut in the "Holocaust Tower," a giant concrete room virtually devoid of light and sound. *(Lindenstr. 9. U6 to Kochstr. or U1, 6, or 15 to Hallesches Tor. Open daily 10am-10pm. €5, students €2.50.)*

▣ ENTERTAINMENT

Berlin has one of the most vibrant cultural scenes in the world. Reservations can be made by calling the box office. Always ask about student discounts; most theaters and concert halls offer up to 50% off, but only if you buy at the *Abendkasse* (evening box office), which generally opens 1hr. before performances. Other ticket outlets charge 15-18% commissions and don't offer student discounts. There's also a ticket counter in the **KaDeWe** department store, Tauentzienstr. 21. (☎217 77 54. Open M-F 10am-8pm, Sa 10am-4pm). Most theaters and operas close from mid-July to late August.

CONCERTS, OPERA, AND DANCE

Berlin reaches its musical zenith during **Berliner Festwochen**, lasting almost all of September and drawing the world's best orchestras and soloists. The **Berliner Jazztage** in November features top-notch jazz musicians. For info about either, contact Berliner Festspiele (☎254 890; www.berlinerfestspiele.de). In mid-July, the **Bachtage** is a week of classical music, while every Saturday night in August the **Sommer Festspiele** turns the Ku'damm into a concert hall with punk, steel-drum, and folk groups. Look for concert listings in the pamphlets *Konzerte und Theater in Berlin und Brandenburg* (free), *Berlin Programm* (€1.50), *Zitty*, or *Tip*.

▨ **Berliner Philharmonisches Orchester,** Herbert Von Karajanstr. 1 (☎25 48 81 32). U2: *Potsdamer Pl.* and walk up Potsdamer Str. It may look bizarre, but this big yellow building is acoustically perfect. The *Berliner Philharmoniker* is one of the world's finest orchestras. It's tough to get a seat; check an hour before concert time or write 8 weeks in advance. Tickets start at €7 for standing room, €15 for seats. Performs early Sept.-May. Box office open M-F 3-6pm, Sa-Su 11am-2pm.

Konzerthaus (Schauspielhaus am Gendarmenmarkt), Gendarmenmarkt 2 (☎20 30 90; www.konzerthaus.de). U2: *Stadtmitte.* The opulent home of Berlin's symphony orchestra. Last-minute tickets are somewhat easier to come by. No performances mid-July through August. Box office open M-Sa 11am-7pm, Su noon-4pm.

Deutsche Oper Berlin, Bismarckstr. 35 (☎343 84 01). U2: *Deutsche Oper.* Berlin's best and youngest opera, featuring newly commissioned works as well as German and Italian classics. Tickets €10-110. 25% student discounts. Box office open M-Sa 11am until 1hr. before performance, Su 10am-2pm. Open Sept.-June.

Deutsche Staatsoper, Unter den Linden 7 (☎20 35 45 55). U6: *Französische Str.* Eastern Berlin's leading opera company is led by Daniel Barenboim (also the conductor of the Chicago Symphony Orchestra). Tours on some Sa-M—check ahead for times. Tickets €5-200. Student tickets €10 1 hr. before show. Box office open M-F 11am-7pm, Sa-Su 2-7pm, and 1hr. before performance. Performs Sept. to mid-July.

THEATER

The pamphlets *Kultur!news, Berlin Programm, 030, Zitty,* and *Tip* have theater listings. In addition to the world's best German-language theater, Berlin also has a lively English-language scene. A number of private companies called "off-theaters" also occasionally feature English-language plays. As with concert halls, look out for summer closings (*Theaterferien* or *Sommerpause*).

▨ **Deutsches Theater,** Schumannstr. 13a (☎28 44 12 25). U6: *Friedrichstr.* Go north on Friedrichstr., turn left on Reinhardtstr., and then right on Albrechtstr., which curves into Schumannstr. Even western Berlin admits it: this is the best theater in Germany. The **Kammerspiel** (☎28 44 12 26) stages smaller, provocative productions. Tickets €4-36, students €8. Box office for both open M-Sa 11am-6:30pm, Su 3-6:30pm.

Hebbel-Theater, Stresemannstr. 29 (☎25 90 04 27). U1: *Hallesches Tor.* The most avant of the avant-garde theaters in Berlin draws talent from all over the world. Committed to producing in the original language, this venue brings in the playwrights to collaborate with the actors. Tickets €11-23, students €11. Box office open daily 4-7pm.

Friends of Italian Opera, Fidicinstr. 40 (☎691 12 11). U6: *Pl. der Luftbrücke.* The name of Berlin's leading English-language theater is a joking reference to the mafia in *Some Like It Hot.* A smaller, less subsidized venue, this stage still produces new, experimental works. Tickets €8-15. Box office opens at 7pm. Most shows at 8pm.

FILM

Berlin is a movie-loving town—it hosts the international **Berlinale** film festival (Feb. 5-15, 2004), and on any night you can choose from over 150 films. *O.F.* next to a movie listing means original version (i.e., not dubbed); *O.m.U.* means original version with German subtitles. Check *Tip* or *Zitty* for theater schedules. Prices are reduced M-W at most theaters. Bring a student ID for discounts. English-language films screen at the **Odeon,** Hauptstr. 116 (☎78 70 40 19. U4: *Rathaus Schöneberg.*) and **Cinestar,** in the Sony Center at Potsdamer Platz 4 (☎20 66 62 60. U2: *Potsdamer Pl.*).

⬛ SHOPPING

The seven-story **KaDeWe department store** on Wittenbergpl. at Tauentzienstr. 21-24, is the largest department store on the continent. The name is an abbreviation of *Kaufhaus des Westens* (Department Store of the West); for product-starved East Germans who flooded Berlin in the days following the opening of the Wall, KaDeWe *was* the West. (☎212 10. Open M-F 9:30am-8pm, Sa 9am-4pm.) The **Kurfürstendamm,** near *Bahnhof Zoo,* has almost every kind of shop imaginable. The classified *Zweite Hand* (second-hand; €2), appears Tu, Th and Sa, and has ads for anything anyone wants to resell: plane tickets, silk dresses, cats, and terrific deals on **bikes.** Kreuzberg's strip for used clothing and cheap antiques is on **Bergmannstraße.** *(U7: Gneisenaustr.)*

⬛ NIGHTLIFE

Berlin's nightlife is absolute madness. Bars typically open around 6pm and get going around midnight, just as the clubs are opening their doors. Bar scenes wind down anywhere between 1am and 6am; meanwhile, dance floors fill up at clubs that groove until dawn, when a variety of after-parties and 24hr. cafes keep up the perpetual motion. From 1-4am, take advantage of the **night buses** and **U-Bahn** 9 and 12, which run all night on F and Sa. The best sources of info about bands and dance venues are *Tip* (€2.50) and the superior *Zitty* (€2.30), available at all newsstands, or the free *030,* distributed in hostels, cafes and bars.

Kreuzberg's reputation as the dance capital of Germany is challenged by clubs sprouting up in **Mitte, Prenzlauer Berg,** southern **Friedrichshain,** and near **Potsdamer Platz** in East Berlin. The largest bar scene sprawls down pricey **Oranienburger Straße** in Mitte. Prenzlauer Berg, originally the edgy alternative to trendy Mitte, has become more expensive, especially around **Kollwitzplatz** and Kastanienallee. Still, areas around Schönhauser Allee and Danziger Str. keep the dream alive, such as the "LSD" zone of Lychener Str., Schliemannstr., and Dunckerstr. **Friedrichshain** has edgier venues and a lively bar scene along Simon-Dach-Str. and Gabriel-Max-Str. Raging dance venues aimed at the young are scattered between the car dealerships and empty lots of Mühlenstr. In western Berlin, gay life centers around **Nollendorfplatz.** The Ku'damm is where businessmen and middle-aged tourists drink.

Try to hit the techno **Love Parade,** usually held in the third weekend of July, when over a million ravers ecstatically converge. Prices are astronomical during this weekend of hedonism and insanity. Counter-movements such as the Hate Parade and the Fuck Parade can provide interesting, cheap party alternatives—ask around. It's also worth mentioning that Berlin has de-criminalized marijuana possession of up to 8g, although in effect the police can arrest you for any amount if they feel the need. Exercise discretion.

BARS AND CLUBS

MITTE

■ **Tresor/Globus,** Leipziger Str. 126a. U2 or night bus N5, N29, or N52 to *Potsdamer Pl.* One of the best techno venues in Berlin. Downstairs former bank vaults flicker in strobe light as ravers sweat to hard-core techno; upstairs the music is slower. Cover W €3, F €7, Sa €7-11. Open W and F-Sa 11pm-6am.

Zosch, Tucholskystr. 30. U6: *Oranienburger Tor.* The bright, laid-back bar on the ground floor is like a living room. The basement has live music, fiction and poetry readings, and another, darker bar. Dixieland jazz W. Open M-F from 4pm, Sa-Su from noon.

WMF, Karl-Marx-Allee 34. U5: *Schillingstr.* In a former East German cabaret, its double-dancefloors fill with electroloungers Th and Sa. Gay night Su. Cover €7-13. Open Th and Sa from 11pm, Su from 10pm.

2BE-Club, Ziegelstr. 23. U6: *Oranienburger Tor.* Reggae and hip-hop in a huge space. F, Sa ladies free until midnight. Cover €8. Open F-Sa from 11pm.

Strandbar Mitte, Monbijioustr. 3. S3, 5, 7, 9, or 75 to *Hackescher Markt.* In Monbijoupark, across from the Bodemuseum. There's a difference between gimmicks and really awesome gimmicks, and Strandbar's miniature outdoor beach, spread with countless beach chairs, is in the second category. Open in summer only, daily from 10pm.

SCHÖNEBERG

■ **Slumberland,** Goltzstr. 24. U1: *Nollendorfpl.* See it to believe it: Palm trees, rotating African art, and a sand floor. The secret to the bittersweet frappes is instant coffee crystals. Open Su-Th 6pm-2am, F 6pm-5am, Sa 11am-5am.

Metropol, Nollendorfpl. 5 (☎217 368 11). U1: *Nollendorfpl.,* or night buses #N5, N19, N26, N48, N52, or N75. Don't tell someone to meet you here without specifying a room and a floor. **Tanz Tempel,** the central dance venue, is vast: 650,000 watts of light, 35,800 watts of sound, and DJs who aren't afraid to use them. Music and hours vary.

KREUZBERG

■ **Freischwimmer,** vor dem Schlesischen Tor 2. U1: *Schlesischen Tor.* A mess of waterside tables tangled in rose vines—some indoors, some outdoors, some with chubby sofas, some in boats. M poetry reading followed by a party. F a roll of the die determines the cover charge (€1-6). Open M-F from noon, Sa-Su from 11am.

■ **SO36,** Oranienstr. 190 (☎61 40 13 06). U1, 12, or 15 to *Görlitzer Bahnhof* or night bus #N29 to *Heinrichpl.* Berlin's best mixed club, with a hip hetero, gay, and lesbian clientele. A massive dance packs in a friendly crowd for techno, hip-hop, and ska—often live. Cover for parties €4-8, concerts €7-18. Open from 11pm.

Wild at Heart, Wiener Str. 20 (☎611 70 10). U1: *Görlitzer Bahnhof.* Shrines to Elvis, Chinese lanterns, flaming booths, tiki torches, glowing tigers, and other glittery kitsch. The crowd is pierced and punked. Gritty music every night. Open daily from 8pm.

Muvuca, Mehringhof, Gneisenaustr. 2a (☎693 01 75). U6: *Mehringdamm* or night bus #N4, N19, or N76. A bar, performance space, Afro-Brazilian eatery, and club run by a socialist collective in a steel and concrete courtyard. Also the site of political meetings, lesbian events, and an anarchist bookstore. Open Su and Tu-Sa 3pm-late.

GERMANY

FRIEDRICHSHAIN

Astro-Bar, Simon-Dach Str. 40. Plastic retro space robots and loud electronica. Open daily from 6pm.

Dachkammer Bar (DK), Simon-Dach Str. 39. U5: *Frankfurter Tor.* Rustic themed, with lots of brick, wood, and comfortable nooks. Snacks from €4. Mixed drinks €5-7. Open M-F noon-late, Sa-Su 10am-late.

Paule's Metal Eck, Krossener Str. 15 (☎291 1624; www.paules-metal-eck.de). U5: *Frankfurter Tor.* At the corner of Simon-Dach Str. How do you make your bar stand out on the strip? Chihuahua skeletons! A well-executed fake heavy metal bar—don't let the hooded Goth monk over the door scare you off. Open noon until late.

PRENZLAUER BERG

Morgenrot, Kastanianallee 85. U2: *Eberswalder Str.* By day it's a vegetarian restaurant, by night it serves frosty vodka shots. Th-Su vegetarian brunch buffet 11am-4pm. Open Su and Th-Sa 11am-1am, T-W 3pm-1am, F-Sa until 3am.

August Fengler, Lychener Str. 11 (☎44 35 66 40). U2: *Eberswalder Str.* This hip, homey cafe-bar is very un-Prenzlberg. DJs W-Th, live music F-Sa (reggae, funk, house, jazz, Latin). Open daily from 7pm, music from 10pm.

KulturBrauerei, Knaackstr. 97 (☎441 92 69; www.kulturbrauerei.de). U2: *Eberswalder Str.* Enormous party space in a former East German brewery. This expansive village of *Kultur* houses everything from the popular clubs **Soda** and **Kesselhaus** to a Russian theater to upscale cafes and an art school. Music includes hard-core *Ostrock,* disco, techno, reggae, *Schlager* and more. Cover varies wildly—€1.50-16 or more.

CHARLOTTENBURG (SAVIGNYPLATZ)

Quasimodo, Kantstr. 12a. U2: *Zoologischer Garten.* Beneath a huge cafe, this concert venue showcases soul and jazz. Cover €7-24. Open M-F from 5pm, Sa-Su from 2pm.

A-Trane, Bleibtreustr. 1 (☎313 25 50; www.a-trane.de). S3, 5, 7, 9, or 75 to *Savignypl.* There's little chat: the jazz fans are here for the music. Cover €8-15. Doors open at 9, musicians play 10pm-2am weeknights, later on weekends. Usually closed M and Su.

GAY AND LESBIAN NIGHTLIFE

Berlin is one of the most gay-friendly cities on the continent. The main streets of Nollendorfplatz, including Goltzstr., Akazienstr., and Winterfeldtstr., have mixed bars and cafes, while the "Bermuda Triangle" of Motzstr., Fuggerstr., and Eisenacherstr. is more purely gay. **Mann-o-Meter,** Bülowstr. 106, at the corner of Else-Lasker-Schüler-Str., has info on nightlife. (☎216 80 08. Open M-F 5-10pm and Sa-Su 4-10pm.) **Spinnboden-Lesbenarchiv,** Anklamer Str. 38, is the lesbian equivalent. Take U8 to *Bernauer Str.* (☎448 58 48. Open W and F 2-7pm.) For up-to-date event listings, pick up the free *Siegessäule, Sergej* (for men), or *Blattgold* (for women). The second half of June culminates in the **Christopher Street Day** (CSD) parade, a six-hour-long street party drawing more than 250,000 revelers (June 26, 2004). The weekend before sees the smaller **Lesbisch-schwules Stadtfest** at Nollendorfpl.

SCHÖNEBERG

▨ **Hafen,** Motzstr. 19. U1: *Nollendorfpl.* All its art was made by one of the eight owners, who take turns tending the bar. Mostly male but not restricted. The weekly pub quiz (at 10pm) is in English the first M of each month. Open daily 8pm-late.

Heile Welt, Motstr. 5. U1: *Nollendorfpl.* Despite the recent addition of two enormous, quiet inner sitting rooms, the clientele still packs the bar and spills into the street. Mostly male crowd during "prime time," more mixed in the early evening and early morning. Open 6pm-4am.

KREUZBERG

Rose's, Oranienstr. 187 (☎615 65 70). U1: *Görlitzer Bahnhof.* Marked only by "Bar" over the door. It's Liberace meets Cupid meets Satan. A friendly, mixed gay and lesbian clientele packs this intense and claustrophobic party spot at all hours of the night. Margaritas €4. Open daily 10pm-6am.

Schoko-Café, Mariannenstr. 6 (☎615 15 61). Lesbian central; a bright and colorful cafe with billiards, Turkish baths, a cultural center, and innumerable other women-only services. Dancing every second Sa of the month (from 10pm) and cultural events every weekend. Friendly and laid-back. Open daily from 5pm.

◪ DAYTRIPS FROM BERLIN

KZ SACHSENHAUSEN. The small town of Oranienburg, just north of Berlin, was home to the Nazi concentration camp Sachsenhausen, where more than 100,000 Jews, communists, intellectuals, Roma, and homosexuals were killed between 1936 and 1945. The **Gedenkstätte Sachsenhausen,** a memorial preserving the remains of the camp, was opened by the DDR in 1961. It including some of the original cramped barracks, the cell block where "dangerous" prisoners were kept in solitary confinement and tortured, and a pathology wing where Nazis experimented on inmates. *(Str. der Nationen 22. S1: Oranienburg (40min.). Follow the signs from Stralsunderstr., turn right on Bernauer Str., left on Str. der Einheit, and right on Str. der Nationen (20min.). ☎03301 20 00. Free. Audio tour rental €3.50. Open mid-Mar. to mid-Oct. 8:30am-6pm; mid-Oct. to mid-Mar. 8:30am-4pm.)*

POTSDAM. Visitors disappointed by Berlin's distinctly unroyal demeanor can get their Kaiserly fix in nearby Potsdam, the glittering city of Friedrich II (the Great). The 600-acre ◪**Park Sanssouci** is Friedrich's testament to the size of his treasury and the diversity of his aesthetic tastes. For info on the park, stop by the **Visitor's Center** at the windmill. *(Open May-Oct. daily 8:30am-5pm; Nov.-Feb. 9am-4pm.)* **Schloß Sanssouci,** the park's main attraction, was Friedrich's answer to Versailles. German tours are limited to 40 people and leave every 20min., but the final tour (5pm) usually sells out by 2pm, so come early. The tourist office leads English-language tours of the main Schloß only. *(Open Apr.-Oct. Su and Tu-Sa 9am-5pm; Nov.-Mar. Su and Tu-Sa 9am-4pm. Required tour €8, students €5.)* The exotic gold-plated **Chinesisches Teehaus,** complete with a rooftop Buddha toting a parasol, contains 18th-century *chinoiserie* porcelain. Next door is the **Bildergalerie,** whose collection of Caravaggio, van Dyck, and Rubens crams a long hall. *(Open mid-May to mid-Oct. Su and Tu-Sa 10am-12:30pm and 1-5pm. €2, students €1.50. Tour €1 extra.)* The stunning **Sizilianischer Garten** is perhaps the park's most intricate garden. At the opposite end of the park is the largest of the four castles, the 200-room **Neues Palais.** *(Open Apr.-Oct. Sa-Th 9am-5pm; Nov.-Mar. 9am-4pm. €6, students €5; €1 less in winter.)*

Potsdam's second park, **Neuer Garten,** contains several royal residences. At **Schloß Cecilienhof,** built in the style of an English Tudor manor, exhibits document the **Potsdam Treaty,** which was signed here in 1945. It was supposed to be the "Berlin Treaty," but the capital was too bombed-out to accommodate the Big Three. *(Take bus #692 to Schloß Cecilienhof. Open Su and Tu-Sa 9am-5pm. €3, students €2. Tour €1 extra.)* The garden also contains the huge, marbled **Marmorpalais,** and odd little buildings like a replica of an Egyptian pyramid. *(Marmorpalais open Apr.-Oct. Su and Tu-Sa 10am-5pm; Nov.-Mar. Sa-Su 10am-4pm. €2, students €1.50. Tour €1 extra.)*

GERMANY

EASTERN GERMANY

Saxony (*Sachsen*) is known primarily for Dresden and Leipzig, the largest cities in Eastern Germany after Berlin. However, the entire region offers fascinating historical and cultural diversity. The castles around Dresden testify to the decadence of Saxony's Electors, while boxy socialist monuments elsewhere recall the GDR aesthetic. Saxony is also home to the Sorbs, Germany's only national minority, who lend a Slavic feel to many of the region's eastern towns.

DRESDEN   ☎ 0351

The stunning buildings of Dresden's *Altstadt* look ancient, but most are newly reconstructed—the Allied bombings of February 1945 that claimed over 40,000 lives destroyed 75% of the city center. Its Baroque architecture, world-class museums, and *Neustadt* nightlife make Dresden (pop. 479,000) one of the most celebrated cities its size; backpackers traveling from Berlin to Prague often stop over.

▐ TRANSPORTATION

Flights: Dresden's **airport** (DRS; ☎ 881 33 60) is 9km from the city. S2 runs there from both train stations (20min., 2 per hr. 4am-10:30pm, €1.50.)

Trains: Nearly all trains stop at both the **Hauptbahnhof** in the Altstadt and **Bahnhof Dresden Neustadt** across the Elbe. Trains to: **Berlin** (3hr., 1 per hr., €30); **Budapest** (11hr., every 2hr., €64); **Frankfurt** (7hr., 2 per hr., €70); **Leipzig** (1½hr., 1-2 per hr., €17); **Munich** (7 hr., 1 per hr., €27); **Prague** (2½hr., 12 per day, €20); and **Warsaw** (8hr., 8 per day, €27). Buy tickets from the machines in the main halls of both stations or pay less at the *Reisezentrum* desk.

Public Transportation: Most of Dresden is manageable on foot, but **streetcars** cover the whole city. Single ride €1.50; 4 or fewer stops €1. Day pass €4; weekly pass €14. Tickets are available from *Fahrkarten* dispensers at major stops and on the streetcars. For info and maps, go to one of the **Verkehrs-Info** stands in front of the *Hauptbahnhof* or at Postpl. (Open M-F 7am-7pm, Sa 8am-6pm, Su 9am-6pm). Most major lines run hourly after midnight—look for the moon sign marked "*Gute-Nacht-Linie.*"

Taxis: ☎ 211 211 or ☎ 888 88 88.

Ride-Sharing: Mitfahrzentrale, Dr.-Friedrich-Wolf-Str. 2 (☎ 194 40). On Slesischen Pl., across from Bahnhof Neustadt. Open M-F 9am-8pm, Sa-Su 10am-2pm.

▐ ORIENTATION AND PRACTICAL INFORMATION

Dresden is bisected by the **Elbe** river 60km northwest of the Czech border. The **Hauptbahnhof** is on the same side as the **Altstadt,** south of the river. Many of Dresden's main attractions are between **Altmarkt** and the Elbe. Nightlife is to the north in the **Neustadt,** around Albertplatz.

Tourist Office: There are two main branches: On Prager Str. 3, near the *Hauptbahnhof* (open M-F 9am-7pm, Sa 9am-4pm), and Theaterpl. in the Schinkelwache in front of the Semper Oper (☎ 49 19 20. Open M-F 10am-6pm, Sa-Su 10am-4pm.) Call city hotlines for general info (☎ 49 19 21 00), reservations (☎ 49 19 22 22), tours (☎ 49 19 21 40), and advance ticket purchases (☎ 49 19 22 33).

Currency Exchange: ReiseBank, in the *Hauptbahnhof.* €1-3 commission, depending on the amount; 1-1.5% for traveler's checks. Open M-F 8am-7pm, Sa 9am-12pm, 12:30-4pm, Su 9am-1pm. Other banks are on Prager Str.

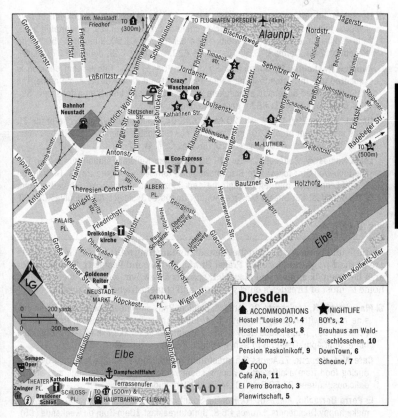

Dresden

▲ ACCOMMODATIONS
Hostel "Louise 20," 4
Hostel Mondpalast, 8
Lollis Homestay, 1
Pension Raskolnikoff, 9

★ NIGHTLIFE
BOY's, 2
Brauhaus am Wald-
  schlösschen, 10
DownTown, 6
Scheune, 7

🍴 FOOD
Café Aha, 11
El Perro Borracho, 3
Planwirtschaft, 5

GERMANY

Laundromat: "Crazy" Waschsalon, 6 Louisenstr. Wash €2.50, dry €0.50 per 10min. Open M-Sa 7am-11pm.

Emergency: Police ☎ 110. **Ambulance** and **Fire** ☎ 112.

Pharmacy: Apotheke Prager Straße, Prager Str. 3 (☎ 490 30 14). Open M-F 8:30am-7pm, Sa 8:30am-4pm. The *Notdienst* sign outside lists 24hr. pharmacies.

Internet Access: In the bar at **Hostel Mondpalast,** Louisenstr. 77. €3.50 per hr. Open daily 8am-1am. **Groove Station,** Katharinenstr. 11-13. €3 per hr. Open daily 1pm-late.

Post Office: Hauptpostamt, Königsbrücker Str. 21/29 (☎ 819 13 73), in Neustadt. Open M-F 8am-7pm, Sa 9am-1pm. Address mail to be held: Firstname SURNAME, *Post-lagernde Briefe,* Hauptpostamt, **D-01099** Dresden, Germany.

🏠 ACCOMMODATIONS

The *Neustadt* is home to a number of hostels that give revelers proximity to clubs and bars and have late check-out times. Quieter hostels and pricier hotels can be found around the *Altstadt,* closer to the sights. Reservations are a must anywhere.

GERMANY

▨ **Hostel Mondpalast,** Louisenstr. 77 (☎563 40 50). With a guestbook full of rave reviews, this hostel has all a backpacker could desire: Good prices, comfortable beds, a large kitchen, a social dining room, and a bar. Sheets €1.50. Internet €3.50 per hr. Reception 24hr. Dorms €13.50-16; singles €29, with bath €39; doubles €37/50. ❷

Pension Raskolnikoff, Böhmische Str. 34 (☎804 57 06). This 6-room pension is squeezed into the same building as the restaurant and gallery of the same name. The distinctly relaxed bohemian atmosphere is a perfect escape from the hostel scene. Singles €31; doubles €41; €8 for each extra person. ❸

Hostel "Louise 20," Louisenstr. 20 (☎889 48 94). Climb the ladder to one of the 20 beds in the dorm attic (€10) in Dresden's newest hostel. Sheets €2.50. 5-bed room €15; 3-4 bed room €16; singles €26; doubles €37. ❶

Lollis Homestay, Seitenstr. 2A (☎799 30 25). From Neustadt station turn left on Dr.-Friedrich-Wolf-Str.; follow it to Bischofsweg and turn left under the tracks. Go right on Rudolf-Leonardstr. and left through the park. Cozy as a German *WG* (shared student flat). Breakfast €3. Sheets €2. Free laundry. Dorms €13; singles €25; doubles €34. ❶

▌ FOOD

It's difficult to find anything in the Altstadt not targeting tourists; the cheapest eats are at the *Imbiß* stands along **Prager Straße** and around **Postplatz**. The Neustadt area between **Albertplatz** and **Alaunplatz** spawns a new bar every few weeks and is home to most of Dresden's quirky, ethnic, and student-friendly restaurants.

▨ **Planwirtschaft,** Louisenstr. 20. Attracts political Reds and Greens with neo-German cuisine made with ingredients fresh from local farms. Inventive soups, fresh salads (€3.50-6.50), and entrees from stuffed eggplant to fresh lake fish (€7-10). Breakfast buffet until 4pm. Open Su-Th 9am-midnight, F-Sa 9am-1am. ❸

Café Aha, Kreuzstr. 7. Across the street from Kreuzkirche. Promotes fair trade by introducing food from a different devloping country each month. Often exotic and always delicious. Entrees €3.50-8.40. Open daily 10am-midnight. ❷

El Perro Borracho, Alaunstr. 70. Flowing Spanish wines, *Sekt, sangria,* and tasty *tapas* make happy Dresdeners. Entrees €6-8. Buffet breakfast 10am-3pm on weekends (€8). Open M-F 11:30am-2am, Sa-Su 10am-3am. ❸

▌ SIGHTS

The electors of Sachsen once ruled nearly all of central Europe from the banks of the Elbe. Destroyed during WWII and partly rebuilt during Communist times, the *Altstadt* carries the city's legacy as one of the continent's major cultural centers.

ZWINGER. The extravagant collection of August the Strong, Prince Elector of Saxony and King of Poland, is housed in the magnificent Zwinger palace. One of the most successful examples of Baroque design, the palace narrowly escaped destruction in the 1945 bombings. The northern wing was designed by Gottfried Semper, revolutionary activist and master architect. The palace is now home to Dresden's finest museums (see Museums, below).

SEMPER-OPER. Dresden's famed opera house luxuriates in the same style as the northern wing of the Zwinger palace. Painstaking restoration has returned the building to its original state, making it one of Dresden's major attractions. Tour the interior any day—or just go to an opera. *(Theaterpl. 2. Check the main entrance for tour times, usually M-F every 30min. 11am-3pm. €5, students €3.)*

DRESDENER SCHLOß. Once the proud home of August the Strong, this palace will regain the lion's share of its notoriety in 2004, when the ▧**Grünes Gewölbe** (Green Vault) returns. From a collection of rare medieval chalices to the most lavish Baroque jewels, the vault dazzles the eyes with some of the finest metal and gem work in Europe. The 100m tall ▧**Hausmannsturm** hosts a collection of sobering photographs of the city after the bombings that, combined with the 360° view from the tower, convey the enormity of the reconstruction project. *(Open Su and Tu-Sa 10am-6pm. €3.50, students and seniors €2.)* To meet the rulers of Saxony from 1123 to 1904, stop by the **Fürstenzug** (Procession of Electors) along Augustsstr., a 102m mural made of 24,000 tiles of Meißen china.

KREUZKIRCHE. After being leveled three times—by fire in 1669; in 1760 by the Thirty Years War; and again in 1897 by fire—the *Kreuzkirche* survived WWII despite the flames that ruined its interior. The tower offers a bird's-eye view of downtown. *(An der Kreuzkirche 6. Open in summer M-Tu and Th-F 10am-5:30pm, W and Sa 10am-4:30pm, Su noon-5:30pm; in winter M-Sa 10am-3:30pm, Su noon-4:30pm. Free. Tower €1.)* The world-class **Kreuzchor** boys' choir is still singing after all these years. *(Concerts Sa 6pm. €4-31, students €3-23.)*

▥ MUSEUMS

After several years of renovations, Dresden's museums are once again ready to compete with the best in Europe. If you plan on visiting more than one in a day, consider a **Tageskarte** (€10, students and seniors €6), which gives one-day admission to the Albertinum museums, the Schloß, most of the Zwinger, and more.

ZWINGER. Through the archway from the Semper-Oper, ▧**Gemäldegalerie Alte Meister** has a world-class collection of predominantly Italian and Dutch paintings from 1400 to 1800. Cranach the Elder's luminous *Adam* and *Eve* paintings, Rubens's *Leda and the Swan*, and Raphael's *Sistine Madonna* are good company. *(Open Su and Tu-Sa 10am-6pm. €6, students €3.50. Tours F and Su at 11am and 4pm, €0.50.)* The nearby **Rüstkammer** shows shiny but deadly toys from the court of the Wettin princes: Ivory-inlaid guns, chain mail, and the wee armor of the Wettin toddlers. *(Open Su and Tu-Sa 10am-6pm. €1.50, students and seniors €1; covered by admission to the Gemäldegalerie Alte Meister.)* With over 20,000 pieces, the **Porzellansammlung** boasts the largest collection of European porcelain in the world. *(Open Su-W and F-Sa 10am-6pm. €1.50, students and seniors €1.)*

ALBERTINUM. The **Gemäldegalerie Neue Meister** picks up in the 19th century where the Alte Meister gallery leaves off, with such German and French Impressionists as Degas, Monet, Renoir, and hometown hero Caspar David Friedrich. Check out Otto Dix's renowned *War* triptych, along with the Expressionist and *Neue Sachlichkeit* works. *(Open Su-W and F-Sa 10am-6pm. €6, students and seniors €3.50.)* The immense **Skulpturensammlung** collection of classical sculpture was rescued from the basement during the 2002 floods, and will likely fill the void left by the departure of the Grünes Gewölbe in December 2003.

DEUTSCHES HYGIENEMUSEUM. The world's first public health museum is famous for its "Glass Man," a transparent human model with illuminated organs, and its rotating exhibits. *(Lingnerpl. 1; enter from Blüherstr. www.dhmd.de. Open Su and Sa 10am-6pm, Tu-F 9am-5pm. €2.50, students €1.50. Special exhibits €4, students €2.)*

▧ ENTERTAINMENT

For centuries, Dresden has been a focal point of theater, opera, and music. Although most theaters break from mid-July to early September, open-air festivals bridge the gap; movies screen during **Filmnächte am Elbufer** in July and August at 9pm for around €6. (Office at Alaunstr. 62. ☎89 93 20.) Like other area palaces, the **Zwinger** has classical concerts on summer evenings. (Shows start at 6:30pm.)

Opera's finest perform at **Sächsische Staatsoper (Semper-Oper)**, Theaterpl. 2. Getting tickets (€3-74.50) takes work; call ahead. (☎491 17 05. Box office at Schinkelwache open M-F 10am-6pm, Sa 10am-1pm, and 1hr. before performances.) Orchestra's best hold forth at **Kulturpalast**, Am Altmarkt (☎486 66 66), the civic center which is also home to the **Dresdner Philharmonie** (☎486 63 06. Tickets at Schloßstr. 2. Main entrance open M-F 10am-7pm, Sa 10am-2pm.) For musical theater and operetta from Lerner to Sondheim, head to **Staatsoperette Dresden**, Pirnaer Landstr. 131 (☎207 990. Tickets €4-19. Discounted Tu-Th. Ticket office open M 11am-4pm, Tu-Th 10am-7pm, F 11am-7pm, Sa 4-7pm, Su 1hr. before curtain. For more cutting-edge theater, witness **projekttheater dresden**, Louisenstr. 47 (☎8 10 76 10. Tickets €11, students €7. Box office open 8pm, shows at 9pm.)

■ NIGHTLIFE

Ten years ago, the area north of Albertpl. was a maze of gray streets lined with crumbling buildings. Now a spontaneous, alternative community has sprung up in the 50 bars crammed onto Königsbrücker Str., Bischofsweg, Kamenzerstr., and Albertpl. *Kneipen Surfer* (free at Neustadt hostels) describes every bar.

DownTown, Katharinenstr. 11. Constantly packed. The music is loud, seating is rare, and the crowd is enthusiastic. The evening here begins upstairs at the bar, billiard hall, and tattoo parlor. Expect pop, Latin, and electronic music. Cover €3.50, students €2.50. Open Tu, Th-Sa 10pm-5am.

Brauhaus am Waldschlösschen, am Brauhaus 8b. Tram 11 to *Waldschlösschen* or walk 25min. up Baunitzerstr. On a hill overlooking the Elbe and the Dresden skyline, this brewery proves Bavaria doesn't have a monopoly on great beer gardens. Beer by the liter (€4.60) and classic German entrees (€6-9).

Scheune, Alaunstr. 36. From Albertpl., walk up Königsbrücker Str. and turn right onto Katharinenstr.; take a left onto Alaunstr. The granddaddy of the *Neustadt* bar scene. Club opens at 8pm. Cover varies. Indian cafe open M-F 5pm-2am, Sa-Su 10am-2pm.

BOY's, Alaunstr. 30, just beyond the Kunsthof Passage. A half-naked devil mannequin guards one of Dresden's popular gay bars. Drinks €2.70-6. Open daily 8pm-3am.

■ DAYTRIP FROM DRESDEN

MEIßEN. In 1710, the Saxon elector contracted severe *Porzellankrankheit* (the porcelain "bug," which still afflicts tourists today) and turned the city's defunct castle into Europe's first porcelain factory. The building was once more tightly guarded than KGB headquarters to prevent competitors from learning its techniques; today, anyone can tour the **Staatliche Porzellan-Manufaktur,** Talstr. 9. Peruse finished products in the **Schauhalle** (€4.50, students €4), but the real fun is the **Schauwerkstatt** (show workshop), in which porcelain artists paint perfectly detailed flowers before your incredulous eyes. (Open May-Oct. daily 9am-6pm; Nov.-Apr. 9am-5pm. €3. English headsets available.) Narrow, romantic alleyways lead up to the **Albrechtsburg** castle and cathedral. (Open Mar.-Oct. daily 10am-6pm; Nov.-Feb. 10am-5pm. €3.50, students €2.50.) From the train station, walk straight onto Bahnhofstr. and follow it over the Elbbrücke. Cross the bridge, continue straight to the Markt, and turn right onto Burgstr. Next door looms the **Meißener Dom,** a Gothic cathedral featuring four 13th-century statues by the Naumburg Master, a triptych by Cranach the Elder, and the metal grave coverings of the Wettins. (Open Apr.-Oct. daily 9am-6pm; Nov.-Mar. 10am-4pm. €2, students €1.50.)

Reach Meißen from Dresden by train (40min. €4.50). The **tourist office**, Markt 3, across from Frauenkirche, finds private rooms for a €3 fee. (☎(03521) 419 40. Open Apr.-Oct. M-F 10am-6pm, Sa-Su 10am-4pm; Nov.-Mar. M-F 10am-5pm, Sa 10am-3pm.) **Postal Code:** 01662.

LEIPZIG   ☎0341

Leipzig (pop. 493,000) is one of the few German university cities large enough to have a life outside the academy, but small enough to feel the influence of its students. Every corner is packed with cafes, cabarets, street-musicians, and second-hand stores. Once home to Bach and Mendelssohn, Wagner and Nietzsche, Goethe and Leibniz, central Leipzig is compact and navigible.

TRANSPORTATION AND PRACTICAL INFORMATION. Leipzig lies on the Berlin-Munich line. **Trains** run to: Berlin (2-3hr., 3 per hr., €26); Dresden (1½hr., 3 per hr., €17); Frankfurt (5hr., 2 per hr., €62); and Munich (7hr., 3 per hr., €68). To find the **tourist office**, Richard-Wagner-Str. 1, cross Willy-Brandt-Pl. in front of the station and turn left at Richard-Wagner-Str. (☎710 42 60. Open M-F 9am-7pm, Sa 9am-4pm, Su 9am-2pm.) **Postal Code:** 04109.

ACCOMMODATIONS AND FOOD. To reach **Hostel Sleepy Lion ❷**, Käthe-Kollwitz-Str. 3, take streetcar #1 (dir.: Lausen) to *Gottschedstr.* Run by young locals, it draws an international crowd. All rooms have showers and bath. (☎993 94 80. Sheets €2. **Internet** €2 per hr. Reception 24hr. Dorms €14; singles €24; doubles €36; quads €60.) **Kosmos Hotel ❸**, Gottschedstr. 1, is a 12min. walk from the train station. Cross the street and turn right onto Richard-Wagner-Str.; when it ends, cut left through the parking lot and small park. At the end of the park, keep left on Dittrichring and it'll be ahead on the right. This funky hotel is part of a larger complex that includes a nightclub and restaurant. (☎233 44 20. Breakfast €5. Reception daily 8am-11pm. Singles from €30; doubles from €50.)

The *Innenstadt*, especially **Grimmaischestraße**, is full of *Imbiß* stands, bistros, and bakeries. Outside the city center, **Karl-Liebknecht-Straße** (streetcar #10 or 11 to *Kochstr.*) is packed with cheap *Döner* stands and cafes that double as bars. Vegetarian **Avocado ❸**, Karl-Liebknecht-Str. 79, does big things with goat cheese, forest berries, and its namesake fruit. (Open M-Th and Su 11:30am-1am, F 11:30am-2am, Sa 4pm-2am.) **Zur Pleißenburg ❷**, Schulstr. 2, down Burgstr. from the Thomaskirche, serves hearty fare. (Open daily 9am-5am.) There's a **market** on Richard-Wagner-Pl. at the end of the Brühl. (Open Tu and F 9am-5pm).

SIGHTS AND NIGHTLIFE. The heart of Leipzig is the **Marktplatz**, a cobblestoned square guarded by the slanted 16th-century **Altes Rathaus**. Head down Grimmaischestr. to the **Nikolaikirche**, where massive weekly demonstrations led to the fall of the GDR. (Open M-Sa 10am-6pm, Su after services. Free.) Backtrack to the *Rathaus* and follow Thomasg. to the **Thomaskirche;** Bach's grave lies beneath the floor in front of the altar. (Open daily 9am-6pm. Free.) Just behind the church is the **Johann-Sebastian-Bach-Museum,** Thomaskirchof 16. (Open daily 10am-5pm. €3, students €2. Free English-language audio tours.) Head back to Thomasg., turn left, then turn right on Dittrichring to reach Leipzig's most fascinating museum, the **Museum in der "Runden Ecke,"** Dittrichring 24, which displays stunningly blunt exhibits on the history, doctrine, and tools of the *Stasi* (secret police). Ask for an English brochure in the office. (Open daily 10am-6pm. Free.) Outside the city ring, the **Völkerschlachtdenkmal** memorializes the 1813 Battle of Nations against Napoleon. Climb the 500 steps for a fabulous view. (Streetcar #15 from the train station to *Völkerschlachtdenkmal.* Open daily Apr.-Oct. 10am-6pm; Nov.-Mar. 10am-5pm. Free. To ascend €3, students €2.)

The **Gewandhaus-Orchester,** Augustuspl. 8, has been a major international orchestra since 1843. Guest orchestras are sometimes free. (☎ 127 02 80. €12-40, 20% student discount.) Free magazines *Fritz* and *Blitz* and the superior *Kreuzer* (€1.50 at newsstands) fill you in on nightlife. **Barfußgäßchen,** a street just off the Markt, serves as the see-and-be-seen nightlife area for everyone from students to *Schicki-mickis* (yuppies). Just across Dittrichring on **Gottschedstraße** and **Bosestraße** is a similar scene with a slightly younger crowd and slightly louder music. Leipzig university students spent eight years excavating a series of medieval tunnels so they could get their groove on in the ■**Moritzbastei,** Universitätsstr. 9, which has multi-level dance floors and relaxed bars in cavernous rooms with vaulted brick ceilings. (Cover €4, students €2.50; higher for concerts. Cafe open daily 2pm-midnight. Disco open W and F until late.)

WITTENBERG ☎ 03491

The Protestant Reformation began here in 1517 when Martin Luther nailed his *95 Theses* to the door of the Schloßkirche; Wittenberg (pop. 48,000) has been fanatical about its native heretic ever since. All the major sights lie around **Collegienstraße.** The ■**Lutherhalle,** Collegienstr. 54, chronicles the Reformation through letters, texts, art, and artifacts. (☎ 420 30. Open Apr.-Oct. daily 9am-6pm; Nov.-Mar. Su and Tu-Sa 10am-5pm. €5, students €3.) The **Schloßkirche** allegedly holds Luther's body and a copy of the *95 Theses.* The tower offers a sumptuous view of the countryside. (Down Schloßstr. Church open M-Sa 10am-5pm, Su 11:30am-5pm. Free. Tower open M-F noon-4pm, Sa-Su 10am-4pm. €1, students €0.50.)

Trains leave for Berlin (1½hr., every 2hr., €17) and Leipzig (1hr., every 2hr., €9). From the station, follow the street curving right and continue until Collegienstr., the start of the **pedestrian zone.** The **tourist office,** Schloßpl. 2, provides maps, leads tours (€6), and books rooms. (☎ 49 86 10. Open Mar.-Oct. M-F 9am-6pm, Sa 10am-3pm, Su 11am-4pm; Nov.-Feb. M-F 10am-4pm, Sa 10am-2pm, Su 11am-3pm.) The **Jugendherberge (HI)** ❷ is in the castle across from the tourist office. (☎ 40 32 55. Breakfast included. Sheets €3.50. Reception 3-10pm. Dorms €15, under-27 €12.) Cheap eats lie along the Collegienstr.-Schloßstr. strip. **Postal Code:** 06886.

WEIMAR ☎ 03643

While countless German towns leap at any excuse to build memorial *Goethehäuser* (proclaiming that Goethe slept here, Goethe ate here, Goethe once asked for directions here), Weimar (pop. 63,500) features the real thing; the **Goethehaus** and **Goethe-Nationalmuseum,** Frauenplan 1, present the preserved private chambers where the poet entertained, wrote, and ultimately died after 50 years in Weimar. (Open April-Oct. Su and Tu-Sa 9am-6pm; Nov.-Mar. 10am-4pm. Expect a wait on summer weekends. €6, students €4.50.) The **Neuesmuseum,** Weimarpl. 4, has fascinating rotating exhibits of modern art, including an interactive "Terror orchestra," composed of knives, nails, and a hammer and sickle. (Open Apr.-Sept. Su and Tu-Sa 10am-6pm; Oct.-Mar. 10am-4:30pm. €3, students €2.) South of the town center in the **Historischer Friedhof,** Goethe and Schiller rest together in the basement of the **Fürstengruft.** Schiller, who died in an epidemic, was originally buried in a mass grave. Later, Goethe combed through the remains until he identified Schiller and had him interred in a tomb. Skeptics argued that Goethe was mistaken, but a team of Russian scientists verified his claim in the 1960s. (Cemetery open Mar.-Sept. daily 8am-9pm; Oct.-Feb. 8am-6pm. Tomb open April to mid-Oct. M and W-Su 9am-6pm; mid-Oct. to mid-Mar. M and W-Su 10am-4pm. €2, students €1.50.)

Trains run to: Dresden (3½hr., 2 per hr., €30); Frankfurt (3hr., every hr., €40); and Leipzig (1½hr., 2 per hr., €21). To reach **Goetheplatz** (the center of the *Altstadt*) from the station, follow Carl-August-Allee downhill to Karl-Liebknecht-Str., which leads into Goethepl. (15min.). The **tourist office,** Marktstr. 10, across from the *Rathaus,* hands out free maps, books rooms for a €2.55 fee, and offers German-language **walking tours.** The Weimarer Wald desk has lots of info on **outdoor activities** in the area. (☎240 00. Open Apr.-Oct. M-F 9:30am-6pm, Sa-Su 9:30am-3pm; Nov.-Mar. M-F 10am-6pm, Sa-Su 10am-2pm.) To get to the student-run ⚑**Hababusch Hostel ❶,** Geleitstr. 4, follow Geleitstr. from Goethepl.; after it takes a sharp right, you'll come to a statue on your left. The entrance to the Hababusch is behind the statue. Expect a laid-back atmosphere in the heart of Weimar. (☎85 07 37. Reception 24hr. Dorms €10; singles €15; doubles €24.) In a lovely *Jugendstil* mansion, **Jugendherberge Germania (HI) ❷,** Carl-August-Allee 13, has convenience written all over it. (☎85 04 90. Breakfast and sheets included. Internet access. Dorms €20, under-27 €17.) A combination cafe and gallery, **ACC ❸,** Burgpl. 1-2, is popular with students and vegetarians. (Open daily noon-1am.) The daily **produce market,** at Marktpl., has groceries. (Open M-Sa 7am-5pm.)

⚑ DAYTRIP FROM WEIMAR: BUCHENWALD. During WWII, 250,000 Jews, Roma (Gypsies), homosexuals, communists, and political opponents were imprisoned at the Buchenwald labor camp. Although it was not intended as an extermination camp, over 50,000 died here due to harsh treatment by the SS. The **Nationale Mahnmal und Gedenkstätte Buchenwald** (National Monument and Memorial) has two principal sights. **KZ-Lager** refers to the remnants of the camps itself. The large storehouse documents both the history of Buchenwald (1937-1945) and of Nazism in general. The East German **Mahnmal** (monument) is on the other side of the hill; go up the main road that bisects the two large parking lots or take the footpath uphill from the old Buchenwald *Bahnhof* and then continue on the main road. The camp **archives** are open to anyone searching for records of family and friends between 1937 and 1945. Schedule an appointment with the curator. (Archives ☎(03643) 43 01 54; library (03643) 43 01 60. Outdoor camp area open daily until sundown.) Sadly, the suffering at Buchenwald did not end with liberation—Soviet authorities used the site as an internment camp, **Special Camp. No. 2,** where more than 28,000 Germans—mostly Nazi war criminals and opponents of the communist regime—were held until 1950; an exhibit detailing this period opened in 1997.

The best way to reach the camp is by **bus** #6 from Weimar's train station or Goethepl. Check the schedule carefully; some #6 buses go to *Ettersburg* rather than *Gedenkstätte Buchenwald.* (20min.; M-Sa every hr., Su every 2hr.) Buses back to Weimar stop at the *KZ-Lager* parking lot and at the road by the *Glockenturm* (bell tower). There is an **info center** near the bus stop at Buchenwald, which offers a walking tour (€3) and shows an excellent video with English subtitles every hour. (Open May-Sept. Su and Tu-Sa 9am-6pm; Oct.-Apr. 9am-4:30pm.)

EISENACH ☎03691

Birthplace of Johann Sebastian Bach, Eisenach (pop. 44,000) is also home to one of Germany's most treasured national symbols, ⚑**Wartburg castle.** In 1521, the castle protected Martin Luther (disguised as a bearded noble named Junker Jörg) after his excommunication. Much of the castle's interior is not authentically medieval, but the Wartburg is still enchanting and the view from its south tower is spectacular. (Open Mar.-Oct. daily 8:30am-5pm; Nov.-Feb. 9am-3:30pm. Required German tour €6, students and children €3.) According to local tradition, the actual location of Bach's birth in 1685 was the **Bachhaus,** Frauenplan 21. Every 40min., a guide gives a presentation on Bach's life in German and English, complete with musical interludes. (Open Apr.-Sept. M noon-5:45pm, Tu-Su 9am-5:45pm; Oct.-Mar. M 1-4:45pm, Tu-Su 9am-4:45pm. €2.50, students €2.) Bach was baptized at the 800-year-old **Georgenkirche,** just off the Markt, where members of

GERMANY

ON THE MENU

THE BEST *WURST*

So you're finally in Germany and itching to get your teeth into your first authentic German *Wurst*. With over 1500 varieties, you'll have plenty of choices. All have one thing in common: German law mandates that sausages can only be made of meat and spices—if it has cereal filling, it's not *Wurst*.

Bockwurst: This tasty sausage is common roasted or grilled at street stands, and is usually served dripping with ketchup and mustard in a soft *Brötchen*. Although *Bock* means billy-goat, this *Wurst* is made of finely ground veal with parsley and chives. Complement your Bockwurst with some Bock beer.

Thüringer Bratwurst: Similar to the Bockwurst both in content and presentation, the Bratwurst has a little pork too, plus ginger and nutmeg.

Frankfurter: Unlike the American variety (whose origin is believed to be the *Wienerwurst*), the German Frankfurter can only have this name if made in Frankfurt. It's made of lean pork ground into a paste and then cold smoked, which gives it that orange-yellow coloring.

Knockwurst: Shorter and plumper, this sausage is served with sauerkraut. It's made of lean pork and beef, and a healthy dose of garlic. Pucker up!

Weißwurst: Cream and eggs give this "white sausage" its pale coloring. Weißwurst goes with rye bread and mustard.

his family were organists for 132 years. (Open M-Sa 10am-12:30pm and 2-5pm, Su after services.) Just up the street is **Lutherhaus,** Lutherpl. 8, Martin's home in his school days. (Open Apr.-Oct. daily 9am-5pm; Nov.-Mar. 10am-5pm. €2.50.)

Trains run frequently to Weimar (1hr., 2 per hr., €11). The **tourist office,** Markt 2, sells maps (€2), offers daily city tours (2pm, €3), and books rooms for free. From the train station, follow Bahnhofstr. through the tunnel and angle left until you turn right onto the pedestrian Karlstr. (☎ 194 33. Open M 10am-6pm, Tu-F 9am-6pm, Sa-Su 10am-2pm.) To reach the recently renovated **Jugendherberge Arthur Becker (HI) ❷,** Mariental 24, take Bahnhofstr. from the station to Wartburger Allee, which runs into Mariental. (☎ 74 32 59. Breakfast included. Reception daily 8am-11pm. Dorms €18, under-27 €15.) For groceries, head to **Edeka supermarket** on Johannispl. (Open M-F 8am-6:30pm, Sa 8am-12:30pm.) Near the train station, **Café Moritz ❷,** Bahnhofstr. 7, serves Thüringian specialties (€3-9) and sinful ice cream delicacies. (Open May-Oct. M-F 8am-9pm, Sa-Su 10am-9pm; Nov.-Apr. M-F 8am-7pm, Sa-Su 10am-7pm.) **Postal Code:** 99817.

NORTHERN GERMANY

Once a favored vacation spot for East Germans, Mecklenburg-Vorpommern, the northeasternmost portion of Germany, has suffered economic depression in recent years. To the west, Schleswig-Holstein, which borders Denmark, maintains close ties with Scandinavia. Portly Hamburg is by turns rich and radical. To the south, Bremen is Germany's smallest state.

HANOVER (HANNOVER)　　　☎ 0511

Despite its relatively small size, Hanover (pop. 516,000) rivals any European city with its art, culture, and landscape. Broad avenues, enormous pedestrian zones, and endless parks and gardens make the city an example of all that is good in urban planning. The gems of Hanover are the three bountiful ◾**Herrenhausen gardens.** The largest, the geometrically trimmed **Großer Garten,** holds the **Große Fontäne,** one of Europe's highest-shooting fountains. (Fountain spurts M-F 11am-noon and 3-5pm, Sa-Su 11am-noon and 2-5pm. Garden open Apr.-Oct. 9am-8pm; Nov.-Mar. 8am-dusk. €2.50.) On the outskirts of the *Altstadt* stands the spectacular **Neues Rathaus;** take the elevator up the tower for a thrilling view of the city. (Open May-Sept. M-F 8am-10pm, Sa-Su 10am-10pm. Elevator €2.) The nearby ◾**Sprengel Museum,** Kurt-Schwitters-Pl., hosts the best of 20th-century art—

including Dalí, Picasso, and Magritte. (Open Su and W-Sa 10am-6pm, Tu 10am-8pm. Permanent collection €3.30, students €2; with special exhibits €6, students €3.50.) **Kestner-Museum,** Trammpl. 3, majors in decorative arts, with a focus on chairs. (Open Su, Tu and Th-Sa 11am-6pm, W 11am-8pm. €2.60, students €1.50. F free.)

Trains leave at least every hour for: Amsterdam (4½-5hr., €40); Berlin (2½hr., €40); Frankfurt (3hr., €80); Hamburg (1½hr., €25); and Munich (9hr., €130). To reach the **tourist office,** Ernst-August-Pl. 2, head out the main entrance of the train station; facing the large rear of the king's splendid steed, turn right. (☎ 16 84 97 00. Open M-F 9am-6pm, Sa 9am-2pm.) ❚**Jugendherberge Hannover (HI) ❷,** Ferdinand-Wilhelm-Fricke-Weg. 1, is far from the city center, but definitely worth the trek. Take U3 or 7 to *Fischerhof.* From the stop, backtrack 10m, turn right, cross the tracks, and walk on the path through the school's parking lot; follow the path as it curves, and cross the street. Go over the red footbridge and turn right. (☎ 131 76 74. Breakfast included. Reception daily 7:30am-1am. Dorms €19-30, under-27 €16-28.) To reach **CityHotel am Thielenplatz ❹,** Thielenpl. 2, take a left onto Joachimstr. from the station and go one block to Thielenpl. (☎32 76 91 93. Breakfast included. Check-out 11:30am. Singles €40, with shower €57; doubles with shower €75. Weekends cheaper.) **Jalda ❷,** Limmerstr. 97, serves Greek and Middle Eastern dishes for €4-8. (Open M-Th and Su 11:30am-midnight, F-Sa 11:30am-1am.) **Uwe's Hannenfaß Hanover ❷,** Knochenhauerstr. 36, in the center of the *Altstadt,* serves traditional German fare for €5-7 and great house brews for €3. (Open Su-Th 4pm-2am, F 4pm-4am, Sa noon-4am.) There's a **Spar supermarket** by the *Lister Meile* U-Bahn stop. (Open M-F 7am-7pm, Sa 8am-2pm.) **The Loft,** Georgstr. 50b, is packed with students on the weekends. (Disco night F and ladies night Sa have €3.50 covers. Open W-Sa from 8pm.) **Postal Code:** 30159.

HAMBURG ☎040

The largest port city in Germany, Hamburg (pop. 1,700,000) radiates an inimitable recklessness. Hamburg gained the status of Free Imperial City in 1618 and proudly retains its autonomy as one of Germany's 16 *Länder* and one of only three German city-states. Restoration and riots determined the post-WWII landscape, but today Hamburg has become a haven for contemporary artists and intellectuals as well as party-goers who live it up in Germany's self-declared "capital of lust."

▐ TRANSPORTATION

Trains: The *Hauptbahnhof* has hourly connections to: **Berlin** (2½hr., €37); **Copenhagen** (4½hr., €67); **Frankfurt** (5hr., €57); **Hanover** (2¼hr., €25); **Munich** (6hr., €96); and runs frequently to **Amsterdam** (5½, €65). Two other stations, **Dammtor** (near the university) and **Altona** (to the west) service the city; frequent trains and the S-Bahn connect the 3 stations. 24hr. **lockers** available for €1-2 per day.

Buses: The **ZOB** is on Steintorpl. across from the *Hauptbahnhof,* between McDonald's and the Museum für Kunst und Gewerbe. To: **Berlin** (3¼hr., 8 per day, €23); **Copenhagen** (5½hr., 2 per day, €42); **Paris** (12½hr., 1 per day, €61). Open M-F 9am-8pm, Sa 9:30am-1:30pm and 4-8pm, Su 4-8pm.

Public Transportation: HVV operates an efficient U-Bahn, S-Bahn, and bus network. Most single tickets within the downtown cost €1, but prices vary depending on where you go and what transport you take. 1-day (€5) and 3-day (€13) tickets are not as cost effective as the **Hamburg Card** (see below). Buy tickets at the orange *Automaten.*

Bike Rental: Fahrradladen St. Georg, Schmilinskystr. 6, off Lange Reihe towards the Außenalster. (☎24 39 08. €8 per day. Open M-F 10am-7pm, Sa 10am-1pm.)

GERMANY

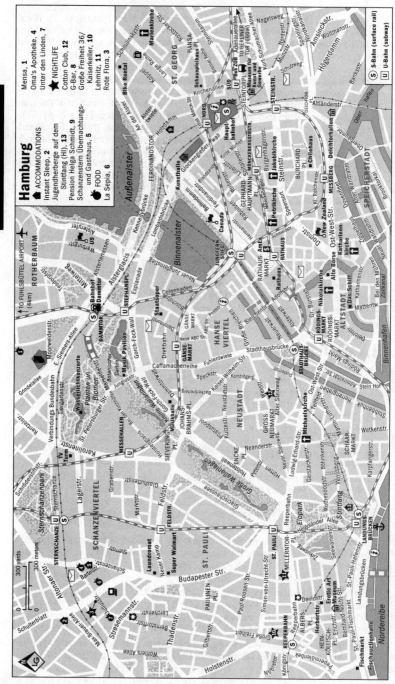

Hamburg

▲ ACCOMMODATIONS
Instant Sleep, 2
Jugendherberge auf dem
  Stintfang (HI), 13
Pension Helga Schmidt, 9
Schanzenstern Übernachtungs-
  und Gasthaus, 5

● FOOD
La Sepia, 6

Mensa, 1
Oma's Apotheke, 4
Unter den Linden, 7

★ NIGHTLIFE
Cotton Club, 12
G-Bar, 8
Große Freiheit 36/
  Kaiserkeller, 10
Lehmitz, 11
Rote Flora, 3

Ⓢ S-Bahn (surface rail)
Ⓤ U-Bahn (subway)

ORIENTATION AND PRACTICAL INFORMATION

Hamburg's city center sits between the Elbe River and the two city lakes, **Außenalster** and **Binnenalster**. Most major sights lie between the **St. Pauli Landungsbrücken** port area in the west and the *Hauptbahnhof* in the east. **Mönckebergstraße**, Hamburg's most famous shopping street, runs all the way to Rathausmarkt. North of downtown, the **university** dominates the **Dammtor** area and sustains a vibrant community of students and intellectuals. To the west of the university, the **Schanzenviertel** is a politically active community home to artists, squatters, and a sizeable Turkish population. At the south end of town, an entirely different atmosphere reigns in **St. Pauli**, where the raucous **Fischmarkt** (fish market) is surpassed only by the wilder **Reeperbahn**, home to Hamburg's infamous sex trade and its best discos.

Tourist Offices: The **Hauptbahnhof office,** in the Wandelhalle near the Kirchenallee exit (☎30 05 12 01), books rooms for a €4 fee. Open daily 7am-11pm. The **St. Pauli Landungsbrücken office,** between piers 4 and 5 (☎300 512 03), is less crowded. Both offices supply free English maps and sell the **Hamburg Card**, which provides unlimited access to public transportation, reduced admission to most museums, and discounts on bus and boat tours. (1-day card €7, 3-day card €15.)

Currency Exchange: ReiseBank, on the 2nd fl. of the *Hauptbahnhof* near the Kirchenallee exit. Exchanges money for a 4.5% fee. Open daily 7:30am-10pm.

Gay and Lesbian Resources: The center of the gay community is in St. Georg. Pick up the free **hinnerk** magazine or the Hamburg "Gay Map."

Laundromat: Schnell und Sauber, Grindelallee 158, in the university district. Take S21 or 31 to *Dammtor*. Wash €3.50. Dry €1 per 15min. Open daily 7am-10:30pm.

Emergency: Police: ☎110. **Fire** and **Ambulance:** ☎112.

Pharmacy: The staff at the **Senator-Apotheke,** Hachmannpl. 14 (☎32 75 27), speaks English. Exit the *Hauptbahnhof* on Kirchenallee. Open M-F 7am-8pm, Sa 8am-6pm.

Internet Access: Teletime, Schulterblatt 39. €0.50 per 10min. Open M-Sa 10am-midnight. **Spiele-Netzwerk,** Kleine Schäferkamp. €4 per hr. Open daily 10am-2am.

Post Office: At the Kirchenallee exit of the *Hauptbahnhof*, 20097 Hamburg. Open M-F 8am-8pm, Sa 9am-6pm. Address mail to be held: Firstname SURNAME, *Postlagernde Briefe*, Post Hamburg-Hauptbahnhof, **20099** Hamburg, GERMANY.

ACCOMMODATIONS

The dynamic **Sternschanze** area has the city's two best backpacker hostels. More expensive hotels line the **Binnenalster** and eastern **Außenalster**. Small, relatively cheap pensions line **Steindamm** and the area around the *Hauptbahnhof*, although prostitutes and wannabe Mafiosi prowl these streets. **Lange Reihe** has equivalent options in a cleaner neighborhood. For longer stays, try **Mitwohnzentrale Homecompany,** Schulterblatt 112 (☎194 45; www.homecompany.de).

◪ **Schanzenstern Übernachtungs- und Gasthaus,** Bartelsstr. 12 (☎439 84 41). S21 or U3 to *Sternschanze*, turn left onto Schanzenstr., right on Susannenstr., and left onto Bartelsstr. In an electrifying neighborhood of students, working-class Turks, and left-wing dissenters, the hostel maintains order and a tasteful decor. Dorms €17; singles €33; doubles €55; triples €60; quads €73; quints €91. ❷

◪ **Instant Sleep,** Max-Brauer-Allee 277 (☎43 18 23 10). S21 or U3 to *Sternschanze*. Everyone is part of a big happy family in this backpacker hostel; rooms are often left open while guests lounge together, read, or cook dinner in the communal kitchen. Bike rental €4 per 6hr. Sheets €2. Internet €1 for 15min. Reception daily 9am-2pm. Dorms €15; singles €26; doubles €42; triples €57. ❷

GERMANY

Pension Helga Schmidt, Holzdamm 14 (☎28 21 19). Welcoming pension only 2 blocks from the *Hauptbahnhof*. Some two room suites; all rooms with TV and phone. Cheaper rooms share a hall shower. Singles €35-37; doubles €55-65; triples €82. ❸

Jugendherberge auf dem Stintfang (HI), Alfred-Wegener-Weg 5 (☎31 34 88). Take U3 or S1, 2, or 3, to *Landungsbrücke*, then head up the hill on the wooded path. Clean and well-furnished rooms look out on the woods or the harbor. Breakfast included. Reception daily 12:30pm-12:30am. Curfew 2am. Dorms €21-24, under-27 €19-22. ❸

▯ FOOD

As you'd expect, seafood abounds in Hamburg. **Sternschanze** offers Turkish fruit and falafel stands and avant-garde cafes, while slightly cheaper establishments abound in the **university** area, especially along **Rentzelstraße.** The Portuguese community lends its own take on seafood between the Michaelskirche and the river.

▨ La Sepia, Schulterblatt 36, is a fine Portuguese restaurant with the city's best and most reasonably priced seafood. Lunch €4-6. Dinner €8-14. Open daily 11am-3am. ❸

Unter den Linden, Juliusstr 16. Read complimentary papers over Milchkaffe (€3.20), breakfast (€4-7), or enormous salads (€4-6) in a relaxed atmosphere beneath the linden trees. M-F 11am-11pm, Sa-Su 10am-11pm. ❷

Oma's Apotheke, Schanzenstr. 87. Retro ambiance and portions large enough to make grandma proud. German, Italian, and American cuisine. *Schnitzel* platter €7.50. Hamburger with a pound of fries €6.60. Open M-Th and Su 9am-1am, F-Sa 9am-2am. ❷

Mensa, Von-Melle-Park 7. S21 to *Dammtor.* Massive plates of cafeteria food and a bulletin board of university events. Meals €1.50-3 with student ID; non-students add €0.70. Open M-Th 10am-5:30pm, F 10am-4:30pm. ❶

▢ SIGHTS

ALTSTADT. The gargantuan 18th-century **Michaelskirche** is the symbol of Hamburg. Its tower, accessible by foot or elevator, is the only one of the city's six spires that may be climbed. *(Church open June-Oct. daily 11am-4:30pm, Nov.-May M-F 11am-4:30pm. Organ music Apr.-Aug. daily at noon and 5pm. Tower €3.)* The seat of government, the **Rathaus** is the most richly-ornamented building in Hamburg. The plaza in front hosts political demonstrations and medieval fairs. *(Tours in English every hr. M-Th 10:15am-3:15pm, F-Su 10:15am-1:15pm. €1.)* The spire of hallowed (and hollowed) **Nikolaikirche** pierces the heavens with its dark reminder of war. *(History exhibition open M-F 11am-5pm, Sa-Su 11am-6pm. €2.)* Hamburg's shopping strip, **Mönkebergstraße,** stretches from the *Rathaus* to the *Hauptbahnhof* and is punctuated by two spires. The first belongs to **St. Petrikirche,** the oldest church in town. *(Open M-Tu and Th-F 10am-6:30pm, W 10am-7pm, Sa 10am-5pm, Su 9am-9pm. Free concerts W 5:15pm.)* The second, **St. Jakobikirche,** is known for its 14th-century Arp-Schnittger organ. *(Open M-Sa 10am-5pm.)*

ALSTER LAKES AND PLANTEN UN BLOMEN. To the west of the Alster lies **Planten un Blomen,** a manicured expanse which includes the largest Japanese Garden in Europe. *(Open 7am-11pm. Free.)* There are also nightly **Wasserlichtkonzerte,** with a choreographed play of fountains and underwater lights. *(May-Aug. daily 10pm; Sept. 9pm.)* North of the city center, the two **Alster lakes,** bordered by tree-lined paths, provide further refuge from crowded Hamburg.

ST. PAULI LANDUNGSBRÜCKEN. Hamburg's harbor lights up at night with ships from all over the world. At the **Fischmarkt,** charismatic vendors haul in and hawk huge amounts of fish, produce, and other goods. *(U- or S-Bahn to Landungsbrücken or S-Bahn to Königstr. Open April-Oct. Su 5-10am, Nov.-Mar. Su 7-10am.)*

REMEMBERING THE HOLOCAUST. An idyllic agricultural village east of Hamburg provided the backdrop for the **KZ Neuengamme,** where Nazis killed 55,000 prisoners through slave labor. Banners inscribed with the names of the victims hang in the **Haus des Gedenkens,** and **Walther-Werke** has the recorded testimony of survivors. *(Jean-Doldier-Weg 39. S21 to Bergedorf, then bus #227 to Jean-Doldier-Weg. Open May-Oct. Su and Sa 10am-6pm, Tu-F 10am-5pm; Oct.-Mar. Su and Tu-Sa 10am-5pm.)* Amidst warehouses, **Gedenkstätte Bullenhuser** is a memorial to 20 Jewish children brought here from Auschwitz for "testing" and murdered by the S.S. only hours before Allied troops arrived. Visitors plant a rose for the children in the garden behind the school. *(Bullenhuser Damm 92. S21 to Rothenburgsort. Follow the signs to Bullenhuser Damm along Ausschlaeger Bildeich and across a bridge. Open Su 10am-5pm and Th 2-8pm. Free.)*

MUSEUMS. Most museums are closed on Mondays. The first-rate ⊠**Hamburger Kunsthalle,** Glockengießerwall 1, presents the best art—from medieval to postmodern. *(Open Su, Tu-W and F-Sa 10am-6pm, Th 10am-9pm. €7.50, students €5.)* **Museum für Kunst und Gewerbe,** Steintorpl. 1, brims with handicrafts, china, and some of the oldest pianos in the world. *(Open Su and Tu-Sa 10am-6pm, Th 10am-8pm. €8.20, students and seniors €4.)* One of the largest of its kind in Europe, the **Erotic Art Museum,** Nobistor 10a, bares all—from the Kama Sutra to Picasso to truly shocking. *(Open Su-Th 10am-midnight, F-Sa 10am-2am. €8. Under 16 not admitted.)*

🎵 🎭 ENTERTAINMENT AND NIGHTLIFE

The **Staatsoper,** Große Theaterstr. 36, houses one of the best opera companies in Germany; the associated **ballet company** is the acknowledged dance powerhouse of the nation. (☎35 68 68. U1 to *Stephanspl.* Open M-Sa 10am-6:30pm.) **Orchestras** abound—the Philharmonie, the Norddeutscher Rundfunk Symphony, and Hamburg Symphonia all perform at the **Musikhalle** on Johannes-Brahms-Pl. (U2 to *Gänsemarkt.*) Traditional **jazz** swings at the **Cotton Club.** On Sunday mornings, good and bad alike play at the **Fischmarkt.** The **West Port Jazz Festival,** Germany's largest, runs in mid-July; call the Koncertskasse (☎32 87 38 54) for info. The most anticipated festival is the **G-Move** (May 25, 2004), dubbed the "Love Parade of the North." Check www.g-move.com for details.

The infamous **Reeperbahn,** is the spinal cord of **St. Pauli;** it's lined with sex shops, strip joints, and the best bars and clubs in town. Though the Reeperbahn is reasonably safe, it is not recommended for women to venture into the adjacent streets. **Herbertstraße,** Hamburg's "official" prostitution strip, runs parallel to the Reeperbahn, and is open only to men over 18. The prostitutes flaunting their flesh on Herbertstr. are licensed professionals required to undergo health inspections, while the streetwalkers are venereal roulette wheels. Unlike St. Pauli, the trendy streets of **Schanzenviertel** are more cafe than club and more leftist than lustful. The **gay scene** is in classy **St. Georg,** near Berliner Tor. In general, clubs open and close late, with some techno and trance clubs remaining open all night.

⊠ **Rote Flora,** Schulterblatt 71. This looming mansion of graffiti serves as the nucleus of the autonomist scene. Beer €1.50. Weekend cover from €3-5. Cafe open M-F 6-10pm. Music starts at around 10pm. Crowds come at midnight.

GERMANY

■ **Große Freiheit 36/Kaiserkeller,** Große Freiheit 36 (☎31 77 780). Everyone from Ziggy Marley to Matchbox Twenty stomps about on the big stage upstairs. Live music or DJs usually 10:30pm-5am. Cover €5-6, more for live music. Often entry until 11pm is free—get your hand stamped and return later.

Lehmitz, Reeperbahn 22. Friendly students and hardcore punks gather around the clock for €2 beers. Live, thrashing music W and weekends. Open 24hr.

Cotton Club, Alter Steinweg 10. U3 to *Rödingsmarkt*. New Orleans, dixie, swing, and big band jazz in a warmly lit setting. Cover €5 for Hamburg bands, around €10 for guest bands. Shows start at 8:30pm. Open M-Th 8pm-midnight and F-Sa 8pm-1am.

G-Bar, Lange Reihe 81. Men in skin-tight shirts serve beer (€2-3) and mixed drinks (€7) with a smile in this comfortable, neon-lit gay bar. Open daily noon-2am.

LÜBECK   ☎0451

Lübeck (pop. 213,000) is easily Schleswig-Holstein's most beautiful city—you'd never guess that most of it was razed in WWII. In its heyday it was the capital of the Hanseatic league, controlling trade across Northern Europe. Although no longer a center of political and commercial influence, Lübeck still churns out delicious marzipan and red-blond Dückstein beer.

▣◪ TRANSPORTATION AND PRACTICAL INFORMATION. Trains run to Berlin (3½hr., 1 per hr., €35) and Hamburg (45min., 2 per hr., €9). Ryanair **flies** cheaply from London to Lübeck (LBC). A privately owned, expensive tourist office is in the train station. The **tourist office** in the *Altstadt*, at Breite Str. 62, is better. (☎122 54 20. Open M-F 9:30am-7pm, Sa-Su 10am-3pm.) **Postal Code:** 23552.

▮▯ ACCOMMODATIONS AND FOOD. To reach ▨**Rucksack Hotel ❶,** Kanalstr. 70, walk past the *Holstentor* from the station, turn left on An der Untertrave and right on Beckergrube; the hostel is on the corner of Kanalstr. (☎70 68 92. Breakfast €3. Sheets €3. Reception daily 10am-1pm and 4-9pm. Dorms €13; doubles with bath €40; quads €60, with bath €68.) The **Baltic Hotel ❹,** Hansestr. 11, is across the street from the station. (☎855 75. Breakfast included. Reception daily 7am-10pm. Singles €35-45; doubles €58-65; triples from €80.) Lübeck's specialty is **marzipan,** a delectable candy made from almonds. Stop by the famous confectionery ▨**I.G. Niederegger Marzipan Café ❶,** Breitestr. 89, for marzipan in the shape of pigs, jelly-fish, and even the town gate. (Open M-F 9am-7pm, Sa 9am-6pm, Su 10am-4pm.) **Tipasa ❷,** Schlumacherstr. 12, serves pizza, pasta, and vegetarian dishes, and runs a *Biergarten* in back. (Open M-Th and Su noon-1am, F-Sa noon-2am.)

◪ SIGHTS. Between the station and the *Altstadt* stands the massive **Holstentor,** one of Lübeck's four 15th-century gates and the city's symbol. The museum inside deals in equal parts trade and torture. (Open Apr.-Sept. daily 10am-5pm; Oct.-Mar. closed M. €4, students €2.) The city skyline is dominated by the twin brick towers of the **Marienkirche,** a gigantic church housing the largest mechanical organ in the world. (Open in summer daily 10am-6pm; off-season 10am-4pm. Organ concerts Th and Sa at 6:30pm. €3.50, students €2.50.) The **Dom,** on Domkirchhof, shelters a majestic crucifix and is guarded by the trademark lion statue. (Open Apr.-Sept. daily 10am-6pm; Mar. and Oct. 10am-5pm; Nov. 10am-4pm; Dec.-Feb. 10am-3pm. Free. Organ concerts July-Aug. F and Su at 5pm. €3-6, students €1-3.) For a sweeping view of the spire-studded *Altstadt*, take the elevator to the top of **Pet-rikirche.** (Church open daily 11am-4pm. Tower open Apr.-Oct. 9am-7pm. €2, students €1.20.) The ▨**Museum für Puppentheater,** Kolk 16, is the largest private puppet collection in the world. (Open daily 10am-6pm. €3, students €2.50.) Dance afloat the **"body and soul"** boat in the water at the corner of Kanalstr. and Höhe Glockenstr. (Cover usually €4. Open Tu and Sa 10pm-late, F 10:30pm-late.)

SCHLESWIG ☎04621

With a harbor full of sailboats and a shoreline sprinkled with cafes, Schleswig (pop. 25,000) is a sea town with a royal history. Celebrating 1200 years since its founding as Haithabu, Viking ships set sail to Schleswig for the **Opinn Skjold** festival on the first weekend in August. By the harbor, the 18th-century **Schloß Gottorf** and surrounding buildings comprise the **Landesmuseen,** six museums with enough Danish, Dutch, and German art to fill twenty. The surrounding park is an **outdoor sculpture museum.** (All museums open daily 10am-6pm. €5, students €2.50.) Scale the 240 steps of the **St. Petri Dom** for a striking view of town. (Open May-Sept. M-Sa 9am-5pm, Su 1:30-5pm; Oct.-Apr. M-Sa 10am-4pm, Su 1:30-5pm. €1.)

Schleswig centers around its **bus terminal** rather than its train station. Single rides (€2). The **train station** is 20min. south of the city center; take bus #1, 2, 3, 6, or 7 from the stop outside the bus station. The **tourist office,** Plessenstr. 7, is up the street from the harbor; from the ZOB, walk down Plessenstr. toward the water. (☎98 16 16; room reservations ☎98 16 17. Open May-Sept. M-F 9:30am-5:30pm, Sa 9:30am-12:30pm; Oct.-Apr. M-Th 10am-4pm, F 10am-1pm.) The **Jugendherberge (HI)** ❶, Spielkoppel 1, is close to the center of town. Take bus #2 from either the train or bus station to *Schwimmhalle;* the hostel is across the street. (☎238 93. Breakfast included. Reception daily 7am-1pm and 5-11pm. Curfew 11pm. Dorms €17, under-27 €14; singles €20, under-27 €18.) Nurse cloudy brews at **Asgaard-Brauerei** ❸, Königstr. 27, with descendants of Eric the Red. (Meals €9-10. Open M-Th 5pm-midnight, F 5pm-2am, Sa 11am-2am, Su 11am-midnight.) **Postal Code:** 24837.

CENTRAL AND WEST GERMANY

Lower Saxony (*Niedersachsen*), which stretches from the North Sea to the hills of central Germany, has foggy marshland and broad agricultural plains inland. Just south of Lower Saxony, North Rhine-Westphalia is the most heavily populated and economically powerful area in Germany. While the region's squalor may have inspired the philosophy of Karl Marx and Friedrich Engels, the area's natural beauty and the intellectual energy of Cologne and Düsseldorf inspired the muses of Goethe, Heine, and Böll.

DÜSSELDORF ☎0211

As Germany's fashion hub and multinational corporation base, the rich city of Düsseldorf (pop. 571,000) crawls with German patricians and would-be aristocrats. The nation's "Hautstadt"—a pun on *Hauptstadt* (capital) and the French *haute,* as in *haute couture*—is a stately metropolis with an *Altstadt* that features the best nightlife along the Rhine.

TRANSPORTATION AND PRACTICAL INFORMATION. Trains run to: Amsterdam (2hr., every hr., €39); Berlin (4½hr., every hr., €93); Frankfurt (2½hr., 3 per hr., €32); Hamburg (3½hr., every hr., €63); Munich (6hr., 2 per hr., €98); and Paris (4½hr., 7 per day, €87). Düsseldorf's S-Bahn is integrated into the mammoth regional **VRR** *(Verkehrsverbund Rhein-Ruhr)* system, which connects most surrounding cities. For schedule info, call ☎582 28. The S-Bahn is the cheapest way to get to Aachen and Cologne. On the **public transportation system,** single tickets cost €1-7, depending on distance traveled. The *Tagesticket* (€6.35-17.50) lets up to five people travel for 24hr. on any line. To reach the **tourist office,** Immermannstr. 65, head straight and to the right from the train station; look for the Immermanhof building. It books rooms for a €4 fee. (☎172 02 22. Open M-F 8:30am-6pm, Sa 9am-12:30pm.) The **post office,** Konrad-Adenauer-Pl., **40210** Düsseldorf, is just to the right of the tourist office. (Open M-F 8am-6pm, Sa 9am-2pm.)

GERMANY

⚄ ◨ ACCOMMODATIONS AND FOOD. It's not unusual for hotels in Düsseldorf to double their prices during trade fairs, which happen from August to April. **Jugendgästehaus Düsseldorf (HI) ❷**, Düsseldorfer Str. 1, is just over the Rheinknie-brücke from the *Altstadt*. Take U70, 74, 75, 76, or 77 to *Luegpl.*, then walk 500m down Kaiser-Wilhelm-Ring. (☎55 73 10. Reception daily 7am-1am. Curfew 1am; doors open every hr. 2-6am. Dorms €20; singles €32; doubles €50.) To reach **Hotel Schaum ❸**, 63 Gustav-Poengsen-Str., exit left from the train station on Graf-Adolf-Str., take your first left, and follow the tracks to Gustav-Poengsen-Str. (☎311 65 10. Breakfast included. Singles from €30; doubles from €50.) **Hotel Komet ❹**, Bismarckstr. 93, is straight down Bismarckstr. from the train station and offers bright but snug rooms. (☎17 87 90. Singles from €40; doubles from €55.) To camp at **Kleiner Torfbruch ❶**, take any S-Bahn to *Düsseldorf Geresheim*, then bus #735 (dir.: Stamesberg) to *Seeweg*. (☎899 20 38. €4 per person, €5 per tent.) For a cheap meal, the endless eateries in the *Altstadt* can't be beat; rows of pizzerias, *Döner* stands, and Chinese diners reach from Heinrich-Heine-Allee to the banks of the Rhine. **A Tavola ❸**, Wallstr. 11, has bottomless bread baskets and meticulously prepared pastas. (Open daily noon-3pm and 6-11pm.) The local outlet of the Czech brewery, **Pilsner Urquell ❷**, Gragenstr. 6, specializes in meaty eastern European fare. (Open M-Sa noon-1am, Su 4pm-midnight.) **Otto Mess** is a popular grocery chain; the most convenient location is at the eastern corner of Karlspl. in the *Altstadt*. (Open M-F 8am-8pm, Sa 8am-4pm.)

◪ SIGHTS. The glitzy **Königsallee** (the "Kö"), just outside the *Altstadt*, embodies the vitality and glamor of wealthy Düsseldorf. Midway up is the awe-inspiring **Kö-Galerie,** a marble-and-copper shopping mall showcasing one haughty store after another. (10min. down Graf-Adolf-Str. from the train station.) The Baroque **Schloß Benrath** in the suburbs of Düsseldorf was originally built as a pleasure palace and hunting grounds for Elector Karl Theodor. Strategically placed mirrors and false exterior windows make the castle appear larger than it is, but the enormous French gardens still dwarf it. (S6 (dir.: Köln) to *Schloß Benrath*. Open Su and Tu-Sa 10am-6pm, W until 8pm. Tours every 30min. €4, students €1.75.) The **Heinrich-Heine-Institut** is the official shrine of Düsseldorf's melancholic son. (Bilker Str. 12-14. Open Su and Tu-F 11am-5pm, Sa 1-5pm. €2, students €1.) At the upper end of the Kö is the **Hofgarten park,** the oldest public park in Germany. At the east end of the park, the 18th-century **Schloß Jägerhof** houses the **Goethemuseum.** (Jakobistr. 2. Streetcar #707 or bus #752 to *Schloß Jägerhof*. Open Su and Tu-F 11am-5pm, Sa 1-5pm. €2, students and children €1.) The **Kunstsammlung Nordrhein-Westfalen,** within the black glass edifice west of the Hofgarten, houses works by Expressionists, Surrealists, Picasso, and hometown boy Paul Klee. (Grabbepl. 5. U70, 75, 76, 78, or 79 to *Heinrich-Heine-Allee;* walk north two blocks. Open Su and Sa 11am-6pm, Tu-F 10am-6pm, first W of month until 10pm. €3, students €1.50.)

◪ NIGHTLIFE. Folklore holds that Düsseldorf's 500 pubs make up *die längste Theke der Welt* (the longest bar in the world). Pubs in the *Altstadt* are standing-room-only by 6pm; by nightfall it's nearly impossible to see where one pub ends and the next begins. **Bolkerstraße** is jam-packed with street performers. *Prinz* (€3) gives tips on the scene; it's often free at the youth hostel. *Facolte* (€2), a gay and lesbian nightlife magazine, is available at newsstands. **Pam-Pam,** Bolkerstr 34, plays house, rock, pop, and plenty of American music. (Open F-Sa 10pm-dawn.) **Zur Ül,** Ratinger Str. 16, is the quintessential German pub. (Open M-F 9am-1am, Sa-Su 10am-3am.) **Unique,** Bolkerstr. 30, lives up to its name, drawing a younger, trendier crowd to its red-walled interior. (Cover €5. Open W-Sa 10pm-late.)

AACHEN
☎ 0241

Once the capital of Charlemagne's Frankish empire, modern Aachen (pop. 246,000) is a trove of historical treasures and a thriving forum for up-and-coming European artists. The three-tiered dome and dazzling blue-gold mosaics of the **Dom** are in the center of the city; Charlemagne's remains lie in the reliquary behind the altar. (Open M-Sa 11am-7pm, Su 12:30-7pm, except during services.) Around the corner is the **Schatzkammer,** Klosterpl. 2, a treasury of reliquaries containing John the Baptist's hair and ribs, splinters and nails from the cross, and Christ's scourging robe. A silver bust of Charlemagne holds his skull. (Open M 10am-1pm, Tu-W and F-Su 10am-6pm, Th 10am-9pm. €2.50, students €2.) The **Ludwigforum für Internationale Kunst,** Jülicherstr. 97-109, houses a rotating collection of cutting-edge art. (Open Tu and Th 10am-5pm, W and F 10am-8pm, Sa-Su 11am-5pm. Free tours Su 11:30am and 3pm. €3, students €1.50.)

Trains run to Brussels (2hr., every 2hr., €20) and Cologne (1hr., 2-3 per hr., €11). The **tourist office,** on Friedrich-Wilhelm-Pl. in the Atrium Elisenbrunnen, runs tours and finds rooms for free. From the station, head up Bahnhofstr.; turn left onto Theaterstr.; which becomes Theaterpl., then turn right onto Kapuzinergraben, which becomes Friedrich-Wilhelm-Pl. (☎ 180 29 60. Open M-F 9am-6pm, Sa 9am-2pm.) The **Euroregionales Jugendgästehaus (HI) ❸,** Maria-Theresia-Allee 260, feels more like a hotel than a hostel. From the station, walk left on Lagerhausstr. until it intersects Karmeliterstr. and Mozartstr., then take bus #2 (dir.: Preusswald) to *Ronheide.* (☎ 71 10 10. Breakfast included. Curfew 1am. Dorms €21; singles €34; doubles €52.) **Hotel Drei König ❸,** Büchel 5, on the corner of Marktpl., is just steps from the *Rathaus.* (☎ 483 93. Breakfast included. Reception daily 8am-11pm. Singles €45, with bath €65; doubles €65/75; triples €100.) **Pontstraße,** off Marktpl., and the pedestrian zone have a lot of great restaurants. The Mexican cocktail bar and restaurant **Sausalitos ❸,** Markt 47, has become Aachen's most popular place to eat. (Entrees €6-13. Open daily noon-1am.) **Postal Code:** 52064.

COLOGNE (KÖLN)
☎ 0221

Although most of inner Cologne (pop. 968,000) was destroyed in WWII, the magnificent Gothic *Dom* survived 14 bombings and remains Cologne's main attraction. Today, the city is the largest in North Rhine-Westphalia and its most important cultural center, with a full range of world-class museums and theaters.

▐▀ TRANSPORTATION

Flights: Flights depart from **Köln-Bonn Flughafen** (CGN); a shuttle to **Berlin** leaves hourly. Bus #170 to the airport leaves from stop #3 at the train station (20min; daily 5:30-6:30am every 30min., 6:30am-8pm every 15min., 8-11pm every 30min.; €4.80).

Trains: To: **Amsterdam** (3hr., €46); **Berlin** (5hr., 1-2 per hr., €67); **Brussels** (2½hr., €43); **Düsseldorf** (40min., 2 per hr., €7); **Frankfurt** (2hr., 3 per hr., €32); **Hamburg** (5hr., 3 per hr., €67); **Munich** (4hr., 1 per hr., €72).

Ride-Sharing: Citynetz **Mitfahrzentrale,** Maximinstr. 2 (☎ 194 40). Turn left from the back of the train station. Open daily 9am-7pm.

Ferries: Köln-Düsseldorfer (☎ 208 83 18) begins its popular Rhine cruises here. Sail upstream to **Koblenz** (€33) or **Bonn** (€11). Eurail valid on most trips.

Public Transportation: VRS (Verkehrsverbund Rhein-Sieg), downstairs in the train station, has free maps of the S- and U-Bahn, bus, and streetcar lines.

Bike Rental: Kölner Fahrradverleihservice, Markmannsgasse (☎ 0171 629 87 96), in the *Altstadt* on the Rhine. €2 per hr., €10 per day. Open daily 10am-6pm.

GERMANY

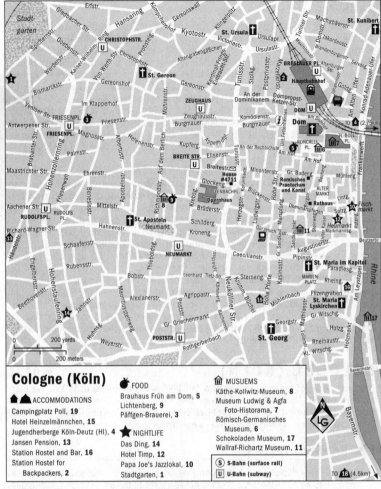

Cologne (Köln)

🛖▲▲ ACCOMMODATIONS
Campingplatz Poll, **19**
Hotel Heinzelmännchen, **15**
Jugendherberge Köln-Deutz (HI), **4**
Jansen Pension, **13**
Station Hostel and Bar, **16**
Station Hostel for
  Backpackers, **2**

🍴 FOOD
Brauhaus Früh am Dom, **5**
Lichtenberg, **9**
Päffgen-Brauerei, **3**

★ NIGHTLIFE
Das Ding, **14**
Hotel Timp, **12**
Papa Joe's Jazzlokal, **10**
Stadtgarten, **1**

🏛 MUSEUMS
Käthe-Kollwitz-Museum, **8**
Museum Ludwig & Agfa
  Foto-Historama, **7**
Römisch-Germanisches
  Museum, **6**
Schokoladen Museum, **17**
Wallraf-Richartz Museum, **11**

Ⓢ S-Bahn (surface rail)
Ⓤ U-Bahn (subway)

🔷❄❓ ORIENTATION AND PRACTICAL INFORMATION

Cologne stretches across the Rhine, but nearly all sights and the city center can be found on the western side. The *Altstadt* is split into **Altstadt-Nord,** near the **Hauptbahnhof,** and **Altstadt-Süd,** south of the **Severinsbrücke** (bridge).

Tourist Office: Verkehrsamt, Unter Fettenhennen 19 (☎ 194 33), across from the entrance to the *Dom,* provides free city maps and books rooms for a €3 fee. Open May-Oct. M-Sa 9am-9pm, Su 10am-6pm; Nov.-Apr. M-Sa 8am-9pm, Su 9:30am-7pm.

Currency Exchange: Reisebank, in the train station. Open daily 7am-9pm.

Bi-Gay-Lesbian Resources: Schulz Schwulen-und Lesbenzentrum, Kartäuserwall 18 (☎ 93 18 80 80), near Chlodwigpl. Info, advice, and cafe. The tourist office also offers the *Gay City Map* with listings of gay-friendly hotels, bars, and clubs.

Police: ☎110. **Fire** and **ambulance:** ☎112.

Pharmacy: Apotheke im Hauptbahnhof, near Gleis 12 (☎139 11 12), in the train station. Open M-F 6am-8pm, Sa 9am-8pm.

Internet access: Galeria Kaufhof, Hohe Str. 41 3rd fl. €1.50 per 30min.

Post Office: at the corner of Breite Str. and Tunisstr. in the WDR-Arkaden shopping gallery. Address mail to be held: Postlagernde Briefe für Firstname SURNAME, Hauptpostamt, **50667** Köln, GERMANY. Open M-F 8am-8pm, Sa 8am-4pm.

ACCOMMODATIONS

Hotels fill up in spring and fall when conventions come to town, and the two hostels are often booked from June to September. The **Mitwohnzentrale,** Im Ferkulum 4, arranges apartments for longer stays. (☎194 45. Open M-F 9am-1pm and 2-4pm.)

Jansen Pension, Richard-Wagner-Str. 18 (☎25 18 75). U1, 6, 7, 15, 17, or 19 to *Rudolfpl.* Owned by a welcoming English couple and featuring beautiful high-ceilinged rooms in Victorian style. Breakfast included. Singles €31-39; doubles €57. ❸

Hotel Heinzelmännchen, Hohe Pforte 5 (☎21 12 17). Bus #132 to *Waidmarkt.* Or walk down the Hohe Str. shopping zone until it becomes Hohe Pforte. Fairy-tale pictures decorate this family-run hotel. Rooms with TV. Breakfast included. Reception 6am-10pm. Singles €34-38; doubles €60; triples from €70. Discounts for stays over 2 nights. ❸

Station Hostel and Bar, Rheing. 34-36 (☎23 02 47). Clean rooms, a popular bar, and English-speaking staff. Free Internet. Reception 24hr. Reserved rooms held until 6pm. Singles €27; doubles €42; triples €57; quads €70. ❸

Station Hostel for Backpackers, Marzellenstr. 44-48 (☎912 53 01). From the station, walk 1 block along Dompropst-Ketzer-Str. and take the first right on Marzellenstr. Abuzz with backpackers and reggae beats. Breakfast €1.50-2.50. Sheets €1.50. Internet €0.50, plus €0.05 per min. Reception 24hr. Check-in 2pm. Check-out noon. 4- to 6-bed dorms €15-16; singles €27; doubles €40; triples €54. ❷

Jugendherberge Köln-Deutz (HI), Siegesstr. 5a (☎81 47 11), just over the Hohenzollernbrücke. S6, 11, or 12 to *Köln-Deutz.* Exit the station, walk down Neuhöfferstr., and take the 1st right; the hostel is in a courtyard. Newly renovated rooms. Breakfast included. Free laundry. Reception 11am-1am. Curfew 1am. Call ahead. Dorms €20. ❸

Campingplatz Poll, Weidenweg (☎83 19 66), on the Rhine, southeast of the *Altstadt.* U16 to *Marenberg* and cross the Rodenkirchener Brücke. Reception daily 8am-noon and 5-8pm. Open mid-Apr. to Oct. €4.50 per person; €2.50 per tent or car. ❶

FOOD

Cologne cuisine includes scrumptious *Rievekoochen* (slabs of fried potato dunked in applesauce) and smooth Kölsch beer. Cheap restaurants line **Zülpicherstraße,** and **Weidengasse** in the Turkish district. Mid-priced ethnic restaurants toe the perimeter of the *Altstadt,* particularly from **Hohenzollernring** to **Hohenstaufenring.** German eateries surround the **Domplatz.** An open-air **market** on **Wilhelmsplatz** takes over the Nippes neighborhood in the morning. (Open M-Sa 8am-1pm.)

Brauhaus Früh am Dom, Am Hof 14 (☎258 03 97). A trip to Cologne isn't complete without a visit. The Kölsch is cheap (€1.35) and the specialties regional (€4-18). Open daily 8am-midnight, menu until 11:45pm. ❸

Lichtenberg, Richmondstr. 13. U12: *Neumarkt.* Chandeliers and a color-coded library provide decor at this hip cafe. Sandwiches €3-4. Open daily 9am-1am. ❷

Päffgen-Brauerei, Friesenstr. 64. Take U6 to *Friesenplatz*. Local favorite since 1883. Kölsch (€1.25) is brewed on the premises and consumed in cavernous halls or in the 600-seat *Biergarten*. Meals €2-16. Open daily 10am-midnight. ❸

🄖 SIGHTS

■ **DOM.** Whether illuminated in a pool of eerie blue floodlighting or eclipsing the sun with its colossal spires, the *Dom*, Germany's greatest cathedral, is the first thing to greet travelers as they enter the city. A chapel inside on the right houses a 15th-century **triptych** that depicts the city's five patron saints. Behind the altar in the center of the choir is the **Shrine of the Magi,** the most sacred element of the cathedral, which reportedly holds the remains of the Three Kings. Before exiting the choir, stop in the **Chapel of the Cross** to admire the 10th-century **Gero crucifix,** which is the oldest intact sculpture of a crucified Christ with his eyes shut. *(Cathedral open daily 6am-7pm. Free. Tours in English M-Sa 10:30am and 2:30pm, Su 2:30pm. €4, children €2.)* Fifteen minutes and 509 steps bring you to the top of the **Südturm** tower. *(Open May-Sept. 9am-6pm; Nov.-Feb. daily 9am-4pm; Mar.-Apr. and Oct. 9am-5pm. €2, students €1.)* Catch your breath at the **Glockenstube,** a chamber with the tower's nine bells, about three-quarters of the way up.

MUSEUMS. ■**Heinrich-Böll-Platz** houses two complementary collections: the **Museum Ludwig,** which spans Impressionism through Dalí, Lichtenstein, and Warhol; and the **Agfa Foto-Historama,** which chronicles photography through the last 150 years, including a rotating display of Man Ray's works. *(Bischofsgartenstr. 1. Open Su and Sa 11am-6pm, Tu 10am-8pm, W-F 10am-6pm. €6.40, students €3.20.)* The galleries of the **Wallraf-Richartz Museum** are lined with masterpieces from the Middle Aged to the Post-Impressionist. *(Martinstr. 39. From the Heumarkt, take Gürzenichtstr. 1 block to Martinstr. Open Su and Sa 11am-6pm, Tu 10am-8pm, W-F 10am-6pm. €5.10, students €2.60.)* The **Römisch-Germanisches Museum** displays a large array of artifacts documenting the daily lives of Romans rich and poor. *(Roncallipl. 4. Open Su and Tu-Sa 10am-5pm. €3, students €2.)* Four words about the ■**Schokoladen Museum** (Chocolate Museum): Willy Wonka made real. It presents every step of chocolate production from the rainforests to the gold fountain that spurts streams of silky chocolate. Resist the urge to drool and wait for the free samples. *(Rheinauhafen 1a, near the Severinsbrücke. From the train station, head for the river, walk along the Rhine heading right, go under the Deutzer Brücke, and take the 1st footbridge. Open M-F 10am-6pm, Sa-Su 11am-7pm. €5.50, students €3.)* The **Käthe-Kollwitz-Museum** houses the world's largest collection of sketches, sculptures, and prints by the brilliant 20th-century artist-activist. *(Neumarkt 18-24. On the top fl. in the Neumarkt-Passage. U12, 14, 16, or 18 to Neumarkt. Open Su and Sa 11am-6pm, Tu-F 10am-6pm. €2.50, students €1.)*

HOUSE #4711. The fabled **Eau de Cologne,** once prescribed as a drinkable curative, gave the town worldwide recognition. Today the house where it was born, labeled #4711 by a Napoleonic system that abolished street names, is a boutique whose fountain flows freely with the scented water. The gallery upstairs has a full history of the fragrance. *(Glockeng., at the intersection with Tunisstr. From Hohe Str., turn right on Brückenstr., which becomes Glockeng. Open M-F 9:30am-8pm, Sa 9:30am-4pm.)*

RÖMISCHES PRAETORIUM UND KANAL. The excavated ruins of the former Roman military headquarters display remains of Roman gods and an array of rocks left by early inhabitants. *(From the Rathaus, take a right toward the swarm of hotels and then a left onto Kleine Budeng. Open Su and Sa 11am-4pm, Tu-F 10am-4pm. €1.50, students €0.75.)*

🎵 📷 ENTERTAINMENT AND NIGHTLIFE

Cologne explodes in celebration during **Karneval**, a week-long pre-Lenten festival made up of 50 neighborhood processions in the days before Ash Wednesday. **Weiberfastnacht**, Feb. 19, 2004, is the first major to-do; the mayor mounts the platform at Alter Markt and abdicates leadership to the city's women, who then find their husbands at work and chop off their ties. The weekend builds up to the out-of-control parade on **Rosenmontag** (Feb. 23, 2004), where everyone gets and gives a couple dozen *Bützchen* (Kölsch dialect for a kiss on the cheek). While most revelers nurse their hangovers on Shrove Tuesday, pubs and restaurants set fire to the straw scarecrows hanging out of their windows. For more info, pick up the Karneval booklet at the tourist office.

Roman mosaics dating back to the third century record the wild excesses of the city's early residents; they've toned it down only a bit since. The best way to know what you'll get is to pick up the monthly magazine *Kölner* (€1). The closer to the Rhine or *Dom* you venture, the more quickly your wallet gets emptied. After dark in **Hohenzollernring**, crowds of people move from theaters to clubs and finally to cafes in the early morning. Students congregate in the **Bermuda-Dreieck** (Bermuda Triangle), bounded by Zülpicherstr., Zülpicherpl., Roonstr., and Luxemburgstr. The center of gay nightlife runs up Matthiasstr. to Mühlenbach, Hohe Pforte, Marienpl., and the Heumarkt area by **Deutzer Brücke**. Radiating westward from Friesenpl., the **Belgisches Viertel** has slightly more expensive bars and cafes.

🍴 **Papa Joes Jazzlokal**, Buttermarkt 37. Papa Joe's reputation for great jazz and good times is legendary. Drinks are pricey, but a Kölsch (€3.60) goes a long way. Grab some peanuts when the sack comes around. Open daily 7pm-3am.

Stadtgarten, Venloerstr. 40. Take U6, 15, 17, or 19 to *Friesenplatz*. Two clubs for the price of one. Downstairs spins techno and house; upstairs, the concert hall is renowned for its live jazz recordings. Cover €4-5. Open M-Th 9pm-1am. F-Sa 9pm-3am.

Das Ding, Hohenstaufenring 30. Smoky and very *noir*. A popular bar and disco for students with varied music and dirt-cheap drink specials (under €1). Cover around €4. Open M and W 9pm-2am, Tu and Th-Su 9pm-3am.

Hotel Timp, Heumarkt 25 (www.timp.de). This outrageous gay-friendly club and hotel has become a virtual institution in Cologne for travesty theater. Shows daily 1-4am. No cover, but your first drink is €8 weeknights or €13 on weekends.

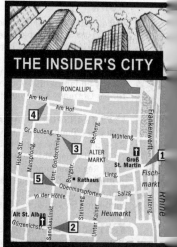

THE INSIDER'S CITY

KUNST, KULTUR, AND KOLSCH

Forever in the shadow of the magnificent Dom, the area surrounding Cologne's *Altstadt* is underappreciated by most sightseers. But not you.

1 Most of the **Fischmarkt's** colorful *Rheinisch* facades are restorations, but the riverside atmosphere and jolly accordionists are originals.

2 The 15th-century **Gürzenich** hall is still used for festivities. (*Martinstr. 29.* ☎ *92 58 99 90.*)

3 Give thanks for the advent of Roman plumbing at this **sewer** ruin. (*At the intersection of Unter Goldschmied and Kleine Budengasse.*)

4 The **Brauhaus Früh am Dom** has served the best *Kölsch* in town since the 19th century. (*Am Hof 12.* ☎ *258 03 97.*)

5 Though your vision may be blurry from all that beer, don't fret; so is the art at **Wallraf-Richartz-Museum**. (*Martinstr. 39.*)

BONN ☎ 0228

Once derisively called *Hauptdorf* (capital village) just because it wasn't Berlin, Bonn (pop. 306,000) became the capital of West Germany by chance because Konrad Adenauer, the first chancellor, resided in its suburbs. In 1999, the *Bundestag* packed up and moved back to Berlin, allowing Bonn to be itself again. Today, the streets of the *Altstadt* bustle with notable energy, and Bonn's well-respected university and museums bolster the cultural scene. Bonn is also fast becoming a center for Germany's computer-technology industry and hip cyber-culture.

■ ■ TRANSPORTATION AND PRACTICAL INFORMATION. Trains run to: Cologne (20min., 5 per hr., €5); Frankfurt (2hr., 1 per hr., €25); and Koblenz (1hr., 2 per hr., €8). The **tourist office** is at Windeckstr. 2, near the cathedral off Münsterpl. (☎ 194 33. Open M-F 9am-6:30pm, Sa 9am-4pm, Su 10am-2pm.) Consider buying the **Bonn Regio Welcome Card** (1-day €9, 2-day €14, 3-day €19), which covers transportation (M-F after 9am, Sa-Su 24hr.) and admission to more than 20 museums in Bonn and the surrounding area. The **post office** is at Münsterpl. 17. (Open M-F 9am-8pm, Sa 9am-4pm.) **Postal Code:** 53111.

■ ■ ACCOMMODATIONS AND FOOD. Take bus #621 (dir.: Ippendorf Altenheim) to *Jugendgästehaus* to reach the super-modern **Jugendgästehaus Bonn-Venusberg (HI) ❸**, Haager Weg 42. (☎ 28 99 70. Breakfast included. Laundry €5. Curfew 1am. Dorms €21; singles €34; doubles €48.) Closer to the city center, **Hotel Bergmann ❸**, Kasernenstr. 13 (☎ 63 38 91) is a small family-run hotel. Follow Poststr. from the station, turn left at Münsterpl. on Vivatsgasse, then right on Kasernenstr. (☎ 63 38 91. Bath on each floor. Breakfast included. Singles €35; doubles €50.)

The **market** on Münsterpl. teems with vendors selling meat, fruit, and vegetables. At the end of the day voices rise and prices plummet. (Open M-Sa 8am-6pm.) There is also a **supermarket** in the basement of the Kaufhof department store on Münsterpl. (Open M-F 9:30am-8pm, Sa 9am-4pm.) Cheap eats are available at **Mensa ❶**, Nassestr. 11, a 15min. walk from the station along Kaiserstr. (Open M-F noon-2pm and 5:30-7:30pm, Sa noon-2pm.) **Cafe Blau ❷**, Franziskanerstr. 5, across from the university, will sate your hunger without devouring your cash supply. (Chicken or pasta platters €3-5. Open daily 10am-1am.)

■ ■ SIGHTS AND NIGHTLIFE. Bonn's lively pedestrian zone is littered with historic nooks. ■**Beethovenhaus,** Beethoven's birthplace, hosts a fantastic collection of the composer's personal effects, from his primitive hearing aids to his first violin. (Bonng. 20. Open Apr.-Oct. M-Sa 10am-6pm, Su 11am-4pm; Nov.-Mar. M-Sa 10am-5pm, Su 11am-4pm. €4, students €3.) In its governmental heyday, the transparent walls of the **Bundestag** were meant to symbolize the government's responsibility to the public. (Take U16, 63, or 66 to *Heussallee/Bundeshaus* or bus #610 to *Bundeshaus*.) Students study within the **Kurfürstliches Schloß,** the huge 18th-century palace now serving as the center of Bonn's **Friedrich-Wilhelms-Universität.** To reach Bonn's other palace, follow Poppelsdorfer Allee to the 18th-century **Poppelsdorfer Schloß,** which boasts beautifully manicured **botanical gardens.** (Gardens open Apr.-Oct. M-F 9am-6pm, Su 10am-5pm; Nov.-Mar. M-F 9am-4pm. Free.) The Welcome Card (see Practical Information, above) provides admission to most of Bonn's **Museum Mile.** To start your museum-crawl, take U16, 63, or 66 to *Heussallee* or *Museum König.* ■**Haus der Geschichte** (House of History), Willy-Brandt 4, examines post-WWII German history through interactive exhibits. (Open Su and Tu-Sa 9am-7pm. Free.) One block away, **Kunstmuseum Bonn,** Friedrich-Ebert-Allee 2, houses a superb selection of Expressionist and modern German art. (Open Su, Tu and Th-Sa 10am-6pm, W 10am-9pm. €5, students €2.50.)

For club and concert listings, pick up *Schnüss* (€1). The ■Jazz Galerie, Oxfordstr. 24, hosts jazz and rock concerts as well as a jumping bar and disco. (Cover €3-5. Open Su and Tu-Th 9pm-3am, F-Sa 9pm-4am.) **Pantheon**, Bundeskanzlerpl., caters to eclectic tastes with a disco, concerts, and stand-up comedy; follow Adenauerallee out of the city to Bundeskanzlerpl. (Cover €6.50-8. Open M-Sa 11pm-4am.) **Boba's Bar**, Josephstr. 17, is one of Bonn's most popular gay and lesbian nightspots. (Open Su and Tu-Sa 8pm-3am.)

KASSEL ☎ 0561

Napoleon III was dragged to Kassel (pop. 195,000) as a prisoner of Prussian troops, but today, folks visit this edgy city of their own free will. From Bahnhof Wilhelmshöhe, take streetcar #1 to ■Wilhelmshöhe, a hillside park in a time warp. Inside, **Schloß Wilhelmshöhe** is a dressed-down version of the Residenz in Würzburg (p. 490), but more authentically furnished. Uphill, **Schloß Löwenburg** was built by Wilhelm in the 18th century with stones deliberately missing to look like a crumbling medieval castle—he was obsessed with the year 1495 and fancied himself a time-displaced knight. (Both castles open Mar.-Oct. Su and Tu-Sa 10am-5pm; Nov.-Feb. Su and Tu-Sa 10am-4pm. Required tours every hr. €3.50, students €2.50.) All of the park's paths lead up to **Herkules**, Kassel's emblem; visitors can climb up onto Herkules's pedestal and, if they're brave enough, into his club. (Access to the base of the statue free. Pedestal and club open mid-Mar. to mid-Nov. daily 10am-5pm. €2, students €1.25.) The **Brüder-Grimm-Museum**, Schöne Aussicht 2, exhibits Jacob and Wilhelm's handwritten copy of *Kinder- und Hausmärchen*. (Open daily 10am-5pm. €1.50, students €1.)

Kassel has two train stations, Bahnhof Wilhelmshöhe and the Hauptbahnhof; most trains stop only at Wilhelmshöhe. **Trains** run to: Düsseldorf (3½hr., 1 per hr., €37); Frankfurt (2hr., 3 per hr., €27); Hamburg (2½hr., 3 per hr., €51); and Munich (4hr., 1 per hr., €88). The **tourist office,** in Bahnhof Wilhelmshöhe, has free maps and books rooms for a €4 fee. (☎70 77 07. Open M-F 9am-6pm, Sa 9am-1pm.) To reach **Jugendherberge am Tannenwäldchen (HI) ❷**, Schenkendorfstr. 18, take streetcar #4 from the Wilhelmshöhe station to Annastr., backtrack on Friedrich-Ebert-Str., and make a right on Querallee, which becomes Schenkendorfstr. (☎77 64 55. Breakfast included. Sheets €4. Reception daily 9am-11:30pm. Curfew 12:30am. Dorms €19, under-26 €18. HI members only.) For **Hotel Kö78 ❸**, Kölnische Str. 78, follow the directions to the Jugendherberge, then walk up Annastr. from the stop and turn right onto Kölnische Str. (☎716 14. Breakfast included. Reception daily 7am-10pm. Singles €32, with shower €41-46; doubles €51/61-75.) **Friedrich-Ebert-Straße,** the upper part of **Wilhelmshöher Allee,** and the area around **Königsplatz** all have supermarkets and cafes sprinkled amongst clothing stores. **Postal Code:** 34117.

FRANKFURT AM MAIN ☎ 069

Frankfurt's role as home to the central bank of the European Union lends it a glitzy vitality—international offices, shiny skyscrapers, and expensive cars define every intersection. Equally important is its role as a major transportation hub for all of Europe. Indeed, Frankfurt (pop. 641,000) first made its appearance as a crossing point for the Main River—the Franks forded the river in early times; the city's name literally means *ford of the Franks*. Today, the city spends more on cultural attractions and tourism than any other German city. Visitors are drawn by the selection of museums and exhibits—and, of course, the highly trafficked transportation routes that make Frankfurt a likely stop on your itinerary.

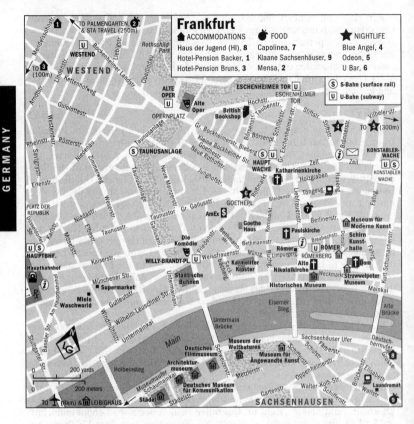

Frankfurt

🏠 ACCOMMODATIONS
Haus der Jugend (HI), **8**
Hotel-Pension Backer, **1**
Hotel-Pension Bruns, **3**

🍴 FOOD
Capolinea, **7**
Klaane Sachsenhäuser, **9**
Mensa, **2**

⭐ NIGHTLIFE
Blue Angel, **4**
Odeon, **5**
U Bar, **6**

Ⓢ S-Bahn (surface rail)
Ⓤ U-Bahn (subway)

TRANSPORTATION

Flights: Flughafen Rhein-Main (FRA; ☎(0180) 53 72 46 36), is connected to the *Hauptbahnhof* (main train station) by S8 and 9 (every 15min., buy tickets for €3 from the green machines marked *Fahrkarten* before boarding).

Trains: Call ☎(0180) 599 66 33 for schedules, reservations, and info. Frequent trains leave the Hauptbahnhof for: **Amsterdam** (4hr., 2 per hr., €80); **Berlin** (5-6hr., 2 per hr., €58-86); **Cologne** (2½hr., 3 per hr., €29-51); **Hamburg** (5hr., 2 per hr., €81); **Munich** (3½-4½hr., 2 per hr., €65); **Paris** (6-8hr., 2 per hr., €59-73).

Public Transportation: Runs daily until about 1am. Single-ride tickets (€1.65, rush hour €1.95) are valid for 1hr. in one direction, including transfers. **Eurail** is valid only on S-Bahn. The **Tageskarte** (day pass; valid until midnight of the day of purchase) provides unlimited transportation on the S-Bahn, U-Bahn, streetcars, and buses; buy from machines in any station (€4.60, children €2.70).

⊞ 🔢 ORIENTATION AND PRACTICAL INFORMATION

The *Hauptbahnhof* lies at the end of Frankfurt's red light district; from the station, the **Altstadt** is a 20min. walk down Kaiserstr. or Münchener Str. To the north, the commercial heart of Frankfurt lies along **Zeil**. Cafes, stores, and services cluster in **Bockenheim** (U6 or 7 to Bockenheimer Warte). Across the Main, **Sachsenhausen** draws pub-crawlers and museum-goers (U1, 2, or 3 to Schweizer Pl.).

Tourist Office: (☎21 23 88 00), in the *Hauptbahnhof*, sells the **Frankfurt Card** (1-day €6.15, 2-day €9.75), which allows unlimited travel on all trains and buses and gives 50% off admission to many sights. Open M-F 8am-9pm, Sa-Su and holidays 9am-6pm.

Laundromat: Schnell & Sauber, Wallstr. 8, near the hostel in Sachsenhausen. Wash €3, dry €0.50 per 15min. Soap included. Open M-Sa 6am-11pm.

Emergency: Police: ☎110. **Fire** and **Ambulance:** ☎112.

Pharmacy: (☎23 30 47), in the Einkaufs passage of the train station. Open M-F 6:30am-9pm, Sa 8am-9pm, Su and holidays 9am-8pm. **Emergencies** ☎192 92.

Internet Access: Alpha, in the *Hauptbahnhof*'s casino, by track 24. €0.50 per 6min. Open M-Sa 6am-1am, Su 8am-1am. **CybeRyder Internet Café,** Töngesgasse 31. €2.50 per 30min. Open M-Th 9am-11pm, F-Sa 9am-midnight, Su 11am-11pm.

Post Office: Main branch, Zeil 90 (☎13 81 26 21), inside the Karstadt department store. U- or S-Bahn to Hauptwache. Open M-Sa 9:30am-8pm. Address mail to be held: Firstname SURNAME, *Postlagernde Briefe*, Hauptpostamt, **60313** Frankfurt, GERMANY.

▟ ACCOMMODATIONS

🛏 **Hotel-Pension Bruns,** Mendelssohnstr. 42, 2nd fl. (☎74 88 96; www.brunsgallus-hotel.de). Take U4 to Festhalle. In the wealthy Westend area near the *Uni*, Bruns has nine Victorian rooms with high ceilings, hardwood floors, cable TV, and breakfast in bed. Ring the bell. Showers €1.50. Doubles €46-52; triples €63. ❹

Haus der Jugend (HI), Deutschherrnufer 12 (☎610 01 50). Take bus #46 from the main train station to Frankensteiner Pl. Turn left along the river. In the museum district. Popular with student groups. Breakfast included. Reception 24hr. Check-in after 1pm. Curfew 2am. Reservations recommended. Dorms from €20, under-27 €15. ❷

Hotel-Pension Backer, Mendelssohnstr. 92 (☎74 79 92). Take U6 or 7 to Westend. Cheap, clean, and near the city center. Breakfast included. If you're on a tight budget, ask for room #1 (€10). Singles €25; doubles €40; triples €45. ❸

🍴 FOOD

The cheapest meals surround the university in **Bockenheim** and nearby parts of Westend, and pubs in **Sachsenhausen** serve food at a decent price. Just a few blocks from the youth hostel is a fully stocked **HL Markt,** Dreieichstr. 56 (open M-F 8am-8pm, Sa 8am-4pm); an **Alim Markt,** Münchener Str. 37, is close to the *Hauptbahnhof* (open M-F 8:30am-7:30pm, Su 8am-2pm). At ◨**Capolinea** ❸, Ziegelgasse 5, the chef *is* the menu: He creates fresh Italian pastas or bruschetta (€8-10) as you like it. (Open M-Sa 2pm-1am, Su 6pm-1am.) The student **Mensa** ❶ has two floors of cheap cafeteria food. (U6 or 7 to Bockenheimer Warte. Follow signs for Palmengarten Universität. Open M-F 11am-6:30pm.) Let the 5th generation of the Wagner family feed you homemade *Ebbelwei* (€1.40) and Frankfurt specialties (€7-15) at **Klaane Sachsenhäuser** ❸, Neuer Wallstr. 11. (Open M-Sa

4pm-midnight.) **Kleinmarkthalle,** on Haseng. between Berliner Str. and Töngesg., is a three-story warehouse with bakeries, butchers, and fruit and vegetable stands. Cutthroat competition pushes prices way down. (Open M-F 7:30am-6pm, Sa 7:30am-4pm.)

👁 SIGHTS

Much of Frankfurt's historic splendor lives on only in memories and in reconstructed monuments, since Allied bombing left everything but the cathedral completely destroyed. At the center of the *Altstadt* is ▧**Römerberg Square** (U-Bahn to Römer), home to half-timbered architecture and a medieval fountain of justice that once spouted wine. At the west end, the gables of **Römer** have marked the site of Frankfurt's city hall since 1405; upstairs, the Kaisersaal, an imperial banquet hall, is adorned with portraits of the 52 German emperors from Charlemagne to Franz II. (Open daily 10am-1pm and 2-5pm. €2.) Next to the Römer stands the only building that survived the bombings, the red sandstone **Dom,** which contains several elaborate altarpieces. A new viewing tower is scheduled to open in 2004. (Open Su and Sa 11am-5pm, Tu-F 10am-5pm.) Across Braubachstr. from the Römerberg, **Paulskirche** holds a conference center and a memorial to the trials and tribulations of German democracy. (Open daily 10am-5pm. Free.) A few blocks away is the **Museum für Moderne Kunst,** a triangular building (dubbed "the slice of cake") displaying an array of modern art. (Domstr. 10. Open Su and Tu-Sa 10am-5pm, W 10am-8pm. €5, students €2.50. W free.) The ▧**Städel,** Schaumainkai 63, has important paintings from nearly every period of the Western tradition. (Open Su, Tu and F-Sa 10am-5pm, W-Th 10am-8pm. €6, students €5. Tu free.) Only Goethe-fanatics will be awestruck by his reconstructed first house, the **Goethehaus.** (Großer Hirschgraben 23. Open Apr.-Sept. M-F 9am-6pm, Sa-Su 10am-4pm; Oct.-Mar. M-F 9am-4pm, Sa-Su 10am-4pm. €5, students €2.50.) A simpler and more peaceful afternoon can be spent at the **Palmengarten,** in the northwest part of town. (Siesmayerstr. 61. U6 or 7 to Bockenheimer Warte. Open Feb.-Oct. daily 9am-6pm; Nov.-Jan. 9am-4pm. €5, students €2.50.)

🎵 🎭 ENTERTAINMENT AND NIGHTLIFE

Frankfurt's theater and opera are first-rate. The **Alte Oper,** Opernpl. (☎134 04 00; U6 or 7 to Alte Oper), offers a full range of classical music. The **Städtische Bühne,** Untermainanlage 11 (☎21 23 71 33; U1, 2, 3, or 4 to *Willy-Brandt-Pl.*), hosts ballets and operas. The **English Theatre,** Kaiserstr. 52 (☎24 23 16 20) puts on comedies and musicals in English. Shows and schedules are listed in *Fritz* and *Strandgut* (free). For info on tickets at most venues, call **Frankfurt Ticket** (☎134 04 00).

Frankfurt has a number of thriving discos and prominent techno DJs, mostly in the commercial district between **Zeil** and **Bleichstraße.** Wear something dressier than jeans if you plan to get past the selective bouncers. In an old subway station, **U Bar,** on Roßmarkt, features Frankfurt's best DJs. (Cover €6-15. Open M-F 10pm-10am, Sa-Su 10pm-6am.) **Odeon,** Seilerstr. 34, packs its two floors with students and house, soul, and hip hop. (Th drinks half-price until midnight and free buffet from 11:30pm. Cover €5, students €3. Open Tu-Sa from 10pm.) **Blue Angel,** Brönnerstr. 17, is a Frankfurt institution and one of the liveliest gay men's clubs around. Ring the bell to be let in. (Cover €5. W and Su free. Open daily 11pm-4am.) For more drinks and less dancing, head to the **Alt-Sachsenhausen** district between Brückenstr. and Dreieichstr., home to a huge number of rowdy pubs and taverns. The complex of cobblestoned streets centering on **Grosse** and **Kleine Rittergaße** teems with cafes, bars, restaurants, and Irish pubs.

SOUTHWEST GERMANY

The Rhine and Mosel river valleys are a feast as much for the eyes as the mouth—the Mosel curls downstream to the Rhine Gorge, a soft shore of castle-backed hills, while dozens of vineyards provide Germany's best wines. Just a bit farther south, the hinterlands of the Black Forest contrast with its modern cities.

RHINE VALLEY (RHEINTAL)

The Rhine River runs from Switzerland to the North Sea, but in the popular imagination it exists only in the 80km Rhine Valley, a region prominent in historical legends, sailors' nightmares, and poets' dreams. The river flows north from Mainz (easily accessible from Frankfurt) through Bacharach and Koblenz to Bonn.

⌐ TRANSPORTATION

Two different **train** lines (one on each bank) traverse the Rheintal; the line on the west bank stays closer to the water and provides superior views. Though full of tourists, **boats** are probably the best way to see the sights; the **Köln-Düsseldorfer (KD) Line** covers the Mainz-Koblenz stretch four times per day in summer.

MAINZ. Once the greatest Catholic diocese north of the Alps, Mainz's colossal sandstone **Martinsdom** stands as a memorial to its former ecclesiastic power. (Open Mar.-Oct. Su 1-3pm and 4-6pm, Tu-F 9am-6pm, Sa 9am-2pm; Nov.-Feb. M-F 9am-5pm, Sa 9am-4pm, Su 12:45-3pm and 4-5pm. Free.) The Gothic **Stephanskirche,** south of the Dom, holds stunning stained-glass windows created by artist Marc Chagall. (Stephansberg. Open daily 10am-noon and 2-5pm. Free.) Johannes Gutenberg, the father of movable type, is immortalized at the **Gutenberg-Museum,** which contains a replica of his original press. (Liebfrauenpl. 5, across from the Dom. Open Su 11am-3pm, Tu-Sa 9am-5pm. €3, students €1.50.)

   Trains run to: Frankfurt (30min., €6); Heidelberg (1hr., €17); and Koblenz (1hr., €17). **KD ferries** (☎06131 23 28 00) depart from the wharves on the other side of the *Rathaus.* The **tourist office** arranges **tours** (2hr.; July-Aug. daily 2pm, May and Oct. W and F-Sa 2pm; €6) and gives free maps. (☎06131 28 62 10. Open M-F 9am-6pm, Sa 10am-3pm.) To reach the **Jugendgästehaus (HI) ❷,** Otto-Brunfels-Schneise 4, take bus #62 (dir.: Weisenau), 63 (dir.: Laubenheim), or 92 (dir.: Ginsheim) to Viktorstift/Jugendherberge and follow the signs. All rooms are clean and come with a private bath. (☎06131 853 32. Breakfast included. Reception daily 7am-10pm. Dorms €17; doubles €44.) On the edge of the *Altstadt,* **Der Eisgrub-Bräu ❷,** Weißliliengaße 1a, serves breakfast (€2.90), lunch buffets (€5.10), and its own house beer. (Open Su-Th 9am-1pm, F-Sa 9am-2pm.) For groceries, try **Super 2000,** Am Brand 41, under the Sinn-Leffers department store. (Open M-F 9:30am-8pm, Sa 9am-4pm). **Postal Code:** 55001.

BACHARACH. Bacharach ("Alter of Bacchus") lives up to its name, with *Weinkeller* and *Weinstuben* (wine cellars and pubs) tucked between every other half-timbered house. Try some of the Rhine's best wines and cheeses at **Die Weinstube,** Oberstr. 63. (Open daily from noon.) Nearby is the 14th-century **Wernerkapelle,** the remains of a red sandstone chapel that took 140 years to build but only a few hours to destroy during the Palatinate War of Succession in 1689. The **tourist office,** Oberstr. 45, and the *Rathaus* share a building at one end of the town center. (☎91 93 03. Open Apr.-Oct. M-F 9am-5pm, Sa 10am-4pm; Nov.-Mar. M-F 9am-noon.) Hostels get no better than ▧**Jugendherberge Stahleck (HI) ❷,** a gorgeous 12th-century castle that provides a panoramic view of the Rhine Valley. The steep 15min. hike to the hostel is worth every step. Call ahead; they're usually full by 6pm. Make a right out of the station pathway, turn left at the Peterskirche, and take any of the marked paths leading up the hill. (☎ 12 66. Breakfast included. Curfew 10pm. Dorms €14.20; doubles €36.) At █**Café Restaurant Rusticana** ❸, Oberstr. 40, a lovely German couple serves up three-course meals (€6-11) and lively conversation. (Open May-Oct. M-W and F-Su 11:30am-9:30pm.) **Postal Code:** 55422.

LORELEI CLIFFS AND CASTLES. Though sailors were once lured to these cliffs by the infamous Lorelei maiden, her hypnotic song is now superfluous; today, hordes of travelers are seduced by scenery alone. The charming towns of **St. Goarshausen** and **St. Goar,** on either side of the Rhine, host the spectacular **Rhein in Flammen** fireworks celebration at the end of every summer (September 19, 2004). St. Goarshausen, on the east bank, provides access by foot to the Lorelei statue and the cliffs. Directly above the town, the fierce **Burg Katz** (Cat Castle) eternally stalks its prey, the smaller **Burg Maus** (Mouse Castle). Burg Maus offers daily falconry demonstrations at 11am and 2:30pm; call ☎ 76 69 for info or visit St. Goarshausen's **tourist office**, Bahnhofstr. 8. (☎ (06771) 76 69. Open Su-M and Sa 9:30am-noon and M, Th and F 2-4pm.) **Trains** run to St. Goarshausen from Cologne (1hr., €18) and Mainz (1hr., €8). The "Lorelei V" **ferry** (M-F 6am-11pm, Sa-Su from 7am; €1, round-trip €1.50) crosses the river to **St.Goar,** which has a spectacular view. St. Goar's **tourist office**, Heerstr. 6, is in the pedestrian zone. (☎ (06741) 333. Open M-F 8am-12:30pm and 2-5pm, Sa 10am-noon.) To reach **Jugendheim Loreley** ❷, on the St. Goarshausen side of the Rhine, walk from the cliffs past the parking gate down the road a few hundred meters and turn left. (☎ (06771) 26 19. Breakfast included. Curfew 10pm. Dorms €16.) **Postal Code:** 56329.

KOBLENZ   ☎ 0261

Koblenz (pop. 108,000) has long been a strategic hotspot; in the 2000 years since its birth, the city has hosted every empire seeking to conquer Europe. The city centers around the **Deutsches Eck** (German Corner), a peninsula at the confluence of the Rhine and Mosel rivers that purportedly witnessed the birth of the German nation in 1216. The **Mahnmal der Deutschen Einheit** (Monument to German Unity) to the right is a tribute to Kaiser Wilhelm I. The █**Museum Ludwig im Deutschherrenhaus,** Danziger Freiheit 1, behind the *Mahnmal*, features contemporary French art. (Open Su 11am-6pm, Tu-Sa 10:30am-5pm. €2.50, students €1.50.) Head across the river to the **Festung Ehrenbreitstein,** a fortress at the highest point in the city. Today, it's a youth hostel. (Non-hostel guests €1.05, students €0.60. Tours €2.10.) **Trains** run to: Bonn (30min., 4 per hr, €8); Cologne (1hr., 4 per hr., €13.50); Frankfurt (2hr., 1-2 per hr., €17); Mainz (1hr., 3 per hr., €13.50); and Trier (2hr., 1-2 per hr., €16). Directly across from the station is the **tourist office**, Bahnhofpl. 7. (☎ 30 38 80. Open May-Oct. M-F 9am-7pm, Sa-Su 10am-7pm; Nov.-Apr. M-F 9am-6pm, Sa-Su 10am-6pm.) The best value in town is **Hotel Jan van Werth** ❸, Van-Werth-Str. 9, a classy, familyrun, English-speaking establishment. From the station, walk up Bahnhofstr. to the market district and take a right on Van-Werth-Str. (☎ 365 00. Breakfast included. Reception daily 6:30am-10pm. Singles from €23, with bath €41; doubles from €53/70; triples €60.) **Jugendherberge Koblenz (HI)** ❷, within the fortress, offers breathtaking views of the Rhine and Mosel. Take bus #9 from the stop by the train station on Löhrstr. to *Charlottenstr.* Then take the chairlift up (Mar.-Sept. daily 9am-5:50pm, roundtrip €6), or continue along the Rhine side of the mountain on the main road, following the DJH signs, and take the footpath up. (☎ 97 28 70. Breakfast included. Reception daily 7:15am-10pm. Curfew 11:30pm. Dorms €16; doubles €37.) **Ferries** (€1) cross the Mosel to **Campingplatz Rhein-Mosel** ❶, Am Neuendorfer Eck. (☎ 827 19. Reception daily 8am-10pm. Open Apr.-Oct. 15. €4 per person, €2.50 per site.) **Marktstübchen** ❷, Am Markt 220, serves authentic German food at budget prices. (Open Su-Tu and Th 11am-midnight, W 11am-2pm, F 4pm-1am, Sa 11am-1am.) **Postal Code:** 65068.

TRIER ☎ 0651

The oldest town in Germany, Trier (pop. 100,000) has weathered over two millennia in the Mosel Valley. Founded by the Romans, Trier reached its zenith in the 4th century as the capital of the Western Roman Empire and a center for Christianity. A one-day **combination ticket** (€6.20, students €3.10) provides access to all the city's Roman monuments. The most impressive is the massive 2nd-century **Porta Nigra** (Black Gate), one of the best preserved city gates of the ancient world. (Open Apr.-Sept. daily 9am-6pm; Oct.-Mar. 9am-5pm. €2.10, students €1.60.) The nearby **Dom** shelters the *Tunica Christi* (Holy Robe of Christ) and the tombs of many archbishops. (Open Apr.-Oct. daily 6:30am-6pm; Nov.-Mar. 6:30am-5:30pm. Free.) The enormous **Basilika** was originally the location of Emperor Constantine's throne room. (Open M-Sa 10am-6pm, Su noon-6pm. Free.) Near the southeast corner of the city walls are the 4th-century **Kaiserthermen** (Emperor's baths), most memorable for the gloomy underground passages remaining from their ancient sewer network—avoid contact with the walls. (Open daily 9am-5pm. €2.15, students €1.60.) A 10min. walk uphill along Olewiger Str. brings you to the **amphitheater;** once the site of bloody gladiatorial games, it's now a stage for city productions. (Open daily 9am-5pm. €2.10, students €1.60.)

Trains run to Koblenz (1¾hr., 2 per hr., €16). From the station, walk down Theodor-Haus-Allee or Christophstr. to reach the **tourist office,** in the shadow of the Porta Nigra. (☎97 80 80. Open Apr.-Oct. M-Sa 9am-6pm, Su 10am-3pm; Nov.-Dec. and Mar. M-Sa 9am-6pm, Su 10am-1pm; Jan.-Feb. M-F 10am-5pm, Sa 10am-1pm. English city tours Sa 1:30pm. €6, students €5.) The **Jugendhotel/Jugendgästehaus Kolpinghaus ❷,** Dietrichstr. 42, one block off the Hauptmarkt, is in an unbeatable location. (☎97 52 50. Breakfast included. Sheets €2.50. Dorms €15; singles €22; doubles €42.) Squeezed into the passageway by Miss Maple's, **Astarix ❷,** Karl-Marx-Str. 11, serves excellent tortellini and pizza from €4. (Open M-Th 11:30am-1am, F-Sa 11:30am-2am, Su 2pm-1am.) The **Plus supermarket,** Brotstr. 54, is near the Hauptmarkt. (Open M-F 8:30am-8pm, Sa 8:30am-4pm.) **Postal Code:** 54292.

HEIDELBERG ☎ 06221

Sun-drenched Heidelberg (pop. 141,000) and its crumbling castle once lured writers and artists, including Twain, Goethe, and Hugo. Today, legions of camera-toting fannypackers fill the length of Hauptstr., where postcards and T-shirts sell like hotcakes and every sign is posted in four lan guages. But even mass tourism can't mar the experience of Heidelberg's beautiful hillside setting, Germany's oldest university, and its enviable nightlife.

▐ TRANSPORTATION

Trains run to: Frankfurt (50min., 2 per hr., €13) and Stuttgart (40min., 1 per hr., €16); other trains run regularly to towns in the Neckar Valley. On Heidelberg's **public transportation** system, single-ride tickets cost €2; day passes (€5) are available from the tourist office. The Rhein-Neckar-Fahrgastschifffahrt (☎201 81), in front of the *Kongresshaus*, runs **ferries** all over Germany and provides round-trip Neckar cruises to **Neckarsteinach** (3hr., Easter-Oct. 9:30am-3:30pm, €9.50).

▐ ORIENTATION AND PRACTICAL INFORMATION

Most of Heidelberg's attractions are in the eastern part of the city, along the south bank of the Neckar. From the train station, take any bus or streetcar to Bismarckpl., then walk east down **Hauptstraße,** the city's spine, to the **Altstadt.** The **tourist office,**

GERMANY

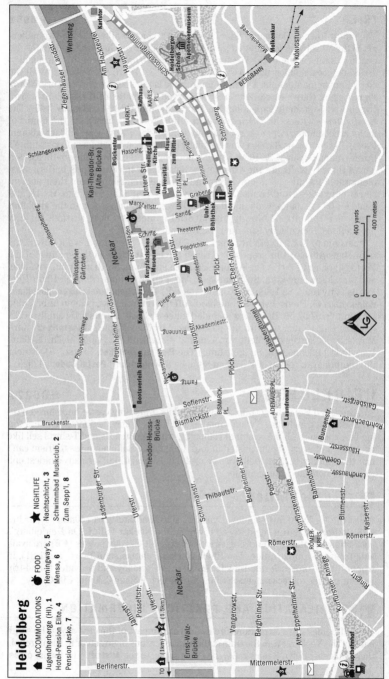

Heidelberg

▲ ACCOMMODATIONS
Jugendherberge (HI), **1**
Hotel-Pension Elite, **4**
Pension Jeske, **7**

● FOOD
Hemingway's, **5**
Mensa, **6**

★ NIGHTLIFE
Nachtschicht, **3**
Schwimmbad Musikclub, **2**
Zum Sepp'l, **8**

in front of the station, books rooms for a €2.50 fee and a small deposit. (☎ 13 88 121. Open Apr.-Oct. M-Sa 9am-7pm, Su 10am-6pm; Nov.-Mar. M-Sa 9am-6pm.) They also sell the 2-day **Heidelberg Card,** which includes unlimited public transit and admission to most sights (€12). Check your email at **Mode Bredl,** Hauptstr. 90, near Bismarckpl. (€3 per 30min. Open M-F 10am-7pm, Sa 10am-6pm.) The **post office** is at Sofienstr. 8-10. (Open M-F 9am-6:30pm, Sa 9:30am-1pm.) **Postal Code:** 69155.

ACCOMMODATIONS AND FOOD

In summer, reserve rooms ahead or arrive early in the day to spare yourself a headache. To reach the **Jugendherberge (HI) ❷,** Tiergartenstr. 5, take bus #33 (dir.: Zoo-Sportzentrum). Next to the Heidelberg Zoo, one of the biggest in Europe, this hostel also teems with wildlife—schoolchildren. The rooms are large and the basement is a pub. (☎ 65 11 90. Breakfast and sheets included. Reception daily until 11:30pm. Lockout 9am-1pm. Curfew 11:30pm; stragglers admitted every ½hr. until 2am. Reserve at least a week ahead. Dorms €18, under-27 €15. HI members only.) For rooms with more personality and privacy, head to **Pension Jeske ❸,** Mittelbadgasse 2, in the *Altstadt.* Take bus #33 (dir: Ziegelhausen) to *Rathaus/Kornmarkt.* (☎ 237 33. Doubles €50, with bath €60; triples €60/90; quints €100. Cash only.) At **Hotel-Pension Elite ❹,** Bunsenstr. 15, all rooms have high ceilings, bath, and TV. From the train station, take streetcar #1 to *Poststr.* (☎ 257 34. Breakfast included. *Let's Go* discounted rates: singles €51; doubles €61; triples €72; quads €83.)

Most of the restaurants on and around Hauptstr. are expensive but the *Imbiße* (fast food stands) are reasonably priced. Just outside this central area, historic student pubs offer good values as well. To reach the student **Mensa ❶,** in the stone fortress on Marstallstr., take bus #35 to *Marstallstr.* You'll find cheap cafeteria fare. (€4, with student ID €2; €1.50 plate deposit; CampusCard required for lunch. Open M-F 11:30am-10pm.) The mood is **Hemingway's Bar-Café-Meeting Point ❷,** Fahrtg. 1, is embodied in the "Ernie" (€5)—a dessert consisting of a shot of brandy and a cigar. (Lunch menu €4.10. Open Su-Th 9am-1am, F-Sa 9am-3am.)

SIGHTS

HEIDELBERGER SCHLOß. The jewel in the crown of an already striking city, the castle stands careful watch over the armies (of tourists) that dare approach Heidelberg. Since 1329 it has housed the Prince Electors, whose statues decorate the facade in front of the entrance. Over a period of almost 400 years, the castle's residents commissioned their own distinctive additions, resulting in the conglomeration of styles you see today. The castle **wine cellar** houses the **Großer Faß,** the largest wine barrel ever made, which holds 221,726L. *(Grounds open daily 9am-6pm. €2.50, students €1.50. English tours every 15min. €3.50, students €2.50.)* The *Schloß* is accessible by the **Bergbahn,** one of Germany's oldest cable cars. *(Take bus #11 (dir.: Karlstor) to Bergbahn/Rathaus. Trams leave the parking lot next to the bus stop every 10min. Open 9am-8pm. Round-trip €3.50.)*

UNIVERSITÄT. Heidelberg is home to Germany's oldest and most prestigious university, established in 1386. More than 20 Nobel laureates have called the university home, and it was here that sociology became a legitimate academic subject. The **Museum der Universität Heidelberg** traces the university's long history in a building containing **Alte Aula,** Heidelberg's oldest auditorium. Before 1914, students were exempt from prosecution by civil authorities thanks to the principle of academic freedom; instead, the crimes of naughty youths were tried and punished by the faculty in the **Studentenkarzer** jail. *(Grabeng. 1. Open Apr.-Oct. M-Sa 10am-4pm; Nov.-Mar. Tu-F 10am-2pm. Museum and Studentenkarzer €2.50, students €2.)*

GERMANY

MARKTPLATZ. The center of the *Altstadt* is the cobblestoned *Marktplatz*, where accused witches and heretics were burned at the stake in the 15th century. Some of Heidelberg's oldest structures border the square: the 14th-century **Heiliggeist-kirche** (Church of the Holy Spirit) and the 16th-century **Haus Zum Ritter,** opposite the church. *(Church open M-Sa 11am-5pm, Su 1-5pm. Free. Church tower €0.50.)*

PHILOSOPHENWEG. A high path opposite the Neckar from the *Altstadt*, the Philosophenweg (Philosopher's Way) offers the best views of the city. On the top of Heiligenberg (Holy Mountain) lie the ruins of the 9th-century **St. Michael Basilika,** the 13th-century **Stefanskloster,** and an **amphitheater** built under Hitler in 1934 on the site of an ancient Celtic gathering place. *(To get to the path, take streetcar #1 or 3 to Tiefburg, or use the steep spur trail 10m west of the Karl-Theodor-Brücke.)*

🔊 NIGHTLIFE

Most popular nightspots fan out from the **Marktplatz.** On the Neckar side of the Heiliggeistkirche, **Unter Straße** boasts the most concentrated—and congested—collection of bars in the city. **Hauptstraße** also harbors a fair number of venues.

Nachtschicht, in Landfried-Komplex (☎ 43 85 50; www.nachtschicht.com). University students jam to a variety of music in a basement resembling an old factory. Cover €3.50; M and F students €1.50. Open M and Th-Sa 10pm-4am; W 10pm-3am.

Zum Sepp'l, Hauptstr. 213. This age-old student lair, accented by stained glass windows, hosts a loud crowd and piano player M-Tu and F-Sa. Open M-F 5:30pm-midnight, Sa-Su 11am-2:30pm and 5:30pm-1am.

Schwimmbad Musikclub, Tiergartenstr. 13. Convenient for hostelers, but a trek for others. Four levels of live music, dancing, and movies. Open W-Sa 8pm-3am.

🎆 DAYTRIP FROM HEIDELBERG: NECKARSTEINACH. Fourteen kilometers upstream from Heidelberg, Neckarsteinach is a fishing village made famous by its four picture perfect, nearly untouristed castles. The two westernmost castles stand in romantic ruin, while the two to the east are privately occupied and not open to visitors. All lie within 3km of one another along the north bank of the Neckar river and can be reached by foot via the **Burgenweg** (castle path). From the train station, turn right on Bahnhofstr., turn left on Hauptstr., and follow the bend in the road; a red stone cross marks the beginning of the *Schloßsteige* (Castle Stairs), a brick path leading upward to the Burgenweg. Fireworks light the sky above the town on the second Saturday after Pentecost in June and on the last Saturday in July for the **Vierburgenbeleuchtung** (four-castle lighting).

Trains connecting Heidelberg to Heilbronn run through the Neckar valley, a thickly-forested stretch running north through Bad Wimpfen, Burg Guttenberg, Hirschhorn am Neckar, and Neckarsteinach. Castles dot the hilltops of the valley and form part of the Burgenstraße (Castle Road), which stretches from Mannheim to Prague. Local **buses** also traverse the Neckar Valley; often these are faster than the infrequent trains. Schedules are posted at bus stops. The **tourist office,** Hauptstr. 15, has a list of **private rooms.** (☎ 06229 920 00. Open M-Tu and Th-F 8:30am-12:30pm and 2:30-6pm, W 8:30am-12:30pm, Sa 8:30am-1pm.) **Postal Code:** 69239.

STUTTGART   ☎ 0711

Forget about *Lederhosen*—Porsche, Daimler-Benz, and a host of other corporate thoroughbreds keep Stuttgart (pop. 587,000) speeding along in the fast lane. After almost complete destruction in WWII, Stuttgart was rebuilt in a thoroughly modern and uninspiring style. The city does have amazing **mineral baths** (*Mineralbäder*), fueled by western Europe's most active mineral springs. **Mineralbad**

Leuze, Am Leuzebad 2-6, has indoor and outdoor thermal pools. Take U1, or streetcar #2 to *Mineralbäder.* (☎216 42 10. Open daily 6am-9pm. 2hr. soak €6.40, students €4.80.) The superb ▓**Staatsgallerie Stuttgart,** Konrad-Adenauer-Str. 30-32, houses an excellent collection of modern art in the new wing. (Open Su, Tu-W and F-Sa 10am-6pm; Th 10am-9pm. €4.50, students €3. W free.) The **Mercedes-Benz Museum,** Mercedesstr. 137, is a must for car-lovers. Take S1 to *Daimlerstadion.* (Open Su and Tu-Sa 9am-5pm. Free.)

Stuttgart has direct **trains** to most major German cities, including: Berlin (6hr., 2 per hr., €103); Frankfurt (1½hr., 2 per hr., €43); and Munich (2½-3½hr., 2-3 per hr., €36-43). The tourist office, **tips 'n' trips,** Lautenschlagerstr. 22, has **Internet** (€3 per hr., W free) and info on the Stuttgart scene. (☎222 27 30. Open M-F noon-7pm, Sa 10am-2pm.) The **post office** is in the station. (Open M-F 8:30am-6pm, Sa 8:30am-12:30pm.) To reach the **Jugendherberge Stuttgart (HI) ❷,** Haußmannstr. 27, take streetcar #15 to *Eugenspl.* and go downhill on Kernerstr. (☎24 15 83. Breakfast included. Sheets €3.10. Reception 24hr. Lockout 9:30am-1pm. Dorms €16, under-26 €14.) **Hotel Espenlaub ❹,** Charlottenstr. 27, has pricey but well-equipped rooms. Take streetcar #15 or U5, 6, or 7 to *Olgaeck.* (☎21 09 10. Breakfast included. Singles €44, with bath €62; doubles €51/87; triples €74/98. MC/V.) The pedestrian zone between Pfarrstr. and Charlottenstr. has many reasonably priced restaurants, while Rotebühlpl. is filled with fast food joints. Nightlife clusters around Eberhardstr., Rotebühlpl., and Calwer Str. **Suite 212,** Theodor-Heuss-Str. 15, has DJs and videotechnique on weekends. (Open M-Th 11am-2am, F-Sa 11am-5am, Su 2pm-2am.) **Postal Code:** 70173.

CONSTANCE (KONSTANZ)   ☎07531

Located on the **Bodensee** (Lake Constance), the charming city of Constance (pop. 79,000) has never been bombed; part of the city extends into Switzerland, and the Allies were leery of accidentally striking neutral territory. Now one of Germany's favorite vacation spots, its narrow streets wind around beautiful Baroque and Renaissance facades, gabled and turreted 19th-century houses gleam with a confident gentility along the river promenades, and a palpable jubilation fills the streets. The **Münster** has a 76m Gothic spire and a display of ancient religious objects, but it's being renovated through 2005. (Open M-F 10am-6pm, Sa-Su noon-5pm.) Wander down **Seestraße,** near the yacht harbor on the lake, or **Rheinsteig,** along the Rhine, for picturesque promenades. Constance boasts a number of **public beaches;** all are free and open May to Sept. **Freidbad Horn** (bus #5), the largest and most crowded, sports a nude sunbathing section modestly enclosed by hedges.

Trains run from Constance to most cities in southern Germany. BSB **ferries** leave hourly from Constance for all ports around the lake. Buy tickets on board or in the building, Hafenstr. 6, behind the train station. (☎28 13 89. Open Apr.-Oct. daily 7:45am-6:35pm.) The friendly but tiny **tourist office,** Bahnhofspl. 13, to the right of the train station, provides free walking maps and finds rooms for a €2.50 fee. (☎13 30 30. Open Apr.-Oct. M-F 9am-6:30pm, Sa 9am-4pm, Su 10am-1pm; Nov.-Mar. M-F 9:30am-6pm.) In the center of town, **Pension Gretel ❸,** Zollernstr. 6-8, offers bright rooms. In summer, call at least a month ahead. (☎45 58 25. Breakfast included. Singles €29-36; doubles €49-64, with bath €59-74; triples €75-93; quads €87-113. Extra bed €18.) To reach the newly renovated **Jugendherberge Otto-Moericke-Turm (HI) ❷,** Zur Allmannshöhe 18, take bus #4 from the train station to *Jugendherberge;* turn back and head uphill on Zur Allmannshöhe. (☎322 60. Breakfast included. Sheets €3.10. Reception Apr.-Oct. daily 3-10pm; Nov.-Mar. 5-10pm. Lockout 9:30am-noon. Call ahead. Dorms €18, under-26 €15. HI members only.) Camp by the waterfront at **DKV-Campingplatz**

Bodensee ❶, Fohrenbühlweg 45. Take bus #1 to *Staad* and walk for 10min. with the lake to your left. (☎330 57. Reception closed daily noon-2:30pm. Showers included. €4 per person, €4 per tent.) For groceries, head to the basement of the **Karstadt** department store, on Augustinerpl. (Open M-F 9:30am-8pm, Sa 9am-4pm.) **Postal Code:** 78462.

BLACK FOREST (SCHWARZWALD)

The Black Forest owes its name to the eerie gloom that prevails under its ever-green canopy. Once inspiration for the Grimm Brothers' *Hansel and Gretel*, today the region lures hikers and skiers with more than just gingerbread.

▣ TRANSPORTATION

The gateway to the Black Forest is **Freiburg,** accessible by **train** from Stuttgart and Basel, Switzerland. Most visitors explore the area by bike, as public transportation is sparse. Rail lines encircle its perimeter, but only two **train** lines cut through the region. **Bus** service is more thorough, although slow and infrequent.

FREIBURG IM BREISGAU. Freiburg (pop. 208,000) may be the metropolis of the Schwarzwald, but it has yet to succumb to the hectic pace of city life. Its pride and joy is the majestic **Münster**, a stone cathedral with a 116m spire and a tower whose bell is the oldest in Germany. (Open M-Sa 9:30am-5pm, Su 1-5pm. Tower €1, students €0.50.) The surrounding hills brim with fantastic **hiking** trails; maps (€3.50-6) are available in the tourist office, and paths are clearly marked. **Mountain biking** trails also traverse the hills; look for signs with bicycles to guide you.

Trains run to Basel (1hr., 3 per hr., €9-16) and Stuttgart (2hr., every hr., €38). The **tourist office,** Rotteckring 14, two blocks down Eisenbahnstr. from the station, has maps and books *Privatenzimmer* (rooms in private homes); these are usually the most affordable accommodations in Freiburg itself. (Open June-Sept. M-F 9:30am-8pm, Sa 9:30am-5pm, Su 10am-noon; Oct.-May M-F 9:30am-6pm, Sa 9:30am-2pm, Su 10am-noon.) To reach the **Jugendherberge (HI) ❷,** Kartäuserstr. 151, take bus #1 to *Lassbergstr.* Take a left and then a right onto Fritz-Geiges-Str., and follow the signs. (☎(0761) 676 56. Breakfast included. Dorms €22, under-27 €19; doubles €48.) The **Freiburger Markthalle ❷,** next to the Martinstor, is home to food-stands serving ethnic specialties for €3-7. (Open M-F 7am-7pm, Sa 7am-4pm.) **Brennessel ❸,** Eschholzstr. 17, behind the train station, stuffs patrons with everything from ostrich-steak to pancakes. (Open M-Sa 8am-1am, Su 5pm-1am.) **Postal Code:** 79098.

TRIBERG. The residents of touristy Triberg (pop. 5,000) brag about the **Gutacher Wasserfall**, the highest in Germany, a series of bright cascades tumbling over moss-covered rocks for 163m. It's more of a mountain stream than a waterfall, but the hike itself is idyllic. (Park open 9am-7pm. €1.50, students €1.20.) Nearby Schoach's claim to the world's two largest cuckoo clocks is less tenuous. The signs for **Wallfahrtskirche** lead to the small pilgrimage church, **Maria in der Tanne,** where the pious have, according to legend, been miraculously cured since the 17th century.

Trains run to Freiburg (2-2½hr., 1-2 per hr., €16-25). The **tourist office,** Luisenstr. 10, is on the ground floor of the *Kurhaus;* from the station, turn right and follow the signs, or take any bus to *Marktpl.* (☎(07722) 95 32 30. Open May-Sept. M-F 9am-5pm, Sa 10am-noon; Oct.-Apr. M-F 9am-5pm.)

BAVARIA (BAYERN)

Bavaria is the Germany of Teutonic myth, Wagnerian opera, and the Brothers Grimms' fairy tales. From the Baroque cities along the Danube to mad King Ludwig's castles high in the Alps, the region draws more tourists than any other part of the country. Most foreign notions of Germany are tied to this land of *Biergarten* and *Lederhosen*. Mostly rural, Catholic, and conservative, it contrasts sharply with the rest of the country. Local authorities still use Bavaria's proper name, *Freistaat Bayern*, and its traditions and dialect have been preserved. Residents have always been Bavarians first and Germans second.

> **REMINDER** HI-affiliated hostels in Bavaria generally do not admit guests over age 26 except in families or groups of adults with young children.

MUNICH (MÜNCHEN)   ☎089

The capital and cultural center of Bavaria, Munich (pop. 1,228,000) is a sprawling, relatively liberal metropolis in the midst of conservative southern Germany. World-class museums, handsome parks and architecture, a rambunctious arts scene, and an urbane population combine to create a city of astonishing vitality. *Müncheners* party zealously during *Fasching*, Germany's Mardi Gras (Jan. 7-Mar. 4, 2004), shop with abandon during the Christmas Market (Nov. 28-Dec. 24, 2004), and consume unfathomable quantities of beer during the legendary **Oktoberfest** (Sept. 19-Oct. 4, 2004).

▐ TRANSPORTATION

Flights: Flughafen München (☎97 52 13 13). S8 runs between the airport and the *Hauptbahnhof* (40min., every 10min., €8 or 8 stripes on the *Streifenkarte*).

Trains: Munich's **Hauptbahnhof** (☎22 33 12 56) is the transportation hub of southern Germany, with connections to: **Amsterdam** (9hr., every hr., €143); **Berlin** (8hr., every hr., €141, or €103 via Leipzig); **Cologne** (6hr., every hr., €101); **Frankfurt** (3½hr., every hr., €76); **Hamburg** (6hr., every hr., €138); **Paris** (10hr., 3 per day, €105); **Prague** (7hr., 2 per day, €60); **Salzburg** (1¾hr., 1 per hr., €25); **Vienna** (5hr., every hr., €59); and **Zurich** (5hr., 4 per day, €61). For 24hr. schedules, fare info, and reservations (in German), call ☎(01805) 99 66 33. **EurAide,** in the station, provides free train info and sells train tickets. **Reisezentrum** info counters open daily 6am-10:30pm.

Public Transportation: MVV, Munich's public transport system, runs Su-Th 5am-12:30am, F-Sa 5am-2am. The S-Bahn to the airport starts running at 3:30am. Eurail, InterRail, and German railpasses are valid on the S-Bahn, but *not* on the U-Bahn, streetcars, or buses.

Tickets: Buy tickets at the blue vending machines and **validate them** in the blue boxes marked with an E before entering the platform. If you jump the fare (*schwarzfahren*), you risk a €30 fine.

Prices: Single ride tickets €2, valid for 3hr. **Kurzstrecke** (short trip) tickets are good for 2 stops on U or S, or 4 stops on a streetcar or bus (€1). A **Streifenkarte** (10-strip ticket; €9) can be used by more than 1 person. Cancel 2 strips per person for a normal ride, or 1 strip per person for a *Kurzstrecke;* beyond the city center, cancel 2 strips per additional zone. A **Single-Tageskarte** (single-day ticket) is valid for 1 day of unlimited travel until 6am the next day (€4.50). The **3-Day Pass** (€11) is also a great deal. Passes can be purchased at the **MVV office** behind tracks 31 and 32 in the *Hauptbahnhof*, or at any of the *Kartenautomats*. Ask at tourist offices about the **Munich Welcome Card** (1-day €6.50, 3-day €15.50), which gives public transportation and various other discounts.

GERMANY

Munich

♦ ACCOMMODATIONS
4 You.München, 7
Campingplatz Thalkirchen, 26
Creatif Hotel, 8
Euro Youth Hotel, 19
Hotel Helvetia, 20
Hotel Kurfplaz, 17
Hotel-Pension am Markt, 23
Jugendhotel
  Marienherberge, 18
Jugendlager Kapuzinerhölzl, 6
Pension am Kaiserplatz, 3
Pension Frank, 2
Pension Locarno, 11

● FOOD
Café Hag/Confiserie
  Retenhäfen, 15
Dukatz im Literaturhaus, 14
Gollier, 25
Schelling Salon, 1
Schwimmkrabbe, 27
Shoya, 21

🍺 BEER GARDENS
Augustinerkeller, 9
Hirschgarten, 10
Hofbräuhaus, 22

★ BARS
Nachtcafe, 12
Reitschule, 4
Sausalitos, 24

NIGHTLIFE
Ballhaus, 5
Bei Carla, 28
Kunstpark Ost, 29
Nachtwerk, Club,
  and Tanzlokal, 16
Soul City, 13

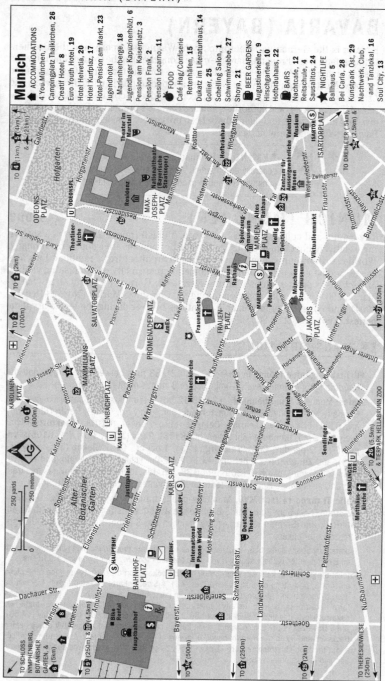

Ride-Sharing: McShare Treffpunkt Zentrale, Klenzestr. 57b or Lämmerstr. 6 (☎194 40; www.mitfahrzentrale.de). Open daily 8am-8pm. At the same location, **Frauenmitfahrzentrale,** arranges ride shares for women only. Open M-F 8am-8pm.

Hitchhiking: *Let's Go* does not recommend hitchhiking as a safe mode of transportation. Those looking to share rides scan the bulletin boards in the **Mensa,** Leopoldstr. 13. Otherwise, hitchers try *Autobahn* on-ramps; those who stand behind the blue sign with the white auto **may be fined.** Hitchhikers going to Salzburg take U1 or 2 to Karl-Preis-pl. Those heading to Nürnberg and Berlin take U6 to Studentenstadt and walk 500m to the Frankfurter Ring. Those heading to the Bodensee and Switzerland take U4 or 5 to Heimeranpl., then bus #33 to Siegenburger Str.

Taxis: Taxi-Zentrale (☎216 11 or 194 10) has large stands in front of the train station and every 5-10 blocks in the city center. Women can request a female driver.

Bike Rental: Radius Bikes (☎59 61 13), at the far end of the *Hauptbahnhof,* behind the lockers opposite tracks 30-36. €3 per hr., €14 per day. Deposit €50, passport, or credit card. 10% student, Eurail, and Munich Welcome Card discount. Open July-Aug. M-F10am-6pm, Sa-Su 9am-8pm; May-Oct. daily 10am-6pm. **Aktiv-Rad,** Hans-Sachs-Str. 7 (☎26 65 06). U1 or 2 to Frauenhofer Str. €12-20 per day. Open M-F 10am-1pm and 2-6:30pm, Sa 10am-1pm.

ORIENTATION

Munich's center is a circle split into four quarters by one horizontal and one vertical line. The east-west and north-south thoroughfares cross at Munich's epicenter, the **Marienplatz,** and connect the traffic rings at **Karlsplatz** (called **Stachus** by locals) in the west, **Isartorplatz** in the east, **Odeonsplatz** in the north, and **Sendlinger Tor** in the south. In the east beyond the Isartor, the **Isar River** flows north-south past the city center. The **Hauptbahnhof** (main train station) is just beyond Karlspl. to the west of the Ring. To get to Marienpl. from the station, use the main exit and head across Bahnhofpl.; keep going east through Karlspl., and Marienpl. will be straight ahead. Or, take any S-Bahn to Marienpl.

The **University** is north of Munich's center, next to the budget restaurants of the **Schwabing** district. East of Schwabing is the **English Garden;** west of Schwabing is the **Olympiapark.** South of town is the **Glockenbachviertel,** filled with all sorts of night hotspots, including many gay bars. The area around the train station is rather seedy, dominated by hotels and sex shops. Oktoberfest is held on the large, open **Theresienwiese,** southeast of the train station on the U4 and 5 lines.

PRACTICAL INFORMATION

Several publications help visitors navigate Munich. The most comprehensive is the monthly English-language *Munich Found* (€3), available at newsstands and bookshops, which provides a list of services, events, and museums.

TOURIST, FINANCIAL, AND LOCAL SERVICES

EurAide (☎59 38 89), along track 11 (room 3) of the *Hauptbahnhof,* near the Bayerstr. exit. Books train tickets for free, explains the public transport, and sells maps (€1) and tickets for English tours of Munich. Pick up the free brochure *Inside Track.* Open June-Sept. daily 7:45am-12:45pm and 2-6pm; May 7:45am-12:45pm and 2-4:30pm; Oct. 7:45am-12:45pm and 2-4pm; Nov.-Apr. 8am-noon and 1-4pm.

Main Tourist Office: (☎23 39 65 00), on the front (east) side of the train station, next to the SB-Markt on Bahnhofpl. Books rooms for free with a 10-15% deposit, sells English city maps (€0.30), and offers the **Munich Welcome Card.** Open M-Sa 9:30am-6:30pm, Su 10am-6pm. **Branch office** just inside the entrance to the Neues Rathaus on Marienpl. Open M-F 10am-8pm, Sa 10am-4pm.

Discover Bavaria (☎25 54 39 88), Hochorückenstr., near the rear entrance of the Hofbräuhaus. Helps find rooms for free, rents bikes, and dispenses coupons for a variety of activities. Also sells tickets for the hugely popular Mike's Bike Tours of Munich, Neuschwanstein, and Dachau. Open Apr.-Sept. daily 8:30am-9pm.

Consulates: Canada, Tal 29 (☎219 95 70). Open M-Th 9am-noon and 2-5pm, F 9am-noon and 2-3:30pm. **Ireland,** Dennigerstr. 15 (☎20 80 59 90). Open M-F 9am-noon. **South Africa,** Sendlinger-Tor-Pl. 5 (☎23 11 63 37). Open M-F 9am-noon. **UK,** Bürkleinstr. 10, 4th fl. (☎21 10 90). Open M-F 8:30am-noon and 1-3pm. **US,** Königinstr. 5 (☎288 80). Open M-F 8-11am.

Currency Exchange: ReiseBank, in front of the train station on Bahnhofpl. Open M-Sa 7:30am-7:15pm, Su 9:30am-4:45pm.

Bi-Gay-Lesbian Resources: Gay services information (☎260 30 56). **Lesbian information** (☎725 42 72). Phone staffed M and W 2:30-5pm, Tu 10:30am-1pm, Th 7-9pm. Also see **Gay and Lesbian Munich** (p. 484).

Laundromat: SB Waschcenter, Paul-Heyse-Str. 21, near the train station. Turn right on Bayerstr., then left on Paul-Heyse-Str. Wash €4, dry €0.60 per 10min. Open daily 7am-11pm. **Kingsgard Waschsalon,** Amalienstr. 61, near the university. Wash €3, dry €1.50. Open M-F 8am-6:30pm, Sa 9am-1pm.

EMERGENCY AND COMMUNICATIONS

Police: ☎110. **Ambulance** and **Fire:** ☎112. **Medical service:** ☎192 22.

Pharmacy: Bahnhofpl. 2 (☎59 41 19 or 59 81 19), on the corner outside the train station. Open M-F 8am-6:30pm, Sa 8am-2pm.

Internet Access: Easy Everything, on Bahnhofspl. next to the post office. Prices depend on demand (max. €3 per hr.). Open 24hr. **Internet Cafe,** Marienpl. 20, serves cocktails and food all night. €1 per 30min. Open 24hr.

Post Office: Bahnhofpl. The yellow building across the street from the main train station exit. Open M-F 7:30am-8pm, Sa 9am-4pm. **Postal Code:** 80335.

♠ ACCOMMODATIONS AND CAMPING

Munich's accommodations usually fall into one of three categories: Seedy, expensive, or booked solid. During times like Oktoberfest, when prices usually jump 10-15%, only the latter exists. In summer, book a few weeks in advance or start calling before noon. At most of Munich's hostels you can check in all day, but try to start your search before 5pm. Don't even think of sleeping in any public area, including the *Hauptbahnhof*; police patrol all night long.

HOSTELS AND CAMPING

▓ **Euro Youth Hotel,** Senefelderstr. 5 (☎59 90 88 11). From the Bayerstr. exit out of the *Hauptbahnhof,* make a left on Bayerstr. and a right on Senefelderstr. Friendly and well-informed English-speaking staff. Breakfast buffet €4.90. Laundry facilities (wash €2.80, dry €1.30. Reception 24hr. Dorms €18; singles €45; doubles €48, with private shower, telephone, and breakfast €72; triples €63; quads €84. ❷

4 You München, Hirtenstr. 18 (☎ 552 16 60), 200m from the *Hauptbahnhof*. Ecological youth hostel with restaurant and bar. Wheelchair accessible. Breakfast buffet €4.35. 12-bed dorms €17; 4-, 6-, or 8-bed dorms €21-29; singles €34; doubles €48. ❷

Jugendlager Kapuzinerhölzl ("The Tent"), In den Kirschen 30 (☎ 141 43 00). Streetcar #17 from the *Hauptbahnhof* (dir.: Amalienburgstr.) to *Botanischer Garten* (15min.). Follow the signs straight on Franz-Schrank-Str. and turn left at In den Kirschen. Sleep with 250 fellow campers under a big tent on a wooden floor. Laundry €2. Lockers €4. Internet €1 for 15min. Kitchen available. Reception 24hr. Reservations only for groups over 15, but rarely full. Open June-Aug. €8.50 gets you a foam pad, blankets (you can also use your sleeping bag), a shower, and breakfast. Actual beds €11. Camping available for €5.50 per campsite plus €5.50 per person. ❶

Jugendhotel Marienherberge, Goethestr. 9 (☎ 55 58 05), less than a block from the train station. **Open only to women.** Reduced prices for those under 26. Staffed by merry nuns, the rooms are spacious, cheery, and spotless. Breakfast included. Laundry €1.50. Reception daily 8am-midnight. Curfew midnight. 6-bed dorms €22, over-25 €27; singles €25/30; doubles €40/50; triples €60/75. ❸

Campingplatz Thalkirchen, Zentralländstr. 49 (☎ 723 17 07). U1 or 2 to Sendlinger Tor, then U3 to Thalkirchen, and change to bus #57 (20min.). From the bus stop, cross the busy street on the left and take a right onto the footpath. The entrance is down the tree-lined path on the left. Well-run, crowded grounds with jogging and bike paths, TV lounge, groceries, and a restaurant. Showers €1. Laundry facilities (wash €4, dry €0.25 per 11min.). Open mid-Mar. to late Oct. €4.40 per person, €8 per tent. ❶

HOTELS AND PENSIONS

▨ **Hotel Helvetia,** Schillerstr. 6 (☎ 590 68 50), at the corner of Bahnhofspl. Just beyond the Vereinsbank, to the right as you exit the station. A friendly hotel with newly renovated rooms. Free Internet. Breakfast included. Laundry €6. Reception 24hr. Singles €30-35; doubles €40-55, with shower €50-65; triples €55-69; quads €72-90. ❸

▨ **Creatif Hotel,** Lammerstr. 6 (☎ 55 57 85). Take the Arnulfstr. exit out of the station, hang a quick right, turn left on Hirtenstr., then right on Lammerstr. Uniquely modern rooms, all with bath, telephone, and TV. Internet €1 per 30min. Reception 24hr. Singles €30-40; doubles €40-65. Extra bed €10. ❸

Pension am Kaiserplatz, Kaiserpl. 12 (☎ 34 91 90). U3 to Münchener Freiheit. Take the escalator to Herzogstr., then turn left; it's 3 blocks to Viktoriastr. Take a left at Viktoriastr.; it's at the end of the street on the right. A few blocks from nightlife central—a good location if you doubt your sense of direction after a couple of beers. Motherly owner offers elegant rooms, each one in its own style, from Victorian to modern. Breakfast included and served in-room. Reception 7am-8pm. Singles €31, with shower €47; doubles €53/57; triples €63/66; quads €84; quints €105; 6-bed rooms €126. ❸

Pension Locarno, Bahnhofspl. 5 (☎ 55 51 64). Cozy rooms, all with cable TV and phone. Reception daily 7:30am-5pm. Singles €38; doubles €57; triples €69; quads €81. ❸

Hotel Kurfplaz, Schwanthaler Str. 121 (☎ 540 98 60). Exit on Bayerstr. from the station, turn right and walk 5-6 blocks down Bayerstr., veer left onto Holzapfelstr., and make a right onto Schwanthaler Str. Or, take streetcar #18 or 19 to Holzapfelstr. and walk from there. TV, phone, and bath in all rooms. Breakfast included. Internet €3 per 30min. Reception 24hr. Singles from €50; doubles from €100. ❹

Hotel-Pension am Markt, Heiliggeiststr. 6 (☎ 22 50 14), smack dab in the city center, off the Viktualienmarkt. Take any S-Bahn to Marienpl., then walk past the Altes Rathaus and turn right down the little alley behind the Heiliggeist Church. Small but spotless rooms are wheelchair-accessible. Breakfast included. Reception (3rd fl.) daily 7am-9pm. Singles €38, with shower €66; doubles €68/87-92; triples €100/123. ❹

GERMANY

Pension Frank, Schellingstr. 24 (☎28 14 51). U3 or 6 to Universität. Take the Schelling-str. exit, then the 1st right onto Schellingstr. Rooms with balconies in a great location for cafe and bookstore aficionados. Breakfast included. Reception daily 7:30am-10pm. 3- to 6-bed dorms €25; singles €35-40; doubles €52-55. ❸

▶ FOOD

For an authentic Bavarian lunch, grab a *Brez'n* (pretzel) and spread it with *Leber-wurst* (liverwurst) or cheese. **Weißwürste** (white veal sausages) are another native bargain. Don't eat the skin of the sausage; just slice it open and eat the tender meat. **Leberkäs** is a slice of a pinkish, meatloaf-like compound of ground beef and bacon, and **Leberknödel** are liver dumplings, usually served in soup.

The vibrant **Viktualienmarkt,** south of Marienpl., is Munich's gastronomic center. It's fun to browse, but don't plan to do any budget grocery shopping here. (Open M-F 10am-8pm, Sa 8am-4pm.) Birthplace of the **beer garden,** Munich's progeny are everywhere. The university district off **Ludwigstraße** is Munich's best source of inexpensive and filling meals. Many reasonably priced restaurants and cafes cluster on **Schellingstraße, Amalienstraße,** and **Türkenstraße** (U3 or 6 to Universität.)

IN THE CENTER

▧ **Dukatz im Literaturhaus,** Salvatorpl. 1 (☎291 96 00). Any *Münchener* will tell you this is the place to see and and be seen. The home for small artists serves gourmet food (€6-8) to complement creative drink options (€2-4). Sip a cup of coffee and people watch—not only are entrees among the best in the city, they're also among the most expensive (€16-22). Open daily noon-2:30pm and 6:30-10:30pm. ❹

▧ **Marché,** Neuhauser Str., between Karlspl. and Marienpl. The top floor offers cafeteria-style food; downstairs, chefs prepare every food imaginable, including great vegetarian selections. You'll get a food card that will be stamped for each item taken; pay at the end. Bottom floor open 11am-10pm; top floor 8am-11pm, until 10pm in off-season. ❷

Café Hag/Confiserie Retenhäfen, Residenzstr. 25-26, across from the Residenz. Specializes in a delectable array of cakes and sweets (€2-4). Serves breakfast (€4-8) and entrees (€5-8). Open M-F 8:45am-7pm, Sa 8am-6pm. ❷

Shoya, Orlandostr. 5, across from the Hofbräuhaus. The most reasonable Japanese restaurant in town. Fill up on rice dishes (€7-9), teriyaki (€4-8), and sushi (€4-10) as you Saki-bomb to Japanese music. Open daily 10:30am-midnight. ❸

ELSEWHERE

Schelling Salon, Schellingstr. 54 (☎272 07 88). Bavarian *Knödel* and billiards since 1872. Rack up at the same tables where Lenin, Rilke, and Hitler once played. Breakfast €3-5. Traditional German entrees €4-11. A free **billiard museum** displays a 200-year-old Polish noble's table and the history of pool back to the pharaohs. Museum open Su night. Restaurant open Su-M and Th-Sa 6:30am-1am. ❸

Gollier, Gollierstr. 83. U4 or 5, S7 or 27 to Heimeranpl. Delicious vegetarian fare €6-11. Open Tu-F 11:30-3pm and 5pm-midnight, Sa 5pm-midnight, Su 10am-midnight. ❸

Schwimmkrabbe, Ickstattstr. 13. U1 or 2 to Frauenhoferstr. This family-run Turkish restaurant is popular with locals. Appetizers €4-9. Meals €8-18. Open daily 5pm-1am. ❹

◉ SIGHTS

MARIENPLATZ. The **Mariensäule,** an ornate 17th-century monument to the Virgin Mary, was built to commemorate the city's survival during the Thirty Years' War. At the neo-Gothic **Neues Rathaus,** the **Glockenspiel** chimes with a display of jousting knights and dancing coopers. *(Daily 11am and noon; in summer also 5pm.)* At 9pm, a mechanical watchman marches out and the Guardian Angel escorts the *Münchner Kindl* (Munich Child) to bed. Be careful; this is a likely spot for pickpocketing. The Neues Rathaus tower offers a sweeping view. *(Tower open M-F 9am-7pm, Sa-Su 10am-7pm. €1.50.)* On the face of the **Altes Rathaus** tower, to the right of the Neues Rathaus, are all but one of Munich's coats of arms—the local government refused to include the swastika-bearing arms from the Nazi era.

PETERSKIRCHE AND FRAUENKIRCHE. Across from the Neues Rathaus is the 12th-century **Peterskirche**, the city's oldest parish church. More than 300 steps scale the tower to a spectacular view of Munich. *(Open daily 10am-7pm. €1.50, students €1.)* From the Marienpl., take Kaufingerstr. one block toward the *Hauptbahnhof* to the onion-domed towers of the 15th-century **Frauenkirche**—one of Munich's most notable landmarks and now the symbol of the city. *(Towers open Apr.-Oct. M-Sa 10am-5pm. €3, students €1.50.)*

RESIDENZ. Down the pedestrian zone from Odeonspl., the richly decorated rooms of the **Residenz** (Palace), built from the 14th to 19th centuries, form the material vestiges of the Wittelsbach dynasty. Behind the Residenz, the beautifully landscaped **Hofgarten** shelters the lovely temple of Diana. The **Schatzkammer** (treasury) contains jeweled baubles, crowns, swords, china, ivory work, and other trinkets. *(Open Apr. to mid-Oct. daily 9am-6pm; mid-Oct. to Mar. 10am-4pm. €4, students €3.)* The **Residenzmuseum** comprises the former Wittelsbach apartments and State Rooms, a collection of European porcelain, and a 17th-century court chapel. The 120 portraits in the **Ahnengalerie** trace the royal lineage in an unusual manner back to Charlemagne. *(Max-Joseph-pl. 3. U3-6 to Odeonspl. Residenz museum open same hours as Schatzkammer. €4, students €3. Combination ticket €7, students €5.50.)*

ENGLISCHER GARTEN. Extending from the city center is the vast **Englischer Garten** (English Garden), Europe's largest metropolitan public park. On sunny days, all of Munich turns out to bike, play badminton, ride horseback, or swim in the Eisbach. The garden includes a Japanese tea house, a Chinese pagoda, a Greek temple, and good old German beer gardens. **Nude sunbathing** areas are designated FKK (*Frei-Körper-Kultur*) on signs and park maps. Daring *Müncheners* surf the rapids of the Eisbach, which flows artificially through the park.

SCHLOß NYMPHENBURG. After 10 years of trying for an heir, Ludwig I celebrated the birth of his son in 1662 by erecting an elaborate summer playground. **Schloß Nymphenburg**, in the northwest of town, hides a number of treasures. Check out Ludwig's "Gallery of Beauties;" whenever a woman caught his fancy, he would have her portrait painted—a scandalous hobby considering many of the women were commoners. Four manors and a few lakes also inhabit the grounds. Finally, learn about the means of 17th-century royal travel in the **Marstallimuseum.** *(Streetcar #17 to Schloß Nymphenburg. All attractions open Apr. to mid-Oct. daily 9am-6pm; late Oct. to Mar. 10am-4pm. Museum and Schloß open Su and Tu-Sa 9am-noon and 1-5pm. Schloß €3.50, students €2.50. Each manor €3/2. Museum €2.50/2. Entire complex €7.50/6.)*

OLYMPIAPARK. Built for the 1972 Olympic Games in Munich, the **Olympiapark** contains the architecturally daring, tent-like **Olympia-Zentrum** and the **Olympia Turm** (tower), the highest building in Munich at 290m. Two **tours** in English are available: The "Adventure Tour" of the entire park (Apr.-Oct. daily 2pm, €7) or a tour of just the soccer stadium (Mar.-Oct. daily 11am, €5). The Olympiapark also hosts various events all summer, ranging from concerts to flea markets to bungee jumping. *(U3 to Olympiazentrum. Tower open daily 9am-midnight. €3, students €2. Info Pavilion (Besucherservice) open M-F 10am-6pm, Sa 10am-3pm.)*

GERMANY

🏛 MUSEUMS

Munich is the supreme museum city—many of the city's offerings would require days for exhaustive perusal. The *Münchner Volkshochschule* (☎48 00 62 29) offers tours of many city museums for €6. A **day pass** to all of Munich's state-owned museums is sold at the tourist office and many larger museums (€15). All state-owned museums are **free on Sunday.**

■ **PINAKOTHEK DER MODERNE.** The newest and largest addition to Munich's world of art offers four museums in one. Paintings, drawings, architecture, and design occupy the large building created by *Münchener* Stephan Braunfels. Lose yourself in the works of Picasso, Dalí Matisse, Warhol, and others. *(Barerstr. 40. U2 to Königspl. Take a right at Königspl., and a left after 1 block onto Meiserstr. Open Su and Tu-Sa 10am-5pm. €5, students €3.50. Day pass for all 3 Pinakotheke €12.)*

■ **DEUTSCHES MUSEUM.** One of the largest and best museums of science and technology, with fascinating displays, including a mining exhibit that winds through a labyrinth of recreated subterranean tunnels. The museum has over 50 departments covering 17km. *(Museuminsel 1. S1 or 8 to Isartor or streetcar #18 to Deutsches Museum. Open daily 9am-5pm. €7.50, students €3. Guidebooks €4.)*

ALTE PINAKOTHEK AND NEUE PINAKOTHEK. Commissioned in 1826 by King Ludwig I, the world-renowned **Alte Pinakothek** houses Munich's most precious art, including works by da Vinci, Rembrandt, and Rubens. The **Neue Pinakothek** next door displays paintings and sculptures of the 19th to 20th centuries, including van Gogh, Cézanne, and Manet. *(Barerstr. 27-29. U2 to Königspl. Each open W, F, Sa-Su 10am-5pm; Tu-Th 10am-8pm. Each €5, students €3.50; combination ticket €8/5.)*

BMW MUSEUM. The ultimate driving museum features a fetching display of past, present, and future BMW products. The English brochure *Horizons in Time* guides you through the spiral path to the top of the museum. *(Petuelring 130. U3 to Olympiazentrum. Take the Olympiaturm exit and walk a block up Lerchenauer Str.; the museum will be on your left. Open daily 9am-5pm. €3, students €2.)*

ZAM: ZENTRUM FÜR AUSSERGEWÖHNLICHE MUSEEN. Munich's Center for Unusual Museums brazenly corrals—under one roof—such treasures as the Peddle-Car Museum and the Museum of Easter Rabbits. *(Westenriederstr. 41. Any S-Bahn or streetcar #17 or 18 to Isartor. Open daily 10am-6pm. €4, students €3.)*

🎭 🎦 ENTERTAINMENT AND NIGHTLIFE

Munich's cultural cache rivals any in the world. Sixty theaters of various sizes are scattered throughout the city; styles range from dramatic classics at the **Residenztheater** and **Volkstheater** to comic opera at the **Staatstheater am Gärtnerplatz** to experimental works at the **Theater im Marstall** in Nymphenburg. Munich's **opera festival** (in July) is held in the ■**Bayerische Staatsoper** (Bavarian National Theater), Max-Joseph-pl. 2. (Tickets ☎21 85 19 20; recorded info ☎21 85 19 19. Streetcar #19 to Nationaltheater or U3-6 to Odeonspl. Standing-room and student tickets €4-10, sold 1hr. before performance at the side entrance on Maximilianstr. Box office open M-F 10am-6pm, Sa 10am-1pm. No performances Aug. to mid-Sept.) *Monatsprogramm* (€1.50) and *Munich Found* (€3) both list schedules for Munich's stages, museums, and festivals. Munich reveals its bohemian face in scores of small fringe theaters, cabaret stages, and art cinemas in **Schwabing.**

Munich's nightlife is a curious collision of Bavarian *Gemütlichkeit* ("warmth") and trendy cliquishness. The odyssey begins at one of Munich's beer gardens or beer halls, which generally close before midnight and are most crowded in the early evening. The alcohol keeps flowing at cafes and bars, which, except for Friday and Saturday nights, close their taps at 1am. Discos and dance clubs, sedate before midnight, throb relentlessly until 4am. The trendy spots along **Leopoldstraße** in **Schwabing** attract tourists from all over Europe. Many of these venues require you to at least attempt the jaded hipster look, and the Munich fashion police generally frown on shorts, sandals, and t-shirts.

GERMANY

BEER GARDENS (BIERGÄRTEN)

The six great Munich labels are *Augustiner, Hacker-Pschorr, Hofbräu, Löwenbräu, Paulaner,* and *Spaten-Franziskaner;* but most restaurants and *Gaststätte* have picked a side and only serve one brewery's beer. There are four main types of beer served in Munich: **Helles** (light), **Dunkles** (dark), **Weißbier** (cloudy blond beer made from wheat instead of barley), and **Radler** ("cyclist's brew;" half beer and half lemon soda). Saying *"Ein Bier, bitte"* will get you a liter, known as a *Maß* (€4-6). Specify if you want only a *halb-Maß* (€3-4).

■ Augustinerkeller, Arnulfstr. 52, at Zirkus-Krone-Str. Any S-Bahn to Hackerbrücke. Founded in 1824, Augustiner is viewed by most *Müncheners* as the finest beer garden in town. Lush grounds, 100-year-old chestnut trees, and the delicious, sharp Augustiner beer (*Maß* €5.70) support their assertion. Open daily 10:30am-1am.

Hirschgarten, Hirschgarten 1. Streetcar #17 (dir.: Amalienburgstr.) to Romanpl. The largest beer garden in Europe (seating 9000) is boisterous and pleasant but somewhat remote, near Schloß Nymphenburg. *Maß* €5.30. Open daily 9am-midnight.

Hofbräuhaus, Platzl 9, 2 blocks from Marienpl. Many tables are reserved for locals— some even keep their personal steins in the hall's safe. To avoid tourists, go in the early afternoon. *Maß* €6. *Weißwürste* with pretzel €3.70. Open daily 9am-midnight.

BARS

■ Nachtcafe, Maximilianspl. 5. U4 or 5 or any S-Bahn to Karlspl. Live jazz, funk, soul, and blues until the wee hours. Very *schicki-micki* (yuppie). Things don't get rolling until midnight. No cover, but prices are outrageous; do your drinking beforehand. Very picky dress code on weekends. Live music 11pm-4am. Open daily 9pm-6am.

Reitschule, Königinstr. 34. U3 or 6 to Giselastr. A sleek bar with marble tables, as well as a cafe with a beer garden out back. *Weißbier* €3. Open daily 9am-1am.

Sausalitos, Im Tal 16. Any U-Bahn to Marienpl. Mexican bar and restaurant hopping with a 20-something crowd. Drinks €6-9. Open daily 11am-late.

CLUBS

■ Kunstpark Ost, Grafinger Str. 6. U5 or any S-Bahn to Ostbahnhof; follow signs for the Kunstpark Ost exit. A huge complex containing 40 different venues swarming with parties. Try the standard **MilchBar** (open M, W-F); the psychedelic-trance **Natraj Temple** (open F-Sa); the alternative cocktail bar and disco **K41** (open nightly, Th 80s night); or the risque South American rock bar **Titty Twister** (open W-Sa). Hours, cover, and themes vary—check www.kunstpark.de for details.

Nachtwerk, Club, and Tanzlokal, Landesberger Str. 185. Streetcar #18 or 19 or bus #83 to Lautensackstr. **Nachtwerk** spins mainstream dance tunes for sweaty crowds in a packed warehouse. **Club** offers a 2-level dance floor just as tight and swinging as its neighbor. **Tanzlokal** (open F-Sa) has hip-hop on F. Beer €2.50 at all venues. Cover €5.50. Open daily 10pm-4am.

Ballhaus, Domagkstr. 33, in the Alabamahalle. U6 to Heide. Free shuttle from there to the club. On a former military base in Schwabing with 3 other discos. Start out in the beer garden, which opens 8pm. **Alabama** serves free drinks all night Sa and until 1am F (open F 9pm-4am, Sa 10pm-5am). **Tempel Club** has typical pop music (open Sa 10pm-4am) and **Schwabinger Ballhouse** plays international jams. (Drinks €1.50-3. Cover €8. Open F-Sa 10pm-5am.)

GAY AND LESBIAN MUNICH

Although Bavaria has the reputation of being less welcoming to homosexuality, Munich sustains a respectably vibrant gay nightlife. The center of the gay scene is in the **Glockenbachviertel,** stretching from the area south of the Sendlinger Tor through the Viktualienmarkt/Gärtnerpl. area to the Isartor. *Our Munich*, Munich's gay and lesbian leaflet, is available at the tourist office, while *Sergej* is available at many gay locales, including **Max&Milian Bookstore,** Ickstattstr. 2 (open M-F 10:30am-2pm and 3:30-8pm, Sa 11am-4pm).

▓ **Bei Carla,** Buttermelcherstr. 9. Any S-Bahn to Isartor. Walk 1 block south on Zweibrück-enstr., take a right on Rumfordstr., turn left on Klenzestr., then left again onto Butter-melcherstr. One of Munich's best-kept secrets. Open M-Sa 4pm-1am, Su 6pm-1am.

Soul City, Maximilianspl. 5, at the intersection with Max-Joseph-Str. Purportedly the big-gest gay disco in Bavaria; music ranges from disco to Latin to techno. Straights always welcome. Cover €5-13. Open W-Sa 10pm-late.

▶ DAYTRIPS FROM MUNICH

DACHAU. *"Arbeit Macht Frei"* ("work will set you free") was the first thing prisoners saw as they entered Dachau; it's written over the gate of the Jourhaus, formerly the only entry to the camp. Dachau was primarily a work camp (rather than a death camp, like Auschwitz). During the war, prisoners made armaments in Dachau because the SS knew that the Allies would not bomb a concentration camp. Although Dachau has a gas chamber, it was never actually used because the prisoners purposely made mistakes and worked slowly in order to delay completion. Once tightly packed barracks are now, for the most part, only foundations; however, survivors ensured that at least two barracks would be reconstructed to teach future generations about the 206,000 prisoners who were interned here from 1933 to 1945. The walls, gates, and cre-matorium have been restored since 1962 in a chillingly sparse memorial to the victims of Dachau. The museum, located in the former administrative buildings, examines pre-1930s anti-Semitism, the rise of Nazism, the establishment of the concentration camp system, and the lives of prisoners through photographs, documents, and artifacts. The thick guide (€26) translates the propaganda posters, SS files, documents, and letters. Most exhibits are accompanied by short captions in English. A **short film** (22min.) is screened in English at 11:30am, 2pm, and 3:30pm. A new display in the Bunker, the concentration camp's prison and torture chamber, chronicles the lives of the camp's prisoners and the barbarism of SS guards. Lengthy (2hr.) **tours** in English leave from the museum. (June-Aug. daily 12:30pm; Sept.-May Sa-Su 12:30pm. Free, but donation requested. Camp open Su and Tu-Sa.)

From Munich, take S2 (dir.: Petershausen) to Dachau (20min.; €4, or 4 stripes on the Streifenkarte), then bus #724 (dir.: Kraütgarten) or 726 (dir.: Koperni-kusstr.) to KZ-Gedenkstätte (10min.; €1, or 1 stripe on the Streifenkarte).

GARMISCH-PARTENKIRCHEN   ☎08821

The **Zugspitze** (2964m), Germany's tallest mountain, is the main attraction in Garmisch-Partenkirchen (pop. 28,000). There are three ways to conquer it, and all of them are weather-dependent. You can take the **cog railway** from the **Zugspitzbahnhof** (behind the Garmisch main station) to *Eibsee* (1¼hr., every hr. 8:15am-3:15pm), then continue on the **Gletscherbahn** or the steeper **Eibsee Seilbahn** cable car to the top (1½hr., every hr. 8am-3:15pm, round-trip with train and either cable car €42). Experienced climbers can make the semi-technical ascent in 10-12hrs., although surrounding peaks may be of more interest.

From Garmisch-Partenkirchen, **trains** run to Munich (1½hr., 1 per hr., €14) and Innsbruck (1½hr., 1 per hr., €10). **Buses** #1084 and 9606 go to Füssen (2hr., 6-7 per day, €7). To get to the **tourist office,** Richard-Strauss-Pl. 2, turn left on Bahnhofstr. from the train station and turn left again onto Von-Brug-Str.; it's the pink building on the square. The staff distributes maps and will help find rooms for free. (☎18 07 00. Open M-Sa 8am-6pm, Su 10am-noon.) To reach ▨**Naturfreundehaus ❶,** Schalmeiweg 21, from the station, walk straight on Bahnhofstr. as it becomes Ludwigstr., follow the bend to the right and turn left on Sonnenbergstr., and continue straight as this becomes Prof. Michael-Sachs-Str. and then Schalmeiweg (25min.). At this cozy hostel, you can sleep in attic lofts with up to 16 other backpackers. (☎43 22. Kitchen use €0.50. Reception daily 6-8pm. Loft dorm beds €8; 3- to 5-bed dorms €10.) **HL Markt,** at the intersection of Bahnhofstr. and Von-Brug-Str., sells groceries. (Open M-F 8am-8pm, Sa 7:30am-4pm.) **Postal Code:** 82467.

THE CHIEMSEE   ☎08051

The region's dramatic crescent of mountains and its picturesque islands, forests, and marshland have lured visitors for 2000 years. Today, prices have risen and the area has been overrun by resorts for the German *nouveaux riches.* Prien, the largest lake town, offers easy access to resort paradises Aschau and Sachrang, ski areas of the Kampenwand, and the surrounding curtain of mountains.

PRIEN AM CHIEMSEE. Located on the southwestern corner of the Chiemsee, Prien is a good base for exploring the islands. **Trains** depart from the station, a few blocks from the city center, for Munich (1hr., every hr., €12.40) and Salzburg (50min., 1 per hr., €9). **Ferries** run from Prien to Herreninsel and Fraueninsel (every 40min., 7:15am-7:30pm, €6-7). To get to the ferry port, turn right from the main entrance of the Prien train station and follow Seestr. for 20min., or hop on the green *Chiemseebahn* steam train from the station (10am-6pm, every hr., round-trip €4). The **tourist office,** Alte Rathausstr. 11, dispenses maps and books private rooms for free. (☎690 50. Open M-F 8:30am-6pm, Sa 8:30am-noon.) The **Jugendherberge (HI) ❷,** Carl-Braun-Str. 66, is a 20min. walk from the station; go right on Seestr. and turn left on Staudenstr., which becomes Carl-Braun-Str. (☎687 70. Breakfast, showers, and lockers included. Reception 8-9am, 5-7pm, and 9:30-10pm. Open early Feb.-Nov. Dorms €16.) To reach **Campingpl. Hofbauer ❶,** Bernauer Str. 110, from the station, turn left on Seestr., left again at the next intersection, and then walk 25min. along Bernauerstr. heading out of town. (☎41 36. Showers included. Reception 7:30-11am and 2-8pm. Open Apr.-Oct. €6 per person, €5.10 per campsite.) Grab a cheap meal at **Bäckerei/Cafe Müller ❷,** Marktpl. 8. (Open M-F 6:30am-6pm, Sa 6:30am-12:30pm, Su 7:30-10:30am.)

HERRENINSEL AND FRAUENINSEL. Ludwig's palace on ▨**Herreninsel** (Gentlemen's Island), **Königsschloß Herrenchiemsee,** is a shameless attempt to be larger, better, and more extravagant than Louis XIV's Versailles. Ludwig bankrupted Bavaria building this place—a few unfinished rooms (abandoned after funds

YOUR OWN WAY

CASTLES OF GERMANY

So **Neuschwanstein** (p. 491) whet your appetite and you want to tour like Teutonic nobility?

10. Jugendherberge Stahleck, Bacharach. Hostels don't get any better than this: Stay in a 12th-century castle overlooking the Rhine for €15 per night (p. 467).

9. Schloß Gottorf, Schleswig. A former Viking stronghold now holds six museums (p. 455).

8. Moritzburg, Dresden. A huge palace full of hunting trophies on a custom-made island (p. 440).

7. Wilhelmshöhe, Kassel. A mad prince, artificial ruins, and a 350 ft. statue of Hercules (p. 463).

6. Heidelberger Schloß, Heidelberg. This fortress guards Germany's oldest university and largest wine barrel (p. 469).

5. Burg Rheinfels, St. Goar. Bring a candle to explore the ruined underground passages (p. 468).

4. Schloß Hohenschwangau, Füssen. The royal bedroom is inlaid with thousands of crystals to replicate the night sky (p. 490).

3.Schloß Sanssouci, Potsdam. A French-named English garden near Germany's capitol (p. 439).

2. Wartburg, Eisenach. Deep in the Thuringian forest, this fortress inspired Bach, Goethe, Martin Luther, and Wagner (p. 447).

1. Schloß Linderhof, Oberommergau. The hunting lodge for a king who has everything: Complete with mosque, half-ton chandeliers and a man-made grotto.

ran out) contrast greatly with the completed portion of the castle. (Open Apr.-Sept. daily 9am-6pm; Oct. 9:40am-5pm; Nov.-Mar. 9:40am-4pm. Required tour €5.50, students €4.50.) **Fraueninsel** (Ladies' Island) is home to the **Klosterkirche** (Island Cloister), the convent that complemented the monastery on Herreninsel. The nuns make their own marzipan, beeswax candles, and five kinds of liqueur, all sold in the convent shop. The 8th-century **Cross of Bischofhofen** and other religious artifacts are displayed in the Michaelskapelle above the **Torhalle** (gate), the oldest surviving part of the cloister. (Open May-Oct. 11am-5pm. €2.)

BERCHTESGADEN. The area's natural beauty and the sinister attraction of **Kehlsteinhaus** ("Eagle's Nest"), Hitler's mountaintop retreat, draw world travelers to the town. The stone resort house, now a restaurant, has a spectacular view from the 1834m peak. From the train station, take bus #38 to *Kehlstein Busabfahrt* (7am-6pm, every 45min.); then catch bus #49 to *Kehlstein Parkpl.* (June-Oct. every 30min. 9:30am-4pm, €15.) Be sure to reserve your spot for the return bus when you get off. (Open May-Oct. daily except heavy snow days.) **Trains** run every hr. to Munich (3hr., €25) and Salzburg (1hr., €6.60). The **tourist office,** Königsseerstr. 2, opposite the station, has tips on **hiking** trails in the Berchtesgaden National Park. (☎96 71 50. Open mid-June to Oct. M-F 8:30am-6pm, Sa 9am-5pm, Su 9am-3pm; Nov. to mid-June M-F 8:30am-5pm, Sa 9am-noon.) To get to the **Jugendherberge (HI) ❷,** Gebirgsjägerstr. 52, turn right from the station, left on Ramsauer Str., right on Gmündbrücke, and left up the steep gravel path. You can also take bus #39 (dir.: Strub Kaserne). (☎943 70. Breakfast included. Reception 6:30-9am and 5-7pm. Check in until 10pm. Curfew midnight. Closed Nov.-Dec. 26. Dorms €16.) For groceries, stop by the **Edeka Markt,** Königsseerstr. 22. (Open M-F 7:30am-6pm, Sa 7:30am-noon.) The nearby **Bäckerei-Konditorei Ernst,** Königseer Str. 10, has fresh bread and pastries. (Open M-F 6:30am-6pm, Sa 6:30am-noon.) **Postal Code:** 83471.

⚑ HIKING NEAR BERCHTESGADEN. From Berchtesgaden, the 5½km path to the **Königssee**—which winds through fields of flowers, across bubbling brooks, and past several beer gardens—affords a heart-stopping view of the Alps. From the train station, cross the street, turn right, and take a quick left over the bridge. Walk to the right of and past the green-roofed building (but not up the hill) and take a left onto the gravel path near the stone wall, then follow the Königssee signs. Alternatively, take bus #41

from the bus station to *Königssee* (round-trip €3.70). Once you arrive in König-
stein, walk down Seestr. and look for the *Nationalpark Informationstelle* to
your left, which has hiking info. To explore the **Berchtesgaden National Park,** take
bus #46 from Berchtesgaden (15min., 6:10am-7:25pm, €2.10). Get off at *Neu-
hausenbrücke* in Ramsau, and head to the **tourist office,** Im Tal 2, for hiking maps.
(☎ (08657) 98 89 20. Open July-Sept. M-Sa 8am-noon and 1-5pm, Su 9am-noon and
2-5pm; Oct.-June M-F 8am-noon and 1-5pm.)

PASSAU   ☎ 0851

This beautiful 2000-year-old city (pop. 51,000) embodies the ideal image of Old-
World Europe. The capstone of Passau is the Baroque **Stephansdom,** Dompl.,
where cherubs sprawl across the ceiling and the world's largest church organ,
with 17,774 pipes, looms above the choir. (Open in summer daily 6:30am-7pm;
off-season 6:30am-6pm. Free. Organ concerts May-Oct. M-F noon, Th also 7:30pm.
€3-5, students €1-3.) Behind the cathedral is the **Residenz,** home to the **Domschatz,**
an extravagant collection of gold and tapestries. (Enter through the back of the
Stephansdom, to the right of the altar. Open Easter-Oct. M-Sa 10am-4pm. €1.50,
students €0.50.) The heights of the river during various floods are marked on the
outside wall of the 13th-century Gothic **Rathaus.** (Open Apr.-Oct. daily 10am-4pm.
€1.50, students €1.) Over the Luitpoldbrücke is the former palace of the bishopric, now home to the **Cultural History Museum.** (Open Apr. to Oct. M-F 9am-5pm,
Sa-Su 10am-6pm; Nov.-Mar. Su and Tu-Sa 9am-5pm. €4, students €2.50.)

   Trains depart for: Frankfurt (4½hr., every 2hr., €65); Munich (2hr., every 2hr.,
€27); Nuremberg (2hr., every 2hr., €31); and Vienna (3½hr., 1 per hr., €31). To get
to the **tourist office,** Rathauspl. 3, follow Bahnhofstr. from the train station to Ludwigspl., and bear left downhill across Ludwigspl. to Ludwigstr., which becomes
Rindermarkt, Steinweg, and finally Große Messerg.; continue straight on
Schusterg. and turn left on Schrottg. (☎ 95 59 80. Open Easter to mid-Oct. M-F
8:30am-6pm, Sa-Su 9:30am-3pm; mid-Oct. to Easter M-Th 8:30am-5pm, F 8:30am-
4pm.) High above the Danube in a castle, the **Jugendherberge (HI) ❷,** Veste Oberhaus
125, is 30min. from the station. Cross the bridge downstream from the *Rathaus*
and follow the signs. (☎ 49 37 80. Breakfast included. Dorms €16.) Closer to the
center, the homey **Pension Rößner ❸,** Bräug. 19, is downstream from the *Rathaus.*
(☎ 93 13 50. Breakfast included. Singles €35; doubles €50-60.) The student district
around **Innstraße,** parallel to the Inn River, is lined with good, cheap places to eat.
Pick up groceries at **Normas supermarket,** Bahnhofstr. 16b. Get meat, baked goods,
sandwiches, and salads at **Schmankerl Passage ❷,** Ludwigstr. 6. (Open M-F
7:30am-6pm, Sa 7:30am-2pm.) **Postal Code:** 94032.

REGENSBURG   ☎ 0941

Regensburg (pop. 127,000) is teeming with students and the places that feed,
souse, and engage them in their idle hours. The city is reputed to have more cafes
and bars per square meter than any other city in Europe. The **Dom St. Peter** dazzles
with richly colored stained glass. Inside, the **Domschatz** (Cathedral Treasury) displays gold and jewels purchased by the bishops, as well as the preserved hand of
Bishop Chrysostomus, who died in AD 407. (Open Apr.-Oct. daily 6:30am-6pm;
Nov.-Mar. 6:30am-5pm. Free.) A few blocks away, the **Rathaus** served as capital of
the Holy Roman Empire until 1803. Downriver from Regensburg, **Walhalla** is an
imitation Parthenon honoring Ludwig I's favorite Germans. Take the ferry or bus
#5 from Albertspl. to *Donaustauf Walhallastr.* **⬛Historische Wurstküche,** Thun-
dorfer Str., an 850-year-old beer garden, is ideal for sipping brew (0.5L €2.60)
while watching ships drift by on the Danube. Check bulletin boards around campus for student parties, which are usually free and open to all.

Trains to: Munich (1½hr., every hr., €20); Nuremberg (1-1½hr., 1-2 per hr., €14); and Passau (1-1½hr., every hr., €17). The **tourist office** is in the *Altes Rathaus*. From the station, walk down Maximilianstr., turn left on Grasg., turn right at the end onto Obere Bachg., and follow it for 5 blocks. (☎507 44 10. Open Apr.-Oct. M-F 9am-6pm, Sa 9am-4pm, Su 9:30am-4pm; Nov.-March M-F 9am-6pm, Sa 9am-4pm, Su 9:30am-2:30pm.) To get to the **Jugendherberge (HI) ❷**, Wöhrdstr. 60, walk from the station to the end of Maximilianstr., turn right on Pflugg., and then left at the *Optik* sign onto tiny Erhardig.; at the end, take the steps down, walk left over the bridge, and veer right onto Wöhrdstr. Or, take bus #3, 8, or 9 (€1.50) from the station. (☎574 02. Breakfast included. Reception daily 3pm-midnight. Dorms €17.) **Hinterhaus ❷**, Rote-Hahnen-Gasse 2, serves cheese and meat dishes. (Entrees €4-9. Open daily 6pm-1am.) There's a **supermarket** in the basement of Galeria Kaufhof, on Neupfarrpl. (Open M-F 9am-8pm, Sa 9am-4pm.) **Postal Code:** 93047.

NUREMBERG (NÜRNBERG)   ☎0911

Nuremberg (pop. 491,000) once hosted massive Nazi rallies; the Allies later chose it as the site of the post-war tribunals. Today, townspeople have forged a new image for their city as the *Stadt der Menschenrechte* (City of Human Rights). Locally, Nuremberg is known more for its Christmas market (Nov. 26-Dec. 24, 2004), toy fair, sausages, and gingerbread than its politics.

🖛🔂 TRANSPORTATION AND PRACTICAL INFORMATION. Trains go to: Berlin (6hr., every 2hr., €78-120); Frankfurt (3½hr., 2 per hr., €36-55); Munich (2½hr., 2 per hr., €38); and Stuttgart (2¾hr., 6 per day, €28). DB Reisezentrum, located in the central hall of the station, sells tickets. (Open daily 6am-9:30pm.) The **tourist office**, Königstr. 93, books rooms for free. Walk through the tunnel from the station to the *Altstadt* and take a right. (☎233 61 31. Open M-Sa 9am-7pm.) **Internet** is available at **Flat-s,** on the second floor of the train station. (€1 per 15min. Open M-Th 7am-11pm, F-Su 24hr.) **Postal Code:** 90402.

🖛🔂 ACCOMMODATIONS AND FOOD. 🏠Jugendgästehaus (HI) ❸, Burg 2, is in a castle above the city. From the tourist office, follow Königstr. through Lorenzerpl. and over the bridge to the Hauptmarkt. Head toward the fountain on the left and go right on Burgstr., then head up the hill. (☎230 93 60. Reception 7am-1am. Dorms €20.) When in town, Hitler would stay at **Deutscher Hof ❹**, Frauentorgraben 29, only 400m from the station. (☎249 40. Breakfast included. Singles €39, doubles €52.) In the southwest corner of the *Altstadt*, **🍴Zum Goldener Stern ❷**, Zirkelschmiedgasse 26, is the oldest bratwurst kitchen in the world. (Six bratwurst €6. Open daily 11am-10pm.) **Sushi Glas ❸,** Kornmarkt 7, next to the National Museum, attracts a chic yuppie crowd with delicious Japanese specialties. (Open M-W noon-11pm, Th-Sa noon-midnight, Su 6-11pm.) **Edeka,** Hauptmarkt 12, near Frauenkirche, sells groceries. (Open M-F 8:30am-7pm, Sa 8am-3pm.)

🔂🔂 SIGHTS AND ENTERTAINMENT. Allied bombing left little of old Nuremberg for posterity, but its churches, castle, and other buildings have all been reconstructed. The walled-in **Handwerkerhof** near the station is more medieval than mall; head up Königstr. for the real sights. Take a detour to the left for the pillared **Straße der Menschenrechte** ("Avenue of Human Rights") as well as the **Germanisches Nationalmuseum,** Kartäuserg. 1, which chronicles German art from pre-history to the present. (Open Su, Tu and Th-Sa 10am-6pm, W 10am-9pm. €5, students €4. W 6-9pm free.) Across the river is the **Hauptmarktplatz,** site of the annual **Christmas market.** Hidden in the fence of the **Schöner Brunnen** (Beautiful Fountain) in the Hauptmarkt is a seamless gold-colored ring; spinning it brings good luck. Walk uphill to the **Rathaus;** the **Lochgefängnisse** (dungeons) beneath contain medieval torture instruments. (Open Su and Tu-Sa 10am-4:30pm. Required tours every 30min. €2, students €1.) Atop the hill, the **Kaiserburg** (emperor's fortress), Nuremberg's symbol, offers the best vantage point of the city. (Open Apr.-Sept. daily 9am-6pm; Oct.-Mar. 10am-4pm. Required tours every 30min. €5, students €4.)

The ruins of **Reichsparteitagsgelände,** site of the Nazi Party Congress rallies, remind visitors of Nuremberg's darker history. On the far side of the lake is the **Tribüne,** the marble platform where throngs gathered to hear Hitler. The "Fascination and Terror" exhibit, in the ▣**Kongresshalle,** at the north end of the park, covers the rise of the Third Reich and the war crimes trials. (Open M-F 9am-6pm, Sa-Su 10am-6pm. €5, students €2.50.) To reach the park, take S2 to *Dutzendteich,* then take the middle of three exits, go down the stairs, and turn left. Walk past the lake on your left, turn left, then turn right to reach the Kongresshalle. On the other side of town, Nazi leaders faced Allied judges during the historic Nuremberg war crimes trials, held in room 600 of the **Justizgebäude,** Fürtherstr. 110. (Take U1 to *Bärenschanze.* Tours Sa-Su 1, 2, 3, and 4 pm. €2, students €1.)

Nuremberg's nightspots are clustered around the *Altstadt;* the most popular are in the west, near the river. **Cine Città,** Gewerbemuseumspl. 3, packs in 16 bars and cafes, 17 cinemas, an IMAX theater, and a disco. Take the U-Bahn to *Wöhrder Wiese.* (Open M-Th and Su until 3am, F-Sa until 4am.) **Frizz,** Weißgerberg. 37, swings to oldies and 80s rock. (Cover men €2. Women free. Open M and Th 8pm-2am, F-Sa 8pm-4am.)

ROMANTIC ROAD

Groomed fields of sunflowers and wheat, vineyards, rolling hills, and dense forests checker the landscape between Würzburg and Füssen. It's beauty was not lost on the German tourist industry, which christened the area the Romantic Road (*Romantische Straße*) in 1950; it's now the most traveled route in Germany.

▣ TRANSPORTATION

Europabus runs daily at 10am from bus platform #13 in Würzburg to Füssen via Rothenburg ob der Tauber. (Reservations ☎089 59 38 89; www.euraide.de/romantic. 10% student discount, 60% Eurail and German Railpass discount.) A more flexible and economical way to travel the Romantic Road is by the frequent trains that connect all the towns.

ROTHENBURG OB DER TAUBER. Rothenburg (pop. 12,000) is *the* Romantic Roadstop. After the Thirty Years' War, the town had no money to modernize; it remained unchanged for 250 years. When it became a tourist destination at the end of the 19th century, new laws protected the integrity of the medieval *Altstadt;* today, Rothenburg is probably your only chance to see a walled medieval city without a single modern building. After the war, the conquering general promised to spare the town from destruction if any local could chug a wine keg (3.25L). The mayor successfully met the challenge, then passed out for several days. The **Meistertrunk** is reenacted each year, and the town clock performs a slow motion version every hour over the Marktpl. For other fascinating tidbits of Rothenburg history, take the 1hr. English tour led by the ▣**night watchman,** which starts from the Rathaus. (Easter-Christmas daily 8pm. €3.)

The 60m tower of the Renaissance **Rathaus,** on Marktpl., provides a panoramic view of the town. (Open Apr.-Oct. daily 9:30am-12:30pm and 1-5pm; Nov. and Jan-Mar. noon-3pm, Dec. Sa-Su only noon-3pm. €1.) The ■**Medieval Crime Museum,** Burgg. 3, exhibits tools of torture for anyone who can stomach the thought of iron-maiden justice. (Open Apr.-Oct. daily 9:30am-6pm; Nov. and Jan.-Feb. 2-4pm; Dec. and Mar. 10am-4pm. €3, students €2.) Head to **Christkindlmarkt** (Christ Child Market), Herrng. 2, and **Weihnachtsdorf** (Christmas Village), Herrng. 1, which houses a **Christmas Museum** documenting the evolution of gift-giving. (Open Jan. to mid-May M-F 9am-6:30pm, Sa 9am-4pm; mid-May to Dec. also Su 11am-6pm.)

Trains run to and from Steinach (15min., €1.75), where you can transfer to trains for Würzburg and Munich. The **Europabus** leaves from the *Busbahnhof*, next to the train station. The **tourist office,** Marktpl. 2, books rooms. (☎404 92. Open May-Oct. M-F 9am-noon and 1-6pm, Sa 10am-3pm; Nov.-Apr. M-F 9am-noon and 1-5pm, Sa 10am-1pm.) The cheery, spacious rooms of **Gasthof Goldene Rose ❸,** Spitalgasse 28, are on the main street. (☎(09861) 46 38. Singles €21-23; doubles €36-62.) Many other private rooms are not registered with the tourist office; look for *Zimmer frei* signs and knock on the door to inquire. **Postal Code: 91541.**

WÜRZBURG. The university town of Würzburg is surrounded by vineyard slopes and bisected by the Main River. In 1895, Wilhelm Conrad Röntgen discovered X-rays here and was awarded the first Nobel Prize. Inside the striking **Fortress Marienburg** are the 11th-century **Marienkirche,** the 40m **Bergfried watchtower,** above the Hole of Fear dungeon, and the **Fürstengarten,** built to resemble a ship. Outside the main fortress is the castle arsenal, which now houses the **Mainfränkisches Museum.** (Take bus #9 from the station to *Festung*, or walk 40min. toward the castle on the hill. Tours depart from the main courtyard Apr.-Oct. Tu-F 11am, 2, and 3pm, Sa-Su every hr. 10am-4pm. €2, students €1.50. Museum open Apr.-Oct. Su and Tu-Sa 9am-6pm; Nov.-Mar. 10am-4pm. €2.50/2.) The **Residenz** houses the largest ceiling fresco in the world; the **Residenzhofkirche** inside is a Baroque fantasy of gilding and pink marble. (Open Apr. to mid-Oct. daily 9am-6pm, Th until 8pm; mid-Oct. to Mar. 10am-4pm. €4, students €3. English tours Sa-Su 11am and 3pm.) **Trains** arrive from: Frankfurt (2hr., 2 per hr., €19); Munich (3hr., every hr., €39); Nuremberg (1hr., 2 per hr., €15); and Rothenburg ob der Tauber (1hr., every hr., €9). The **tourist office,** in the yellow Haus zum Falken on the Marktpl., provides maps and helps find rooms. (☎(0931) 37 23 98. Open Apr.-Oct. M-F 10am-6pm, Sa-Su 10am-2pm; Nov.-March M-F 10am-6pm, Sa 10am-2pm.) **Postal Code: 97070.**

FÜSSEN. With its position at the foot of the Romantic Road, in the foothills of the Bavarian Alps, the name Füssen (feet) is apt for this little town. The main attraction of Füssen is its proximity to Ludwig's famed **Königsschlösser** (p. 491). Within the town, the inner walls of the **Hohes Schloß** (High Castle) courtyard feature arresting *trompe-l'oeil* windows and towers, and the **Staatsgalerie** in the castle shelters a collection of regional art. (Open Apr.-Oct. Su and Tu-Sa 11am-4pm; Nov.-Mar. Su and Tu-Sa 2-4pm. €2.50, students €2.) Inside the **Annakapelle,** macabre paintings depict everyone from the Pope and Emperor to the smallest child engaged in the *Totentanz* (death dance), a public frenzy of despair that overtook Europe during the plague. (Open Apr.-Oct. Su and Tu-Sa 10am-5pm; Nov.-Mar. Su and Tu-Sa 1-4pm. €2.50, students €2.)

Trains run to Munich (2hr., every 2hr., €19). Füssen can also be reached by **bus** #1084 or 9606 from Garmisch-Partenkirchen (2¼hr., 5 per day, €7). To get from the train station to the **tourist office,** Kaiser-Maximilian-Pl. 1, walk the length of Bahnhofstr. and head across the roundabout to the big yellow building on your left. The staff finds **rooms** for free and sells hiking maps. (☎08362 93 85 32. Open Apr.-Sept. M-F 8:30am-6:30pm, Sa 9am-12:30pm, Su 10am-noon; Oct.-Mar. M-F 9am-5pm, Sa 10am-noon.) **Postal Code:** 87629.

KÖNIGSSCHLÖßER (ROYAL CASTLES). King Ludwig II, a zany visionary and fervent Wagner fan, used his cash to create fantastic castles. In 1886, a band of nobles and bureaucrats deposed Ludwig, declared him insane, and imprisoned him. Three days later, the King and a loyal advisor were mysteriously discovered dead in a nearby lake. The fairy tale castles that framed Ludwig's life and the enigma of his death still captivate tourists today. The glitzy ◪**Schloß Neuschwanstein** is Germany's most clichéd tourist attraction and was the inspiration for Disney's Sleeping Beauty Castle. The completed chambers (63 remain unfinished) include a Byzantine throne room, a small artificial grotto, and an immense *Sängersaal* (singer's hall) built expressly for performances of Wagnerian operas. For the fairy godmother of all views, hike 10min. up to ◪**Marienbrücke**, a bridge that spans the gorge and waterfall behind the castle. Ludwig summered in the bright yellow, neo-Gothic **Schloß Hohenschwangau** across the valley. (Both open Apr.-Sept. daily 9am-6pm; Oct.-Mar. 10am-4pm. Mandatory tours €7 per castle; combination ticket €13.) Tickets can be purchased at the **Ticket-Service Center,** Alpseestr. 12 (☎08362 93 08 30), about 100m south of the Hohenschwangau bus stop.

From Füssen, hop on **bus** #73 or 78 marked Königsschlösser, which departs from the train station (10min., 2 per hr., €1.40). It drops you in front of the info booth (open daily 9am-6pm); the Ticket-Service Center is a short walk uphill on Alpseestr. Separate paths lead up to both Hohenschwangau and Neuschwanstein. A *Tagesticket* (€5.60; buy from the bus driver) gives unlimited regional bus use.

GREECE (Ελλας)

A land where sacred monasteries are mountainside fixtures, three-hour seaside siestas are standard issue, and dancing on tables until daybreak is a summer rite—Greece's treasures are impossibly varied. Much of the history of the Western world owes its character to the philosophical, literary, artistic, and athletic mastery of the ancient Greeks. Schoolkids still dream of Hercules and Medusa, only to long later for Greece's island beaches and its gorgeous natural landscape, once the playground of a pantheon of gods. The all-encompassing Greek lifestyle is a mix of high speed traveling and sun-inspired lounging: Old men hold lively debates in town *plateias*, mopeds skid through the streets around the clock, and unpredictable schedules force a go-with-the-flow approach to life.

FACTS AND FIGURES

Official Name: Hellenic Republic.

Capital: Athens.

Major Cities: Thessaloniki.

Population: 10,600,000.

Land Area: 131,940 sq. km.

Time: GMT+2.

Language: Greek.

Religion: Eastern Orthodox (98%).

DISCOVER GREECE

Make the sprawl of **Athens** (p. 496) more manageable by hitting the highlights: the **Acropolis,** the **National Museum,** a sunset atop **Lycavittos,** a night clubbing in **Glyfada,** and a trip to **Cape Sounion;** during the summer of 2004, drop by the **Olympic Games.** Greece's second-largest and less-touristed city, **Thessaloniki** (p. 510), home to both trendy shopping and some of Byzantium's most precious ruins, will give you a taste of authentic Greek life. Spend a few days on the lovely island of **Corfu** (p. 515), immortalized by Edward Lear, Oscar Wilde, and sun-hungry partiers, or indulge in hedonism for nights on end on **Mykonos** (p. 518) or **Ios** (p. 520). For a quieter trip, climb up to the cliffside monasteries of **Meteora** (p. 514), commune with the ancient gods at **Mount Olympus** (p. 514), and hike through Europe's longest gorge, **Samaria** (p. 522). Finally, reflect on your travels at the awe-inspiring **Temple of Apollo** on the sacred isle of **Delos** (p. 519).

ESSENTIALS

WHEN TO GO

June through August is high season in Greece; consider visiting during May or September, when the weather is equally beautiful but the crowds thinner. The low season, from mid-September through May, offers cheaper airfares and lodging, but many sights and accommodations have shorter hours or close altogether. Ferries and trains run considerably less frequently, although ski areas at Mt. Parnassos, Mt. Pelion, and Metsovo beckon winter visitors.

DOCUMENTS AND FORMALITIES

VISAS. EU citizens do not need a visa. Citizens of Australia, Canada, New Zealand, the UK, and the US do not need a visa for stays of up to 90 days, though they are ineligible for employment. Citizens of South Africa need a visa for stays of any length.

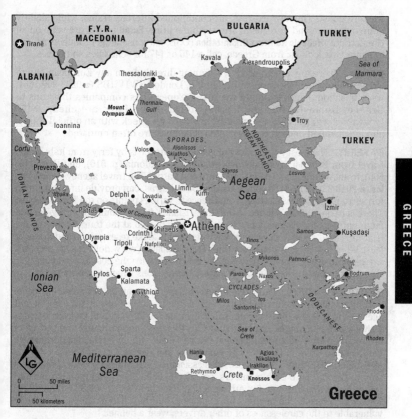

GREECE

EMBASSIES. Foreign embassies in Greece are in Athens (p. 496). For Greek embassies at home, contact: **Australia,** 9 Turrana St., Yarralumla, Canberra, ACT 2600 (☎02 6273 3011); **Canada,** 80 MacLaren St., Ottawa, ON K2P 0K6 (☎613-238-6271; www.greekembassy.ca); **Ireland,** 1 Upper Pembroke St., Dublin 2 (☎01 676 7254); **South Africa,** 1003 Church St., Hatfield, Arcadia-Pretoria 0028 (☎12 437 3523); **UK,** 1a Holland Park, London W11 3TP (☎020 7229 3850); and **US,** 2221 Massachusetts Ave. N.W., Washington, D.C. 20008 (☎202-939-1300; www.greekembassy.org).

TRANSPORTATION

BY PLANE. The domestic service offered by **Olympic Airways,** Syngrou 96-100, Athens 11741 (☎2810 114 4444; www.olympic-airways.gr), has increased greatly. Their website lists information for every office around the globe. A 1hr. flight from Athens (€60-90) can get you to almost any island in Greece. Even in the low season, remote destinations are serviced several times per week, while developed areas may have several flights per day.

BY TRAIN. Greece is served by a number of international train routes that connect Athens, Larissa, and Thessaloniki to most European cities. Train service within Greece, however, is limited and sometimes uncomfortable, and no lines go to the western coast. The new express, air-conditioned intercity trains, while slightly more expensive and infrequent, are worth the price. **Eurail** passes are valid on all Greek trains. **Hellenic Railways Organization** (OSE; www.osenet.gr) connects Athens to major Greek cities; from Greece, call ☎145 or 147 for schedules and prices.

BY BUS. There are almost no buses running directly from any European city to Greece. **Busabout,** 258 Vauxhall Bridge Rd., London SW1V 1BS (☎0207 950 1661; www.busabout.com), is one of the few European bus companies that runs to Greece. Domestic bus service is extensive and fares are cheap. **KTEL** (www.ktel.org) runs most domestic buses; always check with an official source about scheduled departures, as posted schedules are often outdated.

BY FERRY. The most popular way of getting to Greece is by ferry from Italy. Boats travel from Brindisi, Italy, to Corfu (p. 515), Kephalonia (p. 516), and Patras (p. 506), from Ancona, Italy (p. 681), to Corfu and Patras. The travel agency **Manolopoulos** (☎2610 223 621), at Othonos Amalias 35 in Patras, can provide information on ferries to Italy. Ferries also run from Greece to various points on the Turkish coast. There is frequent ferry service to the Greek islands, but schedules are irregular and faulty information is common. Check schedules posted at the tourist office or the *limenarcheio* (port police), or at www.ferries.gr. Make reservations and arrive at least 1-2hr. before your departure time. **Flying Dolphins** (www.dolphins.gr) provides extensive hydrofoil service between the islands at twice the cost and speed as ferries; their routes are listed in the **Transportation** sections where appropriate.

BY CAR AND MOPED. Cars are a luxury in Greece, a country where public transportation is nonexistent after 7pm. Ferries charge a transport fee for cars. Rental agencies may quote low daily rates that exclude the 20% tax and **Collision Damage Waiver** (CDW) insurance; expect to pay €20-40 per day for a rental. Foreign drivers are required to have an **International Driving Permit** and an **International Insurance Certificate** to drive in Greece. The **Automobile and Touring Club of Greece** (ELPA), Messogion 395, Athens 11527, provides assistance and offers reciprocal membership to foreign auto club members. (☎210 606 8800. 24hr. emergency roadside assistance ☎104. Info line for Athens ☎174; elsewhere ☎210 606 8838. Open M-F 7am-3pm.) **Mopeds** can be great for exploring, but they also make you extremely vulnerable to the carelessness of other drivers; wear a helmet.

TOURIST SERVICES AND MONEY

EMERGENCY   **Police:** ☎100. **Hospital:** ☎106. **Ambulance:** ☎166.

TOURIST OFFICES. Tourism in Greece is overseen by two national organizations: The **Greek National Tourist Organization** (GNTO) and the **tourist police** *(touristiki astinomia)*. The GNTO, Tsoha 7, Athens (☎210 870 7000. www.gnto.gr), known as the **EOT** in Greece, can supply general information about the country's sights and accommodations. The tourist police (24hr. info ☎171) deal with local and immediate problems: Bus schedules, accommodations, lost passports, etc. They are open long hours and are willing to help, but their English may be limited.

MONEY. The official currency of Greece is the **euro**. The Greek drachma can still be exchanged at a rate of 340.75dr to €1. For exchange rates and more information on the euro, see p. 14. If you're carrying more than €1000 in cash when you enter Greece, you must declare it upon entry. A bare-bones day in Greece, staying at hostels, campgrounds, or *domatia* (rooms to let), and buying food at supermarkets or outdoor food stands, costs about €35. A day with more comforts, like accommodation in a nicer *domatia* or budget hotel, and eating one meal per day in a restaurant, runs €50. There is no **tipping** anywhere except restaurants. Generally, **bargaining** is expected for street wares and in other informal venues, but shop owners whose goods are tagged will consider bargaining rude and disrespectful. The European Union imposes a **value-added tax** (VAT) on goods and services purchased within the EU, which is included in the price. For more info, see p. 16.

COMMUNICATION

PHONE CODES	**Country code: 30. International dialing prefix: 00.** The city code must always be dialed, even when calling from within the city. From outside Greece, dial int'l dialing prefix (see inside back cover) + 30 + local number.

TELEPHONES. The only way to use the phone in Greece is with a prepaid phone card. You can buy the cards at *peripteros* (streetside kiosks) in denominations of €3, €12, and €25. Time is measured in minutes or talk units (100 units=30min. of domestic calling). A calling card is the cheapest way to make international phone calls. To place a call with a calling card, contact your service provider's Greek operator: **AT&T** ☎00 800 1311; **British Telecom** ☎00 800 4411; **Canada Direct** ☎00 800 1611; **Ireland Direct** ☎00 155 1174; **MCI** ☎00 800 1211; **Sprint** ☎00 800 1411. Cell phones are an increasingly popular option; for more info, see p. 36.

MAIL. To send a letter weighing up to 50g within Europe costs €0.85; to send to anywhere else in the world costs €0.90. Mail sent to Greece from the Continent generally takes at least 3 days to arrive; from Australia, the US, and South Africa airmail will take 5-10 days. Address mail to be held according to the following example: First Name SURNAME, Corfu Town Post Office, Corfu, Greece 8900, POSTE RESTANTE.

INTERNET ACCESS. The availability of the Internet in Greece is rapidly expanding. In all big cities, most small cities and large towns, and most of the touristed islands, you will be able to find Internet access. Expect to pay €3-6 per hour. For lists of cybercafes in Greece, check out http://dmoz.org/Computers/Internet/Cybercafes/Greece/.

ACCOMMODATIONS AND CAMPING

GREECE	❶	❷	❸	❹	❺
ACCOMMODATIONS	under €10	€10-25	€26-40	€41-70	over €70

Lodgings in Greece are a bargain. Tourist offices usually maintain lists of inexpensive accommodations. A bed in a **hostel** averages around €7. Those not currently endorsed by HI are in most cases still safe and reputable. In many areas, **domatia** (rooms to let) are an attractive and perfectly dependable option. Often you'll be approached by locals as you enter town or disembark from your boat, a practice that is common, but theoretically illegal. Prices vary; expect to pay €12-20 for a single and €25-35 for a double. Always negotiate with *domatia* owners before settling a price, and never pay more than you would for a hotel in town. If in doubt, ask the tourist police; they may set you up with a room and conduct the negotiations themselves. **Hotel** prices are regulated, but proprietors may try to push you to take the most expensive room. Budget hotels start at €15 for singles and €25 for doubles. Check your bill carefully, and threaten to contact the tourist police if you think you are being cheated. Greece hosts plenty of official **campgrounds,** which run about €4.50 per person, plus €3 per tent. Discreet freelance camping on beaches—though illegal—is common in July and August but may not be the safest way to spend the night.

FOOD AND DRINK

GREECE	❶	❷	❸	❹	❺
FOOD	under €5	€5-10	€11-15	€16-25	over €25

Penny-pinching carnivores will thank Zeus for lamb, chicken, or beef *souvlaki*, stuffed into a pita to make *gyros* (yee-RO). Vegetarians can also eat their fill on the cheap, with *horiatiki* (Greek salad) and savory pastries like *tiropita* (cheese pie) and *spanakopita* (spinach and feta pie). Frothy, iced coffee *frappés* take the edge off the summer heat. *Ouzo*, a powerful, licorice-flavored spirit, is served with *mezedes*, which are snacks of octopus, cheese, and sausage.

Breakfast, served only in the early morning, is generally very simple: A piece of toast with *marmelada* or a pastry. Lunch, a hearty and leisurely meal, can begin as early as noon but is more likely eaten sometime between 2 and 5pm. Dinner is a drawn-out, relaxed affair served late. A Greek restaurant is known as a *taverna* or *estiatorio*; a grill is a *psistaria*. Many restaurants don't offer printed menus.

HOLIDAYS AND FESTIVALS

Holidays: Feast of St. Basil/New Year's Day (Jan. 1); Epiphany (Jan. 6); 1st Monday in Lent (Feb. 23); Greek Independence Day (Mar. 25); Easter (Apr. 11); St. George's Day (Apr. 23); Labor Day (May 1); Ascension (May 20); Pentecost (May 30); Feast of the Assumption of the Virgin Mary (Aug. 15); The Virgin Mary's Birthday (Sept. 8); Feast of St. Demetrius (Oct. 26); Ohi Day (Oct. 28); Christmas Day (Dec. 25).

Festivals: Three weeks of **Carnival** feasting and dancing (starting Feb. 2) precede Lenten fasting. April 23 is **St. George's Day,** when Greece honors the dragon-slaying knight with horse races, wrestling matches, and dances. The **Feast of St. Demetrius** (Oct. 26) is celebrated with particular enthusiasm in Thessaloniki.

ATHENS (Αθηνα) ☎210

Ancient ruins sit quietly amid hectic modern streets as tacit testaments to Athens's rich history, while the Acropolis looms larger than life, a perpetual reminder of ancient glory. Byzantine churches recall an era of foreign invaders, when the city was ruled from Macedonia, Rome, and Constantinople. But the packs of mopeds in Pl. Syndagma prove that Athens refuses to become a museum—over the past two centuries, democracy has revived the city in a wave of madcap construction. The 2004 Olympic Games, to be held in Athens, promises an array of modern landmarks to stand proudly alongside the city's ancient ones.

▮ TRANSPORTATION

Flights: Eleftherios Venizelou (ATH; ☎210 353 0000; www.aia.gr), Greece's new international airport operates as one massive, yet easily navigable terminal. Arrivals are on the ground floor, departures are on the 2nd. The new **suburban rail,** expected to be finished by summer 2004 for the Olympic Games, will serve the international airport from the city center in 30min. 4 bus lines run from the airport to Athens, Piraeus, and Rafina.

Trains: Hellenic Railways (OSE), Sina 6 (☎210 362 4402; www.ose.gr). **Larisis Train Station** (☎210 529 8837) serves northern Greece and Europe. Ticket office open daily 5am-midnight. Take trolley #1 from El. Venizelou (also known as Panepistimiou) in Pl. Syndagma (every 10min. 5am-midnight, €0.50). Trains depart for **Thessaloniki** (7hr., 5 per day, €15). **Peloponnese Train Station** (☎210 513 1601) serves **Olympia** (express: 5½hr., 2 per day, €4.40); **Patras** (4¼hr., 2 per day, €5.30) as well as major towns in the Peloponnese. From Larissis, exit to your right and go over the footbridge.

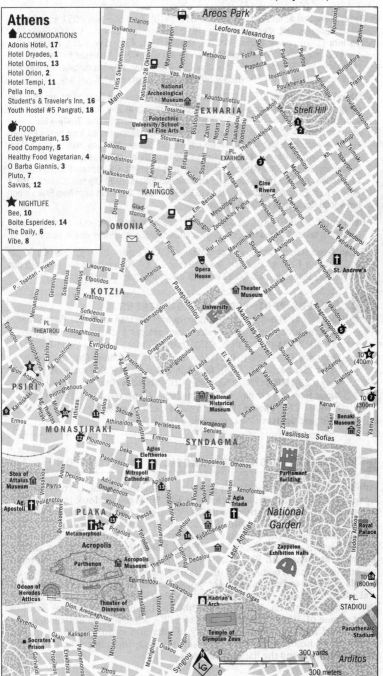

Athens

🏠 ACCOMMODATIONS
Adonis Hotel, **17**
Hotel Dryades, **1**
Hotel Omiros, **13**
Hotel Orion, **2**
Hotel Tempi, **11**
Pella Inn, **9**
Student's & Traveler's Inn, **16**
Youth Hostel #5 Pangrati, **18**

🍴 FOOD
Eden Vegetarian, **15**
Food Company, **5**
Healthy Food Vegetarian, **4**
O Barba Giannis, **3**
Pluto, **7**
Savvas, **12**

⭐ NIGHTLIFE
Bee, **10**
Boite Esperides, **14**
The Daily, **6**
Vibe, **8**

GREECE

Areos Park

0   300 yards
0   300 meters

Buses: Terminal A: Kifissou 100 (☎210 512 4910). Take blue bus #051 from the corner of Zinonos and Menandrou near Pl. Omonia (every 15min., €0.50). Buses to: **Corinth** (1½hr., every 45min., €5.70); **Corfu** (10hr., 4 per day, €28); **Patras** (3hr., every 30 min., €13); **Thessaloniki** (6hr., 11 per day, €28). **Terminal B:** Liossion 260 (☎210 831 7153, M-F only). Take blue bus #024 from Amalias outside the National Gardens (45min., every 20min., €0.50). Buses to **Delphi** (3hr., 6 per day, €11).

Public Transportation: KTEL (ΚΤΕΛ) **buses** around Athens and its suburbs are blue and designated by 3-digit numbers. Buy bus/trolley tickets at any street kiosk. Hold on to your ticket—you can be fined €18-30 by police if caught without one. **Trolleys** are yellow and crowded, sporting 1- or 2-digit numbers; they are distinguished from buses by their electrical antennae. The Athens **Metro** consists of 3 lines. **M1** runs from northern Kifissia to the port of Piraeus. **M2** runs from Sepolia to Dafni. **M3** runs from Ethniki Amyna to Monastiraki in central Athens. Trains run 5am-midnight. Buy tickets (€0.30-0.60) in any station. **Tram:** 2 trams are under construction for the 2004 Olympic Games. **Line 1** will run from Zappeio in Athens Centre to Helliniko. **Line 2** will run from Neo Faliro along the Apollo Coast until Glyfada Square.

Car Rental: Try the places on **Singrou**. €35-50 for a small car with 100km mileage (including tax and insurance). Up to 50% student discount. Prices rise in summer.

Taxis: Meters start at €0.80, with an additional €0.30 per km; midnight-5am €0.50 per km. There's a €2 surcharge from the airport and a €0.70 surcharge for trips from bus and railway terminals, plus €0.30 for each piece of luggage over 10kg.

PIRAEUS PORT: FERRIES FROM ATHENS

The majority of ferries from Athens leave from the town of Piraeus Port. Ferries sail to nearly all Greek islands (except the Sporades and Ionian Islands). Ferries to Crete: **Hania** (9½hr., daily, €18); **Iraklion,** (14hr., 3 per day, €21-26); and **Rethymno** (11hr., daily, €22). Additional ferries to: **Chios** (9hr., daily, €19); **Hydra** (3hr., every hr., €15); **Ios** (7½hr., 2-5 per day, €17); **Lesvos** (12hr., daily, €23); **Milos** (7hr., 2-5 per day, €16); **Mykonos** (6hr., 2-5 per day, €17); **Naxos** (6hr., 2-5 per day, €17); **Paros** (6hr., 2-5 per day, €17); **Poros** (2½hr., every hr., €14); **Rhodes** (15hr., 2-5 per day, €27); **Santorini** (9hr., 2-5 per day, €19); and **Spetses** (4½hr., every hr., €21).

ORIENTATION AND PRACTICAL INFORMATION

Athenian geography mystifies newcomers and natives alike. If you lose your bearings, ask for directions back to well-lit **Syndagma** or look for a cab; the **Acropolis** serves as a reference point, as does **Mt. Lycavittos**. Athens's suburbs occupy seven hills in southwest Attica, near the coast. Syndagma, the central *plateia* containing the Parliament building, is encircled by the other major neighborhoods. Clockwise, they are **Plaka, Monastiraki, Psiri, Omonia, Exarhia, Kolonaki,** and **Pangrati.** Plaka, the center of the old city and home to many accommodations, is bounded by the city's two largest ancient monuments—the **Temple of Olympian Zeus** and the Acropolis. Omonia is the site of the city's central subway station. Two parallel avenues, **Panepistimiou** and **Stadiou,** connect Syndagma to Omonia. Omonia's neighbor to the east, progressive Exarhia, sports some of Athens's most exciting nightlife, while nearby Kolonaki, on the foothills of Mt. Lycavittos, has plenty of glitz and swanky shops. Pangrati, southeast of Kolonaki, is marked by several Byzantine churches, a park, the **Olympic Stadium,** and the **National Cemetery.**

Tourist Office: Tsohas 7 (info booth ☎210 870 7181; main desk ☎210 870 7000; www.gnto.gr.), off of Vas. Sophias in Ambelokipi. Bus, train, and ferry schedules and prices; lists of museums, embassies, and banks; brochures on travel throughout Greece; and an indispensable Athens map. Open M-F 9am-3:30pm. ▧**Philippis Tours,** Akti Tzelepi 3 (☎210 411 7787 or 210 413 3182; filippistours@hotmail.com). Open daily 5:30am-10:30pm. From the Metro, take a left, and walk 200m until you come to Karaskaiki Square. Walk toward the water; it's on the left side of the cluster of offices. Sells ferry and plane tickets, helps with accommodations, rents cars, exchanges money, and stores baggage (free for the day with *Let's Go*).

Banks: National Bank of Greece, Karageorgi Servias 2 (☎210 334 0015), in Pl. Syndagma. Open M-Th 8am-2pm, F 8am-1:30pm; open for **currency exchange** only M-Th 3:30-5:20pm, F 3-6:30pm, Sa 9am-3pm, Su 9am-1pm. Currency exchange available 24hr. at the **airport,** but exchange rates and commissions may be unfavorable.

American Express: Ermou 7 (☎210 322 3380), in Pl. Syndagma. Cashes traveler's checks commission-free, exchanges money, and provides travel services for cardholders. Open M-F 8:30am-4pm, Sa 8:30am-1:30pm.

Laundromats: Most *plintirios* have signs reading "Laundry." **National,** Apollonos 17, in Syndagma. Wash and dry €4.50 per kg. Open M-Th 4:30-8:30pm, F 8am-8pm.

Emergencies: Police: ☎100. **Medical:** ☎105 from Athens, 101 elsewhere; line open daily 2pm-7am. **Ambulance:** ☎166. **Fire:** ☎199. **AIDS Help Line:** ☎210 722 2222. *Athens News* lists emergency hospitals. Free emergency health care for tourists.

Tourist Police: Dimitrakopoulou 77 (☎171). English spoken. Open 24hr.

Pharmacies: Identified by a **green cross** hanging over the street. Many are open 24hr.; check *Athens News* for the day's emergency pharmacy.

Hospitals: Emergency hospitals on duty ☎106. **Geniko Kratiko Nosokomio** (Public State Hospital), Mesogion 154 (☎210 720 1211). **Ygeia,** Erithrou Stavrou 4 (☎210 682 7904), is a private hospital in Maroussi. "Hospital" is *nosokomio* in Greek.

Internet Access:

Berval Travel Internet Access, Voulis 44A (☎210 331 1294), in Plaka near Pl. Syndagma. €6 per hr., students €5 per hr. Open daily 9:30am-8pm.

Bits 'n Bytes Internet, Akademias 78 in Exarhia (between Em. Benaki and Zoodochou Pigis), Kapnikareas 19 in Plaka, Chremonidou 17 in Pangrati. (☎210 382 2545 or 210 330 6590; www.bnb.gr). Fast-connected flat screens in air-conditioned, black-lit joints. Midnight-9am €1.50 per hr., 9am to midnight €2.50 per hr.

easyInternet Cafe, Filellinon 2 (☎210 331 3034) in Syndagma. On the 2nd floor above the Everest fast food eatery, directly across from Pl. Syndagma. 40 high speed, flat screen computers. Rates range from €0.80 to €3 per hr.

Internet Cafe, Stournari 49, in Omonia (☎210 383 8808; www.intergraphics.gr) on 7th floor. Gaze at the city below while checking email (€2 per hr.). Open M-F 9am-9:30pm, Sa 10am-2pm.

Ivis Travel Internet Services, Mitropoleos 3 (☎210 324 3365 or 210 324 3543; fax 210 322 4205). On the 2nd floor of the building across the street from the post office in Syndagma. €2 per hr., €1 min. Open daily 8:30am-10:30pm.

Arcade Internet Cafe, Stadiou 5 (☎210 324 8105; sofos1@ath.forthnet.gr), just up Stadiou from the *plateia* in Syndagma, in a shopping center about 15m from the main thoroughfare. €3 per hr., €0.50 every additional 10min. €1 min. Open M-Sa 9am-11pm, Su 11am-8pm.

Post Office: Syndagma (☎210 322 6253), on the corner of Mitropoleos. Open M-F 7:30am-8pm, Sa 7:30am-2pm. Branch offices in Omonia, at Aiolou 100, and Exarhia, at the corner of Zaimi and K. Deligiani. **Postal Code:** 10022.

GREECE

ACCOMMODATIONS

The **Greek Youth Hostel Association,** Damareos 75 in Pangrati, lists hostels in Greece. (☎210 751 9530; y-hostels@ote.net.gr. Open daily M-F 9am-3pm.) The **Hellenic Chamber of Hotels,** Stadiou 24 in Syndagma, provides info and makes reservations for all types of hotels throughout Greece. Reservations require a cash deposit; you must contact them at least one month in advance and inform them of the length of your stay and the number of people. (☎210 323 7193; grhotels@ote-net.gr. Open May-Nov. M-F 8:30am-1:30pm.)

Student's and Traveler's Inn, Kydatheneon 16 (☎210 324 4808), in Plaka. Unrivaled location and lively atmosphere with A/C, 24hr. restaurant, and around-the-clock cyber cafe. Reserve ahead and arrive on time. Co-ed dorms €17-22; singles €40, with private bath €50; doubles €58/70; triples €75/90; quads €100/120. ❷

Pella Inn, Karaiskaki 1 (☎210 325 0598), in Monastiraki. Walk 10min. down Ermou from Pl. Syndagma; it's two blocks from the Monastiraki subway station. Features a large terrace with impressive views of the Acropolis. Free luggage storage. Dorms €15; doubles €40-50; triples €60; quads €80. ❷

Adonis Hotel, Kodrou 3 (☎210 324 9737), in Plaka. From Syndagma, follow Filellinon; turn right on Nikodimou and left onto Kodrou. A family hotel with a delightful rooftop lounge. Reserve far in advance. All rooms with bath. In summer, singles €41; doubles €56; triples €84. Off-season €29/43/62. A/C €10 extra per person. Discounts for longer stays. ❸

Hotel Tempi, Aiolou 29 (☎210 321 3175), in Monastiraki. Simple rooms with fans. Front-facing rooms are brighter. Luggage storage. Laundry service. Check-out 11am. Singles €32; doubles €42, with bath €48; triples €60. Off-season 20% discount. ❸

Hotel Orion, Em. Benaki 105 (☎210 382 7362), in Exarhia. From Pl. Omonia, walk up Em. Benaki or take bus #230 from Pl. Syndagma. Orion rents small rooms with shared baths. Sunbathers relax on the rooftop. Internet €3 per hr. Laundry €3. Singles €25; doubles €35; triples €40. Bargain for better prices. ❸

Hotel Dryades, Dryadon 4 (☎210 382 7116), in Exarhia. Elegant Dryades offers some of Athens's nicest budget accommodations, with large rooms and private baths. Internet €3 per 30hr. Singles €35; doubles €50; triples €60. ❸

Youth Hostel #5 Pangrati, Damareos 75 (☎210 751 9530). From Omonia or Pl. Syndagma, take trolley #2 or 11 to Filolaou. There's no sign for this cheery hostel, just a green door. Owners speak English. Hot showers €0.50 for 7min. Sheets €0.75; pillowcases €0.50. Laundry €3. Quiet hours 2-5pm and 11pm-7am. Dorms €9. Bring a sleeping bag to stay on the roof (€6). ❶

Hostel Aphrodite, Einardou 12 (☎210 881 0589 or 210 883 9249; www.hostelaphrodite.com), in Omonia. Small, clean rooms with A/C. Free luggage storage. Internet access €6 per hr. Laundry €11 per 6kg. Reception 24hr. Dorms €17; doubles €45; triples €60; quads €72. ❷

Hotel Omiros, Apollonos 15 (☎210 323 5486), near Pl. Syndagma. Relatively spacious rooms have A/C and private baths. Breakfast included. Call ahead. Singles €50; doubles €75; triples €93; quads €111. Bargain for student discounts. ❹

FOOD

Athens offers a mix of fast-food stands, open-air cafes, side-street *tavernas,* and intriguing restaurants. Cheap food abounds in **Syndagma** and **Omonia.** Pick up groceries at the markets on **Nikis** in **Plaka.**

ATHENS 2004

- ◙ **Eden Vegetarian Restaurant,** Lysiou 12 (☎210 324 8858), in Plaka. Fantastic dishes like *boureki* pie (zucchini with feta; €5), as well as flavorful mushroom *stifado* with onions and peppers (€8.80). Open Su-M and W-Sa noon-midnight. ❷

- ◙ **Savvas,** Mitropoleos 86 (☎210 324 5048), right off of Plateia Monastiraki, across from the flea market. A budget eater's dream with heavenly, cheap *gyros* (€1.30); just don't sit down—prices skyrocket if you do. *Souvlaki* plate €6.50. Open 8am-4am. ❶

- ◙ **O Barba Giannis,** Em. Benaki 94, in Exarhia. From Syndagma, walk up Stadiou and make a right on Em. Benaki. Delicious traditional Greek food and outstanding service. *Moussaka* €5.30. Stuffed tomatoes and peppers €4. Ask about the day's choices. In summer, open M-Sa noon-1:30am, Su noon-5:30pm. ❶

- **Pluto,** Plutarchou 38 (☎210 724 4713), in Kolonaki. Chic, warm ambience with an international menu. Try the grilled eggplant with feta and tomatoes (€9) or strawberry meringue (€9). Open M-Sa 12:30pm-3am. ❸

- **Food Company,** Anagnostopoulou 47 (☎210 361 6619), in Kolonaki. Translates the casual, gourmet lunch into an art. Try the lentil salad with goat cheese, parsley, and tomato (€4). Open daily noon-11:30pm. ❸

- **Healthy Food Vegetarian Restaurant,** Panepistimiou 57 (☎210 321 0966), in Omonia. Serves huge portions of wholesome, fresh Greek food. Open M-Sa 8am-10pm, Su 10am-4pm. ❷

◉ SIGHTS

ACROPOLIS

Looming majestically over the city, the Acropolis complex has been the heart of Athens since the 5th century BC. Although each Greek *polis* had an *acropolis* ("high point of the city"), the buildings atop Athens's central peak outshone their imitators and continue to awe visitors today. Visit as early in the day as possible to avoid crowds and the broiling midday sun. (*☎210 321 0219. Open in summer daily 8am-7pm; off-season 8am-2:30pm. Admission includes access to all of the sights below the Acropolis including Hadrian's Arch, the Olympian Temple of Zeus, and the Agora within a 48hr. period; tickets can be purchased at any of the sights. €12, students €6.)*

TEMPLE OF ATHENA NIKE. This tiny cliff-side temple was raised during the Peace of Nikias (421-415 BC), a respite from the Peloponnesian War. The temple, known as the "jewel of Greek architecture," is

---

DOG DAYS IN ATHENS

In the 1990s, an influx of refugees from unstable Balkan states prompted many Greeks to buy guard dogs. When local anxieties receded, unwanted pets were released into the streets. By 2001, Athens's stray canine population was estimated to be over 3000, and increasing all the time. The animals have become so accustomed to city life that the furry quadrupeds can be seen standing patiently at crosswalks, waiting for the lights to turn green.

On the eve of the Olympic Games, the city has been consumed by spirited debates over how to control this problem. On New Year's Day in 2003, over 60 canine carcasses were found strewn about a city park, the result of a nasty incident of rogue poisoning. Some, believing Olympic conspirators planned the extermination in preparation for the Games, banded together in demonstrations of unprecedented size.

On June 26, 2003, the Athens 2004 Committee announced a new initiative for dealing with the ever burgeoning canine population. The plan involves collecting, vaccinating, and neutering stray animals, before releasing them back onto the city streets. While the debate continues over the fate of Athens's stray population, one thing is certain: these days, more time and energy has been going to the dogs—which may be a good thing.

ringed by eight miniature Ionic columns and once housed a statue of the winged goddess of victory, Nike. One day, in a paranoid frenzy, the Athenians were seized by a fear that Nike would flee the city and take peace with her, so they clipped the statue's wings. The remains of the 5m-thick **Cyclopean wall,** predating the Classical Period, lie below the temple.

PARTHENON. The **Temple of Athena Parthenos** (Athena the virgin), more commonly known as the Parthenon, keeps vigil over Athens and the modern world. Ancient Athenians saw their city as the capital of civilization, and the **metopes** (scenes in the open spaces above the columns) on the sides of the Parthenon celebrate Athens's rise. On the far right of the south side—the only side that has not been defaced—the Lapiths battle the Centaurs; on the east side, the Olympian gods defeat the giants; the north depicts the victory of the Greeks over the Trojans; and the west depicts their triumph against the Amazons.

ERECHTHEION. The Erechtheion, to the left of the Parthenon, was completed in 406 BC, just before Sparta defeated Athens in the Peloponnesian War. The building takes its name from the snake-bodied Erechtheus; the eastern half is devoted to the goddess of wisdom, Athena, the western half to the god of the sea, Poseidon.

ACROPOLIS MUSEUM. The museum, which neighbors the Parthenon, houses a superb collection of sculptures, including five of the original Caryatids that supported the south side of the Erechtheion. In Room VIII, notice the space that has been left for the British return of the large part of the Parthenon frieze that was taken: The Elgin marbles. The statues seem to be replicas, but a close look at the folds of their drapery reveals delicately individualized detail. *(Open in summer Su and Tu-Sa 8am-7pm, M 11am-7pm; off-season Su and Tu-Sa 8am-2pm, M 11am-2pm.)*

ELSEWHERE ON THE ACROPOLIS. The southwest corner of the Acropolis looks down over the reconstructed **Odeon of Herodes Atticus,** a functional theater dating from the Roman period (AD 160). See the *Athens News* for a schedule of concerts and plays. *(Entrance on Dionissiou Areopagitou. ☎ 210 323 2771. Purchase tickets at the door or by phone.)*

OTHER SIGHTS

AGORA. The Agora served as the city's marketplace, administrative center, and hub of daily life from the 6th century BC to AD 500. Here, the debates of Athenian democracy raged; Socrates, Aristotle, Demosthenes, Xenophon, and St. Paul all preached here. Today, visitors have free reign over what is now an archaeological site. The 415 BC ▨**Hephaesteion,** on a hill in the northwest corner of the Agora, is the best-preserved classical temple in Greece, flaunting **friezes** depicting Hercules's labors and Theseus's adventures. The **Stoa of Attalos** was a multi-purpose building filled with shops and home to informal gatherings of philosophers. Reconstructed in the 1950s, it now houses the **Agora Museum,** which contains relics from the site. According to Plato, Socrates's first trial was held at the recently excavated **Royal Stoa,** to the left of the Adrianou exit. *(Enter the Agora off Pl. Thission, from Adrianou, or as you descend from the Acropolis. Open daily 8am-7:20pm. €4, students and EU seniors €2. Under-18 and EU students free.)*

KERAMEIKOS. The Kerameikos's rigidly geometric design is quickly noticeable upon entering the grounds; the site includes a large-scale cemetery and a 40m-wide boulevard that ran through the Agora and the Diplyon Gate and ended at the sanctuary of **Akademos,** where Plato founded his academy. The **Oberlaender Museum** displays finds from the burial sites; it houses an excellent collection of highly detailed pottery and sculpture. *(Northwest of the Agora. From Syndagma, walk* *toward Monastiraki on Ermou for 1km. Open Su and Tu-Sa 8:30am-3pm. €2, students and EU seniors €1. Under-18 and EU students free.)*

TEMPLE OF OLYMPIAN ZEUS AND HADRIAN'S ARCH. Right in the center of downtown Athens, you'll spot the traces of the largest temple ever built in Greece. The 15 Corinthian columns of the Temple of Olympian Zeus mark where it once stood. Started in the 6th century BC, it was completed 600 years later by Roman emperor Hadrian, who attached his name to the effort by adding an arch to mark the boundary between the ancient city of Theseus and Hadrian's own new city. *(Vas. Olgas at Amalias, across from the National Garden. Open Su and Tu-Sa 8:30am-3pm. Temple €2, students and EU seniors €1. Under-18 and EU students free. Arch free.)*

OLYMPIC STADIUM. The Panathenaic Olympic Stadium is wedged between the National Gardens and Pangrati, carved into a hill. The site of the first modern Olympic Games in 1896, the stadium seats 75,000 and will serve as both the finish line of the Marathon events and the venue for the sport of archery during the **2004 Summer Olympics.** A new Olympic stadium sits in the northern suburb of Irini; take the M1 Metro line right to it. *(On Vas. Konstantinou. From Syndagma, walk up Amalias 15min. to Vas Olgas, then follow it left. Alternatively, take trolley #2, 4, or 11 from Syndagma. Open daily 8am-8:30pm. Free.)*

OLYMPIC SPORTS COMPLEX (OCO). The Athens Olympic sports complex, located about 10km north of the center of Athens, is in the residential northern suburb of Marousi, also the headquarters of Greece's major marketing and advertising industries. Everything in OCO seems to have been constructed on an elephant's scale; the complex will host nine of the Games's 28 sports. *(Take the blue line 3 to Neratziotissa; change to Metro green line 1 from Omonia toward Kifisia to Eirini.)*

FALIRO COASTAL ZONE OLYMPIC COMPLEX (FCO). The three new (or newly refurbished) sites of the Faliro Coastal Zone Olympic Complex feature beautiful gardens, walkways and a state-of-the-art marina. Faliro will host four of the Games's 28 sports. *(From Zappeio, take tram line 1; switch to tram line 2 at the junction on Poseidonos, and continue in the opposite direction the last stop (Neo Faliro). Alternatively, take Metro green line 1 toward Piraeus.)*

HELLINIKON OLYMPIC COMPLEX (HCO). Located at the site of the old airport, the Hellinikon Olympic Complex is one of the flattest areas in the Attican peninsula and offers solid wind protection. At the 2004 Olympic Games, the Hellinikon will host seven sports. *(Take tram line 1 from Zappeio to the last stop, Helliniko.)*

ATHENS 2004

THE PLEBS' GAMES

The Olympic Committee might be keener on advertising VIP packages to bring in the big bucks, but there *are* bargains to be found when it comes to the 2004 Olympic Games. One of the most exciting and historically significant events on the schedule, the Athens 2004 Marathon, will be entirely *tzamba* (free). After a 108-year hiatus, the Olympic Marathon will return to Greece to follow the original Marathon route, forged by heroic Phidippides in 490 BC.

To witness the event, find a spot anywhere alongside the runners' path, from a little after where they begin to a little before the finish line. While some pay to watch at the Marathon Finish line and others pay to watch the Marathon's three-second start, anyone willing to wait has the option of viewing the runners from any vantage point along Phidippides' original path. You could even run on the sidewalk alongside your favorite star to share in their agony or lend a little support.

The women's race begins at 6pm on August 22nd; the men's at 6pm on August 29th. The road cycling (men's Aug. 14 12:45pm; women's Aug. 15 3pm) and sailing (in 14 sessions on Aug. 14-26 and 28) events can also be viewed free of charge.

AROUND SYNDAGMA. Be sure to catch the changing of the guard in front of the **Parliament** building. Every hour on the hour, two *evzones* (guards) wind up like toy soldiers, kick their tasselled heels in unison, and fall backward into symmetrical guardhouses on either side of the **Tomb of the Unknown Soldier.** Athens's endangered species—greenery and shade—are preserved in the **National Gardens.** Women should avoid strolling here alone.

MT. LYCAVITTOS. Of Athens's seven hills, Lycavittos is the largest and most central. Ascend at sunset to catch a glimpse of Athens's densely packed rooftops in waning daylight and watch the city light up for the night. At the top is the **Chapel of St. George,** a popular spot for weddings. A leisurely stroll around the church provides a view of Athens's panoramic expanse.

▨ NATIONAL ARCHAEOLOGICAL MUSEUM. This astounding collection deserves a spot on even the most packed itinerary. The museum's highlights include the archaeologist Heinrich Schliemann's treasure, the **Mask of Agamemnon,** the death mask of a king who lived at least three centuries earlier than Agamemnon himself. *(Patission 44. Take trolley #2, 4, 5, 9, 11, 15, or 18 from the uphill side of Syndagma, or trolley #3 or 13 from the north side of Vas. Sofias. Open Apr.-Oct. Su and Tu-Sa 8am-7pm, M 12:30-7pm; Nov.-Mar. 8am-5pm; holidays 8:30am-3pm. €6, students and EU seniors €3. Nov.-Mar. Su and holidays free.)*

NATIONAL GALLERY. The National Gallery (a.k.a. Alexander Soutzos Museum) exhibits the work of Greek artists, with periodic international displays. The permanent collection includes works by El Greco, as well as drawings, photographs, and sculpture gardens. *(Vas. Konstantinou 50. Set back from Vas. Sofias, by the Hilton. ☎ 210 723 5857. Open M and W-Sa 9am-3pm, Su 10am-2pm. €6.50, students and seniors €3.)*

GOULANDRIS MUSEUM OF NATURAL HISTORY. This museum exhibits an impressive array of taxidermied Greek birds and mammals, as well as an overview of insect, reptile, mollusk, and plant biology. *(Levidou 13. Open Su-Th and Sa 9am-2:30pm. €3; students and children 5-18 years €1.20. Children under 5 free.)*

🎵 🎭 ENTERTAINMENT AND NIGHTLIFE

The weekly *Athens News* (€1) gives locations, hours, and phone numbers for events, as well as news and ferry information. The **Athens Flea Market,** adjacent to Pl. Monastiraki, is a jumble of second-hand junk and valuable antiques. Sunday is the best day, when it is open from 8am-1pm. Summertime performances are staged in **Lycavittos Theater** as part of the **Athens Festival,** which has included acts from the Greek Orchestra to Pavarotti to the Talking Heads. The **Festival Office,** Stadiou 4, sells tickets. (☎ 210 322 1459. Open M-Sa 8am-4pm, Su 9am-2pm and 6-9pm. Tickets €10-110. Student discounts available.) The cafe/bar flourishes throughout Athens, especially on **Haritos** in **Kolonaki.** In summertime, chic Athenians head to the seaside clubs of **Glyfada,** past the airport. **Privilege, Venue,** and **Prime,** all along Poseidonos, are perfect places to enjoy the breezy night air. (Dress well; no shorts. Drinks €4-10. Cover €10-15.) Take the A3 or the B3 bus from Vas. Amalias to Glyfada (€0.75), and then catch a cab from there to your club. Taxis to Glyfada run about €8, but the return trip typically costs more.

▨ Vibe, Aristophanous 1, just beyond Plat. Iroön in Monastiraki. Unusual lighting makes for a great atmosphere. Open Su and Tu-Sa 9:30pm-5am.

Boite Esperides, Tholou 6, at the end of Mnisskleous. Young bouzouki players and honey-voiced Greek girls "sing about love and the moon." Ouzo €7.50. Cover €7.50. Open Su and Tu-Sa 10pm-4am.

Bee, at the corner of Miaoli and Themidos, off Ermou; a few blocks from the heart of Psiri in Monastiraki. DJs spin while the friendly staff keeps the booze flowing. Drinks €3-9. Open Su and Tu-Th noon-3am, F-Sa noon-6am.

The Daily, Xenokratous 47. Kolonaki's chic student population converges here to imbibe, listen to Latin and reggae, and watch sports on TV. Fabulous outdoor seating and open-air bar. Drinks €3-6. Open daily 9am-2am.

⚡ DAYTRIPS FROM ATHENS

TEMPLE OF POSEIDON. The **Temple of Poseidon** has been a dazzling white landmark for sailors at sea for centuries. The original temple was constructed around 600 BC, destroyed by the Persians in 480 BC, and rebuilt by Pericles in 440 BC; 16 Doric columns remain. The temple sits on a promontory at ◼**Cape Sounion,** 65km from Athens. (Open daily 10am-sunset. €4, students €2. EU students free.) Two **bus** routes run to Cape Sounion from Athens; the shorter and more scenic route begins at the Mavromateon 14 stop near Areos Park (2hr., every hr., €4.30).

MARATHON. Immediately after running 42km to spread word of the Athenian victory in the 490 BC battle of Marathon, **Phidippides** collapsed and died. Today, runners trace the route between Athens and Marathon twice per year, beginning at a commemorative plaque. The town is just south of **Marathonas Olympic Complex,** which will be the venue for two of the 28 sports during the 2004 Olympic Games. With a car, you can explore nearby sights and beaches. At **Ramnous,** 15km northeast, lie the ruins of the **Temple of Nemesis,** goddess of divine retribution, and **Thetis,** goddess of law and justice. **Schinias** to the north and **Timvos Marathonas** to the south are popular beaches. **Buses** leave Athens for Marathon from the Mavromateon 29 station (1½hr., every hr. 5:30am-10:30pm, €2.50).

DELPHI. Troubled denizens of the ancient world journeyed to the **Oracle of Delphi,** where the priestess of Apollo related the cryptic advice of the gods. Head east out of town to reach the site. (Open 7:30am-6:45pm. Museum closed for renovations until 2004. Site €6, students €3. EU students free.) **Buses** leave Athens for Delphi from Terminal B, Liossion 260 (3hr., 6 per day, €11). Delphi's **tourist office,** Pavlou 12, is in the town hall. (☎ 22650 82 900. Open M-F 8am-2:30pm.) If you spend the night, stay at **Hotel Sibylla ❷,** Pavlou 9, which has rooms with wonderful views and private baths at the best prices in town. (☎ 22650 82 335. Singles €15; doubles €22; triples €27.)

THE PELOPONNESE (Πελοποννεσος)

A hand-shaped peninsula stretching its fingers into the Mediterranean, the Peloponnese is rich in history and folklore that contribute to its otherworldly atmosphere. The majority of Greece's most significant archaeological sites reside here, including Olympia, Mycenae, Messene, Corinth, Mystras, and Epidavros. A world apart from the islands, the serenely beautiful and sparsely populated Peloponnese remembers 5000 years of continuous habitation, making it a bastion of Greek village life.

🌙 FERRIES TO ITALY AND CRETE

Boats sail from Patras to destinations in Italy, including Brindisi, Trieste, Bari, Ancona, and Venice. **Manolopoulous,** Othonos Amalias 35, in Patras, sells tickets. (☎ 2610 223 621. Open M-F 9am-8pm, Sa 10am-3pm, Su 5pm-8pm.) Questions about departures from Patras should be directed to the Port Authority (☎ 2610 341 002).

PATRAS (Πατρας) ☎ 2610

Sprawling Patras (pop. 155,000) Greece's third-largest city and one of the official cities for the 2004 Olympic Games, serves largely as a transport hub for island-bound tourists. During **Carnival** (mid-Jan. to Ash Wednesday), this port city becomes one gigantic dance floor consumed by pre-Lenten madness. During the 2004 Olympics, the **Pampeloponnisiako Stadium,** known around the city as the "Jewel of Patras," will host swimming and soccer events and serve as the athletic training halls. To get there, take bus #7 (20 min., €1) from outside Europa Center. Follow the water to the west end of town to reach **Agios Andreas,** the largest Orthodox cathedral in Greece, which houses magnificent frescoes and St. Andrew's holy head. (Dress modestly. Open daily 7am-dusk.) Sweet black grapes are transformed into Mavrodaphne wine at the ▨**Achaïa Clauss Winery,** the country's most famous vineyard. Take bus #7 (30min., €1) from the intersection of Kolokotroni and Kanakari. (Open daily May-Sept. 11am-8pm; Oct.-Apr. 9am-8pm. Free samples. In summer, free English tours every hr. noon-5pm.)

Trains (☎ 2610 639 110) leave from Othonos Amalias for: Athens (3½-5hr., 8 per day, €10); Kalamata (5½hr., 2 per day, €5); and Olympia (1½hr., 8 per day, €3-6) via Pyrgos. KTEL **buses** (☎ 2610 623 886) leave from Othonos Amalias for: Athens (3hr., 33 per day, €13); Ioannina (4hr., 4 per day, €16); Kalamata (4hr., 2 per day, €15); Thessaloniki (8hr., 3 per day, €30); and Tripoli (4hr., 2 per day, €11). **Ferries** go to: Corfu (6-8hr., daily, €21-25); and Italy (see p. 515). The **tourist office** is on Othonos Amalias, between 28 Octovriou and Astingos (☎ 2610 461 740. Open daily 8am-10pm.) The **Pension Nicos ❷,** Patreos 3, is cheery and conveniently located. (☎ 2610 623 757. Singles €20; doubles €35; triples €50. Cash only.) The friendly, cafeteria-style ▨**Europa Center ❶,** on Othonos Amalias, serves cheap, large portions. (Entrees €3-7.) **Postal Code:** 26001.

OLYMPIA (Ολυμπια) ☎ 26240

In ancient times, every four years city-states would call truces and travel to Olympia for a pan-Hellenic assembly which was as much about peace and diplomacy as about athletic ability. Modern Olympia (pop. 42,500), though set among meadows and shaded by cypress and olive trees, is anything but relaxed. As the 2004 Olympic Games rapidly approach, this small town is in a frenzy, ready to show the world proudly where it all began. The ancient **Olympic arena,** whose central sanctuary was called the **Altis,** draws hordes of tourists. The gigantic **Temple of Zeus** dominates **Ancient Olympia,** although ▨**Hera's Temple,** dating from the 7th century BC, is better preserved. The ▨**Archaeological Museum** has an impressive sculpture collection that includes the **Nike of Paionios** and the **Hermes of Praxiteles.** Maps, available at the site (€2-4), are essential for navigation. (Site open in summer daily 8am-7pm. Museum open M noon-3pm, Tu-Su 8am-7pm. Site or museum €6, both €9; students and seniors €3/€5. Under-18 and EU students free.) The **Museum of the Olympic Games,** or the **Sports Museum,** on Angerinou, two blocks uphill from Kondili, houses a collection of Olympic paraphernalia that includes a silver medal from the 1996 games in Atlanta. (☎ 26240 22 544. Open M-Sa 8am-3:30pm, Su 9am-4:30pm. €2. Children and EU students free.)

Buses run to Tripoli (4hr., 2-3 per day, €8). The **tourist office,** on Kondili, is on the east side of town toward the ruins. (☎ 26240 23 100. Open M-F 9am-4pm.) To reach the **Internet Cafe** (☎ 26240 22 578), turn off Kondili with the youth hostel on your right and walk uphill two blocks. (€3 per hr., €1.50 minimum. Open daily 9:30am-2am.) The friendly **Youth Hostel ❶,** Kondili 18, is cheap. (☎ 26240 22 580. Free hot showers. Check-out 10:30am. Dorms €8; doubles €20.) **New Olympia ❹,** on the road that leads diagonally to the train station, has spacious rooms with A/C, TVs, and large private baths. (☎ 26240 22 506. Buffet breakfast included. Singles €25-52;

doubles €45-70; triples €90.) **Minimarkets,** bakeries, and fast-food establishments line **Kondili.** Restaurants on Kondili are overpriced, but a walk toward the railroad station or up the hill leads to inexpensive *tavernas.* **Postal Code:** 27065.

TRIPOLI (Τριπολη) ☎ 2710

The transportation hub of Arcadia, Tripoli (pop. 22,000) is crowded and fast-paced; the *plateias* and huge city park are a break in the city's otherwise urban landscape. The **Archaeological Museum** on Evangelistrias, Pl. Ag. Vasiliou, has a large prehistoric collection, including pottery, jewelry, and weaponry from the Neolithic to the Mycenaean periods. **Trains** arrive from: Athens (4hr., 3 per day, €6); Corinth (2½hr., 4 per day, €3); and Kalamata (2½hr., 2 per day, €5). **Buses** arrive at Pl. Kolokotronis, east of the center of town, from Athens (3hr., 14 per day, €11) and Nafplion (1hr., 5 per day, €3.70). Buses arrive at the KTEL Messenia and Laconia depot, across from the train station, from Kalamata (1½hr., 10 per day, €5.50) and Sparta (1hr., 8 per day, €3.70). **Arcadia Hotel ❸,** in Pl. Kolokotronis, offers old-fashioned rooms with unique color schemes, A/C, and private bath. (☎ 2710 225 551. Singles €30-50; doubles €45-72; triples €80-85.) Try the goat with mushrooms in egg and lemon sauce (€8.20) at ▓**Klimataria ❸,** on Eth. Antistasis, four blocks past the park as you walk from Pl. Petriou. (☎ 2710 222 058. Entrees €10-12.) **Postal Code:** 22100.

KALAMATA (Καλαματα) ☎ 27210

Kalamata (pop. 50,000) flourishes as a port and beach resort, and also serves as a useful transport hub. Take a bus from Kalamata (1hr., M-Sa 2 per day, €2) to **Ancient Messini** in nearby **Mavromati,** one of Greece's most impressive archaeological sites. (Open daily 8am-8pm. Free.) To reach the train station, walk toward the waterfront in Pl. Georgiou, turn right on Frantzi at the far end of the *plateia,* and walk a few blocks to Sideromikou Stathmou. **Trains** run to: Athens (6½hr., 3 per day, €7) via Tripoli (2½hr., €2.80); Corinth (5¼hr., €5.60); and Patras (5½hr., 3:19pm, €5). **Buses** leave from the station on Artemidos to: Athens (4hr., 12 per day, €16); Patras (4hr., 2 per day, €15); Sparta (2hr., 2 per day, €2.80); and Tripoli (2hr., €5.50). **Tourist information** is available at **D.E.T.A.K.,** Polivou 6, just off Aristomenous near the Old Town. (☎ 27210 21 700. Open M-F 7am-2:30pm.) **Hotel Nevada ❷,** Santa Rosa 9, off Faron one block up from the water, offers large, wildly decorated rooms with shared baths and kitchen. (☎ 27210 82 429. Singles €11-14; doubles €16-19; triples €19-24.) Good meals can be found along the waterfront. Before leaving town, sample the famous Kalamata olives and figs. The immense **New Market,** across the bridge from the bus station, has an assortment of meat, cheese, and fruit shops, and a daily farmer's market. **Postal Code:** 24100.

SPARTA (Σπαρτη) AND MYSTRAS (Μυστρας) ☎ 27310

Citizens of today's Sparta (pop. 12,500) make olive oil, not war. Pleasant public gardens and broad, palm-lined boulevards make Sparta hospitable, and it is by far the best base for exploring the Byzantine ruins of Mystras. **Ancient Sparta** is only a 1km walk north down Paleolougou. **Buses** from Sparta go to: Areopolis (1½hr., 2 per day, €4.60); Athens (3½hr., 8 per day, €14) via Corinth (2½hr., €8.30) and Tripoli (1hr., €3.70); and Monemvasia (2hr., 3 per day, €6.80). To reach the town center from the bus station, walk about 10 blocks west on Lykourgou; the **tourist office** is in the *plateia.* (☎ 24 852. Open M-F 8am-2pm.) **Hotel Cecil ❸,** Paleologou 125, 5 blocks north of Lykourgou toward Ancient Sparta, on the corner of Paleologou and Thermopilion, has pleasant rooms with A/C, phones, private baths, and TVs. (☎ 24 980. Reservations recommended. Singles €28-33; doubles €33-38.)

GREECE

Mystras, 4km from Sparta, was once the religious center of all Byzantium and the locus of Constantinople's rule over the Peloponnese. Its extraordinary hillside ruins comprise a city of Byzantine churches, chapels, and monasteries. Modest dress is required at the functioning convent. (Open in summer daily 8am-7pm; off-season 8:30am-3pm. €5. Children and EU students free.) **Buses** leave from the station and from the corner of Lykourgou and Leonidou in Sparta for the top of the ruins (20min., 11 per day, €0.90).

GYTHION (Γυθειο) AND AREOPOLIS (Αρεοπολη)   ☎27330

Near sand and stone beaches, Gythion is the liveliest town in Mani and a good base for visiting other villages. A tiny causeway to the left of the waterfront as you face inland connects it to the island of **Marathonisi,** where Paris and Helen consummated their ill-fated love. **Buses** in Gythion leave from the north end of the waterfront, to the right as you face inland, for: Athens (4hr., 6 per day, €17) via Tripoli (2hr., €6.50); Corinth (3hr., €12); Kalamata (2hr., 2 per day, €6.20) via Itilo (1hr., €3); and Sparta (1hr., €3). **Moto Makis Rent-A-Moped,** on the waterfront near the causeway, rents wheels for exploring. (☎27330 25 111. €16 per day. Open daily 8:30am-1:30pm and 4:30-8:30pm.) ⚑**Xenia Karlaftis Rooms ❷,** on the water 20m from the causeway, rents spacious rooms with private baths. (☎27330 22 719. Singles €15; doubles €22; triples €30.) **Postal Code:** 23200.

Although **Areopolis** neighbors both the sea and the mountains, its buildings dominate the scenery: stone tower houses and cobbled streets are framed by the dramatic purple peaks of the Taygetus. Just 11km from Areopolis, the unusual **Vlihada Cave,** part of a subterranean river, is cool, quiet, and strung with tiny crystalline stalagmites; a bus (€0.90) runs from Areopolis at 11am and returns at 12:45pm. (Open daily 8am-3pm. Mandatory 30min. tours. €12, students €7.) **Buses** stop in Areopolis's main *plateia* and go to Athens (6hr., 4 per day, €18) via Gythion (45min., €1.80) and Sparta (2hr., €6.50). To reach **Tsimova ❷,** which rents narrow rooms with tiny doors and windows typical of tower houses, turn left at the end of Kapetan Matapan, the road leading to the Old Town. (☎27330 51 301. Singles €25-32; doubles €35-60.) **Postal Code:** 23062.

MONEMVASIA (Μονεμβασια) AND GEFYRA (Γεφυρα) ☎27320

Despite the tourists, an otherworldly quality shrouds the island of Monemvasia. No cars or bikes are allowed on the island, and pack horses bear residents' groceries into the city. Narrow streets hide tiny doorways and flowered courtyards. At the edge of the cliffs perches the **Agia Sofia,** a 12th-century church; to get there, navigate the maze of streets to the inland edge of town, where a path climbs the side of the cliff to the tip of the rock. Stay in more modern and less expensive **Gefyra,** a 15min. walk down the main road and across the causeway from Monemvasia. An orange **bus** runs between the causeway and Monemvasia's gate (every 15min., 8am-midnight, €0.30). Three **buses** per day leave for: Athens (6hr., €20); Corinth (5hr., €15); Sparta (2½hr., €6.80); and Tripoli (4hr., €11). ⚑**Hotel Akrogiali ❷,** Iouliou 23, has private baths, TVs, and a shared fridge. (☎27320 61 360. Singles €20-23; doubles €28-35.) ⚑**To Limanaki ❶,** in Gefyra, serves exceptional Greek food, including excellent *pastitsio* (€4) and *moussaka* (€5).

NAFPLION (Ναυπλιο)   ☎27520

Beautiful old Nafplion (pop. 10,000) glories in its fortresses, Venetian architecture, and nearby pebble beaches. The town's crown jewel is the 18th-century **Palamidi fortress,** which provides spectacular views of the town and harbor. To get there, walk or take a taxi (€3) up the 3km road; or climb the grueling 999 steps up from Plizoidhou, across the park from the bus station. (Open in summer daily 8am-

6:45pm; off-season 8:30am-5:45pm. €4, students €2.) To reach **Bouboulinas,** the waterfront promenade, from the station, go left and follow Syngrou to the harbor and the **Old Town.** Nafplion's small, pebbly beach **Arvanitia** is along the road that curves around the left-hand side of Palamidi; if it gets too crowded on a hot day, follow the footpath for lovely private coves.

Buses leave from Syngrou, near the base of the Palamidi fortress, for Athens (3hr., every hr., €9) via Corinth (2hr., €4). The **tourist office** is on 25 Martiou across from the telephone office. (☎27520 24 444. Open daily 9am-1pm and 4-8pm.) For the Old Town rooftop views from **Dimitris Bekas' Domatia ❷,** turn up the stairs on Kokkinou, following the sign for rooms off Staikopoulou; climb to the top and go up 50 steps. (☎27520 24 594. Singles €16; doubles €20-22.) **To Fanaria ❷,** above the *plateia* on Staikopoulou in a trellised alleyway, serves tantalizing entrees in an intimate atmosphere. (Soups €2.50-3; fish dishes €6-8.) **Postal Code:** 21100.

🛂 DAYTRIPS FROM NAFPLION: MYCENAE AND EPIDAVROS. The head of the Greek world from 1600 to 1100 BC, **Mycenae** (Μυκηνες) was once ruled by the legendary Agamemnon, leader of the attacking forces in the Trojan War. Excavations of ancient Mycenae have persisted for 130 years, turning the area into one of the most visited sites in Greece. Today, backpackers and senior citizens stampede to the famed ruins. The imposing **Lion's Gate,** the portal into the ancient city, has two lions carved in relief above the lintel and is estimated to weigh some 20 tons. The **Tomb of Agamemnon** (also known as the Treasury of Atreus) is the large and impressive *tholos.* (Both sites open Apr.-Sept. daily 8am-7pm; Oct.-Mar. 8am-5pm. €6, students €3. Keep your ticket or pay twice.) The only direct **bus** to Mycenae is from Nafplion (45min., 5 per day, €1.80) via Argos (30min., €0.90). Join the ranks of Claude Debussy, William Faulkner, Allen Ginsberg, and Virginia Woolf by staying at **Belle Helene Hotel ❸,** which doubles as a bus stop on the main road. (☎27510 76 225. Singles €20-30; doubles €40-50; triples €50-55.)

The grandest structure at the ancient site of **Epidavros** (Επιδαυρος) is the **Theater of Epidavros,** built in the early 2nd century BC. The incredible acoustics allow you to stand at the top row of seats—14,000 seats back—and hear a match lit on stage. Near the theater and on the road to the sanctuary's ruins is Epidavros's **museum.** (☎27520 22 009. Open daily 8am-7pm. Ticket office open daily 7:30am-7pm, during festival season also F-Sa 7:30am-9pm. €6, students €3.) From late June to mid-Aug., the **Epidavros Theater Festival** brings performances of classical Greek plays on Friday and Saturday nights. Shows are at 9pm; purchase tickets at the site or by calling the Athens Festival Box Office. (☎210 322 1459. Tickets €17-40, students €9.) **Buses** arrive in Epidavros from Nafplion (45min., 3 per day, €2).

CORINTH (Κορινθος) ☎27410

Most visitors to the Peloponnese travel to the ruins of **Ancient Corinth,** at the base of the **Acrocorinth.** Majestic columns have endured through the ages around the courtyard of the **Temple of Apollo,** down the stairs to the left of the excellent **Archaeological Museum.** The 2-3hr. hike to the **fortress** at the top of the Acrocorinth is strenuous and dangerous; instead, take a taxi to the summit (☎27410 31 464, €6), which will wait an hour before the drive back down (€10). Explore the surprisingly intact remains of the **Temple to Aphrodite,** where disciples were initiated into the "mysteries of love." (☎27410 31 207. Open summer Tu-F 8am-7pm, Sa-Su 8:30am-3pm; off-season daily 8am-5pm. Museum and site €6, students €3.)

In **New Corinth,** which is both a transportation hub and the logical base for viewing the ruins, **buses** leave from Terminal A, past the train station, for Athens (1½hr., 29 per day, €6). Buses run from Terminal B, on Koliatsou, halfway through the park, to Ancient Corinth (20min., 8 per day 8:10am-9:10pm, €1). Buses leave

Terminal C, **Argolis Station** (☎27410 24 403), at the intersection of Eth. Antistasis and Aratou, for: Argos (1hr., €3.20); Mycenae (45min., €2.40); and Nafplion (1½hr., €4). **Trains** go from the station on Demokratias to Athens (normal: 2hr., 7 per day, €2.60; express: 1½hr., 7 per day, €5.70). The **tourist police**, Ermou 51, are located in the city's park and provide tourists with maps, brochures, and other assistance. (☎27410 23 282. Open daily 8am-2pm.) The newly renovated **Hotel Apollon ❷**, Damaskinou 2, in New Corinth, has TVs, A/C, and Internet access. (☎27410 25 920. Singles €40; doubles €60.)

NORTHERN AND CENTRAL GREECE

The last additions to the Greek state, northern and central Greece have a harsh continental climate that makes for a life distinct from that of its Mediterranean counterparts. Forgotten mountain-goat paths lead to glorious vistas, overlooking silvery olive groves, fruit-laden trees, and patchwork farmland.

THESSALONIKI (Θεσσαλονικη) ☎2310

Thessaloniki (pop. 1,830,000), a jumble of ancient, Byzantine, European, Turkish, Sephardic, and contemporary Greek culture and history, fans out from its hilltop fortress toward the Thermaic Gulf. From its peak, the fortress overlooks the Old Town's placid streets which stretch down to the city's long, congested avenues. Golden mosaics, frescoes, and floating domes still gleam in the industrial city's Byzantine churches. Most travelers spend a couple of days in Thessaloniki checking out the sights, going to clubs, and enjoying the tranquility of countryside hikes.

▐▀ TRANSPORTATION

Ferries: Buy tickets at **Karacharisis Travel and Shipping Agency,** Koundouriotou 8 (☎2310 524 544; fax 2310 532 289), across from the Olympic Airways Office. Open M-F 8:30am-8:30pm, Sa 8:30am-2:30pm. During high season, from mid-June to early Sept., ferries travel to **Chios** (20hr., Su 1am, €31; 9hr., W 9:30am, €62) via **Lesvos** (14hr., Su, €31; 6½hr., W, €62); **Iraklion** (24hr.; Tu 3pm, Th 7:30pm, Sa midnight; €41) via **Mykonos** (15hr., 3 per week, €31); **Naxos** (16hr., 1 per week, €29); **Paros** (17½hr., 2 per week, €31); **Santorini** (19½hr., 3 per week, €33); **Skiathos** (4hr., 2 per week, €16); **Skopelos** (6½hr., 3 per week, €17); **Kos** (20hr., 1 per week, €39), **Samos** (16hr., 2 per week, €32), and **Rhodes** (24hr., 1 per week, €46).

Trains: Main Terminal (☎2310 517 517), on Monastiriou in the western part of the city. Take any bus down Egnatia (€0.50). To **Athens** (8hr., 5 per day, €15). The **Travel Office** (☎2310 598 112) can provide updated schedules.

Buses: Most **KTEL** buses leave from one central, dome-shaped bus station west of the city center. To: **Athens** (☎2310 595 495; 6hr., 11 per day, €28); **Corinth** (☎2310 595 405; 7½hr., 11:30pm, €32); **Patras** (☎2310 595 425; 7hr., 3 per day, €30).

Flights: The **airport** (☎2310 408 400), 16km east of town, can be reached by **bus #78** or from the train station or Pl. Aristotelous, or by **taxi** (€10). There's an EOT **tourist office** branch (☎2310 985 215) at the airport. The **Olympic Airways** office at Koundouriotou 3 (☎2310 368 311), is open M-F 8am-3:45pm. Call for reservations (☎2310 368 666; M-Sa 8am-4:30pm). To: **Athens** (1hr., 9 per day, €90); **Chios** (3hr., 4 per week, €60); **Corfu** (50min., 2 per week, €64); **Iraklion** (2hr., 2 per day, €109); **Lesvos** (2hr., daily, €63); **Rhodes** (3hr., daily, €116); and **Samos** (1hr., 4 per week, €70).

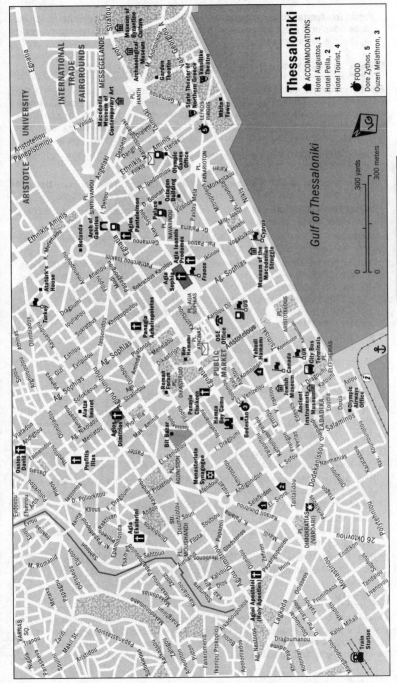

Thessaloniki

▲ ACCOMMODATIONS
Hotel Augustos, **1**
Hotel Pella, **2**
Hotel Tourist, **4**

● FOOD
Dore Zythos, **5**
Ouzeri Melathron, **3**

GREECE

Gulf of Thessaloniki

300 yards
300 meters

Public Transportation: Local buses cost €0.50 and run throughout the city. Buy tickets at *periptera* or at depot ticket booths. **Taxis** (☎2310 551 525) have specific queues at Ag. Sophia and Mitropoleos.

ORIENTATION AND PRACTICAL INFORMATION

Egnatia, an old Roman highway, runs down the middle of town and is home to the cheapest hotels. Running parallel to the water, the main streets are **Ermou, Tsimiski, Mitropoleos,** and **Nikis,** which runs along the waterfront. Inland from Egnatia is **Agios Dimitriou** and the **Old Town** beyond. Intersecting these and leading into town are I. Dragoumi, El. Venizelou, Aristotelous, Ag. Sophias, and Eth. Aminis.

Tourist Office: EOT, inside the port at the Passenger Terminal (☎2310 222 935). Open M-Sa 7:30am-3pm.

Banks: Banks with **currency exchange** and 24hr. **ATMs** line Tsimiski, including **National Bank,** Tsimiski 11 (☎2310 230 783). Open M-Th 8am-2pm, F 8am-1:30pm.

Tourist Police: Dodekanissou 4, 5th fl. (☎2310 554 871). Free maps and brochures. Open 24hr. For the **local police,** call ☎2310 553 800 or 100.

Telephones: OTE, Karolou Diehl 27 (☎134), at the corner of Ermou, 1 block east of Aristotelous. Open M-F 7am-3pm, W also 7pm-9pm.

Internet Access: There are several small Internet cafes along the western end of Egnatia. **Interspot Cafe,** Tsimiski 43, inside the mall, offers access for €1.50 per hr. **E-Global,** Egnatia 105, one block east of Arch of Galerius, sports over 50 terminals. €2-3 per hr. Open 24hr. **Meganet Internet Cafe,** 5 Pl. Navarinou, overlooking the Palace of Galerius, offers access for €2 per hr. Open 24hr. The **British Council,** Eth. Aminis 9, offers **free access.** Open M-F 9am-1pm.

Post Office: Aristotelous 27, just below Egnatia. Open M-F 7:30am-8pm, Sa 7:30am-2pm, Su 9am-1:30pm. A **branch** office (☎2310 229 324), on Eth. Aminis near the White Tower, is open M-F 7am-8pm. Both offer *Poste Restante.* **Postal Code:** 54101.

ACCOMMODATIONS

Most budget hotels cluster along the western end of Egnatia, between Pl. Dimokratias (500m east of the train station) and Aristotelous. Egnatia can be noisy and gritty, but you'll have to pay more elsewhere.

Hotel Atlantis, Egnatia 14 (☎2310 540 131). Offers standard budget furnishings and well-maintained hallway bathrooms. Singles and doubles €20, with bath €30. ❷

Hotel Augustos, El. Svoronou 4 (☎2310 522 955). Walking down the western end of Egnatia, turn north at the Argo Hotel; Augustos is 20m straight ahead. Cozy rooms. Singles with bath €25; doubles €30, with bath €40; triples with bath €50. ❷

Hotel Pella, Dragoumi 63 (☎2310 524 221). North on Dragoumi 2 blocks up from west Egnatia's budget strip. Comfortable rooms with desk, TV, telephone, and bath. Singles €35; doubles €50. ❸

Hotel Tourist, Mitropoleos 21 (☎2310 270 501). An excellent location. Rooms with TV, telephone, A/C, and bath. Singles €50; doubles €70; triples €90. ❹

FOOD

Ouzeri can be found in tiny streets off Aristotelous; the innovative places a block down from Egnatia between Dragoumi and El. Venizelou cater to a younger clientele. **Ouzeri Melathron** ❷, Karypi 21-34, in an alleyway at El. Venizelou 23, has a humorous menu and delicious food. (Entrees €3.50-12.) A meal at **Dore Zythos** ❷,

Tsiroyianni 7, behind the grassy triangular plot across from the White Tower, includes sea breezes, superb views, and an avant-garde menu. Try the €7 *its pilaf* for an Anatolian treat. (Entrees €6-8.)

SIGHTS AND ENTERTAINMENT

The streets of modern Thessaloniki are littered with the reminders of its significance during both the Byzantine and Ottoman empires. **Agios Dimitrios,** on Ag. Dimitriou north of Aristotelous, is the city's oldest and most famous church. Although most of its interior was gutted in a 1917 fire, some lovely mosaics remain. (Open daily 6am-10pm.) South of Egnatia, on the square that bears its name, the magnificent domed **Agia Sophia** features a splendid ceiling mosaic of the Ascension. (Open daily 7am-1pm and 5-7pm.) Originally part of a palatial complex designed to honor the Roman Caesar Galerium, the **Rotunda** became the church **Agios Georgiou** in late Roman times. Its walls were once plastered with some of the city's most brilliant mosaics; unfortunately, very few remain. (Open Su and Tu-Sa 8am-7pm.) A colonnaded processional once led south to the **Arch of Galerius,** on the eastern end of Egnatia, which commemorates the Caesar's 397 AD Persian victory. Further west down Egnatia, don't miss **Bey Hamami,** a perfectly preserved 15th-century bath house that served the Ottoman governor and his retinue. (Open daily 8am-9pm. Free.) The **Heptapyrgion,** a 5th-century Byzantine fortress, is the main attraction of the city's modest acropolis. (Open Su and Tu-Sa 8am-7pm.)

All that remains of a 15th-century Venetian seawall, the **White Tower** presides over the eastern edge of the waterfront like an overgrown chess piece. (Tower open M 12:30-7pm, Tu-Su 8am-7pm. Free.) Thessaloniki's **Archaeological Museum,** at the western end of Tsimiski, across from the International Helexpo Fairgrounds, is full of discoveries gleaned from Neolithic tombs, mosaics from Roman houses, and a dazzling display of Macedonian gold. (Open Su and Tu-Sa 8am-7pm, M 12:30-7pm; off-season reduced hours. €4, students €2. EU students free.) Just across the street at Stratou 2, the **Museum of Byzantine Culture** displays an impressive array of artifacts from both the Early and Middle Byzantine eras, from church mosaics and elaborate tombs to 1500-year-old personal effects. (Open Su and Tu-Sa 8am-7pm, M 12:30-7pm; off-season reduced hours. €4, students and seniors €2. EU students and under-18 free.)

There are four main hubs for late-night fun: The bars and cafes of the **Ladadika** district, the renovated mill factories of **Mylos** behind the harbor, the waterfront's cafes, and the open-air discos near the airport exit (€8-9 by taxi). **Rodon 2000,** 11km east of the city along the main highway, is a sophisticated hot spot filled with Greek music. (€10 cover includes 1 drink.)

DAYTRIP FROM THESSALONIKI

VERGINA. The tombs of Vergina (Βεργινα), final home to ancient Macedonian royalty, lie only 30km from Thessaloniki. The principal sight is the **Great Tumulus,** a huge, man-made mount 12m tall and 110m wide. Check out the bones of **Alexander IV,** son of Alexander the Great, as well as the magnificent **Tomb of Philip II,** Alexander's father. Visitors can stroll into the mound and check out its magnificent burial treasures, intricate gold work, and brilliant frescoes. (Open Su and Tu-Sa 8am-7pm, M noon-7pm; off-season Su and Tu-Sa 8am-7pm. €8, students €4.) **Buses** run from Thessaloniki (1hr., every hr., €4.60) to Veria. From Veria, take the bus to Vergina's *plateia* (20min., 8 per day, €1); follow the signs to the sights.

MOUNT OLYMPUS (Ολυμπος)   ☎ 23520

The impressive height (nearly 3000m) and formidable slopes of the Thermaic Gulf's Mt. Olympus so awed the ancients that they proclaimed it the dwelling place of the gods. A network of well-maintained **hiking** trails now makes the summit accessible to anyone with sturdy legs and a taste for the divine. Two approaches to the peaks begin near **Litochoro** (elev. 340m); the first and most popular starts at **Prionia** (elev. 1100m), 18km from the village, and takes one full day round-trip. The second, a longer and more picturesque route, begins at **Diastavrosi** (also called **Gortsia;** elev. 1300m), 14km away. There is no bus to the trailheads from Litohoro, so you'll have to walk, drive, or take a taxi (from Prionia €20). Unless you're handy with a crampon and an ice axe, make your ascent between May and October. **Mytikas,** the tallest peak, is inaccessible without special equipment before June.

Trains (☎ 23520 22 522) run to the Litochoro station from Athens (6hr., 4 per day, €15) and Thessaloniki (1½hr., 4 per day, €3); a **taxi** from the train station to the town costs around €6. KTEL **buses** (☎ 23520 81 271) run from Athens (5½hr., 3 per day, €25) and Thessaloniki (1½hr., 17 per day, €6). The **tourist office** is on Ag. Nikolaou by the park. (☎ 23520 83 100. Open July-Nov. 8:30am-2:30pm and 5-9pm.) The EOS-run ▓**Spilos Agapitos ❷** ("Refuge A" or "Zolotas") is about 800m below **Skala** and Mytikas peaks. The English-speaking staff dispenses info over the phone to prospective hikers and can also help reserve spots in other refuges. (☎ 23520 81 800; zolotam@hol.gr. Meals 6am-9pm. Lights out 10pm. Open mid-May to late-Oct. Dorms €10, members €8. €4.20 to **camp** nearby and use facilities.) **Camp** at **Olympus Zeus ❷** (☎ 23520 22 115; sites from €11) on the beach about 5km from town.

METEORA (Μετεωρα)   ☎ 24230

The iron-gray pinnacles of the Meteora rock formations are stunning, offering astonishing views of fields, mountains, and monolithic stone. These wonders of nature are bedecked with 24 gravity-defying, frescoed Byzantine monasteries. (Dress modestly. Open Apr.-Sept. Sa-Su and W 10am-12:30pm and 3:30-5pm; hours vary during the rest of the week. €2 per monastery.) The **Grand Meteoron Monastery** is the oldest, largest, and most touristed of the monasteries. It houses a **folk museum** and the 16th-century **Church of the Transfiguration,** whose dome features a *Pantokrator* (a central image of Christ). To escape the hordes of tourists, venture to **Roussanou,** to the right after the fork in the road. Visible from most of the valley, it is one of the most spectacularly situated monasteries in the area.

Buses leave for Meteora from the fountain in **Kalambaka,** the most popular base for exploring the sight (2 per day, €0.80). **Trains** leave Kalambaka for Athens (4hr., 3 per day, €19.10) and Thessaloniki (5hr., 3 per day, €10.50). **Buses** depart for Athens (5hr., 8 per day, €20) and Patras (6hr., Tu and Th 9:45am and 3pm, €19.40). The large rooms at **Koka Roka ❷** offer views of Meteora; from the central *plateia,* follow Vlachara to its end, bear left, and follow the signs. (☎ 24230 24 554. Singles €15; doubles €27, with bath €32; triples with bath €42.) **Postal Code:** 42200.

IOANNINA (Ιωαννινα)   ☎ 26510

On the shores of Lake Pamvotis lies Epirus's capital and largest city, Ioannina (pop. 100,000). While perhaps not captivating, the city does serve as a useful transport hub between Greece and Italy. Aside from local finds, the highlights of the city's **Archaeological Museum,** off Averof, near the city center, are the lead tablets used by ancients to inscribe their questions to the oracle at Dodoni. (Open Su and Tu-Sa 8:30am-3pm. €2, students free.) Catch a boat from the waterfront (10min., €1) for **Nisi** ("The Island") to explore Byzantine monasteries and the **Ali Pasha Museum** (Open daily 8am-10pm. €0.75).

Buses run from the terminal at Zossimadon 4 to Athens (6½hr., 10 per day, €27) and Thessaloniki (7hr., 6 per day, €22). To reach the **tourist office,** walk 500m down Leoforos Dodoni; the office is on the left, immediately after the playground. (☎26510 46 662. Open July-Sept. M-F 7:30am-2:30pm and 5-8:30pm, Sa 9am-1pm; Oct.-June M-F 7:30am-2:30pm.) **Hotel Tourist ❸,** Kolleti 18, on the right a few blocks up Averof from the kastro, offers baths, telephones, TV, and A/C. (☎26510 25 070. Singles €30; doubles €40; triples €50.) **Postal Code:** 45110.

▶ DAYTRIP FROM IOANNINA: DODONI. Ancient Dodoni (Δωδώνη), the site of mainland Greece's oldest oracle, is at the base of a mountain 22km southeast of Ioannina. According to myth, **Zeus** answered queries here from the roots of a giant oak tree. There is also a large 3rd-century **amphitheater** at the site (currently undergoing restoration). **Buses** to Dodoni run from Ioannina's smaller station at Bizaniou 21 (30min.; M, W, F 6:30am and 3:30pm; €1.70). Ask to be let off at the theater. The return bus passes by at about 4:45pm; alternatively, you can hire a **taxi** (at least €15).

IONIAN ISLANDS (Νησια Του Ιουιου)

Just to the west of mainland Greece, the Ionian Islands are renowned for their medley of rugged mountains, rolling farmland, shimmering olive groves, and pristine beaches, all surrounded by an endless expanse of clear, blue water. The islands are a favorite among vacationing Brits, Italians, and Germans, as well as ferry-hopping backpackers heading to Italy.

◖ FERRIES TO ITALY

To catch a ferry to Italy, buy your ticket at least a day ahead; be sure to find out if the port tax (€5-6) is included. **International Tours** (☎26610 39 007) and **Ionian Cruises** (☎26610 31 649), both located across the street from the old port on Venizelou, can help with your scheduling woes. Ferries go from Corfu to: Ancona (20hr., daily, €58); Bari (9hr., daily, €46); Brindisi (6-7hr., 3 per day, €30); Trieste (24hr., 4 per week, €52); and Venice (24hr., daily, €57). Schedules vary; call ahead.

CORFU (KERKYRA; Κερκυρα)　　☎26610

Ever since Homer's Odysseus washed ashore and praised its lush beauty, the seas have brought a multitude of conquerors, colonists, and tourists to verdant Corfu. Those who stray from the beaten path, however, will still encounter unspoiled, uncrowded beaches.

CORFU TOWN AND ENVIRONS. Corfu Town (pop. 31,000) enchants with its two fortresses, various museums, churches, and winding streets. South of Corfu Town is the exquisite **Achillion Palace;** take a bus to Gastouri (30min.; M-Sa 6 per day, Su 4 per day; €0.90). The lovely **Paleokastritsa** beach, where Odysseus supposedly washed ashore, lies west of town; take a KTEL bus to Paleokastritsa (45min.; M-Sa 7 per day, Su 5 per day; €1.60). A short walk from there will bring you to the hilltop monastery **Panagia Theotokos.** KTEL buses also run from Corfu Town to **Agios Gordios** (45min.; M-Sa 5 per day, Su 3 per day; €1.50), home to impressive rock formations, a beach, and the **Pink Palace Hotel ❷,** which is immensely popular with American and Canadian backpackers. The Palace has an impressive list of amenities, including tennis courts, a nightclub, massages (€11), clothing-optional cliff-diving (€15), and various water sports. They also run buses to Athens (€38 from Pink Palace, €47 from Athens), that bypass Patras. (☎26610 53 103; www.thepinkpalace.com. Breakfast, dinner, and ferry pick-up included. **Internet** €2 per 30min. Rooms €19, with A/C and bath €25.)

Ferries run from Corfu Town to Italy (see above) and Patras (6-7hr., 1-2 per day, €25), and high-speed **catamarans** run to Kephalonia (3hr., W and Sa 9am, €38). KTEL inter-city green buses depart from between I. Theotaki and the New Fortress; blue municipal buses leave from Pl. San Rocco. The EOT **tourist office** is at the corner of Rizopaston Voulefton and I. Polila. (☎26610 37 520. Open M-F 8am-1:30pm. Free maps and info.) **The Association of Owners of Private Rooms and Apartments,** I. Polila 24 (☎26610 26 133), has a complete list of rooms in Corfu Town. **Hotel Hermes ❸,** G. Markorka 14, centrally located across the bend from the police station, has a verdant entrance and low rates. (☎26610 39 268. Singles €28, with bath €33; doubles €33/€44; triples €50.) **To Paradosiakon ❶,** Odos Solomou 20, serves traditional food highly recommended by locals. (Open daily 11am-midnight. Entrees €4.10-8.50.) **Restaurant Rex ❸,** Kapodistriou 66, one block back from the Spianada, has long been famed as one of the town's best. (Entrees €7.40-14.) The undisputed epicenter of Corfu Town's nightlife is the **Disco Strip,** on Eth. Antistaseos, 2km west of New Port. **Postal Code:** 49100.

KEPHALONIA (Κεφαλονια) ☎26710

Mountains, subterranean lakes and rivers, caves, forests, and more than 250km of sand-and-pebble coastline make Kephalonia (pop. 32,000) a nature lover's paradise. Its profound beauty, fought over by the Byzantine, Ottoman, and British Empires draws and humbles a diverse crowd. **Argostoli,** the capital of Kephalonia and Ithaka, is a lively city packed with pastel buildings that climb the hills from the calm waters of the harbor. Argostoli offers good shopping and nightlife, as well as easy access to other points on the island. **Buses** leave from the south end of the waterfront for Sami (2 per day, €3) and Fiskardo (2hr., 2 per day, €4). **Internet** is available at **Cafeland,** on Andrea Choida in Argostoli. (☎26710 24 064. €5 per hour, €2.50 min. Open daily 9am-11pm.) **Hotel Tourist ❸,** on the waterfront near the bus station, is a great deal. (☎26710 22 510. All rooms have balconies. Singles €30-36; doubles €46-52.) 🖾**Mister Grillo ❷,** near the port authority, offers large portions and live Greek music. (Vegetarian options. Entrees €6-14.)

Sami is 24km from Argostoli on the east coast. Stunning views stretch in every direction, from the waves crashing on the beach to the green hills cradling the town. Sami is close to the underground **Melissani Lake** and **Drogarati Cave,** a large cavern filled with stalactites and stalagmites. (Cave open daily until nightfall. €3, children €1.50.) **Fiskardo,** at the northern tip of the island, is the most beautiful of Kephalonia's towns; take a bus from either Sami (1hr., 10:15am, €3) or Argostoli (2hr., 2 per day, €4). Buses from Fiskardo stop at the turn-off for 🖾**Myrtos Beach,** one of Europe's best. (Beach 4km from turn-off.) **Ferries** run from Sami to: Patras (2½hr., 2 per day, €12); and Brindisi, Italy (July-Sept. daily, €35). **Hotel Kyma ❷,** in Sami's main *plateia*, has spacious rooms. (☎26740 22 064. Singles €18-28; doubles €26-55; triples €31-66.) **Postal Code:** 28100.

THE SPORADES (Σποραδες)

Circling into the azure Aegean, the Sporades form a family of enchanting sea maidens. From wild Skiathos to sophisticated Skopelos to quiet Alonnisos, the islands have beckoned to visitors for millennia. Ancient Athenians and Romans, early Venetians, and modern-day tourists have all basked on their sunlit shores and trod their shaded forests.

TRANSPORTATION

To get to most of the Sporades from Athens, take the bus to Agios Konstantinos (2½hr., every hr., €11), where **Hellas Lines** (☎22 209) operates **ferries** to: Alonnisos (5½hr., 2 per week, €14); Skiathos (2hr., 2 per day, €21); and Skopelos (3hr., 2 per day, €27). **Flying Dolphins** leave Agios Konstantinos for: Alonnisos (2¾hr., 1-5 per day, €27); Skiathos (1½hr., 1-5 per day, €21); and Skopelos (2½hr., 1-5 per day, €27). Ferries also shuttle between the islands (see below).

SKIATHOS (Σκιαθος) ☎24270

Having grown up almost overnight from an innocent island daughter to a madcap dancing queen, Skiathos (local pop. 5,000; summer pop. over 50,000) is the tourism hub of the Sporades. Buses leave the port in Skiathos Town for the southern beaches (every 15min., €1.10). The bus route ends in Koukounaries, near the lovely, pine-wooded ◪**Koukounaries Beach and Biotrope** and the nude **Banana Beach** and **Little Banana Beach.** Indulge at the countless bars in **Plateia Papadiamantis** or along **Polytechniou** and **Evangelistra,** then dance all night long at the clubs on the eastern side of the waterfront. Hellas Lines **ferries** (☎24270 22 209) run to Alonnisos (2hr., 1-2 per day, €8) and Skopelos (1½hr., 1-3 per day, €5.40). *Domatia* are the best deal in town. The **Rooms to Let Office,** in the wooden kiosk by the port, provides a list of available rooms. (☎24270 22 990. Open daily 9am-8pm.) The rooms at ◪**Australia Hotel ❷,** in an alley on Evangelistra off Papadiamantis, have A/C, private baths, fridges, and balconies. (Singles €20; doubles €25-30; triples €36; in Aug. prices increase.) **Primavera ❷** has delicious Italian food. (Entrees €5-10. Open daily 6:30pm-12:30am.) **Postal Code:** 37002.

SKOPELOS (Σκοπελος) ☎24240

Skopelos (pop. 6,000) sits between the whirlwind of Skiathos and the wilderness of Alonnisos featuring the best elements of both. Hikes and moped rides lead to numerous monasteries, bright beaches, and white cliffs. Buses leave from the right of the waterfront (as you face the sea) for beaches near **Stafylos, Milia,** and **Loutraki.** At night, the waterfront strip closes to traffic and crowds swarm the streets in search of the tastiest *gyros* and the most authentic Greek *taverna.* Hellas Lines (☎22 767) runs **ferries** to: Alonnisos (30min., 1-2 per day, €4.10); Skiathos (1hr., 3-4 per day, €5.50); and Thessaloniki (1 per week, €40). **Thalpos Travel Agency,** 5m to the right of Galanatsiou along the waterfront, provides tourist info. (☎22 947. Open May-Oct. daily 10am-2pm and 6-10pm; Nov.-Apr. info available by phone.) The **Rooms and Apartments Association** can provide a list of current *domatia.* (☎24 567. Open daily 10am-2pm and 6-10pm.) **Pension Sotos ❷,** on the waterfront at the corner of Galanatsiou, has a fantastic location and unbeatable prices. (☎22 549. Singles €22; doubles €32; triples €55.) **Plateia Platanos** abounds with fast, cheap food. **Postal Code:** 37003.

ALONNISOS (Αλοννησος) ☎24240

Of the 20-odd islands within Greece's new **National Marine Park,** only Alonnisos (pop. 2,000) is inhabited. **Hikers** take to the highland trails in the north; pick up *Alonnisos on Foot* (€9) in **Patitiri** for walking routes. In the south, endless beaches satisfy sun-seeking souls; many are accessible from the island's main road. A 1½hr. walk from Patitiri takes you to **Votsi;** locals dive off the 15-20m cliffs near **Votsi Beach.** Beautiful **Hora** (Χωρα; Old Town) is ideal for both hikers and beachgoers. A **bus** runs between Hora and Patitiri (every hr., €1). **Ferries** run to Skiathos (2hr., 2 per day, €6) and Skopelos (30min., 1-2 per day, €4.10). **Alonissos Travel,** in the center of the waterfront, exchanges currency, finds rooms, books excursions, and sells ferry tickets. (☎65 188. Open daily 8am-11pm.) **Panorama ❷**, down the first alley on the left from Ikion Dolophon, rents bright rooms and studios. (☎65 240. All rooms with bath. Singles €25; doubles €40; 2-bedroom suite with kitchen €40-60.) Locals adore the *ouzeri* **To Kamaki ❶**, on the left side of Ikion Dolophon, past the National Bank. The octopus salad (€8.50) is delicious. (Open daily 11am-2am.) **Postal Code:** 37005.

THE CYCLADES (Κυκλαδες)

When people wax rhapsodic about the Greek islands, chances are they're talking about the Cyclades. Whatever your idea of Greece—cobblestone streets and whitewashed houses, breathtaking sunsets, scenic hikes, all-night revelry—you'll find it here. Although most islands are mobbed in the summer, each has quiet villages and untouched spots.

▊ TRANSPORTATION

Ferries run from: Athens to Mykonos, Naxos, and Santorini; Crete to Naxos and Santorini; and Thessaloniki to Naxos and Ios. Frequent ferries also run between each of the islands in the Cyclades. See below for all ferry information. High-speed ferries and **hydrofoils** typically cover the same routes at twice the cost and speed.

MYKONOS (Μυκονος)   ☎22890

Coveted by pirates in the 18th century, Mykonos is still lusted after by those seeking revelry and excess. Nightlife, both gay and straight, abounds on this island, the expensive playground of chic sophisticates. Ambling in colorful alleyways at dawn or dusk is the cheapest and most exhilarating way to experience the island, especially **Mykonos Town**. All of Mykonos's beaches are nudist, but the degree of bareness varies. **Plati Yialos, Paradise Beach,** and **Super Paradise Beach** are the most daring; **Elia** is a bit tamer. Buses run south from South Station to Plati Yialos (every 30min., €1), where *caïques* (little boats) go to the other beaches (around €1.50); direct buses also run to Paradise from South Station (every 30min., €1) and to Elia from North Station (30min., 8 per day, €1). After 11pm, wild dancing and irresistible hedonism are the norm at **Pierro's** on Matogianni (beer €5). The **Skandinavian Bar** on the waterfront has something for everyone in its two-building party complex. (Beer and shots €3-4. Open Su-F 8:30pm-3am, Sa 8:30pm-4am.)

Ferries run to: Naxos (3hr., 1-2 per day, €7.10); Santorini (6hr., 3 per week, €14); and Tinos (45min., 3 per day, €4). The helpful **tourist police** are located at the ferry landing. (☎22890 22 482. Open daily 8am-11pm.) Most budget travelers bed down at Mykonos's several festive campsites, which offer a myriad of sleeping options beyond the standard plot of grass. There are **information offices** on the dock, one for **hotels** and one for **camping**. (Hotels ☎22890 24 540; open daily 9am-midnight. Camping ☎22890 23 567; open daily 9am-midnight.) **Hotel Philippi ❷**, Kalogera 25, across from Zorzis Hotel, provides cheerful rooms with bath, fridge, and A/C around a bountiful garden. (☎22890 22 294; chriko@otenet.gr. Open Apr.-Oct. Singles €35-60; doubles €45-75). The lively ▊**Paradise Beach Camping ❶**, 6km from the village, is directly on the beach. (☎22890 22 852. €5-7 per person, €2.50-3 per tent, 2-person beach cabin €20-45.) Cheap *creperies* and *souvlaki* joints are on nearly all of Mykonos's streets. **Appaloosa ❸**, one block from Taxi Square on Mavrogeneous, serves mostly Mexican selections. (Entrees €9-11. Open daily 8pm-1:30am.) **Postal Code:** 84600.

⚅ DAYTRIP FROM MYKONOS: DELOS. Delos (Δηλος) is the sacred center of the Cyclades. The **archaeological site,** which occupies much of the small island, takes several days to explore completely, but its highlights can be seen in about three hours. From the dock, head straight to the **Agora of the Competaliasts;** continue in the same direction and turn left onto the wide **Sacred Road** to reach the **Sanctuary of Apollo,** a collection of temples built from Mycenaean times onward. On the right is the biggest and most famous, the **Great Temple of Apollo.** Continue 50m past the end of the Sacred Road to the beautiful **Terrace of the Lions.** The **museum,** next to the cafeteria, contains an assortment of archaeological finds. (Open Su and Tu-Sa 8:30am-3pm. €5, students €2.) A path from the museum leads to the summit of **Mt. Kythnos** (112m), from which Zeus watched Apollo's birth. Excursion **boats** leave the dock near Mykonos Town for Delos (35min., 3 per day, round-trip €10).

PAROS (Παρος) ☎ 22840

Paros is famed for its slabs of pure white marble, used for many of the great statues and buildings of the ancient world. Today's visitors know the island for its tall mountains and long, golden beaches. Behind the commercial surface of **Parikia** (pop. 3,000), Paros's port and largest city, flower-filled streets wind through archways and past one of the most treasured basilicas of the Orthodox faith, the **Panagia Ekatontapiliani** (Church of Our Lady of 100 Gates). Tradition holds that only 99 of the church's 100 doors are visible—when the 100th appears, Constantinople will again belong to the Greeks. (Dress modestly. Open daily 7am-10pm. Free.) Just 10km south of town is the shady, spring-fed ⚅**Valley of the Butterflies** (a.k.a. *Petaloudes*), where rare *Panaxiaquadripunctaria* moths congregate during the mating season from June to late September. Take the bus from Parikia to Aliki (10min., 8 per day, €0.90) and ask to be let off at Petaloudes. Follow the signs 2km up the road. (Open June-Sept. daily 9am-8pm. €1.50.) The **Parian Experience,** along the waterfront, is a pulsating party complex with a spacious central courtyard and four simultaneous tunes. Follow the spotlight and crowds to the far end of the harbor. (☎ 22840 21 113. Beer €2-3. Mixed drinks €5-6. €3 discount on first drink.)

Ferries sail to Ios (2½hr., 7-9 per day, €8.30) and Santorini (3½hr., 7-9 per day, €12). The **tourist police** are on the *plateia* behind the telephone office. (☎ 22840 21 673. Open daily 7am-2:30pm.) Turn left at the dock and take a right after the cemetery ruins to reach the pleasant **Rena Rooms ❷.** (☎ 22840 22 220. Doubles €18-39; triples €27-45. 20% discount for *Let's Go* readers.) The psychedelic **Happy Green Cow ❸,** a block off the *plateia* behind the National Bank, serves tasty vegetarian fare. (Entrees €8-12. Open Apr.-Nov. daily 7pm-midnight.) **Postal Code:** 84400.

NAXOS (Ναξος) ☎ 22850

The ancients believed Naxos (pop. 18,500), the largest of the Cyclades, was the home of Dionysus. Olive groves, wineries, small villages, and chalky white ruins fill its interior, while sandy beaches line its shores. **Naxos Town,** the capital, is crowned by the **Kastro,** a Venetian castle now home to two museums. The ⚅**Venetian Museum** features evening concerts with traditional Greek music, dancing, and shadow theater. (Open daily 10am-4pm and 7-11pm. €5, students and seniors €3.) The **Archaeological Museum** occupies the former Collège Français, which educated Nikos Kazantzakis, author of *The Last Temptation of Christ* and *Zorba the Greek.* (Open Su and Tu-Sa 8:30am-2pm. €3, students €2.) The **Mitropolis Museum,** next to the Orthodox Church, is an architectural achievement in itself, built around the excavated site of a 13th-century BC settlement. (Open Su and Tu-Sa 8:30am-3pm. Free.) The 6th-century BC **Portara** archway, visible from the waterfront, is one of the few archaeological sites in Greece where you can actually climb all over the ruins. To experience the island fully, it's essential to escape

Naxos Town. A bus goes from the port to the beaches of **Agia Georgios, Agios Prokopios, Agia Anna,** and **Plaka** (every 30min., €1.20). Buses also run from Naxos Town to **Apiranthos,** a beautiful village with narrow, marble paths (1hr., €2.10). To get to the **Tragea** highland valley, an enormous, peaceful olive grove, take a bus from Naxos Town to Halki (30min., 6 per day, €1.20).

Ferries go from Naxos Town to: Athens (6½hr., 2 per day, €17); Ios (1hr., daily, €8.20); Kos (7hr., 1 per week, €16); Mykonos (3hr., daily, €9); Paros (1hr., 4 per day, €5.50); Rhodes (13hr., 1 per week, €20); Santorini (3hr., 3 per day, €13); and Thessaloniki (14hr., 1 per week, €30). The **tourist office** is 300m up from the dock, by the bus station. (☎22850 24 358. Open daily 8am-11pm.) **Irene's Pension ❷,** about 100m from Ag. Giorgios, is near the center of the town. (☎22850 23 169. All rooms with A/C. Call ahead. Singles €15; doubles €20-30; triples €25-35; 5-person apartments €40-50.) **Panorama ❸,** in Old Naxos, has rooms with fans and fridges. (☎22850 22 330. Doubles from €25.) Naxos has three **camping ❶** options along the beach; look for representatives along the dock. (€5 per person, plus a small tent fee.) **Postal Code:** 84300.

IOS (Ιος)   ☎22860

Ios (pop. 2,000) has everything your mother warned you about—swimming less than 30 minutes after a meal, dancing in the streets, and drinking games all day long on the beach. The **port** (Yialos) is at one end of the island's sole paved road; the **village** (Hora) sits above it on a hill; but the beaches are the place to be. Most spend their days at **Mylopotas Beach,** a 20min. walk downhill from Ios town or a bus ride from the port or village (every 10-20min. 7:20am-midnight, €1). Sunning is typically followed by drinking; **Dubliner,** near the basketball courts, is a good place to start. On Thursday nights, €24 buys you pizza, a drink, and cover immunity at five bars that comprise the ultimate pub crawl. Head up from the *plateia* to reach the **Slammer Bar** for tequila slammers (€3), then run with the pack to **Red Bull** for shots (€2.40). Grind to techno at **Scorpion Disco,** the island's largest club, as you stumble your way back to the beach. (Cover after 1am.) Only a few hours later, crowds begin to gather at the beach, where **Mylopotas Water Sports Center** offers rental and lessons for windsurfing, water-skiing, and snorkeling (€14-40).

Ferries go to: Naxos (1¾hr., at least 3 per day, €8.20) and Santorini (1¼hr., 3 per day, €6.20). The main **tourist office** is next to the bus stop. (☎22860 91 343. Open daily 8am-midnight.) In the village, take the uphill steps to the left in the *plateia* and take the first left to reach ▨**Francesco's ❶,** where you'll find spectacular harbor views and a terrace bar. (☎22860 91 706; www.francescos.net. Dorms €8-14; doubles €10-25.) On the end of Mylopotas Beach, ▨**Far Out Camping ❶** has a pool, plenty of tents, parties, and activities, including bungee jumping. (☎22860 92 301. Open Apr.-Oct. Tent rental €4-7.50; small cabins from €5; bungalows €7-18.) ▨**Ali Baba's ❷,** next to Ios Gym, offers delicious pad thai (€8.50) and burgers (€5.50). On a narrow street off the main church's *plateia,* **Lord Byron's ❸** serves a unique blend of Greek and Smirniki food. (Entrees €9-15.) **Postal Code:** 84001.

SANTORINI (Σαντορινη)   ☎22860

Whitewashed towns balanced on cliffs, black-sand beaches, and deeply scarred hills make Santorini's landscape nearly as dramatic as the volcanic explosion that created it. Despite all the kitsch in touristy **Fira** (pop. 2,500), the island's capital, nothing can ruin the pleasure of wandering the town's cobblestoned streets, browsing its craft shops, and taking in the sunset from its western edge. On the southwestern side of the island, the excavations at **Akrotiri,** a late Minoan city, are preserved under layers of volcanic rock. (Open Su and Tu-Sa 8:30am-3pm. €5, students €3.) Buses run to Akrotiri from Fira (30min., 16 per day, €1.30). Frequent buses also leave Fira for the black-sand **beaches** of Perissa (15min., 30 per day, €0.90) and Kamari (20min., 2-3 per hr., €0.90) to the southeast. The bus stops before Perissa in Pyrgos; from there, you can hike (40min.) to the **Profitis Ilias Monastery,** whose lofty location provides an island panorama, and continue an extra 1½hr. to the ruins of **Ancient Thira.** (Open Su and Tu-Sa 8:30am-2:30pm.)

Ferries from Fira run to: Ios (1½hr., 3-5 per day, €6.30); Iraklion (4hr., daily, €14); Mykonos (7hr., 2 per week, €13); Naxos (4hr., 4-8 per day, €11); and Paros (4½hr., 3-5 per day, €12). Most ferries depart from Athinios harbor; frequent buses (30min., €1.50) connect to Fira. Head 300m north from the *plateia* in Fira to reach the friendly **Thira Youth Hostel ❶,** in an old monastery. (☎22860 22 387. Open Apr.-Oct. Dorms €8-12; doubles €20-40.) Take a bus from Fira to **Oia** (25min., 30 per day, €0.90) for more options; the impeccable rooms at █**Youth Hostel Oia ❷** are a good choice. (☎22860 71 465. Breakfast included. Open May-Oct. Dorms €12-14.) The cheery and colorful **Mama's Cyclades Cafe ❷,** north of Fira on the road to Oia, serves up a big breakfast special. (☎22860 23 032. Entrees €5-8. Open daily 8am-midnight.) **Postal Code:** 84700.

CRETE (Κρητη)

According to a Greek saying, a Cretan's first loyalty is to his island, his second to his country. Since 3000 BC, Crete has maintained an identity distinct from the rest of Greece, first expressed in the language, script, and architecture of the ancient Minoans. Despite this insular mind-set, residents are friendly to visitors who come to enjoy their island's inexhaustible trove of mosques, monasteries, mountain villages, gorges, grottoes, and beaches. Crete is divided into four main prefectures: Iraklion, Hania, Rethymno, and Lasithi.

▉ TRANSPORTATION

Olympic Airways (☎2810 288 073) and **Air Greece** connect Athens to: Sitia (2-3 per week, €83) in the east; Iraklion (45min., 13-15 per day, €84) in the center; and Hania (4 per day, €53) in the west.

IRAKLION (Ηρακλιον)   ☎2810

Iraklion (pop. 132,000) is Crete's capital and primary port. The chic locals live life in the fast lane, which translates into an urban brusqueness unique among the cities of Crete and the most diverse nightlife on the island. Iraklion's main attraction after Knossos (p. 522) is the superb ▉**Archaeological Museum,** off Pl. Eleftherias. By appropriating major finds from all over the island, the museum has amassed a comprehensive record of the Neolithic and Minoan stages of Cretan history. (Open M noon-7pm, Tu-Su 8am-7pm. €6, students €3, EU students free.) A maze of streets between **Plateia Venizelou** and **Plateia Eleftherias** houses Iraklion's night spots; visit Korai for classy cafes or D. Boufor for posh clubs.

From Terminal A, between the old city walls and the harbor, **buses** leave for Agios Nikolaos (1½hr., 20 per day, €5). Buses leave across from Terminal A for Hania (3hr., 17 per day, €11) and Rethymno (1½hr., 17 per day, €6). The **tourist police** are on Dikeosinis 10. (☎2810 283 190. Open daily 7am-10pm.) **Gallery Games Net,** Korai 14, has **Internet** access. (☎2810 282 804. €3 per hr.) **Rent a Room Hellas ❶,** Handakos 24, two blocks from El Greco Park, has large dorm rooms and a spectacular view. (☎2810 288 851. Dorms €9; doubles €25; triples €36.) The **open-air market** near Pl. Venizelou has stalls piled high with fruit, vegetables, cheeses, and meats. (Open M, W and Sa 8am-2pm, Tu and Th-F 8am-2pm and 5-9pm.) **Prassein Aloga ❷**, Handakos 21, serves fresh Mediterranean dishes in its tree-lined courtyard. (Entrees €6-10. Open M-Sa noon-midnight). **Postal Code:** 71001.

🔁 DAYTRIP FROM IRAKLION: KNOSSOS. At Knossos (Κνωσσος), the most famous archaeological site in Crete, excavations have revealed the remains of the largest and most complicated of Crete's **Minoan palaces.** Sir Arthur Evans, who financed and supervised the excavations, eventually restored large parts of the palace in Knossos; his work often crossed the line from preservation to artistic interpretation, but the site is nonetheless impressive. (Open in summer daily 8am-7pm; off-season 8am-5pm. €6, students €3; In off-season, Su free.) To reach Knossos from Iraklion, take **bus** #2 from Augustou 25 (€1).

RETHYMNO (Ρεθυμνο) ☎ 28310

Crete's many conquerors—Venetians, Ottomans, and even Nazis—have had a profound effect in Rethymno (pop. 25,000). Arabic inscriptions adorn the walls of the narrow streets, minarets highlight the skyline, and the 16th-century **Venetian Fortezza** stands watch over the scenic harbor. Bring a picnic and explore the fortress ruins. (Open M-Th and Sa-Su 8:30am-7pm. €2.90.) Cloistered beaches, steep gorges and stunning hikes await in the nearby town of **Plakias.** (4 buses from Rethymno per day, €3.30). The **Rethymno-Hania bus station** (☎ 28310 22 212) is south of the fortress on the water, with service to Hania (1hr., 16 per day, €5.60) and Iraklion (1½hr., 17 per day, €6). Climb the stairs behind the bus station, turn left on Ig. Gavriil, which becomes Kountouriotou, and turn left on Varda Kallergi to reach the waterfront and the **tourist office,** on El. Venizelou. (☎ 28310 29 148. Open M-F 9am-2pm.) To get from the station to the friendly **Youth Hostel ❶**, Tombazi 41-45, walk down Ig. Gavriil, take the first left at Pl. Martiron; Tombazi is the first right. (☎ 28310 22 848. Breakfast €1.70. Internet €1 per 15 min. Reception 8am-noon and 5-9pm. Dorms €7.) **Postal Code:** 74100.

HANIA (Χανια) ☎ 28210

The **Venetian lighthouse** marks the entrance to Hania's (pop. 70,000) stunning architectural relic, the **Venetian Inner Harbor.** The inlet has retained its original breakwater and arsenal; the lighthouse was restored by the Egyptians during their occupation of Crete in the late 1830s. A day is best spent meandering among the narrow Venetian buildings and Ottoman domes on the lively waterfront.

Ferries arrive in the nearby port of Souda; buses connect from the port to Hania's supermarket on Zymvrakakidon (15min., €1). **Buses** (☎ 28210 93 306) leave from the station on the corner of Kydonias and Kelaidi for Rethymno (17 per day, €5.60). The **tourist office,** Korkidi 16, is just off P. 1866. (☎ 28210 36 155. Open M-F 8am-2pm.) To get to ▓**Hotel Fidias ❷**, Sarpaki 6, walk toward the harbor on Halidon and turn right onto Athinagora, which then becomes Sarpaki. (☎ 28210 52 494. Dorms €7-13; singles €13-20; doubles €15-23.) ▓**Anaplous ❷**, near the harbor on Sifaka, is an open-air bistro that serves *pilino*, a pork and lamb creation. (*Pilino* €25; serves three. Entrees €6-8. Open daily 6pm-1am.) **Postal Code:** 73100.

🔁 HIKING NEAR HANIA: SAMARIA GORGE. The most popular excursion from Hania and Iraklion is the 5-6hr. hike down ▓**Samaria Gorge** (Φαραγγι τηϖ Σαμαριαϖ), a spectacular 16km ravine extending through the White Mountains. Sculpted by rainwater over 14 million years, the gorge—the longest in Europe—retains its allure despite having been trampled by thousands of visitors. Rare native plants peek out from sheer rock walls, wild *agrimi* goats clamber about the hills, and golden eagles and endangered griffin vultures circle overhead. (Open

May to mid-Oct. daily 6am-6pm. €3, children under-15 and organized student groups free.) For more info, call **Hania Forest Service** (☎28210 92 287). The trail starts at **Xyloskalo;** take the 6:15am or 8:30am **bus** from Hania to Xyloskalo (1½hr., €5.20) for a day's worth of hiking. The 1:45pm bus from Hania will put you in **Omalos,** ready for the next morning. The trail ends in **Agia Roumeli,** on the southern coast, where you can hop on a **boat** to Hora Sfakion (1¼hr., 3-4 per day, €4.40) or take a return bus to Hania (4 per day, €5.20).

SITIA (Σητεια)   ☎28430

Sitia (pop. 8,500) makes a great base for exploring Crete's east coast. Skip the town's own beach and head to the beautiful **Vai Beach** and its palm tree forest, a 1hr. bus ride away via Palaikastro (€2.10). To reach the **Valley of Death,** a Minoan burial ground that's great for hiking, take a bus from Sitia via Palaikastro and Zakros (1hr., 2 per day, €3.80). The **Minoan Palace** rests at the end of the valley. (Open daily 8am-3pm. €3, students and seniors €2. EU students free.) After midnight, everyone in Sitia heads to **Hot Summer,** 1km down the road to Palaikastro, where a swimming pool replaces the traditional dance floor.

Ferries leave Sitia for: Athens (16-17hr., 5 per week, €24) via Agios Nikolaos (1½hr., €6.30); Karpathos (5hr., €16); and Rhodes (12hr., €22). From the center of town, head east along the water; the **tourist office** will be on your left. (☎28430 28 300. Open M-F 9:30am-2:30pm and 5:30-8:30pm.) **Venus Rooms to Let ❷,** Kondilaki 60, looks out on scenic views; walk up on Kapetan Sifi from the main *plateia* and turn right after the telephone office. (☎28430 24 307. Doubles €25, with bath €30; triples €30/€36.) The **Cretan House ❷,** K. Karamanli 10, off the *plateia* and on the waterfront, serves Cretan meals for €5-8. Ask for the "Cretan Viagra" to heat up your night. (*Staka* €3.30. Open daily 9am-1am.) **Postal Code:** 72300.

EASTERN AEGEAN ISLANDS

The intricate, rocky coastlines and unassuming port towns of the **Northeast Aegean Islands** enclose thickly wooded mountains and unspoiled villages and beaches. Despite their proximity to the Turkish coast and a noticeable military presence, the Northeast Aegean Islands dispense a taste of undiluted Greek culture. **The Dodecanese** are the farthest Greek island group from the mainland. Closer to Asia Minor than to Athens, these islands have experienced more invasions than the central parts of the country—eclectic architecture is the most visible legacy of these comings and goings.

SAMOS (Σαμος)   ☎22730

Visitors frequently stop in Samos en route to Kuşadası and the ruins of Ephesus on the Turkish coast. *Tavernas* line the crescent-shaped harbor of Samos Town while red roofs speckle the hillsides of **Vathy,** the residential part of town. The ▧**Archaeological Museum,** which sits behind the municipal gardens, houses a comprehensive collection from the Temple of Hera. (Open Su and Tu-Sa 8:30am-3pm. €3, seniors and students €2, EU students free.) The ancient city of **Pythagorion,** once the island's capital, is 14km south of Vathy. Near the town are the magnificent remains of Polykrates's 6th-century BC engineering project, the **Tunnel of Eupalinos,** which supplied water to the city from a natural spring 1.3km away. (Open Su and Tu-Sa 8:45am-2:45pm. €4, students €2. EU students free.) Buses go from Samos Town to Pythagorion (20min., €1.20). Polykrates's greatest feat was the **Temple of Hera,** in Heraion, a 30min. bus ride (€1.60) from Pythagorion. (Open Su and Tu-Sa 8:30am-3pm. €3, students €2.)

Ferries arrive in Samos from: Chios (5hr., 3 per week, €11); Mykonos (6hr., 3 per week, €18); Naxos (6hr., 6 per week, €38); and Rhodes (1 per week, €24). The **tourist office** is on a side street a block before Pl. Pythagoras. (☎22730 28 530. Open July-Aug. M-Sa 7am-2:30pm.) Once an old monastery, **Pension Avli** ❸, Areos 2, offers an elegant, shady courtyard. (☎22730 22 939. Doubles with bath €25-30; triples available.) **Postal Code:** 83100.

CHIOS (Χιος)   ☎22710

Pine-speckled hills lend an untamed feel to the interior of Chios (pop. 50,000), which offers its visitors charming villages and hot, sandy shores. **Pyrgi,** 25km from Chios Town, is one of Greece's most striking villages, with black-and-white geometric designs covering its buildings. Farther south lies **Emborio** beach, where beige cliffs accentuate the black stones and blue water below. **Buses** run from Chios Town to Pyrgi (4 per day, €2.20). **Ferries** go from Chios Town to: Mykonos (1 per week, €14); Rhodes (2 per week, €28); Samos (4hr., 2 per week, €11); and Tinos (2 per week, €15). To reach the **tourist office,** Kanari 18, turn off the waterfront onto Kanari and walk toward the *plateia.* (☎22710 44 344. Open May-Oct. M-F 7am-2:30pm and 6-10pm, Sa-Su 9am-2pm and 6-10pm; Nov.-Mar. M-F 7am-2:30pm.) The hospitable owners at ◪**Chios Rooms** ❷, Leofores 114, offer large rooms and sparkling-clean bathrooms. (☎22710 20 198. Singles €18-22; doubles €23-25, with bath €30; triples with bath €35.) **Postal Code:** 82100.

LESVOS (Λεσβος)   ☎22510

Lesvos's (pop. 100,000) cosmopolitan, off-beat culture incorporates horse breeding, *ouzo,* and leftist politics. Huge, geographically diverse, and far from the mainland, the island attracts visitors who spend weeks exploring its therapeutic hot springs, monasteries, petrified forest, sandy beaches, mountain villages, and seaside cliffs. Most travelers pass through the modern **Mytilini,** the capital and central port city. At the new ◪**Archaeological Museum,** 8 Noemvriou, visitors can walk on preserved mosaic floors dating from Lesvos's Neolithic past. (Open Su and Tu-Sa 8am-3pm. €3, students €2. Under-18 and EU students free.) Only 4km south of Mytilini along El. Venizelou, the village of **Varia** is home to two excellent museums. **Theophilos Museum** features the work of the neo-primitivist Greek painter Theophilos Hadzimichali. (Open Su and Tu-Sa 9am-2:30pm and 6-8pm. €2. Students and under-18 free.) **Musée Tériade** displays lithographs by Chagall, Matisse, Miró, and Picasso. (Open Su and Tu-Sa 9am-2pm and 5-8pm. €2. Students and children free.) The artist colony of **Molyvos** has a quiet charm and is more affordable than the capital; take a bus from Mytilini (1½hr., 5-6 per day, €4.70). **Eftalou** has beautiful pebble and black sand beaches, accessible by frequent buses from Molyvos. A 20-million-year old petrified forest 4km from **Sigri,** one of only two such forests in the world, has fossilized trunks preserved in amazingly precise detail. For more info, call the main parks office in Mytilini. (☎22510 40 132. Park open late July to Aug. daily 8am-7pm; Sept. to early July 8am-4pm. €2. Under-15 free.)

Ferries go from Mytilini to: Chios (3hr., 1-2 per day, €12); Limnos (5hr., 6 per week, €15); and Thessaloniki (13hr., 1 per week, €12). Book ferries at **NEL Lines,** Pavlou Koudourioti 67 (☎22510 46 595), on the far right side of the waterfront facing inland. The **tourist police,** on Aristarchou near the ferry docks, offer brochures and advice. (☎22510 22 776. Open daily 7am-2:30pm.) Mytilini *domatia* are plentiful and well advertised. Be sure to negotiate; doubles should run €20-23. ◪**Nassos Guest House** ❷, on the hill just into Molyvos, offers cheerful rooms with balconies and a shared kitchen. (☎22510 71 432. Doubles €22-30; triples €24-34; discounts for longer stays.) **Postal Code:** 81100.

RHODES (Ροδος)   ☎ 22410

The undisputed tourism capital of the Dodecanese, the island of Rhodes (pop. 99,000) has retained a sense of serenity in the sandy beaches along its east coast, the jagged cliffs skirting its west coast, and the green mountains dotted with villages in its interior. The island's most famous sight is one that doesn't exist: the **Colossus of Rhodes,** a 35m bronze statue of Helios was one of the Seven Wonders of the Ancient World. While recent historians have debated the exact stance of the statue, legend says it straddled the island's harbor until it was destroyed by an earthquake in 237 BC. The **Old Town,** constructed by the Knights of St. John, lends **Rhodes Town** a medieval flair. At the top of the hill, a tall, square tower marks the entrance to the pride of the city, the **Palace of the Grand Master,** which features moats, drawbridges, battlements, and 300 rooms. (☎ 22410 25 500. Open Su and T-Sa 8:30am-3pm. €6, students €3. EU students free.) The beautiful halls and courtyards of the **Archaeological Museum,** dominating the **Plateia Argykastrou,** shelter small treasures, including the exquisite *Aphrodite Bathing* from the first-century BC. (Open T-Su 8:30am-2:30pm. €3, students €1.50.) Nightlife in the Old Town focuses around the street of **Militadou,** off Apelou. **Orfanidou,** in the New Town, is popularly known as **Bar Street.** Fifteen kilometers south of the city, **Faliraki** is frequented by rowdy drinkers and beach bathers. Buses run to Faliraki from Rhodes Town (20 per day, €1.60).

Ferries leave Rhodes Town for: Athens (1-4 per day, €30); Karpathos (3 per week, €15); Kos (1-2 per day, €15); Patmos (1-2 per day, €29); Samos (1 per week, €22); and Sitia, Crete (3 per week, €22). There is a **Greek National Tourist Office (EOT)** up Papgou, a few blocks from Pl. Rimini, at Makariou. ▮**Mama's Pension ❶,** Menekleous 28, has a kitchen, a *taverna* with live music, and balcony views. (☎ 22410 25 359. Laundry €3. Dorms €10; doubles €25.) The **Rhodes Youth Hostel ❶,** Ergiou 12, has a cool, quiet courtyard; to reach it, turn onto Fanouriou from Sokratous and follow the signs. (☎ 22410 30 491. Free luggage storage. Dorms €6; doubles and triples €20.) Fresh shellfish is the specialty at **Nireas ❷,** Sophokleous 22, in the Old Town. Try the *fouskes* (sea snails; €7.50), a local treat. (☎ 22410 21 703. Entrees €6-8. Open daily 7:30pm-late.) **Postal Code:** 85100.

KOS (Κως)   ☎ 22420

While the beaches of **Kos Town** (pop. 12,500) draw a young party crowd, rural Kos attracts the traveler in search of serene mountain villages. At the sanctuary of ▮**Asclepeion,** 4km southwest of Kos Town, Hippocrates opened the world's first medical school in the 5th century BC. In the summer, mini-trains (15 min., every hr., €.50-1.20.) run there from Kos Town. (Open Su and Tu-Sa 8am-6:30pm. €3, students €2.) The island's best beaches stretch along Southern Kos to Kardamene and are all accessible by bus; stops are by request. **Agios Theologos,** south of Limionas, is a pebbly beach perfect for night swimming. Most bars are located in **Exarhia,** in the Old City past Pl. Platonou, or along **Porfirou,** between Averof and Zouroundi. Runway models loom on giant television screens at the **Fashion Club,** Kanari 2, the hottest spot in town. (Cover €10, includes 1 drink. Open daily 11pm-4am.) The **Hamam Club,** inland from the Pl. Diagoras taxi station, is a former bathhouse turned dance club. **Heaven,** on Zouroudi, opposite the beach, is a large, popular disco. (Open Su-Th 10am-4am, F-Sa 10am-dawn.) The island of **Nisryos,** with an active volcano and beaches black with volcanic rock, is an idyllic daytrip; DANE Sea Lines **ferries** run from to Nisryos from **Kos** (1.5 hr., 2 per week, €7.40).

Ferries run to: Athens (11-15hr., 2-3 per day, €16); Patmos (4hr., 1-2 per day, €10); and Rhodes (4hr., 2-3 per day, €16). The **Greek National Tourist Office (EOT)** is at Vas. Georgiou 1. (☎ 22420 24 460. Open M-F 8am-2:30pm and 5:30-8:30pm.) Take the first right off Megalou Alexandrou to get to ▮**Pension Alexis ❷,** Irodotou 9, where the hospitable owners offer their guests every service. (☎22420 28 798. Doubles €20-22; triples €28-33.) **Studios Nitsa ❷**, Averof 47, has small rooms with bath and A/C. Take Averof inland from Akti Koundourioti. (☎22420 25 810. Doubles €20.) **Postal Code:** 85300.

PATMOS (Πατμος)   ☎22470

Given that it has recently become a favorite destination of the rich and famous, and that it has also been declared a "Sacred Island" by ministerial decree, Patmos (pop. 25,000) has an interesting blend of visitors. The white houses of **Hora** and the majestic walls of the sprawling **Monastery of St. John the Theologian** are visible from anywhere on the island. (Dress modestly. Monastery open daily 8am-1pm; also Tu, Th, Su 4-6pm.) Buses from **Skala**, the port town, run to Hora (10min., 11 per day, €1); alternatively, take a taxi (€3) or tackle the steep hike. The **Apocalypsis Monastery,** a complex of interconnected buildings between Skala and Hora, is built on the site where St. John stayed while on Patmos. Most visitors come to Patmos to see the **Sacred Grotto of the Revelation,** adjacent to the church of St. Anne, the cave where St. John dictated the Book of Revelation. (Dress modestly. Open daily 8am-1pm; Tu, Th, Su also 4-6pm.)

Ferries arrive in Skala from: Kos (4hr., 2-3 per day, €9.70); Rhodes (8hr., daily, €11); Samos (6 per week, €6); and Thessaloniki (22hr., 1 per week, €37). The **tourist office** is opposite the dock. (☎22470 31 666. Open daily 9am-9pm.) *Domatia* are offered by locals who meet the ferries; expect to pay €15-20 for singles and €20-30 for doubles. To reach **Stefanos Flower Camping at Meloi ❶**, 1.5km northeast of Skala, follow the waterfront road as it wraps along the port. The campground is on the left at the bottom of the hill. (☎22470 31 821. €5 per person.) **To Kyma ❸**, near the campground at Meloi Beach, serves freshly prepared fish. (Fish €20-40 per kg. Open daily 6:30pm-2am.) **Postal Code:** 85500.

HUNGARY
(MAGYARORSZÁG)

After 1100 years of repression and renewal, Hungary now appears at ease with its new-found capitalist identity. The country's social and economic keystone may still be Budapest, but travelers who skip the countryside for a whirlwind tour of the capital will miss rolling hills with wine valleys to the north, a rough-and-tumble cowboy plain to the south, and a beach resort to the east.

FACTS AND FIGURES

Official Name: Republic of Hungary.

Capital: Budapest.

Major Cities: Eger, Szombathely, Debrecen, Pécs.

Population: 10,300,000 (90% Magyar, 4% Roma, 3% German, 2% Serb).

Land Area: 92,340 sq. km.

Time Zone: GMT +1.

Language: Hungarian (Magyar).

Religions: Roman Catholic (68%), Calvinist (21%), Lutheran (5%), other (6%).

DISCOVER HUNGARY

Budapest (p. 531), Hungary's capital, is quickly being discovered as Central Europe's most cosmopolitan city. Sail down the river to reach the relaxed villages of the **Danube Bend** (p. 541) nearby. In Southern Transdanubia, **Eger** (p. 544) is home to one of Hungary's most important castles, and the vibrant wine cellars of the Valley of the Beautiful Women are a stone's throw away. Don't miss charming **Győr** (p. 546), which overflows with cultural treasures, and the nearby **Archabbey of Pannonhalma** (p. 546). **Lake Balaton** (p. 547), the Hungarian summer capital, hosts a kitschy beach scene. **Keszthely** (p. 548), on the lake's western end, has a stunning palace and provides an escape from the thonged throngs of **Siófok** (p. 547).

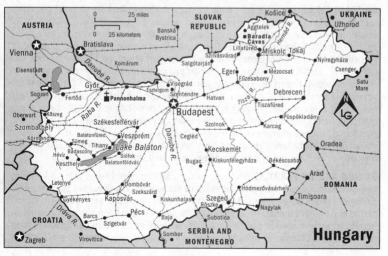

ESSENTIALS

WHEN TO GO

Temperatures are most pleasant from May to September. Because Budapest never feels crowded, even in the high season, time your visit to coincide with some of the summer festivals. Fall and spring, though a bit chillier, can be quite nice as well. Avoid visiting in winter, as it tends to get very cold.

DOCUMENTS AND FORMALITIES

VISAS. Citizens of Canada, Ireland, South Africa, the UK, and the US can visit without visas for 90 days, provided their passport does not expire within six months of their journey's end. Australians and New Zealanders must obtain 90-day tourist visas from a Hungarian embassy or consulate. Visas cost: Single-entry US$40; double-entry US$75; multiple-entry US$180; and 48hr. transit US$38. Border officials are generally quite efficient; there is no border fee. Visa extensions are rare; apply at a Hungarian police station.

EMBASSIES. All foreign embassies in Hungary are in Budapest (see p. 531). Hungarian embassies at home include: **Australia,** 17 Beale Crescent, Deakin, ACT 2600 (☎02 6282 3226); **Canada,** 299 Waverley St., Ottawa, ON K2P 0V9 (☎613-230-2717; www.docuweb.ca/hungary); **Ireland,** 2 Fitzwilliam Pl., Dublin 2 (☎01 661 2903; fax 01 661 2880); **New Zealand,** 37 Abbott St., Wellington, 6004 (☎04 973 7507; www.hungarianconsulate.co.nz); **South Africa,** 959 Arcadia St., Hatfield 0083; mail to: P.O. Box 27077, Sunnyside 0132 (☎012 430 3020); **UK,** 35 Eaton Pl., London SW1X 8BY (☎020 7235 5218; www.huemblon.org.uk); and **US,** 3910 Shoemaker St. NW, Washington, D.C. 20008 (☎202-362-6730; www.hungaryemb.org).

TRANSPORTATION

BY PLANE. Several international airlines fly into Budapest (BUD); the national airline, **Malév,** has daily direct flights from New York and London.

BY TRAIN. Most trains (*vonat*) pass through Budapest and are generally reliable and cheap. Book international tickets in advance. Consult www.elvira.hu for schedules and fares. **Eurail** is valid in Hungary. Students and those under 26 may be eligible for a 30% discount on train fares; ask ahead and be persistent. An **ISIC** card gets discounts at IBUSZ, Express, and station ticket counters. Flash your card and say "*diák*" (DEE-ahk; student). *Személyvonat* trains are slow; *Gyorsvonat* (listed on schedules in red) cost the same and are twice as fast. Large towns are accessible by the blue *Expressz* lines. Air-conditioned *InterCity* trains are fastest. A seat reservation (*potegy*) is required for trains labeled "R." While you can board an *InterCity* train without a reservation, the fine for doing so is 1000Ft, and purchasing the reservation on board will double the price of the ticket. Some basic vocabulary words are: *Érkezés* (arrival), *indulás* (departure), *vágány* (track), *állomás* or *pályaudvar* (station, abbreviated *pu.*), and *peron* (platform).

BY BUS AND BY FERRY. The cheap, clean, and crowded bus system links many towns that have rail connections only to Budapest. The **Erzsébet tér** station in Budapest posts schedules and fares. *InterCity* tickets are purchased on board; arrive early to get a seat. In larger cities, tickets for local transportation must be bought from newsstands; punch the ticket on board or face a fine. In smaller cities, pay on board. A **ferry** goes from Budapest to Vienna; contact Utinform ☎1 322 3600.

TOURIST SERVICES AND MONEY

EMERGENCY	Police, Ambulance, and Fire: ☎112.

TOURIST OFFICES. Tourinform has branches in most cities, and is the most useful tourist service in Hungary. They can't make reservations, but they'll check on vacancies, usually in university dorms and private *panzió*. Tourinform should be your first stop in any Hungarian town, as they always stock maps and tons of local info, and employees generally speak both English and German. Most **IBUSZ** offices throughout the country book private rooms, exchange money, sell train tickets, and charter tours. Pick up the pamphlet *Tourist Information: Hungary* and the monthly entertainment guides *Programme in Hungary* and *Budapest Panorama* (all free and in English).

MONEY. The **forint** (Ft) is divided into 100 *fillérs*, which are quickly disappearing from circulation. Inflation is currently around 5.3%, so expect prices to increase over the next year. The maximum legal commission for cash-to-cash exchange is 1%. Never change money on the street. Currency exchange machines have excellent rates, but tend to be slow. **OTP Bank** and **Postabank** offices have the best rates for exchanging traveler's checks. **Credit cards** are accepted at expensive hotels and shops. Rounding up the bill as a **tip** is standard etiquette. In restaurants, hand the tip to the server when you pay; it's rude to leave it on the table. Foreigners are expected to tip 15%, although locals never give more than 10%. Bathroom attendants generally get 30Ft.

FORINTS	AUS$1 = 151.88FT	100FT = AUS$0.66
	CDN$1 = 169.30FT	100FT = CDN$0.59
	EUR€1 = 256.68FT	100FT = EUR€0.40
	NZ$1 = 136.08FT	100FT = NZ$0.73
	UK£1 = 370.97FT	100FT = UK£0.27
	US$1 = 235.70FT	100FT = US$0.42
	ZAR1 = 32.25FT	100FT = ZAR3.10

COMMUNICATION

PHONE CODES	**Country code: 36. International dialing prefix: 00.** From outside Hungary, dial int'l dialing prefix (see inside back cover) + 36 + city code + local number.

TELEPHONES. For intercity calls, wait for the tone and dial slowly; enter ☎06 before the phone code. International calls require red phones or new, digital-display blue phones, which unfortunately tend to cut you off after three to nine minutes. Phones often require phone cards (*telefonkártya*), available at kiosks, train stations, and post offices. Direct calls can be made from Budapest's phone office. International carriers include: **AT&T Direct** (☎06 800 01111), **British Telecom** (☎800 89 0036), **Canada Direct** (☎06 800 01211), and **MCI Worldphone** (☎06 800 06111).

MAIL. The Hungarian mail system is somewhat reliable; airmail (*légiposta*) takes 5-10 days to the US and the rest of Europe, and two weeks to Australia, New Zealand, and South Africa. Postage costs around 36Ft for domestic mail and 140-150Ft for international. If you're mailing to a Hungarian citizen, the family name precedes the given name. For *Poste Restante*, address mail to be held: SURNAME Firstname, *Poste Restante*, Városház u. 18, 1052 Budapest, HUNGARY.

HUNGARY

INTERNET ACCESS. Internet access is available throughout Hungary (usually 150-300Ft per hr.). The Hungarian keyboard differs significantly from English-language keyboards. When you first log on, go to the lower right-hand corner of the screen and look for the *"Hu"* icon; click here to switch the keyboard setting to *"Angol."*

LANGUAGES. Hungarian, a Finno-Ugric language, is related distantly to Turkish, Estonian, and Finnish. After Hungarian and German, English is the most commonly spoken language. For Hungarian basics, see p. 1056.

ACCOMMODATIONS AND CAMPING

HUNGARY	❶	❷	❸	❹	❺
ACCOMMODATIONS	under 2000Ft	2000-3000Ft	3001-6000Ft	6001-10,000Ft	over 10,000Ft

Many travelers stay in **private homes** booked through tourist agencies, who may try to foist their most expensive rooms on you. Singles are scarce—it's worth finding a roommate, as solo travelers often pay for a double room. Outside Budapest, the best offices are region-specific (e.g. EgerTourist in Eger). After staying a few nights, you can make arrangements directly with the owner, saving yourself a 20-30% commission. **Panzió** (pensions), run out of private homes, are common, although not always cheap. **Hotels** exist in some towns, but most have disappeared. **Hostelling** is becoming more attractive, although it is rare outside Budapest; HI cards are increasingly useful. Many hostels can be booked through Express, the student travel agency, or through a regional tourist office. From June to August, **university dorms** become hostels; inquire at Tourinform. More than 300 **campgrounds** throughout Hungary are open from May to September. Tourist offices offer the annual booklet *Camping Hungary* for free. For more info and maps, contact Tourinform in Budapest (p. 533).

FOOD AND DRINK

HUNGARY	❶	❷	❸	❹	❺
FOOD	under 400Ft	400-800Ft	801-1300Ft	1301-2800Ft	over 2800Ft

Hungarian food is more flavorful and varied than standard Eastern European fare. Paprika, Hungary's chief agricultural export, colors most dishes red. In Hungarian restaurants (*vendéglő* or *étterem*), begin your meal with *halászlé*, a deliciously spicy fish stew. Alternatively, try *gyümölcsleves*, a cold fruit soup topped with whipped cream. The Hungarian national dish is *bográcsgulyás* (goulash), a beef stew with dumplings and paprika. *Borjúpaprikás* is veal with paprika and potato-dumpling pasta. Vegetarians can find recourse in the tasty *rántott sajt* (fried cheese) and *gombapörkölt* (mushroom stew) on most menus. In a *cukrászda* (confectionery), you can satisfy your sweet tooth cheaply. *Túrós rétes* is a chewy pastry pocket filled with sweetened cottage cheese. *Somlói galuska* is a rich, rum-soaked sponge cake of chocolate, nuts, and cream. *Unicum*, advertised as the national drink, is a fine herbal liqueur that Habsburg kings used to cure digestive ailments. Hungary also produces a diverse array of fine wines.

SAFETY AND SECURITY

Medical assistance is easily obtained in Budapest, where most hospitals have English-speaking doctors; embassies carry a list of Anglophone doctors. Outside Budapest, try to bring a Hungarian speaker with you. **Tourist insurance** is valid—and often necessary—for many medical services. Tap water is usually clean and drinkable. Public toilets vary in cleanliness: Pack toilet paper, soap, and a towel, and be prepared to pay the attendant 30Ft. Men's rooms are labeled *Férfi*, and women's *Női*. *Gyógyszertar* (pharmacies) are usually well-stocked with Western brands. Violent crime in Hungary is low, but in larger cities, especially Budapest, foreign tourists are favored targets of petty thieves and pickpockets. Although Hungarian laws are tolerant of homosexuality, travelers may experience serious discrimination, especially outside of Budapest—discretion is wise.

HOLIDAYS AND FESTIVALS

Holidays: National Day (Mar. 15); Easter (Apr. 11-12); Labor Day (May 1); Pentecost (May 30-31); Constitution Day (Aug. 20); Republic Day (Oct. 23); All Saints' Day (Nov. 1); Christmas (Dec. 25-26).

Festivals: Hotels and tourist offices have English-language guides to Budapest's many summer festivals (p. 540). In June and July, Budapest's Ferencvaros Festival is a diverse celebration of music. At the end of June, the **Budapest Farewell Festival** includes parades and concerts in celebration of the day the last Russian soldier left the country. For more info, check out www.fesztivalvaros.hu.

BUDAPEST   ☎ 1

Ten times larger than any other Hungarian city, Budapest (pop. 1,900,000) is reassuming its place as a major European capital. Originally two separate cities, Budapest was created in 1872 with the joining of Buda and Pest, soon becoming the most important Habsburg city after Vienna. World War II ravaged the city, but the Hungarians rebuilt it from rubble with the same pride they retained while weathering the Soviet occupation. Neon lights and legions of tourists may draw attention away from the city's cultural and architectural gems—but beneath it all beats a truly Hungarian heart.

TRANSPORTATION

Flights: Ferihegy Airport (BUD; ☎296 9696). **Malév** (Hungarian Airlines; reservations ☎235 3888). From the airport, the cheapest way to reach the city center is to take bus #93 (20min., every 15min. 4:55am-11:20pm, 106Ft), and then take the M3 to Köbanya-Kispest (15min. to Deák tér in downtown Pest).

Trains: There are three main stations: **Keleti pu., Nyugati pu.,** and **Déli pu.** (International ☎461 5500, domestic 461 5400; www.mav.hu). Most international trains arrive at Keleti Pályaudvar, but some from Prague go to Nyugati pu. Each station has schedules for the others; for a complete listing of Hungarian rail schedules, see ▨ www.bahn.de. To: **Berlin** (12hr., daily, 22,900Ft); **Bucharest** (14hr., 4 per day, 17,400Ft); **Prague** (8hr., 5 per day, 14,000Ft); **Vienna** (3hr., 17 per day, 7000Ft); **Warsaw** (11hr., 2 per day, 13,950Ft). Reservation fees 700-2000Ft. The daily **Orient Express** stops on its way from Paris to Istanbul. Purchase tickets at the **International Ticket Office,** Keleti pu. (Open daily 8am-6pm.) Or, try **MÁV Hungarian Railways,** VI, Andrássy út 35 and at all stations. (☎ 461 5500. Open M-F 9am-5pm. For student or under-26 discount on tickets, say, "*diák*".)

Buses: Most buses to Western Europe leave from **Volánbusz main station,** V, Erzsébet tér (☎117 2966; international tickets ☎485 2162, ext. 211). M1, 2, or 3: Deák tér. Open M-F 6am-6pm, Sa-Su 6am-4pm. Buses to much of Eastern Europe depart from **Népstadion,** Hungária körút 48/52 (☎252 1896). M2: Népstadion. To: **Berlin** (14½hr., 5 per week, 19,900Ft); **Prague** (8hr., 4 per week, 6990Ft); **Vienna** (3-3½hr., 5 per day, 5790Ft).

HUNGARY

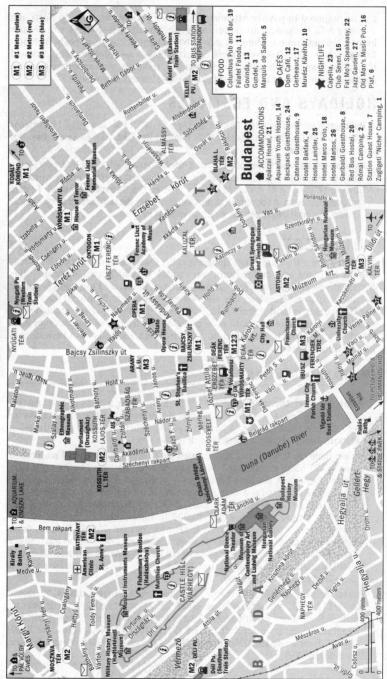

Budapest

● ACCOMMODATIONS
Apáczai Hostel, **21**
Aquarium Youth Hostel, **14**
Backpack Guesthouse, **24**
Caterina Guesthouse, **9**
Hostel Bakfark, **4**
Hostel Landler, **25**
Hostel Marco Polo, **18**
Hostel Martos, **26**
Garibaldi Guesthouse, **8**
Red Bus Hostel, **20**
Római Camping, **2**
Station Guest House, **7**
Zugligeti "Niche" Camping, **1**

● FOOD
Columbus Pub and Bar, **19**
Falafel Faloda, **11**
Govinda, **13**
Gundel, **3**
Marquis de Salade, **5**

● CAFÉS
Dom Café, **12**
Gerbeaud, **17**
Művész Kávéház, **10**

★ NIGHTLIFE
Capella, **23**
Club Seven, **15**
Fat Mo's Speakeasy, **22**
Jazz Garden, **27**
Old Man's Music Pub, **16**
Piaf, **6**

Map legend:
M1 #1 Metro (yellow)
M2 #2 Metro (red)
M3 #3 Metro (blue)

Commuter Trains: The **HÉV commuter railway** station is at Batthyány tér, across the river from the Parliament, 1 Metro stop past the Danube in Buda. Trains head to **Szentendre** (45min., every 15min. 5am-9pm, 268Ft). Purchase tickets at the station for transport beyond the city limits.

Public Transportation: Subways, buses, and **trams** are cheap, convenient, and easy to navigate. The **Metro** has three lines: yellow (M1), red (M2), and blue (M3). Pick up free **route maps** from hostels, tourist offices, and train stations. Night transit ("É") runs midnight-5am along major routes; buses #7É and 78É follow the M2 route, #6É follows the 4/6 tram line, and #14É and 50É follow the M3 route. **Single-fare tickets** for all public transport (one-way on one line 120Ft) are sold in Metro stations, in *Trafik* shops, and by sidewalk vendors. Punch them in the orange boxes at the gate of the Metro or on buses and trams; punch a new ticket when you change lines, or face a 1500-3000Ft fine. Day pass 925Ft, 3-day 1850Ft, 1-week 2250Ft.

Taxis: Beware of scams; check that the meter is on, and inquire about the rates. **Budataxi** (☎233 3333) charges 135Ft per km if you call. **Fötaxi** (☎222 2222), **6x6 Taxi** (☎266 6666), and **Tele 5 Taxi** (☎355 5555) are also reliable.

■ ORIENTATION

Originally Buda and Pest, two cities separated by the **Danube River** (Duna), modern Budapest preserves the distinctive character of each. On the west bank, **Buda** has winding streets, breathtaking vistas, a hilltop citadel, and the Castle District. On the east bank is the city's bustling commercial center, **Pest,** home to shopping boulevards, theaters, Parliament (Országház), and the Opera House. Three main bridges join the two halves: **Széchenyi Lánchíd,** slender **Erzsébet híd,** and green **Szabadság híd.** Just down the north slope of Várhegy (Castle Hill) is **Moszkva tér,** the tram and local bus hub. **Batthyány tér,** opposite Parliament in Buda, is the starting point of the HÉV commuter railway. The city's Metro lines converge at **Deák tér,** next to the main international bus terminal at **Erzsébet tér.** Two blocks west toward the river lies **Vörösmarty tér** and the main pedestrian shopping zone **Váci utca.**

Addresses in Budapest begin with a Roman numeral representing one of the city's 23 **districts.** Central Buda is I; central Pest is V. To navigate Budapest's often-confusing streets, a **map** is essential; pick one up at any tourist office or hostel.

∎ PRACTICAL INFORMATION

TOURIST AND FINANCIAL SERVICES

Tourist Offices: All sell the **Budapest Card** (Budapest Kártya), which provides discounts, unlimited public transport, and museum admission (2-day 3950Ft, 3-day 4950Ft). Your first stop should be **Tourinform,** V, Vigadó u. 6 (☎235 4481; www.hungarytourism.hu). M1: Vörösmarty tér. Walk toward the river from the Metro. Open 24hr. **Vista Travel Center,** Paulay Ede 7 (☎429 9950; www.vista.hu), arranges tours and accommodations. Open M-F 9am-8pm, Sa 10am-4pm. ▓ **Budapest in Your Pocket** (www.inyourpocket.com; 750Ft) is an up-to-date guide of the city.

Embassies: Australia, XII, Királyhágó tér 8/9 (☎457 9777; www.ausembbp.hu). M2: Déli pu., then bus #21 or tram #59 to Királyhágó tér. Open M-F 9am-noon. **Canada,** XII, Budakeszi út 32 (☎392 3360; www.canadaeuropa.gc.ca/hungary). Entrance at Zugligeti út. 51-53. Take bus #158 from Moszkva tér to the last stop. Open M-F 8:30-11am and 2-3:30pm. **South Africa,** II, Gárdonyi Géza út 17 (☎392 0999; emergency ☎(0620) 955 8046; www.sa-embassy.hu). **UK,** V, Harmincad u. 6 (☎266 2888), near the intersection with Vörösmarty tér. M1: Vörösmarty tér. Open M-F 9:30am-12:30pm

and 2:30-4:30pm. **US,** V, Szabadság tér 12 (☎475 4400; emergency ☎266 28 88 93 31; www.usis.hu). M2: Kossuth tér. Walk 2 blocks down Akademia and turn on Zoltán. Open M-F 8:15am-5pm. **New Zealand** and **Irish** nationals contact the UK embassy.
Currency Exchange: The best rates are at banks. **Citibank,** V, Vörösmarty tér 4 (☎374 5000). M1: Vörösmarty tér. Cashes traveler's checks for no commission and provides MC/V cash advances (passport required).
American Express: V, Deák Ferenc u. 10 (☎235 4330; travel@amex.hu). M2 or 3: Deák tér. Open M-F 9am-5:30pm, Sa 9am-2pm. Cardholders can have mail delivered here.

LOCAL SERVICES

Luggage Storage: Lockers at all three train stations. 150-300Ft.

English-Language Bookstore: Libri Konyvpalota, VII, Rakoczi u. 12 (☎267 6258), is probably the best choice. Open M-F 10am-7:30pm, Sa 10am-3pm. M2: Astoria. MC/V.

Bi-Gay-Lesbian Resources: GayGuide.net Budapest (☎(0630) 932 3334; www.budapest.gayguide.net), maintains a comprehensive website and runs a hotline (daily 4-8pm) with info for gay tourists and gay-friendly accommodations lists.

EMERGENCY AND COMMUNICATIONS

Emergency: ☎112 connects to all. **Police:** ☎107. **Ambulance:** ☎104. **Fire:** ☎105.

Tourist Police: V, Vigadó u. 6 (☎235 4479). M1: Vörösmarty tér. Walk toward the river from the Metro to reach the station, just inside Tourinform. Open 24hr.

24hr. Pharmacies: II, Frankel Leó út 22 (☎212 4406); **III,** Szentendrei út 2/a (☎388 6528); **IV,** Pozsonyi u. 19 (☎389 4079); **VI,** Teréz krt. 41 (☎311 4439); **VII,** Rákóczi út 39 (☎314 3695). At night, call the number on door or ring the bell.

Medical Assistance: Falck (SOS) KFT, II, Kapy út 49/b (☎200 0100 and 275 1535). Open 24hr. The US embassy (see **Embassies,** above) lists English-speaking doctors.

Telephones: Most phones require **phone cards,** available at newsstands, post offices, and Metro stations. 50-unit card 800Ft, 120-unit card 1800Ft. Domestic operator ☎191; info ☎198; international operator ☎190; info ☎199.

Internet Access: Cybercafes are everywhere, but access can get expensive and long waits are common. Try a wired hostel. **Ami Internet Coffee,** V, Váci u. 40 (☎267 1644; www.amicoffee.hu). M3: Ferenciek tér. 200Ft per 10min., 400Ft per 30min., 700Ft per hr. Open daily 9am-2am. **Eckermann,** VI, Andrássy út 24 (☎269 2542). M1: Opera. Free. Open M-F 8am-10pm, Sa 9am-10pm.

Post Office: V, Városház u. 18 (☎318 4811). Open M-F 8am-9pm, Sa 8am-2pm. Address mail to be held: SURNAME Firstname, *Poste Restante,* V, Városház u. 18, **1052** Budapest, HUNGARY. **Branches** include: Nyugati pu.; VI, Teréz krt. 105/107 and Keleti pu.; VIII, Baross tér 11/c. Open M-F 8am-9pm, Sa 8am-2pm.

▌ ACCOMMODATIONS AND CAMPING

Call ahead in summer. Travelers arriving at Keleti pu. will be swarmed with hawkers; be cautious and don't believe all promises of special discounts, but keep an open mind if you need a place to stay.

ACCOMMODATION AGENCIES

Private rooms, slightly more expensive than hostels (2000-5000Ft per person; less with longer stays), usually offer what hostels can't: Peace, quiet, and private showers. Arrive early, bring cash, and haggle.

IBUSZ, V, Ferenciek tér (☎485 2767; accommodation@ibusz.hu). M3: Ferenciek tér. Doubles 5000Ft; triples 5000-6000Ft. 1800Ft surcharge if staying fewer than 4 nights. Open M-Th 8:15am-4pm, F 8:15am-3pm. ❸

Non-Stop Hotel Service, V, Sütő u. 2 (☎318 3925). M1, 2, or 3: Deák tér. Bus #7 from Keleti pu. Rooms in Pest from 6000Ft. Open 24hr. ❹

YEAR-ROUND HOSTELS

Budapest's hostels are backpacker social centers, each with its own quirks. You may find some hostel common rooms as exciting as the city's expat bars and clubs, and especially if you're traveling alone, they're a great place to whip up instant friends. Many hostels are now run by the **Hungarian Youth Hostels Association,** which operates from an office in Keleti pu. Their representatives wear Hostelling International T-shirts and will—along with legions of competitors—accost you as you get off the train. Take the free transport; it doesn't commit you.

▨ **Backpack Guesthouse**, XI, Takács Menyhért u. 33 (☎209 8406; backpackguest@hotmail.com), in Buda, 12min. from central Pest. From Keleti pu., take bus #7 or 7a toward Buda; get off at Tétenyi u. and walk back under the railway bridge to a sharp left turn. Take the 3rd right at Hamzsabégi út. With a common room full of movies, music, and cheap beer, hostel life doesn't get much better. Internet access 15Ft per min. Reception 24hr. Reserve ahead. Dorms 2800Ft; doubles 6600Ft. ❷

▨ **Red Bus Hostel**, V, Semmelweis u. 14 (☎266 0136; www.redbusbudapest.hu), in Pest. New spacious dorms in the heart of downtown Pest. Free luggage storage. Internet access 12Ft per min. Breakfast included. Laundry 1000Ft. Reception 24hr. Check-out 10am. 10-bed dorms 2700Ft; singles 6000Ft; doubles 7000Ft; triples 10,000Ft. ❷

Hostel Martos, XI, Stoczek u. 5/7 (☎209 4883; reception@hotel.martos.bme.hu), in Buda. From Keleti pu., take bus #7 to *Móricz Zsigmond Körtér* and walk 300m toward the river on Bartók Béla út. Turn right on Bertalan Lajos and take the 3rd right on Stoczek u.; the hostel is on the corner. A short walk to the outdoor clubs along the river. Free Internet access and satellite TV. Reserve ahead. Singles 4000Ft; doubles 5000Ft, with shower 8000Ft; triples 7500Ft; 2- to 4-bed apartments with bath 15,000Ft. ❸

Aquarium Youth Hostel, VII, Alsoérdósor u. 12 (☎322 0502; aquarium@budapesthostels.com), in Pest. A hidden gem—there are no signs outside. Ring buzzer. Close to Keleti pu. and the Metro. Free Internet access and kitchen. Laundry 1200Ft. Reception 24hr. 4- to 5-bed dorms 2500Ft; doubles 8000Ft. ❷

Station Guest House (HI), XIV, Mexikói út 36/b (☎221 8864; www.stationguesthouse.hu), in Pest. From Keleti pu., take bus #7 or night bus #78É 4 stops to *Hungária körút*, walk under the railway pass, and take an immediate right on Mexikói út. Free billiards, live music, and a friendly staff. Internet access 20Ft per min. Reserve ahead. Attic 1900Ft; dorms 2400Ft; quads 2700Ft. All prices drop 100Ft with each night you stay, up to 5 nights. ❶

Hotel Marco Polo, VII, Nyár u. 6 (☎413 2555; www.marcopolohostel.com), in Pest. M2: Astoria or M2: Blaha Lujza tér. Newly renovated, luxurious, and spotless. Internet access 500Ft per 30min. Reception 24hr. Book 1-2 days ahead in summer. Dorms 5000Ft; singles 13,900Ft; doubles 17,000Ft. 10% HI and ISIC discount. ❸

SUMMER HOSTELS

Many university dorms moonlight as hostels during July and August. The majority are clustered around Móricz Zsigmond Körtér in district XI.

Hostel Bakfark, II, Bakfark u. 1/3 (☎413 2062), in Buda. M2: Moszkva tér. Comfortable dorms with lofts instead of bunks. Check-out 10am. Call ahead. Open mid-June to late-Aug. Dorms 3300Ft. 10% HI discount. ❸

Apáczai Hostel, V, Papnövelde 4/6 (☎267 0311), in Pest. Great location, clean rooms, and a friendly staff. Open late-June to late-Aug. Dorms 2700Ft; doubles 4300Ft. 10% HI discount. ❸

HUNGARY

Hostel Landler, XI, Bartók Béla út 17 (☎463 3621), in Buda. Take bus #7 or 7A across the river and get off at Géllert; take Bartók Béla út away from the river. Comfy dorms. Check-out 9am. Open July 5-Sept. 5. Singles 5850Ft; triples 11,700Ft; quads 15,600Ft. 10% HI discount. ❸

GUESTHOUSES

Guesthouses and private rooms add a personal touch for about the same price as hostels. Owners will usually pick travelers up from the train station or airport.

Garibaldi Guesthouse, V, Garibaldi u. 5 (☎302 3456; garibaldiguest@hotmail.com). M2: Kossuth tér. Charming Ena lets spacious rooms in her apartment and other suites in the building. Some have kitchenette, TV, and shower. Rooms from 3500Ft per person; apartments 6000-10,000Ft. Reduced prices for longer stays. ❸

Caterina Guesthouse and Hostel, VI, Andrássy út 47, 3rd fl., apt. #18; ring bell #11 (☎342 0804; www.extra.hu/caterin), in Pest. M1: Oktogon, or trams #4 and 6. Spotless rooms with fresh linens. Reception 24hr. Check-out 9am. Lockout 10am-2pm. Reserve by email. Dorms 2800Ft; doubles 9000Ft; triples 11,400Ft. ❷

CAMPING

Római Camping, III, Szentendrei út 189 (☎368 6260). M2: Batthyány tér. Take HÉV to Római fürdő; walk 100m toward river. Communal showers and kitchen. Breakfast 880Ft. Laundry 800Ft. Electricity 600Ft. Tents 1950Ft per person; bungalows 1690-15,000Ft. Each person must also pay a personal fee (990Ft, children 590Ft). Tourist tax 3%. 10% HI discount. MC/V. ❷

Zugligeti "Niche" Camping, XII, Zugligeti út 101 (☎/fax 200 8346; www.camping-niche.hu). Take bus #158 from Moszkva tér to Laszállóhely, the last stop. Restaurant. Communal showers. Electricity 450Ft. 850Ft per person. Tents 500Ft, large tents 900Ft. Cars 700Ft, caravans 1800Ft. MC/V. ❶

🍴 FOOD

Explore the cafeterias beneath "Önkiszolgáló Étterem" signs for something cheap (meat dishes 300-500Ft) or seek out a neighborhood kifőzés (kiosk) or vendéglő (vendor) for a real taste of Hungary. Corner markets, many of which have 24hr. windows, stock basics. The king of them all, the ▩**Grand Market Hall,** IX, Fővam tér 1/3, next to Szabadság híd (M3: Kálvin tér), was built in 1897; it now boasts 10,000 square meters of stalls, making it a tourist attraction in itself. For a wide array of ethnic restaurants, try the upper floors of **Mammut Plaza,** just outside of the *Moszkva tér* Metro stop in Buda, or the **West End Plaza,** accessible from the *Nyugati* Metro stop in Pest.

RESTAURANTS

▩ **Columbus Pub and Restaurant,** V, Danube prominade below the chain bridge (☎266 9013). If you feel you've neglected the beautiful Danube, enjoy a meal on this moored ship. Open daily noon-1am. AmEx/MC/V. ❸

▩ **Govinda,** V, Vigyázó Ferenc u. 4 (☎269 1625). An Indian vegetarian restaurant, complete with yoga classes. The best deals are the meal plates (big plate 1450Ft, small plate 1150Ft, student plate 520Ft). Yoga classes Sept.-June M 5-6:30pm (500Ft). Open M-Sa noon-9pm. AmEx/MC/V. ❷

▩ **Gundel,** XIV, Allatkerti út 2 (☎468 4040). The most famous restaurant in Hungary. Many think the 7-course meal is worth the splurge (13,000-17,500Ft), but there are also delicious sandwiches outside for 400-600Ft. Su brunch buffet 11:30am-3pm (400Ft). Open daily noon-4pm and 6:30pm-midnight. AmEx/MC/V. ❹

Falafel Faloda, VI, Pauley Ede u. 53 (☎351 1243; www.falafel.hu). M1: Opera. From the Metro, cross Andrássy, head straight on Hajós u., and turn left on Pauley Ede. Make-your-own falafel with tons of ingredients. Falafel 490Ft. Salad 480-580Ft. Open M-F 10am-8pm, Sa 10am-6pm. ❷

Robinson Mediterranean-style Restaurant and Cafe, Városligeti tér (☎422 0222). This spectacularly scenic restaurant overlooking the lake in City Park is infused with charm. Serves favorites like pan-roasted goose liver (2100Ft) and paprika veal (2200Ft). Vegetarian options available. Entrees 1200-5800Ft. Open daily noon-midnight. ❹

Marquis de Salade, VI, Hajós u. 43 (☎302 4086). M3: Arany János. At the corner of Bajcsy-Zsilinszky út, 2 blocks from the Metro. Huge menu with dishes from Azerbaijan, France, India, Italy, Japan, and Hungary. Entrees 1200-2500Ft. Open daily noon-midnight. Cash only. ❹

CAFES

Once the haunts of the literary, intellectual, and cultural elite—as well as political dissidents—the city's cafes boast histories as rich as the pastries they serve.

Dom Cafe, I, Szentháromság tér. Atop Castle Hill, with astonishing views of the Danube and Pest. Beer and coffee start at 350Ft. Pastries and sandwiches also served. Open daily 10am-7pm. ❶

Gerbeaud, V, Vörösmarty tér 7 (☎429 9000). M1: Vörösmarty tér. Perhaps Budapest's largest and most famous cafe, this institution has been serving its layer cakes (590Ft) and homemade ice cream (75Ft) since 1858. Open daily 9am-9pm. ❶

Muvész Kávéház, VI, Andrássy út 29 (☎352 1337). M1: Opera. Diagonally across from the Opera. Before or after a show, stop in for a slice of rich cake (290Ft) and a cup of cappuccino (260Ft) at the polished stone tables. Open daily 9am-11:45pm. ❶

◉ SIGHTS

In 1896, Hungary's 1000th birthday bash prompted the construction of what are today Budapest's most prominent sights. Among the works commissioned by the Habsburgs were **Heroes' Square** (Hősök tér), **Liberty Bridge** (Szbadság híd), **Vajdahunyad Castle** (Vajdahunyad vár), and continental Europe's first **Metro** system. Slightly grayer for wear, war, and Communist occupation, these monuments attest to the optimism of a capital on the verge of its Golden Age. See the sights, learn your way around the city, and meet other travelers with **Absolute Walking & Biking Tours.** Their basic tour (3½hr.; 4000Ft, under-27 3500Ft) meets May 16-Sept. 30 daily at 9:30am and 1:30pm on the steps of the yellow church in Deák tér and at 10am and 2pm in Heroes' Sq. They also hold off-season tours Oct.-Jan. 6 and Feb.-May 15 that leave at 10:30am from Deák tér and at 11am from Heroes' Sq. You can also choose from a range of specialized tours that focus on everything from communist Hungary to pub-crawling Budapest. (☎211 8861; www.budapesttours.com. Specialized tours 2½-5½hr., 4000-5000Ft.) **Boat tours** of Budapest can also be taken from Vigadó tér piers 6-7. The *Danube Legend,* which runs in the evening, costs 4200Ft (950Ft with Budapest Card). The *Duna Bella,* the daytime boat, costs 3600Ft (850Ft with Budapest Card).

BUDA

On the east bank of the Danube, **Buda** sprawls between the base of **Castle Hill** and southern **Gellért Hill,** rambling into Budapest's main residential areas. Older than Pest, Buda is filled with parks, lush hills, and islands.

CASTLE DISTRICT. Towering above the Danube on Castle Hill, the Castle District has been razed three times in its 800-year history, most recently in 1945. With its winding, statue-filled streets, breathtaking views, and hodge-podge of architec-

HE HIDDEN DEAL

BUCK-NAKED
IN BUDAPEST

The city's baths were first built n 1565 by a Turkish ruler who eared that a siege would prevent he population from bathing. Thanks to his anxiety, there's noth- ng to keep budget travelers from bathing, either: The range of ser- vices—from mud baths to mas- sage—is cheap enough to warrant ndulgence without guilt.

Although first-time bathers may be intimidated at first, guests at Budapest's baths always receive the royal treatment. Upon arrival, you will probably be handed a bizarre apron no bigger than a dish-rag, which modesty requires that you tie around your waist. In general, women set the apron aside as a towel, while men keep theirs on; bring a bathing suit just n case. Customs vary greatly by establishment, so just do as the ocals do—nothing is more con- spicuous than a Speedo-clad tour- st among naked natives.

Cycle through the sauna and thermal baths a couple times, then enter the massage area. For a good scrubbing, try the sanitary massage (vízi); if you're a tradi- tionalist, stick to the medical mas- sage (orvosi). Most baths provide a much-needed rest area once the process is complete. Refreshed, smiling, and somewhat sleepy, tip the attendant, lounge over mint tea, and savor your afternoon of guilt-free pampering. (Baths and pools 700-2000Ft, massages 1000- 1500Ft.)

tural styles, the UNESCO-protected district now appears much as it did in Habsburg times. Although the reconstructed **Buda Castle** *(Vár)* now houses a number of fine museums (p. 539), bullet holes in the palace facade recall the 1956 Uprising. *(M1, 2, or 3: Deák tér. From the Metro, take bus #16 across the Danube and up to the castle. Alternatively, take the Metro to M2: Moszkva tér and walk up to the hill on Várfok u. Vienna Gate, or hop on bus #16. Becsi kapu marks the castle entrance.)* Beneath Buda castle are the **Castle Labyrinths** (Budvári Labirinths), caverns that allow for spooky trips through the subterranean world of the city. *(Úri u. 9. ☎212 0207. Open daily 9:30am-7:30pm. 900Ft, students 700Ft.)*

MATTHIAS CHURCH. The multi-colored roof of Matthias Church (Mátyás templom) is one of Budapest's most popular sights. The church was converted into a mosque in 1541, then reconverted 145 years later when the Habsburgs defeated the Turks. Ascend the spiral staircase to reach the gold-heavy exhibits of the **Museum of Ecclesiastical Art.** *(On Castle Hill. High mass 7, 8:30am, 6pm; Su also 10am and noon. Open M-Sa 9am-5pm, Su 1pm-5pm. Museum 400Ft, students 200Ft. Free.)*

GELLÉRT HILL. When King Stephen, the first Christian Hungarian monarch, was coronated, the Pope sent Bishop Gellért to convert the Magyars. The hill got its name (Gellért-hegy) when those unconvinced by his message hurled the good bishop to his death from the top. The **Liberation Monument** (Szabadság Szobor), created to honor Soviet soldiers who died "liberating" Hungary, looks over Budapest from atop the hill. The view from the adjoining **Citadel,** built as a symbol of Habsburg power after the foiled 1848 revolution, is especially spectacular at night. At the base of the hill sits Budapest's most famous Turkish bath (p. 541), the **Gellért Hotel and Baths.** *(Take tram #18 or 19, or bus #7, to Hotel Gellért; follow Szabó Verjték u. to Jubileumi Park, continuing on the marked paths to the summit. Or, take bus #27 to the top; get off at Búsuló Juhász and walk 5min. to the peak.)*

PEST

Constructed in the 19th century, the winding streets of Pest now host cafes, corporations, and monuments. The crowded **Belváros** (Inner City) is based around the swarming pedestrian boulevards **Váci utca** and **Vörösmarty tér.**

■ PARLIAMENT. Standing 96m tall, a number that symbolizes the date of Hungary's millennial anniversary, the palatial Gothic Parliament (Országház) was modeled after the UK's, right down to the riverside location and churchly facade. The **Hungarian crown jewels,** housed here since 1999, were moved from the National Museum to the center of the Cupola Room amidst national controversy because of the cost of the security required to move them. *(M2: Kossuth Lajos tér. English tours M-F 10am, noon, 2, 2:30, 5, and 6pm; Sa-Su 10am only—come early. 2000Ft, students 1000Ft. Purchase tickets at gate #10 and enter at gate #12.)*

GREAT SYNAGOGUE. The largest synagogue in Europe and the second-largest in the world after Temple Emmanuel in New York City, Pest's Great Synagogue (Zsinagóga) was designed to hold 3000 worshippers. The Moorish building has been under renovation since 1988, and much of its artwork is blocked from view. In the garden is a **Holocaust Memorial** that sits above a mass grave for thousands of Jews killed near the end of the war. The Hebrew inscription reads: "Whose pain can be greater than mine?" with the Hungarian words "Let us Remember" beneath. Each leaf of this enormous metal tree bears the name of a family that perished, but the memorial represents only a fraction of the sufferers. Next door, the **Jewish Museum** (Zsidó Múzeum) documents Hungary's rich Jewish past. *(M2: Astoria. At the corner of Dohány u. and Wesselényi u. Open May-Oct. M-Th 10am-5pm, F 10am-1pm, Su 10am-2pm; Nov.-Apr. M-F 10am-3pm, Su 10am-1pm. Synagogue and museum 600Ft, students with ISIC 200Ft.)*

ST. STEPHEN'S BASILICA. The city's largest church (Sz. István Bazilika) was decimated by Allied bombs in WWII. Its neo-Renaissance facade is still undergoing reconstruction, but the ornate interior attracts both tourists and worshippers. The **Panorama Tower** offers an amazing 360° view. The oddest attraction is St. Stephen's mummified right hand, one of Hungary's most revered religious relics; a 100Ft donation dropped in the box will light up the hand. *(M1-3: Deák tér. Mass M-Sa 7, 8am, 6pm; Su 8:30, 10am, noon, 6pm. Basilica and museum open May-Oct. M-Sa 9am-5pm; Nov.-Apr. M-Sa 10am-4pm. Tower open June-Aug. daily 9:30am-6pm; Sept.-Oct. 10am-5:30pm; Apr.-May 10am-4:30pm. Basilica and museum free. Tower 500Ft, students 400Ft.)*

ANDRÁSSY ÚT AND HEROES' SQUARE. Hungary's grandest boulevard, Andrássy út, extends from Erzsébet tér in downtown Pest to **Heroes' Square** (Hősök tere) to the northeast. The **Hungarian State Opera House** (Magyar Állami Operaház), whose gilded interior glows on performance nights, is a vivid reminder of Budapest's Golden Age. If you can't see an opera, take a tour. *(Andrássy út 22. M1: Opera. Daily English-language tours 3 and 4pm; 2000Ft, students 1000Ft. 20% Budapest Card discount.)* At the Heroes' Sq. end of Andrássy út, the **Millenium Monument** (Millenniumi emlékmű) commemorates the nation's most prominent leaders. Also right off Heroes' Sq. is the **Museum of Fine Arts** (see below).

CITY PARK. The City Park (Városliget) is home to a zoo, a circus, a run-down amusement park, and the lakeside **Vajdahunyad Castle**, whose collage of Romanesque, Gothic, Renaissance, and Baroque styles is intended to chronicle the history of Hungarian architecture. Outside the castle broods the hooded statue of King Béla IV's **anonymous scribe,** to whom we owe much of our knowledge of medieval Hungary. Rent a **rowboat** or **ice skates** on the lake next to the castle, or a **bike-trolley** to navigate the shaded paths. The main road through the park is closed to automobiles on weekends, making the park especially peaceful. *(M1: Széchenyi Fürdő. Park open Apr.-Aug. daily 9am-6pm; Sept.-Mar. 9am-3pm. Pedal boat rentals May-Aug. daily 10am-10pm. Rowboat rental May-Aug. daily 10am-9:30pm. Ice skate rental Oct.-Feb. daily 10am-2pm and 4-8pm.)*

🏛 MUSEUMS

▇ MUSEUM OF FINE ARTS. A spectacular collection of European art is housed in the magnificent Museum of Fine Arts (Szépművészeti Múzeum). These are paintings you've never seen in books but should not miss, especially those in the El Greco room. *(XIV, Heroes' Sq. M1: Hősök tere. Open Su and Tu-Sa 10am-5:30pm. 500Ft, students 200Ft. Free English tours Tu-F 11am. Camera 300Ft, video 1500Ft.)*

NATIONAL MUSEUM. At the National Museum (Nemzeti Múzeum), a well laid-out, extensive exhibition on the second floor chronicles the history of Hungary, extending from the founding of the state through the 20th century. The first floor is reserved for temporary exhibits. *(VIII, Múzeum krt. 14/16. M3: Kálvin tér. ☎ 338 2122; www.origo.hnm.hu. Open Mar. 15-Oct. 15 Su and Tu-Sa 10am-6pm; Oct. 16-Mar. 14 Su and Tu-Sa 10am-5pm; last admission 30min. before closing. 800Ft, students 400Ft.)*

STATUE PARK. After the collapse of Soviet rule, the open-air Statue Park museum (Szoborpark Múzeum) was created from statues removed from Budapest's parks and squares. The indispensable English guidebook (1000Ft) explains the statues' past and present locations. *(XXII, on the corner of Balatoni út and Szabadkai út. Take express bus #7 from Keleti pu. to Étele tér and then take the Volán bus from terminal #2 to Diósd (15min., every 10min.). Open in good weather Mar.-Nov. daily 10am-dusk; Dec.-Feb. weekends and holidays only. 600Ft, students 400Ft.)*

MUSEUM OF APPLIED ARTS. (Iparművészeti Múzeum). The Art Nouveau building of the Museum of Applied Arts was designed for Hungary's 1896 millenium celebration. Inside is an eclectic collection of impressive hand-crafted objects, including Tiffany glass and furniture, as well as excellent temporary exhibits highlighting specific crafts. *(IX, Üllői út 33-37. M3: Ferenc körút. Open Mar. 15-Oct. Su and Tu-Sa 10am-6pm; Nov.-Mar. 14 Su and Tu-Sa 10am-4pm. 600Ft, students 300Ft.)*

BUDA CASTLE. Leveled by the Nazis and later by the Soviets, the reconstructed Buda Castle (see **Castle District**, p. 537) now houses several museums. Wing A contains the **Museum of Contemporary Art** (Kortárs Művészeti Múzeum), as well as the smaller **Ludwig Museum** upstairs, which is devoted to Warhol, Lichtenstein, and other masters of modern art. Wings B-D hold the **Hungarian National Gallery** (Magyar Nemzeti Galéria), a collection of the best in Hungarian painting and sculpture. *(Wings A-D open Su and Tu-Sa 10am-6pm, Th open until 8pm. Wing A 800Ft, students 400Ft. Wings B-D 600/300Ft.)* Artifacts from the 1242 castle are in the **Budapest History Museum** (Budapesti Történeti Múzeum) in Wing E. *(I, Szent György tér 2. M1-3: Deák tér. Take bus #16 across the Danube to the top of Castle Hill. Wing E open mid-May to mid-Sept. daily 10am-6pm; mid-Sept. to Oct. and Mar. to mid-May M and W-Su 10am-6pm; Nov.-Feb. M and W-Su 10am-4pm. 600Ft, students 300Ft.)*

🎵 ENTERTAINMENT

Budapest Program, Budapest Panorama, Pesti Est and the essential *Budapest in Your Pocket* (750Ft) are the best English-language entertainment guides, listing everything from festivals to cinemas to art showings. All are available at most tourist offices and hotels. The "Style" section of the *Budapest Sun* (www.budapestsun.com; 300Ft) has a comprehensive 10-day calendar and film reviews. (Tickets 550-1000Ft; cinema schedules change on Th.) Many of the world's biggest shows pass through Budapest. Prices are reasonable; check the **Music Mix 33 Ticket Service**, V, Váci ú. 33. (☎317 77 36. Open M-F 10am-6pm, Sa 10am-1pm.)

THEATER, MUSIC, AND DANCE. The ◼**State Opera House** (Magyar Allami Operaház), VI, Andrássy út 22, one of Europe's leading performance centers, epitomizes the splendor of Budapest's Golden Age. (M1: Opera. ☎332 8197, box office ☎353 0170. Tickets 800-8700Ft. Box office open M-Sa 11am-7pm, Su 4-7pm; cashier closes at 5pm on non-performance days.) The **National Dance Theatre** (Nemzeti Táncszínház), Színház u. 1-3, hosts a variety of shows—modern, alternative, Latin, ballet—but the Hungarian folklore is the most popular. (On Castle Hill. ☎/fax 201 4407, box office ☎375 8649; www.nemzetitancszinhaz.hu. Most shows 7pm.) Performances in the lovely **Városmajor Open-Air Theater**, XII, Városmajor, include musicals, operas, and ballets. Walk up the big stairs, turn right on Várfok u. and left on Csaba u., then right on Maros u. and left on Szamos u. (M1: Moszkva tér. ☎375 5933. Open June 27-Aug. 18. Box office open Su-M and Th-Sa 3-6pm.) For an eclectic line up of music, go to **Buda Park Stage**, XI, Kosztolányi Dezső tér. (☎466 9894. Tickets 90-350Ft. Box office at V, Vörösmarty tér 1. Open M-F 11am-6pm.)

THERMAL BATHS. To soak away the city grime, sink into a hot, relaxing thermal bath. First built in 1565, their services—from mud baths to massages—are quite cheap. **Széchenyi**, XIV, Állatkerti u. 11/14, is a welcoming bath with beautiful pools. (M1: Hősök tér. Open May-Sept. daily 6am-7pm; Oct.-Apr. M-F 6am-7pm, Sa-Su 6am-5pm. 1700Ft. to enter, 900Ft returned if you leave within 2hr., 600Ft within 3hr., and 300Ft within 4hr.; keep your original receipt. 15min. massage 1200Ft.) Famous **Gellért**, XI, Kelenhegyi út 4/6, one of the most elegant baths, has a rooftop sundeck and an outdoor wave pool. Take bus #7 or tram #47 or 49 to Hotel Gellért, at the base of Gellért-hegy. (Thermal bath and pool 2000Ft. Pools open daily 6am-7pm, Sa-Su 6am-5pm. 15min. massage 1500Ft., pedicure 1200Ft, foot massage 700Ft. Open M-F 6am-7pm, Sa-Su 6am-5pm.)

NIGHTLIFE

All-night outdoor parties, elegant after-hours clubs, the nightly thump and grind—Budapest has it all. Pubs and bars bustle until 4am, but the streets themselves are empty and poorly lit. Upscale cafes and restaurants in **VI, Ferencz Liszt tér** (M2: Oktogon) attract Budapest's hip youth.

Undergrass, VI, Ferencz Liszt tér 10. M1: Oktogon. The hottest spot in Pest's trendiest area. A soundproof glass door divides a hip bar from a packed disco. Cover F 300Ft, Sa 1000Ft. Open F-Sa 10pm-4am.

Piaf, VI, Nagymező u. 25. A much-loved lounge, and a good place to meet fellow travelers. Knock on the door to await the approval of the club's matron. Cover 600Ft, includes 1 beer. Open Su-Th 10pm-6am, F-Sa 10pm-7am, but don't come before 1am.

Capella, V, Belgrád rakpart 23 (www.extra.hu/capellacafe). With glow-in-the-dark graffiti and an underground atmosphere, this spot draws a mixed gay and straight crowd. Cover 1000-1500Ft. Open Su and Tu-Sa 9pm-5am. The owners also run the three-level **Limo Cafe** down the street. Open daily noon-5am.

Club Seven, Akácfa u. 7. M2: Blaha Lajos tér. This upscale underground music club is a local favorite and features a casino. Cover for men Sa-Su 2000Ft, women free.

Old Man's Music Pub, VII, Akácfa u. 13. M2: Blaha Lujza tér. Arrive early for daily blues and jazz from 9-11pm, then relax in the restaurant (open 3pm-3am) or hit the dance floor (11pm-late). Open M-Sa 3pm-4:30am.

Jazz Garden, V, Veres Páiné u. 44a. Although the "garden" is actually a vaulted cellar with Christmas lights, the effect works well. Beer 420-670Ft. Live jazz daily at 9pm. Open Su-F noon-1am, Sa noon-2am.

Fat Mo's Speakeasy, V, Nyári Pal u. 11. M3: Kálvin tér. 14 varieties of draft beer (350-750Ft). Live jazz Su-W 9-11pm. W-Sa DJ after midnight. Open M-F noon-2am, Sa noon-4am, Su 6pm-2am.

DAYTRIPS FROM BUDAPEST: THE DANUBE BEND

North of Budapest, the Danube sweeps in a dramatic arc called the Danube Bend (Dunakanyar), deservedly one of the most beloved tourist attractions in Hungary.

SZENTENDRE. Narrow cobblestone streets in Szentendre (pop. 23,000) brim with upscale art galleries and pricey restaurants. Head up **Church Hill** (Templom-domb) in Fő tér, above the town center, for an amazing view from the 13th-cen-

> ❗ **NIGHTLIFE SCAM.** There have been reports of a mafia-organized scam involving English-speaking Hungarian women who approach foreign men and suggest that they buy her a drink. The bill, accompanied by imposing men, can be US$1000 for a single drink. If he claims not to have money, they conveniently have an ATM inside the bar. The US Embassy (see Embassies, p. 533) has advised against patronizing a number of establishments in the Váci u. area. More importantly, if a women asks you to come to a bar with her in that area, politely refuse, or take her to a bar of your choice—not the one she suggests. Always check drink prices before ordering at places you are not sure about. The names of these establishments change faster than a two-bit hustle. For the most current list of establishments about which complaints have been received, check with the US Embassy in Budapest or view their list on the web at www.usembassy.hu/conseng/announcements.html. If you are taken in, call the police. You'll probably still have to pay, but get a receipt to issue a complaint at the Consumer Bureau.

tury Roman Catholic church. The **Czóbel Museum,** to the left of the church at Templom tér 1, exhibits the work of Béla Czóbel, Hungary's foremost post-Impressionist painter, including his bikini-clad "Venus of Szentendre." Some English info is provided. (Open Su and Tu-Sa 10am-6pm. 350Ft, students 150Ft.) The popular **Margit Kovács Museum,** Vastagh György u. 1, off Görög u., which branches from Fő tér, displays whimsical ceramic sculptures and tiles by the 20th-century Hungarian artist. (Open Mar.-Oct. daily 10am-6pm; Nov. daily 9am-5pm; Dec.-Feb. Su and Tu-Sa 10am-5pm. 550Ft, students 250Ft.) The real thriller at the **Szabó Marzipan Museum and Confectionery,** Dumtsa Jenő u. 12, is the 80kg white chocolate statue of Michael Jackson. (Open daily 10am-6pm. Desserts 120-1000Ft. Museum 300Ft) The ▧**National Wine Museum** (Nemzeti Bormúzuem), Bogdányi u. 10, is a cellar exhibit of wines from all the wine-making regions in Hungary. (Open daily 10am-10pm. Wine tasting 1500Ft for 8 samples and admission to the exhibition. Exhibition 100Ft.)

HÉV commuter trains travel to Szentendre from Budapest's Batthyány tér (45min., every 10-15min., 335Ft). **Buses** run to: Budapest's Árpád híd Metro station (30min., every 20-40min., 220Ft); Esztergom (1½hr., 476Ft); and Visegrád (45min., 246Ft). The HÉV and bus stations are 10min. from Fő tér; descend the stairs past the end of the HÉV tracks, go through the underpass, and head up Kossuth u. At the fork, bear right onto Dumtsa Jenő u., which leads to the town center. **MAHART boats** leave from a pier 20min. north of the town center. With the river on the right, walk along the water to the sign. **Tourinform,** Dumtsa Jenő u. 22, between the town center and the station, has free maps. (☎(026) 31 79 65; www.szentendre.hu. Open Mar. 16-Oct. 15 M-F 9am-4:30pm, Sa-Su 10am-2pm; Oct. 16-Mar. 15 M-F 9:30am-4:30pm.) Restaurants are expensive; it's often cheaper to dine in Budapest or Visegrád. Enjoy a pastry (from 350Ft) and cappuccino (from 350Ft) while being serenaded by the opera-singing owners of ▧**Nostalgia Cafe ❷,** Bogdányi u. 2. (Open Su and Th-Sa 10am-10pm.) **Kedvenc Kifőzde ❶,** Bükköspart 21, is a tiny diner with incredible food. (Entrees 300-460Ft. Open M-F noon-5pm, Sa noon-3pm.)

VISEGRÁD. Host to the royal court in medieval times, Visegrád was devastated when the Habsburgs destroyed its 13th-century **citadel** in a struggle against the freedom fighters. This former Roman outpost gives a dramatic view of the Danube and surrounding hills. Hike a strenuous 30min. up Kalvária út, or take the local bus (10-15min.; 9:30am, 12:30, and 3:30pm; 100Ft). Sprawling across the foothills above Fő út are the ruins of King Matthias's **Royal Palace** (Királyi Pal-

ota); impressive exhibits inside include a computerized reconstruction of the original castle. (Open Su
and Tu-Sa 9am-5pm. 500Ft, students 250Ft.) The
palace grounds relive their glory days of parades,
jousting, and music during the **Viségrad Palace
Games** (☎(026) 209 34 59) in mid-July. At the end of
Salamontorony u., the **King Matthias Museum**, inside
Solomon's Tower (Alsóvár Salamon Torony), displays artifacts from the palace ruins. (Open Apr.-
Oct. Su and Tu-Sa 9am-5pm. 460Ft, students 230Ft.
Su students free.)

Buses run to Budapest's Árpád híd Metro station
(1½hr., 30 per day, 421Ft). The tourist office, **Visegrád
Tours**, Rév út 15, has maps (300Ft) for sale. (☎(026)
39 81 60. Open Apr.-Oct. daily 8am-7pm; Nov.-Mar. M-
F 10am-4pm.) Pick up the basics across the street at
CBA Élelmiszer supermarket. (Open M 7am-6pm, Tu-F
7am-7pm, Sa 7am-3pm, Su 7am-noon.) **Gulás Csárda
❸**, Nagy Lajos u. 4, is a cozy family restaurant.
(Entrees 950-1990Ft. Open daily noon-10pm.)

ESZTERGOM. In Esztergom, a millennium of religious history revolves around a solemn hilltop **cathedral**, whose crypt holds the remains of Hungary's
archbishops. The **cupola** (200Ft) offers the best
view of the Danube Bend. The **Cathedral Treasury**
(Kincstáv) to the right of the main altar has Hungary's most extensive collection of ecclesiastical
treasures. To the left of the altar is the red marble
Bakócz Chapel, a masterwork of Renaissance Tuscan
craftsmanship. (Open Mar.-Oct. daily 9am-4pm; Nov.-
Dec. M-F 11am-3:30pm, Sa-Su 10am-3:30pm. English-
language guidebook 100Ft. Cathedral free.)

Trains go to Budapest (1½hr., 22 per day, 436Ft).
From the station, turn left on the main street, Baross
Gábor út, and make a right onto Kiss János Altábor-
nagy út, which becomes Kossuth Lajos u., to reach
the square. **Buses** run to Szentendre (1½hr., every
hr., 476Ft) and Visegrád (45min., every hr., 316Ft).
From the bus station, walk up Simor János u. toward
the street market to reach Rákóczi tér. MAHART
boats depart from the pier at Gőzhajó u. on Primas
Sziget Island for: Budapest (4hr.; 3 per day; 1200Ft,
students 600Ft); Szentendre (2¾hr.; every hr.; 980Ft,
students 490Ft); and Visegrád (1½hr.; every hr.;
700Ft, students 350Ft). **Grantours**, Széchenyi tér 25,
at the edge of Rákóczi tér, sells maps (200Ft-500Ft)
and arranges accommodations. (☎(033) 41 70 52;
grantour@mail.holop.hu. Open July-Aug. M-F 8am-
6pm, Sa 9am-noon; Sept.-June M-F 8am-4pm, Sa
9am-noon.) **Csülök Csárda ❷**, Batthány út 9, offers
fine Hungarian cuisine. (Entrees 480-1800Ft. Open
daily noon-midnight.)

THE INSIDER'S CITY

MARGIT ISLAND

**Outdoor enthusiasts will find
plenty to do in this gorgeous oasis
north of Budapest. Catch the #26
or 26A bus in Pest at Nyugati pu.,
and take it to the Grand Hotel on
the island.**

1 Lounge by the fountain with
Speedo-clad Hungarians, grab
a snack, and jump on the tram-
polines (200Ft per 5min.).

2 Rent a pedal car (1800Ft per
hr.).

3 Splash in the pools and scream
down the slides at Palatinus
Strandfürdo.

4 Walk through the statue park,
where Hungary's cultural icons
are immortalized, and visit the
convent ruins.

5 See a show at the theater—pay
to enter or listen as the music
carries across the island.

6 Walk through the rose gardens
and enter the mini-zoo.

7 End with a historical tour of the
celebrated Grand Hotel.

SOUTHERN TRANSDANUBIA

Once the southernmost portion of the Roman province Pannonia, Southern Transdanubia is framed by the Danube to the west, the Dráva River to the south, and Lake Balaton to the north. Known for its rolling hills, mild climate, and sunflower fields, the region is also filled with magnificent Habsburg architecture.

PÉCS
☎072

Pécs (PAYCH; pop. 180,000), at the foot of the Mecsek mountains, is blessed with a pleasant climate and gorgeous vistas and architecture. Outdoor activities in the surrounding region and an intense nightlife fueled by university students make Pécs an attractive weekend spot. There's nothing mass-produced at the ▨Zsolnay Museum, where a family workshop has hand-crafted the world-famous Zsolnay porcelain since the mid-19th century. (Káptalan u. 2. Walk up Szepessy I. u. behind the Mosque Church and turn left at Káptalan u. Open Su 10am-4pm, Tu-Sa 10am-6pm. 600Ft, students 300Ft. Photographs 400Ft, video 800Ft.) At nearby Széchenyi tér stands the Mosque of Ghazi Kassim (Gázi Khasim Pasa dzsámija). Now a church once more, the building was once a Turkish mosque built on the site of an earlier church; this fusion of Christian and Muslim traditions has become an emblem of the city. (Open Apr. 16-Oct. 14 M-Sa 10am-4pm, Su 12:30-4pm; Oct. 15-Apr. 15 10am-noon, Su open for services only at 9:30am, 10:30am, and 11:30am. Free; donations requested.) Walk downhill from Széchenyi tér on Irgalmasok u. to Kossuth tér to reach the stunning 1869 synagogue, which has intricate paintings covering the ceiling and a fabulous Ark of the Covenant. (Open Su-F 10-11:30am and noon-5pm. 200Ft, students 100Ft.)

To reach the train station, just south of the historic district, take bus #30, 32, or 33 from the town center. Trains run to Budapest (3½hr., 16 per day, 1918-2338Ft), as do buses (4½hr., 7 per day, 2088Ft). Tourinform, Széchenyi tér 9, sells maps and phone cards. (☎21 26 32. Open June 16-Sept. 30 M-F 9am-7pm, Sa-Su 10am-6pm; Oct.-May reduced hours.) Private rooms are a good budget option in the town center. Also in the center, ▨Pollack Mihály Students' Hostel ❶, Jokai u. 8, has spotless bedrooms and bathrooms, kitchen facilities, and lounging areas. (☎315 846. Call ahead. Dorms 1800Ft.) Szent Mór Kollégium ❶, 48-as tér 4, offers affordable university dorm rooms. From the main terminal, take bus #21 to 48-as tér. (☎50 36 10. Curfew midnight. Call ahead. Open July-Aug. 30. Dorms 1300Ft.) Pécs's restaurants, cafes, and bars are among the city's biggest attractions. ▨Cellarium Étterem ❸, Hunyadi út 2, is a Hungarian restaurant housed in a wine cellar. (Entrees 950-3200FT.) Afiúm ❸, Irgalmasok u. 2, has a delicious Italian and Hungarian menu with many veggie options. (Entrees 830-1950Ft. Open M-Sa 11am-1am, Su 11am-midnight.) At night, chill with the artsy crowd at ▨Cafe Dante, Janus Pannonis u. 11, in the same building as the Csontváry Museum. (Beer 290-390Ft. Open daily 10am-1am; later on weekends.) Postal Code: 7621.

EGER
☎036

The siege of Eger Castle in 1553 and István Dobó's subsequent defeat of the Ottoman army figure prominently in Hungarian lore. The key to victory was rumored to be the strengthening powers of local Egri Bikavér (Bull's Blood) wine. The legacy lives on today in the vibrant cellars of the Valley of the Beautiful Women and in the historical monuments scattered throughout the city. Close enough to Budapest to do in a daytrip but bustling enough to spend days there, Eger (EGG-air; pop. 58,200) continues to seduce visitors with its quaint cobblestone streets, delicious delicacies, and infectious friendliness.

[E] [?] TRANSPORTATION AND PRACTICAL INFORMATION. Budapest direct **trains** (2hr., 6 per day, 1036-1242Ft) split in Hatvan; make sure you're in the correct car. From the station, turn right on Deák Ferenc út., walk 10min., go right on Kossuth Lajos u., left on Széchenyi u., and right on Érsek u. to reach **Dobó tér**, the main square (20min.). **TourInform**, Bajcsy-Zsilinszky u. 9, has lodging info. (☎51 77 15; www.ektf.hu/eger. Open June-Sept. M-F 9am-7pm, Sa-Su 10am-6pm; Sept.-June M-F 9am-5pm, Sa 9am-1pm.) **OTP Bank**, Széchenyi u. 2, grants AmEx/MC/V advances, cashes AmEx Traveler's Cheques without commission, and has an **ATM**. (☎31 08 66. Open M-Tu and Th 7:45am-5pm, W 7:45am-6pm.) **Postal code:** 3300.

[?] [C] ACCOMMODATIONS AND FOOD. Private rooms are best (about 2000Ft); look for "zimmer frei" or "szòba eladò" on signs outside the main square, particularly on Almagyar u. and Mekcsey István u. near the castle. **Eger Tourist**, Bajcsy-Zsilinszky u. 9, next to TourInform, arranges private rooms which cost about 3000Ft. (☎51 70 00. Open M-F 9am-5pm.) **Lukács Vendégház ❷**, Bárány u. 10, located just next to Eger Castle, has its own garden, an outdoor seating area, and large, comfortable rooms. (☎/fax 411 567. Rooms 1800-2600Ft.) **Hotel Minaret ❹**, Knézich K. u. 4, is centrally located and offers a beauty and massage center, swimming pool, and gym. (☎/fax 410 233. All rooms include satellite TV. Singles 7750Ft; doubles 10500Ft; triples 12750Ft; quads 14500Ft. Nov.-Mar. 1000Ft less.) Take bus #5, 11, or 12 north to the Shell station (20min.) to reach **Autós Caravan Camping ❶**, Rákóczi u. 79. (Apr. 15-Oct. 15, open daily 9am-10pm. 900Ft, students 700Ft.) **Széchenyi u.** is lined with restaurants. **🖾Dobos ❶**, Széchenyi u. 6, offers a mouth-watering selection of pastries and desserts. (Confections 100-180Ft. Ice cream 80Ft. Open daily 9:30am-9pm.) **Gyros Étterem Sérozc ❶**, Széchenyi u. 10, serves gyros (350-380Ft) in a bright, well-kept setting that offers patio seating in the summer. In the Valley of the Beautiful Women, crowds dine in the courtyard of **Kulacs Csárda Borozó's ❸**. (Entrees 950-1600Ft. Open Su and Tu-Sa noon-10pm.) There is an **ABC supermarket** between Sandor u. and Szt. Janos u. (Open M-F 6am-7pm, Sa 6am-1pm.)

[G] [?] SIGHTS AND FESTIVALS. Dobó István and his men repelled the attacking Ottoman army from medieval **Eger Castle**, which features subterranean barracks, catacombs, a crypt, and a wine cellar. One ticket covers the picture gallery, the **Dobó István Vármúzeum**, which displays artifacts and weapons, and the **dungeon exhibition**. (Castle open daily 8am-8pm. Wine cellars open daily 10am-7pm. Museums open Mar.-Oct. Su and Tu-Sa 9am-5pm; Nov.-Feb. 9am-3pm. Castle 200 Ft, students 100Ft. Wine cellars free; 140Ft per tasting. English tour 400Ft. All three museums Su and T-Sa 500Ft, students 250Ft; M 250Ft/120Ft.) The **Lyceum**, at the corner of Kossuth Lajos u. and Eszterházy tér., houses an astronomical museum and a *camera obscura* that projects a live image of the surrounding town onto a table. (Open Apr.-Oct. Su and Tu-Sa 9:30am-1:30pm; Oct.-Dec. and Mar.-Apr. Su 9:30am-1:30pm, Th-F 9:30am-1pm, Sa 9:30am-1:30pm. 350Ft, students 200Ft.)

After a morning exploring Eger's historical sights, spend the afternoon or evening in the wine cellars of the **🖾Valley of the Beautiful Women** (Szépasszonyvölgy). To reach the wine cellars, start on Széchenyi u. with Eger Cathedral to your right. Turn right on Kossuth Lajos u., left on Deák Ferenc út. (ignore the sign directing you otherwise), and right on Telekessy u.; continue until you arrive at Szépasszonyvölgy (20 min.). Most of the 25 open cellars consist of little more than a tunnel and a few tables and benches, but each has its own personality: Some are hushed while others burst with Hungarian and Roma singalongs. (0.1L 50-80Ft, 1L 350Ft. Open from 9am, closing times vary; Jul.-Aug. some stay open until midnight.)

In summer, **open-air baths** offer a break from the sweltering city heat. (Open May-Sept. M-F 6am-7pm, Sa-Su 8:30am-7pm; Oct.-Apr. daily 9am-7pm. 500Ft, students 350Ft.) The city celebrates its heritage with daily performances of opera and early court music during the **Baroque Festival** (late July to mid-Aug.).

▷ DAYTRIP FROM EGER: SZILVÁSVÁRAD. Perfect for an outing from Eger, Szilvásvárad (SEAL-vash-vah-rod) attracts both horse and nature lovers. **Horse shows** (800Ft) kick into action on most weekends in the arena on Szalajka u. **Lipicai Stables** is the stud farm for the town's famed Lipizzaner breed. From the park entrance on Egri út., turn left on Enyves u., then follow signs to the farm. (☎35 51 55. Open daily 8:30am-noon and 2-4pm. 80Ft to visit.) Many farms offer **horseback riding,** especially in the summer. **Péter Kovács,** Egri út. 62 (☎35 53 43), rents horses (2000Ft per hr.). For **hiking,** head to the nearby **Bükk mountains** and **Szalajka valley.** A 45min. walk along the green trail will lead you to the most popular attraction, the **Fátyol waterfall;** 30min. past the falls is the **Istálósk cave,** the Stone Age home to a bear-worshipping cult. **Bike rentals** and cycling maps are available on Szalajka u.

Szilvásvárad can be reached by **train** (1hr., 7 per day, 262Ft) or **bus** (45min., every 30-60min., 316Ft) from Eger. From the train station (Szilvásvárad-Szalajkavölgy), follow Egri út. to Szalajka u. directly to the national park. There is no bus station in town; just get off at the second stop on Egri út. near Szalajka u. where the road bends sharply. Szilvásvárad has no tourist office; visit Eger's **Tourinform** (see p. 545) before heading out.

GYŐR ☎096

In the unspoiled, far western region of Őrség, lively Győr (DYUR; pop. 130,000) overflows with religious monuments, well-kept museums, and 17th- and 18th-century architectural gems. From the train station, go right until you come to the bridge; turn left just before the underpass, then cross the street to reach pedestrian **Baross Gabor utca.** Walking uphill on Czuczor Gergely u., one street to the right of Baross Gabor u., will lead you to the striking **Ark of the Covenant statue** (Frigylada szobov) and **Chapter Hill** (Káptalandomb). At the top of the hill is the **Episcopal Cathedral** (Székesegyház), which holds the **Weeping Madonna of Győr;** legend says that the icon wept blood for persecuted Irish Catholics on St. Patrick's Day in 1697. The **Diocesan Library and Treasury** (Egyházmegyei Kincstáv), Káptalandomb 26, hidden in an alley off the cathedral's square, displays priceless jewels and more religious art. (English captions. Open Su and Tu-Sa 10am-4pm. 300Ft, students 150Ft.) For contemporary art, head to the **Imre Patkó collection** at Széchenyi tér 4, down Czuczor Gergely u. from the statue; enter at Stelczera u. (Open Su and Tu-Sa 10am-6pm. 240Ft, students 120Ft.) Across the river from the town center is the huge and popular **water park,** Cziráky tér 1, with thermal springs. From Bécsi Kapu tér, take the bridge over the small island and make the first right on the other side, then go right again onto Cziráky tér. (Open daily 8am-7pm. 550Ft, students 400Ft.) At night, music and young people spill from cellar bars onto Győr's streets. The fabulous patio at **Komédiás Biergarten,** Czuczor Gergely u. 30, invites drinking and laughing crowds. (Beer 250-420Ft. Open M-Sa 11am-midnight.)

Frequent **trains** go to Budapest (2½hr., 26 per day, 1160-1480Ft) and Vienna (2hr., 13 per day, 4450Ft). **Buses** run to Budapest (2½hr., every hr., 1300Ft). The train station is 3min. from the city center; the underpass that links the rail platforms leads to the bus station. The **Tourinform kiosk,** Árpád u. 32, at the corner with Baross Gabor u., provides free maps and arranges lodgings. (☎ 31 17 71. Open June-Aug. M-F 8am-8pm, Sa-Su 9am-6pm.) ◪**Katalin's Kert ❸,** Sarkantyú köz 3, off Bécsi Kapu tér, has huge modern rooms with private baths. (☎/fax 45 20 88. Singles 5800Ft; doubles 7500Ft.) **Matróz Restaurant ❷,** Dunakapu tér 3, off

Jedlik Ányos u. facing the river, fries up succulent fish. (Entrees 500-1100Ft. Open Su-Th 9am-10pm, F-Sa 9am-11pm.) **John Bull Pub ❸**, Aradi u., offers a break from the Hungarian diet. (Entrees 810-1500Ft. Open daily 10am-midnight.) **Kaiser's supermarket** is at the corner of Arany János u. and Aradi vértanúk. (Open M 7:30am-7pm, Tu-F 6:30am-7pm, Sa 6:30am-2pm.) **Postal Code:** 9021.

◪ DAYTRIP FROM GYŐR: ARCHABBEY OF PANNONHALMA. Visible at a distance from Győr, the hilltop Archabbey of Pannonhalma (Pannonhalmi Főapátság) has seen ten centuries of destruction and rebuilding since it was established in AD 996 by the Benedictine order. The UNESCO World Heritage site features an opulent, treasure-filled library, a 13th-century basilica, and frequent classical concerts. **Pax Tourist,** to the left of the entrance, leads tours and has concert info. (☎57 01 91; pax@osb.hu. Hungarian tour with English text every hr.; English tours in summer 11am and 1pm. Hungarian tour 1000Ft, students 300Ft; English tour 2000/1000Ft.) To reach Pannonhalma from Győr, take the **bus** from stand #11 (45min., 7 per day, 263Ft). Ask for Pannonhalma vár and look for the huge gates, or you may end up in the town 1km away.

LAKE BALATON

A retreat since Roman times, the warm Lake Balaton drew the European elite in the 19th-century and is now a budget paradise for German and Austrian students. Be aware that storms can roll in quickly—when the yellow lights on tall harbor buildings speed up to one revolution per second, swimmers must get out of the water.

SIÓFOK. Tourist offices are more densely packed in Siófok than in any other Hungarian city, reflecting the influx of lake-bound vacationers who flock here every summer. Most attractions in Siófok pale in comparison with the **Strand**, a series of park-like lawns running to the concrete shoreline (some sections 200-400Ft per person). Bars and nightclubs line the lakefront, and **disco boats** push off at 9pm. Right in the center of the Strand is the ◪**Renegade Pub**, Petőfi Sétány 3, a casual bar and dance club that draws a large crowd. (Open June-Sept. daily 8pm-5am.) **Palace Disco,** Deák Ferenc Sétány 2, is a party complex with discos, bars, and restaurants. (Mixed drinks 980-1750Ft. Cover 1500-2500Ft. Pizzeria open 11am-5am. Disco open May-Sept. 10pm-5am.)

Trains go to Budapest (2½hr., every hr., 926Ft). **Express buses** (gyorsjárat) head to Budapest (1½hr., 9 per day, 1320Ft) and Pécs (3hr., 4 per day, 2456Ft). **Tourinform,** Fő u. at Szabadság tér, in the base of the water tower across from the train station, helps find rooms and has free maps. (☎(084) 31 53 55; www.siofok.com. Open July-Aug. M-Sa 8am-8pm, Su 9am-6pm; Sept.-June M-F 9am-4pm.) Take a quick bus or train ride to Balatonszéplak felsö to reach ◪**Villa Benjamin Youth Hostel ❷**, Siófoki u. 9, which has garden rooms and a beach bungalow feel. (☎(084) 350 704. Kitchen available. Single 2500Ft, double 5000Ft, triple 7500Ft. 4- to 6-person apartment 3500Ft per person; 8- to10-person house 3500Ft per person.) **Hotel Park ❺**, Batthány u. 7, has modern rooms right by the Strand. (☎(084) 31 05 39. Reception 24hr. July-Aug. doubles 10,000-15,000Ft; Sept.-June 8000-10,000Ft.)

TIHANY. With its scenic hikes, charming cottages, and panoramic views, the Tihany peninsula is the pearl of Lake Balaton. The **Benedictine Abbey** (Bencés Apátság) draws over a million visitors annually to its luminous frescoes, gold-leaf Baroque altars, and a crypt housing one of Hungary's earliest kings. (Open Mar.-Oct. daily 9am-6pm. 300Ft, students 150Ft. Su free.) The well-marked **hiking** trails across the peninsula take only an hour or two. The green-line trail runs past the

Hermit's Place (Barátlakások), where the cells and chapel hollowed out by 11th-century Greek Orthodox hermits are still visible. MAHART **ferries** go to Tihany from Siófok (1-1¼hr.; every hr.; 800Ft, students 400Ft). To reach the town from the ferry pier and neighboring Strand, walk underneath the elevated road and follow the "Apátság" signs up the steep hill to the abbey.

KESZTHELY. At the lake's west tip, the resort of Keszthely (KEST-HAY), once the playground of the powerful Austro-Hungarian Festetics family, is now home to an agricultural college and year-round thermal springs. The ▧**Helikon Palace Museum** (Helikon Kastélymúzeum) in the **Festetics Palace** (Kastély) is a storybook Baroque palace with a 90,000-volume library, extravagantly furnished chambers, an exotic arms collection, and a porcelain exhibit. From Fő tér, follow Kossuth Lajos u. toward Tourinform until it becomes Kastély u. (Open Su and Tu-Sa 9am-6pm. 1700Ft, students 800Ft.) The **Strand,** on the coast to the right as you exit the train station, attracts crowds with its giant slide, kayaks, paddle boats, and volleyball nets. From the center, walk down Erzsébet u. as it curves right into Vörösmarty u.; after the train tracks, go through the park on the left to get to the beach. (Open May 15-Sept. 15 daily 8:30am-7pm. 400Ft, after 4pm 240Ft.)

Express trains run between Keszthely and Budapest (3hr.; 13 per day; 1556Ft, reservations 400Ft). From the train station, take Mártirok u., which ends in Kossuth Lajos u., and turn left to reach the main square, Fő tér. **Tourinform,** Kossuth Lajos u. 28, on the palace side of Fő tér, gives out free maps and info and helps find rooms. (☎(083) 31 41 44. Open July-Aug. M-F 9am-8pm, Sa-Su 9am-6pm; Oct.-June M-F 9am-5pm, Sa 9am-1pm.) **Kiss-Máte Panzió ❸,** Katona J u. 27, offers spacious central rooms. (☎(083) 319 072. Kitchen available. Free laundry. Doubles 3000Ft per night for 2 or more nights, 5000Ft for 1 night only.) **Castrum Camping ❶,** Móra Ferenc u. 48, has large sites and tennis courts. (☎(083) 31 21 20. 900Ft per person. July-Aug. 600Ft per tent; Sept.-June 480Ft per tent.) ▧**Corso Restaurant ❸,** Erzsébet Királyné u. 23, in the Abbázia Club Hotel, serves fish from Balaton. (Entrees 650-1600Ft. Open M-Sa 7am-11pm.) **Oázis-Reform Restaurant ❶,** Rákóczi tér 3, is a vegetarian's lunch-time heaven. (Buffet 210Ft per 100g. Open M-F 11am-4pm, Sa 11am-2pm.)

ICELAND (ÍSLAND)

Born from the collision of the European and North American continents, Iceland's landscape is uniquely warped and contorted, having been forged by the tempers of still-active volcanoes and raked by the slow advance and retreat of timeless glaciers. Nature is the country's greatest attraction—few other places offer visitors the chance to walk across lava-filled moonscapes, dodge warm water shooting from geysers, and sail across a glacial lagoon filled with icebergs. Civilization has made a powerful mark on Iceland; the geothermal energy that causes numerous earthquakes also provides hot water and electricity to Iceland's settlements, and a network of roads carved through seemingly inhospitable terrain connects even the smallest villages to larger cities. A booming tourist industry attests to the fact that physical isolation has not set the country behind the rest of Europe. However, Iceland's island status has allowed it to achieve a high standard of living without damaging its pristine natural surroundings and deeply rooted sense of community.

FACTS AND FIGURES

Official Name: Ísland.

Capital: Reykjavík.

Major Cities: Hafnarfjörður, Höfn, Ísafjörður, Vík.

Population: 280,000.

Land Area: 100,000 sq. km.

Time Zone: GMT.

Language: Icelandic; English is widely spoken.

Religions: Evangelical Lutheran (93%).

DISCOVER ICELAND

Spend a day exploring the heart of **Reykjavík** (p. 553), then daytrip to the peerless natural wonders of **Gullfoss, Geysir,** and the **Blue Lagoon** (p. 558). Straddle two continents in **Þingvellir National Park** (p. 559), then sail to the ruggedly beautiful **Westman Islands** (p. 559) for a first-hand look at the type of volcanic activity that formed mainland Iceland only 14 million years ago.

ICELAND

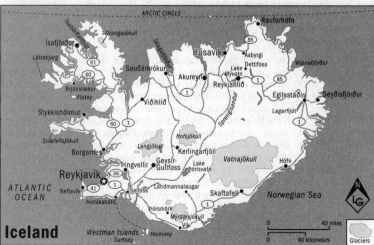

ESSENTIALS

WHEN TO GO

High season hits in July, when the interior opens up, snow almost disappears, and all the bus lines are running. In summer, the sun dips below the horizon for a few hours each night, but the sky never truly gets dark and it's warm enough to camp and hike. With warm clothing you could travel as late as October, but in winter there is very little sun, and finding transportation is difficult. The temperature rarely gets higher than 16°C (60°F) in summer or dips below -6°C (20°F) in winter.

DOCUMENTS AND FORMALITIES

VISAS. South Africans need a visa for stays of any length. Citizens of Australia, Canada, the EU, New Zealand, and the US do not need a visa for stays of up to 90 days, but this three-month period begins upon entry into any Nordic country; for more than 90 days in any combination of Denmark, Finland, Iceland, Norway, and/or Sweden, you will need a visa.

EMBASSIES. Foreign embassies in Iceland are in Reykjavík (p. 555). Icelandic embassies at home include: **Canada,** 360 Albert St., Ste. 710, Ottawa, ON KIR 7X7 (☎ 613-482-1944; www.iceland.org/ca); **UK,** 2A Hans St., London SW1X 0JE (☎ 020 7259 3999; www.iceland.org.uk); and **US,** 1156 15th St. NW, Ste. 1200, Washington, D.C. 20005 (☎ 202-265-6653; www.iceland.org/us).

TRANSPORTATION

BY PLANE. Icelandair (US ☎ 800-223-5500; UK ☎ 020 7874 1000; www.icelandair.net) flies to Reykjavík year-round from the US and Europe. Icelandair provides free stopovers of up to three days on all transatlantic flights; it also offers some student discounts, including half-price standby flights. Domestic **Flugfélag Islands** (☎ 750 30 30; eyjaflug.is) flies between Reykjavík and Iceland's other major towns; tickets can be issued at BSÍ Travel (see p. 553). Another option is the **Air/Bus Rover,** offered jointly by the domestic air carriers and BSÍ Travel (June-Sept.; from 8000Ikr). Weather can ground flights; leave yourself time for delays.

BY BUS. Iceland has no trains; although flying is faster and more comfortable, buses are usually cheaper and provide a closer look at the terrain. **Destination Iceland** (☎ 591 10 00; www.dice.is), which has offices in the Reykjavík bus terminal, coordinates schedules and prices. Schedules are available at hostels and tourist offices. Their main brochure lists all bus schedules and is a must for anyone traveling the **Ring Road,** the loop that circles Iceland. Buses run daily on each segment from mid-June to August, but bus frequency drops dramatically in the off season. The going is slow, since some roads are unpaved. The circle can be rushed through in three days, but ten days is a much more adequate time frame.

The **Full Circle Passport** lets travelers circle the island at their own pace on the Ring Road (available mid-May to Sept.; 21,000Ikr). However, it allows travel only in a continuous direction, so travelers must move either clockwise or counter-clockwise around the country. For an extra 10,000Ikr the pass (which has no time limitation) provides access to the Westfjords in the island's extreme northwest. The **Omnibus Passport** gives a period of unlimited travel on all scheduled bus routes, including non-Ring roads (1-week 23,000Ikr, 2-week 33,000Ikr, 3-week 42,500Ikr, 4-week 47,000Ikr; off-season reduced prices). Both passes give 5% discounts on many ferries, campgrounds, farms, *Hótel Edda* sleeping-bag dorms, and guided bus tours.

BY FERRY. The best way to see Iceland's rugged shores is on the **Norröna** car and passenger ferry (☎562 63 62; fax 552 94 50) that circles the North Atlantic via: Seyðisfjörður, East Iceland; Tórshavn in the Faroe Islands; and Hanstholm, Denmark (runs mid-May to Aug.; 7 days, students 42,500Ikr). From Tórshavn, you can continue on to Bergen or return to Seyðisfjörður. **Eimskip** (reservations ☎585 40 70) offers more expensive ferry rides on cargo ships from Reykjavík to Immingham, Rotterdam, and Hamburg.

BY CAR. Travelers using cars have the most freedom. Iceland is overflowing with car rental (*bílaleiga*) companies. Prices average about 5000Ikr per day and 40Ikr per km after the first 100km for smaller cars, but are substantially higher for 4-wheel-drive vehicles (ask about special package deals). **Ragnar Bjarnason**, Staðarbakka 2 (☎557 42 66; fax 557 42 33), offers the lowest rates. You are required to keep your headlights on at all times, wear a seatbelt, and drive only on marked roads. Iceland recognizes foreign driver's licenses, but you may need to purchase insurance for the rented car (750-2000Ikr).

BY BIKE AND BY THUMB. Cycling is gaining popularity, but ferocious winds, driving rain, and narrow roads make it a difficult mode of tranport. Buses will carry bikes for a 5000-7000Ikr fee, depending on the distance covered. Trekking is extremely arduous; well-marked trails are rare, but several suitable areas await the truly ambitious. Ask the tourist office in Reykjavík for maps and more info. Hitchhikers sometimes try the roads in summer, but sparse traffic and harsh weather exacerbate the inherent risks. Nevertheless, determined hitchhikers can find rides with relative ease between Reykjavík and Akureyri; hitchhiking is harder in the east and the south. *Let's Go* does not recommend hitchhiking.

TOURIST SERVICES AND MONEY

EMERGENCY	Police: ☎112. Ambulance: ☎112. Fire: ☎112.

TOURIST OFFICES. Tourist offices in large towns have schedules, maps, and brochures; check at hotel reception desks in smaller towns for local info. The free brochure *Around Iceland* (accommodation, restaurant, and museum listings for every town in the country), *The Complete Iceland Map*, and the BSÍ bus schedule are all must-haves. Reykjavík's tourist office maintains a helpful website (www.tourist.reykjavik.is), as does the US tourist board (www.goiceland.org).

MONEY. Iceland's monetary unit is the **króna** (plural: krónur), which is divided into 100 rarely used *aurar*. There are 1Ikr, 5Ikr, 10Ikr, 50Ikr, and 100Ikr coins; notes are in denominations of 500Ikr, 1000Ikr, 2000Ikr, and 5000Ikr. Costs are high; on average, a night in a hostel might cost 1750Ikr, a budget hotel 6500-8500Ikr, and a budget restaurant meal 1000-2000Ikr. **Tipping** is not customary in Iceland. **Value-added tax (VAT)** is included in all posted prices; refunds are available upon departure for purchases of 4000Ikr or more (p. 16).

BUSINESS HOURS. Stores are generally open Monday to Friday 9am-5pm (6pm in summer) and Saturday mornings.

ICELANDIC KRÓNUR		
	AUS$1 = 46.98IKR	100IKR = AUS$2.12
	CDN$1 = 58.98IKR	100IKR = CDN$1.70
	EUR€1 = 89.80IKR	100IKR = EUR€1.11
	NZ$1 = 48.09IKR	100IKR = NZ$2.08
	ZAR1 = 11.03IKR	100IKR = ZAR9.07
	UK£1 = 129.77IKR	100IKR = UK£0.77
	US$1 = 82.58IKR	100IKR = US$1.21

COMMUNICATION

TELEPHONES. Telephone (*sími*) offices are often in the same building as post offices. Pay phones take phone cards or 10Ikr, 50Ikr, or 100Ikr pieces; local calls cost 20Ikr. For the best prices, make calls from telephone offices; otherwise use a prepaid phone card. Mobile phones are an increasingly popular alternative (p. 36). To make an international call, insert a phone card or dial direct (see numbers below). To reach the operator, call ☎ 118 (59Ikr per min.). International direct dial numbers include: **AT&T,** ☎ 800 90 01; **British Telecom,** ☎ 800 90 44; **Canada Direct,** ☎ 800 90 10; **Ireland Direct,** ☎ 800 93 53; **MCI,** ☎ 800 90 02; **Sprint,** ☎ 800 90 03; **Telecom New Zealand Direct,** ☎ 800 199 64; **Telkom South Africa,** ☎ 800 199 27; and **Telstra Australia,** ☎ 800 199 61.

PHONE CODES	**Country code: 354. International dialing prefix: 00.** There are no city codes in Iceland. From outside Iceland, dial int'l dialing prefix (see inside back cover) + 354 + local number.

MAIL. Mailing a postcard or letter from Iceland costs 80Ikr to Australia, Canada, New Zealand, the US, or South Africa; 55Ikr to Europe. Post offices (*póstur*) are generally open Monday to Friday 9am-4:30pm. See p. 556 for info on *Poste Restante*.

INTERNET ACCESS. Internet access is widespread in Iceland, although in small towns it may only be available in public libraries.

ACCOMMODATIONS AND CAMPING

ICELAND	❶	❷	❸	❹	❺
ACCOMMODATIONS	500-1500Ikr	1501-3000Ikr	3001-5000Ikr	5001-10000Ikr	over 10000Ikr

Iceland's 27 **HI youth hostels** are invariably clean and uniformly priced at 1500Ikr for members and 1850Ikr for nonmembers. Pick up the free *Hostelling in Iceland* brochure at tourist offices. **Sleeping-bag accommodations** (*svefnpokapláss;* beds with no sheets or blankets included) are often the only option on farms, at summer hostels, and in guesthouses (*gistiheimili*); they are usually relatively cheap (p. 556). In early June, many schoolhouses become *Hótel Eddas*, which have sleeping-bag accommodations. Staying in a tiny farm or hostel can be the highlight of a trip, but the nearest bus may stop 20km away and run once a week. Many remote lodgings will pick up tourists in the nearest town for a small fee. In cities and nature reserves, **camping** is permitted only at designated campsites. Outside of official sites, camping is free but discouraged; watch out for *Tjaldstœði Bönnuð* (No Camping) signs, and always ask at the nearest farm before you pitch a tent. Use gas burners; Iceland has no firewood, and it is illegal to burn the sparse vegetation. Official campsites (summer only) range from rocky fields with cold water taps to the sumptuous facilities in Reykjavík (around 700Ikr). Many offer discounts for students and bus-pass holders.

FOOD AND DRINK

ICELAND	❶	❷	❸	❹	❺
FOOD	under 800Ikr	801-1200Ikr	1201-2000Ikr	2001-3500Ikr	over 3500Ikr

Traditional foods include *lundi* (puffin) on the Westman Islands, *rjúpa* (ptarmigan) around Christmas, and *selshreifar* (seal flippers) during the *Þorra matur* (Thorri or Mid-Winter Feast). Fish, lamb, and chicken are the most common components of authentic dishes, although more adventurous diners can try *svið* (singed and boiled sheep's head), *hrútspungur* (ram's testicles), or *hákarl* (rotten shark meat that has been buried underground), all of which are traditional dishes consumed during the Thorri Feast. International cuisine also has a strong presence in Iceland, and Italian, American, and Asian fare can usually be found even in smaller towns. Food is very expensive in Iceland; a *cheap* restaurant meal will cost at least 800Ikr. Grocery stores are the way to go; virtually every town has a couple of them. Gas stations usually run a grill and sell snacks. Bonus and Netto are cheaper alternatives to the more ubiquitous Hagkaup and 10-11 chains. Iceland has some of the purest water in Europe. Beer costs 500-600Ikr at most pubs, cafes, and restaurants. The national drink is *Brennivín*, a type of schnapps known as "the Black Death." The rarely enforced drinking age is 20.

HOLIDAYS

Holidays: New Year's Day (Jan. 1); Good Friday (Apr. 8); Easter (Apr. 11-12); Labor Day (May 1); Ascension Day (May 20); Whit Sunday and Monday (May 30-31); National Day (June 17); Commerce Day (Aug. 5); Christmas Eve and Day (Dec. 24-25); Boxing Day (Dec. 26); New Year's Eve (Dec. 31).

REYKJAVÍK

Reykjavík's character more than makes up for its modest size. Bold, modern architecture complements a backdrop of snow-dusted purple mountains, and the city's refreshingly clear air is matched by its sparkling streets and gardens. Quiet during the week, the world's smallest metropolitan capital comes alive on weekends.

▐ TRANSPORTATION

Flights: All international flights arrive at **Keflavík Airport** (KEF), 55km from Reykjavík. From the main exit, catch a **Flybus** (☎ 562 10 11, departs 30min. after every arrival, 1000Ikr) to the domestic **Reykjavík Airport** (REK) or Hótel Loftleiðir; from the hotel, you can take Flybus minivans to your hostel or hotel (free) or bus #7 (M-F every 20min. until 7pm, after 7pm and Sa-Su every hr.; 220Ikr) downtown to *Lækjartorg*. Flybus minivans running to the airport stop at Hótel Loftleiðir (2hr. before each departure), and Grand

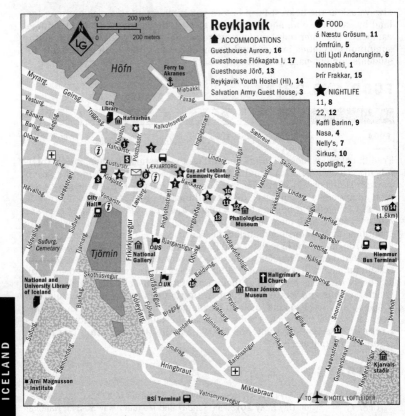

Reykjavík

🏠 ACCOMMODATIONS
Guesthouse Aurora, **16**
Guesthouse Flókagata I, **17**
Guesthouse Jörð, **13**
Reykjavik Youth Hostel (HI), **14**
Salvation Army Guest House, **3**

🍴 FOOD
á Næstu Grösum, **11**
Jómfrúin, **5**
Litli Ljoti Andarunginn, **6**
Nonnabiti, **1**
Þrír Frakkar, **15**

⭐ NIGHTLIFE
11, **8**
22, **12**
Kaffi Barinn, **9**
Nasa, **4**
Nelly's, **7**
Sirkus, **10**
Spotlight, **2**

Hótel Reykjavík (2½hr. before each departure). Most hostels and guesthouses can arrange pick-ups. The **Omnibus pass** covers Flybus; get a refund at Destination Iceland (see below) or Reykjavík Excursions (in the Hótel Loftleiðir).

Buses: Umferðarmiðstöð (BSÍ Station), Vatnsmýrarvegur 10 (☎552 23 00), off Hringbraut near Reykjavík Airport. Walk 15-20min. south along Tjörnin from the city center, or take bus #7 (every 20min., 220lkr). Open daily 7am-10pm; tickets sold 7:30am-8pm. **Destination Iceland** (☎591 10 00; www.dice.is) is inside the bus terminal. Open June-Aug. M-F 7:30am-6pm, Sa-Su 7:30am-2pm; Sept.-May M-F 9am-5pm.

Public Transportation: Strætisvagnar Reykjavíkur (Strato; ☎540 27 00) operates yellow city buses (220lkr). Pick up SVR's helpful city map and bus schedule at its terminals. Tickets are sold at four terminals; the two major terminals are **Lækjartorg** in the center of town (open M-F 7am-11:30pm, Sa 8am-11:30pm, Su 10am-11:30pm) and **Hlemmur,** farther east on Hverfisg. (open M-Sa 8am-11pm, Su noon-11pm). Buy packages of 9 adult fares (1500lkr) or 20 senior fares (1800lkr), or buy tickets on the bus (exact change only). Ask the driver for a free transfer ticket (*skiptimiði;* valid for 45min.). Buses run M-Sa 7am-midnight, Su and holidays 10am-midnight.

Taxis: BSR, Skogarhild 18 (☎561 00 00). 24hr. service. BSÍ Station 600-700lkr; Keflavík Airport 7500lkr. **Hreyfill,** Fellsmuli 26-28 (☎588 55 22).

Car Rental: Hertz (☎505 06 00), in the Reykjavík Airport. 10,000-37,400Ikr per day. **Berg**, Bíldshöfða 10 (☎577 60 50; www.carrental-berg.com). Under 100km 4800-6900Ikr per day, unlimited mileage 8850-13,600Ikr per day. **Átak**, 200 Kópavogur, south of Reykjavík (☎554 60 40; www.atak.is). Under 100km 6200-7950Ikr per day; unlimited mileage 8900-11,900Ikr per day.

Bike Rental: At the youth hostel campsite (p. 556). 800Ikr per 6hr., 1500Ikr per day. **Reykjavík Travel Service** (see below). 700Ikr per 3hr., 1100 per 6hr., 1600Ikr per day.

Hitchhiking: Hitchhiking is uncommon but not difficult in Iceland. Those looking for a ride generally head to the east edge of town. *Let's Go* does not recommend hitchhiking.

◤◢ ORIENTATION AND PRACTICAL INFORMATION

Lækjartorg is Reykjavík's main square and a good base for navigation. **Lækjargata** leads from the southern end of Lækjartorg to **Tjörnin** (the pond), which lies halfway between the square and BSÍ Station. Reykjavík's main thoroughfare extends out from Lækjartorg, changing names from **Austurstræti** to **Bankastræti** and then **Laugavegur** as it moves west to east. City maps are available at the tourist office or around town, and the monthlies *What's On in Reykjavík* and *Reykjavík This Month* provide info about exploring the city (both free).

TOURIST, FINANCIAL, AND LOCAL SERVICES

Tourist Office: Upplýsingamiðstöð Ferðamála í Íslandi, Bankastr. 2 (☎562 30 45; www.visitreykjavik.is), at Lækjartorg and Bankastr. **Branches** at Keflavík airport and City Hall. Open June-Aug. daily 8:30am-6pm; Sept.-May M-F 9am-5pm, Sa-Su 10am-2pm. All sell the **Reykjavík Card**, which allows unlimited public transportation and free entry to several sights. (1-day 1000Ikr, 2-day 1500Ikr, 3-day 2000Ikr. See p. 557 for participating establishments.) ■**Reykjavík Travel Service**, Lækjarg. 2 (☎511 24 42; www.icelandvisitor.com) rents **bikes** and has **Internet** access (250Ikr per 30min.). Open June-Aug. daily 9am-10pm; Sept.-May M-Sa 10am-6pm.

Embassies: Canada, Túng. 14 (☎533 55 50; fax 533 55 51). Open M-F 9am-noon. **UK**, Laufásvegur 31 (☎550 51 00; fax 550 51 05). Open M-F 9am-noon. **US**, Laufásvegur 21 (☎562 91 00; fax 562 91 10). Open M-F 8am-12:30pm and 1:30-5pm.

Banks: Most banks are open M-F 9:15am-4pm, and some have extended hours on Thursdays until 6pm. On weekends, try the **BSÍ Station** (mid-May to mid-Sept.). ATM machines in the city operate 24hr., and the tourist office also exchanges money.

Luggage Storage: At BSÍ Station, next to ticket window. 500Ikr per day. Open M-F 7:30am-7pm, Sa-Su 7:30am-4pm.

Gay and Lesbian Services: Laugavegur 3, 4th fl. (☎552 78 78; www.gayiceland.com). Includes library and cafe. Offices open M-F 2-4pm; library open M and Th 8-11pm; cafe open M and Th 8-11:30pm, Sa 9-11:30pm.

Laundromat: Þvottahusið Emla, Barónsstíg. 3. 1700Ikr per load. Open M-F 8am-6pm.

EMERGENCY AND COMMUNICATIONS

Emergency: ☎112.

Police: Hverfisg. 113-115 (☎569 90 20). Station at Tryggvag. 19 (☎569 90 25).

Pharmacies: Lyf og Heilsa, Haaleitisbraut 68 (☎581 21 01). Open M-F 8am-midnight, Sa-Su 10am-midnight. **Lyfja Apótek**, Laugavegur 16 (☎552 40 45). Open M-F 9am-7pm, Sa 10am-4pm.

ICELAND

Medical Assistance: National Hospital at Fossvogur (☎525 17 00), on Hringbraut, has a 24hr. emergency ward. From the center of town, take bus #3 southeast.

Telephones: Phones require either coins or a phone card (500 or 1000Ikr; available at the tourist office, post office, and most convenience stores). For local calls insert at least 30Ikr. Phones accept 10, 50, or 100Ikr coins. International assistance: ☎115.

Internet Access: In **City Hall,** Tjörnin. Free 20min. slots. Open M-F 10:30am-6pm, Sa-Su noon-6pm. **Ground Zero,** Vallarstr. 4. 300Ikr per 30min. Open daily 11am-1am. **K-Lanið,** Laugavegur 103. 250Ikr per 30min., 1000Ikr per day. Open daily 10am-11pm.

Post Office: Íslandspóstur, Pósthússtr. 5 (☎580 11 01), at Austurstr. Address mail to be held: Firstname SURNAME, *Poste Restante,* ÍSLANDSPÓSTUR, Pósthússtr. 5, **101** Reykjavík, ICELAND. Open M-F 9am-4:30pm.

ACCOMMODATIONS

Many *gistiheimili* (guesthouses) offer "sleeping-bag accommodations" (bed and pillow in a dorm room; add 300-500Ikr for a blanket). Hotels cost at least 5500Ikr. Call ahead for reservations, especially between mid-June and August.

■ **Hjálpræðisherinn Gisti-og Sjómannaheimili** (Salvation Army Guest and Seamen's Home), Kirkjustr. 2 (☎561 32 03; www.guesthouse.is), in a pale yellow house north of Tjörnin, at the corner of Kirkjustr. and Tjarnarg. Great location and friendly staff. Kitchen available. Breakfast 800Ikr. Laundry 700Ikr. May-Sept. sleeping-bag accommodations 1900Ikr, blanket 400Ikr; singles 4200Ikr; doubles 5900Ikr; triples 7400Ikr; quads 9000Ikr. Oct.-Apr. reduced prices. ❷

Guesthouse Flókagata 1, Flókag. 1 (☎552 11 55; guesthouse@eyjar.is). From Hallgrímur's Church, head down Egilsg. and turn left onto Snorrabraut. Pristine rooms. Breakfast included. Reception 24hr. May-Sept. sleeping-bag accommodations 2700Ikr; singles 7200Ikr; doubles 10,500Ikr. Extra bed 3200Ikr. 10% Oct.-Apr. discount. ❷

Reykjavík Youth Hostel (HI), Sundlaugavegur 34 (☎553 81 10; info@hostel.is). Take bus #5 from Lækjarg. to Sundlaugavegur. Far from the center of town, but next to Laugardalslaug. Kitchen available. Sheets 500Ikr. Laundry 300Ikr. Internet 200Ikr per 15min. Flybus pickup 1000Ikr. Reception 8am-11pm; ring bell after hours. Dorms 1550Ikr; doubles 3000Ikr. Nonmembers add 350Ikr. ❷

Guesthouse Jörð, Skólavörðustíg 13a (☎562 17 39; fax 562 17 35). Just 2 blocks uphill from Laugavegur. Convenient guesthouse with spacious, comfortable rooms. Reserve ahead. Breakfast 600Ikr. Singles 4000Ikr; doubles 6000Ikr. ❹

Guesthouse Aurora, Freyjug. 24 (☎552 55 15; fax 551 48 94). Head south on Njarðarg. from Hallgrímur's Church and turn right onto Freyjug.; Aurora is the purple house. In a quiet neighborhood 10min. from the city center. Rustically homey, perfect for couples. Kitchen available. Breakfast included. Laundry 250Ikr. July-Aug. singles 6000Ikr; doubles 8000Ikr; triples 10,000Ikr; Sept.-June reduced prices. ❹

Reykjavík Youth Hostel Campsite (☎568 69 44), next to the youth hostel. Take bus #5 from the city center. Campsite in a huge field next to Laugardalslaug. Friendly staff. Bus from the campsite to BSÍ Station at 7:30am (200Ikr). Reception open 10am-1pm and 3-8pm. Laundry 200Ikr. Free showers. Electricity 300Ikr. Open mid-May to mid-Sept. 700Ikr per person; 2-bed cabins 3800Ikr. ❶

FOOD

An authentic Icelandic meal featuring seafood, lamb, or puffin costs upwards of 1000Ikr, but is worth the splurge at least once. ■**á Næstu Grösum** ❷, Laugavegur 20B, serves delicious vegetarian fare in a soothing environment. (Daily special

1290Ikr. Open M-F 11:30am-10pm, Sa noon-10pm, Su 5-10pm.) **Jómfrúin ❶**, Lækjarg. 4, offers delectable, meticulously prepared open sandwiches (half-sandwich from 530Ikr, full sandwich 990-1680Ikr) that are almost too pretty to eat. (Open Apr.-Sept. daily 11am-10pm; Oct.-Mar. 11am-6pm. **Litli Ljoti Andarunginn ❷**, Lækjarg. 6B, has a fish buffet (1990Ikr) that is the most affordable way to sample the Arctic's delicacies. (Catch of the day 1090Ikr. Open Su-Th 11am-1am, F-Sa 11am-3am.) **Þrir Frakkar ❹**, Baldursgötu 14, offers an authentic, but pricey, taste of Iceland, with specials including whale, cod, herring, and puffin. (Starters 1320-1490Ikr. Entrees 1880-2990Ikr. Lunch M-F 11:30am-2:30pm, dinner daily 6-10pm.) Cheap fast-food joints are easy to find in the area west of Lækjartorg, especially on **Hafnarstræti** and **Tryggvagata**. The best of them is **Nonnabiti ❶**, Hafnarstr. 11, an Icelandic-style sandwich shop. (Sandwiches 580-660Ikr. Open Su-Th 10am-2am, F-Sa 10am-5:30am.) Get groceries on **Austurstræti, Hverfisgata**, or **Laugavegur**.

◉ SIGHTS

A stunning domed gallery on Sigtún houses **Ásmundarsafn**, a collection of Sveinsson's sculptures, and one of the three branches of the Reykjavík Art Museum. **Kjarvalsstaðir**, on Flókag., and **Hafnarhús**, on Tryggvag., comprise the other two branches and exhibit modern works. (Take bus #5 to *Ásmundarsafn*. All open May-Sept. daily 10am-4pm; Oct.-Apr. 1-4pm. Kjarvalsstaðir and Hafnarhús open M-Tu and Th-Su 10am-5pm, W 10am-7pm. Combination ticket 500Ikr.) **Listasafn Íslands** (National Gallery of Iceland), Fríkirkjuvegur 7, on the east shore of Tjörnin, displays small exhibits of traditional Icelandic art. (Open Su and Tu-Sa 11am-5pm.) **Laugardalslaug**, on Sundlaugavegur, next to the youth hostel campground, is the largest of Reykjavík's geothermally heated pools. (Take bus #5 to *Laugardalslaug*. Open M-F 6:50am-9:30pm, Sa-Su 8am-8pm. 220Ikr, children 100Ikr.)

City Hall, on the north end of Tjörnin, is home to a raised relief map of Iceland as well as rotating exhibits. (Open M-F 8am-7pm, Sa-Su 10am-6pm. Free.) East of Lækjartorg is the bizarre 🖾**Phallological Museum**, Laugavegur 24, a collection of Arctic and Icelandic mammal members sure to humble any man. (Open Tu-Sa 2-5pm. 400Ikr.) Turn off Laugavegur onto Skólavörðustígur to reach **Hallgrímskirkja**; the steeple is Reykjavík's highest point and provides a good sense of the city's layout. (Open daily 9am-6pm. Services Su 11am. Elevator to the top 300Ikr.) The **Einar Jónsson Museum** houses 300 of the prolific sculptor's works. (Open June-Sept. Su and Tu-Sa 2-5pm; Sept.-Nov. and Feb-May Sa-Su 2-5pm. 400Ikr, children 200Ikr.)

🥾 HIKING

South of the city lies the **Heiðmörk Reserve**, a large park and sports complex with the best hiking trails and picnicking spots in the Reykjavík area; however, there is no direct public transportation. (Take bus #10 or 11, and ask the driver to let you off at Lake Elliðavatn; from there, you can walk or bike 3-4km south to the reserve.) Pleasant **Viðey Island**, home to Reykjavík's oldest house and Iceland's second-oldest church, has been inhabited since the 10th century. (To reach Sundahöftn harbor, take bus #4 east of the city center. A **ferry** departs daily at 1, 2, and 3pm. 500Ikr, children 250Ikr.) Across the bay from Reykjavík looms **Mt. Esja**, which you can ascend via a well-maintained trail (2-3hr.). While the trail is not difficult, hikers are often assaulted by rain, hail, and snow, even in summer. (Take bus #10 or 110 to *Artún* and transfer to bus #20, exiting at *Mógilsá*. Bus #20 runs only once every 1-2hr.; consult SVR city bus schedule before departing.)

NIGHTLIFE

Although quiet on weeknights, Reykjavík reasserts its reputation as a wild party town each weekend; in few other places on earth can you step out of a club at 3am to a sky that has barely dimmed to twilight. To avoid vicious drink prices and cover charges, most Icelanders pregame at home and then hit the clubs just before covers kick in. Only designated liquor stores can sell alcohol; **Nelly's**, Þingholtsstr. 2, sells the cheapest beer in town. (Open Su-Th noon-1am, F-Sa noon-6am.) Most cafes turn into boisterous bars on weekend nights, and crowds happily bar-hop along vibrant **Austurstræti, Tryggvagata,** and **Laugavegur.**

Sirkus, Klapparstígur 30. An outdoor patio and upstairs room make Sirkus the undisputed place to relax in Reykjavík. Beer 550Ikr. Open M-Th 5pm-1am, F-Sa 5pm-5:30am, Su 7pm-1am.

11, Laugavegur 11. Only place in Reykjavík to find a jukebox, foosball, and great rock music. Upstairs lounge. Open Su-Th 4pm-1am, F-Sa 4pm-5am.

22, Laugavegur 22. Upstairs disco, downstairs bar. A solid starter for Laugavegur bar-hopping. 500Ikr cover after 1am. Open Su-Th 11:30am-1am, F-Sa noon-5:30am.

Nasa, Viðausturvöll 18. Reykjavík's most extreme dance club. Open F-Sa 11pm-4am.

Kaffi Barinn, on Bergstaðastr. near Laugavegur. Cafe by day, bar by night, mecca for the city's young artists. Coffee 200-250Ikr. Beer 550Ikr. Food served noon-6pm. Live DJ Th-Sa. Open M-Th 11am-1am, F-Sa 11am-5am, Su 1pm-1am.

Spotlight, Hafnarstr. 17, just down from the SVR Lækjartorg bus station. A self-proclaimed "straight-friendly" gay bar. Spotlight welcomes anyone and everyone to its all-night raves. Beer 600Ikr. Open Su and Tu-W 9pm-1am, F-Sa 9pm-6am.

DAYTRIPS FROM REYKJAVÍK

Iceland's true attractions are its mesmerizing natural wonders. **Iceland Excursions** runs the popular **Golden Circle** tour, which stops at Hveragerði, Kerið, Skálholt, Geysir, Gullfoss, and Þingvellir National Park. (☎562 10 11. 9-10hr. 5500Ikr.) **Highlanders** offers exciting off-road tours in super jeeps that can traverse rivers, crags, and even glaciers. (☎568 30 30; www.hl.is. 10,500-17,500Ikr.)

BLUE LAGOON. Southwest of Reykjavík lies paradise: a vast pool of geothermally heated water in the middle of a lava field. Though the lagoon attracts a few too many tourists, its unique concentrations of silica, minerals, and algae are soothing enough to rejuvenate any crowd-weary traveler. Bathers may further indulge in a steam bath, a skin-soothing mud facial, or massage (1200Ikr per 10min.). The lagoon rents towels (300Ikr) and bathing suits (250Ikr) if you've forgotten yours. (Open 9am-10pm. 1200Ikr; locker included.) **Buses** arrive from BSÍ station in Reykjavík. (5 per day 10am-6pm; last return 8pm. 850Ikr each way.)

GULLFOSS AND GEYSIR. A glacial river plunging over 30m creates Gullfoss, the "Golden Falls." The greatest attraction besides the falls themselves is the stunning view of the surrounding mountains, plains, cliffs, and glaciers from atop the hill adjacent to the falls. Only 9km away is the **Geysir** area, a rocky, rugged tundra with steaming pools of hot water scattered throughout the area. The energetic **Strokkur** erupts every 5-10min., reaching heights up to 20m. BSÍ runs a round-trip **bus** to both sites (departs Reykjavík June-Aug. daily 8:30am and 12:30pm, Sa also 5pm; Sept.-May M-Sa 9:30am, Su 12:30pm; 3800Ikr).

ÞINGVELLIR NATIONAL PARK. Þingvellir National Park straddles the divide between the **European** and **North American tectonic plates.** Stand with one foot on each continent, but don't linger too long—the plates are moving apart at a rate of about one inch per year. The **Öxará River,** slicing through lava fields and jagged fissures, leads to the **Drekkingarhylur** (Drowning Pool), where adulterous women were once drowned, and to **Lake Þingvallavatn,** the largest lake in Iceland. Not far from the Drekkingarhylur lies the site of **Alþing** (ancient parliament), where, for almost nine centuries, Icelanders gathered in the shadow of the **Lögberg** (Law Rock) to discuss matters of blood, money, and justice. A **bus** runs from Reykjavík to Þingvellir's **information center.** (☎482 26 60. Open May-Sept. daily 8:30am-8pm. Bus May 20-Sept. 10 daily 1:30pm, return 4:50pm. 900Ikr.)

LANDMANNALAUGAR AND ÞÓRSMÖRK

Nestled among the rivers, glaciers, lava fields, and colorful mountains of southern Iceland, Landmannalaugar and Þórsmörk (Thor's Woods) offer countless **hikes,** including a 5-day trek between the two. The 52km trail poses a number of challenges, including volatile weather conditions, even in the middle of the summer. **Ferðafélag Íslands** (Iceland Touring Association) runs guided hikes. (☎568 25 33; www.fi.is). Excellent walks include a 2hr. loop through the volcanoes and bubbling hot springs from Landmannalaugar, as well as the walk from Þórsmörk to the peak of **Valahnjukur,** which overlooks a web of rivers and ash fields. Weary travelers can soak in Landmannalaugar's soothing **thermal spring.**

Austurleið SBS (☎552 23 00; www.austurleid.is) runs **buses** daily from Reykjavík to Landmannalaugar (4hr.; June to mid-Sept. 8:30am, return 2:30pm; round-trip 7900Ikr) and Þórsmörk (3½hr.; June to mid-Sept. daily 8:30am, return 3:30pm; 6400Ikr). Landmannalaugar has a **lodge ❶** and **campsite ❶** run by Ferðafélag Íslands. (☎854 11 92. Showers 100Ikr. Camping 600Ikr; huts 1700Ikr.) In Þórsmörk, **Húsadalur Lodge ❶** offers comfortable accommodations and helpful hiking tips. (☎852 55 06. Kitchen available. Laundry 500Ikr. Showers 250Ikr, with sauna 350Ikr. Camping 500Ikr per person; sleeping-bag dorms 1400Ikr; singles 1600Ikr; 5-person cabin with kitchen 5900Ikr.)

WESTMAN ISLANDS (VESTMANNAEYJAR)

Jutting from the depths of the North Atlantic, the black cliffs off the Westman Islands are the most recent products of the volcanic fury that created Iceland. In 1973, the fiery **Eldfell** volcano tore through the northern section of **Heimaey,** the only inhabited island, spewing lava and ash in a surprise eruption that forced the population to flee overnight. When the eruption ceased five months later, a third of the town's houses had been destroyed, but the island itself had grown by the same amount. Visitors can still feel the heat of the cooling lava. The **Volcanic Show** cinema runs a fascinating documentary about the eruption. (Shows mid-June to Aug. daily 11am, 3:30, 9pm; Sept. to mid-June 11am and 3:30pm. 600Ikr, children 300Ikr.) Head to the **aquarium** on Heiðarvegur, to see some of the island's sea creatures. A combination ticket (450Ikr) also grants admission to the **Folkmuseum,** in the town hall, which re-creates 19th-century Heimaey. (Both open May-Sept. daily 11am-5pm; Sept.-Apr. Sa-Su 3-5pm. 300Ikr each.) Though fewer than 15 square kilometers, the island offers several spectacular **hikes.** Scenic spots include the cliff's edge at **Há** and the puffin colony at **Stórhöfði.** Both volcanic peaks await experienced hikers, but strong winds often make for rough going. The three-day **Þjóðhátíð** (People's Feast) draws Reykjavík's livelier citizens to the island for an annual festival of drinking and dancing during the first weekend in August.

Flugfélag Islands (Air Iceland) has daily **flights** from Reykjavík Airport. (☎570 30 30. One-way from 5700Ikr.) A slower but much cheaper option is the Herjólfur **ferry** (☎481 28 00) departing from Þorlákshöfn. (3hr. In summer Su-F noon and 7:30pm, Sa noon only; return Su-F 8:15am and 4pm, Sa 8:15am only. 1700Ikr.) **Buses** go from BSÍ Station to the dock in Þorlákshöfn 1hr. before departure (750Ikr). The **tourist office** is in the central harbor. (☎481 35 55; www.eyjar.is/ eyjar. Open May-Sept. M-F 8am-4pm, Sa 10am-4pm, Su 11am-4pm; Oct.-Apr. M-F 8am-4pm.) ⬛**Guesthouse Hreiðreið and Bolið ❷**, Faxastigur 33, is just past the cinema on Heiðarvegur. (☎699 89 45. Sleeping-bag accommodations 1700Ikr; singles 3500Ikr; doubles 5600Ikr.) **Guesthouse Sunnoholl ❷**, Vestmannabraut 28, offers rooms in a house behind Hótel Þorshamar. (☎481 29 00. Sleeping-bag accommodations 2700Ikr; singles 3900Ikr.) The **campground ❶**, 10min. west of town on Dalvegur, has showers and a kitchen. (☎692 69 52. 500Ikr per person.) Get groceries at **Krónan** on Strandavegur. (Open daily noon-7pm.)

REPUBLIC OF IRELAND AND NORTHERN IRELAND

Travelers who come to Ireland with their heads filled with poetic imagery will not be disappointed—this largely agricultural and sparsely populated island still looks as it did when Celtic bards roamed the land. Windswept scenery is found all along the coast, and untouched mountain chains stretch across the interior bogland. The landscape is punctuated with pockets of civilization, ranging in size from one-street villages to large cities; Dublin and Belfast are cosmopolitan centers whose international populations greatly influence their immediate surroundings. Some fear this threatens the native culture, but the survival of traditional music, dance, and storytelling proves otherwise. The Irish language lives on in small, secluded areas known as *gaeltachts*, as well as on road signs, in national publications, and in a growing body of modern literary works. While non-violence usually prevails in Northern Ireland, recent negotiations hope to ensure peace for future generations. Although the Republic and Northern Ireland are grouped together in this chapter for geographical reasons, no political statement is intended.

FACTS AND FIGURES: REPUBLIC OF IRELAND

Official Name: Éire.

Capital: Dublin.

Major Cities: Cork, Galway, Limerick.

Population: 4,000,000.

Land Area: 70,280 sq. km.

Time Zone: GMT.

Languages: English, Irish.

Religion: Roman Catholic (91.6%).

DISCOVER IRELAND

Take time to explore the thousand-year-old **Dublin** (p. 566), a bastion of literary history and the stomping-ground of international hipsters. Wander the grounds of Trinity College, catch a film in Temple Bar, and down a pint or two at one of the city's seemingly infinite pubs. A walk through **Belfast** (p. 590) will give you a glimpse of Northern Ireland's rich, complicated history. **Giant's Causeway** (p. 597), also in the North, is a unique formation of rocks rising out of the sea called by some the 8th natural wonder of the world. In **Donegal Town** (p. 589), visitors get a taste of traditional Irish music, commonly called *trad*, before clambering the **Slieve League** (p. 589), Europe's tallest seacliffs. Devotees of W.B. Yeats shouldn't miss the region surrounding **Sligo** (p. 589), the poet's home town, which inspired many of his more famous poems. **Galway** (p. 586) is an artsy student town that draws the island's best musicians. The legendary scenery of the **Ring of Kerry** (p. 582) and the exquisite mountains and lakes of **Killarney National Park** (p. 581) will satisfy any nature lover.

ESSENTIALS

WHEN TO GO

Irish weather is subject to frequent changes but relatively constant temperatures. The southeastern coast is the driest and sunniest, while western Ireland is considerably wetter and cloudier. May and June are the sunniest months, July and August the warmest. December and January have the worst weather. Take heart when you wake to clouded, foggy mornings—the weather usually clears by noon. Make sure you bring rain gear, regardless of the season.

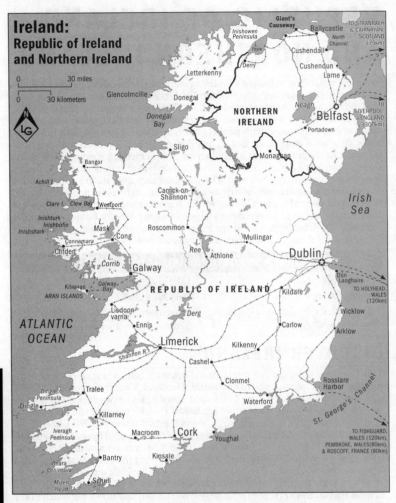

Ireland:
Republic of Ireland
and Northern Ireland

0   30 miles

0   30 kilometers

DOCUMENTS AND FORMALITIES

VISAS. Citizens of Australia, Canada, the EU, New Zealand, South Africa, and the US do not need a visa for stays of up to 90 days.

EMBASSIES. All embassies for the Republic of Ireland are in Dublin (p. 566). For Irish embassies at home, contact: **Australia,** 20 Arkana St., Yarralumla, Canberra ACT 2600 (☎062 73 3022); **Canada,** Suite 1105, 130 Albert St., Ottawa, ON K1P 5G4 (☎613-233-6281); **New Zealand,** Honorary Consul General, 6th fl., 18 Shortland St. 1001, Auckland 1 (☎09 302 2867; www.ireland.co.nz); **South Africa,** 1st fl., Southern Life Plaza, 1059 Shoeman St., Arcadia 0083, Pretoria (☎012 342 5062); **UK,** 17 Grosvenor Pl., London SW1X 7HR (☎020 7235 2171); and **US,** 2234 Massachusetts Ave. NW, Washington, D.C. 20008 (☎202-462-3939).

TRANSPORTATION

BY PLANE. Flying to London and connecting to Ireland is often easier and cheaper than flying direct. A popular carrier to Ireland is its national airline, **Aer Lingus** (☎081 836 5000; US ☎800-474-74247; www.aerlingus.ie), which has direct flights to the US, London, and Paris. **Ryanair** (☎081 836 3030; www.ryanair.ie) is a smaller airline that offers a "lowest-fare guarantee." The web-based phenomenon **easyJet** (UK ☎08706 000 000; www.easyjet.com) has recently began flying from Britain to Belfast. **British Airways** (UK ☎0845 773 3377; Republic ☎800 626 747; US ☎800-247-9297; www.british-airways.com) flies into most Irish airports daily.

BY TRAIN. Iarnród Éireann (Irish Rail; ☎01 836 3333; www.irishrail.ie) is useful only for travel to urban areas. The **Eurail** pass is accepted in the Republic but not in Northern Ireland. The **BritRail** pass does not cover travel in Northern Ireland or the Republic, but the month-long **BritRail+Ireland** pass works in both the North and the Republic, with rail options and round-trip ferry service between Britain and Ireland (€400-570). **Northern Ireland Railways** (☎028 9066 6630; www.nirailways.co.uk) is not extensive but covers the northeastern region well; the major line connects Dublin to Belfast. A valid **Northern Ireland Travelsave** stamp (UK£6), affixed to the back of an ISIC card, will get you up to 33% off all train fares and 15% off bus fares over UK£1.45 in the North. The **Freedom of Northern Ireland** ticket allows unlimited travel by train and Ulsterbus (1-day UK£11, 3-day UK£27.50, 7-day UK£40).

BY BUS. Bus Éireann (☎01 836 6111; www.buseireann.ie), the national bus company, reaches Britain and the Continent by working in conjunction with ferry services and the bus company **Eurolines** (www.eurolines.com). Most buses leave from Victoria Station in London (to Belfast: 15hr., €49/UK£31, round-trip €79/UK£51; Dublin: 12hr., €42/UK£27, round-trip €69/UK£45); other major city stops include Birmingham, Bristol, Cardiff, Glasgow, and Liverpool. Services run to Cork, Derry, Galway, Limerick, Tralee, and Waterford, among others. Discounted fares are available in the low-season, as well as for people under 26 or over 60. Bus Éireann operates both long-distance Expressway buses, which link larger cities, and local buses, which serve the countryside and smaller towns.

 Ulsterbus (☎028 9033 3000; Belfast ☎028 9032 0011; www.ulsterbus.co.uk) runs extensive routes throughout Northern Ireland. The **Irish Rover** pass covers both Bus Éireann and Ulsterbus services (3 of 8 consecutive days €60/UK£90, children €33/UK£50; 8 of 15 €135/UK£200, children €75/UK£113; 15 of 30 €195/UK£293, children €110/UK£165). The **Emerald Card** offers unlimited travel on Ulsterbus, Northern Ireland Railways, Bus Éireann Expressway, and many local services; for more info, see www.buseireann.ie (8 of 15 consecutive days €168/UK£108, children €84/UK£54; 15 of 30 €290/UK£187, children €145/UK£94).

BY FERRY. Ferries, more economical than air travel, journey between Britain and Ireland several times per day (€28-55/UK£18-35). Weeknight travel promises the cheapest fares. **An Óige** (HI) members receive up to a 20% discount on fares from Irish Ferries and Stena Sealink, while **ISIC cardholders** with the **TravelSave stamp** receive a 15-17% discount on Stena Line and Irish Ferries. Ferries run from Cork to South Wales and Roscoff, France (see p. 578), and from Rosslare Harbour to Pembroke, Wales, and Roscoff and Cherbourg, France (p.575).

BY CAR. Drivers in Ireland use the left side of the road, and their steering wheels are on the right side of the car. Petrol (gasoline) prices are high. Be particularly cautious at roundabouts—give way to traffic from the right. **Dan Dooley** (☎062 53 103, UK ☎0181 995 4551, US ☎800-331-9301; www.dandooley.com) is the only company that will rent to drivers between 21 and 24, though such drivers incur an

IRELAND

added surcharge. Prices are €150-370/UK£95-235 (plus VAT) per week, including insurance and unlimited mileage. If you plan to drive a car while in Ireland for longer than 90 days, you must have an **International Driving Permit (IDP).** If you rent, lease, or borrow a car, you will need a **green card** or **International Insurance Certificate** to certify that you have liability insurance and that it applies abroad. It is always significantly less expensive to reserve a car from the US than from Europe.

BY BIKE, FOOT, AND THUMB. Much of Ireland's countryside is well suited for **biking,** as many roads are not heavily traveled. Single-digit N roads in the Republic and M roads in the North are more busily trafficked; try to avoid these. Ireland's mountains, fields, and heather-covered hills make **walking** and **hiking** a joy. The **Wicklow Way** has hostels within a day's walk of each other. Locals do not recommend **hitchhiking** in Northern Ireland, where it is illegal along motorways; some caution against it in Co. Dublin. *Let's Go* does not recommend hitchhiking.

TOURIST SERVICES AND MONEY

EMERGENCY	Police: ☎999. Ambulance: ☎999. Fire: ☎999.

TOURIST OFFICES. Bord Fáilte (the Irish Tourist Board; ☎01 602 4000; www.ireland.travel.ie) operates a nationwide network of offices. Most tourist offices book rooms for a small fee and a 10% deposit, but many fine hostels and B&Bs are not on the board's central list. The **Northern Ireland Tourist Board** (☎028 9023 1221; www.discovernorthernireland.com) offers similar services.

MONEY. On January 1, 2002, the **euro** (€) replaced the Irish pound (£) as the unit of currency in the Republic of Ireland. Legal tender in Northern Ireland is the **British pound;** for more info, see p.142. Northern Ireland has its own bank notes, identical in value to English and Scottish notes. Although all of these notes are accepted in Northern Ireland, Northern Ireland notes are not accepted in Britain. As a general rule, it is cheaper to exchange money in Ireland than at home.

If you stay in hostels and prepare your own food, expect to spend anywhere from €20-34/UK£12-22 per person per day. Some restaurants in Ireland figure a service charge into the bill; some even calculate it into the cost of the dishes themselves. The menu often indicates whether or not service is included. Most people working in restaurants, however, do not expect a tip, unless the restaurant is targeted exclusively toward tourists. In those incidences, consider leaving 10-15%, depending upon the quality of the service. Tipping is very uncommon for other services, such as taxis and hairdressers, especially in rural areas. In most cases, people are usually happy if you simply round up the bill to the nearest euro. The European Union imposes a **value-added tax (VAT)** on goods and services purchased within the EU, which is included in the price; for more info, see p. 16.

COMMUNICATION

PHONE CODES	**Country code:** 353 (Republic); 44 (Northern Ireland; dial 048 from the Republic). **International dialing prefix:** 00. From outside the Republic of Ireland, dial int'l dialing prefix (see inside back cover) + 353 + city code + local number.

TELEPHONES. Both the Irish Republic and Northern Ireland have public phones that accept coins (€0.20/UK£0.15 for about 4min.) and pre-paid phone cards. In the Republic, dial ☎114 for an international operator, 10 for a national operator, or

11850 for a directory. Mobile phone are an increasingly popular and economical alternative (p. 36). International direct dial numbers in the Republic include: **AT&T,** ☎800 550 000; **British Telecom,** ☎800 550 144; **Canada Direct,** ☎800 555 001; **MCI,** ☎800 551 001; **New Zealand Direct,** ☎800 550 064; **Telkom South Africa,** ☎800 550 027; and **Telstra Australia,** ☎800 550 061. In Northern Ireland, call ☎155 for an international operator, 100 for a national operator, or 192 for a directory. International direct dial numbers in Northern Ireland include: **AT&T,** ☎0800 013 0011; **Canada Direct,** ☎0800 890 016; **MCI,** ☎800 551 001; **New Zealand Direct,** ☎0800 890 064; **Telkom South Africa,** ☎0800 890 027; **Telstra Australia,** ☎0800 856 6161. For more info on making calls to and from Northern Ireland, see p.590.

MAIL. In the Republic, postcards and letters up to 25g cost €0.40 domestically and to the UK, €0.45 to the Continent, and €0.60 to any other international destination. Airmail letters take about 6-9 days between Ireland and North America and cost €0.80. Dublin is the only place in the Republic with postal codes. Even-numbered codes are for areas south of the Liffey, odd-numbered are for those north. The North has the same postal system as the rest of the UK (p.143). Address *Poste Restante* according to the following example: Firstname SURNAME, *Poste Restante*, Enniscorthy, Co. Wexford, Ireland. The mail will go to a special desk in the central post office, unless you specify otherwise.

INTERNET ACCESS. Internet access is available in cafes, hostels, and most libraries. One hour of web time costs about €4-6/UK£2.50-4; an ISIC card often earns you a discount. Look into a county library membership in the Republic (€2.50-3), which gives unlimited access to participating libraries and their Internet terminals. Online listings of cybercafes in Ireland and Britain include the **Cybercafe Search Engine** (http://cybercaptive.com) and **Cybercafes.com** (www.cybercafes.com).

ACCOMMODATIONS AND CAMPING

THE REPUBLIC	❶	❷	❸	❹	❺
ACCOMMODATIONS	under €15	€15-24	€25-39	€40-54	over €55

A **hostel** bed will average €12-18 in the Republic and UK£7-12 in the North. **An Óige** (an OYJ), the **HI** affiliate, operates 32 hostels countrywide. (☎01 830 4555; www.irelandyha.org. One-year membership €25, under-18 €10.50.) Many An Óige hostels are in remote areas or small villages and were designed primarily to serve hikers, long-distance bicyclists, anglers, and others seeking nature, and do not offer the social environment typical of other European hostels. The North's HI affiliate is HINI (Hostelling International Northern Ireland; formerly known as **YHANI**). It operates only eight hostels, all comfortable. (☎028 9031 5435; www.hini.org.uk. One-year membership UK£13, under-18 UK£6.) A number of hostels in Ireland belong to **Independent Holiday Hostels** (**IHH;** ☎01 836 4700; www.hostels-ireland.com). Most of the 140 IHH hostels have no lockout or curfew, accept all ages, require no membership card, and have a comfortable atmosphere that generally feels less institutional than that at An Óige hostels; all are Bord Fáilte-approved. Numerous **B&Bs,** in virtually every Irish town, can provide a luxurious break from hostelling; expect to pay €20-30/UK£12-20 for singles and €35-50/UK£22-32 for doubles. "Full Irish breakfasts" are often filling enough to get you through to dinner. **Camping** in Irish State Forests and National Parks is not allowed; camping on public land is permissible only if there is no official campsite nearby. Sites cost €5-13, depending on the level of luxury. Northern Ireland treats its campers royally; there are well-equipped campsites throughout (£3-8). For more info on price ranges in Northern Ireland, see p.590.

IRELAND

FOOD AND DRINK

THE REPUBLIC	❶	❷	❸	❹	❺
FOOD	under €5	€5-9	€10-14	€15-19	over €20

Food in Ireland is expensive, but the basics are simple and filling. Find quick and greasy staples at chippers (fish 'n' chip shops) and takeaways (takeout joints). Most pubs serve food like Irish stew, burgers, soup, and sandwiches. Soda bread is delicious and keeps well, and Irish cheeses are addictive. Guinness, a rich, dark stout, is revered in Ireland with a zeal usually reserved for religion. Known as "the dark stuff" or "the blonde in the black skirt," it was once recommended as food for pregnant mothers, and its head is so thick that you can stand a match in it. Irish whiskey, which Queen Elizabeth claimed was her only true Irish friend, is sweeter than its Scotch counterpart. Irish monks invented whiskey, calling it *uisce beatha*, meaning "water of life." For info on price ranges in the North, see p.590.

HOLIDAYS AND FESTIVALS

Holidays: Holidays for the Republic of Ireland include: New Year's Day (Jan. 1); St. Patrick's Day (Mar. 17); Good Friday; Easter Monday (Apr. 12); and Christmas (Dec. 25-26). There are Bank Holidays in the Republic and Northern Ireland during the summer months; check at tourist offices for dates. Northern Ireland has the same national holidays as the Republic; it also observes Orange Day (July 12).

Festivals: All of Ireland goes green for **St. Patrick's Day** (Mar. 17th). On **Bloomsday** (June 16), Dublin celebrates James Joyce's *Ulysses* (p. 573).

DUBLIN ☎01

In a country known for its relaxed pace and rural sanctity, Dublin stands out for its boundless energy and international flair. The city and its suburbs, home to one-third of Ireland's population, are at the vanguard of the country's rapid social change. In an effort to stem international and rural emigration, vast portions of the city have undergone renovation and redevelopment, funded by the deep pockets of the EU. Dublin may hardly look like the rustic "Emerald Isle" promoted on tourist brochures, but its people and history still embody the charm and warmth that have made the country famous.

▐ TRANSPORTATION

Flights: Dublin Airport (DUB; ☎814 1111). Dublin **buses** #41, 41B, and 41C run from the airport to Eden Quay in the city center with stops along the way (every 20min., €1.60). The **Airlink shuttle** (☎844 4265) runs non-stop to Busáras Central Bus Station via O'Connell St. (20-25min., every 10min., €5) and on to Heuston Station (50min., €4.50). A **taxi** to the city center costs roughly €15-20.

Trains: The **Iarnród Éireann** travel center, 35 Lower Abbey St. (☎836 6222; www.irishrail.ie), sells tickets for **Irish Rail.** (Open M-Sa 9am-6pm, Su 10am-6pm.) **Connolly Station,** Amiens St. (☎702 2358), is north of the Liffey and close to Busáras Central Bus Station. Buses #20, 20A, and 90 go from the station to destinations south of the river, and the DART (see below) runs to Tara on the south quay. Trains to: **Belfast** (2hr., 5-8 per day, €29); **Sligo** (3hr., 3-4 per day, €22); **Wexford** (3hr., €17). Heuston Station (☎703 2132) is south of Victoria Quay, west of the city center (25min. walk from Trinity College). Buses #26, 51, 90, and 79 go to the city center. Trains to: **Cork** (3hr., 6-11 per day, €43); **Galway** (2½hr.; 4-5 per day; €21, F and Su €28); **Limerick** (2½hr., 9 per day, €34); **Waterford** (2½hr., 3-4 per day, €17).

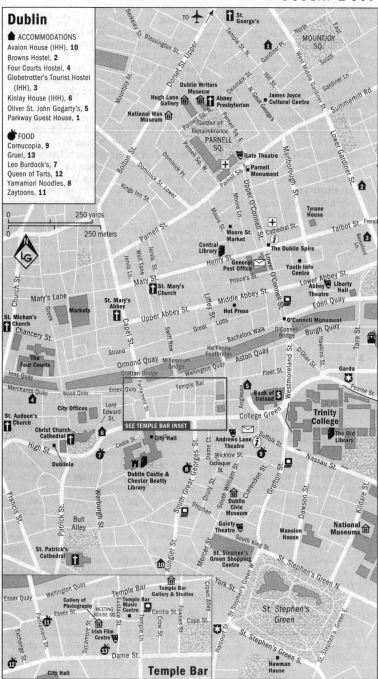

Dublin

🏠 **ACCOMMODATIONS**
Avalon House (IHH), **10**
Browns Hostel, **2**
Four Courts Hostel, **4**
Globetrotter's Tourist Hostel (IHH), **3**
Kinlay House (IHH), **6**
Oliver St. John Gogarty's, **5**
Parkway Guest House, **1**

🍴 **FOOD**
Cornucopia, **9**
Gruel, **13**
Leo Burdock's, **7**
Queen of Tarts, **12**
Yamamori Noodles, **8**
Zaytoons, **11**

0   250 yards
0   250 meters

IRELAND

Temple Bar

Buses: Info is available at the **Dublin Bus Office,** 59 O'Connell St. (☎872 0000); the Bus Éireann window is open M-F 9am-5pm, Sa 10:30am-2pm. Buses arrive at **Busáras Central Bus Station** (☎836 6111), on Store St., directly behind the Customs House and next to Connolly Station. Bus Éireann runs to: **Belfast** (3hr., 6-7 per day, €18); **Derry** (4¼hr., 5-6 per day, €18); **Donegal Town** (4¼hr., 5-6 per day, €15); **Galway** (3½hr., 13 per day, €13); **Limerick** (3½hr., 7-13 per day, €15); **Rosslare Harbour** (3hr., 7-10 per day, €14); **Sligo** (4hr., 4-5 per day, €14); **Waterford** (3hr., 10 per day, €10); **Wexford** (2¾hr., 7-10 per day, €10).

Ferries: Irish Ferries, 2-4 Merrion Row (☎638 3333; www.irishferries.com), is open M-F 9am-5pm, Sa 9:15am-12:45pm. Ferries arrive from **Holyhead, UK** at the **Dublin Port** (☎607 5665), from which buses #53 and 53A run every hr. to Busáras (Tickets €1). **Norse Merchant Ferries** also dock at the **Dublin Port** and run a route to **Liverpool, UK** (7½hr.; 1-2 per day; €25-40, with car €105-170); booking for Norse Merchant is only available from **Gerry Feeney,** 19 Eden Quay (☎819 2999). **Stena Line** ferries arrive from **Holyhead** at the Dún Laoghaire ferry terminal (☎204 7777); DART (see below) trains run from Dún Laoghaire to the Dublin city center. Dublin Bus also runs connection buses timed to fit the ferry schedules (€2.50-3.20).

Public Transportation: Dublin Bus, 59 O'Connell St. (☎873 4222). Open M 8:30am-5:30pm, Tu-F 9am-5:30pm, Sa 9am-1pm. The smaller **City Imp** buses run every 8-15min. Dublin Bus runs the **NiteLink** service to the suburbs (M-W at 12:30am and 2am; Th-Sa, every 20min. from 12:30am-4:30am; €4). **Travel Wide** passes offer unlimited rides for a day (€5) or a week (€18). **DART** trains serve the suburbs and the coast (every 10-15min., 6:30am-11:30pm; €0.75-1.70).

Taxis: National Radio Cabs, 40 James St. (☎677 2222). €2.75 plus €1.35 per mi. before 10pm, €1.80 per mi. after 10pm. €1.50 call-in charge.

Car Rental: Budget, 151 Lower Drumcondra Rd. (☎837 9611), and at the airport. In summer from €40 per day, €200 per week; off-season €38/165. Min. age 23.

Bike Rental: Cycle Ways, 185-6 Parnell St. (☎873 4748). Open M-W and F-Sa 10am-6pm, Th 10am-8pm. €20 per day, €80 per week; deposit €200.

■✴🏠 ORIENTATION AND PRACTICAL INFORMATION

The **River Liffey** forms a natural boundary between Dublin's North and South Sides. Heuston Station and the more famous sights, posh stores, and upscale restaurants are on the **South Side.** Connolly Station and the majority of hostels and the bus station cling to the **North Side.** The North Side hawks merchandise cheaper than in the more touristed South. It also has the reputation of being rougher, especially after sunset. The streets running alongside the Liffey are called **quays** (KEYS); each bridge over the river has its own name, and streets change names as they cross. If a street running parallel to the river is split into "Upper" and "Lower," then the "Lower" is always the part of the street closer to the mouth of the Liffey. **O'Connell Street,** three blocks west of the Busáras Central Bus Station, is the primary link between north and south Dublin. **Henry Street** and **Mary Street** comprise a pedestrian shopping zone that intersects with O'Connell after the **General Post Office** (GPO), two blocks from the Liffey. **Fleet Street** becomes **Temple Bar** one block south of the Liffey. **Dame Street** runs parallel to Temple Bar until **Trinity College,** which defines the southern edge of the district. Trinity College is the nerve center of Dublin's cultural activity, with legions of bookshops and student-oriented pubs.

TOURIST, FINANCIAL, AND LOCAL SERVICES

Tourist Information: Main Office, Suffolk St. (☎(1850) 230 330). From Connolly Station, turn left down Amiens St., take a right onto Lower Abbey St., and continue until O'Connell St. Turn left, cross the bridge, and walk past Trinity College; Suffolk St. is on the right. Books rooms for a €4 fee plus a 10% non-refundable deposit. Open July-Aug. M-Sa 9am-8:30pm, Su 11am-5:30pm; Sept.-June M-Sa 9am-5:30pm. The **Northern Ireland Tourist Board,** 16 Nassau St. (☎679 1977 or (1850) 230 230), books accommodations in the North. Open M-F 9:15am-5:30pm, Sa 10am-5pm.

Embassies: Australia, 2nd fl., Fitzwilton House, Wilton Terr. (☎676 1517; www.australianembassy.ie); **Canada,** 65/68 St. Stephen's Green (☎478 1988); **South Africa,** 2nd fl., Alexandra House, Earlsfort Terr. (☎661 5553); **United Kingdom,** 29 Merrion Rd., Ballsbridge (☎205 3700; www.britishembassy.ie); **United States,** 42 Elgin Rd. (☎668 8777). **New Zealanders** should contact their embassy in London.

Banks: Bank of Ireland, AIB, and **TSB** branches with currency exchange and 24hr. **ATMs** cluster on Lower O'Connell St., Grafton St., and in the Suffolk and Dame St. areas. Most bank branches are open M-F 10am-4pm, Th 10am-5pm.

American Express: Suffolk St., in the main tourist office (☎605 7709). Currency exchange; no commission for AmEx Traveler's Cheques. Open M-Sa 9am-5pm.

Luggage Storage: Connolly Station. €2.50 per item per day. Open M-Sa 7:40am-9:20pm, Su 9:10am-9:45pm. **Heuston Station.** €2-5 per item, depending on size. Open daily 6:30am-10:30pm.

Laundry: The Laundry Shop, 191 Parnell St. (☎872 3541), near Busáras. Wash and dry €8-12. Open M-F 8am-7pm, Sa 9am-6pm, Su 11am-5pm.

EMERGENCY AND COMMUNICATIONS

Emergency: ☎999 or 112; no coins required.

Police (*Garda*): Dublin Metro Headquarters, Harcourt Terr. (☎666 9500); Store St. Station (☎666 8000); Fitzgibbon St. Station (☎666 8400).

Pharmacy: O'Connell's, 56 Lower O'Connell St. (☎873 0427). Open M-Sa 7:30am-10pm, Su 10am-10pm. Branches throughout the city, including two on Grafton St.

Hospital: St. James's Hospital (☎453 7941), on James St. Served by bus #123. **Mater Misericordiae Hospital** (☎830 1122), on Eccles St., off Lower Dorset St. Served by buses #10, 11, 13, 16, 121, and 122.

Internet Access: The Internet Exchange, 146 Parnell St. (☎670 3000). €4 per hour. €2.50 per hr. with €5 membership. Open daily 9am-10:30pm.

Post Office: General Post Office (GPO; ☎705 7000), on O'Connell St. Even-numbered postal codes are for areas south of the Liffey, odd-numbered are for the north. *Poste Restante* pick-up at the *Post Restante* window. Open M-Sa 8am-8pm, Su 10am-6:30pm. **Postal Code:** Dublin 1.

▋ ACCOMMODATIONS

Reserve accommodations at least a week in advance, especially during Easter, other holidays, and the summer. **Hostel** dorms range from €10-24 per night. Quality **B&Bs** blanket Dublin and the surrounding suburbs, although prices have risen with housing costs; most charge €20-40 per person.

HOSTELS

Dublin's hostels lean toward the institutional, especially in comparison to their more personable country cousins. The beds south of the river fill up fastest; they also tend to be more expensive than those to the north.

▧ **Four Courts Hostel,** 15-17 Merchants Quay (☎672 5839), near O'Donovan Rossa Bridge. First-rate hostel with clean rooms (most with showers) and a really friendly staff. Breakfast included. Internet €1 per 10 min. Dorms €15-22; doubles €54-65. ❷

Globetrotter's Tourist Hostel (IHH), 46-7 Lower Gardiner St. (☎878 0700). A dose of luxury for the weary in these beautifully designed rooms. Beds are snug, but there's plenty of room to store your stuff. Irish Breakfast included. Internet access. Dorms €19-22; singles €60-67; doubles €102-110. ❷

Avalon House (IHH), 55 Aungier St. (☎475 0001). With good location close to many nightlife spots, Avalon House hums with the energy of transcontinental travelers. Large but not overwhelming, Avalon has top-notch security for its guests. Breakfast included. Internet access. Dorms €15-30; singles €30-37; doubles €56-70. ❷

Kinlay House (IHH), 2-12 Lord Edward St. (☎679 6644). Snuggle into the soft couches in the TV room, or gaze at Christ Church Cathedral from your room window. Kinlay House offers nice rooms that offer a crash course on Irish culture with the many icon posters lining the walls. Breakfast included. Laundry €7. Internet €1 per 15min. Dorms €15-26; singles €40-46; doubles €50-60. ❷

Brown's Hostel, 89-90 Lower Gardiner St. (☎855 0034). Glistening decor with TVs, closets, and A/C in every room. Dorms are named after Irish rivers; be sure to ask for the Shannon room. Breakfast included. Internet access. Dorms €13-25. ❶

Oliver St. John Gogarty's Temple Bar Hostel, 18-21 Anglesea St. (☎671 1822). Joyce once roomed here with Gogarty. The location is unbeatable if you're frolicking in Temple Bar. Internet access. Laundry €4. Dorms €13-23; doubles €46-56; triples €63-75. ❶

BED AND BREAKFASTS

B&Bs with a green shamrock sign out front are registered and approved by Bord Fáilte. On the North Side, B&Bs cluster along **Upper** and **Lower Gardiner Street,** on **Sheriff Street,** and near **Parnell Square.**

Mona's B&B, 148 Clonliffe Rd. (☎837 4147). Gorgeous house run for 37 years by Ireland's loveliest proprietress. Homemade brown bread accompanies the full Irish breakfast. Singles €35; doubles €66. Open May-Oct. ❸

Parkway Guest House, 5 Gardiner Pl. (☎874 0469). Rooms are high-ceilinged and tidy, and the location is perfectly central. Ask the proprietors for some restaurant and pub advice. Irish breakfast included. Singles €32; doubles €52-60, with bath €60-70. ❸

Mrs. Bermingham, 8 Dromard Terr. (☎668 3861), on Dromard Ave. Take the #2 or 3 bus and get off at Tesco. Soft, comfortable beds. One room has a lovely bay window overlooking the garden. Singles €28; doubles with bath €52. Open Feb.-Nov. ❸

CAMPING

Most campsites are far away from the city center, and while it may seem convenient, camping in **Phoenix Park** is both illegal and unsafe.

Camac Valley Tourist Caravan & Camping Park, Naas Rd., Clondalkin (☎464 0644), near Corka gh Park. Accessible by bus #69 (35min. from city center, €1.50). Food shop and kitchen facilities. Laundry €4.50. Hikers €7; 2 people with car €15. ❶

Shankill Caravan and Camping Park, (☎282 0011). The DART and buses #45 and 84 from Eden Quay run to Shankill. €2 per person. €9 per tent. Showers €1. ❶

▣ FOOD

Dublin's **open-air markets** sell fresh and cheap fixings. On Saturdays, a gourmet open-air market takes place in Temple Bar at the Meeting House Square. The cheapest **supermarkets** around Dublin are the **Dunnes Stores** chain, with branches at St. Stephen's Green (open M-W and F-Sa 8:30am-7pm, Th 8:30am-9pm, Su noon-6pm), the ILAC Centre off Henry St., and North Earl St. **Temple Bar** has creative eateries catering to every budget.

Cornucopia, 19 Wicklow St. (☎671 2840). If you can find the space, sit down for a rich meal (about €8.50) or snack (€2). Portions at this vegetarian hotspot are huge. Open M-W and F-Sa 8:30am-8pm, Th 9am-9pm. ❷

Queen of Tarts, 3 Cork Hill (☎670 7119). This little red gem offers homemade pastries, scones, cakes, and coffee. Continental breakfast €4-6. Open M-F 7:30am-6pm, Sa 9am-6pm, Su 10am-6pm. ❷

Zaytoons, 14-15 Parliament St. (☎677 3595). Persian food served on big platters of warm bread. Excellent chicken kebab (€6.50). Open M-Sa noon-4am. ❷

Gruel, 68 Dame St. (☎670 7119). Come for a sit-down or takeaway meal made by a world-class chef. Lunch changes daily; go F for roast lamb with apricot chutney (€6). Dinners €6-12. Open daily 8:30am-9:30pm. ❸

Yamamori Noodles, 71-72 S. Great Georges St. (☎475 5001). Exceptional Japanese cuisine. Entrees €12-14. Open M-W and Su 12:30-11pm, Th-Sa 12:30-11:30pm. ❸

Leo Burdock's, 2 Werburgh St. (☎454 0306), up from Christ Church Cathedral. The real deal for fish and chips. A holy ritual for many Dubliners. Takeaway only. Fish €4. Chips €1.50. Open M-Sa noon-midnight, Su 4pm-midnight. ❶

🔘 SIGHTS

Most of Dublin's sights lie less than 2km from O'Connell Bridge. The **Historical Walking Tour** provides a 2hr. crash course in Irish history, stopping at a variety of sights. Meet at Trinity College's front gate. (☎878 0227. Tours May-Sept. M-F 11am and 3pm; Sa-Su 11am, noon, and 3pm. Oct.-Apr. F-Su noon. €10, students €8.)

TRINITY COLLEGE AND ENVIRONS. The British built Trinity College in 1592 as a Protestant religious seminary that would "civilize the Irish and cure them of Popery." Jonathan Swift, Robert Emmett, Thomas Moore, Edmund Burke, Oscar Wilde, and Samuel Beckett are just a few of the famous Irishmen who studied here. Look for bullet holes from the Easter Rising that still mar the stone entrance. *(Between Westmoreland and Grafton St. The main entrance is on College Green. Pearse St. runs along the north edge of the college, Nassau St. to its south. Grounds open 24hr. Free.)* **Trinity College Walking Tour** is run by students and concentrates on University lore. *(June-Sept. daily 10:15am-3:40pm; Mar.-May weekends only. Tours leave roughly every 45min. from the info booth inside the front gate. Includes admission to the Old Library. €7, students €6.)* **The Old Library** holds a priceless collection of ancient manuscripts, including the magnificent **Book of Kells,** 9th-century illustrated volumes of the Gospels. *(From Trinity's main gate, go straight; the library is on the south side of Library Sq. Open June-Sept. M-Sa 9:30am-5pm, Su noon-4:30pm; Oct.-May M-Sa 9:30am-5pm, Su noon-4:30pm. €6, students and seniors €5.)* The area south of **College Green,** off-limits to cars, is a pedestrian haven. Grafton's **street performers** range from string octets to jive limboists.

KILDARE STREET AND TEMPLE BAR. The ▧**Natural History Museum** displays fascinating examples of classic taxidermy, including enormous Irish deer skeletons *(Upper Merrion St. Open Su 2-5pm and Tu-Sa 10am-5pm. Free.)* The **National Museum of Archaeology and History,** Dublin's largest museum, has extraordinary artifacts spanning the last two millennia, including the **Tara Brooch,** the **Ardagh Hoard,** and other Celtic gold work. Don't miss the bloody vest of nationalist **James Connelly.** *(Kildare St., adjacent to Leinster House. Open Su 2-5pm and Tu-Sa 10am-5pm. Free.)* The **National Gallery** has a collection of over 2400 paintings, including canvases by Bruegel, Caravaggio, Goya, El Greco, Rembrandt, and Vermeer. *(Merrion Sq. West. Open M-W and F-Sa 9:30am-5:30pm, Th 10am-8:30pm, Su noon-5pm. Free.)* The **National Library** chronicles Irish history and exhibits literary goodies in its entrance room. A genealogical research room can help families trace the thinnest roots of their

Irish family tree, which will inevitably reach back to the kings of Ireland. *(On Kildare St. Open M-W 10am-9pm, Th-F 10am-5pm, Sa 10am-1pm. Free.)* West of Trinity, between Dame St. and the Liffey, the **Temple Bar** neighborhood has rapidly become one of Europe's hottest night spots. Narrow cobblestone streets link cafes, theaters, rock venues, and vintage stores. The government-sponsored Temple Bar Properties spent over €40 million to build a fleet of arts-related attractions. Among the most inviting are: **The Irish Film Centre,** which screens art house film *(6 Eustace St.),* Ireland's only **Gallery of Photography** *(Meeting House Sq.),* and the **Temple Bar Gallery & Studios** *(5-9 Temple Bar).*

DAME STREET AND THE CATHEDRALS. King John built **Dublin Castle** in 1204 on top of the Viking settlement of *Dubh Linn.* For 700 years after its construction, it was the seat of British rule in Ireland. As part of the independence movement, fifty insurgents died at the castle's walls on Easter Monday, 1916. Since 1938, each president of Ireland has been inaugurated here. *(On Dame St., at the intersection of Parliament and Castle St. Open M-F 10am-5pm, Sa-Su 2-5pm. €4.50, students and seniors €3.50. Grounds free.)* **St. Patrick's Cathedral,** Ireland's largest, dates to the 12th century, although Sir Benjamin Guinness remodeled much of it in 1864. Jonathan Swift spent his last years as Dean of St. Patrick's, and his crypt is above the south nave. *(On Patrick St. Take bus #49, 49A, 50, 54A, 56A, 65, 65B, 77, or 77A from Eden Quay. Open Mar.-Oct. daily 9am-6pm; Nov.-Feb. Sa 9am-5pm, Su 9am-3pm. €4. Students, seniors, and children free.)* Sitric Silkenbeard, King of the Dublin Norsemen, built a wooden church on the site of the **Christ Church Cathedral** around 1038; Strongbow rebuilt it in stone in 1169. Further additions were made in the following century and again in the 1870s. Now stained glass sparkles above the raised crypts, and fragments of ancient pillars are scattered about like bleached bones. *(At the end of Dame St., across from the castle. Take bus #50 from Eden Quay or 78A from Aston Quay. Open daily 9:45am-5:30pm except during services. Suggested donation €3.)*

GUINNESS BREWERY AND KILMAINHAM. Guinness brews its black magic at the St. James Gate Brewery, next door to the ⬛**Guinness Storehouse.** In 1759, farsighted Arthur Guinness signed a 9000-year lease for the original 1759 brewery. The lease is displayed in the Storehouse's atrium, an architectural triumph that rises seven floors around a center shaped like a pint glass. View the exhibit on Guinness's infamously clever advertising, then give in and drink. *(St. James's Gate. From Christ Church Cathedral, follow High St. west through its name changes: Commarket, Thomas, and James. Take bus #51B or 78A from Aston Quay or #123 from O'Connell St. Open Apr.-Sept. daily 9:30am-7pm; Oct.-Mar. 9:30am-5pm. €12, students €8, seniors and children €5.30.)* Almost all of the rebels who fought in Ireland's struggle for independence from 1792 to 1921 spent time at **Kilmainham Gaol.** Tours wind through the chilly limestone corridors of the prison and end in the haunting execution yard. *(Inchicore Rd. Take bus #51 or 79 from Aston Quay or #51A from Lower Abbey St. Open Apr.-Sept. daily 9:30am-4:45pm; Oct.-Mar. M-F 9:30am-4pm, Su 10am-4:45pm. €4.40, students and children €1.90.)*

O'CONNELL ST. AND PARNELL SQUARE. O'Connell St. is Dublin's biggest shopping thoroughfare, and at 45m it was once Europe's widest street as well. Statues of Irish leaders such as **Daniel O'Connell, Charles Parnell,** and **James Larkin** adorn the street's traffic islands. One monument you won't see is **Nelson's Pillar,** a free standing pillar that remembered Trafalgar and stood outside the General Post Office for 150 years. In 1966 the IRA commemorated the 50th anniversary of the Easter Rising by blowing the admiral out of the water. Follow O'Connell St. to get to Parnell Sq., home of **The Hugh Lane Municipal Gallery of Modern Art.** In the early 20th century, Dubliners refused to finance the museum that was to hold American artist Lane's collection of French Impressionist paintings; although the gallery was eventually constructed, Yeats lamented his city's provincial attitude in a string of poems. *(Par-*

nell Sq. Buses #3, 10, 11, 13, 16, and 19 all stop near the gallery. Open Su 11am-5pm, Tu-Th 9:30am-6pm, F-Sa 9:30am-5pm. Free.) The city's rich literary heritage comes to life at **The Dublin Writers' Museum,** which displays rare editions, manuscripts, and memorabilia of Beckett, Brendan Behan, Patrick Kavanagh, Sean O'Casey, Shaw, Swift, Wilde, and Yeats. (18 Parnell Sq. North. Open June-Aug. M-F 10am-6pm, Sa 10am-5pm, Su 11am-5pm; Sept.-May M-Sa 10am-5pm. €5.50, students and seniors €5. Combined ticket with James Joyce Centre €8.) Nearby, the **James Joyce Cultural Centre** features a wide range of Joyceana, including portraits of the individuals who inspired his characters. Call for info on lectures, walking tours, and Bloomsday events. (35 N. Great Georges St., past Parnell St. ☎878 8547. Open July-Aug. M-Sa 9:30am-5pm, Su 11am-5pm; Sept.-June M-Sa 9:30am-5pm, Su 12:30-5pm. €4, students and seniors €3.)

SMITHFIELD AND ELSEWHERE. At the **Old Jameson Distillery,** learn how science, grain, and tradition come together to create the golden fluid called **whiskey.** Be quick to volunteer in the beginning and you'll get to sample a whole tray of different whiskeys. Even the unchosen are blessed, however, with a glass of firewater at the end. (Bow St. From O'Connell St., turn onto Henry St. and continue straight as the street dwindles to Mary St., then Mary Ln., then May Ln.; the warehouse is on a cobblestone street on the left. Tours daily 9:30am-5:30pm. €7, students and seniors €4.) **Phoenix Park,** Europe's largest enclosed public park, is most famous for the 1882 Phoenix Park murders. The Invincibles, a nationalist splinter group, stabbed the Chief Secretary of Ireland, Lord Cavendish, and his Under-Secretary 180m from the **Phoenix Column.** The 712-hectare park incorporates the President's residence (Áras an Uachtaraín), cricket pitches, polo grounds, and grazing deer. **Dublin Zoo,** Europe's largest, is in the park. It contains 700 animals and the world's biggest egg. (Take bus #10 from O'Connell St. or #25 or 26 from Middle Abbey St. Park open 24hr. Free. Zoo open M-Sa 9:30am-6:30pm, Su 10:30am-6:30pm. Closes at sunset in winter. €10, students €8.)

🎵🎭 ENTERTAINMENT AND NIGHTLIFE

Whether you fancy poetry or punk, Dublin is equipped to entertain you. The free *Event Guide* is available at the tourist office and Temple Bar restaurants. The **Abbey Theatre,** 26 Lower Abbey St., was founded in 1904 by Yeats and Lady Gregory to promote Irish culture and modernist theater. Synge's *Playboy of the Western World* was first performed here in 1907. Abbey Theatre is now Ireland's national theater. (☎878 7222. Box office open M-Sa 10:30am-7pm. Tickets €12-25; M-Th students €10.) **St. Patrick's Day** (Mar. 17) and the half-week leading up to it host a carnival of concerts, fireworks, street theater, and intoxicated madness. (☎675 3205; www.paddyfest.ie.) By the time the city sobers up, **Bloomsday** (June 16), the day of Leopold Bloom's journey in Joyce's *Ulysses*, rolls around and the party starts up again. The James Joyce Cultural Centre (☎873 1984) sponsors a reenactment of the funeral and wake, a lunch at Davy Byrnes, and a Guinness breakfast.

Trad (traditional music) is an important element of the Dublin music scene—some pubs in the city center have sessions nightly. The best pub for *trad* is ⬛**Cobblestones** (☎872 1799), on King St. North, in Smithfield.

PUBS

James Joyce once proposed that a "good puzzle would be to cross Dublin without passing a pub." A radio station once offered €125 to the first person to solve the puzzle. The winner explained that you could take any route—you'd just have to visit them all on the way. *Let's Go* recommends beginning your journey at the gates of Trinity College, moving onto Grafton St., stumbling onto Camden St., teetering down S. Great Georges St., and, finally, triumphantly crawling into the Temple Bar area. Then again, any port in a storm; drink where ye may.

HE LOCAL STORY

THE PERFECT PINT

Bartender Glenn, of a local Dublin Pub, helps Let's Go resolve the most elusive question of all...

G: *What's the most important thing about pouring a pint*

A: The most important thing is to have the keg as close to the tap as possible. The closer, the better.

G: And why's that?

A: Well, you don't want the Guinness sitting in a long tube while you wait to pour the next pint. You want to pull it straight out of the keg, without any muck in between.

G: Does stopping to let the Guinness settle make a big difference?

A: Well, you can top it straight off if you want, but you might get too big a head with that. You don't want too small or big a head, so if you stop ¾ of the way, you can adjust the pint until the head is perfect. A true Guinness lover will taste the difference.

G: Because of the head?

A: No, because of the gas. If you pull the Guinness straight from the tap and get a big head, it means you've gotten too much gas. It kills the taste.

G: Anything else to look for?

A: Good Guinness leaves a healthy film on the glass. If it doesn't, you didn't get a good Guinness.

G: Well, Glenn, you sure make pouring pints sound like an art form.

A: Oh aye, but only with Guinness—everything else you just chuck into a glass and hand out.

The Stag's Head, 1 Dame Ct. This beautiful Victorian pub has stained glass, mirrors, and yes, you guessed it, evidence of deer decapitation, all enjoyed by a largely student crowd. Excellent food abounds. Entrees about €10. Food served M-F noon-3:30pm and 5-7pm, Sa 12:30-2:30pm. Open M-W 11:30am-11:30pm, Th-Sa 11:30am-12:30am.

Whelan's, 25 Wexford St., down S. Great Georges St. The stage venue in back hosts big-name *trad* and rock groups, with live music every night at 9:30pm (doors open 8pm). Cover €7-12. Open for lunch daily 12:30-2:30pm. Pub open W-Sa until late.

The Brazen Head, 20 North Bridge St., off Merchant's Quay. Dublin's oldest and one of its liveliest pubs. Brazen Head was established in 1198. The courtyard is quite the pickup scene on summer nights. Open late.

The Porter House, 16-18 Parliament St. The largest selection of international beers in the country, Porter House also serves 8 self-brewed stouts, ales, and porters. Excellent sampler tray includes a sip of stout made with oysters (€9). Open M-W 10:30am-11:30pm, Th-F 10:30am-1:30am, Sa 10:30am-2am, Su 12:30-11pm.

Mulligan's, 8 Poolbeg St., behind Burgh Quay. Upholds its reputation as one of the best pint-pourers in Dublin. Try to collect all 6 Guinness coasters to learn how. A taste of the typical Irish pub: Low-key and nothing fancy.

Davy Byrnes, 21 Duke St., off Grafton St. A lively, middle-aged crowd fills the pub in which Joyce sets the "Cyclops" chapter of *Ulysses*. Open M-W 11am-11:30pm, Th-Sa 11am-12:30am, Su 11am-11pm.

CLUBS

The PoD, 35 Harcourt St. Spanish-style decor meets hard core dance music. The brave venture upstairs to **The Red Box,** a separate, more intense club with a warehouse atmosphere. Cover €10-20; Th and Sa €7 with ISIC; Th ladies free before midnight. Cover skyrockets when big-name DJs play. Open until 3am.

Rí-Rá, 1 Exchequer St. Good music that steers clear of pop and house extremes. Two floors, several bars, lots of nooks and crannies. Cover €7-10. Open daily 11pm-2am.

Gaiety, S. King St., just off Grafton St. This elegant theater shows its wild side late night, with DJs and live music from salsa to soul. Cover from €10. Open F-Sa midnight-4am.

The George, 89 S. Great Georges St. Dublin's first and most prominent gay bar. All ages gather throughout the day to chat and drink. Hosts frequent theme nights. Dress well—no effort, no entry. Cover €8-10 after 10pm. The nightclub is open W-Su until 2am.

⚡ DAYTRIPS FROM DUBLIN

HOWTH. Howth (rhymes with "both") dangles from the mainland in Edenic isolation, fewer than 16km from Dublin. A 3hr. **cliff walk** circles the peninsula, passing heather and thousands of seabird nests. The best section of the walk is a 1hr. hike between the harbor and the lighthouse at the southeast tip. To get to the trailhead from town, turn left at the DART station and follow Harbour Rd. around the coast for about 20min. Just offshore is **Ireland's Eye,** a former sanctuary for monks that has become an avian refuge. **Ireland's Eye Boat Trips,** on the East Pier, jets passengers across the water. (☎(01) 831 4200. Round-trip €8, students and children €4.) To reach the private **Howth Castle,** a charmingly awkward patchwork of architectural styles, turn right as you exit the DART station and then left after 400m, at the entrance to the Deer Park Hotel. To get to Howth, take a northbound DART **train** to the end of the line (30min., 6 per hr., €1.50). Turn left out of the station to get to the **tourist office,** in the Old Courthouse on Harbour Rd. (☎844 5976. Open May-Aug. M 11am-1pm, Tu-F 11am-1pm and 1:30-5pm.)

BOYNE VALLEY. The thinly populated Boyne Valley hides Ireland's greatest archaeological treasures. Along the curves of the river between Slane and Drogheda lie no fewer than 40 crypt-like passages constructed by the Neolithics around the 4th millennium BC. **Newgrange** is the most spectacular; a roof box over the entrance allows a solitary beam of sunlight to shine directly into the tomb for 17min. on the winter solstice, a breathtaking experience that is simulated on the tour. You may only enter Newgrange by admission at ▓**Brú na Bóinne Visitors Centre,** near Donore on the south side of the River Boyne, across from the tombs. (☎(041) 988 0300. Open June to mid-Sept. daily 9am-7pm; late Sept. and May 9am-6:30pm; Oct. and Mar.-Apr. 9:30am-5:30pm; Nov.-Feb. 9:30am-5pm. Center and 1hr. tour €6, students €3.50.) A group of enormous, well-preserved Norman castles—including **Trim Castle,** conquered by Mel Gibson in *Braveheart*—overlooks **Trim** proper on the River Boyne. (Open May-Oct. daily 10am-6pm. Tours every 45min. Limited to 15 people; sign up upon arrival in Trim. Grounds only €1.20. Tour and grounds €3.10, students €1.20.)

SOUTHEAST IRELAND

A base first for the Vikings and then the Normans, the Southeast echoes a fainter Celtic influence than the rest of Ireland. Town and street names in this region reflect Norse, Norman, and Anglo-Saxon influences rather than Gaelic ones. The Southeast's busiest attractions are its beaches, which draw admirers to the coastline stretching from Kilmore Quay to tidy Ardmore.

⚓ FERRIES TO FRANCE AND BRITAIN

Irish Ferries (☎053 33 158) sails from Rosslare Harbour to Pembroke, Wales (4hr., every day, €28-38) and Roscoff and Cherbourg, France (18hr., every other day). **Eurail** passes grant passage on ferries to France. **Stena Line** (☎053 61 567) runs from Rosslare Harbour to Fishguard, Wales (3½hr., €28-35).

THE WICKLOW MOUNTAINS ☎0404

Over 600m tall, carpeted in fragrant heather and pleated by sparkling rivers, the Wicklow summits are home to grazing sheep and scattered villages. Smooth glacial valleys embrace two lakes and the monastic ruins that epitomize the romantic image of pristine rural Ireland. Public transportation is severely limited, so driving is the easiest way to get around. **Glendalough,** a verdant, blessed valley renowned as a medieval monastic village, is most accessible, and draws a steady stream of coach tours from Dublin. The **National Park Information Office,** between the two lakes, is the best source for hiking advice. (☎45 425. Open May-Aug. daily 10am-6pm; Apr.-Sept. Sa-Su 10am-dusk.) **St. Kevin's Bus Service** (☎(01) 281 8119) arrives in Glendalough from St. Stephen's Green in Dublin (2 per day, round-trip €15). The **tourist office** is across from the Glendalough Hotel. (☎45 688. Open from mid-June to Sept. M-Sa 10am-1pm and 2-5:30pm.) Good beds can be found at ■**The Glendaloch Hostel (An Óige/HI) ❷,** 5min. up the road from the tourist office. Excellent security and an in-house cafe make it by far the best option in the area. (☎45 342. Irish breakfast included. Laundry €5. **Internet** access. Dorms €20-22; singles €23-24; doubles €46-48; off-season €3 discount.) For more affordable food, B&Bs, and groceries, head to **Laragh,** 1.5km up the road.

ROSSLARE HARBOUR   ☎053

Rosslare Harbour is a useful departure point for Wales or France. **Trains** run from the ferry port to Dublin (3hr., 3 per day, €19) and Limerick (2½hr., 1-2 per day, €17) via Waterford (1¼hr., €8.50). **Buses** run from the same office to: Cork (3-5 per day, €9); Dublin (3hr., 10-12 per day, €14); Galway (4 per day, €23) via Waterford; Limerick (3-5 per day, €19); and Tralee (2-4 per day, €23). The Rosslare-Kilrane **tourist office** is 1.5km from the harbor on Wexford Rd. in Kilrane. (☎33 622. Open daily 11am-6pm.) If you need to stay overnight, try ■**Mrs. O'Leary's Farmhouse ❷,** off N25 in Kilrane. Call for pickup. (☎33 134. Singles €30, off-season €27.)

KILKENNY   ☎056

Ireland's best-preserved medieval town, Kilkenny (pop. 25,000) is also a center of great nightlife; nine churches share the streets with 80 pubs. **Tynan Walking Tours** provide the down-and-dirty on Kilkenny's folkloric tradition; hour-long tours depart from the tourist office. (☎(87) 265 1745. €6, students €5.) The 13th-century ■**Kilkenny Castle** housed the Earls of Ormonde from the 1300s until 1932. The basement shelters the **Butler Gallery's** modern art exhibitions. (☎21 450. Open June-Aug. daily 9:30am-7pm; Sept. 10am-6:30pm; Oct.-Mar. 10:30am-12:45pm and 2-5pm; Apr.-May 10:30am-5pm. Required tour €4.50, students €2.) Climb the narrow 30m tower of **St. Canice's Cathedral,** up the hill off Dean St., for a panoramic view of the town and its surroundings. (☎64 971. Open Easter-Sept. M-Sa 9am-6pm, Su 2-6pm; Oct.-Easter M-Sa 10am-4pm, Su 2-4pm.) Start your pub crawl at either the top of **John Street** or the end of **Parliament Street.**

    Trains (☎22 024) arrive at Dublin Rd. from Dublin (2hr., €16) and Waterford (45min., €8). **Buses** (☎64 933) arrive at Dublin Rd. and the city center from: Cork (3hr., 2-3 per day, €16); Dublin (2hr., 5-6 per day, €10); Galway (5hr., 3-6 per day, €19); Limerick (2½hr., 2-4 per day, €14); Rosslare Harbour (2hr., 2-3 per day, €7); and Waterford (1½hr., 2 per day, €6.40). The **tourist office** is on Rose Inn St. (☎51 500. Open Mar.-Sept. M-F 9am-6pm, Sa 10am-6pm; Oct.-Feb. M-F 9am-5pm.) **B&Bs** are concentrated on **Waterford Road.** Stay in former royal quarters at the 15th-century ■**Foulksrath Castle (An Óige/HI) ❶,** in Jenkinstown, 12.5km north of town on the N77. Buggy's Buses run to the hostel from the Parade (20min., M-Sa 2 per day, €2) in Kilkenny. (☎67 674. Dorms €11-12.) **Pordylo's ❹,** on Butterslip Ln. between Kieran St. and High St., has excellent world cuisine, including many vegetarian options. (Entrees €17-23. Open daily 6-11pm.) A **Dunnes supermarket** is on Kieran St. (☎61 655. Open M-Tu and Sa 8:30am-7pm, W-F 8:30am-10pm, Su 10am-6pm.)

WATERFORD   ☎ 051

A skyline of huge metal silos and harbor cranes greets visitors to Waterford. Fortunately, behind this industrial facade lies a city with 10 centuries of fascinating history. Waterford is Ireland's oldest city, founded in AD 914 by the grandson of Viking Ivor the Boneless as a refuge for his longships. Today, traces of early Vadrafjord are still visible in the city's streets, though her harbor is now filled with massive freighters instead of Viking warships. The highlight of Waterford is the **⬛Waterford Crystal Factory,** 3km away on N25 (the Cork road). One-hour tours allow you to witness the transformation of molten glass into polished crystal. Catch the City Imp minibus outside Dunnes on Michael St. and request a stop at the factory (10-15min., every 15-20min., €1.20) or take city bus #1 (2 per hr., €1.20), which leaves across from the Clock Tower. (☎332 500. Gallery open Mar.-Oct. daily 8:30am-6pm; Nov.-Feb. 9am-5pm. Tours Mar.-Oct. daily 8:30am-4pm; Nov.-Feb. M-F 9am-3:15pm. Tours €6.50, students €3.50.) **Reginald's Tower,** at the end of The Quay, has guarded the city's entrance since the 12th century. (☎873 501. Open June-Sept. daily 9:30am-6:30pm; Oct.-May 10am-5pm. €2, students €1.) To get a taste of Vadrafjord, head to **Waterford Treasures** at the Granary, which contains an impressive collection of Viking artifacts as well as the only extant item of Henry VIII's clothing, a velvet hat. (☎304 500. Open June-Aug. M-F 9am-9pm, Sa 9am-6pm, Su 11am-5pm; May and Sept. M-Sa 9:30am-6pm, Su 11am-6pm; Oct.-Apr. M-Sa 10am-5pm, Su 11am-5pm. €6, students €4.50.) The Quay is crowded with pubs; try **T&H Doolan's,** on George's St., which has been serving crowds for 300 years. (Pub food €13-19. *Trad* nightly at 9:30pm.)

Trains (☎876 243) leave from The Quay across the bridge for: Dublin (2½hr., M-F 5-6 per day, €17-21); Kilkenny (40min., 3-5 per day, €8); Limerick (2¼hr., M-Sa 2 per day, €16); and Rosslare Harbour (1hr., M-Sa 2 per day, €10). **Buses** depart from The Quay for: Cork (2½hr., 10-13 per day, €15); Dublin (2¾hr., 6-12 per day, €10); Galway (4¾hr., 5-6 per day, €19); Kilkenny (1hr., daily, €8); Limerick (2½hr., 6-7 per day, €15); and Rosslare Harbour (1¼hr., 3-5 per day, €13). The **tourist office** is on The Quay, across from the bus station. (☎875 823. Open M-F 9am-6pm, Sa 10am-6pm.) Allow Mrs. Ryan of **Beechwood ❷,** 7 Cathedral Sq., to invite you into her charming house. Rooms look directly onto Christ Church Cathedral. (☎876 677. Doubles €50.) **⬛Haricot's Wholefood Restaurant ❷,** 11 O'Connell St., serves innovative home-cooked meals. The menu changes constantly and is often vegetarian-friendly. (Entrees €8-10. Open M-F 10am-8pm, Sa 10am-6pm.)

CASHEL   ☎ 062

Cashel sits at the foot of the 90m **⬛Rock of Cashel** (a.k.a. **St. Patrick's Rock**), a huge limestone outcropping topped by medieval buildings. (Open Mar.-Sept. daily 9:30am-5:30pm; Oct.-Feb. M-F 9:30am-5:30pm. Free.) Down the cow path from the Rock lie the ruins of **Hore Abbey,** built by Cistercian monks and presently inhabited by sheep. The **GPA-Bolton Library,** on John St., houses ecclesiastical texts and rare manuscripts, including a 1550 edition of Machiavelli's *Il Principe* and the world's smallest book. (☎62 511. Call for tours.) The internationally acclaimed **Brú Ború Heritage Centre,** at the base of the Rock, stages traditional music and dance performances; participation is encouraged. (☎61 122. Performances mid-June to mid-Sept. Tu-Sa 9pm. €15, with dinner €35.) **Bus Éireann** (☎61 333) leaves from the Bake House on Main St. for: Cork (1½hr., 6 per day, €12); Dublin (3hr., 6 per day, €16); and Limerick (1hr., 5 per day, €12). The **tourist office** is in the City Hall on Main St. (☎61 333. Open June-Sept. M-F 9am-6pm, Su 10am-6pm.) Just out of town on Dundrum Rd. is the outstanding **⬛O'Brien's Farmhouse Hostel ❶.** (☎61 003. Laundry €8-10. Dorms €15; doubles €50. **Camping** €7.50 per person.)

SOUTHWEST IRELAND

With a dramatic landscape that ranges from lakes and mountains to stark, ocean-battered cliffs, Southwest Ireland is a land rich in storytellers and history-makers. Outlaws and rebels once lurked in the hidden coves and glens now overrun by visitors. If the tourist mayhem is too much for you, you can always retreat to the placid stretches along the Ring of Kerry and Cork's southern coast.

◀ FERRIES TO FRANCE AND BRITAIN

Swansea-Cork Ferries (☎021 427 1166) go between Cork and Swansea, South Wales (10hr., daily, €30-43). **Brittany Ferries** (☎021 427 7801) sail from Cork to Roscoff, France (14hr., €50-100).

CORK CITY   ☎021

Cork (pop. 150,000), the country's second-largest city, serves as the center of the sports, music, and arts scenes in southwest Ireland. Cork is a great place to eat and sleep for those who want to explore the surrounding countryside, but the city itself is well worth its own visit.

▨ ▮ TRANSPORTATION AND PRACTICAL INFORMATION

Cork is compact and pedestrian-friendly. **St. Patrick's Street** becomes **Grand Parade** to the west; to the north it crosses **Merchant's Quay,** home of the bus station. Across **St. Patrick's Bridge,** to the north, **McCurtain Street** runs east to **Lower Glanmire Road** and the train station, before becoming the N8 to Dublin, Waterford, and Cobh. Downtown action concentrates on the vaguely parallel **Paul Street, Oliver Plunkett Street,** and St. Patrick's Street. Their connecting north-south avenues are overflowing with shops, and all are largely pedestrian and easy to traverse.

Trains: Kent Station (☎450 6766), on Lower Glanmire Rd., across the river from the city center. Open M-Sa 6:30am-8:00pm, Su 7:50am-8pm. Connections to: **Dublin** (3hr., 5-7 per day, €52); **Killarney** (2hr., 4-7 per day, €26); **Limerick** (1½hr., 4-7 per day, €26); **Tralee** (2½hr., 3 per day, €31).

Buses: (☎450 8188), Parnell Pl., 2 blocks east of St. Patrick's Bridge on Merchant's Quay. Info desk open daily 9am-6pm. **Bus Éireann** (☎450 8188, www.buseireann.ie) goes to: **Dublin** (4½hr., 5-6 per day, €20-33); **Galway** (4hr., 4-7 per day, €17-27); **Killarney** (2hr., 10-13 per day, €13-21); **Limerick** (2hr., 14 per day, €14-21); **Rosslare Harbour** (4hr., 3 per day, €19-30); **Sligo** (7hr., 5 per day, €23-37); **Tralee** (2½hr., 12 per day, €14-22); **Waterford** (2¼hr., 13 per day, €15-23).

Public Transportation: City buses crisscross the city and its suburbs every 10-30min. (M-Sa 7:30am-11:15pm, Su 10am-11:15pm; from €0.95). From downtown, catch buses along St. Patrick St., across from the Father Matthew statue.

Tourist Office: (☎425 5100), on Grand Parade, along the Lee's south channel. Open June-Aug. M-F 9am-6pm, Sa 9am-5:00pm; Sept.-May M-Sa 9:15am-5:30pm.

Banks: Ulster Bank Limited, 88 St. Patrick's St. (☎427 0618). Open M 10am-5pm and Tu-F 10am-4pm. **Bank of Ireland,** 70 St. Patrick's St. (☎427 7177). Open M 10am-5pm, Tu-F 10am-4pm. Most banks in Cork have 24hr. **ATMs.**

Emergency: ☎999; no coins required. **Police** (Garda): (☎452 2000), on Anglesea St.

Pharmacies: Regional Late Night Pharmacy (☎434 4575), on Wilton Rd., opposite the Regional Hospital on bus #8. Open M-F 9am-10pm, Sa-Su 10am-10pm. **Phelan's Late Night,** 9 Patrick St. (☎427 2511). Open M-Sa 9am-10pm, Su 10am-10pm.

Hospital: Mercy Hospital (☎ 427 1971), on Grenville Pl. €25 fee for emergency room access. **Cork Regional Hospital** (☎ 454 6400), on Wilton St., on the #8 bus.

Internet Access: ▒**Web Workhouse** (☎ 434 3090), on Winthrop St., near the post office. €2.50-5 per hr. Open daily 24hr.

Post Office: (☎ 427 2000), on Oliver Plunkett St. Open M-Sa 9am-5:30pm.

▐ ACCOMMODATIONS

B&Bs are clustered along **Patrick's Hill,** on **Glanmire Road** rising upward from St. Patrick's Bridge, and on **Western Road** near University College.

▒ **Sheila's Budget Accommodation Centre (IHH),** 4 Belgrave Pl. (☎ 450 5562; www.sheilashostel.ie). At the intersection of Wellington St. and York St. Helpful, energetic staff. Breakfast €3.20. Internet €1 per 20min. 24hr. reception desk is also a general store. Check-out 10am. Dorms €15-16; singles €30; doubles €40-50. ❶

▒ **Clare D'Arcy B&B,** 7 Sidney Place, Wellington Rd. (☎ 450 4658; www.darcysguesthouse.com). From St. Patrick's Bridge, start up St. Patrick's Hill, turning right onto Wellington Rd. A luxurious guesthouse with an elegant Parisian interior. Doubles €80. ❹

Cork International Hostel (An Óige/HI), 1-2 Redclyffe, Western Rd. (☎ 454 3289). A 15min. walk from Grand Parade. Bus #8 stops across the street. Immaculate and spacious bunk rooms in a stately brick Victorian townhouse. All rooms with bath. Breakfast €3.50. Internet €1 per 10min. Reception 10:30am-midnight. Dorms €17-19; doubles €44; under-18, reduced prices. ❷

Kinlay House (IHH), on Bob and Joan Walk (☎ 450 8966). To the right of Shandon Church. Offers family-sized rooms and a warm atmosphere. Breakfast included. Laundry €7. Internet €1 per 15min. Dorms €14; singles €25-30; triples €54; quads €72. ❶

▐ FOOD

Delicious restaurants and cafes abound on the lanes connecting Patrick St., Paul St., and Oliver Plunkett St. **Tesco** (☎ 427 0791), on Paul St., is the biggest grocery store in town. (Open M-W and Sa 8:30am-8pm, Th-F 8:30am-10pm.)

▒ **Quay Co-op,** 24 Sullivan's Quay (☎ 431 7660). Delicious vegetarian and vegan meals. Soup €2.80. Entrees around €6.50. Open M-Sa 9am-9pm. ❷

▒ **Tribes,** Tuckey St. (☎ 427 6070). Keep Bishop Lucy Park on your left and walk to the end of Oliver Plunkett St. The only late-night coffee shop in town. Sandwiches and burgers around €6. Open M-W noon-12:30am, Th-Sa noon-4:30am. ❷

Amicus, 14A French Church St. (☎ 427 6455). A sophisticated decor. Artistic, delicious dishes. Meals around €15-20. Open M-Sa 10am-10:30pm and Su noon-9pm. ❹

▐ ▐ SIGHTS AND NIGHTLIFE

Cork's sights are loosely divided into several districts, but all can be reached by foot. Pick up the *Cork Area City Guide* at the tourist office (€2) for a good overview of local sights and times. Built in 1845, ▒**University College Cork (UCC)** offers a collection of brooding Gothic buildings, manicured lawns, and sculpture-studded grounds that make for a great afternoon walk or picnic. (☎ 490 3000; www.ucc.ie). ▒**Fitzgerald Park,** across the walkway from UCC's front gate, is the other must-see in Cork, with beautiful rose gardens and art exhibits courtesy of the **Cork Public Museum.** (☎ 427 0679. Museum open M-F 11am-1pm and 2:15-5pm, Su 3-5pm. Students and seniors free.) **St. Anne's Church (Shandon's Church),** across the river to the north, has earned the nickname "the four-faced liar," because the tower's four clocks are notoriously out of sync with one another. Walk up Shandon St. and take a right down the unmarked Church St. (Open June-Sept. M-Th and Sa 10am-5:30pm. €4, students and seniors €3.50.) The **Cork City Gaol** offers multimedia tours of the former prison; cross the bridge at the western end of Fitzgerald Park, turn right on Sunday's Well Rd., and follow the signs. (Open daily Mar.-Oct. 9:30am-6pm; Nov.-Feb. 10am-5pm. €5, students €4; includes audio tour.)

The lively streets of Cork make finding entertainment easy; try Oliver Plunkett St., **Union Quay,** and **South Main Street.** for pubs and live music. To keep on top of the scene, check out *List Cork,* free at local shops. Unless otherwise noted, establishments listed close M-Th 11:30pm, F-Sa 12:30am, and Su 11pm. ◪**The Lobby,** 1 Union Quay, gave some of Ireland's most famous folk acts their big breaks; it features nightly live music with a view of the river. (Occasional cover €2.50-6.40. Closes M-Th 11:30pm, F-Sa 12:30am, and Su 11pm.) ◪**Half Moon,** on Academy Ln. to the left of the Opera House, is the most popular dance club in Cork. (18+. Cover €9. Open daily until 2am. Purchase tickets from the box office across the street.) At **An Spailpín Fanac,** 28 South Main St., live *trad* complements the decor of this 224-year-old pub. (Closes M-Th 11:30pm, F-Sa 12:30am, and Su 11pm.) At classy **Bodega,** 46-49 Cornmarket St., off the northern end of Grand Parade in a striking converted warehouse, patrons relax with glasses of wine on velvet couches. (Closes M-Th 11:30pm, F-Sa 12:30am, and Su 11pm.)

▣ DAYTRIPS FROM CORK

BLARNEY. Tourists eager for quintessential Irish scenery and a cold kiss head northwest of Cork to see **Blarney Castle** and its legendary **Blarney Stone,** which confers the gift of persuasion upon those who smooch it while leaning over backwards. The top of the castle provides an airy and stunning view of the countryside. Try to come early in the morning to avoid the ubiquitous crowds. (☎438 5252. Open June-Aug. M-Sa 9am-7pm, Su 9:30am-5:30pm; Sept. M-Sa 9am-6:30pm, Su 9:30am-dusk; May M-Sa 9am-6:30pm, Su 9:30am-5:30pm; Oct.-Apr. M-Sa 9am-6pm or dusk, Su 9:30am-5pm or dusk. €4.50, students and seniors €3, children €1.50.) **Buses** run from Cork to Blarney (10-16 per day, round-trip €4.50).

KINSALE. Affluent tourists come to eat at Kinsale's expensive, famed restaurants, known as the **Good Food Circle,** but the town's other attractions are cheap. Follow the coastal **Scilly Walk** 30min. from the end of Pearse St. to reach the star-shaped, 17th-century **Charles Fort,** which offers spectacular views of the town and its watery surroundings. (☎477 2263. Open mid-Mar. to Oct. M-F 10am-6pm; Nov. to mid-Mar. Sa-Su 10am-5pm, M-F by appointment. €3.50, students €1.25.) **Buses** arrive on the pier, at the Esso station, from Cork (40min., 5-11 per day, round-trip €6.50). The **tourist office,** on Emmet Pl., is on the waterfront. (☎477 2234. Open Mar.-Nov. M-Sa 9am-7pm.) Local fishermen roast their catch at ◪**The Spaniard ❸,** a pub with delicious entrees (€7-14).

SCHULL AND THE MIZEN HEAD PENINSULA ☎028

The seaside hamlet of Schull is an ideal base for exploring the craggy and beach-laden southwest tip of Ireland. A calm harbor and numerous shipwrecks make it a diving paradise; the **Watersports Centre** rents gear. (☎28 554. Open Apr.-Oct. M-Sa 9:30am-6pm.) The coastal road winds past the **Barley Coast Beach** and continues on to **Mizen Head.** The Mizen becomes more scenic and less populated the farther west you go from Schull; **Betty Johnson's Bus Hire** offers tours of the area. (☎28 410. Call ahead. €12.) In summer, **ferries** (☎28 138) depart from Schull for Cape Clear Island (June-Sept. 2-3 per day, round-trip €12). **Buses** arrive in Schull from Cork

(1-3 per day, €12) and Goleen (1-3 per day, €3.10). There is no other public transportation on the peninsula. Confident **cyclists** can daytrip to Mizen Head (29km from Schull). The immaculate **Schull Backpackers' Lodge (IHH)** ❶, on Colla Rd., has **hiking** and **biking** maps and info. (☎28 681. Bike rental €10 per day. Dorms €12; singles €18; doubles €36.) **The Courtyard** ❷, on Main St., has delicious options for breakfast and lunch; the fruit scones (€0.60) and the sandwiches on fresh ciabatta (€7-9.50) are both worth a try. (Open M-Sa 9:30am-6pm.)

CAPE CLEAR ISLAND ☎028

Although the scenery visible from the ferry landing at Cape Clear Island (*Oileán Chléire*) is desolate and foreboding, the main industry of this beautiful island is farming. Cape Clear provides asylum for gulls, petrels, cormorants, and of course their attendant flocks of ornithologists; the **Cape Clear Bird Observatory** (☎39 181), on North Harbour, is one of the most important observatories in Europe, and offers bird-watching and ecology courses. Those more interested in lovebirds should head to the **Marriage Stones**, on the northeast corner of the island, which were often visited by those seeking the gift of fertility. If the stones fail you, console yourself at **Cléire Goats** (☎39 126), on the steep hill between the harbor and the heritage center, where you can sample rich and delicious goat's milk ice cream for €1.50. **Ferries** (☎28 138) go to Schull (45min., 1-3 per day, round-trip €11.50). There is an **information office** in the pottery shop by the pier that provides a pamphlet detailing the island's sights. (☎39 100. Open July-Aug. 11am-1pm and 3-6pm; Sept. and June 3-6pm.) **Cléire Lasmuigh (An Óige/HI)** ❶ is a 10min. walk from the pier; follow the main road and keep left. (☎39 198. June-Sept. dorms €11-13.) To reach **Cuas an Uisce Campsite** ❶, walk 5min. uphill from the harbor and bear right before Ciarán Danny Mike's; it's on the left. (☎39 136. Open June-Sept. Tent and one person €10; under-16 €7.50.) Groceries are available at **An Siopa Beag**, on the pier. (Open July-Aug. daily 11am-9pm; June 11am-6pm; Sept.-May 11am-4:30pm.)

KILLARNEY AND KILLARNEY NATIONAL PARK ☎064

The town of Killarney is just minutes from some of Ireland's most glorious natural scenery. The 95 sq. km national park outside of town blends forested mountains with the famous **Lakes of Killarney.** Five kilometers south of Killarney on Kenmare Rd. is **Muckross House,** a massive 19th-century manor with a garden that blooms brilliantly each year. A path leads to the 20m high **Torc Waterfall,** the starting point for several short trails along the beautiful **Torc Mountain.** Walk or drive to the 14th-century **Ross Castle,** the last stronghold in Munster to fall to Cromwell's army, by taking a right on Ross Rd. off Muckross Rd., 3km from Killarney. Alternatively, the footpaths from Knockreer (out of town on New St.) are more scenic. (Open June-Aug. daily 9am-6:30pm; May and Sept. 10am-6pm; Oct. and mid-Mar. to Apr. 10am-5pm. €5, students €2.) Bike around the **Gap of Dunloe,** which borders **Macgillycuddy's Reeks,** Ireland's highest mountain range, or hop on a boat from Ross Castle to the head of the Gap (1½hr., €12; book at the tourist office). From **Lord Brandon's Cottage,** on the Gap, head left over the stone bridge, continue cycling 3km to the church, and then turn right onto a winding road. Huff the 2km to the top, and your reward is an 11km coast downhill through the park's most breathtaking scenery. The 13km ride back to Killarney (bear right after Kate Kearney's Cottage, turn left on the road to Fossa, and turn right on Killorglin Rd.) passes the ruins of **Dunloe Castle,** demolished by, you guessed it, Cromwell's armies.

Trains (☎31 067 or (1890) 200 493) arrive at Killarney station, off East Avenue Rd., from: Cork (2hr., 4 per day, €20); Dublin (3½hr., 4 per day, €52); and Limerick (3hr., 4 per day, €20). **Buses** (☎30 011) leave from Park Rd. for: Belfast (2-4 per day, €30); Cork (2hr., 10-14 per day, €13); and Dublin (6hr., 5-6 per day, €20). **O'Sullivan's,** on

Bishop's Ln., rents **bikes.** (☎31 282. Free locks and maps. Open daily 8:30am-6:30pm. €12 per day, €70 per week.) The staff at the **tourist office,** Beech St., is extremely helpful. (☎31 633. Open July-Aug. M-Sa 9am-8pm, Su 10am-1pm and 2:15-6pm; June and Sept. M-Sa 9am-6pm, Su 10am-1pm and 2:15-6pm; Oct.-May M-Sa 9:15am-1pm and 2:15-5:30pm.) The immense and immaculate **Neptune's (IHH) ❶,** on Bishop's Ln., up the first walkway off New St. on the right, has an ideal location and professional staff. (☎35 255. Breakfast €2.50. Dorms €11-17; singles €25-35; doubles €16-19.) **Orchard House B&B ❸,** on Fleming's Ln., is near the town center and an unbeatable deal; small rooms are compensated by a lovely proprietress and good amenities. (☎31 879. Singles €25-30; doubles €45-60.) For a delicious variety of quality vegetarian and meat dishes, try ▊**The Stonechat ❸,** on Fleming's Ln. The low-key but sophisticated atmosphere makes this the best restaurant in Killarney. (Lunch €7-9. Dinner €11-14. Open M-Sa 11am-5pm and 6-10pm.) ▊**The Grand ❷,** on High St., brings together locals and tourists for fantastic food and live music. (Open daily 7pm-3am.)

RING OF KERRY   ☎066

The Southwest's most celebrated peninsula offers picturesque villages, fabled ancient forts, and rugged mountains. Although tour buses often hog the roads, rewards await those who take the time to explore the landscape on foot or by bike.

▐ TRANSPORTATION

The term "Ring of Kerry" usually describes the entire **Iveragh Peninsula,** though it technically refers to the ring of roads circumnavigating it. Hop on the circuit run by **Bus Éireann,** based in Killarney and stopping at the major towns on the Ring (mid-June to Aug., 2 per day), including Cahersiveen (from Killarney 2½hr., €11.50) and Caherdaniel (from Cahersiveen 1hr., €4.30).

CAHERSIVEEN. Although best known as the birthplace of patriot Daniel O'Connell, Cahersiveen (CAR-sah-veen) serves as an excellent base for jaunts to Valentia Island, the Skelligs, and local archeological sites. The ruins of **Ballycarbery Castle,** once held by O'Connell's ancestors, are past the barracks on Bridge St. and over the bridge, off the main road to the left. About 200m past the castle turn-off stands a pair of Ireland's best-preserved stone forts, **Cahergall Fort** and **Leacanabuaile Fort.** The **tourist office** is directly across from the bus stop, next to the post office. (☎947 2589. Open June to mid-Sept. M-F 9:30am-1pm and 2-5:30pm.) The welcoming **Sive Hostel (IHH) ❶** is at 15 East End, Main St. (☎947 2717. Laundry €5.10. Dorms €10.50; doubles €25-32. **Camping** €5 per person.) **O'Shea's B&B ❸,** next to the post office on Main St., boasts comfortable rooms, some with impressive views. (☎947 2402. Singles €25-30; doubles €50.) **Main Street** has several pubs that harken back to the early 20th century, when establishments served as both watering holes and as the proprietor's main business, be it general store, blacksmithy, or leather shop.

Quiet ▊**Valentia Island** is a fantastic daytrip. The little roads of this unspoiled gem are perfect for biking or light hiking. Bridges on either end of the island connect it to the mainland; alternatively, a **ferry** runs during the summer (3min.; Apr.-Sept. 8:15am-10pm, Su 9am-10pm; €1.50, with bike €2.50) from **Reenard Point,** 5km west of Cahersiveen. A taxi to the ferry dock from Cahersiveen is about €7. Another recommended daytrip is to the **Skellig Rocks,** about 13km off the shore of the Iveragh Peninsula. From the boat, **Little Skellig** may appear snow-capped; it's actually covered with 24,000 pairs of crooning birds. Climb 630 steps to reach a **monastery** built by 6th-century Christian monks, whose beehive-like dwellings are still intact. The hostel and campground in Cahersiveen can arrange the **ferry** ride (about 1hr.) for €32-35, including a ride to the dock.

CAHERDANIEL. There's little in the village of **Caherdaniel** to attract the Ring's droves of buses. But nearby **Derrynane National Park,** 2.5km along the shore from the village, holds 3km of gorgeous beach ringed by picture-perfect dunes. Follow the signs for **Derrynane House,** once the residence of Daniel O'Connell. (Open May-Sept. M-Sa 9am-6pm, Su 11am-7pm; Apr. and Oct. Su and Tu-Sa 1-5pm; Nov.-Mar. Sa-Su 1-5pm. €3, students €1.50.) Guests are made to feel at home at **The Travellers' Rest Hostel ❶.** (☎947 5175. Breakfast €4. Dorms €12.50; singles €16.)

DINGLE PENINSULA ☎066

For decades, the Ring of Kerry's undertouristed counterpart has remained more laden with ancient sites than with tour buses. Only recently has the Ring's tourist blitz begun to encroach upon the spectacular cliffs and sweeping beaches of the Irish-speaking Dingle peninsula. Many visitors explore the area by bike, an especially attractive option given the scarcity of public transportation.

◼ TRANSPORTATION. Dingle Town is most easily reached by Bus Éireann from Tralee (1¼hr., 4-6 per day, €8.60); other routes run from Dingle to: Ballydavid (Tu and F 3 per day, round-trip €4.80); Ballyferriter (M-Sa 2 per day, €4.80); and Dunquin (M-Sa 2 per day, €4.80).

DINGLE TOWN. Lively Dingle Town, adoptive home of **Fungi the Dolphin** (now a major focus of the tourist industry), is a good base for exploring the peninsula and a fabulous tourist town in its own right. **Sciúird Archaeology Tours** leave from the pier for 3hr. whirlwind bus tours of the area's ancient spots. (☎915 1606. 2 per day, €15; book ahead.) **Moran's Tours** runs great trips to Slea Head, passing through majestic scenery and stopping at historic sites. (☎915 1155. 2 per day, €15; book ahead.) The **tourist office** is on Strand St. (☎915 1188. Open mid-June to mid-Sept. M-Sa 9am-7pm, Su 10am-5pm; late Sept. to early June daily 9:30am-5:30pm.) **◙Ballintaggart Hostel (IHH) ❶,** 25min. east of town on Tralee Rd. in a gorgeous stone mansion, is supposedly haunted by the murdered wife of the Earl of Cork. For the less supernaturally-inclined, Ballintaggart's draws are its enormous bedchambers, cobblestone courtyard, and elegant common rooms. (☎915 1454. Dorms €13-20; doubles €48. **Camping** €11 per tent, €13 per van.) The laid-back **Grapevine Hostel ❶,** on Dykegate St., is just a brief stagger from Dingle's finest pubs. Rooms are small but comfy, and the staff is very accommodating. (☎915 1434. Dorms €13-15.)

VENTRY, SLEA HEAD, AND DUNQUIN. By far the most rewarding way to see Slea Head and Dunquin's cliffs and crashing waves is to **bike** along the predominantly flat **Slea Head Drive.** Past Dingle Town toward Slea Head sits the village of **Ventry** (Ceann Trá), home to a sandy **beach** and the **◙Celtic and Prehistoric Museum,** 6km from Dingle Town, a massive collection that ranges from sea worm fossils to Millie, a 50,000-year-old woolly mammoth. (☎915 9191. Open Mar.-Nov. daily 9:30am-5:30pm; call ahead Dec.-Feb. €5, students €3.50.) While in Ventry, stay at the marvelous **Ballybeag Hostel ❶,** a secluded, yet convenient, place to unwind. A free shuttle runs to Dingle Town 7 times per day. (☎915 9876. Bike rental €7. Laundry €2. Dorms €10; singles €15.)

North of Slea Head and Ventry, the scattered settlement of Dunquin (Dún Chaoin) consists of stone houses, a pub, and little else. Past Dunquin on the road to Ballyferriter, the **◙Great Blasket Centre** has outstanding exhibits about the isolated Blasket Islands. (☎915 6444. Open July-Aug. daily 10am-7pm; Easter-June and Sept.-Oct. 10am-6pm. €3.50, students €1.30.) At **An Óige Hostel (HI) ❶,** on the Dingle Way across from the turnoff to the Blasket Centre, each bunk has an ocean view. (☎915 6121. Breakfast €3. Reception 9-10am and 5-10pm. Lockout 10am-5pm. Dorms €13-15; doubles €32.) **Kruger's ❸,** the westernmost pub in Europe, features pub grub, music sessions, and great views. (☎915 6127. Entrees €7-13.)

IRELAND

TRALEE. Tralee (pop. 20,000) is a good departure point for the Ring of Kerry or the Dingle Peninsula, with the hustle and bustle appropriate for the economic and residential capital of County Kerry. ■**Kerry the Kingdom,** in Ashe Memorial Hall on Denny St., features a high-tech history of Ireland from 8000 BC to the present. (☎712 7777. Open mid-Mar. to Oct. daily 9:30am-6pm; Nov. noon-4:30pm. €8, students €6.50.) During the last week of August, the nationally-known **Rose of Tralee Festival** brings a horde of lovely Irish lasses to town to compete for the title "Rose of Tralee." **Trains** depart from the station on Oakpark Rd. for: Cork (2½hr., 3-4 per day, €25); Dublin (4hr., 3-4 per day, €52); Galway (5-6hr., 3 per day, €52); and Killarney (40min., 4 per day, €7.50). **Buses** leave from the train station for: Cork (2½hr., 10-14 per day, €14); Galway (9-11 per day, €17); Killarney (40min., 5-14 per day, €6); and Limerick (2¼hr., 9 per day, €13). To get from the station to the **tourist office** in Ashe Memorial Hall, head down Edward St., turn right on Castle St., and then left on Denny St. The well-informed staff provides free maps. (☎712 1288. Open July-Aug. M-Sa 9am-7pm, Su 9am-6pm; May-June and Oct. M-Sa 9am-6pm; Nov.-Apr. M-F 9am-5pm.) **Westward Court (IHH) ❷,** Mary St., has spotless dorms and quality showers. (☎718 0081. Breakfast included. Curfew 3am. Dorms €17; singles €24; doubles €44.) **Whitehouse Budget Accommodations and B&B ❸,** Boherboy St., offers incredibly clean rooms with hardwood floors. Relax in the adjoining pub with *trad* on Thursdays. (☎710 2780. Dorms €19; singles €30; doubles €50.)

WESTERN IRELAND

Even Dubliners will tell you that the west is the "most Irish" part of Ireland; in many remote areas you'll hear Gaelic as often as English. The potato famine that plagued the island was most devastating in the west—entire villages emigrated or died. The region still has less than half of its 1841 population. Though miserable for farming, the land from Connemara north to Ballina is great for hiking and cycling, and for those who enjoy the isolation of mountainous landscapes.

LIMERICK   ☎061

Although its 18th-century Georgian streets and parks are both regal and elegant, 20th-century industrial and commercial developments have cursed Limerick (pop. 80,000) with a featureless urban feel. In the past century, what little attention Limerick has received has mostly focused on its squalor—a tradition exemplified by Frank McCourt's celebrated memoir *Angela's Ashes.* Despite the stigma, Limerick is a city on the rise and a fine place to stay en route to points west. The **Hunt Museum,** in the Custom House on Rutland St., has been recognized for its outstanding and diverse collection; among its treasures are a gold crucifix given by Mary Queen of Scots to her executioner and a coin reputed to be one of the infamous 30 pieces of silver paid to Judas by the Romans. (☎312 833. Open M-Sa 10am-5pm, Su 2-5pm. €6, students and seniors €5.) Limerick's student population adds spice to the nightlife scene. The area where **Denmark Street** and **Corn Market Row** intersect is a good place to quench your thirst or listen to live music. **Dolan's,** on Dock Rd., hosts nightly *trad* and rambunctious local patrons.

   Trains (☎315 555) leave Parnell St. for: Cork (2½hr., 5-6 per day, €20); Dublin (2hr., 7-10 per day, €37); Ennis (2 per day, €8); Killarney (2½hr., 3-5 per day, €22); and Waterford (2hr., 1-2 per day, €15). **Buses** (☎313 333) leave the train station for: Cork (2hr., 14 per day, €14); Derry (6½hr., 3 per day, €24); Donegal (6hr., 4 per day, €22); Dublin (3½hr., 13 per day, €15); Ennis (45min., 14 per day, €7.50); Galway (2hr., 14 per day, €14); Killarney (2½hr., 3-6 per day, €14); Rosslare Harbour (4hr., 3 per day, €19); Tralee (2hr., 8 per day, €14); and Waterford (2½hr., 7 per day, €15). The **tourist office** is on Arthurs Quay. From the station, walk down Davis

St., turn right on O'Connell St., then left at Arthurs Quay Mall. (☎361 555. Open July-Aug. M-F 9am-6pm, Sa-Su 9am-5:30pm; Sept. and May-June M-Sa 9:30am-5:30pm; Oct.-Apr. M-F 9:30am-5:30pm, Sa 9:30am-1pm.) A number of **B&Bs** can be found on Ennis St. or O'Connell St. **Cherry Blossom Budget Accommodation ❶**, several blocks south of the Daniel O'Connell statue, has comfortable and relatively spacious rooms, quality bathrooms, and serves a delicious breakfast. (☎469 449. Singles €20; doubles €40.) Next door, **Alexandra House B&B ❸**, O'Connell St., is a red brick townhouse with a pleasant interior and sunlit upstairs bedrooms. (☎318 472. Irish breakfast included. Singles €26; shared rooms €24-32 per person.) **Dolan's ❷** (see above) is Limerick's best choice for evening meals, serving traditional pub fare. (☎314 483. Entrees €6-10. Kitchen open during pub hours.) **Furze Bush Cafe Bistro ❷**, on the corner of Catherine St., offers delicious crepes (€11.50) and sandwiches (€7) in an eccentric atmosphere. (☎411 733. Open June-Aug. M-Sa 10:30am-5pm; Sept.-May M-W 10:30am-5pm, Th-Sa 10:30am-5pm and 7-10pm.)

ENNIS AND DOOLIN ☎065

Ennis's proximity to Shannon Airport and the Burren makes it a common stopover for tourists, who come for a day of shopping followed by a night of pub crawling. At ◪**Cruises Pub**, on Abbey St., local musicians appear nightly for cozy *trad* sessions in one of the oldest buildings in Co. Clare (est. 1658). Those with eclectic tastes should stop by **Glor**, a state-of-the-art music center that features nightly performances of both *trad* and more contemporary music, along with film, theater, and dance performances. (☎684 3103. Box office open M-Sa 9:30am-5:30pm. Tickets €12-22.) **Trains** leave from Station Rd. for Dublin (1-2 per day, €27). **Buses** also leave from Station Rd. for: Cork (3hr., every hr., €14); Dublin (4hr., every hr., €14); Galway (1hr., 5 per day, €10); Limerick (40min., every hr., €6.70); and Shannon Airport (40min., every hr., €7). The **tourist office** is on Arthur's Row, off O'Connell Sq. (☎28 366. Open July-Sept. daily 9am-1pm and 2-6pm; Apr.-June and Oct. M-Sa 9:30am-1pm and 2-6pm; Nov.-Mar. M-F 9:30am-1pm and 2-6pm.) **Abbey Tourist Hostel ❶**, Harmony Row, overflows with flowers, and its rooms are clean and comfortable. (☎682 2620; www.abbeytouristhostel.com. Curfew Su-W 1:30am, Th 2:30am, F-Sa 3am. Dorms €12-15; singles €25; doubles €38.)

Something of a shrine to Irish music, the little village of **Doolin** draws thousands every year to its three pubs. The pubs are commonly known by the mnemonic **MOM**: ◪**McDermott's** (in the Upper Village), **O'Connor's** (in the Lower), and **McGann's** (Upper). All have *trad* sessions nightly at 9:30pm. The ◪**Cliffs of Moher**, 10km south of town, feature a 200m vertical drop into the sea. Take the bus from Doolin (#50; 15min., 1-3 per day). **Buses** leave from Doolin Hostel for Dublin via Ennis and Limerick (#15; 2 per day) and Galway (#50; 1½hr., 1-5 per day). Almost every house on the main road is a **B&B** in Doolin. **Aille River Hostel (IHH) ❶**, halfway between the Upper and Lower villages, has a friendly atmosphere and a gorgeous location. Check out the unofficial beer garden out front, next to the Aille River. (☎707 4260. **Internet** €6 per hr. Dorms €12; doubles €27. **Camping** €6.)

THE BURREN ☎065

Limestone, butterflies, ruined castles, and labyrinthine caves make the Burren, which covers 260 sq. km, a unique geological experience. ◪**Burren Exposure**, between Kinvara and Ballyvaughn on N67, gives a soaring introduction to the region through films shown on a wall-to-wall screen. (☎707 7277. Open 10am-6pm. Tickets €5, children €3.) The Burren town of **Lisdoonvarna** is synonymous with its **Matchmaking Festival**, a month-long *craic*-and-snogging celebration that attracts over 10,000 singles each September. The **Hydro Hotel ❹** has information on the festival and its own nightly music. (☎707 4005. Open Mar.-Oct. €45 per person.) The

Burren is difficult to get around; the surrounding tourist offices (at Kilfenora, Ennis, Corofin, and the Cliffs of Moher) have detailed maps of the region. Hikers can set out on the 40km **Burren Way**, a trail from Liscannor to Ballyvaughan marked by yellow arrows. **Bus Éireann** (☎682 4177) connects Galway to towns in and near the Burren a few times a day in summer but infrequently during winter. In **Bally-vaughan,** stay at **O'Brien B&B ❸**, above a pub and restaurant on Main St., which has pleasing rooms, a plethora of fireplaces, and a hearty Irish breakfast. (☎707 7292. Single €20; doubles €40.) **Fallon's B&B ❸**, in **Kinvara** on the **Quay,** offers spacious rooms. (☎637 483. Breakfast €8-10. Open Apr.-Nov. Singles €35; doubles €60.)

GALWAY CITY   ☎091

In the past few years, County Galway's reputation as Ireland's cultural capital has brought flocks of young Celtophiles to Galway City (pop. 70,000). Given the 13,000 university students from Galway's two major universities, the large transient population of Europeans in their twenties, and the waves of international backpackers that arrive daily, it is no surprise that Galway is the fastest growing city in Europe. During the day, Galway's greatest draw is its close proximity to the Clare Coast and Connemara; as a starting point for seeing the west, Galway can't be beat. At night, however, the city itself becomes the center of attention, with a mesmerizing pub universe and an incredible music scene.

⌨🚻 TRANSPORTATION AND PRACTICAL INFORMATION. Trains (☎561 444) leave from Eyre Sq. for Dublin (3hr., 4-5 per day, €21-30) via Athlone (€11-14). Transfer at Athlone for lines to all other cities. **Bus Éireann** (☎562 000) leaves from Eyre Sq. for: Belfast (7hr., 2-3 per day, €28); Cork (4¼hr., 13 per day, €16); Donegal (4hr., 4 per day, €16); and Dublin (4hr., every hr., €12). The main **tourist office,** on Forster St., is a block south of Eyre Sq. Ask for the free *Galway Tourist Guide* to avoid paying for your info. (☎537 700. Open July-Aug. daily 9:30am-7:45pm; May-June and Sept. 9am-5:45pm; Oct.-Apr. Su-F 9am-5:45pm, Sa 9am-12:45pm.) Check email at **Neatsurf,** 7 St. Francis St. (☎533 976. €0.75 per 10min.)

🛏🍴 ACCOMMODATIONS AND FOOD. ◙Sleepzone ❷, Bóthar na mBán, northwest of Eyre Sq., takes the "s" out of "hostel." With a huge kitchen, big rooms, and free Internet before 10am and after 8pm, Sleepzone offers extremely comfortable stays. (☎566 999. Dorms €17-20; singles €40; doubles €54. Weekend and off-season rates vary.) ◙**Salmon Weir Hostel ❶,** 3 St. Vincent's Ave., has a homey feel that is reinforced by the laid-back staff and the affable guests. (☎561 133. Laundry €6. Curfew 3am. Dorms €9-15; doubles €35.) For a hip eatery with outstanding food, try **Anton's ❶,** just over the bridge near the Spanish Arch. The scrambled eggs with smoked salmon (€5) is delicious. (☎528 067. Open M-F 8am-6pm, Sa 10am-5pm.) **McDonagh's ❷,** 22 Quay St., has been serving up fish and chips for over a century. The restaurant boasts an incredible selection of seafood dishes. (☎561 011. Takeaway fish fillet and chips €5.60. Open daily noon-midnight; takeaway Su 5-11pm.) On Saturdays, an **open-air market** sets up on Market St. (Open Sa 8am-5pm.)

◙🏴 SIGHTS AND NIGHTLIFE. The **Nora Barnacle House,** 8 Bowling Green, was once the home of James Joyce's life long companion. Today, a friendly staff happily discusses their favorite author while pointing out his original love letters to Ms. Barnacle. (Open mid-May to mid-Sept. W-F 10am-1pm and 2-5pm; off-season by appointment. Admission €2.50.) The Lynch family ruled Galway from the 13th to the 18th century; their elegant 1320 mansion, **Lynch's Castle,** now houses the Allied Irish Bank. A small display recalls the story of an elder Lynch who hanged his own son, thus giving his name to executions performed without legal authority. The castle is in front of the Church of St. Nicholas on Market St. (Exhibit open M-F 10am-4pm, Th until 5pm. Free.) Drift down the **Corrib** for great views of the city, the countryside, and nearby castles. In mid-July, the **Galway Arts Festival** (☎583 800) attracts scores of *trad* musicians, rock groups, theater troupes, and filmmakers.

The pubs along **Quay Street** tend to cater to tourists and students, while the pubs on **Dominick Street** (across the river from the Quay) are popular with locals. ◼**The King's Head**, on High St., has three floors and nightly rock. Galway's best live music is hidden at the back of ◼**Roisín Dubh** ("The Black Rose"), on Dominick St. (Occasional cover €5-20.) **The Crane**, 2 Sea Rd., is a great place to hear nightly *trad*.

ARAN ISLANDS (OILEÁIN ÁRANN)   ☎099

On the westernmost edge of County Galway, isolated from the mainland by 32km of swelling Atlantic, lie the spectacular Aran Islands (*Oileán Árann*). Their fields are hatched with a maze of limestone, the result of centuries of farmers piling stones into thousands of meters of walls. The tremendous cliff-top forts of the early islanders give the illusion of having sprung from the limestone itself. Of the dozens of ruins, forts, churches, and holy wells that rise from the stony terrain of **Inishmore** (*Inis Mór;* pop. 900), the most amazing is the **Dún Aengus** ring fort, where concentric stones circle a sheer 100m drop. The **Inis Mór Way** is a mostly paved route that passes the majority of the island's sights and is great for biking; pick up a map at the tourist office (€2). Windswept **Inishmaan** (*Inis Meáin;* pop. 300) and **Inisheer** (*Inis Oírr;* pop. 300), the smallest island, also feature paths that pass by the islands' incomparable ruins.

Island Ferries (☎(091) 561 767) go from **Rossaveal**, west of Galway, to Inishmore (2-3 per day) and Inisheer (2 per day). **Queen of Aran II** (☎566 535), based in the islands, also leaves from Rossaveal for Inishmore (4 per day; round-trip €19, student €12). Both companies run **buses** to Rossaveal, which depart from Kinlay House, on Merchant St. in Galway, 1½hr. before ferry departure (€6, students €5). Ferries to Inishmore arrive at **Kilronan**. The **tourist office** stores luggage (€1), changes money, and finds accommodations. (☎61 263. Open July-Sept. daily 10am-6:45pm; Oct. 10am-5pm; Nov.-Mar. 10am-4pm.) ◼**Mainistir House (IHH)** ❶, less than 2km from town on the main road, is a sprawling hostel that was once a haven for musicians and writers. Don't miss the nightly vegetarian buffet (€12), an excellent place to meet other travelers. (☎61 169. Bike rental €10 per day. Laundry €6. Dorms €12; singles €20; doubles €32.) The **Spar Market** in Kilronan functions as an unofficial community center. (Open in summer M-Sa 9am-8pm, Su 10am-6pm; off-season M-Sa 9am-8pm, Su 10am-5pm.)

CONNEMARA

Connemara, a largely Irish-speaking region, is composed of a lacy net of inlets and islands, a gang of inland mountains, and desolate stretches of bog. This thinly populated region of northwest County Galway harbors some of Ireland's most breathtaking scenery, from rocky offshore islands to the green slopes of the area's two major mountain ranges, the **Twelve Bens** and the **Maamturks.**

CLIFDEN (AN CLOCHÁN)   ☎095

Busy, English-speaking Clifden has more amenities than its old-world, Irish-speaking neighbors. Clifden's proximity to the scenic bogs and mountains of Connemara attracts crowds of tourists, who use it as a base for exploring the region. The **Connemara Walking Centre,** on Market St., runs tours of the bogs and explores the history, folklore, and geology of Connemara. (☎21 379. Open Mar.-Oct. M-Sa 10am-6pm. 1-2 tours per day. €19-32.) **Bus Éireann** goes from the library on Market St. to

IRELAND

Galway via Oughterard (2hr., 1-6 per day, €9) and Westport via Leenane (1½hr., late June to Aug. M-Sa, 1-3 per day). Michael Nee runs a bus from the courthouse to Galway (June-Sept. 2 per day, €11). Rent a **bike** at **Mannion's,** on Bridge St. (☎21 160. €9 per day, €60 per week; deposit €20. Open Su 10am-1pm and 5-7pm, M-Sa 9:30am-6:30pm.) The **tourist office** is on Galway Rd. (☎21 163. Open July-Aug. M-Sa 9am-6pm, Su noon-4pm; June M-Sa 10am-6pm; Sept.-Oct. and Mar.-May M-Sa 10am-5pm.) **B&Bs** are everywhere and start at €25 per person. **Clifden Town Hostel (IHH) ❶,** on Market St., has great facilities and spotless rooms in a 180-year-old house near the pubs. (☎21 076. Call ahead Nov.-Feb. Dorms €12-15; doubles €32-34; triples €32; quads €56-60.) Tranquil **Shanaheever Campsite ❶** is 1.5km outside Clifden on Westport Rd. (☎21 018. Showers. Laundry €6. €12 per person with tent or trailer.) Most restaurants in Clifden are attached to pubs and serve the standard fare. **Cullen's Bistro & Coffee Shop ❸,** Market St., is family-run, and cooks up hearty meals and delicious desserts. (☎21 983. Thick Irish stew €13. Open daily 11am-10pm.) **SuperValu supermarket** is on Market St. (Open M-F 9am-7pm, Su 10am-6pm.)

CONNEMARA NATIONAL PARK ☎095

Connemara National Park occupies 12.5 square kilometers of mountainous countryside that thousands of birds call home. Bogs constitute much of the park's terrain, often thinly covered by a deceptive screen of grass and flowers; be prepared to get muddy. The **Snuffaunboy Nature** and **Ellis Wood trails** are easy 20min. hikes. Trails lead from the back of the Ellis Wood trail and along Bog Road onto **Diamond Hill.** Although erosion control efforts have kept Diamond Hill trail closed for the past 2 years, it's worth a call to the Visitors Centre (see below) to check if it's reopened; the 2hr. hike rewards hikers with views of the bog, the harbor, and the forest. Experienced hikers often head for the **Twelve Bens** (*Na Benna Beola;* the Twelve Pins), a rugged range that reaches 2200m heights. (The range is not recommended for solo or beginning hikers.) A tour of all 12 bens takes experienced hikers about 10hr. **Biking** the 65km circle through Clifden, Letterfrack, and the Inagh Valley is truly captivating, but only appropriate for fit bikers. A guidebook mapping out 30min. walks (€6.40) is available at the **Visitors Centre,** where the staff helps plan longer hikes. They'll also explain the differences between hummocks and tussocks. (☎41 054. Open July-Aug. daily 9:30am-6:30pm; June 10am-6:30pm; May and Sept. 10am-5:30pm. €2.50, students €1.25.) Hikers often base themselves at the **Ben Lettery Hostel (An Óige/HI) ❶,** in Ballinafad. (☎51 136. Dorms €10-12.)

WESTPORT ☎098

Palm trees and steep hills lead down to Westport's busy Georgian streets. Nearby, the conical **Croagh Patrick** rises 650m over Clew Bay. The summit has been revered as a holy site for thousands of years. St. Patrick worked here in AD 441, praying for 40 days and nights to banish snakes from Ireland. Climbers start their excursion from the 15th-century **Murrisk Abbey,** several kilometers west of Westport on R395 toward Louisburgh. Buses go to Murrisk (2-3 per day); for groups, cabs (☎27 171) are cheaper and more convenient. Sheep calmly rule **Clare Island,** a desolate but beautiful speck in the Atlantic. Take a bus to Roonah Pier, 29km from Westport, and then a ferry to the island. (Bus departs from Westport's tourist office at 10am and returns by 6pm; €25 for bus and ferry combined.) **Matt Molloy's,** on Bridge St., is owned by a member of the Irish band the Chieftains and has nightly *trad.* (Open M-W 12:30-11:30pm, Th-Sa 12:30pm-12:30am, Su 12:30-11pm.)

Trains arrive at the Altamont St. Station (☎25 253), a 5min. walk up the North Mall, from Dublin (2-3 per day, €21-23) via Athlone. **Buses** leave Mill St. for Galway (2hr., 4-8 per day, €12). The **tourist office** is on James St. (☎25 711. Open daily 9am-5:45pm.) **B&Bs** cluster on **Altamont Road** and **The Quay.** A conservatory and garden grace ▧The Granary Hostel ❶, a 25min. walk from town, just at the bend in The Quay. (☎25 903. Open Apr.-Sept. Dorms €10.) Altamont House ❶, Altamont St., has award-winning breakfasts and incredible hospitality that have kept travelers coming back for 36 years. (☎25 226. Singles €25, with bath €27; doubles €50/44.) Restaurants are concentrated on Bridge Street. The SuperValu supermarket is on Shop St. (Open M-Sa 8:30am-9pm, Su 10am-6pm.)

NORTHWEST IRELAND

The farmland of the upper Shannon stretches northward into County Sligo's mountains, lakes, and ancient monuments. A mere sliver of land connects Co. Sligo to Co. Donegal, the second-largest and most remote of the Republic's counties. Donegal's *gaeltacht* is a storehouse of genuine, unadulterated Irish tradition.

SLIGO   ☎071

Since the beginning of the 20th century, Sligo has seen a literary pilgrimage of William Butler Yeats devotees; the poet spent summers in town as a child and set many of his poems around Sligo Bay. Sligo Town, the commercial center, is an excellent base from which to explore Yeats's haunts. The well-preserved 13th-century Sligo Abbey is on Abbey St. (Open Apr.-Oct. daily 10am-6pm; Nov.-Mar. reduced hours. €1.90, students €0.70.) The Model Arts Centre and Niland Gallery, on the Mall, houses one of the finest collections of modern Irish art. (Open June-Oct. Su noon-5:30pm and Tu-Sa 10am-5:30pm; Sept.-Apr. Tu-Sa 10am-5:30pm. Free.) Yeats is buried in Drumcliffe Churchyard, on the N15, 6.5km northwest of Sligo. Buses from Sligo to Derry stop at Drumcliffe (10min., 3-7 per day, round-trip €4). Over 70 pubs crowd the main streets of Sligo. The trendy ▧Shoot the Crows, on Grattan St., has fairies and skulls dangling from the ceiling.

Trains (☎69 888) go from Lord Edward St. to Dublin (3 hr., 4 per day, €22) via Carrick-on-Shannon and Mullingar. From the same station, buses (☎60 066) head to: Belfast (4hr., 2-3 per day, €22); Derry (3hr., 4-7 per day, €15); Dublin (3-4hr., 4-5 per day, €14); Galway (2½hr., 4-6 per day, €12); and Westport (2½hr., 1-4 per day, €13). Turn left on Lord Edward St., then follow the signs right onto Adelaid St. and around the corner to Temple St. to find the tourist office. (☎61 201. Open June-Aug. M-Sa 9am-7pm, Su 10am-6pm; Oct.-May M-F 9am-5pm.) B&Bs cluster on Pearse Road, on the south side. Eden Hill Holiday Hostel (IHH) ❶, off Pearse Rd., has Victorian decor and a friendly staff. From the town center, follow Pearse Rd., turn right at the Marymount sign, and take another right after one block. (☎43 204. Laundry facilities Dorms €13.) A Tesco supermarket is on O'Connell St. (☎62 788. Open M-Tu and Sa 8:30am-7pm, W-F 8:30am-9pm, Su 10am-6pm.)

COUNTY DONEGAL AND SLIEVE LEAGUE   ☎073

Tourists are a rarity in County Donegal. Its geographic isolation in the northwest has spared it from the widespread deforestation of the rest of Ireland; vast wooded areas engulf many of Donegal's mountain chains, while the coastline alternates between beaches and cliffs. Travelers use Donegal Town as the gateway to the county. Buses (☎21 101) stop outside the Abbey Hotel on The Diamond and run to Dublin (4hr., 5-7 per day, €14) and Galway (4hr., 3-4 per day, €14). With your back to the Abbey Hotel, turn right; the tourist office, on Quay St., is just outside of The Diamond. (☎21 148. Open July-Aug. M-Sa 9am-6pm, Su noon-4pm; Sept.-Oct. and Easter-June M-F 9am-5pm, Sa 10am-2pm.) ▧Donegal Independent Town Hostel (IHH) ❶, on Killybegs Rd., is family-run and has a homey atmosphere. (☎(97) 22 805. Call ahead. Dorms €10.50; doubles €24. Camping €6.)

The **Slieve League Peninsula**'s rocky cliffs, Europe's highest, jut to the west of Donegal Town. The cliffs and mountains of this sparsely populated area harbor coastal hamlets, untouched beaches, and dramatic scenery. **Glencolmcille** (glen-kaul-um-KEEL), on the western tip of the peninsula, is a parish of several tiny villages wedged between two monstrous cliffs. The villages are renowned for their handmade products, particularly sweaters. On sunny days, visitors to the **Silver Strand** are rewarded with stunning views of the gorgeous beach and rocky cliffs; the trek along the Slieve League coastline begins here. Bus Éireann **buses** run from Donegal Town to Glencolmcille and Dungloe, stopping in tiny **Kilcar** (1-3 per day), the gateway to Donegal's *gaeltacht* and a commercial base for many Donegal tweed weavers. Many Slieve League hikers stay in Kilcar, where they can comfortably drive, bike, or hike to the mountains. The fabulous **Derrylahan Hostel (IHH) ❶** is 3km from Kilcar on the coast road to Carrick; call for pickup. (☎38 079. Laundry €7. Dorms €10; singles €14; doubles €28. **Camping** €6.) In Glencolmcille, sleep at the hillside **Dooey Hostel (IHO) ❶**, which has an ocean view and a beautiful garden. (☎30 130. Dorms €9.50; doubles €21. **Camping** €5.50.)

NORTHERN IRELAND

FACTS AND FIGURES: NORTHERN IRELAND	
Official Name: Northern Ireland.	**Time Zone:** GMT.
Capital: Belfast.	**Language:** English.
Population: 1,700,000.	**Religions:** Protestant (40%), Roman Catholic (40%), other (20%).
Land Area: 14,160 sq. km.	

Despite its best efforts to present an image of reconciliation and progress in recent years, Northern Ireland still often finds itself associated with the specter of its difficult past. While the aftermath of the Troubles is undeniably visible in much of the North, the sectarian strife that caused it has slowly abated. Today, acts of violence and extremist fringe groups are less prominent than the division in civil society that sends Protestants and Catholics to separate neighborhoods, separate stores, separate pubs, and often separate schools, with separate, though similar, traditional songs and slang. The 1998 Good Friday Agreement, which granted Home Rule to Northern Ireland with the hope of resolving some of the region's struggles, has been struggling itself. London briefly took the reins again in the summer of 2001, and both sides renewed their efforts to make their country as peaceful as it is beautiful. While everyday life in Northern Ireland may be divided, its landscape and society are for the most part quiet and peaceful.

N. IRELAND	❶	❷	❸	❹	❺
ACCOMMODATIONS	under £12	£12-19	£20-29	£30-44	over £45
FOOD	under £3	£3-5	£6-9	£10-14	over £15

PHONE CODES	The regional code for all of Northern Ireland is 028. From outside Northern Ireland, dial int'l dialing prefix (see inside back cover) + 44 (from the Republic, 048) + 28 + local number.

BELFAST ☎028

Belfast (pop. 330,000), the second-largest city on the island, is the focus of the North's cultural, commercial, and political activity. Acclaimed writers and the annual arts festival in November support Belfast's reputation as a thriving artistic center, with art galleries, coffee shops, and black-clad sub-cultural connoisseurs all contributing to that view. West Belfast's famous sectarian murals are now perhaps the most informative source on the effects of what the locals call "the Troubles." Despite the violent associations conjured by the name Belfast, the city feels more neighborly than most international (and even Irish) visitors expect.

Belfast

🏠 **ACCOMMODATIONS**
The Ark (IHH), **7**
Arnie's Backpackers (IHH), **5**
Belfast Hostel (HINI), **3**
Botanic Lodge, **8**
Camera Guest House, **9**

🍴 **FOOD**
Azzura, **1**
Benedict's, **4**
Bookfinders, **6**
St. George's Market, **2**

▐ TRANSPORTATION

Flights: Belfast International Airport (BFS; ☎9442 4848; www.belfastairport.com), in Aldergrove. **Airbus** (☎9033 3000) runs from the airport to the Europa and Laganside bus stations (M-Sa every 30min., Su about every hr.; £6). **Trains** connect the **Belfast City Airport** (Sydenham Halt), at the harbor, to Central Station (£1).

Trains: Central Station (☎9066 6630), on East Bridge St., runs trains to: Derry (2hr., 3-9 per day, £8.20) and Dublin (2hr., 5-8 per day, £20). **Centrelink** buses run from the station to the city center (free with rail tickets).

Buses: Europa Station (☎9066 6630), off Great Victoria St., serves the north coast, the west, and the Republic. Buses to Derry (1¾hr., 7-19 per day, £7.50) and Dublin (3hr., 6-7 per day, £12). **Laganside Station** (☎9066 6630), Donegall Quay, serves Northern Ireland's east coast. **Centrelink** buses connect both stations with the city center.

Ferries: SeaCat (☎(08705) 523 523; www.seacat.co.uk) leaves for: Heysham, England (4hr., Apr.-Nov. 1-2 per day); the Isle of Man (2¾hr., Apr.-Nov. M, W, F daily); and Troon, Scotland (2½hr., 2-3 per day). Fares £10-30 without car.

Local Transportation: The red **Citybus Network** (☎9066 6630) is supplemented by **Ulsterbus's** suburban "blue buses." Travel within the city center £1.10, students and children 55p. **Centrelink** buses traverse the city (every 12min., M-F 7:25am-9:15pm, Sa 8:35am-9:15pm; £1.10, free with bus or rail ticket). Late **Nightlink** buses shuttle to small towns outside the city (F-Sa 1 and 2am; £3, payable on board).

Taxis: Value Cabs (☎9080 9080). Residents of West and North Belfast use the huge **black cabs;** some are metered, and some follow set routes.

▐ ▐ ORIENTATION AND PRACTICAL INFORMATION

Buses arrive at the Europa bus station on **Great Victoria Street.** To the northeast is the **City Hall** in Donegall Square. South of the bus station, Great Victoria St. meets **Dublin Road** at **Shaftesbury Square;** this stretch of Great Victoria St. between the bus station and Shaftesbury Sq. is known as the **Golden Mile** for its high-brow establishments and Victorian architecture. **Botanic Avenue** and **Bradbury Place** (which becomes **University Road**) extend south from Shaftesbury Sq. into the **Queen's Uni-**

versity area, where cafes, pubs, and budget lodgings await. To get to Donegall Sq. from Central Station, turn left, walk down East Bridge St., turn right on Oxford St., and make your first left on **May Street,** which runs into Donegall Sq.; or, take the Centrelink bus. Divided from the rest of Belfast by the **Westlink Motorway,** working-class **West Belfast** has been more politically volatile; the area is best seen by day. The Protestant neighborhood stretches along **Shankill Road,** just north of the Catholic neighborhood, which is centered around **Falls Road.** The two are separated by the **peace line.** During the week, the area north of City Hall is essentially deserted at night, and it's a good idea to use taxis after dark.

Tourist Office: The Belfast Welcome Centre, 47 Donegall Pl. (☎9024 6609). Has an incredibly helpful and comprehensive free booklet on Belfast and info on surrounding areas. Open June-Sept. M 9:30am-7pm, Tu-Sa 9am-7pm, Su noon-5pm; Oct.-May M 9am-5:30pm, Tu-Sa 9am-7pm.

Banks: Banks and **ATMs** are on almost every corner. **Bank of Ireland,** 54 Donegall Pl. (☎9023 4334). Open M-F 9am-4:30pm.

Laundry: Globe Drycleaners & Launderers, 37-39 Botanic Ave. (☎9024 3956). About £3-4 per load. Open M-F 8am-9pm, Sa-Su noon-6pm.

Emergency: ☎999; no coins required. **Police,** 65 Knock Rd. (☎9065 0222).

Hospitals: Belfast City Hospital, 9 Lisburn Rd. (☎9032 9241). From Shaftesbury Sq., follow Bradbury Pl. and take a right at the fork. **Royal Victoria Hospital,** 12 Grosvenor Rd. (☎9024 0503). From Donegall Sq., take Howard St. west to Grosvenor Rd.

Internet Access: Belfast Central Library, 122 Royal Ave. (☎9050 9150). £1.50 per 30min. Open M and Th 9am-8pm, Tu-W and F 9am-5:30pm, Sa 9:30am-1pm.

Post Office: Central Post Office, 25 Castle Pl. (☎9032 3740). *Poste Restante* mail comes here. Open M-Sa 9am-5:30pm. **Postal Code:** BT1 1NB. Branch offices: **Botanic Garden,** 95 University Rd., across from the university (☎9038 1309; **Postal Code:** BT7 1NG); **Botanic Avenue,** 1-5 Botanic Ave. (☎9032 6177; **Postal Code:** BT2 7DA). Branch offices open M-F 8:45am-5:30pm, Sa 10am-12:30pm.

⚑ ACCOMMODATIONS

Despite a competitive hostel market, Belfast's fluctuating tourism and rising rents have shrunk the number of available cheap digs. Most budget accommodations are located near Queen's University, south of the city center, which is convenient to pubs and restaurants. Take **Citybus** #69, 70, 71, 83, 84, or 86 from Donegall Sq. to areas in the south. B&Bs occupy virtually every house between **Malone Road** and **Lisburn Road,** just south of Queen's University.

▨ **Arnie's Backpackers (IHH),** 63 Fitzwilliam St. (☎9024 2867). From Bradbury Pl., fork left onto University Rd.; Fitzwilliam St. is on the right. Friendly atmosphere in the comfort of an antiquated building with a drawing room to match. Dorms £7-9.50. ❶

▨ **Camera Guesthouse,** 44 Wellington Park (☎9066 0026). A pristine and light-filled family-run guesthouse. Offers a fabulous breakfast, with a wide selection of organic options and teas. Singles £25, with bath £40; doubles £48/55. July discounts available. ❸

Belfast Hostel (HINI), 22 Donegall Rd. (☎9031 5435), off Shaftesbury Sq. Clean and inviting interior is highlighted by colorful rooms and floors. Books tours of Belfast and Giant's Causeway. Breakfast £2. Laundry £3. Reception open 24hr. Dorms £8.50-10.50; singles £17; triples £33. Expect higher prices on the weekend. ❶

The Ark (IHH), 18 University St. (☎9032 9626. Follow the Great Victoria St. through Shaftsbury Sq., taking Botanic Ave., and then make a right on University St.; look for the blue grating on the right. The Ark has nice dorm rooms with a bustling, well-stocked kitchen to boot. They also book tours of Belfast (£8) and Giant's Causeway (£16). Weekend luggage storage. Laundary £4. Internet access £1 per 20min. Curfew 2am. Coed Dorms £8.50-9.50; doubles £32. ❶

Botanic Lodge, 87 Botanic Ave. (☎9032 7682). Offers B&B comfort surrounded by many eateries and a short walk to the city center. All rooms with sink and TV, some with bath. Singles £25, with bath £35; doubles £40/45. ❸

🍴 FOOD

Dublin Road, Botanic Avenue, and the **Golden Mile** have a high concentration of restaurants. 📖**Azzura** ❷, 8 Church Ln., has gourmet pizzas, pastas, and sandwiches, with options for both veggie and meat lovers. (Entrees under £4. Open M-Sa 9am-5pm.) **Benedict's** ❷, 7-21 Bradbury Pl., is located in a swanky restaurant, but that doesn't mean you need to pay extravagant prices for their great meals. Come between 5:30-7:30pm, and as part of their "Beat the Clock" gimmick the time you order becomes the price you pay. (Open M-Sa 7-10am, noon-2:30pm, and 5:30-10:30pm; Su 5:30-9pm.) Mismatched dishes mingle with counter-culture paraphernalia at **Bookfinders** ❶, 47 University Rd. (Sandwiches under £3. Open M-Sa 10am-5:30pm.) Find fruits and vegetables at **St. George's Market,** on East Bridge St., between May St. and Oxford St. (Open F 8am-2pm and Sa 6am-noon.)

👁 SIGHTS

DONEGALL SQUARE. The most dramatic and impressive piece of architecture in Belfast is appropriately its administrative and geographic center, the **Belfast City Hall.** Its green copper dome is visible from any point in the city. Check out the forboding **Queen Victoria statue** in front of the main entrance. (1hr. tour June-Sept. M-F 11am, 2pm, and 3pm.; Sa 2:30pm; Oct.-May M-F 11am and 2:30pm; Sa 2:30pm. Free.) The **Linen Hall Library,** 52 Fountain St., contains a collection of documents related to the Troubles in the North. (Open M-F 9:30am-5:30pm, Sa 9:30am-4pm.)

CORNMARKET AND ST. ANNE'S CATHEDRAL. North of the city center, this shopping district envelops eight blocks around **Castle Street** and **Royal Avenue.** Relics of old Belfast remain in the **entries,** or tiny alleys. **St. Anne's Cathedral,** also known as the **Belfast Cathedral,** was begun in 1899. Each of its pillars names one of Belfast's professions: Agriculture, Art, Freemasonry, Healing, Industry, Music, Science, Shipbuilding, Theology, and "Womanhood." (Donegall St. Open M-Sa 10am-4pm.)

THE DOCKS AND EAST BELFAST. Belfast's newest mega-attraction, **Odyssey,** 2 Queen's Quay, a gigantic center that houses five different science attractions, promises to bring back the hordes to this previously dilapidated industrial area. (☎9045 1055.) The best feature is the **W5 Discovery Centre,** a science and technology museum that beckons geeks of all ages to play with pulley chairs, laser harps, and robots. (Open M-Sa 10am-5pm, Su noon-5pm; £5.50, students and seniors £4.)

THE GOLDEN MILE. This strip along Great Victoria St. contains many of Belfast's jewels. Of these, the **Grand Opera House** is the city's pride and joy, sadly making it a repeated bombing target for the IRA. Recently, it was restored to its original splendor at enormous cost, only to be bombed again. However, more peaceful times have allowed the Grand Opera House to flourish. Enjoy the current calm either by attending a performance or by taking a tour on Saturdays. (Tours 11am; £3, seniors and children £2. Box office open M-Sa 8:30am-6pm.) If opera is not your thing, visit the popular **Crown Liquor Saloon,** 46 Great Victoria St., a showcase of carved wood, gilded ceilings, and stained glass recently restored by the National Trust. Finally, check in to the **Europa Hotel,** which has the dubious distinction of being "Europe's most bombed hotel," having survived 32 blasts.

WEST BELFAST AND THE MURALS. West Belfast is not a "sight" in the traditional sense. The streets display political **murals,** which you will come across quickly as you wander among the houses. Be discreet if photographing the murals. It is illegal to photograph military installations; do so and your film may be confiscated. The Protestant Orangemen's **marching season** (July 4-12) is a risky time to visit the area, since the parades are underscored by mutual antagonism. Cab tours provide a fascinating commentary detailing the murals, paraphernalia, and sights on both sides of the peace line. Michael Johnston of **Black Taxi Tours** has made a name for himself with his witty, objective presentations. (☎0800 052 3914; www.belfasttours.com. £9 per person for groups of 3 or more.)

ENTERTAINMENT AND NIGHTLIFE

Belfast's cultural events and performances are covered in the monthly *Arts Council Artslink* (free at the tourist office). The **Grand Opera House,** on Great Victoria St., stages a mix of opera, ballet, musicals, and drama. Buy tickets at the box office, 2-4 Great Victoria St. (☎9024 1919. Tickets from £12.50.) The **Queen's University Festival** (☎9066 7687) in November draws film, opera, and other musical performances. For more, consult *The List,* available in the tourist office and hostels.

Pubs close early; start crawling while the sun's still up. In Cornmarket, begin with an afternoon pint at Belfast's oldest pub, **White's Tavern,** Winecellar Entry, off High St., where great *trad* music can be found. (Open M-Sa 11:30am-11pm.) North of Donegall Sq., **Katy Daly's Pub** is a high-ceilinged, wood-paneled, antique pub with a young crowd. Catch the local bands that frequent it Tuesday to Thursday and Saturday. If you're still standing, stumble to the **Apartment,** 2 Donegall Sq. West, where Belfast's beautiful people come for pre-clubbing cocktails. (21+ after 6pm. Open M-F 8am-1am, Sa 9am-1am, Su noon-midnight.) Near the **Queen's University** area, **The Botanic Inn (the "Bot")** is almost an official extracurricular for its student regulars. (20+. Cover £2. Open daily 11:30am-1am.)

Explore the club scene at the **Milk Club Bar,** 10-14 Tomb St., which is packed with people letting loose to pop hits. (Open daily noon-3am.) Socialites head to **The Fly,** 5-6 Lower Crescent, a fun vodka lounge with three floors on which to relax. (Open M-Th 9pm-1:30am, F-Sa 9pm-1:45am.) **The Kremlin,** 96 Donegall St., is Belfast's hottest gay spot. Free Internet upstairs is upstaged by free condoms downstairs. (Bar open M-Th 4pm-3am, F-Su 1pm-3am.)

DERRY (LONDONDERRY) ☎028

Modern Derry is in the middle of a determined and largely successful effort to cast off the legacy of its political Troubles. Although the landscape was razed by years of bombings and violence still erupts occasionally during the marching season (July 4-12), recent years have been relatively peaceful, and today's rebuilt city looks sparklingly new. Derry's **city walls,** 5.5m high and 6m thick, erected between 1614 and 1619, have never been breached—hence Derry's nickname "the Maiden City." The raised portion of the wall past New Gate was built to protect **St. Columb's Cathedral,** off Bishop St., the symbolic focus of the city's Protestant defenders. (Open Easter-Oct. M-Sa 9am-5pm; Nov.-Mar. M-Sa 9am-4pm. Suggested donation £1.) At Union Hall Place, just inside Magazine Gate, the **Tower Museum**'s engaging exhibits recount Derry's history. (Open July-Aug. M-Sa 10am-5pm, Su 2-5pm; Sept.-June Tu-Sa 10am-5pm. £4.20, students £1.60.) West of the city walls, Derry's residential neighborhoods—both the Protestant **Waterside** and **Fountain Estate** as well as the Catholic **Bog-**

side—display brilliant murals. After dark, check out ▓**Mullan's,** 13 Little James St., an incredible pub with stained-glass ceilings and bronze lion statues. (Open M-Sa 10am-2am, Su noon-12:30am.)

Trains (☎7134 2228) arrive on Duke St., Waterside, from Belfast (2½hr., 4-9 per day, £8.20). A free Rail-Link bus connects the **train station** and the **bus station,** on Foyle St., between the walled city and the river. **Ulsterbus** (☎7126 2261) goes to Belfast (1½-3hr., 6-16 per day, £8) and Dublin (4¼hr., 4-6 per day, £11). The **tourist office** is at 44 Foyle St. (☎7126 7284. Open July-Sept. M-F 9am-7pm, Sa 10am-6pm, Su 10am-5pm; Nov.-Easter M-F 9am-5pm; Easter-June and Oct. M-F 9am-5pm, Sa 10am-5pm.) Go down Strand Rd. and turn left on Asylum Rd. just before the RUC station to reach the friendly ▓**Derry City Independent Hostel ❶,** 4 Asylum Rd. (☎7137 7989. Breakfast included. Free **Internet** access. Dorms £9; singles £13; doubles £26.) At **The Saddler's House (No. 36) ❸,** 36 Great James St., the friendly owners welcome you into their lovely Victorian home, where great breakfasts can be found. (☎7126 9691. Singles £25; doubles £45.) There is a **Tesco supermarket** in the Quayside Shopping Centre just a short walk from the walled city along Strand Rd. (Open M-Th 9am-9pm, F 8:30am-9pm, Sa 8:30am-8pm, Su 1-6pm.) **Postal Code:** BT48.

GLENS OF ANTRIM ☎028

Glaciers left nine deep scars in the mountainous coastline of northeastern County Antrim. Over the years, water collected in these glens, fostering lush flora not usually found in Ireland. The glens and their mountains and waterfalls are best visited as daytrips from the villages of Glenarm and Cushendall.

▐ **TRANSPORTATION. Ulsterbus** (☎9032 0011) #162 runs from Belfast to Glenarm (1-7 per day, £3-6) and sometimes continues to Waterfoot, Cushendall, and Cushendun (2-4 per day). Bus #150 runs from Ballymena to Glenariff (M-Sa 5 per day, £2.60), then to Waterfoot, Cushendall, and Cushendun (3-5 per day, £4.30).

GLENARM. Lovely Glenarm was once the chief dwelling place of the MacDonnell Clan. The village is comprised of centuries-old houses and is a starting point for several short walks. The huge arch at the top of Altmore St. marks the entrance to **Glenarm Forest,** where trails trace the river's path. (Open daily 9am-dusk.) The **tourist office** is in the town council building. (☎2884 1087. **Internet** £4 per hr. Open M 10am-4pm, Tu-F noon-7pm, Su 2-6pm.) **Riverside B&B ❷,** Toberwine St., has quaint rooms with lovely baths. (☎2884 1474. £18 per person.)

THE HIDDEN DEAL

THE EMERALD ISLE'S GOLDEN EGG

Many of Ireland's most touristed sights—its national parks, museums, monuments and gardens—are owned and operated by the Irish Department of Arts and Heritage. While this government-run department keeps the price of admission to these sights quite low, the accumulated cost of visiting each can grow too high for the ordinary budget traveler to afford.

Recently, the Department of Heritage has started to offer discount cards to those wishing to visit multiple sights. Their **Dúchas Heritage Discount Card** may just be Ireland's greatest hidden deal. Not only does the ticket give you access to all of the sights owned and operated by the Department of Heritage, it also gives you one full year of access so that you can return again at your leisure.

There are ten sights in Dublin alone, including the Casino, Kilmainham Gaol, St. Audeon's Church, and the Royal Hospital Kilmainham. Other sights around Ireland include a slew of castles and ruins. The average price to visit one sight is between €2.50-5, so the card—at €19—is a steal.

The Irish Heritage Discount Card. €19.05, students and children €7.62, seniors €12.70, families €45.72. For more info call ☎01 647 2461; or within Ireland ☎1850 600 601; www.heritageireland.ie/en/HeritageCard.

GLENARIFF. Antrim's broadest (and arguably most beautiful) glen, Glenariff lies 6.5km south of Waterfoot along Glenariff Rd., in the large **Glenariff Forest Park.** Bus #150 stops at the park entrance (3-5 per day); if you're walking from Waterfoot, you can enter the park 2.5km downhill of the entrance by taking the road that branches left toward the Manor Lodge Restaurant. The stunning 5km ⊠**Waterfall Trail** follows the fern-lined Glenariff River from the park entrance to the Manor Lodge. (☎2175 8769. Open daily 10am-dusk. £1.50 per pedestrian, £3 per car.)

CUSHENDALL. Cushendall, nicknamed the capital of the Glens, houses a variety of goods, services, and pubs unavailable elsewhere in the region. The **tourist office,** 25 Mill St., is near the bus stop at the northern end of town. (☎2177 1180. Open July-Sept. M-F 10am-5:30pm, Sa 10am-4:30pm; Oct. to mid-Dec. and Feb.-June Tu-Sa 10am-1pm.) A warm welcome and huge rooms await at ⊠**Glendale ❷,** 46 Coast Rd., south of town overlooking the sea. (☎2177 1495. £18 per person.)

CUSHENDUN. This minuscule, picturesque seaside village is 8km north of Cushendall on A2. Its white-washed and black-shuttered buildings sit next to a vast beach with wonderful, murky **caves** carved within red sea cliffs. Visitors can choose between the immaculate **B&B ❸** and **camping barn ❶** at Drumkeerin, just west of town on the A2 at 201a Torr Rd. (☎2176 1554. B&B singles £20; doubles £35. Camping barn £8.) **Mary McBride's ❶,** 2 Main St., used to hold the *Guinness Book of World Records* title "smallest bar in Europe"—until it expanded. (☎2176 1511. Steak-and-Guinness pie £5. Food served daily noon-9pm.)

CAUSEWAY COAST ☎028

Past Cushendun, the northern coast becomes even more dramatic. Sea-battered cliffs tower 185m over white beaches before giving way to the spectacular geology of **Giant's Causeway,** for which the region is named. Thousands of visitors swarm to the site today, but few venture beyond the visitors center to the stunning and easily accessible coastline that stretches beyond.

▐ **TRANSPORTATION. Ulsterbus** (☎7043 334) #172 runs between Ballycastle and Portrush along the coast (1hr., 3-7 per day, £3.50). The Antrim Coaster #252 runs from Belfast to Portstewart via most small towns along the coast (2 per day). The open-topped Bushmills Bus traces the coast between Coleraine, 8km south of Portrush, and the Causeway (July-Aug. 7 per day).

BALLYCASTLE AND ENVIRONS. The Causeway Coast leaves the sleepy glens behind when it hits **Ballycastle,** a bubbly seaside town that shelters tourists bound for Giant's Causeway. **Ulsterbus** #162A goes to Cushendall via Cushendun (50min., M-F daily, £3), and #131 goes to Belfast (3hr., M-Sa 5-6 per day, £6.10). The **tourist office** is in Sheskburn House, 7 Mary St. (☎2076 2024. Open July-Aug. M-F 9:30am-7pm, Sa 10am-6pm, Su 2-6pm; Sept.-June M-F 9:30am-5pm.) Sleep at the friendly and comfortable **Castle Hostel (IHH) ❶,** 62 Quay Rd. (☎2076 2337. Dorms £7.50.)

Just off the coast of Ballycastle, bumpy, boomerang-shaped **Rathlin Island** ("Fort of the Sea") is home to more puffins (pop. 20,000) than people (pop. 100). A **minibus** drives to the **Kebble Bird Sanctuary,** 7km from the harbor (20min., every 45min., £2.80). Caledonian MacBrayne (☎2076 9299) **ferries** run to the island from the pier at Ballycastle, up the hill from Quay Rd. (45min., 1-3 per day, round-trip £8.40).

Eight kilometers west of Ballycastle, the modest village of **Ballintoy** attracts the crowds on their way to the tiny **Carrick-a-rede Island.** From the mainland, cross the fishermen's rope bridge (about 2m wide) over the dizzying 30m drop to rocks and sea below; be extremely careful in windy weather. A sign marks the turn-off for the bridge from the coastal road east of Ballintoy. The island's **Larrybane sea cliffs** are home to a variety of species of gulls. The **Sheep Island View Hostel (IHH) ❶** is at 42A Main St. in Ballintoy. (☎2076 9391. Continental breakfast £3. Laundry £2. Dorms £10. **Camping** £5 per person.)

GIANT'S CAUSEWAY. Geologists believe that the unique rock formations found at ▨**Giant's Causeway** were formed some 60 million years ago. Comprised of over 40,000 perfectly symmetrical hexagonal basalt columns, the site resembles a large descending staircase that leads out from the cliffs to the ocean's floor below. Ulsterbuses #172 to Portrush, the #252 Antrim Coaster, and the Bushmills Bus all drop off visitors at the **Giant's Causeway Visitors Centre.** A minibus (£1.20) runs from the center to the columns. (Causeway open 24hr. Free. Visitors Centre open July-Aug. daily 10am-7pm; June 10am-6pm; Sept.-Oct. 10am-5pm; Nov.-Feb. 10am-4:30pm; Mar-Apr. M-F 10am-5pm, Sa-Su 10am-5:30pm; May daily 10am-5:30pm.)

ITALY (ITALIA)

One of the few countries whose very geography seems active—it resembles a boot poised to kick Sicily clear across the Mediterranean—Italy has never been inclined to sit back quietly. After bursting onstage as the base for the ambitious Roman empire, it became persecutor and popularizer of an upstart religion called Christianity and later served as center to the artistic and philosophical Renaissance. Today it has emerged as a world power that has changed governments more than 50 times since World War II. Countless invasions have left the land rich with examples of nearly every artistic era; Egyptian obelisks, Etruscan huts, Greek temples, Augustan arches, Byzantine mosaics, Renaissance *palazzi*, Baroque fountains, and postmodern superstructures sprawl across its 20 regions. From perfect pasta to the creation of pizza, Italy knows that the quickest way to a country's happiness is through its stomach. Italy is also the champion of romance—passionate lovers shout their *amore* from the rooftops of southern Italy and Venice. Somewhere between the leisurely gondola rides and the frenetic nightclubs, you too will fall in love with Italy.

FACTS AND FIGURES

Official Name: Italian Republic.

Capital: Rome.

Major Cities: Florence, Milan, Naples, Venice.

Population: 57,000,000.

Land Area: 301,230 sq. km.

Time Zone: GMT+1.

Language: Italian; some German, French and Slovenian.

Religions: Roman Catholic (98%).

DISCOVER ITALY

The ideal place to begin any Italian voyage is **Rome** (p. 603), where you can view the rubble of the toga-clad empire, the cathedrals of high Christianity, and the art of the Renaissance. Shoot north to Umbria and shun worldly wealth à la Saint Francis in **Assisi** (p. 679) before checking out the black-and-white *duomo* of stunning **Siena** (p. 676) and the medieval towers of **San Gimignano** (p. 676). Continue northward to enchanting **Florence** (p. 667), where burnt-orange roofs shelter works by Renaissance masters. The famous Leaning Tower is, of course, in **Pisa** (p. 678). Visit the mysterious shroud at **Turin** (p. 647) before heading to gritty **Genoa** (p. 657), which is no postcard darling but has personality and palaces. Nearby, explore the five colorful fishing villages of **Cinque Terre** (p. 661) on the Italian Riviera. Away from the coast, the nightlife in fashionable **Milan** (p. 649) is unrivaled, as is the beauty of **Lake Como** (p. 656). Dreamy **Verona** (p. 645) makes it easy to indulge your romantic, star-crossed side, while nearby **Trent,** (p. 648) in the Dolomites, offers year-round skiing. In **Venice** (p. 633), misty mornings give way to mystical *palazzi*. Move inland to sample the culinary delights of **Bologna** (p. 663), then satisfy pizza cravings at its birthplace in **Naples** (p. 681). A daytrip to **Pompeii** (p. 686) reveals Roman remains buried in the eruption of Mt. Vesuvius in AD 79. Sail to captivating **Capri** (p. 688) and the **Amalfi Coast** (p. 687), framed by crystal-blue waters. Take the ferry from Naples to vibrant **Palermo** (p. 689), the perfect start to an exploration of Sicily. Round out your tour of Italy at the spectacular **Aeolian Islands** (p. 691), with Stromboli's simmering volcano and beaches of ebony sand.

Italy

ESSENTIALS

WHEN TO GO

Traveling to Italy in late May or early September, when the temperature drops to a comfortable 77°F (25°C), will assure a calmer and cooler vacation. Also keep weather patterns, festival schedules, and tourist congestion in mind. Tourism enters overdrive in June, July, and August: Hotels are booked solid, with prices limited only by the stratosphere. During *Ferragosto*, a national holiday in August, all Italians take their vacations and flock to the coast like well-dressed lemmings; northern cities become ghost towns or tourist-infested infernos. Though many visitors find the larger cities enjoyable even during the holiday, most agree that June and July are better months for a trip to Italy."

ITALY

DOCUMENTS AND FORMALITIES

VISAS. Citizens of Australia, Canada, the EU, New Zealand, South Africa, and the US do not need a visa for stays of up to 90 days. Those wishing to stay in Italy for more than three months must apply for a *permesso di soggiorno* (residence permit) at a police station (*questura*).

EMBASSIES. Foreign embassies are in Rome (p. 603). For Italian embassies at home, contact: **Australia,** 12 Grey St., Deakin, Canberra ACT 2600 (☎02 6273 3333; www.ambitalia.org.au); **Canada,** 275 Slater St., 21st fl., Ottawa, ON K1P 5H9 (☎613-232-2401; www.italyincanada.com); **Ireland,** 63 Northumberland Rd., Dublin (☎01 660 1744; www.italianembassy.ie); **New Zealand,** 34 Grant Rd., Wellington (☎006 4473 5339; www.italy-embassy.org.nz); **South Africa,** 796 George Ave., Arcadia 0083, Pretoria (☎012 430 55 41; www.ambital.org.za); **UK,** 14 Three Kings Yard, London W1K 4EH (☎020 73 12 22 00; www.embitaly.org.uk); and **US,** 3000 Whitehaven St. NW, Washington, D.C. 20008 (☎202 612 4400; www.italyemb.org).

TRANSPORTATION

BY PLANE. Rome's international airport, known as both Fiumicino and Leonardo da Vinci, is served by most major airlines. You can also fly into Milan's Malpensa or Linate airports or Florence's Amerigo Vespucci airport. **Alitalia** (US ☎800-223-5730; UK 870 544 8259; www.alitalia.com) is Italy's national airline and may offer low-season youth fares.

BY TRAIN. The Italian State Railway **Ferrovie dello Stato,** or **FS** (national information line ☎147 88 80 88; www.fs-on-line.com), offers inexpensive and efficient service. There are several types of trains: The *locale* stops at every station on a particular line; the *diretto* makes fewer stops than the *locale;* and the *espresso* stops only at major stations. The air-conditioned *rapido,* an **InterCity** (IC) train, zips along but costs a bit more. Tickets for the fast, pricey **Eurostar** trains require reservations. If you are under 26 and plan to travel extensively in Italy, the **Carta verde** should be your *first* purchase. The card (€26) is valid for one year and gives a 15% discount on state train fare. **Eurail** is valid without a supplement on all trains except Eurostar. For a couple or a family, an **Italian Kilometric Ticket** (€117-181; good for 20 trips or 3000km), can pay off. Otherwise, railpasses are seldom cost effective since regular fares are cheap. For more info, contact the **Italian State Railways** in the US (☎212 730 2121).

BY BUS. Intercity buses serve countryside points inaccessible by train and occasionally arrive in more convenient places in large towns. For city buses, buy tickets in *tabacchi* or kiosks and validate them on board to avoid a fine.

BY FERRY. Portside ferries in Bari, Brindisi, and Ancona (p. 681) connect Italy to Greece. Boats from Trieste (p. 646) serve the Istrian Peninsula down to Croatia's Dalmatian Coast. Ferries also connect Italy's islands to the mainland. For Sardinia, boats go from Genoa (p. 657), La Spezia (p. 662), and Naples (p. 681). Travelers to Sicily (p. 689) take the ferry from Naples (p. 681) or Reggio di Calabria.

BY CAR. There are four kinds of roads: *Autostrada* (superhighways; mostly tollroads); *strade statali* (state roads); *strade provinciali* (provincial); and *strade communali* (local). Italian driving is frightening; congested traffic is common in large cities and in the north. On three-lane roads, be aware that the center lane is for passing. **Mopeds** (€20-31 per day) can be a great way to see the islands and the more scenic areas of Italy, but can be disastrous in the rain and on rough roads. Call the **Automobile Club Italiano** (ACI) at ☎116 if you break down.

BY BIKE AND BY THUMB. Bicycling is a popular national sport, but bike trails are rare, drivers are often reckless, and, except in the Po Valley, the terrain is challenging. *Let's Go* does not encourage hitchhiking. It can be particularly unsafe in Italy, especially in areas south of Rome or Naples.

TOURIST SERVICES

EMERGENCY	Police: ☎ 112. Ambulance: ☎ 113. Fire: ☎ 115.

TOURIST OFFICES. In provincial capitals, look for the **Ente Provinciale per il Turismo** (EPT) or **Azienda di Promozione Turistica** (APT) for info on the entire province and the town. Local tourist offices, **Informazione e Assistenza ai Turisti** (IAT) and **Azienda Autonoma di Soggiorno e Turismo** (AAST), are generally the most useful. **Italian Government Tourist Board** (ENIT) has offices in: **Australia,** Level 26, 44 Market St., Sydney NSW 2000 (☎ 02 9262 1666); **Canada,** 175 E. Bloor St., #907 South Tower, Toronto, ON M4W 3R8 (☎ 416 925 4882); **UK,** 1 Princes St., London WIR 2AY (☎ 020 7399 3562); **US,** 630 Fifth Ave., #1565, New York, NY 10111 (☎ 212 245 5618). Visit www.enit.it for a comprehensive list of all ENIT locations.

MONEY. On January 1, 2002, the **euro** (€) replaced the **lira** as the unit of currency in Italy. For more information, see p. 14.

BUSINESS HOURS. Nearly everything closes from around 1 to 3 or 4pm for *siesta*. Most museums are open 9am-1pm and 3-6pm; some are open through lunch, however. Monday is often their *giorno di chiusura* (day of closure).

COMMUNICATION

	Country code: 39. International dialing prefix: 00.
PHONE CODES	The city code must always be dialed, even when calling from within the city. From outside Italy, dial int'l dialing prefix (see inside back cover) + 39 + city code + local number (drop the leading zero).

TELEPHONES. Pre-paid phone cards, available from *tabacchi*, vending machines, and phone card vendors, carry a certain amount of time depending on the card's denomination (€5, €10, or €20). International calls start at €1.05 and vary depending on where you are calling. A collect call is a *contassa a carico del destinatario* or *chiamata collect.* For info on purchasing and using a **cell phone** in Italy, see p. 36. International direct dial numbers include: **AT&T,** ☎ 172 10 11; **British Telecom,** ☎ 172 00 44; **Canada Direct,** ☎ 172 10 01; **Ireland Direct,** ☎ 172 03 53; **MCI,** ☎ 172 10 22; **Sprint,** ☎ 172 18 77; **Telecom New Zealand,** ☎ 172 10 64; **Telkom South Africa,** ☎ 172 10 27; **Telstra Australia,** ☎ 172 10 61.

MAIL. Airmail letters sent from Australia, North America, or the UK to Italy take anywhere from three to seven days. Since Italian mail is notoriously unreliable, it is usually safer and quicker to send mail express (*espresso*) or registered (*raccomandata*). *Fermo Posta* is Italian for *Poste Restante.*

INTERNET ACCESS. Though Italy had initially lagged behind in constructing the information superhighway, it's now playing the catch-up game like a pro. While Internet cafes are still rare in rural and industrial cities, "Internet points" such as bars and even laundromats are becoming common in well-touristed areas. Rates range from €5-8 per hour. For free Internet access, try the local universities and libraries. For a list of Italian cyberspots, check www.cybercaptive.com.

ITALY

LANGUAGE. Any knowledge of Spanish, French, Portuguese, or Latin will help you understand Italian. The tourist office staff usually speaks some English. For a traveler's survival kit of basic Italian, see p. 1054.

ACCOMMODATIONS AND CAMPING

ITALY	❶	❷	❸	❹	❺
ACCOMMODATIONS	under €15	€16-25	€26-40	€41-60	over €60

Associazione Italiana Alberghi per la Gioventù (AIG), the Italian hostel federation, is a Hosteling International (HI) affiliate, though not all Italian hostels (*ostelli per la gioventù*) are part of AIG. A full list is available from most **EPT** and **CTS** offices and from many hostels. Prices start at about €13 per night for dorms. Hostels are the best option for solo travelers (single rooms are relatively scarce in hotels), but curfews, lockouts, distant locations, and less-than-perfect security detract from their appeal. Italian **hotel** rates are set by the state. Hotel owners will need your passport to register you; don't be afraid to hand it over for a while (usually overnight), but ask for it as soon as you think you will need it. Hotel singles (*camera singola*) usually start at around €26-31 per night, and doubles (*camera doppia*) start at €36-42. A room with a private bath (*con bagno*) usually costs 30-50% more. Smaller **pensioni** are often cheaper than hotels. Be sure to confirm the charges before checking in; Italian hotels are notorious for tacking on additional costs at check-out time. The **Azienda di Promozione Turismo** (APT), provides lists of hotels that have paid to be listed; some of the hotels we recommend may not be on the list. **Affitta-camere** (rooms for rent in private houses) are another inexpensive option. For more info, inquire at local tourist offices. There are over 1700 **campsites** in Italy; the **Touring Club Italiano,** C. Italia 10-20122, Milan (☎02 852 61; fax 53 59 95 40) publishes numerous books and pamphlets on the outdoors. Rates average €4.20 per person or tent, and €3.70 per car.

FOOD AND DRINK

ITALY	❶	❷	❸	❹	❺
FOOD	under €5	€6-10	€11-15	€16-25	over €25

Breakfast in Italy often goes unnoticed; lunch is the main feast of the day. A *pranzo* (full meal) is a true event, consisting of an *antipasto* (appetizer), a *primo* (first course of pasta or soup), a *secondo* (meat or fish), a *contorno* (vegetable side dish), and then finally *dolce* (dessert or fruit), a *caffè*, and often an after-dinner liqueur. If you don't have a big appetite, you can buy authentic snacks for a picnic at *salumeria* or *alimentari* (meat and grocery shops). A bar is an excellent place to grab a quick bite. They usually offer *panini* (hot and cold sandwiches), drinks with or without alcohol, and *gelato*. Grab a lighter lunch at an inexpensive *tavola calda* (hot table), *rosticceria* (grill), or *gastronomia* (serving hot prepared dishes). *Osterie, trattorie*, and *ristoranti* are, in ascending order, fancier and more expensive. Many restaurants offer a fixed-price tourist menu *(menù turistico)* that includes *primo, secondo*, bread, water, and wine. Italian dinner is typically a lighter meal. In the north, butter and cream sauces dominate, while Rome and central Italy are notoriously spicy regions. Farther south, tomatoes play a significant role. Coffee is another rich and varied focus of Italian life; for a standard cup of *espresso*, request a *caffè; cappuccino* is the breakfast beverage. *Caffè macchiato* (spotted coffee) has a touch of milk, while *latte macchiato* is heavier on the milk and lighter on the coffee. Wines from the north of Italy, such as the Piedmont's *Asti Spumante* or Verona's *Soave*, tend to be heavy and full-bodied; stronger, fruitier wines come from southern Italy. Almost every shop sells Italy's greatest contribution to civilization: *Gelato* (ice cream).

HOLIDAYS AND FESTIVALS

Holidays: New Year's Day (Jan. 1); Epiphany (Jan. 6); Easter Sunday and Monday (Apr. 11 and 12); Liberation Day (Apr. 25); Labor Day (May 1); Assumption of the Virgin (Aug. 15); All Saints' Day (Nov. 1); Immaculate Conception (Dec. 8); Christmas Day (Dec. 25); and Santo Stefano (Dec. 26).

Festivals: The most common excuse for a local festival is the celebration of a religious event—a patron saint's day or the commemoration of a miracle. Most include parades, music, wine, obscene amounts of food, and boisterousness. **Carnevale,** held in February during the 10 days before Lent, energizes Italian towns; in Venice, costumed Carnevale revelers fill the streets and canals. During **Scoppio del Carro,** held in Florence's P. del Duomo on Easter Sunday, Florentines set off a cart of explosives, following a tradition dating back to medieval times. On July 2 and August 16, **Il Palio** hits Siena (p. 676) with a bareback horse race around the central *piazza*.

ROME (ROMA)

Centuries of sporadic growth transformed Rome from a fledgling city-state to the capital of the Western world. At its zenith, the glory of Rome transcended human imagination and touched upon the divine; from its legendary founding in the shadows of pre-history, to the demi-god emperors who reveled in human form, to the modern papacy's global political influence, earthly ideas have proved insufficient to capture the Eternal City. Looking at Rome today, the phrase "decline and fall" seems preposterous—though Rome no longer dictates the course of Western history, its claim upon the modes of culture remains firmly intact. Style. Art. Food. Passion. These form Rome's new empire, tying the city to the living moment, rather than relegating it to stagnate in a museum case.

Today, while the Colosseum crumbles from industrial pollution, Romans celebrate their city: Concerts animate the ancient monuments, children play football around the Pantheon, and august *piazze* serve as movie houses for the latest Hollywood costume dramas. In a city that has stood for nearly three thousand years, Rome's glory is not dimmed, merely altered.

■ INTERCITY TRANSPORTATION

Flights: da Vinci International Airport (FCO; ☎06 659 51), known as **Fiumicino,** handles most flights. The **Termini line** runs nonstop to Rome's main station, **Termini Station** (30min., 2 per hr., €20). After hours, take the blue **COTRAL bus** to Tiburtina from the ground floor outside the main exit doors after customs (€4.50). From Tiburtina, take bus #40N to Termini. Most charter flights arrive at **Ciampino** (CIA; ☎06 79 49 41). To get to Rome, take the CO.TRA.L bus (every 30min., €1) to Anagnina station.

Trains: From Termini Station to: **Bologna** (2¾-4¼hr., €33); **Florence** (2-3hr., €25); **Milan** (4½-8hr., €47); **Naples** (2-2½hr., €18); **Venice** (5hr., €43). Trains arriving in Rome between midnight and 5am arrive at **Stazione Tiburtina** or **Stazione Ostiense,** which are connected to Termini by the #40N and 20N-21N buses.

ITALY

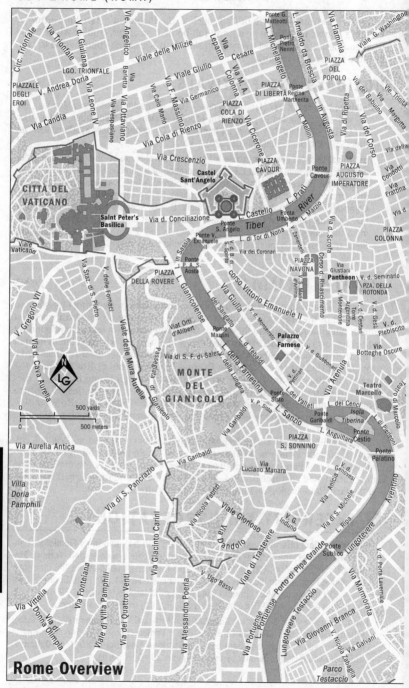

Rome Overview

ITALY

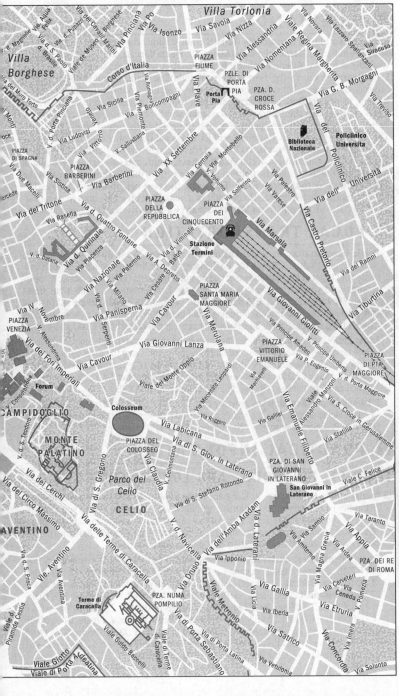

⚡ ORIENTATION

Located two blocks north of the **Termini** train station, **Via Nazionale** is the central artery connecting **Piazza della Repubblica** with **Piazza Venezia,** home to the immense wedding-cake-like **Vittorio Emanuele II monument.** A few blocks west of P. Venezia, **Largo Argentina** marks the start of **Corso Vittorio Emanuele,** which leads to Centro Storico, the medieval and Renaissance tangle of sights around the **Pantheon, Piazza Navona, Campo dei Fiori,** and **Piazza Farnese.** From P. Venezia, V. dei Fori Imperiale leads southeast to the **Forum** and **Colosseum,** south of which are the ruins of the **Baths of Caracalla** and the **Appian Way,** and the neighborhoods of southern Rome: The Aventine, Testaccio, Ostiense, and EUR. **Via del Corso** stretches from P. Venezia north to **Piazza del Popolo.** To the east, fashionable streets border the **Piazza di Spagna** and, to the northeast, the **Villa Borghese.** South and east are the **Fontana di Trevi, Piazza Barberini,** and the **Quirinal Hill.** Across the Tiber to the northwest is the **Vatican City,** and, to the southwest, **Trastevere,** the best neighborhood for wandering. It's impossible to navigate Rome without a map. Pick up a free map from a tourist office. The invaluable **Roma Metro-Bus map** (€4.20) is available at newsstands.

⬛ LOCAL TRANSPORTATION

Public Transportation: The 2 **Metropolitana** subway lines (A and B) meet at Termini and run 5:30am-11:30pm. **Buses** run 6am-midnight (with limited late-night routes); validate your ticket in the machine when you board. Buy tickets (€0.80) at *tabacchi,* newsstands, and station machines; they're valid for 1 Metro ride or unlimited bus travel within 75min. of validation. **BIG daily tickets** (€4) and **CIS weekly tickets** (€16) allow for unlimited public transport, including Ostia but not Fiumicino. For a short stay, buy the €11 3-day tourist pass. Be careful; pickpocketing is rampant on buses and trains.

Taxis: Easily located at stands, or flag them down in the street. Ride only in yellow or white taxis, and make sure your taxi has a meter (if not, settle the price before you get in the car). **Surcharges** apply at night (€2.60), on Su (€1), and when heading to or from Fiumicino (€7.25) or Ciampino (€5.50). Fares run about €7.75 from Termini to the Vatican City; between city center and Fiumicino around €35.

Bike and Moped Rental: Bikes generally cost €3 per hr. or €8 per day, but the length of a "day" varies according to the shop's closing time. In summer, try the stands on V. del Corso at P. di San Lorenzo and V. di Pontifici. (Open daily 10am-7pm.)

⬛ PRACTICAL INFORMATION

TOURIST, FINANCIAL, AND LOCAL SERVICES

Tourist office: Enjoy Rome, V. Marghera 8a (☎06 445 18 43; www.enjoyrome.com). From the middle concourse of Termini, exit right, with the trains behind you; cross V. Marsala and follow V. Marghera 3 blocks. Full-service travel agency, booking transportation, tours, a guide, and lodgings throughout Italy. Open Apr.-Oct. M-F 8:30am-7pm, Sa 8:30am-2pm; Nov.-Mar. M-F 9:30am-6:30pm, Sa 9am-2pm.

Foreign Consulates: Australia, V. Alessandria 215 (☎06 85 27 21; emergency 800 877 790). Services around the corner at C. Trieste 25. Open M-F 8:30am-12:30pm and 1:30-5:30pm. **Canada,** V. Zara 30 (☎06 44 59 81; www.canada.it). Open M-F 8:30am-4:30pm. **Ireland,** P. Campitelli 3 (☎06 697 91 21; fax 06 69 79 12). Open M-F 10am-12:30pm and 3-4:30pm. **New Zealand,** V. Zara 28 (☎06 441 71 71; fax 06 440 29 84). Open M-F 8:30am-12:45pm and 1:45-5pm. **South Africa,** V. Tanaro 14 (☎06 85 25 41; fax 06 85 25 43). Open M-F 8:30am-4:30pm. **UK,** V. XX Settembre 80/A (☎06 482 54 41; www.grbr.it). Open M-F 8:30am-4:30pm. **US,** V. Veneto 119/A (☎06 467 41; www.usembassy.it/mission). Open M-F 8:30am-5:30pm.

American Express: P. di Spagna 38 (☎06 676 41; lost cards ☎06 722 82). Open Aug. M-F 9am-6pm, Sa 9am-12:30pm; Sept.-July M-F 9am-7:30pm, Sa 9am-3pm.

Luggage Storage: In train station Termini, by track 1.

Bisexual, Gay, and Lesbian Resources: Arci-Gay, V.d. Minzoni 18 (☎051 649 30 55; www.arcigay.it). Membership card (€10) gains admission to gay clubs. **Coordinamento Lesbico Italiano,** V.S. Francesco di Sales 1a (☎06 686 42 01), off V.d. Lungara in Trastevere. **Circolo Mario Mieli di Cultura Omosessuale,** V. Corinto 5 (☎06 541 39 85; www.mariomieli.it). M: B-San Paolo. Walk 1 block to Largo Beato Placido Riccardi, turn left, and walk 1½ blocks to V. Corinto. Open Sept.-July M-F 9am-1pm and 2-6pm.

Laundromat: OndaBlu, V. La Mora 7 (☎800 86 13 46). Locations throughout Rome. Wash €3.20 per 6.5kg load; dry €3.20 per 6.5kg load. Open daily 8am-10pm.

EMERGENCY AND COMMUNICATIONS

Police: ☎113. **Carabinieri:** ☎112. **Emergency:** ☎118. **Fire:** ☎115.

24hr. Pharmacies: Farmacia Internazionale, P. Barberini 49 (☎06 487 11 95). MC/V. **Farmacia Piram,** V. Nazionale 228 (☎06 488 07 54). MC/V.

Hospitals: International Medical Center, V. G. Amendola 7 (☎06 488 23 71; nights and Su 06 488 40 51). Call first. Paramedic crew on call, referral service to English-speaking doctors. General visit €68. Open M-Sa 8:30am-8pm; on-call 24hr. **Rome-American Hospital,** V. E. Longoni 69 (☎06 225 51 for 24hr. service; 22 552 90 for appointments; www.rah.it). Laboratory services, HIV tests, and pregnancy tests. No emergency room. On-call 24hr.

Internet Access: Internet cafes are located throughout the city.

Trevi Tourist Service: Trevi Internet, V.d. Lucchesi 31-32 (☎/fax 06 69 20 07 99). €2.50 per hr., €4 for 2hr. Open daily 9:30am-10pm.

Splashnet, V. Varese 33 (☎06 49 38 20 73), 3 blocks north of Termini. €1.50 per hr. Open in summer daily 9am-1am; off-season daily 9am-11pm.

Freedom Traveller, V. Gaeta 25 (☎06 47 82 38 62; www.freedom-traveller.it). Run by a youth hostel. €2.60 per hr. with card; otherwise €4.13. Open daily 9am-midnight.

Internet Café, V. Cavour 213 (☎06 47 82 30 51). €3.20 per hr. Open daily 9am-1am.

Post Office: Main Post Office (Posta Centrale), P. San Silvestro 19 (☎06 679 50 44 or 06 678 07 88; fax 06 678 66 18). Open M-F 9am-6:30pm, Sa 9am-2pm. **Branch** at V.d. Terme di Diocleziano 30 (☎06 481 82 98), near Termini.

▛ ACCOMMODATIONS

Rome swells with tourists around Easter, from May through July, and in September. Prices vary widely with the time of year, and a proprietor's willingness to negotiate increases with length of stay, number of vacancies, and group size. Termini is swarming with hotel scouts. Many are legitimate and have IDs issued by tourist offices; however, some imposters have fake badges and direct travelers to rundown locations with exorbitant rates, especially at night.

CENTRO STORICO

If being a bit closer to the sights is worth it to you, then choosing Rome's medieval center over the area near Termini may be worth the higher prices.

Albergo del Sole, V.d. Biscione 76 (☎06 68 80 68 73; fax 06 689 37 87). Off Campo dei Fiori. 61 comfortable, modern rooms with phone, fan, TV, and fantastic antique furniture. English spoken. Check-out 11am. Parking garage €15-18. Singles €65, with bath €83; doubles €95/110-140. ❺

ITALY

Albergo Pomezia, V.d. Chiavari 13 (☎/fax 06 686 13 71; www.hotelpomezia.it). Off C. V. Emanuele II, behind Sant'Andrea della Valle. 3 floors of recently renovated, clean, and quiet rooms with fans. Breakfast included. Handicapped-accessible room on the first floor. Singles €60-105; doubles €80-125; triples €100-160. AmEx/MC/V. ❹

Albergo della Lunetta, P.d. Paradiso 68 (☎06 686 10 80; fax 689 20 28). The 1st right off V. Chiavari from C. V. Emanuele II behind Sant'Andrea della Valle. Clean, well-lit rooms; some face a small, fern-filled courtyard. Great location between Campo dei Fiori and P. Navona. Reservations recommended (with credit card or check). Singles €55, with bath €65; doubles €85/110; triples €115/145. MC/V. ❺

Albergo Abruzzi, P.d. Rotonda 69 (☎06 97 84 13 51). A mere 200 ft. from the Pantheon. Some rooms have a terrific view. Communal bath; rooms have sinks. Singles €75/150; doubles €115/195; triples €170/240. ❺

Hotel Navona, V.d. Sediari 8 1st fl. (☎06 686 42 03; www.hotelnavona.com). Take V.d. Canestrari from P. Navona, cross C. del Rinascimento, and go straight. This recently refurbished building has been used as a *pensione* for over 150 years, and counts Keats and Shelley among its guests. Check-out 10:30am. Breakfast included. A/C €15. Singles €84; doubles €110; triples €150. ❺

BORGO AND PRATI (NEAR THE VATICAN CITY)

While not the cheapest in Rome, the *pensioni* near the Vatican have all of the sobriety and quiet that one would expect from a neighborhood with this kind of nun-to-tourist ratio.

▨ Colors, V. Boezio 31 (☎06 687 40 30; www.colorshotel.com). M: A-Ottaviano, or take a bus to P. Risorgimento. V. Cola di Rienzo to V. Terenzio. Wonderful English-speaking staff and guests. 18 beds in rooms painted with a bravado that would put Raphael to shame. Internet €3 per hr. Flower-filled terrace and kitchen open 7:30am-11pm. Coed dorm beds €20; doubles €73-89; triples €83-104. Credit card required for private room reservations; for dorm beds, call at 9pm the night before. ❷

Hotel Florida, V. Cola di Rienzo 243 (☎06 324 18 72; www.hotelfloridaroma.it), on the 1st-3rd floors, reception on 2nd. Floral carpets, bedspreads, and wall decorations. English-speaking staff. A/C (€10 per night), TV, phone, and hair dryer in each of the 18 rooms. Singles €65-82; doubles €90-113; triples €110-135; quads €130-150. Call ahead to reserve; ask about discounts. 5% discount for cash payment. AmEx/MC/V. ❸

Hotel Pensione Joli, V. Cola di Rienzo 243, 6th fl. (☎06 324 18 54; www.hoteljoliroma.com), at V. Tibullo, scala A. A *pensione* with nice beds, ceiling fans, and views of the Vatican. Located on a busy shopping street, Joli also offers rooms that face an interior courtyard. All 18 rooms save a few singles have private baths and telephones. TV available with advance notice. Breakfast 7am-9am. Singles €53, with bath €67; doubles €90-100-; triples €135; quads €165; quints €190. AmEx/MC/V. ❹

Hotel Lady, V. Germanico 198, 4th fl. (☎06 324 21 12; www.hotellady.supereva.it), between V. Fabbio Massimo and V. Paolo Emilio. The 8 rooms, some with beautiful loft-style open wood-work ceilings and tile floors, lack A/C but are cool in the summer. Spacious common room. All rooms with sinks and desks. Singles without bath €75; doubles €90, with bath €100; triples €120. Prices quoted include a *Let's Go* discount, so mention it when you reserve. AmEx/MC/V. ❺

TRASTEVERE

Trastevere is a beautiful old Roman neighborhood famous for its separatism, medieval streets, and pretty-far-from-the-tourist-crowd charm. Hotels here are scattered, most of them too pricey for budget travelers, but the area does offer great nightlife and a location near the Vatican.

Hotel Carmel, V. G. Mameli 11 (☎06 580 99 21; www.hotelcarmel.it). Take a right onto V. E. Morosini (V. G. Mameli), off V.d. Trastevere. A short walk from central Trastevere. This simple hotel has 9 small rooms with bath. A comfortable atrium-like sitting room leads to a lovely garden terrace with breakfast seating. Breakfast included. Singles €80; doubles €100; triples €120; quads €150. AmEx/MC/V. ❺

Hotel Trastevere, V. Luciano Manara 25 (☎06 581 47 13; fax 588 10 16). Take a right off V.d. Trastevere onto V.d. Fratte di Trastevere, which becomes V. Luciano Manara. This homey establishment overlooks P.S. Cosimato. Neighborhood murals give way to 9 simple and airy rooms with bath, TV, and phone. English spoken. Breakfast included. Singles €77; doubles €98-103; triples €129; quads €154. Short-term apartments for 2-6 people with little kitchens and loft beds available. AmEx/D/MC/V. ❺

TERMINI AND SAN LORENZO

Welcome to budget traveler and backpacker central. While Termini is chock-full of traveler's services, the area south of Termini is a little sketchy at night.

▨ **Pensione Fawlty Towers,** V. Magenta 39, 5th fl. (☎/fax 06 454 359 42; www.fawltytowers.org). Exit Termini to the right, cross V. Marsala onto V. Marghera, and turn right onto V. Magenta. The flower-filled terrace provides a peaceful respite from Termini. Common room with satellite TV, library, refrigerator, microwave, and free Internet access. Frequently full, but the reception will help find a room elsewhere. Check-out 9am for dorms, otherwise 10am. Reserve by fax or email. English-speaking staff. No curfew. Dorms €18-20, with bath €23-25; singles €44/51; doubles €62/77; triples €82/90. ❷

▨ **Hotel Papa Germano,** V. Calatafimi 14a (☎06 48 69 19; www.hotelpapagermano.com). From the middle concourse of Termini, exit right; turn left onto V. Marsala, which becomes V. Volturno. V. Calatafimi is the 4th cross-street on the right. Clean rooms with TV and outstanding service. English, French, and Spanish spoken. Internet access €2.60 per hr. Check-out 11am. Dorms €18-25; singles €23-40; doubles €45-70, with bath €52-93; triples €54-78/72-105. Prices vary depending on season. Nov.-Mar. 10% discount. AmEx/MC/V. ❷

Hotel Des Artistes, V. Villafranca 20 (☎06 445 43 65; www.hoteldesartistes.com). From the middle concourse of Termini, exit right, turn left onto V. Marsala, right onto V. Vicenza, and then left onto the 5th cross-street. 3-star, 40-room hotel with clean, elegant rooms. Amenities include a rooftop terrace (open until 1am) and lounge with satellite TV. Free Internet access.

THE LOCAL STORY

OIL TAKES THE HIGH ROAD

Fabio Parpelli, 27, is the owner and sommelier at Apicius, an oleoteca and wine shop.

LG: How did you get interested in olive oil and wine?

A: I always had good oil at home. My mother taught me a lot. For wine, it started when I was young (about 15). I preferred wine to beer, which I guess is uncommon for young people. I went to stores to buy wines, and tasted the difference. Then I started to study it. I went to the AIS, the only Italian sommelier school in the world that's accredited.

LG: What are some of the challenges of opening a new store in Italy?

A: Well, I think you need to start with an idea of what you want. I wanted to showcase oil, because people usually don't care about it. Until 2 or 3 years ago, people bought bad stuff. I saw that other wine shops sold oil, but they didn't showcase it like they did with their wines. My mother was like a "sommelier" for oil, and so I learned from her. I am very particular about it. When I go into a restaurant, I have to know what I'm using.

LG: What makes a good oil?

A: A good olive oil comes from a small farm that presses olives from their own region, like they did a long time ago.

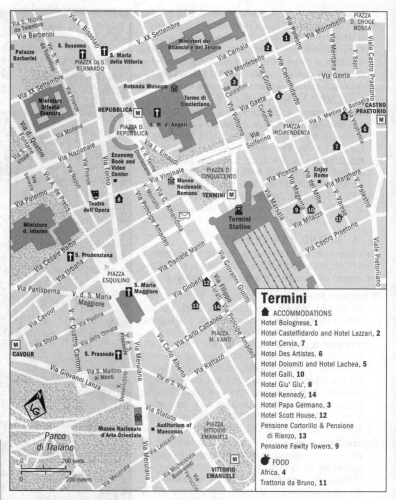

Termini

🏠 ACCOMMODATIONS
Hotel Bolognese, **1**
Hotel Castelfidardo and Hotel Lazzari, **2**
Hotel Cervia, **7**
Hotel Des Artistes, **6**
Hotel Dolomiti and Hotel Lachea, **5**
Hotel Galli, **10**
Hotel Giu' Giu', **8**
Hotel Kennedy, **14**
Hotel Papa Germano, **3**
Hotel Scott House, **12**
Pensione Cortorillo & Pensione di Rienzo, **13**
Pensione Fawlty Towers, **9**

🍴 FOOD
Africa, **4**
Trattoria da Bruno, **11**

Breakfast included for rooms with a bathroom, otherwise a steep €12. Check-out 11am. Singles €52-62, with bath €99-149; doubles €59-84/109-159; triples €75-112/139-179; quads €96-126/149-199. Off-season prices 20-30% less. €15 discount with cash payment. AmEx/MC/V. ❹

Hotel Dolomiti and **Hotel Lachea**, V.S. Martino della Battaglia 11 (☎06 495 72 56; www.hotel-dolomiti.it). From the middle concourse of Termini, exit right, turn left onto V. Marsala and right onto V. Solferino (V.d. Battaglia). This aging *palazzo* houses two new 3-star hotels with the same reception (on 2nd fl.) and management. Bar and breakfast room. Rooms with bathrooms have satellite TV, minibars, safes, hair-dryers, and A/C. Some with balcony. Breakfast €6. Internet access €2.60 per 30min. A/C €13 per night. Check-out 11am. Check-in 1pm. Singles €37-42, with bath €55-67; doubles €55-68/75; triples €60-73/88; quads €115-135. ❺

Hotel Bolognese, V. Palestro 15 (☎/fax 06 49 00 45). From the middle concourse of Termini, exit right. Walk down V. Marghera and take the 4th left on V. Palestro. In a land of run-of-the-mill *pensioni*, this place is spruced up by the artist-owner's impressive paintings. Some rooms have balconies. Check-out 11am. Singles €31, with bath €43; doubles €47/55; triples €55/70. ❸

Hotel Cathrine, V. Volturno 27 (☎06 48 36 34). From the middle concourse of Termini, exit right, and turn left onto V. Marsala, which becomes V. Volturno. 2 common bathrooms serve the 8 spacious singles and doubles with sinks. There are more rooms at the modern **Affittacamere Aries,** V. XX Settembre 58/a (☎06 42 02 71 61; www.affi-camerearies.com). Breakfast €2. *Let's Go* discount available, depending on season. Singles €35-45; doubles €47-62, with bath €52-72. Extra bed €15. ❹

Hotel Cervia, V. Palestro 55 (☎06 49 10 57; www.hotelcerviaroma.com). From Termini, exit onto V. Marsala, head down V. Marghera, and take the 4th road on the left. Common TV room, breakfast room with bar, and clean rooms. Rooms with bath include breakfast; otherwise, it's €5. Check-out 11am. Singles €35, with bath €45; doubles €60/95; triples €75/95. In summer, dorm beds available for €20. Ask about the *Let's Go* discount. AmEx/MC/V. ❷

Hotel Galli, V. Milazzo 20 (☎06 445 68 59; www.albergogalli.com). From Termini's middle concourse, exit right. Take a right on V. Marsala and the first left on V. Milazzo. 12 clean rooms with tile floors and wrought-iron beds. Kind and helpful family owners. All rooms have bath, phone, TV, A/C, fridge, and safe. Breakfast included. Singles €50; doubles €80; triples €90; quads €110. 10% discount off-season. AmEx/MC/V. ❹

VIA XX SETTEMBRE AND ENVIRONS

Dominated by government ministries and private apartments, this area is less noisy and touristy than the nearby Termini.

🖼 **Pensione Monaco,** V. Flavia 84 (☎/fax 06 420 141 80). Go north up V. XX Settembre, turn left onto V. Quintino Sella, and then right onto V. Flavia. The 11 sun-lit rooms, all with bathroom, are kept remarkably clean. Comfortable mattresses and a bright courtyard. Check-out 9am. *Let's Go* discount prices: Singles €37; doubles €60; triples €75; quads €100. 10% discount off-season. ❸

Pensione Tizi, V. Collina 48 (☎06 482 01 28; fax 06 474 32 66). A 10min. walk from the station. Go north up V. XX Settembre, and turn left onto V. Servio Tullio, then right onto V. Flavia, and left on V. Collina. Or take bus #360 or 217. Marble floors and inlaid ceilings adorn spacious and recently renovated rooms. Check-out 11am. Singles €45; doubles €55, with bath €65; triples €80/90; quads €100/110. ❹

Hotel Castelfidardo and **Hotel Lazzari,** V. Castelfidardo 31 (☎06 446 46 38; www.castelfidardo.com). 2 blocks off V. XX Settembre. Both run by the same friendly family. Renovated rooms with soothing pastel walls. 3 floors of modern, comfortable rooms. Check-out 10:30am. English spoken. Singles €44, with bath €55; doubles €64/74; triples €83/96; quads with bath €110. AmEx/MC/V. ❹

SOUTH AND WEST OF TERMINI

Esquilino (south of Termini) is home to many cheap hotels close to the major sights. The neighborhood west of Termini is slightly more inviting, with busy streets and lots of shopping.

🖼 **Pensione di Rienzo,** V. Principe Amedeo 79a (☎06 446 71 31; fax 06 446 69 80). A tranquil, family-run retreat with spacious rooms that overlook a courtyard. Extremely friendly English-speaking staff. 20 rooms, with balconies, TVs, and baths. Breakfast €7. Check-out 10am. Singles without bath €20-50; doubles €23-60, with bath €25-70. Prices vary with season. MC/V. ❷

■ **Pensione Cortorillo,** V. Principe Amedeo 79a, 5th fl. (☎06 446 69 34; www.hotelcortorillo.it). TVs and A/C in all 14 rooms, and a cheap lobby phone. Breakfast included. Check-out 10am. Singles €30-70, with bath €40-100; doubles €40-80/50-120. Prices vary with season. AmEx/D/MC/V. ❸

Hotel Kennedy, V. Filippo Turati 62-64 (☎06 446 53 73; www.hotelkennedy.net). Classical music in the bar, leather couches and a large color TV in the lounge. Private bath, satellite TV, phone, and A/C. Hearty all-you-can-eat breakfast included. Check-out 11am. Reservations by fax or email only. Singles €60-80; doubles €85-129; triples €100-149. 10% *Let's Go* discount. AmEx/D/MC/V. ❺

Pensione Sandy, V. Cavour 136 4th fl. (☎06 488 45 85; www.sandyhostel.com). Just past the intersection of V.S. Maria Maggiore. Next door to the Hotel Vallet. Free Internet, sheets, and individual lockers (bring a lock) in each room. Simple, hostel-style rooms, usually for 3-5 people. Dorms €12-18. ❶

Hotel Scott House, V. Gioberti 30 (☎06 446 53 79; www.scotthouse.com). Each one of the 34 clean and comfortable rooms features a private bath, A/C, phone, safe box, satellite TV, and brightly painted walls. Breakfast included. Check-out 11am. Singles €35-68; doubles €63-98; triples €75-114; quads €88-129; quints €100-140. Prices vary with season. AmEx/MC/V. ❸

Hotel Il Castello, V. Vittorio Amedeo II 9 (☎06 77 20 40 36; www.ilcastello.com). M: A-Manzoni. Walk down V. San Quintino and take the first left. Spartan rooms, but an eager staff. Continental breakfast €3. Check-out 10:30am. Dorms €20; singles (none with bath) €26-37; doubles €45-82; triples €55-92. MC/V. ❷

Hotel Giu' Giu', V.d. Viminale 8 (☎06 482 77 34; www.hotelgiugiu.com). The air-conditioned rooms of this elegant but fading *palazzo* will make you forget the hustle and bustle of Rome. Pleasant breakfast area and 12 quiet rooms. English spoken. Breakfast €7. Check-out 10am. Singles (none with bath) €30-40; doubles €50-70, with bath €60-70; triples with bath €90-105; quads with bath €120-140. ❸

RELIGIOUS HOUSING

Don't automatically think cheap; some of the most popular religious accommodations run up to €155 for a single. A few still require letters of introduction from local dioceses, but most are open to people of all religious backgrounds. Most are single-sex with early curfews, church services, and light chores.

■ **Domus Nova Bethlehem,** V. Cavour 85/A (☎06 478 244 1 or 06 478 825 11; www.suorebambinogesu.it). Walk down V. Cavour from Termini, past P.d. Esquilino on the right. A clean, modern, and centrally located hotel. Curfew 1am. All rooms come with A/C, private bath, safe, TV, and phone. Breakfast included. Singles €70; doubles €100; triples €129; quads €148. AmEx/MC/V. ❺

Santa Maria Alle Fornaci, P.S. Maria alle Fornaci 27 (☎06 393 676 32; ciffornaci@tin.it). Facing St. Peter's Basilica, take a left (through a gate in the basilica walls) onto V.d. Fornace. Take the 3rd right onto V.d. Gasperi, which leads to P.S. Maria alle Fornaci. This *casa per ferie,* in the Trinitarian tradition of hospitality, has 54 rooms, each with a private bath and phone. Simple, small, and clean. No curfew. Breakfast included. Singles €50; doubles €80; triples €110. AmEx/MC/V. ❹

WOMEN'S HOUSING

YWCA Foyer di Roma, V. C. Balbo 4 (☎06 488 04 60). From Termini, take V. Cavour, turning right onto V. Torino and then the 1st left onto V. C. Balbo. The YWCA (pronounced EEV-kah and known as the *Casa per Studentesse*) is a pretty, clean, and secure hostel. Breakfast included. Tell reception by 10am if you want lunch (served 1-2pm; €11). Reception 7am-midnight. Curfew midnight. Check-out 10am. Singles €37, with bath €47; doubles €62/74; triples €78; quads €104. Extra bed €26. ❸

🖸 FOOD

Traditional Roman cuisine is not generally ranked among the best in Italy, but the city has excellent restaurants specializing in both regional Italian and international cuisine. Lunch is typically the main meal, although some Romans now eat lunch on the go during the week. Restaurants tend to close between 3 and 7:30pm.

ANCIENT CITY

Despite its past glory, this area has yet to discover the noble concept of "affordable food." But along **Via dei Fori Imperiali,** several restaurants offer decent prices.

▨ **I Buoni Amici,** V. Aleardo Aleardi 4 (☎06 70 49 19 93). From the Colosseum, take V. Labicana to V. Merulana. Turn right, then left onto V.A. Aleardi. The food is worth the walk. Choices include the *linguine all'astice* (linguini with lobster sauce; €6.50). Cover €1. Open M-Sa noon-3pm and 7-11:30pm. AmEx/D/MC/V. ❷

Taverna dei Quaranta, V. Claudia 24 (☎06 700 05 50), off P.d. Colosseo. Shaded by the trees of Celian Park, outdoor dining at this corner *taverna* is a must. The menu changes weekly and often features the sinfully good *oliva ascolane* (olives stuffed with meat and fried; €4). Reservations suggested, especially for a table outside. Open daily 12:30-3:30pm and 7:45pm-midnight. AmEx/D/MC/V. ❷

CENTRO STORICO

The twisting streets of Rome's historic center offer many hidden gems, especially just off the main *piazze.*

▨ **Pizzeria Baffetto,** V.d. Governo Vecchio 114 (☎06 686 16 17). At the intersection of V.d. Governo Vecchio and V. Sora. Once a meeting place for 60s radicals, Baffetto now overflows with hungry Romans—be prepared to wait a long time for an outdoor table. Pizza €4.50-7.50. Open daily 8-10am and 6:30pm-1am. Cash only. ❶

Trattoria dal Cav. Gino, V. Rosini 4 (☎06 678 34 34), off V.d. Campo Marzio across from P. del Parlamente. The very affable Gino will greet you at the door. *Tonnarelli alla ciociala* (€7) is the house specialty. *Primi* €6-7. *Secondi* under €20. Reservations accepted. Open M-Sa 1-3:30pm and 8-10:30pm. Cash only. ❸

CAMPO DEI FIORI AND THE JEWISH GHETTO

▨ **Trattoria da Sergio,** V.d. Grotte 27 (☎06 654 66 69). Take V.d. Giubbonari and your 1st right. Sergio offers Roman ambience and hearty portions. Try the *Spaghetti Matriciana* (with bacon and spicy tomato sauce; €6). Reservations suggested. Open M-Sa 12:30-3pm and 6:30-11:30pm. MC/V. ❷

▨ **Zampano',** P.d. Cancelleria 83 (☎06 689 70 80), between C. V. Emanuele II and the Campo. This *hostaria* is running out of room for all the awards it has won. Offers creative pizzas (€7-9) and over 200 wines. *Primi* €7-8. *Secondi* €12-13. Finish with a savory dessert (€4.50-6). Open daily noon-2:30pm and 7:30-11pm. AmEx/MC/V. ❷

Trattoria Da Luigi, P.S. Cesarini 24 (☎06 686 59 46), near Chiesa Nuova. Enjoy cuisine such as the delicate *carpaccio di salmone fresco con rughetta* (€8). Bread €1. Open Tu-Su noon-3pm and 7pm-midnight. AmEx/MC/V. ❷

PIAZZA DI SPAGNA

Although the upscale P.d. Spagna might appear to have little in common with Termini, they both share one thing: Tons of bad, bad food. The difference is that you'll pay €10 more for the atmosphere here. The best food is closer to the Ara Pacis, across V.d. Corso, away from the throngs of tourists.

▨ **Trattoria da Settimio all'Arancio,** V.d. Arancio 50-52 (☎06 687 61 19). Take V.d. Condotti from P.d. Spagna, the 1st right after V.d. Corso, then the 1st left. Order the fried artichokes (€4.50), although the less inhibited might try the squid's ink risotto (€7.50). Bread €1. Open M-Sa 12:30-3pm and 7:30-11:30pm. AmEx/MC/V. ❷

▨ **Vini e Buffet,** P. Toretta 60 (☎06 687 14 45). From V.d. Corso, turn into P.S. Lorenzo in Lucina. Take a left on V. Campo Marzio, then a quick right onto V. Toretta. Popular salads are creative and fresh—the *insalata con salmone* (€8.50) is delightful. Reservations recommended. Open M-Sa 12:30-3pm and 7-11pm. ❷

Il Brillo Parlante, V. Fontanella 12 (☎06 324 33 34), near P. del Popolo. The wood-burning oven, fresh ingredients, and excellent wine attract many lunching Italians. Pizza €5-7.75. Open Su and Tu-Sa 12:30-5:30pm and 7:30pm-1am. MC/V. ❷

BORGO AND PRATI (NEAR THE VATICAN CITY)

Establishments near the Vatican serve mediocre sandwiches at hiked-up prices, but just a few blocks northeast, food is much better and reasonably priced.

▨ **Franchi,** V. Cola di Rienzo 204 (☎06 687 46 51; www.franchi.it). Delicacies include various croquettes (€1.10), marinated munchies (anchovies, peppers, olives, and salmon, all sold by the kg.), and pastas (vegetarian lasagna or *cannellini* stuffed with ricotta and beef; €5.50). Open M-Sa 8:15am-9pm. AmEx/MC/V. ❷

Cacio e Pepe, V. Giuseppe Avezzana 11 (☎06 321 72 68). From P. Mazzini take V. Settembrini to P. dei Martiri di Belfiore, then left on V. Avezzana. Great pasta for cheap; no wonder it has been a neighborhood favorite since 1964. All the homemade pasta is delicious, but yes, the *Cacio e Pepe* is their specialty. Lunch under €10. Full dinner around €15. M-F 8-11:30pm, Sa 12:30-3pm. Reservations accepted. Cash only. ❷

TRASTEVERE

Perhaps one of the best places to enjoy a meal in Rome, Trastevere has fabulous, largely undiscovered restaurants.

▨ **Pizzeria San Calisto,** P.S. Calisto 9a (☎06 581 82 56). Right off P.S. Maria in Trastevere. Simply the best pizza in Rome. Gorgeous thin crust pizzas so large they hang off the plates (€4.20-7.80). Open Tu-Su 7pm-midnight. MC/V. ❶

Ristorante a Casa di Alfredo, V. Roma Libera 5-7 (☎06 588 29 68). Try the *gnocchi tartufo e gamberi* (€8) to start and the grilled calamari (€10.50) or the *filetto a pepe verde* (€13) as a main dish. Open daily noon-3pm and 7:30-11:30pm. AmEx/MC/V. ❸

TERMINI

Tourist traps abound; avoid the torturous €8 "quick lunch" advertised in windows.

▨ **Africa,** V. Gaeta 26-28 (☎06 494 10 77), near P. Independenza. Excellent Eritrean/Ethiopian food. The meat-filled *sambusas* (€2.50) are a flavorful starter; both the *zighini beghi* (roasted lamb in a spicy sauce; €8) and the *misto vegetariano* (mixed veggies; €6) make fantastic entrees. Cover €1. Open M-Sa 8pm-midnight. MC/V. ❷

Trattoria da Bruno, V. Varese 29 (☎06 49 04 03). From V. Marsala, next to the train station, walk 3 blocks down V. Milazzo and turn right onto V. Varese. Start with the *tortellini con panna e funghi* (with cream and mushrooms; €6.50). For dessert: The best *crépes* in town. Open daily noon-3:30pm and 7-10:15pm. Closed Aug. AmEx/MC/V. ❷

SAN LORENZO

Rome's funky university district, San Lorenzo, offers many good, cheap eateries. From Termini, walk south on V. Pretoriano to P. Tiburtino, or take bus #492. Women may find the walk a little uncomfortable at night.

ITALY

Il Pulcino Ballerino, V.d. Equi 66-68 (☎06 494 12 55). Take a right off V. Tiburtina. Dishes include *conchiglione al "Moby Dick"* (shells with tuna, cream, and greens). Open M-Sa 1-3:30pm and 8pm-midnight. Closed mid-Aug. AmEx/MC/V. ❷

Il Tunnel, V. Arezzo 11 (☎06 44 23 68 08). From M: B-Bologna, walk down V.d. Provincie, take the 4th right onto V. Padova, and the 2nd left onto V. Arezzo. A bit of a trek, but the locals love it. All pasta dishes (€4-10) are made fresh and the *bisteca alla Fiorentina* is unrivaled in Rome (priced by weight, around €15 per person). Open Tu-Su noon-3pm and 7pm-midnight. Closed Aug. MC/V. ❸

Arancia Blu, V.d. Latini 65 (☎06 445 41 05), off V. Tiburtina. *Tonnarelli con pecorino romano e tartufo* (pasta with sheep cheese and truffles; €6.20) or fried ravioli stuffed with eggplant and smoked *caciocavallo* with pesto sauce (€8.50) make excellent meals. Extensive wine list. Open daily 8:30pm-midnight. ❷

TESTACCIO

This working-class southern neighborhood is the center of Roman nightlife, and eateries here offer food made of just about every animal part imaginable.

La Cestia, V. di Piramide Cestia 69. M: B-Piramide. Walk across P. di Porta San Paolo to V. di Piramide Cestia; the restaurant is on the right. Pasta €4.20-7.20. *Secondi* €6.20-11. Open Tu-Su 12:30-3pm and 7:30-11pm. D/MC/V. ❸

Trattoria da Bucatino, V. Luca della Robbia 84-86 (☎06 574 68 86). Take V. Luigi Vanvitelli off V. Marmorata, then the 1st left. The animal entrails you know and love, and plenty of gut-less dishes as well. Heaping mounds of *tripe alla romana* (€7). Pizza €4-7. Cover €1.50. Open Tu-Su 12:30-3:30pm and 6:30-11:30pm. Closed Aug. MC/V. ❷

DESSERT AND COFFEE

Cheap *gelato* is as plentiful on Roman streets as leather pants. Look for *gelato* with very muted (hence natural) colors. Coffee (*espresso*) is Italian for "wash away those early-morning hostel lockout blues."

San Crispino, V.d. Panetteria 42 (☎06 679 39 24). Near the Trevi Fountain. Facing the fountain, turn right onto V. Lavatore and take your 2nd left; it is inset on the right. Crispino is almost universally acknowledged as the best *gelato* in Rome. Every flavor is made from scratch. Cups €1.70-6.30. **Branch** at V. Acaia 56 (☎06 70 45 04 12), in Appio. Both open M, W-Th, and Su noon-12:30am; F-Sa noon-1:30am.

THE LOCAL STORY

THE AGE OF JANUARIUS

Dr. Luigi Garlaschelli is an organic chemist at the University of Pavia who, in his spare time, investigates the authenticity of blood relics .

LG: Can you explain the ubiquitousness of relics in Italian churches?
A: In the Middle Ages, it was believed that they would protect the city from its enemies. [Relics include] the feather of the Archangel Michael, the milk of the Virgin Mary, and the fingernails and blood of Christ.
LG: What was your first project?
A: My first work was on the blood of St. Januarius, which is contained in a small vial kept in the duomo in Naples. Januarius was beheaded in 305 AD. The relic appeared in the Middle Ages, 1000 years later. Normally blood taken from a living body will clot only once; the "miracle" of this blood is that it liquefies twice a year during religious ceremonies.
LG: How does that work?
A: Well, using an iron salt, which exists naturally near active volcanoes (like Vesuvius, near Naples, active at the time of the discovery of the blood), kitchen salt, and techniques available in the Middle Ages, we were able to make a substance of the same color and properties as the reputed blood of St. Januarius. The matter would be closed were we to open the vial and take a sample. But, of course, the vial is sealed.

The Old Bridge, V.d. Bastioni di Michelangelo (☎06 39 72 30 26), off P. del Risorgimento, perpendicular to the Vatican museum walls. Huge cups and cones (€1.50-3) filled with your choice of 20 homemade flavors. Open M-Sa 9am-2am, Su 3pm-2am.

Giolitti, V.d. Uffici del Vicario 40 (☎06 699 12 43). 2 blocks north of the Pantheon, find V.d. Maddelena and walk to its end; V.d. Uffici del Vicario is on the right. Makes wonderful *gelato* in dozens of flavors (€1.55-2.60), as well as ices laden with fresh fruit. Festive and crowded at night. Open daily 9am-1am. AmEx/D/MC/V.

Pasticceria Ebraica Boccione, Portico d'Ottavia 1 (☎06 687 86 37). Little fanfare, just long lines of locals who line up for what they all acknowledge to be the best pastries in Rome. *Torta Riccotta Vicciole* and *Torta Ricotta Cioccolate* are the most famous of their creations (€10.30 per kg.). Open Su-Th 8am-8pm, F 8am-5:30pm.

Bar Giulia (a.k.a. Caffe Peru), V. Giulia 84 (☎06 686 13 10), near P.V. Emmanuele II. Giulia serves what may be the cheapest (and most delicious) coffee in Rome (€0.70), and they'll add your favorite liqueur at no extra charge. Open M-Sa 4am-9:30pm.

ENOTECHE (WINE BARS)

Roman wine bars range from laid-back and local to chic and international. They often serve excellent food to accompany your bottle.

■ **Bar Da Benito,** V.d. Falegnami 14 (☎06 686 15 08), off P. Cairoli in the Jewish Ghetto. A *tavola calda* lined with bottles and hungry patrons. Wine from €1; bottles from €5.50. One hot pasta prepared daily (€4.50), along with fresh *secondi* like *prosciutto* with vegetables (€5). Open M-Sa 6:30am-7pm; lunch noon-3:30pm. Closed Aug.

Cul de Sac, P. Pasquino 73 (☎06 68 80 10 94), off P. Navona. Specialty *pates* (such as pheasant and mushroom; €5.40) are exquisite, as are the scrumptious *escargot alla bourguigonne* (€5.10). Open M 7pm-12:30am, Tu-Sa noon-4pm and 6pm-12:30am.

Enoteca Cavour 313, V. Cavour 313 (☎06 678 54 96). A short walk from M: B-Cavour. Wonderful meats and cheeses (€8-9 for a mixed plate) listed by region or type, many fresh salads (€5-7), and rich desserts (€3-5). Massive wine list (€11-260). Open M-Sa 12:30-2:30pm and 7:30pm-1am; kitchen closes 12:30am. Closed Aug.

◉ SIGHTS

Rome wasn't built in a day, and it's not likely that you'll see any substantial portion of it in twenty-four hours, either. Ancient temples and forums, Renaissance basilicas, 280 fountains, and 981 churches—there's a reason, according to Robert Browning, that "everyone sooner or later comes round by Rome."

ANCIENT CITY

What Rome lacks in a "downtown" it more than makes up for in ruins—the downtown Cicero and Catullus knew. The **Umbilicus Urbis,** literally "navel of the world," marked the center of the known universe. And who said Romans were egocentric?

ROMAN FORUM. Here, the pre-Romans founded a thatched-hut shantytown in 753 BC. The entrance ramp leads to V. Sacra, Rome's oldest street, near the **Basilica Aemilia,** built in 179 BC, and the area once known as the Civic Forum. Next to the Basilica stands the Curia (Senate House); it was converted to a church in AD 630 and restored by Mussolini. The broad space in front of the **Curia** was the Comitium, where male citizens came to vote and representatives of the people gathered for public discussion. Bordering the Comitium is the large brick Rostrum (speaker's platform) erected by Julius Caesar in 44 BC, just before his death. The hefty **Arch of Septimius Severus,** to the right of the Rostrum, was dedicated in AD 203 to celebrate Caesar's victories in the Middle East. The **market square** holds a number of shrines and sacred precincts, including the *Lapis Niger* (Black Stone), where Romulus was supposedly murdered by Republican senators. Below the Lapis Niger are the underground ruins of a 6th-century BC altar and the oldest known Latin inscription in Rome. In the square, the **Three Sacred Trees of Rome**—olive, fig, and grape—have been replanted by the Italian state. The newest part of the Forum is the Column of Phocas, erected in AD 608. The three great temples of the **Lower Forum** have been closed off for excavations; however, the eight columns of the 5th-century BC **Temple of Saturn**, next to the Rostrum, have been restored. Around the corner, rows of column bases are all that remain of the **Basilica Julia,** a courthouse built by Julius Caesar in 54 BC. At the far end, three marble columns mark the massive podium of the recently restored **Temple of Castor and Pollux,** built to celebrate the Roman defeat of the Etruscans. The circular building is the **Temple of Vesta,** where Vestal Virgins tended the city's sacred fire, keeping it lit for more than a thousand years.

In the Upper Forum lies the **House of the Vestal Virgins.** For 30 years, the six virgins who officiated over Vesta's rites lived in seclusion here from the ripe old age of seven. Near here, V. Sacra runs over the Cloaca Maxima, the ancient sewer that still drains water from the otherwise marsh-like valley. V. Sacra continues out of the Forum proper to the Velia and the gargantuan Basilica of Maxentius. The middle apse of the basilica once contained a gigantic statue of Constantine with a bronze body and marble head, legs, and arms. The uncovered remains, including a 2m foot, are displayed at the Palazzo dei Conservatori on the Capitoline Hill. V. Sacra leads to an exit on the other side of the hill to the Colosseum; the path that crosses before the **Arch of Titus** heads to the Palatine Hill. *(M: B-Colosseo, or bus to P. Venezia. Main entrance is on V.d. Fori Imperiali, at Largo C. Ricci, between P. Venezia and the Colosseum. Open in summer daily 9am-6:30pm; off-season daily 9am-3:30pm. Guided tour €3.50; audioguide in English, French, German, Italian, Japanese, or Spanish; €4.)*

THE PALATINE HILL. The best way to attack the Palatine is from the stairs near the Forum's **Arch of Titus.** Throughout the garden complex, terraces provide breathtaking views. Farther down, excavations continue on the 9th-century BC village, the **Casa di Romulo.** To the right of the village is the podium of the 191 BC **Temple of Cybele.** The stairs to the left lead to the **House of Livia,** which is connected to the **House of Augustus** next door. Around the corner, the long, spooky **Cryptoporticus** connected Tiberius's palace with the buildings nearby. The path around the House of Augustus leads to the vast ruins of a giant palace and is divided into two wings. The solemn **Domus Augustana** was the private space for the emperors; the adjacent wing, the sprawling **Domus Flavia,** once held a gigantic octagonal fountain. Between the Domus Augustana and the Domus Flavia stands the **Palatine Antiquarium,** the museum that houses the artifacts found during the excavations of the Palatine Hill. *(30 people admitted every 20min. starting at 9:10am. Free.)* Outside on the right, the palace's east wing contains the curious **Stadium of Domitian,** or *Hippodrome*, a sunken oval space once surrounded by a colonnade but now decorated with fragments of porticoes, statues, and fountains. The **Arch of Constantine** lies between the Colosseum and the Palatine Hill, marking the tail end of the V. Sacra. One of the best-preserved monuments in the area, it commemorates Constantine's victory over Maxentius at the Milvian Bridge in AD 315. *(The Palatine rises to the south of the Forum. Open in summer daily 9am-7:15pm; off-season 9am-4pm; sometimes closes M-F 3pm, Su and holidays noon. Ticket to the Palatine Hill and the Colosseum €8. 7-day ticket book good for entrance to the 4 Musei Nazionali Romani, the Colosseum, the Palatine Hill, the Terme di Diocleziano, and the Crypti Balbi; €20.)*

FORI IMPERIALI. Across the street from the Ancient Forum are the **Fori Imperiali,** a conglomeration of temples, basilicas, and public squares constructed in the first and second centuries. Excavations will proceed through 2003, so the area is closed off, but you can still get free views by peering over the railing from V.d. Fori Imperiali or V. Alessandrina. Built between AD 107 and 113, the **Forum of Trajan** included a colossal equestrian statue of Trajan and an immense triumphal arch. At one end of the now-decimated forum, 2500 carved legionnaires march their way up the almost perfectly preserved ▨**Trajan's Column,** one of the greatest extant specimens of Roman relief-sculpture. The crowning statue is St. Peter, who replaced Trajan in 1588. The gray tufa wall of the **Forum of Augustus** commemorates Augustus's victory over Caesar's murderers in 42 BC. The aptly named **Forum Transitorium** (also called the **Forum of Nerva**) was a narrow, rectangular space connecting the Forum of Augustus with the Republican Roman Forum. The only remnant of **Vespatian's Forum** is the mosaic-filled **Church of Santi Cosma e Damiano** across V. Cavour, near the Roman Forum. *(Open daily 9am-6:30pm.)*

THE COLOSSEUM. This enduring symbol of the Eternal City—a hollowed-out ghost of marble that dwarfs every other ruin in Rome—once held as many as 50,000 spectators. Within 100 days of its opening in AD 80, some 5000 wild beasts perished in the arena (from the Latin word for sand, *harena*, which was put on the floor to absorb blood). The floor (now partially restored) covers a labyrinth of brick cells, ramps, and elevators used to transport wild animals from cages up to arena level. Beware the men dressed as gladiators: They want to take a picture with you for €5. *(M: B-Colosseo. Open May-Oct. daily 9am-6:30pm; Nov.-Apr. 9am-4pm.)*

DOMUS AUREA. This park houses just a portion of Nero's "Golden House," which once covered a huge chunk of Rome. After deciding that he was a god, Nero had architects build a house worthy of his divinity. The Forum was reduced to a vestibule of the palace; Nero crowned it with the 35m Colossus, a huge statue of himself as the sun. *(On the Oppian Hill. From the Colosseum, walk up V.d. Domus Aurea and make the 1st left. Reservations ☎06 39 96 77 00. Open M and W-Su 9am-7:45pm. Groups of 30 admitted every 20min. €5.)*

VELABRUM. The **Velabrum** is a flat flood plain south of the Jewish Ghetto. At the bend of V. del Portico d'Ottavia, a shattered pediment and a few ivy-covered columns are all that remain of the once magnificent **Portico d'Ottavia.** The stocky, gray **Teatro di Marcello** next door is named for Augustus's nephew, whose early and sudden death remains a mystery. Farther down V. di Teatro di Marcello, **Chiesa di San Nicola in Carcere** incorporates three Roman temples originally dedicated to Juno, Janus, and Spes. *(☎06 686 99 72. Open Sept.-July M-Sa 7:30am-noon and 4-7pm.)* Across the street, the **Chiesa di Santa Maria in Cosmedin** harbors some of Rome's most beautiful medieval decorations. The Audrey Hepburn film *Roman Holiday* made the portico's relief, the ▨**Bocca della Verità,** famous; according to legend, the hoary face will chomp on the hand of a liar. *(Open daily 10am-1pm and 3-7pm. Portico open daily 9am-7pm.)*

CAPITOLINE HILL. Home to the original capitol, the **Monte Capitolino** still serves as the seat of the city government. Michelangelo designed its **Piazza di Campidoglio,** now home to the **Capitoline Museums** (see p. 618). Stairs lead up to the rear of the 7th-century **Chiesa di Santa Maria in Aracoeli.** The gloomy **Mamertine Prison,** consecrated the **Church of San Pietro in Carcere,** lies down the hill from the back stairs of the Aracoeli. Saint Peter, imprisoned here, baptized his captors with the waters that flooded his cell. *(Open daily 9am-12:30pm and 2:30-6:30pm. Donation requested.)* At the far end of the *piazza,* opposite the stairs, lies the turreted **Palazzo dei Senatori,** the home of Rome's mayor. *(To get to the Campidoglio, take any bus that goes to P. Venezia. From P. Venezia, walk around to the right to P. d'Aracoeli, and take the stairs up the hill.)*

CENTRO STORICO

PIAZZA VENEZIA AND VIA DEL CORSO. The **Via del Corso** takes its name from its days as Rome's premier racecourse, running between P. del Popolo and the rumbling P. Venezia. **Palazzo Venezia** was one of the first Renaissance *palazzi* built in the city; Mussolini used it as an office and delivered his famous orations from its balcony, but today it's little more than a glorified traffic circle dominated by the **Vittorio Emanuele II monument.** Off V. del Corso, the picturesque **Piazza Colonna** was named for the colossal **Colonna di Marco Aurelio,** designed in imitation of Trajan's column. Off the northwest corner of the *piazza* is the **Piazza di Montecitorio,** dominated by Bernini's **Palazzo Montecitorio,** now the seat of the Chamber of Deputies. The opulent **Il Gesu,** mother church of the Jesuit order, makes few concessions towards poverty, chastity, or obedience. *(Take V.C. Battisti from P. Venezia, which becomes V.d. Plebiscito before entering P.d. Gesu. Open daily 6am-12:30pm and 4-7:15pm.)*

THE PANTHEON. Architects still wonder how this 2000-year-old temple was erected; its dome—a perfect half-sphere made of poured concrete without the support of vaults, arches, or ribs—is the largest of its kind. The light that enters the roof was used as a sundial to indicate the passing of the hours and the dates of equinoxes and solstices. In AD 606, it was consecrated as the **Church of Santa Maria ad Martyres.** *(In P. della Rotonda. Open M-Sa 8:30am-7:30pm, Su 9am-6pm.)*

PIAZZA NAVONA. Originally a stadium built in AD 86, the *piazza* once hosted wrestling matches, track and field events, and mock naval battles (in which the stadium was flooded and filled with fleets skippered by convicts). Each of the river god statues in Bernini's **Fountain of the Four Rivers** represents one of the four continents of the globe (as known then): The Ganges for Asia, the Danube for Europe, the Nile for Africa (veiled, since the source of the river was unknown), and the Río de la Plata for the Americas. The **Church of Sant'Agnese in Agone** dominates the *piazza*'s western side. *(Open daily 9am-noon and 4-7pm.)*

OTHER SIGHTS. In front of the temple, the *piazza* centers on Giacomo della Porta's late-Renaissance fountain and an Egyptian obelisk added in the 18th century. Around the left side of the Pantheon, another obelisk marks the center of tiny **Piazza Minerva.** Behind the obelisk, the **Chiesa di Santa Maria sopra Minerva** hides some Renaissance masterpieces, including Michelangelo's *Christ Bearing the Cross,* Antoniazzo Romano's *Annunciation,* and a statue of St. Sebastian recently attributed to Michelangelo. The south transept holds the famous **Carafa Chapel,** home to a brilliant fresco cycle by Filippino Lippi. *(Open M-Sa 7am-7pm, Su 7am-1pm and 3:30-7pm.)* From the upper left-hand corner of P. della Rotonda, V. Giustiniani goes north to intersect V. della Scrofa and V. della Dogana Vecchia at the **Church of San Luigi dei Francesi,** home to three of Caravaggio's most famous paintings: *The Calling of St. Matthew, St. Matthew and the Angel,* and *Crucifixion.* *(Open Su-W and F-Sa 7:30am-12:30pm and 3:30-7pm, Th 7:30am-12:30pm.)*

CAMPO DEI FIORI

Campo dei Fiori lies across C. V. Emanuele II from P. Navona. During papal rule, the area was the site of countless executions; now the only carcasses that litter the *piazza* are the fish in the colorful produce **market** (M-Sa 6am to 2pm). South of the Campo lie P. Farnese and the huge, stately **Palazzo Farnese,** the greatest of Rome's Renaissance *palazzi.* To the east of the *palazzo* is the Baroque facade of the **Palazzo Spada** and the collection of the **Galleria Spada** (p. 591).

THE JEWISH GHETTO. The Jewish community in Rome is the oldest in Europe—Israelites came in 161 BC as ambassadors from Judas Maccabei, asking for help against invaders. The Ghetto, the tiny area to which Pope Paul IV confined the Jews

ITALY

ITALY

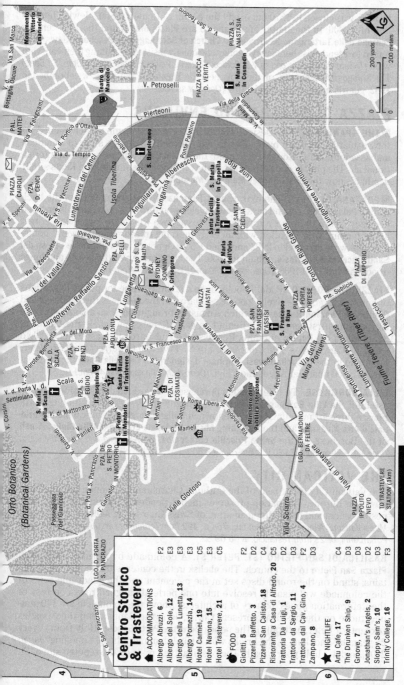

Centro Storico & Trastevere

▲ ACCOMMODATIONS

Albergo Abruzzi, 6	F2
Albergo del Sole, 12	E3
Albergo della Lunetta, 13	E3
Albergo Pomezia, 14	E3
Hotel Carmel, 19	C5
Hotel Navona, 15	E3
Hotel Trastevere, 21	C5

❖ FOOD

Giolitti, 5	F2
Pizzeria Baffetto, 3	D2
Pizzeria San Calisto, 18	C4
Ristorante a Casa di Alfredo, 20	C5
Trattoria Da Luigi, 1	D2
Trattoria da Sergio, 11	D3
Trattoria dal Cav. Gino, 4	F2
Zampano, 8	D3

★ NIGHTLIFE

Artu Cafe, 17	C4
The Drunken Ship, 9	D3
Groove, 7	D3
Jonathan's Angels, 2	D2
Sloppy Sam's, 10	D3
Trinity College, 16	F3

ITALY

in 1555, was closed in 1870 but is still the center of Rome's vibrant Jewish population of 16,000. In the center of the ghetto are **Piazza Mattei** and the 16th-century **Fontana delle Tartarughe.** Nearby is the **Church of Sant'Angelo in Pescheria;** Jews were forced to attend mass here every Sunday and quietly resisted by stuffing their ears with wax. *(Toward the eastern end of V.d. Portico d'Ottavia. Prayer meetings W 5:30pm, Sa 5pm.)* The **Sinagoga Ashkenazita,** on the Tiber near the Theater of Marcellus, was bombed in 1982; guards now search all visitors. *(Open for services only.)*

PIAZZA DI SPAGNA AND ENVIRONS

■**THE SPANISH STEPS.** Designed by an Italian, funded by the French, named for the Spaniards, occupied by the British, and currently under the sway of American ambassador-at-large Ronald McDonald, the **Scalinata di Spagna** exude an international air. The pink house to the right of the Steps was the site of John Keats's 1821 death; it's now the **Keats-Shelley Memorial Museum.**

■**FONTANA DI TREVI.** The extravagant **Fontana di Trevi** emerges from the back wall of **Palazzo Poli.** Legend says that a traveler who throws a coin into it is ensured a speedy return to Rome; a traveler who tosses two will fall in love there. Forget about funding your vacation with an early morning treasure hunt: Several homeless men were arrested in 2002 and fined €500. Opposite is the Baroque **Chiesa dei Santi Vincenzo e Anastasio,** rebuilt in 1630. The crypt preserves the hearts and lungs of popes from 1590-1903. *(Open daily 7:30am-12:30pm and 4-7pm.)*

PIAZZA DEL POPOLO. P. del Popolo, once a favorite venue for public executions of heretics, is now the lively "people's square." In the center is the 3200-year-old **Obelisk of Pharaoh Ramses II,** which Augustus brought back as a souvenir from Egypt in the first century BC. Behind an early-Renaissance shell, the **Church of Santa Maria del Popolo** contains Renaissance and Baroque masterpieces. Two exquisite Caravaggios, *The Conversion of St. Paul* and *Crucifixion of St. Peter*, are found in the **Cappella Cerasi.** Raphael designed the **Cappella Chigi** for the great Renaissance financier Augustino Chigi. *(Open daily 7am-noon and 4-7pm.)*

VILLA BORGHESE. To celebrate his purchase of a cardinalship, Scipione Borghese built the **Villa Borghese** north of P.d. Spagna and V.V. Veneto. Its huge park houses three art museums: World-renowned **Galleria Borghese,** stark **Galleria Nazionale d'Arte Moderna,** and the intriguing **Museo Nazionale Etrusco di Villa Giulia.** North of the Borghese are the **Santa Priscilla catacombs.** *(M: A-Spagna and follow the signs. Open M-F 9:30am-6pm, Sa-Su 9:30am-7pm. €8.50.)*

THE VATICAN CITY

The Vatican City is the seat of the Catholic Church and was once the mightiest power in Europe. The nation preserves its independence by running a separate postal system and maintaining an army of Swiss Guards. *(M: A-Ottaviano or A-Cipro/ Musei Vaticani. Alternatively, catch bus #64 or 492 from Termini or Largo Argentina, 62 from P. Barberini, or 23 from Testaccio.* ☎*06 69 82.)*

BASILICA DI SAN PIETRO (ST. PETER'S). A colonnade by Bernini leads from **Piazza San Pietro** to the church. The **obelisk** in the center is framed by two fountains; stand on the round discs set in the pavement and the quadruple rows of the colonnade will visually resolve into one perfectly aligned row, courtesy of the Reformation popes' battery of architects. Above the colonnade are 140 statues; those on the basilica represent Christ, John the Baptist, and the Apostles (except for Peter, naturally). The pope opens the **Porta Sancta** (Holy Door) every 25 years by knocking in the bricks with a silver hammer; the last opening was in 2000, so don't hold your breath. The basilica itself rests on the reputed site of St.

Peter's tomb. To the right, Michelangelo's *Pietà* has been protected by bullet-proof glass since 1972, when an axe-wielding fiend smashed Christ's nose and broke Mary's hand. Arnolfo di Cambio's *Peter*, in the central nave of the basilica, was not originally malformed, but centuries' worth of pilgrims rubbing his foot have crippled him. The climb to the top of the **Dome** might very well be worth the heart attack it will undoubtedly cause. An elevator will take you up about 300 of the 330 stairs. *(Dress modestly—no shorts, skirts above the knee, sleeveless shirts, or sundresses allowed. Multilingual confession available. Open daily 7am-7pm. Mass M-Sa 9, 10, 11am, noon, and 5pm; Su 9, 10:30, 11:30am, 12:10, 1, 4, and 5:30pm. Dome: From inside the basilica, exit the building, and re-enter the door to the far left with your back to the basilica. €4, by elevator €5. Open Apr.-Sept. daily 7am-5:45pm; Oct.-Mar. 7am-4:45pm.)*

■ **SISTINE CHAPEL.** Ever since its completion in the 16th century, the **Sistine Chapel** (named for its founder, Pope Sixtus IV) has served as the chamber in which the College of Cardinals elects new popes. The frescoes on the side walls predate Michelangelo's ceiling; on the right, scenes from the life of Moses complement parallel scenes of Christ's life on the left. Each section of the ceiling depicts a story from Genesis. It appears vaulted but is actually flat. Contrary to legend, Michelangelo did not paint flat on his back, but standing up and craning backward, and he never recovered from the strain to his neck and eyes. In his *Last Judgment,* on the altar, the figure of Christ as judge hovers in the upper center. *(Admission included with Vatican Museums, p. 625.)*

CASTEL SANT'ANGELO. Built by **Hadrian** (AD 117-138) as a mausoleum for himself, this hulking mass of brick and stone has served the popes as a fortress, prison, and palace. When the city was wracked with the plague in 590, Pope Gregory saw an angel sheathing his sword at the top of the complex; the plague abated soon after, and the edifice was rededicated to the angel. It now contains a **museum of arms and artillery** and offers an incomparable view of Rome and the Vatican. *(Walk along the river with St. Peter's behind you and the towering castle to your left; follow the signs to the entrance. Open Su and Tu-Sa 9am-7pm. €5.)*

TRASTEVERE

Right off the **Ponte Garibaldi** stands the statue of the famous dialect poet G.G. Bellie. On V. di Santa Cecilia, behind the cars, through the gate, and beyond the courtyard full of roses is the **Basilica di Santa Cecilia in Trastevere;** Carlo Maderno's famous statue of Santa Cecilia lies under the altar. *(Open M-Sa 8am-12:30pm and 4:15-6:30pm; Su 9:30-10am, 11:15-noon, and 4:15-6:30pm.)* From P. Sonnino, V. della Lungaretta leads west to P.S. Maria in Trastevere, home to numerous stray dogs, expatriates, and the **Chiesa di Santa Maria in Trastevere,** built in the 4th century. *(Open M-Sa 9am-5:30pm, Su 8:30-10:30am and noon-5:30pm.)* North of the *piazza* are the Rococo **Galleria Corsini,** V. della Lungara 10, and, across the street, the **Villa Farnesina,** the jewel of Trastevere. Atop the Gianicolo hill is the **Chiesa di San Pietro in Montorio,** built on the spot once believed to be the site of St. Peter's upside-down crucifixion. Next door in a small courtyard is Bramante's tiny ■**Tempietto,** constructed to commemorate the site of Peter's martyrdom. Rome's **botanical gardens** contain a **garden for the blind** as well as a rose garden that holds the bush from which all the world's roses are supposedly descended. *(Church and Tempietto open daily 9:30am-12:30pm and 4-6pm.)*

NEAR TERMINI

The sights in this urban part of town are concentrated northwest of the station and to the south, near P. V. Emanuele II.

ITALY

PIAZZA DEL QUIRINALE AND VIA XX SETTEMBRE. Several blocks south of P. Barberini and northeast of P. Venezia, the statues of Castor and Pollux, Rome's protectors, flank yet another obelisk that served as part of Sixtus V's redecoration plan. The **Church of Sant'Andrea al Quirinale,** full of Bernini's characteristic jolly cherubs, highlights the artist's ability to combine architecture and painting for a single, coherent effect—even if that effect is as overdone as most Baroque work. *(Open Sept.-July M and W-Su 8am-noon and 4-7pm; Aug. M and W-Su 8am-noon.)* A Counter-Reformation facade by Maderno marks **Santa Susanna,** the American parish in Rome. The Mannerist frescoes by Croce are worth a look. *(Open daily 9am-noon and 4-7pm.)*

BASILICA OF SANTA MARIA MAGGIORE. As one of the five churches in Rome granted extraterritoriality, this basilica, crowning the Esquiline Hill, is officially part of Vatican City. To the right of the altar, a marble slab marks the **tomb of Bernini.** The 14th-century mosaics in the **loggia** recount the story of the August snowfall that showed the pope where to build the church. *(Dress code strictly enforced. Open daily 7am-7pm. Loggia open daily 9:30am-1pm. Tickets in souvenir shop €2.70.)*

SOUTHERN ROME

The area south of the center is a great mix of wealthy and working-class neighborhoods and is home to the city's best nightlife and some of its grandest churches.

CAELIAN HILL. Southeast of the Colosseum, the Caelian, along with the Esquiline, is the biggest of Rome's seven original hills and home to some of the city's greatest chaos. Split into three levels, each from a different era, the **Church of San Clemente** is one of Rome's most intriguing churches. A fresco cycle by Masolino dating from the 1420s graces the **Chapel of Santa Caterina.** *(M: B-Colosseo. Turn left out of the station and walk east on V. Fori Imperiali. Open M-Sa 9am-12:30pm and 3-6pm, Su and holidays 10am-12:30pm and 3-6pm. €3.)* The immense **Chiesa di San Giovanni in Laterano** was the seat of the pope until the 14th century; founded by Constantine in AD 314, it's Rome's oldest Christian basilica. The two golden reliquaries over the altar contain the heads of St. Peter and St. Paul. Across the street is the **Scala Santa,** which houses what are believed to be the 28 steps used by Jesus outside Pontius Pilate's house. *(Dress code enforced. M: A-San Giovanni or bus #16 from Termini. Open daily 7am-12:30pm and 3:30-7:30pm. €2; museum €1.)*

APPIAN WAY. Since burial inside the city walls was forbidden during ancient times, fashionable Romans made their final resting places along the Appian Way. At the same time, early Christians secretly dug maze-like catacombs under the ashes of their persecutors. *(M: A-San Giovanni. Take bus #218 from P. di S. Giovanni to the intersection of V. Ardeatina and V.d. Sette Chiese.)* **San Callisto,** V. Appia Antica 110, is the largest catacomb in Rome, with nearly 22km of subterranean paths. Its four levels once held 16 popes, St. Cecilia, and 500,000 other Christians. *(Take the private road that runs northeast to the entrance to the catacombs. Open Mar.-Jan. Th-Tu 8:30am-noon and 2:30-5:30pm.)* **Santa Domitilla** houses an intact 3rd-century portrait of Christ and the Apostles. *(Facing V. Ardeatina from the exit of S. Callisto, cross the street and walk up V.d. Sette Chiese. Open Feb.-Dec. M and W-Su 8:30am-noon and 2:30-5pm.)* **San Sebastiano,** V. Appia Antica 136, once held the bodies of Peter and Paul. *(Open Dec.-Oct. M-Sa 8:30am-noon and 2:30-5:30pm. Adjacent church open daily 8am-6pm.)*

AVENTINE HILL. The ▨**Roseto Comunale,** Rome's official rose garden, is host to the annual Premio Roma, the worldwide competition for the best blossom. Entries are sent in May. *(On both sides of V.d. Valle Murcia, across the Circus Maximus from the Palatine Hill. Open daily 8am-7:30pm.)* The **Giardini degli Aranci** nearby is also a pleasant place for an afternoon stroll. *(Open daily dawn to dusk.)* The **Church of Santa**

Sabina and its accompanying monastery were home to St. Dominic, Pius V, and St. Thomas Aquinas, and dates from the 5th century. *(At the southern end of Parco Savello. Open daily 6:30am-12:45pm and 3:30-7pm.)* V.S. Sabina continues along the crest of the hill to **Piazza dei Cavalieri di Malta,** home of the crusading order of the Knights of Malta. Through the ▓keyhole in the pale yellow gate, the dome of St. Peter's is perfectly framed by hedges.

EUR. EUR (AY-oor) is an Italian acronym for the 1942 Universal Exposition of Rome, which Mussolini planned as a showcase of Fascist achievement. The center of the area is **Piazza Guglielmo Marconi.** According to legend, when St. Paul was beheaded at the **Abbazia delle Tre Fontane (Abbey of the Three Fountains),** his head bounced three times, creating a fountain at each bounce. *(M: B-Laurentina. Walk north on V. Laurentina and turn right on V. di Acque Salve; the abbey is at the bottom of the hill. Open daily 8am-1pm and 3-7pm.)*

🏛 MUSEUMS

Etruscans, emperors, popes, and *condottiere* have been busily stuffing Rome full of artwork for several millennia, leaving behind a city teeming with galleries. Museums are generally closed holidays, Sunday afternoons, and all day Mondays.

VATICAN MUSEUMS. More or less the content of every art book you've ever seen. The four color-coded routes displayed at the entrance are the only way to see the museums, but route C is the most comprehensive. The **Egyptian Museum** contains a small, high-quality sample of Egyptian and pseudo-Egyptian statuary and paintings. The walk through the entire gallery comes out in the **Belvedere Courtyard,** with its gigantic bronze pinecone, and a view of the **Tower of the Winds,** where Queen Christina of Sweden lived briefly before insisting on more comfortable accommodations. The **Pio-Clementine Museum** is the western world's finest collection of antique sculpture, and features, among other wonders, the Apollo Belvedere. Minor galleries (Candelabra, Tapestries, Maps) abound, and a trip to the Vatican without a sojourn in the ▓Raphael Rooms is no trip at all. The **Stanza della Segnatura** and its companions hold the *School of Athens* and a number of famous frescoes. The **Pinacoteca,** the Vatican's painting collection, spans eight centuries. *(Walk north from the right hand side of P.S. Pietro along the wall of the Vatican City for about 10 blocks. ☎06 69 88 49 47. Open M-F 8:45am-4:45pm, Sa 8:45am-1:45pm. Last entrance 1hr. before closing. €10. Free last Su of the month 8:45am-1:45pm. Plan to spend at least 4-5hr.)*

GALLERIA BORGHESE. The exquisite Galleria's **Room I,** on the right, houses Canova's sexy statue of **Paolina Borghese** portrayed as Venus triumphant. The next rooms display the most famous sculptures by Bernini: a magnificent **David,** crouching with his slingshot; **Apollo and Daphne;** the weightless body in **Rape of Proserpina;** and weary-looking Aeneas in **Eneo e Anchise.** Don't miss six **Caravaggio** paintings, including his *Self Portrait as Bacchus* and *St. Jerome,* which grace the side walls. The collection continues in the pinacoteca upstairs, accessible from the gardens around the back by a winding staircase. **Room IX** holds Raphael's **Deposition** while Sodoma's *Pietà* graces **Room XII.** Look for self portraits by Bernini, del Conte's Cleopatra and Lucrezia, Rubens's **Pianto sul Cristo Morto,** and Titian's **Amor Sacro e Amor Profano.** *(M: A-Spagna; take the exit labeled "Villa Borghese," walk to the right past the Metro stop to V. Muro Torto and then to P. Porta Pinciana; Viale del Museo Borghese is ahead and leads to the museum. Open daily 9am-7pm. Entrance every hr., visits limited to 2hr. Tickets (including reservation, tour, and bag charge) €8. Audio guide €5. Open M-F 9am-6pm, Sa 9am-1pm.)*

CAPITOLINE MUSEUM. This collection of ancient sculpture is one the largest in the world. The Palazzo Nuovo contains the original statue of **Marcus Aurelius** that once stood in the center of the piazza. The collections continue across the piazza in the Palazzo dei Conservatori. See fragments of the **Colossus of Constantine** and the famous **Capitoline Wolf,** an Etruscan statue that has symbolized the city of Rome since antiquity. At the top of the stairs, the **pinacoteca's** masterpieces include Bellini's *Portrait of a Young Man,* Titan's *Baptism of Christ,* and Rubens's *Romulus and Remus Fed by the Wolf,* and Caravaggio's *St. John the Baptist* and *Gypsy Fortune-Teller.* (*On Capitoline Hill behind the Vittorio Emanuele II monument.* ☎ *06 39 96 78 00. Open Su and Tu-Sa 9am-8pm. €7.80. Guidebook €7.75, audio guide €4. Guided tours in Italian Sa 5pm, Su at noon and 5pm.*)

EUR MUSEUMS. All of the museums splayed around Mussolini's obelisk are small and manageable, and serve as a break from the usual decadent Classical and Renaissance offerings of Rome's more popular museums. The intimidating facade of the **Museo della Civilita Romana** gives way to a number of scale models of life in ancient Rome. See how the Longobards overran the remains of the Empire in the **Museo dell'Alto Medioevo,** a collection of weapons, jewelry, and household items from Late Antiquity. The **Museo Nazionale delle Arti e Tradizioni Popolari** contains such incongruent items as a Carnevale costume and a wine press. The skull of the famous Neanderthal Guattari Man, discovered near Circeo, is found at the **Museo Preistorico ed Etnografico Luigi Pigorini.** (*M: B-EUR-Palasport or B-EUR-Fermi. Walk north up V. Cristoforo Colombo. Civilita Romana: Open Tu-Sa 9am-6:45pm, Su and holidays 9am-1:30pm. €6.20. Alto Medioevo: Open Tu-Su 9am-8pm. €2. Nazionale delle Arti e Tradizioni Popolari: Open Tu-Su 9am-8pm. Closed holidays. €4. Preistorico ed Etnografico Luigi Pigorini: Open daily 9am-8pm. €4. All museums: under-18 and over-65 free.*)

OTHER RECOMMENDED COLLECTIONS. Montemartini, Rome's first power plant, was converted to hold displaced sculpture from the Capitoline Museums in the 1990s. (*V. Ostiense 106. M: B-Piramide. Open Su and Tu-Sa 9:30am-7pm. €4.20.*) The **Doria Pamphilj** family, whose relations with Pope Innocent X coined the term "nepotism," still owns its stunning private collection. Titian's *Salome* and Velasquez's portrait of Innocent X alone are worth the visit. (*P. del Collegio Romana 2. Open M-W and F-Su 10am-5pm. €7.30, students and seniors €5.70. Audioguide included.*) After overdosing on "artwork" and "culture," get your aesthetic stomach pumped at the one museum dedicated to crime and punishment, the **Museo Criminologico.** Etchings like *A Smith Has His Brains Beaten Out With a Hammer* hang on the walls along with terrorist, spy, and druggie paraphernalia. (*V. del Gonfalone 27. Open Tu-Th 9am-1pm and 2:30-6:30pm, F-Sa 9am-1pm. €2; under-18 and over-65 €1.*)

🎭 ENTERTAINMENT

Unfortunately, Roman entertainment just ain't what it used to be. Back in the day, you could swing by the Colosseum to watch a man get mauled by a bear; today, Romans seeking diversion are more likely to go to a nightclub than fight a wild beast to the death. Check *Roma C'è* (which has an English-language section) or *Time Out,* available at newsstands, for club, movie, and events listings.

THEATER AND CINEMA

The **Festival Roma-Europa** in late summer brings a number of world-class acts to Rome (consult www.romace.it for more information), but for year-round performances of classic Italian theater, **Teatro Argentina,** Largo di Torre Argentina 52, is the grand matriarch of all Italian venues. (☎ 06 68 80 46 01. Box office open M-F 10am-2pm and 3-7pm, Sa 10am-2pm. Tickets around €10-26, depending on performance; students €10-21. AmEx/D/MC/V.) **Teatro Colosseo,** V. Capo d'Africa 5a, usually features work by foreign playwrights translated into Italian, but also hosts an English theater night. (☎06 700 49 32. M: B-Colosseo. Box office open Tu-Sa 6-9:30pm. Tickets €10-20. Students €7.80. Closed in summer.)

Most English-language films are dubbed into Italian; check newspapers or *Roma C'è* for listings with a **v.o.** or **I.o.** These indicate that the film is in the original language. For a sure bet, pay a visit to **Il Pasquino,** P. Sant-Egidio 10, off P.S. Maria in Trastevere. Three different screens show English films, and the program changes daily. (☎06 580 36 22. €6.20, students €4.20.)

MUSIC

Founded by Palestrina in the 16th century, **Accademia Nazionale di Santa Cecilia** remains the best in classical music performances. Concerts are held at the Parco della Musicain, V. Pietro di Coubertin, 30, (☎06 80 82 058; http://www.musicaper-roma.it/) near P. del Popolo. Box office open 9am-6pm. Regular season runs Oct.-June. €9, students €5. Alexanderplatz Jazz Club, V. Ostia 9, is the current residence of that je ne sais quoi that was expatriate life in Italy during the 50s. Read messages on the wall from old jazz greats, and be prepared to move outside during the summer to the Villa Celimontana. (☎06 39 74 21 71. M: A-Ottaviano, near the Vatican City. Required tessera €6.20. Open Sept.-June daily 9pm-2am. Shows start at 10pm.) The Cornetto Free Music Festival Roma Live attracts acts like Pink Floyd, The Cure, and the Backstreet Boys at a number of venues throughout the city during the summer. (☎06 592 21 00; www.bbecom.it. Shows start at 9:30pm.)

SPECTATOR SPORTS

While other spectator sports may exist in Rome, it's *calcio* (football) that brings the scantily-clad fans and the large-scale riots that the world knows and loves. Rome has two teams in Italy's Serie A: **A.S. Roma** and **S.S. Lazio.** Games are played at the Stadio Olimpico in the Foro Italico (M: A-Ottaviano to bus #32). *Tifosi*, as hardcore fans are called, arrive hours or sometimes days ahead of time for big games, to drink, sing, and taunt rivals. Tickets can be bought at the stadium box office, but are easier to obtain at the **A.S. Roma Store,** P. Colonna 360. (☎06 678 65 14; www.asroma.it. Open daily 10am-10pm, tickets sold 10am-6:30pm. Tickets start at €15.50. AmEx/MC/V.) Italy is also one of the hosts to the **6 Nations Cup,** Europe's premier Rugby Union tournament. Visitors will find that despite rising interest, good seats are readily available from mid-February through March at the Flaminio Stadium. (Metro A: Flaminio. Then take the #2 tram to the V. Tiziano stop. For more info visit www.6-nations-rugby.com.)

▗ SHOPPING

Everything you need to know about Italian fashion is summed up in one simple phrase: *la bella figura.* It describes a beautiful, well-dressed, put-together woman, and it is very, very important in Rome. Think whole picture: tinted sunglasses, Ferragamo suit, Gucci pumps with six-inch heels, and, stuffed in your Prada bag, a *telefonino* with a signature ring. For men, a single gorgeous black suit will do the trick. If you're not a Telecom heir or heiress, there are still ways to purchase grace and aplomb. Sales happen twice a year, in mid-January and mid-July, and a number of boutiques, while not as fashionable as their counterparts on the Via Condotti, won't require the sale of a major organ, or even a minor one.

BOUTIQUES

No matter what anti-capitalist mantra you may espouse, you know you've secretly lusted after that Versace jacket. So indulge. If you spend over €155 at one store, you are eligible for a tax refund. (As if you needed another incentive to splurge.)

Dolce & Gabbana, V.d. Condotti 52 (☎06 69 92 49 99). Open M-Sa 10am-7:30pm.

Prada, V.d. Condotti 88-95 (☎06 679 08 97). Open M-Sa 10am-7pm, Su 2-8pm.

Salvatore Ferragamo, Men: V.d. Condotti 64-66 (☎06 678 11 30). Women: V.d. Condotti 72-74 (☎06 679 15 65). Open M 3-7pm, Tu-Sa 10am-7pm.

Bruno Magli, V.d. Gambero 1 (☎06 679 38 02). Open M-Sa 10am-7:30pm.

Gucci, V.d. Condotti 8 (☎06 678 93 40). Open M 3-7pm, Tu-Sa 10am-7pm, Su 2-7pm.

CHEAP AND CHIC

Designer emporiums such as **David Cenci,** V. Campo Marzio 1-7 (☎06 699 06 81; open M 4-8pm, Tu-F 9:30am-1:30pm and 4-8pm, Sa 10am-8pm); **Antonelo & Fabrizio,** C.V. Emanuele 242-243 (☎06 68 80 27 49; open daily in summer 9:30am-1:30pm and 4-8pm; off-season 3:30-7:30pm); and **Discount dell'alta Moda,** V. Agostino Depretis 87 (☎06 47 82 56 72; open M 2:30-7:30pm, Tu-Sa 9:30am-7:30pm) stock many lines of designer clothes and shoes—sometimes at half their normal prices.

▨ **Diesel,** V.d. Corso 186 (☎06 678 39 33). Off V.d. Condotti. Also at V.d. Babuino 95. *The* label in retro fashion is surprisingly high-octane. Prices are cheaper than elsewhere in the world, so it's worth the visit. Open M-Sa 10:30am-8pm, Su 3:30-8pm.

Mariotti Boutique, V.d. Frezza 20 (☎06 322 71 26). This elegant boutique sells clothes for the modern, sophisticated woman. Prices are steep; watch for the significant sales. Open M-F 10am-7:30pm, Sa 10am-2pm.

MISCELLANEOUS

▨ **Alcozer,** V.d. Carozze 48 (☎06 679 13 88). Near P. di Spagna. Gorgeous old-world jewelry at decent prices. Earrings from €20; a jeweled crucifix Lucrezia Borgia would've been proud of for €65. Open M 2-7:30pm, Tu-Sa 10am-7:30pm.

▨ **Materozzoli,** P.S. Lorenzo in Lucina 5, off V.d. Corso (☎06 68 89 26 86). This old-world *profumeria* carries everything from the exclusive Aqua di Parma line to shaving brushes. Hard-to-find perfumes and colognes. Open M 3:30-7:30pm, Tu-Sa 10am-1:30pm and 3:30-7:30pm. Closed Aug. 10-28.

Campo Marzio Penne, V. Campo Marzio 41 (☎06 68 80 78 77). Fountain pens (from €12) and leather goods, in addition to brightly-colored journals and photo albums (from €25). The small address books (€7) make great presents. Open daily 10am-1pm and 2-7pm.

Tedeschi Roma, V. Nazionale 106 (☎06 679 55 75). Good selection of luggage and other bags, convenient to Termini. Large backpacks around €100. Open M-F 10am-7:30pm, Sa 10:30am-2pm. AmEx/MC/V.

Disfunzioni Musicali, V. degli Etruschi 4 (☎06 446 19 84), in San Lorenzo. CDs, cassettes, and LPs available, including excellent selections of rock, avant-garde classical, jazz, and ethnic. Open M 3-8pm, Tu-Sa 10:30am-8pm.

◪ NIGHTLIFE

PUBS

Exactly why the Irish pub became the *de facto* form of Roman nightlife is unclear, but that's the way it is. Rome has more pubs than Dublin, and more are on the way. Not all of Rome's pubs are Irish; some claim to be English, Scottish, American, or Brazilian, and some are distinctly Roman. Nationality is in the eye of the drinker.

▨ **Jonathan's Angels,** V.d. Fossa 14-16. West of P. Navona. Not since Pope Julius II has there been a case of Roman megalomania as severe as that of Jonathan, whose face serves as the theme for the decor in this bar. Medium beer on tap €5; delicious cocktails €8. Open M-F 5pm-2am, Sa and Su 3pm-2am.

▨ **Trinity College,** V.d. Collegio Romano 6. Off V.d. Corso near P. Venezia. Offers degrees in such diverse curricula as Guinness, Harp, and Heineken. Tuition €5. Happy Hour noon-8pm. Classes held every day 11am-3am. AmEx/MC/V.

▨ **Il Simposio,** V.d. Latini 11. Off V. Tiburtina. Chances are good that on any given night a splattered painter will be hard at work beautifying a discarded refrigerator. With cocktails from €3.50 and a glass of *fragolino* for €2.75, even starving artists can afford the place. Open daily 9pm-2am. Closed late July-Aug.

The Nag's Head, V. IV Novembre 138b. Dance floor inside; live music twice a week. Guinness €5; cocktails €8. Cover €5; F and Sa men €7.80; no cover Su. Open in summer daily 8pm-2am; winter noon-2am. MC/V.

Nuvolari, V. degli Ombrellari 10. Off V. Vittorio. This cocktail bar (serving beer and tropical drinks) also functions as an *enoteca* with wine by the glass (€3.50), a diverse wine list, and the usual salads (choose from 30 at €6 each) and meat and cheese platters (€7.50). Open M-Sa 8pm-2am.

Friend's, V. Piave 71. From P. Independenza take V. Goito, then cross V. XX Settembre onto Via Piave. Plenty of outdoor seating and stainless steel interior. Chill music and all manner of cocktails (€5.50). Beer €4-4.50. Happy Hour 7-9:30pm. Open M-Sa 7:30am-2am, Su 6pm-2am. AmEx/V/MC.

Artu Cafe, Largo Fumasoni Biondi 5. Good selection of drinks. Enjoy specialty cocktails made with fresh juices (€6.20-7.20). Beer €4.50. Wine €3-5.50. Free *apertivi* buffet 6:45-9pm. Open Tu-Su 6pm-2am. MC/V.

Pub Hallo'Ween, P. Tiburtino 31, at the corner of V. Tiburtina and V. Marsala. Plastic skulls and fake spiders and spiderwebs. Beer €3.70-4.20. Mixed drinks €4.20-5.20. Open Sept.-July M-Sa 8:30pm-2:30am, Su 5pm-2:30am.

Shanti, V. dei Conciatori 11. From M: Piramide, head down V. Ostiense; take second street on the right. Yes, these surely are some of the best cocktails (€6-7) to be had in Rome. Great hookahs (€2.60 per person). Belly dancing Sept.-Mar. W-F 11pm-1am. Open Sept.-July daily 9pm-1am. Closed on Su in July.

ketumbar, V. Galvani 24. A taste of New York decadence in the middle of Italy. It even doubles as a Japanese restaurant (sushi plates €18-36). Wear black; everyone else will. Open Sept.-July M-Sa 8pm-3am. AmEx/MC/V.

Mount Gay Music Bar, V. Galvani 54. Grab a pillow on the floor and sip your cocktail (€8) alongside Rome's young and beautiful. Open daily 11pm-6am. MC/V.

The Proud Lion Pub, Borgo Pio 36. The outside of the pub says "Rome, Borgo Pio," but the beer and scotch says "Hey, I don't forget my Highland roots." Beer and mixed drinks €4. Single malts €4.50-5. Open M-Sa 8:30-late.

The Drunken Ship, Campo dei Fiori 20-21. Because you're tired of meeting Italians. Because you feel the need to have an emotion-free fling with a kindred spirit. Because you're proud to be an American, dammit. Happy Hour daily 5-8pm. W 9-10pm power hour (all you can drink; €6). Open daily 11am-2am. AmEx/MC/V.

Sloppy Sam's, Campo dei Fiori 9-10. The identical twin of the Drunken Ship. Note that once home, wistful stories about that "special someone" you "befriended" at Sloppy Sam's will probably be regarded cynically. Beer €3.50. Shots €2.50. Ask about theme nights. Happy Hour 4-8pm. Open M-F 4pm-2am, Sa-Su 11am-2am. AmEx/MC/V.

Night and Day, V.d. Oca 50. Off V. di Ripetta near P. del Popolo. Don't even think of coming until the rest of the bars close. At 2am, Italians who don't let dawn stop their fun stream in. Buy a membership card (€5) for discounts on drinks. Beer €3-5, Guinness €4.50. Happy Hour until midnight. Open daily 7pm-6am. Closed part of Aug.

ITALY

1 COLOSSEUM. The bad news: millions of Christians, contrary to a number of Hollywood movies, did not meet their unfortunate ends within these partially deteriorated walls. The good news: at least 5000 wild animals did, during the stadium's inaugural festivities in AD 80. Titus's grand addition to the principle of bread and circuses may look like a heap of sun-bleached rock today (thanks in no small part to Julius II's not-so-clandestine pillaging during the Renaissance), but in its

TIME: 3-4hr. walk; longer if you visit the museums along the way.

DISTANCE: about 8km.

SEASON: A sunny day is preferable; bring lots of water.

A highlights tour of ancient Rome

youth, it was an engineering marvel, containing, among other things, a system of awnings that protected the bloodthirsty populace from the inconveniences of sun and rain. Allow an extra 20min. if you plan to make the climb to the upper tiers of the structure, or stride confidently across the new wooden walkway—just don't look down (p. 618).

2 SANTA MARIA IN ARACOELI. The archetypal Roman Church. In the first century AD, the Romans worshipped the spirit of money in the guise of Jupiter Moneta. Later, piety replaced productivity, and the mint originally located here became a meeting place for the Franciscans, who were generally uninterested in making money. In the meantime, the Sibyl once quartered within the walls of the old temple informed Augustus that although he did enjoy divine status, one greater than even he would come to rule Rome. In response, the emperor erected the Ara Coeli, or the altar to heaven (p. 618).

3 IL GESU. Historically, the Jesuits were an order known throughout Europe for their commitment to evangelism and their love of extravagant luxury items. The Gesu is the living incarnation of both strains, built in 1584 but left undecorated for more than 100 years (the prescient founders of the Order apparently realized that only Baroque could provide the gilded opulence that such a project required). The Chapel of St. Ignatius and its crowning piece of artistic achievement, the altar topped with an enormous globe of lapis lazuli, are rendered almost unholy by their grandeur, but the real triumph of the church is Baciccia's Triumph of the Holy Name of Jesus, in which sinners, cast from the communion of souls, appear to be hurtling from heaven towards the observers on the ground (p. 619).

4 TEATRO DI MARCELLO. Arranging a walk past the Marcello on a summer evening is a rewarding enterprise: some of Rome's best classical musicians often use the crumbling structure as a venue for concerts in nice weather. Without venturing too far into the stark, dusty collection of ruins, one can visit the oldest building in Rome permanently designated as a theater (p. 618).

5 ISOLA TIBERINA. A stroll around this island, enclosed by the Romans with travertine marble so that it would resemble a ship, is a good way to cross the Tiber on the way to Trastevere. The first structure on the island was a temple to Aesculapius, son of Apollo and god of medicine. During the plague of 293 BC, a statue of him was brought from Greece to the island, which has been dedicated to healing ever since. The Fatebenefratelli (literally "do good brothers") Hospital and San Bartolomeo, Holy Roman Emperor Otto III's church of choice, are both located on the grounds.

6 CASTEL SANT'ANGELO. The popes often used this former site of Hadrian's mausoleum as an escape from the pressures, problems, and riots that often plagued St. Peter's. The wealth of the Vatican was often stored here when the Holy Roman Emperors decided that a little trip to the south was the perfect way to fill their coffers. The lower building served as quarters for some of Rome's more rowdy residents, including the boastful autobiographer and

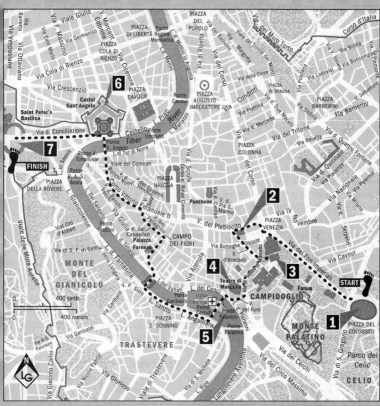

sometime artist Benvenuto Cellini, heretical monk Giordano Bruno, and Beatrice Cenci, accused of incest and patricide and memorialized by Shelley's *The Cenci*. The papal apartments are worth a look, especially the Camera d'Amore e Psiche (p. 623).

7 PIAZZA SAN PIETRO.   Far too often, tourists eager to rub flesh with millions of other pensive pilgrims in the Sistine Chapel rush past Bernini's masterpiece without a second look. The artist is undoubtedly taking the proverbial route of disgruntled dead people and turning over in his grave; his work was meant to awe the Protestant heretics who came to Rome in order to talk politics with the pope. A set of four colonnades crowned by 140 distinct saints was part of the visual effect planned by Bernini, in addition to the sensation of leaving the narrow streets of the medieval quarter for the comparative openness of the square. Mussolini ruined the characteristic Baroque metaphor (darkness into light) by constructing the Via di Conciliazione, but the square, and the obelisk placed in the middle by Sixtus V, are nonetheless impressive to even the biggest heretic in the crowd (p. 622).

CLUBS

Although Italian discos can be a flashy, sweaty good time, the scene changes as often as Roman phone numbers. Check *Roma C'è* or *Time Out*. Rome has fewer gay establishments than most cities its size, but those it has are solid and keep late hours. Many gay establishments require an **ARCI-GAY pass** (€10 yearly), available from **Circolo di Cultura Omosessuale Mario Mieli** (☎ 06 541 39 85).

Chic and Kitsch, V.S. Saba 11a. Uniting the elegant with the eclectic; music (often House or a variant) is selected by resident DJ Giuliano Marchili. Cover: men €13, women €10 includes 1st drink. Open Sept.-July Th-Sa 11:30pm-4am.

Groove, V. Savelli 10. Look for the black door. Lose it to acid jazz, funk, soul, and disco. F-Sa 1-drink min. (€5.16). Open W-Su 10pm-2am. Closed most of Aug.

Alien, V. Velletri 13-19. One of the biggest discos in Rome. As of this writing, the comfy chill-out room had not yet reached 1987. Cover varies (about €15, including a drink). Open Tu-Su 11pm-5:30am. In summer, moves to Fregene.

Piper, V. Tagliamento 9. A popular club that occasionally hosts gay nights. 70s, rock, and disco, as well as house and underground. Gay friendly all the time. Cover €10-18, includes 1st drink. Open F-Sa 11pm-4:30am; in summer Sa-Su 11pm-4:30am.

Black Out, V. Saturnia 18. From the Colosseum, take V. Claudia (V.d. Navicella/V. Gallia) southeast; turn right on V. Saturnia. Punk and Britpop. Occasional bands. Cover €8 (includes 1 drink). Open Sept. to mid-June Th-Su 11pm-4am.

Il Giardini di Adone, V.d. Reti 38a. Off V.d. Sabelli. Though it fancies itself a "spaghetti-pub," the happy students who frequent this little place would remind you that tables are properly used for dancing, not for eating linguine. Cover €6, includes 1st drink. Open Sept. to late July Su and Tu-Sa 8pm-3am.

Charro Cafe, V. di Monte Testaccio 73. So you wanted to go to Tijuana, but got stuck in Rome. Weep no more, *mis amigos:* make a run for Charro, home of the €2.60 tequila. Open daily midnight-3am.

Aquarela, V. di Monte Testaccio 64. You want pottery shards? You got pottery shards. A fine example of urban renewal, Roman-style. Entrance €10, includes 1st drink. Open Su and Tu-Sa 8:30pm-4am.

L'Alibi, V. di Monte Testaccio 40/44. Traditionally a gay club, L'Alibi now draws a mixed crowd. Its two floors host drag queen shows and hip DJs alike. The roof garden, decorated with leopard prints, plays chill music and serves cocktails (€8). Cover F-Sa €13-15. Open W-Su midnight-5am.

Coyote, V. di Monte Testaccio 48b. The newly-opened club sports a Tex-Mex look and caters to the homesick American tourist. Hosts Italian DJs. Its spacious terrace is a welcome escape from the revelry inside. Open daily 9pm-4am.

Radio Londra Caffè, V. di Monte Testaccio 65b. Packed with an energetic, good-looking, young crowd. Pint of beer €4-5. Pizza, *panini,* and hamburgers €4.20-5.20. 1-year membership required (€8; includes one free drink). Open M-Sa 9pm-3am.

Classico Village, V. Libetta 3. M: B-Garbatella. Exit onto V. Argonauti and take a left on V. Libetta. Women probably don't want to travel alone in this area at night. One of the best-known *centri sociali* in Rome—your one-stop shop for all things countercultural. Hosts live music, films, art exhibits, poetry readings, African cuisine tastings, and more. Hours and cover vary (€8-10).

⚡ DAYTRIPS FROM ROME

PONZA. As the largest of the Pontine Islands, Ponza was also the most susceptible to pirate attacks, which were frequent until the arrival of the fierce and wealthy Bourbon monarchs in 1734. The laid-back island lifestyle has resulted in a happy disregard for signs, street names, and maps. *Isole Pontine*, a comprehensive guide to the islands, is available at newsstands for €6.20. Beaches are the reason for the season in Ponza. **Cala dello Schiavone** and **Cala Cecata** (on the bus line) are the best and most accessible spots. The most spectacular views on the island are available at **Chiaia di Luna**, an expansive, rocky beach set at the bottom of a 200m tufo cliffside. Another point of sunbathing interest is the **Piscine Naturale,** just a quick ride through Ponza's hillside. Take the bus to Le Foma and ask to be let off at the Piscine. Cross the street and make your way down the long, steep path. Spiny sea urchins line the rocks, so take caution. From Rome, take the **train** from Termini to Anzio (1hr., every hr. 6am-11pm, €2.90) and then the Linee Vetor hydrofoil from Anzio to Ponza. (1hr., €20-23). Ticket office in Anzio is on the quay (☎06 984 50 85; www.vetor.it). Pro Loco **tourist office** is on V. Molo Musco, at the far right of the port, next to lighthouse, in the red building. (☎07 718 00 31; prolocoponza@libero.it. Open in summer M-Sa 9am-1pm and 4-8:30pm, Su 9am-1pm.)

FRASCATI. Patrician villas dotting the hillside are a testament to the peculiar power of Frascati, and, possibly, of its superb dry white wines. The sculpture-filled gardens of the **Villa Aldobrandini** dominate the hills over P. Marconi, while a 1km walk up on F. Massaia leads to the tiny **Chiesa dei Cappuccini.** A sign above the door announces that you need reservations for marriages, but the **Ethiopian Museum** next door requires no such foresight. It houses a collection of weapons, handmade crafts, and the death mask of the cardinal who collected the artifacts while doing missionary work. (Open daily 9am-noon and 4-6pm. Free.) The town of **Tusculum** was an ancient resort for the who's who of ancient Roman society, including Cicero and Cato. From the entrance of the Villa Aldobrandini, turn right onto V. Tusculo, which climbs 5km over winding country roads to reach the ruins of the collection of villas. The town is a 15min. **bus** ride from Anagnina Station; the bus driver will let you off at the depot in P. Marconi, the town center.

THE VENETO

From the rocky foothills of the Dolomites to the fertile valleys of the Po River, the Veneto region has a geography as diverse as its historical influences. Once loosely linked under the Venetian Empire, these towns retained their cultural independence, and visitors are more likely to hear regional dialects than standard Italian when neighbors gossip across their geranium-bedecked windows. The tenacity of local culture and custom may be a pleasant surprise for those who come expecting only mandolins and gondolas.

VENICE (VENEZIA)   ☎041

There is a mystical quality to Venice's (pop. 265,000) decadence. Her lavish palaces stand proudly on a steadily sinking network of wood, treading in the clouded waters of age-old canals lapping at the feet of her abandoned front doors. Venice's labyrinthine streets lead to a treasury of Renaissance art, housed in scores of palaces, churches, and museums that are themselves architectural delights. But the same streets that once earned the name *La Serenissima* (Most Serene) are now saturated with visitors, as Venice grapples with an economy reliant on the same tourism that forces more and more of the native population away every year. Still, Romanticism dies hard, and the sinking city persists beyond the summer crowds and polluted waters, united by winding canals and the memory of a glorious past.

ITALY

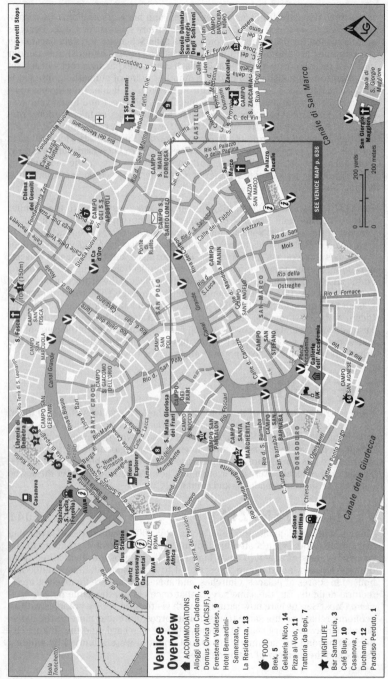

SEE VENICE MAP p. 636

Venice Overview

▲ ACCOMMODATIONS
Alloggi Gerotto Calderan, **2**
Domus Civica (ACISJF), **8**
Foresteria Valdese, **9**
Hotel Bernardini-
Semenzato, **6**
La Residenza, **13**

● FOOD
Brek, **5**
Gelateria Nico, **14**
Pizza al Volo, **11**
Trattoria da Bepi, **7**

★ NIGHTLIFE
Bar Santa Lucia, **3**
Café Blue, **10**
Casanova, **4**
Duchamp, **12**
Paradiso Perduto, **1**

ITALY

▐ TRANSPORTATION

The **train station** is on the northwest edge of the city; be sure to get off at **Santa Lucia,** *not* Mestre on the mainland. Buses and boats arrive at **Piazzale Roma,** just across the Canal Grande from the train station. To get from either station to **Piazza San Marco** or the **Ponte di Rialto** (Rialto Bridge), take *vaporetto* #82 or follow the signs for the 40min. walk—from the train station, exit left on Lista di Spagna.

Flights: Aeroporto Marco Polo (VCE; ☎041 260 61 11; www.veniceairport.it), 10km north of the city. Ticket office open daily 5:30am-9:30pm. Take the **ATVO shuttlebus** (☎041 520 55 30) from the airport to P. Roma (30min., every hr., €2.70).

Trains: Stazione Santa Lucia, northwest corner of the city. Open daily 3:45am-12:30am. **Info office** at the left as you exit the platforms. Open daily 7am-9pm. To: **Bologna** (2hr., every hr., €8); **Florence** (3hr., every 2hr., €27); **Milan** (3hr., 1-2 per hr., €13); **Rome** (4½hr., 5 per day, €36-45).

Buses: ACTV (☎041 528 78 86), in P. Roma. Local buses and boats. **ACTV long-distance carrier** runs buses to **Padua** (1½hr., every 30min, €3.50).

Public Transportation: The **Canal Grande** can be crossed on foot only at the Scalzi, Rialto, and Accademia *ponti* (bridges). Most **vaporetti** (water buses) run 5am-midnight, the *Notte* line 11:30pm-5:30am. Single-ride €3.10. 24hr. *biglietto turistico* pass €9.30, 3-day €18.10 (€13 with Rolling Venice Card), 7-day €31. Buy tickets from booths in front of *vaporetti* stops, self-serve dispensers at the ACTV office in P. Roma and the Rialto stop, or from the conductor. Pick up extra *non timbrati* (non-validated) tickets for when the booths aren't open. Validate them yourself before boarding to avoid a fine. **Lines #82** (faster) and **#1** (slower) run from the station down Canale Grande and Canale della Giudecca; **line #52** goes from the station through Canale della Giudecca to Lido and along the city's northern edge, then back to the station; **line #12** runs from Fondamente Nuove to Murano, Burano, and Torcello.

▐▐ ORIENTATION AND PRACTICAL INFORMATION

Venice spans 118 bodies of land in a lagoon and is connected to the mainland by a thin causeway. The city is a veritable labyrinth and can confuse even its natives, most of whom simply set off in a general direction and then patiently weave their way. If you follow their example by ungluing your eyes from your map and going with the flow, you'll discover some of the unexpected surprises that make Venice spectacular. A few tips will help you to orient yourself. Locate the following landmarks on a map: **Ponte di Rialto** (the bridge in the center), **Piazza San Marco** (central south), **Ponte Accademia** (the bridge in the southwest), **Ferrovia** (the train station, in the northwest), and **Piazzale Roma** (directly south of the station). The Canal Grande winds through the city, creating six *sestieri* (sections): Cannaregio, Castello, Santa Croce, San Polo, San Marco, and Dorsoduro. Within each *sestiere*, there are no street numbers—door numbers in a section form one long, haphazard set, consisting of around 6000 numbers. While these boundaries are nebulous, they can give you a general sense of location. **Cannaregio** is in the north and includes the train station, Jewish ghetto, and Cà d'Oro; **Castello** extends east toward the Arsenale; **San Marco** fills in the area between the Ponte di Rialto and Ponte Accademia; **Dorsoduro,** across the bridge from S. Marco, stretches the length of Canale della Giudecca and up to Campo S. Pantalon; **San Polo** runs north from Chiesa S. Maria dei Frari to the Ponte di Rialto; and **San Croce** lies west of S. Polo, across the Canal Grande from the train station. If *sestiere* boundaries prove too vague, Venice's **parrochie** (parishes) provide a more defined idea of where you are; *parrochia* signs, like *sestiere* signs, are painted on the sides of buildings.

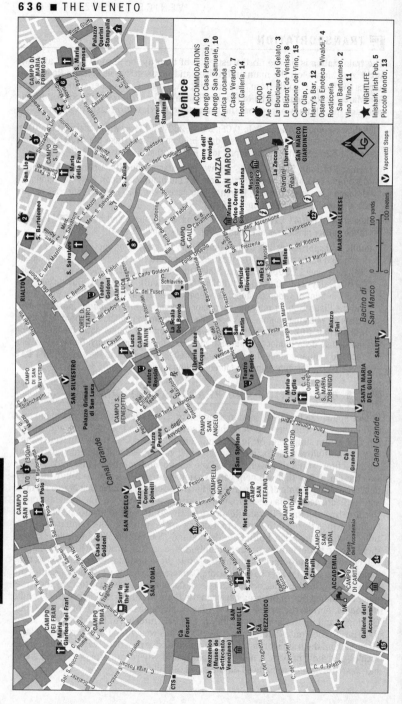

Venice

▲ ACCOMMODATIONS
Albergo Casa Petrarca, 9
Albergo San Samuele, 10
Antica Locanda
  Casa Verardo, 7
Hotel Galleria, 14

🍴 FOOD
Ae Oche, 1
La Boutique del Gelato, 3
Le Bistrot de Venise, 8
Cantinone del Vino, 15
Cip Ciap, 6
Harry's Bar, 12
Osteria Enoteca "Vivaldi," 4
Rosticceria
  San Bartolomeo, 2
Vino, Vino, 11

★ NIGHTLIFE
Inishark Irish Pub, 5
Piccolo Mondo, 13

▼ Vaporetti Stops

TOURIST, FINANCIAL, AND LOCAL SERVICES

Tourist Office: APT, Calle della Ascensione, S. Marco 71/F (☎/fax 041 529 87 40; www.tourismovenezia.it), directly opposite the Basilica. Open M-Sa 9:30am-3:30pm. The APT desk at the nearby **Venice Pavilion,** Giardini E Reali, S. Marco 2 (☎041 522 51 50) sells ACTV tickets. Open daily 9am-6pm.

AVA (☎041 171 52 88), in the train station, next to the tourist office. Makes same-day room reservations for a €1 fee. Open daily 9am-10pm. **Branch** offices in P. Roma (☎041 523 13 79) and the airport (☎041 541 51 33). Call for advance reservations.

Rolling Venice Card: Offers discounts on transportation and at over 200 restaurants, cafes, hotels, museums, and shops. Ages 14-29 only. Tourist office provides list of participating vendors. Cards cost €3 and are valid for one year from date of purchase. The card is sponsored by ACTV and can be purchased at the **ACTV VeLa** office (☎041 274 76 50) in P. Roma. Open daily 8:30am-6pm. The card is also available at any APT tourist office, and ACTV VeLa kiosks next to the Ferrovia, Rialto, S. Marco, and Vallaresso *vaporetto* stops.

Budget Travel: CTS, Fondamenta Tagliapietra Dorsoduro, 3252 (☎041 520 56 60; www.cts.it). From Campo S. Barnaba, cross the bridge and follow the road through the piazza. Turn left at the foot of the large bridge. Sells discounted student plane tickets and issues ISIC cards. English spoken. Open M-F 9:30am-1:30pm and 2:30-6pm.

Currency Exchange: Money exchangers charge high prices for service. Use banks whenever possible and inquire about fees beforehand. The streets around S. Marco and S. Polo are full of banks and ATMs. Many 24hr. automatic change machines, outside banks and next to ATMs, offer low commissions and decent rates.

EMERGENCY AND COMMUNICATIONS

Emergency: ☎113. **Ambulance:** ☎118.

Police: ☎113 or 112. **Carabinieri (tourist police):** Campo S. Zaccaria, Castello 4693/A (☎041 27 41 11). **Questura,** V. Nicoladi 24 (☎041 271 55 11). Contact the Questura if you have a serious complaint about your hotel.

Pharmacy: Farmacia Italo Inglese, Calle della Mandola, S. Marco 3717 (☎041 522 48 37), Follow C. Cortesia out of Campo Manin. Open M-F 9am-12:30pm and 3:45-7:30pm, Sa 9am-12:30pm. Late-night and weekend pharmacies rotate; check the list posted in the window of any pharmacy.

Hospital: Ospedale Civile, Campo S.S. Giovanni e Paolo, Castello (☎041 529 41 11).

Internet Access:

Casanova, Lista di Spagna, Cannaregio 158/A (☎041 275 01 99). This hip bar has Internet access on 4 modern, high-speed computers. €7 per hr., students €4. Internet 9am-11:30pm.

Surf In the Net, Calle del Campanile, S. Polo 2898A (☎041 244 02 76). From *vaporetto:* S. Tomà, take Calle del Traghetto, and turn left. €7 per hr., students €5. Open M-Sa 10am-10pm, Su 11am-10pm.

Net House, in Campo S. Stefano, S. Marco 2967-2958 (☎041 227 11 90). €9 per hr., with ISIC or Rolling Venice €6. M-Th 8am-2am, F-Su 24hr.

Post Office: Poste Venezia Centrale, Salizzada Fontego dei Tedeschi, S. Marco 5554 (☎041 271 71 11), off Campo S. Bartolomeo. Open M-Sa 8:30am-6:30pm. **Postal Codes:** S. Marco: 30124; Castello: 30122; S. Polo, S. Croce, and Cannaregio: 30121; Dorsoduro: 30123.

♦ ACCOMMODATIONS

Plan to spend more for a room in Venice than anywhere else in Italy. Always agree on a price before booking, and if possible, make reservations at least one month ahead. Religious institutions around the city offer both dorms and private rooms during the summer for about €25-70. Options include **Casa Murialdo,** Fondamenta Madonna dell'Orto, Cannaregio 3512 (☎041 71 99 33); **Casa Capitania,** S. Croce 561 (☎041 520 30 99; open June-Sept.); **Patronato Salesiano Leone XIII,** Calle S. Domenico, Castello 1281 (☎041 240 36 11); **Domus Cavanis,** Dorsoduro 896 (☎041 528 73 74), near the Accademia Bridge; **Ostello Santa Fosca,** Cannaregio 2372 (☎041 71 57 75); **Instituto Canossiano,** F. delle Romite, Dorsoduro 1323 (☎041 240 97 11); and **Instituto Ciliota,** Calle Muneghe S. Stefano, S. Marco 2976 (☎041 520 48 88).

CANNAREGIO AND SANTA CROCE
The station area, around the Lista di Spagna, has some of Venice's best budget accommodations. Although a 20min. *vaporetto* ride and a 30min. walk from most major sights, at night the streets bustle with young travelers and students.

▨ **Alloggi Gerotto Calderan,** Campo S. Geremia 283 (☎041 71 55 62; www.casagerottocalderan.com). 34 big, bright rooms. Check-out 10am. Curfew 12:30am for dorms, 1am for private rooms. Reserve at least 15 days in advance. Dorms €21; singles €41, with bath €46; doubles €75/93; triples €84/93. ❷

▨ **Hotel Bernardi-Semenzato,** Calle dell'Oca, Cannaregio 4366 (☎041 522 72 57; mtpepoli@tin.it). From *vaporetto*: Cà d'Oro, turn right on Strada Nuova, left on tiny Calle del Duca, then right on Calle dell'Oca. Antiques decorate a renovated annex. Curfew 1am; exceptions made. Singles without bath €30; doubles with bath €95; triples €115; quads €130. 10% Rolling Venice discount on larger rooms. AmEx/MC/V. ❸

Ostello di Venezia (HI), Fondamenta Zitelle, Giudecca 87 (☎041 523 82 11; www.hostelbooking.com). Take *vaporetto* #82, 41, or 42 to Zitelle. Turn right alongside canal. Large and efficient, with a sweeping view of the water. Must book through website; do not call to reserve. Reception 7-9:30am and 1:30-11:30pm. Lockout 9:30am-1:30pm. Curfew 11:30pm. HI members only; cards for sale. Dorms €17. MC/V. ❷

Istituto Canosiano, Ponte Piccolo, Giudecca 428 (☎041 522 21 57). Take *vaporetto* #82 or 41 to Palanca, and cross the bridge on the left. Women only. 35 beds. Sheets included. Reception 3pm-curfew. Lockout noon-3pm. Strict curfew 10:30pm; in winter 10pm. Large dorms €15. ❶

SAN MARCO AND SAN POLO
Surrounded by exclusive shops, souvenir stands, scores of *trattorie* and *pizzerie*, and many of Venice's most popular sights, these accommodations are pricey options for those in search of Venice's showy side.

▨ **Albergo San Samuele,** Salizzada S. Samuele, S. Marco 3358 (☎/fax 041 522 80 45, www.albergosansamuele.it). Follow Calle delle Botteghe from Campo S. Stefano and turn left on Salizzada S. Samuele. A crumbling stone courtyard leads to this charming deal. Great location 2min. from *vaporetto* #82 (San Samuele) and 10min. from P.S. Marco. Clean, well-decorated rooms, some with gorgeous balcony views of S. Marco's red rooftops. Singles €26-45; doubles €36-75, with bath €46-105; triples €135. ❸

Albergo Casa Petrarca, Calle Schiavine, S. Marco 4386 (☎/fax 041 520 04 30). From Campo S. Luca, follow C. Fuseri, take 2nd left and then a right. Tiny hotel has 7 small but bright, white rooms. Cheery sitting room with rows of English books and a quaint breakfast room. All rooms with A/C. Singles €45; doubles with bath €90. ❹

Domus Civica (ACISJF), Campiello Chiovere Frari, S. Polo 3082 (☎041 72 11 03; fax 041 522 71 39). From the train station, cross Ponte Scalzi and turn right. Turn left on Fondamenta dei Tolentini and left through the courtyard onto Corte Amai. The hostel is to the right, after the bridge. Simple student housing. Strict curfew 11:30pm. Open June-Sept. 25. Singles €30; doubles €54; triples €81. 15% Rolling Venice discount. ❸

CASTELLO

Castello is arguably the most beautiful part of Venice, and, as it houses the largest number of Venetians, also the most authentic. A room on the second or third floor with a view of red rooftops and the sculpted skyline is worth the inevitability of getting lost in some of the most narrow and tightly clustered streets in the city.

■ **Foresteria Valdese,** Castello 5170 (☎041 528 67 97; www.diaconiavaldese.org/venezia). From Campo S. Maria Formosa, take Calle Lunga S. Marial; it's immediately over the 1st bridge. Frescoed ceilings ornament the 18th-century Palazzo Cavagnis, a guest house of Venice's largest Protestant church. Reception daily 9am-1pm and 6-8pm. Lockout 10am-1pm. Closed 3 weeks in Nov. Dorms €21; doubles €56, with bath €74; quads with bath €102. €1 Rolling Venice discount. MC/V. ❷

La Residenza, Campo Bandiera e Moro Castello 3608 (☎041 528 53 15; www.venicelaresidenza.com). From *vaporetto*: Arsenal, turn left on Riva degli Schiavoni and right on C. del Dose into the *campo*. Luxurious hotel with palatial lobby. Singles €60-95; doubles €100-155. MC/V. ❺

Antica Locanda Casa Verardo, Castello 4765 (☎041 528 61 27; www.casaverardo.it). From the Basilica, take C. Canonica, turn right before the bridge and left over the bridge on Ruga Giuffa into S. Filippo e Giacomo. Follow C. della Chiesa left out of the *campo* until reaching a bridge. Hotel is on the other side. Richly colored rooms in a 15th-century *palazzo*. Singles without A/C €60-75; doubles €80-165. AmEx/MC/V. ❺

DORSODURO

Spartan facades and still canals trace the quiet, wide streets of Dorsoduro. Here, art museums draw visitors to canal-front real estate, while the interior remains a little-visited residential quarter. Situated near the Grand Canal between Chiesa dei Frari and Ponte Accademia, most hotels here tend to be pricey.

Hotel Galleria, Rio Terra Antonio Foscarini, Dorsoduro 878/A (☎041 523 24 89; www.hotelgalleria.it), on the left facing the Accademia museum. Oriental rugs and art prints lend an elegance appropriate to its location on the Grand Canal. Breakfast in bed included. Singles €70; doubles without bath €95-145. AmEx/MC/V. ❻

Locanda Cà Foscari, Calle della Frescada, Dorsoduro 3887b (☎041 71 04 01; valtersc@tin.it), in a quiet neighborhood. From *vaporetto:* San Tomà, turn left at the dead end, cross the bridge, turn right, then turn left on the alley. Murano glass chandeliers and a private garden embellish this simple, family-run hotel. Closed end of Nov.-Jan. 1. Singles €60; doubles €70-90; triples €87-110; quads €108-130. MC/V. ❹

CAMPING

Plan on at least a 20min. boat ride from Venice. In addition to these listings, the **Litorale del Cavallino,** on the Lido's Adriatic side, has multiple beach campsites.

Camping Miramare, Lungomare Dante Alighieri 29 (☎041 96 61 50; www.camping-miramare.it). A 40min. ride on *vaporetto* #14 from P.S. Marco to Punta Sabbioni. Campground is 700m along the beach on the right. 3-night min. stay in high season. Reserve ahead for bungalows with A/C. Open Apr. 1 to Nov. 2. €5 per person, €6 per tent. Bungalows €35 plus €5.50 per person. 15% Rolling Venice discount. ❶

Camping Fusina, V. Moranzani 79 (☎041 547 00 55; www.camping-fusina.com), in Malcontenta. From Mestre, take bus #1. Restaurant, *pizzeria,* laundromat, ATM, Internet access, and satellite TV on premises. Call ahead to reserve cabins. Free hot showers. €4 per person, €7 per tent, €14 per car. Cabins: singles €19; doubles €26. ❶

ITALY

◪ FOOD

In Venice, dining well on a budget requires exploration. The best and most afford-able restaurants are hidden in the less-traveled alleyways. For an inexpensive and informal option, visit any *osteria* or *bacario* in town and create a meal from the vast array of **cicchetti** (meat- and cheese-filled pastries; €1-3), tidbits of seafood, rice, meat, and *tramezzini* (triangular slices of soft white bread with any imagin-able filling). The key ingredients of Venetian cuisine come fresh from the sea. *Spa-ghetti al vongole* (pasta with fresh clams and spicy vegetables) is served on nearly every menu. Good local wines include the sparkling white *prosecco della Marca* or the red *valpolicella*. **BILLA supermarket,** Strada Nuova, Cannaregio 3660, is near Campo Apostoli. (Open M-Sa 8:30am-8pm, Su 9am-8pm. AmEx/MC/V.)

RESTAURANTS

■ **Le Bistrot de Venise,** Calle dei Fabbri, S. Marco 4685 (☎041 523 66 51; www.bistrot-devenise.com). Scrumptious, beautifully presented pasta dishes prepared from 14th-century recipes are overshadowed only by the service. *Primi* from €12. *Secondi* from €17. Service 15%. 10% Rolling Venice discount. Open daily noon-3pm and 7pm-1am. AmEx/MC/V. ❺

Trattoria da Bepi, Cannaregio 4550 (☎041 528 50 31). This traditional Venetian res-taurant, family-run for 38 years, has copper pots dangling from the ceiling. *Primi* €7-10.50. *Secondi* €9.50-18. Open M-W and F-Su noon-3pm and 7-10pm. MC/V. ❹

Brek, Lista di Spagna, Cannaregio 124A (☎041 244 01 58). Italian fast-food chain whips up pasta and salad dishes from an extensive array of ingredients. Perfect for a meal on the go. Menu and prices change daily. 10% Rolling Venice discount. *Primi* €2.90-3.90. *Secondi* €4-7. Open daily 8-10:30am and 11:30am-10:30pm. ❷

Vino, Vino, Ponte delle Veste, S. Marco 2007A. Dark, no-frills wine bar has over 350 vari-eties of wine. Seafood-focused menu changes daily. *Primi* €5. *Secondi* €9. Open Su-F 10:30am-midnight, Sa 10am-1am. 15% Rolling Venice discount. ❸

Cip Ciap, Calle Mondo Novo, Castello 5799a (☎041 523 66 21). Huge, delicious pizzas from €4.20, with smaller *margherita* for €2.30. Also sold by the slice. Try the *disco vol-ante* (literally, flying saucer), made like a calzone and stuffed with mushrooms, egg-plant, ham, egg, and salami (€6.50). Open M and W-Su 9am-9pm. ❷

Trattoria Al Vecio Canton, Castello, 4738/a (☎041 528 51 76). Tavern-style *trattoria* is famous for its pizza. Try the *Al Vecio Canton* (topped with tomatoes, cheese, olive oil, garlic, and a spritz of lemon; €6). Open M and W-Su noon-3pm and 7pm-midnight. ❸

Rosticceria San Bartolomeo, Calle della Bissa, S. Marco 5424/A (☎041 522 35 69). A smorgasbord of sandwiches, pasta, and *cicchetti* to be enjoyed on the go or in a win-dow booth. Full-service restaurant upstairs serves lunch. Entrees from €5.90. *Panini* from €1.10. Cover for restaurant €1.30. Open daily 9:30am-9:30pm. AmEx/MC/V. ❶

Harry's Bar, Calle Vallaresso, S. Marco 1323 (☎041 528 57 77). Founded in 1931 by Bostonian Harry Cipriani who believed that Venice suffered a lack of bars, this cafe has been pouring pricey drinks to tourists and notables like Ernest Hemingway, Katharine Hepburn, and Robert DeNiro ever since. Open daily 10:30am-11pm. MC/V. ❹

Pizza al Volo, Campo S. Margherita, Dorsoduro 2944 (☎041 522 54 30). Students and locals come for delicious, cheap pizza. Slices from €1.30. Pizza from €3.40. Gigantic pizza for 2 from €6.30. Open daily 11:30am-4pm and 5:30pm-1:30am. ❶

Cantinone del Vino, Fondamente Meraviglie, Dorsoduro 992. A spectacular display of wines, ranging in price from €3-200 a bottle. Enjoy a glass (from €0.70) at the bar with some *cicchetti* (from €1). Open M-Sa 8am-2:30pm and 3:15-8:30pm. ❷

ITALY

Ae Oche, S. Croce 1552a/b (☎041 524 11 61). From Campo S. Giacomo da L'Orio, take Calle del Trentor. Not for the indecisive: Over 100 types of pizza (€3.50-10) and a crowd who can take them on. Open daily noon-3pm and 7pm-midnight. MC/V. ❶

Osteria Enoteca "Vivaldi," S. Polo 1457 (☎041 523 81 85). Friendly tavern-style restaurant. *Primi* €8-10. *Secondi* from €10. Cover €1.50. Service 10%. Open daily 11:30am-2:30pm and 6:30-10:30pm. AmEx/MC/V. ❸

GELATERIE

▒ **La Boutique del Gelato,** Salizzada S. Lio, Castello 5727 (☎041 522 32 83). Huge cones, gigantic quality and miniscule prices. Single scoop €0.80, 2 scoops €1.30. Open daily 10am-8pm, July-Aug. until 10:30pm.

Gelateria Nico, Fondamenta Zattere, Dorsoduro 922. Great view of the Giudecca Canal. Try the Venetian specialty *gianduiotto al passagetto* (a slice of dense chocolate-hazelnut ice cream dunked in whipped cream; €2.30). *Gelato* €0.80-6.50. Open daily 6:45am-11pm.

🅖 SIGHTS

AROUND PIAZZA SAN MARCO

▒ **BASILICA DI SAN MARCO.** The interior of this glittering church sparkles with both 13th-century Byzantine and 16th-century Renaissance mosaics. Behind the altar screen is the **Pala D'Oro,** a gem-encrusted relief covering the tomb of Saint Mark. To the right of the altar is the **tesoro** (treasury), a hoard of gold and relics from the Fourth Crusade. Steep stairs in the atrium lead to the **Galleria della Basilica,** which offers a staggering perspective on the interior mosaics, a tranquil vista of the exterior *piazza*, and an intimate view of the original bronze *Horses of St. Mark.* St. Mark's is worth the long lines; visit in the early morning for the shortest wait, or at dusk for the best natural illumination of the mosaics. *(Basilica open daily 9:30am-4:30pm. Dress code enforced. Free. Pala D'Oro open daily 9:45am-5pm. €1.50. Treasury open M-Sa 9:45am-5pm. €2. Galleria open daily 9:45am-5pm. €1.50.)*

▒ **PALAZZO DUCALE.** Once the home of Venice's *doge* (mayor), the Palazzo Ducale now houses one of Venice's best museums. Within the palace lie the *doge*'s private apartments and the magnificent state rooms of the Republic. Climb the richly decorated **Scala d'Oro** (Golden Staircase) to reach the **Sala del Maggior Consiglio** (Great Council Room), dominated by Tintoretto's *Paradise*, the largest oil painting in the world. Passages lead through the courtrooms of the much-feared Council of Ten and the even-more-feared Council of Three, crossing the Ponte dei Sospiri (Bridge of Sighs) and continuing into the prisons. *(Wheelchair accessible. Open Apr.-Oct. daily 9am-7pm; Nov.-Mar. 9am-5pm €11, students €5.50.)*

▒ **PIAZZA SAN MARCO.** In contrast to the narrow, labyrinthine streets that wind through most of Venice, P.S. Marco is a magnificent expanse of light and space. Enclosing the *piazza* are the unadorned 16th-century Renaissance **Procuratie Vecchie** (Old Treasury Offices), the more ornate 17th-century Baroque **Procuratie Nuove** (New Treasury Offices), and the smaller Neoclassical **Ala Napoleonica,** sometimes called the *Procuratie Nuovissime* (Newer Treasury Offices), which Napoleon constructed when he took the city in 1797. The brick **campanile** (96m) across the *piazza* stands on Roman foundations. *(Campanile open daily 9am-9pm. €6.)*

CHIESA DI SAN ZACCARIA. Dedicated to the father of John the Baptist and designed by (among others) Coducci in the late 1400s, this Gothic-Renaissance church holds one of the masterpieces of Venetian Renaissance painting, Giovanni Bellini's *Virgin and Child Enthroned with Four Saints*. *(Vaporetto: S. Zaccaria. From P.S. Marco, turn left along the water, cross the bridge, and turn left on Calle Albanesi. Take a right and go straight. Open daily 10am-noon and 4-6pm. Free.)*

AROUND THE PONTE DI RIALTO

CANAL GRANDE. The Canal Grande loops through Venice, and the splendid facades of the palazzi that crown its banks testify to the city's history of immense wealth. Although their external decorations vary, the palaces share the same basic structure. *(Vaporetto #82 or 1: P.S. Marco.)*

PONTE DI RIALTO. The Ponte di Rialto (1588-1591) arches over the Canal Grande, symbolizing Venice's commercial past. Antonio da Ponte created this image that graces postcards throughout the city. *(Vaporetto: Rialto.)*

CHIESA DI SAN GIACOMO DI RIALTO (SAN POLO). Between the Ponte Rialto and surrounding markets stands Venice's first church, diminutively called "San Giacometto." Across the *piazza*, a statue called *il Gobbo* (the hunchback) supports the steps. Once the podium from which officials made announcements, it was at the foot of this sculpture that convicted thieves, forced to run naked from P.S. Marco and lashed all the way by bystanders, could finally collapse. *(Vaporetto: Rialto. Cross bridge and turn right. Church open daily 10am-5pm. Free.)*

SAN POLO

■ **BASILICA DI SANTA MARIA GLORIOSA DEI FRARI.** Within the cavernous brick walls of this church rest outstanding paintings by masters of the Renaissance. Titian's *Assumption* (1516-1518) on the high altar marks the height of the Venetian Renaissance. In the Florentine chapel to the right is Donatello's *St. John the Baptist* (1438), a wooden Renaissance sculpture. *(Vaporetto: S. Tomà. Follow signs back to Campo dei Frari. Open M-Sa 9am-6pm, Su 1-6pm. €2.)*

SCUOLA GRANDE DI SAN ROCCO. Venice's most illustrious *scuola*, or guild hall, stands as a monument to painter Jacopo Tintoretto. The *scuola* commissioned Tintoretto to complete all of the building's paintings, a task that took 23 years. *(Behind Basilica dei Frari in Campo S. Rocco. Open daily 9:30am-5:30pm. €5.50, students €4.)*

DORSODURO

■ **GALLERIE DELL'ACCADEMIA.** The Accademia houses the most extensive collection of Venetian art in the world. At the top of the double staircase, **Room I,** topped by a ceiling full of cherubim, houses Venetian Gothic art, with a luxurious use of color that influenced Venetian painting for centuries. Among the enormous altarpieces in **Room II,** Giovanni Bellini's *Madonna Enthroned with Child, Saints, and Angels* stands out for its lush serenity. **Rooms IV** and **V** display more Bellinis and **Giorgione's** enigmatic *La Tempesta*. In **Room XX,** works by Bellini and Carpaccio display Venetian processions and cityscapes so accurately that scholars use them as "photos" of Venice's past. *(Vaporetto: Accademia. Open M 8:15am-2pm, T-Su 9:15am-7:15pm. €6.50.)*

■ **COLLEZIONE PEGGY GUGGENHEIM.** Guggenheim's Palazzo Venier dei Leoni now displays works by Brancusi, Marini, Kandinsky, Picasso, Magritte, Rothko, Ernst, Pollock, and Dalí. The Marini sculpture *Angel in the City*, in front of the *palazzo*, was designed with a detachable penis. Guggenheim occasionally modified this sculpture so as not to offend her more prudish guests. *(Calle S. Cristoforo, Dorsoduro 710. Vaporetto: Accademia. Turn left and follow the yellow signs. Open Su-M and W-F 10am-6pm, Sa 10am-10pm. €8, €5 with Rolling Venice card.)*

CHIESA DI SAN SEBASTIANO. The painter Veronese hid here when he fled Verona in 1555 after allegedly killing a man, and filled the church with some of his finest works. His breathtaking *Stories of Queen Esther* covers the ceiling. *(Vaporetto: S. Basilio. Open M-Sa 10am-5pm. €2.)*

CASTELLO

CHIESA DI SANTISSIMI GIOVANNI E PAOLO. This immense church is the final resting place of 25 *doges*, its walls lined with monuments to them and other honored citizens. Outside stands the bronze **statue of Bartolomeo Colleoni,** a mercenary who left his inheritance to the city on the condition that a monument to him be erected in front of S. Marco. The city, unwilling to honor him in such a grand space, decided to pull a fast one and place the statue in front of the Scuola di San Marco. *(Vaporetto: Fond. Nuove. Turn left, then right onto Fond. dei Mendicanti. Open M-Sa 7:30am-12:30pm and 3:30-7pm, Su 3-6pm. Free.)*

CHIESA DI SANTA MARIA DEI MIRACOLI. Among the most stunning Venetian churches, this Renaissance jewel was designed by the Lombardos in the late 1400s. *(From S.S. Giovanni e Paolo, cross Ponte Rosse. Open M-Sa 10am-5pm, Su 1-5pm. €2.)*

GIARDINI PUBLICI AND SANT'ELENA. Those who long for trees and grass can stroll through the Public Gardens, installed by Napoleon, or bring a picnic lunch to the shady lawns of Sant'Elena. *(Vaporetto: Giardini or S. Elena. Free.)*

CANNAREGIO

JEWISH GHETTO. In 1516, the *doge* forced Venice's Jewish population into the old cannon-foundry area, creating the first Jewish ghetto in Europe; the word "ghetto" is the Venetian word for "foundry." The oldest *schola* (synagogue), **Schola Grande Tedesca** (German Synagogue), shares a building with the **Museo Ebraica di Venezia** (Hebrew Museum of Venice) in the Campo del Ghetto Nuovo. *(Cannaregio 2899/B. Vaporetto: S. Marcuola. Hebrew Museum open June-Sept. Su-F 10am-7pm; Oct.-May 10am-4:30pm. €3, students €2. Entrance to synagogues by guided tour only (40min.). English tours leave from the museum every hr. June-Sept. 10:30am-5:30pm; Oct.-May 10:30am-3:30pm. Museum and tour €8, students €6.50.)*

CÀ D'ORO AND GALLERIA GIORGIO FRANCHETTI. The most spectacular facade on the Canal Grande and the premiere example of Venetian Gothic, the Cà d'Oro, built between 1425 and 1440, now houses the Giorgio Franchetti collection. For the best view of the palace, take the *traghetto* across the canal to the Rialto Markets. *(Vaporetto: Cà d'Oro. Open M-Su 9am-2pm. €3.50, students €2.50.)*

GIUDECCA AND SAN GIORGIO MAGGIORE

BASILICA DI SAN GIORGIO MAGGIORE. Standing on its own monastic island, S. Giorgio Maggiore contrasts sharply with most other Venetian churches. Palladio ignored the Venetian fondness for color and decorative excess, constructing an austere church of simple dignity. Ascend the elevator to the top of the **campanile** for a breathtaking view. *(Vaporetto: S. Giorgio Maggiore. Open M-Sa 10am-12:30pm and 2:30-4:30pm. Basilica free. Campanile €3.)*

ISLANDS OF THE LAGOON

BURANO. In this traditional fishing village, fishermen haul in their catch every morning as their black-clad wives sit in the doorways of the fantastically colored houses, creating unique knots of Venetian lace. The small **Scuola di Merletti di**

ITALY

Burano (Lace Museum) displays their handiwork. *(A 40min. boat ride from Venice. Vaporetto #12: Burano from either S. Zaccaria or Fond. Nuove. Museum in P. Galuppi. Open Su-M and W-Sa 10am-5pm. €4.)*

MURANO. Famous for its glass since 1292, the island of Murano affords visitors the chance to see the glass-blowing process. The **Museo Vetrario** (Glass Museum) houses a splendid collection that includes pieces from Roman times. Farther down the street is the 12th-century **Basilica di Santa Maria e San Donato.** *(Vaporetto #12 or 52: Faro from S. Zaccaria. Museo Vetrario: Fond. Giustian 8. ☎ 041 73 95 86. Open M-Tu and Th-Su 10am-5pm. €5, students €3. Basilica open daily 8am-noon and 4-7pm. Free.)*

LIDO. The Lido is now mostly a summer beach town, complete with cars, blaring radios, and beach bums. Head for the **public beach,** which features an impressive shipwreck at the southern end. *(Vaporetto: Lido.)*

■ NIGHTLIFE

Venetian nightlife is quieter and more relaxed than that of other major Italian cities. Most locals would rather spend an evening sipping wine or beer and listening to string quartets in P.S. Marco than gyrating in a disco, but Venice does have a few hot dance spots. Student nightlife is concentrated around **Campo Santa Margherita** in Dorsoduro and the areas around the **Lista di Spagna** in Cannaregio.

■ **Paradiso Perduto,** Fondamenta della Misericordia 2540. Students and locals flood this unassuming bar with conversation and laughter, while the young waitstaff doles out large portions of *cicchetti* (mixed plate €11). Live jazz Su. Open Th-Su 7pm-2am.

■ **Café Blue,** S. Pantalon, Dorsoduro 3778. Let Johnny from Liverpool flip ice cubes into your drink at this lively, friendly bar. Free Internet available. Live jazz F and Su evening during the winter. Open in summer noon-2am; off-season 9:30am-2am.

Piccolo Mondo, Accademia, Dorsoduro 1056/A. Dance-happy students, locals, and tourists keep the party going at this small, but popular *discoteca* where such notables as Michael Jordan, Mick Jagger, and Prince Albert of Monaco have strutted their stuff. Drinks from €7. Open nightly 10pm-4am. AmEx/MC/V.

Duchamp, C. Santa Margherita 3019. Lively place with plenty of outdoor seating for the social, student-heavy crowd that congregates here. Beer €4.30. Wine €1.30. Open Su-F 9pm-2am, Sa 5pm-2am.

Casanova, Lista di Spagna, Cannaregio 158/A. This modern, stylish club claims to be the only real disco in Venice, and modestly-sized crowds mean there's always plenty of room on the dance floor. Enthusiastic dancers make up for the lack of numbers, shaking things up until closing. Cover €10 F-Sa includes 1 drink. Open daily 10pm-4am.

Inishark Irish Pub, Calle Mondo Novo Castello 5787. Most creative and authentic-looking Irish pub in Venice. Guinness €4.20. Open Tu-Su 6pm-1:30am.

Bar Santa Lucia, Lista di Spagna, Cannaregio 282/B. This tiny bar stays crowded and noisy long into the night with a mix of Italians and tourists. A few outdoor tables available. Guinness €5. Wine €2.10. Open M-Sa 6pm-2am.

PADUA (PADOVA) ☎ 049

Ancient Padua (pop. 205,000) was a wealthy center of commerce, but centuries of barbarian attacks and natural disasters left few of her architectural treasures intact. Padua's university, founded in 1222 and second in seniority only to Bologna's, brings book-toting students to the city's statue-lined *piazze*. The ■**Cappella degli Scrovegni,** P. Eremitani 8, contains Giotto's breathtaking 38-panel fresco cycle, illustrating the lives of Mary and Jesus. Buy tickets at the attached **Musei Civici Erimitani,** which displays an overwhelming art collection, including a beautiful crucifix by Giotto that once adorned the Scrovegni Chapel. (Open Feb.-Oct. daily 9am-7pm; Nov.-Jan. 9am-6pm. €9, students €4.) Thousands of pilgrims are drawn to Saint Anthony's jawbone and well-preserved tongue on display at the **Basilica di Sant'Antonio,** in P. del Santo, a medieval conglomeration of eight domes filled with beautiful frescoes. (Dress code enforced. Open Apr.-Sept. daily 9am-12:30pm and 2:30pm-7pm; Nov.-Mar. reduced hours. €2, students €1.50.) From the basilica, follow signs to **Orto Botanico,** V. Orto Botanico 18, which tempts visitors with water lilies, medicinal herbs, and a 417-year-old palm tree that still offers shade. (Open daily Apr.-Sept. 9am-1pm and 3-6pm; Oct.-Mar. M-F 9am-1pm. €4, students €1.) Next to the **duomo,** in P. Duomo, lies the 12th-century **Battistero,** with a dome covered in frescoes. (Open M-Sa 7:30am-noon and 3:45-7:45pm, Su 7:45am-1pm and 3:45-8:30pm. €2.50, students €1.50.) Ancient buildings from the university are scattered throughout the city, especially near **Palazzo Bó.** At night, much of the action is nearby. The **Highlander Pub,** V.S. Martino 69, is a particularly popular Scotch-Irish establishment. (Open daily 7pm-2am.)

Trains depart from P. Stazione for: Bologna (1½hr., 1-2 per hr., €6); Milan (2½hr., 1-2 per hr., €17); Venice (30min., 3-4 per hr., €2.30); and Verona (1hr., 1-2 per hr., €4.50). **Buses** (☎049 820 68 11) leave from P. Boschetti for Venice (45min., 2 per hr., €2.20). The **tourist office** is in the train station (☎049 875 20 77. Open M-Sa 9am-7pm, Su 8:30am-12:30pm.) Follow the main street through town from the train station and turn right on V. Rogati. Go to V. Aleardi and turn left; walk to the end of the block and **Ostello Città di Padova (HI) ❶,** V. Aleardi 30, will be on the left. (☎049 875 22 19. **Internet** €5.20 per hr. Reception daily 7-9:30am and 2:30-11pm. Curfew 11pm. Reserve at least 1 week in advance. Dorms €14.) **Locanda la Perla ❸,** V. Cesarotti 67, has large, airy rooms in a great location. (☎049 87 55 89 39. Closed last 2 weeks in Aug. Singles €28, doubles €38.) Join a lively crowd at **Pizzeria Al Borgo ❷,** V.L. Belludi 56, near the Basilica di S. Antonio. (Pizzas from €3.70. Cover €2. Open Su and W-Sa noon-3pm and 7-11:30pm.) **Postal Code:** 35100.

VERONA ☎045

A glorious combination of majestic Roman ruins, colorful Venetian facades, and orange rooftops, Verona (pop. 245,000) is one of the most beautiful cities in Northern Italy. Gazing at the town from one of its many bridges at sunset sets the tone for romantic evenings befitting the home of *Romeo and Juliet.* Meanwhile, its artistic and historical treasures fill days with rewarding sightseeing.

⎘⎘ TRANSPORTATION AND PRACTICAL INFORMATION. Trains (☎045 800 08 61) go from P. XXV Aprile to: Bologna (2hr., every hr., €5.80); Milan (2hr., every hr., €7); Trent (1hr., every 2 hr., €4.70); and Venice (1¾hr., every hr., €6). From the train station, walk 20min. up **Corso Porta Nuova,** or take bus #11, 12, 13, 72, or 73 (weekends take #91, 92, or 93) to Verona's heart, the **Arena** in **Piazza Brà.** The **tourist office** is left of the *piazza.* (☎806 86 80. Open M-Sa 9am-7pm, Su 9am-3pm.) **Internet Train,** V. Roma 17/a, has modern, high-speed computers. (€2.50 per 30min. Open M-F 11am-10pm, Sa-Su 2-8pm.). **Postal Code:** 37100.

⎘⎙ ACCOMMODATIONS AND FOOD. Reserve hotel rooms ahead, especially in opera season (June-Sept.). The **⎘Ostello della Gioventù (HI) ❶,** Villa Francescatti, Salita Fontana del Ferro 15, is in a renovated 16th-century villa with gorgeous gardens; from the station, take bus #73 or night bus #90 to P. Isolo, turn right, and follow the yellow signs uphill. (☎045 59 03 60. Lockout 9am-5pm. Curfew 11pm; flexible for opera-goers. No reservations. Dorms €13.)

ITALY

To get to **Locanda Catullo ❹**, V. Catullo 1, walk to V. Mazzini, turn onto V. Catullo, and turn left on Vco. Catullo. (☎045 800 27 86. July-Sept. 3-night min. stay. Singles €40; doubles €55-65; triples €81-96.) Verona is famous for its wines, such as the dry white *soave* and red *valpolicella*. Prices in **Piazza Isolo** are cheaper than those in P. delle Erbe. **Cantore ❸**, V. A. Mario 2, near P. Brà, boasts delicious pizza and pasta dishes. (☎045 803 18 30. Primi €6.80. Secondi €8. Cover €1.50. AmEx/MC/V.) **Pam supermarket** is at V. dei Mutilati 3. (Open M-Sa 8am-8pm and Su 9:30am-1pm and 3-7pm.)

◨ **SIGHTS.** The physical and emotional heart of Verona is the majestic, pink-marble, first-century ◧**Arena** in P. Brà. (Open M 1:45-6:30pm, Tu-Su 8:30am-6:30pm. €3.10, students €2.10.) From P. Brà, V. Mazzini leads to the markets and stunning medieval of **Piazza delle Erbe,** the former Roman forum. The 83m ◧**Torre dei Lambertini,** in P. dei Signori, offers a stunning view of Verona. (Open M 1:30-5:30pm, Tu-Su 8:30am-7:30pm. €2.60, students €2.10.) The **Giardino Giusti,** V. Giardino Giusti 2, is a magnificent 16th-century garden with a labyrinth of mythological statues. (Open daily 9am-8pm. €5.) The della Scala fortress, **Castelvecchio,** down V. Roma from P. Brà, is filled with walkways, parapets, and an art collection that includes Pisanello's *Madonna and Child.* (Open M 1:30-7:30pm, Tu-Su 8:30am-7:30pm. €5, students €4. Thousands of tourists have immortalized **Casa di Giulietta** (Juliet's House), V. Cappello 23, although the dell Cappello (Capulet) family never really lived there. A balcony overlooks a courtyard full of tourists waiting to rub the bronze statue of Juliet. (Open M 1:30-7:30pm, Tu-Su 8:30am-7:30pm. €3.10, students €2.10.) From late June to early September, tourists and singers from around the world descend on the Arena for the city's annual **Opera Festival.** (☎045 800 51 51. General admission Su-Th €19.50, F-Sa €21.50.)

FRIULI-VENEZIA GIULIA

Friuli-Venezia Giulia traditionally receives less than its fair share of recognition, but it has served as inspiration to a number of prominent literary figures. James Joyce lived in Trieste for 12 years, during which he wrote most of *Ulysses;* Ernest Hemingway drew part of the plot for *A Farewell to Arms* from the region's role in World War I; and Freud and Rilke both worked and wrote here. The city of Trieste attracts large numbers of tourists to the cheapest beach resorts on the Adriatic.

TRIESTE (TRIEST)   ☎040

A long-disputed piece of real estate among Italians, Austrians and Slavs, Trieste (pop. 230,000) finally became part of Italy in 1954, yet it still remains divided between its Slavic and Italian origins. While Trieste's fast-paced center, with Gucci-clad locals and bustling quays, is undeniably urban, the colors of the surrounding Carsoian hillside and the tranquil Adriatic Sea temper the metropolis with stunning natural beauty. The **Città Nuova,** a grid-like pattern of streets lined with crumbling Neoclassical palaces, centers around the **Canale Grande.** Facing the canal from the south is the striking Serbian Orthodox **Chiesa di San Spiridione.** (Dress modestly. Open Tu-Sa 9am-noon and 5-8pm.) The ornate **Municipio** complements the **Piazza dell'Unità d'Italia,** the largest *piazza* in Italy. Take bus #24 to the last stop (€0.90) to reach the 15th-century Venetian **Castello di San Giusto,** which presides over **Capitoline Hill,** south of P. Unità (the city's historical center), and includes a museum. From P. Goldoni, you can ascend the hill by the **Scala dei Giganti** (Steps of the Giants), a daunting 265-step climb. (☎040 31 36 36.

Castle open daily 9am-sunset; free. Museum open daily 9am-1pm; €1.60.) **Piazza della Cattedrale** overlooks the sea and downtown Trieste. The archaeological **Museo di Storia e d'Arte**, V. Cattedrale 15, is down the hill past the *duomo*. (☎040 37 05 00. Open Su and Tu-Sa 9am-1pm. €1.70.)

Trains leave P. della Libertà 8, down C. Cavour from the quays, for Budapest, Hungary (12hr., 2 per day, €73) and Venice (2hr., 2 per hr., €8.20). The APT **tourist office** is at P. dell'Unità d'Italia 4/E, near the harbor. (☎040 347 83 12; fax 040 347 83 20. Open M-Sa 9am-7pm.) **Hotel Alabarda ❸**, V. Valdirivo 22, is near the city center. All rooms have high ceilings and satellite TV. From P. Oberdan, head down V. XXX Ottobre, and turn right onto V. Valdirivo. (☎040 63 02 69; www.hotelalbarda.it. **Internet** access €5.20 per hr. Singles €32-34, with bath €47; doubles €44-49/67. AmEx/MC/V.) To get from the station to **Ostello Tegeste (HI) ❶**, V. Miramare 331, 4km away just south from Castle Miramare, take bus #36 (€0.90), which leaves from across V. Miramare, and ask for the Ostello stop. From there, walk along the Barcola, following the seaside road toward the castle which has a charming view of the Adriatic Sea. (☎/fax 040 22 41 02. Reception daily 8am-11:30pm. Dorms €12. Nonmembers add €3.) For cheap food, stop by **Euro Spesa** supermarket at V. Valdirivo 13/F, off C. Cavour. (Open M-Sa 8am-8pm.) **Postal Code:** 34100.

PIEDMONT (PIEMONTE)

Piedmont has been a politically influential region for centuries, as well as a producer of fine food and wine, which *Piedmontese* insist is the best in Italy, and thus internationally. After native-born Vittorio Emanuele II and Camillo Cavour united Italy, Turin served as the capital from 1861 to 1865.

TURIN (TORINO)   ☎011

Turin's (pop. 860,000) elegance is the direct result of centuries of urban planning—graceful, church-lined avenues lead to spacious *piazze*. At the same time, Turin vibrates with modern economic energy as headquarters of the **Fiat Auto Company** and future host of the **2006 Winter Olympics**. The city is also home to one of the more famous relics of Christianity: the **Holy Shroud of Turin** is housed in the **Cattedrale di San Giovanni**, behind the **Palazzo Reale**. The church is undergoing restoration, but remains open. (Open daily 7am-12:30pm and 3-7pm. Free.) The **Museo Egizio**, in the **Palazzo dell'Accademia delle Scienze**, V. dell'Accademia delle Scienze 6, boasts a world-class collection of Egyptian artifacts. (Open Su, Tu and F-Sa 8:30am-2pm; W-Th 2-7:30pm. €4, ages 18-25 €2. Under-18 and over-65 free.) One of Guarini's great Baroque palaces, the **Palazzo Carignano**, V. dell'Accademia delle Scienze 5, houses the **Museo Nazionale del Risorgimento Italiano**, commemorating the 1706-1846 unification of Italy. (Open Su and Tu-Sa 9am-7pm. €4.25, students €2.50.) Begun as a synagogue in 1863, the **Mole Antonelliana**, V. Montebello 20, dominates Turin's skyline. (Open Su and Tu-F 10am-8pm, Sa 10am-11pm. Elevator to the observation deck €3.60.) The **Museo dell'Automobile**, C. Unita d'Italia 40, documents the evolution of the automobile, including prototype models of the Ford, Benz, Peugeot, and homegrown Fiat. From the station, head south along V. Nizza. (Open Su and Tu-Sa 10am-7pm. €2.70.)

Trains leave Porta Nuova on C. Vittorio Emanuele (☎011 531 327) for: Genoa (2hr., every hr., €8); Milan (2hr., every hr., €8); Rome (4½hr., 5 per day, €38); and Venice (4½hr., 3 per day, €31). The **tourist office**, P. Castello 161, has free maps. (☎011 53 51 81. Open M-Sa 9:30am-7pm, Su 9:30am-3:30pm.) To get to the clean and comfortable **Ostello Torino (YHI) ❶**, V. Alby 1, take bus #52 (bus #64 on Su) from Stazione Porto Nuova to the 2nd stop past the Po river. Turn right onto C. Lanza, follow the signs to V. Gatti and climb 200m up the winding road. (☎011 660 29 39; hostelto@tin.it. Reception 7-10am and 3:30-11pm. Curfew 11:30pm; ask for a key if you go out. Closed Dec. 20-Feb. 1. Dorms €12.) **Hotel Canelli ❷,** V.S. Dalmazzo 5b, has clean rooms in a quiet neighborhood. From the train station, take bus #52 to *Cernaia*, turn right down V. Gianone, and then turn left onto V.S. Dalmazzo. (☎011 53 71 66. Singles €24; doubles €32, triples €39.) Turin has grown into one of the great international centers of chocolate; Ferrero Rocher and Nutella are two of its more famous progeny. **Via Mazzini** has cheap fruit, cheese, and bread shops, along with a number of inexpensive eateries. **Postal Code:** 10100.

THE DOLOMITES (DOLOMITI)

With their sunny skies and powdery, light snow, the Dolomites offer immensely popular downhill skiing. These amazing peaks, which Le Courbusier once called "the most beautiful natural architecture in the world," are also fantastic for hiking and rock climbing.

TRENT ☎0461

Between the Dolomites and the Veneto, Trent (pop. 105,000) offers an affordable sampling of northern Italian life with superb restaurants and spectacular hikes set against dramatic scenery. The **Piazza del Duomo,** Trent's center and the heart of its social life, contains the city's best sights. The **Fontana del Nettuno** stands, trident in hand, in the center of the *piazza.* Nearby is the **Cattedrale di San Vigilio,** named for the patron saint of Trent. (Open daily 9:30am-12:15pm and 2:30-7:30pm.) Walk down V. Belenzani and head right on V. Roma to reach the well-preserved **Castello del Buonconsiglio,** which has a series of frescoes depicting medieval life. (Open daily 10am-6pm. €5, students and seniors €2.50.) **Monte Bondone** rises majestically over Trent, making a pleasant daytrip or overnight excursion. Catch the **cable car** (☎0461 38 10 00; every 30min., €0.80) to **Sardagna** on Mt. Bondone from V. Lung'Adige Monte Grappa, between the train tracks and the river.

    Trains (☎0461 98 36 27) leave V. Dogana for: Bologna (3hr., 13 per day, €11); Bolzano (45min., 2 per hr., €3); Venice (3hr., 5 per day, €11); and Verona (1hr., every hr., €4.70). Atesina **buses** (☎0461 82 10 00) go from V. Pozzo, next to the train station, to Riva del Garda (1hr., every hr., €3). The **tourist office,** V. Manci 2, offers advice on biking, skiing, and hiking. Turn right as you exit the train station and turn left on V. Roma, which becomes V. Corsi. (☎0461 98 38 80; www.apt.trento.it. Open daily 9am-7pm.) The central and clean **Hotel Venezia ❸** is at P. Duomo 45. (☎/fax 0461 23 41 14. Breakfast €5.20. Singles €40; doubles €59. MC/V.) From the station, turn right on V. Pozzo and left on V. Torre Vanga to get to **Ostello Giovane Europa (HI) ❶,** V. Torre Vanga 11, a white building with new rooms and clean bathrooms. (☎0461 26 34 84; fax 0461 22 25 17. Reception 7:30am-11pm. Check-out 10am. Curfew 11:30pm. Dorms €13; singles €25; doubles €40.) Around P. Duomo there are several cafes and a produce market. **Postal Code:** 38100.

BOLZANO ☎0471

In the tug-of-war between Austrian and Italian cultural influences, Bolzano (pop. 100,000) leans toward Austria's side. The town's prime location beneath vineyard-covered mountains makes it a splendid base for hiking or skiing in the Dolomites. Artwork and numerous frescoes fill the Gothic **duomo,** off P. Walther. (Open M-F 9:45am-noon and 2-5pm, Sa 9:45am-noon.) The fascinating **South Tyrol Museum of**

Archaeology, V. Museo 43, near Ponte Talvera, houses the 5000-year-old **Ice Man.** (☎ 0471 98 06 48. Open Tu-F 10am-6pm, Th until 7pm. €8, students €5.50.) **Trains** (☎ 0471 97 42 92) leave P. Stazione for: \ (3hr., 3 per day, €21); Trent (45min., 2 per hr., €3); and Verona (2hr., 1-2 per hr., €6.80). Walk up V. Stazione from the train station to reach the **tourist office,** P. Walther 8. (☎ 0471 30 70 00; fax 0471 98 01 28. Open M-F 9am-6:30pm, Sa 9am-12:30pm.) **Croce Bianca ❸,** P. del Grano 3, is around the corner from P. Walther. Its homey rooms are the most centrally located budget accommodations in town. (☎ 0471 97 75 52. Singles €28; doubles €47.) Sample some of Bolzano's Austrian-influenced fare around P. Walther and along V. Grappoli. **Postal Code:** 39100.

LOMBARDY (LOMBARDIA)

Over the centuries, Roman generals, German emperors, and French kings have vied for control of Lombardy's fertile soil and strategic location. The disputing powers failed to rob Lombardy of her prosperity; the region remains the wealthiest in Italy. While Milan may bask in the cosmopolitan spotlight, equally important are the rich culture and beauty of Bergamo, Mantua, and the foothills of the Alps.

MILAN (MILANO)   ☎ 02

Since its days as capital of the western Roman Empire from AD 286 to 402, Milan (pop. 1,300,000) has embraced modern life more forcefully than any other major Italian city. The pace of life is quick, and *il dolce di far niente* (the sweetness of doing nothing) is an unfamiliar taste. Although Milan's growth has brought petty crime and drugs, the city remains on the cutting edge of finance, fashion, and fun.

▐ TRANSPORTATION

Flights: Malpensa Airport (MXP; ☎ 02 74 85 22 00), 45km from town. Handles intercontinental flights. **Malpensa Express** leaves Cadorna Metro station for the airport (45min., €9). **Linate Airport** (LIN; ☎ 02 74 85 22 00), 7km away, covers Europe. Take bus #73 from MM1: P.S. Babila (€1).

Trains: Stazione Centrale (☎ (01) 47 88 80 88), in P. Duca d'Aosta on MM2. Info office open daily 7am-9:30pm. Every hour to: **Florence** (2½hr., €22); **Genoa** (1½hr., €8); **Rome** (4½hr., €39); **Turin** (2hr., €8); and **Venice** (3hr., €13).

Buses: Stazione Centrale. Intercity buses tend to be less convenient and more expensive than trains. **SAL, SIA, Autostradale,** and other carriers leave from P. Castello and nearby (MM1: Cairoli) for **Bergamo,** the **Lake Country,** and **Turin.**

Public Transportation: The **Metro** (Metropolitana Milanese, or **MM**) runs 6am-midnight. **ATM buses** handle local transportation. Ticket booths (toll-free ☎ 800 01 68 57) are open M-Sa 7:15am-7:15pm. Single-fare tickets €1, day passes €3, 2-day €5.50.

◢◤ ▐ ORIENTATION AND PRACTICAL INFORMATION

The layout of the city resembles a giant target, encircled by a series of ancient concentric city walls. In the outer rings lie suburbs built during the 1950s and 60s to house southern immigrants. Within the inner circle are four central squares: **Piazza Duomo,** at the end of V. Mercanti; **Piazza Cairoli,** near the Castello Sforzesco; **Piazza Cordusio,** connected to Largo Cairoli by V. Dante; and **Piazza San Babila,** the business and fashion district along C. Vittorio Emanuele. The **duomo** and **Galleria Vittorio Emanuele** constitute the bull's-eye, roughly at the center of the downtown

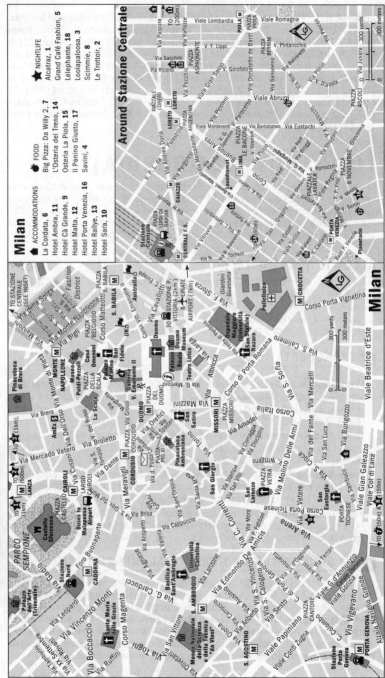

Milan

⌂ ACCOMMODATIONS
La Cordata, **6**
Hotel Ambra, **11**
Hotel Cà Grande, **9**
Hotel Malta, **12**
Hotel Porta Venezia, **16**
Hotel Rallye, **13**
Hotel Sara, **10**

🍴 FOOD
Big Pizza: Da Willy 2, **7**
L'Osteria del Treno, **14**
Osteria La Piola, **15**
Il Panino Giusto, **17**
Savini, **4**

★ NIGHTLIFE
Alcatraz, **1**
Grand Café Fashion, **5**
Lelephante, **18**
Loolapaloosa, **3**
Scimmie, **8**
Le Trottoir, **2**

Around Stazione Centrale

Milan

circle. Radiating from the center are two large parks, the Giardini Pubblici and the Parco Sempione. From the colossal **Stazione Centrale** train station, farther northeast, you can take a scenic ride on bus #60 or the more efficient commute on subway line #3 to the downtown hub. **Via Vito Pisani,** which leads to the mammoth **Piazza della Repubblica,** connects the station to the downtown area.

Tourist Office: APT, V. Marconi 1 (☎02 72 52 43 00; www.milanoinfotourist.com), in the Palazzo di Turismo in P. Duomo. Pick up the comprehensive *Milano e Milano* as well as *Milano Mese* for info on activities and clubs. Open M-Sa 9am-1pm and 3-6pm, Su 9am-1pm and 3-5pm.

American Express: V. Larga 7 (☎02 72 00 36 93), on the corner of V. dell'Orso. Walk through the Galleria, across P. Scala, and up V. Verdi. Holds mail free for AmEx members for 1 month, otherwise €5 per month. Handles wire transfers for AmEx cardholders. Also **exchanges currency.** Open M-F 9am-5:30pm.

Emergencies: ☎118. **Toll-free Operator:** ☎12. **Medical Assistance:** ☎38 83.

Police: ☎113 or 02 772 71. **Carabinieri** (tourist police): ☎112.

Hospital: Ospedale Maggiore di Milano, V. Francesco Sforza 35 (☎(025) 50 31).

24hr. Pharmacy: Galeria at Stazione Centrale. (☎(026) 69 07 35).

Internet Access: Enjoy Internet, V. le Tunisia 11 (☎02 36 55 08 05). €2 per hr. Open M-Sa 9am-midnight, Su 9:30am-11:30pm.

Post Office: V. Cordusio 4 (☎02 72 10 41). Address mail to be held: First Name SUR-NAME, *In Fermo Posta,* Ufficio Postale Centrale di Piazza Cordusio 4, Milano **20100,** ITALY. Open M-F 8:30am-7:30pm, Sa 8:30am-1pm.

▐ ACCOMMODATIONS

Every season in Milan is high season—except August. A single room in a decent establishment for under €35 is a real find. For the best deals, try the city's southern periphery or the areas south and east of the train station. When possible, make reservations well ahead of time.

▓ **Hotel Sara,** V. Sacchini 17 (☎02 20 17 73; www.hotelsara.it). MM1/2: Loreto. From Loreto take V. Porpora; the 3rd street on the right is V. Sacchini. Recently renovated, on a peaceful street, and all rooms with bath. Free Internet access. Singles €45-55; doubles €68-85; triples €93-110. AmEx/MC/V. ●

Hotel Ca Grande, V. Porpora 87 (☎02 26 14 40 01; www.hotelcagrande.it). Take tram #33 from Stazione Centrale; it runs along V. Porpora and stops at V. Ampere, near the front door. Spotless rooms over a beautiful garden. Internet €3 per hr. Reception 24hr. Singles €45, with bath €55; doubles €65/75. AmEx/MC/V. ●

Hotel Rallye, V. Marcello 59 (☎/fax 02 29 53 12 09). MM1: Lima. Walk along V. Vitruvio 2 blocks to V. Marcello and turn left. Homey rooms with phone and TV. Spacious doubles, free parking, and complimentary breakfast under an apricot tree in the garden. Singles €30, with bath €35; doubles €51/67. AmEx/D/MC/V. ●

Hotel Porta Venezia, V. B. Castaldi 26 (☎02 29 41 42 27; fax 02 20 24 93 97). MM1: P. Venezia. Walk down C. Venezia for 2 blocks, then turn right onto V. B. Castaldi. Simple and tidy rooms come with TV and fan. Singles €31-42, with bath €36-47; doubles €41-62/51-77. MC/V. ●

Hotel Ambra, V. Caccianino 10 (☎02 266 54 65). MM1/2: Loreto. V. Caccianino is about a block up on the right from Ca' Grande. Set off on a quiet side street; offers 19 rooms, all with bath, TV, telephone, and balcony. Breakfast €3. Reserve ahead. Singles €42; doubles €68; triples €91. Student discounts July-Aug. AmEx/MC/V. ●

La Cordata, V. Burigozzo 11 (☎02 58 31 46 75; fax 58 30 35 98; www.lacordata.it). MM3: Missori. From P. Missori, take the tram 2 stops to Italia (Lusardi), walk same direction for 1 block, and turn right on V. Burigozzo. Entrance is around the corner from La Cordata camping store. Founded by a group of educators in the 1980s as a non-profit cooperative, this hostel of sky-blue walls and whimsical murals houses mostly college-aged backpackers. Rooms have bath. Loose curfew 11:30pm. Dorms €16. ❷

Hotel Malta, V. Ricordi 20 (☎02 204 96 15; www.hotelmalta.it). MM1/2: Loreto. From Stazione Centrale, take tram #33 to V. Ampere and backtrack along V. Porpora to V. Ricordi. Reserve ahead. Singles €36; doubles €73. ❹

Camping Citta di Milano, V. G. Airaghi 61 (☎02 48 20 01 34). From Stazione Centrale take the Metro to MM1/3: Duomo or MM1/2: Cadorna; from either of these, take bus #62 towards D'Angelli and get off at Vittoria Caldera. Closed Dec.-Jan. Laundry €4.50. €13 per person. ❶

🍴 FOOD

Like its fine *couture*, Milanese cuisine is sophisticated and sometimes over-priced. Specialties include *risotto giallo* (rice with saffron), *cotoletta alla milanese* (breaded veal cutlet with lemon), and *cazzouela* (a mixture of pork and cabbage). *Pasticcerie* and *gelaterie* crowd every block. Sample the Milanese favorite, *panettone*, an Italian fruitcake. **Peck,** off V. Orefici near the P. Duomo, V. Cantu 3, has sold delectables like *foie gras* and black forest ham since 1883. (Open M 3-7:30pm, Tu-Sa 8:45am-7:30pm.) **Supermarket Pam,** V. Piccinni 2, is off C. Buenos Aires. (Open Su and Tu-Sa 8:30am-9pm, M 3-9pm.)

Savini, Galleria Vittorio Emanuele II (☎02 72 00 34 33). Opposite the McDonald's—in every way. Italian writer Castellaneta once said, "Savini is as much a part of Milan as the Galleria and La Scala." Pay dearly for exquisite food, superb service, and most of all, bragging rights. *Primi* €14-20. *Secondi* €21-29. Cover €7. Open M-Sa 12:30-2:30pm and 7:30-10:30pm. AmEx/DC/MC/V. ❺

Osteria del Treno, V.S. Gregorio 46/48 (☎02 670 04 79). MM2/3: Centrale F.S. Hearty and reasonably priced food; self-service lunch and *Primi* go for €4.20. *Secondi* €6.50. In the evening the restaurant is sit-down and prices rise by a euro or two. Open Su-F noon-2:30pm and 7-10:30pm. ❷

Osteria La Piola, V. le Abruzzi 23 (☎02 29 53 12 71). Feast on homemade pasta and flavorful Lombardian cuisine at this *osteria con cucina* (tavern with a kitchen). *Primi* €8-9.50. *Secondi* €12-15. Open M-Sa 12:30-2:30pm and 7:30-11pm. AmEx/D/MC/V. ❹

Il Panino Giusto, V. Malpighi 3 (☎02 29 40 92 97). From MM1: Porta Venezia, turn onto V. Piave, and then take a left on V. Malpighi. Gourmet sandwiches are some of the best in Milan (€3.80-7). ❶

Big Pizza: Da Willy 2, V. G. Borsi 1, along V. A. Sforza (☎02 83 96 77). This student favorite takes its name seriously: Witness the chefs shoving pies of epic proportions into the stone oven. Pizza €5-8. Open M-F 11am-midnight, Sa-Su 6pm-midnight. ❷

👁 SIGHTS

DUOMO. The Gothic *duomo* is the geographical and spiritual center of Milan. More than 3400 statues, 135 spires, and 96 gargoyles grace the third-largest church in the world. Climb or ride to the top of the cathedral from outside the north transept, where you will find yourself surrounded by a fantastic field of turrets, spires, and statues. (*MM1: Duomo. Open Mar.-Oct. daily 7am-7pm; Nov.-Feb. 9am-4:15pm. Free. Roof open daily 9am-5:30pm. €3.50, with elevator €5.*)

ITALY

TEATRO ALLA SCALA. Known simply as La Scala, this is the world's most renowned opera house. Singer Maria Callas became a legend in this 18th-century Neoclassical building. The theater is currently closed for renovation until the end of 2004. *(P. della Scala, at the opposite end of the galleria from the duomo. Open daily 9am–6pm. €5.)* The **Museo Teatrale alla Scala** includes memorabilia from poster art to a plaster cast of Toscanini's hand. *(C. Magenta 71. MM1: Conciliazione. Open daily 9am–6pm. €5, students €4.)*

GALLERIA VITTORIO EMANUELE II. On the left as you face the *duomo*, a glass barrel vault covers a five-story arcade of cafes and shops. Beautiful mosaics representing different continents sieged by the Romans adorn the floors and walls. Once considered the drawing room of Milan, the statue-bedecked Galleria is now a graceful mall that radiates elegance. *(Open M-Sa 10am-11pm, Su 10am-8pm.)*

PINACOTECA DI BRERA. The Brera Art Gallery presents one of Italy's most impressive collections of paintings, with works by Caravaggio, Bellini, and Raphael. *(V. Brera 28. Open Su and Tu-Sa 8:30am-7:15pm. €6.20.)*

CASTELLO SFORZESCO. Restored after heavy bomb damage in 1943, the enormous Castello Sforzesco is one of Milan's best-known monuments. Inside are the **Musei Civici** (Civic Museums), which include the **Museo Degli Instrumenti Musicali** (Musical Instruments Museum) and the **Museo d'Arte Applicata** (Applied Arts Museum). The ground floor contains a sculpture collection most renowned for Michelangelo's unfinished *Pietà Rondanini*. *(MM1: Cairoli. Open Su and Tu-Sa 9:30am-7:30pm. Free.)*

CHIESA DI SANTA MARIA DELLE GRAZIE. The church's Gothic nave is dark and elaborately patterned with frescoes. Next to the church entrance, in what was once the dining hall, is the **Cenacolo Vinciano (Vinciano Refectory),** home to one of the most important pieces of art in the world: **Leonardo da Vinci's Last Supper.** *(P. di S. Maria delle Grazie 2, on C. Magenta, off V. Carducci. MM1: Cadorna Cairoli. ☎ 02 89 42 11 46. Reservations required. Open Su and Tu-F 8am-7:30pm, Sa 8am-11pm. Last Supper €6.50.)*

BASILICA DI SANT'AMBROGIO. A prototype for Lombard-Romanesque churches throughout Italy, Sant'Ambrogio is the most influential medieval building in Milan. The 4th-century **Cappella di San Vittore in Ciel D'Oro,** with exquisite 5th-century mosaics adorning its cupola, lies through the 7th chapel on the right; enter, walk a few paces, and then turn left. *(MM1: Sant'Ambrogio. Open M-Sa 7:30am-noon and 2:30-7pm, Su 3-7pm. Free.)*

NAVIGLI DISTRICT. The "Venice of Lombardy," the Navigli district comes alive at night. Complete with canals, footbridges, open-air markets, and cafes, this area once constituted part of a medieval canal system used to transport tons of marble for the *duomo* that linked Milan to various northern cities and lakes. *(Outside the MM2: Porta Genova station, through the Arco di Porta Ticinese.)*

BASILICA DI SANT'EUSTORGIO. Founded in the 4th century to house the bones of the Magi, the church lost its original function when the dead wise men were spirited off to Cologne in 1164. The triumph of the church is the **Portinari Chapel,** one of the great masterpieces of early Renaissance art. *(P.S. Eustorigio 3, down C. Ticinese from S. Lorenzo Maggiore. Tram #3. Open Su-M and W-Sa 9:30am-noon and 3:30-6pm. Cappella open Su and Tu-Sa 4:30-6:30pm.)*

CHIESA DI SAN LORENZO MAGGIORE. The oldest church in Milan, San Lorenzo Maggiore testifies to the city's 4th-century greatness. To its right lies the **Cappella di Sant'Aquilino,** which contains a 5th-century mosaic of a beardless Christ among his apostles. *(On C. Ticinese. MM2: Porta Genova, then tram #3 from V. Torino. Open daily 7:30am-6:45pm. Cappella €2. Students €1.)*

PINACOTECA AMBROSIANA. The Ambrosiana's 23 rooms display exquisite works from the 14th through 19th centuries, including paintings by Botticelli, Leonardo, Raphael, Caravaggio, Titian, and Breugel. *(P. Pio XI 2. ☎02 86 46 29 81. Follow V. Spadari off V. Torino and make a left onto V. Cantù. Open Tu-Su 10am-5:30pm. €7.50.)*

■ ▶ SHOPPING AND NIGHTLIFE

If Milan's status as a world-famous fashion capital has lured you here for shopping, don't despair about the prices. If you can tolerate the stigma of being an entire season behind, purchase your famous designer duds from *blochisti* (wholesale clothing outlets), such as **Monitor** on V. Monte Nero (MM3: Porta Romana, then tram #9 or 29) or the well-known **Il Salvagente**, V. Bronzetti 16, off C. XXII Marzo (bus #60 from MM1: Lima or MM2/3: Stazione Centrale). The clothing sold along **Corso Buenos Aires** is more affordable—all the stores are open 10am-12:30pm and 2:30-7pm. Winter sales begin January 10. Shop in late July for end-of-the-summer sales (20-50% off) and a glimpse of the new fall lines. Hard-core window shoppers should head to the world-famous ▓fashion district between **Corso Vittorio Emanuele** near the *duomo* and **Via Monte Napoleone** off P. San Babila. The dresses come straight from the designers and the selection is more up-to-date than anywhere else in the world, including New York and Tokyo. Expect to find high-class places to buy perfume, glasses, leather goods, shoes, and jewelry.

   Milan Oltre is a festival of drama, dance and music; call the **Ufficio Informazione del Comune** (☎02 86 46 40 94) for more details. Milan's increasingly popular **Carnevale**, which spans the three days after Ash Wednesday, is the longest festival in Italy. The revelry centers around the *duomo* and spreads throughout the city. Milan's nightlife resembles the sophisticated city: The vibrant, the mellow, the chic, and the wild all live within a few Metro stops. The **Navigali district** is a particularly popular area for nightlife.

▓ **Le Trottoir**, near V. Brera. From MM2: Lanza, take V. Tivoli to the C. Garibaldi intersection. A lively atmosphere with live bands nightly. Open daily 7pm-2:30am.

▓ **Scimmie**, V. Sforza 49. A legendary, energetic bar. Different theme every night and frequent concerts; fusion, jazz, soul, and reggae dominate. Open daily 8pm-3am.

   Alcatraz, V. Valtellina 25. MM2: Porta Garibaldi. Take V. Ferrari and go right on C. Farni. After the train tracks, turn left on V. Valtellina. Biggest club and indoor concert venue in Milan. Cover €14 includes 1 drink. Open F-Sa 11pm-3am.

   Loolapaloosa, C. Como 15. A wild crowd will have you dancing on the tables. €6 cover includes 1st drink. Open Su-Th 6pm-3am.

   Grand Café Fashion, C. Porta Ticinese, near V. Vetere. A bar/restaurant/dance club with a stunningly beautiful crowd and velour leopard-print couches. €7.80 cover includes 1 drink. Open Su and Tu-Sa 6pm-4am.

   Lelephante, V. Melzo 22. MM2: Porta Venezia; walk up C. Buenos Aires and turn right on V. Melzo. Vaguely 60s gay club with lava lamps. Open Su and Tu-Sa 6:30pm-2am.

MANTUA (MANTOVA)   ☎0376

Mantua (pop. 100,000) owes its literary fame to its celebrated son, the poet Virgil. Its grand *palazzi* and graceful churches come thanks to the Gonzaga family who, after ascending to power in 1328, imported well-known artists to change Mantua's small-town image. Once the largest palace in Europe, the opulent ▓**Palazzo Ducale** towers over **Piazza Sordello**, sheltering the Gothic **Magna Domus** and **Palazzo del Capitano**. Inside, check out a breathtaking array of frescoes, gardens, and facades. Outside the *palazzo*, signs point to the **Castello di San Giorgio**

(1390-1406), a formidable fortress before its absorption into the *palazzo* complex. (*Palazzo* open Su and Tu-Sa 8:45am-6:30pm. €6.50, students €3.25, children and seniors free.) In the far south of the city, down V.P. Amedeo, through P. Veneto, and down Largo Parri, lies the **Palazzo di Te**, built by Giulio Romano in 1534 as a suburban retreat for Federico II Gonzaga. It is widely considered the finest building in the Mannerist style. (Open M 1-6pm, Tu-Su 9am-6pm. €8, students €2.50.) Just south of P. Sordello is the 11th-century Romanesque **Piazza delle Erbe;** opposite the *piazza* is Leon Alberti's **Chiesa di Sant'Andrea,** Mantua's greatest contribution to the Italian Renaissance and one of the first monumental Classical constructions since Imperial Rome. (*Piazza* open daily 10am-12:30pm and 2:30-4:30pm, *Chiesa* open daily 8am-noon and 3-6:30pm. Both free.)

Trains go from P. Don E. Leoni to Milan (2hr., 9 per day, €8) and Verona (40min., 17 per day, €2.30). From the train station, head left on V. Solferino, through P.S. Francesco d'Assisi to V. Fratelli Bandiera, and right on V. Verdi to reach the **tourist office,** P. Mantegna 6, next to Chiesa Sant'Andrea. (☎0376 32 82 53; www.aptmantova.it. Open M-Sa 8:30am-12:30pm and 3-6pm, Su 9:30-12:30pm.) Charming **Hotel ABC ❸,** P. Don E. Leoni 25, is opposite the station. (☎0376 32 33 47; fax 0376 32 23 29. Breakfast included. Singles €44-66; doubles €66-99; triples €77-110.) **Antica Osteria ai Ranari ❷,** V. Trieste 11, down V. Pomponazzo near Porta Catena, specializes in regional dishes. (☎0376 32 84 31. *Primi* €5-7. *Secondi* €5-9. Closed for 3 weeks July-Aug. Open Su and Tu-Sa noon-2pm and 7-11:30pm.) **Postal Code:** 46100.

BERGAMO   ☎035

Bergamo's (pop. 110,000) two sections reflect its colorful history: while the *città alta* (upper city) reveals its origins as a Venetian outpost, the *città bassa* (lower city) is a modern metropolis packed with Neoclassical buildings. **Via Pignolo,** in the *città bassa*, winds past a succession of handsome 16th- to 18th-century palaces. Turning left onto V.S. Tomaso and then right brings you to the **Galleria dell'Accademia Carrara,** which holds works by van Dyck, Rubens, and Titian. (Open Apr.-Sept. Su and Tu-Sa 10am-1pm and 3-6:45pm; Oct.-Mar. 9:30am-1pm and 2:30pm-5:45pm. €2.60.) From the Galleria, the cobbled **Via Noca** ascends to the medieval *città alta* through the 16th-century **Porta S. Agostino.** Stroll down V. Porta Dipinta to V. Gambito, which ends in **Piazza Vecchia,** an ensemble of medieval and Renaissance buildings flanked by restaurants and cafes at the heart of the *città alta.* Head through the archway near P. Vecchia to P. del Duomo, and see the fresco-laden **Cappella Colleoni.** (Open Apr.-Oct. daily 9am-12:30pm and 2-6:30pm; Nov.-Feb. Su and Tu-Sa 9am-12:30pm and 2:30-4:30pm.) Immediately left of the Cappella Colleoni is the ◪**Basilica di Santa Maria Maggiore,** a 12th-century basilica with an ornate Baroque interior and tapestries depicting biblical scenes. (Open daily Apr.-Oct. 9am-12:30pm and 2:30-6pm; Nov.-Mar. reduced hours.) Climb the **Torre Civica** (Civic Tower) for a marvelous view of Bergamo. (Open May to mid-Sept. Su-Th 10am-8pm, F-Sa 10am-10pm; mid-Sept. to Apr. reduced hours. €1.)

The train station, bus station, and many budget hotels are in the *città bassa.* **Trains** (1hr., every hr., €3.65) and **buses** (every 30min. €4.10) pull into P. Marconi from Milan. To get to the **tourist office,** V. Aquila Nera 2, in the *città alta*, take bus #1a to the top of the *città alta*. (☎035 24 22 26; www.apt.bergamo.it. Open daily 9am-12:30pm and 2-5:30pm.) To get from the train station to **Ostello della Gioventù di Bergamo (HI) ❶,** V.G. Ferraris 1, take bus #9 to *Comozzi*, then #14 to *Leonardo da Vinci* and walk up the hill. (☎/fax 035 36 17 24. Internet €5.20 per hr. Lockout 10am-2pm. Curfew midnight. Dorms €14. HI members only. MC/V.) **Locanda Caironi ❷,** V. Torretta 6B, off V. Gorgo Palazzo, is in a

ITALY

quiet residential neighborhood. Take bus #5 or 7 from V. Angelo Maj. (☎ 24 30 83. Singles €20; doubles €38. MC/V.) The friendly, student-run **Cooperativa Città Alta ❶**, has fast service and tasty cuisine. (☎035 21 85 68. Open daily noon-midnight.) **Postal Code:** 24122.

THE LAKE COUNTRY

When Italy's monuments and museums start to blur together, escape to the natural beauty of the northern Lake Country, where clear water laps at the foot of the encircling mountains. A youthful crowd descends upon Lake Garda, with its watersports by day and thriving club scene at night; palatial hotels line Lake Maggiore's sleepy shores; and Lake Como's urbane shore hosts three excellent hostels.

LAKE COMO (LAGO DI COMO)

Although a heavenly magnificence lingers over the reaches of Europe's deepest lake (410m), peaceful Lake Como is more than a figment of your imagination. *Bougainvillea* and lavish villas adorn the lake's craggy backdrop, warmed by the sun and cooled by lakeside breezes. Como, the largest city on the lake, makes an ideal transportation hub. For excellent **hiking** and stunning views, head from the far end of Lungo Lario Trieste up to Brunate. **Trains** roll into Stazione San Giovanni (☎0147 88 80 88) from Milan (1hr., every 30min. 4:45am-11:35pm, €4.85) and Venice (4hr., every hr. 4:45am-7:55pm, €22). To get from the train station to the **tourist office**, P. Cavour 16, walk down the steps, turn left on V. Fratelli Ricchi after the little park, and turn right on Viale Fratelli Rosselli, which leads to P. Cavour via Lungo Lario Trento. (☎031 26 97 12; www.lakecomo.org. Open M-Sa 9am-1pm and 2:30-6pm, Su 9:30-1pm.) **Ostello Villa Olmo (HI) ❶**, V. Bellinzona, 2 behind Villa Olmo, offers clean rooms, great food, and discounts on various sights in Como. From the train station, walk 20min. down V. Borgo Vico, which becomes V. Bellinzona. (☎/fax 031 57 38 00. hostellocomo@tin.it. Breakfast included. Reception 7-10am and 4-11:30pm. Lockout 10am. Strict curfew 11:30pm. Open Mar-Nov. Reserve ahead. Dorms €15.)

LAKE MAGGIORE (LAGO MAGGIORE)

Lacking the frenzy of its eastern neighbors, Lake Maggiore combines similar temperate mountain waters and idyllic shores. The romantic resort town **Stresa** is only an hour from Milan by **train** (every hr., €5.10). The local **tourist office** is in the ferry building at the dock, in P. Martini. (☎/fax 0323 30 150. Open daily 10am-12:30pm and 3-6:30pm.) To reach **Orsola Meublé ❷**, V. Duchessa di Genova 45, turn right from the station, walk downhill to the intersection and turn left. The affordable blue-tiled rooms have cement balconies. (☎0323 31 087; fax 93 31 21. Breakfast included. Singles €15, with bath €30; doubles €30/40. AmEx/D/MC/V.)

🔁 **DAYTRIP FROM LAKE MAGGIORE: BORROMEAN ISLANDS.** Stresa is a perfect stepping-stone to the gorgeous Borromean Islands. Daily excursion tickets (€10) allow you to hop back and forth between Stresa and the three islands—**Isola Bella, Isola Superiore dei Pescatori,** and **Isola Madre.** The islands boast lush, manicured botanical gardens and elegant villas. The opulent, Baroque ▨**Palazzo e Giardini Borromeo,** on Isola Bella, features six meticulously designed rooms with priceless masterpieces, tapestries and sculptures. The 10 terraced gardens, punctuated with statues and topped by a unicorn, rise up like a large wedding cake. (Open Mar.-Sept. daily 9am-5:30pm; Oct. 9am-5pm. €8.50.)

LAKE GARDA (LAGO DI GARDA)

Garda has staggering mountains and breezy summers. **Desenzano,** the lake's southern transport hub, is only 30min. from Verona, 1hr. from Milan, and 2hr. from Venice. Sirmione and Gardone Riviera, easily accessible by bus and boat, are best explored as daytrips, as accommodations are scant and pricey.

SIRMIONE. Sirmione's beautiful 13th-century castle and Roman ruins make for a leisurely day or a busy afternoon. **Buses** run every hour from Verona (1hr., €2.70). *Battelli* (water steamers) run until 8pm to: Desenzano (20min., €3); Gardone (1¼hr., €5.40); and Riva (4hr., €7.80). The **tourist office,** V. Guglielmo Marconi 2, is in the disc-shaped building. (☎030 91 61 14. Open Apr.-Oct. daily 9am-9pm; Nov.-Mar. reduced hours.) The **Albergo Grifone ❸,** V. Bocchio 4, has country-style rooms, all with bath, and lake views. (☎030 91 60 14; fax 030 91 65 48. Reserve ahead. Singles €32; doubles €55.) **Postal Code:** 25019.

RIVA DEL GARDA. Riva's calm pebble beaches are Lake Garda's compromise for the budget traveler. Travelers **swim, windsurf, hike,** and **climb** near the most stunning portion of the lake, where cliffs crash into the water. Riva is accessible by **bus** (☎0464 55 23 23) from Trent (2hr., 10 per day, €3.20) and Verona (2hr., 11 per day, €5). **Ferries** (☎030 914 95 11) leave from P. Matteoti for Gardone (€6.60). The **tourist office,** Giardini di Porta Orientale 8, is near the water. (☎0464 55 44 44; fax 52 03 08. Open M-Sa 9am-noon and 3-6pm, Su 10am-noon and 4-6:30pm.) Snooze at the fabulous **Locanda La Montanara ❷,** V. Montanara 20, off V. Florida. (☎/fax 0464 55 48 57. Breakfast €5. Singles €16; doubles €32-35; triples €49.) **Postal Code:** 38066.

ITALIAN RIVIERA (LIGURIA)

The Italian Riviera stretches 350km along the Mediterranean between France and Tuscany, forming the most famous and most touristed area of the Italian coastline. Genoa divides the crescent-shaped strip into the **Riviera di Levante** ("rising sun") to the east and the **Riviera di Ponente** ("setting sun") to the west. The elegant coast beckons with lemon trees, almond blossoms, and turquoise seas. Especially lovely is the **Cinque Terre** area, just to the west of **La Spezia.**

▐ TRANSPORTATION

The coastal towns are linked by the main **rail** line, which runs west to Ventimiglia (near the French border) and east to La Spezia (near Tuscany), but slow local trains can make short trips take hours. Frequent intercity **buses** pass through all major towns, and local buses run to inland hill-towns. **Boats** connect most resort towns. **Ferries** go from Genoa to Olbia, Sardinia and Palermo, Sicily.

GENOA (GENOVA)　　　　　　　　　　☎010

Genoa (pop. 640,000), city of grit and grandeur, has little in common with its resort neighbors. A Ligurian will tell you, *"Si deve conosceria per amaria"* (you have to know her to love her). While lacking the intimacy of a small-town resort, Genoa more than makes up for it in its rich cultural history and extravagant sights. Since falling into decline in the 18th century, modern Genoa has turned its attention from industry and trade to the restoration of its bygone splendor, and is once again claiming its position among Italy's most important cultural centers.

ITALY

▪ TRANSPORTATION. C. Columbo Internazionale airport (GOA), in Sesti Ponente, services European destinations. Take **Volabus** #100 from Stazione Brignole to the airport (every 30min., €2) and get off at *Aeroporto*. Most visitors arrive at one of Genoa's two **train stations: Stazione Principe,** in P. Acquaverde, or **Stazione Brignole,** in P. Verdi. **Trains** go to Rome (5hr., 9 per day, €33) and Turin (2hr., 19 per day, €9). AMT **buses** (☎010 558 24 14) run throughout the city. One-way tickets (€1) are valid for 1½hr.; all-day passes cost €3. **Ferries** depart from the Ponte Assereto arm of the port; buy tickets at **Stazione Marittima** in the port.

▪▪ ORIENTATION AND PRACTICAL INFORMATION. To get to the center of town, **Piazza de Ferrari,** from Stazione Principe, take **Via Balbi** to **Via Cairoli,** which becomes **Via Garibaldi,** and turn right on **Via XXV Aprile** at P. delle Fontane Marose. From Stazione Brignole, turn right onto **Via Fiume,** and right onto **Via XX Settembre.** Or, take bus #19, 20, 30, 32, 35, or 41 from Stazione Principe or bus #19 or 40 from Stazione Brignole to P. de Ferrari in the center of town. The **centro storico** (historic center) contains many of Genoa's monuments. The **tourist office** is on Porto Antico, in Palazzina S. Maria. From the aquarium, walk toward the complex of buildings to the left. (☎010 24 87 11; www.genovatouristboard.net. Open M-Sa 9am-1pm and 2-6pm.) Log on to the **Internet** at **APCA,** V. Colombo 35r. (☎/fax 010 58 13 41. €5.40 per hr. Open M-F 9am-noon.) **Postal Code:** 16121.

▪▪ ACCOMMODATIONS AND FOOD. Ostello per la Gioventù (HI) ❶, V. Costanzi 120, has a cafeteria, TV, and a view of the city far below. From Stazione Principe, take bus #35 to V. Napoli and transfer to #40, which runs to the hostel. From Stazione Brignole, pick up bus #40 (every 15min.) and ask to be let off at the *ostello*. (☎/fax 010 242 24 57. Breakfast included. Reception 7-11am and 3:30pm-12:30am. No curfew. HI members only. Dorms €13.) **Hotel Balbi ❸,** V. Balbi 21/3, offers large, ornate rooms. (☎/fax 010 25 23 62. Breakfast €4. Singles €30, with bath €45; doubles €55/70; triples €75/85. AmEx/MC/V.) **Camping** is popular; check the tourist office for availability, or try **Genova Est ❶** on V. Marcon Loc Cassa. Take the train from Stazione Brignole to the suburb of Bogliasco (10min., 6 per day, €1); a free bus (5min., every 2hr. 8:10am-6pm) will take you from Bogliasco to the campsite. (☎010 347 20 53. Electricity €1.80 per day. Laundry €3.50 per load. €4.70 per person, €9.60 per tent.) **◾Trattoria da Maria ❷,** V. Testa d'Oro 14r, off V. XXV Aprile, has new selections every day, with a three-course *menu* for €8. (☎010 58 10 80. Open Su-F noon-2:30pm and 7-9:30pm.)

▪▪ SIGHTS AND ENTERTAINMENT. Genoa boasts a multitude of *palazzi* built by its famous merchant families. These are best seen along **Via Garibaldi,** on the edge of *centro storico,* and **Via Balbi,** in the heart of the university quarter. The 17th-century **Palazzo Reale,** V. Balbi 10, 10min. west of V. Garibaldi, is filled with Rococo rooms bathed in gold and upholstered in red velvet. (Open Su and Th-Sa 9am-7pm, Tu-W 9am-1:30pm. €4, ages 18-25 €2, under-18 and seniors free.) Follow V. Balbi through P. della Nunziata and continue to L. Zecca, where V. Cairoli leads to **Via Garibaldi,** the most impressive street in Genoa, bedecked with elegant *palazzi* that once earned it the names "Golden Street" and "Street of Kings." The **Galleria di Palazzo Bianco,** V. Garibaldi 11, exhibits Ligurian, Dutch, and Flemish paintings. Across the street, the 17th-century **Galleria Palazzo Rosso,** V. Garibaldi 18, has magnificent furnishings in a lavishly frescoed interior. (Both open Su 10am-6pm, Tu-Sa 9am-7pm. €3.10 each, €5.20 for both. Su free.) The **Villetta Di Negro,** on the hill farther down V. Garibaldi, contains waterfalls, grottoes, and terraced gardens. From P. de Ferrari, take V. Boetto to P. Matteotti for the ornate **Chiesa di Gesù.** (Open daily 7:15am-12:30pm and 4-

7:30pm.) Head past the Chiesa di Gesù down V. di Porta Soprana to V. Ravecca to reach the medieval twin-towered **Porta Soprana,** the supposed boyhood home of **Christopher Columbus.** Off V.S. Lorenzo lies the **San Lorenzo Duomo,** a church in existence since the 9th century, which boasts a striped Gothic facade with a copiously decorated main entrance and 9th-century carved lions. (Open M-Sa 8am-7pm, Su 7am-7pm.) The **centro storico,** the eerie and beautiful historical center bordered by the port, V. Garibaldi, and P. Ferrari, is a mass of winding and confusing streets containing some of Genoa's most memorable monuments, including the **duomo** and the medieval **Torre Embraici.** However, a dangerous night scene makes visiting the centro storico best confined to weekdays when stores are open. From P. Matteotti, go down V.S. Lorenzo toward the water, turn left on V. Chiabrera and left on V. di Mascherona to reach the ⧉**Chiesa S. Maria di Castello,** a labyrinth of chapels, courtyards, cloisters, and crucifixes. (Open daily 9am-noon and 3-6pm.) Kids and ocean-lovers will adore the massive **aquarium** on Porto Antico to the right of the APT tourist office. (Open July-Aug. daily 9:30am-11pm; Sept.-June reduced hours. €12.)

RIVIERA DI PONENTE

FINALE LIGURE ☎019

A beachside plaque proclaims the town of Finale Ligure (pop. 15,000) the place for "*Il riposo del popolo*" (the people's rest). From bodysurfing in choppy waves to browsing through chic boutiques to scaling the 15th-century ruins of **Castello di San Giovanni,** *riposo* takes many forms in Finale Ligure. The city is divided into three sections: **Finalpia** to the east, **Finalmarina** in the center, and **Finalborgo** further inland. The train station and most sights are in Finalmarina. Skip the packed beaches in town and walk east along V. Aurelia through the first tunnel, turning right for a less populated **free beach.** Climb the tough trail to the ruins of **Castel Govone** for a spectacular view. Enclosed within ancient walls, **Finalborgo,** the historic quarter of Finale Ligure proper, is a 1km walk or short ACTS bus ride up V. Bruneghi from the station. **Pilade,** V. Garibaldi 67, features live jazz on Friday nights. (☎019 69 22 20. Open daily 10am-2am.) The towns near Finale Ligure are also worth exploring. SAR **buses** run from the train station to **Borgo Verezzi** (10min., every 15min., €1.50).

Trains leave from P. Vittorio Veneto for Genoa (1hr., every hr., €3.80). The IAT **tourist office,** V.S. Pietro 14, gives out free maps. (☎019 68 10 19; fax 019 68 18 04. Open M-Sa 9am-12:30pm and 3:30-6:30pm, Su 9am-noon.) Check email at **Net Village Internet Cafe,** near the train station. (☎019 681 62 83. Open daily 8:15am-midnight. €5.50 per hr.) ⧉**Castello Wuillerman (HI) ❶,** on V. Generale Caviglia, is well worth the hike. From the train station, cross the street and turn left onto V. Raimondo Pertica, then left onto V. Rossi. After passing a church on the left, take a left onto V. Alonzo, and trudge up the daunting steps to a red-brick castle with a stunning view of the sea. (☎019 69 05 15; hostelfinaleligure@libero.it. Breakfast and sheets included. Internet access €4.50 per hr. Reception daily 7-10am and 5-10pm. Curfew 11:30pm. Email reservations. HI members only. Dorms €11.) **Albergo San Marco ❸,** V. della Concezione 22, has spotless rooms, many with balconies. From train station, walk straight ahead down V. Saccone, and turn left on V. della Concezione. (☎019 69 25 33; fax 681 6187. Open Easter-late Sept. Singles €33-39; doubles €45-57. Extra bed €10. AmEx/DC/MC/V.) **Camping Del Mulino ❶,** on V. Castelli, has a restaurant and mini-market on the premises. Take the Calvisio bus from the station to the Boncardo Hotel and follow the brown and yellow signs to the campsite entrance. (☎019 60 16 69. Reception Apr.-Sept. 8am-8pm. €4.50-6 per person, €5-7 per tent.) Cheap restaurants lie along **Via Rossi, Via Roma,** and **Via**

Garibaldi. Fill up on huge portions of delicious pasta at **Spaghetteria Il Posto ❷**, V. Porro 21. The **Coop supermarket** is at V. Dante Alighieri 7. (Open M-Sa 8:30am-7:30pm, Su 9am-1pm. MC/V.) **Postal Code:** 17024.

RIVIERA DI LEVANTE

CAMOGLI. Postcard-perfect Camogli shimmers with color. Sun-faded peach houses crowd the hilltop, red and turquoise boats bob in the water, piles of fishing nets cover the docks, and bright umbrellas dot the dark stone beaches. **Trains** to Genoa (40min., 38 per day, €1.50) and La Spezia (1½hr., 24 per day, €3.50). Golfo Paradiso **ferries**, V. Scalo 3 (☎0185 77 20 91; www.golfoparadiso.it), near P. Colombo, go to Portofino (round-trip €16) and Cinque Terre (round-trip €20). Buy tickets on the dock, call ahead for the schedule. Turn right from the station to find the **tourist office**, V. XX Settembre 33, which helps find rooms. (☎0185 77 10 66. Open M-Sa 9am-12:30pm and 3:30-7pm, Su 9am-1pm.) Exit the train station, walk down the stairway to the right, and look for the blue sign for the ⚑**Albergo La Camogliese ❹**, V. Garibaldi 55, near the beach. (☎0185 77 14 02; fax 0185 77 40 24. **Internet** access €1 per 30min. Singles €51-59; doubles €69-80. 10% *Let's Go* discount with cash payment. AmEx/MC/V.) **Postal Code:** 16032.

SANTA MARGHERITA LIGURE. Santa Margherita Ligure was a calm fishing village until the early 20th century, when it fell into favor with Hollywood stars. Today, glamour and glitz paint the shore, but the serenity of the town's early days still lingers. If ocean waves don't invigorate your spirit, try the holy water in seashell basins at the **Basilica di Santa Margherita**, at P. Caprera. **Trains** go from P. Federico Raoul Nobili, at the top of V. Roma, to Genoa (40min., 2-4 per hr., €2.10) and La Spezia (1½hr., 2 per hr., €4). Tigullio **buses** (☎0185 28 88 34) go from P.V. Veneto to Camogli (30min., 1-2 per hr., €1.20) and Portofino (20min., 3 per hr., €1.50). Tigullio **ferries**, V. Palestro 8/1b (☎0185 28 46 70), has tours to Cinque Terre (July-Sept. 1 per day W, Th and Sa, €20) and Portofino (every hr., €3.50). Turn right from the train station on V. Roma, left on C. Rainusso, turn left and take a hard right onto V. XXV Aprile from Largo Giusti to find the **tourist office**, V. XXV Aprile 2b, which arranges lodging. (☎0185 28 74 85; fax 0185 28 30 34. Open M-Sa 9am-12:30pm and 3-7:30pm, Su 9:30am-12:30pm and 4:30-7:30pm.) ⚑**Hotel Terminus ❹**, P. Nobili 4, is to left as you exit station. The spacious rooms in this 18th-century building give breathtaking view of sea. (Singles €50, with bath €65; doubles with bath €85; triples €105; quads €116. AmEx/MC/V.) **Trattoria Baicin ❸**, V. Algeria 9, has the best pesto in town. (☎0185 28 67 63. Open Su and Tu-Sa noon-3pm and 7pm-midnight. AmEx/MC/V.) **Postal Code:** 16032.

PORTOFINO. As long as you don't buy anything, princes and paupers alike can enjoy the curved shores and tiny bay of Portofino. A 1hr. walk along the ocean road offers the chance to scout small rocky **beaches.** The area's only sandy beach, **Paraggi** (where the bus stops) is a small strip. In town, follow the signs uphill from the bay to escape to the cool interior of the **Chiesa di San Giorgio.** A few minutes up the road toward the **castle** is a serene garden with sea views. (Open daily 10am-7pm; off-season reduced hours. €3.50.) To get to town, take the bus to *Portofino Mare* (not *Portofino Vetta*). From P. Martiri della Libertà, Tigullio **buses** go to Santa Margherita (3 per hr., €1.50); buy tickets at the green kiosk. **Ferries** also go to Camogli (2 per day, €7) and Santa Margherita (every hr. 10:30am-4pm, €3.50). The **tourist office**, V. Roma 35, is on the way to the waterfront from the bus stop. (☎0185 26 90 24. Open daily 10:30am-1:30pm and 2-7:30pm.) **Postal Code:** 16034.

CINQUE TERRE ☎ 0187

The five bright fishing villages of Cinque Terre are as soothing as they are beautiful. A vast expanse of dazzling turquoise sea laps against the *cittadine* that cling to a stretch of terraced hillsides and steep crumbling cliffs. Tourists journey from around the world to hike between the five villages, climbing through vineyards along dry stone cliffs with breathtaking views of the surrounding seas. Each of these five villages—Monterosso, Vernazza, Corniglia, Manarola, and Riomaggiore—invites the traveler to explore its own unique character. Despite the increasing tourism, the towns of the Cinque Terre still feel untouched by time.

E TRANSPORTATION. Trains run along the Genoa-La Spezia line. A **Cinque Terre Tourist Ticket** (€4.20) allows unlimited trips among the five towns and to La Spezia. Monterosso is the most accessible. From the station on V. Fegina, the north end of town, trains run to: Florence (3½hr., every hr., €8), via Pisa (2½hr., every hr., €4.40); Genoa (1½hr., every hr., €3.60); La Spezia (20min., every 30min., €1.20); and Rome (7hr., every 2hr., €27). Frequent local trains connect the 5 towns (5-20min., every 50min., €1-1.50). Monterosso can also be reached by **ferry** from La Spezia (1hr., 2 per day, €18).

▚▐ ORIENTATION AND PRACTICAL INFORMATION. The five villages stretch along the shore between Levanto and La Spezia, connected by trains, roads (although cars are not allowed inside the towns) and footpaths that traverse the rocky shoreline. **Monterosso** is the first town and the largest, containing most of the services for the area, followed by picturesque **Vernazza,** cliffside **Corniglia,** and the quiet towns of **Manarola** and **Riomaggiore.** The Pro Loco **tourist office** V. Fegina 38 is in Monterosso, below the train station, provides information and accommodations service. (☎0187 81 75 06; fax 0187 817 825. Open Apr.-Oct. M-Sa 9am-noon, 2:30-6:30pm, Su 9am-noon.) **Postal Code:** 19016 for Monterosso, 19018 for Corniglia and Vernazza, 19017 for Manarola and Riomaggiore.

▐◖ ACCOMMODATIONS AND FOOD. Most hotels are in Monterosso, and they fill quickly during the summer. Try the tourist office for help finding the more plentiful *affitacamere* (private rooms). The ▨**Albergo Della Gioventù-Ostello "Cinque Terre" ❷,** V. B. Riccobaldi 21 is in Manarola. Turn right from train station and continue up the hill 300m. The new hostel is both beautiful and mod-

THE HIDDEN DEAL

LIFE'S A BEACH

In 1873, the first Italian railroad split through the **Guvano** valley surrounding the hill town of Corniglia. Abandoned in 1968, the track left behind a long tunnel that cuts through the mountainside, rendering a sparkling cove and secluded beach newly accessible to the town's inhabitants. Before long, young men and women made the discovery, and soon they turned it into a lawless haven, building bonfires by the tunnel and basking in the buff.

In the 1990s, the local government gave the area over to a group of agricultural workers who cleaned up the beaches, planted vineyards along the coast, and began charging a small entrance fee. The workers are awaiting a license from the state to provide lifeguarding services and sell food and supplies to adventurous swimmers. Though newly scrubbed and supervised, Guvano hasn't lost its naturalist charm. Tourists who discover the tunnel can strut their stuff with the locals down the two pristine coves and take brisk, nude dips in the sea.

To reach Guvano, take a left from the Corniglia train station. Pass the stairs and turn left down the ramp on the other side of the tracks. At the bottom of the ramp, turn right, heading toward town. A 15min. walk through the dark tunnel (don't go alone) delivers you to the cove. Open July-Aug. daily 9am-7pm; June and Sept. Sa-Su 9am-7pm. €5.

ern with incredible views. (☎0187 92 02 15; www.hostel5terre.com. Breakfast €3.50. Curfew 1am, in winter midnight. Reserve in advance. Dorms €17-20. AmEx/DC/MC/V.) **Hotel Gianni Franzi ❸**, P. Marconi 1, in Vernazza, is run by the town's oldest *trattoria* (below) and has lovely antique rooms. (☎0187 82 10 03; www.giannifranzi.it. Single €38; double €58-62, with bath €75; triple €96. AmEx/DC/MC/V.) **Hotel Souvenir ❸**, V. Gioberti 24, in Monterosso, is friendly and family-run. (☎/fax 0187 81 75 95. Breakfast €5. Rooms €35 per person, students €25.) For private rooms in Riomaggiore, call **Mar-Mar ❸**, V. Malborghetto 8 (☎/fax 0187 92 09 32; www.marmar.5terre.com), an established *affita-camere* organization that rents doubles (€50-80) and nice dorms (€20 per person). Cinque Terre has excellent food—Vernazza is reputed to have the best. **Tratorria Gianni Franzi ❸**, P. Marconi 1, is famous for its pesto. (☎0187 82 10 03. *Primi* €4-11. *Secondi* €5-16. Open Su-Tu and Th-Sa noon-3pm, 7:30-9:30pm. AmEx/DC/MC/V.)

◉▯ SIGHTS AND ENTERTAINMENT. The best sightseeing in Cinque Terre consists of exploring the five villages and the gorgeous paths that connect them. Monterosso has the Cinque Terre's largest **free beach,** in front of the historic center, sheltered by a cliff cove. The 17th-century **Chiesa Del Convento dei Cappuccini** perched on a hill in the center of town, yields the most expansive vistas. (Open daily 9am-noon and 4-7pm.) The hike between Monterosso and Vernazza is considered the hardest of the four, with steep climbs over dry, rugged cliffs. The trail winds its way through terraced vineyards and past hillside cottages before descending steeply into town. From there, the trip to Corniglia offers breathtaking views of the sea, olive groves and scents of rosemary, lemon and lavender. Near Corniglia, the secluded **Guvano Beach,** accessed through a tunnel, is popular for nude sunbathing. (Open July-Aug. daily 9am-7pm; June and Sept. Sa-Su 9am-7pm. €5). The subsequent hike to youthful and vibrant Manarola lacks the picturesque vegetation of the previous two, but retains the sweeping, open views of the turquoise sea. The most famous of the Cinque Terre hikes, the **Via dell'Amore,** between Manarola and Riomaggiore, smallest of the five towns, is a slate-paved walk that features a stone tunnel painted with love scenes. All together the hikes generally take about five hours, not including time spent exploring the towns themselves. At night, the most popular towns are Monterosso, Manarola, and Riomaggiore. In Monterosso, **Il Casello,** V. Lungo Fessario 70, brings in the backpacking crowd with thumping music and a location near the beach—making it far enough from the town to be the only bar open past 1am. (Beer and mixed drinks from €2.50. **Internet** access €1 per 15min. Open daily 11am-3am.)

LA SPEZIA. A departure point for Corsica and an important transport hub for Cinque Terre, La Spezia is among Italy's most beautiful ports, with regal palms lining the promenade and citrus trees growing in the parks. The unique collection of the **Museo Navale,** in P. Chiodo, features diving suits from WWII, gargantuan iron anchors, and tiny replicas of Egyptian, Roman, and European vessels. (Open M-Sa 8:30am-1pm and 4:15-9:45pm, Su 8:30am-1:15pm. €1.60.) La Spezia lies on the Genoa-Pisa **train** line. Navigazione Golfo dei Poeti, V.d. Minzoni 13 (☎0187 73 29 87) offers **ferries** that stop in each village of Cinque Terre (one-way €11; round trip M-Sa €19, Su €22). The **tourist office,** V. Mazzini 45, is at the port. (☎0187 77 09 00. Open M-Sa 9:30am-1pm and 3:30-7pm, Su 9:30am-1pm.) **Albergo Il sole ❹**, V. Cavalloti, off V. Prione, offers spacious rooms. (☎0187 73 51 64. Singles €25-36; doubles €39-55; triples €53-74. AmEx/MC/V.) **Postal Code:** 19100.

EMILIA-ROMAGNA

Go to Florence, Venice, and Rome to sightsee; come to Emilia-Romagna to eat. Italy's wealthy wheat- and dairy-producing region covers the fertile plains of the Po River Valley, and celebrates the finest culinary traditions on the peninsula. The Romans originally settled here, but the towns later fell under the rule of great Renaissance families whose names adorn every *palazzo* and *piazza* in the region.

BOLOGNA   ☎051

Home to Europe's oldest university and rich, flavorful cuisine, Bologna (pop. 500,000) has been known since ancient times as the *grassa* (fat) and *dotta* (learned) city. Today, academic liberalism drives political activism—minority groups, student alliances, and the national gay organization all find a voice (and listening ears) in Bologna. All eyes, however, are on Bologna's art. Priceless works inhabit numerous museums and churches, whose 700-year-old porticoes line wide, straight streets.

▛▊ TRANSPORTATION AND PRACTICAL INFORMATION. Bologna is a rail hub for all major Italian cities and the Adriatic coast. **Trains** leave the northern tip of the walled city for: Florence (1½hr., every 2hr., €5-7); Milan (3hr., 2 per hr., €10); Rome (4hr., every hr., €22); and Venice (2hr., every hr., €10). **Buses** #25 and 30 run between the train station and the historic center at **Piazza Maggiore** (€1). The **tourist office**, P. Maggiore 1, is next to the Palazzo Comunale. (☎051 648 76 07; www.comune.bologna.it/bolognaturismo. Open M-Sa 10am-2pm and 3-7pm, Su 10am-2pm.) **Postal Code:** 40100.

▛▐ ACCOMMODATIONS AND FOOD. The sparklingly clean **Albergo Panorama ❹**, V. Livraghi 1, 4th fl., has a prime location. Follow V. Ugo Bassi from P. Maggiore and take the third left. (☎051 22 18 02. Singles €50; doubles €65; triples €80. AmEx/MC/V.) **Ostello due Torre San Sisto (HI) ❶**, V. Viadagola 5, is off V. San Donato, in the Località di San Sisto, 6km from the center of town. Walk down V. dell'Indipendenza from the station, turn right on V. della Mille, and take bus #93 from across the street to San Sisto. (☎051 22 49 13. Reception 7:30-9am, 3:30-11pm. Lockout 10am-3:30pm. Curfew 11:30pm. Dorms €14; doubles €30.) All rooms at **Pensione Marconi ❸**, V. Marconi 22, are clean and include bathrooms. Turn right from the train station and turn left on V. Amendola, which becomes V. Marconi. (☎051 26 28 32. Singles €45; doubles €70; triples €93.)

Don't leave without sampling Bologna's signature *spaghetti alla bolognese*. Scout **Via Augusto Righi, Via Piella,** and **Via Saragozza** for traditional *trattorie*. A **PAM** supermarket, V. Marconi 26, is by the intersection with V. Riva di Reno. (Open M-Sa 7:45am-8pm.) Locals chat over plates of pasta at **▧Trattoria Da Maro ❷**, V. Broccaindosso 71b, between Strada Maggiore and V.S. Vitale. (☎051 22 73 04. *Primi* €5-6. *Secondi* €5-7. Open Tu-Sa noon-2:30pm and 8-11pm.) **Ristorante Clorofilla ❷**, Strada Maggiore 64C, is a hip, primarily vegetarian spot. (☎051 23 53 43. Salads and hot dishes €5-8. Open M-Sa 12:15-2:45pm and 7:30-11pm.)

◐ ▟ SIGHTS AND ENTERTAINMENT. Forty kilometers of porticoed buildings line the streets of Bologna in a mix of Gothic, Renaissance, and Baroque styles. The tranquil **▧Piazza Maggiore** flaunts both Bologna's historical and modern wealth. The cavernous Gothic interior of the city's *duomo*, **Basilica di San Petronio**, was meant to be larger than Rome's St. Peter's, but the jealous Church leadership ordered that the funds be used instead to build the nearby Palazzo

ITALY

Archiginnasio. It hosted both the Council of Trent (when it wasn't meeting in Trent) and the 1530 ceremony in which Pope Clement VII gave Italy to the German King Charles V. The pomp and pageantry of the exercises at the church allegedly inspired a disgusted Martin Luther to reform religion in Germany. (Open M-Sa 7:15am-1pm and 2-6pm, Su 7:30am-1pm and 2-6:30pm.) The **Palazzo Archiginnasio,** behind S. Petronio, was once a university building; the upstairs theater was built in 1637 to teach anatomy to students. (☎051 27 68 11. Open daily 9am-1pm. Closed 2 weeks in Aug.) On the northern side of P. Maggiore is the **Palazzo de Podestà,** remodeled by Fioravanti's son Aristotle, who later designed Moscow's Kremlin. Next to P. Maggiore, **Piazza del Nettuno** contains Giambologna's famous 16th-century fountain, *Neptune and Attendants.* From P. Nettuno, go down V. Rizzoli to **Piazza Porta Ravegana,** where seven streets converge to form Bologna's medieval quarter. Two towers that constitute the city's emblem rise magnificently from the *piazza;* you can climb the 498 steps of the **Torre degli Asinelli** for a breathtaking view of the city. (Open daily 9am-6pm. €3.) From V. Rizzoli, follow V.S. Stefano to Piazza Santo Stefano, where four of the original seven churches of the Romanesque **Piazza Santo Stefano Church Complex** remain. Bologna's patron saint, San Petronio, lies buried under the pulpit of the **Chiesa di San Sepolcro.** (Open daily 9am-noon and 3:30-6pm.) Take Strada Maggiore to P. Aldrovandi to reach the remarkably intact **Chiesa di Santa Mari dei Seru,** whose columns support an unusual combination of arches and ribbed vaulting. (Open daily 7am-1pm and 3:30-8pm. The **Pinacoteca Nazionale,** V. delle Belle Arti 56, off V. Zamboni, traces the history of Bolognese artists. (☎051 420 94 11. Open Su and Tu-Sa 9am-6:30pm. €6, students €3, seniors and under-18 free.)

Bologna's hip student population ensures raucous nighttime fun. **Cluricaune,** V. Zamboni 18/b, is an Irish bar packed with students who flock to its pool table and dart boards. (Pints €4.20. Happy Hour 7-10:30pm features €2.50 pints. Open Su-F 11pm-3am, Sa 4pm-3am.) **Cassero,** in the Porta Saragozza, is a lively gay bar packed with men and women. (Drinks €3-6. Open daily 10pm-2am.)

PARMA ☎0521

Famous for its *parmigiano* cheese and *prosciutto* ham, Parma's (pop. 200,000) artistic excellence is not confined to the kitchen. 16th-century Mannerist painting came into full bloom here, and native Giuseppe Verdi resided in Parma while composing some of his greatest works. From P. Garibaldi, follow Strada Cavour toward the train station and take the third right on Strada al Duomo to reach the 11th-century Romanesque **duomo,** in P. del Duomo, which is filled with masterpieces. Most spectacular is the dome, where Correggio's *Virgin* ascends to a golden heaven in a spiral of white robes, pink *putti,* and blue sky. The pink-and-white marble **baptistery** was built between the Romanesque and Gothic periods. (*Duomo* open daily 9am-noon and 3-7pm. Baptistery open daily 9am-12:30pm and 3-7pm. €2.70, students €1.50.) Behind the *duomo* is the frescoed dome of the **Chiesa di San Giovanni Evangelista,** P.S. Giovanni, designed by Correggio. (Open M-Sa 8am-11:45am and 3-6:45pm, Su 8am-12:45pm and 3-7:45pm.) From P. del Duomo, follow Strada al Duomo across Strada Cavour, walk one block down Strada Piscane, and cross P. della Pace to reach the 17th-century **Palazzo della Pilotta,** an artistic treasure chest that houses the **Galleria Nazionale.** (Open Su and Tu-Sa 8:30am-2pm. €6, students €3.)

Parma is on the Bologna-Milan rail line. **Trains** go from P. Carlo Alberto della Chiesa to: Bologna (1hr., 2 per hr., €4.20); Florence (3hr., 7 per day, €15); and Milan (1½hr., every hr., €7). Walk left from the station, turn right on V. Garibaldi, and turn left on V. Melloni to reach the **tourist office,** V. Melloni 1a. (☎0521 21 88 89; fax 0521 23 47 35. Open M-Sa 9am-7pm, Su 9am-1pm.) From the station, take bus #9 (€0.75) and get off when the bus turns left on V. Martiri della Libertà for the **Ostello Cittadella (HI) ❶**, on V. Passo Buole, in a corner of a 15th-century fortress with a campground beside it. (☎0521 96 14 34. 3-night max. stay. Lockout 9:30am-5pm. Curfew 11pm. Open Apr.-Oct. HI members only. Dorms €9. Camping €6.50 per person, €11 per site.) **Albergo Leon d'Oro ❸**, V. Fratti 4, off V. Garibaldi, is clean and only two blocks from the train station. (☎0521 77 31 82. Singles €33; doubles €50. AmEx/MC/V.) Look near **Via Garibaldi** for fragrant Parma cuisine. **Pizzeria La Duchessa ❷**, P. Garibaldi 1/B is an excellent *trattoria* with a large variety of pastas and thick-crust pizzas. (☎0521 23 59 62. Pizza €4.20-9.50. *Primi* €5.50-8. *Secondi* €6.50-15. Cover €1.30-1.55. Open Su and Tu-Sa 10am-2pm and 7pm-12:30am. MC/V.) **K2**, Borgo Cairoli 23, next to the Chiesa di San Giovanni Evangelista, has great *gelato*. (Cones from €1.50. Open M-Tu and Th-Su 11am-midnight.) **Dimeglio supermarket** is at V. XXII Luglio 27c. (Open M-W and F-Sa 8:30am-1pm and 4:30-8pm, Th 8:30am-1pm.) **Postal Code:** 43100.

RAVENNA   ☎0544

Ravenna's (pop. 130,000) 15 minutes of historical fame came and went 14 centuries ago, when Justinian and Theodora, rulers of the Byzantine Empire, headquartered their campaign to restore order in the anarchic west here. Take V. Argentario from V. Cavour to reach the 6th-century **◪Basilica di San Vitale**, V.S. Vitale 17. An open courtyard overgrown with greenery leads to the brilliant, glowing mosaics inside; those of the Emperor and Empress adorn the lower left and right panels of the apse. Behind S. Vitale, the city's oldest and most intriguing mosaics cover the glittering interior of the **Mausoleo di Galla Placidia**. (☎0544 21 62 92. Open Apr.-Sept. daily 9am-7pm; Oct.-Mar. 9:30am-5:30pm.) Take bus #4 or 44 across from the train station (€0.70) to Classe, south of the city, to see the astounding mosaics at the **◪Chiesa di Sant'Apollinare**. (Open M-Sa 8:30am-7:30pm, Su 9am-1pm. €2. Su free.) Much to Florence's dismay, Ravenna is also home to the **Tomb of Dante Alighieri**. In the adjoining **Dante Museum**, his heaven and hell come alive in etchings, paintings, and sculptures. From P. del Popolo, cut through P. Garibaldi to V. Alighieri. (☎0544 302 52. Tomb open daily 9am-7pm. Free. Museum open Apr.-Sept. Su and Tu-Sa 9am-noon and 3:30-6pm; Oct.-Mar. reduced hours. €2.)

Trains (☎0544 21 78 84) leave P. Farini for Ferrara (1hr., every hr., €4) and Bologna (1hr., every 1-2hr., €4). Follow V. Farini from the station to V. Diaz, which runs to the central P. del Popolo and the **tourist office**, V. Salara 8. (☎0544 354 04. Open Apr.-Sept. M-Sa 8:30am-7pm, Su 10am-4pm; Oct.-Mar. reduced hours.) Take bus #1 or 70 from V. Pallavicini at the train station (1-4 per hr., €0.70) to reach **Ostello Dante (HI) ❶**, V. Nicolodi 12. (☎/fax 0544 42 11 64. Breakfast included. Reception 7-10am and 5-11:30pm. Lockout 10am-5pm. Curfew 11:30pm. Dorms €13. MC/V.) Walk down V. Farini, and go right at P. Mameli for the renovated **Albergo Al Giaciglio ❸**, V. Rocca Brancaleone 42. (☎0544 394 03. Breakfast €2-5. Singles €33-36; doubles €42-52; triples €55-65. MC/V.) **Piazza del Popolo** has a number of good restaurants nearby. **Postal Code:** 48100.

FERRARA   ☎0532

Rome has its mopeds, Venice its boats, and Ferrara (pop. 135,000) has its bicycles. Old folks, young folks, and babies perched precariously on handlebars whirl through Ferrara's jumble of major thoroughfares and twisting medieval roads. Take a deep breath of fresh air, hop on a bike, and explore the city.

◪❼ TRANSPORTATION AND PRACTICAL INFORMATION. Trains go to: Bologna (30min., 1-2 per hr., €2.80); Padua (1hr., every hr., €4); Ravenna (1hr., 1-3 per hr., €4); Rome (3-4hr., 7 per day, €31); and Venice (2hr., 1-2 per hr., €6). ACFT

ITALY

(☎0532 59 94 92) and GGFP **buses** leave V. Rampari S. Paolo or the train station for Bologna (1½hr., 15 per day, €3.30) and Ferrara's beaches (1hr., 12 per day, €4-5). To get to the center of town, turn left out of the train station, and then veer right on **Viale Costituzione.** This road becomes Viale Cavour and runs to the **Castello Estense** (1km). Or, take bus #2 to *Castello* or bus #1 or 9 to the post office (every 20min., €0.85). The **tourist office** is in Castello Estense. (☎0532 20 93 70. Open M-Sa 9am-1pm and 2-6pm, Su 9:30am-1pm and 2-5:30pm.) Rent **bikes** at **Pirani e Bagni,** P. le Stazione 2. (€7 per day. Open daily 6:30am-1pm and 3:30-7pm.) **Postal Code:** 44100.

▐▐ ACCOMMODATIONS AND FOOD. Ferrara has plenty of inexpensive and comfortable accommodations. **◪Pensione Artisti ❷,** V. Vittoria 66, near P. Lampronti, is in the historic center of Ferrara and has a pleasant, attentive staff. (☎0532 76 10 38. Singles €21; doubles €38, with bath €55.) Walk down C. Ercole I d'Este from the *castello,* or take bus #4c from the station to the *castello* to reach the central **Ostello della Gioventù Estense (HI) ❶,** C. B. Rossetti 24, with simple, clean rooms. (☎/fax 0532 20 42 27. Breakfast €1.60. **Internet** access. Reception 7-10am and 5-11:30pm. Lockout 10am-5pm. Curfew 11:30pm. Dorms €13.) **Hotel de Prati ❹,** V. Padiglioni 5, is a lovely three-star hotel. (☎0532 24 19 05; www.hoteldeprati.com. Singles €47-70; doubles €70-105; suites €110-140. AmEx/MC/V.) Gorge on local specialties such as triangular meat ravioli served in a broth, or the traditional *Ferrarese* dessert of luscious *pampepato,* chocolate-covered almond and fruit cake. Try delicious *panini* with one of 600 varieties of wine at **Osteria Al Brindisi 11 ❸,** V.G. degli Adelardi 9b, which has wined and dined the likes of Copernicus and Pope John Paul II since opening in 1435. (☎0532 20 91 42. Open Su and Tu-Sa 8:30am-1am.) For picnic supplies, stop by the **Mercato Comunale** on V. Garibaldi. (Open daily 8am-1pm.)

◎♫ SIGHTS AND ENTERTAINMENT. Bike the tranquil, wooded concourse along the city's well-preserved 9km **medieval wall,** which begins at the far end of C. Giovecca. The imposing **◪Castello Estense** stands precisely in the center of town. C. della Giovecca lies along the former route of the moat's feeder canal, separating the medieval section from the part planned by the d'Este's architect. (☎0532 29 92 33. Open Su and Tu-Sa 9:30am-5pm. €7, students €6.) From the *castello,* take C. Martiri della Libertà to P. Cattedrale and the **Duomo San Romano,** which contains the **Museo della Cattedrale.** (*Duomo* open M-Sa 7:30am-noon and 3-6:30pm, Su 7:30am-12:30pm and 4-7:30pm. Museum open Su and Tu-Sa 9am-1pm and 3-6pm. €4.20, students €2.) From the *castello,* cross Largo Castello to C. Ercole I d'Este and walk to the corner of C. Rossetti to reach the gorgeous **Palazzo Diamanti,** built in 1493. Inside, the **Pinacoteca Nazionale** holds many of the best works of the Ferrarese school. (Open Su 9am-1pm, Tu-W and F-Sa 9am-2pm, Th 9am-7pm. €4, students €2.) Follow C. Ercole I d'Este behind the *castello* and go right on C. Porta Mare to find the **Palazzo Massari,** C. Porta Mare 9, which houses both the **Museo d'Arte Moderna e Contemporanea Filippo de Pisis,** and, upstairs, the spectacular **Museo Ferrarese dell'Ottocentro/Museo Giovanni Boldini.** (Both open Su and Tu-Sa 9am-1pm and 3-6pm. Joint ticket €6.70, student €4.20) **Postal Code:** 44100.

TUSCANY (TOSCANA)

The vision of Tuscany has inspired countless artists, poets, and hordes of tourists. Its rolling hills, prodigious olive groves, and cobblestone streets beg visitors to slow their frenetic pace, sip some wine, and relax in fields of brilliant sunflowers. Tuscany fostered some of Italy's, and the world's, greatest cultural achievements under the tender care—and devious machinations—of the powerful Médici family, gaining eternal eminence in the arts for its staggering accomplishments during a scant half-century. Today, tourists flock to Tuscany to witness the glory that was, and the wonder that still is, *Toscana*.

FLORENCE (FIRENZE)   ☎055

The rays of the setting sun shimmer over a sea of burnt-orange roofs and towering domes to reveal the breathtaking concentration of beauty in Florence (pop. 376,000). Once a busy 13th-century wool- and silk-trading town, Florence took a decidedly different path under Médici rule. By the mid-15th century, the city was the undisputed European capital of art, architecture, commerce, and political thought. Present-day Florence is a vibrant mix of young and old: Street graffiti quotes Marx and Malcolm X, businessmen whiz by on Vespas, and children play soccer in front of the *duomo*.

⌐ TRANSPORTATION

Flights: Amerigo Vespucci Airport (FLR; ☎055 31 58 74), in Peretola. The **ATAF** bus #62 connects the train station to the airport (€1).

Trains: Santa Maria Novella Station, across from S. Maria Novella. Trains depart every hr. for **Bologna** (1hr., €7.80), **Milan** (3½hr., €22), and **Rome** (3½hr., €15-22); and less frequently to **Siena** (1½hr., 10 per day, €5.30) and **Venice** (3hr., 4 per day, €19).

Buses: SITA, V.S. Caterina da Siena 15r (☎055 28 46 61). Run to **San Gimignano** (1½hr., 14 per day, €5.70) and **Siena** (1½hr., 2 per day, €6.50). **LAZZI,** P. Adua, 1-4r (☎35 10 61) sends buses to **Pisa** (every hr., €5.80).

Public Transportation: ATAF (☎055 565 02 22), outside the train station, runs orange city buses (6am-1am). 1hr. tickets €1, 3hr. €1.80, 24hr. €4, 3-day €7.20. Buy tickets at any newsstand, *tabacchi,* or automated ticket dispenser before boarding. Validate your ticket using the orange machine on board or risk a €50 fine.

Taxis: ☎055 43 90, 055 47 98, or 055 42 42. Outside the train station.

Bike/Moped Rental: Alinari Noleggi, V. Guelfa 85r (☎055 28 05 00). Bikes €12-18 per day, mopeds €28-55 per day.

◼◼ ◼◼ ORIENTATION AND PRACTICAL INFORMATION

From the train station, a short walk on V. dei Panzani and a left on V. dei Cerretani leads to the **duomo,** the center of Florence. Major arteries radiate from the *duomo* and its two *piazze*. A bustling walkway, **Via dei Calzaiuoli** runs south from the *duomo* to **Piazza Signoria.** V. Roma leads from P.S. Giovanni through **Piazza della Repubblica** to the **Ponte Vecchio** (Old Bridge), which spans the Arno River to the **Oltrarno** district. Note that most streets change names unpredictably. For guidance through Florence's tangled center, grab a **free map** from the tourist office. Sights are scattered throughout Florence, but few lie beyond walking distance.

TOURIST, FINANCIAL, AND LOCAL SERVICES

Tourist Office: Informazione Turistica, P. della Stazione 4 (☎055 21 22 45), across the *piazza* from the main exit. Info on entertainment and cultural events. Be sure to ask for a free map with a street index. Open daily 8:30am-7pm.

Consulates: UK, Lungarno Corsini 2 (☎055 28 41 33). Open M-F 9:30am-12:30pm and 2:30-4:30pm. **US,** Lungarno Amerigo Vespucci 38 (☎055 239 82 76), at V. Palestro, near the station. Open M-F 9am-12:30pm. Others are in Rome or Milan.

ITALY

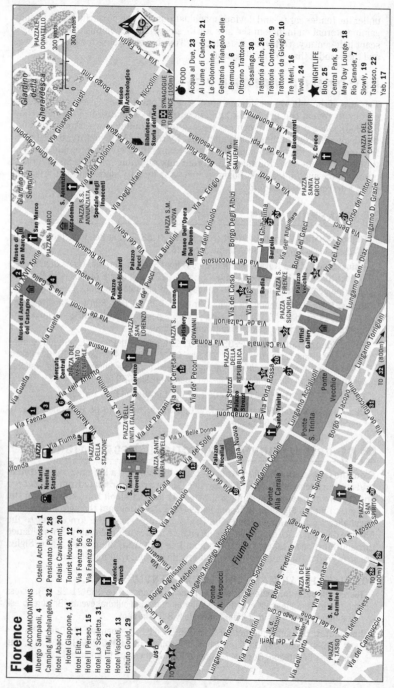

Florence

ACCOMMODATIONS
Albergo Sampaoli, **4**
Camping Michelangelo, **32**
Hotel Abaco/
Tourist House, **12**
Hotel Elite, **11**
Hotel Il Perseo, **15**
Hotel La Scaletta, **31**
Hotel Tina, **2**
Hotel Visconti, **13**
Istituto Gould, **29**
Ostello Archi Rossi, **1**
Pensionato Pio X, **28**
Relais Cavalcanti, **20**
Via Faenza 56, **3**
Via Faenza 69, **5**

FOOD
Acqua al Due, **23**
Al Lume di Candela, **21**
Le Colonnine, **27**
Gelateria Triangolo delle Bermuda, **6**
Oltrano Trattoria Casalinga, **30**
Trattoria Anita, **26**
Trattoria Contadino, **9**
Trattoria da Giorgio, **10**
Tre Merli, **16**
Vivoli, **24**

★ NIGHTLIFE
Blob, **25**
Central Park, **8**
May Day Lounge, **18**
Rio Grande, **7**
Slowly, **19**
Tabasco, **22**
Yab, **17**

ITALY

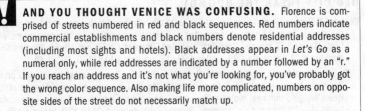

AND YOU THOUGHT VENICE WAS CONFUSING. Florence is comprised of streets numbered in red and black sequences. Red numbers indicate commercial establishments and black numbers denote residential addresses (including most sights and hotels). Black addresses appear in *Let's Go* as a numeral only, while red addresses are indicated by a number followed by an "r." If you reach an address and it's not what you're looking for, you've probably got the wrong color sequence. Also making life more complicated, numbers on opposite sides of the street do not necessarily match up.

Currency Exchange: Local banks offer the best rates. Most are open M-F 8:20am-1:20pm and 2:45-3:45pm. 24hr. **ATMs** abound.

American Express: V. Dante Alighieri 20-22r (☎055 509 81). From the *duomo*, walk down V. dei Calzaiuoli and turn left on V. dei Tavolini. Mail held free for AmEx customers, otherwise €1.55. Open M-F 9am-5:30pm, Sa 9am-12:30pm.

EMERGENCY AND COMMUNICATIONS

Emergency: ☎113. **Fire:** ☎115. **Police:** ☎055 497 71. **Medical Emergency:** ☎118

24-Hour pharmacies: Farmacia Comunale (☎055 28 94 35), at the train station by track #16. **Molteni,** V. dei Calzaiuoli 7r (☎055 28 94 90).

Internet Access: Walk down almost any busy street and you'll find an Internet cafe.

Internet Train. 15 locations listed on www.internettrain.it, including near the train station and *duomo*. €4 per hr., students €3. Most open M-F 9am-midnight, Sa 10am-8pm, Su noon-9pm.

Libreria Edison, P. Repubblica 27r, has great atmosphere and coffee upstairs. €2.50 per hr. Open daily 10am-8pm.

Post Office: V. Pellicceria (☎055 21 61 22), off P. della Repubblica. Address mail to be held: Firstname SURNAME, *In Fermo Posta*, L'Ufficio Postale, V. Pellicceria, Firenze, **50100** ITALY. Open M-F 8am-7pm, Sa 8:15am-noon.

ACCOMMODATIONS

Lodgings in Florence generally don't come cheap. **Consorzio ITA,** in the train station by track #16, can find rooms for a €2.50-7.75 fee (☎055 28 28 93. Open daily 8:45am-8pm). Because of the constant stream of tourists in Florence, it is best to make reservations (*prenotazioni*) in advance, especially if you plan to visit during Easter or summer.

HOSTELS

Ostello Archi Rossi, V. Faenza 94r (☎055 29 08 04; fax 055 230 26 01). Exit left from the station on V. Nazionale and take the 2nd left on V. Faenza. Patio packed with young travelers. Breakfast €1.60. Laundry €5.20. Free Internet access. Lockout 11:30am-2pm. Curfew 1am. No reservations; in summer, arrive before 8am. Dorms €18-21. ❷

Istituto Gould, V. dei Serragli 49 (☎055 21 25 76), in the Oltrarno. Take bus #36 or 37 from the train station to the 2nd stop across the river. Spotless rooms. Reception M-F 9am-1pm and 3-7pm, Sa 9am-1pm, Su check-out only. Singles €30, with bath €35; doubles €44/50; triples €56/63; quads €72/80. MC/V. ❸

Pensionato Pio X, V. dei Serragli 106 (☎/fax 055 22 50 44). Follow directions to Istituto Gould, and walk a few blocks farther; it's on the right. Don't be fazed by the construction in the courtyard. Rooms are nothing fancy, but are very clean and larger than average. Check-out 9am. Curfew midnight. Dorms €16. ❶

ITALY

OLD CITY (NEAR THE DUOMO)

▨ **Hotel Il Perseo,** V. de Cerretani 1 (☎055 21 25 04; www.hotelperseo.com), en route to the *duomo* from the station, opposite the Feltrinelli bookstore. Immaculate rooms with fans. Bar and TV lounge. Breakfast included. Internet €1.50 per 15min. Singles €50; doubles €73, with bath €93; triples €97/120; quads €118/140. MC/V. ❹

Relais Cavalcanti, V. Pellicceria 2 (☎055 21 09 62; www.relaiscavalcanti.com). Supreme location just steps from P. della Repubblica, near the central post office. Beautiful gold-trimmed rooms with antique painted wardrobes and large, immaculate baths. Ask for the *Let's Go* discount. Singles €80; doubles €110-120; triples €155. ❺

AROUND PIAZZA SANTA MARIA NOVELLA

▨ **Hotel Elite,** V. della Scala 12 (☎055 21 53 95). Exit right from the train station onto V. degli orti Oricellari and turn left on V. della Scala. Brass glows in this hotel's lovely rooms. Breakfast €6. Singles €60-75; doubles €90; triples €110; quads €120. ❺

▨ **Hotel Abaco,** V. dei Banchi 1 (☎/fax 055 238 19 19). From train station, cross to the back of S. Maria Novella church. Walk past church into P.S. Maria Novella and go left onto V. dei Banchi. Seven beautiful rooms, each named after a Renaissance great, feature reproductions of the honored artist's most famous work on the walls. Breakfast included. A/C €5 extra. Laundry €7. Free Internet access. Ask for the *Let's Go* discount. Singles €63; doubles €70, with bath €85. MC/V. ❺

Hotel Giappone, V. dei Banchi, 1 (☎055 21 00 90; fax 29 28 77; www.hotelgiappone.com). Follow directions to Hotel Abaco. 10 clean rooms in a central location. All rooms with phone, TV, A/C and Internet jacks. Singles €45, with shower €47, with bath €55; doubles €65/72/85. Extra bed €26. MC/V. ❹

Hotel Visconti, P. Ottaviani 1 (☎/fax 055 21 38 77). Exit the train station from the left and cross behind the church into P.S. Maria Novella, and walk to the left until you reach tiny P. Ottaviani. Look for huge Grecian nudes. Breakfast included. Singles €40; doubles €60; triples €80; quads €90. ❹

Tourist House, V. della Scala 1 (☎055 26 86 75). Extremely friendly proprietors also run Hotel Giappone. Comfortable rooms with bath and TV, some with A/C. Singles €67; doubles €83; quads €124. AmEx/MC/V. ❺

AROUND PIAZZA SAN MARCO

▨ **Hotel Tina,** V.S. Gallo 31 (☎055 48 35 19; hoteltina@tin.it). From P.S. Marco, follow V. XXII Aprile and turn right on V.S. Gallo. *Pensione* with high ceilings, new furniture, and amicable owners. Singles €44; doubles €60-75; triples €83. ❹

Albergo Sampaoli, V.S. Gallo 14 (☎055 28 48 34; www.hotelsampaoli.it). Helpful reception and a large common area with patterned tile floors and ornate wooden furniture. All with fans, some with balconies. Free Internet (30min.). Singles €45, with bath €60; doubles €65/84. AmEx/MC/V. ❹

AROUND VIA NAZIONALE

Via Faenza 56 houses 5 separate *pensioni,* some of the best deals in the city. From the train station, exit left onto V. Nazionale, walk 1 block, and turn left on V. Faenza.

Pensione Azzi (☎055 21 38 06) has large rooms and a terrace. Breakfast included. Singles €45, with bath €55; doubles €62/80. AmEx/MC/V. ❹

Locanda Paola (☎055 21 36 82) has doubles with views of the surrounding hills. Flexible 2am curfew. Doubles €62. ❹

Albergo Merlini (☎055 21 28 48; www.hotelmerlini.it) has some rooms with views of the *duomo.* Curfew 1am. Doubles €65, with bath €75; triples €90; quads €98. AmEx/MC/V. ❺

Albergo Marini (☎055 28 48 24) boasts spotless rooms. Breakfast €5. Singles €48, with bath €75; doubles €65/96; triples €86/117. ❹

Albergo Armonia (☎055 21 11 46) decorates its rooms with film posters. Singles €42; doubles €65; triples €90; quads €100. ❹

Via Faenza 69 houses no-frills hotels. Same directions as for Via Faenza 56.

Locanda Giovanna (☎055 238 13 53) has basic, well-kept rooms with garden views. Singles €40; doubles €60, with bath €70; triples €80/85. ❹

Hotel Nella/Pina (☎055 265 43 46) has 14 basic rooms and Internet access. Singles €47; doubles €62. AmEx/MC/V. ❹

OLTRARNO

🏨 **Hotel La Scaletta,** V. Guicciardini 13b (☎055 28 30 28). Turn right onto V. Roma from the *duomo,* cross Ponte Vecchio and walk on V. Guicciardini. Has views of Boboli gardens. Breakfast included. Reception open until midnight. Singles €51, with bath €93; doubles €120; 10% *Let's Go* discount when you pay cash. MC/V. ❹

CAMPING

Campeggio Michelangelo, V. Michelangelo 80 (☎055 681 19 77), beneath Piazzale Michelangelo. Take bus #13 from the bus station (15min.; last bus 11:25pm). Crowded, but a great view of Florence. Open Apr.-Nov. €7 per person, €4.70 per tent, €4.30 per car. ❶

🍴 FOOD

Florence's hearty cuisine originated in the peasant fare of the countryside. Specialties include *bruschetta* (grilled bread soaked with olive oil and garlic and topped with tomatoes and basil, anchovy, or liver paste) and *bistecca alla Fiorentina* (thick sirloin steak). Wine is a Florentine staple, and genuine *chianti classico* commands a premium price; a liter costs €3.70-5.20 in Florence's *trattorie,* while stores sell bottles for as little as €2.60. The local dessert is *cantuccini di prato* (almond cookies made with egg yolks) dipped in *vinsanto* (a rich dessert wine made from raisins). Florence's own Buontalenti family supposedly invented *gelato;* true or not, you must sample it. For lunch, visit a *rosticceria gastronomia,* peruse the city's pushcarts, or pick up fresh produce or meat at the **Mercato Centrale,** between V. Nazionale and S. Lorenzo. (Open June-Sept. M-Sa 7am-2pm; Oct.-May M-F 7am-2pm, Sa 7am-2pm and 4-8pm.) To get to **STANDA supermarket,** V. Pietrapiana 1r, turn right

THE BIG SPLURGE

A VERY NICE CHIANTI

Tuscan rains have swamped the highway, forcing Chianti residents to take clever side-street routes to home and market; even so, on these tiny back roads we don't pass a single car. We make our way to a small hilltop home where a family prepares our lunch, then swing by a private vineyard unannounced. The manager emerges, and he and our guide exchange cordial waves. Meet Silvio, native and connoisseur of the Chianti region, and host of a unique tour through this land of wine and olives. A long-time friend to many Chianti residents, Silvio has a special rapport with families and vineyard owners. At one home, he borrows a set of keys to the tiny, fresco-filled *chiesa* in the family's private yard. Along the way, he instructs his guests in wine-tasting technique and recounts significant dates and facts with ease. Silvio's day-long tours are each custom designed; he will arrange cooking lessons with a Chianti family or simply host lengthy treks through fields of sunflowers. This increasingly popular part of Tuscany is filled with tour opportunities, but Silvio's is distinctly enthusiastic, leisurely and personal. For those who seek a genuine understanding of Chianti and all its richness, this is a special, and comparatively affordable experience.

€420 for 2 people. For info contact italyinfo1@yahoo.com.

on V. del Proconsolo, take the first left on Borgo degli Albizi, and continue straight through P.G. Salvemini; it will be on the left. (Open M-Sa 8am-9pm, Su 9:30am-1:30pm and 3:30-6:30pm.)

OLD CITY (THE CENTER)

■ **Trattoria Anita,** V. del Parlascio 2r (☎055 21 86 98), just behind the Bargello. Dine by candlelight, surrounded by expensive wine bottles on wooden shelves. Traditional Tuscan fare—filling pastas and an array of meat dishes from roast chicken to beefsteak Florentine. *Primi* €4.70-5.20. *Secondi* from €5.20. Fantastic lunch *menu* €5.50. Cover €1. Open M-Sa noon-2:30pm and 7-10pm. AmEx/MC/V. ❷

■ **Acqua al Due,** V. Vigna Vecchia 40r (☎055 28 41 70), behind the Bargello. Popular with young Italians. Serves Florentine specialties, including an excellent *assaggio* (€7.50). *Primi* €6.70. *Secondi* from €7-19. Cover €1. Reserve ahead. Open daily 7pm-1am. ❸

Al Lume di Candela, V. delle Terme 23r (☎055 265 65 61), halfway between P.S. Trinità and P. della Signoria. Candlelit tables illuminate the bright yellow walls of this restaurant that serves Tuscan, Venetian, and southern Italian favorites. *Primi* €6-8. *Secondi* €9.60-12. Open daily noon-2:30pm and 7-11pm. AmEx/MC/V. ❸

Le Colonnine, V. dei Benci 6r, north of the Ponte alle Grazie. Delicious traditional fare. Pizza €4.70. Pasta from €7. Famous *paella* for 2 could feed a small army (€18). Open daily noon-3:30pm and 6:30pm-midnight. ❷

PIAZZE SANTA MARIA NOVELLA AND DEL MERCATO CENTRALE

■ **Tre Merli,** entrances on V. del Moro 11r and V. dei Fossi 12r (☎055 28 70 62). Beautiful red mushroom lights shine on booths for a candlelit meal. *Primi* €7.50-14. *Secondi* €12-19. Cover €2. Lunch *menu* €12. Open daily 11am-11pm. AmEx/MC/V. ❸

■ **Trattoria da Giorgio,** V. Palazzuolo 100r. Generous portions. *Menu* €8-9. Expect a wait. Open M-Sa noon-3:30pm and 7pm-12:30am. ❷

Trattoria Contadino, V. Palazzuolo 71r (☎055 238 2673). Filling, home-style meals. Offers fixed price *menu* only that includes *primi, secondi*, bread, water, and .25L of house wine for €9.50. Open M-Sa noon-2:30pm and 6-9:30pm. AmEx/MC/V. ❷

OLTRARNO

■ **Oltrarno Trattoria Casalinga,** V. Michelozzi 9r (☎055 21 86 24), near P.S. Spirito. Basic Tuscan dishes and specialties. Good quality for the price. *Primi* €4-6. *Secondi* €5-9. Cover €1.50. Open M-Sa noon-2:30pm and 7-10pm. ❸

GELATERIE

■ **Vivoli,** V. della Stinche 7, behind the Bargello. A renowned Florentine *gelateria* with a huge selection of the self-proclaimed "best ice cream in the world." Cups from €1.50. Open Su and Tu-Sa 9:30-1am; 7:30am-1am.

■ **Gelateria Triangolo delle Bermuda,** V. Nazionale 61r. Blissful *crema venusiana* has hazelnut, caramel, and meringue. Cones €1.60. Open daily 11am-midnight.

◉ SIGHTS

There's enough to see in the center of Florence alone to keep a visitor occupied for years; if you're in the city for only a few days, hit the highlights. Plan well, as the city's art museums are spectacular, but exhausting and expensive. Florence's museums run €3.10-8.50 per venue, and no longer offer student discounts. In summer, watch for **Sere al Museo,** evenings when certain museums are free from 8:30-11pm. Also, many of Florence's churches are treasuries of great art.

PIAZZA DEL DUOMO

■ **THE DUOMO (CATTEDRALE DI SANTA MARIA DEL FIORE).** The red brick of Florence's *duomo*, the **Cattedrale di Santa Maria del Fiore,** at the center of P. del Duomo, is visible from virtually every part of the city. Filippo Brunelleschi drew from long-neglected classical methods to come up with his revolutionary double-shelled construction that utilized self-supporting interlocking bricks in order to construct the enormous dome. The *duomo* claims the world's third longest nave, trailing only St. Peter's in Rome and St. Paul's in London. *(Open M-Sa 10am-4:45pm, Su 1:30-4:45pm. Mass daily 7am-12:30pm and 5-7pm.)* Climb the 463 steps inside the dome to ■**Michelangelo's lantern,** which offers an unparalleled view of the city. *(Open M-F 8:30am-7pm, Sa 8:30am-5:40pm. €6.)* The 82m high **campanile,** next to the *duomo,* also has beautiful views. *(Open daily 8:30am-7:30pm. €6.)*

BATTISTERO. The *battistero* (baptistery) next to the *duomo,* built between the 5th and 9th centuries, was the site of Dante's christening; its Byzantine-style mosaics inspired the details of his *Inferno.* The famous **bronze doors** were a product of intense competition among Florentine artists; Ghiberti was commissioned to forge the last set of doors. The products, reportedly dubbed the ■**Gates of Paradise** by Michelangelo, exchanged his earlier 28-panel design for 10 large, gilded squares, each of which employs mathematical perspective to create the illusion of deep space. Under restoration since a 1966 flood, they will soon be housed in the Museo dell' Opera del Duomo. *(Open M-Sa noon-7pm, Su 8:30am-2pm. €3.)*

MUSEO DELL'OPERA DEL DUOMO. Most of the *duomo*'s art resides behind the cathedral in the Museo dell'Opera del Duomo. Up the first flight of stairs is a late *Pietà* by Michelangelo, who, according to legend, destroyed Christ's left arm with a hammer in a fit of frustration; soon after, a diligent pupil touched up the work, leaving visible scars on parts of Mary Magdalene's head. The museum also houses four frames from the baptistery's *Gates of Paradise. (P. del Duomo 9, behind the duomo. Open M-Sa 9am-6:30pm, Su 9am-1pm. €6.)*

PIAZZA DELLA SIGNORIA AND ENVIRONS

From P. del Duomo, the bustling **Via dei Calzaiuoli,** one of the city's oldest streets, runs south through crowds and chic shops to P. della Signoria.

PIAZZA DELLA SIGNORIA. The destruction of powerful Florentine families' homes in the 13th century created an empty space that cried out *"piazza!"* With the construction of the Palazzo Vecchio in 1299, the square became Florence's civic and political center. In 1497, religious leader and social critic Savonarola convinced Florentines to light the **Bonfire of the Vanities,** a grand roast in the square that consumed some of Florence's best art. A year later, disillusioned citizens sent Savonarola up in smoke on the same spot, marked today by a granite disc. Monumental sculptures cluster in front of the *palazzo,* including a copy of Michelangelo's *David.* The awkward *Neptune* to the left of the Palazzo Vecchio so revolted Michelangelo that he insulted the artist: "Oh Ammannato, Ammannato, what lovely marble you have ruined!" The graceful 14th-century **Loggia dei Lanzi,** built as a stage for civic orators, displays world-class sculpture free of charge.

PALAZZO VECCHIO. Arnolfo del Cambio designed this fortress-like *palazzo* in the late-13th century as the governmental seat. It later became the Médici family home; in 1470, Michelozzo decorated the ■**courtyard** in Renaissance style. Inside are works by Michelangelo, da Vinci, and Bronzino. The **Monumental Apartments,** which house the *palazzo*'s extensive art collections, are accessible as a museum.

The **Activities Tour,** well worth the extra €2 (students €1) on top of the cumulative ticket, includes the **Secret Routes,** which reveal hidden stairwells and chambers, and **Invitation to Court,** a reenactment of court life. *(☎055 276 84 65; tours ☎055 276 82 24. Call ahead for tour reservations. Monumental Apartments €6, ages 18-25 €4.50. Palazzo €5.70. Courtyard free. June-Sept. M and F 9am-11pm, Tu-W and Sa 9am-7pm, Th and Su 9am-2pm; Oct.-May M-W and F-Sa 9am-7pm, Th and Su 9am-2pm.)*

◼**THE UFFIZI.** Vasari designed this palace in 1554 for the offices (*uffizi*) of Duke Cosimo's administration; today, it houses more first-class art per square inch than any other museum in the world. Botticelli, da Vinci, Michelangelo, Raphael, Titian, Giotto, Fra Angelico, Caravaggio, Bronzino, Cimabue, della Francesca, Bellini, even Dürer, Rubens, and Rembrandt—you name it, they have it. To avoid disappointment at the museum, note that a few rooms are usually closed each day and famous works often go on temporary loan, so not all works will be available for viewing. A sign outside the ticket office lists the *sale* that will be closed for the day; ask if they will reopen the next day. *(Extends from P. della Signoria to the Arno River. ☎055 21 83 41. Open Su, Tu-Sa 8am-7pm. €8.50.)*

PONTE VECCHIO. From the Uffizi, follow V. Georgofili left and turn right along the river to reach the nearby **Ponte Vecchio** (Old Bridge). The oldest bridge in Florence, it replaced an older Roman version in 1345. In the 1500s, the Médici kicked out the butcheries and tanneries that lined the bridge and installed goldsmiths and diamond-carvers instead. The view of the bridge from the neighboring Ponte alle Grazie at sunset is breathtaking, and the bridge itself buzzes with pedestrians and street performers, particularly at night.

BARGELLO. The heart of medieval Florence lies in this 13th-century fortress between the *duomo* and P. della Signoria. Once the residence of the chief magistrate and later a brutal prison with public executions in the courtyard, it was restored in the 19th century and now houses the sculpture-filled **Museo Nazionale.** Donatello's bronze *David*, the first freestanding nude since antiquity, stands opposite the two bronze panels of the *Sacrifice of Isaac*, submitted by Ghiberti and Brunelleschi in the baptistery door competition. Michelangelo's early works, including *Bacchus*, *Brutus*, and *Apollo*, are on the ground floor. *(V. del Proconsolo 4, between duomo and P. della Signoria. ☎055 238 86 06. Open daily typically 8:15am-1:50pm. Closed 2nd and 4th M of each month, though hours and off days vary by month. €4.)*

SAN LORENZO AND FARTHER NORTH

BASILICA DI SAN LORENZO. The Médici, who lent the city the funds to build the church (designed in 1419 by Brunelleschi), retained artistic control over its construction. The family cunningly placed Cosimo Médici's grave in front of the high altar, making the entire church his personal mausoleum. Michelangelo designed the exterior but, disgusted by Florentine politics, he abandoned the project to study architecture in Rome. *(☎055 21 66 34. Open daily M-Sa 10am-5pm. €2.50.)*

To reach the ◼**Cappelle dei Médici** (Médici Chapels), walk around to the back entrance on P. Madonna degli Aldobrandini. The **Cappella dei Principi** (Princes' Chapel) is a rare example of Baroque style in Florence, while the **Sacrestia Nuova** (New Sacristy) shows Michelangelo's work and holds two Médici tombs. *(Open daily 8:15am-5pm. Closed the 2nd and 4th Su and the 1st, 3rd, and 5th M of every month. €6.)*

◼**ACCADEMIA.** Michelangelo's triumphant **David** stands in self-assured perfection in a rotunda designed specifically for it. In the hallway stand Michelangelo's four *Slaves*; the master left these statues intentionally unfinished, chipping away just enough to liberate the "living stone." *(V. Ricasoli 60, between churches of S. Marco and S.S. Annunziata. Wheelchair accessible. Open Su and Tu-Sa 8:15am-6:50pm. €6.50.)*

PIAZZA SANTA CROCE AND ENVIRONS

▧ **CHIESA DI SANTA CROCE.** The thrifty Franciscans ironically built the city's most splendid church. Among the luminaries buried here are Machiavelli, Galileo, Michelangelo (who rests in the right aisle in a tomb designed by Vasari), and humanist Leonardo Bruni, shown holding his precious *History of Florence.* Note also Donatello's gilded *Annunciation. (Open M-Sa 9:30am-5:30pm, Su and holidays 3-5:30pm.)* Intricate *pietra serena* pilasters and statues of the evangelists by Donatello grace Brunelleschi's small **Cappella Pazzi**, at the end of the cloister next to the church, a humble marvel of perfect proportions and lovely decorations, among them Luca della Robbia's *tondi* of the apostles and Brunelleschi's moldings of the evangelists. *(Enter through the Museo dell'Opera. Open Su-Tu and Th-Sa 10am-7pm. €2.60.)*

THE OLTRARNO

Historically disdained by downtown Florentines, the far side of the Arno remains a lively and unpretentious quarter, even in high season.

PALAZZO PITTI. Luca Pitti, a wealthy banker of the 15th century, built his *palazzo* east of P.S. Spirito against the Boboli hill. The Médici acquired the *palazzo* and the hill in 1550 and expanded in every way possible. Today, it houses six museums, including the ▧ **Galleria Palatina.** The galleria was one of only a few public galleries when it opened in 1833 and today houses Florence's most important art collection after the Uffizi. Works by Raphael, Titian, Andrea del Sarto, Caravaggio, and Rubens line the walls. Other museums display Médici family treasures, costumes, porcelain, carriages, and *Apartamenti Reale* (royal apartments)—lavish reminders of the time when the *palazzo* was the royal House of Savoy's living quarters. *(Open Su and Tu-Sa 8:15am-6.50pm. €6.50.)*

BOBOLI GARDENS. With geometrically sculpted hedges, contrasting groves of holly and cypress trees, and bubbling fountains, the elaborate gardens are an exquisite example of stylized Renaissance landscaping. A large oval lawn is just up the hill from the back of the palace, with an Egyptian obelisk in the middle and marble statues in freestanding niches dotting the hedge-lined perimeter. *(Open June-Aug. daily 8:15am-7:30pm; Sept.-May reduced hours. €4.)*

🎵 ENTERTAINMENT

In June, the *quartieri* of Florence turn out in costume to play their own medieval version of soccer, known as **calcio storico,** in which two teams of 27 players face off over a wooden ball in one of the city's *piazze.* These games often blur the line between athletic contest and riot. Tickets (around €16) are sold at the box office across from P.S. Croce. Check with the tourist office for times and locations of matches. The **Festival of San Giovanni Battista,** on June 24, features a tremendous fireworks display in P. Michelangelo beginning around 10pm. May starts the summer music festivals with the classical **Maggio Musicale.** The **Estate Fiesolana** (June-Aug.) fills the Roman theater in nearby Fiesole with concerts, opera, theater, ballet, and film events. September brings the **Festa dell'Unità,** a concert series at Campi Bisenzia (take bus #30). The **Festa del Grillo** (Festival of the Cricket), is on the first Sunday after Ascension Day, May 22, when crickets in tiny wooden cages are sold in the Cascine park and then released into the grass.

NIGHTLIFE

For info on hot nightlife, consult the monthly *Firenze Spettacolo* (€2). Begin your nighttime *passeggiata* along V. dei Calzaiuoli and end it with coffee or *gelato* in a ritzy cafe on **Piazza della Repubblica,** where singers prance about the stage in front of **Bar Concerto.** In the Oltrarno, **Piazza San Spirito** has plenty of bars and restaurants, and live music in summer.

May Day Lounge, V. Dante Alighieri 16r. Aspiring artists display their work on the walls of this eclectic lounge. Play Pong on the early 1980s gaming system or sip mixed drinks (€4.50-6.50) to the beat of the background funk. Beer €4.50. Happy Hour 8-10pm. Open daily 8pm-2am.

Rio Grande, V. degli Olmi 1, near Parco delle Cascinè. Among locals and tourists alike, this is the most popular of Florence's discos. Cover €16; includes 1 drink. Special nights include soul, hip-hop, house, and reggae. Open Tu-Sa 11pm-4am. AmEx/MC/V.

Central Park, in Parco della Cascinè. Open-air dance floor pulses with hip-hop, reggae, and rock. Mixed drinks €8. Open M-Tu and Th-Sa 11pm-late. AmEx/MC/V.

Blob, V. Vinegia 21r, behind the Palazzo Vecchio. DJs, movies, foosball, and an evening bar buffet. Mixed drinks €6. 2-for-1 Happy Hour 6-10pm. Open daily until 4am.

Yab, V. Sassetti 5. Another dance club seething with American students and locals. With classic R&B and reggae on Mondays. A very large dance floor is packed by midnight. Mixed drinks €5. Open daily 9pm-1am.

Slowly, V. Porta Rossa 63r. Posh leather booths, sleek black barstools and tables, blaring pop-jazz to a silent four-screen TV, and small mood candles. Lively but casual. Mixed drinks €7. Coffee €3-5. Open daily 7pm-2:30am. MC/V.

Tabasco Gay Club, P.S. Cecilia 3r from Palazzo Vecchio. Smoke machines and strobe lights on dance floor. Florence's popular gay disco caters primarily to men. 18+. Cover €13, includes 1st drink. Open Tu-Su 10pm-4am. AmEx/MC/V.

SIENA
☎ 0577

Many travelers rush from Rome to Florence, ignoring gorgeous, medieval Siena (pop. 60,000). The Sienese have a rich history in arts, politics, and trade. One of their proudest celebrations is **Il Palio,** (p. 677) a wild horse race among the city's 17 competing *contrade* (districts).

TRANSPORTATION AND PRACTICAL INFORMATION. Trains leave P. Rosselli hourly for Florence (1½hr., 12 per day, €5.30) and Rome (3hr., 16 per day, €17) via Chiusi. TRA-IN/SITA **buses** (☎ 0577 20 42 45) depart from P. Gramsci and the train station for Florence (every hr., €6.50) and San Gimignano (8 per day, €5). From the train station, cross the street and take TRA-IN/SITA buses #3, 4, 7-10, 14, 17, or 77 into the center of town at **Piazza del Sale** or **Piazza Gramsci** (€0.90). The central APT **tourist office** is at Il Campo 56. (☎ 0577 28 05 51; fax 27 06 76. Open daily mid-Mar. to mid-Nov. 8:30am-7:30pm; mid-Nov. to mid-Mar. 8:30am-1pm and 3-7pm.) **Prenotazioni Alberghiere,** in P.S. Domenico, finds rooms for a €2 fee. (☎ 0577 28 80 84. M-Sa 9am-7pm.) Check email at **Internet Train,** V. di Citta 121. (€5.20 per hr. Open M-Sa 10am-8pm, Su noon-8pm.) **Postal Code:** 53100.

ACCOMMODATIONS AND FOOD. Finding a room in Siena can be difficult from Easter to October. Book months ahead if coming during *Il Palio*. The tastefully furnished **Albergo Tre Donzelle** ❸ is at V. Donzelle 5. (☎ 0577 28 03 58; fax 0577 22 39 38. Curfew 1am. Singles €33; doubles €45-60. AmEx/MC/V.) Take bus #15 from P. Gramsci to reach the **Ostello della Gioventù "Guidoriccio" (HI) ❶**, V. Fiorentina 89, in Località Lo Stellino. (☎0577 522 12. Curfew midnight. Reserve ahead. Dorms €13. MC/V.) **Hotel Alma Domus ❸**, V. Camporegio 37, behind S. Domenico, has spotless rooms with views of the *duomo*. (☎0577 441 77; fax 0577 476 01. Curfew 11:30pm. Singles €42; doubles €55; triples €70; quads €85.) To **camp** at **Colleverde ❶**, Strada di Scacciapensieri 47, take bus #3 or 8 from P. del Sale. (☎0577 28 00 44. Open mid-Mar. to mid-Nov. €8 per person, €8 per tent.)

Siena specializes in rich pastries, of which the most famous is *panforte*, a confection of honey, almonds, and citron; indulge in this treat at **Bar/Pasticceria Nannini**, V. Banchi di Sopra 22-24, the oldest *pasticceria* in Siena. Next to Santuario di S. Caterina is the divine **Osteria La Chiacchera ❷**, Costa di S. Antonio 4, which serves hearty pasta dishes. (☎0577 28 06 31. *Secondi* €4.80-7. Open M, W-Su 12-3:30pm and 7-midnight.) **Consortio Agrario supermarket,** V. Pianigiani 5, is off P. Salimberi. (Open M-F 8am-7:30pm.)

🎫🎵 SIGHTS AND ENTERTAINMENT. Siena offers two **biglietto cumulativi** (cumulative tickets)—the first is good for five days (€7.50) and allows entry into the Museo dell'Opera Metropolitana, baptistery, and Piccolomini library; the second is valid for seven days (€16) and covers four more sights, including the Museo Civico. Both may be purchased at any of the included sights. Siena radiates from **Piazza del Campo (Il Campo),** a shell-shaped brick square designed for civic events. At the top of Il Campo is the **Fonte Gaia,** still fed by the same aqueduct used in the 1300s. At the bottom, the **Torre del Mangia** clock tower looms over the graceful Gothic **Palazzo Pubblico**. Inside the *palazzo*, the **Museo Civico** contains excellent Gothic and early Renaissance paintings; also check out the **Sala del Mappamondo** and the **Sala della Pace.** (*Palazzo,* museum, and tower open Mar.-Oct. daily 10am-7pm; Nov.-Feb. reduced hours. Tower €5.50; museum €6.50, students €4; combined ticket with tower €9.50.) From the *palazzo,* take the right-side stairs and cross V. di Città for Siena's Gothic **duomo.** The apse would have been left hanging in mid-air save for the construction of the lavishly decorated **baptistery** below. (Open mid-Mar. to Oct. M-Sa 7:30am-7:30pm, Su 2-7:30pm; Nov. to mid-Mar. 7:30am-5:30pm and 2:30-5pm, Su 2-5:30pm. Free except when floor is uncovered in Sept. €4-5.50.) The **Libreria Piccolomini,** off the left aisle, holds frescoes and 15th-century scores. (Same hours as *duomo.* €1.50.) The **Museo dell'Opera della Metropolitana,** to the right of the *duomo,* houses overflow art. (Open mid-Mar. to Sept. daily 9am-7:30pm; Nov. to mid-Mar. reduced hours. €5.50.)

Siena's **Il Palio** (July 2 and Aug. 16) is a traditional bareback horse race around the packed P. del Campo. Arrive three days early to watch the five trial runs and to pick a *contrada* to root for. At *Il Palio,* the jockeys take about 90 seconds to tear around Il Campo three times. To stay in Siena during the Palio, book rooms at least four months in advance, especially budget accommodations—call the APT (see above) in March or April for a list of rented rooms.

🔲 DAYTRIP FROM SIENA: SAN GIMIGNANO. The hilltop village of San Gimignano looks like an illustration from a medieval manuscript. The city's famous 14 towers, which are all that survive of its original 72, earned San Gimignano its nickname as the *Città delle Belle Torri* (City of Beautiful Towers). The **Museo Civico,** on the 2nd floor of **Palazzo del Popolo,** houses an amazing collection of artwork. Within the museum is the entrance to the **Torre Grossa,** the tallest remaining tower; climb its 218 steps for a panoramic view of Tuscany. (Open Mar.-Oct. daily 9:30am-7pm; Nov.-Feb. 10am-7pm. €5, students €4.) Not for the faint of heart, **Museo Della Tortura,** V. del Castello 1, off P. Cisterna, offers a morbidly fascinating history of torture from Medieval Europe to the present. (Open Apr.-Oct. daily 10am-8pm; Nov.-Mar. 10am-6pm. Entrance €8, students €5.50.)

TRA-IN buses leave P. Montemaggio for Siena (1hr., every hr., €5.20) and Florence (1½hr., every hr., €6) via Poggibonsi. From the bus station, pass through the *porta*, climb the hill, following V.S. Giovanni to the city center **Piazza della Cisterna**, which runs into P. del Duomo and the **tourist office**, P. del Duomo 1. (☎0577 94 00 08; fax 0577 94 09 03. Open Mar.-Oct. daily 9am-1pm and 3-7pm; Nov.-Feb. 9am-1pm and 2-6pm.) Accommodations are pricey in San Gimignano—*affitte camere* (private rooms) are a good alternative, with doubles from €50. The tourist office and the **Associazione Strutture Extralberghiere,** P. della Cisterna 6, both find private rooms. (☎0577 94 08 09. Open Mar.-Nov. daily 9:30am-7:30pm.) From the bus stop, enter through Porta S. Giovanni for the quaint **Camere Cennini Gianni ❹,** V.S. Giovanni 21. The reception is at the *passticceria* at V.S. Giovanni 88. (☎0577 94 19 62; www.sangiapartments.com. Reserve ahead. Singles €45; doubles €55; triples €65; quads €75.) **Postal Code:** 53037.

PISA   ☎050

Tourism hasn't always been Pisa's (pop. 96,000) prime industry: during the Middle Ages, the city was a major port with its own Mediterranean empire. But when the Arno River silted up and the tower started leaning, the city's power and wealth declined accordingly. Today the city seems resigned to welcoming tourists and myriad t-shirt and ice cream vendors to the **Piazza del Duomo,** also known as the **Campo dei Miracoli** (Field of Miracles), a grassy expanse enclosing the tower, *duomo*, baptistery, Camposanto, Museo delle Sinopie, and Museo del Duomo. An **all-inclusive ticket** to the Campo's sights–excluding the tower–costs €10.50. Begun in 1173, the famous **Leaning Tower** began to tilt when the soil beneath suddenly shifted. In June of 2001, a multi-year stabilization effort was completed; the tower is presently considered stable. Tours of 30 visitors are permitted to ascend the 300 steps once every 30 minutes. (Make reservations at adjacent tourist office. Tours depart July-Aug. daily 8:30am-10:30pm, 8:30am-7:30pm Sept.-June. €15.) Also on the Campo, the dazzling **duomo,** a treasury of art, is considered one of the finest Romanesque cathedrals in the world. (Open daily 10am-7:30pm. €2.) Next door is the **baptistry,** whose precise acoustics allow an unamplified choir to be heard 2km away. (Open late Apr. to late Sept. daily 8am-8pm; Oct.-Mar. 9am-6pm. €6.) The adjoining **Camposanto,** a cloistered cemetery, has Roman sarcophagi and a series of haunting frescoes by an unidentified 14th-century artist known only as the "Master of the Triumph of Death." (Open late Apr. to late Sept. daily 8am-7:30pm; Mar. and Oct. 9am-5:40pm; Nov.-Feb. 9am-4:40pm. €6.) The **Museo delle Sinopie,** across the *piazza* from the Camposanto, displays preliminary fresco sketches discovered during post-WWII restoration. Behind the tower is the **Museo dell'Opera del Duomo.** (Both open late Apr.-Sept. daily 8am-7:20pm; Oct.-Apr. reduced hours. €6.)

Trains (☎147 808 88) leave Piazza della Stazione, in the southern part of town, for: Florence (1hr., every hr., €4.90); Genoa (2½hr., €7.90); and Rome (3hr., 12 per day, €24). The **tourist office** is to the left after you exit the train station. (☎050 422 91; www.turismo.toscana.it. Open Apr.-Oct. M-Sa 9am-7pm, Su 9:30am-3:30pm; Nov.-Mar. reduced hours.) To reach the Campo from the train station, take **bus** #3 (€0.75). The **Albergo Helvetia ❸,** V. Don G. Boschi 31, off P. Archivescovado, has large, clean rooms 2min. from the *duomo*. (☎050 55 30 84. Singles €35; doubles €45.) **Centro Turistico Madonna dell'Acqua ❶,** V. Pietrasantina 15, is behind an old Catholic sanctuary 2km from the Tower. Take bus #3 from station (4 per hr., last bus 9:45pm; ask driver to stop at *ostello.* ☎050 89 06 22. Sheets €1. Dorms €15; doubles €42; triples €54; quads €64. MC/V.) Cheap dining options line **Corso Italia,** south of the river, and **Via Santa Maria,** as long as you're not too close to the *duomo*, where prices skyrocket. Try the heavenly *risotto* at the lively ▧**ll Paiolo**

❶, V. Curtatone e Montanara 9. (*Menù* with *primi* and *secondi* €4-6. Open M-F 12:30-3pm and 7:30pm-1am, Sa-Su 7:30pm-2am.) Get groceries at **Superal,** V. Pascoli 6, just off C. Italia. (Open M-Sa 8am-8pm.) **Postal Code:** 56100.

UMBRIA

Umbria is known as the "Green Heart of Italy," a land rich in natural beauty, from wild woods and fertile plains to craggy gorges and tiny villages. Christianity transformed Umbria's architecture and regional identity, turning it into a breeding ground for saints and religious movements; it was here that St. Francis of Assisi shamed the extravagant church with his humility.

PERUGIA   ☎075

Perugia (pop. 150,000) may boast the most polite people in Italy. With its gorgeous countryside, big-city vitality, and world-renowned chocolate, this city's residents have much to smile about. Perugia's most popular sights frame **Piazza IV Novembre.** In its center, the **Fontana Maggiore** is adorned with sculptures and bas-reliefs by Nicolà and Giovanni Pisano. At the end of the *piazza*, the imposing Gothic **duomo** houses the purported wedding ring of the Virgin Mary. (Open M-Sa 9am-12:45pm and 4-5:15pm, Su 4-5:45pm.) The 13th-century **Palazzo dei Priori** presides over the *piazza* and houses the impressive **⊠Galleria Nazionale dell'Umbria,** C. Vannucci 19. (Open daily 8:30am-7:30pm. Closed 1st M each month. €6.50.) At the end of town past the Porta S. Pietro, the **⊠Basilica di San Pietro,** on Borao XX Guigo, has a beautiful garden. (Open daily 8am-noon and 3:30-6:30pm.)

Trains leave **Perugia FS** in P.V. Veneto, Fontiveggio, for: Assisi (25min., every hr., €1.60); Florence (2½hr., 7 per day, €8); and Rome (2½hr., 6 per day, €11) via Terontola or Foligno. From the station, take bus #6, 7, 9, 13d, or 15 to the central P. Italia (€0.80), then walk down C. Vannucci to P. IV Novembre and the **tourist office,** P. IV Novembre 3. (☎075 572 33 27; fax 075 573 93 86. Open M-Sa 8:30am-1:30pm and 3:30-6:30pm, Su 9am-1pm.) **⊠Ostello della Gioventù/Centro Internazionale di Accoglienza per la Gioventù ❶,** V. Bontempi 13, has clean rooms and panoramic views. From the tourist office, walk down C. Vannucci past the *duomo* and P. Danti, take the farthest street directly through P. Piccinino, and turn right on V. Bontempi. (☎/fax 075 572 28 80; www.ostello.perugia.it. Sheets €1.50. Lockout 9:30am-4pm. Curfew midnight. Open mid-Jan. to mid-Dec. Dorms €12. MC/V/ AmEx.) **Albergo Anna ❹,** V. dei Priori 48, off C. Vannucci, has cozy 17th-century rooms with great views. (☎/fax 075 573 63 04. Singles €40, with bath €45; doubles €46/€60; triples €70/€85. AmEx/MC/V.) Local favorite **Trattoria Dal Mi Cocco ❸,** provides prompt service and ample food at a reasonable price. (*Menu* €13. Open Tu-Su 1-3pm and 8:45pm-midnight. MC/V.) The **COOP,** P. Matteotti 15, has groceries. (Open M-Sa 9am-8pm.) **Postal Code:** 06100.

ASSISI   ☎079

The undeniable jewel of Assisi (pop. 25,000) is the 13th-century **⊠Basilica di San Francesco.** The subdued art of the lower church celebrates St. Francis' modest lifestyle, while Giotto's renowned *Life of St. Francis* fresco cycle decorates the walls of the upper church, paying tribute to his sainthood and consecration. A no shorts or tank tops dress code is strictly enforced. (Lower basilica open daily 6:15am-6:45pm. Upper basilica open daily 8:30am-6:45pm.) The dramatic fortress **Rocca Maggiore** towers above the town, offering panoramic view of the countryside. (Open daily 10am-dusk. €1.70, students €1.) The pink and white **Basilica of Santa Chiara** houses St. Francis's tunic, sandals, and crucifix. (Open daily 9am-noon and 2-7pm.)

From the station near the Basilica Santa Maria degli Angeli, **trains** go to: Ancona (2hr., 8 per day, €7); Florence (2½hr., 13 per day, €9); and Rome (2½hr., 11 per day, €9). **Buses** run from P. Unita D'Italia to Florence (2½hr., 7am, €6.40) and Perugia (1½hr., 12 per day, €2.70). From P. Matteotti, follow V. del Torrione, bear left in P.S. Rufino, and take V.S. Rufino to **Piazza del Comune,** the town center, and location of the **tourist office.** (☎ 079 81 25 34; www.umbria2000.it. Open M-F 8am-2pm and 3:30-6:30pm, Sa 9am-1pm and 3:30-6:30pm, Su 9am-1pm.) The lovely ▨ **Camere Martini** ❷, V.S. Gregorio 6, has lots of amenities and a friendly atmosphere. (☎/fax 075 81 35 36; cameremartini@libero.it. Singles €23-25; doubles €32-36; triples €48-52; quads €57.) **Ostello Fontemaggio** ❶, V. per L'Eremo delle Carceri 8, has a variety of rooms, camping and a market. Take V. L'Eremo from P. Matteotti about 1.5km. (☎ 075 81 36 36; fax 075 81 37 49. Curfew 11pm. Camping €5; dorms €18.50; singles €36; doubles €52; quads €86.) **Postal Code:** 06081.

ORVIETO
☎ 0763

Perched on a plateau of volcanic rock, **Orvieto** (pop. 25,000) has a view of the rolling farmlands of Umbria that provides a perfect complement to a glass of its famous *Orvieto Classico* wine. Below the surface, caves and tunnels attest to the town's long history; Etruscans began burrowing into the hillside in the 7th century BC. Six hundred years of labor went into the construction of the breathtaking ▨ **Duomo,** whose spires, sculptures, and mosaics remain the pride and joy of Orvieto to this day. The **Capella della Madonna di San Brizio,** off the right transept, houses the dramatic Apocalypse frescoes of Luca Signorelli, whose compositions inspired Michelangelo. (Duomo open M-Sa 7:30am-12:45pm and 2:30-7pm, Su 2:30-6:45pm. Modest dress required. Capella open Apr.-Sept. M-Sa 10am-12:45pm and 2:30-7:15pm, Su 2:30-6pm; Oct.-Mar. reduced hours. €3.) **Underground City Excursions** offers the most complete tour of the ancient Etruscan city buried beneath modern Orvieto. (☎ 0763 34 48 91. Four 1hr. tours leave the tourist office daily 11:30-5:45pm. €5.50, students €3.50.)

Trains run hourly to Florence (2½hr., €9.70) and Rome (2½hr., €7). From the train station, take a shuttle to the tourist office at P. del Duomo 24. (☎ 0763 34 17 72; fax 0763 34 44 33. Open M-F 8:15am-1:50pm and 4-7pm, Sa 10am-1pm and 4-7pm, Su 10am-noon and 4-6pm.) Walk up V. Duomo to reach **Hotel Posta** ❸, V. Luca Signorelli 18, situated in a grand old building with antique decorations. (☎ 0763 34 19 09. Singles €31; doubles €44.) For free tasting of *Orvieto Classico* or another wine that piques your interest, try **Cantina Freddano,** C. Cavour 5. (☎ 0763 30 82 48. Open daily 9:30am-7:30pm. Bottles from €4.) **Postal Code:** 05018.

THE MARCHES (LE MARCHE)

In the Marches, green foothills separate the gray shores of the Adriatic from the Apennine peaks, and traditional hill towns from umbrella-laden beaches. Inland towns, easily accessible by train, rely on agriculture and preserve the region's historical legacy in the architectural remains of Gauls and Romans.

URBINO
☎ 0722

With picturesque stone dwellings scattered along steep city streets and a turreted palace ornamenting its skyline, Urbino (pop. 15,000) encompasses all that is classic Italy. The city's most remarkable monument is the imposing Renaissance **Palazzo Ducale,** in P. Rinascimento, though its facade is more thrilling than its interior. The central courtyard is the essence of Renaissance balance and proportion; to the left, stairs lead to the former private apartments of the

Duke, which are now home to the **National Gallery of the Marches.** (Open M 8:30am-2pm, Tu-F and Su 8:30am-7:15pm, Sa 8:30am-10:30pm. €4, students €2.) Walk back across P. della Repubblica and continue onto V. Raffaello to Raphael's birthplace, the **Casa di Rafaele,** V. Raffaello 57, now a museum that contains a reproduction of his earliest work, *Madonna e Bambino.* (Open M-Sa 9am-1pm and 3-6pm, Su 10am-1pm. €3.)

Bucci **buses** (☎0722 13 24 01) go from Borgo Mercatale to Rome (5hr., daily, €19). Blue SOBET **buses** (☎0722 223 33) run to P. Matteotti and the train station in Pesaro, which sends trains on to Ancona (1hr., 4-10 per day, €2.10). From there, a short walk uphill on V.G. Mazzini leads to **P. della Repubblica,** the city center. The **tourist office,** V. Puccinatti 35, is opposite the palace. (☎0722 26 13; fax 0722 24 41. Open M-F 9am-1pm and 3-6pm. Hours change frequently.) **Pensione Fosca ❷,** V. Raffaello 67, has large rooms five doors down from Rafael's birthplace. (☎32 96 22. Singles €21; doubles €40; triples €43.) **Hotel San Giovanni ❷,** V. Barocci 13, has simple, clean rooms. (☎0722 28 27. Open Aug.-June. Singles €23, with bath €33; doubles €34/50.) **Margherita supermarket** is at V. Raffaello 37. (Open M-Sa 7:30am-2pm and 3-8pm.) **Postal Code:** 61029.

ANCONA ☎071

Ancona (pop. 100,000) is Italy's major transportation hub for those heading east. Though industry and transportation are the main functions of this busy town, the old city provides a pleasant atmosphere for those passing through town. The **Piazzale del Duomo,** atop Monte Guasco, offers a view of the red rooftops of the town below. (Open M-Sa 8am-noon and 3-6pm, Su hours vary with mass schedule.) **Ferries** leave Stazione Marittima for Greece, Croatia, and northern Italy. **Adriatica** (☎071 50 211; www.adriatica.it), **Jadrolinija** (☎071 20 43 05; www.jadrolinija.tel.hr/jadrolinija), and **SEM Maritime Co.** (☎071 20 40 90; www.sem.hr) run to Croatia (from €37). **ANEK** (☎071 207 23 46; www.anek.gr) and **Blue Star** (Strintzis) (☎071 207 10 68; www.strinzis.gr) ferries go to Greece (from €50). Departure times and frequency vary, so consult a schedule ahead of time. Schedules and tickets are available at the Stazione Marittima. **Trains** arrive at P. Rosselli from: Bologna (2½hr., 1-2 per hr., €12); Milan (5hr., 1-2 per hr., €21); Rome (3-4hr., 9 per day, €15); and Venice (5hr., 3 per day, €15). Take bus #1/4 (€0.80) along the port past Stazione Marittima and up C. Stamira to reach P. Cavour, the city center. The **tourist office** in Stazione Marittima provides ferry info. (☎071 20 11 83. Open June-Sept. Su-M 8am-2pm, Tu-Sa 8am-8pm.) From the train station, cross the *piazza,* turn left, then take the first right and make a sharp right behind the newsstand to reach the **Ostella della Gioventù ❶,** V. Lamaticci 7. (☎071 42 257. Reception daily 6:30-11am and 4:30pm-midnight. Dorms €13.) **CONAD supermarket** is at V. Matteotti 115. (Open M-Sa 8-1:30pm and 5-7:30pm.) **Postal Code:** 60100.

SOUTHERN ITALY

South of Rome, the sun gets brighter, the meals longer, and the passion more intense. The introduction to the *mezzogiorno* (Southern Italy) begins in Campania, the fertile cradle of the Bay of Naples and the Gulf of Salerno. The shadow of Mt. Vesuvius hides the famous ruins of Pompeii, lost to time and a river of molten lava, while the Amalfi Coast cuts a dramatic course down the lush Tyrrhenian shore. The region remains justly proud of its open-hearted populace, strong traditions, classical ruins, and relatively untouristed beaches.

ITALY

NAPLES (NAPOLI)   ☎081

Italy's third-largest city, Naples (pop. 1,000,000) is also its most chaotic—shouting merchants flood markets, and summer traffic jams clog the broiling city. Striving to shed its bad reputation, Naples has made many improvements in recent years despite continuing problems with poverty and unemployment, including increased efforts to maintain its numerous architectural and artistic treasures. Public art and artisan's workshops abound, as well as some of Italy's most colorful *trattorie*, and of course, Neapolitan *pizzarie*—peerless throughout the world.

▐ TRANSPORTATION

Flights: Aeroporto Capodichino, V. Umberto Maddalena (NAP; ☎081 789 61 11), northwest of the city. Connects to all major Italian and European cities. A CLP **bus** (☎081 531 16 46) leaves from P. Municipio (20min., 6am-10:30pm, €1.55).

Trains: Ferrovie dello Stato goes from Stazione Centrale to: **Brindisi** (5hr., 5 per day, €19); **Milan** (8hr., 13 per day, €50); **Rome** (2hr., 34 per day, €9.60). **Circumvesuviana** (☎081 772 24 44), heads for **Herculaneum** (€1.55) and **Pompeii** (€1.90).

Ferries: Depart from **Molo Angioino** and **Molo Beverello,** at the base of P. Municipio. From P. Garibaldi, take tram #1; from P. Municipio, take the R2 bus. **Caremar,** Molo Beverello (☎081 551 38 82), goes frequently to **Capri** and **Ischia** (both 1½hr., €5). **Tirrenia Lines,** Molo Angioino (☎081 720 11 11), goes to **Palermo, Sicily,** and **Cagliari, Sardinia.** Schedules and prices change frequently, so check *Qui Napoli* (free at the tourist office).

Public Transportation: Giranapoli tickets (€0.80 per 1½hr., full-day €2.35) are valid on **buses, Metro, trams,** and **funiculars.**

Taxis: Free (☎081 551 51 51) or **Napoli** (☎081 556 44 44). Only take metered taxis.

▐ ▐ ORIENTATION AND PRACTICAL INFORMATION

The main train and bus terminals are in the immense **Piazza Garibaldi** on the east side of Naples. From P. Garibaldi, broad **Corso Umberto I** leads southwest to P. Bovi, from which V. de Pretis leads left to **Piazza Municipio,** the city center, and **Piazza Trieste e Trento** and **Piazza Plebiscito.** Below P. Municipio lie the **Stazione Marittima** ferry ports. From P. Trieste e Trento, **Via Toledo** (also known as **Via Roma**) leads through the Spanish quarter to **Piazza Dante.** Make a right into the historic **Spaccanapoli** neighborhood, which follows **Via dei Tribunali** through the middle of town. While violence is rare in Naples, theft is fairly common, so exercise caution.

Tourist Offices: EPT (☎081 26 87 79), at Stazione Centrale. Helps with hotels and ferries. Grab ▨ **Qui Napoli,** a monthly tourist publication full of schedules and listings. Open M-Sa 9am-8pm. **Branch** at Stazione Mergellina.

Consulates: Canada, V. Carducci 29 (☎081 40 13 38). **South Africa,** C. Umberto 1 (☎081 551 75 19). **UK,** V. dei Mille 40 (☎081 423 89 11). **US,** P. della Repubblica (☎081 583 81 11, emergency 03 37 94 50 83), at the west end of Villa Comunale.

Currency Exchange: Thomas Cook, at the airport (☎081 551 83 99). Open M-F 9:30am-1pm and 3-6:30pm.

Emergency: ☎113. **Police:** ☎113 or 081 794 11 11. English spoken.

Hospital: Cardarelli (☎081 747 28 59), on the R4 line. **Ambulance:** ☎081 752 06 96.

Internet Access: Internet Point, V. Toledo 59A, across from the Bank of Naples (☎081 497 60 90). €2 per hr. Open daily 9:30am-8:30pm. **Internetbar,** P. Bellini 74 (☎081 29 52 37). €3 per hr. Open M-Sa 9am-2am, Su 8am-2am.

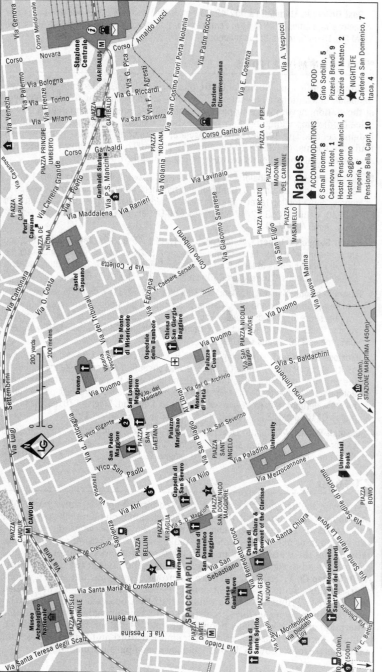

Naples

▲ ACCOMMODATIONS
6 Small Rooms, 8
Casanova Hotel, 1
Hostel Pensione Mancini, 3
Hostel Soggiorno
Imperia, 6
Pensione Bella Capri, 10

🍴 FOOD
Gino Sorbillo, 5
Pizzeria Brandi, 9
Pizzeria di Matteo, 2

★ NIGHTLIFE
Cafeteria San Domenico, 7
Itaca, 4

ITALY

Post Office: P. Matteotti (☎552 42 33), at V. Diaz on the R2 line. Address mail to be held: First name, SURNAME, *In Fermo Posta*, P. Matteotti, Naples **80100**, ITALY. Open M-F 8:15am-6pm, Sa 8:15am-noon.

▌ ACCOMMODATIONS

Although Naples has some fantastic bargain lodgings, especially near **Piazza Garibaldi**, be cautious when choosing a room. Avoid hotels that solicit customers at the station, never give your passport until you've seen the room, agree on the price *before* unpacking, be alert for unexpected costs, and gauge how secure a lodging seems. The **ACISJF/Centro D'Ascolto**, at Stazione Centrale, helps women find safe rooms. (☎081 28 19 93. Open M-Tu and Th 3:30-6:30pm.) Rooms are scarce in the historic district between P. Dante and the *duomo*.

■ **Casanova Hotel,** C. Garibaldi 333 (☎081 26 82 87; www.hotelcasanova.com). From P. Garibaldi, continue down C. Garibaldi and turn right before V. Casanova. Clean, airy rooms, and a rooftop terrace. Breakfast €4. Reserve ahead. Singles €23-26, with bath €26-30; doubles €38-42/47-52; triples €55-68; quads €69-78. 10% *Let's Go* discount. AmEx/MC/V. ❸

■ **Hostel Soggiorno Imperia,** P. Miraglia 386 (☎081 45 93 47). Take the R2 from the train station, walk up V. Mezzocannone through P.S. Domenico Maggiore, and enter the 1st set of green doors to the left on P. Miraglia. Clean rooms in a 16th-century *palazzo*. Call ahead. Dorms €16; singles €30; doubles €42; triples €60. ❷

Hostel Pensione Mancini, V. Mancini 33 (☎081 553 67 31; www.hostelpensionemancini.com), off the far end of P. Garibaldi from the train station. Multilingual, friendly owners share their encyclopedic knowledge of Naples. Spacious, newly renovated rooms. Check-in and check-out noon. Dorms €18; singles €35; doubles €45, with bath €55; triples €80; quads €90. ❷

Pensione Bella Capri, V. Melisurgo 4, door B, 6th fl. (☎081 552 94 94; www.bellacapri.it), at corner of V. Cristofor Colombo, across street from the port. Take the R2 bus to the end of V. de Pretis, cross the street, and turn onto V. Melisurgo. From courtyard enter door B and go to the 6th floor. Less-expensive alternative to the high-priced hotels on the waterfront, with great views of Vesuvius and the port. Singles €70; doubles €80; triples €110; quads €120. 10% *Let's Go* discount. AmEx/MC/V. ❺

6 Small Rooms, V. Diodato Lioy 18 (☎081 790 13 78), up from P. Monteolovieto. Larger rooms than its name suggests in a friendly atmosphere. There is no sign; look for the name on the call button. Dorms €16; singles €21. ❷

▐ FOOD

If you ever doubted that Neapolitans invented pizza, Naples's *pizzerie* will take that doubt, beat it into a ball, throw it in the air, spin it on their collective finger, punch it down, cover it with sauce and mozzarella, and serve it *alla margherita*. Neapolitans also serve up incomparable seafood, the best of which is, naturally, along the waterfront. For pizza try the historic district; for cafes and *gelaterie* head to **Via Toledo**. As former customer Bill Clinton can attest, ■**Pizzeria Di Matteo ❶**, V. Tribunali 94, draws a crowd of students and pizza connoisseurs to this small, pre-eminent eatery. (Open M-Sa 9am-midnight.) ■**Gino Sorbillo ❶**, V. Tribunali 32, is a family affair that boasts a grandfather who invented the *ripieno al forno* (calzone) and 21 pizza-making children in this generation alone. (Open daily noon-3:30pm and 7-11:30 pm.) **Pizzeria Brandi ❷**, Salita S. Anna di Palazzo 1, counts Luciano Pavarotti and Isabella Rossellini among its patrons. (Cover €1.55. Open daily noon-3pm and 7pm-late.)

👁 SIGHTS

■ **MUSEO ARCHEOLOGICO NAZIONALE.** This world-class collection contains exquisite treasures from Pompeii and Herculaneum, including the outstanding "Alexander Mosaic." The sculpture collection is also quite impressive. *(From M: P. Cavour, turn right and walk 2 blocks. Open Su-M and Th-Sa 9am-7:30pm. €6.50.)*

SPACCANAPOLI. This east-west neighborhood overflows with gorgeous architecture, meriting at least a 30min. meander. From P. Dante, walk through Porta Alba and P. Bellini before turning on V. dei Tribunali, where the churches of **San Lorenzo Maggiore** and **San Paolo Maggiore** lie. Turn right on V. Duomo and turn right again on V.S. Biago to stroll past the **University of Naples** and the **Chiesa di San Domenico Maggiore,** where, legend has it, a painting spoke to St. Thomas Aquinas. *(In P.S. Domenico Maggiore. Open M-F 8:30am-noon and 5-8pm, Sa-Su 9:30am-1pm and 5-7pm. Free.)*

DUOMO. The main attraction of the 14th-century *duomo* is the **Cappella del Tesoro di San Gennaro.** A beautiful 17th-century bronze grille protects the high altar, which holds a gruesome display of relics including the saint's head and two vials of his coagulated blood. Supposedly, disaster will strike if the blood does not liquefy on the celebration of his *festa*; miraculously, it always does. *(3 blocks up V. Duomo from C. Umberto I. Open M-F 9am-noon and 4:30-7pm, Sa-Su 8am-3:30pm and 5-7:30pm.)*

MUSEO AND GALLERIE DI CAPODIMONTE. This museum, in a royal *palazzo*, is surrounded by a pastoral park and sprawling lawns. The true gem is the amazing **Farnese Collection,** which displays works by Bellini and Caravaggio. *(Take bus #16 from the Archaeological Museum and get off when you see the gate to the park on your right. The park has 2 entrances, the Porta Piccola and the Porta Grande. Open Su and Tu-F 8:30am-7:30pm. €7.50, after 2pm €6.50.)*

PALAZZO REALE AND CASTEL NUOVO. The 17th-century **Palazzo Reale** contains opulent royal apartments, the **Museo di Palazzo Reale,** and a fantastic view from the terrace of the **Royal Chapel.** The **Biblioteca Nazionale** stores 1.5 million volumes, including the scrolls from the **Villa dei Papiri** in Herculaneum. The **Teatro San Carlo** is reputed to top the acoustics in Milan's La Scala. *(Take bus R2 from P. Garibaldi to P. Trieste e Trento and go around to the P. Plebiscito entrance. Open M and W-Su 9am-8pm. €4.20.)* From P. Trieste e Trento, walk up V. Vittorio Emanuele III to P. Municipio for the five-turreted **Castel Nuovo,** built in 1286 by Charles II of Anjou. The double-arched entrance commemorates the arrival of Alphonse I of Aragon in Naples. Inside, admire the **Museo Civico.** *(Open M-Sa 9am-7pm. €5.)*

🎵 🍷 ENTERTAINMENT AND NIGHTLIFE

Piazza Vanvitelli in Vomero draws young people to relax and socialize. **Piazza San Domenico Maggiore** is another hotspot. Take the funicular from V. Toledo or bus C28 from P. Vittoria. Outdoor bars and cafes are a popular choice in **Piazza Bellini,** near P. Dante. **Itaca,** P. Bellini 71, mixes eerie trance music with dark decor. (Mixed drinks from €6. Open daily 10am-3am.) **Cafeteria San Domenico,** in P.S. Domenico Maggiore is packed every night with throngs of Neapolitan university students. (Shots €3-4. Mixed drinks €4.50-5.50. Open daily 7am-2am.) **ARCI-Gay/Lesbica** (☎ 081 551 82 93) has info on gay and lesbian club nights.

ⓝ DAYTRIPS FROM NAPLES

Mount Vesuvius, the only active volcano on the European continent, looms over the area east of Naples. Its infamous eruption in AD 79 buried the nearby Roman city of **Ercolano** (Herculaneum) and neighboring **Pompei** (Pompeii).

POMPEII. Since 1748, excavations have unearthed a stunningly well-preserved picture of Roman daily life. The site hasn't changed much since then, and neither have the victims, whose ghastly remains were partially preserved by plaster casts in the hardened ash. Walk down V.d. Marina to reach the colonnaded ■**Forum,** which was once the civic and religious center of the city. Exit the Forum through the upper end by the cafeteria, and head right on V. della Fortuna to reach the ■**House of the Faun,** where a bronze dancing faun and the spectacular Alexander Mosaic (today in the Museo Archeologico Nazionale) were found. Continue on V. della Fortuna and turn left on V. dei Vettii to reach the **House of the Vettii,** on the left, and the most vivid frescoes in Pompeii. Back down V. dei Vettii, cross V. della Fortuna to V. Storto, turn left on V. degli Augustali, and take a quick right to reach a small **brothel** (the Lupenar), still popular after 2000 years. V. dei Teatri, across the street, leads to the oldest standing **amphitheater** in the world (80 BC), which once held up to 12,000 spectators. To get to the ■**Villa of the Mysteries,** the complex's best-preserved villa, head west on V. della Fortuna, right on V. Consolare, and all the way up Porta Ercolano. (Archaeological site open daily 8:30am-7:30pm. €10.)

Take the Circumvesuviana **train** (☎081 772 24 44) from Naples's Stazione Centrale to Pompeii (dir.: Sorrento; 2 per hr., €2.20). To reach the site, head downhill and take your first left to the west (Porta Marina) entrance. To reach the **tourist office,** V. Sacra 1, walk right from the station and continue to the bottom of the hill. (Open M-F 8am-3:30pm, Sa 8am-2pm.) Food at the on-site cafeteria is expensive, so bring lunch.

HERCULANEUM. Herculaneum is 500m downhill from the *Ercolano* stop on the Circumvesuviana **train** from Naples (dir.: Sorrento; 20min., €1.90). Stop at the **tourist office,** V. IV Novembre 84 (☎081 88 12 43), to pick up a free map. The city is less excavated than Pompeii because it was buried much deeper and a modern city sits on top; highlights include the **House of Deer.** (Open daily 8:30am-7:30pm. €10.)

MOUNT VESUVIUS. You can peer into the only active volcano on mainland Europe at Mt. Vesuvius. Trasporti Vesuviani **buses** (buy ticket on board; roundtrip €3.10) run from the Ercolano Circumvesuviana station to the crater. Although Vesuvius hasn't erupted since March 31, 1944 (and scientists say volcanoes should erupt every 30 years), experts deem the trip safe.

CASERTA. Few palaces, no matter how opulent, can hold a candle to Caserta's glorious ■**Reggia**—often referred to as "The Versailles of Naples." A world apart from the brutality of Pompeii, the palace and grounds resonate with a passion for art and beauty. When Bourbon King Charles III commissioned the palace in 1751, he intended it to rival Louis XIV's famously spectacular abode. Completed in 1775, the vast expanse of lush lawns, fountains, sculptures, and carefully pruned trees culminates in a 75m man-made waterfall—the setting for the final scene of the 1977 *Star Wars.* To the right are the English Gardens, complete with fake ruins inspired by Pompeii and Paestum. The **palazzo** boasts 1200 rooms, 1742 windows, and 34 staircases, whose furnishings and decorations are equally grandiose. The Reggia is directly opposite the train station. (Open Su and Tu-Sa 9am-7:30pm. €6.) **Trains** run from Naples (40min., 35 per day, €2.70).

AMALFI COAST

Tucked between the jagged rocks of the Sorrentine peninsula and the azure waters of the Adriatic, the Amalfi Coast has many alluring aspects. Its lush lemon groves bask in the sun, its local population is spirited and lively, and its monuments reflect the area's history as a maritime powerhouse, yet its oldest attribute—the area's natural beauty—remains the region's prime attraction.

⧉ TRANSPORTATION. The coast is accessible from Naples, Sorrento, Salerno, and the islands by ferry and blue SITA buses. **Trains** run directly to Salerno from Naples (45min., 42 per day, €5-10) and Rome (2½-3hr., 19 per day, €22-33). Trains also run to Sorrento from Naples (1hr., 29 per day, €3). **Buses** link Paestum and Salerno (1hr., every hr. 7am-7pm, €2.80). From Salerno, Travelmar (☎089 87 31 90) runs **ferries** to Amalfi (35min., 6 per day, €3.60) and Positano (1¼hr., 6 per day, €5.30). From Sorrento, Linee Marittime Partenopee (☎081 807 18 12) ferries (40min., 5 per day 8:30am-4:50pm, €6.50) and **hydrofoils** (20min., 17 per day 7:20am-5:40pm, €9.50) run to Capri.

AMALFI AND ATRANI. Breathtaking natural beauty surrounds the narrow streets and historic monuments of Amalfi. Visitors crowd P. del Duomo to admire the elegant 9th-century **Duomo di Sant'Andrea** and the nearby **Fontana di Sant'Andrea,** a marble nude with water spouting from her breasts. **A'Scalinatella ❶,** P. Umberto 12, has hostel beds and regular rooms all over Amalfi and Atrani. (☎089 87 19 30. Dorms €10-21; doubles €26-50, with bath €40-80.) The tiny beachside village of Atrani is a 15min. walk around the bend from Amalfi. The **Path of the Gods,** a spectacular 3hr. hike, follows the coast from Bomerano to Positano. The 2hr. hike to **Ravello** via Scalla also makes a for a pleasant trip. **Postal Code:** 84011.

RAVELLO. Perched atop 330m cliffs, Ravello has provided a haven for many celebrity artists over the years. The Moorish cloister and gardens of **Villa Rufolo,** off P. Duomo, inspired Boccaccio's *Decameron* and Wagner's *Parsifal.* (Open daily 9am-8pm. €4.) Classical music **concerts** are performed in the gardens of the Villa Rufolo; call the *Società di Concerti di Ravello* (☎089 85 81 49) for more info. The small road to the right leads to the impressive **Villa Cimbrone,** whose floral walkways and gardens hide temples and statue-filled grottoes. The area also offers magnificent views. (Open daily 9am-7:30pm. €4.50.) **Hotel Villa Amore ❹,** V. dei Fusco 5, has 12 tidy rooms and a garden overlooking the cliffs and sea. (☎/fax 089 85 71 35. Singles €48-60; doubles €74-85. MC/V.) **Postal Code:** 84010.

POSITANO. Today, Positano's most frequent visitors are the wealthy few who can afford the pricey *Positanese* lifestyle, yet the town has its charms for the budget traveler. To see the large *pertusione* (hole) in **Montepertuso,** one of three perforated mountains in the world, hike 45 min. uphill or take the bus from P. dei Mulini. Positano's **beaches** are also popular; the beach at **Fornillo** is a nicer, quieter alternative to the area's main beach, **Spaggia Grande.** The **tourist office,** V. del Saraceno 4, is below the *duomo.* (☎089 87 50 67. Open M-Sa 8am-2pm and 3-8pm; reduced hours off-season.) **Ostello Brikette ❷,** V.G. Marconi 358, 100m up the main coastal road to Sorrento from Viale Pasitea, has incredible views from two large terraces. (☎089 87 58 57. Dorms €22; doubles €70.) Prices in the town's restaurants reflect the high quality of the food. For a sit-down dinner, thrifty travelers head toward the beach at Fornillo.

SORRENTO. The most heavily touristed town on the peninsula, lively Sorrento makes a convenient base for daytrips around the Bay of Naples. The **tourist office,** L. de Maio 35, is off P. Tasso. (☎081 807 40 33. Open Apr.-Sept. M-Sa 8:45am-

ITALY

7:45pm; Oct.-Mar. reduced hours.) Halfway to the free **beach** at **Punta del Capo** (bus A), **Hotel Elios ❷**, V. Capo 33, has comfy rooms. (☎081 878 18 12. Open Apr.-Oct. Singles €25-30; doubles €45-55.) It's easy to find good, affordable food in Sorrento. **Davide**, V. Giuliani 39, off C. Italia, two blocks from P. Tasso, has divine *gelato* and masterful *mousse.* (Open daily 10am-midnight.) After 10:30pm, a crowd gathers for drinks in the rooftop lemon grove above **The English Inn,** C. Italia 56. (Open daily 9am-1am.) **Postal Code:** 80067.

SALERNO AND PAESTUM. Industrial **Salerno** is best used as a base for daytrips to nearby **Paestum,** the site of spectacularly preserved **Doric temples,** including the **Temple of Ceres** and the **Temple of Poseidon,** as well as a **museum** with artifacts taken from the sites. (Temples open daily 9am-7:30pm. Museum open daily 9am-6:30pm. Reduced hours for both off-season. Both closed 1st and 3rd M each month. €6.50 includes both sites.) To reach the clean and comfortable **Ostello Per La Gioventù ❷**, V. Canali, take C. Emanuele into the old district, where it becomes V. dei Mercanti, and head left onto V. Canali. (☎089 23 47 76. Lockout 10:30am-3pm. Curfew 12:30am. Dorms €16; doubles €50.) **Postal Code:** 84100.

BAY OF NAPLES ISLANDS   ☎081

CAPRI. There are two towns on the island of Capri—**Capri proper,** near the ports, and **Anacapri,** higher up the mountain. Visitors flock to the renowned **Blue Grotto,** a sea cave whose waters shimmer with neon-blue light. (Open daily 9am-5pm. Boat tour €8.50.) In the summer months crowds and prices increase; the best times to visit are in the late spring and early fall. **Buses** departing from V. Roma make the trip up the mountain to Anacapri every 15 min. until 1:40am. Away from the throngs flitting among Capri's expensive boutiques, Anacapri is home to budget hotels, spectacular vistas, and quiet mountain paths. Upstairs from P. Vittoria in Anacapri, **Villa San Michele** sports lush gardens, ancient sculptures, and a remarkable view. (Open daily 9:30am-6pm. €5.) To appreciate Capri's Mediterranean beauty from higher ground, take the chairlift up **Monte Solaro** from P. Vittoria. (Open Mar.-Oct. daily 9:30am-4:45pm. Round-trip €5.50.) For those who prefer cliff to coastline, Capri's hiking trails lead to stunning panoramas; try the short but strenuous hike to the ruins of Emperor Tiberius's **Villa Jovis,** the largest of his 12 Capri villas. Always the gracious host, Tiberius tossed those who displeased him over the precipice. The view from the **Cappella di Santa Maria del Soccorso,** built onto the villa, is unrivaled. (Open daily 9am-6pm.) In the evenings, dressed-to-kill Italians come out for Capri's nightlife; bars around **Piazza Umberto** in Capri proper keep the music pumping late, while cheaper Anacapri caters to a younger crowd.

Caremar (☎081 837 07 00) **ferries** run from Marina Grande to Naples (1¼hr., 6 per day, €8.50) and Sorrento (50min., 3 per day, €6.50). LineaJet (☎081 837 08 19) runs **hydrofoils** to Naples (40min., 10 per day, €11.50) and Sorrento (20min., €8.50). Ferries and hydrofoils to Ischia and Amalfi run with much less frequency and regularity; check with the lines at Marina Grande for details. The Capri **tourist office** (☎081 837 06 34) sits at the end of Marina Grande; in Anacapri, it's at V. Orlandi 59 (☎081 837 15 24), to the right of the P. Vittoria bus stop. (Both open June-Sept. M-Sa 8:30am-8:30pm; Oct.-May M-Sa 9am-1:30pm and 3:30-6:45pm.) **Alla Bussola di Hermes ❷**, V. Traversa La Vigna 14, in Anacapri, has a friendly proprietor and some of the best deals on the island. (☎081 838 20 10; bus.hermes@libero.it. Dorms €20-24 per person; doubles €50-65. AmEx/MC/V.) For more convenient access to the beach and the center of Capri, stay at the **Bed and Breakfast Tirrenia Roberts ❹**, V. Mulo 27. Walk away from P. Umberto on V. Roma and take the stairs on your right just before the fork. (☎ 081 837 61 19. Reserve well in advance. Doubles €80-105.) Bear right at the fork to reach **Dimeglio supermarket.** (Open M-Sa 8:30am-1:30pm and 5-9pm.) **Postal Codes:** Capri: 80073; Anacapri: 80021.

ISCHIA. Augustus fell in love with Capri's fantastic beauty in 29 BC, but later swapped it for its more fertile neighbor. Ischia, just across the bay, offers sandy beaches, natural hot springs, ruins, forests, vineyards, and lemon groves. Orange SEPSA **buses** #1, CD, and CS (every 20 min.; €1.20, day pass €4.80) depart from the ferry landing and follow the coast in a circular route, stopping at: **Ischia Porto,** a port formed by the crater of an extinct volcano; **Casamicciola Terme,** with a crowded beach and legendary thermal waters; **Lacco Ameno,** the oldest Greek settlement in the western Mediterranean; and popular **Forio,** home to lively bars. The **Motella Gardens,** V. Calese 39, feature acres of tropical plants, man-made streams and gorgeous views of Ischia. (Open daily 9am-7pm. €8).

Caremar **ferries** (☎ 081 98 48 18) arrive from Naples (1½hr., 14 per day, €6.20). Alilauro (☎ 081 18 88, www.alilauro.it) runs **hydrofoils** to Sorrento (6 per day; call ahead for prices and schedule). The **tourist office** is on Banchino Porto Salvo, in the main port. (☎ 081 507 42 31; fax 081 507 42 30. Open in summer daily 8am-2pm and 3-8pm; off-season reduced hours.) **Pensione Di Lustro ❸,** V. Filippo di Lustro 9, is near the beach. (☎ 081 99 71 63. Singles €34; doubles €50-65.) The **Ostello "Il Gabbiano" (HI) ❷,** Strada Statale Forio-Panza, 162, is accessible by buses #1, CS, and CD. The hostel has beach access as well as a friendly staff. (☎ 081 90 94 22. Lockout 9:30am-1pm. Curfew 2am. Open Apr.-Sept. Dorms €16.) **Camping Internazionale ❶** is at V. Foschini 22, 15min. from the port. Take V. Alfredo de Luca from V. del Porto; bear right on V. Michele Mazzella at P. degi Eroi. (☎ 081 99 14 49; fax 99 14 72. Open May-Sept. €6-9 per person, €3-10 per tent.) **Postal Code:** 80077.

SICILY (SICILIA)

Sicily is a land of sensuous sunshine and sinister shadows. Ancient Greek influences lauded the golden island as the second home of the Gods; now eager tourists seek it as the home of *The Godfather.* While the *Cosa Nostra* remains a presence in Sicily, it makes up only the smallest part of the vivacious and varied culture.

▣ TRANSPORTATION

Tirrenia Ferries (☎ 091 33 33 00) offers extensive service. From southern Italy, take a **train** to Reggio di Calabria, then a NGI or Meridiano **ferry** (40min.; NGI: 10-12 per day, €0.55; Meridiano: 11-15 per day, €1.55) or Ferrovie Statale **hydrofoil** (☎ 096 586 35 40) to Messina, Sicily's transport hub (25min., 12 per day, €2.60). Ferries also go to Palermo from Sardinia (14hr., €42) and Naples (10hr., 2 per day, €38). **SAIS Trasporti** (☎ 091 617 11 41) and SAIS **buses** (☎ 091 616 60 28) serve destinations throughout the island. **Trains** head to Messina directly from Naples (4½hr., 7 per day, €22) and Rome (9hr., 7 per day, €30). Trains continue west to Palermo (3½hr., 15 per day, €11) via Milazzo.

PALERMO   ☎ 091

From twisting streets lined with ancient ruins to the shrinking shadow of organized crime, gritty Palermo (pop. 700,000) is a city whose recent history provides shade and texture to a rich cultural heritage. To get to the magnificent **Teatro Massimo,** where the climactic opera scene of *The Godfather: Part III* was filmed, walk up V. Maqueda past the intersection of Quattro Canti and C. Vittorio Emanuele. (Open Su and Tu-Sa 10am-5:30pm. €3.) Up C. Vittorio Emanuele, the **Palazzo dei Normanni**

LA FAMIGLIA

Powerful because people owed them favors, strong because they supported one another, and feared because they did not hesitate to kill offenders, the Sicilian Mafia founded a brutal tradition that has dominated life since the late 19th century. The Mafia system has its roots in the *latifondi* (agricultural estates) of rural Sicily, where land managers and salaried militiamen protected their turf and people. Today, Sicilians avoid the topic, referring to the Mafia as *Cosa Nostra* (Our Thing). At a grass-roots level, the Mafia is said to have long controlled public works infrastructure, and farmers for years have lived in fear of land seizure and extortion. The Mafia was reported to have capitalized upon a drought in the summer of 2002 by stealing water from private wells and public water systems. Recent local resistance includes a farmers' group, Libera, that sells what it calls "anti-Mafia pasta," made from wheat grown on land seized from the Mafia by the government. Another jailed Mafia don's estate has been converted to a cooperative olive oil production site. Since the mid-80s, government efforts to curtail Mafia influence have had some success. Dozens of members of Mafia strongholds like the Corleone, mythologized by *The Godfather* films, have been arrested, and in August 2002, Palermo police confiscated an estimated £500 million in Mafia property.

contains the ▧**Cappella Palatina,** full of incredible golden mosaics. (Open M-Sa 9am-noon and 3-4:45pm, Su 9-10am and 11:15am-1pm.) The morbid **Cappuchin Catacombs,** in P. Cappuccini, are only for the strong of stomach. Eight thousand corpses and twisted skeletons line the underground labyrinth. To get there, take buses #109 or 318 from Stazione Centrale to P. Indipendenza and then transfer to bus #327. (Open M-Su 9am-noon and 3-5:30pm. €1.50.)

Trains leave Stazione Centrale, in P. Giulio Cesare, at V. Roma and V. Maqueda, for Florence (16hr., 3 per day, €46) and Rome (11hr., 8 per day, €42). All four **bus** lines run from V. Balsamo, next to the train station. After purchasing tickets, ask exactly where your bus will arrive and its logo. Ask at an **AMAT** or **Metro** information booth for a combined Metro and bus map. The **tourist office,** P. Castelnuovo 34, is opposite Teatro Politeama; from the train station, take a bus to P. Politeama, at the end of V. Maqueda. (☎091 605 83 51; www.palermotourism.com. Open June-Sept. M-F 8:30am-2pm and 2:30-6pm, Sa-Su 9am-1pm; Oct.-May. M-F 2:30-6pm.) Homey **Hotel Regina ❷,** C. Vittorio Emanuele 316, is off V. Maqueda. (☎091 611 42 16; fax 091 612 21 69. Singles €21, with bath €35; doubles €40/50.) The area around **Teatro Massimo** has a variety of cheap restaurants. **Postal Code:** 90100.

SYRACUSE (SIRACUSA)   ☎0931

Never having regained the glory of its golden Grecian days, the modern city of Syracuse (pop. 130,000) takes pride in its extraordinary ruins. Syracuse's one-time role as one of the most powerful cities in the Mediterranean is still evident in the **Archaeological Park,** on the north side of town, which includes several sites. The enormous **Greek theater** is where 20,000 spectators watched Aeschylus premiere his *Persians.* To reach the well-preserved 2nd-century **Roman amphitheater,** follow C. Gelone until it meets V. Teocrito, then walk left down V. Augusto. (Open in summer daily 9am-7pm; off-season reduced hours. €4.50.) More ruins lie over the Ponte Umbertino on **Ortigia,** the serene island on which the Greeks first landed. The ruined **Temple of Apollo** has a few columns still standing, but those at the **Temple of Diana** are much more impressive. Those who prefer tans to temples take bus #21, 22, or 24 to **Fontane Bianche,** a glitzy beach with plenty of discos.

Trains leave V. Francesco Crispi for Messina (3hr., 16 per day, €8.30) and Rome (12hr., 5 per day, €38). Interbus **buses,** V. Trieste 28 (☎0931 667 10), leave for Palermo (3hr., 5 per day, €14). To get from the train station to the **tourist office,** V.S. Sebastiano 43, take

V.F. Crispi to C. Gelone, turn right on V. Teocrite, then left on V.S. Sebastiano; it's on the left. (☎0931 048 12 32. Open M-F 8:30am-1:30pm and 3:30-6:30pm, Sa 8:30am-1:30pm.) **Hotel Centrale ❷,** C. Umberto I 141, has clean rooms with astounding sea views. (☎0931 605 28. Singles €17; doubles €26; triples €35-37.) For cheap food, try places on **Via Savoia** and **Via Cavour,** or the open-air **market** in Ortigia, on V. Trento, off P. Pancali. (Open M-Sa 8am-1pm.)

AEOLIAN ISLANDS (ISOLE EOLIE)

Homer thought the Aeolian Islands to be the second home of the gods, and indeed, these last few stretches of unspoiled seashore border on the divine. Sparkling seas, smooth beaches, and fiery volcanoes testify to the area's stunning beauty.

▐▀ TRANSPORTATION

The archipelago lies off the Sicilian coast, north of **Milazzo,** the principal and least expensive departure point. Hop off a **train** from Palermo (3hr., €9.20) and onto an orange AST **bus** for the port (10min., every hr., free). Siremar (☎98 60 11) and Navigazione Generale Italiana (NGI; ☎98 30 03) **ferries** depart for Lipari (2hr., €6.20); Stromboli (5hr., €9.90); and Vulcano (1½hr., €5.70). **Hydrofoils** *(aliscafi)* make the trip in half the time, but cost twice as much. Both have ticket offices on V.d Mille facing the port in Milazzo. Ferries visit the islands less frequently from Molo Beverello port in Naples.

LIPARI. Lipari, the largest and most developed of the islands, is renowned for its amazing beaches and stunning hillside views. To reach the popular beaches of **Spiaggia Bianca** and **Porticello,** take the Lipari-Cavedi bus a few kilometers north to Canneto; Spiaggia Bianca is *the* spot for topless (and sometimes bottomless) sunbathing. Lipari's other offerings include a splendidly rebuilt medieval **castello,** the site of an ancient Greek acropolis. The fortress shares its hill with an **archaeological park,** the **San Bartolo church,** and the superb ◪**Museo Archeologico Eoliano,** up the stone steps off V. Garibaldi. (Open May-Oct. daily 9am-1:30pm and 4-7pm; Nov.-Apr. M-Su 9am-1:30pm and 3-6pm. €4.50.) The **tourist office,** C. Vittorio Emanuele 202, is near the ferry dock. (☎090 988 00 95; www.net-net.it/aasteolie. Open July-Aug. M-F 8am-2pm and 4:30-9:30pm, Sa 8am-2pm; Sept.-June reduced hours.) **Casa Vittorio ❷,** Vico Sparviero 15, is on a quiet street in the center of town. Rooms range from singles to a five-person penthouse. (☎090 981 15 23. €15-40 per person.) **Camp** at **Baia Unci ❶,** V. Marina Garibaldi 2, 2km from Lipari at the entrance to the hamlet of Canneto. (☎090 981 19 09. www.campeggitalia.it/sicilia/baiaunci. Reserve for Aug. Open mid-Mar. to mid-Oct. €8-12 per person, with tent.) Stock up at **UPIM supermarket,** C. Vittorio Emanuele 212. (Open M-Sa 8am-10pm.) ◪**Da Gilberto ❶,** V. Garibaldi 22-24, is known for its sandwiches. (☎090 981 27 56. Sandwiches from €3.50. Open 7am-4am; off-season 7am-2am.) **Postal Code:** 98050.

VULCANO. Black beaches, bubbling seas, and natural mud spas attract visitors from around the world to Vulcano. A steep 1hr. **hike** to the inactive **Gran Cratere** (Grand Crater) snakes between the volcano's noxious yellow fumaroles. On a clear day, you can see all the other islands from the top. The therapeutic **Laghetto di Fanghi** (Mud Pool) is just up V. Provinciale to the right from the port. If you would prefer not to bathe in sulfuric radioactive mud, you can step gingerly into the scalding waters of the **acquacalda,** where underwater volcanic outlets make the sea percolate like a jacuzzi, or visit the nearby black sands and clear waters of **Sabbie Nere.** (Follow the signs off V. Ponente.) To get to Vulcano, take the 10min. **hydrofoil** from the port at nearby Lipari (10min., 8 per day, €2.50). For more info, see the tourist office at V. Provinciale 41. (☎985 20 28. Open July-Aug. daily 8am-1:30pm and 3-5pm.) For **private rooms** *(affittacamere)*, call ☎985 21 42. The Lipari tourist office also has information on Vulcano. **Postal Code:** 98050.

STROMBOLI. If you find luscious beaches and hot springs a bit tame, a visit to Stromboli's active **volcano,** which spews orange cascades of lava and molten rock about every 10min. each night, will quench your thirst for adventure. **Hiking** the *vulcano* on your own is **illegal** and **dangerous,** but **Magmatrek** offers tours, which also should be taken at your own risk. The group runs a 4hr. afternoon trek to the lower crater that emerged in December 2002 from a new subterranean magma tunnel that broke through the volcano's crust along the side. As of summer 2003, treks to the top are illegal, but once the situation stabilizes, Magmatrek will resume their 6-7 hour excursions to the pinnacle. (☎/fax 986 57 68. Tours depart from V. Vittorio Emanuele. €13.50.) Bring sturdy shoes, a flashlight, snacks, water, and warm clothes; don't wear contact lenses, as the wind sweeps ash and dust everywhere. **Siremar** (☎090 986 011) runs an infrequent **ferry** from Milazzo to Stromboli, and boat rentals are readily available. From July to September, you won't find a room without a reservation; your best bet may be one of the non-reservable *affitta-camere*. Expect to pay €15-30 for a room. The best value is ▨**Casa del Sole ❷,** on V. Giuseppe Cincotta, off V. Regina at the end of town. At the church of St-Bartholomew, take a right down the stairs and go straight down the alley. Large rooms face a shared terrace. (☎090 986 017. Open Mar.-Oct. €23, off-season reduced prices.) **Postal Code:** 98050.

SARDINIA (SARDEGNA)

When the vanity and cultivation of mainland Italy starts to wear thin, when one more church interior will send you into the path of the nearest speeding Fiat, Sardinia's savage coastline and rugged people will be a reality check for your soul. D. H. Lawrence sought respite here from the "deadly net of European civilization," and he found his escape among the wild horses, wind-carved rock formations, and pink flamingos of this remote island.

▐ TRANSPORTATION

Tirrenia **ferries** (☎081 317 29 99; www.tirrenia.it) run to **Olbia** from Civitavecchia, just north of Rome (6hr., 4 per day, from €30), and Genoa (9hr., 6 per week, from €28). They also chug to **Cagliari** from Civitavecchia (15-18hr., 2 per day, from €26); Genoa (20hr., July-Sept. 2 per week, from €37); Naples (16hr., Jan.-Sept. 1 per week, €26); and Palermo (13½hr., 1 per week, from €24). **Trains** run from Cagliari to Olbia (4hr., daily, €13) via Oristano (1½hr., 16 per day €4.55) and to Sassari (4hr., 2 per day, from €12). From Sassari, trains run to Alghero (40min., 11 per day, €1.80). PANI **buses** connect Cagliari to Oristano (1½hr., €5.80).

CAGLIARI   ☎070

Cagliari combines the bustle and energy of a modern Italian city with the endearing rural atmosphere of the rest of the island. Its Roman ruins, medieval towers, and cobblestone streets contrast with the regal tree-lined streets and sweeping beaches downtown. Climb Largo Carlo Felice to reach the city's impressive **duomo,** P. Palazzo 3, with dazzling gold mosaics topping each of its entryways. Open daily 8am-12:30pm and 4-8pm.) The 2nd-century **Roman ampitheater** comes alive with concerts, operas, and classic plays during the summer **arts festival** in July and August. If you prefer to sun-worship, take city bus P, PQ, or PF to **Il Poetto** beach (20min., €0.80), which has pure white sand and turquoise water. The **tourist office** is on P. Matteotti. (☎070 66 92 55; fax 070 66 49 23. Open in summer M-Sa 8:30am-1:30pm and 2:30-7:30pm; off-season reduced hours.) **Albergo Palmas ❷,** V. Sardegna 14 is the town's best budget option. Cross V. Roma and turn right; take the first left on Largo Carlo Felice, and turn right onto V. Sardegna. (☎070 65 16 79. Singles €21; doubles €31-37. AmEx/MC/V.) **Postal Code:** 09100.

ALGHERO   ☎079

Vineyards, ruins, and horseback rides are all a short trip away from Alghero's palm-lined parks and twisting medieval streets. The nearby ▨**Grotte di Nettuno,** an eerie, stalactite-filled 70-million-year-old cavern complex in Capo Caccia, can be reached by bus (1hr., 3 per day, round-trip €1.80). Visitors descend 632 steps between massive white cliffs. (Open Apr.-Sept. daily 9am-7pm; Oct. 10am-4pm; Nov.-Mar. 8am-2pm. €10.) The **tourist office,** P. Porta Terra 9, is to the right from the bus stop. (☎079 97 90 54. Open Apr.-Oct. M-Sa 8am-8pm, Su 10am-1pm; Nov.-Mar. M-Sa 9am-1pm.) To get to **Hotel San Francesco ❸,** V. Machin 2, walk straight from the tourist office and take the 3rd right. (☎079 98 03 30; www.sanfrancesco-hotel.com. Singles €35-43; doubles €62-77. MC/V.) **Postal Code:** 07041.

ORISTANO AND THE SINIS PENINSULA   ☎0783

The town of Oristano is an excellent base for excursions to the nearby Sinis Peninsula. From the train station, follow V. Vittorio Veneto straight to P. Mariano, then take V. Mazzini to P. Roma to reach the town center (25min.). Rent a moped or car to explore the tranquil beaches, stark white cliffs, and ancient ruins on the mystical Sinis Peninsula. At the tip, 17km west of Oristano, lie the ruins of the ancient Phoenician port of **Tharros.** Take the ARST bus to *San Giovanni di Sinis* (dir.: Is Arutas; 40min., 5 per day, €1.50). Slightly to the north off the road to Cuglieri is **S'Archittu,** where people leap from a 15m limestone arch into the waters of a rocky inlet. ARST buses go to S'Archittu (30min., 7 per day, €1.45). The secluded white quartz sands of **Is Arutas** are well worth the trip. The ARST bus to Is Arutas runs only during July and August (50min., 5 per day, €1.50). The **tourist office,** V. Vittorio Emanuele 8, provides maps. (☎/fax 0783 30 32 12. Open M-F 9am-12:30pm and 4:30-8pm, Sa 9am-12:30pm.) **Piccolo Hotel ❸,** V. Martignano 19, on a quiet side street in the historic center, is spacious and tastefully decorated. (☎0783 71 500. Singles €31; doubles €52.) **Postal Code:** 09170.

ITALY

LATVIA (LATVIJA)

At the Baltic crossroads, Latvia has been caught for hundreds of years in international political struggles. The country has been conquered and reconquered so many times that the year 2004 will only be Latvia's 35th year of independence—ever. National pride, however, abounds, from patriotically renamed streets to a rediscovery of native holidays predating even the Christian invasions. Rīga, Latvia's only large city, is a Westernized capital luring more and more international companies, while the rest of the country is mostly a provincial expanse of green hills dominated by tall birches and pines, dairy pastures, and quiet towns.

FACTS AND FIGURES

Official Name: Republic of Latvia.

Capital: Rīga.

Population: 2,400,000.

Land Area: 64,589 sq. km.

Time Zone: GMT +2.

Languages: Lettish, Lithuanian, Russian.

Religions: Lutheran, Roman Catholic, Russian Orthodox.

ESSENTIALS

DOCUMENTS AND FORMALITIES

VISAS. Irish, UK, and US citizens can visit Latvia for up to 90 days without a visa. Citizens of Australia, Canada, New Zealand, and South Africa need 90-day visas, obtainable at a Latvian consulate. Apply for extensions at the Department of Immigration and Citizenship in Rīga, Raiņa bul. 5 (☎721 91 81).

EMBASSIES. All foreign embassies are in Rīga (p. 696). For Latvian embassies at home, contact: **Australia**, P.O. Box 23 Kew, VIC 3101 (☎03 9499 6920; fax 03 9499 7008); **Canada**, 280 Albert St., Ste. 300, Ottawa, ON K1P 5G8 (☎613-238-6014;

Latvia

www.magmacom.com/~latemb); **UK,** 45 Nottingham Pl., London W1M 3FE (☎020 7312 0040; fax 7312 0042); and **US,** 4325 17th St. NW, Washington, D.C. 20011 (☎202-726-8213; www.latvia-usa.org).

TRANSPORTATION

Air Baltic, SAS, Finnair, and Lufthansa, among others, fly into Rīga (RIX). **Trains** link Latvia to Berlin, Lviv, Moscow, Odessa, St. Petersburg, Tallinn, and Vilnius. **Eurail** is not valid. Trains are cheap and efficient, but stations aren't well marked—always carry a map. The **suburban rail** system renders the entire country a suburb of Rīga, and is a better choice than buses for daytrips from the capital. Latvia's quicker **bus** network reaches Prague, Tallinn, Vilnius, and Warsaw. **Ferries** run to Rīga from Stockholm, Sweden and Kiel, Germany. **Hitchhiking** is common, but hitchhikers may be expected to pay. *Let's Go* does not recommend hitchhiking.

TOURIST SERVICES AND MONEY

EMERGENCY	**Police:** ☎02. **Ambulance:** ☎03. **Fire:** ☎01.

Tourist offices are scarce; look for a green "i." Private offices such as **Patricia** (p. 698) are more helpful. The Latvian **Lat** is divided into 100 *santims*. Inflation is around 3%. It's often hard to exchange currencies other than US dollars and euros. There are many **ATMs** in Rīga and in large towns, most linked to Cirrus, Master-Card, and Visa. Larger businesses, restaurants, and hotels accept MasterCard and Visa. Traveler's checks are harder to use; both AmEx and Thomas Cook can be converted in Rīga, but elsewhere, Thomas Cook is a safer bet.

LATS		
	AUS$1 = 0.37 LVL	1LVL = AUS$2.68
	CDN$1 = 0.42 LVL	1LVL = CDN$2.40
	EUR€1 = 0.63 LVL	1LVL = EUR€1.58
	NZ$1 = 0.33 LVL	1LVL = NZ$3.00
	ZAR1 = 0.08 LVL	1LVL = ZAR12.73
	UK£1 = 0.91 LVL	1LVL = UK£1.10
	US$1 = 0.58 LVL	1LVL = US$1.74

COMMUNICATION

PHONE CODES	**Country code:** 371. **International dialing prefix:** 00. From outside Latvia, dial int'l dialing prefix (see inside back cover) + 371 + city code + local number.

TELEPHONES AND INTERNET ACCESS. If a number is six digits long, dial a 2 before the number; if it's seven digits, you needn't dial anything before the number. To call abroad from an analog phone, dial 1, then 00, then the country code. From a digital phone, simply dial 00, then the country code. Most telephones take cards (available in 2, 3, 5, or 10Ls denominations) from post offices, telephone offices, kiosks, and state stores. The phone system has been undergoing changes; phone offices and *Rīga in Your Pocket* have the latest info. **International** calls can be made from telephone offices or booths. International access codes include **AT&T Direct** (☎800 2 288) and **MCI WorldPhone** (☎800 8888). **Internet access** is readily available in major cities and towns and averages 0.5Ls per hr.

MAIL. Ask for *gaisa pastu* to send something by airmail. Letters abroad cost 0.40Ls, postcards 0.30Ls. For *Poste Restante*, address mail to be held: Firstname SURNAME, *Poste Restante*, Stacijas laukums 1, Rīga, LV-1050 LATVIA.

LANGUAGES. Heavily influenced by German, Russian, Estonian, and Swedish, Lettish is one of two languages (the other is Lithuanian) in the Baltic language group. Russian is in disfavor in the countryside but is more widespread in Rīga. Many young Latvians study English. Older Latvians tend to know some German.

ACCOMMODATIONS AND FOOD

LATVIA	❶	❷	❸	❹	❺
ACCOMMODATIONS	under 8Ls	8-14Ls	15-19Ls	20-24Ls	over 24Ls
FOOD	under 2Ls	2-3Ls	4-5Ls	6-7Ls	over 7Ls

College **dormitories,** which open to travelers in the summer, are often the cheapest places to sleep. In Rīga, Patricia (p. 698) arranges **homestays** and **apartment** rentals for around 10Ls per night. There are very few budget-range (3-15Ls) hotels. Latvian food is heavy and starchy, but tasty. Rīga is one of the easiest places to find vegetarian options in all the Baltics. Tasty national specialties include the holiday dish *zirņi* (gray peas with onions and smoked fat), *maizes zupa* (bread soup usually made from corn bread and full of currants, cream, and other goodies), and the warming *Rīgas* (or *Melnais*) *balzams* (a black liquor great with ice cream, Coke, or coffee). Dark rye bread is a staple. Try *speķa rauši*, a warm pastry, or *biezpienmaize*, bread with sweet curds. Latvian beer is stellar, especially *Porteris* and other offerings from the Aldaris brewery.

HOLIDAYS

Holidays: New Year's Day (Jan. 1); Good Friday (Mar. 29); Catholic Easter (Mar. 31); Labor Day (May 1); Ligo (Midsummer Festival; June 23); Independence Day (Nov. 18); Ziemsvetki (Christmas; Dec. 25-26); New Year's Eve (Dec. 31).

RĪGA ☎82

More Westernized and cosmopolitan than the rest of Latvia, sprawling Rīga feels strangely out of place as the capital of a small, struggling country. Despite its abundance of casinos, Rīga envisions itself as the "Paris of the East." Striving to become a major European cultural and social center, the self-proclaimed capital of the Baltics has been working hard to rebuild since the fall of the USSR.

The phone code in Rīga is 2 for all 6-digit numbers; there is no phone code for 7-digit numbers. Info: ☎800 80 08. Latvian operator: ☎116. International operator: ☎115. Directory services: ☎118, 722 22 22, or 777 07 77.

▐ TRANSPORTATION

Flights: Lidosta Rīga (RIX; ☎720 70 09), 8km southwest of Vecrīga. Take **bus** #22 from Gogol iela (0.20Ls).

Trains: Centrālā Stacija (Central Station), Stacijas laukums (☎583 30 95), down the street from the bus station. Long-distance trains depart from the larger building to the left; destinations include: **Moscow** (18hr., 2 per day, 25Ls); **St. Petersburg** (13hr., daily, 22Ls); and **Vilnius** (8hr., 2 per day, 9-11Ls).

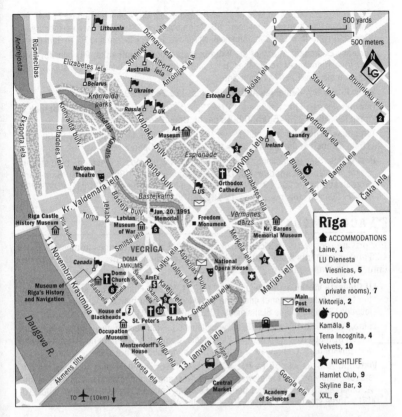

Rīga

▲ ACCOMMODATIONS
Laine, 1
LU Dienesta
  Viesnicas, 5
Patricia's (for
  private rooms), 7
Viktorija, 2

● FOOD
Kamāla, 8
Terra Incognita, 4
Velvets, 10

★ NIGHTLIFE
Hamlet Club, 9
Skyline Bar, 3
XXL, 6

Buses: Autoosta, Prāgas 1 (☎900 00 09), 200m from the train station, across the canal from the Central Market. To: **Kaunas** (5-6hr., 2 per day, 5.20Ls); **Minsk** (10-12hr., 3 per day, 7Ls); **Tallinn** (4-6hr., 8 per day, 7-8.50Ls); **Vilnius** (5hr., 4-6 per day, 4.5-6Ls). **Ecolines** (☎721 45 12; www.ecolines.lv), in the bus station, sends buses to **Prague** (25½hr.; 1 per week; 36Ls, students 24Ls).

✤ ? ORIENTATION AND PRACTICAL INFORMATION

The city is divided in half by **Brīvības bulvāris,** which leads from the outskirts to the **Freedom Monument** in the center, becoming **Kaļķu iela** and passing through **Vecrīga** (Old Rīga). To reach Vecrīga from the train station, turn left on Marijas iela and then right on any of the small streets beyond the canal. For good info, pick up the free *Rīga This Week* at major hotels or the Tourist Information Center.

Tourist Office: Tourist Information Center, Rātslaukums 6 (☎703 79 00; www.rigatour-ism.com), in the town square, next to the House of Blackheads. Sells maps and provides advice and brochures. Open daily 9am-7pm; off-season 10am-7pm.

Embassies and Consulates: Australia, Alberta iela 13 (☎733 63 83; acr@latnet.lv). Open Tu 10am-noon and Th 3-5pm. **Canada,** Doma laukums 4, 3rd and 4th fl. (☎783 01 41; riga@dfaitmaeci.gc.ca). Open Tu and Th 10am-1pm. **Ireland,** Brīvības iela 54 (☎702 52

59; fax 702 52 60). Open M-Tu and Th-F 9:30am-noon. **UK,** Alunāna iela 5 (☎777 47 00; www.britain.lv). Open M-F 9am-noon. **US,** Raiņa bul. 7 (☎721 00 05; www.usembassy.lv). Open M-Tu and Th 9-11:30am. American citizen hrs. M, W, F 2-4pm and Tu, Th 9am-noon.

Currency Exchange: At any of the **Valutos Maiņa** kiosks. **Unibanka,** Pils iela 23, gives MC/V cash advances and cashes AmEx and Thomas Cook traveler's checks, both without commission. Open M-F 9am-5pm.

24hr. Pharmacy: Kamelijas Aptieka, Brīvības iela 74 (☎729 35 14).

Internet Access: Elik, Kaļķu iela 11 (☎722 70 79), in the center of Vecrīga; **branch** at Čaka iela 26 (☎728 45 06). 0.50Ls per hr. Open 24hr.

Telephone Office: Brīvības bul. 19 (☎701 87 38). Open M-F 7am-11pm, Sa-Su 8am-10pm. **Branch** at the post office by the train station. Open 24hr.

Post Office: Stacijas laukums 1 (☎701 88 04; www.riga.post.lv), near the train station. *Poste Restante* at window #9. Open M-F 8am-8pm, Sa 8am-6pm, Su 8am-4pm. **Branch** at Brīvības bul. 19. Address mail to be held: Firstname SURNAME, *POSTE RESTANTE,* Stacijas laukums 1, Rīga, **LV-1050** LATVIA.

▌ ACCOMMODATIONS

For private rooms, try **Patricia,** Elizabetes iela 22, which arranges homestays from €25 and apartments from €40. (☎728 48 68; www.rigalatvia.net. Open M-F 9:15am-6pm, Sa-Su 11am-1pm.)

LU Dienesta Viesnicas, Basteja bul. 10 (☎721 62 21). From the bus station, go under the tracks, take the tunnel under the highway, and bear right on Aspazijas bul. Great location. Student rooms 8Ls; singles 10Ls, with bath 20Ls; doubles 16/30Ls. ❷

Laine, Skolas iela 11 (☎728 88 16; www.laine.lv). From Vecrīga, take Brīvības bul., turn left on Dzirnava iela, then right on Skolas iela. Comfortable modern hotel. Some rooms with private bath. Call ahead. Singles 35-40Ls; doubles 45-50Ls. ❺

Viktorija, A. Caka iela 55 (☎701 41 11; reservation@hotel-viktorija.lv). From the bus station, follow Mariajas iela away from the river, and continue as Mariajas merges into A. Caka. Fits a wide range of budgets. Economy rooms: Singles 8-12Ls; doubles 10-17Ls. Three star rooms: Singles 30Ls; doubles 40Ls. ❷

▐ FOOD

Look for 24-hour food and liquor stores along **Elizabetes iela, Marijas iela,** and **Ģertrūdes iela.** The **Centrālais Tirgus** (Central Market) is one of the largest in Europe; prices are low, but remember to haggle anyway. (Open daily 8am-6pm.)

Terra Incognita, Blaumaņa iela 27. Restaurant, art gallery, and venue for spirited African drumming. Entrees 2.30-3.70Ls. Live music W-Sa 8pm. Cover 1Ls some nights. Open M noon-11pm, Tu-Sa 11am-11pm. ❷

Velvets, Skārņu iela 9, just off Kaļķu iela in Vecrīga. A stylish French restaurant with outside seating and a dance floor in back. Entrees 1-6.65Ls. Open Su-Th 10am-2am, F-Sa 10am-4am. ❶

Kamāla, Jauniela iela 14, around the corner from the Dome Cathedral. Serves Indian vegetarian cuisine in a decadent setting. Entrees 2-4Ls. Open M-Sa noon-11pm, Su 2-10pm. ❷

▐ SIGHTS

FREEDOM MONUMENT AND ENVIRONS. Take time to savor the winding streets and unusual architecture of Vecrīga (Old Rīga). In the center stands the beloved **Freedom Monument** (Brīvības Piemineklis), affectionately known as "Milda." *(At the* *corner of Raiņa bul. and Brīvības bul.*) Continuing along Kaļķu iela from the Freedom Monument toward the river, you'll see one of the few Soviet monuments not torn down: the **Latvian Riflemen Monument** (Latviešu Strēlnieku Laukums), which honors Lenin's famous bodyguards. Rising behind the statues are the black walls of the ◙**Occupation Museum** (Okupācijas muzejs), Strēlnieku laukums 1, where the initial Soviet occupation is depicted so vividly that you can almost hear the Red Army marching through the streets of Rīga. *(Open May-Sept. daily 11am-6pm; Oct.-Apr. Tu-Su 11am-5pm. Free; donations accepted.)* Just beyond the museum stands the **House of Blackheads** (Melngalvju nams) Rātslaukums 7. Built in 1344 and completely destroyed by the Nazis and the Soviets, the unusual and magnificent building was reconstructed in 1999 in honor of Rīga's 800th birthday, and is now used for meetings and concerts. *(Open Su and Tu-Sa 10am-5pm. 1Ls, students 0.5Ls.)*

ELSEWHERE IN VECRĪGA. Follow Kaļķu iela from the Freedom Monument and turn right on Šķūņu iela to reach the cobblestone **Dome Square** (Doma laukums), home of the 13th-century **Dome Cathedral** (Doma baznīca), the largest cathedral in the Baltics. *(Open Tu-F 1-5pm, Sa 10am-2pm. 0.50Ls, students 0.10Ls.)* Behind the cathedral is the **Museum of Rīga's History and Navigation** (Rīgas Vēstures un Kugnie-cības Muzejs), Palasta iela 4. Housed in a 13th-century monastery, the permanent collection traces the history of the city. *(Open May-Sept. Su and W-Sa 10am-5pm; Oct.-Apr. 11am-5pm. 1.20Ls, students 0.40Ls. English tours 3/2Ls.)* From the top of the dark 123m spire of **St. Peter's Church** (Sv. Pētera baznīca), you can see the entire city and the Baltic Sea. *(On Skāmu iela, off Kaļķu iela. Open in summer Su and Tu-Sa 10am-6pm; off-season 10am-5pm. Church free. Tower 1.60Ls, students 1Ls.)* The magnificent neoclassical **State Museum of Art** (Valsts mākslas muzejs), Kr. Valdemāra iela 10a, displays 18th- to 20th-century Latvian art and hosts occasional concerts. *(Near the intersection of Elizabetes iela and Kr. Valdemāra iela. Open Apr.-Oct. Su-M, W, and F-Sa 11am-5pm, Th 11am-7pm; Oct.-Apr. Su-M and W-Sa 11am-5pm. 0.50Ls, students 0.40Ls. English tours 5Ls.)* The newer areas of Rīga feature fantastic **Art Nouveau** (*Jugendstil*) architecture. Elaborately adorned buildings dot the city; most are on Alberta iela, and others are on Elizabetes iela and Strēlnieku laukums.

BASTEJKALNS. The ruins of the old city walls lie in Bastejkalns, a central park near the old city moat (Pīlsētas kanāls). Across and around the canal, five red stone slabs stand as memorials to those killed on January 20, 1991, when Soviet special forces stormed the Interior Ministry on Raiņa bul. At the north end of Bastejkalns, on Kr. Valdemāra iela, sits the **National Theatre**, where Latvia first declared its independence on November 18, 1918. *(Open daily 10am-7pm.)*

🎵 🎭 ENTERTAINMENT AND NIGHTLIFE

Rīga offers the best and widest array of music and performance art in the Baltics. Theaters close from mid-June to August, but the Opera House and Dome Cathedral host special summer events. The **Latvian National Opera** performs in the **Opera House**, Aspazijas bul. 3 (☎722 58 03; www.opera.lv), where Richard Wagner once presided as director. The **Latvian Symphony Orchestra** (☎722 48 50) has frequent concerts in the Great and Small Guilds off Filharmonija laukums. Smaller ensembles perform throughout the summer in **Wagner Hall**, Vāgnera iela 4 (☎721 08 17). At the **Dome Cathedral,** popular organ concerts (ērģeļmūzikas koncerts) employ the world's third-largest organ. Buy tickets at *koncertzales kase*, opposite the main entrance at Doma laukums 1 (☎721 32 13), or in Wagner Hall. The **Rīga Ballet** carries on the proud dancing tradition of native star Mikhail Baryshnikov. The **ticket offices** at Teātra 10/12 (☎722 57 47; open daily 10am-7pm) and Amatu iela 6 (☎721 37 98), on the first floor of the Great Guild, serve most local concerts.

The night scene is centered in **Vecrīga;** for a mellow alternative to its many 24hr. casinos and *diskotekas*, relax with locals at a beer garden. ⬛**Skyline Bar,** Elizabetes iela 55, on the 26th floor of the Reval Hotel Latvija, has the best view in the city. (Open Su-Th 3pm-2am, F-Sa 3pm-3am.) The classy **Hamlet Club,** Jāņa Sēta 5, in the heart of Vecrīga, has live jazz most nights from 9:30 or 10pm. (Cover 2.50Ls. Open M-Sa 7pm-2am.) The gay bar and club **XXL,** A Kalniņa iela 4, is off K. Barona iela; buzz to be let in. (www.xxl.lv. Cover Tu-Sa 1-5Ls. Open daily 6pm-6am.)

🞐 DAYTRIPS FROM RĪGA

JŪRMALA. Boardwalks and sun-bleached, powder-fine sand cover the narrow spit of Jūrmala. Visitors, including the Soviet elite, have been drawn to its warm waters since the 19th century. The coastal towns between **Bulduri** and **Dubulti** are popular for sunning and swimming, but Jūrmala's social center is **Majori,** where masses file to the crowded beach or wander along **Jomas iela,** a pedestrian street lined with cafes, restaurants, and shops. The **commuter rail** runs from Rīga to Jūrmala (every 30min. 5am-11:30pm, 0.51Ls). **Public buses** (0.18Ls) and **microbuses** (0.20-0.30Ls) string together Jūrmala's towns. From the train station in Majori, cross the road, walk through the cluster of trees in the small park, and turn right. The **tourist office** is at Jomas iela 42. (☎(877) 642 76; www.jurmala.lv. Open in summer daily 10am-7pm; off season 10am-5pm.) After a long day at the beach, sip a cocktail at **Slavu ❸,** Jomas iela 57; the upstairs lounge becomes a disco after 9pm. (Entrees 2-12.85Ls. Open M-Th 11am-1am, F-Su 11am-2am.)

SIGULDA. Situated in **Gaujas Valley National Park,** Sigulda feels refreshingly distant from hectic Rīga. For English tours of the park, visit the **Gaujas National Park Center,** Baznicas iela 3. (☎(79) 713 45. Open M 9:30am-6pm. Tours 20Ls per group. Call ahead.) The area offers great biking, bobsledding, bungee jumping, horseback riding, and hot-air ballooning, as well as skiing in winter; **Makars Tourism Agency,** Peldu 1, can arrange all kinds of outdoor excursions. (☎(79) 924 49 48; www.makars.lv.) The restored brick fortifications of ⬛**Turaida Castle** (Turaidas Pils), Turaidas iela 10, across the river from Sigulda and 2km down the road, are visible throughout the Gauja valley and from surrounding hilltops. Climb the steep staircase of the main tower for a scenic view of the region. (Tower open daily 8am-9pm.) Take Turaidas iela 10-15min. back down the hill to reach the legendary **caves** of Sigulda. Inscriptions and coats of arms from as early as the 16th century cover the chiseled mouth of **Gutman's Cave** (Gūtmaņa ala). On a ridge to the right of Gaujas iela, on the near side of the gorge, is the **Sigulda Dome** palace, behind which lie the remains of 13th-century **Sigulda Castle** (Siguldas pilsdrupas). The immense ruins form the backdrop for the renowned **Sigulda Opera Festival** in late July.

Trains run from Rīga on the Rīga-Lugaži commuter rail line (1hr., 15-20 per day, 0.80Ls). From the station, walk up Raiņa iela to the center. Continue as it turns into Gaujas iela, which, after the Gaujas Bridge, becomes the steep Turaidas iela and passes Turaida Castle. **Bus #12** runs directly to Turaida Castle (at least 1 per hour, 0.20Ls). The **Sigulda Tourist Information Center,** Pils iela 6, in Hotel Sigulda, gives out free maps and brochures and arranges accommodations. (☎(79) 713 35; www.sigulda.lv. Open May-Oct. daily 10am-7pm; Nov.-Apr. 10am-5pm.) **Hotel Sigulda ❹,** Pils iela 6, in the center of town near the bus station, is an original late 19th-century stone building with a modern addition completed in 2001. (☎(79) 722 63; www.hotelsigulda.lv. Breakfast included. Singles 24Ls; doubles 30Ls.) ⬛**Pilsmuižas Restorāns ❸,** Pils iela 16, inside Sigulda Dome, serves delicious and generous portions. For a great view, ask to go to the roof. (Entrees 3-10Ls. Open daily noon-2am.) For a huge, inexpensive meal, try **Trīs Draugi ❶,** Pils iela 9. (Open M-Sa 8am-10pm, Su 9am-8pm.)

LIECHTENSTEIN

PHONE CODES **Country code: 423. International dialing prefix: 00.**

A tourist brochure for Liechtenstein amusingly mislabeled the already tiny 160 sq. km country as an even tinier 160 sq. m; that's about how much most tourists see of the world's only German-speaking monarchy. Enter Liechtenstein by **bus** from **Sargans** or **Buchs** in Switzerland, or from **Feldkirch**, Austria (20min., 4SFr). A cheap, efficient **Post Bus** system links all 11 villages (short trips 3SFr, long trips 4SFr; students half-price; SwissPass valid). Remember to carry your passport when traveling. The **official language** is German (see p. 1055); the **currency** is the Swiss franc. **Police:** ☎117. **Medical emergencies:** ☎144. **Postal Code:** FL-9490.

SYMBOL	❶	❷	❸	❹	❺
ACCOMMODATIONS	under 16SFr	16-35SFr	36-60SFr	61-120SFr	over 120SFr
FOOD	under 9SFr	9-15SFr	16-24SFr	25-34SFr	over 34SFr

VADUZ AND LOWER LIECHTENSTEIN. As the national capital, Vaduz (pop. 5,000) attracts the most visitors of any village in Lichtenstein. Above town, the 12th-century **Schloß Vaduz** (Vaduz Castle) is home to Hans Adam II, Prince of Liechtenstein. The interior is off-limits to the masses; however, you can hike up to the

castle for a closer look and a phenomenal view of the whole country. The 15min. trail begins down the street from the tourist office, heading away from the post office. Across the street from the tourist office is the **Kunstmuseum Liechtenstein,** Städtle 32. Mainly focusing on modern art, the museum boasts paintings by Dalí, Kandinsky, and Klee, as well as rotating special exhibits and installations. (Open Su, Tu-W and F-Sa 10am-5pm, Th 10am-8pm. 8SFr, students and seniors 5SFr.) Liechtenstein's national **tourist office,** Städtle 37, one block up the hill from the Vaduz Post Bus stop, stamps passports (2SFr), sells **hiking maps** (8-16SFr), and gives hiking advice. (☎232 14 43. Open July-Sept. M-F 8am-5:30pm, Sa-Su 9am-5pm; Oct.-June M-F 8am-noon and 1:30-5:30pm.) Budget lodgings in Vaduz are few and far between, but nearby **Schaan** is more inviting. Liechtenstein's sole **Jugendherberge ❷,** Untere Rüttig. 6, is in Schaan. From Vaduz, take

LIECHTENSTEIN

bus #1 to *Mühleholz*, walk toward the intersection with traffic lights, and turn left down Marianumstr. Walk 5min. and follow the signs to this spotless pink hostel on the edge of a farm. (☎232 50 22. Breakfast included. Reception daily 5-10pm. Check-out 10am. Open Feb.-Oct. Dorms 30SFr; doubles 40SFr.) Your best bet for a cheap meal is **Migros supermarket,** Aulestr. 20, across from the tour bus parking lot in Vaduz. (Open M-F 8am-1pm and 1:30-7pm, Sa 8am-6pm.)

UPPER LIECHTENSTEIN. Just when it seems that the roads cannot possibly become any narrower or steeper, they do—welcome to Upper Liechtenstein. These heights are where the real character and beauty of Liechtenstein lie. Even if you're in the country for one day, take the short bus trip to **Triesenberg** or **Malbun** (30min. from Vaduz) for spectacular views of the Rhine Valley below. **Triesenberg** (take bus #10), the principal town, is spanned by a series of switchbacks and foothills 800m above the Rhine. The **tourist office** (☎262 19 26) shares a building with the **Walser Heimatmuseum,** which chronicles the history of the region. (Both open June-Aug. Su 2-5pm, Tu-F 1:30-5:30pm, Sa 1:30-5pm; Sept.-May Tu-F 1:30-5:30pm, Sa 1:30-5pm. Museum 2SFr.) For great hiking, take bus #34 to *Gaflei* (20min., every hr). **Malbun** sits in an alpine valley in the southeastern corner of Liechtenstein. It is undoubtedly the hippest place in the principality, home to approachable people, plenty of hiking, and affordable ski slopes (day-pass 33SFr). Contact the **tourist office** for more info. (☎263 65 77. Open June-Oct. and mid-Dec. to mid-Apr. M-Sa 9am-noon and 1:30-5pm.) The best place to stay for hiking and skiing access is **Hotel Alpen ❸,** which is close to the bus stop and tourist office. (☎263 11 81. Reception daily 8am-10pm. Open mid-May to Oct. and mid-Dec. to Apr. In summer 45-65SFr per person; in winter add 10SFr.)

LITHUANIA (LIETUVA)

Once part of the largest country in Europe, stretching into modern-day Ukraine, Belarus, and Poland, Lithuania shrank significantly in the face of oppression from tsarist Russia, Nazi Germany, and the Soviet Union. The first Baltic nation to declare its independence from the USSR in 1990, Lithuania has become more Western with every passing year and now stands on the verge of joining the European Union. The spectacular capital city of Vilnius welcomes hordes of tourists into the largest Old Town in Europe, recently covered in a bright new coat of paint. In the other corner of the country, the mighty Baltic Sea washes up against Palanga and the towering dunes of the Curonian Spit.

FACTS AND FIGURES

Official Name: Republic of Lithuania.
Capital: Vilnius.
Major Cities: Klaipėda, Šiauliai.
Population: 3,600,000.

Land Area: 65,200 sq. km.
Time Zone: GMT +2.
Language: Lithuanian, Polish, Russian.
Religions: Roman Catholic (80%).

ESSENTIALS

DOCUMENTS AND FORMALITIES

VISAS. Citizens of South Africa and the US do not need a visa for visits up to 30 days; Australia, Canada, Ireland, and New Zealand 90 days; and UK up to 180 days. Citizens of South Africa who have visas from Estonia or Latvia can use those to enter Lithuania, otherwise, 90-day visas are required. Obtain visas from embassies or consulates: Single-entry visas cost US$10 (valid for 90 days); multiple-entry visas US$20 (valid for 90 days); 49hr. transit visas US$5. Visas are not available at the border. **Visa extensions** are granted in Lithuania by the Migration Services.

EMBASSIES. Foreign embassies are in Vilnius (p. 708). Embassies at home include: **Australia,** 40B Fiddens Wharf Rd., Killara 2071, NSW (☎02 9498 2571); **Canada,** 130 Albert St. Ste. 204, Ottawa, ON K1P 5G4 (☎613-567-5458; www.lithuanianembassy.ca); **New Zealand,** 28 Heather St., Parnell, Auckland (☎09 379 6639; fax 307 2911); **UK,** 84 Gloucester Pl., London W1U 6AU (☎020 7486 6401; fax 7486 6403); **US,** 2622 16th St. NW, Washington, D.C. 20009 (☎202-234-5860; www.ltembassyus.org).

TRANSPORTATION

Finnair, LOT, Lufthansa, SAS, and other, smaller, airlines fly into Vilnius. **Trains** are more popular for long-distance travel. Two major lines cross Lithuania: One runs north-south from Latvia through Šiauliai and Kaunas to Poland; the other runs east-west from Belarus through Vilnius and Kaunas to Kaliningrad. Domestic **buses** are faster, more common, and only a little more expensive than the often-crowded trains. Whenever possible, try to catch an express bus to your destination. They are typically direct and can be up to twice as fast. Vilnius, Kaunas, and Klaipėda are easily reached by train or bus from Belarus, Estonia, Latvia, Poland, and Russia. **Ferries** connect Klaipėda with Århus, Denmark and Kiel, Germany.

Lithuania

Baltic Sea

LATVIA

KALININGRAD REGION (RUSSIA)

Curonian Split

Curonian Lagoon

POLAND

BELARUS

Europas Centras (Geographical Center of Europe)

0   40 miles
0   40 kilometers

TOURIST SERVICES AND MONEY

Litinterp is generally the most helpful organization for travel info; they reserve accommodations, usually without a surcharge. Vilnius, Kaunas, Nida, Palanga, and Klaipėda each have an edition of the *In Your Pocket* series, available at news-stands and some hotels. The unit of currency is the **Lita** (1Lt=100 *centas*), plural *Litai*. In February 2002 the *Lita* was fixed to the euro at €1 to 3.4528Lt. Prices are stable, with inflation hovering at just under 1%. Except in Vilnius, exchange bureaus near the train station usually have worse rates than banks; it's often diffi-cult to exchange currencies other than US dollars and euros. Most banks cash **trav-eler's checks** for a 2-3% commission. **Vilniaus Bankas,** with outlets in major cities, accepts major credit cards and traveler's checks for a small commission. Be aware that most places don't take credit cards. **ATMs** are readily available in most cities.

PHONE CODES   **Country code: 370. International dialing prefix: 810.** From outside Lithuania, dial int'l dialing prefix (see inside back cover) + 370 + city code + local number.

LITAI		
AUS$1 = 2.03LT		1LT = AUS$0.49
CDN$1 = 2.27LT		1LT = CDN$0.44
EUR€1 = 3.45LT		1LT = EUR€0.29
NZ$1 = 1.82LT		1LT = NZ$0.55
UK£1 = 4.96LT		1LT = UK£0.20
US$1 = 3.14LT		1LT = US$0.32
ZAR1 = 0.43LT		1LT = ZAR2.33

COMMUNICATION

MAIL AND TELEPHONES. Airmail (*oro pastu*) letters abroad cost 1.70Lt (postcards 1.20Lt) and usually take about one week to reach the US. For *Poste Restante*, address mail to be held: Firstname SURNAME, Centrinis Paštas, Gedimino pr. 7, Vilnius LT-2000, LITHUANIA. There are two kinds of **public phones:** Rectangular ones accept magnetic strip cards and rounded ones accept chip cards. Both are sold at phone offices and kiosks in denominations of 3.54, 7.08, and 28.32Lt. Calls to Europe cost 5.80Lt and to the US 7.32Lt. Most countries can be dialed directly. Dial 8, wait for the second tone, dial 10, then enter the country code and number. International direct dialing numbers include: **AT&T, ☎**8 80 09 28 00; **British Telecom, ☎**8 80 09 00 44; and **Canada Direct, ☎**8 80 09 10 04.

ACCOMMODATIONS AND FOOD

LITHUANIA	❶	❷	❸	❹	❺
ACCOMMODATIONS	under 30Lt	30-80Lt	81-130Lt	131-180Lt	over 180Lt
FOOD	under 11Lt	11-20Lt	21-30Lt	31-40Lt	over 40Lt

Lithuania has several **youth hostels.** HI membership is nominally required, but an LJNN guest card (10.50Lt at any of the hostels) will suffice. The head office is in Vilnius. Their *Hostel Guide* is a handy booklet with info on bike and car rentals, hotel reservations, and maps. **Litinterp,** with offices in Vilnius, Kaunas, and Klaipėda, assists in finding homestays or apartments for rent. **Camping** is gaining popularity, but is vigorously restricted by law to marked campgrounds. Lithuanian cuisine is heavy and sometimes greasy. Keeping a vegetarian or kosher diet will prove difficult, if not impossible. Restaurants serve various types of *blynai* (pancakes) with *mėsa* (meat) or *varškė* (cheese). Good Lithuanian beer flows freely; *Kalnapis* is common. Lithuanian vodka (*degtinė*) is also very popular.

SAFETY AND SECURITY

Lithuania's **crime rate** is generally lower than most of Europe. Vilnius is one of the safer capitals in Europe, although street crime does occur on occasion. Lithuanian police are generally helpful but understaffed, so your best bet for English-speaking assistance is still your **consulate.** Pharmacies are everywhere and carry most medical supplies and German or French brands of tampons, condoms, and toiletries. Drink bottled mineral water, and **boil tap water** for 10 minutes before drinking. A triangle pointing downward indicates men's **bathrooms;** an upward triangle indicates women's bathrooms. Many restrooms are nothing but a hole in the ground.

HOLIDAYS

Holidays: New Year's Day (Jan. 1); Independence Day (Feb. 16); Restoration of Independence (Mar. 11); Easter (Apr. 11-12); May Day (May 1); Day of Statehood (July 6); Feast of the Assumption (Aug. 15); All Saints' Day (Nov. 1); Christmas (Dec. 25-26).

VILNIUS ☎5

Encouraging new businesses and foreign investment, Vilnius (pop. 579,000) was the leading force in Lithuania's recent ascension to the EU. Founded in 1321 after a prophetic dream by Grand Duke Gediminas, Vilnius grew and flourished throughout the centuries despite numerous foreign occupations. Scarred but not destroyed by WWII, the Holocaust, and the iron grip of the Soviet Union, Vilnius today remains a rich cultural and commercial center.

▐ TRANSPORTATION

Flights: Vilnius Airport (VNO; *Vilniaus oro uostas*), Rodūnės Kelias 2 (info ☎2 30 66 66, booking ☎2 75 26 00), is 5km south of the city. Take bus #1 or 2 to the Old Town.

Trains: Geležinkelio Stotis, Geležinkelio 16 (☎2 33 00 86; www.litrail.lt). Domestic tickets are sold to the left of the entrance, and international tickets (reservations for Western Europe ☎2 69 37 22) to the right. Open daily 6-11am and noon-6pm. All international trains (except those heading north) pass through Belarus, requiring a Belarussian visa (p. 108). To: **Berlin** (22hr., daily, 317Lt); **Minsk** (5½hr., 2 per day, 57Lt); **Moscow** (17hr., 3 per day, 128Lt); **Rīga** (7½hr., daily, 72Lt); **St. Petersburg** (18hr., 3 per day, 110Lt); **Warsaw** (8hr., 2 per day, 115Lt).

Buses: Autobusų Stotis, Sodų 22 (☎290 16 61; reservations ☎216 29 77), opposite the train station. **Eurolines** (☎269 00 00; www.eurolines.com) and **Varta Buses** (☎273 02 19; www.5ci.net/varta) serve Western Europe. Windows #13-15 serve destinations outside the former Soviet Union. Open daily 7am-8pm. To: **Kaliningrad** (8hr., 2 per day, 38Lt); **Minsk** (5hr., 8 and 9am, 22Lt); **Rīga** (6hr., 5 per day, 30-40Lt); **Tallinn** (11hr., 6am and 8:45pm, 90Lt); **Warsaw** (8hr., 9am and 9:30pm, 80Lt).

Public Transportation: Buses and **trolleys** run daily 6am-midnight. Buy tickets at any kiosk (0.80Lt) or from the driver (1Lt). Tickets are checked frequently; always punch them on board to avoid the hefty fine. Monthly passes available for students (5Lt).

Taxis: Vilnius' cheapest companies are **Fiakvas** (☎70 57 05) and **Kortesa** (☎73 73 73). About 1.65Lt per km; negotiate price with driver in advance.

▐▐ ORIENTATION AND PRACTICAL INFORMATION

The **train** and **bus stations** are across from each other. **Geležinkelio** runs right from the train station to **Aušros Vartų,** which leads downhill through the **Aušros Vartai** (Gates of Dawn) and into the **Senamiestis** (Old Town). Aušros Vartų becomes Didžioji and then Pilies before reaching the base of Gediminas Hill. Here, the **Gediminas Tower** of the Higer Castle presides over **Arkikatedros Aikštė** (Cathedral Square) and the banks of the river Neris. **Gedimino,** the commercial artery, leads west from the square in front of the cathedral.

Tourist Offices: Tourist Information Center, Didžioji 31 (☎/fax 262 07 62; www.vilnius.lt), in the Town Hall, provides info about travel and events and sells *Vilnius in Your Pocket* (8Lt). Open in summer M-F 9am-7pm; off-season M-F 10am-6pm. **Branch,** Vilniaus 22 (☎262 96 60). Open M-F 9am-noon and 12:45-7pm.

LITHUANIA

TO KGB PRISON/ MUSEUM OF THE
GENOCIDE VICTIMS (400m),
PARLIAMENT & *Canada* (1km)

Kalnų park

TO ❶

K. Širvydo

Tilto

T. Vrublevskio

Lithuanian
National
Museum

Gediminas Tower

Gedimino pr.

Lietuvos Nacionalinis
Dramos Teatras

Arkikatedra
Bazilika

Clock Tower

CATHEDRAL
SQUARE

Restoration of
the Royal Palace

Gedimino
Castle
Hill

St. Michael's
Church

Totorių

Vilniaus

Jogailos

Australia

Supermarket

Labdarių

Odminių

Gediminas
Statue

Šventaragio

TAXI

B. Radvilaitės

TO ❷

Islandijos

Gaon Museum

i

L. Stuokos-Gucevičiaus

Skapo

DAUKANTO
SQUARE

VILNIUS
UNIVERSITY

Adam Micklewicz
Memorial
Apartment

❸

St. Anne's & Benedictine Monstery
(Šv. Onos ir Bernadinų baznycia)

Sereikiškės
park

Bernardinų

Pilies

Maironio

Palangos

Liejyklos

Benediktinų

President's
Palace

St. John's
(Šv. Jono)

Šv. Mykolo

St. Michael's
(Šv. Mykolo)
and
Architecture
Museum

TO BUST OF FRANK
ZAPPA (50m),
US (400m)

Šv. Ignoto

Totorių

Universiteto

Šv. Jono

Literatų

Rusų

Klaipėdos

St. Catherine's

i

Vilniaus

Dominikonų

Stiklių

Gaono

Švarco

France

Latako

Vilnia R.

Lithuanian Theatre
Music and Cinema
Museum

❺

AmEx

Žydų

Didžioji

Vilnius
Picture
Gallery

Bokšto

Užupio

Traku

Prancikonų

Šv. Mikalojaus

❻

Vokiečių

TAXI

Savičiaus

Maironio

Aukštaičių

Maironio

Lydos

Žemaitijos

Ašmenos

Town Hall &
Lithuania Artists' Center

i

St. Casimir's Church
(Šv. Kazimiero baznycia)

Kudrų

Bokšto

Naugarduko

Kėdainių

Šiaulių

Mėsinių

Rūdninkų

Didžioji

Šv. Kazimiero

Artillery
Bastion
(Basteja)

Ligoninės

Etmonų

Subačiaus

N
LG

Karmelitų

Visų

Arklių

Pasažo

National
Philharmonic

Church of the
Holy Spirit

A. Strazdelio

Šv. Dvasios

M. Daukšos

Pylimo

Šv. Stepono

Gėlių

TAXI

Šventųjų

St. Theresa's
(Šv. Teresės)

Aušros Vartų

Gates of Dawn
(Aušros Vartai)

K. Vanagėlio

Bazilijonų

Vilnius

🏠 ACCOMMODATIONS
Litinterp, **3**
Mikotel, **8**
Old Town Hostel (HI), **9**

🍎 FOOD
Finjan, **6**
Ritos Smuklė, **1**

☕ CAFÉS
Skonis Ir Kvapas, **5**

⭐ NIGHTLIFE
Club Gravity, **2**
Gero Viskio Baras, **4**
SoHo, **7**

TO PANERIAI
MEMORIAL
(15km)

Sodų

F. Šopeno

Geležinkelio

❾

❽

0   150 yards
0   150 meters

TO
(5km)

Budget Travel: Lithuanian Student and Youth Travel, V. Basanavičiaus 30, #13 (☎222 13 73). Great deals for travelers under 27. Open M-F 8:30am-6pm, Sa 10am-2pm.

Embassies: Australia, Vilniaus 23 (☎/fax 212 33 69; aust.con.vilnius@post.omnitel.net). Open M, W, F 11am-2pm. **Canada,** Gedimino pr. 64 (☎49 68 53; vilnius@canada.lt). Open M, W, F 9am-noon. **Russia,** Latvių 53/54 (☎72 17 63; visas ☎72 38 93; rusemb@rusemb.lt). Open M-F 8am-noon. **UK,** Antakalnio 2 (☎12 20 70; www.britain.lt). Open M-F 8:30-11:30am. **US,** Akmenų 6 (☎66 55 00; www.usembassy.lt). Open M-Th 8:30-11:30am.

Currency Exchange: Pabex Bankas, Geležinkelio 6, left of the train station. Open 24hr. **Vilniaus Bankas,** Vokiečių 9, cashes traveler's checks. Open M-F 8am-6pm.

24hr. Pharmacy: Gedimino Vaistinė, Gedimino pr. 27 (☎61 01 35).

Medical Assistance: Baltic-American Medical & Surgical Clinic, Antakalnio 124 (☎234 20 20; www.baclinic.com), at Vilnius University Hospital. Open 24hr.

Internet Access: V002, Ašmenos 8 (☎279 18 66). 8Lt per hr. Open 24hr. **Klubas Lux,** Svitrigailos 5 (☎233 37 88). 8am-6pm 3Lt per hr., 6pm-8am 10Lt per hr. Open 24hr.

Post Office: Centrinis Paštas, Gedimino 7 (☎262 54 68; www.post.lt), west of Arkikatedros aikštė. *Poste Restante* at the window "iki pareikalavimo." Address mail to be held: Firstname SURNAME, Centrinis Paštas, Gedimino pr. 7, Vilnius **LT-2000,** LITHUANIA. 0.50Lt to pick up mail. Open M-F 7am-7pm, Sa 9am-4pm.

▐ ACCOMMODATIONS

▓ **Litinterp,** Bernardinų 7/2 (☎12 38 50; www.litinterp.lt). Spacious rooms with clean shared baths. Breakfast included. Reception M-F 8:30am-5:30pm, Sa 9am-2pm. Call ahead. Singles 80-120Lt; doubles 140-160Lt. 5% ISIC discount. MC/V. ❸

Mikotel, Pylimo 63 (☎60 96 26; www.travel.lt/mikotel). From the train station, go right and then take a left onto Pylimo. Private, cheerful rooms with shower. Friendly staff. Kitchen available. Singles 180Lt; doubles 240Lt. MC/V. ❺

Old Town Hostel (HI), Aušros vartų 20-15a (☎62 53 57), 100m south of the Gates of Dawn. A good place to meet fellow travelers. Free Internet access. Reservations recommended. Dorms 32Lt, nonmembers 34Lt; apartments for around 60Lt. MC/V. ❷

▐ FOOD

IKI supermarkets, which stock foreign brands, are all over Vilnius. The IKI at the bus station is the closest branch to the Old Town. (Open daily 8am-10pm.) Locals and students linger at **Finjan ❸,** Vokiečių 18, sampling a mix of Lebanese, Israeli, and Egyptian cuisine. (Entrees 24-45Lt. Belly dancer Th-Sa nights. Open daily 11am-midnight.) Take tram #12, 13, or 17 to **Ritos Smuklė** (Rita's Tavern), Žirmūnų 68, a well-known traditional Lithuanian tavern with live folk music Wednesday-Saturday 8pm-10pm. (Entrees 15-30Lt. Open daily 10am-midnight.) The cafe **Skonis Ir Kvapas ❶,** Trakų 8, has exotic teas (2.50-10Lt) and serves breakfast, dessert, and light meals all day. (Open M-F 8:30am-11pm, Sa-Su 9:30am-11pm.)

◉ SIGHTS

SENAMIESTIS. The 16th-century **Aušros Vartai** (Gates of Dawn) guard the Senamiestis (Old Town). After the gates, enter the first door on the right to ascend to the 17th-century **chapel** (Koplyčia), packed with locals praying to the gilded Virgin Mary icon. Around the corner is **St. Theresa's Church** (Šv. Teresės bažnyčia), known for its Baroque sculptures, multicolored arches, and frescoed ceiling. A few steps farther down, a gateway leads to the bright 17th-century **Church of the Holy Spirit** (Šv. Dvasios bažnyčia), the seat of Lithuania's Russian Orthodox Archbishop. The street merges with the pedestrian Pilies and leads to the main entrance of **Vilnius University** (Vilniaus Universitetas), at Pilies and Šv. Jono. Founded in 1570, the university is the oldest in Eastern Europe. Further north on Pilies is **Arkikatedros aikštė** (Cathedral Square); its **cathedral** contains the ornate **Chapel of St. Casimir** (Šv. Kazimiero koplyčia), the royal mausoleum. From behind the cathedral, walk up the Castle Hill path to **Gedimino Tower** for a great view of Vilnius' spires. Off Pylimo, between Kalinausko 1 and 3, is the continent's most random monument: A 4-meter steel shaft topped with a bust of the late freak-rock legend **Frank Zappa**.

THE OLD JEWISH QUARTER AND GENOCIDE MEMORIAL. Vilnius was once a center of Jewish life comparable to Warsaw and New York, with a Jewish population of 100,000 (in a city of 230,000) at the start of WWII. Nazi persecution left only 6,000 survivors and only one of pre-war Vilnius's 105 **synagogues**, at Pylimo 39. The **Genocide Memorial**, Agrastų 15, is in **Paneriai**, 10min. away by train (0.90Lt). Head right from the train station and follow Agrastų to the memorial. Between 1941 and 1944, 100,000 people, including 70,000 Jews, were shot, burned, and buried here. The memorials, at pits that served as mass graves, are connected by paved paths. Return by bus #8, on the other side of the tracks. *(Open M and W-Sa 11am-6pm. Free.)* The **Holocaust Museum**, locally called "The Green House," tracks the destruction of Vilnius's Jewish community. *(Pamėnkalnio 12. Open M-Th 9am-5pm, F 9am-4pm. Donations requested.)* For info on the Jewish Quarter or on locating ancestors, visit the **Jewish Cultural Centre.** *(Šaltinių 12. ☎241 88 09. Open daily 9am-6pm.)*

MUSEUM OF GENOCIDE VICTIMS. Once a royal court for Tsar Nicholas II, this building was used as a Gestapo headquarters during WWII and later became home to the KGB in Vilnius. The isolation cells, torture chambers, and execution room are disturbing, but the exhibition is eloquent and informative. *(Aukų 2a, at the intersection with Gedimino. Open May 15-Sept. 15 Su and Tu-Sa 10am-6pm; Sept. 16-May 14 Su and Tu-Sa 10am-4pm. 2Lt.)*

🎵🎭 ENTERTAINMENT AND NIGHTLIFE

Summer is full of festivals, including the National Philharmonic's **Vilniaus Festivalis** that starts in late May (www.filharmonija.lt/vilniausfestivalis); check *Vilnius in Your Pocket* or the Lithuanian morning paper *Lietuvos Rytas* for more info on performances. Vilnius has a vibrant nightlife, whether you prefer a mellow pub or a raging dance floor. For info on gay nightlife, check the **Lithuanian Gay and Lesbian Homepage** (www.gayline.lt). 🏳️‍🌈**Club Gravity**, Jasinkio 16, is an ultra-modern techno club. (Cover 25Lt. Open Th-Sa 10pm-6am.) **Broadway,** Mėsinių 4, is a popular bar with the hottest dance floor in the Old Town. (Open M noon-3am, Tu noon-4am, W-Sa noon-5am.) In the center of town, **Gero Viskio Baras,** Pilies 34, is a three-floor bar. (Basement cover men 5Lt, women free. Open Su-Th 10am-3am, F-Sa 10am-5am.) **SoHo,** Aušros Vartų 7, is a new bar with a music-filled courtyard. (Live music most F-Sa nights. Open Su-Th 10am-2am, F-Sa 10am-3am. MC/V.)

🗺️ DAYTRIPS FROM VILNIUS

TRAKAI CASTLE. Trakai Castle has inspired legends since its construction in the 15th century. In 1665, the Russians accomplished what 15th-century Germans could not—plundering the town and razing the castle. Perhaps out of a sense of guilt, the Soviets began restoring the castle in 1955, and now the red-brick structure towers over beautiful lakes and woods. Climb the spiral staircase in the watchtower to the third floor for a magnificent view of the medieval courtyard below. Across from the tower, the **City and Castle History Museum** chronicles the history of Trakai and Lithuania. (Museum open daily 10am-7pm. 8Lt, students 4Lt. Tours 40/20Lt.) The castle also forms a dramatic backdrop for a summer concert series (www.trakaifestival.lt). Paddle boats and waterbikes are available for rent by the footbridge to the castle. Trakai, 28km west of Vilnius, is accessible by **bus.** (30min.; every hr. 6:45am-9:30pm; 2.90Lt, buy tickets on board.) The last bus back usually departs by 9pm.

KAUNAS. Kaunas (pop. 378, 900), easily accessible from Vilnius, is considered the cradle of Lithuanian culture. At the end of **Laisvės,** the main pedestrian boulevard, is the sumptuous, domed **St. Michael the Archangel Church.** (Open M-F 9am-3pm, Sa-Su 8:30am-2pm. Free.) Nearby is the **Museum of Exiles and Political Prisoners** (Tremties ir Rezistencijos Muziejus), Vytauto 46. The curator was once an exile herself; find someone to translate her tours. (Open W-Sa 10am-4pm. Donation requested.) Also at this end of Laisvės is the **Devil Museum** (Velnių Muziejus), V. Putvinskio 64, which displays more than 2000 depictions of devils in various media. (Open Su and Tu-Sa 10am-5pm. Closed last Tu of the month. 5Lt, students 2.50Lt.) Take microbus #46 across the Neris River to IX Fortas (2-5 per hr. 6am-9pm) to reach the **Ninth Fort,** which was used as a Nazi death camp; 64 men escaped on Christmas Day, 1943, but most were later caught. (Open Su-M and W-Sa 10am-6pm. Museum 2Lt, students 1Lt.) To reach Kaunas from Vilnius, take a **train** (2hr., 11 per day, 9.80Lt) or **bus** (1½hr., every 30min., 12Lt). The **Tourist Information Center** is at Laisvės 36. (☎32 34 36; visit.kaunas.lt. Open M-F 9am-6pm, Sa-Su 9am-12:15pm and 1-6pm.) ▨**Litinterp ❸,** Gedimino 28, arranges private rooms. (☎/fax 22 87 18; www.litinterp.lt. Reserve ahead. Open M-F 8:30am-5:30pm, Sa 9:30am-3pm. Singles 80-120Lt; doubles 140-160Lt.) **Žalias Ratas ❷,** Laisvės 36b, is an excellent traditional tavern. (Entrees 5-28Lt. Open daily 11am-midnight. MC/V.)

KLAIPĖDA ☎846

Guarding the Curonian Spit is Klaipėda (pop. 194,000), Lithuania's third-largest city. Strategically located on the tip of the Neringa peninsula, it was briefly the Prussian capital in the 19th century, and was later handed to France in the 1919 Treaty of Versailles. In WWII, the city served as a German U-boat base before being industrialized by the Soviets after the war. On mainland Klaipėda, the **Clock Museum** (Laikrodžių Muziejus), Liepų 12, displays every conceivable kind of time-keeping device. From S. Daukanto, turn right on H. Manto and left on Liepų (Open Su and Tu-Sa noon-6pm. 4Lt, students 2Lt. English tour 40Lt.) **Klaipėda Drama Theater** (Klaipėdos Dramos Teatras), Teatro aikštė, on the other side of H. Manto, was one of Wagner's favorite haunts. (Tickets ☎31 44 53. Open Su and Tu-Sa 11am-2pm and 4-7pm.) The main attraction in **Smiltynė,** across the lagoon, is the ▨**Maritime Museum, Aquarium, and Dolphinarium** (Lietuvos Jūrų Muziejus), Smiltynė 3, in an 1860s fortress. (www.juru.muziejus.lt. Open June-Aug. Su and Tu-Sa 10:30am-5pm; off-season 10:30am-3:30pm. 8Lt, students 4Lt.) Forest paths lead west 500m to the **beaches.** The best bars line H. Manto. **Kurpiai,** an excellent jazz club, is at Kurpių 1a. (Live jazz 9:30pm. Cover F-Sa 5-10Lt. Open daily noon-3am.) **Memelis,** Žvejv 4, on the river across the street from the ferry port, is part brewery, part dance club, part bar. (Open M 11am-midnight, Tu-W 11am-2am, Th 11am-3am, F-Sa 11am-4am, Su noon-midnight.)

Buses (☎41 15 47; reservations ☎41 15 40) go from Butkų Juzės 9 to: Kaunas (3hr., 14 per day, 28Lt); Palanga (30-40min., 23 per day, 2.50-3Lt); and Vilnius (4-5hr., 10-14 per day, 41Lt). **Ferries** (☎31 42 17; info ☎31 11 57) run from Old Castle Port, Žveju 8, to Smiltynė (10min., every 30min., free) and connect with microbuses to Nida (1hr., 7Lt). The staff at the **tourist office,** Turgaus 5-7, has free maps and arranges tours. (☎41 21 86; www.klaipeda.lt. Open M-F 8:30am-6:30pm, Sa 9am-3:30pm, Su 10am-2pm.) **Litinterp ❸**, S. Šimkaus 2¼, arranges rooms. (☎31 14 90. Singles 90-120Lt; doubles 140-180. Off-season 20-40Lt less. Open M-F 8:30am-5:30pm, Sa 9:30am-3:30pm.) ▨**Klaipėda Traveller's Guesthouse (HI) ❷**, Butkų Juzės 7-4, 50m from the bus station, has spacious dorms, hot showers, and a friendly staff. (☎21 18 79; oldtown@takas.lt. Dorms 32Lt. Nonmembers add 2Lt.) Heading away from the Danė River on Tiltų, make a left on Kulių Vartų, then turn left onto Bangu to reach **Aribė Hotel ❹**, Bangų 17a, a modern hotel with private bathrooms. (☎49 09 40; vitetur@klaipeda.omnitel.net. Singles 140Lt; doubles 180Lt; luxury suite 260Lt. Off-season 20Lt less.) **PEDA ❷**, Targaus 10, a cafe-cum-gallery encourages you to sip coffee (2Lt) or enjoy a wide range of entrees (10-16Lt) while admiring the works of Lithuanian metal sculptor Vytautas Karčiauskas. (☎41 07 10. Open M-Sa 10am-midnight.) **IKI supermarket** is at M. Mažvyado 7/11. (Open daily 8am-10pm.) **Postal Code:** LT-5800.

▸▸ **DAYTRIPS FROM KLAIPĖDA: NIDA AND PALANGA.** Windswept white sand dunes have long drawn summer vacationers to **Nida,** only 3km north of the Kaliningrad region on the Curonian Spit. From the remains of the town's immense sundial on the highest of the ▨**Drifting Dunes of Parnidis,** you can look down on the Curonian Lagoon and the Baltic. Take a walk along the beach or through the forest paths to see surreal mountains and sheets of white sand from the dunes blowing gracefully into the sea. From the center of town, follow the promenade by the water and bear right on Skruzdynės to reach the **Thomas Mann House** (Thomo Manno Namelis) at #17. Mann built the cottage in 1930 and wrote *Joseph and His Brothers* here, but had to abandon it when Hitler invaded. (Open June-Aug. Su and Tu-Sa 10am-6pm; Sept.-May Tu-Sa 11am-5pm. 2Lt, students 0.50Lt.) From Naglių 18e, **microbuses** (☎(8469) 524 72) run to Smiltynė (1hr., every 30-60min., 7Lt). The **Tourist Info Center,** Taikos 4, opposite the bus station, arranges private rooms for a 5Lt fee and offers free **Internet** access. (☎(8469)523 45. Open June 1-Sept. 1, M-F 10am-8pm, Sa 10am-6pm, Su 10am-3pm. Off-season open M-F 9am-1pm and 2-6pm, Sa-Su 10am-3pm.)

The largest park in the country, over 20km of shoreline, and an exuberant nightlife make **Palanga** (pop. 18,000) the hottest summer spot in Lithuania. While the beach is the main attraction, Palanga's pride and joy is the **Amber Museum** (Gintaro muziejus) in a mansion in the Botanical Gardens. The collection consists of 15,000 pieces of amber that have primeval flora and fauna trapped inside. (Open June-Aug. Su 10am-7pm, Tu-Sa 10am-8pm; Sept.-May daily 11am-4:30pm. 5Lt, students 2.50Lt.) Palanga's main streets are **Vytauto,** which runs parallel to the beach and passes the bus station, and **J. Basanavičiaus,** which runs perpendicular to Vytauto, ending at the boardwalk. Pedestrian **Meilės alėja** runs south of the pier along the beach, becoming **Birutės alėja** in the Palanga Park and Botanical Garden. Vytauto and J. Basanavičiaus g. are lined with cafes and restaurants that have outdoor seating. **Buses** (☎(8460) 533 33) from Klaipėda (30min., every 30min., 2.50Lt) arrive at Kretinjos 1. Info is available in a **tourist office** (☎(8460) 488 11; palangaturinfo@is.lt) to the right of the station; they also book private rooms by email.

LITHUANIA

LUXEMBOURG

Too often overlooked by budget travelers, the tiny Grand Duchy of Luxembourg boasts impressive fortresses and castles as well as beautiful hiking trails. Established in 963, the original territory was called *Lucilinburhuc*, named for the "little fortresses" that saturated the countryside after successive waves of Burgundians, Spaniards, French, Austrians, and Germans had receded. Today, Luxembourg has become a notable European Union member and a prominent international financial center. Judging by their national motto, *"Mir welle bleiwe wat mir sinn"* ("We want to remain what we are"), it seems that the Luxembourgians are pleased with their accomplishments.

FACTS AND FIGURES

Official Name: Grand Duchy of Luxembourg.
Capital: Luxembourg City.
Population: 430,000.
Land Area: 2,600 sq. km.

Time Zone: GMT +1.
Languages: French, German, Luxembourgian.
Religions: Roman Catholic (90%).

DISCOVER LUXEMBOURG

Luxembourg City (p. 715) is one of Europe's most romantic capitals. Your next stop should be **Vianden** (p. 719), whose gorgeous chateau and outdoor opportunities make it well worth an overnight stay. If you have time to linger, head out into the Ardennes to hike and bike around **Diekirch** (p. 719).

ESSENTIALS

WHEN TO GO

Anytime between May and mid-Oct. is a good time to visit. Luxembourg has a temperate climate with less rain than Belgium. Temperatures average 17°C (64°F) in summer, and 0°C (32°F) in winter.

DOCUMENTS AND FORMALITIES

VISAS. EU citizens do not need a visa. Citizens of Australia, Canada, New Zealand, and the US do not need a visa for stays of up to 30 days. South Africans need a visa for stays of any length. Contact your embassy for more info.

EMBASSIES AND CONSULATES. All foreign embassies are in Luxembourg City (p. 716). Embassies and consulates in other countries include: **Australia,** Level 18, Royal Exchange Bldg., 56 Pitt St., Sydney NSW 2000 (☎(02) 92 41 43 22; fax 92 51 11 13). **Canada,** 3706 St. Hubert St., Montréal, PQ H2L 4A3 (☎514-849-2101). **South Africa,** P.O. Box 357, Lanseria 1748 (☎(011) 659 09 61). **UK,** 27 Wilton Crescent, London SW1X 8SD (☎(020) 7235 6961; fax 7235 9734). **US,** 2200 Massachusetts Ave. NW, Washington, D.C. 20008 (☎202-265-4171; fax 328-8270).

TRANSPORTATION

BY PLANE. The Luxembourg City airport (LUX) is serviced by **Luxair** (☎479 81, reservations ☎4798 42 42) and by flights from the UK and throughout the continent. Cheap last-minute flights on Luxair are available at www.luxair.lu.

BY TRAIN AND BUS. A **Benelux Tourrail Pass** allows five days of unlimited **train** travel in a one-month period in Belgium, The Netherlands, and Luxembourg (p. 54). The **Billet Réseau** (€4.50, book of 5 €17.50), a network ticket, is good for one day of unlimited bus and train travel. Even better is the **Luxembourg Card** (p. 718), which includes unlimited transportation. International train routes to Luxembourg include: Brussels (1¾hr.; p. 116) and Liège (2½hr.) in Belgium; Koblenz (2¼hr.; p. 468) and Trier (45min.; p. 469) in Germany; and Metz in France (45min.).

BY BIKE AND THUMB. Hiking and **biking trails** run between Luxembourg City and Echternach, from Diekirch to Echternach and Vianden, and elsewhere. Bikes aren't permitted on buses, but are allowed on many trains for free. *Let's Go* does not recommend **hitchhiking** as a safe means of transport.

TOURIST SERVICES AND MONEY

EMERGENCY	Police: ☎112. Ambulance: ☎112. Fire: ☎112.

TOURIST OFFICES. For general info, contact the **Luxembourg National Tourist Office,** P.O. Box 1001, L-1010 Luxembourg (☎(352) 42 82 82 10; www.etat.lu/tourism). The **Luxembourg Card,** available from Easter to October at tourist offices, hostels, and many hotels and public transportation offices, provides unlimited transportation on national trains and buses and includes admission to 40 tourist sites (1-day €9, 2-day €16, 3-day €22). The **All-in-One Ticket** covers five museums over three days (€7 at the Municipal Tourist Office).

MONEY. On January 1, 2002, the **euro** (€) replaced the **Luxembourg Franc** as the unit of currency in Luxembourg. The Luxembourg Franc can still be exchanged at a rate of 40LF to €1. For exchange rates and more info on the euro, see p. 14. The European Union imposes a **value-added tax (VAT)** on goods and services purchased within the EU (p. 16). Luxembourg's VAT (15%) is already included in most prices. Luxembourg's refund threshold (US$85) is lower than most other EU countries; refunds are usually 13% of the purchase price. The cost of living in Luxembourg is moderate to high. **Service** (15-20%) is included in the price; tipping extra for exceptional service is optional. Tip taxi drivers 10%.

BUSINESS HOURS. Most **banks** are open M-F 8:30am-4:30pm, and most **shops** are open M-Sa 10am-6pm, with shorter hours on Sunday. However, some banks and shops close at noon for two hours, especially in the countryside.

COMMUNICATION

PHONE CODES	Country code: 352. International dialing prefix: 00. Luxembourg has no city codes.

TELEPHONES. There are no city codes; from outside the country, dial 352 plus the local number. Most public phones accept phone cards, which are sold at post offices and newspaper stands. **Mobile phones** are an increasingly popular and economical alternative (p. 36). International direct dial numbers include: **AT&T,** ☎8002 0111; **British Telecom,** ☎0800 89 0352; **Canada Direct,** ☎800 2 0119; **Ireland Direct,** ☎0800 353; **MCI,** ☎8002 0112; **Sprint,** ☎0800 0115; **Telecom New Zealand,** ☎800 20064.

MAIL. Mailing a postcard or a letter (up to 50g) within Luxembourg costs €0.59, within the EU €0.74, and to the rest of the world €1.12.

LANGUAGES. French and German are the administrative languages; since a referendum in 1984, *Letzebuergesch*, a mixture of the two, is the national language. French is most common in the city, while German is more common in smaller towns. English is commonly spoken as a second, third, or fourth language.

ACCOMMODATIONS AND CAMPING

LUXEMBOURG	❶	❷	❸	❹	❺
ACCOMMODATIONS	under €12	€12-16	€17-30	€31-40	over €40

Luxembourg's 12 **HI youth hostels** (*Auberges de Jeunesse*) are often filled with school groups. Contact **Centrale des Auberges de Jeunesse Luxembourgeoises** (☎26 29 35 00; www.youthhostels.lu) for info. **Hotels** generally cost €25-50 or more per night, depending on amenities; make sure to negotiate the price beforehand. Luxembourg is a **camping** paradise; most towns have campsites close by.

FOOD AND DRINK

LUXEMBOURG	❶	❷	❸	❹	❺
FOOD	under €5	€6-9	€10-14	€15-20	over €21

Luxembourgish cuisine combines elements of French and German cooking in a recipe all its own. Regional specialties include **Judd mat Gaardenbounen** (smoked neck of pork with beans), **Gromperenkichelchen** (potato cakes), and **Kéiskuch** (cheesecake). **Reisling wines** are produced in the Moselle valley.

HOLIDAYS AND FESTIVALS

Holidays: New Year's Day (Jan. 1); Carnival (Feb. 23); Easter (Apr. 11); Easter Monday (Apr. 12); May Day (May 1); Ascension Day (May 20); Whit Sunday and Monday (May 30-31); Grand Duke's Birthday Celebration (June 23); Assumption Day (Aug. 16); All Saints' Holiday (Nov. 1); Christmas (Dec. 25); and Saint Stephen's Day (Dec. 27).

Festivals: Luxembourg City hosts the Luxembourg City Fête (Sept. 6).

LUXEMBOURG CITY

With a medieval fortress perched on a cliff that overlooks lush green river valleys, and high bridges stretching over the downtown area, Luxembourg City (pop. 84,000) is one of the most beautiful and dramatic capitals in Europe.

▌ TRANSPORTATION

Flights: Findel International Airport (LUX), 6km from the city. Bus #9 (€1.20) is cheaper than the Luxair bus (€3.70) and runs the same route every 10-20min.

Trains: Gare CFL, av. de la Gare (toll-free info ☎ 49 90 49 90; www.cfl.lu), 15min. south of the city center. To: **Amsterdam** (6hr.; every hr.; €45, under-26 €35); **Brussels** (2¾hr., every hr., €25/14); **Ettelbrück** (25min., 2 per hr., €4.60); **Frankfurt** (4½hr., every hr., €46); **Paris** (4hr., every 2hr., €42/31).

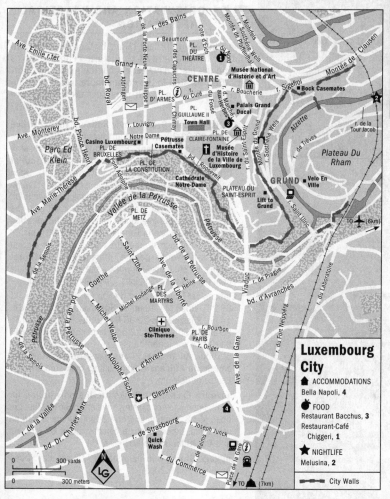

LUXEMBOURG

Luxembourg City

🏠 ACCOMMODATIONS
Bella Napoli, 4

🍎 FOOD
Restaurant Bacchus, 3
Restaurant-Café
   Chiggeri, 1

⭐ NIGHTLIFE
Melusina, 2

▬▬▬ City Walls

O WORK, ALL PLAY

;O HENRI, IT'S YOUR BIRTHDAY

Its petite size doesn't stop Luxembourg from throwing a colossal dusk-till-dawn fête to honor the birthday of its ruling monarch. It's not actually current Grand Duke Henri's birthday; the date, June 23, was set when his grandmother, Duchess Charlotte, deemed her January birthdate inopportune for an outdoor celebration of a suitable size.

The action begins in the early evening of June 22nd with a lengthy procession through the old city. At 11pm, fireworks rip through the air, illuminating the city's graceful bridges against the night sky. The procession may have ended—but the real party is just getting started. In an instant, the tiny alleys and narrow streets of this fairy-tale capital are magically transformed into impromptu bars and dance floors. A steady stream of alcohol and universal desire to get down saturate the tiny capital.

The rising sun traditionally breaks up the party, as disheveled revelers stumble to the Place d'Armes for breakfast. Although June 23rd is the official holiday, most Luxembourgers spend the day catching up on sleep missed the night before. The holiday's highlight, for those who can get out of bed, is watching Grand Duke Henri stroll, often with family and without visible security, through the center of what once again feels like a small town.

Buses: Within the city, buy a *billet courte distance* (short-distance ticket; 1hr. €1.20, package of 10 €9.20) or a *billet réseau* (day pass; €4.60, package of 5 €19). Tickets are valid on buses and trains throughout the country; a day pass is the most economical option for intercity travel. Buses run until midnight; night buses offer limited service.

Taxis: Colux Taxis, ☎48 22 33. €2.04 per km. 10% premium 10pm-6am.

Bikes: Rent from **Vélo en Ville,** 8 r. Bisserwé (☎47 96 23 83), in the Grund. Open daily 10am-noon and 1-8pm. €13 per half-day, €20 per day. Under-26 20% discount.

ORIENTATION AND PRACTICAL INFORMATION

Five minutes by bus and 15min. by foot from the train station, Luxembourg City's historic center revolves around the **place d'Armes.** Facing the municipal tourist office, located in the commemorative Town Hall, turn right down r. Chimay to reach **Boulevard Roosevelt.**

Tourist Offices: Grand Duchy National Tourist Office (☎42 82 82 20; www.etat.lu/tourism), in the train station. Open June-Sept. 8:30am-6:30pm, Oct.-May 9:15am-12:30pm and 1:45-6pm. **Municipal Tourist Office,** pl. d'Armes (☎22 28 09; www.ont.lu). Open Apr.-Sept. M-Sa 9am-7pm, Su 10am-6pm; Oct.-Mar. M-Sa 9am-6pm, Su 10am-6pm. Also, look for the helpful, yellow-shirted **"Ask Me"** representatives all over the city—they give out free tourist info. **Centre Information Jeunes,** 26 pl. de la Gare (☎26 29 32 00), inside Galerie Kons across from the train station, is a great service for young people, providing free **Internet** access for students (1hr. max.) and info on everything from hostels to finding jobs. Open M-F 10am-6pm.

Embassies: Ireland, 28 r. d'Arlon (☎45 06 10; fax 45 88 20). Open M-F 10am-12:30pm and 2:30-5pm. **UK,** 14 bd. Roosevelt (☎22 98 64; fax 22 98 67). Open M-F 9am-12:30pm. **US,** 22 bd. Emmanuel Servais (☎46 01 23; www.amembassy.lu). Open M-F 8:30am-5:30pm. **Australians, Canadians, New Zealanders,** and **South Africans** should contact their embassies in France or Belgium.

Currency Exchange: Banks are the only option for changing money or cashing traveler's checks. Most are open M-F 8:30am until 4 or 4:30pm. All are closed on weekends. Expect to pay a commission of €5 for cash and €8.30 for traveler's checks.

Luggage Storage: In train station. €3 per day. Open daily 6:30am-9:30pm.

Laundromat: Quick Wash, 31 r. de Strasbourg. €10. Open M-Sa 8:30am-6:30pm.

Emergency: Police: ☎113. **Ambulance:** ☎112.

Pharmacy: Pharmacie Goedert, 5 pl. d'Armes (☎22 33 99). Open M 1-6:15pm, Tu-F 8am-6:15pm, Sa 8am-12:30pm. Check pharmacy window for night info.

Medical Services: Doctors and pharmacies on call: ☎112. **Clinique Ste-Therese,** r. Ste-Zithe 36 (☎49 77 61 or 49 77 65).

Internet Access: Center Information Jeunes has free Internet access for students. **Cyber-Grund,** 2 r. Saint Ulric (☎26 20 39 55), in the Grund. €2 per 30min., €3 per hr. (50% discount Tu-F 12:30-3:30pm.) Open Tu-F 12:30-6:30pm, Sa 1:30-5pm. **Sp@rky's,** 11a av. Monterey (☎20 12 23), at the pl. d'Armes. €0.10 per min. Open M-Sa 7am-1am.

Post Office: 38 pl. de la Gare, across the street and left of the train station. Open M-F 6am-7pm, Sa 6am-noon. Address mail to be held: Firstname SURNAME, *Poste Restante,* **L-1009** Luxembourg G-I Gare, LUXEMBOURG. **Branch office,** 25 r. Aldringen, near the pl. d'Armes. Open M-F 7am-7pm, Sa 7am-5pm.

■ ACCOMMODATIONS

Hotels are cheaper near the train station than in the city center, but are often a splurge nonetheless. The **Youth Hostel (HI) ❷,** 2 r. du Fort Olisy, is the only real budget option. Take bus #9, then head under the bridge and turn right down the steep path. (☎22 19 20; luxembourg@youthhostels.lu Breakfast and sheets included. Reception 24hr. Dorms €17; singles €25; doubles €39. Nonmembers add €3.) **Bella Napoli ❹,** 4 r. de Strasbourg, has simple rooms with bath. (☎48 46 29. Breakfast included. Reception daily 8am-midnight. Singles €38; doubles €45; triples €60.) Take bus #5 to **Camping Kockelscheuer ❶.** (☎47 18 15. Showers included. Open Easter-Oct. €3.50 per person, €4 per site.)

■ FOOD

Although the area around the pl. d'Armes teems with a mix of fast-food joints and upscale restaurants, there are affordable and appealing alternatives. **Restaurant-Café Chiggeri ❸,** 15 r. du Nord, serves divine French food in a fun and funky atmosphere. (☎22 82 36. Entrees €11-14. Open M-Th 8am-1am, F-Sa 8am-3am, Su 10am-1am.) **Restaurant Bacchus ❷,** 32 r. du Marché-aux-Herbes, serves excellent pizza and pasta (€7.40-12) in a homey environment. (☎47 13 97. Open Su and Tu-Sa noon-10pm.) Get groceries at **Supermarché Boon,** across from the train station. (Open M-F 8am-8pm, Sa 8am-6pm, Su 8am-noon.)

■ SIGHTS

Luxembourg City is compact enough to be explored without a map; by wandering around you'll bump into most of the major sights. The most spectacular views of the city can be seen from any of the three major bridges connecting to the city center and from **place de la Constitution.** For guidance, follow the signs pointing out the **Wenzel Walk.** It leads visitors through 1000 years of history as it winds around the old city, from the **chemin de la Corniche** down into the casemates.

FORTRESSES AND THE OLD CITY. The 10th-century **Bock Casemates** fortress, part of Luxembourg's original castle, looms over the Alzette River Valley and offers a fantastic view of the **Grund** and the **Clausen.** Of the original 23km, 17 remain today, parts of which are used by banks, schools, and private residences. *(Entrance on r. Sigefroi, just past the bridge leading to the hostel. Open Mar.-Oct. daily 10am-5pm. €1.75, students €1.50.)* The **Pétrusse Casemates** were built by the Spanish in the 1600s to reinforce the medieval structures and were later improved by the Austrians. In the 19th century, a second ring of fortification was extended and a third was begun around the expanding city, lending Luxembourg the nickname "Gibraltar of the North." *(On pl. de la Constitution. Open July-Sept. Tours every hr. 11am-4pm. €1.75, students €1.50.)* Stroll down through the green **Pétrusse** valley, or catch one of the tourist trains that meander through the city and the valley. *(Trains ☎651 16 51. Mid-Mar. to Oct. every 30min. 10am-6pm except 1pm. €6.50.)*

MUSEUMS. The eclectic collection at the **Musée National d'Histoire et d'Art** chronicles the influences of the various European empires, from ancient to contemporary, that controlled Luxembourg. *(Marché-aux-Poissons, at r. Boucherie and Sigefroi. ☎479 33 01; www.mnha.lu. Open Su and Tu-Sa 10am-5pm. €5, students €3.)* Ignore its name; the only gamble at the **Casino Luxembourg** is on the changing exhibits. *(41 r. de Notre Dame, near pl. de la Constitution. Exhibition info ☎22 50 45; www.casino-luxembourg.lu. Open M and W-Su 11am-6pm, Th until 8pm. €4, under-26 €3. Under-18 free.)*

OTHER SIGHTS. Built as the city hall in 1574, the Renaissance **Palais Grand Ducal** lies in the heart of the downtown area and became the official city residence of the Grand Duke in 1890. *(Required tours mid-July to Aug. M-F afternoons and Sa mornings; tickets sold at the Municipal Tourist Office. Reservations ☎22 28 09. English-language tours available. €5.45.)* Nearby, the 17th-century **Cathédrale de Notre Dame** and houses the tomb of John the Blind, the 14th-century King of Bohemia and Count of Luxembourg. *(Open M-F 9am-6:15pm, Sa 9am-6:30pm, Su 9am-10:30am and noon-6pm. Free.)*

🎵📷 ENTERTAINMENT AND NIGHTLIFE

At night, the **place d'Armes** comes to life. Pick up a copy of *Nico* for a list of nightlife action and events. Nightlife centers on the valley in the **Grund** (by the bottom of the elevator lift on pl. du St-Esprit) and the **Clausen** area. On weekends, dance the night away at **Melusina,** 145 r. de la Tour Jacob *(☎43 59 22)*, a cafe-by-day that becomes a popular student nightspot when the sun sets. *(Entrees €7.40-17. Open M-Th 11:30am-2pm and 7-11pm, F-Sa 11:30am-2pm and 7pm-3am.)* On the eve of the **Grand Duke's birthday** (June 23), the city shuts down to honor their beloved Duke with a dusk-til-dawn fiesta filled with fireworks, alcohol, and fun.

THE ARDENNES

Six decades ago, the Battle of the Bulge (1944) mashed Luxembourg into the mud. Today, quiet towns, looming castles, and pleasant hiking trails are powerful draws.

ETTELBRÜCK. Ettelbrück's (pop. 7,000) position on the main railway line between Liège, Belgium, and Luxembourg City makes it the transportation hub for the Ardennes. The **General Patton Memorial Museum,** 5 r. Dr. Klein, commemorates Luxembourg's liberation during WWII. *(☎81 03 22. Open July to mid-Sept. daily 10am-5pm; mid-Sept. to June Su 2-5pm. €2.50.)* **Trains** go to: Clervaux (30min., every hr.); Diekirch (5min., every 20-40min.); and Luxembourg City (25min., 2 per hr.). **Buses** go to Diekirch (10min., every 15-40min., €1.60). To get to the city center from the station, go left on r. du Prince Henri, continue right at the fork, then turn left on Grand Rue and follow it to pl. de l'Église. The **tourist office** is in the train station. (☎81 20 68; site@pt.lu. Open July-Aug. M-F 9am-noon and 1:30-5pm, Sa 10am-noon and 2-4pm; Sept.-May closed Sa.) To get to **Ettelbrück Hostel (HI) ❷**, r. G. D. Josephine-Charlotte, head left out of the station and follow the signs. (☎81 22 69; ettelbruck@youthhostels.lu. Breakfast and sheets included. Lockout 10am-5pm. Dorms €15.) **Camping Kalkesdelt ❶** is at 22 r. du Camping. (☎81 21 85. Open Apr.-Oct. Reception daily 7:30am-noon and 2-10pm. €4.30 per person, €4 per site.) **Delhaize grocery** is close to the center of town. (Open M-F 8am-7pm, Sa 8am-6pm.)

DIEKIRCH. Diekirch (pop. 6,000) was evacuated during WWII in the face of imminent German attack. Today, the only invaders are backpackers and outdoorsy-types. The **National Museum of Military History,** 10 Bamertal, showcases moving relics from WWII's Battle of the Bulge. (☎80 89 08. Open Apr.-Oct. daily 10am-6pm; Jan.-Mar. and Nov.-Dec. daily 2-6pm. €5, students €3.) Rent **bikes** at **Speicher Sport,** 56 r. Clairefontaine (☎80 84 38; speibike@pt.lu. €10 per half-day, €15 per day.) Call ahead to rent **canoes** from **Outdoor Center,** 10 r. de la Sûre. (☎86 91 39. From €17.50 per day.) **Trains** head to Luxembourg City (35min., 2 per hr.) via Ettelbrück (5min.). **Buses** run to: Echternach (40min., every hr.); Ettelbrück (2 per hr., €4.60); and Vianden (#570; 20min., every hr.). To get to the **tourist office,** 3 pl. de la Liberation, turn left out of the station; at the fork, and follow r. du Pont to Grand Rue to pl. de la Liberation. (☎80 30 23; www.diekirch.lu. Open July-Aug. M-F 9am-5pm, Sa-Su 10am-noon and 2-4pm; off-season reduced hours.) **Au Beau-Séjour ❺**, 12 Esplanade, is pricey, but convenient. (80 34 03; beausejour.@pt.lu. Reception daily 8am-midnight. Singles €50; doubles €72.) Pitch your tent at **Camping de la Sûre ❶**, 34 rte. de Gilsdorf. (☎80 94 25; tourisme@diekirch.lu. Open Apr.-Sept. €4.80 per person, €4.30 per tent.) **Match supermarket** is off r. Alexis Heck. (Open M-Th 8:30am-7:30pm, F 8:30am-8pm, Sa 8am-6pm.)

VIANDEN. The village of Vianden (pop. 2,000), is home to one of the most impressive castles in Western Europe. Ride the ■ **télésiège** up to the **chateau,** a mix of Carolingian, Gothic, and Renaissance architecture, filled with armor, furniture, and tapestries. (☎83 41 08. Chateau open Apr.-Sept. daily 10am-6pm. €4.50, students €3.50. Télésiège ☎83 43 23. Open July-Aug. daily 10am-6:30pm; off-season reduced hours. €2.75, students €1.50.) The **Maison Victor Hugo,** 37 r. de la Gare, housed the author of *Les Misérables* during his exile from France. (☎26 87 40 88; www.victor-hugo.lu. Open Jan.-Oct. Su and Tu-Sa 11am-6pm.) **Hikers** enjoy Vianden's many trails; some also **bike** to Diekirch (13km) and Echternach (30km).

Buses head to Ettelbrück (#570; 30min., 2 per hr., €2.40) via Diekirch (20min.). The **tourist office,** 1 r. du Vieux Marché is next to the main bus stop. (☎83 42 57; www.tourist-info-vianden.lu. Open M-F 8am-noon and 1-6pm, Sa 10am-2pm, Su 2-4pm.) To reach the **Youth Hostel (HI) ❷**, 3 Montée du Château, follow Grande Rue away from the river up the hill; turn onto Montée du Château. (☎83 41 77; vianden@youthhostels.lu. Breakfast and sheets included. Reception daily 8-10am and 5-9pm. Lockout 10am-5pm. Curfew 11pm. Open May-Dec. Dorms €15. Nonmembers add €3.) Relax by the fountain at **Hotel Berg en Dal ❸**, 3 r. de la Gare. (☎83 41 27; info@hotel-bergendal.com. Breakfast included. Singles €34, with shower €37, with bath €52; doubles €38/48/74.) **Camp op dem Deich ❶**, r. Neugarten, alongside the Our river, is 5min. downstream from the tourist office. (☎83 43 75. Open Apr.-Sept. €4 per person, €4.50 per site.)

CLERVAUX. You'll see more faces in Clervaux's **chateau** than in the tiny town (pop. 1,000); the castle houses Edward Steichen's moving ☒**Family of Man,** an exhibit of 500 photos from 68 countries, depicting milestones of human life, emphasizing the common bonds of the human experience. (☎92 96 57. Open Mar.-Dec. Su and Tu-Sa 10am-6pm. €7, students €3.50.) To get to the chateau and the **Benedictine Abbey,** turn left out of the train station. (Abbey open daily 9am-7pm. Free.) Trains run to: Ettelbrück (25min., every 30min.); Luxembourg City (50min., every hr.); and Liège, Belgium (1¾hr., every 2hr.). The **tourist office,** in the castle, finds rooms. (☎92 00 72; www.tourisme-clervaux.lu. Open July-Aug. daily 9:45-11:45am and 2-6pm; off-season reduced hours.) **Camping Officiel ❶,** 33 Klatzewe, is near the river. (☎92 00 42. Open Apr.-Nov. €4.30 per person, €4.30 per tent.)

MOROCCO المغرب

Morocco has carved its identity out of a host of influences. At the crossroads of Africa, Europe, and the Middle East, it combines Arab culture and Islamic religion, African history and landscape, European influences and ties, and languages of all three. At the same time, the country teeters between the past and present as both an ancient civilization descended from nomadic tribes and a modern nation that struggled against imperial powers for its sovereignty. For travelers weary of another visit to a Spanish cathedral, a short excursion to Morocco can unexpectedly become the highlight of the trip. Excitement and adventure do not need to be planned or paid for lavishly: just step outside your hotel door and wander down an ancient medina street for an introduction to the Islamic and African city. While Morocco is only a few hours from Europe, it's an entirely different world.

FACTS AND FIGURES

Official Name: Kingdom of Morocco.

Capital: Rabat.

Major Cities: Agadir, Casablanca, Fez, Marrakesh, Tangier.

Population: 30,000,000.

Land Area: 446,500 sq. km.

Time Zone: GMT.

Languages: Arabic (official), French, Berber Dialects.

Religion: Islam (98.7%).

DISCOVER MOROCCO

Spend as little time as possible in **Tangier** (p. 725); instead, discover the charm of the brilliant white medina and beaches of **Asilah** (p. 725). **Fez** (p. 727) is easily accessible and best epitomizes traditional Morocco. Jimi Hendrix and Cat Stevens discovered the enchantment of **Essaouira** (p. 728) three decades ago,

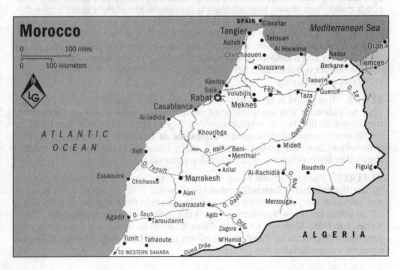

Morocco

0 ——— 100 miles
0 ——— 100 kilometers

Mediterranean Sea

SPAIN • Gibraltar

Tangier • Tetouan
Asilah • Al Hoceima • Oran
Chefchaouen • • Nador
• Ouazzane • Berkane • Tiemcen
Kénitra • Taourirt
Salé • Volubilis • Fèz • Guercif
Rabat • • Taza
Casablanca • Meknès
Al-Jadida •
Khouriga
Safi • • Midelt
O. Rbia • Beni-
• Memmal • • Boudnib • Figuig
Essaouira • • Azilal • Al-Rachidia
Chichaoua • **Marrakesh**
• Asni • Merzouga
Ouarzazate • Agdz
Agadir • O. Sous Taroudannt • Zagora
Tiznit • Tafraoute • M'Hamid
↓ TO WESTERN SAHARA   Oued Drâa

ATLANTIC OCEAN

ALGERIA

and while hippie expats have mostly gone home, the city's easygoing charm remains. For those seeking a little more action, **Marrakesh** (p. 729) never disappoints; a visit to the city's main square will unveil mystics, acrobats, snakecharmers, and storytellers.

ESSENTIALS

> **NOTE.** Due to the May 2003 Casablanca bombings, *Let's Go* did not send a researcher for the 2004 edition. However, factual information has been updated.

DOCUMENTS AND FORMALITIES

VISAS. EU citizens do not need a visa. Citizens of Australia, Canada, Ireland, New Zealand, South Africa, the UK, and the US do not need a visa for stays up to six months. Citizens of South Africa need a visa in addition to a passport for entry.

EMBASSIES. Foreign embassies in Morocco are in Rabat. Moroccan embassies at home include: **Australia,** 11 West St., North Sydney, NSW 2060 (☎612 9957 6717; fax 612 9923 1053); **Canada,** 38 Range Rd., Ottawa, ON K1N 8J4 (☎613-236-7391; www.ambassade-maroc.ottawa.on.ca); **South Africa,** 799 Schoeman St., Arcadia 0083; P.O. Box 12382, Hatfield 0028 Pretoria (☎27 12 343 0230; fax 27 343 0613); **UK,** 49 Queens Gate Gardens, London SW7 5NE (☎44 20 7581 5001; fax 44 20 7225 3862); and **US,** 1601 21st St. NW, Washington, D.C. 20009 (☎202-462-7979; fax 202-265-0161).

TRANSPORTATION

BY PLANE. Royal Air Maroc (Casablanca ☎022 31 41 41 or 022 33 90 00; US ☎800-344-6726; UK ☎07 439 43 61), Morocco's national airline, flies to and from most major cities in Europe, including Madrid and Lisbon. For more info on flying to Morocco from Europe, see p. 43.

BY TRAIN. Trains in Morocco are fairly reliable, prompt, and faster and more comfortable than buses. Second-class train tickets are slightly more expensive than corresponding CTM bus fares; first-class tickets cost around 20% more than second-class. The main line runs from Tangier to Marrakesh via Rabat and Casablanca. A spur with the main line at Sidi Kasem connects Fez, Meknes, and points east. There is one nightly *couchette* train between Fez and Marrakesh. **Interrail** is valid in Morocco, but **Eurail** is not. Fares are so low, however, that Interrail is generally not worth buying.

BY BUS. Bus travel is less frequent and less reliable than in Spain or Portugal. Plan well ahead if you are thinking of using buses as your method of transport; they're not all that fast or comfortable, but they're extremely cheap and travel to nearly every corner of the country. **Compagnie de Transports du Maroc** (CTM), the state-owned line, has the best buses. In many cities, CTM has a station separate from other lines; reservations are usually unnecessary.

BY FERRY. For travel from Spain to Morocco, the most budget-minded route is by sea. Spanish-based **Trasmediterranea** (Spain ☎902 45 46 45; www.trasmediterranea.es/homei.htm) runs ferries on a shuttle schedule from **Algeciras** (☎956 65 62 44) to **Ceuta,** known within Morocco as Sebta (☎956 50 94 11), and **Tangier.** "Fast" ferries run from Algeciras to Ceuta. **Comarit** (☎956 66 84 62; www.comarit.com) runs from Algeciras to Tangier and offers **vehicle transport.** Check online for Comarit's unpredictable weekly schedule.

BY CAR AND BY TAXI. Taxis are dirt-cheap by European standards. Make sure the driver turns the meter on. There is a 50% surcharge after 8pm. Drivers may stop for other passengers or pick you up with other passengers in the car; if you are picked up after the meter has been started, note the initial price. *Grand taxis,* typically beige or dark-blue Mercedes sedans, congregate at a central area in town and won't go until they are filled with passengers going in the same direction. Rent a car in Morocco only for large group travel or travel to areas inaccessible by Moroccan bus lines.

BY THUMB. Almost no one in Morocco **hitchhikes,** although flagging down buses and trains can feel like hitchhiking. *Let's Go* does not recommend hitchhiking.

TOURIST SERVICES AND MONEY

TOURIST OFFICES. Tourist offices in Morocco tend to be few and far between. However, existing offices have lists of available accommodations and an official tour-guide service. *Let's Go* does not recommend hiring unofficial guides. The official website for tourism in Morocco is www.tourism-in-morocco.com.

MONEY. Do not try the **black market** for currency exchange—you'll be swindled. As in Europe, **ATMs** are the best way to change money. Also know that it is very difficult to change currency back upon departure. **Taxes** are generally included in the price of purchases. **Tipping** a small amount after restaurant meals, while certainly not necessary, is a nice gesture given the extreme degree of poverty of many Moroccan citizens. **Bargaining** is definitely a legitimate part of the Moroccan shopping experience—it is most commonly accepted in outdoor markets. Do not try to bargain in supermarkets or established stores.

DIRHAM (DH)		
US $1= 9.82DH	1DH=US $0.10
CDN $1= 7.01DH	1DH=CDN $0.14
EUR €1= 10.66DH	1DH=EUR €0.09
UK £1= 15.42DH	1DH=UK £0.06
AUS $1= 6.38DH	1DH=AUS $0.16
NZ $1= 5.71DH	1DH=NZ $0.18

COMMUNICATION

PHONE CODES	**Country code:** 212. **International dialing prefix:** 00. From outside Morocco, dial int'l dialing prefix (see inside back cover) + 212 + city code + local number.

Morocco has recently invested hundreds of millions of dollars into modernizing its telephone system, resulting in markedly improved services. **Pay phones** accept only phone cards, which are available at post offices, but are usually in denominations too large to be practical. Entrepreneurial Moroccans hang around phone banks and let you use their phone cards. You pay for the units used—typically 2dh per unit, a rate not much worse than doing it yourself. To use the card, insert and dial 00. Once the dial tone turns into a tune, dial the number. **Air mail** (*par avion*) can take anywhere from a week to a month to reach the US or Canada (about 10dh for a slim letter, 4-7dh for postcards). Less reliable **surface mail** (*par terre*) takes up to 2 months. **Express mail** (*recommandé* or *exprès postaux*), is slightly faster than regular air mail and more

MOROCCO

reliable. Post offices and some *tabacs* sell **stamps.** For very fast service (2 days to the US), your best bet is DHL (www.dhl.com), which has drop-off locations in most major cities, or FedEx (www.fedex.com). Cybercafes are common in major cities and more touristed towns.

ACCOMMODATIONS AND CAMPING

MOROCCO	❶	❷	❸	❹	❺
ACCOMMODATIONS	under 60dh	60-100dh	101-150dh	151-200dh	over 200dh

The **Federation Royale des Auberges de Jeunesse** (FRMAJ) is the Moroccan Hosteling International (HI) affiliate. Beds cost 30-40dh per night, and there is a surcharge for nonmembers. **Camping** is popular and cheap (about 15dh per person), especially in the desert, mountains, and beaches. Like hotels, conditions vary widely. You can usually expect to find restrooms, but electricity is not as readily available. Use caution if camping unofficially, especially on beaches, as theft is a problem.

FOOD AND DRINK

MOROCCO	❶	❷	❸	❹	❺
FOOD	under 40dh	40-60dh	61-80dh	81-110dh	over 110dh

Moroccan chefs lavish aromatic and colorful spices on their dishes—pepper, ginger, cumin, saffron, honey, and sugar are culinary staples. The distinctive Moroccan flavor comes from a unique blend of spices known as *ras al-hanut*. However, no matter how delicious everything may seem, be prepared to get sick at least once, as Morocco is full of things to which tourists are not immune. Taking extra precautions may help. Bottled mineral water is the way to go, as is peeling all fruits and vegetables. The truly vigilant may avoid salads as well, or ensure that their vegetables are washed in purified water. Most food sold on the street, especially meat, can be quite risky and should be regarded as such.

SAFETY AND SECURITY

EMERGENCY Police: ☎ 19. **Highway services:** ☎ 177.

Visitors should be suspicious of people offering free food, drinks, or cigarettes, as they have been known to be drugged. Avoid unofficial tour guides in large cities like Tangier and Fez. Women should dress conservatively and never travel alone. Travelers should drink only bottled or boiled water, and should avoid tap water, fountain drinks, and ice cubes. It's also advisable to only eat fruit and vegetables that are cooked and that you have peeled yourself. Stay away from food sold by street vendors, and check to make sure that dairy products have been pasteurized. There is only a slight malaria risk in Morocco, but it would still be wise to take extra precaution against insect bites and consider getting a vaccine before leaving.

HOLIDAYS

Holidays: New Year's Day (Jan. 1); Independence Manifesto (Jan. 11); 'Eid al-Adha (Feb. 12); Islamic New Year (Mar. 5); Labor Day (May 1); Reunification Day (Aug. 14); Anniversary of the King's and the People's Revolution (Aug. 20); Young People's Day (Aug. 21); Anniversary of the Green March (Nov. 6); Ramadan (begins Oct. 26); Independence Day (Nov. 18); 'Eid al-Fitr (Nov. 24-27).

TANGIER طنجة ☎ 039

For travelers venturing out of Europe for the first time, disembarking in Tangier (pop. 500,000), Morocco's main port of entry, can be a distressing experience. Many visitors' stories make the city out to be a living nightmare, but for the determined traveler, it can be surprisingly pleasant. If you have a few extra hours, learn about Tangier's international past at the ■Old American Legation, 8 r. d'America. (Open M-F 10am-1pm and 3-5pm. Small donation suggested.) Or, visit the opulent palace-turned-museum Dar al-Makhzen (open Su and W-Sa 9am-12:30pm and 3-5:30pm; 10dh) and the hectic markets in the Grand Socco. In the evening, sip mint tea in front of the Café de Paris, 1 pl. de France, which hosted countless rendez-vous between secret agents during WWII. Coming from the Grand Socco, look to the left. (Open daily 7am-11:30pm.)

Flights arrive at the Royal Air Maroc, pl. de France (☎37 95 08), from Barcelona, London, Madrid, Marrakesh, and New York. Trains leave from Mghagha Station (☎95 25 55), 6km from the port, for Asilah (1hr., 4 per day, 13dh). Buses leave from av. Yacoub al-Mansour, 2km from the port entrance at pl. Jamia al-Arabia, for Fez (6hr., 11 per day, 63dh) and Marrakesh (10hr., 3 per day, 115dh). The CTM Station (☎93 11 72) near the port entrance offers posher (and pricier) bus service to the same destinations. Ferries, 46 av. d'Espagne (☎94 26 12), head to Algeciras (2½hr., every hr. 7am-9pm, 210dh). You'll need a boarding pass, available at any ticket desk, and a customs form (ask uniformed agents). The tourist office, 29 bd. Pasteur, has a list of accommodations. (☎94 80 50. Open M-F 8:30am-7:30pm.) Expect to pay around 50-60dh for a single and 80-100dh for a double. The most convenient hostels cluster near rue Mokhtar Ahardan off the Petit Socco; from the Grand Socco, take the first right down r. al-Siaghin. Hôtel El Muniria (Tanger Inn) ❸, r. Magellan, has spacious rooms and hot showers. From the port, walk south along the pedestrian walkway, take the first right after Hôtel Biarritz, and follow r. Magellan uphill. (☎93 53 37. Singles 100dh; doubles 130dh.) Grab lunch for less than 15dh at the Brahim Abdelmalek ❶, 14 r. de Mexique.

ASILAH أصيلة ☎ 039

Just a short trip from Tangier, Asilah offers sandy shores and a brilliant white medina. During the first two weeks in August, Asilah hosts an international art festival; year-round peaceful Asilah remains an ideal spot for soaking up the sun. The stunning ■medina is bound by heavily fortified 15th-century Portuguese walls. Bab Kasaba, the gate off r. Zallakah, leads past the Grand Mosque. Take a stroll along the enclosed ■Paradise Beach, an hour's walk from the medina. Or, take a horse-drawn wagon (round-trip 150-200dh).

Trains (☎41 73 27) run to Marrakesh (9hr., 3 per day, 101-150dh) and Tangier (40min., 4 per day, 14-20dh). The train station is a 25min. walk from town on the Asilah-Tangier highway, past a strip of campgrounds; a taxi to or from town costs about 10dh. Buses go to: Fez (4hr., 3:45 and 7:45pm, 55dh); Marrakesh (9hr., 5pm, 130dh); and Tangier (1hr., 12:15 and 4:15pm, 10dh). Grand taxis bound for Tangier pick up passengers in pl. Mohammed V (12dh). The bulk of Asilah's restaurants, accommodations, and cafes are on rue Zallakah, off pl. Mohammed V. Hôtel Sahara ❷, 9 r. Tarfaya, a block inland from av. Mohammed V and two blocks before pl. Mohammed V, has immaculate rooms. (☎41 71 85. Hot showers 5dh. Singles 98dh; doubles 126dh; triples 186dh; quads 252dh.) Av. Hassan II holds the town market.

CHEFCHAOUEN شفشوان ☎ 039

High in the Rif Mountains, but easily accessible from Tangier or Fez, Chefcha-ouen (pop. 30,000) refreshes weary travelers with its cool mountain air. Its steep ■medina is one of Morocco's best. Enter through Bab al-Ain and walk

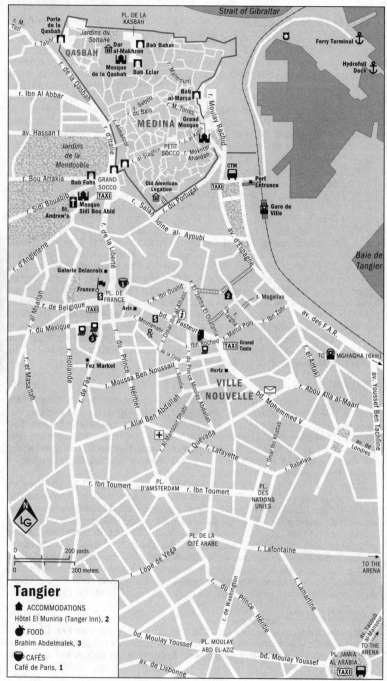

Tangier

uphill toward pl. Uta al-Hammam, the center of the medina. In the *place* stands the 16th-century **Grand Mosque** and its red-and-gold minaret, as well as a 17th-century *kasbah*. (Open daily 9am-1pm and 3-6:30pm. 10dh.) Chefchaouen's **souq** operates Mondays and Thursdays outside the medina and below both av. Hassan II and av. Allal ben Abdalallah. The town makes a spectacular base for **hiking;** follow the Ras al-Ma river upstream into the hills for a few kilometers. For a quick view of the city from the hills, hike following signs for the *ville nouvelle.*

   Buses (☎98 95 73) run to Fez (5hr., 1:15 and 3pm, 45-55dh) and Tangier via Tetouan (28-33dh). From the bus station, head up the steep hill and turn right after several blocks onto the large road, which leads to the circular pl. Mohammed V; walk 20min. to the center of town. Cross the *place* and continue east on **avenue Hassan II.** Chefchaouen has no tourist office. A slew of budget hotels are on **Bab al-Ain** and **place Uta al-Hammam,** uphill in the medina. The best of the lot is ▨**Hotel Andalus** ❶, 1 r. Sidi Salem, directly behind Credit Agricola on pl. Uta al-Hammam. (☎98 60 34. Singles 30dh; doubles 60dh; triples 90dh; quads 120dh; terrace 20dh.)

FEZ فاس ☎055

No visit to Morocco is complete without visiting Fez's bustling, colorful medina. Artisans bang out sheets of brass, donkeys strain under crates of Coca-Cola, children balance trays of dough on their heads, and tourists struggle to stay together. Founded in the 8th century, Fez rose to prominence with the construction of the Qairaouine, a university-mosque complex. Post-independence Fez has been somewhat eclipsed by Rabat (the political capital), Casablanca (the economic capital), and Marrakesh (the tourist capital), yet it remains at the artistic, intellectual, and spiritual helm of the country.

▤ TRANSPORTATION. Flights arrive at **Aérodrome de Fès-Saïs** (☎62 47 12), 12km out of town on the road to Immouzzèr. **Royal Air Maroc** (RAM), 54 av. Hassan II (☎62 55 16), flies to Casablanca, Marrakesh, Paris, and Tangier. **Trains** (☎93 03 33) leave from the intersection of av. Almohades and r. Chenguit for Marrakesh (9hr., 7 per day, 171-255dh) and Tangier (5hr., 4 per day, 96-141dh). **CTM buses** (☎73 29 92) run to: Chefchaouen (4hr., 2 per day, 50dh); Marrakesh (8hr., 2 per day, 130dh); and Tangier (6hr., 3 per day, 85dh). Buses stop near pl. d'Atlas, at the far end of the *ville nouvelle.* From pl. Florence, walk 15min. down bd. Mohammed V, turn left onto av. Youssef ben Tachfine, and take the first right at pl. d'Atlas.

▰▨ ORIENTATION AND PRACTICAL INFORMATION. Fez is large and spread out but still manageable. Essentially three cities in one, the main areas of Fez are: The fashionable **ville nouvelle,** a couple kilometers from the medina; Arab **Fez al-Jdid** (New Fez), which sits next to the medina and contains both the Jewish cemetery and the palace of Hassan II; and the enormous medina area of **Fez al-Bali** (Old Fez). Hire an official local guide at the Syndicat d'Initiative **tourist office,** pl. Mohammed V. (☎62 34 60. Half-day with guide 150dh, full-day 250dh. Open M-F 8:30am-noon and 2:30-6:30pm, Sa 8:30am-noon.) Access the **Internet** at **Soprocon,** off pl. Florence. (10dh per hr. Open daily 9am-11pm.)

▮▯ ACCOMMODATIONS AND FOOD. Rooms in the *ville nouvelle* are close to local services and more comfortable than those in the medina. The cheapest lodgings and eateries surround **boulevard Mohammed V,** between av. Mohammed al-Slaoui near the bus station and av. Hassan II near the post office. **Hôtel du Commerce ❶**, pl. Alaouites, by the Royal Palace in Fez al-Jdid, has friendly owners and comfortable rooms. (☎62 22 31. Cold showers. Singles 50dh; doubles 90dh.) **Hôtel Central ❶**, 50 r. Brahim Roudani, off pl. Mohammed V, has clean rooms with nice furnishings. (☎62 23 33. Singles 59dh, with shower 89dh; doubles 89/119dh; triples 150/180dh.) Budget rooms fill the **Bab Boujeloud** area. **Hôtel Cascade ❶**, 26 Serrajine Boujeloud, is popular with both backpackers and families. (☎63 84 42. 50dh per person; terrace 20dh.)

Cheap sandwich dives, cafes, and juice shops line both sides of bd. Mohammed V. For those in search of local eats, sort through stalls of fresh food at the central market on bd. Mohammed V, two blocks up from pl. Mohammed V. (Open daily 7am-1pm.) **Restaurant des Jeunes ❶**, 16 r. Serrajine, next to Hôtel Cascade by Bab Boujeloud, serves inexpensive Moroccan specialties. (Entrees 25-30dh. Open daily 6am-midnight.)

⊙ ♫ SIGHTS AND ENTERTAINMENT. Hiring an official guide at the Syndicat d'Initiative (see tourist office, above) will save you time, discourage hustlers, and provide detailed explanations; make sure to nail down an itinerary and price beforehand. Fez's **medina** is the handicraft capital of the country and exports goods around the world. With over 9000 streets and nearly 500,000 residents, the crowded medina is also possibly the most difficult to navigate in all of Morocco. Its narrow, frenzied streets contain fabulous mosques, *madrassas*, and *souqs*. At the head of the main thoroughfare, Tala'a Kebira, is the spectacular ▧**Bou Inania Madrasa,** a school built in 1326 for teaching the Qur'an and other Islamic sciences. *(Undergoing renovation; reopening date uncertain. Normally open daily 9am-5:30pm. 10dh.)* Back on Tala'a Kebira is the **attarine ("spice") souq,** perhaps the most exotic market. Walking through the market leads to **Zaouia Moulay Idriss II,** the resting place of the Islamic saint credited with founding Fez. Non-Muslims are not allowed to enter but can peer in. The Tala'a Kebira ends at Madrasa al-Attarine, which dates from 1324. Exiting the *madrasa*, turn left, and then left again; a few meters down is a little opening into the **Qairaouine mosque,** which holds up to 20,000 worshippers. Non-Muslims may not enter through the portal. Continue with the mosque to your right to reach pl. Seffarine, known for its fascinating **metal souq,** which deafens travelers with incessant cauldron-pounding. In Fez al-Jdid, the gaudy **Dar al-Makhzen,** former palace of Hassan II, borders pl. Alaouites. Tourists may enter the grounds but not the palace. The **jewelers' souq** glitters at the top of Grande Rue des Merinides. Cackling chickens and salty fish are sold at the **covered market,** inside Bab Smarine at the entrance to Fez al-Jdid proper.

ESSAOUIRA الصويرة ☎044

In the late 1960s, the arrival of Jimi Hendrix and Cat Stevens triggered a mass hippie migration to Essaouira, and over the next decade, the city achieved international fame as an expat enclave. Though most of the hash smoke has cleared, Essaouira remains one of Morocco's most enchanting communities.

🖃 ⊉ TRANSPORTATION AND PRACTICAL INFORMATION. Supratours **buses** (☎47 53 17) run from Bab Marrakesh to **Marrakesh** (2½hr., 6:10am and 4pm, 55dh) and various other destinations. The Syndicat d'Initiative **tourist office** is on r. de Caire. (☎47 50 80. Open M-F 9am-noon and 2:30-6:30pm.) **Internet** access is available at **Mogador Informatique,** av. Oqba ben Nafil, 3rd fl. (10dh per hr. Vague hours; usually daily 9am-midnight.)

⚠️🏠 ACCOMMODATIONS AND FOOD. Though once Morocco's best-kept secret, Essaouira has lost its anonymity; reservations may be necessary in the summer. From pl. Moulay Hassam, facing Credit du Maroc, make a left on r. Skala, take the right just before the archway to reach the beautiful **Hôtel Cap Sim ❹**, 11 Ib Rochd. (☎78 58 34. Singles and doubles 158dh, with shower 258dh.) **Hôtel Smara ❷**, 26 r. Skala, next to Banque Populaire, is a mere 100m away from the ocean. (☎47 56 55. Singles 62dh; doubles 94dh, with ocean view 124dh; triples 156dh; quads 196dh.) **Hôtel Souiri ❷**, 37 r. Attarine, off r. Sidi Mohammed Ben Abdallah, is comfortable and worth the extra dirhams. (☎47 53 39. Singles 95dh, with shower 220dh; doubles 150/310dh; triples 225/375dh. MC/V.)

Informal dining, mostly geared toward tourists, is common near the port and **place Moulay Hassan.** At the many 🔲**port fish grilles,** fried sardines (with fish, bread, and tomatoes; 20dh) and grilled shrimp (25dh) are sure bets. The so-called **Berber cafes,** near Porte Portugaise and off av. l'Istiqlal, have low tables, straw mats, and fresh fish *tajine* and couscous (20dh). Establish prices before eating. For outstanding Moroccan food at reasonable prices, try **Restaurant Laayoune ❷**. (4 set *menú* 45-72dh. Open daily noon-4pm and 7-11pm.)

🔲⛰️ SIGHTS AND OUTDOORS. Buttressed by formidable ramparts, dramatic, sea-sprayed **Skala de la Kasbah,** up the street from Hôtel Smara and away from the main square, is the nicer of Essaouria's two *skalas* (forts). Visitors can go up the large turret- and artillery-lined wall to see cannons facing the sea. Follow the sound of pounding hammers and the scent of *thuya* wood to the **carpenters' district,** comprised of cell-like niches set in the **Skala Stata de la Ville.** On sale are unique masks and statues, as well as the more typical drums, chess sets, and desk tools. For an overview of Essaouira's goods, go to the cooperative **Afalkai Art,** 9 pl. Moulay Hassan (open daily 9am-8pm), and browse the many shops lining **rue Abd al-Aziz al-Fechtaly,** off r. Sidi ben Abdallah.

Though infamous for its winds, the wide **beach** of Essaouira is still one of Morocco's finest. To get there, head to the port and veer left. Just offshore from Essaouira are the famed Purple Isles, named for the dye factories, used to color Julius Caesar's cape, located on the islands around 100 BC. Visiting the Isles requires permission from the tourist office, which can take a couple of days.

MARRAKESH مراكش ☎044

Founded in 1062, the imperial city of Marrakesh has been exerting an unshakable grip on visitors for centuries. Djema'a al-Fna, the centrally-located main square, is home to boxers, musicians, snake-charmers, acrobats, storytellers, dentists, and mystics. Marrakesh's *souqs* and craftwork are some of Morocco's best, and the bustling city is generally more tourist-friendly than the rest of the country.

📧❓ TRANSPORTATION AND PRACTICAL INFORMATION

Flights arrive at **Aéroport de Marrakesh Menara** (RAK; ☎44 79 10), 5km south of town. Bus #11 runs from the airport to the Koutoubia Mosque (7am-10pm, 3dh). **Trains** run from av. Hassan II (☎44 65 69) to Fez (8hr., 6 per day, 225dh) and Tangier (8hr., 3 per day, 188dh). **Buses** (☎43 39 33) run from outside the medina walls by Bab Doukkala to Essaouira (8 per day) and other destinations. Most of the excitement, as well as budget food and accommodations, centers around the **Djema'a al-Fna** and the **medina** streets directly off it. The **bus** and **train stations** are in **Guéliz** (*ville nouvelle*) down av. Mohammed V; from the Djema'a al-Fna, walk to the towering Koutoubia Minaret and turn right. Bus #1 runs between the minaret and the heart of the Guéliz (1.50dh). Or, take one of the many *petits taxis* (10dh)

MOROCCO

MOROCCO

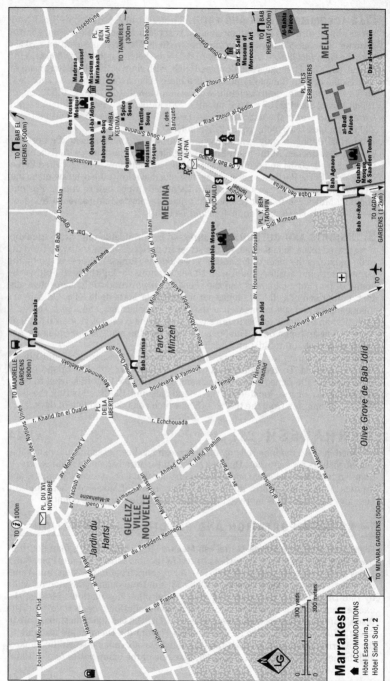

Marrakesh

▲ ACCOMMODATIONS
Hôtel Essaouira, **1**
Hôtel Sindi Sud, **2**

or horse-drawn carriages (15dh, sometimes more at night). The **tourist office,** av. Mohammed V (☎ 43 61 79), is at pl. Abdel Moumen ben Ali. Walk 35min. from the Djema'a al-Fna or take a *petit taxi* (15dh). Many tobacco shops sell better maps (15dh), although **official guides** (full day 150dh), a worthwhile option in Marrakesh, can be booked here. (Open in summer daily 7:30am-3pm; off-season 8:30am-noon and 2:30-6:30pm.) Many good **Internet** cafes are on Bab Agnaou, the pedestrian mall off the Djema'a al-Fna. **Cyber Bab Agnaou, Cyber Mohammed Yassine,** and **Hanan Internet Cyber Cafe** each charge 10dh per hr. (Open daily 8am-11pm.)

> Marrakesh's petit taxi drivers are notorious for taking "scenic" routes. Make sure the meter's on and have a clear sense of how to get to your destination.

ACCOMMODATIONS AND FOOD

Most of Marrakesh's inexpensive accommodations are near the Djema'a al-Fna. Many places allow you to sleep on the rooftop terrace for about 20dh. To reach **Hôtel Essaouira ❶,** 3 Derb Sidi Bouloukat, from the Djema'a al-Fna, walk just beyond Café de France, take the first right after the Hôtel de France, and look for signs. (☎ 44 38 05. Hot showers 5dh. Singles 40dh; doubles 80dh; terrace 25dh.) **Hôtel Sindi Sud ❶,** 109 Riad Zitoun El Quduim, is just off the intersection with Derb Sidi Bouloukat, across from Hôtel Essaouira. Popular with American Peace Corps workers, it has clean, well-furnished rooms and a nice indoor courtyard. (☎ 44 33 37. Hot shower and breakfast included. 40dh per person; terrace 25dh.)

For delicious dinner bargains, head for the **food stalls** in the Djema'a al-Fna; try the *harira* (spicy bean soup; 2dh) and *kebab* (skewered meat; 2dh). On the other end of the price spectrum, Marrakesh also has many **"palace restaurants"** where music, liquor, and huge portions combine for a memorable, if expensive, evening (300-600dh per person). Two **markets** peddle fresh produce along the fortifications surrounding the city. **Star Foods ❶,** off pl. Abdel Boumem Ben Ali, in Gueliz, serves American and Moroccan dishes. (Open daily 8:30am-11pm.)

SIGHTS

■ DJEMA'A AL-FNA. The Djema'a al-Fna (Assembly of the Dead) is one of the world's most frantically exotic squares, where sultans once beheaded criminals and displayed the remains. While snake-charmers and monkey-handlers entice tourists, the vast majority of the audience are townspeople from outlying villages. Villagers consult potion dealers and fortune tellers; crowds encircle preachers, storytellers, and musicians; women have their children blessed by mystics; and promoters encourage bets on boxing matches between young boys (and girls). Come here for wonderful food and the chance to watch the spectacle.

■ MEDINA AND SOUQS. The best place in Morocco to buy spices, Marrakesh's medina is also where you'll find the most colorful iron and sheepskin lampshades. Enter the medina from the Djema'a al-Fna, directly across from the Café de France. Berber blankets and yarn pile the alleyways of the **fabric souq.** Head through the first major orange gateway and make a quick right to the Zahba Qedima, a small plaza containing the **spice souq,** complete with massive sacks of saffron and cumin as well as the apothecaries' more unusual remedies—goat hoof for hair loss, ground-up ferrets for depression, and live chameleons for sexual frustration. Try **Chateau des Souks** for Berber rugs and carpets. (*44 Souk Semmarine.*) At **Herboristerie Avenzoar,** listen to fascinating explanations of the healing qualities of herbs and spices in fluent English. (*78 Derb N'Khel, off the Rahba Kedima.*)

MOROCCO

AL-BAHIA PALACE. The ruthless late-19th-century vizier Si Ahmad Ibn Musa, also known as Ba Ahmad, constructed this palace and named it al-Bahia (The Brilliance). Its impressive ceilings are beautifully preserved. *(Open Sa-Th 8:30-11:45am and 2:30-5:45pm, F 8:30-11:30am and 3-5:45pm. 10dh.)*

MADRASA BEN YOUSSEF. In 1565, Sultan Moulay Abdallah al-Ghalib raised the Madrasa ben Youssef in the medina center. It reigned as the largest Qur'anic school in the Maghreb until closing in 1960. *(Open June-Aug. Tu-Su 9am-1pm and 2:30-6pm; Sept.-May Tu-Su 9am-6:30pm. 20dh, under-18 10dh.)*

OTHER SIGHTS. The 19th-century palace **Dar Si Said** was built by Si Said, brother of Grand Vizier Ba Ahmed, and houses the **Museum of Moroccan Art,** which features splendid Berber carpets, pottery, jewelry, Essaouiran ebony, and Saadian woodcarving. (Open Su-M, W, and Sa 9-11:45am and 2:30-5:45pm, F 9-11:30am and 3-5:45pm. 10dh.) The **Museum of Marrakesh** features exhibits on Moroccan culture. (Open daily 9am-6pm. 30dh, students 10dh.)

◙ NIGHTLIFE

Most travelers hang around the Djema'a al-Fna, or the overlooking terrace cafes, for most of the night. Locals and tourists alike enjoy the bars at the **Tazi** (☎44 27 87) and **Foucauld** (☎44 54 99) hotels. (*Spéciale Flag* 15dh. Cover 50dh. Both bars open at 9pm.) The city's largest club is **Paradise,** at the far end of Guéliz.

THE NETHERLANDS
(NEDERLAND)

The Dutch say that although God created the rest of the world, *they* created The Netherlands. The country is a masterful feat of engineering; since most of it is below sea level, vigorous pumping and many dikes were used to create dry land. What was once the domain of seaweed is now packed with windmills, bicycles, and tulips. The Netherlands's wealth of art and its canal-lined towns draw as many travelers as do the unique hedonism and perpetual partying of Amsterdam.

FACTS AND FIGURES

Official Name: The Kingdom of The Netherlands.

Capital: Amsterdam.

Major Cities: Amsterdam, Maastricht, Rotterdam, Utrecht.

Population: 16,000,000.

Land Area: 41,526 sq. km.

Time Zone: GMT + 1.

Language: Dutch.

Religions: Catholic (31%), Protestant (21%), Muslim (4%), unaffiliated (40%).

DISCOVER THE NETHERLANDS

Roll it, light it, then smoke it in **Amsterdam** (p. 737), a hedonist's dream, with chill coffeeshops and peerless museums. Clear your head in the rustic Dutch countryside; the amazing **Hoge Veluwe National Park** (p. 760), southeast of Amsterdam, shelters within its 30,000 wooded acres one of the finest modern art museums in Europe. Beautifully preserved **Leiden** (p. 756) and **Utrecht** (p. 759), less than 30 minutes away, delight visitors with picturesque canals. International politics and museums abound in **The Hague** (p. 757); for more innovative art and architecture, step into futuristic **Rotterdam** (p. 758). An afternoon in **Delft** (p. 758) provides a dose of small-town Dutch charm. Visit the sand dunes and isolated beaches of the tiny **Wadden Islands** (p. 762), a cyclist's paradise.

ESSENTIALS

WHEN TO GO

The ideal time to visit is between mid-May and early October, when day temperatures are generally 20-31°C (70-80°F), with nights around 10-20°C (50-60°F). It can be quite rainy; bring an umbrella. The tulip season runs from April to mid-May.

DOCUMENTS AND FORMALITIES

VISAS. South Africans need a visa for all visits. Citizens of Australia, Canada, the EU, New Zealand, and the US do not need visas for stays less than 90 days.

EMBASSIES. All foreign embassies and most consulates are in The Hague (p. 757). The US has a consulate in Amsterdam (p. 737). For Dutch embassies at home: **Australia,** 120 Empire Circuit, Yarralumla Canberra, ACT 2600 (☎02 62 73 31

The Netherlands

Schiermonnikoog
Terschelling   Ameland
Vlieland   Wadden Islands
Texel   Waddenzee
Leeuwarden   Groningen
Harlingen   Heerenveen
Den Helder   Assen
Hoorn   Hoogeveen
Alkmaar   Meppel
North Sea   Zaanse Schans   Edam   Vecht R.
Haarlem   Zwolle
Zandvort-aan-Zee   Amsterdam
Noordwijk-aan-Zee   Aalsmeer   IJssel R.
Scheveningen   Lisse   Apeldoorn
The Hague   Leiden   Utrecht   Amersfoort   De Hoge Veluwe
Hoek van Holland   Delft   Rijn R.
Gouda   Arnhem
Rotterdam   Waal R.   Nijmegen
Maas R.   Rhine R.
TO HARWICH, ENGLAND   Breda
AND HULL, ENGLAND
Eindhoven   GERMANY
Antwerp   Maas R.
BELGIUM   Roermond
Brussels   Cologne
Maastricht
TO NEWCASTLE-UPON TYNE, ENGLAND
IJsselmeer

0   25 miles
0   25 kilometers

11; www.netherlandsembassy.org.au); **Canada,** 350 Albert St., Ste. 2020, Ottawa ON K1R 1A4 (☎6130-237-5030; www.netherlandsembassy.ca); **Ireland,** 160 Merrion Rd., Dublin 4 (☎012 69 34 44; www.netherlandsembassy.ie); **New Zealand,** P.O. Box 840, at Ballance and Featherston St., Wellington (☎04 471 63 90; netherlandsembassy.co.nz); **South Africa,** 825 Arcadia St., Pretoria, P.O. Box 117, Pretoria (☎012 344 3910; www.dutchembassy.co.za); **UK,** 38 Hyde Park Gate, London SW7 5DP (☎020 75 90 32 00; www.netherlands-embassy.org.uk); and **US,** 4200 Linnean Ave., NW, Washington, D.C. 20008 (☎202-244-5300; www.netherlands-embassy.org).

TRANSPORTATION

BY PLANE. Continental, Delta, KLM/Northwest, Martinair, Singapore Airlines, and **United** serve Amsterdam's sleek, glassy Schiphol Airport (AMS).

BY TRAIN. The national rail company is the efficient **Nederlandse Spoorwegen** (NS; Netherlands Railways; www.ns.nl). Train service tends to be faster than bus service. *Sneltreins* are the fastest; *stoptreins* make the most stops. One-way tickets are called *enkele reis;* normal round-trip tickets, *retour;* and same-day round-trip tickets (valid only on day of purchase, but cheaper than normal round-trip tickets), *dagretour.* **Eurail** and **InterRail** are valid in The Netherlands. The **Holland Rail-**

pass (US$52-98) is good for three or five travel days in any one-month period. Although available in the US, the Holland Railpass is cheaper in The Netherlands at DER Travel Service or RailEurope offices. **One-day train passes** cost €35, which is about the equivalent of the most expensive one-way fare across the country. The fine for a missing ticket on Dutch trains is a whopping €90.

BY BUS. A nationalized fare system covers city buses, trams, and long-distance buses. The country is divided into zones; the number of strips on a *strippenkaart* (strip card) required depends on the number of zones through which you travel. A trip between destinations in the same zone costs one strip; a trip that traverses two zones requires two strips. On buses, tell the driver your destination and he or she will cancel the correct number of strips; on trams and subways, stamp your own *strippenkaart* in either a yellow box at the back of the tram or in the subway station. Train and bus drivers sell tickets, but it's cheaper to buy in bulk at public transit counters, tourist offices, post offices, and some tobacco shops and news-stands. *Dagkarten* (day passes) are valid for unlimited use in any zone (€5.20, children and seniors €3.60). Unlimited-use passes are valid for one week in the same zone (€21, seniors and children €13; requires a passport photo and picture ID). Riding without a ticket can result in a €30 fine.

BY CAR. The Netherlands has well-maintained roadways. North Americans and Australians need an International Driver's License; if your insurance doesn't cover you abroad, you'll also need a green insurance card. Driving in the Netherlands is expensive. Fuel comes in two types; some cars use benzene (€1.50 per liter), while others use gasoline (€0.90 per liter). The **Royal Dutch Touring Association** (ANWB) offers roadside assistance to members. For more information, contact the ANWB at Wassenaarseweg 220, 2596 EC The Hague (☎(070) 314 71 47).

BY BIKE AND BY THUMB. Cycling is the way to go in The Netherlands—distances between cities are short, the countryside is absolutely flat, and most streets have separate bike lanes. Bikes run about €7 per day or €30 per week. Bikes are some-times available at train stations and hostels, and *Let's Go* also lists bike rental shops in many towns. For more info, try www.visitholland.com. Hitchhiking is somewhat effective, but there is cutthroat competition on the roads out of Amster-dam. *Let's Go* does not recommend hitchhiking.

TOURIST SERVICES AND MONEY

EMERGENCY	Police: ☎112. Ambulance: ☎112. Fire: ☎112.

TOURIST OFFICES. VVV (vay-vay-vay) tourist offices are marked by triangular blue signs. The website www.visitholland.com is also a useful resource.

MONEY. On January 1, 2002, the **euro** (€) replaced the guilder (NLG) as the unit of currency in The Netherlands. For more information, see p. 14. A bare-bones day trav-eling in The Netherlands will cost €30-35; a slightly more comfortable day will run €50-60. Service charges are always included in bills for hotels, shopping, and res-taurants. Tips for services are accepted and appreciated but not necessary. Taxi drivers are generally tipped 10% of the fare.

COMMUNICATION

TELEPHONES. Pay phones require a Chipknip card, which can be bought at hostels, train stations, and tobacconists for as little as €4.50. Even when using a calling card, a Chipknip card is necessary to gain access to the phone system.

THE NETHERLANDS

PHONE CODES	**Country code:** 31. **International dialing prefix:** 00. From outside The Netherlands, dial int'l dialing prefix (see inside back cover) + 31 + city code + local number.

Mobile phones are an increasingly popular and economical alternative (p. 30). For directory assistance, dial ☎09 00 80 08; for collect calls, dial ☎06 04 10. International dial direct numbers include: AT&T ☎0800 022 91 11; Australia Direct ☎0800 022 20 61; BT Direct ☎0800 022 00 44; Canada Direct ☎0800 022 91 16; Ireland Direct ☎0800 02 20 353; MCI WorldPhone Direct ☎0800 022 91 22; NZ Direct ☎0800 022 44 64; Sprint ☎0800 022 91 19; Telekom South Africa Direct ☎0800 022 02 27.

MAIL. Post offices are generally open Monday to Friday 9am-6pm, and some are also open Saturday 10am-1:30pm; larger branches may stay open later. Mailing a postcard or letter (up to 20g) in the EU or a postcard outside of Europe costs €0.54; letters to outside of Europe cost €0.75. Mail takes 2-3 days to the UK, 4-6 to North America, 6-8 to Australia and New Zealand, and 8-10 to South Africa. Address mail to be held according to the following example: Firstname SUR-NAME, *Poste Restante*, Museumplein Post Office, 1071 DJ Amsterdam, NL.

INTERNET ACCESS. Email is easily accessible within The Netherlands. In small towns, if Internet access is not listed, try the library or even your hostel.

ACCOMMODATIONS AND CAMPING

NETHERLANDS	❶	❷	❸	❹	❺
ACCOMMODATIONS	under €30	€30-49	€50-69	€70-100	over €100

VVV offices supply accommodation listings and can almost always reserve rooms in both local and other areas (fee around €2). **Private rooms** cost about two-thirds as much as hotels, but they are hard to find; check with the VVV. During July and August, many cities add a tourist tax of €1.15 to the price of all rooms. The country's best values are the 34 **HI youth hostels,** run by **Stayokay International Hostels,** formerly the Dutch Youth Hostel Federation (NJHC). Hostels are divided into four price categories based on quality. Most are exceedingly clean and modern. The VVV has a list of hostels, and the useful *Jeugdherbergen* brochure describes each one (both free). For more information, contact Stayokay at P. O. Box 9191, 1006 AD, Amsterdam (☎010 264 60 64; www.stayokay.com). **Camping** is available across the country, but many sites are crowded and trailer-ridden in summer.

FOOD AND DRINK

NETHERLANDS	❶	❷	❸	❹	❺
FOOD	under €7	€7-10	€11-14	€15-20	over €20

Traditional Dutch cuisine is usually hearty, heavy, meaty, and wholesome. Expect a lot of bread and cheese for breakfast and lunch, and generous portions of meats and fishes for dinner. Popular seafood choices include all sorts of grilled fish and shellfish, fish stews, and raw herring. To round out a truly authentic Dutch meal (especially in May and June), ask for white asparagus, which can be a main dish on its own, served with potatoes, ham, and eggs. The Dutch conception of a light snack often includes *tostjes* (piping hot grilled cheese sandwiches, occasionally with ham), *broodjes* (sandwiches), *oliebollen* (doughnuts), or *poffertjes* (small pancakes). Colonial history has brought Surinamese and Indonesian cuisine to The Netherlands, followed closely by near-relatives from other South American and Asian countries. Indonesian cuisine is probably one of the safest bets for vegetarians. Wash it all down with a small, foamy glass of Heineken or Amstel.

HOLIDAYS AND FESTIVALS

Holidays: New Year's Day (Jan. 1); Good Friday (Apr. 9); Easter Sunday and Monday (Apr. 11 and 12); Liberation Day (May 5); Ascension Day (May 9); Whitsunday and Whitmonday (June 3-4); Christmas Day (Dec. 25); Boxing Day (Dec. 26; also called Second Christmas Day).

Festivals: Koninginnedag (Queen's Day; Apr. 30) turns the country into a huge carnival. The **Holland Festival** (in June) features more than 30 productions in a massive celebration of the arts. **Bloemen Corso** (Flower Parade; first Sa in Sept.) runs from Aalsmeer to Amsterdam. Many historical canal houses and windmills are open to the public for **National Monument Day** (2nd Sa in Sept.). The **Cannabis Cup** (November) celebrates the magical mystery weed that brings millions of visitors to Amsterdam every year.

AMSTERDAM ☎020

Amsterdam is not merely the city of garish sin. While the aroma of marijuana smoke does waft out of coffeeshops and prostitutes do pose provocatively behind windows bathed in red light, there is much to savor beyond the city's fabulous excess. Amsterdam has long been a center of varied openness—the same culture of acceptance that tolerates cannabis use and a commercial sex trade has also turned the city into an immigrant capital; countless refugees from Spain to Surinam have called this city home, giving it a multicultural richness rivaled by few places on earth. A Golden Age of art flourished in Amsterdam, and art remains in many forms—Rembrandt's shadowy portraits, Vermeer's luminous women, and the post-Impressionist swirls of van Gogh's brush. And here, history breathes. Renaissance canal houses perch on enchanting waterways, while subtle remnants of WWII Nazi occupation litter the streets. Accordingly, this supremely relaxed capital of northern Europe is alluring for all sorts of guests: Eagerly experimenting youth, pot pilgrims, businesspeople, art aficionados, and history buffs. They all serve as a reminder that, though Amsterdam *is* a place for indulging desires, the best trip to Amsterdam isn't necessarily the one you won't remember.

▐▘ TRANSPORTATION

Flights: Schiphol Airport (AMS; ☎(0800) 72 44 74 65). Light rail **sneltrains** connect the airport to Centraal Station (20min., every 10min., €3).

Trains: Centraal Station, Stationspl. 1, at the northern end of the Damrak (☎09 00 92 92, €0.30 per min.; www.ns.nl). To: **Brussels** (2½-3hr., 1-2 per hr., €40); **Groningen** (2½hr., 2 per hr., €25); **Haarlem** (20min., 1-2 per hr., €3.10); **Leiden** (35min., 1-6 per hr., €6.60); **Paris** (4hr., 8 per day, €87); **Rotterdam** (1hr., 1-4 per hr, €12); **The Hague** (50min., 1-4 per hr., €8.50); **Utrecht** (30min., 3-6 per hr., €5.60).

Buses: Trains are quicker, but the **GVB** (see below) will direct you to a bus stop for domestic destinations not on a rail line. **Muiderpoort** (2 blocks east of Oosterpark) sends buses east; **Marnixstation** (at the corner of Marnixstr. and Kinkerstr.) west; and the **Stationsplein depot** north and south.

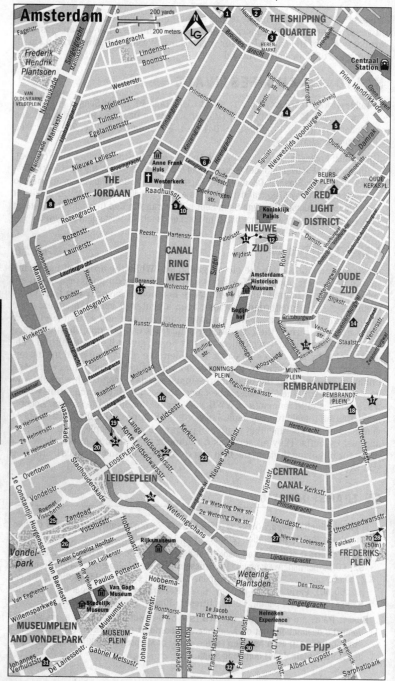

Public Transportation: GVB (☎09 00 92 92, €0.30 per min.) Stationspl. In front of Centraal Station. Open M-F 7am-9pm, Sa-Su 8am-9pm. **Tram, Metro,** and **bus** lines radiate from Centraal Station. Trams are most convenient for inner-city travel; the Metro leads to farther-out neighborhoods. Normal public transportation runs daily 6am-12:30am; from 12:30am-6am, night buses traverse the city—pick up a schedule at the GVB. *Strippenkart* are used on all public transportation in Amsterdam; two strips (€1.40) will get you to almost all sights within the city center and is good for unlimited transportation for one hour. *Strippenkart* are cheaper when bought in bulk (up to bundles of 45) and are available everywhere, especially at newsstands and VVV offices.

Bike Rental: Bike rental runs about €5-12 per day, plus a €30-100 deposit. Try **Frederic Rent a Bike,** Brouwersgr. 78 (☎624 55 09; www.frederic.nl), in the Shipping Quarter. Bikes €10 per day, which includes lock and theft insurance. Reserve online. AmEx/MC/V required for deposit, but pay in cash only.

✴ ORIENTATION

Welcome to Amsterdam, the "Venice of the North," whose confusing neighborhoods can be easily explored through its guiding canals. In Amsterdam, water runs in concentric circles, radiating from Centraal Station, the starting point for most visitors. The **Singel** runs around the **Centrum,** which includes the **Oude Zijd,** the infamous **Red Light District,** and the **Nieuwe Zijd.** In a space not even a kilometer in diameter, brothels, bars, clubs, and tourists abound under wafting marijuana smoke. The next three canals are the **Herengracht,** the **Keizersgracht,** and the **Prinsengracht,** lined by streets of the same name. The land around them is known as the **Canal Ring,** home to beautiful canal houses and classy nightlife, including bars and traditional *bruin cafes.* In the eastern end of the Canal Ring, **Rembrandtplein** is the city's gay district and home to some raucous nightlife, while in the western end, at the corner of Leidsegrt. and Singelgrt., **Leidseplein** boasts some of the city's best restaurants and nightlife. Just over the Singelgrt., **Museumplein** is home to the city's most deservedly famous art museums as well as the sprawling **Vondelpark.** Farther out lie the more residential Amsterdam neighborhoods: To the west the **Jordaan, Oud-West,** and **Westerpark;** to the east **Plantage** and the **Jodenbuurt;** and to the south **De Pijp.** Though these districts are populated by dense housing, they still boast excellent eateries and brilliant museums.

THE NETHERLANDS

Amsterdam

🛏 ACCOMMODATIONS
City Hotel, **18**
Euphemia Budget Hotel, **27**
Flying Pig Downtown, **5**
The Flying Pig Palace, **26**
The Golden Bear, **16**
Hans Brinker Hotel, **23**
Hemp Hotel, **28**
Hotel Bema, **20**
Hotel Brouwer, **4**
Hotel Clemens, **9**
Hotel de Stadhouder, **29**
Hotel Winston, **7**
Ramenas Hotel, **1**
The Shelter Jordan, **8**

StayOkay Amsterdam
  Stadsdoelen, **14**
StayOkay Amsterdam
  Vondelpark, **25**
Weichmann Hotel, **10**

🍴 BEST OF FOOD
Cafe De Pijp, **30**
Eat at Jo's, **19**
Harlem: Drinks and
  Soulfood, **3**
Lunchcafe Nielson, **13**
Zagros, **32**

☕ BEST OF COFFEESHOPS
Abraxas, **12**
Barney's Coffeeshop, **2**
Grey Area, **7**

⭐ BEST OF NIGHTLIFE
Bourbon Street Jazz
  & Blues Club, **22**
Cafe de Jaren, **15**
The iT, **17**
Melkweg, **21**
NL Lounge, **11**
Paradiso, **24**

⚡ PRACTICAL INFORMATION

TOURIST, FINANCIAL, AND LOCAL SERVICES

Tourist Office: VVV, Stationspl. 10 (☎(0900) 400 40 40, €0.55 per min.), to the left when exiting Centraal Station. Room booking fee €3. Open M-F 9am-5pm. **Branches** inside Centraal Station (open M-Sa 8am-7:45pm, Su 9am-5pm) and Leidsepl. 1 (open M-Th 9am-6pm, F-Sa 9am-7pm, Su 9am-5pm).

Budget Travel: Eurolines, Rokin 10 (☎560 87 88; www.eurolines.nl). Books coach travel throughout Europe. Open M-F 9:30am-5:30pm, Sa 10am-4pm.

Consulates: All foreign embassies are in **The Hague** (p. 757). **American Consulate,** Museumpl. 19 (☎575 53 09; open M-F 8:30am-11:30pm). **British Consulate,** Koningslaan 44 (☎676 43 43; open M-F 9am-noon, and 2-5:30pm).

American Express: American Express, Damrak 66, offers the best rates, no commission on AmEx Traveler's Checks, and a €4 flat fee for all non-euro cash and non-AmEx Traveler's Checks. Open M-F 9am-5pm, Sa 9am-noon.

Bi-Gay-Lesbian Resources: COC, Rozenstr. 14 (☎626 30 87; www.cocamsterdam.nl), is a social network and main source of info. Open M-Tu and Th-F 10am-5pm, W 10am-8pm. **Gay and Lesbian Switchboard** (☎623 65 65) takes calls daily 10am-10pm.

Laundromat: Aquarette, Oudebrugsteeg 22 (☎638 13 97), off Damrak just south of Centraal Station. Self-service 5kg load for €5, dry €1 per 12min. Go to Continental Hotel across the street for doorkey. Open daily 8am-9:30pm. Cash only.

EMERGENCY AND COMMUNICATIONS

Emergency: Medical, Police, and Fire ☎112; no coins required.

Police: Headquarters, Elandsgr. 117 (☎08 00 88 44), at the intersection with Marnixstr. Call here for the **Rape Crisis Deparment.**

Crisis Lines: General counseling at **Telephone Helpline** (☎675 75 75). Open 24hr. **Rape crisis hotline** (☎612 02 45) staffed M-F 10:30am-11pm, Sa-Su 3:30-11pm. For **drug counseling,** call **Jellinek Clinic** (☎570 22 22). Open M-F 9am-5pm.

Medical Assistance: For hospital care, **Academisch Medisch Centrum,** Meibergdreef 9 (☎566 91 11), is easily accessible by bus #59, 60, 120, or 158 from Centraal Station (ask the driver to announce the medical center). **Kruispost Medisch Helpcentrum,** Oudezijds Voorburgwal 129 (☎624 90 31), is a walk-in clinic offering first aid only to non-insured travelers daily 7am-9pm. For 24hr. medical help, call the English-speaking **Centrale Doktorsdienst** (☎592 34 34). **STD Line,** Groenburgwal 44 (☎555 58 22), offers phone counseling. Free testing clinic if you call ahead. Open for calls M-F 8am-noon, 1-4pm.

24hr. Pharmacy: A hotline (☎694 87 09) will direct you to the nearest pharmacy.

Internet Access: Internet access in Amsterdam leaves much to be desired; the best bet may be a cozy coffeeshop. Try **easyEverything,** Reguliersbreestr. 22 and Damrak 34. (€1 generally buys 26min., but varies according to demand. Open 24hr.) Other cafes include **The Mad Processor,** Bloemgr. 82. (€3 per hr; open daily noon-2am) and **Free World,** Nieuwendijk 30 (€1 per 30min; open M-Th and Su 9am-1am, F-Sa 9am-3am).

Post Office: Singel 250, at Radhuisstr. Address mail to be held: Firstname, SURNAME, *Poste Restante,* Singel 250, Amsterdam, THE NETHERLANDS. Open M-W and F 9am-6pm, Th 9am-8pm, Sa 10am-1:30pm.

ACCOMMODATIONS

Accommodations near **Centraal Station** often take good security measures due to the chaos of the nearby Red Light District. Hostels and hotels near **Museumplein** toward the south and the **Jordaan** out to the west are quieter and safer. Both locations are close to bars, coffeeshops, AND museums and are a mere 2min. by tram from the heart of the city. Museumpl. is also very close to the bustling Leidsepl. The accommodations in the **Red Light District** (surrounded by the Oude Zijd) are often bars with beds over them. Before booking a bed there, consider just how much noise and drug use you can tolerate from your neighbors.

OUDE ZIJD, NIEUWE ZIJD, AND THE RED LIGHT DISTRICT

StayOkay Amsterdam Stadsdoelen, Kloveniersburgwal 97 (☎624 68 32; www.hostel-booking.com). Clean, drug-free lodgings in a quiet corner of Centrum. Bar on site. Kitchen available. Breakfast and sheets included. Laundry facilities available. Internet €1 per 12min. Reception 7am-1am. Dorms €22; €2.50 HI discount. MC/V. ❶

Hotel Winston, Warmoesstr. 129 (☎623 13 80; www.winston.nl). Rooms painted by local artists and designers make every room feel like an installation art piece. Club downstairs. Singles €60-72; doubles €74-96; triples €113-128. AmEx/MC/V. ❹

Anna Youth Hostel, Spuistr. 6 (☎620 11 55). By far the most beautiful hostel in the city. The quiet, drug-free ambience is surprising given its central location in the Nieuwe Zijd. Sheets and lockers included. 2-night min. stay on weekends. Reservations recommended. Closed during part of Dec. Dorms €16-18; doubles €70-80. AmEx/MC/V. ❶

Flying Pig Downtown, Nieuwendijk 100 (☎420 68 22; www.flyingpig.nl). Helpful and professional staff, great location, and colorful decor—a perennial favorite among backpackers. Kitchen available. Breakfast and sheets included. Key deposit €10. Dorms €21-27; singles and doubles €76. AmEx/MC/V. ❶

Hotel Brouwer, Singelgr. 83 (☎624 63 58; www.hotelbrouwer.nl). Eight gorgeously restored rooms each named after a Dutch painter: Rembrandt, Vermeer, and others. Breakfast included. Singles €50; doubles €85. Cash and traveler's checks only. ❷

SHIPPING QUARTER, CANAL RING WEST, AND THE JORDAAN

Hotel Clemens, Raadhuisstr. 39 (☎624 60 89; www.clemenshotel.nl). A gem with renovated, elegant suites. Internet and safe in all rooms. Breakfast €7. Key deposit €20. Book well in advance. Min. stay 3 nights on weekends. Singles €55; doubles €70-75, deluxe €110; triples €125/150. Cash only for budget rooms. AmEx/MC/V. ❷

Wiechmann Hotel, Prinsengr. 328-332 (☎626 33 21; www.hotelwiechmann.nl). Three restored canal houses with spacious rooms. Breakfast included. Singles €70-90; doubles with bath €125-135; triples and quads €170-230. MC/V. ❸

Ramenas Hotel, Haarlemmerdijk 61 (☎624 60 30; www.amsterdamhotels.com). Ramenas's rooms are ascetic, but they get the job done. Breakfast included. Reservations via website. Doubles €64-80; triples €96-120; quints €160-200. MC/V. ❶

The Shelter Jordan, Bloemstr. 179 (☎624 47 17; www.shelter.nl). Religious, but not proselytizing, this companionable Christian hostel is a treasure. No smoking or alcohol. Age limit 35. Breakfast included. Lockers €5; free storage for larger bags. Internet €0.50 per 20min. Curfew 2am. Dorms €16.50-18. MC/V. ❶

THE LOCAL STORY

HEMP, PH.D

Lorna Clay volunteers at **⬛ Cannabis College** (p. 748), the city's foremost authority on all things related to marijuana, hashish, and hemp. *Lets Go* got her very informed opinion about cannabis in Amsterdam:

...In the 60s, originally the coffeeshops were known as teahouses. You couldn't buy cannabis, but you could go and buy tea and smoke it there. Then, when the licenses came out, it was just to provide a bit more choice for people and take it away from the criminals. Right off, there only used to be about four or five coffeeshops here, and that was fine for the people that lived here. Then, since the late 70s, Amsterdam's become a mecca for smokers.

...Unfortunately, Amsterdam has seen a big amount of drug tourism and that's been exploited by a lot of horrible owners. They think 'I can sell [tourists] bad cannabis and they'll never come back, and that's fine because I've made my money.' There's 281 coffeeshops in Amsterdam and I can recommend you 15, honestly... a lot of the owners don't even smoke. A good thing to look out for are the members of the BCD--basically a union of coffeeshops. We can give you a BCD map.

LEIDSEPLEIN AND MUSEUMPLEIN

⬛ **StayOkay Amsterdam Vondelpark,** Zandpad 5 (☎589 89 96; www.stayokay.com/vondelpark). A palatial, slightly corporate, hostel with many amenities. Breakfast and sheets included. Lockers €2.50. Internet €0.50 per min. Reception 7:30am-midnight. Reserve well in advance. Dorms €21-25; quads €26-28. €2.50 HI discount. MC/V. ❶

⬛ **Quentin Hotel,** Leidsekade 89 (☎626 21 87). You don't have to sacrifice style to get budget accommodations. Each room bears a distinctive motif. Continental breakfast €7. Reception 24hr. Singles €40, with facilities €65; smaller "economy" doubles with facilities €80, regular doubles €100; triples €133. AmEx/MC/V with 5% surcharge. ❷

⬛ **Hotel Bema,** Concertgebouw 19b (☎679 13 96; www.bemahotel.com). Charming 7-room hotel with skylights, a friendly staff, and funky neo-hippie style. Breakfast included. Reception 8am-midnight. Singles €50-65; doubles €68-85; triples €85-120; quads €105-160. AmEx/MC/V with 5% surcharge. ❷

Flying Pig Palace, Vossiusstr. 46-47 (☎400 41 87; www.flyingpig.nl). Laid-back, friendly attitude with views of the park. Ages 18-35 only. Sheets included. Free Internet. Reception 8am-9pm. Dorms €20-38; doubles €63-66. AmEx/MC/V. ❶

Hans Brinker Hotel, Kerkstr. 136 (☎622 06 87; www.hans-brinker.com). Really a massive hostel, with spartan, clean rooms. Guest-only bar. No visitors. Breakfast included. Free Internet. Key deposit €5. Reception 24hr. Dorms €29-35; singles €52; doubles €58-75; triples €90; quads €96. AmEx/MC/V. ❶

CENTRAL CANAL RING AND REMBRANDTPLEIN

⬛ **Hemp Hotel,** Frederikspl. 15 (☎625 44 25; www.hemp-hotel.com). Only 5 rooms, but each is lovingly done up to celebrate one of the world's major hemp-producing regions: Afghanistan, the Caribbean, India, Morocco, and Tibet. Everything is made of hemp—bedclothes, curtains, and even soap. Single €50; doubles €65-70. ❸

Euphemia Budget Hotel, Fokke Simonszstr. 1-9 (☎622 90 45; www.euphemiahotel.com). Welcoming, quiet, and bright budget digs in a former monastery. Gay friendly. Continental breakfast €5. Internet €1 per 15min. Reception 8am-11pm. Dorms €23; doubles €46; triples €69. AmEx/MC/V with 5% surcharge. ❶

The Golden Bear, Kerkstr. 37 (☎624 47 85; www.goldenbear.nl). Opened in 1948, The Golden Bear may be the oldest openly gay hotel in the world. Mainly male couples frequent the hotel, though lesbians are welcome as well. Breakfast included. Singles €57-99; double €78-112. AmEx/MC/V. ❸

City Hotel, Utrechtsestr. 2 (☎627 23 23; www.city-hotel.nl). Classy, spacious accommodations above a pub right on the Rembrandtpl. Rooms immaculately kept. Breakfast included. Reception 24hr. Doubles €80-90, doubles with facilities €90-100; triples €105-135; quads €140-180. AmEx/DC/MC/V. ❹

DE PIJP, JODENBUURT, AND THE PLANTAGE

▨ **Bicycle Hotel,** Van Ostadestr. 123 (☎679 34 52; www.bicyclehotel.com). Clean digs, spotless bathrooms, and a leafy garden. Bicycle-friendly hotel with a bike garage, trip recommendations, and bike decor. Breakfast included. Free Internet. Double €68-70, with bath €99; triples €90/120; quads with bath €120. Cash only. ❷

Hotel Pension Kitty, Plantage Middenlaan 40 (☎622 68 19). Look out for the small sign. Gentle 80-year-old proprietress provides for those seeking a peaceful respite. Grandmotherly warmth and wonderful tranquility abound. No children. Singles €50; doubles €60-70; triples €75. Cash only. ❷

Hotel De Stadhouder, Stadhouderskade 76 (☎671 84 28). Well-kept rooms, some with patios or canal views. Breakfast and sheets included. Singles €35-65; doubles €40-85; triples €75-100; quads €110/95; quints €125/85. AmEx/MC/V with 5% surcharge. ❸

🍴 FOOD

Many cheap restaurants cluster around **Leidseplein**, **Rembrandtplein**, and the **Spui**. Cafes, especially in the Jordaan, serve inexpensive sandwiches (€1.50-4) and good meat-and-potatoes fare (€5.50-9). Bakeries line **Utrechtsestraat**, south of Prinsengr. Fruit, cheese, flowers, and even live chickens fill the **markets** on **Albert Cuypstraat**, behind the Heineken brewery. (Open M-Sa 9am-6pm.)

NIEUWE ZIJD AND OUDE ZIJD

▨ **In de Waag,** Nieuwmarkt 4 (☎452 77 72; www.indewaag.nl) In the late 1400s, this castle served as the eastern entrance to the city. Today, sandwiches and salads (€4-8.50) are served on the patio for lunch. At night, the restaurant lights 250 candles and patrons pack the medieval behemoth for richly flavored Italian, French, and Norwegian specialties. Entrees €17-22. Open M-Th and Su 10am-midnight, F-Sa 10am-1am; often open until 3am on busy evenings. ❷

...If a company doesn't even distinguish on their menu between bio or hydro, it's not worth buying. Bio is when weed's grown in soil and hydro is when it's grown in water. Usually when you're growing hydro, you're filling it with artificial chemical nutrients. Good quality coffeeshops will sell good quality hydro but in bad quality coffeeshops, they don't flush the chemicals out of their plants so you get high off the harmful chemicals.

...[In a coffeeshop] don't ask: what's the strongest? It's difficult for someone to answer, because what's strongest for one is not strongest for someone else. Ask them for their most flavorsome, not their strongest. Ask them what they recommend. Never go in and ask for a name because it depends on who grows the particular plant, not the strain. For example, White Widow—it's just been made famous by the name. You will find they will bump up the price. Never ever be afraid to ask the guy or the girl about their weed. Just like if you walk into a wine bar, you want to ask advice about wine. If they give you [a hard time], honestly, turn around and walk straight out... Don't give them your business.

...Know the difference between Sativa and Indica. Sativa will get you high and giggly and energized and that is something that "Haze" or "Kali Mist" will do. When you smoke the Indica, that gets you really stoned and relaxed, and that's like "Afghani Shiva" or "Buddha." The choice is: Do you want to get high or stoned?

Pannenkoekenhuis Upstairs, Grimburgwal 2 (☎626 56 03). This tiny nook boasts the city's best pancakes (€5-9). Open M-F noon-7pm, Sa noon-6pm, Su noon-5pm. ❶

Ristorante Caprese, Spuistr. 259-261 (☎620 00 59). Excellent Italian food accompanied by smooth jazz. Open daily 5-10:45pm. No reservations. ❸

Theehuis Himalaya, Warmoesstr. 56 (☎626 08 99; www.himalaya.nl). The back room houses a Buddhist-themed *theehuis* that serves light vegetarian and vegan lunches as well as 40 varieties of tea. Tasty *tostis* €3-3.50. Pies €3-3.25. Open M 1-6pm, Tu-W and F-Sa 10am-6pm, Th 10am-8:30pm, Su 12:30-5pm. AmEx/MC/V. ❶

Aneka Rasa, Warmoesstr. 25-29 (☎626 15 60). Find elegance amid the seediness of the Red Light District. Indonesian *rijsttafel* (rice table) €16-27 per person. Open daily 5-10:30pm. AmEx/MC/V. ❸

SHIPPING QUARTER, CANAL RING WEST, AND THE JORDAAN

▨ **Harlem: Drinks and Soulfood,** Haarlemmerstr. 77 (☎330 14 98). High-class fusion cuisine blends American-style soul food with Cajun and Caribbean flavors. Entrees €12-17. Soups and sandwiches €4-5. Open M-Th 10am-1am, F-Sa 10am-3am, Su 11am-1am. Kitchen closes 10pm. MC/V. ❸

▨ **Lunchcafe Nielson,** Berenstr. 19 (☎330 60 06). A bright ray of light in an already shining neighborhood. Brilliant breakfast and lunch served all day (€4-10). Open Tu-F 8am-5pm, Sa 8am-6pm, Su 9am-5pm; kitchen closes 30min. before restaurant. ❶

Bolhoed, Prinsengr. 60-62 (☎626 18 03). The best in vegetarian and vegan fare—fresh, flavorful, and lovingly prepared. Pastas, casseroles, and Mexican dishes €12.50-15. Fresh-squeezed juices as well as organic and vegan desserts around €4. Dinner reservations a must. Open M-F and Su 11am-10pm, last reservation 9pm. Cash only. ❸

Cinema Paradiso, Westerstr. 186 (☎623 73 44). Cavernous former cinema with purist Italian food and candle-lit charm. Antipasti €4-10. Pasta €9-15. No reservations; be prepared for a wait. Open Su and Tu-Sa 6-11pm; kitchen closes 11pm. AmEx/MC/V. ❷

Wolvenstraat 23, Wolvenstr. 23 (☎320 08 43). At this trendy spot, lunch means sandwiches (€2-5.20), salads (€6), and omelets (€3-4) and dinner means Cantonese cuisine (around €10). Lunch menu 8am-3:30pm, dinner 6-10:30pm. Open M-Th 8am-1am, F 8am-2am, Sa 9am-2am, Su 10am-1am. Cash only. ❷

LEIDSEPLEIN AND MUSEUMPLEIN

▨ **Eat at Jo's,** Marnixstr. 409 (☎624 17 77; www.melkweg.nl), inside Melkweg. Multi-ethnic menu that changes daily. Soups (€3.40) and numerous vegetarian options (entrees €10) earn raves. Open Su and W-Sa noon-9pm. Cash only. ❶

Cafe Vertigo, Vondelpark 3 (☎612 30 21; www.vertigo.nl). Vertigo's expansive, tree-lined terrace is the perfect place to relax. Skip the pricier dinner menu in favor of the lunch sandwiches (€4) and tasty pastries (€2). Open daily 10am-1am. MC/V. ❶

Bojo, Lange Leidsedwarsstr. 51 (☎622 74 34). Popular Indonesian eatery with stalwart Javanese chow. Dishes €5.80-11. Try the mini *rijstaffel* sampler (€10.50). Open M-Th 4pm-2am, F 4pm-4am, Sa noon-4am, Su noon-2am. MC/V. ❸

CENTRAL CANAL RING AND REMBRANDTPLEIN

▨ **Maoz Falafel** Regulierbreestr. 45 (☎624 92 90). Great falafels with all-you-can-stack self-serve salad bar (for any size) make this the best budget deal in the city. Small falafel €2.50. Other locations: Outside Centraal Station; Muntpl. 1; Leidsestr. 85; Ferdinand Bolstr. 67. Open daily at least 11am-11pm; hours vary by location. ❶

Lanskroon, Singel 385 (☎623 77 43). The city's best traditional Dutch pastries and wonderful sorbet. Open Su 10am-5pm, Tu-F 8am-5:30pm, Sa 8am-5pm. Cash only. ❶

Coffee and Jazz, Utrechtsestr. 113 (☎624 58 51). Dutch-Indonesian fusion: Fruity *pannenkoeken* (€4.50-7) share the menu with tender lamb and chicken *satay* (€7-9). Locals say this is the best coffee in town. Open Tu-F 9:30am-8pm, Sa 10am-4pm. ❷

DE PIJP, JODENBUURT, AND THE PLANTAGE

▨ **Cafe De Pijp,** Ferdinand Bolstr. 17-19 (☎670 41 61). Stylish, but affordable with flavorsome fusion food. Soup of the day €3.90. Appetizers €7.90. Entrees €13-15. Cocktails €5. Open M-Th and Su noon-1am, F-Sa noon-3am. Cash only. ❸

▨ **Zagros,** Albert Cuypstr. 50 (☎670 04 61). Great Kurdish cuisine influenced by the 5 countries spanned by Kurdistan—Armenia, Iran, Iraq, Syria, and Turkey—in a plain but appealing candlelit atmosphere. Hearty, lamb-heavy menu (€10-14) but plenty of veggie options. Open daily 3pm-midnight. AmEx/MC/V. ❷

Cafe Latei, Zeedijk 143 (☎625 74 85). Unique cafe-*cum*-curiosities-shop, with all-day continental breakfast (€6.40). Large sandwiches about €3. Fresh juices €2-4. Call for special food events. Open M-F 8am-6pm, Sa 9am-6pm, Su 11am-6pm. ❶

Abe Veneto, Plantage Kerklaan 2 (☎639 23 64). This homey Italian eatery has food and prices to make any traveler happy. A dizzying selection of freshly made pizzas (€4.50-9.50), pastas (€6.50-9.50), and salads (most under €5). Wine by the bottle or the carafe (half carafe €6.50). Takeout available. Open daily noon-midnight. Cash only. ❷

◉ SIGHTS

Amsterdam is fairly compact, so tourists can easily explore the area from the Rijksmuseum to the Red Light District on foot. For those not inclined to pedestrian navigation, the tram system will get you to any of the city's major sights within minutes from any destination (p. 739). For a peaceful trip, **Museumboot Canal Cruise** allows you to hop on and off along its loop from the VVV to the Anne Frank Huis, the Bloemenmarkt, the Rijksmuseum, Waterloopl., and the old shipyard. (Every 30min. Day ticket €14.30; €12.50 after 1pm.)

OUDE ZIJD, THE RED LIGHT DISTRICT, AND NIEUWE ZIJD

THE RED LIGHT DISTRICT. No trip to Amsterdam would be complete without witnessing the notorious spectacle that is the Red Light District. After dark, the area actually takes on a red radiance—sex theaters throw open their doors, and the main streets are thick with people gawking at the unabashed openness of the window prostitutes; **Warmoesstraat** and **Oudezijds Achterburgwal** boast wall-to-wall brothels. There are also **sex shows,** in which actors perform strictly choreographed fantasies on stage for 1hr.; the most famous live sex show takes place at **Casa Rosso,** Oudezijds Achterburgwal 106-108, where €25 will buy you admission to 8 or 9 consecutive acts and complimentary drinks. The Casa's **marble penis fountain** across from the theater is the Red Light District's most recognizable landmark. (☎627 89 54; www.janot.com. Open daily M-Th 8pm-2am, F-Sa 8pm-3am.)

BEGIJNHOF. You don't have to take vows to enter this secluded courtyard—the 14th-century home of the Beguines, a sect of religiously devoted laywomen—but you will have to get up early. Begijnhof's peaceful, rose-lined gardens, beautifully manicured lawns, and tree-lined walkways afford a much-needed respite from the bustling excesses of the Nieuwe Zijd. The oldest house in Amsterdam, **Het Houten Huys** (The Wooden House), is located on the premises. *(Open July-Aug. daily 8-11am; Sept.-May 9am-5pm. Free. Het Houten Huys ☎ 623 55 54. Open M-F 8-10am. Free.)*

OUDE KERK. The "old church" may come as a welcome, wholesome shock, smack in the middle of the otherwise lurid Red Light District. Oude Kerk is a stunning structure, with an enormous interior and magnificent stained-glass windows. The earliest parish church built in Amsterdam, it is now a center for cultural activities, hosting photography and modern art exhibitions. At the head of the church is the massive Vater-Müller organ, which was built in 1724 and is still played for public concerts. *(Oudekerkspl. 23. ☎ 625 82 84; www.oude-kerk.nl. Open M-Sa 11am-5pm, Su 1-5pm. €4, students €3. Additional admission for exhibitions.)*

NIEWMARKT. On the border between the Oude Zijd and the Jodenbuurt, Niew-markt is worth a visit simply to take a look at the Waag, Amsterdam's largest surviving medieval building. Dating from the 15th century, the Waag was one of Amsterdam's fortified city gates and later housed the Surgeons Guild's amphi-teater. Public dissections and private anatomy lessons were once held there, as Rembrandt's *The Anatomy Lesson of Dr. Tulp* famously depicts.

DAM SQUARE AND KONINKLIJK PALEIS. The **Koninklijk Paleis** (Royal Palace) was completed in 1655 and functioned as the town hall until Louis Napoleon had it renovated and remodeled in 1808 to better serve the function of a royal residence. Today Queen Beatrix still uses the building for official receptions though she makes her home in The Hague. The palace's indisputable highlight is the **Citizen's Hall,** designed to replicate the universe in a single room. Across the large Dam Square is the Dutch **Nationaal Monument,** unveiled on May 4, 1956, to honor Dutch victims of WWII. Inside the 21m white stone obelisk is soil from all twelve of Holland's provinces as well as from the Dutch East Indies. *(Koninklijk Paleis ☎ 620 40 60; www.kon-paleisamsterdam.nl. Palace open June-Aug. daily 12:30-5pm; off-season hours vary. €4.50, children and seniors €3.60. Under-6 free.)*

CANAL RING WEST AND THE JORDAAN

WESTERKERK. This stunning Protestant church was designed by Roman Catholic architect Hendrick de Keyser and completed in 1631. It stands as one of the last structures built in the Dutch Renaissance style, which can be distinguished by its use of both brick and stone. Rembrandt is believed to be buried here, though the exact spot of his resting place has not yet been located. Climb the **Westerkerkstoren** tower in a 45min.-1hr. tour for a great view of the city. *(Prinsengr. 281. ☎ 624 77 66. Open July-Aug. M-Sa 11am-3pm; Sept. and Apr.-June M-F 11am-3pm. Tours every hr. €3.)*

HOMOMONUMENT AND PINK POINT. Homomonument serves as a tripartite memorial to men and women persecuted for their homosexuality, and since 1987 has stood in the center of Amsterdam as a testament to the strength and resilience of the homosexual community. Karin Daan's design, three pink granite triangles, allude to the signs homosexuals were required to wear in Nazi concentration camps. The Homomonument's neighbor, **Pink Point,** stands as a reminder of everything vibrant and fun about gay life in Amsterdam. The kiosk is a clearinghouse for information on homosexual happenings. Pick up free listings of BGL bars, clubs, restaurants, and cultural life. *(Both in front of Westerkerk. Pink Point: ☎ 428 10 70; www.pinkpoint.org. Open Apr.-Sept. daily noon-6pm.)*

LEIDSEPLEIN AND MUSEUMPLEIN

LEIDSEPLEIN. Leidseplein proper is a crush of street musicians, blaring neon lights, and open-air urinals. Daytime finds the square packed with shoppers, smokers, and drinkers lining the sidewalks around the square. When night falls, tourists and locals emerge in packs of skin-tight jeans and greased-down hair. **Max Euweplein,** a square along Weteringschans named for the famous Dutch chess master, sports an enormous chess board with people-sized pieces.

VONDELPARK. With meandering walkways, green meadows, several ponds, beautifully maintained rose gardens and a 1.5km paved path for bikers and skaters, this English-style park is a lovely meeting place for children, seniors, soccer players, and stoners. Named after one of Holland's great writers, Joost van den Vondel, Vondelpark is home to an open-air theater—**The Openluchttheater** (☎ 673 14 99; www.openluchttheater.nl)—where visitors can enjoy free concerts during the summer. (*In the southwestern corner of the city, outside the Singelgr. A short walk across the canal and to the left from the Leidsepl. www.vondelpark.org.*)

CENTRAL CANAL RING AND REMBRANDTPLEIN

CENTRAL CANAL RING. You haven't seen Amsterdam until you've spent some time wandering in the Central Canal Ring, the city's highest rent district and arguably its most beautiful. Collectively, **Prinsengracht** (Prince's canal), **Keizersgracht** (Emperor's canal), and **Herengracht** (Gentlemen's canal) are known as the *grachtengordel* (literally "canal girdle"). The Ring is home to some of Amsterdam's most important and breathtaking architecture, particularly on a stretch of the Herengrt. between Leidsegrt. and Vijzelstr. that is known as the **Golden Bend** by virtue of its wide, lavish homes. (*Over the Singel and just south of Centrum.*)

REMBRANDTPLEIN. Rembrandtplein proper consists of a grass rectangle surrounded by scattered flowerbeds. A bronze likeness of the famed master, **Rembrandt van Rijn,** overlooks the scene, but it's what surrounds the greenery that makes this neighborhood unforgettable. Litters of bars and cafes are all packed with lively night owls. In the evening, Rembrandtpl. competes with Leidsepl. for Amsterdam's hippest nightlife, with a concentration of gay hotspots. South and west of the square lies **Reguliersdwarsstraat,** fittingly dubbed "the gayest street in Amsterdam," where good-looking men abound. (*In the northeast corner of the Central Canal Ring, just south of the Amstel.*)

DE PIJP, JODENBUURT, AND THE PLANTAGE

HEINEKEN EXPERIENCE. Beer is not made in the Heineken Brewery but plenty is served. The factory stopped producing here in 1988 and has turned the place into an amusement park devoted to their green-bottled beer. In the "Experience," visitors guide themselves past holograms, virtual reality machines, and other multimedia treats. A visit includes three beers and a souvenir glass. (*Heinekenpl.* ☎ 523 96 66; www.heinekenexperince.com. Open Su, Tu-Sa 10am-6pm; last entry at 5pm. Under-18 must be accompanied by a parent. €7.50.)

PORTUGEES-ISRAELIETISCHE SYNAGOGE. This beautifully maintained Portuguese synagogue dates to 1675, when it was founded by Jews fleeing the Spanish Inquisition. Since then, it has remained largely unchanged and still holds services. (*Mr. Visserpl. 1-3.* ☎ 624 53 51; www.esnoga.com. Open Apr.-Oct. M-F and Su 10am-4pm; Nov.-Mar. M-Th and Su 10am-4pm, F 10am-3pm. €5, under-15 €4.)

HOLLANDSCHE SCHOUWBURG. This historic building stands today as one of the region's most enduring symbols of freedom, a moving testament to Dutch life before, during, and after Hitler. Hollandsche Schouwburg was founded as a Dutch theater on the edge of the old Jewish quarter. It later underwent a metamorphosis in 1941, when Nazi occupiers converted it into the Joodsche Schouwburg, the city's sole establishment to which Jewish performers and Jewish patrons were granted access. Not long after, the building was changed into an assembly point for Dutch Jews who were to be deported to transit camps in the north. Now Hollandsche Schouwburg houses a memorial to Holocaust victims. (*Plantage Middenlaan 24.* ☎ *626 99 45; www.jhm.nl. Open daily 11am-4pm; closed on Yom Kippur. Free.*)

🏛 MUSEUMS

OUDE ZIJD, THE RED LIGHT DISTRICT, AND NIEUWE ZIJD

MUSEUM AMSTELKRING "ONS' LIEVE HEER OP SOLDER" ("OUR LORD IN THE ATTIC"). A secret enclave of virtue and piety hides in this 17th-century secret church, built during the Alteration for Catholics who were forbidden to practice their faith. Amstelkring, which once masqueraded as a shop front, contains a stunning little chapel which spans the attics of three adjacent buildings. (*Oudezijds Voorburgwal 40.* ☎ *624 66 04; www.museumamstelkring.nl. Open M-Sa 10am-5pm, Su and holidays 1-5pm. €6, students €4.50, under-18 €1.*)

THE VICES. If it's weed that interests you, far and away your best bet is the staggeringly informative ▓**Cannabis College,** Oudezijds Achterburgwal 124. The center for "higher" education offers info on everything from the uses of medicinal marijuana to facts about the War on Drugs to the creative applications of industrial hemp. For a curated taste of the seaminess that runs down Amsterdam's underbelly, your best bet is to head to the **Amsterdam Sex Museum,** Damrak 18, less than a five-minute walk from Centraal Station. The low admission fee won't leave you feeling burned if you find that walls plastered with pictures of bestiality and S&M are not your thing. (*Cannabis College open daily 11am-7pm. Free. Sex Museum open daily 10am-11:30pm. €2.50.*)

NIEUWE KERK. The extravagant 15th-century brick-red "new church" at the heart of the Nieuwe Zijd now serves a triple role as religious edifice, historical monument, and art museum. Through 2004, the originally Catholic church will open its doors to rotating exhibits from the Stedelijk collection's depository while the Stedelijk is being renovated. (*Adjacent to Dam Sq., beside Koninklijk Palace.* ☎ *638 69 09; www.nieuwekerk.nl. Open M-W, F, and Su, 10am-6pm; Th 10am-10pm. Organ recitals June-Sept. Su 8pm and Th 12:30pm. €8, ages 6-15 and seniors €6.*)

CANAL RING WEST AND THE JORDAAN

▓**ANNE FRANK HUIS.** A visit to the Anne Frank House is a must for everyone, whether or not you've read the famous diary. The museum chronicles the two years the Frank family and four other Jews spent hiding in the annex of this warehouse on the Prinsengr. The rooms are no longer furnished, but personal objects in display cases and text panels with excerpts from the diary bring the story of the eight inhabitants to life, and the magazine clippings and photos that Anne used to decorate her room still hang on the wall. Footage of interviews with Otto Frank, Miep Gies (who supplied the family with food and other necessities), and childhood friends of Anne provide further information and details. Arrive before 10am and after 4pm for the shortest lines. *(Prinsengr. 267. ☎ 556 71 00; www.annefrank.nl. Open Apr.-Aug. daily 9am-9pm; Sept.-Mar. daily 9am-7pm. Closed on Yom Kippur. Last admission 30min. before closing. €6.50, ages 10-17 €3. Under-10 free.)*

BIJBELS MUSEUM. The Bible Museum presents info both on the contents and history of the Bible and on the cultural context in which it was written. The collection includes the first Bible ever printed in The Netherlands. *(Herengr. 366-368. ☎ 624 24 36; www.bijbelsmuseum.nl. Open M-Sa 10am-5pm, Su 11am- 5pm. €5, children €2.50.)*

MUSEUMPLEIN

◪ VAN GOGH MUSEUM. This architecturally breathtaking museum houses the largest collection of van Goghs in the world and a diverse group of 19th-century paintings by contemporaries like Gaugin and friend Emile Bernard. Don't miss the substantial collection of Impressionist, post-Impressionist, Realist, and Symbolist art. *(Paulus Potterstr. 7. ☎ 570 52 52; www.vangoghmuseum.nl. Open daily 10am-6pm; ticket office closes 5:30pm. €9, ages 13-17 €2.50. Under-12 free. Audio guides €4.)*

◪ STEDELIJK MUSEUM OF MODERN ART. The Stedelijk has amassed a world-class collection that is on par with the Tate Modern or the MoMA. The museum is slated to close in January 2004 for up to three years of renovations, though this repair work may be delayed. If it does undergo renovations, the museum will exhibit selections from its collection in venues around Amsterdam, like the **CoBrA Museum** and the **Nieuwe Kerk** (p. 748); check the website for more up-to-date information. *(Paulus Potterstr. 13. ☎ 573 27 45; recorded info 573 29 11; www.stedelijk.nl. Open daily 11am-5pm. €7; ages 7-16, over-65 and groups over 15 €3.50. Under-7 free.)*

◪ RIJKSMUSEUM AMSTERDAM. The "State Museum" has long been known as Amsterdam's preeminent destination for art from the Dutch Golden Age. Even though the main building of the museum will close for renovations in December 2003, the Rijksmuseum is still a mandatory Amsterdam excursion. During restoration, the smaller Philips Wing will remain open to show masterpieces of 17th-century painting, including works by Frans Hals, Rembrandt van Rijn, Jan Steen, and Johannes Vermeer. Unfortunately, while the museum undergoes renovation, much of the collection will not be on display, but you may be able to catch a glimpse of some of the museum's holdings on loan at venues around the city. For details on the locations that will temporarily hold the Rijksmuseum's collection, check the website. *(Stadhouderskade 42. ☎ 674 70 00; www.rijksmuseum.nl. Open daily 10am-5pm. €8.50. Under-18 free. Audio guides €3.50.)*

CENTRAL CANAL RING

DE APPEL. This contemporary art museum houses a brilliant permanent collection and welcomes compelling, cutting-edge temporary exhibits that make even the Stedelijk look old-fashioned. *(Nieuwe Spiegelstr. 10. ☎ 625 56 51; www.deappel.nl. Open Su and Tu-Sa 11am-6pm. €2.)*

FOAM PHOTOGRAPHY MUSEUM. Inside a traditional canal house, Foam stages a fearless exploration of modern photography. Every genre of the photographed image is fair game—from the purely aesthetic to the overtly political, from fashion photography to historical exhibits. *(Keizersgr. 609. ☎ 551 65 00; www.foam.nl. Open daily 10am-5pm. €5, students with ID €4. Cafe open Su and W-Sa 10am-5pm.)*

JODENBUURT AND PLANTAGE

JOODS HISTORISCH MUSEUM. In the heart of Amsterdam's traditional Jewish neighborhood, the Jewish Historical Museum aims to celebrate Jewish culture and document the religion's cultural legacy. Through exhibits by Jewish artists and galleries of historically significant Judaica, the museum presents The Netherlands's most comprehensive picture of Jewish life—photographs, religious artifacts, texts, artwork, and traditional clothing remain in the permanent collection. *(Jonas Daniel Meijerpl. 2-4. ☎626 99 45; www.jhm.nl. Open daily 11am-5pm. Closed Yom Kippur. €6.50, seniors and ISIC holders €4, ages 13-18 €3, ages 6-12 €2. Audio Tour €1.)*

MUSEUM HET REMBRANDT. Dutch master Rembrandt van Rijn's house at Waterloopl. is the home of the artist's impressive collection of 250 etchings. See the inhumanly claustrophobic box-bed in which Rembrandt slept and tour the studio in which he mentored promising painters. *(Jodenbreestr. 4. ☎520 04 00; www.rembrandthuis.nl. Open M-Sa 10am-5pm, Su 1-5pm. €7, with ISIC €5. Under-6 free.)*

🎵 ENTERTAINMENT

The **Amsterdams Uit Buro** (AUB), Leidsepl. 26, is stuffed with fliers, pamphlets, and guides to help you sift through current events; pick up the free monthly *UITKRANT* at any AUB office to see what's on. The AUB also sells tickets and makes reservations for just about any cultural event. (☎09 00 01 91, €0.55 per min.; www.uitlijn.nl. AUB office open M-W, F-Sa 10am-6pm, Th 10am-9pm, Su noon-6pm.) The VVV **tourist office,** Stationspl. 10, has a theater desk that can also make reservations. (☎(0900) 400 40 40, €0.55 per min. Open M-Sa 10am-5pm.) If you're thirsty for more info on bars, coffeeshops, gay life, and other events, pick up *Shark* (www.underwateramsterdam.com; print versions available throughout the city).

CONCERTS. In the summer, the Vondelpark Openluchttheater hosts free performances of all sorts every Wednesday through Sunday. (☎673 14 99; www.openluchttheater.nl.) The **Royal Concertgebouw Orchestra,** one of the world's finest orchestras, plays in the **Concertgebouw,** Concertgebouwpl. 2-6. Take tram #316 to Museumpl. (☎671 83 45; www.concertegebouw.nl. Tickets from €7. Sept.-June, those under 27 can get last minute tickets for anything that isn't sold out for €7. Free lunchtime concert W 12:30pm, no tickets necessary. Ticket office open daily 10am-7pm. Guided tours Su at 9:30am; €7.)

FILM. Check out www.movieguide.nl for movie listings. In the Vondelpark, head left from the main entrance on Stadhouderskade to see what's on at the stately **Filmmuseum** independent movie theater. (☎589 14 00; www.filmmuseum.nl. Info center open M-F from 10am; Sa-Su box office opens 1hr. prior to first showing. €6.30-7, students and seniors €5.) **The Movies,** Harlemmerstr. 159, is the city's oldest movie theater. (☎624 57 90. €7.50, students and seniors €6.50.)

🌿 COFFEESHOPS AND SMART SHOPS

COFFEESHOPS

The coffee at coffeeshops in Amsterdam is rarely the focal point. Places calling themselves coffeeshops sell pot or hash or will let you buy a drink and smoke your own stuff. Look for the green-and-white "Coffeeshop BCD" sticker that certifies a coffeeshop's credibility. Although Amsterdam is known as the **hashish** capital of the world, **marijuana** is increasingly popular. Technically, pot is illegal in The Netherlands; soft drugs are merely tolerated. It is unlikely you'll be punished (though your drugs will be confiscated) if you are carrying 5g of marijuana or hash at any given time. Any more, and you will be treated as a **dealer** by the cops. Harder drugs like cocaine and heroin will be severely punished. For info on the legal ins and outs, call the **Jellinek clinic** (☎570 23 55). If your questions pertain only to matters of cannabis or hemp, try the **Cannabis College** (p. 748).

If you do decide to partake, it's a good idea not to get too caught up in Amsterdam's narcotic quirk; use common sense, and remember that any experimentation with drugs can be dangerous. **Never buy drugs from street dealers,** because you have no way of knowing if they are laced drugs with other, more harmful drugs. Coffeeshops are licensed to sell cannabis, and the good ones regulate the quality of their product very carefully. When you walk into a coffeeshop, ask for a menu. Above all, **don't smoke in public;** though many Dutch smoke cigarettes, puffing a joint in places outside coffeeshops is considered very impolite, and is an easy way to single yourself out as a tourist. If you want to smoke at a bar, ask permission first.

Marijuana in The Netherlands is incredibly potent; you'll likely need to smoke less to get the same high than marijuana from your home county. Unless otherwise noted, pre-rolled joints are rolled with tobacco, which makes smoking harsher on the lungs; however, pure pre-rolled pot joints are sometimes available. Almost no one smokes out of pipes; while some places provide bongs, usually only tourists use them. Dutch marijuana is the most common and costs anywhere from €3-12 per gram; most coffeeshops sell bags in set amounts (€6, 12, etc.). Staff at coffeeshops are accustomed to explaining the different kinds of pot on the menu. When you move from one coffeeshop to another, you must either buy drugs from the shop or buy a drink if you want to stay and smoke your own stash.

Hashish is made of the resin crystals extracted from the flowers of the cannabis plant. It can run from €4-30 per gram. Typically, the cost of the hash is proportional to its quality and strength. Black hash hits harder than blonde.

Spacecakes, Spaceshakes, and **Space Sweets** are cakes and sweets made with hash or weed; hash chocolate, popsicles, and bonbons are also available. Because they need to be digested, they take longer to affect you (up to 1hr.) and longer to rinse out; don't eat another brownie if you don't feel effects immediately.

SMART SHOPS

Smart shops, which peddle a variety of **"herbal enhancers"** and **hallucinogens** that walk the line between soft and hard drugs are also legal. **Magic mushrooms** start to work thirty minutes to an hour after consumption and act on your system for four to eight hours. Different types give different highs; consult a smart shop owner on what sort of mushroom is appropriate for you. Never look for mushrooms in the wild and never buy from a street dealer; it's extremely difficult to tell the difference between poisonous mushrooms and hallucinogenic mushrooms. Don't mix hallucinogens with alcohol; if you have a bad trip, call ☎122 to go to the hospital—you won't be arrested, and they've seen it all before.

WHERE TO GO...

Don't smoke at shops right at Centraal Station. Try these instead:

▨ **Barney's Coffeeshop,** Haarlemmerstr. 102. Get a greasy breakfast with your big fat joint. Three-time "best marijuana strain" winner at the Cannabis Cup. Open daily 7am-7pm.

▨ **Abraxas,** J. Roelensteeg 12-14. Amsterdam's most beautiful coffeeshop. Casual, sophisticated, no-pressure atmosphere. Open daily 10am-1am.

▨ **Grey Area,** Oude Leliestr. 2. Where coffeeshop owners go for the best. One of the only owner-operated spots left in the city. The Yankee expat behind the counter will be happy to lend you one of the coffeeshop's bongs. Open Su and Tu-Sa noon-8pm.

The Dolphins, Kerkstr. 39. Enter the beautiful world of coral reefer madness at this ocean-themed coffeeshop. Open M-Th and Su 10am-1am, F-Sa 10am-3pm.

Yo Yo, 2e van der Heijdenstr. 79. So warm it makes smoking nearly wholesome. Famous apple pie, good coffee, and of course, great smokeables. Open daily noon-7pm.

Bluebird, Sint Antoniesbreestr. 71. Fun spot with a vast menu that includes samples of weed and hash for inspection. Open daily 9:30am-1am.

Paradox, 1e Bloemdwarsstr. 2. The owners match the feel of this place: Colorful, free-spirited, and ready to have a good time. Weed, hash, and awesome veggie burgers (€3.50). Kitchen closes at 3pm. Coffeeshop open daily 10am-8pm.

La Tertulia, Prinsengrt. 312. Leafy plants everywhere make for a relaxing time. *Smoker's Guide* praises the special Hawaiian haze. Open Tu-Sa 11am-7pm.

Hill Street Blues, Warmoesstr. 52. Don't let the loud rock music blaring into the street drive you away; it's all about leisurely comfort inside. If you don't want to smoke, the bar serves cheap beer (€2.50). Open M-Th and Su 9am-1am, F-Sa 9am-3am.

Dampkring, Handboogstr. 29. Deep blue, chill subterranean space with experienced, but unpretentious patrons. Open M-Th 10am-1am, F-Sa 10am-2am, Su 11am-1am.

■ NIGHTLIFE

The **Leidseplein** and **Rembrandtplein** are the liveliest nightspots, with coffeeshops, loud bars, and tacky clubs galore, but in all locations, bars frequently become more clubby as the night goes on—check listings. Near Leidseplein, pricey discos abound on **Prinsengracht,** near **Leidsestraat,** and on **Lange Leidsedwarsstraat.** Some clubs charge a membership fee in addition to normal cover. Amsterdam's finest cafes are the old, dark, wood-paneled *bruine cafe* (brown cafes) mainly on the **Jordaan;** those lining **Prinsengracht** usually have outdoor seating. In Amsterdam, the concept of a completely "straight" nightlife versus a "gay" nightlife does not really apply. Essentially all establishments are gay-friendly and have a mixed-orientation crowd. Around Rembrandtpl., gay bars almost exclusively for men line **Amstelstraat** and **Reguliersdwarsstraat. Kerkstraat,** five blocks north of Leidseplein, is a gay hotspot. Pick up a wallet-sized *Clu* guide, free at cafes and coffeeshops, for a club map of the city, and *Gay and Night*, a monthly magazine, for more info.

BARS AND CAFES

■ **Café de Jaren,** Nieuwe Doelenstr. 20-22. This fabulous 2 floor cafe's air of sophistication doesn't quite mesh with its budget-friendly prices. It's a bona fide student haunt as well. Cocktails and beer €1.80-3.10. Open M-Th and Su 10am-1am, F-Sa 10am-2am.

■ **NL Lounge,** Nieuwezijds Voorburgwal 169. This is the unmarked destination where some of Amsterdam's slickest, best-dressed, and most savvy insiders hang out. Cocktails (€6). Music varies, but at 1am, the beat invariably switches over to trippy techno. No cover. Open M-Th and Su 10pm-3am, F-Sa 10pm-4am.

Lux, Marnixstr. 403. Kitschy but classy with red plush walls and leopard-print curtains. There's not much dancing, but DJs spinning Th-Su will get you pumped to go hit the clubs later on. Beer €2. Cocktails €4. Open M-Th and Su 8pm-3am, F-Sa 8pm-4am.

Absinthe, Nieuwezijds Voorburgwal 171. With layers of magenta leather couches, Absinthe, bathes in purple light and trancy music. May be more touristy than you'd like. Open M-Th and Su 8pm-3am, F-Sa 8pm-4am.

Cafe de Wilde Zee, Haarlemmerstr. 32. Elegant, black-clad literati congregate in this maroon-colored wine bar to sip Italian espressos (€1.70), and great wines (€2.60-3 per glass), and converse to cool jazz. Open M-Tu 11am-8pm, W-Su 11am-1am.

Cafe Kalkhoven, Prinsengrt. 283. "Old Amsterdam" in all its brown, wooden glory: Old oak barrels on the wall behind the bar, darkly painted ceilings, and food choices all have a markedly Dutch flavor. *Tostis (*ham and cheese sandwich) and *appeltas* (apple strudel) both €1.80. Heineken pint €4. Open daily 11am-1am.

Arc Bar, Reguliersdwarsstr. 44. A hip, cutting-edge spot done up in leather. Cocktails €6.50-7.50. Black tabletops in front are lowered to form dancing platforms later in the evening. Open M-Th and Su noon-1am, F-Sa noon-3am.

Montmartre, Halvemaarsteg 17. Rococo interior bedecked with flowers and rich draperies houses some of the wildest gay parties in the city. Voted best gay bar in Amsterdam by *Gay Krant* 6 years running. Open M-Th and Su 5pm-1am, F-Sa 5pm-3am.

CLUBS AND DISCOS

The iT, Amstelstr. 24. This club is the reason why others in Rembrandtpl. are sometimes empty. Amsterdam's beauties come here to dance the night away. Beer €4. Cocktails €7.50. Cover €15. Open Su, Th 11pm-4am; F-Sa, 11pm-6am.

Dansen Bij Jansen, Handboogstr. 11-13. *The* student dance club in Amsterdam, popular with locals from the University of Amsterdam and backpackers. You must show a student ID or be accompanied by a student. A great way to meet local university kids. Beer €1.70-3.30. Cocktails from €3.30. Open M-Th and Su 11pm-4am, F-Sa 11pm-5am.

Escape, Rembrandtpl. 11. Party animals pour into this massive venue—one of Amsterdam's hottest clubs. 2 floors with 6 bars, where scenesters groove to house, trance, disco, and dance classics. Dress well. Beer €2.30. Cocktails €7.50. Cover €10-15. Open Su and Th 11pm-4am, F-Sa 11pm-5am. Cash only.

Meander, Voetboogstr. 3b. Smoky atmosphere, constant din, and dense crowds make for a raucous, high-energy good time. M student night, F-Sa disco. Beer €1.80. Cover €2.50-5. Open M-Th and Su 9pm-3am, F-Sa 9pm-4am.

De Beetles, Lange Leidsedwarsstr. 81. A drink house with a sometimes-hopping dance floor and a mixed crowd. Su reggae, Th rock night, Sa oldies and dance classics. No cover F before midnight; after midnight, €5 includes a €2 drink. Beer and soda €2. Hard liquor €3.50-5. Open Su-Th 9pm-4am, F-Sa 9pm-5am. Cash only.

Cockring, Warmoestr. 90. Somewhere between a sex club and a disco. Dark room in the back where anything goes. Men only. No cover, except for special parties, when it runs around €5. Open M-Th and Su 11pm-4am, F-Sa 11pm-5am.

LIVE MUSIC

Melkweg, Lijnbaansgrt. 234a (☎531 81 81; www.melweg.nl). Legendary nightspot in an old milk factory, it's one-stop shopping for live music, food (see **Eat At Jo's,** p. 744), films, and dance parties. Concert tickets €9.50-22 plus €2.50 monthly membership fee. Box office open M-F 1-5pm, Sa-Su 4-6pm; show days from 7:30pm to end of show.

Paradiso, Weteringschans 6-8 (☎626 45 21; www.paradiso.nl). When big-name rock, punk, new-wave, hip-hop, and reggae bands come to Amsterdam, they almost invariably play in this former church. Tickets €5-25; additional mandatory monthly membership fee €2.50. Open until 2am.

Bourbon Street Jazz & Blues Club, Leidsekruisstr. 6-8 (☎623 34 40; www.bourbonstreet.nl). A slightly older crowd comes for blues, soul, funk, and rock bands. Check the web or posting in the window for events. Beer €2.50. Cover Su and Th €3; F-Sa €5. Free with entry at 10-10:30pm. Open M-Th and Su 10pm-4am, F-Sa 10pm-5am.

THE NETHERLANDS

▓ DAYTRIPS FROM AMSTERDAM

TULIP COUNTRY: AALSMEER AND LISSE. Easily accessible by bus, quietly quaint Aalsmeer is home to the world's largest flower auction. With an impressive trading floor that rivals the area of 150 football fields, the **Bloemenveiling Aalsmeer,** Legmeerdijk 313, acts as a central market where growers sell over 19 million flowers annually; the world price of flowers is determined here. (☎ 297 39 21 85; www.vba-aalsmeer.nl. Open M-F 7:30-11am. €4.) From Amsterdam's Centraal Station, take **bus** #172 (45min., every 15min., 5 strips). Arrive before 9am to witness the busiest trading; buses begin leaving Amsterdam at 6:10am.

To see even more flowers, check out the town of Lisse in late spring. The **Keukenhof Gardens** become a kaleidoscope of color as over 7 million bulbs come to life. Now the world's largest flower garden, Keukenhof boasts impeccably kept grounds and even a petting zoo. (☎ 252 46 55 55; www.keukenhof.nl. In 2004, open Mar. 25-May 20 daily 8am-7:30pm; tickets on sale until 6pm. €12.) **The Zwarte Tulip Museum** details the historical cultivation and scientific evolution of "bulbiculture." Many call the ongoing quest for the *zwarte* (black) tulip impossible, since the color does not exist naturally. (☎ 252 41 79 00. Open Su and Tu-Sa 1-5pm. €3.) Take a **train** from Amsterdam's Centraal Station to Leiden (30min., every 30min. until 2:45am, round-trip €12), then catch **bus** #50 or 51 to Lisse (5 strips).

ZAANSE SCHANS. Unleash your inner tourist for a day in delightful Zaanse Schans, a 17th-century town on the River Zaan. In the 1950s, the people of the Zaan region were concerned that industrialization was destroying their historic landmarks, so they transported the prized sights to this pretty plot of land. Duck-filled canals, working windmills, and restored houses make Zaanse Schans feel like a museum village, although a handful of people actually live and work here. The lovely **De Kat Windmill,** Kalverringdijk 29, has been grinding plants into artists' pigments since 1782. (Open Apr.-Oct. daily 9am-5pm; Nov.-Mar. Sa-Su 9am-5pm. €2.) The oldest oil mill in the world is the **De Zoeker Windmill.** (Open Mar.-Oct. daily 9:30am-4:30pm. €2.) The **Cheesefarm Catharina Hoeve** offers free samples of its homemade wares as well as a tour of its workshop. (Open daily 8am-6pm.) Watch craftsmen mold blocks of wood into comfy clogs at **Klompenmakerij de Zaanse Schans,** or see where the ubiquitous Albert Heijn supermarket craze started at the original shop, now the **Albert Heijn Museumwinkel.** Next door you can stop by the **Museum van het Nederlandse Uurwerk** (Museum of the Dutch Clock), Kalverringdijk 3, to view the oldest working pendulum clock in the world. (Open Apr.-Oct. daily 10am-1pm, 2-5pm. €2.30.) The pint-sized **Museum Het Noorderhuis** features original costumes from the Zaan region. (Open July-Aug. daily 10am-5pm; Sept.-Oct. and Mar.-June Su and Tu-Sa 10am-5pm; Nov.-Feb. Sa-Su 10am-5pm. €1.)

From Amsterdam, take the *stoptrein* (dir: Alkmaar) and get off at Koog Zandijk (20min., €2.25). From there, follow the signs across a bridge to Zaanse Schans (12min.). An **information center** is at Schansend 1. (☎ 616 82 18; www.zaanseschans.nl. Open July-Aug. daily 8:30am-5:30pm, off-season 8:30am-5pm.)

HAARLEM ☎ 023

Haarlem's narrow cobblestone streets, rippling canals, and fields of tulips make for a great escape from the urban frenzy of Amsterdam. Most visitors come to Haarlem (pop. 150,000) for its Renaissance facades, medieval architecture, and incredible museums, but the city possesses more than just this antiquated charm.

Haarlem also bustles with a relaxed energy that befits its urban size. Coffeeshops, bars, and the most restaurants per capita of any Dutch city ensure that there is fun to be had even after the sun goes down.

TRANSPORTATION AND PRACTICAL INFORMATION. Reach Haarlem from Amsterdam by **train** from Centraal Station (20min.; €3.10, same-day round-trip €5.50) or by **bus** #80 from Marnixstr. (2 per hr., 2 strips). The VVV **tourist office,** Stationspl. 1, just to your right when you walk out of the train station, finds private rooms (from €18.50) for a €5 fee. (☎(090) 06 16 16 00; www.vvvzk.nl. Open in summer M-F 9am-5:30pm, Sa 10am-3:30pm; off-season Sa 10am-2pm.)

ACCOMMODATIONS AND FOOD. Walk to the Grote Markt and take a right to reach **Joops Innercity Apartments ❶,** Oude Groenmarkt 20, a centrally located hotel with elegant rooms. (☎532 20 08. Reception M-Sa 7am-11pm, Su 8am-10pm. Singles €28-75; doubles €55-100; triples €95; quads €120.) **Hotel Carillon ❷,** Grote Markt 27, is ideally located right on the town square, to the left of the Grote Kerk. Despite their small size, most rooms include a shower, phone, and TV, and all are extremely clean. (☎531 0591; www.hotelcarillon.com. Breakfast included. Reception 7:30am-1am. Singles €30, with bath €55; doubles €55/71; triples €92.) Take bus #2 (dir.: Haarlem-Noord; every 10min. until 6pm, every 15min. 6pm-12:30am) to stay at **Stayokay Haarlem ❶,** Jan Gijzenpad 3. Stayokay is packed with amenities and is home to a laid-back crowd. (☎537 3793; www.stayokay.com/haarlem. Breakfast included. Dorms €22-25, off-season €19-22.) To **camp** at **De Liede ❶,** Lie Over 68, take bus #2 (dir.: Zuiderpolder) and walk 10min. (☎535 8666. Single with tent €6, each additional person €2.90. Cash only.) For cheap meals, try cafes in the **Grote Markt** or **Botermarkt;** many offer outdoor patios. ■**Grand Café Doria ❷,** Grote Houtstr. 1a, right in the Grote Markt, specializes in great Italian fare on an outdoor patio. (☎531 3335. Entrees €6-20. Open Su-Th 9am-midnight, Sa-F 9am-2am. ■**Lambermon's ❸,** Spaarne 96, offers Haarlem's best *haute cuisine*. The menu changes nightly, but always mixes fish, meat, and vegetarian options. (☎542 7804. Entrees €8. Due to small portions, entrees are usually ordered in groups of 4. Open daily 6:30-10:30pm. Reservations necessary.)

SIGHTS AND MUSEUMS. The action centers on the **Grote Markt,** Haarlem's vibrant main square. To get there from the train station, head south along Kruisweg, which becomes Kruisstr. and then Barteljorisstr. The ■**Grote Kerk,** at the opposite end of the Grote Markt, houses a mammoth Müller organ once played by Handel and Mozart. In the nearby **Dog Whipper's Chapel,** check out artist Frans Hals' tomb, marked only by a lantern. (Open M-Sa 10am-4pm. €1.50. Guided tours €2.) Having met the man, now see his work. From the front of the church, take a right on to Warmoestr. and walk three blocks to the ■**Frans Hals Museum,** Groot Heiligland 62, which houses a collection of Golden Age paintings in a 17th-century almshouse and orphanage. (Open Su noon-5pm, Tu-Sa 11am-5pm. €5.40. Under-19 free.) A 2min. walk toward the train station from the Grote Markt is the moving ■**Corrie Ten Boomhuis,** Barteljorisstr. 19, which served as the headquarters for Corrie Ten Boom's movement to protect Jews during WWII. The savior of an estimated 800 lives, Corrie was caught and sent to a concentration camp but survived to write *The Hiding Place,* which was later made into a film. The **Teyler's Museum,** Spaarne 16, is The Netherlands's oldest museum, and contains an eclectic assortment of scientific instruments, paintings, and drawings, including works by Michelangelo and Rembrandt; from the church, turn left onto Damstr. and follow it until Spaarne. (Open Su noon-5pm, Tu-Sa 10am-5pm. €5.50.) The **De Hallen Museum,** Grote Markt 16, displays exhibits of modern art housed in a former abattoir. (☎511 5775. Open Su noon-5pm, Tu-Sa 11am-5pm. €4. Under-19 free.)

THE NETHERLANDS

▶ DAYTRIPS FROM HAARLEM: ZANDVOORT AND BLOEMENDAAL. A mere seven miles from Haarlem, the seaside town of **Zandvoort** draws sun-starved Nederlanders to its miles of sandy beaches. To find the shore from the train station, follow the signs to the Raadhuis, then head west along Kerkstr. For a different feel, walk 30min. to hip **Bloemendaal,** which has been transformed from a quiet, family-oriented oceanside town to one of the best beach parties in Holland. The hippie-style club ◼**Woodstock 69** hosts **Beach Bop** the last Sunday of every month (www.beachbop.info), although lower-profile parties go on other nights of the week. The town's clubs, including **Republic, De Zomer,** and **Solaris,** are open only in summer, generally from April to September.

Trains arrive in Zandvoort from Haarlem (10min., round-trip €2.75). The VVV **tourist office,** Schoolpl. 1, is just east of the town square, off Louisdavidstr. (☎571 7947; www.vvvzk.nl. Open M-Sa 9am-5:15pm.) The **Hotel Noordzee ❷,** Hogeweg 15, has cheerful rooms replete with shower and TV just 100m from the beach. (☎571 3127. Doubles €45-65.)

LEIDEN
☎071

Home to one of the oldest and most prestigious universities in Europe, Leiden brims with bookstores, windmills, gated gardens, hidden walkways, and some truly outstanding museums. Rembrandt's birthplace and the site of the first **tulip** cultivation, The Netherlands's third-largest city serves as a gateway to flower country. Follow the signs from the train station to the spacious and modern ◼**Museum Naturalis,** which explores the history of earth and its inhabitants, providing scientific and anthropological explanations of fossils, minerals, animals, evolution, and astronomy. (☎568 76 00. Open July-Aug. daily 10am-6pm; Sept.-June Su and Tu-Sa 10am-6pm. €8.) Collecting the world's heritage since 1837, the ◼**Rijksmuseum voor Volkenkunde** (National Museum of Ethnology), Steenstr. 1, has on display Inca sculptures, Chinese paintings, and African bronzes that were all acquired during the height of Dutch imperial power. The museum also houses impromptu re-creations and modern interpretations of past societies in its lush gardens. (☎516 88 00. Open Su and Tu-Sa 10am-5pm. €6.50.) The **Rijksmuseum van Oudheden** (National Antiquities Museum), Rapenburg 28, holds the restored Egyptian Temple of Taffeh, a gift removed from the reservoir basin of the Aswan Dam. (☎516 31 63. Open Su noon-5pm, Tu-F 10am-5pm, Sa noon-5pm. €6.) Sharing a main gate with the Academy building is the university's 400-year-old garden, the **Hortus Botanicus,** Rapenburg 73, where the first Dutch tulips were grown. Its grassy knolls alongside the **Witte Singel** canal make it an ideal picnic spot. (☎527 72 49. Open Apr.-Nov. daily 10am-6pm; Dec.-Mar. M-F and Su 10am-4pm. €4.) Scale steep staircases to inspect the inside of a functioning 18th-century windmill at the **Molenmuseum "De Valk",** 2e Binnenvestgrt. 1. (☎516 53 53. Open Su 1-5pm, Tu-Sa 10am-5pm. €2.50.) The **Museum De Lakenhal,** Oude Singel 32, exhibits works by Rembrandt and Jan Steen. (☎516 53 60. Open Su noon-5pm, Tu-F 10am-5pm., Sa noon-5pm. €4. Under-18 free.)

Leiden is easily reached by **train** from Amsterdam's Centraal Station (30min., every 30min. until 2:45am, round-trip €12) or The Hague (20min., every 30min. until 3:15am, €4.20). The VVV **tourist office,** Stationsweg 2d, a 5min. walk from the train station, sells maps (€3) and walking tour brochures (€2), and helps find hotel rooms for a €2.30 fee for the first person, €1.80 fee for each additional person. (☎090 02 22 23 33; www.leiden.nl. Open M 11am-5:20pm, T-F 10am-5:20pm, Sa 10am-4:30pm.) The **Hotel Pension Witte Singel ❷,** Witte Singel 80, 5min. from Hortus Botanicus, has immaculate rooms that overlook gorgeous canals and gardens. (☎512 45 92; wvanvriel@pensione-ws.demon.nl. Singles from €31; doubles from €47.) Locals and students pack the popular **de Oude Harmonie ❷,** Breestr. 16, just off Rapenburg, where candlelight and stained glass set the mood. (Entrees €6-13. Open M-Th noon-1am, F-Sa noon-2am, Su 3pm-1am.) **Super de Boer supermarket** is opposite the train station. (Open M-F 7am-9pm, Sa 9am-8pm, Su noon-7pm.)

THE HAGUE (DEN HAAG) ☎070

In many senses, The Hague (pop. 450,000) is Amsterdam's all-business brother; there are precious few coffeeshops amidst The Hague's intimidating collection of historically significant buildings and monuments. William II moved the royal residence to The Hague in 1248, prompting the creation of Parliament buildings, museums, and sprawling parks. Today, countless diplomats fill designer stores, merging rich history with a bustling metropolis.

◨⊘ TRANSPORTATION AND PRACTICAL INFORMATION. Trains come from Amsterdam (50min., €8) and Rotterdam (25min., €3.50) to both of The Hague's major stations, **Centraal Station** and **Holland Spoor.** Trams #1, 9, and 12 connect the two stations. The VVV **tourist office,** Kon. Julianapl. 30, just outside the north entrance to Centraal Station and right next to the Hotel Sofitel, books rooms for a €5 fee and sells detailed city maps (€2). Hotel booking by computer is available 24hr. (☎090 03 40 35 05; www.denhaag.com. Open June-Sept. M and Sa 10am-5pm, Tu-F 9am-5:30pm, Su 11am-5pm; Oct.-May M and Sa 10am-5pm, Tu-F 9am-5:30pm.) Most foreign **embassies** are in The Hague: **Australia,** Carnegielaan 4, 2517 KH (☎310 82 00; open M-F 8:45am-4:30pm); **Canada,** Sophialaan 7, 2514 JP (☎311 16 00; open M-F 9am-1pm and 2-5:30pm); **Ireland,** 9 Dr. Kuyperstr., 2514 BA (☎363 09 93; call for hours); **New Zealand,** Carnegielaan 10, 2517 KH (☎346 93 24; open M-F 9am-12:30pm and 1:30-5:30pm); **South Africa,** Wassenaarseweg 40, 2596 CJ (☎392 45 01; open daily 9am-noon); **UK,** Lange Voorhout 10, 2514 ED (☎427 04 27; call for hours); **US,** Lange Voorhout 102, 2514 EJ (☎310 92 09; open M-F 8am-4:30pm).

┏╔ ACCOMMODATIONS AND FOOD. The StayOkay City Hostel Den Haag ❷, Scheepmakerstr. 27, is near Holland Spoor; turn right from the station, follow the tram tracks, turn right at the big intersection, and Scheepmakerstr. is 3min. down on your right. From Centraal Station, take tram #1 (dir.: Delft), 9 (dir.: Vrederust), or 12 (dir.: Duindrop) to *Rijswijkseplein* (2 strips); cross to the left in front of the tram, cross the intersection, and Scheepmakerstr. is straight ahead. StayOkay is a huge modern hostel that features private baths and a helpful staff. (☎315 78 88; www.njhc.org/denhaag. In-house restaurant/bar. Breakfast included. Dorms €23; singles €47; doubles €61.) Budget takeaway places line **Lage Poten** and **Korte Poten** near the Binnenhof. **◪Cafe de Oude Mol ❷,** Oude Molstr. 61, a few blocks from Grote Halstr., serves up delicious *tapas,* all from €3-5. (☎345 16 23. Open M-W 5pm-1am, Th-Sa 5pm-2am, Su 5pm-1am.)

◷╝ SIGHTS AND ENTERTAINMENT. The Hague has served as the seat of Dutch government for 800 years; recently, it has also become headquarters for the international criminal justice system. Andrew Carnegie donated the **Peace Palace** (Het Vredespaleis) at Carnegiepl., the opulent home of the International Court of Justice. (www.vredespaleis.nl. Take tram #7 or 8 north from the Binnenhof. Tours M-F 10, 11am, 2, and 3pm. Book through the tourist office. €3.50, under-13 €2.30.) For snippets of Dutch politics, visit the **Binnenhof,** The Hague's Parliament complex. Near the entrance of the Binnenhof, the 17th-century **Mauritshuis,** Korte Vijverberg 8, features an impressive collection of Dutch paintings, including works by Rembrandt and Vermeer. (www.mauritshuis.nl. Open Su 11am-5pm, Tu-Sa 10am-5pm. €7. Under-18 free.) Tours leave from Binnenhof 8a and visit the 13th-century **Ridderzaal** (Hall of Knights) as well as the chambers of the States General.

(Open M-Sa 10am-4pm, last tour leaves at 3:45pm. Tour €5. Entrance to courtyard free.) The impressive modern art collection at the **Gemeentemuseum,** Stadhouderslaan 41, displays Piet Mondrian's *Victory Boogie Woogie*. Take tram #10 from Holland Spoor or bus #4 from Centraal Station. (Open Su 11am-5pm, Tu-Sa 11am-5pm. €7.50.) For vibrant nightlife, prowl the Strandweg in nearby **Scheveningen.**

DELFT
☎015

The lillied canals and stone footbridges that still line the streets of Delft (pop. 95,000) offer the same images that native Johannes Vermeer immortalized in paint over 300 years ago. It's best to visit on Thursdays and Saturdays, when townspeople flood the marketplace. The town is renowned for **Delftware,** blue-on-white earthenware developed in the 16th century. Watch Delftware being made from scratch at **De Candelaer,** Kerkstr. 13a-14, located in the center of town. (Open 9am-6pm.) To see a larger factory, take Tram #1 to *Vrijenbanselaan* and enjoy a free demonstration at **De Delftse Pauw,** Delftweg 133. (Open Apr.-Oct. daily 9am-4:30pm; Nov.-Mar. M-F 9am-4:40pm, Sa-Su 11am-1pm.) Built in 1381, the **Nieuwe Kerk** holds the restored mausoleum of Dutch liberator Willem of Orange. Climb the tower, which holds a 36-bell carillon and offers a magnificent view of old Delft. (Church open Apr.-Oct. M-Sa 9am-6pm; Nov.-Mar. M-F 11am-4pm, Sa 11am-5pm. €2.50. Tower closes 1hr. earlier. €2.) **Nusantra Museum,** St. Agathapl. 4-5, is post-colonialism at its best, housing a small but gorgeous collection of objects from former Dutch colonies. All information is in Dutch, but the friendly staff can answer your questions. (Open Su 1-5pm, Tu-Sa 10am-5pm. €3.50.) Founded in 1200, the **Oude Kerk** has a rich history and a 75m tower that leans 2m out of line. (Open Apr.-Oct. M-Sa 9am-6pm; Nov.-Mar. 11am-4pm, Sa 11am-5pm. €2.50.)

The easiest way into Delft is the 15min. ride on **tram** #1 from The Hague (2 strips) to Delft station. **Trains** also arrive from Amsterdam (1hr., €9). The **Tourist Information Point,** Hippolytusbuurt 4, near the Stadhuis, has lots of free maps and books rooms for free. (☎215 40 15, phone service €0.30 per minute; www.delft.nl. Open M 10am-4pm, T-F 9am-6pm, Sa 9am-5pm, Su 10am-4pm.) There aren't any rock-bottom budget accommodations in Delft; your best bet is to sleep in The Hague, which is 8min. away and has much better deals. **Delftse Hout Recreation Area ❷** has campsites and cabins; take #64 to the end of the line. (☎213 00 40; www.tours.nl/delftsehout. Reception May to mid-Sept. 8:30am-8pm; mid-Sept. to Apr. 9am-6pm. 2-person tent €22.) Restaurants line **Volderstraat** and **Oude Delft.**

ROTTERDAM
☎010

The second-largest city in The Netherlands and the busiest port city in the world, Rotterdam (pop. 590,000) lacks the quaint, classic feel that characterizes much of The Netherlands. After it was bombed in 1940, experimental architects replaced the rubble with striking (some say strikingly ugly) buildings, creating an urban, industrial conglomerate. Artsy and innovative, yet almost decrepit in its hyper-modernity, the Rotterdam that arose from the ashes—filled with museums, parks, and creative architecture—is now one of the centers of cultural activity in Europe.

🖃🚉 TRANSPORTATION AND PRACTICAL INFORMATION. Trains run to: Amsterdam (1¼hr., €12); The Hague (25min., €3.60); and Utrecht (45min., €7.50). The VVV **tourist office,** Coolsingel 67, opposite the *Stadhuis*, books rooms for a €2 fee. (Open M-Th 9:30am-6pm, F 9:30am-9pm, Sa 9:30am-5pm.)

🏠🍴 ACCOMMODATIONS AND FOOD. If you've grown tired of Europe, escape to the Middle East, Africa, or South America in one of the many themed rooms of **Hotel Bazar ❸,** Witte de Withstr. 16. For the best value, book the South

American floor, which comes with a charming private garden. (☎206 51 51. Singles €60-100; doubles €65-120.) To reach the **StayOkay Rotterdam (HI) ❷**, Rochussenstr. 107-109, take the Metro to *Dijkzigt;* at the top of the Metro escalator, exit onto Rochussentr. and turn left. (☎436 57 63. Breakfast and sheets included. Reception 7am-midnight. Dorms €23; singles €31; doubles €52.) Chinese food and schwarma await along **Witte de Withstraat**, where you can easily grab a meal for under €5. Try **Lijbaan** for its array of pubs, bars, and all their accompanying culinary charm. **Bazar ❷**, on the 1st floor of the hotel of the same name, shines with glittering colored lights, bright blue tables, and amazing Middle Eastern fusion cuisine. (☎206 51 51. Sandwiches and some entrees €4. Open M-Th 8am-1am, F 8am-2am, Sa 10am-2am, Su 10am-midnight.)

◉ ♫ SIGHTS AND ENTERTAINMENT. The **Netherlands Architecture Institute**, Museumpark 18-20, is one of the most extraordinary buildings in Rotterdam. The multi-leveled glass and steel construction—which traverses a man-made pool and looks out onto the Museumpark—is home to several exhibition spaces, a world-class archive, and a permanent display on Dutch architecture. (Open Su 11am-5pm, Tu-Sa 10am-5pm. €7, students and seniors €5.) For a dramatic example of Rotterdam's eccentric designs, check out the **Kijk-Kubus** (Cube Houses) by Piet Blom. Take tram #1 or the Metro to *Blaak*, turn left, and look up. (Open Mar.-Dec. daily 11am-5pm; Jan.-Feb. F-Su 11am-5pm. €1.80.) Brush up on your knowledge of van Gogh, Magritte, Rembrandt, Rothko, Rubens, and Rubinstein across the street at the **Museum Boijmans van Beuningen**, Museumpark 18-20. (M: Eendractspl. or tram #5. Open Su 11am-5pm and Tu-Sa 10am-5pm. €7.) Restored to its medieval splendor after its bombing, **St. Laurenskerk**, Grote Kerkpl. 15, is home to the largest mechanical organ in Europe. (Open Tu-Sa 10am-4pm. Free.) Step aboard the *De Buffel*, a restored 19th-century turret ship, at the **Maritiem Museum**, Leeuvehaven 1, or peruse hundreds of intricately detailed model ships. (Open July-Aug. M-Sa 10am-5pm, Su 11am-5pm; Sept.-June Su 11am-5pm and Tu-Sa 10am-5pm. €3.50.) Make sure to swing by the powerful **Zadkine Monument**, to the left of the museum. Known as the Monument for the Destroyed City and erected only 11 years after the bombing, it depicts a man with a hole in his heart writhing in agony. **Museumpark** features sculptures, mosaics, and monuments designed by some of the world's foremost artists and architects; take tram #5 to reach the outdoor exhibit.

Coffeeshop-hop along **Oude Binnenweg** and **Nieuwe Binnenweg**, or dance the night away at ▨**Off_Corso**, Kruiskade 22, Rotterdam's hottest club phenomenon. (Beer €2. Mixed drinks €6. Cover €6, €4 with student ID. Open Th-Sa 11pm-5am.)

UTRECHT   ☎030

Sitting roughly in the center of The Netherlands, Utrecht (pop. 250,000) is a national hub that draws visitors with its lively festivals, numerous museums, young nightlife, and winding, tree-lined canals. Get info on churches and museums at **RonDom**, Dompl. 9, the Utrecht visitor's center for cultural history. Then make your first stop the awe-inspiring **Domkerk** (Dom Church), which was started in 1254 and finished 250 years later. Initially a Roman Catholic cathedral, the Domkerk has held Protestant services since 1580. (Open May-Sept. M-F 10am-5pm, Sa 10am-3:30pm, Su 2-4pm; Oct.-Apr. M-F 11am-4pm, Sa 11am-3:30pm, Su 2-4pm. Free.) The **Domtoren**, the tallest tower in The Netherlands, was attached to the cathedral until a medieval tornado blew away the nave. (Tickets at RonDom. Daily July-Aug. every 30min. 10am-4:30pm; Sept.-June every hr. 10am-4pm. €6.)

Trains from Amsterdam (30min., 3-6 per hr., €5.60) arrive in the Hoog Catharijne. To get to the VVV **tourist office**, Vinkenbrugstr. 19, follow the signs to Vredenberg, which leads to the town center. (☎(0900) 128 87 32; info@vvvutrecht.nl. Open M-W

(vertical text in right margin) THE NETHERLANDS

and F 9:30am-6:30pm, Th 9:30am-9pm, Sa 10:30am-5pm, Su 10am-2pm.) Near the corner of Lucasbolwerk and Nobelstr., **B&B Utrecht City Centre ❶**, Lucasbolwerk 4, offers a kitchen, sauna, piano, and home video system to its guests. (☎(0650) 43 48 84; www.hostelutrecht.nl. Breakfast 24hr. Free Internet. Dorms €16; singles €55; doubles €65; triples €85; quads €100.) Slightly farther from the city, the same owners run **B&B Utrecht ❶**, Egelantierstr. 25. Take bus #3 to Watertoren (€1), cross the street and head to Anemoonstr., then go two blocks to the end and turn left. The street turns into Egelantierstr. and the hostel is on your left. (☎(0650) 43 48 84; www.hotelinfo.nl. Breakfast 24hr. Free Internet. Dorms €12; singles €40; doubles €45; triples €70; quads €85.) For a pastoral setting perfect for recharging, try **Stayokay Ridderhofstad Rhijnauwen (HI) ❷**, Rhijnauwenselaan 14, in nearby Bunnik. Take bus #40, 41, or 43 from Centraal Station (10-15min., round-trip €4.20), and tell the driver to let you off at Bunnik. From the stop, cross the street, backtrack, turn right on Rhijnauwenselaan, and it's 0.5km down the road. The hostel offers bike rentals and a small bar. (☎656 12 77. Breakfast included. Dorms July-Aug. weeknights €22, weekends €23; doubles €52; triples €64-77; quads €78-€94.) Look for cheap meals along **Nobelstraat.**

Nightlife in Utrecht thrives seven days a week. If you're looking for a great time, try **De Winkel van Sinkel**, Oude Gracht 158, the city's most popular nightspot. (Open Su-F 11am-2am, Sa 11am-5am.) **'t Oude Pothuys**, Oudegr. 279, has live music every night until 3am in a candle-lit, converted cellar. (Open daily 10pm-3am.) Students party at fraternity-run **Woolloo Moollo** on Janskerkhof 14 once the rest of Utrecht has shut down. (Student ID required. Cover varies. Open W-Sa 11pm-late.)

HOGE VELUWE NATIONAL PARK   ☎0318

The impressive **Hoge Veluwe National Park** (HO-geh VEY-loo-wuh) is a 13,565-acre preserve of woods, heath, dunes, red deer, and wild boars. (☎59 16 27; www.hogeveluwe.nl. Park open June-July daily 8am-10pm; May and Aug. 8am-9pm; Sept. 9am-8pm; Apr. 8am-8pm; Oct. 9am-7pm; Nov.-Mar. 9am-5:30pm. €5, children 6-12 €2.50; 50% discount May-Sept. after 5pm.) Deep in the park, the **Rijksmuseum Kröller-Müller** has troves of van Goghs from the Kroller-Muller family's outstanding collection, as well as key works by Giacometti, Gris, Mondrian, Picasso, and Seurat. The museum's striking **sculpture garden,** one of the largest in Europe, has exceptional works by Bourdelle, Rodin, and Serra. (www.kmm.nl. Open Tu-Su 10am-5pm, sculpture garden closes at 4:30pm. €5, children €2.75.) Take one of the free **bikes** in the park and get a map (€2) at the **visitor's center** to explore over 33km of paths. (☎(055) 378 81 19. Open daily 10am-5pm.)

Arnhem (15km from the park) is a good base for exploration; **bus** #107 comes from Arnhem to the park's northwestern Otterlo entrance. Contact the park or either **tourist office** for more information. (☎(0900) 202 40 75; www.vvvarnhem.nl.) To get to the **Stayokay Hostel ❷**, Diepenbrocklaan 27, take bus #3 from the station to Rijnstate Hospital; as you face the hospital turn right, then left on Catte-poelseweg. About 150m ahead, turn right up the brick steps, and at the top turn right. Rooms are exceptionally clean, service is friendly, and the reading room and bar make for a peaceful entree into the park. (☎(026) 442 01 14; www.stay-okay.com/arnhem. Breakfast included. Reception 8am-11pm. Dorms €22-23; singles €30-31; doubles €53-55; triples €72-76; quads €91-96.)

MAASTRICHT   ☎043

Situated on a narrow strip of land between Belgium and Germany, Maastricht's strategic location has made it a frequent target of military conquest throughout history. More recently, however, it has been a symbol of international cooperation, as the Maastricht Treaty created the European Union in 1991. Home of the prestigious **Jan van Eyck Academie of Art,** Maastricht (pop. 125,000) is known for its abundance of art galleries and antique stores. The striking ⊠**Bonnefantenmuseum,** Ave. Ceramique 250, contrasts Maastricht's traditional Dutch brickwork with its futuristic (and slightly dated) rocketship design. The museum houses permanent collections of archaeological artifacts, medieval sculpture, Northern Renaissance painting, and contemporary art. (www.bonnefanten.nl. Open Su and Tu-Sa 11am-5pm. €7.) Despite its recent status as the birthplace of modern European unity, Maastricht has seen its share of interstate rivalries; centuries of foreign threats culminated in an innovative subterranean defense system. The ⊠**Mount Saint Peter Caves**'s 20,000 underground passages were used as a siege shelter as late as WWII and contain inscriptions and artwork by generations of inhabitants. Access to the caves is possible only with a tour guide at two locations: the **Northern System** (Grotten Noord), Luikerweg 71 (tours in Dutch and English available depending on guide; €3.30); and the **Zonneberg Caves,** Slavante 1 (☎325 21 21. €3.30).

The train station is on the east side of town, across the river from most of the action. **Trains** arrive from Amsterdam (2½hr., 2 per hr., €24). To get from the train station to the VVV **tourist office,** Kleine Staat 1, walk straight on Station Str., cross the bridge, go one more block, take a right, and walk down a block; the office will be on the right. (☎325 21 21. Open May-Oct. M-Sa 9am-6pm, Su 11am-3pm; Nov.-Apr. M-F 9am-6pm, Sa 9am-5pm.) **Le Virage ❹,** Cortenstr. 2-2b, offers spotless suites with a bedroom, living room, kitchenette, and bathroom above a cafe. Reception is open Su and Tu-Sa 8am-midnight, but hours can be spotty, so make sure you plan your stay in advance. (Breakfast €9. Double apartments €90; triples €112; quads €136.) Spend the night on the centrally located **Botel ❷,** Maasboulevard 95, a boat with tiny cabins and a cozy deckroom lounge. Try to get the rooms above-deck; they're the same price, but much cheerier. (☎321 90 23. Singles €27-30; doubles €41-43; triples €60.) To get from the train station to **City-Hostel de Dousberg (HI) ❶,** Dousbergweg 4, take bus #11 on weekdays, bus #33 on weeknights after 6pm, and bus #8 or 18 on weekends. (☎346 67 77; www.dousberg.nl. Breakfast included with HI membership. Dorms €22-25; triples €75.) Cheap food can be found around the central **Vrijthof** area. For entertainment info, check out the free *Uit in Maastricht,* found in the tourist office. **Night Live,** Kesselkade 43, is a church converted to a disco. (Cover €4-6. Open Th-Sa 11pm-6am.)

GRONINGEN   ☎050

Groningen, easily the most happening city in the northern Netherlands, pulses with new life. More than half of the city's 170,000 inhabitants are under 35, fueling to Groningen's reputation as a frenetic party city. The town's spectacular ⊠**Groninger Museum,** housed in a vibrant, almost entropic building, exhibits both modern art and traditional paintings. The multicolored galleries create a futuristic laboratory atmosphere for their contemporary art exhibits. (www.groningermuseum.nl. Open July and Aug. M 1-5pm, Tu-Su 10am-5pm; Sept.-June SU and Tu-Sa 10am-5pm. €7, seniors €6, children €3.50.) Admire the city from atop the Grote Markt's **Martinitoren Tower,** which weathered the German attacks during WWII. (Open Apr.-Oct. daily 11am-5pm; Nov.-Mar. noon-4pm. €2.50, under-12 €1.50.) Cool off at **Noorderplantsoen,** a fountain-filled park that serves as host space to the huge **Noorderzon Festival** of art in late August, Groningen's annual cultural climax.

Trains roll in from Amsterdam (2½hr., every 30min., €24). To reach the VVV **tourist office,** Grote Markt 25, turn right as you exit the station, walk along the canal, turn left at the first bridge, head straight through the Herepl. on Herestr., cross Gedempte Zuiderdiep, and keep on Herestr. until it hits the **Grote Markt.** (☎05 03 13 97 41; www.vvvgroningen.nl. Open July-Aug. Su 11am-3pm, M-W and F 9am-6pm, Th 9am-8pm, Sa 10am-5pm; Sept.-June M-W and F 9am-6pm, Th 9am-

8pm, Sa 10am-5pm.) Hang out with a fun crowd at **Simplon Jorgerenhotel ❶**, Boterdiep 73-2. Take bus #1 from the station (dir.: Korrewegwijk) to Boterdiep; the hostel is through the yellow- and white-striped entranceway. (☎313 52 21; www.xs4all.nl/~simplon. Breakfast €4. Free lockers with deposit. Lockout noon-3pm. All-female dorm available. Dorms €11.40; singles €30; doubles €43; triples €62; quads €80.) ☒**Ben'z ❷**, Peperstr. 17, in the heart of Groningen's party district, is a unique dining experience. Dinner is served upon Turkish cushions in a Bedouin tent, while *nargilas* (water pipes) abound. (Student menu €7.60-9.10. Cash only.) For cheap pitchers of beer and shoulder-to-shoulder packed bars, head to the southeastern corner of the Grote Markt on **Poelestraat** and **Peperstraat**. Billing itself as the "club for the international pop underground," **Vera**, Oosterstr. 44, is a center for live music and cinema that draws an unmissable party every night. Pick up a copy of *VeraKrant*, the newsletter in the box outside, for hours and a schedule of events. The intimate, candlelit **Jazzcafé de Spieghel**, Peperstr. 11, has two floors of live jazz, funk, or blues every night. (Wine €2.20. Open daily 8pm-4am.) **Postal Code:** 9725.

WADDEN ISLANDS (WADDENEILANDEN)

Wadden means "mudflat" in Dutch, but sand is the defining characteristic of these islands: Gorgeous beaches hide behind ridges covered in golden grass. Deserted, tulip-lined bike trails carve through vast, flat stretches of grazing land to the sea. Sleepy and isolated, these islands are truly Holland's best-kept secret.

▉ TRANSPORTATION

The islands arch clockwise around the northwestern coast of The Netherlands: Texel (closest to Amsterdam), Vlieland, Terschelling, Ameland, and Schiermonnikoog. To reach **Texel,** take the train from Amsterdam to **Den Helder** (1½hr., €11), then grab bus #33 (2 strips), and a ferry to 't Hoorntje, the island's southernmost town (20min., every hr. 6:30am-9:30pm, round-trip €4). **Buses** depart from the ferry dock to various locales throughout the island, though the best way to travel is to rent a **bike** from **Verhuurbedrijf Heijne,** opposite the ferry dock. (From €4.50 per day. Open Apr.-Oct. daily 9am-8pm; Nov.-Mar. 9am-6pm.) To reach the other islands from Amsterdam, grab a **train** from Centraal station to Harlingen Haven (3hr., €26). From Harlingen, **ferries** (☎(0517) 49 15 00; www.doeksen.nl) depart for Terschelling (1-2 hr., 3-5 per day, €18).

TEXEL. The largest of the Wadden Islands, Texel boasts stunning beaches and museums. **Beaches** lie near De Koog, on the western side of the island. **Nude beaches** beckon the uninhibited; you can bare it all near paal 9 (2km southwest of Den Hoorn) or paal 27 (5km west of De Cocksdorp). Say hi to the playful *zeehonden* (seals) at the **EcoMare Museum and Aquarium**, Ruijslaan 92, in De Koog. (www.ecomare.nl. Open daily 9am-5pm. €7, under-13 €3.50.) The staff can also arrange group tours of the surrounding **nature reserves;** make sure to ask for a guide who speaks English.

A **Texel Ticket** (€3.90) allows one day of unlimited travel on the island's bus system. (Runs mid-June to mid-Sept.). The VVV **tourist office**, Emmaln 66, is located just outside Den Burg, about 300m south of the main bus stop; look for the blue signs. (☎02 22 31 47 41; www.texel.net. Open July-Aug. Su 10am-1:30pm, M-Th 9am-6pm, F 9am-9pm, Sa 9am-5:30pm; Sept.-June M-Th 9am-6pm, F 9am-9pm, Sa 9am-5:30pm.) **Campgrounds** cluster south of De Koog and near De Cocksdorp; the tourist office can provide any info you may need.

TERSCHELLING. With 80% of the island covered by protected nature reserves, Terschelling (pop. 4,500) offers secluded **beaches** and green pastures spotted with cows and horses. To explore the island's striking scenery, rent a **bike** from **Haantjes Fietsverhuur,** W. Barentzskade 23 and other locations around the island. (☎ 44 29 29. Bikes at €4.50 per day, €20 per week.)

Both tours can also be booked at the VVV **tourist office,** W. Barentzkade 19, which sits opposite the ferry landing. (☎ (0562) 44 30 00. Open M-Sa 9:30am-5:30pm.) The **Terschelling Hostel (HI) ❶,** van Heusdenweg 39, is located just out of town on the waterfront. (☎ (0562) 44 23 38; www.stayokay.com/terschelling. Breakfast and sheets included. Laundry €7. Reception daily 9am-10pm. Dorms €18-21; ask for the backpacker special.) The best place to grab a bite is in the island's main village, Terschelling West. ◪**The Heartbreak Hotel ❷,** Oosterend, one of Terschelling's best food experiences, also doubles as a shrine to Elvis. Serving great diner-style food (Burning Love Burger €4), the restaurant also hosts free rock n' roll groups every night in July and August. **Zeezicht ❷,** Wm. Barentszkade 20, has enormous dinner portions (€12-16.50) and a sweeping view of the ocean. (Kitchen closes at 9:30pm. Open daily 10am-midnight.) A wild set floods Terschelling on summer nights; head to **Braskoer,** Torenstr. 32, to join a younger crowd on a sweaty, packed dance floor. (Beer €3. Cover €5. Open 10am-2am.) To relax, kick back at **Cafe De Zeevaart,** Torenstr. 22. (Beer €1.80. Open daily 10am-2am.)

NORWAY (NORGE)

Norway is blessed with an abundance of natural beauty, from its rugged fjords to turquoise rivers and glacier-capped mountain ranges. The long Nordic history manifests itself in an intimate relationship with the sea. The country's original seafarers, the Vikings, dominated a realm that spanned from the British Isles to Southern Europe. The late 19th century saw Norway's artistic reputation rise with luminaries like Edvard Munch and Henrik Ibsen. In the years since World War II, Norway has developed into a modern welfare state. Although prices and taxes are among the world's highest, they translate into unparalleled social services, little class stratification, and a high standard of living. As a result of Norway's prosperity and low crime rate, visitors encounter a safe and easy place to travel and can focus their attention on the country's main attraction—the breathtaking scenery.

FACTS AND FIGURES

Official Name: Kingdom of Norway.

Capital: Oslo.

Major Cities: Bergen, Stavanger, Tromsø, Trondheim.

Population: 4,525,000.

Land Area: 307,000 sq. km.

Time Zone: GMT +1.

Language: Norwegian; Swedish and English widely spoken.

Religions: Evangelical Lutheran (86%).

DISCOVER NORWAY

Cosmopolitan **Oslo** (p. 769), the first stop on most itineraries, swarms with lively cafes and museums. After you've exhausted the capital, head south to charming, seaside **Stavanger** (p. 777) or hop on the scenic **Oslo-Bergen rail line** (p. 783) to fjord country. At the end of the line lies **Bergen** (p. 778), a relaxed, coastal city with pointed gables lining its wharf. If you only have a day to see the fjords, spend it exploring **Sognefjord** (p. 778); the **"Norway in a Nutshell"** tour (p. 784) gives a glorious glimpse of fjord country. With more time, continue on the fjord circuit to **Geirangerfjord** (p. 787) and **Jostedalsbreen Glacier** (p. 787), or explore the mountains of **Jotunheimen National Park** (p. 786). The adventurous head north of the Arctic Circle to stay in colorful fishermen's shacks in the isolated **Lofoten Islands** (p. 790).

ESSENTIALS

WHEN TO GO

Oslo averages 18°C (63°F) in July and -4°C (24°F) in January. In the north, average temperatures drop and it is wetter than the south and east; Bergen and the surrounding mountains, in particular, see more than their share of rain. For a few weeks around the summer solstice (June 21), the area north of Bodø basks in the midnight sun. You stand the best chance of seeing the **Northern Lights** from above the Arctic Circle (Nov.-Feb.). Skiing is best just before Easter.

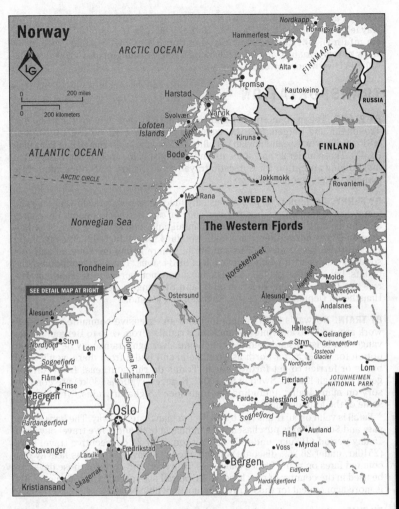

Norway

ARCTIC OCEAN

Nordkapp
Honningsvåg
Hammerfest

FINNMARK

Alta

Tromsø
Kautokeino

RUSSIA

Harstad

Svolvær
Narvik

Lofoten
Islands

Vestfjord

Kiruna

FINLAND

ATLANTIC OCEAN

Bodø

ARCTIC CIRCLE

Jokkmokk

Rovaniemi

Mo i Rana

SWEDEN

Norwegian Sea

The Western Fjords

Norsekehavet

Hareyfjord

Molde
Moldefjord

Ålesund
Åndalsnes

Trondheim

Ostersund

Hellesylt
Geiranger
Geirangerfjord
Stryn
Josteoal
Glacier
Nordfjord

SEE DETAIL MAP AT RIGHT

Ålesund

Nordfjord
Stryn

Lom

Fjærland

JOTUNHEIMEN
NATIONAL PARK

Lom

Sognefjord

Flåm
Finse

Glomma R.

Lillehammer

Førde
Balestrand
Sogndal

Sognefjord

Bergen

Oslo

Flåm
Aurland

Voss
Myrdal

Hardangerfjord

Stavanger
Larvik
Fredrikstad

Bergen

Eidfjord

Kristiansand
Skagerrak

Hardangerfjord

DOCUMENTS AND FORMALITIES

VISAS. Citizens of Australia, Canada, the EU, New Zealand, and the US do not need a visa for stays of up to 90 days, but this period begins upon entry into any Nordic country; for more than 90 days in any combination of Denmark, Finland, Iceland, Norway, and Sweden, you will need a visa. South Africans need a visa for stays of any length.

EMBASSIES AND CONSULATES. Foreign embassies are in Oslo (p. 772). Norwegian embassies at home include: **Australia** and **New Zealand,** 17 Hunter St., Yarralumla, Canberra ACT 2600 (☎26 273 34 44; www.canberra.mfa.no); **Canada,** Ste. 532, 90 Sparks St., Ottawa, ON K1P 5B4 (☎613-238-6571; www.embnoway.ca); **Ireland,** 34 Molesworth St., Dublin 2 (☎01 662 18 00; www.nor-way.ie); **South Africa,** 1166 Park St., Hatfield, 0083 (☎12 342 61 00; www.pretoria.mfa.no); **UK,** 25 Belgrave Sq., London SW1X 8QD (☎020 7591 5500; www.norway.org.uk); and **US,** 2720 34th St. NW, Washington, D.C. 20008 (☎202-421-7333; www.norway.org/embassy).

TRANSPORTATION

BY PLANE. The main international airport is in Oslo, though a few flights land at Trondheim and Bergen. **SAS** (US ☎800-221-2350; UK ☎845 6072 7727; Norway ☎815 20 400; www.scandinavian.net) flies to Norway, as do **Finnair** and **Icelandair** (p. 45). Those under 25 and students under 32 qualify for special youth fares that make flying an option for domestic travel (from 100kr). SAS offers domestic standby tickets (*sjanse billetter*).

BY FERRY. Car ferries (*ferjer*) are usually much cheaper (and slower) than the many passenger express boats (*hurtigbat* or *ekspressbat*) cruising the coasts and fjords; both often have student, Scanrail, and InterRail discounts. The **Hurtigruten** (www.hurtigruten.com) takes six days for the incredible voyage from Bergen to Kirkenes on the Russian border; there is one northbound and one southbound departure daily from each of its 34 stops. There are no railpass discounts, but students get 50% off. The most common ports for international ferries are Oslo, Bergen, Kristiansand, and Stavanger; destinations include: Hanstholm, Denmark; Newcastle, England; and Iceland.

BY TRAIN. Norway's train system includes an extensive commuter train network around Oslo and long-distance lines running from Oslo to Bergen, to Stavanger via Kristiansand, and to Trondheim. Overnight trains may be your best option for travel as far north as Trondheim and Bodø; from there, you'll need buses or ferries to get farther north. Trains do run southeast from Narvik, going through Kiruna, Sweden (p. 1009). Seat reservations (30kr) are compulsory on many trains, including the high-speed Signatur trains, which cover some of the long-distance lines.

　　Eurail is valid on all trains run by the Norwegian State Railway. The **Norway Railpass** and **Scanrail pass** purchased in Scandinavia both allow five travel days in a 15-day period (1620kr, under-26 25% discount) or 21 consecutive travel days (2510kr, under-26 25% discount) of unlimited rail travel, as well as heavily discounted fares on many ferries and buses. However, only three of those days can be used in the country of purchase, so a Scanrail pass purchased at home (p. 51) is more economical for those traveling mostly within Norway.

BY BUS. Buses can be quite expensive, but are the only land option north of Bodø and in the fjords. **Norway Bussekspress** (☎23 00 24 40; www.nor-way.no) operates 75% of the domestic bus routes and publishes a free timetable (*Rutehefte*) containing schedules and prices, available at bus stations and on buses. Scanrail and InterRail pass holders are entitled to a 50% discount on most bus routes, and students get a 35% discount—be insistent, and follow the rules listed in the Norway *Bussekspress* booklet. Bus passes, valid for one (1375kr) or two (2200kr) weeks, are good deals for those exploring the fjords or the north.

BY CAR. Citizens of Canada, the EU, or the US need only a valid driver's license in their home country to drive in Norway. Insurance is required and is usually included in the price of rental. Roads in Norway are in good condition, although blind curves are common and roads are frighteningly narrow in some places. Drivers should remember to be cautious, especially on mountain roads and in tunnels. Driving around the fjords can be frustrating, as only Nordfjord has a road completely circumnavigating it; there are numerous car ferries, but check timetables in advance to connect with the boats. Rental cars are expensive, but can be more affordable than trains and buses for groups. Vehicles are required to keep headlights on at all times. For more info on driving a car in Europe, see p. 59.

BY BIKE AND BY THUMB. Biking is becoming increasingly common. The beautiful scenery is rewarding for cyclists, although the hilly terrain can be rough on bikes. Contact **Syklistenes Landsforening** (☎22 41 50 80) for maps, suggested routes, and other info. **Hitchhiking** is notoriously difficult in Norway. Some successfully hitchhike beyond the rail lines in northern Norway and the fjord areas of the west, but many others try for hours and end up exactly where they started. Hitchhikers should bring several layers of clothing, rain gear, and a warm sleeping bag. *Let's Go* does not recommend hitchhiking as a safe means of transport.

TOURIST SERVICES AND MONEY

EMERGENCY	Police: ☎110. Ambulance: ☎113. Fire: ☎112.

TOURIST OFFICES. Virtually every town and village has a **Turistinformasjon** office; look for a white lower-case "i" on a square green sign. In July and the first half of August, almost all tourist offices are open daily; most have reduced hours the rest of the year. For more info, contact the **Norwegian Tourist Board,** P.O. Box 722 Sentrum, NO-0105, Oslo; street address: Stortorvet 10 (☎24 14 46 00; www.ntr.no).

MONEY. The Norwegian **krone** (plural: kroner) is divided into 100 rarely used øre. Coins come in 50 øre, as well as 1kr, 5kr, 10kr, and 20kr denominations; bills are in 50kr, 100kr, 200kr, 500kr, and 1000kr denominations. Banks and large post offices change money, usually for a commission but at good rates. Prices are sky-high throughout all of Norway. As a general rule, more isolated areas have even higher prices; the Lofoten Islands are especially pricey. **Tipping** is not essential, but it is customary to tip 5-15% for restaurant service. A 15% service charge is often included in hotel bills. Refunds for the 10-17% **value-added tax (VAT)** are available for single-item purchases of more than 300kr in a single store (p. 16).

NORWEGIAN KRONE		
AUS$1 = 4.97KR	10KR = AUS$2.01
CDN$1 = 5.46KR	10KR = CDN$1.83
EUR€1 = 8.31KR	10KR = EUR€1.20
NZ$1 = 4.45KR	10KR = NZ$2.25
ZAR1 = 1.02KR	10KR = ZAR9.80
UK£1 = 12.00KR	10KR = UK£0.83
US$1 = 7.64KR	10KR = US$1.31

BUSINESS HOURS. Business hours are short in summer, especially on Fridays and in August, when Norwegians vacation. Shop hours are Monday to Friday 10am-5pm, Saturday 10am-2pm; hours may be extended on Thursday. Banks are generally open Monday to Wednesday and Friday 8am-3pm, Thursday 8am-5pm.

COMMUNICATION

PHONE CODES	**Country code: 47. International dialing prefix: 095.** There are no city codes in Norway. From outside Norway, dial int'l dialing prefix (see inside back cover) + 47 + local number.

COMMUNICATION. There are three types of **public phones;** the black and gray phones accept 1kr, 5kr, 10kr, and 20kr coins; green phones accept only phone cards; and red phones accept coins, phone cards, and major credit cards. All calls, including international direct dial calls, usually require at least 5kr. Buying a **phone card** (*telekort;* 40kr, 90kr, or 140kr at Narvesen Kiosks and post offices) is more economical. **Pay phones** cost twice as much as calls from private lines; prices drop between 5pm and 8am. **Mobile phones** are an increasingly popular and economic option; for more info, see p. 36. To make domestic **collect calls,** dial ☎117; international collect calls, ☎115. International direct dial numbers include: **AT&T,** ☎800 190 11; **British Telecom,** ☎800 190 44; **Canada Direct,** ☎800 191 11; **Ireland Direct,** ☎800 193 53; **MCI,** ☎800 199 12; **Sprint,** ☎800 198 77; **Telecom New Zealand,** ☎800 140 58; **Telkom South Africa Direct,** ☎800 199 27; **Telstra Australia,** ☎800 199 61.

MAIL. Mailing a postcard or letter within Norway costs 5.50kr; to Sweden or Finland 7kr; within Europe 9kr; to regions outside Europe 10kr.

INTERNET ACCESS. There are a good number of Internet cafes in Oslo and Bergen. Smaller cities might have one or two Internet cafes, but most have a public library open on weekdays that offers free Internet access in 15-30min. time slots.

LANGUAGE. Norwegian is fairly similar to the Nordic languages of Swedish and Icelandic. Sami is spoken by the indigenous people of northern Norway. Most Norwegians speak flawless English. For Norwegian phrases, see p. 1057.

ACCOMMODATIONS AND CAMPING

NORWAY	❶	❷	❸	❹	❺
ACCOMMODATIONS	under 200kr	201-350kr	351-500kr	501-650kr	over 650kr

HI youth hostels (*vandrerhjem*) are run by **Norske Vandrerhjem,** Dronninggsgt. 26, in Oslo (☎23 13 93 00; www.vandrerhjem.no). Beds run 85-180kr; another 40-60kr usually covers breakfast. Sheets typically cost 40-60kr per stay. Usually only rural or smaller hostels have curfews, and only a few are open year-round. Most open in mid- to late June and close after the third week in August. Most tourist offices book **private rooms** and last-minute hotel rooms for a fee (25-35kr).

Norwegian law allows free **camping** anywhere on public land for up to two nights, provided that you keep 150m from all buildings and fences and leave no trace behind. **Den Norske Turistforening** (DNT; Norwegian Mountain Touring Association) sells excellent maps (60-70kr), offers guided hiking trips, and maintains about 350 **mountain huts** (*hytter*) throughout the country. (☎22 82 28 00; www.turistforeningen.no. Membership cards available at DNT offices, huts, and tourist offices; 365kr, under-25 175kr. 65-170kr per night. Nonmembers add 50kr.) Staffed huts, open around Easter and from late June to early September, serve meals. Unstaffed huts are open from late February until mid-October; if you're a member, you can pick up entrance keys (100kr deposit) from DNT and tourist offices. Official campgrounds charge about 110-125kr for one or two people in a tent. Some also have cabins (450-800kr).

FOOD AND DRINK

NORWAY	❶	❷	❸	❹	❺
FOOD	under 60kr	60-135kr	136-200kr	201-300kr	over 300kr

Eating in Norway is pricey; markets and bakeries are the way to go. The supermarket chains Rema 1000 and Rimi generally have the best prices (usually open M-F 9am-8pm, Sa 9am-6pm). You can also join Norwegians at outdoor markets for cheap seafood and fruit. Many restaurants have inexpensive *dagens ret* (dish of the day; 70-80kr); otherwise, you'll rarely spend less than 100kr on a full Norwegian meal. Eating at cafes (65-85kr) can also save you money without compromising quality; all-you-can-eat buffets and self-service *kafeterias* are other inexpensive options. Fish in Norway—cod, salmon, and herring—is fresh and relatively inexpensive. Norway also grows divine berries. National specialties include *ost* (cheese); *kjøttkaker* (pork and veal meatballs) with boiled potatoes; and, for more adventurous carnivores, reindeer, ptarmigan, and *hval* (whale meat). Around Christmas, you can also delight in a special meal of *lutefisk* (dried fish soaked in water and lye). Beer is very expensive in bars (45-60kr for 0.5L), and cheapest in supermarkets. Alcohol is almost exclusively available in bars and government-run liquor stores. You must be 18 to buy beer, 20 to buy wine and alcohol.

HOLIDAYS AND FESTIVALS

Holidays: New Year's Day (Jan. 1); Easter Sunday and Monday (Apr. 11-12); May Day (May 1); National Independence Day (May 17); Ascension Day (May 20); Christmas Eve and Day (Dec. 24-25); Boxing Day (Dec. 26); New Year's Eve (Dec. 31).

Festivals: The **Bergen Festival** in May offers world-class performances in music, dance, and theater. The **Norwegian Wood** rock festival (www.norwegianwood.no) in early June in Oslo features big-name rock bands, while Kristiansand's week-long **Quart** music festival (www.quart.no) in early July attracts acts from Moby to Beck to Ben Harper. **Midsummer Night** (St. Hansaften), June 23, the longest day of the year, is celebrated with bonfires and huge parties. For more info about Norway's festivals, visit www.norwayfestivals.com.

OSLO

The Viking capital of Oslo has grown into an eclectic city of 500,000. Amidst the city's ethnic communities and growing diversity remains a strong tie to its Nordic past and cultural identity. Its urban edge is typified by classy cafes, cool boutiques, and tight, trendy clothing; its natural charm lies in the pine-covered hills to the north and the blue waters of Oslofjord in the south. In winter, the short days and blue dusks may remind you of the gloomier works of natives Edvard Munch and Henrik Ibsen; come summer, Oslo's only drawback is its rooftop prices.

TRANSPORTATION

Flights: The high-speed **FlyToget** train runs between **Gardermoen Airport** (GEN; ☎815 50 250) and various stops in downtown Oslo (20min.; M-F every 10min., Sa-Su every 20min.; 4:45am-midnight from Oslo S, 5:34am-12:34am from airport; 110-180kr, students 55-90kr). White **Flybussen** make the same trip daily from 4:15am-midnight (40min.; every 20min.; 100kr, round-trip 150kr), with pickup and drop-off at bus and train stations and the Radisson SAS Scandinavia.

Trains: Oslo Sentralstasjon (Oslo S; ☎81 50 08 88). Trains run by **NSB** (www.nsb.no). *Minipriser* (40% discount) available to major cities if you book 5-7 days ahead. Trains run to: **Bergen** (6-7hr., 4-6 per day, 657kr); **Copenhagen** (8hr.; 2 per day; 1158kr, under-26 809kr); **Stockholm** (6hr.; 4 per day; 1014kr, under-26 709kr); **Trondheim** (6-7hr., 2-5 per day, 730kr). Mandatory reservations for regular trains and *signatur* trains to Bergen, Kristiansand, Stavanger, and Trondheim (41-71kr). Scanrail pass (p. 51) covers train tickets, but not reservations.

Buses: Norway Busekspress, Schweigårdsgt. 8 (☎81 54 44 44). Follow the signs from the train station through the Oslo Galleri Mall to the Bussterminalen Galleriet. Schedules available at the info office. 25-50% student discount on tickets to major cities.

Ferries: Color Line (☎22 94 44 00). To **Hirtshals, Denmark** (12hr., 7:30pm, from 580kr) and **Kiel, Germany** (20hr., 1:30pm, from 1430kr). 50% student discount mid-Aug. to mid-June. **DFDS Seaways** (☎22 41 90 90) goes to **Helsingborg, Sweden** (14hr.) and **Copenhagen, Denmark** (16hr.) daily at 5pm (both from 750kr). Color Line departs 20min. west of train station, DFDS from 10min. south.

Public Transportation: Trafikanten (☎177), in front of train station. Tourist office offers comprehensive schedules. **Bus, tram, subway,** and **ferry** 30kr per ride, 20kr in advance; 750kr fine for traveling without valid ticket. **Dagskort** (day pass) 60kr; **Flexi-card** (8 trips) 140kr; **7-day Card** 160kr (M-F 7am-8pm, Sa-Su 8am-6pm). Tickets also available at Narvesen kiosks and Automat machines. The **Oslo Pass** (see Tourist Office, below) grants unlimited public transport. Late-night service midnight-5am (44kr).

Bikes: For info on cycling, contact **Syklistenes Landsforening,** Storgt. 23d (☎22 41 50 80) for maps and suggested routes (M-W and F 10am-5pm, Th 10am-7pm, Sa 10am-2pm). Also, see www.bike-norway.com. Tourist info centers sell cards (50kr) for 1-day rental of bikes on racks around the city.

Hitchhiking: Those heading south (E-18 to Kristiansand and Stavanger) take bus #31 or 32 to *Maritim*. Hitchers to Bergen take bus #161 to the last stop; to Trondheim, metro #5 or bus #32 or 321 to *Grorud*; to **Sweden,** local train (dir.: Ski) to *Nordstrand* or bus #81, 83, or 85 to *Bekkelaget*. *Let's Go* does not recommend hitchhiking.

✚🔢 ORIENTATION AND PRACTICAL INFORMATION

At Oslo's center is **Slottsparken,** which lies just beside **Oslo University** and the **National Theater,** and surrounds the **Royal Palace.** The city's main street, **Karl Johans Gate,** runs through the heart of town to **Oslo Sentralstasjon** ("Oslo S") at the eastern end. Don't be confused by "gate," the Norwegian word for "street." The harbor is south of the city; the **Bygdøy** peninsula farther southwest. Parks are scattered throughout Oslo, especially north of the Nationaltheatret. An excellent network of public trams, buses, and subways makes transportation through the outskirts quick and simple.

Tourist Offices: Main Tourist Office, Fridtjof Nansenspl. 5 (☎23 14 77 00; www.visitoslo.com). From Oslo S, walk 15min down Karl Johans gt., turn left on Roald Amundsens gt., office on right just before City Hall. Sells the **Oslo Pass,** which covers public transit and admission to nearly all sights (1-day 190kr, 2-day 280kr, 3-day 370kr), and books hotels (45kr fee). Open daily June-Aug. 9am-7pm; Sept. and May M-Sa 9am-5pm; Oct.-Apr. M-F 9am-4pm. **Branch** at Oslo S also books last-minute pensions (45kr fee). Open May-Aug. daily 8am-11pm; Sept. M-Sa 8am-11pm; Oct.-Apr. M-Sa 8am-5pm. ▓ **Use It,** Møllergt. 3 (☎22 41 51 32; http://unginfo.oslo.no/useit) is an info center with free **Internet** terminals. They book accommodations for free, help plan travel elsewhere in Norway, and put out the invaluable *Streetwise Budget Guide to Oslo.* Go up Karl Johans gt. from Oslo S and turn right onto Møllergt.; it's on the left. Open July-Aug. M-F 9am-6pm; Sept.-June M-F 11am-5pm, Th until 6pm.

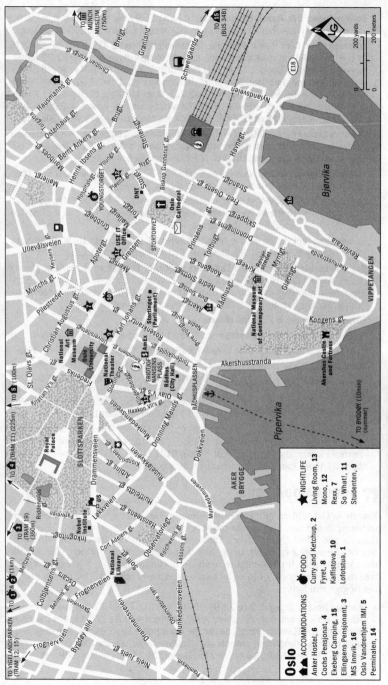

Oslo

ACCOMMODATIONS
Anker Hostel, **6**
Cochs Pensjonat, **4**
Ekeberg Camping, **15**
Ellingsens Pensjonant, **3**
MS Innvik, **16**
Oslo Vandrerhjem IMI, **5**
Perminalen, **14**

🍴 **FOOD**
Curry and Ketchup, **2**
Fyret, **8**
Kaffistova, **10**
Lofotstua, **1**

★ **NIGHTLIFE**
Living Room, **13**
Mono, **12**
Rexx, **7**
So What!, **11**
Studenten, **9**

TO VIGELANDSPARKEN
(TRAM 12, 15)

TO 1 & 2 (1km)
TO 3 (TRAM 19) (350m)
TO 4 (TRAM 11) (225m)
TO 5 (100m)

TO MUNCH MUSEUM (750m)
TO 15 (BUS 34B)
TO BYGDØY (10min) (summer)

Royal Palace
SLOTTSPARKEN
National Library
Nobel Institute
National Theater
Oslo University
National Art Museum
Stortinget (Parliament)
Rådhus (City Hall)
FRIDTJOF NANSENS PLASS
RÅDHUSPLASSEN
Oslo Cathedral
USE IT Office
YOUNGSTORGET
STORTORVET
National Museum of Contemporary Art
Akershus Castle and Fortress
AKER BRYGGE
VIPPETANGEN
Bjørvika
Pipervika
DNT
AmEx

E18

Budget Travel: STA Travel, Karl Johans gt. 8 (☎81 55 99 05; www.statravel.no), a few blocks up from Oslo S. Books student airfares. Open M-F 10am-5pm, Sa 11am-3pm.

Embassies and Consulates: Australia, Jermbanetorg. 2 (☎22 47 91 70; fax 22 42 26 83). Open M-F 9am-noon and 2-4pm. **Canada,** Wergelandsveien 7 (☎22 99 53 00; www.canada.no). Open June-Aug. M-F 8:00am-3:30pm, Sept.-May M-F 8:30am-4:45pm. **Ireland,** Radisson SAS Hotel, Haakon VII's gt. 1 (☎22 01 72 00). **South Africa,** Drammensveien 88c (☎23 27 32 20). Open M-F 8am-12:30pm and 1-4pm. **UK,** Thomas Heftyes gt. 8 (☎23 13 27 00; www.britain.no). Open M-F 8:30am-4pm. **US,** Drammensveien 18 (☎22 44 85 50; www.usembassy.no). Open M-F 8:30am-5pm.

Currency Exchange: Available at AmEx office, the main post office, the banks and hotels along Karl Johans gt., and the branch of Nordea Bank in Oslo S. Open May-Sept. M-F 7am-7pm, Sa-Su 8am-5pm; Oct.-Apr. M-F 7am-7pm, Sa 8am-5pm.

American Express: Fridtjof Nansens pl. 6 (☎22 98 37 35), across from City Hall. Open M-F 9am-4:30pm, Sa 10am-3pm; July-Aug. also Su 11am-3pm.

Luggage Storage: Lockers at the train station. 7-day max. 20-45kr per 24hr. Open M-F 9am-3pm. Some hostels offer luggage storage; bags can be left in the Use It office (see Tourist Offices, above) for an afternoon or night.

Laundromat: Look for the word *myntvaskeri.* **Selva AS,** Ullevålsveien 15. Wash 40kr, dry 30kr. Open daily 8am-9pm. *The Streetwise Budget Guide* lists others.

Gay and Lesbian Services: The **Landsforeningen for Lesbisk og Homofil fri gjøring** (LLH), Nordahl Breuns gt. 22. (☎23 32 73 73; www.llh.no). Open June-Aug. M-F 8am-3pm, Sept.-May 8am-4pm. Cafe W 6pm-9pm. Sells *Blikk* (50kr), a monthly newspaper with attractions and nightlife listings. Appointments recommended.

Emergency: Police: ☎112. **Ambulance:** ☎113. **Fire:** ☎110.

Pharmacy: Jernbanetorvets Apotek (☎23 35 81 00), opposite the train station.

24hr. Medical Assistance: Oslo Kommunale Legevakt, Storgt. 40 (☎22 11 80 80).

Internet Access and Library: Free terminals at **Use It** and public libraries—including the stately **Deichmanske Library,** Henrik Ibsensgt. 1. Sign up for free 15min. slots. Open June-Aug. M-F 10am-6pm, Sa 9am-2pm; Sept.-May M-F 10am-8pm, Sa 9am-3pm. **Studenten,** Karl Johans gt., is conveniently located. 20kr per 15min., 30kr per 30min., 55kr per hr. Open M-Tu 11am-11pm, W-Sa 11am-9pm, Su noon-11pm.

Post Office: Main post office at Kirkegt. 20 (☎23 35 86 90). From Oslo S, head down Karl Johans gt. and turn left on Kirkegt. Address mail to be held: Firstname SURNAME, *Poste Restante,* Oslo Sentrum Post Handel **0101** Oslo 1, NORWAY. Open M-F 9am-5pm, Sa 10am-2pm. Other branches near the city center.

ACCOMMODATIONS

Hostels in Oslo fill up quickly in the summer—make reservations, especially if traveling in a group. The **private rooms** arranged by Use It (see above), Møllergt. 3, are a good deal (from 125kr). **Pensions** (*pensjonater*) are centrally-located, but can be more expensive since they do not offer dorm options. Check with the tourist office for last-minute deals on accommodations. You can **camp** for free in the forest north of town as long as you avoid public areas; try the end of the Sognsvann line.

■ **Anker Hostel,** Storgt. 55 (☎22 99 72 00; booking 22 99 72 10; www.ankerhostel.no). Walk 15min. from the city center or take tram #10, 11, 12, 13, or 17 to Hausmanns gt.; it's 100m up Storgt., behind the Anker Hotel. Clean, comfortable rooms with a kitchenette. Friendly and sociable staff. Breakfast 60kr. Sheets 40kr. Laundry 100kr. Internet 30kr per 30min. Reception 24hr. Dorms 135-155kr; doubles 370kr. ❶

Perminalen, Øvre Slottsgt. 2 (☎23 09 30 81; perminalen@statenskantiner.no). Clean rooms only 5min. from the heart of Oslo. Breakfast included. Internet 15kr per 15min. Key deposit 50kr. Reception 24hr. Dorms 280kr; singles 495kr; doubles 650kr. ❷

Cochs Pensjonat, Parkveien 25 (☎23 33 24 00; www.cochs.no), at Hegdehaugsveien. From the train station, walk 25min. or take tram #11 or 19 to the end of the park. Quiet rooms next to the Slottsparken. Reception on 2nd fl. Singles 380kr, with bath and kitchenette 480-520kr; doubles 520/620-680kr; quads 900kr. ❸

Oslo Vandrerhjem IMI (HI), Staffeldgt. 4 (☎22 98 62 00; www.vandrerhjem.no). Walk 20min. down Karl Johans gt., staying to the right of Slottsparken, and turn right on Linstows gt. Or take tram #17 or 18 to *Holberg pl.* Open June to mid-Aug. Breakfast included. Sheets 50kr. Towels 20kr. Internet 20kr per 30min. Reception 24hr. Singles 295kr; doubles 470kr; triples 670kr; quads 790kr. Nonmembers add 25kr. ❹

MS Innvik, Langkaia 49 (☎22 41 95 00; www.msinnvik.no). A botel just south of Oslo S. Cross the large white overpass and head right along the harbor. Small but well-kept rooms. Live music Sa in summer. Breakfast included. Laundry free. Reception 24hr. Singles 300kr; doubles 600kr. Extra bed 200kr. ❷

Ellingsens Pensjonat, Holtegt. 25 (☎22 60 03 59; ep@tiscali.no). Take tram #19 to *Briskeby.* From the intersection of Holtegt. and Uranienborgveien, walk away from the church; it's an unmarked off-white house on the right. Reception M-F 7:30am-10:30pm, Sa-Su 8am-10:30pm. Singles 300kr; doubles 490kr, with bath 590kr. Cash only. ❷

Ekeberg Camping, Ekebergveien 65 (☎22 19 85 68). 3km from town. Take bus #34A or 34B (10min.). Cooking facilities, grocery store (open daily 8am-9pm), and laundry (wash and dry 40kr). Electricity 35kr. Free showers. Reception daily 7:30am-11pm. Open May 23-Aug. Two people with tent 130kr, with car 200kr; extra person 40kr. ❶

▶ FOOD

Visitors should have no problem finding authentic Norwegian meals or dishes from any part of the globe, but they may have trouble affording them. **Grocery stores** may be the best option; look for **Rema 1000** or **Kiwi,** two chains that dot the city. **Lunch buffets,** offered by most restaurants in the city center, are the cheapest way to eat out; lower-budget fast food is common in the ethnic **Grønland** district east of the train station and around **Oslo S.**

Kaffistova, at the intersection of Rosenkrantz gt. and Kristian IV gt. Quiet, convenient cafeteria-style eatery with traditional Norwegian meat, fish, porridges, and desserts. Vegetarian options. Sandwiches 50-60kr. Entrees 85-160kr. Open M-F 9:30am-8pm, Sa-Su 10:30am-5pm. ❷

Lofotstua, Kirkeveien 40. One of Oslo's best fish restaurants. The only place in town serving whale and seal. Entrees from 150kr. Open M-F 3-10pm. ❷

Fyret, Youngstorg. 6. Down the stairs at the intersection of Møllergt. and Pløens gt. Small restaurant and bar serves fresh meat, shellfish, and Oslo's oldest and largest *aquavit* selection. Open M-Sa 11am-2pm, Su 2pm-10pm. Live jazz M 8pm. ❸

Curry & Ketchup, Kirkeveien 51. Traditional Indian food, including naan and tikka masala. Generous portions 75-100kr. Open daily 1-11pm. ❷

◉ SIGHTS

Although some of Oslo's greatest sights, including the tree-lined streets and free parks that dot the city, are free, others come at a hefty price. Fortunately, several major museums are free, and others drop the admission price with the Oslo Pass.

■VIGELANDSPARKEN. Inside the larger **Frognerparken,** the 80-acre **Vigeland-sparken** is home to over 200 of Gustav Vigeland's creative sculptures depicting each stage of the human life cycle. A favorite among visitors and locals for its serene, yet intense atmosphere, the park includes evocative works such as a towering granite monolith of intertwining bodies. *(Entrance on Kirkeveien. Take bus #20 or tram #12 or 15 to Vigelandsparken. Open 24hr. Free.)*

ART MUSEUMS. The **Munch Museum** *(Munch-museet)* displays rotating exhibits of over 20,000 paintings, prints, drawings, and watercolors that Edvard Munch bequeathed to the city of Oslo before his death in 1944. *(Tøyengt. 53. Take the subway to Tøyen, or walk 10min. northeast from the train station. Open June to mid-Sept. daily 10am-6pm; mid-Sept. to May M-F 10am-4pm, Sa-Su 11am-5pm. 60kr, students 30kr. Free with Oslo Pass.)* Munch's most famous work, **■The Scream** *(Shrik),* is housed at the **National Art Museum** *(Nasjonalgalleriet),* which also displays an impressive collection of Norwegian and foreign works. *(Universitetsgt. 13. Open M, W, and F 10am-6pm, Th 10am-8pm, Sa-Su 11am-4pm. Free.)* Next door at **Oslo University,** several gigantic murals by Munch grace the walls of a concert hall. *(Enter through the door by the columns off Karl Johans gt. Open mid-June to mid-Aug. M-F 10am-2:45pm. Free.)* For modern works, head to the **Contemporary Art Museum** *(Museet for Samtidskunst)* in Bankplassen, behind Askerhus Fortress. Spacious halls display circulating works from the museum's permanent collection, as well as temporary exhibits. *(Take bus #60 or tram #10, 12, 13, 15, or 19 to Koongens Gt. Open Su 11am-5pm, Tu-W and F 10am-5pm, Th 10am-8pm, Sa 11am-4pm. 40kr, students and seniors 20kr. Under-16 free. Th free.)*

AKERSHUS CASTLE AND FORTRESS. Originally built in 1299, Christian IV transformed this waterfront complex into a Renaissance palace complete with dungeons, underground passages, and vast halls, between 1637 and 1648. *(Take bus #60 to Bankplassen or tram #10 or 15 to Christiania torv. Fortress complex open daily 6am-9pm. Free. Castle open May to mid-Sept. M-Sa 10am-4pm, Su 12:30-4pm. 30kr; students, seniors, and children 10kr. Free with Oslo Pass. Tours M-Sa 11am, 1, 3pm; Su 1 and 3pm. Frequent performances in the evening.)* The castle grounds also house the powerful **Hjemmefrontmuseet** (Resistance Museum), which documents Norway's efforts to subvert Nazi occupation. *(Open mid-June to Aug. M, W, F, and Sa 10am-5pm, Tu and Th 10am-6pm, Su 11am-5pm; Sept. to mid-June closes 1-2hr. earlier. 25kr; students, seniors, and children 10kr.)*

BYGDØY. The Bygdøy peninsula is right across the inlet from downtown Oslo; although mainly residential, it boasts some of the city's best museums and a few beaches. In summer, a public ferry leaves from pier 3 in front of City Hall for Bygdøy. *(10min.; runs late-May to mid-Aug.; every 15-30min. M-F 7:45am-8:45pm, Sa-Su 8:45am-8:45pm; 20kr, seniors and children 10kr. Ferry info ☎177; www.boatsightseeing.com. Or, take bus #30 from the National Theater or Oslo S to Folkemuseet or Bygdøynes.)* Uphill from the ferry port is the **Norsk Folkmuseum,** one of Europe's largest open-air museums, which traces everyday life in an architectural context since 1200. Nearby, the **Viking Ship Museum** showcases three massive wooden vessels promoted as the best-preserved of their kind. *(Walk up the hill leading away from the dock and follow signs to the right (10min.), or take bus #30 to Folkemuseet or Vikingskipshuset. Folkmuseum open mid-May to mid-Sept. daily 10am-6pm; mid-Sept. to mid-May M-F 11am-3pm, Sa-Su 11am-4pm. 75kr, students and seniors 45kr. Viking Ship open May-Sept. daily 9am-6pm; Oct.-Apr. 11am-4pm. 40kr, students and children 20kr. Under-7 free.)* More recent exploits at sea are chronicled at the **Fram Museum,** home to the enormous polar ship "Fram," and the **Kon-Tiki Museum,** which details Norwegian Thor Heyerdahl's daring 1947 ocean crossing from South America to Polynesia. *(10min. walk toward Bygdøynes, or bus #30b. Fram open mid-June to Aug. daily 9am-6:45pm; Sept. to early June 11am-3:45pm. 35kr, students 25kr, children 20kr. Kon-Tiki open June-Aug. daily 9:30am-5:45pm; Apr.-May and*

Sept. 10:30am-5pm; Oct.-Mar. 10:30am-4pm. 30kr, students 20kr. Both museums free with Oslo Pass.) On the southwestern side of Bygdøy are two popular beaches. **Huk** appeals to a younger crowd, while **Paradisbukta** is more family-oriented. The stretch of shore between them is a nude beach. *(Take bus #30 or walk south for 25min. from the Bygdøynes ferry stop.)*

OTHER SIGHTS. The annual Nobel Peace Prize ceremony takes place each year on the 10th of December in the huge main ballroom of the **Rådhus** (City Hall). Upstairs there are several exhibits, including an evocative Per Krohg mural, depicting Oslo through the seasons, that covers every inch of wall and ceiling in a long, narrow room. *(South of the National Theater and Karl Johans gt. on Fridtjof Nansens pl., near the harbor. May-Aug. daily 9am-5pm, Sept.-May 9am-4pm. 40kr, under-12 free. Free with Oslo Pass. June-July Tours daily 10am, noon, 2pm; Aug.-May M-F 10am, noon, 2pm.)* The **Royal Palace,** on a hill at the western end of Karl Johans gt., is open to the public via guided tours, but tickets sell out well in advance. *(Open late-June to mid-Aug. Tours in English daily 2, 2:20pm. Purchase tickets at any post office, ☎81 33 31 33 to reserve. 80kr, students 70kr.)* You can watch the changing of the guard daily at 1:30pm in front of the palace. *(Tram #12, 15, or 19, or bus #30-32 or 45 to Slottsparken. Free.)* For a great panorama of Oslofjord and the city, head to the mighty ski jump Holmenkollen and explore 4000 years of skiing history at the world's oldest **Ski Museum,** Kongeveien 5. A simulator recreates the adrenaline rush of a leap off a ski jump and a 4min., 130kph downhill ski run. *(Take subway #1 on the Frognerseteren line to Holmenkollen. It's a 10min. walk uphill. Open June-Aug. daily 9am-8pm; Sept. and May 10am-5pm; Oct.-Apr. 10am-4pm. Museum 50kr, children 25kr. Free with Oslo Pass. Simulator 45kr.)*

🎵 📷 ENTERTAINMENT AND NIGHTLIFE

The monthly *What's On in Oslo* (free at tourist offices), chronicles the current opera, symphony, and theater. **Filmenshus,** Dronningens gt. 16 (☎22 47 45 00), is the center of Oslo's indie film scene. In addition to the countless bars along **Karl Johans gate** and in the **Aker Brygge** harbor complex, Oslo boasts a number of nightclubs and cafes featuring DJs and live music.

    Mono, Pløens gt. 4, plays rock and alternative music with frequent concerts. (Beer 46kr. Su-Th 20+, Fr-Sa 22+. Cover for concerts 50kr. M-Sa 3pm-3am, Su 6pm-3am. **So What!,** Grensen 9, delivers metal, with an open courtyard in the summer. (Beer 46kr. 4-5 concerts per week. Fr-Sa 22+. Cover 50-150kr. M-F 2pm-3am, Sa noon-3am, Su 6pm-3am.) A few blocks away, the dance floor and bar at the recently-opened **Rexx,** Grensen 7, have become a local favorite on weekends. (Beer 57kr. 24+. Cover Sa 100kr. Fr-Su 10pm-3am). All are a 5min. walk from Karl Johans gt. Top-40 hits attract partygoers to the bar and dance floor of **Studenten,** on the corner of Karl Johans gt. and Universitetsgt. (Beer 50kr. Cover F-Sa 50kr after 9:30pm. Open M-Sa 11am-3am, Su noon-3am.) **Living Room,** Olav V's gt. 1, stays busy seven days a week with hip-hop, reggae, and house. (Beer 50kr. Open mic W. 24+; cover 50-80kr F-Sa. Open M-Sa 10pm-3:30am.) For a mellow vibe, head to the cafe-by-day, bar-by-night lounges along **Thorvald Meyers Gate** in Grüner Løkka.

📷 DAYTRIPS FROM OSLO

The nearby islands of inner **Oslofjord** offer cheap, delightful daytrips. The ruins of a **Cistercian Abbey,** as well as a rocky southern shore perfect for picnicking, lie on the landscaped island of **Hovedøya,** while **Langøyene** has Oslo's best **beach.** Take bus #60 (22kr) from City Hall to **Vippetangen** to catch a ferry to either island. An hour from Oslo by ferry, **Drøbak** has traditional wooden houses. The **ferry** (☎ 22 08 40 00 or 177) to Drøbak leaves from in front of the Rådhus. Ask the tourist office about cross-country ski rental. **The Wilderness House** (*Villmarkshuset*), Christian Krohgs gt. 16, rents canoes and kayaks on the Akerselva river (☎ 22 05 05 22; www.schlytter.no. Open M-F 10am-6pm, Sa 10am-3pm. 1-2hr. 200kr; full weekend 650kr.)

LILLEHAMMER

Lillehammer (pop. 19,000), a small city set in a valley at the edge of a lake, retains an unmistakable air of former glory from its days as host of the 1994 Winter Olympics. The **Norwegian Olympic Museum** in Olympic Park traces the history of the modern Olympic Games from their inception in 1896. From the train station, it's a 15-20min. walk; head two blocks uphill, turn left on Storgt., turn right on Tomtegt., go up the stairs, and follow the road uphill to the left. Or, take bus #5 to Sigrid Undsetsveg (5min., 17kr). The museum is in the farther dome. (Open late May to mid-Aug. daily 10am-6pm; late Aug. to mid-May Tu-Su 11am-4pm. 60kr, students 50kr, children 30kr.) You can climb up the endless steps of an Olympic **ski jump,** or give your spine a jolt on a **bobsled simulator** at the bottom of the hill. (Open mid-June to mid-Aug. daily 9am-8pm; early June and late Aug. 9am-5pm; Sept. and Mar-May 11am-4pm. Ski jump 15kr. Simulator 40kr, students 30kr. Combination ticket including chairlift ride 65/45kr.)

  Trains run to Oslo (2½hr.; every 2hr.; 265kr, children 133kr) and Trondheim (4½hr.; 6 per day; 543kr, children 272kr). **Lillehammer Tourist AS,** in the station, has good info on hiking and attractions. (☎ 61 28 98 00; www.lillehammertourist.no. Open mid-June to mid-Aug. M-Sa 9am-7pm, Su 11am-6pm; mid-Aug. to mid-June M-F 9am-4pm, Sa 10am-2pm.) The comfy **Lillehammer Vandrerhjem (Mary's Guest House) ❷** is on the top floor of the train station. (☎ 61 24 87 00; www.marysguesthouse.no. Breakfast included. Sheets 60kr. Internet 20kr per 15min. Reception 24hr. Dorms 200kr; singles 490kr; doubles 700kr.) Most restaurants are around the pedestrian section of **Storgata,** two blocks uphill from the station.

SOUTHERN NORWAY

Norway's southern coast substitutes serenity for drama, creating the premier summer holiday destination for Norwegian couples and families. *Skjærgard,* archipelagos of water-worn rock, hug the shore, stretching southward from Oslo to the pleasant beaches past Kristiansand. Fishing, hiking, rafting, and canoeing are popular in summer, while cross-country skiing reigns in winter.

KRISTIANSAND

Kristiansand's (pop. 62,000) best-known attraction is ▨**Dyreparken,** "the living park," which contains a zoo, an amusement park, and a circus. The zoo, 11km east of Kristiansand, is one of Europe's best; its newly acquired Siberian tigers are not to be missed. Take bus #1 (dir.: Sørlandsparken) from the tourist office. (Open June-late Aug. daily 10am-7pm; late Aug.-May M-F 10am-3pm, Sa-Su 10am-5pm; 225kr, children 195kr, seniors 150kr; off-season reduced rates.) **Posebyen,** the old town just two blocks from Markensgt., is worth meandering through. The **Skerries,** a group of tiny islands and fjords, are just off the coast. (Ferry 2½hr.; departs noon from Nupen Park in East Harbor; round-trip 150kr, children 100kr.)

  Trains run to Oslo (4½-5½hr.; 5 per day; 518kr, students 466kr) and Stavanger (3hr.; 8 per day; 347-388kr, students 302kr). Color Line **ferries** (☎ 81 00 08 11) sail to Hirsthals, Denmark (2½-4hr.; 2-5 per day; in summer M-F 400kr, Sa-Su

440kr; off-season 190-280kr; students 50% off). The **tourist office,** opposite the train station at Henrik Wegerlandsgt. and Vestre Strandgt, can arrange elk safaris in local forests. (☎38 12 13 14. **Internet** 15kr per 15min. Open mid-June to mid-Aug. M-Sa 8:30am-6pm, Su noon-6pm; mid-Aug. to mid-June M-F 8:30am-3:30pm.) The **Kristiansand Youth Hostel (HI) ❶,** Skansen 8, is 25min. from the harbor and train station. Walk away from the water until you reach Elvegt., turn right, then turn left onto Skansen. (☎38 02 83 10. Breakfast included. Kitchen, lockers, and laundry facilities available. Sheets 50kr. Reception June-Aug. 24hr.; Sept.-May 5-11pm. Dorms 185kr; singles 395kr; doubles 430kr. Nonmembers add 25kr.) Few restaurants in Kristiansand are cheap, even by Norwegian standards; look around **Markensgata** for reasonable options. **Postal Code:** 4601.

STAVANGER

A delightful port town with colorful wooden houses, cobblestone streets, and a lively fish market, Stavanger (pop. 110,000) is known for its cultural history and its proximity to great hikes. On the western side of the harbor is **Gamle Stavanger,** a neighborhood maintained in its 19th-century state. The 1125 **Stavanger Domkirke,** surrounded by the park at the pond's northern end, solemnly dominates the modern town center. (Open June-Aug. 11am-7pm; Sept.-May Tu-Th, Sa 11am-4pm.) A short walk down Kirkegt. from the church, the modern, architecturally innovative **Norsk Oljemuseum** (Norwegian Petroleum Museum) explains the driving force behind Norway's powerful oil industry. (Open June-Aug. daily 10am-7pm; Sept.-May M-F 10am-4pm, Su 10am-4pm. 75kr; students, seniors, and children 35kr.) One of Norway's postcard darlings, **Pulpit Rock** (Preikestolen), in nearby **Lysefjord,** boasts a magnificent view from an altitude of 600m. Take the ferry to Tau (4 per day; 32kr), catch the waiting bus (mid-June to Aug. only; 50kr, children 25kr), and hike up the marked trail (1½-2hr.).

Fjordline **ferries** (☎55 54 88 00; www.fjordline.com) go to Newcastle, England (17-20hr., 2-3 per week, from 1000kr), departing and arriving at a terminal on the western side of the harbor. There is a ferry **customer center** on Fiskepirterminalen. (☎51 86 87 87. Open M-F 9am-3pm.) The **tourist office,** Rosenkildetorg. 1, books accommodations (30kr fee) and provides info about bike rental, as well as routes in and around the city. (☎51 85 92 00; www.visitstavanger.com. Open June-Aug. daily 9am-8pm; Sept.-May M-F 9am-4pm, Sa 9am-2pm.)

NO WORK, ALL PLAY

MIND YOUR PINTS AT QUART

Kristiansand is normally a quiet town of about 60,000 people; the first week of each July, however, 20,000 music fans flood in for the five-day **Quart Festival,** a time of world-class concerts, movie premieres, and endless partying. Unlike similar European rock festivals, Quart possesses a neighborly, down-to-earth quality, thanks to the fact that it is relatively undiscovered outside of Northern Europe. The crowds packing concert are almost entirely Scandinavian despite the festival's widespread appeal.

A group of Kristiansand residentsstarted the festival in 1992; by 1996, it had grown to its present size. Each year, about 100 groups perform on the various stages. The 2003 line-up featured artists as diverse as the Roots, Coldplay, the Cardigans, the Flaming Lips, and breakout act Junior Senior.

The 2004 program and ticket info can be found online at www.quart.no. A 5-day pass is pricey (1500kr), but individual day passes (400kr) allow you to catch just your favorite acts. Plan far in advance if you're hoping to attend the festival; passes almost always sell out, and sleeping arrangements should be booked at least two months in advance. The two official **Quart Camps ❶** are the best option for a few hours of sleep each night. (200kr per tent, 60kr per person.)

To reach **Tone's Bed and Breakfast ❷**, Peder Claussøns gt. 22, from the train station, turn left on St. Olav's gt. along the pond, turn left onto Haakon VII's gt., go up the stairs, head right on Ovre Kleivegt. to Lokkeveien, turn right and take the first left onto the unmarked Peder Claussøns gt. One of the cheaper bed and breakfasts in town, Tone's provides cozy rooms and generous hospitality. (☎/fax 51 52 42 07. Breakfast included. Free laundry upon request. Singles 280kr; doubles 450kr.) Inexpensive restaurants can be found throughout the small streets behind the church. The **market** opposite the cathedral sells fresh Norwegian strawberries and other regional foods. (Open M-F 8am-5pm, Sa varying hours.) **Postal Code:** 4001.

THE FJORDS AND WEST COUNTRY

Spectacular views and charming towns await at the end of the scenic train ride from Oslo to **Bergen**. From the rugged peaks of **Jotunheim National Park** to the humbling depths of **Sognefjord,** western Norway possesses a dramatic natural grandeur irresistible to all types of travelers.

▮ TRANSPORTATION

Although transportation around the fjords can be complicated, the scenery through the window is half the fun. Plan your route ahead of time, as lines and times vary from day to day. Call **☎177** for regional transportation info; tourist offices, boat terminals, and bus stations can also help plan routes. **Bergen** is the major port serving the region; **HSD express boats** (☎55 23 87 80; ticket office at Strandkaiterminalen) run to Stavanger, and points south of the city, while **Fylkesbaatane** (☎55 90 70 71; tickets also at Strandkaiterminalen) sails north into Sognefjord. Almost all fjord towns connect via **bus** to Bergen (p. 778).

BERGEN

Situated between steep mountains and the waters of the Puddefjorden, Bergen (pop. 200,000) bills itself as the "Gateway to the Fjords." Despite being Norway's second-largest metropolis, the city has a compact downtown that is easily accessible on foot. Many prefer Bergen's west-coast feel to the rush of Oslo and the east.

▮ TRANSPORTATION

Trains: ☎81 50 08 88. The station is a 7-10min. walk south of the harbor. Trains run to: **Myrdal** (2½hr., 5-8 per day, 197-237kr); **Oslo** (6½hr.; 4-5 per day; 653kr, Minipriser discount 367kr if reserved at least a day in advance); **Voss** (1¼hr., 15 per day, 138kr).

Buses: Busstasjon, Strømgtn. 8. Inside the Bergen Storsenter mall at the corner of Strømgt. and Fjøsangermeien (☎177, outside Bergen ☎55 55 90 70). Serves: **Ålesund** (10hr., 1-2 per day, 545kr); **Oslo** (11hr., 1-3 per day, 640kr); **Trondheim** (14hr., daily, 805kr). 25% student discount and 50% InterRail and Scanrail discount.

Ferries: The **Hurtigruten,** or Coastal Steamer (☎81 03 00 00; www.hurtigruten.com) begins its journey up the coast from **Bergen** and stops in **Ålesund,** the **Lofoten Islands, Tromsø,** and **Trondheim,** as well as other towns and fjords to the north (Apr.-May daily 8pm, 495-4598kr; June-Sept. daily 8pm, 561-5212kr; Oct.-Apr. daily 10:30pm, 400-2616kr; 50% student discount). **Flaggruten** (☎51 86 87 80) boats head southward to Stavanger (4hr.; 1-2 per day; 590kr, students 350kr; 50% InterRail and Scanrail dis-

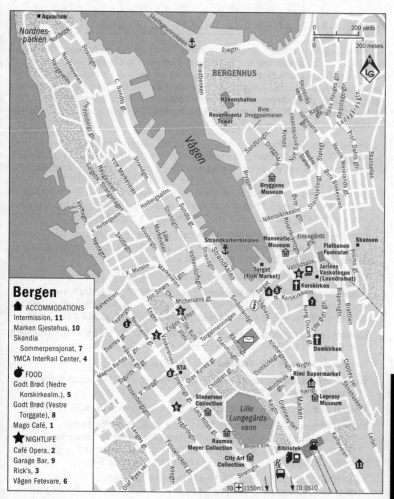

Bergen

🏠 ACCOMMODATIONS
Intermission, 11
Marken Gjestehus, 10
Skandia
 Sommerpensjonat, 7
YMCA InterRail Center, 4

🍴 FOOD
Godt Brød (Nedre
 Korskirkealm.), 5
Godt Brød (Vestre
 Torggate), 8
Mago Café, 1

⭐ NIGHTLIFE
Café Opera, 2
Garage Bar, 9
Rick's, 3
Vågen Fetevare, 6

counts.) **Fjord Line,** on Skoltegrunnskaien (☎55 54 88 00; www.fjordline.com), sends ships to **Hanstholm, Denmark** (16hr.; 3-4 per week; mid-June to mid-August M-Th 820kr, F-Su 920kr, children 410/460kr; off-season reduced prices), and **Newcastle, England** (20-22hr.; 2-3 per week; mid-June to early Aug. M-W 1100kr, Th-Su 1250kr, children 550/625kr; off-season from 500kr). **Smyril Line,** Slottsgt. 1, 5th fl. (☎55 59 65 20; www.smyril-line.no), departs Tu at 3pm for: the **Faroe Islands** (24hr.; mid-June to early July from 1160kr; off-season from 880kr); **Iceland** (45hr., from 2100/1560kr); the **Shetland Islands** (12hr., from 820/620kr, 25% student discount). All international ferries, except the Hurtigruten, depart from **Skoltegrunnskaien,** a 10-15min. walk past Bryggen along the right side of the harbor.

Public Transportation: Buses are 10kr in city center, 23kr outside. Free bus #100 goes from the bus station to the Galleriet shopping mall on Torgalmenningen by the harbor.

✳ 🛈 ORIENTATION AND PRACTICAL INFORMATION

Central Bergen is small enough for visitors to explore on foot. Using the **Torget** (fish market) by the harbor as a basis for navigation, the city can be broken down into a few basic areas. North of the Torget where the main street **Bryggen** curves around the harbor, is the touristy old city; southwest of the Torget is **Torgalmenningen**, the city's main shopping street. More authentic parts of Bergen lie down Torgalmenningen, past **Håkons gaten** and **Nygårdsgaten**. The train and bus stations are about 10min. south of the Torget.

Tourist Office: Vågsalmenningen 1 (☎55 55 20 00; www.visitbergen.com), just past the Torget. Books private rooms, has free copies of the *Bergen Guide*, and helps visitors plan travel through the fjords. The **Bergen Card** grants free museum admission and unlimited public transportation (1-day 165kr, children 70kr; 2-day 245/105kr). Open June-Aug. daily 8:30am-10pm; May and Sept. 9am-8pm; Oct.-Apr. M-Sa 9am-4pm. **DNT,** Tverrgt. 4-6 (☎55 33 58 10), off Marken, sells maps 77-99kr) and provides comprehensive hiking info. Open M-W and F 10am-4pm, Th 10am-6pm.

Currency Exchange: At banks near the harbor (generally open M-W and F 9am-3pm, Th 9am-5:30pm) and the post office. After hours, the tourist office will change currency at a rate less favorable than the bank rate, but without commission.

Luggage storage: At train and bus stations. 20-40kr per day.

Budget Travel: STA Travel, Vaskerelven 32 (☎81 55 99 05; bergen@statravel.no). Take Torgalmenningen southwest from the Torget; turn left on Vaskerelven. Sells discounted tickets for international flights and books accommodations. Open M-F 10am-5pm.

Laundry: Jarlens Vaskoteque, Lille Øvregt. 17. Wash 45kr; dry 5kr per 15min. Detergent 5kr. Open M-Tu and F 10am-6pm, W-Th 10am-8pm, Sa 10am-3pm.

Emergency: Police: ☎112. **Ambulance:** ☎113. **Fire:** ☎110.

Pharmacy: Apoteket Nordstjernen (☎55 21 83 84), on 2nd fl. of the bus station. Open M-Sa 8am-midnight, Su 9:30am-midnight.

Medical Assistance: 24-hour Accident Clinic, Vestre Strømkai 19 (☎55 32 11 20).

Internet Access: Bibliotek (public library), Strømgt. 6, at the intersection of Strømgt. and Vestre Strømkaien. Free 15min. slots. Open May-Aug. M-Th 10am-6pm, Fr 10am-4:30pm, Sa 10am-3pm. **CyberHouse,** Vetrlidsalm. 13, between the Torget and the funicular. 20kr per 30min. Open M-F and Su 9am-midnight, Sa 24hr.

Post Office: Småstrandgt. (☎55 54 15 00). Open M-F 8am-6pm, Sa 9am-3pm. Address mail to be held: Firstname SURNAME, *Poste Restante*/P.O. Box 1372, 5811 Bergen, NORWAY. *Poste Restante* office open M-F 8am-3pm, Sa 9am-3pm.

⌂ ACCOMMODATIONS

In the summer, it's best to reserve ahead. The tourist office books **private rooms** for a 30kr fee (singles 200-300kr; doubles 375-600kr). You can **camp** for free on the far side of the hills above town.

Intermission, Kalfarveien 8 (☎55 30 04 00; www.intermissionhostel.com). Friendly staff and communal atmosphere. Breakfast 30kr. Kitchen available. Laundry free. Internet 15kr per 30min. Reception Su-Th 7-11am and 5pm-midnight, F-Sa until 1am. Lockout 11am-5pm. Curfew Su-Th midnight, F-Sa 1am. Open mid-June to mid-Aug. Dorms 100kr. **Camping** in backyard 70kr. ❶

NORWAY

YMCA InterRail Center, Nedre Korskirkealm. 4 (☎ 55 31 72 52; fax 55 31 35 77). Ideal location with supermarket next door. Kitchen available. Reception 7am-midnight. Lockout 11am-3:30pm. Dorms 125kr; 4- to 6-person room 160-175kr per person. Nonmembers add 25kr. ❶

Skandia Sommerpensjonat, Kong Oscars gt. 22 (☎ 55 21 00 35; www.skandiapensjonat.no). Spacious, sunny, and functional rooms in convenient location. Laundry 30kr. Reception 8am-midnight. Open mid-June to mid-Aug. Singles 375kr; doubles 500kr, with kitchen 600kr; triples with kitchen 700kr. ❸

Marken Gjestehus, Kong Oscars gt. 45 (☎ 55 31 44 04; markengjestehus@smisi.no). Immaculate rooms, some with nice views of the nearby mountains. Breakfast 55kr. Kitchen available. Sheets 45kr. Laundry 15kr. Reception May-Sept. daily 9am-11pm; Oct.-Apr. 9am-7pm. Dorms 30kr; 6-person dorms 165kr; 4-person dorms 190kr; singles 340kr; doubles 440kr. ❶

🗂 FOOD

Bergen's culinary centerpiece is the **fish market** that springs up on the Torget; it's sometimes unclear, however, whether fish or tourists are the main haul. (Open M-F 7am-5pm, Th 7am-7pm, Sa 7am-4pm.) **Godt Brød** ❶, Vestre Torggt. 6 and Nedre Korskirkealm. 12, prepares the best sandwiches in town (25-49kr). The N. Korskirkealm. location has outdoor seating. (V. Torggt.: Open M-F 8am-6pm, Sa 8am-4:30pm. N. Korskirkealm.: Open M-F 7:15am-6pm, Sa 7:15am-3:30pm, Su noon-4pm.) For creative, satisfying fare in a quieter part of town, head to the **Mago Cafe** ❷, Neumanns gt. 5. (Vegetarian options. Entrees from 129kr, meat dishes from 215kr. Open May-Aug. daily 6-11pm; Sept.-April 1-10pm.)

🔆 SIGHTS

BRYGGEN AND BERGENHUS. Gazing down the right side of the harbor from the Torget yields a view of **Bryggen's** signature pointed gables. This row of medieval buildings, with its narrow alleys and projecting balconies, has weathered numerous fires and the explosion of a Nazi munitions ship, surviving to be listed by UNESCO as one of the world's most significant examples of the history and culture of the Middle Ages. The **Bryggens Museum** displays archeological artifacts and depicts Norwegian life in the Middle Ages. *(Dreggsalm. 3, behind a small park at the end of the Bryggen houses. Open May-Aug. daily 10am-5pm; Sept.-Apr. M-F 11am-3pm, Sa noon-3pm, Su noon-4pm.*

THE BIG SPLURGE

HAVE YOU KAYAKED A FJORD LATELY?

Taking a ferry through the fjords is picturesque; pulling yourself in a tiny kayak up to the base of a cliff hundreds of meters high, peering up at a seemingly endless expanse of rock, is surreal and mind-boggling. You're no longer simply passing through the towering landscape—you're swallowed up by it.

Nordic Ventures arranges a variety of outdoor activities, from quick afternoon tours to paragliding to overnight camping trips in Nærøyfjord and Osefjord. Among these, the day-long sea kayaking excursion offers a perspective unlike any hike or boat ride, as it takes its participants into the middle of expansive waters, to the base of waterfalls, and past some of the area's most remote villages.

The trip, at 890kr, may put a dent in your budget but is well worth sacrificing a few meals. Moreover, the scrumptious fjordside lunch is enough to keep you full for several days. In addition to experienced, affable guides, the tour provides all necessary equipment and instruction.

Nordic Ventures is located behind the Park Hotel in Voss. (☎ 56 51 00 17; www.nordicventures.com. 1-day tour 890kr, 2-day 1395kr. Open May to mid-Oct. daily 9am-7pm; mid-Oct. to Apr. 10am-5pm. MC/V.)

30kr, students 15kr.) English-language walking tours of Bryggen begin at the Bryggens Museum and travel down to the Hanseatic Museum. *(1½hr.; June-Aug. daily 11am and 1pm; 70kr, under-10 free.)* Not included in the tour is the city fortress, **Bergenhus**. On its grounds stand **Rosenkrantz Tower**, in late medieval splendor, and the cavernous 13th-century **Håkonshallen**, which is all that remains of the ancient royal residence. *(Walk along the harbor away from the Torget. Mid-May to Aug. hall and tower open daily 10am-4pm; Sept. to mid-May tower open Su noon-3pm, hall open M-W and F-Su noon-3pm, Th 3-6pm. Guided tours every hr. in summer. 20kr, students and children 10kr.)*

MUSEUMS. Three branches of the **Bergen Art Museum** line the west side of the Lille Lungegårdsvann. The **City Art Collection** and **Rasmus Meyers Collection** display Norway's masterpieces, including paintings by Dahl, Tidemand, and Munch; the **Stenersen Collection** has a more international collection with contemporary, abstract works by Miró and Picasso. *(Lars Hilles gt. 10, Rasmus Meyers allé 3 and 7. Open mid-May to mid-Sept. daily 11am-5pm; mid-Sept. to mid-May Su and Tu-Sa 11am-5pm. 50kr for all 3 museums, children 35kr; temporary exhibits 15kr.)*

⚠ THE OUTDOORS

A vast archipelago spreads westward from the only side of Bergen not bordered by towering mountains. **Hiking** trails surrounding the city are well kept and easily accessible. The **Fløibanen funicular** runs up **Mt. Fløyen** to a spectacular lookout point. (Runs June-Aug. M-F 7:30am-midnight, Sa 8am-midnight, Su 9am-midnight; Sept.-May closes at 11pm. Round-trip 50kr, children 25kr.) At the summit, you'll find terrific views and plenty of tourists, as well as several well-marked **trailheads** that lead through an equally striking, less-crowded landscape dotted by mammoth boulders, springy moss, pristine waterfalls, and quiet ponds, occasionally opening up to stunning landscape vistas. A 4hr. trek from Fløyen leads to the top of **Mt. Ulriken**, the highest peak above Bergen, and a panoramic view over the city, fjords, mountains, and nearby islands. A **bus/cable car combination** also runs to the top of Mt. Ulriken from the city center. (Cable car runs May-Sept. daily every 7min. 9am-10pm; Oct.-Apr. 10am-5pm. 70kr, children 35kr.) Pick up **maps** of the hills above Bergen at the DNT office (p. 780).

🎵🍷 ENTERTAINMENT AND NIGHTLIFE

Bergen doesn't pick up until late on weekend nights; many locals pre-game at home before heading to the bars and clubs. To get away from the touristy harborside bars, take Torgallm. to **Nygårdsgaten,** home to an array of pubs and cafes. Bergen's cafes are a relaxing nightlife option. **🍷Vågen Fetevare,** Kong Oscars gt. 10, is the best of them, drawing locals with board games, quality coffee (15-33kr), and inexpensive food. (Open M-Th 8am-11pm, F 8am-8pm, Sa 9am-6pm, Su 11am-11pm.) **Rick's,** Veiten 3, is a huge club with packed venues including a stage, dance floor, and several bars. (☎55 55 31 31. Occasionally 26+. Cover 80kr F-Sa. Open Su-Th 10pm-3am, F-Sa 10pm-3:30am.) **Garage Bar,** at the corner of Nygårdsgt. and Christies gt., is Bergen's most popular alt-rock and metal pub. (20+. Cover 30kr after 1am. Open M-Th 1pm-3am, F-Sa 1pm-3:30am, Su 3pm-1am.) **Café Opera,** Engen 18, is a mellow cafe that serves light meals and drinks; a DJ steps it up after 11pm. (Open Su-M noon-12:30am, Tu-Th noon-3am, F-Sa noon-3:30am.)

The city pulls out all the stops in late May for two simultaneous festivals: the annual **Bergen International Festival,** a 12-day program of music, ballet, folklore, and drama (May 19-May 31, 2004), and the **Night Jazz Festival** (late May to early Jun.)

🔁 DAYTRIP FROM BERGEN

HARDANGERFJORD. South of Bergen, the steep banks of Hardangerfjord are lined with orchards and waterfalls. Local tourist offices distribute the free *Hardanger Guide*, which provides detailed info about transportation and accommodations. At Bergen's tourist office, find more info on **Hardanger Sunnhordlandske Dampskipsselskap** (HSD), which offers a variety of day cruises through the fjord, with stops at larger towns. (☎81 52 21 20; www.hsd.no. From 250kr. Mid-May to mid-Sept. Tours to Eidfjord, Lofthus, Ulvik, and Utne from 395kr.) Most tours depart from platforms #4 or 21 at Bergen's bus station. **Bergen Fjord Sightseeing** offers tours of all the area's fjords. (☎55 25 90 00; www.bergen-fjordsightseeing.no. May-Aug. From 300kr.)

EIDFJORD

Stampeding hikers can be heard in beautiful Eidfjord (pop. 1050), a tiny town tucked into the fjord 45km southeast of Voss, as they pass through this gateway to **Hardangervidda,** Norway's largest national park. Near the harbor lies the austere 14th-century **Eidfjord Old Church** (open July-Aug. M-F 9am-3:30pm). A 1½hr. walk along a trail from the harbor leads to a **Viking Burial Place** on top of a plateau in **Hereid.** Pick up a free map of the walking trail from the tourist office (see below) and then head out along Simadalvegen. After passing the bridge, turn right and walk along the river; follow the path as it goes by the lake and winds uphill. Also popular is a **mini-tour** that goes to the **Hardangervida Nature Center** and continues through the mountains to **Vøringstossen,** one of Norway's most famous waterfalls. (Mid-June to mid-Aug. daily. Departs after ferry arrival. 185kr; children 105kr.)

To get to Eidfjord from Bergen take a **bus/ferry** combo transferring at Norheimsund (4¼hr., Su-F 7:30am, 300kr). Since this route is only one way, the most straightforward return trip is a **bus/ferry/bus** combo through Voss (3hr., 7:15am and 1:10pm, from 225kr). HSD also offers a full-day tour of Eidfjord from Bergen. (☎55 96 69 00. Mid-May to mid-Sept. Leave Bergen 8:40am, return 7pm. 590kr, children 390kr). Ask at the **tourist office,** Simadalsvn. 2, for info about the area's fantastic hikes. (☎53 67 34 00; www.eidfjordinfo.no. Open mid-June to mid-Aug. M-F 9am-6pm, Sa-Su noon-6pm; May to mid-June and mid-Aug. to Sept. M-F 8:30am-4pm; Oct.-Apr. M-F 10am-4pm.) They also rent **bikes** (full-day 150kr, half-day 100kr) and can help you find a hut. For a spectacular lakeside location on the fjord, try 🏕**Saebø Camping ❶**, 7km from town. Buses leave from the HSD station across the street from the tourist office; ask the driver to let you off at the campground. (☎53 66 59 27. Open mid-May to mid-Sept. Electricity 25kr. Showers 5kr per 2min. 65kr per person and tent, 90kr per car. Cabins 240-600kr.)

ALONG THE OSLO-BERGEN RAIL LINE

The seven-hour rail journey from Oslo to Bergen is one of the most famous scenic rides in the world. From Oslo, there are stops at Finse, Myrdal (the transfer point for the Flåm railway), and Voss, before the train finally pulls into Bergen.

🏔**FLÅM AND THE FLÅM RAILWAY.** The spectacular railway connecting Myrdal, a stop on the Oslo-Bergen line, to the tiny fjord town of Flåm is one of Norway's most celebrated attractions. The railway is an incredible feat of engineering, descending almost 864m in 55min. as it winds through tunnels and past rushing waterfalls. The centerpiece of the ride is **Kjosfossen falls,** where the train stops for an incomparable view. Alternatively, a 20km **hike** (4-5hr.) on well-tended paths from Myrdal to Flåm allows for extended lingering and free camping amid the rainbow-capped waterfalls and snowy mountain vistas. Taking the train uphill to Myrdal opens up a wonderful bike ride back to Flåm. For bike rental and more detailed info inquire at the tourist office (see below). Flåm sits in a valley at the edge of **Aurlandsfjord,** an inlet off Sognefjord. During the day, the tiny town is heavily touristed; when Flåm empties out in the low season, the stunning surroundings make this a terrific place to spend a night or two. **Trains** cover the railway in each direction (55min.; 8-10 per day; 30kr, round-trip 210kr). The **tourist office** is in the large building beside the train station. (☎57 63 21 06. Open June-Aug. daily 8:30am-8pm; May and Sept. 8:45am-5pm.) The rest of the year, the main tourist office in Aurland handles all Flåm questions. (Open M-F 8am-4pm. **Bikes** 30kr per hr., 175kr per day.) From Flåm, there are daily express boats to Aurland, Balestrand, and Bergen, and ferries to Gudvangen (inquire at the tourist office for up-to-date schedules).

NORWAY IN A NUTSHELL. The immensely popular "Norway in a Nutshell" tour (☎ 81 56 82 22; www.nsb.no) combines a ride along the stunning **rail** line between Myrdal and Flåm (55min.; 8-10 per day; 125kr, round-trip 205kr), a **cruise** through the narrowest branches of Sognefjord between Gudvangen and Flåm (2hr.; 1-4 per day; 180kr, round-trip 220kr; 50% student and InterRail discount), and a twisting **bus** ride over the mountains from Gudvangen to Voss (1¼hr., 8-10 per day, 70kr). The tour is unguided and extremely flexible, allowing "nutshellers" to customize the trip, completing it in one day or taking stopovers at transfer points. The three-part excursion can be done as a round-trip from Oslo, Bergen, or Voss, or as a side-trip while going from one city to the other. Each version starts with a train to Myrdal and continues to Flåm; most tours also include Gudvangen, Voss, or both. At the end, you have the choice of returning to Oslo or Bergen, or further exploring the heart of the country. **Tickets** can be bought separately for each leg of the journey while traveling, or purchased in advance as a package from tourist offices or train stations in Oslo and Bergen. The cheapest route is a round-trip loop from Voss (450kr); those from Bergen and Oslo are more pricey (Bergen 705-865kr; Oslo 1435-1815kr). Railpass holders and students may be able to get a better deal by purchasing individual tickets along the way.

FINSE. Outdoor enthusiasts hop off at Finse and hike north for several days down the Aurlandsdal Valley to **Aurland,** 10km from Flåm. Be sure to ask about trail conditions at the Finse rail station or the DNT in Oslo or Bergen before you set off; the trails are usually snow-free and accessible between early July and late September. You can sleep in DNT *hytte,* all spaced a day's walk apart along the trail to Aurland. For maps, prices, and reservations, inquire at the **DNT** in Oslo (☎22 82 28 00) or Bergen (☎55 33 58 10).

VOSS. Stretched along a glassy lake that reflects snow-capped mountains, Voss (pop. 13,000) is an adventurer's dream. The **Extreme Sport Week** (www.extremsportveko.com) in late June, the world's largest competition of its kind, with over 1000 participants from 30 countries, features challenges in the air and water, as well as clinics for interested spectators, a free trial day for paragliding, and nightly concerts around the town. In winter, skiing is plentiful; in summer, Voss is a base for kayaking, paragliding, horseback riding, and white-water rafting. Book activities through **Nordic Ventures** (☎56 51 00 17; www.nordicventures.com) or the next-door **Voss Rafting Center** (☎56 51 05 25; www.vossrafting.no), both located behind the Park Hotel in the corner of a mini-mall. (Nordic Ventures: Open May to mid-Oct. daily 9am-7pm; mid-Oct. to Apr. 10am-5pm. Voss Rafting: Open May-Oct. M-F 9am-5pm, Sa 9am-7pm.) If you'd prefer to keep your feet on the ground, take a 30min. walk to the ethereal **Bordal Gorge,** where water rushes in a narrow path lined by overhanging rocky cliffs. Turn left from the train station, walk along the shore and turn right onto the gravel path; after crossing the bridge, turn right and follow the signs to *Bordalgjelet.*

Trains leave for Oslo (5½-6hr., 7 per day, 568kr) and Bergen (1¼hr., 16 per day, 138kr). The central train station is a few minutes west of downtown. To get to the **tourist office,** Hestavangen 10, turn left as you exit the station and bear right at the fork by the church. (☎56 52 08 00. Open June-Aug. M-Sa 9am-7pm, Su 2-7pm; Sept.-May M-F 9am-3:30pm.) Turn right as you exit the station and walk along the lakeside road to reach Voss's modern, well-equipped █Youth Hostel (HI) ❷, home to a sauna and a terrific view. (☎56 51 20 17. Canoe, rowboat, bike, and kayak rental. Breakfast included. Reception 24hr. Dorms 195kr; singles 420kr; doubles 540kr. Nonmembers add 25kr.) Those set on **camping** should head left from the station, stick to the lake shore, and turn right onto the gravel path at the church. **Voss Camping ❶** is at the end. (☎56 51 15 97. Reception May-Sept. daily 8am-10pm. 1 person with tent 95kr, additional person 15kr. 5-person cabin 400kr.) Pick up groceries at **Kiwi** supermarket, on the main street just past the post office. (Open M-F 9am-9pm, Sa 9am-6pm.) **Postal Code:** 5701.

SOGNEFJORD

The slender fingers of Sognefjord, the longest and deepest fjord in Europe, reach all the way to the foot of the Jotunheimen Mountains in central Norway. Sognefjord is a short, stunning ride north of the rail line running west from Oslo, or a quick boat trip from Bergen. **Fylkesbaatane** (☎55 90 70 70) sends boats on daytrips to towns on Sognefjord and back to Bergen, and offers day tours of Sognefjord and the Flåm valley. The boats depart from Strandkaiterminalen; buy tickets there or at Bergen's tourist office. Transportation is certain to be confusing and frustrating due to the limited number of bus routes and difficulty of obtaining accurate info, especially on weekends; allow plenty of time and consult tourist offices for help in planning a route.

BALESTRAND. Balestrand (pop. 1,500) is an ideal base for exploration of Sognefjord. **Jostedalen Breførarlag** (☎57 68 32 50; www.bfl.no) runs everything from one-hour outings to full-day jaunts (140-600kr), and **Breheimsenteret** (☎57 68 32 50) has recently begun organizing guided kayaking trips in the glacier's frigid fjords. In front of the ferry docks, **Sognefjord Akvarium** gives a glimpse of the rarely seen marine life of the fjords. (Open late June to mid-Aug. daily 9am-10pm; May to late June and mid-Aug. to early Sept. 10am-6pm. 60kr, children 30kr.) **Hiking** in the area immediately around Balestrand is excellent, with several clear, color-coded trails guaranteeing exquisite views. From the harbor, head uphill, turn left, and walk along the main road for 7-10min.; turn right on Sygna and follow the signs. The trails, described at the trailhead, range from simple walks to arduous treks for experienced hikers. On a clear day, the 972m peak **Raudmelen,** about a 5hr. hike, offers an expansive 360° view of the surrounding landscape.

Express boats connect Bergen and Balestrand (4hr.; 2 per day; 355kr, students 177kr). For trail maps and other info, stop by the **tourist office** near the quay. (☎57 69 12 55. Open mid-June to mid-Aug. M-F 7:30am-7pm, Sa-Su 8am-1pm and 4-6pm; May to mid-June and mid-Aug. to Sept. daily 10am-3pm. **Internet** 20kr per 15min.) **Askelund ❶,** 1km past the brown church on the coastal road, welcomes

NORWAY

guests with low-key, comfortable rooms in an old schoolhouse right on the fjord. (☎57 69 12 02; www.askelund.no. Breakfast 90kr. Kitchen available. Singles 200kr; doubles 300kr; triples 400kr.) The **Kringsjå Hotel and Youth Hostel (HI)** ❶ is 100m up the hill behind town. (☎57 69 13 03. Breakfast included. Kitchen available. Laundry 15kr. Open July to mid-Aug. Dorms 190kr; doubles 520kr. Nonmembers add 20kr.) **Sjøtun Camping** ❶, also on the way to Askelund, has tent sites and huts. (☎57 69 12 23. Open June to early Sept. 20kr per person; 30kr per tent; cabins 150-325kr.)

🔢 **DAYTRIP FROM SOGNEFJORD: FJÆRLAND AND FJÆRLANDSFJORD.** With Balestrand perched at its mouth, Fjærlandsfjord branches off from Sognefjord in a thin northward line to the tiny town of **Fjærland,** resting beneath looming Jostedalsbreen. The **Glacier Museum** (Norsk Bremuseum), 3km outside town, Fjærland's main point of interest, screens a beautiful panoramic film about Jostedalsbreen and the surrounding national park. (Open June-Aug. daily 9am-7pm; Apr.-May and Sept.-Oct. 10am-4pm. 80kr, students 40kr.) **Ferries** run between Balestrand and Fjærland (1¼hr.; 2 per day; 147kr, students 75kr). Buses (120kr) shuttle passengers to the Glacier Museum, whisk them to view two offshoots of Jostedalsbreen, then return them to the harbor. From the Glacier Museum, **buses** connect to: Ålesund (6hr., 6 per day, 353kr); Førde (1¼hr., 9 per day, 110kr); Sogndal (30min., 6 per day, 86kr); and (2½hr., 4 per day, 163kr). The **tourist office,** near the harbor, helps solve transportation woes, rents bikes (25kr per hr., 125kr per day), and provides hiking maps. (☎57 69 32 33. Open daily 9:30am-5:30pm.)

LOM AND JOTUNHEIMEN NATIONAL PARK

Somewhere between the offshoots of the western fjords and the remote towns of the interior lies the vast, unadulterated landscape that comprises Jotunheimen National Park. Used by hunters and fishermen for thousands of years, the park's craggy mountains and tranquil lakes began to attract visitors to the untamed landscape in the 19th century as Romanticism pervaded Norway. In 1862, poet Aasmund Olavsson christened the region the "Jotunheimen," home of the giants.

LOM. The tiny town of Lom (pop. 2,500) has grown into a convenient hub for excursions further into the park. Steeped in tradition, Lom's residents continue to worship at the 12th-century **Stave Church,** which boasts intricate woodcarvings and an impressive painting collection. (Open mid-June to mid-Aug. daily 9am-8pm; mid-May to mid-June and mid-Aug. to mid-Sept. 10am-4pm. 40kr. Children free.) The nearby **Mountain Museum** (*Fjellmusuem*), focusses on Jotunheim itself. (Open June 15-Aug. 15 M-F 9am-9pm, Sa-Su 10am-8pm; early June and late Aug. M-F 9am-6pm, Sa-Su 10am-5pm; Sept. and May M-F 9am-4pm, Sa-Su 10am-5pm; Oct.-Apr. M-F 9am-4pm. 60kr, students 40kr, under-12 free.) Jotunheimen offers endless opportunities for exploration, including the popular trek to the summit of **Galhøpiggen,** northern Europe's tallest mountain, and the **Memurubu-Gjendsheim** trail from Henrik Ibsen's *Peer Gynt.* Ask at the tourist office for the best location from which to base your excursions; several focal points in the park include **Juvashytta, Krossbu, Leirvassbu,** and **Spiterstulen.**

Buses run to: Bergen (8½hr., 2 per day, 505kr); Oslo (6-6½hr., 3-5 per day, 475kr); Sogndal (3½hr., 2 per day, 200kr); and Trondheim (5½hr., 2 per day, 370kr). From the bus station, turn left and cross the bridge to reach the church, museum, and tourist office. The **tourist office,** in the same building as the museum, provides crucial transportation info, suggests outdoor activities for all levels, and directs travelers to the hostels and campgrounds dotting the park. (☎61 21 29 90; www.visitlom.com. Open same hours as the Mountain museum.) Take the bus from Lom (8:40am, 1:30, 4:15pm; 32kr, students 24kr) to reach

Bøverdalen Vandrerhjem (HI). Twenty kilometers from Lom, it's the closest hostel, with simple, cabin-like rooms and an adjoining campground and grocery store. (☎61 21 20 64; boeverdalen.hostel@vandrerhjem.no. Breakfast 60kr. Kitchen available. Reception 8am-10pm. Open June-Sept. Dorms 105kr; singles 200kr; doubles 255kr. Camping 25kr per person; 100kr per tent; cabins 360kr.)

NORDFJORD AND JOSTEDALSBREEN

Although Nordfjord itself places third compared to Geirangerfjord and Sognefjord, its icy 800km expanse of Jostedalsbreen (Jostedal glacier) is becoming an increasingly popular destination for guided excursions. The glacier is difficult to miss as it winds through mountain passes in frozen cascades of luminous blue. Adventurous travelers should note that it is dangerous to venture onto the glacier without a guide, as all glaciers have hidden soft spots and crevices.

STRYN (BRIKSDALSBREEN). Stryn (pop. 6,700) is wedged between the mountains near the inner end of Nordfjord. It's not an attraction in and of itself, but it provides a good base for glacier walks and other outdoor excursions. **Briksdal Breføring** (☎57 87 68 00; www.briksdalsbre.no) and the especially good **Olden Aktiv** (☎57 87 38 88; www.briksdalsbreen.com) run a variety of glacier tours for different fitness and skill levels (230-400kr; reserve ahead). ▧**Melkevoll Bretun ❶** is a particularly good glacier-side lodge with nice, well-equipped rooms and an unbelievable open-air cave-dorm; as warm as the reindeer skins may keep you, make sure to bring a sleeping bag. (☎57 87 38 64; fax 57 87 38 90. Cave-dorm 90kr; 4- to 6-person cabins 370-690kr.) **Bus/train** combos connect to Trondheim, Lillehammer, and Oslo via Otta (3hr., 3 per day, 260kr); **buses** go to Ålesund (5½-6hr., 2-4 per day, 220kr). The **tourist office,** Perhusveien 19, past the Esso station, sells maps (30kr) and recommends hikes. (☎57 87 40 40; www.nordfjord.no. **Internet** 15kr per hr. Open July daily 8:30am-8pm; June and Aug. 8:30am-6pm; Sept.-May M-F 8:30am-3:30pm.) To reach the **Youth Hostel (HI) ❶** from the bus station, turn left onto Setrevegen, head up the hill and look for the signs. (☎57 87 11 06; stryn.hostel@vandrerhjem.no. Breakfast included. Laundry 20kr. Reception 8-11am and 4-11pm. Lockout 11am-4pm. Open June-Aug. only. Dorms 170kr; singles 250kr; doubles 400kr, with bath 500kr. Nonmembers add 25kr.) **Stryn Camping ❶** is in the center of town. (☎57 87 11 36; 57 87 20 25. Showers 15kr. Reception 8am-11pm. 90kr per person and tent. 4- to 6-person cabins 350-690kr.)

GEIRANGERFJORD

Only 16km long, Geirangerfjord is lined with narrow cliffs and waterfalls that make it one of the prettiest places in Norway. While cruising through the iridescent turquoise water, watch for the Seven Sisters waterfalls and the Suitor geyser opposite them. Geirangerfjord can be reached from the north via the famous Trollstigen road from Åndalsnes, or by the bus from Ålesund that stops in Hellesylt.

GEIRANGER. Tiny Geiranger (pop. 330) is situated at Geirangerfjord's glorious eastern end. An endpoint of the famous Trollstigen road splintered by sheer inclines, the town is one of Norway's most visited destinations. Even the tourists don't overwhelm the picture-perfect area. **Hiking** abounds in this charmed country; you can walk right behind **Storseter Waterfall** (3hr.), peer down from the overhanging **Flydalsjuvet Cliff** (1½hr.), catch a view of the Seven Sisters waterfalls from **Skageflå Farm** (5hr.), and tromp in the snow at the mile-high **Dalsnibba Mountain.**

NORWAY

Each hike has its own starting point, which may require a short bus ride. One kilometer uphill to the right of the tourist office is the modern **Fjord Center**, which houses an informative exhibit about the history of fjord life and shows a slide show following the region through the seasons. (Open mid-May to Aug. daily 10am-10pm; Sept. 10am-6pm. 75kr, children 35kr.) **Buses** run directly to Ålesund (3hr.; M-Sa 7:20am and 12:45pm, Su 6pm; 169kr), but getting to Lillehammer, Oslo, or Trondheim requires connecting through Åndalsnes (3hr.; 1 and 6:10pm; 146kr, 50% InterRail and Scanrail discount). For hiking maps and travel help, head to the **tourist office**, up from the ferry landing. They can also help find private rooms. (☎70 26 30 99; www.geiranger.no. Open mid-June to Aug. daily 9am-7pm, mid-May to mid-June 9am-4pm.) **Vinjebakken Hostel ❶** is in a home up on the main road behind town; head to the church and look for the sign. (☎70 26 32 05. Breakfast 40kr. Sheets 30kr. Laundry. Reception 24hr. Curfew midnight. Reserve ahead. Open June-Sept. Dorms 130kr. Cash only.) **Geiranger Camping ❶** is by the water, 100m from the town center. (☎70 26 31 20. Showers 10kr. Electricity 25kr. Open mid-May to early Sept. 14kr per person; 60kr per tent, 92kr with car.)

ÅLESUND

The largest city between Bergen and Trondheim, Ålesund (OH-les-oond; pop. 40,000) is renowned for its lovely architecture and oceanside location. The best view of the city and the distant mountains is 418 steps away at the ◪**Aksla** viewpoint. Follow hordes of children to the **Atlantic Sea Park,** where the innovative tanks are submerged in the ocean and illuminated by natural daylight. To reach the park, take bus #13 or 18 (10min., 6-7 per day, 22kr) from St. Olavs pl. or in front of the tourist office to *Atlanterhavsparken.* (Open mid-June to mid-Aug. Su-F 10am-7pm, Sa 10am-4pm; mid-Aug. to mid-June M-Sa 11am-4pm, Su noon-5pm. 85kr, students and seniors 70kr, children 55kr.) Step into a time machine at the centrally located **Art Nouveau Center,** in the old "Apothek" building, which surveys architectural changes following the fire that destroyed the city in 1904. (Open early June-Aug. M-Sa 10am-5pm, Su noon-5pm; Sept.-May Su noon-4pm, Tu-Sa 11am-3pm. 40kr, students and seniors 30kr, children 20kr.) There are Viking burial mounds and a 12th-century marble church on the nearby island of **Giske.** Bus #64 travels through the tunnel connecting Giske to the mainland (20min.; M-F 8 per day, Sa 5 per day; 45kr, students 30kr).

Buses go to Stryn (3½hr., 1-2 per day, 220kr) via Hellesylt (2½hr., 3 per day, 145kr) and Trondheim (8hr., 2 per day, 485kr). There is also a bus/train combo to Trondheim; a bus runs to Åndalsnes (2½hr., 3 per day, 172kr) and connects with a waiting train (4hr., 4 per day, 476kr). The luxurious **Hurtigruten** also heads to Trondheim; considering that it may save a night's accommodation, it can be an affordable alternative. (Departs daily at 6:45pm, arrives in Trondheim at 8:15am; 905kr, students 453kr.) The **tourist office,** on Keiser Wilhelms gt. in the city hall has **Internet** access (10kr per 10min.) and books accommodations for a 30kr fee. (☎70 15 76 00. Open June-Aug. M-F 8:30am-7pm, Sa 9am-5pm, Su 11am-5pm; Sept.-May M-F 9am-4pm.) It's a 5-7min. walk from the bus station to the enjoyable **Ålesund Vandrerhjem ❶**, Parkgt. 14, where you can shack up in triple-decker bunk beds. Head down Keiser Wilhelms gt., keeping the water on your right, turn left onto Rådstugt. and head uphill to Parkgt; the hostel will be around the corner to the right. (☎70 11 58 30; eaaa@online.no. Breakfast included. Kitchen available. Laundry. Open May-Sept. Reception 8:30-11am and 3:30pm-midnight. Lockout 11am-3:30pm. Dorms 150kr; singles 390kr; doubles 510kr. Nonmembers add 25kr.) **Volsdalen Camping ❶** is 2km along the main highway, next to a beach. Take bus #13, 14, 18, or 24 (20kr) to *Volsdalen,* turn right off the highway, follow the road downhill, turn left at the bottom and right across the overpass; it'll be 200m down on the left.

NORWAY

(☎70 12 58 90. Reception M-Sa 8am-11pm, Su 8am-10pm. Open May-Aug. 100kr per tent; cabins 300-500kr.) You can grab a bite to eat at any of the area's many supermarkets, as well as the casual, artistic cafes dotting the town center.

TRONDHEIM

A thousand years ago, Viking kings turned Trondheim (then Nidaros) into Norway's seat of power. Today, the city is a leading technological center whose vivacity stems from its 25,000 university students.

TRANSPORTATION AND PRACTICAL INFORMATION. Trains go to: Bodø (11hr., 3 per day, 798kr); Oslo (6½hr.; M-F 5 per day, Sa-Su 3 per day; 730kr, minipriser discount 430kr); and Stockholm (11hr., 2 per day, 500kr). The **Hurtigruten** sails to Stamsund, in the Lofoten Islands (p. 790; 31½hr.; departs daily at noon, arrives in Stamsund 7:30pm the next day; 1799kr, students 900kr). **Buses** leave the train station for: Ålesund (7¼hr., 2-3 per day, 485kr); Bergen (14hr., 2 per day, 805kr); and Oslo (9¾hr., 4 per week, 610kr). Trondheim is bike-friendly; the city keeps 300 serviceable bikes parked at stations in town (20kr deposit). Maps showing the stations' locations are available at the **tourist office**, Munkegt. 19. To get there from the train station, cross the bridge, walk six blocks down Søndregt., turn right on Kongensgt., and look to your left as you approach the rotary. (☎73 80 76 60; www.visit-trondheim.com. Open July-early Aug. M-F 8:30am-8pm, Sa-Su 10am-6pm; mid-May to June and early Aug.-late Aug. M-F 8:30am-6pm, Sa-Su 10am-6pm; late Aug. to mid-May M-F 9am-4pm.) **DNT**, Sandgt. 30, has maps and hiking info. (☎73 92 42 00. Open M-F 8am-4pm, Th until 6pm.) **Postal Code:** 7400.

ACCOMMODATIONS AND FOOD. ▣InterRail Centre ❶, Elgesetergt. 1, in the Studentersamfundet, is a lively hostel 10-12min. from the tourist office. Cross the roundabout to Kongensgt., turn left onto Prinsens gt., and the hostel will be on your left after the bridge. (☎73 89 95 38; tirc@stud.ntnu.no. Free **Internet** access. Breakfast included. Dinner 45kr. Sheets 30kr. Open late June to mid-Aug. Sleeping-bag dorms 115kr.) For more peaceful lodging, take Lillegårdsbakken, off Øvre Bakklandet, uphill to **Singsaker Sommerhotell ❶**, Rogertsgt. 1. (☎73 89 31 00; http://sommerhotell.singsaker.no. Breakfast included. Sheets 35kr. Open June to mid-Aug. Sleeping-bag dorms 150kr; singles 375-480kr; doubles 570-680kr; triples 780kr.) There's a cluster of enjoyable cafes around the Torget. **Rema 1000 supermarket** is on the main square. (Open M-F 8am-9pm, Sa 9am-8pm.)

SIGHTS. Most sights are concentrated in the south end of town around the gigantic **Nidaros Cathedral,** easily the main attraction. With intricate ornamentation and an evocative presence, the 11th-century cathedral is the site of all Norwegian coronations and the repository of the crown jewels. (Open July-late Aug. M-F 9am-6pm, Sa 9am-2pm, Su 1-4pm; May-June and late Aug. to mid-Sept. M-F 9am-3pm, Sa 9am-2pm, Su 1-4pm; mid-Sept. to Apr. M-F noon-2:30pm, Sa 11:30am-2pm, Su 1-3pm. 40kr, children 20kr). The **Rustkammeret** (Army Museum) and **Hjemmefrontmuseet** (Resistance Museum) are located in the same complex. (Museums open June-Aug. M-F 9am-3pm, Sa-Su 11am-4pm; Mar.-May and Sept.-Nov. Sa-Su 11am-4pm. Free with cathedral admission ticket.) The image of Olav Tryggvason, who founded Trondheim in AD 997, watches over the town from a pillar in the **Torget,** the main market square. Across the **Gamle Bybro** (Old Town Bridge), the **old district's** former fishing houses have been transformed into chic galleries and cafes. On the hill above the old district, **Kristiansten Fortress** yields a splendid view; take the bike lift up from the base of the Old Town Bridge. (Key-card available at the tourist office or adjacent cafes. 100kr deposit.)

FARTHER NORTH

LOFOTEN ISLANDS

A jumble of emerald mountains, mirror-like waters, and colorful villages, the Lofotens prove that there is more to Norwegian beauty than fjords. As late as the 1950s, isolated fishermen lived in *rorbuer*, wooden shacks along the coast; today, Lofoten residents gladly greet travelers who come to fish under the midnight sun.

▐ TRANSPORTATION

To get to the Lofoten Islands from Trondheim, take the **Hurtigruten** to Stamsund (31½hr.; departs daily at noon, arrives at 7:30pm the next day; 1799kr, student discount 50%) or take a **train** to Bodø (11hr., 2-3 per day including a night train, 798kr; reservations mandatory) and then either a **car ferry** to Moskenes (3-4hr.; 4-7 per day; 127kr, children 63kr), an **express boat** to Svolvær (3½hr.; 1 per day Su-F; 257kr, student discount 50%), or the **Hurtigruten** to Svolvær (6hr., daily 3pm, 383kr) via Stamsund (4½hr., 356kr). Bodø's tourist office and bus and express boat terminal, are down Sjogt. from the train station. (Tourist office open June-Aug. M-F 9am-8pm, Sa 10am-8pm, Su noon-8pm; Sept.-May M-W and F 9am-4pm, Th 9am-6pm, Sa 10am-3pm.) Within the islands, **local buses** are the main form of transport; pick up the invaluable *Lofoten Trafikklag* timetable at the tourist office.

MOSKENES AND FLAKSTAD. Travelers are drawn to the jagged mountains and quaint fishing villages on Moskenes and Flakstad, two islands linked by a bridge. **Ferries** from Bodø dock in Moskenes, the southernmost of the large Lofotens. The **tourist office**, by the ferry landing, offers tours (5hr., 590kr) that take you through the **Maelstrom,** one of the most dangerous ocean currents in the world, past the abandoned fishing hamlet of **Hell,** to the ancient **Refsvika caves** to view their 3000-year-old drawings. (☎76 09 15 99; www.lofoten-info.no. **Internet** 15kr per 15min. Open early June-Aug. daily 10am-6pm; Sept.-May. M-F 10am-2pm.) Visitors to Moskenes usually head 5km south to **Å** (OH), a tiny but well-known fishing village at the end of the E10 highway. **Buses** depart from the tourist office 5-15min. after boat landings. In Å, pick up a free map at the bus station's service center. (Open June-late Aug. 11am-4:30pm.) Six unconnected buildings comprise the exceptional ▨**Norsk Fiskeværsmuseum,** which re-creates life in an old-fashioned fishing village. (Open mid-June to mid-Aug. daily 10am-5:30pm; mid-Aug. to mid-June M-F 10am-3pm. 40kr, students 30kr.) **Å Hamna Rorbuer As ❶,** is in the town center. (☎76 09 11 21. June-Sept. reception 24hr. Reserve ahead. 2- to 4-person dorms 100kr.) Or, **camp** for free on the shores of the lake behind town.

VESTVÅGØY. Farther north is Vestvågøy, an island worth visiting just to stay at the seaside ▨**Justad youth hostel (HI) ❶.** A 15min. walk from the ferry dock, in the hamlet of **Stamsund,** the bustling hostel is paradise for those looking to fish and hike; long-time owner Roar, however, is the biggest draw of all. (☎76 08 93 34; fax 76 08 97 39. Fishing gear and rowboats 100kr deposit. Bikes 100kr per day. Laundry 30kr. Showers 5kr per 5min. Open mid-Dec. to mid-Oct. Dorms 90kr; doubles 300kr; *rorbuer* 450-650kr.) Hiking in the area is great, most notably the trek to the peak of **Stein Tinden** (500m), where the midnight sun can be seen all through June (round-trip 6hr.). Another good option is the peak at **Justad Tinden** (732m; round-trip 6-7hr.), which provides a panoramic view of the Lofoten Islands and northern Scandinavia. Between June 14-27, borrow a rowboat and paddle out about 300m for the best lowland chance at seeing the **midnight sun**. On clear nights between late August and March, Stamsund is a good place to see the **Northern Lights**.

TROMSØ

Norway's "northern capital," Tromsø has always been recognized for its sophisticated culture and hospitable residents. Pleasant and easy to walk around, Tromsø provides those heading to Nordkapp a final dose of Norwegian city-life. **Polaria,** Hjarlmar Johansens gt. 12, is a sleek, interactive museum and aquarium focused on Arctic ecosystems; watch the bearded seals strut their stuff at the daily feeding. (Open May–Aug. daily 10am-7pm; Sept.-Apr. noon-5pm. Seal meals 12:30 and 3:30pm. 75kr, seniors 60kr, students 55kr.) Across the bridge, the **Arctic Cathedral** contains one of the largest stained-glass windows in Europe. (Open June to mid-Aug. M-Sa 10am-8pm, Su 1-8pm. 22kr. Concerts June-Aug. 11:30pm. 70kr. Services Su 11am.) The **Tromsø University Museum** delves into geology, zoology, and Sami culture in its informative exhibit, with a scientific explanation of the extraordinary **Northern Lights.** (Take bus #28 from city center. Museum open mid-June to mid-Aug. daily 9am-8pm; mid-May to mid-June and mid-Aug. to mid-Sept. 9am-6pm; mid-Sept. to mid-May M-F 9am-3:30pm, Sa-Su 11am-5pm. 30kr, children 15kr.)

The **Hurtigruten** comes to Tromsø from Stamsund, in the Lofoten Islands (departs 7:30pm, arrives 2:30pm the next day; 968kr, student discount 50%). **Buses** go to Narvik (4½hr.; 2-3 per day; 320kr, student and railpass discount 50%), which has transportation links to Finland and Sweden. The **tourist office,** Storgt. 63, books private rooms for a 25kr fee. (☎77 61 00 00; www.destinasjon-tromso.no. Open June-Aug. M-F 10am-6pm, Sa-Su noon-5pm; Sept.-May reduced hours.) To reach **Tromsø Vandrerhjem (HI) ❶,** Åsgårdveien 9, from the tourist office, turn right and walk two blocks down Storgt., take another right on Fr. Langes gt., and take bus #26 for 10-15min. (☎77 65 76 28; tromso.hostel@vandrerhjem.no. Sheets 60kr. Reception 8-11am and 5-11pm. Open late June to mid-Aug. Dorms 150kr.) The mountainside **Tromsø Camping ❶,** across the river, has comfortable cabins and convenient access to outdoor activities. Take bus #20 or 24 to *Kraftforsyninga*, walk back across the red bridge, turn left, and follow the road 400m. (☎77 63 80 37; www.tromsocamping.no. Electricity 30kr. Reception 7am-11pm. Tents 150kr; 2- to 6-person cabins 400-950kr.) Affordable food, killer cappucino (29kr), board games, and free **Internet** access are available at ▨**Amtmandens Datter ❷,** Grønne gt. 81. (Open June-Aug. Su-Th 3pm-1:30am, F 3pm-3am, Sa noon-3am; Sept.-May M-Sa noon-3am, Su 3pm-3am.)

POLAND (POLSKA)

Caught at the threshold of East and West, Poland's moments of freedom have always been brief. From 1795 to 1918, the country simply did not exist on any map of Europe. Ravaged in World War II and then suppressed by Stalin and the USSR, Poland has at long last been given room to breathe, and its residents are not letting the opportunity slip by. The most prosperous of the "Baltic tigers," Poland now has a rapidly increasing GDP and a new membership in NATO, and will become a member of the EU in 2004. Although capitalism has brought with it rising crime and unemployment, the Poles are also using their new wealth to explore their cultural roots and to repair buildings destroyed in the wars.

FACTS AND FIGURES

Official Name: Republic of Poland.
Capital: Warsaw.
Major Cities: Gdańsk, Kraków, Lublin.
Population: 38,600,000.

Land Area: 312,685 sq. km.
Time Zone: GMT +1.
Language: Polish.
Religions: Roman Catholic (95%).

DISCOVER POLAND

Over 19 million visitors flock annually to Poland's spectacular castles, museums, villages, and beaches. The vibrant, glamorous capital, **Warsaw** (p. 796), gives testimony to Poland's resiliency. Much-adored **Kraków** (p. 805), the only Polish city to make it through the 20th century unscathed by natural disaster or war, has a magnificent castle and perfectly preserved Old Town. To the south, in the heart of the High Tatras, **Zakopane** (p. 811) boasts ear-popping hikes, music festivals, and Tatran folk culture. **Gdańsk** (p. 816), where World War II began, was also the base of Poland's anti-Communist Solidarity movement in the 1980s. On the Baltic Coast, **Sopot** (p. 819) shelters Poland's best beaches, while **Malbork** (p. 819) has the biggest brick castle in the world.

ESSENTIALS

WHEN TO GO

Winter temperatures average -3 to -6°C (20-26°F), while summer temperatures range from 16-19°C (61-66°F). Visit the Tatras between November and February to ski, or in August to hike. Elsewhere, summer and autumn are the best times to visit, as winter can be dreary.

DOCUMENTS AND FORMALITIES

VISAS. Citizens of Ireland and the US can travel to Poland without a visa for up to 90 days, UK citizens for up to 180 days. Australians, Canadians, New Zealanders, and South Africans need visas (180-day single-entry €60, students €45; multiple-entry €100/75; 48hr. transit €20/15). To extend your stay, apply to the regional government branch (*voi vodine*) of the city you are staying in, or at the **Ministry of Internal Affairs** at ul. Stefana Batorego 5, Warsaw 02-591 (☎ 022 621 02 51).

EMBASSIES. All foreign embassies are in Warsaw (see p. 798) and Kraków (p. 806). Polish embassies at home include: **Australia,** 7 Turrana St., Yarralumla ACT 2600 Canberra (☎ 06 273 1208 or 06 273 1211; ambpol@clover.com.au); **Canada,**

Poland

443 Daly St., Ottawa, ON K1N 6H3 (☎613-789-0468; polamb@hookup.com); **Ireland,** 5 Ailesbury Rd., Ballsbridge, Dublin 4 (☎01 283 0855; fax 01 269 8309); **New Zealand,** 17 Upland Rd., Kelburn, Wellington (☎04 712 456; polishembassy@xtra.co.nz); **South Africa,** 14 Amos St., Colbyn, Pretoria 0083 (☎012 432 631; amb.pol@pixie.co.za); **UK,** 47 Portland Pl., London W1N 4JH (☎020 7580 4324; http://home.btclick.com/polishembassy); **US,** 2640 16th St. NW, Washington, D.C. 20009 (☎202-234-3800; www.polandembassy.org).

TRANSPORTATION

BY PLANE. LOT (www.lot.com) flies into Warsaw's modern Okęcie Airport (WAW) from London, New York, Chicago, and Toronto, among other cities.

BY TRAIN. Trains are generally faster and more convenient than buses. Be alert—stations are not announced and can be poorly marked. Stations have boards that list towns alphabetically and posters that list trains chronologically. For a complete **timetable,** see www.pkp.pl. *Odjazdy* (departures) are in yellow, *przyjazdy* (arrivals) in white. **InterCity** and **ekspresowy** (express) trains are listed in red with an "IC" or "Ex" before the train number. *Pośpieszny* (direct; also in red) are almost as fast. *Osobowy* (in black) are the slowest but are 35% cheaper than *pośpieszny*. All InterCity, *ekspresowy*, and some *pośpieszny* trains require seat reservations (indicated by a boxed R on the schedule); ask the clerk for a *miejscówka* (myay-TSOOF-kah; reservation). Allot time for long, slow lines or buy your ticket in advance at the station or an Orbis office. On board, the *konduktor* sells surcharged tickets. Tickets are valid only for the day they are issued. **Eurail** passes are not valid in Poland. While Polish students and seniors can buy *ulgowy* (half-price) tickets, foreign travelers are not eligible for discounts; there is a hefty fine for traveling with an *ulgowy* ticket without Polish ID. Tickets cost 20% less on Sundays. **BIJ-Wasteels** tickets and **Eurotrain** passes, sold at Almatur and Orbis, give under-26 travelers 40% off international tickets.

BY BUS AND BY FERRY. PKS buses are cheapest and fastest for short trips. Like trains, there are *pośpieszny* (direct; marked in red) and *osobowy* (slow; in black) buses. Purchase advance tickets at the station and expect long lines. Tickets for many routes can be bought only from the driver. In the country-side, PKS markers (steering wheels that look like upside-down, yellow Mercedes-Benz symbols) indicate bus stops; drivers will also often stop if you flag them down. Traveling with a backpack can be a problem if the bus is full, since there are no storage compartments. The private **Polski Express** has more luxurious buses, but service is limited. **Ferries** run from Sweden and Denmark to Gdańsk (see p. 61).

BY TAXI AND BY THUMB. Arrange cabs by phone rather than hailing one on the street. Taxi drivers generally try to gouge foreigners; arrange the price before getting in or be sure the meter's on. The going rate is 1.50-2zł per km. Hand-waving is the accepted sign for hitchhiking. Although it is legal in Poland, *Let's Go* does not recommend hitchhiking.

TOURIST SERVICES AND MONEY

EMERGENCY	Police: ☎997. Ambulance: ☎999. Fire: ☎998.

TOURIST OFFICES. City-specific offices are generally more helpful than the larger chains. All offices provide free info in English and should be of some help with accommodations. **Orbis** (www.orbis-use.com), the state-sponsored travel bureau staffed by English speakers, operates luxury hotels and sells transportation tickets. **Almatur** (www.almatur.com.pl), the Polish student travel organization, sells ISIC cards, arranges dorm rooms in summer, and sells student tickets. Both provide maps and brochures, as do **PTTK** and **IT** (*Informacji Turystycznej*) bureaus.

MONEY. The Polish złoty (plural *złote*) is composed of 100 *grosze*. For cash, private **kantor** offices offer better exchange rates than banks. **Bank PKO SA** also has fairly good exchange rates; they cash **traveler's checks** and give MasterCard and Visa **cash advances** for a small commission. **ATMs** are almost everywhere. Budget accommodations rarely, if ever, accept **credit cards**, but some restaurants do.

BUSINESS HOURS. Business hours tend to be Monday to Friday 8am-4pm and Saturday 9am-2pm. Saturday hours vary, as some shops distinguish "working" (*pracująca*) Saturdays from "free" (*wolna*) ones, when hours are shorter. Very few stores are open on Sunday. Museums are generally open Tuesday to Sunday 10am-4pm and banks Monday to Friday 9am to 3 or 6pm.

ZŁOTE		
AUS$1 = 2.58ZŁ		1ZŁ = AUS$0.39
CDN$1 = 2.87ZŁ		1ZŁ = CDN$0.35
EUR€1 = 4.36ZŁ		1ZŁ = EUR€0.23
NZ$1 = 2.31ZŁ		1ZŁ = NZ$0.43
UK£1 = 6.29ZŁ		1ZŁ = UK£0.16
US$1 = 4.00ZŁ		1ZŁ = US$0.25
ZAR1 = 0.55ZŁ		1ZŁ = ZAR1.83

COMMUNICATION

PHONE CODES	Country code: 48. International dialing prefix: 00. From outside Poland, dial int'l dialing prefix (see inside back cover) + 48 + city code + local number.

TELEPHONES AND INTERNET ACCESS. Most public phones use cards, which come in several denominations, are sold at post offices, Telekomunikacja Polska offices, and most kiosks. To make a **collect call,** write the name of the city or country and the number plus "*Rozmowa 'R'*" on a slip of paper and hand it to a post office clerk. International access codes include: **AT&T Direct** (☎00 800 111 11 11); **Australia Direct** (☎00 800 611 11 61); **BT Direct** (☎00 800 89 0036); **Canada Direct** (☎00 800 111 41 18); **MCI WorldPhone** (☎00 800 111 21 22); **Sprint** (☎00 800 111 31 15); and **Telkom SA WorldCall** (☎00 800 271 11 27). Most mid-sized towns have an **Internet** cafe, and larger cities have several. The cost is about 3-8zł per hour.

MAIL. Mail service is generally efficient; airmail (*lotnicza*) reaches the US in about 2 weeks. Letters abroad cost about 2.20zł, depending on weight. When picking up *Poste Restante*, you may have to pay a small fee (1.10zł) or show your passport. Address mail to be held: Firstname SURNAME, *Poste Restante*, ul. Świętokrzyska 31/33, Warsaw 1, 00-001 POLAND.

LANGUAGES. Polish varies little across the country; the exceptions are Kaszuby, which has a Germanized dialect, and Karpaty, where the highlanders' accent is extremely thick. In western Poland and Mazury, German is the most commonly known foreign language, although many Poles in big cities, especially students, speak English.

ACCOMMODATIONS AND FOOD

POLAND	❶	❷	❸	❹	❺
ACCOMMODATIONS	under 45zł	45-65zł	66-80zł	81-120zł	over 120zł
FOOD	under 8zł	8-17zł	18-30zł	31-45zł	over 45zł

Private rooms (around 20-60zł per night) are available in most towns but are not regulated; tourist offices can usually help you find reputable renters. **PTSM** is the national organization of **youth hostels** (*schroniska młodzieżowe*), which average 15-40zł per night. Call at least a week in advance. **University dorms** transform into spartan budget housing in July and August; these are an especially good option in Kraków. **PTTK** runs a number of hotels called **Dom Turysty,** which have multi-bed rooms as well as budget singles and doubles. **Hotels** generally cost 80-120zł per night. **Campsites** average €3 per person; **bungalows** are also often available (about €5). *Polska Mapa Campingów* lists all campsites.

POLAND

Polish staples include meat, potatoes, cabbage, and butter. Meals always begin with soup, often *barszcz* (clear broth), *chłodnik* (a cold beet soup with buttermilk and hard-boiled eggs), *kapuśniak* (cabbage soup), or *żurek* (barley-flour soup loaded with eggs and sausage). Hearty main courses include *gołąbki* (cabbage rolls stuffed with meat and rice), *kotlet schabowy* (pork cutlets), *naleśniki* (cream-topped crepes filled with cottage cheese or jam), and *pierogi* (stuffed dumplings). Poland bathes in beer, vodka, and spiced liquor. Żywiec is the most popular strong beer; EB is its excellent, gentler brother. The Wyborowa, Żytnia, and Polonez brands of Wódka usually decorate private bars, while Belweder (Belvedere) is Poland's most prized alcoholic export.

SAFETY AND SECURITY

Public restrooms (up to 0.70zł) are marked with an upward-pointing triangle for men and a circle for women. Pharmacies are well-stocked, and at least one in each large city stays open 24hr. Avoid state hospitals. There are usually **clinics** in major cities with private, English-speaking doctors; expect to pay 50zł per visit. **Tap water** is theoretically drinkable, but bottled mineral water, available carbonated (*gazowana*) or flat (*nie gazowana*), will spare you from some unpleasant metals and chemicals. Always be on your guard against pickpockets, especially at big train stations and on crowded public buses and trams.

HOLIDAYS AND FESTIVALS

Holidays: New Year's Day (Jan. 1); Easter (Apr. 11-12); Labor Day (May 1); Constitution Day (May 3); Corpus Christi (June 10); Assumption Day (Aug. 15); Independence Day (Nov. 11); Christmas (Dec. 25-26).

Festivals: Kraków is Poland's festival capital, especially in summer. The most notable include the **International Short Film Festival** (late May), the **Festival of Jewish Culture** (early July), and the **Jazz Festival** (Oct.-Nov.).

WARSAW (WARSZAWA)   ☎ 022

According to legend, Warsaw (pop. 1,640,000) was founded when the fisherman Wars netted a *syrena* (mermaid, now the city's emblem). She begged him to release her and told him that if he and his wife established a city on the spot, she would protect it forever. She and the city's motto, *contemnire procellas* (to defy the storms), have been put to the test in the city's long history. Over the past millennium, invaders from the north, east, and west have all taken a shot at this fiercely proud capital city, which has been swallowed by neighboring empires more than once. Most recently, World War II saw two-thirds of the population killed and 83% of the city destroyed. It took decades to rebuild the ravaged capital, but Warsaw's inclusion on UNESCO's World Heritage list in 1980 shows the authenticity of its restoration as a beautiful city and a national emblem.

▌ TRANSPORTATION

Flights: Port Lotniczy Warszawa-Okęcie ("Terminal 1"), ul. Żwirki i Wigury. (☎650 41 00). Take bus #175 (bus #611 after 10:40pm) for a 20min. ride to the city center. Buy tickets (2.40zł) at the *Ruch* kiosk in the departure hall. Open M-F 6am-10pm.

Trains: Warszawa Centralna, al. Jerozolimskie 54 (☎94 36), is the most convenient of Warsaw's 4 train stations. Services include: a **cafe, 24hr. pharmacy, ATM, telephones, baggage check,** and a **post office (urząd poctowy).** The **IT office** can help with schedules and translations. Yellow signs list departures (*odjazdy*); white signs list arrivals (*przyjazdy*). English is rare; write down where and when you want to go, then ask *"Który peron?"* ("Which platform?"). Domestic trains to: **Gdańsk** (4hr., 12 per day, 43-117zł); **Kraków**

(2½-5hr., 10 per day, 55-101zł); **Łódź** (1½-2hr., 10 per day, 27-40zł); **Lublin** (2½hr., daily, 19-92zł); **Poznań** (2½-3hr., 15 per day, 42-114zł); **Radom** (1½-2hr., 9 per day, 25-66zł); **Toruń** (2½-4½hr., 7 per day, 35-105zł); **Wrocław** (4½hr., 9 per day, 45-125zł). International trains to: **Berlin** (6hr., 4 per day, 160zł); **Bratislava** (8hr., 2 per day, 230zł); **Bucharest** (26½-28hr., 2 per day, 550zł); **Budapest** (11hr., 2 per day, 280zł); **Minsk** (11hr., 3 per day, 190zł); **Moscow** (22hr., daily, 300zł); **Prague** (9-11hr., 2 per day, 270-310zł); **St. Petersburg** (27-30hr., 2 per day, 300zł); **Vilnius** (11hr., daily, 200zł).

Buses: Both PKS and Polski Express buses serve Warsaw.

Polski Express, al. Jana Pawła II (☎620 03 20), in a kiosk adjacent to Warszawa Centralna. A private company offering very competitive, fast, comfortable domestic bus service. To: **Gdańsk** (6hr., 2 per day, 68zł); **Kraków** (8hr., 2 per day, 60zł); **Wrocław** (6hr., 3 per day, 65zł).

PKS Warszawa Zachodnia, al. Jerozolimskie 144 (☎822 48 11; domestic info and reservations ☎94 33; international info ☎823 55 70), in same building as Warszawa Zachodnia train station. Take bus #508, E5, 127, 130, or 517 to the center. State run PKS serves many of the same domestic destinations as Polski Express as well as international destinations.

Centrum Podróży AURA, al. Jerozolimskie 144, at the Zachodnia train station (☎823 55 70) is possibly your best bet for international destinations. Buses depart for **Prague** (11½ hr.; M, W, F; 100zł). Open M-F 9am-6pm, Sa 9am-2pm.

Public Transportation: (☎94 84; www.ztm.waw.pl). **Trams, buses,** and **Metro** run 4:30am-11pm. 2.40zł, with ISIC 1.25zł; extra ticket required for large baggage. **Day pass** 7.20/3.70zł. **Weekly pass** 26/12zł. Punch the ticket (on the end marked by the arrow and *"tu kasować"* in the machines on board. Bus #175 runs from the airport to Stare Miasto via Warszawa Centralna and ul. Nowy Świat. Warsaw's single **Metro** line runs north-south through the center. Two **sightseeing bus routes,** #100 (weekend only) and 180 (weekday only) have been added for tourists.

Taxis: Try **MPT Radio Taxi** (☎919), **Euro Taxi** (☎96 62), or **Halo Taxi** (☎96 23). Call for pickup to avoid overcharging. State-run cabs with a mermaid logo tend to be safer. The meter begins at 5-6zł, plus 1.80-3zł per km. MPT accepts MC/V.

◪ ORIENTATION

The main part of Warsaw lies west of the **Wisła River**. Although the city is large, its grid layout and efficient public transportation system make it easy to navigate and explore. The main east-west thoroughfare is **al. Jerozolimskie.** Several north-south avenues, including **ul. Marszałkowska,** a major tram route, intersect this main drag. **Warszawa Centralna,** the busiest train station, is set in the thick of the city at the intersection of al. Jerozolimskie and **al. Jana Pawła II.** A stone's throw away, the gargantuan **Pałac Kultury i Nauki** (Palace of Culture and Science) looms above **pl. Defilad** (Parade Square); its clock tower, visible from most anywhere near the city center, serves as an orientation point. To the east of these landmarks lies **Rondo Charles de Gaulle.** Intersecting the traffic circle at al. Jerozolimskie, the **Trakt Królewski** (royal way) takes different names as it runs north/south. Going north it first becomes **Nowy Świat** (New World Street) and then **ul. Krakówskie Przedmieście** as it leads into **Stare Miasto** (Warsaw's restored old city). Going south, it becomes **al. Ujazdowskie** as it runs past embassy row, more palaces, and **Łazienki Park.**

◪ PRACTICAL INFORMATION

TOURIST, FINANCIAL, AND LOCAL SERVICES

Tourist Offices: Informacji Turystyczna (IT), al. Jerozolimskie 54 (☎94 31; www.warsawtour.pl), in Warszawa Centralna. Provides maps, currency exchange, and hotel reservations. English-language *Warsaw Insider* (6zł) sold in kiosks outside the office. Open daily May-Sept. 8am-8pm; Oct.-Apr. 8am-6pm. **Branches** at ul. Krakowskie Przedmieście 89, opposite Pl. Zamkowy (open daily May-Sept. 9am-8pm; Oct.-Apr. 9am-6pm); al. Jerozolimkie 144, at the Western Station (open daily 9am-5pm); and in the departure terminal of the airport (open daily May-Sept. 8am-8pm; Oct.-Apr. 8am-6pm).

Budget Travel: Almatur, ul. Kopernika 23 (☎826 35 12; fax 826 45 92), off ul. Nowy Świat. Discount airfare. ISIC cards 44zł. Open M-F 9am-7pm, Sa 10am-3pm. **Orbis,** ul. Bracka 16 (☎827 07 30; fax 827 76 05), entrance on al. Jerozolimskie near ul. Nowy Świat. Sells plane, train, ferry, and international bus tickets. Open M-F 8am-6pm, Sa 9am-3pm. **STA,** ul. Kruzca 41/43 (☎622 62 64; www.eria.pl). Open daily 10am-6pm.

Embassies: Most are near ul. Ujazdowskie. **Australia,** ul. Nowogrodzka 11 (☎521 34 44). Open M-Tu and Th 9am-1pm and 2-4pm, W and F 9am-1pm. **Canada,** al. Matejki 1/5 (☎584 31 00). Open M-F 10am-noon and 1-3pm. **South Africa,** ul. Koszykowa 54 (☎625 62 28). Open M-F 9am-noon. **UK,** ul. Emilii Plator 28, 2nd fl. (☎625 30 30). Open M-F 10:30am-4:30pm. **US,** al. Ujazdowskie 29/31 (☎628 30 41; www.usinfo.pl). Open M and W-F 9am-noon, Tu 9am-3pm.

Currency Exchange: 24hr. ATM machines accepting Cirrus, Maestro, Plus, etc. are abundant. Except at tourist sites, *Kantori* have the best rates for exchanging both currency and traveler's checks. **24hr. exchange** is available at Warszawa Centralna station. **Bank PKO S.A.,** pl. Bankowy 2 (☎635 05 00), in the blue glass skyscraper, and ul. Grójecka 1/3 (☎658 82 17), in Hotel Sobieski, cash AmEx/V **traveler's checks** for 1-2% commission and give MC/V **cash advances.** Open M-F 8am-6pm, Sa 10am-2pm.

American Express: al. Jerozolimskie 65/79 (☎630 69 52/53). Will send and receive **Western Union** money transfers. Open M-F 9am-7pm, Sa 10am-6pm. **Branch** at ul. Sienna 39 (☎581 51 53). Open M-F 9am-6pm.

Luggage Storage (Kasa Bagażowa): At Warszawa Centralna train station, below the main hall. 4zł per item per day. Optional insurance is 2.25zł per 50zł of value. Open 24hr. Or, in Zachodnia Station train station, 4zł for a large pack. Open daily 7am-7pm.

Laundromat: ul. Karmelicka 17 (☎831 73 17). Take bus #180 or 516 from ul. Marszałkowska toward Żoliborz, get off at ul. Anielewicza, and go back 1 block to ul. Karmelicka. Some English spoken. Detergent 3zł. Wash and dry 26.60zł. Open M-F 9am-5pm, Sa 9am-1pm. Call 1 day ahead to make a reservation.

EMERGENCY AND COMMUNICATIONS

Emergency: Police: ☎997. **Ambulance:** ☎999. **Fire:** ☎998.

24hr. Pharmacy: Apteka Grabowskiego (☎825 69 86), at Warszawa Centralna.

Medical Assistance: Centrun Medyczne LIM, al. Jerozolimskie 65/79 (24hr. emergency info ☎458 70 00; ambulance ☎430 30 30), at the Marriott. English-speaking doctors. 85zł for an appointment. Open M-F 7am-9pm, Sa 8am-8pm, Su 9am-1pm. **Branch** at ul. Domaniewski 41 (☎458 70 00). Open M-F 7am-9pm, Sa 8am-8pm. **Central Emergency Station,** ul. Hoża 56 (☎999) also has a 24hr. ambulance.

Telephones: At the post office and in scattered booths throughout city. Phones only accept cards (available at the post office). **Directory assistance:** ☎913.

Internet Access: e-cafe, ul. Zlota 9 (☎828 38 88), opposite Galeria Centrum, inside the Kino Relax complex. 8zł per hr. Open daily 10am-9pm. **Piękna Internet Pub,** ul. Piękna 68A (☎622 33 77; www.piekna.pl). Beer 5zł. 2zł per 30min. Open M-F 10am-11pm, Sa noon-midnight, Su noon-11pm. **Internet Access Office Center,** ul. Freta 17 (☎831 38 54; www.verso.pl), at the corner of Świętokrzyska. Open M-F 8am-8pm, Sa 9am-5pm, Su 10am-4pm.

Post Office: Ul. Świętokrzyska 31/33 (☎827 00 52). Take a ticket from the computer at the entrance. For stamps and letters, push "D"; for packages, push "F"; for **Poste Restante,** inquire at window #42 in the room to the left of the main hall. Address mail to be held: Firstname SURNAME, *Poste Restante,* ul. Świętokrzyska 31/33, Warsaw 1, **00 001** POLAND. Open 24hr. *Kantor* (currency exchange) open daily 7am-10pm.

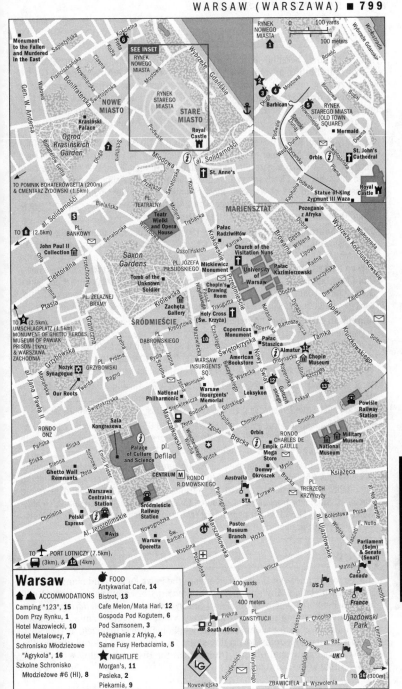

POLAND

Warsaw

ACCOMMODATIONS

Camping "123", 15
Dom Przy Rynku, 1
Hotel Mazowiecki, 10
Hotel Metalowcy, 7
Schronisko Młodzieżowe
  "Agrykola", 16
Szkolne Schronisko
  Młodzieżowe #6 (HI), 8

FOOD

Antykwariat Cafe, 14
Bistrot, 13
Cafe Melon/Mata Hari, 12
Gospoda Pod Kogutem, 6
Pod Samsonem, 3
Pożegnanie z Afryką, 4
Same Fusy Herbaciarnia, 5

NIGHTLIFE

Morgan's, 11
Pasieka, 2
Piekarnia, 9

ACCOMMODATIONS AND CAMPING

In summer, rooms become scarce and prices rise; call ahead, particularly for hostels. For help finding **private rooms**, consult the **Office of Private Quarters** (Biuro Kwater Prywatnych), ul. Krucza 17, off al. Jerozolimskie, near Hotel Syrena. (☎628 75 40. Singles 79zł, 68zł per night for 3 or more nights; doubles 110/96zł. Open M-Sa 9am-6pm, Su 2-6pm.) The **IT** (p. 797) maintains a list of accommodations in the city and can also arrange stays in **university dorms**. (25-30zł. Available July-Sept.)

Dom Przy Rynku, Rynek Nowego Miasta 4 (☎/fax 831 50 33; www.cityhostel.net). Take bus #175 from the center to Franciszkańska; turn right on Franciszkańska, then right into the *Rynek* (main square); the hostel will be down the hill on your left. In the summer, this school for disadvantaged children makes money for supplies and furniture by transforming into one of Warsaw's most charming and spotless budget accommodations. TV room, and kitchenette. Reception 24hr. Flexible lockout for cleaning 10am-5pm. Open July-Aug. only. Dorms 45zł per person. ❷

Szkolne Schronisko Młodzieżowe #6 (HI), ul. Karolkowa 53a (☎632 88 29; www.ptsm.com.pl/ssmnr6). Take tram #12 or 24 west from al. Jerozolimskie or the train station to D. T. Wola. Turn right out of the underpass, walk half a block towards the city on al. Solidarnosci, and turn left on ul. Karolkowa. Easy tram access to Stare Miasto. Clean bathrooms and a cafe. Sheets 5zł. Internet access 6-10pm (5zł per hour). Reception 6-10am and 5-11pm. Lockout 10am-5pm. Curfew 11pm. Dorms 31.50zł, singles with bath and kitchen 130zł. Nonmembers add 3.50zł. ❶

Schronisko Młodzieżowe "Agrykola," ul. Myśliwiecka 9 (☎622 91 10; www.hotelagrykola.pl). Near Łazienki Park. Take bus #151 from the train station, or bus #107, 420, or 520 from Marszałkowska to Rozbrat. Continue as it turns into Myśliwiecka, then turn right at the path that leads to the Castle. Part sports complex. Inline skate rental 6zł per hr. Dorms 35zł; singles 274zł; doubles with bath 329zł. MC/V. ❶

Hotel Metalowcy, ul. Długa 29 (☎831 40 21, ext. 29). Take any tram north along ul. Marszałkowska to pl. Bankowy, walk toward the tram, and turn right on Długa. Great location near Stare Miasto. Singles 75zł; doubles 114zł; quads with bath 206zł. ❸

Hotel Mazowiecki, ul. Mazowiecka 10 (☎/fax 827 23 65; www.mazowiecki.com.pl), off ul. Świętokrzyska, next to Stare Miasto. Newly renovated bathrooms. Singles 150zł, with bath 210zł; doubles 200/270zł. Weekend discount 20%. ❺

Camping 123, ul. Bitwy Warszawskiej 15/17 (☎/fax 823 37 48), by Warszawa Zachodnia. Take bus #508, 127, 130, or 517 to "Zachodnia," walk to the traffic circle and turn left on Bitwy Warszawskiej. Close to the city center yet secluded by a buffer of trees and parkland. Swimming pool and tennis courts. Guarded 24hr. English spoken. Open May-Sept. Electricity 10zł. 10zł per person, per tent, and per vehicle. Singles 40zł; doubles 70zł; triples 100zł; quads 120zł. ❶

FOOD

Countless food stands dot the square beneath the **Pałac Kultury,** and many more lie under the **train station.** Any milk bar *(bar mleczny)* or cafeteria *(stołowki)* will dish up a decent, inexpensive meal. **24hr. grocery stores,** often called *delikatesy,* are by the central train station and at ul. Nowy Świat 53. (Open 7am-5am.) Those plucky enough to cook for themselves will delight in **Domowy Okruszek,** ul. Bracka 3, just south of Aleje Jerozolimskie, a tiny store, that sells ready-to-cook dishes like *naleśniki* (pancakes) and *pierogi* (dumplings) for 15-20zł per kilo. (☎628 70 77. Open M-Sa 10am-6pm, Su 10am-3pm.)

Gospoda Pod Kogutem (Under the Rooster), ul. Freta 48 (☎635 82 82). A shining star in Stare Miasto. Enjoy local food in the rustic interior or, during the summer, outside along ul. Freta. Beer 6zł. Entrees 15-40zł. Open daily 11am-midnight. MC/V. ❸

Pożegnanie z Afryka, ul. Freta 4/6, ul. Ostrobranmska 75c, and ul. Dobra 56/66. Brews incredible coffee (8-15zł). Indoor tables are worth the wait. Cafe open M-Th 10am-9pm, F-Su 10am-10pm. Store open M-F 11am-7pm, Sa-Su noon-5pm. ❷

Pod Samsonem, ul. Freta 3/5 (☎831 17 88). Between Stare Miasto and Nowe Miasto. Hearty Polish cuisine that could satisfy even Samson's appetite. Entrees 10-35zł. Vegetarian entrees 12-15zł. Open daily 10am-11pm. AmEx/MC/V. ❷

Pod Gołebiami, ul. Piwna 4a (☎635 01 56). A perfect stop for a quick and delectable lunch and the best *naleśniki* (Polish crepes; 12-15zł) in town. Entrees 8-29zł. Open daily 10am-11pm. AmEx/MC/V for orders over 50zł. ❷

Bistrot, ul. Foksal 2 (☎827 87 07), at the end of the street through the gates. Specializes in delicious international gourmet cuisine. Romantic stone terrace, classy atmosphere, and formal waitstaff make it worth the splurge. Entrees 38-86zł. Open M-F 11am-midnight, Sa-Su noon-10pm. AmEx/MC/V. ❸

Cafe Melon/Mata Hari, ul. Nowy Świat 52 (☎620 98 29). Incredibly cheap vegetarian Indian dishes served on edible plates. Takeout available. Open M-Sa noon-8pm. ❶

Bar Złota Kurka Mleczny, ul. Marszałkowska 55/73, just north of pl. Konstytucji. Ultra low prices and long lunch lines for "rations" that include all the traditional favorites such as *bigos* (3.50zł), *naleśniki* (2.50zł), *kotlet* (4.50zł), *flaki* (tripe; 4.70zł), and soups (1.00zł). This subsidized communist era "milk bar" represents the last of a dying breed. An experience that may cast a few doubts on your free-market ways. ❶

Antykwariat Cafe, ul. Żurawia 45 (☎629 99 29), 2 blocks south of Rondo Charles de Gaulle. Comfy, plush chairs welcome lingerers. Coffees 5-17zł. Also serves tea, wine, cocktails, and desserts. Open M-F 11am-11pm, Sa-Su 1-11pm. ❶

Same Fusy Herbaciarnia, ul. Nowomiejska 10 (☎635 90 14), in Stare Miasto. Earthy teahouse in a forest-themed cellar. 150 varieties of tea (5zł per cup; 10-35zł per pot; iced teas 6-11zł per glass). Open M-F 11am-11pm, Sa-Su 11am-late. ❶

THE LOCAL STORY

AN IRISHMAN IN WARSAW

Thomas Morgan is the owner of the popular Morgan's Pub in Warsaw.

LG: This is a unique space for a pub—in a castle, under a Chopin museum.

A: Yeah, it's a great place. Upstairs, people don't even know there's a pub down here, which is good, since we don't bother them.

LG: So, why Poland?

A: Well, it wasn't planned. I was working in another pub and I got bored with that, so I opened up this place a couple years ago.

LG: Do you speak Polish?

A: (*Laughs.*) Very badly! Most of the time I have no idea what customers are saying or singing, but as long as they're having a good time, that's all I care about.

LG: Morgan's has become something of a legend here in Warsaw. Do you expect to stay here long?

A: Yeah, as long as we're doing well, I'll stick around. Poles are great—love to sing, always telling stories. But too impatient—just like the Irish!

LG: Does the Guinness sell well, or do the Poles stick to local brews?

A: It sells really well. To be honest, I don't really like the stuff. But I don't want to disappoint them, so I play along.

(*Imitates drinking and grimaces, but then smiles and gives a thumbs up.*)

(*Morgan's, ul. Okólnik 1. Guinness 15zl. Open daily 10am-late.*)

👁 SIGHTS

Razed beyond recognition during WWII, Warsaw was almost entirely rebuilt from the rubble. Thanks to impressive renovations, buildings have been nearly restored to their pre-war state. Because sights are so spread out, the new tourist buses are a blessing. **Route #100** begins at Plac Zamkowy and runs along Plac Teatralny, ul. Marszalkowska, al. Ujazdowskie, Łazienki Park, and back up the Royal Way, then loops through Praga before returning to Plac Zamkowy. **Route #180** runs south from Wilanów past Łazienki and up the Royal Way before turning west to the Jewish Cemetery.

STARE MIASTO. Warsaw's postwar reconstruction shows its finest face in the narrow cobblestone streets and colorful facades of **Stare Miasto** (Old Town). *(Take bus #175 or E3 from the city center to Miodowa.)* The landmark **Statue of King Zygmunt III Waza,** constructed in 1644 to honor the king who transferred the capital from Kraków to Warsaw, towers over the entrance to Stare Miasto. To the right stands the impressive **Royal Castle** (Zamek Królewski), the royal residence since the late 16th century. When it was plundered and burned by the Nazis in September 1939, many Varsovians risked their lives hiding priceless works in the hope they might one day be returned. Today the palace houses the 🖼**Royal Castle Museum,** which has paintings, artifacts, and the stunning Royal Apartments. *(Pl. Zamkowy 4. Route 1 open M 11am-4pm, Tu-Sa 10am-4pm. 8zł; students 3zł. Route 2 (Royal Apartments) open M 11am-6pm, Tu-Sa 10am-6pm. 14zł, students 7zł. Su highlights tour 11am-6pm; free.)* Across ul. Świętojańska sits Warsaw's oldest church, **St. John's Cathedral** (Anrchi-Katedra św. Jana), decimated in the 1944 Uprising but rebuilt after the war. (Open daily 10am-1pm and 3-5:30pm. Entrance to crypts 1zł.) Ul. Świętojańska leads to the restored Renaissance and Baroque **Rynek Starego Miasta** (Old Town Square); the mermaid statue sits in the center. Ul. Krzywe Koło starts in the northeast corner of the *Rynek* and leads to the restored **Barbican** (*barbakan*), a rare example of 16th-century Polish fortification and a popular spot to relax. The *barbakan* opens onto ul. Freta, the edge of **Nowe Miasto** (New Town). Nobel prize-winning physicist and chemist **Marie Curie** was born at ul. Freta 16.

TRAKT KRÓLEWSKI. The Trakt Królewski (Royal Way) begins at the entrance to the Stare Miasto on pl. Zamkowy and stretches 4km south toward Kraków, Poland's former capital. On the left as you leave pl. Zamkowy looms the 15th-century **St. Anne's Church** (Kościół św. Anny). Rebuilt in Baroque style, its most striking feature is a gilded altar. *(Open daily dawn-dusk.)* Frederick Chopin spent his childhood in the neighborhood near ul. Krakowskie Przedmieście. He gave his first public concert in **Pałac Radziwiłłów,** ul. Krakowskie Przedmieście 46/48, the building guarded by four stone lions; it is now known as **Pałac Namiestnikowski,** the Polish presidential mansion. **Pałac Czapskich,** where Chopin wrote some of his best-known works, was his last home before he left for France in 1830; today, the palace houses his preserved Drawing Room (Salonik Chopinów) and the Academy of Fine Arts. *(ul. Krakówskie Przedmieście 5; the entrance is on the left. Open M-F 10am-2pm. 3zł, students 2zł.)* Chopin died abroad at the age of 39 and was buried in Paris, but his heart belongs to Poland; it now rests in an urn in **Holy Cross Church** (Kościół św. Krzyża), next to the Academy. For more Chopin relics, visit the **Frederick Chopin Museum** (Muzeum Fryderyka Chopina), which has a collection of original letters, scores, paintings, and keepsakes, including the great composer's last piano and a section of his first polonaise, penned when he was seven years old. *(ul. Okólnik 1; enter from ul. Tamka. Open May-Sept. M, W, F 10am-5pm, Th noon-6pm, Sa-Su 10am-2pm; Oct-Apr. M-W and F-Sa 10am-2pm, Th noon-6pm. 8zł, students 4zł. Audio guides 4zł.)*

POLAND

The Royal Way continues down fashionable **ul. Nowy Świat.** Turn left just after Rondo Charles de Gaulle to reach Poland's largest museum, the **National Museum** (Muzeum Narodowe), which has an impressive art collection. *(Al. Jerozolimskie 3. Open July-Aug. Su and Tu-Sa 10am-4pm; Sept.-June. Tu-W and F 10am-4pm, Th noon-5pm, Sa-Su 10am-5pm. 8zł, students 6zł, Sa free.)* Farther down, the Royal Way turns into al. Ujazdowskie and runs alongside sprawling **Łazienki Park.** Farther into the park is the striking Neoclassical **Palace on Water** (Pałac na Wodzie or Pałac na Wyspie), which houses rotating art exhibits. *(Take bus #116, 180, or 195 from ul. Nowy Świat or #119 from the city center to Bagatela. Park open daily dawn-dusk. Palace open Su and Tu-Sa 9:30am-4pm. 11zł, students 8zł.)* Just north of the park, off ul. Agrykola, the exhibitions in the **Center of Contemporary Art** (Centrum Sztuki Współczesnej), al. Ujazdowskie 6, break all aesthetic barriers. *(Open M-Th and Sa-Su 11am-5pm, F 11am-9pm. 10zł, students 5zł.)*

THE FORMER WARSAW GHETTO AND SYNAGOGUE. Still referred to as the Ghetto, the modern **Muranów** ("walled") neighborhood north of the city center holds few traces of the nearly 400,000 Jews who made up one-third of the city's population prior to WWII. The **Umschlagplatz**, at the corner of ul. Dzika and ul. Stawki, was the railway platform where the Nazis gathered 300,000 Jews for transport to death camps. *(Take tram #35 from ul. Marszałkowska to Dzika.)* With the Umschlag pl. monument to your left, continue down Stawki and turn right on ul. DuBois, which becomes ul. Zamenhofa; you will pass a stone monument marking the location of the command bunker of the 1943 Ghetto Uprising. Farther on, in a large park to your right, the large **Monument of the Ghetto Heroes** (Pomnik Bohaterów) pays homage to the leaders of the uprising. Continue along ul. Zamenhofa for two blocks and then take a right on Dzielna. On the corner of Dzielna and al. Jana Pawall, the **Museum of Pawiak Prison** (Muzeum Więzienia Pawiaka) exhibits photographs and artifacts, including the artwork and poetry of many former prisoners. Over 100,000 Polish Jews were imprisoned here from 1939-1944; 37,000 were executed and 60,000 were transferred to concentration camps. *(ul. Dzielna 24/26. Open Su 10am-4pm., W 9am-5pm, Th and Sa 9am-4pm, F 10am-5pm. English captions. Donation requested.)* Follow al. Jana Pawall, take a left on ul. Anielewicza, and continue for five blocks to reach the **Jewish Cemetery** (Cmentarz Żydowski), in the western corner of Muranów. The thickly wooded cemetery is the final resting place of 250,000 Varsovian Jews. *(Tram #22 runs from the city center to Cm. Żydowski. Open Apr.-Oct. M-Th 10am-5pm, F 9am-1pm, Su 11am-4pm; Nov.-Mar. M-Th 10am-3pm, F 9am-1pm, Su 11am-3pm. 4zł.)* The beautifully reconstructed **Nożyk Synagogue** (Synagoga Nożyka) is a living remnant of Warsaw's Jewish heritage. The only synagogue to survive the war, today it serves as the spiritual home for the few hundred observant Jews who remain in Warsaw. *(ul. Twarda 6. From the city center, take any tram along ul. Jana Pawlall to Rondo Onz. Turn right on ul. Twarda (5min.) and left at the Jewish Theater (Teatr Żydowski). Services ☎ 620 43 24. Open Su-F 10am-7pm. 5zł.)*

ELSEWHERE IN CENTRAL WARSAW. The center of Warsaw's commercial district, southwest of Stare Miasto near the Warszawa Centralna train station, is dominated by the 70-story Stalinist **Palace of Culture and Science** (Pałac Kultury i Nauki) on ul. Marszałkowska. Locals claim the view from the top is the best in Warsaw—partly because it's the only place from which you can't see the building itself. Below is **plac Defilad** (Parade Square), Europe's largest square. Adjacent to **Saxon Garden** (Ogród Saski) is the **John Paul II Collection,** with works by Dalí, Gogh, Goya, Rembrandt, van Renoir, and others. *(Pl. Bankowy 1. Open May-Oct. Su and Tu-Sa 10am-5pm; Nov.-Apr. 10am-4pm. 8zł, students 4zł.)*

🎵 🎷 ENTERTAINMENT AND NIGHTLIFE

For the latest schedule of performances, call the tourist info line (☎94 31). Inquire about concerts at the **Warsaw Music Society** (Warszawskie Towarzystwo Muzyczne), ul. Morskie Oko 2. (☎849 56 51. Take tram #4, 18, 19, 35, or 36 to Morskie Oko from ul. Marszałkowska.) The **Warsaw Chamber Opera** (Warszawska Opera Kameralna), al. Solidarności 76B (☎831 22 40), hosts a Mozart festival each year in early summer. **Łazienki Park** hosts free performances at the **Chopin Monument** (Pomnik Chopina) on Sundays. (May-Oct. noon and 4pm.) **Teatr Wielki**, pl. Teatralny 1 (☎826 32 88; www.teatrwielki.pl), Warsaw's main opera and ballet hall, offers performances almost daily (tickets 10-100zł.). **Sala Kongresowa** (☎620 49 80), on the train station side of the Pałac Kultury, hosts jazz and rock concerts with famous international bands; enter from ul. Emilii Plater. **Warsaw Summer Jazz Days** (☎620 12 19) take place annually in June. **Teatr Dramatyczny** (☎620 21 02), in the Pałac Kultury, has a stage for large productions and a studio theater playing more avante-garde works. **Kinoteka** (☎826 1961), in the Pałac Kultury, shows recent hollywood blockbusters in a wonderfully surreal Stalinist setting. Head to **Kino Lab**, ul. Ujazdowskie 6, for independent films. (☎628 12 71.)

In the evening, Warsaw is full of energy. Cafes (*kawiarnie*) around Stare Miasto and ul. Nowy Świat continue serving until late into the night, and a large variety of pubs attract crowds with live music. In summer, large outdoor beer gardens complement the pub scene. Kiosks sell *Gazeta Wyborcza*, a magazine that lists gay nightlife info. **⚑Morgan's**, ul. Okólnik 1, is a friendly Irish joint with live music on weekends and a mean shepherd's pie (Pie 20zł. Guinness 15zł. Open daily 10am-late.) **⚑Piekarnia**, ul. Młocinska 11 (☎636 49 79), has a packed dance floor and expert DJs. (Cover F 20zł, Sa 25zł. Open F-Sa 10pm-late.) **Pasieka**, ul. Freta 7/9, specializes in mead, an alcoholic honey brew that singes your throat but leaves a sweet, soothing aftertaste. (Open daily 10am-10pm.)

🗺 DAYTRIPS FROM WARSAW

ŻELAZOWA WOLA. Twisting paths wind through the expansive, well-maintained gardens of **Frederick Chopin's birthplace.** (Cottage and park 10zł, students 5zł. Park only 4zł, students 2zł. Open May-Sept. Su and Tu-Sa 9:30am-5:30pm; Oct.-Apr. Su and Tu-Sa 9:30am-4pm.) From May to September, Polish musicians perform free **concerts** of Chopin's works. (Su at 11am and 3pm.) Concert schedules are posted throughout Warsaw and are also available at Warsaw's Chopin Museum (see p. 802). The **Wyszogród bus** runs from Warsaw (1hr., 3 per day, 9zł). Take one of the first two buses, since no direct buses return after 4:30pm.

WILANÓW. In 1677, King Jan III Sobieski bought the sleepy village of Milanowo, had its existing mansion rebuilt into a Baroque palace, and named the new residence Villa Nova (Wilanów). Since 1805, **Pałac Wilanowski** has functioned both as a public museum and as a residence for the highest-ranking guests of the Polish state. Surrounded by elegant, formal gardens, the palace is filled with lovely frescoed rooms, portraits, and extravagant royal apartments. English signs along the way allow you to break off from the slow-moving Polish-language tour to explore on your own. (☎842 81 01. Take bus #180 from ul. Krakowskie or, alternately, take bus #516 or 519 from ul. Marszałkowska south to Wilanów; the road leading to the palace is across the street to the right. Palace open mid-June to mid-Sept. M and W-Sa 9:30am-2:30pm; Su 9:30am-4:40pm; mid-Sept. to mid-June M and W-Su 9:30am-4pm. 15zł, students 8zł. English tours 120zł; (5 or fewer people); 24zł per person (6-35 people). Gardens open M and W-F 9:30am-dusk. 3zł, students 2zł.)

KRAKÓW

☎012

Home to 100,000 students and scores of museums, galleries, and underground pubs, Kraków (KRAH-koof; pop. 745,000) is the highlight of Poland. Although it emerged only recently as a trendy international hot spot, the city has always figured prominently in Polish history. Wedged between the notorious Stalinist-era Nowa Huta steelworks to the east and the Auschwitz-Birkenau death camp 70km to the west, Kraków endured much darkness in the 20th century. Earlier, the city protected centuries of Central European kings and astounding architectural achievements, many of which still stand in the colorful Stare Miasto (Old Town).

◪ TRANSPORTATION

Flights: Balice Airport (KRK; ☎411 19 55; tickets 411 67 00; airport@lotnisko-balice.pl), 15km west of the center. Connected to the main train station by northbound bus #192 (40min.) or 208 (1hr.). A taxi to the center costs 30-50zł.

Trains: Kraków Główny, pl. Kolejowy 1 (☎624 54 39; info 624 15 35). To: **Bratislava** (8hr., daily, 167zł); **Budapest** (11hr., daily, 227zł); **Gdańsk** (dir.: Gdynia; 7-10hr., 3 per day, 52-100zł); **Kyïv** (22hr., daily, 149zł); **Lviv** (12½hr., daily, 126zł); **Prague** (9hr., daily, 226zł); **Vienna** (8½hr., 2 per day, 183zł); **Warsaw** (4½-5hr., 3 per day, 45-70zł); and **Zakopane** (3-5hr., 4 per day, 30zł).

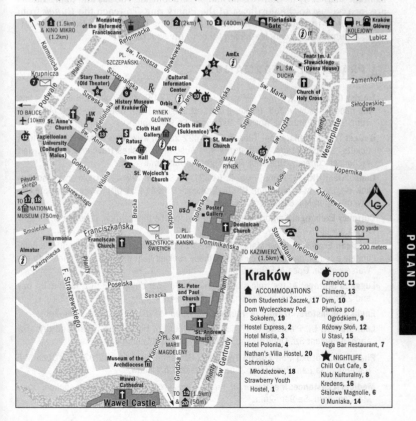

Kraków

FOOD
Camelot, 11
Chimera, 13
Dym, 10
Piwnica pod Ogródkiem, 9
Różowy Słoń, 12
U Stasi, 15
Vega Bar Restaurant, 7

⌂ ACCOMMODATIONS
Dom Studentcki Żaczek, 17
Dom Wycieczkowy Pod Sokołem, 19
Hostel Express, 2
Hotel Mistia, 3
Hotel Polonia, 4
Nathan's Villa Hostel, 20
Schronisko Młodzieżowe, 18
Strawberry Youth Hostel, 1

★ NIGHTLIFE
Chill Out Cafe, 5
Klub Kulturalny, 8
Kredens, 16
Słalowe Magnolie, 6
U Muniaka, 14

POLAND

Buses: On ul. Worcella (☎93 16), directly across from Kraków Główny. To: **Warsaw** (6hr., 3 per day, 40zł); **Wrocław** (6½hr., 2 per day, 35zł); and **Zakopane** (2hr., 33 per day, 10zł). **Sindbad**, in the main hall, sells international tickets (☎421 02 40). To: **Budapest** (11hr., 1 per week, 100zł); **Prague** (9hr., 2 per week, 98zł); and **Vienna** (9hr, 7 per week, 115zł).

Public Transportation: Buy **bus** and **tram** tickets at kiosks labeled *Ruch* (2.20zł) or from the driver (2.50zł) and punch them on board. Large backpacks need their own tickets. Day pass 9zł; week 22zł. Night buses (from 11pm) 4zł.

Taxis: Barbakan Taxi (☎96 61, toll-free 0800 400 400); **Euro Taxi** (☎96 64); **Express Taxi** (☎96 29); **Radio Taxi** (☎919); **Wawel Taxi** (☎96 66).

■ ORIENTATION

The true heart of the city is the huge **Rynek Główny** (Main Marketplace), in the center of **Stare Miasto** (Old Town). The **Planty gardens** and a ring of roads including **Basztowa, Dunajewskiego, Podwale,** and **Westerplatte** encircle Stare Miasto. The gigantic **Wawel Castle** looms South of the *Rynek*. The **Wisła** (VEE-swa) river snakes past the castle and borders the old Jewish village of **Kazimierz,** which is accessible from the market by ul. Starowiślna and ul. Stradomska. The **bus** and **train** stations are located just to the northeast of the Planty ring. To reach the *Rynek* from either, follow the *"do centrum"* signs through the underpass to the Planty gardens. A number of streets lead from there to the square.

⁊ PRACTICAL INFORMATION

Tourist Offices: MCI, Rynek Główny 1/3 (☎421 77 06; www.mcit.pl). Sells maps and the handy *Kraków in Your Pocket* guide (5zł, English 10zł). Open May-Sept. M-F 9am-7pm, Sa 9am-2pm; Oct.-Apr. M-F 9am-5pm, Sa 9am-1pm.

Budget Travel: Orbis, Rynek Główny 41 (☎422 28 85; www.orbis.krakow.pl). Sells train tickets, arranges trips to Wieliczka and Auschwitz, cashes traveler's checks, and exchanges currency. Open M-F 9am-7pm, Sa 9am-3pm.

Consulates: UK, św. Anny 9, 4th fl. (☎421 70 30; fax 422 42 64; ukconsul@bci.krakow.pl). Open M-F 9am-2pm. **US,** ul. Stolarska 9 (☎424 51 00; www.usconsulate.krakow.pl). Open M-F 8:30am-5pm.

Currency Exchange: *Kantory,* except those around the train station, have the best rates. **ATMs** are all over the city.

American Express: Ul. św. Marka 25 (☎423 12 02; www.americanexpress.pl). Predominately a tourist agency but can direct those seeking help with traveler's checks to the Warsaw office. Open M-F 9am-5pm.

Luggage Storage: At the train station. 1% of value per day plus 3.90zł for the 1st day and 2zł per bag for each additional day. Open 24hr.

English Bookstore: Szawal, ul. Krupnicza 3. Open M-F 10am-7pm, Sa 10am-2pm.

Laundromat: Ul. Piastowska 47, in the basement of Hotel Piast. Wash and dry 15zł each, detergent 3zł. Open Tu and Th 11am-4pm, Sa 11am-2pm.

Pharmacy: Apteka Pod Żółtym Tygrysem, Szczepańska 1 (☎422 92 93). Open M-F 8am-8pm, Sa 8am-3pm. Lists 24hr. pharmacies in window.

Medical Assistance: Medicover, ul. Krótka 1 (☎/fax 616 10 00). English spoken. Open M-F 8am-8pm, Sa 9am-2pm.

Telephones: At the post office and opposite the train station at ul. Lubicz 4. Open 24hr. Phone cards sold at **Telekomunikacja Polska,** ul. Wielpole 2 (☎421 64 57). Open M-F 9am-7pm, Sa 10am-2pm.

Internet Access: ▨ **Enter Internet Cafe,** ul. Baztowa 23/1 (☎429 42 25). 8-11am 2zł per hr., 11am-11pm 3zł per hr. Open daily 8am-10pm. **Cafe Tera,** Rynek Główny (☎431 21 84). 3zł per hr. Open 24hr.

Post Office: Ul. Lubicz 4. *Poste Restante* at counter #5. Open M-F 7am-8pm, Sa 2-8pm for letters, 2-4pm for packages. Address mail to be held: Firstname SURNAME, *Poste Restante,* Kraków 1, **31-075,** POLAND.

◪ ACCOMMODATIONS

Call ahead in summer. **Travel Agency Jordan,** ul. Pawia 8 (☎422 60 91; www.jordan.krakow.pl) arranges private rooms. (Open M-F 8am-6pm, Sa 9am-2pm. Singles 65-100zł; doubles 130-160zł; triples 180-240zł. AmEx/MC/V.)

▨ **Nathan's Villa Hostel,** ul. św. Agnieszki 1 (☎422 35 45; www.nathansvilla.com). The newest hostel in Kraków. Full kitchen. Breakfast, storage, sheets, and laundry included. Reception 24hr. Check in before midnight. Dorms 50zł. ❷

▨ **Hostel Express,** ul. Wrocławska 91 (☎/fax 633 88 62; www.express91.pl). Spacious bungalows, spotless baths, kitchens, and washing machines (7zł per load). Reception 24hr. Check-in 3pm. Check-out 10am. Quiet hours 10pm-6am. 6-bed dorms 29zł; doubles 70zł; triples 99zł. MC/V. ❶

Schronisko Młodzieżowe (HI), ul. Oleandry 4 (☎633 88 22). Cheap dorms in a good location. Call ahead. Kitchenette and TV room. Cafeteria open daily 8am-6pm. Reception 6pm-midnight. Flexible lockout 10am-5pm. Curfew midnight. Dorms 20-32zł. ❶

Strawberry Youth Hostel, ul. Racławicka 9 (☎294 53 63 or 294 63 64; www.strawberryhostel.com). Well-kept student dorm open during July and Aug. only. TV room and kitchen available. Dorms 40zł. ❶

Dom Wycieczkowy Pod Sokołem (Vacation Home Under the Falcon), ul. Sokolska 17 (☎292 01 99; sokoldw@inetia.pl), across the river from Kazimierz. Reception 24hr. Check-out 10am. Dorms 40zł. ❶

Dom Studencki Żaczek, ul. 3 Maja 5 (☎633 19 14; www.zaczek.com.pl). A 10min. walk from the heart of Kraków, the excellent location and clean rooms make up for the thumping disco downstairs. Check-in 2pm. Check-out 10am. Singles 75zł, with bath 95zł; doubles 85/150zł; triples 105/165zł; quads 120zl; quints with bath 225zł. ❸

Hotel Polonia, ul. Basztowa 25 (☎422 12 33; www.hotel-polonia.com.pl). Right across from the train station and a 5min. walk from Rynek Główny. Elegant rooms. Breakfast 17zł, included for rooms with baths. Reception 24hr. Check-in 2pm. Check-out noon. Singles 99zł, with bath 268zł; doubles 119/319zł; triples 139/380zł; apartments 484zł. MC/V. ❹

Hotel Mistia, ul. Szlak 73a (☎633 29 26; www.mistia.org.pl). Soviet-style exterior belies excellent rooms inside. Call ahead. Reception upstairs. Check-in 2pm. Check-out 10am. Singles with bath 143zł; doubles with sink 98-116zł, with bath 143-166zł; triples with bath 166-179zł. MC/V. ❺

◪ FOOD

Many restaurants, cafes, and grocery stores are located on and around the *Rynek.* More grocery stores surround the bus and train stations.

POLAND

■ **U Stasi,** ul. Mikoajska 16 (☎421 50 84). Home-cooked meals draw local connoisseurs and enlightened tourists. Fruit-filled pierogi 2.10-5.40zł. Traditional meat dishes 6-12zł. Open until the food runs out (usually by 3-4pm in the summer). ❷

Vega Bar Restaurant, ul. Krupnicza 22 (☎430 08 46). Soups, salads, and delightful vegetarian cuisine 2-5zł. 36 varieties of tea 2.50zł each. **Branch** at ul. św. Gertrudy 7 (☎422 34 94). Both open daily 9am-9pm. MC/V. ❶

Dym (Smoke), ul. św. Jana 5 (☎429 66 61). Sophisticated locals gather for the best coffee in town (4.50zł) or to chat over a beer (5.50zł). Open daily 10am-midnight. ❶

Camelot, ul. św. Tomasza 17 (☎421 01 23). A legend in Stare Miasto. Cafe serves sandwiches (3-6zł) and salads (19-21zł). Cabaret F 9pm. Open daily 9am-midnight. ❶

Bar Kanapkowy "Zapiecek," ul. Floriańska 20 (☎422 13 45). An Italian twist on Polish hot sandwiches with a wide array of toppings. Open M-Sa 10am-10pm. ❷

Różowy Słoń (Pink Elephant), ul. Szpitalna 38 (☎422 14 16), near the train station, just opposite Teatr Słowackiego. **Branch** at ul. Straszewskiego 24. Convenient fast-food joint known for its *naleśniki* (5.20zł). Open M-Sa 9am-9pm, Su 10am-9pm. ❶

Restauracja Samoobsługowa "Polakowski," ul. Miodowa 39 (☎421 21 17). Old-fashioned Polish cooking served in home-style restaurant. Full meals 10-15zł. Soup 4zł. Open daily 10am-10pm. ❷

Chimera, św. Anny 3 (☎423 21 78). Cellar and romantic ivy garden. The oldest and most famous salad joint in town. Salad 7-10zł. Open daily 9am-10pm. ❷

Piwnica Pod Ogródkiem (Cellar Under the Garden), ul. Jagiellońska 6 (☎292 07 63). A blend of French and Polish fare, from savory *gallettes* (10-12zł) to sweet crepes (6-8zł). Beer 6zł. Open daily noon-midnight. ❷

◉ SIGHTS

STARE MIASTO. In center of Stare Miasto is Rynek Główny, a sea of cafes and bars, surrounded by multi-colored row houses. Nearby, **Collegium Maius** of Kraków's ■**Jagiellonian University** (Uniwersytet Jagielloński) was established in 1364, making it the second oldest institution of higher learning in Eastern Europe (after Prague's Charles University). Among its celebrated alumni are astronomer Mikołaj Kopernik (Copernicus) and painter Jan Matejko. Formerly used for lectures and for professors' quarters, the Collegium was opened as a museum in 1964. *(At ul. Jagiellońska 15. Walk down św. Anny in the corner of the Rynek near the Town Hall and turn left onto Jagiellońska. ☎422 05 49. Open M-F 10am-3pm, Sa 11am-2pm. University Museum (30min.) 10zł, students 5zł; all rooms (60min.) 15/10zł. Sa free. English tour of all rooms daily at 1pm.)* A trumpet call blares from the towers of **St. Mary's Church** (Kościół Mariacki) once in each direction every hour; its abrupt ending recalls the near-destruction of Kraków in 1241, when the invading Tartars are said to have shot down the trumpeter as he tried to warn the city. The church, which has a stunning blue and gold interior, encases the world's oldest Gothic altarpiece, a 500-year-old treasure once dismantled by the Nazis. *(At the corner of the Rynek closest to the train station. Open daily 11:30am-6pm. Altar ticket 4zł, students 2zł.)* In the middle of the *Rynek*, the yellow Italianate **Cloth Hall** (Sukiennice) houses vendors hawking souvenirs and a gallery of the **National Museum** that displays Polish paintings and sculptures. *(Open Su, Tu-W, and F-Sa 10am-3:30pm, Th 10am-6pm. 7zł, students 4zł. Su free.)* Ul. Floriańska runs from the **Barbakan** and **Floriańska Gate,** the old entrance to the city, to the *Rynek*. The Barbakan and the Gate are the only remnants of the city's medieval fortifications. From the *Rynek*, walk down Grodzka and turn right one block to reach the vibrantly colored **Franciscan Church,** which houses Stanisław Wyspiański's amazing stained-glass window, *God the Father. (Open daily until 7:30pm.)*

AROUND WAWEL CASTLE. ▓**Wawel Castle** (Zamek Wawelski) is one of Poland's finest architectural works and arguably *the* sight to see in Poland. Begun in the 10th century but remodeled during the 1500s, the castle contains 71 chambers, including a magnificent sequence of 16th-century tapestries commissioned by the royal family. *(Most rooms open Tu and F 9:30am-4pm, W-Th and Sa 9:30am-3pm, Su 10am-3pm; State Rooms and Treasury 12zł, students 7zł; Royal Chambers 12/7zł.)* Next door is **Wawel Cathedral** (Katedra Wawelska), where Kraków native Karol Wojtyła was archbishop before he became Pope. Earlier ages saw Poland's monarchs crowned and buried here. The steep wooden stairs from the church lead to **Sigismund's Bell** (Dwon Zygmunta). The climb affords a great view of the city. *(Open May-Sept. M-Sa 9am-5pm, Su 12:15-5:15pm; Oct.-Apr. M-Sa 9am-3pm, Su 12:15-5:15pm. Tombs and bell 8zł, students 4zł.)* The entrance to **Dragon's Den** (Smocza Jama) is in the southwest corner of the complex. Legend says that a shepherd left a poisoned sheep outside the cave; the dragon took the bait and got so thirsty it drank itself to death at the Wisła river. *(Open Apr.-Oct. daily 10am-5pm. 3zł.)*

KAZIMIERZ. South of Stare Miasto lies Kazimierz, Kraków's 600-year-old **Jewish quarter.** On the eve of WWII, 68,000 Jews lived in the Kraków area, many of them in Kazimierz, but occupying Nazis forced most out. All were deported by March 1943, many to the nearby Płaszów (where parts of *Schindler's List* were filmed) and Auschwitz-Birkenau concentration camps. Today, Kazimierz is a focal point for the 5000 Jews remaining in Poland and serves as a starting place for those seeking their roots. *(The walk from the Rynek leads down ul. Sienna by St. Mary's Church; ul. Sienna turns into Starowislna. After 1km, turn right onto Miodowa, then take the 1st left onto Szeroka. Or, take tram #3, 13, or 24 toward Bieżanow Nowy from the train station.)* The tiny **Remuh Synagogue** is surrounded by **Remuh's Cemetery,** one of Poland's oldest Jewish cemeteries, with graves dating back to the plague of 1551-52 and a wall constructed from tombstones recovered after the Nazi occupation. *(Ul. Szeroka 40. Open Su-F 9am-6pm. 5zł, students 2zł. Services F dusk and Sa morning.)* Back on Szeroka is the **Old Synagogue,** Poland's oldest synagogue, which houses a museum of sacred art. *(Ul. Szeroka 24. Open Apr. 8-Oct. 13 Su and Tu-Sa 9am-5pm; Nov.-Mar. M 10am-2pm, W-Th and Sa-Su 9am-3:30pm, F 10am-5pm. 6zł, students 4zł. M free.)* **The Center for Jewish Culture,** in the former Bene Emenu prayer house, organizes cultural events and arranges heritage tours. *(Rabina Meiselsa 17, just off pl. Nowy. Open M-F 10am-6pm, Sa-Su 10am-2pm.)*

🎵 🎭 ENTERTAINMENT AND NIGHTLIFE

The **Cultural Information Center,** ul. św. Jana 2, sells the comprehensive monthly guide *Karnet* (3zł; www.karnet.krakow2000.pl) and tickets for upcoming events. (☎421 77 87. Open M-F 10am-6pm, Sa 10am-4pm.) Summer festivals are especially abundant, including the **International Short Film Festival** (late May), **Children's Day Celebrations** (early June), the **Floating of Wreaths on the Wisła** (June), **Festival of Jewish Culture** (early July), the **Street Theater Festival** (early July), and the **Jazz Festival** (Oct.-Nov.). The opera performs at **J. Słowacki Theater,** pl. św. Ducha 1. (☎422 40 22; www.slowacki.krakow.pl. Box office open M-Sa 11am-2pm and 3-7pm, Su 2hr. before each performance.) The **Stary Teatr** has several stages in the city. (Tickets at pl. Szczepański 1. ☎422 40 40. Open Tu-Sa 10am-1pm and 5-7pm.)

At night, cozy pubs come alive in the brick basements of 14th-century buildings near the *Rynek*. ▓**Stalowe Magnolie,** ul. św Jana 15, is where locals relax and listen to live jazz Tu-Th and contemporary rock on the weekends. (Beer 6-10zł. Mixed drinks14-25zł. Open Tu-W 7pm-1am, Th-Su 7pm-3am.) **Klub Kulturalny,** ul. Szewska 25, replete with blue lights and pulsing music, espouses a laid-back attitude. (Beer 5.50zł. Open M-F noon-3am.) **Kredens,** Rynek Główny 12, is a casual club packed with multinational party-goers. (21+. Cover F-Sa 5zł. Open daily 5pm-

3am.) **Faust,** Rynek Główny 6, has closed-circuit cameras and TV sets that let you witness the crowd go wild as you chat with friends at a candle-lit table. (Beer 4zł. Disco W-Sa. F-Sa cover 5zł. Open Su-Th noon-1am, F-Sa noon-4am.) At night, **Chill Out Café,** ul. św. Jana 15, becomes a hip bar; furniture disappears as the dancing ensues. (Beer 6zł. Smoothies 8zł. DJ Th-Su. Open M-W 11am-1am, Th-Su 11am-3am.) **Soho,** ul. Szpitalna 34, has East Asian decor and a light atmosphere perfect for a quiet evening before the disco and electronic music urge party-goers to hit the dance floor. (Beer 5zł. Occasional concerts and shows. Disco F-Sa from 9pm. Gay friendly. 18+. Open daily 3pm-late.) **Jazz Club "U Muniaka,"** ul. Floriańska 3, is the home of Kraków's jazz scene. (Shows M-Sa 9:30pm. M-W 10zł, students 5zł. Th-Sa 20/10zł. Open Su-W 3pm-midnight, F-Sa 3pm-1am.)

■ DAYTRIPS FROM KRAKÓW

AUSCHWITZ-BIRKENAU. An estimated 1½ million people, mostly Jews, were murdered—and thousands more suffered unthinkable horrors—in the Nazi concentration camps at **Auschwitz** (in Oświęcim) and **Birkenau** (in Brzezinka). The gates over the smaller **Konzentrationslager Auschwitz I** are inscribed with the ironic dictum *"Arbeit Macht Frei"* ("Work Makes You Free"). Tours begin at the **museum** at Auschwitz; as you walk past the remnants of thousands of lives—suitcases, shoes, glasses, and thousands of kilos of women's hair—the sheer enormity of the evil committed comes into focus. A 15min. English-language **film,** with footage shot by the Soviet Army that liberated the camp on January 27, 1945, is shown at 11am and 1pm. (Open June-Aug. daily 8am-7pm; closes earlier Sept.-May. Free. 3½hr. English tour daily at 11:30am. 25zł.)

The larger, starker Konzentrationslager Auschwitz II-Birkenau is located in the countryside 3km from the original camp. A 30min. walk along a well-marked route or a quick **shuttle** ride from the parking lot of the Auschwitz museum (every hr. 11:30am-5:30pm, 2zł) will get you there. Birkenau was built later in the war, when the Nazis developed a more brutally efficient means of exterminating the massive numbers of people brought to Auschwitz. Little is left of the camp today; most was destroyed by retreating Nazis who tried to conceal the genocide. The train tracks, reconstructed after the liberation, lead to the ruins of the crematoria and gas chambers, where a memorial pays tribute to all those who died in the Auschwitz system. Near the monument lies a pond that is still gray from the ashes deposited there half a century ago.

Auschwitz Jewish Center and Synagogue features exhibits on pre-war Jewish life in the town of Oświęcim, films based on survivors' testimonies, genealogy resources, and a reading room. To get there, take bus #1, 3-6, or 8 from the train station to the town center, get off at the first stop after the bridge, and backtrack to Pl. Ks. Jana Skarbka, or take a taxi (about 17zł.). Tours of Auschwitz are available. (Pl. Ks. Jana Skarbka 5. ☎844 70 02; www.ajcf.pl. Open Apr.-Sept. daily 8:30am-8pm; Oct.-Mar. Su-F 8:30am-6pm.)

Buses from Kraków's central bus station go to **Oświęcim** (1½hr., 5 per day, 10zł). The bus back to Kraków leaves from the stop on the other side of the parking lot; turn right out of the museum to reach it. Less convenient **trains** leave from Kraków Główny (1¾hr., 3 per day, 8.70zł) and from Kraków Płaszów, south of the town center. Buses #2-5, 8, 9, and 24-29 connect the Oświęcim train station to the Muzeum Oświęcim stop; or, walk right as you exit the station, walk a block, turn left onto ul. Więźniów Oświęcimia, and walk 1.6km to Auschwitz.

WIELICZKA. A 1000-year-old **salt mine** sits at ul. Daniłowicza 10 in the tiny town of Wieliczka, 13km southeast of Kraków. Pious Poles carved the immense underground complex of chambers out of salt; in 1978, UNESCO declared the mine one of the 12 most priceless monuments in the world. The most spectacular cavern is **St. Kinga's Chapel,** complete with salt chandeliers, an altar, and relief works. (☎278 73 66; www.kopalnia.pl. Open Apr.-Oct. daily 7:30am-7:30pm; Nov.-Mar. 8am-4pm. Tours 38zł, students 28zł.) Most travel companies, including **Orbis** (p. 798), organize trips to the mines, but the cheapest way to go is on the private **minibuses,** such as "Lux-Bus," which depart from between the train and bus stations (30min., every 15min., 2zł). Look for *"Wieliczka"* marked on the door. In Wieliczka, follow the path of the former tracks, then the *"do kopalni"* signs.

LUBLIN   ☎081

Unlike most cities in Poland, Lublin (pop. 400,000) survived WWII with cobblestones and medieval buildings intact. The 14th-century **Lublin Castle** (Zamek Lubelski), in the *Rynek* of the **Stare Miasto** (Old Town), was used as a Gestapo jail during the Nazi occupation. The adjacent **Holy Trinity Chapel** contains stunning Russo-Byzantine frescoes. (Castle museum open Su 9am-5pm and W-Sa 9am-4pm. 5zł, students 3zł. Chapel open M-Sa 9am-3:30pm, Su 9am-4:30pm. 6zł, students 4zł. Entry to both 9/5zł) Take eastbound bus #28 from the train station, trolley #153 or 156 from al. Racławickie, or walk on Droga Męczenników Majdanka (Road of the Martyrs of Majdanek; 30 min.) to Zamość in order to reach **Majdanek,** the second-largest concentration camp during WWII. Nazis did not have time to destroy the camp, so the original structures still stand. (☎744 26 48; www.majdanek.pl. Open May-Sept. Su and Tu-Sa 8am-6pm; Mar.-Apr. and Oct.-Nov. Su and Tu-Sa 8am-3pm. Free. Children under 14 not permitted. Tours 100zł per group; call ahead. English guidebooks 7zł.)

Trains (☎94 36) run from pl. Dworcowy 1 to: Berlin (13hr., daily, 158-234zł); Kraków (4hr., 4 per day, 43zł); Warsaw (3hr., 14 per day, 32zł); and Wrocław (9½hr., 3 per day, 48zł). The **tourist office,** ul. Jezuica 1/3, is near the Kraków Gate. (☎532 44 12; loit@inetia.pl. Open May-Aug. M-Sa 9am-6pm, Su 10am-3pm; Sept.-Apr. M-F 9am-5pm, Sa-Su 10am-3pm.) From the bus station, walk through Zamkowy Square, past the castle, and through the gate to reach **⊠Domu Rekolekcyjnym ❶,** ul. Podwale 15, an old rectory with comfortable rooms. (☎532 41 38; j.halasa@kuria.lublin.pl. No curfew. Dorms 20-40zł.) Lublin's eateries cluster near **ulica Krakówskie Przedmieście,** and a dozen beer gardens are spread throughout Stare Miasto. **Café Szeroka 28 ❸,** ul. Grodzka 21, has a great view of the castle and live Klezmer on Saturday. (Entrees 30zł. Open Su-Th 11am-11pm, F-Sa 11am-late.) The *naleśniki* (Polish crepes; 4-12zł) at **Naleśnikarnia/Kawiarnia "Zadora" ❶,** Rynek 8, are excellent. (Open daily 10am-late.) **Postal Code:** 20-950.

ZAKOPANE   ☎018

Poland's premier year-round resort is set in a valley surrounded by jagged Tatran peaks and alpine meadows. During peak seasons (Jan.-Feb. and June-Sept.), Zakopane swells with skiers and hikers who come for the magnificent **Tatra National Park** (Tatrzański Park Narodowy). (3zł, students 1.50zł.) The bus station is on the corner of ul. Kościuszki and ul. Jagiellońska, across from the train station. **Buses** (☎201 46 03) go to: Kraków (2-2½hr., 25 per day, 8zł); Poprad, Slovakia (2¼hr., mid-June to Sept. Su and W-Sa, 15zł); and Warsaw (8½hr., 2 per day, 53zł). A private **express line** runs between Zakopane and Kraków (2hr., 15 per day, 10zł); buses leave from a stop on ul. Kościuszki, 50m toward the center from the station. **Trains** (☎201 45 04) go to Kraków (3-4hr., 22 per day, 19zł) and Warsaw (6-9hr., 8 per day, 46-80zł). Walk down ul. Kościuszki, which intersects the central ul. Krupówki (15min.). **Tourist Agency Redykołka,** ul. Kościeliska 1, gives info on private rooms (30-50zł) and runs English-language tours. (☎201 32 53; www.tatratours.pl. Open

M-Sa 9am-5pm, Sa 9am-1pm.) *Pokój, noclegi,* or *Zimmer* signs indicate private rooms. **Schronisko Morskie Oko ❶**, by the Morskie Oko lake, is a gorgeous hostel in an ideal hiking location. Take a bus (45min., 11 per day, 4zł) from the station to *Palenice Białczańska* or a direct minibus (20min., 5zł) from opposite the bus station. (☎207 76 09. Reserve well in advance. June-Oct. 3-to 6-bed dorms 41zł, 8- to 12-bed dorms 31zł, Nov.-June 33/23zł.) **PTTK Dom Turysty ❶**, ul. M. Zaruskiego 5, is a large chalet in the center of town. From the bus station, walk down ul. Kościuszki, which turns into ul. M. Zaruskiego. (☎206 32 07. Curfew midnight. Dorms 18-30zł.) Most restaurants are expensive; the **Delikatesy** grocery store on ul. Krupówki 41, however, is cheap. (Open M-Sa 7am-8pm.) **Postal Code:** 34-500.

🔲 **HIKING NEAR ZAKOPANE.** The best place to start hiking is **Kuźnice,** south of central Zakopane. Walk from the train station along ul. Jagiellońska, which becomes ul. Chałubińskiego, then continue down ul. Przewodników Tatrzańskich to the trailheads (45min.). Alternatively, catch the Kasprowy Wierch **cable car,** (1987m) which runs between Zakopane and Kuźnice. (Round-trip 28zł, students 18zł. Open July-Aug. 7am-7pm; June and Sept. 7:30am-4pm; Oct. 7:30am-3pm.) The trails are well-marked, but pick up the tourist map *Tatrzański Park Narodowy* (7zł) at a kiosk or bookstore before hiking.

🔲 **Valley of the Five Polish Tarns** (Dolina Pięciu Stawów Polskich; full-day) is an intense, beautiful hike. It starts at Kuźnice and follows the blue trail to Hala Gąsienicowa. After several steep ups and downs, the blue trail ends at Morskie Oko. From here, it's 2km farther down to a parking lot in Palenica Białczańska, where buses return to Zakopane.

Mt. Giewont (1894m; 6½hr.) has a silhouette that looks like a man lying down. It's crowded and the final ascent is steep, so be careful. From Kuźnice, take the moderately difficult blue trail (7km) to the peak for a view of Zakopane, the Tatras, and Slovakia.

Sea Eye (Morskie Oko; 1406m; 5-6hr.) is a dazzling glacial lake. Take a bus from the Zakopane station (45min., 11 per day, 4zł), or a private minibus (30-40min., 5zł) from opposite the station to Palenica Białczańska. Hike the popular 18km round-trip on a paved road, or take a horse and carriage (round-trip 1½hr.; 30zł up, 15zł down).

WROCŁAW ☎071

Wrocław (pop. 657,000), the capital of Dolny Śląsk (Lower Silesia), straddles the Oder River. During World War II, it became *Festung Breslau,* one of the last Nazi battlegrounds en route to Berlin. After suffering heavily under Communist control, Wrocław's architecture has been rejuvenated over the past ten years by local officials. Today, fewer scars are visible and Wrocław captivates visitors with the antique grace of its 19th-century buildings and lush parks. The gothic **Ratusz** (Town Hall) towers over the **Rynek** (main square) in the heart of the city. The beautiful central street **Ulica Świdnicka** runs by the *Rynek.* Entering the rotunda that contains the 🔲**Racławice Panorama,** ul. Purkyniego 11, is like stepping right onto a battlefield; the painting depicts the 18th-century peasant insurrection led by Tadeusz Kościuszko against the Russian occupation. To reach the exhibit, face away from the *Ratusz,* bear left onto Kuźnicza, and turn right onto Kotlarska, which becomes ul. Purkyniego. (Open Su and Tu-Sa 9am-4pm. 19zł, students 15zł.) Just across the street is the massive **National Museum** (Muzeum Narodowe), pl. Powstańców Warszawy 5, which has permanent modern art exhibits. (Open Sa-Su 10am-6pm, W and F 10am-4pm, Th 9am-4pm. 15zł, students 10zł.) The center of Wrocław's cultural life, the **Uniwersytet Wrocławski** (Wrocław University), houses many architectural gems. Climb the **mathematical tower** at pl. Uniwersytecki 1 for a sweeping view of the city. (Open Su-Tu and Th-Sa 10am-3pm. 4zł, students 2zł.) Across the Oder river lies the serene **Cathedral Square** (Plac Katedralny). With your back to the *Ratusz*, take any street until you hit ul. Piaskowy; take a left over Pia-kowsky bridge to **Cathedral Island,** then a right onto Tumski bridge to pl. Kate-dralny to reach the 13th-century **Cathedral of St. John the Baptist** (Katedra Św. Jana Chrzciciela), whose spires dominate the skyline. (Open daily 10am-6pm. Donation suggested.) Students crowd into ▨**REJS Pub,** ul. Kotlarska 32a. (Beer 3.50zł. Open M-Sa 9:30am-late, Su 11am-late.)

Trains, ul. Piłsudskiego 105 (☎368 83 33), go from Wrocław Głowny to: Berlin (6¼hr., 2 per day, 184zł); Dresden (4½hr., 4 per day, 158zł); Kraków (6¼hr., 14 per day, 61zł); Poznań (3¼hr., 25 per day, 32zł); Prague (5¼hr., 2 per day, 128zł); and Warsaw (4¼hr., 12 per day, 45zł). **Buses,** generally slower than trains, leave from behind the train station. From the train station, turn left on ul. Piłsudskiego, take a right on ul. Świdnicka, and go past Kościuszki pl. over the Fosa river to reach the *Rynek.* **IT,** Rynek 14, can help find rooms in student dorms. (☎344 11 09; fax 344 29 62. Open M-F 10am-6pm, Sa 9am-2pm.) Surf the web at **Internet Klub Navig@tor Podz-iemia,** ul. Kuźnicza 11/13. (3zł per hr. Open daily 9am-10pm.) The cheerful ▨**Youth Hostel Mlodziezowy Dom Kultury im. Kopernika (HI) ❶,** ul. Kołłątaja 20, is opposite the train station on the road perpendicular to ul. Piłsudskiego. (☎343 88 56. Lockout 10am-5pm. Curfew 10pm. Call ahead. Dorms 22zł; doubles 29zł. Discount after two nights.) **Bazylia ❶,** ul. Kuźniczna 42, is a traditional Polish milk bar serving cheap nourishing meals. (Open M-F 7am-7pm, Sa 8am-5pm.) **Postal Code:** 50 900.

KARPACZ
☎075

Karpacz (pop. 8000) is a beautiful gateway to **Karkonosze National Park** (Karkonoski Park Narodowy; 3zł, students 1.50zł; 3-day pass 6/3zł), where several 2¼-3hr. trails lead to **Pod Śnieżka** (1394m) on **Śnieżka** (Mt. Snow; 1602m), the highest peak in the Czech Republic; the Polish-Czech border runs across the summit. The Kopa chair lift also runs to Pod Śnieżka. (Follow the black trail from Hotel Biały Jar to the lift, on the left. Runs June-Aug. daily 8:30am-5:30pm; Sept.-May 8am-4pm. Before 1pm 17zł, students 14zł; round-trip 22/18zł. After 1pm 15/10zł; round-trip 18/13zł.)

PKS **buses** from Jelenia Góra (45min., every 30min.-1hr., 5.20zł) stop at eight points throughout Karpacz (2.20zł). **Trains** from Jelenia Góra run to Kraków (7¾hr., 3 per day, 42zł); Póznan (5½hr., 2 per day, 30zł); and Wrocław (2hr., 29 per day, 24zł). Get off the PKS bus at *Karpacz Bachus* and head uphill to the Karpacz **tourist office,** ul. 3-go Maja 52, for maps, **currency exchange,** and info about various outdoor activities. (☎761 95 47. Open M-F 9am-5pm, Sa 9am-4pm; July-Aug. also open Su 10am-4pm.) The office also makes reservations for accommodations at **D.W. Szczyt ❶,** ul. Na Śnieżkę 6, at the Karpacz Wang stop. (Singles 25zł; doubles 50zł.) The gro-cery store **Delikatesy,** ul. 3-go Maja 29, is near the tourist office. (Open M-Sa 8:30am-9pm, Su 10am-6pm.) **Postal Code:** 58-540.

POZNAŃ
☎061

International trade fairs throughout the year (except Dec., July, and Aug.) fill Poznań (pop. 600,000), the capital of Wielkopolska (Greater Poland), with tourists and businessmen. Opulent 15th-century merchant homes surround the Renais-sance **Town Hall** (*Ratusz*), a multi-colored gem with an ornately painted ceiling. (Open M-Tu and F 10am-4pm, W noon-6pm, Th and Sa 9am-4pm, Su 10am-3pm. Museum 5.50zł, students 3.50zł. Sa free.) The **National Museum** (Muzeum Naro-dowe), ul. Marcinkowskiego 9, contains a marvelous collection of 13th- to 19th-century paintings. (Open Su 10am-4pm, Tu 10am-6pm, W 9am-5pm, Th and F-Sa 10am-5pm. 10zł, students 6zł. Sa free.) The **Museum of Musical Instruments** (Muzeum Instrumentów Muzycznych), Stary Rynek 45, holds a fascinating display of antique and foreign instruments, including one of Chopin's pianos. (Open Su 11am-3pm, Tu-Sa 11am-5pm. 5.50zł, students 3.50zł. Sa free). Sculpted ceilings and columns spiral heavenward in the **Parish Church of the City of Poznań of St. Mary Magdalene,** at the end of ul. Świętosławska off Stary Rynek. (Free concerts M-Sa 12:15pm.) On the outskirts of town stands the first Polish cathedral, the **Cathedral of St. Peter and St. Paul** (Katedra Piotra i Pawła). In the **Golden Chapel** (Kaplica Złota) are the tombs of Prince Mieszko I and his son Bolesław Chrobry, the first king of Poland. (Open daily 9am-4pm. Entrance to crypt 2.50zł, students 1.50zł.)

Trains (☎866 12 12) go from Poznań Główny, Ul. Dworcowa 1, to: Berlin (3½hr., 7 per day, 138zł); Kraków (5hr., 10 per day, 45-79zł); and Warsaw (3hr., 23 per day, 57-87zł). To reach **Stary Rynek** (Old Market), take any tram heading down św. Marcin (to the right) from the end of ul. Dworcowa, and get off at ul. Marcinkowskiego. **Centrum Informacji Turystycznej** (CIT), Stary Rynek 59/60 (☎852 61 56), provides free maps and accommodation info. (Open June-Aug. M-F 9am-6pm, Sa 10am-4pm; Sept.-May M-F 9am-5pm, Sa 10am-2pm.) 🏠**Przemysław ❶,** ul. Głogowska 16, arranges **private rooms** near the city center. (☎866 35 60; przemyslaw@przemyslaw.com.pl. Singles 42zł; doubles 64zł. During fairs 26-32zł more. Open M-F 8am-6pm, Sa 10am-2pm; open 2hr. later during trade fairs. Closed some Saturdays July-Aug.) **Bar Mleczny "Przysmak" ❶,** ul. Podgorna 2, has salads and pasta downstairs and heartier meals upstairs. (Open M-F 9am-9pm, Sa 10am-7pm.) For tickets and info on cultural events, contact **Centrum Informacji Miejskiej,** ul. Ratajczka 44, next to the Empik Megastore. (☎94 31. Open M-F 10am-7pm, Sa-Su 10am-5pm.) **Postal Code:** 61-890.

TORUŃ   ☎056

Toruń (pop. 210,000) bills itself as the birthplace and childhood home of Mikołaj Kopernik, also known as Copernicus. Even before the local genius came to fame, his hometown was known far and wide as "beautiful red Toruń" for its impressive brick and stone structures. **Stare Miasto** (Old Town), on the right bank of the Wisła River, was constructed by the Teutonic Knights in the 13th century. The 14th-century **Town Hall** (*Ratusz*) that dominates **Rynek Stromiejski** (Old Town Square) is one of the finest examples of monumental burgher architecture in Europe. (Town Hall museum open May-Aug. Tu-W, Sa noon-6pm; Th, Su 10am-4pm. Sept.-Apr. Su and Tu-Sa 10am-4pm. 6zł, students 4zł. Su free. Medieval tower open May-Sept. Su and Tu-Sa. 6zł, students 4zł.) The birthplace of the man who "stopped the sun and moved the earth" is at ul. Kopernika 15/17; the meticulously restored **Dom Kopernika** features historical artifacts and an interesting sound-and-light show. (Open Tu, Th, Sa noon-6pm; W, F, Su 10am-4pm. Show every 30min. House 7zł, students 5zł. Show 8/5zł. Both 12/8zł.) A city-wide revolt in 1454 led to the destruction of the **Teutonic Knights' Castle,** but the ruins on ul. Przedzamcze are still impressive. (Open daily 9am-8pm. 1zł, students 0.5zł.) The 15m **Leaning Tower** (Krzywa Wieża), ul. Krzywa Wieża 17, was built in 1271 by a Teutonic Knight being punished for breaking the Order's rule of celibacy. The **Cathedral of St. John the Baptist and St. John the Evangelist** (Bazylika Katedralna pw. św. Janów), at the corner of ul. Żeglarska and św. Jana, is the most impressive of the many Gothic churches in the area. (Open Jan. 4-Oct. M-Sa 8:30am-5:30pm, Su 2-5:30pm. 2zł, students 1zł.) From there, it's a short walk across the *Rynek* to the slender stained-glass windows of the **Church of the Virgin Mary** (Kościół św. Marii) on ul. Panny Marii. (Open 8am-5pm. Free.) The pub 🏠**Miś,** in the basement at św. Ducha 6, has an artsy reputation, but patrons gather here for laid-back foosball and darts. (Beer 4zł. Live music daily. DJ F-Sa. Open daily 6pm-late.)

The **train station,** across the Wisła River from the city center at ul. Kujawska 1, serves: Gdańsk (3¼hr., 7 per day, 36zł); Łódz (1¾hr., 4 per day, 32zł); and Warsaw (2¾hr., 6 per day, 37zł). **Dworzec PKS buses,** ul. Dąbrowskiego 26, leave for Berlin

(9½hr., daily, 120zł); Gdańsk (3½hr., 2 per day, 31zł); and Warsaw (4hr., 9 per day, 36zł). **Polski Express buses** leave from the Ruch Kiosk just north of pl. Teatralny for Kołobrzeg (6¾hr., daily, 43zł) and Warsaw (3½hr., 15 per day, 34-37zł). The IT **tourist office,** Rynek Staromiejski 1, offers helpful advice in English and helps find lodgings. From the train station, take city bus #22 or 27 to Plac Rapackiego, the first stop across the river, and head through the park; the office is on your left. (☎621 09 31; www.it.torun.pl. Open May-Dec. M and Sa 9am-4pm, Tu-F 9am-6pm, Su 9am-1pm; Sept.-Apr. closed Su.) Check email at **Hacker Pubi,** ul. Podmurna 28. (4zł per hr. Open M-Th 9am-midnight, F 9am-2am, Sa 10am-3am, Su 1-11pm.)

■**Hotel Trzy Korony** ❹, Rynek Staromiejski 21, has an amazing location. (☎/fax 622 60 31. Reception 24hr. Singles 90zł, with bath 150zł; doubles 110/190zł; triples 140/230zł; apartments 250zł.) **Hotel "Gotyk"** ❺, ul. Piekary 20, has beautiful rooms with Internet access. (☎658 40 00; gotyk@ic.torun.pl. Reception 24hr. Singles 150zł; doubles 250-300zł; apartments 300-350zł.) To reach the student-filled **PTTK Dom Turystyczny** ❶, ul. Legionów 24, from the *Rynek*, follow ul. Chelmińska past pl. Teatralny; take the second right after the park and turn left onto ul Legionów. (☎/fax 622 38 55. Dorms 30zł; singles 70zł; doubles 80zł; triples 99zł.) ■**U Sołtysa** ❷, ul. Mostowa 17, serves hearty Polish food. (Pierogi 9.50-12zł. Open daily noon-midnight.) There's a 24hr. **grocery store** at ul. Chełmińska 22. **Postal Code:** 87 100.

ŁÓDŹ
☎042

Łódź (WOODGE; pop. 813,000) once held the largest Jewish ghetto in Europe. Since it doubled as a Nazi textile factory during World War II, the ghetto was a valuable source of labor, and its 70,000 residents were not deported to death camps until 1944. Of those, 20,000 survived, and the Red Army saved another 800 from mass execution. The **Jewish cemetery** (Cmentarz Żydowski), which has an entrance on ul. Zmienna, is the largest in Europe, with over 200,000 graves. Near the entrance is a memorial to the Jews killed in the Łódź ghetto; signs lead the way to the **Ghetto Fields** (Pole Ghettowe), which are lined with the faintly marked graves of those who died there. (Take tram #1 from ul. Kilinskiego north to *Strykowska Inflancka* at the end of the line (20min.). Continue up the street, take a left on ul. Zmienna, and enter through the small gate in the wall on your right. Open May-Sept. M-F and Su 9am-5pm; Oct.-Apr. M-F and Su 9am-3pm. 4zł. Free for those visiting the graves of relatives.) The **Jewish Community Center** (Gmina Wyznaniowa Żydowska), ul. Pomorska 18, in the center of town, has info about those buried in the cemetery. (Open M-F 10am-2pm. Services daily.) Łódź also happens to be the second-largest city in Poland. Its main thoroughfare, **ulica Piotrkowska,** is a bustling pedestrian shopping drag by day and a lively pub land by night.

Trains run to Kraków (3¼hr., daily, 41zł) and Warsaw (2hr., 19 per day, 28zł) from the Łódź Fabryczna station, pl. B. Sałacinskiego 1, and to Gdańsk (7½hr., 2 per day, 45zł) and Wrocław (3¾hr., 5 per day, 39zł) from Łódź Kaliska station, al. Unii 1. Polski Express **buses** also depart from Łódź Fabryczna station to Kraków (5hr., 3 per day, 31zł) and Warsaw (2½hr., 5 per day, 24zł). **IT,** al. Kościuszkiul 88, has tourist and lodging info. (☎/fax 638 59 56; cit@uml.lodz.pl. Open M-F 8:30am-4:30pm, Sa 9am-1pm.) **Postal Code:** 90-001.

KOŁOBRZEG
☎094

Long known as the "Pearl of the Baltic," Kołobrzeg (koh-WOH-bzheg), with its excellent beaches and healing **salt springs,** was voted Poland's most popular holiday resort in 2001. The glamour of the modern city belies its history; in March, 1945, the Poles battled fiercely with the Nazis over the port, and although most of the city was destroyed, the Poles ultimately triumphed. They threw a wedding ring into the Baltic to symbolize Poland's claims on Kołobrzeg, and a **monument** near the beach now commemorates the event, which is known as "Poland's marriage to the sea" (Zaślubiny z Morzem). The nearby 1745 **lighthouse** offers an expansive view of the Baltic. (Open July-Aug. daily 10am-sunset; Sept.-June 10am-5pm. 3zł, students 2zł.) The **Museum Oręża Polskiego,** ul. Emilii Gierczak 5, features an impressive array of military paraphernalia. (Open Su-Tu and Th-Sa 9:30am-5pm, W 9:30am-6pm. 6zł, students 3zł. Free W noon-6pm.) The **Gallery of Modern Art** (Galeria Sztuki Współczesniej), in the Town Hall, ul. Armii Krajowej 12, displays an exquisite collection of Polish crafts and artwork. (Open Su and Tu-Sa 10am-5pm. 4zł, students 2zł.)

Dworzec PKP trains (☎352 35 76) run from ul. Kolejowa to: Gdynia (3½hr., 8 per day, 39zł); Kraków (11½hr., 5 per day, 51zł); Poznań (6hr., 5 per day, 40zł); Warsaw (8hr., 9 per day, 49-83zł); and Wrocław (7¾hr., 3 per day, 51zł). Dworzec PKS buses (☎352 39 28) depart from next door for: Gdańsk (6hr., daily, 40zł); Gdynia (5hr., 2 per day, 35zl); Poznań (5hr., 4 per day, 45zl); and Warsaw (11hr., 5 per day, 65zl). To reach the city center from the stations, take ul. Dworcowa, turn left onto ul. Armii Krajowej, the main thoroughfare, and continue to the Town Hall (15min.). Reaching the beach can be tricky; free English info and maps are available at the CIT **tourist office,** ul. Dworcowa 1, opposite the stations. (☎352 79 39; www.kolobrzeg.turystyka.pl. Open June-Aug. daily 7am-7pm; Sept.-May M-F 7am-3pm.) **Private rooms** are the best lodging options; look for locals with *"wolne pokoje"* signs at the stations. **PTTK ❶,** in the tower at ul. Dubois 20, can also help. (☎/fax 352 32 87. 20-50zł. Open M-Sa 9am-4pm.) **Jadłodajnia Całoroczna ❷,** ul. Budowlana 28, is a delightful milk bar hidden off the main square. From the Town Hall, turn left on ul. Armii Krajowej, turn right on Budowlana, and pass under the arch; enter through the back. (Meals 12-15zł. Open daily 10am-7pm.) **Postal Code:** 78-100.

GDAŃSK   ☎058

The strategic location of Gdańsk (pop. 481,000) on the Baltic Coast at the mouth of the Wisła River has put it at the forefront of Polish history for more than a millennium. As the free city of Danzig, it was treasured by Poles as the "gateway to the sea" during years of occupation in the 18th and 19th centuries. During WWII, it was the site of the first casualties and the Germans' last stand; by the early 1980s, it was in the spotlight as the birthplace of Lech Wałęsa's Solidarity trade union. Efficient transport makes it the perfect starting point to explore Malbork, Sopot, and Gdynia, with which Gdańsk forms the Tri-City area (Trójmiasto).

▐ TRANSPORTATION

Trains: Gdańsk Główny, ul. Podwale Grodzkie 1 (☎94 36). To: **Kołobrzeg** (2¾hr., 8 per day, 41zł); **Kraków** (7hr., 9 per day, 42zł); **Poznań** (4½hr., 7 per day, 42-73zł); **Warsaw** (4hr., 18 per day, 46-78zł); and **Wrocław** (6-7hr., 6 per day, 47-80zł). **SKM trains** (☎628 57 78) run to **Gdynia** (35min.; 4zł, students 2zł) and **Sopot** (20min.; 2.80/1.40zł) every 10min. during the day and less frequently at night.

Buses: ul. 3-go Maja 12 (☎302 15 32), behind the train station, connected by an underground passage. **Kołobrzeg** (6hr., daily, 47zł); **Kraków** (10¾hr., daily, 65zł); **Łódz** (8hr., 4 per day, 44zł); **Malbork** (1hr., 8 per day, 10-13zł); **Toruń** (2½hr., 4 per day, 31zł); and **Warsaw** (5¾hr., 7 per day, 55zł).

Ferries: (☎301 49 26; www.zegluga.gda.pl). Depart from under the Green Gate from May-Sept. to: **Gdynia** (1¾-2hr.; 2 per day; 39zł, students 28zł, round trip 54/37zł.) and **Sopot** (45-60min.; 5 per day; 33zł, students 22zł, round-trip 46/32zł). Apr.-Oct. to **Westerplatte** (50min.; every hr. 10am-6pm; 34zł, students 18zł).

Local Transportation: Buses and **trams** cost 1.10-3.30zł; day pass 6.20zł. Night buses 3.30zł; night pass 5.50zł. Large baggage needs a ticket.

Taxis: Super Hallo Taxi: ☎301 91 91. **Hallo Taxi:** ☎91 97. Both 1.80zł per km.

✳ 🔃 ORIENTATION AND PRACTICAL INFORMATION

While Gdańsk technically sits on the Baltic Coast, its center is 5km inland. From the **Gdańsk Główny** train station, the center lies just a few blocks southeast, bordered on the west by **Wały Jagiellońskie** and on the east by the **Motława River.** Take the underpass in front of the train station, go right, exit the shopping center, and then turn left on **ulica Heweliusza.** Turn right on **ulica Rajska** and follow the signs to **Główne Miasto** (Main Town), turning left on **ulica Długa.** Ul. Długa becomes **Długi Targ** as it widens near **Motława** and opens into the area that houses most of the city's sights. Gdańsk has several suburbs, all north of Główne Miasto.

Tourist Offices: PTTK Gdańsk, ul. Długa 45 (☎301 91 51; www.pttk-gdansk.com.pl), in Główne Miasto. Open June-Aug. M-F 9am-6pm; May-Sept. M-F 9am-6pm, Sa-Su 9am-3pm. **Branch** (☎328 52 89) kiosk outside the train station. Open daily 10am-6pm.

Budget Travel: Orbis, ul. Podwale Staromiejskie 96/97 (☎301 45 44; orbis.gdansk-pod@pbp.com.pl). International and domestic tickets. Open M-F 9am-6pm, Sa 10am-3pm. AmEx/MC/V. **Almatur,** ul. Długi Targ 11, 2nd fl. (☎301 29 31; www.alma-tur.gda.pl), in Główne Miasto. Sells **ISIC** cards (52zł), offers hostel info, and books international air and ferry tickets. Open M-F 10am-5pm, Sa 10am-2pm.

Currency Exchange: The train station has a 24hr. *kantor* with decent rates. **Bank Pekao S.A.,** ul. Garncarska 31 (☎801 365 365) cashes traveler's checks for 1% commission and provides MC/V cash advances for no commission. Open M-F 9am-5pm and first and last Sa of every month 10am-2pm.

24hr. Pharmacy: Apteka Plus, at the train station (☎763 10 74). Ring the bell at night.

Internet Access: Internet Cafe, ul. Karmelicka 1, in the foyer of cinema "Krewetka" across ul. Podwale Grodzkie from the train station. 5zł per hr. Open daily 9am-1am.

Post Office: ul. Długa 23/28 (☎301 88 53). For *Poste Restante* use the back entrance on ul. Pocztowa. Open M-F 8am-8pm, Sa 9am-3pm. Address mail to be held: Firstname SURNAME, *Poste Restante*, Gdańsk 1, **80-801**, POLAND.

🔃 ACCOMMODATIONS

Reserve ahead, especially in summer. Or, get a **private room** through **Grand-Tourist,** ul. Podwale Grodzkie 8, downstairs in the City Forum shopping complex, connected to the train station by an underground passage. (☎301 26 34. Singles 43-60zł; doubles 75-100zł. Open July-Aug. daily 8am-8pm; Sept.-June M-Sa 10am-6pm.)

Dizzy Daisy Hostels, ul. Gnilna 3 (☎301 39 19; www.hostel.pl). If they don't intercept you at the train station, take the pedestrian tunnel underneath ul. Podwale Grodzkie. Take the last staircase on the left exiting the tunnel and walk beside the Holiday Inn until you see a passage on your right that will lead to ul. Rajska. Cross ul. Rajska to ul. Gnilna. Take a left onto ul. Łagiewniki and another left on ul. Wałowa. The entrance to the hostel is off the courtyard of ul. Wałowa 21. Prices are negotiable. All rooms have shared bath. Checkout 11am. No curfew. Open July-Aug. Dorms 50zł; singles 100zł; doubles 100zł; triples 150zł. 10% discount with ISIC or Euro 26 cards. Amex/V/MC. ❷

Dom Aktora, ul. Stragarniarska 55/56 (☎301 61 93; fax 301 59 01). Combines European luxury and a home-style feel just a few steps from Długi Targ. Breakfast included. Singles 200zł; doubles 250zł; apartments 300-400zł. ❺

Dom Studencki Angielski, ul. Chlebnicka 13/16 (☎301 28 16), 1 block off Długi Targ. Amazing location and unbeatable prices, but don't expect luxury. Sleeping bags required. Curfew midnight. Open July-Aug., but closed first week of Aug. Dorms 30zł, students 27zł. ❶

Schronisko Młodzieżowe (HI), ul. Grunwaldzka 244 (☎/fax 341 33 06). From the train station, take tram #6 or 12 north (to the left facing away from the station) and get off 14 stops later at Abrahama (unmarked); you'll see several tram garages on the left (20-25min.). Continue in the direction of the tram and turn right on ul. Abrahama. Walk several blocks, then turn right again on Grunwaldzka; the hostel entrance is by the track. Built only 5 years ago, it has immaculate rooms and bathrooms. The only down side is the remote location. Lockout 10am-5pm. Reception 24hr. Curfew midnight. 2-bed dorms 30zł, students 36zł per person, with bath 44/50zł per person; 4-bed dorms 20/24zł per person; apartments 90zł. ❶

◨ FOOD

▨**La BoMba ❶,** ul. Rybackie Pobrzeże 5/7, is a tiny creperie with a creative menu. (Crepes 4.50-15zł. Open June-Aug. daily 10am-10pm; Sept.-May 11am-9pm.) Try the *szarlotka* (apple pie; 5zł) at **Cafe Kamienica ❷,** ul. Mariacka 37/39, in the shadow of St. Mary's Church. (Tea 4zł. Coffee 5zł. Entrees 12-19zł. Open June-Sept. 9am-midnight; Oct.-May 10am-10pm.) Find delicious peirogies (10-20zł) stuffed with everything from soy to caviar at **Pierogarnia u Dzika ❷,** ul. Piwna 59/60. (Open daily 10am-10pm.) **Bar Pod Ryba ❶,** Długi Targ 35/38/1, has huge stuffed baked potatoes as well as good fish and chips. (Entrees 6-15zł. Open July-Aug. daily 11am-10pm; Sept.-June 11am-7pm.) For fresh produce, try **Hala Targowa** on ul. Pańska, just off Podwale Staromiejskie. (Open M-F 9am-6pm, first and last Sa of the month 9am-3pm.)

◉ SIGHTS

DŁUGI TARG. The heart of **Główne Miasto** (Main Town) is the handsome square Długi Targ (Long Market), where the 16th-century facade of **Arthur's Court** (Dwór Artusa) faces out onto **Neptune Fountain** (Fontanna Neptuna). The court features a magnificent Renaissance interior and spiraling carved-wood staircase. Next to the fountain, where ul. Długa and Długi Targ meet, is the 14th-century **Town Hall** (*Ratusz*), which houses a branch of the **Gdańsk History Museum** (Muzeum Historii Gdańska) and its amazing collection of amber. *(Court and museum open June-Sept. Su 11am-6pm, M 10am-3pm, Tu-Sa 10am-6pm; Oct.-May Su 11am-4pm, Tu-Sa 10am-4pm. Each 6zł, students 3zł. W free.)* A block toward the train station is the **Church of the Blessed Virgin Mary** (Kościół Najświętszej Marii Panny), which has an intricate 15th-century astronomical clock. Climb the 405 steps to the steeple for a fantastic vista. *(Open June-Aug. M-Sa 9am-5:30pm, Su 1-5:30pm; off-season hours vary. 3zł, students 1.50zł.)*

ELSEWHERE IN GŁÓWNE MIASTO. The **National Museum** (Muzeum Narodowe Gdańsku) has a large collection of 16th- to 20th-century art and furniture. *(Signs lead from opposite the Town Hall down Lawnicza and Żabi Kruk, under Podwale Przedmiejskie, and right on Toruńska. Open June to mid-Sept. Tu-F 9am-4pm, Sa-Su 10am-5pm; mid-Sept. to May Su and Tu-Sa 9am-4pm. 8zł, students 4zł.)* The **Memorial to the Defenders of the Post Office Square** (Obroń ców Poczty) honors the postal workers who bravely defended themselves on September 1, 1939, at the start of WWII. *(From Podwale Staromiejskie, take Olejarna and turn right at the sign for Urzad Poctowy Gdańsk 1. Open M and W-F 10am-4pm, Sa-Su 10:30am-2pm. 3zł, students 2zł.)* Cobblestone ul. Mariacka, with Gdańsk's famous stone porch steps and gaping dragon's-head gutter-spouts, leads to riverside ul. Długie Pobrzeże. The huge **Gothic Harbor Crane** (Żuraw), part of **Central Maritime Museum** (Centralne Muzeum Morskie), is to the left. The other two branches lie across the river: One on land, the other is on board the ship *Sol dek. (All branches open June-Aug. daily 10am-6pm; Sept.-May Su and Tu-Sa 9:30am-4pm. Museums and ferry 12zł, students 7zł.)* The flags of Lech Wałęsa's trade union *Solidarność* (Solidarity) fly high once again at the **Gdańsk Shipyard** (Stocznia Gdańska) and at the **Solidarity Monument,** on pl. Solidarności, north of the city center at the end of ul. Wały Piastowskie.

WESTERPLATTE. When Germany attacked Poland on September 1, 1939, the little island fort guarding Gdańsk's harbor gained the unfortunate distinction of being the first target of WWII. Its defenders held out bravely for a week until lack of food and munitions forced them out. **Guardhouse #1** has been converted into a museum. *(Take bus #106 or 606 south from the train station to the last stop (20-25min. every 25-40min.) Open May-Sept. daily 9am-6pm. 2zł, students 1.50zł.)* The path beyond the museum passes the bunker ruins and, farther up, the massive **Memorial to the Defenders of the Coast** (Pomnik Obrońców Wybrzeża). Giant letters below spell out "Nigdy Więcej Wojny" ("No More War"). On March 31, 1945, Westerplatte also became the site of the Germans' last resistance.

⚑ NIGHTLIFE

Długi Targ hums at night as crowds of all ages pack its pubs, clubs, and beer gardens. Local magazines like *City* list events and venues in the Tri-City area. Eclectically decorated █**Latajacy Holender Pub,** ul. Waly Jagiełłońskie 2/4, is toward the end of ul. Dluga in the basement of the LOT building. (Beer 6zł. Coffee 4zł. Open daily noon-midnight.) The new **Blue Cafe,** ul. Chmielna 103/104, just across the first bridge at the end of Długi Targ, has occasional live music and an illuminated dance floor. (Beer 5-12zł. Open daily 11am-late.)

⚑ DAYTRIPS FROM GDAŃSK

MALBORK. Malbork (pop. 40,000) is home to the largest brick **castle** in the world, built by the Teutonic Knights. The castle's treasures include spectacular collections of amber and weapons. The best point from which to see the entire castle is across the river, on the other side of the complex from the train and bus stations. Facing away from the station, walk right on ul. Dworcowa and turn left at the fork. Turn the corner to the roundabout and cross to ul. Kościuszki, then veer right on ul. Piasłowska and follow signs for the castle. (☎ (055) 647 09 76; www.zamek.malbork.com.pl. Castle open May-Sept. Su and Tu-Sa 9am-7pm; Oct.-Apr. 9am-3pm. 22zł, students 13zł. 3hr. tour in Polish included. Courtyards, terraces, and moats open May-Sept. daily 9am-8pm; Oct.-Apr. 9am-4pm. 6zł, students 4zł. English guide books (7zł) are sold at kiosks. Call ahead for an English tour (12zł). Both **trains** (40-60min., 36 per day, 15zł) and **buses** (1hr., 8 per day, 9.20-12.40zł) run from Gdańsk to Malbork.)

SOPOT. Sopot (pop. 50,000) is Poland's premier seaside spa town. The most popular golden sands lie at the end of **ulica Bohaterów Monte Cassino,** which is lined with cafes, pubs, and discos. (Beach open M-F 2.50zł, Sa-Su 3.30zł.) The SKM **commuter rail** connects Sopot to Gdańsk (20min.; every 10min.-60min.; 2.80zł, students 1.40zł). Ul. Dworcowa begins at the train station and leads to the pedestrian ul. Bohaterów Monte Cassino, which runs along the sea to the 512m pier (*molo*). **Ferries** (☎ 551 12 93) go from the end of the pier to: Gdańsk (1hr.; daily; round-trip 46zł, students 32zł); Gdynia (35min., 4 per day, 45/34zł); and Westerplatte (35min.;

2 per day, 34/22zł). The IT **tourist office,** ul. Dworcowa 4, by the train station, arranges rooms. (☎(058) 550 37 83. Accommodations bureau open June-Sept. 15 daily 10am-5pm; Sept. 16-May M-F 10am-3pm. Singles 39-46zł; doubles 62-78zł; triples 90zł.)

GDYNIA. Prosperous Gdynia is Poland's major port. The highlight of the massive pier off Skwer Kościuzki is the destroyer **Błyskawica** (Lightning), where sailors lead tours. (Open Su and Tu-Sa 10am-12:30pm and 2-4pm. 4zł, students 2zł.) The 1909 sailboat **Dar Pomorza** (Gift of Pomerania), once known as the "fastest and most beautiful ship of the seas," has taken first honors at the Cutty Sark Tall Ships Contest. (Open June-Aug. daily 10am-6pm; Sept.-May 10am-4pm. 5zł, students 3zł. June-Aug. Sa free.) The gargantuan **Museum of Oceanography and Aquarium** (Muzeum Oceanograficzne i Akwarium Morskie) sits at the end of the pier. (www.mir.gdynia.pl/akw. Open daily 9am-7pm. 8.50zł, students 5zł.) The beach stretches to the right of the pier.

SKM Commuter trains run every 10min. from platform #1 at Gdynia Główna (☎94 36) to Gdańsk (35min.; 4zł, students 2zł) and Sopot (15min.; 2.80/1.40zł). The IT **tourist office,** pl. Konstytuciji 1, in the train station, has free maps and accommodation lists. (☎(058) 628 54 66. Open May-Sept. M-F 8am-6pm, Sa 9am-4pm, Su 9am-3pm; Oct.-Apr. M-F 10am-5pm, Sa 10am-4pm.) Any of the roads running away from the train station on your right will take you toward the waterfront. Gdynia's most intimate pub is ⯀**Cafe Strych,** pl. Kaszubski 76, at the end of ul. Jana z Kolna. (Live piano music Su and Th-F 6:30-10:30pm. Open June-Aug. daily 4pm-1am; Sept.-May Su and Tu-Sa noon-midnight.)

PORTUGAL

In the era of Christopher Columbus, Vasco da Gama, and Magellan, Portugal was one of the world's most powerful nations, ruling a wealthy empire that stretched from Africa to America to Asia. Today, it is often overshadowed by its larger neighbor Spain. But while it shares the beaches, nightlife, and strong architectural heritage of the Iberian Peninsula, Portugal is culturally and geographically unique. It contains some of the most pristine wilderness areas in all of Europe, and some villages in the northeast have not changed in over 800 years. Despite ongoing modernization, Portugal's rich, age-old traditions seem destined to stay—rows of olive trees give way to ancient castles, and Porto's wines are as fine as ever.

FACTS AND FIGURES

Official Name: Portuguese Republic.
Capital: Lisbon.
Major Cities: Coimbra, Porto.
Population: 10,084,000.
Land Area: 91,951 sq. km.
Time Zone: GMT.
Language: Portuguese.
Religion: Roman Catholic (94%).

DISCOVER PORTUGAL

Most tours start in charmingly sophisticated **Porto** (p. 840), home to its namesake dessert wine, and continue on to the thriving university town of **Coimbra** (p. 838). The rich history and constant action of **Lisbon** (p. 824) are not to be missed, nor is a climb to the nearby castles of **Sintra** (p. 831). **Lagos** (p. 835) has a wild nightlife and a spectacular coast that may be impossible to leave, but those who escape are rewarded by the glorious beach **Praia da Rocha** (p. 837).

ESSENTIALS

WHEN TO GO

Summer is high season, but the southern coast draws tourists March through November. In the low season, many hostels cut their prices by 50% or more, and reservations are seldom necessary. But while Lisbon and some of the larger towns (especially Coimbra with its university) burst with vitality year-round, many smaller towns virtually shut down, and sights cut their hours nearly everywhere.

DOCUMENTS AND FORMALITIES

VISAS. Citizens of Australia, Canada, Ireland, New Zealand, the UK and the US can travel without visas for up to 90 days. As of August 2003, citizens of South Africa need a visa in addition to a valid passport for entrance to Portugal.

EMBASSIES. Most foreign embassies are in Lisbon (p. 825). For Portuguese embassies at home, contact: **Australia,** 23 Culgoa Circuit, O'Malley, ACT 2606, mailing address P.O. Box 9092, Deakin, ACT 2600 (☎612 6290 1733); **Canada,** 645 Island Park Dr., Ottawa, ON K1Y OB8 (☎613 729 0883); **South Africa,** 599 Leyds St., Muckleneuk, Pretoria 0002 (☎27 012 341 5522); **UK,** 11 Belgrave Sq., London SW1X 8PP (☎44 20 7235 5331); and **US,** 2125 Kalorama Rd. NW, Washington, D.C. 20008 (☎202 328 8610). **New Zealanders** should refer to the Australian embassy.

TRANSPORTATION

BY PLANE. Most international airlines serve Lisbon; some serve Porto, Faro, and the Madeiras. **TAP Air Portugal** (Lisbon ☎218 43 11 00; US and Canada ☎800 221 7370; UK ☎845 601 09 32; www.tap.pt) is Portugal's national airline, serving all domestic locations and many major international cities. **Portugália** (www.pga.pt) is a smaller Portuguese airline that flies between Faro, Lisbon, Porto, all major Spanish cities, and other Western European destinations.

BY TRAIN. Caminhos de Ferro Portugueses (☎808 208 208; www.cp.pt) is Portugal's national railway, but for long-distance travel outside of the Braga-Porto-Coimbra-Lisbon line, buses are a better option. The exception is around Lisbon, where local trains are fast and efficient. Trains often leave at irregular hours, and posted schedules (*horarios*) aren't always accurate; check station ticket booths upon arrival. Unless you own a Eurail, **round-trip tickets** must be used before 3am the following day. Don't ride without a ticket; if you're caught *sem bilhete* you'll be fined exorbitantly. Though there is a Portugal Flexipass, it is rarely worth buying.

BY BUS. Buses are cheap, frequent, and connect just about every town in Portugal. **Rodoviária** (national info ☎213 54 57 75), the national bus company, has recently been privatized. Each company name corresponds to a particular region of the country, such as Rodoviária Alentejo or Minho e Douro, with notable exceptions such as EVA in the Algarve. Be wary of non-express buses in small regions like Estremadura and Alentejo, which stop every few minutes. Express coach service (*expressos*) between major cities is especially good; inexpensive city buses often run to nearby villages.

BY CAR. Portugal has the highest rate of automobile accidents per capita in Western Europe. The new highway system (IP) is quite good, but off the main arteries, the narrow, twisting roads are difficult to negotiate. Speed limits are ignored, recklessness is common, and lighting and road surfaces are often inadequate. Buses are safer options. Moreover, parking space in cities borders on nonexistent. **Gas** prices are high by North American standards—€0.60-0.90 per liter. Portugal's national automobile association, the **Automóvel Clube de Portugal** (ACP), Shopping Center Amoreiras, Lojas 1122, Lisbon (☎213 71 20), provides breakdown and towing service and first aid.

BY THUMB. Hitchhikers are rare in Portugal. Rides are easiest to come by at gas stations near highways and rest stops. *Let's Go* does not recommend hitchhiking.

TOURIST SERVICES AND MONEY

EMERGENCY	Dial ☎ 112 for police, medical, or fire.

TOURIST OFFICES. The official tourism website is www.portugalinsite.pt. When in Portugal, stop by municipal and provincial tourist offices for maps and advice.

MONEY. On January 1, 2002, the **euro** (€) replaced the **escudo** as the unit of currency in Portugal. For more info, see p. 14. **Taxes** are included in all prices in Portugal and are not redeemable like those in Spain, even for EU citizens. **Tips** are customary only in fancy restaurants or hotels. Some cheaper restaurants include a 10% service charge; if they don't and you'd like to leave a tip, round up and leave the change. Taxi drivers do not expect a tip unless the trip was especially long. **Bargaining** is not customary in shops.

COMMUNICATION

PHONE CODES	**Country code: 351. International dialing prefix: 00.** From outside Portugal, dial int'l dialing prefix (see inside back cover) + 351 + local number.

TELEPHONES. Pay phones are either coin-operated or require a phone card. The basic unit for all calls is €0.10. Telecom phone cards are most common in Lisbon and Porto. Credifone cards are sold at drugstores, post offices, and locations posted on phone booths, and are most useful outside these two big cities. City codes all begin with a 2, and local calls do not require dialing the city code. **Calling cards** probably remain the best method of making international calls. For info on using a **cell phone** in Portugal, see p. 36.

MAIL. Air mail (*via aerea*) can take from one to two weeks (or longer) to reach the US or Canada. It is slightly quicker for destinations in Europe and longer for Australia, New Zealand, and South Africa. **Surface mail** (*superficie*), for packages only, takes up to two months. **Registered** or **blue mail** takes five to eight business days but is roughly three times the price of air mail. **EMS** or **Express Mail** will probably get there in three to four days for more than double the blue mail price.

INTERNET ACCESS. Cybercafes are common in cities and most smaller towns. When in doubt, try the library, where there is often at least one computer with Internet access.

ACCOMMODATIONS AND CAMPING

SYMBOL	❶	❷	❸	❹	❺
ACCOMMODATIONS	under €15	€15-25	€26-35	€36-50	over €50

Movijovem, Av. Duque de Ávila 137, 1069 Lisbon (☎707 20 30 30; www.pousadasjuventude.pt), the Portuguese Hostelling International affiliate, oversees the country's HI hostels. All bookings can be made through them. A bed in a *pousada da juventude* (not to be confused with plush *pousadas*) costs €10-15 per night; slightly less in the low season. To reserve a bed in the high season, obtain an **International Booking Voucher** from Movijovem (or your country's HI affiliate) and send it from home to the desired hostel four to eight weeks in advance. In the low season (Oct.-Apr.), double-check to see if the hostel is open. **Hotels** tend to be pricey. When business is weak, try bargaining down in advance. **Quartos** are rooms in private residences, similar to Spain's *casas particulares*. These rooms may be the

PORTUGAL

only option in smaller towns or the cheapest one in bigger cities; tourist offices can usually help you. There are over 150 official **campgrounds** (*parques de campismo*) with an array of amenities. Police are strict about illegal camping—especially near official campgrounds. Tourist offices stock the free *Portugal: Camping and Caravan Sites*, an official campgrounds guide. Or, write the **Federação Portuguesa de Campismo e Caravanismo,** Av. Coronel Eduardo Galhardo 24D, 1199-007 Lisbon (☎218 12 68 90; www.fpcampismo.pt).

FOOD AND DRINK

SYMBOL	❶	❷	❸	❹	❺
FOOD	under €6	€6-10	€11-15	€16-25	over €25

Dishes are seasoned with olive oil, garlic, herbs, and sea salt, but few spices. The fish selection includes *chocos grelhados* (grilled cuttlefish), *linguado grelhado* (grilled sole), and *peixe espada* (swordfish). Portugal's renowned *queijos* (cheeses) are made from the milk of cows, goats, and ewes. For dessert, try *pudim*, or *flan* (caramel custard). The hearty *almoço* (lunch) is eaten between noon and 2pm and *jantar* (dinner) is served between 9pm and midnight. *Meia dose* (half-portions) are often adequate; full portions may satisfy two. The *prato do dia* (special of the day) or *ementa* (menu) of appetizer, bread, entree, and dessert is filling. *Vinho do porto* (port) is a dessert in itself. *Madeira* wines have a unique "cooked" flavor. Coffees include *bica* (black espresso), *galão* (with milk, served in a glass), and *café com leite* (with milk, in a cup).

HOLIDAYS AND FESTIVALS

Holidays: New Year's Day (Jan. 1); Good Friday (Apr. 9); Easter (Apr. 11); Liberation Day (Apr. 25); Labor Day (May 1); Feast of the Assumption (Aug. 15); Republic Day (Oct. 5); All Saints' Day (Nov. 1); Feast of the Immaculate Conception (Dec. 8); Christmas (Dec. 25).

Festivals: All of Portugal celebrates **Carnival** (Mar. 4) and **Holy Week** (Apr. 4-11). Coimbra holds the **Burning of the Ribbons** festival in early May, and Lisbon hosts the **Feira Internacional de Lisboa** in June. Coimbra's **Feira Popular** takes place the 2nd week of July. For more information on Portuguese festivals, see www.portugal.org.

LISBON (LISBOA)   ☎21

Once the center of the world's richest and farthest-reaching empire, Lisbon (pop. 1,971,000) hit its peak at the end of the 15th century when Portuguese navigators pioneered explorations of Asia, Africa, and South America. Aching with *saudade* for its past, the city works to preserve its rich history, continually renovating its monuments and meticulously maintaining its black-and-white mosaic sidewalks, pastel facades, and cobbled medieval alleys. In 1998, Lisbon hosted the World Expo, sparking a citywide face-lift and beginning a movement to reclaim its place as one of Europe's grandest cities.

▐ TRANSPORTATION

Flights: Aeroporto de Lisboa (LIS; ☎218 41 35 00), on the city's northern edge. **Buses** #44 and 45 (15-20min., every 12-15min., €1) and the express **AeroBus** #91 (15min., every 20min., €1) go to Pr. dos Restauradores from outside the terminal. A **taxi** to downtown costs about €6, plus a €1.50 luggage fee.

Trains: Caminhos de Ferro Portuguêses (☎800 20 09 04; www.cp.pt). Four main stations, each serving different destinations. Portuguese trains are usually quite slow; buses are often a better choice.

Estação do Barreiro, across the Rio Tejo, goes south. Station accessible by ferry from the Terreiro do Paço dock off Pr. do Comércio (30min., every 30min., price included in train ticket). Trains to **Évora** (2½hr., 7 per day, €7.50) and **Lagos** (5½hr., 5 per day, €14).

Estação Cais do Sodré (☎213 47 01 81), to the right of Pr. do Comércio when walking from Baixa. M: Cais do Sodré. To **Estoril** and **Cascais** (30min., every 20min., €1).

Estação Rossio (☎213 46 50 22), serves points west. M: Rossio or Restauradores. To **Sintra** (45min., every 15-30min., €1.30) via **Queluz** (€0.80).

Estação Santa Apolónia (☎218 88 40 25), on Av. Infante Dom Henrique, east of the Alfama on the Rio Tejo, runs the international, northern, and eastern lines. Take bus #9, 39, 46, or 90 to Pr. dos Restauradores and Estação Rossio. To: **Coimbra** (2½hr., 8 per day, €16); **Madrid** (10hr., 10pm, €52); **Porto** (4½hr., 8 per day, €21).

Buses: Arco do Cego, Av. João Crisóstomo, around the block from M: Saldanha. All "Saldanha" buses (#36, 44, 45) stop in the *praça* (€0.60). Fast **Rede Expressos** buses (☎213 10 31 11; www.rede-expressos.pt) go to many destinations, including: **Coimbra** (2½hr., 16 per day, €9.40); **Évora** (2hr., 13 per day, €9.80); **Lagos** (5hr., 9 per day, €15); **Porto** (4hr., 7 per day, €14), via **Leiria.**

Public Transportation: CARRIS (☎213 61 30 00; www.carris.pt) operates **buses, trams,** and **funiculars** (each €1); *passe turistico* (tourist pass) good for unlimited CARRIS travel. 1-day pass €2.40, 3-day pass €5.70, 4-day pass €10, 7-day pass €15. The **Metro** (☎213 55 84 57; www.metrolisboa.pt) covers downtown and the modern business district. Individual tickets €0.65; book of 10 tickets €5.10. **Trains** run daily 6:30am-1am; some stations close earlier.

Taxis: Rádio Táxis de Lisboa (☎218 11 90 00), **Autocoope** (☎217 93 27 56), and **Teletáxis** (☎218 11 11 00) all line up along Av. da Liberdade and Rossio.

ORIENTATION AND PRACTICAL INFORMATION

The city center is **Baixa,** the old business area, between **Bairro Alto** and **Alfama.** Baixa's grid of mostly pedestrian streets is bordered to the north by Rossio (a.k.a. Praça Dom Pedro IV), adjacent to **Praça dos Restauradores** (at the tourist office and airport bus stop); **Avenida da Liberdade** runs north, uphill from Pr. dos Restauradores. At the Baixa's southern end is the **Praça do Comércio,** on the **Rio Tejo** (River Tagus). Along the river are the Expo '98 grounds, now called the **Parque das Nações** (Park of Nations), and the fast-growing **Alcântara** and **Docas** (docks) districts. **Alfama,** a labyrinth of narrow alleys and stairways beneath the Castelo de São Jorge, is the city's oldest district. Across Baixa from Alfama is **Bairro Alto** and its upscale shopping district, the **Chiado,** which is traversed by R. do Carmo and R. Garrett, near much of the city's nightlife.

TOURIST, FINANCIAL, AND LOCAL SERVICES

Tourist Offices: Palácio da Foz, Pr. dos Restauradores (☎213 46 33 14). M: Restauradores. The mother of all Portuguese tourist offices, this houses info about the entire country. The **Welcome Center,** Pr. do Comércio (☎210 31 28 10), is the office for the city of Lisbon. Both offices open daily 9am-8pm. Office at the **Aeroporto de Lisboa** (☎218 45 06 60) is just outside the baggage claim area. Open daily 8am-2am.

Embassies: Australia, Av. da Liberdade 200-2 (☎213 10 15 00; austemb@oninet.pt); **Canada,** Av. da Liberdade 198-200, 3rd fl. (☎213 16 46 00; lsbon-cs@dfait-maeci.gc.ca); **Ireland,** R. Imprensa à Estrela, 4th fl. (☎213 92 94 40; fax 97 73 63); **New Zealand** (consulate), R. do S. Felix 13-2 (☎213 50 96 90); **South Africa,** Av. Luis Bivar 10 (☎213 19 22 00; safrica@mail.eunet.pt); **UK,** R. São Bernardo 33 (☎213 92 40 00; www.uk-embassy.pt); **US,** Av. das Forças Armadas (☎217 27 33 00; www.american-embassy.pt).

PORTUGAL

American Express: Top Tours, Av. Duque de Loulé 108 (☎213 19 42 90). M: Marquês de Pombal. Exit the Metro stop and walk up Av. da Liberdade toward the Marquês de Pombal statue, then turn right; the office is 2 blocks up on the left side of the street. Handles all AmEx functions. English spoken. Open M-F 9:30am-1pm and 2:30-6:30pm.

Luggage Storage: Estação Rossio and **Estação Santa Apolónia.** Lockers €4.50 for 24hr. Open daily 6:30am-1am.

English Bookstore: Livraria Británica, R. Luís Fernandes 14-16 (☎213 42 84 72), in the Bairro Alto. Open M-F 9:30am-7pm.

Laundromat: Lavatax, R. Francisco Sanches 65A (☎218 12 33 92). Wash, dry, and fold €2 per 5kg. Open M-F 8:30am-1pm and 3-7pm, Sa 8:30am-1pm.

EMERGENCY AND COMMUNICATIONS

Emergency: ☎112. **Ambulance:** ☎219 42 11 11.

Police: R. Capelo 13. ☎213 46 61 41. English spoken.

24hr. Pharmacy: Call directory assistance ☎118. Rotates; check the list posted on the door of any pharmacy.

Medical Services: Hospital Inglês, R. Saraiva de Carvalho 49 (☎213 95 50 67). **Cruz Vermelha Portuguesa,** R. Duarte Galvão 54 (☎217 71 40 00).

Internet Access: Web C@fe, R. Diário de Notícias 126 (☎213 42 11 81). €2 per 15min., €2.50 per 30min., €4 per hr. Open daily 4pm-2am. **Abracadabra,** Pr. Dom Pedro IV 66. €1 per 15min., €3 per hr. Open daily 8am-9:30pm. **Cyber.bica,** R. Duques Bragança 7 (☎213 22 50 04), close to Lgo. Chiado, down R. Raiva de Andrade. €0.80 per 15min., €3 per hr. Open M-Th 11am-midnight, F 11am-2am.

Post Office: Marked by red *Correios* signs. **Main** office (☎213 23 89 71), Pr. dos Restauradores. Open daily 8am-7pm. **Branch** office (☎213 22 09 21) at Pr. do Comércio. Open M-F 8:30am-6:30pm. Credit cards not accepted. **Postal Code:** 1100 for central Lisbon.

■ ACCOMMODATIONS

Several hotels are in the center of town on **Avenida da Liberdade,** while many convenient budget hostels are in **Baixa** along the **Rossio** and on **Rua da Prata, Rua dos Correeiros,** and **Rua do Ouro.** Lodgings near the **Castelo de São Jorge** are quieter and closer to the sights. If central accommodations are full, head east to the hostels along **Avenida Almirante dos Reis.** At night, be careful in Baixa, Bairro Alto, and especially Alfama; many streets are isolated and poorly lit.

Casa de Hóspedes Globo, R. Teixeira 37 (☎/fax 213 46 22 79), across from the Parque São Pedro de Alcântara. From the park entrance, cross the street and go 1 block on Tv. da Cara, then turn right onto R. Teixeira. Popular with young travelers. All rooms newly renovated with phones. Laundry €10 per load. Singles €20, with bath €23; doubles with bath €30; triples with bath €40. ●

Pousada da Juventude de Lisboa (HI), R. Andrade Corvo 46 (☎213 53 26 96). M: Picoas. Exit the Metro station, turn right, and walk 1 block; the hostel is on your left. HI card required. Due to finish renovations in March 2004. June-Sept. dorms €15; doubles with bath €35. Oct.-May dorms €13; doubles €25. MC/V. ❶

Pensão Londres, R. Dom Pedro V 53, 2nd-5th fl. (☎213 46 22 03; www.pensaolondres.com.pt). From the top of the Elevador Glória, turn right onto R. São Pedro de Alcântara and continue past the park; the *pensão* is on the corner of R. da Rosa. All rooms with phone, some with panoramic views of the city. Breakfast included. Singles €29, with bath €48; doubles €40/67; triples €76; quads €86. MC/V. ❸

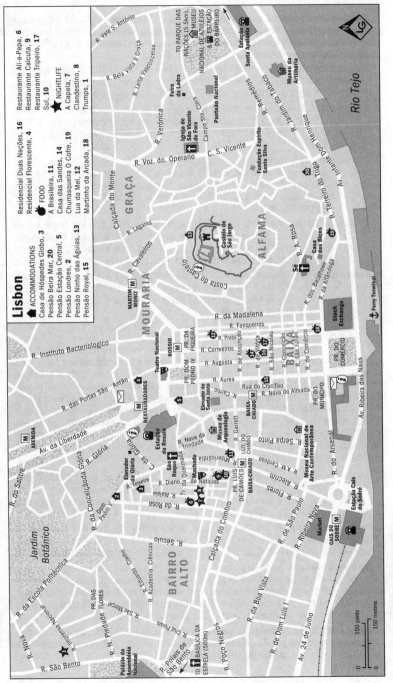

Lisbon

ACCOMMODATIONS
Casa de Hóspedes Globo, **3**
Pensão Beira Mar, **20**
Pensão Estação Central, **5**
Pensão Londres, **2**
Pensão Ninho das Águias, **13**
Pensão Royal, **15**

Residencial Duas Nações, **16**
Residencial Florescente, **4**

FOOD
A Brasileira, **11**
Casa das Sandes, **14**
Churrasqueira O Cofre, **19**
Lua da Mel, **12**
Martinho da Arcada, **18**

Restaurante Ali-a-Papa, **6**
Restaurante Calcuta, **9**
Restaurante Tripeiro, **17**
Sul, **10**

★ **NIGHTLIFE**
A Capela, **7**
Clandestino, **8**
Trumps, **1**

PORTUGAL

Pensão Estação Central, Calçada da Carmo 17, 2nd-3rd fl. (☎213 42 33 08), a block from the central station, across the Lg. Duque Cadaval. M: Rossio. Small, plain rooms in a central location. Rooms without full bath have shower. June-Sept. singles €15, with bath €20; doubles €30/35. Oct.-May €5 less. ❷

Pensão Beira Mar, Lgo. do Terreiro do Trigo 16 (☎218 87 15 28). Probably the cheapest option in Alfama for solo travelers. Rooms with river views cost a bit more. June-Aug. singles €15; doubles €30-40; quads €60. Oct.-May €10/15-20/40. ❶

Pensão Royal, R. do Crucifixo 50, 3rd fl. (☎213 47 90 06). M: Baixa/Chiado. Take a right out of the station on R. do Crucifixo; it's on the left before the intersection with R. São Nicolau. This new *pensão* offers airy rooms with hardwood floors, TV, and bath. May-Oct. dorms €15; singles €20; doubles €30. Nov.-Apr. €5 less. ❶

Residencial Duas Nações, R. da Vitória 41 (☎213 46 07 10), on the corner of R. Augusta, 3 blocks from M: Baixa/Chiado. Hotel-style lodging with large rooms that look out onto the main pedestrian street of Baixa. Breakfast included. May-Sept. singles €20, with bath €35; doubles €25/45; triples with bath €55. Oct.-Apr. €15/30/20/40/45. AmEx/MC/V. ❷

Residencial Florescente, R. Portas de Santo Antão 99 (☎213 42 66 09), 1 block from Pr. dos Restauradores. M: Restauradores. Marble baths and rooms with French doors and small terraces. All rooms with phone and TV. June-Sept. singles €25, with bath €40; doubles €30/45-60; triples €45/60. Oct.-May €5 less. AmEx/MC/V. ❸

Pensão Ninho das Águias, Costa do Castelo 74 (☎218 85 40 70), behind the Castelo. From Pr. da Figueira, take R. da Madalena to Largo Adelino Costa, then head uphill to Costa do Castelo. Canary-filled garden looks out over the old city. Singles €25; doubles €38, with bath €40; triples €50. ❸

🗋 FOOD

Lisbon has some of the best wine and least expensive restaurants of any European capital. Dinner costs about €10 per person; the *prato do dia* (daily special) is often only €5. Head to the **Calçada de Sant'Ana** and **Rua dos Correeiros** to find small, authentic restaurants that cater to locals. The city's culinary specialties include *amêjoas à bulhão pato* (steamed clams), *creme de mariscos* (seafood chowder with tomatoes), and *bacalhau cozido com grão e batatas* (cod with chickpeas and boiled potatoes, doused in olive oil). Snack on surprisingly filling and incredibly cheap Portuguese pastries; *pastelarias* (pastry shops) are everywhere. For groceries, look for any **Pingo Doce** supermarket. (Most open M-Sa 8:30am-9pm.)

Lua da Mel, R. Prata 242, on the corner of R. Santa Justa. If it can be caramelized, this diner-style pastry shop has done it. Pastries €0.60-1. Try the house specialty *Lua da Mel*. They also serve affordable meals (€7-9), and the daily specials are a great value (€5-6). Open M-Sa 7am-midnight. ❶

Restaurante Tripeiro, R. dos Correeiros 70A, serves some of the best Portuguese meals to be found on the lower streets of Baixa. Specializes in fish but also offers large portions of non-seafood dishes. Entrees €6-9. Open M-Sa noon-3pm and 7-10pm. ❷

Martinho da Arcada, Pr. do Comércio 3, just outside the *praça*, to the far right with your back to the river. Founded in 1782, this is the oldest restaurant in Lisbon. Contains photos and poems of the restaurant's most celebrated regular, the renowned Portuguese poet Fernando Pessoa. Adjacent cafe has excellent lunch specials. Entrees €11-15. *Pratos do dia* €4. Open M-Sa 7am-10pm. AmEx/MC/V. ❷

Antiga Confeitaria de Belém, R. de Belém 84-92. Since 1837, this pastry shop has served world-famous *pastéis de Belém;* only 3 people are privy to the secret recipe. Most pastries sold in one day: 52,000. *Pastéis* €0.80. ❶

Churrasqueira O Cofre, R. dos Bacalhoeiros 2C-D, at the foot of the Alfama near Pensão Estrela. A display case at the entrance shows everything available for grilling. Entrees €6-11. Open daily 9am-midnight, meals noon-4pm and 7-11:30pm. AmEx/MC/V. ❷

Sul, R. do Norte 13. Dark-wood paneling, tree-trunk bar stools, and candlelight give this restaurant and wine bar a romantic feel. Food tastes as good as it looks. Converts to a bar at 10pm. International entrees €7.50-14. Open Su and Tu-Sa 7:30pm-midnight. ❸

Restaurante Calcuta, R. do Norte 17, near Lg. Camões. Indian restaurant with wide selection of vegetarian entrees (€5). Meat entrees €6.50-9. Fixed price *menú* €13. Open M-F noon-3pm and 7-11pm, Sa-Su 7-11pm. AmEx/MC/V. ❷

Restaurante Ali-a-Papa, R. da Atalaia 95. Serves generous helpings of traditional Moroccan food in a quiet atmosphere. Vegetarian options. Entrees €7.50-12. Open M-Sa 7-11pm. AmEx/MC/V. ❷

A Brasileira, R. Garrett 120-122. A former romping ground of early 20th century poets and intellectuals, the *esplanade* out front is a hot gathering spot day and night. Mixed drinks €5. Specialty is *bife à brasileira* (€11). Open daily 8am-2am. ❸

Casa das Sandes, R. da Vitória 54, between R. dos Correeiros and R. Augusta. This restaurant's baguette sandwiches are becoming a local tradition. Outdoor terrace seating. Large sandwich €3-5. Open daily 10am-10pm. ❶

🄖 SIGHTS

BAIXA. Start at the heart of Lisbon, the **Rossio** (also known as the **Praça Dom Pedro IV**). Once a cattle market, the site of public executions, a bullfighting arena, and a carnival ground, the *praça* is now the domain of drink-sipping tourists and honk-happy traffic, which whizzes around a statue of Dom Pedro IV. Past the train station, an obelisk and a sculpture of the "Spirit of Independence" in the **Praça dos Restauradores** commemorate Portugal's independence from Spain in 1640. The *praça* is the start of **Avenida da Liberdade,** Lisbon's most imposing, elegant promenade. Modeled after the wide boulevards of 19th-century Paris, this shady, mile-long thoroughfare ends at **Praça do Marquês do Pombal.** On the other side of the Rossio from Pr. dos Restauradores, the **Baixa's** grid of pedestrian streets and wide mosaic sidewalks invites wandering. From the Baixa, all roads lead to **Praça do Comércio,** on the banks of the Rio Tejo, where government ministries are housed.

BAIRRO ALTO. From the Baixa, walk uphill to the *bairro* or view the neighborhood from on high in the **Elevador de Santa Justa,** a 1902 elevator in a Gothic wrought-iron tower. (*Elevator runs M-F 7am-11pm, Sa-Su 9am-11pm.*) **Praça Camões,** which adjoins **Largo Chiado** at the top of R. Garrett, is a good place to rest and orient yourself while sightseeing. To reach R. Garrett, turn left from the Rossio and take R. do Carmo uphill; it's the first street on the right. Half-mad Maria I, desiring a male heir, made fervent religious vows promising God anything if she were granted a son. When a baby boy was finally born, she built the exquisitely ornate 🄑**Basílica da Estrela.** (*On Pr. da Estrela. Take tram #28 from Pr. do Comércio. Open daily 8am-12:30pm and 3-7:30pm. Free.*) For a perfect picnic, walk up R. Misericórdia to the shady **Parque de São Pedro de Alcântara.** The **Museu Nacional de Arte Antiga** hosts a large collection of Portuguese art as well as a survey of European painting dating back as far as the 12th century and ranging from Gothic primitives to 18th-century French masterpieces. (*R. das Janelas Verdes, Jardim 9 Abril. 30min. down Av. Infante Santo from the Elevador de Santa Justa. Buses #40 and 60 stop to the right of the museum exit. Open Su and W-Sa 10am-6pm, Tu 2-6pm. €3, students €1.50. Su before 2pm free.*)

ALFAMA. Lisbon's medieval quarter slopes in tiers from the **Castelo de São Jorge,** facing the Rio Tejo. Between Alfama and Baixa is the **Mouraria** (Moorish quarter), established after the Crusaders expelled the Moors in 1147. Walking is the best way to explore the neighborhood: From Pr. do Comércio, follow R. da Alfândega two blocks, climb up R. da Madalena, turn right after the church on Largo da Madalena, walk down R. de Santo António da Sé, and follow the tram tracks to the richly ornamented **Igreja de Santo António.** *(Open daily 8am-7pm. Mass daily 11am, 5 and 7pm.)* Follow brown and yellow signs to the 5th-century ▧**Castelo de São Jorge,** a Visigoth castle expanded by the Moors that offers a spectacular ocean view. *(Open daily Apr.-Sept. 9am-9pm; Oct.-Mar. 9am-6pm. Free.)*

SÃO SEBASTIÃO. Home to Lisbon's first *El Corte Inglés,* this section of town is home to two excellent museums. The ▧**Museu Calouste Gulbenkian** houses oil tycoon Calouste Gulbenkian's collection, including an extensive array of ancient art as well as more modern European pieces. *(Av. Berna 45. M: São Sebastião. Bus #18, 46, or 56. Open Su and Tu-Sa 10am-6pm. €3. Students free.)* The adjacent **Centro de Arte Moderna** has a sizeable modern art collection and beautiful gardens. *(On R. Dr. Nicolau Bettencourt. Open Su and Tu-Sa 10am-5pm. €3. Students free.)*

BELÉM. A pseudo-suburb of Lisbon, Belém showcases the opulence of the Portuguese empire with well-maintained museums and historical sites. King Dom Manuel I established the **monastery** in 1502 to give thanks for Vasco da Gama's successful voyage to India. *(Take tram #15 from Pr. do Comércio (15min.), bus #28 or 43 from Pr. Figueira (15min.), or the train from Estação Cais do Sodré (10min.). From the train station, cross the tracks and the street, then go left. The Mosteiro dos Jerónimos is to the right, through the public gardens. Open Su and Tu-Sa 10am-5pm. €3, students €1.50. Su 10am-2pm free.)* Take the underpass beneath the highway to the ▧**Torre de Belém** (10min.), with views of Belém, the Rio Tejo, and the Atlantic beyond. Surrounded by ocean, it's accessible only by bridge. *(Open Su and Tu-Sa 10am-6pm. €3, students €1.50.)*

▧ **PARQUE DAS NAÇÕES (PARK OF NATIONS).** The government took a chance on the former Expo '98 grounds, spending millions to convert it into the Parque das Nações. The gamble paid off—the futuristic park is constantly packed. Take the Metro to Oriente and enter through the **Centro Vasco da Gama.** The biggest attraction is the ▧**Oceanário,** the largest oceanarium in Europe. The 145m **Torre Vasco da Gama** offers spectacular views of the city. *(Shopping mall open daily 10am-midnight. Oceanarium open Apr.-Sept. daily 10am-7pm; Oct.-Mar. 10am-6pm. €9, under-13 €5. Torre open daily 10am-8pm. €2.50, under-18 €1.30.)*

ENTERTAINMENT

Agenda Cultural and *Follow Me Lisboa* have information on arts events and bullfights; both are free at kiosks in the Rossio, on R. Portas de Santo Antão, and at the tourist office. Lisbon's trademark is **fado,** an art combining singing and narrative poetry that expresses sorrowful *saudade* (nostalgia and yearning). The Bairro Alto has many *fado* joints off R. da Misericórdia and on streets by the Igreja de São Roque, but the prices alone may turn a knife in your heart. Various bars offer free performances. **Machado,** R. Norte 91, is one of the larger *fado* restaurants and features well-known *cantadeiras.* (Entrees €19-30. Min. purchase €15. Open Su and Tu-Sa 8pm-3am; *fado* starts at 9:15pm. AmEx/MC/V.)

NIGHTLIFE

Bairro Alto is the first place to go for nightlife, where a plethora of small bars and clubs fills the side streets. In particular, **Rua do Norte, Rua do Diário Notícias,** and **Rua Atalaia** have many small clubs packed into three short blocks, making clubhopping as easy as crossing the street. Several gay and lesbian clubs are found between **Praça de Camões** and **Trav. da Queimada,** as well as in the **Rato** area near the edge of Bairro Alto. During the later hours, **Avenida 24 de Julho** and the **Rua das Janelas Verdes** in the **Santos** area have some of the most popular bars and clubs. Newer hot spots include the area along the river across from the **Santa Apolo'nia** train station. There's no reason to arrive before midnight; crowds flow in around 2am and stay until dawn.

📷 **Lux,** Av. Infante D. Henrique A. Take a taxi to the area across from the St. Apolo'nia train station. In a class of its own, Lux continues to be the hottest spot in Lisbon since its opening in 1998. Beer €1.50-2.50. Min. purchase €10. Open Tu-Sa 6pm-6am; arrive after 2am.

📷 **Speakeasy,** Docas de St. Amaro, between the *Santos* and *Alcântara* stops, next to the river. More of a concert with waiters and beer than a bar, Speakeasy is Lisbon's premiere jazz and blues center. Live shows every night, with famous national and international performers once a month. Beer €3. Open M-Sa 8pm-4am.

Salsa Latina, Gare Marítima de Alcântara, across the parking lot from the cluster at Doca de Santo Amaro. Sophisticated crowds come for the live salsa on weekends. Terrace with a view of the river. Min. purchase €10. Open M-Th 8-11pm, F-Sa 8pm-4am.

Trumps, R. Imprensa Nacional 104B, in the Bairro Alto. Lisbon's biggest gay club features several bars in addition to a massive dance floor. Min. purchase €10. Open Su and Tu-Th 11:30pm-4:30am, F-Sa midnight-6:30am.

Clandestino, R. da Barroca 99. Cavernous bar with messages scrawled by former patrons on its rock walls. Beer €1.50. Mixed drinks €3. Open Su and Tu-Sa 10pm-2am.

A Capela, R. Atalaia 45. A spacious bar with gold walls and red velvet cushions. Popular in the late hours. Beer €3. Mixed drinks €5. Open daily 9pm-2am.

▶ DAYTRIPS FROM LISBON

SINTRA. With fairy-tale castles, enchanting gardens, and spectacular mountain vistas, Sintra (pop. 20,000) is a favorite among backpackers. Perched on the mountain overlooking the Old Town, the **Castelo dos Mouros** provides stunning views of the mountains and coast. Follow the blue signs 3km up the mountain or take bus #434 (15min., every 30min., day pass €4), which runs to the top from the tourist office. The awestruck are also usually sunstruck; a bottle of water is recommended. (Open June-Sept. 9am-8pm; Oct.-May 9am-7pm. €3, seniors €1.) A mix of Moorish, Gothic, and Manueline styles, the **Palácio Nacional de Sintra,** in Pr. da República, was once the summer residence of

THE LOCAL STORY

SUCH SWEET SORROW

Lisbon's trademark is fado, *an art combining singing and narrative poetry. The Bairro Alto has several fado joints off R. da Misericórdia and on streets by the Igreja de São Roque. Here, fado singer Sara Reis describes her interpretation of the musical genre for* Let's Go.

Fado *comes from the Latin,* fatum, *which means destiny. It's a feeling that is born with us. Either you understand it or you don't. I do because I was born in the middle of* fadistas. *At home I never heard Rock 'n' Roll, and by the time I reached age 7, I was already singing* fado. *To feel* fado *in its totality is to understand life— its love, death, birth, passion, hatred. It's very complex. In order to really feel* fado, *you have to have reached a certain level of maturity and suffering. There you have it.* Fado *is nostalgia. In my opinion, it is one of the most revolutionary kinds of music. It was created by and for the people...I have already heard young girls no older than 16 sing about life in a way that would move you with emotion. And, on the other hand, I've heard old* fado *singers 50 years old sing from here (points to her head). It all depends on the sensibility and ability of the person.*

Moorish sultans and their harems. (☎219 10 68 40. Open Su-Tu and Th-Sa 10am-5:30pm. Buy tickets by 5pm. €3, seniors €1.50.) Farther uphill is the **Palácio da Pena**, a Bavarian castle decorated with Arabic minarets, Gothic turrets, Manueline windows, and a Renaissance dome. (Open July-Sept. Su and Tu-Sa 10am-6:30pm; Oct.-June Su and Tu-Sa 10am-5pm. €5, seniors and students €3.50.)

Trains (☎219 23 26 05) arrive at Av. Dr. Miguel Bombarda from Lisbon's Estação Rossio (45min., every 15min. 6am-2am, €1.30). **Stagecoach buses** leave from outside the train station for Cascais (#417; 40min., every hr. 7:20am-8:30pm, €2.80) and Estoril (#418; 40min., every hr. 6:50am-midnight, €2.50). Down the street, **Mafrense buses** go to Ericeira (50min., every hr. 7:30am-8:30pm, €2.30). The **tourist office**, Sintra-Vila Pr. da República 23, is in the historic center. From the bus station, turn left on Av. Bombarda, which becomes the winding Volta do Duche. Continue straight into the Pr. da República; the tourist office is to the left. (☎219 23 11 57. Open June-Sept. daily 9am-8pm; Oct.-May 9am-7pm.) To reach the **Pousada da Juventude de Sintra (HI) ❶**, on Sta. Eufémia, take bus #434 from the train station to São Pedro (15min., €1.20), and then hike 2km, or hail a taxi (weekdays €9; weekends €10) in front of the train station. (☎219 24 12 10. Reservations recommended. June 16-Sept. 15 dorms €11 per person; doubles €24, with bath €25. Sept. 16-June 15 €8.50/20/24. Members only. MC/V.)

ESTORIL AND CASCAIS. Glorious beaches draw sun-loving tourists and locals alike to Estoril (pop. 24,000) and neighboring Cascais (pop. 33,000). For the beach-weary, the marvelous (and air-conditioned) **Casino Estoril**, Europe's largest casino, is a welcome relief. (☎214 66 77 00; www.casino-estoril.pt. No swimwear, tennis shoes, jeans, or shorts. Slots and game room 18+. Passport required. Open daily 3pm-3am.)

Trains from Lisbon's Estação do Sodré stop in Cascais via Estoril (30min., every 20min. 5:30am-2:30am, €1.10). Estoril and Cascais are only a 20min. stroll along the coast or Av. Marginal from each other. **Bus #418** to Sintra departs from Av. Marginal, in front of Estoril's train station (35min., every hr. 6:10am-11:40pm, €2.30). From the station, cross Av. Marginal and head to the Estoril **tourist office**, which is to the left of the Casino on Arcadas do Parque, for a free map of both towns. (☎214 66 38 13. Open M-Sa 9am-7pm, Su 10am-6pm.) Ask for help finding a room at the Cascais **tourist office**, Av. Dos Combatantes da Grande Guerra 25. From the Cascais train station, cross the square and take a right onto Av. Valbom. Look for a small sign at Av. Dos Combatantes. (☎214 86 82 04. Open M-Sa 9am-7pm, Su 10am-6pm.)

MAFRA. Sleepy Mafra (pop. 11,300) is home to one of Portugal's most impressive sights and one of Europe's largest historical buildings, the **Palácio Nacional de Mafra.** The massive 2000-room palace, including a cathedral-sized church, a monastery, and a library, took 50,000 workers 30 years to complete. (Open Su-M and W-Sa 10am-5pm; last entrance 4pm. €3, students and seniors €1.50. Under-14 and Su 10am-1:30pm free. Daily 1hr. tours in English 11am and 2:30pm.) The entrance to the recently renovated **tourist office** is inside the palace compound. (☎261 81 71 70. Open M-F 9am-7pm, Sa-Su 9:30am-1pm and 2:30-6pm.) Frequent Mafrense **buses** run from Lisbon's Campo Grande (M: Campo Grande) to Mafra (1-1½hr., every hr., €2.80) and stop in front of the palace.

ERICEIRA. Primarily a fishing village, Ericeira is known for its spectacular beaches and surfable waves. The main beaches, **Praia do Sul** and **Praia do Norte**, crowd quickly; for something more secluded, stroll down the Largo da Feira toward Ribamar until you reach the stunning sand dunes of **Praia da Ribeira d'Ilhas**. Frequent Mafrense **buses** run from Lisbon's Campo Grande (M: Campo Grande) to Ericeira (1½hr., every hr., €4.) and from Mafra to Ericeira (25min., every hr., €1.50). If you stay, ask about rooms at the **tourist office,** R. Eduardo Burnay 46. (☎261 86 31 22. Open July-Sept. daily 9:30am-midnight; Oct.-June Sa 9:30am-10pm, Su-M 9:30am-7pm.)

CENTRAL PORTUGAL

Jagged cliffs and whitewashed fishing villages line the Costa de Prata of Estremadura, with beaches that rival even those in the Algarve. In the fertile region of the Ribatejo (Banks of the Tejo), lush greenery surrounds historic sights.

LEIRIA ☎244

Capital of the surrounding district and an important transport hub, prosperous and industrial Leiria (pop. 43,000) fans out from a fertile valley, 22km from the coast. Chosen to host the Euro 2004 soccer finals, Leiria is preparing itself for the crowds that will flood the city. The city's most notable sight is its **Castelo de Leiria,** a granite fort built by Dom Afonso Henriques atop the crest of a volcanic hill after he snatched the town from the Moors. The terrace opens onto a panoramic view of the town and river. (Castle open Apr.-Sept. M-F 9am-6:30pm, Sa-Su 10am-6:30pm; Oct.-Mar. M-F 9am-5:30pm, Sa-Su 10am-5:30pm. €1.) Nearby **beaches** include **Vieira, Pedrógão,** and **São Pedro de Muel,** all accessible by bus.

Leiria makes a practical base for exploring the nearby region. **Trains** (☎88 20 27) run from the station 3km outside town to Coimbra (2hr., 6 per day, €3.60) and Lisbon (1¾hr., 9 per day, €7.60-8.50). **Buses** (☎81 15 07), just off Pr. Paulo VI, next to the main park and near the tourist office, run to: Batalha (20min., 9 per day, €1.20-2); Coimbra (1hr., 11 per day, €6.50); Lisbon (2hr., 11 per day, €7.80); Porto (3½hr., 10 per day, €11); and Tomar (1½hr., 6 per day, €3.10-6.70). Buses also run between the train station and the **tourist office** (15min., every hr. 7am-7:20pm, €0.80), in the Jardim Luís de Camões. (☎244 84 87 70. Open May-Sept. daily 10am-1pm and 3-7pm; Oct.-Apr. 10am-1pm and 2-6pm.) If you're going to spend the night, try **Pousada da Juventude de Leiria (HI) ❶,** on Largo Cândido dos Reis 9. (☎/fax 83 18 68. Dorms €8.50-11; doubles €21-27.) **Postal Code:** 2400.

TOMAR ☎249

For centuries, the Knights Templar plotted crusades from a celebrated convent-fortress high above the small town of Tomar (pop. 22,000). The ▨**Convento de Cristo** complex, built by the Moors, was the Knights' powerful and mysterious headquarters. The **Claustro dos Felipes** is a Renaissance masterpiece. (☎31 34 81. Complex open June-Sept. daily 9am-6pm; Oct.-May 9am-5pm. €3. Under-14 free.) **Trains** (☎72 07 55) run from Av. Combatentes da Grande Guerra, at the southern edge of town, to: Coimbra (2½hr., 8 per day, €5.60-6.40); Lisbon (2hr., 18 per day, €5.60-6.40); and Porto (4½hr., 7 per day, €8.50-9.50). Rodoviária Tejo **buses** (☎968 94 35 50) leave from Av. Combatentes da Grande Guerra, by the train station, for: Coimbra (2½hr., 7am, €9.20); Leiria (1hr.; M-F 7:15am and 5:45pm, Sa 7am; €3.10); Lisbon (2hr., 4 per day, €6.50); and Porto (4hr., 7am, €12). From the bus or train station, head down Av. General Bernardo Faria toward the city three blocks; turn left and follow Av. Cândido Madureira to the **tourist office.** (☎32 24 27. Open July-Sept. daily 10am-8pm; Oct.-June 10am-6pm.) **Postal Code:** 2300.

BATALHA ☎244

The centerpiece of Batalha is the gigantic ▨**Mosteiro de Santa Maria da Vitória.** Built by Dom João I in 1385, the complex of cloisters and chapels remains one of Portugal's greatest monuments. To get to the monastery, enter through the church.

(Open Apr.-Sept. daily 9am-6pm; Oct.-Mar. 9am-5pm. €3, under-25 €1.50. Under-14 and Su before 2pm free.) **Buses** run from across from the monastery to: Leiria (20min., 10 per day, €1.20-1.50); Lisbon (2hr., 6 per day, €6.60); and Tomar (1½hr.; 8am, noon, and 6pm; €3). The **tourist office,** on Pr. Mouzinho de Albuquerque, stands opposite the monastery. (☎76 51 80. Open May-Sept. daily 10am-1pm and 3-7pm; Oct.-Apr. 10am-1pm and 2-6pm.) **Postal Code:** 2440.

NAZARÉ
☎262

In Nazaré (pop. 10,000), it's hard to tell where authenticity stops and tourism begins. Fishermen in traditional garb go barefoot while the day's catch dries in the hot sun. But if Nazaré is part theater, at least it puts on a good show—and everyone gets front row seats on its glorious **beach.** For an evening excursion, take the **funicular** (3min., every 15min. 7:15am-9:30pm, €0.70), which runs from R. Elevador off Av. da República to the **Sítio,** a clifftop area replete with uneven cobbled streets, weathered buildings, and wonderful views of the town and ocean. Around 6pm, fishing boats return to the **port** beyond the far left end of the beach; head over to watch fishermen at work and eavesdrop as local restaurateurs bid for the most promising catches at the **fish auction** (M-F 6-9:30pm). **Cafes** in Pr. Souza Oliveira teem with people after midnight. Nazaré is on the revolving schedule that brings **bullfights** to a different city in the province each summer weekend. (Usually Sa 10pm; tickets from €27.)

Nazaré is only accessible by **bus** (☎800 20 03 70). Buses run to: Coimbra (2hr., 5 per day 6:25am-7:25pm, €8.80); Lisbon (2hr., 8 per day 6:50am-8pm, €7.30); Porto (3½hr., 7 per day 6:25am-7:25pm, €9); and Tomar (1½hr. 3 per day 7am-5:10pm, €5). The **tourist office** is beachside on Av. da República. (☎56 11 94. Open July-Aug. daily 10am-10pm; Sept. 10am-8pm; Oct.-Mar. 9:30am-1pm and 2:30-6pm; Apr.-June 10am-1pm and 3-7pm.) Try Pr. Dr. Manuel de Arriaga and Pr. Sousa Oliveira for the best deals on accommodations. **Vila Turística Conde Fidalgo ❸,** Av. da Independência Nacional 21-A, is three blocks uphill from Pr. Sousa Oliveira. (☎/fax 55 23 61. July singles €30; doubles €35; Aug. €40/45. Sept.-June singles €15-20; doubles €25-30.) For **camping,** head to **Vale Paraíso ❶,** on Estrada Nacional 242, 2.5km out of town; they also rent bungalows and apartments. Take the bus (10min., 12 per day 7am-7pm) to Alcobaça or Leiria. (☎56 18 00. June-Sept. €4 per person, €3-5 per tent, €3 per car. Oct.-May €3/2.50-3.70/2.50.) Supermarkets line **Rua Sub-Vila,** parallel to Av. da República. **Postal Code:** 2450.

ÉVORA
☎266

Named a UNESCO World Heritage site, Évora (pop. 44,000) is justly known as the "Museum City." Moorish arches line the streets of this picture-perfect town, which boasts a Roman temple, an imposing cathedral, and a 16th-century university.

⌨🎫 TRANSPORTATION AND PRACTICAL INFORMATION. Trains (☎266 70 21 25) run from Av. dos Combatentes de Grande Guerra to Lisbon (2½hr., 5 per day, €8.10) and Porto (6½hr., 3 per day, €14). **Buses** (☎266 76 94 10) go from Av. Sebastião to Lisbon (3hr., every 1-1½hr., €8.80) and Faro (4½hr., 4 per day, €12). The **tourist office** is at Pr. Giraldo 65. (☎266 70 26 71. Open Apr.-Sept. M-F 9am-7pm, Sa-Su 9am-5:30pm; Oct.-Mar. daily 9am-6pm.) Free **Internet** access is available at **Instituto Português da Juventude,** R. da República 105. (Open M-F 9am-11pm.) **Postal Code:** 7000.

🏠🍴 ACCOMMODATIONS AND FOOD. *Pensões* cluster around **Praça do Giraldo.** Take a right out of the tourist office, and then the first right onto R. Bernardo Mato to get to the warm **Casa Palma ❷,** R. Bernardo Mato 29A, which has quality rooms at competitive prices. (☎266 70 35 60. Singles €15, with bath €25; doubles €25/30.) Or, cross Pr. Giraldo and take a right on R. da República, then turn left on R. Miguel Bombarda to reach **Pousada da Juventude (HI) ❶**, R. Miguel Bombarda 40, which has a terrace with a view of the city. (☎266 74 48 48; fax 266 74 48 43. June 16-Sept. 15 dorms €13; doubles with bath €35. Sept. 16-June 15 €10/28.) Many budget restaurants are near Pr. Giraldo, particularly along **Rua Mercadores.** The cozy **Restaurante Burgo Velho ❷**, R. de Burgos 10, serves large portions of local dishes. (Entrees €5-9. Open M-Sa noon-3pm and 7-10pm.) From Pr. Giraldo, walk up R. 5 de Outubro and take a right onto R. Diogo Cão to reach the only real Italian restaurant in Évora, **Pane & Vino ❷**, Páteo do Salema. (Entrees €5-8. Open Su and Tu-Sa noon-3pm and 6:30-11pm.)

◨ ◨ SIGHTS AND ENTERTAINMENT. Attached to the pleasant **Igreja Real de São Francisco,** the bizarre █**Capela dos Ossos** (Chapel of Bones) was built by three Franciscan monks using the bones of 5000 people. From Pr. Giraldo, follow R. República; the church is on the right and the chapel is around back to the right of the main entrance. (Open M-Sa 9am-1pm and 2:30-6pm, Su 10am-1pm. €1.) According to legend, the second-century **Templo Romano,** on Largo Conde do Vila Flor, was built for the goddess Diana. Facing the temple is the **Igreja de São João Evangelista;** its interior is covered with dazzling tiles. (Open Su and Tu-Sa 10am-12:30pm and 2-6pm. €2.50.) From Pr. Giraldo, head up R. 5 de Outubro to the colossal 12th-century **cathedral;** the 12 apostles on the doorway are masterpieces of medieval Portuguese sculpture. Climb the stairs of the cloister for an excellent view of the city. The **Museu de Arte Sacra,** above the nave, has religious artifacts. (Cathedral open daily 9am-12:30pm and 2-5pm. Cloisters open daily 9am-noon and 2-4:30pm. Museum open Su and Tu-Sa 9am-noon and 2-4:30pm. Cathedral free. Cloisters and museum €2.50.) A country fair accompanies the **Feira de São João** festival the last week of June. After sunset, head to █**Jonas,** R. Serpa Pinto 115, to discover a cavernous underground lounge with a mellow bar. (Open M-Sa 10:30am-3am.)

ALGARVE

Nearly 3000 hours of sunshine per year have transformed the Algarve, a desert on the sea, into a popular vacation spot. In July and August, sun-seeking tourists mob the resorts, packing the bars and discos from sunset until way past dawn. In the off season, the resorts become pleasantly de-populated.

LAGOS   ☎282

As the town's countless international expats will attest, Lagos (pop. 17,400) is a black hole: Come for two days and you'll stay for two months. Lagos keeps you soaking in the view from the cliffs, the sun on the beach, and the drinks at the bars.

◨ ◨ TRANSPORTATION AND PRACTICAL INFORMATION

Running the length of the channel, Avenida Descobrimentos is the main road that carries traffic to and from Lagos. From the train station, walk through the pastel pink marina and cross over the channel on the pedestrian suspension bridge, then turn left onto Av. Descobrimentos. From the bus station, walk straight until you hit Av. Descobrimentos, then turn right. After 15m, take another right onto R. Porta de Portugal to reach Praça Gil Eanes, the center of the old town.

PORTUGAL

Trains: ☎282 79 23 61. Across the river (over the pedestrian suspension bridge) from the main part of town. To **Évora** (6hr., 8:20am and 5:15pm, €13) and **Lisbon** (4-4½hr., 5-6 per day, €14).

Buses: The **EVA** bus station (☎282 76 29 44), off Av. Descobrimentos, is across the channel from the train station. To: **Lisbon** (5hr., 12 per day, €15) and **Sagres** (1hr., 17 per day, €2.80).

Tourist Office: R. Vasco de Gama (☎282 76 30 31), a 25min. walk from the bus station. Open July-Aug. M-Sa 10am-8pm; Sept.-June M-F 10am-6pm.

Emergency: ☎112. **Police:** (☎282 76 29 30), R. General Alberto Silva.

Medical Services: Hospital (☎282 77 01 00), R. Castelo dos Governadores.

Internet Access: The Em@il Box (Ciaxa de Correio), R. Cândido dos Reis 112 (☎282 76 89 50). €3.50 per hr. Open M-F 9:30am-8pm, Sa-Su 10am-3pm.

Post Office: R. Portas de Portugal (☎282 77 02 50), between Pr. Gil Eanes and the river. Open M-F 9am-1pm and 3-6pm. **Postal Code:** 8600.

■ ACCOMMODATIONS

In the summertime, *pensões* (and the youth hostel) fill up quickly and cost a bundle. Reserve rooms over a week in advance. Rooms in *casas particulares* run around €15-20 per person in summer.

▨ **Pousada da Juventude de Lagos (HI),** R. Lançarote de Freitas 50 (☎282 76 19 70; www.hostalbooking.com), off R. 25 de Abril. Friendly staff and lodgers congregate in the courtyard. Breakfast included. In summer, book through the central **Movijovem** office (☎213 59 60 00). June 16-Sept. 15 dorms €15; doubles with bath €42. Sept. 16-June 15 €10/28. MC/V. ❶

▨ **Olinda Teresa Maria Quartos,** R. Lançarote de Freitas 37 (☎282 08 23 29; cell 966 32 40 41), across the street from the youth hostel. Offers doubles or dorm rooms with shared kitchen, terrace, and bath. If the owner is not in, check at the youth hostel. June 16-Sept. 15 dorms €15; doubles €24. Sept. 16-June 15 €10/30. ❶

Residencial Rubi Mar, R. Barroca 70 (☎282 76 31 65; fax 282 76 77 49), off Pr. Gil Eanes toward Pr. Infante Dom Henrique. July-Oct. doubles €40, with bath €45; quads €75. Nov.-June €28/33/50. Prices vary, call ahead. ❹

Residencial Lagosmar, R. Dr. Faria da Silva 13 (☎282 76 37 22), up from Pr. Gil Eanes. Friendly 24hr. reception. July-Aug. singles €60; doubles €70; extra bed €22. June and Sept. €35/40/13. Mar.-May and Oct. €30/35/11. Nov.-Feb. €22/25/9. ❺

Residencial Caravela, R. 25 de Abril 8 (☎282 76 33 61), just up the street from Pr. Gil Eanes. Singles €24; doubles €33, with bath €36; triples €50. ❷

Camping Trindade (☎282 76 38 93), just outside of town. Follow Av. Descobrimentos toward Sagres. The way most Europeans experience the Algarve. €3 per person; €3.50 per tent, €4 per car. ❶

Camping Valverde (☎282 78 92 11), 6km outside Lagos and 1.5km west of Praia da Luz. Showers, grocery, and pool. €4.80 per person, €4 per tent, and €6 per car. ❶

◖ FOOD

Peruse multilingual menus around **Praça Gil Eanes** and **Rua 25 de Abril.** Hordes of backpackers enjoy €3.50 meals at ▨**Casa Rosa** ❶, Tv. Ferrador 22. (Open daily 6pm-midnight.) For Mediterranean cuisine, head to **Mediterraneo** ❸, R. Senhora da Graça 2. (Entrees €7.50-9. Open Tu-Sa.) **Mullen's** ❷, R. Cândido dos Reis 86, serves Portuguese and international cuisine. Try the spicy *frango grelhado*. (Entrees €7-

10. Open noon-2:30pm, 7:30-10pm and midnight-2am). The morning **market,** on Av. Descobrimentos, 5min. from the town center, is cheap (open Sa). **Supermercado São Toque,** R. Portas de Portugal 61, is opposite the post office. (Open July-Sept. M-F 9am-8pm, Sa 9am-7pm; Oct.-June M-F 9am-7:30pm, Sa 9am-7pm.)

🏖 🏄 BEACHES AND NIGHTLIFE

Flat, smooth sand can be found at **Meia Praia,** across the river from town. Hop on the 30-second ferry near Pr. República (€0.50). For beautiful cliffs with less-crowded beaches and caves, follow Av. Descobrimentos toward Sagres to the **Praia de Pinhão** (20min.). A bit farther, **Praia Dona Ana** features the sculpted cliffs and grottos that grace the majority of Algarve postcards.

The streets of Lagos pick up as soon as the sun dips down, and by midnight the city's walls are shaking. The area between **Praça Gil Eanes** and **Praça Luis de Camões** is filled with cafes. For late-night bars and clubs, try R. Cândido dos Reis, R. do Ferrador, and the intersection of R. 25 de Abril, R. Silva Lopes, and R. Soeiro da Costa. Staggered Happy Hours make drinking easy, even on the tightest of budgets. **⬛Three Monkeys,** R. Lançarote de Freitas, one of the newest bars, quickly becomes packed. (Open daily 1pm-2am. Beer €2-3. Mixed drinks €4.) **Eddie's,** R. 25 de Abril 99, is an easy-going bar popular with backpackers. (Beer €2. Open M-Sa 4pm-2am, Su 8pm-2am.) **Taverna Velha** (The Old Tavern), R. Lançarote de Freitas 34, down the street from Pousada da Juventude, is the only air-conditioned bar in Lagos. (Beer €1.25-2.50. Open M-Sa 4pm-2am, Su 8pm-2am.) **Whyte's Bar,** R. Ferrador 7, has a live DJ and the 9 Deadly Sins shot-drinking contest. (Beer €3. Mixed drinks €2.50-3.50. Open daily July-Sept. 7pm-2am, Oct.-June 8pm-2am.)

⬛ DAYTRIPS FROM LAGOS

SAGRES. Marooned atop a desert plateau at the most southwestern point in Europe, desolate Sagres and its cape were once considered the edge of the world. Near the town lurks the **⬛Fortaleza de Sagres,** the fortress where Prince Henry stroked his beard, decided to map the world, and founded his famous **school of navigation.** (Open May-Sept. daily 10am-8:30pm; Oct.-Apr. 10am-6:30pm. €3, under-25 €1.50.) Six kilometers west lies the dramatic **Cabo de São Vicente,** where the second-most powerful lighthouse in Europe shines over 100km out to sea. To get there on weekdays, take the bus from the bus station on R. Comandante Matos near the tourist office (10min.; 11:15am, 12:30 and 4:15pm; €1). Alternatively, hike 1½hr. past the several fortresses perched atop the cliffs. The most notable **beach** in the area is **Mareta,** at the bottom of the road from the town center. The nearby coves of **Salema** and **Luz** are intimate and picturesque. At night, a young crowd fills lively **Rosa dos Ventos,** famous for its *sangria,* in Pr. República. (Beer €1. Open Su-Tu and Th-Sa 10am-2am.) EVA **buses** (☎282 76 29 44) run from Lagos (1hr., 17 per day, €2.60). The **tourist office,** on R. Comandante Matoso, is up the street from the bus stop. (☎282 62 48 73. Open Tu-Sa 9:30am-1pm and 2-5:30pm.)

PRAIA DA ROCHA. A short jaunt from Lagos, this grand beach is perhaps the very best the Algarve has to offer. With vast expanses of sand, surfable waves, rocky red cliffs, and plenty of secluded coves, Praia da Rocha has a well-deserved reputation and the crowds to match. From Lagos, take a bus to Portimão (40min., 14 per day, €1.80), then switch to the Praia da Rocha bus (10min., every 30min. 7:30am-8:30pm, €1.30). The **tourist office** is at the end of R. Tomás Cabreina. (☎282 41 91 32. Open May-Sept. daily 9:30am-7pm; Oct.-Apr. M-F 9:30am-12:30pm and 2-5:30pm, Sa-Su 9:30am-12:30pm.)

PORTUGAL

TAVIRA ☎ 281

Tavira (pop. 11,000) invites its visitors with whitewashed houses and cobblestone streets. The **Castelo de Tavira,** begun in the Neolithic period and later improved by the Phoenicians, Moors, and Christians, sits next to **Igreja de Santa Maria do Castelo.** (Castle open M-F 8am-5pm and Sa-Su 10am-7pm. Church open daily 9:30am-12:30pm and 2-5pm. Free.) ▓**Moinha da Rocha** is a beautiful hidden waterfall located 5km outside of town at the source of the Rio Gilão. To reach the golden shores of **Ilha da Tavira,** an island 2km away, take the ferry from the end of Estrada das 4 Aguas (round-trip €1.20).

Trains (☎281 32 23 54) leave Tavira for Faro (40min., 15-20 per day, €1.80) and Vila Real de Santo António (30min., 9-13 per day, €1.20). EVA **buses** (☎281 32 25 46) leave from the station upriver from Pr. República for Faro (1hr., 12-13 per day, €2.50). The town is a short 5-10min. walk down Av. Dr. Teixeira de Azevedo from the train station, or you can catch the local **TUT bus** to the town center (10min., every 30min., €0.50). **Postal Code:** 8800.

FARO ☎ 289

The Algarve's capital, largest city, and transportation hub, Faro (pop. 55,000) is untouristed despite its charm. Its **cidade velha,** a medley of museums, handicraft shops, and ornate churches, begins at the **Arco da Vila,** a stone arch. In Largo Carmo is the **Igreja de Nossa Senhora do Carmo** and its **Capela dos Ossos** (Chapel of Bones), a macabre bonanza of bones and skulls "borrowed" from the adjacent cemetery. (Open May-Sept. daily 10am-1pm and 3-6pm; Oct.-Apr. M-F 10am-1pm and 3-5pm, Sa 10am-1pm. Chapel €0.80. Church free.) Faro's **beach** hides on an islet off the coast. Take bus #16 from the bus station or the stop in front of the tourist office (5-10min., every hr., €1).

Trains (☎289 82 64 72) run from Largo Estação to: Évora (5hr., 9am and 5:30pm, €11); Lagos (2hr., 6 per day 8am-9pm, €4.10); and Lisbon (5-6hr., 6 per day 7:20am-11pm, €14). **EVA buses** (☎289 89 97 00) go from Av. República to: Lagos (2hr., 8 per day 7:30am-5:30pm, €4) and Tavira (1hr., 11 per day 7:15am-7:30pm, €2.40). **Renex** (☎289 81 29 80), across the street, provides express long-distance bus service to: Braga (8½hr., 8 per day 5:30am-1:30am, €21); Lisbon (4hr., 11-15 per day 5:30am-1:30am, €15); and Porto (7½hr., 6-13 per day 5:30am-1:30am, €20). From the stations, turn right down Av. República along the harbor, then turn left past the garden to reach the **tourist office,** R. da Misericórdia 8, at the entrance to the old town. (☎289 80 36 04. Open May-Sept. daily 9:30am-7pm; Oct.-Apr. 9:30am-5:30pm.) Travelers sleep easy at **Pousada da Juventude (HI) ❶,** R. Polícia de Segurança Pública, opposite the police station. (☎/fax 289 82 65 21. Dorms €9.50; doubles €23, with bath €27. AmEx/MC/V.) Enjoy coffee and the local marzipan at cafes along **Rua Conselheiro Bívar** and **Praça Dr. Francisco Gomes.**

NORTHERN PORTUGAL

The unspoiled Costa da Prata (Silver Coast), the plush greenery of the interior, and the rugged peaks of the Serra Estrela comprise the Three Beiras region. Beyond trellised vineyards, *azulejo*-lined houses grace charming streets.

COIMBRA ☎ 239

Home to the country's only university from the mid-16th to the early 20th century, vibrant Coimbra (pop. 103,000) continues to be a mecca for backpackers and youth around the world.

☎☑ TRANSPORTATION AND PRACTICAL INFORMATION. Trains (☎808 20 82 08) from other regions stop only at Estação Coimbra-B (Velha), 3km northwest of town, while regional trains stop at both Coimbra-B and Estação Coimbra-A (Nova), two blocks from the lower town center. A train connects the two stations, departing after trains arrive (4min., €0.70). Trains run to Lisbon (3hr., 23 per day, €8.50-9.50) and Porto (2hr., 21 per day, €5.60-9.40). **Buses** (☎239 82 70 81) go from Av. Fernão Magalhães, past Coimbra-A on the university side of the river, to Lisbon (2½hr., 17 per day, €9.40) and Porto (1½hr., 10 per day, €8.10). From the bus station, turn right, follow the avenue to Coimbra-A, then walk to Largo Portagem to reach the **tourist office.** (☎239 85 59 30. Open June-Sept. M-F 9am-7pm, Sa-Su 10am-1pm and 2:30-5:30pm; Oct.-May M-F 9am-6pm, Sa-Su 10am-1pm and 2:30-5:30pm.) Check **email** at **Central Modem,** Escada de Quebra Costas, down the stairs from Lg. da Sé Velha. (€0.60 per 15min. Open M-F 11am-11pm.) **Postal Code: 3000.**

☎☑ ACCOMMODATIONS AND FOOD. With both newly renovated and older rooms, **Residencial Vitória ❷,** R. da Sota 11-19, across from Coimbra-A has prices to suit any budget. (☎239 82 40 49; fax 84 28 97. Reception 24hr. Singles €10-25; doubles €20-40; triples €45. MC/V.) **Residência Lusa Atenas ❸,** Av. Fernão Magalhães 68, between Coimbra-A and the bus station, next to Pensão Avis, has rooms with bath, phone, A/C, and cable TV in a classic aristocratic building. (☎239 82 64 12. Reception 8am-midnight. July-Aug. singles €20-25; doubles €30-40; triples €45-50; quads €50-60. Sept.-Apr. €18-20/25-30/38-40/40-50. May-June €20/30/38/50.) The best cuisine in Coimbra lies off Pr. 8 de Maio around **Rua Direita,** on the side streets between the river and Largo Portagem, and around **Praça República** in the university district. **Supermercado Minipreço,** R. António Granjo 6C, is in the lower town center. (Open M-Sa 8:30am-8pm, Su 9am-1pm and 3-7pm.)

☎☑ SIGHTS AND ENTERTAINMENT. Take in the sights in **Old Town** by climbing from the river up the narrow stone steps to the university. Begin your ascent at the **Arco de Almedina,** a remnant of the Moorish town wall, one block uphill from Largo da Portagem. The looming 12th-century Romanesque **Sé Velha** (Old Cathedral) is at the top. (Open M-Th 10am-noon and 2-7:30pm, F-Su 10am-1pm. Cloister €0.75.) Follow signs to the late 16th-century **Sé Nova** (New Cathedral), built by the Jesuits (open Tu-Sa 9am-noon and 2-6:30pm; free), just a few blocks from the

THE LOCAL LEGEND

FOWL PLAY?

One evening many years ago, a rich landowner hosted a magnificent banquet. The evening turned sour when he discovered that someone had stolen his silver. He accused an innocent guest, who was tried in court and, with a great deal of evidence against him, declared guilty and sentenced to death. The accused man maintained his innocence and pleaded with the town magistrate for one last chance to save himself. Moved by the man's resoluteness, the magistrate agreed. Upon seeing a tray with a roasted rooster on it, the man declared, "If I am innocent, the cock will crow!"

And crow it did. Just before being hanged, the prisoner's life was spared.

The legendary rooster, known as *O Galo de Barcelos,* has become the national symbol of Portugal, representing honesty, integrity, trust, and honor. Today, the Portuguese commemorate the merciful animal with hundreds of rooster statues and statuettes. Vendors sell rooster key chains and trinkets decorated with red and yellow flowers and hearts; likewise, artisans create roosters with original patterns and coloring that are displayed in homes and museums. Though the Portuguese no longer call upon *O Galo* in desperate times, they continue to respect and value the bird who, when faced with an opportunity to speak for justice, certainly was no chicken.

16th-century **University of Coimbra.** The **Porta Férrea** (Iron Gate), off R. São Pedro, opens onto the old university, whose buildings constituted Portugal's royal palace when Coimbra was the kingdom's capital. (Open May-Sept. daily 9am-7:30pm; Oct.-Apr. 9:30am-12:30pm and 2-5:30pm.) The stairs to the right lead to the **Sala dos Capelos,** which houses portraits of Portugal's kings, six of whom were Coimbra-born. (Open daily 9:30am-12:30pm and 2-5:30pm. €2.50.) The **university chapel** and the mind-boggling, entirely gilded 18th-century **Biblioteca Joanina** (University Library) lie past the Baroque clock tower. (Open May-Sept. daily 9am-7:30pm; Oct.-Apr. 9:30am-noon and 2-5:30pm. €2.50. Students free. Ticket to all university sights €4; buy tickets in the main quad.) Cross the bridge in front of Largo Portagem to find the 14th-century **Convento de Santa Clara-a-Velha** and the 17th-century **Convento de Santa Clara-a-Nova.** (Closed indefinitely for renovations and repairs.)

Nightlife in Coimbra gets highest honors. **Bar Quebra Costas,** R. Quebra Costas, blasts jazz and funk. (☎239 821 661. Beer €1-3. Mixed drinks €4-5. Open daily noon-4:00am.) The recently renovated **Pitchclub,** Lgo. da Sé Velha 4-8, one of Coimbra's newest dance spots, pulses with house, Brazilian, African, and pop. (Beer €1. Mixed drinks €2.50. Open June-Sept. 15 M-Sa 11am-4am; Sept. 16-May M-Sa 9pm-4am.) **Via Latina,** R. Almeida Garrett 1, around the corner and uphill from Pr. República, is hot in all senses of the word. (Beer €1.50. Open M-Sa 11pm-7am.) In early May, university graduates burn the narrow ribbons they got as first-years and get wide ones in return during Coimbra's week-long **Queima das Fitas.**

PORTO (OPORTO)   ☎22

Porto (pop. 264,200) is famous for its namesake product—a strong, sugary wine. Developed by English merchants in the early 18th century, the port industry is at the root of the city's successful economy. But there's more to Porto than just port; the country's second-largest city retains traditional charm with granite church towers, orange-tiled houses, and graceful bridges, and also hosts a sophisticated lifestyle that won Porto its title as a Cultural Capital of Europe in 2001.

TRANSPORTATION AND PRACTICAL INFORMATION. Most trains pass through Porto's main station, Estação Campanhã (☎225 36 41 41), on R. da Estação. **Trains** run to: Coimbra (2hr., 17 per day, €5.60); Lisbon (3½-4½hr., 14 per day, €15-21); and Madrid (13-14hr., daily 6:10pm, €60). Estação São Bento (☎222 00 27 22), Pr. Almeida Garrett, located one block off Pr. Liberdade, is the terminus for trains with local and regional routes. Rede Expresso **buses,** R. Alexandre Herculano 366 (☎222 05 24 59), in the Garagem Atlântico, travel to Coimbra (1½hr., 11 per day, €7.50) and Lisbon (4hr., 12 per day, €14). REDM, R. Dr. Alfredo Magalhães 94 (☎222 00 31 52), two blocks from Pr. República, sends buses to Braga (1hr., 9-26 per day, €3.30). Buy tickets for the **intracity buses** and **trams** from small kiosks around the city, or at the **STCP office,** Pr. de Almeida Garrett 27, downhill and across the street from Estação São Bento (pre-purchased single ticket €0.60, day pass €2.10). The **tourist office,** R. Clube dos Fenianos 25, is off Pr. da Liberdade. (☎223 39 34 72. Open July-Sept. daily 9am-7pm; Oct.-June M-F 9am-5:30pm, Sa-Su 9:30am-4:30pm.) Check **email** at **Portweb,** Pr. Gen. Humberto Delgado 291, near the tourist office. (€1.20 per hour. Open M-Sa 10am-2am, Su 3pm-2am.) The **post office** is on Pr. Gen. Humberto Delgado. (☎223 40 02 00. Open M-F 8:30am-9pm, Sa-Su 9am-6pm.) **Postal Code:** 4000.

ACCOMMODATIONS AND FOOD. For good accommodation deals, look west of **Avenida dos Aliados** or on **Rua Fernandes Tomás** and **Rua Formosa,** perpendicular to Av. dos Aliados. Popular with young travelers from around the world, **Pensão Duas Nações ❷,** Pr. Guilherme Gomes Fernandes 59, offers a variety of rooms at low rates. (☎222 08 96 21. Internet €0.50 per 15min. Reserve ahead. Singles €13, with bath €20; doubles €22/25-30; triples €30/35; quads €40/45.) From the tourist office, climb the hill past the Igreja de Trinidade and turn left on the second street to reach **Hospedaria Luar ❷**, R. Alferes Malheiro 133, which offers spacious rooms with private baths. (☎222 08 78 45. Singles €20-25; doubles €25-30.) **Pensão Douro ❶**, R. do Loureiro 54, offers huge rooms close to the river. (☎222 05 32 14. Singles €12, with bath €15-20; doubles €18/20-30.) Take bus #6, 50, 54, or 87 (at night #50 or 54) from Pr. Liberdade to **camp** at **Prelada ❶**, on R. Monte dos Burgos, in Quinta da Prelada, 4km from the town center. (☎228 31 26 16. Reception 8am-11pm. €3 per person, €3-3.50 per tent, €2.60 per car.) Look near the river in the **Ribeira** district on C. Ribeira, R. Reboleira, and R. Cima do Muro for great restaurants. The **Confeitaria Império ❶**, R. de Santa Catarina 149-151, serves excellent pastries and inexpensive lunch specials. (Open M-Sa 7:30am-8:30pm.) Across the street, the **Majestic Café ❷**, R. de Santa Catarina 112, is the oldest, most famous cafe in Porto. (Open M-Sa 9:30am-midnight.)

◙ ⬛ SIGHTS AND ENTERTAINMENT. Your first brush with Porto's rich stock of fine artwork may be the celebrated collection of *azulejos* (tiles) in the **São Bento train station**. Walk past the station and uphill on Av. Afonso Henriques to reach Porto's pride and joy, the 12th- to 13th-century Romanesque **cathedral**. (Open M-Sa 9am-12:30pm and 2:30-6pm, Su 2:30-6pm. Cloister €1.30.) From the station, follow signs downhill on R. Mouzinho da Silveira to R. Ferreira Borges and the ⬛ **Palácio da Bolsa** (Stock Exchange), the epitome of 19th-century elegance. The ornate **Sala Árabe** (Arabian Hall) took 18 years to decorate. (Open Apr.-Oct. daily 9am-7pm; Nov.-Mar. 9am-1pm and 2-6pm. Tours every 30min. €5, students €3.) Next door, the Gothic **Igreja de São Francisco** glitters with an elaborately gilded wooden interior, belying the thousands of human bones stored under the floor. (Open daily 9am-6pm. €3, students €1.50.) Up R. dos Clérigos from Pr. Liberdade rises the **Torre dos Clérigos** (Tower of Clerics), adjacent to the 18th-century **Igreja dos Clérigos**, which is adorned with Baroque carvings. (Tower open Aug. 9:30am-7pm; Sept.-July daily 9:30am-1pm and 2:30-7pm. €1. Church open M-Th 10am-noon and 2-5pm, Sa 10am-noon and 2-8pm, Su 10am-1pm. Free.) From there, head up R. da Restauração, turn right on R. Alberto Gouveia, and go left on R. Dom Manuel II to reach the **Museu Nacional de Soares dos Reis**, R. Dom Manuel II 44. This former royal residence now houses an exhaustive collection of 19th-century Portuguese painting and sculpture. (Open Su and W-Sa 10am-6pm, Tu 2-6pm. €3, students €1.50.) Bus #78 from Av. dos Aliados runs several kilometers out of town to the **Museu de Arte Contemporânea,** which hosts an exhibit of contemporary art and an impressive park with sculpted gardens and fountains. (Open Tu-W, F and Sa 10am-7pm; Th 10am-10pm; Su 10am-8pm. Park closes at 7pm. Museum and park €5. Su before 2pm free.) To get to Porto's rocky and polluted (but popular) **beach,** in the ritzy Foz district, take bus #1 from the São Bento train station.

But we digress—back to the wine. Fine and bounteous port wines are available for tasting at 20-odd **port wine cellars,** usually *gratuito* (free). The cellars are across the river in **Vila Nova da Gaia;** from the Ribeira district, cross the lower level of the large bridge. Most cellars are open daily 10am-6pm. With costumed guides, **Sandeman,** Lgo. Miguel Bombardo 3, is a good place to start (tours €2.50). ⬛ **Taylor's,** R. do Choupelo 250, has a terrace with views of the city and no entrance fee.

BRAGA   ☎253

Braga (pop. 160,000) originally served as the capital of a region founded by Celtic tribes in 300 BC. The city's beautiful gardens, plazas, museums, and markets earned it the nickname "Portuguese Rome." In Portugal's oldest **cathedral,** the treasury showcases the archdiocese's most precious paintings and relics, including a collection of *cofres cranianos* (brain boxes), one of which contains the 6th-century cortex of São Martinho Dume, Braga's first bishop. (Cathedral and treasury open June-Aug. daily 8:30am-6pm; Sept.-May 8:30am-5pm. Cathedral free. Treasury €2.) Braga's most famous landmark, **Igreja do Bom Jesús**, is actually 5km outside of town. To visit Bom Jesús, take the bus labeled "#02 Bom Jesús" from in front of Farmacia Cristal, 571 Av. da Liberdade (€1.10). At the site either take the 285m ride on the antique funicular (8am-8pm; €1), or walk 25-30min. up the granite-paved pathway that leads to a 365-step zig-zagging staircase.

Buses (☎253 61 60 80) leave Central de Camionagem for: Coimbra (3hr., 6-9 per day, €8); Guimarães (1hr., every 30min., €2); Lisbon (5¼hr., 8-9 per day, €12); and Porto (1¾hr., every 45min., €3.80). The **tourist office** is on 1 Av. da Liberdade. (☎253 26 25 50. Open July-Sept. M-F 9am-7pm, Sa-Su 9am-12:30pm and 2-5:30pm; Oct.-June M-F 9am-7pm, Sa 9am-12:30pm and 2-5:30pm.) **Postal Code:** 4700.

▶ DAYTRIP FROM BRAGA: GUIMARÃES. Ask any Portugal native about the city of Guimarães (pop. 60,000), and they will tell you it was the birthplace of the nation. It is home to one of Portugal's most gorgeous palatial estates, the ☒**Paço dos Duques de Bragança** (Ducal Palace), which is modeled after the manor houses of northern Europe. Guimarães is best reached by **bus** from Braga. REDM buses (☎253 51 62 29) run frequently between the cities (40min., €2.20). The **tourist office** is on Alameda de São Dâmaso 83, facing Pr. Toural. (☎253 41 24 50. Open June-Sept. M-Sa 9:30am-7pm; Oct.-May M-Sa 9:30am-6pm.)

VIANA DO CASTELO   ☎258

Situated in the northwestern corner of the country, Viana do Castelo (pop. 20,000) is one of the loveliest coastal cities in all of Portugal. Visited mainly as a beach resort, Viana also has a lively historic district centered around the **Praça da República.** Diagonally across the plaza, granite columns support the flowery facade of the **Igreja da Misericórdia.** Known for its *azulejo* interior, the ☒**Monte de Santa Luzia,** overlooking the city, is crowned by magnificent Celtic ruins and the **Templo de Santa Luzia,** an early 20th-century neo-Byzantine church. The view from the hill is fantastic. For more views of the harbor and ocean, visit the **Castelo de São Tiago da Barra,** built by Felipe I of Spain. Viana do Castelo and the surrounding coast feature excellent beaches. The most convenient are **Praia Norte,** at the end of Av. do Atlántico at the west end of town, and **Praia da Argaçosa,** on Rio Lima.

Trains (☎258 82 13 15) run from the station at the top of Av. Combatentes da Grande Guerra to Porto (2hr., 13-14 per day, €4.10). **Buses** run to: Braga (1½hr., 4-9 per day, €3.20); Lisbon (5½hr., 2-3 per day, €18); and Porto (2hr., 4-9 per day, €3.50-6). The **tourist office**, R. do Hospital Velho, at the corner of Pr. Erva, has a helpful English-speaking staff and offers maps and accommodation listings. (☎258 82 26 20. Open Aug. daily 9am-7pm; May-July and Sept. M-Sa 9am-1pm and 2:30-6pm, Su 9:30am-1pm; Oct.-Apr. M-Sa 9am-12:30pm and 2-5pm.) The ☒**Pousada de Juventude de Viana do Castelo (HI) ❶**, R. de Limia, off of R. da Argaçosa, is right on the marina, off Pr. de Galiza; its balconies have great views. (☎258 80 02 60. Reception 8am-midnight. Checkout 10:30am. Reservations recommended. Mid-June to mid-Sept. dorms €13, doubles with bath €35; mid-Sept. to mid-June €10/28.)

ROMANIA (ROMÂNIA)

Devastated by the lengthy reign of Nicolae Ceauşescu, Romania today suffers from the effects of a sluggish economy. Some Romanians are eager to Westernize while others retreat to the countryside to live as their ancestors have for centuries. The resulting state of flux, combined with a largely-undeserved reputation for poverty and crime, has discouraged many foreigners from visiting. But travelers who dismiss Romania do themselves an injustice—it is a country rich in history, rustic beauty, and hospitality.

FACTS AND FIGURES

Official Name: Romania.
Capital: Bucharest.
Major Cities: Braşov, Bucharest, Cluj-Napoca, Constanţa.
Population: 22,500,000.
Land Area: 230,340 sq. km.

Time Zone: GMT +2.
Languages: Romanian (official), Hungarian, German.
Religions: Romanian Orthodox (70%), Catholic (6%), Protestant (6%).

DISCOVER ROMANIA

Romania is blessed with snowy peaks, a superb stretch of Black Sea coast, and culturally rich cities—all at half the price of similar attractions in Western Europe. The vast and hectic capital, **Bucharest** (p. 847), has good museums, expanses of green parks, myriad historical monuments, and a hip night scene. For a hefty dose of Transylvanian vampire mythology, visit the legendary castle of Count Dracula at **Bran** (p. 854). Nearby **Braşov** (p. 853) provides access to the trails and slopes of the Transylvanian Alps. **Cluj-Napoca** (p. 852), Romania's cultural center and student capital, is the most diverse city in the country. For a holier take on Romania, visit the secluded **Bukovina Monasteries** (p. 855) near Gura Humorului.

ESSENTIALS

WHEN TO GO

As Romania experiences fairly extreme summers and winters, spring and fall are the best times to visit. Winters can be very cold, especially in the mountains, and there is often a lot of precipitation. The coasts are more moderate.

DOCUMENTS AND FORMALITIES

VISAS. Citizens of Australia, New Zealand, and South Africa need visas to enter Romania. Citizens of the EU (including Ireland and the UK) can stay without visas for 90 days. US citizens do not need visas for stays of up to 30 days. Americans staying longer than 30 days and others with visas who wish to stay longer than 90 days can obtain a **visa extension** at police headquarters in large cities or at Bucharest's passport office, Str. Luigi Cazzavillan 11. Apply early to allow the bureaucratic process to run its slow, frustrating course.

EMBASSIES. Foreign embassies in Romania are in Bucharest (p. 847). Romanian embassies abroad include: **Canada,** 655 Rideau St., Ottawa, ON K1N 6A3 (☎613-789-5345; romania@cyberus.ca); **Ireland,** 74 Ailesbury Rd., Ballsbridge,

Dublin 4 (☎01 269 2852; fax 269 2122); **South Africa,** 117 Charles St., Brooklyn, Pretoria; mail to: P.O. Box 11295, Brooklyn, 0181 (☎012 466 941; fax 012 466 947); **UK,** 4 Palace Green, Kensington, London W8 4QD (☎020 7937 9666; fax 020 7937 8069); and **US,** 1607 23rd St. NW, Washington, D.C. 20008 (☎202-332-4848; www.roembus.org).

TRANSPORTATION

BY PLANE. Numerous airlines fly into Bucharest; **TAROM** (Romanian Airlines), which is in the process of updating its aging fleet, flies direct from Bucharest to New York, Chicago, and major European cities (☎21 201 4000; www.tarom.ro). Bucharest's **Otopeni International Airport** (OTP) has improved its ground services but is still far from ideal.

BY TRAIN. Trains, a better option for international travel than buses, head daily to Western Europe via Budapest. **Interrail** is accepted, but **Eurail** is not. **CFR** (Che-Fe-Re) offices in larger towns sell international and domestic tickets up to 24hr. before departure. After that, only train stations sell tickets. The English-language timetable *Mersul Trenurilor* (also available online at www.cfr.ro; L12,000) is very useful. Schedule info is available at ☎221. International trains (often blue) are usually indicated by "i" on timetables. *InterCity* trains ("IC" on timetables) stop only at major cities. *Rapid* trains (green) are the next fastest; *Accelerat* trains (red) have four digits starting with "1" and are slower. There is little difference between first class (*clasa întâi;* cars marked with a "1" on the side; 6 people per compartment) and second class (*clasa dova;* 8 people), except on *personal* trains (black), where first class is markedly better. On an **overnight train,** shell out for first class in a *vagon de dormit* (sleeping carriage). The best mode to exit the country is by direct train from Bucharest to the capital city of a neighboring country.

BY BUS. Buses connect major cities in Romania to Athens, Prague, and various cities in Western Europe. Since plane and train tickets to Romania are often expensive, buses are a good—if slow—option. It is best to take a domestic train to the border and catch an international bus from there. Buying tickets straight from

ROMANIA

the carrier saves you from paying commission. Use the local bus system only if there is no other option; look for signs for the *autogară* (bus station) in each town. **Minibuses** are good for short distances.

BY THUMB. *Let's Go* does not recommend hitchhiking. If you do, hold your palm out as if waving. Know that drivers expect a payment similar to the price of a train ticket for the distance traveled. Never hitchhike at night.

TOURIST SERVICES AND MONEY

EMERGENCY	Police: ☎955. Ambulance: ☎961. Fire: ☎981.

TOURIST OFFICES. Most tourist offices are intended for Romanians traveling abroad, and much of the country has poor resources for foreign travelers. If you want info, the best idea is to walk into the most expensive hotel in town and pretend to be important. **Cluj-Napoca,** however, operates numerous tourist offices.

LEI		
	AUS$1 = L21,564	L100,000 = AUS$4.63
	CDN$1 = L24,011	L100,000 = CDN$4.16
	EUR€1 = L36,446	L100,000 = EUR€2.74
	NZ$1 = L19,310	L100,000 = NZ$5.18
	UK£1 = L52,625	L100,000 = UK£1.90
	US$1 = L33,445	L100,000 = US$2.99
	ZAR1 = L4,571	L100,000 = ZAR21.87

MONEY. The Romanian unit of currency is the *leu,* plural **lei** (abbreviated "L"). Banknotes come in the denominations L10,000, L50,000, L100,000, and L500,000. Pay for everything in *lei* to avoid rip-offs and to save your reliable currency for emergencies and bribes. Private exchange bureaus litter the country, but few take credit cards or traveler's checks. Shop around for good rates. US dollars are preferred, although euros can usually be exchanged as well. **ATMs,** which generally accept MasterCard, and less frequently Visa, exchange *lei* at reasonable rates. It is customary to give inexact change for purchases, generally rounding to the nearest L500; this usually suffices as a tip in restaurants.

COMMUNICATION

PHONE CODES	Country code: 40. International dialing prefix: 00. From outside Romania, dial international dialing prefix (see inside back cover) + 40 + city code + local number.

TELEPHONES AND INTERNET ACCESS. Nearly all public phones are orange and accept **phone cards,** although a few archaic blue phones take L500 coins. Cards (L50,000, L100,000, and L200,000) are available at telephone offices, major Bucharest Metro stops, and some post offices and kiosks. Rates per minute run: L10,000 to neighboring countries, L14,000 to most of Europe, and L18,000 to the US. Orange phones in major cities will operate in English when you press "i." Local calls cost L595 per minute and can be made from any phone; a busy signal may just indicate a connection problem. To make a phone call *prin commandă* (with the help of the operator) at the telephone office, write down the destination, duration, and phone number for your call. Pay up front, and ask for the rate per minute. For general info, call ☎931; for the operator, call ☎930. **Internet cafes** are easy to find in most large cities; rates are around L10,000-20,000 per hour.

MAIL. Request *par avion* for airmail, which takes 2-3 weeks to reach international destinations. Mail can be received general delivery through *Poste Restante;* address mail to be held: Firstname SURNAME, *Poste Restante,* Str. Nicolae Iorga 1, Braşov 2200, ROMANIA.

LANGUAGES. Romanian is a Romance language; those familiar with French, Italian, Spanish, or Portuguese should be able to read signs. German and Hungarian are widely spoken in Transylvania. German and French are second languages for the older generation, English for the younger.

ACCOMMODATIONS AND CAMPING

ROMANIA	❶	❷	❸	❹	❺
ACCOMMODATIONS	under L400,000	L400,000-700,000	L701,000-1,000,000	L1,001,000-2,000,000	over L2,000,000

While some **hotels** charge foreigners 50-100% more than natives, lodging is still relatively cheap (€6-20). Youth hostels are usually nicer than one-star hotels, two-star establishments are decent, and three-star places are good but expensive. **Private accommodations** are generally the best option; be aware that renting "together" means sharing a bed. Rooms run US$5-12 per person in the countryside and at least US$15 in big cities, sometimes including breakfast and other amenities. Visit the room and fix a price before accepting. Many towns allow foreign students to stay in **university dorms** at low prices, but they may be hard to find if you don't speak Romanian. **Campgrounds** are crowded and often have intolerable bathrooms. Relatively cheap **bungalows** are generally full in summer, so reserve in advance.

FOOD AND DRINK

ROMANIA	❶	❷	❸	❹	❺
FOOD	under L70,000	L71,000-110,000	L111,000-150,000	L151,000-200,000	over L200,000

Lunch usually starts with a soup, called *supă* or *ciorbă,* followed by a main dish (typically grilled meat) and dessert. Soups can be very tasty; try *ciorbă de perişoare* (vegetables and ground meatballs) or *supă cu găluşte* (fluffy dumplings). Pork comes in several cuts, of which *muşchi* and *cotlet* are the best quality. For dessert, *clătite* (crepes), *papanaşi* (doughnuts with jam and sour cream), and *tort* (creamy cakes) are all fantastic. Some restaurants charge by weight (usually 100g) rather than by portion. *Garnituri,* the extras that come with a meal, are usually charged separately, even down to that dollop of mustard. As a rule, you will pay for everything the waiter puts in front of you. "Fast food" means precooked and microwaved. Check expiration dates on everything you buy.

SAFETY AND SECURITY

Most public restrooms lack soap, towels, and toilet paper; carry a roll with you. *Farmacies* sometimes have what you need; *antinevralgic,* sometimes called "tylenol," is for headaches, *aspirină* or *piramidon* for colds and the flu, and *saprosan* for diarrhea. There are some American medical clinics in Bucharest with English-speaking doctors; pay in cash.

HOLIDAYS AND FESTIVALS

Holidays: New Year's (Jan. 1-2); Epiphany (Jan. 6); Easter (Apr. 20-21); Labor Day (May 1); National Unity Day (Dec. 1); Christmas (Dec. 25-26).

Festivals: Summer festivals abound in Transylvania. Sibiu's many festivals include the **International Theatre Festival** in early June. Sighişoara holds a huge **medieval festival** in the 2nd week of July, while Braşov hosts the **International Chamber Music Festival.**

BUCHAREST (BUCUREŞTI)   ☎ 021

Bucharest (pop. 2,000,000) was a fabled beauty on the Orient Express, until Communist dictator Nicolae Ceauşescu rose to power and spent 25 years systematically replacing the grand boulevards and Ottoman ruins with wide highways and concrete blocks. Although Bucharest is no longer the beautiful *Micul Paris* (Little Paris) it once was, historic neighborhoods, secluded parks, and a thriving club scene keep the capital lively.

▛ TRANSPORTATION

Flights: Otopeni Airport (OTP; ☎204 10 00), 16km from the city. Bus #783 to Otopeni leaves from Piaţa Unirii with stops throughout the city center. Buy **domestic tickets** at the **TAROM office,** Spl. Independenţei 7 (☎337 04 00). Open M-F 9am-7pm, Sa 9am-1pm.

Trains: Gara de Nord (☎223 08 80) is the main station. Bus route #85 or M1: Gara de Nord. L4000 to enter the station for non-ticket-holders. Buy tickets at least 1hr. before departure for domestic travel, 2hr. for international travel. To: **Brasov** (3-4hr., 12 per day, L160,000); **Budapest** (12-16hr., 5 per day, L2,000,000); **Cluj-Napoca** (8-12hr., 5 per day, L272,000); **Iaşi** (6-7hr., 4 per day, L272,000); **Krakow** (24-30hr., daily, L2,500,000); **Sofia** (12-14hr., 2 per day, L1,300,000). Domestic tickets sold at **CFR,** Str. Domniţa Anastasia 10-14 (☎313 26 43; www.cfr.ro). Inside Gara de Nord, **Wasteels** (☎222 78 44; www.wasteelstravel.ro) books international tickets and gives helpful info in English. Open M-F 8am-6pm, Sa 8am-2pm.

Buses: Filaret, Cuţitul de Argint 2 (☎335 11 40). M2: Tineretului. South of the center. To **Athens,** buy ticket from **Ager Agency** (☎336 67 83). To **Istanbul,** catch a **Toros** (☎223 18 98; daily) or a **Murat** (☎224 92 93; 2 per day) bus from outside Gara de Nord (both L1,250,000; including a shuttle to Filaret). **Double T,** Calea Victoriei 2 (☎313 36 42), a Eurail affiliate, or **Eurolines Touring,** Str. Ankara 6 (☎230 03 70; fax 315 01 66), can get you to Western Europe.

Public Transportation: Buses, trolleys, and **trams** run daily 5:30am-11:30pm. Tickets (L7000) sold at kiosks only; validate on board or face a fine. All **express buses** except #783 take only magnetic cards (L30,000 for two trips). Pick pocketing is a problem during peak hours. The **Metro** offers reliable and less-crowded service to major points. (Open daily 5am-11:30pm. Magnetic cards L16,000 for 2 trips, L50,000 for 10 trips.)

Taxis: The official rate is L6000, plus L4000-5000 per km. Only use taxis that have a company name, a phone number, and a rate-per-km posted in the window. Drivers rarely speak English, so carry directions to your hotel or hostel written in Romanian. Reliable companies include **Meridien** (☎94 44 or 98 88), **ChrisTaxi** (☎94 61 or 94 66), and **Taxi2000** (☎94 94).

▞ ▐ ORIENTATION AND PRACTICAL INFORMATION

Bucharest's main street changes its name from **Strada Lascăr** to **Bulevardul General Magheru** to **Bulevardul Nicolae Bălcescu** to **Bulevardul I.C. Brătianu** as it runs north-south through the city's four main squares: **Piaţa Victoriei, Piaţa Romană, Piaţa Universităţii,** and **Piaţa Unirii.** The **train station,** Gara de Nord, lies along the M1 line. To reach the city center from the station, take the M1 (dir.: Dristor) one stop to Piaţa

Victoriei, then change to the M2 (dir.: Depoul IMGB). Go one stop to get to Piața Romana, two stops for Piața Universității, or three stops for Piața Unirii. The ever helpful *Bucharest In Your Pocket* (L80,000) is available at metro stations, museums, bookstores, and hotels.

Emergency: Police: ☎955. **Ambulance:** ☎961. **Fire:** ☎981.

Tourist Info: Private tourist offices litter the city, but hotels and hostels are usually better sources of info.

Embassies and Consulates: Australia, Bd. Unirii 74, 5th fl. (☎320 98 26). M2: Piața Unirii, then bus #104, 123, or 124 to Lucian Blaga. Open M-Th 9:30am-12:30pm. **Canada,** Str. Nicolae Iorga 36 (☎307 50 63). M2: Piața Romană. Open M-Th 8am-2pm. **Ireland,** Str. V. Lascăr 42-44, 6th fl. (☎210 89 48). M2: Piața Romană. Open M-F 10am-noon. **UK,** Str. Jules Michelet 24 (☎312 03 03). M2: Piața Romană. Open M-Th 8:30am-1pm and 2-5pm, F 8:30am-1:30pm. **US,** Str. Tudor Arghezi 7-9 (☎210 40 42, ext. 403 or 318; after hours 210 01 49). M2: Piața Universității. Citizens of **New Zealand** should contact the UK embassy. Citizens of **South Africa** should contact the South African embassy in Budapest (p. 533).

Currency Exchange: Exchange agencies are everywhere. **Banca Comercială Română,** in Piața Victoriei and Piața Universității (☎315 82 99; www.bcr.com), gives good rates, and exchanges AmEx Traveler's Cheques for 1.5% commission. Open M-F 8:30am-5:30pm, Sa 8:30am-12:30pm. Changing money on the street is almost always a scam.

American Express: Marshall Tourism, Bd. Magheru 43, 1st fl., #1 (☎212 97 87). M2: Piața Romană. Books hotel rooms and flights, but does not cash traveler's checks. Open M-F 9am-5pm.

Luggage Storage: At Gara de Nord. Holds small (L25,000) or large (L50,000) bags in exchange for your passport number. Use it only in a pinch. Open 24hr.

24hr. Pharmacy: Sensiblu pharmacies (☎203 90 09) are everywhere.

Telephones: Phone cards (L80,000 or L135,000) are good for domestic and some international calls. Place collect calls at **Romtelecom,** Calea Victoriei 35 (☎313 36 35). M2: Piața Universității. Open 24hr.

Internet Access: Internet cafes abound. Try **P-C Net Café,** Calea Victoriei 136 (☎315 51 86). M2: Piața Romană. Fax, xerox, printing, and phones for international calls. 13 computer stations. M-F 6am-11pm L40,000 per hr., M-F 11pm-6am and all day Sa-Su L28,000 per hr. Minimum L10,000. Open 24hr.

Post Office: Str. Matei Millo 10 (☎315 90 30). M2: Piața Universității. Open M-F 7:30am-8pm, Sa 7:30am-2pm. *Poste Restante* nearby, next to Hotel Carpați. Address mail to be held: Firstname SURNAME, *Poste Restante,* Str. Matei Millo 10, Bucharest **70700** ROMANIA.

▌ ACCOMMODATIONS

Renting private rooms is not common. You won't go wrong with either of Bucharest's two youth hostels, but avoid "representatives" you meet at Gara de Nord.

▧ **Elvis's Villa,** Str. Avram Iancu 5 (☎312 16 53; www.elvisvilla.ro). M2: Piața Universității. Or, from Gara de Nord, take trolley bus #85 to the Calea Moșilor stop. Continue along Bd. Carol I and turn right at the park onto Str. Sfântul Ștefan. When you reach a playground, turn left on Str. Avram Iancu. New hostel run by a friendly Aussie-Kiwi couple. A/C and comfy mattresses. Laundry facilities, Internet access, and breakfast included. Reservations recommended. €12 per day, €72 per week. ❷

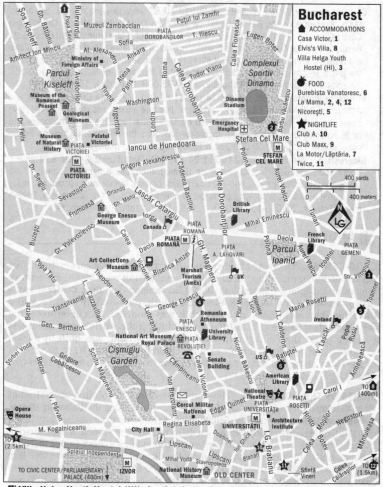

Bucharest

🏠 **ACCOMMODATIONS**
Casa Victor, **1**
Elvis's Villa, **8**
Villa Helga Youth
    Hostel (HI), **3**

🍴 **FOOD**
Burebista Vanatoresc, **6**
La Mama, **2, 4, 12**
Nicoreşti, **5**

⭐ **NIGHTLIFE**
Club A, **10**
Club Maxx, **9**
La Motor/Lăptăria, **7**
Twice, **11**

ROMANIA

🏠 **Villa Helga Youth Hostel (HI),** Str. Salcâmilor 2 (☎610 22 14). M2: Piaţa Romană. Or, take bus #86, 79, or 133 from Gara de Nord to Piaţa Gemeni. Continue 1 block on Bd. Dacia and turn right on Str. Viitorului. Romania's first hostel. Breakfast and laundry included. Kitchen available. Internet access L30,000 per hr. Reservations recommended in summer. US$10 per day, US$60 per week. ❶

Casa Victor, Str. Emanoil Porumbaru 44 (☎222 57 23). M2: Piaţa Aviatorilor. A touch of casual luxury. Transportation to and from the airport or train station included (call ahead). Singles €40-55; doubles €70; apartment €80-90. ❹

🍴 FOOD

Open-air markets selling meat, cheese, flowers, and oodles of fresh fruits and vegetables are all over Bucharest—try the one at **Piaţa Amzei,** next to Piaţa Romană.

▨ **La Mama,** Str. Barbu Văcărescu 3 (☎212 40 86; www.lamama.ro). M1: Ştefan cel Mare. **Branches** at Str. Del Veche 51 (☎320 52 13). M1: Piaţa Muncii. Off of Calea Călăraşilor; and at Str. Episcopiei 9 (☎312 97 97). M2: Piaţa Universităţii. Off of Piaţa Revoluţiei. Motto: "Like at mom's house." Top-notch Romanian food served in a pleasant building with elegant decor. Probably the most acclaimed restaurant in the city, for the price. Try the *sarmale*, a stuffed-cabbage-like Romanian dish. No jeans or shorts. Reservations recommended. Entrees L70,000-95,000. Open daily 10am-2am. ❷

Burebista Vanatoresc, Str. Batistei 14 (☎211 89 29). M2: Piaţa Universităţii. Make a right off of Bd. Nicolae Bălcescu. Taxidermy, live folk music, and bear-skin rugs drive home the rustic theme of this self-styled hunter's restaurant. The fun atmosphere and large portions—bear is the house specialty—make this the place for higher-end Romanian cuisine. Entrees L100,000-230,000. Open daily noon-midnight. ❸

Nicoreşti, Str. Maria Rosetti 40 (☎211 24 80). M2: Piaţa Romană. Head east on Bd. Dacia and continue 2 blocks past Piaţa Gemeni, then take a right on Toamnei. Take your pick of the shady patio, pub-like downstairs, or more formal main entrance to enjoy traditional meals, from suckling pig to bread crumbed brain, at fabulous prices. English menu. Entrees L50,000-100,000. Open M-Sa 11am-11pm, Su 1-11pm. ❶

◉ SIGHTS

CIVIC CENTER. To create his ideal Socialist capital, Ceauşescu destroyed five sq. km of Bucharest's historical center, demolishing over 9000 19th-century houses and displacing more than 40,000 Romanians. The **Civic Center** (Centru Civic) lies at the end of the 6km-long Bd. Unirii, purposefully built 1m wider than the Champs-Elysées, after which it was modeled. Its centerpiece, the ▨**Parliamentary Palace** (Palatul Parlamentului), is the world's second-largest building (after the Pentagon in Washington, D.C.) and was built by 20,000 workers using wood and marble exclusively from Romania. *(M1 or 3: Izvor. Enter off Calea Izvor, on the right side of the building as seen from Bd. Unirii. Open daily 10am-4pm. Tours L100,000, students L50,000.)*

SIGHTS OF THE REVOLUTION. The first shots of the Revolution were fired at **Piaţa Revoluţiei** on December 21, 1989. The square contains the **University Library,** the **National Art Museum,** and the **Senate Building** (formerly Communist Party Headquarters), on whose balcony Ceauşescu delivered his final speech. A white marble triangle with the inscription *"Glorie martirilor nostri"* (Glory to our martyrs) commemorates the rioters who overthrew the dictator. *(M2: Piaţa Universităţii. With Hotel Intercontinental on your left, turn right on Bd. Regina Elisabeta and then take a right on Calea Victoriei.)* **Piaţa Universităţii** houses memorials to victims of both the 1989 revolution and the protests of 1990. Crosses that honor the fallen line the center of Bd. Nicolae Bălcescu—the black cross marks the spot where the first victim died. In June of 1990, the piaţa was again gripped by student riots. Ceauşescu's replacement, Ion Iliescu, bused in over 10,000 miners to put down the protest, killing 21 students. Iliescu is now the president once again, and although this time he was democratically elected, anti-Iliescu graffiti persists on the walls of **Bucharest University** and of the **Architecture Institute.** *(M2: Piaţa Universităţii. Behind the fountain.)*

MUSEUMS. The ▨**Village Museum** (Muzeul Satului), Şos. Kiseleff 28-30, is a unique open-air replica of a rural village. *(M2: Aviatorilor. Open Su and Tu-Sa 9am-8pm. L40,000, students L15,000.)* The **National Art Museum** (Muzeul Naţional de Artă), Calea Victoriei 49-53, in Piaţa Revoluţiei, has works by Monet, van Eyck, El Greco, and Romania's most famous painter, Nicolae Grigorescu. *(M2: Piaţa Universităţii. Open in summer Su and W-Sa 11am-7pm; off-season Su and W-Sa 10am-6pm. For both gal-*

leries L120,000, students L60,000; one gallery L80,000/L40,000.) The **Museum of the Romanian Peasant** (Muzeul Ţăranului Român), Şos. Kiseleff 3, captures Romanian rural life. *(M2 or 3: Piaţa Victoriei. Open Su and Tu-Sa 10am-6pm, last entrance 5pm. L50,000, students L15000.)* The **National History Museum** (Muzeul Naţional de Istorie al României), Calea Victoriei 12, offers a thorough look at Romanian history. *(M2: Piaţa Universităţii. Open in summer Su and W-Sa 10am-6pm; off-season 9am-5pm. L30,000, students L15,000.)*

OTHER SIGHTS. Several of modern Bucharest's most fashionable streets, including **Calea Victoriei, Şoseauna Kiseleff, Bulevardul Aviatorilor,** and **Bulevardul Magheru,** are sights in and of themselves. The side-streets just off Piaţa Victoriei and Piaţa Dorobanţilor brim with villas and houses typical of beautiful 19th-century Bucharest. The only remaining part of Bucharest's **old center** lies west of Bd. Brătianu and south of Bd. Regina Elisabetha, in the vicinity of Str. Lipscani and Str. Gabroveni.

 ## ENTERTAINMENT AND NIGHTLIFE

Bucharest often hosts huge **rock festivals** (Michael Jackson once greeted screaming fans here with "Hello, Budapest!"). **Theater** and **opera** performances are cheap (L10,000-150,000); tickets go on sale at each theater's box office two Saturdays before performances. However, there are no shows June-September.

At night, pack a map and cab fare—streets are poorly lit and public transportation stops at 11:30pm. **La motor/Lăptăria,** Bd. Bălcescu 2, on top of the National Theater, has a lively terrace. (M2: Piaţa Universităţii. Open daily noon-2am.) **Twice,** Str. Sfânta Vineri 4, has two dance floors. (M2: Piaţa Universităţii. Cover for men L100,000; women free. Open daily 9pm-5am.) **Club A,** Str. Blănari 14, easily Bucharest's most famous nightspot, has absurdly cheap drinks. (M2: Piaţa Universităţii. F-Sa Cover for men L50,000; women L20,000. Open daily 8pm-5am.) **Club Maxx,** Str. Independenţei 290, an excellent *discotecă,* attracts a university crowd. (M1: Grozăveşti. Cover L30,000. Students free. Open daily 10pm-late.)

SINAIA ☎ 0244

Sinaia (sih-NAI-uh; pop. 15,000) first made its mark in the late 1880s as an alpine getaway for Romania's royal family. Although the construction of opulent ■**Peleş Castle** was completed in 1873, it

THE LOCAL STORY

CONFESSIONS OF A CABBIE

Alexandru Dan Alistar works for Taxi-Leone in Bucharest. His taxi fare meter was running throughout this interview.

LG: Is it true that there's a taxi mafia in Bucharest?

A: Yes, I believe there is. They charge you 5, 10, or 15 times more when they realize you don't speak Romanian. We call them pirate cabs.

LG: Are they concentrated in any particular area?

A: Outside the terminal in Otopeni and the train station in Gara de Nord. From the airport to the city center, they'll charge 1 or 2 million lei (*shakes his head*).

LG: Are you surprised that I think 95% of the cabs in Bucharest are crooked?

A: No. That's what most people think.

LG: Do you have any advice for tourists?

A: From the airport, cross the bridge to the parking lot and take the elevator to ground level—there are honest cabs there. Call companies that are known to be honest. Travel in cabs with tall radio antennas. 90% of the time that means they work for a company and are honest. But pirate cabs have lots of tricks.

LG: What do you think the future is like for cabs in Bucharest?

A: In my opinion, they are becoming more honest. But there are dead leaves in any tree.

has central heating, electric lights, and an elevator. (Open Su and Th-Sa 9am-5pm, W noon-5pm; last entrance 4:15pm. L90,000; students L40,000.) The equally striking █Pelişor Castle, built in the early 20th century, was decorated by Ferdinand's wife, Queen Maria, in the Art Nouveau style. (Open Su and Th-Sa 9am-5pm, W noon-5pm. L50,000; students L25,000.) The nearby **Bucegi Mountains** are good for hiking in the summer and skiing in the winter. A *telecabina* (cable car) to the mountains leaves from behind Hotel New Montana, Bd. Carol I 24. (Round-trip L90,000-170,000.)

   Trains go to Braşov (1hr., 22 per day, L92,000) and Bucharest (2hr., 19 per day, L175,000). To get to the center of town, climb the second set of stone steps across from the station. When the staircase forks, bear right and follow Bd. Carol I into town. **Vila Camelia ❷,** Str. Spâtar Mihai Cantacuzinu 5, is close to the center. From the train station, head left on Bd. Carol I and then right at the town monument onto Str. Aosta. When Str. Aosta forks, bear right. (☎31 17 54. Singles L200,000-300,000; doubles L300,000-400,000.) **Liliana ❷,** Str. Mânăstirii 7, serves tasty Romanian and international dishes. (Entrees L60,000-90,000. Open daily 8am-11pm.) There is an **open-air market** at Piaţa Unirii. (Open daily 7am-9pm.) Sheep cheese, a traditional local treat, can be found at **Piaţa Centrală** in the market; ask for *brânză de copac* (BRIN-zuh day co-PAHK). **Postal Code:** 2180.

TRANSYLVANIA (TRANSILVANIA)

Though the name evokes images of a dark land filled with black magic and vampires, Transylvania is actually a relatively Westernized region of green hills and mountains that gently descend from the Carpathians to the Hungarian Plain. The vampire legends do, however, take root in the region's architecture: Transylvanian buildings are tilted, jagged, and more sternly Gothic than any others in Europe.

CLUJ-NAPOCA   ☎0264

Cluj-Napoca (pop. 400,000) is Transylvania's student center and unofficial capital. Colorful, relaxed, and relatively Western (with a sizable Hungarian minority), the city is a good starting point for a journey farther into Transylvania or north to Maramureş. The 80m Gothic steeple of the Catholic **Church of St. Michael** (Biserica Sf. Mihail) pierces the skyline in **Piaţa Unirii.** The **Franciscan Church** (Biserica Franciscanilor), founded on a Roman temple site, has a Baroque interior. (Open M-F 8am-5pm, Sa-Su 9am-3pm.) Take Bd. Ferdinand across the river, turn left on Str. Dragalina, and climb the stairs to your right to reach **Cetătuie Hill,** where a dazzling view awaits. To visit the serene **Botanical Garden** (Grădină Botanica), return to Piaţa Unirii; with your back to the statue, take a right on Str. Napoca, then turn left on Str. Coh. Bilaşcu. (Open daily 9am-8pm. L15,000.) Kick back with students enjoying rock, jazz, and techno at **Music Pub,** Str. Horea 5. (Live music F-Sa 9 or 10pm. Open in summer daily 6pm-3am; off-season M-Sa 9am-4am, Su noon-4am.)

   Trains run to: Braşov (5-7hr., 3 per day, L222,000); Bucharest (8-13hr., 5 per day, L272,000); Budapest (6½-7hr., 2 per day, L1,130,000); Sibiu (4hr., daily, L186,000); and Timişoara (6hr., 4 per day, L232,000). **Local buses** and **trams** run 5am-10pm; buy tickets (2 trips L15,000) at **RATUC** kiosks. There are **ATMs** along Bd. Ferdinand. Check email at the **Net Zone Internet Cafe,** Pta. Muzeului 5. (7am-10pm L12,000 per hr.; 10pm-7am L6,000 per hr. Open 24hr.) **Retro Youth Hostel ❶,** Str. Potaissa 13, has handsomely decorated dorm-style rooms next to the university. (☎45 04 52; www.retro.ro. Breakfast €2. Dorms €10.) **Hotel Vladeasa ❷**, Bd. Regele Ferdinand 20, has a good location and clean, simple rooms. (☎19 44 29. Singles L650,000; doubles L900,000.) **▨Roata ❶**, Str. Alexandru Ciura 6a, off Str. Emil Isac, is a traditionally-themed Romanian restaurant. (Entrees L60,000-200,000. Open Su-M 1pm-midnight, Tu-Sa noon-midnight.) **Postal Code: 3400.**

▨ DAYTRIP FROM CLUJ-NAPOCA: SIGHIŞOARA. Vlad Ţepeş, the model for Bram Stoker's *Dracula* (see Bran, p. 854) was born in enchanting Sighişoara (see-ghee-SHWAH-rah; pop. 39,000). Surrounded by mountains and crowning a green hill, its gilded steeples and old clock tower have survived centuries of attacks, fires, and floods. The **Citadel** (Cetate), built by the Saxons in 1191, is now a tiny medieval city-within-a-city. Enter through the **Clock Tower** (Turnul cu Ceas), off Str. O. Goga, passing through the museum and to the top for a great view. (Open in summer M 10am-3:30pm, Tu-F 9am-6:30pm, Sa-Su 9am-3:30pm; off-season Su-M and Sa 10am-3:30pm, Tu-F 9am-3:30pm. L30,000; students L15,300.) The second weekend in July is the huge **medieval festival,** and a **Folk Art Festival** takes place in the third week of August. **Trains** run to Bucharest (5hr., 8 per day, L280,000) and Cluj-Napoca (3½hr., 8 per day, L234,000). To reach the center, turn right on Str. Libertătii and the first left onto Str. Gării; veer left at the Russian cemetery, turn right, cross the footbridge over river Târana Mare, and walk down Str. Morii. **Sighişoara Tour,** Str. Teculescu 1, has maps. From the train station, take a left on Str. 1 Decembrie 1918. (☎(0265) 77 69 77. Open M-F 8am-3pm, Sa-Su 8-11am.) From the station, take a right to reach **▨Nathan's Villa Hostel ❶**, Str. Libertatii 10. (☎(0265) 77 25 46. Bike rental US$5. US$10.)

BRAŞOV
☎0268

Braşov (pop. 353,000) is an ideal starting point for trips into the mountains. A *tele-cabina* (cable car) goes up **Muntele Tâmpa;** to reach it from **Piaţa Sfatului,** walk down Apollonia Hirscher, make a left on Str. Castelui, a right on Suişul Castelui, and head up the steep stairs to the off-white building on the right. (Cable car runs M noon-6pm, Tu-F 9:30am-6pm, Sa-Su 9:30am-7pm. Round-trip L40,000.) Trails on Aleea T. Brediceanu lead to the **Weaver's Bastion** and other medieval ruins. Braşov itself is a picturesque town with peaceful side-streets. Beyond the square along Str. Gh. Bariţiu, Romania's most celebrated Gothic church, the Lutheran **Black Church** (Biserica Neagră), earned its name when it was charred by fire in 1689. (Open M-Sa 10am-5pm. L20,000; students L10,000.) Piaţa Sfatului, Str. Republicii, and **Piaţa Unirii** are nice areas to take a stroll. The box office at Str. Republicii 4 sells tickets for **operas** and for the summer **International Chamber Music Festival.** (☎47 18 89. Open M-F 10am-5pm, Sa 10am-1pm. L50,000-200,000.)

Trains go to: Bucharest (3-4hr., 13 per day, L195,000); Cluj-Napoca (5-6hr., 5 per day, L300,000); Iaşi (9-10hr., daily, L272,000); and Sibiu (4hr., 7 per day, L145,000). Buy tickets at **CFR,** Str. Republicii 53. (☎47 70 18. Open M-F 8am-7pm, Sa 10am-1pm.) To get to town from the station, take bus #4 (dir.: Piaţa Unirii) to Piaţa Sfat-ului (10min.); get off in front of the Black Church. Maps are at kiosks on Str. Republicii. For a **private room** expect to pay €8-10. **Kismet Dao Villa Hostel ❶**, Str. Democraţiei 2b, formerly known as Elvis' Villa Hostel, is plush and new. From Piaţa Unirii, walk up Sra. Bâlea and take the first right onto Str. Democraţiei. (☎51 42 96. Apr.-Dec. dorms €10, doubles €25; Jan.-Mar. dorms €8.) For Romanian and Mexican food with free shots of *pălinkă*, head to **Bella Musica ❶**, Str. G. Bariţu 2. (Entrees L65,000-200,000. Open daily noon-midnight.) **Taverna ❷**, Str. Politehnicii 6, has excellent Romanian, Hungarian, and Italian fare. (Entrees L80,000-250,000. Open daily noon-midnight.) **Postal Code: 2200.**

DAYTRIP FROM BRAŞOV: BRAN. Vlad Ţepeş Dracula, the model for the villain-hero of Bram Stoker's famed novel *Dracula*, once lived in Bran. The exploits of the real Dracula make those of his fictional counterpart pale in comparison. His father (also Vlad) was a member of the Order of the Dragon, a society that defended Catholicism from infidels, hence the name by which he ruled: Vlad Dracul ("Dragon"). As a local governor of the Wallachia region, Vlad Ţepeş protected the Bran pass from the Turks, and he became infamous for impaling his enemies. When the Turks invaded Wallachia in 1462, they were met by some 20,000 of their kinsmen impaled outside Dracula's territory. Horrified, the Turks retreated. While Ţepeş may have been a guest at **Bran Castle,** he did not actually live there—in fact, Stoker himself never even visited Romania. (Castle open Su and Tu-Sa 9am-5pm. L60,000; students L20,000.) From Braşov, take city bus #5 or 9 to Autogară 2 (officially Gară Bartolomeu; 45min., every 30min. 7am-6pm, L18,000), to reach Bran. Get off at the big souvenir market or at the "Cabana Bran Castle—500m" sign. Then take the main road back toward Braşov and take the first right to get to the castle.

SIBIU ☎0269

Sibiu (SEE-bee-oo; pop. 170,000), the ancient capital of Transylvania, is a city of medieval monuments and colorfully ornate houses. The nearby **Făgăraş Mountains** offer some of the best hiking in Romania. Begin by taking the train from Sibiu to Ucea (1½hr., 4 per day, L25,000), where a bus connects to Victoria (25min., 7 per day, L20,000). From there, many itineraries are possible. The range can also be reached after a day's hike from the sleepy town of Avrig (from Sibiu: 1hr., 7 per day, L54,000). **Libraria Friedrich Schiller** in Sibiu sells maps and guides to the mountains in Romanian and in English (L70,000-200,000). Hiking season lasts from July to mid-September. Be prepared for cold temperatures year-round, and know that parts of the range can be very challenging. In case of **emergency,** or for expert help planning your trip, contact **Salvamont,** Nicolae Balcescu 9 (☎21 64 77), located down the alley. Sibiu has many **summer festivals,** including the International Theatre Festival in early June and the Medieval Festival in late August. And **Summer Fest** rages from June 15-September 15 near Piaţa Unirii with free open-air concerts Thursday and Friday nights.

Trains from Sibiu run to: Braşov (3½hr., 7 per day, L145,000); Bucharest (6hr., 4 per day, L222,000); and Cluj-Napoca (4hr., daily, L186,000). Buy tickets at **CFR,** Str. N. Bălcescu 6. (Open M-F 7:30am-7:30pm.) **Buses** go to Bucharest (5hr., 5 per day, L200,000) and Cluj-Napoca (3½hr., 9 per day, L110,000). From the stations, take Str. General Magheru and turn right onto Str. Avram Iancu to reach **Piaţa Mare,** the main square. **Hotel Pensiune Leu ❶,** Str. Moş Ion Roată 6, has spotless rooms. Walk along Str. S. Brukenthall from Piaţa. Mare until it ends and continue down the staircase on the right. At the bottom, follow the road as it makes a left-hand U-turn onto Str. Moş Ion Roată. (☎21 83 92. Dorms L300,000; singles L400,000; doubles L600,000.) Don't be fooled by the no-frills decor of **Kon-Tiki ❶,** Str. Tudor Vladimescu 10; locals love it and so will you. (☎22 03 50. Entrees L24,000-60,000. Open M-F 10am-10pm, Su noon-midnight.) To reach the **outdoor market,** follow the directions to Hotel Pensiune Leu, but walk straight instead of turning onto Str. Moş Ion Roată. (Open dawn-dusk.) **Postal Code:** 2400.

TIMIŞOARA ☎0256

Timişoara (pop. 334,000), Romania's westernmost city, is one of the country's largest and liveliest. The city was the starting place for the 1989 revolution that overthrew the Communist regime; anti-Ceauşescu protestors gathered in **Piaţa Victoriei.** At one end of the square stands the **Metropolitan Cathedral,** designed in Moldavian folk style with a rainbow-tiled roof. (Open daily 6:30am-8pm.) Across the square is the **National Theater** (Teatrul Național) and the **Opera House** (Opera Timișoara); the opera box office is down the street, on Str. Mărășești. (Open Sept.-May daily 10am-1pm and 5-7pm.) Nearby in **Huniade Castle** is the **Banat Museum** (Muzeul Banatului), which traces Timișoara's history. (Open Su and Tu-Sa 10am-4:30pm. L10,000, students L5000.) **Trains** run from Timișoara Nord to: Brașov (9hr., daily, L280,000); Bucharest (8hr., 5 per day, L440,000); Budapest (5hr., 3 per day, L895,000); Cluj-Napoca (7hr., 4 per day, L240,000). **Trams** #1, 8, and 11, and **trolley-buses** #11 and 14 go to the city center (2 trips L14,000). **Libraria Mihai Eminescu,** in Piața Victoriei, sells maps and English books. (Open M-F 9am-7pm, Sa 9am-1pm.) ⬛**Hotel Cina Banatul ❸,** Str. Craiului 4, is clean and centrally located. (☎49 01 30. Singles L900,000; doubles L1,200,000.) There are many good restaurants in and around Piața Victoriei in the center of town. **Postal Code:** 1900.

MOLDAVIA AND BUKOVINA

Eastern Romania, known as Moldavia (Moldova), extends from the Carpathians to the Prut River. Starker than Transylvania but more developed than Maramureș, Moldavia also boasts the distinctive painted monasteries of Bukovina (Bucovina).

IAȘI ☎0232

Iași (YAHSH; pop. 340,000) rose to prominence in the 19th century as the home of the Junimea Society, a literary club whose members filled the city with Neo-classical architecture. Bd. Ștefan cel Mare leads south from the main square, **Piața Unirii,** past the gorgeous 1637 **Trei Ierarchi church,** whose walls display Moldavian and Turkish patterns in raised relief. The boulevard then continues to the massive, neo-Gothic ⬛**Palace of Culture** (Palatul Culturii), which contains historical, ethnographic, polytechnic, and art museums. (Open Su and Tu-Sa 10am-5pm. Each museum L15,000; students L10,000.) North of Piața Unirii, Bd. Copou leads from Piața Eminescu past some of the most beautiful buildings in Iași to **Copou Park.** Inside the park is the **Eminescu Museum,** which exhibits some of the great Romanian poet's documents. (Open Su and Tu-Sa 10am-5pm. L10,000.)

Trains go from Str. Silvestru to: Brașov (6hr., daily, L272,000); Bucharest (7½hr., 6 per day, L372,000); Cluj-Napoca (9hr., 4 per day, L272,000); Constanța (8hr., daily, L272,000); and Timișoara (14hr., 3 per day, L360,000). **CFR,** Piața Unirii 9/11, sells train tickets. (☎14 52 69. Open M-F 8am-8pm.) **Buses** leave from **Iași Vest,** Str. Moara de Foc 15, for Brașov (8hr., daily, L230,000). **Libraria Junimea,** Piața Unirii 4, sells maps. (Open M-F 8:30am-8pm, Sa 9am-4pm, Su 9am-2pm.) **Hotel Continental ❷,** Str. Cuza Vodă 4, has a good location and private baths. Coming from the train station, continue one intersection past Piața Unirii. (☎21 18 46. Singles L550,000; doubles L690,000, with bath L830,000.) ⬛**Bolta Rece ❶,** Str. Rece 10, serves Iași's best traditional dishes. Take Str. Cuza Vodă out of Piața Unirii and turn left on Str. Brătianu; at Bd. Independenței, turn right, take an immediate left onto Str. M. Eminescu, then turn left onto Str. Rece. (Entrees L32,000-75,000. Open daily 8am-midnight.) **Postal Code:** 6600.

BUKOVINA MONASTERIES

Built 500 years ago by Moldavia's ruler, Ștefan cel Mare (Stephen the Great) and his successors, Bukovina's painted monasteries are hidden among green hills and farming villages. The exquisite structures mix Moldavian and Byzantine architecture with Romanian Christian images. Taking an organized tour from Gura Humorului or Suceava is often the best way to see the monasteries. Dress modestly.

ROMANIA

GURA HUMORULUI
☎0230

Within walking distance of the Humor and Voroneț monasteries, small Gura Humorului is an ideal base. For info and **car tours**, visit the ◙**Dispecerat de Cazare**, at the end of Str. Câmpului on Str. Voroneț; from the train station, head left off Str. Ștefan cel Mare. The office also arranges villa rooms. (☎23 88 63. Open Mar.-Nov. 11am-9pm. Tours €30-35 per car.) **Trains** go to: Bucharest (6hr., daily, L272,000); Cluj-Napoca (5hr., 4 per day, L186,000); Iași (3hr., 4 per day, L166,000); and Suceava (1hr., 9 per day, L25,000). To reach the town center from the station, make a right onto Str. Ștefan cel Mare and continue over the bridge. ◙**Pensiunea Casa Ella ❶**, Str. Cetații 7, off Bd. Bucovina, offers soft beds and home-cooked meals. (☎23 29 61. Meals L75,000-150,000. Singles L350,000; doubles L500,000.) The more luxurious **Villa Fabian ❷** is across Str. Voroneț from Dispecerat de Cazare. (☎23 23 87. Singles €15; doubles €25.) **Postal Code:** 5900.

🔃 **DAYTRIPS FROM GURA HUMORULUI: THE HUMOR, MOLDOVIȚA, AND VORONEȚ MONASTERIES.** Bukovina's oldest frescoes are at **Humor,** which is known for a depiction of the life of the Virgin Mary on the south wall. The mural, based on a poem by the patriarch of Constantinople, shows Mary saving Constantinople from a Persian attack in 626. From Gura Humorului, walk right on Ștefan cel Mare from the train or bus station to the center of town. At the fork near a park on the right, take Str. Manasteria Humorului to the left and continue 6km to the monastery. (Open daily 8am-8pm. L40,000; students L20,000. Cameras L60,000.)

The largest monastery, **Moldovița,** has the best-preserved frescoes. Painted in 1537, the frescoes portray the Last Judgment, Jesse's Tree, and a monumental Siege of Constantinople. In the first room is a calendar depicting a saint for each day of the year. (Open daily 7am-9pm. L40,000; students L20,000. Cameras L60,000.) Take a **train** from Gura Humorului to Vama (20min., 9per day, L39,000) and continue to Vatra Moldoviței (35min., 3 per day, L24,000).

The restoration of the 1488 **Voroneț** has been delayed while preservationists attempt to reproduce its distinctive pigment, Voroneț Blue. Its incredible frescoes include a depiction of the Last Judgment on the west wall, painted in five tiers and crossed by a river of fire from hell. Take a **bus** from Gura Humorului (15min., mid-Sept. to mid-June M-F 3 per day, L10,000). Or, walk left from the Gura Humorului train station, turn left again onto Cartierul Voroneț, and continue 5km down the scenic road. (Open daily dawn-dusk. L40,000; students L20,000. Cameras L60,000.)

SUCEAVA
☎0230

The capital of Moldavia under Ștefan cel Mare, Suceava has many noteworthy museums, as well as the grand 1388 **Citadel of the Throne** (Cetatea de Scaun). Climb the ramparts for a spectacular view. Take a taxi (5min., L30,000) from the main square, Piața 22 Decembrie. (Open in summer daily 8am-8pm; off-season 9am-5pm. L10,000; students L5000.) At night, two of the citadel's terraces serve food and drinks. (Entrees L35,000-100,000. Terraces open daily 8am-10:30pm.)

Trains depart for: Brașov (8hr., daily, L272,000); Bucharest (6hr., 7 per day, L372,000); Cluj-Napoca (6hr., 4 per day, L222,000); Gura Humorului (1hr., 10 per day, L58,000); Iași (2hr., 8 per day, L145,000); and Timișoara (14hr., 3 per day, L360,000). Buy tickets at **CFR**, Str. N. Bălcescu 4. (☎21 43 35. Open M-F 7am-7pm.) **Buses** run from the intersection of Str. N. Bălcescu and Str. V. Alecsandri to: Bucharest (8hr., 4 per day, L226,000); Cluj-Napoca (7hr., daily, L185,000); Gura Humorului (1hr., 10 per day, L30,000); and Iași (3hr., 4 per day, L100,000). **Libraria**

Cipiran Porumbescu, Aleea Ion Grămadă 5, sells maps (L70,000. Open M-F 7am-7:30pm, Sa 9am-6pm.) **Hotel Suceava ❷,** Str. N Bălcescu 4, in Piața 22 Decembrie, has large rooms with private baths. (☎52 10 72. Singles L650,000; doubles L900,000.) **Postal Code:** 5800.

🖅 DAYTRIP FROM SUCEAVA: PUTNA. Constructed around 1469, pure-white **Putna** was the first of 38 monasteries founded by Ștefan cel Mare, who built one church for each battle he won. He left the monastery's location up to God: climbing a nearby hill (now marked with a cross) to the left of the monastery, he shot an arrow into the air. A slice of the oak it struck is on display at the museum, along with manuscripts, icons, and tapestries. (Museum open daily 9am-8pm. L40,000; students L5000. No cameras.) The tomb of Ștefan cel Mare is in Putna's church. (Monastery and church open daily 6am-8pm. Free.) **Trains** from Suceava run a scenic route to Putna (2½hr., 5 per day, L31,000). Exit the platform to the right, take a left at the first intersection, and keep walking.

RUSSIA (РОССИЯ)

More than a decade after the fall of the Soviet Union, vast Russia stumbles along with no clear direction; former Communists run the state, while impoverished pensioners long for a rose-tinted Soviet past. Heedless of the failing provinces, cosmopolitan Moscow gorges on hyper-capitalism, while majestic St. Petersburg struggles to remain one of Europe's major cultural centers. Although traveling here can be a bureaucratic nightmare, Russia is in many ways the ideal destination for a budget traveler—inexpensive and well served by public transportation, with hundreds of monasteries, kremlins, and churches.

FACTS AND FIGURES

Official Name: Russian Federation.

Capital: Moscow.

Major Cities: St. Petersburg, Ulan Ude, Vladivostok.

Population: 145,000,000.

Land Area: 16,995,800 sq. km.

Time Zone: GMT +3.

Language: Russian.

Religions: Unaffiliated (74%), Russian Orthodox (16%), Muslim (10%).

DISCOVER RUSSIA

Moscow (p. 862) is more than memories of revolution: The spires of St. Basil's are more brilliant in real life than in photos, and the collections of the Kremlin are mind-boggling. The cultural glory of **St. Petersburg** (p. 874) is reflected in Europe's largest art collection at the Hermitage, the opulence of the Summer and Winter Palaces, and one of the world's best ballet companies.

ESSENTIALS

DOCUMENTS AND FORMALITIES

BEFORE YOU GO. In August 1999, the US State Department issued a travel advisory regarding the bringing of Global Positioning Systems (GPS), cellular phones, and other radio transmission devices into Russia. Failure to register such devices can (and does) result in search, seizure, and arrest.

VISAS. Citizens of Australia, Canada, Ireland, New Zealand, South Africa, the UK, and the US all require a visa to enter Russia; you need an **invitation** stating your itinerary and dates of travel to get a visa. Many hotels will **register** your visa for you on arrival, as should the organizations listed below. Some travel agencies in Moscow and St. Petersburg will also register your visa for approximately €30. As a last resort, you'll have to climb into the 7th circle of bureaucratic hell known as the central **OVIR** (ОВИР) office (in Moscow: UVIR; УВИР) to register. To obtain a visa, you may apply in person or by mail to a Russian embassy or consulate; travel agencies that advertise discounted tickets to Russia can often provide visas as well. **Visa assistance** (€30-45) is available at www.visatorussia.com. The following organizations can issue invitations and/or visas for tourists:

Info Travel, 387 Harvard St., Brookline, MA 02146 (☎617-566-2197; info-study@aol.com). Invitations and visas to Russia start at €145.

Russia House provides invitations and visas for €250. In the **US:** 1800 Connecticut Ave. NW, Washington, D.C. 20009 (☎202-986-6010; www.russiahouse.org). In **Russia:** 44 Bolshaya Nikitskaya, Moscow 121854 (☎095 290 34 59).

Host Families Association (HOFA), 5-25 Tavricheskaya ul., 193015 St. Petersburg, Russia (☎812 275 19 92; www.hofa.us).

Red Bear Tours/Russian Passport, 401 St. Kilda Rd., Ste. 11, Melbourne 3004, Australia (☎613 98 67 38 88; www.travelcentre.com.au).

EMBASSIES. All foreign embassies are in Moscow (p. 865); many consulates are also in St. Petersburg (p. 878). Russian embassies at home include: **Australia,** 78 Canberra Ave., Griffith ACT 2603 (☎026 295 90 33; fax 06 295 1847); **Canada,** 285 Charlotte St., Ottawa, ON K1N 8L5 (☎613-235-4341); **Ireland,** 186 Orwell Rd., Rathgar, Dublin 14 (☎/fax 01 492 35 25); **New Zealand,** 57 Messines Rd., Karori, Wellington (☎04 476 61 13; visas ☎04 476 67 42; eor@netlink.co.nz); **South Africa,** Butano Building, 316 Brooke St., Menlo Park 0081, Pretoria; mail to: P.O. Box 6743, Pretoria 0001 (☎012 362 13 37; www.icon.co.za/rusco); **UK,** 5 Kensington Palace Gardens, London W8 4QX (☎02 07 12 29 36 28; visas ☎02 07 12 29 80 27; dom.harhouse1@harhouse1.demon.co.uk); and **US,** 2650 Wisconsin Ave. N.W., Washington, D.C. 20007 (☎202-298-5700; www.russianembassy.org).

RUSSIA

TRANSPORTATION

BY PLANE. Most major international carriers fly into **Sheremetyevo-2** (SVO) in Moscow or **Pulkovo-2** (LED) in St. Petersburg. **Aeroflot** (www.aeroflot.org) is the most commonly used domestic airline.

BY TRAIN. If you take a train that passes through Belarus, you will need a US$40 **transit visa** (p. 108). For **domestic travel,** trains are best; weekend trains between Moscow and St. Petersburg can sell out a week in advance, so buy your ticket ahead of time. There are four classes of train cars: *Lyuks* (люкс) has two beds; second-class *kupeyny* (купейный) has four bunks; and *platskartny* (плацкартный) has 52 shorter, harder bunks. Aim for bunks 1-33; bunks 34-37 are next to the restrooms, and bunks 38-52 get hot in summer. **Women** traveling alone can try to buy out a *lyuks* compartment for security, or can travel *platskartny* and depend on the crowds to shame would-be harassers. Riding *platskartny* is also a good idea on the theft-ridden St. Petersburg-Moscow line, as you will be less conspicuous. *Elektrichka* (commuter rail; marked on signs as пригородные поезда; *prigorodnye poezda*) has its own platforms; buy tickets at the *kassa*.

BY BUS. Buses, cheaper than trains, are better for shorter distances, but are often crowded and overbooked; don't hesitate to eject people who try to sit in your seat.

BY TAXI AND BY THUMB. In Russia, hailing a taxi is a lot like hitchhiking and should be treated with equal caution. Most drivers who stop will be private citizens. Those seeking a ride should stand off the curb and hold out a hand into the street, palm down; when a car stops, riders tell the driver their destination before getting in; he will either refuse the destination altogether or ask *skolko?* ("how much?"), leading to protracted negotiations. Non-Russian speakers will get ripped off unless they manage a firm agreement on the price—if the driver agrees without asking for a price, you must ask *skolko* yourself (sign language works too). Never get into a car that is already carrying a passenger.

TOURIST SERVICES AND MONEY

EMERGENCY   Police: ☎ 02. **Ambulance:** ☎ 03. **Fire:** ☎ 01.

TOURIST OFFICES. There are two types of Russian tourist offices—those that only arrange tours and those that offer general travel services. Offices of the former type are often unhelpful, but those of the latter are often eager to help, especially with visa registration. Big hotels are a good resource for maps and info.

MONEY. The **ruble** was revalued in 1998, losing three zeros; the old currency is gradually being phased out. You'll have no problem changing rubles back at the end of your trip (just keep exchange receipts), but don't exchange large sums at once, as the rate is unstable. Never exchange money on the street; find an *Obmen Valyuty* (Обмен Валюты; currency exchange) to exchange euros or US dollars. You must show your passport when you exchange money. **Banks** offer the best combination of good rates and security; main branches usually accept traveler's checks and give cash advances on credit cards, most often Visa. **ATMs** (банкомат; *bankomat*), linked to all major networks and credit cards, can be found all over most cities. Banks, large restaurants, ATMs, and currency exchanges often accept major credit cards, especially Visa. Although in most places you must pay in rubles, it's wise to keep €20 on hand. A budget day will run you between €30-40. In St. Petersburg and Moscow, a 5-10% **tip** is becoming customary.

BUSINESS HOURS. Most establishments, even train ticket offices and "24hr. stores," close for a lunch break, and most also close at least 30 minutes earlier than posted—if they choose to open at all.

RUBLES		
	AUS$1 = 19.7R	10R = AUS$0.51
	CDN$1 = 22R	10R = CDN$0.45
	EUR€1 = 33.5R	10R = EUR€0.30
	NZ$1 = 17.62R	10R = NZ$0.57
	ZAR1 = 4.13R	10R = ZAR2.40
	UK£1 = 48.2R	10R = UK£0.21
	US$1 = 30.5R	10R = US$0.33

COMMUNICATION

PHONE CODES	**Country code: 7. International dialing prefix:** 810. From outside Russia, dial int'l dialing prefix (see inside back cover) + 7 + city code + local number.

TELEPHONES AND INTERNET ACCESS. Calling is expensive, so email is your best bet for keeping in touch. **Internet** cafes are common in Moscow and St. Petersburg (from 30-60R per hr.). Direct international calls can be made from telephone offices in St. Petersburg and Moscow; calls to Europe run €1-1.50 per minute, and to the US and Australia about US$1.50-2. Telephones that use tokens are becoming obsolete; the new card phones, which often have instructions in English, are quickly replacing them. **Phonecards** are sold at central telephone offices, Metro stations, and newspaper kiosks; at a telephone office or Metro station, the attendant will ask you, "На улицу?" (Na ulitsu; "On the street?") to distinguish between cards for the phones in the station or in an office and for outdoor public phones. For 5-digit numbers, insert a "2" between the dialing code and the phone number.

MAIL. Service is much more reliable for outgoing mail than for incoming. Letters to the US will arrive as soon as a week after mailing, although letters to other destinations take 2-3 weeks. Airmail is indicated by *avia* (авиа). Send your mail certified (заказное; 16R) to reduce the chance of it being lost. Regular letters to the US cost 7R; postcards cost 5R. *Poste Restante* is "Письмо До Востребования" (Pismo Do Vostrebovania); address mail to be held: SURNAME Firstname, 103 009 Москва, Письмо До востребования, RUSSIA.

LANGUAGE. Familiarize yourself with the **Cyrillic alphabet** (p. 1051); it will make getting around and getting by immeasurably easier. For some basic Russian words and phrases, see p. 1059.

ACCOMMODATIONS

RUSSIA	❶	❷	❸	❹	❺
ACCOMMODATIONS	under 400R	400-700R	701-1200R	1201-2000R	over 2000R

Homestays, arranged through a tourist office, are often the cheapest (50-100R per night) and best option in the country. Only Moscow and St. Petersburg have **hostels,** which average around US$18-25. Reserve well in advance, especially in summer. Expect to pay 300-450R for a single in a budget **hotel.** There are several classes of rooms. *Lux,* usually two-room doubles with TV, phone, fridge, and bath, are the most expensive. *Polu-lux* rooms are singles or doubles with TV, phone, and bath. The lowest-priced rooms are *bez udobstv* (без удобств), which are singles with a sink. Most hotels only accept cash, and hot water (and sometimes all water) is only on for a few hours a day. **University dorms** offer cheap rooms, but don't expect sparkling bathrooms or reliable hot water. Some accept foreign students (€5-10 per night); make arrangements through an institute from home.

FOOD AND DRINK

RUSSIA	❶	❷	❸	❹	❺
FOOD	under 70R	70-150R	151-300R	301-500R	over 500R

Russian dishes are often both delectable and disgusting; tasty *borscht* sometimes comes with *salo* (pig fat). The largest meal of the day, *obed* (обед; lunch), includes: *salat* (салат; salad), usually cucumbers and tomatoes or beets and potatoes with mayonnaise or sour cream; *sup* (суп; soup); and *kuritsa* (курица; chicken) or *myaso* (мясо; meat), often called *kotlyety* (котлеты) or *beefshteaks* (бифштекс). Ordering a few *zakuski* (закуски; small appetizers) instead of a main dish can save money. *Blini* (stuffed crepes), *shashlyki* (шашлыки; skewered meat), and *kvas* (квас), a dark-brown alcoholic drink, are sold on the streets.

SAFETY AND SECURITY

Water in much of Russia is drinkable in small doses, but not in Moscow and St. Petersburg; boil it to be safe. Russian bottled water is often mineral water—you may prefer to boil or filter your own. For medical emergencies, leave the country or go to the **American Medical Centers** in Moscow (p. 866) or St. Petersburg (p. 878), which have American doctors. Traveler's **health insurance** is essential (p. 22). Reports of **crime** against foreigners are on the rise, particularly in cities. Although it is hard to look Russian (especially with a big pack), try not to flaunt your nationality. Reports of mafia warfare are scaring off tourists, but shops are more likely targets than individuals. Due to the recent eruption of violence in the Northern Caucasus, avoid the Dagestan and Chechnya regions.

HOLIDAYS AND FESTIVALS

Holidays: New Year's (Jan. 1-2); Orthodox Christmas (Jan. 7); Defenders of the Motherland Day (Feb. 23); International Women's Day (Mar. 8); Orthodox Easter (Apr. 11); Labor Day (May 1-2); Victory Day (May 9); Independence Day (June 12); Day of Accord and Reconciliation (Nov. 7); Constitution Day (Dec. 12).

Festivals: From June 21-July 11, when the sun barely touches the horizon, St. Petersburg and Moscow celebrate the **White Nights** with concerts and fireworks.

MOSCOW (MOCKBA)   ☎8095

While St. Petersburg is Russia's "window on the West," Moscow (pop. 9,000,000) is the window into the very heart of the nation. When Communism swept through Moscow, it leveled most of the capital's golden domes and left behind massive buildings, crumbling outskirts, and countless statues of Lenin. But things change quickly in this audacious city, and in the midst of its debauchery and corruption, Moscow is recreating itself using the same resourcefulness that helped it engineer—and then survive—the most ambitious social experiment in history.

▐ TRANSPORTATION

Flights: International flights arrive at **Sheremetyevo-2** (SVO; Шереметьево-2; ☎578 90 05). Take the van under the "автолайн" sign in front of the station to M2: Rechnoy Vokzal (Речной Вокзал; 20min., every 10min. 7am-10pm, 15R). Or, take bus #551 or

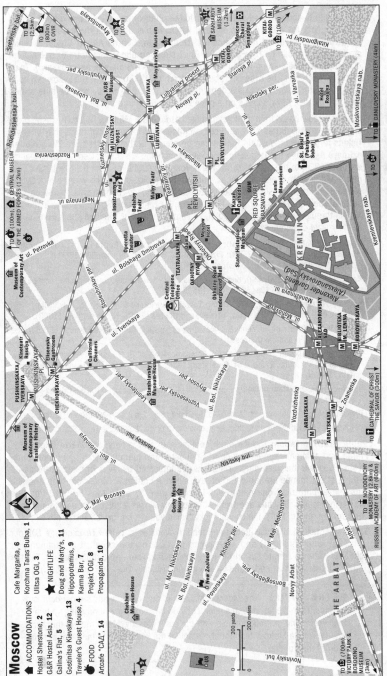

RUSSIA

MOSCOW

▲ ACCOMMODATIONS
Hostel Sherstone, **2**
G&R Hostel Asia, **12**
Galina's Flat, **5**
Gostinitsa Kievskaya, **13**
Traveler's Guest House, **4**

🍴 FOOD
Artcafe "САД", **14**

Cafe Margarita, **6**
Korchma Taras Bulba, **1**
Ulitsa OGI, **3**

★ NIGHTLIFE
Doug and Marty's, **11**
Hippopotamus, **9**
Karma Bar, **7**
Projekt OGI, **8**
Propaganda, **10**

851 to M2: Rechnoy Vokzal or bus #517 to M8: Planyornaya (Планёрная; 10R). Buses run 24hr., but the Metro closes at 1am. Purchase bus tickets at the kassa (касса) at **Tsentralnyy Aerovokzal** (Центральный Аэровокзал; Central Airport Station), Leningradskiy pr. 37, corpus 6 (☎941 99 99), 2 stops on almost any tram or trolley from M2: Aeroport (the sign on front of bus should say "Центральный Аэровокзал"). **Taxis** to the center tend to be expensive; bargain down to US$30 or less. The yellow taxi company has fixed prices. Go to the departures level to find cars; you may be able to find US$15-20 rides. Always agree on a price before getting into the car.

Trains: Moscow has 8 train stations arranged around the M5 line. Due to financial problems, many train routes are being cut, so prices and frequency of trains may change. Tickets for longer trips within Russia can be bought at the **Tsentralnoye Zheleznodorozhnoye Agenstvo** (Центральное Железнодорожное Агенство; Central Train Agency; ☎266 93 33), to the right of Yaroslavskiy Vokzal (see above). Your ticket will have your name and seat on it and tell you at which station *(vokzal)* to catch your train. A Cyrillic schedule of trains, destinations, departure times, and *vokzal* names is posted on both sides of the hall. (*Kassa* open M-F 8am-9pm, Sa 8am-7pm, Su 8am-6pm.) If you buy tickets through **Intourist** or your hotel, you'll pay more, but you'll be spared the hassle of the *vokzal* experience.

Belorusskiy Vokzal (Белорусский), pl. Tverskoi Zastavy 7. To: **Berlin** (27hr., daily, 3500R); **Minsk** (10hr., 3-4 per day, 750R); **Prague** (35hr., daily, 2860R); **Vilnius** (16hr., 1-2 per day, 1950R); and **Warsaw** (21hr., 2 per day, 2520R).

Kazanskiy Vokzal (Казанский), Komsomolskaya pl. 2 (Комсомольская), opposite Leningradskiy Vokzal. Serves: **Kazan** (12hr., 2 per day, 1950R).

Kievskiy Vokzal (Киевский), pl. Kievskovo Vokzala (Киевского Вокзала). To: **Kyiv** (14hr., 4 per day, 950R); **Lviv** (26hr., 2 per day, 1100R); and **Odessa** (25-28hr., 1-2 per day, 1100R).

Kurskiy Vokzal (Курский), ul. Zemlyanoy Val 29/1 (Земляной Вал), serves **Sevastopol** (26hr., 1-2 per day, 1100R) and the **Caucasus.**

Leningradskiy Vokzal (Ленинградский), Komsomolskaya pl. 3. M1 and 5: Komsomolskaya. To: **Helsinki** (13hr. daily, 2720R); **St. Petersburg** (8hr., 10-15 per day, 700R); and **Tallinn** (14hr., daily, 1550R).

Paveletskiy Vokzal (Павелецкий), Paveletskaya pl. 1 (Павелецкая), serves the **Crimea** and eastern **Ukraine.**

Rizhskiy Vokzal (Рижский), Pr. Mira 79/3. To **Rīga** (16hr., 2 per day, 2050R) and **Estonia.**

Yaroslavskiy Vokzal (Ярославский), Komsomolskaya pl. 5a, begins the Trans-Siberian Railroad.

Public Transportation: Though often confusing to newcomers, the **Metro** (Метро) is large and efficient—a masterpiece of Stalinist urban planning. Trains run daily 6am-1am. Passages between lines or stations are indicated by signs of a man walking up stairs; street names are indicated on exit signs. A station serving more than one line may have more than one name. Buy token-cards (7R, or 10 trips for 50R) from the *kassy* in stations. Buy **bus** and **trolley** tickets from kiosks labeled "проездные билеты" or from the driver (10R). Punch your ticket when you get on, or risk a 100R fine.

Taxis: Most taxis do not use meters and tend to overcharge. **Yellow Taxis** charge 10R per km (15R after midnight) and are easy to pick out on the street. It is common and cheaper to hail a private car on the street by holding your arm out horizontally. Tell the driver your destination and agree on a price first (usually 50-100R across town).

METRO MANIA. The Moscow Metro has one of the world's most confusing systems. To make navigation easier, *Let's Go* has created a numbering system for each Metro line that coordinates with the color Moscow Metro map in this guide. When asking a Metro attendant about any of the lines, refer to the color or name, and not the number.

ORIENTATION AND PRACTICAL INFORMATION

A series of concentric rings radiates outward from the **Kremlin** (Кремль; Kreml) and **Red Square** (Красная Площадь; Krasnaya ploshchad). The outermost **Moscow Ring Road** marks the city limits, but most sights lie within the smaller **Garden Ring** (Садовоуе Кольцо; Sadovoe Koltso). Main streets include **Ulitsa Tverskaya** (Тверская), which extends north along the Metro's green line, and **Arbat** (Арбат) and **Novyy Arbat** (Новый Арбат), which run west parallel to the blue lines. Familiarize yourself with the Cyrillic alphabet and orient yourself using the Metro. English and Cyrillic maps (35-60R) are at kiosks all over the city. Be careful when crossing streets, as drivers are notoriously oblivious to pedestrians; use the underpass (*perekhod*; переход) at most intersections.

> **PAYING IN RUSSIA.** Due to the fluctuating value of the Russian ruble, some establishments list their prices in US dollars. For this reason, some prices in this book may also appear in US dollars, but be prepared to pay in rubles.

TOURIST, FINANCIAL, AND LOCAL SERVICES

Tourist Office: Intourist, Milyutinskiy per. 13/1 (Милютинскии; ☎924 31 01). M1 or 6: Turgenyevskaya. Open M-Sa 10am-7pm.

Budget Travel: Student Travel Agency Russia (STAR), Baltiyskaya ul. 9, 3rd fl. (Балтийская; ☎797 95 55; www.startravel.ru). M2: Sokol. ISICs, discount plane tickets, and hostel booking. Open M-F 10am-7pm, Sa 11am-4pm.

Embassies: Australia, Podkoloniy per. 10 (☎956 60 70). M6: Kitai Gorod. (Китай Город). M3 or 5: Smolenskaya/Park Kultury (Смоленская/Парк Культуы). Open M-F 9am-12:30pm and 1:15-5pm; visas M-F 9:30am-12:30pm. **Canada,** Starokonyushennyy per. 23 (Староконюшенный; ☎105 60 00; fax 232 99 50). M1: Kropotkinskaya or M4: Arbatskaya (Арбатская). Open M-F 8:30am-1pm and 2-5pm. **Ireland,** Grokholskiy per. 5 (Грохольский; ☎937 59 11, consular section 937 59 02). M5 or 6: Prospekt Mira. Open M-F 9:30am-1pm and 2:30-5:30pm. **New Zealand,** ul. Povarskaya 44 (Поварская; ☎956 35 79). M7: Barikadnaya (Барикадная). Open M-F 9am-5:30pm. Consular section (☎956 26 42) open M-F 9:30am-10:30am and 4pm-5pm. **South Africa,** Bolshoy Strochenovskiy per. 22/25 (Большой Строченовский; ☎230 68 69; fax 230 68 65). Open M-F 8:30am-5pm. Consular section open M-F 8am-noon. **Ukraine,** Leontyevskiy per. 18 (Леонтьевский; ☎229 10 79, visas ☎229 34 22), off ul. Tverskaya. M2: Tverskaya (Тверская). Open M-F 9am-1pm and 2pm-6pm. **US,** Novinskiy 19/23 (Новинский; ☎728 50 00; www.usia.gov/posts/moscow.html). M5: Krasnoprenenskaya (Краснопресненская). Flash a US passport and cut the long lines. Open M-F 9am-6pm. Consular section (☎728 55 60); open M-F 9am-noon. **American Citizen Services** (☎728 55 77, after-hours emergency ☎728 50 00; fax 728 50 84) connects citizens to various organizations and arranges annual July 4th celebrations. Open M-F 9am-noon and 2-4pm.

Currency Exchange: *Moscow Express Directory,* free in most luxury hotels, lists banks and places to buy and cash traveler's checks. Usually only main branches of large banks will change traveler's checks or issue cash advances. Nearly every bank and hotel has an **ATM;** avoid machines protruding from buildings; they work erratically, and withdrawing cash on busy streets makes you a target for muggers.

American Express: ul. Usacheva 33 (☎933 84 00). M1: Sportivnaya. Use the exit at the front of the train, turn right, and turn right again after the Global USA shop onto Usacheva. Open M-F 9am-6pm.

English Bookstore: Anglia British Bookshop, Vorotnikovskiy per. 6 (Воротниковский). Large selection. ISIC discount. AmEx/MC/V. Open M-F 10am-7pm, Sa 10am-6pm, Su 11am-5pm.

HE LOCAL LEGEND

COPS AND ROBBERS

A word to the wise: Register our visa within three days of arrival in every Russian city you visit, especially Moscow. Hotels will usually register you automatically upon check-in, but a hostel can register you only if they issued our invitation. Your other options are visiting the OVIR office or paying a hotel around €50 to do it for ou. In Moscow, your best bet is **Visa House** (☎ 721 10 21; www.visahouse.com. €30).

Why go to all this trouble? The Moscow *militsia* (police) loves to ake advantage of naive travelers with unregistered visas, waiting around tourist sights demanding o see documents. You may stand out particularly if you are Asian, have darker skin, or look the least bit Chechen. When the police discover an unregistered visa, they give a long, imperious spiel about how they will take the traveler down to the police station, where he will spend a long time, pay a large fine, and be unpleasantly lectured by both the Russians and his own consulate.

In reality, the fine for an unregistered visa is often as low as 00R and is not such a big deal, but most foreigners don't know his. "This visa is not my problem; t is your problem," the crooked cop says in well-rehearsed English. "So what is it worth to you o fix?" Resist the easy bribe; they'll give up once they realize hey can't milk anything from you.

Laundromat: California Cleaners, Maly Gnezdnikovsky per. (Малы Гнездниковскы). M2, 7, or 9: Pushkinskaya. Wash and dry 150R per kg. Pick-up and delivery 150R; free for loads of 10kg or more. Open M-Sa 11am-9pm, Sa 11am-7pm.

EMERGENCY AND COMMUNICATIONS

Emergency: Police: ☎02. **Ambulance:** ☎03. **Fire:** ☎01.

24hr. Pharmacies: Look for "круглосуточно" (*kruglosutochno;* always open) signs. Ul. Tverskaya 25 (☎299 24 59 or 299 79 69). M2: Tverskaya/Mayakovskaya. Ul. Zemlyanoi Val 25 (☎917 12 85). M5: Kurskaya. Kutozovskiy Prospekt 24 (Кутозовский; ☎249 19 37). M4: Kutuzovskaya (Кутузовская).

Medical Assistance: American Medical Center (AMC), Prospekt Mira 26 (☎933 77 00). M5 or 6: Prospekt Mira. From the Metro, turn left on Grokholskiy per. Walk-in medical care US$175 per visit. Open 24hr. AmEx/MC/V. **American Clinic,** Grokholskiy per. 31 (☎937 57 57; www.klinik.ru). M5 or 6: Prospekt Mira. See directions for AMC. American board-certified doctors; family, internal, and pediatric services. Consultations US$98. House calls US$160. Open 24hr. MC/V. **European Medical Clinic,** Spiridoniyevskiy Per. 5 (☎787 70 00; www.emcmos.ru) offers psychiatric, pediatric, gynecological, and dental care. Consultations US$120. Open 24hr.

Internet Access: Timeonline, on the bottom level of the Okhotnyy Ryad underground mall. M1: Okhotnyy Ryad. At night, enter through the Metro underpass. Over 100 computers in the center of the city. 40-70R per hr., depending on time of day. Student discount 6R per hr. Open 24hr. **Kutkushka** (Куткушка), ul. Rozhdedestvenka 6/9/20. M7: Kuznetskiy Most. Fast connections 60R per hr. Open daily 11am-midnight.

Telephones: Moscow Central Telegraph (see Post Offices, below). To call abroad, go to the 2nd hall with telephones. Prepay at the counter for the amount of time you expect to talk, or buy a prepaid phonecard. Collect calls and calling card calls not available. Calls to the US 9-20R per min., to Europe 12-35R per min. **Local calls** require phone cards, available at some Metro stops and kiosks. Dial ☎09 for directory assistance.

Post Offices: Moscow Central Telegraph, ul. Tverskaya 7, a few blocks uphill from the Kremlin. M1: Okhotnyy Ryad. International mail at window #23; faxes at #11-12; telegram service available. Open M-F 8am-2pm and 3pm-8pm, Sa-Su 7am-2pm and 3pm-7pm. **Poste Restante** at window #24, although they may send you to the main post office at Myasnitskaya 26 (Мясницкая). **Postal Code:** 103 009.

ACCOMMODATIONS

The lack of backpacking culture in Moscow results in slim pickings and over-priced rooms. Women standing outside major rail stations rent **private rooms** (сдаю комнату; sdayu komnatu) or **apartments** (сдаю квартиру; sdayu kvartiru)—be sure to haggle. US-based **Moscow Bed and Breakfast ❸** rents apartments in the city center. (US ☎603-585-3347; jkates@top.monad.net. Reserve ahead. Singles US$35; doubles US$52.)

Galina's Flat, ul. Chaplygina 8, #35 (Чаплыгина; ☎921 60 38; galinas.flat@mtu-net.ru). M1: Chistyye Prudy. Take Chistoprudny bul. (Чистопрудный) past the statue of Griboedov and turn left onto Kharitonevskiy per. (Харитоньевский), then take the 2nd right on Chaplygina. Go through the courtyard at #8, curve around the building to the right, and enter by the "Уникум" sign. Homey apartment with cats. Hot showers. Kitchen facilities. Call ahead. Dorms US$10; doubles US$30; discounts for longer stays. Airport pickup US$25-30, drop-off US$20-25. ❶

Traveler's Guest House (TGH), Bolshaya Pereyaslavskaya ul. 50, 10th fl. (Большая Переславская; ☎971 40 59; www.infinity.ru/tgh). M5 or 6: Prospekt Mira. Take the 2nd right across from Prospekt Mira 61, walk to the end of the *pereleuk*, and go left on B. Pereyaslavskaya. TGH is in a white high-rise on the right. While it's not the cheapest or most central option, this hostel attracts a large crowd. English-speaking staff. Kitchen available. Luggage storage 10R. Laundry service 130R per 3kg. Internet access 1R per min. Airport transport US$30. Visa invitations US$50, guests US$30. Singles US$44; doubles US$54, with bath US$59; dorms US$22. Nonmembers add US$1. ❹

G&R Hostel Asia, Zelenodolskaya ul. 3/2 (Зеленодольская; ☎378 28 66; www.hos-tels.ru). M7: Ryazanskiy Prospekt (Рязанский Проспект). On the 15th fl. of the gray building with "Гостиница" on top. Near the Metro, this hotel features clean rooms and a helpful staff. Internet access 2R per min. Visa invitations US$35, US$30 if you prepay for 1 night. Airport transport US$35. Reception 8am-midnight. Dorms US$17. Singles US$24; doubles US$39; triples US$53. Nonmembers add US$1. MC/V. ❷

Gostinitsa Kievskaya (Гостиница Киевская), Kievskaya ul. 2 (☎240 14 44). M3, 4, or 5: Kievskaya. Beside the train station, with a good market just outside. Simple, comfy rooms all with telephone and TV. Singles must be booked in advance (30% added to first night's stay for reservation). Singles 660R, with bath 1100R; doubles 700/1050R; luxury suite 1500R. ❷

Hostel Sherstone, Gostinichny pr. 8 (Гостиничны; ☎797 80 75). M9: Vladykino. Walk along the railway turning left from the metro as far as the overpass, then take a left and go past a post office. The hostel is at the end of the street on the 3rd fl. on your left opposite the kiosks. Farther from the center, but has lots of rooms, all with showers. Breakfast included. Internet access 2R per min. Visa support $30. Dorms US$17. Singles US$35; doubles US$22. $1 discount for HI & EURO<26 youth card (not ISIC). ❷

FOOD

Restaurants range from the expensive to the outrageous; kiosk fare is a cheap alternative. Restaurants serving local cuisine are often more affordable, and many higher-priced places now offer business lunch specials (бизнес ланч; typically available noon-3pm; US$4-8). Russians tend to eat in late evening; avoid crowds by eating earlier.

RUSSIA

RESTAURANTS

▨ **Cafe Margarita** (Кафе Маргарита), Malaya Bronaya ul. 28 (Малая Вроная; ☎299 65 34), at the intersection with Malyy Kozikhinskiy per. (Малый Козихинский). M2: Mayakovskaya. Take a left on Bolshaya Sadovaya, then another left on Malaya Bronaya. An excellent Russian cafe-restaurant that is very popular with locals. Entrees 250-450R. Live piano after 8pm (cover 100R). Open daily 1pm-midnight. ❹

Ulitsa OGI (Улица ОГИ), Petrovka 26/8 (Петровка; ☎200 68 73). M7: Kuznetsky Most. Pass through the arch and walk straight for 50m. This well-kept secret serves delicious Russian and European food. The Gallic trout (230R) is superb. Salads 90-350R. Entrees 230-400R. Business lunch 250R. Open daily 8am-11pm. MC/V. ❸

Artcafe "САД" (Арткафе), B. Tolmachevskiy per. 3 (Толмачевский; ☎239 91 15), across from ul. Krymskiy Val. M2, 6 or 8: Tretyakovskaya. Understated decor in a courtyard dining area. Excellent bread and several varieties of tea (70R per pot). Salads 100-400R. Entrees 150-360R. Open daily 10am-midnight. ❸

Korchma Taras Bulba (Корчма Тарас Бульва), Sadovaya-Samotechnaya ul. 13 (☎200 00 56). M9: Tsvetnoy Bulvar (Цветной Бульвар). Up Tsvetnoy Bulvar. Delicious Ukrainian specialities. Try the restaurant's eponymous *taras bulba* (cheese, with a hint of vegetables). Entrees 140-300R. Open 24hr. MC/V. ❸

MARKETS AND SUPERMARKETS

Vendors bring everything from a handful of cherries to an entire produce section to Moscow's **markets.** A visit is worthwhile just for the sights: Sides of beef, grapes, and pots of flowers crowd together in a visual bouquet. Impromptu markets spring up around Metro stations; some of the best are at Turgenyevskaya and Kuznetsky most. Vendors arrive around 10am and leave by 8pm. Bring your own bag. **Eliseevskiy Gastronom** (Елисеевский), ul. Tverskaya 14 (☎209 07 60), is Moscow's most famous supermarket, although it was closed for renovation in 2003. (Open M-Sa 8am-9pm, Su 10am-8pm.) There are other supermarkets all over the place; look for "продукти" (produkty; food products) signs.

◉ SIGHTS

Visitors can choose between 16th-century churches and Soviet-era museums, but there's little in between. Because St. Petersburg was the tsar's seat for 200 years, Moscow has no grand palaces, and while the city's art museums contain the very best Russian works, they have virtually no foreign pieces. Although the Soviet regime destroyed 80% of the city's pre-revolutionary splendor, there are still enough sights to occupy visitors for over a week.

THE KREMLIN

The Kremlin (Кремль; Kreml) is the geographical and historical center of Moscow. Here, Ivan the Terrible reigned and Stalin ruled the lands behind the Iron Curtain. Napoleon simmered at this fortress while Moscow burned, and the USSR was dissolved here in 1991. The glory and the riches of the Russian Empire are all on display in the Kremlin's Armory and in its magnificent churches. Besides the sights listed below, the only other place in the triangular complex visitors are allowed to enter is the **Kremlin Palace of Congresses,** the white square monster built by Khrushchev in 1961 for Communist Party Congresses; today, it's a theater. English-speaking guides offer tours of the complex at typically outrageous prices; haggle away. *(Complex open M-W and F-Su 10am-5pm. Buy tickets in Alexander Gardens, on the west side of the Kremlin.)*

ARMORY MUSEUM AND DIAMOND FUND. (Оружейная и Вьставка Алмазного Фонда; Oruzheynaya i Vystavka Almaznovo Fonda.) At the southwest corner of the Kremlin complex, the Armory Museum exemplifies the opulence of the Russian court. Among all the imperial thrones, coaches, and crowns are the legendary **Fabergé Eggs** in room 2, each revealing an intricate jewelled miniature. The Diamond Fund, in an annex of the Armory, has even more glitter, including a 190-carat diamond given to Catherine the Great by her lover Gregory Orlov. Soviet-era finds, including the world's largest chunks of platinum, are also on display. *(The Armory lets in groups for 1½hr. visits at 10am, noon, 2:30, and 4:30pm. Diamond Fund open 10am-1pm and 2-6pm. Armory 350R, students 175R. Diamond Fund 350R, students 250R.*

CATHEDRAL SQUARE. Russia's most famous golden domes can be seen in Cathedral Square. The church closest to the Armory is the **Annunciation Cathedral** (Благовещенский Собор; Blagoveshchensky Sobor), which guards luminous icons by Andrei Rublev and Theophanes the Greek. The square **Archangel Cathedral** (Архангельский Собор; Arkhangelsky Sobor), gleaming with vivid icons and metallic coffins, is the final resting place for many of the tsars who preceded Peter the Great, including Ivans III (the Great) and IV (the Terrible), as well as Mikhail Romanov. The 15th-century **Assumption Cathedral** (Успенский Собор; Uspenskiy Sobor), at the center of the square, was used by Napoleon as a stable in 1812. Nearby are the small **Patriarch's Palace** (Патриарший Дворец; Patriarshiy Dvorets), which now houses a museum, and the even smaller **Church of the Deposition of the Robe.** To the right of Assumption Cathedral the **Belltower of Ivan the Great** (Колокольня Ивана Великого; Kolokolnya Ivana Velikovo) now houses temporary exhibits. Directly behind the belltower is the **Tsar Bell** (Царь-колокол; Tsarkolokol), the world's largest. It has never rung and probably never will—a 1737 fire caused an 11½-ton piece to break off. *(All cathedrals 250R, students 125R.)*

AROUND RED SQUARE

RED SQUARE SIGHTS. The 700m-long Red Square (Красная площадь; Krasnaya Ploshchad) has been the site of everything from a giant farmer's market to public hangings, from Communist parades to a renegade Cessna landing. On one side is the Kremlin and on the other is **GUM,** once a market and the world's largest purveyor of Soviet "consumer goods," now an upscale shopping mall. Also flanking the square are **St. Basil's Cathedral,** the **State Historical Museum,** the **Lenin Mausoleum,** and the pink-and-green **Kazan Cathedral.**

ST. BASIL'S CATHEDRAL. (Собор Василия Блаженного; Sobor Vasiliya Blazhennovo.) There is no more familiar symbol of Moscow than the colorful onion domes of St. Basil's Cathedral. Commissioned by Ivan the Terrible to celebrate his 1552 victory over the Tatars in Kazan, it was completed in 1561. The cathedral bears the name of a holy fool, Vasily (Basil in English), who correctly predicted that Ivan would murder his own son. The labyrinthine interior—unusual for Orthodox churches—is filled with both decorative and religious frescoes. *(M3: Ploshchad Revolutsii (Площадь Революции). Open daily 11am-6pm. Buy tickets from the kassa to the left of entrance, then proceed upstairs. 100R, students 50R.)*

LENIN'S TOMB. (Мавзолей В.И. Ленина; Mavzoley V.I. Lenina.) Lenin's likeness can be seen in bronze all over the city, but here he appears in the eerily luminescent flesh. In the glory days, this squat red structure was guarded fiercely, and the wait to get in took three hours. Today's line is still long, and the guards are still stone-faced, but the atmosphere is characterized by curiosity rather than reverence. Entrance to the mausoleum also gives access to the **Kremlin wall,** where Stalin, Brezhnev, Andropov, Gagarin, and John Reed (author of *Ten Days That Shook the World*) are buried. *(Open Tu-Th and Sa-Su 10am-1pm.)*

RUSSIA

NORTH OF RED SQUARE

Just outside the main gate to Red Square is an elaborate gold circle marking **Kilometer 0,** the spot from which all distances from Moscow are measured. Don't be fooled by this tourist attraction—the real Kilometer 0 sits underneath the Lenin Mausoleum. Just a few steps away, the **Alexander Gardens** (Александровский Сад; Aleksandrovskiy Sad) are a green respite from the pollution of central Moscow. At the north end of the gardens is the **Tomb of the Unknown Soldier** (Могила Неизвестного Солдата; Mogila Neizvestnovo Soldata), where an **eternal flame** burns in memory of the catastrophic losses suffered in WWII, known in Russia as the Great Patriotic War. To the west is **Manezh Square** (Манежная площадь; Manezhnaya Ploshchad), only recently converted into a pedestrian area. The famous **Moscow Hotel**—which may be demolished and rebuilt under Mayor Luzhdoz's city renovation plans—overlooks the square and separates it from the older, smaller **Revolution Square** (Площадь Революции; Ploshchad Revolyutsii). Both squares are connected in the north by **Okhotnyy Ryad** (Охотный Ряд; Hunters' Row). Across Okhotnyy Ryad from the Moscow Hotel is the **Duma,** the lower house of Parliament, and across from Revolution Square is **Theater Square** (Театральная площадь; Teatralnaya Ploshchad), home of the **Bolshoy** and **Malyy Theatres.** More posh hotels, chic stores, and government buildings line **Tverskaya Street,** which starts at Manezh Square and runs northwest. Tverskaya, home to some of Moscow's richest residents, is the closest the city gets to having a main street. The glass domes on Manezh Square provide sunlight to the ritzy **Okhotnyy Ryad underground mall.** *(Open daily 11am-11pm. Enter directly from the square or through the underpass.)*

CHURCHES, MONASTERIES, AND SYNAGOGUES

CATHEDRAL OF CHRIST THE SAVIOR. (Храм Христа Спасителя; Khram Khrista Spasitelya.) The city's most controversial landmark is the enormous, gold-domed Cathedral of Christ the Savior. Stalin demolished Nicholas I's original cathedral on this site to make way for a gigantic Palace of the Soviets, but Khrushchev abandoned the project and built an outdoor pool instead. In 1995, after the heated pool's water vapors damaged paintings in the nearby Pushkin Museum, mayor Yury Luzhkov and the Orthodox Church won the battle for the site and built the cathedral in a mere two years. As for where they got the money—let's just say it was a miracle. *(M1: Kropotkinskaya; between ul. Volkhonka (Волхонка) and the Moscow River. Open daily 10am-5pm. Service schedule varies. Cathedral free, but donations welcome.)*

NOVODEVICHY MONASTERY AND CEMETERY. (Новодевичий Монастырь.) Moscow's most famous monastery is hard to miss thanks to its high brick walls, golden domes, and tourist buses. In the center, the **Smolensk Cathedral** (Смоленский Собор; Smolenskiy Sobor) shows off Russian icons and frescoes. As you exit the gates, turn right and follow the exterior wall back around to the **cemetery** (кладбище; kladbishche), a pilgrimage site that holds the graves of such famous figures as Bulgakov, Chekhov, Gogol, Mayakovsky, Shostakovich, and Stanislavsky. *(M1: Sportivnaya. Take the Metro exit that does not lead to the stadium, turn right, and walk several blocks. ☎246 85 26. Open M and W-Su 10am-5:30pm; kassa closes at 4:45pm. Closed 1st M of each month. Cathedral closed on humid days; call in advance. English tour 300R. Grounds 40R, students 20R. Smolensk Cathedral and special exhibits 93R each, students 53R. Cemetery open in summer daily 9am-7pm, off-season 9am-6pm. 30R.)*

DANILOVSKY MONASTERY. (Даниловский.) The seat of the Patriarch, head of the Russian Orthodox Church, is at Danilovsky. An enormous mosaic of a stern-looking man, which watches over visitors, marks the Patriarch's office. The white exterior is complemented by stunning grounds and long-robed monks; unfortunately, visitors can enter only the church and the small museum, both to the left of the main entrance. *(M9: Tulskaya (Тульская). From the square, follow the trolley tracks down Danilovsky val., away from the gray buildings. Open daily 6:30am-7pm. Services M-F 6, 7am, and 5pm; Sa-Su 6:30, 9am, and 5pm. Museum open W and Su 11am-1pm and 1:30-4pm.)*

MOSCOW CHORAL SYNAGOGUE. Constructed in the 1870s, the synagogue is a break from the city's ubiquitous onion domes. Though it functioned during Soviet rule, all but the bravest Jews were deterred by KGB agents who photographed anyone who entered. Today, more than 200,000 Jews officially live in Moscow and services are increasingly well attended, but occasional graffiti is a sad reminder that anti-Semitism in Russia is not dead. *(M6 or 7: Kitai-Gorod. Go north on Solyanskiy Proyezd (Солянский Проезд) and take the first left. Open daily 8am-9pm. Su-Th services 8:30am and 8pm, F service 7:30pm, Sabbath services 9am and 10am.)*

CHURCH OF ST. NICHOLAS OF THE WEAVERS. (Церковь Николы в Хамовниках; Tserkov Nikoly v Khamovnikakh.) The maroon-and-green trim of the Church of St. Nicholas of the Weavers gives it the appearance of a giant gingerbread house. Enter off ul. Lva Tolstovo (Льва Толстого) for the best view of the low ceilings and vivid interior. *(M1 or 5: Park Kultury. Open daily 8am-8pm. Services M-Sa 8am and 5pm; Su 7, 10am, and 5pm.)*

OTHER SIGHTS

MOSCOW METRO. (Московское Метро.) The beautiful Moscow Metro stations are each unique, and those inside the Circle Line have sculptures, stained glass, elaborate mosaics, and unusual chandeliers. Especially noteworthy stations include Kievskaya, Komsomolskaya, Mayakovskaya, Mendeleevskaya, Novoslobodskaya, Ploshchad Revolutsii, and Rimskaya. *(Open daily 6am-1am.)*

THE ARBAT. Now a commercial pedestrian shopping arcade, the Arbat was once a showpiece of *glasnost* and a haven for political radicals, Hare Krishnas, street poets, and *metallisty* (heavy metal rockers). Some of the old flavor remains in the street performers and guitar-playing teenagers. Intersecting but nearly parallel to the Arbat runs the bigger, newer, and uglier **Novy Arbat**, lined with gray high-rises, foreign businesses, and massive Russian stores. *(M3: Arbatskaya or Smolenskaya.)*

VICTORY PARK. (Парк Победы; Park Pobedy.) On the left past the **Triumphal Arch,** which celebrates the victories of 1812, is Victory Park, which was built as a lasting monument to WWII. It includes the gold-domed **Church of St. George the Victorious** (Храм Георгия Победоносного; Khram Georgiya Pobedonosnova) and the impressive **Museum of the Great Patriotic War** (Музей Отечественной Войны; Muzey Otechestvennoy Voyny). *(M4: Kutuzovskaya.)*

KOLOMENSKOYE SUMMER RESIDENCE. (Коломенское.) The tsars' summer residence sits on a wooded slope above the Moskva River. The centerpieces of the grounds are the cone-shaped, 16th-century **Assumption Cathedral** (Успенский Собор; Uspensky Sobor) and the seven blue-and-gold cupolas of the nearby **Church of Our Lady of Kazan** (Церковь Казанской Богоматери; Tserkov Kazanskoy Bogomatyeri). The most notable of the park's several small museums is Peter the Great's 1702 log cabin. *(M2: Kolomenskaya; follow the exit signs to "кмузею Коломенское." Turn right out of the Metro and walk down the tree-shaded path, through the small black gate, and uphill on the left-most path (10min). Museums open Su and Tu-Sa 10am-5:30pm. Each museum 90R, students 45R.Grounds open Apr.-Oct. daily 7am-10pm; Nov.-Mar. 9am-9pm. Free.)*

RUSSIA

▥ MUSEUMS

Moscow's museum scene remains the most patriotic and least Westernized part of the city. Large government museums and small galleries alike proudly display Russian art, and dozens of historical and literary museums are devoted to the nation's past. They want you to see it thoroughly, too—*babushki* spill their wealth of knowledge on visitors and yell at those who breeze through exhibits too quickly, and entry into museums stops well before closing time. Ticket prices are much higher (nearly 80% more) for foreigners than for natives.

▨ **STATE TRETYAKOV GALLERY.** (Третьяковская Галерея; Tretyakovskaya Galereya.) A treasure chest of 18th- to early 20th-century Russian art, the museum also displays a magnificent collection of icons, including works by Andrei Rublyov and Theophanes the Greek. *(M8: Tretyakovskaya (Третьяковская). Exiting the Metro, turn left and then left again, followed by an immediate right on Bolshoy Tolmachevsky per. Walk 2 blocks and turn right on Lavrushinsky per. Open Su and Tu-Sa 10am-7:30pm. Kassa closes at 6:30pm. For an English tour call ☎ 953 52 23. 640R. Gallery 225R, students 130R.)*

▨ **NEW TRETYAKOV GALLERY.** (Государственная Третьяковская Галерея; Gosudarstvennaya Tretyakovskaya Galereya.) The new gallery picks up chronologically where the first Tretyakov leaves off, displaying the greatest Russian art of the 20th century. Behind the gallery and to the right is a graveyard for fallen statues, including decapitated Lenins and Stalins, as well as sculptures of Gandhi, Einstein, and Niels Bohr. From outside the gallery, you can also get a good view of the metal statue of **Peter the Great** that towers over the Moscow River. Zurab Tsereteli, a favorite of mayor Yuri Luzhkov, built the statue in 1997 for Moscow's 850th anniversary, but Muscovites have despised the 100m-tall monstrosity from the start. *(Ul. Krymsky Val 10 (Крымский Вал). M5 and 6: Oktyabraskaya. Walk toward the big intersection at Kaluzhskaya pl. and turn right onto ul. Krymskiy. Open Su and Tu-Sa 10am-7:30pm; kassa closes at 6:30pm. Gallery 225R, students 130R.)*

PUSHKIN MUSEUM OF FINE ARTS. (Музей Изобразительных Искусств им. А.С. Пушкина; Muzey Izobrazitelnykh Iskusstv im. A.S. Pushkina.) The museum houses Moscow's most important collection of non-Russian art, with major Renaissance, Egyptian, and classical works as well as superb pieces by Van Gogh, Chagall, and Picasso. *(Ul. Volkhonka 12 (Волхонка). M1: Kropotkinskaya. Open Su and Tu-Sa 10am-7pm; kassa closes at 6pm. 190R, students 60R.)*

KGB MUSEUM. (Музей КГБ; Muzey KGB.) The museum documents the history and strategies of Russian secret intelligence from the reign of Ivan the Terrible to the present. Enjoy the guide's intriguing anecdotes, followed by the opportunity to quiz a current FSB agent. *(Ul. Bul. Lubyanka 12. M1: Lubyanka. It's the building behind the concrete behemoth that towers over the northeast side of the square. Pre-arranged tours only; Patriarshy Dom Tours (☎ 795 09 27) leads 2hr. group tours of the museum, from US$15.)*

STATE HISTORICAL MUSEUM. (Государственный Исторический Музей; Gosudarstvennyi Istoricheskii Muzey.) This comprehensive collection traces Russian history from the Neanderthals through Kyivan Rus to modern Russia. Highlights include ancient idols and jewelry, elaborate medieval icons, and paintings of various historical figures. *(Krasnaya pl. 1/2. M1: Okhotnyy Ryad. Entrance to the right just inside Red Square. Open Su 11am-8pm, W-Sa 10am-6pm; kassa closes 1hr. earlier. Closed 1st M of each month. Museum 150R, students 75R.)*

CENTRAL MUSEUM OF THE ARMED FORCES. (Центральный Музей Вооруженных Сил; Tsentralnyy Muzey Vooruzhennykh Sil.) The museum exhibits a large collection of weapons, uniforms, and artwork from the time of Peter the Great to modern day. *(Ul. Sovetskoy Armii 2 (Советской Армии). M5: Novoslobodskaya. Walk down ul. Seleznevskaya (Селезневская) to the rotary (10min.). Turn left after the theater and bear right at the fork. Open Su and W-Sa 10am-5pm. Call ahead for an English tour; 300R. Museum 30R, students 10R.)*

HOMES OF THE LITERARY AND FAMOUS

■ **PUSHKIN LITERARY MUSEUM.** (Литературный Музей Пушкина; Literaturny Muzey Pushkina.) If you've never seen Pushkin-worship first-hand, this large collection of Pushkin memorabilia will either convert or frighten you. *(Ul. Prechistenka 12/2 (Пречистенка). Entrance on Khrushchevsky per. M1: Kropotkinskaya. Open Su and Tu-Sa 11am-7pm; kassa closes at 6pm. 25R, students 10R.)*

MAYAKOVSKY MUSEUM. (Музей им. В. В. Маяковского; Muzey im V. V. Mayakovskovo.) A walk-through work of Futurist art, the museum was created as a poetic reminder of Mayakovsky's ideas, life, and death. *(Lubyansky pr. 3/6 (Лубянский). M1: Lubyanka. Behind a bust of Mayakovsky on ul. Myasnitskaya (Мясницкая). Open Su-Tu and F-Sa 10am-6pm, Th 1-9pm. 60R.)*

TOLSTOY MUSEUM. (Музей Толстого; Muzey Tolstovo.) This museum in the neighborhood of Tolstoy's first Moscow residence displays original texts, paintings, and letters related to his masterpieces. *(Ul. Prechistenka 11 (Пречистенка). M1: Kropotkinskaya. Open Su and Tu-Sa 11am-7pm; kassa closes at 6pm. Closed last F of the month. 70R, students 30R.)*

GORKY MUSEUM-HOUSE. (Музей-дом Горкого; Muzey-dom Gorkovo.) The museum is a pilgrimage site as much for its Art Nouveau architecture as for its collection of Maxim Gorky's possessions. *(Ul. Malaya Nikitskaya 6/2 (Малая Никитская). M3: Arbatskaya; cross Novy Arbat, turn right on Merelyakovsky per. (Мереляковский), and cross the small park. Open W and F noon-7pm, Th and Sa-Su 10am-5pm. Closed last Th of the month. Donation requested.)*

▐▲ ENTERTAINMENT

From September to June, Moscow boasts some of the world's best theater, ballet, and opera, along with excellent orchestral performances. Advance tickets are often very cheap (US$2-5), and can be purchased from the *kassa* inside each theater or from "Театральные" kiosks throughout the city.

Bolshoy Theater (Большой Театр), Teatralnaya pl. 1 (☎292 00 50; www.bolshoi.ru). M2: Teatralnaya. Home to both the opera and the world-renowned ballet companies. *Kassa* open Su-W and F-Sa 11am-3pm and 4-7pm, Th 11am-3pm and 4-9pm. Performances Sept.-June daily at noon and 7pm. Tickets 20-3500R. MC/V.

Maly Teatr (Малый Театр), Teatralnaya pl. 1/6 (☎923 26 21). M2: Teatralnaya. Just right of the Bolshoy. Different Russian productions daily. *Kassa* open daily noon-3pm and 4-7pm. Sept.-June daily performances at 7pm. Tickets 20-300R.

Moscow Operetta Theater (Оперетты Театр), ul. Bolshaya Dmitrovka 6 (Большая Дмитровка; ☎292 12 37; www.operetta.org.ru), to the left of the Bolshoy. M2: Teatralnaya. Shows M-Th 7pm, F-Su 6pm, and some daytime performances. *Kassa* open M-Th noon-3pm and 4-7pm, F-Su noon-3pm and 4-6pm. Tickets 30-300R.

▐◕ NIGHTLIFE

Moscow's bacchanalian nightlife is the most varied, expensive, and dangerous in Eastern Europe. Many of the more interesting clubs enjoy flaunting their exclusivity and their cover charges; more sedate, inexpensive venues attract bohemians and absinthe-seeking students. Check the weekend editions of *The Moscow Times* or *The Moscow Tribune* for club reviews and music festival listings. The Friday pull-out section of *The Moscow Times*, the nightlife section of *The eXile* (www.exile.ru), and *The Beat* have weekly calendars and up-to-date restaurant, bar, and club reviews.

■ **Propaganda** (Пропаганда), Bolshoy Zlatoustinskiy per. 7 (Большой Златоустинский). M6 or 7: Kitai Gorod. Dance to good house without feeling like you're in a meat market. Beer 70R. Cover Sa-Su 100R. Open daily noon-6am.

Projekt OGI (Проект ОГИ), 8/12 Potapovskiy per., bldg. 2 (Потаповский). M1: Chistye Prudy. Head down bul. Chistoprudny (Чистопрудный), take the 1st right, then the 1st left onto Potapovsky per. Cheap, exceptional food and wine and a unique, colorful atmosphere. Cover 150-300R. Open 24hr.

Doug and Marty's Boar House, Zemlyanoi val. 26 (Земляной). M3: Kurskaya, opposite the train station. This American-style bar is packed with patrons on weekends. Happy Hour 6-9pm. 50% discount on food noon-9pm. Beer 90-145R. Cover men 150R, women 100R. Open daily noon-6am. AmEx/MC/V.

Hippopotamus (Гиппопотам), ul. Mantulinskiy 5/1 (Мантулинский). M7: Ulitsa 1905 Goda. Cross the intersection and walk down Tryokhgorny Val. Go right onto Shmitovskiy per., take the 1st left onto ul. 1905 Goda, and turn right onto ul. Mantulinskiy. Plays hip-hop, R&B, and soul. Beer US$2-3. Mixed drinks US$2-5. Cover men US$8, women US$4. Open Su and W-Sa 10pm-6am.

Karma Bar, ul. Pushechnaya 3. M: Kuznetzky Most. Walk through the archway on your left and turn right onto ul. Pushechnaya. Spins crowd-pleasing dance music. Amazing club dancers. Su hip-hop night. Beer 100-140R. Vodka 80-150R. Mixed drinks 180R. Cover F-Sa men 200R, women 100R. Open Su and Th-F 7pm-6am, Sa 9pm-6am.

■ DAYTRIP FROM MOSCOW: SERGIEV POSAD

Russia's most famous pilgrimage point, Sergiev Posad (Сергиев Посад; pop. 200,000) attracts believers to several churches huddled around its main sight: **St. Sergius's Trinity Monastery** (Свято-Троицкая Сергиева Лавра; Svyato-Troitskaya Sergieva Lavra). After decades of state-propagated atheism, the stunning monastery, founded circa 1340, is again a thriving religious center. The splendid **Assumption Cathedral** (Успенский Собор; Uspenskiy Sobor) was modeled after its namesake cathedral in Moscow's Kremlin. The magnificent frescoes of the **Refectory** (Трапезная; Trapeznaya) and the gilded Andrei Rublyov icons at **Trinity Cathedral** (Троицкий Собор; Troitskiy Sobor) are equally colorful and captivating. (Monastery open daily 9am-6pm.) **Commuter trains** *(elektrichki)* run to *Sergiev Posad* from Moscow's Yaroslavskiy Vokzal (1½-2hr., every 20-50min., round-trip 61R). To get to the monastery from the station, turn right and look for the domes, cross the street, and walk down the road until you see the city (10-15min.).

ST. PETERSBURG (САНКТ-ПЕТЕРБУРГ) ☎8812

The splendor of St. Petersburg's wide boulevards and bright facades is exactly what Peter the Great envisioned when he founded his "window on the West." The shutters were closed, however, when St. Petersburg (pop. 4,200,000) became the birthplace of the February Revolution of 1917 that turned Russia in to a Communist State. Sophisticated and majestic, the city has inspired the artistic genius of greats such as Dostoevsky, Gogol, Tchaikovsky, and Stravinsky, as well as the revolutionary dreams of Lenin and Trotsky.

▣ TRANSPORTATION

Flights: The main airport, **Pulkovo** (LED; Пулково), has 2 terminals: Pulkovo-1 (☎ 104 38 22) for domestic flights, and Pulkovo-2 (☎ 104 34 44) for international flights. From M2: Moskovskaya, take bus #39 to Pulkovo-1 (25min.) or bus #13 to Pulkovo-2 (20min.). Hostels can arrange a taxi (usually US$30-35).

Trains: Central Ticket Offices (Центральные Железнодорожные Кассы; Tsentralnye Zheleznodorozhnye Kassy), Canal Griboedova 24 (Грибоедого). International tickets at windows #4-6. Purchase tickets from **Intourist** offices at any of St. Petersburg's train stations on the day of departure. Check your ticket to see from which station your train leaves. Open M-Sa 8am-8pm, Su 8am-6pm.

Finlyandsky Vokzal (Финляндский Вокзал; Finland Train Station; ☎ 168 76 87). M1: pl. Lenina (Ленина). To **Helsinki** (6hr., 2 per day, 1375R).

Moskovsky Vokzal (Московский Вокзал; Moscow Train Station; ☎ 168 45 97). M1: pl. Vosstaniya (Восстания). To **Moscow** (5-8hr., 12-15 per day, 600-1200R) and **Novgorod** (3-4hr., 2 per day, 66R).

Vitebsky Vokzal (Витебский Вокзал; Vitebsky Train Station; ☎ 168 58 07). M1: Pushkinskaya (Пушкинская). To: **Kaliningrad** (26hr., daily); **Kyiv** (25hr., 2 every 2 days, 506-637R); **Odessa** (36hr., daily, 654R); **Rīga** (13hr., daily, 887R); **Tallinn** (9hr., daily, 350R); **Vilnius** (14hr., every 2 days, 647R).

Buses: nab. Obvodnovo Kanala 36 (Обводного Канала; ☎ 166 57 77). M4: Ligovsky pr. Take tram #19, 25, 44, or 49 or trolley #42 to the stop just across the canal. Facing the canal, turn right and walk 2 blocks. The station will be on your right, behind a derelict building. Surcharge for advance tickets. One-way tickets only. Open daily 6am-8pm.

Local Transportation: The efficient, cheap **Metro** (Метро) is the deepest in the world, and it's generally busy, especially 8-9am and 5-6pm. **Tokens** (жетон; zheton) cost 7R. Stock up, as lines are often long and cutting is common. For **buses, trams,** and **trolleys,** buy tickets (6R) from the driver. All run daily 6am-midnight. Licensed private **minibuses** (Маршрутки, Marshrutki), following a set route through the city, cost more (10R-14R) but move much more quickly through traffic and will stop on request.

Taxis: Marked cabs are 11R per km; add 35R if you call ahead. Many people hail private cars, which are usually cheaper but less safe, and negotiate the fare before getting in.

✴ ⓘ ORIENTATION AND PRACTICAL INFORMATION

The city center lies on mainland St. Petersburg between the south bank of the **Neva River** and the **Fontanka Canal.** The easiest way to get around the city is by using the Metro. Most major sights, including the Hermitage and the three main cathedrals, are on or near **Nevsky prospekt** (Невский Проспект), the city's main street; **Moscow Train Station** (Московский Вокзал; Moskovsky Vokzal) is near the midpoint. Trolleys #1, 5, and 22 run along Nevsky pr. On the north side of the Neva River is the **Petrograd Side** archipelago, where the **Peter and Paul Fortress** stands.

Museums and sights often charge several times more for "foreigners" than for Russians. To avoid paying the higher price, hand the cashier the exact amount for a Russian ticket, and say *adeen* (one). Walk as if you know where you are going, and do not keep your map, camera, or *Let's Go* in plain view. Dress like a local, and try to speak Russian when you can.

RUSSIA

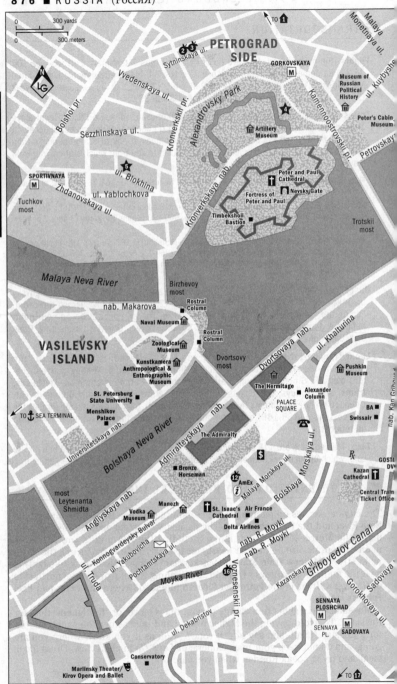

PETROGRAD SIDE

GORKOVSKAYA M

Museum of Russian Political History

Peter's Cabin Museum

Sytninskaya ul.

Wedenskaya ul.

Kronverkskii pr.

Alexandrovsky Park

Kamennoostrovskii pr.

Petrovskay

Sezzhinskaya ul.

Artillery Museum

Bolshoi pr.

ul. Blokhina

Peter and Paul Cathedral

Nevsky Gate

SPORTIVNAYA M

Zhdanovskaya ul.

ul. Yablochkova

Fortress of Peter and Paul

Kronverkskaya nab.

Tuchkov most

Timbeksholi Bastion

Trotskii most

Malaya Neva River

Birzhevoy most

nab. Makarova

Rostral Column

Naval Museum

Rostral Column

VASILEVSKY ISLAND

Zoological Museum

Dvortsovy most

Dvortsovaya nab.

ul. Khalturina

Kunstkamera Anthropological & Enthnographic Museum

Pushkin Museum

St. Petersburg State University

The Hermitage

Alexander Column

PALACE SQUARE

BA

TO ⚓ SEA TERMINAL

Menshikov Palace

Swissair

Universitetskaya nab.

Bolshaya Neva River

Admiralteyskaya nab.

nab. Kan Griboyeo

R⟋

GOSTI DV

Kazan Cathedral

The Admiralty

Central Train Ticket Office

Angliyskaya nab.

most Leytenanta Shmidta

Bronze Horseman

Manezh

$

Bolshaya Morskaya ul.

Malaya Moskaya ul.

Bolshaya Morskaya ul.

AmEx ⓘ

Vodka Museum

St. Isaac's Cathedral

Air France

Delta Airlines

Konnogvardeyskiy Bulvar

ul. Yakubovicha

Pochtamtskaya ul.

nab. R. Moyki

nab. R. Moyki

ul. Truda

Moyka River

Voznesenskii pr.

Kazanskaya ul.

Griboyedov Canal

Gorokhovaya ul.

Sadovaya

ul. Dekabristov

SENNAYA PLOSHCHAD M

SENNAYA PL.

SADOVAYA M

Conservatory

Marlinsky Theater/ Kirov Opera and Ballet

TO 17

300 yards
300 meters

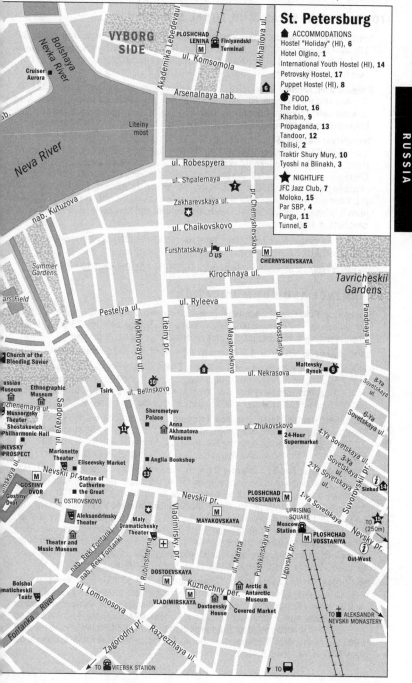

St. Petersburg

🏠 ACCOMMODATIONS
Hostel "Holiday" (HI), 6
Hotel Olgino, 1
International Youth Hostel (HI), 14
Petrovsky Hostel, 17
Puppet Hostel (HI), 8

🍴 FOOD
The Idiot, 16
Kharbin, 9
Propaganda, 13
Tandoor, 12
Tbilisi, 2
Traktir Shury Mury, 10
Tyoshi na Blinakh, 3

⭐ NIGHTLIFE
JFC Jazz Club, 7
Moloko, 15
Par SBP, 4
Purga, 11
Tunnel, 5

RUSSIA

TOURIST, FINANCIAL, AND LOCAL SERVICES

Tourist Office: Ost-West Contact Service, ul. Mayakovskovo 7 (Маяковского; ☎327 34 16; www.ostwest.com). M3: Mayakovskaya. Resourceful staff arranges homestays (US$20 in center; US$15 elsewhere), hotel rooms, tours, and theater tickets. Visa invitations and registrations US$35-50. Open M-F 10am-6pm.

Budget Travel: Sindbad Travel (FIYTO), ul. 3-ya Sovetskaya 28 (3-я Советская; ☎324 08 80; www.sindbad.ru), in the International Hostel. Arranges tickets and adventure trips. Student discounts on flights. Open M-F 9:30am-8pm, Sa-Su 10am-5pm. **Branch** office at nab. Universitetskaya 11 (Университетская наб; ☎/fax 324 08 80). Open M-F 10am-6pm.

Consulates: Canada, Malodetskoselsky pr. 32 (Малодетскосельский; ☎325 84 48; fax 325 83 93). M2: Frunzenskaya. Open M-F 9am-1pm and 2-5pm. **UK,** pl. Proletarskoi Diktatury 5 (Пролетарской Диктатуры; ☎320 32 00; www.britain.spb.ru). M1: Chernyshevskaya. Open M-F 9:30am-1pm, 2pm-5:30pm. **US,** ul. Furshtatskaya 15 (Фурштатская; ☎331 26 00; 24hr. emergency ☎331 28 88; acs_stpete@state.gov). M1: Chernyshevskaya. Open M-F 9am-5:30pm. Services for US citizens (fax 331 28 46) open 9:30am-1:30pm. Citizens of **Australia, Ireland,** and **New Zealand** can use the UK consulate in an emergency.

Currency Exchange: Look for "Обмен валюты" (obmen valyuty) signs everywhere. **Sperbank** (☎329 87 87). Dumskaya ul. 1 (right at M2: Nevsky pr.).

American Express: Ul. Malaya Morskaya 23 (☎326 45 00). Open M-F 9am-5pm.

EMERGENCY AND COMMUNICATIONS

Emergency: Police: ☎02. **Ambulance:** ☎03. **Fire:** ☎01. Multilingual police office for crimes against foreigners at ul. Zakharevskaya 19 (Захаревская; ☎278 30 14). M1: Chernyshevskaya. In the event of a crime, contact your consulate for help.

24hr. pharmacy: Nevsky pr. 22. Stocks Western medicines and toiletries. MC/V.

Medical Assistance: British-American Family Clinic, Grafsky Pereulok 7 (Графски пер; ☎327 60 30), on the corner of Vladmirsky pr. Expat staff offers primary care services and evaluations. Consultation with Western doctor US$90, with a Russian doctor US$60. Students with ISIC get a 30% reduction on these fees. Open 24hr.

Telephones: Central Telephone and Telegraph (Междугородный Междуяродный Телефон; Mezhdugorodny Mezhduyarodny Telefon) is located at Bolshaya Morskaya 28. **Branch** offices can be found at Nevsky pr. 27, Nevsky pr. 88, Nevsky pr. 107, Kronversky pr. 21, and Moskovsky Vokzal b.o. 3-ya Linya 8. Open daily 8am-10pm.

Internet Access: Red Fog Internet Cafe, ul. Kazanskaya 30-32 (☎595 41 39). M2: Nevsky pr. Walk toward the Admiralty as far as the Kazan Cathedral; turn left onto Kazanskaya ul. and follow it to ul. Kazanskaya 30. 8:30am-11:30pm 40R per hour; 11:30pm-8:30am 100R per hr. Open 24hr. **Consay Internet Salon,** Ligovsky pr. 63 (☎164 57 42). M1: pl. Vosstaniya. On your left as you go out Ligovsky pr. from pl. Vosstaniya. 6am-11pm 33R-48R per hr.; 11pm-6am 150R; student discount. Offers widest variety of services, including translation (5R per page), printing (3-60R per page; varies with paper type, size, and number of sheets), CD writing, and individual assistance (80R per hr.). ISIC discount 10% (9am-3pm 15%). Open 24hr.

Post Office: Ul. Pochtamtskaya 9 (Почтамтская; ☎312 83 02). From Nevsky pr., go west on ul. Malaya Morskaya, which becomes ul. Pochtamtskaya. It's about 2 blocks past St. Isaac's Cathedral on the right, before an overhanging arch. **Currency exchange** and **telephone** service. International mail at windows #24-30. *Poste Restante* held up to 1 month at windows #1 and 2. Address mail to be held: SURNAME Firstname, **190 000** Санкт-Петербург, Главпочтамт, Писмо До Востребования, RUSSIA. Open M-Sa 9am-7:45pm, Su 10am-5:45pm.

⚑ ACCOMMODATIONS

Puppet Hostel (HI), ul. Nekrasova 12 (Некрасова; ☎272 54 01; www.hostelling-russia.ru). M3: Mayakovskaya. Take the 2nd left on Nekrasova; the hostel is next to the Bolshoy Puppet Theater, on the 4th fl. Friendly, English-speaking staff and clean, simple rooms. Breakfast included. Check-out noon. No curfew. Apr.-Sept. dorms US$19; doubles US$48; Oct.-Mar. US$16/42. US$1 HI/ISIC discount. ❷

International Youth Hostel (HI), ul. 3-ya Sovetskaya 28 (☎329 80 18; ryh@ryh.ru). M1: pl. Vosstaniya. Walk 3 blocks down Suvorovsky pr. (Суворовский), then turn right on ul. 3-ya Sovetskaya. Great location in a pleasant neighborhood. Breakfast included. Internet access 1R per min. Laundry US$4 for 5kg. Check-out 11am. No curfew. Dorms US$19, with ISIC US$18, with HI US$17. ❷

Hostel "Holiday" (HI), nab. Arsenalnaya 9 (Арсенальная; ☎327 10 70; www.hostel.spb.ru). M1: pl. Lenina. Exit at Finlyandsky Vokzal, turn left on ul. Komsomola (Комсомола) and right on ul. Mikhailova (Михаилова). At the end of the street turn left onto nab Arsenalnaya. View across the glittering Neva River makes up for a slightly less convenient location. Breakfast included. Internet access 150R per hr. Call ahead. May-Sept. 3- to 5-bed dorms US$14; singles US$37; doubles US$38; Sept.-Apr. dorms US$12/$29/$30. HI/ISIC discount US$1, US$2 after 5 days. MC/V. ❷

Petrovsky Hostel, ul. Baltiskaya 26 (Балтийская; ☎252 53 81; fax 252 65 12). M1: Narvskaya. Facing the Triumphal Arch from the Metro station, turn left on Stachek pr.; when you reach the square, go left on ul. Baltiskaya. The hostel is a few blocks ahead in the Petrovsky College building. Though a trek from the center, this hostel's clean, comfortable rooms and low prices attract many guests. Kitchen, common room with TV, and a few private luxury rooms with bath, TV, and phone. Reception 9am-5pm. Check-in 24hr. 2- to 5-bed dorms 200R; *luks* rooms 400-800R. ❶

Hotel Olgino (Отель Ольгино), Primorskoye Shosse 18 (Приморское Шоссе; ☎238 36 71; fax 238 37 63). M4: Staraya Derevnya. From the Metro, take bus #110 (20-25 min.). Considerable luxury at an uninflated price. Offers banya, bowling, horseback riding, billiards, snow-biking, and disco-dancing. Check-out noon. Call ahead. Camping US$12. Singles US$50; doubles US$116-132; luxury rooms US$162-184. ❹

⚐ FOOD

Russian food is not known for innovation; most menus offer the staples of pike, sturgeon, beef, and sausage. Markets stock a wide range of items; don't be afraid to bargain. The **covered market,** Kuznechny pr. 3 (Кузнечьный), just around the corner from M1: Vladimirskaya, and the **Maltsevsky Rynok** (Мальцевский Рынок), ul. Nekrasova 52 (M1: pl. Vosstaniya), at the top of Ligovsky pr. (Лиговский), are the largest and most exciting. For groceries, try **24 Super Market,** at the corner of ul. Zhukovskovo and ul. Vosstaniya. (M3: pl. Vosstaniya. Open 24hr.)

> **!** Note that there is no effective water purification system in St. Petersburg, making exposure to **giardia** (p. 21) very likely, so boil tap water, use iodine, or buy bottled water.

Kharbin (Харбин), ul. Nekrasova 58 (☎279 99 90). M1: pl. Vosstaniya. Walk all the way down Ligovsky pr., passing the Oktyabrsky Hotel on your right. Chinese culinary delights. Divine salads (40-150R) and delicious entrees (90-400R). Open daily 1-11pm. MC/V. ❷

Propaganda, nab. Reki Fontanka 40. M2: Gostiny Dvor. Soviet-themed restaurant with snappy service. Meat and seafood menu. Entrees 150-350R. Open daily noon-5am. 20% discount from noon-3am. ❸

Tbilisi (Тбилиси), ul. Sytninskaya 10. M2: Gorkovskaya. Some of Russia's best Georgian cuisine. Entrees 40-260R. Live music from 8pm. Open daily noon-midnight. ❷

The Idiot (Идиоть), nab. Reki Moyki 82 (Реки Мойки; ☎315 16 75). M2: Sennaya pl. Turn right on Grivtsova pr. and walk toward the Moyka and Admiralty, then turn left on nab. Reki Moiki. The Idiot is on the left just past the bridge to Isaakyevskaya pl. Vegetarian Russian cuisine is worth the wait. Entrees 20-250R, plus a 10% service charge. Happy Hour 6:30-7:30pm. Open daily 11am-1am. No credit cards. ❷

Traktir Shury Mury, ul. Belinskovo 8 (Белинсково). M2: Gostiny Dvor or M1: Vladimir-skaya. Romantic country bistro serving delightful and inexpensive traditional dishes. Entrees 100-200R. Open 11am-late. MC/V. ❸

Tandoor (Тандур), Voznesensky pr. 2 (Вознесенский; ☎312 38 86). M2: Nevsky pr. On the corner of Admiralteysky pr. (Адмиралтейский), at the end of Nevsky pr. Tandoor makes it easy to forget that Russia is just outside. Vegetarian options. Lunch special M-F noon-5pm US$10. Dinner US$15-18. Open daily noon-11pm. AmEx/D/MC. ❹

Tyoshi na Blinakh, ul. Sytninskaya 16 (Сытнинская; ☎232 76 69). Great for lunch on the run. Salads, meat dishes, and *blini* (pancakes) stuffed with fillers ranging from proletarian cabbage (26R) to bourgeois caviar (45R). Open daily 10am-9pm. ❶

◉ SIGHTS

■ **THE HERMITAGE.** The State Hermitage Museum (Эрмитаж; Ermitazh) houses the world's largest art collection. The collection, which began with 255 paintings bought by Catherine the Great in 1764, now rivals the Louvre and the Prado in architectural, historical, and artistic significance. The **Winter Palace** (Зимний Дворец; Zimny Dvorets) was commissioned in 1762. The complex later expanded to include the Small Hermitage (Малый; Maly Ermitazh), the Large Hermitage (Большой; Bolshoy Ermitazh), the Hermitage Theater (Эрмитажный Театр; Ermitazhny Teatr), and the New Hermitage (Новый; Novy Ermitazh). The tsars lived with their collections in the complex until 1917, when the museum was nationalized. It is impossible to absorb the whole museum in a day or even in a week; only 5% of the three-million-piece collection is on display at a time. English floor plans are available at the info desk near the *kassa*.

Palace Square (Дворцовая Площадь; Dvortsovaya Ploshchad), the huge, windswept expanse in front of the Winter Palace, has witnessed many turning points in Russia's history. Catherine took the crown here after overthrowing Tsar Peter III, her husband; years later, Nicholas II's guards fired into a crowd of peaceful demonstrators on "Bloody Sunday," which precipitated the 1905 revolution; and Lenin's Bolsheviks seized power from the provisional government during the storming of the Winter Palace in October 1917. The 700-ton **Alexander Column,** held in place by its massive weight alone, commemorates Russia's defeat of Napoleon in 1812. Across the bridge from the Hermitage, **Vasilevsky Island** splits the Neva River in two; most of its sights lie on the eastern edge in the **Strelka** neighborhood. The area closest to the Hermitage was a center for sea trade and now houses many of the city's best museums. *(nab. Dvortsovaya 34 (Дворцовая). M2: Nevsky pr. Exiting the Metro, turn left and walk down Nevsky pr. to the Admiralty. The Hermitage is to the right; enter on the river side. Open Su and Tu-Sa 10:30am-6pm; cashier and upper floors close 1hr. earlier. Camera fee 100R. Long lines; come early. 320R. Students free.)*

■ ST. ISAAC'S CATHEDRAL. Glittering, intricately carved masterpieces of iconography are appropriately housed under the awesome dome of **St. Isaac's Cathedral** (Исаакиевский Собор; Isaakievsky Sobor), a 101.5m tall exemplar of 19th-century architecture. On a sunny day, the 100kg of pure gold coating the dome is visible for miles. The 360° view of the city from atop the **colonnade** is stunning. *(M2: Nevsky pr. Exiting the Metro, turn left and walk almost to the end of Nevsky pr.; turn left onto ul. Malaya Morskaya. Open daily 11am-7pm. 250R, students 125R. Colonnade open daily 11am-6pm. 100R, students 50R. Last entry 1hr. before closing. The kassa is to the right of the main entrance. Foreigners buy tickets inside.)*

PETER AND PAUL FORTRESS. Across the river from the Hermitage stand the walls and golden spire of the Peter and Paul Fortress (Петропавловская Крепость; Petropavlovskaya Krepost). Construction of the fortress, supervised by Peter the Great himself, began on May 27, 1703, which is considered the birthday of St. Petersburg. The fortress was intended as a defense against the Swedes, but was later used as a prison for political dissidents. Inside, the **Peter and Paul Cathedral** (Петропавловский Собор; Petropavlovsky Sobor) glows with rosy marble walls and a breathtaking Baroque partition covered with intricate iconography. The cathedral holds the remains of Peter the Great and his successors. Before the main vault sits the **Chapel of St. Catherine the Martyr.** The bodies of the last Romanovs—Tsar Nicholas II and his family—were entombed here on July 17, 1998, on the 80th anniversary of their murder at the hands of the Bolsheviks. Condemned prisoners awaited their common fate at **Trubetskoy Bastion** (Трубецкой Бастион), where Peter the Great held and tortured his first son, Aleksei. Dostoevsky, Gorky, Trotsky, and Lenin's older brother also spent time here. *(M2: Gorkovskaya. Exiting the Metro, turn right on Kamennoostrovsky pr. (Каменноостровский), the street in front of you (there is no sign). Continue to the river and cross the wooden bridge to the island fortress. Open Su-M and Th-Sa 10am-5pm, Tu 10am-4pm; closed last Tu of each month. A single ticket covers most sights (120R, students 60R) at the kassa in the "boathouse" in the middle of the complex or in the smaller kassa to the right, just inside the main entrance.)*

ALEKSANDR NEVSKY MONASTERY. A major pilgrimage site and peaceful strolling ground, Aleksandr Nevsky Monastery (Александро-невская Лавра; Aleksandro-Nevskaya Lavra) became one of four Orthodox monasteries to receive the highest monastic title of *lavra* in 1797. The **Artists' Necropolis** (Некрополь Мастеров Искусств; Nekropol Masterov Uskusstv) is the permanent resting place of Fyodor Dostoyevsky and composers Tchaikovsky, Rimsky-Korsakov, and Mussorgsky. The nearby **Lazarus Cemetery** (Лазаревское Кладбище; Lazarevskoye Kladbishche), also known as the 18th-century Necropolis, is the city's oldest burial ground. The **Church of the Annunciation** (Благовещенская Церковь; Blagoveshchenskaya Tserkov), farther along the central stone path on the left, holds the remains of war heroes and is the original burial place of the Romanovs, who were moved to Peter and Paul Cathedral in 1998. The active **Holy Trinity Cathedral** (Свято-Троицкий Собор; Svyato-Troitsky Sobor), teeming with priests and devout *babushki*, is at the end of the path. *(M3/4: pl. Aleksandra Nevskovo. The 18th-century Necropolis lies behind and to the left of the entrance; the Artists' Necropolis is behind and to the right. Dress modestly. Grounds open daily 6am-10pm, cathedral open daily 6am-8pm, 18th-century Necropolis open 9:30am-5:45pm, Artists' Necropolis open 9:30am-6pm. Admission to both cemeteries 60R, students 30R.)*

ALONG NEVSKY PROSPEKT. Many sights cluster around the western end of vibrant Nevsky pr., the city's 4.5km main thoroughfare. Unfortunately, there is no Metro station immediately nearby; one was built, but after the station was completed, local residents refused to allow the construction of an entrance or exit connecting it to the surface. The **Admiralty** (Адмиралтейство; Admiralteystvo) towers over the surrounding gardens and most of Nevsky pr. The golden spire of this former naval headquarters was painted black during WWII to disguise it from German artillery bombers. In the park to the left of the Admiralty is the **Bronze Horseman** statue of Peter the Great, one of the most widely recognized symbols of the city; copies are all over Russia. *(M2: Nevsky pr. Exit the Metro and walk to the end of Nevsky pr. toward the golden spire.)* Walking back east on Nevsky pr., the enormous, Roman-style **Kazan Cathedral** (Казанский Собор; Kazansky Sobor) looms to the right. *(M2: Nevsky pr. Open daily 8:30am-7:30pm. Free.)* Half a block down, looking up Canal Griboyedova to the left, you can see the brilliantly colored ▧**Church of the Bleeding Savior** (Спас На Крови; Spas Na Krovi), which sits on the site of the 1881 assassination of Tsar Aleksandr II. *(In summer, open Su-Tu and Th-Sa 10am-7pm; off-season 11am-7pm; kassa closes at 6pm. 250R, students with ID 125R, under-7 free.)* The 220-year-old **Merchants' Yard** (Гостиный Двор; Gostiny Dvor) is to the right. *(M3: Gostiny Dvor. Open daily 10am-9pm.)* Nearby **Ostrovskovo Square** (Островского) houses the historic Aleksandrinsky Theater and an impressive monument to Catherine the Great. Much farther down Nevsky pr. is **Uprising Square** (Площадь Восстания; Ploshchad Vosstaniya), where the bloodiest confrontations of the February Revolution of 1917 took place. *(M1: pl. Vosstaniya.)*

SUMMER GARDENS AND PALACE. The long, shady paths of the Summer Gardens and Palace (Летний Сад и Дворец; Letny Sad i Dvorets) are a lovely place to rest and cool off. Peter's small **Summer Palace**, in the northeast corner, has decor reflecting his diverse tastes, with everything from Spanish and Portuguese chairs to Dutch tile and German clocks. **Mars Field** (Марсово Поле; Marsovo Pole), a memorial to the victims of the Revolution and the Civil War (1917-1919), extends next to the Summer Gardens. *(M2: Nevsky Prospekt. Turn right on nab. Kanala Griboyedova (Канала Грибоедова), pass the Church of the Bleeding Savior, cross the Moyka, and turn right on ul. Pestelya (Пестеля). The palace and gardens will be on your left, just after the next small canal. Garden open May-Oct. daily 10am-9:30pm. 12R, students 10R; Nov.-Apr. daily 10am-8pm. Free. Palace open May-Oct. M and W-Su 11am-6pm; closed last M of the month. Palace signs in English. 100R, students 50R, free the 3rd. Th of the month.)*

MUSEUMS. The ▧**Russian Museum** (Русский Музей; Russky Muzey) boasts the world's second largest collection of Russian art. *(M3: Gostiny Dvor. Down ul. Mikhailovskaya past the Grand Hotel Europe. Open M and W-Su 10am-6pm; kassa closes 1hr. earlier. 240R, students 120R.)* The **Pushkin Museum** (Музей Пушкина; Muzey Pushkina) displays the personal effects of Russia's adored poet and tells the tragic story of his last days. *(M2: Nevsky pr. Walk toward the Admiralty and turn right onto nab. Reki Moyki. Follow the canal; the museum is the yellow building on the right. Open Su-M and W-Sa 10:30am-5pm. Closed last F of the month. Camera 50R. 80R, 40R without tour; students 20/10R.)* **Dostoyevsky House** (Дом Достоевского; Dom Dostoyevskovo) is where the author wrote *The Brothers Karamazov.* *(M1: Vladimirskaya. On the corner of ul. Dostoevskovo, just past the market. Open Su and Tu-Sa 11am-6pm. Closed last W of each month. Kassa closes 5:30pm. 80R, students 40R.)* The **Museum of Russian Political History** (Музей Политической Истории России; Muzey Politicheskoi Istorii Rossii) has a vast collection of Soviet propaganda and artifacts from WWII. *(M2: Gorkovskaya. Go down Kamennoostrovsky toward the mosque and turn left on Kuybysheva. Open Su-W and F-Sa 10am-6pm. 80R, students 40R.)* The **Russian Vodka Museum** (Музей Водки; Muzey Vodki) is the world's first and, to date, only museum devoted to vodka. It features exhibits about the history of vodka, and the cafe offers a chance for hands on learning. *(Konnogvardeysky bul. 5. From the Manezh, walk 1 block toward the river and go left on Konnogvardeysky bul. The museum is one block down on the right. Open daily 11am-10pm. 50R. Vodka shots 20-60R. MC/V.)*

✴ ♫ FESTIVALS AND ENTERTAINMENT

Throughout the month of June, when the evening sun barely touches the horizon, the city holds a series of outdoor concerts as part of the famed **White Nights Festival.** Watch the bridges over the Neva River go up at 1:30am, but remember to walk on the side of the river where your hotel is located—the bridges don't go back down until 4:30-5:30am, though some are down briefly from 3 to 3:20am.

The city of Tchaikovsky, Prokofiev, and Stravinsky continues to live up to its reputation as a mecca for the performing arts. Tickets to world-class performances are often as little as 100R. You could try to save a fair bit of money by buying Russian tickets from scalpers, but you'll have to pose as a Russian to get into the performance. The **Mariinsky Teatr** (Мариинский; a.k.a."Kirov"), Teatralnaya pl. 1 (Театральная), can be reached by M4 (dir.: Sadovaya) or Bus #3, 22, or 27. Widely known as one of the most famous ballet halls in the world, the Mariinsky Teatr premiered Tchaikovsky's *Nutcracker* and *Sleeping Beauty*, and Baryshnikov, Nizhinsky, Nureyev, and Pavlova all started here. In June, the theater hosts the **White Nights Festival.** Tickets go on sale 20 days in advance. (☎326 41 41. 160-3200R for foreigners. *Kassa* open Su and Tu-Sa 11am-3pm and 4-9pm.) **Musorksorgsky Opera and Ballet Theater** (Театр Имены Муссоргского), pl. Iskusstv 1, is open July-Aug., when Mariinsky is closed. (☎595 42 82. Bring your passport. Tickets 240-1800R for foreigners. *Kassa* open Su-M and W-Sa 11am-7pm, Tu 11am-6pm.) **Shostakovich Philharmonic Hall,** ul. Mikhailovskaya 2, opposite the Russian Museum, has both classical and modern concerts. (☎110 42 57. M3: Gostiny Dvor. Tickets from 480-800R. *Kassa* open daily 11am-3pm and 4-7:30pm.) **Aleksandrinsky Teatr** (Александринский Театр), pl. Ostrovskovo 2, attracts famous Russian actors and companies. (☎311 15 33. M3: Gostiny Dvor. Tickets 70-680R. *Kassa* open daily noon-6pm.)

▣ NIGHTLIFE

▩ **JFC Jazz Club,** ul. Shpalernaya 33 (Шпалерная). M1: Chernyshevskaya. Showcases exciting local jazz. Cover 100-150R. Open daily 7-11pm.

Par SBP, 5B Alexandrovsky Park. M2: Gorkovskaya. Exit the Metro and bear right, walking through the park toward the fortress. Progressive club spinning underground house. Beer and vodka from 30R. Cover 100-500R. Open Su and Th-Sa from 11pm.

Tunnel, ul. Blokhina 16. M2: Gorkovskaya. Located in a former bomb shelter, this spacious techno club has an excellent sound system. Beer and vodka 40R. Cover 120-250R. Open Th-Sa midnight-8am.

Moloko (Молоко; Milk), Perekupnoy pr. 12. Off Nevskiy pr., halfway between M1: pl. Vosstaniya and M3/4: pl. Aleksandra Nevskovo. A mecca of live music featuring the best St. Petersburg bands. Beer 25R. Cover 70-120R. Open Su and Tu-Sa 7pm-midnight; music starts at 8pm.

Purga, Reki Fontanka 11. M3: Gostiny Dvor. Walk toward pl. Vosstaniya on Nevskiy pr. and make a left on Reki Fontanki (don't cross the Fontanka). Without taking itself too seriously, this cafe provides very well for its loyal and varied clientele. Beer 60R. Food 60-250R. Open daily noon-6am.

▨ DAYTRIPS FROM ST. PETERSBURG

PETERHOF. Peterhof (Петергоф) is the largest and the best-restored of the Russian palaces. It was burned to the ground during the Nazi retreat, but Soviet authorities provided the staggering sums needed to rebuild it. The gates open onto the **Lower Gardens,** a perfect place for a picnic along the shores of the Gulf of Finland. (Open May-Sept. M-F 10am-5pm, Sa-Su 10am-6pm; Oct.-Apr. 9am-5pm; last entrance 1hr. earlier. 200R, students 125R.) Wanting to create his own Versailles, Peter started building the first residence at the **Grand Palace** (Большой Дворец; Bolshoy Dvorets) in 1714; his daughter Empress Elizabeth and later Catherine the Great expanded and remodeled it. (Open Su and Tu-Sa 10:30am-6pm. Closed last Th of the month. 380R, students 190R.) The elegant, gravity-powered fountains of the **Grand Cascade** shoot from the palace into the Grand Canal. To enter the impressive stone grotto underneath the fountains, buy tickets just outside the palace. (Grotto open Su and Tu-Sa 11am-4:30pm; *kassa* 10:30am-noon and 2-4:15pm. 100R, students 50R.) The Grand Palace was saved for special occasions—Peter actually lived at **Monplaisir.** (Open Su, Tu, and Th-Sa 10:30am-6pm; *kassa* closes at 5pm. Closed third Tu of the month. 190R, students 95R.) Next door is the **Catherine Building** (Екатерининский Корпус; Ekaterininsky Korpus), where Catherine the Great laid low while her husband was being overthrown on her orders. (Open Su-W and F-Sa 10:30am-5pm. 100R, students 50R.)

Take the **train** from Baltiysky station (Балтийский; M1: Baltiyskaya; 35min., every 10-50min., 32R). Tickets are sold at the office (Пригородная касса; *prigorodnaya kassa*) in the courtyard. Get off at Novy Peterhof. From the station, take any van (5min.; 10R) or bus (10min.; 7R) to Petrodvorets (*Петродворец*; Peter's Palace) and get off when you see the palace. Or, in summer, take the **hydrofoil** from the quay on nab. Dvortsovaya (Дворцовая) in front of the Hermitage (30-35min.; every 40-60min. 9:30am-6pm; 400R, students 300R.)

TSARSKOYE SELO (PUSHKIN). About 25km south of St. Petersburg, Tsarskoye Selo (Tsar's Village) surrounds Catherine the Great's summer residence, a gorgeous azure, white, and gold Baroque palace overlooking extensive, English-style parks. The area was renamed "Pushkin" during the Soviet era, although the train station, Detskoye Selo (Детское Село; Children's Village), kept its old name. (Open Su-M and W-Sa 10am-6pm. 400R, students 200R.) The palace overlooks sprawling **parks** where Catherine once rambled with her dogs, who some believed she loved more than her own children. (Open May-Sept. daily 9am-11pm; Oct.-Apr. 10am-11pm. 70R, students 35R. Free after 6pm.) In summer, a ferry runs across the Great Pond to the **Island Pavilion.** (Ferry every 40min. noon-6pm; round-trip 200R, students 100R. All buildings open May-Sept.) The **Cold Bath Pavilion,** which contains the exotic Agate Rooms, stands in front of the palace to the left. (Open Su and W-Sa 10am-5pm. 160R, students 80R.) Across the street from the palace, the **lycée** schooled a 12-year-old Pushkin. His classrooms and spartan dorm room can still be seen through hordes of awestruck Russians. (Open Su-M and W-Sa 10:30am-5:30pm. 80R, students 20R.) The *elektrichka* runs from Vitebsky Station (M1: Pushkinskaya). All **trains** from platforms 1-3 go to Pushkin, the first stop that looks like a real station (30min.). From the station, take bus #371 or 382 to the end (10min., 5R). To find the stop, watch for the palace through the trees to the right.

SLOVAK REPUBLIC
(SLOVENSKA REPUBLIKA)

After centuries of nomadic invasions and Hungarian domination, as well as 40 years of Soviet rule, the Slovak Republic has finally emerged as an independent nation. While still part of Czechoslovakia, the country rejected Communism in the 1989 Velvet Revolution, then split from its Czech neighbor in 1993. The Slovak Republic is now stuck in a state of flux between industry and agriculture, with many rural Slovaks still sticking to their peasant traditions while their children flock to the city. Meanwhile, budget travelers are discovering its castle ruins and spectacular terrain, made even more attractive by the country's low prices.

FACTS AND FIGURES

Official Name: Slovak Republic.

Capital: Bratislava.

Population: 5,400,000.

Land Area: 48,845 sq. km.

Time Zone: GMT +1.

Languages: Slovak, Hungarian.

Religions: Roman Catholic (60%), Protestant (8%), atheist (10%), other (22%).

DISCOVER THE SLOVAK REPUBLIC

The Slovak Republic is an outdoor-lover's paradise. In the west, the relatively deserted **Low Tatras** near **Liptovský Mikuláš** (p. 893) offer everything from day hikes in the range's wooded foothills to overnight treks above the tree line. One of the best—and cheapest—mountain playlands in Europe, the snow-capped **High Tatras** near **Starý Smokovec** (p. 892) are filled with German and Slovak tourists. Farther south, **Slovenský Raj National Park** (p. 893) contains miles of ravine-crossing, cliff-climbing, and mountain treks, as well as ice caves ripe for spelunking. The often-overlooked capital, **Bratislava** (p. 888), has its own man-made treasures, including a ruined castle towering over the Danube.

ESSENTIALS

DOCUMENTS AND FORMALITIES

VISAS. Citizens of South Africa and the US can visit the Slovak Republic without a visa for up to 30 days; citizens of Australia, Canada, Ireland, New Zealand, and the UK can visit for 90 days. To apply for a visa, contact an embassy or consulate in person or by mail; processing may take up to 30 days, and prices vary with exchange rate (30-day single-entry €32; 90-day multiple-entry €67; 180-day multiple-entry €90). Travelers must also register their visa within three days of entering the country; most hotels do so automatically. If you intend to stay longer or get a visa extension, notify the Office of Border and Alien Police.

EMBASSIES. All foreign embassies are in Bratislava (p. 888). Slovakian embassies at home include: **Australia,** 47 Culgoa Circuit, O'Malley, Canberra, ACT 2606 (☎06 290 1516; www.slovakemb-aust.org); **Canada,** 50 Rideau Terrace, Ottawa, ON K1M 2A1 (☎613-749-4442; www.slovakembassy.com); **Ireland,** 20 Clyde Rd., Ballsbridge, Dublin 4 (☎01 660 0012 or 660 0008); **South Africa,** 930 Arcadia St., Arcadia, Pretoria, P.O. Box 12736, Hatfield, 0028 (☎012 342 2051; fax 342 3688); **UK,** 25

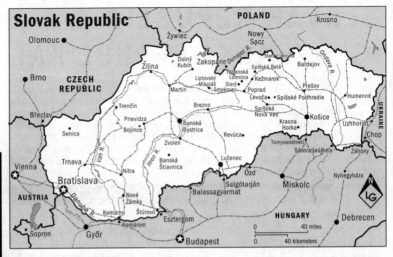

Kensington Palace Gardens, London W8 4QY (☎ 020 7243 0803; www.slovakembassy.co.uk); and **US**, 2201 Wisconsin Ave. NW, Ste. 250, Washington, D.C. 20007 (☎ 202-237-1054; www.slovakembassy-us.org).

TRANSPORTATION

BY PLANE. Entering the country through Bratislava's international airport (BTS) can be inconvenient and expensive. Flying to Vienna and then taking a bus or train into the Slovak Republic is cheaper and takes about the same amount of time.

BY TRAIN. ŽSR (www.zsr.sk) is the national train company; **Cestovný poriadok** (58Sk), the master schedule, is available at every info desk, and is also printed on a large, round board in stations. **EastRail** is valid in the Slovak Republic, but **Eurail** is not. Tickets must be bought before boarding the train, except in the tiniest towns. Large stations have **BIJ-Wasteels** offices, which sell discounted tickets to those under 26. Fast *InterCity* and *EuroCity* trains are more expensive. If a boxed R appears on the timetable, a reservation (*miestenka;* 7Sk) is required; if you board without a reservation, expect to pay a fine. Reservations are also recommended for *expresný* (express) trains and first-class seats, but are not necessary for *rychlík* (fast), *spešný* (semi-fast), or *osobný* (local) trains. First and second class are both relatively comfortable.

BY BUS. In many hilly regions, **ČSAD** or **SAD** buses are the best—and sometimes only—option. Except for long trips, buy tickets on the bus. Schedule symbols include: **X,** weekdays only; **a,** Saturdays and Sundays only; **r** and **k,** excluding holidays. Numbers refer to the days of the week on which the bus runs—1 is Monday, 2 is Tuesday, and so forth. *"Premava"* means including and *"nepremava"* is except; following those words are often lists of dates (day, then month).

BY BIKE AND BY THUMB. The Slovaks love to ride **bikes,** especially in the Tatras, the western foothills, and Šariš. VKÚ publishes color maps of most regions (70-80Sk). *Let's Go* does not recommend **hitchhiking,** which is legal, but neither convenient nor common; if you hitchhike, write your destination on a sign.

TOURIST SERVICES AND MONEY

EMERGENCY	Police: ☎123. Ambulance: ☎233. Fire: ☎23.

TOURIST OFFICES. The main tourist offices form a loose conglomeration called **Asociácia Informačných Centier Slovenska** (AICS); look for the green logo. The offices, often with English-speaking staff, are invariably in or near the town's main square; for the nearest location, dial ☎186. The **Slovakotourist** travel agency can help arrange transportation and accommodations.

MONEY. One hundred *halér* make up one **Slovak koruna** (Sk). Inflation is currently around 8%. **Banks** are usually the best—and often the only—places to change money. **Všeobecná Úverová Banka** (VÚB), which has offices in even the smallest towns, cashes American Express Traveler's Cheques for a 1% commission, and often gives MasterCard cash advances. Many **Slovenská Sporiteľňa** bureaus handle Visa cash advances. There are 24hr. **ATMs** in all but the smallest towns. The most commonly accepted credit cards are MasterCard and Visa. Tipping is common in restaurants; as there are no exact rules, most people simply round up. Do not try to bargain in the Slovak Republic; it is especially rude when foreigners do so.

SLOVAK REPUBLIC

SLOVAK KORUNA		
AUS$1 = 24.72SK		10SK = AUS$0.40
CDN$1 = 27.56SK		10SK = CDN$0.36
EUR€1 = 41.95SK		10SK = EUR€0.24
NZ$1 = 22.08SK		10SK = NZ$0.45
UK£1 = 60.25		10SK = UK£0.17
US$1 = 38.20SK		10SK = US$0.26
ZAR1 = 5.21SK		10SK = ZAR1.92

COMMUNICATION

PHONE CODES	**Country code: 421. International dialing prefix:** 00. From outside the Slovak Republic, dial int'l dialing prefix (see inside back cover) + 421 + city code + local number.

TELEPHONE AND INTERNET ACCESS. Card phones are common and are much better than the coin-operated variety. Purchase cards (100-500Sk) at kiosks; buy the "GlobalPhone" card to make international calls. International direct access numbers include: **AT&T,** ☎00 42 70 01 01; **British Telecom,** ☎080 00 44 01; **Canada Direct,** ☎08 00 00 01 51; and **MCI,** ☎08 00 00 01 12. **Internet** access is common even in small towns; Internet cafes usually offer the cheapest and fastest connections.

MAIL. The Slovak Republic has an efficient mail service. International mail takes two to three weeks, depending on the destination. Almost every post office (*pošta*) provides **Express Mail Services,** but use a *colnice* (customs office) to send packages abroad. When sending mail *Poste Restante*, put a "1" after the city name to indicate the main post office; address mail to be held: Firstname SURNAME, *Poste Restante*, Nám. SNP 35, 81000 Bratislava 1, SLOVAK REPUBLIC.

LANGUAGES. Slovak, closely related to Czech, is a complex Slavic language. Attempts to speak it are appreciated. English is often spoken at tourist offices and by Bratislava's youth. Elsewhere, people are more likely to know German. Russian is often understood, but not always welcome.

ACCOMMODATIONS AND CAMPING

SLOVAK REPUBLIC	❶	❷	❸	❹	❺
ACCOMMODATIONS	under 250Sk	250-500Sk	501-800Sk	801-1000Sk	over 1000Sk

Foreigners often must pay up to twice as much as Slovaks for the same room. Finding cheap accommodations in Bratislava before the student dorms open in July is impossible, and without reservations, the outlook in Slovenský Raj and the Tatras can be bleak. In other regions, it's not difficult to find a bed as long as you call ahead. A tourist office or Slovakotourist agency can usually help. **Juniorhotels (HI),** though uncommon, are a step above the usual hostel. **Hotels** are rarely full, and prices fall dramatically outside Bratislava and the High Tatras. **Pensions** (*penzióny*) are smaller and less expensive than hotels. **Campgrounds** lurk on the outskirts of most towns, and many offer bungalows. Note that camping in national parks is illegal. In the mountains, **chaty** (mountain huts/cottages) range from a friendly bunk and outhouse for 200Sk per night to plush quarters for 600Sk.

FOOD AND DRINK

SLOVAK REPUBLIC	❶	❷	❸	❹	❺
FOOD	under 120Sk	120-190Sk	191-270Sk	271-330Sk	over 330Sk

The national dish, *bryndžové halušky*, is a plate of dumpling-like pasta smothered in a thick sauce of sheep or goat cheese, often flecked with bacon. *Knedlíky* (dumplings) frequently accompany entrees, but it is possible to opt for *zemiaky* (potatoes) or *hranolky* (fries) instead. Note that a *syrový burger* (cheeseburger) is made of only cheese, and hamburgers are made from ham. *Koláčky* (pastry) is baked with cheese, jam or poppy seeds, and honey. Enjoy flavorful wines at a *vináreň* (wine hall); the western Slovak Republic produces the celebrated full-bodied *Modra*. *Pivo* (beer) is served at a *pivnica* or *piváreň* (tavern). The favorite Slovak beer is *Zlatý Bažant*, a light, slightly bitter Tatran brew.

SAFETY AND SECURITY

Tap water varies in quality and appearance but is generally safe. *Drogerie* (drugstores) stock Western brand names: Bandages are *obväz*, aspirin *aspirena*, tampons *tampony*, and condoms *kondómy*. The Slovak Republic is friendly toward **lone women travelers,** though they may encounter stares. **Minority** travelers with darker skin may be mistaken for the stigmatized Roma (Gypsies) and are thus advised to exercise caution. **Homosexuality** is not always tolerated.

HOLIDAYS

Holidays: Independence Day (Jan. 1); Epiphany (Jan. 6); Good Friday (Apr. 9); Easter (Apr. 11); May Day (May 1); Sts. Cyril and Methodius Day (July 5); Anniversary of Slovak Uprising (Aug. 29); Constitution Day (Sept. 1); Our Lady of the Seven Sorrows (Sept. 15); All Saints' Day (Nov. 1); Christmas (Dec. 24-26).

BRATISLAVA   ☎02

One of only two regions in Eastern Europe with living standards above the European Union average, Bratislava (pop. 450,000) surprises those who take the time to discover it. While villages, vineyards, and castles lace the outskirts of the booming city, inside, its streets are lined with shops, restaurants, and cafes.

Since the Velvet Revolution of 1989, the collapse of Communism, and the dissolution of Czechoslovakia in 1993, quality of life in Bratislava has risen above that in other cities in the region.

▐ TRANSPORTATION

Trains: Bratislava Hlavná stanica. To get downtown, take tram #2 to the sixth stop. International tickets at counters #5-13. **Wasteels** (☎ 52 49 93 57; www.wasteels.host.sk) sells discounted tickets to those under 26. Open M-F 8:30am-4:30pm. To **Prague** (4½-5½hr., 3 per day, 750-838Sk) and **Warsaw** (8hr., daily, 1456Sk).

Buses: Mlynské nivy 31 (☎ 55 42 16 67). Take trolley #202 to the center, or turn right on Mlynské nivy and continue to Dunajská, which leads to Kamenné nám. and the center of town. To: **Berlin** (12hr., daily, 1200Sk); **Budapest** (4hr., daily, 550Sk); **Prague** (4¾hr., 5 per day, 410Sk); **Vienna** (1½hr., every 1-2 hr., 380Sk); and **Warsaw** (13hr., daily, 670Sk). More reliable than trains for domestic transport. Check ticket for bus number (č. aut.) since several different buses may depart from the same stand.

Public Transportation: Tickets for daytime **trams** and **buses** (4am-11pm) are sold at kiosks and orange ticket machines in bus stations (10min. ticket 14Sk, 30min. 16Sk, 1hr. 22Sk). **Night buses**, marked with black and orange numbers in the 500s, require 2 tickets (midnight-4am). Stamp your ticket on board or face a 1200Sk fine. **Tourist passes** are sold at kiosks: 1-day pass 80Sk, 2-day 150Sk, 3-day 185Sk, 7-day 275Sk.)

Taxis: BP (☎ 16 999); **FunTaxi** (☎ 16 777); **Profi Taxi** (☎ 16 222).

Hitchhiking: Those hitching to **Vienna** cross Most SNP and walk down Viedenská cesta. This road also heads to **Hungary** via Győr, though fewer cars head in that direction. Hitchikers to **Prague** take bus #21 from the center to Patronka. For destinations within the Slovak Republic, take tram #2 or 4 to Zlaté Piesky. Hitchhiking is legal (except on major highways), but Let's Go does not recommend it.

▐✦▐ ORIENTATION AND PRACTICAL INFORMATION

The **Dunaj** (Danube) runs west-east through the city, which is a stone's throw from the borders of Austria and Hungary. The city center lies between **Námestie Slovenského Národného Povstania** (Nám. SNP; Slovak National Uprising Square) and the river. Suché mýto leads from Nám. SNP to **Kamenné Námestie** (Stone Square).

Tourist Office: Bratislavská Informačná Služba (BIS), Klobúčnicka 2 (☎ 16 186; www.bratislava.sk/bis), books private rooms and hotel rooms for a 50Sk fee, sells maps (60Sk) and a pass to four major museums (75Sk), and gives tours. Open June-Oct. 15 M-F 8:30am-7pm, Sa-Su 10am-6pm; Oct. 16-May M-F 8am-6pm, Sa 9am-2pm.

Embassies: For a list of all local consulates and embassies, check www.foreign.gov.sk. Citizens of **Australia** and **New Zealand** should contact the British Embassy in an emergency. **Canadians** and **South Africans** should consult their embassies in **Vienna**. **Ireland,** Mostová 2 (☎ 59 30 96 11; mail@ireland-embassy.sk). Open M-F 9am-12:30pm. **UK,** Panská 16 (☎ 59 98 20 00; www.britishembassy.sk). Visa office open M-F 9-11am. **US,** Hviezdoslavovo nám. 4 (☎ 54 43 08 61, emergency 0903 70 36 66; www.usembassy.sk). Open M-F 8am-4:30pm. Visa office open M-F 8-11:30am.

Currency Exchange: Ľudová Banka, Jesenkého 2 (☎ 54 41 89 84; www.luba.sk) cashes AmEx/V **traveler's checks** for a 1% commission and offers MC/V **cash advances.** Open M-F 7am-9pm. 24hr. MC/V **ATMs** are at the train station and throughout the city center.

Emergency: Police: ☎ 158. **Ambulance:** ☎ 155. **Fire:** ☎ 150.

SLOVAK REPUBLIC

Pharmacy: Lekáreň Pod Manderlom, Nám. SNP 20 (☎54 43 29 52), on the corner of Štúrova and Laurinská. Open M-F 7:30am-7pm, Sa 8am-5pm, Su 9am-5pm. 24hr. emergency service; ring bell after hours.

Internet Access: On-Line Internet Café, Obchodná 2. 1Sk per min. Open M-F 9:30am-midnight, Sa 10am-midnight, Su 10am-11pm. **Internet Centrum,** Michalská 2. 1Sk per min. Open daily 9am-midnight.

Post Office: Nám. SNP 34 (☎59 39 33 30). Open M-F 7am-8pm, Sa 7am-6pm, Su 9am-2pm. *Poste Restante* open M-F 7am-8pm, Sa 7am-2pm. Address mail to be held: Firstname SURNAME, POSTE RESTANTE, Nám. SNP 35, **81000** Bratislava 1, SLOVAK REPUBLIC.

ACCOMMODATIONS

In July and August, several **university dorms ❶** open as hostels; they are sometimes run-down but are quite cheap (from 150Sk; BIS, above, has a list). Pensions or **private rooms** (see BIS, above) are an inexpensive and comfortable alternative.

Slovenská Zdravotnicka Univerzita, Limbová 12 (☎59 37 01 00; www.szu.sk). From the train station take bus #32 or the electric cable bus #204 five stops to *Nemocnica Kramárel.* Clean and comfortable. Breakfast 35Sk. Reception 24hr. Check-out 11am. Singles 600Sk; doubles 700Sk; apartments 1000-1200Sk. ❸

Družba, Botanická 25 (Dorms: ☎60 29 92 61; fax 65 43 36 80; recepcia@sdjdr.uniba.sk. Hotel: ☎65 42 00 65; www.ubytujsa.sk). Take tram #1 from the train station (dir.: *Pri Kríži*) to *Botanická Záhrada.* Facing the departing tram, it's to the left. Družba is one of the more luxurious student dorms. Clean rooms with shared baths open July 5-Aug. 25. Singles and doubles open year-round. **Dorms:** Reception 24hr. Dorms 315Sk, students 130Sk. **Hotel:** Reception M-Th 7am-3:30pm, F 7am-1pm. Singles 590Sk; doubles 840Sk. ❷

Ubytovacie Zariadenie Zvárač, Pionierska 17 (☎49 24 67 61; www.vuz.sk). Take tram #3 from the train station or #5 or 11 from the city center (dir.: *Raca-Komisárky*) to *Pionierska.* Backtrack to the intersection, then turn right. Newly refurbished, comfortable rooms. Reception 24hr., ring bell after midnight. Check-in noon. Check-out 10am. Singles 600-800Sk; doubles 850-1050Sk. MC/V. ❸

FOOD

The grocery store **Tesco Potraviny** is at Kamenné nám. 1. (Open M-F 8am-9pm, Sa 8am-7pm, Su 9am-7pm.) The square in front of Tesco is full of fast food stalls.

Chez David, Zámocká 13 (☎54 41 38 24). The only kosher restaurant in Bratislava. Offers kosher and vegetarian favorites such as falafel (67Sk). Entrees 67-197Sk. Open M-Th, Su 11:30am-10pm, F 11:30am-3pm. ❷

City Restaurant, Obchodna 58. Upstairs, to the left. Try the *syrový karbonátok.* Soups 9-12Sk. Entrees 41-80Sk. Open M-F 11am-3:30pm. ❶

Vegetariańska Kuchynva, Nám. 1. Mája 3. Though the grocery-store atmosphere is far from cozy, the international and Slovak salads tickle the taste buds. Salads 7-26Sk per 10g. Open M-F 7am-7pm. ❶

SIGHTS

NÁMESTIE SNP AND ENVIRONS. With the exception of Devín Castle, most of the city's major attractions are in **Old Bratislava** (Stará Bratislava). From Nám. SNP, which commemorates the bloody 1944 Slovak National Uprising against fascism, walk down Uršulínska to reach the Baroque **Primate's Palace** (Primaciálny Palác).

Bratislava

⌂ ACCOMMODATIONS
Družba, **9**
Slovenská Zdravotnicka
 Univerzita, **1**
Ubytovacie Zariadenie
 Zvárat, **2**

🍴 FOOD
Chez David, **7**
City Restaurant, **5**
Vegetanańska Kuchyňa, **3**

★ NIGHTLIFE
1. Slovak Pub, **4**
Jazz Café, **8**
KGB, **6**

SLOVAK REPUBLIC

Napoleon and Austrian Emperor Franz I signed the Peace of Pressburg in the palace's **Hall of Mirrors** (Zrkadlová Sieň) in 1805. *(Primaciálné nám. 1. Open Su and Tu-Sa 10am-5pm. 30Sk, students free.)* Turn left down Kostolná as you exit the palace to reach **Hlavné námestie.** On your left as you enter the square is the **Town History Museum** (Muzeum Histórie Mesta) which has an impressive 1:500 scale model of Bratislava in 1945-1955. *(Open Tu-F 10am-5pm, Sa-Su 11am-6pm. 30Sk, students 10Sk.)* Continue to the opposite end of the square and take a left onto Rybárska Brana to **Hviezdoslavovo námestie,** where the gorgeous 1886 **Slovak National Theatre** (Slovenské Národné Divadlo) is located. Go through the square, take Mostová, and turn left at the Danube to reach the **Slovak National Gallery,** which displays artwork from the Gothic and Baroque periods as well as some modern sculptures. *(Rázusovo nábr. 2. www.sng.sk. Open Su and Tu-Sa 10am-5:30pm. 80Sk, students 40Sk.)* With the Danube on your left, continue to the gaudy neon-lit **Nový Most** (New Bridge), designed by the Communist government in the 1970s. Backtrack from the bridge and turn left on Rigoleho, continue straight onto Strakova (which becomes Ventúrska, then Michalská), and pass through **St. Michael's Tower** (Michalská Brána), Bratislava's last remaining medieval gateway. Keep going as Michalská becomes Župnénám and take a left onto Kapucínska; take the pedestrian bridge over the highway to reach the **Museum of Jewish Culture** (Múzeum Zidovskej Kultúry). *(Židovská 17. Open Su-F 11am-5pm. 200Sk, students 50Sk.)*

CASTLES. Visible from much of the city, the four-towered **Bratislava Castle** (Bratislavský hrad) is the city's defining landmark. The castle burned in 1811 and was bombed during World War II; what's left today is a Communist-era restoration. Its towers provide fantastic views of the Danube. To reach the castle, start beneath Nový Most and climb the stairs to Židovská; turn right on Zámocké schody and head uphill. *(Castle open Apr.-Sept. daily 9am-8pm; Oct.-Mar. 9am-6pm. Free. Museum open Tu-Su 9am-5pm. Last entrance 4:15pm. Museum 60Sk, students 30Sk.)* The ruins of **Devín Castle** sit above the Danube and Morava Rivers, a stone's throw from Austria. Take bus #29 from below Nový Most to the last stop, 9km west of Bratislava. Originally a Celtic fortification, the castle was held by the Romans, Slavs, and Hungarians before it was destroyed by Napoleon's armies in 1809. A museum highlights the castle's history. *(Museum open July-Aug. Tu-F 10am-5pm, Sa-Su 10am-6pm; May-June and Sept.-Oct. Tu-Su 10am-5pm. 40Sk, students 10Sk.)*

♫ 🎭 ENTERTAINMENT AND NIGHTLIFE

The regular theater season is September through June. BIS (p. 889) has the monthly *Kam v Bratislave*, which provides film, concert, and theater schedules. The ballets and operas at the **Slovak National Theatre,** Hviezdoslavovo nám. 1, draw crowds from neighboring Austria. (☎54 43 30 83; www.snd.sk. Box office open Sept.-June M-F 8am-5:30pm, Sa 9am-1pm. Tickets 100-200Sk.) The **Slovak Philharmonic** (Slovenská Filharmónia) plays regularly at Medená 3; the box office is around the corner at Palackého 2. (☎54 43 33 51; www.filharm.sk. Box office open Sept.-June M-Tu and Th-F 1-7pm, W 8am-2pm. Tickets 100-200Sk.)

By day, **Hlavné námestie** features souvenir stands and free outdoor concerts; by night, it fills with strolling couples and local teens warming up for an evening out. A small circular sign with a beer mug is all that marks **Krcma Gurmanov Bratislavy** (KGB), Obchodna 52, one of Bratislava's most popular pubs. (Beer 20-60Sk. Open M-Th 11am-1:30am, F 11am-3:30am, Sa 3:30pm-1:30am, Su 3:30-11pm.) **1. Slovak Pub,** Obchodná 62, is a gigantic restaurant with an outdoor terrace by day and a popular local pub with a quiet, sophisticated crowd by night. (Entrees 50-120Sk. Beer 20-25Sk. Open M-Th 10am-midnight, F-Sa 10am-2am, Su noon-midnight.) Set in the heart of the old town, **Jazz Café,** Ventúrska 5, has celebrated cocktails and live jazz. (Beer 40Sk. Live jazz Th-Sa 9pm-1am. Cafe open daily 10am-2am. Club open daily 2pm-2am.)

THE TATRA MOUNTAINS (TATRY)

The mesmerizing High Tatras, which span the border between the Slovak Republic and Poland, offer hundreds of hiking and skiing trails along the highest Carpathian peaks (2650m). One of the most compact ranges in the world, the High Tatras feature sky-scraping hikes, glacial lakes, and deep snows. Cheap mountain railways and accommodations add to the allure for the budget hiker.

 The Tatras are a great place to hike, but many of the hikes are extremely demanding and require experience, even in summer. In winter, a guide is almost always necessary. For current conditions, check **www.tanap.sk.**

STARÝ SMOKOVEC. Spectacular trails run from Starý Smokovec, the High Tatras' most central resort. To reach **Hrebienok** (1285m), which leads to hiking country, ride the funicular (June 28-Sept. 12 90Sk up, 40Sk down, 100Sk round-trip; Sept. 13-June 27 70/40/80Sk). Or, from the funicular station behind the train station, hike 35min. up the green trail. The green trail continues 20min. north from Hrebienok to the foaming **Cold Stream Waterfalls** (Volopáday studeného potoka). From the falls, take the red trail, which connects with the eastward blue trail to **Tatranská Lomnica** (1¾hr.). The hike to **Little Cold Valley** (Malá studená dolina) is also fairly relaxed; take the red trail (40min.) from Hrebienok to **Zamkovského chata** (hut) ❶ (☎(052) 442 26 36; rooms 290Sk per person) and onto the green trail (2hr.) which climbs above the tree-line to a high lake and **Téryho chata** ❶ (☎(052) 442 52 45; rooms 280Sk per person).

TEŽ **trains** arrive from Poprad (30min., every hr., 18Sk). **Buses** to many Tatran resorts stop in a parking lot to the right of the train station. Head uphill on the road that runs just left of the train station, then veer left across the main road. The **Tatranská Informačná Kancelária,** in Dom Služieb, has weather info and sells hiking maps, including the essential *VKÚ sheet #113*. (Open July-Aug. M-F 8am-5:30pm, Sa-Su 8am-1pm; Sept.-June M-F 9am-4:30pm, Sa 8am-1pm.) Most budget accommodations are down the road in **Horný Smokovec**. From the station, turn right on the main road and walk 5min. to **Hotel Šport** ❷, which has a cafe, sauna, pool, and massage parlor. (☎(052) 442 23 61. Reserve ahead. July-Aug. singles 390Sk, doubles 680Sk, extra person 280Sk; Dec. 26-Jan. 1 700/1130/480Sk; Sept.-June 280/500/180Sk.)

ŠTRBSKÉ PLESO. The 1975 Interski Championship was held at placid Štrbské Pleso (Štrbské Lake). Many beautiful **hikes** begin from the town, but just one lift runs in summer, hoisting visitors to **Chata pod Soliskom** (1840m), which overlooks the lake and the valleys behind Štrbské Pleso. (One-way 90Sk, round-trip 130Sk. Open 8:30am-4pm.) The challenging but rewarding yellow route heads from the east side of the lake (follow the signs to Hotel Patria) out along **Mlynická dolina** to mountain lakes and **Vodopády Skok** (Waterfalls). It then crosses **Bystré Sedlo** (Saddle; 2314m) and circles **Štrbské Solisko** (2302m) before returning to Štrbské Pleso (8-9hr.). TEŽ **trains** arrive from Starý Smokovec (30min., every 30min., 20Sk).

LIPTOVSKÝ MIKULÁŠ. Liptovský Mikuláš (pop. 33,000) is a good springboard for hiking in the **Low Tatras** (Nízke Tatry). To scale **Mt. Ďumbier,** the region's tallest peak (2043m), catch an early bus from platform #11 at the bus station to Liptovský Ján (25-30min., every hr., 13-16Sk), then follow the blue trail up the Štiavnica River to the **Svidovské Sedlo** (5hr.). Next, bear left on the red trail to the ridge, which leads to the summit (45min.). Descend the ridge and follow the red sign to neighboring peak **Chopok** (2024m), the second-highest in the range. From Chopok, it's a winding walk down the blue trail to the **bus** stop behind the Hotel Grand at Otupné (1¾hr.). **Trains** from Bratislava to Liptovský Mikuláš (4hr., 12 per day, 330Sk) are cheaper and more frequent than buses. Get to the town center by following Štefánikova toward the gas station at the far end of the lot, then turn right onto Hodžu. The **tourist office,** Nám. Mieru 1, in the Dom Služieb complex on the north side of town, books private rooms (245-400Sk) and sells dozens of hiking maps. (☎(044) 552 24 18; www.lmikulas.sk. Open June 15-Sept. 15 and Dec. 15-Mar. 31 M-F 8am-7pm, Sa 8am-2pm, Su noon-6pm; off season reduced hours.) **Hotel Kriváň** ❷, Štúrova 5, is across from the tourist office. (☎(044) 552 24 14. Singles 300Sk, with bath 400Sk; doubles 480/600Sk.)

SLOVENSKÝ RAJ. Southeast of the Nízke Tatry is the less-touristed Slovenský Raj (Slovak Paradise) National Park, filled with forested hills, deep ravines, and fast-flowing streams. The excellent trail guide **VKÚ sheet #4** is available at many hotels. The **Dobšinská Ice Caves** (Dobšinská ľadová jaskyňa) are composed of 110,000 cubic meters of water still frozen from the last Ice Age. Tours cover 475m of the cave, passing hall after hall of frozen columns, gigantic ice wells, and hardened waterfalls. To get there from **Dedinky** (pop. 400), the largest town on Slovenský Raj's southern border, take the **train** for two stops (15min.; 7am, 11:15am, and 2:30pm; 11Sk). The road from the caves' train station leads 100m out to the main road. Turn left, and the cave parking lot is 250m ahead. From there, the blue trail (20min., 20Sk) leads up a steep incline to the caves. (www.ssj.sk. Open July-Aug. Su and Tu-Sa 9am-4pm; mid-May to June and Sept. Su and Tu-Sa 9am-2pm. 120Sk, students 100Sk.)

The **bus** to Poprad (dir.: Rožňava; 1hr., 6 per day, 57Sk) stops at a junction 2km south of Dedinky. Watch for the huge blue road signs at the intersection, just before the bus stop. From the intersection, walk down the road that the bus did *not* take, turn right at the next intersection, cross the dam after the train station, turn left, and walk 10min. to Dedinky. *Privat, ubytowanie,* or *zimmer frei* signs indicate **private rooms** (200-300Sk). **Penzión Pastierňa ❷,** Dedinky 42, offers tasteful rooms with shared baths. (☎ 058 798 11 75. Breakfast 40-60Sk. Reception daily 8:30am-9:30pm. Check-out 11am. 2- to 4-bed rooms 300Sk.)

SLOVENIA
(SLOVENIJA)

Slovenia, the most prosperous of Yugoslavia's breakaway republics, revels in its newfound independence and has quickly separated itself from its neighbors. With a hungry eye turned toward the West, Slovenia is now using liberal politics and a high GDP to gain entrance into coveted alliances like the EU and NATO. Fortunately, modernization has not adversely affected the tiny country's natural beauty and diversity: You can still have breakfast on an Alpine peak, lunch under the Mediterranean sun, and dinner in a Pannonian vineyard.

FACTS AND FIGURES

Official Name: Republic of Slovenia.
Capital: Ljubljana.
Population: 2,000,000.
Land Area: 20,151 sq. km.

Time Zone: GMT +1.
Language: Slovenian.
Religions: Roman Catholic (71%), atheist (5%), other (24%).

DISCOVER SLOVENIA

Any visit should start in youthful **Ljubljana** (p. 898), which has the majesty of the Habsburg cities and a cafe scene on par with Paris or Vienna. **Lake Bled** (p. 901) and **Lake Bohinj** (p. 902) in the Julian Alps are traversed by miles of hikes that range from casual to treacherous. In winter, the Alps allow for very snowy, steep, and relatively cheap skiing.

ESSENTIALS

DOCUMENTS AND FORMALITIES

VISAS. Australian, Canadian, Irish, New Zealand, UK, and US citizens can visit without visas for up to 90 days. South Africans need visas (3-month single-entry or 5-day transit €24; 3-month multiple-entry €46). Apply in your home country.

EMBASSIES. Foreign embassies are in Ljubljana (p. 898). Embassies at home include: **Australia,** Level 6, Advance Bank Center, 60 Marcus Clarke St. 2608, Canberra ACT 2601 (☎06 243 4830; fax 6243 4827); **Canada,** 150 Metcalfe St. Ste. #2101, Ottawa, ON K2P 1P1 (☎613-565-5781; fax 565-5783); **New Zealand,** Eastern Hutt Rd., Pomare, Lower Hutt, Wellington (☎04 567 0027; fax 567 0024); **UK,** 11 Little College St., London SW1P 3SJ (☎020 7222 5400; fax 7222 5277); **US,** 1525 New Hampshire Ave. NW, Washington, D.C. 20036 (☎202-667-5363; www.embassy.org/slovenia).

TRANSPORTATION

BY PLANE. Commercial flights arrive at the Ljubljana Airport (LJU). **British Airways** flies direct to Slovenia, and other major lines offer connections to Slovenia's national carrier, **Adria Airways** (☎(386) 14 31 81 55; www.adria.si). Flying to Vienna and taking the train to Ljubljana is cheaper but more time-consuming.

BY TRAIN. Trains are cheap, clean, and reliable. First and second classes do not differ much; save your money and opt for the latter. For most international destinations, travelers under 26 can get a 20% discount; check at the Ljubljana station (look for the BIJ-Wasteels logo). Domestic tickets are 30% off for ISIC holders—ask for a *"popust"* (discount). *Vlak* means train, *prihodi vlakov* means arrivals, and *odhodi vlakov* means departures. Schedules usually list trains by direction; look for those that run *dnevno* (daily).

BY BUS. Slovenia's bus network is extensive. Though usually more expensive than trains, buses are often the only option in mountainous regions. Tickets are sold at the station or on board. Put your luggage in the passenger compartment if it's not too crowded; all large backpacks cost 220Sit extra.

BY BOAT, CAR, BIKE, OR THUMB. In the summer, a regular **hydrofoil** runs between Venice and Portorož. When not traveling by bus or train, most Slovenes transport themselves by **bike;** most towns have a rental office. For those traveling by car, the emergency number for the **Automobile Association of Slovenia** is ☎987. *Let's Go* does not recommend hitchhiking, which is uncommon in Slovenia.

TOURIST SERVICES AND MONEY

EMERGENCY	Police and Fire: ☎112. Ambulance: ☎113.

TOURIST OFFICES. The main tourist organization is **Kompas.** Tourist offices, which can usually help with accommodations, are located in most major cities and tourist spots. Staffs generally speak English, German, or, on the coast, Italian.

MONEY. The national currency is the **Slovenian tolar** (Sit). Inflation is currently around 7%, so expect some changes in prices. Rates vary, but tend to be better at **exchange offices;** post offices have the worst rates. **ATMs** are common. Major credit cards are not accepted consistently, but American Express Traveler's Cheques and Eurocheques usually work. **Tipping** is not expected, but rounding up is appreciated; 10% is sufficient for good service. Bargaining is often considered offensive.

TOLARS	AUS$1 = 139SIT	100SIT = AUS$0.72
	CDN$1 = 155SIT	100SIT = CDN$0.65
	EUR€ = 235SIT	100SIT = EUR€0.42
	NZ$1 = 124SIT	100SIT = NZ$0.81
	ZAR1 = 29SIT	100SIT = ZAR3.42
	UK£1 = 338SIT	100SIT = UK£0.30
	US$1 = 214SIT	100SIT = US$0.47

COMMUNICATION

PHONE CODES	Country code: 386. International dialing prefix: 00. From outside Slovenia, dial int'l dialing prefix (see inside back cover) + 386 + city code + local number.

TELEPHONES AND INTERNET ACCESS. Slovenia is **changing** all of its numbers. Correct numbers may differ from those at the time of publication; however, changed numbers should direct you to the new number in English and Slovenian. All phones now take **phone cards,** which are sold at post offices, kiosks, and gas stations (750Sit per 50 impulses; 1 impulse yields 1½min. to the US). Most international telecommunications companies do not have international direct dialing numbers in Slovenia. Dial ☎115 for collect calls assisted by an English-speaking operator. Calling the US costs over US$6 per minute; try the phones at the post office. **Internet access** is very common throughout the country.

MAIL. Airmail (ask for *letalsko*) takes 1-2 weeks to reach North America, Australia, New Zealand, and South Africa. To the US, letters cost 105Sit and postcards cost 95Sit; to the UK, 100/90Sit; to Australia and New Zealand, 110/100Sit. For *Poste Restante*, address mail to be held: Firstname SURNAME, *Poste Restante*, Slovenska 32, 1000 Ljubljana, SLOVENIA.

LANGUAGES. Slovenian is a Slavic language using the Latin alphabet. Most young people speak some English, but the older generation (especially in the Alps) is more likely to understand German (in the north) or Italian (along the Adriatic). Serbian and Croatian are also commonly spoken.

ACCOMMODATIONS AND CAMPING

SLOVENIA	❶	❷	❸	❹	❺
ACCOMMODATIONS	under 1000Sit	1000-3500Sit	3501-5000Sit	5001-6000Sit	over 6000Sit

Pensions, the most common form of lodgings, usually have private singles as well as inexpensive triples and dorms. Youth **hostels** and student dormitories are cheap (2500-3000Sit), but generally open only in summer (June 25-Aug. 30). While hostels are often the cheapest and most fun option, **private rooms** are the only budget lodgings on the coast and at Lake Bohinj; inquire at the tourist office or look for *Zimmer frei* or *Sobe* signs. Prices vary according to location, but rarely exceed €30, and most rooms are very comfortable. **Campgrounds** can be crowded but are in excellent condition. Camp only in designated areas in order to avoid fines.

FOOD AND DRINK

SLOVENIA	❶	❷	❸	❹	❺
FOOD	under 400Sit	400-800Sit	801-1200Sit	1201-1600Sit	over 1600Sit

For homestyle cooking, try a *gostilna* or *gostisče* (both refer to a restaurant with a country flavor). Meals start with *jota*, a soup with potatoes, beans, and sauerkraut. *Svinjska pečenka* (roast pork) is tasty, but vegetarians should look for *štruklji*—large, slightly sweet dumplings. Pizzerias usually have meatless dishes. A favorite dessert is *potica*, a pastry with a rich filling (usually walnut). The country's wine-making tradition dates from antiquity. *Renski Rizling* and *Šipon* are popular whites, while *Cviček* and *Teran* are well-known reds. Good beers include *Lasko* and *Union*. For something stronger, try the fruit brandy *žganje*. The most enchanting alcoholic concoction is *Viljamovka*, distilled by monks who manage to fit a full pear inside the bottle.

SAFETY AND SECURITY

Tap water is safe to drink everywhere. **Medical facilities** are of high quality, and most have English-speaking doctors. UK citizens receive free medical care with a valid passport; other foreigners must pay cash. **Pharmacies** are also stocked to Western standards. *Obliž* means band-aids; *tamponi*, tampon; and *vložki*, sanitary pads. **Crime** is rare, and even in the largest cities, overly friendly drunks and bad drivers are the greatest public menace. There are few **minorities** in Slovenia; while incidents of discrimination are uncommon, minority travelers may encounter curious stares, especially in rural areas. **Homosexuality** is legal, but may elicit unsure or unfriendly reactions from the middle-aged and elderly or outside of urban areas.

HOLIDAYS AND FESTIVALS

Holidays: New Year's (Jan. 1-2); Culture Day (Prešeren Day; Feb. 8); Easter (Apr. 11-12); National Resistance Day (Apr. 27); Labor Day (May 1-2); Pentecost (May 30); National Day (June 25); Assumption (Aug. 15); Reformation Day (Oct. 31); Remembrance Day (Nov. 1); Christmas (Dec. 25); Independence Day (Dec. 26).

Festivals: The **International Summer Festival** (July-Sept.) in Ljubljana is an extravaganza of opera, theater, and classical music.

LJUBLJANA
☎ 061

While the city itself is small, Ljubljana (pop. 280,000) possesses a mysteriously complex character woven through the many layers of its colorful past. According to legend, Ljubljana was founded when Jason and the Argonauts sailed into the Ljubljana River and slew the horrible Ljubljana dragon. Today's bridge dragons guard both sides of the river, surrounded by a mix of Baroque monuments, Art Nouveau facades, and modern high rises.

▐ TRANSPORTATION

Trains: Trg O.F. 6 (☎291 33 32). To: **Budapest** (9hr., daily, 10,000Sit); **Trieste** (3hr., 2-3 per day, 4400Sit); **Venice** (6hr., 3 per day, 7900Sit); **Vienna** (5-6hr., 2 per day, 11,600Sit); and **Zagreb** (2hr., 9 per day, 2452Sit).

Buses: Trg O.F. 4 (☎090 42 30), by the train station. **Zagreb** (3hr., 3 per day, 2920Sit).

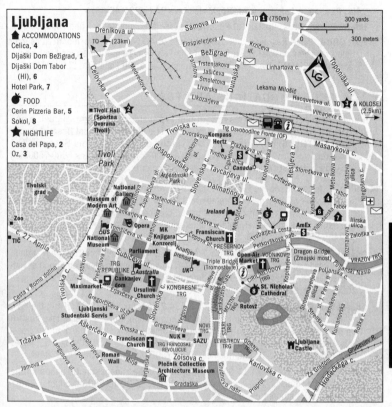

Ljubljana

🏠 ACCOMMODATIONS
Celica, 4
Dijaški Dom Bežigrad, 1
Dijaški Dom Tabor
(HI), 6
Hotel Park, 7

🍴 FOOD
Cerin Pizzeria Bar, 5
Sokol, 8

⭐ NIGHTLIFE
Casa del Papa, 2
Oz, 3

SLOVENIA

Public Transportation: Buses run until midnight. Drop 230Sit in change in the box beside the driver or buy 170Sit tokens (žetoni) at post offices and kiosks. Daily passes (660Sit) sold at **Ljubljanski Potniški Promet,** Trdinova 3.

🔳 🛈 ORIENTATION AND PRACTICAL INFORMATION

The train and bus stations are on **Trg Osvobodilne Fronte** (Trg O.F. or O.F. Square). Turn right as you exit the train station, then left on **Miklošičeva cesta** and follow it to **Prešernov Trg,** the main square. Cross the **Tromostovje** (Triple Bridge) over the **Ljubljanica River** to **Stare Miasto** (Old Town) at the base of the castle hill.

Tourist Office: Tourist Info Center (TIC), Stritarjeva 1. English brochures and free maps. (☎306 12 15; www.ljubljana.si. Open June-Sept. daily 8am-9pm; Oct.-May 8am-7pm.)

Embassies and Consulates: Australia, Trg Republike 3 (☎425 42 52). Open M-F 9am-1pm. **Canada,** Miklošičeva 19 (☎430 35 70; fax 430 35 77). Open M-F 9am-1pm. **UK,** Trg Republike 3 (☎200 39 10; fax 425 01 74). Open M-F 9am-noon. **US,** Prešernova 31 (☎200 55 00; fax 200 55 55). Open M-F 8am-5pm.

Currency Exchange: 24hr. MC/V **ATM**s can be found throughout the city.

Luggage storage: At the train station; look for garderoba. 400Sit per day. Open 24hr.

24hr. Pharmacy: Lekarna miklošič, Miklošičeva 24 (☎231 45 58).

Internet: Free access upstairs at **Pizzeria Bar** (see Accommodations and Food, below).

Post Office: *Poste Restante,* Slovenska 32 (☎426 46 68) held for 1 month at counter labeled *"izročitev pošiljk."* Open M-F 7am-8pm, Sa 7am-1pm. Address mail to be held: Firstname SURNAME, *Poste Restante,* Slovenska 32, **1000** Ljubljana, SLOVENIA.

ACCOMMODATIONS AND FOOD

Finding cheap accommodations in Ljubljana is easier in July and August, when university dorms open their doors to travelers. The **Slovene National Hostel Association** (PZS; ☎231 21 56) provides info about youth hostels throughout Slovenia. The **TIC ❷** can help you find **private rooms** (singles 3000-4500Sit; doubles 5000-7500Sit.) There is a daily **tourist tax** (160Sit) at all establishments.

▨ **Celica,** Metelkova 8, opened in June 2003. With your back to the train station, walk left down Masarykova, then right on Metelkova. Look for the red and yellow building on your left. Local and foreign artists have transformed this former military prison into an incredibly creative living space. Bar, cafe, Internet access, and cultural arts programs. Reception 24hr. 2500-5000Sit. ❷

Dijaški Dom Tabor (HI), Vidovdanska 7 (☎234 88 40). Go left from the train station, right on Resljeva, left on Komenskega, and left on Vidovdanska. Clean and popular with backpackers. Breakfast included. Free Internet access. Open June 25-Aug. 25. Singles 3200-4600Sit. ❷

Dijaški Dom Bežigrad, Kardeljeva pl. 28 (☎534 28 67; fax 534 28 64). From the train station, cross the street and turn right; at the intersection with Slovenska, take bus #6 (Črnuče) or #8 (Ježica) and get off at *Stadion* (5min.), then walk 1 block to the crossroads. Clean, comfortable rooms. Negotiable check-out. Open June 20-Aug. 25. Singles 3500Sit, with shower 3960Sit; doubles 4660/7000Sit; triples 6800/7800Sit. ❸

Hotel Park, Tabor 6 (☎433 13 06; fax 433 05 46). The cheapest hotel option for the off-season backpacker. Knowledgeable staff. Singles 6700-10,500Sit; doubles 8300-12,500Sit. 10% student discount. ❺

Maximarket on Trg Republike has a basement **grocery store.** (Open M-Th 9am-8pm, F 9am-10pm, Sa 8am-3pm.) ▨**Sokol ❸**, Ciril Metodov Trg 18, serves Slovenian delicacies. (Open M-Sa 9am-midnight.) **Cerin Pizzeria Bar ❷**, Trubarjeva 52, has free Internet access upstairs. (Open M-F 10am-11pm, Su noon-10pm.)

SIGHTS AND ENTERTAINMENT

A good way to see the city is to meet in front of the *rotovž* (city hall), Mestni Trg 1, for the two-hour **walking tour** in English and Slovenian. (June-Sept. daily 5pm; July-Aug. also Su 11am. 1200Sit, students 600Sit.) A short walk from the *rotovž* down Stritarjeva across **Tromostovje** (Triple Bridge), which majestically guards Stare Miasto, leads to the main square, **Prešernov Trg,** with its pink 17th-century **Franciscan Church** (Frančiškanska cerkev). Cross the bridge back to Stare Miasto and take a left; continue along the river and you'll see Vodnikov Trg, where **Zmajski most** (Dragon Bridge) stretches back across the Ljubljanica. On the far side of Vodnikov Trg, the narrow path Studentovska leads uphill to **Ljubljana Castle** (Ljubljanski Grad), which has a breathtaking view of Ljubljana. (Open May-Oct. daily 10am-9pm; Nov.-Apr. 10am-7pm. 400-700Sit.) Cross the Dragon Bridge back to Resljeve cesta, turn left on Tubarjea cesta, continue to Prešernov trg, take a left onto Wolfova (which becomes Gosposka), then take a right onto Zoisova cesta and a left onto Emonska ul. Across a bridge is the **Plečnik Collection** (Plečnikova zbrika), Karunova 4, which shows the works of Ljubljana's most famous architect. (Open Tu and Th 10am-2pm. 600Sit, students 300Sit.) Walking back from the museum, take a left onto Zoistova and a right onto Slovenska. After the Ursuline Church, take a left to find **Trg Republike,** home to the national Parliament, the large Maximarket, and Cankarjev Dom, the city's cultural center.

The **Ljubljana International Summer Festival** (mid-June to mid-September) has musical, operatic, and theatrical performances. **Casa del Papa,** Celovška 54a pays homage to Hemingway and Key West, while the downstairs club pulsates with Cuban beats, serves up Cuban cocktails, and sells Cuban cigars. (Open M-Sa noon-midnight, Su noon-11pm.) Popular **Oz,** Smartinska 152, is a trendy disco and bar that offers a varied music selection. (Open Su-W 9am-1am, Th-Sa 6pm-5am.)

▶ DAYTRIP FROM LJUBLJANA: ŠKOCJANSKE CAVES

ŠKOCJANSKE CAVES. Škocjanske is an amazing system of UNESCO-protected ▓**caverns** with limestone formations and a 120m gorge created by the Reca River. Be prepared; this physically demanding trip is for the truly adventurous. (☎(057) 63 28 40; www.gov.si/parkskj. Tours June-Sept. daily 10am-5pm; Oct.-May 10am, 1, and 3pm. 2200Sit, students 1200Sit.) **Trains** run from Ljubljana to Divača (1½hr., 10 per day, 1370Sit). Follow signs out of town to the ticket booth (40min.).

BLED ☎04

Alpine hills, snow-covered peaks, a turquoise lake, and a stately castle make Bled (pop. 6,000) one of Slovenia's most striking destinations. The **Church of the Assumption** (Cerkev Marijinega Vnebovzetja) stands on the island in the center of the lake. To get there, you can rent a boat (1000-2500Sit per hr.), hop on a gondola (round-trip 1800Sit), or even swim. High above the water perches the picture-perfect 16th-century **Bled Castle** (Blejski grad), which houses a museum detailing the history of the Bled region. (Open daily 8am-8pm. 800Sit, students 700Sit.) ▓**Blejski Vintgar,** a 1.6km gorge traced by the waterfalls and rapids of the Radovna River, carves through the rocks of the **Triglav National Park** (Triglavski Narodni). To see the 16m **Šum Waterfall,** go over the hill on Grajska cesta and turn right at the bottom. After 100m, turn left and follow the signs for Vintgar.

Trains from Ljubljana arrive at the Lesce-Bled station, about 4km from Bled (1hr., 11 per day, 920Sit). **Intercity buses** run directly from Ljubljana (1½hr., every hr., 1260Sit). The **tourist office,** cesta Svobode 11, sells maps (1100-1400Sit) of Bled and the local trails. (☎578 05 00. Open in summer M-Sa 8am-7pm, Su 11am-6pm; off-season M-Sa 9am-7pm, Su and holidays 11am-4pm.) To find **private rooms,** look for *Sobe* signs on Prešernova cesta and Ljubljanska. ▓**Bledec Youth Hostel (HI) ❸,** Grajska cesta 17, was just renovated. From the bus station, turn left and follow the street to the top, bearing left at the fork. (☎574 52 50. Reception 24hr. Reserve ahead July-Aug. 3700Sit. Nonmembers 3860Sit.) To get to **Camping Bled ❷,** Kidričeva 10c, from the bus station, walk downhill on cesta Svobode, then turn left and walk along the lake for 25min. (☎575 20 00; info@camping.bled.si. Reception 24hr. Open Apr.-Oct. 1370-1790Sit.) A **Mercator supermarket** is in the complex at Ljubljanska cesta 13. (Open M-Sa 7am-8pm, Su 8am-noon.) **Postal Code:** 4260.

LAKE BOHINJ (BOHINJSKO JEZERO)   ☎04

Although it is only 30km southwest of Bled, Bohinjsko Jezero (BOH-heen-sko YEH-zeh-roh) feels worlds away. The three farming villages that border the lake, Ribčev Laz, Stara Fužina, and Ukranc, retain a traditional Slovene atmosphere. Surrounded by **Triglav National Park,** the glacial lake is Slovenia's center for alpine tourism. Hikes from the lake's shores range from casual to nearly impossible. Trails are marked with a white circle inside a red circle; look for the blaze on trees and rocks. Maps are available at the tourist office (see below). The most popular and accessible destination is **Savica Waterfall** (Slap Savica). Take a bus from Ribčev Laz to Bohinj-Zlatorog, get off at Hotel Zlatorog, and follow signs uphill (1hr. to trailhead at Koča pri Savici, then 20min. to waterfall).

The nearest town is **Bohinjska Bistrica,** 6km to the east. **Trains** from Ljubljana (2½hr., 8 per day, 1440Sit) pass through Jesenice. **Buses** from Ljubljana (2hr., every hr., 1620Sit) pass through Bled (35min., 680Sit) and Bohinjska Bistrica (15min., every hr., 360Sit) on their way to the lake; they stop at Hotel Jezero in Ribčev Laz or at Hotel Zlatorog in Ukanc, on the other side of the lake. The **tourist office,** Ribčev Laz 48, sells maps, arranges accommodations, and plans guided excursions. (☎574 60 10; tdbohinj@bohinj.si. Open July-Aug. daily 8am-8pm; Sept.-June M-Sa 8am-6pm, Su 9am-3pm.) To reach **AvtoCamp Zlatorog ❷,** Ukanc 2, take the bus to Hotel Zlatorog and backtrack a bit. (☎572 34 82. May-Sept. and July-Aug. 2150Sit; May-June and Sept. 1400Sit. Tourist tax 154Sit.) The restaurant ▧**Gostišče Kramar ❷,** Stara Fužina 3, offers outstanding views of the lake. (Entrees 200-900Sit. Open Su-Th 11am-midnight, F-Sa 11am-9pm.) A **Mercator supermarket** is next to the tourist office. (Open M-F 7am-8pm, Sa 7am-8pm.) **Postal Code:** 4265.

SPAIN (ESPAÑA)

Fiery flamenco dancers, noble bullfighters, and a rich history blending Christian and Islamic culture set Spain apart from the rest of Europe and draw almost 50 million tourists each year. The raging nightlife of Madrid, Barcelona, and the Balearic Islands has inspired the popular saying "Spain never sleeps," yet the afternoon siestas of Andalucía attest the country's laid-back, easy-going approach to life. Spain houses stunning Baroque, Mudejar, and Mozarabic cathedrals and palaces; hangs the works of Velasquez, Dalí, and Picasso on its hallowed walls; and offers up a backyard of beauty with long sunny coastlines, snowy mountain peaks, and the dry, golden plains wandered by Don Quixote. You can do Spain in one week, one month, or one year. But you must do it at least once.

FACTS AND FIGURES

Official Name: Kingdom of Spain.

Capital: Madrid.

Major Cities: Barcelona, Granada, Seville, Valencia.

Population: 40,000,000.

Land Area: 499,542 sq. km.

Time Zone: GMT+1.

Language: Spanish (Castilian), Catalan, Valencian, Basque, Galician dialects.

Religions: Roman Catholic (94%).

DISCOVER SPAIN

Begin in **Madrid** (p. 908), enjoying its unique blend of art, architecture, and cosmopolitan life; after days of soaking up art and nights of dancing 'til dawn, take your bleary-eyed self to the austere palace of **El Escorial** (p. 920) and the twisting streets of **Toledo** (p. 921), once home to El Greco. Head into the Don Quixote territory of central Spain, to the famed university town of **Salamanca** (p. 925), then to the heart of bullfights and flamenco in **Seville** (p. 934). Visit the stunning mosque in **Córdoba** (p. 929) and the world-famous Alhambra in **Granada** (p. 944). The ethereal beaches of the **Costa del Sol** stretch along the Mediterranean; delay your return to earth in posh **Marbella** (p. 943). Move up along the east coast to **Valencia** (p. 949) and indulge in *paella* and oranges. The gem of the northeast is **Barcelona** (p. 952), where you can tour the bizarre Modernista architecture and even crazier nightlife. Moving westward into Basque Country, **San Sebastián** (p. 974) entertains with beaches and fabulous *tapas* bars; **Bilbao** (p. 977), home of the incredible Guggenheim museum, is only a daytrip away. Finish up with a stop at the 24-hour party that is **Ibiza** (p. 980).

ESSENTIALS

WHEN TO GO

Summer is high season for the coastal and interior regions. In many parts of the country, high season includes *Semana Santa* (Holy Week; mid-April) and festival days. Tourism peaks in August; the coastal regions overflow while inland cities empty out, leaving behind closed offices, restaurants, and lodgings. Traveling in the low season has the advantage of noticeably lighter crowds and lower prices, but smaller towns virtually shut down, and tourist offices and sights cut their hours nearly everywhere.

Spain

Golfo de Vizcaya
San Sebastián
FRANCE
La Coruña Oviedo
Bilbao Guernica
Santiago de
Compostela
ANDORRA
León
Pamplona Jaca
Astorga
Burgos
Figueres
Miño
Valladolid
Girona
Zamora
Duero
Zaragoza
Barcelona
Salamanca Segovia
Sigüenza
Sitges
Menorca
Ávila El Escorial
Ciudadela Mahón
Béjar
Tajo
TO MENORCA →
PORTUGAL
Madrid
Balearic
Toledo
Cuenca
Golfo de
Sea
Aranjuez
Valencia
Palma
Cáceres
Trujillo
Mallorca
Guadiana
Valencia
ISLAS BALEARES
Badajoz
Mérida
Júcar
Ibiza Ibiza
Zafra
Formentera
Alicante
Guadalquivir
Córdoba
Seville
Granada
Mediterranean Sea
Golfo de
Cádiz
Jerez de
Málaga
la Frontera
ALGERIA
Cádiz
Marbella
ATLANTIC
Algeciras Gibraltar
OCEAN
Strait of Gibraltar
0   100 miles
0   100 kilometers
MOROCCO

SPAIN

DOCUMENTS AND FORMALITIES

VISAS. EU citizens do not need a visa. Citizens of Australia, Canada, New Zealand, South Africa, the UK, and the US do not need a visa for stays of up to 90 days. As of August 2003, citizens of South Africa need a visa in addition to a valid passport for entrance into Spain.

EMBASSIES. Foreign embassies are in Madrid (p. 912); all countries have consulates in Barcelona (p. 956). Australia, the UK, and the US also have consulates in Seville (p. 934). Another Canadian consulate is in Málaga; UK consulates are also in Alicante, Bilbao, Ibiza, Málaga, and Palma de Mallorca; more US consulates are in Las Palmas and Valencia. For Spanish embassies at home, contact: **Australia,** 15 Arkana St., Yarralumla, ACT 2600, mailing address P.O. Box 9076, Deakin, ACT 2600 (☎612 6273 3918; www.embaspain.com); **Canada,** 74 Stanley Ave., Ottawa, ON K1M 1P4 (☎613-747-2252; www.docuweb.ca/SpainInCanada); **Ireland,** 17A Merlyn Park, Ballsbridge, Dublin 4 (☎353 269 1640); **South Africa,** 169 Pine St., Arcadia, P.O. Box 1633, Pretoria 0083 (☎27 12 344 3875); **UK,** 39 Chesham Pl., London SW1X 8SB (☎44 207 235 5555); and **US,** 2375 Pennsylvania Ave. NW, Washington, D.C. 20037 (☎202-738-2330; www.spainemb.org).

TRANSPORTATION

BY PLANE. Airports in Madrid and Barcelona handle most international flights; Seville also has a major international airport. Iberia (US and Canada ☎800-772-4642; UK ☎45 601 28 54; Spain ☎902 40 05 00; South Africa ☎11 884 92 55; Ireland ☎1 407 30 17; www.iberia.com), the national carrier, serves all domestic locations and all major international cities. For more info on flying to Spain, see 43.

BY TRAIN. Spanish trains are clean, relatively punctual, and reasonably priced, but tend to bypass many small towns. Spain's national railway is **RENFE** (www.renfe.es). Avoid *transvía*, *semidirecto*, or *correo* trains—they are very slow. *Alta Velocidad Española* (AVE) trains are the fastest between Madrid, Córdoba, and Seville. *Talgos* are almost as fast; there are lines from Madrid to Algeciras, Cádiz, Huelva, and Málaga. *Intercity* is cheaper, but still fairly fast. *Estrellas* are slow night trains with bunks. *Cercanías* (commuter trains) go from cities to suburbs and nearby towns. There is rarely a good reason to buy a **Eurail** if you are planning on traveling only within Spain and Portugal. Trains are cheap, so a pass saves little money; moreover, buses are an easier and more efficient means of traveling around Spain. However, there are several RailEurope passes that cover travel within Spain. (US ☎1-800-4EURAIL; www.raileurope.com.) **Spain Flexipass** offers three days of unlimited travel in a two-month period (first-class €211, 2nd-class €164). The **Iberic Railpass** is good for three days of unlimited first-class travel in Spain and Portugal (€217). The **Spain Rail 'n' Drive** pass is good for three days of unlimited first-class train travel and two days of unlimited mileage in a rental car (€250-343).

BY BUS. In Spain, buses are cheaper and provide far more comprehensive routes than trains. In addition, bus routes also provide the only public transportation to many isolated areas. Spain has numerous private companies; the lack of a centralized bus company may make itinerary planning an ordeal. **ALSA** (☎902 42 22 42; www.alsa.es) serves Madrid, Asturias, Castilla y León, and Galicia, as well as international destinations in France, Italy, Morocco, Poland and Portugal. **Auto-Res/Cunisa, S.A.** (☎902 02 09 99; www.auto-res.net) serves Madrid, Castilla y León, Extremadura, Galicia, and Valencia.

BY CAR. Gas prices average €1.50-1.60 per liter. Speeders beware: police can "photograph" the speed and license plate of your car and issue a ticket without pulling you over. **Renting a car** in Spain is cheaper than in many other Western European countries. Try **Atesa** (☎902 10 01 01; www.atesa.es), Spain's largest national rental agency. The Spanish automobile association is **Real Automóbil Club de España** (RACE), C. José Abascal 10, Madrid (☎915 94 74 75).

BY BIKE AND BY THUMB. With hilly terrain and extremely hot summer weather, hiking is difficult. Renting a bike should be easy, especially in the flatter southern region. Hitchers report that Castilla y León, Andalucía, and Madrid are long, hot waits. The Mediterranean Coast and the islands are much more promising, but *Let's Go* does not recommend hitchhiking.

TOURIST SERVICES AND MONEY

EMERGENCY	**Emergency:** ☎112. **Local Police:** ☎092. **National Police:** ☎091. **Ambulance:** ☎124.

TOURIST OFFICES. The Spanish Tourist Office operates an extensive official website (www.tourspain.es) and has 29 offices abroad. Municipal tourist offices, called *oficinas de turismo*, are a good stop to make upon arrival in a town; they usually have free maps and region-specific advice for travelers.

MONEY. On January 1, 2002, the **euro** (€) replaced the **peseta** as the unit of currency in Spain. For more info, see p. 14. As a general rule, it is cheaper to exchange money in Spain than at home. **Santander Central Hispano** often provides good exchange rates. **Tipping** is not very common in Spain. In restaurants, all prices include a service charge. Satisfied customers occasionally toss in some spare change—usually no more than 5%—but this is purely optional. Many people give train, airport, and hotel porters €1 per bag; taxi drivers sometimes get 5-10%. **Bargaining** is common only at flea markets and with street vendors.

Spain has a 7% **value-added tax,** known as IVA, on all restaurants and accommodations. The prices listed in *Let's Go* include IVA unless otherwise mentioned. Retail goods bear a much higher 16% IVA, although listed prices are usually inclusive. Non-EU citizens who have stayed in the EU fewer than 180 days can claim back the tax paid on purchases at the airport. Ask the shop where you made the purchase to supply you with a tax return form.

HEALTH AND SAFETY

While Spain is a relatively stable country, travelers should beware that there is some terrorist activity; the militant Basque separatist group **ETA** has carried out attacks on government officials and tourist destinations. Though the attacks are ongoing, the threat is relatively small. Travelers should be aware of current levels of tension in the region and exercise appropriate caution. Recreational **drugs** are illegal in Spain. Any attempt to buy or sell marijuana could land you in jail or with a heavy fine.

COMMUNICATION

PHONE CODES	**Country code: 34. International dialing prefix: 00.** From outside Spain, dial int'l dialing prefix (see inside back cover) + 34 + local number.

TELEPHONES. The central Spanish phone company is *Telefónica.* The best way to make local calls is with a phone card, issued in denominations of €6 and €12 and sold at tobacconists (*estancos* or *tabacos*) and most post offices. You can also ask tobacconists for calling cards known as *Phonepass.* (To US, €6 per hr.) The best way to call home is with an international calling card issued by your phone company. For info on using a **cell phone** in Spain, see p. 36.

MAIL. Air mail (*por avión*) takes five to eight business days to reach the US or Canada; service is faster to the UK and Ireland and slower to Australia and New Zealand. Standard postage is €0.70 to North America. Surface mail (*por barco*), while less expensive than air mail, can take over a month, and packages take two to three months. Registered or express mail (*registrado* or *certificado*) is the most reliable way to send a letter or parcel home and takes four to seven business days. Address mail to be held (*Poste Restante*) according to the following example: SURNAME, First Name; Lista de Correos; City Name; Postal Code; SPAIN; AIR MAIL.

INTERNET ACCESS. Email is easily accessible within Spain and much quicker and more reliable than the regular mail system. An increasing number of bars offer Internet access for a fee of €1.20-4.50. Cybercafes are listed in most towns and all cities. In small towns, if Internet access is not listed, check the library or the tourist office. The website www.tangaworld.com lists nearly 200 cybercafes in Spain.

ACCOMMODATIONS AND CAMPING

SYMBOL	❶	❷	❸	❹	❺
ACCOMMODATIONS	under €15	€16-25	€26-35	€36-50	over €50

The cheapest and barest options are *casas de huéspedes* and *hospedajes*, while *pensiones* and *fondas* tend to be a bit nicer. All are essentially just boarding houses. Higher up the ladder, *hostales* generally have sinks in bedrooms and provide sheets and lockers, while *hostal-residencias* are similar to hotels in overall quality. The government rates *hostales* on a two-star system; even establishments receiving one star are typically quite comfortable. The system also fixes *hostal* prices, posted in the lounge or main entrance. **Red Española de Albergues Juveniles** (REAJ), C. Galera 1a, Seville 41001 (☎954 21 68 03; www.reaj.com), the Spanish Hostelling International (HI) affiliate, runs 165 youth hostels year-round. Prices depend on location (typically some distance away from the town center) and services offered, but are generally €9-15 for guests under 26 and higher for those 26 and over. Breakfast is usually included; lunch and dinner are occasionally offered at an additional charge. Hostels usually lock guests out around 11:30am and have curfews between midnight and 3am. As a rule, don't expect much privacy—rooms typically have four to 20 beds in them. To reserve a bed in high season (July-Aug. and during festivals), call in advance. A national **Youth Hostel Card** is usually required. **Campgrounds** are generally the cheapest choice for two or more people. Most charge separate fees per person, per tent, and per car; others charge for a *parcela* (a small plot of land), plus per-person fees. Tourist offices can provide more info, including the *Guía de Campings*.

FOOD AND DRINK

SYMBOL	❶	❷	❸	❹	❺
FOOD	under €6	€6-10	€11-15	€16-25	over €25

Spanish food has tended to receive less international attention than the country's beaches, bars, and discos. Taste often ranks above appearance, preparation is rarely complicated, and many of the best meals are served not in expensive restaurants but in private homes or streetside bars. All of this has started to change as Spanish food becomes increasingly sophisticated and cosmopolitan, but fresh local ingredients are still an integral part of the cuisine, varying according to each region's climate, geography, and history. Most experts, in fact, argue that one can speak of Spanish food only in local terms. Spaniards breakfast lightly and wait for a several-course lunch, served between 2 and 3pm. Supper at home (*la cena*) tends to be light while eating out begins anywhere between 9pm and midnight. Some restaurants are "open" from 8am until 1 or 2am, but most serve meals only from 1 to 4pm and from 8pm until midnight. Prices for a full meal start at about €4 in the cheapest *bar-restaurantes*. Many places offer a *plato combinado* (main course, side dishes, bread, and sometimes a beverage) or a *menú del día* (two or three set dishes, bread, beverage, and dessert) for roughly €5-9. If you ask for a *menú*, this is what you may receive; *carta* is the word for menu. *Tapas* (savory meats and vegetables cooked according to local recipes) are truly tasty and in some regions complimentary with beer or wine. *Raciones* are large *tapas* served as entrees. *Bocadillos* are sandwiches on hunks of bread. Spanish specialties include *tortilla de patata* (potato omelette), *jamón serrano* (smoked ham), *calamares fritos* (fried squid), *arroz* (rice), *chorizo* (spicy sausage), *gambas* (shrimp), *lomo* (pork), *paella* (steamed saffron rice with seafood, chicken, and vegetables), and *gazpacho* (cold tomato-based soup). Vegetarians should learn the phrase "*yo soy vegetariano*" (I am a vegetarian) and specify that means no *jamón* (ham) or *atún* (tuna). *Vino blanco* is white wine and *tinto* is red. Beer is *cerveza;* Mahou and Cruzcampo are the most common brands. *Sangría* is red wine, sugar, brandy, and fruit.

HOLIDAYS AND FESTIVALS

Holidays: New Year's Day (Jan. 1); Epiphany (Jan. 6); Maundy Thursday (Apr. 8); Good Friday (Apr. 9); Easter (Apr. 11); Labor Day (May 1); Assumption Day (Aug. 15); National Day (Oct. 12); All Saints' Day (Nov. 1); Constitution Day (Dec. 6); Feast of the Immaculate Conception (Dec. 8); Christmas (Dec. 25).

Festivals: Nearly everything closes during festivals. Almost every town has several, and in total there are more than 3000. All of Spain celebrates **Carnaval** March 4; the biggest parties are in Cataluña and Cádiz. Valencia hosts the annual **Las Fallas** in mid-March. From April 4-11, the entire country honors the Holy Week, or **Semana Santa.** Seville's **Feria de Abril** takes place in late April. Pamplona's **San Fermines** (Running of the Bulls) breaks out from July 6 to 14. For more fiesta info, see www.tourspain.es, www.SiSpain.org, or www.planetware.com/national/E/HOLIDAYS.HTM.

MADRID ☎91

After Franco's death in 1975, young *madrileños* celebrated their liberation from totalitarian repression with raging, all-night parties in bars and on streets across the city. This revelry became so widespread that it defined an era, and *la Movida* (the Movement) is recognized as a world-famous nightlife renaissance. While the newest generation is too young to recall the Franco years, it has kept the spirit of *la Movida* alive. Not particularly cognizant of the city's historic landmarks nor preoccupied with the future, young people have taken over the streets, shed their parents' decorous reserve, and captured the present. Bright lights and a perpetual stream of cars and people blur the distinction between 4pm and 4am, and infinitely energized party-goers crowd bars and discos until dawn. Madrid's sights and culture equal its rival European capitals and have twice the intensity.

✈ INTERCITY TRANSPORTATION

Flights: All flights land at **Aeropuerto Internacional de Barajas** (MAD; general info ☎913 05 83 43, 44, 45, or 46), 20min. northeast of Madrid. The Barajas **Metro** line connects the airport to all of Madrid (€1.10). Another option is the green **Bus-Aeropuerto #89** (look for EMT signs just outside the airport doors), which leaves the national and international terminals and runs to the city center (every 15min., €2.50). The bus stops underground beneath the Jardines del Descubrimiento in Plaza de Colón. Serving national and international destinations, **Iberia** is at Santa Cruz de Marcenado 2, M: San Bernardo. (Office ☎915 87 47 47. 24hr. reservations and info ☎902 40 05 00. Open M-F 9:30am-2pm and 4-7pm.)

Trains: Two *Largo Recorrido* (long distance) **RENFE** stations connect Madrid to the rest of Europe. Call RENFE (☎913 28 90 20; www.renfe.es) for reservations and info. Try the **Main Office,** C. Alcalá 44, at Gran Vía (M: Banco de España) for schedules.

Estación Chamartín: 24hr. info international ☎934 90 11 22, domestic ☎902 24 02 02; Spanish only. M: Chamartín. Bus #5 runs to Sol (45min.). Ticket windows open 8am-10:30pm. Most *cercanías* (local) trains stop at Atocha and Chamartín. To: **Barcelona** (7-10½hr., 10 per day, €33-44); **Lisbon** (9½hr., 10:45pm, €48-67); **Paris** (13½hr., 7pm, €119-131).

Estación Atocha: ☎913 28 90 20. M: Atocha-Renfe. Ticket windows open 7:15am-10pm. Trains to Andalucía, Castilla y León, Castilla-La Mancha, El Escorial, Extremadura, Sierra de Guadarrama, Toledo, and Valencia. AVE service (☎915 34 05 05) to **Córdoba** (1¾hr., 20 per day, €35-47) and **Seville** (2½hr., 20 per day, €57-64).

Intercity Buses: Numerous private companies, each with its own station and set of destinations, serve Madrid; many buses pass through the **Estación Sur de Autobuses.**

Estación Sur de Autobuses: C. Méndez Álvaro (☎914 68 42 00). M: Méndez Álvaro. Info open daily 7am-11pm. **Continental-Auto** (☎915 27 29 61) to **Toledo** (1½hr.; every 30min.; €4).

Estación Auto Res: C. Fernández Shaw 1 (☎902 02 09 99). M: Conde de Casal. To: **Cuenca** (3hr.; M-F 8-10 per day, Sa-Su 5-6 per day 8am-8pm; €9); **Salamanca** (2½-3hr., 20 per day, €10-15); **Trujillo** (3¼hr., 11-12 per day, €14); **Valencia** (4-5hr., 14 per day 1am-2pm, €20-24).

Estación La Sepulvedana: Po. de la Frontera 16 (☎915 30 48 00). M: Príncipe Pío (via extension from M: Ópera). To **Segovia** (1½hr., every 30min. 6:30am-10:15pm, €5.60).

Empressa Larrea: ☎915 30 48 00. To **Ávila** (1½hr.; M-F 8 per day, Sa-Su 4 per day; €6.30).

▪ ORIENTATION

Marking the epicenter of both Madrid and Spain, **"Kilometro 0"** in **Puerta del Sol** ("Sol" for short) is within walking distance of most sights. To the west are the **Plaza Mayor,** the **Palacio Real,** and the **Ópera** district. East of Sol lies **Huertas,** the heart of cafe, theater, and museum life, which is centered around Pl. Santa Ana and bordered by C. Alcalá to the north, Po. Prado to the east, and C. Atocha to the south. The area north of Sol is bordered by **Gran Vía,** which runs northwest to **Plaza de España.** North of Gran Vía are three club and bar-hopping districts, linked by Calle de Fuencarral: **Malasaña, Bilbao,** and **Chueca.** Modern Madrid is beyond Gran Vía and east of Malasaña and Chueca. East of Sol, the tree-lined thoroughfares **Paseo de la Castellana, Paseo de Recoletos,** and **Paseo del Prado** split Madrid in two, running from Atocha in the south to **Plaza Castilla** in the north, passing the Prado, the fountains of **Plaza Cibeles,** and **Plaza Colón.** Refer to the **color map** of Madrid's Metro. Madrid is safer than its European counterparts, but Sol, Pl. España, Pl. Chueca, and Malasaña's Pl. Dos de Mayo are still intimidating late at night. As a general rule, travel in groups, avoid the parks and quiet streets after dark, and always watch for thieves and pickpockets in crowds.

▪ LOCAL TRANSPORTATION

Public Transportation: Madrid's **Metro** (☎902 44 44 03; www.metromadrid.es) puts most major subway systems to shame. Individual Metro tickets cost €1.10, a **bonotransporte** (ticket of 10 rides for Metro or bus system) is €5.20. Buy both at machines in any Metro stop, *estanco* (tobacco shop), or newsstand. Keep your ticket; Metro officials often board and ask to see them, and travelers without tickets get fined. **Bus** info ☎914 06 88 10 (Spanish only). 6am-midnight, €1.10. *Buho* (owl), the **night bus** service, runs every 20min. midnight-3am, every hr. 3-6am, and is the cheapest form of transportation for late-night revelers. Look for buses N1-20.

Taxis: Call ☎914 05 12 13, 914 47 51 80, or 913 71 37 11. A *libre* sign in the window or a green light indicates availability. Base fare €1.40, plus €0.70-0.90 per km.

▪ PRACTICAL INFORMATION

TOURIST, FINANCIAL, AND LOCAL SERVICES

Tourist Offices: Municipal, Plaza Mayor 3 (☎/fax 913 66 54 77), will be expanding and relocating to a location across the Plaza Mayor. M: Sol. Open M-Sa 10am-8pm, Su 10am-3pm. **Regional/Provincial Office of the Comunidad de Madrid,** Duque de Medinacelia 2 (☎914 29 49 51; www.comadrid.es/turismo). **Branches** at Estación Chamartín and the airport.

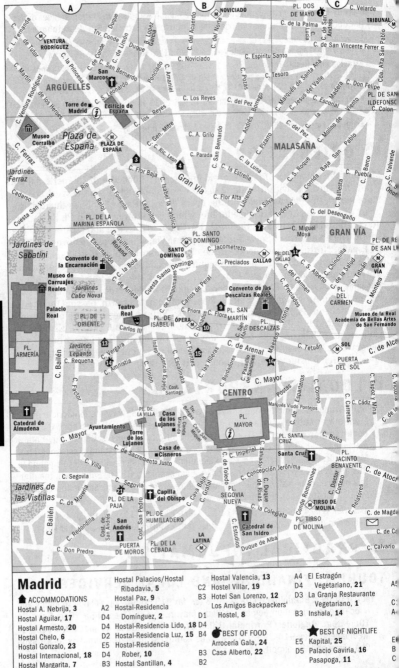

Madrid

ACCOMMODATIONS
Hostal A. Nebrija, 3
Hostal Aguilar, 17 D4
Hostal Armesto, 20 D4
Hostal Chelo, 6 E5
Hostal Gonzalo, 23 E5
Hostal Internacional, 18 D4
Hostal Margarita, 7 B3

Hostal Palacios/Hostal
Ribadavia, 5 C2
Hostal Paz, 9 B3
Hostal-Residencia
Domínguez, 2 A2
Hostal-Residencia Lido, 18 D4
Hostal-Residencia Luz, 15 D2
Hostal-Residencia
Rober, 10 B4
Hostal Santillan, 4 E5

Hostal Valencia, 13 B3
Hostel Villar, 19 B2
Hotel San Lorenzo, 12 C2
Los Amigos Backpackers'
Hostel, 8 D1

BEST OF FOOD
Arrocería Gala, 24 B3
Casa Alberto, 22 B2

El Estragón A4
Vegetariano, 21 D4
La Granja Restaurante D3
Vegetariano, 1 B3
Inshala, 14

BEST OF NIGHTLIFE
Kapital, 25 E5
Palacio Gaviria, 16 D5
Pasapoga, 11 B3

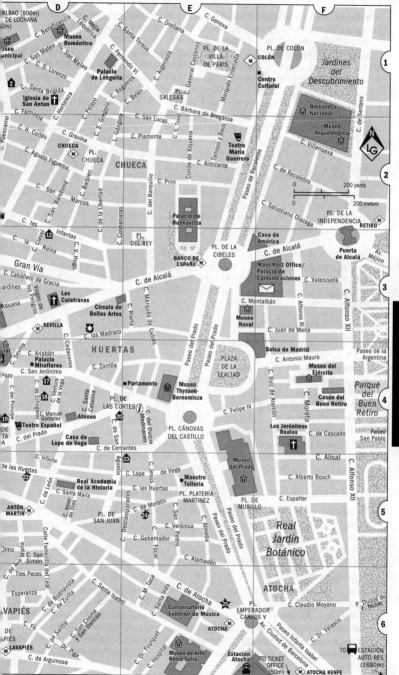

SPAIN

Websites: www.comadrid.es/turismo; www.madrid.org; www.tourspain.es; www.cronica-madrid.com; www.guiadelocio.com; www.madridman.com; www.red2000.com/spain/madrid; www.descubremadrid.munimadrid.es.

Budget Travel: Viajes TIVE, C. Fernando el Católico 88 (☎915 43 74 12; fax 915 44 00 62). M: Moncloa. Exit the Metro at C. Isaac Peral, walk straight down C. Arcipreste de Hita, and turn left on C. Fernando el Católico; it'll be on your left. Organizes group excursions and language classes. Lodgings and student residence info. ISIC €6; HI card €5, over-30 €11, non-Spaniards €19. Open M-F 9am-2pm. Arrive early to avoid long lines.

Embassies: Australia, Pl. Descubridor Diego de Ordás 3 (☎914 41 60 25; www.embaustralia.es). **Canada,** C. Núñez de Balboa 35 (☎914 23 32 50; www.canada-es.org). **Ireland,** Po. Castellana 46, 4th fl. (☎914 36 40 93; fax 914 35 16 77). **New Zealand,** Pl. Lealtad 2, 3rd fl. (☎915 23 02 26; fax 915 23 01 71). **South Africa,** Claudio Coello 91, 6th fl. (☎914 36 37 80; fax 915 77 74 14). **UK,** C. Fernando el Santo 16 (☎917 00 82 00; fax 917 00 82 72). **US,** C. Serrano 75 (☎915 87 22 00; www.embusa.es).

Currency Exchange: In general, credit and ATM cards offer the best exchange rates. Avoid changing money at airport and train station counters; they tend to charge exorbitant commissions on horrible rates. **Santander Central Hispano** charges no commission on cash or traveler's checks up to €600. **Main branch,** Pl. Canalejas 1 (☎915 58 11 11). M: Sol. Follow C. San Jeronimo to Pl. Canalejas. Open Apr.-Sept. M-F 8:30am-2pm; Oct.-Mar. M-Th 8:30am-4:30pm, F 8:30am-2pm, Sa 8:30am-1pm.

American Express: Pl. Cortés 2 (traveler services ☎917 43 77 40; currency exchange ☎917 43 77 55). M: Banco de España. Traveler services open M-F 9am-7:30pm, Sa 10am-2pm; currency exchange M-F 9am-7:30pm, Sa 9am-2pm. 24hr. Express Cash machine outside.

LOCAL SERVICES

Luggage Storage: Barajas Airport. Follow the signs to *consigna.* One day €3; 2-15 days €3-5 per day; after day 15, €0.60-1.40 per day. **Estación Chamartín** and **Estación Atocha.** Lockers €2.40-4.50 per day. Open daily 6:30am-10:15pm.

Bi-Gay-Lesbian Resources: Most establishments in the Chueca area carry *Shanguide,* a free guide to gay nightlife in Spain. **Colectivo de Gais y Lesbianas de Madrid (COGAM),** C. Fuencarral 37 (☎/fax 915 22 45 17). M: Gran Vía. Provides a wide range of services and activities, including an HIV support group (M-F 6-10pm). Reception daily M-Sa 5:30-9pm. Free counseling M-Th 7-9pm.

Laundromat: Lavandería Ondablu, C. León 3 (☎913 69 50 71). M: Antón Martín, Sol, or Sevilla. Open daily 9am-10:30pm. Just up the street is **Lavandería Cervantes,** C. León, 6. Wash €2, dry €1. Open daily 9am-9pm.

EMERGENCY AND COMMUNICATIONS

Emergency: ☎112. **Ambulance:** ☎061. **National police:** ☎091. **Local police:** ☎092.

Police: C. de los Madrazo 9 (☎915 41 71 60). M: Sevilla. From C. Alcalá take a right onto C. Cedacneros and a left onto C. de los Madrazo. To report crimes committed in the **Metro,** go to the office in the Sol station (open daily 8am-11pm). **Guardia Civil** (☎062 or 915 34 02 00). **Protección Civil** (☎915 37 31 00).

Rape Hotline: ☎915 74 01 10. Open M-F 10am-2pm and 4-7pm.

Medical Services: Equipo Quirúrgico Municipal No. 1, C. Montesa 22 (☎915 88 51 00). M: Manuel Becerra. **Hospital Ramón y Cajal,** Ctra. Colmenar Viejo (☎913 36 80 00). Bus #135 from Pl. Castilla. For non-emergency concerns, **Anglo-American Medical Unit,** Conde de Aranda 1, 1st fl. (☎914 35 18 23), is quick and friendly.

Internet Access: New Internet cafes are surfacing everywhere. While the average is a reasonable €2 per hr., small shops in apartments charge even less; keep a lookout.

■ **Easy Everything,** C. Montera 10 (☎915 21 18 65; www.easyeverything.com). M: Sol. From the Plaza del Sol, look for C. Montera, which goes toward Gran Vía. Open daily 8am-1am, with hundreds of computers, fast connections, good music, and a cafe. Access from €0.50.

Conéctate, C. Isaac Peral 4 (☎915 44 54 65; www.conectate.es). M: Moncloa. Over 300 flat-screens and some of the lowest prices in Madrid. Open 24hr.

Yazzgo Internet, Gran Vía 84 & 69 (☎915 22 11 20; www.yazzgo.com). M: San Bernado or Pl. de España. Also locations at Puerta del Sol 6, Gran Vía 60, Estación Chamartín, and Estación Méndez Álvaro. A growing chain; check their website for new locations. Most branches open daily 8:30am-10:30pm; Gran Vía 69 branch open 8:30am-1am.

Post Office: Palacio de Comunicaciones, C. de Alcala 51, on Pl. Cibeles (☎902 19 71 97). M: Banco de España. Windows open M-Sa 8:30am-9:30pm, Su 9am-2pm for stamp purchases, certified mail, telex, and fax service. **Poste Restante** (Lista de Correos) at windows 80-82; passport required. **Postal Code:** 28080.

⌐ ACCOMMODATIONS

Make reservations for summer visits. Expect to pay €17-€50 per person, depending on location, amenities, and season. Tourist offices provide information about the 13 or so **campsites** within 50km of Madrid. **Centro,** the triangle between Puerta del Sol, Opera, and Plaza Mayor, is full of *hostales,* but you'll pay for the prime location. The cultural hotbed of **Huertas,** framed by C. San Jeronimo, C. las Huertas, and C. Atocha, is almost as central and more fun. Festive **Malasaña** and **Chueca,** bisected by C. Fuencarral, host cheap rooms in the heart of the action, but the sleep-deprived should beware; the party doesn't quiet down for rest. *Hostales,* like temptations, are everywhere among **Gran Vía's** sex shops and scam artists.

EL CENTRO: SOL, ÓPERA, AND PLAZA MAYOR

■ **Hostal Paz,** C. Flora 4, 1st and 4th fl. (☎915 47 30 47). M: Ópera. Located on a quiet street, parallel to C. Arenal, off C. Donados or C. Hileras. Peaceful rooms with large windows are sheltered from street noise and lavished with amenities. Reservations advised. Singles €20; doubles €30-36; triples €45. MC/V. ❷

■ **Hostal-Residencia Luz,** C. Fuentes 10, 3rd fl. (☎915 42 07 59 or 915 59 74 18; fax 42 07 59), off C. Arenal. M: Ópera. Neck and neck with Hostal Paz for the best digs in Madrid. Newly redecorated rooms with hardwood floors and elegant furniture ooze comfort. Singles €15; doubles €34-39; triples €39-45. ❷

Hostal-Residencia Rober, C. Arenal 26, 5th fl. (☎915 41 91 75). M: Ópera. Brilliant balcony views down Arenal. Singles with double bed and shower €24, with bath €34; doubles with bath €39; triples with bath €59. Discounts for longer stays. ❸

Hostal Valencia, Pl. Oriente 2, 3rd fl. (☎915 59 84 50). M: Ópera. Narrow glass elevator leads to elegant rooms. Singles €42; doubles €72; master suite €92. ❹

Los Amigos Backpackers' Hostel, C. Campomanes 6, 4th fl. (☎915 47 17 07; www.losamigoshostel.com), off Pl. de Isabel II. M: Ópera. One of very few standard hostels in Madrid. Brightly decorated dorms and clean shared baths. Kitchen and festive common room. Breakfast included. Sheets €5. Laundry €5. Internet €1 per 30min. 24hr. reception. Dorms €15 (includes breakfast). MC/V. ❷

HUERTAS

■ **Hostal Gonzalo,** C. Cervantes 34, 3rd fl. (☎914 29 27 14; fax 914 20 20 07). M: Antón Martín. Off C. León, which is off C. Atocha. A budget traveler's dream: renovated rooms, pristine baths, TVs, and fans in the summer. Singles €38; doubles €47; triples €60. ❸

Hostal Internacional, C. Echegaray 5, 2nd fl. (☎914 29 62 09). M: Sol. Rooms renovated in 2002. Nice common room. Singles €25-30; doubles €40. ❸

SPAIN

Hostal-Residencia Lido, C. Echegaray 5, 2nd fl. (☎914 29 62 07). M: Sol or Sevilla. Across from Internacional, Lido showcases new rooms with comfy beds, TVs, and complete baths. Singles €22-25, with bath €25-30; doubles €35-40. ❷

Hostal Villar, C. Príncipe 18, 1st-4th fl. (☎915 31 66 00; www.arrakis.es/~h-villar). M: Sol. From the Metro, follow C. San Jerónimo and turn right on C. Príncipe. Feels secluded despite its busy location. Singles €22, with bath €25; doubles €30/40; triples €42/56. ❷

Hostal Aguilar, C. San Jerónimo 32, 2nd fl. (☎914 29 59 26 or 914 29 36 61; www.hostalaguilar.com). M: Sol or Sevilla. Clean and expansive rooms with A/C and safe. Hemingway purportedly spent many nights in room 107. Singles €33; doubles €45; triples €60; quads €73. MC/V. ❸

Hostal Sardinero, C. Prado 16, 3rd fl. (☎914 29 57 56, ☎/fax 914 29 41 12), a few blocks from Plaza Santa Ana. An upscale hostel with all the creature comforts of a hotel, sparkling rooms have A/C, TV, safe, and private baths. Singles €50; doubles €60. 24hr. reception. MC/V. ❹

Hostal Armesto, C. San Agustín 6, 1st fl. (☎914 29 90 31). M: Antón Martín. In front of Pl. Cortés. This *hostal* offers exceptional hospitality and a quiet night's sleep. All rooms with private bath and A/C. Older crowd. Singles €45; doubles €50; triples €54. ❹

GRAN VÍA

Hostal A. Nebrija, Gran Vía 67, 8th fl., elevator A (☎915 47 73 19). M: Pl. España. Pleasant, spacious rooms offering magnificent views of the city landscape. Singles €26; doubles €36; triples €49. AmEx/MC/V. ❸

Hostal Santillan, Gran Vía 64, 8th fl. (☎/fax 915 48 23 28). M: Pl. España. Friendly management. Simple rooms all have showers, sinks, TVs, fans, and safes. Singles €30; doubles €45; triples €60. MC/V. ❸

Hostal Margarita, Gran Vía 50, 5th fl. (☎/fax 915 47 35 49). M: Callao. Simple rooms with large windows and TV; most with street views. Singles €25; doubles €36, with bath €38; triples with bath €48. MC/V. ❷

MALASAÑA AND CHUECA

▨ **Hostal-Residencia Domínguez,** C. Santa Brígida 1, 1st fl. (☎/fax 915 32 15 47). M: Tribunal. Go down C. Fuencarral toward Gran Vía, turn left on C. Santa Brígida, and climb up a flight. Hospitable young owner ready with tips on local nightlife. English spoken. Singles €22, with bath €30; doubles with bath and A/C €40. ❷

Hostal Chelo, C. Hortaleza 17, 3rd fl. (☎915 32 70 33; www.chelo.com). M: Gran Vía. Great location, hospitable and helpful staff. Rooms are spacious, with complete bath. Singles €30; doubles €38. ❸

Hostal Palacios and **Hostal Ribadavia,** C. Fuencarral 25, 1st-3rd fl. (☎915 31 10 58 or ☎915 31 48 47). M: Gran Vía. Both run by the same cheerful family. Singles €20, with bath €30; doubles €30/36; triples €45/51. AmEx/MC/V. ❷

Hotel San Lorenzo, C. Clavel 8 (☎915 21 30 57; www.hotel/sanlorenzo.com). M: Gran Vía. From the Metro, walk down Gran Vía and make a left on C. Clavel. New furniture, modern bathrooms, and soundproof windows. Reservations recommended. Singles €50; doubles €75-85. AmEx/MC/V. ❹

◘ FOOD

In Madrid, it's not hard to fork it down without forking over too much. Most restaurants offer a *menú del día*, which includes bread, one drink, and one choice from each of the day's selection of appetizers, main courses, and desserts (€7-9). Many small eateries line **Calles Echegaray, Bentura de la Vega,** and **Manuel Fernández González** in Huertas; **Calle Agurrosa** at Lavapiés has some funky outdoor cafes, and there are good restaurants up the hill toward Huertas; **Calle Fuencarral** in Gran Vía is lined with cheap eats. **Bilbao,** the area north of Glorieta de Bilbao, is the place to go for ethnically diverse culinary choices. Bars along **Calle Hartzenbusch** and **Calle Cisneros** offer cheap *tapas*. Keep in mind the following essential buzz words for quicker, cheaper *madrileño* fare: *bocadillo* (a sandwich on a long, hard roll, €2-2.80); *ración* (a large *tapa*, served with bread €2-3.80); and *empanada* (a puff pastry with meat fillings, €1.30-2). Vegetarians should check out the *Guía del Ocio*, which has a complete listing of Madrid's vegetarian havens under the section *"Otras Cocinas,"* or the website www.mundovegetariano.com. For **groceries**, **%Dia** and **Simago** are the cheapest supermarket chains. More expensive are **Mantequerías Leonesas, Expreso,** and **Jumbo.**

■ **Inshala,** C. Amnistia 10 (☎915 48 26 32). M: Ópera. Eclectic menu filled with delicious Spanish, Mexican, Japanese, Italian, and Moroccan dishes. Weekday lunch *menú* €8. Dinner *menú* €8-€15. Reservations strongly recommended for both lunch and dinner. Open M-Th noon-2pm, F-Sa until 3am. ❸

■ **Arrocería Gala,** C. Moratín 22 (☎914 29 25 62). Down the hill from C. Atocha on C. Moratín. The decor is as colorful and varied as the house *paella* (€14). Reserve on weekends. Open daily 1:30-5pm and 9-11pm. ❸

■ **El Estragón Vegetariano,** Pl. de la Paja 10 (☎913 65 89 82). M: La Latina. Perhaps the best medium-priced restaurant—of any kind—in Madrid, with vegetarian food that could convert even the most die-hard carnivores. Try the delicious *menú* (M-F €9; Sa-Su and evenings €18). Open daily 1:30-4:30pm and 8pm-1am. AmEx/MC/V. ❹

■ **La Granja Restaurante Vegetariano,** C. San Andrés 11 (☎915 32 87 93), off Pl. 2 de Mayo. M: Tribunal or Bilbao. Dimmed yellow lights glow above intricately tiled walls in this Arabic-themed restaurant. Youthful crowd, friendly owner, and big portions. *Menú* €7.50. Open daily 1:30-4:15pm and 8:30pm-midnight. MC/V. ❷

■ **Casa Alberto,** C. Huertas 18 (☎914 29 93 56). M: Antón Martín. Interior dining room decorated with bullfighting and Cervantine relics; Cervantes wrote the second part of *El Quijote* here. The *tapas* are all original house recipes. Get the feel of their *gambas a ajillo* (shrimp with garlic and hot peppers; €8.40) or the *canapés* (€2). Sit-down dinner is a bit pricey. Open Tu-Sa noon-5:30pm and 8pm-1:30am. AmEx/MC/V. ❸

■ **Los Gabrieles,** C. Echegaray 17 (☎914 29 62 61). M: Sol. The tiled mural at the back depicts famous artists—from Velázquez to Goya—as stumble-drunks. Serves *tapas* by afternoon and drinks by night. Flamenco Tu night. Open daily 1pm-late. ❶

Café de Oriente, Pl. Oriente 2 (☎915 47 15 64). M: Ópera. An old-fashioned cafe with a spectacular view of the Palacio Real from the *terraza*, especially at night when floodlights illuminate the facade. Specialty coffees (€1.80-6) live up to their price. Open Su-Th 8:30am-1:30am, F-Sa until 12:30am. ❷

Al-Jaima, Cocina del Desierto, C. Barbieri 1 (☎915 23 11 42). M: Gran Vía or Chueca. Lebanese, Moroccan, and Egyptian food in intimate North African setting. Specialties include the *pastela*, couscous, *shish kebabs*, and *tajine* (€4-8). Open daily 1:30-4pm and 9pm-midnight. Dinner reservations recommended. AmEx/MC/V. ❷

Osteria Il Regno di Napoli, C. San Andrés 21 (☎914 45 63 00). From Glorieta de Bilbao, head one block down C. Carranza, then turn left onto C. San Andrés. Delicious Italian cuisine in a hip environment. Lunch *menú* €10; dinner entrees €8-12. Reservations recommended. Open M-F 2-4pm and 9pm-midnight, Sa 9pm-midnight, Su 2-4pm. AmEx/MC/V. ❷

Restaurante Casa Botín, C. de Cuchilleros 17 (☎913 66 42 17), off Plaza Mayor. The "oldest restaurant in the world," founded in 1725, serves filling Spanish dishes (€7-25). Reservations recommended. Lunch daily 1-4pm, dinner 8pm-midnight. ❸

Café-Botillería Manuela, C. San Vicente Ferrer 29 (☎915 31 70 37). M: Tribunal. Inviting atmosphere with upbeat music and occasional impromptu piano playing. Specialty international cocktails (€3-5), coffees (€3.50-4.50), and *tapas* menu (€2-8). Open July-Aug. Su and Tu-Sa 6pm-2:30am, Sept.-June daily 4pm-2am. ❷

Ananias, C. Galileo 9 (☎914 48 68 01). M: Argüelles. From C. Alberto Aguilera, take a left onto C. Galileo. Swirling waiters serve Castilian dishes with a flourish. Entrees €7-15. Open Su 1-4pm; M-Tu and Th-Sa 1-4pm and 9pm-midnight. AmEx/MC/V. ❸

La Finca de Susana, C. Arlaban 4 (☎913 69 35 57). M: Sevilla. Probably the most popular lunch place in Madrid; fine dining at an extremely low price (*menú* €7). Be prepared to wait in line. Open daily 1-3:45pm and 8:30-11:45pm. ❷

◉ SIGHTS

Madrid, as large as it may seem, is a walker's city. The word *paseo* refers to a major avenue, but literally means "a stroll." The municipal tourist office's *Plano de Transportes*—which marks monuments as well as bus and Metro lines—is indispensable.

EL CENTRO: SOL, ÓPERA, AND PLAZA MAYOR

PUERTA DEL SOL. Kilómetro 0, the origin of six national highways, marks the center of the city (and the country) in the most chaotic of Madrid's plazas. Puerta del Sol (Gate of Sun) blazes with taxis, bars, and street performers. The statue **El Oso y el Madroño,** a bear and strawberry tree, is a popular meeting place. *(M: Sol.)*

PLAZA MAYOR. Juan de Herrera, architect of El Escorial, also designed this plaza. Its elegant arcades, spindly towers, and open verandas, erected for Felipe III in 1620, came to define "Madrid-style" architecture and inspired every peering *balcón* thereafter. Toward evening, Plaza Mayor awakens as *madrileños* resurface, tourists multiply, and cafes fill with lively patrons. Live flamenco performances are a common treat. *(M: Sol. From Pta. Sol, walk down C. Mayor. The plaza is on the left.)*

CATEDRAL DE SAN ISIDRO. Designed in the Jesuit Baroque style at the beginning of the 17th century, the cathedral received San Isidro's remains in 1769. During the Civil War, rioting workers burned the exterior and damaged much of the cathedral—only the primary nave and a few Baroque decorations remain from the original. *(M: Latina. From Pta. Sol, take C. Mayor to Plaza Mayor, cross the plaza, and exit onto C. Toledo. Open for Mass only.)*

PLAZA DE LA VILLA. Plaza de la Villa marks the heart of what was once old Madrid. Though only a few medieval buildings remain, the plaza still features a stunning courtyard (around the statue of Don Alvara de Bazón), beautiful tilework, and eclectic architecture. Across the plaza is the 17th-century **Ayuntamiento (Casa de la Villa),** designed in 1640 by Juan Gomez de Mora as both the mayor's home and the city jail. *(M: Sol. From Pta. Sol, go down C. Mayor, past Plaza Mayor.)*

AROUND THE PALACIO REAL. This amazingly luxurious palace was built for the first Bourbon King, Felipe V, to replace the Alcázar after it burned down. It took 40 years to build, and the decoration of its 2000 rooms with 20km of tapestry dragged on for a century. *(M: Sol. From Pta. Sol, take C. Mayor and turn right on C. Bailén. Open Apr.-Sept. M-Sa 9am-6pm, Su 9am-3pm; Oct.-Mar. M-Sa 9:30am-5pm, Su 9am-2pm. €7, students €3.30. Tours €8. W free for EU citizens.)* The palace faces **Plaza de Oriente,** a sculpture garden. Most of its statues were designed for the palace roof, but were placed in this shady plaza after the queen had a nightmare about the roof collapsing. *(From Pta. Sol, take C. Arenal to the plaza. Free.)* Next door to the palace is the **Cathedral de Nuestra Señora de la Almudena,** begun in 1879 and finished a century later. The cathedral's modern interior stands in contrast to the gilded Palacio Real. *(M: Sol. From Pta. Sol, go down C. Mayor and it's just across C. Bailén. Open daily 9am-9pm. Free.)*

HUERTAS, GRAN VÍA, MALASAÑA, CHUECA, AND ARGÜELLES

East of Pta. del Sol, **Huertas** reflects its literary ilk, from famed authors' houses to legendary cafes. The neighborhood was home to Cervantes, Góngora, Calderón, and Moratín and enjoyed a fleeting return to literary prominence when Hemingway hung out here. *(M: Sol.)* **Gran Vía,** which stretches from Pl. de Callao to Pl. de España, is the busiest street in Madrid; massive skyscrapers, fast-food joints, and bustling stores grace this chaotic thoroughfare. *(M: Callao and Pl. España.)* **Malasaña** and **Chueca** lie at the core of Madrid's alternative scene; the area between C. de Fuencarral and C. de San Bernardo, north of Gran Vía, boasts avant-garde architecture, chic eateries, and the city's hippest fashion. Out of the way in **Argüelles,** Goya's frescoed dome in the beautiful **Ermita de San Antonio de la Florida** arches above his buried corpse. *(M: Príncipe Pío. From the Metro, go left on C. de Buen Altamirano, walk through the park, and turn left on Po. Florida; the Ermita is at the end of the street. Open Open Tu-F 10am-2pm and 4-8pm, Sa-Su 10am-2pm. Free.)* The **Temple de Debod,** Spain's only Egyptian temple, was built by Pharaoh Zakheramon in the 4th century BC. *(M: Ventura Rodríguez. From the Metro, walk down C. Ventura Rodríguez into the Parque de la Montaña; the temple is on the left. Open April 1-Sept. 31 Tu-F 2pm and 4-8pm, Sa-Su 10am-2pm; Oct. 1-March 31 Tu-F 9:45am-1:15pm and 4:15-5:45pm, Sa-Su 9:45am-1:45pm. Free.)* The **Faro de Moncloa,** a 92m-tall metal tower, offers views of the city. *(Av. Arco de la Victoria. Open Su and Tu-Sa 10am-2pm and 5-8pm. To ascend the tower adults €1, over-65 and under-11 €0.50.)*

OTHER SIGHTS

▨ RETIRO

Join an array of vendors, palm-readers, soccer players, and sunbathers in what Felipe IV converted from a hunting ground into a *buen retiro* (nice retreat). The finely landscaped 300-acre Parque del Buen Retiro is centered around a rectangular lake and a magnificent monument to King Alfonso XII. Dubbed **Estanque Grande,** this central location is popular among casual rowers. Built by Ricardo Velázquez to exhibit Filipino flowers, the exquisite steel-and-glass **Palacio de Cristal** hosts a variety of art shows. *(Open Apr.-Sept. M and W-Sa 11am-8pm, Su 11am-6pm; Oct.-Mar. M and W-Sa 10am-6pm, Su 10am-4pm. Closed Tu. Free.)* All artists should dream of having their art displayed in the **Palacio de Velázquez,** with its billowing ceilings, marble floors, and ideal lighting. *(Past the Estanque, turn left on Paseo del Venezuela. Open Apr.-Sept. M and W-Sa 11am-8pm, Su 11am-6pm; Oct.-Mar. M and W-Sa 10am-6pm, Su 10am-4pm. Closed Tu. Free.)* Avoid venturing into the park alone after dark.

EL PARDO

Built as a hunting lodge for Carlos I in 1547, El Pardo was enlarged by generations of Habsburgs and Bourbons. El Pardo gained attention in 1940 when Franco made it his home, in which he resided until his death in 1975. It is renowned for its collection of tapestries—several of which were designed by Goya—but the palace also holds paintings by Velázquez and Ribera. *(Take bus #601 (15min., €1) from the stop in front of the Ejército del Aire building. M: Moncloa. Palace open Apr.-Sept. M-Sa 10:30am-6pm, Su 9:20am-1:40pm; Oct.-Mar. M-Sa 10:30am-5pm, Su 9:50am-1:40pm. Required 45min. guided tour in Spanish. €3, students €1.50. W EU citizens free.)*

🏛 MUSEUMS

Madrid's great museums need no introduction. If you're not a student and plan on visiting the big three, your best bet is the **Paseo del Arte** ticket (€7.70), which grants admission to the Museo del Prado, Museo Thyssen-Bornemisza, and Museo Centro de Arte Reina Sofía. The pass is available at all three museums.

▓ MUSEO DEL PRADO

One of Europe's finest museums, the walls of the Prado are graced by Goya's "black paintings" and Velázquez's *Las Meninas*. As a result of the Spanish Habsburgs' long reign over the Netherlands, the museum has an extraordinary collection of Flemish paintings by Van Dyck, van der Weyden, Albrecht Dürer, Pieter Brueghel the Elder, and Rubens. Other notable collections include works by: Titian, Raphael, Botticelli, Bosch, and El Greco. (*M: Banco de España. On Po. Prado at Pl. Cánovas del Castillo. http://museoprado.mcu.es. Open Su and Tu-Sa 9am-7pm. €3, students €1.50. Under-18, over-65, and Su free.*)

▓ MUSEO NACIONAL CENTRO DE ARTE REINA SOFÍA

The centerpiece of this 20th-century collection is Picasso's masterwork *Guernica*, depicting the agony of the Nazi bombing of the Basque town of Guernica for the Fascists during the Spanish Civil War. Works by Miró, Julio González, Juan Gris, and Dalí illustrate the essential role of Spanish artists in Cubism and Surrealism. (*M: Atocha. C. Santa Isabel 52, opposite Estación Atocha at the south end of Po. Prado. Open M and W-Sa 10am-9pm, Su 10am-2:30pm. €3, students €1.50. Sa after 2:30pm, Su, and holidays free.*)

▓ MUSEO THYSSEN-BORNEMISZA

This 18th-century palace houses a fabulous art collection accumulated by generations of the Austro-Hungarian magnates. The museum surveys it all, parading canvases and sculptures by many of the greats, including El Greco, Titian, Caravaggio, Picasso, Rothko, Hopper, Renoir, Klee, Chagall, and Dalí. To view the collection in chronological order and observe the evolution of styles and themes, begin on the top floor and work down. (*M: Banco de España. Bus #6, 14, 27, 37, or 45. On the corner of Po. Prado and C. San Jerónimo. www.museothyssen.org. Open Su and Tu-Sa 10am-7pm. Last entrance 6:30pm. €4.80, students with ISIC and seniors €3. Under-12 free.*)

MUSEO DE AMÉRICA

This under-appreciated museum documents the cultures of America's pre-Columbian civilizations and the legacy of the Spanish conquest. (*M: Moncloa. Av. Reyes Católicos 6, next to the Faro de Moncloa. Open Su and Tu-Sa 9:30am-3pm. €3, students €1.50. Under-18, over-65, and Su free.*)

🎭 ENTERTAINMENT

▓ **EL RASTRO (FLEA MARKET).** For hundreds of years, El Rastro has been a Sunday morning tradition. The market begins in La Latina at Pl. Cascorro off C. Toledo and ends at the bottom of C. Ribera de Curtidores. Get lost in the insanity and find anything from jewelry and jeans to antique tools and pet birds. El Rastro is open Sundays and holidays from 9am to 2pm.

CLASSIC CAFES. Spend an afternoon lingering over a *café con leche* and soak up Madrilenian culture in historic cafes. At ▓**Café Gijón**, Po. Recoletos 21 (*M: Colón*), a 115-year-old literati hangout, thought-provoking conversation makes good coffee well worth the price. *(Open daily 7am-1:30am, F-Sa until 2am.)* Or, gaze at the Palacio Real from the ritzy **Café de Oriente**, Pl. Oriente 2. *(M: Ópera. Open Su-Th 8:30am-1:30am, F-Sa until 12:30am.)*

MUSIC AND FLAMENCO. Anyone interested in live entertainment should stop by the **Círculo de Bellas Artes,** C. Alcala 42 (*M: Sevilla or Banco de España.* ☎913 60 54 00; *www.circulobellasartes.com*). Their magazine, *Minerva*, is indispensable. Check the *Guía del Ocio* for information on the city-sponsored movies, plays, and concerts. **Flamenco** in Madrid is tourist-oriented and expensive. A few nightlife spots are authentic, but pricey. **Casa Patas,** C. Cañizares 10, is good quality for less than usual. (☎*913 69 04 96; www.casapatas.com. M: Antón Martín.*) At **Corral de la Morería,** C. Morería 17, shows start at 9:45pm and last until 2am. (☎*913 65 84 46. M: Ópera or La Latina. Cover €30.*)

SPORTS. Spanish sports fans go ballistic for **fútbol** (soccer to Americans). Every Sunday and some Saturdays from September to June, one of two local teams plays at home. **Real Madrid** plays at Estadio Santiago Bernabéu, Po. Castellana 104. (☎*914 57 11 12. M: Lima.*) **Atlético de Madrid** plays at Estadio Vicente Calderón, C. Virgen del Puerto 67. (☎*913 66 47 07. M: Pirámides or Marqués de Vadillos. Tickets €18-42.*) **Corridas** (bullfights) are held during the Festival of San Isidro and every Sunday from March to October; they are less frequent the rest of the year. **Plaza de las Ventas,** C. Alcalá 237, east of Madrid, is Spain's largest bullfighting ring. (☎*913 56 22 00; www.las-ventas.com. M: Ventas. Tickets €5-92.*)

▓ NIGHTLIFE

Spaniards average one hour less sleep a night than other Europeans, and *madrileños* claim to need even less than that. Proud of their nocturnal offerings—they'll say with a straight face that Paris or New York bored them—they don't retire until they've "killed the night" and a good part of the morning. As the sun sets, *terrazas* and *chiringuitos* (outdoor cafes/bars) spill across sidewalks. *Madrileños* start in the *tapas* bars of **Huertas,** move to the youthful scene in **Malasaña,** and end at the crazed parties of **Chueca** or late-night clubs of **Gran Vía.** Students fill the streets of **Bilbao** and **Moncloa.** Madrid's gay scene, centered on **Plaza Chueca,** is fantastic. Most clubs don't heat up until around 2am; don't be surprised by a line waiting outside at 5:30am. The *entrada* (cover) can be as high as €12, but usually includes a drink. Bouncers on power trips love to make examples; dress well to avoid being overcharged or denied. Women may not be charged at all.

▓ **Ananda,** Estación Atocha 2, Esq. Av. Ciudad de Barcelona. Large outdoor terraza equipped with multiple bars and a 20-something crowd. Check out the white room indoors for a dance. W and Su transform Ananda into a Sundance party packed with crowds to rival weekend nights. Cover €10. Mixed drinks €8. Open daily 11pm-dawn.

▓ **Palacio Gaviria,** C. Arenal 9. M: Sol or Ópera. A grand red carpet leads to two huge ballrooms-turned-club-spaces with dancers and blazing light shows; it's the most exceptional of Madrid's grandiose *discotecas.* Cover €9-15. Open M-W 11pm-4am, Th 10:30pm-6am, F-Sa 11pm-6am, Su 9pm-2:30am.

▓ **Pasapoga,** Gran Vía 37. M: Callao. Around the corner from Pl. Callao. Gay nightlife explodes here on the weekends, especially on Saturdays. Beautiful interior, beautiful people. Cover €15. Open Su and Tu-Sa 6pm-dawn.

▓ **Kapital,** C. Atocha 125. M: Atocha. *Thumba la casa* (bring down the house) on 7 floors of *discoteca* insanity. Dress to impress the bouncer. Cover €12, includes 1 drink. Mixed drinks €9. Open Th-Su midnight-6am and afternoons F–Su 5:30-11pm.

El Café de Sheherezade, C. Santa María 18. M: Antón Martín. Surrounded by Middle Eastern music and decor, groups cluster around *pipas* (pipes; €7-10) that filter sweet smoke through whiskey or water. Open in summer Su-Th 6pm-2:30am, F-Sa 6pm-3:30am; off-season Su-Th 5pm-2am, F-Sa 5pm-3am.

Acuarela, C. Gravina 10. M: Chueca. A welcome alternative to the club scene. Buddhas and candles surround antique furniture, inspiration for good conversation and a good buzz. Coffees and teas €2-6. Liqueur €4. Open daily 3pm-3am.

Why Not?, C. San Bartolome 7. M: Chueca. Small, downstairs bar packed almost every night of the week with a wild, mixed crowd. Open daily 10pm-6am.

Suite, Virgen de los Peligros 4, off C. de Alcalá. M: Sevilla. Classy restaurant, bar, and club boasts nouveau *tapas* by day and sleek drinks (€6) by night. Mixed crowd. Open daily 1-5pm and 8pm-3:30am.

⌦ DAYTRIPS FROM MADRID

EL ESCORIAL. The **Monasterio de San Lorenzo del Escorial** was a gift from Felipe II to God, the people, and himself, commemorating his victory over the French at the battle of San Quintín in 1557. Near the town of **San Lorenzo,** El Escorial is filled with artistic treasures, two palaces, two pantheons, a church, and a magnificent library. Don't come on Monday, when the complex and most of the town shut down. To avoid crowds, enter via the gate on C. Floridablanca, on the west side. The adjacent **Museo de Arquitectura and Pintura** chronicles the construction of El Escorial and includes masterpieces by Bosch, El Greco, Titian, Tintoretto, Velázquez, Zurbarán, and van Dyck. The **Palacio Real,** lined with 16th-century *azulejos* (tiles), includes the majestic **Salón del Trono** (Throne Room), Felipe II's spartan 16th-century apartments, and the luxurious 18th-century rooms of Carlos III and Carlos IV. The macabre **Panteón Real** is filled with tombs of monarchs and glitters with gold-and-marble designs. (Complex ☎918 90 59 03. Open Apr.-Sept. Su-Tu-Sa 10am-6pm; Oct.-Mar. 10am-5pm. Last admission 1hr. before closing. Monastery €7, students and seniors €3.50.) Autocares Herranz **buses** arrive from Madrid's Moncloa Metro station. (50min.; every 15min. M-F 7am-11:30pm, Sa 9am-10pm, Su 9am-11pm; last return 1hr. earlier; €3.)

EL VALLE DE LOS CAÍDOS. In a valley of the Sierra de Guadarrama, Franco built the overpowering **Santa Cruz del Valle de los Caídos** (Valley of the Fallen) as a memorial to those who died during the Civil War. The granite cross was meant to honor only those who died "serving *Dios* and *España*" (ie., the Fascist Nationalists). Many of those forced to build the monument died during its construction. Beneath the high altar, underneath the cross, lies the body of Franco himself. It is accessible only via El Escorial. (Mass M-Sa 11am; Su 11am, 12:30, 1, and 5:30pm. Entrance gate open Su and Tu-Sa 10am-6pm. €5, seniors and students €2.50. EU citizens free on W. Funicular to the cross €2.50.) An Autocares Herranz **bus** runs to the monument from El Escorial, C. Juan de Toledo. (20min.; Su and Tu-Sa 3:15pm, return 5:30pm; round-trip plus admission €7.70.)

CENTRAL SPAIN

Medieval cities and olive groves fill Castilla La Mancha, the land south and east of Madrid. Castilla y León's dramatic cathedrals stand testament to its glorious history. Farther west, bordering Portugal, stark Extremadura was birthplace to hundreds of world-famous explorers.

CASTILLA LA MANCHA

Although Castilla La Mancha is one of Spain's least-developed regions, you don't need Don Quixote's imagination to fall in love with this battered, windswept plateau; its austere beauty surfaces through its tumultuous history, gloomy medieval fortresses, and awesome crags.

TOLEDO
☎925

Cossío called Toledo (pop. 66,000) "the most brilliant and evocative summary of Spain's history." Today, the city may be marred by armies of tourists and caravans of kitsch, but this former capital of the Holy Roman, Visigoth, and Muslim empires remains a treasure trove of Spanish culture. The city's numerous churches, synagogues, and mosques share twisting alleyways, emblematic of a time when Spain's three religions coexisted peacefully.

TRANSPORTATION AND PRACTICAL INFORMATION. Trains arrive at Po. Rosa 2 (☎902 24 02 02) from Madrid's Estación Atocha (1-1½hr., 9-10 per day, €5-5.50). **Buses** (☎925 21 58 50) depart from Av. Castilla La Mancha, 5min. from the Puerta de Bisagra, the city gate (5½hr., M-F 3pm, €17; buy ticket on the bus). Take

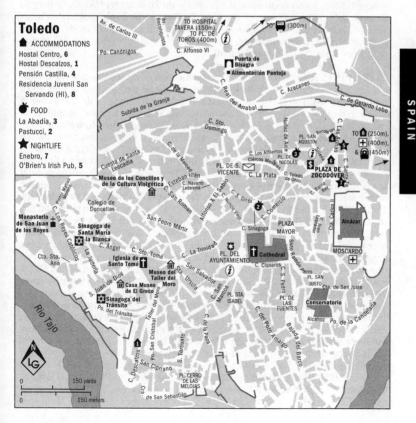

Toledo

🏠 ACCOMMODATIONS
Hostal Centro, **6**
Hostal Descalzos, **1**
Pensión Castilla, **4**
Residencia Juvenil San
Servando (HI), **8**

🍴 FOOD
La Abadía, **3**
Pastucci, **2**

⭐ NIGHTLIFE
Enebro, **7**
O'Brien's Irish Pub, **5**

SPAIN

bus #5 or 6 from the right of the train station to Pl. de Zocodóver (€0.80), follow C. Armas downhill as it changes names and leads through the Puerta Nueva de Bisagra gates, and cross the intersection to reach the **tourist office**. (☎925 22 08 43. Open July-Sept. M-Sa 9am-7pm, Su 9am-3pm; Oct.-June M-F 9am-6pm, Sa 9am-7pm, Su 9am-3pm.) Surf the **Internet** at **Zococentro**, C. Silleria 14, located just off Pl. de Zocodóver. (☎925 22 03 00. Open in summer 10:30am-7pm, off-season 10:30am-6pm.) **Postal Code:** 45070.

▐▌▌ ACCOMMODATIONS AND FOOD. The ▨**Residencia Juvenil San Servando (HI) ❶**, on Castillo San Servando, uphill from the train station, sits inside a 14th-century castle. (☎925 22 45 54. Dorms €11, under-26 €8.50. Members only.) **Hostal Centro ❸**, C. Nueva 13, toward C. Comercio on Pl. de Zocodóver, offers clean, spacious rooms in a central location. (☎925 25 70 91. Singles €30; doubles €42; triples €60. MC/V.) From Pl. de Zocodóver, take C. Armas downhill, then the first left up C. Recoletos to get to **Pensión Castilla ❷**, C. Recoletos 6. (☎925 25 63 18. Singles €15; doubles with bath €25.) Down the steps off Po. del Tránsito, near the Sinagoga del Tránsito, you'll find the high-class **Hostal Descalzos ❸**, C. Descalzos 30. (☎925 22 28 88. Apr.-Oct. singles €30-42; doubles €47-53. Oct.-Mar. €25-36/40-45. MC/V.) Try Toledo's marzipan delights at the *pastelerías*, or have a square meal at ▨**La Abadía ❷**, Pl. San Nicolás 3. (Lunch *menú* €8.50. Open M-Th 8am-12:30am, F 8am-1:30am, Sa-Su noon-1:30am.) From Pl. de Zocodóver, take C. Comercio through the underpass to reach the cheerful **Pastucci ❶**, C. Sinagoga 10. (Pastas €5.50-8. Small pizza €6.10-8.50. 10% discount with a *Let's Go* guide. Open in summer M-Th 12:15pm-midnight, F-Su noon-4pm and 8pm-midnight; off-season daily noon-4pm and 7pm-midnight. MC/V.)

◩▐ SIGHTS AND NIGHTLIFE. A vast collection of museums, churches, synagogues, and mosques lies within the city walls; despite well-marked streets, you'll probably get lost. Toledo's grandiose ▨**cathedral,** southwest of Pl. de Zocodóver at the Arco de Palacioz, boasts five naves, delicate stained glass, and unapologetic ostentation. (Open daily 10am-noon and 4-6pm.) Toledo's most formidable landmark, the ▨**Alcázar,** Cuesta Carlos V 2, uphill from Pl. de Zocodóver, has been a stronghold of Romans, Visigoths, Moors, and Spaniards. Today, it houses a national military museum. (Open Su and Tu-Sa 9:30am-2pm. €2. W free.) El Greco spent most of his life in Toledo, and several of his works are displayed throughout town. His famous **El entierro del Conde de Orgaz** (*Burial of Count Orgaz*) is housed on the west side of town in the **Iglesia de Santo Tomé**, Pl. Conde 1. (Open Mar.-Oct. 15 daily 10am-6:45pm; Oct. 16-Feb. 10am-5:45pm. €1.50.) Downhill and to the left lies the **Casa Museo de El Greco,** C. Samuel Leví 2, which houses 19 works by the master. (Open Su 10am-2pm, Tu-Sa 10am-2pm and 4-6pm. €2.40; students, under-18, and over-65 free. Sa-Su afternoons free.) The simple exterior of the 14th-century **Sinagoga del Tránsito**, on C. Samuel Leví, hides ornate Mudéjar plasterwork and an intricate wooden ceiling. (Open Su 10am-2pm, Tu-Sa 10am-2pm and 4-6pm. €2.40; under-18 and students €1.20. Sa after 4pm and Su free.) The 12th-century **Sinagoga de Santa María la Blanca,** down the street to the right, was built as a mosque and then used as the city's main synagogue until its conversion to a church in the early 16th century. (Open June-Aug. daily 10am-2pm and 3:30-7pm; Sept.-May 10am-2pm and 3:30-6pm. €1.50.) At the western edge of the city resides the Franciscan **Monasterio de San Juan de los Reyes,** commissioned by Isabella and Ferdinand; the cloister is covered with the initials of the *Reyes Católicos*. (Open Apr.-Sept. daily 10am-1:45pm and 3:30-6:45pm; Oct.-Mar. 10am-2pm and 3:30-6pm. €1.50.)

For nightlife, head through the arch and to the left from Pl. de Zocodóver to **Calle Santa Fé**, which brims with beer and local youth. **Enebro**, on Pl. Santiago Balleros off C. Cervantes, serves free *tapas* in the evenings. (Open daily 11am-4pm and 7pm-1:30am.) For more upscale bars and clubs, try **Calle Sillería** and **Calle Alfile-ritos**, west of Pl. de Zocodóver. **O'Brien's Irish Pub**, C. Armas 12, has live music on Thursdays. (Open Su-Th noon-2:30am, F-Sa noon-4am.)

CUENCA
☎ **969**

Cuenca (pop. 50,000) is a hilltop city flanked by two rivers and the stunning rock formations they created. The enchanting ▓**old city** safeguards most of Cuenca's unique charm, including the famed *casas colgadas* (hanging houses) that dangle high above the Río Huécar, on C. Obispo Vaero off Plaza Mayor. Cross the San Pablo bridge to **Hoz del Huécar** for a spectacular view of the *casas* and cliffs. Many of the *casas* house museums; on Pl. Ciudad de Ronda is the excellent **Museo de Arte Abstracto Español.** (Open Tu-F 11am-2pm and 4-6pm, Sa 11am-2pm and 4-8pm, Su 11am-2pm. €3, students and seniors €1.50.) The perfectly square **Cathedral de Cuenca** sits in the Plaza Mayor. (Open daily 9am-2pm and 4-6pm. Free.)

Trains (☎902 24 02 02) run to Madrid (2½-3hr., 5-6 per day, €9) and Valencia (3-4hr., 3-4 per day, €10). **Buses** (☎22 70 87) depart from C. Fermín Caballero for: Barcelona (9hr., 1-2 per day, €30); Madrid (2½hr., 8-9 per day, €8.20-11); and Toledo (2½hr., 3 per day, €10). To get to Plaza Mayor from either station take a left onto C. Fermín Caballero, following it as it becomes C. Cervantes and C. José Cobo and then bearing left through Pl. Hispanidad. The **tourist office** is in Plaza Mayor. (☎23 21 19; www.aytocuenca.org. Open July-Sept. M-Sa 9am-9pm, Su 9am-2pm; Oct.-June M-Sa 9am-2pm and 4-6pm, Su 9am-2pm.) ▓**Posada de San José ❷**, C. Julián Romero 4, a block up from the left side of the cathedral, has gorgeous views and a friendly staff. (☎21 13 00. July-Nov. and F-Sa year-round singles €20, with bath €41; doubles €31/61; triples with sink €42; quads with bath €97. *Semana Santa* increased prices; off-season reduced prices.) To reach **Pensión Tabanqueta ❸**, C. Trabuco 13, head up C. San Pedro from the cathedral past Pl. Trabuco. (☎21 12 90. Singles €12; doubles €24; triples €36.) Budget eateries line **Calle Cervantes** and **Calle República Argentina.** Grab groceries at **%Día,** on Av. Castilla La Mancha and Av. República Argentina. (Open M-Th 9:30am-2pm and 5:30-8:30pm, F-Sa 9am-2:30pm and 5:30-9pm.) **Postal Code:** 16004.

CASTILLA Y LEÓN

Castilla y León's cities rise like green oases from a desert of burnt sienna. The aqueduct of Segovia, the majestic Gothic cathedrals of Burgos and León, the slender Romanesque belfries along Camino de Santiago, the sandstone of Salamanca, and the city walls of Ávila have emblazoned themselves as regional and national images.

SEGOVIA
☎ **921**

Legend has it that the devil built Segovia's (pop. 56,000) famed aqueduct in one night, in an effort to win the soul of a Segovian water-seller named Juanilla. Devil or not, Segovia's attractions and winding alleyways entice their share of Spanish and international tourists, as well as students seeking to practice their *español*. In the 12th and 13th centuries, Segovia had more Romanesque monuments than anywhere else in Europe. Today, its remaining cathedrals and castles represent Castilla at its finest——a labyrinthine town of twisted alleys and old-town charm. However, pleasure has its price: food and accommodations are more expensive than in Madrid. In the Sierra de Guadarrama, 88km northwest of Madrid, Segovia is close enough to the capital to be a daytrip but definitely warrants a longer stay.

SPAIN

☎❷ TRANSPORTATION AND PRACTICAL INFORMATION. Trains (☎921 42 07 74), Po. Obispo Quesada, run to Madrid (2hr.; 7-9 per day M-F 5:55am-8:55pm, Sa-Su 8:55am-8:55pm; €5). **Buses** run from Estacionamiento Municipal de Autobuses, Po. Ezequiel González 12, at the corner of Av. Fernández Ladreda. **La Sepulvedana** (☎921 42 77 07) sends buses to Madrid (1½hr.; M-F every 30min. 6am-9:30pm, Sa 7:30am-9:30pm, Su 8:30am-10:30pm; €6). **Linecar** (☎921 42 77 06) sends buses to Salamanca (3hr.; 4 per day M-F 8:50am-5:45pm; Sa 8:50am, 1:30, 5:45pm; Su 5:45pm; €8.50). From the train station, take any bus (€0.70) to the **Plaza Mayor**, the city's historic center and site of the regional **tourist office**. Segovia is impossible to navigate without a map, so pick one up here. (Open June-Aug. Su-Th 9am-8pm, F-Sa 9am-9pm; Sept.-May M-F 9am-2pm and 5-7pm, Sa-Su 9am-2pm and 5-8pm.) The Po. del Salón **bus** (M-F every 30min. 7:45am-10:15pm) runs directly to the steps of **Puerta del Sol**. To access the **Internet**, try **Locutorio Mundo 2000**, Pl. de Azoguejo 4, between Horno de Asar and the Jimena clothing store. (€0.90 per 30min., €1 per 1 hr. Open daily 11am-11pm.)

☎❶❖ ACCOMMODATIONS AND FOOD. Reservations are a must for any of Segovia's hotels, especially those in or around major plazas. Budget travelers should prepare to pay €21 or more for a single and arrive early to ensure space. The pensiones are significantly cheaper, but rooms tend to be on the less comfortable side of "basic." To reach **⬛Hospedaje El Gato ❷**, Pl. del Salvador 10, which has beautiful rooms and individual bathrooms, TV, and A/C, follow the aqueduct up the hill, turning left on C. Ochoa Ondategui; it meets San Alfonso Rodríguez which leads into Pl. del Salvador. (☎921 42 32 44; fax 921 43 80 47. Doubles €35; triples €49.) **Hotel Las Sirenas ❸**, C. Juan Bravo 30, down C. Cervantes, has luxurious rooms with TV, shower, telephone, and A/C. (☎921 46 26 63; fax 921 46 26 57. Singles €36-45, with bath €42-50; doubles with bath €55-65. AmEx/MC/V.) For a fortifying experience, try the stone walls and rustic rooms of the **Pensión Ferri ❶**, C. Escuderos 10, off the Plaza Mayor. (☎921 46 09 57. Showers €2. Singles €13; doubles €19.) From Pl. Azoguejo, follow the aqueduct down C. Teodosio and turn left; around the bend and up the slope is **Hostal Don Jaíme ❷**, Ochoa Ondátegui 8. This *hostal* has rooms with wood paneling and large mirrors. (☎921 44 47 87. Singles €22, with bath €30; doubles with bath €40; triples with bath €50. MC/V.) **Camping Acueducto ❶**, C. Borbón 49/Ctra. Nacional 601, km 112, is 2km toward La Granja. Take the AutoBus Urbano (€0.70) from Pl. Azoguejo to Nueva Segovia. (☎/fax 921 42 50 00. Open *Semana Santa*-Sept. €4.30 per person, per tent, and per car.)

Sample Segovia's famed lamb, *cochinillo asado* (roast suckling pig), or *sopa castellana* (soup with bread, eggs, and garlic), but steer clear of pricey Plaza Mayor and Pl. Azoguejo. Buy groceries at **%Día**, C. Gobernador Fernández Giménez 3, off C. Fernández Ladreda. (Open M-Th 9:30am-8:30pm, F-Sa 9am-9pm). At the casual but classy **⬛Bar-Meson Cueva de San Esteban ❸**, C. Vadelaguila 15, off Pl. Esteban and C. Escuderos, the owner knows his wines, and the service is friendly. (☎921 46 09 82. Lunch *menús* M-F €8, Sa-Su €10. Entrees €7-14. Wines €1-3. Open daily 10am-midnight. MC/V.) At **⬛Mesón El Cordero ❸**, C. del Carmen 4-6, spreads of wine, meats, and other specials are a feast for the eyes and the stomach. (Selection of *menús* from €9. Entrees €9-15. Open M-Sa 12:30-4:30pm and 8pm-midnight, Su 12-6pm.) For tasty vegetarian options (€3.60-9) as well as meat entrees (€6-10), try **Restaurante La Almuzara ❷**, C. Marqués del Arco 3, past the cathedral. (Open Tu 8pm-midnight, W-Su 12:45-4pm and 8pm-midnight.)

◎❐ SIGHTS AND ENTERTAINMENT. Segovia rewards the wanderer. Its picturesque museums, palaces, churches, and streets beg closer observation. The serpentine **⬛Roman aqueduct**, built in 50 BC, commands the entrance to the old city.

Supported by 128 pillars that span 813m and reach a height of 29m near Pl. Azoguejo, the two tiers of 163 arches were constructed out of some 20,000 blocks of granite—without any mortar to hold them together. This spectacular feat of engineering, restored by the monarchy in the 15th century, can transport 30 liters of water per second and was used until the late 1940s. The **cathedral**, commissioned by Carlos V in 1525, towers over the Plaza Mayor. Inside, the **Sala Capitular,** nicknamed "The Lady of all Cathedrals," displays intricate tapestries. (Open Apr.-Oct. daily 9am-6:30pm; Nov.-Mar. 9:30am-6pm. €2.) The **Alcázar,** a late-medieval castle and site of Isabel's coronation in 1474, dominates the northern end of the old quarter. In the **Sala de Solio** (throne room), an inscription reads: *Tanto monta, monta tanto* ("she mounts, as does he"). Get your mind out of the gutter—this simply means that Ferdinand and Isabella had equal authority as sovereigns. The 140 steps up a nausea-inducing spiral staircase to the top of the **Torre de Juan II** (80m high) afford a marvelous view of Segovia and the surrounding plains.

Though the city isn't particularly known for its sleepless nights, native Segovians know how to party. Packed with bars and cafes, the **Plaza Mayor** is the center of nightlife. Club headquarters are on **Calle Ruiz de Alda,** off Pl. Azoguejo. You can count on a party every night at **La Luna,** C. Puerta de la Luna 8, where a young crowd downs cheap shots and Heineken. (Shots €1. Beer €1.50. Open daily 4:30pm-4am.) From June 24-29, Segovia celebrates a **fiesta,** complete with free open-air concerts, dances, and fireworks, in honor of San Juan and San Pedro.

⚡DAYTRIP FROM ˙SEGOVIA: LA GRANJA DE SAN ILDEFONSO. The royal palace and grounds of **La Granja,** 9km southeast of Segovia, were commissioned by Philip V, the first Bourbon King. Of the four royal summer retreats (the others being El Pardo, El Escorial, and Aranjuez), this "Versailles of Spain" is by far the most extravagant. Marble, lace curtains, lavish crystal chandeliers, and a world-class collection of Flemish tapestries enliven the palace, while manicured gardens and a forest envelop it. (Open daily Apr.-Sept. Tu-Su 10am-6pm; Oct.-Mar. Tu-Sa 10am-1:30pm and 3-5pm, Su 10am-2pm. €5, students and EU seniors €2.50. W free for EU citizens. Mandatory guided tours in Spanish depart every 15min.) **Buses** run to La Granja from Segovia (20min., 9-12 per day, round-trip €1.50).

SALAMANCA ☎923

For centuries, the gates of Salamanca (pop. 152,600) have welcomed scholars, saints, rogues, and royals. The bustling city is famed for its exquisite silver filigree and golden sandstone architecture as well as its university—the oldest in Spain, and once one of the "four leading lights of the world" along with the universities of Bologna, Paris, and Oxford.

🏛🚆 TRANSPORTATION AND PRACTICAL INFORMATION. Trains run from Po. de la Estación (☎902 24 02 02) to Lisbon (6hr., 4:50am, €35) and Madrid (2½hr., 5-6 per day 6am-7:50pm, €14). **Buses** run from Av. Filiberto Villalobos 71-85 (☎923 23 67 17) to: Barcelona (11hr.; daily 7:30am and noon, Su and F 4pm; €39); León (2½hr.; M-F 3 per day 11am-6:30pm, Sa 11am, Su 10pm; €11); Madrid (3hr., M-Sa 16 per day, €10-15); and Segovia (3hr., 2 per day, €9). Visit the **tourist office** at Plaza Mayor 32. (☎923 21 83 42. Open M-Sa 9am-2pm and 4:30-6:30pm, Su 10am-2pm and 4:30-6:30pm.) Access the **Internet** at **CiberPlaza,** Plaza Mayor 10. (Open daily. 10:30am-9pm, €1.20 per hr. and 9pm-2am €0.90 per hr.)

🛏🍴 ACCOMMODATIONS AND FOOD. Reasonably priced *hostales* and *pensiones* cater to the floods of student visitors, especially off Plaza Mayor and C. Meléndez. **Pensión Las Vegas ❷,** C. Meléndez 13, 1st fl., has friendly owners and

TVs. (☎923 21 87 49. Singles with shower €18; doubles €24, with bath €30-36; triples with bath €45. MC/V.) At **Pensión Villanueva ❶**, C. San Justo 8, 1st fl., Sra. Manuela shares local lore and gossip. Exit Plaza Mayor via Pl. Poeta Iglesias, cross the street, and take the first left. (☎923 26 88 33. Singles €13; doubles €26.) **Hostal Anaya ❷**, C. Jesús 18, is steps away from Plaza Mayor. (☎923 27 17 73. Singles €24; doubles with shared bath €36, with private bath €42; triples €54; quads €72.) Albertur buses shuttle **campers** from Gran Vía (every 30min.) to the first-class **Regio ❶**, 4km toward Madrid on Ctra. Salamanca. (☎923 13 88 88. €3 per person, €5.50 per tent, €2.90 per car.) Cafes and restaurants surround **Plaza Mayor**, where three course meals run about €8. **El Patio Chico ❷**, C. Meléndez 13, is crowded at lunch and dinner, but the large and delicious portions are worth the wait. (*Menú* €11. Entrees €4-8. *Bocadillos* €2-3. Open daily 1-4pm and 8pm-midnight.) **Mesón Las Conchas ❸**, R. Mayor 16, is the quintessential *bar español*. (*Menú* €10.50. *Raciones* €6-14. Open daily 1-4pm and 8pm-midnight. MC/V.) **Champion**, C. Toro 64, has a downstairs supermarket. (Open M-Sa 9:15am-9:15pm.)

⑤ SIGHTS. The ▧**Plaza Mayor**, designed by Alberto Churriguera, has been called one of the most beautiful squares in Spain. Between its 88 sandstone arches hang medallions with bas-reliefs of famous Spaniards, from El Cid to Franco. Walk down R. Mayor to Pl. San Isidro to reach the 15th-century **Casa de las Conchas** (House of Shells), one of Salamanca's most famous landmarks, adorned with over 300 large scallop halves chiseled in sandstone. From Plaza Mayor follow R. Mayor, veer right onto R. Antigua, then left onto C. Libreros to enter the ▧**Universidad**, founded in 1218. The university's 16th-century entryway is one of the best examples of Spanish Plateresque, named for the delicate filigree work of *plateros* (silversmiths). Hidden in the sculptural work lies a tiny frog; according to legend, those who can spot the frog will be blessed with good luck and even marriage. Inside the Patio de Escuelas Menores, the University Museum contains the **Cielo de Salamanca**, a 15th-century fresco of the zodiac. (Open M-F 9:30am-1:30pm and 4-7:30pm, Sa 9:30am-1:30pm and 4-7pm, Su 10am-1:30pm. €2.40, students and seniors €1.20.) Continue down R. Mayor to Pl. Anaya to reach the *vieja* (old) and *nueva* (new) cathedrals. Begun in 1513 to accommodate the growing tide of Catholics, the spindly spired late-Gothic **Catedral Nueva** wasn't finished until 1733. The **Catedral Vieja**, built in 1140, has a striking cupola with depictions of apocalyptic angels separating the sinners from the saved. The **museum** in the back houses the Mudéjar Salinas organ, one of the oldest organs in Europe. (*Nueva:* open Apr.-Sept. daily 9am-2pm and 4-8pm; Oct.-Mar. 9am-1pm and 4-6pm. Free. *Vieja:* cloister and museum open Apr.-Sept. daily 10am-1:30pm and 4-7:30pm. €3, students €2.25, children €1.50.) **Casa Lis Museo Art Nouveau y Art Deco**, C. Gibraltar 14, behind the cathedrals, houses Miguel de Lis's eclectic art nouveau and Art Deco collection. Exhibits range from elegant fans signed by noteworthies like Salvador Dalí to racy sculptures of animals and people in compromising positions. (Open Apr.-Oct. 15 Tu-F 11am-2pm and 5-9pm, Sa-Su 11am-9pm; Oct. 16-Mar. Tu-F 11am-2pm and 4-7pm, Sa-Su 11am-8pm. €2.10, students €1.50. Tu mornings free.)

🎭🎵 ENTERTAINMENT AND NIGHTLIFE. According to Salamantinos, Salamanca is the best place in Spain to party; it is said that there is one bar for every one hundred people living in the city. There are *chupiterias* (shot bars), *barres*, and *discotecas* on nearly every street, and while some close at 4am, others go all night. Nightlife centers on **Plaza Mayor** and spreads out to Gran Vía, C. Bordadores, and side streets. **Calle Prior** and **Rúa Mayor** are also full of bars. Intense partying occurs off **Calle Varillas**. Begin at ▧**Bar La Chupitería**, Pl. Monterrey (at the intersection of C. Prior and Bordadores), which serves inexpensive shots (€0.90 each) and slightly larger *chupitos* (€1 each). Students also pregame at **Duende Bar,** Pl. San Juan Bautista 7, for *litros* of beer or *sangría* (€3 each). Drink to modern funk and jazz at **Birdland,** C. Azafranal 57. At **Cum Laude,** C. Prior 5, the dance floor is a replica of Plaza Mayor. Disco beats draw visitors and locals alike to **Gatsby,** C. Bordadores 6, where the walls display African masks and macabre decor. Or, try **Camelot,** C. Bordadores 3, a monastery-turned-club.

⚑ DAYTRIP FROM SALAMANCA: ZAMORA. Perched atop a rocky cliff over the Río Duero, Zamora (pop. 70,000) is an intriguing mix of the modern and the medieval; 15th-century palaces harbor Internet cafes and luxury hotels. Zamora's foremost monument is its Romanesque **cathedral,** built between the 12th and 15th centuries. Highlights include its intricately carved choir stalls (complete with seated apostles laughing and singing) and the main altar, an ornate structure of marble, gold, and silver. Inside the cloister, the **Museo de la Catedral** features the priceless 15th-century *Black Tapestries*, which tell the story of Achilles's defeat during the Trojan War. (☎980 53 06 44. Cathedral and museum open Su and Tu-Sa 10am-2pm and 5-8pm. Mass daily at 10am, also Sa 6pm and Su 1pm. Cathedral free, museum €2.) All in all, twelve handsome Romanesque churches remain within the walls of the old city, gleaming in the wake of recent restoration. Most visitors follow the **Romanesque Route,** a self-guided tour of all of the churches available from the **tourist office,** 6 Pl. Arias Gonzalo. (☎987 53 36 94. Open Apr.-Sept. daily 10am-2pm and 4-7pm, Oct.-Mar. 10am-2pm and 5-8pm.) The **⬛Museo de Semana Santa,** in sleepy Pl. Santa María La Nueva 9, is a rare find. Hooded mannequins stand guard over elaborately sculpted floats depicting the stations of the *Vía Crucis*. (Open M-Sa 10am-2pm and 5-8pm, Su 10am-2pm. €2.70.) Linea Regular **buses** run from Avenida Alfonsa Peña to Salamanca. (1hr., 10-15 per day, €3.60.)

LEÓN
☎987

Formerly the center of Christian Spain, today León (pop. 145,000) is best known for its 13th-century Gothic **⬛cathedral,** arguably the most beautiful in Spain. Its spectacular stained-glass windows have earned the city the nickname *La Ciudad Azul* (The Blue City) and alone warrant a trip to León. The cathedral's **museum** displays gruesome wonders, including a sculpture depicting the skinning of a saint. (Cathedral open in summer daily 8:30am-2:30pm and 5-7pm; off-season 8:30am-1:30pm and 4-7pm. Free. Museum open in summer daily 9:30am-1:30pm and 4-6:30pm; off-season M-F 9:30am-1pm and 4-6pm, Sa 9:30am-1:30pm. €3.50.) The **Basílica San Isidoro,** dedicated in the 11th century to San Isidoro of Seville, houses the bodies of countless royals in the impressive *Panteón Real*. From Pl. Santo Domingo, walk up C. Ramón y Cajal; the basilica is up the flight of stairs on the right just before C. La Torre. (Open M-Sa 9am-1:30pm and 4pm-6:30pm, Su 9am-1:30pm. €3.) For nearby bars, discos, and techno music, head to the *barrio húmedo* (drinker's neighborhood) around **Plaza de San Martín** and **Plaza Mayor.** After 2am, the crowds weave to **Calle Lancia** and **Calle Conde de Guillén,** both heavily populated with discos and bars.

Trains (☎902 24 02 02) run from Av. Astorga 2 to Madrid (4½hr.; M-Sa 6 per day, Su 2 per day; €22-32). **Buses** (☎987 21 00 00) leave from Po. Ingeniero Sáenz de Miera for Madrid (4½hr.; M-F 12 per day 2:30am-10:30pm, Sa-Su 8 per day 2:30am-7:30pm; €18-30). Av. Palencia (a left out of the main entrance of the bus station and then a right onto the bridge, or a right out of the main entrance of the train station) leads across the river to **Plaza Glorieta Guzmán el Bueno,** which after the rotary becomes **Avenida de Ordoño II** and leads to León's cathedral and the adjacent **tourist office,** Pl. Regla 3. (☎987 23 70 82. Open M-F 9am-2pm and 5-7pm, Sa-Su 10am-2pm and 5-8pm.) Many accommodations cluster on **Avenida de Roma, Avenida Ordoño II,** and **Avenida República Argentina,** which lead into the old town from Pl. Glorieta Guzmán el Bueno. **Hostal Orejas ❸,** C. Villafranca 6, 2nd fl., is just down Av. República Argentina from Pl. Glorieta Guzmán el Bueno. Each brand-new room comes with bath, shower, and cable TV. (☎987 25 29 09; janton@usarios.retecal.es. Free Internet access. Singles €30; doubles €39-49; triples €62; extra bed €10.) Inexpensive eateries fill the area near the cathedral and on the small streets off C. Ancha; also check **Plaza San Martín,** near Plaza Mayor. **Postal Code:** 24004.

◪ DAYTRIP FROM LEÓN: ASTORGA. Astorga's fanciful ▨**Palacio Episcopal,** designed by Antoni Gaudí in the late-19th century, now houses the **Museo de los Caminos.** (☎987 61 88 82. Open July-Sept. Su 10am-2pm, Tu-Sa 10am-2pm and 4-8pm; Oct.-June Su 11am-2pm, Tu-Sa 11am-2pm and 4-6pm. €2.50.) Opposite the *palacio* is Astorga's cathedral and museum. (Both open daily 10am-2pm and 4-8pm. Cathedral free. Museum €2.50.) Astorga is most easily reached by **bus** from Po. Ingeniero Saenz de Miera in León (45min.; M-F 16 per day 6am-9:30pm, Sa-Su 6-7 per day 8:30am-8:30pm; €3).

EXTREMADURA

Arid plains bake under the intense summer sun, relieved only by scattered patches of glowing sunflowers. This land of harsh beauty and cruel extremes hardened New World conquistadors such as Hernán Cortés and Francisco Pizarro.

TRUJILLO
☎927

The gem of Extremadura, hill-perched Trujillo (pop. 10,000) is an enchanting old-world town. It's often called the "Cradle of Conquistadors" because the city produced over 600 explorers of the New World. Scattered with medieval palaces, Roman ruins, Arabic fortresses, and churches of all eras, Trujillo is a glorious hodgepodge of histories and cultures. Its most impressive monument is its tallest: A 10th-century **Moorish castle** that offers a panoramic view of the surrounding plains. The **Plaza Mayor** was the inspiration for the Plaza de Armas in Cuzco, Perú, which was constructed after Francisco Pizarro defeated the Incas. Festooned with stork nests, **Iglesia de San Martín** dominates the northeastern corner of the plaza. (Open M-Sa 10am-2pm and 4:30-7:30pm, Su 10am-2pm and 4:30-7pm. €1.30. Mass M-Sa at 7:30pm, Su 1 and 7:30pm. Free.)

Buses run from the corner of C. de las Cruces and C. del M. de Albayada to Madrid (2½hr., 14-16 per day, €14). To get to Plaza Mayor, turn left up C. de las Cruces as you exit the station, right on C. de la Encarnación, then left on C. Chica; turn left on C. Virgen de la Guia and right on C. Burgos, continuing on to the Plaza (15min.). The **tourist office** is across the plaza and posts info in its windows when closed. (☎927 32 26 77. Open June-Sept. daily 9:30am-2pm and 4:30-7:30pm; Oct.-May 9:30am-2pm and 4-7pm.) **Camas Boni ❶,** C. Domingo Ramos 117, is off Plaza Mayor on the street directly across from the church. (☎927 32 16 04. Singles €12; doubles €21, with bath €30.) Try **Hostal Trujillo ❷,** C. de Francisco Pizarro 4-6. From C. de las Cruces, turn right on C. de la Encarnación, then right again onto C. de Francisco Pizarro. (☎/fax 927 32 22 74; www.hostaltrujillo.com. Singles €24; doubles €40.) The **Plaza Mayor** teems with tourist eateries. **Meson Alberca ❹,** C. Victoria 8, has an interior garden and an excellent three-course *menú* for €14-19. (Open Su-Tu and Th-Sa 11am-5pm and 8:30pm-1am.) **Postal Code:** 10200.

SOUTHERN SPAIN (ANDALUCÍA)

Andalucía is all that you expect Spain to be—flamenco shows, bullfighting, tall pitchers of *sangría*, white-washed villages, and streets lined with orange trees. The Moors arrived in AD 711 and bequeathed the region with far more than the flamenco music and gypsy ballads proverbially associated with southern Spain, sparking the European Renaissance and reintroducing the wisdom of Classical Greece and the Near East. Under their rule, Seville and Granada reached the pinnacle of Islamic arts and Córdoba matured into the most culturally influential Islamic city. Despite (or perhaps because of) the poverty and high unemployment in their homeland, Andalucians have always maintained a passionate, unshakable dedication to living the good life. The never-ending *festivales*, *ferias*, and *carnavales* of Andalucía are world-famous for their extravagance.

CÓRDOBA ☎ 957

Charming Córdoba (pop. 310,000), perched on the south bank of the Rio Guadalquivir, was once the largest city in Western Europe. Córdoba remembers its heyday with amazingly well-preserved Roman, Jewish, Islamic, and Catholic monuments; the city's mosques, synagogues, and cathedrals accentuate each other with their befuddling proximity. Today, springtime festivals, flower-filled patios, and a steady nightlife make it one of Spain's most beloved cities.

⌐ TRANSPORTATION

Trains: Plaza de las Tres Culturas, Av. América (☎957 24 02 02). To: **Cádiz** (2½-3½hr., 5 per day, €16-32); **Madrid** (2-4hr., 22-31 per day, €24-47); **Málaga** (2-3hr., 10-12 per day, €13-19); and **Seville** (45-60min., 20-29 per day, €7-24).

Buses: Estación de Autobuses, Av. América (☎957 40 40 40), across from the train station. **Alsina Graells Sur** (☎957 27 81 00) covers most of Andalucía. To: **Cádiz** via Seville (4-5hr.); **Granada** (3hr., 8-9 per day, €11); **Málaga** (3-3½hr., 5 per day, €11); and **Seville** (2hr., 10-13 per day, €9). **Bacoma** (☎957 45 65 14) runs to **Barcelona** (10hr., 3 per day, €69). **Secorbus** (☎902 22 92 92) sends cheap buses to **Madrid** (4½hr., 6-7 per day, €11). **Empresa Rafael Ramírez** (☎957 42 21 77) runs buses to nearby towns and camping sites.

◼◼ ◼ ORIENTATION AND PRACTICAL INFORMATION

Córdoba is split into two parts: the **old city** and the **new city.** The modern and commercial northern half extends from the train station on Av. de América down to **Plaza de las Tendillas,** the center of the city. The old section in the south is a medieval maze known as the **Judería** (Jewish quarter). The easiest way to reach the old city from the adjacent train and bus stations is to take bus #3 to **Campo Santo de los Mártires** (€0.80). Or to walk (20min.), exit left from the station, cross the parking plaza and make a right onto Av. de los Mozárabes. When you reach the Roman columns, turn left and cross Gta. Sargentos Provisionales. Make a right on Paseo de la Victoria and continue until you reach Puerto Almodovar and the old city.

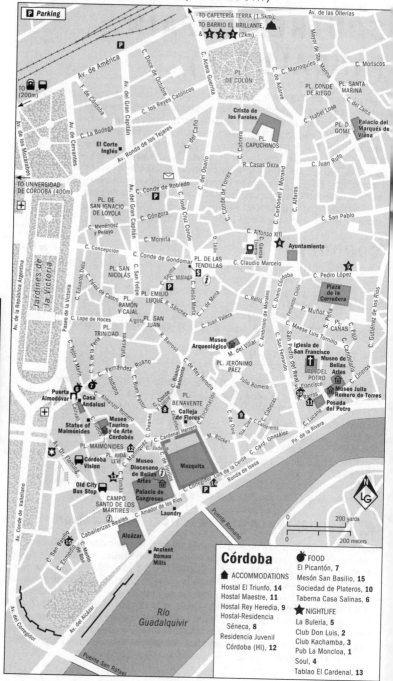

Córdoba

ACCOMMODATIONS

Hostal El Triunfo, 14
Hostal Maestre, 11
Hostal Rey Heredia, 9
Hostal-Residencia
Séneca, 8
Residencia Juvenil
Córdoba (HI), 12

FOOD

El Picantón, 7
Mesón San Basilio, 15
Sociedad de Plateros, 10
Taberna Casa Salinas, 6

NIGHTLIFE

La Bulería, 5
Club Don Luis, 2
Club Kachamba, 3
Pub La Moncloa, 1
Soul, 4
Tablao El Cardenal, 13

SPAIN

Tourist Offices: Oficina Municipal de Turismo y Congresos, currently in Pl. de las Tendillas and Campo Santo de los Martires (☎957 20 05 22) while the old office at Pl. Judá Leví, next to the youth hostel, undergoes renovations. Open M-F 8:30am-2:30pm. **Tourist Office of Andalucía,** C. Torrijos 10 (☎957 47 12 35), in the Junta de Andalucía, across from the Mezquita. From the train station, take bus #3 along the river until a stone arch appears on the right. Office is 1 block up C. Torrijos. General information on Andalucía. Open May-Sept. M-F 9:30am-8pm, Sa 10am-7pm, Su 10am-2pm; Oct.-Apr. M-F 9:30am-6pm, Su 10am-2pm.

Currency Exchange: Santander Central Hispano, Pl. de las Tendillas 5 (☎957 49 79 00). No commission up to €600. Open M-F 8:30am-2pm.

Emergency: ☎092. **Police:** Av. Doctor Flemming 2 (☎957 59 45 80).

Ambulance: urgent ☎902 505 061, main line ☎957 767 359.

Medical Assistance: Emergencies ☎061. **Red Cross Hospital,** Po. de la Victoria (urgent ☎957 22 22 22, main line 957 42 06 66). M-F 9am-1:30pm and 4:30-5:30pm.

24hr. Pharmacy: On a rotating basis. Refer to the list posted outside the pharmacy in Pl. Tendillas or the local newspaper.

Internet Access: In the old city, try **NavegaWeb,** Pl. Judá Leví 1 (☎957 29 30 89. €1.20 per hr.) Enter through the HI youth hostel. In the new city, check out **e-Net,** C. Garcia Lovera 10 (☎957 48 14 62). Leave Pl. Tendillas on C. Claudio Marcelo, take 2nd left. €1.20 per hr. Open daily 9am-2pm and 5-10pm.

Post Office: C. Cruz Conde 15 (☎957 47 97 96), 2 blocks up from Pl. Tendillas. **Lista de Correos.** Open M-F 8:30am-8:30pm, Sa-Su 9:30am-2pm. **Postal Code:** 14070.

ACCOMMODATIONS AND CAMPING

Most accommodations cluster around the whitewashed walls of the Judería, and in old Córdoba between the Mezquita and C. de San Fernando, a quieter and more residential area. Call up to several months before *Semana Santa* and summer.

Residencia Juvenil Córdoba (HI), Pl. Judá Leví (☎957 29 01 66; informacion@inturjoven.junta.andalucia.es), unbeatable location in the Judería and a 2min. walk from the Mezquita. A backpacker's utopia. Internet cafe inside hostel. Reception 24hr. Reservations recommended. Under-26 €14; over-26 €18. ❶

Hostal El Triunfo, Corregidor Luis de la Cerda 79 (☎957 49 84 84; www.htriunfo.com), across from the southern side of the Mezquita. All rooms have A/C, phone, TV, bath, and a safe. Singles €27-40; doubles €46-59. ❸

Hostal-Residencia Séneca, C. Conde y Luque 7 (☎/fax 957 47 32 34). Follow C. Céspedes 2 blocks from the Mezquita. Beautiful garden courtyard. Breakfast included. Reservations recommended. Singles with sink €21-22, with bath €31-34; doubles €32-36/41-43; triples €40-48/54-58. ❷

Hostal Rey Heredia, C. Rey Heredia 26 (☎957 47 41 82). From C. Cardenal Herrero on the northeast side of the Mezquita, take C. Encarnación to C. Rey Heredia; turn right and the hostel will be half a block down on the right. Singles €12; doubles €24. ❶

Hostal Maestre, C. Romero Barros 4-5 (☎/fax 957 47 53 95), off C. San Fernando. Immaculate and pleasantly decorated rooms. All with private bath, most with TV. 2 pretty courtyards. Singles €22; doubles €33; triples €42. ❷

Camping Municipal, Av. Brillante 50 (☎957 40 38 36). From the train station, turn left on Av. América, left on Av. Brillante, and walk uphill for about 20min; or, take bus #10 or 11 from Av. Cervantes. Pool, supermarket, restaurant, and laundry service. Camping equipment for rent. 1 person and tent €8; 2 people and tent €12. ❶

◘ FOOD

The Mezquita area attracts nearly as many high-priced eateries as tourists to fill them, but a five-minute walk in any direction yields local specialties at reasonable prices. Córdobans converge on the outdoor *terrazas* between **Calle Severo Ochoa** and **Calle Dr. Jiménez Díaz** for drinks and *tapas* before dinner. Cheap eateries cluster farther away from the Judería in **Barrio Cruz Conde**, around **Avenida Menéndez Pidal** and **Plaza Tendillas**. Regional specialties include *salmorejo* (a gazpacho-like cream soup) and *rabo de toro* (bull's tail simmered in tomato sauce). **El Corte Ingles,** Av. Ronda de los Tejeres 30, has a grocery store. (Open M-Sa 10am-10pm.)

▨ **El Picantón,** C. F. Ruano 19, 1 block from the Puerta de Almodóvar. Take ordinary *tapas*, pour on *salsa picante*, stick it in a roll, and you've got lunch (€1-3). There's nothing else as cheap or as filling. Open daily 10am-3:30pm and 8pm-midnight. ❶

Sociedad de Plateros, C. San Francisco 6 (☎957 47 00 42), between C. San Fernando and Pl. Potro. A Córdoba mainstay since 1872. Entrees €2.60-6.20. Kitchen open 1-4pm and 8pm-midnight. Open June-Aug. M-Sa 8am-4:30pm and 8pm-midnight; Sept.-May Su and Tu-Sa 8am-4:30pm and 8pm-midnight. MC/V. ❶

Taberna Casa Salinas, Puerto Almodóvar (☎957 29 08 46). A few blocks from the synagogue, up C. Judíos and to the right. Romantic outdoor patio. (€3.60-8.40.) Open M-Sa 11:30am-4:30pm and 8:30pm-12:30am, Su 11:30am-4:30pm. Closed in Aug. ❷

Mesón San Basilio, C. San Basilio 19. The locals love it, and so will you. Dine on one of two floors surrounding a breezy patio or have a drink at the bar. *Menús* M-F €6.50, Sa-Su €10. Entrees €6.50-14. Open daily 1-4pm and 8pm-midnight. AmEx/MC/V. ❷

◉ SIGHTS

Built in AD 784, Córdoba's famous ▨**Mezquita** is considered the most important Islamic monument in the Western world. Visitors enter through the **Patio de los Naranjos,** an arcaded courtyard featuring carefully spaced orange trees and fountains; inside the mosque, 850 pink-and-blue marble and alabaster columns support hundreds of striped arches. At the far end of the Mezquita lies the **Capilla Villaviciosa,** where Caliphal vaulting appeared for the first time. In the center, intricate marble Byzantine mosaics—a gift from Emperor Constantine VII—shimmer across the arches of the **Mihrab,** which houses a gilt copy of the Qur'an. Although the town rallied violently against the proposed erection of a **cathedral** in the center of the mosque, after the Crusaders conquered Córdoba in 1236 the towering **crucero** (transept) and **coro** (choir dome) were built. (☎957 47 05 12. Transept closed for renovations. Open July-Oct. daily 10am-7pm; Apr.-June M-Sa 10am-7:30pm, Su and holidays 2-7:30pm; Nov.-Mar. daily 10am-6pm. €6.50. Under-10 free.)

The **Judería** is the historic area northwest of the Mezquita. Just past the statue of Maimonides, the small **Sinagoga,** on C. Judíos, is one of Spain's few remaining synagogues, a solemn reminder of the 1492 expulsion of the Jews. (Open M-Sa 10am-2pm and 2:30-5:30pm, Su 10am-1:30pm. €0.50. EU citizens free.) To the south, along the river, is the ▨**Alcázar,** constructed for Catholic monarchs in 1328 during the conquest of Granada. Ferdinand and Isabella bade Columbus *adios* here and the building later served as Inquisition headquarters. (Open July-Aug. Tu-Su 8:30am-2:30pm; May-June and Sept. Tu-Sa 10am-2pm and 5:30-7:30pm, Su 9:30am-2:30pm; Oct.-Apr. Tu-Sa 10am-2pm and 4:30-6:30pm, Su 9:30am-2:30pm.) The **Museo Taurino y de Arte Cordobés,** on Pl. Maimónides, highlights the history of the bullfight. (Open July-Aug. Tu-Sa 8:30am-2:30pm, Su 9:30am-2:30pm; Sept.-June Tu-Sa 10am-2pm and 5:30-7:30pm, Su 9:30am-2:30pm. €3, students €1.50. F free.) There is a **combined ticket** for the Alcázar, Museo Taurino y de Arte Cordobés, and the **Museo Julio Romero,** which displays Romero's sensual portraits of Córdoban women (€7.10, students €3.60).

ENTERTAINMENT AND NIGHTLIFE

For the latest cultural events, pick up a free copy of the *Guía del Ocio* at the tourist office. Hordes of tourists flock to see the flamenco dancers at the **Tablao El Cardenal,** C. Torrijos 10, facing the Mezquita. The price is high, but a bargain compared to similar shows in Seville and Madrid. (€18 includes 1 drink. Shows M-Sa 10:30pm.) **La Bulería,** C. Pedro López 3, is even less expensive. (€11 includes 1 drink. Daily 10:30pm.) Close to town is ◼**Soul,** C. Alfonso XIII 3, a hip and relaxed bar with cozy tables and dreadlock-sporting bartenders. (Beer €1.20. Mixed drinks €4.50. Open Sept.-June 9am-3am.) Starting in June, the **Barrio Brillante,** uphill from Av. América, is packed with young, well-dressed *córdobeses* hopping between packed outdoor bars and dance clubs. Bus #10 goes to Brillante from the train station until about 11pm, but the bars don't wake up until around 1am (most stay open until 4am); a lift from **Radio Taxi** (☎957 76 44 44) should cost €4-6. If you're walking, head up Av. Brillante, passing along the way **Pub BSO,** C. Llanos de Pretorio and **Brujas Bar** right around the corner. Once in Barrio Brillante, where C. Poeta Emilia Prados meets C. Poeta Juan Ramón Jiménez, stop at **Cafetería Terra** before hitting the bars. A string of popular nightclubs run along Av. Brillante, including **Pub La Moncloa, Club Don Luis,** and **Club Kachamba.**

Of Córdoba's festivals, floats, and parades, **Semana Santa** in early April is the most extravagant. During the **Festival de los Patios** in the first two weeks of May, the city erupts with classical music concerts, flamenco dances, and a city-wide patio decorating contest. Late May brings the **Feria de Nuestra Señora de la Salud** (*La Feria*), a week of colorful garb, live dancing, and nonstop drinking.

◼ DAYTRIP FROM CÓRDOBA: MADINAT AL-ZAHRA

Legend says that Madinat al-Zahra was built by Abd al-Rahman III for his favorite concubine, Zahra. The ruins of this 10th-century medina, considered one of the greatest cities of its time, were discovered in the mid-19th century and excavated in the early 20th century. Today, it's one of Spain's most impressive archaeological finds. (Open May to mid-Sept. Tu-Sa 10am-8:30pm, Su 10am-2pm; mid-Sept. to Apr. Su and Tu-Sa 10am-2pm. €1.50. EU citizens free.) **Córdoba**

THE HIDDEN DEAL

CLEAN IN CÓRDOBA

Under the caliphate, Arab culture flowered in Córdoba, complete with marketplaces (*souks*), public fountains, and public baths (*baños árabes*, or *hammam* in Arabic). As Catholics did not have a tradition of public bathing, most of these baths were abandoned, destroyed, or left to ruin after *la Reconquista*, which ended in the 14th century.

In recent past, many baths around the country have been restored and opened for public usage, allowing visitors to escape temporarily to 11th century Andalucía. The rich Arabic decor, combined with gracious service, make the Córdoban baths a fine spot to relax and wash away your travels. Like any traditional Arab bath, there is a dressing room, cold room, temperate room, and two hot rooms. You can proceed through the rooms in ceremonial order or choose your own sudsy adventure. For further indulgence, try a massage or tea in the tea-drinking room, which offers music, Moorish pastries, and even belly dancing. *Baños Árabes, Hammam, Medin Caliphal. C. Corredor Luis de la Cerda 51, 14003.* ☎*957 48 47 46, fax 47 99 17;* *medinacaliphal@grupoandalus.com. Open daily. Baths every other hour from 10am-midnight. One bath €12; four baths €34; bath, massage, aromatherapy, and tea €21; bath and massage with student ID €16. Reservations required.*

Vision, C. Doctor Maranon 1, offers transportation and a 2½hr. guided visit to the site in English. (☎957 76 02 41. €18.) Reaching Madinat Al-Zahra takes some effort if you don't go with an organized tour. The O8 **bus** leaves every hour from Av. República Argentina in Córdoba for Cruce Madinat Al-Zahra; from there, walk 45min. to the palace. (☎957 25 57 00. €0.80.) A taxi from Córdoba should cost about €26.

SEVILLE (SEVILLA)   ☎954

Site of a Roman acropolis, capital of the Moorish empire, focal point of the Spanish Renaissance, and guardian of traditional Andalusian culture, the charming and romantic Seville (pop. 700,000) never disappoints. Flamenco, *tapas*, and bullfighting are at their best here, and Seville's cathedral is among the most impressive in Spain. But it's the city's infectious, vivacious spirit that defines it, and fittingly, the local *Semana Santa* and *Feria de Abril* celebrations are among the most extravagant in all of Europe.

▐ TRANSPORTATION

Flights: All flights arrive at **Aeropuerto San Pablo** (SVQ; ☎954 44 90 00), 12km out of town on Ctra. Madrid. A taxi ride to the town center costs about €13. **Los Amarillos** (☎954 98 91 84) runs a bus to the airport from outside the Hotel Alfonso XIII at the Pta. Jerez (1-2 per hr. 6:15am-11pm, €2.30).

Trains: Estación Santa Justa (☎954 41 41 11), on Av. Kansas City. Near Pl. Nueva is the **RENFE** office, C. Zaragoza 29 (☎954 54 02 02). Open M-F 9am-1:15pm and 4-7pm. **AVE** trains run to **Córdoba** (45min., 18-20 per day, €15-17) and **Madrid** (2½hr., 18-20 per day, €62). **Talgo** trains run to: **Barcelona** (12hr., 3 per day, €53); **Cádiz** (2hr., 7-12 per day, €8.10); **Córdoba** (1½hr., 6 per day, €8); **Granada** (3hr., 5 per day, €17); **Málaga** (2½hr., 4-7 per day, €14); **Valencia** (8½hr., 4 per day, €36).

Buses: The old bus station at Prado de San Sebastián, C. Manuel Vázquez Sagastizabal (☎954 41 71 11), mainly serves Andalucía:

Transportes Alsina Graells (☎954 41 88 11). To: **Córdoba** (2hr., 10-12 per day, €9); **Granada** (3hr., 10 per day, €16); **Málaga** (3hr., 11 per day, €13).

Transportes Comes (☎954 41 68 58). To **Cádiz** (1½hr., 14 per day 7am-10pm, €9.40) and **Jerez de la Frontera** (1½hr., 9-10 per day 9am-10pm, €5.70).

Los Amarillos (☎954 98 91 84). To **Arcos de la Frontera** (2hr., 8am and 4:30pm, €6.40) and **Marbella** (3hr., 3 per day 8am-8pm, €14).

Linesur (☎954 98 82 20). To **Jerez de la Frontera** (1½hr., 8-12 per day 6am-9pm, €5.40), with connections to **Algeciras** (5hr., 7 per day 6:30am-9pm, €14).

Public Transportation: TUSSAM (☎900 71 01 71), the city bus network. Most lines run every 10min. (6am-11:15pm) and converge on Pl. Nueva, Pl. Encarnación, or in front of the cathedral. Night service departs from Pl. Nueva (every hr. midnight-2am). Fare €1, *bonobús* (10 rides) €4.50. Particularly useful are C3 and C4, which circle the center, and 34, which hits the youth hostel, university, cathedral, and Pl. Nueva.

Taxis: TeleTaxi (☎954 62 22 22). **Radio Taxi** (☎954 58 00 00). Base rate €2.20, Su 25% surcharge. Extra charge for luggage and night taxis.

▐✦ ▐ ORIENTATION AND PRACTICAL INFORMATION

The **Río Guadalquivir** flows roughly north to south through the city. Most of the touristed areas of Seville, including the **Barrio de Santa Cruz** and **El Arenal,** are on the east bank. The **Barrio de Triana,** the **Barrio de Santa Cecilia, Los Remedios,** and the Expo '92 fairgrounds occupy the west bank. The cathedral, next to Barrio de Santa Cruz, is Seville's centerpiece. If you're disoriented, look for the conspicuous

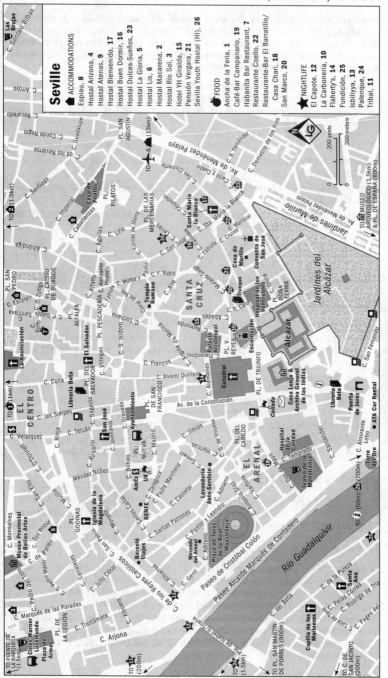

Seville

▲ ACCOMMODATIONS
Espiau, **8**
Hostal Arizona, **4**
Hostal Atenas, **9**
Hostal Bienvenido, **17**
Hostal Buen Dormir, **16**
Hostal Dulces-Sueños, **23**
Hostal La Gloria, **5**
Hostal Lis, **6**
Hostal Macarena, **2**
Hostal Río Sol, **3**
Hotel YH Giralda, **15**
Pensión Vergara, **21**
Sevilla Youth Hostal (HI), **26**

🍴 FOOD
Ancha de la Feria, **1**
Café-Bar Campanario, **19**
Habanita Bar Restaurant, **7**
Restaurante Coello, **22**
Restaurante-Bar El Barratillo/
Casa Chari, **18**
San Marco, **20**

★ NIGHTLIFE
El Capote, **12**
La Carbonería, **10**
Flaherty's, **14**
Fundición, **25**
Isbiliyya, **13**
Palenque, **24**
Tribal, **11**

SPAIN

Giralda (the minaret-turned-belltower). **Avenida de la Constitución,** home of the tourist office, runs alongside the cathedral. **El Centro,** a busy commercial pedestrian zone, lies north of the cathedral, starting where Av. Constitución hits **Plaza Nueva,** site of the Ayuntamiento. **Calle Tetuan,** a popular street for shopping, runs northward from Pl. Nueva through El Centro.

Tourist Offices: Centro de Información de Sevilla, Po. de las Delicias 9 (☎954 23 44 65; www.turismo.sevilla.org), near the university and the river. The main office for Seville. English spoken. Maps, info on flamenco and hostels. Open M-F 8am-7pm. **Turismo Andaluz, S.A.,** Av. Constitución 21B (☎954 22 14 04; fax 22 97 53), 1 block from the cathedral. Info on all of Andalucía. English spoken. Open M-F 9am-7pm, Sa 10am-2pm and 3-7pm, Su 10am-2pm. **Info booths** at the train station and Pl. Nueva.

Currency Exchange: Santander Central Hispano, C. la Campaña 19 (☎902 24 24 24). Open M-F 8:30am-2pm, Sa 8:30am-1pm.

American Express: Pl. Nueva 7 (☎954 21 16 17). Open M-F 9:30am-1:30pm and 4:30-7:30pm, Sa 10am-1pm.

Luggage Storage: At Pr. San Sebastián bus station (€1 per bag per day; open 6:30am-10pm) and the train station (€3 per day).

Bi-Gay-Lesbian Resources: COLEGA (Colectiva de Lesbianas y Gays de Andalucía) (☎954 50 13 77; www.colegaweb.net). Pl. Encarnación 23, 2nd fl. Look for the sign in the window; the door is not marked. Open M-F 10am-2pm.

Laundromat: Lavandería Auto-servicio, C. Castelar 2 (☎954 21 05 35). Wash and dry €6. Open M-Sa 9:30am-1:30pm and 5-8:30pm.

Emergency: Medical: ☎061. **Police:** Po. Concordia (local ☎092; national ☎091).

24hr. Pharmacy: Check list posted at any pharmacy for those open 24hr.

Medical Assistance: Red Cross (☎913 35 45 45). **Ambulatorio Esperanza Macarena** (☎954 42 01 05). **Hospital Universitario Virgen Macarena** (☎954 24 81 81), Av. Dr. Fedriani. English spoken.

Internet Access: Seville Internet Center, C. Almirantazgo 2, 2nd fl., across from the cathedral. €3 per hr., €1.80 per hr. with prepaid cards. Open M-F 9am-10pm, Sa-Su 10am-10pm. **CiberBoston,** C. San Fernando 23. €2 per hr.; Sa special €1 per hr. Open M-F 9am-1am, Sa-Su noon-midnight. **The Email Place,** C. Sierpes 54. €2.20 per hr. Open June-Sept. M-F 10am-10pm, Sa-Sa noon-9pm; Oct.-May M-F 10am-11pm, Sa-Su noon-9pm.

Post Office: Av. Constitución 32 (☎954 21 64 76), opposite the cathedral. *Lista de Correos* and fax. Open M-F 8:30am-8:30pm, Sa 9:30am-2pm. **Postal Code:** 41080.

▐ ACCOMMODATIONS

Rooms vanish and prices soar during *Semana Santa* and the *Feria de Abril;* reserve ahead. The narrow streets east of the cathedral around **Calle Santa María la Blanca** are full of cheap, centrally located hostels. Hostels by the **Plaza de Armas** bus station, mostly on C. Gravina, are convenient for visits to **El Centro** and the lively C. Betis on the west bank of the river.

▨ **Espiau,** C. Pérez Galdós 1A (☎954 21 06 82), between Pl. Alfalfa and Pl. Encarnación. Friendly Spanish and British couple keep the most beautiful *hostal* in town. Rooms with high ceilings and full-length tiled mirrors surround huge, sunny living room. Singles €22; doubles €42, with bath €48; triples €54. Discounts for longer stays. ❷

▨ **Pensión Vergara,** C. Ximénez de Enciso 11, 2nd fl. (☎954 21 56 68), at C. Mesón del Moro. Beautiful rooms of varying size with lace bedspreads, antique-style furniture, and a sitting room with book swap. Singles, doubles, triples, and quads available; all have fans. Towels provided on request. €18 per person. ❷

■ **Hostal Lis,** C. Escarpín 10 (☎954 21 30 88), in an alley near Pl. Encarnación. Cozy, tiled rooms in a traditional Sevilian house. Owner is in the process of adding A/C to all rooms and a rooftop terrace. Free Internet access. Laundry service. Singles with shower €21; doubles with bath €42; triples with bath €63. MC/V. ❷

■ **Hostal Macarena,** C. San Luis 91 (☎954 37 01 41). Curtains, tiles, wooden furniture, and quilted bedspreads make Macarena's rooms homey and welcoming. All rooms with A/C. Singles €20; doubles €30, with bath €40; triples €51. MC/V. ❷

Hostal Buen Dormir, C. Farnesio 8 (☎954 21 06 82). Quilted bedspreads, tiled walls, and sunny rooms, all with A/C, make Hostal "Good Sleep" one of the best deals in town. Rooftop terrace. Laundry €6. Singles €18; doubles €30, with shower €35, with bath €40; triples with shower €50, with bath €55. ❷

Hostal Arizona, C. Pedro del Toro 14 (☎954 21 60 42), off C. Gravina. Some rooms have balconies. Mar.-Oct. singles €20; doubles €30, with bath €36. Nov.-Apr. €15/30/36. Prices higher for *Semana Santa* and *Feria*. ❶

Hotel YH Giralda, C. Abades 30 (☎954 22 83 24). This 2-star hotel features spacious, sparkling, mauve-and-white painted rooms. Simplistic, modern, but trendy style with iron-post beds and marble-floored patio. All rooms with private bath, A/C, and Internet jacks. July 15-Oct. and Dec. doubles €80; Nov. and Jan.-July 14 €65. AmEx/MC/V. ❹

Hostal Dulces-Sueños, C. Puerta de la Carne 21 (☎954 41 93 93). Comfortable rooms, some with A/C. Prices with *Let's Go*: Singles €20; doubles €40, with bath €50; one triple with bath €65. ❷

Hostal Atenas, C. Caballerizas 1 (☎954 21 80 47; fax 22 76 90), near Pl. Pilatos. Slightly pricier than other options, but with good reason—all sunny, orange-painted rooms come with private baths and A/C. Singles €29; doubles €55; triples €70. Prices higher during *Semana Santa* and *Feria*. MC/V. ❸

Hostal Bienvenido, C. Archeros 14 (☎954 41 36 55), off C. Santa Maria la Blanca. Simple, but cheap rooms. 5 rooftop rooms surround a social patio; downstairs ones overlook an inner atrium. Very international backpacker crowd. Singles €20; doubles €30-37 depending on room; triples and quads €15-16 per person. ❷

Hostal La Gloria, C. San Eloy 58, 2nd fl. (☎954 22 26 73), at the end of a lively shopping street. Spotless rooms. One of the best deals in the center. Singles €18; doubles €30, with bath €36; limited triples available €45. *Semana Santa* and *Feria* prices substantially higher. ❷

Hostal Río Sol, C. Márquez de Parada 25 (☎954 22 90 38), 1 block from Pl. de Armas bus station. Circular staircase leads to cheap and clean rooms. Singles €15, with bath €21; doubles with bath, TV, and A/C €43. MC/V. ❷

Sevilla Youth Hostel (HI), C. Isaac Peral 2 (☎954 61 31 50; reservas@inturjoven.junta-andalucia.es). Take bus #34 across from the tourist office near the cathedral; the 5th stop is behind the hostel. Isolated and difficult to find. A/C. Many private baths. Breakfast included. Mar.-Oct. dorms €17, under-26 €13; Nov.-Feb. €15, under-26 €11. ❶

Camping Sevilla, Ctra. Madrid-Cádiz km 534 (☎954 51 43 79), near the airport. From Pr. San Sebastián, take bus #70 (stops 800m away at Parque Alcosa). Hot showers, supermarket, and pool. €3 per person, €3 per car, €2.50 per tent. ❶

🍴 FOOD

Seville, which claims to be the birthplace of *tapas*, keeps its cuisine light. *Tapas* bars cluster around **Plaza San Martín** and along **Calle San Jacinto.** Popular venues for *el tapeo* (*tapas*-barhopping) are **Barrio Santa Cruz** and **El Arenal.** Locals imbibe Seville's own Cruzcampo beer, a light, smooth pilsner. **Mercado del Arenal,** near the bullring on C. Pastor y Leandro, has fresh meat and produce. (Open M-Sa 9am-2pm.) For a supermarket, try **%Día,** C. San Juan de Ávila, near El Corte Inglés. (Open M-F 9:30am-2pm and 6:30-9pm, Sa 9am-1pm.)

■ **Restaurante-Bar El Baratillo/Casa Chari,** C. Pavía 12 (☎954 22 96 51), on a tiny street off C. Dos de Mayo. Hospitable owner will help you practice your Spanish. Order at least an hour in advance for the *tour-de-force*: Homemade *paella* (vegetarian options available) with a jar of wine, beer, or *sangría* (2 jars €18). *Menú* €4-9. Open M-F 10am-10pm, Sa 10am-5pm; stays open later when busy. ❷

■ **Habanita Bar Restaurant,** C. Golfo 3 (☎606 71 64 56; www.andalunet.com/habanita), on a tiny street off of C. Perez Galdos, next to Pl. Alfalfa. Exquisite Cuban fare, including yucca and *tostones* (fried bananas). Full or half-entree €4.80-10. Open daily 12:30-4:30pm and 8pm-12:30am. Closed Su night. MC/V. ❶

■ **San Marco,** C. Mesón del Moro 6 (☎954 21 43 90), several blocks from the cathedral. Amazing pizzas, pastas, and Italian desserts in an 18th-century house and 17th-century Arab baths. Other locations in equally impressive settings at C. Betis 68 (☎954 28 03 10), and at C. Santo Domingo de la Calzada 5 (☎954 58 33 43). Entrees €5-7.50. Open Su and Tu-Sa 1:15-4:30pm and 8:15pm-12:30am. MC/V. ❷

Ancha de la Feria, C. Feria 61 (☎954 90 97 45). Snack on delicious homemade *tapas* in this bright and airy local bar/restaurant. Old sherry barrels line the walls and ceiling. *Tapas* €1.50-2. *Raciones* from €4. Great *menú del día* €5.80, served M-F afternoons only. Open Tu-Sa 9am-4pm and 9pm-1am, Su 9am-4pm. ❶

Café-Bar Campanario, C. Mateos Gago 8 (☎954 56 41 89), ½ block from the cathedral, on the right. Newer and shinier than most *tapas* bars. Mixes the best (and strongest) jugs of *sangría* around (½L €7.30, 1L €9.70). *Tapas* €1.50-2. *Raciones* €6-8.40. Open daily 10:30am-12:30am. ❷

Restaurante Coello, C. Doncella 8 (☎954 42 10 82), on a tiny street off C. Santa María la Blanca. Dine in the bright yellow interior or outside on the narrow cobblestone street. Splurge on their delicately prepared *a la carte* meat and fish entrees (€10-15). *Menú* €8. Appetizers €4-10. Open daily noon-midnight. MC/V. ❸

◉ SIGHTS

■ **THE CATHEDRAL.** To clear space for Seville's most impressive sight, Christians demolished an Almohad mosque in 1401, leaving only the **Patio de Los Naranjos** (orange trees) and the famed **La Giralda** minaret. Along with its siblings in Marrakesh and Rabat, La Giralda is one of the oldest and largest surviving Almohad minarets. The **cathedral**—the third-largest in the world—took over 100 years to complete and is the largest Gothic edifice ever constructed. The **retablo mayor** (altarpiece) is a golden wall of intricately wrought disciples and saints. Circle the choir to view the **Sepulcro de Cristóbal Colón** (Columbus's tomb). His coffin-bearers represent the grateful kings of Castilla, León, Aragón, and Navarra. The cathedral's **Sacristía Mayor** museum holds Riberas, Murillos, and a glittering Corpus Christi icon. The neighboring **Sacristía de los Cálices** (or **de los Pintores**) displays canvases by Zurbarán and Goya. In the corner of the cathedral are the perfectly oval **cabildo** (chapter house) and **Sala de Las Columnas.** *(Entrance by the Pl. de la Virgen de los Reyes. Open M-Sa 11am-5pm, Su 2:30-6pm. Tickets sold until 1hr. before closing. €6, students €1.50. Su and under-12 free. Mass held M-Sa 8:30, 10am, noon; Su 8:30, 10, 11, noon, 1pm.)*

■ **ALCÁZAR.** The imposing 9th-century walls of the Alcázar date from the Moorish era, as does the exquisitely carved **Patio de las Muñecas** (Patio of the Dolls). Of the later Christian additions to the palace, the most exceptional is the **Patio de**

las Doncellas (Maid's Court), which has ornate archways and complex tile-work. The astonishing, golden-domed **Salón de los Embajadores** is where Ferdinand and Isabella welcomed Columbus back from America. In 1987, UNESCO named it a World Heritage site. *(Pl. Triunfo 7. Open Tu-Sa 9:30am-7pm, Su 9:30am-5pm. €5. Students, seniors, over-65, and under-16 free. Audio guides €3.)*

■ **MUSEO PROVINCIAL DE BELLAS ARTES.** This museum contains Spain's finest collection of works by painters of the Seville school, notably Murillo, Valdés Leal, and Zurbarán, as well as El Greco and Dutch master Jan Breughel. The building itself is a work of art; take time to sit in its shady gardens. *(Pl. Museo 9, off C. Alfonso XII. Open Tu 3-8pm, W-Sa 9am-8pm, Su 9am-2pm. €1.50. EU citizens free.)*

PLAZA DE TOROS DE LA REAL MAESTRANZA. Home to one of the two great bullfighting schools (the other is in Ronda), Plaza de Toros de la Real Maestranza fills to capacity for weekly fights and the 13 *corridas* of the *Feria de Abril*. The museum inside has costumes, paintings, and antique posters. *(Open non-bullfight days 9:30am-7pm, bullfight days 9:30am-3pm. Tours every 20min., €4.)*

BARRIO DE SANTA CRUZ. King Fernando III forced Jews fleeing Toledo to live in the Barrio de Santa Cruz, now a neighborhood of weaving alleys and courtyards. Beyond C. Lope de Rueda, off C. Ximénez de Enciso, is the **Plaza de Santa Cruz.** South of the plaza are the **Jardines de Murillo,** a shady expanse of shrubbery. Pl. Santa Cruz's church houses the grave of the artist Murillo, who died after falling from a scaffold while painting ceiling frescoes in a Cádiz church. Nearby, **Iglesia de Santa María la Blanca,** built in 1391, contains Murillo's *Last Supper*. *(Church open M-Sa 10-11am and 6:30-8pm, Su 9:30am-2pm and 6:30-8pm. Free.)*

LA MACARENA. This area northwest of El Centro is named for the Virgin of Seville. A stretch of 12th-century **murallas** (walls) runs between the Pta. Macarena and the Pta. Córdoba on the Ronda de Capuchinos. At the west end is the **Basílica Macarena,** whose venerated image of *La Virgen de la Macarena* is paraded through town during *Semana Santa*. A **treasury** within glitters with the virgin's jewels and other finery. *(C. Béquer 1. Basilica open M-Sa 9am-2pm and 5-9pm, Su 9:30am-2pm and 5-9pm. Free. Treasury open daily 9:30am-2pm and 5-8pm. €3, students and over-65 €1.50. Sa free.)* Toward the river is the **Iglesia de San Lorenzo y Jesús del Gran Poder,** with Montañés's remarkably lifelike sculpture *El Cristo del Gran Poder*. Worshipers kiss Jesus's ankle

THE HIDDEN DEAL

THE BARGAIN OF SEVILLE

Seville is home to gorgeous *artesanía* and hundreds of people anxious to sell it. Avoid the overpriced tourist shops by the cathedral, and head to the specialty stores for authentic merchandise.

1. **Abanicos de Sevilla,** Pl. San Francisco 7. Largest selection of hand-painted fans in town. Open June-Aug. M-F 9:30am-1:30pm and 5-8:30pm, Sa 9:30am-2pm; Sept.-May M-Sa 9:30am-1:30pm and 5-8:30pm. MC/V.

2. **Martian Cerámica Sevillana,** C. las Sierpes 74. Colorful hand-painted ceramics, all made in Seville. Tiny trays and vases start at €3; larger ones cost €20-30. Open M-Sa 10am-2pm and 5-8:30pm. MC/V.

3. **Artesanía Textil,** C. las Sierpes 70. Authentic, hand-sewn silk shawls. Prices start at €56. Open June-Aug. M-F 10am-1:30pm and 5:15-8:15pm, Sa 10am-1:30pm; Sept.-May M-Sa 10am-1:30pm and 5:15-8:15pm. MC/V.

4. **Diza,** C. Tetuán 5. Fans, some dating back to the 19th-century, from €4. June-Aug. M-F 9:30am-1:30pm and 5-8:30pm, Sa 9:30am-2pm; Sept.-May M-Sa 9:30am-1:30pm and 5-8:30pm. MC/V.

5. **Trajes Sevillanos,** Modas Muñoz, C. Cerrajería 5. Colorful, high-quality *flamenco* costumes (from €120) and accessories (fans, flowers). Open M-F 10am-1:30pm and 5-8:30pm, Sa 10am-1:30pm. MC/V.

through an opening in the bulletproof glass for luck. *Semana Santa* culminates in a procession honoring the statue. *(Pl. San Lorenzo. Open M-Th 8am-1:30pm and 6-9pm, F 7:30am-10pm, Sa-Su 8am-2pm and 6-9pm. Free.)*

🎵 📷 ENTERTAINMENT AND FESTIVALS

The tourist office distributes *El Giraldillo*, a free monthly magazine with complete listings on music, art exhibits, theater, dance, fairs, and film. Get your flamenco fix at **Los Gallos**, Pl. Santa Cruz 11, on the west edge of Barrio Santa Cruz. (Cover €27, includes 1 drink. Shows daily 9 and 11:30pm.) If you're going to see a **bullfight** somewhere in Spain, Seville is probably the best place to do it; the bullring here is generally considered the most beautiful in the country. The cheapest place to buy bullfight tickets is at the ring on Po. Marqués de Contadero; or try the booths on C. Sierpes, C. Velázquez, or Pl. Toros (€18-75). Seville's world-famous 🟦**Semana Santa** (Holy Week; Apr. 13-20 in 2004) festival, during which penitents in hoods guide candle-lit processionals, lasts from Palm Sunday to Good Friday. During the last week of April, the city rewards itself for its Lenten piety with the **Feria de Abril** (Apr. 27-May 2 in 2004).

📷 NIGHTLIFE

Seville's reputation for gaiety is tried and true—most clubs don't get going until well after midnight, and the real fun often starts after 3am. Popular bars can be found around **Calle Mateos Gago** near the cathedral, **Calle Adriano** by the bullring, and **Calle Betis** across the river in Triana.

🟦 **La Carbonería,** C. Levies 18, off C. Santa María La Blanca. Popular bar with free live flamenco and a massive outdoor patio replete with banana trees, picnic tables, and guitar-strumming Romeos. *Tapas* €1.50-2. Beer €1.50. Mixed drinks €4.50. Open July-Aug. M-Sa 8pm-4am, Su 8pm-2:30am; Sept.-May M-Sa 8pm-4am, Su 7pm-3am.

🟦 **El Capote,** next to Pte. Isabel II, at C. Arjona and C. Reyes Católicos. Popular summertime bar, full of tables overlooking the river. Young *sevillanos* and tourists mingle amidst upbeat live music or recorded American and Latin pop. Beer €1.50 during the day, €2 at night. Mixed drinks €5. Open June-Sept. 15 daily noon-4am.

Flaherty's, C. Alemanes 7, across from the cathedral. Friendly, sprawling Irish pub popular among tourists, ex-pats, and foreign and local students. 4 beers on tap, including Guinness. Serves international food daily until 11:30pm. *Entrees* and sandwiches €5-10. Beer €2. Mixed drinks €4.60. Open daily 11am-3am.

Tribal, next to Pte. de la Barqueta. Popular *discoteca,* playing American hip-hop and Latin favorites. Outdoor patio overlooking the river. W hip-hop nights are the most popular with backpacker crowd. Beer €3.50. Mixed drinks €5.50. No cover before 1am. After 1am cover €6-10, includes 1 drink. Open W-Sa 10pm-6am.

Palenque, Av. Blas Pascal, on the grounds of Cartuja '93. Gigantic dance club, complete with 2 dance floors and a small ice skating rink (€3, including skate rental). F-Sa dress to impress. Mainly *sevillano* university crowd. Beer €3. Mixed drinks €5. Cover €7 F-Sa. Open June-Sept. Th-Sa midnight-7am.

Fundición, C. Betis 49-50, at the end of the hallway. Popular bar among American exchange students. American music and decor fill the huge interior. Beer €2.50. Mixed drinks €5. Open M-Sa 10pm-5am. Closed July 15-Aug. 30.

Isbiliyya, Po. de Colon 2, across from Pte. Isabel II. Popular riverfront gay, straight, and lesbian bar with outdoor seating and an ample dance floor. Beer €2-2.50. Open daily 8pm-6am.

▌ DAYTRIPS FROM SEVILLE

CÁDIZ. Founded by the Phoenicians in 1100 BC, Cádiz (pop. 155,000) is thought to be the oldest inhabited city in Europe. **Carnaval** is perhaps Spain's most dazzling party (Feb. 19-29 in 2004), but year-round the city offers golden sand **beaches** that put its pebble-strewn eastern neighbors to shame. **Playa de la Caleta** is the most convenient, but better sand awaits in the new city; take bus #1 from Pl. España to Pl. Glorieta Ingeniero (€0.80), or walk along the *paseo* by the water (20-30min. from behind the Cathedral) to reach ▨**Playa de la Victoria,** which has earned the EU's *bandera azul* for cleanliness. Back in town, the gold-domed, 18th-century **cathedral** is considered the last great cathedral built by colonial riches. To get there from Pl. San Juan de Dios, follow C. Pelota. (Cathedral and museum open Tu-F 10am-1:30pm and 4:30-7:30pm, Sa 10am-1:30pm. €3.) From the train station, walk two blocks past the fountain with the port on your right, and look left for **Plaza San Juan de Dios,** the town center.

Transportes Generales Comes **buses** (☎956 22 78 11) arrive at Pl. Hispanidad from Seville (2hr., 11-14 per day, €9.40). From the bus station, walk 5min. down Av. Puerto with the port on your left; Pl. de San Juan de Dios will be after the park on your right. The **tourist office** is at #11 Pl. de San Juan de Dios. (☎ 956 24 10 01. Office open M-F 9am-2pm and 5-8pm. Kiosk in front of office open June-Sept. Sa-Su and holidays 10am-1pm and 5-7:30pm; Oct.-May 10am-1:30pm and 4-6pm.) Most *hostales* huddle in and around Pl. de San Juan de Dios and around the harbor. **Hostal Marques ❷,** C. Marques de Cádiz 1, off Pl. de San Juan de Dios, offers clean and spacious rooms with balconies that surround an enclosed inner courtyard. (☎956 28 58 54. Singles €18; doubles €25, with bath €35; triples €35.)

ARCOS DE LA FRONTERA. With castles and Roman ruins at every turn, Arcos (pop. 33,000) is a historic and romantic gem. Wander the winding alleys of ruins and hanging flowers in the **old quarter,** and marvel at the stunning view from ▨**Plaza Cabildo.** In the square is the **Basilica de Santa María de la Asunción,** a mix of Baroque, Renaissance, and Gothic styles. To reach the old quarter from the bus station, exit left, follow the road and turn left, and continue 20min. uphill on C. Muñoz Vásquez as it changes names. **Buses** (☎956 70 49 77) run from C. Corregidores to Cádiz (1½hr., 6 per day, €4.60) and Seville (2hr., 7am and 5pm, €6.20). The **tourist office** is on Pl. Cabildo. (☎956 70 22 64. Open Mar. 15-Oct. 15 M-Sa 10am-2pm and 4-8pm; Oct. 16-Mar. 14 M-Sa 10am-2pm and 3:30-7:30pm.) **Pensión Callejon de las Monjas ❷,** C. Dean Espinosa 4, shaded by the Iglesia de Sta. María, offers a restaurant, barbershop, and hostel with spotless rooms and A/C. (☎956 70 23 02. Singles €18, with bath €22; doubles €27/33, with large terrace €39; quads €66.) Cheap cafes and *tapas* bars huddle along the bottom end of **C. Corredera** between the bus station and the old quarter.

RONDA. Picturesque Ronda (pop. 38,000) has all the charm of a small, medieval town with the amenities and cultural opportunities of a thriving city. Ancient bridges, picturesque views, and old dungeons — not to mention the famed bullring — attract many visitors to Ronda, the birthplace of modern bullfighting. A precipitous 100m gorge, carved by the Río Guadalevín, dips below the **Puente Nuevo,** opposite Pl. España. The views from the Puente Nuevo, and its neighboring **Puente Viejo** and **Puente San Miguel,** are unparalleled. Bullfighting aficionados charge over to Ronda's **Plaza de Toros,** Spain's oldest bullring (est. 1785) and cradle of the modern *corrida.* Descend the steep stairs of the **Casa Del Rey Moro** into the 14th-century water mine for an otherwordly view of the river ravine.

Trains (☎902 24 02 02) depart from Av. Alferez Provisional for: Algeciras (2hr., 4 per day, €5.80); Granada (3hr., 3 per day, €11); Madrid (4½hr., 2 per day, €49); and Málaga (2hr., 7:50am, €7.55). **Buses** (☎952 18 70 61) go from Pl. Concepción García Redondo 2, near Av. Andalucía, to: Cádiz (3hr., 3 per day, €11.50); Málaga (2½hr., 9 per day, €7.60); Marbella (1½hr., 5 per day, €4.30); and Seville (2½hr., 3-5 per day, €9). The **tourist office** is at Pl. España 1. (☎952 87 12 72. Open Sept.-May M-F 9am-7pm, Sa-Su 10am-2pm.; June-Aug. M-F 9am-8pm, Sa-Su 10am-2pm.) **Pensión La Purisima ❶**, C. Sevilla 10, offers bright rooms. (☎952 87 10 50. Singles €15; doubles €28-30, with bath €30-33; triples with bath €45.) **Postal Code:** 29400.

GIBRALTAR

PHONE CODES   ☎350 from the UK or the US; ☎9567 from Spain.

From the morning mist just off the southern shore of Spain emerges the Rock of Gibraltar. Bastion of empire and Jerusalem of Anglophilia, this rocky peninsula is among history's most contested plots of land. Ancient seafarers called "Gib" one of the Pillars of Hercules, believing it marked the end of the world. After numerous squabbles between Moors, Spaniards, and Turks, the English successfully stormed Gibraltar in 1704 and have remained in possession ever since.

📱🔟 TRANSPORTATION AND PRACTICAL INFORMATION. Buses arrive in the Spanish border town of **La Línea** from: Algeciras (40min., every 30min., €1.60); Cádiz (3hr., 4 per day, €10); and Granada (5hr., 2 per day, €17). From the bus station, walk directly toward the Rock; the border is 5min. away. Once through Spanish customs and Gibraltar's passport control, catch bus #9 or 10 or walk across the airport tarmac into town (20min.). Stay left on Av. Winston Churchill when the road forks at Corral Lane; Gibraltar's **Main Street,** a commercial strip lined with most services, begins at the far end of a square, past the Burger King on the left.

The **tourist office,** Duke of Kent House, Cathedral Sq., is across the park from the Gibraltar Museum. (☎450 00; tourism@gibraltar.gi. Open M-F 9am-5:30pm.) Although **euros** are accepted almost everywhere (except pay phones and public establishments), the **pound sterling (£)** is preferred. Merchants sometimes charge a higher price in euros than in the pound's exchange equivalent. Change is often given in English currency rather than euros. As of press date, **1£ = €1.45.**

📷 SIGHTS. About halfway up the Rock is the infamous **Apes' Den,** where barbary monkeys cavort on the sides of rocks, the tops of taxis, and the heads of tourists. At the northern tip of the Rock facing Spain are the **Great Siege Tunnels.** Originally used to fend off a combined Franco-Spanish siege at the end of the American Revolution, the underground tunnels were later expanded during WWII to span 33 miles. The eerie chambers of **St. Michael's Cave,** located 0.5km from the siege tunnels, were cut into the rock by thousands of years of water erosion. (Cable car to above sights every 10min. daily 9:30am-5:15pm. Combined admittance ticket, including one-way cable car ride, £7.50/€12.50.)

🍴🏠 ACCOMMODATIONS AND FOOD. Gibraltar is best seen as a daytrip. The few accommodations in the area are often full, especially in the summer, and camping is illegal. **Emile Youth Hostel Gibraltar ❷**, Montague Bastian, behind Casemates Sq., has bunkbeds in cheerfully painted rooms with clean communal bathrooms. (☎511 06. Breakfast included. Lock-out 10:30am-4:30pm. Dorms and singles £15/€25; doubles £30/€50.) International restaurants are easy to find, but you may choke on the prices. **The Viceroy of India ❸** serves both vegetarian and meat dishes. (Entrees £4-10. Open M-F noon-3pm and 7-11pm, Sa 7-11pm. MC/V.) For groceries, try the **Checkout** supermarket on Main St., next to Marks & Spencer. (Open M-F 8:30am-8pm, Sa 10am-6pm, Su 1am-3pm. MC/V.)

ALGECIRAS   ☎956

Hidden beyond Algeciras's (pop. 101,000) seedy port is a more serene old neighborhood, worthy of a visit for those with a few hours to spare. However, for most itinerary-bound travelers, this is a city seen only in transit. RENFE **trains** (☎902 24 02 02) run from C. Juan de la Cierva to Granada (4hr., 3 per day, €16) and Ronda (1½hr., 4 per day, €5.80). Empresa Portillo **buses** (☎956 65 43 04) leave from Av. Virgen del Carmen 15 for: Córdoba (6hr., 2 per day, €20); Granada (4hr., 4 per day, €18); Málaga (3hr., 8-9 per day, €9.40); and Marbella (1hr., 8-9 per day, €5.20). Transportes Generales Comes (☎956 65 34 56) goes from C. San Bernardo 1 to Cádiz (2½hr., 10 per day, €8.60). La Línea runs to: Gibraltar (45min., every 30min. 7am-9:45pm, €1.60); Madrid (8hr., 4 per day, €23); and Seville (4hr., 5 per day, €14.30). To reach the **ferries** from the bus and train stations, follow C. San Bernardo to C. Juan de la Cierva and turn left at its end; the port entrance will be on your right. The **tourist office** is on C. Juan de la Cierva. (☎956 57 26 36. Open M-F 9am-2pm.) Hostels cluster around **Calle José Santacana.** Clean rooms all with phones, TV, and bathrooms can be found at **Hostal Residencia Versailles ❷**, C. Moutero Rios 12, off C. Cayetano del Toro (☎/fax 956 65 42 11. Singles with shower €18; doubles €30.) **Postal Code:** 11203.

COSTA DEL SOL

The Costa del Sol mixes rocky beaches with chic promenades and swank hotels. While some spots have been over-developed and can be hard on the wallet, the coast's stunning natural beauty has elsewhere been left untouched. Summer brings swarms of tourists, but nothing takes away from the main attraction: eight months of spring and four months of summer.

MÁLAGA. Once celebrated by Hans Christian Andersen, Málaga (pop. 550,000) is the largest Andalucian city on the coast and the birthplace of Pablo Picasso. Today this transportation hub offers a charming *casco antiguo* (old town) and beautiful nearby beaches like the whitewashed Nerja. (Buses run from Málaga, 1½hr., 12-18 per day, €3.20.) The **Alcazaba,** the city's most imposing sight, exudes a medieval tranquility and offers views of the harbor. (Open June-Aug. Su and Tu-Sa 9:30am-8pm; Sept.-May Tu-Sa 8:30am-7pm. €1.80, students €.60). Málaga's breathtaking **cathedral,** C. Molina Larios 4, blends Gothic, Renaissance, and Baroque styles and contains more than 15 side chapels. (☎952 22 03 45. Open M-F 10am-6:45pm, Sa 10am-5:45pm. €3.)

Buses run from Po. Tilos (☎952 35 00 61), one block from the RENFE station along C. Roger de Flor, to: Cádiz (5hr., 5 per day, €18); Córdoba (3hr., 5 per day, €11); Granada (2hr., 17 per day, €8.10); Madrid (7hr., 12 per day, €18); Marbella (1½hr., every hr., €4.20); and Seville (3hr., 11-12 per day, €14). The **tourist office** is at Av. Cervantes 1 (☎/fax 952 60 44 10. Open M-F 8:15am-2pm and 4:30-7pm, Sa-Su 9:30am-1:30pm). **Hostal La Palma ❷**, C. Martínez 7, off C. Marqués de Larios, has a great family atmosphere and rooms with A/C, mini-terraces and private baths. (☎952 22 67 72. Singles €21-25.) **Vegetariano Cañadú ❶**, Pl. de la Merced 21, serves hearty meatless entrees. (☎952 22 90 56. Open Su-Th 1:30-4pm and 8-11pm, F-Sa 1:30-4pm and 8pm-midnight. AmEx/MC/V.) **Postal Code:** 29080.

MARBELLA. Like your vacation spots shaken, not stirred? Scottish smoothie Sean Connery and a host of other jet-setters choose **Marbella** (pop. 116,000; 500,000+ in summer) as their vacation home. While there may be more yachts here than hostels, it's still possible to have a budgeted good time. The beaches beckon with 320 days of sunshine per year, but no visit would be complete without a stroll through the *casco antiguo* (old town), a maze of cobblestone streets and white-washed facades trimmed with wild roses. With 22km of beach, Marbella offers a variety of settings. Stroll the 7km from Marbella center to chic and trendy **Puerto Banús**, where beautiful, clean beaches are buffered by white yachts. Beaches to the east of the port are popular with British backpackers; those to the west attract a more posh crowd.

From the station atop Av. Trapiche (☎952 76 44 00), buses go to: Algeciras (1½hr., 17 per day, €5.20); Cádiz (4hr., 6 per day, €14); Granada (3½hr., 7 per day, €13); Madrid (7½hr., 7 per day, €20); Málaga (1½hr., 2 per hr., €4.20); and Seville (4hr., 2-3 per day, €14). The **tourist office** is on Pl. Naranjos. (☎952 82 35 50. Open June-Aug. M-F 9:30am-9pm, Sa 10am-2pm.) The area in the *casco antiguo* around Pl. Naranjos offers quick-filling hostels. Once a 17th-century inn run by monks for traveling pilgrims, today ▨**Hostal del Pilar ❶**, C. Mesoncillo 4, is centrally located off of C. Peral and is clean and comfortable. (☎952 82 99 36. Dorms €15.) The excellent **Albergue Juvenil (HI) ❶**, Av. Trapiche 2, downhill from the bus station, has a social atmosphere and huge pool. (☎952 77 14 91. June 15-Sept. 15 Dorms €18, under-26 €14; Apr.-June 15, Sept. 15-Oct. 15 €16/12; Nov.-Mar. €12/9.) ▨**El Gallo**, C. Lobatas 44, offers local cuisine in huge portions. (*Tapas* from €1.50. Entrees €2.50-8. Open Su-M and W-Sa 1-4:30pm and 7-11:30pm.) Nightlife in Marbella begins and ends late. A mellow ambience suffuses the ▨**Townhouse Bar**, C. Alamo 1, tucked down an alley off C. Nueva. Ask for a shot (€1.50) of Apple Pie. (Open daily 10pm-3am.) **Postal Code:** 29600.

GRANADA ☎958

Legend says that in 1492, when Moorish ruler Boabdil fled Granada (pop. 240,000), the last Muslim stronghold in Spain, his mother berated him for casting a longing look back at the Alhambra. "You do well to weep as a woman," she told him, "for what you could not defend as a man." A spectacular palace celebrated by poets and artists throughout the ages, the Alhambra continues to inspire melancholy in those who must leave its timeless beauty. The Albaicín, an enchanting maze of Moorish houses and twisting alleys, is Spain's best-preserved Arab quarter and the only part of the Muslim city to survive the *Reconquista*.

▣ TRANSPORTATION

Trains: RENFE Station, Av. Andaluces (☎902 24 02 02). To: **Algeciras** (5-7hr., 3 per day 7am-6pm, €16); **Madrid** (5-6hr., 7:55am and 4:40pm, €28-44); **Seville** (4-5hr., 4 per day 8am-9pm, €17).

Buses: Major bus routes originate from the **bus station** on the outskirts of Granada on Ctra. Madrid, near C. Arzobispo Pedro de Castro. **Alsina Graells** (☎958 18 54 80) runs to **Córdoba** (3hr., 10 per day 7:30am-8pm, €11) and **Seville** (3hr., 10 per day 7:30am-8am, €16). **ALSA** (☎902 42 22 42) goes to **Alicante** (6hr., 8 per day, €23), **Barcelona** (14hr., 7 per day, €57), and **Valencia** (10hr., 7 per day, €35). All ALSA buses run 2:15am-11:30pm.

Public Transportation: From the bus station take bus #10 to the youth hostel, C. de Ronda, C. Recogidas, or C. Acera de Darro or bus #3 to Av. Constitución, Gran Vía, or Pl. de Isabel la Católica. From Pl. Nueva catch #30 to the Alhambra or #31 to the Albaicín. Rides €0.85, *bonobus* (10 tickets) €5. Free map at tourist office.

⊞ 🛈 ORIENTATION AND PRACTICAL INFORMATION

The geographic center of Granada is the small **Plaza de Isabel la Católica**, at the intersection of the city's two main arteries, **Calle de los Reyes Católicos** and **Gran Vía de Colón**. To reach Gran Vía and the **cathedral** from the train station, walk three blocks up Av. Andaluces and take bus #3-6, 9, or 11 from Av. Constitución; from the bus station, take bus #3. Two blocks uphill on C. Reyes Católicos sits **Plaza Nueva**. Downhill on C. Reyes Católicos lies Pl. Carmen, site of the **Ayuntamiento** and Puerta Real. The **Alhambra** commands the steep hill above Pl. Nueva.

Tourist Office: Oficina Provincial, Pl. Mariana Pineda 10 (☎958 24 71 28; www.dipgra.es). From Pta. Real, turn right onto C. Angel Ganivet, then take a right 2 blocks later to reach the plaza. Open M-F 9am-8pm, Sa 10am-7pm, Su 10am-4pm.

American Express: C. Reyes Católicos 31 (☎958 22 45 12), between Pl. de Isabel la Católica and Pta. Real. Open M-F 9am-1:30pm and 2-9pm, Sa 10am-1pm.

Luggage Storage: At the train station. €3.

Laundromat: C. La Paz 19. From Pl. Trinidad, take C. Alhóndiga, turn right on C. La Paz, and walk 2 blocks. Wash €5, dry €1 per 15min. Open M-F 10am-2pm and 5-8pm.

Emergency: ☎ 112. **Police:** C. Duquesa 21 (☎958 24 81 00). English spoken.

Medical Assistance: Clínica de San Cecilio, C. Dr. Oloriz 16 (☎958 28 02 00 or 27 20 00), on the road to Jaén. **Ambulance:** ☎958 28 44 50.

Internet Access: Net (☎958 22 69 19) has 2 locations: Pl. de los Girones 3 and C. Buensucesco 22, 1 block from Pl. Trinidad. €0.75 per hr. Both open M-F 9am-11pm, Sa-Su 10am-11pm.

Post Office: Pta. Real (☎958 22 48 35; fax 22 36 41), on the corner of Carrera del Darro and C. Angel Ganivet. **Lista de Correos** and **fax** service. Wires money M-F 8:30am-2:30pm. Open M-F 8am-9pm, Sa 9:30am-2pm. **Postal Code:** 18009.

⌂ ACCOMMODATIONS

Hostels line **Cuesta de Gomérez, Plaza Trinidad**, and **Gran Vía**. Call ahead during *Semana Santa*.

▧ **Hostal Venecia**, Cuesta de Gomérez 2, 3rd fl. (☎958 22 39 87), on the corner of Pl. Nueva. Wake up to a soothing cup of tea and a hint of incense. Singles €15; doubles €26; triples €39. ❶

▧ **Hospedaje Almohada**, C. Postigo de Zarate 4 (☎958 20 74 46). From Pl. Trinidad, follow C. Duquesa and take a right on C. Málaga; it's the red door with the small sign on your right. A successful experiment in communal living. Dorms €14; singles €16; doubles €30; triples €40. ❶

Hostal Residencia Britz, Cuesta de Gomérez 1 (☎/fax 958 22 36 52), on the corner of Pl. Nueva. Singles €18; doubles €28, with bath €38. Show the reception your copy of *Let's Go* for a 6% discount. MC/V. ❷

Hostal Antares, C. Cetti Meriém 10 (☎958 22 83 13), on the corner of C. Elvira, 1 block from the cathedral. TV and A/C. Singles €18; doubles €30, with bath €36. ❷

Albergue Juvenil Granada (HI), Ramon y Cajal 2 (☎958 00 29 00). From the bus station take #10. Across from "El Estadio de la Juventud," on the left. Dorms €14-16, under-26 €10-12. Non-members add €3.50. ❶

Hostal Macia Plaza, Pl. Nueva 4 (☎958 22 75 36), located on the plaza. Carpeted rooms with marble baths, phone, and A/C. Singles €47; doubles €70; triples €90. ❹

Hostal-Residencia Lisboa, Pl. Carmen 29 (☎958 22 14 13 or 22 14 14; fax 22 14 87). Take C. Reyes Católicos from Pl. de Isabel la Católica; Pl. Carmen is on the left. Singles €18, with bath €30; doubles €27/€40; triples €33/€50. MC/V. ❷

◗ FOOD

Cheap North African cuisine can be found around the Albaicín, while more typical *menú* fare awaits in Pl. Nueva and Pl. Trinidad. The adventurous eat well in Granada—try *tortilla sacromonte* (omelette with calf's brains, bull testicles, ham, shrimp, and veggies). Feast on sumptuous seafood at ⬛ **El Ladrillo II ❷**, C. Panaderos 13. (Entrees €6-12. Open daily 12:30pm-1:30am. MC/V.) ⬛ **Naturi Albaicín ❷**, C. Calderería Nueva 10, serves excellent vegetarian cuisine in a serene Moroccan ambience. (No alcohol served. *Menú* €7-8.30. Open M-Th and Sa-Su 1-4pm and 7-11pm, F 7-11pm.) Get groceries at **Supermercado T. Mariscal,** C. Genil, next to El Corte Inglés. (Open M-F 9:30am-2pm and 5-9pm, Sa 9:30am-2pm.)

◉ SIGHTS

⬛ **THE ALHAMBRA.** From the streets of Granada, the Alhambra appears simple, blocky, faded—but up close, it's an elaborate and detailed piece of architecture, magically uniting water, light, wood, stucco, and ceramics to create a fortress-palace of rich aesthetic and symbolic grandeur. The age-old saying holds true: "If you die without seeing the Alhambra, you have not lived." The first Nasrid King Alhamar built the fortress **Alcazaba,** the section of the complex with the oldest recorded history. A dark, spiraling staircase leads up to a 360° view of Granada and the mountains. Follow signs to the *Palacio Nazaries* to see the stunningly ornate **Alcázar,** a 14th-century royal palace full of dripping stalactite archways, multicolored tiles, and sculpted fountains. Ferdinand and Isabella restored the Alcázar after they drove the Moors from Spain, but two generations later, Emperor Carlos V demolished part of it to make way for his **Palacio de Carlos V;** although incongruous with such Moorish splendor, many consider it one of the most beautiful Renaissance buildings in Spain. Over a bridge are the vibrant blossoms, towering cypresses, and streaming waterways of ⬛**El Generalife,** the sultan's vacation retreat. *(Take C. Cuesta de Gomérez off Pl. Nueva (20min). Or take the cheap, quick Alhambra-Neptuno microbus from Pl. Nueva (every 5min., €0.85). Open Apr.-Sept. daily 8:30am-8pm; Oct.-Mar. M-Sa 9am-5:45pm. Nighttime visits June-Sept. Tu, Th, and Sa 10-11:30pm; Oct.-May Sa 8-10pm. All visits €8. Limited visitors each day; get there early. Alcázar entry only during the time specified on ticket. BBVA books tickets in advance (☎902 22 44 60. www.alhambratickets.com).*

THE ALBAICÍN. A labyrinth of steep streets and narrow alleys, the Albaicín was the only Moorish neighborhood to escape the torches of the *Reconquista* and remains a quintessential part of Granada. After the fall of the Alhambra, a small Muslim population remained here until their expulsion in the 17th century. The abundance of North African cuisine and the construction of a mosque near Pl. San Nicolás attest to the persistence of Islamic influence in Andalucía. Spectacular sunsets over the surrounding mountains can be seen from C. Cruz de Quirós, above C. Elvira. Although generally safe, the Albaicín is disorienting and should be approached with caution at night. *(Bus #12 runs from beside the cathedral to C. Pagés at the top of the Albaicín.)*

OTHER SIGHTS. Downhill from the Alhambra's Arab splendor, the **Capilla Real,** Ferdinand and Isabella's private chapel, exemplifies Christian Granada. The sacristy shelters Isabel's private art collection, the first Christian banner to flutter in triumph over the Alhambra, and the glittering royal jewels. *(Both open M-Sa 10:30am-1pm and 4-7pm, Su 11am-1pm and 4-5pm. €2.50.)* Ferdinand and Isabella began the construction of the adjacent **cathedral** in 1523 upon the foundation of an Arab

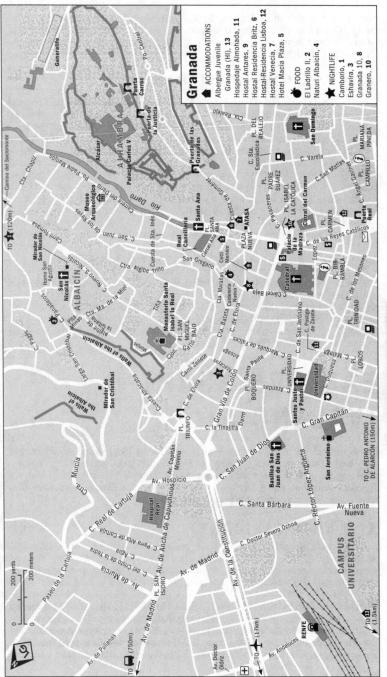

Granada

▲ ACCOMMODATIONS
Albergue Juvenile
Granada (HI), 13
Hospedaje Almohada, 11
Hostal Antares, 9
Hostal Residencia Britz, 6
Hostal-Residencia Lisboa, 12
Hostal Venecia, 7
Hotel Macia Plaza, 5

◆ FOOD
El Ladrillo II, 2
Naturi Albaicín, 4

★ NIGHTLIFE
Camborio, 1
Eshavira, 3
Granada 10, 8
Granero, 10

S P A I N

mosque. Completed in 1704, it was the first purely Renaissance cathedral in Spain, and its Corinthian pillars support an astonishing 45m vaulted nave. *(Open Apr.-Sept. M-Sa 10:45am-1:30pm and 4-7pm, Su 4-7pm; Oct.-Mar. M-Sa 10:30am-1:30pm and 3:30-6:30pm, Su 11am-1:30pm. €2.50.)*

🎵 🎭 ENTERTAINMENT AND NIGHTLIFE

The *Guía del Ocio*, sold at newsstands (€1), lists clubs, pubs, and cafes. The most boisterous nightspots belong to **Calle Pedro Antonio de Alarcón,** running from Pl. Albert Einstein to Ancha de Gracia, while hip new bars and clubs line **Calle Elvira** from Cárcel to C. Cedrán. **Gay bars** cluster around Carrera del Darro. A smoky, intimate setting awaits at **Eshavira,** C. Postigo de la Cuna, in an alley off C. Azacayes, between C. Elvira and Gran Vía; it's the place to go for flamenco and jazz. (☎958 29 08 29. 1 drink min.) Highwaymen once roamed the caves of Sacromonte; now, scantily clad clubbers can as well at **Camborio,** Camino del Sacromonte 48. (€4.50 cover F-Sa. Open Tu-Sa 11pm-dawn.) **Granero,** Pl. Luis Rosales, near Pl. de Isabel la Católica, is a New-Age barn bulging with grooving Spanish yuppies. (Open daily 10pm-dawn.) **Granada 10,** C. Carcel Baja 3, is a movie theater by evening and a raging dance club by night. (Cover Th-Sa €6, includes 1 drink. Open daily.)

🏔 HIKING AND SKIING NEAR GRANADA: SIERRA NEVADA

The peaks of **Mulhacén** (3481m) and **Veleta** (3470m), Spain's highest, sparkle with snow and buzz with tourists for most of the year. **Ski** season runs from December to April. The rest of the year, tourists hike, parasail, and take jeep tours. Call **Cetursa** (☎958 24 91 11) for info on outdoor activities. The Autocares Bonal **bus** (☎958 27 31 00), between the bus station in Granada and Veleta, is a bargain (9am departure, 5pm return; €5.40).

EASTERN SPAIN (VALENCIA)

Valencia's rich soil and famous orange groves, fed by Moorish irrigation systems, have earned it the nickname *Huerta de España* (Spain's Orchard). Dunes, sandbars, jagged promontories, and lagoons mark the grand coastline, while lovely fountains and pools grace carefully landscaped public gardens in Valencian cities. The famed rice dish *paella* was born in this region.

ALICANTE (ALICANT)   ☎965

Sun-drenched Alicante has it all: relaxing beaches, fascinating historical sites, and an unbelievable collection of bars and port-side discos. High above the rows of bronzed beach-goers, the ancient *castillo*, spared by Franco, guards the tangle of streets in the cobblestone *casco antiguo*.

🚆 🚌 TRANSPORTATION AND PRACTICAL INFORMATION. RENFE **trains** (☎902 24 02 02) run from Estación Término on Av. Salamanca, at the end of Av. Estación, to: **Barcelona** (4½-6hr., 9 per day, €43-67); **Madrid** (4hr., 9 per day, €36); and **Valencia** (1½hr., 10 per day, €9-32). Trains from **Ferrocarriles de la Generalitat Valenciana,** Estació Marina, Av. Villajoyosa 2 (☎965 26 27 31), on Explanada d'Espanya, serve the

Costa Blanca. **Buses** run from C. Portugal 17 (☎965 13 07 00), to: **Barcelona** (7hr., 13 per day, €34); **Granada** (6hr., 9 per day, €23); and **Madrid** (5hr., 9 per day, €23). The **tourist office** is on Rbla. de Méndez Nuñez 23. (☎965 20 00 00. Open June-Aug. M-F 10am-8pm; Sept.-May M-F 10am-7pm, Sa 10am-2pm and 3-7pm.) Use the **Internet** at **Fundación Bancaja**, Rbla. Méndez Nuñez 4, on the corner of C. San Fernando, 2nd fl. (Open M-F 10am-2pm and 5-9pm, Sa 9am-2pm.) **Postal Code:** 03070.

⌐⌐ ACCOMMODATIONS AND FOOD. The ▧**Habitaciones México ❶**, C. General Primo de Rivera 10, off the end of Av. Alfonso X El Sabio, has a friendly atmosphere and small, cozy rooms. (☎965 20 93 07. Free Internet access. Singles €12-15; doubles €27; triples €33.) **Hostal Les Monges Palace ❷**, C. San Agustín 4, behind the Ayuntamiento, up the hill from Pl. Santísima Faz., is luxurious, with bath, TV, and sometimes A/C. (☎965 21 50 46. Singles €24-35; doubles €27-29; triples €44-46.) Take bus #21 to camp at **Playa Mutxavista ❶**. (☎965 65 45 26. June-Sept. €4 per person, €12 per tent; Oct.-May €2/8.) Try the family-run *bar-restaurantes* in the *casco antiguo*, between the cathedral and the castle steps. ▧**Kebap ❶**, Av. Dr. Gadea 5, serves heaping portions of Middle Eastern cuisine. (Open daily 1-4pm and 8pm-midnight.) Buy basics at **Supermarket Mercadona**, C. Alvarez Sereix 5, off Av. Federico Soto. (Open M-Sa 9am-9pm.)

◐⌐ SIGHTS AND ENTERTAINMENT. The ancient Carthaginian **Castell de Santa Bárbara,** complete with drawbridges, dark passageways, and hidden tunnels, keeps silent guard over Alicante's beach. A paved road from the old section of Alicante leads to the top, but most people take the **elevator** rising from a hidden entrance on Av. Jovellanos, just across the street from Playa Postiguet, near the white pedestrian overpass. (Castle open Apr.-Sept. daily 10am-7:30pm; Oct.-Mar. 9am-6:30pm. Elevator €2.40.) The **Museu de Arte del Siglo XX La Asegurada,** Pl. Santa María 3, at the east end of C. Mayor, showcases modern art pieces, including works by Picasso and Dalí. (Open mid-May to mid-Sept. T-F 10am-2pm and 5-9pm, Sa-Su 10:30am-2:30pm; mid-Sept. to mid-May T-F 10am-2pm and 4-8pm, Sa-Su 10:30am-2:30pm.) Alicante's **Playa del Postiguet** attracts beach lovers, as do nearby **Playa de San Juan** (TAM bus #21, 22, or 31) and **Playa del Mutxavista** (TAM bus #21). (Buses depart every 15min., €0.80.) Most begin their night bar-hopping in the *casco antiguo;* the complex of bars that overlook the water in Alicante's **main port** and the discos on **Puerto Nuevo** tend to fill up a little later. For an even crazier night, the **Trensnochador** night train (July-Aug. F-Sa every hr. 9pm-5am, Su-Th 4 per night 9pm-5am; round-trip €0.90-4.20) runs from Estació Marina to *discotecas* and other stops along the beach, where places are packed until dawn. Try **Pachá, Ku, KM,** and **Space** (open nightly until 9am) at the *Disco Benidorm* stop. During the hedonistic **Festival de Sant Joan** (June 20-29), *fogueres* (satiric effigies) are erected around the city and then burned in the streets during *la Cremà*; afterwards, firefighters soak everyone during *la Banyà*, and the party continues until dawn.

VALENCIA
☎**963**

Stylish and cosmopolitan, Valencia (pop. 750,000) presents a striking contrast to the surrounding orchards and mountain range. Valencia seems to possess all the best of its sister cities: the bustling energy of Madrid, the vibrant spirit of Alicante, the off-beat sophistication of Barcelona, the friendly warmth of Seville. Despite its cosmopolitan style, Valencia retains a small-town charm.

⌐⌐ TRANSPORTATION AND PRACTICAL INFORMATION. Trains arrive at C. Xàtiva 24 (☎963 52 02 02). **RENFE** (24hr. ☎902 24 02 02) runs to: Alicante (2-3hr., 9 per day, €10-25); Barcelona (3hr., 12 per day, €34); and Madrid (3½hr., 9 per day,

€18-37). **Buses** (☎963 49 72 22) go from Av. Menéndez Pidal 13 to: Alicante via the Costa Blanca (4½hr., 13 per day, €13-15); Barcelona (4½hr., 15 per day, €21); Madrid (4hr., 13 per day, €20-24); and Seville (11hr., 4 per day, €41-48). Bus #8 (€0.90) connects to Pl. Ayuntamiento and the train station. Trasmediterránea **ferries** (☎902 45 46 45) sail to the Balearic Islands (p. 979).

The main **tourist office**, C. Paz 46-48, has branches at the train station and Pl. Ayuntamiento. (☎963 98 64 22. Open M-F 9am-7pm and Sa 10am-7pm.) **Internet** access is at **Ono**, C. San Vicente 22, around the corner from Pl. Ayuntamiento. (☎963 28 19 02. €1.80 per 45 min. 9am-2pm, €1.80 per 30 min. 2-10pm, €1.80 per hour 10pm-1am. Open M-Sa 9am-1am, Su 10am-1am.) The **post office** is at Pl. Ayuntamiento 24. (Open M-F 8:30am-8:30pm, Sa 9:30am-2pm.) **Postal Code:** 46080.

⛏️🏠 ACCOMMODATIONS AND FOOD. The best lodgings are around **Plaza del Ayuntamiento** and **Plaza del Mercado**. The **Home Youth Hostel ❶**, C. Lonja 4, is directly behind the Lonja, on a side street off Pl. Dr. Collado. Brightly painted rooms, a spacious common living room, and a kitchen create a homey atmosphere for road-weary guests. (☎963 91 62 29; www.likeathome.net. Laundry €5.50. Internet €0.50 per 15min. Dorms €14; singles €21; doubles €32; triples €48; quads €64.) **Hostal Alicante ❷**, C. Ribera 8, is centrally located on the pedestrian street off Pl. Ayuntamiento. Its clean, well-lit rooms and firm beds are hugely popular with backpackers. (☎963 51 22 96. Singles €20, with bath and A/C €28; doubles €29/37. MC/V.) From Pl. Ayuntamiento, turn right at C. Barcas, left at C. Poeta Querol, and take the second right onto C. Salvá to reach **Pensión Paris ❷**, C. Salvá 12, which has spotless, sunny rooms with balconies. (☎963 52 67 66. Singles €18; doubles €27, with shower €30; triples €34/39.) To get to **Hostal Antigua Morellana ❸**, C. En Bou 2, walk past Pl. Dr. Collado; it's on the small streets behind the Lonja. Quiet and comfortable rooms with bath and A/C cater to an older crowd. (☎/fax 963 91 57 73. Singles €30; doubles €45.)

Paella is the most famous of Valencia's 200 rice dishes; try as many of them as you can before leaving. Buckets of fresh fish, meat, and fruit (including Valencia's famous oranges) are sold at the **Mercado Central,** on Pl. Mercado. (Open M-Sa 7am-3pm.) For groceries, stop by the basement of **El Corte Inglés,** C. Colon, or the fifth floor of the C. Pintor Sorilla building. (Open M-Sa 10am-10pm.)

◙ SIGHTS. Touring Valencia on foot is a good test of stamina. Most of the sights line Río Turia or cluster near Pl. Reina, which is linked to Pl. Ayuntamiento by C. San Vicente Mártir. EMT bus #5, dubbed the **Bus Turistic** (€1), makes a loop around the old town sights. Head toward the beach along the riverbed off C. Alcalde Reig. or take bus #35 from Pl. Ayuntamiento to reach the modern, airy, and thoroughly fascinating **▨Ciudad de las artes y las ciencias**. This mini-city has created quite a stir; it's become the fourth biggest tourist destination in Spain. The complex is divided into four large attractions, only two of which are currently completed: **Palau de les Arts** and **L'Oceanografic** will not open until at least 2004. The **▨Museu de Les Ciencias Principe Felipe** is an interactive playground for science and technology fiends; **L'Hemisfèric** has an IMAX theater and planetarium. (www.cac.es. Museum open June 15-Sept. 15 daily 10am-9pm, Sept. 16-June 14 M-F and Su 10am-8pm, Sa 10am-9pm. €6, M-F students €4.30. IMAX shows €6.60, M-F students €4.80.) The 13th-century **▨cathedral,** in Pl. Reina, was built on the site of an Arab mosque. The **Museo de la Catedral** squeezes several treasures into three tiny rooms. (Cathedral open in summer daily 7:30am-1pm and 4:30-8:30pm; off-season reduced hours. Free. Museum open Mar.-Nov. M-Sa 10am-1pm and 4:30-6pm; Dec.-Feb. 10am-1pm €1.20.) Across the river, the **Museu Provincial de Belles Artes,** on C. Sant Pius V, displays superb 14th- to 16th-century Valencian art. Its collection includes El Greco's *San Juan Bautista*, Velázquez's self-portrait, and a slew of works by Goya. (Open Su and Tu-Sa 10am-8pm. Free.) West across the old river, the **Institut Valenciá d'Art Modern** (IVAM), C. Guillem de Castro 118, has works by 20th-century sculptor Julio González. (Open Su and Tu-Sa 10am-10pm. €2.10, students €1. Su free.)

🔊 🎵 ENTERTAINMENT AND NIGHTLIFE. The most popular **beaches** are **Las Arenas** and **Malvarrosa**—buses #20, 21, 22, and 23 all pass through. To get to the more attractive **Salér,** 14km from the center of town, take an Autobuses Buñol **bus** (☎963 49 14 25) from the corner of Gran Vía de Germanias and C. Sueca (25min., every 30min. 7am-10pm, €0.90). Bars and pubs abound in the El Carme district. Follow C. Bolsería out of Pl. Mercado, bearing right at the fork, to guzzle *agua de Valencia* (orange juice, champagne, and vodka) in Pl. Tossal. **Carmen Sui Generis,** C. Caballeros 38, is an upscale lounge in an 18th-century palace with eclectic decor and chic clientele. (Cocktails €5-6. Open W-Sa 11pm-3am.) The loud **Cafe Negrito,** Pl. del Negrito 1, off C. Caballeros, is wildly popular with locals. (Small pitcher of *agua de Valencia* €6. Open daily 10pm-3am.) **Rumbo 144,** Av. Blasco Ibañez 144, plays a wide variety of music, from Spanish pop to house. (Cover €9. Open Th-Sa midnight-7am.) For more info, consult the weekly *Qué y Dónde* (€1), available at newsstands, or the weekly entertainment supplement *La Cartelera* (€0.80). The most famed festival in Valencia is **Las Fallas** (Mar. 12-19), which culminates with the burning of gigantic (up to 30m) papier-mâché effigies.

COSTA BLANCA

You could while away a lifetime touring the charming resort towns of the Costa Blanca. The "white coast" that extends through Dénia, Calpe, and Alicante derives its name from its fine white sands. ALSA **buses** (☎902 42 22 42) run from Valencia to: Alicante (2-4hr., 12-15 per day, €13-15); Altea and Calpe (3-4½ hr., 8-10 per day 6am-5pm, €9.40-11); and Gandía (1 hr., 9-11 per day, €5.10). From Alicante buses run to: Altea (1¼hr., 11 per day, €3.80) and Calpe (1½hr., 11 per day 6:30am-8pm, €5.95). Going to **Calpe** (Calp) is like stepping into a Dalí landscape. The town cowers beneath the **Peñón d'Ifach** (327m), which drops straight to the sea, making it one of the most picturesque coastal settings in Spain. Peaceful **Gandía** has fine sand **beaches.** The **tourist office,** Marqués de Campo, is opposite the train station. (☎962 87 77 88. Open June-Aug. M-F 9:30am-1:30pm and 4:30-7:30pm, Sa 10am-1:30pm; Sept.-May M-F 9:30am-1:30pm and 4-7pm, Sa 10am-1pm.) Buses depart from outside the

ON THE MENU

RICE IS NICE

Paella is known throughout the world as a quintessentially Spanish dish, but any *valenciano* can tell you where it all started—here. From the region's rice fields to the factories where it is carefully processed to the tables of the best restaurants, rice is the spice of life in Valencia. The techniques of preparation have been perfected for years by rice cultivators, processors, and *paelleros* (traditionally male). And don't call it all *paella;* there are hundreds of different rice dishes, each distinct in ingredients and preparation.

Paella, for example, is the Valenciano word for the typical pan in which the rice *paella* dish (originally called *arroz en paella*) is cooked. *Arroz a banda,* while similar to *paella,* is traditionally a more humble dish enjoyed by fishermen, who cook the fish separately (*a banda*) from the rice, saffron, garlic, and tomato.

If you prefer your rice baked, try *arroz al horno,* very popular in la Ribera and la Huerta for its mixes of meats and vegetables and slightly less complicated recipe. If you don't prefer rice at all, try *fideuá,* the cousin of *paella,* made with noodles instead of rice. Whichever you choose, you are certain not to be disappointed, so long as you go for the authentic version. Avoid the more touristy restaurants bearing pictures of pre-made *paellas* on sandwich boards; what you see is what you get, and it's not the real thing.

train station for **Platja de Piles** (M-Sa 4-9 per day, €0.80). To sleep at the fantastic **Alberg Mar i Vent (HI) ❶** in Platja, follow the signs down C. Dr. Fleming. The beach is out the back door. (☎962 83 17 48. Sheets €1.80. 3-day max. stay, flexible if uncrowded. Curfew Su-F 2am, Sa 4am. Closed until March 2004 for renovations. Dorms €9-11, under-26 €6-9.)

NORTHEAST SPAIN

Northeastern Spain encompasses the country's most avidly regionalistic areas and is home to some of its best cuisine. Cataluña is justly proud of its treasures, from mountains to beaches to hip Barcelona. However, Cataluña isn't the only reason to head northeast. The area is also home to the glorious mountains of the Pyrenees, the running bulls of Navarra, the industrious cities of Aragón, the beautiful coasts of Basque Country, and the crazy parties of the Balearic Islands.

CATALUÑA

From rocky Costa Brava to chic Barcelona, the prosperous Cataluña is graced with the nation's richest resources. Catalán is the official language (though most everyone is bilingual), and local cuisine is lauded throughout Spain.

BARCELONA ☎93

Barcelona loves to indulge in the fantastic. From the urban carnival that is Las Ramblas to buildings with no straight lines, from wild festivals to even wilder nightlife, the city pushes the limits of style and good taste in everything it does—and with amazing results. The center of the whimsical and daring *Modernisme* architectural movement, and once home to the most well-known Surrealist painters—Salvador Dalí, Pablo Picasso, and Joan Miró—even Barcelona's art is grounded in an alternate reality. In the quarter-century since Spain was freed from Franco's oppressive regime, Barcelona has led the autonomous region of Cataluña in the resurgence of a culture so esoteric and unique it is puzzling even to the rest of Spain. The result is a vanguard city where rooftops drip toward the sidewalk, serpentine park benches twist past fairy-tale houses, and an unfinished cathedral captures imaginations around the world.

✈ INTERCITY TRANSPORTATION

Flights: El Prat de Llobregat Airport (BCN; ☎932 98 38 38), 12km southwest of Barcelona. To get to the central Pl. Catalunya, take the **Aerobus** (40min.; every 15min.; to Pl. Catalunya M-F 6am-midnight, Sa-Su 6:30am-midnight; to the airport M-F 5:30am-11:15pm, Sa-Su 6am-11:20pm; €3.30) or a RENFE **train** (40min.; every 30min.; from airport 6:10am-11:15pm, from Estació Barcelona-Sants 5:30am-11:20pm; €2.20).

Trains: Barcelona has 2 main train stations. For general info about trains and train stations, call ☎902 24 02 02. **Estació Barcelona-Sants,** in Pl. Països Catalans (M: Sants-Estació) is the main terminal for domestic and international traffic. **Estació França,** on Av. Marquès de l'Argentera. M: Barceloneta. Services regional destinations, including Girona Tarragona and Zaragoza, and some international arrivals.

Ferrocarrils de la Generalitat de Cataluña (FGC; ☎932 05 15 15; www.fgc.catalunya.net), has commuter trains with main stations at Pl. Catalunya and Pl. Espanya.

RENFE (☎902 24 02 02; international ☎934 90 11 22; www.renfe.es). RENFE has extensive service in Spain and Europe. Popular connections include: **Bilbao** (8-9hr., 5 per day, €30-32); **Madrid** (7-8hr., 7 per day, €31-42); **San Sebastián** (8-9hr., 5 per day, €31); **Seville** (11-12hr., 6 per day, €47-51); **Valencia** (3-5hr., 15 per day, €28-32). International destinations include **Milan, Italy** (via Figueres and Nice), and **Montpellier, France** with connections to Geneva, Paris, and various stops along the French Riviera. 20% discount on round-trip tickets.

Buses: Most buses arrive at the **Barcelona Nord Estació d'Autobuses**, C. Ali-bei 80 (☎932 65 61 32). M: Arc de Triomf. **Sarfa** (☎902 30 20 25; www.sarfa.com) goes to **Cadaqués** (2½hr., 11:15am and 8:25pm, €16) and **Tossa del Mar** (1½hr., 10 per day, €8). **Linebús** (☎932 65 07 00) travels to **Paris** (13hr.; M-Sa 8pm; €80, under-26 reduced prices), southern France, and Morocco. **Alsa Enatcar** (☎902 42 22 42; www.alsa.es) goes to: **Alicante** (9hr., 3 per day, €33); **Madrid** (8hr., 13 per day, €22); **Naples** (24hr., 5:15pm, €113); **Valencia** (4hr., 16 per day, €21); **Zaragoza** (3½-4½hr., 20 per day, €18).

Ferries: Trasmediterránea (☎902 45 46 45), in Estació Marítima-Moll Barcelona, Moll de Sant Bertran. In the summer months only to: **Ibiza** (10-11hr., daily M-Sa, €46); **Mahón** (10½hr., daily starting mid-June, €46); **Palma** (3½hr., daily, €65).

■ ORIENTATION

Barcelona's layout is simple. Imagine yourself perched on Columbus's head at the **Monument a Colom** (on Passeig de Colom, along the shore), viewing the city with the sea at your back. From the harbor, the city slopes upward to the mountains. From the Monument a Colom, **Las Ramblas**, the main thoroughfare, runs from the harbor up to **Plaça de Catalunya** (M: Catalunya), the city's center. The **Ciutat Vella** (Old City) is the heavily touristed historical neighborhood, which centers around Las Ramblas and includes the Barri Gòtic, La Ribera, and El Raval. The **Barri Gòtic** is east of Las Ramblas (to the right, with your back to the sea), enclosed on the other side by **Vía Laietana**. East of V. Laietana lies the maze-like neighborhood of **La Ribera**, which borders Parc de la Ciutadella and the Estació França (train station). To the west of Las Ramblas (to the left, with your back to the sea) is **El Raval**. Beyond La Ribera—farther east, outside the Ciutat Vella—is **Poble Nou** and **Port Olímpic**, with its twin towers (the tallest buildings in Barcelona) and an assortment of discos and restaurants. Beyond El Raval (to the west) rises **Montjuïc**, crammed with gardens, museums, the 1992 Olympic grounds, and a stunning castle. Directly behind your perch on the Monument a Colom is the **Port Vell** (Old Port) development, where a wavy bridge leads across to the ultra-modern shopping and entertainment complexes **Moll d'Espanya** and **Maremàgnum**. Beyond the Ciutat Vella is **l'Eixample**, the gridded neighborhood created during the expansion of the 1860s, which runs from Pl. Catalunya toward the mountains. **Gran Vía de les Corts Catalanes** defines its lower edge, and the **Passeig de Gràcia**, l'Eixample's main street, bisects the neighborhood. **Avinguda Diagonal** marks the border between l'Eixample and the **Zona Alta** ("Uptown"), which includes Pedralbes, Gràcia, and other older neighborhoods in the foothills. The peak of **Tibidabo,** the northwest border of the city, offers the most comprehensive view of Barcelona.

▐ LOCAL TRANSPORTATION

Public Transportation: ☎010. Pick up a *Guia d'Autobusos Urbans de Barcelona* for Metro and bus routes. **Buses** run 5am-10pm and cost €1 per ride. The **Metro** (☎934 86 07 52; www.tmb.net) runs M-Th 5am-midnight, F-Sa 5am-2am, Su and holidays 6am-midnight. Buy tickets at vending machines and ticket windows. Tickets cost €1.10 per *sencillo* (ride). A **T1 Pass** (€5.80) is valid for 10 rides on the bus or Metro; a **T-DIA Card** entitles you to unlimited bus and Metro travel for 1 (€4.40) or 3 days (€11.30).

Barcelona

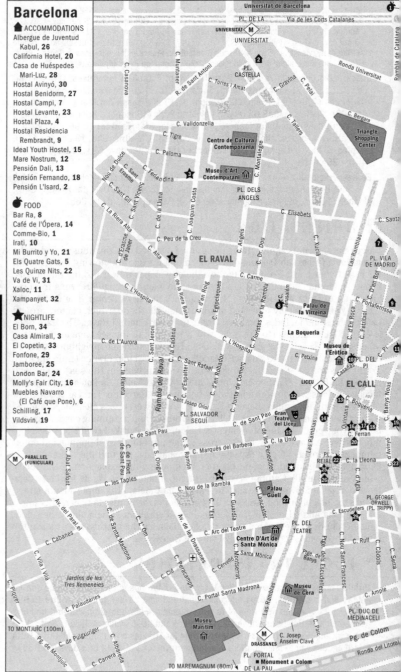

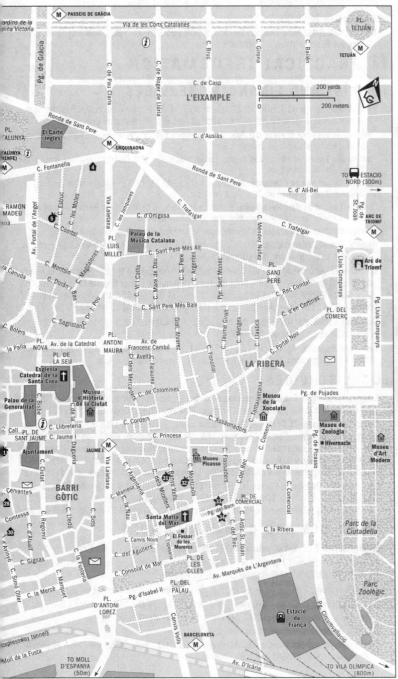

ardins de la
eina Victoria

PASSEIG DE GRÀCIA

Via de les Corts Catalanes

PL.
TETUÁN

C. Bruc

C. Girona

C. Bailén

TETUÁN

Pg. de Gràcia

C. de Pau Clars

C. de Roger de Llúria

C. de Casp

L'EIXAMPLE

0   200 yards
0   200 meters

N

PL.
ALUNYA

El Corte
Ingles

Ronda de Sant Pere

URQUINAONA

C. d'Ausiàs

ALUNYA
(ENFE)

C. Fontanella

Ronda de Sant Pere

TO ESTACIO
NORD (300m)

4

C. d' Alí-Bei

Pg. de
St. Joan

ARC DE
TRIOMF

RAMON
MADEU
ana

C. Estruc

C. les Moles

Via Laietana

C. les Jonqueres

C. d'Ortigosa

C. Trafalgar

C. Méndez Núñez

C. Trafalgar

Av. Portal de l'Àngel

5

C. Comtal

PL.
LUIS
MILLET

Palau de la
Música Catalana

C. Sant Pere Més Alt

C. S.-Pere

C. Argentes

PL.
SANT
PERE

Arc de
Triomf

Pg. Lluís Companys

C. Montsio

C. Magdalenes

C. Vi i Catlls

C. Mare de Deu

Pje. Sert Munec

C. Rec Comtal

la Canuda

C. Duran i Bas

C. Dr. J. Pou

C. Sant Pere Més Baix

PL. DEL
COMERÇ

C. d'en Cortinas

Pg. Lluís Companys

C. Boters

C. Sagristans

PL.
ANTONI
MAURA

Av. de
Francesc Cambó

Gral. Alvarez

C. Jaume Giralt

C. Metges

C. Clàstics

C. Portal Nou

la Palla

PL.
NOVA

Av. de la Catedral

C. Avellà

C. Tantarrantana

LA RIBERA

PL. DE
LA SEU

C. dels Mercaders

C. de Colomines

Esglèsia
Catedral de la
Santa Creu

Museu
d'Història
de la Ciutat

C. de la

C. Corders

Museu
de la
Xocolata

Pg. de Pujades

Palau de la
Generalitat

C. Bisbe

C. Assaonadors

C. Comerç

Museu de
Zoologia

Call

C. Llibreteria

C. Princesa

C. Comerç

Hivernacle

Museu
d'Art
Modern

PL. DE
SANT JAUME

C. Jaume I

JAUME I

Pg. de Picasso

Ajuntament

C. Ciutat

Via Laietana

C. l'Argenteria

Daguena

Museu
Picasso

C. Flassaders

C. Montcada

C. Rec

C. Fusina

BARRI
GÒTIC

Cervantes

28

C. Regomir

C. Lledó

C. Sots

31

32

Banys Vells

C. Antic St. Joan

C. Comercial

Parc de la
Ciutadella

Comtessa

30

C. d'Avuall

C. Manresa

C. dels Mirallers

C. la Nau

Santa Maria
del Mar

PL. DE
COMERCIAL

Avinyó

C. Simó Oller

C. Gignàs

C. Canvis Nous

C. dels Aguilers

El Fossar
de les
Moreres

Pg. del Born

C. del Rec

C. la Ribera

C. la Mercè

C. Manuel

C. Consolat de Mar

PL. DEL
PALAU

PL. DE
LES
OLLES

Av. Marquès de L'Argentera

Parc
Zoològic

Canvis Vells

PL.
D'ANTONI
LOPEZ

Pg. d'Isabel II

Estació
de
França

Pg. Circumvallació

expressway tunnel)

Moll de la Fusta

TO MOLL
D'ESPANYA
(50m)

BARCELONETA

Av. D'Icària

TO VILA OLÍMPICA
(800m)

SPAIN

Taxis: ☎933 30 03 00.

Car Rental: Avis/Auto Europe, Casanova 209 (☎932 09 95 33). Will rent to ages 21-25 for an additional fee of about €5 a day.

🔢 PRACTICAL INFORMATION

TOURIST AND FINANCIAL SERVICES

Tourist Offices: (☎010, 906 30 12 82, or 933 04 34 21; www.barcelonaturisme.com.) Barcelona has 4 main tourist offices and numerous mobile information stalls.

Informacio Turistica at Plaça Catalunya, Pl. Catalunya 17S. M: Catalunya. The biggest, best, and busiest tourist office. Open daily 9am-9pm.

Informacio Turista at Plaça Sant Jaume, Pl. Sant Jaume 1, off C. Ciutat. M: Jaume I. Open M-Sa 10am-8pm, Su 10am-2pm.

Oficina de Turisme de Catalunya, Pg. Gràcia 107 (☎932 38 40 00; www.gencat.es/probert). M: Diagonal. Open M-Sa 10am-7pm, Su 10am-2pm.

Estació Central de Barcelona-Sants, Pl. Països Cataláns, in the Barcelona-Sants train station. M: Sants-Estació. Open M-F 4:30am-midnight, Sa-Su 5am-midnight.

Aeroport El Prat de Llobregat, in the international terminal. Open daily 9am-9pm.

Budget Travel Offices: Usit, Ronda Universitat 16 (☎934 12 01 04; www.unlimited.es). Open M-F 10am-8:30pm, Sa 10am-1:30pm.

Consulates: Australia, Gran Vía Carlos III 98, 9th fl. (☎933 30 94 96); **Canada,** Elisenda de Pinos 8 (☎932 04 27 00); **New Zealand,** Traversa de Gràcia 64, 4th fl. (☎932 09 03 99); **South Africa,** Teodora Lamadrid 7-11 (☎934 18 64 45); **UK,** Av. Diagonal 477 (☎933 66 62 00; www.ukinspain.com); **US,** Pg. Reina Elisenda 23 (☎932 80 22 27).

Currency Exchange: ATMs give the best rates; the next best rates are available at banks. General banking hours are M-F 8:30am-2pm.

American Express, Pg. Gràcia 101 (☎933 01 11 66). M: Diagonal. Open M-F 9:30am-6pm, Sa 10am-noon. Also at Las Ramblas 74. Open daily 9am-8pm.

LOCAL SERVICES

Luggage Storage: Estació Barcelona-Sants. M: Sants-Estació. Large lockers €4.50. Open daily 5:30am-11pm. **Estació França.** M: Barceloneta. Open daily 7am-10pm.

Department Store: El Corte Inglés, Pl. Catalunya 14 (☎933 06 38 00). M: Catalunya. Behemoth department store. **Free map** of Barcelona at the info desk. Has English books, salon, cafeteria, supermarket, and the *oportunidades* discount department. Open M-Sa and first Su of every month 10am-10pm. **Branches:** Av. Portal de l'Angel 19-2 (M: Catalunya); Av. Diagonal 471-473 (M: Hospital Clìnic); Av. Diagonal 617 (M: Maria Cristina).

Laundromat: Tintorería Ferrán, C. Ferrán 11. M: Liceu. Open M-F 9am-8pm. **Tintorería San Pablo,** C. San Pau 105 (☎933 29 42 49). M: Paral·lel. Wash, dry, and fold €10; do-it-yourself €7.30. Open July-Sept. M-F 9am-2pm; Oct.-June M-F 9am-2pm and 4-8pm.

EMERGENCY AND COMMUNICATIONS

Emergency: ☎112. **Local police:** ☎092. **National police:** ☎091. **Medical:** ☎061.

Police: Las Ramblas 43 (☎933 44 13 00), across from Pl. Reial and next to C. Nou de La Rambla. M: Liceu. Multilingual officers. Open 24hr.

24hr. Pharmacy: Rotates; check any pharmacy window for the nearest on duty.

Hospital: Hospital Clìnic, Villarroel 170 (☎932 27 54 00). M: Hospital Clìnic. Main entrance at the intersection of C. Roselló and C. Casanova.

Internet Access:

■ **easyEverything,** Las Ramblas 31. M: Liceu. About €1.20 per 40min. Open 24hr. Branch at Ronda Universitat 35, right next to Pl. Catalunya.

Bcnet (Internet Gallery Café), Barra de Ferro 3, right down the street from the Picasso museum. M: Jaume I. €3 per hr., 10hr. ticket €20. Open daily 10am-1am.

Cybermundo Internet Centre, Bergara 3 and Balmes 8. M: Catalunya. Just off Pl. Catalunya, behind the Triangle shopping mall. Allows uploading of disks. €1 per hr. Open daily 9am-1am.

Workcenter, Av. Diagonal 441. M: Hospital Clínic or Diagonal. Another branch is at C. Roger de Lluria 2. M: Urquinaona. €0.60 per 10min. Open 24hr.

Post Office: Pl. de Antoni López (general info ☎902 197 197). M: Jaume I or Barceloneta. Fax and **lista de correos.** Open M-F 8:30am-9:30pm. A little shop in the back of the post office building, across the street, wraps packages for mailing (about €2). Shop open M-Sa 9am-2pm and 5-8pm. **Postal Code:** 08003.

ꘐ ACCOMMODATIONS

The area between Pl. Catalunya and the water—the **Barri Gòtic, El Raval,** and **La Ribera**—offers budget beds, but reservations are a must. Last-minute travelers can crash in **Gràcia** or **l'Eixample,** outer boroughs with more vacancies.

LOWER BARRI GÒTIC

⊠ **Hostal Levante,** Baixada de San Miguel 2 (☎933 17 95 65; www.hostallevante.com). M: Liceu. The best deal in Barri Gòtic. Singles €30; doubles €50-60. MC/V. ❸

⊠ **Pensión Fernando,** C. Ferran 31 (☎/fax 933 01 79 93; www.barcelona-on-line.es/fernando). M: Liceu. Fills from walk-in requests. Dorms with lockers. In summer dorms €19, with bath €20; doubles €45/58; triples with bath €68. MC/V. ❷

Hostal Benidorm, Las Ramblas 37 (☎933 02 20 54). M: Drassanes. The best value on Las Ramblas, with phones and complete baths in each of the very clean rooms, balconies overlooking Las Ramblas, and excellent prices. Singles €30; doubles €45-53; triples €65; quads €75; quints €85-90. ❸

Casa de Huéspedes Mari-Luz, C. Palau 4 (☎/fax 933 17 34 63; pensionmariluz@menta.net). M: Liceu. Tidy 4- to 6-person dorm rooms and a few comfortable doubles. Reservations require a credit card. In summer dorms €16; doubles €41. Off-season reduced prices. MC/V. ❷

Hostal Avinyó, C. Avinyó 42 (☎933 18 79 45; www.hostalavinyo.com). M: Drassanes. Rooms with couches, high ceilings, fans, safes, and stained-glass windows. Singles €22; doubles €34, with bath €47; triples €48/66. ❷

Albergue de Juventud Kabul, Pl. Reial 17 (☎933 18 51 90; www.kabul-hostel.com). M: Liceu. Legendary among backpackers; squeezes in up to 200 frat boys at a time. Key deposit €10. Laundry €2.50. No reservations. Dorms €20. ❷

California Hotel, C. Rauric 14 (☎933 17 77 66). M: Liceu. Enjoy one of the 31 clean, sparkling rooms, all with TV, phone, full bath, and A/C. Convenient location. Singles €52; doubles €82; triples €102. AmEx/MC/V. ❹

UPPER BARRI GÒTIC

Between C. Fontanella and C. Ferran, accommodations are pricier but more serene than in the lower Barri Gòtic. Early reservations are obligatory in summer. The nearest Metro stop is Catalunya, unless otherwise specified.

⊠ **Hostal-Residencia Rembrandt,** C. Portaferrissa 23 (☎/fax 933 18 10 11; hostrembrandt@yahoo.es). M: Liceu. Biggest rooms in the area; ask for a balcony. Fans €2 per night. Singles €25, with bath €35; doubles €42/50; triples €60/65. MC/V. ❸

⊠ **Hostal Plaza,** C. Fontanella 18 (☎/fax 933 01 01 39; www.plazahostal.com). Savvy, super-friendly Texan owners; fun, brightly painted rooms with wicker furniture; and great location. Laundry €9. Internet €1 per 15min. Singles €60, with bath €75; doubles €65/75; triples €86/96. 10% discount Nov. and Feb. AmEx/MC/V. ❺

SPAIN

Hostal Campi, C. Canuda 4 (☎/fax 933 01 35 45; hcampi@terra.es). A great bargain with large balconies. Call ahead to reserve 9am-8pm. Prices vary, but generally doubles €42, with bath €49; triples €58/68. ❷

Hotel Lloret, Las Ramblas 125 (☎933 17 33 66). M: Catalunya. New rooms include large bathrooms, tasteful furniture, A/C, heat, TV, and phone. Worth the cost. Singles €45-48; doubles €75-81; triples €89-95; quads €105. AmEx/MC/V. ❹

Pensión Dalí, C. Boquería 12 (☎933 18 55 90; pensiondali@wanadoo.es). M: Liceu. Designed as a religious house by Domènech i Montaner and originally run by a friend of Dalí. All rooms have TVs. In the high season, doubles €47, with bath €53; triples with bath €75; quads with bath €85. MC/V. ❹

Mare Nostrum, Las Ramblas 67 (☎933 18 53 40; fax 934 12 30 69). M: Liceu. The swankiest hotel on the strip. All rooms have A/C and satellite TV. Breakfast included. Singles €57, with bath €72; doubles €66/76; triples €88/100; quads €99/114. ❺

EL RAVAL

Be careful in the areas near the port and farther from Las Ramblas.

🏠 **Pensión L'Isard,** C. Tallers 82 (☎/fax 933 02 51 83). M: Universitat. A clean find with enough closet space for even the worst over-packer. Singles €20; doubles €36, with bath €52; triples €52. ❷

🏠 **Ideal Youth Hostel,** C. la Unió 12 (☎933 42 61 77; www.idealhostel.com). M: Liceu. One of the best deals in the city. Breakfast included. Free Internet access in the swanky lobby area. Sheets €2.50. Laundry €4. Dorms €16. ❷

L'EIXAMPLE

🏠 **Hostal Residencia Oliva,** Pg. de Gràcia 32, 4th fl. (☎934 88 01 62 or 934 88 17 89; www.lasguias.com/hostaloliva). M: Pg. de Gràcia. Elegant wood-worked bureaus, mirrors, ceilings, and a light marble floor give this hostel a classy ambience. Singles €26; doubles €48, with bath €55; triple with bath €78. ❸

🏠 **Pensión Fani,** València 278 (☎932 15 36 45). M: Catalunya. Oozes quirky charm. Rooms rented by month; single nights also available. Singles €280 per month; doubles €500 per month; triples €780 per month. One-night stay €20 per person. ❷

🏠 **Hostal Eden,** C. Balmes 55 (☎934 52 66 20; http://hostaleden.net). M: Pg. Gràcia. Modern rooms are equipped with TVs and fans; most have big, new bathrooms. May-Oct. singles €29, with bath €39; doubles €39/60. Nov.-Apr. singles €23/32; doubles €29/45. AmEx/MC/V. ❸

Hostal Qué Tal, C. Mallorca 290 (☎/fax 934 59 23 66; www.quetalbarcelona.com), near C. Bruc. M: Pg. Gràcia or Verdaguer. This quality gay-and-lesbian friendly hostel has one of the best interiors in the city. Singles €39; doubles €58, with bath €78. ❹

GRÀCIA

🏠 **Hostal Lesseps,** C. Gran de Gràcia 239 (☎932 18 44 34). M: Lesseps. Spacious, classy rooms sport red velvet wallpaper. All 16 rooms have a TV and bath; 4 have A/C (€5.60 extra). Singles €38; doubles €60; triples €75; quads €90. MC/V. ❹

Pensión San Medín, C. Gran de Gràcia 125 (☎932 17 30 68; www.sanmedin.com). M: Fontana. Embroidered curtains and ornate tiling adorn this family-run pensión. Common room with TV. Singles €30, with bath €39; doubles €48/60. MC/V. ❸

Albergue Mare de Déu de Montserrat (HI), Pg. Mare de Déu del Coll 41-51 (☎932 10 51 51; www.tujuca.com). This gorgeous 220-bed hostel is a great way to meet other backpackers. Breakfast included. Flexible 3-day max. stay. Dorms €18, under-26 €14. Members only. AmEx/MC/V. ❶

SPAIN

CAMPING

El Toro Bravo, Autovía de Castelldefells km 11 (☎936 37 34 62; www.eltorobravo.com). Offers beach access, laundry facilities, currency exchange, 3 pools, 2 bars, a restaurant, and a supermarket. Reception 8am-7pm. Electricity €4. Open Sept.-June 14. €5 per person, €5 per site, €5 per car. AmEx/MC/V. ❶

▣ FOOD

The *Guia del Ocio* (available at newsstands; www.guiadelociobcn.es; €1) is an invaluable source of culinary suggestions. **Port Vell** and **Port Olímpic** are known for seafood. The restaurants on **Calle Aragó** by Pg. Gràcia have great lunchtime *menús*, and the **Passeig de Gràcia** has beautiful outdoor dining. Gràcia's **Plaça Sol** and La Ribera's **Santa Maria del Mar** are the best places to head for *tapas*. If you want to live cheap and do as the Barcelonese do, buy your food fresh at a *mercat* (marketplace). For wholesale fruit, cheese, and wine, head to **La Boqueria** (Mercat de Sant Josep), outside M: Liceu. For groceries, try **Champion Supermarket,** Las Ramblas 11. (M: Liceu. Open M-Sa 10am-10pm.)

BARRI GÒTIC

▨ **Café de l'Opera,** Las Ramblas 74 (☎933 17 75 85). M: Liceu. A drink here used to be a post-opera bourgeois tradition. Hot chocolate €1.70. *Churros* €1.20. *Tapas* €2-4. Salads €2-8. Open Su 10am-2:30am, M-Th 9am-2:30am, F-Sa 9am-2:45am. ❷

▨ **Mi Burrito y Yo,** C. del Pas de l'Ensenyanca 2 (☎933 18 27 42). M: Jaume I. Not a Mexican joint (burrito here means "little donkey"), but rather inviting and lively. Live music 9:30pm. Entrees €12-20. Open daily 1pm-midnight. AmEx/MC/V. ❹

▨ **Les Quinze Nits,** Pl. Reial 6 (☎933 17 30 75). M: Liceu. One of the most popular restaurants in Barcelona, with nightly lines. Delicious Catalán entrees at unbeatable prices (€3-7). No reservations. Open daily 1-3:45pm and 8:30-11:30pm. AmEx/MC/V. ❶

Els Quatre Gats, C. Montsió 3 (☎933 02 41 40). M: Catalunya. Picasso's old hangout. Entrees €12-18. Live piano and violin 9pm-1am. Open daily 1pm-1am, Closed Aug. AmEx/MC/V. ❸

Irati, C. Cardenal Casañas 17 (☎933 02 30 84). M: Liceu. An excellent Basque *tapas* bar. Keep your toothpicks to figure out your bill. Bartenders pour *sidra* (cider) behind their backs. Entrees €13-20. Open daily noon-1am. AmEx/MC/V. ❹

Xaloc, C. de la Palla 13-17 (☎93 301 19 90). M: Liceu. This classy delicatessen is centered around a butcher counter with pig legs hanging from the high ceiling. Meat and poultry sandwiches on tasty baguettes €3-7. Open daily 9am-midnight. AmEx/MC/V. ❶

ELSEWHERE IN BARCELONA

▨ **Xampanyet,** C. Montcado 22 (☎933 19 70 03). M: Jaume I. This *tapas* bar serves house *cava* at a colorful bar. Glasses €1. Bottles €7 and up. Open Sept.-July Tu-Sa noon-4pm and 7-11:30pm, Su 7-11:30pm. ❶

▨ **Va de Vi,** C. Banys Vells 16 (☎933 19 29 00). M: Jaume I. Romantic, medieval wine bar in a 16th-century building. Wine €1.60-4 per glass. Cheeses €4-16. *Tapas* €2-13. Open Su-Th 6pm-2am, F-Sa 6pm-3am. ❷

▨ **Bar Ra,** Pl. Garduña (☎933 01 41 63). M: Liceu. This place exudes cool. Dinner by reservation. Excellent duck (€10) and vegetarian lasagna (€8). Open M-Sa 9pm-midnight, Su brunch noon-6pm. AmEx/MC/V. ❷

El Racó d'en Baltá, C. Aribau 125 (☎934 53 10 44). M: Hospital Clínic. Offers creative Mediterranean dishes. Fish and meat entrees €12-17. Open Su 9-10:45pm, Tu-Sa 1-3:30pm and 9-10:45pm, F-Sa until 11pm. AmEx/MC/V. ❸

Thai Gardens, C. Diputació 273 (☎934 87 98 98). M: Catalunya. Extravagant decor. Weekday *menú* €11. Pad thai €6. Entrees €9-14. Open Su-Th 1-4pm and 8pm-midnight, F-Sa 1:30-4pm and 8pm-1am. ❸

Comme-Bio, Av. Gran Vía 603 (☎933 01 03 76). The antithesis of traditional Catalán food, this place has hummus, tofu, and yogurt. Restaurant and small grocery store. Veggie pizzas, pasta, and rice €9. Salads €6-8. Open daily 9am-11:30pm. ❷

◎ SIGHTS

Barcelona is defined by its unique *Modernisme* architecture. The tourist areas are **Las Ramblas,** a bustling avenue smack in the city center, and the **Barri Gòtic,** Barcelona's "old city." But don't neglect vibrant La Ribera and El Raval, the upscale Modernist avenues of l'Eixample, the panoramic city views from Montjuïc and Tibidabo, Gaudí's Park Güell, and the harborside Port Olímpic. The **Ruta del Modernisme** pass is the cheapest and most flexible option for those with a few days and an interest in seeing all the biggest sights. Passes (€3.60; students, over-65, and groups of 11 or more €2.60) are good for a month and give holders discounts on entrance to Palau Güell, La Sagrada Família, Palau de la Música Catalana, Casa-Museu Gaudí, Fundació Antoni Tàpies, the Museu d'Art Modern, tours of El Hospital de la Santa Creu i Sant Pau, tours of the facades of La Manzana de la Discòrdia, and other attractions. You can purchase passes at **Casa Amatller,** Pg. Gràcia 41. (☎934 88 01 39; www.rutamodernisme.com. M: Pg. de Gràcia.)

LAS RAMBLAS

Las Ramblas, a pedestrian-only median strip, is a cosmopolitan cornucopia of street performers, fortune-tellers, human statues, vendors, and artists, all for the benefit of the visiting droves of tourists. A stroll along this bustling avenue can be an adventure at almost any hour, day or night. The wide, tree-lined thoroughfare dubbed Las Ramblas is actually composed of five (six if you count the small Rambla de Mar) distinct ramblas (promenades) that together form one boulevard, about 1km long, starting at Pl. Catalunya and the **Font de Canaletes** (more a pump than a fountain)—visitors who wish to eventually return to Barcelona are supposed to sample the water. Halfway down Las Ramblas, **Joan Miró**'s pavement mosaic brightens up the street. Pass the **Monument a Colom** on your way out to the Rambla de Mar and a beautiful view of the Mediterranean.

GRAN TEATRE DEL LICEU. Once one of Europe's leading stages, the Liceu has been ravaged by anarchists, bombs, and fires. It is adorned with palatial ornamentation, gold facades, sculptures, and grand side rooms—including a fantastic Spanish hall of mirrors. *(Las Ramblas 51-59, by C. de Sant Pau. Office open M-F 2-8:30pm and 1hr. before performances. ☎934 85 99 13. Tours M-F 10am, by reservation only. €5.)*

MONUMENT A COLOM. Ruis i Taulet's Monument a Colom towers at the port end of Las Ramblas. Nineteenth-century *Renaixença* enthusiasts convinced themselves that Columbus was Catalán, from a town near Girona. The fact that Columbus points proudly toward Libya, not the Americas, doesn't help the claim; historians agree that Columbus was from Italy. Take the elevator to the top to enjoy a stunning view. *(Portal de la Pau. M: Drassanes. Elevator open daily June-Sept. 9am-8:30pm; Oct.-Mar. M-F 10am-1:30pm and 3:30-6:30pm, Sa-Su 10am-6:30pm; Apr.-May M-F 10am-2pm and 3:30-7:30pm, Sa-Su 10am-7:30pm. €1.80, children and over-65 €1.20.)*

Suggested Time: 5hr.

Distance: 3.2km (2 mi.)

When to go: A weekday morning.

Start: M: Liceu, L3.

End: M: Drassanes, L3.

No visit to Barcelona is complete (or even possible) without traversing the famous Las Ramblas. Translated as "The Promenades," Las Ramblas is a series of five individual walkways strung together. Although they are generally referred to as one collective rambla, each has its own distinct character and plenty of built-in entertainment.

1 GRAN TEATRE DEL LICEU. Get off the Metro at Liceu, you can't miss it. Start your morning with the 10am guided tour of Barcelona's premier stage, and bask in the history of one of Europe's greatest opera houses (tours M-F; see p. 960)

2 LA BOQUERIA. Check out the famous market housed in an all-steel Modernist structure. Choose a late-morning snack from this wondrous bounty of fresh food (see p. 948).

3 PALAU DE LA VIRREINA. Wander in the courtyard of this 18th-century Rococo palace and see if any exhibitions are going on. If not, visit the building's Cultural Events Office or admire the upscale souvenirs in the giftshop .

4 PLAÇA CATALUNYA. Now you've come to the city's main hub. Every tourist wanders through at least once; can you tell by the crowds? The busy *plaça* makes a great place to people-watch or just relax. Check out the enormous El Corte Inglés and do some serious shopping (see p. 956). It is also where the old city meets the new; turn south to catch the rest of this walking tour, or continue farther north to l'Eixample (see p. 963).

5 MUSEU DE L'ERÒTICA. Swing back around the *plaça* and head back down the left side of Las Ramblas. If you dare, check out Spain's only erotica museum.

6 CAFÉ DE L'OPERA. Enjoy a cup of coffee at the famous cafe (see p. 959). But don't expect to order to go; Europeans like to enjoy their coffee by sipping it leisurely.

7 MUSEU DE CERA. Peruse over 300 different wax recreations of famous politicians, celebrities, fictional characters, and European royalty. While many of the figures are difficult to recognize, the scenes of death in the horror room are straightforward enough to appreciate.

8 MONUMENT A COLOM. End your tour with a visit to the 60m statue of the man Spanish cities love to claim as their own, Christopher Columbus. Sevilla purports that he is buried in their city (he's not). Barcelona claims that he was born in Catalunya (he wasn't). Christopher Columbus may have been elusive in birth and death, but at least Barcelona has captured the prophet in a moment of inspiration, pointing valiantly, heroically, epically...the wrong way. You can take an elevator to the top of the statue for a stunning view of the city (see p. 960).

WALKING TOUR

BARRI GÒTIC

While the ancient cathedrals and palaces gives the impression that this neighborhood's time has passed, the area is still very much alive, as evident in the ever-crowded streets. As the oldest part of Barcelona, the Barri Gòtic came into existence well before the inception of the grid layout (found in l'Eixample), which took form during Roman times and continued to develop during the medieval period.

ESGLÉSIA CATEDRAL DE LA SANTA CREU. This cathedral is one of Barcelona's most popular monuments. Beyond the choir are the altar with the bronze cross designed by Frederic Marès in 1976 and the sunken Crypt of Santa Eulalia, one of Barcelona's patron saints. The cathedral museum holds Bartolomé Bermejo's *Pietà*. Catch a performance of the sardana in front of the cathedral on Sunday after Mass. *(M: Jaume I. In Pl. Seu, up C. Bisbe from Pl. St. Jaume. Cathedral open daily 8am-1:30pm and 4-7:30pm. Cloister open 9am-1:15pm and 4-7pm. Elevator to the roof open M-Sa 10:30am-12:30pm and 4:30-6pm. €1.40. Mass Su noon and 6:30pm. Choir area open M-F 9am-1pm and 4-7pm, Sa-Su 9am-1pm. €1. English audioguide €1.)*

PLAÇA DE SANT JAUME. Plaça de Sant Jaume has been Barcelona's political center since Roman times. Two of Cataluña's most important buildings have dominated the square since 1823: The **Palau de la Generalitat,** the headquarters of Cataluña's government, and the **Ajuntament,** the city hall. *(Generalitat open 2nd and 4th Su of every month 10:30am-1:30pm. Closed Aug. Mandatory tours in Catalán, Spanish, or English every 30min. starting at 10:30am. Free. Ajuntament open Su 10am-1:45pm. Free.)*

LA RIBERA

This neighborhood has recently evolved into Barcelona's bohemian nucleus, with art galleries, chic eateries, and exclusive bars.

■ **MUSEU PICASSO.** The most-visited museum in Barcelona traces the development of Picasso as an artist, with the world's best collection of work from his formative Barcelona period. *(C. Montcada 15-19. M: Jaume I. Open Tu-Sa 10am-8pm, Su 10am-3pm. €5, students and seniors €2.50. Under-16 free. First Su of each month free.)*

■ **PALAU DE LA MÚSICA CATALANA.** In 1891, the Orfeó Catalán choir society commissioned Modernist Luis Domènech i Montaner to design this must-see concert venue. The music hall glows with tall stained-glass windows, an ornate chandelier, marble reliefs, intricate woodwork, and ceramic mosaics. Concerts given at the Palau include symphonic and choral music in addition to more modern pop, rock, and jazz. *(C. Sant Francese de Paula 2. ☎932 95 72 00; www.palaumusica.org. M: Jaume I. Mandatory tours in English every hr. Reserve 1 day in advance. Open daily Aug. 10am-6pm; Sept.-July 10am-3:30pm. €5, students and seniors €4. Check the Guía del Ocio for concert listings. Concert tickets €6-150. MC/V.)*

■ **MUSEU DE LA XOCOLATA (CHOCOLATE MUSEUM).** Arguably the most delectable museum in Spain, with gobs of information about the history, production, and ingestion of chocolate. Perhaps more interesting are the exquisite chocolate sculptures, particularly the edible version of La Sagrada Família. A small cafe offers workshops on cake baking and chocolate tasting. *(Pl. Pons i Clerch. M: Jaume I. Open M and W-Sa 10am-7pm, Su 10am-3pm. €3.80, students and seniors €3.30. Reservations required. Workshops from €6.)*

SANTA MARIA DEL MAR. This 14-century architectural wonder was built in a quick 55 years. Standing 13m apart, the supporting columns span a width greater than any other medieval building in the world. It's a fascinating example of the limits of Gothic architecture—were it 2ft. taller, the roof would collapse from structural instability. *(Pl. Santa Maria 1. M: Jaume 1. Open M-Sa 9am-1:30pm and 4:30-8pm, Su 9am-2pm and 5-8:30pm. Free.)*

PARC DE LA CIUTADELLA. Host of the 1888 Universal Exposition, the park harbors several museums, well-labeled horticulture, the wacky Cascada fountains, a pond, and a zoo. Buildings of note include Domènech i Montaner's Modernista **Castell dels Tres Dragons** (now the Museu de Zoología), the geological museum, and Josep Amergós's **Hivernacle.** In the **Parc Zoològic** *(M: Ciutadella. Open May-Aug. 9:30am-7:30pm; Apr. and Sept. 10am-7pm; Mar. and Oct. 10am-6pm; Nov.-Feb. 10am-5pm. €12.)* ◼**Floquet de Neu** (a.k.a. *Copito de Nieve;* Little Snowflake), the world's only known albino gorilla, lounges in the sun. The nearby **Museu d'Art Modern** houses a potpourri of works by 19th-century Catalán artists. *(Pl. D'Armes. Open Tu-Sa 10am-7pm, Su 10am-2:30pm. €3, students €2. First Th of every month free.)*

EL RAVAL

◼**PALAU GÜELL.** Gaudí's Palau Güell (1886)—the Modernist residence built for patron Eusebi Güell (of Park Güell fame)—has one of Barcelona's most spectacular interiors. Güell spared no expense on this house, considered to be the first where Gaudí's unique style truly showed. *(C. Nou de La Rambla 3-5. M: Liceu. Open Mar.-Oct. Su 10am-2pm, M-Sa 10am-8pm, last tour at 6:15pm; Nov.-Dec. M-Sa 10am-6pm. €3, students €1.50. Mandatory tour every 15min.)*

MUSEU D'ART CONTEMPORANI (MACBA). This monstrosity of a building was constructed with the idea that sparse decor would allow the art to speak for itself. The MACBA has received worldwide acclaim for its focus on avant-garde art between the two world wars, as well as Surrealist and contemporary art. *(Pl. dels Angels 1. M: Catalunya. Open July-Sept. M, W, and F 11am-8pm; Th 11am-9:30pm; Sa 10am-8pm; Su 10am-3pm. Oct.-June M and W-F 11am-7:30pm, Sa 10am-8pm, Su 10am-3pm. €7, students €3. Under-17 free.)*

L'EIXAMPLE

The Catalán Renaissance and the growth of Barcelona during the 19th century pushed the city past its medieval walls and into modernity. Ildefons Cerdà drew up a plan for a new neighborhood where people of all social classes could live side by side; however, l'Eixample (pronounced luh-SHOMP-luh) did not thrive as a utopian community but rather as a playground for the bourgeois. Despite the gentrification, the original Modernist architecture remains truly idealistic.

◼**LA SAGRADA FAMÍLIA.** Although Antoni Gaudí's unfinished masterpiece is barely a shell of the intended finished product, La Sagrada Família is without a doubt the world's most visited construction site. Despite the fact that only eight of the eighteen planned towers have been completed (and those the shortest, at that) and the church still doesn't have an "interior," millions of people make the touristic pilgrimage to witness its work-in-progress majesty. Of the three proposed facades, only the Nativity Facade was finished under Gaudí. A furor has arisen over recent additions, especially sculptor Josep Subirachs's Cubist Passion Facade, which is criticized for being inconsistent with Gaudí's plans. *(C. Mallorca 401. M: Sagrada Família. Open Apr.-Sept. daily 9am-8pm, elevator open 9:30am-7:45pm; Oct.-Mar. 9am-6pm, elevator open 9:30am-5:45pm. Entrance €8, students €5. Cash only. ◼Guided tours Apr.-Sept. daily every hour 11am-5pm; Oct. 11am-3pm; Nov.-Mar. Su-M and F-Sa 11am-1pm. €3.)*

◼**LA MANZANA DE LA DISCÒRDIA.** A short walk from Pl. Catalunya, the odd-numbered side of Pg. de Gràcia between C. Aragó and Consell de Cent is popularly known as *la manzana de la discòrdia* (block of discord), referring to the stylistic clashing of three buildings. Regrettably, the bottom two floors of **Casa Lleó i Morera,** by Domènech i Montaner, were destroyed to make room for a fancy store, but you can buy the **Ruta del Modernisme pass** there and take a short tour of the upper floors, where sprouting flowers, stained glass, and legendary doorway sculptures adorn the interior. Puig i Cadafalch opted for a geometric, Moorish-influenced pattern on the facade of **Casa Amatller** at #41. Gaudí's balconies ripple like water, and tiles sparkle in blue-purple glory on **Casa Batlló**, #43. The most popular interpretation of Casa Batlló is that the building represents Cataluña's patron Sant Jordi (St. George) slaying a dragon; the chimney plays the lance, the scaly roof is the dragon's back, and the bony balconies are the remains of his victims. (*Open M-Sa 9am-2pm, Su 9am-8pm. €8, students €6.*)

■ **CASA MILÀ (LA PEDRERA).** Modernism buffs argue that the spectacular Casa Milà apartment building, an undulating mass of granite popularly known as *La Pedrera* (the Stone Quarry), is Gaudí's most refined work. Note the intricate iron-work around the balconies and the irregularity of the front gate's egg-shaped window panes. The roof sprouts chimneys that resemble armored soldiers, one of which is decorated with broken champagne bottles. Rooftop tours provide a closer look at these Prussian helmets. The winding brick attic has been transformed into the **Espai Gaudí**, a multimedia presentation of Gaudí's life and works. (*Pg. Gràcia 92. Open daily 10am-8pm. €7; students and over-65 €3.50. Free guided tours in English M-F 4pm, Sa-Su 11am.*)

WATERFRONT

■ **L'AQUÀRIUM DE BARCELONA.** Barcelona's aquarium—the largest in Europe—is an aquatic wonder, featuring a large number of octopi and penguins. The highlight is a 75m glass tunnel through an ocean tank of sharks and sting rays, as well as one two-dimensional fish. (*Moll d'Espanya, next to Maremàgnum. M: Drassanes. Open July-Aug. daily 9:30am-11pm; Sept.-June 9:30am-9pm. €13, students €12, under-12 and seniors €9.*)

■ **TORRE SAN SEBASTIÀ.** One of the easiest and best ways to view the city is on these cable cars, which span the entire Port Vell, connecting beachy Barceloneta with mountainous Montjuïc. The full ride, which takes about 10min. each way and makes an intermediate stop at the Jaume I tower near Colom, gives an aerial perspective of the entire city. (*Pg. Joan de Borbo. M: Barceloneta. In Port Vell, as you walk down Joan de Borbo and see the beaches to the left, stay right and look for the high tower. To Jaume I round-trip €7.50; to Montjuïc one-way €7.50, round-trip €9.50. Open daily 11am-8pm.*)

VILA OLÍMPICA. The Vila Olímpica, beyond the east side of the zoo, was built to house 15,000 athletes and entertain millions of tourists for the 1992 Summer Olympics. It's home to several public parks, a shopping center, and business offices. In the area called **Barceloneta,** beaches stretch out from the port. (*M: Ciutadella/Vila Olímpica. Walk along the waterfront on Ronda Litoral toward the two towers.*)

MONTJUÏC

Throughout Barcelona's history, whoever controlled Montjuïc (Hill of the Jews) controlled the city. Dozens of rulers have modified the **fortress,** built atop an ancient Jewish cemetery; Franco made it one of his "interrogation" headquarters, rededicating it to the city in 1960. A huge stone monument expresses Barcelona's (forced) gratitude for its return; the three statues symbolize the three seas surrounding Spain. (*M: Espanya, then bus #50 (every 10min.) from Av. Reina María Cristina.*)

■ **FUNDACIÓ MIRÓ.** Designed by Miró's friend Josep Luís Sert and tucked into the side of Montjuïc, the Fundació links interior and exterior spaces with massive windows and outdoor patios. Skylights illuminate an extensive collection of statues and paintings from Miró's career. His best-known pieces in the museum include *El Carnival de Arlequin, La Masia,* and *L'or de L'azuz.* Room 13 displays experimental work by young artists. The Fundació also sponsors music and film festivals. *(Av. Miramar 71-75. Take the funicular from M: Paral·lel. Open July-Aug. Tu-W and F-Sa 10am-8pm, Th 10am-9:30pm, Su 10am-2:30pm; Oct.-June Tu-W and F-Sa 10am-7pm, Th 10am-9:30pm, Su 10am-2:30pm. €7.20, students and seniors €4.)*

■ **MUSEU NACIONAL D'ART DE CATALUNYA (PALAU NACIONAL).** Designed by Enric Catá and Pedro Cendoya for the 1929 International Exposition, the beautiful Palau Nacional has housed the Museu Nacional d'Art de Catalunya (MNAC) since 1934. Its main hall is a public event space, while the wings are home to the world's finest collection of Catalán Romanesque art and a wide variety of Gothic pieces. The Romanesque frescoes, now integrated as murals into dummy chapels, were salvaged in the 1920s from their original, less protected locations in northern Cataluña's churches. The museum's Gothic art corridor displays paintings on wood, the medium of choice during that period. The chronological tour of the galleries underlines the growing influence of Italy over Cataluña's artistic development, and ends with a breathtaking series of paintings by Gothic master Bernat Martorell. Behind the building, the **Fonts Luminoses** (the Illuminated Fountains) are dominated by the central **Font Mágica,** which are employed in weekend laser shows during the summer. *(From M: Espanya, walk up Av. Reina María Cristina, away from the two brick towers, and take the escalators to the top. Open Su 10am-2:30pm, Tu-Sa 10am-7pm. €4.80; with temporary exhibits €6; temporary exhibits only €4.20. 30% discount for students and seniors.)*

■ **CASTELL DE MONTJUÏC.** A visit to this historic fortress and its ■**Museum Militar** is a great way to get an overview of the city's layout and history. From the castle's exterior *mirador,* gaze over the city. Enjoy coffee at the cafe while cannons stare you down. *(From M: Paral·lel, take the funicular to Av. Miramar and then the Teleféric de Montjuïc cable car to the castle. Teleféric open M-Sa 11:15am-9pm. One-way €3.20, round-trip €4.50. Or, walk up the steep slope on C. Foc, next to the funicular station. Open Mar. 15-Nov. 15 9:30am-8pm; Nov. 16-Mar. 14 9:30am-5pm. Castle and mirador €1.)*

ZONA ALTA

■ **PARK GÜELL.** This fantastic park was designed entirely by Gaudí but—in typical Gaudí fashion—was not completed until after his death. Gaudí intended Park Güell to be a garden city with dwarfish buildings and sparkling ceramic-mosaic stairways. Two mosaic staircases flank the park, leading to a towering Modernist pavilion that Gaudí originally designed as an open-air market. The longest park bench in the world, a multicolored serpentine wonder made of tile shards, decorates the top of the pavilion. In the midst of the park is the **Casa-Museu Gaudí.** *(Bus #24 from Pl. Catalunya stops at the upper entrance. Park free. Open May-Sept. daily 10am-9pm; Mar.-Apr. and Oct. 10am-7pm; Nov.-Feb. 10am-6pm. Museum open daily Apr.-Sept. 10am-8pm; Oct.-Mar. 10am-6pm. €4, students €3.)*

■ **MUSEU DEL FÚTBOL CLUB BARCELONA.** A close second to the Picasso Museum as Barcelona's most-visited museum, the FCB museum merits all the attention it gets. Sports fans will appreciate the storied history of the team. The high point is the chance to enter the stadium and take in the enormity of Camp Nou. *(C. Aristides Maillol, next to the stadium. M: Collblanc. Enter through access gates 7 or 9. Open M-Sa 10am-6:30pm, Su 10am-2pm. €5, under-13 €3.50.)*

♫ 🎭 ENTERTAINMENT AND FESTIVALS

For tips on entertainment, nightlife, and food, pick up the *Guía del Ocio* (www.guiadelociobcn.es) at any newsstand. Most of Barcelona's galleries are in **La Ribera** around C. Montcada. Grab face paint to join Barça at the Nou Camp stadium for **fútbol**. (☎ 934 96 36 00. Box office C. Aristedes Maillol 12-18.) Join in the ⊠**sardana**, Cataluña's regional dance, in front of the cathedral after mass on Sundays (noon and 6:30pm). Bullfights are held at the **Plaça de Toros Monumental,** on C. Castillejos 248. (☎ 932 45 58 04. Tickets €16-90.) Take advantage of **Barceloneta** or **Poble Nou's** easy access to the Mediterranean. The **Festa de Sant Jordi** (St. George; Apr. 24) celebrates Cataluña's patron saint with a feast. Men give women roses, and women give men books. On August 15-21, city folk jam at Gràcia's **Festa Mayor;** lights blaze in *plaças* and music plays all night. On September 11, the **Fiesta Nacional de Cataluña** brings traditional costumes, dancing, and Catalán flags hanging from balconies.

◪ NIGHTLIFE

BARRI GÒTIC

In this neighborhood, cookie-cutter *cervecerías* and *bar-restaurantes* can be found every five steps. The Barri Gòtic is perfect for chit-chatting your night away, sipping *sangría*, or scoping out your next dance partner.

Fonfone, C. Escudellers 24. M: Liceu or Drassanes. Atmospheric lighting and cool sounds draw 1-3am crowds. Different DJs every night from all over the world. Beer €3.20. Mixed drinks €6. Open Su-Th 9:30pm-2:30am, F-Sa 9:30pm-3am.

Molly's Fair City, C. Ferran 7. M: Liceu. The place to go if you're looking to meet English-speaking tourists in the Barri Gòtic, guzzling pricey but strong mixed drinks. Guinness on tap €5. Bottled beer €4. Mixed drinks €7. Open Su-Th 8pm-2:30am, F-Sa 7pm-3am.

Jamboree, Pl. Reial 17. M: Liceu. In the corner immediately to your right coming from Las Ramblas. What was once a convent now serves as one of the city's most popular live music venues. Daily jazz or blues performances. Cover M-F €6, Sa-Su €9-12; includes 1 drink. Open daily 11pm-1am. Upstairs, the attached club **Tarantos** hosts flamenco shows (€25). Open M-Sa 9:30pm-midnight.

Schilling, C. Ferran 23. M: Liceu, L3. One of the more chill and spacious bars in the area. Mixed gay and straight crowd. Excellent *sangría* (pitcher €14). Mixed drinks €5. Wine and beer €2. Open daily 10am-2:30am.

Vildsvin, C. Ferran 38. M: Liceu. Oysters and international beers (€4-8) are the specialties at this Norwegian bar. *Tapas* €3-5. Desserts €3.50-5. *Entrees* €8-14. Open M-Th 9am-2am, F-Sa 9am-3am. AmEx/MC/V.

LA RIBERA

El Copetin, Pg. del Born 19. M: Jaume I. Cuban rhythm infuses everything in this casual nightspot. *Mojitos* €5. Open Su-Th 7pm-2:30am, F-Sa 7pm-3am.

El Born, Pg. del Born 26. M: Jaume I. Sit at the marble counter over the basins where fish were once sold or follow spiral staircase upstairs for a meal. Fondues €12-15. Excellent cocktails €4-6. Open Su-Th 6pm-2am, F-Sa 6pm-3am.

EL RAVAL

These streets are densely packed with a place for every variety of bar-hopper—Irish pubbers, American backpackers, absinthe aficionados, social drinkers, lounge lizards, and foosball maniacs will find themselves at home in El Raval.

⊠ **Casa Almirall,** C. Joaquim Costa 33. M: Universitat. This cavernous space, with weathered couches, is Barcelona's oldest bar, founded in 1860. The staff will walk you through your first glass of *absenta* (absinthe; €4.50)—and cut you off after your second. Beer €2. Mixed drinks €5. Open Su-Th 6:30pm-2:30am, F-Sa 6:30pm-3am.

Muebles Navarro (El Café que pone), C. la Riera Alta 4-6. Enjoy the mellow ambience and watch friends get friendlier as they sink into the comfy couches together. Beer and wine €2-3. Mixed drinks €5-7. Open Tu-Th 6pm-2am, F-Sa 6pm-3am.

London Bar, C. Nou de la Rambla 34, off Las Ramblas. M: Liceu. Rub shoulders with unruly, fun-loving expats at this Modernist tavern. Live music nightly. Beer, wine, and absinthe €2-3. Open Su and Tu-Th 7:30pm-4:30am, F-Sa 7:30pm-5am. AmEx/MC/V.

L'EIXAMPLE

L'Eixample has upscale bars and some of the best gay nightlife in Europe, as evidenced by the area's nickname, "Gaixample."

■ **Buenavista Salsoteca,** C. Rosselló 217. FGC: Provença. This over-the-top salsa club manages to attract a laid-back, mixed crowd. Free salsa and merengue lessons W-Th at 10:30pm. F-Sa cover €9, includes 1 drink. Open W-Th 11pm-4am, F-Sa 11pm-5am, Su 8pm-2am.

■ **Dietrich,** C. Consell de Cent 255. M: Pg. Gràcia. A rather unflattering painting of Marlene Dietrich in the semi-nude greets a mostly gay crowd. Nightly drag/strip/dance shows. Beer €3.50. Mixed drinks €5-8. Open Su-Th 10:30pm-2:30am, F-Sa 10:30pm-3am.

La Fira, C. Provença 171. M: Hospital Clìnic. Bartenders serve a hip crowd dangling from carousel swings and surrounded by creepy fun-house mirrors. DJs spin funk, disco, and oldies. Open M-Th 10pm-3am, F-Sa 10pm-4:30am, Su 6pm-1am.

Fuse, C. Roger de Llúria 40. M: Tetuán or Pg. Gràcia. A cutting-edge Japanese-Mediterranean restaurant, cocktail bar, dance club. Mixed gay and straight crowd. Beer €3. Mixed drinks €6. Restaurant open M-Sa 8:30pm-1am. Bar open Th-Sa 1-3am. MC/V.

POBLE NOU AND PORT OLÍMPIC

L'Ovella Negra (Megataverna del Poble Nou), C. Zamora 78. *The* place to come for the first few beers of the night. Foosball games on the 2nd floor are nearly as intense as the real-life FCB/Real Madrid rivalry. Large beers €2. Cocktails from €2. Kitchen open until 12:30am. Open F-Sa 5pm-3am, Su 5-10:30pm.

Club Danzatoria, C. Ramon Trias Fargas 24. The sleek interior makes this one of the hottest places in town. All house music all the time. Cover €15, includes 1 drink. Open Su and Th-Sa midnight-late.

MAREMAGNUM

Barcelona's biggest mall has a split personality. At night, the complex turns into a tri-level maze of clubs, each playing its own music for a plethora of tourists and the occasional Spaniard. This is not the most "authentic" experience in Barcelona, but it is an experience. No one charges cover; clubs make their money from exorbitant drink prices. Be aware that catching a cab at the end of the night can be extremely difficult; consider leaving clubs 30min. before they close.

MONTJUÏC

Lower Montjuïc is home to Barcelona's epic "disco theme park," **Poble Espanyol,** Av. Marqués de Comillas. Fall in love with the craziest disco experience in all of Barcelona at some of the most popular (and surreal) discos: **La Terrazza** (an outdoor madhouse; open July-Aug. Su midnight-6am; Sept.-June Su and Th-Sa midnight-6am), **Torres de Ávila** (with speedy glass elevators; open Th-Sa midnight-6:30am), and ■**Tinta Roja** (for tango lovers; open July-Aug. Tu-Th 7pm-1:30am, F-Sa 8pm-3am; Sept.-June also Tu-Th). Dancing starts at 1am and ends after 8am.

ZONA ALTA

The area around C. de Marià Cubí has great nightlife, undiscovered by tourists, but you'll have to take a taxi. For more accessible fun in Gràcia, head to Pl. Sol.

SPAIN

■ **Otto Zutz,** C. Lincoln 15 (www.ottozutz.com). FGC: Pl. Molina. Groove to house, hip-hop, and funk while Japanimation lights up the top floor. Beer €5. Cover €15, includes 1 drink; email ahead for a discount. Open Tu-Sa midnight-6:30am.

■ **D_Mer,** C. Plató 13. FCG: Muntaner. A blue-hued heaven for lesbians of all ages. A touch of class, a dash of whimsy, and a ton of fun. Cover €6, includes 1 drink. Beer €3.50, Mixed drinks €6. Open Th-Sa 11pm-3:30am.

Bar Marcel, C. Santaló 42. When midnight strikes, locals pack the place in search of cheap booze. Certainly not the fanciest bar in the neighborhood, but possibly the most loved. Beer €1.60. Mixed drinks €5. Prices vary. Open daily 8pm-3am.

▶ DAYTRIPS FROM BARCELONA

MONTSERRAT. An hour northwest of Barcelona, the mountain of Montserrat is where a wandering 9th-century mountaineer had a blinding vision of the Virgin Mary. In the 11th century, a monastery was founded to worship the Virgin, and the site has since evolved into a major pilgrimage center. The **monastery**'s ornate **basilica** is above Pl. Creu. To the right of the main chapel is a route through the **side chapels** that leads to the 12th-century Romanesque **La Moreneta** (the black Virgin Mary), Montserrat's venerated icon. (Walkway open July-Sept. daily 8-10:30am and noon-6:30pm. Nov.-June M-F 8-10:30am, noon-6:30pm, and 7:30-8:15pm. Sa-Su 8-10:30am and noon-6:30pm.) In Pl. Santa María, the **Museo de Montserrat** exhibits a sweeping range of art, from an Egyptian mummy to several Picassos. (Open July-Sept. M-F 10am-7pm, Sa-Su 9:30am-7pm; Nov.-June M-F 10am-6pm, Sa-Su 9:30am-6:30pm. €5.30, students and over-65 €4.50.) The **Santa Cova funicular** descends from Pl. Creu to paths that wind along to ancient hermitages. (Apr.-Oct. daily every 20min. 10am-6pm; Nov.-Mar. Sa-Su 10am-5pm. Round-trip €2.50.) Take the **St. Joan funicular** up for more inspirational views. (Apr.-Oct. daily every 20min. 10am-6pm; Nov.-Mar. M-F 11am-5pm, Sa-Su 10am-5pm. Round-trip €6.10; joint round-trip ticket with the Sta. Cova funicular €7, students and over-65 €6.20.) The dilapidated **St. Joan monastery** and **shrine** are only 20min. from the highest station. The real prize is **St. Jerónim** (1235m), about 2hr. from Pl. Creu (1hr. from the terminus of the St. Joan funicular); after walking 45min., take the sharp left at the little old chapel.

FGC **trains** (☎932 05 15 15) to Montserrat leave from M: Espanya in Barcelona (1hr.; every hr. 8:35am-6:36pm; round-trip including cable car €12); get off at Aeri de Montserrat, not Olesa de Montserrat. From the base of the mountain, the Aeri cable car runs up to the monastery. (July-Aug. every 15min. daily 9:20am-6:30pm; Mar. and Oct. 9:20am-1:40pm and 2:20-6:40pm. Schedules change frequently; call ☎938 77 77 01 to check. €4. Free with FCG.)

THE COSTA BRAVA: FIGUERES AND CADAQUÉS. The Costa Brava's jagged cliffs cut into the Mediterranean Sea from Barcelona to the French border. Though rugged by name, the Brave Coast is tamed in July and August by the planeloads of Europeans dumped onto its once-tranquil beaches.

In 1974, Salvador Dalí chose his native, beachless **Figueres** (pop. 37,000), 36km north of Girona, as the site to build a museum to house his works, catapulting the city into instant fame. His personal tribute is undeniably a masterpiece—and the second most popular museum in Spain. The ■**Teatre-Museu Dalí** is in Pl. Gala. From La Rambla, take C. Girona, which becomes C. Jonquera, and climb the steps. The museum parades the artist's erotically nightmarish landscapes and bizarre installations. (☎972 67 75 00; www.salvador-dali.org. Open July-Sept. 9am-7:15pm; Oct.-June daily 10:30am-5:15pm. Call ahead about night hours during the summer. €9, students €6.50.) Trains (☎902 24 02 02) run to Barcelona

(2hr., 23 per day, €8.10) and Girona (30min., 23 per day, €2.40). **Buses** (☎972 67 33 54) run from Pl. Estació to: Barcelona (2¼hr., 2-6 per day, €13); Cadaqués (1¼hr., 2-5 per day, €3.60); and Girona (1hr., 2-6 per day, €3.60). The **tourist office** is in Pl. Sol. (☎972 50 31 55. Open July-Aug. M-Sa 9am-8pm, Su 9am-3pm; Apr.-June and Oct. M-F 9am-3pm and 4:30-8pm, Sa 9:30am-1:30pm and 3:30-6:30pm; Sept. M-Sa 9am-8pm; Nov.-Mar. M-F 9am-3pm.) **Hostal La Barretina ❷**, C. Lasauca 13, is a lesson in luxury. (☎972 67 64 12. Singles €23; doubles €39. AmEx/MC/V.) **Postal Code:** 17600.

The whitewashed houses and rocky beaches of **Cadaqués** (pop. 1,800) have attracted artists, writers, and musicians—not to mention tourists—ever since Dalí built his summer home here. **◨Casa-Museu Salvador Dalí**, Port Lligat, Dalí's home until 1982, holds with a lip-shaped sofa and pop-art miniature Alhambra. Follow the signs to Port Lligat (bear right with your back to the Statue of Liberty) and then to the Casa de Dalí. (☎972 25 10 15. Open June 15-Sept. 15 daily 10am-8:15pm; Sept. 16-Nov. and Mar. 15-June 14 Su and Tu-Sa 10am-5:10pm. Tours are the only way to see the house; make reservations 1-2 days in advance. Ticket office closes 45min. earlier. €8, students €5.) **Buses** arrive from: Barcelona (2½hr., 11:15am and 4:15pm, €16); Figueres (1hr., 5-7 per day, €4); and Girona (2hr., 1-2 per day, €7). With your back to the Sarfa office at the bus stop, walk right along Av. Caritat Serinyana; the **tourist office**, C. Cotxe 2, is off Pl. Frederic Rahola, opposite the *passeig*. (☎972 25 83 15. Open July-Aug. M-Sa 9:30am-1:30pm and 4-8pm, Su 10:30am-1:30pm; Sept.-June M-Sa 9am-2pm and 4-7pm.) **Postal Code:** 17488.

GIRONA

A world-class city patiently waiting to be noticed, Girona (pop. 70,500) is really two cities in one: A hushed medieval masterpiece on one riverbank and a thriving, modern metropolis on the other. Though founded by the Romans, the city owes more to the renowned *cabalistas de Girona*, who for centuries spread the teachings of Kabbalah (mystical Judaism) in the West. Still a cultural center and university town, Girona is a magnet for artists, intellectuals, and activists.

Most sights are in the old city, across the river from the train station. The **Riu Onyar** separates the new city from the old. The **Pont de Pedra** bridge connects the two banks and heads into the old quarter by way of C. Ciutadans, C. Peralta, and C. Força, which lead to the cathedral and **◨El Call**, the medieval Jewish neighborhood. A thriving community in the Middle Ages, El Call was virtually wiped out by the 1492 Inquisition and mass expulsion and conversion. The entrance to **Centre Bonastruc Ça Porta,** the site of the last synagogue in Girona (today a museum), is off C. Força, about halfway up the hill. (Center and museum open May-Oct. M-Sa 10am-8pm, Su 10am-3pm; Nov.-Apr. M-Sa 10am-6pm, Su 10am-3pm. Museum €2, students €1.) Uphill and around the corner to the right on C. Força, the Gothic **cathedral** rises a record-breaking 90 Rococo steps from the plaza below. The **Tesoro Capitular** within contains some of Girona's most precious possessions, including the **Tapis de la Creació,** a 15th-century tapestry depicting the creation story. (Both open Mar.-Sept. Su-M 10am-2pm, Tu-Sa 10am-2pm and 4-7pm; Oct.-Mar. Su-M 10am-2pm, Tu-Sa 10am-2pm and 4-6pm. Tesoro and cloister €3.) **La Rambla** and **Plaza de Independéncia** are the places to see and be seen in Girona. The expansive, impeccably designed **Parc de la Devesa** explodes with *carpas*, temporary outdoor bars. Bars in the old quarter draw crowds in the early evening. **Café la Llibreria,** C. Ciutadans 15, serves cocktails (€3.60) and *tapas* (€3) to intellectual types. (Open M-Sa 8:30am-1am, Su 8:30am-midnight. MC/V.)

RENFE **trains** (☎972 24 02 02) depart from Pl. de Espanya to Barcelona (1½hr., 24 per day, €5) and Figueres (30-40min., 23 per day, €2.10). **Buses** (☎972 21 23 19) depart from just around the corner. The **tourist office,** Rambla de la Libertat 1, is on the other side. (☎972 22 65 75. Open in summer M-F 9am-

3pm, Sa 9am-2pm; off-season M-F 9am-7pm, Sa 9am-2pm.) Most budget accommodations are in the old quarter and are well-kept and reasonably priced. The **Pensió Viladomat ❷**, C. Ciutadans 5, has well-furnished rooms. (☎972 20 31 76. Singles €16; doubles €32, with bath €55.) Girona abounds with innovative cuisine; **Calle Cort Reial** is the best place to find good, cheap food. **La Crêperie Bretonne ❶**, C. Cort Reial 14, is potent proof of Girona's proximity to France. (☎972 21 81 20. Open Su 8pm-midnight, Tu-Sa 1-4pm and 8pm-midnight. MC/V.) Pick up groceries at **Caprabo,** C. Sequia 10, a block from C. Nou off Gran Vía. (Open M-Sa 9am-9pm.) **Postal Code:** 17070.

THE PYRENEES ☎973

The jagged green mountains, Romanesque churches, and tranquil towns of the Pyrenees draw hikers and skiers in search of outdoor adventures. Spectacular views make driving through the countryside an incredible experience in and of itself. Without a car, transportation is tricky, but feasible.

VAL D'ARAN. Some of the Catalán Pyrenees' most dazzling peaks cluster around Val d'Aran, in the northwest corner of Cataluña. The Val d'Aran is best known for its chic ski resorts: the Spanish royal family's favorite slopes are those of **Baquiera-Beret.** The **Auberja Era Garona (HI) ❶**, Ctra. de Vielha s/n, a few kilometers away in the lovely town of **Salardú,** is accessible by shuttle bus (€0.80) in high-season from Vielha. (☎973 64 52 71; eragarona@aran.org. Breakfast included. May-June and Sept.16-Nov. €12, under-26 €11. Dec.-Apr. Sa and Su and *Semana Santa* €19/16; Dec.-Apr. M-F and July-Sept. 15 €16/13.) While you're in town, don't miss Salardú's impressive 13th-century **church,** or the church's incredible garden view. For skiing info, contact the **Oficeria de Baquiera-Beret** (☎973 64 44 55; fax 64 44 88).

The biggest town in the valley, **Vielha** (pop. 7,000) welcomes hikers and skiers to its lively streets with every service the outdoorsy type might desire. It's only 12km from Baquiera-Beret; **shuttle buses** connect the two during July and August (schedules at the tourist office). Alsina Graells **buses** (☎973 27 14 70) also run to Barcelona (5½hr., 5:30am and 1:30pm, €24). The **tourist office,** C. Sarriulèra 10, is one block upstream from the *plaça.* (☎973 64 01 10; fax 64 03 72. Open daily 9am-9pm.) Several inexpensive *pensiones* cluster at the end of C. Reiau, off Pg. Libertat (which intersects Av. Casteiro at Pl. Sant Antoni); try **Casa Vicenta ❷** at C. Reiau 3. (☎973 64 08 19. Dec.-*Semana Santa* and July 15-Sept. 15 Singles €25; doubles €40. Off-season €18/30. Closed Oct. and Nov.)

PARQUE NACIONAL DE ORDESA. The beauty of Ordesa's Aragonese Pyrenees will enchant even the most seasoned traveler; its well-maintained trails cut across idyllic forests, jagged rock faces, snow-covered peaks, rushing rivers, and magnificent waterfalls. Pay a cyber visit to www.ordesa.net for more info about the park. The **Visitor Center** is on the left, 1.8km past the park entrance. (Open Apr.-Sept. 15 daily 9am-1:30pm and 3-6pm.) The **Soaso Circle** is the most practical hike; frequent signposts clearly mark the 5hr. journey, which can be cut to a 2hr. loop. Enter the park through the village of **Torla,** where you can buy the indispensable *Editorial Alpina* guide (€7.50). La Oscense (☎974 35 50 60) sends a **bus** from Jaca to Sabiñánigo (20min., 2-3 per day, €1.30). Sabiñánigo is also easily accessible by **train;** all trains on the Zaragoza-Huesca-Jaca line stop here. From there, Compañía Hudebus (☎974 21 32 77) runs to Torla (55min., 1-2 per day, €2.50). During the high season, a bus shuttles between Torla and Ordesa (15min., 6am-7pm, €2). Off-season, you'll have to hike the 8km to the park entrance or catch a Jorge Soler **taxi** (☎974 48 62 43; €12), which also offers van tours for up to 8 people. To exit the park area, catch the bus as it passes through Torla at 3:30pm on its way back to Sabiñánigo. In the park, many *refugios* (mountain huts) allow overnight stays. In Torla, ascend C. Francia one block to reach **Refugio L'Atalaya ❶**, C. Francia 45 (☎974 48 60 22), and **Refugio Lucien Briet ❶** (☎974 48 62 21), across the street. (Both €8 per person.) Stock up at **Supermercado Torla**, on C. a Ruata. (Open May-Oct. daily 9am-2pm and 5-8:30pm; Nov.-Apr. closed Su.)

JACA. For centuries, pilgrims bound for Santiago would cross the Pyrenees into Spain, spend the night in Jaca (pop. 14,000), and be off the next morning. They had the right idea; Jaca is a great launching pad for the exploring the Pyrenees. RENFE **trains** (☎974 36 13 32) run from C. Estación to Madrid (7hr., Su-F 1:45pm, €24) and Zaragoza (3hr., daily 7:30am and 6:45pm, €8.50). La Oscense **buses** (☎974 35 50 60) run to Pamplona (2hr., every hr., €5.50) and Zaragoza (2hr., 3-4 per day, €9.50). The **tourist office**, Av. Regimiento de Galicia 2, is one block down from Pl. de Cortes de Aragón. (☎974 36 00 98; www.aytojaca.es. Open July-Aug. M-F 9am-2pm and 4:30-8pm, Sa 9am-1:30pm and 5-8pm, Su 10am-1:30pm; Sept.-June M-F 9am-1:30pm and 4:30-7pm, Sa 10am-1pm and 5-7pm.) From the bus station, cross the park and head right past the church to the next plaza to find **Hostal Paris ❷**, San Pedro 5, one of the best deals in town. (☎974 36 10 20; www.jaca.com/hostalparis. July 15-Sept. 15 and *Semana Santa* singles €19; doubles €30; triples €41. Sept. 16-July 14 €18/28/38.) **Postal Code:** 22700.

NAVARRA

Bordered by Basque Country to the west and Aragón to the east, Navarra's villages—from the rustic Pyrenean pueblos on the French border to bustling Pamplona—are seldom visited apart from the festival of *San Fermines*, and greet non-bullrunning tourists with enthusiasm and open arms.

PAMPLONA (IRUÑA)   ☎948

While the lush parks, impressive museums, and medieval churches of Pamplona (pop. 200,000) await exploration, it's an annual, eight-minute event that draws visitors from around the world. Since the publication of Ernest Hemingway's *The Sun Also Rises*, hordes of travelers have come the week of July 6-14 to witness and experience *San Fermines*, the legendary "Running of the Bulls."

▐▐ TRANSPORTATION AND PRACTICAL INFORMATION. RENFE **trains** (☎902 24 02 02) run from off Av. San Jorge to Barcelona (6-8hr., 3-4 per day 12:25pm-12:55am, €29) and Madrid (5hr., 7:15am and 6:10pm, €35). **Buses** go from C. Conde Oliveto, at C. Yanguas y Miranda, to: Barcelona (5½hr.; 8:30am, 4:30pm, and 1am; €20); Bilbao (2hr., 4-6 per day 7am-7pm, €11); Madrid (5hr.; 4-7 per day M-Th and Sa 8am-7:30pm, F and Su 8am-9:30pm; €22); San Sebastián (1hr., 7-12 per day 7am-11pm, €5.50); and Zaragoza (2-3hr., 6-8 per day 7:15am-8:30pm, €11). From Pl. del Castillo, take C. San Nicolás, turn right on C. San Miguel, and walk through Pl. San Francisco to get to the **tourist office**, C. Hilarión Eslava 1. (☎948 20 65 40; www.cfnavarra.es. Open during *San Fermines* daily 8am-8pm; July-Aug. M-Sa 9am-8pm, Su 10am-2pm; Sept.-June M-F 10am-2pm and 4-7pm, Sa 10am-2pm.) During *San Fermines*, **store luggage** at the Escuelas de San Francisco, the big stone building at the end of Pl. San Francisco. (€2 per day. Open 24hr.) Check **email** at **Kuria.Net**, C. Curia 15. (€3 per hr. Open during *San Fermines* daily 9am-11pm; rest of year M-Sa 10am-10pm, Su 1-10pm.) **Postal Code:** 31001.

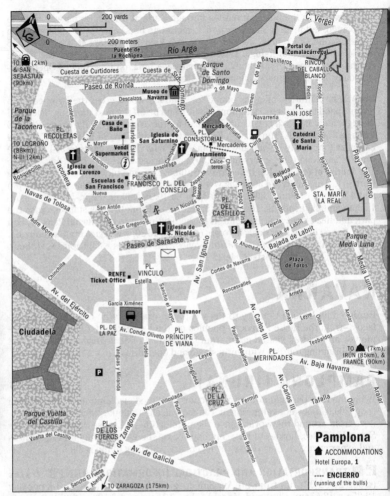

Pamplona

▲ **ACCOMMODATIONS**
Hotel Europa, **1**

---- **ENCIERRO**
(running of the bulls)

ACCOMMODATIONS AND FOOD. And now, a lesson in supply and demand: Smart *San Ferministas* take the bull by the horns and book their rooms up to a year (or at least two months) in advance to avoid paying rates up to four times higher than those listed here. Beware of hawkers at the train and bus stations—quality and prices vary tremendously. Check the newspaper *Diario de Navarra* for **casas particulares.** Many roomless folks are forced to fluff up their sweatshirts and sleep on the lawns of the Ciudadela or on Pl. de los Fueros, Pl. del Castillo, or the banks of the river. Be careful—if you can't store your backpack (storage fills fast), sleep on top of it. During the rest of the year, finding a room in Pamplona is no problem. Budget accommodations line C. San Nicolás and C. San Gregorio off Pl. del Castillo. **Hotel Europa ❺,** C. Espoz y Mina 11, off Pl. del Castillo, offers bright, luxurious rooms away from the noise of C. San Nicolás.

One good night's sleep is worth the price. Reservations are recommended, especially for *San Fermines*. (☎948 22 18 00. Year-round singles €65; doubles €74. MC/V.) To reach the impressive 18th-century mansion of **Pensión Santa Cecilia ❷**, C. Navarrería 17, follow C. Chapitela, take the first right onto C. Mercaderes, and make a sharp left. (☎948 22 22 30. *San Fermines* dorms €45. Otherwise singles €20; doubles €30; triples €35. MC/V.) To get to **Camping Ezcaba ❶** in Eusa, take city bus line 4-1 from Pl. de las Merindades (4 per day, €0.70). (☎948 33 03 15. *San Fermines* €9 per person, per tent, or per car. Otherwise €3.50 per person, per tent or per car. AmEx/MC/V.) Look for food near Pensión Santa Cecilia, above **Plaza San Francisco,** and around **Paseo Ronda.** Check out **Calles Navarrería** and **Paseo Sarasate** for *bocadillo* bars. **Vendi Supermarket,** at C. Hilarión Eslava and C. Mayor, has groceries. (Open M-F 9am-2pm and 5:30-7:30pm, Sa 9am-2pm.)

◎◪ SIGHTS AND NIGHTLIFE. Pamplona's rich architectural legacy is reason enough to visit during the 51 other weeks of the year. The restored 14th-century Gothic **cathedral** is at the end of C. Navarrería. (Open M-F 10am-1:30pm and 4-7pm, Sa 10am-1:30pm. Guided tours €4.) The walls of the pentagonal **Ciudadela** once humbled Napoleon; today the Ciudadela hosts free exhibits and summer concerts. Follow Po. Sarasate to its end, and take a right on Navas de Tolosa; take the next left onto C. Chinchilla, and follow it to its end. (Open M 9:30am-9:30pm; Su and Tu-Sa 7:30am-9:30pm. closed for *San Fermines*. Both free.) Throughout the year, **Plaza del Castillo** is the heart of the social scene. Hemingway's favorite haunt was the **Café-Bar Iruña,** immortalized in *The Sun Also Rises*. (*Menú* €10. Open M-Th 8am-11pm, F 8am-2pm, Sa 9am-2am, Su 9am-11pm.) A young crowd boozes up at bars in the *casco antiguo*, around **Calles de Jarauta, San Nicolás,** and **San Gregorio** before hitting the **Travesia de Bayona,** a plaza of bars and *discotecas* off Av. Bayona.

> **!** Although Pamplona is usually very safe, crime skyrockets during *San Fermines*. Beware of assaults and muggings, do not walk alone at night, and take care in the *casco antiguo*.

▦ LOS SAN FERMINES (JULY 6-14). Visitors overcrowd the city as Pamplona delivers an eight-day frenzy of parades, bullfights, parties, dancing, fireworks, concerts, and wine. Pamplonese, clad in white with red sashes and bandanas, literally throw themselves into the merry-making, displaying obscene levels of both physical stamina and tolerance for alcohol. The "Running of the Bulls," called the *encierro*, is the highlight of *San Fermines;* the first *encierro* takes place on July 7 at 8am and it's repeated at 8am every day for the next seven days. Hundreds of bleary-eyed, hungover, hyper-adrenalized runners flee from large bulls as bystanders cheer from barricades, windows, balconies, and doorways. Both the bulls and the mob are dangerous; terrified runners react without concern for those around them. Hemingway had the right idea: Don't run. Instead, arrive at the bullring around 6:45am to watch the *encierro*. Tickets for the Grada section of the ring are available before 7am (M-F €3.60, Sa-Su €4.20). You can watch for free, but the free section is overcrowded, making it hard to see and breathe. To participate in the bullring excitement, line up by the Pl. de Toros well before 7:30am and run in *before* the bulls are in sight. **Be very careful; follow the tourist office's guidelines for running.** To watch a bullfight, wait in the line that forms at the bullring around 8pm. As one fight ends, the next day's tickets (€15-70) go on sale. Once the running ends, insanity spills into the streets and gathers steam until nightfall, when it explodes with singing in bars, dancing in alleyways, spontaneous parades, and a no-holds-barred party in Pl. del Castillo, Europe's biggest open-air dance floor.

BASQUE COUNTRY (PAÍS VASCO)

Basque Country's varied landscape resembles a nation complete in itself, combining cosmopolitan cities, verdant hills, industrial wastelands, and quaint fishing villages. Many believe that the strongly nationalistic Basques are the native people of Iberia, as their culture and language cannot be traced to any known source.

SAN SEBASTIÁN (DONOSTIA)   ☎943

Glittering on the shores of the Cantabrian Sea, coolly elegant San Sebastián (pop. 180,000) is known for its world-famous beaches, bars, and scenery. Locals and travelers down *pintxos* (*tapas*) and drinks in the *parte vieja* (old city), which claims the most bars per square meter in the world. Residents and posters lend a constant reminder: You're not in Spain, you're in Basque Country.

▐ TRANSPORTATION

Trains: RENFE, Estación del Norte (☎902 24 02 02), on Po. Francia, on the east side of Puente María Cristina. Info office open daily 7am-11pm. To: **Barcelona** (9hr., Su-F 10:45am and 11pm, €33); **Madrid** (8hr., 3 per day, €41); **Zaragoza** (4hr., daily 10:45am, €19).

Buses: PESA, Av. Sancho el Sabio 33 (☎902 10 12 10), runs to **Bilbao** (1¼hr., every 30min., €7.50). **Continental Auto,** Av. Sancho el Sabio 31 (☎943 46 90 74), goes to **Madrid** (6hr., 7-9 per day, €25). **La Roncalesa,** Po. Vizcaya 16 (☎943 46 10 64), runs to **Pamplona** (1hr., 9 per day, €5.50). **Vibasa,** Po. Vizcaya 16 (☎943 45 75 00), goes to **Barcelona** (7hr., 3 per day, €23).

Taxis: Santa Clara (☎943 36 46 46), **Vallina** (☎943 40 40 40), or **Donostia** (☎943 46 46 46). Taxis to **Pamplona** take about 45min. and cost around €83.

◼◼ ◪ ORIENTATION AND PRACTICAL INFORMATION

The **Río Urumea** splits San Sebastián. The city center, most monuments, and the two most popular beaches, Playa de la Concha and Playa de Ondaretta, line the peninsula on the west side of the river. At the tip of the peninsula sits **Monte Urgull.** On the east side of the river, Playa de la Zurriola attracts a younger surfing and beach crowd. Inland lies the *parte vieja* (old city), San Sebastián's restaurant, nightlife, and budget accommodation nexus, where you'll find the most tourists. South of the *parte vieja*, at the base of the peninsula, is the commercial district. The **bus station** is south of the city center on Pl. Pío XII, while the RENFE **train station, Barrio de Gros,** and **Playa de la Zurriola** are across the river from the *parte vieja* east of the city. The river is spanned by four bridges: Puentes Zurriola, Santa Catalina, María Cristina, and de Mundaiz (listed north to south). To get to the *parte vieja* from the train station, head straight to Puente María Cristina, cross the bridge, and turn right at the fountain. Continue four blocks north to Av. Libertad, then take a left and follow it to the port; the *parte vieja* fans out to the right and Playa de la Concha sits to the left.

Tourist Office: Municipal: Centro de Atracción y Turismo, C. Reina Regente 3 (☎943 48 11 66; fax 943 48 11 72), in front of Puente de la Zurriola. From the train station, turn right immediately after crossing Puente María Cristina and continue until reaching Puente de la Zurriola; the office is on the left. From the bus station, follow Av. Sancho el Sabio. At Pl. Centenario, bear right onto C. Prim, follow the river until the 3rd bridge (Puente de la Zurriola), and look for the plaza on your left. Open June-Sept. Su 10am-2pm, M-Sa 8am-8pm; Oct.-May Su 10am-2pm, M-Sa 9am-1:30pm and 3:30-7pm.

Hiking Information: Izadi (☎943 29 35 20), C. Usandizaga 18, off C. Libertad. Sells hiking guides. Open M-F 10am-1pm and 4-8pm, Sa 10am-1:30pm and 4:30-8pm.

Luggage Storage: At the **train station.** €3 per day. Buy tokens at the ticket counter. Open daily 7am-11pm.

Laundromat: Lavomatique, C. Iñigo 14, off C. San Juan in the *parte vieja.* 4kg wash €3.80, dry €2.70. Open M-F 9:30am-2pm and 4-8pm, Sa-Su 10am-2pm.

Emergency: ☎ 112. **Municipal police:** C. Easo (☎943 45 00 00).

Medical Services: Casa de Socorro, Bengoetxea 4 (☎943 44 06 33).

Internet Access: Zarr@net, C. San Lorenzo 6 (☎943 43 33 81). €0.05 per min., €3 per hr. Also sells phone cards.

Post Office: Po. Francia 13 (☎943 44 68 26), near the RENFE station, just over the Santa Catalina bridge and to the right; look for the yellow trim on the left side of the street. Open M-F 8:30am-8:30pm, Sa 9:30am-2pm. **Postal Code:** 20006.

▗ ACCOMMODATIONS

Desperate backpackers will scrounge for rooms in July and August, particularly during *San Fermines* (July 6-14) and *Semana Grande* (starts Su the week of Aug. 15); September's film festival is just as booked. Budget options center in the *parte vieja* and by the cathedral. The tourist office has lists of accommodations and most hostel owners know of *casas particulares.*

THE PARTE VIEJA

▨ **Pensión Amaiur,** C. 31 de Agosto 44, 2nd fl. (☎943 42 96 54). From Alameda del Boulevard, follow C. San Jerónimo to its end, turn left. Friendly owner and uniquely decorated rooms. Internet €1 per 18min. July-Sept. and *Semana Santa* dorms €25; May-June and Oct. €22; Nov.-Apr. €18. MC/V. ❷

Pensión San Lorenzo, C. San Lorenzo 2 (☎943 42 55 16), off C. San Juan. Bright, sunny doubles with TV and refrigerator. July-Aug. doubles €45; June and Sept. €36; Oct.-May €24. ❷

Pensión Larrea, C. Narrica 21, 2nd fl. (☎943 42 26 94). Spend time with Mamá and Papá, as the friendly owners are often called, in this comfortable and welcoming *pensión.* July-Aug. singles €24; doubles €36; triples €50. Sept.-June €18/30/45. ❷

Hospedaje Alai, C. 31 de Agosto 16, 3rd fl. (☎943 42 48 06). Comfortable bunks and clean bathrooms. Closed Oct.-May. July-Aug. dorms €25; June and Sept. €12. ❶

Pensión Puerto, C. Puerto 19, 2nd fl. (☎943 43 21 40), off C. Mayor. Spotless rooms with comfy beds. July-Aug. singles €30; June and Sept. €20-22; Oct.-May €18. ❸

OUTSIDE THE PARTE VIEJA

Most of these places tend to be quieter but just as close to the port, beach, bus and train stations, and no more than 5min. from the *parte vieja.*

Pensión La Perla, C. Loyola 10, 2nd fl. (☎943 42 81 23), on the street directly ahead of the cathedral. English spoken. Private baths and TVs. July-Sept. singles €28-30; doubles €40. Oct.-June €24/32. ❸

S P A I N

Pensión Easo, C. San Bartolomé 24 (☎943 45 39 12; www.pension-easo.com). Head toward the beach on C. San Martín, turn left on C. Easo, and right on C. San Bartolomé. July-Sept. 15 singles €33, with bath €49; doubles €42/61. June and Sept. 15-30 singles €27/40; doubles €33/45. Oct.-May singles €25/33; doubles €30/40. ❸

Pensión Urkia, C. Urbieta 12, 3rd fl. (☎943 42 44 36), located on C. Urbieta between C. Marcial and C. Arrasate. Borders the Mercado de San Martín. All rooms with bath. July-Sept. singles €25; doubles €43; triples €60. Oct.-June €22/30/45. ❸

Pensión Añorga, C. Easo 12 (☎943 46 79 45), at C. San Martín. Shares entryway with 2 other *pensiones*. Spacious rooms have wood floors and comfy beds. July-Aug. singles €25; doubles €34, with bath €43. Sept.-June singles €19; doubles €25/32. ❷

Albergue Juvenil la Sirena (HI), Po. Igueldo 25 (☎943 31 02 68), at the far west end of the city. Take bus #24 or 27 to Av. Zumalacárregui; from there, take Av. Brunet and turn left at its end. Clean rooms, multilingual staff. Breakfast included. Curfew Sept.-May Su-Th midnight, F-Sa 2am. July-Aug. €15, under-25 €13. May 6-Jun. 7 and Apr. 8-31 €12/14. Oct.-Mar. €12/13-15. MC/V. Members only. ❶

🔋 FOOD

Pintxos (*tapas*; around €1.50 each), chased down with the fizzy regional white wine *txacoli*, are a religion here; bars in the *parte vieja* spread an array of enticing tidbits on bread. The entire *parte vieja* seems to exist for no other purpose than to feed. The chef at ▨**Kursaal** ❷, Po. Zurriola 1, is a legend among locals; enjoy an elegant lunch on the breezy, outdoor patio. (*Menú* €13-16.) ▨**Arrai Txiki** ❶, C. del Campanario 3, cooks up delicious, healthy cuisine, including an array of vegetarian options, in a simple, elegant setting. (Entrees €3-6. Open Su-M and W-Sa 1-4pm and 8-11pm.) **Mercado de la Bretxa,** Alameda del Boulevard at C. San Juan, sells fresh produce. (Open M-Sa 9am-9pm.) **Super Todo Todo,** Alameda del Boulevard 3, across the street from the Mercado de la Brexta, also sells groceries. (Open M-Sa 8:30am-9pm, Su 10am-2pm.)

🔲🔋 SIGHTS AND BEACHES

San Sebastián's most attractive sight is the city itself, with its green walks, grandiose buildings, and placid bay. The views from ▨**Monte Igueldo,** west of the center, are the best in town: by day, the countryside meets the ocean in a line of white and blue, and by night the flood-lit **Isla Santa Clara** seems to float on a ring of light. The walk up the mountain is along a narrow road; you're better off taking the funicular (€0.85). Across the bay from Monte Igueldo, the gravel paths on **Monte Urgull** wind through shady woods, monuments, and stunning vistas. The overgrown **Castillo de Santa Cruz de la Mota** tops the summit with 12 cannons, a chapel, and the statue of the *Sagrado Corazón de Jesús* blessing the city. (Open May-Sept. daily 8am-8pm; Oct.-Apr. 8am-6pm.) Directly below the hill, on Po. Nuevo in the *parte vieja*, the serene **Museo de San Telmo** resides in a Dominican monastery strewn with Basque funerary relics, and the main museum beyond the cloister displays a fascinating array of pre-historic Basque artifacts, a few dinosaur skeletons, and a piece of contemporary art. (Open Su 10:30am-2pm, Tu-Sa 10:30am-8:30pm. Free.) The gorgeous **Playa de la Concha** curves from the port to the **Pico del Loro,** the beak-shaped promontory home to the Palacio de Miramar. The virtually flat beach disappears during high tide. Sunbathing crowds jam onto the smaller and steeper **Playa de Ondarreta,** beyond the Palacio de Miramar, and surfers flock to **Playa de la Zurriola,** across the river from Mt. Urguel. **Picnickers** head for the alluring Isla de Santa Clara in the center of the bay, either by rented rowboat or public motorboat ferry (5min., June-Sept. every 30min., round-trip €2).

🎵 🎭 ENTERTAINMENT AND NIGHTLIFE

For info on **theater** and special events, pick up the weekly *Kalea* (€1.40) from tobacco stands or newsstands. The *parte vieja* pulls out all the stops in July and August, particularly on **Calle Fermín Calbetón,** three blocks in from Alameda del Boulevard. During the year, when students outnumber backpackers, nightlife tends to move beyond the *parte vieja*. Keep an eye out for discount coupons on the street. **Ostadar,** C. Fermín Calbetón 13, attracts locals and tourists alike with its happening dance mix. (Beer €1.80. Mixed drinks €4.50.) **Zibbibo,** Pl. Sarriegi 8, is a hip club with a dance floor and a blend of hits and techno. (Open daily 2pm-4am.) **Akerbeltz,** C. Koruko Andra Mari 9, is a sleek, local bar. (Open M-Th 3pm-2:30am, F-Sa 3pm-3:30am.)

BILBAO (BILBO) ☎944

Bilbao (pop. 370,000) is a city transformed; what was once industry is now new, avant-garde, and futuristic. 20th-century success showered the city with a new subway system, a new bridge, a stylish riverwalk, and other additions designed by renowned international architects. But above all else, the shining Guggenheim Museum has most powerfully fueled Bilbao's rise to international prominence.

🏛 🛈 TRANSPORTATION AND PRACTICAL INFORMATION. Trains (☎902 24 02 02) arrive at the Estación de Abando del Norte, Pl. Circular 2, from Barcelona (9-11hr., Su-F 10:45pm, €43); Madrid (6-9hr., Su-F 4:30 and 8:45pm, €38); and Salamanca (5½hr., 2pm, €24). From Pl. Circular, head right around the station and cross Puente del Arenal to reach Pl. Arriaga, the entrance to the *casco viejo* and Pl. Nueva. Most **bus** companies leave from the Termibús terminal, C. Gurtubay 1 (☎944 39 50 77; M: San Mamés), on the west side of town, for: Barcelona (7¼hr., 4 per day, €35); Madrid (4-5hr.; M-F 10-18 per day, Su 2 per day; €23); Pamplona (2hr., 4-6 per day, €11); and San Sebastián (1¼hr., every hr., €8). The **tourist office** is on C. Rodriguez Arias 3. (☎944 79 57 60; www.bilbao.net. Open M-F 9am-2pm and 4-7:30pm, Sa 9am-2pm, Su 10am-2pm.) Surf the **Internet** at **Ciberteca,** C. José Maria Escuza 23, on the corner of C. Simón Bolívar. (€.60 per 10min., €2.10 per hr. Open M-Th 8am-10pm, F-Sa 8am-midnight, Su 10am-10pm.) **Postal Code:** 48008.

🛏 🍴 ACCOMMODATIONS AND FOOD. During **Semana Grande** (Aug. 17-25) rates are higher than those listed below. **Plaza Arriaga** and **Calle Arenal** have budget accommodations galore, while upscale hotels line the river or are in the new city off **Gran Vía.** Large rooms with private bath and A/C are available at **Hotel Arriaga ❹,** C. Ribera 3. (☎944 79 00 01; fax 79 05 16. Singles €39; doubles €60; triples €72. AmEx/V.) To reach **Pensión Méndez ❷,** C. Santa María 13, 4th fl., take C. Bidebbarrieta from Puente del Arenal; after two blocks, take a right onto C. Perro, then turn right on C. Santa María. Rooms are insulated from the raging nightlife below. (☎944 16 03 64. Singles €25; doubles €33.) To get to **Pensión Ladero ❷,** C. Lotería 1, 4th fl., from Puente del Arenal, take C. Corre; after three blocks, take a right onto C. Lotería. This *pensión* has modern common bathrooms and winter heating. (☎944 15 09 32. Singles €18; doubles €30.) **Restaurante Vegetariano Garibolo ❷,** C. Fernández del Campo 7, serves creative vegetarian meals. (*Menú* €9.75. Open M-Sa 1-4pm. MC/V.) **Mercado de la Ribera,** on the bank of the river in the *casco viejo*, is the biggest indoor market in Spain. (Open M-Th and Sa 8am-2:30pm; F 8am-2:30pm and 4:30-7:30pm.) Pick up groceries at **Champión,** Pl. Santos Juanes. (Open M-Sa 9am-9:30pm.)

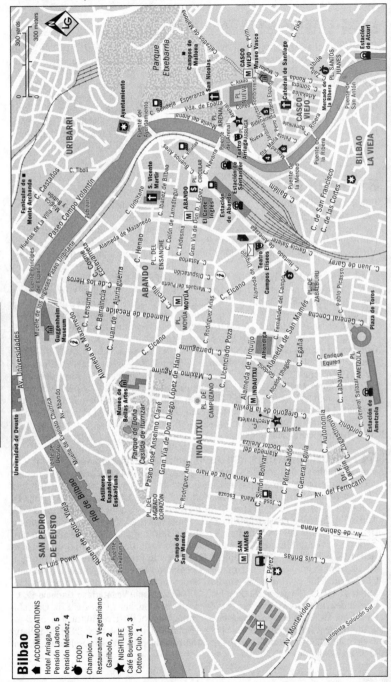

Bilbao

▲ ACCOMMODATIONS
Hotel Arriaga, 6
Pensión Ladero, 5
Pensión Méndez, 4

🍴 FOOD
Champion, 7
Restaurante Vegetariano
Garibolo, 2

★ NIGHTLIFE
Café Boulevard, 3
Cotton Club, 1

◎ ♫ **SIGHTS AND ENTERTAINMENT.** Frank O. Gehry's ⊠**Guggenheim Museum Bilbao,** Av. Abandoibarra 2, can only be described as breathtaking. Lauded by the international press, it has catapulted Bilbao into cultural stardom. The building's undulating curves of glistening titanium, limestone, and glass resemble an iridescent scaly fish. The museum currently hosts rotating exhibits culled from the Guggenheim Foundation's collection. (☎944 35 90 00; www.guggenheim-bilbao.es. Open July-Aug. daily 10am-8pm; Sept.-June Tu-Su 10am-8pm. €10, students €4.20. Under-12 free. Guided tours in English Tu-Su 11am, 12:30, 4:30, and 6:30pm. Sign up 30min. before tour at the info desk. Audio tour €3.70.) The often overshadowed **Museo de Bellas Artes,** Pl. Museo 2, hordes an impressive collection of 12th- to 21st-century art, including works by Gauguin and Picasso. To get there, take C. Elcano to Pl. Museo, or bus #10 from Puente del Arenal. (Open Tu-Sa 10am-8pm, Su 10am-2pm. €4.50, students €3. Under-12 free and W free.)

Revelers spill into the streets of *casco viejo*, especially on **Calle Barrenkalea.** A young crowd parties along **Calle Licenciado Poza** on the west side of town. For a more mellow scene, people-watch at the elegant 19th-century **Café Boulevard,** C. Arenal 3. **The Cotton Club,** C. Gregorio de la Revilla 25, decorated with over 30,000 beer caps, draws a huge crowd on Friday and Saturday nights. (Open M-Th 4:30pm-3am, F-Sa 6:30pm-6am, Su 6:30pm-3am.) The massive blowout fiesta in honor of *Nuestra Señora de Begoña* takes place during **Semana Grande,** a nine-day party beginning the Saturday after August 15.

▶ **DAYTRIP FROM BILBAO: GUERNICA (GERNIKA).** Founded in 1366, Guernica (pop. 15,600) long served as the ceremonial seat of the Basque country. On April 26, 1937, the Nazi "Condor Legion" released an estimated 29,000kg of explosives on Guernica, obliterating 70% of the city in three hours. The nearly 2000 people who were killed in the bombings were immortalized in Pablo Picasso's stark masterpiece *Guernica*, now in Madrid's Museo Reina Sofía (see p. 918). **Trains** (☎902 543 210; www.euskotren.es) roll in from Bilbao (45min., every 45min., €2). To reach the **tourist office,** C. Artekalea 8, from the train station, walk two blocks up C. Adolfo Urioste and turn right on C. Barrenkalea. Turn left at the alleyway; the office will be on your right. (☎946 25 58 92; www.gernika-lumo.net. Open July-Sept. M-Sa 10am-7pm, Su 10am-2pm; Oct.-June M-Sa 10am-2pm and 4-7pm, Su 10am-2pm.) The office can direct you to several memorial sites, including the newly renovated ⊠**Gernika Peace Museum,** Pl. Foru 1, which features an exhibition chronicling the bombardment. **Postal Code:** 48300.

BALEARIC ISLANDS

Every year, discos, ancient history, and beaches—especially beaches—draw nearly two million of the hippest Europeans to the *Islas Baleares*.

▛ **TRANSPORTATION**

Flights are the easiest way to get to the islands. Those under 26 often get discounts from **Iberia** (☎902 40 05 00; www.iberia.com), which flies to Palma de Mallorca and Ibiza from Barcelona (40min., €60-120) and Madrid (1hr., €150-180). **Air Europa** (☎902 24 00 42; www.air-europa.com) and **SpanAir** (☎902 13 14 15; www.span-air.com) offer budget flights to and between the islands. Most cheap round-trip **charters** include a week's stay in a hotel; some companies called *mayoristas* sell leftover spots on package-tour flights as "seat-only" deals.

Ferries to the islands are less popular. **Trasmediterránea** (☎902 45 46 45; www.trasmediterranea.com) departs from Barcelona's Estació Marítima Moll and Valencia's Estació Marítima for Mallorca, Menorca, and Ibiza (€38-58). **Buquebus** (☎902 41 42 42) goes from Barcelona to Palma (4hr., 2 per day, €49). Between islands, **ferries** are the most cost-efficient way to travel. **Trasmediterránea** (see above) sails from Palma to Mahón (6½hr., Su only, €23) and Ibiza (2½hr., 7am daily, €37). **Car** rental costs about €36 per day, **mopeds** €18, and **bikes** €6-10.

MALLORCA   ☎971

A favorite of Spain's royal family, Mallorca has been popular with the in-crowd since Roman times. Lemon groves and olive trees adorn the jagged cliffs of the northern coast, and lazy beaches sink into calm bays to the east. The capital of the Balearics, **Palma** (pop. 323,000) embraces conspicuous consumption and pleases with its well-preserved old quarter, colonial architecture, and local flavor.

The tourist office (see below) distributes a list of over 40 nearby **beaches**, many a mere bus ride away; one popular choice is **El Arenal** (*Platja de Palma;* bus #15), 11km southeast of town toward the airport. When the sun sets, **La Bodeguita del Medio,** C. Vallseca 18, keeps its crowd dancing to Cuban rhythms. (Open Su-W 8pm-1am, Th-Sa 8pm-3am.) Follow the Aussie accents down C. Apuntadores to the popular **Bar Latitude 39,** C. Felip Bauza 8, a self-proclaimed "yachtie" bar. (Open M-Sa 7pm-3am.) Palma's clubbers start their night in the *bares-musicales* lining the **Paseo Marítimo** strip; try salsa-happy **Made in Brasil,** Po. Marítimo 27 (open daily 8pm-4am) or dance-crazy **Salero,** Po. Marítimo 31 (open daily 8pm-6am). The bars and clubs around **El Arenal** overflow with fashion-conscious German disco-fiends, but braving them is well worth the price at **Riu Palace,** one block from the beach. (Cover €15, includes unlimited free drinks. Open daily 10pm-6:30am.) When the bar scene fades at 3am, partiers migrate to Palma's *discotecas.* **Tito's Palace,** Po. Marítimo, is the city's hippest disco. (Cover €15-18. Open daily 11pm-6am.)

From the airport, take bus #1 to **Plaza Espanya** (15min., every 20min., €1.80). To reach the **tourist office,** C. Sant Dominic 11, from Pl. Reina, take C. Conquistador to C. Sant Dominic. (☎971 72 40 90. Open M-F 9am-8pm, Sa 9am-1:30pm.) **Branches** are in Pl. Reina and the Pl. Espanya. **Hostal Cuba ❷,** C. San Magí 1, offers spotless rooms with high ceilings and wood furniture. From Pl. Joan Carles I, turn left and walk down Av. Jaume III, cross the river, and turn left on C. Argentina; the hostel is several blocks down. (☎971 73 81 59. Singles €20; doubles €36.) **Hostal Apuntadores ❶,** C. Apuntadores 8, is in the middle of the action, less than a block from Pl. Reina. (☎971 71 34 91. Dorms €14; singles €25; doubles €33.) Those on a budget tend to head to the side streets off **Passeig Born,** to the cheap cafes along **Avenida Joan Miró,** or to the carbon-copy pizzerias along **Paseo Marítimo.** For groceries, try **Servicio y Precios,** on C. Felip Bauzá. (Open M-F 8:30am-8:30pm, Sa 9am-2pm.)

IBIZA   ☎971

Perhaps nowhere on Earth does style rule over substance (or substances over style) more than on the island of Ibiza (pop. 84,000). Once a 60s hippie enclave, Ibiza has long abandoned her roots for new-age decadence. None of Ibiza's beaches is within quick walking distance of **Eivissa** (Ibiza City), but **Platja de Talamanca, Platja des Duros, Platja d'en Bossa,** and **Platja Figueredes** are at most a 20min. bike ride away; buses also leave from Av. Isidor Macabich 20 for Platja d'en Bossa (every 30min., €0.75). One of the most beautiful beaches near Eivissa is **Playa de Las Salinas,** where the nude sunbathers are almost as perfect as the crystal-blue water and silky sand. The crowds return from the beaches by nightfall, arriving at the largest party on Earth. The bar scene centers around **Calle Barcelona,** while **Calle Virgen** is the center of gay nightlife. The island's █**discos** (virtually all a mixed gay/straight crowd) are world-famous. Refer to *Ministry in Ibiza* or *DJ*, free at many hostels, bars, and restaurants, for a full list of nightlife options. The **Discobus** runs to and from all the major hot spots (leaves Eivissa from A. Isidoro Macabich every hr. 12:30am-6:30am; schedule available at tourist office and hotels. €1.50). According to the Guinness Book of World Records, wild ■**Privilege** is the world's largest club. It can fit up to 10,000 bodies, has more than a few bars, and is the place to be Monday nights. (Cover from €40. Open June-Sept. daily midnight-7am.) At **Amnesia**, on the road to San Antonio, you can forget who you are and who you came with. (Foam parties W and Su; cream and MTV parties Th. Cover from €40. Open daily midnight-7am.) Elegant **Pachá**, on Pg. Perimitral, is a 15min. walk or a 2min. cab ride from the port. (Cover €50. Open daily midnight-7:30am.) Cap off your night in **Space**, which starts hopping around 8am, peaks mid-afternoon, and doesn't wind down until 5pm. (Cover €30-40.)

The local paper *Diario de Ibiza* (www.diariodeibiza.es; €0.75) features an *Agenda* page with everything you need to know about Ibiza. The **tourist office**, C. Antoni Riquer 2, is on the water. (☎971 30 19 00. Open M-F 9:30am-1:30pm and 5-7:30pm, Sa 10:30am-1pm.) Email friends about your crazy night while washing the beer out of your clothes at **Wash and Dry**, Av. España 53. (☎971 39 48 22. Wash and dry €4.20 each. Internet €5.40 per hr. Open M-F 10am-3pm and 5-10pm, Sa 10am-5pm.) The letters **"CH"** *(casa de huespedes)* mark many doorways; call the owners at the phone number on the door. **Hostal Residencia Sol y Brisa ❷**, Av. B. V. Ramón 15, parallel to Pg. Vara de Rey, has clean rooms, a central location, and a social atmosphere. (☎971 31 08 18; fax 30 30 32. Singles €24; doubles €42.) **Hostal La Marina ❸**, Puerto de Ibiza, C. Barcelona 7, is across from Estació Marítima, right in the middle of a raucous bar scene. (☎971 31 01 72. Singles €30-62; doubles €41-150.) **Hostal Residencia Ripoll ❸** is at C. Vicente Cuervo 14. (☎971 31 42 75. July-Sept. singles €30; doubles €42; 3-person apartments with patio, kitchen, and TV €78.) For a supermarket, try **Spar**, on the corner of C. d'Avicenna and Pl. des Parc. (Open M-Sa 9am-9pm.)

MENORCA   ☎971

Menorca's (pop. 72,000) 200km coastline of raw beaches, rustic landscapes, and well-preserved ancient monuments draws ecologists, photographers, and wealthy young families. Unfortunately for those on a budget, the island's unique qualities and ritzy patrons have resulted in elevated prices. Atop a

THE LOCAL LEGEND

PRELUDE TO A BREAKUP

Two of Mallorca's most famous vacationers were the Polish composer Frédéric Chopin and his lover, French novelist George Sand, who visited during the winter of 1838-39. Though intended to be a honeymoon of sorts, the excursion was doomed from the outset. Chopin, suffering from tuberculosis, was constantly in pain and prone to black moods. Sand, a passionate free-thinker, felt trapped on the island. The presence of the couple, along with Sand's two children from a previous marriage, caused a stir among the townsfolk, who tormented them through the windows of cells #2 and 4 of the Cartoixa Real, where they stayed. Sand documents these incidents in her book *Un Hiver a Majorque* (A Winter in Mallorca), referring to the local villagers as "barbarians and monkeys." Despite (or because of) the less than ideal circumstances, Chopin produced some of his greatest pieces while on the island. At the winter's end the two realized their personalities were too divergent for the relationship to last. In February of 1839, they boarded the same ship which had taken them to Mallorca less than four months before and, once on the Spanish mainland, parted forever.

steep bluff, **Mahón** (pop. 25,000) is the main gateway to the island. The popular **beaches** outside Mahón are accessible by bus. Transportes Menorca **buses** leave from C. Josep M. Quadrado for ■**Platges de Son Bou** (6 per day, €1.80), which offers 4km of gorgeous beaches on the southern shore. Autocares Fornells buses leave C. Vasallo in Mahón for the breathtaking views of sandy **Arenal d'en Castell** (30 min., 3-5 per day, €1.70), while TMSA buses go to touristy **Cala'n Porter** (7 per day, €1.10) and its whitewashed houses, orange stucco roofs, and red sidewalks. A 10min. walk away, the ■ **Covas d'en Xoroi,** caves residing on cliffs high above the sea, are inhabited by a network of bars during the day, and a popular disco at night. (Bar cover €5, includes one drink. Open Apr.-Oct. daily 10:30am-9pm. Disco cover €15. Open daily 11pm-late.)

The **tourist office** is at Sa Rovellada de Dalt 24. (☎971 36 37 90. Open M-F 9am-1:30pm and 5-7pm, Sa 9am-1pm.) **Posada Orsi ❷** is at C. de la Infanta 19; from Pl. s'Esplanada, take C. Moreres, which becomes C. Hannover; turn right at Pl. Constitució, and follow C. Nou through Pl. Reial. (☎971 36 47 51. Breakfast included. Singles €15-21; doubles €26-35, with shower €30-42.) To get to **Hostal La Isla ❷**, C. de Santa Catalina 4, take C. Concepció from Pl. Miranda. (☎/fax 971 36 64 92. Singles €25; doubles €40.)

NORTHWESTERN SPAIN

Northwestern Spain is the country's best-kept secret; its seclusion is half its charm. Rainy **Galicia** hides mysterious Celtic ruins, and on the northern coast tiny **Asturias** allows access to the dramatic Picos de Europa mountain range.

GALICIA (GALIZA)

If, as the Galician saying goes, "rain is art," then there is no gallery more beautiful than the Northwest's misty skies. Often veiled in silvery drizzle, it is a province of fern-laden eucalyptus woods, slate-roofed fishing villages, and endless white beaches. Locals speak *gallego,* a linguistic hybrid of Castilian and Portuguese.

SANTIAGO DE COMPOSTELA   ☎981

Santiago (pop. 140,000) has long drawn pilgrims eager to gaze at one of Christianity's holiest cities. The cathedral marks the end of the *Camino de Santiago*, a pilgrimage believed to halve one's time in purgatory. Today, sunburnt pilgrims, street musicians, and hordes of tourists fill the streets.

■**7** **TRANSPORTATION AND PRACTICAL INFORMATION. Trains** (☎981 52 02 02) run from R. Hórreo to Madrid (8hr.; M-F 1:45 and 10:25pm, Sa 10:30pm, Su 9:45am, 1:45, and 10:30pm; €36). A schedule is printed daily in *El Correo Gallego*. To reach the city, take bus #6 to Pr. Galicia or walk up the stairs across the parking lot from the main entrance, cross the street, and bear right onto R. Hórreo, which leads to Pr. Galicia. **Buses** (☎981 58 77 00) run from R. de Rodríguez (20min. from downtown) to: Bilbao (11¼hr., 9am and 9:30pm, €39); Madrid (8-9hr., 4 per day, €31); and San Sebastián (13½hr., 8am and 5:30pm, €44). From the station, take bus #10 to Pr. Galicia. The **tourist office** is at R. do Vilar 43. (☎981 58 40 81. Open M-F 10am-2pm and 4-7pm, Sa 11am-2pm and 5-7pm, Su 11am-2pm.) Check **email** at **CyberNova 50,** R. Nova 50. (9am-10pm €1.20 per hr., 10pm-1am €1 per hr. Open daily 9am-1am.) **Postal code:** 15701.

🏠🍴 ACCOMMODATIONS AND FOOD. Nearly every street in the *ciudad vieja* houses at least one or two *pensiónes*. **Rúa Vilar** and **Rúa da Raíña** are the liveliest and most popular streets. 🏠**Hospedaje Ramos ❶**, R. da Raíña 18, 2nd fl., above **O Papa Una** restaurant, is in the center of the *ciudad vieja*. (☎981 58 18 59. Singles €14; doubles €25.) **Hospedaje Santa Cruz ❷**, R. Vilar 42, 2nd fl., is close to a myriad of bars and restaurants. (☎981 58 28 15. Singles €15; doubles €25, with bath €40.) Renovated in 2003, **Hostal Barbantes ❸**, Pr. de Fonseca 5, lets big rooms, each with bath. (☎981 57 65 20. Singles €40; doubles €60.) **Hospedaja Fonseca ❶**, R. de Fonseca 1, 2nd fl., offers colorful, sunny rooms with kitchen, TV, and winter heating. (☎981 57 24 79. Singles €12-15; doubles €24-30; triples €36-45; quads €48-60.) Take bus #6 or 9 to get to **Camping As Cancelas ❶**, R. 25 de Xullo 35, 2km from the cathedral on the northern edge of town. (☎981 58 02 66. €4.40 per person, €4.70 per car or per tent.) Bars and cafeterias line the streets, offering a variety of inexpensive *menús;* most restaurants are on R. do Vilar, R. do Franco, R. Nova, and R. da Raíña. Santiago's **market**, between Pl. San Felix and Convento de San Augustín, is a sight of its own right. (Open M-Sa 7:30am-2pm.) **Supermercado Lorenzo Froiz**, Pl. do Toural, is one block from Pr. de Galicia. (Open M-Sa 9am-3pm and 4:30-9pm, Sa 9am-3pm and 5-9pm.)

🎯🎭 SIGHTS AND NIGHTLIFE. Santiago's cathedral has four facades, each a masterpiece from a different era, with entrances opening to four different plazas: Praterías, Quintana, Obradoiro, and Inmaculada. The southern **Praza das Praterías** is the oldest of the facades; the Baroque **Obradoiro** encases the Maestro Mateo's **Pórtico de la Gloria,** considered the crowning achievement of Spanish Romanesque sculpture. The remains of **St. James** (Santiago) lie beneath the high altar in a silver coffer. Inside the **museum** are gorgeous 16th-century tapestries and two poignant statues of the pregnant Virgin Mary. (Cathedral open daily 7am-7pm. Museum open June-Sept. M-Sa 10am-1:30pm and 4-7:30pm, Su 10am-1:30pm; Mar.-June M-Sa 10:30am-1:30pm and 4-6:30pm, Su 10:30am-1:30pm; Oct.-Feb. M-Sa 11am-1pm and 4-6pm, Su 11am-1pm. Museum and cloisters €5, students €3.) Those curious about the Camino de Santiago can head to the 🏠**Museo das Peregrinacións,** Pl. de San Miguel Dos Agros. (Open Su 10:30am-1:30pm, Tu-F 10am-8pm, Sa 10:30am-1:30pm and 5-8pm. In most of summer free. Off-season €2.40.)

NO WORK, ALL PLAY

HOLD YOUR HORSES

Over 100,000 wild horses inhabit the Galician hills, where they have roamed for nearly 4000 years. Once used as cart-pullers, few are domesticated today. Still, the age-old branding rituals are celebrated each July during *A Rapa das Bestas* ("The Shearing of the Beasts").

"Here, we fight horses for tradition," says one rider, a sweaty, blood-speckled bandana across his hairline. The blood may not be his; for the past two hours he's straddled, head-locked, tail-pulled, herd-surfed, tackled, branded, been kicked and bitten, and—most importantly—sheared numerous feisty steeds. The struggle between man and beast is central to Spanish culture, most famously (and controversially) played out between matador and bull. *A Rapa* gives a new face to the traditional dynamic.

Before the festivities begin, Galician men comb the mountains and valleys gathering wild horses. Then, brave souls, wielding scissors, fight their way into the writhing sea of animals, wrestle one horse at a time to submission, and send thick crops of shiny hair flying to the ground—to be collected later by children as souvenirs.

At night, crowds looking for post-pilgrimage consumption flood cellars throughout the city. Take R. Montero Ríos to the bars and clubs off **Praza Roxa** to party with local students. ◨**Casa oas Crechas,** Vía Sacra 3, just off Pr. da Quintana, is a smoky pub with a witchcraft theme. (Beer €2. Open daily 4pm-2am or later.) **Xavestre,** R. de San Paolo de Antaltares 31, is packed with 20-somethings. (Mixed drinks €5. Open daily 11am-late.) Students dance the night away at **La Quintana Cafe,** Pr. da Quintana 1. (Beer €3-5. Mixed drinks €4. Open daily 10am-late.)

◨ **DAYTRIP FROM SANTIAGO: O CASTRO DE BAROÑA.** South of the town of **Noia** is a little-known treasure of historical intrigue and mesmerizing natural beauty: The seaside remains of the 5th-century Celtic fortress of ◨**O Castro de Baroña.** Its foundations dot the isthmus, ascending to a rocky promontory above the sea and then descending to a crescent **beach,** where clothing is optional. Castromil **buses** from Santiago to Muros stop in Noia (1hr.; M-F 15 per day, Sa 12 per day, Su 8 per day; €3) and Hefsel buses from Noia to Riveira stop at O Castro—tell the driver your destination (30min.; M-F 14 per day, Sa 7 per day, Su 11 per day; €1.30).

ASTURIAS

Spaniards call the tiny land of Asturias a *paraíso natural* (natural paradise). Surrounded by centuries of civilization, its impenetrable peaks and dense alpine forests have remained untouched. Unlike the rest of the country, travelers don't come here to see the sights; they come here to brave them.

PICOS DE EUROPA

This mountain range is home to **Picos de Europa National Park,** the largest national park in Europe. The most popular trails and peaks lie near the **Cares Gorge** (Garganta del Cares). For a list of mountain *refugios* (cabins with bunks but no blankets) and general park info, contact the **Picos de Europa National Park Visitors' Center** in Cangas de Onís. (☎/fax 985 84 86 14. Open May-Sept. M-F 9am-2pm and 5-6:30pm, Sa 9am-2pm and 4-6:30pm, Su 9am-2:30pm; Oct.-Apr. M-Sa 9am-2pm and 4-6:30pm, Su 9am-2:30pm.)

CANGAS DE ONÍS. During the summer months the streets of Cangas (pop. 6,285) are packed with mountaineers and vacationing families looking to spelunk and hang glide in the Picos de Europa National Park. Cangas itself is, if not particularly thrilling, a relaxing town rich in history. The **tourist office,** Jardines del Ayuntamiento 2, is just off Av. de Covadonga, across from the bus stop. (☎985 84 80 05. Open May-Sept. daily 10am-10pm; Oct.-Apr. 10am-2pm and 4-7pm.) ALSA, Av. de Covadonga 18 (☎985 84 81 33), in the Pícaro Inmobiliario building across from the tourist office, runs **buses** to Madrid (7hr., 2:35pm, €26) via Valladolid (5hr., 2 per day, €145).

SWEDEN
(SVERIGE)

Described by a former prime minister as *folkhemmet* ("the people's home"), Sweden has a strong sense of national solidarity and a warm culture that is welcoming to travelers. The Swedish concept of *lagom* ("moderation") implies that life should be lived somewhere between wealth and poverty—in the 20th century, this ideal was translated into a successful experiment with egalitarian socialism that is still in place today. For many, Sweden's greatest draw is its striking landscape, stretching from the mountainous Arctic reaches of northern Lapland to the flat farmland and white beaches of Skåne and Småland in the south. Dalarna, Värmland, and Norrland evoke images of quiet woods and rustic Midsummer celebrations, while the capital city of Stockholm shines as a cosmopolitan center.

FACTS AND FIGURES

Official Name: Kingdom of Sweden.
Capital: Stockholm.
Major Cities: Gothenburg, Malmö.
Population: 8,876,000.

Land Area: 411,000 sq. km.
Time Zone: GMT +1.
Language: Swedish.
Religions: Lutheran (87%).

DISCOVER SWEDEN

The natural starting point for any tour of Sweden is the vibrant chain of islands that constitutes **Stockholm** (p. 989), arguably one of the most attractive capitals in Europe. Leave time to visit **Skärgård** (p. 998), the city's lovely archipelago, and the nearby university town of **Uppsala** (p. 998). The island of **Gotland** (p. 1000), in the Baltic Sea, invites travelers to bike and camp amid its timeless landscape, medieval sites, and gorgeous beaches. In the south, **Malmö** and **Lund**'s (p. 1003) intimate cafes, student-driven nightlife and eclectic cultural mix attract a young crowd. On the west coast, Sweden's second-largest city, **Gothenburg** (p. 1004), counterbalances the capital's fast-paced atmosphere with a laid-back attitude and elegant cafe culture. In **Kiruna** in **Lapland** (p. 1009), you can explore Sami culture and vast stretches of Arctic wilderness.

ESSENTIALS

WHEN TO GO

The best time to visit Sweden is in the summer, when temperatures average 20°C (68°F) in the south and 16°C (61°F) in the north. If you go in winter, bring heavy cold-weather gear; temperatures are frequently below -5°C (23°F). The midnight sun is best seen between early June and mid-July.

DOCUMENTS AND FORMALITIES

VISAS. South Africans need a visa for stays of any length. Citizens of Australia, Canada, the EU, New Zealand, and the US do not need a visa for stays of up to 90 days, but this three-month period begins upon entry into any Nordic country; for more than 90 days in any combination of Denmark, Finland, Iceland, Norway, and/or Sweden, you will need a visa.

EMBASSIES AND CONSULATES. Foreign embassies in Sweden are in Stockholm (p. 989). Swedish embassies at home include: **Australia,** 5 Turrana St., Yarralumla, Canberra, ACT 2600 (☎ 62 70 27 00; www.embassyofsweden.org.au); **Canada,** 377 Dalhousie St., Ottawa, ON K1N 9N8 (☎ 613-241-8553; www.swedishembassy.ca);

Ireland, 12-17 Dawson St., Dublin 2 (☎671 58 22; www.swedishembassy.ie); **New Zealand,** P.O. Box 12538, Wellington (☎04 499 98 95); **South Africa,** P.O. Box 13477, Hatfield, 0028 (☎12 426 64 00; sweden@iafrica.com); **UK,** 11 Montagu Pl., London W1H 2AL (☎020 79 17 64 00; www.swedish-embassy.org.uk); and **US,** 1501 M St. NW, Washington, D.C. 20005 (☎202-467-2600; www.swedish-embassy.org).

TRANSPORTATION

BY PLANE. Most international flights land in Stockholm, although domestic flights also connect to northern Sweden. **Scandinavian Airlines** (SAS; ☎(08) 797 4000; www.scandinavian.net) offers youth fares (ages 12-25) on flights within Scandinavia (round-trip from 750kr; 50kr discount for Internet booking).

BY TRAIN. Statens Järnväger (SJ), the state railway company, runs reliable trains throughout the southern Sweden. Seat reservations (20-50kr) are required on some trains (indicated by an R, IN, or IC on the schedule) and are recommended on all other routes. Reservations are also mandatory on the new high-speed **X2000** trains; they are included in the ticket price but are not included in railpasses. In southern Skåne, private **pågatågen** trains service Helsingborg, Lund, Malmö, and Ystad; **InterRail** and **Scanrail** passes are valid. Northern Sweden is served by two main rail routes: The coastal **Malmbanan** runs north from Stockholm through Boden, Umeå, and Kiruna to Narvik, Norway; in summer, the privately run **Inlandsbanan** (☎63 19 44 12; www.inlandsbanan.se) travels an inland route from Mora to Gällivare. The 35min. trip over the **Øresund bridge** connecting Malmö to Copenhagen is the fastest way arrive from continental Europe. Schedules are online at www.samtrafiken.se. **Eurail** is valid on all trains in Sweden. A **Scanrail pass** purchased in Scandinavia allows five travel days in a 15-day period (2040kr, under-26 1530kr) or unlimited travel for 21 consecutive days (3160/2370kr) throughout Scandinavia, and free or discounted ferry rides. Only three of those days can be used in the country of purchase, however, so a Scanrail pass purchased at home is more economical for those traveling mostly in Sweden (p. 51).

BY BUS. In the north, buses may be a better option than trains. **Swebus** (☎(08) 546 30 00; www.swebus.se) is the main company; its **Swebus Express** serves southern Sweden only. **Bus Stop** (☎(08) 440 85 70) reserves tickets for buses from Stockholm. Bus tickets are treated as an extension of the rail network and can be bought from state railways or on board. Express buses offer discounts for children, seniors, and students. Bicycles are not allowed on buses.

BY FERRY. Ferries cross from Malmö (p. 1002) to Copenhagen. Ystad (p. 1004) sends boats to Bornholm, Denmark. Ferries from Gothenburg (p. 1004) serve Frederikshavn, Denmark; Kiel, Germany; and Newcastle, England. From Stockholm (p. 989), ferries run to the Åland Islands, Gotland, Turku, and Helsinki. RG Line ferries (☎(090) 18 52 10) connect Umeå (p. 1008) and Vaasa, Finland.

BY CAR. Swedish roads are remarkably uncrowded and in good condition. Unleaded gas costs an average of 10kr per liter. When gas stations are closed, look for pumps marked *sedel automat*, which operate after hours. Renting a car within Sweden averages 300-500kr per day. Special discounts abound, particularly if you opt for a fly/drive package (p. 57) or if you rent for an extended period.

BY BIKE AND THUMB. Sweden is a biker's heaven; paths cover most of the country, and the hostel-spotted **Sverigeleden bike route** makes a complete circuit through Sweden. Contact STF (p. 988) for info. **Hitchhiking** is uncommon in Sweden; *Let's Go* does not recommend hitchhiking as a safe means of transport.

TOURIST SERVICES AND MONEY

TOURIST OFFICES. Nearly every village and town has a tourist office. For more info, consult the **Swedish Tourist Board** (www.visit-sweden.com).

MONEY. The unit of Swedish currency is the **krona** (plural: kronor), divided into 100 *öre*. Bills come in denominations of 20kr, 50kr, 100kr, and 500kr; coins come in 1kr and 5kr, and 10 and 50 *öre*. Many post offices are also banks. Although a gratuity is usually added to the bill, **tipping** is becoming more common; a 10-15% tip is now considered standard. Tip 10% for taxis. The **value-added tax (VAT)** in Sweden is 25%; refunds can be had on purchases over 200kr (p. 16).

SWEDISH KRONOR		
US$1 = 8.51KR	10KR = US$1.17
CDN$1 = 6.08KR	10KR = CDN$1.65
UK£1= 13.38KR	10KR = UK£0.75
AUS$1 = 5.54KR	10KR = AUS$1.81
NZ$1 = 4.95KR	10KR = NZ$2.02
ZAR1 = 1.14KR	10KR = ZAR8.79
EUR€1 = 9.26KR	10KR = EUR€1.08

BUSINESS HOURS. Banks are usually open Monday to Friday 10am-3pm. Stores generally stay open Monday to Friday 10am-7pm, Saturday and Sunday noon-4pm. Museums open Tuesday to Sunday anywhere from 10am-noon and close between 4 and 6pm. Some are open until 9pm on Tuesday or Wednesday.

COMMUNICATION

PHONE CODES	**Country code:** 46. **International dialing prefix:** 009. From outside Sweden, dial int'l dialing prefix (see inside back cover) + city code + local number.

TELEPHONES. Most payphones only accept *Telefonkort* (phone cards); buy them at newsstands and post offices in 30, 60, or 120 units (35kr, 60kr, and 100kr). **Mobile phones** are an increasingly popular and economical alternative; for more info, see p. 36. International direct dial numbers include: **AT&T,** ☎020 79 56 11; **British Telecom,** ☎020 79 91 44; **Canada Direct,** ☎020 79 90 15; **Ireland Direct,** ☎020 79 93 53; **MCI,** ☎020 79 59 22; **Sprint,** ☎020 79 90 11; **Telecom New Zealand,** ☎020 79 90 64; **Telkom South Africa,** ☎020 79 90 27; and **Telstra Australia,** ☎020 79 90 61.

MAIL. Mailing a postcard or letter from Sweden to Australia, Canada, New Zealand, the US, or South Africa costs 10kr.

LANGUAGE. Almost all Swedes speak some English; most under 50 are fluent. For basic Swedish words and phrases, see p. 1060.

ACCOMMODATIONS AND CAMPING

SWEDEN	❶	❷	❸	❹	❺
ACCOMMODATIONS	under 150kr	151-225kr	226-350kr	351-500kr	over 500kr

Youth hostels (*vandrarhem*) cost about 110-200kr per night. The 315 HI-affiliated hostels run by the **Svenska Turistföreningen** (STF) are invariably top-notch. Nonmembers pay 45kr extra per night. Most hostels have kitchens, laundry facilities, and common areas. To reserve ahead, call the hostel directly or contact the STF headquarters in Stockholm (☎(08) 463 22 70); all sell **Hostelling International** (HI) membership cards (175kr) or offer guest cards. Tourist offices often book beds in hostels for no fee, and can help find private rooms (200-350kr). Private hotels are very good as well. More economical hotels are beginning to offer reduced-service rooms at prices competitive with hostels. STF also manages **mountain huts** in the northern wilds (155-240kr). Many **campgrounds** (80-110kr per site) also offer *stugor* (cottages) for around 85-175kr per person. International Camping Cards are not valid in Sweden; **Swedish Camping Cards,** available at all SCR campgrounds, are virtually mandatory. You may camp for free for one or two nights anywhere as long as you respect the flora, fauna, and the owner's privacy, and remove all garbage. Pick up *Right (and Wrongs) of Public Access in Sweden* from tourist offices, or call the **Swedish Environmental Protection Agency** (☎(08) 698 10 00).

FOOD AND DRINK

SWEDEN	❶	❷	❸	❹	❺
FOOD	under 50kr	51-75kr	76-125kr	126-200kr	over 200kr

Restaurants can be expensive in Sweden, but supermarkets, **saluhallen** (food halls), outdoor fruit and vegetable markets, and kebab stands (45-65kr) make budget eating relatively easy. Most restaurants offer affordable **dagens ratt** (55-70kr), daily lunch specials. Breakfast usually consists of bread, coffee, and muesli with **filmjölk,** a very thin yogurt. Traditional Swedish fare is based around meat and potatoes, but the country's growing diversity has made ethnic and vegetarian cuisine quite common, especially in cities. Other than the weak beer (*lättöl;* under 3.5% alcohol), alcoholic beverages can be purchased only at state-certified Systembolaget liquor stores and in licensed bars and restaurants. A real beer (*starköl*) costs 10-15kr in stores and 30-50kr in city pubs. You must be 20 to buy alcohol. The drinking age is 18, but many bars have age restrictions as high as 25.

HOLIDAYS AND FESTIVALS

Holidays: New Year's Day (Jan. 1); Epiphany (Jan. 5-6); Easter Sunday and Monday (Apr. 11-12); Valborg's Eve (Apr. 30); May Day (May 1); Ascension Day (May 29); Whit Sunday and Monday (May 30-31); National Day (June 6); All Saints' Eve and Day (Nov. 2-3); Christmas (Dec. 24-25); Boxing Day (Dec. 26); New Year's Eve (Dec. 31).

Festivals: Midsummer (June 21-23) incites family frolicking and bacchanalian dancing around Midsummer poles. July and August bring two special festivals, the **Surström-ming** (rotten herring) and **Crayfish** celebrations.

STOCKHOLM   ☎08

Stockholm advertises itself as "the most beautiful city in Europe," and it may be hard to dispute the assertion. Trees, water, and architecture seem to have found harmony on this collection of islands. Yet Stockholm's attractiveness only begins with its beauty. It is a city acutely aware of its heritage as a model of social democracy; busts of laborers, not politicos, adorn the city hall, where female politicians outnumber the men, and the subways are decorated with world-class art.

SWEDEN

TRANSPORTATION

Flights: Arlanda Airport (ARN; ☎797 60 00), 45km north of the city. **Flygbussar** shuttles (☎686 37 87) run between Arlanda and the bus station (40min., every 10min. 4am-10pm, 80kr; SL and Stockholm Cards not valid), as do **Arlanda Express** trains (☎(020) 22 22 24; 20min.; every 15min, 5am-midnight; 140kr, students 80kr). **Bus** #583 runs to T-bana: Märsta (10min., 35kr or 5 coupons; SL Card valid); T-Centralen is 40min. farther by T-bana. Flygbussar also operates shuttles to **Vasteras Airport** (VST; ☎021 80 56 10) that leave 2½hr. before a corresponding RyanAir departure (100kr).

Trains: Centralstation (☎(0771) 75 75 75). T-bana: T-Centralen. To: **Copenhagen** (5-6hr.; 5-6 per day; 627kr, under-25 462kr); **Gothenburg** (3-5hr., 16-19 per day, 542/328kr); **Oslo** (5-7hr., 5-6 per day, 562/392kr). See p. 987 for info on reservations.

Buses: Cityterminalen, above Centralstation. **Terminal Service** (☎762 59 97) to airport (80kr) and Gotland ferries (70kr). **Biljettservice** (☎762 59 79) and **Bus Stop** (☎440 85 70) handle longer routes. To: **Copenhagen** (10hr., 3 per day, 380kr); **Gothenburg** (7hr.; 7 per day; 350kr, under-25 285kr); **Malmö** (8½hr., 2 per day, 435/345kr).

Ferries: Silja Line, Kungsg. 2 (☎22 21 40), sails overnight to Finland: **Helsinki** (16hr., daily, 446kr); **Mariehamn** (5hr., 2 per day, 99kr); **Turku (Åbo)** (12hr., 2 per day, 220-370kr). To get to the terminal, take T-bana to *Gärdet* and follow "Värtahamnen" signs, or take the Silja bus (20kr) from Cityterminalen. 50% Scanrail discount; free with Eurail. **Viking Line** sails to: **Helsinki** (15hr.; daily; 285-377kr); **Mariehamn** (5½hr., daily, 104/52kr); **Turku (Åbo)** (12hr., 2 per day, 130-307/65-79kr). Viking Line terminal is at Stadsgården on Södermalm. T-bana: Slussen. **Tallink** (☎666 60 01; www.tallink.se) ferries sail to **Tallinn** (16hr.; daily; from 410kr, off-season 300kr). Shuttle buses (20kr) run from Cityterminalen to the Tallink port. See p. 1000 for info on ferries to **Gotland.**

Public Transportation: T-bana (*Tunnelbana*; subway) runs 5am-12:30am. Nightbuses (which cover many of the same routes as the daytime buses) run 12:30am-5:30am. Most destinations cost 2 coupons (20kr, 1hr. unlimited bus/subway transfer). *Rabattkuponger*, books of 20 coupons (110kr), are sold at Pressbyrån news agents. The **SL Turistkort** (Tourist Card) is valid on all public transportation. 1-day 80kr; 3-day 150kr. The **Stockholmskortet** (Stockholm Card), available at Sweden House and Centralstation, offers use of public transportation, admission to 70 museums and attractions, and discounts on boat tours. 1-day 220kr, under-17 60kr; 2-day 380/120kr; 3-day 540kr. **SL Office,** Sergels Torg (☎600 10 00) offers transportation info. T-bana: T-Centralen. Open M-F 7am-6:30pm, Sa-Su 10am-9pm.

Taxis: Many cabs have fixed prices; ask beforehand. 435kr from airport to Centralstation. **Taxi Stockholm** (☎15 00 00); **Taxicard** (☎97 00 00); **Taxikurir** (☎30 00 00).

Bike Rental: Sjöcaféet (☎660 57 57), on Djurgårdsbron. Bikes and in-line skates 250kr per day. Open daily 9am-9pm.

Hitchhiking: Waiting on highways is illegal in Sweden, and hitchhiking is uncommon. Hitchhikers going south take the T-bana *Kungens Kurva*; those going north take bus #52 to *Sveaplan* and stand on Sveav. *Let's Go* does not recommend hitchhiking.

ORIENTATION AND PRACTICAL INFORMATION

This compact city spans seven small islands (linked by bridges and the T-bana) at the junction of **Lake Mälaren** to the west and the **Baltic Sea** to the east. The large northern island is divided into two sections: **Norrmalm**, home to Centralstation and the shopping district on Drottningg., and **Östermalm**, which boasts the elegant **Strandvägen** waterfront and vibrant nightlife fanning out from **Stureplan**. The mainly residential western island, **Kungsholmen**, holds grassy beaches and the

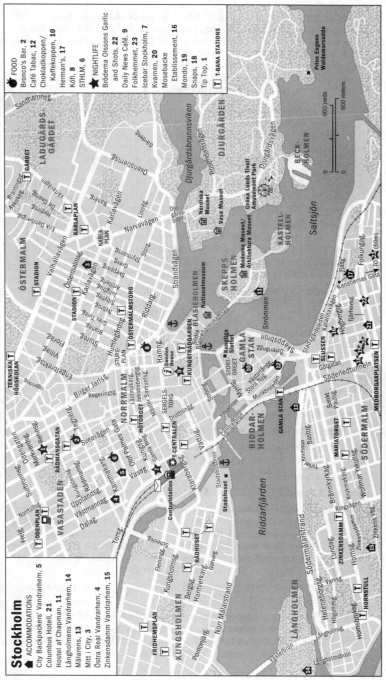

Stockholm

🏠 ACCOMMODATIONS
City Backpackers' Vandrarhem, **5**
Columbus Hotell, **21**
Hostel af Chapman, **11**
Långholmens Vandrarhem, **14**
Mälarens, **13**
Mitt i City, **3**
Östra Real Vandrarhem, **4**
Zinkensdamm Vandrarhem, **15**

🍴 FOOD
Bronco's Bar, **2**
Café Tabac, **12**
Chokladkoppen/
   Kaffekoppen, **10**
Herman's, **17**
Kofi, **8**
STHLM, **6**

★ NIGHTLIFE
Bröderna Olssons Garlic
   and Shots, **9**
Daily News Café, **22**
Folkhemmet, **23**
Icebar Stockholm, **7**
Kvarnen, **20**
Mosebacke
   Etablissement, **16**
Mondo, **19**
Snaps, **18**
Tip Top, **1**

🇹 T-BANA STATIONS

SWEDEN

majestic Stadhuset (City Hall). The southern island of **Södermalm** retains an old neighborhood feel in the midst of a budding cafe culture. Nearby **Långholmen** is a nature preserve, as is much of the eastern island **Djurgården**. At the center of these five islands is **Gamla Stan** (Old Town). Gamla Stan's neighbor (via Norrmalm) is **Skeppsholmen**, an island of museums. The city's streets are easy to navigate: each begins with the number one at the end closest to the City Palace in Gamla Stan; the lower the numbers, the closer you are to Gamla Stan.

Tourist Offices: Sweden House, Hamng. 27, temporarily located in the basement of the Kulturhuset in Sergels Torg until Feb. 2004 (☎789 24 90; www.stockholmtown.com). From Centralstation, walk up Klarabergsg. to Sergels Torg (the plaza with the 50ft. glass tower) and bear right on Hamng. A vital resource for travelers. Friendly, multilingual agents. Sells the **SL** and **Stockholm Cards.** Arranges and sells tickets for theater, concerts, and excursions. Open June-Aug. M-F 8am-7pm, Sa 9am-5pm, Su 10am-4pm; Sept. and May M-F 9am-6pm, Sa-Su 10am-4pm; Oct.-Apr. M-F 9am-6pm, Sa-Su 10am-3pm. The **HotellCentralen** (☎789 24 25; hotels@stoinfo.se), books rooms for a 50kr fee. Open June-Aug. daily 8am-8pm; Sept.-May 9am-6pm, Su noon-4pm.

Embassies: Australia, Sergels Torg 12, (☎613 29 00; www.sweden.embassy.gov.au). **Canada,** Tegelbacken 4 (☎453 30 00; www.canadaemb.se). **Ireland,** Ostermalmsg. 97 (☎661 80 05; fax 660 13 53). **South Africa,** Linnég. 76 (☎24 39 50; www.southafricanemb.se). **UK,** Skarpög. 6-8 (☎671 30 00; www.britishembassy.com). **US,** Daghammarskjölds Väg 31 (☎783 53 00; www.usemb.se).

Currency Exchange: Forex in Centralstation (☎248 800; open daily 7am-9pm), **Cityterminalen** (☎21 42 80; open M-F 7am-10pm, Sa 8am-5pm), and **Sweden House** (☎20 03 89; open M-F 8am-7pm, Sa-Su 9am-5pm). 15-20kr commission.

American Express: Norrlandsg. 21 (☎411 05 40). T-bana: Östermalmstorg. No fee to cash AmEx Traveler's Cheques, 20kr for cash. Open M-F 9am-5pm, Sa 9am-1pm.

Luggage Storage: Lockers available at Centralstation. 20-60kr per 24hr.

Gay and Lesbian Services: RFSL, Sveav. 57-59 (☎457 13 20; www.rfsl.se). T-bana: Rådmansg. Located above Tip Top, a popular gay club (p. 996). Open M-F 9am-5pm. Occasional evening activities; call for a schedule. *Queer Extra (QX)* and the **QueerMap,** available at Sweden House, give info about Stockholm's gay hot spots.

Emergency: Ambulance, fire, and **police:** ☎112.

Pharmacy: Look for the green and white "Apoteket" signs. **Apoteket C. W. Scheele,** Klarabergsg. 64, at the overpass over Vasag. T-bana: T-Centralen. Open 24hr.

Medical Assistance: ☎32 01 00.

Hospitals: Karolinska, ☎517 700 00. **Sankt Göran,** ☎587 100 00.

Internet Access: Stadsbiblioteket (library), Odeng. 59, in the annex. T-bana: Odenplan. 10min. free. Open M-Th 11am-7pm, F 9am-7pm, Sa-Su 11am-5pm. **Sweden House** (above) provides free terminals. **Nine,** Odeng. 44. T-bana: Odenplan. Turn left on Odeng. 45kr per hr. Open M-Th 10am-1am, F-Sa 10am-midnight, Su 11am-1am. **Cafe Access IT,** in the basement of the Kulturhuset. 1kr per min. or 25kr per 30min. Open M 11am-6pm, Tu-F 10am-7pm, Sa 10am-5pm, Su 11am-4pm.

Telephones: Buy phone cards at **Pressbyrån** stores. 50 (50kr) or 120 (100kr) units. **Directory assistance:** ☎079 75. 15kr per min.

Post Office: Main office is at the entrance to the blue line at T-bana: T-Centralen (☎781 46 82). Open M-F 8am-6:30pm, Sa 11am-2pm. Address mail to be held: Firstname SURNAME, *Poste Restante,* **10110** Stockholm 1, SWEDEN. **Branch** in Centralstation (☎781 24 25). Open M-F 7am-10pm, Sa-Su 10am-7pm.

ACCOMMODATIONS AND CAMPING

Summer demands reservations, and many HI hostels limit stays to five nights. If you haven't booked ahead, arrive around 8am. Stockholm's several **botels** (boathostels) are a novel solution to space issues, but they can be cramped and noisy—request a room on the water side of the boat. Note that many independent (non-HI) hostels are hotel/hostels; specify if you want to stay in a dorm-style hostel, or risk paying hotel rates. There are also various **B&B booking services**, including the **Bed & Breakfast Agency** (☎ 643 8028; www.bba.nu; open 9am-5pm). **Campers** should bring insect repellent to ward off the infamous Swedish mosquitoes. If you don't have a **Swedish Camping Card** (p. 988), sites will sell you one for 90kr. An SL bus pass (or Stockholm Card) is the cheapest way to get to the more remote campsites.

City Backpackers' Vandrarhem (SVIF), Upplandsg. 2A (☎20 69 20; www.citybackpackers.se). From Centralstation, go left on Vasag. and bear right on Upplandsg. Dorm rooms are on the small side, but a friendly staff and great amenities available more than compensate. Sauna 20kr. Kitchen available. Sheets 50kr. Laundry 50kr. Free Internet. Reception 9am-noon and 2-7pm. Dorms 170-200kr; doubles 490kr. ❷

Hostel af Chapman/Skeppsholmens Vandrarhem (HI/STF), Flaggmansvägen 8, on Skeppsholmen (☎463 22 66; www.stfchapman.com). From T-bana: T-Centralen, take bus #65 to the parking lot or walk 20min. along the waterfront over the Skeppsh. Olmsbron bridge. Modern on-shore hostel and unusually roomy 19th-century botel. Great view of Gamla Stan. Breakfast 55kr. Kitchen available. Sheets 30kr. Laundry 35kr. Internet 1kr per min. Reception 24hr. Lockout 11am-3pm. Botel curfew 2am. Dorms 125-155kr; botel doubles 185kr. Non-members add 45kr. ❶

Långholmens Vandrarhem (HI), Långholmsmuren 20 (☎668 05 10; www.langholmen.com). T-bana: Hornstull. Walk north on Långholmsg., turn left onto Högalidsg., and turn right to cross to the island on Långholmsbron. Turn left and follow the yellow wall. Located on the tranquil Långholmen, this former prison has dorm-style "cells" and rooms, all with abundant character. Kitchen, cafe, pub, and laundry. Breakfast 65kr. Sheets 40kr. Reception 24hr. Check-out 10am. Book far in advance. Dorms 185-210kr; nonmembers add 45kr. Hotel rooms from 600kr in summer; off-season 725kr. ❷

Hostel Mitt i City, Västmannag. 13 (☎21 76 30; www.stores.se/hostal.htm). T-bana: T-Centralen. Turn left up Vasag. and bear left on Västmannag. for 3 blocks. Reception on 5th fl. Bright, basic rooms and a helpful staff. Breakfast included. Sheets 50kr. Reception 24hr. Dorms 195kr; doubles 590kr; quads 980kr.❷

Zinkensdamm Vandrarhem (HI), Zinkens Väg 20, in Södermalm (☎616 81 00; www.zinkensdamm.com). T-bana: Zinkensdamm. Head south on Ringv. 3 blocks, then turn right and head down Zinkens Väg. Kitchen, restaurant, and laundry. Bike rental (100kr per day). Reception 24hr. Dorms 165kr. Nonmembers add 45kr. ❷

Columbus Hotell (SVIF), Tjärhovsg. 11 in Södermalm (☎50 31 12; www.columbus.se). T-bana: Medborgarpl. From Medborgarpl. (facing Mondo), turn left onto Tjärhovsgtn. Clean rooms in a well-located ex-brewery. Singles from 595kr; doubles from 795kr. ❺

Mälarens, Södermälarstrand, Kajplats 6 (☎644 43 85; www.rodabaten.nu). T-bana: Gamla Stan. Take Centralbron across the river and walk 100m to the right along the shore—it's the red boat. Small rooms and maritime decor. Extensive breakfast 55kr. Reception 8am-11pm. Dorms 185kr; singles 400kr; doubles 450kr; quads 860kr. ❷

SWEDEN

Östra Real Vandrarhem (SVIF), Karlavägen 79, in Östermalm (☎664 11 14; realostra@hotmail.com). T-bana: Karlaplan. Exit toward Karlaplan, turn right, and then take the second right onto Karlavägen. This school fills its classrooms with beds in the summer. Friendly common rooms, but few amenities. Kitchen available. Sheets 45kr. Reception 8:30am-9pm. Curfew M-Th 1am, F-Sa 3am. Open mid-June to mid-Aug. 7- to 10-bed dorms 125kr; 4- to 6-bed dorms 150kr; doubles 450kr). ❶

Ängby Camping, Blackebergsv. 24, on Lake Mälaren (☎37 04 20; www.angbycamping.se). T-bana: Ängbyplan. Go downstairs, turn left on Färjestadsvägen, and bear left at the fork; it's at the bottom of the road. Wooded campsite with swimming area, walking paths. Reception in summer 7am-11pm; off-season 8am-10pm. 115kr per couple with tent; 80kr per extra person. RVs 165kr, with electricity 190kr. Cabins 300-675kr. ❶

Bredäng Camping, Stora Sällskapets Väg, near Lake Mälaren (☎97 70 71; www.camping.se/plats/A04). T-bana: Bredäng. Turn left onto Stora Sällskapets Väg under tunnel and follow the street 700m, past Ålgrytevägen; hostel reception is on the left, camping reception on the right. Reception 7am-10pm. Open mid-Apr. to late Oct. Campground: single tents 85-95kr; group tents 165-180kr; 4-bed cottage 450kr; RV hookups 30kr. Hostel: singles 140kr; doubles 380kr; quads 500kr; cabins 630-830kr. ❶

🍴 FOOD

Your best budget bet is to fuel up on the all-you-can-eat breakfasts offered by most hostels, then track down lunch specials (*dagens rätt*; 45-90kr). Cafes line **Götgatan** and **Skånegatan** in Södermalm; many cheap eateries are on **Odengatan** in Vasastaden. The Swedes (who are second in the world in per capita coffee consumption) have elevated the act of drinking coffee in a sidewalk cafe into an art form, even inventing their own term for it: "*fika*". Upscale **Birger Jarlsgatan** in Ostermalmtorg is great for people-watching. **Grocery stores** are easy to find around any T-bana station—popular chains include Coop and Vivo. The huge **Östermalms Saluhall,** Nybrogtn., 31 (T-bana: Östermalmstorg), contains bustling fish and meat markets and various restaurants serving Swedish dishes. (M-Th 9:30am-6pm, F 9:30am-6:30pm, Sa 9:30am-2pm.) There's a bustling **fruit market** at Hötorg. (M-Sa 7am-6pm).

■ **Herman's,** Fjällg. 23A, in Södermalm. T-bana: Slussen. Surprisingly good vegetarian fare, served buffet-style, with phenomenal views of Stockholm off the Söder cliffs. Lunch 68-75kr, dinner 98kr. Open in summer daily 11am-11pm; off-season M-F 11am-9pm, Sa-Su noon-10pm. ❷

Café Tabac, Stora Nyg. 46. T-bana: Gamla Stan. Cafe by the waterfront with delicious salads (68-84kr) and huge panini sandwiches (46-60kr). ❸

STHLM, Drottningg. 73c. 7 blocks north of T-Centralen. Urbane cafe on Vasastaden's main pedestrian avenue. Beautifully presented salads, pastas, and sandwiches (45-75kr), all in ample portions, and tempting desserts. Open M-F 8am-8pm, Sa 10am-8pm, Su 10am-6pm. ❷

Kófi, Birger Jarlsg. 11. T-bana: Östermalmstorg. The chic decor and upscale location of this cafe conceal the relatively inexpensive sandwiches served inside. Open in summer daily 7am-1am; off-season 7am-11pm. ❶

Bronco's Bar, Tegnérgtn. 16. T-bana: Rådmansgtn. Large servings of traditional Swedish and American fare (60-80kr) in an unpretentious atmosphere. Open M-F 11am-midnight, Sa 1pm-midnight. Pub open daily 5pm-midnight. ❷

Chokladkoppen and **Kaffekoppen,** Stortorg. 18-20. T-bana: Gamla Stan. Light meals (34-65kr) and generous desserts (from 34kr). Open in summer daily 9am-11pm; off-season Su-Th 9am-10pm. ❶

◎ SIGHTS

Stockholm's bridges and frequent open spaces make it an extremely walkable city. Its parks—especially **Ekoparken,** the world's first urban national park—set it apart from all other European cities. The best way to get a taste of Stockholm's neighborhoods and rich street life is to explore by foot, hopping on the T-bana (sometimes called the longest art exhibit in the world) to get to more remote places.

GAMLA STAN (OLD TOWN). Originally, Stockholm was composed of just this one small island in the center of the city, through which earlier generations controlled Baltic trade routes. Today the island is dominated by the **Kungliga Slottet** (Royal Palace), one of the largest palaces in all of Europe and the winter home of the Swedish royal family. The massive complex contains various museums, including the extravagant **Royal Apartments** and the lavishly decorated **Rikssalen** (State Hall) and **Slottskyrkan** (Royal Chapel). In the former royal wine cellar, the **Skattkammaren** (Royal Treasury) now houses enough jewel-encrusted accessories to make a thief drool, while the nearby **Livrustkammaren** (Armory) presents an extensive collection of swords, suits of armor, and carriages that look like they came straight out of *Cinderella*. The **Gustav III Antikmuseum,** one of Europe's oldest museums, has extensive collection of statues, while the **Museum Tre Konor** contains the remains of the original 13th-century castle. In 2004, the palace celebrates its 250th anniversary. *(www.royalcourt.se. Open mid-May to Aug. daily 10am-4pm; Sept.-Apr. Su and Tu-Sa noon-3pm. Each attraction 70kr, students 35kr; combination ticket (excluding armory) 110/65kr. English-language tours included.)* Adjacent to the palace, on the **Stortorget** (town square) lies the **Storkykan** (Royal Church), where royals gets married and where winners of the Nobel Peace Prize speak after accepting their awards. Be sure not to miss the statue of Saint George slaying the dragon. Next door, the small but informative **Nobelsmuseum** traces the controversies and contributions of the Nobel Prize and its winners through various multimedia exhibits. *(www.nobel.se/nobelmuseum. Open mid-May to mid-Sept. M and W-Su 10am-6pm, Tu 10am-8pm; mid-Sept. to mid-May Tu 11am-8pm, W-Su 11am-5pm. 50kr, students 40kr, children 7-18 20kr, under-7 free.)* Near the square are Gamla Stan's main pedestrian streets: **Västerlånggatan,** which can be a bit overrun with tourists, and nearby **Stora Nygatan** and **Österlånggatan,** which are quieter and good for window-shopping. *(T-bana: Gamla Stan, or take bus #46 or 55. Tours of Gamla Stan June-Aug. 2 per day. Meet at the Royal Opera House. 85kr.)*

KUNGSHOLMEN AND STADSHUSET. The imposing brick facade of the **Stadshuset** (City Hall) towers on the tip of the island of Kungsholmen. Inside, be sure not to miss the council room, whose roof was built in the shape of an inverted Viking ship. Nobel Prize winners dine in the poorly-named Blue Hall (the hall is actually all brick), then dance the night away under millions of mosaic tiles in the dazzling Gold Room. At 106m, the panorama of the city provided by the adjacent **Stadsjustornet** (City Hall Tower) is unparalleled in Stockholm. *(Hantverkarg. 1. T-bana: T-Centralen. Walk toward the water and turn right on Stadshusbron. June-Aug. daily 10, 11am, noon, 2pm, 3pm; Sept.-Apr. 10am, noon; May 10am, noon, 2pm. Tours required. 50kr, under-12 free. Tower open May-Sept. daily 10am-4:30pm. 20kr.)*

BLASIEHOLMEN AND SKEPPSHOLMEN. On Blasieholmen, a short peninsula jutting out from Norrmalm, is the **Nationalmusem,** Stockholm's major art museum. It displays art from the likes of Rembrandt, Renoir, and Rodin, as well as national treasures by Carl Larsson, Anders Zorn, and Eugen Jansson, and a retrospective on Swedish design. *(www.nationalmuseum.se. T-bana: Kungsträdgården. The museum is on the left before Skeppsh. Olmsbron bridge. Open Tu 11am-8pm, W-Su 11am-5pm. 75kr, students*

60kr, under-16 free. W reduced prices.) The **Moderna Museet** and the **Arkitektur Museet,** across the bridge on Skeppsholmen, are scheduled to reopen in early 2004; see www.modernamuseet.se and www.arkitekturmuseet.se. for more info.

DJURGÅRDEN. Djurgården is a lush national park in the heart of the city, a perfect place for a long walk or a summer picnic. It is also home to **Skansen,** a popular open-air museum featuring 150 historical buildings, handicrafts, and a zoo. The homes, extracted from different periods of Swedish history, are inhabited by costumed actors. *(Bus #44 or 47 from Drottningg. and Klarabergsg. in Sergels Torg. Park and zoo open daily June-Aug. 10am-10pm; Sept.-Apr. 10am-4pm; May 10am-8pm. Historical buildings open daily May-Aug. 11am-5pm; Sept.-Apr. 11am-3pm. 60kr, off-season 30kr.)* Before the entrance to Skansen is the haunting **⬛Vasa Museet,** which houses a salvaged warship that sank on its 1628 maiden voyage before even leaving the harbor. *(Galärvarvet. Take bus #44, 47, or 69. Open June 10-Aug. 20 daily 9:30am-7pm; Aug. 21-June 9 M-Tu and Th-Su 10am-5pm, W 10am-8pm. 70kr, students 40kr.)* Next door, the **Nordiska Museet** (Nordic Museum) presents an exhibit on Swedish history and culture from the Viking age to the modern era. *(Djurgårdsvägen 6-16. Bus #44, 47, or 69. Open June 24-Aug. daily 10am-5pm; Jan.-June 23 Tu 10am-5pm, W 10am-9pm, and Th-Sa 10am-5pm. 60kr, students 30kr. Under-18 free.)* On the far side of the island, **Prins Eugens Waldemarsudde,** former home of the full-time prince and part-time painter, contains its namesake's major works and personal collection. The seaside grounds also boast a beautiful sculpture garden. *(Prins Eugen Väg 6. Bus #47. Open May-Aug. Su and Tu-Sa 11am-5pm, Th until 8pm; Sept.-Apr. 11am-4pm. 60kr.)*

ENTERTAINMENT AND FESTIVALS

Stockholm offers a number of venues for theater and music, many of which are small establishments that can be found by looking through *What's On,* available at the tourist office (p. 992). There are also a number of larger, more widely known performance spots. The six stages of the national theater, **Dramaten,** Nybroplan (☎667 06 80), feature Swedish- and English-language performances of works by August Strindberg and other playwrights (50-260kr). Check out **Backstage** for more experimental material. The **Kulturhuset** (Culture House), an arts complex built in the 60s, provides "high culture," ranging from art galleries to performance spaces to a comic book collection, at publicly appealing prices. (☎50 83 15 08.) The **Operan,** Jakobs torg 2 (☎24 82 40) stages operas and ballets. (135-460kr. Student, obstructed-view, and rush-ticket discounts.) The imposing **Konserthuset** at Hötorg. (☎10 21 10) is home to the Stockholm Philharmonic (100-270kr, 15% student discount.) Pop music venues include the **Globen** arena (☎600 34 00; 250-500kr), **Skansen** (☎5789 0005), and the stage at **Gröna Lund,** Djurgården's huge outdoor Tivoli amusement park (☎670 76 00; concerts late Apr.-early Sept. at 7:30pm). In summer, **Kungsträdgården** hosts several free outdoor concerts; also look for signs about **Parkteatern,** a summer-long program of free theater, dance, and musical productions in different parks around the city. Visit Sweden House or call Biljett-Direkt (☎(07) 7170 7070) for tickets to events and performances.

Stockholm's festivals include the world-class **Stockholm Jazz Festival** (mid- to late July; ☎556 924 40; www.stockholmjazz.com); **Strindberg Festival** (late Aug. or early Sept.; ☎34 14 01; www.strindberg.stockholm.se/festivalen); and the gay **Stockholm Pride** (late July or early Aug.; ☎33 59 55; www.stockholmpride.org).

NIGHTLIFE

For a city where "night" barely exists during the summer, Stockholm knows a thing or two about nightlife. In posh, upscale Östermalm (T-bana: Östermalmtorg), celebrities party with beautiful people until 5am. Expect long lines outside nearly every club. High up on the cliffs across the river, Södermalm's nightlife is a little less glitzy and a little more student-friendly, with a diverse mix of bars and clubs. A grab bag of nightlife options lines **Sveavägen** and the **Vasastaden** area (T-bana: Odenplan or Rådmansgtn.). Stockholm is cozy enough to walk between all three areas, and Stockholm's night buses cover most of the city. Alcohol is expensive at bars (35-55kr) but cheaper (10-15kr per 0.5L) at **Systembolaget** state liquor stores. (Most open M-F 9am-6pm.) For info about Stockholm's **gay scene**, pick up *QX (Queer Extra)* or the QueerMap, for entertainment and nightlife listings.

Daily News Café, Kungsträdgården, next to Sweden House. (☎21 56 55). T-bana: T-Centralen. Delivers live and house music to a slick but friendly clientele. Music changes nightly; call for a schedule. Cover 60-90kr. Open Su-Th 9pm-3am, F-Sa 9pm-5am.

Mondo, Medborgarpl. 8. T-bana: Medborgarpl. On the left across from the station. This massive complex (5 bars, 4 dance floors, and 3 stages) is frequently packed with well-dressed young Swedes listening to live rock, hip-hop, or reggae. Definitely the newest star in Södermalm. Drinks from 50kr.

Tip Top, Sveav. 57. T-bana: Rådmansg. Walk one block left of the station. This trendy gay club's large dance floor draws a mixed crowd on the weekends. Beer 44kr, mixed drinks 68kr. Cover 70kr F-Sa after 9pm. Open M-Sa 5pm-3am.

Icebar Stockholm, Vasaplan 4. (☎505 635 51) T-bana: T-Centralen. Inside the Nordic Seahotel. The coldest (although perhaps too touristy to be the coolest) bar in Stockholm. Inside, everything—from the glasses to the tables to the bar itself—is carved out of ice. Wear warm clothing. Cover 125kr, includes drinks. Open M-Sa 3pm-midnight, Su 3-9pm. Reservations mandatory, call M-F 9am-5pm for a 45min. booking.

Bröderna Olssons Garlic and Shots, Folkungag. 84. T-bana: Medborgarpl. Walk 3 blocks up Folkungag. Quirky bar with an electric atmosphere. 101 unique shots (35kr). Trademark garlic-flavored beer 48kr. Open daily 5pm-1am.

Mosebacke Etablissement, Mosebacke Torg 3. T-bana: Slussen. Take the Katarina lift to *Söder Heights.* Eclectic array of live music and a terrace with a spectacular view. Beer 43kr, mixed drinks 62kr. 20+. Cover 50-100kr. In summer, terrace open daily 11am-1am. Bar and club Th-Sa 8pm-1am; off-season 5pm-1am.

Snaps, Medborgarpl. T-bana: Medborgarpl. The free-standing yellow house across from the station. Basement dance floor (jungle, reggae, and dance music). Beer 42kr, mixed drinks from 64kr. Women 23+, men 25+. Open in summer Su-M 3pm-midnight, Tu-Sa 3pm-3am; off-season M 3pm-midnight, Tu-W 3pm-2am, Th-Sa 3pm-3am.

Folkhemmet, Renstiernas G. 30. T-bana: Medborgarpl. Down-to-earth locals' bar. Beer 39kr, mixed drinks 79kr. DJ every night from 8pm. 21+. Open daily 5pm-1am.

Kvarnen, Tjärhovsg. 4. T-bana: Medborgarpl. A 200-year-old beer hall along with a new cocktail bar, **H2O,** and dance club, **Eld.** 23+. Kvarnen open M-F 11am-3am, Sa-Su 5pm-3am. H2O open M-F 11am-3am, Sa 5pm-3am. Eld open W-Su 10pm-3am.

DAYTRIPS FROM STOCKHOLM

Stockholm is situated in the center of an archipelago, where the mainland gradually crumbles into the Baltic. The islands in either direction—east toward the Baltic or west toward Lake Mälaren—are well worth exploration. Visit the **Excursion Shop** in Sweden House (p. 992) for more info. **Ferries** to the archipelago leave from in front of the Grand Hotel on the **Stromkajen** docks between Gamla Stan and Skeppsholmen (T-Bana: Jakobskyrka) or the **Nybrohamnen** docks (T-Bana: Östermalmstorg; walk down Birger Jarlsg. toward the water).

LAKE MÄLAREN. The island of **Björkö** on Lake Mälaren is home to **Birka,** where the Vikings established the country's first city and where Christianity first reached Sweden in AD 829. The island now holds a Viking museum as well as fascinating

SWEDEN

excavation sites and burial mounds. A **ferry** departs Stockholm from the Stadshus-bron docks next to the Stadshuset. (1-1¾hr. July-Aug. 10am and 2pm, return 3:30 and 6:30pm; Sept. and May 10am, return 3:30pm. Guided tour, museum admission, and round-trip ferry 200kr.)

It should come as no surprise that the main characters who figure in **Drott-ningholm Palace** (Swedish for "Queen's Island Palace") tend to be queens them-selves. Occupying the location of a former palace built for Queen Katerina Jagellonica, the new palace was built by Queen Hedwig Eleanora and, after completion, served as a wedding gift for Queen Lovisa Ulrika. Inside, lavishly-appointed Rococo and Baroque interiors open up onto sprawling English and Baroque gardens, perfect for a summer picnic. Be sure not to miss the palace's theater, the oldest theater with functioning stage equipment, or **Kina Slott,** the pseudo-Chinese-styled pavilion built in secret by Gustav III for his wife. The **Museum de Vries,** containing the world's largest collection of the Dutch sculp-tor's works, is also nearby. (Palace open May-Aug. daily 10am-4:30pm, Sept. noon-3:30pm. 60kr, students 30kr. Mandatory guided tour for theater 60/30kr. Kina Slott open May-Aug. daily 11am-4:30pm, Sept. noon-3:30pm. 50/25kr. Com-bined Palace and Kina Slott ticket 90/45kr. De Vries museum 50/25kr.) Strömma Kanalbolaget **ferries** depart from Stadshusbron from May to early Sept. (1hr; M-F every hr., Sa-Su more frequently.) Or, take the **subway** to T-bana: Brommaplan, then take **bus** #177 or #301-323.

THE ARCHIPELAGO (SKÄRGÅRD). The wooded islands of the Stockholm archi-pelago grow rockier and increasingly dramatic closer to the Baltic. The archipel-ago is perfect for picnicking and hiking; the water is very cold but swimmable on its many beaches. The **Waxholmsbolaget ferry company** (☎679 58 30) serves even the tiniest islands and offers the 16-day **Båtluffarkortet card** (385kr), good for unlimited boat travel. The Excursion Shop at Sweden House (p. 992) sells the ferry pass and has info on hostels and camping, as well as kayak and canoe rentals. Overnight stays in the area's 20 **hostels** must be booked months ahead, but the odd night may be available on short notice. There are **hostels** on **Möja** in the outer archipelago (☎571 647 20) and **Vaxholm,** closer to Stockholm (☎541 322 40). Consult Sweden House for listings. Or, enjoy **free camping** courtesy of the law of public access (p. 992) on almost any island except Sandhamn. (Some islands are also in military protection zones and are not open to foreigners.)

Vaxholm, a mere hour away by ferry or bus, is overwhelmingly the most popular island in the archipelago to visit, and can be thronged with Swedish daytrippers and tourists at times, especially in the middle of the summer. The island itself has an old fortress to explore, beaches to swim in, and sidewalk cafes galore. Alterna-tively, you can rent a boat on Vaxholm (☎541 377 90) and explore some of the qui-eter surrounding islands. Ferries depart in front of the Grand Hotel almost every 30min. (55kr each way). Among the many other islands in the archipelago, **Utö** has great bike paths; **bike rental** and ferry packages are available from Sweden House or on the island itself. **Sandhamn,** three hours from Stockholm, is ideal for swim-ming and **sailing,** while **Finnhamn,** also a two- to three- hour boat ride, has excellent hiking in addition to its coastal features. The labyrinth north of Landsort on **Öja** is reputed to bring luck to fishermen. Take the *pendeltag* (commuter train) from Stockholm to Nynashamn, then ride bus #852 to Ankarudden and hop the ferry to Landsort (55kr; 2hr.).

UPPSALA ☎018

Uppsala (pop. 120,000), the most biker-friendly town in Sweden, houses the 20,000 students of Sweden's oldest university in a beautiful urban setting of grand churches and footbridges. Uppsala's main attraction is the towering

Domkyrka, the largest cathedral in Sweden, whose towers, at 118.7m, are as tall as the cathedral is long. Many famous Swedes, ranging from the philosopher Emanuel Swedenborg to the scientist Carolus Linneaus, are buried here. (Open daily 8am-6pm. Tours in English June 24-Aug. M-Sa 2pm. Free.) During the summer, the cathedral holds choral music concerts (call ☎ 18 72 01 for a schedule). Across from the Domkyrka, the **Gustavianum** houses the university's collection of artifacts and scientific curiosities, and presents a short history of the university itself. Be sure not to miss the **Anatomical Theater** built on the top floor of the building, where public dissections were conducted from the late 17th century onwards. (Open June 25-Aug. 25 11am-5pm; Aug. 26-June 24 Su and Tu-Sa 11am-4pm. 40kr, students 30kr.) A walk through the center of town along the Fyrisån River is an excellent way to get a taste of the city's flourishing gardens and cafes. For an aerial view, walk away from the river on Drottningg. and take the path up to the castle, which also houses an art museum. (W-F noon-4pm, Sa-Su 11am-5pm.) The **Universitetsbiblioteket** (University Library), at the foot of the castle, has an exhibition hall and a popular cafe, a promising spot for meeting students. (Library open Aug. 19-June 15 M-F 9am-8pm, Sa 10am-5pm, Su 11am-4pm; June 16-Aug. 18 reduced hours. May 14-Sept. 16 20kr, Sept. 17-May 13 free.) Uppsala's most famous resident, botanist Carl Linneaus, lived across the river on Svarbäcksgtn.; his house is now a museum commemorating his contributions to science and Sweden. (House open June-Sept. Su and Tu-Sa noon-4pm. 25kr. Gardens open May-Sept. 9am-7pm, 20kr.) **Gamla Uppsala,** 4km north of the city center, is now little more than a collection of Viking burial mounds. Archaeologists believe, that the site once contained a pagan temple where human and animal sacrifices were performed. Nearby is **Gamla Uppsala Kyrka,** one of Sweden's oldest churches. (Open Apr.-Sept. daily 9am-6pm; Oct.-Mar. 9am-4pm. Free.) Nearby, a new museum, the **Gamla Uppsala Historiskt Centrum,** outlines the area's history and excavation. (Open May-Aug. 20 daily 10am-5pm; Aug. 21-Sept. 10am-4pm. 50kr, students 40kr, under-16 free.) Take bus #2, 20, 24, or 54 (16kr) north from Dragarbrunnsg. Two hours from Uppsala is **Skokloster,** a dazzling Baroque palace that is accessible by boat. (Open May-Aug. daily 11am-4pm. Entrance and tour 65kr, students 50kr. Boat departs Su and Tu-Sa 11:30am from Islandsbron on Östra Åg. and Munkg.; returns 5:15pm. Roundtrip 115kr.) Uppsala's students drive a lively night scene. You'll find students lounging on terraces along the river and bars in and around **Stortorget,** especially on **Sysslomansgatan, Västra Ågatan,** and the pedestrian areas of **Svartbäcksgatan** and **Kungsgatan.** Many bars require student ID for entry.

   Trains go to Stockholm (40min.; every 30min., less frequently on weekends; 70kr, under-25 55kr) via Arlanda Airport. To get from the station to the **tourist office,** Fyristorg 8, walk right on Kungsg., left on St. Persg., and across the bridge. (☎ 27 48 00. Open in summer M-F 10am-6pm, Sa 10am-3pm, Su noon-4pm; off-season closed Su.) Around the corner from the tourist office is **Internet Horna,** Drottning. 3, on the first floor of the city newspaper office. (20kr per 30min. Open M-F 9:30am-5:30pm, Sa 10:30am-2:30pm.) For renovated rooms in a lovely pastoral setting, try **Sunnersta Herrgård (HI) ❸,** Sunnerstav. 24, 6km south of town. Take bus #20, 25, 50, or 802 (20kr) from Dragarbrunnsg. to Herrgårdsv., cross the street, walk two blocks down the path behind the kiosk, and walk 50m to the left. (☎ 32 42 20. Breakfast 65kr. Reception June-Aug. M-F 8-10am and 5-9pm; Sept.-May M-F 7:30am-8pm, Sa-Su 7:30-10am. Singles 330kr; doubles 360kr; triples 540kr. Nonmembers add 45kr.) **Fyrishov Camping ❶,** Idrottsg. 2, off Svartbäcksg., is 2km from the city center. Take bus #4 or 6 (bus #50 or 54 at night; 10min.) to Fyrishov. (☎ 27 49 60. Reception 7am-10pm. Tents 130kr; 4- to 5-bed huts 450-800kr. Swedish Camping Card required.) **Postal Code:** 75101.

GOTLAND   ☎0498

Gotland, Sweden's largest island, is 150km south of Stockholm. Famed for white-sand beaches, green meadows dotted with old stone churches, and its medieval capital of Visby, Gotland's timeless landscape is best seen at a leisurely pace.

▐ TRANSPORTATION. Destination Gotland **ferries** (☎20 10 20; www.destinationgotland.se) sail to Visby from **Nynäshamn,** south of Stockholm (3-5hr.), and **Oskarshamn,** north of Kalmar (2½-4hr.). Fares are highest on weekends and in summer, and cheapest for early-morning and late-night departures. (June-Aug. 2-5 per day; Oct.-May 1-3 per day. 150-475kr, students 95-300kr; 40% Scanrail discount.) To get to Nynäshamn from **Stockholm,** take the Båtbussen **bus** from Cityterminalen (1hr.; leaves 1¾hr. before ferry departures; 75kr, 100kr on bus) or the **Pendeltåg** from Centralstation (1hr.; 60kr, SL passes and *rabattkuponger* valid). To get to Oskarshamn, hop on a bus (1¾hr., 69kr) or train from **Kalmar.** If you're planning your trip from Stockholm, **Gotland City,** Kungsg. 57A, books ferries and has tourist info. (☎08 406 1500. Open June-Aug. M-F 9:30am-6pm, Sa 10am-2pm; Sept.-May M-F 9:30am-5pm.) **Skyways** (☎08 797 7639; www.skyways.se) offers numerous daily **flights** from Stockhom's Arlanda and Bromma airports (35min., 6-7 per day from each airport, fares from 350kr), while **Gotlandsflyg** (☎22 22 22; www.gotlandsflyg.se) flies four times daily from Bromma as well (fares from 300kr).

To explore the island, pick up a bus timetable at the ferry terminal or at the Visby **bus station,** Kung Magnusväg 1, outside the wall north of the city. (☎21 41 12. Bus 59kr, bikes 40kr extra.) **Cycling** along Gotland's extensive paths and bike-friendly motorways is the best way to explore its flat terrain; bike rental shops are all over the island, especially in Visby and Klintehamn.

VISBY. The sleepy village of Visby (pop. 21,500) seems straight out of a fairy tale. Its medieval wall encloses knotted cobblestone streets and crumbling churches. Don't miss the opportunity to wander the winding streets; small alleys often lead to beautiful vistas of the town and the sea. The town awakens in August for **Medeltidsveckan,** a re-creation of the town's medieval past complete with costumes and tournaments (between the 31st and 32nd Sundays of the year, generally the first or second week in August).

From the ferry terminal, walk 10min. to the left to get to the **tourist office,** Hamng. 4. (☎20 17 00. Open mid-June to mid-Aug. daily 8am-7pm; May to mid-June M-F 8am-5pm, Sa-Su 10am-4pm; mid-Aug. to Apr. M-F 8am-4pm.) Dozens of **bike rental** shops surround the ferry terminal; prices generally start at 65kr per day for a 3-speed bike. **Gotlandsresor,** Färjeleden 3, 75m to the right of the ferry terminal, will help you book ferries, rent bikes, and find private rooms. (☎04 98 20 12 60; www.gotlandsresor.se. Open June-Aug. daily 6am-10pm; Sept.-May 8am-6pm.) **Private rooms** generally cost about 240-290kr for singles and 380-430kr for doubles. ◪**Visby Fängelse Vandrarhem ❷,** Skeppsbron 1, is 300m to the left as you exit the ferry terminal. You'll recognize it by the barbed wire atop its yellow walls, the only remnants of the 19th-century prison that preceded this airy, whimsically decorated hostel. (☎20 60 50. Reception in summer M-F 2-6pm; off-season 11am-2pm. Call ahead if arriving at another time. Reserve ahead. Dorms 170-200kr; doubles 400-550kr; triples 600-825kr; quads 800-1100kr.) Outdoor bars and cafes are everywhere in Visby, but especially around the ruins of the church in **Stora Torget** and down by the harbor. **Postal Code:** 62101.

ELSEWHERE ON GOTLAND. Great daytrips from Visby during the high season include visits to the popular **Tofta** beach 15km south (bus #31, 30min.); the calcified cliffs of **Hoburgen,** at the island's southernmost tip (bus #11, 3hr.); and the physics-defying monoliths on **Fårö**, off the northern tip of the island (bus #23, 2hr.). **Gotlandsresor** (see above) has info on over 30 hostels, campgrounds, and bike rentals elsewhere on Gotland. The friendly **Fårögarden (STF) Hostel ❶**, 17km north of the ferry terminal, is a warm retreat in Fårö's gorgeous countryside. Stay on the bus from the ferry terminal and ask to get off at the hostel. Guests can borrow bikes free of charge. (☎22 36 39. Open May-Aug. Reception 8am-noon and 5-7pm. Dorms 85kr; doubles 260kr; quads 520kr. Nonmembers add 45kr.) You can also take advantage of the right of public access and **camp**.

SOUTHERN SWEDEN

This mild region is graced with flat beaches, wide fields of waving grass, and Swedish summer homes. **Halland** and the southwest **Småland** coastline, between Västervik and Kalmar, are especially popular.

KALMAR   ☎0480

Although Kalmar (pop. 33,000) is no longer at the center of Scandinavian politics, the city still retains a certain dignity and undeniable beauty. Perched elegantly across from downtown Kalmar is its greatest attraction, the 16th-century **Kalmar Slott**. Once an important center for Scandinavian politics, today the Renaissance-style palace hosts art exhibits and displays on castle life. (Open July daily 10am-6pm; June and Aug. 10am-5pm; Apr.-May and Sept. 10am-4pm; Oct.-Mar. 11am-3:30pm. 70kr, students 40kr; Oct.-Mar. reduced prices.) The castle hosts an annual **Renaissance Festival** in late June and early July (☎45 06 62 for info and tickets), and a **Medieval Festival** in late July. Adjoining the castle's seaside grounds is the tree-lined **Kyrkogarden** cemetery. The **Kalmar Konstmuseum**, down the street at Slottsvagan 1D, is a center for modern Swedish art and design. (Open daily 11am-5pm, Th until 8pm. 40kr, students 30kr.) While the **Läns Museum**, Skeppsbrog. 49, does not contain a fully-restored ship like Stockholm's Vasa Museum, it displays many intriguing relics from the wreckage of the 17th-century warship Kronan, which sank in a battle against the Danes. (Open mid-June to mid-Aug. daily 10am-6pm; mid-Aug. to mid-June Tu-F 10am-4pm, Sa-Su 11am-4pm. 50kr, students 25kr, under-18 free.) In the center of town, Kalmar's light-filled **Domkyrkan** is a beautiful example of a 17th-century baroque church.

   Trains and **buses** arrive south of town, across the bay from the castle. Trains go to: Gothenburg (2-5 per day, 395/275kr); Malmö (7 per day, 380/265kr); and Stockholm (2 per day, 475/335kr). Buses run directly to Stockholm (3 per day; 315kr, students 250kr). The new **tourist office**, Ölandskajen 9, offers info on nearby sights, books hotel and private accommodations, and provides free **Internet** access. From the train station, turn right onto Stationsg., and then turn right at the McDonald's onto Ölandskajen. (☎41 77 00; www.kalmar.se/turism. Open July M-F 9am-8pm, Sa-Su 10am-5pm; June and Aug. M-F 9am-7pm, Sa-Su 10am-4pm; Sept.-May M-F 9am-5pm.) To hike the 1km from the tourist office to the modern **Vandrarhem Svanen (HI) ❷**, Rappeg. 1, on the island of Ängö, head north on Larmg., turn right on Södra Kanalg., cross the bridge, and turn left on Ängöleden; it will be on the right. (☎129 28. Breakfast 55kr. Sheets 45kr. Laundry 25kr. Internet access. Reception mid-June to mid-Aug. M-F 7am-10pm, Sa-Su 7:30am-9pm; mid-Aug. to mid-June M-F 7am-9pm, Sa-Su 7:30am-9pm. Dorms 190kr. Nonmembers add 45kr.) Alternatively, the **Söderportshotellet ❹**, Slottsvägen 1, between the Konstmuseum and Kalmar Slott, rents student housing during the summer months. (☎125 01. Breakfast included. Open June 15-Aug. 15.

SWEDEN

Singles 395kr; doubles 595kr.) Seaside **Stensö Camping ❶** is 2km south of Kalmar; take bus #3. (☎888 03. Electricity 30kr. Tents and RVs 105-135kr. Cabins 400kr. Mid-Aug. to mid-June reduced prices.) **Larmtorget** is the best place to find cheap restaurants. **Postal Code:** 39101.

❷ DAYTRIP FROM KALMAR: ÖLAND AND GLASRIKET. Visible from Kalmar's coast, the long, thin island of **Öland** stretches over 100km of green fields and white sand beaches. The royal family roosts here on holiday; Crown Princess Victoria's birthday, Victoriadagen (July 14), is celebrated island-wide. Commoners fill the **beaches** of Löttorp and Böda in the north and Grönhögen and Ottenby in the south. A UNESCO World Heritage site, **Southern Öland**'s expansive fields, ancient graveyard, and wooden windmills make for scenic bike trips. **Buses** #101 and 106 go from Kalmar's train station to Borgholm, the island's main town (30min., 45kr); bus #106 continues to Löttorp and Böda (77kr), while bus #103 goes to Grönhögen and Ottenby (53kr). Öland's **tourist office** (☎04 85 56 06 00) is outside Färjestaden; follow signs from the first bus stop after the bridge on all buses.

In the towns surrounding Kalmar, collectively dubbed **Glasriket** (Kingdom of Crystal), artisans craft some of the world's most exquisite hand-blown glassworks. **Bus** #138 (1hr., 100kr) passes workshops at **Orrefors** and **Kosta Böda**. (☎04 81 341 95 or 04 78 345 00. Both open M-F 9am-6pm, Sa 10am-4pm, Su noon-4pm.)

MALMÖ ☎040

Owing in part to its proximity to Copenhagen and mainland Europe, Malmö (pop. 265,000), Sweden's third-largest city, has an ethnic and cultural diversity unmatched elsewhere in Sweden. The city has been re-energized by the completion of the Øresund bridge to Denmark, which cut the travel time between Malmö and Copenhagen to under 30min. Intimate and full of outdoor cafes, **Lilla Torg**, which adjoins the larger **Stortorget** on one side, is great for people-watching and is known as the best meeting place in Sweden. **Möllevångstorget,** in the diverse neighborhood of **Möllevången,** has a lively open-air market, laid-back local bars, and lots of affordable ethnic restaurants.

🖪🖬 TRANSPORTATION AND PRACTICAL INFORMATION. The train station and harbor lie north of the Old Town. **Trains** arrive from: Copenhagen (35min., every 20min., 80kr); Gothenburg (3½hr.; every hr.; 430kr, students 305kr); and Stockholm (4½hr., every hr., 720/505kr). The **tourist office** in the train station books rooms for a 70kr fee. (☎34 12 00. Open June-Aug. M-F 9am-8pm, Sa-Su 10am-5pm; May and Sept. M-F 9am-6pm, Sa-Su 10am-3pm; Oct.-Apr. M-F 9am-6pm, Sa 10am-2pm.) **Cityroom** (☎79 59 94) also books rooms. **Internet** access can be found at the **Cyberspace Cafe,** four blocks down Engelbrektsg. (☎23 81 28; cyberspace-cafe.net. 22kr per 30min. Open M-F 10am-10pm, Sa-Su noon-10pm.) **Postal Code:** 20110.

🖬🖸 ACCOMMODATIONS AND FOOD. Vandrarhem Malmö (HI) ❷, Backav. 18, is out of the way but well-kept. Roadside rooms are quite loud; ask for a room on the yard. From the train station or harbor, cross the canal and Norra Vallg. and take bus #21 to Vandrarhemmet. (☎82 220; www.malmohostel.com. Breakfast 50kr. Kitchen available. Sheets 40kr. Reception May-Aug. 8-10am and 4-10pm; Sept.-Apr. 8-10am and 4-8pm. Dorms 130kr; singles 285kr; doubles 350kr; triples 450kr. Nonmembers add 45kr.) **Hotel Pallas ❸,** across from the train station at Norra Vallg. 74, is a bit pricier but has a great location. (☎611 50 77. In-room breakfast 30kr. Singles 355kr; doubles 395-475kr. Cash only.) Nightlife resides in the bars on Lilla Torg and Möllevangstorg. and the clubs around Stortorg. With its diverse population, expect to get as wide a range of ethnic food in Malmö as anywhere in Sweden. **Gök Boet ❶**, Lilla torg. 3, serves sandwiches and cafe food (35-45kr) at very reasonable prices and turns into a popular bar at night. (Open Su-Th 11am-midnight; F-Sa 11am-2am; Su 11am-11pm.) Next door, the Lilla Torg **Saluhallen** has numerous restaurants and markets that offer a variety of global cuisines. (Open M-Sa 10am-6pm; Su 10am-3pm.)

SIGHTS AND ENTERTAINMENT

The **Form Design Center,** Lilla Torg 9, hosts rotating exhibits on the cutting edge of Swedish design. (☎664 51 50; www.scandinaviandesign.com. Open Su noon-4pm, T-W and F 11am-5pm, Th 11am-6pm, Sa 10am-4pm. Closed Su-M in July. Free.) The all-white, stunningly designed **Malmö Konsthall,** St. Johannesg. 7, exhibits challenging but accessible modern art. (☎34 12 94. Open M-Tu and Th-Su 11am-5pm, W 11am-9pm. Guided tours daily at 2pm. Free.) Surrounded by a beautiful park in Malmö's West End, **Malmöhus Castle** houses three museums, all under the same auspices. Inside the castle itself, the **Malmös Museer** documents the city's history, while the **Konstmuseet** displays Swedish and international artwork from the 15th century to today. Down the road, the **Tekniska och Sjöfartsmuseum** (Technology and Maritime Museum) has various exhibits on Sweden's extensive naval history and technology. Be sure not to miss the chance to go inside the **U3 Submarine,** which served in Sweden's navy from 1943 to 1964. On Sunday and Tuesday afternoons, former servicemen stand by and give firsthand accounts of the submarine and share old war stories. (☎34 44 37. Open June-Aug. daily 10am-4pm; Sept.-May noon-4pm. 40kr, students 20kr.) For a completely different cultural experience, walk along the **Ribersborg beach** to the **Kallbadhuset,** a natural swimming bath and sauna, where locals are known to break through the ice to go swimming in winter. In summer, it hosts jazz and poetry evenings. (☎26 03 66. Open May-Aug. M-F 8:30am-7pm; Sept.-Apr. M-F noon-7pm, Sa-Su 9am-4pm. 35kr.)

LUND   ☎046

What Oxford and Cambridge are to England, Lund (pop. 72,500) and Uppsala are to Sweden. **Lund University**'s antagonism toward its scholarly northern neighbor in Uppsala has inspired countless pranks, drag shows, and drinkfests in Lund's bright streets. With its vibrant student life and proximity to major cities like Malmö and Copenhagen, Lund makes an excellent alternative base for exploring Skåne or just a nice daytrip. The town's Romanesque cathedral, **St. Laurentius,** is an impressive 900-year-old reminder of the time when Lund was the religious center of Scandinavia; its floor-to-ceiling astronomical clock rings in the hour at noon and 3pm, and its 7074-pipe organ is Sweden's largest. To find the cathedral from the train station, walk straight across Bang. and Knut den Storestorg, then turn left on Kyrkog. (Open M-Sa 8am-6pm, Su 9am-6pm.) The **University** campus is a calm stroll across the park from the cathedral; find events info at **Student Info,** Sang. 2, in the Student Union. (☎38 49 49; af.lu.se. Open Sept.-May M-F 10am-4pm.) **Kulturen,** across the street from the Student Union at the end of Sankt Anneg. on Tegnerplastén, is an expansive, engrossing open-air museum with 17th- and 18th-century homes, churches, and historical displays. (Open mid-Apr. to Sept. daily 11am-5pm; Oct. to mid-Apr. Su and Tu-Sa noon-4pm. 50kr.) Lund's thriving nightlife revolves around the "nations," student clubs that throw parties and generally serve as social centers; stop by Student Info for tips on getting a guest pass. Students should not have much trouble getting into the nations, but others may have more difficulty. The best options that don't require a pass are **Stortorget,** Stortorg. 1, a bar and nightclub (22+, 20+ with student ID. Bar open Su-W 11:30am-midnight, Th 11:30am-1am, F-Sa 11:30am-2am. Nightclub open Th-Sa 11pm-3am.), and **Palladium,** Stora Söderg. 13 (50kr cover. Bar open Aug. to mid-June 11:30am-10pm; nightclub open Th-Sa 10pm-3am). **Mejerlet,** Stora Söderg. 64, and art-house theater and bar, is also popular with students (☎211 00 23). Be warned—many establishments of all sorts close during the summer, when school is out of session.

Lund is easily accessible from Malmö on most SJ **trains** and by local **pågatågen** (10min.; 1-5 per hr.; 34kr, railpasses valid). Trains also run to: Gothenburg (3hr., every hr., 430/300/190kr); Kalmar (3hr., every 2hr., 380/265/170kr); and Stockholm (4-6hr.; every 1-2hr.; 585-1045kr, students 410-730kr). The **tourist office,** Kyrkog. 11, books rooms for a 50kr fee. (☎35 50 40. Open June-Aug. M-F 10am-6pm, Sa-Su 10am-2pm; May and Sept. M-Sa only; Oct.-Apr. M-F only.) The delightful but cramped **Hostel Tåget (HI)** ❶, Vävareg. 22, is housed in a 1940s train. Take the overpass to the park side of the station. (☎14 28 20. Breakfast 50kr. Sheets 50kr. Reception Apr.-Oct. daily 8-10am and 5-8pm; Nov.-Mar. 8-10am and 5-7pm. Call ahead. Dorms 120kr. Nonmembers add 45kr.) To get to **Källby Camping** ❶, take bus #1 (dir.: Klostergården) 2km south of the city center. (☎35 51 88. Open mid-June to Aug. 45kr per tent, 160kr per RV.) Budget food can be found on Stortorg. and Stora Söderg. as well as at the open-air **market** at Mårtenstorg. (open daily 7am-2pm) and the adjoining **Saluhallen** (open M-F 9:30am-3pm, Sa 9am-3pm). **Postal Code:** 22101.

YSTAD   ☎0411

When first seen from the windows of the train, Ystad (pop. 26,000) appears to be nothing more than a ferry port for those heading on to **Bornholm,** Denmark (p. 285). Just a few blocks inland, though, Ystad's cobblestone pathways and half-timbered houses are worth peek. Many theorize that the stone formation **Ales Stenar** (Ale's Stones) once served as a solar calendar; its stones are aligned with the positions of the sun at the solstices. Take bus #322 to get there (30min., 3 per day, 23kr).

Bornholms Trafikken (☎130 13) **ferries** sail to Bornholm (1½-2½hr., up to 6 per day in summer, 180kr). **Trains** pull in from Malmö (45min., every hr., 70kr). The **tourist office** across from the station offers 15min. of free **Internet** access. (☎57 76 81. Open mid-June to mid-Aug. M-F 9am-7pm, Sa 10am-7pm, Su 11am-6pm; mid-Aug. to mid-June M-F 9am-5pm.) The train station houses the **Vandrarhemmet Stationen (SVIF)** ❷, a sunny hostel perfectly located for those passing through. (☎070 857 79 95. Sheets 60kr. Bikes 10kr. Reception June-Aug. 9-10am and 5-7pm; Oct.-May 5-6pm. Doubles 360kr; triples 540kr; quads 720kr.) **Saluhallen supermarket** is off the main square. (Open daily 8am-9pm.) **Postal Code:** 27101.

GOTHENBURG (GÖTEBORG)   ☎031

If Stockholm is "the Venice of the North," then Gothenburg (YO-teh-boree; pop. 460,000) is its Milan. The industrial center of Sweden and home to such companies as Volvo, Gothenburg is surprisingly relaxed. With top-notch museums, vibrant street life, and beautiful parks, Gothenburg has something to please every traveler.

🖩🛈 TRANSPORTATION AND PRACTICAL INFORMATION. Trains go from Central Station to: Malmö (2¾-3¾hr., 12 per day, 305-430kr); Oslo (4hr.; 3 per day; 397kr, under-26 279kr); and Stockholm (3-5½hr.; 15 per day; 570-680kr, under-26 400-475kr). Stena Line **ferries** (☎704 00 00) sail to Frederikshavn, Denmark (2-3¼hr.; 10 per day; 100-200kr, 50% Scanrail, InterRail, or Eurail discount) and Kiel, Germany (13½hr.; daily; in summer 650-750kr, off-season 330-490kr). DFDS Seaways (☎65 06 50) sails to Newcastle, England (22-25hr.; daily; 525-1175kr, 25% under-26 discount). The **tourist office,** Kungsportspl. 2, books rooms for a 60kr fee and sells the **Göteborg pass,** which includes public transit and admission to various attractions, although it may not be worth it for those who plan to see fewer than 3 or 4 sights. From the station, cross Drottningtorg. and follow Östra Larmag. from the right of the Radisson. (☎61 25 00. 1-day pass 175kr, 2-day pass 295kr. Open late June to early Aug. daily 9am-8pm; off-season reduced hours.) The stylish **stadsbibliotek** (city library), in Götapl., provides free **Internet** access. (Open M-F 10am-8pm, Sa 11am-5pm.) **Postal Code:** 40401.

▛▟ ACCOMMODATIONS AND FOOD. Gothenburg's hostels are mainly in the west end of the city. The well-run ▧**Masthuggsterrassen ❶,** Masthuggsterrassen 8, has a welcoming atmosphere; ask for a room with a harbor view. Take tram #3, 9, or 11 to *Masthuggstorget,* cross the square diagonally onto Angra Långg., walk up the stairs, and follow the signs along the terrace. (☎42 48 20; fax 42 48 21. Breakfast 55kr. Kitchen available. Sheets 55kr. Laundry 20kr. Reception 8-10am and 5-8pm. Dorms 150kr; doubles 380kr; quads 540kr.) The elegant **Hotel Flora ❹,** Grönsakstorg. 2, is the best budget option in the center of town. Take tram #1, 7, or 9 to *Grönsakstorget.* (☎13 86 16; www.hotelflora.nu. Breakfast included. Reception 24hr. Singles 415kr; doubles 575kr.) Pitch your tent at **Kärralund Camping ❶,** on Olbersg. Catch tram #5 to Welandersg., then go east on Olbersg. (☎84 02 00. Reception May-Aug. 7am-11pm; Sept.-Apr. reduced hours. Tents 60-120kr.)

Affordable restaurants and cafes are easy to find on Linnég., Viktoriag., and Vasag., and around Haga. ▧**Solrosen ❶,** Kaponjarg. 4a, a mellow vegetarian restaurant, is a neighborhood institution. (Salad bar 45kr. Daily specials 65kr. Open M-F 11:30am-1am, Sa 2pm-1am. Kitchen closes at 9pm.) Cafes on Kungsportsavenyn are abundant but pricey; try the popular **Eva's Paley ❷,** Kungsportsavenyn 39, known for huge portions and great people-watching. (Lunch buffet 52kr. Happy Hour F 4-7pm. Open M-Th 8am-11pm, F 8am-2:30am, Sa 10am-12:30am, Su 10am-11pm.) The **Saluhallen,** Kungstorg., is a covered market with a great selection of groceries. (Open M-F 9am-6pm, Sa 9am-2pm.)

▣▐ SIGHTS AND ENTERTAINMENT. Just across Drottningtorg. and the Hamn canal from the train station is the bustling shopping district of **Inom Vallgraven.** Tree-lined paths wind through **Tradgardsforeningens Park.** The city's main drag, **Kungsportsavenyn** (known simply as **Avenyn**), stretches from **Kungsportsplatsen** to **Götaplatsen,** the site of Carl Milles's famous **sculpture fountain** of Poseidon. The size of Poseidon's manhood caused an uproar when the design was unveiled; it was later modified. In the same square, the imposing edifice of the **Konstmuseet** contains three top-notch museums. The Konstmuseet itself has an impressive collection of Swedish and international painters. The adjacent **Konsthall** displays modern and contemporary art, while the **Hasselblad Center** hosts rotating exhibits. (All open Tu and Th 11am-6pm, W 11am-9pm, F-Su 11am-5pm. 40kr. Under-20 free.) Nearby, the **Röhsska Museum,** Vasag. 37-39, is dedicated to that most Swedish of the arts: design. Its exhibits cover everything from 4000-year-old Chinese crafts to modern Scandinavian furniture. (Open Su and W-Sa noon-5pm, Tu noon-9pm. 40kr. Under-20 free.) The **Göteborgs Operan,** Lilla Bommen, an architectural marvel that mimics a ship at full mast, is en route to the **Göteborg Maritime Centrum,** which features a number of docked ships that you can board. (Opera in session in winter; purchase tickets at ☎13 13 00 or at the box office. Maritime center open July-Aug. daily 10am-8pm; June and Sept. 10am-6pm; Oct.-Nov. and Mar.-May 10am-4pm.

60kr.) The **Stadsmuseet,** Norra Hamng. 12, houses
exhibits on the history of the city from the Vikings
to post-industrial rebirth. (Open May-Aug. daily
10am-5pm; Sept.-Apr. Su, Tu and Th-Sa 10am-5pm,
W 10am-8pm. 40kr, students 10kr.) The expansive
Botanical Gardens, Carl Skottsbergs Gata 22a, make
for a wonderful stroll.

One canal farther to the west lie two of Gothenburg's most appealing small neighborhoods, the
relatively untouristed **Haga** district, a formerly
working-class neighborhood that is now lined with
art galleries, bookstores, and cafes. Southwest of
the Haga and Linnéstan, parts the lush
Slottsskogsparken, a path leads up from Stig-
bergssliden to the hilltop **Masthuggskyrkan,** an
intriguing brick church with a timber ceiling that
suggests the inside of Viking ship; the view of the
city is gorgeous. A short trip from the mainland of
Gothenburg, **Göteborgs Skärgård** is a summer paradise for beach-goers and sailors. Take tram #11 to
Saltholmen, then catch a ferry (50min., every hr.)
to reach the secluded **beach** on **Vrångö** island.

Gothenburg has a thriving theater and classical
music scene—pick up *What's on in Göteborg* at the
tourist office. Posh nightclubs line **Kungsportsavenyn;**
especially popular are **Nivå, Deep,** and **Valand.** ◪**Nefertiti,** Hvitfeldtspl. 6, is an intimate jazz bar that transforms into a dance club after 1am. (Cover 70kr for
club; 120kr for concerts. Open Th-Sa 9pm-4am.)
Locals and expats mix it up at **Joe Farelli's,** Kungs-
sportsavenyn 12. (Open Su-Th noon-1am; F-Sa noon-
3am.) Across the canal on Nya Allén, striking **Tragar'n**
has a dance floor and an outdoor bar. (21+. Cover
80kr. Open Th 11pm-3am, F-Sa 11pm-5am.) **Gretas,**
Drottninggtn. 35, is a popular gay bar. Many clubs
have gay or lesbian nights; contact the **RFSL** (p. 992)
for info.

▶ DAYTRIP FROM GOTHENBURG: VARBERG.
Between Gothenburg and Malmö beckon the expansive beaches of Varberg and its spectacular **fortress.**
(Tours mid-June to mid-Aug. every hr. 11am-4pm.
40kr.) The shallow **Apelviken** bay offers some of the
best surfing and windsurfing in Northern Europe.
Follow the *Strandpromenaden* (boardwalk) along
the beach 2km south of town. **Surfer's Paradise,**
Söderg. 22 (☎03 40 67 70 55), rents gear and gives
tips. **Trains** arrive from Gothenburg (1hr., 100-200kr)
and Malmö (2½hr., 300-500kr). To get from the station to the **tourist office,** in Brunnsparken, walk four
blocks right on Västra Vallg. (☎03 40 887 70. Open
mid-June to mid-Aug. M-Sa 9am-7pm, Su 3-7pm; mid-
Aug. to mid-June M-F 9am-6pm.) **Postal Code:** 43201.

DALARNA

Three hours west of Stockholm, Dalarna is the seat of Sweden's folk culture, home to spirited Midsummer celebrations and the national symbol, the Dala horse.

MORA. An excellent base for exploring Dalarna, bright and compact Mora (pop. 19,000) sits on the western shore of Lake Siljan. The 310km **Siljansleden bike trail** skirts the shore of the lake, and a 340km **walking trail** traverses pastures, forests, small lakes, and lovely mountain scenery. The legendary red wooden **dalahäst** (Dala horses) are hand-made in **Nusnäs,** 10km east of Mora (bus #108; 15min., 15kr). On the first Sunday in March, Mora serves as the terminus of the **Vasaloppet,** the most popular cross-country skiing race in the world. The route can be hiked in summer. **Trains** run to Östersund (7hr.; daily 3:30pm; 600kr, under-26 300kr) and Stockholm (4hr., 7 per day, 275kr). The **tourist office,** in Mora's train station, books rooms (135-155kr) for a 25kr fee. (☎02 50 59 20 20. Open mid-June to mid-Aug. M-F 9am-7pm, Sa-Su 10am-5pm; mid-Aug. to mid-June M-F 9am-5pm.) The **Stadsbibliotekt,** off Kyrkogtn. at Köpmang. 4, has **Internet** access. (20k per hr. Open M-F 10am-7pm, Sa 10am-2pm). The homey **Vandrarhem Mora (STF) ❶,** Fredsg. 6, is 500m from the train station; turn left on the main road and turn right on Fredsg. (☎02 50 381 96. Breakfast 60kr. Kitchen available. Sheets 60kr. Reception 8-10am and 5-7pm. Dorms 140kr; doubles 320kr. Nonmembers add 45kr.) There is an **ICA supermarket** on Kyrkog. (Open M-Sa 9am-8pm, Su 11am-8pm.) **Postal Code:** 79201.

ÖSTERSUND. The hilly lakeside town of Östersund (pop. 42,000), is a required stopover for travelers on the *Inlandsbanan* or those headed to Trondheim, Norway. Lake Storsjön is perfect for boating and swimming; watch out for the fabled resident **monster,** which is "spotted" every year by lucky eyewitnesses and unlucky swimmers. The steamer *S/S Thomée* runs cruises and monster-spotting tours. (☎063 14 40 01. 65-95kr.) Rent a **bike** at **Cykelogen,** Kyrkg. 45 (☎063 12 20 80; open M-F 10am-1pm and 2-6pm, Sa 10am-2pm; 100kr per day), and pedal over the footbridge to **Frösön Island,** once thought to be the home of Viking gods. **Trains** run to Stockholm (6hr.; 4 per day; 530kr, under-26 370kr) and Trondheim (5½hr.; 2 per day; 270kr, under-14 135kr). From June 24-Aug. 3, the *Inlandsbanan* runs to Mora (7hr., 6:45am, 300kr) and Gällivare, Lapland (15hr., 485kr). The **tourist office,** Rådhusg. 44, books rooms for free. From the train station, walk up the hill on your left and continue down Prästg.; hang a right one block up Postgränd. (☎063 14 40 01. Open June 24-Aug. 8 M-Sa 9am-9pm, Su 9am-7pm; Aug. 9-June 23 reduced hours.) Wild strawberries grow on the thatched roofs of whimsical log cabins at the **Frösötornets Härbärge ❶** hostel. Take bus #5 from the cit m y center. (☎063 51 57 67. **Internet** access. Reception 9am-9pm. Call ahead. Open May-Oct. Dorms 125kr.) Stock up at the **Hemköp supermarket** at Kyrkg. 56. (Open M-F 8am-8pm, Sa 9am-6pm, Su noon-4pm.) **Postal Code:** 83101.

GULF OF BOTHNIA

The Gulf of Bothnia is best known for its natural attractions: sprawling forests, stark ravines, endless lakes, and miles of pristine coastline. Yet its cities—quieter, and friendlier than their southern counterparts—maintain an allure all their own.

GÄVLE. An hour and a half north of Stockholm, Gävle (pop. 90,000) is the first stop on the way to northern Sweden. Just south of the train station lie the cobblestoned streets and 17th-century houses of **Gamle Gefle,** the only part of Gävle that survived a ravaging 19th-century fire. In downtown Gävle, the **Konstcentrum,** Kyrkogtn. 24, hosts rotating contemporary art exhibits. (Open Su noon-3pm, W-F noon-5pm, Sa noon-3pm.) **Trains** run from Gävle to Stockholm (up to 20 per day, 100-270kr) and Sundsvall (7 per day). Across from the train station, the **tourist office,** Drottningg. 37, has **Internet** access. (☎ 026 14 74 30. Open M-F 9am-6pm, Sa 9am-2pm, Su 11am-4pm.) Located in the middle of Gamle Gefle, the **Vandrarhem Gävle (STF) ❶,** Södra Rådmansg. 1, has well-lit rooms and a pleasant courtyard. From the train station, turn left, cross the canal, turn right onto Södra Strandg., turn left at the library, go through the square and up the stairs; the hostel is on the left. (☎026 62 17 45. Breakfast 55kr. Kitchen available. Sheets 55kr. Reception 8-10am and 5-7pm. Dorms 125kr. Nonmembers add 45kr.)

ÖRNSKÖLDSVIK. Örnsköldsvik (urn-SHULDS-vik; "Ö-vik" to locals; pop. 28,000) is off the main train route, and is a superb base for fishing, or **hiking.** The 127km **Höga Kusten Leden** (High Coast Trail), a UNESCO world heritage site, winds along to most dramatic section of Sweden's Baltic coast. Several day hikes are also nearby, including the easy **Yellow Trail** loop (6km). You'll find the trailhead on Hantverkareg.; from the tourist office, walk uphill on Nyg. and turn right. **Buses** run from Örnsköldsvik to: Östersund (4½hr., 1-3 per day, 252kr); Sundsvall (2hr., 6-7 per day, 140kr); and Umeå (2hr., 7 per day, 107kr). The **tourist office,** Nyg. 18, books rooms for a 40kr fee. (☎06 60 125 37. Open mid-June to mid-Aug. M-F 9am-7pm, Sa-Su 10am-3pm; mid-Aug. to mid-June M-F 10am-5pm.) To get there, walk up the steps behind the bus station, follow Fabriksg., and turn left on Nyg. The town **library,** Lasarettsg. 5, offers free **Internet** access. (Open M-Th 10am-6pm, F 10am-5pm, Sa 10am-2pm.) **STF Vandrarhem Örnsköldsvik (HI) ❶,** Högsnäsgården pl. 1980, is outside town in a gracious country house. The last bus to the hostel (#421; 25kr) leaves by 9pm. (☎06 60 702 44. Reception 9-10am and 5-7pm. 130kr. Nonmembers add 45kr.) Pick up groceries at **Hemköp** on Stortorg. (Open M-F 10am-7pm, Sa 10am-3pm, Su noon-4pm.) **Postal Code:** 89101.

UMEÅ. Umeå (OOM-eh-oh; pop. 106,000), the largest city in northern Sweden, is a fast-growing university town surrounded by beautiful countryside. The 30km **Umeleden bike and car trail** snakes past old hydropower stations, ancient rock-carvings, an arboretum, and **Baggböle Herrgård,** a delightful cafe in a 19th-century mansion. (Open June-Aug. Su and Tu-Sa noon-7pm.) A bridge upriver allows for a 15km loop. **Cykel och Mopedhandlaren,** Kungsg. 101, rents and repairs **bikes.** (☎14 01 70. 70kr per day, 195kr per week. Open M-F 9:30am-5:30pm, Sa 10am-1pm.) The **Tavelsjöleden** (24km) and **Isälvsleden** (60km) trails are the best of the area's hikes.

 Trains go to Gothenburg (14½hr., 2 per day, 355kr) and Luleå (4½hr., 2 per day, 255kr). Regular trains do not run north from Umeå, but the private Connex trains connect to Kiruna, Luleå, and Narvik, Norway. Ybuss **buses** (☎(0200) 33 44 44) run to Stockholm (10hr.; daily; 330kr, students 240kr), and Norrlands Kusten (☎(020) 51 15 13) sends buses north to Luleå (4hr., 250kr) and Kiruna (9½hr., 400kr). The bus terminal is across from the train station. RG Line **ferries** (☎090 18 52 00) sail to Vasa, Finland (4hr.; daily; 360kr, students 270kr). The harbor is 20km south of Umeå; buses leave from the tourist office an hour before departure. To get to the **tourist office,** Renmarkstorg. 15, walk straight down Rådhusesplanaden from the train station and turn right on Skolg. (☎090 16 16 16; www.umea.se. Open mid-June to late Aug. M-F 8am-7pm, Sa 10am-4pm, Su noon-4pm; late Aug. to Sept. M-F 10am-5pm, Sa 10am-2pm; May to mid-June M-F 10am-6pm, Sa 10am-2pm; Oct.-Apr. M-F 10am-5pm.) The nondescript **Youth Hostel (HI) ❶,** V. Esplanaden 10, is to the left off Skolg. (☎090 77 16 50. Breakfast 50kr. Sheets 45kr. Reception M-F 8am-noon and 5-8pm, Sa-Su 8-10am and 5-8pm. Dorms 120kr, with bath 140-155kr. Nonmembers add 45kr.) Take Holmsund bus #124 from Vasaplan to **Ljumvikens Camping ❶**. (☎ 09 04 17 10. 75kr per tent.) Nightlife in Umeå centers around its students, who spend nights at the bars along **Rådhusgata** and **Kungsgata. Postal Code:** 90101.

LULEÅ. At the mouth of the **Lule Älv** lies the quiet university town of Luleå (LOOL-eh-oh; pop. 70,000). The **Norbottens Museum,** Storgtn. 2, holds exhibitions on Swedish and Sami history. (Open Tu-F 10am-4pm, Sa-Su noon-4pm. Free.) Nearby is **Gammelstad,** a UNESCO World Heritage site. Going to church used to require a full day's travel in winter; 15th-century farmers built hundreds of tiny cottages here to house their families before making the trip home. (Bus #32; 23kr. Church open June-Aug. daily 9am-6pm; Sept.-May M-F 10am-2pm. In summer, English tours every hr. 10am-4pm. 30kr.) The mostly uninhabited **Luleå archipelago** awaits exploration by ferry, canoe, or kayak.

Trains run to Kiruna (4hr., 4 per day, 160kr) and Umeå (4½hr., 2 per day, 255kr). The **tourist office,** Storg. 43b, books private rooms (120-450kr) for free. From the train station, cross Prästg. and follow it to the right, walk diagonally across the park, cross Hermalingsg., and tromp up Storg. to get there. (☎ 09 02 29 35 00. Open June to mid-Aug. M-F 9am-7pm, Sa-Su 10am-4pm; mid-Aug. to May M-F 10am-6pm, Sa 10am-2pm.) The Luleå **Youth Hostel and Mini-Hotel ❶**, Sandviksg. 26, has small but clean rooms. From the tourist office, walk down Storg., turn left onto Rådhusg., and follow it until the highway; the hostel is 50m to the right. (☎ 09 02 22 26 60. Reception daily 9-10am and 5-7pm. Dorms 150kr; singles 175kr; doubles 350kr.) **Storgatan** is full of cafes that convert from a laid-back daytime atmosphere to an energetic night scene. **Postal Code:** 97101.

LAPLAND (SÁPMI)

Lapland has been called "Europe's last wilderness." Hundreds of miles of mountains, forests, and lakes extend in all directions, much of landscape untouched and even unexplored. In addition to its raw beauty, Lapland is also rich in the culture of the Sami, descendants of prehistoric Scandinavians, who now use helicopters and snowmobiles to tend their herds of reindeer.

▐ TRANSPORTATION

There are two **rail** routes to Lapland. The **coastal route** runs from Stockholm through Boden, Umeå, and Kiruna to Narvik, Norway, along the **Malmbanan** (ore railway). From Midsummer (June 24) to early August, the privately run **Inlandsbanan** (p. 987) runs north from Mora. For info, see www.connex.se or contact **Din resebyrå** in Umeå (☎ (090) 14 28 90) or **Centralens resebyrå** in Kiruna (☎ (0980) 660 15). **Buses,** most of which do not accept railpasses, are the only transportation to smaller towns. Call ☎ (020) 47 00 47 for schedules. Two trains per day travel from Luleå to Narvik, **Norway** (6½hr.), stopping in Gällivare, Kiruna, and Abisko.

KIRUNA. The only large town in Lapland, Kiruna (pop. 23,000) is an industrial center in the wilderness, where Sami culture exists beside cutting-edge research facilities. The world's largest **mine** put Kiruna on the map. Tours descend 540m to an old mining level, now an informative museum. (Every hr. 9am-4pm. 195kr.) Scientists at **ESRANGE,** a space center 40km outside Kiruna, study the aurora borealis and the ozone layer. (4hr. tours depart from the tourist office June-Aug. M-F 9:30am. 190kr.) Kiruna is also a useful gateway to

╡E BIG SPLURGE

PARAD*ICE* HOTEL

Rising out of the Torne River in ₃uburban Jukkasjärvi, the Icehotel ∩ay well be the world's most ∪nusual lodging; the bragging ∩ights alone are worth the cost. ⸰ach year, halls are reconstructed ∍ntirely out of ice, with translucent ∍illars supporting cavernous ceil-ngs and awe-inspiring ice chande-iers suspended from above. The ∍emperature, a toasty -5°C, is sur-∍risingly manageable. Guests ₃leep swathed in fur on ice beds, ∍nd are awoken (or revived) each ∩orning with a hot cup of lingen-∍erry juice.

Amenities include an **ice ∍hurch**, which hosts weddings, ∩he **Absolut Icebar**, where unique ∪rinks are served *in* the rocks, and ∩he **Ice Globe Theater,** a replica ∍f Shakespeare's original con-₃tructed entirely—you guessed it—∍ut of ice. For those interested in ∩ore active pursuits (or perhaps ∪st dissatisfied with the furni-∪ure), the hotel arranges every-∩hing from dogsledding runs to the ∍irport to ice-sculpting lessons.

In the warmer months, the **Ice-∩otel Art Center,** a 10,000 sq. ft. ∩reezer, keeps the icebar and ∩any sculptures intact, offering ₃ummer visitors a glimpse of Juk-∢asjärvi's winter wonderland.

(☎668 99; www.icehotel.com. ∃rom Kiruna, take bus #501. Break-∍ast and sauna included. Jan.-Mar. ₃ingles 2320kr; doubles 2490kr. ⸰ec. and Apr. reduced prices. Non-∢uest visits 100kr, students 80kr.)

▨**Abisko National Park,** which contains **Kebnekaise,** Sweden's tallest mountain, and serves as the northern endpoint of the 450km **Kungsleden** (Royal Trail). In addition to the stunning **Icehotel,** the neighboring town of Jukkasjärvi has one of the first churches used to convert the Sami. (Open 8am-10pm. Free.) Feast on reindeer stew in an authentic *kata* (tent), at the **Sami culture museum.** (Open daily 10am-6pm.)

Buses run to Jokkmokk (185kr) and Luleå (5-6hr., 4 per day, 230kr). Connex **trains** run to Luleå (5-6hr., 4 per day, 160kr) and north to Abisko and Riksgränsen, as well as Narvik, Norway. **Flights** to Stockholm depart from Kiruna Flygplats. (KRN; ☎09 80 28 48 10. 2-3 per day; 500kr, students 300kr.) The Kiruna-Lapland **tourist office** is in the **Folkshuset** in the town center. Walk straight from the train station, follow the footpath through the tunnel, and then walk up to the top5 of the hill. The agents can arrange dog-sled excursions in winter. (☎09 80 188 80; www.lappland.se. **Internet** 50kr per 30min. Open June-Aug. M-F 8:30am-9pm, Sa-Su 8:30am-6pm; Sept.-May M-F 9am-5pm, Sa 10am-4pm.) The **Yellow House Hostel ❶,** Hantverkareg. 25, has a sauna and spacious rooms. (☎09 80 137 50. Breakfast 50kr. Sheets 50kr. Dorms 120kr; singles 300kr; doubles 200kr.) From the tourist office, walk uphill and turn left onto Vänortsg., which turns into Steinholtzg., which then turns into Hantverkareg. **Postal Code:** 98135.

SWITZERLAND
(SCHWEIZ, SVIZZERA, SUISSE)

The unparalleled natural beauty of Switzerland entices outdoor enthusiasts from around the globe to romp in its Alpine playground. Three-fifths of the country is dominated by mountains: The Jura cover the northwest region bordering France, the Alps stretch gracefully across the entire lower half of Switzerland, and the eastern Rhaetian Alps border Austria. While the stereotypes of Switzerland as a "Big Money" banking and watch-making mecca are to some extent true, its energetic youth culture belies its staid reputation. Although the country is not known for being cheap, the best things—warm Swiss hospitality and the highest peaks in Europe—remain priceless.

FACTS AND FIGURES

Official Name: Swiss Confederation.

Capital: Bern.

Major Cities: Basel, Geneva, Zurich.

Population: 7,300,000 (65% German, 18% French, 10% Italian).

Land Area: 41,290 sq. km.

Time Zone: GMT + 1.

Languages: German, French, Italian.

Religions: Roman Catholic (46%), Protestant (40%), none (9%).

DISCOVER SWITZERLAND

Skydive, bungee-jump, and river raft your way to adrenalized happiness in **Interlaken** (p. 1027) and the **Jungfrau Region,** the adventure capital of the world. The mighty Alps peak in **Zermatt** (p. 1029), home of the Matterhorn and year-round hiking and skiing. Ease off your mountain high in comfortable **Lucerne** (p. 1024), and then explore cutting-edge, consumer-culture **Zurich** (p. 1019). To the west, stroll

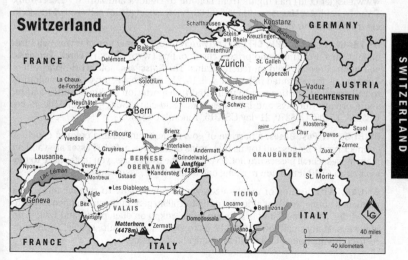

the quiet squares of **Geneva** (p. 1030), *the* international city and a symbol of diversity in this polyglot nation. If you have enough time, hit the Jazz Festival in **Montreux** (p. 1036) and taste the *dolce vita* in Italian Switzerland with stops at **Locarno** (p. 1038) and **Lugano** (p. 1037).

ESSENTIALS

WHEN TO GO

November to March is ski season; prices in eastern Switzerland double and travelers need reservations months in advance. The situation is reversed in the summer, when the flatter, western half of Switzerland fills up. Sights and accommodations are cheaper and less crowded in the shoulder season (May-June and Sept.-Oct.); call ahead to check if the Alpine resort areas will be open then.

DOCUMENTS AND FORMALITIES

VISAS. EU citizens do not need a visa. Citizens of Australia, Canada, New Zealand, South Africa, and the US do not need a visa for stays of up to 90 days.

EMBASSIES. Most foreign embassies are in **Bern** (p. 1015). Swiss embassies at home include: **Australia,** 7 Melbourne Ave., Forrest, Canberra, ACT 2603 (☎(02) 61 62 84 00); **Canada,** 5 Marlborough Ave., Ottawa, ON K1N 8E6 (☎613-235-1837); **Ireland,** 6 Ailesbury Rd., Ballsbridge, Dublin 4 (☎(353) 12 18 63 82); **New Zealand,** 22 Panama St., Wellington 6001 (☎(04) 472 15 93); **South Africa,** P818 George Ave., Arcadia 0083, 0001 Pretoria (☎(012) 430 67 07); **UK,** 16-18 Montagu Pl., London W1H 2BQ (☎(020) 76 16 60 00); and **US,** 2900 Cathedral Ave. NW, Washington, D.C. 20008 (☎202-745-7900).

TRANSPORTATION

BY PLANE. Major international airports for overseas connections are in Bern (BRN), Geneva (GVA), and Zurich (ZRH). From the UK, **easyJet** (☎(0870) 600 00 00; www.easyjet.com) has flights from London to Geneva and Zurich (UK£47-136). From Ireland, **Aer Lingus** (☎(01) 886 32 00; www.aerlingus.ie) sells round-trip tickets from Dublin to Geneva for €100-300.

BY TRAIN. Federal (**SBB, CFF**) and private railways connect most towns, with frequent trains. For times and prices, check online (www.sbb.ch). **Eurail, Europass,** and **Interrail** are all valid on federal trains. The **SwissPass,** sold worldwide, offers five options for unlimited rail travel: 4, 8, 15, 21, or 30 consecutive days. In addition to rail travel, it entitles you to unlimited transportation within 36 cities and on some private railways and lake steamers. (2nd-class 4-day pass US$160, 8-day US$225, 15-day US$270, 21-day US$315, 1-month US$350.)

BY BUS. PTT Post Buses, a barrage of government-run banana-colored coaches, connect rural villages and towns that trains don't service. **SwissPasses** are valid on many buses; **Eurail** passes are not. Even with the SwissPass, you might have to pay a bit extra (5-10SFr) if you're riding one of the direct, faster buses.

BY CAR. With armies of mechanized road crews ready to remove snow at a moment's notice, roads at altitudes of up to 1500m generally remain open throughout winter. The speed limit is 50kph in cities, 80kph on open roads, and 120kph on highways. Many small towns forbid cars to enter; some require special permits, or restrict driving hours. Call ☎140 for roadside assistance.

BY BIKE. Cycling, though strenuous, is a splendid way to see the country; most train stations rent bikes and let you return them at another station. The **Touring Club Suisse**, Chemin de Blandonnet 4, Case Postale 820, 1214 Vernier (☎(022) 417 27 27; www.tcs.ch), is a good source of maps and route descriptions.

TOURIST SERVICES AND MONEY

EMERGENCY	Police: ☎117. Ambulance: ☎144. Fire: ☎118.

TOURIST OFFICES. The **Swiss National Tourist Office,** marked by a standard blue "i" sign, is represented in nearly every town in Switzerland; most agents speak English. The tourist info website for Switzerland is www.myswitzerland.com.

MONEY. The Swiss monetary unit is the **Swiss Franc (SFr/CHF),** which is divided into 100 *centimes* (called *Rappen* in German Switzerland). Coins come in 5, 10, 20, and 50 *centimes* and 1, 2, and 5SFr; bills come in 10, 20, 50, 100, 500, and 1000SFr. Switzerland is not the cheapest destination; if you stay in hostels and prepare your own food, expect to spend 45-100SFr per day. As a general rule, it's cheaper to exchange money in Switzerland than at home. There is **no value-added tax (VAT),** although there are frequently tourist taxes of a few SFr for a night at a hostel. **Gratuities** are automatically factored into prices; however, it is polite to round up your bill 1-2SFr as a nod of approval for good service.

SWISS FRANCS		
AUS$1 = 0.90SFR		1SFR = AUS$1.11
CDN$1 = 1.01SFR		1SFR = CDN$0.99
EUR€1 = 1.54SFR		1SFR = EUR€0.65
NZ$1 = 0.80SFR		1SFR = NZ$1.24
ZAR1 = 0.19SFR		1SFR = ZAR5.19
UK£1 = 1.41SFR		1SFR = UK£0.71
US$1 = 2.23SFR		1SFR = US$0.45

COMMUNICATION

PHONE CODES	**Country code:** 41. **International dialing prefix:** 00. From outside Switzerland, dial int'l dialing prefix (see inside back cover) + 41 + city code + local number.

TELEPHONES. Whenever possible, use a calling card for international phone calls, as the long-distance rates for national phone services are often exorbitant. For info about using cell phones abroad, see p. 36. Most pay phones in Switzerland accept only prepaid phone cards. Phone cards are available at kiosks, post offices, and train stations. Direct dial access numbers include: **AT&T,** ☎0800 89 00 11; **British Telecom,** ☎0800 55 25 44; **Canada Direct,** ☎0800 55 83 30; **Ireland Direct,** ☎0800 40 00 00; **MCI,** ☎0800 89 02 22; **Sprint,** ☎0800 89 97 77; **Telecom New Zealand,** ☎0800 55 64 11; **Telkom South Africa,** ☎0800 55 85 35.

MAIL. Airmail from Switzerland averages 4-7 days to North America, although times are more unpredictable from smaller towns. Domestic letters take 1-3 days. Address mail to be held according to the following example: Firstname SURNAME, *Postlagernde Briefe*, CH-8021 Zürich, SWITZERLAND.

LANGUAGES. German, French, Italian, and Romansch are the national languages. Most urban Swiss speak English fluently. For basic German words and phrases, see p. 1055; for French, see p. 1054; for Italian, see p. 1057.

SWITZERLAND

ACCOMMODATIONS AND CAMPING

SWITZERLAND	❶	❷	❸	❹	❺
ACCOMMODATIONS	under 16SFr	16-35SFr	36-60SFr	61-120SFr	over 120SFr

There are **hostels** (*Jugendherbergen* in German, *Auberges de Jeunesse* in French, *Ostelli* in Italian) in all big cities and in most small towns. **Schweizer Jugendherbergen** (SJH; www.youthhostel.ch) runs HI hostels in Switzerland, where beds are usually 20-34SFr. Non-HI members can stay in any hostel but usually pay a surcharge. The more informal **Swiss Backpackers** (SB) organization (www.backpacker.ch) has 31 hostels for the young, foreign traveler interested in socializing. Most Swiss **campgrounds** are not isolated areas but large plots glutted with RVs. Prices average 6-9SFr per person and 4-10SFr per tent site. **Hotels** and **pensions** tend to charge at least 50-75SFr for a single room, 80-150SFr for a double. The cheapest have *Gasthof*, *Gästehaus*, or *Hotel-Garni* in the name. **Privatzimmer** (rooms in a family home) run about 25-60SFr per person. Breakfast is included at most hotels, pensions, and *Privatzimmer*.

FOOD AND DRINK

SWITZERLAND	❶	❷	❸	❹	❺
FOOD	under 9SFr	9-15SFr	16-24SFr	25-35SFr	over 35SFr

Switzerland is not for the lactose-intolerant. The Swiss are serious about dairy products, from rich and varied **cheeses** to decadent **milk chocolate**—even the major Swiss soft drink, rivella, is dairy. Swiss dishes vary from region to region and what your waiter brings you is most likely related to the language he is speaking. Bernese *Rösti*, a plateful of hash-brown potatoes (sometimes flavored with bacon or cheese), is prevalent in the German regions; cheese or meat **fondue** is popular in the French part. Try Valaisian *raclette*, made by melting cheese over a fire, scraping it onto a baked potato, and garnishing it with meat or vegetables. **Supermarkets** Migros and Co-op double as self-serve cafeterias; stop in for a cheap meal as well as groceries. Each canton has its own local beer—it's relatively cheap, often less expensive than Coca-Cola.

HIKING AND SKIING. Nearly every town has **hiking trails;** consult the local tourist office. Lucerne (p. 1024), Interlaken (p. 1027), Grindelwald (p. 1029), and Zermatt (p. 1029) offer particularly good hiking opportunities. Trails are usually marked with either red-white-red markers (only sturdy boots and hiking poles needed) or blue-white-blue markers (mountaineering equipment needed). **Skiing** in Switzerland is often less expensive than in North America if you avoid pricey resorts. **Ski passes** run 30-50SFr per day, 100-300SFr per week; a week of lift tickets, equipment rental, lessons, lodging, and *demi-pension* (breakfast plus one other meal) averages 475SFr. **Summer skiing** is less common than it once was but is still available in a few towns, such as Zermatt and Saas Fee.

HOLIDAYS AND FESTIVALS

Holidays: New Year's Day (Jan. 1-2); Good Friday (Apr. 9); Easter Monday (Apr. 12); Labor Day (May 1); Swiss National Day (Aug. 1); Christmas (Dec. 25-26).

Festivals: Two raucous festivals are the **Fasnacht** (Carnival; Mar.) in Basel and the **Escalade** (early Dec.) in Geneva. Music festivals occur throughout the summer, including **Open-Air St. Gallen** (late June) and the **Montreux Jazz Festival** (July).

GERMAN SWITZERLAND

The cantons in northwest Switzerland are gently beautiful, with excellent museums, a rich Humanist tradition, and charming old town centers. Previously thought of as a financial mecca, the region has begun to change its image with the growing popularity of Interlaken and the cultural attractions of Lucerne.

BERN ☎031

The city (pop. 127,000) has been Switzerland's capital since 1848, but don't expect fast tracks, power politics, or men in suits—the Bernese prefer to focus on the lighter things in life, nibbling the local Toblerone chocolate and lolling along the banks of the serpentine Aare.

▣ TRANSPORTATION. The Bern-Belp **airport** (BRN; ☎960 21 11) is 20min. from the city; a **bus** departs from the train station 50min. before each flight (10min., 14SFr). **Trains** leave the station at Bahnhofpl. for: Basel (1¼hr., 4 per hr., 34SFr); Berlin (8hr., 14 per day, 245SFr); Geneva (2hr., 3 per hr., 47SFr); Interlaken (50min., every hr., 23SFr); Lucerne (1½hr., every 30min., 32SFr); Milan (3½hr., 6 per day, 72SFr); Munich (6hr., 4 per day, 117SFr); Paris (4½hr., 4 per day, 109SFr); Zurich (1¼hr., every 30min., 45SFr). 25% under-27 discount on international fares. **Bike** rental is available from the **Bernrollt Kiosk** at the train station. (Free, but ID and a 20SFr deposit required. Same-day return. Open May-Oct. 7:30am-9:30pm.)

◪ PRACTICAL INFORMATION. Most of medieval Bern lies in front of the train station and along the Aare River. The **tourist office**, at the station, offers daily **city tours** (14-27SFr) in summer by bus, foot, or raft. (☎328 12 12. Open June-Sept. daily 9am-8:30pm; Oct.-May M-Sa 9am-6:30pm, Su 10am-5pm.) Get online in the basement of **Jäggi Bücher**, on Bubenbergpl., in the Loeb department store. 2 computers allow 20min. of free **Internet**; 4 other terminals cost 5SFr per 30min. (Open M-W and F 9am-6:30pm, Th 9am-9pm, Sa 8am-4pm.) The **post office**, Schanzenpost 1, is a block from the train station. (Open M-F 7:30am-9pm, Sa 8am-4pm, Su 5-9pm.) Address mail to be held: Firstname SURNAME, *Postlagernde Briefe*, Schanzenpost 3000, Bern, SWITZERLAND. **Postal Codes:** CH-3000 to CH-3030.

▥▢ ACCOMMODATIONS AND FOOD. From the station, turn left on Spitalg., left on Kornhauspl., and right on Rathausg. to reach **▨Backpackers Bern/Hotel Glocke ❷**, Rathausg. 75. Shoot pool and watch CNN. (☎311 37 71. Internet access. Reception daily 8-11am and 3-10pm. Dorms 29SFr; singles 75SFr; doubles 120SFr, with bath 150SFr. MC/V.) To get to the **Jugendherberge (HI) ❷**, Weiherg. 4, go down Christoffelg. from the station, take the stairs to the left of the park entrance, go down the steep slope, and turn left on Weiherg. (☎311 63 16. Breakfast included. Reception Feb.-Dec. daily 7-10am and 5pm-midnight. Dorms 30SFr; overflow mattresses 22SFr. Nonmembers add 6SFr. MC/V.)

Almost every *Platz* overflows with cafes and restaurants. Try one of Bern's hearty specialties: *Gschnätzlets* (fried veal, beef, or pork), *Suurchabis* (a kind of sauerkraut), or Toblerone chocolate. **Fruit** and **vegetable markets** sell produce daily at Bärenpl. and every Tuesday and Saturday on Bundespl. (Open May-Oct. 8am-6pm). Across Lorrainebr., **Restaurant du Nord ❸**, Lorrainestr. 2, draws a diverse crowd with creative dishes. (Meat entrees 22-32SFr. Pasta plates from 17SFr, Su night Indian specials. Open M-F 8am-12:30am, Sa-Su 9am-12:30am. MC/V.) **Manora ❶**, Bubenbergpl. 5A, near the station, is a self-service chain with nutritious, cheap food. (Open M-Sa 6:30am-10:45pm, Su 8:30am-10:45pm.)

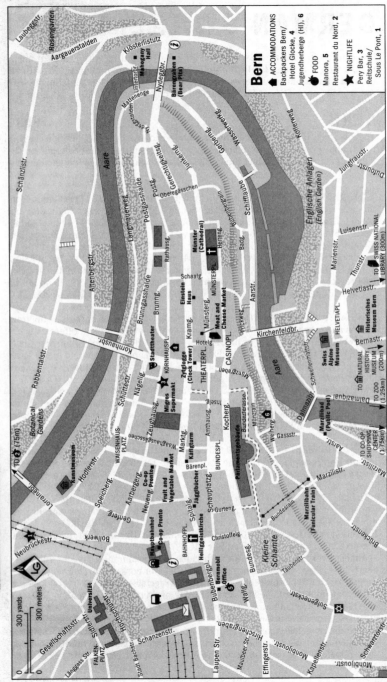

Bern

■ ACCOMMODATIONS
Backpackers Bern/
Hotel Glocke, 4
Jugendherberge (HI), 6

● FOOD
Manora, 5
Restaurant du Nord, 2

★ NIGHTLIFE
Pery Bar, 3
Reitschule/
Sous Le Pont, 1

⑥ **SIGHTS.** The massive █**Bundeshaus,** seat of the Swiss government, dominates the Aare. (45min. tour every hr. M-Sa 9-11am and 2-4pm. Free.) From the Bundeshaus, Kocherg. leads to the Protestant **Münster** (cathedral), which has a fantastic view from its 100m spire. (Open Easter-Oct. Su 11:30am-4:30pm, Tu-Sa 10am-5pm; Nov.-Easter Su 11am-2pm, Tu-F 10am-noon and 2-4pm, Sa 10am-noon and 2-5pm. Tower 3SFr.) Several steep walkways lead from the Bundeshaus to the █**Aare River;** on hotter days, locals dive from the banks for a ride in the swift current. Only experienced swimmers should join in. Bern's **Kunstmuseum,** Hodlerstr. 8, includes the world's largest Paul Klee collection and a smattering of other 20th-century art. (Open Su and W-Sa 10am-5pm, Tu 10am-9pm. 15SFr, students and seniors 10SFr; 7/5SFr for Klee collection only.) The **Bernisches Historische Museum,** Helvetiapl. 5, gives you roots. (Open Su, Tu and Th-Sa 10am-5pm, W 10am-8pm. 13SFr, students 8SFr, under-16 4SFr.) **Albert Einstein's House,** Kramg. 49, where he conceived the theory of general relativity, is now filled with his photos and letters. (Open Feb.-Nov. Tu-F 10am-5pm, Sa 10am-4pm. 3SFr, students 2SFr.)

█▉ **ENTERTAINMENT AND NIGHTLIFE.** Luminaries such as Bob Dylan, Elvis Costello, and Björk have played at the **Gurten Festival** in July (www.gurtenfestival.ch); jazz-lovers flock to the **International Jazz Festival** (www.jazzfestivalbern.ch) in early May. The orange grove at **Stadgärtnerei Elfnau** (tram #19 to Elfnau) has free Sunday concerts in summer, and from mid-July to mid-August **OrangeCinema** (www.orange-cinema.ch) screens recently released films in the open air.

At night, the fashionable linger in the *Altstadt's* bars and cafes while leftists gather under the gargoyles of the Lorrainebrücke. **Pery Bar,** Schmiedenpl. 3, is a classic see-and-be-seen bar. (Open M-W 5pm-1:30am, Th 5pm-2:30am, F-Sa 5pm-3:30am.) The **Reitschule,** Neubrückstr. 8, is a cultural center for Bern's counterculture; **Sous le Pont** serves beer (3.50SFr), indie rock, and hip-hop. From Bollwerk, head left before Lorrainebrücke through the cement park. (Open Tu 11:30am-12:30am, W-Th 11:30am-2:30pm and 6pm-12:30am, F 11:30am-2:30pm and 6pm-2:30am, Sa 6pm-2:30am.)

BASEL (BÂLE) ☎061

Situated on the Rhine near France and Germany, Basel is home to a large medieval quarter as well as one of the oldest universities in Switzerland—graduates include Erasmus and Nietzsche. Visitors encounter art from Roman times through the 20th century and are serenaded by musicians on every street corner.

█▉ **TRANSPORTATION AND PRACTICAL INFORMATION.** Basel has three **train stations:** the French SNCF and Swiss SBB stations on Centralbahnpl., near the *Altstadt;* and the German DB station across the Rhine. **Trains** leave from the SBB for: Bern (1¼hr., every hr. 5:50am-11:50pm, 34SFr); Geneva (3hr., every hr. 6:20am-8:45pm, 71SFr); Lausanne (2½hr., every hr. 6am-10:30pm, 60SFr); and Zurich (1hr., every 15-30min. 4:40am-midnight, 30SFr). Make international connections at the SNCF or DB stations. To reach the **tourist office,** Schifflände 5, from the SBB station, take tram #1 to Schifflände; the office is on the river, near the Mittlere Rheinbrücke. (☎268 68 68. Open M-F 8:30am-6pm, Sa-Su 10am-4pm.) For **bi-gay-lesbian** information, stop by **Arcados,** Rheing. 69, at Clarapl. (☎681 31 32. Open Tu-F noon-7pm, Sa 11am-4pm.) To reach the **post office,** Rüdeng 1., take tram #1 or 8 to Marktpl. and backtrack one block, away from the river. (Open M-W and F 7:30am-6:30pm, Th 7:30am-8pm, Sa 8am-noon.) **Poste Restante:** Postlagernde Briefe für Firstname SURNAME, Rüdengasse, **CH-4001** Basel, Switzerland.

■▢ ACCOMMODATIONS AND FOOD. Basel's shortcoming is its lack of cheap lodgings. Call ahead to ensure a spot at the only hostel in town, the **Jugendherberge (HI) ❷**, St. Alban-Kirchrain 10. Take tram #2 to Kunstmuseum; turn right on St. Alban-Vorstadt and follow the signs. (☎272 05 72. Breakfast included. Laundry 7SFr. Internet 10SFr per hr. Reception Mar.-Oct. 7-10am and 2-11pm; Nov.-Feb. 2-11pm. Check-out 10am. Mid-Feb. to Sept. dorms 29-31SFr; singles 79SFr; doubles 98SFr. Nov. to mid-Feb. 2.50SFr less. Nonmembers add 6SFr. AmEx/MC/V.) To reach **Hotel Steinenschanze ❹**, Steinengraben 69, from the SBB, turn left on Centralbahnstr. and follow signs for Heuwaage; go up the ramp under the bridge to Steinengraben and turn left. (☎272 53 53. Breakfast included. Reception 24hr. Singles 110-180SFr, with ISIC 60SFr per night for up to 3 nights; doubles with shower 160-250SFr, 100SFr. AmEx/MC/V.)

Barfüsserpl., Marktpl., and the streets connecting them are especially full of restaurants. **Wirtshaus zum Schnabel ❷**, Trillengässlein 2, serves tasty German fare. (Open M-Sa 9am-midnight. AmEx/MC/V.) Vegetarians can dine at **Restaurant Gleich ❸**, Leonhardsberg 1. (Open M-F 9am-9:30pm.) Groceries are available at **Migros supermarket,** in the SBB station. (Open M-F 6am-10pm, Sa-Su 7:30am-10pm.)

◪ SIGHTS. Groß-Basel (Greater Basel), and the train station are separated from **Klein-Basel** (Lesser Basel) by the Rhine. The very red **Rathaus** brightens Marktpl. in Groß-Basel with its blinding facade and gold and green statues. Behind the Marktpl. is the 775-year-old **Mittlere Rheinbrücke** (Middle Rhine Bridge), which connects the two halves of Basel. At the other end of Marktpl. is a spectacular **Jean Tinguely Fountain,** also known as the **Fasnachtsbrunnen.** Behind Marktpl. stands the red sandstone **Münster,** where you can visit the tomb of Erasmus or climb the tower for a spectacular view of the city. (Open Easter-Oct. 15 M-F 10am-5pm, Sa 10am-4pm, Su 1-5pm; Oct. 16-Easter M-Sa 11am-4pm, Su 2-4pm. Free. Tower closes 30min. before the church. 3SFr.)

▦▯ MUSEUMS AND ENTERTAINMENT. Basel has over 30 museums; pick up the comprehensive museum guide at the tourist office. The **Basel Card,** available at the tourist office, provides admission to all museums as well as discounts around town. (24hr. card 25SFr, 48hr. card 33SFr, 72hr. card 45SFr.) The ◪**Kunstmuseum,** St. Alban-Graben 16, houses outstanding collections of old and new masters; admission also gives access to the **Museum für Gegenwartskunst** (Modern Art), St. Alban-Rheinweg 60. (Kunstmuseum open Tu and Th-Su 10am-5pm, W 10am-7pm. Gegenwartskunst open Tu-Su 11am-5pm. 10SFr, students 8SFr; first Su of every month free.) At ◪**Museum Jean Tinguely,** Grenzacherstr. 214a, everything rattles and shakes in homage to the Swiss sculptor's vision of metal and movement. Take tram #2 or 15 to Wettsteinpl. and then bus #31 or 36 to Museum Tinguely. (Open W-Su 11am-7pm. 7SFr, students 5SFr.) The **Fondation Beyeler,** Baselstr. 101, is one of Europe's finest private art collections, housing works by nearly every major artist. Take tram #6 to Fondation Beyeler. (Open daily 9am-8pm. M-F 16SFr, Sa-Su 20SFr; students 5SFr daily. 12SFr after 6pm daily.)

In a year-round party town, Basel's carnival, or **Fasnacht,** still manages to distinguish itself. The festivities commence the Monday before Lent with the *Morgestraich*, the 600-year-old, 72hr. parade beginning at 4am. The goal is to scare away winter—it rarely succeeds. During the rest of the year, head to **Barfüsserplatz** for an evening of bar-hopping. ◪**Atlantis,** Klosterberg 10, is a multi-level, sophisticated bar with reggae, jazz, and funk. (Open Tu-Th 11am-midnight, F 11:30am-4am, Sa 6pm-4am.) **Brauerei Fischerstube,** Rheing. 45, brews the delectably sharp ◪*Hell Spezial* ("light special") beer. (Open M-Th 10am-midnight, F-Sa 10am-1am, Su 5pm-midnight. Full dinner menu from 6pm.)

ZURICH (ZÜRICH)

☎01

Battalions of executives charge daily through the world's largest gold exchange and fourth-largest stock exchange, keeping Zurich's upper-crust boutiques thriving. Once a focal point of the Reformation, 20th-century Zurich (pop. 363,000) enjoyed an avant-garde radicalism that attracted progressive thinkers; while James Joyce wrote *Ulysses*, an exiled Vladimir Lenin read Marx and dreamt of revolution. A walk through Zurich's student quarter immerses you in an energetic counter-culture, only footsteps away from the Bahnhofstr. shopping district.

▐ TRANSPORTATION

Flights: Kloten Airport (☎816 25 00) is a major stop for Swiss International Airlines (☎084 885 20 00). Daily connections to Frankfurt, Paris, London, and New York. Trains connect the airport to the *Hauptbahnhof* in the city center (every 10-20min. 5am-midnight, 5.40SFr; Eurail and SwissPass valid).

Trains: Bahnhofpl. To: **Basel** (1hr., 1-2 per hr., 30SFr); **Bern** (1¼hr., 1-2 per hr., 45SFr); **Geneva** via **Bern** (3hr., every hr. 6am-10pm, 76SFr); **Lucerne** (1hr., 2 per hr. 6am-midnight, 20SFr); **Milan** (4hr., every hr. 6:30am-10pm, 72SFr); **Munich** (5hr., every hour 6am-10pm, 86SFr); **Paris** (5hr., every hour 6:30am-midnight, 133SFr); **Salzburg** (5hr., every hour 6am-7pm, 97SFr); **Vienna** (9hr., every hour 6am-6pm, 124SFr). Under-26 discount on international trains.

Public Transportation: Trams criss-cross the city, originating at the *Hauptbahnhof*. Tickets for rides longer than 5 stops cost 3.60SFr and are valid for one hour (press the blue button on automatic ticket machines); rides less than 5 cost 2.10SFr (yellow button). Policemen won't hesitate to fine you (60SFr) if you try to be a *Schwarzfahrer* (Black Rider) and ride for free. If you plan to ride several times, buy a 24hr. **Tageskarte** (7.20SFr), which is valid on trams, buses, and ferries. **Night buses** run from city center to outlying areas (F-Su 1am-4am).

Bike Rental: One day bike loans are free at **Globus** (☎079 336 36 10); **Enge** (☎079 336 36 12); and **Hauptbahnhof** (☎210 13 88), at the very end of track 18. With passport and 20SFr deposit. Open daily May-Oct 7:00am-9:30pm.

Hitchhiking: Though *Let's Go* does not recommend hitchhiking and the practice is illegal on highways, hitchhikers to Basel, Geneva, or Paris often take tram #4 to *Werdhölzli* or bus #33 to *Pfingstweidstr.* Those bound for Lucerne, Italy, and Austria report taking tram #9 to *Bahnhof Wiedikon* and walking down Schimmelstr. to Silhölzli. For Munich, hitchhikers have been seen taking S1 to *Wiedikon* and catching rides at Seebahnstr.

✵ ▐ ORIENTATION AND PRACTICAL INFORMATION

Zurich is in north-central Switzerland, close to the German border, on some of the lowest land in the country. The **Limmat River** splits the city down the middle on its way to the **Zürichsee**. On the west side of the river are the **Hauptbahnhof** and **Bahnhofstraße.** Two-thirds of the way down Bahnhofstr. lies **Paradeplatz**, the town center. On the east side of the river is the University district, which stretches above the narrow **Niederdorfstraße** and pulses with bars, hip restaurants, and hostels.

Tourist Offices: Main office (☎215 40 00; free hotel reservation service ☎215 40 40), in the main train station. An electronic hotel reservation board is at the front of the station. Open May-Oct. M-Sa 8am-8:30pm, Su 8:30am-6:30pm; Nov.-Mar. M-Sa 8:30am-7pm, Su 9am-6:30pm. For bikers and backpackers, the **Touring Club der Schweiz** (TCS), Alfred-Escher-Str. 38 (☎286 86 86), offers maps and travel info.

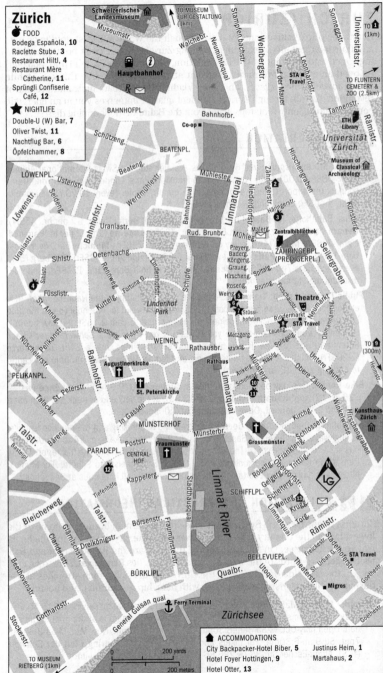

Zürich

🍎 FOOD
Bodega Española, 10
Raclette Stube, 3
Restaurant Hiltl, 4
Restaurant Mère
  Catherine, 11
Sprüngli Confiserie
  Café, 12

★ NIGHTLIFE
Double-U (W) Bar, 7
Oliver Twist, 11
Nachtflug Bar, 6
Öpfelchammer, 8

🏠 ACCOMMODATIONS
City Backpacker-Hotel Biber, 5   Justinus Heim, 1
Hotel Foyer Hottingen, 9   Martahaus, 2
Hotel Otter, 13

Currency Exchange: At the main train station. Cash advances with DC/MC/V and photo ID; 200SFr minimum. Open daily 6:30am-10pm. **Credit Suisse,** Bahnhofstr. 53. 2.50SFr commission. Open daily 6am-10pm.

Bi-Gay-Lesbian Organizations: Homosexuelle Arbeitsgruppe Zürich (HAZ), Sihlquai 67 (☎271 22 50). Offers a library, meetings, and the free newsletter *InfoSchwül.* Open Su noon-2pm and 6-11pm, Tu-F 7:30-11pm.

Laundromat: Speed Wash Self Service Wascherei, Weinbergstr. 37 (☎242 99 14). Wash and dry 10.20SFr per 5kg. Open M-Sa 7am-10pm, Su 10:30am-10pm.

Emergencies: Police, ☎117. **Fire,** ☎118. **Ambulance,** ☎144.

24-Hour Pharmacy: Bahnhofpl. 15 at the main station (☎225 42 42).

Internet Access: The **ETH Library,** Ramistr. 101 (☎631 21 35), in the *Hauptgebäude*, has three free computers. Take tram #6, 9, or 10 to *ETH*, enter the main building, and take the elevator to floor H. Open M-F 8:30am-9pm, Sa 9am-2pm. **Quanta Virtual Fun Space,** Limmatquai 94 (☎260 72 66), at the corner of Muehleg. and Niederdorfstr. Open daily 9am-midnight. **Internet Café,** Uraniastr. 3, (☎210 33 11) in the Urania Parkhaus. 5SFr per 20min. Open M-Sa 9am-midnight, Su 11am-11pm. **Telefon Corner,** downstairs in the station. 6SFr per hr. Open daily 8am-10pm.

Post Office: Main office, Sihlpost, Kasernestr. 97, just behind the station. Open M-F 6:30am-10:30pm, Sa 6am-8pm, Su 11am-10:30pm. Address mail to be held: First-name, LASTNAME, Sihlpost, Postlagernde Briefe, **CH-8021** Zurich, SWITZERLAND.

▚ ACCOMMODATIONS

The few budget accommodations in Zurich are easily accessible public transportation. Reserve at least a day in advance, especially in the summer.

▨ **Martahaus,** Zähringerstr. 36 (☎251 45 50). Popular with American college students. Breakfast included. Reception 24hr. Checkout noon. Dorms 38SFr; singles in summer 85SFr, off-season 114SFr; doubles 98/135SFr; quads 200SFr. With private bath add 30-60SFr. The owners also run the nearby **Luther pension,** a **women-only** residence. Dorms 30SFr, singles 50SFr. ❸

Hotel Foyer Hottingen, Hottingenstr. 31 (☎256 19 19). Take tram #3 to *Hottingenpl.* Only a block from the Kunsthaus. In-house chapel. Woman-only and mixed dorms. Breakfast, lockers, and kitchen included. Reception daily 7am-11pm. 11-bed dorm 35SFr; singles 70SFr, with bath 105SFr; doubles 110/150SFr; triples 140/190SFr; quads 180SFr. MC/V. ❷

Justinus Heim Zürich, Freudenbergstr. 146 (☎361 38 06). Take tram #9 to *Seilbahn Rigiblick,* then take the hillside funicular up to the end. Quiet, private rooms. Breakfast included. Reception daily 8am-noon and 5-9pm. Singles 35-50SFr, with shower 60SFr; doubles 80SFr-100SFr; triples 120-140SFr; rates reduced for multi-week stays. ❸

The City Backpacker-Hotel Biber, Niederdorfstr. 5 (☎251 90 15). With the Niederdorf nightlife outside, you may not even need to use your bunk-bed. Lockers available; bring a lock. Sheets 3SFr; towels 3SFr. Internet 12SFr per hr. Reception daily 8am-noon and 3-10pm. Checkout 10am. Dorms 29SFr; singles 66SFr; doubles 88-92SFr. MC/V. ❷

Hotel Otter, Oberdorfstr. 7 (☎251 22 07), and the swanky **Wuste Bar** below it attracts not-so-starving-artists. Shared bathrooms. Rooms have TV, phone, fridge, and sink. Breakfast included. Reception 8am-4pm in hotel, 4pm-midnight in bar. Laundry 15 SFr. Singles 100SFr; doubles 130-160SFr. AmEx/MC/V. ❹

▟ FOOD

Zurich's 1300 restaurants run the gamut. The cheapest meals are available at *Würstli* stands for about 5SFr. For heartier appetites, Zurich prides itself on *Geschnetzeltes mit Rösti,* thinly-sliced veal (often liver or kidney) in cream sauce with hash-brown potatoes. Check out the *Swiss Backpacker News* (found at the tourist office, Hotel Biber, and Martahaus) for info on budget meals in Zurich. The **farmer's markets** at Burklipl. (Tu and F 6am-11am) and Rosenhof (Th 10am-8pm and Sa 10am-5pm) sell fruit, flowers, and veggies.

■ **Bodega Española,** Münsterg. 15. Catalan delights served by charismatic waiters since 1874. Egg-and-potato tortilla dishes 15.50SFr. Yummy *tapas* 4.80SFr. Kitchen open noon-2pm and 6-10pm. Open daily 10am-midnight. AmEx/DC/MC/V. ❷

■ **Sprüngli Confiserie Café,** Paradepl., is a Zurich landmark, founded by one of the original Lindt chocolate makers. Pick up a handful of the bite-size Luxemburgerli (8SFr per 100g), try the homemade ice cream, or eat a full meal (20-26SFr). Confectionary open M-F 7:30am-8pm, Sa 8am-4pm. Cafe open M-F 7:30am-6:30pm, Sa 8am-6pm, Su 9:30am-5:30pm. AmEx/DC/MC/V. ❸

Restaurant Mère Catherine, Nägelihof 8. Hidden on a small street near the Großmünster, in a building constructed in 1565. Serves provençal French dishes (starting at 22SFr). Vegetarian options. Daily fish special from the Zürichsee. Open Su-W 11:30am-10pm, Th-Sa 11:30am-10:30pm. ❸

Restaurant Hiltl, Sihlstr. 28. Munch carrot sticks with the vegetarian elite. All-day salad buffet (3.90SFr per 100g; 15SFr for large salad), and Indian buffet at night (same price). Open M-Sa 7am-11pm, Su 11am-11pm. AmEx/DC/V/MC. ❷

Raclette Stube, Zähringerstr. 16. Family-oriented Swiss restaurant. All-you-can-eat *raclette* 33SFr per person. Open daily from 6pm to about 11pm. ❹

⊙ SIGHTS AND MUSEUMS

It's virtually inconceivable to start a tour of Zurich anywhere but the stately **Bahnhofstraße,** the causeway of capitalism. At the Zürichsee end of Bahnhofstr., **Bürkliplatz** is a good place to explore the lakeshore. On the other side of the river, the pedestrian zone continues on Niederdorfstr. and Münsterg., where shops run from the ritzy to the raunchy. **Spiegelgasse** was once home to Goethe, Buchner, and Lenin. **Fraumünster, Grossmünster,** and **St. Peterskirche** straddle the Limmat River.

■ **KUNSTHAUS ZÜRICH.** The largest privately-funded museum in Europe houses a collection ranging from 21st century American pop art to religious pieces. Works by Dalí, van Gogh, Gaughin, Dali, Picasso, Rubens, Rembrandt, Renoir, and Munch highlight a museum that is itself a compelling reason to come to Zurich. Renovations from Feb.-Aug. 2004 may reduce the number of works on display. *(Heimpl. 1. Take tram #3, 5, 8, or 9 to Kunsthaus. www.kunsthaus.ch. English audio tours and brochures. Bag storage required. Open Su and F-Sa 10am-5pm, Tu-Th 10am-9pm. Admission 12SFr. Students and seniors 6SFr. W free. Free tours W 6:30pm and Sa 3pm.)*

FRAUMÜNSTER. This 13th-century cathedral's Gothic style is juxtaposed with **Marc Chagall's** stained-glass windows, which depict Chagall's interpretations of stories from the Old and New Testament. Outside the church on Fraumünsterstr., a mural decorating the courtyard's archway pictures Felix and Regula (the decapitated patron saints of Zurich) with their heads in their hands. *(Right off Paradepl. Open daily May-Sept. 9am-6pm; Oct. and Mar.-Apr. 10am-5pm; Nov.-Feb. 10am-4pm.)*

GROSSMÜNSTER. The twin Neo-Gothic towers of this mainly Romanesque church can best be viewed on the bridge near the Fraumünster. Considered to be the mother church of the Swiss-German Reformation movement, it has become a symbol of Zurich. *(Church open daily Mar. 15-Oct. daily 9am-6pm; Nov.-Mar. 14 10am-5pm. Tower open Mar.-Oct. daily 1:30-5pm; Nov.-Feb. Sa-Su 9:15am-5pm. Tower 2SFr.)*

ST. PETERSKIRCHE. St. Peterskirche has the largest clock face in Europe. *(Open M-F 8am-6pm, Sa 8am-4pm, Su 10-11am.)* Roman baths dating from the first century are visible beneath the iron stairway. *(Down Thermeng. from St. Peter's.)*

MUSEUM RIETBERG. In contrast to the Kunsthaus, Rietberg presents Asian, African, and other non-European art, housed in two mansions in Rieter-Park. **Park-Villa Rieter** features Chinese, Japanese, and Indian paintings; **Villa Wesendonck** stores most of the permanent sculpture collection. Renovations will close Park-Villa Rieter from spring 2004-2006, while Villa Wesendonck will remain open. *(Gablerstr. 15. Take tram #7 to Museum Rietberg. Villa Wesendonck open Su and Tu-Sa 10am-5pm. Audio guide 5SFr. Park-Villa Rieter open Su 10am-5pm, Tu-Sa 1-5pm. 6SFr, students 3SFr.)*

🎵 🖼 ENTERTAINMENT & NIGHTLIFE

Niederdorfstraße is the epicenter of Zurich's nightlife. Beware the "night club"—it's a euphemism for strip club. Because of this, women may not want to walk alone in this area at night. Other hot spots include Münsterg. and Limmatquai, both lined with overflowing cafes and bars. Beer in Zurich is pricey (from 6SFr), but a number of cheap bars have established themselves on Niederdorfstr. near Muhleg. After July 18, the **Orange Cinema,** an open-air cinema at Zürichhorn (take tram #4 to *Fröhlichstr.*) attracts huge crowds to its lakefront screenings. For more nightlife info, check **ZüriTipp** (www.zueritipp.ch) or the posters that decorate the streets at Bellevuepl. or Hirschenpl.

Double-U (W) Bar, Niederdorfstr. 21, on the 1st floor of Hotel Schafli. Popular with locals and students. Beer (from 10SFr) and mixed drinks (from 14SFr) rise 2SFr in price after midnight. Open Su-F 4pm-2am, Sa 4pm-4am. AmEx/DC/V/MC.

Nachtflug Bar, Café, and Lounge, Stuessihofstatt 4. A popular outdoor bar where locals mix with backpackers. Occasional live music. Wine from 7SFr. Beer from 4.90SFr. Cold *tapas* and fresh-squeezed juices (6SFr). Open M-Th 11am-midnight, F-Sa 11am-2am.

Oliver Twist, Rindermarkt 6, welcomes soccer fans and ex-pats in a pub atmosphere that's only somewhat contrived. Beer from 6.50SFr. Wine from 5.50SFr. Pub grub noon-10pm. English breakfast (15.50SFr) available during major sporting events. Open M-Sa 11:30am-midnight.

Öpfelchammer, Rindermarkt 12. This popular Swiss wine bar has low ceilings and wooden crossbeams covered with initials and messages from 200 years of merry-makers. Those who climb the rafters and drink a free glass of wine from the beams get to engrave their names on the furniture. It's harder than it looks. Wine 3-5SFr. Open Tu-Sa 11am-12:30am. Closed from mid-July to mid-August. AmEx/V/MC/DC.

STEIN AM RHEIN   ☎052

The tiny medieval *Altstadt* of Stein am Rhein (pop. 3,000) is postcard-perfect, with traditional Swiss architecture framed by hills and river. All the houses of the square date back to the 15th century, and are marked by detailed facade paintings depicting the animal or scene after which each house is named. The 12th-century establishment of the **Kloster St. George** first made Stein am Rhein prominent. You can reach the Benedictine monastery by heading up Chirchhofpl. from the Rathauspl. Less austere is the vibrant **Festsaal,** whose yellow-and-green-tiled floor is off-limits to feet. As lights are few and dim, try to go when it is bright outside for the best view of delicate paintings and engravings. (☎741 21 42. Open Mar.-Oct. Su and Tu-Sa 10am-5pm. 3SFr, students 1.50SFr.) The **Rathaus,** at the corner of Rhig. and Rathauspl., is more stately.

Trains connect Stein am Rhein to Konstanz (40min., 1 per hr. 6:24am-midnight, 10SFr) via Kreuzlingen. **Boats** (☎634 08 88) depart for Schaffhausen (1¼hr., 4 per day, 20SFr); Konstanz (2½hr., 4 per day, 24SFr); and other Bodensee towns. The

HE HIDDEN DEAL

A BED OF STRAW

If crisply-made hotel beds have grown bland, consider making like Heidi and bedding down in an authentic Swiss barn. Started ten years ago to provide back-to-the-roots lodging for cost-conscious Swiss families on vacation, the *Schlaf im Stroh* (sleep in straw) program now involves 240 farms in rural northeastern Switzerland.

Though plots are as hygienic as everything else in Switzerland, bring bug spray and a jacket to ward off pre-dawn chill. Call ahead to tell the host about allergies you have (believe it or not, substantial accommodations can be made). Ammenities range from donkey rides to craft demonstrations, and the sunrises are riveting.

In the vicinity of Stein am Rhein, *Let's Go* recommends the barn run by Frau Ullman, her son, Christian, and their amiable St. Bernard, Leila, who tends the chicken coop.

Contact Frau Ullman through the Stein am Rhein tourist office. To get to her barn, ride the local train to Eschenz. Press the button to get off—the train won't stop if you don't. From the station, make a left; take the bike path and follow the signs. The stay includes a 'farmer's breakfast' with tea from the lindenberry tree and chocolate milk courtesy of the cows. Shower 2SFr. Guests 16+ 20SF; children 11-15 pay by their age; 10 and under 10SFr.) For other barns, check www.abenteuer-stroh.ch/en.

tourist office, Oberstadt. 3, lies on the other side of the *Rathaus.* (☎742 20 90. Open July-Aug. M-F 9:30am-noon and 1:30-5pm, Sa 9:30am-noon and 1:30-4pm, Su 10:30am-12:30pm.; Sept.-June M-F 9:30am-noon and 1:30-5pm.) The family-oriented **Jugendherberge (HI) ❷** is at Hemishoferstr. 87. From the train station, take the bus (#7349, dir.: Singen) to *Strandbad* and walk 5min. farther in the same direction. By foot, the hostel is an enjoyable 20min. stroll along the Rhein from town. (☎052 741 12 55. Breakfast, showers, and sheets included. Reception 8-10am and 5-10pm. Curfew 10:30pm; keys available. Open Mar.-Nov. Dorms 25SFr; doubles 60SFr; family rooms 30SFr per person. Nonmembers add 6SFr. AmEx/DC/MC/V.) The waitresses at the **Rothen Ochsen Wine Bar ❶**, Rathauspl. 9, are dedicated to preserving the traditions of this wooden hall, built in 1466—the oldest public house in the town. Though full meals are not available, their regional soups, appetizers, and wines are sustenance enough. (☎741 23 28. Open Su 10:30am-6pm, Tu-Sa 11:30am-11:30pm.) **Postal Code:** CH-8260.

LUCERNE (LUZERN) ☎041

Lucerne (pop. 60,000) is the Swiss traveler's dream come true. The old city is engaging, the lake is placid, and sunrise over the famous Mt. Pilatus has hypnotized hikers and artists—including Twain, Wagner, and Goethe—for centuries.

🖪🔃 TRANSPORTATION AND PRACTICAL INFORMATION. Trains leave Bahnhofpl. for: Basel (1¼hr., 1-2 per hr. 4:40am-11:50pm, 29SFr); Bern (1½hr., 1-2 per hr. 4:40am-11:50pm, 30SFr); Geneva (3½hr., every hr. 4:40am-9:55pm, 64SFr); Interlaken (2hr., every hr. 6:30am-7:35pm, 26SFr); Lausanne (2½hr., every hr. 4:40am-9:55pm, 56SFr); Lugano (3hr., every hr. 6:40am-10:15pm, 56SFr); and Zurich (1hr., 2 per hr. 4:55am-11:10pm, 20SFr). VBL **buses** depart from in front of the station and provide extensive coverage of Lucerne (1 zone 2.40SFr, 2 zones 3.60SFr, 3 zones 5.60SFr; day pass 9SFr); route maps are available at the tourist office. The **tourist office,** in the station, offers free city guides, makes reservations, and sells the **Visitor's Card.** (☎227 17 17. Open May-Oct. daily 9am-6:30pm; Nov.-Apr. M-F 8:30am-5:30pm, Sa-Su 9am-6pm.) **C&A Clothing,** on Hertensteinstr. at the top of the *Altstadt,* has two free but busy **Internet** terminals. (Open M-W 9am-6:30pm, Th-F 9am-9pm, Sa 8:30am-1pm.) The **post office** is by the train station. Address mail to be held: Firstname SURNAME, *Postlagernde Briefe*, Hauptpost, **CH-6000** Luzern 1, SWITZERLAND. (Open M-F 7:30am-6:30pm, Sa 8am-noon.)

ⵏⵉ ACCOMMODATIONS AND FOOD. Inexpensive beds are limited, so call ahead. To reach ◪**Backpackers ❷**, Alpenquai 42, turn right from the station on Inseliquai and follow it until it turns into Alpenquai (20min.); the hostel is on the right. (☎360 04 20. Bikes 16SFr per day. Internet 10SFr per hr. Reception daily 7:30-10am and 4-11pm. Dorms 27-33SFr.) Until 1998, **Hotel Löwengraben ❷**, Löwengraben 18, was a prison; now it's a trendy, clean hostel with a bar, a restaurant, and dance parties every summer Saturday. (☎417 12 12. Breakfast 11SFr. Dorms 40SFr; singles 110-160SFr; doubles 160-220SFr.) **Markets** along the river sell cheap, fresh goods on Tuesday and Saturday mornings. There's a **Migros supermarket** at the train station. (Open M-W and Sa 6:30am-8pm, Th-F 6:30am-9pm, Su 8am-8pm.)

◪▨ SIGHTS AND NIGHTLIFE. The *Altstadt*, across the river over Spreuer-brücke from the station, is famous for its frescoed houses; the best examples are those on Hirschenpl. and Weinmarkt. The 14th-century **Kapellbrücke**, a wooden-roofed bridge, runs from left of the train station to the *Altstadt* and is decorated with Swiss historical scenes; further down the river, the **Spreuerbrücke** is decorated by Kaspar Meglinger's eerie *Totentanz* (Dance of Death) paintings. On the hills above the river, the **Museggmauer** and its towers are all that remain of the medieval city's ramparts. Three of the towers are accessible to visitors and provide panoramas of the city; walk along St. Karliquai, head uphill to the right, and follow the brown castle signs. (Open daily 8am-7pm.) To the east is the magnificent **Löwen-denkmal** (Lion Monument), the dying lion of Lucerne, which is carved into a cliff on Denkmalstr. The ◪**Picasso Museum,** Am Rhyn Haus, Furreng. 21, displays 200 intimate photographs of Picasso as well as a large collection of his lesser-known works. From Schwanenpl., take Rathausquai to Furreng. (Open Apr.-Oct. daily 10am-6pm; Nov.-Mar. 11am-5pm. 8SFr, students 5SFr.) The ◪**Verkehrshaus der Schweiz** (Swiss Transport Museum), Lidostr. 5, has interactive displays on all kinds of vehicles, but the real highlight is the warehouse of trains. Take bus #6, 8, or 24 to *Verkehrshaus*. (Open Apr.-Oct. daily 10am-6pm; Nov.-Mar. 10am-5pm. 21SFr, students 19SFr, with Eurail 14SFr.)

Lucerne's nightlife is more about lingering than club-hopping, although the candle-lit **Club 57,** Haldenstr. 57, has DJs spin on the weekends. (Beer 4-6SFr. Open daily 8pm-2:30am, F-Sa until 4am.) The mellower **Jazz Cantine,** Grabenstr. 8, is a product of the Jazz School of Lucerne. (Sandwiches 6-8SFr. Open M-Sa 7am-12:30am, Su 4pm-12:30am.) Lucerne attracts big names for its two jazz festivals: **Blue Balls Festival** (July 23-31, 2004) and **Blues Festival** (Nov. 8-14, 2004.)

▨ DAYTRIPS FROM LUCERNE: MT. PILATUS AND RIGI KULM. The view of the Alps from the top of **Mt. Pilatus** (2132m) is absolutely phenomenal. For the most memorable trip, catch a boat from Lucerne to Alpnachstad (1½hr.), ascend by the world's steepest **cogwheel train,** then descend by cable car to Krienz and take the bus back to Lucerne (entire trip 80SFr; with Eurail or SwissPass 40-43SFr). For less money and more exercise, take a train or boat to Hergiswill and hike up to Fräkmüntegg (3hr.), then get on the cable car at the halfway point (23SFr round-trip, with Eurail 19SFr.) Fräkmüntegg also operates central Switzerland's longest *Rodelbahn* course; for 7SFr, you whizz down the hillside on a plastic slide that achieves surprising speeds. Across the sea from Pilatus soars the **Rigi Kulm** (1800m), which has a magnificent view of the lake; watching the sunrise from the summit is a Lucerne must. **Ferries** run from Lucerne to Vitznau, where you can catch a cogwheel train to the top. You can also conquer Rigi on foot; it's 5hr. from Vitznau to the top. Return by train, take the cable car from Rigi Kaltbad to Weggis, and head back to Lucerne by boat (round-trip 87SFr; with Eurail 29SFr).

S W I T Z E R L A N D

GRAUBÜNDEN

The largest, least populous, and highest of the Swiss cantons, Graubünden's rugged gorges, fir forests, and eddying rivers give the region a wildness seldom found in ultra-civilized Switzerland. Visitors should plan their trips carefully, especially in ski season, when reservations are absolutely required. Beware: Almost everything shuts down in May and June.

DAVOS ☎ 081

Davos (pop. 12,000) sprawls along the valley floor under seven mountains laced with chair-lifts and cable cars. Originally a health resort, the city catered to such *fin de siècle* giants as Robert Louis Stevenson and Thomas Mann, who, while in Davos, wrote *Treasure Island* and *The Magic Mountain*. The influx of tourists in recent decades has given the city an impersonal feel, but the thrill of carving down the famed run from Weißfluhgipfel to Kublis (a 2000m vertical drop) may make up for it. Europe's largest natural **ice rink** (22,000sq. m), between Platz and Dorf, has figure skating, ice dancing, hockey, speed skating, and curling. (☎415 36 04. Open Dec. 15-Feb. 15. M-W and F-Sa 10am-4pm; Th 10am-4pm and 8-10pm. 5SFr. Skate rental 6.50SFr.) For joggers, birdwatchers, and the aspiring windsurfer, the **Davosersee** is the place to be. (Take bus #1 to *Flueelastr.* and follow the yellow signs to the lake.) At the Davosersee Surfcenter, board rentals are 30SFr per hr., 60SFr per day. Classes are also available. (Open mid-June to mid-Sept. daily 11am-6:30pm.) Davos provides direct access to two mountains—**Parsenn** and **Jakobshorn**—and four skiing areas. Parsenn, with long runs and fearsome vertical drops, is the mountain around which Davos built its reputation. (www.fun-mountain.ch. Day pass 60SFr.) Jacobshorn has found a niche with the younger crowd since the opening of a snowboarding park with two half-pipes. (Day pass 55SFr.) In the valley run 75km of cross-country trails, one of which is lit at night. In the summer, ski lifts connect to **hikes,** such as the 2hr. **Panoramweg.** To get a little culture with your sweat, visit the **Kirchner Museum,** on the Promenade. It houses an extensive collection of Ernst Ludwig Kirchner's artwork, whose harsh colors and long figures defined 20th-century German Expressionism. (Take the bus to *Kirchner Museum.* Open Su and Tu-Sa 10am-6pm; Sept.-Dec. 24 and Easter-July 7 Su and Tu-Sa 2-6pm. 10SFr, students 5SFr.)

Davos is accessible by **train** from Chur (1½hr., 7 per day, 25SFr) via Landquart or from Klosters (25min., 2 per hr., 8.60SFr) on the Rhätische Bahn lines. The town is divided into two areas, Davos-Dorf and Davos-Platz, each with a train station; Platz has the tourist office, post office, and most places of interest to budget travelers. Dorf is closer to the Davosersee. **Buses** (2.70SFr) run between the two train stations and stop near major hotels and the hostel on the Davosersee. The main **tourist office,** Promenade 67, is up the hill from the *Platz* station. (☎415 21 21. Open Dec. to mid-Apr. and mid-June to mid-Oct. M-F 8:30am-6:30pm, Sa 9am-5pm, and Su 10am-noon, 3-5:30pm; mid-Oct. to Dec. and mid-Apr. to June M-F 8:30am-1:45pm, Sa-Su 8:30am-noon.) At Jakobshorn Ski Mountain's **Snowboardhotel Bolgenschanze ❸**, Skistr. 1, dorm rooms are sold as a package with ski passes (☎414 90 20; www.fun-mountain.ch. Reception Su and M-Th 8:30-11am and 4-7pm. Check-out 10am. Free **Internet** for guests. 1-night, 2-day ski-pass 125-135SFr; weekend 175-185SFr; 6-night, 7-day pass 570SFr. AmEx/MC/V.) **Postal Code:** CH-7270.

KLOSTERS ☎ 081

Davos's sister resort, Klosters, lies across the Gotschna and Parsenn mountains. Though Klosters is 10min. from Davos by train, it's a world away in atmosphere. While Davos makes every effort to be cosmopolitan, Klosters capitalizes on its natural serenity and cozy chalets. Most ski packages include mountains from both towns, and Klosters's main lift leads to a mountain pass where one can ski down to either. In summer, Klosters has better access to fantastic biking trails. **Ski passes** for the Klosters-Davos region run 121SFr for 2 days and 279SFr for 6 days (including public transportation). The **Madrisabahn** leaves from Klosters-Dorf (1-day pass 46SFr, 6-day pass 249SFr). The **Grotschnabahn** gives access to Parsenn and Strela in Davos and Madrisa in Klosters (1-day pass 57SFr, 6-day pass 308SFr). Summer cable car passes (valid on Grotschna and Madrisabahnen) are also available (6-day pass 120SFr). **Bananas,** operated out of Duty Boardsport, Bahnhofstr. 16, gives snowboard lessons. (☎422 66 60. Lessons 70SFr per 4hr. Board and shoes 31SFr per day.) **Ski rental** is also available at **Sport Gotschna,** across from the tourist office. (☎422 11 97. Skis and snowboards 38SFr per day plus 10% insurance, 5 days 123SFr; boots 19/69SFr. Open M-F 8am-noon and 2-6:30pm, Sa 8am-12:30pm and 2-6pm, Su 9am-noon and 3-6pm.) On the luscious green valley floor, **hikers** can make a large loop, from Klosters's Protestant church on Monbielstr. to Monbiel. The route continues to an elevation point of 1488m and turns left, passing through **Bödmerwald, Fraschmardintobel,** and **Monbieler Wald** before climbing to its highest elevation of 1634m and returning to Klosters via **Pardels.** Several adventure companies offer a variety of activities including **river rafting, canoeing, horseback riding, paragliding,** and **glacier trekking.**

Klosters-Platz and Klosters-Dorf are connected to Chur by **train** via Landquart (1¼hr., every hr. 5:30am-9:30pm, 19SFr). The same line connects Klosters and Davos (30min., every hr. 5:30am-11:30pm, 9SFr.) The main **tourist office,** in Platz by the station, sells area hiking (16SFr) and biking (7.50SFr) maps. (Open daily 10am-5pm.) **Andrist Sport** on Gotschnastr, rents **bikes.** (☎410 20 80. 38SFr per day, 6 days 130SFr. Open M-F 9am-noon and 2-6:30pm, Sa 8am-noon and 2-6pm.) To get to **Jugendherberge Soldanella (HI) ❷,** Talstr. 73., from the station, go left uphill past Hotel Alpina to the church, then cross the street and head up the alleyway to the right of the Kirchplatz bus station sign. Walk 10min. along the gravel path. This massive, renovated chalet has a comfortable reading room, couches on a flagstone terrace, and friendly English-speaking owners. (☎422 13 16. Breakfast included. Open mid-Dec. to mid Apr. and late June to mid-Oct. Reception 7-10am and 5-10pm. Checkout 10am. Dorms 28SFr; singles 39SFr; doubles 70SFr. Family rooms 39SFr per person. Nonmembers add 6SFr. AmEx/DC/MC/V.) **Postal Code:** CH-7250.

JUNGFRAU REGION

The Jungfrau area has attracted tourists for hundreds of years with glorious hiking trails and snow-capped peaks. From Interlaken, the valley splits at the foot of the Jungfrau: The eastern valley contains Grindelwald and the western valley holds many smaller towns. The two valleys are divided by an easily hikeable ridge.

INTERLAKEN   ☎ 033

Interlaken (pop. 21,000) lies between the Thunersee and the Brienzersee at the foot of the largest mountains in Switzerland. With easy access to these natural playgrounds, Interlaken has earned its rightful place as one of Switzerland's prime tourist attractions and its top outdoor adventure spot.

◪◪ TRANSPORTATION AND PRACTICAL INFORMATION. The *Westbahnhof* (☎826 47 50) and *Ostbahnhof* (☎828 73 19) have **trains** to: Basel (5:30am-10:30pm, 56SFr); Bern (6:35am-10:30pm, 24SFr); Geneva (5:30am-9:30pm, 63SFr); Lucerne

(5:30am-8:35pm, 26SFr); Lugano/Locarno (5:30am-4:35pm, 87SFr); and Zurich (5:30am-10:30pm, 62SFr). The *Ostbahnhof* also sends trains to Grindelwald (June-Sept. every 30min., Sept.-May every hr. 6:35am-10:35pm; 9.80SFr).

The **tourist office**, Höheweg 37, in Hotel Metropole, has free maps. (☎826 53 00. Open July-Aug. M-F 8am-6pm, Sa 8am-5pm, Su 10am-noon and 5-7pm; Sept.-June M-F 8am-noon and 1:30-6pm, Sa 9am-noon.) Both train stations rent **bikes.** (30SFr per day. Open daily 6am-7pm.) For **snow and weather info,** call ☎828 79 31. In case of emergency, call the **police** ☎117 or the **hospital** ☎826 26 26. **Postal Code:** CH-3800.

▐ ▐ ACCOMMODATIONS AND FOOD. ▨**Backpackers Villa Sonnenhof ❷**, Alpenstr. 16, diagonally across the Höhenmatte from the tourist office, is friendly and low-key. (☎826 71 71. Mountain bikes 28SFr per day. Breakfast and lockers included. Laundry 10SFr. **Internet** 10SFr per hr. Reception 7:30-11am and 4-10pm. Dorms 29-32SFr; doubles 82-88SFr; triples 111-120SFr. 5SFr extra for balcony. AmEx/MC/V.) **Balmer's Herberge ❷**, Hauptstr. 23. Switzerland's oldest private hostel (since 1945) is thoroughly American: It is a place to party, not relax. Services include mountain bike rental (35SFr per day), nightly movies, TV, free sleds, and a bar. (☎822 19 61. Breakfast included. **Internet** (20SFr per hr.). Reception summer 6:30am-noon and 4-10pm, winter 6:30-10am and 4:30-10pm. Dorms 20-24SFr; doubles 68SFr; triples 90SFr; quads 120SFr.) **Swiss Adventure Hostel ❷,** in the tiny town of Boltigen, has made this quiet valley a sporty alternative to the party scene in Interlaken. A free shuttle runs to and from Interlaken each day (40min.). Its adventure company offers the same activities as the Interlaken companies, but with a more personal touch. (☎773 73 73. Dorms 20SFr; double with shower 70SFr; quad with shower 100SFr. Special deals if combined with adventure sports.) **Happy Inn ❷**, Rosenstr. 17, lives up to its name with a friendly staff. From *Westbahnhof*, turn left towards the tourist office, then right on Rosenstr. at Centralpl. (☎822 32 25. Reception 7am-6pm. Call early for rooms. Dorms 22SFr; singles 38SFr; doubles 76SFr.) Most hostels serve cheap food, and there are **Migros supermarkets** by both train stations. (Open M-Th 8am-7pm, F 8am-9pm, Sa 7:30am-5pm.)

▟ ▟ OUTDOORS AND HIKING. Interlaken offers a wide range of adrenaline-pumping activities. **Alpin Raft** (☎823 41 00), the most established company in Interlaken, has qualified, personable guides and offers: paragliding (150SFr); canyoning (110-195SFr); river rafting (95-109SFr); skydiving (380SFr); bungee jumping (125-165SFr); and hang gliding (180SFr). All prices include transportation to and from any hostel in Interlaken. A number of horse and hiking tours, as well as rock-lessons, are also available upon request. **Outdoor Interlaken** (☎826 77 19) offers rock-climbing lessons (89SFr per half-day) and **white-water kayaking** tours (155SFr per half-day). The owner of **Skydiving Xdream,** Stefan Heuser, has been on the Swiss skydiving team for 17 years. (Skydiving 380SFr. ☎079 75 93 48 34. Open Apr.-Oct.)

> **!** Interlaken's adventure sports industry is thrilling, but accidents do happen. On July 27, 1999, 19 tourists were killed by a sudden flash flood while canyoning. Be aware that you participate in all adventure sports at your own risk.

Interlaken's most traversed trail climbs to the **Harder Kulm** (1310m). From the *Ostbahnhof*, head toward town, take the first road bridge right across the river, and follow the yellow signs that later give way to white-red-white markings on the rocks. From the top, signs lead back down to the *Westbahnhof*. A funicular runs from the trailhead near the *Ostbahnhof* to the top from May-Oct. (2½hr. up, 1½hr. down. May to mid-Oct. 14SFr, round-trip 21SFr; 25% Eurailpass and SwissPass discount.) For flatter **trails,** turn left from the train station and left before the bridge, then follow the canal over to the nature reserve on the shore of the Thunersee. The trail winds up the Lombach river and through pastures at the base of the Harder Kulm back toward town (3hr.).

GRINDELWALD ☎033

Grindelwald (pop. 4,500), the launching point to the only glaciers accessible by foot in the Bernese Oberland, crouches beneath the north face of the Eiger. The town has all kinds of hikes, from easy valley walks to challenging peaks for top climbers. The **Bergführerbüro** (Mountain Guides Office), in the sports center near the tourist office, sells hiking maps and coordinates glacier walks, ice climbing, and mountaineering. (☎853 12 00. Open June-Oct. M-F 9am-noon and 2-5pm.) The **Lower Glacier** *(Untere Grindelwaldgletscher)* hike is moderately steep (5hr.). To reach the trailhead, walk up the main street away from the station and follow the signs downhill to Pfinstegg. Hikers can either walk the first forested section of the trail (1hr.), following signs up to Pfinstegg., or take a funicular to the Pfinstegg. hut (July to mid-Sept. 8am-7pm; mid-Sept. to June 8am-4pm; 9.80SFr). From the hut, signs lead up the glacier-filled valley to Stieregg., a hut that offers food.

The **Jungfraubahn** runs to Grindelwald from Interlaken's *Ostbahnhof* (40min., 6:35am-10:30pm, 9.80SFr). The **tourist office**, located in the Sport-Zentrum to the right of the station, provides chairlift information and a list of free guided excursions. (☎854 12 12. Open July-Aug. M-F 8am-6pm, Sa 8am-7pm, Su 9-11am and 2-6pm; Sept.-June M-F 8am-noon and 2-6pm, Sa 8am-noon and 2-5pm.) **Hotel Hirschen ❹**, to the right of the tourist office, offers comfortable beds and a bowling alley. (☎854 84 84. Breakfast included. Reception daily 8am-10pm. Singles 90-135SFr; doubles 150-220SFr.) To reach the **Jugendherberge (HI) ❷**, head left out of the train station for 400m, then cut uphill to the right just before Chalet Alpenblume and follow the steep trail all the way up the hill. (☎853 10 09. Breakfast included. Reception daily 7:30-10am and 3pm-midnight. Dorms 28-30SFr; doubles 70SFr, with toilet and shower 101SFr. Nonmembers add 6SFr. AmEx/MC.) **Hotel Eiger ❷**, near the tourist office, is a huge complex of middle crust eateries and bars. (Open 8:30am-1:30am.) There's a **Co-op supermarket** on Hauptstr., across from the tourist office. (Open M-F 8am-6:30pm, Sa 8am-4pm.) **Postal Code:** CH-3818.

VALAIS

The Valais occupies the deep and wide glacial gorge traced by the Rhône River. Though its mountain resorts can be over-touristed, the region's spectacular peaks and skiing, hiking, and climbing make fighting the traffic worthwhile.

ZERMATT AND THE MATTERHORN ☎027

The shape of the valley blocks out most of the great Alpine summits that ring Zermatt, allowing the monolithic **Matterhorn** (4478m) to rise alone above town. The area has attained mecca status with Europe's longest **ski** run, the 13km trail from Klein Matterhorn to Zermatt, and more **summer ski trails** than any other Alpine ski resort. A one-day ski pass for any of the area's mountains runs 60-77SFr. The **Zermatt Alpine Center,** which houses both the **Bergführerbüro** (Mountain Guide's Office; ☎966 24 60) and the **Skischulbüro** (Ski School Office; ☎966 24 66), is located past the post office from the station; the Bergführerbüro provides ski passes, four-day weather forecasts, and info on guided climbing. (Open July-Sept. M-F 8:30am-noon and 3:30-7pm, Sa 3:30-7pm, Su 10am-noon and 3:30-7pm; late Dec. to mid-May daily 5-7pm.) Rental prices for skis and snowboards are standardized throughout Zermatt (28-50SFr per day, 123-215SFr per week). **Freeride Film Factory** (☎213 38 07) offers custom **hiking, biking,** and **climbing** expeditions (160-250SFr) that come with a videotape of your trek. ■**The Pipe Surfer's Cantina,** on Kirchstr., has the craziest "beach parties" in the Alps. Don't leave without downing a shot of Moo (6SFr), their specialty caramel vodka. (www.gozermatt.com/thepipe. Happy Hour daily 7-8pm. Open daily 3:30pm-2:30am.)

To preserve the Alpine air, cars and buses are banned in Zermatt; the only way in is the hourly **BVZ** (Brig-Visp-Zermatt) rail line, which connects to Lausanne (73SFr). The **tourist office,** in the station, sells hiking maps for 26SFr. (☎966 81 00. Open mid-June to mid-Oct. M-F 8:30am-6pm, Sa 8:30am-6:30pm, Su 9:30am-noon and 4-6:30pm; mid-Oct. to mid-Dec. and May to mid-June M-F 8:30am-noon and 1:30-6pm, Sa 8:30am-noon; mid-Dec. to Apr. 8:30am-noon and 1:30-6:30pm, Sa 8:30am-6:30pm, Su 9:30am-noon and 4-6:30pm.) **Hotel Bahnhof ❷,** on Bahnhofstr. to the left of the station, provides hotel housing at hostel rates. (☎967 24 06. Dorms 30SFr; singles 59SFr, with shower 71SFr; doubles 86-96SFr. MC/V.) Treat yourself to filling Swiss fare at **Walliserkanne ❸,** on Bahnhofstr. next to the post office. (Open 9am-midnight. AmEx/MC/V.) Pick up groceries at the **Co-op Center,** opposite the station. (Open M-F 8:15am-12:15pm and 1:45-6:30pm, Sa 8:15am-12:15pm and 1:45-6pm.) **Postal Code:** CH-3920.

FRENCH SWITZERLAND

All around Lac Léman, hills sprinkled with villas and blanketed by patchwork vineyards seem tame and settled—until the haze clears. From behind the hills surge rough-hewn mountain peaks with the energizing promise of unpopulated wilderness and wide, lonely expanses.

GENEVA (GENÈVE)   ☎022

A stay in Geneva will likely change your definition of diversity. As the most international city in Switzerland, Geneva is a brew of 178,000 unlikely neighbors: wealthy businessmen speed past dreadlocked skaters in the street while nuclear families stroll by artists squatting in abandoned factories; only one-third of the city's residents are natives of the canton. Birthplace of the League of Nations and current home to dozens of multinational organizations (including the Red Cross and the United Nations), Geneva emanates worldliness.

✈ INTERCITY TRANSPORTATION

Flights: Cointrin Airport (GVA; ☎717 71 11, flight info ☎799 31 11) is a hub for **Swiss Airlines** (☎(0848) 85 20 00) and also serves **Air France** (☎827 87 87) and **British Airways** (☎(0848) 80 10 10). Several direct flights per day to Amsterdam, London, New York, Paris, and Rome. Bus #10 runs to the Gare Cornavin (15min., every 5-10min., 2.20SFr). The train provides a shorter trip (6min., every 10min., 4.80SFr).

Trains: Trains run approximately 4:30am-1am. **Gare Cornavin,** pl. Cornavin, is the main station. To: **Basel** (2¾hr., every hr., 71SFr); **Bern** (2hr., every hr., 47SFr); **Interlaken** (3hr., every hr., 63SFr); **Lausanne** (40min., every 20-30min., 19SFr); **Montreux** (1hr., 2 per hr., 29SFr); **Zurich** (3½hr., every hr., 76SFr). Ticket counter open M-F 8:30am-6:30pm, Sa 9am-5pm. **Gare des Eaux-Vives** (☎736 16 20), on av. de la Gare des Eaux-Vives (tram #12 to *Amandoliers SNCF*), connects to France's regional rail through **Annecy** (1½hr., 6 per day, 14SFr) or **Chamonix** (2½hr., 4 per day, 24SFr). Ticket office open M-F 9am-6pm, Sa 11am-5:45pm.

TO COINTRIN
AIRPORT
(1.5km)

0   300 yards
0   300 meters

r. Ferrier

r. J. Ch. Amat
r. Rothschild
r. des Buis
r. J.A. Gautier

quai Woodrow Wilson

Coop

r. du Prieuré

r. du Môle

r. de Berne

r. de Bâle

r. de l'Ancien Port

r. de Lausanne

r. de Zurich

Diologal

r. de la Navigation

PL. DE
LA NAVIGATION

r. du Léman

r. de Monthoux

r. de Fribourg

r. de Neuchâtel

r. de Berne

Rossi

r. de Sismondi

A. Vincent

Lavseul

r. des Pâquis

r. A. Gevray

r. de la Cloche

r. des Gares

PL. MONT-
BRILLANT

Gare
Cornavin

PL. DE
CORNAVIN

bd. J. Fazy

r. de Cornavin

r. de Chantepoulet

r. de Constance

r. A. Vaillin

r. de Genus

r. Rousseau

r. de Coutance

Terraux-
du-Temple

Basilique
de
Notre-Dame

r. de la Taponnière

r. des Alpes

Thalberg

Pécolat

Ami-Lévrier

PL. DES
ALPES

Adhémar-Fabri

Alpine
Garden

François-
Bonivard

du Mont-Blanc

AMEX

SQUARE DU
MONT-BLANC

Mont-Blanc Pier

quai du Mont-Blanc

Philippe Plantamour

American
Library

Pâquis Pier

Lac Léman

Jet d'Eau

PL. DES
BERGUES

r. du Cendrier

Kléberg

quai des Bergues

Pont des Bergues

Île
Rousseau

Pont du Mont-Blanc

Promenade du Lac

TO
(4 km)

quai Gustav Ador

Promenade du Lac

PL. DE ST. GERVAIS

Rhône

Pont de la Machine

Pont de l'Ile

PL.
RHÔNE

Coop

PL. DE
LA
FUSTERIE

r. du Rhône

PL. DU
LAC

Jardin
Anglais

quai Général Guisan

r. du Mont

PL.
BEL-AIR

r. de Commerce

r. de la Confédération

PL. DU
MOLARD

PL.
LONGEMALLE

r. Versonnex

r. de la Scie

av. Pictet-de-Rochemont

r. des Eaux-Vives

r. de la Corraterie

r. de la Cité

r. de la Rôtisserie

r. du Marché

r. de la Croix d'Or

r. Neuve

r. de la Fontaine

r. du Port

r. du Prince

r. d'Italie

r. de Rive

STA
Travel

r. Verdaine

r. du Vieux Collège

P. Fatio

bd. Helvétique

PL. DES
EAUX-
VIVES

ROND-
POINT
DE RIVE

PL.
DU
PRÉ-
L'EVEQUE

r. de la Terrassière

bd. de Théâtre

Didoy

r. de la Terrasse

Grand-Rue

r. Jean Calvin

r. des Granges

rampe de la Treille

Musée J.-
Barbier-Mueller

Maison
Tavel

Old
Arsenal

Puits-St-Pierre

St-Pierre

r. de l'Hôtel-de-Ville

PL. DE
MADELEINE

PL. DU BOURG-
DE-FOUR

r. des Chaudronniers

Hôtel
de Ville

r. de la Croix-Rouge

Reformer's
Wall

Promenade des Bastions

University

Parc des
Bastions

PL.
NEUVE

r. Général Dufour

r. de Candolle

r. de Carouge

Pleine de
Plainpalais

ROND-POINT DE
PLAINPALAIS

PL. DE LA
TACONNERIE

PL. DE LA
CROIX-ROUGE

Théodore-de-Bèze

E. Dumont

Musée d'Art
et d'Histoire

Prom. de
St. Antoine

Russian
Orthodox
Church

r. Ferdinand Hodler

r. du Glacis-de-Rive

r. A. Lachenal

r. de Villereuse

rte. de Malagnou

Parc de
Malagnou

TO
(2.5km)

St-Léger

cours des
Bastions

r. de l'Athénée

bd. Helvétique

r. Jacques-Dalcroze

PL. DES
PHILOSOPHES

bd. des Philosophes

PL.
CLAPARÈDE

bd. des Tranchées

St-Victor

Le Fort

Bellot

Charles-Galland

rte. de Florissant

r. de Contamines

Petit-
Palais

av. Henri-Dunant

r. de Carouge

G. Favon

St-Léger

J. Senebier

Geneva

ACCOMMODATIONS
Auberge de Jeunesse (HI), **2**
Camping Point-à-la-Bise, **7**
Cité Universitaire, **11**
City Hostel Geneva, **1**
Hôtel de la Cloche, **3**

FOOD
Les Armures, **9**
Les Brasseurs, **4**
Chocolaterie Micheli, **12**
La Crise, **5**
Restaurant Manora, **6**
Le Rozzel, **8**

★ **NIGHTLIFE**
La Clémence, **10**

▐ LOCAL TRANSPORTATION

Carry your passport with you at all times; the French border is never more than a few minutes away and buses frequently cross it. Ticket purchasing is largely on the honor system, but you may be fined 60SFr for evading fares. Much of the city can be explored on foot.

Public Transportation: Geneva has an efficient bus and tram network. **Transport Publics Genevois** (☎308 34 34), next to the tourist office in Gare Cornavin, provides *Le Réseau* (a free map of bus routes) and inexpensive timetables. Open M-Sa 7am-7pm, Su 10am-6pm. **Day passes** 6SFr-12SFr. Stamp multi-use tickets before boarding. Buses run roughly 5:30am-midnight; **Noctambus** (3SFr, 1:30-4:30am) runs when the others don't. SwissPass valid on all buses; Eurail not valid.

Taxis: Taxi-Phone (☎331 41 33). 6.80SFr plus 2.90SFr per km. Taxi from airport to city 30SFr, max. 4 passengers (15-20min.).

Bike Rental: Geneva has well-marked bike paths and special traffic lights for spoked traffic. For routes, get *Itineraires cyclables* or *Tours de ville avec les vélos de location* from the tourist office. Behind the station, **Genève Roule**, pl. Montbrillant 17 (☎740 13 43), has free bikes available (50SFr deposit; hefty fine if bike is lost or stolen). Slightly nicer neon bikes from 5SFr per day. Open daily 7:30am-9:30pm.

Hitchhiking: Those headed to Germany or northern Switzerland take bus #4 to *Jardin Botanique*. Those headed to France take bus #4 to *Palettes*, then line D to *St. Julien*. *Let's Go* does not recommend hitchhiking.

✴ ▐ ORIENTATION AND PRACTICAL INFORMATION

The labyrinthine cobbled streets and quiet squares of the historic *vieille ville*, around **Cathédrale de St-Pierre,** make up the heart of Geneva. Across the **Rhône River** to the north, banks and five-star hotels gradually give way to lakeside promenades, **International Hill,** and rolling parks. Across the **Arve River** to the south lies the village of **Carouge,** home to student bars and clubs (take tram #12 or 13 to *pl. du Marché*).

TOURIST, FINANCIAL, AND LOCAL SERVICES

Tourist Offices: Main office, r. du Mont-Blanc 18 (☎909 70 00), in the Central Post Office Building. From Cornavin, walk 5min. toward the Pont du Mont-Blanc. Staff books hotel rooms for a 5SFr fee, leads walking tours, and offers free city maps. Open July-Aug. daily 9am-6pm; Sept.-June M-Sa 9am-6pm. During the summer, head for **Centre d'Accueil et de Renseignements** (☎731 46 47), an office-in-a-bus parked in pl. Mont-Blanc, by the Metro Shopping entrance to Cornavin Station. Lists free performances and makes hotel reservations. Open mid-June to mid-Sept. daily 9am-9pm.

Consulates: Australia, chemin des Fins 2 (☎799 91 00). **Canada,** av. de l'Ariana 5 (☎919 92 00). **New Zealand,** chemin des Fins 2 (☎929 03 50). **South Africa,** r. de Rhône 65 (☎849 54 54). **UK,** r. de Vermont 37 (☎918 24 26). **US,** r. Versonnex 7 (☎840 51 60; recorded info 840 51 61).

Currency Exchange: ATMs offer the best rates. **Gare Cornavin** has good rates with no commission on traveler's checks, makes cash advances on credit cards (min. 200SFr), and arranges Western Union transfers. Open M-Sa 6:50am-7:40pm, Su 6:50am-6:40pm. Western Union desk open daily 7am-7pm.

Bi-Gay-Lesbian Resources: Dialogai, r. de la Navigation 11-13 (☎906 40 40). From Gare Cornavin, turn left, walk 5min. down r. de Lausanne, and turn right onto r. de la Navigation. Resource group with programs from support groups to outdoor activities. Mostly male, but women welcome.

Laundromat: Lavseul, r. de Monthoux 29. Wash 5SFr, dry 1SFr per 10min. Open daily 7am-midnight.

EMERGENCY AND COMMUNICATIONS

Emergency: Police: ☎117. **Ambulance:** ☎144. **Fire:** ☎118.

Medical Assistance: Hôpital Cantonal, r. Micheli-du-Crest 24 (☎372 33 11). Bus #1 or 5 or tram #12. Door #2 is for emergency care, door #3 for consultations. For info on walk-in clinics, contact the **Association des Médecins** (☎320 84 20).

Internet Access: Point 6, r. de Vieux-Billard 7a, off r. des Bains (☎800 26 00). 5SFr per hr. Open daily noon-midnight. **Connections Net World,** r. de Monthoux 58. 3SFr per 30min., 5SFr per hr. Copier available. Open M-Sa 9:30am-2:30am, Su 1pm-2am.

Post Office: Poste Centrale, r. de Mont-Blanc 18, a block from Gare Cornavin. Open M-F 7:30am-6pm, Sa 8:30am-noon. Address mail to be held: Firstname SURNAME, *Poste Restante*, Genève 1 Mont-Blanc, **CH-1211,** Geneva, SWITZERLAND.

▐ ACCOMMODATIONS

Geneva is a cosmopolitan city, and its 5-star hotel system is geared toward the international banker. Luckily for the budget traveler, the seasonal influx of university students and interns has created a second network of hostels, pensions, and university dorms moonlighting as summer hotels. The indispensable *Info Jeunes* lists about 50 options; *Let's Go* lists the highlights below. The tourist office publishes *Budget Hotels*, stretching the definition to 120SFr per person. Even for short stays, reservations are a must.

City Hostel Geneva, r. Ferrier 2 (☎901 15 00). TV room and kitchen. Sheets 3SFr. Internet 8SFr per hr. Reception daily 7:30am-noon and 1pm-midnight. Check-out 10am. Single-sex dorms 25SFr; singles 55SFr; doubles 80SFr. MC/V. ❷

Auberge de Jeunesse (HI), r. Rothschild 28-30 (☎732 62 60). Restaurant, kitchen facilities (1SFr per 30min.), TV room, lockers, and library. Breakfast included. Laundry 6SFr. Internet 7SFr per hr. 6-night max. stay. Reception June-Sept. daily 6:30-10am and 2pm-midnight; Oct.-May 6:30-10am and 4pm-midnight. Lockout 10am-3pm. Dorms 25SFr; doubles 70SFr, with bath 80SFr; quads 110SFr. MC/V. ❷

Cité Universitaire, av. Miremont 46 (☎839 22 11). Take bus #3 (dir.: Crets-de-Champel) from the station to the last stop. TV rooms, restaurant, disco (Th and Sa, free to guests), and a small grocery shop. Hall showers. Reception M-F 8am-noon and 2-10pm, Sa 8am-noon and 6-10pm, Su 9-11am and 6-10pm. Check-out 10am. Dorm lockout 11am-6pm. Dorm curfew 11pm. Dorms (July-Sept. only) 20SFr; singles 49SFr; doubles 66SFr; studios with kitchenette and bathroom 75SFr. ❷

Hôtel de la Cloche, r. de la Cloche 6 (☎732 94 81), off quai du Mont-Blanc in a converted mansion. Breakfast included. Reception daily 8am-10pm. Singles 65-70SFr; doubles 85-95SFr; triples 110-140SFr; quads 140SFr. AmEx/MC/V. ❹

Camping Pointe-à-la-Bise, Chemin de la Bise (☎752 12 96). Take bus #8 to Rive, then bus E north to Bise and walk 10min. to the lake. Reception daily 8am-noon and 2-9pm. Open Apr.-Sept. 6.20SFr per person, 9SFr per site. No tents provided. Beds 15SFr. 4-person bungalows 60SFr. ❶

▐ FOOD

You can find anything from sushi to *paella* in Geneva, but you may need a banker's salary to foot the bill. Do-it-yourselfers can pick up basics at *boulangeries*, *pâtisseries*, or at the ubiquitous supermarkets. Many supermarkets also have attached cafeterias; try the **Co-op** on the corner of r. du Commerce and r. du Rhône, in the Centre Rhône Fusterie. (Open M 9am-6:45pm, Tu-W and F 8:30am-6:45pm, Th 8:30am-8pm, Sa 8:30am-5pm.) There are extensive dining options in the old city near the cathedral, but you'll pay for the location. In the **Les Paquis** area, bordered by the r. de Lausanne and Gare Cornavin on one side and the Quais Mont-Blanc and Wilson on the other, are a variety of relatively cheap ethnic foods. Around **pl. du Cirque** and **plaine de Plainpalais** are cheap, student-oriented tea rooms. To the south, the village of **Carouge** is known for its cozy pizzerias and funky brasseries.

▨ **Chocolaterie Micheli,** r. Micheli-du-Crest 1 (☎329 90 06). Take tram #13 to *Plainpalais* and walk up bd. des Philosophes until it intersects r. Micheli-du-Crest. Confectionary masterpieces abound in this chocolate store and cafe *par excellence.* Open Tu-F 8am-7pm, Sa 8am-5pm. MC/V. ❶

Le Rozzel, Grand-Rue 18. Take bus #5 to *pl. Neuve,* then walk up the hill past the cathedral on r. Jean-Calvin to Grand-Rue. Large dinner crepes (4-18SFr). Dessert crepes (5-9SFr). Open M 7am-4pm, Tu-W 7am-7pm, Th-F 7am-10pm, Sa 9am-10pm. ❷

Restaurant Manora, r. de Cornavin 4, to the right of the station in the Placette department store. This huge self-serve restaurant has a varied selection and free water (rare in Switzerland). Entrees from 8SFr. Open M-Sa 7:30am-9:30pm, Su 9am-9:30pm. ❶

Les Armures, r. due Puits-St-Pierre 1, near the main entrance to the cathedral. Elegance in the heart of the *Altstadt.* Fondue 24-26SFr. Pizza 14-17SFr. Entrees run to 45SFr. Open M-F 8am-midnight, Sa 11am-midnight, Su 11am-11pm. ❹

Les Brasseurs, pl. Cornavin 20. Go left from the station. Serves *flammeküchen,* an Alsatian specialty similar to thin crust pizza but topped with cream and onions (11.60-23SFr), and home-brewed towers of beer (31SFr for 2L). Kitchen open 11:30am-2pm and 6-10:45pm. Open M-W 11am-1am, Th-Sa 11am-2am, Su 5pm-1am. ❸

La Crise, r. de Chantepoulet 13. Small but popular snack bar dishes out tasty quiches and soups at reasonable prices. Open M-F 6am-3pm and 5-8pm, Sa 6am-3pm. ❷

◉ SIGHTS

The city's most interesting historical sites are in a dense, easily walkable space. The tourist office offers 2hr. walking tours. (Mid-June to Sept. M-Sa 10am; Oct. to mid-June Sa 10am. 12SFr, students and seniors 8SFr.)

VIEILLE VILLE. From 1536 to 1564, Calvin preached at the **Cathédrale de St-Pierre.** The **north tower** provides a commanding view of the old town. *(Open June-Sept. daily 9am-7pm; Oct.-May M-Sa 10am-noon and 2-5pm, Su 11am-12:30pm and 1:30-5pm. Tower 3SFr.)* Ruins, including a Roman sanctuary and a 4th-century basilica, rest in an **archaeological site** below the cathedral. *(Open June-Sept. Su 10am-5pm, Tu-Sa 11am-5pm; Oct.-May Su 10am-noon and 2-5pm, Tu-Sa 2-5pm. 5SFr, students 3SFr.)* At the west end of the *vieille ville* sits the 14th-century **Maison Tavel,** which now houses a history museum. *(Open Su and Tu-Sa 10am-5pm. Free.)* Across the street is the **Hôtel de Ville** (town hall), where world leaders met on August 22, 1864, to sign the Geneva Convention that still governs war conduct today. The **Grand-Rue,** which begins at the Hôtel de Ville, is lined with medieval workshops and 18th-century mansions; plaques commemorate famous residents like Jean-Jacques Rousseau, who was born at #40. Below the cathedral, along r. de la Croix-Rouge, the **Parc des Bastions** stretches from pl. Neuve to pl. des Philosophes and includes **Le Mur des Réformateurs** (Reformers' Wall), a sprawling collection of bas-relief figures of the Reformers themselves. The park's center walkway leads to the ▨**Petit-Palais,** Terrasse St-Victor 2, a beautiful mansion containing art by Chagall, Gauguin, Picasso, and Renoir, as well as themed exhibitions. *(Bus #36 to Petit Palais or #1, 3, or 5 to Claparède. Open M-F 10am-6pm, Sa-Su 10am-5pm. 10SFr, students 5SFr.)*

WATERFRONT. As you descend from the cathedral to the lake, medieval lanes give way to wide quais and chic boutiques. Down quai Gustave Ador, the **Jet d'Eau,** Europe's highest fountain, spews a spectacular 7-ton plume of water 440ft into the air. The **floral clock** in the nearby **Jardin Anglais** pays homage to Geneva's watch industry. It's probably Geneva's most overrated attraction and was once the most hazardous—the clock had to be cut back almost 1m because tourists, intent on taking the perfect photograph, repeatedly backed into oncoming traffic. On the north shore, the beach **Pâquis Plage,** quai du Mont-Blanc 30, is popular with locals. *(Open 9am-8:30pm. 2SFr.)*

INTERNATIONAL HILL. The International Red Cross building contains the moving ▨**International Red Cross and Red Crescent Museum,** Av. de la Paix 17. *(Bus #8 or F to Appia or bus V or Z to Ariana. Open M and W-Su 10am-5pm. 10SFr, students 5SFr.)* The nearby European headquarters of the **United Nations** is in the same building that sheltered the now-defunct League of Nations. The constant traffic of international diplomats (often in handsome non-Western dress) provides more excitement than the dull guided tour. *(Open July-Aug. daily 10am-5pm; Apr.-June and Sept.-Oct. daily 10am-noon and 2-4pm; Nov.-Mar. M-F 10am-noon and 2-4pm. 8.50SFr, seniors and students 6.50SFr.)*

♫ ▨ ENTERTAINMENT AND NIGHTLIFE

Genève Agenda, available at the tourist office, is your guide to fun, with event listings ranging from major festivals to movies (be warned—a movie runs about 16SFr). In July and August, the **Cinelac** turns Genève Plage into an open-air cinema screening mostly American films. Free **jazz concerts** take place in July and August in Parc de la Grange. Geneva hosts the biggest celebration of **American Independence Day** outside the US (July 4), and the **Fêtes de Genève** in early August is filled with international music and fireworks. The best party is **L'Escalade** in early December, which lasts a full weekend and commemorates the dramatic repulsion of invading Savoyard troops.

　　Place Bourg-de-Four, in the *vieille ville* below the cathedral, attracts students and professionals to its charming terraces and old-world atmosphere. **Place du Molard,** on the right bank by the pont du Mont-Blanc, offers terrace cafes and big, loud bars and clubs. **Les Paquis,** near Gare Cornavin and pl. de la Navigation, is the city's red-light district, but it also has a wide array of rowdy, low-lit bars, many with an ethnic flavor. **Carouge,** across the river Arve, is a student-friendly locus of nightlife activity. Generations of students have eaten at the famous ▨**La Clémence,** pl. du Bourg-de-Four 20. (Open M-Th 7am-12:30am, F-Sa 7am-1:30am.)

LAUSANNE　　　　　　　　　　　　　　　　　　　　　☎021

The unique museums, distinctive neighborhoods, and lazy Lac Léman waterfront of Lausanne (pop. 125,000) make it well worth a stay. In the *vieille ville,* two flights of medieval stairs lead to the Gothic **Cathédrale.** (Open July to mid-Sept. M-F 7am-7pm, Sa-Su 8am-7pm; mid-Sept. to June daily 8am-5:30pm.) Below the cathedral is the **Hôtel de Ville,** on pl. de la Palud, the meeting point for guided tours of the town. (Tours M-Sa 10am and 3pm. 10SFr, students free. English available.) The ▨**Collection de l'Art Brut,** av. Bergières 11, is filled with disturbing and original sculptures, drawings, and paintings by artists on the fringe—institutionalized schizophrenics, uneducated peasants, and convicted criminals. Take bus #2 or 3 to *Jomini.* (Open July-Aug. daily 11am-6pm; Sept.-June Tu-F 11am-1pm and 2-6pm, Sa-Su 11am-6pm. 6SFr, students 4SFr.) The **Musée Olympique,** Quai d'Ouchy 1, is a high-tech temple to modern Olympians with an extensive video collection, allowing visitors to relive almost any moment of the games. Take bus #2 to *Ouchy.* (Open May-Sept. M-W and F-Su 9am-6pm, Th 9am-8pm; Oct.-Apr. closed Mondays.

14SFr, students 9SFr.) In Ouchy, several booths along quai de Belgique and pl. de la Navigation rent **pedal boats** (10SFr per 30min.) and offer water skiing or wake boarding on **Lake Léman** (30SFr per 15min.).

Trains leave from pl. de la Gare 9 for: **Basel** (2½hr., every hr. 5:25am-9:25pm, 68SFr); **Geneva** (50min., every 20min. 4:55am-12:45am, 19SFr); **Montreux** (20min., every 30min. 5:25am-2:25am, 10SFr); **Paris** (4hr., 4 per day 7:35am-5:50pm, 71SFr); and **Zurich** (2½hr., 3 per hr. 5:25am-10:25pm, 65SFr). The **tourist office** in the train station reserves rooms. (☎613 73 73. Open daily 9am-5pm.) Home of the world's oldest hotel school, Lausanne has a well-deserved reputation for service-industry excellence. ◪**Lausanne Guesthouse & Backpacker ❷**, chemin des Epinettes 4, is conveniently located and has comfortable rooms. Head left and downhill out of the station on W. Fraisse; take the first right on chemin des Epinettes. (☎601 80 00. Sheets for dorms 5SFr. Reception daily 7am-noon and 3-10pm. 4-bed dorms 29SFr; singles 80SFr, with bathroom 88SFr; doubles 86/98SFr. MC/V.) **Camping de Vidy ❶**, chemin du Camping 3, has a restaurant (open May-Sept. 7am-11pm) and supermarket. Take bus #2 (dir.: Bourdonnette) to *Bois-de-Vaux*, cross the street, follow chemin du Bois-de-Vaux past Jeunotel and under the overpass. (☎622 50 00. Showers included. Electricity 3-4SFr. Reception July-Aug. daily 8am-9pm; Sept.-June 8:30am-12:30pm and 4-8pm. 6.50SFr per person, 8-12SFr per tent; 1- to 2-person bungalow 54SFr; 3- to 4-person bungalow 86SFr.) Restaurants, cafes, and bars cluster around **place St-François** and the *vieille ville*, while *boulangeries* sell cheap sandwiches on every street and grocery stores abound. Stop by **Le Barbare ❶**, Escaliers du Marché 27, for a sandwich (7SFr), omelette (8-10SFr), or pizza (12SFr) after trekking to the cathedral. (☎312 21 32. Open M-Sa 8:30am-midnight.)

MONTREUX
☎021

Montreux (pop. 22,500) is a resort town past its Jazz Age heyday. Fortunately, the music still swings; world-famous for drawing and discovering exceptional talent, the ◪**Montreux Jazz Festival** erupts for 15 days starting the first Friday in July (www.montreuxjazz.com; tickets 49-79SFr). Luminaries Neil Young, Bob Dylan, Paul Simon, and Miles Davis have all played here. If you can't get tickets, come anyway for the **Jazz Off,** 500 hours of free, open-air concerts by fledgling bands. The **Château de Chillon,** a gloomy medieval fortress on a nearby island, is one of the most visited attractions in Switzerland. It features all the comforts of home: prison cells, a torture chamber, and a weapons room. Take the CGN **ferry** (14SFr) or bus #1 (2.80SFr) to Chillon. (Open Apr.-Sept. daily 9am-6pm; Mar. and Oct. 9:30am-5pm; Nov.-Feb. 10am-4pm. 9SFr, students 7SFr.)

Trains leave the station on av. des Alpes for: Bern (1½hr., 2 per hr. 5:30am-11pm, 37SFr); Geneva (1hr., 2 per hr. 5:30am-11:30pm, 26SFr); and Lausanne (20min., 3-5 per hr. 5:25am-midnight, 9.80SFr). Descend the stairs opposite the station, head left on Grand Rue for 5-10min., and look to the right for the **tourist office,** on pl. du Débarcadère. (☎962 84 84. Open mid-June to mid-Sept. M-F 9:30am-6pm, Sa-Su 10am-5pm; mid-Sept. to mid-June M-F 8:30am-5pm, Sa-Su 10am-3pm.) Cheap rooms in Montreux are scarce year-round and almost nonexistent during the jazz festival, so book ahead. ◪**Riviera Lodge ❷**, pl. du Marché 5, in the neighboring town of Vevey, is worth the commute. Take bus #1 to Vevey (20min., every 10min., 2.80SFr). From the bus stop, head away from the train station on the main road to the open square on the water. Guests get a pass for discounts and free activities in the area, such as waterskiing and a ride up the Vevey funicular. (☎923 80 40. Sheets 5SFr. Laundry 7SFr. **Internet** 7SFr per hour. Reception daily 8am-noon and 5-8pm. Call ahead if arriving late. 4- to 8-bed dorms 24SFr; doubles 80SFr. MC/V.) To get to **Hôtel Pension Wilhelm ❸**, r. du Marché 13-15, take a left on av. des Alpes from the Montreux station, walk uphill 3min., and take a left on r. du Marché.

(☎963 14 31. Breakfast included. Reception daily 7am-10pm. Open Mar.-Sept. Singles 60SFr, with shower 70SFr; doubles 100/120SFr.) Grand Rue and ave. de Casino have reasonably priced markets. **Marché de Montreux,** pl. du Marché, is an open-air food market. (F 7am-1pm.) There's a **Co-op supermarket** at Grand Rue 80. (Open M-F 8am-12:15pm and 2-6:30pm, Sa 8am-5pm.) **Postal Code:** CH-1820.

ITALIAN SWITZERLAND

Ever since Switzerland won the Italian-speaking canton of Ticino (Tessin in German and French) from Italy in 1512, the region has been renowned for its mix of Swiss efficiency and Italian *dolce vita*—no wonder the rest of Switzerland vacations here among jasmine-laced villas painted the bright colors of Italian gelato.

LUGANO   ☎091

Set in a valley between two mountains, Lugano (pop. 114,000) draws plenty of visitors with its seamless blend of religious beauty, artistic flair, and natural spectacle. The frescoes of the 16th-century **Cattedrale San Lorenzo,** just south of the train station, are still vivid despite their advanced age. The most spectacular fresco in town, however, is the gargantuan *Crucifixion* in the **Chiesa Santa Maria degli Angiuli,** to the right of the tourist office. Armed with topographic maps and trail guides (sold at the tourist office), hikers can tackle the nearby mountains, **Monte Bré** (933m) and **Monte San Salvatore** (912m), or the more rewarding **Monte Boglio** (5hr.). Alpine guides at the **ASBEST Adventure Company,** V. Basilea 28 (☎966 11 14), offer everything from snowshoeing and skiing (full-day 90SFr) to paragliding (170SFr) and canyoning (from 90SFr).

Trains leave P. della Stazione for: Locarno (1hr., every 30min. 5:30am-midnight, 17SFr); Milan (45min., every hr. 7am-9:45pm, 21SFr); and Zurich (3hr., 1-2 per hr. 6am-8:35pm, 60SFr). The **tourist office** is across from the ferry station at the corner of p. Rezzonico. (☎913 32 32. Open July-Aug. M-F 9am-7:30pm, Sa 9am-10pm, Su 10am-4pm; Apr.-May and Sept.-Oct. M-F 9am-7:30pm, Sa 9am-5:30pm, Su 10am-4pm; Nov.-Mar. M-F 9am-12:30pm and 1:30-5pm.) ▨**Hotel Montarina** ❷, Via Montarina 1, is a palm-tree-enveloped hostel with a swimming pool, kitchen, and

NO WORK, ALL PLAY

DO YOU SCHWING?

A summer in Switzerland would not be complete without the institution that is the annual *Schwingfest,* an event dedicated to the arcane sport of *Schwingen.* A form of wrestling, *Schwingen* features two male *Schwingers* faced off in a Sägemuhlring (a ring of sawdust). The men wear leather over shorts with loops on the back which the other *Schwinger* must grip for leverage at all times. As a *Schwinger,* your goal in life is to throw your opponent down on his back, and to stay within the circle while doing so; matches last around five minutes.

The earliest known reference to the sport is a 13th-century stone carving in the cathedral of Lausanne, which depicts two over shirt-wearing strongmen at loggerheads. The sport's origins lie in Alpine farming regions where farmhands would compete to see who was the strongest, and everyone presumably wore suspenders. Today, the men are still distinguished by the roots of their training: *Sennen* are farmers and wear traditional blue workshirts; *Turnen* are gym-trained athletes and wear only white.

The *Schwingfest* itself includes more Swiss tradition than just wrestling. Normally, the playing of an *Alphorn* kicks off the first bout, and flag throwers, yodel choirs and a beer-and-sausage tent provide entertainment on the side lines. Check www.esv.ch for info on the *Fest* nearest you.

terrace. (☎966 72 72. Sheets 4SFr. Laundry 4SFr. Reception daily 8am-10pm. Open Mar.-Oct. Dorms 25SFr; singles 70-80SFr; doubles 100SFr, with bath 120SFr.) The **Migros supermarket,** Via Pretoria 15, also has a food court. (Open M-W and F 8am-6:30pm, Th 8am-9pm, Sa 7:30am-5pm.) **Postal Code:** CH-6900.

LOCARNO ☎091

A Swiss vacation spot, Locarno (pop. 48,000) gets over 2200 hours of sunlight per year—more than anywhere else in Switzerland. For centuries, visitors have journeyed here solely to see the orange-yellow **Church of Madonna del Sasso** (Madonna of the Rock), founded in 1487. A 20min. walk up the smooth stones of the Via al Sasso leads to the top, passing life-size wooden niche statues along the way. Hundreds of heart-shaped medallions on the church walls commemorate acts of Mary's intervention in the lives of worshipers who have journeyed here. (Grounds open 6:30am-7pm.) Each August (Aug. 4-14, 2004), Locarno swells with pilgrims of a different sort; its world-famous **film festival** draws 150,000 movie-lovers.

   Trains run from P. Stazione to: Lucerne (2½hr., every 30min. 6am-9pm, 54SFr); Lugano (50min., every 30min. 5:30am-midnight, 17SFr); and Milan via Bellinzona (2hr., every hr. 5am-9:25pm, 34SFr). The **tourist office,** on P. Grande in the *Kursaal* (casino), makes hotel reservations. (☎791 00 91. Open M-F 9am-6pm, Sa 10am-6pm, Su 2:30-6pm.) To reach **Pensione Città Vecchia ❷,** Via Toretta 13, turn right onto Via Toretta from P. Grande. (☎751 45 54. Breakfast included. Reception daily 8am-9pm. Check-in 1-6pm. Dorms 29-37SFr; doubles 70-80SFr; triples 120SFr.) The rooms of **Garni Sempione ❸,** Via Rusca 6, are set around an enclosed courtyard. To reach the hotel, walk to the end of the P. Grande, turn right onto Via della Motta, and take the left fork onto Via Rusca. (☎751 30 64. Breakfast included. Reception 8am-9pm. Singles 60SFr, with shower 65SFr; doubles 110/120SFr; triples 150/170SFr; quads 160SFr. AmEx/DC/MC/V.) Left of the station, **Ristorante Manora ❶,** Via della Stazione 1, is good, cheap, self-service dining. Salad bar 4.50-10SFr. Pasta buffet 8.50-10SFr. Meat *Menüs* 10.50-16.50SFr. Open Nov.-Feb. M-Sa 8am-9pm, Su 8am-9pm; Mar.-Oct. M-Sa 8am-10pm, Su 8am-9m. Get groceries at the **Aperto** in the station. (Open daily 6am-10pm.) **Postal Code:** CH-6600.

UKRAINE (УКРАЇНА)

Translated literally, "Ukraine" means "borderland," and the country has occupied this precarious position for most of its history. Vast and fertile, and perpetually tempting to invaders, newly independent Ukraine is now caught between overbearing Russia on one side and a bloc of *nouveau riche* countries on the other. The country offers fascinating, uncrowded museums, wonderful castles, and the magnificent, spirited Black Sea coast. With no beaten path from which to stray, Ukraine rewards travelers with a challenging but unique experience.

FACTS AND FIGURES

Official Name: Ukraine.

Capital: Kyiv.

Major cities: Kyiv, Lviv, Odessa.

Population: 49,000,000.

Land Area: 603,700 sq. km.

Time Zone: GMT +2.

Languages: Ukrainian, Russian, Tatar.

Religions: Ukrainian Orthodox (85%).

DISCOVER UKRAINE

Start any trip to Ukraine in **Kyiv** (p. 1043); once the seat of the Kyivan Rus dynasty, the modern city's park-covered environs and riverside vistas are a breathtaking backdrop to its incomparable mix of urban rush and provincial charm. The country's undiscovered jewel is **Lviv** (p. 1047), in western Ukraine. Khrushchev gave **Yalta** (p. 1049) to Ukraine, and the Russians didn't object—unfortunately for them, they didn't realize how much sun and fun they were losing. Farther west is **Odessa** (p. 1048), a former USSR party town.

ESSENTIALS

WHEN TO GO

The best time to visit is between May and September, when it's warmer. Spring and early fall can be unpredictable; snow flurries are always possible. Winter is bitterly cold. Along the Black Sea, summers are hot and winters are mild.

DOCUMENTS AND FORMALITIES

VISAS. Travelers from Australia, Canada, Ireland, New Zealand, South Africa, the UK, and the US must have a visa. (Processing fee €45; single-entry €30; double-entry €60; multiple-entry €120; transit €15. Fees are waived for American students with proper documents.) Citizens of Australia, New Zealand, and South Africa need an **invitation,** but citizens of Canada, the EU, and the US do not. **International Management Services** also arrange invitations; fax the request a month in advance. (US ☎ 757-573-8362; fax 757-622-4693; Ukraine ☎/fax 044 516 2433; www.travel-ims.com.) When proceeding through **customs** you will be required to declare all valuables and foreign currency above €1000 (including traveler's checks). It is illegal to bring Ukrainian currency into Ukraine. Foreigners arriving at Kyiv's Borispol airport must buy a health insurance policy (€23 per week), which is essentially an entry tax and does not provide health care coverage. **Offices of Visas and Registration** (OVIR; ОВІР), in Kyiv at blv. Tarasa Shevchenka 34 (Тараса Шевченка; ☎(044) 224 9051), and in police stations in smaller cities, extend visas. Do not lose the paper given to you when entering the country to supplement your visa; it is required to leave the country.

EMBASSIES AND CONSULATES. All foreign embassies are in Kyiv (p. 1044). Ukrainian embassies at home include: **Australia,** Ste. 306-7 Edgecliff Centre, 203-233 New South Head Road, Edgecliff NSW 2027 (☎02 9328 5429; fax 9328 5164); **Canada,** 331 Metcalfe St., Ottawa, ON K2P 0J9 (☎613-230-2961; www.infoukes.com/ukremb); **South Africa,** 398 Marais Brooklyn, Pretoria; mail to: P.O. Box 57291, Arcadia, 0181 (☎012 461 946; fax 461 944); **UK,** 78 Kensington Park Rd., London W11 2PL (☎020 7727 6312; 7792 1708); **US,** 3350 M St. NW, Washington, D.C. 20007 (☎202-333-0606; www.ukremb.com).

TRANSPORTATION

BY PLANE. Ukraine International Airlines (US ☎800-876-0114; in Kyiv ☎(044) 461 5050 or 234 4528; www.ukraine-international.com) flies to Kyiv (KBP and IEV), Lviv (LWO), and Odessa (ODS) from a number of European capitals. Several other international carriers also fly to Kyiv, generally once or twice per week.

BY TRAIN. Trains run frequently from Ukraine's neighboring countries, and are the best way to travel. Be prepared for a two-hour stop at the border. On most trains within Ukraine there are three classes: *Platzkart, coupé,* and *SV.* Paying the extra two dollars for *coupé* can make a big difference.

BY BUS. Buses cost about the same as trains, but are often much shabbier, except for modern **AutoLux** (АвтоЛюкс) buses. Schedules are generally reliable, but low demand can cause cancellations. Buy tickets at the *kasa* (box office); if they are sold out, go directly to the driver, who might be able to find an extra seat.

BY TAXI AND BY THUMB. In cities, private minibuses called *marshrutke* run along the same routes as public transportation; they are faster but slightly more expensive. **Taxi** drivers may try to gouge foreigners, so negotiate the price beforehand. **Hitchhiking** is uncommon; if you must, hold a sign with your destination. *Let's Go* does not recommend hitchhiking.

TOURIST SERVICES AND MONEY

EMERGENCY	Police: ☎02. Ambulance: ☎03. Fire: ☎01.

TOURIST OFFICES. There is no state-run tourist office. Local travel agencies often have English-speaking staffs. Remnants of the Soviet **Intourist** can be found in some hotels, but their employees usually don't speak English.

MONEY. The *karbovanets* (Krb; a.k.a. *kupon*) has been replaced with the **hryvnia** (гривна; hv; plural *hryvny*), each worth 100,000 *karbovantsi*. The best exchange rates are at **Obmin Valyut** (Обмін Валют) kiosks in the center of most cities. Western Union and ATMs are everywhere. Traveler's checks can be changed into US dollars for small commissions. Most banks will give Visa and MasterCard cash advances for a high commission. The lobbies of fancier hotels usually exchange US dollars at lousy rates. Private money changers lurk near legitimate kiosks, ready with brilliant schemes for ripping you off; do not exchange money with them—it's illegal. Although locals don't usually leave tips, most expats give 10%. Accommodations in Ukraine average €10-20; meals run €5-7.

HRYVNY		
AUS$1 = 2.93HV	1HV = AUS$0.34
CDN$1 = 3.42HV	1HV = CDN$0.29
EUR€1 = 5.24HV	1HV = EUR€0.19
NZ$1 = 2.49HV	1HV = NZ$0.40
UK£1 = 8.26HV	1HV = UK£0.12
US$1 = 5.33HV	1HV = US$0.19
ZAR1 = 0.50HV	1HV = ZAR1.99

COMMUNICATION

PHONE CODES	Country code: 380. International dialing prefix: 810. From outside Ukraine, dial int'l dialing prefix (see inside back cover) + 380 + city code + local number.

TELEPHONES. Telephones are stumbling toward modernity. The easiest way to make international calls is with **Utel.** Buy a Utel phonecard (sold at most Utel phone locations) and dial the number of your international operator. Alternatively, call at the central telephone office—estimate how long your call will take, pay at the counter, and they'll direct you to a booth. Calling can be expensive, but you can purchase a 30-minute Ukrainian international calling card for 15hv. Local calls from gray payphones generally cost 10-30hv. For an English-speaking operator, dial ☎8 192. International access codes include: **AT&T Direct** (☎8 100 11); **Canada Direct** (☎ 8 100 17); **MCI WorldPhone** (☎8 100 13).

MAIL. Mail is cheap and quite reliable (about 10 days to North America). The easiest way to mail letters is to buy pre-stamped envelopes at the post office. For *Poste Restante*, address envelope to be held: Firstname SURNAME, До Запитание, Ul. Sadovaya 10, 270015 Odessa, UKRAINE.

INTERNET ACCESS. Email is the easiest and cheapest way of communicating with the outside world. Internet cafes are just beginning to make their presence known throughout Ukraine. You'll be able to find at least one in each major city. Otherwise, several post offices offer Internet access at decent prices.

UKRAINE

LANGUAGES. It's extremely difficult to travel without knowing some Ukrainian or Russian. In Kyiv, Odessa, and the Crimea, Russian is more common than Ukrainian (although all official signs are in Ukrainian). In Transcarpathia, Ukrainian is preferred—people will speak Russian only if they know you are not Russian.

ACCOMMODATIONS AND FOOD

UKRAINE	❶	❷	❸	❹	❺
ACCOMMODATIONS	under 55hv	55-105hv	106-265hv	266-480hv	over 480hv
FOOD	under 11hv	11-27hv	28-54hv	55-105hv	over 105hv

There are no youth hostels, and budget accommodations are usually in unrenovated Soviet-era buildings. Not all **hotels** accept foreigners, and those that do often charge them many times more than what a Ukrainian would pay. Although room prices in Kyiv are astronomical, singles run anywhere from 5hv to 90hv in the rest of the country. More expensive hotels aren't necessarily nicer; in some hotels, women lodging alone may be mistaken for prostitutes. Standard hotel rooms include a TV, phone, and a refrigerator. You will be given a *vizitka* (визитка; hotel card) to show to the hall monitor (дежурная; dezhurnaya) to get a key; surrender it on leaving the building. Valuables should never be left unattended; ask at the desk if there's a safe. Hot water is a rarity—ask before checking in. **Private rooms** can be arranged through overseas agencies or bargained at the train station. Most cities have a **campground,** but camping outside of designated areas is illegal, and enforcement is merciless.

There are few choices between fancy restaurants and **stolovayas** (cafeterias), dying bastions of cheap, hot food. Old *stolovaya* food can knock you out of commission for hours, but a good *stolovaya* meal is a triumph of the human spirit. Vegetarians can create their own meals from **potatoes, mushrooms,** and **cabbage** sold at markets; bring your own bag. State food stores are classified by content: *hastronom* (гастроном) sell packaged goods; *moloko* (молоко) milk products; *ovochi-frukty* (овочі-фрукты) fruits and vegetables; *myaso* (мясо) meat; *hlib* (хліб) bread; *kolbasy* (колбаси) sausage; and *ryba* (риба) fish. Tea is a popular national drink, as is the beer-like *kvas*.

SAFETY AND SECURITY

While Ukraine is neither violent nor politically volatile, it is poor. Keep a low profile and watch your belongings. Pickpocketing and wallet scams are the most common crimes; instances of armed robbery and assault have been reported. Do not exchange money on the street. Do not accept drinks from strangers as this could result in your being drugged and robbed. Credit card and ATM fraud are endemic; avoid using credit or ATM cards while in Ukraine. Be careful crossing the street— drivers do not stop for pedestrians.

Water is bad and hard to find in bottled form; it's best to boil it or learn to love brushing your teeth with soda. Fruits and vegetables from open markets are generally safe, although storage conditions and pesticides make thorough washing imperative. Meat purchased at public markets should be checked very carefully and cooked thoroughly. Embassy officials say that Chernobyl-related radiation poses minimal risk to short-term travelers, but the region should be given a wide berth. Public toilets are disgusting; pay toilets are cleaner and sometimes have toilet paper, but bring your own anyway. Pharmacies are quite common and carry basic Western products.

HOLIDAYS

Holidays: New Year's (Jan. 1); Orthodox Christmas (Jan. 7); Women's Day (Mar. 8); Good Friday (Apr. 9); Easter (Apr. 11-12); Labor Day (May 1-2); Victory Day (May 9); Holy Trinity (June 6); Constitution Day (June 28); Independence Day (Aug. 24).

KYIV (КИЇВ)   ☎ 8044

Straddling the wide Dniper River and layered with hills, Kyiv (pop. 2,600,000) greets visitors with golden-domed churches, winding streets, and a sprawling old town. The cradle of Slavic-Orthodox culture, and once the USSR's third-largest city, Kyiv has been struggling to adjust to its new role as the capital of an independent and nationalist Ukraine. Though development is proving to be a slow process, extensive construction and remodeling projects promise great changes to come.

▐ TRANSPORTATION

Flights: Boryspil International Airport (KBP; Бориспіль; ☎296 72 43), 30km southeast of the capital. **Polit** (Полит; ☎296 73 67) sends buses from Boryspil to Ploscha Peremohi and the train station. Buy tickets on the bus (every 30min.-1hr.; 8-10hv). A taxi to the center costs 70-100hv.

Trains: Kyiv-Pasazhyrskyy (Київ-Пасажирський), pl. Vokzalna (☎005). MR: Vokzalna (Вокзальна). Trains are better than buses for long-distance travel. Purchase tickets (a passport is required) in the main hall. An info kiosk (Довидка; dovydka) is in the center of the main hall. Open daily 6:30am-11pm. There is an **Advance-Ticket Office** next to Hotel Express, blv. Shevchenka 38, straight up vul. Kominternu from the train station. Many travel agencies also book train tickets. To: **Bratislava** (18hr., daily, 405hv); **Budapest** (24hr., daily, 532hv); **Lviv** (10hr., 20 per day, 53hv); **Minsk** (12-13hr., daily, 98hv); **Moscow** (15-17hr., 20 per day, 130-190hv); **Prague** (35hr., daily, 530hv); **Sevastopol** (20hr., 2 per day, 59hv); **Warsaw** (17hr., 2 per day, 395hv).

Buses: Tsentralny Avtovokzal (Центральний Автовокзал), pl. Moskovska 3 (Московська; ☎250 99 86), is 10min. past Libidska, the last stop on the MG line. Go right and then left out of the Metro; take trolleybus #4 or walk 100m down the big highway and follow it to the right for 500m.

Public Transportation: The 3 intersecting lines of the **Metro**—blue (MB), green (MG), and red (MR)—are efficient but limited. Purchase blue tokens (0.50hv), good on all public transport, at the "каса" (kasa). "Вхід" (vkhid) indicates an entrance, "перехід" (perekhid) a walkway to another station, and "вихід у місто" (vykhid u misto) an exit onto the street. **Trolleys, buses,** and **marshrutki** (private vans numbered with bus routes) go where the Metro doesn't. Bus tickets are sold at kiosks; punch your ticket on board to avoid a 10hv fine. Marshrutki tickets (1hv) are sold on board. Public transport runs 6am-midnight, although some buses go later.

❋ ▐ ORIENTATION AND PRACTICAL INFORMATION

Most attractions and services lie on the west bank of the Dniper River. Three Metro stops from the train station is the main avenue **vulitsa Khreshchatyk** (Хрещатик; MR line). The center of Kyiv is vul. Khreshchatyk's fountained **Independence Sq.** (Майдан Незалежності; Maydan Nezalezhnosti; on the MB line).

Tourist Office: Kyiv still lacks official tourist services. Representatives of various agencies at the airport offer vouchers, excursion packages, hotel arrangements, and other services. Try **Carlson Wagonlit Travel**, vul. Ivana Franka 34/33, 2nd fl. (☎238 61 56).

Open M-F 9am-6pm. Or, head to **Yana Travel Group,** vul. Saksahanskoho 42 (Саксаганського; ☎246 62 13; www.yana.kiev.ua). Open M-F 9am-7pm, Sa 10am-5pm, Su 10am-3pm. Students and youth should try **STI Ukraine,** vul. Priorizna 18/1 #11 (☎490 59 60; www.sticom.ua). Open M-F 9am-9pm, Sa 10am-4pm.

Embassies: Australia, vul. Kominternu 18/137 (Комінтерну; ☎/fax 235 75 86). Open M-Th 10am-1pm. **Canada,** vul. Yaroslaviv Val 31 (Ярославів Вал; ☎464 11 44; fax 464 11 33). Open M-Th 8:30am-noon. **South Africa,** vul. Chervonoarmiyska 9/2 (Червоноармійська; ☎227 71 72 or 227 36 22; fax 220 72 06). Open M-F 9:30am-12:30pm. **UK,** vul. Desyatynna 6 (Десятинна; ☎462 00 11; fax 462 00 13). **Consular section** at vul. Mazepy 6 (мазепи; ☎290 73 17 or 290 79 47). Open M-F 9am-noon. **US,** vul. Yu. Kotsyubynskoho 10 (Ю. Коцюбинського; ☎490 40 00; www.usinfo.usemb.kiev.ua). **Consular section** on vul. Pymonenka (ьпимоненка; ☎490 44 22; fax 216 33 93). From the corner of Independence Sq. and Sofyevska (Софиевска), take trolley #16 or 18 for 4 stops. Continue on vul. Artema (Артема) until it curves to the right, then take the first right onto vul. Pymonenka. Call ahead for an appointment. Open M-Th 9am-6pm.

Medical Assistance: Ambulance: ☎03. The **American Medical Center,** vul. Berdycherska 1 (Бердичерска; ☎/fax 490 76 00; www.amcenters.com), has English-speaking doctors. Open 24hr. AmEx/MC/V.

Internet Access: Cyber Cafe (Кібер Кафе), Prorizna 21 (Прорізна; ☎228 05 48). Centrally located. 10hv. per hr. Open daily 9am-11pm. The main **post office** also houses 2 Internet cafes. Walk through the doors to the right of the entrance and up the stairs. 10hv per hr. Pay in advance. Open M-Sa 8am-9pm, Su 9am-7pm.

Telephones: Myzhmisky Perehovorny Punkt (Мижміський Переговорний Пункт), at the post office. **Telefon-Telefaks** (Телефон-Телефакс), around the corner (enter on vul. Khreshchatyk). Both open 24hr. **Public telephones** (Таксофон; Taksofon) work only with phone cards, available at the post office. **English operator:** ☎8192.

Post Office: vul. Khreshchatyk 22 (☎228 11 67) next to Independence Sq. Address mail to be held: Firstname SURNAME, *Poste Restante,* **01001** Київ-1, Почтамт до Воетребоваиия, UKRAINE. Open M-Sa 8am-9pm, Su 9am-7pm.

🏠 ACCOMMODATIONS AND FOOD

Hotels are geared toward high-paying customers, and foreigners often pay twice as much as Ukrainians. People at the train station, and occasionally outside of hotels, offer **private rooms** (US$5 and up). A list of pricier private rooms can be found in the *Kyiv Post* (www.kyivpost.com). The savvy traveler's best bet for budget accommodations is the telephone service **Okean-9** (Океан; ☎443 61 67). Tell them your price and preferred location and they'll reserve you a room for free. The only catch is that the friendly staff has rather spotty English. (Open M-F 9am-5pm, Sa 9am-3pm.) **Hotel Druzba ❷** (Дрчжбый Народю), blv. Druzhby Narodiv 5 offers spacious rooms in a convenient location. From MB: Lybidska (Либідська), take a left on blv. Druzhby Narodiv and walk 200m to the hotel. (☎268 34 06; fax 268 33 87. Shower, phone, TV, and fridge. Singles 136hv; doubles 205hv.) **Hotel Express ❸** (Експрес), blv. Shevchenka 38/40, is straight up vul. Kominternu from the train station and offers clean, inexpensive rooms. (☎239 89 95. Breakfast included. Internet access 4lv per 30min. Singles 145hv; doubles 260hv.) **Hrazhdanskyy Aviatskyy Instytut Student Hotel ❶** (Гражданский Авіатский), vul. Nizhinska 29E (Ніжінська), is a good deal if you don't mind the trek. From behind MR: Vokzalna, turn right into the passageway leading to the trams. Take tram #1 or 1K to Гарматна (*Harmatna;* 6 or 7 stops) and get off at Індустріальна (*Industrialna*). Backtrack 1½ blocks, turn right on vul. Nizhinska, cross at the first intersection, and follow the stairs into the complex. Keep the first building on your right as you walk diagonally to block "Д." After passing Д on the right, look for the "Готел НАУ" (Hotel NAU) sign above. (☎484 90 59. Check-out noon. Singles 45hv, with private bath, TV, and fridge 98hv; doubles 82/160hv.) **Dykanka ❸** (Диканька), vul. Malyshka 4a (Малишка, ☎558 96 52), serves traditional food. Exit the metro to the left, turn right and walk diagonally through the park, and then turn right onto the busy street and walk 30m. (MR: Darnytza (Дарница). Entrees 24-160hv. Open daily noon-1am. MC/V.) **Taras ❷** (Тарас), in the Taras Shevchenko Park, offers a large, creative menu in a pleasant atmosphere. (☎235 21 32. Open 10am-last customer.) **Korchma pid Osokorom ❶** (Корчма під Осокором), vul. Mykhaylivsky 20b (Михайлівська), is an intimate cafe serving traditional food. (English menu. Entrees 5-9hv. Open daily 10am-10pm.)

👁 SIGHTS

VULITSA KHRESHCHATYK AND ENVIRONS. Broad and commercial **vulitsa Khreshchatyk** (Хрещатик) begins at the intersection with blv. Shevchenka and goes up to **Independence Sq.** (Maydan Nezalezhnosti), which is filled with fountains and covers an underground shopping mall. *(MR: Khreshchatyk.)* **Khreshchaty Park,** past the silver **Friendship of the Peoples Arch,** contains a historical monument celebrating Prince Volodymyr, who converted Kyivan Rus to Christianity.

VULITSA VOLODYMYRSKA: ST. SOPHIA TO GOLDEN GATE. The enormous **St. Sophia Monastery** complex was the religious center of Kyivan Rus and is still the focal point of Ukrainian nationalism. The monastery's golden onion domes, decorated facades, and exquisite Byzantine mosaics and frescoes make it one of the main attractions in Kyiv. *(MG: Zoloty Vorota or trolley #16 from Maydan Nezalezhnasti. Grounds open daily 10am-7:30pm. 1hv. Museum open Su-Tu and F-Sa 10am-6pm, W 10am-5pm. 10hv, with camera 20hv; students 4hv.)* The **Golden Gate** (Золоти Ворота; Zoloty Vorota) marks the entrance to the city and houses a small museum; next to it is a statue of Yaroslav the Wise. Several other small churches are scattered throughout the area, especially along vul. Tryokhsvyatytelska.

ANDRIYIVSKYY PATH AND THE PODIL DISTRICT. Full of cafes, vendors, and galleries, the cobblestone **Andriyivskyy path** (Андріївский узвіз; Andriyivskyy uzviz) can be reached by funicular from the subway or by walking from Mikhaylivska Sq. *(MB: Poshtova. Funicular operates daily 6:30am-11pm, every 5min., 0.50hv.)* The ▨**Museum of One Street,** Andriyivskyy 2b, creatively covers the history of Kyiv's most famous street. *(Open Su and Tu-Sa noon-6pm. 3hv. English tour 25hv.)* Climb the gray steps at the corner of Desyatinna and vul. Volodymyrska to see the ruins of **Tithe Church** (Десятинна Церква; Desyatinna Tserkva), the oldest stone church of Kyivan Rus, and the **National Museum of Ukrainian History.** *(Open Su-Tu and Th-Sa 10am-5pm. 5hv.)* Nearby is the impressive 18th-century **St. Andrew's Cathedral.** The path spills out into the church-filled **Podil** district, which was the center of Kyiv in the 10th and 11th centuries. Just east of the *ploscha,* the **Chernobyl Museum,** Provulok Khoryva 1, details the legacy of the nuclear disaster and features a multimedia tour. *(Open M-F 10am-6pm, Sa 10am-5pm. Closed last M of each month. 5hv., students 1hv.)*

BABYN YAR. The monument at **Babyn Yar** is a moving tribute to the first victims of the Nazis in Ukraine. The statue, a group of interlocking figures falling to their deaths, is accompanied by a plaque stating that 100,000 Kyivans died at Babyn Yar; the current estimate of victims—mostly Jews—is twice that figure. *(MG: Dorohozhychi. In the park near the TV tower, at the intersection of vul. Oleny Telihy and vul. Melnykova.)*

UKRAINE

KYIV-PECHERY MONASTERY. Kyiv's oldest and holiest religious site, the mysterious **Kyiv-Pechery Monastery** (Києво-Печерська Лавра; Kyivo-Pecherska Lavra) deserves a full day of exploration. In addition to several museums, the complex houses the 12th-century **Holy Trinity Gate Church,** the **Refectory Church,** and the fascinating ▨**caves** where saints and the monastery's monks lie mummified and entombed. Buy a candle to help you navigate the caves. *(MR: Arsenalna. Turn left as you exit the Metro and walk 10min. down vul. Sichnevoho Povstaniya. Monastery open daily 9am-7pm. Entrance 10hv, students 5hv. Museums open daily 10am-5pm. Each museum 5-6hv, students 3hv. Caves open daily 8am-2pm. Dress modestly.)*

🎵 📷 ENTERTAINMENT AND NIGHTLIFE

In summer, shopping at the weekend bazaars is an experience in itself (MB: Respublykanskyy Stadion and MR: Vokzalna). In May, a two-week theater festival leads to **Kyiv Days,** when stages for drama, folklore, jazz, and rock performances are set up all over town. The famed **Kyiv International Film Festival** comes to Kyiv in July.

During the soccer season from late spring to fall, don't miss **Dynamo Kyiv,** one of the top teams in Europe. From European Sq., walk down vul. Hrushevskoho to the *kasa* in front of Dynamo Stadium (tickets 5-20hv). On hot summer days, locals sun on the beaches of ▨**Hydropark** (Гідропарк), an **amusement park** and **beach** on an island in the Dniper (MR: Hidropark). The **National Philharmonic,** vul. Volodymyrsky 2, grooves the old-fashioned way. (☎228 16 97. *Kasa* open Su and Tu-Sa noon-3pm and 4-7pm.) **Shevchenko Opera and Ballet Theater,** on vul. Volodymyrsky, puts on several shows each week at noon and 7pm. (MR: Teatralna. ☎224 71 65. *Kasa* open M 11am-3pm, Su and Tu-Sa 11am-3pm and 4:30-7pm.)

Check out *What's On* (www.whatson-kiev.com) and the *Kyiv Post* (www.kyivpost.com) for entertainment listings and the latest nightspots. Through an unmarked door to the left of the courtyard at vul. Khreshchatyk 44, you'll find Kyiv's jazz mecca, **Artclub 44.** (150 kinds of whisky. Beer from 8hv. Live music daily. Cover from US$2. Open 10am-late.) **O'Brien's Pub,** vul. Mykhaylivska 17a (Михайлівська; ☎229 15 84), off Independence Sq., is full of expats, and has the most relaxed drinking atmosphere around. (Satellite TV, and darts. Billiards 7hv per game. Beer 7-22hv. Tea 4hv. Live music Th-Sa 9-11:30pm, Th Irish, F-Sa blues, pop, and rock. Open daily 8am-2am.) At **Caribbean Club,** vul. Kominternu 4

(Комінтерну), Cuban barmen mix Cuban cocktails (30-50hv) and other libations (9hv and up) to salsa music. (No sports attire. Cover for men 30hv, women 20hv. Open 9pm-late.) **Androhyn,** vul. Harmatna 26/2, MR: Shulyavska, is one of the few gay clubs in town. (Cover 15-25hv. Open Th-Su 8pm-8am.)

LVIV (ЛЬВІВ) ☎80322

Lviv (pop. 800,000) was the toy of empires for ages—Poland conquered it, Austria rebuilt it, and the Soviet Union neglected it for fifty years in fear of its "decadent" Western ways. Now, more affordable than Kyiv and teeming with energy, Lviv rewards visitors with its steeple-filled center, striking castle, and ornate theater. Meander down its cobblestone streets, sip coffee in a romantic cafe, and watch Lviv come into its own before your eyes.

TRANSPORTATION AND PRACTICAL INFORMATION. Trains (☎748 20 68) go from pl. Vokzalna (Вокзальна) to: Bratislava (18hr., daily, 290hv); Brest (11½hr., daily, 70hv); Budapest (13½hr., daily, 330hv); Kraków (7½hr., daily, 136hv); Minsk (14hr., daily, 95hv); Moscow (25hr., 2 per day, 195hv); Prague (24hr., daily, 350hv); and Warsaw (12hr., daily, 200hv). Tickets can be bought at the railway *kasa* at Hnatyuka 20 (Гнатюка. ☎748 52 76. Open daily 8am-2pm and 3-8pm.) The main bus station, vul. Stryyska 189 (Стрийська; ☎63 24 93), sends buses to Kraków (8-9hr., daily, 74hv) and Warsaw (10hr., 4 per day, 82hv). From the bus station, marshrutka #18 goes to the train station, where trams run to town. **Lviv Tourist Info Center,** at vul. Pidvalna 3, distributes info on hotels and restaurants and provides free maps. (☎97 57 51; www.tourism.lviv.ua. Open M-Sa 9am-1pm and 2-6pm.) **Internet Klub,** vul. Dudayeva, has 24hr. high-speed Internet access. (8am-midnight 4hv per hr., midnight-8am 2hv per hr.) **Postal Code:** 79 000.

ACCOMMODATIONS AND FOOD. At the end of pr. Svobody is **Hotel Lviv** ❶, vul. Chornovola 7 (Чорновола). Take tram #6 from the train station to the first stop after the Opera House on the right. Cross the street and walk to the intersection slightly off to your right; turn left and continue across the first busy street to the hotel. (☎79 86 51. Showers 3hv. Spartan singles 40hv, with bath 80hv; doubles 60/116hv.) Take tram #1 from the train station to "Дорошенка" (Doroshenka) and walk another block, heading right at the park, to reach **Hotel George** ❸, pl. Mitskevycha 1. A grand neo-Renaissance exterior belies modest rooms. (☎74 21 82. Breakfast included. Singles 134hv, with bath 147hv; doubles 318/340hv.) **Oselya** ❷ (Оселя), vul Hramyuka 11, serves traditional Ukrainian cuisine and occasionally has live folk music. (☎72 16 01. Entrees 9-18hv. Vegetarian borscht 5.50hv. Open daily 11am-11pm. MC/V.) **Kaktus** ❷ (Кактус), vul. O. Nyzhankivskoho, near Hotel George, has creative peasant cuisine and great breakfasts. (☎74 50 61. Open M-F 7am-11pm, Sa-Su 7am-2am. MC/V.) **Kilikiya** ❷, vul. Virmenska 13, next to the Armenian Cathedral, has peaceful outdoor seating. (☎72 62 01. Entrees 8-37hv. Open daily 11am-11pm. MC/V.) Sip coffee (3hv) amid Renaissance statues in the courtyard of a 16th-century Italian merchant's house at **Italiyskyy Dvoryk** ❶, pl. Rynok 6. (Walk through the museum entrance to reach the cafe. Open daily 11am-8pm.)

SIGHTS AND ENTERTAINMENT. Climb up to **High Castle Hill** (Високий Замок; Vysokyy Zamok), the former site of the Galician King's Palace, for a panoramic view of Lviv. To get there, follow vul. Krivonoca (Кривоноса) from its intersection with Hotny and Halytskono, walk until you pass #39, then take a left down the long dirt road to wind your way up and around the hill counterclockwise. After admiring the view, return to the heart of the city and begin a walking tour from pr. Svobody, which is dominated by the dazzling exterior of the **Theater of Opera and Ballet.** (Театра Опери Та Балету; Teatr Opery Ta Baletu; ☎72 88 60. Tickets from 10hv.) **Ploschad Rynok,** the historic market square, is surrounded by churches and richly decorated merchant homes dating from the 16th to18th centuries. The 19th-century **town hall** is topped with a trident-wielding statue of Neptune. The **History Museum** (Історичний Музей; Istorychnyy Muzey) complex is at pl. Rynok #4, 6, and 24. The revamped displays at #4 recount episodes of Lviv's history that were ignored under the Soviets; in WWII, Ukrainian citizens fought for the Nazis, then for Soviet Russia, and later faced oppression from both sides. King Jan III Sobieski lived at building #6 in the 17th century; museum #24 focuses on earlier Ukrainian history. (Open Su-Tu and Th-Sa 10am-5:30pm. Each museum 3.50hv.) Walk up vul. Staroyevrejska (Old Jewish Road) to reach **Golden Rose Synagogue.** For centuries, Lviv was an important center of Jewish culture, but now only ruins remain; Nazis destroyed the synagogue in 1942. The mystic, 14th century dodecahedric dome of the **Armenian Cathedral** is at vul. Virmenska 7-9. (Open M-F 9am-5pm.) Lviv is renowned for its cafe culture. ▧**Club-Cafe Lyalka** (Клуб-Кафе Лялька), vul. Halytskoho 1, below the Puppet Theater (Театр Лялок; Teatr Lyalok), often has live music or art installations. (Wine 3hv. Cover 7-10hv. Open daily 11am-7am.) **Red Bull Dancing Club,** vul. Ivana Franka 15, is an underground discotheque. (Cover 20hv; includes food and drink. Dancing daily 9pm-3am. Open 11am-9am.)

ODESSA (ОДЕССА) ☎80482

Since its founding by Catherine the Great in 1794, Odessa (pop. 1,100,000) has been blessed by prosperity and cursed with corruption. With French, British, Turkish, Greek, Italian, and Russian influences, life in this port town has always been exciting. Attractive to intellectuals as well as thieves and *mafiosi*, Odessa has captured the imaginations of writers from Aleksandr Pushkin to Isaac Babel, who wrote about Odessa's colorful Jewish mafia in his *Odessa Tales.* Since the collapse of the Soviet Union, many visitors, both Russian and Western, are rediscovering the city's ancient beauty.

TRANSPORTATION AND PRACTICAL INFORMATION. Trains go from pl. Privokzalnaya 2 (Привокзальная), at the north end of ul. Pushkinskaya, to: Kyiv (10hr., 6 per day, 59hv); Moscow (25hr., 2-3 per day, 210hv); and Warsaw (24hr., even-numbered days, 340hv). To reach the bus station, take tram #5 from the train station to the last stop. **Buses** run from ul. Kolontayevskaya 58 (Колонтаевская) to Kyiv (8-10hr., 11 per day, 36hv) and Simferopol (12hr., 2 per day, 40hv). **Ferries** go from Morskoy Vokzal (Морской Вокзал; Sea Terminal), ul. Primorskaya 6 (Приморская) to Istanbul (25hr. or 36hr., 2 per week, US$80-295). **FGT Travel** (also known as Fagot; Фагот), ul. Rishelyevskaya ul. 4, in the wax museum, runs tours and has accommodations info. (☎37 52 01; www.odessapassage.com. Open daily 8:30am-10pm.) **Postal Code:** 65 000.

▣▢ ACCOMMODATIONS AND FOOD. Staying in **private rooms** is cheap (from US$5 per person). From the train station, take trams #3 or 12 to reach the downtown hotels, most near pl. Grecheskaya (Греческая) and ul. Deribasovskaya. **Hotel Spartak ❶** (Спартак), ul. Deribasovskaya 25, has old but clean rooms in a great location. (☎26 89 24. Singles 18-40hv; doubles 24-84hv; triples 36-42hv.) **Passazh ❶** (Пассаж), Preobrazhenskaya ul. 34, has pleasant rooms in a beautiful historic building. (☎22 48 49. Call ahead. Singles 35hv, with bath 67hv; doubles 58/88hv; triples 74/112hv.) **Odessa State University Dormitory #8 ❶,** ul. Dovzhenko 9B

(Довженко), rents spartan rooms in July and August. (Reservations ☎63 05 60, English info ☎23 84 77. Dorms 10hv.) Odessa has many good restaurants and cafes, especially along Deribasovskaya ul. **Kumanets ❸** (Куманець) is at ul. Gavanna 7 (Гаванна) right in the city. (Borscht 10-14hv. Entrees 23-44hv. English menu. Open 11am-midnight.) The **Privoz mega-market** (Привоз), Privoznaya ul., is across from the train station. (Open daily 6am-6pm.)

◙ ♫ SIGHTS AND ENTERTAINMENT. Street performers of all kinds gather on **ulitsa Deribasovskaya.** Turn right on Preobrazhenska, left on Sofiyevskaya (Софиевская), and walk up two blocks to reach the **Odessa Art Museum** (Одеський художеотвеный музей), ul. Sofiyevskaya 5a, where you can explore the grotto below. (☎23 84 62. Museum 2hv; Grotto tour with guide only 2hv plus negotiable guide fee. Open Su-M and W-Sa 10:30am-6pm.) Left off ul. Deribasovskaya onto ul. Yekaterinskaya, the statue of the **Duc de Richelieu,** the city's first governor, looks down the **Potemkin Stairs** (Потемкинская Лестница; Potomkinskaya Lestnitsa) toward the shiny port, **Morskoy Vokzal.** The **Literature Museum** (Литературный Музей; Literaturny muzey), Lanzheronovskaya 2 (Ланжероновская), provides a look at the city's intellectual and cultural heritage. (Open Su and Tu-Sa 10am-5pm. 3.50hv, students 1.50hv.) Turn right from the Literature Museum to reach **ulitsa Pushkinskaya,** Odessa's most beautiful street. The **Pushkin Museum and Memorial** (Литературно-мемориальный музей Пушкина; Literaturno-memorialny muzey Pushkina) at #13 is the former hotel where Pushkin lived during his brief exile (1823-1824) from St. Petersburg. (Open Su and Tu-Sa 10am-5pm. 3hv, students 2hv.) Directly underneath the city is Odessa's main quarry, the world's longest series of ▧**catacombs.** During the Nazi occupation, the resistance was based here; the city has set up an excellent subterranean **museum** in its honor. FGT (see above) gives tours in English. (75hv. Bring a sweater.) Most **beaches** are accessible either by public transportation or on foot. Tram #5 goes to: **Arkadiya** (Аркадия), the most popular on summer nights; **Lanzheron** (Ланжерон), the closest to central Odessa; and **Otrada** (Отрада). Tram #18 goes to **Golden Shore** (Золотой Берег; Zolotoy Bereg) and **Kurortny** (Курортный) beaches. Tram #17 goes to **Chaika** (Чайка) beach.

The **Opera and Ballet Theater** (Театр Оперы и Балета; Teatr Opery i Baleta), at the end of ul. Rishelyevskaya, has daily performances. Buy tickets in advance from the *kasa* to the right of the theater. (Open Su and Tu-Sa 10am-6pm. 10-50hv.) On **ulitsa Deribasovskaya,** restaurants, cafes, and bars stay open late, playing music ranging from Euro-techno to Slavic folk. The open-air discos in **Arkadiya** attract dancing crowds as the summer nights grow warm.

YALTA (ЯЛТА)
☎80654

Yalta is the tsar of Crimean resort towns and the resort town of the tsars. A former respite for the Russian elite, Yalta's beautiful beaches and palatial sanatoria now crawl with the throngs they came here to evade. The ubiquitous blaring of Russian folk-pop attests that the proletariat rules supreme these days. However, the tree-lined streets, cloud-topped mountains, and sparkling sea give visitors a hint of the city that inspired Chekhov, Rachmaninov, and Tolstoy.

◪ ♫ TRANSPORTATION AND PRACTICAL INFORMATION. Buses go from ul. Moskovskaya, to Kyiv (17½hr., daily, 110hv) and Odessa (14½hr., daily, 110hv). To reach the bus station, take tram #5 from the train station to the last stop. **Buses** run from ul. Kolontayevskaya 58 (Колонтаевская) to Kyiv (8-10hr., 11 per day, 36hv) and Simferopol (12hr., 2 per day, 40hv). **Ferries** go to Istanbul (33hr.; Tu-W daily; US$90, round-trip US$160-250). Buy tickets at the Omega window in the front right-hand corner of the Sea Terminal, ul. Rusvelta 5 (Рузевелта). (Open daily 9am-1pm.) Buses run throughout the city (0.40hv). **Eugenia Travel,** ul. Rusvelta 12, offers tours and assists with accommodations. (☎32 81 40; www.eugenia-tours.com.ua/. Open M-F 9am-6pm.) **Postal Code:** 98 600.

⌐⌐ ACCOMMODATIONS AND FOOD. Bus station middlemen often offer unbeatable deals on **private rooms.** A good rate during high season is 30-60hv, but expect to pay more for rooms closer to the water. A *kvartirnoye byuro* (квартирное бюро; housing office) to the right of the trolleybus *kasa*, across the street from the main bus station, can help you find a room as well. (☎34 26 79. Open daily mid-June to Sept. 9am-5pm.) If you plan to stay in a hotel in July or August, make reservations at least a month in advance. **Pension T.M.M. ❸,** 2, ul. Lesi Ukrayinki 16 has views of the sea and its own courtyard. (Singles 110-400hv.) Most of the restaurants that populate nab. Lenina and the passage toward ul. Sadovaya dish out good food, strong beverages, and very high prices. The numerous cafes, on the other hand, serve up decent eats—mostly traditional Ukrainian and Russian fare—at reasonable prices. The **open-air market** opposite the circus, accessible by foot or trolley #1, has a big selection of fresh fruits and vegetables. (Open daily 8am-7pm.) **Siren Cafeteria** (Сирень) ❶, ul. Rusvelta 4, serves tried and true, homestyle Ukrainian food. (Entrees 2.80-10hv. Open daily 7:30am-9pm.)

◙⌐ SIGHTS AND ENTERTAINMENT. For a great view of the city, take the chairlift (канатная дорога; kanatnaya doroga) uphill to the right of the Gastronom on nab. Lenina to the **mock Greek temple,** properly named Olymp. (4hv. Open daily 10am-9pm, off season 10am-5pm.) Chekhov lived in Yalta for the last five years of his life; you can practically retrace his every step by following the monuments and plaques. At ul. Kirova 112, explore the ▨**white dacha** he built in 1899, the garden he planted, the desk at which he wrote *Three Sisters,* *The Cherry Orchard,* and *Lady with a Dog,* and the museum his sister dedicated to him, all remarkably well-preserved. Take bus #8 from Kinoteatr Spartak on ul. Pushkinskaya. The **Nikitskiy Botanical Gardens** (Никицкий Сад; Nikitskiy Sad), founded in 1812, boast over 15,000 species of native and foreign flora. Take bus #34 past Massandra to *arboretum* (15min.) on your left. (Gardens open daily 8am-8pm; off season 9am-4pm. Cactus house open daily 9am-4pm. Gardens 5hv. Cactus house 2hv.) Follow the seashore either way from the harbor to reach one of Yalta's many **beaches.** (Entrance to most city beaches 1.50hv, commercial beaches 2-5hv.) The daily **amusement park** (*lunapark*) on nab. Lenina has a roller coaster (7hv) and bumper cars (12hv). **Organ concerts** take place in the Roman Catholic church, ul. Pushkin-skaya 25. (July-Sept. M-Sa 8pm, Su 5pm; May-June and Oct. M-Sa 7:30pm, Su 5pm. Buy tickets on site.)

Nightlife centers around beachfront bars. **Kaktus** (Кактус; Cactus), upstairs at the Morskoy Vokzal, offers Tex-Mex food, disco music, and various theme nights. (Beer 15hv. Cover 30hv, women free. Open 11am-late.) Get swept off your feet at **Tornado** on nab. Lenina 11, up the stairs through the arch and to the left, by its disco music and occasional laser show. (Beer 8hv. Cover 20hv, after 11pm 30hv; women free until 10pm.)

LANGUAGE BASICS

CYRILLIC ALPHABET

CYRILLIC	ENGLISH	PRONUNCIATION	CYRILLIC	ENGLISH	PRONUNCIATION
А а	a	*ah* as in **Pr**a**gue**	Р р	r	*r* as in **Revolution**
Б б	b	*b* as in **B**osnia	С с	s	*s* as in **Serbia**
В в	v	*v* as in **V**olga	Т т	t	*t* as in **t**ank
Г г	g	*g* as in **G**lasnost	У у	u	*oo* as in B**u**dapest
Д д	d	*d* as in **d**ictatorship	Ф ф	f	*f* as in **F**ormer USSR
Е е	e	*yay* as in **yay!**	Х х	kh	*kh* as in Ba**ch**
Ё ё	yo	*yo* as in **yo!**	Ц ц	ts	*ts* as in Let'**s** Go
Ж ж	zh	*zh* as in mira**g**e	Ч ч	ch	*ch* as in Khrush**ch**ev
З з	z	*z* as in **c**ommunism	Ш ш	sh	*sh* as in Khru**sh**chev
И и	i	*ee* as in Gr**ee**k	Щ щ	shch	*shch* in Khru**shch**ev
Й й	y	*y* as in bo**y** or ke**y**	Ъ ъ	(hard)	(no sound)
К к	k	*k* as in **K**remlin	Ы ы	y	*y* as in s**i**lver
Л л	l	*l* as in **L**enin	Ь ь	(soft)	(no sound)
М м	m	*m* as in **M**acedonia	Э э	e	*eh* as in **R**omania
Н н	n	*n* as in **n**uclear	Ю ю	yu	*yoo* as in **U**kraine
О о	o	*o* as in **Cr**o**atia**	Я я	ya	*yah* as in **Y**aroslavl
П п	p	*p* as in **P**oland			

Belarus, Bulgaria, and the **Ukraine** use variations of the Russian Cyrillic alphabet.

GREEK ALPHABET

SYMBOL	NAME	PRONUNCIATION	SYMBOL	NAME	PRONUNCIATION
α A	alpha	*a* as in **f**a**ther**	ν N	nu	*n* as in **n**et
β B	beta	*v* as in **v**elvet	ξ Ξ	xi	*x* as in mi**x**
γ Γ	gamma	*y* as in **yo** or *g* as in **go**	ο O	omicron	*o* as in **r**o**w**
δ Δ	delta	*th* as in **th**ere	π Π	pi	*p* as in **p**eace
ε E	epsilon	*e* as in **j**e**t**	ρ P	rho	*r* as in **r**oll
ζ Z	zeta	*z* as in **z**ebra	σ (ς) Σ	sigma	*s* as in **s**en**s**e
η H	eta	*ee* as in qu**ee**n	τ T	tau	*t* as in **t**ent
θ Θ	theta	*th* as in **th**ree	υ Y	upsilon	*ee* as in gr**ee**n
ι I	iota	*ee* as in tr**ee**	φ Φ	phi	*f* as in **f**og
κ K	kappa	*k* as in **k**ite	χ X	chi	*h* as in **h**orse
λ Λ	lambda	*l* as in **l**and	ψ Ψ	psi	*ps* as in oo**ps**
μ M	mu	*m* as in **m**oose	ω Ω	omega	*o* as in **go**

CROATIAN

ENGLISH	CROATIAN	PRONOUNCE
Yes/No	Da/Ne	da/neh
Please	Molim	MO-leem
Thank you	Hvala lijepa	HVAH-la leepa
Hello	Dobardan	Do-bar-DAHN
Goodbye	Bog	Bog
Sorry/Excuse me	Oprostite	o-PRO-sti-teh
Help!	U pomoć!	OO pomoch
Police	Policija	po-LEE-tsee-ya
Embassy	Ambasadu	ahm-bah-sah-du

ENGLISH	CROATIAN	PRONOUNCE
Ticket	Kartu	KAR-too
Train/Bus	Vlak/Autobus	vlahk/au-TOH-bus
Station	Kolodvor	KO-lo-dvor
Airport	Zračna luka	ZRA-chna lu-kah
Taxi	Taksi	tahksi
Grocery	Trgovina	TER-goh-vee-na
Hotel	Hotel	hoh-tel
Pharmacy	Ljekarna	lye-KHA-rna
Bathroom	WC	vay-tsay

ENGLISH	CROATIAN	PRONOUNCE
Where is...?	Gdje je?	GDYE je
How do I get to...?	Kako mogu doći do ...?	KAH-ko MO-goo DO-chee do...
How much does this cost?	Koliko to košta?	KO-li-koh toh KOH-shta
Do you have...?	Imate li...?	EEM-a-teh lee
Do you speak English?	Govorite li engleski?	GO-vor-i-teh lee eng-LEH-ski

CZECH

ENGLISH	CZECH	PRONOUNCE
Yes/No	Ano/ne	AH-no/neh
Please	Prosím	PROH-seem
Thank you	Děkuji	DYEH-koo-yih
Hello	Dobrý den	DO-bree den
Goodbye	Nashedanou	NAH sleh-dah-noh-oo
Sorry/Excuse me	Promiňte	PROH-mihn-teh
Help!	Pomoc!	POH-mots
Police	Policie	PO-lits-iye
Passport	Cestovní pas	TSE-stov-neeh
Open/Closed	Otevřeno/Zavřeno	O-te-zheno/ZAV-rzhen-o
Pharmacy	Lékárna	LEE-khaar-nah
Doctor	Lékař	LEK-arzh

ENGLISH	CZECH	PRONOUNCE
Ticket	Lístek	LIS-tek
Train/Bus	Vlak/Autobus	vlahk/OUT-oh-boos
Station	Nádraží	NA-drah-zhee
Airport	Letiště	LEH-tish-tyeh
Taxi	Taxi	TEHK-see
Bank	Banka	BAN-ka
Exchange	Směnárna	smyeh-NAR-na
Grocery	Potraviny	PO-tra-vee-nee
Tourist office	Turistické informace	TOO-rist-it-skeh IN-for-mat-tseh
Center of town	Centrum měšťá	MNEHST-skeh TSEN-troom
Hotel	Hotel	HOH-tel
Bathroom	WC	VEE-TSEE

ENGLISH	CZECH	PRONOUNCE
Where is...?	Kde je...?	k-DEH
How do I get to...?	Jak se dostanu do...?	YAK seh dohs-TAH-noo doh
How much does this cost?	Kolik to stojí?	KOH-lihk STOH-yee
Do you have...?	Máte...?	MAH-teh
Do you speak English?	Mluvíte anglicky?	MLOO-vit-eh ahng-GLIT-ski
I'd like to order...	Prosím...	PROH-seem

DANISH

ENGLISH	DANISH	PRONOUNCE
Yes/No	Ano/ne	AH-no/neh
Please	Vær så venlig	vair soh VEN-li
Thank you	Tak	tahk
Hello	Goddag	go-DAY
Goodbye	Farvel	fah-VEL
Sorry/Excuse me	undskyld	UN-scoold
Help!	Hjælp!	yelp
Police	Politiet	por-lee-TEE-ehth
Embassy	Ambassade	ahm-ba-SA-theh

ENGLISH	DANISH	PRONOUNCE
Ticket	Billet	bill-ETT
Train/Bus	Toget/Bussen	TOE-et/BOO-sehn
Airport	Lufthavns	LAYFD-haown
Departure	Afgang	af-gahng
Market	Marked	mah-GEHTH
City center	Centrum	SEHN-trum
Hotel/Hostel	Hotel/Vandrerhjem	ho-TEL/VAN-drer-yem
Pharmacy	Apotek	ah-por-TIG
Toilet	Toilet	toy-LEHD

ENGLISH	DANISH	PRONOUNCE
Where is...?	Hvor er...?	voa air
How do I get to...?	Hvordan kommer jeg til...?	vo-DAN KOM-ah yai tee
How much does this cost?	Hvad koster det?	va KOS-tor dey
I'd like a...	Jeg vil gerne have en...	yai vi GEHR-neh ha en
Do you speak English?	Taler du engelsk?	TAY-luh dou ENG-elsk

DUTCH

ENGLISH	DUTCH	PRONOUNCE
Yes/No	Ja/Nee	ya/nay
Please/ You're welcome	Alstublieft	ALs-too-bleeft
Thank you	Dank u wel	dank oo vell
Hello	Hallo	hal-LO
Goodbye	Tot ziens	tot zeens
Sorry/excuse me	Neemt u mij niet/Pardon	naymt oo mi neet/par-DON
Help!	Help!	help
Police	Politie	po-LEET-see
Embassy	Ambassade	am-bass-AH-duh
Pharmacy	Apotheek	ah-po-TAYK

ENGLISH	DUTCH	PRONOUNCE
Ticket	Kaartje	KAHRT-yuh
Train/Bus	Trein/Bus	trin/boos
Station	Station	staht-see-ohn
Taxi	Taxi	TAX-ee
Grocery	Kruidenier	krow-duh-EER
Tourist office	VVV	fay-fay-fay
Town Center	Centrum	ZEHN-trum
Hotel	Hotel	ho-TEL
Bathroom	Badkamer	BAT-kah-mer

ENGLISH	DUTCH	PRONOUNCE
Where is...?	Waar is...?	vaar is
How much does this cost?	Wat kost het?	vat kost het
Do you have...?	Heeft u...?	hayft oo
Do you speak English?	Sprekt u Engels?	spraykt oo EN-gels

FINNISH

ENGLISH	FINNISH	PRONOUNCE
Yes/No	Kyllä/Ei	EW-la/ay
Please	Pyydän	BU-dan
Thank you	Kiitos	KEE-tohss
Hello	Hei	hey
Goodbye	Näkemiin	NA-kay-meen
Sorry/Excuse me	anteeksi	ON-take-see
Help!	Apua!	AH-poo-ah
Police	Poliisi	PO-lee-see
Embassy	Suur lähetystöä	SOOHR LA-heh-tüs-ter-ah

ENGLISH	FINNISH	PRONOUNCE
Ticket	Lipun	LEE-pun
Train/Bus	Juna/Bussi	YU-nuh/BUS-si
Boat	Bussi	BOOS-see
Departures	Lähtevät	lah-teh-vaht
Market	Oria	TOH-ree-uh
Hotel/hostel	Hotelli/Retkeilymaja	HO-tehl-lee/
Pharmacy	Apteekki	UHP-teehk-kee
Bathroom	WC	VEE-see
Telephone	Puhelinta	POO-heh-lin-tuh

ENGLISH	FINNISH	PRONOUNCE
Where is...?	Missä on...?	MEESS-ah OWN
How do I get to...?	Miten minä pääsen...?	MEE-ten MEE-na PA-sen
How much does this cost?	Paljonko tämämaksaa?	PA-lee-onk-o teh-meh MOCK-sah
I'd like to buy...	Haluaisin ostaa...	HUH-loo-ay-sin OS-tuh
Do you speak English?	Puhutteko englantia?	POO-hoo-teh-kaw ENG-lan-ti-ah?

FRENCH

ENGLISH	FRENCH	PRONOUNCE
Yes/No	Oui/Non	wee/nohn
Please	S'il vous plaît.	see-voo-PLAY
Thank you	Merci.	mehr-SEE
Hello	Bonjour.	bohn-ZHOOR
Goodbye	Au revoir.	oh re-VWAHR
Excuse me	Excusez-moi!	ex-KU-zay-MWAH
Help!	Au secours!	oh-seh-KOOR
Police	la police	la-poh-LEES
Embassy	l'ambassade	lahm-bah-SADE
passport	le passeport	pass-PORT
Open/Closed	ouvert/fermé	OO-vert/fer-MAY
Pharmacy	la pharmacie	far-ma-SEE
Doctor	le médecin	mehd-SEN

ENGLISH	FRENCH	PRONOUNCE
Ticket	le billet	bee-AY
Train/Bus	le train/le bus	tran/boos
Station	la gare	gahr
Airport	l'aéroport	laehr-O-port
Taxi	le taxi	tax-EE
Bank	la banque	bahnk
Exchange	l'échange	lay-SHANZH
Grocery	l'épicerie	lay-PEES--ree
Tourist office	le bureau de tourisme	byur-OH-de-toor-EE-sm
Town hall	l'hôtel de ville	LO-tel-de-veel
Hotel	l'hôtel	LO-tel
Hostel	l'auberge	LO-berzh
Toilet	les WC	lay-vay-SAY

ENGLISH	FRENCH	PRONOUNCE
Where is...?	Où se trouve...?	OOH-seh-troov
How much does this cost?	Ça fait combien?	sa-FAY-cohm-BEE-ehn
Do you have...?	Avez vous...?	ah-VAY-VOO
Do you speak English?	Parlez-vous anglais?	par-LAY-VOO-an-GLAY
I would like ...	Je voudrais...	zhe-VOO-DRAY

GERMAN

ENGLISH	GERMAN	PRONOUNCE	ENGLISH	GERMAN	PRONOUNCE
Yes/No	Ja/Nein	yah/nain	Ticket	Fahrkarte	FAR-kar-tuh
Please	Bitte	BIH-tuh	Train/Bus	Zug/Bus	tsug/boos
Thank you	Danke	DAHNG-kuh	Station	Bahnhof	BAHN-hohf
Hello	Hallo	HAH-lo	Airport	Flughafen	FLOOG-hahf-en
Goodbye	Auf Wiedersehen	owf VEE-der-zayn	Ferry	Fährschiff	FAYHR-shif
Excuse me	Entschuldigung	ent-SHOOL-di-gung	Bank	Bank	bahnk
Help!	Hilfe!	HIL-fuh	Exchange	Wechseln	VEHK-zeln
Police	Polizei	poh-lit-ZAI	Grocery	Lebensmittel-geschäft	LAY-bens-mit-tel-guh-SHEFT
Embassy	Botschaft	BOT-shaft	Tourist office	Touristbüro	TOR-ist-byur-oh
Open/Closed	Geöffnet/Geschlossen	geh-UHF-net/geh-shlos-sen	Hotel/Hostel	Hotel/Jugendherberge	ho-TEL/YOO-gend-her-BER-guh
Pharmacy	Apotheke	AH-po-TAY-kuh	With shower	Mit Dusche	miht DOO-shuh
Doctor	Arzt	ARTZT	Bathroom	Badezimmer	BAH-deh-tsim-muh

ENGLISH	GERMAN	PRONOUNCE
Where is...?	Wo ist...?	vo ist
How much does that cost?	Wieviel kostet das?	VEE-feel KOS-tet das
Do you have...?	Haben Sie...?	HAB-en zee
Do you speak English?	Sprechen Sie English?	SHPREK-en zee EHNG-lish
I would like...	Ich möchte ...	ish MERK-tuh

GREEK

ENGLISH	GREEK	PRONOUNCE	ENGLISH	GREEK	PRONOUNCE
Yes/No	ναι/οχι	NEH/OH-hee	Train/Bus	τραινο/λεωφορειο	TREH-no/leh-o-fo-REE-o
Please	παρακαλω	pah-rah-kah-LO	Station	σταθμοζ	stath-MOS
Thank you	ευχαριστω	ef-khah-ree-STO	Airport	αεροδρομειο	ah-e-ro-DHRO-mee-o
Hello/Goodbye	Γεια σας	YAH-sas	Taxi	ταξι	tax-EE
Sorry/Excuse me	Συγνομη	sig-NO-mee	Ferry	πλοιο	PLEE-o
Help!	Βοητηεια!	vo-EE-thee-ah	Bank	τραπεζα	TRAH-peh-zah
Police	αστυνομεια	as-tee-no-MEE-a	Exchange	ανταλλασσω	an-da-LAS-so
Embassy	πρεσβεια	prez-VEE-ah	Market	αγορα	ah-go-RAH
Passport	διαβατηριο	dhee-ah-vah-TEE-ree-o	Tourist office	τουριστικο γραψειο	tou-ree-stee-KO graf-EE-o
Open/closed	ανοικτο/κλειστο	ah-nee-KTO/klee-STO	Hotel/Hostel	ξενοδοχειο	kse-no-dho-HEE-o
Pharmacy	φαρμακειο	fahr-mah-KEE-o	Bathroom	τουαλεττα	tou-ah-LET-ta
Doctor	ιατροσ	yah-TROS	Room to let	δωματια	do-MA-shee-ah

For the Greek alphabet, see p. 1051

LANGUAGE BASICS

ENGLISH	GREEK	PRONOUNCE
Where is...?	Που ειναι...?	pou-EE-neh
How much does this cost?	Πσπο κανει?	PO-so KAH-nee
Do you have...?	Εχετε...?	Eh-khe-teh
Do you speak English?	Μιλας αγγλικα?	mee-LAHS ahn-glee-KAH
I'd like ...	Θα ηθελα...	tha EE-thel-ah

HUNGARIAN

ENGLISH	HUNGARIAN	PRONOUNCE
Yes/No	Igen/nem	EE-ghen/nem
Please	Kérem	KAY-rem
Thank you	Köszönöm	KUH-suh-num
Hello	Szervusz	SAIR-voose
Goodbye	Viszontlátásra	Vi-sont-lah-tah-shraw
Excuse me	Elnézést	EL-nay-zaysht
Police	Rendőrséget	REN-dur-shay-get
Passport	Az útlevelemet	oz OOT-lev-el-met
Open/ Closed	Nyitott/Csukott	NYEE-tot/CHOO-kawt
Pharmacy	Gyógyszertár	DYAW-dyser-tar

ENGLISH	HUNGARIAN	PRONOUNCE
Ticket	Jegyet	YED-et
Train/Bus	Vonat/Auto-bussz	VAW-not/auto-boos
Station	Pályaudvar	pa-yo-OOT-var
Airport	Repülőtér	rep-ewlu-TAYR
Bank	Bank	bonk
Exchange	Valutabeváltó	OH-loo-tob-bee-vaal-taw
Grocery	Élelmiszerbolt	ay-lel-mes-er-balt
Tourist office	Utazási iroda	UH-toh-zah-see EE-raw-dah
Hotel	Szálloda	SAH-law-dah
Toilet	W.C.	VAY-tsay

ENGLISH	HUNGARIAN	PRONOUNCE
Where is...?	Hol van...?	hawl von
How much does this cost?	Mennyi ideig tart?	MEN-yee EE-deeg tort
Can I have...?	Kaphatok...?	KAH-fot-tok
Do you speak English?	Beszél angolul?	BAY-sayl ON-gaw-lool

ITALIAN

ENGLISH	ITALIAN	PRONOUNCE
Yes/No	Sì/No	see/no
Please	Per favore/Per piacere	pehr fah-VOH-reh/pehr pyah-CHAY-reh
Thank you	Grazie	GRAHT-see-yeh
Hello	Ciao	chow
Goodbye	Arrivederci	ah-ree-veh-DAIR-chee
Sorry/Excuse me	Mi dispiace/Scusi	mee dees-PYAH-cheh/SKOO-zee
Help!	Aiuto!	ah-YOO-toh
Police	Polizia	po-LEET-ZEE-ah
Embassy	Ambasciata	ahm-bah-shee-AH-tah
Passport	Il passaporto	eel pahs-sah-POHR-toh
Open/Closed	Aperto/Chiuso	ah-PAIR-toh/KYOO-zoh
Pharmacy	Farmacia	far-mah-SEE-ah
Doctor	Medico	MEH-dee-koh

ENGLISH	ITALIAN	PRONOUNCE
Ticket	Biglietto	oon beel-YEHT-toh
Train/Bus	Treno/Autobus	TRAY-no/aow-toh-BOOS
Station	Stazione	lah staht-see-YOH-neh
Airport	Aeroporto	AYR-o-PORT-o
Taxi	Tassì	tahs-SEE
Ferry	Traghetto	eel tra-GHEHT-toh
Bank	Banca	bahn-KAH
Exchange	Cambio	CAHM-bee-oh
Grocery	Alimentari	ah-li-mehn-TA-ri
Tourist office	Azienda Promozione Turistica	ah-tzi-EHN-da pro-mo-tzi-O-nay tur-EES-tee-kah
Hotel/Hostel	Albergo	al-BEHR-go
With shower	Con doccia	kohn DOH-cha
Bathroom	un gabinetto/un bagno	ooh gah-bee-NEHT-toh/oon BAHN-yoh

ENGLISH	ITALIAN	PRONOUNCE
Where is...?	Dov'è...?	doh-VEH
How much does this cost?	Quanto costa?	KWAN-toh CO-stah
Do you have...?	Hai...	HI
Do you speak English?	Parla inglese?	PAHR-lah een-GLAY-zeh
I'd like...	Vorrei...	VOH-ray

NORWEGIAN

ENGLISH	NORWEGIAN	PRONOUNCE
Yes/No	Ja/Nei	yah/nay
Please	Vær så snill	va sho SNEEL
Thank you	Takk	tuhk
Hello	Goddag	gud-DAHG
Goodbye	Ha det	HUH-deh
Sorry/Excuse me	Beklager, tilgi meg/Unnskyld	BEH-KLAH-gehrr til-yee mai/UN-shül
Help!	Hjelp!	yelp
Police	Politi	pohl-ih-TEE
Embassy	Ambassade	uhm-buhs-SAH-do

ENGLISH	NORWEGIAN	PRONOUNCE
Ticket	Billett	BEE-leht
Train/Bus	Toget/Bussen	TOR-go/boosn
Airport	Lufthavn	LUFT-huhvn
Departures	Avgang	av-gang
Market	Torget	TOHR-geh
Hotel/Hostel	Hotell/Vandrerhjem	hoo-TEHL/VAN-drair-yem
Pharmacy	Apotek	uh-pu-TAYK
Bathroom	Do	doo
City center	Sentrum	SEHN-trum

ENGLISH	NORWEGIAN	PRONOUNCE
Where is...?	Hvor er...?	VOOR arr
How do I get to...?	Hvordan kommer jeg til...?	voor-duhn kom-morr yay til
How much is...?	Hvor mye koster det...?	vorr moo-yo KOS-TOR deh...?
Do you speak English?	Snakker du engelsk?	snu-ko du EHNG-olsk

POLISH

ENGLISH	POLISH	PRONOUNCE	ENGLISH	POLISH	PRONOUNCE
Yes/No	Tak/nie	tahk/nyeh	Ticket	Bilet	BEE-leht
Please	Proszę	PROH-sheh	Train/	Pociąg/	POH-chawnk/
Thank you	Dziękuję	jen-KOO-yeh	Bus	Autobus	ow-TOH-booss
Hello	Cześć	cheshch	Bank	Bank	bahnk
Goodbye	Do widzenia	doh veedz-EN-yah	Grocery	Sklep spożywczy	sklehp spoh-ZHIV-chih
Sorry/Excuse me	Przepraszam	psheh-PRAH-shahm	Hostel	Schronisko młodzieżowe	srah-NIHS-kah mwa-jee-eh-SHAH-veh
Help!	Na pomoc!	nah POH-mots	Pharmacy	Apteka	ahp-TEH-ka
Police	Policja	poh-LEETS-yah	Bathroom	Toaleta	toh-uh-LEH-tuh

ENGLISH	POLISH	PRONOUNCE
Where is...?	Gdzie jest...?	g-JEH yest
How much does this cost?	Ile to kosztuje?	EE-leh toh kohsh-TOO-yeh
Do you have...?	Czy są...?	chih sawn
Do you (male/female) speak English?	Czy pan(i) mówi po angielsku?	chih PAHN(-ee) MOO-vee poh ahn-GYEL-skoo

PORTUGUESE

ENGLISH	PORTUGUESE	PRONOUNCE	ENGLISH	PORTUGUESE	PRONOUNCE
Yes/No	Sim/Não	seeng/now	Ticket	Bilhete	beel-YEHT
Please	Por favor	pur fah-VOR	Train/Bus	Comboio/Autocarro	kom-BOY-yoo/OW-to-KAH-roo
Thank you	Obrigado (m)/ Obrigada (f)	oh-bree-GAH-doo/dah	Airport	Aeroporto	aye-ro-POR-too
Hello	Olá	oh-LAH	Exchange	Câmbio	CAHM-bee-yoo
Goodbye	Adeus	ah-DAY-oosh	Market	Mercado	mer-KAH-doo
Sorry/Excuse me	Desculpe	desh-KOOLP	Hotel	Pousada	poh-ZAH-dah
Help!	Socorro!	so-KO-ro!	Pharmacy	Farmácia	far-MAH-see-ah
Police	Polícia	po-LEE-see-ah	Bathroom	Banheiro	bahn-YAY-roo

ENGLISH	PORTUGUESE	PRONOUNCE
Where is...?	Onde é que é ...?	OHN-deh eh keh eh...?
How much does this cost?	Quanto custa?	KWAHN-too KOOSH-tah?
I want...	Quero...	KAY-roo...
Do you speak English?	Fala inglês?	FAH-lah een-GLAYSH?

ROMANIAN

ENGLISH	ROMANIAN	PRONOUNCE
Yes/No	Da/nu	dah/noo
Please/ Thank you	Vă rog/ Mulțumesc	vuh rohg/ mool-tsoo-MESK
Hello	Bună ziua	BOO-nuh zee-wah
Goodbye	La revedere	lah reh-veh-DEH-reh
Sorry	Îmi pare rău	im PA-reh rau
Excuse me	Scuzați-mă	skoo-ZAH-ts muh
Help!	Ajutor!	AH-zhoot-or
Police	Poliție	poh-LEE-tsee-eh

ENGLISH	ROMANIAN	PRONOUNCE
Ticket	Bilet	bee-LEHT
Train/Bus	Trenul Autobuz	TRAY-nool aw-toh-BOOS
Station	Gară	GAH-ruh
Grocery	Alimentar	AH-lee-mehn-tar
Taxi	Taxi	tak-SEE
Hotel	Hotel	ho-TEHL
Bathroom	Toaletă	toh-ahl-EH-tah

ENGLISH	ROMANIAN	PRONOUNCE
Where is...?	Unde e?	OON-deh YEH
How much does this cost?	Cât costă?	kyht KOH-stuh
Do you have...?	Aveți...?	a-VETS
Do you speak English?	Vorbiți englezește?	vor-BEETS ehng-leh-ZESH-te

RUSSIAN

ENGLISH	RUSSIAN	PRONOUNCE
Yes/No	Да/нет	Dah/Nyet pa-ZHAL-u-sta
Please	Пожалуйста	pa-ZHAL-u-sta
Thank you	Спасибо	spa-SEE-bah
Hello	Добрый день	DOH-bri DYEHN
Goodbye	До свидания	da svee-DAHN-ya
Sorry/ Excuse me	Извините	iz-vi-NEET-yeh
Help!	Помогите!	pah-mah-GIT-yeh
Embassy	посольство	pah-SOHL'-stva
Police	милиция	mee-LEE-tsi-ya
Passport	паспорт	PAS-pahrt
Open/Closed	открыт/закрыт	ot-KRIHT/za-KRIHT
Pharmacy	аптека	ahp-TYE-kah

ENGLISH	RUSSIAN	PRONOUNCE
Ticket	билет	bil-YET
Train/Bus	поезд/автобус	PIE-yizt/av-toh-BOOS
Station	вокзал	VOK-zal
Airport	аэропорт	ay-airoh-PORT
Bank	банк	bahnk
Exchange	обмен валюты	ab-MYEhN val-iy-YU-tee
Town center	центр города?	TSEhN-tehr GOR-rah-dah
Grocery	гастроном	gah-stroh-NOM
market	рынок	REE-nohk
Hotel	гостиница	gahs-TEE-nee-tsah
Dorm/Hostel	общежитие	ob-sheh-ZHEE-tee-yeh
Bathroom	туалет	twah-LYET

ENGLISH	RUSSIAN	PRONOUNCE
Where is...?	Где находится...?	gdyeh nah-KHOH-di-tsah
How much does this cost?	Сколько это стоит?	SKOHL'-ka E-ta STOY-it
Do you have...?	У вас есть...?	oo vas YEST'
Do you speak English?	Вы говорите по-английски?	vy ga-va-REE-tyeh pa-an-GLEE-ski
I'd like...	Я хотел(а) бы	ya khah-TYEL(a) bwee

For the Cyrillic alphabet, see p. 1051.

SPANISH

ENGLISH	SPANISH	PRONOUNCE
Yes/No	Si/No	see/noh
Please	Por favor	pohr fah-VOHR
Thank you	Gracias	GRAH-see-ahs
Hello	Hola	OH-lah
Goodbye	Adiós	ah-di-OHS
Sorry/Excuse me	Perdón	pehr-DOHN
Help!	¡Ayuda!	ay-YOOH-duh
Police	Policía	poh-lee-SEE-ah
Embassy	Embajada	em-bah-HA-dah
Passport	Pasaporte	pas-ah-POR-tay
Open/Closed	Abierto(a)/Cerrado(a)	ah-bee-AYR-toh/sehr-RAH-doh
Pharmacy	Farmácia	far-MAH-see-ah
Doctor	Médico	MAY-dee-koh

ENGLISH	SPANISH	PRONOUNCE
Ticket	Boleto	boh-LEH-toh
Train/Bus	Tren Autobús	trehn ow-toh-BOOS
Station	Estación	es-tah-see-OHN
Airport	Aeropuerto	ay-roh-PWER-toh
Taxi	Taxi	tahk-SEE
Ferry	Transbordador	trahns-BOR-dah-dohr
Bank	Banco	BAHN-koh
Exchange	Cambio	CAHM-bee-oh
Grocery	Supermercado	soo-pehr-mer-CHAH-doh
Tourist Office	Oficina de turismo	oh-fee-SEE-nah day toor-EEZ-moh
Hotel/Hostel	Hotel/Hostal	oh-TEL/OH-stahl
Dorm	Dormitorio	dor-mih-TOR-ee-oh
Bathroom	Baño	BAHN-yoh

ENGLISH	SPANISH	PRONOUNCE
Where is...?	Dónde está...?	DOHN-day eh-STA
How much does this cost?	Cuánto cuesta...?	KWAN-toh KWEHS-tah
Do you have...?	Usted tiene....?	ooh-STED tee-EN-ay
Do you speak English?	Habla inglés?	AH-blah een-GLAYS
I'd like...	Me gustaría...	may goos-tah-REE-ah

SWEDISH

ENGLISH	SWEDISH	PRONOUNCE
Yes/No	Ja/Nej	yah/nay
Please	Tack	TOOHK
Thank you	Tack	toohk
Hello	Hej	hay
Goodbye	Adjö	uh-YEHR
Excuse me	Ursäkta mig	oo-SHEHK-tuh MAY
Help!	Hjälp!	yelp
Police	Polisen	poo-LEE-sehn
Embassy	Ambassad	uhm-buh-SAHD

ENGLISH	SWEDISH	PRONOUNCE
Ticket	Biljett	bil-YEHT
Train/Bus	Går/Tåget	gorr/TOR-geht
Ferry	Färjan	FAR-yuhn
Departure	Avgång	UHV-gong
Market	Torghandel	TOH-ree-HUHN-dehl
Hotel/Hostel	Mitt hotell/Vandrarhem	mit hoo-TEHL
Pharmacy	Apotek	uh-poo-TEEK
Toilet	Toalett	too-uh-LEHT
Post office	Posten	POHS-tehn

ENGLISH	SWEDISH	PRONOUNCE
Where is...?	Var finns det...?	vahr FINS deh
How much does this cost?	Hur mycket kostar det?	hurr MUK-keh KOS-tuhr deh
I'd like to buy...	Jag skulle vilja ha...	yuh SKUH-leh vil-yuh HAH
Do you speak English?	Talar du engelska?	TA-luhr du EHNG-ehls-kuh

In June of 2003, 200 would-be European immigrants believed to have embarked from Libya drowned in the rough waters south of Sicily; that same month, 2666 migrants from Africa survived the journey, landing on the isolated Italian island Lampedusa and creating a study in contrasts in the ongoing EU immigration debate. In the annals of European immigration, tragedies of this caliber are far from rare: The Sicily drowning occurred three years to the month after 58 Chinese refugees were asphyxiated in a container lorry at the English port of Dover. Even the illegal immigrants who beat the odds and the border control do not always escape tragic circumstances. Many are forced into black-market labor, such as prostitution, to pay back smugglers for their passage. While it is fairly clear that current EU immigration policies are harmful to refugees, opening the floodgates on legal immigration is not only in the best interests of those seeking entrance—it now appears that the EU needs immigrants as desperately as immigrants need the EU.

Western European birth-rates have crashed to an all-time low, averaging only 1.5 children per woman, and dipping as low as Spain's scant 1.1. At the other end of things, Europe's aging population has become a major strain on its pension systems. French Parliamentarian Elisabeth Guigou reports that, if present demographic trends continue, without relaxing immigration constraints, the mighty new 25-nation European Union will experience a net decline in population of 50 million people by 2050. Even now Europe is facing shortages in both its skilled and unskilled labor pools, making even more apparent its need for immigrants for economic prosperity to continue.

With so much at stake, it may seem confusing to witness the recent immigration policy swing to the political right experienced by much of Europe. Some of the most developed, prosperous nations, such as Germany and France, worry that an influx of immigrants will destabilize their economies and jeopardize publicly-funded medical and social programs. Tensions have been primarily focused on African and Arab ghettos, commonly seen as drags on the welfare state and

feared to be security threats in the wake of September 11. This explosive combination of fear and uncertainty has fueled the popularity of far-right populist political candidates running on anti-immigration platforms, spawning legislation severely restricting legal immigration.

During June-July 2003 at the Thessaloniki Summit, Germany, Britain, and Italy were the most vocal and influential players in the debate over how to manage illegal immigration while integrating legal immigrants. Some leaders, such as German Interior Minister Otto Schily, think agreements with countires of origin are the best way to curbing illegal immigration. Supporters of such efforts point to Italy's bilateral agreements with Lybia, a hub for human trafficking from Africa to Europe, and Albania as models. In the former scenario, Italy will provide technical assistance to Libya, and the two countries will cooperate on offshore patrols. The 1997 Italian-Albanian cooperation deal contains a simplified repatriation scheme, quotas for seasonal workers, and joint patrols in Albanian waters of the Adriatic Sea that separate Italy and the former Stalinist state.

The stage is set for what promises to be an ongoing debate, as Germany leads the fight to retain autonomous control of its border policies while nations like Britain and Italy attempt to institute centralized, EU-wide control of immigration policy and enforcement. For the moment, a stopgap EU program intended to "promote a tolerant and inclusive society by raising awareness of fundamental European values" and to project accurate information about immigrants' culture, traditions, and religion underscores the two-sided complexity of the situation. By educating immigrants in the cultural, social, and political characteristics of their adoptive state—and providing EU citizens with accurate information about immigrants' cultures—there is hope that some of the elements of mistrust and misunderstanding that have plagued the discussion thus far can be mitigated, and that the frustrated desperation that costs the lives of so many refugees will give way to a peaceful, legal, and mutually beneficial solution.

Derek Glanz is currently earning a Ph.D. in political science and was an editor for Let's Go: Spain and Portugal 1998.

Thirteen new countries have applied to become members of the 15-strong EU; ten of them—Cyprus, the Czech Republic, Estonia, Hungary, Latvia, Lithuania, Malta, Poland, the Slovak Republic, and Slovenia—are slated to join in 2004, uniting almost the entire continent into one big, happy, free-market economy. Yet despite real enthusiasm and a widespread sense of the importance of the project, enlargement does have its opponents. The countries that joined the original six-member EU were relatively well-off at the time and came to the table in small, easy-to-digest bites rather than as a ten-course meal. It's proving difficult for the current members to contemplate dividing the spoils of the Union— agricultural subsidies, regional development funds, and chairs at the EU's tables of power— with their neighbors. The candidate countries themselves are not without a number of concerns that make a match with the EU questionable.

The enlargement process began philosophically after the fall of the Berlin Wall but took a decade to pick up any real steam. The hot favorites from the beginning were the large countries closest to the EU—Poland, Hungary, and the former Czechoslovakia—but a little-known contender took the lead in the race to the finish line: Slovenia, which was nearly 100% EU-compliant at the end of 2002. The plucky little country is already looking and acting like the newest member of the club, with new international superhighways and a GDP per capita that's higher than any other applicant in Central or Eastern Europe—higher, even, than some of them combined. While Hungary and the Czech Republic made great strides in the race, the Slovak Republic fell behind due to some messy domestic politics, and Poland proved a bit stubborn; as the largest country to join the EU in this round of enlargement, Poland held out in some negotiations in hope of a better accession package.

After a slow start, Lithuania and Latvia made good progress toward readiness, but still lagged behind their Baltic sister-state, Estonia. Yet despite booming growth and one of Europe's freest economies, Estonian public opinion regarding accession has been cooling off fast. One Eurobarometer survey showed public support for EU membership at a mere 38%—compared to 85% in Romania and 70% in Hungary. Some of this is due to public exhaustion in the wake of the EU's much-delayed plans for their accession, but good old-fashioned scepticism plays a role as well. As one Estonian-on-the-street put it, "We just left a Union, and look where that one got us..."

Romania and Bulgaria are still a bit shy of EU criteria, and analysts say it will be 2010 before they make it to the finish line. Turkey, it seems, has limited prospects for the time being, producing a bit of a quandary over Cyprus. Although the island—divided since 1974 into Greek and Turkish zones of influence—was as prepared a candidate as Slovenia, its accession became quite controversial. Greece insisted that it would veto everyone if Cyprus didn't join in the first wave, while Turkey quietly threatened to do the same in the concurrent NATO enlargement if the EU didn't consider its own application more seriously. The EU, for its part, has always felt that rapid accession may be the best—if not only— solution to the divided island's persistent ethnic problems.

Malta has came back in on the action, having defrosted its earlier application. While it made headway in the last enlargement round, it pulled out of the race before it was over due to a lack of support at home. Norway, though having been officially accepted for membership, never took up the EU's offer, twice holding referenda in which the Norwegian public rejected membership. Referenda—as the Estonian opinion polls show—may prove to be enlargement's Achilles heel. Indeed, the entire project was almost over turned when Ireland refused to ratify the enlargement-centered Treaty of Nice from 2001, temporarily halting all new countries from being admitted to the EU.

And what of that most geographically and linguistically European of nations, Switzerland? Having voted to join the UN this year, some speculate that the EU may be nearing the Swiss horizon. If nothing else, Switzerland's accession would fill the lake-like gap in the map on the front of the €2 coin—although some wags point out that, with Norway still missing from the picture, Sweden and Finland give an altogether different kind of impression. Take a look for yourself the next time you have a jingle in your pocket...

Jeremy Faro is a former Senior Consultant at Interbrand and has worked in the past on Let's Go: Britain & Ireland. *He is currently a master's student in European Studies at Cambridge University.*

INDEX

G

INDEX

Let's Go Phonecard
your global phonecard with more!

JOIN NOW & receive $5 BONUS talk time!*

www.letsgo.ekit.com

- Save up to 70% on calls from over 55 countries
- Family & friends can leave you voicemail messages for FREE
- Choose your own Account Number and PIN
- Recharge your account anywhere, anytime - over the phone or the web

TO JOIN OVER THE PHONE: In the US dial **1-800-706-1333** then press **0** **#** to speak with a Customer Service Consultant. Visit **www.letsgo.ekit.com** for Access Numbers in over 55 countries.

TO JOIN OVER THE WEB: Visit www.letsgo.ekit.com and click 'Join eKit.'

Quote reference code **LGEUR2004** when joining to receive your $5 BONUS.*

Download a full list of Access Numbers and Instructions for your Let's Go Phonecard - **visit www.letsgo.ekit.com** and click on 'User Guide.'

LGO003 Aug03

MAP INDEX

MAP LEGEND

- ■ Point of Interest
- 🏠 Accommodation
- ▲ Camping
- 🍴 Food
- ☕ Café
- 🏛 Museum
- ● Sight
- 🍺 Bar/Pub
- ★ Nightlife

- ✈ Airport
- ⌐ Arch/Gate
- $ Bank
- 🏖 Beach
- 🚌 Bus Station/Stop
- ✪ Capital City
- 🏰 Castle
- ✝ Church
- ⚑ Consulate/Embassy

- ‡ Convent/Monastery
- ⚓ Ferry Landing
- (347) Highway Sign
- ✚ Hospital
- 💻 Internet Café
- 📚 Library/Bookstore
- ⟨M⟩ M Metro Station
- ▲ Mountain
- ☪ Mosque

- ℞ Pharmacy
- ✪ Police
- ✉ Post Office
- ⛷ Skiing
- ✡ Synagogue
- ☎ Telephone Office
- 🎭 Theater
- ℹ Tourist Office
- 🚂 Train Station

Park | Water | Beach | Pedestrian Zone / Stairs | The Let's Go compass always points NORTH.